The Consumer Credit and Sales
Legal Practice Series

DEBTOR RIGHTS LIBRARY

ACCESS TO UTILITY SERVICE

Regulated, De-Regulated and Unregulated Utilities, Deliverable Fuels, and Telecommunications

Fifth Edition

See *page ix* for information about the companion website.

Charles Harak
Olivia Bae Wein
Darlene R. Wong
John Howat

Contributing Authors: Roger Colton, Kay Joslin, Geoff Walsh

National Consumer Law Center®
7 Winthrop Square, 4th Floor Boston, MA 02110 www.consumerlaw.org

About NCLC®	The National Consumer Law Center®, a nonprofit corporation founded in 1969, assists consumers, advocates, and public policy makers nationwide who use the powerful and complex tools of consumer law to ensure justice and fair treatment for all, particularly those whose poverty renders them powerless to demand accountability from the economic marketplace. For more information, go to www.nclc.org.
Ordering NCLC Publications	Order securely online at www.nclc.org, or contact Publications Department, National Consumer Law Center, 7 Winthrop Square, 4th Floor, Boston, MA 02110, (617) 542-9595, FAX: (617) 542-8028, e-mail: publications@nclc.org.
Training and Conferences	NCLC participates in numerous national, regional, and local consumer law trainings. Its annual fall conference is a forum for consumer rights attorneys from legal services programs, private practice, government, and nonprofit organizations to share insights into common problems and explore novel and tested approaches that promote consumer justice in the marketplace. Contact NCLC for more information or see our website.
Case Consulting	Case analysis, consulting and co-counseling for lawyers representing vulnerable consumers are among NCLC's important activities. Administration on Aging funds allow us to provide free consulting to legal services advocates representing elderly consumers on many types of cases. Massachusetts Legal Assistance Corporation funds permit case assistance to advocates representing low-income Massachusetts consumers. Other funding may allow NCLC to provide very brief consultations to other advocates without charge. More comprehensive case analysis and research is available for a reasonable fee. See our website for more information at www.nclc.org.
Charitable Donations and Cy Pres *Awards*	NCLC's work depends in part on the support of private donors. Tax-deductible donations should be made payable to National Consumer Law Center, Inc. For more information, contact Gerald Tuckman of NCLC's Development Office at (617) 542-8010 or gtuckman@nclc.org. NCLC has also received generous court-approved *cy pres* awards arising from consumer class actions to advance the interests of class members. For more information, contact Robert Hobbs (rhobbs@nclc.org) or Rich Dubois (rdubois@nclc.org) at (617) 542-8010.
Comments and Corrections	Write to the above address to the attention of the Editorial Department or e-mail consumerlaw@nclc.org.
About This Volume	This is the Fifth Edition of *Access to Utility Service*. Discard all prior editions and supplements. This book includes a companion website. Continuing developments can be found in periodic supplements to and revised editions of this volume and on the companion website.
Cite This Volume As	National Consumer Law Center, Access to Utility Service (5th ed. 2011).
Attention	*This publication is designed to provide authoritative information concerning the subject matter covered. Always use the most current edition and supplement, and use other sources for more recent developments or for special rules for individual jurisdictions. This publication cannot substitute for the independent judgment and skills of an attorney or other professional. Non-attorneys are cautioned against using these materials to conduct a lawsuit without advice from an attorney and are cautioned against engaging in the unauthorized practice of law.*
Copyright	 ISBN: 978-1-60248-094-0 (this volume) ISBN: 978-0-943116-10-5 (Series) Library of Congress Control Number: 2011942831

About the Authors

Charles Harak is an NCLC staff attorney focusing on low-income energy and utility issues. Mr. Harak previously worked at the office of the Massachusetts attorney general and at the Massachusetts Law Reform Institute, and has worked on utility and housing issues for over 30 years. He is the co-author of this volume's fourth edition and *Guide to the Rights of Utility Consumers.* He currently serves as the treasurer of the board of the Tri-City Community Action Program, and previously served as board president.

Olivia Bae Wein is an NCLC staff attorney focusing on low-income energy and utility issues. She is co-author of this volume's fourth edition and *Guide to the Rights of Utility Consumers.* She serves on the board of directors of the National Low-Income Energy Consortium, co-chairs the LIHEAP Coalition, serves on the steering committee of the Campaign for Safe and Affordable Drinking Water, and served as a member of the U.S. EPA's National Drinking Water Advisory Council's Small Systems Affordability Work Group. She was an Economic Justice Fellow at Consumers Union.

Darlene R. Wong is an NCLC staff attorney with a focus on utility issues affecting low-income consumers. Before joining NCLC, she focused on public utilities regulation at the Pennsylvania Office of Consumer Advocate. She has litigated rate and service quality cases involving issues of rate setting, consumer protection, engineering and environmental concerns relating to water, energy, and telecommunications companies. She is also a contributing author to *Collection Actions* and to *Unfair and Deceptive Acts and Practices 2011 Supplement*.

John Howat, senior policy analyst at NCLC, has been involved with energy programs and policy issues since 1981. He manages state regulatory and legislative projects across the country, providing analysis and expert testimony in support of low-income consumers' access to affordable energy and utility services.

Roger Colton is a principal in the firm of Fisher, Sheehan and Colton, Public Finance and General Economics in Belmont, Massachusetts, a law and economics consulting firm. He formerly was an NCLC staff attorney, assessing utility issues as they affect the poor. He is the author of more than 80 journal articles on utility regulation, fair and affordable housing, and regulatory issues.

Kay Joslin for the last 23 years has been project manager for the LIHEAP Clearinghouse, operated for the U.S. Department of Health and Human Services by the National Center for Appropriate Technology (NCAT), and serves on the board of directors of the National Low Income Energy Consortium. Prior to that, she worked on NCAT's energy efficiency and renewable energy national hotline and held various editorial and reporting positions at newspapers.

Geoff Walsh has been a legal services attorney for over twenty-five years. He is presently a staff attorney with NCLC, and before that he worked with the housing and consumer units of Community Legal Services in Philadelphia and was a staff attorney with Vermont Legal Aid in its Springfield, Vermont office. His practice has focused upon housing and bankruptcy issues. He is a co-author of *Foreclosures* and a contributing author to *Consumer Bankruptcy Law and Practice, Student Loan Law,* and *Truth in Lending 2011 Supplement.*

Acknowledgments

We first want to thank those who worked on prior editions and supplements for this title. In particular, thanks to Margot Saunders, who was an author of the first and second editions. Thanks also to Nancy Brockway, Jerold Oppenheim, Bruce Plenk, Helen Gonzales, Chi Chi Wu, Amy Marshall Mix, Phyllis Kimmel, Gary Klein, Mark Benson, Stacey Greenberg, Steve Patton, John Rao, Tony Rodriguez, Jonathan Sheldon, Stuart Rossman and others too numerous to list. We also appreciate Mike Hanley of the of the Greater Upstate Law Project (New York) and Mac McCreight of Greater Boston Legal Services for their careful review in past years of Chapter 8 (Utility Allowances) and their insights into the convoluted world of subsidized housing.

On this edition, we want to especially thank Allen Agnitti, Kurt Terwilliger, Emily Green Caplan, Mary Kingsley, and James Diaz for their legal research and work on the appendices. Thanks also to Christian Pilhofer and Patricia Weisgerber for legal research. We are also grateful to Dorothy Tan for editorial supervision; Kim Calvi for editorial assistance; Shirlron Williams for assistance with cite checking; Shannon Halbrook and Microsearch for the companion website; Xylutions for typesetting services; and Mary McLean for indexing.

What Your Library Should Contain

The Consumer Credit and Sales Legal Practice Series contains 18 titles, updated annually, arranged into four libraries, and designed to be an attorney's primary practice guide and legal resource in all 50 states. Titles are available individually, as part of a library, or as part of the complete 18-volume series. Each title includes free access to a companion website containing the treatise's appendices, sample pleadings, primary sources, and other practice aids, allowing pinpoint searches and the pasting of text into a word processor. Access remains free as long as purchasers keep their titles current.

Debtor Rights Library

2009 Ninth Edition (Two Volumes), 2011 Supplement, and Companion Website, Including NCLC's Bankruptcy Forms Software

Consumer Bankruptcy Law and Practice: the definitive personal bankruptcy manual, from the initial interview to final discharge, including consumer rights when a company files for bankruptcy. This practice package contains the leading analysis of individual bankruptcy law and such practice aids as the latest Bankruptcy Code, Rules, and fee schedules, a date calculator, over 150 pleadings and forms, software to compute the initial forms, means test data, and a client questionnaire and handout.

2011 Seventh Edition (Two Volumes) and Companion Website

Fair Debt Collection: the basic reference covering the Fair Debt Collection Practices Act and common law, state statutory and other federal debt collection protections. Thousands of unique case summaries cover reported and unreported FDCPA cases by category. The companion website contains sample pleadings and discovery, the FTC Commentary, an index to and the full text of *all* FTC staff opinion letters, and other practice aids.

2010 Third Edition, 2011 Supplement, and Companion Website

Foreclosures: examines RESPA and other federal and state rights to challenge servicer abuses, as well as details on workout options, loan modification, and mediation programs implemented by federal and state governments. The volume also covers standing and substantive and procedural defenses to foreclosure and tactics after the foreclosure sale. Special chapters cover tax liens, land installment sales contracts, manufactured home foreclosures, and other topics.

2010 Seventh Edition, 2011 Supplement, and Companion Website

Repossessions: a unique guide to motor vehicle and mobile home repossessions, threatened seizures of household goods, statutory liens, and automobile lease and rent-to-own default remedies. The volume examines UCC Article 9 and hundreds of other federal and state statutes regulating repossessions.

2010 Fourth Edition, 2011 Supplement and Companion Website

Student Loan Law: collection harassment; closed school, disability, and other discharges; tax intercepts, wage garnishment, and offset of social security benefits; and repayment plans, consolidation loans, deferments, and non-payment of loan based on school fraud.

2011 Fifth Edition and Companion Website

Access to Utility Service: consumer rights as to regulated and unregulated utilities, including telecommunications, terminations, billing errors, low-income payment plans, utility allowances in subsidized housing, LIHEAP, and weatherization.

Credit and Banking Library

2010 Seventh Edition (Two Volumes), 2011 Supplement, and Companion Website

Truth in Lending: detailed analysis of *all* aspects of TILA, the Consumer Leasing Act, the Fair Credit Billing Act, the Home Ownership and Equity Protection Act (HOEPA), and the Credit CARD Act, including the major 2010 amendments. Appendices and the website contain the Acts, Reg. Z, Reg. M, and their official staff commentaries, numerous sample pleadings, rescission notices, two programs to compute APRs, TIL legislative history, and a unique compilation of *all Federal Register* notices and supplementary information on Regulation Z since 1969.

2010 Seventh Edition, 2011 Supplement, and Companion Website

Fair Credit Reporting: the key resource for handling any type of credit reporting issue, from cleaning up blemished credit records to suing reporting agencies and creditors for inaccurate reports. Covers the new FACTA changes, identity theft, creditor liability for failing to properly reinvestigate disputed information, credit scoring, privacy issues, the Credit Repair Organizations Act, state credit reporting and repair statutes, and common law claims.

2009 Fourth Edition, 2011 Supplement, and Companion Website

Consumer Banking and Payments Law: covers checks, telechecks, electronic fund transfers, electronic check conversions, money orders, and credit, debit, payroll, unemployment, and stored value cards. The title also covers banker's right of setoff, electronic transfers of federal and state benefit payments, and a special chapter on electronic records and signatures.

2009 Fourth Edition, 2011 Supplement, and Companion Website

The Cost of Credit: Regulation, Preemption, and Industry Abuses: a one-of-a-kind resource detailing state and federal regulation of consumer credit in all 50 states. Examines numerous types of predatory lending, federal preemption of state law, credit math calculations, excessive credit charges, credit insurance, and numerous other topics.

2009 Fifth Edition, 2011 Supplement, and Companion Website

Credit Discrimination: analysis of the Equal Credit Opportunity Act, Fair Housing Act, Civil Rights Acts, and state credit discrimination statutes, including reprints of all relevant federal interpretations, government enforcement actions, and numerous sample pleadings.

Consumer Litigation Library

2011 Second Edition and Companion Website

Collection Actions: a complete guide to consumer defenses and counterclaims to collection lawsuits filed in court or in arbitration, with extensive discussion of setting aside default judgments and limitations on a collector's post-judgment remedies. Special chapters include the rights of active duty military, and unique issues involving medical debt, government collections, collector's attorney fees, and bad check laws.

2011 Sixth Edition and Companion Website

Consumer Arbitration Agreements: successful approaches to challenge arbitration agreements' enforceability and waivers of class arbitration, the interrelation of the Federal Arbitration Act and state law, class actions and punitive damages in arbitration, implications of NAF's withdrawal from consumer arbitrations, the right to discovery, and other topics.

2010 Seventh Edition, 2011 Supplement, and Companion Website

Consumer Class Actions: makes class litigation manageable even for small offices, including numerous sample pleadings, class certification memoranda, discovery, class notices, settlement materials, and much more. Includes a detailed analysis of the Class Action Fairness Act, class arbitration, state class action rules and case law, and other topics.

Website and 2011 Index Guide: ALL pleadings from ALL NCLC treatises, including Consumer Law Pleadings Numbers One through Seventeen

Consumer Law Pleadings: over *2000* notable pleadings from all types of consumer cases, including predatory lending, foreclosures, automobile fraud, lemon laws, debt collection, fair credit reporting, home improvement fraud, student loans, and lender liability. Finding aids pinpoint desired pleading in seconds, ready to paste into a word processor.

Deception and Warranties Library

2008 Seventh Edition, 2011 Supplement, and Companion Website

Unfair and Deceptive Acts and Practices: the only practice manual covering all aspects of a deceptive practices case in every state. Special sections on automobile sales, the federal racketeering (RICO) statute, unfair insurance practices, the FTC Holder Rule, telemarketing fraud, attorney fees, and many other topics.

2011 Fourth Edition and Companion Website

Automobile Fraud: examination of title law, "yo-yo" sales, odometer tampering, lemon laundering, sale of salvage and wrecked cars, undisclosed prior use, and prior damage to new cars. The website contains numerous sample pleadings and title search techniques.

2010 Fourth Edition, 2011 Supplement, and Companion Website

Consumer Warranty Law: comprehensive treatment of new and used car lemon laws, the Magnuson-Moss Warranty Act, UCC Articles 2 and 2A, mobile home, new home, and assistive device warranty laws, FTC Used Car Rule, tort theories, car repair and home improvement statutes, service contract and lease laws, with numerous sample pleadings.

NCLC's Companion Websites

Every NCLC manual includes a companion website, allowing rapid access to appendices, pleadings, primary sources, and other practice aids. Search for documents by category or with a table of contents or various keyword search options. All documents can be downloaded, printed, and copy-pasted into a word processing document. Pleadings are also available in Word format. Web access is free with each title ordered and remains free as long as a title is kept current.

Website continually subject to update

Consumer Law on the Web: combines *everything* from the 18 other NCLC companion websites. Using *Consumer Law on the Web,* instead of multiple individual companion websites, is often the fastest and most convenient way to pinpoint and retrieve key documents among the thousands available on our individual companion websites.

Other NCLC Publications for Lawyers

Issued 24 times a year

NCLC REPORTS, a four-page newsletter, keeps you up to date 24 times a year with the latest consumer law developments. It is also an essential practice tool, with novel ideas, innovative tactics, and key insights from NCLC's experienced consumer law attorneys. Learn the practice implications of new statutes, regulations, cases and trends.

First Edition and Companion Website

Bankruptcy Basics: A Step-by-Step Guide for Pro Bono Attorneys, General Practitioners, and Legal Services Offices: provides everything attorneys new to bankruptcy need to file their first case, with a companion website that contains software, sample pleadings, and other practice aids that greatly simplify handling a bankruptcy case.

Second Edition and Companion Website

Foreclosure Prevention Counseling: Preserving the American Dream: explains how to obtain a workout, with advice specifically tailored for Fannie Mae, Freddie Mac, subprime, FHA-insured, VA, and Rural Housing Service loans. The book also details new loan modification initiatives from federal and state governments and industry.

Second Edition with CD-Rom

STOP Predatory Lending: A Guide for Legal Advocates: provides a roadmap and practical legal strategy for litigating predatory lending abuses, from small loans to mortgage loans. How to analyze the documents, spot issues, raise legal claims, select defendants, and even craft a community response.

First Edition

Instant Evidence: A Quick Guide to Federal Evidence and Objections: facilitates objection by rule number and includes common objections and motions at every stage of a case—all in under 20 pages! Spiral-bound to lay flat, all pages are laminated, allowing new notations for each trial with a dry-erase pen.

Second Edition with CD-Rom

The Practice of Consumer Law: Seeking Economic Justice: contains an essential overview to consumer law and explains how to get started in a private or legal services consumer practice. Packed with invaluable sample pleadings and practice pointers for even experienced consumer attorneys.

National Consumer Law Center Guide Series are books designed for consumers, counselors, and attorneys new to consumer law:

2010 Edition

NCLC Guide to Surviving Debt: a great overview of consumer law. Everything a paralegal, new attorney, or client needs to know about home foreclosures and mortgage modifications, debt collectors, managing credit card debt, whether to refinance, credit card problems, evictions, repossessions, credit reporting, utility terminations, student loans, budgeting, and bankruptcy.

First Edition

NCLC Guide to the Rights of Utility Consumers: explains consumer rights concerning electric, gas, and other utility services: shut off protections, rights to restore terminated service, bill payment options, weatherization tips, rights to government assistance, and much more.

First Edition

NCLC Guide to Consumer Rights for Domestic Violence Survivors: provides practical advice to help survivors get back on their feet financially and safely establish their economic independence.

First Edition

NCLC Guide to Mobile Homes: what consumers and their advocates need to know about mobile home dealer sales practices and an in-depth look at mobile home quality and defects, with 35 photographs and construction details.

First Edition

Return to Sender: Getting a Refund or Replacement for Your Lemon Car: find how lemon laws work, what consumers and their lawyers should know to evaluate each other, investigative techniques and discovery tips, how to handle both informal dispute resolution and trials, and more.

Visit **www.consumerlaw.org** to order securely online or for more information on all NCLC publications and companion websites, including the full tables of contents, indices, and **web-based searches of the publications' full text**.

About the Companion Website, Other Search Options

The Companion Website

Purchase of any title in NCLC's consumer law practice series includes free access to its companion website. Access remains free with continued subscription to that title. Frequently updated, NCLC companion websites offer the treatises' appendices plus hundreds of additional documents in PDF and Microsoft Word formats—pleadings, forms, statutes, regulations, agency interpretations, legislative and regulatory history, and much more—all easily located with flexible, powerful search tools. Documents can be electronically searched, printed, downloaded, and copy-pasted into a word processor.

Accessing the Companion Website

One-time registration is required to access NCLC companion websites. Once registered, users logging in are granted access to all websites they are authorized to use, with only one username and password required.

Subscribers do *not* need to register more than once.[1] Subscribers purchasing additional NCLC titles are automatically given access to the new websites under their existing username and password. Registering a second time with the same registration number overrides a prior username and password.

To register, go to **www.nclc.org/webaccess**, and click "New users click here to register." Enter the Companion Website Registration Number found on the packing statement or invoice accompanying this publication.[2] Then enter the requested information and click Enter. An email address may be used for the username or a different username may be chosen.

Once registered, go to **www.nclc.org/webaccess**, enter your username and password, and select the desired companion website from the list of authorized sites.

Libraries and others subscribing to the entire 18-volume set can arrange "IP access" so that a username and password are *not* required. Email publications@nclc.org with a list or range of static IP addresses for which access should be permitted *without* the need to enter a username and password.

We encourage users who find mistakes to notify us using the "Report Errors" button, on the left toolbar. Also on the left toolbar, users can click "My Account" to change personal information.

Use of the companion websites with Internet Explorer requires Adobe Reader 7.0 or later or Adobe Acrobat 7.0 or later. Users of other browsers, or those experiencing problems with the websites, should download the latest version of the free Adobe Reader from Adobe's website at www.adobe.com. A link to Adobe's site is provided on the NCLC companion website login page.

Locating Documents on the Companion Website

The companion website provides three options to locate documents.

1. The search page (the home page) offers keyword searches to find documents—either full-text searches of all documents on the website or of only the documents' titles.

- Narrow the search to documents of a certain type (such as federal statutes or pleadings) by making a selection from the "Document Type" menu, and then perform a full text or document title search.
- If unsure of a keyword's spelling, type the first few letters and click "See choices."
- To locate a specific appendix section, select the appendix section number (e.g., A.2.3) or a partial identifier (e.g., A) in the search page's "Appendix" drop-down fields.
- Click Search Hints for a quick reference to special search operators, wildcards, shortcuts, and complex searches. Read this closely, as syntax and search operators may be slightly different from those of other websites.

---

1 If all your subscriptions to NCLC treatises are allowed to lapse, your account may be deleted; if this happens, you must re-register if you subsequently purchase a book.

2 If you cannot locate this number, contact NCLC Publications at (617) 542-9595 or publications@nclc.org.

2. The contents page (click on the "Contents" tab at the top of the page) is a traditional "branching" table of contents. Click a branch to expand it into a list of sub-branches or documents. Each document appears once on this contents tree.

3. The pleading finder page (click on the "Pleading Finder" tab at the top of the page, *if available*) allows pleadings to be located using one or more menus, such as "Type of Pleading" or "Subject." **Select more than one item from a menu, or deselect items, by holding the Ctrl key while clicking.** For example, make one selection from "Type of Pleading–General," one from "Subject," and three from "Legal Claims" to locate all pleadings of that type and subject that contain one or more of the three legal claims selected. If this search produces insufficient results, simply broaden the search by deselecting "Subject" and/or "Legal Claims" to find pleadings of that type in any subject area or based upon any legal claim. This page also includes optional fields to specify terms to be found in the documents' text or titles, to further narrow search results.

Additional software, related websites, and other information can be located by clicking on links found at the left hand toolbar or on the "Search" page. These links bring you to credit math software, search tips, other websites, tables of contents and indices of all NCLC publications, and other practice aids. Some companion websites have "Software" or "Links" tabs at the top of the page, where this material may also be found.

Finding Word Versions of Website Documents

All documents on the website are in PDF format, and can be copied and pasted into a word processor. Pleadings and certain other documents also are available in Word format, facilitating the opening of entire documents in a word processor. After opening the selected PDF file, click at the top of the page on "Word Version, if available." If a Word version is listed as available, click "DOC Download Document" to save the Word file to your computer.

Documents Found on the Website

The companion website to *Access to Utility Service* contains summaries of state utility regulations and state energy assurance programs, as well as numerous pleadings relating to utility law. The site also includes federal statutes and regulations on telecommunications, the LIHEAP program, and the Department of Energy's Weatherization Assistance Program.

Locating Topics in This Treatise

Go to www.nclc.org/keyword to electronically search the full text of every chapter and appendix of this title. While the chapters' complete text is not available online, this web-based search engine specifies each page of this title where a word or phrase is found. Select this title, enter a search term or combination of search terms—such as a case name, a regulation cite, or other keywords—and the page numbers containing those terms are listed. Search results are shown with the surrounding text ("hits in context"), facilitating selection of the most relevant pages.

Locating Topics in Other NCLC Manuals or NCLC REPORTS

The full text of all NCLC treatises and supplements, *NCLC REPORTS*, and other publications can be electronically searched to locate relevant topics as described above. Go to www.nclc.org/keyword, and enter a search term or combination of search terms in a similar fashion to performing a keyword search on one title.

Current tables of contents, indices, and other information for all NCLC titles can be found at www.nclc.org/shop. Click *Publications for Lawyers* and scroll down to the book you want. The PDF documents found there can be quickly searched for a word or phrase.

The Quick Reference at the back of this volume lets you pinpoint the correct treatise and treatise sections or appendices that discuss over 1000 different subject areas. These subject areas are listed in alphabetical order and can also be electronically searched at www.nclc.org/qr.

Finding Pleadings

Pleadings relating to this title are found in PDF and Word format on the companion website; search options are discussed above at "Locating Documents on the Website." Over 2000 pleadings are also available at NCLC's *Consumer Law Pleadings* website using the same search techniques discussed above. Pleadings can also be located using *Consumer Law Pleadings*' index guide, which organizes pleadings by type, subject area, legal claim, title, and other categories identical to those on the website.

Summary Contents

Contents

Chapter 3 Tenant Strategies for Maintaining Service

Chapter 4 Metering Issues: Metering Errors, Master-Metering, Submetering, Prepayment Meters, Advanced Meters

Chapter 5 Payment Issues: Payment, Security Deposits, and Late Charges

Chapter 10 Utility Allowances in Subsidized Housing

Part IV Issues Specific to Low-Income Telecommunications and Water

Chapter 11 Telecommunications

Part V Special Circumstances

Chapter 13 Bankruptcy Issues: When Either the Consumer or Landlord Files for Bankruptcy

Chapter 14 Manufactured Homes and Utility Service

Chapter 15 Due Process Protections for Municipal and REC Customers; Unregulated Deliverable Fuels

Appendix C The Low Income Home Energy Assistance Program (LIHEAP)

Appendix D The Department of Energy's Weatherization Assistance Program

Appendix F Utility Discount Rate Outreach and Enrollment—Sample Legislation and Other Material

Chapter 1 Introduction

1.1 About This Treatise

1.1.1 Introduction

This book takes a broad look at regulated utility companies—gas, electric, water, and telephone—and unregulated companies that deliver home energy products—propane, home heating oil, wood, coal, and kerosene—from the consumer advocate's perspective. Traditionally, many providers of natural gas, electricity, and telephone service have been closely regulated as utilities by the individual state, in terms of price, major investments in new plant, or infrastructure (to widely varying degrees in each state), and service quality. Far fewer water companies have been closely regulated because so many of them are municipally owned. State laws that regulate utilities tend not to cover municipal entities. Rural electric cooperatives also are in large part exempt from state regulation.

Most of the companies that provide "deliverable fuels," such as propane, wood, coal, kerosene, and home heating oil, are not regulated as to the prices they charge, the deposits they may seek, or the terms and conditions of service. When no extensive state regulation applies to a specific form of utility or fuel, existing consumer protection laws of more general applicability become particularly important. Due to the fundamental differences between regulated and unregulated companies and between "delivered fuels" and electricity and gas, these topics are often discussed separately throughout this book.

From the mid-1990s through the early 2000s, there was a trend in states to consider and, in many cases, adopt "deregulation" or "restructuring" of the utilities that have traditionally been closely regulated. Utility deregulation added complexity in two ways. First, there are now largely unregulated companies within the electric, gas, and telephone industries that exist side by side with (and may be corporate affiliates of) traditional regulated companies. It has become even more important to determine the exact nature of the company serving a particular customer. Second, it is harder to learn which rules or regulations apply because, despite the rhetoric of "deregulation," there may now be two sets of regulations that apply to a given industry—a set of traditional regulations that apply to the incumbent company and a new set of less detailed and less extensive regulations that apply to new competitive companies.

The recent growing awareness and concern over climate change has led to a renewed national, regional and state interest in the promotion of conservation and a movement away from fossil-fuel-dependence to an increased interest in renewable fuels. These are trends that will have a profound impact on the affordability and accessibility of essential energy and utility services for low-income consumers.

This treatise attempts, to some extent, to address these industries and issues. It examines the application of utility regulation to the consumer customer, the implications of the current trend toward deregulation, and consumer protections for all types of consumers, regardless of who is providing the utility or energy service.

1.1.2 The Structure of This Treatise

This treatise is organized into four topics: (1)getting and maintaining regulated utility service; (2)keeping utility bills affordable in private and subsidized housing; (3) issues specific to low-income telecommunications and water, and (4) special circumstances.

Chapters 2 through 6, *infra*, cover the topic of getting and maintaining regulated utility service as well as focus on electric, natural gas, water, and telecom service under the jurisdiction of the state public utility commission. Chapter 2 discusses the right to utility service. Chapter 3 explores tenant strategies for maintaining service. Chapter 4 deals with an array of metering issues. Chapter 5 focuses on payment issues, and Chapter 6 examines issues related to utility terminations and consumer protections from disconnection.

Chapters 7 through 10, *infra*, cover the topic of keeping utility bills affordable in private and subsidized housing and focus on federal, state, utility, and private programs and rules to help keep utility bills affordable. Chapter 7 examines utility affordability programs. Chapter 8 describes the federal Low Income Home Energy Assistance Program. Chapter 9 discusses low-income weatherization programs, and Chapter 10 explores utility allowances in publicly owned and subsidized housing.

Chapters 11 and 12, *infra*, cover issues specific to low-income telecommunications and water as well as additional programs and issues specific to these utilities. Chapter 11 discusses telecommunication programs and issues, and Chapter 12 explores the issue of water affordability.

Finally, Chapters 13 through 15, *infra*, cover special circumstances. Chapter 13 focuses on consumer and landlord bankruptcy issues related to utility service. Chapter 14 covers special utility issues related to manufactured housing, and Chapter 15 explores protections for consumers of municipal utility service, cooperatives, and deliverable fuels.

Certain documents are referred to in this treatise and cited by a "Clearinghouse" number. These documents may be ordered from the Sargent Shriver National Center on Poverty Law (formerly known as the National Clearinghouse for Legal Services) by calling (312) 263-3830, ext. 223, or by sending a facsimile to (312) 263-3846. Some documents may be available on the organization's website at www.povertylaw.org. Paper documents cost $10.00 per case plus actual delivery charges.

1.1.3 The Concept of the Public Utility

A "public utility" is a business:

- That is a natural monopoly, typically due to large demands for capital and other barriers to entry,[1] and
- Is affected by the public interest and of great importance to health, welfare, or the economy.[2]

"Public" utilities often are not in fact public, in the sense of being owned or operated by the public, but instead are owned by private stockholders. They are referred to as public not because of the nature of the ownership of the utility but because the utility must offer service to the public on a non-discriminatory basis. Three types of utility providers are referred to as public utilities: the private, investor-owned utility companies just mentioned; utility providers owned by a city, town, or other municipal entity; and rural electric cooperatives (also known as electric membership corporations). Public utilities typically sell gas, electricity, telephone service, or water.[3] Companies that deliver fuels such as propane or home heating oil are not public utilities.

Until recently, gas, electric, telephone, and water service were all regarded as natural monopolies. Utilities were granted a monopoly franchise to serve a particular geographic area on the premise that this would result in overall lower prices for consumers compared to situation in which several companies compete for the same set of customers. In exchange, the franchised utilities had the obligation to serve all customers in that service area. State and federal governments (and sometimes local governments) regulated these enterprises to achieve what the free market could not: the provision of adequate service at reasonable prices to anyone who demands it.[4] The entity regulating public utilities in a state is usually the Public Service Commission or Public Utilities Commission.[5]

Traditional thinking has been that too few companies would choose to compete in an unregulated utility market, resulting in a lack of effective competition over prices and terms.[6] The rationale for regulation is that, if public utilities are not regulated, the probable outcome would be a small number of enterprises (or perhaps one) would dominate the market and set prices at economically unjustified levels—the classic monopoly situation. This would happen for several reasons.

1 Indeed, public utilities are considered to be "natural monopolies" because the service required is sufficiently capital-intensive that one firm can offer it more efficiently than many competing firms. *E.g.*, Alabama Power Co. v. F.C.C., 311 F.3d 1357, 1361 (11th Cir. 2002) (discussing economies of scale and network effects); Generic Hearings Concerning Electric Rate Structure, 36 Pub. Util. Rep. 4th, at 6 (Colo. Pub. Util. Comm'n 1979); City of Calhoun v. North Ga. Elec. Membership Corp., 213 S.E.2d 596 (Ga. 1975) (public utilities often require anti-competitive practices); Weld v. Gas & Elec. Light Comm'rs, 84 N.E. 101, 197 Mass. 556, 558, 559 (1908); City of Boston v. Edison Elec. Illuminating Co., 136 N.E. 113, 242 Mass. 305, 312 (1922); Electric Indus. Restructuring, 160 Pub. Util. Rep. 4th 76, 1995 WL 125596 (Mass. Dep't of Pub. Utils. Feb. 10, 1995); State *ex rel.* Laclede Gas Co. v. Public Serv. Comm'n, 600 S.W.2d 222 (Mo. App. 1980).

2 16 U.S.C. § 824(a).

3 A few states regulate the provision of sewer service, some regulate propane to a very limited extent, and some regulate customer service aspects of cable television companies.

4 *See* Weld v. Gas & Elec. Light Comm'rs, 84 N.E. 101, 102 (Mass. 1908) ("The state, through the regularly constituted authorities, has taken complete control of these corporations so far as is necessary to prevent the abuses of monopoly.").

5 These bodies have different names in different locations. For example, Iowa has a "Utilities Board" and New Mexico has a "Public Regulation Commission." We refer to a public service commission (PSC) or a public utility commission (PUC) generically throughout this treatise, recognizing that other names may be more accurate. For contact information for each state utility commission, go to www.naruc.org and click on the "About NARUC/State Commissions" tabs.

6 There is considerable debate over how many firms in a market constitute adequate competition. *E.g.*, Bruce E. Biewald et al., New England Conference of Pub. Util. Comm'rs, Horizontal Market Power in New England Electricity Markets (1997); J. Kennedy & Assoc., Inc., Office of Pub. Util. Counsel of Tex., Electric Utility Restructuring Issues for ERCOT: Prices, Market Power and Market Structure (1996); Maine Dep't of the Att'y Gen. et al., Market Power in Electricity (1998); William G. Shepherd, *Contestability v. Competition—Once More*, 71 Land Economics 299 (1995); Harry M. Trebing, *Structural Change and the Future of Regulation*, 71 Land Economics 401 (1995).

For example, many observers think that the long-distance telephone market, with its four dominant participants, is not competitive although it is no longer fully treated as a public utility industry. *E.g.*, Harry M. Trebing, Regulatory Assistance Project, Concentration and the Sustainability of Market Power in Public Utility Industries (Mar. 1998).

For one, a plant which produces and supplies a public utility service requires a large amount of fixed equipment and investment before it can begin operating.[7] Only entities with sufficient financial resources can seriously consider entering a public utility business. Because of the large "start-up" expense involved, enterprises have an incentive to recoup costs by maximizing revenue as quickly as possible. Once one company is established and signs up a large number of customers in a given area, it becomes extremely difficult if not impossible for other companies to enter the field. The first company, or the first few companies, quickly dominate the market and set prices at will.

Furthermore, public utilities are considered to be natural monopolies, that is, they return substantial economies of scale. At the outset of the development of the electric, gas, and telephone industries and for decades thereafter, prices declined as the number of customers grew. An unregulated utility would not only be able to recoup its initial investment quickly, but it would also be able to set prices at whatever levels it saw as optimal. Regulation is desirable in these industries as it allows the capture of large economies of scale, but it prevents price-setting at levels above what is fair and reasonable.[8]

Another characteristic that distinguishes public utilities from their unregulated counterparts is the need for "unused capacity,"[9] which in many other industries would be considered unproductive excess capacity. Most utility services—such as communications and electricity—cannot be economically stored. Yet consumers expect and require that these services will be available whenever they wish to use them. Consequently, while other types of companies would simply be able to turn customers away (think of the convenience store that runs out of ice on a hot summer day), public utility facilities must be constructed with excess capacity so as to accommodate peak demands for service. However, periods of peak demand may exist for only a few hours or a few months. At other times, the utility has no use for the capacity it maintains to serve peak demand but is required to have that excess capacity available.

Furthermore, to keep prices reasonable, most utilities do not charge customers the full cost of using energy or services at peak times.[10] In an unregulated environment, firms do not allow this. They may allow shortages in the short run and, in the longer run, raise prices to balance demand with supply. They also discriminate among customers, segmenting the market by charging less to those that are more responsive to price (such as leisure air travelers, who can choose not to travel if the price is too high) in order to fill excess capacity. Thus, some consumers are required to pay higher rates than others. Because of the importance of public utility services to the public welfare and the economy, and the lack of price discipline from competition, the goal of public policy has been to prevent shortages, to outlaw unreasonable prices, and to prohibit discrimination.[11]

Public utilities differ from other providers of necessities—food, shelter, and clothing for instance—in how they relate to the individual consumer as well.[12] For one, most consumer demand for public utility services is relatively inelastic. Because these commodities are indispensable, price increases or decreases have relatively little impact upon consumer demand. This phenomenon, of course, stands in marked contrast to almost all other goods and services the changes in price of which influence consumer purchase patterns. Even when necessities are involved, consumers will choose cheaper cuts of meat or smaller apartments in response to price increases; such choices are more difficult to make in the purchase of utility services. Although recent rate increases have demonstrated that consumer demand for the services of public utilities is not as inelastic as once thought, clearly, consumers will reduce spending on other items before they reduce spending on their heating and water service.[13] Studies have shown that low-income fami-

7 *See generally* Thomas Morgan, James Harrison, & Paul Verkuil, Economic Regulation of Business: Cases and Materials 15–22 (2d ed. 1985).

8 James C. Bonbright, Principles of Public Utility Rates 10 (1961).

Under the typical scenario, a public utility would have to obtain a franchise or certificate of public convenience and necessity from the appropriate authorities prior to entering the market. Once operational, the enterprise would have to supply a minimum level and quality of service to its customers (see discussion of the duties of public utilities below). In addition, the utility would also have to seek permission before ceasing operations and abandoning service.

9 Charles F. Phillips, The Regulation of Public Utilities: Theory and Practice 55, 56 (1993).

10 Some utilities vary price by time of day or season of the year (for example, some gas companies have higher base rates in the winter heating season and flow through the actual cost of procuring gas; some electric companies charge more during the summer months or during peak day-time hours) but, in general, prices are based on average cost for most residential customers.

11 As described in §§ 1.1.4, 1.2.1.3 and 1.2.2.3, *infra*, many legislators and regulators believe that there can be sufficient competition in the generation sector of the electricity market if the monopoly franchise is eliminated and that the resulting competition could discipline prices with little or no regulation. This model of the electric industry leaves unanswered serious questions about which entities or institutions would make sure that there is an adequate supply of electricity at times of peak demand. This model also opens up the possibility of price discrimination against, for example, residential customers, customers with bad credit histories, and those living in remote areas.

12 Charles F. Phillips, The Regulation of Public Utilities: Theory and Practice 57 (1993).

13 However, a study by the National Consumer Law Center found that income *is* an indicator of energy use. Low-income households uniformly use less energy than their average-income neighbors. National Consumer Law Center, Energy and the Poor—The Crisis Continues (1995).

During the summer of 2001, California disproved the conventional wisdom that consumers will not significantly reduce

lies reduce their food expenditures and cut back on other necessities in order to pay higher energy bills during cold winter months.[14]

1.1.4 "Restructuring" and "Deregulation"

Many utility companies and their industries have undergone fundamental changes in organizational and regulatory structure. Once typified by regulatory oversight and protection, utility investment and pricing decision, particularly at the wholesale level, are increasingly guided by market forces and competition. As described more fully in this chapter, utility industry "restructuring" or "deregulation" changes the ways in which utility companies are organized and operated and ways in which customers receive utility service.

At the wholesale level, restructuring involves implementation of what has come to be referred to as "open access," through which natural gas pipeline owners and electricity transmission line owners are required by statute and Federal Energy Regulatory Commission Order to provide access to "transportation" facilities at a fair price. Thus, natural gas producers and electric utility generators are now allowed to compete at the wholesale level without being constrained by discriminatory pricing behavior of pipeline and transmission line owners.

"Electric industry restructuring" generally describes any one of a number of ways of introducing competition between independent power producers and existing monopoly utilities to sell power to retail customers. The key here is the concept of retail competition. Currently, sixteen states plus the District of Columbia have embraced electric restructuring. It is important to note that rapidly-increasing prices, concerns about system reliability, and failure of deregulation to provide customers with viable supplier options prompted legislators in eight states that had initially adopted deregulation to suspend or repeal the legislation.[15]

Since the turn of the century, as the electric industry has evolved, a majority of areas in the country have had a single entity with a monopoly on sales to provide service to retail customers. That entity might be an investor-owned utility (IOU), a municipal utility, or a rural electric cooperative. With the advent of restructuring, those states now allow competitive suppliers to sell electricity directly to retail customers. In such cases, the traditional, "vertically integrated" electric utility structure—in which a single company owns generation, transmission and retail distribution resources—is fundamentally altered. Under restructuring, a company's generation supply resources are sold off or otherwise separated from other company operations and customers are allowed to purchase power from competing suppliers. While state regulatory oversight of distribution functions (for example, maintenance of poles and wires, provision of customer service, metering, and billing) continue, the role played by state regulatory commissions in overseeing retail price of power supply has been drastically diminished.

Thus, under restructuring, customers either take power from an unregulated competitive supplier or through some form of standard or "provider of last resort" service offered by the regulated utility distribution company. Distribution companies meet the energy and peak demand requirements of their standard service customers usually through short-term wholesale market purchases and pass the costs of this procured power along to consumers.

This "market-based" approach to providing retail customers with electricity service subjects customers to the volatility of short-term wholesale market prices. In addition, the approach fails to provide a vast majority of retail customers with the benefits and stability otherwise achievable through asset management, identification of all available supply- and demand-side options to meet customer

their consumption during peak periods (for example, hot summer or cold winter days) even in response to high prices. Faced with skyrocketing prices resulting from the restructuring of its energy markets and from market manipulation by energy traders such as Enron, California funded and launched an emergency conservation program. In the peak month of June 2001, California reduced consumption by 14% compared to June 2000 after adjusting for changes in weather and employment. For the 2001 four-month summer period, consumption was 10% below the same period for 2000. For a further discussion of California's experience and how it could apply to New York's power markets, see C. Komanoff, Riverkeeper/Pace Law Sch./NRDC, Securing Power Through Energy Conservation and Efficiency—Profiting from California's Experience, (May 2002), *available at* www.riverkeeper.org/new/indianpoint/5.7.02Komanoff.doc.

14 *See, e.g.*, Jay Bhattacharya, Thomas DeLeire, Steven Haider & Janet Currie, National Bureau of Econ. Res., Heat or Eat? Cold-Weather Shocks and Nutrition in Poor American Families (June 2002), *available at* www.nber.org/papers/w9004; Deborah A. Frank, M.D., et al., *Heat or Eat: The Low Income Home Energy Assistance Program and Nutritional and Health Risks Among Children Less Than 3 years of Age*, 118 AAP Pediatrics, no.5, at e1293–e1302 (Nov. 2006). *See also* Child Health Impact Working Group, Unhealthy Consequences: Energy Costs and Child Health: A Child Health Impact Assessment of Energy Costs and the Low Income Home Energy Assistance Program (Nov. 2006); *The Climbing Cost of Heating Homes: Why LIHEAP Is Essential: Hearing Before the Senate Comm. on Health, Educ., Labor and Pensions Subcomm. on Children and Families* (Mar. 5, 2008) (statement of Dr. Elizabeth Frank, Director, Grow Clinic for Children at Boston Medical Center), *available at* www.childrenshealthwatch.org/page/Testimony; Mark Nord & Linda S. Kantor, *Seasonal Variation in Food Insecurity Is Associated with Heating and Cooling Costs Among Low-Income Elderly Americans*, J. of Nutrition 2939–2944 (Nov. 2006); National Energy Assistance Directors' Ass'n, National Energy Assistance Survey, *available at* www.neada.org (periodic survey of LIHEAP recipients).

15 *See* www.eia.doe.gov/cneaf/electricity/page/restructuring/restructure_elect.html (map and table summarizing the status of restructuring in each state).

requirements, and the procurement of a portfolio of resources that best meets a defined set of policy and pricing objectives.[16]

In a majority of the states that approved electric utility restructuring, only a small fraction of residential customers received electric supply from a competitive supplier that is lower priced than that provided through the local distribution companies. As a result, in a majority of the deregulated states, the "migration" rate of customers to competitors is very low.[17]

Electric deregulation has in fact not provided long-term rate reduction benefits in any of the states that have adopted deregulation legislation.[18] In addition, many of the states that adopted electric industry restructuring provisions imposed temporary rate caps or freezes to be in effect during the transition to a competitive pricing structure. However, there have been major retail electricity price spikes in states as price caps have expired. Furthermore, with the failure of competition to develop at the wholesale or retail levels, the hoped-for downward turn of retail prices after expiration of transitional price caps has not materialized. In Illinois, when rate caps expired for Commonwealth Edison customers January 2007, residential rates increased by over 22%. Bills for some Ameren residential customers in Illinois rose by as much as 170%. In Texas, after 2002, "prices to beat" offered by incumbent utilities' increased from 67% to 114% depending on the service territory.[19]

1.2 Types of Regulated Utilities

1.2.1 Natural Gas

1.2.1.1 Delivery of Natural Gas to the Consumer

As a source of domestic energy which pre-dates electricity, natural gas has historically been viewed as an economically significant commodity that, in view of the public welfare, has required some form of public control.[20] Today, it is an undeniable fixture on the American energy landscape: natural gas is transported to every area of the country and accounts for about one-quarter of the country's total energy consumption.[21] There are some 1400 local gas distribution companies that collectively serve almost 60 million residential customers.

When consumers adjust the thermostat to help heat their home, they are performing the final act in a continuous chain of economic transactions. The gas service which they enjoy typically has been transported over hundreds and even thousands of miles from its point of origin. First, the gas is gathered in the field, typically in Canada or in a state in the Southwest or Mountain State area. Then it is sold and transported by pipelines to the consumer markets. Finally, the local distribution companies who receive the gas from the pipelines make it available to the public.

Numbering more than 6000, natural gas producers look for and harvest the resource and subsequently sell it to their pipeline customers. In large measure, they are not regulated as public utilities and are generally free to charge whatever prices they feel the market will bear.[22]

The almost one hundred interstate pipelines that purchase gas from producers have historically been the most significant entities within the natural gas industry and the most heavily regulated. Those companies whose transmission contracts cross state lines have been subject to regulation by the federal government. These pipelines (approximately 70), which have operated exclusively intra-state have had to answer to state authorities (with some exceptions). The economic importance of pipelines is derived from the fact that, for over a half century, they have acted in a dual capacity as both sellers and the exclusive transporters of gas. Therefore, if a local gas distribution utility (LDC or local distribution company) wishes to buy gas so that it can supply its residential and business customers, it has no choice but to purchase the gas from a pipeline. Only pipelines have the means and facilities to buy gas from producers and, once they do so, will not transport gas for anyone who did not buy the gas from them. Several recent developments in natural gas regulatory policy have permanently

16 *See* Barbara R. Alexander, U.S. Dep't of Health & Human Servs., Default Service for Retail Electric Competition: Can Residential and Low Income Customers be Protected When the Experiment Goes Awry (Apr. 2002) (full discussion of "portfolio management" and procurement electricity resources for residential electricity customers in states that adopted restructuring), *available at* http://liheap.ncat.org/pubs/barbadefault3.doc.

17 Seth A. Blumsack, Jay Apt, & Lester B. Lave, Lessons from the Failure of U.S. Electricity Restructuring, Electricity J. 15–32 (Mar. 2006).

18 Seth A. Blumsack, Jay Apt, & Lester B. Lave, Lessons from the Failure of U.S. Electricity Restructuring, Electricity J. 15–32 (Mar. 2006).

19 Nancy Brockway, Delaware's Electricity Future: Re-Regulation Options and Impacts, Presented to the Delaware Office and Management and Budget and the Controller General (May 2007), *available at* www.dnrec.delaware.gov (enter "Nancy Brockway" in search box at top left-hand corner of webpage; then click on appropriate link).

20 *E.g.*, Natural Gas Act, 15 U.S.C. §§ 717–717z.

21 Natural gas has provided 22%–24% of the nation's total primary energy since 1953, except when it provided 25%–33% in the period 1957–1984. U.S. Energy Info. Admin., Annual Energy Review database.

22 After a Supreme Court decision in Phillips Petroleum Co. v. Wisconsin, 347 U.S. 672 (1954), which held that producers should be regulated, Congress later passed legislation that overturned the decision. Natural Gas Policy Act of 1978, 15 U.S.C. §§ 3301–3432. *See* Pennzoil Co. v. Federal Energy Regulator Comm'n, 645 F.2d 360 (5th Cir. 1981).

Given the large numbers of producers, few dispute that they operate under very competitive conditions and thus do not require regulation as public utilities.

changed this dynamic and, as a result, new challenges have arisen for residential customers.

Natural gas is received from pipelines by LDCs that then resell it within their service territories. As the vast majority of the 1400 LDCs operate within state boundaries, they are overseen by state utility commissions.[23] These are the companies with which a residential consumer of natural gas must do business.

1.2.1.2 Regulation

Every state and the District of Columbia regulates gas utilities—both LDCs and intrastate pipelines—to some degree.[24] The Federal Energy Regulatory Commission (FERC) regulates wholesale transactions, that is, transactions between pipeline and producer as well as between pipeline and local distribution company.[25]

Although there are individual differences, state public utility commissions (PUCs) generally regulate rates of the regulated portion of a customer's bill, customer service and termination policies and practices, issue certificates of public convenience and necessity for entities that wish to construct facilities and commence service within their respective geographic areas of jurisdiction, and grant permission to intrastate pipelines and local distribution companies to abandon service. Unlike other utility services, there are close substitutes for natural gas (for example, oil and propane for heating, electricity for cooking) so utilities are not required to serve parts of their service territory if they find it uneconomical to do so.[26] To enforce the common law public utility duty to charge "just and reasonable" prices, most state commissions also have the authority to set rates, to require prior notice of any proposed rate changes, to suspend proposed rates, and to launch inquiries into unreasonable proposed rate hikes. As part of their mandate to ensure just and reasonable rates, PUCs will also require the pipelines and LDCs within their reach to provide service in a non-discriminatory manner. Thus, arbitrary classifications among customer groups are subject to challenge.

23 Frank Lindh, Federal Preemption of State Regulation in the Field of Electricity and Natural Gas: A Supreme Court Chronicle, 10 Energy L.J. 277, 306–09 (1989).

24 National Ass'n of Regulatory Util. Comm'rs, Profiles of Regulatory Agencies of the United States and Canada, Yearbook, 1994, 1995 (1995).

Texas was the last to do so. Gas Util. Regulatory Act, Tex. Util. § 102.001 (2003).

25 Natural Gas Act, 15 U.S.C. §§ 717–717z.

26 Many LDCs, however, have tariff provisions or written "line extension policies" that describe at which locations or in which areas the company will provide service to new customers at no installation charge. These tariff provisions or policies may also specify, in more or less detail, the costs of bringing gas service to areas near, but not yet connected to, the company's existing service mains.

1.2.1.3 Gas Restructuring and Impacts on Residential Customers

Culminating with its Order No. 636 issued in April 1992,[27] the FERC instituted a decade-and-a-half-wide-scale deregulation of the interstate pipeline system. In the simplest terms, pipelines have been forced to surrender their traditional monopoly over natural gas sales. Whereas pipeline owners were once able to deny access to other parties who wished to use the pipelines, buy gas from producing well fields or sell gas to end-users, now pipeline owners must provide "open-access" transportation to whomever requests it.

Thus, instead of depending upon the pipeline for both the transportation *and sale* of gas, an LDC, a gas marketer or broker, or a large industrial end-user is only dependent upon the pipeline for transportation. These parties can contract directly with the producer for the sale of its gas and then hire a pipeline to transport the purchased gas to where it is needed.[28]

Residential and small commercial customers may also be able to arrange for a supply of gas directly with a seller, marketer or broker unaffiliated with the LDC. However, less than a majority of states have full "retail access," that is, allowing smaller customers to purchase gas directly and by-pass the LDC.[29] In addition, even in those states that legally allow retail access, there may not be sellers or marketers interested in dealing with small customers.

In creating this regulatory environment in which pipeline customers can "bypass" pipeline facilities to meet their supply needs, the FERC has placed public utility commissions and the consumers that PUCs seek to protect in a tenuous position. Many LDCs have large industrial plants and factories as customers. These customers typically have the resources to either bypass the LDC and construct their own pipeline "spur" to the interstate pipeline or to switch back and forth among energy sources altogether (that is, switch from gas to petroleum or coal depending upon which is cheaper). Most residential consumers, by contrast, do not have these options and are thus captive customers of the LDCs. LDCs typically spread their large, fixed costs (the cost of distribution lines, valves, maintenance equipment, administrative overhead, and so forth) throughout their cus-

27 Order, Regulation of Natural Gas Pipelines After Partial Wellhead Decontrol, 57 Fed. Reg. 13267, FERC Statutes and Regulations ¶ 30,939 (1992) (No. RM87-34-000; Order 636).

28 Charles F. Phillips, The Regulation of Public Utilities: Theory and Practice 711–15 (1993).

In theory, smaller customers can also contract directly with a producer to purchase gas, but this rarely happens.

29 According to the Energy Information Administration, twenty-one states and the District of Columbia had natural gas retail access for residential customers as of December 2007. Energy Info. Admin., What Are Natural Gas Customer Choice Programs?, *at* http://tonto.eia.doe.gov/energy_in_brief/natural_gas_customer_choice.cfm.

tomer base, so any decrease in this base creates pressure to raise rates on remaining customers.[30] Typically, these customers will largely be residential consumers, many of whom do not have the means to easily absorb any rate increases.[31]

1.2.2 Electricity

1.2.2.1 The Electric Power Industry

Virtually every household in America is connected to the electric utility grid. The industry serves almost 125 million residential and 17.5 million commercial customers.[32] Utilities historically generated (or purchased from an affiliate) almost all of the power needed to serve their customers; distributed that electricity over company-owned lines; and performed all related billing and customer service functions. They are therefore often described as "vertically integrated" entities: entities that combine the generation, transmission/distribution, and customer/billing functions in one company.

Electric companies have been subject to regulatory control because they have been considered to be natural monopolies that render a vital service to the public. They received exclusive franchises to operate within a specified territory and the opportunity to earn a reasonable return on invested capital, in exchange for having the obligation to serve all customers without discrimination. However, since the late 1990s, many states have completely or partially severed the generation function from the distribution and billing/customer service functions. Independent generation companies, as well as independent marketers and brokers, may now sell electricity directly to consumer end-users in many states.

The types of organizations that provide electricity to consumers fall into one of three broad categories: investor-owned utilities, publicly owned utilities, and member-owned cooperatives.[33] As policy changes of the last twenty years encouraged the development of non-utility generators, their numbers and the percentage they own of the nation's generating capacity has increased. From 3.5% of total generation in 1978, non-utilities have grown to 30% of generation in 2000.[34] This trend will accelerate as restructured utilities divest their generation capacity, often to non-utility purchasers.

As of 2007, there were more than 3273 electric utilities in the United States, 210 of which are investor-owned utilities (IOUs).[35] These IOUs own over 38% of the nation's generation capacity, own 42% of generation, and serve 71% of ultimate customers.[36] The vast majority of electric utilities neither generate nor transmit electricity on their own and, instead, they purchase electricity at wholesale for distribution to their retail customers. More common now among publicly owned utilities, it will become increasingly true of investor-owned utilities as well.

The 3273 utilities consist of the 210 IOUs mentioned, 2009 publicly owned utilities, and 883 rural electric cooperatives. (There are also nine federal marketing agencies that primarily sell at wholesale to other utilities, but not to end-users, and control approximately 11% of generating capacity.) Of the three categories that sell to end-users, IOUs are the largest sector financially. Despite representing less than 6% of the number of all electric utilities, they possess over one-third of utility-owned generating capacity.[37] IOUs also receive three-quarters of all of the electricity revenues paid by all customers. Publicly owned utilities, which include public power districts, state agencies, and municipal enterprises, constitute roughly two-thirds of the number of all electric utilities but control only 9% of the utility-owned generating capability and receive 13% of total annual electric revenues. Rural electric cooperatives have only 4% of the nation's generation and capacity and obtain 10% of total electric revenues.[38]

1.2.2.2 Regulation

The electric power industry is overseen by independent federal and state regulatory commissions. At the wholesale level, the Federal Energy Regulatory Commission (FERC) has jurisdiction.[39] For retail sales to end-users, individual state public utility commissions (PUCs) determine policy.

30 Harry G. Broadman & Joseph P. Kalt, *How Natural Is Monopoly? The Case of Bypass in Natural Gas Distribution Markets*, 6 Yale J. on Reg. 181, 185–86 (1989). The increase in gas prices for the individual customer can be considerable.

31 This is not as far-fetched as it sounds. In Panhandle E. Pipeline Co., 38 F.E.R.C. ¶ 63,009 at 65,039 (1987), an LDC allocated to its remaining captive users a $51 million loss that was due to a bypass.

32 U.S. Energy Info. Admin., Electricity, Summary Statistics for the United States, tbl. ES1, www.eia.gov/cneaf/electricity/epa/epates.html.

33 *See* § 1.1.3, *supra*.

34 U.S. Energy Info. Admin., Generation and Consumption of Fuels for Electric Generation (May 2003), *at* www.eia.doe.gov/cneaf/electricity/epm/epm_sum.html.

These non-utility generators are not bound by the statutory and common-law duties that govern their regulated counterparts and are in large part operated just like any other private business.

35 U.S. Energy Info. Admin., Electricity Power Industry Overview 2007, *available at* www.eia.doe.gov/cneaf/electricity/page/prim2/toc2.html.

36 *Id.*

37 *Id.*

38 *Id.*

39 The FERC is responsible for regulating non-federal hydroelectric projects on federal waterways and the interstate transmission and sale at wholesale of electricity. Federal Power Act, 16 U.S.C. §§ 797–823d, 824 (regulation of electricity and hydroelectric resources, respectively). *See* Charles F. Phillips, The Regulation of Public Utilities: Theory and Practice 644 (1993).

Most transmission is thus FERC-regulated. However, transmission within Texas is intrastate and thus outside FERC jurisdiction. For a discussion of the need for interstate and intrastate jurisdictional entities to be treated separately for rate purposes,

Although the federal-state dichotomy sharply delineates their powers, the state and federal commissions all follow the classic public utility paradigm in their regulatory approaches.

With the exception of Nebraska, every state and the District of Columbia regulates electricity distribution.[40] State PUCs are generally responsible for issuing licenses or certificates of public convenience and necessity to generation and transmission plants and for granting permission to power companies to abandon service. State commissions also have the authority to set rates, to require prior notice of any proposed rate changes, to suspend proposed rates, and to launch inquiries into unreasonable rate hikes.

In exchange for their monopoly franchises, electric utilities agree to be held accountable to state PUCs representing the interests of ratepayers. PUCs also require the power companies within their reach to provide service in a nondiscriminatory manner. Thus, any arbitrary classification among customer groups is subject to challenge. PUCs set billing, credit, and termination rules and hear consumer complaints in "shut-off" and other cases.[41]

State PUCs have broad authority.[42] Their commissioners may be appointed by the governor or elected by the public, depending on the state. Commissions carry out varying roles ranging from the quasi-judicial to administrative. For example, by conducting an administrative rule-making proceeding, a commission may adopt detailed safety or service standards that the legislature has mandated be adopted. While the commission may allow the public an opportunity to submit comments, it most likely will not allow formal testimony or formally accept evidence. In this capacity, the commission is carrying out an administrative role. However, when the commission sets rates for a particular company, it will almost always hear witnesses, allow cross-examination, accept written documents into evidence, and allow parties to file briefs. Rate-setting hearings are quasi-judicial in that the procedures are similar to a court proceeding. A party that feels harmed by the decision may be able to appeal the decision to a court. Commissions may also adjudicate individual disputes between customers and the companies providing service. PUCs exercise broad discretionary authority over the public utilities that they regulate, but often subject to established rules and procedures.[43]

A significant exception to the PUC regulation of electric utilities is the regulation of rural electric cooperatives. These are primarily self-regulated and are discussed in more detail in this section and at §§ 1.1, *supra*, and 1.3, *infra*.

1.2.2.3 Electric Restructuring and Deregulation

1.2.2.3.1 Restructuring; reliability issues

Electric utility "restructuring" refers to "unbundling" (separation) of the package of supply, transportation, and distribution services traditionally offered by utility companies. The traditional utility company typically owned or controlled generating facilities, high voltage transmission facilities, and the wires, meters, billing, and customer service capabilities that together comprise distribution service. Under restructuring at the retail level, utility companies typically sell off or otherwise functionally separate generating and transmission assets from the distribution function and continue to provide distribution services under the regulatory oversight of the state utility commission.[44]

Congress started the competitive ball rolling in the electric utility industry with the Public Utility Regulatory Policies Act (PURPA) of 1978,[45] which required utilities to purchase wholesale power from certain non-utility power producers.[46] Congress extended wholesale competition with the Energy Policy Act (EPACT) of 1992,[47] which authorized FERC to require wholesale wheeling[48] so competitive

---

see Smyth v. Ames, 169 U.S. 466, 18 S. Ct. 418, 42 L. Ed. 819 (1898), *modified on other grounds*, 171 U.S. 361 (1898).

40 National Ass'n of Reg'l Util. Comm'rs, Profiles of Regulatory Agencies of the United States and Canada, Yearbook, 1991–92, at 352–56 (1992).

All generation and distribution facilities in Nebraska are government-owned. *See* Neb. Rev. Stat. §§ 70-681, 70-1001 to 70-1027, 70-1401 to 70-1423; Sioux City Foundry v. Southern Sioux City, 968 F.2d 777, 781 (8th Cir. 1992) (Nebraska is a public power State).

41 *See* appx. A.1, *infra* (summary of the billing, credit, and termination regulations of a number of states).

42 PUCs are strong players within the state regulatory scene. Their national body, the National Association of Regulatory Commissioners (NARUC), exerts much influence upon the nation's regulatory policies. *See* Charles Stalon & Reinier Lock, *State-Federal Relation in the Economic Regulation of Energy*, 7 Yale J. on Reg. 427, 440 (1990).

43 Proceedings before regulatory agencies may be subject to general provisions of the federal administrative procedure acts, 5 U.S.C. §§ 551–559, or comparable state administrative procedure acts, for example, Mass. Gen. Laws ch. 30A, as well as to federal and state laws governing the particular type of utility proceeding, for example, 16 U.S.C. § 825g (hearings before the Federal Energy Regulatory Commission) and Mass. Gen. Laws ch. 164, § 94G (fuel charge clause hearings). *See* Charles F. Phillips, The Regulation of Public Utilities: Theory and Practice 152, 153 (1993).

44 For the status of the state electric industry restructuring activity, go to www.eia.doe.gov/cneaf/electricity/page/restructuring/restructure_elect.html (status of electricity restructuring by state).

45 16 U.S.C. §§ 2601–2603.

46 Utilities were required to purchase at prices at or below the price at which they could provide power for themselves (known as "avoided cost"). Qualifying Facilities (QFs) included renewables and co-generators meeting defined characteristics. Some states expanded the requirement to include other independent power producers (IPPs, also known as non-utility generators or NUGs). *See, e.g.*, Investigation of the Commission on Its Own Motion, D.P.U. 89-239 (Mass. Dep't of Pub. Util. Nov. 1990).

47 Pub. L. No. 102-486, 102 Stat. 2776 (1988).

48 Wholesale wheeling is the transmission of power from a seller (for example, an IPP or utility) to a buyer using the transmission

generators would not be locked in without a way to transmit their power to their customers. Now, alternative wholesale power producers may sell power to utilities, who in turn resell it to their retail customers along with power that the utilities generate themselves or buy from other utilities.

Prior to deregulation, no entity other than the LDC could sell power directly to retail customers in a given utility's service territory. Restructuring has changed that. In over dozen states, customers can, at least as a matter of law, purchase their power supply from generating companies that are not LDCs or from brokers or marketers acting as middlemen between a generator and the consumer. However, virtually all customers except the very largest industrial customers will still rely on the LDC to distribute that electricity to the customer's premises and to carry out related tasks such as billing and customer service.[49] Furthermore, in many states that legally allow competitive suppliers to sell to consumers, there have been few companies actually willing to sell to residential customers.

As noted, retail competition is now permitted in many states, and customers may buy directly from competitive suppliers. In many of those states, commissions have developed extensive rules and practices regarding the enrollment and billing of customers who choose competitive supply as well as the licensing of competitive suppliers. Those rules and practices address everything from the minutiae of the type of information the customer or competitive supplier must provide the LDC to effectuate a switch in generation supply (much like telephone consumers or their long-distance providers must inform the local telephone company of a change in long-distance carriers), to rules prohibiting "slamming" (unauthorized switching of a customer's competitive supplier), to rules for the billing of charges that a customer incurs with a competitive supplier.[50]

FERC implemented EPACT's wholesale wheeling mandate in its Order 888[51] by requiring utilities to open access to their transmission lines while guaranteeing utilities recovery of prudent costs associated with customers who take advantage of the opportunity to switch suppliers ("stranded costs"). In a related order,[52] FERC imposed standards of conduct to inhibit anti-competitive support of a utility's wholesale power business by its still-regulated transmission business.

These efforts to promote competition among generators, both utility and non-utility, have been promoted as resulting in lower rates for consumers. However, the impact of deregulation on prices, while difficult to measure, has not been demonstrated to be positive. Investment in deregulated generation, without the protections provided by regulatory pre-approval and oversight, has been typified by increased capital costs that lead to higher consumer prices. In addition, "market clearing prices" that flow through to consumers as a result of structures implemented by regional transmission operators such as ISO New England often are much higher than generators' actual costs.

Much of the discussion around "restructuring" in the utility industry refers to changes in the legal structures that support regulation of utility companies: the state laws and commission regulations or decisions allowing for competitive companies to sell electricity and requiring local distribution companies (LDCs) to sell off their own generating assets. However, there has already been a de facto restructuring of the electric industry underway for more than a decade, reflected in significantly reduced staffing levels, cutbacks in maintenance programs, and other efforts to reduce costs and increase profits. In several instances, the operational restructuring has directly affected the reliability of the system.

Between 1986 and 1998, employment at major investor-owned utilities dropped more than one-third, from just under 520,000 to 340,000 employees.[53] Staffing cutbacks went hand-in-hand with cutbacks in scheduled maintenance, routine repairs of damaged equipment, and replacement of obsolete infrastructure. The results have been distribution-related outages of unprecedented scope. Historically, most large-scale outages were caused by the loss of major transmission lines, the lack of adequate generating capacity on peak summer days, and other generation-related problems. For example, the Great Northeast Blackout of 1965 started with the loss of a transmission line on the New York-Canadian border that eventually caused generators across the northeast to go offline, leaving 30 million customers without power for up to thirteen hours.[54]

---

lines of a party that is neither the seller nor buyer. Prior to EPACT, transmission-owning utilities could block sales by independent generators who did not themselves own transmission lines.

49 *See* www.eia.doe.gov/cneaf/electricity/page/prim2/toc2.html.

The fourteen states in which electric utility customers can choose an alternative supplier if it serves the customer's area are Connecticut, Delaware, the District of Columbia, Illinois, Maine, Maryland, Massachusetts, Michigan, New Hampshire, New Jersey, New York, Ohio, Pennsylvania, Rhode Island, and Texas.

50 *See, e.g.*, 220 Mass. Code Regs. § 11.05 ("Competitive Supplier and Electricity Broker Requirements"); Model Terms and Conditions Governing the Relationship Between Electric Utility Distribution Companies, 182 Pub. Util. Rep. 4th 487, 1997 WL 868766 (Mass. Dep't of Telecomms. & Energy Dec. 31, 1997) (Mass. D.T.E. 97-65). *See also* 940 Mass. Code Regs. §§ 19.01–19.07 (Massachusetts attorney general's regulations on retail Marketing and sale of electricity).

51 168 Pub. Util. Rep. 4th 590, 1996 WL 295164 (Fed. Energy Regulatory Comm'n Apr. 24, 1996), *published at* 61 Fed. Reg. 21540 (May 10, 1996) (FERC final rule).

52 Order, Util. L. Rep. P5871, 1996 WL 355534 , No. RM-95-9-000 (Fed. Energy Regulatory Comm'n Apr. 24, 1996), *published at* 61 Fed. Reg. 21737 (May 10, 1996) (FERC final rule).

53 U.S. Energy Info. Admin., The Restructuring of the Electric Power Industry: A Capsule of Issues and Events, DOE/EIA-X037, at 22 (2000).

54 For a brief summary of the great Northeast blackout of 1965 (based on a presentation made by Central Maine Power Com-

The disinvestment in utility infrastructure that occurred during the 1990s resulted in outages that had nothing to do with loss of generating capacity but with the failure of local distribution cables and substations. During the summer of 1999, major outages hit New England, New York City, Long Island, New Jersey, Chicago, and other areas around the country. Investigations by the Department of Energy, the Attorney General of New York, and even some of the utilities involved all identified the failure to conduct routine maintenance and repairs as one of the major causes of these outages.[55] Quite apart from any changes in the laws governing utilities, therefore, the de facto restructuring of the utilities industry, with its emphasis on cutting costs and increasing profits, threatens the reliability of electric supply.[56] In addition, restructuring has been criticized for failing to result in cost-savings for the consumer. A new trend appears to be emerging in which states that have restructured are suspending retail competition (for example, Arkansas, Arizona, California, Montana, Nevada, New Mexico, and Oregon) or have passed legislation that allows the electric utility to once again build their own generation capacity (Delaware, Illinois, and Ohio).[57]

States must establish service quality standards for reliability, telephone response, billing, and a range of other measures to ensure that service after the advent of competition is not degraded from the level established prior to restructuring. No customer should be required to accept a standard of service below that which the customer enjoys under the current system.[58]

1.2.2.3.2 *Customer service, low-income rates, and energy efficiency*

Utilities are corporations. Like other corporations, they cut costs where they can. But restructuring creates new incentives for cost-cutting by introducing the reality or threat of competition and, in some states, by imposing "performance based regulation" schemes that allow companies to capture as profits any cost reductions achieved. Common cost-cutting targets include walk-in customer service offices—often utilized by seniors, immigrants, and others uncomfortable with automated telephone answering systems—and customer service representatives, who help low-income people craft payment arrangements.[59] Companies also cut routine maintenance operations such as tree trimming, inspections of cables, and cleaning of substations.[60]

Most states have statutes and regulations that apply to billing and terminations by local distribution companies (LDCs). These protections do not necessarily apply to competitive suppliers. Some states have chosen to close this regulatory loophole by subjecting all participants in the marketplace, generation suppliers as well as utilities, to similar sets of rules.[61]

Restructuring has allowed the emergence of new players—competitive suppliers, energy marketers and brokers—in the utility marketplace and new business arrangements not previously encountered by regulators. This in turn makes new protections necessary in the following areas:

- The sharing of customer information without specific consent.[62]

---

pany to the IEEE Maine Section), see www.rense.com/general40/95.htm.

55 *See* U.S. Dep't of Energy, Power Outage Study Team, Findings and Recommendations to Enhance Reliability from the Summer of 1999 (Mar. 2000), *available at* http://certs.lbl.gov/pdf/post-final.pdf; Office of the N.Y. Att'y Gen., Con Edison's July 1999 Electric Service Outages: A Report to the People of the State of New York (Mar. 9, 2000); Commonwealth Edison, A Blueprint for Change: Executive Summary for the Investigation Report by Commonwealth Edison to the Illinois Commerce Commission (Sept. 15, 1999) (acknowledging that CommEd had disinvested in its distribution system and needed to spend as much as $2 billion to restore system reliability).

The NSTAR Electric service territory centered in Boston, Massachusetts, also suffered repeated outages during the summer of 2001 due to disinvestment in maintenance and repairs, and NSTAR Electric prepared a thorough report as well. NSTAR Electric Company Report to the Department of Telecommunications and Energy in D.T.E. 01-65 (Oct. 29, 2001) (acknowledging that NSTAR had fallen millions of man-hours behind in routine maintenance).

56 At least one state commission has adopted standards for inspecting, maintaining, and repairing utility infrastructure. Order Instituting Rulemaking for Electric Distribution Facility Standard Setting, R. 96-11-004, Decision 97-03-070 (Cal. Pub. Util. Comm'n Mar. 31, 1997).

57 U.S. Energy Info. Admin., Electricity Power Industry Overview 2007, *available at* www.eia.doe.gov/cneaf/electricity/page/prim2/toc2.html.

58 *See* Mass. Gen. Laws ch. 164, § 1E (mandating the adoption of service quality standards and setting benchmark staffing levels).

The then Department of Telecommunications and Energy (now divided into the Department of Public Utilities and the Department of Telecommunications and Cable) adopted the mandated service quality standards in Docket No. 99-84.

59 *See* Stephanie Luce & Tom Juravich, University of Mass. Amherst Labor Relations Ctr., Stress in the Call Center, A Report on the Worklife of Call Center Representatives in the Utility Industry (Aug. 29, 2002).

60 *See* § 1.2.2.3.1, *supra* (discussion of the reliability impact of cutting back on repairs and maintenance).

61 *E.g.*, Mass. Gen. Laws ch. 164, § 1F(7).

The Massachusetts Department of Telecommunications and Energy passed regulations implementing various consumer protections included in the 1997 Restructuring Act. *See* 220 Mass. Code Regs. § 11.00 ("Rules Governing the Restructuring of the Electric Industry").

The Massachusetts attorney general, under the state's Unfair and Deceptive Acts and Practices statute, Mass. Gen. Laws ch. 93A, also promulgated consumer protection rules at 940 Mass. Code Regs. § 19.00 ("Retail Marketing and Sale of Electricity").

62 The privacy of customer information has become a hotly contested issue in the telephone industry, with companies wanting to share information with affiliates and third parties, while consumers and regulators are more interested in protecting privacy. *See* 47 U.S.C. § 222; 47 C.F.R. §§ 64.2003–.2009

- The application of undesignated partial payments when a shut-off or late charge is imminent.[63]
- Slamming (switching suppliers without customer consent).[64]
- Termination for nonpayment of another entity's bill.
- Ancillary fees, for example, for meter reading or paper (versus e-mail) billing, among other things.
- Protection of discounted rates designed to make service affordable for low-income households. Many states have mandated that, through legislative or commission action, so-called "system benefits" remain after restructuring.[65]

Forcing a utility company to exit the generation business inevitably interferes with "integrated resource planning," which is the process of considering all possible sources to meet customers' needs for power.[66] In fact, public utility or service commissions in restructured states sometimes force regulated companies to take an excessively short-term approach to procuring adequate supply, on the theory that LDCs can stifle competition if they are players in the long-term market.[67]

As a corollary to the decline in integrated resource planning, demand side management (DSM),[68] which is fully funded through utility rates, may slightly increase rates in the short term in order to lower them over time.[69]

Low-income customers simply do not have any disposable income and are unlikely to take advantage of most DSM programs that require co-payments.[70] While it may be desirable to have all participating customers contribute to the cost of energy efficiency equipment or devices installed in their homes, this is simply not possible for most low-income households. Investments in house insulation, weather-stripping, and efficient appliances should be provided to low-income households through "direct install" programs, such as those program funded by utilities that piggy-back on the federal Weatherization Assistance Program.[71]

The move to restructure electricity markets will increase the pressure on LDCs to administer programs that require participating customers to pay. But such programs will fail to serve low-income customers. DSM helps low-income customers reduce bills to manageable levels and thus makes it more likely that these customer will pay their bills on time. Investment in low-income energy efficiency can actually reduce utility bad debt and collection costs.[72]

(rules regarding customer proprietary network information); Order Instituting Rulemaking on the Commission's Own Motion to Establish Consumer Rights and Consumer Protection Rules Applicable to All Telecommunications Utilities, No. R.00-02-004 (Cal. Pub. Utils. Comm'n July 24, 2003) (draft decision of Commissioner Wood).

As part of its stated effort to remove "market barriers" to competition in the electric market, the Massachusetts Department of Telecommunications and Energy (now divided into the Department of Public Utilities and the Department of Telecommunications and Cable) has allowed the sharing of customer information between LDCs and competitive suppliers. Mass. D.T.E. 01-54-A (Oct. 15, 2001); Mass. D.T.E. 01-54-B (July 29, 2002).

63 *See* Mass. D.T.E. 01-28 (Phase II) (Dec. 14, 2001) (issue addressed in notice of inquiry into the rules and procedures by which distribution companies shall provide billing services to customers and competitive suppliers in their service territories).

64 In the telephone industry, "slamming," the unauthorized change of a telephone customer's preferred carrier, has been a problem for consumers ever since it became possible for telephone customers to choose among competing providers. Order Instituting Rulemaking on the Commission's Own Motion to Establish Consumer Rights and Consumer Protection Rules Applicable to All Telecommunications Utilities, No. R.00-02-004, at 101 (Cal. Pub. Utils. Comm'n July 24, 2003) (draft decision of Commissioner Wood).

The Federal Communications Commission has adopted anti-slamming rules, 47 C.F.R. §§ 64.1100–64.1195, as have some states. There are no federal rules regulating the switching of an electric or gas customer from an LDC to a competitive supplier, but some states have adopted anti-slamming laws protecting these customers. *See, e.g.*, Mass. Gen. Laws ch. 164, § 1F(8); 940 Mass. Code Regs., § 19.06(1)(d).

65 *See, e.g.*, Mass. Gen. Laws ch. 164, § 1F(4) (protecting existing discount rates); Tex. Util. Code Ann. § 39.903 (West) (establishing system benefit fund).

66 Integrated resource planning (IRP) requires looking at all generation, transmission, and distribution investments that can help meet future supply needs and control demand. Under IRP, energy efficiency investments that reduce demand are as fully considered as the construction of new power plants that can increase supply. IRP weights the costs and benefits of all possible demand control and supply options. The Regulatory Assistance Project has produced a series of papers that discuss IRP and demand-side options. They can be found at www.raponline.org.

67 *See* Barbara Alexander, National Ctr. for Appropriate Tech., Managing Default Service to Provide Consumer Benefits in Restructured States: Avoiding Short-Term Price Volatility (June 2003) (discussion of how many LDCs are now procuring their supply).

68 DSM investments include weather-stripping, water heater blankets, low-flow water fixtures, replacement of old and inefficient refrigerators and air conditioners, compact fluorescent light bulbs, and industrial process improvements.

69 National Consumer Law Center, The Low-Income Customer As Non-Participant in DSM: What Is to Be Done? (1992).

Due to changes in regulation and business cycle fluctuations, DSM costs can both rise and fall. Additionally, reported effects of DSM can lag behind reported DSM costs such that the two may not always show a direct correlation. *See* U.S. Energy Info. Admin, Electric Power Industry 2008: Year in Review, *available at* www.eia.doe.gov/cneaf/electricity/epa/epa_sum.html.

70 *See, e.g.*, Order, Texas Util. Elec. Co., No. 11735 (Tex. Pub. Util. Comm'n, Dec. 20, 1993).

The Energy Information Administration found that, from 1995 to 1996, the number of electric utilities that reported having DSM programs fell from 1053 to 1003 and that overall spending on DSM programs declined by 21%. Energy Info. Admin., U.S. Electric Utility Demand-Side Management 1996 (Dec. 1997).

71 *See* ch. 9, *infra* (discussion of both the federally funded weatherization program and utility-sponsored efforts).

72 *See* Direct Testimony and Exhibits of Nancy Brockway, on

1.2.2.3.3 "Default" service poses risks for consumers

In every state that has opened up its electricity markets to retail competition, customers who are not on competitive supply are placed on what is variously called "default," "standard offer," "basic," or "provider of last resort" (POLR) service. Under this rate structure, customers are given access to a source of electric generation supply even if no competitive company is willing to offer that supply or if the customer chooses not to switch.

In many states, residential customers in fact have few options but to choose default placement. Enron, which had early on become a licensed competitive supplier in several states, collapsed under the weight of its own chicanery in late 2001/early 2002. Other suppliers, such as Utility.com and Essential.com, that at first solicited residential and small business customers also went bankrupt or stopped doing business as competitive suppliers. In the handful of states that have fully opened their markets to competition, only a fraction of residential customers have switched to competitive supply—ranging from 3% or less in Massachusetts and parts of New York and Pennsylvania, to a maximum of 30% to 35% in the service territory of Duquesne in Pennsylvania.

Depending on the state in which they live, consumers have sometimes been ill-served by default service. In Texas, POLR service is for those who are temporarily without a source of supply—for example, in the midst of switching from one supplier to another—and those who are considered credit risks. These customers have at times charged a premium by providers for service, as much as 40% above rates paid by other customers. In Massachusetts, consumers remain on a more closely regulated rate called standard offer if they have not moved location or been served by a competitive supplier since the opening of the competitive market in 1998; if consumers have moved or been competitively supplied, they are placed on a default service rate. Through 2002, default service proved very volatile and generally more expensive than "standard offer" service. In New York, Consolidated Edison, unlike other utilities in that state, devised a default rate through which wholesale power fuel costs were passed directly onto customers. This resulted in substantially higher rate increases for ConEd's customers than elsewhere in the state.

1.2.3 Water and Sewer

According to the United States Environmental Protection Agency, approximately 15% of households get their drinking water from private wells, streams, or cisterns and approximately 85% get their water from "community water systems."[73] While over 80% of all water/sewer customers are served by large water systems (those serving 10,000 people or more), small water systems (serving fewer than 10,000) make up 93% of the number of community water systems.[74] Approximately 43% of the community water systems are publicly owned; approximately 33% are privately owned; and approximately 24% are ancillary systems.[75] Ancillary systems are a subset of privately owned drinking water systems that include manufactured home parks, where the provision of water is ancillary to the principal business. In contrast to water supply, the vast majority (98%) of wastewater treatment works are publicly owned. However, approximately 25% of households in the nation are not connected to a centralized wastewater treatment facility (for example, use septic tanks or other means of disposing wastewater).[76]

Although most municipally owned water systems are small in size and serve only a tiny pool of customers, some—such as the Los Angeles Department of Water and Power—serve over a million residential and commercial subscribers. In some states, such as Washington and Nebraska, municipal operations are organized as public utility districts and are actual political subdivisions within the state.[77]

A private water utility will typically be regulated quite similarly to an electric or gas utility. A municipal water utility will typically not be regulated by a state commission or other regulatory agency but will be largely unregulated. Such a water utility may, however, be subject to political pressure from consumers because the governing board of the municipal utility will either be elected by the public or appointed by an elected official.

1.3 Regulation by State Utility Commissions

1.3.1 The Governing Statute

The first place to look for the law governing a consumer's relationship with a regulated utility or a competitive provider licensed by the commission is the statutory scheme establishing the state public utilities regulatory commission.

behalf of Low-Income Interveners, *In Re* Tex. Util. Elec. Co. (Revenue Requirement Phase), No. 11735 (Tex. Pub. Util. Comm'n Apr. 1993).

73 U.S. Envtl. Prot. Agency, National Characteristics of Drinking Water Systems Serving Populations Under 10,000, E.P.A. 816-R-99-010 § 2 (1999).

The EPA defines a community water system as serving at least twenty-five year-round residents or having fifteen service connections used by year-round residents.

74 *Id.*

75 U.S. Envtl. Prot. Agency, 1995 Community Water System Survey 7 (1997).

76 U.S. Envtl. Prot. Agency, The Clean Water and Drinking Water Infrastructure Gap Analysis 10 (2002).

77 Charles F. Phillips, The Regulation of Public Utilities: Theory and Practice 650 (1993).

The statutes usually provide for the establishment of a commission or board, define its jurisdiction, and define the entities subject to its oversight. The organic statute of the commission often is the source for provisions such as a complaint mechanism,[78] a mechanism for the commission or attorney general to enforce the public utility law and its orders,[79] a hearing process, and the appeals process.[80]

Often, a statutory scheme will have separate titles or chapters, sometimes widely scattered, that govern utilities providing different types of utility service such as gas, electricity, and telephone. The advocate must find the appropriate chapters because the industry-specific chapters may include additional material regarding commission jurisdiction over the utility in question and may also include rules applicable in customer service cases: restrictions on terminations, deposit rules, rules for tenant utility access when landlords default on the building's bill, and so forth. Important protections for tenants will often be found outside the utility laws, in chapters or titles addressing general landlord-tenant law, manufactured homes, real property, or health and safety requirements.

1.3.2 Commission Rules and Regulations, Unpublished Orders

Many commissions have regulations governing such issues as right to service, deposits, terminations, and the like.[81] In most states, all the regulations promulgated by the PUC will be found in one title or chapter of that state's administrative code or codified regulations. These rules can often be found on the Internet,[82] at law libraries, through the Secretary of State, or directly from the PUC.[83] Commission staff members can be very helpful in obtaining regulations as well.

Developing good relationships with individuals on the staff of the commission is a key component of effective consumer advocacy before any commission. The clerks at the main reception desk, the staff of the Consumer Assistance Division, the people in the docketing office, all can smooth the way to finding documents and learning both the formal and informal rules and practices of the commission. Lawyers in the office of the general counsel can keep you posted on developments that are of interest to consumers. The telecommunications analyst you know by name will spend time explaining some arcane but important point of telecommunications engineering. Individual staffers may have views more in line with your client's interest than the official policy of the commission, and those staffers can be useful in suggesting avenues for relief. The world of public utility practice is a small one, even in large states, and practitioners develop reputations quickly.

Even when a commission has promulgated broad-ranging regulations, these regulations will not cover all relevant procedural or substantive issues that arise in any given case. In every state, there will be a "common law" of the commission's determinations that has been built up through formal "adjudicatory"[84] decisions and other rulings. A

78 For example, see S.D. Codified Laws § 49-34A-26, which provides for investigations of a utility's rates and practices on the commission's own motion or upon a complaint by the governing body of any political subdivision, another public utility, or any twenty-five consumers of the particular utility. As with most such statutes, the commission is not obligated to hold hearings or to take any particular action. Some statutes force a hearing process if certain officials request it or if sufficient numbers of customers join in the complaint.

79 For example, see Conn. Gen. Stat. § 16-10, which allows for the superior court, upon application by the department of public utility control or the attorney general, to enforce any provision of the public utility statute or any order of the department.

80 The Connecticut statutes include good examples of the level of detail that may be found in some states. For example, section 16-259a provides limits on the liability of customers to pay high catch-up bills rendered after a lengthy period of inaccurate bills (such as estimated billings). Section 16-262c contains extensive limitations on the time of day and day of the week during which disconnection is allowed, a winter moratorium on disconnection of "hardship" customers, and a year-round right of hardship customers to payment plans in the event of nonpayment, among other protections. Section 16-262d covers the type and length of advance notice required before disconnection of service, as well as appeal rights and limits on disconnections in hardship cases. Sections 16-262e and 16-262f provide a mechanism for notice to tenants of nonpayment by a landlord of utility bills and the appointment of a receiver in certain such cases.

81 *See, e.g.*, Alaska Admin. Code tit. 3, r. 48.420 (deposits), r. 52.405 (business office standards), r. 52.410 (establishment of permanent service), r. 52.420 (deposits), r. 52.425 (meter readings), r. 52.430 (general billing and collection requirements), r. 52.435 (estimated billings), r. 52.440 (levelized billings), r. 52.445 (deferred payment agreements), 52.450 (disconnection), r. 52.455 (line extensions), r. 52.460 (quality of service), r. 52.465 (meter measurements, adjustment and testing); Fla. Admin. Code Ann. Ann. 25-7.071 (meter readings), 25-7.079 (information to customers), 25-7.083 (customer deposits), 25-7.085 (billing); Mich. Admin. Code r. 460.2116 (general billing and collection rules), r. 460.2119 (information to customers), r. 460.2122 (advising customers of availability of financial assistance to pay utility bills), r. 460.2131–460.2134 (customer deposits).

82 The easiest route for finding state commission regulations is to visit the home page of the National Association of Regulatory Utility Commissioners, pulling down the "About" tab, and then clicking on "State Commissions." This brings up a map of the United States, which links to the home page for each of the fifty state commissions. In many (but by no means all) states, the regulations governing utility companies can be found on the state commission's web page.

83 *See* appx. A.1, *infra* (summaries of PUC customer service regulations from around the country).

84 Most commissions were established before the adoption of that state's Administrative Procedure Act (if the state in fact has an APA). Advocates should check whether the state APA applies to commission proceedings. Even in the absence of an express exemption in the state APA, certain practices of the commission may be deemed not to be governed by the APA's specific terms. *See, e.g.*, Tenn. Code Ann. § 4-5-103(b) (public service com-

commission may treat prior orders in individual cases[85] as having precedential weight in a current case and may follow the earlier rulings under the administrative equivalent of *stare decisis*.

A major problem for advocates who do not spend a great deal of time before PUCs is that PUC decisions are often not published[86] and are rarely digested or indexed. However, with the advent of the Internet, more and more decisions may be researched on commission websites. In addition, specialized legal research tools such as Westlaw and LEXIS are including an increasing number of PUC decisions in their databases, although these services are very expensive. In addition, commission staff members will often help members of the public locate relevant decisions.

1.3.3 Informal Precedent: Unwritten Rules, Word of Mouth

Even when a commission has made an effort to develop a body of precedent on recurring consumer issues, there are often issues that have not been determined by rule or by formal order of the commission but which have been determined by informal precedents consisting of non-binding letter decisions in staff-level dispute resolution proceedings or unwritten practices of the commission in resolving consumer complaints. For example, many commissions have developed informal guidelines for establishing the length of payment plans, that is, how long a payment plan commission staff will allow if a consumer asks the staff to help reach an agreement with the utility. These guidelines may not be written down but simply accumulate over time as the staff mediates between consumers and companies.

Again, access to cooperative staff members is essential for identifying the norms that have been developed. Since by definition these practices have not been adopted formally by the commission, an advocate may not always succeed in arguing that favorable past practices apply in any specific current cases. Conversely, good advocacy can quickly change an unfavorable informal policy, since the commission does not need to open a docket or hold hearings to change informal policies.

1.3.4 Tariffs

Another important source of law governing the relationship of utilities and their customers are the "tariffs" of the utility.[87] Tariffs are detailed multiple-page "books" that state the charges for each class of service and the conditions that apply to the service. They are updated with each rate case decision or other PUC order. Tariffs are often available on the utility's or the commission's website.

The tariff's main purpose is to provide public notice of the utility's commission-approved rates. Laws that prohibit rate discrimination typically forbid the utility to charge any other rate. Many tariffs also often contain customer service provisions, credit and collection rules, and terms governing late fees and deposits. Some tariffs describe the areas in which service will be provided and the charges for extending service into previously unserved areas. Tariffs are treated like contracts between the utility and customer and are accorded the force of law in many states. If, however, a tariff contains illegal provisions, these provisions may be challenged.[88]

Some utilities place their service rules in the tariff, either as a set of "General Rules" or "Terms and Conditions" at the front of the entire set of tariffs or less frequently as specific terms of individual class tariffs. Commissions rarely examine these provisions during rate cases. Once the proposed tariff provisions have been submitted to the commission and allowed to stand without change, they have the legal effect of tariffs explicitly approved by the commission.[89] Advocates should therefore consider reviewing a company's tariffs when a rate case is filed and urge the commission to change rules that are, for example, inconsistent with state law or commission regulations or which simply embody anti-consumer policies.[90]

---

mission statute on preparation of the official record controls; otherwise APA supersedes PSC procedural statutes).

85 A commission may conduct a "generic" or industry-wide investigation into, for example, service terms and conditions and issue an adjudicatory decision that strongly resembles a regulation promulgated under the commission's rulemaking powers. As previously noted, staff can be very helpful in finding relevant decisions that are not as easily found as published regulations.

86 Some states, like California, have reporter systems for publishing decisions, but this is rare. Westlaw and LEXIS carry Public Utilities Reports (a privately-published reporter of utility commission decisions), but that service is selective; PUR carries only some customer service cases. Westlaw and LEXIS carry the orders of a number of commissions (including such leading states as New York, Florida, Michigan, and California, for example), but the commissions choose the cases to be put on the system and, for monetary reasons, often choose not to include customer service cases. One avenue of advocacy could be to push for publication of customer service decisions of the utility commissions in one or more of these forums.

87 *See* Roger Colton & Robert Sable, National Consumer Law Center, A California Advocate's Guide to Telephone Customer Service Issues § 3.2 (1991) (good discussion of tariff issues in the context of one state and one industry).

88 *See* Granbois v. Big Horn County Elec. Coop., 986 P.2d 1097 (Mont. 1999) (REC rule unreasonable); *In re* Tarrant, 190 B.R. 704 (Bankr. S.D. Ga. 1995) (municipal utility rule).

89 Case law varies from state to state on the question of whether the fact that the commission has not reviewed or commented on such provisions leaves them any more vulnerable to collateral attack in a court proceeding.

90 Commissions will sometimes review an entire industry's set of terms and conditions, whether embodied in current tariffs or not, and mandate standard provisions in such areas as deposit rules, penalties for late payments, billing, and so forth. For one example of wide-ranging telecommunications consumer protec-

1.3.5 Dispute Resolution

Public utilities commissions typically have the power to decide individual customer disputes with utilities. The organic statutes often provide for the initiation of complaints against a utility before the commission.[91] Often, however, the standing to bring such a complaint is not accorded to individual complainants.[92] Rather, the statutes often will permit a complaint only if brought by persons or entities representing the general public interest, such as the attorney general, a municipal official, or a group consisting of a minimum number of customers. However, commissions usually have the power to open an investigation on their own motion, which provides authority to hear individual customer complaints. In some states (depending on each state's utility statutes and interpreting case law) and under certain factual circumstances, courts have concurrent jurisdiction to consider matters affecting utility service, especially when the relief requested is equitable in nature.[93] Courts may hold that they, and not the commission, have jurisdiction to award damages for wrongful acts committed by utilities.[94]

Statutes or commission rules frequently provide strict penalties for violation of commission rules. Customers who suffer damages may be able to simultaneously seek recovery of damages in court and also seek penalties before the commission. The penalty, sometimes substantial,[95] would be paid to the state for violation of commission rules or state statutes. Any damages awarded by a court would, of course, go to the consumer.

The doctrine of primary jurisdiction may be invoked to bar judicial relief until a complainant exhausts any remedies available at the public utility commission.[96] If a consumer seeks relief which cannot be granted by the commission but raises issues within the commission's area of expertise, a court may stay proceedings while the commission makes a determination and then proceed to grant what relief is appropriate in light of the commission's decision.[97] A trial court will typically lack jurisdiction to review claims involving the rate-setting process, quality of service, or other matters under the commission's express supervision.[98]

---

tion rules, see the Nov. 2, 2010, CPUC Decision 10-10-034 in docket R.00-02-004 available at http://docs.cpuc.ca.gov/word_pdf/FINAL_DECISION/125959.pdf. For standard terms and conditions applicable to distribution service in Massachusetts, see Mass. D.T.E. 97-65 (1997), *available at* www.env.state.ma.us/dpu/docs/electric/97-65/97-65or2.pdf.

91 *See, e.g.*, Colo. Rev. Stat. § 40-6-108; Ohio Rev. Code Ann. § 4909.24 (West); Or. Rev. Stat. § 756.500.

92 But a state may allow individual suits against a utility to enforce the decisions of the commission or the statutes. For example, S.D. Codified Laws § 49-13-14.1 provides that individuals injured by wrongful acts or omissions of telephone companies may sue for double damages and be awarded attorney fees.

93 *See, e.g.*, Steele v. Clinton Elec. Light & Power Co., 193 A. 613 (Conn. 1937) (fact that a PSC has jurisdiction to hear and determine disputes over charges for service does not deprive equity court of jurisdiction to enjoin the termination of service before payment of a disputed amount); Johnston v. Mid-Michigan Tel. Corp., 290 N.W.2d 146 (Mich. Ct. App. 1980) (court of general jurisdiction did not lack jurisdiction over claim in tort for alleged wrongful termination of service); Hall v. Village of Swanton, 35 A.2d 381 (Vt. 1944) (injunction will ordinarily be granted to prevent a utility company from wrongfully shutting off light, which such corporation is under contract to furnish, on the theory that the remedy at law is inadequate and that the shutting off of the supply would cause irreparable injury). *But see* State *ex rel.* Chesapeake & Potomac Tel. Co. v. Ashworth, 438 S.E.2d 890 (W. Va. 1993) ("Because of the complexity of the issues, we find that the circuit court should have deferred to the PSC.").

Courts frequently stay further court proceedings on complaints filed by customers when it appears that the utility commission can resolve complicated factual or legal issues within the expertise of the commission. *See, e.g.*, Stark Steel v. Michigan Consol. Gas Co., 418 N.W.2d 135 (Mich. Ct. App. 1987) (discussing "primary jurisdiction" of utility commissions).

94 *E.g.*, Lynn v. Houston Lighting & Power, 820 S.W.2d 57 (Tex. App. 1991) (court, not commission, has exclusive jurisdiction over tort damage claims for wrongful disconnection after meter tampering dispute); Stack Steel v. Michigan Consol. Gas Co., 418 N.W.2d 135 (Mich. Ct. App. 1987); City of Newton v. Department of Pub. Utilities, 328 N.E.2d 885 (Mass. 1975).

95 *See, e.g.*, Utah Code Ann. § 54-7-25 (West) (utility violation of any statute or commission rule subject to penalty of $500–$2000 for each offense; for continuing offenses, each day is a separate offense).

96 Northern Ind. Pub. Serv. Co. v. Dozier, 674 N.E.2d 977 (Ind. Ct. App. 1996) (Indiana Utility Regulatory Commission had primary jurisdiction to determine whether customer was unfairly denied gas service based on unpaid bill from former residence that was time-barred by statute of limitations); Whitinsville Water Co. v. Covich, 507 N.E.2d 1059, 1060 (Mass. App. Ct. 1987) (DPU may interpret disputed provisions of a tariff filed by the utility); Massachusetts Elec. Co. v. Doctors Hosp., 413 N.E.2d 779 (Mass. App. Ct. 1980) (staying customer's suit, pending a report from the PUC as to the applicable rate); Rinaldo's Constr. Corp. v. Michigan Bell Tel. Co., 559 N.W.2d 647 (Mich. 1997) (tort claims for money losses due to problems with telephone service must be brought before Michigan PSC; discussing primary jurisdiction). *See also* Travelers Ins. Co. v. Detroit Edison Co., 631 N.W.2d 733 (Mich. 2001) (primary jurisdiction doctrine is not jurisdictional but is not waived even if not timely pleaded by a party).

97 Penny v. Southwestern Bell, 906 F.2d 183 (5th Cir. 1990) (taking jurisdiction of UDAP claim because commission lacked power to award damages for past misconduct; staying proceedings so that commission could determine whether rate discrimination had occurred). *See also* Southwestern Bell Tel. v. Nash, 586 S.W.2d 647 (Tex. App. 1979).

98 Spence v. Boston Edison Co., 459 N.E.2d 80 (Mass. 1983) (rate determinations by the PUC are subject only to appellate review by the Supreme Judicial Court and cannot be challenged directly in courts by private parties); Valentine v. Michigan Bell Tel. Co., 199 N.W.2d 182 (Mich. 1972) (complaint for damages for inadequate service would not lie absent allegations of negligence, gross negligence, fraud, misrepresentation, or some other tort); State *ex rel.* Dayton Power & Light Co. v. Kistler, 385 N.E.2d 1076 (Ohio 1979) (claim of customer that utility discriminated between customers in setting rates). *See also* Stillman & Dolan v. Chesapeake & Potomac Tel. Co., 351 A.2d

State administrative procedures acts may also contain provisions for officials or groups of affected persons to force an agency to undertake a rulemaking proceeding. In Maine, for example, while anyone might petition for the opening of a rulemaking process, upon a petition of 150 voters, an agency is required to hold a public hearing.[99] The first winter disconnect moratorium in Maine was achieved after a commission rulemaking began in response to a petition with 700 signatures. Not only was a public hearing automatically required, but the number of signatories was a powerful signal of broad public interest in the outcome of the hearings.

Many commissions assist customers and utilities in resolving individual disputes by offering the services of staff members as mediators or nonbinding adjudicators. Staff are often located in a division called Consumer Assistance or something similar.[100] In some cases, the process for invoking the assistance of such staff is set forth in rules promulgated by the commission pursuant to the state Administrative Procedures Act.[101]

Occasionally, issues concerning individual customer disputes are reported[102] to or reach the courts on appeal from commission decisions, resulting in judicial determination of the applicable law. Many states require narrow routes for appeal of orders of the public service commission,[103] and collateral attacks may be barred or discouraged by application of the doctrines of primary jurisdiction or exhaustion of administrative remedies discussed previously in this section. To foster the statutory purpose of a unified statewide utilities policy developed by an expert panel, appeals often lie to the supreme court rather than to trial or intermediate appellate courts. Because of the hurdles individual consumers must overcome to file appeals, courts rarely address the appropriateness of commission customer service policies.

Deregulation has affected these practices. Some commissions have looked at how the dispute resolution procedures will be utilized in a deregulated atmosphere.[104] No clear mechanism has emerged, although the provider of last resort, usually the former monopoly utility, will still be subject to commission rules under most proposals. As to other electric service providers, the rules are not so clear.

---

172 (Md. 1976) (legislature established comprehensive utility regulatory scheme). *But see, e.g.*, Lowell Gas Co. v. Attorney Gen., 385 N.E.2d 240, 245 (Mass. 1979) (trial court has jurisdiction over rate challenge to extent complaint alleges fraud in the rate-setting process).

99 Me. Rev. Stat. tit. 5, § 8055.

100 In some cases, staff from the legal division, the staff division charged with responsibility for the industry in question (for example, telecommunications), will handle individual customer complaints.

101 *See, e.g.*, 220 Mass. Code Regs. § 25.02(4) ("investigation and appeal" of customer complaints). *See* appx. A.1, *infra* (summaries of most state customer service regulations).

102 *See, e.g.*, Decision, Muhammad v. Southern Cal. Edison, 999 Cal. Pub. Util. Comm'n LEXIS 110, No. 99-02-026 (Cal. Pub. Utils. Comm'n 1999) (no violation of rules; dismissing customer complaint); Order, *In re* Complaint of Wood Against GTE Fla. Inc. Regarding Serv., 2000 Fla. Pub. Util. Comm'n LEXIS 905, PSC-00-1567-FOF-TL (Fla. Pub. Util. Comm'n 2000); Order, *In re* Complaint of Denson Against Fla. Power Corp. Regarding Improper Billing, 1999 Fla. Pub. Util. Comm'n LEXIS 1036, No. PSC 99-1226-PAA-EI (Fla. Pub. Util. Comm'n 1999) (over-billing charge dismissed).

103 *E.g.*, Mass. Gen. Laws ch. 25, § 5; Ohio Rev. Code Ann. § 4903.12 (West). *See also* Or. Rev. Stat. §§ 756.580–756.610 (appeals first to circuit court, which must not substitute its judgment on the facts for that of commission; appeal thence to court of appeals).

104 For example, the Massachusetts Department of Telecommunications and Energy (now divided into the Department of Public Utilities and the Department of Telecommunications and Cable) produced the rules governing the restructuring of the electric industry, 220 Mass. Code Regs. §§ 11.01–11.08, which includes, *inter alia*, § 11.05(3) ("Billing and Termination of Generation Service").

The Department also produced the model terms and conditions governing the relationship between electric utility distribution companies, customers and competitive suppliers, 182 Pub. Util. Rep. 4th 487, 1997 WL 868766 (Mass. Dep't of Utils./Mass. Dep't of Telecomms. & Energy Dec. 31, 1997).

Separately, the Massachusetts attorney general promulgated rules governing retail marketing and sale of electricity. 940 Mass. Code Regs. § 19.01 (2001).

Other states that have undergone restructuring have also promulgated new rules and regulations, and advocates should check with their state utility commission to make sure they have a current set of relevant customer complaint regulations.

Chapter 2 Right to Utility Service

2.1 Utilities Have a Duty to Furnish Service to All

2.1.1 Introduction

The regulation of private investor-owned utilities has largely been taken over by comprehensive statutory and regulatory schemes in all fifty states. The law governing regulation of municipal utilities and Rural Electric Cooperatives varies from state to state, but common law principles, in some cases, may still apply to the protection of consumers in their disputes with all types of utility providers.[1] Long before the existence of administrative agencies or before the creation of legislatively provided regulatory obligations for public utilities,[2] the common law imposed standards of conduct on business enterprises variously known as public utilities, public service corporations, public callings, and so forth.

The creation of state regulatory agencies that oversee private investor-owned utilities has not necessarily eliminated these common law standards. As a result, common law remedies that existed before the creation of state utility commissions may be available for the protection of utility consumers, just as "old" common law remedies were resurrected decades ago, for example, for purposes of environmental protection.[3]

A utility company's obligations under common law doctrines are generally enforceable in the courts. The duty to serve applies to any company defined as a "public utility" under common law, including municipal utilities and RECs.[4] The general principles of contract law apply to all businesses, whether utilities or free market competitors. However, a court may well look to the statutes under which a state's utility commission was created, as well as the commission's own regulations, in interpreting the current common law principles established in cases decided before the advent of state utility regulation or in contract cases dealing with unregulated parties.

2.1.2 The Common Law Duty to Serve

All public utilities—investor owned, municipal or cooperative—are subject to a common law duty to serve.[5] However, a district court recently held that when there is a statutory duty to serve, the common law duty is superseded and the public utility commission has exclusive jurisdiction over the claim of a utility's breach of its duty to serve.[6] The utility must provide service to any member of the public living within the utility's service area who has applied for service and is willing both to pay for the service and comply with the utility's rules and regulations.[7] The utility must

---

1 "It is respectfully submitted that it is the duty of the courts to vitalize common law rights which have not been codified rather than eradicate them because they have not." Stevenson v. Prairie Power Coop., 794 P.2d 620, 625 (Idaho 1990) (J. Bistline, separate opinion).

2 *See* Francis X. Welch, *The Effectiveness of Commission Regulation of Public Utility Enterprise*, 49 Geo. L.J. 639, 643 (1961).

3 *See* Maloney, *Judicial Protection of the Environment: A New Role for Common-Law Remedies*, 25 Vand. L. Rev. 145 (1972); Wade, *Environmental Protection: The Common Law of Nuisance and the Restatement of Torts*, 8 Forum 165 (1972); Note, *Private Remedies for Water Pollution*, 70 Colum. L. Rev. 734 (1970).

4 *See* §§ 1.1, 1.2, and 1.3, *supra* (discussing status of municipals and RECs as "public utilities"). *See also* Black's Law Dictionary (8th ed. 2004) ("1. A company that provides necessary services to the public, such as telephone lines and service, electricity, and water. Most utilities operate as monopolies but are subject to governmental regulation. . . . 2. A person, corporation, or other association that carries on an enterprise for the accommodation of the public, *the members of which are entitled as a matter of right to use its facilities*." (emphasis added)).

5 United Fuel Gas Co. v. Railroad Comm'n, 278 U.S. 300, 49 S. Ct. 150, 73 L. Ed. 390 (1929); N.Y. *ex rel.* Woodhaven Gaslight Co. v. Public Serv. Comm'n, 269 U.S. 244, 46 S. Ct. 83, 70 L. Ed. 255 (1925); Allen's Creek Props. v. Clearwater, 679 So. 2d 1172 (Fla. 1996).

6 McGee v. East Ohio Gas Co., 2002 WL 484480 (S.D. Ohio Mar. 26, 2002) ("While it may be true that, at some point in history, the duty to serve was a common law duty, Title 49 appears to have superseded the common law."). *But see* Carter v. Buckeye Rural Elec. Coop., 2001 WL 1681104 (S.D. Ohio Sept. 7, 2001) (recognizing case law imposing a duty to serve on a rural electric cooperative).

7 27A Am. Jur. 2d *Energy and Power Sources* § 199 (1996) (duty to serve); 27A Am. Jur. 2d *Energy and Power Sources* § 385 (1996) (failure to furnish or delay in furnishing gas service). *See also* Overman v. Southwestern Bell Tel. Co., 675 S.W.2d 419, 424 (Mo. Ct. App. 1984) ("[a] public utility is obligated by the nature of its business to furnish its service or commodity to the general public, or that part of the public which it has undertaken

render adequate and reasonably efficient service, on reasonable terms, impartially, without unjust discrimination, and at reasonable rates.[8]

In a natural monopoly, regulation is a necessary substitute for competition.[9] Because regulated utilities are not subject to competitive pressures, rates are set by legislatures and administrative communions, subject to court review. These regulations limit utilities to prices that are "just and reasonable."[10]

The duty to serve also prevents utilities from choosing to serve only those customers and areas that will enable them to realize a profit;[11] in contrast to unregulated commercial enterprises, they must also serve unprofitable segments of the market.

Utilities must also provide safe and adequate service to all of their customers.[12] In practical terms, this means that they must provide service twenty-four hours a day and must have the capacity to meet foreseeable increases in customer demand. Such increases would arise not only from periods of peak demand but also from predictable growth in the population of the community served and in the intensity of utility use.

In sum, "[t]he primary duty of a public utility is to serve on reasonable terms all those who desire the service it renders."[13] The common law duty to serve "is one implied at common law and need not be expressed by statute, or contract, or in the charter of the public utility."[14] The common law duty to serve exists independently of federal legislation, state legislation, administrative regulation,[15] or the charter of the public utility.[16]

---

to serve, without arbitrary discrimination . . . *Such duties arise from the public nature of a utility, and statutes providing affirmatively therefor are merely declaratory of the common law.*") (quoting 73B C.J.S. *Public Utilities* § 8, 143–45 (1983) (emphasis added)) (renumbered as *Public Utilities* § 7, at 283, 284. (2004)); Nolte v. City of Olympia, 982 P.2d 659, 667 (Wash. Ct. App. 1999) (as exclusive provider of water and sewer service, city owes public duty to serve all within service area subject to reasonable conditions as allowed by law); Jim Rossi, *The Common Law Duty to Serve and Protection of Consumers in an Age of Competitive Retail Public Utility Restructuring*, 51 Vand. Law Rev. 1233 (Oct. 1998); 26 Am. Jur. 2d *Electricity, Gas and Steam* § 110 (1966) (delay in commencing electric service); 26 Am. Jur. 2d *Electricity, Gas and Steam* § 216 (1966) (delay in commencing gas service); James C. Bonbright, Albert L. Danielsen, & David R. Kamerschen, Principles of Public Utility Rates (2d ed. 1988 Public Utilities Reports); Alfred E. Kahn, The Economics of Regulation, Vol. I: Principles (1970). *See generally* Comment, *Liability of Public Utility for Temporary Interruption of Service*, 1974 Wash. U. L.Q. 344, 346, n.10 (1974) (excellent discussion of scope and ramifications of this duty); Norman Arterburn, *The Origin and First Test of Public Callings*, 75 U. Pa. L. Rev. 411 (1927) (same).

8 *See, e.g.*, Arizona Corp. Comm'n v. Nicholson, 497 P.2d 815, 817 (Ariz. 1972); Southwest Transmission Coop., Inc. v. Arizona Corp. Comm'n, 142 P.3d 1240 (Ariz. Ct. App. 2006). *See also* Carter v. Buckeye Rural Elec. Coop. Inc., 2001 WL 1681104 (S.D. Ohio Sept. 7, 2001). *But see* McGee v. East Ohio Gas Co., 2002 WL 484480, at *8 (S.D. Ohio Mar. 26, 2002) (common law duty to serve now codified in Ohio Rev. Code Ann. § 4905).

9 *See* § 1.1.3, *supra*.

10 Charles F. Phillips, The Regulation of Public Utilities 119 (1984).

11 However, especially in rural areas, there are usually limitations on how far a company will extend service without imposing an extra charge.

12 *See, e.g.*, Van Holten Group v. Elizabethtown Water Co., 577 A.2d 829 (N.J. 1990).

13 City of Mishawaka, Ind. v. American Elec. Power Co., Inc, 465 F. Supp. 1320 (N.D. Ind. 1979) (quoting United Gas Co. v. Railroad Comm'n, 278 U.S. 300, 309, 49 S. Ct. 150, 73 L. Ed. 390 (1929)).

14 64 Am. Jur. 2d *Public Utilities* § 21 (2001) (citations omitted). The duty may well be incorporated into state statutes for regulated utilities, *see* Comment, *Liability of Public Utility for Temporary Interruption of Service*, 1974 Wash. U. L.Q. 344, 345, 346, n.9 (1974), but it exists at common law for those public utilities not covered by statute. The Indiana Supreme Court has noted:

> When the state fails, or does not see fit, to regulate the rates and charges or services by legislation or by creating a commission for the purpose, the public, nevertheless, still has the basic right under the common law to be served in all particulars, without discrimination, and at a reasonable price.

Foltz v. Indianapolis, 130 N.E.2d 650, 656 (Ind. 1955). *Accord* Messer v. Southern Airways Sales Co., 17 So. 2d 679 (Ala. 1944). *See also* Montgomery Ward & Co. v. North Pac. Terminal Co., 128 F. Supp. 475 (D. Or. 1953). *Cf.* Alexander v. Cottey, 801 N.E.2d 651 (Ind. Ct. App. 2004) (holding that trial court should exercise its jurisdiction with respect to common law claims of inmates and others concerning excess charges created by contract between prison officials and phone company).

15 *See, e.g.*, Gibbs v. Consolidated Gas Co. of Balt., 130 U.S. 396 (1889); City of Mishawaka, Ind. v. American Elec. Power Co., 465 F. Supp. 1320 (N.D. Ind. 1979); Messer v. Southern Airways Sales Co., 17 So. 2d 679, 681 (Ala. 1944); Austin View Civic Ass'n v. City of Palos Heights, 405 N.E.2d 1256 (Ill. App. Ct. 1980) (municipality providing utility service is subject to common law duty to serve without unreasonable discrimination; plaintiffs could state a claim for two causes of action, denial of equal protection and violation of common law duty; test to determine whether common law duty was violated was same standard applied to IOUs under Public Utility Act); Morehouse Natural Gas Co. v. Louisiana Pub. Serv. Comm'n, 140 So. 2d 646 (La. 1962); Southwest Gas Corp. v. Public Serv. Comm'n, 474 P.2d 379 (Nev. 1970).

16 64 Am. Jur. 2d *Public Utilities* § 21 (2001) (citations omitted). The duty may well be incorporated into state statutes for regulated utilities, *see* Comment, *Liability of Public Utility for Temporary Interruption of Service*, 1974 Wash. U. L.Q. 344–46, n.9 (1974), but it exists at common law for those public utilities not covered by statute, such as municipally owned utilities or cooperatives. The Indiana Supreme Court has noted:

> when the state fails, or does not see fit, to regulate the rates and charges or services by legislation or by creating a commission for the purpose, the public, nevertheless, still has the basic right under the com-

It is the status of "public utility" that creates a corresponding responsibility to provide service for all who request service and are willing to pay for it.[17] As stated by one court, "such duties arise from the public nature of a utility, and statutes providing affirmatively therefor are merely *declaratory* of the common law."[18] Some public utilities are also common carriers, which must accept all applicants for service at reasonable, posted rates.

The duty to serve is not absolute.[19] Utilities may deny service for good cause but may not act arbitrarily or engage in prohibited discrimination. In general, the same limits apply to refusal to serve, termination of service, and refusal to reconnect service after termination.

2.1.3 State Statutes and PUC Rules and Orders Codify Duty to Serve

Many state statutes have incorporated these "duty to serve" principles,[20] as have utility commissions and courts interpreting statutory obligations of regulated investor-owned utilities,[21] co-ops[22] and municipals.[23]

2.1.4 Effect of Utility Deregulation on Duty to Serve

The duty to serve was imposed to prevent utilities from abusing their monopoly power. As some states moved from regulation to retail competition, some key industry players may no longer be bound by the duty to serve.[24] This deregulation of utility service creates new questions regarding consumer protections.[25] In response to these concerns, nearly all restructuring statutes refer to the need to preserve universal service.[26] State statutes vary, however, as to: how

mon law to be served in all particulars, without discrimination, and at a reasonable price.

Foltz v. Indianapolis, 130 N.E.2d 650, 656 (Ind. 1955). *Accord* Messer v. Southern Airways Sales Co., 17 So. 2d 679 (Ala. 1944). *See also* Montgomery Ward & Co. v. North Pac. Terminal Co., 128 F. Supp. 475 (D. Or. 1953).

17 *Accord* Donnelly v. City of Eureka, Kan., 399 F. Supp. 64 (D. Kan. 1975); Siegel v. Minneapolis Gas Co., 135 N.W.2d 60 (Minn. 1965); Josephson v. Mountain Bell, 576 P.2d 850 (Utah 1978). *See, e.g.*, Denver Welfare Rights Org. v. Public Util. Comm'n, 547 P.2d 239 (Colo. 1976).

18 Overman v. Southwestern Bell Tel. Co., 675 S.W.2d 419, 424 (Mo. Ct. App. 1984) (emphasis added).

19 Northern States Power Co. v. National Gas Co., 606 N.W.2d 613 (Wis. Ct. App. 1999) (no enforceable duty to provide service to manufactured home park where customers in franchise area were satisfied with alternative service).

20 *See, e.g.*, Cal. Pub. Util. Code § 451 (West) (every public utility has an obligation to furnish and maintain adequate, efficient, just, and reasonable service); Ind. Code § 8-1-2-4 (legal duty to provide reasonably adequate service). *See also* McGee v. East Ohio Gas Co., 2002 WL 484480 (S.D. Ohio Mar. 26, 2002) (referencing Ohio Rev. Code Ann. §§ 4905.22, 4905.33, 4905.35 (West)).

21 *See, e.g.*, W. Com Long Distance, Inc. v. Citizens Util. Co. of Cal., 45 Cal. Pub. Util. Comm'n 263 (Cal. Aug. 11, 1992) (restating California statutory mandate that every public utility has an obligation to furnish and maintain "adequate, efficient, just, and reasonable service"); *In re* Peoples Gas & Power Co., 138 Pub. Util. Rep. 4th 320, 1992 WL 409341 (Ind. Utils. Regulatory Comm'n Oct. 21, 1992) (gas company under a legal duty to provide reasonable adequate service pursuant to Ind. Code § 8-1-2-4); Everett v. Baltimore Gas & Elec., 513 A.2d 882 (Md. 1986) (utility has an affirmative duty to provide service to the public), *overruled on other grounds by* Coleman v. Anne Arundel County Police Dep't, 797 A.2d 770 (Md. 2002); *In re* Telecommunications Regulation Within Michigan, *In re* AT&T Commc'ns of Mich., Inc., 116 Pub. Util. Rep. 4th 495, 1990 WL 488907 (Mich. Pub. Serv. Comm'n Oct. 1, 1990) (telephone corporations "required to furnish reasonably adequate service and facilities," citing to Mich. Comp. Laws § 484.103(1) (now Mich. Comp. Laws §§ 484.2202, 484.2315)); *In re* Carolina Power & Light Co., 94 Pub. Util. Rep. 4th 353, 1988 WL 391130 (N.C.U.C. Aug. 5, 1988) (public utilities in North Carolina have a legal duty to provide efficient service, citing to G.S. § 62-131(b)); Monson v. National Fuel Gas Distrib. Corp., 58 Pa. Pub. Util. Comm'n 371 Z-8207989 (Pa. Apr. 19, 1984) (commission found the utility violated its general duty to provide reasonable service). *See also* McGee v. East Ohio Gas Co., 2002 WL 484480 (S.D. Ohio Mar. 26, 2002) ("While it may be true that, at some point in history, the duty to serve was a common law duty, Title 49 appears to have superseded the common law."); Pub. Serv. Co. of Okla. v. Norris Sucker Rods, 917 P.2d 992 (Okla. Civ. App. 1995) (utility company has obligation to provide service at lowest cost to customer after notification of eligibility).

22 Carter v. Buckeye Rural Elec. Coop., 2001 WL 1681104 (S.D. Ohio Sept. 7, 2001) (recognizing case law imposing a duty to serve on a rural electric cooperative and denying motion to dismiss state law claim); Stevenson v. Prairie Power Coop., 794 P.2d 620, 625 (Idaho 1990).

23 Memphis Light, Gas & Water Div. v. Craft, 436 U.S. 1 (1978) (municipal utilities are required to provide certain minimum procedures to protect the right to service when this right is established by state statute or another source).

24 *See, e.g.*, N.Y.P.S.C. Op. 96-12 at pp. 65, *et seq.* (concluding that only the monopoly transmission and distribution company will be subject to the Home Energy Fair Practices Act; codifying utilities' duties towards residential customers).

25 Jim Rossi, *The Common Law Duty to Serve and Protection of Consumers in an Age of Competitive Retail Public Utility Restructuring*, 51 Vand. L. Rev. 1233 (Oct. 1998).

For a list of states that restructured electric service see the Energy Information Agency's webpage at www.eia.gov/cneaf/electricity/page/restructuring/restructure_elect.html.

26 Conn. Gen. Stat. §§ 16-244(8), 16-244i, 16-245r (distribution company has obligation to connect; supplier forbidden to discriminate by geographic area, lawful source of income, or hardship status); Del. Code Ann. tit. 26, § 1010 (existing utilities have obligation to serve during transition, standard offer supplier has duty to serve thereafter); 220 Ill. Comp. Stat. 5/16-101A(c)–(e) (safety, reliability and affordability should not be sacrificed to competitive pressures; consumer protections must ensure safe, reliable, affordable and environmentally safe service.); Me. Rev. Stat. tit. 35-A, § 3214(1) (electricity is a basic necessity to which all residents should have access.); Md. Code Ann., Pub. Util. Cos. §§ 7-501(q) and 512.1 (West) (provisions for universal service program); Mass. Gen. Laws ch. 164, § 1A (restructuring plans must include universal service

prices are set, the method of choosing a "provider of last resort" that must provide service to all takers, and the monopoly company's service obligations after the "transition" period from traditional regulation to competition. Consumer advocates must remain alert to ensure that low-income customers have access to energy at predictable and affordable prices during the current post-transition period.

Most deregulation statutes provide for a "standard offer" or "default" service or both, at least during the transition period. Standard offer combines (or "bundles") generation and distribution service, similar to the product offered by regulated utilities before restructuring. States that restructured created a category of regulated service called default service (also called provider of last resort, or basic generation service) for customers who choose not to shop for a competitive supplier or who cannot get or lose service from a competitive supplier.[27] This type of service is an important means of maintaining service for low-income residential customers as well as preserving other important consumer protections.[28] Default and standard offer service may be provided by the transmission and distribution utility or by another entity to be chosen by the commission, often after competitive bidding. Typically, the default or standard offer supplier is subject to a duty to serve.[29]

Two issues are critical to low-income consumers: the method of pricing these services and the continued availability of services after the transition period. A number of states provided for a freeze or reduction in the price of standard offer (or all residential) service during transition but will move to a market-based mechanism thereafter.[30] Others call for further study of the question whether standard offer or default service will be needed after transition.[31]

Because the duty to serve developed as a curb on abuse of power by natural monopolies, it does not generally apply to competitive service providers. Note, however, that termination by a supplier does not normally result in termination of utility service, because the customer who loses a supplier will in almost all cases automatically default to standard offer or last resort service.[32] Many restructuring statutes, and the regulations that implement them, include consumer protection rules that limit suppliers' power to pick and choose or to terminate. Connecticut, for example, bans geographic redlining, and forbids discrimination by "lawful source of income" or "hardship status."[33]

---

policies.); Nev. Rev. Stat. § 703.151 (commission regulations must provide effective protection of persons who depend upon electric services); N.H. Rev. Stat. Ann. § 374-F:3(V) (electric service is essential and should be available to all customers; distribution provider has duty to serve); N.J. Stat. Ann. § 48:3-50(a)(4) (West) (policy of the state to ensure universal access to affordable and reliable gas and electric service); 66 Pa. Cons. Stat. § 2802(9) (electric service essential to health and well-being; should be available to all "on reasonable terms and conditions"); R.I. Gen. Laws § 39-1-27.3(c) (electricity is an essential service); Tex. Util. Code Ann. § 39.101 (West) (commission must establish consumer protections that entitle customers to safe, reliable and reasonably priced energy); Va. Code Ann. § 56-578 (distributors' duty to connect).

A commitment to universal service is implicit in the detailed provisions for low-income assistance in other statutes, that is, Cal. Pub. Util. Code § 382 (West), Ohio Rev. Code Ann. § 4928.51 to 4928..58 (West), and Or Rev. Stat. § 757.612.

27 *See, e.g.*, 66 Pa. Cons. Stat. § 2807(e); *In re* Delmarva Power & Light Co., 196 Pub. Util. Rep. 4th 387, 1999 WL 1005166 (Del. Pub. Serv. Comm'n Aug. 31, 1999).

28 *See* Barbara Alexander, Default Service for Retail Electric Competition: Can Residential and Low Income Customers Be Protected When the Experiment Goes Awry? (more information on how states have structured their default service), *available on the companion website to this treatise.*

29 Conn. Gen. Stat. § 16-244c; Del. Code tit. 26, § 1010; 220 Ill. Comp. Stat. Ann. §§ 5/16-103(c), (d); Me. Rev. St. Ann. tit. 35-A, § 3212; Md. Code Ann., Pub. Util. Cos. tit. 7-506; Mass. Gen. Laws, ch. 164, § 1B(d); N.Y. P.S.C. Op. 97-5; Ohio Rev. Code Ann. § 4928.35; 66 Pa. Cons. Stat. §§ 2802(16); Tex. Util. Code §§ 39.101 and 39.106.

30 Conn. Gen. Stat. §§ 16-244c (standard offer rates capped at 10% below pre-restructuring rates; standard offer will terminate on Jan. 1, 2004; thereafter, supplier for default service will be chosen by competitive bidding); 220 Ill. Comp. Stat. 5/16-103(c) (during transition, standard offer price must be "consistent with" that available on date of statute; once service found competitive, may charge market-based prices); Md. Code Ann., Pub. Util. Cos. § 7-510(a) (West) (price of standard offer service regulated by commission; obligation to provide standard offer service terminates on July 1, 2003, with certain exceptions); N.H. Rev. Stat. Ann. § 374-F:3(V)(b), (c) (standard offer service to be available for one to five years, should increase in price over time, to encourage consumers to choose supplier; default service is temporary safety net, commission should implement measures to discourage misuse or long-term use); N.J. Stat. Ann. § 48:3-57 (West) (all utilities must offer basic service for first three years, at regulated, cost-based prices; thereafter, board may consider bidding process).

31 Me. Rev. Stat. tit. 35-A, § 3212(4) (standard offer available until Mar. 1, 2005; by December 1, 2002, commission must conclude investigation to determine whether continued availability of standard offer is "necessary and in the public interest").

32 *See, e.g.*, Md. Code Ann., Pub. Util. Cos. § 7-507(e)(6) (West) (commission must make regulations providing for referral by supplier of delinquent customer to standard offer service); Mass. Gen. Laws ch. 164, § 1B(d) (distribution company must provide default service to any customer who, for whatever reason, is no longer receiving service from supplier); N.J. Stat. Ann. §§ 48:3-51, 48:3-57 (West) (define basic service to include services supplied to customers who cannot obtain service for any reason, including nonpayment); *In re* Delmarva Power & Light Co., 196 Pub. Util. Rep. 4th 387, 1999 WL 1005166 (Del. Pub. Serv. Comm'n Aug. 31, 1999); *In re* Pennsylvania Power & Light Co, 1998 WL 985365 (Pa. Pub. Util. Comm'n 1998). *But see* 16 Tex. Admin. Code § 25.483 (retail electric provider has authority to authorize disconnection).

33 Conn. Gen. Stat. § 16-245r. *See also* 220 Ill. Comp. Stat. 5/16-115A (redlining forbidden); N.J. Stat. Ann. § 48:3-85 (West) (ban on discriminatory marketing, including geographic redlining, discrimination against lawful source of income, or receipt of public benefits).

2.2 A Public Utility May Not Deny (or Terminate) Service Based on a "Collateral" Matter

2.2.1 General

Public utilities occasionally seek to impose conditions on consumers requesting (or terminating existing) utility service that have nothing to do with the customer's present utility contract or account. Court decisions, as well as state utility regulations, are generally in accord in holding that a public utility cannot terminate or refuse to render service that it is authorized by its charter to furnish or impose service constraints because of a collateral matter unrelated to that service.[34]

A collateral matter can be defined generally as a dispute that is the subject of a separate transaction, either between the utility and the consumer or between the utility and some other person that is distinct from, and irrelevant to, the utility's immediate duty to furnish a particular service. The definition of "collateral" will vary from state to state, however, and may raise difficult questions of the interaction of commission regulations and state common law.

According to the Iowa Supreme Court, for example, a "collateral" matter is one wherein there is "a wholly separate and independent transaction."[35] Other courts have adopted similar approaches.[36] Water and sewer services are sometimes considered so inter-related that a provider of water service may terminate its service for failure to pay related sewer charges, but water and electric services are generally considered sufficiently unrelated that failure to pay for one cannot form the basis for terminating the other.[37]

Collateral matters may include:

- Nonpayment of unrelated contracts with the utility;
- Nonpayment for services provided by a separate business run by the utility;
- Nonpayment of another person's utility bill;
- Nonpayment of long-distance charges owed to another carrier and added to a local telephone bill;[38] and
- Nonpayment of 900-number (pay-per-call) services added to a local telephone bill.[39]

The common law rule against denying service because of collateral disputes is justified by the status of utilities as quasi-public entities that hold a public franchise and provide an essential service. The common law rule forbids utilities from coercing payment for separate and unrelated obligations by threatening to withhold from the prospective customer the necessities of life. Utilities must use the judicial process, as any other creditor would, to settle a dispute and may not exploit their control over an essential service to punish the consumer for not acceding to their (one-sided) demands.[40]

34 64 Am. Jur. 2d *Public Utilities* § 22 (2001); Annot., *Right of Municipality to Refuse Services Provided by It to a Resident for Failure of Resident to Pay for Other Unrelated Services*, 60 A.L.R.3d 714 (1974). *See also* Owens v. City of Beresford, 201 N.W.2d 890 (S.D. 1972) (municipality cannot refuse to render phone and electric service because of failure to pay for garbage collection, a collateral matter). *Compare* Dale v. City of Morganton, 155 S.E.2d 136 (N.C. 1967) (when acting as an electric utility, a municipality, like a private company, may not refuse to provide service due to a "controversy concerning a matter which is not related to the service sought"), *with* Carolina Water Serv., Inc. v. City of Winston Salem, 161 F.3d 1 (4th Cir. 1998) (unpublished) (water service is interconnected with and not collateral to continued sewage service).

35 Berner v. Interstate Power Co., 57 N.W.2d 55 (Iowa 1953).

Iowa utilities are now constrained by commission regulations from terminating service based on collateral matters. Iowa Admin. Code r. 199-20.14(16) (utility may not terminate service based on failure to pay previous occupant's bill, for merchandise purchased from utility, for a different type or class of service, or for bill of another customer, as a guarantor of that bill).

36 In a case in which a municipality was prohibited from terminating the plaintiff's water service for failure to pay a municipal garbage fee, the Nebraska Supreme Court held that a matter is "collateral" if it is an "independent transaction, not strictly connected with the particular physical service." Garner v. City of Aurora, 30 N.W.2d 917(Neb. 1948).

37 *See* Annot., *Right of Municipality to Refuse Services Provided by It to Resident for Failure of Resident to Pay for Another Unrelated Service*, 60 A.L.R.3d 714 (1974); Annot., *Right to Cut Off Water Supply Because of Failure to Pay Sewer Charge*, 26 A.L.R.2d 1359 (1952).

38 *In re* Local Competition, Universal Serv., and the Non-Traffic Sensitive Access Rate, 181 P.U.R.4th 600, 1997 WL 823992 (Ky. Pub. Serv. Comm'n Nov. 26, 1997) (no denial of local telephone service for nonpayment of toll service); *In re* US W. Commc'n Inc., 153 P.U.R.4th 350, 1994 WL 399182 (Utah Pub. Serv. Comm'n June 28, 1994) (telephone company cannot disconnect local service for failure to pay long-distance charges billed by local company). *Accord In re* Interstate Access Charges for Wyo. Tel. Util., 81 P.U.R.4th 524, 1987 WL 257466 (Wyo. Pub. Serv. Comm'n Feb. 21, 1987). *See also* Wash. Admin. Code §§ 480-120-061(1)(f) (telephone company may deny service because of overdue, unpaid prior obligation to same telecommunications company for same class of service), 480-120-172(4)(c) (nonpayment of interexchange carrier charges shall not be grounds for disconnection of local service, but phone company may restrict long-distance service). *But see* Allstates Transworld Vanlines, Inc. v. Southwestern Bell Tel. Co., 937 S.W.2d 314 (Mo. Ct. App. 1996) (company tariffs have force of law; tariff allowing disconnection of local telephone service for nonpayment of Yellow Pages bill upheld).

39 *See* § 11.6.5.6, *supra*.

40 An example of a case in which the court would not allow the utility to engage in subtle coercion to circumvent the ordinary debt collection process was Elwell v. Atlanta Gas Light Co., 181 S.E. 599 (Ga. Ct. App. 1935) (requiring that a public utility resort to the judicial process to enforce the claim since such process is consistent with principles of "justice" and "fair dealing" and utility should not serve as "both judge and jury" in a dispute). *See also* Wright v. Southern Bell Tel. & Tel. Co., 313 S.E.2d 150 (Ga. Ct. App. 1984) (genuine issue of material fact as to whether telephone company used demand for addi-

2.2.2 Unrelated Contract: Debts from Another Time and Place

2.2.2.1 Introduction

A utility, as a general rule, may not refuse to provide service based on a dispute arising out of a contract separate from the contract to provide the particular service in question. This question often arises when a utility denies service to a customer based on an old debt, such as an old utility bill from a prior residence, or a completely unrelated debt. At common law, a utility could not refuse to enter into a new contract for service because of an old debt, disputed[41] or not, from some other place and time.[42] This common law rule, however, has been significantly modified by regulation in many states. Some commissions have applied this rule in their orders and regulations,[43] but at least thirty states[44] explicitly permit utilities to deny service, or at least require deposits, if customers owe a debt for prior utility services to that company (or in some cases to other specified utilities).

2.2.2.2 Common Law Rule

The common law rationale is that at some point the debt becomes so "unrelated" to the current supply of utility service that utilities lose their right to a special method of collecting the debt. Noting the coercive power that utilities have as monopolies and suppliers of several of life's necessities, courts have tried to prevent abuses. One court reasoned that,

> if in the case at bar the former claim was a past-due indebtedness and was incurred at some other place of residence and was a wholly separate transaction, it must be collected in the usual way in which debts are collectable. . . . The relations of the parties to each other (growing out of their past separate transactions) have no influence upon their rights and obligations in their present transaction. If the [utility] wishes to collect the old bill, it should resort to the usual judicial process in like manner as other creditors are required to do, and not coerce the [consumer] into paying the old bill by denying him gas.[45]

The broad common law rule has been applied by some commissions and upheld by courts, although often in the context of termination.[46] Because the old debts arose under

tional security deposit and subsequent termination of service in a coercive manner).

41 *See* § 6.3.5, *infra* (discussion of utilities' termination rights with regard to disputed debts).

42 *See* Annot. *Right of Public Utility to Deny Service at One Address Because of Failure to Pay for Past Service Rendered at Another*, 73 A.L.R.3d 1292 n.3 (1976) (treating denial of service as encompassing both an initial refusal to render service upon application of the customer and a subsequent discontinuance of service that has been provided). *See also* Walton Elec. Membership Corp. v. Snyder,487 S.E.2d 613 (Ga. Ct. App. 1997), *aff'd*, 508 S.E.2d 167 (Ga. 1998) (cooperative utility liable to member for wrongful disconnection for debt of wife incurred on separate account before marriage); Berner v. Interstate Power Co., 57 N.W.2d 55 (Iowa 1953); Josephson v. Mountain Bell Tel. & Tel. Co., 576 P.2d 850 (Utah 1978) (telephone company may not disconnect an individual's home telephone for failure to pay accounts due on a business telephone). *But see* Soler v. Consolidated Edison Co., 53 A.D.2d 558 (N.Y. App. Div. 1976) (electric company was entitled to terminate service to a residence of a customer because of the customer's failure to make payment in full for electric services furnished to his sole proprietorship business).

43 These rules are often in the context of terminations, although the same principles apply to the initial right to service. Komisarek v. New England Tel. & Tel. Co., 282 A.2d 671 (N.H. 1971) (telephone company's tariff could not reasonably be construed to authorize the termination of a customer's existing service by reason of arrearages as to a discontinued line); Harrell v. Consolidated Edison Co., 398 N.Y.S.2d 522 (N.Y. Sup. Ct. 1977); *In re* Rules and Regulations Governing the Disconnection of Utility Servs., 30-000-004 Vt. Code R. § 3.302(F) (household rule) (a company shall not disconnect or refuse service to a customer due to a delinquent bill owed by another person except when the other person's delinquent bill stems from service to that household and that person is residing in the household). *But see* Carolina Water Serv., Inc. v. City of Winston Salem, 161 F.3d 1 (4th Cir. 1998) (unpublished) (water service is interconnected with and not collateral to continued sewage service); Rivera v. Consolidated Edison Co. of N.Y., Inc., 17 Pub. Util. Rep. 4th 238, 390 N.Y.S.2d 537 (N.Y. 1976) (public utility, as a condition of continued service, may require payment of unpaid bill not only at service recipient's present address but also at former address).

Rules sometimes contain these prohibitions on denying service for this type of collateral matter. *See, e.g.*, Alaska Admin. Code tit. 3, § 52.450(f)(3) (utility may not disconnect for nonpayment of bill related to another class of service at a different service location). *But see, e.g.*, 16 Tex. Admin. Code § 25.23(a)(5) (service may be declined if applicant is indebted to *any* utility for the same kind of service) (emphasis added).

44 Alabama, Alaska, Arizona, Arkansas, Illinois, Indiana, Iowa, Kansas, Kentucky, Louisiana, Maine, Maryland, Massachusetts, Minnesota, Mississippi, Missouri, New Hampshire, New York, Oklahoma, Oregon, Pennsylvania, Rhode Island, South Carolina, South Dakota, Tennessee, Texas, Washington, West Virginia, Wisconsin, Wyoming. *See* appx. A.1, *infra* (under individual state headings, "denial of service" and "deposits").

45 Elwell v. Atlanta, 181 S.E. 599, 601 (Ga. Ct. App. 1935). *See also* Wright v. Southern Bell Tel. & Tel. Co., 313 S.E.2d 150 (Ga. Ct. App. 1984) (company cannot seek to impose additional security deposit and terminate service for nonpayment of that deposit if intent is to coerce payment of debt not owed by plaintiff herself but by relative).

46 Komisarek v. New England Tel. & Tel. Co., 282 A.2d 671 (N.H. 1971) (telephone company's tariff could not reasonably be construed to authorize the termination of a customer's existing service by reason of arrearages as to a discontinued line); Josephson v. Mountain Bell, 576 P.2d 850 (Utah 1978) (company may not disconnect an individual's home telephone for failure to pay accounts due on a business telephone); *In re* Rules & Regulations Governing the Disconnection of Utility Servs.,

separate contracts and remedies, these debts may require judicial action to enforce collection.[47] This approach is not, however, universal. Many states' regulations define certain classes of old debts that may be grounds for refusal of service or imposition of a deposit.[48] Even when the statute of limitations had run on the old debt, one court and commission allowed a utility company to deny service until the old debt had been paid.[49]

2.2.2.3 State Regulations

Many state commissions have narrowed the broad common law rule by permitting utilities to refuse to serve or impose a deposit requirement upon customers who owe certain undisputed debts to utilities.[50] These regulations impose various limitations: same company,[51] same class of service (that is, utility bill of business may not be transferred to owner's residential account[52]), same kind of utility,[53] service within the state for that particular utility,[54] or time limitations.[55] Most of these regulations require the company to offer the consumer some kind of payment arrangement.[56]

Note that utility commission regulations in many states directly impose restrictions on a utility's ability to *terminate* existing service based on collateral matters. The Arkansas regulation is fairly typical and provides that a utility may not terminate service for a customer's:

A. Nonpayment for non-utility merchandise or non-utility services purchased, rented, or leased from or through the utility;
B. Nonpayment for a different kind or class of service; or
C. Nonpayment for service to the same customer but at a separate active account.[57]

It is therefore always important to check if the utility commission has a rule that directly addresses this issue. In states where utility commission regulations do not address the termination of service for collateral matters, it is possible that court decisions have addressed the issue.

2.2.2.4 Past Conduct Defrauding the Utility

It is possible that a utility, particularly a telephone utility, may deny service if it believes the service will be used in the commission of a crime, such as gambling or prostitution.[58] On the other hand, at least one court, in a case with somewhat unusual facts, has held that a utility cannot deny a customer service on the grounds he had allegedly stolen service from the company in the past.[59]

Depending on the facts specific to a case, advocates can argue that the utility should not be allowed to deny service to a customer alleged by the utility to have tampered with utility service. The utility can, instead, protect its interest by requiring an appropriate deposit or other protection against

---

30-000-004 Vt. Code R. § 3.302(B), (F) (prohibits disconnection if debt is more than two years old; prohibits disconnection if debt is for line extensions, special construction or other non-recurring charge; limits disconnection and refusal of service for debts of another). *But see* Rivera v. Consolidated Edison Co., 17 Pub. Util. Rep. 4th 238, 390 N.Y.S.2d 537 (N.Y. 1976) (public utility, as a condition of continued service, may require payment of unpaid bills not only at the service recipient's present address but also at the former address); Soler v. Consolidated Edison Co., 384 N.Y.S.2d 468 (N.Y. App. Div. 1976), *appeal dismissed*, 394 N.Y.S.2d 640 (N.Y. 1977) (electric company was entitled to terminate service to a residence of a customer because of the customer's failure to make payment in full for electric services furnished to his sole proprietorship business).

47 Komisarek v. New England Tel. & Tel. Co., 282 A.2d 671 (N.H. 1971) (commission's finding that past debt was properly due "was immaterial, since a determination of the plaintiff's liability was not sought in the proceedings, and jurisdiction to decide the issue was questionable"); Josephson v. Mountain Bell, 576 P.2d 850 (Utah 1978) ("The defendant is not without other remedies to collect its charges against the separate business entities conducted by plaintiff.").

48 *See* § 2.2.2.3, *infra*.

49 *See* Jackson v. Public Serv. Comm'n, 590 A.2d 517 (D.C. 1991) (finding reasonable the commission's conclusion that expiration of statute of limitations did not bar gas company from enforcing the terms of the tariff amount still on customer's account before service could be reinstated).

50 *See* appx. A.1, *infra* (under specific states and "denial of service" or "deposits").

51 *In re* Wisconsin Power & Light Co., 242 Pub. Util. Rep. 4th 193 (2005) (rules allow company that provides both gas and electricity to combine overdue amounts and take action based on the total). *See, e.g.*, 126-03-003 Ark. Code R. §§ 1.01–8.07 (LexisNexis); N.H. Code Admin. R. Pub. Util. Comm'n 1203.15.

52 *See, e.g.*, Ill. Admin. Code tit. 83, § 280.50. *See also* Brown v. Montana-Dakota Util. Co., 794 N.W.2d 741 (N.D. 2011) (no prohibition on disconnecting services due to unpaid balance when both accounts were for residential services to the same individual); Monroe v. Niagara Mohawk Power Corp., 88 Misc. 2d 876, 388 N.Y.S.2d 1003 (N.Y. City Ct. 1976).

53 *See, e.g.*, Ala. Pub. Serv. Comm'n Rule 12(I) (any utility may decline to serve an applicant or disconnect a customer who is indebted to the utility for similar service at a former location or at the present location); 126-03-003 Ark. Code R. §§ 1.01–8.07 (LexisNexis).

54 *See, e.g.*, 23-020 Wyo. Code R. § 245 (LexisNexis).

55 *See, e.g.*, La. P.S.C. Gen. Order of 12/13/93 (three years); Kan. Corp. Comm. Elec., Natural Gas and Water Billing Standards I D2 (five years); 65-407-81 Code Me. R. § (4)(F) (LexisNexis) (six years).

56 These regulations will be discussed in greater detail in § 6.3.3.3, *infra*.

57 126-03-003 Ark. Code R. § 6.02 (LexisNexis). *See also* Mass. Gen. Laws ch. 164, §§ 124 ("[i]n the event a person is being serviced by gas or electricity at two or more premises at the same time, a gas or electric company may enter only those premises to which the unpaid amount refers"), 124B ("No gas or electric company shall cut off gas or electric service in any home for the reason that a person has failed to pay for an appliance purchased from such company").

58 *See, e.g.*, Annot., *Right or Duty to Refuse Telephone, Telegraph or Other Wire Service in Aid of Illegal Gambling Operations*, 30 A.L.R.3d 1143, § 6(a) (1970).

59 State *ex rel.* Deeney v. Butte Elec. & Power Co., 115 P. 44 (Mont. 1911).

future unauthorized use.[60] Moreover, companies should not be allowed to take punitive action against customers based on unsubstantiated allegations of meter tampering.[61]

Thus the Nevada Commission permits a utility to deny service in the case of fraud committed by the customer,[62] but not in the case of gas and electric service when the conditions "constituting the fraud" have been corrected.[63] A commission may explicitly permit a utility to demand a deposit before reconnecting service in the case of alleged unauthorized use or diversion, when otherwise a deposit demand would not be allowed.[64]

It is important to note that many states have laws making meter-tampering a crime.[65] However, some companies are not very aggressive in seeking criminal penalties against residential (as opposed to business) customers who tamper with utility meters or equipment. In addition, utility commission regulations or a utility's filed tariffs may include provisions addressing the utility's rights in the event that a customer is alleged to have tampered with utility meters or equipment. Advocates working with customers in these situations should carefully review the state's utility statutes and regulations as well as the specific company's tariffs.

2.2.2.5 Separate Business Run by Utility

A second type of matter generally considered collateral is a debt to a separate business run by the utility, such as the sale of appliances or the provision of some optional, unregulated services. Many state regulations specifically forbid the termination or refusal of services for nonpayment of such debts.[66] As restructuring splits up the providers of utility services into various regulated and unregulated entities, a further problem will arise: whether one entity may terminate for nonpayment of another entity's bill. Many state restructuring statutes or regulations forbid the transmission and distribution utility to terminate its services for nonpayment of a generation company's bill (except when the utility is providing bundled standard offer or default service[67]). The generally accepted rule for telecommunications is that a local exchange carrier may not disconnect for nonpayment of long-distance or 900 number (pay per call) services.[68]

The general rule preventing a utility from refusing to provide service for a collateral matter such as a separate business[69] is subject to a significant exception: water and sewer service. These two businesses have become so intertwined in modern times—continuation of water service would necessarily involve the creation of waste water—that there is no definite rule left.

Unlike other utilities, water utilities are often allowed to deny water service for nonpayment of sewer charges and sometimes other service charges, such as garbage collection fees.[70]

60 In Louisville Gas & Electric v. Dulworth, 130 S.W.2d 753 (Ky. 1939), an injunction was granted compelling restoration of service to an alleged tamperer, conditioned upon his paying to the electric company the cost of a device designed to prevent future tampering. The court held that the customer was entitled to notice of the right to continued service with this condition.

61 Roger D. Colton, *Heightening the Burden of Proof in Utility Shutoff Cases Involving Allegations of Fraud*, 33 How. L.J. 137 (1990).

62 Nev. Admin. Code § 704.418(5) (telephone service).

63 Nev. Admin. Code § 704.348.

The distinction between gas and electric service on the one hand and telephone service on the other presumably derives from the greater likelihood that fraudulent use of telephone service can be achieved without changes to the physical equipment but that obtaining unauthorized gas and electric service cannot be accomplished without equipment tampering.

64 Mich. Admin. Code r. 460.2132(1)(d).

65 *See, e.g.*, Mass. Gen. Laws ch. 164, §§ 126, 127.

66 *See, e.g.*, Ill. Admin. Code tit. 83, § 280.50. *But see* Garner v. UGI Utils., Inc., 2005 WL 1651875 (Pa. Pub. Util. Comm'n 2005) (utility's application of overpayment of utility bill to disputed debt for unregulated maintenance and service was permissible when consumer did not specify application of the funds; however, utility fined for unreasonable delays and lack of communication during dispute resolution proceedings); *In re* Wisconsin Power & Light Co., 242 Pub. Util. Rep. 4th 193 (2005) (rules allow company that provides both gas and electricity to combine overdue amounts and take action based on the total).

67 Me. Rev. Stat. tit. 35-A, 3203(14); *In re* PECO Energy Co., 186 Pub. Util. Rep. 4th 388, 1998 WL 456681 (Pa. Pub. Util. Comm'n July 1, 1998). *See also* Commonwealth Edison Co. v. Illinois Commerce Comm'n, 767 N.E.2d 504 (Ill. App. Ct. 2002) (alternative retail supplier using single-billing option not required to bill electric customers for past-due amounts owed for previously supplied bundled service provided by another electric utility). *But see In re* Rochester Gas & Elec. Corp., 239 Pub. Util. Rep. 4th 443 (N.Y. Pub. Serv. Comm'n 2004) (utility may purchase competitive supplier's accounts receivable, then terminate both delivery and commodity supply, following procedures of Home Energy Fair Practices Act, if consumer fails to pay consolidated bill).

Restructuring, and standard offer service, are discussed at § 1.2.2.3, *supra*.

68 *In re* Service Quality Standards, Privacy Protections, and other Consumer Safeguards for Retail Telecomms., 194 Pub. Util. Rep. 4th 353 (Vt. Pub. Serv. Bd. 1999) (board changes its 1986 rule, which had allowed New England Telephone to disconnect local service for nonpayment of long-distance; board notes changes in the market, improved technology, and FCC rule that forbids disconnection of lifeline customers' local service for nonpayment of toll charges). *See also* § 11.6, *infra* (pay-per-call).

69 *See also* Annot., *Right of Municipality to Refuse Services by It to Resident for Failure to Pay for Other Unrelated Service*, 60 A.L.R.3d 707 (1974). *See generally* Note, *Updating a Municipal Utility's Right to Refuse Service, Sebring Utilities Commission v. Home Savings Association*, 508 So. 2d 26 (Fla. Dist. Ct. App. 1987), 17 Stetson L. Rev. 807 (1988).

70 *See, e.g.*, Donnelly v. City of Eureka, Kan., 399 F. Supp. 64 (D. Kan. 1975) (reasoning that courts have consistently held that a city may lawfully discontinue water service for nonpayment of sewer charges); City of Covington v. Sanitation Dist. No. 1 of Campbell & Kenton Counties, 301 S.W.2d 885 (Ky. 1957)

One court decided that the courts tending to prohibit disconnection of water for sewer and other services approach the issue with a functional analysis, focusing on the issue of "unrelated" or "collateral" businesses.[71] The courts that do allow disconnection of water service for nonpayment of sewer service focus on whether this disconnection has a relationship to the goal of public health protection[72] or if the two services are closely linked together. This is the most likely explanation for courts' differing treatment of garbage/water and sewer/water disputes.

Although a majority of jurisdictions permit the disconnection of water service for nonpayment of sewer service, they generally do not require it. Advocates should argue that this action, although permitted, will be devastating to low-income households and detrimental to public health. Other remedies should thus be preferred, such as placing a lien on the property (when permitted) or using the ordinary processes of dunning followed by lawsuit.[73]

(statute authorizing municipal water service to be cut off in the event of unpaid sanitation district sewer service charges was held not to be unconstitutional on any theory of impairment of obligation of contract between city and its water customers, or between the city and its waterworks revenue bondholders, or on any theory of arbitrary discrimination against water customers not paying sewer service charges); Metropolitan Util. Dist. v. City of Omaha, 107 N.W.2d 397 (Neb. 1961) (regulation promulgated by municipal ordinance providing that the water supply be shut off to residents delinquent in the payment of sewer charges is valid and not unreasonable or arbitrary).

This power of water utilities is often specifically authorized by state statute. *See, e.g.*, Cal. Pub. Utils. Code § 779.2 (West) (specifically excepting utility that collects sanitation or sewer charges from rule that no utility may terminate service for indebtedness owed to any other company); Kan. Stat. Ann. § 12-631k; Mo. Rev. Stat. § 250.236 (allowing sewer company to contract with water company to terminate water services for nonpayment of sewer bill). *But see, e.g.*, *In re* Morrilton Water Co., No. U-2792 (Ark. 1977) (water and sewer company may not terminate water service to a customer due to a delinquent sewer bill if the water bill is not delinquent or would not be delinquent if payment had been applied as specified by the customer); Garner v. Aurora, 30 N.W.2d 917 (Neb. 1948) (garbage and utility services are two separate businesses, and utility may not water terminate service to coerce payment for nonpayment of the garbage collection fees even when the collateral services or appliances are "necessary" to the provision of the utility service).

71 Perez v. City of San Bruno, 616 P.2d 1287, 1295, 1296 (Cal. 1980) (citing Garner v. City of Aurora, 149 Neb. 295, 30 N.W.2d 917 (1948)) (garbage collection is "collateral" to water service; thus, disconnection of water service for nonpayment of garbage/sanitation not allowed).

72 Perez v. City of San Bruno, 616 P.2d 1287, 1296 (Cal. 1980) ("in order to encourage and assure the support of all components of the city's public health and sanitation program, it has made the continuance of all of the offered utility services contingent upon the payment for all"); Cassidy v. City of Bowling Green, 368 S.W.2d 318, 320 (Ky. 1963); City of Breckenridge v. Cozart, 478 S.W.2d 162 (Tex. App. 1972).

73 *See* Margot Saunders et al., American Water Works Ass'n Research Found., Water Affordability Programs (1998).

2.2.3 Denial of Service Based on Third Party's Outstanding Debt to the Utility

2.2.3.1 Introduction

Sometimes a utility seeks to deny or terminate service to a customer for a debt that the customer has no connection with or requires as a condition of service that the customer pay the preexisting debt that is owed by a person who lives with the customer. In so doing, the utility is probably in violation of the general common law rule on "collateral matters,"[74] described in § 2.2.2, *supra*. The general common law rule states that a public utility generally may not terminate or refuse to render service because of a collateral matter not related to the service provided. However, at least eighteen states have regulations that permit the denial of service for a limited class of third-party debts.[75] Even so, some of these utility commissions place strict limits on third-party billing. The Connecticut Department of Public Utility Control stated its concerns about third-party liability, as follows:

> State regulations, statutes and Department Decisions clearly limit who the Company can bill for service and under what circumstances. . . . The termination and denial of services are special and severe remedies for nonpayment of a bill, especially as they apply to persons who have not expressly contracted for service, and the Department may proscribe the use of these remedies. . . . Service may not be denied or terminated because of nonpayment by another party. The only exception is marriage [quote from state domestic relations law omitted]. . . . In all other cases, service must be provided to a new applicant without regard to whether a previous customer defaulted on payment, whether the previous customer continues to live at the premises served, or whether

74 Commissions have often followed the common law in this area. *In re* Service Deposit & Termination Practice of Comm'cn Utils., Idaho Admin. Code r. 31.41.01.310 (local residential phone service shall not be terminated due to an unpaid bill for service to another customer or former customer, unless there is a legal obligation to pay, or for any other class of service); *In re* Regulations Governing Termination of Gas & Elec. Serv., 71 P.S.C. 452, Case No. 7413, Order No. 64486 (Md. Oct. 29, 1980) (failure of a gas or electric customer to pay the bill of another customer may not constitute sufficient cause for the company to terminate service to that customer).

75 Alabama, Arkansas, Florida, Kansas, Maryland, Michigan, Montana, New Hampshire, Ohio, Oregon, Rhode Island, South Carolina, South Dakota, Texas, Washington, West Virginia, Wisconsin, Wyoming. *See, e.g.*, State *ex rel.* Missouri Gas Energy v. Public Serv. Comm'n of Missouri, 224 S.W.3d 20 (Mo. Ct. App. 2007) (refusal of service when customer married woman who owed debt; only issue was whether wife was living in customer's household at relevant time). *See* appx. A.1, *infra*.

the new applicant is or was a roommate or a relative other than a spouse.[76]

Similarly, a utility may not withhold service to a new customer until he or she pays the delinquent bill of a prior customer who lived at the same residence.[77]

In the absence of a valid regulation on point,[78] such situations will be governed by state contract law, which generally forbids imposing implied contract or *quantum meruit* liability on one party when an express contract already exists with another.[79] Note that it may be possible for a state regulation that imposes third-party liability on a utility customer to be held as unreasonable if the regulation violates the common law principles articulated above and holds one utility customer liable for the debts of an unrelated party. Regulations held not to be reasonable include permits service disconnection for such collateral matters as nonpayment of a third party's debt[80] and for nonpayment of an unrelated service.[81] Indeed, one court suggested that a company's policy of forcing one person to pay for the debts of another amounted to an unconstitutional invasion of privacy (since it requires monitoring who lives at a particular address and essentially allows the utility to dictate who may live with whom).[82]

2.2.3.2 Former Owner or Occupant of Real Property

A customer who moves into a home may be denied utility service because the prior occupants or owners were in arrears for their utility bill. Many courts and commissions have ordered the utility to provide service in such a situation.[83] Denial of service to applicants who happen to be

76 *In re* Southern Conn. Gas Co., 198 P.U.R.4th 233, 2000 WL 194827 (Conn. Dep't Pub. Util. Control Jan. 28, 2000).

77 Granbois v. Big Horn County Elec. Coop., 986 P.2d 1097 (Mont. 1999) (electric cooperative's practice of making transfer of a membership to a new member contingent upon the new member's full payment of the previous member's delinquent bill held unreasonable and unenforceable). *See also* Bettini v. City of Las Cruces, 485 P.2d 967 (N.M. 1971) (when statute failed to authorize withholding service from subsequent owner, city could not refuse utility service to plaintiff until predecessor in title's debt was paid); Moore v. Metropolitan Utils. Co., 477 P.2d 692 (Okla. 1970); Oliver v. Hyle, 513 P.2d 806 (Or. Ct. App. 1973) (practice of terminating service to tenants who refused to pay arrearages incurred by previous tenants violated due process and equal protection).

78 *See* § 1.3, *supra* (discussing briefly difficult issues of state law concerning scope of power delegated to commissions).

79 *Cf.* California Apartment Assoc. v. City of Stockton, 95 Cal. Rptr. 2d 605 (Cal. Ct. App. 2000) (finding invalid a city ordinance that attempts to impose liability on landlord or subsequent tenant for the unpaid water, sewer, and refuse bills of a tenant). *But cf.* Casteel v. County of San Joaquin, 36 Cal. Rptr. 3d 395 (Cal. Ct. App. 2005) (distinguishing *City of Stockton* case on grounds that, while that case involved a statute prohibiting municipal corporations from recovering overdue utility bills from property owners or subsequent tenants, this case involved statutes expressly authorizing collection from property owners whether or not they contracted for services).

80 *See also* Granbois v. Big Horn County Elec. Coop., 986 P.2d 1097 (Mont. 1999) (REC regulation requiring new occupant of property to pay arrearages of prior occupant was unreasonable; REC not exempt from state's Consumer Protection Act claim). *Contra* First Fed. Sav. & Loan Ass'n of Twin Falls v. East End Mut. Elec. Co., Ltd., 735 P.2d 1073 (Idaho Ct. App. 1987). *See generally Liability of Premises or Their Owner or Occupant for Electricity, Gas or Water Charges, Irrespective of Who Is the User*, 19 A.L.R.3d 1227, 1252 (1968).

81 *See* Annot., *Right of Municipality to Refuse Services Provided by It to Resident for Failure of Resident to Pay for Other Unrelated Services*, 60 A.L.R.3d 714 (1974). *But see* Annot., *Right to Cut Off Water Supply Because of Failure to Pay Sewer Service Charge*, 26 A.L.R.2d 1359 (1952).

82 *In re* Tarrant, 190 B.R. 704 (Bankr. S.D. Ga. 1995).

83 A majority of state regulations explicitly forbid denial or termination for a prior occupant's arrears, including: Arizona, Colorado, Connecticut, Delaware, District of Columbia, Florida, Georgia, Hawaii, Idaho, Illinois, Indiana, Iowa, Kansas, Maine, Maryland, Minnesota, Mississippi, Missouri, Montana, Nevada, New Hampshire, North Carolina, North Dakota, Ohio, Oklahoma, Pennsylvania, Rhode Island, South Carolina, South Dakota, Tennessee, Texas, Washington, West Virginia and Wyoming. *See, e.g.*, Alaska Admin. Code tit. 3, 52.450(f)(1) (utility may not disconnect for delinquency in payment for services rendered to prior customer at premises.); 16 Tex. Admin. Code § 25.23(c)(1) (insufficient grounds to refuse service based on failure to pay the bill of a previous occupant of the premises); appx. A.1, *infra* (summary of each state's regulations). *See also* Golden v. City of Columbus, 404 F.3d 950 (6th Cir. 2005) (city policy of denying water service to tenant if landlord owed city for prior tenant's unpaid water bills violated equal protection); O'Neal v. City of Seattle, 66 F.3d 1064 (9th Cir. 1995) (city policy of denying water service to tenant based on past tenant's unpaid bill violated equal protection; follows Davis v. Weir, 497 F.2d 139 (5th Cir. 1974) and rejects Ransom v. Marrazzo, 848 F.2d 398 (3d Cir. 1988)); *In re* Tarrant, 190 B.R. 704 (Bankr. S.D. Ga. 1995); Price v. South Cent. Bell Tel. Co., 313 So. 2d 184 (Ala. 1975) (public utility company has no right to refuse service to a customer in order to compel that customer to pay the bill of a former subscriber); Alabama Water Co. v. Knowles, 124 So. 96 (Ala. 1929) (in the absence of a statute making a service charge a lien on the premises, a new customer cannot be denied service because some former customer is delinquent); Walton Elec. Membership Corp v. Snyder, 487 S.E.2d 613 (Ga. Ct. App. 1997), *aff'd*, 508 S.E.2d 167 (Ga. 1998); Cascade Motor Hotel, Inc. v. City of Duluth, 348 N.W.2d 84 (Minn. 1984) (municipal utility company's withholding of service until new owner paid indebtedness of former owner is arbitrary and unreasonable); State Bank of Delano v. CenterPoint Energy Res. Corp., 779 N.W.2d 582 (Minn. Ct. App. 2010) (receiver appointed to manage property during foreclosure was not required to pay mortgagor's outstanding utility debts and utility could not disconnect natural gas service to property); State of Mo. *ex rel.* Imperial Util. Corp. v. Borgmann, 664 S.W.2d 215 (Mo. Ct. App. 1983) (because there is no statutory authority enabling utility to charge subsequent customers for unpaid bills of previous customers, provisions in utility's tariff sanctioning collection by threatening to disconnect service or impose lien upon current customer are invalid); McMenamin v. Evesham Mun. Utils. Auth., 249 A.2d 21 (N.J. Super. Ct. Ch. Div. 1969), *aff'd*, 256 A.2d 801 (N.J. Super. Ct. App. Div. 1969); Baylor v.

living in a place for which a third party has not paid the utility bill has been construed by courts to be discriminatory and, when the utility's actions constitute state action (that is, a municipality is involved), this discrimination can rise to the level of a violation of the Equal Protection Clause of the Fourteenth Amendment. As the court stated in *Davis v. Weir*:

> "The fact that a third party may be financially responsible for water service provided under a prior contract is an irrational, unreasonable and quite irrelevant basis upon which to distinguish between other eligible applicants for water service." . . . The Department's actions offend not only equal protection of the law, but also due process.[84]

There are certain important exceptions to this rule. In some states, municipal utilities may impose a lien against real property for unpaid charges. This lien will survive the transfer of the property.[85] Courts have varied in their treatment of rural electric cooperatives, which have occasionally been permitted to require new owners to take over the membership of former owners—along with their unpaid debts.[86]

2.2.3.3 Landlord-Tenant Situations

Sometimes the denial of service results from the delinquency of a landlord, not the prior occupant. This pattern is the second common scenario. Generally utilities are not allowed to deny service in such a situation.[87] The situation has also arisen when an apartment building has only one meter or connection serving several tenants, and the utility tries to refuse (or disconnect) service to one tenant because of the arrears of another.[88] State regulations often prescribe in detail the protections for tenants in case of landlord delinquency. Typically, tenants must be notified, either in person, or by conspicuous posting in common areas and, when possible, given the opportunity to take service in their own names without being required to pay the landlords' arrears.[89] Some states also provide for receivership or rent

---

Philadelphia Elec. Co., 61 Pa. Pub. Util. Comm'n 323, No. F8532525 (Pa. Apr. 17, 1986) (there is a clear prohibition against a utility preconditioning service to a new applicant upon payment for service previously furnished under an account in the name of a person other than the applicant); *In re* Ch. 14 Implementation, 2005 WL 2445959 (Pa. Pub. Util. Comm'n Sept. 9, 2005), *amended by* 2005 WL 4066360 (Pa. Pub. Util. Comm'n Dec. 22, 2005) (tenant not required to pay arrearage of former occupant, but tenant who fails to notify utility upon start of tenancy bears burden of showing move-in date).

84 Davis v. Weir, 497 F.2d 139 (5th Cir. 1974) (quoting Davis v. Weir, 359 F. Supp. at 1027 (N.D. Ga. 1973)).

Davis was a civil rights action brought by a tenant against a city water department challenging the policy of terminating service without notice to the actual user the landlord's refusal to pay a past-due bill. The court held that the city water department's discriminatory rejection of new applications for water service based on the financial obligations of third parties failed to pass Fourteenth Amendment muster under the traditional "rational basis" analysis.

Although *Davis* involved a termination of service, the same reasoning should apply when an applicant first applies for utility service. Lake v. City of Youngstown Div. of Water, No. 4:93CV2559, slip op. (N.D. Ohio July 14, 1994) (holding that a municipal water company's denial of service solely on the basis of a preexisting water bill incurred by a third party at the same address violated equal protection; rejecting utility's arguments that the instant case should be distinguished from *Davis* because it involved an application for new service rather than a termination).

85 Ransom v. Marrazzo, 848 F.2d 398 (3d Cir. 1988) (lien for prior occupant's debt allowed, despite evidence of serious hardship in certain cases, that is, abused woman who moves back into home after abuser is jailed or subjected to restraining order). *Cf.* Missouri *ex rel.* Imperial Util. Corp. v. Borgmann, 664 S.W.2d 215 (Mo. Ct. App. 1983) (no lien for sewer services when no state statute authorized such a lien). *But see* Seattle Mortgage Co. v. Unknown Heirs of Gray, 136 P.3d 776 (Wash. Ct. App. 2006) (public utility district made loan to homeowner for energy-efficiency improvements, placed lien on home; contract allowed termination of service *to borrower* upon default; district not empowered to terminate service to senior lien-holder after foreclosure; district had same rights as any other junior lienholder).

86 First Fed. Sav. & Loan Ass'n of Twin Falls v. East End Mut. Elec. Co., 735 P.2d 1073 (Idaho 1987). *Contra* Walton Elec. Membership Corp. v. Snyder, 508 S.E.2d 167 (Ga. 1998); Granbois v. Big Horn County Elec. Coop., 986 P.2d 1097 (Mont. 1999). *See also* St. John v. Missoula Elec. Coop., Inc., 938 P.2d 586 (Mont. 1997).

87 Davis v. Weir, 497 F.2d 139 (5th Cir. 1974). *See also* Golden v. City of Columbus, 404 F.3d 950 (6th Cir. 2005) (city's policy of denying water service only to those tenants whose predecessors or landlords failed to pay bills violates equal protection); Pilchen v. City of Auburn, 728 F. Supp. 2d 192 (N.D.N.Y. 2010) (enactment of city ordinance established a property interest and "legitimate claim of entitlement" in water service by users, including tenants; city's action of effectively denying tenant water service unless she assumed her landlord's debt did not have a rational basis and therefore violated her right to due process and equal protection); La Nasa v. New Orleans Sewerage & Water Bd., 63 Pub. Util. Rep. 3d 428, 184 So. 2d 622 (La. 1966) (water board may not refuse water service to the owner of a building or his tenants until either of them pay an outstanding bill incurred by a former tenant). *But see* Birmingham Waterworks Co. v. Brooks, 76 So. 515 (Ala. Ct. App. 1917).

88 Jopling v. Bluefield Waterworks & Improvement Co., 74 S.E. 943 (W. Va. 1912) (when a water company contracted directly with a tenant occupying a ground floor of a building to supply him with water, and another tenant, on the second floor, refused to pay water rent, and the water company cut off the supply to the whole building, the tenant on the ground floor was entitled to supply without payment of rent of the second floor tenant). *But see* Birmingham Waterworks Co. v. Edwards, 81 So. 194 (Ala. Ct. App. 1918) (tenant held liable for all charges and arrears for water furnished himself and another tenant through a common pipe).

89 *See, e.g.*, Pilchen v. City of Auburn, N.Y., 728 F. Supp. 2d 192 (N.D.N.Y. 2010) (city's failure to provide written notice to tenant of her right to a hearing prior to deprivation of water

withholding. At least one court has held that a utility could deny service when the tables are turned and it is the landlord who is being refused (or losing) service for delinquent tenant bills.[90]

Whenever a tenant is threatened with loss of utility service due to the landlord's failure to pay the bills, advocates should consult both utility and landlord-tenant law in that state. For example, the state's landlord-tenant laws or the sanitary code may prescribe a list of requirements for habitability—including the provision of heat, light, and water—as well as a variety of remedies for violation, civil and criminal penalties and receivership, among other things.[91]

2.2.3.4 Debt of Roommate or Family Member

In the third common situation, a utility refuses service to an applicant or seeks to disconnect service to a customer because that person is living with a third party who is currently in arrears for utility service. The third party might be a roommate or a family member. This situation often arises when an adult son or daughter must return to the parental home because of unemployment, illness or a failed marriage. In general, again, the rule agreed upon by most commissions is that the utility may not refuse to provide service to one person based on the delinquency of another and may not prevent a customer from living with an individual who has a delinquent utility bill.[92] In at least seventeen states, however, Commission regulations allow a utility to refuse service for certain third party debts.[93] In general, this practice will be permitted if the applicant resided with the delinquent customer at the time the debt was incurred and continues to reside with him or her.[94] These regulations may raise difficult questions, concerning whether the legislature had properly delegated to the commission the power to abrogate the state's common law of contract.

In the absence of a valid regulation, a utility's attempts to impose liability on third parties will be limited by the state's law of contract. One of the most basic doctrines of contract law is that no implied contract can exist with one party when an express contract regarding the same subject matter has been made with another party.[95] Thus, when an applicant enters into an express contract for service, through which the utility agrees to provide service and the applicant agrees to pay for the service provided, liability for that service cannot be imposed on a person not a party to the express

service on three separate occasions as well as failure to provide a written explanation for why tenant could not apply for service in her own name was violation of due process).

90 Chatham v. Jackson, 613 F.2d 73 (5th Cir. 1980) (city's practice of terminating water service to landlord when tenant's bills were delinquent did not violate substantive due process, since it was not arbitrary to coerce owner into paying for services that benefited his property; also, because practice constituted a collection scheme bearing substantial relation to city's valid objective to remain financially sound, practice did not violate landlord's equal protection rights). *Contra* Monroe v. Niagara Mohawk Power Corp., 388 N.Y.S.2d 1003 (N.Y. City Ct. 1976) (when commercial tenant took service in own name, utility was told to look to tenant for payment, and landlord advised utility to terminate if tenant did not pay, landlord not liable).

91 *See, e.g.*, Mass. Gen. Laws ch. 186, § 14 (any owner "required by law or by the express or implied terms of any contract or lease . . . to furnish water, hot water, heat, light, power [or] gas . . . who willfully or intentionally fails to furnish" such utility service" shall be liable for a fine as well as "actual and consequential damages or three month's rent, whichever is greater . . ."); 105 Mass. Code Regs. 410.354 ("owner shall provide the electricity and gas used in each dwelling unit unless . . . a written letting agreement provides for payment by the occupant [and tenant is billed only for his or her own separately-metered] usage).

92 Donovan v. General Tel. Co., 19 Pub. Util. Rep. 3d 49 (Cal. 1957) (telephone company cannot deny service because another member of the household is delinquent); *In re* Tampa Elec. Co., 49 Pub. Util. Rep. 4th 547 (Fla. Pub. Serv. Comm'n 1982) (electric company can hold only the customer of record responsible for the customer's bill and cannot force another person not legally responsible for the debt to pay that debt to obtain or continue service); Walton Elec. Membership Corp. v. Snyder, 508 S.E.2d 167 (Ga. 1998), *aff'g* 487 S.E.2d 613 (Ga. Ct. App. 1997) (cooperative acted tortiously, and punitive damages could be awarded when cooperative threatened to terminate service to member who married another member who was delinquent); Wright v. Southern Bell Tel. & Tel. Co., 313 S.E.2d 150 (Ga. Ct. App. 1984) (termination of service to parents' home was wrongful when used to coerce them into paying son-in-law's debt); Smith v. Tri-County Elec. Membership Corp., 689 S.W.2d 181 (Tenn. Ct. App. 1985) (electric company policy of denying service to a customer when anyone owing on an old bill planned to live in the residence was held unreasonable and arbitrary.); Boone v. Mountain Fuel Supply Co., No. 85-057-04 (Utah Sept. 4, 1985) (practice of denying natural gas service to a new contracting residential customer until the outstanding delinquent balance owed for prior service provided to the roommate of the new customer is paid was held not to be permitted under a natural gas utility's tariff); *In re* Black Hills Power & Light Co., No. 9339, Sub 3 (Wyo. Nov. 27, 1970) (utility service is supplied on an individual basis and cannot be refused because customer's family member is indebted to the company). *See also In re* Brazil, 21 B.R. 333 (Bankr. N.D. Ohio 1982) (ECOA violation to refuse gas service to wife unless husband, who owed arrears, moved out of house); § 6.8, *infra* (regarding landlord requested disconnections). *But see* State *ex rel.* Missouri Gas Energy v. Public Serv. Comm'n of Mo., 224 S.W.3d 20 (Mo. Ct. App. 2007) (Missouri rule: may refuse service if any member of household has outstanding balance).

93 Alabama, Arkansas, Florida, Kansas, Maryland, Michigan, Montana, New Hampshire, Ohio, Oregon, Rhode Island, South Carolina, South Dakota, Texas, Washington, Wisconsin, Utah. *See* appx. A.1, *infra*.

94 *In re* Ch. 14 Implementation, 2005 WL 2445959 (Pa. Pub. Util. Comm'n Sept. 9, 2005), *amended by* 2005 WL 4066360 (Pa. Pub. Util. Comm'n Dec. 22, 2005) (occupant secondarily liable for customer's debt incurred at time when occupant resided with customer).

95 *See, e.g.*, New York Tel. Co. v. Teichner, 329 N.Y.S.2d 689, 692 (N.Y. Dist. Ct. 1972); Vetco Concrete Co. v. Troy Lumber Co., 124 S.E.2d 905 (N.C. 1962); 17 C.J.S. *Contracts* § 6 (1999).

contract,[96] such as a family member or roommate. A similar argument will limit the application of quasi-contract, *quantum meruit* liability.

2.2.3.5 Liability of One Spouse for Another's Bills

The courts and commissions have struggled with the issue of whether a utility should be allowed to deny service to a customer based on a third party's debt to the utility company when the third party is the customer's spouse. The question frequently arises when the bills that are accruing arrearage are in the husband's name and, when the husband leaves because of a divorce or for other reasons, the wife then applies for service in her own name.

Utilities seeking to find one spouse liable for the debts of the other usually look to some variation of the "family expense doctrine" or common law doctrine of necessaries.[97] This doctrine developed under very different economic and social circumstances during the nineteenth century, when husbands generally controlled a family's finances. Under the family expense doctrine, if a husband failed to support his wife and children, his wife could purchase necessities on credit for which the husband would be liable.

Many states now have such a doctrine in place, making both husband and wife legally liable for the payment of family expenses, which would generally include utility service.[98] Thus, if one spouse fails to make payment, the other may be held liable. In an Illinois case in which the decision was based on the Illinois family expense statute, a utility company was found to have lawfully denied service to a woman whose former husband had an outstanding balance—incurred while both were married and living together—with the utility company.[99]

The applicability of this doctrine varies from state to state. Many states do not apply the doctrine to parties who are separated in anticipation of divorce.[100] The doctrine does not apply to unmarried straight or same-sex "couples." If, however, a state authorizes "civil unions," new questions will emerge as to whether these unions should be treated like marriages for purposes of the family expense statutes or the common law doctrine of necessaries. In states that recognize common law marriage,[101] the doctrine's application to common-law couples may be more difficult to ascertain and depends among other things on relevant time periods and if there has been judicial recognition of the marriage. More specific utility statutes or tariffs that limit spousal liability can also be relied upon, under customary rules of statutory construction, to defeat an argument based on the family expense doctrine.

It does seem clear that, if a married couple (or partners in a civil union) reside in a state that applies the family expense doctrine, obtaining service in the name of one spouse when the other has defaulted on a bill becomes more difficult. Note that, in such cases, there are a number of limitations and defenses. In states where the common law doctrine of necessaries imposes liability only on the husband, courts faced with an equal protection challenge must decide whether to extend the obligation to wives[102] or eliminate it altogether.[103] Advocates should argue that the

---

96 "Breach of contract cannot be made the basis of an action for damages against defendants *who did not execute it and who did nothing to assume its obligations*." Gold v. Gibbons, 3 Cal. Rptr. 117, 118 (1960) (emphasis added).

97 *See* Southwestern Bell Tel. Co. v. Bateman, 266 S.W.2d 289 (Ark. 1954) (telephone service cannot be denied on basis that applicant's husband owed telephone company for phone rental, but this fact may be considered in setting amount of deposit). *See also In re* Tarrant, 190 B.R. 704 (Bankr. S.D. Ga. 1995); Walton Elec. Membership Corp. v. Snyder, 487 S.E.2d 613 (Ga. Ct. App. 1997), *aff'd*, 508 S.E.2d 167 (Ga. 1998); Central Ill. Light Co. v. Illinois Commerce Comm'n, 562 N.E.2d 4 (Ill. App. Ct. 1990) (gas and electricity service debts incurred by former and estranged husbands after separation were not a "family expense" for which wives were liable under the Family Expense Act); *In re* Midwest Gas, 161 P.U.R.4th 426, 1995 WL 382766 (Iowa Util. Bd. May 19, 1995) (utility service may or may not be necessary family expense, depending on facts); Tubbs v. Louisiana Power & Light Co., 349 So. 2d 994 (La. Ct. App. 1977) (plaintiff could not recover for damages arising from the discontinuance of electric service when plaintiff never informed the defendant power company that he no longer lived at his marital domicile); State *ex rel.* Missouri Gas Energy v. Public Serv. Comm'n of Mo., 224 S.W.3d 20 (Mo. Ct. App. 2007) (consumer married woman who owed debt; utility could refuse service if she resided in the home at the time the debt was incurred).

98 *See, e.g.*, Utah Admin. Code r. 30-2-9.

99 DiBello v. Illinois Commerce Comm'n, 610 N.E.2d 730 (Ill. App. Ct. 1993) *But see* Central Ill. Light Co. v. Illinois Commerce Comm'n, 562 N.E.2d 4 (Ill. App. Ct. 1990) (gas and electric debts incurred by former and estranged husbands after separation were not a "family expense" for which wives were liable under "Family Expense Act").

100 *See* Central Ill. Light v. Commerce Comm'n, 562 N.E.2d 4 (Ill. App. Ct. 1990).

101 Warren Gen. Hosp. v. Brink, 610 N.E.2d 1128 (Ohio Ct. App. 1992) (Ohio, which recognized common law marriage, made common law spouses liable for each other's necessaries, including last illness expenses).

102 Bartrom v. Adjustment Bureau, 618 N.E.2d 1 (Ind. 1993); St. Francis Reg'l Med. Ctr., Inc. v. Bowles, 836 P.2d 1123 (Kan. 1992); St. Luke's Episcopal-Presbyterian Hosp. v. Underwood, 957 S.W.2d 496 (Mo. Ct. App. 1997); Hulse v. Warren, 777 S.W.2d 319 (Mo. Ct. App. 1989); St. Joseph Hosp. v. Rizzo, 676 A.2d 98 (N.H. 1996); Jersey Shore Med. Center-Fitkin Hosp. v. Estate of Baum, 417 A.2d 1003 (N.J. 1980); Medical Bus. Assocs. v. Steiner, 588 N.Y.S.2d 890 (N.Y. App. Div. 1992); Our Lady of Lourdes Mem'l Hosp., Inc. v. Frey, 548 N.Y.S.2d 109, (N.Y. App. Div. 1989); North Carolina Baptist Hospitals, Inc. v. Harris, 354 S.E.2d 471 (N.C. 1987); Albert Einstein Med. Ctr. v. Gold, 66 Pa. D. & C.2d 347 (Pa. Ct. Com. Pl. 1974); Landmark Med. Ctr. v. Gauthier, 635 A.2d 1145 (R.I. 1994); Richland Mem'l Hosp. v. Burton, 318 S.E.2d 12 (S.C. 1984); Accounts Mgmt., Inc. v. Litchfield, 576 N.W.2d 233 (S.D. 1998); Estate of Stromsted, 299 N.W.2d 226 (Wis. 1980).

103 Emanuel v. McGriff, 596 So. 2d 578 (Ala. 1992); Kent Gen.

crafting of a gender-neutral family expense doctrine is best left to the legislature. Some states recognize a distinction between "provider" and "recipient" spouses, that is, potential obligors or recipients of support.[104] In some states, the spouse who did not incur the debt is only secondarily liable: the creditor may be required to show an attempt to collect from the spouse who is primarily liable,[105] that the secondarily liable spouse was not providing adequate support,[106] or that the resources of the primarily liable spouse are insufficient.[107] Inability to pay is often a defense.[108]

2.3 A Utility May Not Discriminate in Providing Service

2.3.1 Introduction

One of the basic tenets of utility law is that a public utility may not *unjustly* discriminate in its rates, rules or service among its customers. Public utility firms must serve all members of the public on equal terms.[109] Unlike private business concerns, which often discriminate among customers so as to maximize profits, utilities must serve all customers impartially and are forbidden from engaging in discrimination.

This does not mean that utilities may not discriminate at all; indeed, if a reasonable basis exists, they may develop separate customer and rate classifications, as for instance, for the times of day that service is demanded.[110] However, all customers similarly situated must be treated equally.

For low-income advocates, this rule of nondiscrimination can be used as both a sword and a shield. Proactively, it can be the basis for challenging "discriminatory" rules. For example, rules requiring larger deposits for:

- People who rent rather than own their home;
- People who rely on public assistance; or even
- People who have moved more often than others;[111]

might be challenged as having a heavier impact on low-income people, and thus be considered unjust discrimination.[112] On the other hand, the extent to which low-income households are charged different rates than other customers can also be subject to the unjust discrimination challenge.[113]

2.3.2 Basic Rule of Unjust Discrimination

Public utilities are obligated to serve all customers on equal terms—unjust or undue discrimination among customers is forbidden. This duty of nondiscrimination is one of the marks of a "public utility" and it attaches to RECs and municipal utilities as well as investor-owned utilities.[114]

Hosp., Inc. v. Harrison, 1997 WL 33471241 (Del. Ct. Com. Pl. May 2, 1997); Condore v. Prince George's County, 425 A.2d 1011 (Md. 1981); North Ottawa Cmty. Hosp. v. Kieft, 578 N.W.2d 267 (Mich. 1998); Govan v. Medical Credit Serv., Inc., 621 So. 2d 928 (Miss. 1993); Southern New Hampshire Med. Ctr. v. Hayes, 992 A.2d 596, 605 (N.H. 2010) (Hicks, J., concurring); Lichtman v. Grossbard, 533 N.E.2d 1048 (N.Y. 1988); Account Specialists & Credit Collections, Inc. v. Jackman, 970 P.2d 202 (Okla. Civ. App. 1998); Medical Ctr. Hosp. of Vt. v. Lorrain, 675 A.2d 1326 (Vt. 1996); Schilling v. Bedford County Mem'l Hosp., 303 S.E.2d 905 (Va. 1983).

104 Yale Univ. Sch. of Med. v. Scianna, 701 A.2d 65 (Conn. Super. Ct. 1997).

105 Bethany Med. Ctr. v. Niyazi, 890 P.2d 349 (Kan. Ct. App. 1995); Cheshire Med. Ctr. v. Holbrook, 663 A.2d 1344 (N.H. 1995); Trident Reg'l Med. Ctr. v. Evans, 454 S.E.2d 343 (S.C. 1995); Anderson Mem'l Hosp. v. Hagen, 443 S.E.2d 399 (S.C. 1994).

106 Allen v. Keating, 517 N.W.2d 830 (Mich. Ct. App. 1994); Smith v. Hernandez, 794 P.2d 772 (Okla. Civ. App. 1990).

107 St. Francis Reg'l Med. Ctr. v. Bowles, 836 P.2d 1123 (Kan. 1992); Dignity Care Home, Inc. v. Montgomery-Ryan, 246 P.3d 413 (Kan. Ct. App. 2011) (table); Bethany Med. Ctr. v. Niyazi, 890 P.2d 349 (Kan. Ct. App. 1995); Hawley by Cordell v. Hawley, 904 S.W.2d 584 (Mo. Ct. App. 1995); Jersey Shore Med. Center-Fitkin Hosp. v. Estate of Baum, 417 A.2d 1003 (N.J. 1980); Medical Bus. Assocs. v. Steiner, 588 N.Y.S.2d 890 (N.Y. App. Div. 1992); Landmark Med. Ctr. v. Gauthier, 635 A.2d 1145 (R.I. 1994).

108 Porter Mem'l Hosp. v. Wozniak, 680 N.E.2d 13 (Ind. Ct. App. 1997); Medical Bus. Assocs. v. Steiner, 588 N.Y.S.2d 890 (N.Y. App. Div. 1992); Our Lady of Lourdes Mem'l Hosp., Inc. v. Frey, 548 N.Y.S.2d 109 (N.Y. App. Div. 1989).

109 United Fuel Gas Co. v. Railroad Comm'n of Ky., 278 U.S. 300, 49 S. Ct. 150, 73 L. Ed. 390 (1929); Tonto Creek Estates v. Corporation Comm'n, 864 P.2d 1081 (Ariz. Ct. App. 1993).

110 *See* Office of the People's Counsel v. Public Serv. Comm'n of the Dist. of Columbia, 797 A.2d 719 (2002) (commission's approval of a tariff amendment allowing home-based businesses to pay residential rates given great deference when challenged as unjust and discriminatory).

111 *See* Barbara Linden & Anne Wicks, National Science & Law Ctr., Residential Mobility and the Low-Income Consumer (Sept. 10, 1985) (greater mobility of the low-income population).

112 *See Public Utilities and the Poor*, 78 Yale L.J. 448, at 457, 458 (1969) (suggesting that requiring deposits only from non-homeowners would violate the duty of nondiscrimination). *See also* Town of Wickenburg v. Sabin, 200 P.2d 342 (Ariz. 1948) (town may not require enhanced deposit from customer because he lives in tent house rather than a permanent dwelling); *In re* Mountain State Tel. & Tel. Co., 96 Pub. Util. Rep. 3d 338 (Colo. Pub. Util. Comm'n 1972); Poll v. New England Tel., 25 Pub. Util. Rep. 4th 529, 538, 539 (Me. Pub. Util. Comm'n 1970) (blanket policies exempting broad categories of customers based on occupation or class unjustified); 64 Am. Jur. 2d, *Public Utilities* §§ 34, 39 (2001) (no deposit may be required when it will result in discrimination against some customers or when it is enforced against only some customers).

Some of these rules also might fall in the face of a challenge under the Fair Housing Act.

113 *See* § 7.5, *infra*.

114 *See* §§ 1.1, 1.2, 1.3, *supra* (status of RECs and municipal utilities as public utilities). *See also* Inland Real Estate Corp. v. Village of Palatine, 496 N.E.2d 998, 1002 (Ill. App. Ct. 1986) (municipally owned utility systems, though specifically excluded from regulation as public utilities, are required by com-

The obligation to provide nondiscriminatory rates and services is part of the broader "duty to serve." Extremely important to note here is that *all* unjust discrimination is banned, not merely discrimination based on one of the limited categories specified in employment or housing law. Thus discrimination based on sex or race would be improper as would discrimination based on street name, length of service, and so forth, if these were not supported by some evidence to justify the disparate treatment.

The duty to serve is summarized in the "rule under modern industrial conditions" that "the public service company shall serve all with equality."[115] Organizations "which voluntarily undertake to engage in performing a service of a public nature" necessarily and concomitantly undertake "an obligation implied by law to render without discrimination and to all of the public in the area sought to be served, a service reasonably adequate to meet the just requirements of those sought to be served."[116] The reasoning behind the nondiscrimination requirement stems from the fact that public utilities historically held a monopoly status and, "[u]nder conditions of near monopoly, discrimination in price and perhaps service may become profitable to a business . . . [and] customers would be helpless in such a situation."[117]

Every state has some such statutory enactment applying to regulated utilities,[118] as do most utility rules,[119] although the duty to serve without discrimination does not depend on these statutes or rules. "We may conclude that in this country, independently of statutory provisions, all common carriers will be held to the strictest impartiality in the conduct of their business, and that all privileges or preferences given to one customer, which are not extended to all, are in violation of public duty."[120]

As deregulation splits the providers of energy services into monopoly distributors and a variety of non-monopoly entities—free market sellers of electric generation or natural gas, brokers, aggregators, and so forth—advocates will face new challenges. If these new entities are able to discriminate against low-income residential consumers, for example by geographic redlining or the imposition of unreasonable deposit requirements, these consumers will be denied the savings that restructuring provides to others and may be saddled with overpriced energy or, worse, unanticipated price fluctuations or hidden costs. These practices should, whenever possible, be addressed in the restructuring statute and regulations. Advocates should also argue that, insofar as these new entities resemble other competitive enterprises, general UDAP, fair credit, and anti-discrimination statutes should apply. Ideally, the application of these statutes should be made clear in the restructuring statute and regulations.[121] Even with fair and nondiscriminatory conduct by free-market sellers, there will be some low-income consumers who do not or cannot obtain service. Advocates should seek to ensure the continued availability of reasonably priced last resort or standard offer service for this group.[122]

The test for nondiscrimination is whether like customers are treated alike.[123] While a utility may distinguish customers based on "such other material conditions which distin-

---

mon law to serve their customers without unreasonable discrimination in rates or service); Dedeke v. Rural Water Dist. No. 5, Etc., 623 P.2d 1324 (Kan. 1981) (in law and in fact, a rural water district exercises the powers of a public utility—subject to state regulation and control); Owens v. City of Beresford, 201 N.W.2d 890 (S.D. 1972) (discrimination by a municipal utility is not forbidden, but unjust discrimination is forbidden).

115 Charles F. Phillips, Jr., The Regulation of Public Utilities 859 (1993).

116 City of Winter Park v. Southern States Utils., Inc., 540 So. 2d 178 (Fla. Dist. Ct. App. 1989) (citations omitted).

117 Charles F. Phillips, Jr., The Regulation of Public Utilities 119 (1993).

118 *See, e.g.*, Ga. Code. Ann. § 46-3-11 (electric supplies prohibited from having or applying any rate, charge, or service rule or regulation that unreasonably discriminates against or in favor of any member of a class of consumers or any class of consumers); Kan. Stat. Ann. §§ 66-1,189 (telecommunications public utilities) (every unjust or unreasonably discriminatory or unduly preferential rule, regulation, classification, rate, joint rate, toll, charge or exaction is prohibited, unlawful, and void), 66-1,202 (gas public utilities) (same).

119 *See, e.g.*, Fla. Admin. Code Ann. r. 25-7.033(1) (gas), r. 25-6.033 (electric) (utility may adopt additional uniform *non-discriminatory* rules and regulations as it finds necessary).

120 Cook v. Chicago, R.I. & P.R. Co., 46 N.W. 1080 (Iowa 1890).

Indeed, some courts have found statutes establishing a duty of nondiscrimination to be merely declarations of the common law. Hargrave v. Canadian Valley Elec. Coop., 792 P.2d 50, 58 (Okla. 1990) (quoting Consumers' Light & Power Co. v. Phipps, 251 P. 63 (Okla. 1926)) (Oklahoma statute "codifies the common law that 'all persons engaged in a public business have a duty to treat members of all who are similarly situated . . . on equal terms and at reasonable rates' ").

121 *See, e.g.*, *In re* Proposed Policies Governing Restructuring California's Elec. Servs. Industry & Reforming Reg., 184 Pub. Util. Rep. 4th 262, 1998 WL 173314 (Cal. Pub. Util. Comm'n Mar. 26, 1998) (violations of civil rights statute will subject electric service providers to sanctions, including possible loss of license); 65-407-305 Me. Code R. § 4 (LexisNexis) (UDAP violation is per se violation of licensing rules, which may result in loss of license or lesser sanctions).

122 *See* Barbara Alexander, Default Service for Retail Electric Competition: Can Residential and Low Income Customers Be Protected When the Experiment Goes Awry? (more information on how states have structured their default service), *available on the companion website to this treatise*.

123 Municipal utilities, for example, have been allowed to charge residents different rates from *non*-residents, as long as the differences are reasonable. *See, e.g.*, Zepp v. Mayor & Council of Athens, 348 S.E.2d 673, 676 (Ga. Ct. App. 1986) (city has a right to impose different water rates for resident and non-resident customers, but the actual rate is subject to review); Bobrowicz v. City of Chicago, 522 N.E.2d 663, 667 (Ill. App. Ct. 1988) (municipal corporation treated as private utility possessing duty to serve all of its customers without unreasonable discrimination in rates or manner of service; test to determine whether the rates charged by privately owned municipalities are discriminatory is based on factors such as difference in amount of product used, time when used, purpose for which used, or any other relevant factors reflecting differences in costs).

guish them from each other or from other classes,"[124] "laws designed to enforce equality of service and charges and prevent unjust discrimination require the same charge for doing alike and contemporaneous service under the same or substantially similar circumstances or conditions."[125]

To make this determination there must be a comparison between two customers or two groups of customers; claims of discrimination by one customer based on harsh (but not necessarily disparate) treatment by a utility company without such a comparison will probably fail.[126]

Note well that the rule requiring nondiscrimination "does not mean a uniformity of rates or prices for services rendered to the public. A 'public business' cannot be required to charge the same rate for services rendered to different classes or to people differently situated."[127] Only arbitrary discriminations are unjust. A difference in rates based upon a reasonable or fair difference in conditions that justifies a different rate or rule, is not an unjust discrimination.[128]

Discrimination in the rendering of public utility service is governed by the same principles as those governing nondiscrimination in rates.[129] So, for example, to deny service or terminate service to a customer in a manner different from that used with other customers may constitute unlawful discrimination.[130]

A discrimination challenge to a utility's customer service regulation can be broad and wide-ranging. The challenge must assert that the utility's classification of customers based on the challenged regulation categorizes those customers in an arbitrary and irrational fashion.[131] The challenge may address whether customers who are being treated differently evidence "material conditions which distinguish them from each other"[132] as well as whether there are truly "the same or substantially similar circumstances."[133] Thus one case found that charging only new water customers a hook-up fee to pay for costs associated with compliance with a new federal law, the Safe Drinking Water Act, while not assessing any of these costs to existing customers, was unlawful discrimination.[134]

2.3.3 Unjust Discrimination Challenges Based on Status as City Resident

One of the most typical uses of the rule against unjust discrimination is that made by utility customers of municipals who live outside the city boundaries and are charged higher rates than their neighbors within the city lines. The rules prohibiting unjust discrimination in rates and service require municipal providers to serve all customers—both in and out of city boundaries without *unreasonable* discrimination.[135]

However, the test for what is unjust discrimination between residents and non-residents is generally whether the rates are reasonable[136] based on factors such as difference in the amount of product used, the time when used, the purpose for which used, or any other relevant factors reflecting

---

124 Arkansas Natural Gas Co. v. Norton Co., 263 S.W. 775, 776 (Ark. 1924) (including citations therein).

125 Ellsworth Nichols, Public Utility Service and Discrimination 1021–41 (1928). *But see* Liberty Rice Mill, Inc. v. City of Kaplan, 674 So. 2d 395 (La. Ct. App. 1996) (city ordinance restructuring electric utility rate so as to retain large customer and employer threatening to relocate if rate were not reduced, and so as to result in a lower rate relative to plaintiff, was not unreasonable or impermissibly discriminatory).

126 *See* Chase Gardens, Inc. v. Oregon Pub. Util. Comm'n, 886 P.2d 1087 (Or. Ct. App. 1994) (gas company action of placing crop lien on customer's property to collect delinquent bill, destroying credit, and forcing it out of business not discriminatory per commission order since customer unable to show disparate treatment of other customers similarly situated).

127 Hargrave v. Canadian Valley Elec. Coop., 792 P.2d 50, 58 (Okla. 1990).

128 *Id. See also* Fred Nackard Land Co. v. City of Flagstaff, 238 P.2d 149 (Ariz. 2010) (classifications drawn by ordinance establishing charge and credit system to fund city's stormwater management utility were rationally tied to legitimate legislative objectives and did not violate principles of equal protection).

129 Ellsworth Nichols, Public Utility Service and Discrimination 1021–41 (1928).

130 As the court made clear in Choctaw Electric Cooperative v. Redman, 293 P.2d 564 (Okla. 1956), after the plaintiff had done everything required to become a member of the cooperative, the refusal to serve him was considered arbitrary discrimination.

131 *See, e.g.*, Hails & Higgins v. Columbia Gas of Ohio, Inc., 1998 WL 173326 (Ohio Pub. Util. Comm'n 1998) (gas company's "leave on for heat" policy did not discriminate against non-property owners).

132 Arkansas Natural Gas Co. v. Norton Co., 263 S.W. 775, 776 (Ark. 1924) (including citations therein).

133 Ellsworth Nichols, Public Utility Service and Discrimination 1021–41 (1928).

134 Boise Water Corp. to Revise and Increase Rates v. Idaho Pub. Util. Comm'n, 916 P.2d 1259 (Idaho 1996).

135 Zepp v. Mayor & Council of Athens, 348 S.E.2d 673 (Ga. Ct. App. 1986); Bobrowicz v. City of Chicago, 522 N.E.2d 663 (Ill. App. Ct. 1988) ("When a municipal corporation . . . operates a water system for the purpose of selling water to consumers, it is acting in a business capacity and is generally to be treated as if it were a private utility company. At common law, such an enterprise . . . was prohibited from charging exorbitant rates and was required to serve all of its customers without unreasonable discrimination in rates or manner of service.") (citations omitted); Inland Real Estate Corp. v. Village of Palatine, 496 N.E.2d 998, 1002 (Ill. App. Ct. 1986); Mitchell v. City of Wichita, 12 P.3d 402 (Kan. 2000); Spring v. Bradley, 733 A.2d 1038 (Md. Ct. Spec. App. 1999); Township of Meridian v. City of E. Lansing, Mich., 71 N.W.2d 234 (Mich. 1955) (when municipal charges different rates to residents and non-residents, the relevant issue is whether the rates are reasonable); Stepping Stones Assoc. v. City of White Plains, 473 N.Y.S.2d 578 (N.Y. App. Div. 1984), *aff'd in memorandum decision by* 64 N.Y.2d 690474 N.E.2d 1196 (N.Y. 1984); Platt v. Town of Torrey, 949 P.2d 325 (Utah 1997) (town is not precluded from charging non-residents higher rates for water, but rates must be reasonable; party challenging rate has burden or proof).

136 Township of Meridian v. City of E. Lansing, Mich., 71 N.W.2d 234 (Mich. 1955). *See also* Platt v. Town of Torrey, 949 P.2d 325 (Utah 1997) (and citations therein).

differences in costs.[137] Such relevant factors include added costs to extend the system to a new area or the fact that municipal property taxes, which only residents pay, have paid for the system.[138] Even surcharges as much as 50% over the rates charged to city residents, have been found to be reasonable.[139]

2.3.4 *Low-Income Rates Are Not Unjust Discrimination*

Efforts to establish affordability programs for low-income households have often been met with the argument that providing special rates to a class of customers based on their income alone would unjustly discriminate against other customers.[140] At times, this argument has prevailed.[141] However, the argument has also failed on the grounds that low-income customers display other characteristics, such as low usage, which justify setting rates differently; that setting rates which are unaffordable for a portion of the population will result in loss of profits from potential customers; or that utility commissions have some discretion to consider non-cost factors when setting rates.[142]

2.4 Remedies for Refusal to Provide Service

2.4.1 *Dispute Resolution: Regulated Utilities*

A utility's denial of an application for service is a common source of controversy. The first place to turn if an applicant has been refused service is the state public utility commission. Most commissions have some form of informal dispute resolution procedure, generally at no cost to the customer to resolve disputes.[143] If this is not successful, a formal complaint procedure before the commission or an administrative law judge is often provided for in state statute or regulations.

The advantages of this approach are that the cost is usually nothing and the pace of these proceedings, at least at the informal stage, is quick. Formal appeals may take longer but, in general, will still proceed much more quickly than a court case. The remedies, however, are limited. The usual remedy will be a decision ordering the utility to connect service. It may be possible to seek and obtain a penalty for a violation of tariffs or commission rules. These penalties can be quite high (for example, $1000 per day), but the money does not go to the rejected applicant. Instead, it goes to the state, or sometimes into special funds for utility assistance. While such penalties have been awarded from time to time, they are rare. Damages to the applicant will usually not be available.

2.4.2 *Court Remedies and Jurisdiction*

Courts have power to award damages or grant appropriate equitable relief to damaged consumers. Utilities have been found liable for damages for failure to provide service,[144] including compensatory, nominal, and punitive awards when appropriate.[145] Some customers are more interested in eq-

---

137 Bobrowicz v. City of Chicago, 522 N.E.2d 663 (Ill. App. Ct. 1988). *See also* Handy v. City of Rutland, 598 A.2d 114 (Vt. 1990) (city allowed to impose impact fee on extraterritorial users to defray cost of expanding sewage system).

138 *See* Margot Saunders et al., Water Affordability Programs, American Water Works Ass'n Research Found. ch. 8 (1998) (detailed discussion of such cross-subsidization).

139 Mitchell v. City of Wichita, 12 P.3d 402 (Kan. 2000) (finding it was reasonable for municipality to charge a 55% nonresident surcharge for water and sewer service to customers outside the city limits).

140 *See* ch. 7, *infra* (description of these programs).

141 Arkansas Gas Customers, Inc. v. Arkansas Pub. Serv. Comm'n, 118 S.W.3d 109 (Ark. 2003); Nunemaker v. Pacific Tel. & Tel. Co., 80 Pub. Util. Rep. 3d 129 (Cal. 1969); Citizens Action Coal. of Ind., Inc. v. Public Serv. Co. of Ind., 450 N.E.2d 98 (Ind. Ct. App. 1983); Mountain States Legal Found. v. New Mexico State Corp. Comm'n, 687 P.2d 92 (N.M. 1984).

142 *See, e.g.*, U.S. Steel Corp. v. Pennsylvania Pub. Util. Comm'n, 390 A.2d 865, 871 (Pa. Commw. Ct. 1978) ("Certainly there is nothing in Pennsylvania law which now empowers the Commission to require one customer simply to pay another's utility bill; and . . . the utility may not and could not for long be required to provide such subsidy out of its capital. This is not to say, however, that rate structures may not be rearranged from time to time in response to changes in economic conditions—whether general changes or changes especially affecting particular classes of customers."); Pennsylvania Pub. Util. Comm'n v. Pennsylvania Gas & Water Co., 142 Pub. Util. Rep. 4th 302, 1993 WL 193332 (Pa. Pub. Utils. Comm'n Feb. 25, 1993) (evidence of the general customer population as it relates to the affordability of utility service is relevant to setting rates; commission notes that it routinely takes customer's financial circumstances into consideration in dealing with individual inability-to-pay cases and in ordering the creation of Customer Assistance Programs); *In re* PacifiCorp, d.b.a. Utah Power and Light Co. 192 Pub. Util. Rep. 4th 289, 1999 WL 218118 (Utah Pub. Serv. Comm'n Mar. 4, 1999) (sets forth criteria for acceptable Lifeline program and appoints task force to design one); *In re* PacifiCorp, Utah P.S.C. Case 99-035-10 (Lifeline order). *See also* American Hoechest Corp. v. Department of Pub. Utils., 399 N.E.2d 1 (Mass. 1980) (special rate for elderly poor was not unduly or irrationally discriminatory).

143 *See, e.g.*, Utah Admin. Code r. 746-100-2(E), r. 746-100-3(F).

Of course it is important to investigate the basis for the customer's complaint, because sanctions for frivolous litigation in the administrative context are a possibility for abuse of the procedure, much like Rule 11 in a court context. *See* Victor v. GTE Cal., Inc., 1998 WL 242751 (Cal. Pub. Util. Comm'n 1998) (eighteen cases filed with no basis; ALJ ordered to consider sanctions).

144 *See, e.g.*, Central Mo. Elec. Coop. v. Wayne, 18 S.W.3d 46 (Mo. Ct. App. 2000); Danisco Ingredients U.S.A., Inc. v. Kansas City Power & Light Co., 999 S.W.2d 326 (Mo. Ct. App. 1999).

145 *See, e.g.*, Southern Pine Elec. Coop. v. Burch, 878 So. 2d 1120

uitable remedies. This occurs more often, perhaps, in the context of terminations, but a denial of service would present the same issues and a court may issue an injunction requiring the utility to provide service.[146] For example, in the event a utility attempts to violate its legal duty to maintain service pending resolution of a billing dispute, a court may issue an injunction preventing it from carrying out a threat to terminate service.[147] Mandamus, a court order to compel service, may be available;[148] again, this is more common in the context of a customer seeking to have service restored after a wrongful termination, for example, in the event of nonpayment of a disputed bill.[149]

Clearly, under normal rules for injunctions, obtaining relief will be easier in the context of maintaining or restoring the status quo (service) than in obtaining new service when denied. In a recent Indiana case, after holding that the trial court had jurisdiction to grant an injunction ordering the utility to provide service to an applicant who had bypassed the regulatory commission appeals process, and after a discussion of primary jurisdiction, the appeals court found that the customer had not met his burden of proving irreparable harm because he had not introduced evidence to show he was unable to pay the deposit and his old bill or why he waited from July when he first sought service until October ("the brink of winter") to file his case.[150]

These rights to equitable remedies should be available in the courts *regardless* of whether the affected utility is also regulated by the public utility commission.[151] Generally courts have concurrent jurisdiction to consider matters affecting utility service, especially when the relief requested is equitable in nature.[152] Courts do not ordinarily lose their *equity* jurisdiction just because the state has given an administrative agency authority over the business transactions of an industry.[153] Courts may hold that they, and not the commission, have jurisdiction to award damages for wrongful acts of utilities.[154]

(Ala. 2003); Gulf States Utils. Co. v. Low, 79 S.W.3d 561 (Tex. 2002); Southwestern Gas & Elec. Co. v. Stanley, 70 S.W.2d 413 (Tex. 1934). *See also* S.D. Codified Laws § 49-13-14.1 (individuals injured by wrongful acts or omissions of telephone companies may sue for double damages and may be awarded attorney fees).

An example of damages held to be inappropriate is economic damages that a customer sought for harm to his business when a telephone company did not start service in time. California Electronics, Inc. v. Pacific Bell, 41 C.P.U.C.2d 196 (Aug. 7, 1991) (slip opinion) (commission held that, under the statutory mandate, Cal. Pub. Utils. Code § 734, the customer is not entitled to any damages outside of reparation).

146 There is a case involving an injunction to prevent a utility from terminating service. *See, e.g.*, Hall v. Village of Swanton, 35 A.2d 381 (Vt. 1944) (injunction will ordinarily be granted to prevent a public service corporation from wrongfully shutting off electricity on the theory that the remedy at law is inadequate and that shutting off the supply would cause irreparable injury).

147 *See, e.g.*, Coult v. Mayor & Bd. of Aldermen, City of Gretna, 11 So. 2d 424 (La. Ct. App. 1943) ("To permit the City to cut off the water supply of one of its customers on every occasion that there is a dispute concerning its charge for water would result in the denial of the right to have the question of the amount due subject to judicial determination without irreparable loss and damage."); Cedar Graphics, Inc. v. Long Island Power Auth., 826 N.Y.S.2d 396 (N.Y. App. Div. 2006) (preliminary injunction proper when evidence showed likelihood of success on the merits of plaintiff's billing challenge).

148 Plum Creek Dev. Co. v. City of Conway, 512 S.E.2d 106 (S.C. 1999).

149 *See, e.g.*, Home Owners' Loan Corp. v. Logan City, 92 P.2d 346 (Utah 1939) (including cases cited therein).

150 *See* Northern Ind. Pub. Serv. Co. v. Dozier, 674 N.E.2d 977, 990–91 (Ind. Ct. App. 1996).

151 Louisville Gas & Elec. Co. v. Dulworth, 130 S.W.2d 753 (Ky. 1939) (while public utility commission has primary jurisdiction over utilities, it does not have exclusive jurisdiction on complaint made by an individual seeking restoration of service).

152 Steele v. Clinton Elec. Light & Power Co., 193 A. 613 (Conn. 1937) (public service commission's jurisdiction to hear disputes over charges for service does not preclude equity court from enjoining termination of service); Yankee Gas Servs Co. v. Redding Life Care, L.L.C., 2009 WL 1707393 (Conn. Super. Ct. May 28, 2009); Johnston v. Mid-Michigan Tel. Corp., 290 N.W.2d 146 (Mich. Ct. App. 1980) (court of general jurisdiction did not lack jurisdiction over claim in tort for alleged wrongful termination of service); Hall v. Village of Swanton, 35 A.2d 381 (Vt. 1944) (injunction will ordinarily be granted to prevent a public service commission from wrongfully shutting off electricity on the theory that the remedy at law is inadequate and that shutting off the supply would cause irreparable injury). *But see, e.g.*, BPW Plastics Corp. v. Massachusetts Elec. Co., 368 N.E.2d 830 (Mass. App. Ct. 1977) (no court, other than Supreme Judicial Court on direct appeal, may stay rate order of commission).

153 Carter v. Suburban Water Co., 101 A. 771 (Md. 1917) (although public service commission has jurisdiction in cases involving the correctness of charges for water, it could not deprive a court of equity of its original jurisdiction to grant an injunction for refusal to supply water); Steele v. Clinton Elec. Light & Power Co., 193 A. 613 (Conn. 1937). *See also* Louisville Gas & Elec. Co. v. Dulworth, 130 S.W.2d 753 (Ky. 1939) (public utility commission does not have exclusive jurisdiction over complaint made by an individual seeking restoration of service); Stillman & Dolan v. Chesapeake & Potomac Tel. Co., 351 A.2d 172 (Md. Ct. Spec. App. 1976) (legislature established a comprehensive scheme embracing view that commission be the first to hear grievances under procedures carefully designated with judicial review thereafter available; issues involving rates are to be distinguished from those arising from a dispute on a bill, which are appropriate for a court in equity to determine); O'Neal v. Citizens' Pub. Serv. Co. of S.C., 154 S.E. 217 (S.C. 1930); Hall v. Village of Swanton, 35 A.2d 381 (Vt. 1944) (injunction will ordinarily be granted to prevent a public service corporation from wrongfully shutting off electricity on the theory that the remedy at law is inadequate and that shutting off the supply would cause irreparable injury).

154 *E.g.*, Church Mut. Ins. Co. v. Consumers Energy Co., 2008 WL 53773 (W.D. Mich. Jan. 2, 2008) (summary judgment granted on issue of primary jurisdiction; defendant's duty arose in tort, the claim was for property damage not covered by tariffs, and the commission had previously determined that this type of claim did not require special expertise or threaten uniform regulatory treatment); City of Newton v. Massachusetts Dep't of Pub. Util., 328 N.E.2d 885, 9 Pub. Util. Rep. 4th 344 (Mass.

The doctrine of primary jurisdiction may be invoked to bar judicial relief absent first resorting to such remedies as the public utility commission may afford.[155] And trial courts will typically lack jurisdiction to review claims involving the rate setting process, quality of service, or other matters under the commission's express supervision.[156]

Issues concerning individual customer disputes rarely reach the courts on appeal from commission decisions, so there is little reported law in this area. Many states limit challenges to the orders of the public service commission,[157] and collateral attacks may be barred or discouraged by application of the doctrines of primary jurisdiction or exhaustion of administrative remedies. Finally, to foster the statutory purpose of a unified statewide utilities policy developed by an expert panel, appeals often lie to the Supreme Court rather than the trial-level courts.[158]

2.5 Customers Have the Right to Written Notice of Utilities' Rules

A public utility has the general obligation at common law to provide notice of its rates, rules, and regulations—the violation of which may lead to the disconnection of service.[159] At a minimum, this obligation requires the utility to enforce only those policies and regulations that have been committed to writing and that a customer could find if inquiries were made.

At least one court has held that *actual* knowledge of the policies is not required.[160] However, it is likely that an "informal policy" that is not committed to writing, and of which a utility customer could thus not have notice, would not provide an enforceable regulation whose violation can be used to justify a disconnection of service.[161] This argument could be made with regard to municipals and Rural Electric Cooperatives (RECs); since their customer service regulations are not required to be filed with any public agency, there is no reason why a customer of these unregulated utilities should be charged with constructive notice of those service regulations.

Oftentimes, in the case of regulated utilities, commission rules require that the utility provide the customer notice of its rules. For example, the Michigan Public Service Commission rules require utilities to prepare "pamphlets that, in easily understood terms, summarize the rights and responsibilities of its customers." These pamphlets are required to be displayed "prominently" at all utility office locations and

---

1975); Stark Steel v. Michigan Consol. Gas Co., 418 N.W.2d 135 (Mich. Ct. App. 1987); Nevada Power Co. v. Eighth Judicial Dist. Ct., 102 P.3d 578 (Nev. 2004) (claims sounding in tort, contract, and consumer fraud fall within court's original jurisdiction; court properly exercised discretion in refusing to defer primary jurisdiction to PUC); Summit Props., Inc. v. Public Serv. Co. of New Mexico, 118 P.3d 716 (N.M. Ct. App. 2005). *See also* Muise v. GPU, Inc., 753 A.2d 116 (N.J. Super. Ct. App. Div. 2000).

155 Travelers Ins. Co. v. Detroit Edison Co., 631 N.W.2d 733 (Mich. 2001) (doctrine of primary jurisdiction is not an affirmative defense that can be waived); Rinaldo's Constr. Corp. v. Michigan Bell, 559 N.W.2d 647 (Mich. 1997) (tort claims for money losses due to problems with telephone service must be brought before commission; primary jurisdiction discussed); State *ex rel.* Taylor v. Nangle, 227 S.W.2d 655 (Mo. 1950) (commission has primary jurisdiction over claim that utility wrongfully disconnected service; writ of prohibition would lie against trial court to prevent enforcement of injunction obtained by customer who had not sought redress before commission). *See also* Gunter v. Long Island Power Authority/Keyspan, 2011 WL 1225791 (E.D.N.Y. Feb. 15, 2011) (applying the doctrine of primary jurisdiction to the claim that the defendant failed to comply with its own tariff because plaintiff's claims required an application of the Authority's tariff to numerous disputed issues of fact). *But see* Northern Ind. Pub. Serv. Co. v. Dozier, 674 N.E.2d 977, 990–91 (Ind. Ct. App. 1996). *Cf.* City of Galveston v. Flagship Hotel, Ltd., 73 S.W.3d 422 (Tex. App. 2002) (doctrine of primary jurisdiction irrelevant in water shut-off/billing dispute matter because doctrine presupposes concurrent jurisdiction, yet Water Code vested commission with exclusive jurisdiction).

156 Spence v. Boston Edison Co., 459 N.E.2d 80 (Mass. 1983) (trial court lacks jurisdiction over reasonableness of rate in challenge to validity of rate design completely under control of commission); Valentine v. Michigan Bell Tel. Co., 199 N.W.2d 182 (Mich. 1972) (complaint for damages for inadequate service would not lie absent allegations of negligence, gross negligence, fraud, misrepresentation or some other tort); State *ex rel.* Dayton Power & Light Co. v. Kistler, 385 N.E.2d 1076 (Ohio 1979) (claim of rate discrimination).

157 *E.g.*, Mass. Gen. Laws ch. 25, § 5; Ohio Rev. Code Ann. § 4903.12 (West). *But see, e.g.*, Mich. Comp. Laws §§ 460.59, 462.26 (similar to Oregon statute); Or. Rev. Stat. §§ 756.580–756.610 (appeals first to circuit court, which must not substitute its judgment on the facts for that of commission; appeal thence to court of appeals).

158 The state APA may or may not be construed to permit a trial or intermediate level appellate court to review rulemaking decisions, as opposed to adjudications (when the exclusive jurisdiction of the high court to review commission decisions usually survives the enactment of the state APA).

159 Bookstaber v. PECO Energy Co., 99 Pa. Pub. Util. Comm'n 378, 2004 WL 1983032 (Pa. Pub. Util. Comm'n 2004) (utility admonished and fined for failing to communicate to applicant standards for deposits and creditworthiness, and procedure for seeking waiver). *See, e.g.*, Washington Gas Light Co. v. Aetna Cas. & Surety Co., 242 A.2d 802, 804–05 (Md. 1968) (once the utility "receives actual knowledge of a transfer of ownership at a time when the termination of service might present an obvious danger of damage to the premises, it owes an absolute duty *to clearly and unambiguously inform the customer* of its company regulations and policies and what action it intends to take") (emphasis added).

160 Cullinane v. Potomac Elec. Power Co., 147 A.2d 768, 770 (D.C. Mun. App. 1959) ("these rules are binding on both the customer and the utility, and actual knowledge thereof or assent is legally immaterial").

161 Bookstaber v. PECO Energy Co., 99 Pa. Pub. Util. Comm'n 378, 2004 WL 1983032 (99 Pa. Pub. Util. Comm'n 378 2004) (utility ordered to put its credit procedures in writing and make them available to applicants and customers).

mailed to each new customer.[162] Like the Michigan rules, some states' rules take the requirement of publishing notice of utility rules one step further by requiring some standards of clarity.[163] Several even require this information to be printed in Spanish.[164] These pamphlets are sometimes called customers' "Bill of Rights."

A Bill of Rights is both a tool to educate consumers about rights with respect to utility service and a means to apply existing consumer protections from the regulated marketplace to the emerging, competitive marketplace. The National Association of Regulatory Utility Commissioners passed a resolution supporting a Telecommunication Consumer Bill of Rights in response to the unprecedented levels of consumer abuse and fraud occurring as the telecommunications market moves away from monopoly services to a competitive marketplace.[165] The fundamental consumer rights set forth in the NARUC resolution include rights to disclosure, choice, privacy, participation in public policy proceedings, enforcement, accurate bills, freedom from discrimination, and safety. The California's Public Utility Commission initiated a rulemaking in 2000 to establish a Telecommunications Consumers' Bill of Rights and consumer protection rules and has issued a draft decision on the matter.[166]

2.6 The Right to Courteous Treatment

2.6.1 "Special Relationship" Between Utilities and Customers

A "special relationship" exists between utilities and their customers, derived from the powerful bargaining position of the utility vis-à-vis its customers:[167] utilities are generally monopoly providers of service[168] and providers of an essential public service.[169] Because of the bargaining power of utility companies, a public utility is under an enforceable obligation:

(1) To serve all who apply for its service and agree to abide by its reasonable rules and regulations;[170]
(2) To provide non-discriminatory service;[171]
(3) To inform customers of the least-cost rate available;[172] and

162 Mich. Admin. Code r. 460.2145.

163 *See, e.g.*, Fla. Admin. Code Ann. r. 25-24.485(1)(c) (telephone companies) (tariff must be clearly expressed in simple words, sentences and paragraphs, and must avoid unnecessarily long, complicated, or obscure phrases or acronyms so that the customer will understand that for which he or she is contracting).

164 16 Tex. Admin. Code § 25.473(c) requires disclosure statements, enrollment notification notice, and disconnection notice to be provided in Spanish or the language used with marketing the services.

165 *See* NARUC's Resolution on Telecommunications Consumer Bill of Rights, *available at* www.naruc.org/Resolutions/bill_of_rights.pdf.

166 June 6, 2002, Draft Decision of Commissioner Wood, Before the Public Utilities Commission of the State of California, Order Instituting Rulemaking on the Commission's Own Motion to Establish Consumer Rights and Consumer Protection Rules Applicable to All Telecommunication Utilities, Rulemaking 00-02-004 (filed Feb. 3, 2000).

167 *See generally* Comment, *Liability of Public Utility for Temporary Interruption of Service*, 1974 Wash. L. Q. 344, 346, n.10 (1974) (discussing scope and ramifications of the common law duties of "public service corporations"); Gustavas H. Robinson, *The Public Utility Concept in American Law*, 41 Harv. L. Rev. 277 (1928) (same); Norman Arterburn, *The Origin and First Test of Public Callings*, 75 Pennsylvania L. Rev. 411 (1927) (same); Burdick, *The Origin of the Peculiar Duties of Public Service Companies*, 11 Colum. L. Rev. 514 (1911) (same).

168 *See* Dworman v. Consolidated Edison Co., 267 N.Y.S.2d 291, 292 (N.Y. Sup. Ct. 1965), *rev'd*, 271 N.Y.S.2d 363 (N.Y. App. Div. 1966). *See also* Brewer v. Brooklyn Union Gas Co., 228 N.Y.S.2d 177 (N.Y. Sup. Ct. 1962).

169 The availability of these public utility services has been judicially recognized as essential not only to modern convenience but to modern health and welfare as well. The Supreme Court noted in Memphis Gas, Light & Water Div. v. Craft, 436 U.S. 1 (1978), that "utility service is a necessity of modern life; indeed, the discontinuance of water or heating for even short periods of time may threaten health or safety." *Id.* at 18. *See also* Stanford v. Gas Serv. Co., 346 F. Supp. 717, 721 (D. Kan. 1972).

The poor in particular have long been found to be vulnerable to the loss of utility service. J. Kirkwood, *Cash Deposits—Burdens and Barriers in Access to Utility Services*, 7 Harv. C.R.-C.L. L. Rev. 630 (1972); Note, *The Shutoff of Utility Services for Nonpayment: A Plight of the Poor*, 46 Wash. L. Rev. 745 (1971); Note, *Public Utilities and the Poor: The Requirement of Cash Deposits from Domestic Consumers*, 78 Yale L. J. 448 (1969).

170 Boyd v. Board of Trs., Mitchell Pub. Water Dist., 303 N.E.2d 444, 446 (Ill. App. Ct. 1973); Oklahoma City Hotel & Motel Hotel Ass'n Inc. v. Oklahoma City, 531 P.2d 316 (Okla. 1974); 73B C.J.S. *Public Utilities* § 6. *See also* 97 A.L.R. 838, 839 (1994) ("liability of gas, electric or water company for delay in commencing service").

171 *See* Memphis Light Gas & Water Div. v. Craft, 436 U.S. 1 (1978); Arizona Corp. Comm'n v. Nicholson, 497 P.2d 815, 817 (Ariz. 1972) (citations omitted).

According to the Missouri courts, "a public utility is obligated *by the nature of its business* to furnish its service or commodity to the general public, or that part of the public which it has undertaken to serve, without arbitrary discrimination." Overman v. Southwestern Bell Tel. Co., 675 S.W.2d 419, 424 (Mo. Ct. App. 1984) (quoting 73B C.J.S. *Public Utilities* § 8 (1994)) (emphasis added).

172 *See, e.g.*, City of El Dorado v. Arkansas Pub. Serv. Comm'n, 362 S.W.2d 680 (Ark. 1963). *See also* Springfield Township v. Pennsylvania Pub. Util. Comm'n, 676 A.2d 304 (Pa. Commw. Ct. 1996) (utility must compute customer's bill at rate most advantageous to customer given information provided to utility but must have actual knowledge of service conditions before required to compute such rate); Committee of Consumer Servs. v. Public Serv. Comm'n, 595 P.2d 871 (Utah 1979).

This should be distinguished from an obligation to inform customers of the most economic use of power, which obligation does *not* exist.

(4) To use the highest level of care in providing its service.[173]

2.6.2 *Private Remedies for Discourteous Treatment*

Rude, inconsiderate, abusive and demeaning language or conduct by public utility customer service representatives may give rise to a cause of action. This behavior could result in administrative action by a regulatory commission such as revoking a license or ordering changed practices on penalty of sanctions.[174] More practically, this could give rise to a claim for compensation via a breach of contract action against the public utility.

Generally, mental stress such as embarrassment and humiliation that may accompany a breach of contract are not compensable.[175] However, there are three narrow exceptions for which some courts have awarded compensatory or punitive damages for mental stress caused by a breach of contract. These cases include instances when the mental stress is:

(1) Accompanied by or causes bodily injury; or

(2) Is caused intentionally or in a manner that is wanton or reckless;[176] or

(3) When the circumstances surrounding the contract formation suggest that the parties contemplated that a contractual breach would cause mental stress for the non-breaching party.[177]

The cases in which damages for mental stress have been awarded involve instances when a "special relationship" between the contracting parties exists—a relationship for which the law imposes on the breaching party duties that are independent of the contract. Some courts, for example, have found that a railroad or bus company has a duty not only to provide passengers with transportation but to give passengers courteous treatment.[178] That is, the obligation to provide passengers with respectful and courteous treatment is

---

173 *Accord* Washington Gas Light Co. v. Aetna Cas. & Sur. Co., 242 A.2d 802, 804 (Md. Ct. Spec. App. 1968). *See, e.g.*, Kohler v. Kansas Power & Light Co., 387 P.2d 149, 151 (Kan. 1963).

However, the high standard of care imposed in these cases may be a consequence of the particular injury suffered by the plaintiff rather than the status of the defendant as a public utility. *See* DeGraeve v. Southwestern Bell Tel., 687 P.2d 1380, 1382 (Kan. Ct. App. 1984) (utility held to standard of ordinary care in wrongful termination of service case).

174 *See, e.g.*, Investigation on the Commission's Own Motion into the Operations, Practices, and Conduct of America's Tele-Network Corp (ATN), 1998 WL 244230 (Cal. Pub. Util. Comm'n 1998); Investigation on the Commission's own Motion into the Operations, Practices, and Conduct of Brittan Communications Int'l (BCI), 1997 WL 373221 (Cal. Pub. Util. Comm'n 1997); *In re* US W. Comm., Inc., 1999 WL 1132929 (Wyo. Pub. Serv. Comm'n 1999)(investigation and report ordered). *But see* Gerald v. Detroit Edison, 1999 WL 590480 (Mich. Pub. Serv. Comm'n 1999) (commission does not oversee civility or lack of the same experienced by customers).

175 *See* McDermott v. Western Union Tel. Co., 746 F. Supp. 1016 (E.D. Cal. 1990); Selden v. Dinner, 21 Cal. Rptr. 2d 153 (Cal. Ct. App. 1993); Sackett v. St. Mary's Church Soc., 464 N.E.2d 956 (Mass. App. Ct. 1984); Hetes v. Schefman & Miller Law Office, 393 N.W.2d 577 (Mich. Ct. App. 1986); Young v. Abalene Pest Control Servs. Inc., 444 A.2d 514 (N.H. 1982); Fennell v. Nationwide Mut. Fire Ins. Co., 603 A.2d 1064, 1068 (Pa. Super. Ct. 1992), *appeal denied*, 533 Pa. 600, 603 A.2d 1274 (Pa. 1992); Gaglidari v. Denny's Restaurants Inc., 815 P.2d 1362, 1370, 1372, 1376 (Wash. 1991) (holding that damages for mental stress were not recoverable in breach of employment contract regardless of whether breach was wanton or reckless or whether stress was reasonably foreseeable).

Damages for breach of contract are normally intended to compensate the nonbreaching party for pecuniary harm. While mental stress is almost always caused by a breach of contract, it seldom exists independent of the pecuniary loss created by the breach. Thus, compensation for the pecuniary loss is believed to sufficiently resolve the associated mental stress so as to make the mental stress noncompensable. *See* 10 Corbin on Contracts § 1076 (interim ed. 2002).

176 *See* Zamzok v. 650 Park Ave. Corp., 363 N.Y.S.2d 868 (N.Y. Sup. Ct. 1974). *But see* Brown v. Fritz, 699 P.2d 1371, 1377 (Idaho 1985) ("When damages are sought for breach of a contractual relationship, there can be no recovery for emotional distress suffered by a plaintiff. If the conduct of the defendant has been sufficiently outrageous we view the proper remedy to be in the realm of punitive damages."); Hunt v. Mayr, 686 P.2d 74, 78 (Idaho 1984); Valentine v. General Am. Credit Inc., 362 N.W.2d 628, 630 (Mich. 1984). *See generally* Restatement Contracts § 341 (1991); Williston, Williston on Contracts § 1341 at 214–23 (3d. ed. 1994).

177 *See* Ross v. Forest Lawn Mem'l Park, 988, 203 Cal. Rptr. 468 (Cal. Ct. App. 1984); Hatfield v. Max Rouse & Sons Northwest, 606 P.2d 944, 951 (Idaho 1980) (no damages for breach because circumstances surrounding contract formation did not suggest parties contemplated that a contractual breach would cause mental stress); Maere v. Churchill, 452 N.E.2d 694, 697 (Ill. App. Ct. 1983) (no damages unless breach was intentional, wanton, or reckless or when no bodily injury is caused or accompanies breach or when parties did not contemplate that mental stress would result from breach of contract); Guerin v. New Hampshire Catholic Charities, 418 A.2d 224 (N.H. 1980). *But see* Cheney v. Palos Verdes Inv. Corp., 665 P.2d 661 (Idaho 1983); Rasmuson v. Walker Bank & Trust Co., 625 P.2d 1098 (Idaho 1981).

178 The Georgia Supreme Court has found that a public service corporation's duty to provide courteous treatment to its customers derives from its duty to provide "safe and decent" access to its place of business. *See* Crites v. Delta Airlines, Inc., 341 S.E.2d 264, 266 (Ga. 1986).

Crites implicitly reaffirms this notion, first articulated by the Georgia Supreme Court in *Dunn v. Western Union*, that public service corporations have a duty to provide "decent access" that includes "freedom from abuse, humiliation, insult or other unbecoming and disrespectful treatment." Dunn v. Western Union Tel. Co., 59 S.E. 189, 190–91 (Ga. Ct. App. 1907).

Similarly, a New Jersey court has found that a carrier has an obligation to protect its passengers from "abusive and insulting" conduct. Ricci v. American Airlines, 544 A.2d 428 (N.J. Super. Ct. App. Div. 1988). *See also* Southeastern Greyhound Lines v. Klatt, 189 S.W.2d 731 (Ky. 1946); Brown v. Fifth Ave. Coach Lines, Inc., 185 N.Y.S.2d 923 (N.Y. Mun. Ct. 1959); Gebhardt v. Public Serv. Coord. Transp., 137 A.2d 48 (N.J.

implied in the contract to carry passengers.[179] In some jurisdictions, this implied duty may include protecting passengers against violence and insults from the carriers' agents.[180]

Although there is no general rule or description regarding the type of language to which liability may attach, some courts have articulated several factors that may be relevant to the inquiry. These factors include the relationship of the parties, whether the language was provoked and the tone and manner in which the insult or abuse was communicated.[181]

In cases that discuss the nature of the language for which liability is found, the focus of the inquiry is the plaintiff's feelings.[182] In the context of other public service companies, such as carriers, courts have imposed liability for insults, threats and other disrespectful conduct engaged in by the carrier's employees or agents.[183]

Super. App. Div. 1957); Maduro v. American Airlines, 2007 WL 906234 (V.I. Sup. Ct. Feb. 26, 2007) ("a common carrier or other public utility is subject to liability to patrons utilizing its facilities for gross insults which reasonably offend them").

179 *See* Annot., *Recoverability of Compensatory Damages for Mental Anguish or Emotional Distress for Breach of Service Contract*, 54 A.L.R.4th 901, 919 (1987).

180 *Id.*

Other public service corporations that operate under similar constraints include innkeepers, railroads, bus lines, and telecommunication companies. *See generally* J. Geffs, *Part I: Statutory Definitions of Public Utilities and Carriers*, 12 Notre Dame Lawyer 246 (1937); J. Geffs, *Part II: Statutory Definitions of Public Utilities and Carriers*, 12 Notre Dame Lawyer 373 (1937); 74 Am. Jur. 2d §§ 88–92, *Telecommunications, Damages for Mental Anguish* (2002).

It may prove useful to turn to these industries for guidance on claims based on abusive and insulting language and behavior.

181 Cave v. Seaboard Air Line Ry., 77 S.E. 1017, 1020 (S.C. 1913).

As the *Cave* court noted, "when a conductor uses language to a passenger which is calculated to insult, humiliate or wound the feelings of a person of ordinary feelings and sensibilities, the carrier is liable." *Id.*

182 *See, e.g.*, Dunn v. Western Union Tel. Co., 59 S.E. 189, 192 (Ga. Ct. App. 1907).

In *Dunn*, the telegram agent's insulting language was not slanderous—injurious to the plaintiff's reputation—but the language was, however, insulting and humiliating. *See also* Ricci v. American Airlines, 544 A.2d 428 (N.J. Super. Ct. App. Div. 1988) (summary judgment for carrier reversed; plaintiff's claim includes allegations of depression, humiliation, and post-traumatic stress disorder); Brown v. Fifth Ave. Coach Lines, Inc., 185 N.Y.S.2d 923 (N.Y. Mun. Ct. 1959) (plaintiff entitled to recover for humiliation, mortification, and injury to feelings).

183 *See, e.g.*, McAllister v. Greyhound Lines, Inc., 1997 WL 642994 (D.N.J. Oct. 7, 1997) (unpublished) ("[i]t has been accepted as a general legal principle that the relationship between a carrier and a passenger is contractual; the carrier has a duty to protect its passengers from its employee's insulting and abusive language, regardless of whether passage is permitted or refused").

Chapter 3 Tenant Strategies for Maintaining Service

3.1 Introduction

Tenants who pay for utility service through their rent face unique access problems when the landlord is either unable or unwilling to pay the utility bill. Utilities generally terminate service for nonpayment. If tenants seek to have the service renewed in their own name, the utility will often refuse to renew the service until the landlord's past-due bill is paid. This raises the question: must the tenant pay the landlord's past-due bill before establishing service? For a variety of reasons, the answer in most jurisdictions is no.

Another tenant strategy is to pay the utility bill that is in the landlord's name but withhold rent. Alternatively, the tenants can try to force the landlord to pay the bill by bringing a legal action against the landlord to recover tenants' costs associated with having to pay the bill. A landlord in this situation may file for bankruptcy. Surprisingly, this may provide the tenant with more opportunities to keep utility service operating without payment from the tenant.[1]

3.2 Tenant Obtaining Service in Own Name Despite Landlord's Delinquency

3.2.1 Common Law Right to Obtain Service from Utility in Own Name

There is fairly clear development in the common law regarding the inappropriateness of a utility making one customer liable for the debts of another in the absence of a statutory or contractual basis.[2] Public utility commissions have relied on the same concepts to arrive at similar conclusions.[3]

There is also ample case law from various jurisdictions holding that a utility may not deny service to a tenant for the tenant's failure to pay the landlord's past-due utility bill.[4]

---

1 *See* Chapter 13, *infra* (discussing ways a tenant whose landlord is in bankruptcy may retain utility service).

2 *See, e.g.*, Walton Elec. Membership Corp. v. Snyder, 487 S.E.2d 613 (Ga. Ct. App. 1997) (absent contract to assume another's debt, utility may not disconnect customer's service when customer's wife incurred unpaid bill at different address), *aff'd*, Walton Elec. Membership Corp. v. Snyder, 508 S.E.2d 167 (Ga. 1998); Cascade Motor Hotel, Inc. v. City of Duluth, 348 N.W.2d 84 (Minn. 1984) (ordinance allowing a municipal utility to terminate service to a current property owner because of arrearages incurred by former owner was arbitrary and unreasonable); City of Jackson v. Camelot Apartments, 707 So. 2d 191, 194 (Miss. Ct. App. 1998) (new owners not responsible for unpaid balance when title to property conveyed); Yates v. White River Valley Elec. Coop., 414 S.W.2d 808 (Mo. 1967) (in the absence of statutory or contractual authority, company has no right to cut off gas or electricity for payment due from another occupant or owner); Moore v. Metropolitan Util. Co., 477 P.2d 692 (Okla. 1978) ("Absent some legislative authority, a public utility cannot make a tenant responsible for charges incurred by a prior tenant."); Oliver v. Hyle, 513 P.2d 806 (Or. Ct. App. 1973) (ordinance holding subsequent occupants liable for past arrearages was invalid absent statutory authority). *See also* State *ex rel.* Imperial Util. Corp. v. Borgmann, 664 S.W.2d 215 (Mo. Ct. App. 1983); McMenamin v. Evesham Mun. Util. Auth., 249 A.2d 21 (N.J. Super. Ct. Ch. Div. 1969), *aff'd*, 256 A.2d 801 (N.J. Super. Ct. App. Div. 1969); 1 Priest, Principles of Public Utility Regulation 256 (1969); 12 McQuillin, Municipal Corp. *See generally* § 6.4, *infra*.

3 *E.g.*, Donovan v. General Tel. Co., 19 Pub. Util. Rep. 3d 49 (Cal. 1957) (telephone company's unwritten policy to deny service to a member of a household until a delinquent bill of another member of the household has been paid is unreasonable).

4 Alabama Water Co. v. Knowles, 124 So. 96 (Ala. 1929) (tenant cannot be denied service because landlord is in arrears, nor can payment of such arrears be required as a condition of tenant's service); La Nasa v. Sewerage & Water Bd. of New Orleans, 184 So. 2d 622 (La. Ct. App. 1966) (water board may not refuse water service to the owner of a building or his tenants until either of them pays an outstanding bill incurred by a former tenant); Ginnings v. Meridian Waterworks Co., 56 So. 450 (Miss. 1911) (lessee of a single room was entitled to water service for his own use, without having to pay landlord's arrears); Galveston v. Kenner, 240 S.W. 894 (Tex. 1922) (city has duty, upon tenant's request, to install meters for tenant occupying distinct tenement and to collect directly from tenant rather than owner); Waldron v. International Water Co., 112 A. 219 (Vt. 1921) (water company was required to accept tender of payment from some tenants, even though water rents remained uncollected from other tenants and could not require the owner of the property to pay arrears); Jopling v. Bluefield Waterworks & Improvement Co. 74 S.E. 943 (W. Va. 1912) (tenant occupying ground floor space could not be cut off from service despite failure of second floor tenant to pay for water supplied by common pipe serving both floors). *But see* Chatham v. Jackson, 613 F.2d 73 (5th Cir. 1980) (city's practice of termi-

Notice of the intended termination of service to a tenant because of a landlord's overdue bill is generally required.[5]

3.2.2 Utility Statutes with Landlord-Tenant Provisions

A Colorado statute requires the state's Public Utilities Commission to create regulations for the termination of gas and electricity to residential customers. The statute also requires that the tenant be provided prior notice and an opportunity to be heard before service is terminated. No termination can occur if there is a danger to the health or safety of the tenant and an installment payment plan can be arranged.[6]

In Connecticut, when a landlord fails to pay the utility bill, notice of impending termination must be provided to non-customer tenants, and the tenant has the right to have service established in his or her own name if practicable.[7] In addition, the tenant seeking continued service may be exempt from a security deposit requirement.[8] If service in the tenant's name is impractical, the utility is prohibited from terminating service but may initiate a rent receivership action against the landlord.[9] Unless the utility service is separately metered for the tenant's exclusive use, the landlord must pay for the service and the fuel. In the event that the landlord does not make payments on a master meter account and the tenant takes over payments in his or her name, the tenant may deduct the estimated amount associated with other occupants' use of the utility service.[10] Notice of these rights must be provided to the tenants.[11]

In the District of Columbia, there is a statutory prohibition against utility termination without notice affecting tenants who are master metered. The statute provides for opportunity for a payment plan and tenants can have a rent receivership established.[12]

In Florida, tenants are protected by a federal court decision holding that an affected tenant has a due process right to notice of proposed utility termination.[13] Additionally, there is a statutory prohibition against any county terminating or refusing utility service for nonpayment by former occupants of the rental unit.[14] In Miami-Dade County, there is a proposal to establish a bridge acount for tenants when their landlord fails to pay for water and sewer and the service account is therefore closed.[15] Tenants who can pre-pay and deposit a total amount equal to two-and-a-half times the entire multi-unit's average monthly bill would receive continuous service to tenants for six months. This additional time is intended to give tenants the opportunity to seek an injunction or other legal remedies or move to another residence.[16] However, tenants would have to act

nating water service to landlord when tenant's bills were delinquent upheld, despite due process and equal protection challenges); Birmingham Waterworks Co. v. Edwards, 81 So. 194 (Ala. 1919) (tenant held liable for all charges for water furnishing himself and another tenant through a common pipe, all the water furnished being through a single pipe and used in common); Birmingham Waterworks Co. v. Brooks, 76 So. 515 (Ala. 1917) (water company under no duty to furnish a tenant with water through a joint service pipe, when other users on same pipe were in arrears).

5 *See also* Turpen v. City of Corvallis, 26 F.3d 978 (9th Cir. 1994) (disconnection of water service without prior notice to tenant when landlord fails to pay utility bill is unconstitutional); Coghlan v. Starkey, 845 F.2d 566 (5th Cir. 1988) (mere receipt of water for period of time does not create entitlement when tenant did not apply for service); DiMassimo v. City of Clearwater, 805 F.2d 1536 (11th Cir. 1986); Sterling v. Village of Maywood, 579 F.2d 1350 (7th Cir. 1978); Monson v. National Fuel Gas Distribution Corp., 58 Pa. P.U.C. 371 Z-8207989 (Pa. Apr. 19, 1984) (gas utility violated its statutory duty when, upon landlord's failure to pay bill and subsequent termination, utility failed to notify the tenants that service could be continued if tenants estimated thirty-day bill). *Cf.* Midkiff v. Adams County Reg'l Water Dist., 409 F.3d 758 (6th Cir. 2005) (water district's termination of water service to rental property at request of landlord and without notice to tenants was not found to be a substantive due process violation); Rohrbaugh v. Pennsylvania Pub. Util. Comm'n, 727 A.2d 1080, 1085, 1086 (Pa. 1999) (utility company not required to provide notice to non-ratepaying landlord of service disconnection at request of ratepaying tenant). *But see* James v. City of St. Petersburg, Fla., 33 F.3d 1304, 1307 (11th Cir. 1994) (tenant had no legitimate claim to water service when tenant refused to comply with deposit and other service-initiation requirements). *See generally* R. Colton & S. Morrissey, *Tenants' Rights to Pretermination Notice in Cases of Landlord's Nonpayment of Utilities*, 29 Clearinghouse Rev. 277 (1995); § 6.2.6, *infra.*

6 Colo. Rev. Stat. § 40-4-101(3).

7 Conn. Gen. Stat. § 16-262e(a).

8 *See* Conn. Gen. Stat. § 16-262e(a)(2).

9 Conn. Gen. Stat. § 16-262f.

10 Conn. Gen. Stat. §§ 12-262e(a), 12-262e(c).

11 Conn. Gen. Stat. § 12-262e(c)–(e).

12 D.C. Code §§ 42-3302, 42-3303. *See also* Loewinger v. Stokes, 977 A.2d 901 (D.C. 2009) (landlord of property in receivership prohibited under receivership statute from action for possession against tenant for nonpayment of rent); Capitol Terrace v. Shannon & Luchs, 564 A.2d 49 (D.C. 1989).

13 DiMassimo v. City of Clearwater, 805 F.2d 1536 (11th Cir. 1986).

14 Fla. Stat. § 125.485 (applicable to counties). *See also* Fla. Stat. §§ 180.135 (proscribes a municipality's refusal or discontinuance of water service to a tenant for nonpayment of service charges incurred by a former occupant), 180.135(4) (permits municipality to discontinue service to a tenant only when the tenant fails to make timely payment and the municipality provides the tenant with a thirty-day grace period).

15 *See* Memorandum from George M. Burgess to Hon. George A. Martinez and Members, Board of County Comm'rs, Report: Ordinance 10-88 Relating to Section 32-92 of the Miami-Dade County Code Establishing County Policy Providing for Tenants to Receive Water and Sewer Service Through a Bridge Account Not to Exceed 6 Months Where a Rental Multi-Unit Property Is Served By One Meter and Property Owners' Account Is Terminated for Non-Payment (Apr. 13, 2011), www.miamidade.gov/govaction/legistarfiles/Matters/Y2011/110424.pdf.

16 *Id.*

together and be organized to benefit from the proposed policy.[17]

Illinois statutory law restricts the manner in which a utility may terminate service to multifamily buildings. The utility company is required to notify occupants of the date of the proposed termination, which date may not be sooner than ten days after the notice is rendered. The notice must also include a statement of the tenant's right to either pay the utility the amount owed by the landlord and deduct that amount from the rent or to petition the court for appointment of a receiver. The notice must also include the name and telephone number of any legal services agency within the utility's service area where the tenant may obtain free legal assistance.[18]

In Maine, terminations of utility service to tenants for the landlord's nonpayment are only permitted after the tenant has been provided notice and an opportunity to assume responsibility for future service. The tenant is not liable for the landlord's old bill. Payments made by the tenant to the utility can be deducted from the rent.[19] Another statute requires the Utility Commission to have rules regarding when residential customers are subject to utility termination, including prior notice, the right to an installment payment plan and no terminations during a medical emergency.[20]

Massachusetts prohibits the termination of gas or electric service in any unit when the tenant is not the customer of record unless the utility first provides notice and complies with the implementing regulations of the agency charged with regulating the utility service.[21] The same law requires notice to each affected tenant (1) stating the amount due on the account; (2) specifying the date on or after which service will be terminated, which must be no less than 15 and no more than 30 days after the date of the notice; and (3) advising the tenants of their right to pay the amount due, or such portion prescribed by the Department as due under its regulations, to avoid termination and the right to recover any amount so paid from the person to whom rent is paid. Service may not be terminated if the tenant pays the full amount due or such amount as is acceptable to the utility company or deemed sufficient by the Department.

The Department's implementing regulations specify the procedures companies must follow to identify accounts with "landlord customers paying for service to a residential building" and to identify the apartment numbers and addresses of any tenants who may be affected by a planned termination of a landlord-paid account.[22] The regulations also contain more detailed requirements than the statute for providing notice to landlords and, separately, to tenants prior to any termination of a landlord-paid account.[23] The utility must also provide separate notice to the Department's consumer division prior to proceeding with any termination. At any time, the Department "may make inquiry of the parties" of relevant facts, including the amount the tenants have paid to the utility, relative to the size of the total due from the landlord; the number of vacant units in the building; the sources of the tenants' incomes (for example, government assistance); whether the tenants are already engaged in any rent withholding; weather conditions; whether there are any serious illnesses among the tenant households; the age of persons who would be affected by termination; and other factors.[24] In practice, the Department has often ordered service to remain on, based on payment by tenants of something less than the full amount due from the landlord.

In Minnesota, when the utility or other company supplying utility service or home heating oil discontinues service to a tenant due to an owner's failure to pay, the tenants, after notice to the landlord, can have service restored, pay for it directly and deduct it from rent. The tenant must pay only for the most recent billing period.[25] In Minnesota, before a tenant moves into a residential apartment building with a single meter, owners are also required to disclose the total utility cost for the building for each month of the most recent calendar year.[26]

In Missouri, there is a statutory protection against termination of heat-related utility service in master-metered buildings having two or more units. Notice must be provided to tenants at least five days before a shut-off and must include notice of the right to seek a receivership for the building. Either the tenant or the utility company can file for the receivership. No termination of service is allowed if a receivership petition is pending or has been granted.[27]

A New Hampshire statute allows the utility company to provide notice to the property owner (or condo association) of a termination of service to a tenant (or an individual condominium unit) if the owner or association has so requested and the termination occurs between November 1 and April 30 (inclusive).[28] Presumably, notice is provided so as to prevent damage resulting from frozen water pipes.

---

17 *Id.*

The proposal would require that the tenants have a tenant representative and leaves it to the tenants to decide what proportion of the multi-unit's average monthly bill each tenant can and should pay for the bridge account to take effect.

18 765 Ill. Comp. Stat. 735/3.

19 Me. Rev. Stat. tit. 35-A, § 706.

20 Me. Rev. Stat. tit. 35-A, § 704.

21 Mass. Gen. Laws ch. 164, § 124D; 220 Mass. Code Regs. § 25.04 (termination of service to accounts affecting tenants).

The Massachusetts Department of Public Utilities, as successor to the Department of Telecommunications and Energy, now regulates gas and electric service.

22 220 Mass. Code Regs. § 25.04(1), (2).

23 220 Mass. Code Regs. § 25.04(4), (6).

24 220 Mass. Code Regs. § 25.04(7)(d).

25 Minn. Stat. § 504B.215.

26 Kutscheid v. Emerald Sq. Props., Inc., 770 N.W.2d 529 (Minn. Ct. App. 2009) (landlord's provision of average monthly cost for a single unit insufficient).

27 Mo. Rev. Stat. § 441.650.

28 N.H. Rev. Stat. Ann. § 363-B:3.

In New Jersey, when the landlord has failed to pay for utility service, either the tenant or the utility company can bring suit in court; the rent will then be paid to the court and used to correct the situation.[29]

In New York, there is a statutory prohibition against termination of utility service in a multiple dwelling without giving fifteen days notice to the owner, the occupants, the health officer, the mayor and the county executive; occupants must be notified if the cause for the termination is satisfied; the Utility Commission must have rules for tenant payment to prevent termination.[30] There is also a statutory prohibition against termination of utility service to two-family dwellings not separately metered without fifteen days notice to the owner and the occupants; the Utility Commission must have regulations to enable the tenants to prevent termination by making payments.[31] In addition, there are detailed statutory provisions that generally require an owner to eliminate any "shared meter" situations or, in the alternative, pay for the utility service; but there are some exceptions that allow for mutually acceptable arrangements for sharing the costs of the utility service if a shared meter remains in place.[32]

In Pennsylvania, utilities regulated by the public utility commission must give notice to tenants of an impending disconnection due to the landlord's arrearage.[33] Tenants can apply for continued service and can deduct from rent any payments they make for utility service that are made on behalf of the landlord.[34] The regulated utility can also petition a court to appoint a receiver to receive rent payments that can be applied to the utility arrearage.[35]

Pennsylvania has also adopted the Utility Service Tenants Rights Act for customers of municipal utilities and other entities providing utility service that are not regulated by the state commission.[36] The statute provides tenants with a right to individually subscribe for service if no major changes to the distribution system are necessary.[37] It requires that thirty days prior to termination of utility service, notice must be provided to landlords, public agencies, and each residential unit. Also, before a landlord's *voluntary* termination of utility service is effectuated, either the tenant's consent must be obtained, or at the least the utility must have provided notice to the tenants.[38] The tenant has a right to continue or resume service upon paying the landlord's bill due for the last thirty days before notice, continuing the monthly payments as due, and withholding this amount from the rent.[39] These rights cannot be waived.[40]

In Wisconsin, when electricity, gas, or water has a joint meter for two or more rental dwelling units, a statute requires that the owner maintain the account in the name of the owner or the owner's rental agent.[41]

3.2.3 Application of Constitutional Principles

When the terminating utility company is a state actor,[42] constitutional due process requires that the utility provide notice and an opportunity to contest the termination.[43] Due process thus must be followed for any termination by a municipal utility and possibly by an REC but probably not by an investor-owned utility.[44] A number of cases have held that it is unconstitutional for a municipal utility to terminate service to a tenant for the landlord's failure to pay the utility bill.[45]

29 N.J. Stat. Ann. §§ 2A:42-87, 2A:42-88, 2A:42-90, 2A:42-92 (West).

30 N.Y. Pub. Serv. Laws § 33 (McKinney).

31 N.Y. Pub. Serv. Laws § 34 (McKinney).

32 N.Y. Pub. Serv. Laws § 52 (McKinney).

33 66 Pa. Cons. Stat. § 1523(a)(3).

34 66 Pa. Cons. Stat. §§ 1527, 1529.

35 66 Pa. Cons. Stat. § 1533.

36 68 Pa. Stat. Ann. §§ 399.1–399.18 (West).

37 68 Pa. Stat. Ann. § 399.7(b) (West).

38 68 Pa. Stat. Ann. § 399.3 (West).

39 68 Pa. Stat. Ann. §§ 399.7, 399.9 (West).

40 68 Pa. Stat. Ann. § 399.10 (West) (municipal utilities); 66 Pa. Cons. Stat. § 1530 (regulated utilities).

41 Wis. Stat. § 196.643(2).

42 Municipal and other governmental providers are clearly state actors. Memphis Light, Gas & Water Div. v. Craft, 436 U.S. 1 (1978).

Private, investor-owned utilities are another matter. In Jackson v. Metropolitan Edison Co., 419 U.S. 345 (1974), the Court held that there was no state action present when the utility is privately owned, despite the regulation and grant of monopoly power by state. The issue of whether electric membership corporations are covered has not been resolved. *See generally* § 15.1.4, *infra*.

43 *See generally* Memphis Light, Gas & Water Div. v. Craft, 436 U.S. 1 (1978) (termination of utility services implicates a property interest protected by the Fourteenth Amendment's Due Process Clause when applicable state law allows for termination only for cause); Golden v. City of Columbus, 404 F.3d 950 (6th Cir. 2005); O'Neal v. City of Seattle, 66 F.3d 1064 (9th Cir. 1995); DiMassimo v. City of Clearwater, 805 F.2d 1536 (11th Cir. 1986); Sterling v. Village of Maywood, 579 F.2d 1350 (7th Cir. 1978); Davis v. Weir, 497 F.2d 139 (5th Cir. 1974); Koger v. Guarino, 412 F. Supp. 1375 (E.D. Pa. 1976).

44 *See* § 13.2, *infra*.

45 Golden v. City of Columbus, 404 F.3d 950 (6th Cir. 2005) (city violated equal protection clause by denying water service only to tenants whose predecessors or landlords failed to pay water bills); James v. St. Petersburg, 6 F.3d 1457, 1463 (11th Cir. 1993) (actual user of a utility has a protected property interest in water service); DiMassimo v. City of Clearwater, 805 F.2d 1536 (11th Cir. 1986) (pre-termination notice required to actual user of utility service); Koger v. Guarino, 412 F. Supp. 1375 (E.D. Pa. 1976) (city practice of requiring tenants to pay landlord's delinquent water bills to avoid terminations violated due process clause); Davis v. Weir, 328 F. Supp. 317 (N.D. Ga. 1971), *aff'd in part, modified in part*, 497 F.2d 139 (5th Cir. 1974) (city violated equal protection clause by refusing to provide service to tenant until tenant paid landlord's delinquent bill). *See* § 15.1.3.3, *infra*.

3.2.4 Public Utility Commission Rules and Orders

Many public utility commissions have issued rules or orders specifically regarding the termination of utility service supplied by the landlord. Advocates can check with utility commission staff regarding the possibility that such rules or orders have been issued but are not published in a readily accessible place.[46]

3.3 Rent Withholding to Pay Utility Directly for Landlord's Obligation

In some states specific statutes have been adopted that allow tenants to pay overdue utility bills on the landlord's account and deduct the amount of the payment from rent obligations in order to prevent service termination.[47] Many states, by statute[48] or as a common law adjunct to the warranty of habitability,[49] allow the tenant to repair defective conditions and to deduct the cost of repairs from the rent. This remedy is generally broad enough to allow tenants to pay such portion of the landlord's utility arrearage as is necessary to maintain service and to deduct the payment from rent.[50]

In jurisdictions in which an implied warranty of habitability is not recognized, or in which applicable housing codes do not contain a requirement that the landlord supply specific utility services, the advocate must be more creative.

When there is a lease in effect between the landlord and tenant that places the responsibility on the landlord to pay for heat or utility bills, the tenant may use contractual remedies for breach of the landlord's express covenant to pay for utility bills as they come due.[51] The same rule should apply when there is no written lease (or the lease is silent as to utilities) and the landlord rents the property as if utilities were included, or shows the property and utilities are provided.[52]

For example, while courts of North Carolina have construed that state's statutory warranty of habitability provision[53] as not requiring the furnishing of hot water to the unit, they have held that when a landlord implicitly agrees to provide a service to a property by showing the unit with a hot water heater, that service must be adequately provided throughout the tenancy.[54]

The common law, which did not recognize an implied warranty of habitability, did recognize a cause of action for breach of an express warranty to maintain the premises or when a defect was fraudulently concealed from a tenant.[55] The common law also recognized a cause of action for a landlord's failure to maintain those parts of the premises over which the landlord retains exclusive control.[56]

The landlord's responsibility to maintain areas within his or her exclusive control includes a duty to maintain centrally supplied utility and heating services.[57]

3.4 Landlord's Obligation to Tenant to Provide Utility Service

3.4.1 Implied Warranty of Habitability

3.4.1.1 Overview

The implied warranty of habitability, which has been adopted or otherwise given effect in at least forty-seven

46 *See* §§ 6.5.3, 15.1.3.3, *infra*.

47 *See, e.g.*, Conn. Gen. Stat. § 16-262e(e).

48 *See, e.g.*, 765 Ill. Comp. Stat. 735/3; Mass. Gen. Laws ch. 111, § 127L; Tex. Prop. Code Ann. § 92.301 (West). *See generally* James Charles Smith, *Tenant Remedies for Breach of Habitability: Tort Dimensions of a Contract Concept*, 35 U. Kan. L. Rev. 505 (1987) (listing fifteen jurisdictions adopting this remedy).

49 *See* Restatement (Second) of Property: Landlord & Tenant §§ 5.4(2)(c), 11.2.

50 *See, e.g.*, Conn. Gen. Stat. § 16-262e; Tex. Prop. Code Ann. § 92.301(b) (West).

51 McSorley v. Allen, 36 Pa. Super. 271 (Pa. Super Ct. 1908).

52 *See* 49 Am. Jur. 2d *Landlord and Tenant* §§ 579–588 (considerable authority recognizing express warranty to repair). *Cf.* Moldenhauer v. Krynski, 210 N.E.2d 809 (Ill. App. Ct. 1965); Rome v. Johnson, 174 N.E. 716 (Mass. 1931) (breach of express warranty in lease constitutes breach of covenant of quiet enjoyment); Rossiter v. Moore, 370 P.2d 250 (Wash. 1962) (oral agreement to repair enforced).

53 N.C. Gen. Stat. § 42-42(a).

54 Mendenhall-Moore Realtors v. Sedoris, 366 S.E.2d 534, 537 (N.C. Ct. App. 1988); Miller v. C.W. Myers Trading Post Inc., 355 S.E.2d 189 (N.C. Ct. App. 1987). *Compare* Lifter v. Coleman, 480 So. 2d 1336 (Fla. Dist. Ct. App. 1985), *with* Gennings v. Newton, 567 So. 2d 637 (La. 1990) (both interpreting analogous statutory warranties of habitability as requiring the provisions of hot and cold running water).

55 Hatfield v. Palles, 537 F.2d 1245, 1247 (4th Cir. 1976); Blackwell v. DelBosco, 558 P.2d 563, 564 (Colo. 1976); Rome v. Johnson, 174 Mass. 716 (Mass. 1931); Jackson v. Paterno, 108 N.Y.S. 1073 (N.Y. Sup. Ct. 1908), *aff'd*, 112 N.Y.S. 924 (N.Y. App. Div. 1908).

56 *See generally* Robb v. Cineme Francis, Inc, 88 N.Y.S.2d 380 (1949); Annot., *Breach of Covenant of Quiet Enjoyment in Lease*, 41 A.L.R.2d 1414 § 21 (1955) (citing Wood v. Gabler, 70 S.W.2d 110 (Mo. 1934)). *See also* Kinsey v. Zimmerman, 160 N.E. 155 (Ill. 1928); Delamater v. Foreman 239 N.W. 148 (Minn. 1931). *See generally* Annot., *Modern Status of Rule As to Existence of Implied Warranty of Habitability or Fitness for Use of Leased Premises*, 40 A.L.R.3d 646 (1971).

57 *See* Conroy v. 10 Brewster Ave. Corp, 234 A.2d 415 (N.J. 1967); Allen v. William H. Hall Free Library, 26 A.2d 751 (R.I. 1942); Marsh v. Riley, 188 S.E. 748 (W. Va. 1936). *See also* W. Prosser, Torts 406 (4th ed. 1971) (tort liability for landlords' failure to maintain centrally supplied utility and systems as exception to general rule of caveat lessee).

states by the courts,[58] the legislature,[59] or both,[60] is the modern linchpin of remedies for the tenant deprived of utility service for which the landlord is responsible.[61] In addition, many states have adopted specific statutes protecting tenants from utility terminations by landlords.[62] Several states also have special statutes and regulations limiting utility company terminations of service to tenants.[63]

The protection of the warranty of habitability is not confined to conditions that are so gross that the premises are literally uninhabitable; rather, the warranty mandates a standard for the conditions of the leased premises and generally incorporates the conditions promised in the lease agreement. The requirements of the local housing code are also generally included.[64]

3.4.1.2 Application of the Warranty of Habitability

The warranty of habitability is grounded in the twin principles that (1) a landlord is obligated to provide livable and useable residential space in return for the rent and (2) the landlord's material breach of this obligation diminishes the value of the premises and thus the rent owed by the tenant. Under the common law, there was no warranty that required rented residential premises to be reasonably safe or suited for the use intended.[65] The landlord's only duty was

---

58 *See* Javins v. First Nat'l Realty Corp., 428 F.2d 1071 (D.C. Cir. 1994); Green v. Superior Court, 517 P. 2d 1168 (Cal. 1974); Mansur v. Eubanks, 401 So. 2d 1328 (Fla. 1981); Lemle v. Breeden, 462 P.2d 470 (Haw. 1969); Silver Creek Computers, Inc. v. Petra, Inc., 42 P.3d 672 (Idaho 2002); Vanlandingham v. Ivanow, 615 N.E.2d 1361 (Ill. 1993); Jack Spring, Inc. v. Little, 280 N.E.2d 208 (Ill. 1972); Johnson v. Scandia Assoc., Inc., 641 N.E.2d 51 (Ind. Ct. App. 1994), *aff'd on other grounds*, 717 N.E.2d 24 (Ind. 1999); Breezewood Mgmt. Co. v. Maltbie, 411 N.E.2d 670 (Ind. Ct. App. 1980); Mease v. Fox, 200 N.W.2d 791 (Iowa 1972); Steele v. Latimer, 521 P.2d 304, 309–10 (Kan. 1974); Boston Hous. Auth. v. Hemingway, 293 N.E.2d 831 (Mass. 1973); O'Cain v. Harvey Freeman and Sons, Inc., 603 So. 2d 824 (Miss. 1991); Detling v. Edelbrock, 671 S.W.2d 265 (Mo. 1984); Kline v. Burns, 276 A.2d 248 (N.H. 1971); Marini v. Ireland, 265 A.2d 526 (N.J. 1970); Tonetti v. Penati, 367 N.Y.S.2d 804 (N.Y. App. Div. 1975); Glyco v. Schultz, 289 N.E.2d 919 (Ohio Mun. Ct. 1972); Pugh v. Holmes, 405 A.2d 897 (Pa. 1979); Kamarath v. Bennett, 568 S.W.2d 658 (Tex. 1978) (superceded by statute, as noted in Waldon v. Williams, 760 S.W.2d 833 (Tex. App. 1988)); Wade v. Jobe, 818 P.2d 1006, 1010 (Utah 1991); Birkenhead v. Coombs, 465 A.2d 244 (Vt. 1983); Foisy v. Wyman, 515 P.2d 160 (Wash. 1973); Teller v. McCoy, 523 S.E.2d 114 (W. Va. 1978).

59 Ala. Code § 35-9A-204; Alaska Stat. § 34.03.100; Ariz. Rev. Stat. Ann. § 33-1324; Cal. Civ. Code §§ 1941, 1941.1 (West); Colo. Rev. Stat. § 38-12-503; Conn. Gen. Stat. § 47a-7; Del. Code Ann. tit. 25, § 5305; D.C. Mun. Regs. tit. 14, § 301 (implied warranty and other remedies); Fla. Stat. §§ 83.51, 83.56; Ga. Code Ann. § 44-7-13; Haw. Rev. Stat. § 521-42; Idaho Code Ann. § 6-320; Ind. Code § 32-31-8-5; Iowa Code § 562A.15; Kan. Stat. Ann. § 58-2553; Ky. Rev. Stat. Ann. §§ 383.595, 383.625 (West); La. Civ. Code Ann. arts. 2682, 2696; Me. Rev. Stat. tit. 14, § 6021; Md. Code Ann., Real Prop. § 8-211 (West); Mich. Comp. Laws § 554.139; Mass. Gen. Laws ch. 111, §§ 127A–127L, ch. 239, § 8A; Minn. Stat. § 504B.161; Miss. Code. Ann. §§ 89-8-1 to 89-8-27; Mo. Rev. Stat. §§ 441.500, 441.510; Mont. Code Ann. § 70-24-303; Neb. Rev. Stat. § 76-1419; Nev. Rev. Stat. § 118A.290; N.H. Rev. Stat. Ann. § 48-A:14; N.J. Stat. Ann. § 2A:42-88 (West); N.M. Stat. Ann. § 47-8-20; N.Y. Mult. Dwell. Law §§ 78, 301, 302(1)(b) (McKinney); N.Y. Mult. Resid. Law §§ 305, 305-a (McKinney); N.Y. Real Prop. Law § 235-b (McKinney); N.Y. Real Prop. Acts. Law §§ 755, 770 (McKinney); N.C. Gen. Stat. § 42-42; N.D. Cent. Code § 47-16-13.1; Ohio Rev. Code Ann. § 5321.04 (West); Okla. Stat. tit. 41, § 118; Or. Rev. Stat. § 90.320; P.R. Laws Ann. tit. 31, § 4051; R.I. Gen. Laws § 34-18-22; S.C. Code Ann. § 27-40-440; S.D. Codified Laws §§ 43-32-8 to 43-32-9; Tenn. Code Ann. § 66-28-304; Tex. Prop. Code Ann. §§ 92.052, 92.056 (West); Utah Code Ann. §§ 57-22-1 to 57-22-6 (West) (Utah Fit Premises Act, effective Apr. 23, 1990); Vt. Stat. Ann. tit. 9, § 4457; Va. Code Ann. §§ 55-248.13, 55-248.21; Wash. Rev. Code §§ 59.18.060, 59.18.070; W. Va. Code § 37-6-30; Wis. Stat. § 704.07; Wyo. Stat Ann. §§ 1-21-1202, 1-21-1203.

60 *See supra* text accompanying notes 58, 59.

61 Generally, the warranty of habitability requires that the landlord maintain "bare living requirements." Mease v. Fox, 200 N.W.2d 791 (Iowa 1972); Academy Spires, Inc. v. Brown, 268 A.2d 556, 559 (N.J. Dist. Ct. 1970); Park W. Mgmt. Corp. v. Mitchell 47 N.Y.2d 316 (N.Y. 1979) (lease is a sale of both shelter and services); Hilder v. St. Peter, 478 A.2d 202, 208 (Vt. 1984).

This means that the landlord must maintain the premises in a state that is fit for human occupation. Accordingly, substantial compliance with building and housing code standards will generally serve as evidence of the fulfillment of a landlord's duty to provide habitable premises. Green v. Superior Court, 517 P.2d 1168, 1182–83 (Cal. 1974). *See, e.g.*, Lynch v. James, 692 N.E.2d 81, 82 (Mass. App. Ct. 1997) (whether the "scope of the warranty is broader than the minimum standards set out in the State building and sanitary codes" is judicial determination, but warranty is "concerned with the provision, maintenance, and repair of the *physical* facilities vital to the use of the leased premises") (citation omitted).

However, the warranty of habitability does not require that the landlord maintain the premises in perfect condition at all times or avoid minor housing code violations. *See* Javins v. First Nat'l Realty, 428 F.2d 1071, 1082 n.62 (D.C. Cir. 1970); Hinson v. Delis, 102 Cal. Rptr. 661 (Cal. Ct. App. 1972); Marini v. Ireland, 265 A.2d 526 (N.J. 1970).

62 *See, e.g.*, Alaska Stat. § 34.03.180; 765 Ill. Comp. Stat. 735/1.4; Ky. Rev. Stat. Ann. § 383.640 (West); Mass. Gen. Laws ch. 186, § 14; Mont. Code Ann. § 70-24-408; Neb. Rev. Stat. § 76-1427; Okla. St. tit. 41, § 121; 68 Pa. Stat. Ann. § 399.4(b) (West); R.I. Gen. Laws § 34-18-31; Va. Code Ann. § 55-248.23.

63 2 R. Powell, The Law of Real Property § 16B.04[3] (loose-leaf with updates). *See also* § 3.2.2, *supra*.

64 *See, e.g.*, Lynch v. James, 692 N.E.2d 81, 82 (Mass. App. Ct. 1997); Altschuler v. Boston Rent Equity Bd., 425 N.E.2d 781 (Mass. App. Ct. 1981), *aff'd*, 438 N.E.2d 73 (Mass. 1982) ("[h]abitability is a term of art, and the apartment need not be literally uninhabitable to be in violation of the implied warranty of habitability"); Aspon v. Loomis, 816 P.2d 751 (Wash. Ct. App. 1992) (landlord's duty to maintain premises fit for human habitation does not extend beyond duties enumerated in statute). *See also* Javins v. First Nat'l Realty, 428 F.2d 1071 (D.C. Cir. 1970).

65 Robert S. Schoshinski, American Law of Landlord and Tenant § 3.16 (1980 with annual supplements).

not to actively deceive tenants as to a known danger that the tenant did not know about. Otherwise, *caveat lessee* was the rule.[66] The landlord had no duty to repair unless he or she expressly agreed to repair.[67] Breach of the landlord's express agreement to repair did not excuse the tenant from paying rent.[68]

When analyzing state case law relating to the warranty of habitability, certain rental situations require specific analysis. For example, situations involving boarding-house rooming[69] or manufactured-home-lease communities[70] can give rise to warranty of habitability claims and require special analysis. It is also important to distinguish between commercial and residential leases, as some states have developed different laws based on the nature of the lease.[71]

In some states, the habitability concept gave rise to acknowledgment of tenant self-help remedies, including the right to withhold all rent while the unit remained in disrepair and the right to effect repairs and deduct the cost from rent.[72] The baseline of habitability requirements is most often established by housing codes and regulations, so rent withholding directly by a tenant is allowed for self-help enforcement of various housing codes. Thus, the self-help remedy applies to a number of local and statewide codes having as their objects the protection of the health, safety and welfare—including housing or sanitary codes, building codes and a wide range of special legislation and/or regulations.[73]

These tenant self-help remedies for code violations are in addition to criminal proceedings against the landlord and enforcement proceedings by local officials. All such action may occur concurrently, and the tenant generally can proceed for relief for code violations without any action being taken by local officials.

The landlord's liability for a material breach affecting habitability generally runs from the time that notice of the defect is provided to the landlord.[74] When utilities are shut off or threatened to be shut off because of nonpayment by the landlord, the landlord has actual knowledge since the landlord both knows he or she did not pay, and he or she should have received notice from the utility company of the threatened shut-off for nonpayment.

3.4.1.3 Jurisdictions Adopting the Warranty of Habitability

The warranty of habitability is almost universally accepted, either by case law or statute. Arkansas appears to be the only state that does not formally recognize the implied warranty for tenants' housing through a state statute or case law.[75] Advocates in Arkansas, however, can argue that the covenant of quiet enjoyment implied in residential leaseholds comprehends a remedy for a deprivation of landlord-supplied utility service.[76] The warranty of habitability has been established by case decisions in at least eighteen jurisdictions.[77]

---

66 *Id.*

67 *Id.*

68 *See, e.g.*, Detling v. Edelbrock, 671 S.W.2d 265 (Mo. 1984); Kline v. Burns, 276 A.2d 248 (N.H. 1971).

69 *See, e.g.*, Regensburg v. Rzonca 836 N.Y.S. 2d 489 (N.Y. Dist. Ct. 2007).

70 *See generally* ch. 14, *infra*.

71 *See, e.g.*, Commerce Ins. Co. v. Chadwick Med. Assocs. 23 Mass. L. Rptr. 291 (Mass. Super. Ct. 2007).

72 *See* § 3.3, *infra*.

73 *Cf.* Conn. Gen. Stat. § 47a-14h (granting tenants a private course of action to enforce); Mass. Gen. Laws ch. 111, §§ 191 to 199b (lead paint statutes).

Several commentators have studied the ineffectiveness of local code enforcement and have pointed out the need for private remedies. *See* Teitz & Rosenthal, Housing Code Enforcement in New York City (1971); Liberman, Local Administration and Enforcement of Housing Codes (1969); Samuel Basset Abbott, *Housing Policy, Housing Codes and Tenant Remedies: An Integration*, 56 B.U. L. Rev. 1, 49–56 (1976).

74 Berman & Sons v. Jefferson, 396 N.E.2d 981 (Mass. 1979); Detling v. Edelbrock, 671 S.W.2d 265 (Mo. 1984); Teller v. McCoy, 253 S.E.2d 114, 123, 125, 128 (W. Va. 1978) (once notice to the landlord of the existence of the condition is established, liability attached without further regard to the fault of the landlord). *See* Pugh v. Holmes, 384 A.2d 1234, *aff'd as modified*, 405 A.2d 897 (Pa. 1979); Fair v. Negley, 390 A.2d 240, 243 (Pa. 1978); Hilder v. St. Peter, 478 A.2d 202 (Vt. 1984). *See also* Knight v. Hallsthammer, 623 P.2d 268 (Cal. 1981); Leris Realty Corp. v. Robbins, 408 N.Y.S.2d 166 (1981).

In other jurisdictions, liability does not attach until after reasonable time has passed to allow for the landlord to effect repairs.

75 *See* Ark. Code Ann. § 18-16-110; Hall v. Lunsford, 732 S.W.2d 141 (Ark. 1987) (describing trial judge's holding that there is no implied warranty of habitability in Arkansas). *See also* Sanders v. Walker, 767 S.W.2d 526 (Ark. 1989) (time has dissolved any implied warranty of habitability for twenty-year-old premises); Friedman on Leases § 10:1.2 (implied warranty of habitability recognized in sale of new homes but not in leasing).

76 *See* 300 Spring Bldg. v. Matthews, No. CA-89-211 1990, Ark. App. LEXIS 112 (Ark. Ct. App. Feb. 21, 1990) (landlord breached covenant of quiet enjoyment in commercial lease by failing to provide heat, drinking water, and janitorial service); Seymour v. Evans, 608 So. 2d 1141 (Miss. 1992). *See also* Blagg v. Fred Hunt, Inc., 612 S.W.2d 321 (Ark. 1981). *Cf.* Dalrymple v. Fields, 633 S.W.2d 362, 364 (Ark. 1982). *See generally* Note, *Propst v. McNeill: Arkansas Landlord-Tenant law, A Time for Change*, 51 Ark. L. Rev. 575 (1998); Annot., *Breach of Covenant of Quiet Enjoyment in Lease*, 41 A.L.R.2d 1414 (1955).

77 *See, e.g., California:* Knight v. Hallsthammer, 623 P.2d 268 (Cal. 1981); Lehr v. Crosby, 177 Cal. Rptr. 96 (Cal. Ct. App. 1981); Cazares v. Ortiz, 168 Cal. Rptr. 108 (Cal. Ct. App. 1980); Stoiber v. Honeychuck, 162 Cal. Rptr. 194 (Cal. Ct. App. 1980).

District of Columbia: Winchester Mgmt. Corp. v. Staten, 361 A.2d 187 (D.C. 1976); Javins v. First Nat'l Realty Corp., 428 F.2d 1071 (D.C. Cir. 1970).

Illinois: Vanlandingham v. Ivanow, 615 N.E.2d 1361 (Ill. App. Ct. 1993).

Indiana: Johnson v. Scandia Assoc., Inc., 641 N.E.2d 51 (Ind. 1994).

The warranty of habitability has been codified in the twenty-one states that have adopted the Uniform Residential Landlord and Tenant Act (some of these states, such as Washington, Hawaii, Iowa and Kansas, also have adopted the common law implied warranty of habitability).[78] Under the Uniform Residential Landlord and Tenant Act, the landlord is required to comply with all codes, make repairs and do all that is necessary to put and keep premises in a fit and habitable condition and to keep the common areas clean and safe. Additionally, the landlord must maintain all facilities and appliances supplied by the landlord in good and safe working order, including electricity, plumbing, heating, ventilation, air conditioning and elevators. The landlord must also provide for rubbish removal and supply water, reasonable amounts of hot water and reasonable heat in the winter months. Some state courts have held that the statutory obligation is a strict liability statute or that it imposes a higher degree of care than common law.[79]

In addition to the twenty-one jurisdictions that have adopted a form of the Uniform Residential Landlord and Tenant Act, a form of the warranty of habitability has been adopted in all but a handful of the remaining states.[80]

In most jurisdictions, there is no doubt that a termination or threatened termination of utility service due to the landlord's failure to pay his or her utility service constitutes a sufficient threat to the health, safety or welfare of inhabitants to constitute a breach of the warranty.[81]

3.4.1.4 Waiver

The warranty, in most jurisdictions that have adopted it, may not be waived by any provision in the lease or rental agreement.[82]

Pennsylvania: Keck v. Doughman, 572 A.2d 724 (Pa. Super. Ct. 1990); Kuriger v. Cramer, 498 A.2d 1331 (Pa. Super. Ct. 1985). *See also In re* Clark, 96 B.R. 569 (Bankr. E.D. Pa. 1989).

Texas: Waldon v. Williams, 760 S.W.2d 833 (Tex. 1988); Kamarath v. Bennett, 568 S.W.2d 658 (Tex. 1978).

Vermont: Nepveu v. Rau, 583 A.2d 1273 (Vt. 1990); Gokey v. Bessette, 580 A.2d 488 (Vt. 1990).

Washington: Howard v. Horn, 810 P.2d 1387 (Wash. 1991).

West Virginia: Teller v. McCoy, 253 S.E.2d 114 (W. Va. 1979).

Wisconsin: Millikan, Inc. v. Allen, 124 N.W.2d 651 (Wis. 1963); Pines v. Perssion, 111 N.W.2d 409 (Wis. 1961).

78 The following jurisdictions have adopted a form of the URL&TA:

Alabama URL&TA: Ala. Code §§ 35-9A-101 to 35-9A-603.

Alaska URL&TA: Alaska Stat. § 34.03.010 to 34.03.380.

Arizona URL&TA: Ariz. Rev. Stat. Ann. § 33-1301 to 33-1381.

Connecticut URL&TA: Conn. Gen. Stat. §§ 47a-1 to 47a-20.

Florida URL&TA: Fla. Stat. § 83.51.

Hawaii URL&TA: Haw. Rev. Stat. § 521-42.

Iowa URL&TA: Iowa Code §§ 562A.1 to 562A.37.

Kansas URL&TA: Kan. Stat. Ann. §§ 58-2540 to 58-2573.

Kentucky URL&TA: Ky. Rev. Stat. Ann. §§ 383.00 to 383.715 (West).

Michigan URL&TA: Mich. Comp. Laws. §§ 554.601 to 554.616 (Michigan did not adopt the habitability sections of the URL&TA but rather has a separate statute regarding habitability: Mich. Comp. Laws. § 554-139).

Mississippi URL&TA: Miss. Code Ann. §§ 89-8-1 to 89-8-27.

Montana URL&TA: Mont. Code Ann. §§ 70-24-101 to 70-24-442.

Nebraska URL&TA: Neb. Rev. Stat. §§ 76-1401 to 76-1449.

New Mexico URL&TA: N.M. Stat. Ann. §§ 47-8-1 to 47-8-52.

Oklahoma: Okla. Stat. tit. 41, §§ 101 to 136.

Oregon URL&TA: Or. Rev. Stat. §§ 90.100 to 90.940.

Rhode Island URL&TA: R.I. Gen. Laws §§ 34-18-1 to 34-18-56.

South Carolina URL&TA: S.C. Code Ann. §§ 27-40-10 to 27-40-940.

Tennessee URL&TA: Tenn. Code Ann. §§ 66-28-101 to 66-28-516. Shut off of electricity and water violates covenant of quiet enjoyment: Morrison v. Smith, 757 S.W.2d 678 (Tenn. Ct. App. 1988).

Virginia URL&TA: Va. Code Ann. §§ 55-248.2 to 55-248.40.

Washington: Wash. Rev. Code §§ 59.18.010 to 59.18.430, 59.18.900.

79 *See* Jesse v. Lindsley, 233 P.3d 1 (Idaho 2008) (statute imposes strict liability); Giron v. Bailey, 985 A.2d 1003 (R.I. 2009) (Residential Landlord and Tenant Act imposes a higher standard of care and supersedes conflicting common-law rules); Stone v. Linden Real Estate, Inc., 210 P.3d 866 (Okla. Civ. App. 2009) (Residential Landlord and Tenant Act imposes a higher standard of care and supersedes conflicting common law rules unless explicitly stated otherwise).

80 *See supra* text accompanying notes 49, 50.

81 *See, e.g.*, Estate of Romanow v. Heller, 469 N.Y.S.2d 876 (N.Y. Civ. Ct. 1983), *aff'd per curiam*, 513 N.Y.S.2d 347 (N.Y. Sup. Ct. 1987); Parker 72d Assocs. v. Isaacs, 436 N.Y.S.2d 542 (N.Y. Civ. Ct. 1982); Leris Realty Corp v. Robbin, 408 N.Y.S.2d 166 (N.Y. Civ. Ct. 1978) (holding that failure to provide heat and hot water amounted to breach of warranty of habitability); Meader v. Francy, 2001 WL 1117443 (N.Y. J. Ct. Aug. 15, 2001) (failure to provide heat was "very substantial breach" of warranty of habitability); Davidow v. Inwood N. Prof'l Group, 747 S.W.2d 373 (Tex. 1988) (loss of electricity due to landlord's failure to pay bill); Adams v. Gaylock, 378 S.E.2d 297 (W. Va. 1989) (lack of electric service).

82 *See* George Wash. Univ. v. Weintraub, 458 A.2d 43 (D.C. 1983); Collins v. Economic Opportunity of Atlanta, 285 S.E.2d 562 (Ga. Ct. App. 1981); Boston Hous. Auth. v. Hemingway, 293 N.E.2d 831, 843–45 (Mass. 1973); Kline v. Burns, 276 A.2d 248 (N.H. 1971); Semans Family Ltd. P'ship v. Kennedy, 675 N.Y.S.2d 489 (N.Y. Civ. Ct. 1998); Miller v. C.W. Myers Trading Post, Inc., 355 S.E.2d 189 (N.C. Ct. App. 1987); Stone v. Linden Real Estate, Inc., 210 P.3d 866 (Okla. Civ. App. 2009); Fair v. Negly, 390 A.2d 240 (Pa. Super. Ct. 1978); Hilder v. St. Peter, 478 A.2d 202 (Vt. 1984). *Cf.* Wis. Stat. § 704.07 ("agreement to waive the requirements [of statute] in a residential tenancy is void"). *But see* Unif. Residential Landlord & Tenant Act § 1.403(a)(1); Javins v. First Nat'l Realty Corp., 428 F.2d 1071, 1082 (D.C. Cir. 1970); Moorman v. Tower Mgmt. Co., 451 F. Supp. 2d 846 (S.D. Miss. 2006) (lessee can waive warranty at inception of lease); Beltway Mgmt Co. v. Lexington-Landmark Ins. Co., 746 F. Supp. 1145, 1149 (D.C. 1990); P.H. Inv. v. Oliver, 818 P.2d 1018 (Utah 1991) (waiver must be express and is effective only as to specific defects listed); Restatement (Second) Prop. § 5.6 (allowing for written waiver

3.4.1.5 Remedies for Breach of Warranty of Habitability

The full range of contract damages are available for a material breach of the implied warranty of habitability[83] including compensatory and punitive damages, special damages,[84] and in some instances, attorney fees.[85]

General damages such as rent abatement are also available but may be calculated in several different ways.[86] Some courts calculate damages for a material breach of an implied warranty of habitability by determining the difference between the fair rental value of the premises in compliance with all code requirements and the fair rental value in the defective condition.[87] Other courts determine rent abatement by subtracting the fair rental[88] value of the premises in the unrepaired condition from the contract rent.[89] Many courts assess the percentage by which each defect would reduce the overall value of the unit. The percentages for reduction attributable to individual defects are added together; the fair market value of the unit without defects is reduced by the sum of the percentages.[90]

Punitive damages may be awarded when the breach is willful, wanton, or fraudulent.[91] Most important, injunctive relief is generally available to force the landlord to bring the unit in compliance with codes in order to prevent a threat to the health, safety or well-being of the occupants of the unit.[92]

In jurisdictions that subject landlord-tenant relations to state unfair or deceptive act or practices (UDAP) statutes,

---

of warranty provisions in lease, if not unconscionable). *See generally* James Charles Smith, *Tenant Remedies for Breach of Habitability: Tort Dimensions of a Contract Concept*, 35 U. Kan. L. Rev. 505, 517 (1987).

83 *See, e.g.*, Javins v. First Nat'l Realty Corp., 428 F.2d 1071, 1082 (D.C. Cir. 1970); Steele v. Latimer, 521 P.2d 304 (Kan. 1974); King v. Moorehead, 495 S.W.2d 65, 75–76 (Mo. Ct. App. 1973); Hilder v. St. Peter, 478 A.2d 202, 209 (Vt. 1984); Teller v. McCoy, 253 S.E.2d 114 (W. Va. 1978). *See also* Pugh v. Holmes, 384 A.2d 1234 (Pa. Super. Ct. 1977), *aff'd as modified*, 405 A.2d 897 (Pa. 1979).

84 *See* Mease v. Fox, 200 N.W.2d 791, 797 (Iowa 1972); Restatement (Second) of Property, Landlord & Tenant § 10.2 (1977) (special damages are available when a breach of warranty of habitability causes personal injury, property damages, relocation expenses, or other similar injuries, and such results are reasonably foreseeable).

85 *See, e.g.*, Mass. Gen. Laws ch. 239, § 8A, ch. 186, § 14.

86 *See* Note, *An Update on Contract Damages When the Landlord Breaches the Implied Warranty of Habitability: Suratt v. Newton and Allen v. Simmons*, 69 N.C. L. Rev. 1699, 1705 (1991).

87 *See* Boston Hous. Auth. v. Hemingway, 293 N.E.2d 831, 843–45 (Mass. 1973); Miller v. C.W. Meyers Trading Post, Inc., 355 S.E.2d 189, 194 (N.C. Ct. App. 1987). *See also* Green v. Superior Court, 517 P.2d 1168, 1183 (Cal. 1974); Glasoe v. Trinkle, 479 N.E.2d 915 (Ill. 1985); Roeder v. Nolan, 321 N.W.2d 1, 5 (Iowa 1982); Mease v. Fox, 200 N.W.2d 791, 797 (Iowa 1972); Kline v. Burns, 276 A.2d 248 (N.H. 1971); Hilder v. St. Peter, 478 A.2d 202, 209 (Vt. 1984); Teller v. McCoy, 253 S.E.2d 114, 128 (W. Va. 1978). *Cf.* Surratt v. Newton, 393 S.E.2d 554, 560 (N.C. Ct. App. 1990).

88 *See* James Charles Smith, *Tenant Remedies for Breach of Habitability: Tort Dimensions of a Contract Concept*, 35 Kan. L. Rev. 505, 518–23 (1987); Cazares v. Ortiz, 168 Cal. Rptr. 108 (Cal. App. Dep't Super. Ct. 1980).

89 *See, e.g.*, Welborn v. Society for the Propagation of the Faith, 411 N.E.2d 1267, 1271 (Ind. Ct. App. 1980); Poncz v. Loftin, 911, 607 N.E.2d 765, 766 (Mass. App. Ct. 1993) ("appropriate measure of damages in cases involving premises which are uninhabitable is the difference between the rental value of the premises as warranted (the agreed rent), less the fair value of the premises in their defective condition" plus reasonable cost to tenant of remedying the defect); King v. Moorehead, 495 S.W.2d 65, 76 (Mo. Ct. App. 1973); Kline v. Burns, 276 A.2d 248, 252 (N.H. 1971); Berzito v. Gambino, 308 A.2d 17, 22 (N.J. 1973); Park W. Mgmt. Corp. v. Mitchell, 391 N.E.2d 1288, 1295 (N.Y. 1978); Stone v. Gordon, 621 N.Y.S.2d 220 (3d App. Div. 1995); Bay Park One Co. v. Crosby, 442 N.Y.S.2d 837, 838 (N.Y. Sup. Ct. 1981); Lane v. Kelly, 643 P.2d 1375, 1377 (Or. Ct. App. 1982); Beausang v. Bernotas, 442 A.2d 796, 799 (Pa. Super. Ct. 1982); Fair v. Negley, 390 A.2d 240, 242 (Pa. Super. Ct. 1978); Birkenhead v. Coombs, 465 A.2d 244, 246 (Vt. 1983).

90 Cazares v. Ortiz, 168 Cal. Rptr. 108 (Cal. App. Dep't Super. Ct. 1980); Vanlandingham v. Ivanow, 615 N.E.2d 1361 (Ill. App. Ct. 1993); McKenna v. Begin, 362 N.E.2d 548, 551–53 (Mass. App. Ct. 1977). *See* Note, *An Update on Contract Damages When the Landlord Breaches the Implied Warranty of Habitability: Suratt v. Newton and Allen v. Simmons*, 69 N.C. L. Rev. 1699 (1991); Annot., *Measure of Damages for Landlord's Breach of Implied Warranty of Habitability*, 1 A.L.R. 4th 1182 (1980). *See also* Winchester Mgmt. Corp. v. Staten, 361 A.2d 187 (D.C. 1976); Timber Ridge Town House v. Dietz, 338 A.2d 21, 24–25 (N.J. Super. Ct. Law Div. 1975); Academy Spires, Inc. v. Brown, 268 A.2d 556, 561 (N.J. Dist. Ct. 1970); Goldner v. Doknovitch, 388 N.Y.S.2d 504 (N.Y. App. Term 1976); Whiteball Hotel v. Gaynor, 470 N.Y.S.2d 286, 288–89 (N.Y. Civ. Ct. 1978); Whitehouse Estates, Inc. v. Thomson, 386 N.Y.S.2d 733, 734–35 (N.Y. Civ. Ct. 1976); Pugh v. Holmes, 384 A.2d 1234, 1241–42 (Pa. Super. Ct. 1978), *aff'd*, 405 A.2d 897 (Pa. 1979). *See generally* Rest. (Second) Prop. § 11.1 (1976).

91 Minjak Co. v. Randolph, 528 N.Y.S.2d 554 (N.Y. App. Div. 1988) (upholding award of punitive damages for performing repairs without regard to tenants' safety); E. 89th Partners v. Simon, 434 N.Y.S.2d 886 (N.Y. Civ. Ct. 1980) (awarding punitive damages for clear pattern of withholding services in breach of implied warranty of habitability); Hilder v. St. Peter, 478 A.2d 202 (Vt. 1984). *See also* Kuiken v. Garrett, 51 N.W.2d 149 (Iowa 1953). *But see* Drs. Sellke & Conlon, Ltd. v. Twin Oaks Realty, Inc., 173, 491 N.E.2d 912 (Ill. App. Ct. 1986); Miller v. C.W. Myers Trading Post, Inc., 355 S.E.2d 189, 195 (N.C. Ct. App. 1987) (punitive damages not recoverable in action on breach of an implied warranty of habitability when breach neither constitutes nor is accompanied by tortious conduct).

92 *See, e.g.*, Fla. Stat. § 83.67; Mass. Gen. Laws ch. 186, § 14, ch. 239, § 8A; Vt. Stat. Ann. tit. 9, §§ 4463, 4464; Javins v. First Nat'l Realty Corp., 428 F.2d 1071, 1082 n.16 (D.C. Cir. 1970); Hemetek v. Standish (*In re* Bush), No. 89-20949 ch. 7, Adv. Pro. No. 90-0010, Clearinghouse No. 44,838A (Complaint) (Bankr. S.D. W. Va. Feb. 2, 1990); *In re* Clark, 96 B.R. 569, 572 (Bankr. E.D. Pa. 1989); Dugan v. Milledge, 494 A.2d 1203 (Conn. 1985); Jack Spring Inc. v. Little, 280 N.E.2d 208 (Ill. 1992).

additional UDAP remedies may be obtained for the landlord's breach of the implied warranty of habitability, and the landlord's violation of state or local housing codes may constitute a per se UDAP violation.[93] In many instances, punitive damages for intentional infliction of emotional distress may also be available.[94]

The failure to provide basic utilities, such as heat or hot water, has been held to be a substantial violation of the warranty of habitability resulting in substantial rent abatements.[95]

3.4.1.6 Serious Code Violations Violate Warranty of Habitability

Many areas of the country will have a state-wide or local housing code that sets forth the minimum standards for rental of residential real estate.[96] Housing codes generally provide minimum standards for the provision of utility and other essential housing services. Often the codes define whose responsibility it will be to obtain and pay for such services.[97] A landlord's failure to substantially comply with applicable building and housing code standards that materially affect health and safety constitute a breach of the warranty of habitability.[98]

Housing codes provide the baseline for determining the contents of the implied warranty (together with local building and fire codes). However, the warranty may not always be confined to housing code violations,[99] although a few jurisdictions do confine the warranty to a breach of the codes. For example, in the District of Columbia, the warranty was breached by failure to provide hot water but not by a failure to provide air conditioning in summer, although the lease promised air conditioning. This was because air conditioning was not required by the D.C. housing code.[100]

3.4.2 *Specific Statutory Protection Against Landlord Allowing Utility Termination*

3.4.2.1 General

Many jurisdictions, including those that have adopted the Uniform Residential Landlord and Tenant Act have specific provisions that provide a tenant with a remedy against a utility shut-off.[101] Wrongful termination of utility service will entitle a tenant to actual damages,[102] as well as reason-

---

93 *See, e.g.*, Allen v. Simmons, 394 S.E.2d 478, 484 (N.C. Ct. App. 1990) (landlord's attempt to collect rent for premises that were in violation of the housing code was sufficient to permit the jury to decide whether the landlord's conduct constituted a violation of the state's unfair trade practices statute). *See generally* National Consumer Law Center, Unfair and Deceptive Acts and Practices § 3.2 (7th ed. 2008 and Supp.).

94 Wolfberg v. Hunter, 432 N.E.2d 467 (Mass. 1982); 49 Prospect St. Tenants Ass'n v. Sheva Gardens, 547 A.2d 1134 (N.J. Super. Ct. App. Div. 1988); Borders v. Newton, 315 S.E.2d 731 (N.C. Ct. App. 1984). *See also In re* Clark, 96 B.R. 569, 572 (Bankr. E.D. Pa. 1989); Haddad v. Gonzalez, 576 N.E.2d 658 (Mass. 1991); and Dorgan v. Loukes, 473 N.E.2d 1151 (Mass. App. Ct. 1985) (all allowing damages for emotional distress due to defective conditions in rented premises be recovered under UDAP statute). *See generally* Annot., *Tenant Recovery for Emotional Distress Under URLTA*, 6 A.L.R.4th 528 (1981).

95 *See* § 3.4.1.1, *supra*.

96 Statewide codes include: Cal. Health & Safety Code §§ 17910 to 17998.3 (West); Iowa Code § 364.17 (applicable to all cities with 15,000 or more people); 105 Mass. Code Regs. § 410 (LexisNexis); Mich. Comp. Laws §§ 125.1502a to 125.1531.

Many large communities have local housing codes.

97 Most city codes have used one of a number of Model Housing Codes, for example, Southern Standard Housing Code, Southern Building Code Congress, Building Officials and Code Administrator's Basic Housing Code (2d ed. 1970), or U.S. Public Health Service, APHA-PHS Recommended Maintenance and Occupancy Ordinance. *See generally* Samuel Basset Abbott, *Housing Policy, Housing Codes, and Tenant Remedies—An Integration*, 56 B.U.L. Rev. 1, 34–79 (1976).

98 *See* Smith v. David, 176 Cal. Rptr. 112 (Cal. Ct. App. 1981); Hilder v. St. Peter, 478 A.2d 202 (Vt. 1984).

The Massachusetts Sanitary Code has detailed provisions addressing when the owner must pay for gas, electricity, and heating oil. *See* 105 Mass. Code Regs. §§ 410.354 (owner must pay utilities unless separately metered solely for the tenant's individual use), 410.180 and 410.190 (owner required to supply and pay for water and hot water; except tenant can be required to pay for fuel for hot water if in a written lease agreement), 410.201 (regarding when owner or tenant must pay for heat) (LexisNexis).

Curtailing or shutting off utility services is prohibited. 105 Mass. Code Regs. § 410.620 (LexisNexis).

Shutting off required utility and heat services is a material breach of the Code, entitling tenant to damages for breach of implied warranty of habitability. 105 Mass. Code Regs. § 410.750 (LexisNexis). *See also* Green v. Superior Court, 517 P.2d 1168, 1182–83 (Cal. 1974).

99 Boston Hous. Auth. v. Hemingway, 293 N.E.2d 831 (Mass. 1973); Detling v. Edelbrock, 671 S.W.2d 265 (Mo. 1984); Pugh v. Holmes, 384 A.2d 1234, *aff'd*, 405 A.2d 897 (Pa. 1979).

100 Winchester Mgmt. Corp. v. Staten, 361 A.2d 187 (D.C. 1976). *See also* Jackson by Jackson v. Wood, 726 P.2d 796 (Kan. 1986).

101 *See, e.g.*, Alaska Stat. § 34.03.180; Ariz. Rev. Stat. Ann. § 33-1364; Cal. Civ. Code § 789.3 (West); Conn. Gen. Stat. §§ 47a-7, 47a-13, 16-262e; Fla. Stat. § 83.67; 765 Ill. Comp. Stat. 735/1.4, 735/2.1, 735/3; Minn. Stat. § 504B.221; N.H. Rev. Stat. Ann. §§ 540-A-3, 540-A-4; N.M. Stat. Ann. § 47-8-36; 68 Pa. Stat. Ann. §§ 339.1 to 399.18 (West); Wash. Rev. Code § 59.18.300.

102 *See* Cal. Civ. Code § 789.3(c) (West) (actual damages and up to $100 for each day without utility service); Fla. Stat. § 83.67 (actual and consequential damages or three months' rent, whichever is greater); Me. Rev. Stat. tit. 14, § 6014 (actual damages or $250, whichever is greater); N.M. Stat. Ann. § 47-8-36; Ohio Rev. Code Ann. § 5321.15 (West); Tex. Prop. Code Ann. § 92.301 (West); Va. Code Ann. § 55-225.2; Wash. Rev. Code § 59.18.300 (actual damages and up to $100 for each day without utility service).

able attorney fees.[103] Wrongful termination or interruption of utility service may subject the landlord to remedies conferred by other laws as well. For example, Maine's statutory law explicitly authorizes a tenant to pursue remedies conferred by other provisions.[104] Some states explicitly prohibit a landlord from terminating or interrupting a tenant's utility service when done so to evict the tenant.[105] Landlords are generally permitted, however, to terminate utilities in emergencies or to make reasonable repairs.

In Massachusetts, a statute prohibits the landlord from (1) willfully or intentionally failing to furnish water, hot water, heat, light, power, gas, telephone service, janitor service or refrigeration service to residential tenants when obligated to so provide by law or agreement; (2) interfering with another who is providing such services; (3) transferring the responsibility for payment of such services to the tenant without the tenant's knowledge and consent; and (4) eviction of the tenant by force without judicial process. Such conduct is a crime and the landlord is liable for at least three months rent.[106] Other laws require the utility to notify the tenant prior to terminating service to the unit because of the landlord's failure to pay for the service and provide limits on terminations of service during winter months due to financial hardship or to households that include infants, or elderly, or seriously ill persons.[107]

Under Massachusetts law, the landlord is subject to a fine of no less than twenty-five dollars and no more than three hundred dollars or by imprisonment of up to six months. The landlord is also liable to the tenant for actual and consequential damages or three months' rent, whichever is greater. The tenant must give the landlord notice of the breach and then the tenant can (a) procure utility service directly and deduct the actual costs of doing so from the rent, (b) recover damages for the diminution of the fair rental value, or (c) obtain reasonable substitute housing during the period of noncompliance that excuses the tenant from paying rent and obligates the landlord to pay for the rent for the substitute housing up to the amount of the original rent.[108] Other laws may allow the tenant to procure utility service directly and deduct the cost of doing so from the rent—so long as the landlord is given notice of the violation as specified in the statute[109]—or to simply withhold rent to reflect the diminished value of the premises.[110]

In Connecticut, the landlord's failure to provide essential utilities constitutes a breach of the rental agreement. This breach entitles the tenant to give notice to the landlord that the termination shall be treated as a breach and to obtain substitute housing and recover the cost of the substitute housing up to the amount of the rent.[111] The tenant may also obtain utility service independently from the utility company and deduct the cost of securing such service from the rent.[112] Accordingly, the utility company may not terminate service to a tenant for the nonpayment of a delinquent account owed by the landlord without (1) notifying the tenant that it intends to take such action and (2) providing the tenant an opportunity to receive service in the tenant's name *without paying the debt owed by the landlord.*[113]

Similarly, many other states have laws that impose civil[114] or criminal[115] liability upon a landlord's failure to provide utility service to the rental units when the landlord is billed for the service. In Minnesota, for example, the tenant is entitled to treble damages or $500, whichever is greater, and reasonable attorney fees.[116] Other laws provide for self-help remedies against the landlord in the form of rent withholding, or the right to pay the utility directly and deduct the amount of the payment from the rent.[117]

---

103 *See* Fla. Stat. § 83.67; Me. Rev. Stat. tit. 14, § 6014; Ohio Rev. Code Ann. § 5321.15 (West); Tex. Prop. Code Ann. § 92.301 (West); Va. Code Ann. § 55-225.2; Wash. Rev. Code § 59.18.300.

104 Me. Rev. Stat. tit. 14, § 6014.

105 *See, e.g.*, Cal. Civ. Code § 789.3(a) (West) (landlord cannot terminate or interrupt utility service when doing so to terminate occupancy under the lease); Nev. Rev. Stat. § 118B.150 (manufactured home parks); Ohio Rev. Code Ann. § 5321.15 (West) (prohibiting a landlord from terminating or interrupting utility service to either a tenant in rightful possession or a tenant who no longer has a right to possession of the premises, for the purpose of recovering possession of the residential premises).

106 Mass. Gen. Laws ch. 186, § 14.

107 Mass. Gen. Laws ch. 164, §§ 124A, 124D–124F.

108 Mass. Gen. Laws ch. 186, § 14, ch. 111, § 127L, ch. 164, § 124D.

109 Mass. Gen. Laws ch. 111, § 127L.

110 Mass. Gen. Laws ch. 239, § 8A.

111 Conn. Gen. Stat. §§ 47a-7, 47a-13.

112 Conn. Gen. Stat. §§ 47a-7, 47a-13.

113 Conn. Gen. Stat. § 16-262e (emphasis added).

114 *See, e.g.*, Fla. Stat. § 83.67 (greater of three months' rent or actual damages); Me. Rev. Stat. tit. 14, § 6014; Minn. Stat. § 504B.221 (greater of treble damages or $500); Nev. Rev. Stat. § 118A.380 (1); N.Y. Real Prop. Laws §§ 235, 235-a (McKinney); Okla. Stat. tit. 41, § 121(C).

115 *See* Ga. Code Ann. § 44-7-14.1 (upon willful or knowing suspension of service); State v. Elmwood Terrace Inc., 204 A.2d 379 (N.J. 1964).

116 Minn. Stat. § 504B.221.

The tenant is entitled to actual damages unless (1) the tenant failed to notify the landlord of the interruption or (2) the landlord, after receiving notice, makes a good faith effort to reinstate service or has taken other remedial action or (3) the interruption was for the purpose of repairing or correcting faulty or defective equipment or protecting the health and safety of the occupants, and the services were reinstated or a good faith effort was undertaken to reinstate services.

117 *See, e.g.*, Ariz. Rev. Stat. Ann. § 33-1364 (pay and deduct); Conn. Gen. Stat. § 16-262e; Del. Code Ann. tit. 25, §§ 5307, 5308 (rent withholding); 765 Ill. Comp. Stat. 735/01–735/3 (pay and deduct, rent receivership); Me. Rev. Stat. tit. 14, § 6024-A (pay and deduct), tit. 35-A, § 706; Minn. Stat. § 504B.215; N.M. Stat. Ann. § 47-8-36 (rent withholding); N.Y. Pub. Serv. Law §§ 33, 34 (McKinney) (pay and deduct); N.Y. Real Prop. Law § 235-a (McKinney); Tex. Prop. Code Ann. § 92.301 (West) (pay and deduct).

3.4.2.2 State-by-State Analysis

The Uniform Residential Landlord and Tenant Act in Alaska requires the landlord to supply running water, and reasonable amounts of hot water and heat at all times, insofar as energy conditions permit,[118] except when heat and water are within the exclusive control of the tenant and supplied by a direct public utility connection.[119] When the landlord willfully or negligently fails to provide utilities, after notice the tenant can obtain the utility service directly and deduct the cost from the rent, or the tenant can recover as damages a rent abatement, or the tenant can obtain substitute housing, abate the rent due to the original landlord, and receive damages for the increased cost up to the amount of the rent.[120]

Similarly, California by statute prohibits the landlord from willfully interrupting or terminating any utility service, and there is a statutory penalty up to $100 a day for doing so.[121] The landlord must repair conditions making the premises uninhabitable and the water, heating, gas and electric facilities must be in good working order.[122]

In Delaware, when the landlord substantially fails to provide water, heat or hot water, after notice the tenant can deduct two-thirds of the rent due each day the utility service is not provided. Also, for any failure to supply utility service, the tenant can obtain substitute housing and abate the rent; the landlord is also liable for additional expenses up to half of the amount of the abated rent.[123] Additionally, the landlord must comply with all codes, maintain the premises in habitable condition and supply water, hot water and heat when it is required by the rental agreement.[124]

Florida has a statutory prohibition against the landlord terminating utility service, directly or indirectly, whether the landlord controls or pays or not, and the landlord is liable for actual and consequential damages or three months rent. A violation of these provisions is automatically deemed to meet the "irreparable harm" requirement for obtaining an injunction.[125]

By contrast, in Georgia there is a criminal prohibition against landlords knowingly and willfully suspending utility service to tenants.[126]

In Maine, there is a statutory prohibition against the landlord willfully causing termination of utility service; the landlord is liable for the greater of actual damages or $250 and reasonable attorney fees.[127] Another statute requires the landlord to pay for the utilities in his name; if the landlord fails to pay, the tenant can pay for the utilities directly and deduct the cost from the rent.[128] There is also a statute that prohibits the landlord from having the tenant pay for electricity that is not solely used by the tenant's unit, unless the written lease has express consideration such as stated rent reduction; for violating this mandate, the landlord is liable for the greater of actual damages or $250, plus reasonable attorney fees.[129]

In Michigan, the tenant is protected from unlawful interference with a possessory interest and is entitled to actual damages or $200 for each occurrence of such interference. Interference expressly includes termination or interruption of essential utility services.[130]

Minnesota landlords are liable for treble damages or $500 when they cause the interruption of utility service.[131] Intentional interruption of utilities by the landlord is also a misdemeanor.[132]

In Nevada, when the landlord is obligated under lease or this statute to provide utilities or other essential services, the landlord is liable when he willfully or negligently fails to so provide after written notice and forty-eight hours. The tenant can recover, in addition to actual damages, the cost of obtaining utility service or the cost of obtaining alternate housing.[133] For a willful interruption of essential services, the landlord is liable for actual damages up to $1000.[134] Finally, the written rental agreement must state both the landlord's and the tenant's duties as to utilities.[135]

In New Hampshire, the landlord is prohibited from directly or indirectly causing the termination of any utility service being supplied to the tenant, whether or not the utility service is under the control of the landlord.[136] While the statute specifies some particular utilities such as water, heat, light, electricity, gas, telephone, sewerage, elevator, and refrigeration, the protection includes other utilities as well.[137]

In New York, it is a crime for the landlord to willfully or intentionally fail to provide required utilities; the tenant can deduct the cost of obtaining utility service from the rent payments.[138] When utility service has been discontinued due to the landlord's arrearage, the tenant cannot be evicted

118 Alaska Stat. § 34.03.100(a)(5).
119 *Id.*
120 Alaska Stat. § 34.03.180.
121 Cal. Civ. Code § 789.3 (West); Kinney v. Vaccari, 612 P.2d 877 (Cal. 1980).
122 Cal. Civ. Code §§ 1941, 1941.1 (West).
123 Del. Code Ann. tit. 25, § 5308.
124 Del. Code Ann. tit. 25, § 5305.
125 Fla. Stat. § 83.67. *See also* DiMassimo v. City of Clearwater, 805 F.2d 1536 (11th Cir. 1986).
126 Ga. Code Ann. § 44-7-14.1.
127 Me. Rev. Stat. tit. 14, § 6014.
128 Me. Rev. Stat. tit. 14, § 6024-A.
129 Me. Rev. Stat. tit. 14, § 6024.
130 Mich. Comp. Laws § 600.2918.
131 Minn. Stat. § 504B.221.
132 Minn. Stat. § 504B.225.
133 Nev. Rev. Stat. § 118A.380(1).
134 Nev. Rev. Stat. § 118A.390(1).
135 Nev. Rev. Stat. § 118A.200(2)(j).
136 N.H. Rev. Stat. Ann. § 540-A:3.
137 Lally v. Flieder, 986 A.2d 652 (N.H. 2009) (protection against utility termination includes cable service).
138 N.Y. Pub. Serv. Law §§ 33, 34 (McKinney); N.Y. Real Prop. Law § 235-a (McKinney).

for nonpayment of rent until the landlord pays the utility arrearage and service is restored.[139] The landlord is liable for compensatory and punitive damages for a failure to provide the required utilities.[140]

In Oklahoma, the tenant can reduce the rent, and the landlord is liable for the cost of procuring replacement utility service and, after written notice, for the willful or negligent failure to supply utility service.[141] In Virginia, there is a statutory prohibition against the landlord willfully diminishing service to a tenant by interrupting the delivery of gas, water, or other essential service. The tenant's remedies include an order requiring the resumption of utility service or termination of the rental agreement, as well as actual damages and attorney fees.[142]

3.4.3 Protection Against Reprisal

To protect all of these rights adopted for the benefit of tenants, most states have prohibited retaliation by the landlord against the tenant. The tenant is protected against eviction, termination of the tenancy, decrease of services and utilities and/or a refusal to re-rent. In addition to common law cases prohibiting such reprisals, many states have statutes protecting tenants from retaliation.

Many states statutes prohibit, *inter alia*, any reprisal against the tenant for exercising rights or complaining about the landlord's conduct. There is a presumption of reprisal for a termination of tenancy, a rent increase, or an alteration of the terms of tenancy (for example, requiring that the tenant now pay for the utilities directly) when the landlord so acts within six months of the tenant's complaints. Statutory damages may include one to three months' rent, treble damages, and attorney fees.[143] Tenants are similarly protected against retaliation in other states.[144]

Similarly, several other jurisdictions recognize the tenuous position of a tenant who receives utility service that is billed to the landlord and provide for special notice or termination limitations as to individuals or periods in which utility termination is likely to cause severe hardship.[145] Of course, tenants should generally be entitled to service in their own name without regard to any arrearage of the landlord.[146]

139 N.Y. Real Prop. Acts Law § 756 (McKinney).

140 N.Y. Real Prop. Law §§ 235, 235-a (McKinney).

141 Okla. Stat. tit. 41, § 121(C).

142 Va. Code Ann. § 55-225.2.

143 *See, e.g.*, Mass. Gen. Laws ch. 186, § 18. *See also* California Retaliation Protection, Cal. Civ. Code. § 1942.5 (West); Delaware Statutory Tenant Protection, Del. Code Ann. tit. 25, § 5316; Maine Statutory Tenant Protections, Me. Rev. Stat. tit. 14, §§ 6001–6015; Michigan Statutory Tenant Protection, Mich. Comp. Laws §§ 554.139, 600.2918 (protection for tenant against unlawful ejection).

144 State statutes providing tenant protection include: Nev. Rev. Stat. § 118A.510; N.J. Stat. Ann. § 2A:42-10.10 (West); N.Y. Real Prop. Law § 223-b (McKinney); Ohio Rev. Code Ann. § 5321.02 (West); Tex. Prop. Code Ann. §§ 92.001–92.020 (West); Vt. Stat. Ann. tit. 9, § 4465; Washington Statutory Tenant Protections-Residential Landlord-Tenant Act: Wash. Rev. Code §§ 59.18.240, 59.18.250; Wis. Stat. § 704.45. *See also* 68 Pa. Stat. Ann. § 250.205 (West) (Pennsylvania protects tenants who participate in tenants' organizations or associations).

145 D.C. Code §§ 42-3302, 42-3303 (notice, payment plan, rent receivership); 765 Ill. Comp. Stat. 735/0.01 to 735/5 (ten days' notice, rent receivership); 220 Ill. Comp. Stat. 5/8-201 to 5/8-203, 5/8-205 to 5/8-207 (winter moratorium: no termination of service for heat during winter months); Iowa Code § 476.20 (notice, winter moratorium for poor consumers); Mass. Gen. Laws ch. 164, §§ 124A, 124D to 124H (notice to tenants, opportunity to maintain service by paying current bills, winter moratorium, moratorium or service termination for infants, elderly, seriously ill); Me. Rev. Stat. tit. 35-A, §§ 704, 706 (notice and opportunity to assume service, no termination during medical emergency); Mich. Comp. Laws § 400.1161, 400.1210 (no termination to certain low-income households); Minn. Stat. § 504B.215 (notice, tenants may maintain service by paying most recent billing period); Mo. Rev. Stat. § 441.650 (notice, rent receivership, moratorium on termination while receivership application pending); Neb. Rev. Stat. §§ 70-1603, 70-1605, 70-1606, 70-1612 (seven days' notice, moratorium on termination for ill or disabled consumers); N.J. Stat. Ann. § 2A: 42-87, 42-88, 42-90, 42-92 (West) (rent receivership); N.Y. Pub. Serv. Law §§ 33, 34 (McKinney) (fifteen days' notice); Tenn. Code Ann. § 65-32-104 (notice to "user," opportunity to make payments).

146 *See, e.g.*, United States v. Springwood Vill., 168 F. Supp. 885 (S.D.N.Y. 1958); Price v. South Cent. Bell Tel. Co., 313 So. 2d 184 (Ala. 1975); Alabama Water Co. v. Knowles, 124 So. 96 (Ala. 1929); Ginnings v. Meridan Water Works Co., 56 So. 450 (Miss. 1911); McMenamin v. Evesham Mun. Util. Auth., 249 A.2d 21 (N.J. 1969), *aff'd per curiam*, 256 A.2d 801 (N.J. Super. Ct. App. Div. 1969); Baylor v. Philadelphia Elec. Co., 61 Pa. P.U.C. 323 (Pa. Apr. 17, 1986) (No. F-8532525); Galveston v. Kenner, 240 S.W. 894 (Tex. 1922).

Chapter 4 Metering Issues: Metering Errors, Master-Metering, Submetering, Prepayment Meters, Advanced Meters

4.1 Reverse Metering

4.1.1 Typical Fact Patterns

Reverse metering or cross-metering occurs on premises with more than one tenant. Tenant A has been billed for tenant B's use, and tenant B has been billed for A's use. This can happen because tenant A's apartment has been connected to tenant B's meter and *vice versa*.[1] Such a situation often arises as a result of mislabeling of the meter troughs by the developer's electricians when wiring the premises during the building process. The error might also be made by the utility, putting the wrong meter in the meter troughs, despite adequate labeling by the builder's electrician. Or the error can be caused by a billing system mix-up, in which the customer numbers and associated meter readings are reversed by mistake.

When the error is discovered, the utility will correct the match between meters and customers and bill tenant A and tenant B for the correct use (that is, their own use) in the future. The result of such corrected billing will almost invariably be that one of the tenants starts receiving larger bills and the other enjoys smaller bills than previously. This is because the use of the two customers is likely to be different.[2] Until the error was corrected, the customer with the higher use (say, customer B) was billed for the lower use of the other customer (say, customer A). When B's bills start reflecting his or her actual use, it will seem like an increase,[3] and B may not distinguish between such an increase and a rate increase or an increase from a meter that becomes defective. In some cases, B may seek legal help to challenge the new billing (such as by claiming a defective meter).[4]

1 Order, Toon v. Pacific Power & Light Co., Nos. UC-139, 90-236 (Or. Pub. Serv. Comm'n Feb. 20, 1990).

2 Indeed, it would be an extraordinary coincidence if the use was identical. It is likely that a pattern in the differences in use over time can be identified, with one customer generally using more energy and another customer generally using less, for a variety of reasons.

3 Customer A, by contrast, will start seeing much lower bills than he or she is used to.

4 *See* § 4.4, *infra* (discussing high-bill complaints).

More often, B will seek an advocate's help because the utility has also demanded payment of a recomputed back bill. The utility might try to go back at least to when the tenants became customers of the utility and recompute the bills using the actual use for each unit. Tenant A (the one with the lower actual use) will receive a refund. But Tenant B will receive a bill for the difference between the amount paid and the amount that would have been due if B had been billed on B's own use (rather than on A's use).

The amount demanded of the customer who has to pay the difference between actual use and the lower amount billed can be substantial. Reverse metering can go undetected by any of the parties (landlord, tenant A, tenant B, utility) for a long time.[5] The utility's demand that B pay

5 In Hutchins v. Boston Edison Co., No. 1392 (Mass. Dep't Pub. Util. 1983), for example, it was three years before the reverse metering was detected, and the re-bill to "customer B" was $1179. *See also* Illinois Power Co. v. Champaign Asphalt Co., 310 N.E.2d 463 (Ill. App. Ct. 1974) (power company was allowed to recover payment for electricity supplied to an industrial customer over a three-year period in excess of the amount billed and paid for as measured and recorded by a defective transformer and metering equipment when it was found that the company was not at fault in allowing the inaccurate meter to remain in service); Kotsias v. Peoples Gas Light & Coke Co., 114 Pub. Util. Rep. 4th 378, 1990 WL 488808 (Ill. Commerce Comm'n July 6, 1990) (declining, in a billing dispute, to create, as a matter of law, an irrebuttable presumption that all readings from meters that tested within applicable statutory standards were accurate); Kean Inv. Co. v. Michigan Consol. Gas Co., 111 Pub. Util. Rep. 4th 479, 1990 WL 488713 (Mich. Pub. Serv. Comm'n Apr. 12, 1990) (authorized natural gas distribution utility to institute back-billing procedures against the owner of buildings when utility appeared to have used diligent care in making regular inspections and readings of meters in two apartment buildings and had proved allegations of improper bypass of the meters); Northern States Power Co. v. Lynn Food Prods., Inc., 229 N.W.2d 521 (Minn. 1975) (considering evidence introduced by an electric company for nonpayment of service sufficient on which to base an award for damages for service provided but not billed, when it was shown that the meter was defective during the entire period and that the electricity used through one meter that was accurate represented approximately one third of the total energy used by the customer); Norman v. Ohio Pub. Util. Comm'n, 406 N.E.2d 492 (Ohio 1980) (commission rule limiting the utility to one year's

these amounts, and the inclusion of the back-billed amount in the current charges create a risk of shut-off and the associated risk of being unable to obtain service at a new dwelling. Particularly for low-income customers, even a modest back bill can present an urgent problem.

4.1.2 Utility May Generally Collect for Erroneous Undercharge

The general rule first developed in common law and then codified in many state utility regulations is that a utility may collect the amount of an erroneous undercharge.[6] The basic contract doctrine of "mistake" would counsel that in such situations, the burden of the error should lie with the party who: (a) is most capable of preventing the error; and (b) is most capable of bearing the risk of the mistake.[7] Moreover, if there has been a change in position by an innocent party in reliance on the mistake, the other party may be estopped from raising the mistake.[8]

Unfortunately, in the public utility context, most courts refuse to rely on mistake and estoppel in the under-billing context because to do so would violate the strong public policy, as established by statute, against discriminatory rates.[9] As the Tennessee Supreme Court concluded, "if the customer could successfully assert an estoppel defense, it would in effect have received electrical service at a fare far below that charged other users of like services. Besides unjustly enriching the customer, the result would amount to granting it a rate preference. . . ."[10]

It has been held that a utility is required to collect for a mistaken undercharge.[11] Rates when published by the utility become established by law and are akin to statutes.[12] To permit an undercharge would be to disrupt the uniform application of rates.[13] Public utilities assume a statutory[14] and common law[15] duty to provide service at rates that are not discriminatory. This duty prohibits a utility from providing service at a rate less than the one published in its tariffs.[16] Because of this obligation the utility has not only

---

back-billing *ultra vires*); *In re* Valley Util. Co., 73 Pub. Util. Rep. 3d 41 (Ohio 1968) (computation of water bills when a meter is found to be operating inaccurately or ceases to register was required to be estimated, based on the quarterly billing in the same month of the preceding year rather than on the average registration of a new or repaired meter in the opinion of the water company). *Cf.* Cincinnati Gas & Elec. Co. v. Joseph Chevrolet Co., 791 N.E.2d 1016 (Ohio Ct. App. 2003) (while legislature limits back-billing of residential customers to one year, there is no such limit for commercial customers).

6 *See, e.g.*, Haverhill Gas Co. v. Findlen, 258 N.E.2d 294 (Mass. 1970); Memphis Gas, Light & Water Div. v. Auburndale Sch. Sys., 705 S.W.2d 652 (Tenn. 1986); Chesapeake & Potomac Tel. Co. v. Bles, 243 S.E.2d 473 (Va. 1978). *See* Goddard v. Public Serv. Comm'n of Colo., 599 P.2d 278 (Colo. Ct. App. 1979); Shoemaker v. Mountain States Tel. & Tel. Co., 559 P.2d 721 (Colo. Ct. App. 1976); Corp. de Gestion Ste-Foy, Inc. v. Fla. Power & Light Co., 385 So. 2d 124 (Fla. Dist. Ct. App. 1980); Silverman v. Long Island Water Corp., 209 N.Y.S.2d 444 (N.Y. 1960) (a claim of waiver does not lie); Consolidated Edison of N.Y., Inc. v. Jet Asphalt Corp., 522 N.Y.S.2d 124 (N.Y. App. Div. 1987); West Penn Power Co. v. Nationwide Mut. Ins. Co., 228 A.2d 218 (Pa. Super. Ct. 1967). *See also* Empire W. v. Southern Cal. Gas. Co., 528 P.2d 31 (Cal. 1974); Vineland v. Fowler Waste Mfg. Co., 90 A. 1054 (N.J. 1914). *But see* Fla. Stat. § 367.121 (utility may not back-bill customers for any period greater than twelve months for any undercharging that is the result of the utility's mistake; the utility shall allow the customer to pay for the unbilled service over the same time period as the time period during which the under-billing occurred); Fla. Admin. Code Ann. r. 25-7.0851 (same).

7 *See* 7 Corbin on Contracts § 28.44 (2002).

8 *Id.* § 606. *But see* 7 Corbin on Contracts § 28.41 (2002).

9 Haverhill Gas Co. v. Findlen, 258 N.E.2d 294 (Mass. 1970); Rochester Gas & Elec. Corp. v. Greece Park Realty Corp., 600 N.Y.S.2d 985 (N.Y. App. Div. 1993); Consolidated Edison Co. v. Jet Asphalt, 132 A.D.2d 296 (N.Y. App. Div. 1987); West Penn Power Co. v. Nationwide Mut. Ins. Co., 228 A.2d 218 (Pa. 1967); Clarksville Dep't of Elec. v. Mathews Nissan, Inc., 1990 WL 180308, at *3 (Tenn. Ct. App. Nov. 21, 1990) (policy barred defenses of equitable estoppel and stated account); Chesapeake & Potomac Tel. Co. v. Bles, 243 S.E.2d 473 (Va. 1978); Housing Auth. of County of King v. Northeast Lake Wash. Sewer & Water Dist., 784 P.2d 1284, 1287 (Wash. Ct. App.) (though anti-discrimination statute did not apply to government-owned utilities, policy embodied by statute barred defenses of equitable estoppel and laches; customer failed to establish contract defenses of accord and satisfaction and account stated), *op. amended by* 789 P.2d 103 (Wash. Ct. App. 1990). *See also* Mars Express, Inc. v. David Masnik, Inc., 401 F.2d 891, 894 (2d Cir. 1968) (this rule is needed "to preserve the integrity of the filed rates" (citations omitted)); Shoemaker v. Mountain States Tel. & Tel. Co., 559 P.2d 721, 723–24 (Colo. Ct. App. 1976) (holding that to permit an undercharge would be to disrupt the uniform application of rates); Consolidated Edison Co. v. Jet Asphalt, 522 N.Y.S.2d 124 (N.Y. App. Div. 1987); Chesapeake & Potomac Tel. Co. v. Bles, 243 S.E.2d 473, 476 (Va. 1978) ("To permit an undercharge, whether intentionally or inadvertently made, is to grant a preferential rebate to a customer in violation of the statutory mandate.").

10 Memphis Light, Gas & Water Div., Div. of Memphis v. Auburndale Sch. Sys., 705 S.W.2d 652, 654 (Tenn. 1986).

11 *See, e.g.*, Haverhill Gas. Co. v. Findlen, 258 N.E.2d 294 (Mass. 1970). *See also* MCI v. Best Tel. Co., 898 F. Supp. 868 (S.D. Fla. 1994); Albany Oil Mill v. Sumter Elec. Membership Corp. 441 S.E.2d 524 (Ga. Ct. App. 1994).

12 *See, e.g.*, Haverhill Gas Co. v. Findlen, 258 N.E.2d 294 (Mass. 1970); Lee v. Consolidated Edison Co., 413 N.Y.S.2d 826 (N.Y. App. Div. 1978); Northern Wis. Produce Co. v. Chicago & N.W. Ry., 234 N.W. 726 (Wis. 1931).

13 Shoemaker v. Mountain States Tel. & Tel. Co., 559 P.2d 721 (Colo. Ct. App. 1976).

14 *See, e.g.*, Ind. Code § 8-1-2-103; Mass. Gen. Laws ch. 164. *But see e.g.*, N.C. Gen. Stat. § 62-110 (stating that the commission determines whether a utility's rate structure must be uniform).

15 *See, e.g.*, State *ex rel.* Guste v. City Council of New Orleans, 309 So. 2d 290 (La. 1975).

16 *See generally* Richard A. Lord, Williston on Contracts § 6:45 (4th ed. 1991). *But see* Jacksonville Elec. Auth. v. Draper's Egg & Poultry Co., 531 So. 2d 373 (Fla. Dist. Ct. App. 1988) (negotiated settlement of disputed bill is not barred by non-

the right, but also the duty, to collect the undercharge in cases arising from a mistake on the part of the utility.[17] In these instances, the mandatory duties of the public utility to adhere to its tariffs, to avoid discrimination, and to prevent the grant of rebates or other preferences, outweigh the doctrines of mistake and estoppel.[18]

The policy against preferential rate treatment and discriminatory pricing is one of the primary reasons for the institution of public utility regulation.[19]

However, the Georgia Supreme Court overruled previous state precedent to hold that a consumer who had been mistakenly under-billed by his electric utility could assert not only an equitable estoppel defense to collection but also accord and satisfaction and statute of limitations defenses.[20] Though the court acknowledged that the majority of jurisdictions do not allow such defenses in undercharge cases, the court cited fairness and policy reasons supporting its decision:

> It is simply unjust to require an innocent consumer to bear the entire cost of a supplier's mistake when, as here, there is no time limit on back billings. Armed with absolute immunity for an indefinite time, the supplier has little incentive to establish reasonable procedures to guarantee that its meters are properly calibrated or that its bills are computed accurately.[21]

A Pennsylvania court has held that, notwithstanding the general rule that a utility may recover undercharges, a customer who had been under-billed due to the mistake of the utility's meter installer could assert counterclaims of negligence and detrimental reliance.[22]

On the merits, there are several places where an estoppel defense can fail, even aside from the unique problems with utility undercharges as discussed below. First, the action of the party asserting the defense must be causally connected to the statement of the person against whom estoppel is asserted. The statement, in the terms of *Thomason*, must have "induced" the action.[23] If the action would have occurred in any event, there can be no estoppel. Second, the person asserting estoppel must not only have relied on the statements but must have had a *right* to rely on them. If the true state of facts were actually known, or if they could have been discovered by any reasonable effort,[24] estoppel cannot be raised.[25] Finally, as a result of the reliance, there must

---

discrimination public policy), *aff'd in part, rev'd in part*, 557 So. 2d 1357 (Fla. 1990) (settlement is invalid if initial underlying claim—for example, to amount of usage—is found later to be invalid); Cincinnati Gas & Elec. v. Joseph Chevrolet Co., 791 N.E.2d 1016 (Ohio Ct. App. 2003).

17 Goddard v. Public Serv. Co. of Colo., 599 P.2d 278 (Colo. Ct. App. 1979); Shoemaker v. Mountain States Tel. & Tel. Co., 559 P.2d 721 (Colo. Ct. App. 1976); Jacksonville Elec. Auth. v. Draper's Egg & Poultry Co., 557 So. 2d 1357 (Fla. 1990); Corp. de Gestion Ste-Foy, Inc. v. Fla. Power & Light Co., 385 So. 2d 124 (Fla. Dist. Ct. App. 1980); Haverhill Gas Co. v. Findlen, 258 N.E.2d 294 (Mass. 1970); Sigal v. Detroit, 362 N.W.2d 886 (Mich. Ct. App. 1985); Laclede Gas Co. v. Solon Gershman, 539 S.W.2d 574 (Mo. Ct. App. 1976); Rochester Gas & Elec. Corp. v. Greece Park Realty Corp., 600 N.Y.S.2d 985, 986 (N.Y. App. Div. 1993); Memphis Light, Gas & Water Div. v. Auburndale Sch. Sys., Div. of Memphis, 705 S.W.2d 652 (Tenn. 1986); Chesapeake & Potomac Tel. Co. of Va. v. Bles, 243 S.E.2d 473 (Va. 1978).

18 The equitable policy of estoppel may not outweigh these statutory directives. Boone County Sand & Gravel Co. v. Owen County Rural Elec. Coop. Corp., 779 S.W.2d 224, 225 (Ky. Ct. App. 1989).

An example of this type of statute in Kentucky is Ky. Rev. Stat. Ann. § 278.160(2) (West): "No utility shall charge, demand, collect, or receive from any person a greater or less compensation for any service rendered or to be rendered than that prescribed in filed schedules." *See also* Order, May v. Portland Gen. Elec. Co., CCH Util. Law Rptr. § 26752 (Or. Pub. Util. Comm'n Aug. 14, 1992) (No. 92-1168) (no estoppel when twelve years of mistaken under-billing due to incorrect "multiplier"; recovery limited to three years per statute).

The application of these principles in the freight industry has often been discussed. *See, e.g.*, Annot. *Carriers Understatement of Charges Where Discrimination Is Forbidden*, 88 A.L.R.2d 1375 (1963).

The courts rely on freight cases in deciding public utility cases.

19 *See, e.g.*, State *ex rel.* NCUC v. Wilson, 114 S.E.2d 786 (N.C. 1960).

20 Brown v. Walton Elec. Membership Corp., 531 S.E.2d 712 (Ga. 2000).

21 *Id.* at 713. *See also* City of E. Point v. Upchurch Packing Co., 200 S.E. 210, 212 (Ga. Ct. App. 1938) (in suit by utility for undercharges, upholding verdict for customer on grounds that utility was equitably estopped from seeking undercharge because it had set the wrong multiplier on the meter).

22 West Penn Power Co. v. Piatt, 592 A.2d 1306, 1308–09 (Pa. Super. Ct. 1991).

The court reasoned that it was not bound by the precedent of West Penn Power Co. v. Nationwide Mut. Ins. Co., 228 A.2d 218 (Pa. Super. Ct. 1967), in which it upheld a utility's right to recover undercharges, because in that case the defendant had not asserted a meritorious defense. *Id.*

In the present case, the customer argued that he had relied on the utility's bills in passing the costs on to his tenants and was now left unable to recoup the undercharge, an argument that the court found sufficient to withstand the utility's motion for summary judgment. *See* Borough of Mifflinburg v. Hein, 705 A.2d 456 (Pa. Super. Ct. 1997) (discussing of both cases).

23 In one concurring opinion, the proposition was urged that the person against whom estoppel is urged must have intended the inducement to occur. I.X.L. Stores v. Success Markets, 97 P.2d 577, 581 (Utah 1939) (Wolfe concurring).

As a general rule, however, there must only be a reasonable expectation that the person urging estoppel would rely upon the statement. 31 C.J.S. *Estoppel and Waiver* § 78 (1996).

24 I.X.L. Stores v. Success Markets, 97 P.2d 577, 580 (Utah 1939).

25 Note that it has been held that, despite ignorance by a customer of the terms of a tariff provision limiting liability for a utility's error, a tariff provision binds that customer. *See, e.g.*, Hirshemoeller v. National Ice & Cold Storage Co., 294 P.2d 433, 437 (Cal. 1956) (particularly when efforts available to a reasonable and prudent person would have revealed such terms). *See* National Consumer Law Center, A California Advocate's Guide to Telephone Customer Service Issues § 3.2.3 (1991) (discuss-

have been an injurious change of position. If no injury occurs, or if the injury is "speculative,"[26] an estoppel defense will not be available.

However, the prohibition against discrimination in utility rates does not mean that no distinctions can be drawn between customers for the purposes of setting rates and terms of service. Courts have stated that a Commission may reasonably adopt needs-based rate discounts.[27] Low-income discounts are in effect in a number of states.[28] Needs-based arguments for discounted rates have been successful in lowering rates for large industrial customers, who threaten to leave the system if their rates are not reduced, and these rates have not typically been struck down for violation of statutory prohibitions against undue discrimination.[29]

Having said that, it remains true that, in the discussion of back billing for undercharges, courts have held that the policy against undue discrimination is so important to the scheme of regulation that otherwise effective defenses to collection will not prevail in the context of a public utility. Thus, courts have stated that utility negligence in meter reading or billing will not defeat an action for recovery of undercharges.[30] Similarly, it has been held that mistaken misquotation of the rates does not excuse liability for payment or provide grounds for a set-off.[31] Also unavailing in some cases has been the fact that the customer has relied on the lower bills, to his or her detriment.[32] The fact that the utility may have violated a statute requiring accurate meter reading does not per se excuse the customer from making the utility whole for utility service actually delivered.[33] Counterclaims or offsets against the utility, when found to be based on no more than the unavailing defenses against the back billing, have been dismissed.[34]

Public service commission cases generally follow the same logic, with similar holdings. Thus, a mistake in billing or meter reading is generally held not to bar recovery of the undercharge.[35] Public Utility Commissions (PUCs) provide by rule that the utility may re-bill if it has under-billed by mistake.[36]

4.1.3 Limits on Utility's Ability to Collect

Some commissions have promulgated rules that prohibit altogether the "back-billing" of customers when a meter registers lower usage.[37] More frequently, rules prohibit utili-

ing tariff limitations of liability, and the applicability of U.C.C. § 2-302, making exclusions or limitations of liability unconscionable in consumer transactions). *Contra* L.A. Cellular Tel. Co. v. Superior Ct. of L.A. County, 76 Cal. Rptr. 2d 894 (Cal. Ct. App. 1998) (tariff limiting liability enforced when cell phone company did not disclose that its phones did not work well in certain areas, and cell phone customer was seriously injured when she was unable to complete 911 call from high crime area). *But see* Pink Dot, Inc. v. Teleport Comm'cns Group, 107 Cal. Rptr. 2d 392 (Cal. Ct. App. 2001) (tariff cannot restrict liability for fraud and intentional misconduct); Muelder v. Western Greyhound Lines, 87 Cal. Rptr. 297, 310 (Cal. Ct. App. 1970) (tariff limiting liability not applicable when loss caused by utility's gross negligence, unless that person contracted for the service with the knowledge of the limitation and the opportunity to purchase higher liability).

26 *See also* Boone County Sand & Gravel Co. v. Owen County Rural Elec. Coop. Corp., 779 S.W.2d 224 (Ky. Ct. App. 1989); Memphis Light, Gas & Water Div., Div. of Memphis v. Auburndale Sch. Sys., 705 S.W.2d 652, 653 (Tenn. 1986).

27 American Hoechest Corp. v. Department of Pub. Util., 399 N.E.2d 1 (Mass. 1980); Lefkowitz v. Public Serv. Comm'n, 360 N.E.2d 918 (N.Y. 1976); County Comm'nrs Ass'n of Ohio v. Public Util. Comm'n, 407 N.E.2d 534 (Ohio 1980). *But see* Mountain States Legal Found. v. Public Util. Comm'n, 590 P.2d 495 (Colo. 1979); Citizens Action Coalition of Ind. v. Public Serv. Co. of Ind., 450 N.E.2d 98 (Ind. 1983); Mountain States Legal Found. v. New Mexico State Corp. Comm'n, 687 P.2d 92 (N.M. 1984).

28 *See* http://liheap.ncat.org.

Utilities in those states and others may also offer other forms of utility bill assistance, such as customer deposit or late charge waivers, arrearage forgiveness, or bill credit. *See, e.g.*, appx. E, *infra*.

29 *See* J. Stephen Henderson & Robert E. Burns, National Regulatory Research Inst., An Economic and Legal Analysis of Undue Price Discrimination, Columbus Ohio (1989).

30 Fry Trucking Co. v. Shenandoah Quarry, Inc., 628 F.2d 1360 (D.C. Cir. 1980); Illinois Cent. R.R. v. Sankey Bros., 384 N.E.2d 543 (Ill. 1976); Norman v. Public Util. Comm'n of Ohio, 406 N.E.2d 492 (Ohio 1980); Wisconsin Power & Light Co. v. Berlin Tanning & Mfg. Co., 83 N.W.2d 147 (Wis. 1957). *But see* Illinois Power Co. v. Champaign Asphalt Co., 310 N.E.2d 463 (Ill. 1974) (allowing recovery for undercharges from defective transformer and meter when company not at fault in allowing defective meter to remain in service); Laclede Gas Co. v. Solon Gershman Inc., 539 S.W.2d 574 (Mo. Ct. App. 1976); West Penn Power Co. v. Nationwide Mut. Ins. Co., 228 A.2d 218 (Pa. Super. Ct. 1967) (allowing recovery absent evidence of unfairness or mistake).

31 Denver & Rio Grande W. Ry. Co. v. Marty, 353 P.2d 1095 (Colo. 1960); Houston & Tex. Cent. Ry. Co. v. Johnson, 41 S.W.2d 14 (Tex. Civ. App. 1931). *But see* Atchison, Topeka & Santa Fe Ry. Co v. Texas I.G. & O. Co., 811 S.W.2d 685 (Tex. App. 1991).

32 Louisville & Nashville R.R. Co. v. Maxwell, 237 U.S. 94 (1915); Illinois Cent. Gulf R.R. Co. v. Golden Triangle Wholesale Gas Co., 586 F.2d 588 (5th Cir. 1978); I.X.L. Stores Co. v. Success Mkts., 97 P.2d 577 (Utah 1939); Wisconsin Power & Light Co. v. Berlin Tanning & Mfg. Co., 83 N.W.2d 147 (Wis. 1957).

33 Haverhill Gas Co. v. Findlen, 258 N.E.2d 294 (Mass. 1970).

34 *See, e.g.*, MCI v. Best Tel. Co., 898 F. Supp. 868 (S.D. Fla. 1994) (filed rate doctrine barred all equitable and contractual defenses against suit to recover for under-billing for provision of telecommunications services by long-distance company to reseller); Denver & Rio Grande W. Ry. Co. v. Marty, 353 P.2d 1095 (Colo. 1960).

35 *See, e.g.*, Fobert v. Boston Gas Co., D.P.U. No. 20100 (Mass. Dep't Pub. Util. Nov. 29, 1979); Bedford Mktg. Group, Ltd. v. Northwestern Bell Tel. Co., No. F-C-1163 (Neb. Pub. Serv. Comm'n Apr. 12, 1983).

36 *See, e.g.*, Fla. Admin. Code Ann. r. 25-30.340; Mich. Admin. Code r. 460.2125; 16 Tex. Admin. Code § 25.28.

37 *See, e.g.*, Alaska Admin. Code tit. 3, § 52.465; *In re* Regulatory Policy Standards to Fulfill Requirements of the Public Utility

ties from back-billing customers any undercharges that are older than a specified date.[38] And commissions may require that customers be offered a reasonable deferred payment opportunity.[39]

A commission rule may contain the provision that the utility may not disconnect for failure to pay a backbill dating to more than a set time period before the discovery of the error unless the undercharge resulted from meter tampering, bypassing, or diversion by the customer.[40]

While defenses to a back-billing may be rejected in strongly worded court opinions concerning non-discrimination,[41] in practice commissions may take into account equitable considerations (such as comparative fault[42] and detrimental reliance[43]), as well as consideration of utility violation of agency regulations.[44] This is so even in jurisdictions where the judicial precedent appears unbending.[45] Furthermore, while the right to bill for the charges may be clear, the utility's right to terminate service for nonpayment of these arrearages may be questionable.[46]

Both courts and commissions have ruled that, while a utility company may not be required (or even allowed) to waive liability for a bill, companies (of their own initiative or at the direction of the commission) may extend the payment terms for mistaken undercharges or waive late charges.[47]

Regulatory Policies Act of 1978, 7 A.P.U.C. 454 (Alaska 1986) (except in the case of meter tampering, electric utilities cannot back-bill a customer when an inaccurate meter has under-registered usage, as meters are owned and controlled by utility, not customer).

38 Florida, for example, has included this rule in its regulatory scheme: Fla. Admin. Code Ann. r. 25-7.0851 (gas utility may not back-bill customers for any period greater than twelve months for any undercharge in billing that is the result of the utility's mistake); Fla. Admin. Code Ann. r. 25-30.350 (same for water and sewer utilities); Fla. Admin. Code Ann. r. 25-4.110(10) (same for telephone companies); Fla. Admin. Code Ann. r. 25-6.106 (same for electric public utilities); Fla. Admin. Code Ann. r. 25-30.340(3)(a) (not more than twelve months back from the date the customer was notified of a slow meter). *See also In re* United Cities Gas Co., 174 Pub. Util. Rep. 4th 169, 1996 WL 773364 (Ga. Pub. Serv. Comm'n Nov. 25, 1996) (six-month limit on billing for undercharges); Mich. Admin. Code r. 460.2125, adopted in *In re* Consumer Standards & Billing Practices for Electrical & Gas Residential Service, No. U-9754 (Mich. Pub. Serv. Comm'n 1992) (if utility undercharges customer and case does not involve meter tampering or fraud, utility may back-bill for amount of undercharge during twelve-month period immediately preceding discovery of error and shall offer customer reasonable payment arrangements for the amount of the back-bill); Mich. P.S.C. Consumer Standards, Rule 460.2125(2)(b) (no more than twelve months immediately preceding the discovery of the billing error, unless the error was the result of meter tampering or fraud); 16 Tex. Admin. Code § 25.28 (utility may back-bill for amount customer was underbilled, but not to exceed six months generally); 16 Tex. Admin. Code § 7.45(4)(E)(v) (utility service may not be disconnected for failure to pay charges arising from an under-billing occurring due to any misapplication of rates more than six months prior to the current billing).

39 *See, e.g.*, Fla. Admin. Code Ann. r. 25-30.340(3)(a) (customer "may extend the payments of the back-bill over the same amount of time for which the utility issued the backbill"); Mich. Admin. Code r. 460.2125(2) (b) (in cases that do not involve meter tampering or fraud, the utility shall offer the customer "reasonable payment arrangements for the amount of the backbill, taking into account the period of the undercharge"). *See also* Villarino v. Boston Gas Co., D.P.U. No. 87-AD-6 (Mass. Dep't Pub. Util. Oct. 6, 1987) (overcharge for period of seven months; back bill payable over twelve months).

40 *See, e.g.*, Fla. Admin. Code r. 25-30.350 (no back-billing of water and sewer customers for more than twelve months for undercharge resulting from utility's mistake; customers entitled to pay back other undercharges over same period of time as undercharge accrued or other mutually agreeable time period; utility barred from recovering balances from remaining ratepayers); 16 Tex. Admin. Code § 25.28.

41 *See* § 4.1.2, *supra*.

42 *See, e.g.*, MCI v. Best Tel. Co., 898 F. Supp. 868 (S.D. Fla. 1994) (filed rate doctrine barred all equitable and contractual defenses against suit to recover for under-billing for provision of telecommunications services by long-distance company to reseller); Van Buskirk v. Boston Gas Co., D.P.U. No. 3 (Mass. Dep't Pub. Util. 1982) (not allowing back-billing when company at fault for not discovering cross-metering when it installed meters); Kean Inv. Co. v. Michigan Consol. Gas Co., 111 Pub. Util. Rep. 4th 479, 1990 WL 488713 (Mich. Pub. Serv. Comm'n Apr. 12, 1990) (allowing recovery when utility used diligent care in making regular inspections and meter readings); Fergus v. Duke Power Co., No. E-7, Sub 379, (N.C. Pub. Serv. Comm'n Apr. 15, 1982) (no back-billing when customer had made frequent and diligent efforts to bring mistake to company's attention); *In re* New England Tel. & Tel. Co., 111 Pub. Util. Rep. 4th 114, 1990 WL 488671 (Vt. Feb. 9, 1990) (allowing back-billing, but responsibility of customer tied to fact that customer could easily have noticed total lack of billing for long-distance calls).

43 *See, e.g.*, MCI v. Best Tel. Co., 898 F. Supp. 868 (S.D. Fla. 1994) (filed rate doctrine barred all equitable and contractual defenses against suit to recover for under-billing for provision of telecommunications services by long-distance company to reseller); Foley v. Commonwealth Elec. Co., D.P.I. 1523 (Mass. Dep't Pub. Util. Mar. 26, 1985) (company's negligent failure to discover cross-metering in timely manner effectively denied complainant ability to conserve and maintain desired level of use). *Cf. In re* New England Tel. & Tel. Co., 111 Pub. Util. Rep. 4th 114, 1990 WL 488671 (Vt. Feb. 9, 1990) (allowing back-billing, but responsibility of customer tied to fact that customer could easily have noticed total lack of billing for long-distance calls).

44 Foley v. Commonwealth Elec. Co., D.P.I. 1523 (Mass. Dep't Pub. Util. Mar. 26, 1985); Van Buskirk v. Boston Gas Co., D.P.U. No. 3 (Mass. Dep't Pub. Util. 1984).

45 *Cf.* Haverhill Gas Co. v. Findlen, 258 N.E.2d 294 (Mass. 1970); Hutchins v. Boston Edison Co., No. 1392 (Mass. Dep't Pub. Util. 1983).

46 *See* § 6.6, *infra*; Roger D. Colton, *Protecting Against the Harms of the Mistaken Utility Undercharge*, 39 J. of Urb. Affairs, 99 (1991). *See also* 16 Tex. Admin. Code § 7.45 (no disconnection for nonpayment of amount backfilled from period more than six months before customer notification of error, unless undercharge was result of meter tampering, bypass, or diversion on the part of the customer).

47 Boston Edison Co. v. City of Boston, 459 N.E.2d 1231 (Mass. 1984); Howard v. Manchester Gas Co., 68 N.H. P.U.C. 21, D.C.

Commissions may be more inclined to order such relief when the utility was at fault in not identifying the undercharge earlier. Complaint resolution procedures at public service commissions are often separated in practice from the formal establishment of regulatory policy on prices and commission jurisdiction. They may rely heavily on mediation, and staff may prefer jawboning to the formal procedures of adjudication and rate-setting.

4.2 Non-Exclusive Use of Meter

4.2.1 Described

Non-exclusive use refers to a situation in which all or part of a neighbor's unit or the common areas of a building have been connected to the client's meter. The primary issue here is whether the client is responsible for all the metered use and what remedies the client may seek against which parties for any costs the client may have incurred as a result of the draw on the client's meter.

The issues are similar to those that arise when a neighbor or the landlord deliberately taps into the client's line. However, these latter situations are the exception. More frequently, the non-exclusive use arises because the building is not wired for sufficient meters to segregate the use to the meter of each responsible party. It also arises when a landlord requires a tenant to agree to carry the use of some of the common areas or some other unit, as a condition of entering into the tenancy. This requirement typically is imposed merely by the act of renting a unit with common area use connected to the tenant's meter and expecting the tenant to pay the metered charges.

The most common issue to arise is the liability of the customer for the use of the neighbor or landlord. If non-exclusive use is discovered, must the utility pursue payment from the third party who benefited from the use or must the client pay the utility, at the risk of disconnection, and be left to whatever remedies he or she can obtain against the beneficiary of the non-exclusivity of the wiring?

4.2.2 Customer Liability for Others' Use

In keeping with the reasoning discussed in the reverse metering section, one would expect the general rule to be that the client must pay the utility for all metered use and is subject to disconnection for failure to pay, regardless of his or her ability to obtain compensation from the beneficiary. This has been the outcome in some cases.[48] However, in early cases dealing with water service,[49] some courts have held that one tenant cannot be denied service because another tenant refuses to pay for service delivered through a common meter.[50]

82-347, Order No. 16,160 (N.H. Pub. Util. Comm'n Jan. 24, 1983); Weiner v. Bell Tel. Co., 57 Pa. P.U.C. 519 (Pa. Pub. Util. Comm'n July 11, 1983) (C-833446). *See also* Fla. Admin. Code Ann. r. 25-30.340(3)(a) (the customer "may extend the payments of the backbill over the same amount of time for which the utility issued the back-bill"); Mich. Admin. Code r. 460.2125(2) (b) (in cases that do not involve meter tampering or fraud, the utility shall offer the customer "reasonable payment arrangements for the amount of the backbill, taking into account the period of the undercharge"); Villarino v. Boston Gas Co., D.P.U. 87-AD-6 (Mass. Dep't Pub. Util. Oct. 6, 1987) (overcharge for period of seven months; back bill payable over twelve months); Luco v. Bay State Gas Co., D.P.U. 1487 (Mass. Dep't Pub. Util. Aug. 4, 1983) (twenty-nine-month payment plan and deduction from charges owed of amount of fuel assistance claimant relinquished when company took five months to re-bill for twenty-four months of reverse-metering, and claimant lost opportunity to apply for fuel assistance); 16 Tex. Admin. Code § 25.28 ("(c) *Overbilling*. If charges are found to be higher than authorized in the utility's tariffs, then the customer's bill *shall* be corrected. . . .(d) *Underbilling*. If charges are found to be lower than authorized by the utility's tariffs, or if the electric utility failed to bill the customer for service, then the customer's bill *may* be corrected. (1) The electric utility may backbill the customer for the amount that was underbilled. The backbilling bill *shall not* collect charges that extend more than six months from the date the error was discovered unless the underbilling is a result of theft of service by the customer. (2) The electric utility may disconnect service if the customer fails to pay underbilled charges. (3) If the underbilling is $50 or more, the electric utility *shall* offer the customer a deferred payment plan option for the same length of time as that of the underbilling. A deferred payment plan need not be offered to a customer whose underpayment is due to theft of service. (4) The utility *shall not* charge interest on underbilled amounts unless such amounts are found to be the result of theft of service (meter tampering, bypass, or diversion) by the customer, as defined in § 25.126 of this title. Interest on underbilled amounts shall be compounded monthly at the annual rate and shall accrue from the day the customer is found to have first stolen (tampered, bypassed or diverted) the service." (emphasis added)).

48 *See, e.g.*, Kean Inv. Co. v. Michigan Consol. Gas Co., 111 Pub. Util. Rep. 4th 479, 1990 WL 488713 (Mich. Pub. Serv. Comm'n Apr. 12, 1990).

In one case, this principle was held to be so obvious that a tenant was denied a pre-termination hearing when the only grounds for objection was that the water pipe and meter were used in common by more than one apartment. Sims v. Alabama Water Co., 87 So. 688 (Ala. 1921).

However, it is unlikely that a hearing would be denied today on such grounds, given the importance modern interpretations of procedural fairness give to the opportunity to be heard.

49 There are situations in which it is prohibitively expensive or not structurally possible to install separate water meters for each apartment in multifamily buildings. Consider that, with most plumbing installations, in order to meter all water entering an apartment, two or four meters would be required (for example, one cold-water intake in kitchen, one hot-water intake in kitchen, one cold-water intake in bathroom, one hot-water intake in bathroom). At about $170 per meter, the cost quickly becomes prohibitive for most landlords. Salisbury Water Company Filing, Exhibit 2, D.P.U. 87-215 (Mass. Dep't Pub. Util. Jan. 1, 1989).

50 Kelsey v. Board of Fire & Water Comm'n, 71 N.W. 589 (Mich. 1897); Gaines v. Charleston Light & Water Co., 88 S.E. 378

In at least one jurisdiction, administrative action has shifted the risk away from the innocent victim of non-exclusive wiring or metering. In Illinois, under the Illinois Commerce Commission[51] rules and regulations governing the termination of service for nonpayment, the utility was not permitted to bill the victim of an illegal tap but was authorized to pursue the third party that benefited from the tap, whether or not that party was a customer.[52]

A Maryland appellate court held that landlords may be held financially responsible for damages in the amount of the unpaid utility bills of tenants sharing a common meter when one tenant fails to pay for his or her share.[53] Moreover, according to that recent Maryland decision, a landlord breaches the covenant of quiet enjoyment by burdening one tenant with liability for the other tenants' usage when the tenant had no prior knowledge of that burden and did not consent to it.[54] Thus, if the tenant is obligated to the utility in a non-exclusive use case, the tenant may have remedies against the landlord who created or permitted the non-exclusivity.

Michigan Public Service Commission regulations prohibit involuntary disconnection for nonpayment of a bill for an occupied dwelling when the customer, "such as a landlord, has not paid for service used by another person, such as a tenant,"[55] except when, "it is not feasible to provide service to the occupant as a customer without major revision of existing distribution facilities."[56]

In Massachusetts, the state Department of Public Health has issued Sanitary Code regulations that require a landlord to provide and pay for utility service to tenants in all cases of non-exclusive use.[57] This code provision has been interpreted by the Department of Public Utilities to mean that a utility must take service out of the tenant's name, refund all past charges, and bill the landlord, when a violation of the prohibition against non-exclusive use has been certified by an authorized health officer.[58] The Department's interpretation has been upheld on appeal.[59] The rule does not depend on a finding that the landlord intentionally tapped into the tenant's line. Rather, it is a sanction to enforce the requirement of landlord responsibility for utility service absent prescribed protections for tenants.

4.3 Customer's Alleged Meter Tampering

4.3.1 Meter Tampering and Meter Bypass Described

Meter tampering involves making changes to the meter in an effort to cause it to record less use than actually takes place. Meter bypass typically involves attaching to the utility service on the company side of the meter and taking some or all of one's service through this bypass connection, thus causing the meter to register less than the actual use.[60] Less frequently, a neighbor or the landlord intentionally diverts service on the customer side of the meter.

There are four main issues that arise in meter tampering cases. First, may a utility terminate service without advance notice, or without the notice otherwise required by utility or regulatory agency rules, on the grounds that: (a) the customer has allegedly stolen the power and no notice is required to prevent further theft; (b) the customer has violated a utility regulation against meter tampering and that no notice is required in such a case; or (c) an emergency safety risk is presented by a tap into the pipe or line, and no notice is required to deactivate the line in such a case? Second, may a utility disconnect a customer for unauthorized use, including meter tampering or line tapping, without regard to the customer's willingness to pay for any claimed unauthorized use? These two issues are examined in Chapter 6, *infra*. There is also the issue of consumer redress if the allegations of meter tampering are false. In a recent Florida case, a customer lost electric service to his home and business due to allegations of meter tampering based on hearsay evidence and no utility commission investigation. The loss in electric service to the customer's business and home caused crop loss, and the customer subsequently lost his home in foreclosure. The customer sued the utility for gross negligence. A state appellate court in Florida found that the utility commission's authority on this matter does

---

(S.C. 1916). *See also* Jopling v. Bluefield Waterworks Improv. Co., 74 S.E. 943 (W. Va. 1912).

51 In Illinois, the public utilities regulatory functions are carried out by the Commerce Commission.

52 Jones v. Peoples Gas Light & Coke Co., 97 Pub. Util. Rep. 4th 178, 1988 WL 391182 (Ill. Sept. 14, 1988).

53 Legg v. Castruccio, 642 A.2d 906 (Md. Ct. Spec. App. 1994).

54 *Id.*

55 Mich. Admin. Code r. 460.2162(d).

56 *Id.*

57 105 Mass. Code Regs. § 410.354(A) (LexisNexis).

58 The leading case is MacDonald v. Prybuszauckas, D.P.U. 84-86-64 (July 1, 1985).

59 Young v. Patukonis, 506 N.E.2d 1164 (Mass. App. Ct. 1987). *See also* Lezburg v. Rogers, No. 88-P-1029 (Mass. App. Ct. June 12, 1989) (slip opinion) (landlord may not recover these back-billed charges from tenant in civil action). *But see* Poncz v. Loftin, 607 N.E.2d 765 (Mass. App. Ct. 1993) (holding that, in a "Section 93A" (UDAP) action against the landlord for damages for violation of a related section of the State Sanitary Code limiting landlord's rights to insist that utility service be in the tenant's name, only nominal damages would be allowed and no claim could be made for recovery of amounts paid by the tenant to the heating service vendor, because the tenant benefited from the use of the utility service during the time the meter was in the tenant's name in violation of the Code).

60 A related case occurs when a customer who has been disconnected proceeds to reconnect himself without authorization or moves into a premise without service and establishes the connection without authorization.

not preclude a trial court's adjudication of the gross negligence claim for compensatory damages.[61]

Third, to what extent is a tenant (or other customer) liable for unmetered use serving his or her apartment, when the tenant claims not to have known of the alleged meter bypass? Can a utility back-bill a tenant for an estimate of the unmetered use, and can a tenant be disconnected for failure to pay the back bill? Can a tenant be held liable for the costs to the utility of discovering and remedying the meter tap?

The fourth issue concerns the burden of proof a utility must carry to demonstrate the liability of the customer for a meter tampering and to justify termination for alleged tampering. Within this larger topic are the questions of the available presumptions, the standard of evidence in cases of alleged fraud, and the nature of proof that must be shown to establish the amount of unmetered use.

4.3.2 Evidence in Cases of Alleged Fraud

4.3.2.1 Presumption of Responsibility

As a general rule, a utility may obtain the benefits of a presumption that the customer whose service is metered by the tampered meter is responsible for the tampering when seeking to prove the customer's liability in civil suits to recover for unauthorized use or in criminal prosecutions for theft or meter tampering. If, in other words, a person possesses the meter and receives the benefits of utility service obtained through a tampered meter, that person is presumed to be the person who did the tampering.[62] Moreover, the person possessing the tampered meter may be presumed to have engaged in the tampering with the intent to defraud the utility.[63]

The rule, however, is not universal. Some commission regulations, without exceptions for meter tampering cases, place the burden of proof on the utility in all bill disputes.[64] The Florida Supreme Court, in *MacMillan v. State*,[65] declared unconstitutional a meter tampering statute based on a prima facie presumption of intent.[66] According to the Florida court, reliance on the statutory presumption violated due process protections, since the presumption did not meet the "more likely than not" test or the "rational connection" test. Pursuant to these tests, the presumption is irrational unless there is a "substantial assurance" that the presumed fact is "more likely than not" to flow from the proved fact.[67] According to the *MacMillan* court:

> We find that it cannot be said with substantial assurance that the presumed fact the defendant is guilty of violation of [the state meter tampering statute] is more likely than not to flow from the proved fact of possession of the premises or receipt of benefits. Someone in actual possession of property or receiving direct benefits would, more likely than not, not be the guilty person. Such an inference is irrational and arbitrary. Common experience tells us that the device or apparatus tampered with or altered is generally on the outside of a building and accessible to anyone; that the direct benefits from the use of electricity, gas, water, heat, oil, sewer service, telephone service . . . are commonly derived by any occupant of the premises, including family members, business partners, associates, employees and others; and that the billing which would constitute notice of possible alteration is done no more frequently than monthly. Furthermore, there are many ways

61 Ramos v. Florida Power & Light Co., 21 So. 3d 91 (Fla. Dist. Ct. App. 2009).

62 S&D Thrift Stores v. Con Edison, 435 N.Y.S.2d 776 (N.Y. App. Div. 1987), *modified by* 55 N.Y.2d 1013 (1982) (presumption when tampering that tampering done by person receiving service). *See generally* Friedman, *Prosecution for Utility Meter Tampering: Constitutional Limitations on Statutory Presumptions*, 18 Urban L. Annual 297 (1980).

63 Typical language is set forth in Commonwealth of Pa. v. Gallagher, 582 A.2d 1349, 1350 (Pa. Super. Ct. 1990):

> (d) *Inferences*—(1) Any person having possession of or access to the location of a public utility or service measuring device which has been avoided or tampered with so as to inhibit or prevent the accurate measurement of utility service and who enjoys the use of or receives the benefit from the public utility service intended to be metered or measured by the public utility meter or measuring device so avoided or tampered with may be reasonably inferred to have acted to avoid or tamper with the public utility meter or measuring device with the intent to obtain the public utility service without making full compensation therefor.

Another typical statute is set forth in State v. Dixon, 553 A.2d 1, 7 (N.J. 1989) (quoting N.J. Stat. Ann. 2C:20-8(c) (West)) ("The existence of any of the conditions with reference to meters . . . described in this section, is presumptive evidence that the person to whom . . . electricity . . . is being furnished by or through such meters . . . has, with the intent to defraud, created or caused to be created with reference to such meters . . . the conditions so existing."). *See also* Commonwealth v. Deer, 615 A.2d 386 (Pa. 1992) (inference permissible, must be supported by other evidence; here evidence of extensive modifications to defendant's business premises to accommodate illegal tap was sufficient to support conviction).

64 Mich. Admin. Code r. 460.2169(3), 460.2184(3). *Cf.* 4 Colo. Code Regs. § 723-1, Rule 1500 (LexisNexis) (complainant has initial burden of proof in formal proceeding, and burden may be otherwise determined by commission in proceedings other than applications, formal complaints, show cause proceedings, and investigation and suspension proceedings); 10-800-001 Del. Code Regs. § 24(c) (LexisNexis) ("burden of proof shall be on the moving party, except where placed on another party by law or Commission Order"); 26-000-001 Miss. Code R. § 15 (LexisNexis) ("burden of proof shall be carried by the parties in like manner as is required in the courts of record in the state").

65 358 So. 2d 547 (Fla. 1978).

66 *Id.* at 549–50.

67 *Id.* at 549 (quoting Leary v. United States, 395 U.S. 6 (1969)).

> to make an alteration which are so simple in nature that a prankster, a vandal or an angry neighbor could utilize them to cause the one in possession of the premises to receive benefits therefrom without his knowledge and, thereby, subject him to the presumption.[68]

In short, the Florida court simply found it too easy to posit situations in which the customer would be wrongfully accused to uphold the presumption. An amended statute, which created only a permissive inference and required some proof of exclusive control was found acceptable.[69]

In contrast, state courts in both New York[70] and New Jersey[71] have upheld the constitutionality of the use of meter tampering presumptions in criminal cases. Unlike the *MacMillan* court, both of these courts found that the rational basis test for the presumption was met. The most important factor in the *MacMillan* decision was the non-exclusive possession of the meter.[72] Accordingly, while the defendant "possessed" the tampered meter, the meter was in an easily accessible location. While possession of stolen property may be sufficient to raise a presumption of the knowledge that the property was stolen, possession must be *exclusive*.[73] "When others have an equal right and facility of access to property, nonexclusive possession results."[74] So, too, did the court in *Gallagher* find that the accused customer did not necessarily have access to the meter during the time of the tampering.[75]

The flip-side of this issue of possession was presented in *Hamdallah v. Virgin Islands Water and Power Authority* involving an alleged meter tampering.[76] In that case, the federal district court held the meter tampering presumption to be based on a "highly skeptical proposition."[77] The court found that the accused customer had *no* access to the meter.

> In order to monitor the amount of electricity for billing purposes, [the local utility] installs a sealed meter for each of its customers. Hamdallah's meter was in an area where meters were grouped for all tenants of the Plaza. Further, this area was a locked room, the keys to which were in the possession of the landlord and certain representatives of [the utility].[78]

The court in *Louisiana Power Company v. Bourgeois* noted that "the house was occupied by Bourgeois and has been occupied by him ever since—down through the discovery of the devices on April 1, 1975. As noted above, the meter is in a place not freely accessible to any casual passerby and, indeed, the devices are such that they must have been intentionally placed there."[79]

In sum, a utility may engage in the presumption that the possession of a meter with a tampering device was installed by the person in possession. However, the presumption is rebuttable[80] and, in any event, there must be *exclusive* possession for the presumption to arise. In situations in which others have an equal right and facility of access to the property, use of the presumption is inappropriate. As discussed above, however, to demonstrate a right to back-bill a customer for unmetered use in a bypass or tampering situation, it may not be necessary for the utility to show who installed the bypass or tampered with the meter but only to show that the customer benefited from the unmetered utility service in question.[81]

4.3.2.2 Standard of Evidence

The standard of evidence required in any case involving the imposition of sanctions of some type would likely be predicated on the assertion that the tampering at issue involves "fraud" on the part of the customer. Precisely what standard would be required of the utility, therefore, should be governed by the standard required in civil proceedings involving allegations of fraud. This standard will generally entail the use of a "preponderance of the evidence" standard or a "clear and convincing" standard.[82]

---

68 *Id.* at 549–50.

69 Marcolini v. State, 673 So. 2d 3 (Fla. 1996). *Cf.* Ramos v. Florida Power & Light Co., 21 So. 3d 91 (Fla. Dist. Ct. App. 2009) (remanding case alleging negligent disconnection of electricity based on alleged meter tampering when utility commission based decision on hearsay and conducted no evidentiary hearing).

70 People v. McLaughlin, 402 N.Y.S.2d 137 (1978).

71 State v. Curtis, 372 A.2d 612 (N.J. Super. Ct. App. Div. 1977).

72 MacMillan v. State, 358 So. 2d 547, 550 (Fla. 1978).

73 *See, e.g.*, Lewis v. State, 181 So. 2d 357, 358 (Fla. Dist. Ct. App. 1965) ("exclusive possession of stolen property by a defendant soon after a theft is sufficient, when standing alone, to place upon the accused the burden of an explanation, and if he fails to do so, to warrant the jury in convicting him of larceny").

74 Friedman, *Prosecution for Utility Meter Tampering: Constitutional Limitations on Statutory Presumptions*, 18 Urban L. Annual 807 (1980).

75 582 A.2d at 1351–52.

76 1988 WL 59973 (D. V.I. June 9, 1988).

77 *Id.*

78 *Id.*

79 355 So. 2d 597, 599 (La. Ct. App. 1978).

80 Of course, the company must first prove that the meter was defective or bypassed; occasionally a utility will simply fail to present any evidence of tampering. Vaughn v. Boston Gas Co., D.P.U. 1695 (Mass. Dep't of Pub. Utils. Aug. 19, 1985).

The company's evidence that tampering occurred may be rebutted. *See, e.g.*, Mass. Elec. Co. v. LaCroix, D.P.U. 1583 (Mass. Dep't of Pub. Utils. July 23, 1984).

If a customer can rebut the presumption that the meter defects were caused by him or her, the situation becomes in effect a case of erroneous undercharge. Equitable defenses may be available, especially at the informal commission staff level. *See supra* text accompanying notes 31–37.

81 *See* JMA v. State of Fla., 732 So. 2d 27 (Fla. Dist. Ct. App. 1999) (larceny of electrical power overturned for lack of evidence).

82 The Michigan Public Service Commission specifies a standard of "preponderance of evidence" and makes no distinction between fraud allegations and other issues. Mich. Admin. Code

4.3.3 Customer's Liability for the Back Balance

Courts generally hold that a utility may reasonably estimate the unmetered use and bill the customer whose meter was tampered or bypassed for that unmetered use, without alleging or proving that the customer tampered with or bypassed the meter.[83] Some courts rely on a contract theory, reasoning that the customer signed on to pay for all services used, whether metered or not.[84] Other courts point to the fact that the customer benefited from the service and thus find liability on a form of implied contract theory.[85]

Also, decisions and informal guidelines used by public service commission staffs in resolving customer complaints regarding billing and termination for unauthorized use can provide more leeway than court precedent for equitable principles to support less harsh outcomes. While the general rule is also that a utility may back-bill for unmetered use if it proves that the meter was bypassed or altered to register low,[86] mitigating factors may be advanced by the customer. For example, if the utility was in a position to discover the tampering or bypass, or did discover it but took no action to correct it or institute procedures to recover for the unauthorized use, some reduction of the back balance may be required.[87]

It is not uncommon for a utility's tariffs to provide for additional charges to customers who have been determined to have tampered with or bypassed their meters, and these have generally been upheld.[88] A customer charge of $50 to defray such costs was permitted in *In re Dallas Power & Light*.[89]

4.3.4 Calculating the Amount Due for the Unmetered Use

Establishing that the utility has the right to be paid does not complete the utility's case, however, nor does it automatically result in the utility being able to impose a back bill on the customer. The utility must *also* prove the amount of the back bill which is appropriate.

Some courts hold that a "billing analysis" can provide the basis for a determination of the actual consumption used during a period in which full consumption was not recorded by a tampered meter. In *Delaney*, for example, the court simply accepted data comparing the "average monthly readings exclusive of the suspect period" to "the average monthly readings during the suspect period."[90]

Other courts have required the utilities to present further evidence. In *Bourgeois*, for example, the court rejected an attempt to base a recovery on the amount of electricity used in the year previous to the installation of the tampering device in the meter.[91] The utility had argued that the tampering device "diverted all of the current used by an appliance hooked upon that line." The only appliance "drawing current on the wire which did not register in the meter was the air conditioner," the court found. The court then rejected

r. 460.2169(3). *See also* Roger D. Colton, *Heightening the Burden of Proof in Utility Shutoff Cases Involving Allegations of Fraud*, 33 How. L.J. 137 (1990).

83 *See, e.g.*, Sowell v. Douglas County Elec. Membership Corp., 258 S.E.2d 149 (Ga. Ct. App. 1979); Royal Elm Nursing & Convalescent Ctr. v. Northern Ill. Gas Co., 526 N.E.2d 376 (Ill. App. Ct. 1988); New Orleans Pub. Serv., Inc. v. Delaney, 379 So. 2d 842 (La. Ct. App. 1980); Louisiana Power Co. v. Bourgeois, 355 So. 2d 597 (La. Ct. App. 1978). *But see* Everett v. Baltimore Gas & Elec. Co., 513 A.2d 882 (Md. 1986) (utility must prove alleged tampering by clear and convincing evidence to justify termination for nonpayment of back bill), *overruled by* Coleman v. Anne Arundel Co. Police Dep't, 797 A.2d 770 (Md. 2002) (preponderance of evidence standard applies); Kean Inv. Co. v. Michigan Consol. Gas Co., 111 Pub. Util. Rep. 4th 479, 1990 WL 488713 (Mich. Pub. Serv. Comm'n Apr. 12, 1990) (utility had alleged and proven improper bypass).

84 *See, e.g.*, Sowell v. Douglas County Elec. Membership Corp., 258 S.E.2d 149 (Ga. Ct. App. 1979); La. Power Co. v. Bourgeois, 355 So. 2d 597 (La. Ct App 1978).

85 *See, e.g.*, Royal Elm Nursing & Convalescent Ctr. v. Northern Ill. Gas Co., 526 N.E.2d 376 (Ill. App Ct. 1988).

86 *See, e.g.*, 16 Tex. Admin. Code § 25.28(d); Kean Inv. Co. v. Michigan Consol. Gas Co., 111 Pub. Util. Rep. 4th 479, 1990 WL 488713 (Mich. Pub. Serv. Comm'n Apr. 12, 1990).

87 Camiola v. Massachusetts Elec. Co., D.P.U. 1419 (Mass. Dep't Pub. Util. Apr. 27, 1984) (use history and obvious signs of tampering should have alerted company to unmetered use within first three years of eight years of unmetered use; bill partially abated).

88 Louisville Gas & Elec. v. Dulworth, 130 S.W.2d 753 (Ky. 1939) (cost of anti-tampering device); Campbell v. Massachusetts Elec. Co., D.P.U. 525 (Mass. Dep't Pub. Util. Aug. 23, 1982) (repair of meter); Cinelli v. Massachusetts Elec. Co., D.P.U. 20210 (Mass. Dep't Pub. Util. Aug. 1980) (cost of investigation and meter replacement); *In re* Dallas Power & Light, 6 Tex. Pub. Util. Comm'n Bull. 720, No. 3460 (Tex. Feb. 26, 1981) ($50 customer charge).

89 Tex. Pub. Util. Comm'n Bull. 720, No. 3460 (Tex. Pub. Util. Comm'n Feb. 26, 1981). *See also* 30 Tex. Admin. Code § 291.87(o) ("(o) *Equipment damage charges.* A utility may charge for all labor, material, equipment, and all other actual costs necessary to repair or replace all equipment damaged due to negligence, meter tampering or bypassing, service diversion, or the discharge of wastes that the system cannot properly treat. The utility may charge for all actual costs necessary to correct service diversion or unauthorized taps where there is no equipment damage, including incidents where service is reconnected without authority. An itemized bill of such charges must be provided to the customer. A utility may not charge any additional penalty or any other charge other than actual costs unless such penalty has been expressly approved by the commission and filed in the utility's tariff. Except in cases of meter tampering or service diversion, a utility may not disconnect service of a customer refusing to pay damage charges unless authorized to in writing by the executive director.").

90 New Orleans Pub. Serv., Inc. v. Delaney, 379 So. 2d 842 (La. Ct. App. 1980).

91 La. Power Co. v. Bourgeois, 355 So. 2d 597 (La. Ct. App. 1978).

any billing adjustment to be charged to the customer, stating that the utility:

> concludes that that [air-conditioner] was installed in the period of October-November, 1974. The billing period ended April 1975. Defendant [customer] testified that during this period, he spent only a part of his time at home, ordinarily being away at his camp three or four days a week. This is the cold part of the year and a simple statement that an air conditioner would use $10 to $15 electricity per ton per month is not probative. There is no evidence as to how much the air conditioner was used during this period. We agree with the trial judge that to attempt to fix this amount would be speculative.[92]

A similar result was reached by the Illinois Appeals Court in *Royal Elm Nursing and Convalescent Center v. Northern Illinois Gas Company*.[93] As in other cases, the *Royal Elm* court began by noting that Northern Illinois Gas "had to establish only that the customer benefited from that tampering in order to bill the customer for all service usage during the period that the tampered metered remained in use. The question of guilt or innocence never arises."[94] The court, however, denied any adjustment to be charged to the customer. "While we recognize that utility companies are not in the business of providing free service, we are also cognizant of the age-old legal maxim that liability must be established before a penalty is imposed."[95]

The *Royal Elm* court undertook an extensive analysis of the utility's expert's testimony regarding how much service had been used but not billed. The utility had compiled all of the billing data available for Royal Elm and analyzed this data to obtain an estimate of: (1) use per degree day during the heating season; and (2) base use per day during the non-heating season. Based on a comparison of the bills during the time in which the meter did not register full consumption to the bills during which no tampering was evident, the utility developed a billing adjustment.

The court rejected this methodology. Although the expert "recognized that other factors such as patient load, heating patterns, and laundry practice may have precipitated the drops in Royal Elm's gas usage, he completely ignored these factors in reaching his determination. Thus, in effect, [the expert] based his conclusion on the unsupported assumption that all other factors were constant."[96] The court disapproved the commission's finding that to ignore these factors was appropriate.

> In its order, the Commission stated that it was "unreasonable to require [Northern Illinois Gas] to obtain such information from its customer before billing for unmetered service, where a reasonable estimate can be made from a billing history and other available information." In our view, it is even more unreasonable to recognize the likely existence of other factors, yet ignore them, and shift the burden to the consumer to prove that [the utility's] data is erroneous.[97]

The expert's testimony, the court concluded,

> is replete with factual conclusions inferred from evidence that readily leads to inconsistent factual conclusions and is impliedly grounded on the contradicted assumption that, at the time both indicators dropped, "all other things were equal." This assumption is not supported by the evidence. In fact, the evidence clearly indicates that there were a multiple of variables that could have altered both uses.[98]

The court finally said that the utility's expert analysis was subject to dismissal because it was incapable of being rebutted.

> [W]ith respect to the Account Analysis prepared by NI-G from data accumulated by NI-G and interpreted by an NI-G employee, we note the inability of a lay person or his own expert to verify the accuracy of the data on the Analysis. Even in the unlikely event that an NI-G customer kept copies of all his gas bills for the ten-year period a gas meter index is in place,[99] it would be difficult, if not impossible, to correlate the figures on those bills with the NI-G data.

In essence, the court held, "Commission Rule 280.11(c) imposes 'responsibility' for payment of under-registered gas usage on the person or entity who has benefited from the under-registration without any means for the customer to dispute figures used in arriving at his usage or in verifying any increases or decreases. . . . The possible inequities of this rule are readily apparent."[100]

Commission regulations may stipulate that a utility may use one or more methods to estimate actual usage during a period in which meter tampering is alleged to have occurred.[101]

In *Kean Investment Co. v. Michigan Consolidated Gas Co.*,[102] the commission held that the utility must adjust its

92 *Id.*

93 526 N.E.2d 376 (Ill. App. Ct. 1988).

94 *Id.* at 378.

95 *Id.* at 381.

96 *Id.* at 379.

97 *Id.*

98 *Id.* at 380.

99 *Id.* at 377. A gas meter index is the part of the meter that actually registers gas that passes through the meter.

100 *Id.* at 381.

101 *See, e.g.*, 30 Tex. Admin. Code § 291.87 (water utility may estimate bill based on at least twelve consecutive months (or less if customer not served at that site for twelve months) of comparable usage; such history presumed reasonable in case of meter tampering, bypassing, or other service diversion).

102 Kean Inv. Co. v. Michigan Consol. Gas Co., 111 Pub. Util. Rep.

estimate of unmetered use for such factors as conservation that took place at the premises, low occupancy rates, and other factors that would have lowered use.

4.4 Customer Claims of Fast Meter

Bills are typically issued, in part, on the basis of metered usage by a customer.[103] Some water utilities still use so-called "fixture rates," whereby the customer is charged a flat amount per fixture per month, the charge varying with the amount of water the type of fixture is thought to consume on average. However, even water utilities are beginning to meter their customers, as prices rise to the point that metering becomes worth the expense and conservation becomes an important policy objective. Gas and electric utilities have long metered usage. Many jurisdictions require gas or electric companies to use meters as the basis for usage charges.[104]

If a bill looks too high to a customer, the customer may complain to the utility that the meter is inaccurate.[105] Typically, the utility may test the meter at that point. In a number of jurisdictions, the meter must be tested at the request of the customer.[106]

In some jurisdictions, if the meter tests within a certain tolerance, the results are accepted as accurate and the bill is due as rendered.[107] In other cases, if the test shows that the meter is recording too fast by more than 2%, the utility must refund the overcharge.[108] Some commissions give an accurate meter test the weight of an irrebuttable presumption.[109] Other commissions will consider evidence of usage patterns, even in the face of a meter tested and found accurate within the allowed tolerance level.[110] Some commissions allow in so-called "lifestyle" usage evidence but give it less weight than an accurate meter.[111]

Commissions differ as well on the number of months they require a utility to go back in correcting a mistaken overcharge when a meter has been tested and found too fast. Some commissions fix a set period,[112] and some commis-

---

4th 479, 1990 WL 488713 (Mich. Pub. Serv. Comm'n Apr. 12, 1990).

103 *See, e.g.*, 16 Tex. Admin. Code § 25.121 (electric energy must be sold on metered basis).

104 *See, e.g.*, Fla. Admin. Code Ann. r. 25-7.071 (measuring gas service); 16 Tex. Admin. Code § 25.121.

105 *See, e.g.*, Murphy v. Boston Edison Co., D.P.U. 90-AD-8 (Mass. Dep't Pub. Util.).

106 *See, e.g.*, Nev. Admin. Code § 704.343 (a utility must test at the customer's request, and no charge for such test once during any twelve-month period); 16 Tex. Admin. Code § 7.45(7)(B)(iv) (without charge once every four years, and for $15 fee for additional tests if proven accurate in last test).

107 *E.g.*, Fla. Admin. Code Ann. r. 25-30.262 (rule sets forth flow formula for water meters); Nev. Admin. Code § 704.344 (1) (2% tolerance); 16 Tex. Admin. Code § 7.45 (American National Standards Institute, Incorporated Standard C12, adopted for meters—prescribes 2% tolerance, according to public utility commission staff. Telephone communication Aug. 21, 1995). *See also* American National Standard C12-1975 § 8.1.3.4 ("When a test of a watthour meter indicates that the error in registration exceeds 1 percent at either a light load or a heavy load at unity power factor, or exceeds 2 percent at heavy load at approximately 0.5 power factor lag, the percentage registration of the meter shall be adjusted to within these limits of error, as closely as practicable. . . . All meters that are tested shall be left without creep.").

108 *See, e.g.*, Cal. Pub. Util. Comm'n, Gen. Order 103, ¶ VII, § 3a (Adjustment of Bills for Meter Error—Fast Meters) ("When, upon test, a meter is found to be registering more than 2 percent fast, the utility shall refund to the customer the amount of the overcharge based on corrected meter readings for the period the meter was in use but not to exceed a period of six months."); 16 Tex. Admin. Code § 7.45(7) ("utility must correct previous readings consistent with the inaccuracy found in the meter," but rule does not specify if refund calls for reduction of adjusted bill to assumption of 100% accuracy or only to within ANSI tolerance; most utilities refund on assumption correct bill reflects meter if it had been running at 100% accuracy. Telephone communication Aug. 21, 1995). *See also* Villarino v. Boston Gas Co., D.P.U. 86-AD-6 (1987) (when meter tested 2.3% fast, and gas pressure 18% below normal, upon complaint of customer bill adjusted proportionately to extent of deviance; customer liable for balance of adjusted billings on twelve-month payment plan).

109 *See, e.g.*, Dan Mulholland v. California Water Serv. Co., Decision 92-07-013, No. 91-09-004 (Cal. Pub. Util. Comm'n July 1, 1992) (water customer liable for all water service charges as billed, when discrepancy insignificant, despite fact that testing had shown the méter to be running slightly fast; overcharge was refunded to the customer but the entire bill was not removed); Lyons v. Boston Gas Co., D.P.U. 84-86-30 (Mass. Dep't Pub. Util. Jan. 27, 1986) (actual readings from an accurate meter outweigh a customer's impression of usage); Edlin v. Boston Edison Co., D.P.U. 85-13-10 (Mass. Dep't Pub. Util. July 16, 1985) (mere discrepancy between a disputed bill and the billing history does not constitute sufficient evidence to necessitate rejection of meter test); Fetner v. Metropolitan Edison Co., 24 Pub. Util. Rep. 4th 1 (Pa. 1978) (if an electric company's meter is accurate within acceptable standards, the public utility cannot be held responsible for what an individual subscriber claims as unaccountable kilowatt use).

110 Kotsias v. Peoples Gas Light & Coke Co., 114 Pub. Util. Rep. 4th 378, 1990 WL 488808 (Ill. Commerce Comm'n July 6, 1990) (no irrebuttable presumption of meter accuracy even in face of test results; such a presumption would violate due process, and erroneous readings possible even in face of proof of accuracy).

111 *In re* Berry, No. U-6616 (Mich. Pub. Serv. Comm'n Nov. 24, 1981) (customer who contests gas meter readings as excessive has the burden of proving that no unusual conditions caused the meters to register excessive consumption); Monmouth Cold Storage Co. v. Public Serv. Elec. & Gas Co., 51 Pub. Util. Rep. 3d 409 (N.J. 1963) (charges based on actual meter readings taken in the course of business, when the meter is not proven to be inaccurate, are to be given greater weight than assumptions and unsupported assertions as to the probable amount of gas bill).

112 *See, e.g.*, Fla. Admin. Code Ann. r. 25-30.340(2) (one-half the period for which the bill was found to be in error but not to exceed twelve months); Mich. Admin. Code r. 460.2125 (not more than the three years immediately preceding discovery of the billing error, unless the customer is able to establish an

sions make a case-by-case adjudication of the time period for refund, based on considerations of how long the meter was likely to have been recording in error.[113] It has been held that absent statutory authority a commission cannot limit the time period for a refund to a fixed period.[114]

Utility commissions generally discourage customers from claiming that the meter is registering more power than was actually used. The burden of proving that the metered use does not represent actual use is typically on the complaining customer; a meter that is tested and found within the standard of tolerance will support a presumption that the service was accurately measured and billed.[115] But the presumption is generally rebuttable.[116]

earlier date for commencement of the error); 16 Tex. Admin. Code § 7.45(7) (bill adjustment due to meter error dates from six months before the meter was removed for the test or from the time the meter was in service since last tested, but not exceeding six months).

113 *See, e.g.*, Holden Mun. Light Dep't v. Lovett, D.P.U. 85-13-4 (Mass. Dep't Pub. Util. Feb. 28, 1986) (statute of limitations limits period of refund on meter running 23% fast between 1958 and 1984, but statute tolled until discovery of error; refund of excessive charges ordered back to date of installation of meter); Brookline Realty Inv. Corp v. Boston Gas Co., D.P.U. 18554 (Mass. Dep't Pub. Util. Aug. 26, 1976) (meters tested 6% and 8% fast; bills adjusted back to date of meter installation)).

114 Norman v. Ohio Pub. Util. Comm'n, 406 N.E.2d 492 (Ohio 1980).

115 *See, e.g.*, *In re* Berry, No. U-6616 (Mich. Public Serv. Comm'n Nov. 24, 1981); Silvestro v. Massachusetts Elec. Co., D.P.U.I. 91-AD-20 (Mass. Dep't Pub. Util. June 29, 1990); Monmouth Cold Storage Co. v. Public Serv. Elec. & Gas Co., 51 Pub. Util. Rep. 3d 409 (N.J. 1963). *Cf.* Coult v. Mayor & Bd. of Aldermen, City of Gretna, 11 So. 2d 424 (La. 1943) (in an action for an injunction to prevent termination, when city claimed that due to improper functioning of a consumer's water meter consumer had been charged insufficient water rent over a period of months and consumer honestly disputed amount of city's present claim, it was incumbent on city to prove the correctness of amount claimed before termination).

116 Kotsias v. Peoples Gas Light & Coke Co., 114 Pub. Util. Rep. 4th 378, 1990 WL 488808 (Ill. Commerce Comm'n July 6, 1990) (declining in a billing dispute to create, as a matter of law, an irrebuttable presumption that all readings from meters that tested within applicable statutory standards were accurate, because (1) a customer's liability for amounts billed by a utility was a question of both law and fact and, thus, while evidence of a meter's accuracy was properly accorded substantial weight, evidence adduced by customers must also be considered in determining liability; (2) such a presumption could constitute a violation of customers' right to due process of law by depriving them of a reasonable opportunity to present pertinent facts of their cases, because the underlying purpose of the statutory standard was to impose certain operational requirements on utilities and was not to provide an absolute defense in complaint cases before the commission; and (3) commission regulations incorporated a recognition that a meter might erroneously register service usage for reasons unrelated to meter accuracy).

4.5 Billing via Landlords: Master-Metering Cost Allocation Systems

4.5.1 Introduction

This section deals with direct statutory and regulatory controls on the ability of a landlord to charge tenants for energy use in various ways, including the use of allocation devices. The typical problem case arises when the landlord takes service through a single master-meter from the utility, distributes the service through the premises to the tenants, and bills them in some fashion for the costs of the service. When there are no controls on such resale of energy services and when the tenants have no right to insist on individual metering and a direct relationship with the regulated utility, the tenants have little recourse if the landlord charges them more than they would have been charged by the utility or more than the landlord's own cost of purchasing the service. The tenant in such a situation is also without direct regulatory protection from unfair allocations of the building's costs to the tenant's unit. This chapter discusses the regulations and statutes that have been enacted to address potential abuses of master-metering and concludes with a number of theories for legal recourse in the event a state has not adopted an explicit regulatory policy for preventing such abuses.

4.5.2 Statutory and Regulatory Control of Master-Metering

4.5.2.1 Bans on Resale

When electricity and gas service were first extended generally, it was common for landlords to produce electricity or gas (from coal, as opposed to natural gas) or to procure it from a plant situated nearby, for the use of the tenants. Utilities routinely offered "volume discounts" for purchases of large quantities of power or gas and, eventually, much of the self-generation and local generation was abandoned when it was not banned by the statutes defining public utility service.[117] Landlords continued to provide service to their tenants and procured their supplies at the commercial (wholesale) rate from the utility through a single master meter.

After regulation of gas and electric service became pervasive, utilities (via tariff clauses) and their regulatory commissions (by issuing orders or rules) increasingly limited the

117 This history is discussed in Boston Real Estate Bd. v. Department of Public Util., 136 N.E.2d 243 (Mass. 1956) and Campo Corp. v. Feinberg, 110 N.Y.S.2d 250, 252–53 (N.Y. App. Div. 1952).

right of landlords to resell power.[118] The impact of a typical ban on resale is to force a landlord to permit or require individual utility metering of each tenants' unit or to charge for the master-metered service in the rent, without differentiation by the relative use of the tenants and without change when the landlord's costs changed.[119]

The commissions and courts upholding these bans on resale pointed to a number of reasons in support of the limitation on resale:

(a) To prevent the landlord from earning an unfair profit on the arbitrage of the lower bulk (and/or commercial) rate applicable to apartment buildings and the higher retail residential rates for service;[120]

(b) To secure for the utility company and through it the ratepayers generally the revenues from sales to the tenants, thus lowering the overall bills charged by the system;[121]

118 *See, e.g.*, Lewis v. Potomac Elec. Power Co., 64 F.2d 701 (D.C. Cir. 1933) (tariff upheld over, *inter alia*, due process property right claim); Karrick v. Potomac Elec. Power Co., Pub. Util. Rep. 1932C 40 (D.C. Sup. Ct 1931); Fla. Power & Light Co. v. State *ex rel.* Malcolm, 144 So. 657 (Fla. 1932); 1925–1926 Op. Idaho Att'y Gen. 513; Boston Real Estate Bd. v. Department of Pub. Util., 136 N.E.2d 243 (Mass. 1956) (tariff bans resale except by way of "rent inclusion," to wit, recovery of landlord's costs in rent without adjustment for variations in tenant's use); Campo v. Feinberg, 110 N.Y.S.2d 250, 252–53 (N.Y. App. Div. 1952); Baker v. Public Serv. Co. of Okla., 606 P.2d 567 (Okla. 1980). *See also* 4 Colo. Code Regs. § 723-3, Rules 3801–3803 (LexisNexis) (master-meter operators must apply for exemption from rate regulation and show that they are not engaged in resale); Pub. Water Supply Inc. v. DiPasquale, 735 A.2d 378 (Del. 1999), *discussed in* Pub. Water Supply Inc. v. DiPasquale, 802 A.2d 929 (Del. Super. Ct. Feb. 29, 2000) (landlord acting as utility and thus subject to regulations); *In re* Potomac Elec. Power Co., Pub. Util. Rep. 1929B 600 (D.C. Pub. Serv. Comm'n 1929) (gas); D.L. Stokes & Co. Inc. v. Georgia Power Co., 71 Pub. Util. Rep. (N.S.) 15 (Ga. Pub. Serv. Comm'n 1947); *In re* Commonwealth Edison Co., 117 Pub. Util. Rep. 4th 407, 1990 WL 488799 (Ill. C.C. June 28, 1990); *Ex Parte* M.W. Munson Water Works, 80 Pub. Util. Rep. (N.S.) 188 (La. Pub. Serv. Comm'n 1949) (water); Mich. P.S.C. No. U-4717 (Mich. Pub. Serv. Comm'n) (prospective ban of central metering of residential natural gas service, except for central water or space heating systems that are more energy efficient than individual residential heating systems); *In re* Fidelity Natural Gas Co., 168 Pub. Util. Rep. 4th 347, 1996 WL 144340 (Mo. Pub. Serv. Comm'n Jan. 30, 1996) (company required to rewrite its tariff to define "customer" as an "end user" and forbid resale of gas by unregulated affiliate or anyone else); New York Tel. Co. v. P.S.C. of State of N.Y., 731 N.E.2d 1113 (N.Y. 2000) (discussion of Pub. Serv. Comm'n powers); Philadelphia Elec. Co. v. Pennsylvania Pub. Util. Comm'n, 42 Pub. Util. Rep. (N.S.) 126 (Pa. Pub. Util. Comm'n 1942); Dep't of Pub. Serv. of Wash. v. Puget Sound Power & Light Co., 20 Pub. Util. Rep. (N.S.) 457 (Wash. Dep't Pub. Util. 1937). *But see* Public Serv. Comm'n of Md. v. Howard Research & Dev. Corp., 314 A.2d 682 (Md. Ct. Spec. App. 1974) (in case decided before statutory prospective ban on master-metering, no meaningful distinction between landlord charging for, and earning profit through, rent and through separate charge on bill; Pub. Serv. Commission-approved tariff ban on resale overturned); may not discriminate amongst resellers); Compton Adver., Inc. v. Madison-59th Street Corp., 398 N.Y.S.2d 607 (N.Y. Sup. Ct. 1977) (not violative of ban on resale for landlord to impose "rent rider" whereby utilities are charged separately in rental and vary with changes in space rented, equipment used, and utility rate charged to landlord); Holmes Elec. Co. v. Carolina Power & Light Co., 150 S.E. 621, 623 (N.C. 1929) (whether utility may ban resale depends on whether it sells to any resellers); *In re* AMP of Tex., 45 Pub. Util. Rep. 4th 433, 7 Tex. P.U.C. Bull. 589 (Tex. Pub. Util. Comm'n 1982) (when landlord did not submeter and thus was not within purview of PUC rule regulating submetering, landlord was not public utility and landlord's charges to tenant could not be regulated by PUC).

119 *See, e.g.*, Campo Corp. v. Feinberg, 110 N.Y.S.2d 250, 252–53 (N.Y. App. Div. 1952).

Note that, as the court points out, banning resale in the form of separate charges does not prevent the landlord from charging more in rent than needed to cover costs of utilities charged to landlord through master-meter.

120 *See, e.g.*, Boston Real Estate Bd. v. Department of Pub. Util., 136 N.E.2d 243, 245, 15 Pub. Util. Rep. 3d 47 (Mass. 1956); Campo Corp. v. Feinberg, 110 N.Y.S.2d 250, 252–53 (N.Y. App. Div. 1952).

For most gas and electric utilities, from the initiation of monopoly franchises to the present time, the residential unit rates have been higher than the commercial unit rates and, in any event, volume discounts have been offered through the mechanism of declining block rates (the unit rate becomes smaller as the usage is higher). Thus, if a landlord is billed for all the use of a building through a single meter on the commercial rate, the bill has historically been lower than the aggregate bills would have been for each unit billed separately (at the residential rate). Or, if the building is on the residential rate, the bill to the landlord for the entire usage of the building is still likely to be lower than the aggregate bills of the individual tenants would have been, on account of the fact that, under declining block rate structures, more of the usage billed through the single meter would be billed at the lower tail block rates.

Some jurisdictions in the 1980s moved to so-called marginal-cost-based rates and began eliminating declining block rates and increasing the tail block rate, which tends to eliminate the favorable treatment of single-metered buildings. However, a contemporaneous development in rate regulation, whereby commissions began "equalizing rates of return" between the three major rate classes (residential, commercial, and industrial) would tend to raise residential rates and lower commercial rates, offsetting the bill-increasing impact of inclining block rates for apartment buildings charged under commercial rates. *See, e.g.*, W. Mass. Elec. Co., D.P.U. 86-270 (Mass. Dep't Pub. Util. 1987) (discussing marginal-cost ratemaking). *See also In re* Consumers Power Co., 25 Pub. Util. Rep. 4th 167 (Mich. Pub. Serv. Comm'n 1978) (when commercial unit rates are higher than residential unit rates, tariff rule classifying apartment buildings of four or more units as commercial buildings tends to discourage master-metering in large apartment buildings).

121 *See, e.g.*, Lewis v. Potomac Power Co., 64 F.2d 701 (D.C. Cir. 1933); Boston Real Estate Bd. v. Department of Pub. Util., 136 N.E.2d 243, 245, 15 Pub. Util. Rep. 3d 47 (Mass. 1956); Campo Corp. v. Feinberg, 110 N.Y.S.2d 250, 252–53 (N.Y. App. Div. 1952); Pennsylvania Pub. Util. Comm'n v. Duquesne Light Co., 64 Pub. Util. Rep. 3d 162 (Pa. Pub. Util. Comm'n 1966).

(c) To give the tenants the same protections from unfair practices and shut-offs that other end-users enjoy;[122] and
(d) To protect the jurisdiction of the public utilities commission.[123]

Under some statutes, a landlord who provides utility service only to its tenants is not classified as a public utility.[124] Under this view, many states exempted landlords from any regulation in the matter of resale, usually on the grounds that the landlord is not selling service to the public and that the public utility commission could not exert authority over the terms of the relationship between landlord and tenant, even indirectly through a tariff provision limiting a master-metered landlord from reselling the service provided by the utility.[125]

Recently, the U.S. Environmental Protection Agency revised its policy concerning the applicability of the Safe Drinking Water Act to submetered multi-unit properties.[126] In the past, under prior EPA policy, an apartment owner that obtained water through the public water system but then billed tenants separately through submetering was considered to be operating a fully regulated public water system and thus subject to the Safe Drinking Water Act. The new EPA policy regarding the applicability of the Safe Drinking Water Act to submetered properties exempts these residential multi-unit properties in order to promote water conservation.[127]

122 *See, e.g.*, *In re* Submetering of Util. Servs., 10 D.C. P.S.C. 248, No. 859, Order No. 9213 (D.C. Pub. Serv. Comm'n Mar. 14, 1989).

123 *See, e.g.*, Fla. Power & Light Co. v. State *ex rel.* Malcolm, 144 So. 657 (Fla. 1932).

124 I.T.C. v. A.T.T., 1997 WL 599618 (E.D. La. Sept. 16, 1997). *See* Fla. Stat. § 367.022 (water, when cost included in rent); Idaho Code Ann. § 61-119; 220 Ill. Comp. Stat. 25/1.03; N.M. Stat. Ann. § 62-3-4; Wyo. Stat. Ann. § 37-1-101 (landlord exempt except in case of metered or direct sales to tenants).

Note that, when the prohibited activity is described as "resale" of utilities, nonprofits and others who do not make a profit on the transaction may arguably be exempt from the ban and may deliver utility services and charge for them.

125 *See, e.g.*, Antique Vill. Inn, Inc. v. Pacitti, Robins, Anglin, Inc., 390 A.2d 681 (N.J. Super. Ct. Law Div. 1978) (landlord not utility, as not holding out services to public). *See also* Compton Adver., Inc. v. Madison-59th Street Corp., 398 N.Y.S.2d 607 (N.Y. App. Div. 1977) ("rent inclusion" clause allowing separately stated charge for energy use varying with usage permissible despite tariff ban on resale); Michael E. Brooks v. Toledo Edison Co. 169 Pub. Util. Rep. 4th 179, 1996 WL 331201 (Ohio Pub. Util. Comm'n May 8, 1996) (commercial landlord that charged mall tenants separately for electricity without master metering was not a public utility subject to regulation, and utility required to eliminate tariff forbidding resale of power by landlords).

126 68 Fed. Reg. 74233, 74234–35 (Dec. 23, 2003).

127 *See also* Olivia Wein & Charlie Harak, *Soaking Tenants: Billing Tenants Directly for Water and Sewer Services*, NCLC Energy & Util. Update (Fall 2003) (trend to submeter water and dangers of allocation formulas such as ratio-utility billing), *available on the companion website to this treatise*.

4.5.2.2 The Modern Rule: Bans on Master-Metering

The modern trend, developed in the 1970s during the time of the oil embargoes and growing concern over energy costs and energy conservation, has been to require the installation by the regulated utility of individual meters in rental and multifamily dwellings and to require tenants to take service directly from the utility and to pay for it.[128]

One impact of such a requirement is to shield the landlord from the responsibility to provide an energy-efficient building and equipment for the use of the tenants, since the tenant is now responsible for the utility service.[129] Benefits for tenants do exist, however, including eligibility for discounted rates available to low-income tenants as opposed to landlords[130] and potentially greater equity in utility costs between tenants.

Note, however, that individual metering (or, for that matter, submetering) is a benefit for tenants and is more equitable only to the extent each household has actual control over energy use. Given the lack of control over the building stock and major appliances, and the fact that rents

128 *See, e.g.*, Cal. Gov. Code § 39730 (West) (gas and electric); Cal. Pub. Util. Code § 780.5 (West) (gas and electric); Fla. Admin. Code Ann. r. 25-6.049 (requiring individual electric metering after 1980), r. 25-7.071 (requiring individual gas metering after 1986); Ind. Code § 8-1-2-36.5 (references commission rules limiting master-metering); N.C. Gen. Stat. 143-151.42 (after Sept. 1, 1977); Tex. Util. Code Ann. § 184.012 (West) (municipalities may not issue building codes for new residences that are not individually metered); *In re* Investigation on Master Metering for Multiunit Dwellings, 33 Pub. Util. Rep. 4th 482 (Conn. Pub. Util. Comm'n 1980) (prospective only); *In re* Consumers Power Co. (Mich. Pub. Serv. Comm'n 1989) (commission banned central metering in 1977, Case No U-4717; principal factor in imposing the ban was the promotion of gas conservation); Compton Adver., Inc. v. Madison-59th Street Corp., 398 N.Y.S.2d 607 (N.Y. App. Div. 1977) (recites that N.Y. Commission adopted prospective rule requiring individual metering in 1976); Crown Am. Corp. v. Pennsylvania Public Util. Comm'n, 463 A.2d 1257 (Pa. Commw. Ct. 1983) (tariff prospectively barring master-metering upheld over claim by developers that owners grandfathered master-metered buildings would enjoy unfair advantage); *In re* Investigation of Master Metering, 37 Pub. Util. Rep. 4th 110 (S.D. Pub. Util. Comm'n 1980). *See also* Schiavi v. City of Rochester, 880 A.2d 428 (N.H. 2005) (state statute allows owners of manufactured-housing parks to shift from master meter of water to individual meters so that they can be billed directly by municipal water company).

129 *But see, e.g.*, Wis. Stat. § 101.122 (landlords must meet certain energy efficiency standards in rental units).

130 *See, e.g.*, *In re* Investigation on the Commission's Own Motion to Comply with Senate Bill 987 and Realign Residential Rates, Including Baseline Rates, of California Energy Util., 32 Cal. Pub. Util. Comm'n 334 (Cal. Pub. Util. Comm'n July 19, 1989) ((Decision No. 89-07-062) (under low-income ratepayer assistance program providing discounted baseline energy rates to qualifying customers, individually metered and submetered customers would be eligible for the discounts, but unmetered customers would not)).

typically vary within a building based primarily on the number of bedrooms (thus incorporating some variation in implicit energy costs per numbers in the household), the inclusion of energy costs in rent is not necessarily detrimental or inequitable.[131]

In at least two jurisdictions, a landlord is required to reduce the rent to reflect the shift in cost responsibility to the tenant if the landlord voluntarily switches from a master-metering situation to a submeter or individual meter arrangement.[132]

In most cases, statutes or rules banning master-metering grandfather existing buildings, thus permitting master-metering in a large proportion of the housing stock.[133] Some states also provide exceptions allowing master-metering[134] for facilities when providing utility services (such as heating, cooling and/or hot water) centrally by the landlord would be more efficient,[135] for buildings with few units,[136] or for other enumerated types of dwellings.[137]

Similarly, due to the steady increase in the price of water, there have been campaigns to change state laws to allow for the submetering of water.[138] In 1996 the North Carolina

131 *See* § 4.5.3, *infra* (discussing the benefits of tracking payments with household consumption).

132 Md. Code Ann., Pub. Util. Cos. § 7-303 (West) (landlords switching to submetering, except local housing authorities, must calculate savings and flow through to tenants as reduced rents); Tex. Util. Code Ann. § 184.013 (West) (landlord must reduce rents if change to submeter system and landlord had raised rent within previous ninety days due to increased cost of utilities).

133 *See, e.g.*, Cal. Gov't Code § 39730 (West) (permits issued after July 1, 1982); Cal. Pub. Util. Code § 780.5 (West) (same); Fla. Admin. Code Ann. r. 25-6.049 (individual electric metering required after 1980), r. 25-7.071 (individual gas metering required after 1986); N.C. Gen. Stat. § 143-151.42 (after 1977); Tex. Util. Code Ann. § 184.012 (West) (new construction or conversion to condominiums); *In re* Investigation on Master Metering for Multiunit Dwellings, 33 Pub. Util. Rep. 4th 482 (Conn. Pub. Util. Comm'n 1980) (prospective only); Compton Adver., Inc. v. Madison-59th Street Corp., 398 N.Y.S.2d 607 (N.Y. App. Div. 1977) (recites that N.Y. Commission adopted prospective rule requiring individual metering in 1976); Crown Am. Corp. v. Pennsylvania Public Util. Comm'n, 463 A.2d 1257 (Pa. Commw. Ct. 1983) (tariff prospectively barring master-metering upheld over claim by developers that owners grandfathered master-metered buildings would enjoy unfair advantage); *In re* Investigation of Master Metering, 37 Pub. Util. Rep. 4th 110 (S.D. Pub. Util. Comm'n 1980).

134 When a facility falls within one of the exceptions, the landlord may still be subject to limitations on the extent to which he or she may charge what the market will bear for utility service provided by the landlord.

135 Fla. Admin. Code Ann. r. 25-6.049 (central heat, venting, air conditioning, and electrical back-up to storage heat and storage cooling systems); Md. Code Ann., Pub. Util. Cos. § 7-301 (West) (excepting central hot water); N.C. Gen. Stat. § 143-151.42; *In re* Cambridge Assocs., 71 Md. P.S.C. 437, No. 7440 (Phase II), Order No. 64459 (Md. Pub. Serv. Comm'n Oct. 6, 1980) (hearing officer's ruling) (operator of senior citizen complex authorized to use natural gas for central hot water boilers to furnish space heat to residents, when such use found to result in net energy savings over systems using individual meters; statute requiring individual meters outweighed by statutory policy in favor of energy efficiency; statute allows PUC to issue rule to permit central supply when "substantial net savings of energy" and ban does not apply in any event to centralized provision of hot water); *In re* Florian Cos., 212 Pub. Util. Rep. 4th 531, 2001 WL 946442 (N.C. July 5, 2001) (granting gas company's request to master-meter central heating and air conditioning for condominium building, made pursuant to N.C. Gen. Stat. 143-151.42, which requires individual metering unless master metering would conserve energy); *In re* Investigation of Master Metering, 37 Pub. Util. Rep. 4th 110 (S.D. Pub. Util. Comm'n 1980) (master-metering permitted in case of central heating, cooling, ventilation, and hot-water heating systems).

136 *See In re* Investigation on Master Metering for Multiunit Dwellings, 33 Pub. Util. Rep. 4th 482 (Conn. Pub. Util. Comm'n 1980) (multiunit premises only); Crown Am. v. Pennsylvania Public Util. Comm'n, 463 A.2d 1257 (Pa. Commw. Ct. 1983) (ban applies to commercial buildings, including those housing both residences and commercial facilities, with three or more units); *In re* Investigation of Master Metering, 37 Pub. Util. Rep. 4th 110 (S.D. Pub. Util. Comm'n 1980) (three or more units). *See also* Michigan Public Service Commission Standard Rules and Regulations, No. 8, sheet 4.04, Rule 12 (landlords of buildings under thirty units may not resell utilities).

137 *See, e.g.*, Crown Am. v. Pennsylvania Pub. Util. Comm'n, 463 A.2d 1257 (Pa. Commw. Ct. 1983) (when installation of individual meters is "neither feasible nor practical from a financial, technical or engineering point of view or [for] any other valid reason"); *In re* Investigation of Master Metering, 37 Pub. Util. Rep. 4th 110 (S.D. Pub. Util. Comm'n 1980) (buildings constructed, owned, or operated with funds appropriated through the U.S. Department of Housing and Urban Development exempt from commission regulations governing master-metering to extent commission regulations inconsistent with applicable federal regulations). *See also* Mich. Public Service Commission Standard Rules and Regulations, No. 8, sheet 4.04, Rule 12 (manufactured home park owners exempt from rule against landlord resale); *In re* Consumers Power Co., 25 Pub. Util. Rep. 4th 167 (Mich. Pub. Serv. Comm'n 1978) ("practical considerations" affecting metering gas are different from those affecting electricity).

Master-metering is permitted in transient facilities in a number of states: Fla. Admin. Code Ann. r. 25-6.049 (electric service), r. 25-7.071 (gas service) ("specialized-use" facilities such as hospitals, dormitories; overnight campgrounds and marinas); Ind. Code § 8-1-2-36.5 (when building master-metered, landlord must install submetering equipment, except in case of hotels, motels, "or similar transient lodging"); *In re* Investigation of Master Metering, 37 Pub. Util. Rep. 4th 110 (S.D. Pub. Util. Comm'n 1980) (hospitals, nursing homes, transient hotels and motels, dormitories, campgrounds, transient residential facilities, exempt from prospective ban on master-metering in multi-occupancy dwellings).

138 *See* Olivia Wein & Charlie Harak, *Soaking Tenants: Billing Tenants Directly for Water and Sewer Services*, NCLC Energy & Util. Update (Fall 2003) (trend to submeter water and dangers of allocation formulas such as ratio-utility billing), *available on the companion website to this treatise*. *See also* Marc Treitler, National Apartment Ass'n, *Submetering: What You Don't Know Can Cost You*, Units, July 1, 2000 (article cites recent submetering legislative activity in Arizona, Arkansas, California, Florida, Georgia, Nevada, Oklahoma, Oregon, Tennessee, local

legislature, in response to the state apartment association's efforts, changed the state law to allow submetering of water.[139] The state regulations for the resale of water and sewer service to tenants refer to the water and sewer charge as the "variable rent component."[140] The North Carolina legislature added a new subsection to the statute concerning the utility commission's certificate of convenience and necessity that authorized the commission to adopt procedures for the resale of water and sewer in apartments, condos and other similar places.[141] The state legislature clarified the submetering procedure in 2001 by amending the statute to permit the utility commission to adopt submetering procedures that "allow a lessor, pursuant to a written agreement, to allocate the costs for water and sewer on a metered use basis." Furthermore, "the written rental agreement shall specify the monthly rent that shall be the sum of the base rent plus additional rent at a rate that does not exceed the actual purchase price of the water and sewer service to the provider plus a reasonable administrative fee."[142] At the urging of the state's Attorney General's Office and the North Carolina Justice and Community Development Center,[143] the legislature also modified the landlord-tenant laws to protect tenants from eviction for failure to pay their water and sewer submetered bill[144] and to prohibit late fees for water and sewer submetered bills.[145] The landlord is permitted to use the security deposit to recover nonpayment of the water and sewer submetered bills.[146]

In 2000, Georgia's legislature amended its conservation and natural resources code to authorize owners of rental units to submeter or use an allocation formula to charge tenants directly for water and wastewater.[147] The legislation states that the total paid by the tenants cannot exceed that paid by the property owner for the building; that the owner can charge tenants a reasonable fee for establishing, servicing and billing for water; and that the terms of the water and waste-water charges must be disclosed to the tenants prior to any contractual agreement.[148] The legislation had also exempted these property owners from being considered an owner or operator of a public water system.[149] Subsequent legislation removed that exemption in 2002.[150]

4.5.2.3 Flow-Through and Hold-Harmless Rules

When master-metering is permitted, some states have nevertheless established limitations on the scope of the landlord's ability to exact unfair profits from the tenants. Some states or utilities (by tariff approved by the regulatory commission) require the landlord to hold the tenant harmless from the effect of taking service from the landlord rather than the utility. In these jurisdictions, the landlord may not charge the tenants more for the service than they would have been charged had they taken service directly.[151]

---

activity in Chicago and Cleveland, and commission activity in California, South Carolina, Texas and Washington).

139 Chris Helms, *Apartment Water Issue Goes to the City*, Greensboro News & Record, Oct. 14, 2000.

140 *See* 4 N.C. Admin. Code 11.R18-16 (2003) (rescinded Aug. 1, 2004) (variable rent component).

141 1996 N.C. Sess. Laws ch. 753 (S.B. 1183), *codified at* N.C. Gen. Stat. § 62-110(g) (1996).

The statute was amended effective August 1, 2004, to provide for a rate not exceeding the unit consumption rate charged by the supplier of the service and an administrative fee not exceeding a fee authorized by the commission. Certificates of authority issued prior to August 1, 2004, terminated and were deemed to include authority to charge for water or sewer service at the existing rates.

142 2001 N.C. Sess. Laws 2001-502 (H.B. 1061), *codified at* N.C. Gen. St. § 62-110(g) (2001).

143 Apartment Association of North Carolina Final Legislative Report 2001, at 3–4.

144 2001 N.C. Sess. Laws 2001-502 (H.B. 1061), *codified at* N.C. Gen. St. §§ 42-3, 42-26(b) (arrearage in costs for water and sewer services shall not be used as basis for termination of lease).

The amendments to section 42-3 were deleted by Sess. Laws 2004-143 01, effective Aug. 1, 2004.

145 2001 N.C. Sess. Laws 2001-502 (H.B. 1061), *codified at* N.C. Gen. St. § 42-46(d).

146 2001 N.C. Sess. Laws 2001-502 (H.B. 1061), *codified at* N.C. Gen. St. § 42-51.

147 2000 Ga. Laws 831, *codified at* Ga. Code Ann. § 12-5-180.1 (2000).

148 2000 Ga. Laws 831, *codified at* Ga. Code Ann. § 12-5-180.1 (b)(2000).

149 2000 Ga. Laws 831, *codified at* Ga. Code Ann. § 12-5-180.1 (a) (2000).

150 2002 Ga. Laws 954, *codified at* Ga. Code Ann. § 12-5-180.1 (a) (2002).

151 *See, e.g.*, Cal. Pub. Util. Code § 739.5 (West) (master-metered landlord must charge tenants what they would have been charged if they took service directly; utility must set charges to landlord at a level that will provide a sufficient differential to cover reasonable average costs of landlord in providing submeter service, not to exceed average costs to utility of providing services directly); Del. Code Ann. tit. 25, § 5312 (may not charge more than actual cost); Md. Code Ann., Pub. Util. Cos. § 7-301 (West); Minn. Stat. § 327C.04 (manufactured home parks must hold tenants harmless but may only exceed flow-through allocation if landlord suffers loss at flow-through rates); Allegheny Ctr. Assocs. v. Pennsylvania Pub. Util. Comm'n, 228 A.2d 26 (Pa. Super. Ct. 1967) (utility tariff bans resale except when landlord charges tenants same rates utility would have charged "for a like and contemporaneous service"); General Split Corp. v. P. & V. Atlas Corp., 280 N.W.2d 765 (Wis. 1979), *aff'd*, 368 N.W.2d 846 (Wis. Ct. App. 1985) (citing 1963 commission rule requiring resellers to hold tenants harmless). *See also* Boston Real Estate Bd. v. Department of Pub. Util., 136 N.E.2d 243, 245, 15 Pub. Util. Rep. 3d 47 (Mass. 1956) (Boston Edison tariff limits rate for resale to sum of otherwise applicable individual rates, when resale permitted); *In re* Compugas, Inc., 90 Pub. Util. Rep. 4th 450, 1988 WL 391364 (Mich. Pub. Serv. Comm'n Feb. 8, 1988) (when landlord using commercially marketed allocation system to allocate master-metered costs does not charge tenants more than utility charges landlord, neither landlord nor marketer of allocation system is a "public utility" subject to rate regulation; nor does allocation scheme violate tariff ban on resale); *In re* Energy Metering Control Corp., No. U-8122 (Mich. Pub. Serv. Comm'n Apr. 8,

Jurisdictions requiring "hold harmless" rates for resold service may require that the landlord submeter, a practice which ensures that the parties have a basis for calculating what the individual rate would have been had the tenant been individually metered by the utility.[152]

Other jurisdictions require the landlord to flow-through to the tenants the landlord's cost as charged by the utility through the single meter.[153]

Such systems require some basis for apportioning the landlord's costs to the tenants, and submeters may be used for this purpose.[154]

4.5.2.4 Other Tenant Protections

In a number of jurisdictions, statutory provisions subject landlords to further controls, requiring meter accuracy, meter testing, and adequate record-keeping,[155] and provide for commission oversight to mediate complaints by tenants.[156] In some cases, statutes or rules require that tenants have specific notice, as in the case of mandatory lease provisions, of the terms of the master-metering, including the method of allocation and other such information.[157]

Similarly, consumer protection statutes may provide protection if a tenant does not have notice that there is man-

1986) (same). *But see* Michigan Public Service Commission Standard Rules and Regulations, No. 8, Sheet 4.04, Rule 12 (master-metered landlord may charge no more than what would be charged by utility if tenants billed directly).

152 Cal. Pub. Util. Code § 739.5 (West) assumes master-metered facilities will be submetered and requires itemized billings showing submetered use and the otherwise applicable retail rate used to compute the charges payable to the landlord. *See also* Hillsboro Props. v. Public Utils. Comm'n, 108 Cal. App. 4th 246 (Cal. Ct. App. 2003) (affirming PUC decision that city manufactured home rent control ordinance resulted in higher utility charges to tenants of the park in violation of Cal. Pub. Util. Code § 739.5 (West)).

153 *Colorado*: Colo. Rev. Stat. § 38-12-212.7 (landlord must remit to utility all monies collected from each resident for resident's share of charges to landlord, failing which utility may demand deposit from landlord and may sue and recover attorney fees).

Florida: Fla. Admin. Code Ann. r. 25-6.049(9)(b) (master-metered landlord may not collect more in charges from tenants than landlord owes to utility); Fla. Stat. § 367.022 (water and waste water service reseller whose charges do not exceed actual purchase price and who files information on rates with commission exempt from commission regulation); *In re* Procedures Governing Sales of Electricity for Resale, 85 Pub. Util. Rep. 3d 107 (Fla. Pub. Serv. Comm'n 1970) (under tariff permitting resale only if landlord charges no more than amount actually billed by utility, landlord may not add its cost of billing, metering, or other costs to flow-through charges).

Illinois: 765 Ill. Comp. Stat. 740/5.

Indiana: Ind. Code § 8-1-2-36.5(c) (landlord may not pass on late charges).

Maryland: Md. Code Ann., Pub. Util. Comp. § 7-303 (West) (landlord may add $1 administration fee per month per tenant; landlords switching to submetering, except local housing authorities, must calculate savings and flow through to tenants as reduced rents).

Michigan: In re Compugas, Inc., 90 Pub. Util. Rep. 4th 450, 1988 WL 391364 (Mich. Pub. Serv. Comm'n Feb. 8, 1988) (when landlord using commercially marketed allocation system to allocate master-metered costs does not charge tenants more than utility charges landlord, neither landlord nor marketer of allocation system is a "public utility" subject to rate regulation; nor does allocation scheme violate tariff ban on resale); *In re* Energy Metering Control Corp., No. U-8122 (Mich. Pub. Serv. Comm'n Apr. 8, 1986) (same). *But see* Michigan Public Service Commission Standard Rules and Regulations, No. 8, Sheet 4.04, Rule 12 (master-metered landlord may charge no more than what would be charged by utility if tenants billed directly).

See also Minn. Stat. § 327C.04(3) (manufactured home park owners must flow through utility costs, unless flow-through method causes economic loss to landlord); Tex. Util. Code Ann. §§ 124.002 (landlord may not earn profit on gas resale), 184.013 (landlord may submeter electricity in premises that are not banned from master-metering if there is flow-through and must reduce rents if change to submeter system and landlord had raised rent within previous ninety days due to increased cost of utilities), 184.052 (when landlord provides central system water, waste water service, air-conditioning, heat, hot or chilled water, rental agreement must specify that flow-through method will be used to charge tenant) (West). *Cf.* Va. Code Ann. §§ 56-245.3, 55-248.45:1, 55-226.2 (apartment house, office building, shopping center, and manufactured-home park owners who pass through service may impose service charges—including monthly billing, account set-up, and move-out fees—to cover "actual costs of administrative expenses and billing" charged by third-party provider of such services).

154 For example, in Indiana, a master-metered landlord may submeter and then charge tenants separately for utility services. Ind. Code § 8-1-2-36.5(d)(1).

In Delaware, landlords, unless they have metering systems in use prior to July 1976, cannot charge separately for a utility service unless it is separately metered. Del. Code Ann. tit. 25, § 5312.

155 Ind. Code § 8-1.2-36.5(d)(1); Md. Code Ann., Pub. Util. Cos. §§ 7-303 (all submetering equipment subject to same rules as apply to regulated utilities), 7-304 (energy allocation) (West); Tex. Util. Code Ann. §§ 184.013 (electric submetering equipment subject to same rules and standards for accuracy, testing, and record-keeping as meters installed by utilities, 184.052 (West) (owner of apartment house with centrally-supplied utilities must maintain records for inspection by tenants concerning utility consumption, charges assessed by utility, and allocation to tenants). *See also In re* Submetering of Water Serv., 216 Pub. Util. Rep. 4th 466 (Conn. 2001) (approving landlords' request to submeter water service on condition that they not charge tenants more in the aggregate than the tenants' portion of the total bill, excluding common areas, vacant apartments, and owner-occupied areas, and that they abide by the regulations' consumer service standards).

156 Ind. Code § 8-1-2-36.5(d) (1); Md. Code Ann., Pub. Util. Cos. § 7-303(h) (West) (complaints lie with county or municipal landlord-tenant commission or consumer protection agency, if any, and, if not, with Consumer Protection Division of Office of Attorney General or other office or agency designated for tenant's complaints).

157 765 Ill. Comp. Stat. 740/5 (landlord, condominium, or community association must provide tenant with written copy of formula used by landlord for allocating public utility payments among the tenants); Tex. Util. Code Ann. § 184.052 (West).

datory master-metering.[158] Additionally, in a recent case, a tenant successfully argued that the landlord had breached the covenant of quiet enjoyment by having burdened her with another tenant's utility bill without her knowledge or consent.[159]

4.5.3 *Energy Cost Allocation Principles to Determine Tenant Obligation*

4.5.3.1 General

One means of billing tenants of multiple-unit dwellings for energy costs, when a state does not specify the terms of such charges, involves the allocation, rather than the direct measurement, of energy provided to a particular dwelling unit. For example, the allocation of energy costs occurs when a single boiler is used to provide energy for a multiple occupancy building. Since energy consumption is not measured on an individual unit basis under such circumstances, energy costs must either be included as part of the rent or be allocated on some non-measured basis.

When landlords have used submetering or cost allocation techniques to charge tenants for use and are not expressly prevented from taking advantage of a differential between wholesale utility rates they pay (for the bulk purchase registered at the master meter) and the retail utility rates (that would apply if each unit were metered),[160] a number of types of interests are affected. Utilities, public service commissions, consumer advocates, tenant advocates, and conservation advocates have objected for various reasons to such "arbitrage" of utility rates by landlords and the removal of the retail utility sale from regulation. As we have seen, in some states, statutes, public utility commission rules or orders, and utility tariffs have been established, limiting or regulating the practice of resale by a landlord.

The allocation of energy costs differs from both traditional "master-metering" and "submetering" of energy use. In the traditional master-metering situation, a tenant's utility costs are included as an undesignated part of the rent paid for the property. The rent, and therefore the utility charge, does not vary based upon the actual consumption of the tenant.[161] In contrast, submetering involves the placement of individual meters in tenant dwelling units. The property owner directly measures the amount of energy (for example, electricity, natural gas) consumed by the tenant and charges the tenant based on that usage.[162]

The allocation of energy costs stands in contrast to these metered situations. As the Virginia State Corporation Commission viewed it:

> Unlike utility meters or electric and natural gas submeters, energy allocation systems do not directly measure a commodity such as electricity or gas. Instead, such systems usually consist of devices to estimate certain parameters in combination with calculations which utilize those parameters and other assumptions. The result is not a measurement so much as an estimation procedure.[163]

Another definition states:

> Heating cost allocation (HCA) systems are combinations of monitoring devices and accounting procedures designed to allow the energy costs in centrally heated multifamily buildings to be divided among the individual apartments on the basis of use.[164]

The allocation of energy costs within a multifamily building may pose problems to low-income tenants in any number of situations. The allocation of energy costs based upon individual consumption should reasonably reflect the consumption of the rental unit. The allocation of energy costs as a means of promoting energy conservation should only occur under circumstances in which a tenant has control over the energy consumption in the rental property. The use of energy cost allocation methods should be properly disclosed to the tenant prior to the consummation of the rental agreement. In sum, as with many new technologies, energy

158 *See* Legg v. Castruccio, 642 A.2d 906 (Md. 1994) (holding that the landlord commits a deceptive or unfair business practice under the Maryland Consumer Protection Act (Md. Code Ann., Com. Law § 13-102 (West)) by requiring a tenant to obtain utility services measured by a meter that, unknown to the tenant, also services another rental unit).

In *Legg*, the landlord failed to inform the first floor tenant that her utility service, which she established on her own, would include charges for the second floor apartment as well. However, the court dismissed the claim, finding that the tenant had waived her right to recover by remaining on the premises and consenting to the billing arrangement.

159 Legg v. Castruccio, 642 A.2d 906 (Md. 1994).

In this situation, however, the court found that the tenant had waived the right to this remedy by accepting payment from the upstairs tenant, but the case was remanded to determine whether she could overcome the waiver based on her complaints to the landlord.

160 *See* § 4.5.2.1, *supra* (states that limit ability of the landlord to "arbitrage" the differential between the building's rate and the retail rate that the tenant would otherwise pay).

161 Some leases will provide that the rent will escalate as a function of increases in the landlord's utility bill. But, unless the underlying rent component is itself a function of submetering or allocation, the resulting charge after application of the escalator remains unrelated to the tenant's actual usage.

162 The rate at which the usage is charged may vary depending on the latitude landlords have in the particular state.

163 Staff Report, Div. of Energy Regulation, *Ex Parte, In Re: Investigation into the Promulgation Of Standards and Regulations for Energy Allocation Equipment*, No. PUE920067 (Va. State Corp. Comm'n Dec. 11, 1992).

164 M.J. Hewett et al., *Heating Cost Allocation in Multi-Family Buildings: Energy Savings and Implementation Standards*, ASHRAE Transactions, Vol. 95, No. 1, at 1 (1989).

cost allocation systems may be acceptable for low-income tenants, when legal, if proper precautions are taken by the property owners relying upon such systems. What those "proper precautions" are will be operationally defined throughout the discussion below. To the extent that the use of a master-meter between landlord and utility, and check-meters or submeters or some other allocation system between landlord and tenant, the tenant may be deprived of the customer service jurisdiction of the state public utilities commission to resolve complaints and supervise accuracy of the billings.

4.5.3.2 Justification for Use of Energy Cost Allocation to Determine Tenant Liability

According to allocation proponents, it is less costly for tenants to have energy costs allocated than it is for property owners to convert to individually metered electric energy. The Chair of the ASHRAE Committee on "energy cost allocation of comfort HVAC systems for multiple occupancy residential buildings" urges:

> Over the past 20 years, there has been a dramatic shift to electric heat in the multifamily sector, driven largely by landlords' desire to remove variable energy costs from the rent, and the relatively low cost of accomplishing this with individual electric heating systems. In 1975, 19% of the multifamily housing stock nationwide was heated with electricity but, by 1990, the percentage had grown to 34%. During every one of those years, more than 50% of the new multifamily housing built was built with electric heat, while less than a third of new single family housing was.[165]

One result of this is that "tenants, who on average have only about half the income of homeowners, are increasingly being served with a significantly more expensive fuel source."[166]

Proponents state that the allocation of energy costs is one of the more effective means of encouraging tenants to conserve energy. A widely quoted study conducted in New Jersey shows that occupants' energy use habits can cause as much as a two-to-one variation in energy use in identical residences,[167] and the division of responsibility between owners and residents is a major institutional barrier to energy conservation in multifamily buildings.[168] Allocation offers an effective means to realize the behavioral component of energy savings, the argument thus goes. And that argument has some empirical basis. One Minnesota study, for example, measured mean savings of 16% of total gas use (about 20 to 25% of space heating use) in nine buildings.[169]

Allocation proponents posit that charging tenants for energy costs based upon a system of energy use allocations is *more* accurate than including energy costs as part of the rent. Inclusion of energy costs in rent is generally accomplished through flat rate billing, a system under which total energy costs for a multiple unit dwelling is divided by the respective areas in each individual unit. It is thus not surprising that such an allocation system is inherently inaccurate. First, as discussed above, energy use is highly dependent upon individual behavior; usage can vary dramatically even in identical dwellings. Second, usage in particular units within a multiple unit building is dependent upon external factors as much as it is dependent upon the square feet of area. Thus, for example, apartments next to the boiler room may receive "free" heat by conduction through the walls or floor. Moreover, due to wind and stack effects, apartments on the lower floors or windward side routinely heat infiltrating air and "donate" it to their upstairs or leeward neighbors. Finally, apartments vary greatly in their exposure to sun and wind, in the area of their external walls and ceilings, and the like. The square footage of area in an apartment is *one* determinant of the costs of energy of any particular apartment, though certainly not the sole determinant and possibly not the primary determinant.

4.5.3.3 Types of Energy Cost Allocation

Energy costs can be allocated using three primary types of cost allocation equipment. These include:

(1) equipment providing allocations based on measurements of energy use that can be calibrated;

(2) equipment providing allocations based on relative monitoring of energy use; and

(3) equipment providing allocations based on relative thermal comfort.

The *first* type of equipment used in energy cost allocations involves *measurements of energy use that can be calibrated.* This type of system measures and stores the actual thermal output of the heating or cooling system within an individual tenant's unit. The principle underlying use of this equipment is that tenants should be billed based on the proportion of the energy supplied to their unit.

The *second* type of system used involves a *relative monitoring* of energy use. These systems measure and store one or more parameters that are *related* to the thermal output (or input) to an individual living unit. These systems

165 Correspondence, Martha Hewitt, Ctr. for Energy and the Urban Environment, to Michael Ticklin, Chief of Legislative Analysis, New Jersey Dep't of Cmty. Affairs (June 12, 1992).

166 *Id.*

167 Sonderegger, R.C., *Movers and Stayers: The Resident's Contribution to Variation Across Houses in Energy Consumption for Space Heating*, Energy and Buildings, No. 3, at 313–24 (1978).

168 D.L. Bleviss & A.A. Gravitz, Washington D.C.: Energy Conservation Coalition, Energy Conservation and Existing Rental Housing, (1984).

169 M.J. Hewett et al., *Heating Cost Allocation in Multi-Family Buildings: Energy Savings and Implementation Standards*, ASHRAE Transactions, Vol. 95, No. 1 (1989).

cannot, however, measure sufficient parameters to provide a measurement of input or output that can be calibrated.[170] The principle underlying use of this equipment is that tenants should be billed based in *approximate* proportion to the energy supplied to their unit. The use of allocation systems of this type assumes that the parameters that are *not* measured will either be relatively constant as between units, have a negligible impact on energy use as between units, or will vary in such a way as to have the same relative effect on energy use as between units.

The *third* type of system used involves a *monitoring of the relative thermal comfort* of an individual unit. These systems are based on the principle that tenants should be charged in proportion to the level of thermal comfort maintained in their unit. The "comfort" is measured relative to some reference comfort level or to outdoor conditions. Thermal comfort can be measured either by monitoring the setpoint temperature of the thermostat controlling heat delivery to a unit or by monitoring actual space temperature at some representative location within the unit.

In each case, allocation of energy costs cannot result in absolute system accuracy in measuring the actual energy costs of supplying a particular unit. Units in a multifamily building may receive indirect energy from warm distribution pipes, infiltration of warm air from lower units to upper units and the like. The belief is simply that even if not exact, cost allocation generally is more accurate and equitable than inclusion of energy costs in the rent. Finally, the belief is that it is more important for an allocation system to be "equitable" than for it to be "accurate." Such systems are not seeking to measure actual energy consumption, as much as they are seeking to determine relative consumption between units.[171]

170 Examples of approximation devices would include time-based devices, such as equipment that measures the open time on a gas valve, the run time on a fan-coil motor, or the length of time that a heating element is above a certain minimum temperature. Examples also include volume-based devices such as equipment that measures the volume of hot or cold liquid flowing through a heating element. Evaporative allocation devices are a third example. This kind of equipment contains a vial of liquid on the heating element that evaporates at a rate roughly proportional to the temperature of the heating element. A final example of such devices include temperature-based devices. These measure one or more temperatures relating to thermal output. This may measure a temperature at a single point on the heating element, the temperature of the distribution medium (for example, water, air, and so forth) entering and leaving the element, or the temperature of the room air entering and leaving the heating element. This list is exemplary and not comprehensive.

171 The actual costs to the landlord are known and measurable. The cost allocation system seeks to divide up those costs for payment by the respective tenants.

4.5.3.4 Unfair and Deceptive Acts and Practices (UDAP) Challenges to Allocation Systems

State UDAP statutes can be used to challenge retail practices that are "unfair" and "deceptive." Some of the claims that an advocate may wish to consider include claims under the prohibition of "deceptive" practices. These may be highly fact-specific, but it seems likely that many allocation systems would be subject to such challenges. For example, claims by a management company that an energy cost allocation system will result in a reasonable determination of the cost of the use of the utility attributable to an individual unit may well be deceptive.

Claims that an energy cost allocation system is used as a means to promote energy conservation on the part of tenants are deceptive, if the reduced usage by one tenant does not affect the energy consumed in the operation of the master boiler. Remember, this is not simply a master-metering situation. There is a single boiler; it is not clear at all that the boiler's fuel use will decrease as a result of conservation by a single tenant. Indeed, with many boilers, there is a minimum level of use that must be maintained for the boiler to operate at maximum efficiency.

Finally, it may be "deceptive" for the property owner to claim that it is less expensive to the tenants for energy costs to be allocated through an allocation mechanism than it is for such costs to be included in rents but then to refuse to lower the rent once an allocation system is installed.

In addition to claims that the energy cost allocation system is "deceptive," one can argue that it is "unfair" as well. It is unfair, first, to impose the energy cost allocation system as a means to promote conservation unless the tenants have the means by which to control their usage. It is unfair, second, to impose the energy cost allocation system as a means to promote conservation when the reduction of tenant usage will *not* result in reduced bills. It is unfair, finally, to impose the energy cost allocation system as a means to allocate the costs of the usage in individual apartments, when, in fact, the allocated costs include common areas, vacant apartments, office space and the like. Again, this is a fact-specific situation that must be determined.

In an evaluation of energy cost allocation systems in Washington state, it was reported that the UDAP statute was used in a similar fashion in 1986.[172] This report states that in the fall of 1986, the Washington state Attorney General's Office filed a complaint (No. 86-2-20347 8) against the firm installing energy cost allocation devices,[173] the owner of the firm, and the manufacturer of the equipment being installed.[174] The Attorney General alleged violations of the state Unfair Business Practices—Consumer Protection

172 M.J. Hewett & H.L. Emslander, Minneapolis Energy Office, Heating Cost Allocation: An Update on Activities in the U.S. and Europe (Mar. 1988).

173 Monetech, Inc.

174 Synergetics International.

Act.[175] A consent decree was approved by the King County Superior Court in September 1986. Although it may not be construed as an admission of any of the allegations, the consent decree included a number of injunctions against Synergetics, enjoining them from, among other things, representing that the allocation system will perform in a fashion similar to a conversion to individual heating systems; representing that the allocation system measures actual individual energy usage; failing to clearly state that the system is an allocation system, not a measurement system; representing that the system meets any accuracy standards; representing that the tenant can receive a lower energy bill through conservation, without concurrently describing the material factors that will affect each tenant's bill; and failing to give each resident for which an energy bill was estimated an accurate description of the way in which the bill was calculated.[176]

A similar consent decree was approved by the court between the installer of the energy cost allocation system and the state Attorney General's office. This decree contained injunctions similar to those against Synergetics. In addition, however, a second set of injunctions enjoined the installer from: failing to install the system in a workmanlike fashion; failing to maintain the system in good working order; and installing the system in buildings where it "is inappropriate because the heating equipment is either in poor working order or some other consideration exists which would affect the ability of the system to work properly."

Finally, the report notes, an official of the Seattle department of Weights and Measures, which had earlier won a lawsuit holding that the allocation devices were "commercial measurement devices" and thus subject to regulation by the city,[177] stated that cities "could more easily address (heat-cost allocation systems) from the perspective of fair business practices, as the Attorney General's office did, than from the perspective of the technical issues. . . ."[178]

4.5.3.5 Potential Regulations Covering Buildings Where Energy Costs Are Allocated

There may be situations in which low-income advocates may wish to seek prospective regulation of energy cost allocations through local ordinances, state statute, or state agency regulation. The primary purpose of a reliance on energy cost allocation systems is to promote the conservation of energy by tenants. As discussed above, the direct billing of tenant-used energy has been found to result in reductions of energy costs from 10%–25%. Implicit within this observation, however, is the assumption that tenants have control over their energy consumption.

If, due to lack of direct tenant controls (such as functioning apartment-specific thermostats), due to lack of building maintenance, or due to lack of heating and cooling system maintenance, tenants do *not* have effective control over energy consumption, the conservation justification for an energy cost allocation system cannot be fulfilled and such a system should not be implemented. A simple on/off valve does not provide adequate resident control to form a basis for allocation.[179]

Before a tenant rents a particular unit, the prospective tenant should be told of the use of an energy cost allocation system. This notification should include that the tenant will be directly billed for energy costs as determined by an allocation system and of the terms of the billing (such as length of the billing period and the intervals between reading, billing, due date and past due date). Moreover, the prospective tenant should be told that the energy cost allocation system may approximate the relative use of energy in the individual unit, vis-à-vis other units, rather than measuring actual energy consumption.

If the approximate energy use for an individual unit has been determined previously by use of an energy cost allocation system, the prospective tenant should be provided with the highest and lowest monthly energy cost billed to the particular unit in a month,[180] the average monthly energy cost billed to the same unit, and the average monthly energy cost billed to all similar sized leased units within the facility in the preceding twelve months.

Finally, the prospective tenant should be informed of influences on energy usage and costs, including the nature and extent of weatherization; the fuel source, age, type and general maintenance schedule of the heating and cooling system; and other factors affecting energy use. This disclosure should also include information about actions residents can take to decrease energy use.

Remember, every representation that is required of a landlord using an energy cost allocation system may serve as the basis for some type of subsequent legal action to enforce the rights of the tenant. Some representations may become express terms of the contract. Other representations, if they turn out to be in error, might be found to be material misrepresentations in the inducement of the contract.

Maintenance of the building and its heating and cooling system may not only affect the amount of energy consumed by the resident but can affect the equitability of an energy cost allocation system as well. The question raised by building and system maintenance is whether the lack of maintenance renders invalid the assumptions implicit in the

175 Wash. Rev. Code §§ 19.86.010 to 19.86.920.

176 M.J. Hewett & H.L. Emslander, Minneapolis Energy Office, Heating Cost Allocation: An Update on Activities in the U.S. and Europe 6–7 (Mar. 1988).

177 Mass. King County Cause 85-2-15555-6 (1986).

178 M.J. Hewett & H.L. Emslander, Minneapolis Energy Office, Heating Cost Allocation: An Update on Activities in the U.S. and Europe 8 (Mar. 1988).

179 An example of an on/off valve is a manual valve on a radiator.

180 For each month the unit was fully rented.

allocation method. For example, assumptions about the relationship between space temperature in an apartment and space temperature at the thermostat may not be valid if the building and heating and cooling system are not properly maintained. Moreover, assumptions about air and/or water flow within a heating and cooling system must be accurate in order for an energy cost allocation system to be accurate.

If a consumer believes that the bill rendered by an energy cost allocation system does not accurately approximate his or her relative energy consumption, the consumer could very well be in a difficult situation, as it requires time and resources to verify that the building design and level of maintenance are sufficient to assure an equitable allocation with the energy cost allocation system chosen. Submetering rules may provide tenants with the right to know the formula for the allocation and to see the information on which the customer's bill is based. This is also likely to be treated as a landlord-tenant dispute as opposed to a utility service dispute.[181]

4.5.4 Use of Allocation Formulas for Water

With the recent trend to shift rising water bills directly onto tenants, one method of billing is particularly troublesome--the use of water allocation formulas or ratio-utility billing systems (RUBS). The mantra of those advocating for directly shifting the costs of water and sewer bills onto tenants is that it promotes conservation. While there is some merit to this argument in the case of submetering, it is much harder to accept in the case of RUBS. The allocation formulas can be based on factors such as the number of occupants, the number of bedrooms, square footage, and individually metered hot or cold water usage.[182] These are proxies for water usage, and consequently sewer usage, and fail to capture the vast range of actual water usage from household to household. For example, an allocation formula based on the number of occupants does not account for how much time a tenants actually spends in a unit. For example, a tenant who spends much of her time on the road for work will very likely use less water (and thus sewer services) than a tenant who works out of her unit. An allocation based on square footage costs per household could unfairly charge a senior living alone in a two-bedroom unit the same as a young family of four whose one parent and two young children remain at home most of the time. Indeed, under RUBS, a household that makes extra efforts to conserve water will not be paying a water bill that reflects those actual savings. The United States Environmental Protection Agency also expressed its doubts about the conservation claims of RUBS proponents when it declined to include properties billing with RUBS in its recent policy change concerning the applicability of the Safe Drinking Water Act on submetered properties.[183]

In 2003 a Maryland state delegate introduced a bill to ban RUBS, H.B. 976 (Delegates Bobo and James) Residential Landlord and Tenant—Ratio Utility System—Prohibition (2003). The bill was in response to tenants, billed through RUBS, having water bills comparable to single-family homeowners with washing machines, lawns, and pools.[184] RUBS has been described as "terribly arbitrary" by Richard Miller of the Maryland Office of People's Counsel.[185] The National Apartment Association argued that the H.B. 976 was premature, would lead to higher rents and make additional research necessary.[186] The legislation failed to pass in 2003.

A fallback to securing an outright ban on RUBS is to regulate the practice. As noted above, a bill to ban RUBS statewide failed in Maryland, but in November 2003 the Department of Housing and Community Affairs for Montgomery County, Maryland, issued a regulation regarding the practices of landlords using RUBS to allocate water and wastewater costs to tenants. The regulation prescribes the registration of landlords using RUBS, the formulas for calculating bills (including, for example, deductions for common areas that are not separately metered or submetered), the content of the bills and related recordkeeping, and the Department's complaint procedure in the event that a dispute is not first resolved between the landlord and tenant.[187] In October 2003, the Seattle City Council passed

---

181 765 Ill. Comp. Stat. 740/5 (landlord, condominium, or community association must provide tenant with written copy of formula used by landlord for allocating public utility payments among the tenants); Tex. Util. Code Ann. § 184.052 (West) (apartment house rental agreement must include clear description of method of computing allocation of central system utilities or non-submetered master-metered utilities); 22 Va. Admin. Code § 5-305-100 (records for calculating charges for electric or natural gas service must be retained for three years and tenant's submeter or energy allocation readings and billings for lesser of the tenancy or three years must be available for inspection upon tenant's request). *See also* Md. Code Regs. §§ 20.26.03.05, 20.26.03.06 (if complaint to owner of apartment building, condominium, or cooperative is not resolved, owner must advise tenant in writing that a formal complaint about amount billed under energy allocation system may be filed with Consumer Protection Division of the Office of Attorney General).

182 *See, e.g.*, Ariz. Rev. Stat. Ann. § 33-1314.01(F); 30 Tex. Admin Code § 291.122.

183 "Water savings, if any, from RUBS and hot water hybrid billing systems (HWH) are uncertain. At this time, EPA believes that RUBS or other allocation billing systems do not meet the definition of submetering, as used in this policy, *and do not encourage water conservation*." 68 Fed. Reg. 74235 (Dec. 23, 2003) (emphasis added).

184 Liz Kay, *Foes of Unmetered Billing Rebut the Conservation Argument*, Balt. Sun, Mar. 19, 2003; Jason Song, *Delegates to Debate Unmetered Billing Ban*, Balt. Sun, Mar. 18, 2003.

185 As quoted in Liz Kay, *Foes of Unmetered Billing Rebut the Conservation Argument*, Balt. Sun, Mar. 19, 2003.

186 *Id.*

187 Montgomery County Dep't of Hous. & Cmty. Affairs, Ratio

an ordinance that prohibits deceptive and fraudulent practices related to third-part billing for master metered or other unmetered utility service.[188] It defines as a deceptive and fraudulent business practice third-part billing failing to comport with the practices set out in the ordinance. These practices include protection of a tenant's personal information, provision of advance written notice of the billing practice to the tenant (including methodology of the billing), posting of current utility bills for the building, limits on the total charges and on fees, licensing and registration of the third-part billing agent, and a dispute resolution process including filing a complaint with the Office of Hearing Examiner or civil action against the landlord. The ordinance provides for actual damages and a $100 penalty. Attorney fees and a higher penalty are available for deliberate violations.[189] A number of states also regulate submetering and RUBS. In Texas, apartment owners who submeter or use RUBS must adhere to the rules of the Texas Commission on Environmental Quality.[190] Under the submetering and RUBS rules, landlords in Texas must disclose these billing practices and the methodology in the rental agreement as well as the rights of the tenant to contest the bills.[191] Landlords are limited as to which fees can be charged to tenants and cannot make a profit from submetering or use of RUBS.[192]

Advocates fighting the use of RUBS for water should also explore the applicability of the state's UDAP statute.

4.5.5 Advanced Metering Infrastructure and Dynamic Pricing Structures Background

Advanced metering infrastructure (AMI) consists of (1) "smart" electricity, natural gas, or water meters that are capable of monitoring and recording customer usage on an hourly or more frequent basis, (2) a communications network capable of sending usage and pricing information between the utility and the customer, and (3) meter data management systems and software.[193] Some utility companies and other proponents of AMI deployment argue that the technologies are necessary to implement time-of-use pricing, which in turn is needed to send consumers accurate price signals and enable efficient usage of energy resources.[194] In addition to support of time-based rate design, proponents argue that smart meters and AMI enhance efficiency of utility operations through automated meter reading, identification of outages and theft, and capacity for remote service disconnection and restoration.

Real-time or dynamic retail pricing structures are intended to fluctuate according to changes in wholesale prices and thus "enable" consumers to shift usage to low-price periods. Such structures include time-of-use rates (a process by which a customer's usage is recorded on an hourly basis and billed at a set price assigned to each hour); real-time pricing (a customer's usage is recorded on an hourly basis and billed at a price determined by changes in the wholesale spot market price); and critical peak pricing (when usage during the highest peak periods is billed at a very high price). Critical peak pricing may be used in conjunction with time-of-use rates and real-time pricing.[195]

The concept of time-based retail pricing of utility service and deployment of advanced meters or AMI has been proposed or approved in all but six states in the United States.[196] By 2010, utilities had announced plans for deployment of approximately 65 million advanced meters by 2015, representing about one half of all U.S. households.[197]

New federal standards regarding time-based pricing and utility metering are delineated in sections 1251, 1252, and 1254 of the Energy Policy Act of 2005. Key provisions and analysis of these sections is contained on the companion website to this treatise. In addition, the Energy Indepen-

---

Utility Billing System, Reg. No. 3-03AM (Nov. 25, 2003), *available at* www.montgomerycountymd.gov/content/dhca/housing/pdf/rubs%20regulation%203-03AM-clean2.pdf.

188 Seattle, Wash., Mun. Code ch. 7.25 (2003).

189 *Id.*

190 Tex. Water Code Ann. §§ 13.501–13.506 (West).

191 *Id. Cf.* Ariz. Rev. Stat. Ann. §§ 33-1314.01, 33-2107; Va. Code Ann. § 55-226.2.

192 Tex. Water Code Ann. §§ 13.501–13.506 (West).

193 Advanced metering infrastructure incorporates new and rapidly changing technologies. The concept of AMI and proposed applications are also in a state of flux. For definitions of AMI and its components, as well as detailed discussion of the technologies and their applications, see Barbara Alexander, Smart Meters, Real Time Pricing and Demand Response Programs: Implications for Low Income Electric Customers (May 2007), *available at* www.nasuca.org/archive/Alexander%20Smart%20Meter.ppt; Nancy Brockway, National Regulatory Research Inst., Advanced Metering Infrastructure: What Regulators Need to Know About Its Value to Residential Customers (Feb. 2008), *available at* www.energetics.com/MADRI/toolbox/pdfs/vision/Brockway_on_AMI.pdf; Rick Hornby et al., Synapse Energy Economics, Inc., Advanced Metering Infrastructure—Implications for Residential Customers in New Jersey (July 2008), *available at* www.synapse-energy.com/cgi-bin/synapsePublications.pl (enter year of publication, then select title from drop-down list); Federal Energy Regulatory Comm'n, Assessment of Demand Response and Advanced Metering, 2007 Staff Report (Sept. 2007), *available at* www.ferc.gov/legal/staff-reports/09-07-demand-response.pdf.

194 *See, e.g.*, Steven Braithwait, Dan Hansen, & Michael O'Sheasy, Edison Elec. Inst., Retail Pricing and Rate Design in Evolving Markets (July 2007); Itron, Inc., The Critical Role of Advanced Metering Technology in Optimizing Energy Efficiency and Delivery (2005), *available at* www.energetics.com/madri/toolbox/pdfs/vision/critical.pdf.

195 Barbara Alexander, Smart Meters, Real Time Pricing and Demand Response Programs: Implications for Low Income Electric Customers 10, 11 (May 2007).

196 As of July 2011, Missouri, New Hampshire, Rhode Island, Tennessee, Utah, and Wyoming were the only U.S. states that had not approved AMI deployment on at least a pilot basis.

197 Institute for Electric Efficiency, Utility ScaleSmart Meter Deployments, Plans and Proposals (Sept. 2010).

dence and Security Act of 2007 includes provisions directing states to encourage utilities to deploy "smart grid" technologies, including advanced meters, and allow utilities to collect such investments through rates.[198] Furthermore, the 2009 American Recovery and Reinvestment Act included an appropriation of $4.5 billion for electricity grid modernization initiatives, over $2.8 billion of which went for utility grants to install advanced meters.[199]

While Congress and the U.S. Department of Energy have supported deployment of AMI through policy statements and funding initiatives, jurisdiction over retail electric utility rates and operations lies with state public utility commissions.[200] Public utilities commissions in most states have approved at least partial deployment of AMI. However, some commissions in recent decisions have placed financial and consumer protection conditions on such approvals. For example, in Maryland the public service commission rejected Baltimore Gas and Electric Company's request for preapproved, automated recovery of costs associated with AMI deployment. The commission made any future cost recovery contingent upon a showing by the Baltimore Gas and Electric Company that the company had delivered a cost-effective metering system to consumers.[201] In Nevada, after approving deployment of AMI by Nevada Power Company, the public utilities commission issued an order adopting regulations establishing an increased arrearage threshold for disconnection of AMI customers, limited hours for remote disconnection of service, same-day reconnection requirements, temperature-based disconnection protections, and a requirement that elder or disabled customers with advanced electric meters receive a premise visit and in-person notification prior to disconnection of electric service.[202]

4.5.6 AMI and Low-Income Consumers

Adoption of time-based pricing and deployment of AMI technology carry profound ramifications for residential utility customers, particularly those with low incomes. First, the cost of new meters that would replace existing electromechanical devices, along with associated communications and data management capabilities, will place significant upward pressure on rates. Depending on the particular configuration of functionalities and capabilities, AMI can cost between $100 and $525 per meter.[203] Costs for remote meter reading are between $100 and $175 per meter. "Demand response" components, including load control capabilities and communication capabilities to provide customers with pricing information, add an additional $100 to $350 per meter.[204] In fact, investments in AMI will in most cases lead to utility requests for rate increases because savings in utility operating costs typically do not offset the cost of the investment.[205] Furthermore, customer savings from usage reductions during relatively high-priced periods combined with utility operating cost savings are insufficient to justify an AMI investment.[206] To the extent that the significant cost of AMI investments will not be borne by utility shareholders, but instead is be recovered through approved increases in fixed customer charges, low-income customers who typically use less energy than higher-income residential customers will be disproportionately penalized.

In addition to absorbing the costs of purchasing and installing new, expensive meters and related infrastructure, adoption of mandatory time-based pricing structures could result in increased monthly usage costs for low-income residential utility consumers. Time-of-use rates, real-time pricing, and critical peak pricing are based on the theoretical assumptions that consumers will receive timely pricing information and that they will then shift usage from higher-priced periods to lower-priced periods. However, low-income households typically use less home energy than their higher-income counterparts, with consumption concentrated in necessary and non-discretionary end uses such as refrigeration, lighting, and basic heating and cooling. The ability of these households to shift usage to lower-priced off-peak periods without compromising basic health and safety is limited.

Time-based pricing and deployment of AMI will thus likely exert considerable upward pressure on monthly home energy costs borne by low-income consumers. Advanced meters also carry substantial customer service ramifications. A key feature of new metering technology allows utility companies to remotely disconnect and reconnect service without making a premise visit and giving a customer threatened with loss of service a chance to make a payment.

198 Energy Independence and Securities Act, tit. XIII, § 1307, *codified at* 16 U.S.C. § 2621(d).

199 www.cfo.doe.gov/budget/10budget/Content/Highlights/FY2010Highlights.pdf.

200 *See* § 1.2.2.2, *supra*.

201 *In re* Application of Baltimore Gas & Electric Co. for Authorization to Deploy a Smart Grid Initiative and to Establish a Surcharge for Recovery of Costs, No. 9208, Order 83410 (Md. Pub. Serv. Comm'n Apr. 2009).

202 Investigation and Rulemaking Regarding Revisions to the Consumer Bill of Rights Regulations As Impacted by Aspects of Advanced Service Delivery, Order Adopting Temporary Regulations, No. 10-07024 (Pub. Util. Comm'n of Nev. May 2011).

203 Nancy Brockway, National Regulatory Research Inst., Advanced Metering Infrastructure: What Regulators Need to Know About Its Value to Residential Customers 12 (Feb. 2008).

204 Plexus Research Inc., Edison Elec. Inst., Deciding on Smart Meters: The Technology Implications of Section 1252 of the Energy Policy Act of 2005, at xii (Sept. 2005), *available at* www.edisonfoundation.net/iee/reports/deciding_on_smart_meters.pdf.

205 Rick Hornby et. al., Synapse Energy Economics, Inc., Advanced Metering Infrastructure—Implications for Residential Customers in New Jersey 5, 6 (July 2008), *available at* www.synapse-energy.com/cgi-bin/synapsePublications.pl (enter year of publication, then select title from drop-down list).

206 *Id.*

The number of disconnections, with the accompanying adverse impact on customers, will thus likely increase dramatically absent adoption and enforcement of enhanced consumer protections.[207]

Advocates should be skeptical of proposals to replace manual disconnection of service for nonpayment of necessary electric utility service with automated, remote disconnection. This is of particular concern when the practice of establishing personal contact with the customer at the time of disconnection is simultaneously abandoned. The capacity of advanced meters and related infrastructure to allow utilities to remotely disconnect electric service without a precautionary dispatch of field personnel brings up the potential for increased rates of service disconnection and threatens health and safety.

The remote disconnection capabilities of AMI increase the ease and efficiency with which utility companies may disconnect essential electric utility service. By contrast, the number of disconnections of analog meters that may be accomplished by a utility in a given workday is limited by the number of vehicles and field personnel available to manually disconnect service. In proposing deployment of AMI, companies in utility commission proceedings across the country have touted operational cost savings based on the ability to remotely disconnect service to customers for nonpayment, thus ending the need for field personnel and vehicles necessary to disconnect analog meters. Without the physical limitations on shutoffs imposed by the number of field personnel employed by a utility and the number of trucks in its fleet, it is reasonable to expect that rates of disconnection of necessary electric utility service will increase.[208]

Initial experience with AMI deployment in California in 2009 provides evidence of increased disconnection rates stemming from implementation of remote disconnection. Pacific Gas and Electric (PG&E) began remotely disconnecting customers using advanced meters in April 2009. Other major electric utilities in California had not begun implementing remote disconnection at that time. PG&E's disconnection rates spiked subsequent to remote disconnection implementation, while the rates of the other electric utilities remained flat or declined.[209]

207 Barbara Alexander, Smart Meters, Real Time Pricing and Demand Response Programs: Implications for Low Income Electric Customers 16 (May 2007).

208 *See, e.g.*, Potomac Elec. Power Co. & Delmarva Power and Light Co., Request for the Deployment of Advanced Meter Infrastructure, No. 9207 (Md. Pub. Serv. Comm'n, 2009) (referencing to page 13 of direct testimony of William Potts).

209 Division of Ratepayer Advocates, Status of Energy Utility Service Disconnections in California 7 (Nov. 2009).

4.5.7 Advanced Metering Equity Principles

4.5.7.1 General

As state legislatures, regulatory utility commissions, and utility distribution and supply companies consider acquisition and deployment of advanced electric meters, advocates may review proposals and respond based on the extent to which proposals comport with the following guidelines and principles.

4.5.7.2 Maintain Existing Consumer Protections

Utilities should not be permitted to use advanced meters as a means for reducing consumer protections with regard to electric service in general and service disconnection procedures in particular. The notices and warnings that typically are required prior to service disconnection provide important protections for low-income and other vulnerable customers and often avoid negative consequences, from misunderstandings to tragedies.[210]

4.5.7.3 AMI and Prepayment

The implementation of advanced metering should not be used to degrade existing consumer protections in the area of prepayment. The implementation of advanced metering should not lead to new requirements for prepayment of electric service.[211]

4.5.7.4 Analysis of Costs and Benefits

Prior to implementation of advanced meters, states and utilities should conduct detailed analysis of the costs and benefits of a proposed advanced metering program and any attendant rate design changes. This analysis should encompass:

- Bill impact resulting from rate design changes, such as time-of-use and critical peak pricing rates, on different residential and business customer classes;
- Bill impact or other effects on users in various usage and demographic profiles, including low-income consumers, older consumers, consumers with severe health conditions, and other consumers whose electric loads are relatively low or not easily shifted to off-peak times of the day;
- How the cost of additional equipment needed to be purchased or rented by individual ratepayers in order to participate in any voluntary or mandatory utility advanced metering program affects the cost-benefit analysis;

210 *See* appx. A, *infra* (state rules and regulations pertaining to service disconnection notification requirements).

211 *See* § 4.6, *infra* (discussing prepayment metering).

- How the cost of advanced metering included in rates are allocated among the various classes of customers served by the utility; and
- Whether an advanced metering program may lead to a reduced need to build new peaking capacity or transmission and distribution infrastructure or to environmental benefits through decreased fuel use; may reduce the electricity bills of some customers through dynamic pricing options; or may create other system or consumer benefits that offset the costs paid by ratepayers.

4.5.7.5 Pilots Before Full Implementation

To determine costs and benefits of a proposed advanced metering program for a specific location or region, states and utilities should, prior to widespread implementation of advanced meters, consider running a pilot program that is properly designed and includes independent evaluation.

4.5.7.6 Recovery of Prudently Incurred Costs

Utilities should be expected to implement any advanced metering program with prudence and collect at most only the net costs in rates. Any cost overruns, benefit shortfalls, or other negative impact arising from the failure of a utility to implement an advanced metering program in a prudent way should remain the responsibility of utility shareholders, not ratepayers.

4.5.7.7 Least-Cost Means of Achieving Policy Goals

States and utilities should analyze the interaction of proposed advanced metering programs with demand response measures and rate design to determine whether any proposed new infrastructure or program is the most cost-effective way to achieve the stated goals. In particular, states and utilities should consider whether some of the goals expected to be achieved through implementing advanced meters, such as reductions in overall peak electricity loads or in energy usage, could be or already are being accomplished at low net cost to ratepayers in the aggregate through direct load control programs, such as those that offer customers value for interrupting central air conditioning or heat pumps during critical peak hours.

4.5.7.8 No Mandatory Participation in Dynamic Pricing Rate Designs

Implementation of advanced metering should not lead to mandatory or "opt-out" dynamic pricing of electricity usage for residential customers.

4.5.7.9 Security Standards

Any implementation of advanced meters should be administered through specific policies and programs that meet federal and applicable standards for security and protect the privacy of customer usage information, both with respect to usage data derived by the utility for customer billing and information obtained concerning a customer's specific usage of electricity.

4.5.7.10 Consumer Education and Outreach

Any advanced metering program or pilot must be accompanied by a vigorous education and outreach effort to ensure, at a minimum, that participating and non-participating customers are aware of the projected goals and impacts of the program and that participating customers will understand how to utilize equipment provided by the utility and how the deployment would affect them, and to address concerns about privacy of customer usage information.

4.6 Prepaid Utility Service Using Prepayment Meters or Advanced Metering Infrastructure with Remote Disconnection Capability

4.6.1 Introduction

With diminishing regulation and increasing pressure on utility companies to consolidate, utility companies actively strive to reduce levels of outstanding customer debt.[212] In Great Britain, South Africa and, increasingly, the United States and Canada, an arrearage reduction tool favored by industry entails installation and operation of prepayment utility meters or offering prepaid service using advanced meters with remote disconnection and reconnection capabilities. While technologies and payment models vary, prepaid service always entails requiring customers to pay in advance for utility service, with prepaid account balances decreasing as service is delivered. In most instances in which prepaid service is delivered, service is automatically suspended when account balances are depleted.

Proponents argue that prepayment meters provide customers with an added measure of control. However, in reality they are intended to provide utility companies with a means of reducing new arrearages while bypassing the existing state utility consumer protection framework. Furthermore, proliferation of prepayment meters results in an increase in rates of disconnection of low-income households and therefore represents an attack on the ideal of universal

212 *See* § 1.1.4, *supra* (discussing in general deregulation of the utility industry).

access to affordable, reliable utility service. Termination under use of prepayment meters is often "hidden" in that is not accompanied by customer notification and adherence to regulated termination procedures. Finally, the technology is expensive. In a competitive utility environment, it is reasonable to expect that the high cost of prepayment meters will be passed along to ratepayers and that these high costs will be borne by those least able to absorb them.

4.6.2 Prepayment Technologies

Prepaid utility service has traditionally been provided through installation of a dedicated prepayment meter. Prepayment utility meter technology varies widely and has evolved over time. Some systems include display units installed in customers' homes, distribution of plastic magnetic strip cards that are used to "load" the home meter after deposit of funds at "pay center" units or other locations that are placed in various locations around the utility's service area, and a central processor generally located at the utility company's billing facility. The customer display units, if provided, show the dollar amount of credit remaining and oftentimes other information regarding customer energy usage. Some in-home display units include warning alert systems that activate when credit is running low. Pay centers generally accept cash or electronic debit transfers. Customers pay in advance for service, with payment balances decreasing as service is delivered. Service is automatically disconnected if the payment balance is depleted. Service is restored only when additional payment is rendered and the customer returns to load the meter.

Increasingly, with the widespread deployment of advanced metering infrastructure, utility companies are considering delivering prepaid service through AMI rather than through the use of stand-alone prepayment meters that do not allow for time-differentiated pricing. With the cost of AMI already having been approved for many utility companies, the prospect of moving payment-troubled customers to prepaid service without the need to make substantial new capital and systems upgrade investments is particularly attractive.

4.6.3 Experience in Great Britain

Prepayment meters have become commonplace in Great Britain, which began deregulation of its utility industries earlier than the beginning of experiments in the United States. The number of customers using the systems had nearly doubled between 1990 and 1997.[213] Currently, about 6.2 million residential natural gas and electric utility customers in Great Britain use prepayment meters, representing about 13% of all installed residential meters.[214]

Prepayment meters in Great Britain are concentrated disproportionately in lower-income households. In 2010, 60% of electricity and natural gas customers with prepayment meters had annual incomes below £17,500.[215] Furthermore, over half of prepayment meter customers received a means-tested benefit, nearly half had an unemployed head of household, and more than a third had one or more household members with a long-term physical or mental illness or disability.[216]

Not surprisingly, many utility companies have reported a significant decline in the rate of traditional utility-initiated disconnections since the proliferation of prepayment meters in low-income households. However, one study showed that 34% of prepayment meter customers disconnected at least once during the a twelve-month period, usually because of a lack of funds.[217] More recently, research indicated that, among prepayment customers, 16% had "self-disconnected" at least once over the previous year, 22% had sacrificed other necessities to remain connected to utility service, 45% had cut back on energy usage, and 54% had resorted to use of an "emergency credit" to remain connected to service.[218]

4.7 Prepayment Meters in the United States

4.7.1 State Regulations Controlling Use of Prepayment Meters

Several state commissions have promulgated regulations that specify conditions under which utility companies may install prepayment meters. Regulations in Pennsylvania impose the most far-reaching conditions on utilities that propose to install and operate prepayment meters. In Pennsylvania, regulations require that prepayment meters may only be used in cases when the ratepayer is considered to be non-low-income (defined here as gross household income of greater than 150% of federal poverty income guidelines), has outstanding arrears and is requesting a payment plan that is unacceptable to the utility, and service is being delivered to an individually-metered residential dwelling.[219] In addition, Pennsylvania regulations prohibit use of pre-

213 Center for Sustainable Energy & Nat'l Right to Fuel Campaign, Counting the Hidden Disconnected 8–9 (1998).

214 Office of Gas & Elec. Markets, Domestic Suppliers' Social Obligations: 2010 Annual Report 21, 22 (June 2011).

215 Hannah Mummery & Holly Reilly, Consumer Focus, Cutting Back, Cutting Down, Cutting Off: Self-Disconnection Among Prepayment Meter Users 5 (July 2010).

216 *Id.*

217 National Right to Fuel Campaign, Competitive Energy Markets and Low-Income Consumers 56, 57 (2001).

218 Hannah Mummery & Holly Reilly, Consumer Focus Cutting Back, Cutting Down, Cutting Off: Self-Disconnection Among Prepayment Meter Users 17 (July 2010).

219 52 Pa. Code § 56.17.

payment meters unless the ratepayer voluntarily agrees to the installation of the meter, the ratepayer agrees to purchase prepayment cards to maintain service until the outstanding balance is retired, and the utility agrees to furnish the ratepayer with an emergency backup card for usage of at least five days.[220] Finally, Pennsylvania regulations require that utilities opting to use prepayment meters conduct an evaluation, over the first two years, of the degree to which the prepayment program operates efficiently and results in the continuation of utility service at a reasonable cost.[221]

Regulations in Connecticut (natural gas[222]) and Kentucky (natural gas[223]) specify that prepayment meters shall not be installed except when there is no other satisfactory method of collecting payment for utility service. In Florida (natural gas[224]), North Dakota (natural gas[225]), Oregon (natural gas, electricity[226] and water[227]), and Wyoming (electricity[228] and natural gas[229]), prepayment meters may not be used unless authorization is obtained from the public service commission. Regulations in Iowa (natural gas[230] and electricity[231]) and Oklahoma (electricity,[232] natural gas,[233] and water[234]) prohibit use of prepayment meters that are set to produce a rate higher than that which would be obtained through use of a standard meter, except in instances when the public utility commission grants special permission. Mississippi regulations provide for use of prepayment meters at the option of the utility company.[235]

The public utility commission of Texas in April 2011 adopted regulations pertaining to prepaid utility service offered by retail electric providers to customers with advanced metering systems. The regulations include provisions regarding allowable service setup and other fees, disconnection notification and timelines, and customer disclosures.[236]

220 *Id.*
221 *Id.*
222 Conn. Agencies Regs. § 16-11-21.
223 807 Ky. Admin. Regs. § 5:022.
224 Fla. Admin. Code Ann. r. 25-7.059.
225 N.D. Admin. Code 69-09-01-12.
226 Or. Admin. R. 860-023-0010.
227 Or. Admin. R. 860-036-0105.
228 P.S.C. UA-3 Wyo. Code. R. § 302.
229 P.S.C. UA-4 Wyo. Code. R. § 403.
230 Iowa Admin. Code r. 199-19.3(476).
231 Iowa Admin. Code r. 199-20.4(476).
232 Okla. Admin. Code § 165:35-15-18.
233 Okla. Admin. Code § 165:45-5-12.
234 Okla. Admin. Code § 165:65-7-3.
235 26-000-002 Miss. Code R. § 11(D) (LexisNexis).
236 Public Util. Comm'n of Tex., Order Adopting Repeal § 25.498 and New § 25.498 As Approved at the April 14, 2011 Open Meeting, Project No. 38675, Amendments to Customer Protection Rules Relating to Prepaid Service.

4.7.2 Experience in the United States

Salt River Project (SRP), Arizona's second largest electric utility and the third largest municipally owned utility in the United States, operates the SRP M-Power prepayment meter program, the largest program of its kind operating in the United States. The program included 100 customers in 1993 but had grown to 20,000 "budget challenged" participants by April 2002.[237] Currently, over 100,000 customers are enrolled in the Salt River Project program.[238]

Lower-income households make up a majority of SRP prepayment program participants. In 2010, the median household income of M-Power customers was $17,900, and 82% of program participants had household incomes of less than $30,000.[239] SRP does not release data on rates of disconnection among its prepayment customers.[240]

In addition to the SRP M-Power, smaller prepayment electricity programs are offered by utilities in Texas, Oklahoma, and Florida.

4.7.3 Prepayment Meters and Low-Income Utility Consumer Protections

Most U.S. states have adopted a comprehensive regulatory framework that provides low-income utility ratepayers with a range of consumer protections, including limited termination prohibitions, termination notice requirements, and a formal right to dispute a bill or utility practice.[241] A fundamental danger associated with prepayment meters is that they are intended to serve as a means of replacing the disconnection procedures governed by the existing regulatory framework with a technology-based procedure that does not involve regulators. As such, the technology poses a threat to the ideal of universal access to affordable utility service.

237 LIHEAP Clearinghouse, *available at* www.ncat.org/liheap/newslett/39net.htm.
238 Electric Power Research Inst., Paying Upfront: A Review of Salt River Project's M-Power Prepaid Program 1–4 (2010).
239 *Id.* at 4–6.
240 Unfortunately, little is known about the rates of and reasons for "self-disconnections" in the United States prepayment experiments. More research is required to obtain such information.
241 *See* appx. A, *infra* (summarizing utility commission regulations pertaining to utility consumer protections).

Chapter 5 Payment Issues: Payment, Security Deposits, and Late Charges

5.1 Payment

5.1.1 Introduction

There is no entitlement to free utility service.[1] Some arrangement for payment is required to obtain utility service,[2] and some payment is required to continue the service. The utility provider is generally under a statutory and/or regulatory duty to provide requested service and a contractual duty to the customer to continue the service according to the contract and applicable state and local utility regulations. The consumer is under an obligation to pay for the service.[3]

Payment in this context means the delivery or mailing of money or its equivalent (check, money order, credit card authorization, and so forth) by a utility customer or by someone on the customer's behalf in response to a bill sent by the utility company and the receipt and acceptance of the money by the utility company.[4] A customer has the right to a receipt as evidence of payment.[5] Various issues may arise concerning the details of this seemingly simple transaction, potentially leading to the threat of termination of utility service.

5.1.2 Tender of Payment

Ordinarily, utility service is provided upon request on an open account, and a bill for that service is then sent to the customer. Full and timely (by the "due date" printed on the bill) payment by any acceptable method pays this bill and completely discharges the underlying debt.[6]

If a customer attempts to pay a bill but the offer is not accepted by the company, a tender has occurred. A full tender—that is, offering the total amount due in a readily acceptable form—is a defense to late charges or to a threatened shut-off but does not discharge the debt; that is, a *tender* does not pay the bill.[7] Thus, if a customer offers to pay the bill and the offer is refused, the utility company, although it still has the right to collect the bill, should be barred from discontinuing service because of that unpaid bill and from later claiming late charges.

A partial tender, offering an amount less than the full amount of the bill that is rejected, stops neither late charges nor disconnection. An accepted partial payment, however, bars disconnection by the utility for that debt. The balance

1 *See* Morgan v. Kennedy, 331 F. Supp. 861, 864 (D. Neb. 1971) (no constitutional or statutory right to free utility service); Muhammad v. PG&E, 1998 WL 1110494 (Cal. Pub. Utils. Comm'n 1999); *In re* Rules and Regulations Governing the Disconnection of Utility Services, 2 P.U.R.4th 209, 214–15 (Vt. Pub. Serv. Bd. 1973) (customers are required to pay proper utility bills rendered for services provided, and utilities are entitled to discontinue service, under certain circumstances, for the nonpayment of bills).

2 *See* § 5.2, *infra* (deposits).

3 *See* Lamb v. Hamblin, 57 F.R.D. 58, 62 (D. Minn. 1972) (water service is "entitlement" limited to paying customers; no right to free water service); Denver Welfare Rights Org. v. Public Utils. Comm'n, 547 P.2d 239, 246 (Colo. 1976) (right to utility service qualified and dependent upon payment for service); Josephson v. Mountain Bell, 576 P.2d 850, 852 (Utah 1978) (telephone company obligated to provide service to potential customers so long as paid for). *See also* Bricker v. Deason, 655 So. 2d 1110 (Fla. 1995) (customer claim of safety violation by utility not proven; disconnection for nonpayment proper); Carr v. Southern Co., 438 S.E.2d 357 (Ga. 1994) (even when regulated entity defrauded commission to obtain rate, customer must pay rates set by Public Service Commission; otherwise judgment in case would be retroactive rate reduction and invasion of legislative function); § 6.1.1, *infra*. *But see* Popowsky v. Pennsylvania Pub. Utils. Comm'n, 647 A.2d 302 (Pa. Commw. Ct. 1994) (when utility company failed to get approval of its tariff before billing customer, PUC order requiring the customer to pay the bill or face termination was reversed; no bill owed because charges not lawful). *See generally* § 2.2, *supra* (who is the "customer" and thus liable).

4 *See* 60 Am. Jur. 2d *Payment* § 1 (2003); 70 C.J.S. *Payment* § 2 (2005).

5 60 Am. Jur. 2d *Payment* § 6.

6 60 Am. Jur. 2d *Payment* § 136; 70 C.J.S. *Payment* §§ 9, 32 (2005); 13 Corbin on Contracts § 67.3 (2003). *See In re* Carled, Inc., 91 F.3d 811 (6th Cir. 1996) (discussing industry practice concerning "due dates" and payments made after these dates; late payments by debtor to utility company not preferential transfer subject to set-aside by trustee since in ordinary course of business per § 547(c)(2) of Bankruptcy Code).

7 Multach v. Adams, 418 So. 2d 1254, 1255 (Fla. Dist. Ct. App. 1982) (landlord who refused tendered rent not entitled to interest or other damages); 60 Am. Jur. 2d *Payment* § 4 (2003); 13 Corbin on Contracts § 67.6 (2003).

of the debt is still owed, and late charges on the balance may be charged. In one case, disconnection after payment of an entire bill, but not of disputed late charges, subjected a utility to liability for damages for an unlawful disconnection.[8]

5.1.3 Partial Payment

Utilities can accept partial payments.[9] Accepting a partial payment may constitute accord and satisfaction that, under general contract law, also discharges a debt. Accord and satisfaction standards are applicable to utility billings when there is an "honest dispute" as to the bill.[10] If there is no genuine dispute as to the charges, a reduced payment is not accord and satisfaction.[11] However, in one case in which the customer notified the utility of the dispute, submitted a partial payment in the amount the customer believed was owed, designated this as full payment, and the utility kept the money, the bill was considered paid in full and accord and satisfaction reached.[12]

Additional problems arise when partial payments are made in a deregulated market.[13] For example, a utility may bill both for its own transmission and distribution services and for electricity purchased from a competitive electric services provider, or a local exchange carrier (LEC) may bill both for itself and for the long-distance carrier. When this "single bill option" is permitted, the statute or regulations must specify how partial payments are to be applied. However, some states that allow competitors to offer generation supply have come under pressure to change rules that initially provided that the entire amount of any partial payment should first be applied to the distribution company's bill for services. In Massachusetts, for example, the rules initially provided that, "if a Customer pays less than the full amount billed, the Company shall apply the payment first to distribution service and, if any payment remains, it shall be applied to generation service."[14] At the urging of competitive suppliers, the Massachusetts Department of Telecommunications and Energy (DTE) revised its rules to allocate partial payments between the distribution company and competitive supplier:

> The payment should first be allocated to distribution company and supplier charges in proportion to the percentage of the combined arrears represented by each charge. Any remaining payment should be allocated to distribution company and supplier current charges in proportion to the percentage of the combined current charges represented by each charge.[15]

The new rule places both companies on relatively equal footing, with each company receiving partial payment based on the relative amounts owed, respectively, on arrearages and current charges. The DTE was swayed by the arguments of the competitive suppliers that a distribution company should not receive payment on its current charges when the customer is already substantially in arrears in payments to the competitive supplier.

Advocates should be wary of such changes in the rules governing allocation of partial payments. In most states that have restructured, only the distribution company may physically disconnect service.[16] To the extent partial payments are allocated to the competitive supplier, the customer will be that much more behind on the distribution company's bills, making termination of service more likely. In most cases, low-income customers are better off if partial payments are applied first to distribution bills, reducing the likelihood of any disruption in service.

Note, however, that some states allow the competitive supplier, rather than the distribution company, to render a single consolidated bill for both distribution and generation services. One exception is Massachusetts, which only allows distribution companies to render consolidated bills. In Illinois, for example, competitive suppliers may render bills for their own services "and the delivery services provided

8 *See* Trigg v. Middle Tenn. Elec. Membership Corp., 533 S.W.2d 730, 733, 734 (Tenn. Ct. App. 1975).

9 *In re* Wisconsin Elec. Power Co., 175 Pub. Util. Rep. 4th 532, 560, 1997 WL 120654 (Wis. Pub. Serv. Comm'n Feb. 13, 1997) (rule barring partial payments "dated," and elimination of such rule is reasonable).

10 Consolidated Edison Co. of N.Y., Inc. v. Arroll, 322 N.Y.S.2d 420 (N.Y. Civ. Ct. 1971) (meter accuracy dispute; notation on check that cashing check was accord and satisfaction upheld).

11 *In re* Twine, 98 Pub. Util. Rep. 3d 331, 332 (Vt. Pub. Serv. Bd. 1973). *But see* Jones v. Southern Natural Gas Co., 36 So. 2d 34 (La. 1948) (a debt is discharged when creditor accepts partial payment knowing it is not the full amount and intending that the debt be discharged).

12 Consolidated Edison Co. of N.Y., Inc. v. Arroll, 322 N.Y.S.2d 420 (N.Y. Civ. Ct. 1971).

The high volume of checks received and the inability to read the notation on each one was not accepted as a defense for the utility in this case. *See also* Georgia Power v. WHI Atlanta, Inc., 251 S.E.2d 319 (Ga. Ct. App. 1978) (partial payment was accord and satisfaction; no defense that payment clerk not authorized to compromise claims); Vitauts M. Gulbis, *Modern Status of Rule That Acceptance of Check Purporting to Be Final Settlement of Disputed Amount Constitutes Accord and Satisfaction*, 42 A.L.R.4th 12 (1985).

13 *See, e.g.*, *In re* Amendments to Chapter 322, 1999 WL 1131881 (Me. Pub. Utils. Comm'n 1999) (partial payment allocated first to transmission and distribution provider, then to "competitive electricity provider").

14 *In re* Investigation Into the Billing Services Provided by Distribution Companies, Mass. Dep't of Telecomms. & Energy 01-28 (Phase II), at 6 (Dec. 14, 2001) (citing Terms and Conditions, Mass. D.P.U./DTE 97-65, at 54 (1997)).

15 *Id.* at 15.

16 *See, e.g.*, 220 Mass. Code Regs. §§ 11.04(9)(c) (distribution company must provide default service to consumers not otherwise receiving generation supply), 11.04(11) (termination protections), 11.05(3) (competitive supplier may only terminate generation supply).

by the electric utility [distribution company]" to customers.[17] In Illinois, competitive suppliers do not include on their bills distribution company charges for "bundled" services provided prior to the date of initial service rendered by the generation company.[18] Therefore, if the customer makes a partial payment, none of the partial payment would be applied to the costs of bundled distribution and generation service previously rendered by the distribution company. However, any partial payments must be applied "first to the electric utility's tariffed services" if there are distribution charges on the competitive supplier's consolidated bill.[19] Thus, if an Illinois customer makes a partial payment, the distribution company receives an absolute preference for its current charges but no payment on bundled charges rendered before the competitive supplier began serving the customer. Depending on the amounts due to each company and the vintage of those bills, this may place the customer at risk of termination by the distribution company.

As these two contrasting examples demonstrate, restructuring raises a host of new issues for consumers who make partial payments. Advocates should pay close attention to the allocation of partial payments to help ensure that customers are not terminated.

For other examples of settlement with payment of only a portion of the bill, see the discussions at § 7.2, *infra*, and the discussion below of energy assurance programs or arrearage forgiveness plans when a utility bill is considered paid in full without the actual full-dollar payment by the customer of that bill.

5.1.4 Calculating the Date of Payment

Many payment disputes, credit record battles, and potential shut-offs occur in the context of arguments over customers making or failing to make "timely" payments. In the utility context, the bill, usually sent monthly or bi-monthly, establishes the amount due and usually states the due date. The due date is sometimes established by the utility commission or by local regulations or company tariffs.[20] By comparing this due date with the date of payment, customers or advocates can determine if the payment was timely.

In-person payments must be credited on the day they are made. If payment is made by check, the time of payment ordinarily relates back to the date and time when the check is delivered, not when it is cashed.[21] If the check is delivered after hours to the utility and later cashed, payment is as of the date of delivery.[22] Checks received on one day may not be dated as received on the following day for purposes of administrative convenience. For purposes of receiving timely payments, the "day" may not end at 12:00 noon.

If the check is mailed, delivery typically occurs on the date of mailing if the creditor has authorized payment by mail and there is a course of such dealings between the parties.[23] Because nearly all utilities mail bills with return mail envelopes, expecting payments to be made by mail, there should not be a problem in showing such a course of dealings.[24] Generally, "there is a complete delivery of the check at the time of mailing if the check was mailed by the drawer at the direction of the payee, or in response to his request."[25]

A utility must advise the customer if payment must be made before the due date in order to avoid late payment charges. Concern was expressed about one utility's requirement that payment must be made two days before the due date, unless payment was made by direct debit, in order to avoid late payment charges.[26] If a utility's tariff says that the date a bill is paid is determined by the postmark on the envelope, the utility must ensure that it does not use the date on which the payment is logged into its accounts receivable system as the payment date.[27]

---

17 220 Ill. Comp. Stat. § 5/16-118(b) (West).

18 *See* Commonwealth Edison Co. v. Illinois Commerce Comm'n, 767 N.E.2d 504, 506 (Ill. App. Ct. 2002) ("Commission's order provided that alternative retail electric suppliers who utilize the single billing option . . . are not required to bill their electric customers for past-due amounts that the customers may owe ComEd for previously supplied 'bundled' service.").

In this context, "bundled" service refers to the complete package of distribution and generation services that the distribution company provided prior to restructuring.

19 220 Ill. Comp. Stat. § 5/16-118(b) (West).

20 *See In re* Shenandoah Gas Co., 164 Pub. Util. Rep. 4th 351, 1995 WL 628218 (W. Va. Pub. Serv. Comm'n Sept. 18, 1995) (date of payment established in utility company tariff as the date payment is made to the utility company or its authorized collection agency).

21 Scalise v. American Employers Ins. Co., 789 A.2d 1066 (Conn. App. Ct. 2002); Regents of Univ. of N.M. v. Lacey, 764 P.2d 873, 875 (N.M. 1988); Roy v. Mugford, 642 A.2d 688, 690, 691 (Vt. 1994); 6 R. Anderson, Anderson on the Uniform Commercial Code § 3-802:19 (3d ed. 1984); H. Bailey, Brady on Bank Checks § 4.6 (6th ed. 1987).

22 60 Am. Jur. 2d *Payment* § 11 (2003).

23 Nguyen v. Calhoun, 129 Cal. Rptr. 2d 436 (Cal. Ct. App. 2003); Werne v. Brown, 955 P.2d 1053 (Colo. Ct. App. 1998).

24 *But see* Cornwell v. Bank of Am., 274 Cal. Rptr. 322 (Cal. Ct. App. 1990) (supplying payment envelope is not a direction by lender to mail payments).

25 H. Bailey, Brady on Bank Checks § 5.07 (7th ed. 1997). *See* American River Lines, Inc. v. Central Soya Co., 524 F. Supp. 246 (D. Miss. 1981); *In re* Metro Produce, Inc., 80 B.R. 570 (Bankr. N.D. Ga. 1987); Cox v. Gulf Ins. Co., 858 S.W.2d 615, 616 (Tex. App. 1993). *See also* Werne v. Brown, 955 P.2d 1053 (Colo. Ct. App. 1998) (when lease did not specify payment by mail but lessor's address was listed as out-of-state post office box, there was a genuine issue of fact whether payment by mail was specifically authorized so as to make deposit payment rule applicable).

26 *In re* Connecticut Light & Power Co., 229 Pub. Util. Rep. 4th 380, 517, 2003 WL 23112329 (Conn. Dep't of Pub. Utility Control Dec. 17, 2003).

27 *In re* Connecticut Natural Gas Corp., 201 Pub. Util. Rep. 4th 225, 273, 2000 WL 944956 (Conn. Dep't of Pub. Utility Control May 25, 2000).

5.1.5 Other Issues with Checks

There is no payment if a check sent to pay a utility bill bounces,[28] a payment is stopped,[29] or a check is lost in the mail or by the utility company.[30] No payment occurs if a check is received by the creditor but not negotiated, although this seems challengeable under good faith and "fair dealings" arguments.[31] In addition, tariffs may include a returned check charge that could also be added to the customer's bill.[32] But a commission has no jurisdiction to award a customer damages against a telephone company for the bounced check charges that the *bank* assessed the customer in connection with an insufficient funds check used to attempt to pay telephone charges.[33]

28 Gill v. Mercantile Trust Co., 347 S.W.2d 420 (Mo. Ct. App. 1961); 60 Am. Jur. 2d *Payment* § 12 (2003).

29 Noble v. John Hancock Mut. Life Ins. Co., 386 N.E.2d 735, 736 (Mass. App. Ct. 1979).

30 United States v. Johnston, 133 F. Supp. 633 (D. Minn. 1955); Cornwell v. Bank of Am., 274 Cal. Rptr. 322 (App. 1990).

31 *See* § 15.4.1.4, *supra.*

32 *See, e.g., In re* Connecticut Natural Gas Corp., 166 Pub. Util. Rep. 4th 491, 1995 WL 813421 (Conn. Dep't of Pub. Utility Control Oct. 13, 1995) (returned check charge of $19.50 approved, equal to company's actual costs of processing bounced checks); *In re* Bozrah Light & Power Co., 76 Pub. Util. Rep. 4th 697 (Conn. Dep't of Pub. Utility Control 1986) (late charge set at 1% per month given cost of capital of approximately 10%; no late charges for residential hardship customers; $15 bounced check charge approved as equal to bank charge to utility); *In re* Bay State Gas Co., 139 Pub. Util. Rep. 4th 3, 1992 WL 453358 (Mass. Dep't of Pub. Utils. Oct. 30, 1992) (department approved returned check fee of $6.25); *In re* Montana Power Co., 181 Pub. Util. Rep. 4th 397, 1997 WL 823997 (Mont. Pub. Serv. Comm'n Oct. 30, 1997) (bad-check charge of $10 approved); *In re* Toledo Edison Co., 168 Pub. Util. Rep. 4th 193, 1996 WL 190802 (Ohio Pub. Utils. Comm'n Apr. 11, 1996) ($10.00 bad-check fee allowed; reconnection fee kept at $15.00, not raised to $43.90; that amount would cause increased PIPP arrearages and be an impediment to universal service); *In re* Mountain Fuel Supply Co., 165 Pub. Util. Rep. 4th 207, 1995 WL 735721 (Utah Pub. Serv. Comm'n Oct. 17, 1995) (returned check fee raised to $15.00); *In re* Shenandoah Gas Co., 164 Pub. Util. Rep. 4th 351, 1995 WL 628218 (W. Va. Pub. Serv. Comm'n Sept. 18, 1995) (bad-check fee of $10 approved; budget payment plan authorized with reconciliation at last month; 5% late charge approved; 20% discount on rates for SSI, AFDC, AFDC-U, and Food Stamp recipient customers; reconnection fee $15 for company disconnection, $9 times number of months off—but not to exceed $36—for customer-requested disconnection approved); *In re* Wisconsin Elec. Power Co., 175 Pub. Util. Rep. 4th 532, 1997 WL 120654 (Wis. Pub. Serv. Comm'n Feb. 13, 1997) (various charges approved including bounced-check charges and all bank charges plus $10).

33 Filoon v. Pennsylvania Pub. Serv. Comm'n, 648 A.2d 1339 (Pa. Commw. Ct. 1994).

5.1.6 Other Forms of Payment

Payment by money order is the equivalent of payment in cash, unless objected to by the utility company.[34] However, proving a money order has been cashed by the utility company is often an expensive and time-consuming proposition.

Not surprisingly, payment by means of generally accepted forms of money is required. Thus, in two similar cases, utility companies were allowed to disconnect for nonpayment when customers tried to pay in unusual ways. In an Arizona case,[35] the court refused to enjoin termination when the customer paid with an instrument called a "POMC," or Public Office Money Certificate, a promissory note of his own creation that reflected his belief that taxes could only be paid in gold or silver and generally discrediting U.S. currency. The court told him to pay in regular currency or face disconnection.

Similarly, the Washington Utility and Transportation Commission refused to order a utility company to accept bank savings account withdrawal orders called "Transfund Paychecks," which were not negotiable through the normal bank check clearinghouse.[36] In *Matthews v. Pacific Northwest Bell Telephone Company*, the Commission dismissed a complaint seeking to compel the telephone company to accept withdrawal orders in lieu of checks on commercial banks as method of making payment. The Commission stated that "[i]t may be favorably argued that checks, other negotiable instruments and state warrants are themselves not money but, in the world of business and the requirement of practicality, custom has grown to the point that such documents as will flow with expedition and efficiency and will be accepted in due course of business, are acceptable as tender in lieu of money. [The withdrawal orders] have not achieved that status. . . ."[37]

Payments in foreign money, by tendering property or title to personal or real property, or by related methods are generally considered payment only if accepted by the utility company.[38] Likewise, payment of utility bills with services, such as with restaurant meals and drinks, has been disallowed by regulators.[39]

34 Associates Discount Corp v. Gentry, 96 S.E.2d 640 (Ga. Ct. App. 1957); Schmidt v. Hummell, 73 N.E.2d 806 (Ohio Ct. App. 1947); 60 Am. Jur. 2d *Payment* § 32 (2003).

35 Cohn v. Tucson Elec. Power Co., 673 P.2d 334 (Ariz. Ct. App. 1983).

36 Matthews v. Pacific Northwest Bell Tel. Co., 9 Pub. Util. Rep. 4th 463 (Wash. Utils. & Transp. Comm'n 1975).

37 Matthews v. Pacific Northwest Bell Tel. Co., 9 Pub. Util. Rep. 4th 463, 467 (Wash. Utils. & Transp. Comm'n 1975) (utility cannot be compelled to accept anything other than money) (citing Fineson v. McMahon, 120 P.2d 484 (Wash. 1941)).

38 60 Am. Jur. 2d *Payment* § 21 (2003).

39 *In re* Pequot Gas Co., 87 Pub. Util. Rep. 4th 601, 1987 WL 258048 (Conn. Dep't of Pub. Utility Control Mar. 17, 1987) (no

Utilities may require that payments be made in designated forms if customers have previously made inappropriate payments. In Texas, for example, if two or more checks have been returned for insufficient funds within the past twelve months, a utility may require that all future payments be made in cash, by cashier's check, by money order, or by debit/credit card. Similarly, if a debit/credit card payment has been declined two or more times within the past twelve months, utilities may require future payment by cash, cashier's check, or money order.[40] No guidance is given on how a customer may rehabilitate his or her unsatisfactory payment history.

5.1.7 Payments by Others or to Agents

Acceptance of payment on a debt by a third person is equivalent to payment by the debtor.[41] Thus if part or all of a utility bill is paid by a customer's friend, relative, pastor, guardian, social worker or by a governmental or other agency, payment is made as if by the customer himself. A refusal to accept payment by a third party would bring up the issue of good faith and fair dealing.[42]

Payment of utility bills to a utility company employee (such as a worker at the house to disconnect service) or to an authorized utility company agent (such as at a drug store, liquor store, or other community location) is equivalent to paying the utility company directly.[43] This is true even if the utility company never gets the money.[44] A rule that bars payment of past-due bills at a pay station is dated and its elimination is reasonable.[45]

Utilities may be required to provide community payment centers as "an integral dimension of the provision of utility services."[46] However, utilities may charge customers a fee for the use of payment centers. A proposal by one company to charge a 75¢ transaction fee for use of one of its Quick Payment Centers was approved as long as at least one free center was available in every community that had a payment center.[47]

5.1.8 Designating Certain Accounts for Payment/Splitting the Check

It is well established that a debtor has the right to direct the way in which payments are to be applied to debts.[48] Thus, when the same utility provides both gas and electric service, a customer could direct that an entire payment or any fraction go to the electric bill or to the gas bill rather than an equal division between both bills.

Or if a utility customer has other multiple accounts, the customer could direct payment to some accounts and not to others. This was specifically approved in *N.Y. Telephone Co. v. State*,[49] when a state university directed that its payment go only to certain telephone bills and not to pay for disputed third-party billings.

A simple note on the customer's check should suffice to make this direction clear to the utility company: there is no required form of notice to split or direct payments.[50] If the debtor does not direct the payment, the utility company can split or divide it.[51]

---

payment for utility service with goods such as restaurant meals and drinks).

40 *In re* Provider of Last Resort Servs., 220 Pub. Util. Rep. 4th 1, 25, 2002 WL 31045264 (Pub. Utils. Comm'n of Tex. Aug. 23, 2002).

41 60 Am. Jur. 2d *Payment* § 54 (2003).

42 *See* ch. 7, *infra* (payment assistance by government agencies).

43 *See* Wilbanks v. James Talcott, 128 S.E.2d 333, 336 (Ga. Ct. App. 1962); 60 Am. Jur. 2d *Payment* § 59 (2003). *See also* Southwestern States Tel. Co. v. City of Judsonia, 64 Pub. Util. Rep. 3d 125 (Ark. Pub. Serv. Comm'n 1966) (payment contractor—a local bank—is a reasonable method for receiving customer payments).

44 Navrides v. Zurich Ins. Co., 488 P.2d 637, 642 (Cal. 1971) (attorney paid by his client's debtor absconded with check; debtor has fully paid client). *See* Annot., *Discharge of Debtor Who Makes Payment by Delivering Check Payable to Creditor to Latter's Agent, Where Agent Forges Creditor's Signature and Absconds with Proceeds*, 49 A.L.R.3d 843 (1973); Restatement (Second) of Agency § 178.

45 *In re* Wisconsin Elec. Power Co., 175 Pub. Util. Rep. 4th 532, 560, 64 Pub. Util. Rep. 3d 125 (Wis. Pub. Serv. Comm'n 1997).

46 *In re* Washington Gas Light Co., Dist. of Columbia Div., 226 Pub. Util. Rep. 4th 293, 298, 2003 WL 21673716 (D.C. Pub. Serv. Comm'n May 30, 2003), *aff'd*, 856 A.2d 1098 (D.C. 2004).

47 *In re* Entergy Ark., 222 Pub. Util. Rep. 4th 444 (Ark. Pub. Serv. Comm'n 2002).

48 *In re* Securities Groups, 116 B.R. 839, 845 (Bankr. M.D. Fla. 1990); Schreiber v. Armstrong, 374 P.2d 297, 299 (N.M. 1962); Home & City Sav. Bank v. Bilinski, 580 N.Y.S.2d 561, 563 (N.Y. App. Div. 1992); *In re* Interstate Access Charges for Wyoming Tel. Utils., 81 Pub. Util. Rep. 4th 524, 1987 WL 257466 (Wyo. Pub. Serv. Comm'n Feb. 27, 1987) (no disconnection of local service for nonpayment of long-distance charges; partial payments to be applied in following sequence: per direction of customer or, if no direction, first to local basic exchange charges then to intrastate LATA charges, then pro rata among long-distance providers); 60 Am Jur. 2d *Payment* §§ 62, 63 (2003); Corbin on Contracts § 1231.

49 New York Tel. Co. v. State, 496 N.Y.S.2d 655, 658 (N.Y. Ct. Cl. 1985).

50 *See In re* Otis & Edwards, P.C., 55 B.R. 185, 192 (Bankr. E.D. Mich. 1985); Central Nat'l Bank of Canajoharie v. Paton, 439 N.Y.S.2d 619, 621 (N.Y. Sup. Ct. 1981); 60 Am. Jur. 2d *Payment* § 98.

51 Federal Land Bank of St. Louis v. Wilson, 719 F.2d 1367, 1371 (8th Cir. 1983) (FmHA has right to apply proceeds of chattel sale to several loans as it sees fit in absence of direction by debtor). *Cf.* AT&T Corp. v. MerchantWired, 2006 WL 3076671 (S.D. Ind. Oct. 27, 2006) (when written agreement did not specify how payments were to be applied to debtor's account, court employed general rule of first applying funds to earliest indebtedness).

5.1.9 Erroneous Payments Made Under Duress May Be Recovered

Sometimes under threat of disconnection, utility customers pay a bill they do not believe they owe, such as a bill for a previous tenant, a former roommate, or the property owner; a bill for another; or a bill in an improper amount. Such payments are considered to have been made under duress and may be recovered. No actual disconnection need occur to form duress in this context.[52] In establishing duress, "where a threat to discontinue gas and electric service to one's home is made by an official of the utility company, the threat is equal to the deed."[53] Although a utility has the right to disconnect service as a means of collection, it may not use disconnection as a mechanism to coerce customers and to obtain payment that is beyond the amount to which the utility is actually entitled.[54]

5.1.10 Pleading and Burden of Proof As to Payment

If litigation around the issue of payment ensues, payment is an affirmative defense that should be pleaded.[55] Generally the burden of proof as to payment is upon the customer.[56] Receipts showing payment in full or canceled checks are generally presumptive evidence of payment. Payment may also be proved by circumstantial evidence.[57]

5.2 Utility Service May Be Made Contingent Upon Payment of a Security Deposit

5.2.1 General

Because most utilities provide service before receiving payment, they may, within reasonable limits, require a deposit or other assurance of payment from applicants, from customers whose payment performance is unsatisfactory, and from disconnected customers who seek reconnection.[58] The rationale for allowing regulated utilities to collect deposits is simple: "to ensure payment of service bills."[59]

Courts have generally recognized this right.[60] Many commissions, in their rules and regulations or in company tariffs, have explicitly granted public utilities the right to collect deposits.[61] If a customer is unwilling or unable to pay a legitimate deposit, the utility may generally deny or

52 *See* Subin v. City of N.Y., 229 N.Y.S. 628 (N.Y. Mun. Ct. 1928) (water); Monroe v. Niagara Mohawk Power Corp., 388 N.Y.S.2d 1003 (N.Y. City Ct. 1976) (electricity and gas); 70 C.J.S. *Payment* §§ 105–109.

53 Monroe v. Niagara Mohawk Power Corp., 388 N.Y.S.2d 1003 (N.Y. City Ct. 1976).

54 Kean Inv. Co. v. Michigan Consol. Gas Co., 111 Pub. Util. Rep. 4th 470, 475–76, 1990 WL 488713 (Mich. Pub. Serv. Comm'n Apr. 12, 1990).

55 See Fed. R. Civ. P. 8(c) and parallel state court rules.

56 *See* Heart of the Valley Motel v. Edwards, 433 S.E.2d 466, 467 (N.C. Ct. App. 1993), *aff'd*, 441 S.E.2d 550 (N.C. 1994).

57 Ford Motor Credit Co. v. Neiser, 554 N.E.2d 322, 328 (Ill. App. Ct. 1990); 60 Am. Jur. 2d *Payment* § 130.

58 In this fashion, a utility may in effect deny service even though such denial does not occur "directly." Making a deposit a prerequisite to obtaining service, when the deposit is beyond the financial ability of the household to pay, nevertheless constitutes a denial of service, however indirectly. Puckett v. Muldraugh, 403 S.W.2d 252 (Ky. 1966) (dicta); Chrysler Corp. v. Syracuse Suburban Gas Co., 428 N.Y.S.2d 361 (N.Y. App. Div. 1980).

59 Short v. Baltimore Gas & Elec. Co. 63 Pub. Util. Rep. 3d 493 (Md. 1966). *See also* the old case of Elwell v. Atlanta Gas Light Co., 181 S.E. 599 (Ga. Ct. App. 1935) (while a utility may not accelerate or suddenly demand its contractual right to a deposit upon discovery of an old debt, it may request a deposit to secure against future delinquencies).

60 *See* Annot., *Deposit Required by Public Utility*, 43 A.L.R 2d 1262 (1955). *See also* James v. St. Petersburg, 33 F.3d 1304 (11th Cir. 1994) (because neither tenant nor her landlord complied with the city's requirements for initiating service, including paying a deposit, she had no legitimate claim to water service under Florida law, and no 14th Amendment protected property interest); Abbott Laboratories v. Illinois Commerce Comm'n, 682 N.E.2d 340, 347 (Ill. App. Ct. 1997) (Commerce Commission has authority to require deposit); Lill v. Cavalier Rural Elec. Coop., Inc., 456 N.W.2d 527 (N.D. 1990) (REC's requirement that a customer pay $1500 towards cost of connection was not discriminatory in light of REC requirement that all customers requesting hookup pay a deposit or enter into a minimum-service agreement).

61 *See, e.g.*, Fla. Admin. Code r. 25-6.097; 16 Tex. Admin. Code § 25.24(a)(3).

This right is recognized sometimes in a state's statutory scheme. *See, e.g.*, W. Va. Code § 16-13A-9 (all new applicants for service shall deposit a minimum of $50 with the public service district).

Or the right is reflected in a commission's rules. *See, e.g.*, Cullinane v. Potomac Elec. Power Co., 27 Pub. Util. Rep. 3d 384, 147 A.2d 768 (D.C. 1959) (company's right to discontinue service for failure to comply with its regulations requiring a deposit is unaffected by the fact that such an act would result in a foreseeable danger and damage to person or property); Short v. Baltimore Gas & Elec. Co., 63 Pub. Util. Rep. 3d 493 (Md. 1966) (utility acted lawfully in following its own rule by refusing to furnish service at the request of an owner while a tenant remained in the premises receiving the benefit of the service without payment of delinquent charges and a deposit as security for payment of future charges). *But see* Connecticut Light & Power Co. v. Westview Carlton Group, L.L.C., 2006 WL 3719484 (Conn. Super. Ct. Dec. 6, 2006) (describing the limited options available to utility against delinquent landlord; may neither terminate service nor demand a deposit). *See generally* appx. A.1, *infra* (summarizing state regulations governing deposits).

terminate service, although some states make exceptions for hardship customers or the elderly.[62]

The right of a utility to collect a deposit is not absolute, however. The amount of the deposit must be reasonable[63] and the requirement or administration of the deposit may not be unreasonable.[64]

Utilities can enforce their right to collect deposits simply by refusing to provide service.[65] Disputes about the amount of a deposit or the refusal to initiate or restore service without a deposit are usually subject to informal dispute resolution procedures established by many commissions.[66]

5.2.2 Discriminatory Deposit Practices Are Prohibited

5.2.2.1 General

Even with a reasonable level of deposit, a utility may not arbitrarily pick and choose against whom to enforce a deposit requirement.[67] Commission rules[68] as well as state statutes[69] often explicitly prohibit discrimination concerning deposits. A utility may not impose a deposit requirement on certain classes of consumers,[70] for example, on domestic, but not commercial, consumers.[71] Nor may a utility arbitrarily require a deposit from an individual customer in violation of commission regulations, tariffs, or state law.

5.2.2.2 Equal Credit Opportunity Act Prohibitions on Discriminatory Deposits

5.2.2.2.1 General

The Equal Credit Opportunity Act (ECOA)[72] forbids "discrimination"[73] against a person on any "prohibited

62 *See, e.g.*, Conn. Agencies Regs. § 16-262j-1 (may not require deposit of customer unable to pay, i.e., income or below 125% of poverty, recipient of certain means tested benefits, or at risk of deprivation of necessities for customer or dependent children in household if deposit paid); Iowa Admin. Code r. 199-19.4 and 199-20.4 (may not deny service for failure to pay deposit during winter months); Md. Code Regs. § 20.30.02.02 (no deposit if customer is age sixty or over, intends to be primary consumer of service, and owes no outstanding bill); Mich. Admin. Code r. 460.109, 460.110 (no deposit if Department of Human Services is "responsible for making payments," customer secures a guarantor who is a customer in good standing, or applicant is sixty-five years or older and has a satisfactory payment history with any gas or electric provider for the past three years); 39-1-2 Miss. Admin. Code R. 9(2) (LexisNexis) (no deposit from "special customer," that is, aged sixty or over, taking service in own name, with no missed payments in past twelve months).

63 *See* § 5.2.7, *infra.*

64 Thus a public utility may not adopt a rule requiring deposits on the theory that people are generally dishonest or based on retaliatory or spiteful motives or feelings of ill-will toward a consumer. *See, e.g.*, DeLong v. Osage Valley Elec. Membership Coop. Ass'n, 716 S.W.2d 320 (Mo. Ct. App. 1986). *See also* Opinion and Order, David Bookstaber v. PECO Energy Co., No. C-20031314 (Pa. Pub. Util. Comm'n Nov. 18, 2004) (utility ordered to re-evaluate its credit and deposit procedures, put them in writing, and communicate them to applicants and customers).

65 *See, e.g.*, Fla. Admin. Code Ann. r. 25-30.320(2)(e) (2000); 16 Tex. Admin. Code §§ 25.477(a)(6) and 25.478(a)(4).

This right is recognized sometimes in a state's statutory scheme. *See, e.g.*, W. Va. Code § 16-13A-9 (all new applicants for service shall deposit a minimum of $50 with the public service district).

66 *See* the lengthy opinion concerning deposits and waivers, among other topics, in Muhammad v. PG&E, 1998 WL 1110494 (Cal. Pub. Util. Comm'n 1999).

67 Pope v. City of Clearwater, 767 F. Supp. 1147 (M.D. Fla. 1991); Dawes v. Philadelphia Gas Comm'n, 421 F. Supp. 806, 825 (E.D. Pa. 1976). *See also* Cody v. Union Elec. Co., 502 F. Supp. 1298 (E.D. Mo. 1980) (security deposit policy not applied in such a fashion so as to discriminate on basis of race); Pan American World Airways, Inc. v. Florida Pub. Serv. Comm'n, 427 So. 2d 716 (Fla. 1983); 64 Am. Jur. *Public Utilities* §§ 34, 39 (2001) (no deposit required when it will result in discrimination against some customers or when it is enforced against only some customers); Annot., *Deposit Required by Public Utility*, 43 A.L.R.2d 1262 (1955).

68 The Michigan Commission provides an example of such explicit rules, which state that a utility shall not require a deposit based on any of the following: (a) commercial credit standards; (b) income; (c) homeownership; (d) residential location; (e) race; (f) color; (g) creed; (h) sex; (*i*) age; (j) national origin; (k) marital status; (*l*) familial status; (m) disability; and (n) any other criteria not authorized by the rules. Mich. Admin. Code r. 460.108.

69 *See, e.g.*, Cal. Pub. Utils. Code § 453 (prohibiting discrimination in deposit amounts); W. Va. Code Ann. § 16-13A-9 (public service districts/public health) (*all* new applicants for service shall provide deposit) (emphasis added).

70 *See, e.g.*, Town of Wickenburg v. Sabin, 200 P.2d 342 (Ariz. 1948) (town may not require enhanced deposit from customer because he lives in "tent" house rather than a permanent dwelling); *In re* Mountain State Tel. & Tel. Co., 96 Pub. Util. Rep. 3d 321, 338 (Colo. Pub. Util. Comm'n 1972); *In re* Wash. Gas Light Co. 82 Pub. Util. Rep. 3d 225, 227, 228 (D.C. Pub. Serv. Comm'n 1970); Poll v. New England Tel., 25 Pub. Util. Rep. 4th 529, 538, 539 (Me. Pub. Util. Comm'n 1970) (blanket policies exempting broad categories of customers based on occupation or class unjustified). *See also* Note, *Public Utilities and the Poor*, 78 Yale L.J. 448, 457, 458 (1969) (suggesting that a requirement of deposits from non-homeowners only would violate the duty of nondiscrimination).

71 *In re* Washington Gas Light Co. 82 Pub. Util. Rep. 3d 225 (D.C. Pub. Serv. Comm'n 1970); Rogers v. Cincinnati, 23 Ohio Dec. NP 493, 499 (1913) ("a regulation which requires domestic consumers to make quarterly deposits in advance, without requiring the commercial or mercantile consumers to make advance deposits, is unreasonable and arbitrary, and is an abuse of discretion").

72 15 U.S.C. §§ 1691–1691f; Regulation B, 12 C.F.R. § 202.2(m).

73 Reg. B, 12 C.F.R. § 202.2(n).

bases"[74] at "all stages of the credit transaction."[75] Prohibited bases are race, color, religion, national origin, sex, marital status, age (if old enough to contract), receipt of public assistance, or exercise of any right under the Act.[76] Thus, a utility or other seller may not demand a deposit, increase the size of the required deposit, impose other conditions, or use more stringent collection methods than for other customers on the basis of any of these factors.

The ECOA clearly applies to public utility transactions.[77] The ECOA provides a limited exception to certain of its requirements for "public utility credit."[78] However the exemption is very limited and does not authorize discrimination in late fees or other practices by utilities.

The ECOA defines "discriminate against an applicant" for credit as "to treat an applicant less favorably than other applicants."[79] The presence of discrimination in these areas should be determined using an "effects test,"[80] focusing on the results of a practice not the intentions of the utility. This test looks at disparate impacts.[81] The good or bad faith of the defendant, in other words, is irrelevant to any showing that a challenged practice does or does not discriminate against a protected class.[82] The focus, instead, is on discriminatory results.[83] The effects test is used to challenge a pattern or practice that results in discriminatory impacts on particular classes.[84]

It is, of course, important to remember that the term "discriminate" is defined to mean "to treat *less favorably* than." Accordingly, it would always be necessary to show not simply a *different* treatment but a "less favorable" treatment.

5.2.2.2.2 The "prohibited bases"

The ECOA prohibits discrimination based on, *inter alia*, race, color, religion, national origin, sex, marital status, age, and income based in whole or in part on a public assistance program.[85] A "public assistance program" includes "any Federal, State or local government assistance program that provides a continuing, periodic income supplement, whether premised on entitlement or need. . . ."[86] Examples of such programs include, but are not limited to, Temporary Aid to Needy Families (TANF), Supplemental Nutrition Assistance Program (formerly called "food stamps"), rent and mortgage supplement or assistance programs, Social Security and Supplemental Security Income (SSI), and unemployment compensation.[87] Receipt of LIHEAP, of course, would also qualify as receipt of benefits from a public assistance program.

The prohibition on discrimination based on "sex" includes discrimination based on gender-defined occupations.[88] Under this reasoning, affected utilities would be barred from discounting income from certain sources his-

74 15 U.S.C. § 1691(a).

75 Reg. B, 12 C.F.R. § 202.2(m).

76 15 U.S.C. § 1691(a).

77 Official Staff Commentary to Reg. B § 202(3)(a)-2; Midkiff v. Adams County Reg'l Water Dist., 409 F.3d 758 (6th Cir. 2005) (expressly making same assumption as in Golden v. City of Columbus); Golden v. City of Columbus, 404 F.3d 950 (6th Cir. 2005) (court assumes that transaction for water service is a "credit transaction" for purposes of resolving ECOA claim, but no ECOA violation found). *See also* Mick v. Level Propane Gases, Inc., 183 F. Supp. 2d 1014 (S.D. Ohio 2000) (purchase of propane services is "credit transaction"); National Consumer Law Center, Credit Discrimination § 2.2.6.3 (5th ed. 2009 and Supp.) (discussing incidental consumer credit). *But see* Mays v. Buckeye Rural Elec. Coop. Inc., 277 F.3d 873 (6th Cir. 2002) (credit extensions by utility company elements for "incidental credit," and are exempt from compliance with certain provisions of Regulation B). *See generally* Donoghue, *The Equal Credit Opportunity Act and Public Utilities*, 105 Pub. Util. Fortnightly 28 (June 5, 1980); National Consumer Law Center, Credit Discrimination § 2.2.6.2 (5th ed. 2009 and Supp.) (discussing ECOA public utility exemption and see Reg. B, 12 C.F.R. § 202.3(a) and official staff commentary thereto).

78 *See generally* National Consumer Law Center, Credit Discrimination § 2.2.6.2 (5th ed. 2009 and Supp.) (discussing ECOA public utility exemption). *See also* Regulation B, 12 C.F.R. § 202.3(a) and official staff commentary thereto.

79 Regulation B, 12 C.F.R. § 202.2(n). *See also* Carter v. Buckeye Rural Elec. Coop. Inc., 2001 WL 1681104 (S.D. Ohio Sept. 7, 2001) (an "applicant" eligible for protections under the ECOA, within the meaning of the regulation, includes plaintiff whose name was added by utility company to her ex-husband's account without her consent).

80 *See, e.g.*, David C. Hsia, *The Effects Test: New Directions*, 17 Santa Clara L. Rev. 777 (1977); Comment, *Applying the Title VII Prima Facie Case to Title VIII Litigation*, 11 Harv. C.R.-C.L. L. Rev. 128 (1976); Note, *Credit Scoring and the ECOA: Applying the Effects Test*, 88 Yale L.J. 1450 (1979).

81 *See, e.g.*, General Elec. Co. v. Gilbert, 429 U.S. 125, 155 (1976) (Brennan, J., dissenting). *See also* Golden v. City of Columbus, 404 F.3d 950 n.11 (6th Cir. 2005) ("Neither the Supreme Court nor this Court have previously decided whether disparate impact claims are permissible under ECOA. However, it appears that they are.").

82 *See, e.g.*, Griggs v. Duke Power Co., 401 U.S. 424, 432 (1971); United States v. Reddoch, 467 F.2d 897 (5th Cir. 1972); United States v. Hughes Mem'l Home, 396 F. Supp. 544, 548 (W.D. Va. 1975).

83 Note the difference between constitutional and statutory use of the effects test in this regard. "The United States Supreme Court . . . in 1976 . . . proscrib(ed) the non-evidentiary use of disparate impact in constitutional analysis. In so doing, the Court drew a sharp distinction between the constitutional and statutory standards for measuring discrimination." David C. Hsia, *The Effects Test: New Directions*, 17 Santa Clara L. Rev. 777, 787 (1977) (citations omitted). Hsia notes that, "against the restrictive constitutional backdrop, however, the statutory schemes requiring the use of the effects test are increasing." *Id.* at 789, 790.

84 *See* National Consumer Law Center, Credit Discrimination § 4.3 (5th ed. 2009 and Supp.).

85 15 U.S.C. § 1691(a).

Another prohibited basis is the good faith exercise of rights under the federal consumer credit statutes.

86 FRB Official Staff Commentary on Regulation B § 202.2(z)-3.

87 *Id.*

88 *In re* Alden's, Inc., 92 F.T.C. 901 (1978).

torically associated with women, such as part-time employment. Other sources of income traditionally available primarily to women, such as alimony, child support, and separate maintenance agreements may not be discounted automatically.[89]

Use of a "prohibited basis" as a ground for discrimination can occur in any number of ways, all of which are arguably prohibited under the ECOA. For example, a higher deposit is not justified because an applicant receives public assistance, is elderly, or is female. Structuring a due date so that recipients of public assistance would always be late could violate the act. That a former spouse owes a utility bill should have no bearing on an individual's creditworthiness, at least when the applicant did not derive benefit from the delinquent utility bill, and thus has no obligation under state law to repay it.[90] Nor can utilities discriminate against certain communities because of high concentrations of racial or ethnic minorities. Disparate treatment based on whether the customer is a tenant rather than a homeowner or on the length of residence arguably violates the ECOA.

5.2.2.2.3 "All stages of the credit transaction"

The ECOA prohibits discrimination in "all stages of the credit transaction." The implementing regulations define "credit transaction" as including:

> every aspect of an applicant's dealings with a creditor regarding an application for credit, or an existing extension of, credit (including, but not limited to, information requirements; investigation procedures; standards of creditworthiness; terms of credit; furnishing of credit information; revocation, alteration, or termination of credit, and collection procedures).[91]

This definition, of course, assumes that an "application for credit" has been made. The statute defines an applicant as "any person who applies to a creditor directly or indirectly for an extension, renewal, or continuation of credit,"[92] while Regulation B gives a broader definition, including "any person who requests" an extension of credit.[93]

5.2.2.2.4 Enforcement

Private ECOA actions can seek recovery of actual damages.[94] No maximum or minimum amount is placed on recoverable actual damages. Clearly, however, any out-of-pocket expenses would be recoverable as actual damages. Out-of-pocket expenses might include any transportation or communication costs incurred by the customer as a result of the violation, such as extra trips to the utility's office or long-distance phone calls. Taking time from work is also considered an out-of-pocket expense. Additionally, ECOA cases have awarded damages for embarrassment, humiliation and mental distress.[95] "Distress" should include both mental suffering and emotional anguish.

The ECOA also explicitly authorizes punitive damage awards.[96] The statutory criteria for punitive damages include: the actual damages awarded, the frequency and persistence of non-compliance, the creditor's resources, the number of persons adversely affected, and the extent to which non-compliance was intentional. In addition, the ECOA provides for equitable and declaratory relief,[97] costs and attorney fees.[98]

5.2.2.2.5 Parallel state credit discrimination statutes

State credit discrimination or general civil rights statutes may be broad enough to cover extensions of credit by utilities.[99] These statutes may be helpful to low-income consumers in states that restructured the provision of electric and/or natural gas resulting in energy service providers

89 *See, e.g.*, United States v. Amoco Oil Co., Clearinghouse No. 33,836 (D.D.C. 1980) (creditor agreed not to use credit scoring system which allegedly discriminated against women, by giving income from full-time employment or other sources a greater value than "protected sources" commonly associated with women, such as part-time employment, alimony and child support payments). *See also In re* U.S. Federated Dep't Stores Inc., Clearinghouse No. 31,076 (S.D. Ohio 1978) (consent judgment when creditor agreed to stop its practice of refusing to consider part or all of an applicant's income derived from particular sources historically associated with women, such as alimony, child support, separate maintenance payments, and part-time employment).

90 Mays v. Buckeye Rural Elec. Coop. Inc., 277 F.3d 873 (6th Cir. 2002) (as signatory on delinquent joint account, plaintiff demonstrated financial responsibility for the debt); Haynsworth v. South Carolina Elec. & Gas Co., 488 F. Supp. 565 (D.S.C. 1979).

91 Regulation B, 12 C.F.R. § 202.2(m).

92 15 U.S.C. § 1691a.

93 12 C.F.R. § 202.2(e).

94 15 U.S.C. § 1691e.

95 *See, e.g.*, Owens v. Magee Fin. Serv. of Bogalusa, Inc., 476 F. Supp. 758 (E.D. La. 1979); Shuman v. Standard Oil Co. of California, 453 F. Supp. 1150 (N.D. Cal. 1978). *See also* Pena v. Freedom Mortgage Team, Inc., 2007 WL 3223394 (N.D. Ill. Oct. 24, 2007) (damages recoverable under ECOA include mental anguish, humiliation or embarrassment) (citing Anderson v. United Fin. Co., 666 F.2d 1274 (9th Cir. 1982)); Hrubec v. National R.R. Passenger Corp., 829 F. Supp. 1502 (N.D. Ill. 1993).

96 15 U.S.C. § 1691e(b).

97 15 U.S.C. § 1691e(c); 12 C.F.R. § 202.17(b).

98 15 U.S.C. § 1691e(d); 12 C.F.R. § 202.17(b).

99 *See, e.g.*, Mass. Gen. Laws ch. 151B, §§ 4(10) (prohibiting discrimination against public assistance recipients by any person furnishing "credit, services, or rental accommodations"), 4(14) (prohibiting discrimination on the basis of sex, sexual orientation, marital status or age by "any person furnishing credit or services"). *See also* National Consumer Law Center, Credit Discrimination (5th ed. 2009 and Supp.) (listing more completely state credit discrimination laws).

that are outside of commission regulation. The California Public Service Commission, responding to concerns that deregulated electric services providers (ESPs) might use their deposit policy to discriminate, concluded that the state civil rights act will apply to ESPs, as it does to all other businesses. If a provider is found to have violated the act, the California PSC "can open an investigation to determine whether an ESP's registration should be suspended or revoked."[100]

5.2.3 *Who Must Pay a Deposit?*

Many commission rules authorize deposits as one way for new or disconnected customers[101] to obtain service from the utility before payment for the service. These rules usually specify that utilities may evaluate a customer's creditworthiness and, if it is unsatisfactory, may require a deposit.[102] In general, a deposit will be required of customers with a credit record that includes late payments or disconnections.[103]

Typical of many states' rules are Florida's, which state that a public utility may require an applicant for service to establish credit by:

(1) furnishing a guarantor;[104]

(2) furnishing an irrevocable letter of credit from a bank or a surety bond; or

(3) paying a cash deposit.[105]

Other states add other options. In Washington, for example, gas customers can avoid a security deposit if they can show a good service record with the utility company and no more than three delinquency notices; full-time employment for the past twelve months; ownership or purchase of the premises being served; a guarantor; or a credit reference from a similar utility.[106]

5.2.4 *Should Non-Utility Credit History Be Utilized?*

5.2.4.1 Overview

Utilities often use third-party supplied information, such as credit reports, as a basis for cash deposit demands of households deemed to be non-creditworthy. Because of the differences between payment of most other bills and payment of utility bills, however, utility companies may have difficulty justifying deposits for some of these customers.

Research has found that consumers tend to pay their utility bills before paying nearly any other obligation (other than rent or mortgage).[107] As a result, information from a

100 *In re* Proposed Policies Governing Restructuring California's Electric Services Industry and Reforming Regulation, 184 Pub. Util. Rep. 4th 262 (Cal. Pub. Utils. Comm'n 1998).

101 Deposits are generally permitted for current customers if their service has been disconnected for nonpayment or if they owe a substantial amount to the utility. *See, e.g.*, 4 Colo. Code Regs. §§ 723-3:3403(b) (LexisNexis) (electric customers who have previously received service from the utility shall be required to make a new or additional deposit only if previous payment record includes recent or substantial delinquencies), 723-4:4403(b) (same for gas customers), 723-5:5403 (same for water).

102 *In re* Vt. Tel. Co., 182 Pub. Util. Rep. 4th 63 (Vt. Pub. Serv. Bd. 1997) (no deposit required if customer can show no overdrafts on bank account for one year; Equifax check for creditworthiness rejected as "invasive" and not connected to proper criteria; repayment agreement must be offered to cover reconnection charges), *codified at* Vt. Admin. Code § 18-1-3:3.203. *See, e.g.*, California state statutes: Cal. Gov't Code § 60375.5 (West) (requirement for deposit to be based solely upon creditworthiness of applicant); Cal. Pub. Util. Code § 779.5 (West) (decision of electrical, gas, heat, telephone or water corporation to require deposit shall be solely based upon creditworthiness of applicant as determined by the corporation).

103 *See* Mich. Admin. Code r. 460.109(utility may require deposit as condition of providing service to new customer if applicant has prior service account that is delinquent with any electric or gas provider, misrepresents identity or credit standing, fails to provide positive identification information upon request, requests service for a location at which he or she does not reside, engaged in unauthorized use of utility service within last six years, was a household member during a period in which all or part of a delinquent service account was incurred by another household member who still resides with applicant, or sought relief under bankruptcy laws within last six years).

16 Tex. Admin. Code § 25.478(a)(3)(A) allows applicants to establish creditworthiness by showing: if the applicant has been a customer of any utility for the same kind of service within the last two years and during the last year has not had more than one delinquent bill and has never had service disconnected for nonpayment, or can demonstrate satisfactory credit rating (with credit cards, letters of references, and so forth), or furnishes a guarantor in writing.

104 Commission rules may explicitly *require* regulated utilities to allow customers to offer a guarantor instead of a deposit.

105 Fla. Admin. Code Ann. r. 25-7.083(1) (gas service), 25-30.311(1) (water and sewer utilities), 25-4.109(1)(c) (telephone companies).

In Florida, the rule for telephone service adds the following means of establishing credit: if an applicant has been a customer of the utility within the last two years and, during the past year, did not have more than one delinquent bill and has never had service disconnected for nonpayment, Fla. Admin. Code Ann. r. 4.109(1)(a).

106 Wash. Admin. Code § 480-90-113. *See also* Wash. Admin. Code § 480-110-335 (similar rules for water companies).

107 Michael Kiefer & Ronald Grosse, *Why Utility Customers Don't Pay Their Bills*, Pub. Util. Fort. 41 (June 21, 1984); Wisconsin Public Service Corporation: Lifestyle Study: Selected Payment Patterns, at ii (July 1983); Mildred Baker, Utility Collection Customers: Understanding Why They Don't Pay on Time (1989) (representing the interpretations of Washington Gas Company); Market Trends Research Group, Investor Owned Utility Group Credit Customer Survey (1989). *See also* Fisher Sheehan & Colton, Public Fin. and Gen. Economics, *Low-Income Payment Patterns During Iowa's Winter Shutoff Moratorium*, FSC's Law & Economics Insights (Jan./Feb. 2002) (2002 study found that Iowa utilities were able to collect 90% of the revenue billed to LIHEAP recipients during the state winter moratorium).

credit reporting agency that indicates a lack of creditworthiness based on non-utility transactions does not necessarily provide useful information as to a customer's likelihood of paying a home utility bill.[108]

The denial of service, whether direct or indirect (when a customer cannot meet a deposit requirement) for non-utility-related reasons might also be interpreted as a violation of long-standing utility regulatory principles proscribing the denial of service for "collateral" matters.[109] It matters not to other ratepayers whether a household fails to pay its credit card bill, for example, if that household *will* pay its utility bill. Given the fact that nonpayment of non-utility bills has little relevance to whether utility bills will be paid, basic fairness requires that third-party credit information on non-utility transactions not serve as a basis for deposit demands. At least one utility commission has accepted this analysis.[110]

5.2.4.2 Are Credit Scores Fair and Reliable When Determining Access to Utility Services?

Private and public utility companies increasingly rely upon credit scores to assess consumer risk and determine whether consumers will receive utility services and have to pay a deposit for such services.[111] It is difficult to quantify how many utility companies now rely on credit scores to determine access to utility services, but it appears to be a practice that is national in scope. Use of credit scores has existed in the credit context for many years. Mortgage brokers, providers of car loans, and issuers of credit cards have all relied upon credit scores to assess risk and determine whether or not to grant credit and how much to charge for such credit.[112] In the past few years, insurance companies have begun using specialized insurance credit scores to underwrite policies and set rates.[113] Utility company usage of credit scores is a more recent development and has not received as much scrutiny by regulators or the media. As a result, information about the extent of usage of credit scores by utility companies is very limited.

Reliance on credit scores to determine access to utility services raises numerous questions of fairness and appropriateness: Are utility services different than other types of credit transactions and do they therefore warrant a different risk analysis? How are credit scores determined and are they a reliable and accurate means of measuring the likelihood that a consumer will or will not pay his or her utility bill? Do credit scores have a disparate and unfair impact on minority consumers or consumers with low incomes and limited resources? These and other questions relating to the use of credit scores by utility companies should be fully explored before consumers are denied services, forced to pay security deposits, or otherwise asked to pay more for utility services because of their credit scores.

The subsections below discuss a number of issues regarding credit scores and utilities, including how credit scoring works; whether use of credit scores undermines the duty utility companies have to provide services; whether the accuracy of consumer credit files affects the reliability of credit scores; the potential disparate impact on minorities and consumers with low incomes from use of credit scores; how consumers can dispute their credit scores; recent challenges to use of credit scores by utility companies; and appropriate safeguards that should be in place when credit scores are used for access to utility services.

5.2.4.3 How Credit Scoring Works

A credit score is a number generated from a system that numerically weighs or "scores" some or all of the factors considered in the decision to grant credit. There are numerous types of credit scoring systems.[114] In the case of utilities, credit scoring systems have primarily been used in decisions on whether to require a security deposit from applicants for utility services and how large a deposit to demand.

A credit scoring firm will develop a scoring system using a database of credit information, usually consumer credit files, for a large number of consumers.[115]

While the firm may use the consumer credit data or credit histories, the credit scores that are generated will not be the same as those used for credit granting. For example, Equifax has established an Energy Risk Assessment Model (ERAM) to create risk assessment scores specifically for electric and natural gas utility providers. The ERAM model begins with an analysis of utility bill payment from several gas and

108 *See In re* Vt. Tel. Co., 182 Pub. Util. Rep. 4th 63 (Vt. Pub. Serv. Bd. 1997) (Equifax check for creditworthiness rejected as "invasive" and not connected to proper criteria).

109 *See* § 2.2, *supra*.

110 *See In re* Vermont Tel. Co., 182 Pub. Util. Rep. 4th 63 (Vt. Pub. Serv. Bd. 1997).

111 Ill. Admin. Code tit. 83, § 280.50(a) (allows state utility companies to use a credit scoring system and refuse service unless the applicant meets a predetermined score or pays a deposit for services). *See* Telecommunications Energy and Cable Risk Model, *available at* www.experian.com/products/tec_risk_model.html.

112 *See* Brian Deagon, *Fair Isaac's New Scoring Service Attracts Banks*, Investor's Bus. Daily, July 25, 2001; Betty-Lin Fisher, *It Pays to Know the Score: Credit Bureaus Reveal Where You Rank*, Detroit Free Press, Apr. 22, 2002 (quoting Fair Isaac spokesperson); National Consumer Law Center, Fair Credit Reporting § 14.3 (7th ed. 2010).

113 National Consumer Law Center, Fair Credit Reporting § 14.11 (7th ed. 2010).

114 *Id.* § 14.2.2.

115 *Id.* § 14.2.1. *See* www.experian.com/products/tec_risk_model.html; Testimony of Birny Birnbaum for the Public Utility Law Project, Re: Petition of Niagara Mohawk Power Corporation for Authorization to Request Security Deposits from Applicant for Residential Service 2, N.Y.P.S.C. Docket 03-M-0772 (July 24, 2003).

electrical utilities. However, the model also includes over 300 attributes that go beyond just utility bills. These attributes include payment history on credit cards, bank loans, automobile loans, and mortgages; collection case files; bad debt write-offs and others.[116] ERAM then applies these credit attributes to prospective residential customers. Each attribute is assigned a weight or value. A higher value is assigned to accounts that are current, while a lower value is assigned to accounts that are past due. These values are added to form a score from 1 to 999. Under ERAM's logic, the higher the score, the more likely the applicant will pay a utility bill on time. Conversely, the lower the score, the less likely the applicant will pay a utility bill on time.

Experian has also developed a telecommunications, energy and cable (TEC) risk model.[117] This model was developed exclusively from credit information of 2.5 million consumers with at least twelve months of history as wireless subscribers. Consumers are given scores between 1 and 999. The higher the score the greater the risk. This model purportedly predicts the likelihood of future seriously delinquent payment behavior, but it is unclear how much of the data relied upon for this score includes payment histories for utilities such as water, electricity, and gas and how much of the information pertains to other transactions like credit cards and bank loans. Without such information, the accuracy of such a scoring model is questionable with respect to assessing risk for payment of utility bills.

Consultants for utility companies tout credit scores as the answer to mitigating risk, reducing costs, and maximizing revenue.[118] Consultants will advertise that predictive scoring programs help determine which customers will pay their utility bills on a timely basis and which ones "should be targeted on the front end of the application process or as soon as they fall behind." These same consultants are inclined to suggest that utility companies should use their own data to score and segment customer accounts in order to minimize bad debt—sort of a mini-credit reporting system based on internal credit records.

A consumer's score is affected by the type of credit used and/or type of lender; payment history; amounts owed; length of credit history; and whether the credit is new or old. A good credit history does not necessarily equate with a good credit score.[119]

5.2.4.4 Does Use of Credit Scores Undermine the Duty to Provide Service?

The U.S. Supreme Court has held that all public utility providers—investor-owned, municipal, or cooperative—have a common law duty to serve.[120] This duty requires utility companies to provide services to any member of the public within their service area who has applied for services and is willing to pay for the services and comply with the utility's rules and regulations.[121] This duty also encompasses an obligation to render utility services on "reasonable terms, impartially, without unjust discrimination, and at reasonable rates."[122] The duty to serve has been incorporated into many state statutes and is reflected in decisions of utility commissions and courts interpreting statutory obligations of regulated investor-owned utilities, cooperatives, and municipals.[123]

Public utilities have historically been prohibited from refusing to render service that they are authorized to furnish or from imposing service constraints because of some collateral matter unrelated to that service.[124] Several court decisions as well as utility regulations have held that a public utility cannot refuse to render the services it is authorized to furnish, or impose service constraints, because of some collateral matter unrelated to that service.[125] The definition of "collateral" varies from state to state. However, collateral matters that cannot be used as a basis for denying service generally include:

- nonpayment of unrelated contracts with the utility;
- nonpayment for services provided by a separate business run by the utility; and
- nonpayment of another person's utility bill.[126]

There is no question that credit scores are based on credit payment records for services and products other than utilities. With the exception of mortgage obligations, research has shown that consumers are likely to pay their utility bills before other outstanding credit.[127] An argument could be

116 Petition of Columbia Gas of Pennsylvania, Inc. & PPL Electric Utilities Corporation for Limited Waiver of 52 Pa. Code § 56.32(2), Penn. P.S.C. Nos. P-00001807 and P-00001808 (Mar. 8, 2001) (relating to residential deposits).

117 *See* www.experian.com/products/tec_risk_model.html.

118 A simple websearch of "utility credit and collections" will pull up recent conferences and materials on this topic. *See, e.g.*, www.energybiz.com/event/conference/credit-collections-utilities-strategies-and-tactics-effective-utility-credit-collections-management.

119 Testimony of Birny Birnbaum for the Public Utility Law Project, Re: Petition of Niagara Mohawk Power Corporation for Authorization to Request Security Deposits from Applicant for Residential Service 5, N.Y.P.S.C. No. 03-M-0772 (July 24, 2003).

120 United Fuel Gas. Co. R.R. Comm'n of Ky., 278 U.S. 300 (1929); New York *ex rel.* Woodhaven Gaslight Co. v. Public Serv. Comm'n, 269 U.S. 244 (1925).

121 *See* § 2.1.2, *supra*.

122 *See, e.g.*, Arizona Corp. Comm'n v. Nicholson, 497 P. 2d 815, 817 (Ariz. 1972).

123 *See* § 2.1.3, *supra*.

124 64 Am. Jur. 2d *Public Utilities* § 22 (2001); Annot., *Right of Municipality to Refuse Services Provided by It to Resident for Failure of Resident to Pay for Other Unrelated Services*, 60 A.L.R. 3d 714, § 48:3-85 (1974).

125 64 Am. Jur. 2d *Public Utilities* § 22 (2001); Annot., *Right of Municipality to Refuse Services Provided by It to Resident for Failure of Resident to Pay for Other Unrelated Services*, 60 A.L.R. 3d 714, § 48:3-85 (1974).

126 *See* § 2.2.1, *supra*.

127 *See* Roger D. Colton, Customer Deposit Demands by U.S. West: Reasonable Rationales and the Proper Assessment of

made before a utility commission that any denial of service or decision to seek or increase the amount of a security deposit based solely on a credit score is as impermissible as basing access to utility service on the more traditional collateral matters of nonpayment of bills for unrelated services or nonpayment of another person's bills and should be prohibited.[128]

5.2.4.5 Accuracy of Information in Consumer Credit Files Puts into Doubt the Reliability of Credit Scores

Regardless of the model used by utility companies and the firms they rely on for credit scores, if the information in consumer credit files is inaccurate, so too are the consumer credit scores. Several studies have documented the problems with inaccuracies in consumer credit files maintained by credit reporting agencies.[129] In 2002, the Consumer Federation of America and the National Association of Credit Reporting Agencies conducted a comprehensive study of credit scores. Their examination of over 500,000 consumer credit files found that 29% of consumers have credit scores that differ by at least 50 points between credit bureaus, while 4% have scores that differ by at least 100 points.[130] Among the conclusions reached by the CFA with respect to accuracy were: (a) credit scores and information vary significantly among the three national credit reporting repositories; (b) one in five consumers (20.5%) risks being mischaracterized as a poor credit risk due to inaccurate information, while at the same time 22% are likely to have scores too high because creditors do not report to all three national credit reporting repositories; and (c) 10% of consumers risk exclusion from the credit marketplace because of incomplete, duplicate, or mixed credit files.

A study by the Federal Reserve found that among accounts with a significant derogatory piece of information as the most recent addition, almost three-fifths of the reports were not current. The study authors concluded that many of these accounts had been closed or transferred and it was likely that consumers who had paid off delinquent accounts since they were last reported were being penalized.[131] There are several factors in play when relying on credit information to form a basis of a credit score.

Even minor mistakes that would not affect a creditor's judgment can lower a credit score significantly. Consequently, a utility's reliance on credit scores developed from flawed data may violate basic utility principles. Access to utility service cannot be based on unreasonable and unfair terms or conditions.

5.2.4.6 Credit Scores May Have a Disparate Impact on Vulnerable Consumers

Concerns about the bias in credit scores and whether they have a disproportionately negative impact on minorities and others are longstanding. Studies have shown that African-Americans and Latinos are substantially more likely than whites to have credit scores below 620.[132] In addition, minority consumers are also more likely to lack the credit history necessary to even generate a credit score because they are less likely to have used traditional types of credit that scoring companies rely upon to establish credit scores.[133] One study found that 22% of Hispanics did not have enough of a credit history to generate a credit score.[134] This is significant because at least one utility company has sought to automatically impose a deposit requirement when a consumer has no credit score.[135]

Risk, Prepared on Behalf of the Staff of the Washington Utilities and Transportation Commission, No. UT-930482 (Aug. 1994) (citing Michael Kiefer & Ronald Grosse, *Why Customers Don't Pay Their Bills*, Pub. Util. Fort. 41 (June 21, 1984)); Wisconsin Pub. Serv. Corp., Lifestyle Study: Selected Payment Patterns, at ii (July 1983).

128 Concerns about whether deposits that are based on credit scores would receive commission approval may have played a part in Niagara Mohawk's decision to withdraw a request to allow the setting of deposits based on credit scores. *See* The Department of Public Service Staff Statement of Support, in Petition of Niagara Mohawk Power Corporation for Authorization to Request Security Deposits from Applicant for Residential Service 6, N.Y.S.P.S.C. Docket 03-M-0772, *available at* www.pulp.tc/PSCstatement_in_support_FINAL_9-29-03.pdf.

129 *See* National Consumer Law Center, Fair Credit Reporting § 14.8 (7th ed. 2010).

130 Consumer Fed'n of Am. & Nat'l Credit Reporting Ass'n, Credit Score Accuracy and Implications for Consumers 24, (Dec. 17, 2002), *available at* www.consumerfed.org/pdfs/121702CFA_NCRA_Credit_Score_Report_Final.pdf.

131 Robert Avery, Paul Calem, Glenn Canner, & Raphael Bostic, An Overview of Consumer Data and Credit Reporting, Fed. Reserve Bulletin 71 (Feb. 2003).

132 *See* Roberto G. Quercia, Michael A. Stegman, Walter R. Davis & Eric Stein, Performance of Community Reinvestment Loans: Implications for Secondary Market Purchases, in Low Income Homeownership: Examining the Unexamined Goal 363, tbl. 12-7 (2002); Freddie Mac, Automated Underwriting: Making Mortgage Lending Simpler and Fairer for America's Families 27 (Sept. 1996) (African Americans are three times likelier than whites to have a FICO score below 620; Hispanics are twice as likely as whites to have a FICO score below 620).

133 For example, one survey from central Ohio found that African Americans are twice as likely as whites not to have a credit card. Mark A. Fisher, *Minorities Score Lower in "Colorblind" Ratings*, Columbus Dispatch, Apr. 14, 1999, at 5A.

134 *See* Michael Stegman, *et al.*, Presentation to the Research Inst. for Hous. America Conference, Automated Underwriting: Getting to Yes for More Low Income Applicants (Apr. 2001).

A Consumer Federation of America study found that, for the general population, about one in ten consumer credit files did not have enough information to generate a score. Consumer Fed'n of Am. & Nat'l Credit Reporting Ass'n., Credit Score Accuracy and Implications for Consumers 38 (Dec. 17, 2002), *available at* www.consumerfed.org/pdfs/121702CFA_NCRA_Credit_Score_Report_Final.pdf.

135 Petition of Niagara Mohawk Power Corporation for Authoriza-

AARP conducted a survey of credit scoring and mortgage lending, finding inconsistencies between the national credit reporting repositories and concluding that the very poor, less educated and persons living in urban areas may be underrepresented in bureau files.[136] The AARP survey further concluded that minorities may be underrepresented in credit files.[137]

Another study has shown that low-income consumers have lower credit scores as a group. Thirty-three percent of households living in neighborhoods with low family incomes have low credit scores, whereas only 17% of households in high-income neighborhoods have low credit scores.[138] The Federal Reserve Board has also raised concerns about the potential for discriminatory effects of credit scoring and observed that scores "may lack predictive power for the under-represented segments of the overall population."[139]

These shortcomings with credit scores provide opportunities to challenge the use of scores, especially in areas with concentrations of minorities and consumers with low incomes who are likely to be adversely affected by the use of credit scores.

5.2.4.7 What Happens If Consumers Dispute Their Credit Score?

Applicants who are denied access to utility service, charged a higher rate for service or required to pay a deposit for service because of their credit scores are often in the dark as to their right to dispute the accuracy of the score and information upon which it is based. Who do they complain to if they dispute their credit scores or the credit history used to create the scores? What information, if any, does the utility company provide to the consumer regarding how the credit score was determined and how a consumer can dispute the computation of the score or the information upon which the score is based? Until enactment of the Fair and Accurate Credit Transactions Act of 2003 (FACT Act), the Fair Credit Reporting Act (FCRA) specifically exempted credit scores from disclosure. The FACT Act amended the FCRA to require, effective December 1, 2004, the disclosure of credit scores used by a person who makes or arranges a loan.[140] While credit scoring firms have made available to consumers the scores used for granting credit,[141] utility credit scores are not required to be disclosed under the FACT Act or other federal law. This is an area where states can step in and provide for disclosures and enhanced protections for consumers of utility services.

Although credit scores used in the context of utility services are not required to be disclosed under federal law, adverse actions based on credit reports trigger notification requirements under the FCRA[142] and the Equal Credit Opportunity Act (ECOA).[143] The FCRA utilizes the definition of "adverse action" found in the ECOA, that is, a denial or revocation of credit, a change in terms of an existing credit arrangement, or a refusal to grant credit on substantially the same terms as requested.[144] The FCRA also adds that adverse action includes any action taken or determination made in a transaction that is initiated by the consumer and that is adverse to the consumer, so long as the adverse action is based in whole or in part on any information in the consumer's report.[145] The ECOA adverse action notice requires the utility company to include a statement of the reasons for the adverse action or a disclosure of the consumer's right to request a statement of such reasons.[146] Thus the FCRA and ECOA require utilities to provide consumers with notice and an explanation when credit reports, and presumably scores that are based on information in credit reports, are used to require a deposit or charge a higher fee.

Without notice of the adverse action taken, consumers will be unaware that they are being denied service or required to pay a deposit or higher fee for utility services due to a low score that is based on their credit report. In addition, what, if any, action will utility companies take

tion to Request Security Deposits from Applicant for Residential Service, N.Y.P.S.C. Docket 03-M-0772 (July 24, 2003).

136 Neal Walters & Sharan Hermanson, AARP Pub. Policy Inst., Credit Scores and Mortgage Lending 4 (Aug. 2001).

137 *Id.*

138 Brent W. Ambrose, Thomas G. Thibodeau, & Kenneth Temkin, U.S. Dep't of Hous. & Urban Dev., An Analysis of the Effects of the GSE Affordable Goals on Low- and Moderate-Income Families 13 (May 2002).

139 Credit Risk, Credit Scoring, and the Performance of Home Mortgages, Fed. Reserve Bulletin 621, 630 (July 1996).

140 15 U.S.C. § 1681g(a); Pub. L. No. 108-59, § 3 (Dec. 4, 2003); 69 Fed. Reg. 6530 (Feb. 11, 2004).

141 Generic credit scores are available for a fee from the website of Fair Isaac, the major developer of credit scoring models, at www.myfico.com. There is some question as to whether these are the same credit scores as the ones used by creditors.

142 15 U.S.C. § 1681a (k). *See, e.g.*, Baynes v. ALLTEL Wireless of Ala., Inc., 322 F. Supp. 2d 1307 (M.D. Ala. 2004) (consumer stated FCRA claim when utility demanded higher deposit because of information in credit report but failed to provide required adverse action notice). *See generally* National Consumer Law Center, Fair Credit Reporting § 8.4 (7th ed. 2010).

143 15 U.S.C. § 1691(d).

Utility service is considered credit for purposes of the ECOA. *See* Regulation B, 12 C.F.R. § 202.3(a); Official Staff Commentary to Reg. B. § 202.3(a)-2. *See generally* National Consumer Law Center, Credit Discrimination § 2.2.2.3 (5th ed. 2009 and Supp.).

144 15 U.S.C. § 1681a (k) (citing to § 15 U.S.C. § 1691(d)(6)).

145 15 U.S.C. §§ 1681a(k)(1)(B)(iv), 1681m; Baynes v. ALLTEL Wireless of Ala., Inc., 322 F. Supp. 2d 1307 (M.D. Ala. 2004) (demand for higher deposit was adverse action; disclosure requirements triggered). *See* Everson, FTC Informal Staff Opinion Letter (July 28, 1998).

146 15 U.S.C. § 1691(d)(2); Regulation B, 12 C.F.R. 202.9(a)(2); Baynes v. ALLTEL Wireless of Ala., Inc., 322 F. Supp. 2d 1307 (M.D. Ala. 2004) (demand for higher deposit was adverse action; disclosure requirements triggered). *See generally* National Consumer Law Center, Credit Discrimination § 10.5.4.1 (5th ed. 2009 and Supp.).

when consumers seek to challenge the accuracy of the credit score or information upon which the score is based? Consumers will likely face significant hurdles and time delays to: (1) access the information contained in their credit report and (2) have a reinvestigation conducted into the accuracy of the information. In Pennsylvania, the Public Utility Commission initially required utility companies to inform applicants of their credit scores and granted consumers the right to challenge credit scores directly with the utility company. This forward-looking policy was later reversed by the Pennsylvania PUC on the grounds that, since the score served as a "filter" in review of the application and "is not the reason for the credit denial," the credit determination would be based on the applicant's inability to satisfy the creditworthiness standards under Pennsylvania's public utility code.[147] Although consumers could not dispute the credit score with the utility, they could still dispute the denial of credit pursuant to the Pennsylvania PUC's regulations.[148] This change in policy thus made it more difficult for utility applicants to obtain quick resolutions to disputed credit scores through the utility companies, and consumers were forced to resolve their disputes via the credit reporting agency that developed the score, an entity with which the consumer likely has no relationship.

Under the FCRA, consumers must wait up to thirty days (and as many as forty-five) for a credit reporting agency to conduct an investigation into disputed credit information.[149] These timelines hinder the ability of utility consumers to obtain quick and appropriate decisions that are based on accurate and complete information regarding their applications for services. Without an expedited review of the accuracy of the credit score and information upon which the scores are based, consumers will likely face unfair and perhaps illegal denials of access to vitally needed utility services.

5.2.4.8 Recent Challenges to Use of Credit Scores by Utility Companies

There is no case law in which use of credit scores by utility companies has been challenged by consumers and their advocates. However, some challenges have been made at the administrative level. In Albany, residents objected to efforts by Niagara Mohawk Power Corporation to assess security deposits averaging $150.00 to new customers based on credit scores. Niagara Mohawk proposed to assess a security deposit for utility services on new applicants who had a "low" or no credit score as determined by Equifax.[150] Under Niagara Mohawk's proposal, a very large number of consumers would have to pay a deposit. However, only a minority of those required to make a deposit are expected to default.[151] Advocates challenged this proposal, asserting, among other things, that (1) use of scores could unreasonably deny or delay applicants access to essential utility service; (2) credit reports often contain numerous errors, rendering them inappropriate for use in determining access to essential utility services; (3) far too high a percentage of customers would be adversely affected; (4) the proposal erroneously assumes that the absence of a credit score is indicative of poor creditworthiness; and (5) the utility company had overstated the cost effectiveness of credit scores. Opponents to the use of credit scores also pointed out that there is no rational basis to assume that someone is a credit risk just because he or she has not used credit in the past. Under pressure from its opponents, Niagara Mohawk withdrew its proposal and offered a substitute plan that relies primarily on the customer's history of paying utility bills.[152]

In Pennsylvania, two public utility companies sought a waiver to provisions in the state's public utility code that limited the conditions under which a deposit is required for utility service. The companies further sought permission to use Equifax's ERAM credit scoring model in a two-year experiment to reduce uncollectible account expenses.[153] These efforts were challenged by the state's Office of Consumer Advocate (OCA), which was concerned about the number for the cut-off passing score and its uniformity across the utility companies' service territories. OCA was also concerned with the length of the program and recommended quarterly reporting requirements and the provision of data on who passed or failed based on credit scores, who paid or did not pay for deposits based on credit scores, the number of applicants referred to low-income energy assistance programs, and the number of applicants who did not obtain services because they could not pay the deposit.[154] The OCA further requested information on how many applicants challenged their credit scores and found them to be erroneous and, for those customers whose credit scores were used by the utility, the amount of time between the filing of an application for service and when service was actually provided.[155] In the end, the utility companies and the OCA entered into an agreement by which credit scoring was allowed based on a cut-off credit score of 750. If a new

---

147 Order, Petition of Columbia Gas of Pennsylvania, Inc. & PPL Electric Utilities Corp., Penn. Pub. Util. Comm'n Docket P-00001807, P-00001808 (Mar. 8, 2001).

148 *Id.*

149 15 U.S.C. § 1681i(a)(1)(A), (B).

150 Petition of Niagara Mohawk Power Corporation for Authorization to Request Security Deposits from Applicant for Residential Service 4, N.Y.P.S.C. Docket 03-M-0772 (July 24, 2003).

151 *Id.* at 3.

152 *See* www.pulp.tc/html/new_policies.html (Public Utility Law Project's website for current information on the status of this case).

153 Order, Petition of Columbia Gas of Pennsylvania, Inc. & PPL Electric Utilities Corporation for Limited Waiver of 52 Pa. Code § 56.32(2) (Relating to Residential Deposits), No. P-00001807, P-00001808 at 2 n.2 (Penn. Pub. Util. Comm'n Mar. 8, 2001).

154 *Id.*

155 *Id.*

applicant receives a score of 750 or higher, no security deposit would be required. Applicants with scores of 749 or lower would be asked to produce information to demonstrate that they are not an unsatisfactory credit risk. Applicants who were required to pay a deposit based on their credit scores were also required to be referred to the low-income assistance program. If they qualified for the assistance program, the deposit would be waived. The utility companies and the OCA also agreed to reporting requirements, including required reporting of the number of applicants for whom credit scores were requested; the number who received a passing or failing score; and the number of deposits that were obtained from new applicants.[156] The Public Utilities Commission relied upon this agreement to grant the request to use credit scores.

5.2.4.9 Necessary Safeguards When Credit Scores Are Used for Utility Services

Consumer advocates will need to remain vigilant about utility efforts to expand the use of credit scores in requiring security deposits and possibly for other billing issues. Issues of accuracy, reliability, fairness, and efficiency will be paramount in evaluating whether credit scores are appropriate for use in the utility context. With the increase in the availability and dissemination of credit information and the sophistication in which such information is analyzed and used, consumer advocates should ensure that certain safeguards be with place. Such safeguards should include but not be limited to the following:

- Banning the use of credit scores based on their unreliability, potential discriminatory impact, and inherent unfairness when the scores are based on more than utility payment histories;
- Providing consumers with a quick and effective means of assessing and disputing the accuracy of credit scores directly with utility companies, including a requirement to provide the consumer with the credit score used by the utility in setting the deposit or when taking other adverse action;
- Ensuring that information relied upon to create credit scores is accurate to the maximum extent possible; including having consumers review their credit information and dispute inaccurate and obsolete information and being able to do so in a timely manner;
- Ensuring that credit scores are based on utility payment histories rather than consumer credit histories for car loans, credit cards, and other non-utility debts;
- Providing sufficient administrative oversight into the reliability of the credit score models used and how they are applied to utility applicants;
- Providing consumers with effective education materials explaining how credit scores are used and developed, what factors can improve or damage credit scores, and what steps consumers can take to increase their credit scores for utility service purposes;
- Providing consumers, when they are denied utility service or required to pay for more for services, with clear and conspicuous adverse action notices with a statement of reasons for the adverse action, including any requirement that they pay a deposit;
- Ensuring consistency in the credit reporting process so that information furnished to the three national repositories is reported consistently to all three and that each repository reports such information on a consistent basis;
- Evaluating whether use of credit scores for utility services has a disparate impact on minority and low-income consumers, resulting in higher denials of service, higher utility deposit requirements, or other fees.

Many of these protections can be obtained through legislative and administrative advocacy at the local level, since it does not appear that Congress has preempted this field concerning credit scores and utility services.[157]

5.2.5 Full Utility Credit Reporting to Credit Bureaus

5.2.5.1 Overview

In addition to utility use of credit scores to assess consumer risk, some utilities and policy advocates promote utility company reporting of all utility customer payment behaviors and transactions to the major consumer reporting agencies.[158] Proponents of full utility credit reporting contend that it is required to help "thin file" and "no file" consumers to build credit history and gain access to bank loans and other sources of credit. Proponents are also motivated by seeing consumers—even those who struggle to meet monthly financial obligations—move utility bills to the top of monthly "to pay" piles in order to mitigate utility risk.[159] However, it can be shown that such reporting will result in harm to low-income consumers while undermining

156 *Id.*

157 *See* National Consumer Law Center, Fair Credit Reporting § 10.7 (7th ed. 2010).

158 Turner et al., Political & Econ. Research Council, Credit Reporting Customer Payment Data: Impact on Customer Payment Behavior and Furnisher Costs and Benefits (Mar. 2009); Political & Econ. Research Council, The Promise of Non-Financial Data: How Using Energy Utility and Telecoms Payment Data Can Help Millions Build Assets, Policy Brief Vol. 7, No. 1 (Dec. 2006); Turner et al., Political & Econ. Research Council, You Score You Win: The Consequences of Giving Credit Where Credit is Due (July 2008).

159 Turner et al., Political & Econ. Research Council, Credit Reporting Customer Payment Data: Impact on Customer Payment Behavior and Furnisher Costs and Benefits (Mar. 2009).

the policy objectives of state utility consumer protections. Furthermore, problems with consistency of reported data arise as a result of the wide variability in state utility credit and collection rules and energy prices, as well as in the availability of energy efficiency and payment assistance programs. For these reasons many low-income advocates oppose full utility credit reporting—particularly by franchised, monopoly electric and natural gas utility distribution companies—unless it is agreed to by customers on an "opt-in" basis.

5.2.5.2 Traditional Uses of Credit Scores

Credit scores have traditionally been used by prospective creditors and insurance companies to assess risk, determine whether to provide a service, or determine a charge (for example, annual percentage interest rate) for a service.[160] They have provided mortgage and automobile lenders as well as consumer credit and insurance companies with a fast, automated means of making decisions regarding provision and pricing of services. Consumers' credit scores, which are generated by the "big three" nationwide credit reporting agencies based on credit report information supplied by creditors and others, are generated using formulas that are protected as trade secrets. However, it is known that credit scores are based, in order of weighted importance, on payment history, amount owed, extent of indebtedness, length of credit history, new lines of credit, and types of credit.[161] The extent to which a consumer pays his or her bills on time factors most heavily into payment history and generation of a credit score.

5.2.5.3 Nontraditional Uses of Credit Scores

In recent years, a number of "alternative" credit reports and credit scores have been created. While the stated purpose of some alternative credit reports is to help low-income and other underserved consumers who do not have traditional credit histories, many are clearly intended to limit risk of prospective creditors. Alternative credit reports and scores use information such as utility and rent payments. An example of nontraditional credit reporting is performed by Payment Reporting Builds Credit (PRBC), a credit reporting agency that compiles credit histories using rent, utility, insurance, and even daycare monthly payments.[162] Another example is the National Consumer Telecom and Utilities Exchange, managed by the credit reporting giant, Equifax.[163]

5.2.5.4 Utility Credit Reporting—Current Practice

There is no national source of information delineating the details of how each utility company reports consumer payment behaviors. However, many unregulated cell phone and cable companies report all customer payments—both timely and late—to one or more of the credit reporting agencies. Some regulated landline telephone companies also engage in full credit reporting. However, with the exceptions of Detroit Edison Company and Nicor Gas Company, the vast majority of electric and natural gas utility companies only report when a seriously delinquent account has been referred to a collection agency or written off as uncollectible—a tiny percentage of the accounts that are late.[164]

5.2.5.5 Full Reporting by Electric and Gas Utilities—Harm to Low-Income Households

Modifying current electric and gas utility practice by reporting all delinquent accounts would over time have an adverse impact on low-income consumers' credit scores or force those households to go without other necessary goods and services. Nationally, millions of residential utility accounts are in arrears by thirty days or more[165] but are not written off or referred to a collection agency. Furthermore, the 2008 National Energy Assistance Survey indicated that 47% of LIHEAP participants skipped or did not pay a full home energy bill in 2008.[166] For most of these households, full utility credit reporting would result in one or more adverse reports to credit reporting agencies.

New adverse information resulting from full utility credit reporting would have a negative impact on consumer credit scores, which in turn serves to attract a range of predatory lenders. In addition, many prospective landlords, employers, and insurers check credit scores to screen applicants. A

160 Complete discussion and analysis of credit reporting and credit scoring may be found in National Consumer Law Center, Fair Credit Reporting (7th ed. 2010), and Hendricks, Credit Scores and Credit Reports: How the System Works, What You Can Do (2007).

161 Hendricks, Credit Scores and Credit Reports: How the System Works, What You Can Do (2007).

162 Visit www.prbc.com.

163 Visit www.nctue.com.

164 To gain knowledge of current electric and gas utility credit reporting practices, NCLC consulted utility customer service executives, regulators, and state consumer advocates in a broad sampling of states, including California, Iowa, Maine, Massachusetts, New Hampshire, New York, and Ohio. In each case, NCLC was provided with consistent information regarding current electric and gas utility reporting practice.

165 A limited "snapshot" survey by the National Association of Regulatory Utility Commissions' Consumer Affairs Committee identified thirty-nine million overdue residential electric and natural gas utility accounts in May 2008. Sloan et al., Credit Reporting Customer Payment Data: Impact on Customer Payment Behavior and Furnisher Costs and Benefits (Nov. 2008).

166 APPRISE, National Energy Assistance Directors' Association, 2008 National Energy Assistance Survey, at iii (Apr. 2009).

low credit score may thus harm consumers seeking housing, employment, or insurance policies. Fair Isaac Corporation revealed that, for a consumer with a FICO score of 680, a single thirty-day late payment results in the assessment of 60 to 80 credit score "damage points." For a consumer with a "prime" credit score of 780, a single thirty-day late payment results in 90 to 110 damage points.[167] New late payment reports under full utility credit reporting would lower credit scores.

For utility customers whose incomes are insufficient to pay for all necessities, full credit reporting will mean cutting back on non-utility necessities or risking devastation to their credit scores. In the case of older consumers, sacrificing prescribed medicines or compromising indoor temperatures to reduce utility expenditures bring particularly serious threats to health, safety, and general well-being. In general, low-income consumers are far more likely than their higher-income counterparts to be late in paying a home energy bill. Utility payment troubles over the past several years have worsened in light of increased home energy prices and price volatility, deteriorating economic conditions and personal income, and increases in the price of and expenditures for health care and other competing necessities. As a result of these income and expense realities, full utility credit reporting will cause disproportionate harm in low-income households.

Similarly, home energy bill payment troubles are more pronounced in certain households grouped according to circumstances related to income, such as race, household structure, disability status, and health insurance coverage.[168] Therefore, full utility reporting will adversely and disproportionately affect these households as well.

5.2.5.6 Utility Credit Reporting and State Regulatory Consumer Protections

Recognizing that electric and natural gas utility services are necessities of life and that in most cases they are delivered by franchised, monopoly companies, states have adopted regulatory consumer protection frameworks that limit or prohibit disconnection of service to older, seriously ill, or disabled customers who are experiencing financial hardship.[169] Other states limit or prohibit disconnection of service seasonally during harsh-weather months. Still others prohibit disconnection of service when outdoor temperatures or heat indices are forecast to exceed specific thresholds.

These protections are intended to protect vulnerable customers from loss of vital electric and natural gas service during times of financial hardship. They send consumers and utility companies the message that electric and natural gas service is distinct from other goods and services and that access should be protected in order to sustain health and safety. Full utility credit reporting, by threatening consumers with the adverse credit score ramifications of delaying payment even during an emergency, would operate in conflict with the policy objectives of these protections. Suggesting that utility payment behaviors should be fully reported to the credit reporting agencies in the same manner as other financial transactions fails to recognize both the unique nature of utility service and the policy objectives of long-standing consumer protection rules that have been adopted by the regulatory commissions in states across the country.

5.2.5.7 Implementation Concerns—Fairness and Consistency

5.2.5.7.1 General

Credit reporting generally has long been subject to criticisms regarding inaccuracy of reports, the lack of transparency of proprietary "black box" credit score calculation formulas, and the discriminatory treatment of ethnic minority groups.[170] However, the prospect of full utility credit reporting brings a host of additional concerns. Problems with consistency of reported data arise as a result of the wide variability in state utility credit and collection rules, the pricing of residential electric and natural gas service, and the availability of energy efficiency and payment assistance programs. These state-specific rules, pricing conditions, and programs are critical determinants of the extent to which low-income customers are able to make electric and natural gas utility payments in a timely manner. Low-income customers in states with relatively harsh customer service rules, where prices and expenditures for home energy services are high, and where payment assistance through LIHEAP and non-federal discount rate programs is limited, face greater difficulties keeping up with timely payments than do customers in states with more favorable circumstances.

5.2.5.7.2 Customer service rules—bill payment timeframes and deferred payment agreements

Utility customer service rules and regulations, promulgated by state regulatory commissions, include provisions

167 Simon, FICO Reveals How Common Credit Mistakes Affect Scores, CreditCards.com (Nov. 2009).

168 U.S. Census Bureau, 1998 Survey of Income and Program Participation.

169 *See* appx. A, *infra* (state regulation of utilities).

170 *See* National Consumer Law Center, Fair Credit Reporting ch. 4 (accuracy of credit reports), § 14.5 (transparency) (7th ed. 2010).

For analysis of the disparate impact of credit scoring, see, for example, Kabler, Missouri Dep't of Ins., Insurance-Based Credit Scores: Impact on Minority and Low Income Populations in Missouri (Jan. 2004).

regarding bill payment timeframes and establishment of deferred payment agreements. These provisions vary widely across states, and have a tremendous bearing on the extent to which low-income utility customers make timely payments.

State provisions vary with regard to when a bill is considered past due after it is rendered. In Alabama, for example, a bill is due ten days after it is rendered.[171] However, in Alaska a bill is not considered past due for forty days.[172] In Georgia, electric utility customers have forty-five days to pay before a bill is considered late.[173] These varying timeframes create problems in generating and interpreting utility credit reports. In reporting payment of consumer debt, there is a standard thirty-day delinquency guideline. With utility reporting, it is unclear whether the thirty-day reporting guideline will apply irrespective of whether a state has ruled that a customer has more or less time to make a timely bill payment. If not, the question arises as to whether utilities will only report after the state-allowed timeframe has expired, potentially resulting in disparate payment periods within which consumers in different states have to pay before adverse reports are rendered.

In addition to bill payment timeframes, most states have adopted the requirement that utility companies offer residential customers a payment plan, or a deferred-payment agreement, as an alternative to disconnection of service. The terms of these agreements vary considerably between states and even between utility companies operating within a particular state. The structure of these agreements has a bearing on whether past balances will be successfully paid off and on the extent to which limited-income customers will be able to pay current charges in full. Inconsistency can become a problem given these differing agreement requirements, and the extent to which customers who have retained service and are successfully paying off a previous balance under terms of a deferred-payment agreement would be considered "late" for credit reporting purposes must be addressed. Even if the successful payment of arrears under a deferred-payment agreement does not generate adverse credit reporting, there remains the problem of inconsistent interpretation of reports by utilities operating under varying payment agreement guidelines.

5.2.5.7.3 Home energy expenditures

The level of average home energy expenditures in a particular state or region is driven by residential energy prices and weather conditions. Unlike consumer spending on discretionary items, expenditure levels for basic home energy and utility service are based primarily on factors beyond a consumer's control. Full utility credit reporting will not take into account the disparities in necessary home expenditure levels and will tend to penalize customers in states and regions with high energy prices and harsh weather conditions. For example, in the winter of 2009–2010, natural gas winter home heating expenditures in the northeastern census region were projected by the U.S. Energy Information Administration to be more than double those in the western census region.[174] Similarly, there are tremendous home cooling expenditure disparities between states and regions during summer months. Average electricity expenditures in the hot-weather, high-priced state of Texas are nearly double those of the lower-priced and moderate-climate state of Washington. Under full utility credit reporting, customers residing in states with high prices and harsh climates will continue to be forced to spend more for basic service, be more likely to be late or miss a utility payment, and thus be penalized with credit score damage points issued by credit reporting agencies. This disparate treatment will be exacerbated by year-to-year differences. If the upper Midwest experiences an unusually harsh winter, while the New England region has a mild winter, low-income customers in the former will likely fall behind on their utility bills more quickly and in greater numbers. Credit scores that reflect weather patterns rather than creditworthiness are unfair to consumers.

5.2.5.7.4 Availability of low-income energy assistance

Another important factor in determining the extent to which low-income consumers are able to remain current on their monthly electric and natural gas utility bills is the availability of bill payment assistance and energy efficiency programs. Just as there are disparities in state regulatory consumer protections, customer service rules, and home energy expenditure levels, there is also wide variability among states in the resources available to assist low-income households stay current on their utility bills. Full utility credit reporting will not fairly and consistently reflect these energy program disparities. Given the increased likelihood that low-income utility customers who do not have access to meaningful energy assistance will be late or miss utility payments, full utility credit reporting will unfairly penalize low-income consumers living in states where there is limited funding for utility payment assistance and energy efficiency programs.

171 Ala. Pub. Serv. Comm'n Gen. R. 12.

172 Alaska Admin. Code tit. 3, §§ 52.450(b), 52.500(10).

173 Ga. Comp. R. & Regs. 515-3-2-.01.

174 U.S. Department of Energy/Energy Information Administration, Short-Term Energy Outlook (Dec. 2009).

EIA forecast Northeast Census Region natural gas home heating expenditures during the winter of 2009–2010 to average $1123. Average West Census Region expenditures were forecast to be $497.

5.2.6 UCC Limits on Utilities' Power to Demand Deposits or Increased Deposits

The Uniform Commercial Code has been held to apply to the sale of utilities, in metered quantities, to end users.[175] Two sections of the code may apply to a utility's demand for a deposit, or an increase in an existing deposit, from a current customer: section 1-208, which limits the operation of insecurity clauses, and section 2-609, which limits a seller's power to require "assurances" when it fears anticipatory breach.

A utility's demand for a cash deposit can be characterized as a creditor's demand for "collateral or additional collateral," because it deems itself insecure about receiving future payments. UCC § 1-208 provides that an "insecurity clause" may be invoked only if the creditor "in good faith believes that the prospect of payment or performance is impaired."[176] Claims of "insecurity" are highly fact-specific, but courts have generally held that the person asserting the insecurity clause, is not authorized to do so arbitrarily, but must act in good faith, and also have either reasonable grounds or at least probable cause for believing that he is insecure.[177] In the utility context, late payments or other failures to perform by the customer could well justify insecurity under section 1-208.[178] But other events, such as the utility company changing its mind about the need for a deposit or obtaining previously unavailable credit information, would not support a deposit claim.[179] And mere speculation about future concerns, without support, would not justify a deposit. Finally, even a failure to perform, such as making payments late, may not support a finding of insecurity if the utility has accepted the late payments without action before.[180]

Section 2-609 of the UCC provides that when "reasonable grounds for insecurity" arise with respect to one party's performance of a contract of sale, the other party may demand "adequate assurance of due performance" and "if commercially reasonable" may suspend performance if that assurance is not provided.

A utility's demand for a deposit or an increased deposit from a customer may be characterized as a "demand for adequate assurance" in light of a perceived risk of anticipatory breach. This situation will arise when the utility alleges that the customer has given it reason to believe that he or she cannot or will not pay on time, so that a deposit is needed to give "adequate assurance" of payment.

Section 2-609 provides first, that the seller's perception that the customer will anticipatorily breach the contract must be reasonable. Courts have interpreted this to mean that the seller must have some "factually established ground for insecurity" that is "rooted in objective facts" rather than in "purely subjective concerns."[181]

Second, the seller's demand for "adequate assurance" (that is, a deposit, must be reasonable). This raises two issues: (1) is there a need for a cash deposit at all or does some non-cash alternative exist and (2) is the level of cash deposit requested reasonable?

In some situations, advocates might argue that a cash deposit is not needed to give a utility adequate assurances. In particular, receipt of LIHEAP assistance,[182] which provides cash grants to apply toward the payment of home heating bills, reduces the risk of permanent nonpayment in two ways. First, the receipt of LIHEAP makes it more likely that the household will be able to pay its energy bills in a timely and complete fashion. Second, when there is LIHEAP assistance, the risk of *total* nonpayment is *eliminated*, as the utility's risk of loss is reduced by the amount of the LIHEAP benefit.

In addition, there are alternatives to the requirement of deposits that enable utilities to receive adequate assurances. One common method is through the implementation of

175 *See* § 15.4.1.2, *infra*.

176 The term "good faith" under the UCC refers to "honesty in fact," U.C.C. § 1-201(20), and, in the revised Article 9, "the observance of reasonable commercial standards of fair dealing." U.C.C. § 9-102(a)(43).

177 *See, e.g.*, Johnson v. Thayer, 4 N.E.2d 172 (Ohio Ct. App. 1936). *See also* Sackett v. Hall, 478 S.W.2d 381, 384 (Mo. 1972) ("[t]he prevailing view seems to be that an arbitrary power is not conferred but the mortgagee must act reasonably with probable cause to apprehend a loss"); Clayton v. Crossroads Equip. Co., 655 P.2d 1125 (Utah 1982) ("[i]t would be highly inequitable to allow . . . [the secured party] to change its mind once it had accepted that contract simply because it subsequently conducted a more thorough investigation; it is unfair to put the buyer in default based upon information which was apparently available in one of . . . [secured party's] own branch offices at the time that it had accepted plaintiff."); Annot., *Validity, Construction and Application of Insecurity Clause in Chattel Mortgage*, 125 A.L.R. 313, 318 (1940).

178 Ben Franklin Fin. Corp. v. Davis, 589 N.E.2d 857 (Ill. App. Ct. 1992) (late payments); Peoples Bank and Trust Co. v. Cermack, 658 So. 2d 1352 (Miss. 1995).

179 *See* Clayton v. Crossroads Equip. Co., 655 P.2d 1125, 1128, 1129 (Utah 1982).

180 Williamson v. Wanlass, 545 P.2d 1145 (Utah 1976) (late payments accepted; no good faith in acceleration without notice that lateness no longer acceptable).

181 Cole v. Melvin, 441 F. Supp. 193, 203 (D.S.D. 1971). *See also* Top of Iowa Coop. v. Sime Farms, Inc., 608 N.W.2d 454 (Iowa 2000); Land O'Lakes v. Hanig, 610 N.W.2d 518 (Iowa 2000). *See also Adequate Assurance of Performance: Of Risk, Duress, and Cognition*, 69 U. Colo. L. Rev. 71 (1998); R. Robertson, *The Right to Demand Adequate Assurances of Due Performance: U.C.C. Section 2-609 and Restatement (2d) of Contracts Section 251*, 38 Drake L. Rev. 305 (1988–1989).

182 The Low-Income Home Energy Assistance Program (LIHEAP) is a federally funded fuel assistance for low-income customers. 42 U.S.C. §§ 8621–8630.

equal payment plans.[183] Households that participate in these plans present lower risks to utility companies for a number of reasons. Because equal payment plans are often structured to allow households to start payments in the warm weather months, enabling them to build up credit against the time when their higher winter bills exceed their actual payments, the risk of permanent loss due to nonpayment is reduced for any given high winter bill. Additionally, equal payment plans facilitate better household budgeting, thus serving as further assurance that the payment for the utility company will be made. Other alternatives, such as having another person act as a guarantor, may suffice.

In two cases, utilities were authorized to collect a deposit for all residential service applicants who did not provide adequate identification during the application process.[184] Here, providing the requested information would eliminate the need for the deposit.

5.2.7 How Much Deposit Can a Utility Demand?

5.2.7.1 Common Law Rule: Utility May Seek Only a Reasonable Level of Deposit

At common law, a utility's right to seek deposits is limited by a duty to demand only a reasonable amount. No precise formula for calculating reasonableness has emerged. However, the courts generally will not consider a deposit set at an amount totaling one to three estimated (or typical) bills to be excessive.[185]

The right to require an advance payment is not authorization to make an arbitrary or excessive demand. The purpose of a cash deposit, even at common law, was to allow a utility to protect itself against "the loss of revenue through failure of others to pay."[186] A deposit may not be an "enforced loan."[187]

Thus, as one commentator observed, "requiring consumer deposits is sensible only if it actually deters defaults or minimizes losses for the utility company. . . . If deposits do not save utilities and their customers money, they are neither necessary nor reasonable."[188]

The key issue concerning deposits is whether the amount is "reasonable . . . to safeguard the account."[189] Some old cases have held that the deposit amount demanded was unreasonable and excessive.[190] More recently, courts would be likely to defer to utility commission decisions about the reasonableness of deposits, at least as a guide for regulated entities.

5.2.7.2 Regulated Utilities: Deposit Amounts Set by Rules

While the common law principle of reasonableness still applies, commissions, municipals and RECs often have very specific rules on the maximum amount utilities are allowed to require for deposits. Frequently, that amount is related to the amount of the monthly bill. For example, both Alaska and Arkansas have rules tying the amount of deposit to twice the average monthly bill.[191] California allows three months' estimated bill.[192] Similarly, other regulators set the amount of the deposit as a portion of the annual estimated charge for service.[193] Still others use the highest month's bill and charge that or twice that as a deposit. Others set dollar caps.[194] When a customer has had his or her utility service shut off, the deposit rules may be more stringent in some jurisdictions.[195]

---

183 *See* § 6.3.3.1, *infra*.

184 Petition of Consol. Edison Co. of N.Y., Inc., 189 Pub. Util. Rep. 4th 335, 1998 WL 941814 (N.Y. Pub. Serv. Comm'n 1998) (Commission used a cost benefit analysis to conclude that a deposit would reduce the amount of uncollectible accounts for applicants who refused identification and that the deposit could be avoided by providing such information); *In re* PacifiCorp (Utah Power & Light), 192 Pub. Util. Rep. 4th 289, 1999 WL 218118 (Utah Pub. Serv. Comm'n 1999).

185 *See, e.g.*, Southwestern Bell Tel. Co. v. Bateman, 266 S.W.2d 289 (Ark. 1954) (no evidence that deposit demand covering two months' exchange service charges and estimated tolls was unreasonable). *Cf. In re* Spencer, 218 B.R. 290 (Bankr. W.D.N.Y. 1998).

186 Underwood v. Southern Cities Distrib. Co., 157 So. 160, 161 (La. Ct. App. 1934).

187 Barriger v. Louisville Gas & Elec. Co., 244 S.W. 690 (Ky. 1922).

188 Note, *Public Utilities and the Poor: The Requirement of Cash Deposits from Domestic Consumers*, 78 Yale L.J. 448, 453 (1969).

189 Berner v. Interstate Power Co., 57 N.W.2d 55, 56 (Iowa 1953).

Hence, the Arkansas Supreme Court approved a $35 gas deposit because the utility "arrived at the figure of $35 upon the basis of the probable amount of gas that would be consumed thereat and the promptness with which appellant previously met his gas bills." Treadway v. Arkansas La. Gas Co., 120 S.W.2d 378, 379 (Ark. 1938).

190 In Wright v. Philadelphia Co., 16 Pa. Dist. 953 (1906), the plaintiff-gas consumer used a maximum of $8 dollars per month and was current on his payments. The utility threatened to terminate service within thirty days unless a $20 deposit was paid. The court found this excessive.

191 Alaska Admin. Code tit. 3, § 52.420(b). *See also* 16 Tex. Admin. Code § 25.478(d), (e) (deposit may not exceed 1/5 of estimated annual billing or two months' estimated billings); Muhammad v. PG&E, 1998 WL 1110494 (Cal. Pub. Utils. Comm'n 1999) (twice average bill authorized by tariff).

192 Cal. Pub. Util. Code § 394.4(g) (West).

193 West Virginia set this amount at 1/12 of the annual bill for residential service and 1/6 of the annual bill for non-residential accounts. W. Va. Code R. §§ 150-3-4.2, 150-4-4.2, 150-6-2.2, 150-7-4.2.

194 *See In re* PacifiCorp (Utah Power & Light), 192 Pub. Util. Rep. 4th 289, 1999 WL 218118 (Utah Pub. Serv. Comm'n 1999) (deposit set at lesser of $150 of sixty-day peak bill).

195 In Michigan, for example, in restoring service due to shut off for nonpayment, the deposit is no more than twice the average

5.2.7.3 Charging a Particular Customer the Maximum Allowed Deposit May Not Be Reasonable

One means by which utilities over-secure themselves against the risk of loss is to automatically impose maximum permissible deposits. Some public utility commissions, for example, permit a utility to collect a deposit equal to *no more than* twice the average monthly bill for a customer, but the affected utility automatically sets deposits at twice the average bill. Since it is probable that many households do not represent the maximum risk, they should be entitled to a lower deposit.

Similarly, a utility that is allowed to collect a deposit equal to one month's usage may base its deposit demand on the largest monthly bill, perhaps assuming that the largest bill will remain unpaid. There is likely no empirical basis for such an assumption.

Finally, the utility may keep the deposit longer than is necessary to secure payment from a customer who demonstrates reasonable payment history. This practice would also unfairly benefit the utility.

5.2.8 Payment of Deposit in Installments

When a deposit is required of a customer, there is often the possibility of requesting that the deposit be paid in installments to soften the economic blow on low-income consumers. This has been explicitly authorized in some tariffs and commission regulations.[196]

5.2.9 Deposits and Utility Customers in Bankruptcy

Bankruptcy law provides significant protection for utility customers. Once a petition is filed, a utility may not terminate services nor engage in any other collection effort for pre-petition debt and, if service has already been terminated, it must be restored.[197] In return for this protection, the utility is allowed to demand "adequate assurance of payment, in the form of a deposit or other security" for service after the petition date.[198] If the customer disagrees with the amount of security required, she or he may petition the bankruptcy court for modification of the amount. The bankruptcy court is not bound by state regulations or policies, but will consider them as evidence of reasonableness.[199] More on security deposits and bankruptcy can be found at § 13.1, *infra.*

5.2.10 Public Utility Must Pay Interest on Deposits

At common law, as applied to the relationship between a utility and its customers, a utility must pay interest to the customer on the deposit for utility service.[200] Commission rules often specify a minimum amount of interest regulated utilities are required to pay on deposits.[201] Some rules set a

peak-season monthly bill for the premises. Mich. Admin. Code r. 460.111(4), 460.1607(3).

196 *See, e.g., In re* Nova Scotia Power, Inc., 167 Pub. Util. Rep. 4th 250 (N.S. Util. & Review Bd. 1996) (company ordered to advise customers deposit can be paid in equal monthly installments).

197 11 U.S.C. § 366(a); *In re* Whittaker, 882 F.2d 791 (3d Cir. 1989); Citizens Gas & Coke Util. v. Mathews, 2004 WL 2137637 (S.D. Ind. Aug. 13, 2004) (affirming reconnect order); Tarrant v. City of Douglas (*In re* Tarrant), 190 B.R. 704 (Bankr. S.D. Ga. 1995) (when utility refused to restore service after filing of bankruptcy petition and demanded that petitioner pay pre-petition debt, court awarded actual and punitive damages and attorney fees to petitioner). *See also* § 13.1, *infra.*

198 11 U.S.C. § 366(b). *See* Bertrand Pan & Jennifer Taylor, *Sustaining Power: Applying 11 U.S.C. § 366 in Chapter 11 Post-BAPCPA*, 22 Emory Bankr. Dev. J. 371, 380 (2006) (discussing the addition of subsection 366(c), which defines "assurance of payment," in the Bankruptcy Abuse Prevention and Consumer Protection Act of 2005; arguing that the definition limits "the types of security that are acceptable as payment" and "appears to weigh in favor of utilities").

199 *In re* Spencer, 218 B.R. 290 (Bankr. W.D.N.Y. 1998) (utilities' demands for large deposits modified; utility may demand amount of two largest monthly bills in previous twelve month period from bankruptcy petitioners who are in arrears); Lloyd v. Champaign Tel. Co., 52 B.R. 653 (Bankr. S.D. Ohio 1985) (deposit of 2.3 times average monthly bill was reasonable for debtors in arrears, but rounding up of deposit to $150 was unreasonable when such amount would exceed maximum deposit permitted by tariff). *See also In re* Cannon, 2008 WL 2553475 (Bankr. E.D. Wis. June 23, 2008) (no deposit required under circumstances of case; debtor's gross income was below federal income poverty guidelines and applicable state law prohibited the collection of a deposit from such an individual); *In re* Steinebach, 303 B.R. 634 (Bankr. D. Ariz. 2004); *In re* Caldor, Inc., 199 B.R. 1 (Bankr. S.D.N.Y 1996).

200 Annot., *Deposit Required by Public Utility*, 43 A.L.R.2d 1262, §§ 2[a], 4 (1955). *See* Blumberg v. Pinellas County, 836 F. Supp. 839, 845 (M.D. Fla. 1993) (holding that a protected property right existed in the interest generated by utility deposits and that an unconstitutional taking occurred when the county failed to return interest to utility customers).

201 Florida's rules, for example, require public utilities to pay a minimum of 6% per annum, Fla. Admin. Code Ann. r. 25-30.311(4), 25-6.097(4). Michigan's rules specify 7% interest per annum, Mich. Admin. Code r. 460.111(7), 460.1607(5). Texas rules require interest at annual rate equal to the average rate paid over previous twelve months on twenty-six-week Treasury bills, 16 Tex. Admin. Code § 25.478(f); Tex. Util. Code Ann. § 183.003. *See also In re* Sound View Cmty. Media, 1998 WL 1031872 (Conn. Pub. Util. Comm'n 1998) (2.6% per statute); *In re* Determination of Interest Rates on Deposits, 1995 WL 770068 (Idaho Pub. Util. Comm'n 1995) (one-year U.S. treasury bonds as benchmark); *In re* IntraLATA Toll Competition, 122 Pub. Util. Rep. 4th 565 (Ky. Pub. Serv. Comm'n 1991) (carrier that requires a deposit must place these funds in an interest bearing escrow account); *In re* Missouri Pub. Serv., 152 Pub. Util. Rep. 4th 333 (Mo. Pub. Serv. Comm'n 1994) (9% interest on deposits); *In re* PacifiCorp (Utah Power & Light),

fixed interest rate while others tie the rate to some measure of interest rates, such as the prime rate or the rate of return on Treasury bills.[202] The D.C. Public Service Commission, for example, notes that the purpose of a deposit is "to compensate customers in a manner similar to a bank account," and thus favors a flexible rate, which will not become inadequate or excessive when interest rates fluctuate.[203] Municipal utilities often do not have to pay interest on deposits, but local practices vary.[204]

While interest is frequently allowed by regulators, the common utility argument that it should be set low at the same time that the interest rate on late payments should be comparable to credit cards (often 18% per year) should be challenged by consumers as producing an unfair benefit to the utility. If anything, the utility should be required to break even on these deposits and return them to customers along with whatever interest the utility collected while holding them on the customer's behalf.

5.2.11 Deposits Must Be Refunded Within a Reasonable Time

Deposits must be refunded to customers after the customer has demonstrated that he or she is not a risk to the company. The length of time a company can hold a deposit is generally established by regulations or tariff.[205] Few rules exist for RECs or municipal utilities.

5.2.12 Deposit Policies of Restructured Utilities

Restructuring raises additional issues regarding utility deposits. The Maryland Commission concluded that, when a customer chooses a competitive supplier, the utility must adjust its deposits in proportion to the dollar amount of service provided by the utility and refund the "non-utility" portion to the customer.[206] The Commission further required that deposit requirements be "reasonable" and not inconsistent with the deposit provisions of state regulations.[207]

Restructuring presents consumers with a confusing array of entities—free market sellers of generation or natural gas, brokers, and aggregators, and so forth. If these entities use discriminatory or unreasonable deposit policies to exclude low-income consumers, these consumers will be denied many of the benefits of choice and possible savings provided by restructuring. Advocates should argue that because these players resemble all other free market businesses, the various general civil rights, credit discrimination, and UDAP statutes (many of which include exemptions for pervasively regulated monopolies like traditional utility companies) will become applicable. In restructured states, low-income advocates should address the question of what consumer protections apply to deregulated entities. Violations of anti-discrimination or UDAP statutes, for example, could be made per se violations of licensing rules for competitive suppliers, brokers or aggregators.[208] That is, a finding by a court or administrative agency that a licensed seller was guilty of a civil rights or UDAP violation would be grounds for license termination, suspension, or such lesser sanctions as the Commission found appropriate.

5.3 Evaluating and Challenging a Utility's Deposit System

5.3.1 General Economic Considerations: Costs of Deposits

The benefits that deposits provide to utility companies can be summarized as follows:

> Rules adopted by utility companies which permit them to refuse to extend service or to discontinue service to any premises for the failure of a tenant or occupant to furnish a deposit to ensure payment of service bill, appear to be reasonable and necessary to afford a more effective remedy than the time-consuming and costly prosecution of delinquent accounts. Such rules protect not only a utility from those customers who fail to pay their bills, but also other ratepayers who would be burdened with making up the loss of revenue from nonpaying customers.[209]

---

192 Pub. Util. Rep. 4th 289, 1999 WL 218118 (Utah Pub. Serv. Comm'n 1999) (6% rate).

202 *See, e.g., In re* Rules Governing Customer Rights and Responsibilities, 145 Pub. Util. Rep. 4th 311 (D.C. Pub. Serv. Comm'n 1993) (rate of return for one-year Treasury bills); *In re* Mo. Gas Energy, 188 Pub. Util. Rep. 4th 30 (Mo. Pub. Serv. Comm'n 1998) (prime rate plus 1%).

203 *In re* Rules Governing Customer Rights & Responsibilities, 145 Pub. Util. Rep. 4th 311 (D.C. Pub. Serv. Comm'n 1993).

204 *See, e.g.*, Hogan v. Huntsville, 264 So. 2d 155, 158 (Ala. 1972). *See also In re* Municipal Water & Gas Servs., Op. Att'y Gen. No. 2002-0462, 2002 WL 31663393 (Miss. Sept. 13, 2002).

205 *See, e.g.*, 16 Tex. Admin. Code § 25.478(j) (refund provided if in past twelve billings no late payments); Wash. Admin. Code § 480-90-113(10) (deposit refunded after one year of "satisfactory payment," that is, no disconnection and not more than two delinquency notices); Petition of Consol. Edison Co. of N.Y., Inc., 189 Pub. Util. Rep. 4th 335, 1998 WL 941814 (N.Y. Pub. Serv. Comm'n 1998) (one year).

In a related context, an Oklahoma court ordered interest at the US Treasury bill rate to be paid on an over-payment and the over-payment refunded. Public Serv. Co. of Okla. v. Norris Sucker Rods, 917 P.2d 992 (Okla. Ct. App. 1995).

206 *In re* Provision & Regulation of Elec. Serv., 198 Pub. Util. Rep. 4th 43 (Md. Pub. Serv. Comm'n 1999).

207 *Id.*

208 *See, e.g.*, 65-407-305 Me. Code R. 4(k) (LexisNexis).

209 Short v. Baltimore Gas & Elec. Co., 63 Pub. Util. Rep. 3d 493

However, it is crucial to examine the costs of deposits as well, because an onerous and unnecessary deposit that jeopardizes continuing service to a low-income household can pose a serious threat to the home, health, and perhaps even life of the consumer. As the Supreme Court has noted, "[u]tility service is a necessity of modern life; indeed, the discontinuance of water or heating for even short periods of time may threaten health and safety."[210]

5.3.2 *The Function of a Deposit*

A utility's deposit rules and practices can be evaluated within the context of how the utility tries to limit bad debt and uncollectible bills. Bad debt is an expense to the utility that, as with any other expense, a utility should seek to minimize. Reducing bad debt, however, is not an end in itself, especially if the utility spends more on the means to reduce the bad debt than it gains from such an attempt. The goal of a utility should be to minimize net expenses to the ratepayers.

The deposit serves the function of protecting against the risk of nonpayment. A utility's deposit scheme should be subjected to an economic analysis. At least one company, with the approval of its commission, has rejected a universal deposit policy on just such economic grounds.[211]

Conceptually, the risk of loss to a utility is the same as the risk of loss to any other creditor serving debtors who may default. The risk involves all of the different possible types and combinations of default: large, small, partial, total, temporary and permanent. Utility deposit practices, however, often do not differentiate among the different types of risks that consumers may represent to the system. As a result, utilities tend to charge excessive deposits, potentially to the financial detriment of their remaining ratepayers. If this occurs, challenges in rate cases would be appropriate.

5.3.3 *The Costs to Ratepayers of a Deposit*

All ratepayers pay the costs of operating a deposit program in out-of-pocket expenses and any foregone revenues. Out-of-pocket expenses include obtaining credit information, frequently from a "consumer reporting agency." In such instances, the utility must take specific actions to ensure compliance with the terms of the federal Fair Credit Reporting Act.[212] Second, the utility must service the deposits, keeping track of them in such a manner that they can be refunded at the appropriate times and often paying interest on them.[213]

In addition, demanding a deposit from a customer who cannot afford to pay it and thus does not get connected (or reconnected) to the system will result in lost revenues for the utility. To the extent that these revenues would have exceeded the variable cost of delivering the energy (since rates are designed to do just that), another source is lost that contributes towards paying the company's fixed charges. The denial of service can leave the other, paying customers worse off.

For deposits to be cost-effective from a utility's business perspective, they must result in a reduction in uncollectibles at least equal to the cost of obtaining and servicing the deposits. In order for this reduction to occur, the customers from whom deposits are demanded must represent a risk of loss to the utility. If the customer is not considered a potential risk for permanent loss, a deposit collected from that customer may have little connection to the risk of loss. In that instance, to collect a deposit will impose some costs on the system and result in no benefits to offset those costs. Or if a deposit is held too long or is overly costly to administer, it would not be cost effective. If a utility has such a system in place, it should be subject to challenge in a rate proceeding, because the deposit system is costing ratepayers, not benefiting them or the utility company.

5.4 Reconnection Charges

Many utilities charge a fee to reconnect service after disconnection, even though the termination of service may be without fault by the customer. Some commissions have required these charges be waived for wrongful terminations or for some or all low-income customers. For example, in a New York case, the commission approved a settlement agreement that waived the $21 to $28 reconnection charge for any customer who agreed to have their utility bill paid directly by their social services provider or who showed that they were SSI recipients or had received LIHEAP benefits within the prior year.[214]

This approach is important to customers who are on fixed incomes with high utility expenses, as there is often no additional assistance money available to pay reconnect

---

(Md. 1966) (company acted reasonably in refusing to furnish service at the request of the owner of the premises while a tenant continued receiving the benefit of the service without payment of delinquent charges and a deposit as security for payment of future charges).

210 Memphis Light, Gas & Water Div. v. Craft, 436 U.S. 1, 18 (1978).

211 *In re* Minnesota Gas Co., 143 Pub. Util. Rep. 4th 416 (Minn. Pub. Util. Comm'n 1993) (commission agrees with company that collecting a deposit from all customers would cost more to administer than it would save in reducing unpaid bills). *See In re* Collection Policies of Major Gas and Elec. Utilities, 144 Pub. Util. Rep. 4th 86 (N.Y. Pub. Serv. Comm'n 1993) (utilities failed to show that collection of deposit from all new customers would be cost-effective).

212 15 U.S.C. §§ 1681–1681u. *See* § 5.2.4, *supra*.

213 *See* § 5.2.10, *supra* (interest required on deposits).

214 *In re* Consol. Edison of N.Y., Inc., 170 Pub. Util. Rep. 4th 141 (N.Y. Pub. Serv. Comm'n 1996).

charges. If reconnection charges are not waived, no service would be available until receipt of the next monthly income check.

Reconnection costs are often insurmountable to the customer, and may not be reflective of the utilities costs for reconnection, thus an equitable argument for waiver may be successful. The New York Commission found that waiving reconnection fees was part of a utility company's "obligation to take reasonable steps to assist its low-income customers."[215] The Ohio PUC rejected an application to raise reconnection charges from $15.00 to $43.90 on the grounds that it would be an impediment to universal service and increase Percentage of Payment Plan (PIPP) arrearages.[216] When a utility company has installed advanced metering with remote switching (which facilitates remote disconnections and reconnections), the traditional disconnection and reconnection charges should be challenged, as the costs to the utility to disconnect and reconnect are drastically reduced. In a California docket to address electric and gas disconnections, the commission found that remote disconnections and reconnections provide significant cost savings compared to the costs of disconnections and reconnections using field staff.[217]

Some companies charge a different amount for reconnection if the disconnection was customer-requested or company-initiated for nonpayment or other reasons.[218] Others charge differing amounts depending on the type of case or the time of reconnection.[219] Some commissions require that customers be offered a chance to pay these reconnection charges as part of a repayment plan.[220]

5.5 Challenging Late Charges

5.5.1 General

Utilities often seek to impose a late payment charge on those households that do not pay by a designated due date. The names given to these charges do not change their nature. They may be called late payment charges, forfeited discounts, a "net" bill versus a "gross" bill, a penalty, or a late service charge. There is no conceptual difference between the promise of a lower bill for prompt payment and the threat of a higher bill for late payment.

The imposition of such a charge is generally designed to serve either of two purposes: (1) to compensate the utility for expenses incurred as a result of the late payment; or (2) to provide an incentive for households to make timely payments.[221] Some commissions add a third purpose: to prevent subsidization of late payers by timely payers.[222] Unfortunately, utility late payment charges often bear little relation to these stated purposes. However, they have been a fact of life and have been authorized at least since 1915.[223]

215 *See In re* N.Y. State Elec. & Gas Corp., 165 Pub. Util. Rep. 4th 309 (N.Y. Pub. Serv. Comm'n 1995) (reconnection fees waived for all LIHEAP gas or electric customers who had been terminated for nonpayment and reconnected).

Ironically, the same commission, the New York Public Service Commission, also rejected a request that a much reconnection charge ($57.50) be waived for recipients of social services or LIHEAP, in a case involving a different company. *See In re* Nat'l Fuel Gas Distrib. Corp., 164 Pub. Util. Rep. 4th 4 (N.Y. Pub. Serv. Comm'n 1995) (no low-income waiver of $57.50 reconnect charge). *Cf.* South Carolina Elec. & Gas Co., 225 Pub. Util. Rep. 4th 440 (2003) (approves increased reconnection charge, which is slightly less than actual cost of reconnection, but notes that reconnection charges often fall on those least able to afford them).

216 *See In re* Toledo Edison Co., 168 Pub. Util. Rep. 4th 193 (Ohio Pub. Util. Comm'n 1996).

217 *See* Interim Decision Implementing Methods to Decrease the Number of Gas and Electric Utility Service Disconnections, Finding of Fact #17, D.10-07-048 (Cal. Pub. Util. Comm'n Jul. 30, 2010) (in this proceeding, PG&E had stated that the cost of restoring service remotely using smart meters was $8 compared to $66.50 using field staff).

218 *See In re* Shenandoah Gas Co., 164 Pub. Util. Rep. 4th 351 (W. Va. Pub. Serv. Comm'n 1995).

219 *In re* Bay State Gas Co., 139 Pub. Util. Rep. 4th 3 (Mass. Dep't Pub. Util. 1992); *In re* Minnegasco, Inc., 143 Pub. Util. Rep. 4th 416 (Minn. Pub. Util. Comm'n 1993) (reconnection charges of $15 for nonpayment and $50 for all other reasons approved); *In re* Ch. 14 Implementation, 2005 WL 2445959 (Pa. Pub. Util. Comm'n Sept. 9, 2005), *amended by* 2005 WL 4066360 (Pa. Pub. Util. Comm'n Dec. 22, 2005) (reconnection charge varies with customer income and other variables); *In re* Wis. Elec. Power Co., 175 Pub. Util. Rep. 4th 532 (Wis. Pub. Serv. Comm'n 1997) (reconnect charge, $36 during regular hours, $48 at other times); *In re* Cascade Natural Gas Corp., 171 Pub. Util. Rep. 4th 472 (Wash. Pub. Util. Comm'n 1996) (reconnection fee of $16 during regular hours and $32 after hours approved).

220 *In re* Vt. Tel. Co., 182 Pub. Util. Rep. 4th 63 (Vt. Pub. Serv. Bd. 1997) (repayment agreement must be offered to cover reconnection charges).

221 *See, e.g., In re* Potomac Elec. Co., 3 Pub. Util. Rep. 4th 65 (D.C. Pub. Serv. Comm'n 1973) (1% late charge for first month and 1.5% thereafter approved; purpose of late charge: cover administrative expense of collection and compensate for impact on working capital); *In re* Kansas City Power & Light Co., 28 Pub. Util. Rep. 4th 398 (Mo. Pub. Serv. Comm'n 1979) (purposes of late charge: recover additional costs of credit, provide incentive to pay timely, and avoid discrimination against paying customers; 2% late fee approved on first $50, then 1%); Waterbury v. City of Oswego, 674 N.Y.S.2d 530 (N.Y. App. Div. 1998) (municipal utility's 10% late fee upheld when utility statute and regulations did not apply to municipal utility, and purpose of fee was to encourage prompt payment).

222 *In re* Franklin Elec. Light Co., 116 Pub. Util. Rep. 4th 318, 1990 WL 488819 (Vt. Pub. Serv. Bd. Sept. 25, 1990) (compounding of late charges authorized; "non-compounding would likely require overly fastidious accounting and administrative procedures"; 1%-per-month late charge to be added to overdue bill and any prior unpaid late charges; discussion of three purposes of late charges: repay utility for time value of money, send price signals to customers, avoid subsidy by timely bill payers).

223 *See* Southwestern Tel. & Tel. Co. v. Danaher, 238 U.S. 482 (1915) (dismissing complaint for damages by utility customer

5.5.2 Are Late Charges Authorized by PUC?

In twenty-two states and the District of Columbia,[224] utility regulators have established uniform procedures for late payment penalties. In three states, Alabama, Colorado, and Vermont,[225] no late payment penalty is allowed. At least fifteen states have some classes of customers who are exempt from the late charges or for whom special policies apply, such as two late payments per year without penalty.[226] Most importantly, utilities in Kentucky, Massachusetts, New Jersey, Rhode Island, and Texas cannot charge late fees to residential customers. Montana bars late fees for low-income residential customers.[227] Idaho has denied late charges to water companies[228] and to telephone companies on the theory that they bill customers in advance of receiving the service.[229] In reducing a late fee from 1.5% to 1.0% a month, the Utah public service commission observed "that the potential for disconnection may be a sufficient inducement for customers to pay bills on time."[230]

In states that allow late charges on residential accounts, the authorized fees run as high as 5% per month (Missouri, Ohio,[231] and Tennessee), thus the potential for substantial additional amounts owed by low-income utility consumers from this source should not be minimized. Successfully challenging them can be an important boost for such customers.[232] Most late charges are in the range of 1% to 2% per month.[233]

against utility based on alleged discriminatory application of gross/net differential and other late charges).

224 Alabama, Colorado, D.C., Hawaii, Illinois, Indiana, Iowa, Kansas, Maine, Maryland, Michigan, Minnesota, New York, North Carolina, Oklahoma, Oregon, Rhode Island, South Carolina, Tennessee, Texas, Virginia, Washington, and Wisconsin. National Ass'n of Regulatory Util. Comm'rs, 1994–95 Compilation of Utility Regulatory Policy in the U.S. and Canada 457, tbl. 208. *See* appx. A.1, *infra* (summaries of most state customer service regulations).

225 In a 1990 case, the Vermont Public Service Board allowed a 1% late charge in an electric case. *See In re* Franklin Elec. Light Co., 116 Pub. Util. Rep. 4th 318, 1990 WL 488819 (Vt. Pub. Serv. Bd. Sept. 25, 1990) (compounding of late charges authorized; "non-compounding would likely require overly fastidious accounting and administrative procedures"; "1%-per-month late charge to be added to overdue bill and any prior unpaid late charges; discussion of three purposes of late charges: repay utility for time value of money, send price signals to customers, avoid subsidy by timely bill payers).

226 California (one utility), Connecticut, Florida, Georgia, Iowa, Kentucky, Maine, Massachusetts, Michigan, Missouri, Montana, New Hampshire, New Jersey, New York, Ohio, Pennsylvania (one utility), Rhode Island, and Texas. National Ass'n of Regulatory Util. Comm'rs, 1994–95 Compilation of Utility Regulatory Policy in the U.S. and Canada 457, tbl. 208. *See* appx. A.1, *infra*.

227 Maine and Michigan indicate they exempt certain customers, but which class was not specified. *See* National Ass'n of Regulatory Util. Comm'rs, 1994–1995 Compilation of Utility Regulatory Policy in the U.S. and Canada 457, tbl. 208.

228 *In re* Citizens Util. Co., 99 Pub. Util. Rep. 4th 1, 989 WL 418557 (Idaho Pub. Util. Comm'n Jan. 9, 1989).

229 *In re* Silver Star Telecom., 98 Pub. Util. Rep. 4th 222, 1988 WL 391208 (Idaho Pub. Util. Comm'n Nov. 30, 1988).

230 *In re* PacifiCorp d.b.a. Utah Power & Light Co., 192 Pub. Util. Rep. 4th 289, 1999 WL 218118 (Utah Pub. Serv. Comm'n Mar. 4, 1999).

231 *In re* Columbus S. Power Co., 133 Pub. Util. Rep. 4th 525, 1992 WL 205335 (Pub. Utils. Comm'n of Ohio May 12, 1992) (5%-per-month late charge allowed if bill unpaid twenty-one days after mailing; fifteen days proposed unconscionably short).

232 *See also* Annot., *Electricity, Gas or Water Furnished by Public Utility As "Goods" Within Provisions of U.C.C. Art. 2 on Sales*, 48 A.L.R.3d 1060 (1973). *See generally* Jane Mallor, *Utility "Service" Under the Uniform Commercial Code: Are Utilities In for a Shock?*, 56 The Notre Dame Lawyer 89 (1980); Warren Samuels, *Commentary: Utility Late Payment Charges*, 19 Wayne L. Rev. 1151 (1973) (reviews NARUC report on late fees and proposes 1%-per-month charge with one "free" late payment per year); Note, *Determining the Reasonableness of Public Utility Late Charges*, 26 Kan. L. Rev. 559 (1978) (discusses *Jones v. Kansas Gas & Electric Co.* and reviews all pre-1978 cases); 64 Am. Jur. 2d, *Public Utilities* § 28 (1972); Annot., *Validity and Construction of Provision Imposing "Late Charge" or Similar Exaction for Delay in Making Periodic Payments on Note, Mortgage or Installment Sale Contract*, 63 A.L.R.3d 50 (1975).

233 *See In re* Avon Water Co., 2006 WL 733496 (Conn. Dep't of Pub. Util. Control Mar. 13, 2006) (revised late charge of 1% including $2 minimum fee); *In re* Connecticut Natural Gas Corp., 148 Pub. Util. Rep. 4th 239, 1993 WL 590121 (Conn. Dep't of Public Util. Control Dec. 15, 1993); *In re* New York Tel. Co., 63 Pub. Util. Rep. 4th 244 (Conn. Dep't of Pub. Utils. Control 1984) (no late charge allowed if any resident at customer's address is seriously ill and has so certified according to company procedures); *In re* Potomac Elec. Co., 3 Pub. Util. Rep. 4th 65 (D.C. Pub. Serv. Comm'n 1973) (1% late charge for first month and 1.5% thereafter approved; purpose of late charge: cover administrative expense of collection and compensate for impact on working capital); *In re* United Cities Gas Co., 174 Pub. Util. Rep. 4th 169 (Ga. Pub. Serv. Comm'n 1996) (late charges of 1.5% on balances over $20 approved); *In re* Hawaii Elec. Light Co., 54 Pub. Util. Rep. 4th 63 (Haw. Pub. Utils. Comm'n 1983) (1%-per-month late charge approved to avoid subsidization by other customers); *In re* Bay State Gas Co., 139 Pub. Util. Rep. 4th 3, 1992 WL 453358 (Mass. Dep't of Pub. Utils. Oct. 30, 1992) (Department approved late fee on non-gas payments—for example, appliance rental—of 1.5%); *In re* Midwest Energy Coop., 2007 WL 2142065 (Mich. Pub. Serv. Comm'n July 26, 2007) (one-time late payment of 2% approved); *In re* Kan. City Power & Light Co., 28 Pub. Util. Rep. 4th 398 (Mo. Pub. Serv. Comm'n 1979) (purposes of late charge: recover additional costs of credit, provide incentive to pay timely, and avoid discrimination against paying customers; 2% late fee approved on first $50, then 1%); *In re* Montana Power Co., 181 Pub. Util. Rep. 4th 397, 1997 WL 823997 (Mont. Pub. Serv. Comm'n Oct. 30, 1997) (late charge of 1% after sixty days approved; bad-check charge of $10 approved); *In re* New York Tel. Co., 121 Pub. Util. Rep. 4th 117, 1991 WL 501810 (N.Y. Pub. Serv. Comm'n Mar. 7, 1991) (1.5% per month late charge approved, but on advance-billed local service, no late charge until second unpaid bill); Pennsylvania Pub. Util. Comm'n v. General Tel. Co. of Pa., 55 Pub. Util. Rep. 4th 644 (Pa. Pub. Utils. Comm'n 1983) (1%-per-month late charge

Some commissions do not allow charging late fees on the entire bill. For example, in Connecticut, New York Telephone was restricted in its late charges for overdue local service bills, exclusive of long-distance calls and federal, state, or municipal taxes.[234] Other states take a diametrically opposite view and authorize late charges on both the basic utility service and on any other items on the bill.[235] A late fee may not be imposed on a disputed bill.[236] If a bill dispute is resolved in favor of a customer, any assessed late charges must be refunded.[237]

The imposition of late fees is dependent on what bill goes unpaid. West Virginia allows a one-time charge of 10% on the unpaid amount if the bill is not paid within twenty-one days. However, the West Virginia public service commission held that, if the late payment charge applies to the bill only once when it becomes delinquent, and a utility receives payment at a time when both a delinquent bill and current bill are outstanding, the utility is to apply the payment to the current bill first and apply any leftover to the delinquencies.[238] Similarly, the Kentucky commission approved a proposal providing that, when a customer with a past-due balance makes a partial payment sufficient to pay the bill for the current month's usage plus $10 or 5% of the outstanding due balance, whichever is greater, the utility "shall credit the payment to the current month's bill first, then credit the remainder to the past due balance."[239] "Crediting the current month's bill first will eliminate the assessment of a late payment penalty on the current month's bill, and requiring some payment toward the past due balance as a prerequisite for such crediting provides the customer an incentive to reduce the past due balance."[240]

Utilities are seeking and getting approval for more and more fees relating to consumer's delinquencies. For instance, one utility now charges a "warrant fee" of $35 if the company must get a warrant to gain access to the premises to disconnect service.[241] A company went too far, however, when it assessed massive fines on telephone users who did not pay their full bills.[242] Moreover, a utility proposal to charge a fee when payments were made to service personnel in the field to stop a disconnection was rejected as well.[243] One electric company won commission approval for unfounded meter-error claim charges.[244] However, whether cost-justified or not, some fees may not be approved because of their disproportionate impact on low-income customers. In disapproving a proposed increase in the reconnection charge for discontinued service, the Montana public service commission observed that "the customers to whom this charge applies are almost certainly the lowest income customers . . . since they have to pay their arrearages anyway, they are likely suffering some difficulty in getting reconnected. To impose on them yet more cost, such an increase in the reconnection fee might prevent some of these customers from obtaining vital utility service."[245]

Moreover, one utility request for regulatory permission to seek the costs of collection through small claims actions was not approved, with the observation made that the costs of bill collection "are ordinary costs of doing business and should be collectible only if included in the judgment rendered in a case."[246]

Late fees in excess of the charges established by regulation or tariff may be directly challenged in an order-to-show-cause type proceeding before the regulatory authority. There, injunctive relief and/or penalties may be assessed for violation of commission regulations.[247]

---

approved); *In re* Mountain Fuel Supply, 149 Pub. Util. Rep. 4th 36 (Utah Pub. Serv. Comm'n 1994) (12% annual interest rate for past-due accounts approved); *In re* Central Vt. Public Serv. Corp., 113 Pub. Util. Rep. 4th 220, 1990 WL 488660 (Vt. May 31, 1990) (1%-per-month late charge approved since simple to administer and close to company's cost of capital); *In re* Wisconsin Elec. Power Co., 175 Pub. Util. Rep. 4th 532, 1997 WL 120654 (Wis. Pub. Serv. Comm'n Feb. 13, 1997) (various charges approved including late charge of 1% after twenty days). *But see* Waterbury v. City of Oswego, 674 N.Y.S.2d 530 (N.Y. App. Div. 1998) (municipal water utility allowed to charge 10% late fee).

234 *In re* New York Tel. Co., 63 Pub. Util. Rep. 4th 244 (Conn. Dep't of Pub. Utils. Control 1984).

235 *In re* Hawaii Elec. Light Co. Inc., 159 Pub. Util. Rep. 4th 290, 1995 WL 113960 (Haw. Pub. Utils. Comm'n Feb. 10, 1995).

236 *In re* The Detroit Edison Co., 214 Pub. Util. Rep. 4th 278, 305, 2001 WL 1708262 (Mich. Pub. Serv. Comm'n Apr. 26, 2001); *In re* Review of the Commission's Minimum Telephone Service Standards Found in Chapter 4901:1-5 of the Ohio Administrative Code, 2007 WL 2042479 (Pub. Utils. Comm'n of Ohio July 11, 2007) (prohibits late fees on "[a]ny portion of the bill that is in bona fide dispute").

237 *In re* Rules Concerning Residential Gas Util. Serv. Disconnections, 1998 WL 1037589 (Ga. Pub. Serv. Comm'n 1998).

238 *In re* W. Va. Water Co., 231 Pub. Util. Rep. 4th 423, 468, 2004 WL 225496 (W. Va. Pub. Serv. Comm'n Jan. 2, 2004).

239 *In re* Louisville Gas & Elec. Co., 119 Pub. Util. Rep. 4th 431, 460, 1990 WL 488821 (Ky. Pub. Serv. Comm'n Dec. 21, 1990).

240 *Id.*

241 *In re* Bay State Gas Co., 139 Pub. Util. Rep. 4th 3, 1992 WL 453358 (Mass. Dep't of Pub. Utils. Oct. 30, 1992) (department approved; "customer warrant fee" when company must obtain warrant to get access to premises to disconnect, $35 after customer gets specific notice).

242 Commonwealth v. Heggenstaller, 699 A.2d 767 (Pa. Super. Ct. 1997) ($6550 penalty excessive for failing to pay $28.75 in telephone surcharges for 911 service).

243 *In re* Bay State Gas Co., 139 Pub. Util. Rep. 4th 3, 1992 WL 453358 (Mass. Dep't of Pub. Utils. Oct. 30, 1992) ("Field collection fee" of $8.50 rejected).

244 *See In re* PacifiCorp (Utah Power & Light), 192 Pub. Util. Rep. 4th 289, 1999 WL 218118 (Utah Pub. Serv. Comm'n 1999).

245 *In re* Montana-Dakota Util. Co., 222 Pub. Util. Rep. 4th 36, 61, 2002 WL 31991562 (Mont. Pub. Serv. Comm'n Dec. 18, 2002).

246 *In re* Wisconsin Pub. Serv. Corp., 206 Pub. Util. Rep. 4th 1, 30, 2000 WL 33253131 (Wis. Pub. Serv. Comm'n Dec. 22, 2000). *Cf.* Equitable Gas Co. v. Wade, 812 A.2d 715 (Pa. Super. Ct. 2002) (utility not entitled to collect 18% per year interest on past-due bill after it obtained final judgment against customer, since statute on post-judgment interest controlled).

247 Most public utility commissions have statutory authority to

Perhaps the most notable of the cases pursued in this way was a case against Pacific Bell for improperly charging customers late fees for five years by failing to record when payments were received and instead crediting the accounts on the date the payment was processed, sometimes weeks later, resulting in late charges and sometimes disconnection. Some customers who chose to use plain envelopes rather than those provided by the company to make payments were also improperly assessed late charges. The utility was fined $15 million and ordered to return $35 million in late payments and reconnection charges to customers.[248]

5.5.3 No Late Charges When There Is Special Regulatory Protection from Disconnection

Late payment charges are often inappropriate because of special credit and collection protections established by state Public Utility Commission (PUC) regulations. Under many PUC rules, utilities are prohibited from seeking to collect a bill through the disconnection process in a variety of circumstances:

- Most states now have special winter protections, prohibiting disconnection during certain months or when the temperature falls below a certain level.[249]
- Many states prescribe minimum arrears, below which the utility may not disconnect service.[250]
- Many states require utilities to suspend collection activities when a household presents a "medical certificate" indicating that the disconnection of service would present a particular health problem. Frequently, these health problems are tied simply to the presence of the very old or the very young in a household.[251]
- Some states have a general "residential hardship category" and do not permit late charges to be applied against customers who fall into this category.[252]
- Many states have some sort of "time payment plan." It would be improper to charge late fees on overdue charges that have been incorporated into such a plan while the customer is current in payments on that plan.[253]

In these instances of special protections against collection activity, it would be inappropriate to collect any late charge.[254] Because a late charge is designed to compensate the utility for out-of-pocket collection expenses, and the PUC regulations prevent such collection activities, charging a late fee would be compensating the utility for expenses never incurred. Some commissions have refused to authorize late fees on certain utility bills, such as water bills.[255] Thus, when electrical and water bills were combined, no late charges could be assessed.[256]

5.5.4 Late Receipt of Bill and Late Payments by Others As a Defense

Not receiving a bill on time can be a defense to late charges.[257] Late payments by third parties or caused by third parties (for example, fuel funds, charities, or LIHEAP pay-

enforce their own regulations by fines, injunctions, or other remedies. Courts also have equitable powers to create appropriate remedies for violations of regulations or laws. *See, e.g., In re* Crotzer, 147 B.R. 252 (Bankr. N.D. Ala. 1992) (imposing late fees in excess of statutory maximum resulted in creditor's forfeiture of all late fees; to rule otherwise by permitting creditor to retain legal amount would give creditors an incentive to break the law); BellSouth Telecomms., Inc. v. Jacobs, 834 So. 2d 855 (Fla. 2002) (upholding Commission's order that increases from change in tariff on how late charges are assessed violated regulatory statute).

248 The ALJ who heard the case recommended $65 million in rebates and fines. The full commission reduced the final assessment to the $50 million figure. *See* National Ass'n of Regulatory Util. Comm'ns, Bulletin No. 23-1993, at 17, 18 (June 7, 1993); L.A. Times, Apr. 7, 1993, at p.D1 (1993 WL 2327472).

249 *See* appx. A.5, *infra.*

250 In Vermont, for example, a utility may not disconnect for arrears less than $50. Moreover, even absent regulatory directive, some utilities have adopted similar limits as a matter of internal policy. For example, Union Heat, Light, and Power Co. (UHLP) in Kentucky will not disconnect service for less than $50.

251 *See* appx. A.6, *infra.*

252 *In re* Bozrah Light & Power Co., 76 Pub. Util. Rep. 4th 697 (Conn. Dep't of Public Utils. Control 1986) (late charge set at 1% per month given cost of capital of approximately 10%; no late charges for residential hardship customers; $15 bounced-check charge approved as equal to bank charge to utility); *In re* New York Tel. Co., 63 Pub. Util. Rep. 4th 244 (Conn. Dep't of Pub. Utils. Control 1984) (no late charge allowed if any resident at customer's address is seriously ill and has so certified according to company procedures).

253 *See In re* Rulemaking to Amend OAR Chapter 860, Divisions 021 and 034 Relating to Consumer Issues, 1999 WL 719757 (Or. Pub. Utils. Comm'n 1999).

254 *See In re* New York Tel. Co., 63 Pub. Util. Rep. 4th 244 (Conn. Dep't of Pub. Utils. Control 1984) (no late charge allowed if any resident at customer's address is seriously ill and has so certified according to company procedures).

255 *See In re* Barnstable Water Co., Mass. DTE 91-189-A (Mass. Dep't of Telecomms. & Energy July 31, 1992) (extending to water companies the policy expressed in Mass. Gen. Laws ch. 164, § 94D, which strictly prohibits electric and gas companies from imposing late fees on residential accounts).

256 *In re* Citizens Util. Co., 99 Pub. Util. Rep. 4th 1, 1989 WL 418557 (Idaho Pub. Util. Comm'n Jan. 9, 1989) (no late fee allowed on unpaid combined water and electric bills since Idaho commission does not allow late charges on water bills).

257 *See In re* PP&L, Inc., 1999 WL 632770 (Pa. Pub. Utils. Comm'n 1999) (when utility issues bills late, late charges waived); Trigg v. Middle Tenn. Elec. Membership Corp., 533 S.W.2d 730, 733 (Tenn. Ct. App. 1975). *See also* 220 Mass. Code Regs. 25.02(1) ("no bill shall be considered 'due' . . . in less than 45 days from receipt or in the case of gas and electric companies in less time than has elapsed between receipt of such bill and receipt of the most recent previous bill").

ments) should not subject customers to late charges. In a similar context, courts have refused to grant evictions for late payments against tenants who were unable to pay rent on time because welfare checks were delayed and because of other similar circumstances.[258]

5.5.5 *When Liability for Late Fees Terminates*

Generally, late-fee liability ends when the bill, including late fees, is paid either in full or by a negotiated settlement. Additional late fees should not be assessed and, if they are, can be challenged if they are added after the customer has entered a deferred payment agreement,[259] filed for bankruptcy,[260] entered a budget billing plan,[261] enrolled in a percentage-of-payment or affordable payment plan (PIPP),[262] or after the utility writes the bill off as uncollectible.[263]

5.5.6 *Calculation of a Late Charge May Not Involve a "Pyramiding" of Late Charges*

5.5.6.1 Pyramiding Described

One special late charge practice is pyramiding late charges, that is, applying a customer's current payments first to outstanding late charges or overdue amounts—then applying the remainder to the installment that is currently due—or assessing a late charge solely because the consumer did not pay a previous late charge. For example, if a $5 late charge is assessed for failure to pay a $100 bill on time in January, and the consumer later in January pays $100 and pays another $100 in February, a utility company may try to assess a second $5 fee based on the fact that the first $5 late charge is still owing. In this situation, the utility may claim that $5 of the $100 February payment went to the January late charge, such that the February payment is $5 short, and continues to assess monthly late charges even if only the January payment was late. This can easily occur when bills are paid by fuel funds, LIHEAP, or a charity that is willing to pay the underlying bill but not late fees.

258 *See* American Nat'l Bank & Trust Co v. Dominick, 507 N.E.2d 512 (Ill. App. Ct. 1987) (late rent payments because of late welfare checks not material noncompliance with lease); Cincinnati Metro Hous. Auth. v. Green, 536 N.E.2d 1 (Ohio Ct. App. 1987) (stolen money order; circumstances beyond control, promptly informing landlord, and diligent efforts to pay were eviction defense).

259 *See* § 6.6, *infra*.

260 *See* § 12.1, *infra*.

261 *See* § 6.4, *infra*.

262 *See* § 9.2.3, *infra*.

263 *See In re* Franklin Elec. Light Co., 116 Pub. Util. Rep. 4th 318, 1990 WL 488819 (Vt. Pub. Serv. Bd. Sept. 25, 1990).

5.5.6.2 FTC Credit Practices Rule

The Federal Trade Commission has enacted a rule prohibiting precisely the practice described above.[264] The rule makes it unfair "for a creditor, directly or indirectly, to levy or collect any delinquency charge on a payment . . . when the only delinquency is attributable to late fee(s) or delinquency charge(s) assessed on earlier installment(s)."[265] Thus, the FTC Rule would prohibit the type of pyramiding described in the example at the end of § 5.5.6.1, *supra*. However, it does not apply to pyramiding that results from a skipped payment rather than a late payment.[266] For example, if a customer makes no January payment on a bill, the utility may validly apply the February payment to the outstanding January debt and may later attribute the March payment to the February debt, and so on and so forth. Under this accounting method, every payment is viewed as one month late and late charges are validly assessed every month.[267]

Some courts have held that it is unlawful "to add late charges for the initial month that payments were late onto a total balance, and then to compute late charges for each succeeding month on the basis of a figure which included not only all of the payments which were delinquent, a practice itself questionable, but onto a figure which included previously-accrued late charges as well as delinquent payment."[268]

Although this form of pyramiding late charges violates federal regulations, not all utilities are subject to these regulations. Because some utilities are not-for-profit organizations, they are arguably outside the FTC Act's definition of "corporation."[269] Most utilities should be covered however. The FTC Rule sets a standard that might be useful in arguing that such a practice violates a state unfair and deceptive acts and practices law.

264 16 C.F.R. § 444.4.

265 *Id.*

266 *See* Federal Trade Comm'n, Staff Advisory Letter (June 21, 1985), *reprinted in* Consumer Cred. Guide (CCH) 96,257; Federal Trade Comm'n, Staff Advisory Letter (May 31, 1985), *reprinted in* Consumer Cred. Guide (CCH) 96,309.

267 *See* National Consumer Law Center, Unfair and Deceptive Acts and Practices §§ 3.4.5, 6.2 (7th ed. 2008 and Supp.) (thorough treatment of this subject).

268 *In re* Jordan, 91 B.R. 673, 679, 680 (Bankr. E.D. Pa. 1988) (citing Acker v. Provident Nat'l Bank, 512 F.2d 729, 739–42 (3d Cir. 1975) and Haas v. Pittsburgh Nat'l Bank, 526 F.2d 1083, 1094–95 (3d Cir. 1975)). *Cf. In re* Review of the Commission's Minimum Telephone Service Standards Found in Chapter 4901:1-5 of the Ohio Administrative Code, 2007 WL 2042479 (Pub. Utils. Comm'n of Ohio July 11, 2007) (prohibits late fees on "[a]ny previous late payment fees included in the amount due").

269 The term "corporation" is defined to apply only to companies organized to carry on business for profit or for the profit of their members. 15 U.S.C. § 44.

5.5.6.3 The Late Charge Should Not Include Late Charges Imposed More Than Once for the Same Skipped Payment

Another type of pyramiding involves multiple late charges for the same delinquency. That is, if a consumer makes the February, March, and April payments but has never paid the January bill, some creditors assess late charges for the January bill each month. The FTC Rule does not address this type of pyramiding. However, a state retail installment sales act might apply to the utility transaction and specifically address the amount and method of calculating late charges.[270] Many of these acts limit creditors' ability to assess more than one late charge for the same late payment.[271] In those states, these laws would provide the basis for a challenge. Otherwise, a UDAP challenge or a proceeding before the regulatory body might be the only options.

5.5.6.4 No Late Charges on Unpaid Late Charges

The calculation of a late charge that includes, as part of its underlying principal, previously unpaid late fees has often been found unlawful.[272] "The general rule, even as between private persons, is that, in the absence of a contract therefor or some statute, compound interest is not allowed to be computed on a debt."[273] To charge compound interest[274] requires an *express authorization* by the underlying contract.[275] In many jurisdictions, even an agreement to pay interest on interest is void as contrary to public policy.[276] In recent years, however, those prohibitions have been vitiated somewhat with the deregulation of interest rates.[277] *In re Franklin Electric Light Co.*, however, reached the opposite conclusion, finding that "non-compounding would likely require overly fastidious accounting and administrative procedures," and specifically authorized a 1%-per-month late charge that is to be added to the overdue bill and any prior unpaid late charges.[278]

5.5.7 Late Charges Should Not Be Assessed Prematurely

A utility may prematurely levy late payment charges before incurring any expenses. For example, the utility might assess late charges for any payment made after the past-due date—for example, the 15th of the month—but not institute collection activity until a bill is ten days overdue (that is, the 25th of the month). Households making payments during that ten-day interim are paying compensation for collection expenses that were never incurred, and this may be unfairly discriminatory according to utility law principles.

Using this approach, the Kansas Supreme Court, in one of the few reported appellate court cases considering this issue, reversed the Kansas Corporation Commission and threw out the uniform late fees they had approved. The court based its opinion on the failure of the Kansas Corporation Commission to distinguish between customers who are late and cause the company to incur collection costs and those who are late but do not incur collection costs. The court found charging all late customers the same late charge was "discriminatory and unfair." The court also held that any late fee charged must be reasonably related to the "purpose to be achieved."[279] In response, the Kansas Corporation Commission established a two-tier system of late charges, with the higher rate assessed against those customers in situations in which actual collection expenses are incurred.[280]

At least one commission has ordered a telephone company to allow customers to establish a preferred billing date during the month and disallowed late charges for fees billed to third parties in order to minimize late charges.[281] Late charges should not begin to accrue until a reasonable time after mailing of the bill. This period is often set by com-

270 *See, e.g.*, Cal. Civ. Code § 1803.6 (West) (Retail Installment Act); U.C.C.C. § 2.502 (Uniform Consumer Credit Code; Model Code).

271 *See, e.g.*, N.C. Gen. Stat. § 25A-29.

272 *See* Waterman Convalescent Hosp. v. Jurupa Cmty. Servs. Dist., 62 Cal. Rptr. 2d 264 (Cal. Ct. App. 1996) (no pyramiding of late fees allowed); Mich. Admin. Code r. 460.1614 (an electric or gas utility may asses a late charge that is not more than 2%, not compounded, of the portion of the bill that is delinquent). *See generally* 45 Am. Jur. 2d *Interest and Usury* § 57 (1999); 47 C.J.S. *Interest and Usury; Consumer Credit* § 15 (2005).

273 Cherokee Nation v. United States, 270 U.S. 476, 490 (1926). *See also* Brooklyn Sav. Bank v. O'Neil, 324 U.S. 697, 715 (1945).

274 *See* Annot., *What Is "Compound Interest" Within Meaning of Statutes Prohibiting the Charging of Such Interest*, 10 A.L.R.3d 421 (1966).

275 Stovall v. Illinois Cent. Gulf Railroad Co., 722 F.2d 190, 192 (5th Cir. 1984).

276 *See generally* Annot., *Validity of Agreement to Pay Interest on Interest*, 37 A.L.R. 325, 332–34 (1925) (supplemented by 76 A.L.R. 1484, 1485 (1932)).

277 National Consumer Law Center, The Cost of Credit: Regulation, Preemption, and Industry Abuses (4th ed. 2009 and Supp.)

278 *In re* Franklin Elec. Light Co., 116 Pub. Util. Rep. 4th 318, 1990 WL 488819 (Vt. Pub. Serv. Bd. Sept. 25, 1990) (compounding of late charges authorized).

279 Jones v. Kansas Gas & Elec. Co., 565 P.2d 597 (Kan. 1977). *See also* Note, *Determining the Reasonableness of Public Utility Late Charges*, 26 Kan. L. Rev. 595 (1978) (discusses *Jones* and analyzes commercial business practices as a test for reasonableness of late charges).

280 Note, *Determining the Reasonableness of Public Utility Late Charges*, 26 Kan. L. Rev. 595, 606 (1978).

281 Washington Util. & Trans. Comm'n v. U.S. West Commc'ns, 169 Pub. Util. Rep. 4th 417, 1996 WL 350826 (Wash. Utils. & Trans. Comm'n Apr. 11, 1996) (no late charges for local service until past due; customers should be allowed to pick preferred billing date during month to reduce likelihood of charges), *aff'd on other grounds*, 949 P.2d 1337 (Wash. 1997).

mission order, generic rule, or tariffs,[282] most often in the range of twenty to thirty days.[283] At least one state utility commission has found that the period before which late fees are imposed should be longer for bimonthly and quarterly bills than for monthly bills.[284] Moreover, the New York Public Service Commission held that establishing varying payment periods is not prohibited by a statute requiring a utility bill for services.[285]

5.5.8 Usury Challenges

Challenges to utility late charges based on state usury laws have generally not been successful. While utility late fees are generally expressed as a percentage of the overdue bill and thus have the appearance of interest charges, they are different. The analysis used by courts in cases challenging utility late charges on usury grounds has been similar to that described above looking at late fees for consumer loans and mortgages. Courts have uniformly determined that such fees are not interest subject to usury laws at all, sometimes because the fees are not interest, sometimes because they are utility charges not loan charges, and sometimes for other reasons.[286]

5.5.9 The Fair Credit Billing Act

The federal Fair Credit Billing Act (FCBA) provides consumers with a statutory mechanism to challenge billing errors in open-end credit.[287] The key issue is whether the utility charges are exempted under the Truth in Lending Act (of which FCBA is a part).[288] The types of billing errors covered include failing to credit a payment, computational errors, incorrect estimates, and sending a bill to the wrong address.

5.5.10 Credit Discrimination Challenges to Late Charges

Utility rates and services must be reasonable and nondiscriminatory, both under regulatory principles and under federal law. If late fees or other charges are assessed in a

282 *See, e.g.*, 126-03-2 Ark. Code R. § 5.07(C) (LexisNexis) (the amount of a late payment charge shall be set forth in utility's tariff); Ohio Admin. Code 4901:1-15-26(B) (the amount and terms of a late payment charge are set forth in a water and sewer company tariff).

283 *See, e.g.*, 126-03-2 Ark. Code R. § 5.05(B) (LexisNexis) (if utility imposes a late fee, due date shall not be less than twenty-two calendar days after date the bill is mailed). *See In re* Potomac Elec. Co., 3 Pub. Util. Rep. 4th 65 (D.C. Pub. Serv. Comm'n 1973) (1% late charge for first month and 1.5% thereafter approved; purpose of late charge: cover administrative expense of collection and compensate for impact on working capital); *In re* Central Me. Power Co., 8 Pub. Util. Rep. 4th 277 (Me. Pub. Utils. Comm'n 1975) (1% late charge approved; analogy to banks and stores 18% rate inapposite since no disconnection option there); *In re* Kansas City Power & Light Co., 28 Pub. Util. Rep. 4th 398 (Mo. Pub. Serv. Comm'n 1979) (purposes of late charge: recover additional costs of credit, provide incentive to pay timely, and avoid discrimination against paying customers; 2% late fee approved on first $50, then 1%); *In re* Columbus S. Power Co., 133 Pub. Util. Rep. 4th 525, 1992 WL 205335 (Pub. Utils. Comm'n of Ohio May 12, 1992) (5%-per-month late charge allowed if bill unpaid twenty-one days after mailing; fifteen days proposed unconscionably short); *In re* Franklin Elec. Light Co., 116 Pub. Util. Rep. 4th 318, 1990 WL 488819 (Vt. Pub. Serv. Bd. Sept. 25, 1990) (compounding of late charges authorized; "non-compounding would likely require overly fastidious accounting and administrative procedures"; 1%-per-month late charge to be added to the overdue bill and any prior unpaid late charges; discussion of three purposes of late charges: repay utility for time value of money, send price signals to customers, avoid subsidy by timely bill payers); *In re* Wisconsin Elec. Power Co., 175 Pub. Util. Rep. 4th 532, 1997 WL 120654 (Wis. Pub. Serv. Comm'n Feb. 13, 1997) (late charge of 1% approved after twenty days).

284 *In re* Birmingham Util., 226 Pub. Util. Rep. 4th 468, 493, 2003 WL 21961992 (Conn. Dep't of Pub. Utils. Control Aug. 7, 2003).

285 *In re* Retail Access Bus. Rules, 193 Pub. Util. Rep. 4th 143, 152, 1999 WL 548263 (N.Y. Pub. Serv. Comm'n Apr. 15, 1999).

286 *See* Tennyson v. Gas Serv. Co., 506 F.2d 1135 (10th Cir. 1974); Huegel v. City of Easton, 2003 WL 22428435 (E.D. Pa. May 13, 2003) (an interest rate in excess of that allowed by law can be considered usurious only if the rate is imposed as consideration for the creditor's forbearance); Ferguson v. Electric Power Bd. of Chattanooga, 378 F. Supp. 787 (E.D. Tenn. 1974) (Tennessee usury laws not applicable to utility "gross rate" billing charge), *aff'd*, 511 F.2d 1403 (6th Cir. 1975) (table); Mallard v. Forest Heights Water Works, Inc., 580 S.E.2d 602 (Ga. Ct. App. 2003) (evidence that water utility charged a 10% late fee did not create a triable issue on claim of usury); Delich v. Iowa Elec. Light & Power Co., 9 Pub. Util. Rep. 4th 335, 340 (Iowa State Commerce Comm'n 1975); State *ex rel.* Guste v. Council of City of New Orleans, 309 So. 2d 290, 296 (La. 1975) (usury claim denied on grounds that utility sales are consumer credit sales, not loans, and usury laws apply only to loans; no UDAP violation); State *ex rel.* Ashcroft v. Public Serv. Comm'n, 674 S.W.2d 660 (Mo. Ct. App. 1984) (utility late fees not equivalent of interest charged for use of money; late fees apply even to state of Missouri's $100,000 delinquency); Waterbury v. City of Oswego, 674 N.Y.S.2d 530 (N.Y. App. Div. 1998); *In re* City of Binghamton, 521 N.Y.S.2d 140 (N.Y. App. Div. 1987) (no "loan," thus no usury on overdue sewer and water assessments), *appeal dismissed*, 70 N.Y.2d 1002 (N.Y. 1988); Central Hudson Gas & Elec. Corp. v. Napoletano, 101 N.Y.S.2d 57 (N.Y. App. Div. 1950); State *ex rel.* Utilities Comm'n. v. North Carolina Consumers Council, Inc., 198 S.E.2d 98, 100 (N.C. Ct. App. 1973) (charging late fees avoids discrimination against those customers who pay on time, not usury, following Coffelt v. Arkansas Power & Light Co., 451 S.W.2d 881 (Ark. 1970)). *See generally* National Consumer Law Center, The Cost of Credit: Regulation, Preemption, and Industry Abuses § 10.5.2.2 (4th ed. 2009 and Supp.).

287 15 U.S.C. § 1666. *See* National Consumer Law Center, Truth in Lending § 7.9 (7th ed. 2010). *See also* §§ 15.2.1, 15.2.2, *infra*.

288 *See* § 15.2.1, *infra*. *See also* National Consumer Law Center, Truth in Lending § 2.4.6 (7th ed. 2010).

discriminatory fashion in violation of any of the prohibited bases of the federal Equal Credit Opportunity Act (ECOA),[289] a claim has been stated. This statute forbids discrimination "at all stages of the credit transaction" on any prohibited basis, including race, color, religion, national origin, sex, marital status, age (if old enough to contract), receipt of public assistance, or exercise of any right under the act.

For our purposes here:

1. A utility may not impose late fees on households or establish billing and collection schemes that result in the imposition of late fees due to a prohibited basis.
2. A utility may not engage in soft-core dunning procedures, issue past-due "notices," or engage in other accelerated or harsher collection techniques because of a prohibited basis. This would include, for example, threatening or charging late fees or issuing shut-off notices or past-due notices for a smaller "treatment amount" to customers in protected groups.[290]

In many states, state credit discrimination or general civil rights statutes may be broad enough to cover extensions of credit by utilities.[291] These statutes might be helpful in states that have restructured their electric and/or natural gas service, as restructuring removes energy service providers from commission regulation. The California Public Service Commission, responding to concerns that deregulated electric services providers (ESPs) might use their deposit policy to discriminate, concluded that the state civil rights act will apply to ESPs, as it does to all other businesses. If a provider is found to have violated the act, the California PSC "can open an investigation to determine whether an ESP's registration should be suspended or revoked."[292] Maine's licensing rules for competitive providers make violation of the unfair and deceptive acts and practices statute a per se violation of the rules.[293]

289 *See* 15 U.S.C. §§ 1691–1691f.

290 In such a situation, for example, residential customers might generally receive "past due notices" once their bills reach $50 in arrears or sixty days past due, but households that are recipients of public assistance would receive such notices when their bills reach $25 in arrears or thirty days past due.

291 *See, e.g.*, Mass. Gen. Laws ch. 151B, § 4(10) (forbids discrimination against public assistance recipients by any person furnishing "credit, services or rental accommodations"), § 4(14) (forbids discrimination by sex, sexual orientation, marital status, or age by "any person furnishing credit or services"). A more complete listing of state credit discrimination laws is found in National Consumer Law Center, Credit Discrimination (5th ed. 2009 and Supp.).

292 *In re* Proposed Policies Governing Restructuring California's Electric Services Industry and Reforming Regulation, 184 Pub. Util. Rep. 4th 262, 1998 WL 173314 (Cal. Pub. Utils. Comm'n Mar. 26, 1998).

293 65-407-305 Me. Code R. § 4 (LexisNexis).

5.5.11 *Unfair or Deceptive Acts or Practices Statutes*

All states have enacted statutes, commonly called "UDAP" statutes, generally prohibiting deceptive and often unfair or unconscionable practices.[294] These statutes are discussed in detail in § 15.4.2, *infra*. They generally exempt pervasively regulated Investor-owned Utilities (IOUs) but will be applicable to the billing and payment practices of RECs, competitive sellers who bill separately, and possibly municipals. UDAP statutes generally provide important remedies for consumers and are broad enough to reach unfair, oppressive, or deceptive conduct even if it does not violate the letter of a statute or regulation. For example, a UDAP statute might be used to challenge an unregulated utility or competitive service provider that allows an unreasonably short period for payment, imposes exorbitant late fees, or refuses to accommodate consumers on small fixed incomes by adjusting a billing date or providing levelized billing. See § 5.6, *infra*, for a more general discussion of why a late charge can be unfair or deceptive.

5.6 Are Utility Late Charges Fair?

5.6.1 *Introduction*

This section discusses the economic and policy arguments to be used in challenging late fees. Generally these arguments should be raised before the public utilities commission (PUC), since courts often defer to the PUC on the issues of whether a late charge should be imposed at all and the level of any fee allowed.

A potential challenge lies in any case in which late payment charges substantially overstate the actual costs to the utility company of receiving payments late. Excessive late fees allow the utility to make an additional profit above its authorized rate of return. Under regulatory principles, excessive late payment charges thus violate the standard that all utility rates and charges be "cost-based."

5.6.2 *Late Charges Should Only Cover Reasonable and Legitimate Expenses*

The primary purpose of a utility late payment charge is to compensate the utility for expenses associated with delinquent payments.[295] A customer's delinquent payment of a

294 *See generally* National Consumer Law Center, Unfair and Deceptive Acts and Practices (7th ed. 2008 and Supp.).

295 *But see* Low-Income Consumers Union v. Oregon Pub. Util. Comm'n, 946 P.2d 1164 (Or. Ct. App. 1997) (reasonable late fees upheld; failure to match fees exactly with costs of late payments not critical).

utility bill can result in two types of legitimate expenses to the company: the actual out-of-pocket cost of collection activities and the carrying charges associated with receiving payments well after the date that service was provided.

Out-of-pocket expenses might include, for example, the postage and copying costs associated with delivering reminder notices or shut-off notices, the costs of telephone calls to make "personal contact" prior to a shut-off, and the costs of sending an employee to physically terminate the service.

A late payment charge designed to compensate a utility for out-of-pocket collection expenses should be based on a decremental or avoided cost analysis, that is, the costs that the utility would avoid if the payment was made on time. This analysis first calculates the utility's costs *with* the late payment, then calculates the utility's costs *without* the late payment. The difference is then assigned as the late payment charge. The late payment charge should include only the truly decremental expenses: items such as postage and copying of collection and termination notices and the cost of sending out field collectors.[296] In no instance should the late payment charge include general overhead, such as expenses related to management salaries or office buildings, as these costs do not vary with the number of customers who pay late.

Even within a decremental or avoided cost analysis, limits should be placed on the level of late payment fees. Out-of-pocket expenses are generally incurred on a fixed-dollar basis (for example, perhaps $.50 for the postage and copying costs of sending termination notices). Therefore, late payment charges calculated as a percentage of the bill will not match the company's out-of-pocket costs. Out-of-pocket collection expenses do not vary as a function of the size of the customer's arrears. Sending a disconnect notice, for example, would cost the same, whether the customer owes $50 or $500. Accordingly, late payment charges that are based on a percentage of the outstanding bill (for example, 1.5% of the monthly arrears) cannot be justified on the basis of providing compensation for out-of-pocket expenses.[297] For very small arrears, a flat percentage charge is probably inadequate to cover the utility's actual expenses; for very large arrears, a flat percentage charge is likely to over-compensate the company for its costs.

However, a utility may also argue that it is seeking a flat percentage late charge to cover its carrying costs of receiving payments late, rather than simply for the out-of-pocket collection expenses. But this type of carrying cost is built into every company's base rates through a rate case adjustment called the "allowance for cash working capital" or something similar. Utility companies routinely submit "lead-lag" studies in their rate cases that reflect the average lag, in number of days, between the time utility service is provided and the time when payments are received. If the company has properly prepared its lead-lag study, it is already being compensated for the carrying cost of late payments through its regular rates and should not be allowed to add in a late charge. Conversely, if the company is allowed a late charge, its rates should be adjusted to reflect the late charge revenues received from customers who pay late.

To the extent that the utility includes the lag days associated with late payment in its calculation of working capital, it has received compensation for the carrying costs associated with arrears and is not justified in *again* collecting the carrying charges associated with those lag days through a late payment fee.

At least one commission has roundly rejected a company's proposed late charge on the basis that the level of the fee was not justified by the evidence and on the additional grounds that allowing a late charge would result in double recovery of the company's costs. In *In re Mountain Cable Co. d.b.a. Adelphia Cable Communications*,[298] the board affirmed the hearing officer's findings that a "$5.00 late payment fee," when compared to average monthly bills, "equates to a 16.66% monthly rate of interest, or an annual rate of almost 200%. This is an unconscionable rate of interest."[299] The board also affirmed the findings that "[i]t is inappropriate for [the company] to charge a separate cost-based late payment fee if the costs associated with late payment collections were included in the benchmark rates" and that "[c]harging a separate late payment fee essentially results in a double recovery of these costs, once through the benchmark rate and once through the collection of a separate late payment fee."[300]

It is also important to recognize that a late payment fee is *not* the equivalent of interest charged in consumer credit transactions. It is inappropriate for a utility company to impose the high interest rates imposed by credit card issuers and retail merchants. Since many of the commission-authorized late fees are 1.5% per month,[301] a once-common

296 Note that only a small fraction of collection notices result in terminations so that only a very small amount of employee labor expense could reasonably be allocated to the late payment charge.

297 A percentage charge, however, may have another basis, such as compensating the utility for the carrying costs associated with late payment. It is therefore important to identify the utility's alleged purpose for imposing the late payment charge.

298 Nos. 6117–19, 1999 WL 628268 (Vt. Pub. Serv. Bd. May 3, 1999).

299 *Id.* ¶ 92.

300 *Id.* ¶ 110. *See also* United Cable Television of Balt., L.P. v. Burch, 732 A.2d 887 (Md. Ct. Spec. App. 1999).

In this case, the court found that a $5-a-month late fee was a penalty, but the Maryland legislature subsequently enacted detailed regulations governing provisions for late fees. Md. Code Ann., Com. Law § 14-1315 (West).

In most instances, the new law allows late fees up to $5 per month or 10% per month of the amount due, whichever is greater.

301 *See, e.g., In re* Niagara Mohawk Power Corp. Inc., 188 Pub. Util. Rep. 4th 177, 1998 WL 680984 (N.Y. Pub. Serv. Comm'n

level on credit card charges, it appears that this may have been the comparison used in setting these late fees.[302]

Credit card interest rates, along with other late fees that credit card issuers impose, are designed to be the profit center for these companies. But a profit margin is already built into each utility company's rates, including amounts billed but paid late. Also, when credit card interest rates must recover the costs of uncollected accounts and general office overhead, a utility company's overhead costs and costs of uncollectible accounts are already included in rates and in the customer's bills that are subject to collection. Finally, stores and banks do not have the "power to disconnect a vital monopolized service to enforce eventual payment," which results in a greater risk of nonpayment than utilities face.[303]

5.6.3 Late Payment Charge Does Not Induce Prompt Payment

Utility late payment charges are sometimes justified not as a means to gain compensation for expenses but rather as a means to induce prompt payments on the part of customers.[304] If this rationale is proffered, it is a legitimate inquiry as to whether the level of the late payment charge bears any relation to an acceleration in payment dates.[305] Moreover, it is a legitimate inquiry as to whether a late payment charge designed to induce prompt payment is rational in those instances when nonpayment occurs in households who are unable to pay because of chronic poverty. Increasing the bills of low-income households by adding in late charges will provide no inducement to make prompter payments.

Indeed, some utilities have found that they receive more timely payments and more frequent payments by reducing bills to affordable levels rather than by increasing bills as a penalty for late payments. This has been the basis for various programs discussed in § 7.2, *infra*, including percentage of income payment plans (PIPPs), which base utility bills on an affordable percentage of household income.[306]

5.6.4 Late Charges More Favored in the Non-Utility Context

Historically, most discussions of late fees and charges have arisen in the context of loans, whether consumer or mortgage. These cases must be distinguished as covering a different type of transaction—an unregulated loan as opposed to the regulated provision of utility service. The primary question has been whether late charges are interest and thus subject to usury caps or, if not, whether they are reasonable under some other standard.

To the extent that a common law[307] treatment of late fees exists, the general rule is that late fees are distinct, or are excluded, from interest charges because the fees are avoidable or, more precisely, are contingent on the performance

Aug. 26, 1998) (approving 18%-per-year late charge, without discussion).

302 Note that credit card interest rates averaged 13% throughout 2005 and into 2006, according to the national averages reported by Bankrate.com for regular credit cards. Gold and premium cards carried even lower rates. Yet many utility companies still charge 1.5% per month (more than 18% per year compounded) as their late-charge rate.

303 *In re* Central Maine Power Co., 8 Pub. Util. Rep. 4th 277 (Me. Pub. Utils. Comm'n 1975):

> The commission agrees that there should be a late payment charge but feels that one percent is sufficient to cover the cost of late payments. . . . The company's costs both of capital and of short-term debt are well below 12 percent per year, and the administrative costs of this provision will not exceed the difference between the cost of capital and the 12 percent interest we are allowing. Furthermore, the fact that many stores and lending organizations charge 18 percent is not persuasive, for these organizations do not have the power to disconnect a vital monopolized service to enforce eventual payment.

304 *See, e.g.*, *In re* General Tel. Co. of Ohio, 68 Pub. Util. Rep. 4th 212 (Pub. Utils. Comm'n of Ohio 1985) (proposed 1.5% late fee after sixty days rejected as "not providing customers an incentive to pay bills in timely fashion"; thirty-day version rejected as too difficult administratively); *In re* Utah Power & Light Co., 19 Pub. Util. Rep. (N.S.) 369, 372 (Utah Pub. Serv. Comm'n 1937); MacMahon v. Independent Tel. Co., 109 P. 366, 367 (Wash. 1910).

305 *In re* Potomac Elec. Power Co., 3 Pub. Util. Rep. 4th 65, 79 (D.C. Pub. Serv. Comm'n 1973) ("the existing 5 percent late payment charge far exceeds the administrative costs . . . [and] has not accelerated the payment dates of Pepco bills"; 1.5% late charge approved). *Accord In re* Connecticut Light & Power Co., 15 Pub. Util. Rep. 4th 178, 191 (Fed. Power Comm'n 1976) ("[w]hile the inducement to pay bills on time is theoretically appropriate, an arbitrary charge [of 1.5%] is inappropriate. In view of the absence of evidence demonstrating a relationship between costs due to late payments and the level of the proposed late charge, the judge's rejection of the charge is correct."). *See also In re* Buzzards Bay Gas Co., 79 Pub. Util. Rep. (NS) 22, 26 (Mass. Dep't of Pub. Utils. 1949).

306 In 2005, the Massachusetts legislature adopted a law that formally recognizes the advantages of "arrearage management programs" that provide an incentive to low-income households that pay their current bills by the utility writing off a portion of the arrears owed. 2005 Mass. Acts ch. 140, § 17(a) (Nov. 22, 2005). *See* www.massresources.org/arrearage-management.html; appx. A.4, *infra*.

307 The use of the term "common law" here may be somewhat misleading because usury is a statutory offense. Nevertheless, a broadly accepted gloss of usury law has grown from decisions interpreting individual usury statutes. For example, the general principle that usury statutes do not apply when payments to the lender are contingent is not expressly stated in many usury statutes but is still a widely accepted view. The "common law rules" mentioned in this section refer to such generally accepted case law interpretations.

of the borrower.[308] Courts have frequently viewed late payment as a voluntary act of the borrower and the delinquency fee as a consequence of the borrower's voluntary act. These courts have therefore either excluded the late fee from interest[309] or ruled that creditors may validly receive more than the legal interest rate on delinquent payments.[310]

Those courts that exclude the fee from interest typically describe it as a "penalty" designed to encourage prompt payment. The logic here is questionable because the late payment is often not so much a matter of the borrower's voluntary decision as one of economic necessity.[311] In that context, the notion of incentive to pay seems meaningless when the borrower has no funds.

Nonetheless, the common law approach of labeling late fees as penalties rather than interest is widely applied. Challenges to loan late fees are likely to succeed only when the late fees are so large as to obviate the notion that the fee is merely an incentive for prompt payment[312] or when it can be shown that the parties expected late fees to be imposed at the time the contract was created and that the fees are therefore not contingent.[313]

A second justification for the imposition of late fees is that such fees compensate creditors for expenses incurred when payments are made late, such as costs associated with dunning[314] and loss of the use of the principal that was due. Legislation that validates the assessment of non-interest late fees under specified circumstances frequently reflects this justification as well as a legislative desire to limit the assessment of excessive fees. A common statutory formula allows the lender to collect an amount not exceeding a statutory limit (depending on the period of default) as a late fee and restricts the lender to one late fee (or a set number of late fees) per installment regardless of how late the

308 *See, e.g.*, Camilla Cotton Oil Co. v. Spencer Kellogg & Sons, Inc., 257 F.2d 162 (5th Cir. 1958); Bunn v. Weyerhaeuser Co., 598 S.W.2d 54 (Ark. 1980) (stating rule); Hayes v. First Nat'l Bank, 507 S.W.2d 701 (Ark. 1974) (distinguishing late fees from extension fees); Harris v. Guaranty Fin. Corp., 424 S.W.2d 355 (Ark. 1968); O'Connor v. Televideo Sys., Inc., 267 Cal. Rptr. 237 (Cal. Ct. App. 1990); First Am. Title Ins. & Trust Co. v. Cook, 90 Cal. Rptr. 645 (Cal. Ct. App. 1970); Barbour v. Handlos Real Estate & Bldg. Corp., 393 N.W.2d 581 (Mich. Ct. App. 1986); Faverty v. Asmus, 2001 WL 1109045 (Wash. Ct. App. Sept. 21, 2001) ($50 per day late charge provision not usurious even though "seemingly exorbitant" because "excessive interest" came into play only upon a contingency solely within borrower's control); Lew v. Goodfellow Chrysler-Plymouth, Inc., 492 P.2d 258 (Wash. Ct. App. 1971); Union Bank v. Kruger, 463 P.2d 273 (Wash. Ct. App. 1969); Randall v. Home Loan & Inv. Co., 12 N.W.2d 915 (Wis. 1944).

309 *E.g.*, Camilla Cotton Oil Co. v. Spencer Kellogg & Sons, Inc., 257 F.2d 162 (5th Cir. 1958); *In re* Borum, 60 B.R. 516 (Bankr. E.D. Ark. 1986); Tackett v. First Sav. of Ark., 810 S.W.2d 927 (Ark. 1991); Hayes v. First Nat'l Bank, 507 S.W.2d 701 (Ark. 1974); Southwest Concrete Prods. v. Gosh Constr. Corp., 798 P.2d 1247 (Cal. 1990).

This approach has ancient roots in the efforts made by the Roman Catholic Church to collect large fees without violating prohibitions against usury and without giving up the business to non-Church money lenders, often Jews.

310 *See, e.g.*, Ruminant Nitrogen Prods. v. Zittel, 433 N.Y.S.2d 644 (N.Y. App. Div. 1980); Union Bank v. Kruger, 463 P.2d 273 (Wash. Ct. App. 1969). *Cf.* Stuchin v. Kasirer, 568 A.2d 907 (N.J. Super. Ct. App. Div. 1990) (contract providing for post-maturity interest rate higher than legal rate does not render contract usurious, at least provided parties did not contemplate at consummation that loan would not be paid at maturity; court said clause should be examined to determine whether it was an unenforceable penalty); Klapper v. Integrated Agricultural Mgmt. Co., 539 N.Y.S.2d 812 (N.Y. App. Div. 1989) (usury defense inapplicable when terms of note impose higher rate than statutory maximum only after maturity of note).

311 This point was recognized in Begelfer v. Najarian, 409 N.E.2d 167 (Mass. 1980). *See also In re* Brummer, 147 B.R. 552 (Bankr. D. Mont. 1992); Scarr v. Boyer, 818 P.2d 381, 383 (Mont. 1991) ("Usury statutes protect borrowers who lack real bargaining power against overreaching by creditors"; default does not alter this public policy and in fact increases the need; "a debtor who cannot retire a debt compounded by legal interest certainly lacks the resources to pay usurious interest").

312 *See also In re* Graboyes, 371 B.R. 113 (Bankr. E.D. Pa. 2007); Ridgley v. Topa Thrift & Loan Ass'n, 953 P.2d 484 (Cal. 1998). *Cf. In re* Jordan, 91 B.R. 673 (Bankr. E.D. Pa. 1988) (late charge calculated at 1.5% of entire delinquency each month impermissible for several reasons: though creditor's evidence unclear, appears it may have compounded, or pyramided, late charges; excessive late charges constitute additional interest; excessive late charge in relation to creditor's damage is an unenforceable penalty clause; and courts have inherent equitable authority to disallow even non-usurious, contractual interest when amount sought is so disproportionate to damages as to constitute penalty for late payment, especially in light of unequal bargaining power); Garrett v. Coast & Southern Fed. Sav. & Loan Ass'n, 511 P.2d 1197 (Cal. 1973) (liquidated damages analysis; late fee was unrelated to actual damages incurred). *But see* Smith v. Figure World Plus, Inc., 705 S.W.2d 432 (Ark. 1986) (100% late fee was not usurious interest but rather was penalty because charge was a fixed amount and was one-time fee); Chambers v. Myers, 2006 WL 337506 (Ark. Ct. App. Feb. 16, 2006) ($5-per-day late fee on rent in lease upheld; late charge in the nature of a penalty does not render transaction usurious).

313 *See* Bunn v. Weyerhaeuser Co., 598 S.W.2d 54 (Ark. 1980); Metro Hauling, Inc. v. Daffern, 723 P.2d 32 (Wash. Ct. App. 1986) (no contingency when contract modified after default to allow previously unauthorized late charges). *Cf.* Eriksen v. Fisher, 421 N.W.2d 193 (Mich. Ct. App. 1988) (charges for actual, unanticipated late payments are not interest). *But see* Brown v. Investors Mortgage Co., 121 F.3d 472 (9th Cir. 1997) (applying Washington law; late charge not usurious when provided for in original contract and debtor had power to avoid it by prompt payment).

314 *Cf.* Opinion of the Kan. Att'y Gen. No. 88-30, Consumer Credit Guide (CCH) 95,908 (Mar. 3, 1988) (reasonable late charge assessed by cable television company is not interest, so long as actual efforts to collect are made and delinquent users are not offered alternative options for payment).

Most studies show that late charges are, in fact, not regularly billed. *See, e.g.*, Fed. Trade Comm'n, Report of Presiding Officer, Trade Regulation Rule on Credit Practices 192 n.16 (1978).

installment is paid.[315] Many statutes also specify a minimum grace period that must be allowed before a late fee may be imposed.[316]

A few states view late fees as liquidated damages.[317] Contract provisions calling for liquidated damages may be valid if they represent a good faith effort of the parties at the time of contract creation to assess and compensate for the damage that will be caused by a specified breach of contract.[318] However, liquidated damages provisions that go beyond the mere compensation of the injured party and act as punishment[319] for the breach are void. Applying this approach, a late fee calculated as a percentage of an outstanding loan balance, rather than as a percentage of the delinquent amount, may be void as a penalty.[320] California courts, however, have also upheld late fees that are a percentage of the delinquent amount.[321] Furthermore, the creditor must be able to genuinely justify the charge; attrib-

315 *See, e.g.*, Cal. Civ. Code § 1803.6 (West) (Retail Installment Act); U.C.C.C. § 2.502 (Uniform Consumer Credit Code; Model Code). *See also* Md. Code Ann., Com. Law § 14-1315 (West); 16 Tex. Admin. Code § 25.28(b).

316 *See, e.g.*, 24 C.F.R. § 203.25 (FHA-insured loans; 4% late fee allowed on installments more than fifteen days late); 38 C.F.R. § 36.4212(d) (VA-insured loans; 4% late fee allowed on installments more than fifteen days late); Cal. Civ. Code § 1803.6 (West) (ten days); U.C.C.C. § 2.502(1) (Uniform Consumer Credit Code) (ten days).

317 *See* Garrett v. Coast & Southern Fed. Sav. & Loan Ass'n, 511 P.2d 1197 (Cal. 1973); Beasley v. Wells Fargo Bank, N.A., 1 Cal. Rptr. 2d 446 (Cal. Ct. App. 1991); O'Connor v. Televideo Sys., Inc., 267 Cal. Rptr. 237 (Cal. Ct. App. 1990). *See also In re* Union Square Dev. Co., 140 B.R. 544 (D. Colo. 1992) (Colorado law); St. Hilaire & Assocs. v. Harbor Corp., 607 A.2d 905 (Me. 1992) (suggests Maine adopts a liquidated damage analysis; contractual collection charges are enforceable if they are reasonable, reflect actual or anticipated loss, and are not usurious or excessive as to constitute a penalty; interest and attorney fees at issue). *Cf.* Southwest Concrete Prods. v. Gosh Constr., 798 P.2d 1247 (Cal. 1990) (analyzing late fee on other grounds than liquidated damages). *See generally* Annot., *Validity and Construction of Provision Imposing "Late Charge" or Similar Exaction for Delay in Making Periodic Payments on Note, Mortgage, or Installment Sale Contract*, 63 A.L.R.3d 50 (1975).

Note that late fees categorized as liquidated damages may be impervious to challenge in some jurisdictions due to application of the "voluntary payment" doctrine. *See, e.g.*, Telescripps Cable Co. v. Welsh, 542 S.E.2d 640 (Ga. Ct. App. 2000); Dillon v. U-A Columbia Cablevision of Westchester, Inc., 740 N.Y.S.2d 396 (N.Y. App. Div. 2002), *aff'd*, 790 N.E.2d 1155 (N.Y. 2003); McWethy v. Telecomms., 988 P.2d 356 (Okla. Civ. App. 1999); Putnam v. Time Warner Cable of Southeastern Wis., L.P., 649 N.W.2d 626 (Wis. 2002). *But see* Time Warner Entm't Co., L.P. v. Whiteman, 802 N.E.2d 886 (Ind. 2004) (declining to follow "weight of authority" in favor of cable companies and holding that voluntary payment doctrine does not bar claim regarding excessive late fees); TCI Cablevision of Dallas v. Owens, 8 S.W.3d 837 (Tex. Ct. App. 2000) (allowing class certification).

318 *In re* Union Square Dev. Co., 140 B.R. 544 (D. Colo. 1992) (Colorado test is whether parties intend to liquidate damages; damages must be uncertain or difficult to prove and must be a reasonable amount not grossly disproportionate to presumed loss; late fee of 4% of unpaid balloon payment at issue); Beasley v. Wells Fargo Bank, N.A., 1 Cal. Rptr. 2d 446 (Cal. Ct. App. 1991) (late charge calculated to include indirect costs and collection agency expenses did not constitute good faith effort to compensate for damage caused by a specific default) (note that case is informative on methodology in setting fees; that bank seemed to have viewed late and over-the-limit fees as a revenue source probably was a factor in result); MetLife Capital Fin. Corp. v. Washington Ave. Assocs., 732 A.2d 493 (N.J. 1999) (5% late fee on large commercial loan found to be permissible liquidated damages; court reiterated that this was arms-length transaction between sophisticated businesses, both represented by counsel); Westmark Commercial Mortgage Fund IV Teenform Assocs., L.P., 827 A.2d 1154 (N.J. Super. Ct. App. Div. 2003) (following *MetLife*; finding 6% late fee reasonable); Stuchin v. Kasirer, 568 A.2d 907 (N.J. Super. Ct. App. Div. 1990) (appellate court remanded case to trial court to determine whether 15% increase in post-maturity rate was unenforceable penalty; court gave illustrative guidance as to test for whether it was penalty or acceptable recompense, for example, if lender resorted to commercial borrowing to replace lost income, difference between rate of his borrowing and rate he charged as lender might be a measure of damages). *See also* Utility Consumers' Action Network v. AT&T Broadband of S. Cal., 37 Cal. Rptr. 3d 827 (Cal. Ct. App. 2006) (liquidated damages provision of late fee is valid even absent proof of "reasonable endeavor" on part of providers to negotiate with customers). *Cf. In re* Cellphone Termination Fee Cases, 122 Cal. Rptr. 3d 726 (Cal. Ct. App. 2011) (because carrier did not engage in reasonable endeavor to estimate fair compensation for loss sustained in setting early termination fee, fee was void under state law limitation on liquidated damages provisions in consumer contracts).

319 Note that the use of the term "penalty" under a liquidated damages analysis has a very different meaning from that used under the common law usury approach. In many states, late fees are upheld as a "penalty" designed to discourage late payment. However, under a liquidated damages analysis, late fees could be upheld if they constituted a reasonable attempt to compensate a lender for the actual damages that it might incur upon late payment but would be void if they were found to be a "penalty." *See* No. Bloom & Son (Antiques), Ltd. v. Skelly, 673 F. Supp. 1260 (S.D.N.Y. 1987) (sales invoices called for interest at 2% per month on balances unpaid for more than thirty days; given amounts involved, this was impermissible penalty and thus void); Clermont v. Secured Inv. Corp., 102 Cal. Rptr. 340 (Cal. Ct. App. 1972) (late payment fee on loan must be either interest or liquidated damages; here, liquidated damages). *See also* St. Hilaire & Assocs. v. Harbor Corp., 607 A.2d 905 (Me. 1992) (contractual collection charges enforceable if reasonable and not usurious or so excessive as to constitute a penalty; interest and attorney fees at issue).

320 *See* Garrett v. Coast & Southern Fed. Sav. & Loan Ass'n, 511 P.2d 1197 (Cal. 1973). *See also In re* Jordan, 91 B.R. 673 (Bankr. E.D. Pa. 1988) (1.5% monthly late fee calculated on full amount of delinquency impermissible for a variety of reasons, *inter alia*, late charges excessive in relation to creditor's damage an unenforceable penalty; particularly so here, when APR was already over 24%); *In re* Hein, 60 B.R. 769 (Bankr. S.D. Cal. 1986) ($500-per-day late fee was unenforceable penalty).

321 Fox v. Federated Dep't Stores, 156 Cal. Rptr. 893 (Cal. Ct. App. 1979) (upholding 1.5% of installment due late fee). *See also* Comment, *Late-Payment Charges: Meeting the Requirements of Liquidated Damages*, 27 Stan. L. Rev. 1133, 1141 (1975).

uting indirect costs, unrelated overhead costs, and collection agency percentage-based fees do not meet the test for a valid liquidated damages clause.[322] Actual incurred legitimate expenses would.

If a court finds that a liquidated damages clause is actually a penalty clause, the court may refuse to enforce the penalty clause or award damages in this situation.[323] Several recent cases have found cable TV late charges to act as a penalty and therefore have held them unenforceable.[324]

This rule is consistent with section 2-718(1) of the Uniform Commercial Code (UCC), which states that liquidated damages may only be "at an amount which is reasonable in the light of the anticipated or actual harm caused by the breach, the difficulties of proof of loss, and the inconvenience or non-feasibility of otherwise obtaining an adequate remedy. Section 2-719 determines the enforceability of a term that limits but does not liquidate damages."[325]

322 Beasley v. Wells Fargo Bank, N.A., 1 Cal. Rptr. 2d 446 (Cal. Ct. App. 1991). *See also* District Cablevision, L.P. v. Bassin, 828 A.2d 714 (D.C. 2003) (unilateral increase of late fee from $2 to $5 not based on any analysis or estimate of costs actually incurred or anticipated were not valid liquidated damages); Time Warner Entm't Co., L.P. v. Whiteman, 802 N.E.2d 886 (Ind. 2004) (denying summary judgment properly when genuine issue of material fact was raised as to whether or not late fee was grossly disproportionate to damages actually suffered).

323 Beasley v. Wells Fargo Bank, N.A., 1 Cal. Rptr. 2d 446 (Cal. Ct. App. 1991). *See also* District Cablevision, L.P. v. Bassin, 828 A.2d 714 (D.C. 2003); Stroh v. Omni Arabians, Inc., 748 A.2d 1015 (Md. Ct. Spec. App. 2000).

324 *See, e.g.*, United Cable Television of Balt., L.P. v. Burch, 732 A.2d 887 (Md. Ct. Spec. App. 1999) ($5-per-month late fee was penalty); *In re* Mountain Cable Co. d.b.a. Adelphia Cable Co., 1999 WL 628268 (Vt. Pub. Serv. Bd. 1999) (using unconscionability analysis, $5 late fee punitive).

In reaction to the decision in *Burch*, the Maryland legislature enacted detailed regulations governing provisions for late fees. 2000 Md. Laws ch. 59, *codified at* Md. Code Ann., Com. Law § 14-1315 (West). The legislature imposed the new rules retroactively, applying them "to any case pending or filed on or after June 1, 2000" but not to "any case for which a final judgments had been rendered and for which appeals have been exhausted prior to June 1, 2000." 2000 Md. Laws ch. 59, § 6. In most instances, the new law allows late fees up to $5 per month or 10% per month of the amount due. Md. Code Ann., Com. Law § 14-1315 (West).

325 U.C.C. § 2-718.

Chapter 6 Grounds for Termination of Utility Service and Termination Protections

6.1 Grounds for Termination of Service

6.1.1 Nonpayment

The most frequent ground for the termination of utility service is nonpayment of the bill. Public utilities have the right to collect a reasonable price for their services:[1] "While it is the utility's duty to provide service, it is the customer's obligation to promptly pay for such service."[2] The utility may terminate or deny service for the nonpayment of utility bills.[3]

The general rule that utilities have the right to terminate service if a customer has not paid the utility bill has roots in the common law[4] and has been followed by courts at both the federal and state level,[5] as well as by state commissions, in their decisions, rules, and regulations.[6] Many commissions also allow disconnection for failure to make promised payments pursuant to the terms of a deferred payment agreement.[7]

The rationale for allowing utilities to terminate service is ostensibly to provide them with a quick and inexpensive method of enforcing payment, as opposed to bringing individual customers to court. As one court stated, "it would be highly impractical to compel a utility to resort to an infinite number of actions at law to collect small amounts against scattered consumers."[8] One public utility commission has noted that disconnection is not primarily a collection tool but rather a means to avoid future economic losses.[9] Because utilities wield monopoly power and provide a service essential to everyday life, most utility commissions strictly regulate shut-offs to avoid unnecessary harm to customers.[10]

1 *See* Charles F. Phillips, Jr., The Regulation of Public Utilities 199 (1993).

2 Daniel Luch v. GTE Cal., Inc., 41 C.P.U.C.2d 196, (Cal. Pub. Util. Comm'n Aug. 7, 1991) (slip opinion). *See also* Blincoe v. Pacific Tel. & Tel. Co., 60 C.P.U.C. 434 (Cal. Pub. Util. Comm'n 1963) ("[u]tility tariffs contemplate service disconnection for nonpayment of bills").

3 "It is the general rule[] . . . that either a private concern or a municipality furnishing a utility service to the public, such as gas, electricity, or water, may prescribe and enforce a rule or regulation which provides for the shutting off of the service from a consumer who has defaulted in payment therefor." 64 Am. Jur. 2d *Public Utilities* § 48 (2001).

4 Utilities Operating Co. v. Pringle, 177 So. 2d 684 (Fla. Dist. Ct. App. 1965). *See also* Charles F. Phillips, Jr., The Regulation of Public Utilities 559 (1993); Note, *Fourteenth Amendment Due Process in Terminations of Utility Services for Non-Payment*, 86 Harv. L. Rev. 1477, 1480 (1973).

5 *See, e.g.*, Lucas v. Wisconsin Elec. Power Co., 466 F.2d 638, 647 n.15 (7th Cir. 1972) ("It is undisputed that at common law a utility could cut off service for nonpayment of bills."); Masszonia v. Washington, 315 F. Supp. 529, 531 (D.D.C. 1970) ("the obligation of the utilities to terminate service for nonpayment has been recognized as an integral and necessary concomitant of proper rate control"); Snelling v. City of St. Louis Dep't of Pub. Utility—Water Div., 897 S.W.2d 642 (Mo. Ct. App. 1995) (it is well established that a public utility company may adopt and enforce a rule that service will be discontinued due to default in payment).

6 *See, e.g.*, Fla. Admin. Code Ann. r. 25-4.113(1)(f) (utility may discontinue telephone service for nonpayment of bills for telephone service); Mich. Admin. Code r. 460.2161(a) (subject to the requirements of these rules, an electric or gas utility may shut off or terminate service to a residential customer because the customer has not paid a delinquent account that accrued within the last six years); LeBeau v. Green Mountain Power Corp., 100 Pub. Util. Rep. 3d 337 (Vt. 1973) (public utility may disconnect a customer's service for nonpayment of proper bills and charges even in the absence of statutory authority); Vt. Pub. Serv. Bd. R. 3.302 (disconnection of residential gas, electric, telephone and water for nonpayment).

7 *See, e.g.*, Alaska Admin. Code tit. 3, § 52.445(h); Nev. Admin. Code § 704.355(1)(b); N.Y. Comp. Codes R. & Regs. tit. 16, § 11.10; Utah Admin. Code r. 746-200-5(B).

8 Huff v. Electric Plant Bd. of Monticello, 299 S.W.2d 817 (Ky. 1957). *See also* Komisarek v. New England Tel. & Tel. Co., 86 Pub. Util. Rep. 3d 44 (N.H. 1970) (even though a utility company may have the same remedy at law for the collection of delinquent accounts as other businesses have, it also has the remedy of disconnecting service in order to avoid costly collection procedures at law).

9 Houghton v. Bell Tel. Co. of Pa., 55 Pa. P.U.C. 271, No. C-80052011 (Pa. Sept. 18, 1981) (discontinuation of service is a vehicle to prevent loss rather than a collection tool).

10 *See* appx. A.1, *infra* (summary of state utility regulations).

6.1.2 Failure to Pay Deposit

Some regulators allow utilities to disconnect service if a proper deposit is not paid or guarantor provided when due.[11] But other state commissions have refused to allow disconnection of service for nonpayment of a deposit.[12]

6.1.3 Meter Tampering and Other Fraud; Violation of Utility Regulation

A utility may terminate service if the customer has engaged in fraud of any kind, for example, tampering with the meter[13] or misrepresenting one's identity for the purpose of obtaining or evading payment of utility service.[14] In such situations, some regulators allow for the wholesale removal of the meter to prevent continued unauthorized use.[15] The presumptions and standard of evidence in determining whether a consumer is in fact guilty of meter tampering or other fraud is discussed at § 4.3, *supra*. In addition, a utility may prescribe and enforce a rule that provides for terminating service from a customer who has violated a reasonable regulation of the utility.[16]

6.1.4 Failure to Permit Utility Access; Health or Safety Reasons

Many commissions allow disconnection for customer non-cooperation in allowing utility company access to the meter or other equipment. Utility companies are almost always authorized by statute or regulation to disconnect service (without notice to the customer in emergencies) if necessary to protect health or safety or to make repairs.[17] On some occasions, faulty appliances will be shut off or "red-tagged" but service may remain on to operate other equipment that is safe.[18]

6.1.5 Disconnection at Request of Customer

Unless the customer is not the user of the utility service, disconnection at the customer's request should not cause problems and is frequently authorized by regulation or tariffs.[19] Many states regulate landlord-requested shut-offs to ensure that the landlord is not using termination of utilities as a self-help eviction tool.[20]

---

11 *See, e.g.*, Idaho Admin. Code r. 31.21.01.302A.02; Mich. Admin. Code r. 460.2161(b); Oklahoma Corp. Comm'n Regulations 165:55-11-2, *cited in In re* Johnson, 1999 WL 827773 (Okla. Corp. Comm. 1999); Or. Admin. R. 860-021-0305(1)(a).

12 Conn. Gen. Stat. § 16-262j(a); N.D. Admin. Code 69-09-01-18.1(10). *See also In re* Berryman, No. 3971 (Vt. Pub. Serv. Comm'n July 9, 1975).

13 *See, e.g.*, Mich. Admin. Code r. 460.137 (shut-off permitted when the customer or others have caused the unauthorized use, diversion, or interference with the utility service situated or delivered on or about the customer's premises); Passantino v. Consolidated Edison Co. of N.Y., 428 N.E.2d 391 (N.Y. 1981).

14 *E.g.*, Mich. Admin. Code r. 460.2161(f) (shut-off is permitted if the customer has misrepresented his or her identity for the purpose of obtaining utility service).

15 *In re* Wisconsin Elec. Power Co., 175 P.U.R.4th 532, 1997 WL 120654 (Wis. Pub. Serv. Comm'n 1997) ("wrench off" [physical disconnection] policy approved for unauthorized use).

16 Annot., *Right to Cut Off Supply of Electricity or Gas Because of Non-Payment of Service Bill or Charges*, 112 A.L.R. 237 (1938); Annot., *Right to Cut Off Water Supply Because of Non-Payment of Water Bill or Charges for Connections*, 28 A.L.R. 472 (1924); Annot., *Right of Telephone Company to Refuse, or Discontinue, Service Because of Failure to Pay Bills or Other Violation of Conditions of Use*, 70 A.L.R. 894 (1931). *See also* Fla. Admin. Code Ann. r. 25-4.113(1)(a) (telephone); Nev. Admin. Code § 704.418(5); 16 Tex. Admin. Code §§ 26.28(a)(2)(E) (telecommunications), 25.29(b)(3) (electric).

However, at least one commission requires advance commission approval before a utility may disconnect for any reason other than an unpaid bill. 220 Mass. Code Regs. § 25.02(3)(d).

17 *See, e.g.*, Brooklyn Union Gas Co. v. MacGregor's Custom Coach, Inc., 509 N.Y.S.2d 446 (N.Y. App. Term 1986); Or. Admin. R. 860-021-0305(2); *In re* Alsea Props., Inc., 1999 WL 1331300 (Or. Pub. Util. Comm'n 1999). *See also* Mich. Admin. Code r. 460.2161(g) (utility may shut off service because the customer has violated any rules of the utility approved by the commission so as to adversely affect the safety of the customer or other persons or the integrity of the utility system). *Cf.* Stevo v. Frasor, 2011 WL 253963 (N.D. Ill. Jan. 3, 2011) (city permitted to shut off water pursuant to ordinance requiring installation of outdoor meters when ordinance was adopted to protect the safety of meter readers and homeowners and to ensure that bills were based on actual usage).

18 *See* Hegwood v. Virginia Natural Gas, Inc., 505 S.E.2d 372 (Va. 1998) (wrongful death action; gas company did not have duty to shut off entire gas service to residence when defective appliances were shut off and occupants were notified of appliance defects). *But see* Mobile Gas Serv. Corp. v. Robinson, 20 So. 3d 770, 780 (Ala. 2009) (wrongful death action; when gas company observed the same hazardous conditions several times in properties owned by same landlord despite company's red-tag warnings, "the Company could not close its eyes to the known danger posed by its supply of natural gas to the residence in the hope that [the owner] would remedy the defects in the CHU before the CHU was put back into use").

19 Even this seemingly non-controversial scenario can create problems. *See, e.g.*, Sanders v. Dayton Power & Light Co., 1999 WL 920274 (Ohio Pub. Util. Comm'n 1999). *See also* § 6.8, *infra* (landlord requests disconnection of service being used by tenant).

20 Landlord-tenant issues are discussed in Chapter 3, *infra*. Advocates should consult landlord-tenant and utilities law because most states, in some manner, impose requirements on the landlord regarding the provision of heat, light, and water.

6.2 Notice Requirement Prior to Disconnect

6.2.1 *Right to Notice*

Notice requirements for proposed disconnections are commonly found in state statutes, PUC rules and regulations, tariffs, and municipal utility procedures.[21] This notice is constitutionally mandated for municipal utilities,[22] may be mandated for rural electric cooperatives (RECs),[23] but is generally not constitutionally mandated for investor-owned utilities.[24]

At common law, public utility service also cannot be disconnected until after notice is given in accordance with provisions of the contract between the consumer and the utility.[25] A utility's common law right to terminate service to enforce payment is conditional upon its duty to notify the consumer of its intention to do so *prior* to exercising that right.[26] A contract between a public utility and its customer is an agreement to furnish service for an indefinite period of time.[27] An implied term of such a contract is that service will not suddenly be terminated without reasonable notice.[28] Cases have awarded damages for terminating service without notice.[29]

The right to receive notice does not depend upon the right to contest the disconnection of service. "Regardless of whether the plaintiffs had a right to contest the discontinuance of service, they certainly had a right to know that service was being discontinued to enable them to protect themselves from the very damage that did occur."[30]

6.2.2 *Is Notice Required When Termination Is Based on Meter Tampering?*

The common law rule against allowing utilities to terminate service for nonpayment of a disputed bill has also been found to support the right to pre-termination notice in an alleged meter tampering situation. In *Sowell v. Douglas County Electric Membership Corporation*,[31] while the customer was liable for charges as a result of meter tampering, from which he received the direct benefits, the court refused to dismiss a claim for wrongful termination without notice and a hearing.

Similarly, in *Myers v. City of Alcoa*,[32] the city alleged that the customer had unlawfully removed a city electric meter and replaced it with a different meter, and the city disconnected Myers' utility service without notice or a hearing. Relying on the U.S. Supreme Court decision in *Memphis Light, Gas and Water Division v. Craft*,[33] the *Myers* court found that the customer had a property interest in continuing electric service and that such a property interest may not be taken without notice and a pre-termination hearing. The Court rejected the utility's claim that the customer had "no due process right to stolen property, even where the person has no knowledge that the property was stolen."[34]

The *Myers* court examined what it termed the "risk of erroneous deprivation." It noted that at the criminal trial four months after the plaintiff's electric service was disconnected, she had been found not guilty of the theft of electricity. Furthermore, she had "continually claimed lack of knowledge and participation in the removal and replacement of the meter assigned her." Thus, the risk of erroneous deprivation was high for the plaintiff. In addition, there was "nothing in the record from which it can be inferred that Myers refused to pay the reasonable value of an estimated amount of electricity consumed at her residence during the period in question."

The *Myers* court then looked at the *relative* risks and found that the "risk of erroneous deprivation" under the current system is great as to the customer, while virtually a nullity as far as the defendant supplier is concerned, because the Tennessee Code permits the utility to pursue civil remedies, including treble damages, for electricity that has been pirated.

On the other hand, claims by a utility that meter tampering or bypass creates safety risks have been held to justify termination of services without advance notice. In *Hendrickson v. Philadelphia Gas Works*,[35] the court held that no pre-termination notice was necessary when the local utility had cited safety concerns from alleged meter tampering, emphasizing emergency safety concerns, as opposed to the *Myers* case, in which no such emergency factors were involved:

> [E]vidence of meter tampering or diversion of gas through the installation of unauthorized equip-

21 *See, e.g.*, 220 Mass. Code Regs. 25.01–25.06; Mich. Admin. Code r. 460.2163; Nev. Admin. Code § 704.355.

22 *See* § 15.1.2, *infra*.

23 *See* § 15.1.4, *infra*.

24 *See* § 15.1.1, *infra*.

25 BellSouth Telecomm. v. Kerrigan, 55 F. Supp. 2d 1314, 1320 (N.D. Fla. 1999); 28 C.J.S. *Public Utilities* § 29(d), at 567.

26 Carson v. Fort Smith Light & Traction Co., 158 S.W. 129 (Ark. 1913). *See also* 64 Am. Jur. 2d *Public Utilities* § 48 (2001).

27 Cates v. Electric Power Bd., 655 S.W.2d 166, 170 (Tenn. Ct. App. 1983).

28 *Id.* (citing First Flight Assocs., Inc. v. Professional Golf Co., 527 F.2d 931 (6th Cir. 1975)).

29 *See, e.g.*, Mississippi Power Co. v. Byrd, 133 So. 193, 194 (Miss. 1931), *overruled in part by* First Nat'l Bank v. Langley, 314 So. 2d 324 (Miss. 1975).

30 Cates v. Electric Power Bd. of Nashville, 655 S.W.2d 166, 170 (Tenn. Ct. App. 1983).

31 258 S.E.2d 149 (Ga. Ct. App. 1979).

32 752 F.2d 196 (6th Cir. 1985). *See also* Higgins v. Philadelphia Gas Works 54 B.R. 928 (Bankr. E.D. Pa. 1985).

33 436 U.S. 1 (1978).

34 752 F.2d 197 (6th Cir. 1985).

35 672 F. Supp. 823 (E.D. Pa. 1987).

> ment constitutes inherent imminent danger to the health and safety of the serviced premises and occupants, as well as surrounding properties and the general public, requiring immediate remedial action. (citation omitted). . . . *Myers* did not concern imminent danger presented by continuation of the utility service. . . . In *Myers*, the plaintiff's action did not present safety concerns for the customer, the public or the utility. . . . Here, the undisputed evidence is that continuation of service through a tampered meter presented an unacceptable risk of catastrophe. Therefore, termination was a necessary and responsible precaution undertaken by PGW.[36]

The *Hendrickson* court weighed the safety concerns against the plaintiff's need for a pre-termination hearing:

> In the instant case a pre-termination hearing could not have been afforded in advance of the scheduling date of termination. Termination was due to plaintiff's tampering with the meter. The tampering endangered other residents in the area. Thus, termination was a necessary procedural safeguard . . . [which] was a necessary concern of Philadelphia Gas Works which outweighed the plaintiff's need for a pre-termination hearing.[37]

This exception to the general rule requiring notice prior to termination is also found in some states' rules; often utilities *may* be able to disconnect without notice in the event of certain kinds of fraud.[38] But the basis for this lack of notice is often the need to correct a safety hazard, and this particular rationale for avoiding notice may not apply to other types of fraud.

6.2.3 Notice Content

State statutes and commission regulations often impose very specific requirements about what to include in a termination notice. These requirements overlap substantially with what courts have held due process standards to require. Below is an example of the detailed information that may be required in a termination notice:

(a) The name and address of the customer and, if available, the address at which service is provided, if different. Notice to the actual user may also be required.
(b) A clear and concise reason for the proposed shut-off of service.
(c) The date on or after which the utility may shut off service, unless the customer takes appropriate action.
(d) The right of the customer to enter into a payment agreement with the utility if the claim is for an amount that is not in dispute and the customer is presently unable to pay in full.
(e) The right of the customer to file a complaint disputing the claim of the utility before the proposed date of the shut-off of service.[39]
(f) An explanation of the customer's right to request a hearing before a utility hearing officer if the complaint cannot be otherwise resolved and of any requirement that the customer must pay to the utility the non-disputed portion of the bill.
(g) The right of the customer to represent himself or herself, to be represented by counsel, or to be assisted by other persons of his or her choice in the complaint process.
(h) The utility will not shut off service pending the resolution of a complaint that is filed with the utility in accordance with these rules.
(*i*) The telephone number and address of the utility where the customer may make inquiry, enter into a payment agreement, or file a complaint.
(j) The customer should contact a social services agency immediately if the customer believes he or she might be eligible for emergency economic assistance.
(k) The utility will postpone the shut-off of service if a medical emergency exists at the customer's residence.
(*l*) The utility may require a deposit and restoration charge if the utility shuts off service for nonpayment of a delinquent account.
(m) The customer should contact the utility for information about the winter protection plan or some other special plan that may be available to the customer.[40]

---

36 *Id.* at 826, 828–29.

37 Hendrickson v. Philadelphia Gas Works, 672 F. Supp. 823, 830 (E.D. Pa. 1987).

38 *See, e.g.*, Alaska Admin. Code tit. 3, § 52.450(a)(2) (no advance written notice required if utility has evidence of meter tampering or other fraud); Fla. Admin. Code Ann. r. 25-4.113(1)(i) (no advance notice required for discontinuance of telephone service in the event of tampering with the equipment furnished by utility). r. 25-30.320(2)(i), (j) (no advance notice required for discontinuance of telephone service in the event of unauthorized or fraudulent use of service); 220 Mass. Code Regs. § 25.02(3) ("[n]othing in 220 CMR 25.00 shall be construed to prevent termination for reasons of safety, health, cooperation with civil authorities, or any other reason for which termination power is specifically granted in the General Laws"); Nev. Admin. Code §§ 704.350(4) (utility may terminate electric or gas service without prior notice if the acts of the customer or the conditions upon his premises are such as to indicate to the utility his intention to defraud it), 704.418(5) (similar rule in case of telephone service).

39 *See also* Cal. Pub. Util. Code § 10010.1(d)(4) (West) (publicly owned utilities) (detail of information notice shall include procedure to initiate complaint).

40 *See, e.g.*, Alaska Admin. Code tit. 3, § 52.450(c)(1)(D)(i) (notice must advise customer to contact utility for information regarding deferred payment and other procedures to avoid disconnection); Cal. Pub. Util. Code § 10010.1(d) (West) (procedure to obtain information on availability of financial assistance); 16 Tex. Admin. Code § 25.29(k)(5) (disconnection notice for electric service must include a statement notifying the customer that, if they need assistance paying their bill by the

Colorado requires that the notice of discontinuance shall be conspicuous, in easily understood language, and the heading of the notice shall be in capital letters.[41] Some states, including Oregon and Texas, require information to be provided in Spanish or other languages as well as in English.[42]

6.2.4 Timing of Notice

In general, utilities must provide notice reasonably in advance of the proposed shut-off, in order to provide the customer the opportunity to make a payment that would stop the termination or assert some protection against the termination and to permit the customer adequate time to request the assistance of the utility commission. The statutory scheme governing utilities, as well as utility regulations and rules, often specify the minimum number of days prior to disconnecting service when a utility must inform the customer of the impending disconnection.[43] For example:

- In Alaska, rules specify fifteen days' notice be provided to a customer prior to disconnecting service for nonpayment of bills. However, at least 30 days' notice is required for households with seriously ill, elderly, or disabled persons.[44]
- In Florida, a telephone company is required to provide five working days' written notice to the customer, "except in extreme cases."[45]
- In Texas, electric utilities may not disconnect service less than ten days after the notice of disconnection is issued.[46]
- In Connecticut, no public service company or municipal utility may terminate service for nonpayment unless it first gives at least thirteen days' prior notice.[47]
- In Michigan, remote disconnection of service is permitted when the utility makes at least two attempts to contact the customer by phone at least one day before the scheduled shut-off. When the customer has no phone, or no phone contact is made, the utility must leave notice at the premises that service will be shut off on or after the next business day or send notice via first class mail postmarked at least five business days before the scheduled shutoff date. The notice must state that the disconnection will occur remotely.[48]

6.2.5 Method of Providing Notice

Many commissions have specific requirements on the method of providing notice, often requiring utilities to provide notice by first class mail[49] or sometimes by certified mail.[50] Some states specifically require notices of disconnections to be separate from other utility bills, information, or advertisements.[51] In one case, service of notice to a customer's attorney was found wanting.[52] The burden of showing non-receipt of a notice is on the customer if company records demonstrate the notice was sent, in the absence of rules regarding certified notices.[53]

In addition, utility commissions sometimes require companies to ensure that a customer personally receives notice, in hand or by telephone contact, if possible, before disconnecting utility service. For example, in Alaska, in addition to the requirement of written notice, a utility must attempt personal contact with customer by telephone or visit not less than three days prior to disconnection.[54] In Michigan, on at

---

due date or are ill and unable to pay their bill, they may be able to make some alternate payment arrangement, establish deferred payment plan, or possibly secure payment assistance); Vt. Pub. Serv. Bd. R. 3.303(A)(4) (no disconnection if a doctor certifies disconnection will result in immediate and serious health hazard); Vt. Pub. Serv. Bd. R. 3.303(I) (statement that there is no disconnection between November 1 through March 31 if a member of the household is 62 years old or older).

41 *See* 4 Colo. Code Regs. §§ 723-3 (section 3408, electric disconnection notice), 723-4 (section 4408, gas disconnection notice), 723-5 (section 5408, water disconnection notice) (LexisNexis).

42 *See, e.g.*, Or. Admin. R. 860-021-0011(1) (all disconnection notices of energy and large telecommunications utilities shall contain the required information translated into Spanish, Vietnamese, Cambodian, Laotian, and Russian); 16 Tex. Admin. Code §§ 25.29(k)(4) (disconnection notice for electric service must be in English and Spanish), 26.28(a)(7)(d) (disconnection notice for telephone service must be in English and Spanish).

43 *See* appx. A.7, *infra*.

44 Alaska Admin. Code tit. 3, § 52.450(c)(1), (2).

45 Fla. Admin. Code Ann. r. 25-4.113(1)(f).

46 16 Tex. Admin Code §§ 25.29(k)(3), 25.483(l)(3).

47 Conn. Gen. Stat. § 16-262d(a).

48 Mich. Admin. Code r. 460.142.

49 *See, e.g.*, 4 Colo. Code Regs. § 723-3-13(b)(1) (LexisNexis); Mich. Admin. Code r. 460.2163(1) (utility shall not shut off service unless it transmits a notice, by first-class mail, to the customer or personally serves the notice not less than ten days before the date of the proposed shut-off).

Some rules allow more leeway. *See, e.g.*, 16 Tex. Admin. Code § 25.29(k) (proper notice shall consist of a separate mailing or hand delivery).

50 *See, e.g.*, Mont. Admin. R. 38.5.1405 (second notice by first class mail or certified mail if no response to first notice); S.C. Code Ann. Regs. 103-735.1 (notice by certified mail in certain situations before water is shut off).

51 Kansas Corp. Comm'n, Electricity, Natural Gas and Water Billing Standards § IV.E(3). *See also* 16 Tex. Admin. Code § 25.29(k)(2).

52 Columbia Gas of Ohio v. Public Util. Comm'n, 449 N.E.2d 433 (Ohio 1983) (gas termination notice sent to customer's attorney not adequate notice).

53 Allstates Transworld Vanlines, Inc. v. Southwestern Bell Tel. Co., 937 S.W.2d 314, 318 (Mo. Ct. App. 1996).

54 *See, e.g.*, Alaska Admin. Code tit. 3, § 52.450(c)(3). *See also* Cal. Pub. Util. Code § 779.1(b) (West); N.Y. Pub. Serv. Law § 32(3)(b) (McKinney); 52 Pa. Code § 56.93 ("a utility may not interrupt, discontinue or terminate service without personally contacting the ratepayer or a responsible adult occupant at least 3 days prior to the interruption"; requirement can be met by attempting two phone calls to customer); Brooklyn Union Gas

least one day preceding shut-off of service, a utility must make at least two attempts to contact the customer by telephone.[55] In Nevada, a utility may not terminate service to elderly or disabled residential customers without providing notice in person or by telephone at least forty-eight hours prior to disconnection—an additional protection to the requirement of a ten-day written notice.[56] Some states' require that the option of notice to a third party be available when the customer is either elderly or disabled.[57]

In the move to recognize electronic signatures and writings, advocates should be aware that notices of utility disconnections must still be provided in hard copy under federal law. The federal Electronic Signatures in Global and National Commerce Act (E-Sign)[58] has a specific exemption for utility notices of disconnections.[59] Many states' electronic transaction laws also exempt utility disconnections,[60] and those states without the specific exemption for disconnection notices may be preempted by the more protective federal E-Sign.[61]

6.2.6 *Is Notice to Actual User Required? Tenants and Master-Meter Situations*

Often the person who pays for the utility service is not the same person who uses the utility service. The most common situation is one in which a tenant receives utilities as part of the rent, there is one master meter for the building, and the landlord is the utility customer. What happens when the landlord does not pay the utility bill and service is disconnected? Notice to the landlord does not adequately protect the tenant.

Some utility regulations have built-in protections for the utility customer whose landlord is responsible for the bill. Colorado's rule is typical: Service discontinuance notices must be mailed to each individual tenant of a single-metered, multi-unit dwelling,[62] and a utility may be required to post notice of the disconnection in a common area as well.[63] This protection can also be found in the statutes of some states as well.[64] Some go a step further and place the onus on the utility to discover whether they need to provide notice to tenants.[65]

In addition, most commission regulations require more protection than simply providing notice to the tenant that utility service will be shut off because the landlord is in arrears. Utilities are often required to provide the tenant the opportunity to start service in his or her own name without having to pay the back delinquency of the landlord[66] and, if

Co. v. Richy, 475 N.Y.S.2d 981 (N.Y. Civ. Ct. 1984) (utility's application for seizure of gas meters for nonpayment was denied in part due to utility's sole reliance on written notice: "these notices are forwarded to the very people least likely or able to read or respond to them, namely the very sick, the blind, the elderly or the disabled").

55 *See, e.g.*, Cal. Pub. Util. Code §§ 10010.1(b) (municipal corporation that provides utility service shall make reasonable attempt to contact adult by phone or in person at least twenty-four hours prior to termination or, if not possible, posting notice at least forty-eight hours prior to termination), 779.1 (similar rule for electric, gas, heat, or water corporations) (West).

56 *See, e.g.*, Nev. Admin. Code §§ 704.390(1), 704.360(1). *See also* N.Y. Pub. Serv. Law § 32(3) (McKinney).

57 *See, e.g.*, Cal. Pub. Util. Code § 10010.1(c) (West) (public utility shall make available third-party notification service to elderly (65+) or dependent adults). *See also* 4 Colo. Code Regs. § 723-3-13(b)(4) (LexisNexis) (electric) (customers can designate a third party to receive notices of disconnection).

58 Pub. L. No. 106-229, 114 Stat. 464 (2000), *codified at* 15 U.S.C. §§ 7001–7031.

59 15 U.S.C. § 7003(b)(2)(A). *See also* National Consumer Law Center, Credit Discrimination § 11.2.2.2 (5th ed. 2009 and Supp.).

60 *See, e.g.*, Cal. Civ. Code § 1633.3(c) (West).

61 *See* National Consumer Law Center, Banking and Payments Law, § 11.2.2 (4th ed. 2009 and Supp.).

62 *See, e.g.*, 4 Colo. Code Regs. § 723-3, Rule 3408(i) (LexisNexis). *See also* Alaska Admin. Code tit. 3, § 52.450(c)(4)(B) (each tenant served through the master meter must be given individual notice of the pending disconnection at least fourteen days prior to disconnection); Mich. Admin. Code r. 460.2163(3) (in a single-metered dwelling that is used as a residence for five or more families, a utility shall, if possible, mail or deliver a notice of the pending termination to each dwelling unit not less than thirty days before the proposed shut-off of service); 220 Mass. Code Regs. § 25.04 ("Termination of Service to Accounts Affecting Tenants"); N.J. Admin. Code § 14:3-7.14(a); 16 Tex. Admin. Code § 25.29(j) (when a bill for utility services is delinquent for a master-metered apartment complex with five or more residential dwelling units, the utility shall send a notice to the customer).

63 *E.g.*, N.J. Admin. Code § 14:3-7.14 (notice to tenants shall be hand delivered, mailed, or posted in a conspicuous area of the premises); 16 Tex. Admin. Code § 25.29(j)(2) (at least six days after providing notice to customer and at least four days prior to disconnect, the utility shall post a minimum of five notices in conspicuous areas in corridors or other public places of apartment complex).

64 *See, e.g.*, Cal. Gov't Code § 60371(a) (West) (if district furnishes light, heat, water, or power through a master meter or an individual meter to owner of multi-unit building, manufactured home park, or farm labor camp, district shall make every good faith effort to inform actual users when account is in arrears by providing notice that service will be terminated in ten days); Conn. Gen. Stat. § 16-262e(a)(1) (if owner of building is billed directly and utility has actual or constructive knowledge that it does not send bills to occupants, utility shall not terminate service for nonpayment unless utility makes good faith effort to provide notice to occupants of proposed termination).

65 *See, e.g.*, 220 Mass. Code Regs. § 25.04(1), (2) ("Each company shall devise procedures reasonably designed to identify . . . landlord customers paying for service to a residential building. . . . Each company shall devise procedures reasonably designed to identify the number and addresses, including apartment numbers, of tenants who may be affected by a planned termination" of a landlord account); N.J. Admin. Code § 14:3-7.14 (electric, gas, water, and sewer public utilities shall make every reasonable attempt to determine when a landlord-tenant relationship exists at residential premises being serviced).

66 N.J. Admin. Code § 14:3-7.14 (discontinuance of service is prohibited unless the utility has offered tenants continued ser-

so, the notice should inform the customer of this right.[67] Less common are cases holding that a landlord needs to be notified before a tenant-requested disconnection of services takes place, regardless of the landlord's compliance with company procedures for such notification.[68]

6.3 Protections from Disconnection

6.3.1 Protections for Ill, Disabled, or Elderly

The shut-off of utility service can have serious consequences for any customers, but can be particularly devastating to disabled, ill, or elderly people who may be frail. Elderly people are particularly susceptible to the dangers posed by lack of heat or cooling.[69] As a result, some commissions and some utilities on their own have built in restrictions against the shut-off of utility service to disabled and ill customers that can postpone termination for varying lengths of time depending on the medical problems, time of year, and a doctor's opinion.[70]

These regulations usually focus on whether the "discontinuance of service will result in some person residing at that residence becoming seriously ill or more seriously ill . . ."[71] and usually require medical proof of the condition.[72] The protection may be for a limited period of time.[73] These restrictions are generally not limited to elderly customers and generally are available throughout the year.

In California, the utility commission prohibited utilities that had installed smart meters from remotely disconnecting medical baseline and life support customers.[74] The California Commission also approved a settlement between consumer advocates and two utilities to protect the utilities' vulnerable customers, which includes seniors and customers with disabilities, by excluding them from remote disconnections as a strict policy.[75] The Commission also approved a

vice, to be billed to the tenants, unless the utility demonstrates that such billing is not feasible; the continuation of service to a tenant shall not be conditioned upon payment by tenant of any outstanding bills due upon account of any other person). *See also* Cal. Gov't Code § 60371(a) (West); Conn. Gen. Stat. § 16-262e(a)(2); 220 Mass. Code Regs. § 25.04(7).

67 *E.g.*, Cal. Gov't Code § 60371(a) (West) (notice shall inform actual users they have right to become customers without paying amount due).

68 Rohrbaugh v. Philadelphia P.U.C., 663 A.2d 809 (Pa. Commw. Ct. 1995) (utility violated statutory duty to landlord to provide and maintain adequate and reasonable service by disconnecting electricity at tenant's request without first notifying landlord when cold weather caused extensive damage to property after shut-off; landlord's failure to comply with company policy for notification irrelevant), *rev'd*, 727 A.2d 1080 (Pa. 1999).

69 Approximately 50% of all hypothermia-related deaths recorded by the Federal Centers for Disease Control are persons over sixty-four years of age. *See* National Consumer Law Center, The Energy Affordability Crisis of Older Americans (Aug. 1995).

In 2000, approximately 68% of those with heat-related deaths were sixty years old or older. Office of Climate, Water and Weather Services, Heat Related Fatalities by Age and Gender for 2000.

As global warming causes hotter summers, the number of heat-related deaths appears to be on the rise. *See, e.g.*, *130 Deaths Blamed on California Heat Wave*, Wash. Post, July 3, 2006, at A03.

70 A summary of serious illness protection rules is provided in Appendix A.6, *infra*. *See, e.g.*, N.Y. Pub. Serv. Law § 32(3)(a) (gas and electric) (medical emergencies), (3)(b) (special protections for elderly, blind and disabled) (McKinney); Wash. Admin. Code §§ 480-110-355(2) (water) (medical emergencies), 480-120-172(6) (telephone) (medical emergencies); *In re* Florida Power Corp., 1999 WL 397309 (Fla. Pub. Serv. Comm'n May 10, 1999) (medically essential service customer procedures explained). *See also* Brooklyn Union Gas Co. v. Richy, 475 N.Y.S.2d 981 (N.Y. Civ. Ct. 1984) (denying utility's application to seize gas meters for nonpayment, in part because of Legislature's "unequivocal concern" and establishment of special procedures to ensure the continuation of utility services to particular classes of people in winter); National Consumer Law Center, Guide to the Rights of Utility Consumers appx. A-2 (2006) ("Serious Illness and Age-Related Protections") (describing serious illness rules in each state that has such a rule).

Massachusetts has perhaps the most generous serious illness rule in the country in that the customer's doctor may renew the serious illness letter indefinitely as long as the illness persists, and the customer need not show that the utility service is necessary to treat the underlying medical problem or to avoid a worsening of the medical problem. 220 Mass. Code Regs. § 25.03.

71 *See, e.g.*, 16 Tex. Admin. Code § 25.29(g) (disconnection of electricity service for ill and disabled). *See also* 52 Pa. Code § 56.111 (no utility shall terminate, or refuse to restore, service to any premises when any occupant therein is certified by a physician to be seriously ill or affected with a medical condition that will be aggravated by cessation of service or failure to restore service).

72 *See, e.g.*, Cal. Pub. Util. Code § 779(b)(3) (West) (no public utility shall terminate for nonpayment when to do so will be life-threatening to customer on certification of doctor and surgeon and when customer is unable to pay for service and is willing to work out a payment plan); 52 Pa. Admin. Code § 56.111 (to be eligible, customer must be certified by physician to be seriously ill or affected with medical condition that will be aggravated by cessation of service or failure to restore service); 16 Tex. Admin. Code § 25.29(g) (each time customer seeks to avoid termination of service under this rule, customer must have attending physician call or contact utility by date of disconnection and submit a written statement to utility from the physician).

73 *See, e.g.*, 52 Pa. Code § 56.114 (maximum length of time is thirty days for each certification).

74 *See* Cal. Pub. Util. Comm'n, D.10-07-048, Interim Decision Implementing Methods to Decrease the Number of Gas and Electric Utility Service Disconnections (issued Jul. 30, 2010) at 23-24, 30.

75 *See* Cal. Pub. Util. Comm'n, D.10-12-051, Decision Granting Petition to Modify Decision 10-07-048, and Approving Settlement Agreement (issued Dec. 27, 2010) at 8; Joint Motion of San Diego Gas & Electric Company (U 902E), the Southern

settlement provision that any customer of the settling utilities must receive a premise visit before remote disconnections.[76] The Commission is deliberating on whether to apply the last knock policy to the non-settling gas and electric investor owned utilities as well.

6.3.2 *Winter Moratoria and Other Limitations As to Time*

Commissions may limit the days and times of disconnection to those other than Fridays or weekends.[77] There may also be a prohibition on shutting off service during the winter months—a restriction known as a winter moratorium on terminations. Most often the moratorium is limited to certain households that may be low-income, including households with elderly residents, disabled residents, or small children.[78] The authority for such a moratorium may stem either from the state statutory scheme regulating the utility,[79] a utility commission's order or rules, or a company tariff. Typical of these is Iowa's statute, which states that:

> No disconnection may take place from November 1 through April 1 for a resident who is a head of a household and who has been certified to the public utility by the local community action agency as being eligible for either the low-income home energy assistance program or weatherization assistance program.[80]

Some states have temperature-based disconnection moratoria, which are less protective than date-based disconnection moratoria. Temperature-based moratoria only delay disconnections until the temperature has risen or fallen past the specified temperature. Temperature-based moratoria also fail to protect customers disconnected prior to the point where the moratoria become effective. According to Texas rules, an electric utility is restricted from disconnecting service during "extreme weather," hot or cold.[81] Alabama bars disconnections on any day when the forecast low temperature is 32° degrees or below.[82] A much better approach is the requirement that utilities receive commission approval for disconnections during the winter.[83]

Michigan's Winter Protection Plan prohibits utilities from shutting off service to eligible older or low-income customers[84] between the beginning of December through the end of March for nonpayment. The customer pays at least 7% of her estimated annual bill and a portion of arrearages. At the end of the protection period, the customer must pay any amounts still owed in installments from April through November.[85]

Over the past years, utility commissions have adopted formal rules or informal policies to protect customers from termination during periods of extreme hot or cold weather. On October 27, 2005, the California Public Utilities Commission, anticipating "exceptionally high gas prices" in the coming winter, adopted new policies under which "utilities

---

California Gas Company (U 904G), Disability Rights Advocates, the Division of Ratepayer Advocates, the Greenlining Institute, the National Consumer Law Center, and The Utility Reform Network for Adoption of the Settlement Agreement, R.10-02-005 (Sept.9, 2010) at 12-13.

76 *Id.*

77 *In re* Alsea Props., Inc., 1999 WL 1331300 (Or. Pub. Util. Comm'n Nov. 8, 1999) (no non-emergency shut-off on Fridays or holidays or the day before holidays); *In re* Cascade Natural Gas Corp., 171 P.U.R.4th 472, 1996 WL 497437 (Wash. Pub. Util. Comm'n 1996) (no disconnection of service for nonpayment on Fridays or the day before a holiday). *See* appxs. A.1, A.5, *infra*.

78 *See, e.g.*, Mich. Admin. Code r. 460.148, 460.149 (utility shall not shut off service to eligible low-income customer or eligible senior citizen customer who is sixty-five years of age or older for nonpayment during space-heating season, but customer may be required to comply with payment plan and terminated if customer fails to do so); 52 Pa. Code § 56.100 (winter termination procedures); 65-407-81 Me. Code R. § 17 (LexisNexis) (winter disconnection rule). *See also* appx. A.1, *infra* (summarizing in detail most states' customer service regulations).

79 *See, e.g.*, Conn. Gen. Stat. § 16-262c(b) (from November 1 to April 15, electric and gas companies may not terminate in hardship cases); 220 Ill. Comp. Stat. 5/8-201 ("no person should be denied essential utility service during the winter months due to financial inability to pay").

80 Iowa Admin. Code r. 199-19.4(17) (gas), 199-20.4(17) (electricity).

Furthermore, in Iowa, if the utility is informed that a customer's household may qualify for energy assistance or weatherization funds, it cannot disconnect service for thirty days from the application to allow customer time to obtain assistance. Iowa Admin. Code r. 199-19.4(15)(d)(9) (winter energy assistance).

81 16 Tex. Admin. Code § 25.29(i) (electric utilities cannot disconnect on a day when: (1) the previous day's highest temperature did not exceed 32° Fahrenheit and temperature is predicted to remain at or below that level for next twenty-four hours, according to the nearest National Weather Service reports, or (2) National Weather Service issues a heat advisory for any county in electric utility's service territory or when such advisory has been issued on any one of the preceding two calendar days).

82 Alabama Pub. Serv. Comm'n Gen. Rules, Rule 12.B(5) (gas and electric).

83 *See* 52 Pa. Code § 56.100(2).

84 Eligible customers are age sixty-five or older, low-income customers whose household income does not exceed 150% of the poverty level, who receive food stamps, Medicaid, or Michigan's Family Independence Agency cash assistance.

85 *See* www.michigan.gov/mpsc (click on "Consumer Information" link on left side of web page, then on "Inquiry/FAQs," then on "Heating Assistance Programs"). *See also* Minn. Stat. § 216B.096 ("During the cold weather period, a utility may not disconnect and must reconnect utility heating service of a customer whose household income is at or below 50% of the state median income if the customer enters into and makes reasonably timely payments under a mutually acceptable payment agreement with the utility that is based on the financial resources and circumstances of the household; provided that, a utility may not require a customer to pay more than 10% of the household income toward current and past utility bills for utility heating service.").

are prohibited from shutting off service this winter [of 2005–2006] to residential customers that make regular payments of at least 50% of their bills."[86]

On November 21, 2005, the Arkansas Public Service Commission revised its General Service Rule 6.15 (the "Cold Weather rule"), which previously barred electric and gas terminations on days when temperatures are forecast to be 32° or lower. The Arkansas Public Service Commission added a new Rule 6.15.B that additionally prohibits gas utilities from terminating service, between November 1 and March 31, to low-income and elderly households who receive Food Stamps; Women, Infants and Children Assistance (WIC); Transitional Employment Assistance; Medicaid; or LIHEAP (fuel assistance). In order to qualify for the protection, a household must notify the company of receipt of the qualifying public assistance benefits prior to the date of termination; must make minimum payments during the course of the winter (defined as the amount that would otherwise be due under the company's levelized payment plan); and must agree to pay back, prior to the start of the next heating season on November 1, the additional amounts that would have otherwise been due during the winter.[87]

On December 15, 2005, the Missouri Public Service Commission adopted emergency amendments to its winter moratorium rule that reduced the amount of the minimum monthly payments necessary for low-income customers to avoid termination and waived late penalty fees and interest during the moratorium period.[88]

On April 5, 2006, the Ohio Public Utilities Commission extended the coverage period of its 2005–2006 Winter Reconnect Order from April 14, 2006, to April 28, 2006, noting, *inter alia*, the sharp increase in energy prices.[89]

On July 20, 2006, the Texas Public Utility Commission adopted a new rule[90] "due to the extreme and persistent heat."[91] The emergency rule prohibited electricity providers from disconnecting electric service from the date of adoption through September 30, 2006, "for a critical care residential customer[92] or an elderly low-income customer who contacted the utility regarding bill payment or in response to a termination notice" and required the utility to reconnect any such customer who had already had service terminated during the protected period.[93] The rule established parameters for repayment agreements for these critical care and elderly customers but did not require payments to obtain protected status. For low-income customers[94] who were not elderly or critical care customers, the rule prohibited electric utilities from terminating service (or failing to restore service terminated during the protection period) if the customer entered into a deferred payment plan under the parameters established in the regulation.[95]

In October 2008 and October 2009, the Rhode Island Public Utility Commission implemented an emergency rule to address "imminent peril to the health and safety to the public" when customers had been terminated or scheduled for termination from October 5 through December 1. The Commission provided that any such residential customer at risk of no heat for the winter was entitled to restoration of service from their utility, National Grid, if they satisfied the conditions of a payment plan.[96] This payment plan addressed the period immediately preceding and entering into Rhode Island's winter shutoff moratorium that is in effect between November 1 to March 31 and applies to prevent terminations to older, seriously ill, or disabled, or other protected customers.

---

86 Interim Opinion Approving Various Emergency Program Changes in Light of Anticipated High Natural Gas Prices, D. 05-10-044, at 2–3 (Oct. 27, 2005), *available at* www.cpuc.ca.gov/word_pdf/final_decision/50946.pdf.

87 *In re* A Residential Utility Customer Cold Weather Disconnection Rule, No. 05-121-R (Ark. Pub. Serv. Comm'n Nov. 21, 2005), *available at* www.apscservices.info/PDF/05/05-121-r_28_1.pdf.

The Arkansas Public Service Commission's General Service Rules are *available at* www.apscservices.info/Rules/general_service_rules.pdf.

In connection with the new rule, the Arkansas Public Service Commission decided to collect data from the companies to "reevaluate the effect of the revised Rule before the start of the 2006/2007 winter heating season." Ark. Pub. Serv. Comm'n 05-121-R, 2006 WL 2331212 (July 31, 2006).

88 Mo. Code Regs. Ann. tit. 4, § 240-13.055.

Subsequently, several utilities challenged the legality of the emergency regulation, but the court of appeals upheld that regulation. State *ex rel.* Missouri Gas Energy v. Public Serv. Comm'n, 210 S.W.3d 330 (Mo. Ct. App. 2006).

89 *In re* Investigation into Long-Term Solutions Concerning Disconnection of Gas & Elec. Serv. in Winter Emergencies, No. 05-1068-GE-UNC, 2006 WL 870234 (Ohio Pub. Utils. Comm'n Apr. 5, 2006).

90 16 Tex. Admin. Code § 25.50.

91 *In re* Office of Pub. Util. Counsel, 250 P.U.R.4th 151, 2006 WL 2056382 (Tex. Pub. Util. Comm'n July 21, 2006).

92 A "critical care" residential customer is one "for whom an interruption or suspension of electric service will create a dangerous or life-threatening condition," 16 Tex. Admin. Code § 25.497(a)(3).

93 16 Tex. Admin. Code § 25.50(b)(1).

94 Defined as households with incomes at or below 125% of the federal poverty level or that are receiving Food Stamps or medical assistance. 16 Tex. Admin. Code § 25.5(65).

95 16 Tex. Admin. Code § 25.50(b)(2).

Note that this emergency rule was not extended beyond September 2006, and no comparable rule has since been adopted by the Texas commission.

96 *See In Re* Emergency Regulations to the Rules and Regulations Governing Termination of Residential Electric, Gas, and Water Utility Service, No. 1725 (R.I. Pub. Util. Comm'n order entered Oct. 6, 2008, eff. Oct. 5, 2009), *available at* www.ripuc.org/eventsactions/docket/1725-PUC-Ord19779%2810-6-09%29.pdf.

The payment arrangements consisted of a 20%, 15%, or 10% downpayment on arrearages under $1000, arrearages from $1000 to under $2500, and arrearages of $2500 and over, respectively. Balances would be paid over eighteen, twenty-four, and thirty-six months, respectively.

While no commission would ever take the position that low-income households should obtain utility service for free, commissions are increasingly recognizing, through formally adopted regulations and related policies, that customers who pay as much as they can afford should be protected against termination whenever feasible, especially during times of extreme weather. As one commission noted in the context of discussing a utility's obligation to enter into payment plans: "When a consumer is financially unable to pay a balance in full, it is unreasonable for a company to terminate service for nonpayment. Termination in such circumstances serves no apparent purpose other than to punish the customer for being too poor to pay."[97]

6.3.3 *Budget Billing Plans and Deferred Payment Plans*

6.3.3.1 Budget Billing Plans

6.3.3.1.1 Budget billing plans described

In almost all states some or all gas and electric companies offer a form of budget billing plan, sometimes called level payment plan.[98] The rules of many public utility commissions (PUCs) require the utility to offer some sort of payment schedule or budget billing plan to low-income customers.[99]

Such a plan allows customers to divide their anticipated annual utility bill into twelve (sometimes fewer) payments, payable in equal amounts each month throughout the year, to cushion the blow of large winter-heating bills or summer air-conditioning bills. These plans are particularly useful to people on low fixed incomes and are widely used. Most of these plans are designed so that the customer begins in the "off season" to make payments that are larger than the actual bills in those months and to build up a reserve against anticipated higher bills later.

Such plans have been widely approved by regulators. For example, the Florida Public Service Commission approved a budget billing plan, finding that

> [s]uch plans . . . merely provide a different method of paying the same dollar amount for a year's service. Under budget billing, customers would be better able to plan payments during peak use months. Further, an appropriate plan should facilitate payment of low- or fixed-income customers. An additional benefit is realized through a reduction in high bill complaints. . . .[100]

In one case, a court suggested that payment and recoupment problems concerning payment of emergency utility bills by the welfare department might be solved by budget billing.[101] Such plans are widely used by customers. In one case, between 30% to 40% of a utility's residential customers participated.[102]

Generally, a budget bill is an accommodation and, some would argue, an extension of credit after the bill has surpassed the prior payments. Yet the exact nature of a budget billing arrangement is vague.[103] One bankruptcy court likened it to an open-account transaction and found it was not an executory contract.[104] Another court called the agreement to pay the budget figure, to the extent that it exceeded the amount actually due, "legally unenforceable."[105]

Analogous arrangements are few. Perhaps the closest analogy is a mortgage escrow account, established for payment of taxes and insurance, that is balanced at the end of the year. Any surplus is retained in the account and carried over. Any deficit is made up by an increase in monthly payments for the next year.[106] Unfortunately there is little illustrative law. In one case, a mortgage holder was allowed to accelerate a mortgage when the mortgagor was behind in

---

97 Gregory v. New England Tel. & Tel. Co., 2 P.U.R.4th 92 (Vt. Pub. Serv. Bd. 1973).

98 *See* National Regulatory Research Inst., Survey on Budget Billing Participation Conducted for the Joint Economic Committee (Dec. 2005), *available at* www.opportunitystudies.org/repository/File/weatherization/nrri_budget_bill_2005_JEC_report.pdf.

Some water utilities also offer this payment option. *See, e.g., In re* Northern Ind. Pub. Serv. Comm'n, 1999 WL 824597 (Ind. Utils. Regulatory Comm'n 1999). *See also* appx. A.1, *infra.*

99 *See, e.g., In re* Vermont Welfare Rights Org., 326 A.2d 828 (Vt. 1974) (gas and electric companies in Vermont must make available to their customers a "budget plan," a billing procedure averaging estimated utility costs over a yearly period).

100 *In re* Consideration of Lifeline Rates, 43 Pub. Util. Rep. 4th 356, 359 (Fla. Pub. Serv. Comm'n 1981).

101 Achey v. D'Elia, 447 N.Y.S.2d 852, 856 (N.Y. Sup. Ct. 1982).

102 Bay State Gas Co. v. Commissioner of Internal Revenue, 689 F.2d 1, 2 n.3 (1st Cir. 1982).

103 Several courts and commissions have dealt with the question of whether money held in budget billing accounts should be offset against a utility's working capital allowance, as customer deposits are. *See, e.g.,* City of Cleveland v. Public Utils. Comm'n of Ohio, 436 N.E.2d 1366 (Ohio 1982) (upholding the order of the Public Utilities Commission of Ohio that refused to offset average budget billing balance against working capital allowance). *See also* Office of Consumers' Counsel v. Public Utils. Comm'n of Ohio, 513 N.E.2d 243 (Ohio 1987).

104 *In re* Martinez, 92 B.R. 916, 919 (Bankr. D. Colo. 1988).

The utility was also unsuccessful in arguing that budget billing payments that came due and were unpaid between the chapter 13 filing date and the chapter 7 conversion date were administrative expenses under bankruptcy law. The court instead treated them as a prepetition debt under 11 U.S.C. § 348(d).

105 Bay State Gas Co. v. Commissioner of Internal Revenue, 689 F.2d 1, 6 (1st Cir. 1982) (tax court upheld on issue of treating budget billing customers and others the same for accounting purposes).

106 Federal regulation now limits the amount a borrower can be required to keep in such an account, a response to widespread abuse of such accounts. *See* National Consumer Law Center, The Cost of Credit: Regulation, Preemption, and Industry Abuses § 12.2.1.4 (4th ed. 2009 and Supp.).

the escrow account payments.[107] This analysis is not appropriately applied in the utility context, however. With a mortgage, the borrower has agreed to pay the escrow payments as a condition of the contract; failure to make escrow payments is default under the contract. The only obligation a utility customer has to prevent disconnection is to pay the amounts due for service actually delivered.[108]

Since the budget billing plan is essentially an accommodation by the utility and a convenience for the customer based on what the customer is likely to actually owe, a customer's change of circumstances will likely have little effect on the budget billing plan itself. The customer either owes the bill now or later. A sudden decrease in income, worsening of health, damage to the home, or any one of a number of other circumstances that could change for the worse probably will not change the budget plan itself. However such changes will make it more important to consider ancillary measures, such as deferred payment plans and energy assurance plans, to prevent a default on the plan.

6.3.3.1.2 When customer believes the monthly budget amount is too high

The budget billing amount may be set at a level that the customer believes is too high. This can be due to any number of factors, such as computational error, conservation activities undertaken by the household, the plan being based on a previous occupant's usage pattern, or unusual weather during the previous year. Most utilities will review the budget payment amount at a customer's request at any time during the year. This is the course that customers should initially pursue. An automatic review of the budget payment amount every six months is common among utilities (for example, National Grid in Massachusetts); others monitor the payment amounts throughout the year (for example, Mountain Fuel Supply Company) or at year's end.

During the review, unless there are meter inaccuracy complaints, or the customer have recently moved to a new address, the amount of past bills will usually be clear and the issue will focus on estimated bills for upcoming months. It may be useful to use data from comparable residences with similar-sized households, factor in increased energy savings from manufacturers' ratings of new efficient appliances, or extrapolate from a previous residence in order to counter utility projections. The review is most likely to be a fact-intensive negotiation without much law as guidance.

Some states have statutes or regulations that establish parameters for such reviews. In New York state, for example, New York Public Service Law § 38 authorizes budget payment plans. The New York Public Service Commission Rules of Practice at section 11.11 provide that budget bills "be subject to regular review for conformity with actual billings." In other states the utility tariff may be the only arena in which budget billing is even discussed and the tariff is an unlikely source for customer rights.[109]

The method of reconciling over-payments is not uniform either. For example, Mountain Fuel Supply Company issues a money refund at the end of the budget year in the event of an over-payment. Other companies offer only a bill credit. There is little law in this area as well.

6.3.3.1.3 Dealing with "insufficient" budget plan payments

Insufficient payments—that is, payments that appear to be too small to pay the annual bill at the end of the payment year—can be discovered in several ways: as a result of a customer complaint, a scheduled mid-year or end-of-year review, or a substantial deviation between projected and actual payments that is "flagged" by utility company computers. After discovery, usually an increase in the budget payment amount will be demanded for each future month. Customers should argue that such changes can be dealt with at a time and in a manner convenient for the customer, most likely as a small additional charge to be added to the monthly payment over many months or as part of a deferred payment plan. Customers should not automatically accept the utility's likely argument that the monthly budget billing amount should be radically increased to cover the deficit and the prospective shortfall.

Again there is little law in this area to offer guidance. Detrimental reliance analysis should be available: the customer agrees to pay "x" amount of dollars per month and relies on the utility's representations that such payment will ensure service for the year. The utility, with its superior resources, has all the information regarding past usage and the likely costs and has calculated the amount of the payment. It should not now be able to unilaterally change the terms of the contract.

Whether this argument succeeds probably depends on the "changed circumstances" language of the agreement, if any, between the utility and the customer, the language of the tariff or applicable regulation, and the possibility of pointing to utility misconduct as the source of the mistaken amount. Thus, in one Massachusetts case, the company presented a bill for an additional $808 at the end of the winter heating season. The customer refused to pay and

107 *See* Cramer v. Metropolitan Fed. Sav. & Loan Ass'n, 258 N.W.2d 20 (Mich. 1977).

108 *See* § 2.1, *supra.*

109 *See, e.g.*, Lucas County Comm'rs v. Public Utils. Comm'n of Ohio, 686 N.E.2d 501 (Ohio 1997) (unworkable and expensive pilot program for "weather normalized" bills terminated; later suit seeking refunds properly dismissed since utility required to charge at authorized rates); Shenandoah Gas Co., 164 Pub. Util. Rep. 4th 351, 1995 WL 628218 (W. Va. Pub. Serv. Comm'n Sept. 18, 1995) (tariff allows for adjustments "to recognize known changes in customer's consumption pattern, approved changes in rates, or effects of abnormal weather conditions").

sought relief from regulators. The customer proved that the meter was not regularly read and was malfunctioning. The additional charges were waived due to utility negligence.[110]

Delaying the effective date of the increase, phasing it in over time, or allowing installment payments on a retroactive amount owed is supported by analogy in the subsidized-housing context. Two courts have held that, if retroactive assessments are made, the tenants must be given the opportunity to pay in installments and cannot be evicted or have benefits terminated for failure to immediately pay the back amount in full.[111] Congress has also phased in rent increases for subsidized housing tenants when caused by changes in statutes.[112] The philosophy behind each of these actions is similar to that which addresses the underpayment of a budget billing plan: low-income people have little or no discretionary income, therefore repaying money legitimately owed should be done over time to lessen the blow.

For the customer, having part of the arrearage possibly waived and an acknowledged insufficient monthly payment accepted by the public utility is similar to participating in energy assurance programs and percentage-of-income programs.[113] Pressure to change the terms of the budget plan and increase the monthly payments can also be resolved by including in the plan some other type of payment assistance.

6.3.3.2 Fixed Payment Plans

Some states have approved proposals for fixed payment plans, at least on an experimental basis. In approving one such plan, the North Carolina utility commission found that "participating customers will know with certainty the amount of their monthly electric bills for a fixed 12-month period."[114] Similarly, the Oklahoma utility commission approved a "voluntary fixed price program" under which bills might vary depending on weather-induced consumption but would be based on a level price.[115]

110 *In re* Pryor, D.P.U. 19241 (Mass. Dep't of Public Utils. Oct. 25, 1977).

111 *See* Porter v. Shirley, No. C-553151 (Cal. Super. Ct. May 13, 1987), 21 Clearinghouse Rev. 404 (Aug/Sept. 1987) (L.A. County) (Clearinghouse No. 42,480) (public housing authority policy of terminating Section 8 benefits for failure of tenant to repay over-payment within thirty days not enforceable); Regency Park Apartments Gidcumb, No. 896-X-003 (Ky. Cir. Ct. Apr. 3, 1986), 20 Clearinghouse Rev. 282 (July 1986) (Warren Cty.) (Clearinghouse No. 40,788) (no good cause to evict for failure to pay $119 damage charge within fifteen days).

112 *See* National Hous. Law Ctr., HUD Housing Programs: Tenants' Rights, at 3/27 n.274 (2d ed. 1994). *See also* Pub. L. No. 93-383, § 202, 88 Stat. 633 (Aug. 22, 1974); 42 U.S.C. § 1437a note.

113 *See generally* § 7.2, *infra*.

114 *In re* Duke Power Co., a Div. of Duke Energy Corp., 219 Pub. Util. Rep. 4th 124, 126, 2002 WL 1803902 (N.C. Utils. Comm'n July 17, 2002).

115 *In re* Oklahoma Natural Gas Co., 211 Pub. Util. Rep. 4th 230, 241, 2001 WL 1142011 (Okla. Corp. Comm'n July 25, 2001).

6.3.3.3 Deferred Payment Plans

6.3.3.3.1 Introduction

Many utility commissions offer deferred payment agreements (DPAs), a widely used device to counter the problem of delinquent utility bill payments by low-income customers. Thirty-six utility commissions require the utilities they regulate to accept future installment payments of bill arrearages in lieu of disconnection,[116] while thirty-five[117] utility commissions allow an agreement for future installment payments of arrears as a basis for reconnection. For example, Alaska's rules state: "For a residential customer who demonstrates that economic hardship prevents payment in full of a delinquent bill, a utility *may not refuse to restore or continue service* unless the customer refuses to agree to or comply with a deferred payment plan" that meets certain requirements.[118] One court implied that such a plan could also be court ordered.[119] Deferred payment plans have been found to be nondiscriminatory as to other customers.[120]

The rationale for such policies was articulated in 1973 by the Vermont Public Service Board:[121]

> When the customer cannot pay a balance in full, it

116 Alaska, Arizona, Arkansas, California, Colorado, Connecticut, Delaware, Georgia, Idaho, Illinois, Indiana, Iowa, Kansas, Kentucky, Maine, Massachusetts, Michigan, Missouri, Nevada, New Jersey, New York, North Carolina, Ohio, Oklahoma, Oregon, Pennsylvania, Rhode Island, South Carolina, South Dakota, Texas, Utah, Vermont, Virginia, West Virginia (winter only), Wisconsin, and Wyoming. *See* National Ass'n of Regulatory Utility Comm'ns, 1994–1995 Compilation of Utility Regulatory Policy in the U.S. and Canada 464, 465, tbl. 211. *See also* appx. A.1, *infra*.

117 Alaska, Arizona, California, Colorado, Connecticut, Delaware, Georgia, Idaho, Illinois, Indiana (electric), Iowa, Kansas, Kentucky, Maine, Massachusetts, Michigan, Missouri, Nevada, New Jersey, New York, North Carolina, Ohio, Oklahoma, Oregon, Pennsylvania, Rhode Island, South Carolina, South Dakota, Texas, Utah, Vermont, Virginia, West Virginia, Wisconsin, and Wyoming. *See* National Ass'n of Regulatory Utility Comm'ns, 1994–1995 Compilation of Utility Regulatory Policy in the U.S. and Canada 466, 467, tbl. 212.

118 Alaska Admin. Code tit. 3, § 52.445(a) (emphasis added).
In addition, the Alaska rules require the utility to offer a levelized billing option to residential electric heating customers, Alaska Admin. Code tit. 3, § 52.440 (a), which helps low-income and other customers create a more manageable budget during the winter time when bills are extraordinarily high.

119 MCI Comm. Corp. v. Russell, 861 F. Supp. 280 (S.D.N.Y. 1994) (debts owed based on any tariff filed with the FCC may be enforced in federal court; even relatively small collection actions for long-distance charges may be heard by a federal magistrate judge or district judge).

120 Bagley Acquisition Corp. v. Michigan Pub. Serv. Comm'n & Detroit Edison Co., 581 N.W.2d 286 (Mich. Ct. App. 1998).

121 LeBeau v. Green Mountain Power Corp., 100 Pub. Util. Rep. 3d 337, 342–43 (Vt. Pub. Serv. Bd. 1973). *See also* Evelyn Gregory v. New England Tel. & Tel. Co., 2 Pub. Util. Rep. 4th 92, 96 (Vt. Pub. Serv. Bd. 1973).

> would be unreasonable for the company to terminate service for nonpayment, especially where the customer promises to pay all future bills as they become due and a reasonable portion of the back bill in installments. The purpose of permitting utilities to terminate service is to enable them to collect their just and reasonable charges by coercing laggard and unwilling people to pay bills that they owe and are able to pay. However if the customer is unable to pay the bill in question, then termination would serve no useful purpose except to punish the customer for being too poor to pay. Since it would not result in payment of the bill that is owed, termination would be an arbitrary and unreasonable act unrelated to any valid utility function. . . . We rule that in cases where the customer claims inability to pay a back bill in full, the electric utility must continue to serve him if the customer: (1) pays a reasonable portion of the outstanding bill; (2) agrees to pay all future bills as they become due; and (3) agrees to pay a reasonable portion of the back bill until it is fully amortized. . . . This rule protects both the companies' right to be paid and the customer's right to continued service during a personal financial crisis. . . .

The Vermont Public Service Board later clarified that what constitutes a "reasonable portion" will vary from case to case.[122]

As with work-outs of debts in other contexts including common law compositions and extensions[123] and chapter 13 bankruptcy filings, making payments over time to pay large utility bills has a common sense appeal. The Vermont Public Service Board has reasoned: "In the analogous area of civil contempt for nonsupport, the courts hold that it is an abuse of the contempt power to incarcerate a man (sic) for failing to make court-ordered support payments which he is totally unable to meet."[124]

Likewise, with utility bills, inability to pay in full should not be a barrier to right to service. As one commission reasoned, when a customer is financially unable to pay a balance in full, it is unreasonable to terminate service for nonpayment since termination in such circumstances serves no apparent purpose other than to punish the customer for being too poor to pay;[125] especially, as another reasoned, when the customers make a good faith promise to keep up with the bills to the best of their ability.[126] However, one other commission determined that, at least with respect to telephone customers, deferred payment plans are available "only to those customers who demonstrate an ability to pay but only in installments," holding that "only customers who reasonably can pay the bill in installments are entitled to a deferred payment plan."[127]

6.3.3.3.2 Relationship of budget billing plans to deferred payment agreements

Budget payment plans differ from deferred payment plans in that budget bills are established to pay future bills, are usually structured on a twelve-month basis, and may be adjusted during their term. Deferred payment agreements, by contrast, are established to deal with past payment shortfalls and may be structured in a variety of ways.

Thus a customer with an outstanding utility bill who is facing a shut-off is likely to enter into a deferred payment agreement to prevent the shut-off and retire the back bill. Since these plans usually require paying a certain amount of the back bill as well as the current bill to avoid disconnection, minimizing the current bill is important. A budget billing plan may be useful here although, at certain times of the year (for example, summer) it may be more advantageous to apply most resources to the past bill and take on the budget billing payments just as the bills begin to increase. Some commissions require regulated utilities to offer the customer the option of combining deferred payment plans with budget billing plans.[128] The Vermont Public Service Board has held that any customer who applies for budget billing may pay a delinquency under a deferred payment arrangement concurrent with the budget billing plan. The utility must offer budget billing unless it has previously attempted to place the customer on a twelve-month budget

---

122 Evelyn Gregory v. New England Tel. & Tel. Co., 2 Pub. Util. Rep. 4th 92, 96 (Vt. Pub. Serv. Bd. 1973). *See also In re* Rules & Regulations for Tel. Util., 151 Pub. Util. Rep. 4th 64, 66, 1994 WL 202287 (W. Va. Pub. Serv. Comm'n Mar. 29, 1994) (although reasonable time period for typical deferred payment plan may be six months, each situation is different and agreements should be tailored to meet the particular situation; there is no particular limit on length of deferred payment plans; customers have right to appeal reasonableness of deferred payment plan to the commission).

123 *See* 3B Debtor and Creditor Law § 37.02 (Theodore Eisenberg ed.) (loose-leaf with updates).

Generally, an extension is just that, putting off the date of a single payment. A composition may consist of creditors accepting a lesser amount than what was originally due, allowing payment over a longer period of time, or a combination of a reduction and a time extension. This is closer to the typical structure of a DPA.

124 *In re* Rules & Regulations Governing the Disconnection of Util. Servs., 2 Pub. Util. Rep. 4th 209, 219 (Vt. Pub. Serv. Bd. 1973) (citing *Ex parte* Howe, 457 S.W.2d 642 (Tex. App. 1970)).

125 Gregory v. New England Tel. & Tel. Co., 2 Pub. Util. Rep. 4th 92 (Vt. 1973).

126 LeBeau v. Green Mountain Power Corp., 100 Pub. Util. Rep. 3d 337 (Vt. 1973) (it was unreasonable for public utility company to terminate service for nonpayment when customer cannot pay balance in full, especially when customer promises to pay all future bills as they become due and a reasonable portion of back bill in installments).

127 *In re* Rules & Regulations for Tel. Util., 151 Pub. Util. Rep. 4th 64, 66, 1994 WL 202287 (W. Va. Pub. Serv. Comm'n Mar. 29, 1994).

128 *See, e.g.*, Utah Admin. Code r. 746-200-5(A)(4).

billing plan and the customer declined or failed to maintain such a plan in the past.[129]

The deferred payment approach is also the most promising negotiating strategy when dealing with an insufficient budget payment balance. If possible, dealing with this deficit in a large number of small payments may at least postpone the day of reckoning for a customer deep in arrears on a budget billing plan. Of more long-term benefit is an alternative payment arrangement, as discussed more fully in § 7.2, *infra.*

6.3.3.3.3 Form of deferred payment agreements

Some regulators have established very specific procedures for deferred payment agreements. For instance, in Utah, regulated gas and electric utilities are required to have personnel available twenty-four hours each day to reconnect service if the customer, "before reconnection[,] . . . agrees to negotiate and execute a deferred payment agreement and to pay the first installment by visiting the utility's business office within 48 hours after service has been reconnected." There the DPA can include the current bill and any reconnections in the amount to be repaid over time. In addition, the customer can choose the number of months over which to repay the amount in arrears and the monthly payment amount, as long as the customer catches up within twelve months[130] Colorado allows six payments.[131]

Other states authorize deferred payment plans but leave the details to be worked out between the utility and the customer.[132] In these circumstances, the length of the plan and the amount of the payments tend to be much more flexible. For example, in Massachusetts, payment plans must extend over a *minimum* of four months but may be longer.[133] The Massachusetts Public Utilities Commission also looks unfavorably on a "company [that] issues successive estimated bills" resulting in a "large catch-up bill." In circumstances in which a company's "reckless disregard of the requirement to obtain actual meter readings results in high catch-up bills," the Massachusetts PUC both abates a portion of the catch-up and often gives the customer a very long payment plan on the unabated portion, including up to 120 months in one case.[134] The amount of the payments is determined by evaluating a budget for the customer. As a part of the federal Public Utility Regulatory Policies Act of 1978 (PURPA),[135] all states were required to consider "installment payments" in lieu of termination for customers during periods when termination would be especially dangerous to health and when customers cannot pay their bills in a timely way, with special consideration given to older and disabled consumers.[136]

One way to view a deferred payment plan is as a substantial performance of a customer's obligation to pay. According to the Vermont Public Service Board, "based on the fundamental principle that the public utility's duty is to serve the public, is the related rule that the condition of payment for public utility service is satisfied by reasonable performance."[137] The Vermont Public Service Board further analogized the utility's obligation to enter into deferred payment plans to the contractual obligation to mitigate damages.[138]

Utilities are frequently required by regulation to consider specific factors in negotiating deferred payment plans. Standard regulations adopted by utility regulators around the country provide that a utility shall take into account designated factors in deciding what payment plans are "reasonable." These factors include, but are not limited to, "ability to pay."[139] In considering ability to pay, however, one state utility commission has made clear that, in negotiating a deferred payment arrangement, the amount of income is relevant but the "source of income is not ordinarily important."[140]

129 *In re* Citizens Comm'cns d.b.a. Citizens Energy Servs., 220 Pub. Util. Rep. 4th 280, 338, 2002 WL 31103647 (Vt. Pub. Serv. Bd. July 15, 2002).

130 *See* Utah Admin. Code r. 746-200-5.

131 *See In re* Rules Regulating Serv. of Elec. Util., 35 Pub. Util. Rep. 4th 365, 371 (Colo. Pub. Utils. Comm'n 1980).

132 In West Virginia, the customer and the utility work out the amount of payments and the length of the plan. An appeal is possible if these issues cannot be resolved, and termination of service is not allowed during this appeal so long as the current bill is paid. *See In re* Rules & Regulations for Tel. Util., 151 Pub. Util. Rep. 4th 64, 1994 WL 202287 (W. Va. Pub. Serv. Comm'n Mar. 29, 1994) (establishing new DPA procedures—only available to those who can demonstrate "ability to pay" but only in installments).

133 220 Mass. Code Regs. §§ 25.01 (definition of payment plan), 25.03(6) (obligation to offer payment plans); 2005 Mass. Acts ch. 140, § 17 (b).

134 *In re* Myers, D.P.U. 90-AD-26 (Mass. Dep't of Pub. Utils. Oct. 3, 1994) (abating $1220 of $3173 catch-up bill due to negligent failure to read meter and ordering 120-month payment plan on remaining balance of $1953).

135 16 U.S.C. §§ 2601–2645.

136 16 U.S.C. § 2625(g)(2)(b). *See* Dotson v. PG&E, 1995 WL 216862 (Cal. Pub. Utils. Comm'n 1995) (PURPA does not mandate permanent free utility service to low-income or disabled customer; ordering extended payment plan). *See also In re* Ohio Edison Co., 165 Pub. Util. Rep. 4th 22 (Pub. Utils. Comm'n of Ohio 1995) (due to extreme weather conditions, electric customers granted four-month "extended payment" option).

137 Blanche Sorrell v. Franklin Elec. Light Co., 25 Pub. Util. Rep. 4th 142, 146–49 (Vt. Pub. Serv. Bd. 1978).

138 *Id.* at 147 ("[T]he obligation imposed on utilities relating to payment by their customers . . . is similar to the legal duty imposed under contract law to mitigate damages. . . . Clearly the utilities' obligation extends to acceptance of reasonable offers by the customer or third parties which would result in full or partial payments.").

139 *See, e.g.*, Idaho Admin. Code r. 31.21.01.313; Ill. Admin. Code tit. 83, § 280, App. D; 65-407-81 Me. Code R. § 6 (LexisNexis); Mo. Code Regs. Ann. tit. 4, § 240-13.060; Mont. Admin. R. 38.5.1415; 52 Pa. Code § 56.97; Wis. Admin. Code Pub. Serv. Comm'n § 113-0404.

140 *In re* Rules & Regulations Governing the Disconnection of Util. Servs., 2 Pub. Util. Rep. 4th 209, 220 (Vt. Pub. Serv. Bd. 1973).

A West Virginia case demonstrates how the rationale for deferred payment agreements (DPAs) has been undercut by recent changes in the telephone industry. The West Virginia commission found that cellular telephone carriers as well as long-distance carriers need not provide DPAs (or notice of termination) since other alternative providers were available for customers and losses could be more easily avoided.[141] Occasionally a dispute will arise when a negotiated DPA differs from commission termination regulations or a company's tariff. In this case, the regulation takes precedence.[142] A DPA forced upon a customer by threats or coercion may be set aside.[143]

6.3.3.3.4 Partial payment as a substitute for full payment via deferred payments

Deferred payment plans have long been recognized as a means through which public utilities can seek to collect arrears from low-income households. Some public utility commissions, however, recognize that, in cases in which low-income households fell into arrears because they could not pay their past current bills as they came due, it may not be reasonable to expect those households to make any payments in addition to current bills in the future. Under such circumstances, utilities may best serve all their ratepayers by taking what immediate payment they can get from those low-income households rather than requiring those households to perform an impossible task.[144]

In seeking to implement this policy, the utility determination of whether to enter into a long-term deferred payment plan for the "full" amount of the arrears or to take some lesser amount immediately is an economic decision.[145]

A utility may best serve the interests of all its ratepayers by accepting an immediate partial payment of the arrearage rather than extending repayment over a lengthy period of time, especially with the possibility that the customer may fail to make all the payments over that time period. In accepting the smaller immediate payment, the concept of "indubitable equivalence" can be imported from bankruptcy law[146] to the mutual benefit of both the ratepayer and the utility. A utility should accept an immediate lesser payment as satisfaction of arrears if that payment is the functional equivalent of payment "in full" over the long term.

Once the appropriate interest rate has been established, one can compare the value of the smaller payment now with the value of larger total payments over time. This is referred to as the "discount rate." If the total of future payments reduced by the discount rate equals the proposed partial payment now, these courses of action are equivalent. The discount rate accounts for the lost-time value of the stream of deferred payments, that is, it compensates the utility for not having the money to use during the time of the payments as well as for the risk that the deferred payments may not be made.

Well-established mechanisms exist for making this determination. The option that is most appropriate for the utility payment plan process is a U.S. Treasury rate for securities of similar term to the payment plan, as adjusted for risk. Treasury rates are widely publicized in business journals.

Making this argument is worthwhile particularly if the possibility of a one-time payment on behalf of the customer is available now and the customer may not be able to make long-term future payments and keep up with a current bill. Financial assistance in such cases can be obtained from LIHEAP, fuel funds, or any of a variety of sources.

6.3.3.3.5 Renegotiation of plan based on changed circumstances

Unless precluded by commission regulations, there is no legal impediment to attempted renegotiation of a deferred payment agreement in the face of changed circumstances. Even in the face of prohibiting regulations, negotiation with the utility company should be attempted. Some state regulations even require utility companies to amend a deferred payment agreement after notification by the customer of changes beyond the customer's control.[147] West Virginia, for example, allows the renegotiation of a plan upon a showing of a "significant" change in financial circumstances resulting in hardship.[148] The West Virginia Commission declined to establish a standard for "hardship." The

141 *In re* Rules & Regulations for Tel. Util., 151 Pub. Util. Rep. 4th 64, 1994 WL 202287 (W. Va. Pub. Serv. Comm'n Mar. 29, 1994) (exempting cellular phone carriers and interexchange carrier from DPAs and notice of disconnection; telephone service does not raise immediate health and safety concerns like gas or electricity terminations do).

142 Columbia Gas of Ohio v. Public Util. Comm'n, 449 N.E.2d 433 (Ohio 1983) (gas termination notice sent to customer's attorney not adequate notice; when there is conflict between DPA and PUC regulations, regulations prevail).

143 Kean Inv. Co. v. Michigan Consol. Gas Co., 111 Pub. Util. Rep. 4th 470, 1990 WL 488713 (Mich. Pub. Serv. Comm'n Apr. 12, 1990) (DPA set aside because signed under coercion or threat by company).

144 *See* National Consumer Law Center, Understanding Why Customers Don't Pay: The Need for Flexible Collection Practices 2, 44 (1991).

145 Deciding to take less than the full amount is one option in a common law composition. This is different than the usual DPA, when full payment is made but over an extended period, and also different than the "equivalent value" argument made below, although this is another variant of a composition.

146 11 U.S.C. § 1129(b)(2)(A)(i)(II).

147 *See* N.Y. Comp. Codes R. & Regs. tit. 16, § 11.10 (N.Y. Pub. Serv. Comm'n). *See also In re* Rules & Regulations for Tel. Utils., 151 Pub. Util. Rep. 4th 64 (W. Va. Pub. Serv. Comm'n 1994) (renegotiable only if significant changes in financial circumstances).

148 *In re* Rules & Regulations for Tel. Utils., 151 Pub. Util. Rep. 4th 64, 1994 WL 202287 (W. Va. Pub. Serv. Comm'n Mar. 29, 1994) (renegotiable only if significant changes in financial circumstances).

Commission did state that, for a renegotiation to take place, customers would have to pay the current bill and make some payment on the arrearage during the renegotiation period. In declining to limit the number of permissible renegotiations, the West Virginia Commission found that "it will be rare for any customer to legitimately require more than one renegotiation. However, we believe that an occasional customer will suffer more than one major financial set back during the life of a deferred payment plan."[149]

Iowa has perhaps the most favorable renegotiation rule in the country.[150] Companies must offer payment plans in the first instance to any "residential customer [who] cannot pay in full a delinquent bill for utility service." Customers who are either still connected or who have been disconnected less than 120 days must be offered payment plans extending "over at least 12 months." Those who have been disconnected for more than 120 days but who are not in default of a prior agreement must be offered payment plans extending "over at least 6 months." The companies must offer a "second payment agreement" if the customer has made at least two of the payments required under the first agreement. "The second payment agreement shall be for the same term as or longer than the term for the first payment agreement."[151]

This rule acknowledges the reality that many low-income households face. Often, first payment plans are simply too onerous, and the household breaches the plan. When a household makes some but not all of the payments under a payment plan, the utility should be required to consider the possibility that the first plan was not fairly negotiated or that the household's financial circumstances have changed, calling for a longer second payment agreement. The Iowa Utilities Board has also ruled that *all* payments made on a customer's behalf, whether from the customer's own funds or such sources as fuel assistance, count towards the two payments that must be made to qualify under the second payment agreement rules described.[152]

Customers often need the utility to reconsider a prior repayment agreement when someone in the household loses a job or suffers a decrease in government assistance payments. These facts should be stressed in any negotiations regarding a second repayment agreement.

149 *Id.*

150 The "deferred payment plan" rule discussed in this paragraph is Iowa Admin. Code r. 199-19.4(10) (gas utilities). A similar rule for electric companies is found at Iowa Admin. Code r. 199-20.4(11). Several other states informally allow renegotiation of payment agreements if the customer seeks the help of consumer division staff at the PUC, but no state has such a clear, formal rule as Iowa.

151 Iowa Admin. Code r. 199-19.4(10)(c)(2) (emphasis added).

152 *In re* Application of State and Federal Assistance Payments to Meet Requirements of Second Payment Agreement, No. DRU-05-1, at 10–11 (Iowa Utils. Bd. May 17, 2005) ("[t]here should be no consideration of the source of the customer's payment when considering the two consecutive full payments required" in the payment agreement rules).

6.3.3.4 Response to Extraordinary Price Escalation

Consumers may be justified in seeking relief on the timing of a bill payment obligation in the face of extraordinary price increases. State utility commissions have provided relief both with respect to current bill payments and payments toward arrears.

Relief can come in any number of ways. In response to natural gas price spikes from January 2000 to June 2001, the California public utility commission approved replacing a policy mandating the disconnection of service for nonpayment upon an arrearage of $25 with a policy that provided for disconnection only after an arrears of $100.[153] Even with this more flexible disconnection policy, the California public utilities commission stated that the utility would be justified if it "declined to strictly enforce" the policy.[154] Similarly, the proposal of one Rhode Island utility to increase the delinquent balance threshold for utility service terminations from $375 to $500 was approved in light of increased natural gas prices.[155]

The offer of extended payment plans is also a necessary response to high fuel prices. In response to "substantial increases in fuel costs that have driven up the price of electric generation," the Massachusetts Department of Telecommunications and Energy stated that utilities should "expand their budget billing and consumer payment plans during the winter heating season . . . to lessen the effects of rate increases on consumers this winter. . . ."[156] Similarly, the New Jersey commission was quite explicit when it held that a utility "shall offer extended payment plans to their customers above and beyond what they may currently be offering. The length of the payment plan offered shall depend on individual customers but should include plans that allow customers to spread out their payments, without interest, over periods of at least six months."[157]

Not all extended payment plans apply exclusively to utility arrearages. The City of Austin offered a one-time deferred payment arrangement for a six-month term to help make paying bills more manageable for customers when summer electric bills reflected significant increases in the use of air conditioning during July 2009, the hottest month on record for Austin, with temperatures at or above 100° on approximately twenty-six different days.[158] The Public Util-

153 *In re* Southwest Gas Co., 219 Pub. Util. Rep. 4th 421, 434–35, 2002 WL 31094821 (Cal. Pub. Utils. Comm'n Aug. 22, 2002).

154 *Id.* at 434–35.

155 *In re* Providence Gas Co., 209 Pub. Util. Rep. 4th 519, 523, 2001 WL 839022 (R.I. Pub. Utils. Comm'n Apr. 30, 2001).

156 *In re* Standard Offer Serv. Fuel Adjustments, 206 Pub. Util. Rep. 4th 122, 124, 126, 2000 WL 33253133 (Mass. Dep't of Telecomms. & Energy Dec. 4, 2000).

157 *In re* NUI Elizabethtown Gas Co., 205 Pub. Util. Rep. 4th 489, 496, 2000 WL 1911412 (N.J. Bd. of Pub. Utils. Nov. 1, 2000).

158 *See* www.austinenergy.com/About%20Us/Newsroom/Press%20Releases/Press%20Release%20Archive/2009/greenPower.htm.

ity Commission of Ohio approved an "extended payment option to residential customers who are having difficulty paying August 1995 electric bills due to the effect of extreme August weather conditions," allowing for customers to "make payments of August bills, without interest, through December 1995."[159] This Ohio decision is consistent with other decisions addressing payment impacts when extraordinary circumstances give rise to high bills. While high water bills may not be weather-related, the Indiana commission approved a water company policy to adjust up to 50% for a high water bill that resulted from a leak on the consumer's side of the meter if the customer could demonstrate through repair records that prompt corrective action was taken to eliminate the leak.[160]

Though not explicitly tied to the doctrine of "force majeure," the rationale used by utility commissions to approve payment relief is akin to that doctrine. Force majeure is applicable to utility payment situations. In South Carolina, for example, a utility is prohibited from providing more than two successive estimated bills. The South Carolina commission has held that a greater number of successive estimated bills can only be provided "in situations resulting from acts of force majeure," with those situations defined to include "circumstances, beyond the Company's control, that could materially alter the normal course of business."[161]

6.3.4 Default on Deferred Payment Agreements

If a shut-off has been avoided by entering into a deferred payment agreement, defaulting on the agreement will once again put the customer at risk for disconnection. Some states such as Utah allow the utility to terminate if there is any breach of the agreement.[162] Colorado is similar.[163]

At the other extreme, Iowa has perhaps the country's most favorable rules for renegotiating a second payment plan if the customer has partially defaulted on a first payment plan. Iowa's rules require electric and gas companies to enter into second payment plans of at least the same duration as the first plan, if the customer has made at least two consecutive payments on the first plan.[164] The underlying principle appears to be a recognition that the financial circumstances of those customers who need payment plans are usually very shaky and subject to unforeseen changes, such that utility companies should be very flexible in negotiating with customers who have in fact been able to keep up with at least some of the payments due under the first payment agreement.

Other states, including New York, require notice of an opportunity to cure and the time frame for curing or the offer of a new DPA under some circumstances after a breach.[165] Other states require the utility company to act in good faith depending on the reason for the breach and may require another deferred payment plan or other equitable solution to the problem. Utilities in states without specific PUC regulations for DPAs seem more likely to be amenable to such arguments. This is also true for the situation in which customers make partial payments on the deferred agreement and the utility accepts them.

A change in circumstances could always be a basis for arguing that the plan needs to be revised—preferably before a breach but conceivably afterwards—and a basis for restructuring.[166] Waiver or equitable estoppel may also be an available defense if the utility has a pattern of accepting late or partial payments. When a customer missed a payment as part of a PIPP (Percentage of Payment Plan), a court has found that, relying on the utility's past pattern of accepting late payments, notice must be provided before the PIPP can be cancelled.[167]

6.3.5 No Disconnect During Billing Dispute

A significant limitation on utilities' power to terminate service is the general prohibition of disconnection for a

159 *In re* Ohio Edison Co., 165 Pub. Util. Rep. 4th 22, 45, 1995 WL 731792 (Ohio Pub. Utils. Comm'n Oct. 18, 1995).

160 *In re* Indiana-American Water Co., 150 Pub. Util. Rep. 4th 141, 155, 1994 WL 102679 (Ind. Utils. Regulatory Comm'n Feb. 2, 1994). *See also In re* Wisconsin Pub. Serv. Corp., 230 Pub. Util. Rep. 4th 229, 260, 2003 WL 23145651 (Wis. Pub. Serv. Comm'n Dec. 19, 2003) (reasonable to waiver back-billing of less than $50 due to meter errors; however, billing for unbilled revenue less than two years old is required by statute).

161 *In re* Piedmont Natural Gas Co., 223 Pub. Util. Rep. 4th 497, 540–41, 2002 WL 32072495 (S.C. Pub. Serv. Comm'n Nov. 1, 2002).

162 *See* Utah Admin. Code r. 746-200-5(B) (renewal of payment agreement after breach is utility's discretion; however, customer has right to Commission review of the alleged breach). *See also In re* Provision of Elec. Serv., 1998 WL 999897 (Ariz. Dec. 11, 1998) (no requirement of renegotiation after breach of DPA).

163 *See, e.g.*, 4 Colo. Code Regs. § 723-3 (LexisNexis) (section 3404(b)(IV)) (electric payment plan).

164 Iowa Admin. Code r. 199-19.4(10)(c)(2) (gas), r. 199-20.4(11)(c)(2) (electric).

165 N.Y. Pub. Serv. Law § 37 (McKinney) (residential gas, electric, and steam utility service); N.Y. Comp. Codes R. & Regs. tit. 16, § 11.10(e) (deferred payment agreements).

166 New Jersey requires renegotiation of a DPA if the customer's circumstances change significantly. *In re* Parkway Water Co., 1998 WL 310889 (N.J. Bd. of Pub. Utils. May 27, 1998). *See also* 4 Colo. Code Regs. § 723-3-13(e)(10) (LexisNexis); N.Y. Comp. Codes R. & Regs. tit. 16, § 11.10(e) (Home Energy Fair Practices Act).

167 Waterville Gas Co. v. Mason, 639 N.E.2d 1240 (Ohio Ct. App. 1994) (refusing to grant judgment for full $1666 bill when PIPP participant missed one payment; allowing judgment for full bill would lead to termination of service, contrary to public policy; acceptance of late payments constitutes estoppel preventing utility company from demanding full amount).

disputed bill.[168] This rule can be found in court decisions,[169] in statutes,[170] and in commission rules.[171]

At common law, the rule was short and simple, stated this way by a Tennessee court: "An exception to the general rule [that a utility may terminate service for nonpayment] exists when the customer has a bona fide dispute concerning the correctness of the bill."[172] This rule limits the ability of companies to use termination as a collection tool while a dispute is pending.

Courts disagree as to the extent of utilities' right to terminate service as a collection tool rather than a protection from future loss,[173] but most states' courts agree that a utility may not terminate for a disputed bill and, furthermore, that a wrongful termination while a bill is in dispute subjects the utility to damages.[174] As one court noted, there is strong doctrinal precedent for the "disputed bill exception" to the rule allowing termination for nonpayment:

> We think that there can be no dispute about the soundness of the proposition that, when the correctness of a bill of a public service corporation is disputed by one of its customers, and the company, by reason of the failure . . . to pay . . . discontinues its service, it does so at its peril, and, if in the wrong, is liable to compensatory damages in any event and, when the circumstances justify it, to punitive damages. . . .[175]

Courts have fairly uniformly upheld this standard, placing the onus on the utilities for their failure to ensure that the bills in dispute were correct before they employed the heavy-handed collection tool of termination.[176] However, in some jurisdictions, there is limited authority for the proposition that the utility may place the initial burden of paying the bill on the consumer.[177]

If a utility attempts to violate its legal duty to maintain service pending resolution of a billing dispute, a court may issue an injunction preventing it from carrying out a threat to terminate service[178] or may issue a writ of mandamus compelling the utility to restore service after a wrongful

---

168 *See, e.g.*, Wash. Admin. Code § 480-120-172(12) (telephone service may not be disconnected while a dispute is pending, provided amounts not in dispute are paid when due); Wis. Admin. Code Pub. Serv. Comm'n § 134-064(7).

One Maryland court has held that a commercial customer of a water company must pay a disputed amount under protest and then sue for its recovery. Washington Suburban Sanitary Comm'n v. Southern Mgmt. Corp., 472 A.2d 505 (Md. Ct. Spec. App. 1984).

However, the Maryland commission's rules for regulated utilities provide that a utility may not terminate service for nonpayment of a disputed amount. Md. Code Regs. 20.32.01.04(N).

169 *See* Note, *Fourteenth Amendment Due Process in Terminations of Utility Service for Non-Payment*, 86 Harv. L. Rev. 1477, 1479 (1973). *See also* Trigg v. Middle Tenn. Elec. Membership Corp., 533 S.W.2d 730 (Tenn. Ct. App. 1975), *followed by* Memphis Light, Gas & Water Div. v. Craft, 436 U.S. 1, 10 (1978).

Artesian Water Co. v. Cynwyd Club Apartments, 297 A.2d 387 (Del. 1972), is particularly noteworthy in that the court found that the commission abused its discretion in not barring the termination of service when the commission itself had found that there was a bona fide dispute as to the amount due. The customer had alleged that he should not have to pay for water that was corrosive and of substandard quality.

Companies that ignore commission rules regarding collection of disputed bills may be subject to the state's unfair and deceptive trade practices law. *See, e.g.*, Bailey v. Gulf States Utils. Co., 27 S.W.3d 713 (Tex. App. 2000).

170 *See, e.g.*, Cal. Pub. Util. Code § 779(b)(1) (West) (electrical, gas, heat, water corporations) (no utility shall terminate for nonpayment during pendency of investigation by corporation of customer or subscriber dispute or complaint); Conn. Gen. Stat. § 16-262d(c).

171 *See, e.g.*, 220 Mass. Code Reg. § 25.02(3)(d); N.J. Admin. Code § 14:3-7.13(a); 16 Tex. Admin. Code § 25.29(d)(5); 30-000-004 Vt. Code R. § 3.302(B)(3). *See* appx. A.1, *infra* (summaries of most state's customer service regulations).

172 Trigg v. Middle Tenn. Elec. Membership Corp., 533 S.W.2d 730, 733 (Tenn. Ct. App. 1975).

173 *Compare* Barry v. Commonwealth Edison Co., 29 N.E.2d 1014 (Ill. 1940) (when there is a bona fide dispute, right to discontinue service cannot be exercised by utility so as to coerce customer into paying the bill), *and* Houghton v. Bell Tel. Co. of Penn., 55 Pa. P.U.C. 271 (Pa. Pub. Util. Comm'n Sept. 18, 1981) (C-80052011) (discontinuation of service is a vehicle to prevent loss rather than a collection tool), *with* Masszonia v. Washington, 315 F. Supp. 529 (D.D.C. 1970) (obligation of utilities to terminate service for nonpayment is "an integral and necessary concomitant of proper rate control"), Huff v. Electric Plant Bd. of Monticello, 299 S.W.2d 817 (Ky. 1957) (utility may cut off service to any customer who fails to pay his bill after reasonable notice, since it would be impractical to compel the company to resort to numerous actions at law to collect small amounts), *and* Komisarek v. New England Tel. & Tel. Co., 282 A.2d 671 (N.H. 1971) (even though a utility company may have same remedy at law for collection of delinquent accounts as other businesses have, it also has the remedy of disconnecting service in order to avoid costly collection procedures).

174 *See* Trigg v. Middle Tenn. Elec. Membership Corp., 533 S.W.2d 730 (Tenn. Ct. App. 1975). *See also* St. John v. Missoula Elec. Coop., Inc., 938 P.2d 586 (Mont. 1997) (concurring opinion). *But see* Morse v. Pacific Gas & Elec. Co., 314 P.2d 192 (Cal. Ct. App. 1957) (discontinuance of service pursuant to filed rules governing payment of disputed bills is a complete answer to cause of action for damages caused thereby, since rules so filed are conclusively established as reasonable).

175 Birmingham Waterworks Co. v. Davis, 77 So. 927, 928 (Ala. 1918).

176 *See, e.g.*, Berner v. Interstate Power Co., 57 N.W.2d 55 (Iowa 1953); City of Austin v. Schonfeld, 622 S.W.2d 896 (Tex. App. 1981).

177 *See, e.g.*, Morse v. Pacific Gas & Elec. Co., 314 P.2d 192 (Cal. 1957); Womack v. People's Water Serv. Co., 61 So. 2d 785 (Miss. 1953).

178 Steele v. Clinton Elec. Light & Power Co., 193 A. 613 (Conn. 1937); Lawrence v. Atlanta Gas Light Co., 176 S.E. 75 (Ga. Ct. App. 1934); Arnold v. Carolina Power & Light Co., 167 S.E. 234 (S.C. 1933); City of Austin v. Schonfeld, 622 S.W.2d 896 (Tex. Civ. App. 1981); Hall v. Village of Swanton, 35 A.2d 381 (Vt. 1944).

termination.[179] In appropriate situations, a customer may be able to recover damages, including compensatory, nominal, and punitive awards.[180]

These rights to equitable remedies should be available in the courts regardless of whether the affected utility is also regulated by the public utility commission. If there is concurrent jurisdiction with a governmental regulatory agency, courts have held that none of the remedies are exclusive.[181] Courts do not ordinarily lose their equity jurisdiction just because the state has given an administrative agency authority over the business transactions of an industry.[182]

6.3.6 When Customer Is "Ahead" on Level Payment Plan

Many utility customers pay a level amount each month (often called a budget payment), meaning that users sometimes overpay or underpay their actual bill, but the total payments over the year will approximate the actual total yearly bill. If a customer misses a budget payment but is "ahead" of the actual money owed on the bill for the budget year, the utility has no basis to discontinue service. There is scant logic even to discontinue participation in the budget billing plan. After all, the customer has fully paid for service received and then some. While the customer may have breached the terms of the budget billing agreement, the utility has suffered no adverse consequences and, in fact, has had the use of the customer's additional money for some period of time, usually without paying interest.[183] If the customer so chooses, he or she should be reinstated to the budget plan when the delinquent budget amounts are paid. Otherwise the account should be converted to a regular billing arrangement as each bill accrues.

In any particular state, the public utility commission may have rules governing "budget" plans, and those rules might address the situation of a customer who falls behind on the budget payment amounts but has paid more than the actual metered usage to date. Many commissions post their rules on their websites.

6.3.7 No Disconnection Based on Bills from Non-Approved Tariff

Another little-used defense arises when a utility company provides service and bills for that service but has never had the tariff upon which the bill is based properly approved by the appropriate regulatory commission. In that situation, termination for nonpayment of the bill has been denied.[184]

6.3.8 No Disconnection Until Load Limiter Used

One commission allows disconnection only after the utility has installed a load limiter for one week, believing that this will reduce hostility and educate delinquent customers about their electric use.[185] Load limiters have resulted in the loss of life during the winter.[186]

6.3.9 Bankruptcy As a Source of Protection

The U.S. Bankruptcy Code presents one of the strongest sources of consumer rights to deal with utility shut-offs and utilities' unwillingness to restructure utility arrearages.[187] Under the Bankruptcy Code, a consumer may seek to discharge unpayable debts through a variety of mechanisms. Moreover, bankruptcy proceedings provide a forum in which to raise consumer defenses against unjustified creditors'

---

179 Hatch v. Consumers' Co., 104 P. 670 (Idaho 1909), *aff'd*, 224 U.S. 148 (1912); Hiers v. Southeastern Carolinas Tel. Co., 58 S.E.2d 692, 694 (S.C. 1950). *Cf.* Baltimore Gas & Elec. Co. v. Everett, 486 A.2d 248 (Md. Ct. Spec. App. 1985), *rev'd and remanded on other grounds*, 513 A.2d 882 (Md. 1986).

180 *See, e.g.*, Southern Pine Elec. Coop. v. Burch, 878 So. 2d 1120 (Ala. 2003); Brown v. Illinois Iowa Power Co., 52 N.E.2d 722 (Ill. App. Ct. 1943); Haynam v. Laclede Elec. Coop., Inc., 889 S.W.2d 148 (Mo. Ct. App. 1994); LTC Steel Co. v. Duquesne Light Co., 72 P.U.R.4th 605 (Pa. 1986); Trigg v. Middle Tenn. Elec. Membership Corp., 533 S.W.2d 730 (Tenn. Ct. App. 1975); Rusk County Elec. Coop., Inc. v. Flanagan, 538 S.W.2d 498 (Tex. Civ. App. 1976).

181 Steele v. Clinton Elec. Light & Power Co., 193 A. 613 (Conn. 1937); Louisville Gas & Elec. Co. v. Dulworth, 130 S.W.2d 753 (Ky. 1939); Stillman & Dolan, Inc. v. Chesapeake & Potomac Tel. Co., 351 A.2d 172 (Md. Ct. Spec. App. 1976). *But see* Morse v. Pacific Gas & Elec. Co., 314 P.2d 192 (Cal. Ct. App. 1957) (observance of filed rules is complete defense).

182 Steele v. Clinton Elec. Light & Power Co., 193 A. 613 (Conn. 1937) ("[t]he fact that a public service commission has jurisdiction to hear and determine disputes over charges for service does not deprive equity of jurisdiction to enjoin the shutting off of service to coerce payment of a disputed bill").

183 *In re* Idaho Power, 126 P.U.R.4th 536 (Idaho Pub. Util. Comm'n 1991) (electric utility need not pay interest on positive balances in customers' budget billing accounts).

184 Popowsky v. Pennsylvania P.U.C., 647 A.2d 302 (Pa. Commw. Ct. 1994) (when utility company failed to get tariff approved before billing customer, commission order requiring customer to pay bill or face termination was reversed; no bill owed because charges not lawful); GTE N. Inc. v. Public Serv. Comm'n of Wis., 500 N.W.2d 284 (Wis. 1993) (filed rate doctrine precludes billing for service not approved in tariff; refund ordered).

185 *See In re* Kauai Elec., 1999 WL 1066448 (Haw. Pub. Util. Comm'n Oct. 20, 1999).

186 *93-Year-Old-Man Freezes to Death Indoors*, Associated Press, Jan. 26, 2009 (customer of Bay City Electric Light & Power froze to death inside his own home after being put on a service limiter).

187 *See generally* Annot., *Bankruptcy, Debtor's Protection Under 11 U.S.C. Section 316 Against Utility Service Cutoff*, 83 A.L.R. Fed. 207 (1987).

claims. While not every consumer in financial trouble should file for bankruptcy, it is important to know how an individual, along with that individual's creditors, will fare in a bankruptcy proceeding. Such knowledge will not only facilitate a reasoned determination of whether to file for bankruptcy but may also lead to a settlement in the consumer's favor when the creditor realizes it will do even worse if the consumer files for bankruptcy. These issues are discussed in § 13.1, *infra*. A more complete discussion of consumers' rights as bankruptcy debtors is contained in National Consumer Law Center's *Consumer Bankruptcy Law and Practice* (9th ed. 2009 and Supp.).

6.3.10 *Protections for Military Service Personnel*

Many states have adopted their own version of the federal Servicemembers Civil Relief Act (SCRA).[188] A few states that have adopted their own form of SCRA provide very specific protections to those in military service who are responsible for utility bills. For example, the Michigan law provides that the:

> person [on active military service] or his or her immediate household shall not be deprived of or denied heat, water, electricity or gas service by any public utility serving his or her home during the first 90 days of military service by reason of unpaid bills for the commodities.[189]

Ohio law provides:

> No company shall cease to provide electricity to the residential premises of any residential consumer who is deployed on active duty for nonpayment for electricity provided to the residential premises.[190]

Other states do not limit terminations but provide other protections to those in active service, such as the right to cancel wireless phone service without incurring a prepayment penalty.[191]

6.4 Disconnection of Service Based on "Collateral" Matter

6.4.1 *General*

As a general rule, a public utility cannot terminate service because of some collateral matter unrelated to that service. The topic of actions utilities can, or cannot, take in regard to "collateral" matters (including whether termination can be based on collateral matters) is discussed in § 2.2, *supra*.[192]

6.4.2 *Old Utility Debts from a Prior Location*

6.4.2.1 Common Law Rule

At common law, a utility could not refuse to enter into a new contract for service because of an old debt, disputed or not, from some other place and time, such as an old utility bill from a prior residence. This topic is discussed more fully in § 2.2.2, *supra*.

6.4.2.2 State Regulations Often Allow Utility to Deny Service Based on Prior Debt

State regulation may limit the common law approach. At least thirty states explicitly permit utilities to deny service, or at least require deposits, if customers owe a debt for prior utility services to that company (or in some cases to other specified utilities). For example, New Hampshire's statute provides that, if the relevant statute of limitations has not yet run, an outstanding arrearage for prior service may be a basis to deny new service to an applicant for utility service. After the statute of limitations has run, the utility may deny service because of the prior arrearage, for up to three years after the statute has run, if the utility has reasonable, verifiable documentation of its collection efforts during the running of the statute of limitations.[193] In practice, however, it may often be the case that the utility fails to have adequate

---

188 50 U.S.C. app. §§ 501–596 (previously known as the "Soldiers' and Sailors' Civil Relief Act of 1940"). *See* National Consumer Law Center, Foreclosure Prevention Counseling ch. 10 (3d ed. 2010 and Supp.) (more thorough discussion).

189 Mich. Comp. Laws § 32.517. *See also* Mich. Comp. Laws § 460.9 (qualifying customer, namely residential household where income is reduced because customer or customer's spouse is called to full-time active military service, may apply for shut-off protection); Mich. Admin. Code r. 460.143(e).

190 Ohio Rev. Code Ann. § 4933.121(E) (West).
Note that Ohio Rev. Code Ann. § 4933.12(F) (West) provides similar protection regarding natural gas service. *See also* Cal. Mil. & Vet. Code § 827 (West) (utility shut-off protection for qualified customers); 65 Ill. Comp. Stat. 5/11-117-12.2 (covering municipal utilities); 220 Ill. Comp. Stat. 5/8-201.5 (covering utility companies and electric cooperatives); Iowa Code § 476.20(3) (amended in 2010 to provide that "a public utility furnishing gas or electricity shall not disconnect service to a residence in which one of the heads of household is a service member deployed for military service, as defined in section 29A.90, prior to a date ninety days after the end of the service member's deployment, if the public utility is informed of the deployment"); Minn. Stat. § 325E.028 (protections against terminations available to those in military service).

191 *See, e.g.*, Ga. Code Ann. § 46-5-8; La. Rev. Stat. Ann. § 29:418.1.

192 See especially §§ 2.2.1 and 2.2.2, *supra*.

193 *See* N.H. Code Admin. R. Ann. Pub. Utils. Comm'n §§ 1203.15(a)–1203.15(c).

documentation such that the company cannot deny new service based upon the old indebtedness. For a more thorough discussion of this topic, see § 2.2.2, *supra*.

6.4.3 Separate Business Run by Utility

A second type of matter generally considered collateral is a debt to a separate business run by the utility, such as the sale of appliances or the provision of some optional, unregulated services. Many state regulations specifically forbid the termination or refusal of services for nonpayment of such debts and collection fees. This topic is discussed more fully in § 2.2.2.5, *supra*.

6.5 Disconnection Based on Third Party's Debt

6.5.1 General Rule

Sometimes a utility seeks to terminate service for a debt incurred by another person or requires as a condition of continued service that the customer pay the debt owed by a person who lives with the customer. In doing so, the utility may be violating the general common law rule on "collateral" matters described above, that a utility may not terminate service because of some matter not related to the service. Section 2.2.3.1, *supra*, has a fuller discussion of this topic.

6.5.2 Debt Owed by Former Owner or Occupant of Real Property

A utility may seek to deny or terminate service because of arrears owed by a former occupant or owner of the premises. Because the new occupant neither used the services, nor had any control over their use, this practice is especially vulnerable to legal challenge. This topic is discussed more fully in § 2.2.3.2, *supra*.

6.5.3 Landlord-Tenant Situations

Sometimes the termination of service results from the delinquency of a landlord, not the prior occupant. Utilities are generally not allowed to terminate service in such a situation.[194] Landlord-tenant issues are discussed in §§ 2.2.3.3 and 2.4, *supra*.

6.5.4 Debt of Roommate or Family Member

In another common situation, a utility refuses service to an applicant or seeks to disconnect service to a customer because that person is living with a third party who is in arrears for utility service at another location. The third party might be a roommate or a family member. This situation may arise when an adult son or daughter must return to the parental home because of unemployment, illness, or a failed marriage.

In the past, the rule agreed upon by most commissions was that the utility may not refuse to provide service to one person based on the delinquency of another and may not prevent a customer from living with an individual who has a delinquent utility bill.[195] However, there has been an erosion of this protection. To prevent cohabitants from "name-swapping" on accounts with outstanding arrearages in order to maintain service without paying for arrearages, New Hampshire allows utilities under certain circumstances to deny service to a new applicant who lived with the customer in whose name the arrearage accumulated.[196]

6.5.5 Liability of One Spouse for Another's Bills

The courts and commissions have struggled with the issue of whether a utility should be allowed to deny service to a customer based on a third party's debt to the utility company when the third party is the customer's spouse. The question frequently arises when the bills have been in the husband's name for some time, with an arrearage accruing, and the wife then applies for service in her own name when the husband leaves because of a divorce or some other reason. This topic is discussed in more detail in § 2.2.3.5, *supra*.

6.5.6 Does Public Service Commission Have Authority to Hold Third Parties Liable?

6.5.6.1 General

It will be difficult to challenge public service commissions third-party liability rules or tariffs on the basis that they are contrary to common law decisions regarding disconnection for collateral matters. Customers and advocates can try to raise the question of whether such rules or tariffs are within the powers delegated to the commission by the

194 *See* § 2.2.3.3, *supra* (authorities cited therein).
Many state commissions have rules restricting termination of landlord accounts that affect tenants. *See, e.g.*, 220 Mass. Code Regs. § 25.04.

195 *See* § 2.2.3.4, *supra* (authorities cited therein).

196 *See* N.H. Code Admin. R. Ann. Pub. Utils. Comm'n § 1203.15(e).

legislature, but the likelihood of success is greater when it is possible to make policy arguments to protect the health and safety of distinct subpopulations.

Rules that allow a company to deny service based on collateral matters can create serious hardship when, for example, a survivor of abuse is attempting to build a life independent from her abuser but cannot get utility service in her own name, or when an adult child is forced to move back into the parents' home because of illness, unemployment, or a failed marriage and puts the entire household at risk of termination due to unpaid bills at his or her prior address. Because a particular state's rules may permit disconnection or denial even though the applicant or customer of record neither used the services for which payment is demanded nor had any control over their use, these rules may be challenged as having no rational relationship to the legislative purpose. However, it is important to note that many states do allow a utility to deny service to a customer based on the debts of a third party (often a roommate or spouse), and many of those regulations have been on the books for a number of years.[197] It is therefore important, before bringing a challenge to any state's rule, to research carefully whether that rule has been previously subject to any court challenge or interpretation, as well as to research the relevant case law in that state regarding the authority of the commission to adopt regulations.

The authority of a public service commission is grounded in the statute or state constitution that created it.[198] The legislature may, by statute, authorize the utility commission to adopt rules that, without legislative authorization, would appear to abrogate well-established common law principles, including those governing the law of contracts. The legislature may do so by explicitly granting the authority to adopt specific types of rules[199] or by granting the commission broader, more general rulemaking authority.[200] Thus, a regulation may be supported either by an explicit statutory provision or by a more general statement of legislative purpose. Regulations that are not explicitly authorized by the enabling statute must still bear a rational relationship to the legislative purpose.[201]

A utility commission cannot lawfully issue regulations or approve tariffs that are not authorized by the legislature, explicitly or by necessary implication, or that are in contravention of existing law.[202] Thus, it is possible that a commission regulation that holds a person liable for utility bills, when that state's law of contracts would not hold the person so liable, may be subject to challenge.

6.5.6.2 Challenging a Rule Authorizing Termination for a Third-Party Debt

Advocates who wish to challenge a commission rule or tariff authorizing termination of service (or refusal to initiate service) for failure to pay a third party's debt should first raise such a challenge with the commission itself. The commission may acknowledge that such a rule is unfair or unduly onerous and agree to withdraw or modify the rule, even if it believes it had full legal authority to promulgate the rule. It might be possible for an action for an injunction or for a declaratory judgment to be brought in the appropriate state court as well. The asserted grounds for the injunction can be that the customer (or applicant for service) has been paying (or has agreed to pay) all charges for services rendered and that any commission regulation requiring the customer (or applicant) to also pay for service rendered to that customer (or applicant) in the name of a third party is illegal. The utility will defend by citing the commission rule or regulation upon which the termination (or refusal to initiate service) is based, and the commission itself may well intervene on the side of the utility. In order to overcome such a defense, the challenging party must research carefully the scope of that commission's authority to adopt regulations and any cases that have interpreted the extent of the commission's rulemaking authority. In addition, in some cases, specific questions of contract law may arise, and those are addressed below.

6.5.6.3 Contracts Implied in Fact

In response to a challenge to a commission's third-party debt regulation, utilities may argue that such regulations are entirely consistent with that state's common law of contract,

---

197 *See* appx. A.1, *infra*.

198 *See* Union Carbide Corp. v. Public Serv. Comm'n, 428 N.W.2d 322 (Mich. 1988) (Public Service Commission has no inherent or common law powers); *In re* Procedure and Format for Filing Tariffs Under the Michigan Telecommunications Act, 534 N.W.2d 194 (Mich. Ct. App. 1995) (utility commission possesses only that authority specifically granted by statute).

199 *See, e.g.*, Mass. Gen. Laws ch. 164, § 124E (authorizing utility commission to adopt regulations regarding termination of service to customers age sixty-five or older).

200 *See, e.g.*, Mass. Gen. Laws ch. 164, § 76 (granting utility commission "general supervision of all gas and electric companies").

201 *See, e.g.*, Chelmsford Trailer Park, Inc. v. Town of Chelmsford, 469 N.E.2d 1259 (Mass. 1984) (rent control law that authorized board to "regulate evictions" but did not spell out permitted grounds for eviction was sufficient to support regulation setting forth such grounds).

202 *In re* Illinois Bell Switching Station Litig., 641 N.E.2d 440 (Ill. 1994) ("Statutes in derogation of the common law are to be strictly construed in favor of persons sought to be subjected to their operation"); *In re* Midwest Gas, 161 P.U.R.4th 426, 1995 WL 382766 (Iowa Util. Bd. May 19, 1995) (proposed tariff that would make all adults at address jointly and severally liable for utility bills too broad; tariff cannot impose liability beyond contract or common law; Iowa Code § 597.14 provides that "reasonable and necessary expenses of the family" are the joint responsibility of both parents; utility service may or may not be necessary family expense, depending on facts; liability of other adults unreasonable).

because there is an "implied in fact" contract between the customer and the utility.[203] A utility might argue that a person who (i) resides with another person who has contracted for service and is the named customer on the bill and (ii) uses or benefits from the service has an implied-in-fact contract to pay for that service. However, contract principles state that in order for an implied-in-fact contract to arise, the court must find that there was an intention to form a contract even though the intention was never put into words.[204] If the utility has entered into an *express* contract with a different person, the finding of intention cannot be made. A contract cannot be implied in fact when there is an express contract covering the same subject matter.[205]

6.5.6.4 Contracts Implied in Law

In defense to a challenge to a regulation that allows third-party liability for a utility bill, the commission or utility may argue that there is an "implied in law" contract between the customer and the utility and that the regulation is therefore enforceable, as consistent with the common law of contract. A contract implied in law is not a contract at all but an obligation imposed by law to do justice even though it is clear that no promise was ever made or intended.[206] An implied-in-law contract (also known as a "quasi-contract" or the doctrine of "*quantum meruit*") does not create a basis for transferring utility arrears from a third party to an existing customer or applicant for service. For an implied-in-law contract to exist, the utility must show an absence of both an express contract and an implied-in-fact contract. Additionally, the person to be held liable under an implied-in-law contract must have acted wrongfully toward the utility and been unjustly enriched.[207] Merely continuing to use service contracted for by another does not constitute such "wrongful" behavior. Instead, the "wrongful" behavior must involve some behavior such as deceit, oppression, or extortion.[208]

The key requirement for a utility customer (or the customer's advocate) to emphasize is that there must be "unjust" enrichment. As one court clearly stated, "it is not enough to show that goods or services were furnished to another; it must also be shown that the person to whom the goods or services were furnished received a substantial benefit therefrom and that it would be unconscionable to permit him to retain the benefit without paying for its reasonable value."[209]

In this situation, advocates can raise the argument that, if there is an express contract for one person to pay the utility bill, the utility cannot require a third party to pay the bill. That third party has not been unjustly enriched, and it is not unconscionable to allow that third party to have used and benefited from the utility service without paying for it.[210]

6.6 Disconnect to Collect a Mistaken Undercharge

6.6.1 General

The situation sometimes arises that households are billed too little for their utility service. Then, after months or years of undercharges, a mistake is discovered and the household is presented with a large lump sum that is said to be due or disconnection will occur. The mistake often occurs due to simple billing errors, such as improper installation of the meter for one apartment so that it actually reads the usage in a different apartment.

Whether the consumer is obligated to pay the undercharges is discussed at § 4.1.2, *supra*. This section discusses whether nonpayment of this obligated amount can lead to disconnection or whether the utility must pursue payment through other channels, such as a court action.

Some PUCs adopt a middle path of requiring utilities to offer a payment plan so that the obligation can be spread out over a period of months and disconnection would occur only if the consumer became delinquent on that plan.[211]

---

203 Erickson v. Goodell Oil Co., 180 N.W.2d 798 (Mich. 1970) ("contract implied in fact arises under circumstances which, according to the ordinary course of dealing and common understanding of men, show a mutual intention to contract").

204 *See, e.g., In re* Pennsylvania Cent. Transp. Co., 831 F.2d 1221 (3d Cir. 1987) ("An implied-in-fact contract is a true contract arising from mutual agreement and intent to promise, but where the agreement and promise have not been verbally expressed, the agreement is inferred from the conduct of the parties.").

205 New York Tel. Co. v. Teichner, 329 N.Y.S.2d 689 (N.Y. Dist. Ct. 1972) ("[a] situation involving an express contract between two parties generally will not support an implied in fact liability to a third party to the contract to pay for such . . . even though benefits were derived by the third party"; wife not liable for bills rendered in husband's name even when wife was sole occupant of house); 17 C.J.S. *Contracts* §§ 6, 7 (1999).

206 *See* Calamari & Perillo, Contracts § 1.8, at 22 (5th ed. 2003).

207 N.Y. Tel. Co. v. Teichner, 329 N.Y.S.2d 689 (N.Y. Dist. Ct. 1972).

208 *See* Roger D. Colton, *Heightening the Burden of Proof in Utility Shutoff Cases Involving Allegations of Fraud*, 33 How. L. J. 137 (1990).

209 Harold A. Newman Co. v. Nero, 107 Cal. Rptr. 464, 468 (Cal. Ct. App. 1973).

210 New York Tel. Co. v. Teichner, 329 N.Y.S.2d 689 (N.Y. Dist. Ct. 1972).

211 Conn. Gen. Stat. § 16-259a(d) (utility shall establish payment plan that prorates arrearages for service owed for period of time that is no shorter than the period for which customer is being held liable; payment plan shall provide that no payment exceeds 50% of average amount that company charged for each billing period over the previous twelve-month period; utility may require immediate payment of full amount due if customer fails to make timely payments in accordance with payment plan); N.Y. Comp. Codes R. & Regs. tit. 16, § 14.10(a)(1) (utility must provide offer of deferred payment agreement when it renders back-bill exceeding $100 as long as customer's "culpable con-

6.6.2 The Doctrine of Estoppel

The general rule of equitable estoppel may provide protection for customers whose utility service is at risk of being terminated because of a mistaken undercharge. The rule, simply stated, is that "he who, by his language or conduct, leads another to do what he would not otherwise have done, shall not subject such person to loss or injury by disappointing the expectations upon which he acted."[212] The party asserting estoppel need not show any intent to deceive by the other party[213] or any negligence in the statement of erroneous facts. As the New Mexico Supreme Court has emphasized, the necessary element for estoppel is the other party's material change in position in reasonable reliance on the first party's statements or conduct.[214]

Notwithstanding the general estoppel doctrine, as stated above, the principles of utility law prevent the use of an estoppel defense to avoid the *payment* of utility undercharges.[215] However, the estoppel doctrine may be sufficient to force the utility to collect the undercharge through a court action rather than by threatening to terminate service.

The equitable principles incorporated in the doctrines of estoppel and mistake may be applied without violating the utility's obligation to collect its rates as filed. This strategy would allow the utility to collect the under-billing but prohibit the utility from using disconnection of service for nonpayment of the under-billing as a collection device. Advocates should argue that the utility is permitted to use any legitimate collection device, except for the extraordinary and highly coercive use of monopoly power to withhold a necessity. The utility and the customer would thus share the burdens of the utility's mistake.

duct" did not contribute to under-billing); 16 Tex. Admin. Code § 25.28(d)(3) (if under-billing is $50 or more, utility shall offer customer deferred payment plan option for same length of time as that of under-billing; company can back-bill only for most recent six months).

212 I.X.L. Stores v. Success Mkts., 97 P.2d 577, 580 (Utah 1939); National Consumer Law Center, Repossessions § 4.3 (7th ed. 2010).

213 However, there must be: an intent that the statement be acted upon, *see, e.g.*, American Hardware Mut. Ins. Co. v. BIM, Inc., 885 F.2d 132 (4th Cir. 1989); an expectation that it will be relied and acted upon, *see, e.g.*, Shane v. WCAU-TV, CBS Television Stations, Div. of CBS, Inc., 719 F. Supp. 353 (E.D. Pa. 1989); or a foreseeability that it will be relied and acted upon, *see, e.g.*, Wolf Bros. Oil Co. v. International Surplus Lines Ins. Co., 718 F. Supp. 839 (W.D. Wash. 1989).

214 J.R. Hale Contracting Co. v. United N.M. Bank, 799 P.2d 581 (N.M. 1990).

215 *See* § 4.1.2, *supra*.

6.6.3 Mandatory Versus Discretionary Practices

In cases of under-billing, utility companies have the discretion whether or not to terminate the service if the customer cannot pay the corrected bill. Courts are therefore free to apply the doctrine of estoppel, that is, to bar the utility from using termination as a tool to collect a corrected bill after under-billing has been detected. Although under the case law a utility may have an obligation to collect its mistaken undercharges because it has no discretion to charge a lesser rate than that contained in its tariffs, termination is not mandated by statute. In this situation, the equitable doctrine of estoppel does not override the statutory requirements that rates not be less than those contained in the filed tariff.

Accordingly, a utility that has negligently under-billed should, by reason of its negligent or willful mistake, be estopped from disconnecting service. Moreover, even in situations involving no willful misconduct or negligence, the utilities can be prevented from exercising their right to this otherwise discretionary remedy so as to share the consequences of the innocent mistake.[216]

The discretionary nature of disconnections has been discussed in a line of cases in which the issue was whether a utility's termination of service constituted state action. In *Jackson v. Metropolitan Edison Company*, the United States Supreme Court held that utility disconnections did not represent "state action" because such activity was entirely up to the utility.[217] According to the Court, the state had not put its imprimatur on the disconnection of service "by ordering it."[218]

Although the "state action" debate is not directly relevant to the issue at hand, the fact that shut-offs are discretionary, not mandatory, removes them from the traditional undercharge analysis. Even if a utility may not be estopped from performing its mandatory duty to collect its undercharges, it may indeed be estopped from using the discretionary tool of service disconnection in the collection process.

The right to collect an undercharge is not easily challenged, but the manner of collection can nonetheless be regulated. While the utility may have the obligation to collect the undercharge somehow, this does not necessarily mean that it can do so through disconnection of service.

216 "He who, by his language or conduct, leads another to do what he would not otherwise have done, shall not subject such person to loss or injury by disappointing the expectations upon which he acted." IXL Stores v. Success Mkts., 97 P.2d 577, 580 (Utah 1939).

217 419 U.S. 345, 357 (1974).

218 *Id. See also* Taylor v. Consolidated Edison Co., 552 F.2d 39 (2d Cir. 1977); Srack v. Northern Natural Gas Co., 391 F. Supp. 155 (S.D. Iowa 1975); Iowa Citizen/Labor Energy Coal. v. Iowa State Commerce Comm'n, 335 N.W.2d 178 (Iowa 1983).

6.6.4 Past Undercharges As Collateral Matters

Another approach is to argue that the undercharge is a collateral matter and, consistent with the general prohibition against disconnecting utility service for a "collateral" matter, is barred.[219] Courts have recognized the essential nature of utility service and the inherently coercive nature of the disconnection of service as a collection mechanism.[220] Accordingly, the law traditionally bars the use of that mechanism to collect for "collateral" matters.

There is little case law that directly addresses this issue, but amounts due as a result of mistaken past undercharges could be seen as a "collateral" matter. The customer may have made payments in full each month as the bills became due. The utility is not seeking to collect arrears that have arisen due to customer nonpayment; rather, it is seeking to recoup for its own past mistake. A customer should have the right to expect that the utility's monthly billing is accurate and that payment of current bills when rendered satisfies the customer's obligations and will prevent a shut-off.[221] A bill for past undercharges does not represent a bill for services that arises in the ordinary course of monthly customer/utility relations. Accordingly, it is appropriate to prohibit the disconnection of utility service for nonpayment of a bill based on mistaken under-billing.

6.7 Recourse for Wrongful Disconnection

6.7.1 Utility's Failure to Comply with Legal Limitations

Consumers whose utility service has been unlawfully disconnected by a utility company have several different remedies available:

- They may apply for a writ of mandamus[222] or injunction[223] to compel the restoration of service;
- They may seek an injunction to prevent the utility from carrying out a threat to terminate service;[224]
- They may sue for damages;[225] or
- They may file an action before the regulatory commission while simultaneously seeking damages in a court action, seeking an order restoring service and a penalty to be paid to the state pursuant to commission rules or statutes.[226]

Damage actions in court are an alternative means to enforcing utility customer service requirements. These actions serve two purposes. They compensate utility customers who have suffered from the utility's violation of their

219 *See* §§ 2.2, 6.4, *supra*.

220 Spicer v. Baltimore Gas & Elec. Co., 831 A.2d 472 (Md. Ct. Spec. App. 2003); Monroe v. Niagara Mohawk Power Corp., 388 N.Y.S.2d 1003 (N.Y. City Ct. 1976); Trigg v. Middle Tenn. Elec. Membership Corp., 533 S.W.2d 730 (Tenn. Ct. App. 1975).

221 *See, e.g.*, Boston Gas Co. v. Cesaitis, Mass. D.P.U. 84-86-69 (Mass. Dep't of Pub. Util. Mar. 4, 1986).

222 At common law, this was generally true when the situation was the wrongful termination of a bill in dispute. *See, e.g.*, Hatch v. Consumers' Co., 104 P. 670 (Idaho 1909), *aff'd on other grounds*, 224 U.S. 148 (1912); Hiers v. Southeastern Carolinas Tel. Co., 58 S.E.2d 692 (S.C. 1950). *See also* Annot., *Mandamus As Proper Remedy to Compel Service by Public Utility*, 83 A.L.R. 947 (1933).

223 *See, e.g.*, Louisville Gas & Elec. Co. v. Dulworth, 130 S.W.2d 753 (Ky. 1939); La Nasa v. Sewerage & Water Bd. of New Orleans, 184 So. 2d 158 (La. 1966); Southwestern Gas & Elec. Co. v. Stanley, 45 S.W.2d 671 (Tex. App. 1931), *aff'd*, 70 S.W.2d 413 (Tex. 1934). *See also In re* Tarrant, 190 B.R. 704 (Bankr. S.D. Ga. 1995); Sisco v. Luppert, 658 A.2d 886 (Pa. Commw. Ct. 1995).

224 Steele v. Clinton Elec. Light & Power Co., 193 A. 613 (Conn. 1937); Lawrence v. Atlanta Gas Light Co., 176 S.E. 75 (Ga. Ct. App. 1934); Arnold v. Carolina Power & Light Co., 167 S.E. 234 (S.C. 1933); City of Austin v. Schonfeld, 622 S.W.2d 896 (Tex. App. 1981); Hall v. Village of Swanton, 35 A.2d 381 (Vt. 1944).

225 *See, e.g.*, Walton Elec. Membership Corp v. Snyder, 487 S.E.2d 613 (Ga. Ct. App. 1997) (electrical cooperative liable to member for damages for wrongful disconnection), *aff'd*, 508 S.E.2d 167 (Ga. 1998); Huff v. Electric Plant Bd. of Monticello, 299 S.W.2d 817 (Ky. 1957); Haynam v. Laclede Elec. Coop., 889 S.W.2d 148 (Mo. Ct. App. 1994) (affirming award of compensatory and punitive damages for wrongful disconnection of service despite lack of evidence of danger to safety or risk of bodily harm); Trigg v. Middle Tenn. Elec. Membership Corp., 533 S.W.2d 730 (Tenn. Ct. App. 1975) (if customer has bona fide dispute concerning correctness of bill, electric company discontinues services for nonpayment of disputed amount at its peril and, if company is wrong, it is liable for damages); Lynn v. Houston Lighting & Power, 820 S.W.2d 57 (Tex. App. 1991) (court, not PUC, has exclusive jurisdiction over tort damage claims for wrongful disconnection after meter tampering dispute).

However, suits for emotional distress may be difficult. *See* Jackson v. Alabama Power Co., 630 So. 2d 439 (Ala. 1993) (utility found not to have committed tort of "outrage" even though company violated Public Service Commission rules by disconnecting service to customer with asthma who needed electricity to administer her medication and who was hospitalized); DeGraeve v. Southwestern Bell Tel. Co., 687 P.2d 1380 (Kan. Ct. App. 1984) (action for damages for emotional distress denied). *But see* Southern Pine Elec. Coop. v. Burch, 878 So. 2d 1120 (Ala. 2003) (compensatory damages award "for mental distress" ruled not excessive); South Cent. Bell v. Epps, 509 So. 2d 886 (Miss. 1987) (though damages for physical or mental pain and suffering are generally not recoverable for breach of telephone service contract, compensatory damages award of $75,000 not excessive in wrongful disconnection case in which utility had knowledge of special circumstances surrounding account of subscriber who suffered "extreme mental anguish").

226 *See, e.g.*, Utah Admin. Code r. 54-7-25 (utility violation of any statute or commission rule subject to penalty of $500–$2000 for each offense; for continuing offenses, each day is a separate offense).

legal and procedural obligations. Second, the award of damages may provide disincentives to utilities and deter future unlawful disconnections and other violations.

Suit can be brought under at least two alternative theories:[227] (1) breach of contract or (2) tort.[228] "It is generally held that the failure or breach of duty to supply service to one legally entitled thereto is a tort, even if there is also a breach of contract."[229] In such a situation, "a public utility may be held liable in damages for all injuries proximately resulting."[230] This observation extends not only to the disconnection of service but also to a delay in the connection of service. "Where there has been a negligent delay in acting upon an application for the service of a public utility, the utility will be liable on the theory of tort for such damages . . . or, in the absence of affirmative negligence, may be held liable as for a breach of contract."[231] These conclusions have been reached with regard to public utilities furnishing water, gas, and electricity,[232] as well as for telephones service.[233]

227 *See* 9 Am. Jur. Pleadings and Practice Forms (Rev.), *Electricity, Gas and Steam* § 52 (1996) (model complaints). *See also* Cochran v. Appalachian Power Co., 246 S.E.2d 624 (W. Va. 1978) (breach of contract action for wrongful termination when tort statute of limitations expired).

228 *See generally* Roger D. Colton, *Unlawful Utility Disconnections As a Tort: Gaining Compensation for the Harms of Unlawful Shutoffs*, 22 Clearinghouse Rev. 609 (1989). *See also* Tovar v. Southern Cal. Edison Co., 247 Cal. Rptr. 281 (Cal. Ct. App. 1988) (tort damages for landlord's master meter disconnection if proximate causation is shown).

The utility company may also be liable for the intentional tort of trespass if it committed a tortious act, such as causing damage while disconnecting or reconnecting service, even if it was authorized by the customer's nonpayment to go onto the property to perform the shut-off. Snelling v. City of St. Louis, Dep't of Pub. Utilities—Water Div., 897 S.W.2d 642 (Mo. Ct. App. 1995). *See also* DeGraeve v. Southwestern Bell Tel. Co., 687 P.2d 1380 (Kan. Ct. App. 1984) (public utility is held to a standard of ordinary care in wrongful termination of service case); Haynam v. Laclede Elec. Coop., 827 S.W.2d 200 (Mo. 1992), *adopted by* 889 S.W.2d 148 (Mo. Ct. App. 1994) (proof of negligence or intentional action by REC will support tort claim of wrongful disconnection of electrical service).

229 64 Am. Jur. 2d *Public Utilities* § 29 (2001). *See, e.g.*, Walton Elec. Membership Corp. v. Snyder, 508 S.E.2d 167 (Ga. 1998) (breach of contractual duty may also constitute a tort); South E. Ind. Natural Gas Co. v. Ingram, 617 N.E.2d 943 (Ind. Ct. App. 1993) (tort claim would lie for negligent failure to warn greenhouse owners of interruption of service; statute empowering Public Service Commission to regulate utilities did not deprive court of jurisdiction to hear this negligence claim); DeLong v. Osage Valley Elec. Coop. Ass'n, 716 S.W.2d 320 (Mo. Ct. App. 1986).

230 64 Am. Jur. 2d *Public Utilities* § 29 (2001). *See, e.g.*, National Food Stores v. Union Elec. Co., 494 S.W.2d 379 (Mo. Ct. App. 1973).

231 64 Am. Jur. 2d *Public Utilities* § 30 (1972). *See, e.g.*, Smith v. Tri-County Elec. Membership Corp., 689 S.W.2d 181 (Tenn. Ct. App. 1985) (citing Capital Elec. Power Ass'n v. Hinson, 92 So. 2d 867 (Miss. 1957)).

232 64 Am. Jur. 2d *Public Utilities* § 29 (2001).

233 86 C.J.S. *Telecommunications* § 125 (1997). *Accord* South Cent. Bell v. Epps, 509 So. 2d 886 (Miss. 1987).

Note, however, that the *Epps* case was presented as a breach of contract case. South Cent. Bell v. Epps, 509 So. 2d 886, 891 (Miss. 1987).

6.7.2 Disconnections As Torts

6.7.2.1 Duty

The general rule is that a public utility holding a franchise has a duty to serve all members of the public "who apply for and have made the necessary arrangements to receive service, and who pay or offer to pay the price and abide by the reasonable rules and regulations of the company."[234] A supplier of utility service is subject to a duty of exercising reasonable care to fulfill its obligation to provide continuing service.[235]

In other words, in a shut-off situation, a utility must act with the care that a reasonable person would exercise given the consequences of the shut-off. This degree of care is heightened by the recognition that electric, gas, and water services are essentials of life and the deprivation of such services is likely to be detrimental to life, health, and property.[236]

A utility's duty to provide continuous service in some states may extend to persons beyond its "customers," and third parties (particularly tenants who do not directly pay for utility service) may have standing to sue a utility for disconnection-related torts. In states that allow third parties to bring suits in tort for injury or harm arising from a utility termination, it may be sufficient for the claimant to show that he or she has been "affected by the unlawful, prohibited or forbidden conduct" of the utility.[237] If the claimant has

234 Jim Rossi, *The Common Law Duty to Serve and Protection of Consumers in an Age of Competitive Retail Public Utility Restructuring*, 51 Vand. L. Rev. 1233 (Oct. 1998).

235 27A Am. Jur. 2d *Energy and Power Sources* § 199 (1996).

236 *See, e.g.*, Consolidated Edison Co. v. Jones, 444 N.Y.S.2d 1018 (N.Y. Civ. Ct. 1981).

Indeed, a number of utility tort cases indicate that, because of the consequence of the action, a utility owes the "highest standard of care" when seeking to terminate service. Kohler v. Kansas Power & Light Co., 387 P.2d 149, 151 (Kan. 1963). *Accord* Washington Gas Light Co. v. Aetna Cas. & Surety Co., 242 A.2d 802, 804 (Md. Ct. Spec. App. 1968). *But see* DeGraeve v. Southwestern Bell Tel. Co., 687 P.2d 1380 (Kan. Ct. App. 1984) ("highest degree of care" language reserved for cases involving dangerous character of service; "ordinary negligence standard of care" should be applied to wrongful termination of service case).

237 Fawn Lake Ranch Co. v. K.C. Elec. Ass'n, 700 P.2d 564, 566 (Colo. App. 1985). *See also* Lanni v. Rochester Gas & Elec. Corp., 466 N.Y.S.2d 248 (N.Y. City Ct. 1983). *But see* Milliken & Co. v. Consolidated Ed. Co., 644 N.E.2d 268 (N.Y. App. Div. 1994) (no cause of action against utility for four-day loss of power when tenant had no direct contractual relationship with utility).

Note also that the duly-approved tariffs of many utilities include limitation of liability clauses, which may present an

suffered injury in fact to a legally protected interest as contemplated by statutory or constitutional provisions, he or she may bring an action in tort based upon an unlawful shut-off.[238]

This duty of care may be of particular importance to tenants whose utility service is in the landlord's name. Whether or not a tenant has a right to contest a utility shut-off,[239] the obligation of a utility company to exercise "reasonable care" to prevent harm to the users of its services as a result of a shut-off may dictate that notice be provided to tenants. Should a utility company choose not to provide such notice, it would risk facing damages in tort. Indeed, liability for damages on these grounds may arise even if the underlying shut-off is lawful.[240] As stated by a Missouri court, when the utility failed to give notice of an interruption of service, "[t]he right to interrupt service is granted, but the crucial point is that cannot divorce itself from the consequences of its own failure to use ordinary care to avoid harm to its consumers."[241]

6.7.2.2 Breach

Utility companies breach their duty of care to customers and third parties when they fail to act "reasonably" with regard to utility disconnections.[242] Whether the utility has acted reasonably is analyzed on a case-by-case basis. Generally speaking, however, the requirement of reasonableness requires the utility companies to act as a prudent utility company would, given all of the circumstances.[243]

It is reasonable to argue that the disconnection of service in violation of a state statute or administrative regulation requiring either uninterrupted service[244] or specific interruption notice procedures rises to the level of negligence per se.[245] This argument is based upon the reasoning of *Martin v. Herzog*,[246] a case in which the New York court found that violation of a statute setting highway safety standards was negligence per se. In its decision, the court reasoned that "to omit, willfully or heedlessly, the safeguards prescribed by law for the benefit of another that he may be preserved in life or limb, is to fall short of the standard of diligence to which those in organized society are under a duty to conform."[247] The holding that violation of a safety standard is negligence per se has been adopted by the Restatement of Torts[248] and is the majority rule in this country.[249]

The advantage of arguing that violation of shut-off regulations constitutes negligence per se is that it eliminates the issue of "negligence" as an issue in fact.[250] If there is no question of whether the utility did in fact fail to meet a prerequisite to a utility shut-off, the issue of negligence will be disposed of as a matter of law.

While only regulated utilities have statutory standards, this model may be applicable to non-regulated utilities as well. When faced with the actions of an unregulated REC, the existence of certain state PUC shut-off regulations, while not establishing an absolute standard of care, might be

---

additional obstacle to a party seeking recovery for an allegedly illegal or wrongful termination.

238 Fawn Lake Ranch Co. v. K.C. Elec. Ass'n, 700 P.2d 564, 466 (Colo. App. 1985).

239 *See* § 6.5.3, *supra*. *See also* Duhamel, *Rights of the Nonbilled Utility User*, 19 Clearinghouse Rev. 249 (July 1985).

240 *See* Cates v. Electric Power Bd. of Metro. Gov't, 655 S.W.2d 166 (Tenn. Ct. App. 1983) ("regardless of whether the plaintiffs had a right to contest the discontinuance of service, they certainly had a right to know that service was being disconnected to enable them to protect themselves from the damage that did occur"). *See also* Washington Gas Light Co. v. Aetna Cas. & Surety Co., 242 A.2d 802, 804 (Md. Ct. Spec. App. 1968).

241 National Food Stores v. Union Elec. Co., 494 S.W.2d 379, 384 (Mo. Ct. App. 1973).

242 DeGraeve v. Southwestern Bell Tel. Co., 687 P.2d 1380 (Kan. Ct. App. 1984) (public utility is held to a standard of ordinary care in wrongful termination of service case); Haynam v. Laclede Elec. Coop., 827 S.W.2d 200 (Mo. 1992), *adopted by* 889 S.W.2d 148 (Mo. Ct. App. 1994) (proof of negligence or intentional action by REC will support tort claim of wrongful disconnection of electrical service); Central Mo. Elec. Coop. v. Wayne, 18 S.W.3d 46 (Mo. Ct. App. 2000) (tort claim would lie when company breached informal payment arrangement whereby customers were told they need not pay utility bill until settlement of their claims against utility for damages caused by defective equipment furnished by company). *See also* 15 Am. Jur. 2d *Proof of Facts* 125, 142 (1978).

243 *See, e.g.*, Trigg v. Middle Tenn. Elec. Membership Corp., 533 S.W.2d 730 (Tenn. Ct. App. 1975) (utility required to act reasonably when discontinuance of service might present obvious danger to property of customer known to be on vacation).

244 It is likely that no distinction would be made between a state statute and a state agency regulation. Dobbs, The Law of Torts ch. 7, § 134 (2000).

No distinction has been made, for example, between a state statute and a municipal ordinance. *See* Donald Kepner, *Violation of a Municipal Ordinance As Negligence Per Se in Kentucky*, 37 Ky. L.J. 358 (1949).

An administrative regulation has the same force and effect as a statute. *See, e.g.*, Whitley County Rural Elec. Membership Corp. v. Lippincott, 493 N.E.2d 1323, 1327 (Ind. Ct. App. 1986).

245 The negligence per se rule is not universal. In Vermont, for example, violation of a safety statute creates only a rebuttable presumption of negligence. *See, e.g.*, Sheehan v. Nims, 75 F.2d 293 (2d Cir. 1935).

Moreover, in Arkansas, violation of a statute is merely evidence of negligence. *See, e.g.*, Gill v. Whiteside-Hemby Drug Co., 122 S.W.2d 597 (Ark. 1938).

246 228 N.Y. 164 (N.Y. 1920).

247 *Id.*

248 Restatement (Second) of Torts § 288B.

249 *See* Dobbs, The Law of Torts ch. 7, §§ 134, 137–38 (2000).

Some statutes, however, specifically address themselves to the liability question, either establishing or negating that violation of the statute creates liability per se. *See, e.g.*, Section 24 of the Federal Consumer Product Safety Act, 15 U.S.C. § 2072 (1982). *See also* Fleming James, Jr., *Statutory Standards and Negligence in Accident Cases*, 11 La. L. Rev. 95, 103 (1950).

250 *See generally* Stephen Weiner, *The Civil Jury and the Law-Fact Distinction*, 54 Cal. L. Rev. 1867, 1885–86 (1966).

used as evidence of an industry standard reflecting the proper duty of care.[251] A municipal utility's standard of care can be found in cases holding that the utility must comport with the requirements of due process before disconnecting utility service.[252]

6.7.2.3 Causation

As with all negligence causes of action, the utility customer litigant must demonstrate an actual causal relationship between the unlawful utility action and the harm that occurs. As a result, when seeking to bring a subsequent suit in tort, advocates must carefully determine what shut-off requirements have allegedly not been met. A clear causal relationship between the violation and the ensuing harm must be established. For example, in the common situation in which there has been lack of notice, it could be argued that such lack of notice caused a customer to miss the opportunity to pay the bill, get assistance to pay the bill, or enter into an agreed payment plan with the utility company.

To hold the utility company liable for negligence, the disconnection must also constitute the proximate cause of the harm. Whether a disconnection was the proximate cause of the harm to the utility consumer is strictly a question of foreseeability.[253] At the time of its actions, if the utility could reasonably foresee that the shut-off would result in the damages incurred by the consumer, then the proximate cause requirement has been satisfied. Most damages that flow from a wrongful utility shut-off are foreseeable, due to the nature and importance of uninterrupted utility service.

6.7.2.4 Damages

Damages can include compensatory, nominal, and punitive awards when appropriate.[254] In addition, if it is built into the state's statutory scheme, the customer may be entitled to additional damages.[255] A customer whom a public utility has wrongfully terminated is entitled to recover actual damages proximately caused by the wrongful action.[256] These recoverable damages may include the customer's:

- Discomfort, annoyance, and inconvenience;
- Embarrassment and humiliation;
- Temporary loss of use or rental value of property;
- Value of appliances, furniture and other personal property destroyed or damaged;
- Value of food destroyed (for example, in a refrigerator or freezer);
- Incidental expenses (such as motel expenses) directly caused by the shut-off; and
- The cost of obtaining power from another source.[257]

Advocates should also seek reconnection free of charge.[258]

In addition, if the utility acted in "reckless disregard of the rights" of the customer, the utility may also be liable for punitive or exemplary damages.[259] There need be no malice involved in order to recover these damages. As a general rule, in these specific types of cases, "[t]he burden of proof is sustained, once the injured party shows such gross neglect of duty as to evince a reckless indifference of the rights of others on the part of the wrongdoer."[260] The demonstration of "negligence amounting to positive misconduct" is a sufficient basis for the award of punitive damages.[261] However, in order to collect punitive damages in a utility shut-off case,[262] generally there must first be actual damages.[263]

---

251 There would exist no sovereign immunity problems in suing a municipal utility in tort. "[M]unicipal ownership of public utilities . . . must of necessity carry with it the same duty, responsibility and liability on account of tortious conduct that is imposed upon and attaches to private owners of similar enterprises. . . . [T]his rule has been frequently applied with respect to municipal light and power plants, gasworks and waterworks." McQuillin, The Law of Municipal Corporations § 53.100 (3d ed. 2002). *See also id.* § 53.02.

252 *See* § 5.1.3, *supra.*

253 Dobbs, The Law of Torts ch. 10 (2000). *See also* Hill v. Consolidated Edison Corp., 428 N.Y.S.2d 837 (N.Y. Sup. Ct. 1980). *Cf.* Fordham-Coleman v. National Fuel Gas Distrib. Corp., 834 N.Y.S.2d 422 (N.Y. App. Div. 2007) (genuine issue of material fact as to whether gas distributor's failure to provide gas service, based upon prior unsatisfied judgment, was proximate cause of decedent's death from hypothermia).

254 *See, e.g.,* Southern Pine Elec. Coop. v. Burch. 878 So. 2d 1120 (Ala. 2003); Tovar v. Southern Cal. Edison, 247 Cal. Rptr. 281 (Cal. Ct. App. 1988); Rusk County Elec. Coop., Inc. v. Flanagan, 538 S.W.2d 498 (Tex. App. 1976).

255 For example, S.D. Codified Laws § 49-13-14.1 provides that individuals injured by wrongful acts or omissions of telephone companies may sue for double damages and be awarded attorney fees.

256 Haynam v. Laclede Elec. Coop., 889 S.W.2d 148 (Mo. Ct. App. 1994). *Accord* Muise v. GPU, Inc., 851 A.2d 799 (N.J. Super. Ct. App. Div. 2004). *See also* Tegnazian v. Consolidated Edison, Inc., 730 N.Y.S.2d 183 (N.Y. Sup. Ct. 2000) (class action on behalf of residential customers seeking damages from a blackout cannot be maintained because, *inter alia,* whether individual class members have suffered legally cognizable harm, and the extent of any damages, requires individual inquiry).

257 *See* Wrongful Termination of Electric Service, 15 Am. Jur. 2d *Proof of Facts* 125, 147 (1978).

258 *See, e.g.,* Cal. Pub. Utils. Code § 10010.1(f) (West) (municipally owned utilities) (any service wrongfully terminated shall be restored without charge).

259 Wrongful Termination of Electric Service, 15 Am. Jur. 2d *Proof of Facts* 125, 147 (1978).

260 Watkins v. Layton, 324 P.2d 130 (Kan. 1958), *cited with approval in* Kohler v. Kansas Power & Light Co., 387 P.2d 149 (Kan. 1963).

261 DeSalme v. Union Elec. Light & Power Co., 102 S.W.2d 779, 783 (Mo. Ct. App. 1937). *See also* Passantino v. Consolidated Edison Co. of N.Y., 428 N.E.2d 391 (N.Y. 1981).

262 In order to bring a claim for punitive damages, the challenge to a utility shut-off must be brought in tort. Punitive damages do not lie in contract actions. Smith v. Tri-County Elec. Membership Corp., 689 S.W.2d 181 (Tenn. Ct. App. 1985).

263 *See, e.g.,* Haynam v. Laclede Elec. Coop., 827 S.W.2d 200 (Mo. 1992), *adopted by* 889 S.W.2d 148 (Mo. Ct. App. 1994).

6.8 Landlord-Requested Utility Disconnects

6.8.1 General

This section addresses situations in which landlords, who are billed directly for their tenants' utility service, instruct the utility to disconnect service to a tenant's unit because of an underlying dispute between the landlord and the tenant. A landlord who is the customer of record of the utility is thus in control of utility service to the rented premises; the landlord thus has a stranglehold on the tenants. Some landlords may use the threat of service termination to exert pressure when the tenant owes money—for rent, utility service, or other debt—or when the tenant has drawn the attention of governmental agencies, community watchdog groups, or other tenants to the condition of the premises. In particular, this section discusses remedies a tenant may have against the vindictive landlord or the complicit utility company.

The remedies available to a tenant will depend on the nature of the dispute that precipitated the landlord's actions and, to a much greater extent, on the jurisdiction under whose law will govern. In most jurisdictions, the tenant suffering from or facing service termination has remedies against the landlord for damages and, in certain instances, for injunctive relief. Threatened or actual termination of service poses such a danger to most tenants, however, that action must be taken immediately to stop the utility from complying with the landlord's request. Utility policies may also be attacked peremptorily when they allow the threat of service termination to be used by a landlord seeking summary resolution of a dispute or deterrence of the lawful exercise of rights by tenants.

Utility service is a practical necessity of modern life. Thus termination of service effectively facilitates the eviction—constructive or actual—of the tenant, who must choose to either move or live without service.[264] Utility companies generally know if the occupant of the unit receiving utility service is a non-customer tenant, and not the customer of record, because bills for that service are sent to an address other than the service address.[265] A utility that terminates service to the tenant's unit under such circumstances, without giving notice to the tenant and without allowing the tenant to place service in his or her own name, may implicate itself in the landlord's illegal conduct to the extent that the utility's policy will be independently unlawful.

6.8.2 State and Local Laws Placing Obligations on the Utility

Several states' statutes require the utility company to give notice to tenants prior to terminating utility service that is billed to the landlord.[266] Local ordinances may also offer similar protections.[267] Many of these laws apply when the utility terminates service of its own accord; some laws, however, may apply to landlord-ordered service terminations as well.[268]

Even if state law places no obligation on a utility, the tenant may still be able to obtain injunctive relief against the utility based on the landlord's illegal action. This should at least be considered in order to allow the tenant sufficient time to pursue legal remedies against the landlord.[269]

6.8.3 State Statutes Specifically Regulating Landlord's Ability to Order Disconnect

In approximately two-thirds of the states, specific statutes forbid the landlord from terminating utility service to tenants.[270] Civil[271] or criminal penalties may be imposed for

264 *See* Memphis Light, Gas & Water Div. v. Craft, 436 U.S. 1, 18 (1978) (utility service is a necessity of modern life; discontinuing of water or heating for even short periods of time may threaten health and safety); Palmer v. Columbia Gas of Ohio, 342 F. Supp. 241, 244 (N.D. Ohio 1972) (utility termination may have serious effects on health and may even be fatal), *aff'd*, 479 F.2d 153 (6th Cir. 1973); Stanford v. Gas Serv. Co., 346 F. Supp. 717, 721 (D. Kan. 1972); Montalvo v. Consolidated Edison Co., 441 N.Y.S.2d 768, 776 (N.Y. Sup. Ct. 1981), *aff'd in part and modified in part*, 460 N.Y.S.2d 784 (N.Y. App. Div. 1983).

265 Duhamel, *Rights of the Non-Billed Utility User*, 19 Clearinghouse Rev. 247, 253 (July 1985).

266 *See, e.g.*, Cal. Pub. Util. Code §§ 777(a), 10009.1(a) (West); Conn. Gen. Stat. § 16-262e; 765 Ill. Comp. Stat. 735/3-3; Me. Rev. Stat. tit. 35-A, § 706; Mass. Gen. Laws ch. 164, § 124D (gas and electric utilities; opportunity for tenants to put bill in their name and continue service); 68 Pa. Stat. Ann. §§ 399.1 to 399.18 (West) (requiring pre-termination notice to tenants and opportunity to put bill in their name and continue service); 66 Pa. Cons. Stat. §§ 1521 to 1533 (discontinuance of service to leased premises). *But cf.* Rohrbaugh v. Pennsylvania Pub. Util. Comm'n, 663 A.2d 809 (Pa. Commw. Ct. 1995) (utility's termination of service at tenant's request, without notice to landlord and when temperature was below freezing, violated statutory obligation of adequate and reasonable service; landlord's status as mere property owner and not ratepayer did not nullify statutory requirement), *rev'd*, 727 A.2d 1080 (Pa. 1999).

267 *See, e.g.*, Robinson v. Michigan Consol. Gas Co., 918 F.2d 579 (6th Cir. 1990) (discussing Detroit city code); Chandley Enters. v. Evansville, 563 N.E.2d 672 (Ill. App. Ct. 1990) (discussing Evansville municipal ordinance).

268 *See* Mass. Gen. Laws ch. 164, § 124D; 66 Pa. Cons. Stat. § 1523(b).

269 DiMassimo v. City of Clearwater, 805 F.2d 1536 (11th Cir. 1986); Koger v. Guarino, 412 F. Supp. 1375 (E.D. Pa. 1976).

270 *See, e.g.*, Alaska Stat. § 34.03.180; 765 Ill. Comp. Stat. 735/1.4; Ky. Rev. Stat. Ann. § 383.640 (West); Mass. Gen. Laws ch. 186, § 14; Mont. Code Ann. § 70-24-408; Neb. Rev. Stat. § 76-1427; N.H. Rev. Stat. Ann. § 540-A:3(1); Okla. Stat. tit. 41, § 121; 66 Pa. Cons. Stat. § 1523(b); R.I. Gen. Laws § 34-18-31; Tex. Prop. Code Ann. § 92.008 (West); Tex. Admin. Code § 25.29(i); Va. Code Ann. § 55-248.23.

271 Wrongful termination of utility service will often entitle a tenant to damages. *See* Cal. Civ. Code § 789.3(c) (West) (actual dam-

violating these laws.[272] Several states by statute expressly provide for injunctive relief to restore service or to avert a threatened service termination.[273]

6.8.4 State Landlord-Tenant Law Limiting Landlord's Ability to Initiate Disconnect

6.8.4.1 Quiet Enjoyment

The termination of utility service facilitates constructive eviction by rendering the premises uninhabitable.[274] Indeed, in many cases in which landlords order termination of service for an existing tenant, the landlord's actions are intended to force tenants from their units. When the landlord willfully causes utility termination during the course of an ongoing tenancy, the landlord breaches the covenant of quiet enjoyment,[275] which in most jurisdictions is implied in all leases of residential premises.[276]

A breach of the covenant of quiet enjoyment is remedied by an action for damages,[277] and a tenant may seek injunctive relief to enjoin violations of that duty by a landlord.[278]

In a situation in which the landlord causes the utility to terminate service after the tenancy has ended (through termination of the lease, by proper notice, or by operation of law), the tenant's remedies are less clearly defined. In some states, the tenant may be entitled to the benefit of a covenant of quiet enjoyment even while he or she occupies the premises as a tenant at sufferance.[279]

6.8.4.2 Warranties of Habitability

Over the past three decades, a majority of jurisdictions have imposed on property owners an enforceable duty to provide basic habitable premises. In nearly every jurisdic-

ages and up to $100 for each day without utility service); Fla. Stat. § 83.67 (actual and consequential damages or three months' rent, whichever is greater); Me. Rev. Stat. tit. 14, § 6014 (actual damages or $250, whichever is greater); N.M. Stat. Ann. § 47-8-36; Ohio Rev. Code Ann. § 5321.15 (West); Tex. Prop. Code Ann. § 92.301 (West); Va. Code Ann. § 55-225.2; Wash. Rev. Code § 59.18.300 (actual damages and up to $100 for each day without utility service).

Wrongful determination will also entitle a tenant to reasonable attorney fees. *See* Fla. Stat. § 83.67; Ohio Rev. Code Ann. § 5321.15 (West); Tex. Prop. Code Ann. § 92.301 (West) (landlord may be liable to tenant if utility terminates for nonpayment); Va. Code Ann. § 55-225.2; Wash Rev. Code § 59.18.300.

272 Statutes providing for criminal liability of landlords who willfully terminate utility service include Ga. Code Ann. § 44-7-14.1 and Minn. Stat. § 504B.225.

273 *See, e.g.*, Fla. Stat. § 83.67(1); S.D. Codified Laws § 43-32-6; Vt. Stat. Ann. tit. 9, §§ 4463(a), 4464.

274 Davis v. Weir, 497 F.2d 139 (5th Cir. 1974); Koger v. Guarino, 412 F. Supp. 1375 (E.D. Pa. 1976); Lawrence, *District of Columbia Survey: George Washington University v. Weintraub: Implied Warranty of Habitability As a (Ceremonial?) Sword*, 33 Cath. U. L. Rev. 1137, 1154 (1984).

275 1 American Law of Property, § 3.45 (Crasner, ed., 1976). *See, e.g.*, Nielsen v. Wisniewski, 628 A.2d 25 (Conn. App. Ct. 1993) (deprivation of gas and electricity amounted to deprivation of quiet enjoyment); Lowery v. Robinson, 432 N.E.2d 543 (Mass. App. Ct. 1982) (failure to furnish heat during heating season breaches covenant of quiet enjoyment); Johnson v. Grand Cru Prop. One Ltd. P'ship, 49 Pa. D. & C.4th 531 (Pa. Ct. Com. Pl. 2000) (tenants whose electricity had been terminated for nonpayment were certified as class in lawsuit alleging breach of warranty of habitability, breach of covenant of quiet enjoyment, fraud, and negligent misrepresentation among other causes of action); Morrison v. Smith, 757 S.W.2d 678 (Tenn. Ct. App. 1988) (utility termination breaches covenant).

276 1 American Law of Property, §§ 3.45, 3.47–3.52 (Crasner, ed. 1976). *See, e.g.*, Bedell v. Los Zapatistas, 805 P.2d 1198 (Colo. App. 1991) (though it does not recognize an implied warranty of habitability, Colorado does recognize an implied covenant of quiet enjoyment in residential leases that may be breached by interruption of vital utility services); George Wash. Univ. v. Weintraub, 458 A.2d 43, 48 (D.C. 1983); Rittenberg v. Donohoe Constr. Co., 426 A.2d 338 (D.C. 1981) (failure to furnish heat breaches covenant); Cruz Mgmt. Co. v. Thomas, 633 N.E.2d 390 (Mass. 1994); Blackett v. Olanoff, 358 N.E.2d 817 (Mass. 1977); Charles E. Burt, Inc. v. Seven Grand Corp., 163 N.E.2d 4 (Mass. 1959) (failure to furnish heat, light, and power breaches covenant).

277 Hill, Landlord and Tenant Law in a Nutshell 25, 77 (3d ed. 1995).

Damages are generally calculated in the same way as for a breach of an implied warranty of habitability, that is, the value of the premises with services minus its value without the utility service plus associated damages for distress, injury to persons or property, and other consequential damages. *See* Bedell v. Los Zapatistas, 805 P.2d 1198, 1200 (Colo. App. 1991) ("rent is abated to the amount of that proportion of the rent which the fair rental value after the event giving the right to abate bears to the fair rental value before the event"); Whitehouse Estates, Inc. v. Thomson, 386 N.Y.S.2d 733, 735 (N.Y. Civ. Ct. 1976) ("[t]he test is the difference in the value of the apartment with and without the services").

Punitive damages may be recoverable upon a breach of the implied covenant of quiet enjoyment. *See also* Mass. Gen. Laws ch. 186, § 14 (three times monthly rent is minimum damage award for interference with tenant's quiet enjoyment); Nate v. Galloway, 408 N.E.2d 1317 (Ind. Ct. App. 1980); New Summit Ltd. Assocs. v. Nistle, 533 A.2d 1350 (Md. Ct. Spec. App. 1987) (if breach effected with malicious intent); Cruz Mgmt. Co. v. Thomas, 633 N.E.2d 390 (Mass. 1994); Benitez v. Restifo, 641 N.Y.S.2d 523 (N.Y. City Ct. 1996); Bartolomeo v. Runco, 616 N.Y.S.2d 695 (N.Y. City Ct. (1994).

278 Conn. Gen. Stat. § 47a-14h(e)(1); Javins v. First Nat'l Realty, 428 F.2d 1071 (D.C. Cir. 1970); *In re* TM Carlton House Partners, Ltd., 93 B.R. 859 (Bankr. E.D. Pa. 1988); Clore v. Freedman, 319 N.E.2d 18 (Ill. 1974); Pugh v. Holmes, 384 A.2d 1234 (Pa. Super. Ct. 1978), *aff'd*, 405 A.2d 897 (Pa. 1979); Comment, Uniform Residential Landlord Tenant Act § 4.107 (Supp. 1999). *See* Steele v. Latimer, 521 P.2d 304 (Kan. 1974); Jones v. Parker, 40 N.E. 1044 (Mass. 1895).

279 *See, e.g.*, United States v. Bedford Assocs., 548 F. Supp. 732 (S.D.N.Y. 1982), *modified on other grounds*, 713 F.2d 895 (2d Cir. 1983); Brown v. Guerrier, 457 N.E.2d 630 (Mass. 1983); Lawrence v. Osuagwu, 781 N.E.2d 50 (Mass. App. Ct. 2003).

tion, a tenant has a cause of action for breach of the implied warranty of habitability.[280]

Nearly every state that recognizes a landlord's duty to maintain the premises includes within that duty a responsibility to ensure the uninterrupted flow of vital utility services, at least to the extent the provision of those services is part of the lease.[281] A state that may not recognize the failure to provide some utility service as a per se violation of the landlord's implied warranty may nevertheless find that a landlord's interruption of that service breaches his or her express and implied warranties, which become enforceable when the tenant rents the unit on the explicit or implicit understanding that the landlord would supply that service.[282]

Several states have laws imposing civil or criminal liability upon landlords who willfully cause the interruption of utility service to their tenants.[283] Such practices may also constitute an unfair or deceptive commercial practice under many state UDAP provisions.[284]

6.8.4.3 Self-Help Eviction

Many states, including the twenty-one or more states that have adopted a form of the Uniform Residential Landlord Tenant Act,[285] statutorily prohibit self-help eviction.[286] Several states specifically forbid interference with a tenancy by the direct or indirect termination of a tenant's utility service.[287] Thus, in most jurisdictions, self-help eviction by

280 At least forty-seven jurisdictions have adopted or otherwise given effect to an implied warranty of habitability by common law or statute. Smith, *Tenant Remedies for Breach of Habitability*, 35 U. Kan. L. Rev. 505 (1987). *See, e.g.*, Johnson v. Grand Cru Prop. One Ltd. P'ship, 49 Pa. D. & C.4th 531 (Pa. Ct. Com. Pl. 2000) (tenants whose electricity had been terminated for nonpayment were certified as class in lawsuit alleging breach of warranty of habitability, breach of covenant of quiet enjoyment, fraud, and negligent misrepresentation, among other causes of action). *See generally* § 3.4.1, *supra*.

In those states that do not recognize the implied warranty as such, relief may be available based on a theory of express warranty. *See* Mendenhall-Moore Realtors v. Sedoris, 366 S.E.2d 534 (N.C. Ct. App. 1988) (on narrower theory that recognizes landlord's duty to maintain those items that he has promised to provide, including utility service); Marsh v. Riley, 188 S.E. 748 (W. Va. 1936).

On a breach of the covenant of quiet enjoyment, see Bedell v. Los Zapatistas, 805 P.2d 1198 (Colo. App. 1991) and Morrison v. Smith, 757 S.W.2d 678 (Tenn. Ct. App. 1988). For codification of an implied warranty of habitability for provision of utility service on public health grounds, see 105 Mass. Code Regs. § 410.750.

281 *See In re* Clark, 96 B.R. 569, 572 (E.D. Pa. 1989) (full utility service); Javins v. First Nat'l Realty, 428 F.2d 1071, 1074 (D.C. Cir. 1970) (provision of heat and light at heart of warranty of habitability); Bennett M. Lifter, Inc. v. Varnado, 480 So. 2d 1336 (Fla. Dist. Ct. App. 1985) (hot water); Gennings v. Newton, 567 So. 2d 637, 641 (La. Ct. App. 1990) (water); 49 Prospect Street Tenants Ass'n v. Sheva Gardens, 547 A.2d 1134 (N.J. Super. Ct. App. Div. 1988) (heat, water, security); Academy Spires v. Brown, 268 A.2d 556 (N.J. Dist. Ct. 1970) (garbage disposal, elevator, hot water); Whitehouse Estates v. Thomson, 386 N.Y.S.2d 733 (N.Y. Civ. Ct. 1976) (air conditioner, gas stove).

282 Mendenhall-Moore Realtors v. Sedoris, 366 S.E.2d 534, 536–37 (N.C. Ct. App. 1988).

283 *See, e.g.*, Alaska Stat. § 34.03.210; Ariz. Rev. Stat. Ann. § 33-1367; Cal. Civ. Code § 789.3 (West); Conn. Gen. Stat. § 47a-13; 765 Ill. Comp. Stat. 735/2.1; Kan. Stat. Ann. § 58-2563; Ky. Rev. Stat. Ann. §§ 383.640, 383.655 (West); Mass. Gen. Laws ch. 186, § 14; Minn. Stat. §§ 504B.225 (intentional interruption of utility service a misdemeanor), 504B.221 (greater of treble damages or $500, plus attorney fees); Neb. Rev. Stat. § 76-1427; N.M. Stat. Ann. § 47-8-36; N.Y. Real Prop. Acts. §§ 235-a, 756 (stay of eviction proceedings if utilities discontinued) (McKinney); Or. Rev. Stat. § 90.375; Tex. Prop. Code Ann. § 92.301 (West); Va. Code Ann. §§ 55-248.36, 55-248.40; Wash. Rev. Code § 59.18.300. *See also* Bennett M. Lifter, Inc. v. Varnardo, 480 So. 2d 1336 (Fla. Dist. Ct. App. 1982).

284 *In re* Aponte, 82 B.R. 738, 746–47 (E.D. Pa. 1988). *See also* Kingston Square Tenants Ass'n v. Tuskegee Gardens, Ltd., 792 F. Supp. 1566, 1575 (S.D. Fla. 1992); *In re* Clarke, 96 B.R. 569 (E.D. Pa. 1989); Gargano v. Heyman, 525 A.2d 1343 (Conn. 1987) (shutting off electricity to premises of tenant holding over after lease terminated constituted unfair practice); Wolfberg v. Hunter, 432 N.E.2d 467, 472 (Mass. 1982); Stanley v. Moore, 454 S.E.2d 225 (N.C. 1995); Shepard v. Bonita Vista Props., L.P., 664 S.E.2d 388 (N.C. Ct. App. 2008), *aff'd*, 675 S.E.2d 332 (N.C. 2009). *See also* 940 Mass. Code Regs. § 3.17(6)(g). *See generally* National Consumer Law Center, Unfair and Deceptive Acts and Practices §§ 3.2.3, 8.2 (7th ed. 2008 and Supp.).

285 Alaska, Arizona, Florida, Hawaii, Iowa, Kansas, Kentucky, Mississippi, Montana, Nebraska, New Mexico, Oregon, Rhode Island, South Carolina, Tennessee, and Virginia have adopted URLTA. *See* Uniform Law Comm'rs, A Few Facts About the Uniform Residential Landlord Tenant Act; Note, *Propst v. McNeill: Arkansas Landlord-Tenant Law, A Time for Change*, 51 Ark. L. Rev. 575, 597 (1998); Thomley, *The Implied Warranty of Habitability in Residential Leases: Alabama's Unwarranted Position*, 22 Cumberland L. Rev. 73 (1991); Deborah H. Bell, *The Mississippi Landlord-Tenant Act of 1991*, 61 Miss. L.J. 527 (1991).

Note that, in addition to its prohibition of self-help evictions, the URLTA specifically prohibits willful terminations of utility service and allows for damages and injunctive relief as remedies. Uniform Residential Landlord Tenant Act §§ 4.207, 4.107, 4.107 cmt. (Supp. 1991).

As to the legal viability of self-help evictions generally, see Douglas I. Brandon et al., *Special Project, Self-Help: Extrajudicial Rights, Privileges and Immunities in American Society*, 37 Vand. L. Rev. 845 n.640 and text (1984). *See also* McCrory v. Johnson, 755 S.W.2d 566 (Ark. 1988).

286 Uniform Residential Landlord Tenant Act § 4.207; Model Residential Landlord-Tenant Code 2-408. *See also* Mass. Gen. Laws ch. 186, § 14; Whalen v. Taylor, 925 P.2d 462 (Mont. 1996). *See generally* Restatement (Second) Property Landlord and Tenant §§ 14.1, 14.2, stat. notes (1977).

287 *See, e.g.*, Fla. Stat. § 83.67(1); Mass. Gen. Laws ch. 186, § 14; Wash. Rev. Code § 59.18.300. *See also* Badaraco v. Suncoast Towers v. Assocs., 676 So. 2d 502 (Fla. Dist. Ct. App. 1996); Kendall v. Klein, 2006 WL 322362 (Wash. Ct. App. Feb. 13, 2006).

ordering a shut-off of utility service to the tenant is illegal[288] and may be enjoined.[289]

Other states by court decision prohibit self-help dispossession of tenants.[290] Recent decisions suggest an emerging trend towards a total prohibition of self-help evictions by landlords.[291] Since the public policy in these states clearly favors resort to judicial remedies, lease provisions allowing for self-help are void as contrary to public policy.[292]

There appears to be a split in authority in this country over the legality of self-help dispossession. A small minority of decisions may still follow the English rule and permit the landlord to use reasonably necessary force to dispossess; others allow peaceful self-help.[293] However, the "general rule" is that self-help is completely prohibited.[294] Arguably, no American jurisdiction would now allow for self-help evictions from residential tenancies in cases other than when the tenant has vacated the unit and abandoned the tenancy.

Even if a jurisdiction permits peaceful self-help, it is questionable whether termination of utility service would be considered "peaceful self-help." Some states have taken a restrictive approach in which entry is regarded as non-peaceful only when there has been violent forcible entry.[295] Other courts allow dispossession only with a tenant's consent,[296] a view that is effectively a total ban on self-help evictions. Some jurisdictions follow a second approach, which splits the difference: allow only very minimal force to dispossess.[297]

The shut-off of utility service, though indirectly effected, is an act that can be construed as being immediately and powerfully violent.[298] It should in no way be regarded as a peaceful dispossession of the tenant.[299] In addition to damages, punitive damages,[300] and (in some states) attorney fees, injunctive relief may be available in appropriate circumstances to prevent unlawful self-help evictions.[301]

288 *See, e.g.*, Stanley v. Moore, 454 S.E.2d 225 (N.C. 1995); Childers v. Russell, 2002 WL 32757694 (Ohio Ct. Com. Pl. July 10, 2002); James DiPriest, Self-Help Evictions, 25 Clearinghouse Rev. 798, 800 (1991). *See also In re* Aponte, 82 B.R. 738, 743 (E.D. Pa. 1988); Ervin v. Stackhouse, 2010 WL 4910871 (Ala. Civ. App. Dec. 3, 2010) (landlord's failure to secure a writ of possession before disconnecting electrical service could be deemed an unlawful self-help eviction); Gargano v. Heyman, 525 A.2d 1343 (Conn. 1987); Geiger v. Wallace, 664 P.2d 846 (Kan. 1983); Gennings v. Newton, 567 So. 2d 637 (La. Ct. App. 1990); Lally v. Flieder, 986 A.1d 652 (N.H. 2009) (unlawful termination of cable television is "a means of accomplishing a self-help eviction—the very evil the legislature sought to deter").

289 *See, e.g., In re* Aponte, 82 B.R. 738, 743 (E.D. Pa. 1988). *See also* Comment, Uniform Residential Landlord Tenant Act § 4.107 (Supp. 1999).

290 *See, e.g.*, Malcolm v. Little, 295 A.2d 711 (Del. 1972); Mendes v. Johnson, 389 A.2d 781, 787 (D.C. Ct. App. 1978), *overruled in part on other grounds*, 772 A.2d 204 (D.C. 2001) ("[a] tenant has a right not to have his or her possession interfered with except by lawful process, and violation of that right gives rise to a cause of action in tort").

291 Annot., *Right of a Landlord Entitled to Possession to Dispossess a Tenant Without Legal Process*, 6 A.L.R.3d 177, at § 5 (1966 & 1999 Supp.). *See* State v. Main, 764 P.2d 1155 (Ariz. 1988); Roberts v. Roberts, 422 S.E.2d 253 (Ga. Ct. App. 1992); Bass v. Boetel & Co., 217 N.W.2d 804 (Neb. 1974); Coffel v. Clallam County, 794 P.2d 513 (Wash. Ct. App. 1990). *See also* Gorman v. Ratliff, 712 S.W.2d 888 (Ark. 1986); Op. Ark. Att'y Gen. No. 2006-223 (2007) (addressing question of whether rent accountabilities device enabling landlord to cut off utility service for rent nonpayment would violate any laws).

292 *See* DiMassimo v. City of Clearwater, 805 F.2d 1536 (11th Cir. 1986); Lamey v. Masciotra, 78 Cal. Rptr. 344 (Cal. Ct. App. 1969).

293 Spinks v. Taylor, 266 S.E.2d 857 (N.C. Ct. App. 1980), *aff'd in part, rev'd in part, modified in part*, 278 S.E.2d 501 (N.C. 1981). *But see* Stanley v. Moore, 454 S.E.2d 225 (N.C. 1995).

294 Douglas I. Brandon et al., *Special Project, Extrajudicial Rights, Privileges and Remedies in Contemporary American Society*, 37 Vand. L. Rev. 845, 950–51 (1984). The last is the position of the Restatement (Second) Property § 14.1–14.2 (1976).

295 Douglas I. Brandon et al., *Special Project, Extrajudicial Rights, Privileges and Remedies in Contemporary American Society*, 37 Vand. L. Rev. 845, 950–52 (1984).

296 *See, e.g.*, Spinks v. Taylor, 278 S.E.2d 501 (N.C. 1981) (landlord may not take possession of leased premises subject to forfeiture over tenant's objections).

297 In these states, a significant constitutional barrier is raised by sanctioning the deprivation of tenants' property and liberty interests without judicial process. *See also* Swann v. Gastonia Hous. Auth., 675 F.2d 1342 (4th Cir. 1982); Annot., *Modern Views As to Validity Under Federal Constitution of State Prejudgment Attachment, Garnishment and Replevin Procedures, Distraint Procedures Under Landlords' or Innkeepers' Lien Statutes, and Like Procedures Authorizing Summary Seizure of Property*, 18 A.L.R. Fed. 223 (1974 & 1998 Supp.). *Cf.* Fuentes v. Shevin, 407 U.S. 67 (1972) (summary seizure of property under writ of replevin without prior hearing held unconstitutional). *See generally* Annot., *When Is Eviction of Tenant by Private Landlord Conducted "Under Color of the Law" for Purposes of 42 U.S.C.S. § 1983*, 73 A.L.R. Fed. 78 (1985); Restatement (Second) Property, Landlord and Tenant § 12.1, rptr. no. 5 and stat. n.5 (1977).

298 *See* Memphis Light, Gas & Water Div. v. Craft, 436 U.S. 1, 18 (1978). *See also* State v. Elmwood Terrace, Inc., 204 A.2d 379 (N.J. Super. Ct. App. Div. 1964) (discussing criminal liability for failure to provide heat); Op. Ark. Att'y Gen. No. 77-184 (1977) (discussing possible criminal liability for intentional termination of utility service).

299 Gargano v. Heyman, 525 A.2d 1343 (Conn. 1987). *See generally* Earnhardt, *Peaceful Padlocking in a Peaceful World*, 13 N.C. Cent. L. Rev. 195 (1982).

300 DiPriest, *Self-Help Evictions*, 25 Clearinghouse Rev. 798, 800 (1991). *See also* Gennings v. Newton, 567 So. 2d 637, 641 (La. Ct. App. 1990); Pentecost v. Harward, 699 P.2d 696 (Utah 1985) ("Self-help is too likely to lead to a breach of the peace to be permitted, and contractual provisions purporting to authorize it will be void as against public policy."); Mass. Gen. Laws ch. 186, § 14.

301 *See* Mass. Gen. Laws ch. 186, § 14.

In addition to statutes directed specifically at unlawful dispossession, see the statutory note in § 12.1 of Restatement (Second) Property; attempts at unlawful dispossession by means such as terminating utility service may violate state UDAP statutes, providing another avenue to obtaining attorney fees.

6.8.4.4 Prohibitions Against Retaliation and Discrimination As Limits on Landlords' Ability to Terminate Utility Services

Acts of terminating or reducing vital services are often specifically illegal when they are in reprisal for the tenant's exercise of certain delineated remedies, which typically include participation in a tenants' union, rent withholding, or reporting unsafe conditions to the landlord or governmental authorities.[302]

As a result, if a state has a prohibition on retaliatory evictions, even if the law might otherwise allow landlords the option of self-help in the form of terminating vital services, landlords may not pursue such a remedy if they are motivated by a desire to punish or deter the exercise of legally protected rights. Similarly, landlords cannot engage in such activities, even if otherwise permissible, if they intend to discriminate or if discrimination would result from their actions. Intentional discrimination may be proven by a showing that a landlord is taking action against members of a protected group but not those of non-protected groups.[303]

Many states have legislatively enacted protections against retaliation at the state[304] or local level. Other states have developed these protections from the common law; in several of these states, these judicial decisions have later been codified.[305]

Section 5.101 of the Uniform Residential Landlord Tenant Act (URLTA) is representative of the various statutory schemes:

> Section 5.101. [Retaliatory Conduct Prohibited.]
>
> (a) Except as provided in this section, a landlord may not retaliate by increasing rent or decreasing services or by bringing or threatening to bring an action for possession after:
>
> (1) the tenant has complained to a governmental agency . . .; or
>
> (2) the tenant has complained to the landlord of a violation [of the landlord's obligations to maintain the premises]; or
>
> (3) the tenant has organized or become a member of a tenant's union or similar organization.
>
> (b) If the landlord acts in violation of subsection (a), the tenant . . . has a defense in any retaliatory action against him for possession. In an action by or against the tenant, evidence of a complaint within [1] year before the alleged act of retaliation creates a presumption that the landlord's conduct was in retaliation. The presumption does not arise if the tenant made the complaint after notice of a proposed rent increase or diminution of services. "Presumption" means that the trier of fact must find the existence of the fact presumed unless and until evidence is introduced that would support a finding of its nonexistence.
>
> (c) Notwithstanding subsections (a) and (b), a landlord may bring an action for possession if:
>
> (1) the violation of the applicable building or housing code was caused primarily by lack of reasonable care by the tenant, a member of his family, or other person on the premises with his consent; or
>
> (2) the tenant is in default in rent; or
>
> (3) compliance with the applicable building or housing code requires alteration, remodeling, or demolition that would effectively deprive the tenant of the use of the dwelling unit.[306]

Nearly all statutory schemes, like URLTA, delineate the tenant activities that will be protected and, with less specificity, the landlords' responses that may trigger application of the Act. Courts interpreting state statutes that prohibit landlord retaliation have generally limited the protections of the statute to the particular actions clearly falling within that

---

See In re Aponte, 82 B.R. 738 (E.D. Pa. 1988); Gargano v. Heyman, 525 A.2d 1343 (Conn. 1987).

302 *See, e.g.*, Edwards v. Habib, 397 F.2d 687 (D.C. Cir. 1968); Schweiger v. Superior Ct., 476 P.2d 97 (Cal. 1970); Building Monitoring Sys., Inc. v. Paxton, 905 P.2d 1215 (Utah 1995); Gokey v. Bessette, 580 A.2d 488 (Vt. 1990); Murphy v. Smallridge, 468 S.E.2d 167 (W. Va. 1996); Dickhut v. Norton, 173 N.W.2d 297 (Wis. 1970); Uniform Residential Landlord Tenant Act § 5.101; Model Residential Landlord-Tenant Code § 2-407.

About half the states have residential landlord-tenant acts that recognize a cause of action for retaliatory landlord actions.

303 *See* Roger D. Colton & Doug Smith, *Protections for the Low-Income Customer of Unregulated Utilities: Using Federal Fuel Assistance As More Than Cash Grants*, 13 Hamline J. of Pub. L. & Policy, 263 (1992).

For example, a landlord might order a termination of service in response to a late or insufficient payment by an African-American tenant while not responding in the same way to a late or insufficient payment by a white tenant.

304 *See, e.g.*, Cal. Civ. Code § 1942.5 (West); Conn. Gen. Stat. § 47a-20; Del. Code Ann. tit. 25, § 5516; D.C. Code § 42-3505.02; Haw. Rev. Stat. § 521-74; 765 Ill. Comp. Stat. 720/1; Me. Rev. Stat. tit. 14, §§ 6001, 6002; Md. Code Ann., Real Prop. §§ 8-206, 8-208.1, 8-208.2 (West); Mass. Gen. Laws ch. 186, § 18; Mass. Gen. Laws ch. 239, § 2A; Mich. Comp. Laws ch. 600, § 5720; Minn. Stat. § 504B.285; Nev. Rev. Stat. § 118A.510; N.J. Stat. Ann. § 2A:42-10.10 (West); N.C. Gen. Stat. § 42-37.1; Ohio Rev. Code Ann. § 5321.02 (West); Or. Rev. Stat. § 90.385; 68 Pa. Stat. Ann. § 399.11 (West); 35 Pa. Stat. Ann. § 1700-1 (West); R.I. Gen. Laws § 34-20-10; Tex. Prop. Code Ann. § 92.331 (West); Vt. Stat. Ann. tit. 9, § 4465; Va. Code Ann. § 55-248.39; Wash. Rev. Code § 59.18.240; Wis. Stat. § 704.45. *See also* Uniform Residential Landlord Tenant Act §§ 5.101; Model Residential Landlord Tenant Code § 2-407.

305 Edwards v. Habib, 397 F.2d 687, 705 (D.C. Cir. 1968); Markese v. Cooper, 333 N.Y.S.2d 63 (N.Y. Cnty. Ct. 1972); Dickhut v. Norton, 173 N.W.2d 297 (Wis. 1970). *See* Restatement (Second) Property §§ 5.1–5.6 (1977).

306 The URLTA may be found at www.law.upenn.edu/bll/archives/ulc/fnact99/1970s/urlta72.htm. *See also* Restatement (Second) Property, Landlord & Tenant §§ 14.8, 14.9.

statute.[307] Statutes vary to some extent in the kinds of tenant activities to be protected, with those of Maine, Massachusetts, Michigan, New Jersey, and Rhode Island being among the most inclusive. Protections vary to a greater extent with regard to the treatment of evidence suggesting mixed motives[308] and to the strength[309] and duration[310] of any presumption of retaliation.

Landlords can exert significant power over their tenants by starting eviction proceedings. When the power to evict is exercised contrary to state public policy, some states have held that tenants may raise the defense of retaliatory eviction.[311] When a landlord uses his or her power in a way that hurts the health, safety, or well being of a tenant, a court should allow the tenant to bring an action, cross-claim, or defense against the landlord.[312] This should be the case even if the landlord's abuse of power relates to a tenant action that does not fall squarely within the state's landlord-tenant retaliation statute or that does not directly relate to the landlord-tenant relationship. The help of eviction courts should not be enlisted by private parties to defeat the public policies of the state.[313] Moreover, general good faith obligations, such as those contained in URLTA § 1.302, might well result in the landlord being held to a standard of good faith that is much broader in scope than the standard that adheres to cases of retaliatory eviction.

However, courts may find, that state legislatures, by enacting statutes redressing retaliation in the landlord-tenant context, preempt the field and displace any common law remedies that might have emerged in the absence of statutory law on the subject. This would be contrary to the spirit and history of modern landlord-tenant law. The statutory, regulatory, and common law of landlord-tenant relations have existed synergistically. Statutes are often simply codifications or expansions of common law doctrine, while common law often moves in the direction determined by statutes and regulations.[314]

Anti-retaliation statutes were intended to guarantee protection of tenants in certain defined situations. Such statutes are not intended to suppress the development of greater protections in situations not contemplated by these laws.[315]

---

307 *See* Van Buren Apartments v. Adams, 701 P.2d 583 (Ariz. 1984); Visco v. Cody, 547 A.2d 935 (Conn. App. Ct. 1988); Manzaro v. McCann, 519 N.E.2d 1337 (Mass. 1988) (no defense to eviction that landlord was acting in retaliation to tenant's oral complaint regarding illegal lease provisions when state retaliation statute expressly covers only written complaints from tenants to landlords); Frenchtown Villas v. Meadors, 324 N.W.2d 133 (Mich. Ct. App. 1982); Weil v. Kaplan, 643 N.Y.S.2d 312 (N.Y. Dist. Ct. 1996), *aff'd*, 670 N.Y.S.2d 666 (N.Y. App. Term. 1997); Stephanus v. Anderson, 613 P.2d 533 (Wash. Ct. App. 1980).

308 *See* Parkin v. Fitzgerald, 240 N.W.2d 828 (Minn. 1976) (landlord must prove his action to be totally devoid of any retaliatory motive).

For example, the tenant's joining a tenant's union may have coincided with tenant's late payment of rent. The most restrictive view would require the retaliatory motive to be the sole impetus for the action. Dickhut v. Norton, 173 N.W.2d 297 (Wis. 1970). *See also* Gofman v. Almeida, 2006 WL 2729414 (Conn. Super. Ct. Sept. 22, 2006); Alteri v. Layton, 408 A.2d 18 (Conn. Supp. Ct. 1979).

In other jurisdictions, it would be enough if retaliation was a primary factor in the landlord's decision. *See, e.g.* Gokey v. Bessette, 565, 580 A.2d 488 (Vt. 1990) (landlord "should not be surprised that the court would construe as retaliatory his attempt to oust his tenants after four months of contention of the condition of the premises").

309 The Massachusetts statute, for example, requires that the landlord rebut a presumption of retaliation by clear and convincing evidence, which presumption is created upon the landlord's taking adverse action within six months of some protected tenant activity. Mass. Gen. Laws ch. 186, § 18; Mass. Gen. Laws ch. 239, § 2A. *See also* Youssef v. United Mgmt. Co., 683 A.2d 152 (D.C. 1996) (landlord must overcome presumption under statute by clear and convincing evidence). *But see* Houle v. Quenneville, 787 A.2d 1258 (Vt. 2001) (court refuses to read into statute a presumption of retaliation or other burden-shifting provision).

310 Six months to a year is typical. *Compare* Cal. Civ. Code § 1942.5 (West) (180 days), *with* Wash. Rev. Code § 59.18.250 (initiation of eviction by landlord within ninety days after good faith and lawful act by tenant as enumerated in statute creates rebuttable presumption that action is a reprisal or retaliatory action).

311 Barela v. Superior Ct., 636 P.2d 582 (Cal. 1981) (tenant can raise retaliatory eviction claim when eviction initiated shortly after tenant filed complaint with police that landlord molested her child); S.P. Growers Ass'n v. Rodriguez, 552 P.2d 721 (Cal. 1976) (tenant-laborers can raise retaliation claim against landlord when evictions initiated upon heels of labor organizing activities); Custom Parking Inc. v. Superior Ct. of Marin City, 187 Cal. Rptr. 674, 677 (Cal. Ct. App. 1982) (commercial tenant allowed to raise retaliation eviction claim against landlord who was allegedly seeking to coerce false testimony in a civil case); Pohlman v. Metropolitan Trailer Park, 312 A.2d 888 (N.J. Super. Ct. Ch. Div. 1973) (tenants allowed to raise retaliatory eviction claim when they had recently opposed landlord's application for re-zoning); Port of Longview v. International Raw Materials, Ltd., 979 P.2d 917 (Wash. Ct. App. 1999) (commercial tenant allowed to raise retaliatory eviction defense based on exercise of its free speech rights).

312 *See* Robinson v. Diamond Hous. Corp., 463 F.2d 853, 860 (D.C. Cir. 1972); Edwards v. Habib, 397 F.2d 687 (D.C. Cir. 1968).

313 *See* Brown v. Southall Realty, 237 A.2d 834, 837 (D.C. 1968) (no rent due when apartment had substantial conditions violations).

For example, although the state statute does not specifically refer to joining of tenant unions, retaliation against a tenant who joins a tenants union would defeat public policy as expressed in state and federal constitutions in favor of free speech and free association. S.P. Growers Ass'n v. Rodriguez, 552 P.2d 721 (Cal. 1976).

314 *See, e.g.*, 293 N.E.2d 831 (Mass. 1973) ("the [rent withholding] legislation's establishment of policy carries significance beyond the particular scope of each of the statutes involved"; finding that there is an "implied warranty of habitability" based, in part, on existing landlord-tenant statutes such as rent withholding law).

315 Indeed, courts have found that a state is constitutionally bound to honor a retaliation defense to eviction actions because the state would otherwise violate the First Amendment and due

6.8.4.5 State UDAP Statutes As a Remedy Against Vindictive Landlords

State Unfair and Deceptive Acts and Practices (UDAP) statutes may be useful in challenging the actions of vindictive landlords.[316] In many jurisdictions, it is generally a per se UDAP violation to commit an act in violation of state statutes intended for the benefit of consumers, including tenants. Under such provisions, violating state housing codes or engaging in self-help ouster, retaliation, or breach of the warranty of habitability may constitute UDAP violations,[317] with additional remedies available.[318]

UDAP provisions and regulations may specifically identify and prohibit retaliatory evictions,[319] self-help evictions,[320] or utility terminations.[321] Perhaps the most useful of these protections for tenants victimized by actual (or threatened) utility termination come in the form of a state statute's unfair debt collection provisions. Many states, through legislation or judicial decisions, may disallow claims for retaliation[322] or rent-withholding-eviction defenses[323] if the tenant, at the time of the landlord's action, is in default of rent obligations. Unfair debt collection statutes may provide one avenue of relief for tenants when landlords order utility terminations in response to nonpayment of rent.[324]

These statutes frequently also prohibit collection actions that harass or abuse the debtor or may cause damage to people or property. A landlord who uses abusive means—for example, terminating utility services to force payment of rent arrearage or other debts—may run afoul of state laws governing unfair debt collection.[325]

---

process rights of the tenant. Hosey v. Club Van Cortlandt, 299 F. Supp. 501 (S.D.N.Y. 1969); Church v. Allen Meadows Apts., 329 N.Y.S.2d 148, 149 (N.Y. Sup. Ct. 1972) ("[a]ny proceeding for eviction so motivated and retaliatory is unconstitutional in that it seeks to have a state penalize a person for exercising his constitutional rights of free speech") (citing Hosey v. Club Van Cortlandt, 299 F. Supp. 501 (S.D.N.Y. 1969)). *See* Edwards v. Habib, 397 F.2d 687 (D.C. Cir. 1968).

Some courts have found to the contrary, finding no required state action. *See* Weigand v. Afton View Apartments, 473 F.2d 545 (8th Cir. 1973).

316 *See generally* National Consumer Law Center, Unfair and Deceptive Acts and Practices § 8.2 (7th ed. 2008 and Supp.).

However, some states hold that landlord-tenant relations are beyond reach of the UDAP scheme. *Id.* § 2.2.6. *See also* Annot., *Scope and Exemptions of State Deceptive Trade Practice and Consumer Protection Acts*, 89 A.L.R.3d 399 (1979 with annual supps.).

317 *See* Kingston Sq. Tenants Ass'n v. Tuskegee Gardens, Ltd., 792 F. Supp. 1566 (S.D. Fla. 1992); *In re* Aponte, 82 B.R. 738 (Bankr. E.D. Pa. 1988); Hernandez v. Stabach, 193 Cal. Rptr. 350 (Cal. Ct. App. 1983); Wolfberg v. Hunter, 432 N.E.2d 467, 472 (Mass. 1982); Montanez v. Bagg, 510 N.E.2d 298 (Mass. App. Ct. 1987); Love v. Amsler, 441 N.W.2d 555 (Minn. Ct. App. 1989); 49 Prospect St, Tenants Ass'n v. Sheva Gardens, 547 A.2d 1134 (N.J. Super. Ct. App. Div. 1988); Shepard v. Bonita Vista Props., L.P., 664 S.E.2d 388 (N.C. Ct. App. 2008), *aff'd*, 675 S.E.2d 332 (N.C. 2009); Borders v. Newton, 315 S.E.2d 731 (N.C. Ct. App. 1984); § 4.4, *supra*. *Compare In re* Brightful, 1999 WL 812791 (Bankr. E.D. Pa. Oct. 8, 1999), *with In re* Clark, 96 B.R. 569 (Bankr. E.D. Pa. 1989).

318 Including (a) injunctive relief, *see In re* T.M. Carlton House Partners, Ltd., 93 B.R. 859 (Bankr. E.D. Pa. 1988); Hanner v. Classic Auto Body, Inc., 406 N.E.2d 686 (Mass. App. Ct. 1980); National Consumer Law Center, Unfair and Deceptive Acts and Practices § 8.6 (7th ed. 2008 and Supp.); (b) attorney fees, National Consumer Law Center, Unfair and Deceptive Acts and Practices §§ 8.6, 8.8 (7th ed. 2008 and Supp.); and (c) multiple damages, National Consumer Law Center, Unfair and Deceptive Acts and Practices § 8.4 (7th ed. 2008 and Supp.). *See* Montanez v. Bagg, 510 N.E.2d 298 (Mass. App. Ct. 1987) (landlord's knowledge of condition that in fact violates codes requires award of multiple damages); Borders v. Newton, 315 S.E.2d 731 (N.C. Ct. App. 1984).

Actual damages include the reduction in the value of the premises, associated expenses—such as child care, costs of space heaters, among other things—injury to property and to person, and emotional distress. *See In re* TM Carlton House Partners, Ltd., 93 B.R. 859 (Bankr. E.D. Pa. 1988); Haddad v. Gonzalez, 576 N.E.2d 658 (Mass. 1991). *See also* Hilder v. St. Peter, 478 A.2d 202 (Vt. 1984) (damages for emotional distress recoverable for breach of the warranty of habitability); Teller v. McCoy, 253 S.E.2d 114 (W. Va. 1978) (damages for breach of warranty include award for annoyance and inconvenience); Annot., *Tenant's Recovery for Emotional Distress Under ULRTA*, 6 A.L.R.4th 528 (1981); Annot., *Measure of Damages for Landlord's Breach of the Warranty of Habitability*, 1 A.L.R.4th 1182 (1980).

319 *See, e.g.*, 940 Mass. Code Regs. § 3.17 (LexisNexis).

320 *Id.*

321 *Id.* There are cases involving successful claims by tenants under UDAP laws. *See* 49 Prospect St. Tenants Ass'n v. Sheva Gardens, 547 A.2d 1134 (N.J. Super. Ct. App. Div. 1988); Mosley & Mosley Builders v. Landin Ltd., 389 S.E.2d 576 (N.C. Ct. App. 1990); Love v. Pressley, 239 S.E.2d 574 (N.C. Ct. App. 1977). *See also* Hernandez v. Stabach, 193 Cal. Rptr. 350 (Cal. Ct. App. 1983); Shepard v. Bonita Vista Props., L.P., 664 S.E.2d 388 (N.C. Ct. App. 2008), *aff'd*, 675 S.E.2d 332 (N.C. 2009).

322 *See* Mass. Gen. Laws ch. 186, § 18 (no presumption of retaliation in case of nonpayment of rent); Salmonte v. Eilertson, 526 So. 2d 179 (Fla. Dist. Ct. App. 1988) (retaliatory eviction defense inapplicable when tenant is in breach of lease); Frenchtown Villa v. Meadors, 324 N.W.2d 133 (Mich. Ct. App. 1982). *See generally* Uniform Residential Landlord Tenant Act § 5.101; National Consumer Law Center, Fair Debt Collection (7th ed. 2011).

323 *See* Mass. Gen. Laws ch. 239, § 8A (defense available if landlord knew of condition before arrearage, tenant did not cause condition complained of, and condition can be remedied without premises being vacated).

324 *See In re* Aponte, 82 B.R. 738 (E.D. Pa. 1988); Gargano v. Heyman, 525 A.2d 1343 (Conn. 1987).

The availability of unfair debt collection statutes in such actions assumes that the scope of the state's provisions contemplates landlords as creditors. *See* National Consumer Law Center, Unfair and Deceptive Acts and Practices § 8.2 (7th ed. 2008 and Supp.).

325 *In re* Aponte, 82 B.R. 738, 743–44 (Bankr. E.D. Pa. 1988). *See also* Clarkson v. De Cuceres, 105 B.R. 266, 271–72 (Bankr. E.D. Pa. 1989); Gargano v. Heyman, 525 A.2d 1343 (Conn. 1987); McGrath v. Mishara, 434 N.E.2d 1215 (Mass. 1982).

6.8.4.6 Tenants As Third-Party Beneficiaries of Contract Between Landlord and Utility

A landlord contracts with utility companies to provide services to its tenants in order to satisfy contractual[326] and legal obligations to its tenants. A tenant relies on the landlord's provision of utility service by not seeking service in his or her own name or obtaining alternative service while renting from the landlord. Under these circumstances, the tenant may be a third-party beneficiary of the contract between the utility and the landlord, unless that contract explicitly states to the contrary. The tenant may have a right to sue on the contract[327] and may have a property interest sufficient to trigger constitutional due process safeguards.[328] If the tenant is a third-party beneficiary of the landlord-utility company contract, neither the landlord nor the utility is free to modify or terminate the contract without the consent of the tenant.

An intended (not incidental) beneficiary of a contract acquires rights under that contract. At common law, a third party is an intended beneficiary of a contract when recognition of its right to obtain performance is appropriate to effect the intention of the parties, and circumstances indicate that the promisee and promisor intend for the beneficiary to receive the benefits of the promised performance.[329] That is, the common law recognizes the right of a third party to enforce a contract when the intent of the parties to the contract was that the benefit of the promised performance would go to a third party. That the promised performance would satisfy the promisee's duty to the third party is sufficient reason to grant the third party a right to sue on the contract.[330]

In borderline cases, courts look to whether the promisor rendered the promised performance to the beneficiary directly rather than to the promisee. If the performance is rendered directly to the third party, the intent to benefit the third party is beyond doubt.[331] Thus, although "[c]laims based upon a third party beneficiary theory have proven to be difficult ones for courts to entertain because the ideas behind the theory are obscure and elusive,"[332] courts can readily find that a tenant is an intended beneficiary of the contract between the landlord and the utility company to service the unit.[333]

326 Conille v. Pierce, 649 F. Supp. 1133, 1147 (D. Mass. 1986) (contractual nature of urban residential lease includes provision of "a package of goods and services [including] adequate heat, light and ventilation, serviceable plumbing facilities, secure windows and doors, proper sanitation, and proper maintenance") (citation omitted), *vacated on other grounds*, 840 F.2d 105 (1st Cir. Mass. 1988); Javins v. First Nat'l Realty, 428 F.2d 1071, 1075–76 (D.C. Cir. 1981); Mendenhall-Moore Realtors v. Sedoris, 366 S.E.2d 534, 536–37 (N.C. Ct. App. 1988).

327 *See* Restatement (Second) Contracts § 302.

328 *See* Perry v. Sinderman, 408 U.S. 593, 602 (1972); Board of Regents v. Roth, 408 U.S. 564, 568–77 (1972) (express or implied contracts may form basis of protectable property interest under due process clause).

329 Hibbs v. K-Mart Corp., 870 F.2d 435, 441 (8th Cir. 1989) ("Contracting parties must intend that the third party receive a direct and primary benefit."); Restatement (Second) Contracts § 302(1) (1981). *See also* 9 Corbin on Contracts § 776 (interim ed. 2002).

330 *See, e.g.*, Organization of Minority Vendors v. Illinois Gulf Cent. R.R., 579 F. Supp. 574 (N.D. Ill. 1983) (contract need not identify beneficiary so long as intent to benefit group of which beneficiary is member is clear); Dillon v. AFBIC Dev. Corp., 420 F. Supp. 572 (S.D. Ala. 1976), *aff'd in part and rev'd in part on other grounds*, 597 F.2d 556 (5th Cir. 1979); Western Union Tel. Co. v. Massman Constr. Co., 402 A.2d 1275 (D.C. 1979); Oil Capital Racing Ass'n v. Tulsa Speedway, Inc., 628 P.2d 1176 (Okla. Ct. App. 1981).

One commentator opines that there is a direct contract between the utility and the tenant even in master-metered buildings: "Many utilities have rules specifying that service will not be resold without prior . . . approval of the utility. If services were sold by the utility to a landlord, and permission to resell . . . was not given, then the utility's sale of services could be viewed as a de facto direct sale to the nonbilled tenant." Duhamel, *Rights of the Non-billed Utility User*, 19 Clearinghouse Rev. 247, 253 (July 1985). *See also* E. Allan Farnsworth, Contracts § 10.2, at 15 (3d ed. 1991).

331 Cauble v. Mabon Nugent & Co., 594 F. Supp. 985 (S.D.N.Y. 1984) ("Where performance is to be rendered directly to a third party under the terms of an agreement, that party must be considered an intended beneficiary.").

This principle should apply irrespective of whether the utility supplies the tenant's unit directly through individually metered service or to a limited set of tenants through a single meter. It is sufficient that the tenant is a member of an identifiable class intended to benefit from the contract.

332 Moore Constr. Co. v. Clarksville Dep't of Electricity, 707 S.W.2d 1, 7 (Tenn. Ct. App. 1985).

333 Vick v. H.S.I. Mgmt., 507 So. 2d 433 (Ala. 1987) (as an intended beneficiary of contract between power company and landlord to maintain outdoor lights, tenant could maintain an action for negligent maintenance against the company); Forte Hotels v. Kansas City Power & Light Co., 913 S.W.2d 803 (Mo. Ct. App. 1995) (utility could not unreasonably limit its liability to alleged third-party beneficiary of contract between building owner and utility), *overruled in part on other grounds by* 999 S.W.2d 326 (Mo. Ct. App. 1999). *See also* Holbrook v. Pitt, 643 F.2d 1261 (7th Cir. 1981) (tenants are intended beneficiaries of contract between landlord and HUD); Marina Tenants' Ass'n v. Deauville Marina Dev. Co., 226 Cal. Rptr. 321 (Cal. Ct. App. 1986); Zigas v. Superior Ct., 174 Cal. Rptr. 806 (Cal. Ct. App. 1981); Technicable Video Sys. v. Americable, 479 So. 2d 810 (Fla. Dist. Ct. App. 1985); Bush v. Upper Valley Telecable, 524 P.2d 1055 (Idaho 1974) (cable subscriber is third-party beneficiary of rate-setting agreement between cable company and town, and subscriber may sue cable company for damages and injunctive relief upon breach of that agreement); Pond v. New Rochelle Water Co., 76 N.E. 211 (N.Y. 1906) (utility consumer is third-party beneficiary of contract between village and utility company to supply service within given area); Higgins v. New York City Hous. Auth., 702 N.Y.S.2d 502 (N.Y. Civ. Ct. 1999) (public housing tenants are third-party beneficiaries of housing authority's contract with electric utility; holding supported by principles of foreseeability and public policy); Potter v. Carolina Water Co., 116 S.E.2d 374 (N.C. 1960) (breach of contract between water company and municipality). *But see* Midkiff v.

Providing utility service satisfies a contractual duty of the landlord to the tenant, at least in the forty-seven jurisdictions under which a contractual requirement that utility services be provided is implied or whenever the landlord expressly promises that utility service will be provided on the landlord's account. In most jurisdictions, providing utility service to tenants satisfies a landlord's legal obligations as well. The landlord and the utility company generally intend that the service will go to tenants and not to the promisee-landlord.

Thus the tenant as a third-party beneficiary acquires rights under the contract and may sue the contracting parties for equitable relief or damages.[334] Furthermore, neither the landlord nor the utility company is free to modify or rescind the contract without the tenant's consent once the tenant has relied on the contract.[335]

Some courts take it a step further and restrict the ability of the contracting parties to modify or discharge the contract from the time the contract is made, whether or not the beneficiary knows of such a contract.[336] A third approach attaches restrictions on the performance of the contracting parties from the time the beneficiary learns of the contract and consents to it.[337]

An argument can be made that a monopolistic utility company, knowing that tenants are relying on the vital service it provides, should be held tortiously liable for disconnecting service without notice to the tenants or inquiring into their circumstances and for the anticipated consequences of the termination.[338] Thus, at least from the point at which the tenant signs a lease or moves into the apartment with the understanding that the landlord will provide utility service,[339] neither the utility nor the landlord may rescind the contract without the tenant's consent. The tenant may sue the landlord for damages arising from a breach of this contract, and equitable relief may be available to force the re-institution or continuation of utility service in order to maintain the parties' positions and to prevent future harm.

6.8.4.7 Constitutional Protections for Tenants of Public and Subsidized Housing

For tenants in public and subsidized housing, constitutional due process protections generally apply.[340] Moreover, in public and subsidized housing, self-help eviction is prohibited and a "just cause" eviction standard is in effect.[341] Thus, at a minimum, a notice of eviction and a hearing are constitutionally required.[342]

At the county, state, and municipal levels, several jurisdictions have enacted legislation requiring a hearing prior to ouster and a good cause reason for the eviction.[343] A landlord's attempt at self-help eviction by means of a utility service shut-off (and perhaps also the termination itself) may be enjoined in order to preserve the tenant's due process rights.

Adams County Reg'l Water Dist., 409 F.3d 758 (6th Cir. 2005) (residential tenants were not intended beneficiaries of landlord's contractual relationship with regional water district); Williams v. Virgin Islands Water & Power Auth., 672 F.2d 1220 (3d Cir. 1982) (landlord was not third-party beneficiary of contract between power company and tenant, as there was no evidence that either tenant or power company intended for landlord to benefit from contract, and contract would not satisfy any duty owed by tenant to landlord); White v. Southern Cal. Edison, 30 Cal. Rptr. 2d 431 (Cal. Ct. App. 1994) (in absence of contract between utility and consumer expressly providing for service, utility owes no duty to person injured as result of interruption of service to streetlight); Bush v. Upper Valley Telecable, 524 P.2d 1055, 1058 (Idaho 1974); Milliken & Co. v. Consolidated Edison Co., 644 N.E.2d 268 (N.Y. 1994) (commercial tenants who did not have service contracts with utility could not recover from utility for service interruption as third-party beneficiaries of contract between utility and landlord absent express undertaking by utility to supply power for tenants' needs); Strauss v. Belle Realty Co., 482 N.E.2d 34 (N.Y. 1985) (utility is not liable to tenant injured in common area as a result of utility's negligent failure to provide electric service under agreement with owner).

334 9 Corbin on Contracts § 779K (Interim ed. 2002).

335 Restatement (Second) Contracts § 311. *See* Price v. Pierce, 823 F.2d 1114, 1122 (7th Cir. 1987).

336 E. Allan Farnsworth, Contracts § 10.8, at 47 (3d ed. 2004).

337 *Id.*

338 Vick v. H.S.I. Mgmt., 507 So. 2d 433 (Ala. 1987). *See generally* Roger D. Colton, *Utility Disconnections As a Tort: Gaining Compensation for the Victims of Unlawful Utility Shut-Offs*, 22 Clearinghouse Rev. 609 (1988).

339 *See* ch. 3, *supra*.

340 Wright v. City of Roanoke Redevelopment & Hous. Auth., 479 U.S. 418 (1987) (statute and implementing regulations created rights within meaning of 42 U.S.C. § 1983); Swann v. Gastonia Hous. Auth., 675 F.2d 1342 (4th Cir. 1982).

341 *See* 24 C.F.R. §§ 247.6(a), 966.4, 966.50.

342 *See* Thorpe v. Housing Auth. of Durham, 393 U.S. 268, 274–84 (1969); Jeffries v. Georgia Residential Fin. Auth., 678 F.2d 919 (8th Cir. 1982) (finding that Section 8 tenants have constitutionally protected property rights in an expectation of continued occupancy and receipt of rent and utility subsidies); Swann v. Gastonia Hous. Auth., 502 F. Supp. 362, 364–67 (W.D.N.C. 1980), *aff'd*, 675 F.2d 1342 (4th Cir. 1982). *See also* Arnett v. Kennedy, 416 U.S. 134 (1974) (contract that is terminable only for cause gives rise to property interest entitled to constitutional protection).

343 For example, regulations/ordinances of Berkeley and Santa Monica, California, Cambridge, Massachusetts, and certain Maryland counties have, at times, established a just cause eviction requirement. *See also* Fisher v. City of Berkeley, 693 P.2d 261 (Cal. 1984), *aff'd*, 475 U.S. 260 (1986); Nash v. City of Santa Monica, 688 P.2d 894 (Cal. 1984); Flynn v. Cambridge, 418 N.E.2d 335 (Mass. 1981).

New Jersey has enacted a good cause eviction standard at the state level. N.J. Stat. Ann. § 2A:18-61.1 (West). *See generally* Robert S. Schoshinski, American Law of Landlord and Tenant 7:10, at 528–30 (1980 with 2005 supp.).

6.8.4.8 The Fair Housing Act Prohibits Discrimination by Landlords and Utilities

The Fair Housing Act (FHA)[344] proscribes both intentional discrimination and actions that are discriminatory in effect.[345] The FHA applies, *inter alia*, to discrimination in access to property[346] and in the terms, conditions, or privileges of the sale or rental of a dwelling[347] based on race, color, religion, sex, national origin, family status, or disability.[348]

A landlord who terminates utility service to tenants who are members of protected groups may be practicing purposeful discrimination, which is outlawed by the FHA in cases in which the landlord has not taken similar action against members of non-protected groups under the same circumstances.

A landlord who uses the remedy of utility termination to summarily resolve disputes with tenants may also run afoul of the FHA, as such actions may disproportionately affect protected groups. Protected groups may also be more profoundly impacted by utility terminations.[349]

Members of protected groups are disproportionately represented among the ranks of the poor. In general, when utility terminations occur, poor and low-income tenants have less access to transportation, hotels, motels, and restaurants (among other things) that might ease the impact of the utility termination. Inevitably they suffer the greatest impact. In particular, people with disabilities, families with young children, the elderly, and the infirm are likely to suffer disproportionately.[350]

Protected groups, especially African-Americans, Hispanics, and other ethnic minorities, are more likely to live in housing situations that are far from ideal.[351] This holds true for members of minority groups across all income levels and for properties at all rent levels.[352] Thus, when a tenant complains to the landlord about conditions on the premises, and the landlord chooses to retaliate, members of protected groups are more likely to have their utilities terminated by the landlord. A utility policy that gives landlords unchecked power to terminate utility service may be used in ways that disproportionately impacts protected groups.

---

344 42 U.S.C. §§ 3601–3631.

345 *See generally* Trafficante v. Metropolitan Life Ins. Co., 409 U.S. 205, 211–12 (1972); Hamad v. Woodcrest Condo. Ass'n, 328 F.3d 224 (6th Cir. 2003); Resident Advisory Bd. v. Rizzo, 564 F.2d 126 (3d Cir. 1977); Oxford House-Evergreen v. City of Plainfield, 769 F. Supp. 1329, 1343 (D.N.J. 1991); Casa Marie, Inc. v. Superior Ct. of P.R. for Dist. of Arecibo, 752 F. Supp. 1152, 1168 (D. P.R. 1990), *vacated on other grounds*, 988 F.2d 252 (1st Cir. 1993). *See also* Annot., *FHA: Discriminatory Effects*, 100 A.L.R. Fed. 97; 24 C.F.R. §§ 100.90–100.135 (HUD implementing regulations).

346 42 U.S.C. § 3604(b).

347 42 U.S.C. § 3604(b), (f)(1)(2); People Helpers Found. v. City of Richmond, 781 F. Supp. 1132 (E.D. Va. 1992); Meadows v. Edgewood Mgmt. Corp., 432 F. Supp. 334, 335 (W.D. Va. 1977).

348 42 U.S.C. § 3604(b).

The Act is subject to certain exclusions, the most important of which exempts owner-occupied buildings of four units or fewer. 42 U.S.C. §§ 3603(b), 3607.

349 People with disabilities—a protected group—may be especially hard hit by the loss of utility services. *See* Roger D. Colton & Doug Smith, National Consumer Law Center, *Protections for the Low-Income Customer of Unregulated Utilities: Using Federal Fuel Assistance As More Than Cash Grants*, 13 Hamline J. of Pub. L. & Policy, 263 (1992); Note, *The Shut-Off of Utility Services for the Poor*, 46 Wash. L. Rev. 745 (1975); Note, *Public Utilities and the Poor*, 78 Yale L. Rev. 448 (1969).

The poor in general are hard hit by the loss of utility services because they have fewer options for alternative shelter, cooking, and bathing facilities.

350 Myers, Housing Demography 218–50 (1990); Energy Costs, Urban Development and Housing 36–37, 137 (Downs & Bradbury, eds. 1984).

Furthermore, female-headed households are more likely to live in buildings with few (one to five) units. These buildings are far more likely to have utility service provided on the landlord's account. Thus, women and families with young children are likely to suffer disproportionately at the hands of landlords who terminate utility service to resolve disputes with tenants.

351 Energy Costs, Urban Development and Housing 36–37, 137 (Downs & Bradbury, eds. 1984); William Ryan, Blaming the Victim, 164–84 (1970); Reynolds Farley, S.M. Bianchi, & D. Spain, Racial Inequalities in Housing: An Examination of Recent Trends, *cited in* James Momeni, Race Ethnicity and Minority Housing in the United States 23 (1986).

352 Reynolds Farley, S.M. Bianchi, & D. Spain, *Racial* Inequalities in Housing: An Examination of Recent Trends, *cited in* James Momeni, Race Ethnicity and Minority Housing in the United States 23 (1986). *See also* J.T. Darden, Accessibility to Housing: Differential Residential Segregation for Blacks, Hispanics, American Indians and Asians; Goering, Minority Housing Needs and Civil Rights Endorsement, *cited in* James Momeni, Race Ethnicity and Minority Housing in the United States 124, 199–00 (1986); Robert W. Lake, The New Suburbanites: Race and Housing (1981); Peter M. Mieszkowski, Federal Reserve Bank of Boston, Studies of Prejudice and Discrimination in Urban Housing Markets 1–3 (Fall 1979) (special study).

Chapter 7 Utility Affordability Programs: Description and Implementation

7.1 Short-Term or Crisis Energy Payment Assistance

7.1.1 *Fuel Funds*

7.1.1.1 General

A fuel fund is a program that raises private and/or corporate dollars to help low-income households meet their energy needs. While all fuel funds meet this definition, there is tremendous variety among them in organizational structure, sponsorship, operations, and fundraising activities.

Fuel funds are often partnerships between utilities and human service providers to disburse private monies to help low-income households pay their energy bills. The majority of fuel funds have an "energy provider-based structure." These fuel funds may be staffed by or based with the energy provider or utility, with the administrative decisions made by the energy provider.

Fuel funds may also be administered through a local government agency or through an independent nonprofit organization. In many communities, in both urban and rural areas, additional sources of assistance for energy payments can often be found. The Salvation Army, local community action agencies (CAAs), and often houses of worship or other faith-based institutions are known for establishing funds for emergency aid to the poor.

Occasionally these local charities have established special relationships with the utility providers.

Local fuel funds operate generally, but not exclusively, to prevent the disconnection of service for nonpayment. In order to receive assistance in such instances, an applicant must present a notice of pending disconnection. The fuel fund generally requires that the fuel fund's payment, in conjunction with a customer payment or some other resources, will resolve the outstanding arrears.

Even when cash assistance to prevent a utility termination may not be available, assistance with the *deposit* requirements for reconnection might be possible.

For example, some charities have negotiated with their utilities for an agreement whereby the charity agrees to underwrite all or a portion of their client's deposit on a pay-only-after-default basis. In this way, the utility accepts the promise to underwrite the deposit from the charity in lieu of some or all of the deposit required from the household. The charity only has to pay the amount of the promised deposit to the utility if the deposit of the charity's client is actually tapped for payment of the utility bill.

7.1.1.2 Funds Raised

The National Fuel Fund Network (NFFN) consists of over 300 members, including non-profit agencies, utilities, individuals, and government representatives that provide utility bill assistance raised through charitable donations.[1] NFFN reports that successful marketing procedures used for raising money include soliciting donations through customer utility bills. These methods include: bill inserts, solicitations on the cover of the bill, bill contribution check-offs, pledges automatically added to customers' bills, and "round-ups" (through which customers round up the price on their bills to a whole number). One initiative that rural electric cooperatives might explore involves seeking customer donations from their annual patronage capital credits (or patronage capital refunds, as some would refer to them).

The benefits of tapping into refunded money that is flowing back to residential and commercial customers can be substantial. (There is no reason that such an initiative be limited exclusively to residential and commercial customers, but the limitation is mentioned here simply to ease the process of analysis.) Important lessons can be learned from the past experiences of the Colorado Energy Assistance Foundation, which is now known as Energy Outreach Colorado (EOC). EOC generated substantial fuel fund contributions through a solicitation directed toward recapturing customer refunds provided through Public Service Company of Colorado (PSCO). The Colorado initiative recovered $1,126,638 of the $29,657,910 refunds owed to "active" PSCO customers, or about 3.8% of the total refund. While the refund averaged about $35 per customer, the refund donations received averaged about $25 per refund. Nearly

1 A list of NFFN members is available at the NFFN website, www.nationalfuelfunds.org.

one in ten of the total number of customers eligible to receive refunds donated through the program. According to the Colorado fuel fund, the refunds were considered to be "found money," thus making it easier for customers to make the requested donation.

State LIHEAP offices report leveraged non-federal resources each year. According to the LIHEAP Clearinghouse, operated under contract to the federal LIHEAP office, state reports for fiscal year 2009 identified over $121.3 million in leveraged resources from "fuel funds," churches, and other community organizations.[2] This represents a decrease of more than $34 million from the $155.4 million in such resources reported for fiscal year 2007.[3] The fiscal year 2007 figures were an increase from fuel fund resources and church funds reported for fiscal year 2006.[4]

7.1.2 The Emergency Assistance Program and the Repeal of AFDC

The Personal Responsibility and Work Opportunity Reconciliation Act of 1996,[5] commonly referred to as the "welfare reform" law, repealed in its entirety Title IV-A of the Social Security Act, which provided Aid to Families with Dependent Children (AFDC).[6] In its place, the legislation established "Temporary Assistance for Needy Families" (TANF) block grants. AFDC, emergency assistance, and work programs are all folded into this single block grant.

This legislation ended the federal guarantee of public assistance to eligible families with children. Instead, under the new law, states are allowed to deny aid to poor families for any number of reasons; and, if choosing to provide cash assistance to poor families, states will be prohibited from providing aid to families for more than five years.[7]

Under welfare reform, states no longer receive funding specifically for emergency assistance (EA), but they can still use their TANF block grant and their Maintenance of Effort (MOE) funds[8] to fund traditional emergency assistance. During the winter 1999–2000 home heating oil crisis, the Administration urged governors to use TANF to provide emergency heating assistance to very low-income families with children.[9]

Two primary sources of TANF funds can be available to support low-income energy assistance, neither of which provides a long-term stable source for energy assistance.

First, unspent TANF fund balances can be transferred to supplement LIHEAP. As TANF caseloads decreased in the mid-1990s (after "welfare reform" was enacted at the federal level), most states found that they were not spending their entire TANF block grant. These unspent dollars could, however, be retained by the states in an "unobligated fund" for future use on the TANF program or on TANF-type services. In recent years, however, as caseloads have increased and as inflation has reduced the purchasing power of the TANF block grant--the Congressional Research Service estimates that inflation will reduce the purchasing power of the TANF block grant by more than 25% by 2010—states have drawn down their unobligated balances.[10] Today, little of that unspent money remains with the states. Indiana, for example, has a zero balance in its unobligated funds.[11]

Second, states may use some portion of its annual TANF block grant for "non-assistance" program components. Before considering "non-assistance," however, a brief overview of TANF is important.

Like LIHEAP, TANF is a federal block grant program. A block grant program provides states with considerable lati-

---

2 A table showing leveraging dollars can be found at the LIHEAP Clearinghouse website, http://liheap.ncat.org/Supplements/2009/supplement09.htm, and is also reproduced in Appendix E, *infra*.

3 *See* LIHEAP Clearinghouse website, http://liheap.ncat.org/Supplements/2007/supplement07.htm.

4 It is not possible to determine from the LIHEAP Clearinghouse report whether there was an absolute increase in available resources or whether more resources were simply identified for reporting purposes.

5 Pub. L. No. 104-193, § 103, 110 Stat. 2105 (Aug. 22, 1996), *codified at* 42 U.S.C. §§ 601–619.

6 42 U.S.C. §§ 601–619.

7 In addition to the structural changes to the AFDC program, various other changes occurred as a result of the welfare law, including eligibility of legal immigrants for certain programs, and cuts to the food stamp program.

The Center on Budget and Policy Priority's report, *The New Welfare Law*, by David A. Super, Sharon Parrott, Susan Steinmetz, and Cindy Mann (Aug. 13, 1996), provides an excellent overview of provisions of the new welfare law. The Children's Defense Fund and the National Coalition for the Homeless issued a report, *Welfare to What: Early Findings on Family Hardship and Well-Being*, on December 1998. The report reviews data and findings from an array of national and local sources to provide an early look at the effects of the 1996 federal welfare law.

8 The welfare reform law requires states to spend state funds at a level equal to 75% to 80% of their 1994 levels. See Chapter 7 of the 2004 Green Book, produced by the U.S. House Comm. on Ways and Means, for state maintenance of effort (MOE) charts.

9 See letters dated Feb. 18, 2000, from the Secretary of Health and Human Services to the governors of states hardest hit by the home heating oil crisis. *See also* Press Release, The White House, The Clinton-Gore Administration: Working to Mitigate the Effects of High Home Heating Oil Prices (Feb. 28, 2000) (President Clinton announcing he would remind governors that federal law permits states to use TANF to provide emergency heating assistance to very low income families with children).

10 The Congressional Research Service (CRS) has provided a detailed description of the expected loss of TANF purchasing power. Gene Falk, Congressional Research Serv., The Temporary Assistance for Needy Families (TANF) Block Grant: Responses to Frequently Asked Questions, CRS Report to Congress (Aug. 1, 2007).

11 Fred Hash, Advisory Comm. of the Ind. Affordable Hous. & Cmty. Dev. Fund Advisory Comm., The Indiana Affordable Housing and Community Development Fund: Report and Recommendations from the Advisory Committee (June 2006).

tude in deciding how to structure state efforts to accomplish the objectives of the program. With TANF, states may use their TANF allocations to meet any one, or all, of the four objectives of the TANF program. The four statutory objectives for TANF are to "(1) provide assistance to needy families so that children may be cared for in their own homes or in the homes of relatives; (2) end the dependence of needy parents on government benefits by promoting job preparation, work and marriage; (3) prevent and reduce the incidence of out-of-wedlock pregnancies; and (4) encourage the formation and maintenance of two-parent families." The *primary* federal TANF requirement, however, is that funds be used to serve families with children.[12]

Despite the broad discretion granted to the states in their use of TANF funds, Congress has imposed substantial restrictions on the states. To begin, Congress requires that at least half of all TANF recipients must be engaged in some kind of work-related activity for at least thirty hours a week. In addition, Congress requires that no family may receive federally funded TANF assistance for more than five years. Both of these Congressional requirements, however, apply only to "basic" TANF assistance (income supplements and other assistance designed to meet basic needs).

One permitted use of federal funds under the TANF block grant structure involves "other non-assistance." Dollars that are spent on "non-assistance" are exempt from the work requirement and time restrictions imposed on basic TANF assistance. "Assistance" is defined as dollars that are designed to meet ongoing basic needs.[13] The critical term in this definition is "ongoing." Benefits that are designed to address a specific crisis situation or episode of need, which are provided on a one-time basis or for a prospective period that does not exceed four months or intended to meet recurrent or ongoing needs, fall outside the definition of TANF "assistance." More particularly, TANF benefits that are paid toward utility arrears (of any dollar amount and for any number of months) do not invoke the federal restrictions on assistance.[14] According to the Center on Budget and Policy Priorities' discussion of using TANF payments to prevent homelessness,

> as long as benefits are provided to meet a short-term, non-recurrent need, they may be provided more than once during a year. for example, during a single 12-month period, a state can use TANF funds to provide a family with both a rent arrearage payment and funds to repair a car, pay a utility bill, or meet another short-term crisis; this aid would not count against the family's lifetime TANF time limit or trigger the TANF work participation, or child support assignment requirements. States and counties may also make several payments of the same type in a single year as long as each payment is made without the expectation of making additional payments.[15]

Despite the seeming advantage of using TANF block grant dollars to fund this short-term emergency energy assistance, it would be unreasonable for states to look to such dollars as a long-term supplement to its low-income energy assistance funding. Given increasingly tight TANF budgets, the only way for a state to fund "new" energy assistance is for the state to reduce its TANF spending in other areas.

7.1.3 Emergency Shelter Grants (ESG)

The Stewart B. McKinney Homeless Assistance Act provides for the Emergency Shelter Grants (ESG) Program.[16] The program has been funded at approximately $150 million annually since fiscal year 2001. These HUD grants go to state and local governments (who may subcontract with nonprofits) to provide essential services to homeless people and to provide services, including financial assistance, to prevent homelessness. Families are eligible for ESG assistance with utility bills if they have received a termination notice or otherwise are suffering from a problem with their utility account that could lead to homelessness. The statute authorizes payment for provision of utilities, utility deposits, utility payments, and "other activities that are effective at stabilizing individuals and families in their current housing; or quickly moving such individuals and families to other permanent housing."[17]

The regulations specifically describe utility payments as a proper use of the funds for homelessness prevention.[18] The amount of the funds and the agency distributing them are subjects of state or local option. Often these funds must be matched with non-federal dollars.

12 An excellent overview of TANF can be obtained from the Center for Budget and Policy Priorities. Martha Cowen, Center for Budget & Policy Priorities, An Introduction to TANF (Nov. 2005).

13 Mark Greenberg & Hedick Rahmanou, Center for Law & Social Policy, TANF Funding in 2003 (Feb. 2005).

14 *See generally* Barbara Sard, Center on Budget & Policy Priorities, *Using TANF Funds for Housing-Related Benefits to Prevent Homelessness* (Apr. 2001) (more information on the exemptions from federal restrictions on "assistance").

15 CBPP notes that "[d]efining benefits as short-term if they cover a period up to four months, and permitting more than one emergency payment in a 12-month period, are significant changes from the rules that applied to Emergency Assistance (EA) programs under the former Aid to Families with Dependent Children (AFDC) program. Generally, EA benefits were restricted to needs that arose over a 90-day period and could be provided only once in a 12-month period." *Id.*

16 *See* 42 U.S.C. §§ 11371–11378.

17 42 U.S.C. § 11374.

18 24 C.F.R. § 576.3 (definition of "Homeless Prevention").

7.1.4 *FEMA (Federal Emergency Management Agency) Funds*

FEMA, the federal agency responsible for disaster relief,[19] is also responsible for distributing certain McKinney Act funds that may be used for the payment of utility bills. This program, which has no connection to disaster relief, is known as the Emergency Food and Shelter Program (EFSP).[20]

As of March 1, 2003, FEMA became part of the Department of Homeland Security (DHS) and FEMA's funding, which includes EFSP, now falls under DHS. The funding level for fiscal year 2006 for the EFSP was $151.4 million.

Under this program, FEMA allocates money to a national board,[21] which in turn distributes the funds to local governments and nonprofits.[22] A local board composed of homeless providers and other charitable and religious organizations distributes the money. Each local board has wide discretion as to how the funds are used in a community. Often much of this money is used for actual operation of homeless shelters, and only a limited amount is available for assisting individuals with such expenses as utility bills.

EFSP funds are distributed nationally on a formula basis. According to FEMA, the National Board "uses a formula involving population, poverty, and unemployment data to determine the eligibility of a civil jurisdiction." For the most recent round of funding (Phase 29—fiscal year 2011), local jurisdictions qualified for EFSP funding if they met any one of the following criteria:

- The number of unemployed reached 300 or more with a 11.5% rate of unemployment; or
- The number of unemployed was 300 or more with a 14.4% rate of poverty.[23]

One of the eligible uses for EFSP funding is the payment of one month of utility bills for a person in danger of becoming homeless due to an unpaid utility arrears. Other resources such as LIHEAP must have been exhausted, payment must be in arrears, and utility charges, reconnect fees, and late fees—but not deposits—are eligible for payment. A payment from these funds can be made only once per year to each utility serving the family and must guarantee an additional thirty days of service.[24]

7.2 Long-Term Payment Assistance Options

7.2.1 *Introduction*

In addition to LIHEAP assistance and the different forms of emergency assistance, other programs exist that help low-income households pay their energy bills. Some low-income energy assistance takes the form of bill discounts, low-income rates, and/or arrearage forgiveness. These break down into a few distinct categories, based on the approach taken by the assistance programs:

- Rate discount programs;
- Percentage of income payment plans;
- Payment restructuring programs;
- Energy conservation programs. Conservation programs are discussed in Chapter 9, *infra*.

In many cases, these program resources are teamed up with the LIHEAP benefits as well as local resources to create the potential for the household to be self-sufficient. For the best of the programs, the goal is to create a more "affordable" energy burden.[25] In addition, these programs have proven to be effective in reducing arrearages, disconnection, and reconnection, the reduction of which is beneficial for the customer as well as the utility supplying that customer with energy. Evaluations of these programs measure savings obtained through implementing the program: savings on avoided arrearages, disconnect fees and debt, and reconnect fees and debt.

The following discussion sets forth the various options for some of the available programs and the policy basis underlying these programs as they address the problems posed by low-income energy unaffordability. This section provides examples of where these programs have been implemented throughout the country.[26]

19 *See* 42 U.S.C. §§ 5121, 5122.

20 *See* 42 U.S.C. §§ 11331–11335.

21 The national board consists of representatives from FEMA, the United Way of America, the Salvation Army, the National Council of Churches of Christ in the U.S.A., Catholic Charities U.S.A., Council of Jewish Federations, Inc., and the American Red Cross. *See* 42 U.S.C. § 11331.

22 *See* 42 U.S.C. § 11343.

23 *See* www.efsp.unitedway.org/efsp/website/websiteContents/index.cfm?template=qualify.cfm.

In Phase 26—fiscal year 2008, eligibility was based on unemployed numbers of 13,000 with a 3.5% rate of unemployment; between 300 and 12,999 with a 5.5% unemployment rate; or 300 or more with a 11.0% rate of poverty. This is discussed at § 9.1.4 of the 2008 edition of Access to Utilities, available on the companion website to this treatise.

24 *See* 59 Fed. Reg. 3697 (Jan. 26, 1994).

25 "Energy burden" refers to the percentage of a household's income which is used to pay its home energy bill.

26 More detailed information can be found at appendix E of the 2008 edition of Access to Utilities, available on the companion website to this treatise. Appendix E of the 2008 edition provides a brief description, state by state, of the low-income energy assurance programs operating throughout the country.

7.2.2 Low-Income Rate Discount Programs

7.2.2.1 Introduction

Through different variations adopted by utilities throughout the nation, special rate programs have been developed and implemented and are a method of aiding low-income households in attaining affordable utility service. In some of these programs, a discount is taken from the *total energy bill*. However, the bill is actually comprised of two components: a fixed customer service charge and the usage charge. Some programs waive the general customer service charge. Others actually lower the usage rate; in other words, the utility requires fewer dollars per measurement of usage (for example, kWh of electricity or therms of natural gas) from low-income customers.

As compared to percentage of income payment programs, which are discussed in § 7.2.3, *infra*, rate discount programs do not explicitly address a household's ability to pay based on its available income. In this way, program administration can be a relatively easy process. It should be noted, however, that income is often relevant to *eligibility* for a rate discount program.

7.2.2.2 Straight Discount

7.2.2.2.1 Overview

With the straight discount, a specified percentage discount is taken from the total bill. Eligible residential customers receive a flat, or straight, discount on the total utility bill. Thus, if the total bill is $15, a customer receiving a 20% discount would receive a discount of $3 and would pay $12. It does not matter what portion of the total bill is allocated to the usage charge and to the fixed customer service charge. All that matters is the total bill and the percentage discount.

For example, most utilities in California and Massachusetts offer straight discounts off electric and gas bills for qualifying low-income customers.

While this form of assistance may be easier to administer, it is not the best means of targeting energy affordability assistance to the households with the greatest needs. A customer with a home energy burden of 3% would receive the same percentage discount off his or her bill as a customer with a home energy burden of 30%. For the first customer, the discount is probably unnecessary to make the bill affordable; for the latter, the discount is probably insufficient to make the bill affordable.

7.2.2.2.2 The California Alternate Rates for Energy (CARE) discount program

The California Alternative Rate for Energy (CARE) program is a straight discount program. California's rate affordability program for energy utilities was created by statute. Created in 1989, the Low-Income Rate Affordability (LIRA) program was codified into simple language providing that "the commission shall establish a program of assistance to low income electric and gas customers, the cost of which shall not be borne solely by any single class of customers."[27] The program was implemented by the California Public Utilities Commission (CPUC) through a series of orders in a proceeding devoted exclusively to responding to the legislation.[28] The program was subsequently renamed the California Alternate Rate for Energy (CARE) program.[29]

The California CARE program is a simple rate discount. Simplicity has been a goal since the program's inception. As the CPUC noted:

> This program is simple—simple to understand, simple to explain, simple to compute. Simplicity of understanding and explanation will facilitate outreach and explanation by customer service departments and result in a quick start to this program. It confers a noticeable bill decrease on participating customers.[30]

The California low-income rate applies to the state's investor-owned utilities.[31] It allows a rate discount off both

27 Cal. Pub. Util. Code § 739.1(b)(1) (West). The program was created by the "Dills Bill." S.B. 987 (Cal. 1989).

28 Investigation on the Commission's Own Motion to Comply with Senate 987 and Realign Residential Rates, Including Baseline Rates, of California Energy Utilities (Cal. Pub. Util. Comm'n).

The interim opinion, No. D.89-07-062, was issued on July 19, 1989. The final opinion, No. D.89-09-844, was issued on September 7, 1989. An order on the petition for modification, No. D.89-11-018, was issued on September 29, 1989.

29 *See* Cal. Pub. Util. Code § 382(a).

After restructuring the electric industry, the California legislature had prescribed that the "program provided to low-income electricity customers, including but not limited to, targeted energy efficiency services and the California Alternative Rates for Energy program shall be funded at not less than 1996 authorized levels based on an assessment of customer need." *Id.*

30 Final Order at 7, 8, Investigation on the Commission's Own Motion to Comply with Senate 987 and Realign Residential Rates, Including Baseline Rates, of California Energy Utilities, No. D.89-09-044 (Cal. Pub. Utils. Comm'n Sept. 7, 1989).

31 The California Code allows, but does not require, "local publicly-owned electric utilities" to fund energy assistance. Section 385 of the Public Utilities Act provides that "each local publicly owned electric utility shall establish a nonbypassable, usage based charge on local distribution service of not less than the lowest expenditure level of the three largest electrical corporations in California on a percent of revenue basis . . . to fund investments by the utility and other parties in any or all of

consumption and fixed monthly charges.

While program eligibility was initially set at 150% of the federal poverty level,[32] eligibility has since been increased to 200% of the poverty level. The increased eligibility guideline was approved in response to recent increases in natural gas prices. The CPUC considered whether to increase eligibility to either 200% of poverty level or 250% of poverty level. It decided that

> [m]aking CARE discounts available to a broader range of residential customers is an important way to help more customers this winter. Because of the need to protect all customer classes, however, we must exhibit moderation. The utilities would have us extend CARE eligibility only to a subset of those customers earning between 175% and 200% of poverty levels, and this approach would even further limit exposure to other customers. We are persuaded that the elderly and disabled are not the only customers in this income range who will face special challenges this winter and beyond. It would make sense also to include families, many of which may have to choose between buying clothing and paying utility bills. For ease of implementation, it may be better to qualify a broader class of new customers (all of those earning up to 200% of poverty level) than to ask the utilities to invoke a new series of more subtle rules for eligibility.[33]

The CPUC noted that its decision was not without cost. "Although the impact on other customers may be measurable," the CPUC stated, "it is small. We will instruct the utilities to allow all residential customers earning no more than 200% of poverty levels to enroll in the CARE program."[34] California customers who are enrolled in Medicaid, Medical, the Low Income Home Energy Assistance Program, Food Stamps, and other public assistance programs may also be eligible.[35]

The California legislature made several significant policy declarations regarding low-income affordability programs when it enacted state legislation restructuring the electric industry. The legislature determined that it was important for the state utility commission to consider the affordability of energy:

> In order to meet legitimate needs of electric and gas customers who are unable to pay their electric and gas bills and who satisfy eligibility criteria for assistance, recognizing that electricity is a basic necessity and that all residents of the state should be able to afford essential electricity and gas supplies, the commission shall ensure that low-income ratepayers are not jeopardized or overburdened by monthly energy expenditures. Energy expenditures may be reduced through the establishment of different rates for low-income ratepayers, different levels of rate assistance, and energy efficiency programs.[36]

The California legislature provided that, beginning in 2002, the California Public Utility Commission must periodically assess low-income consumers' need for assistance and evaluate effectiveness of energy efficiency and weatherization measures in their homes.[37] The legislature also required the Commission to ensure that, by 2020, low-income energy customers, including renters, have the opportunity to participate in efficiency programs and that the necessary funds are allocated to meet these goals.[38]

The legislature then declared that the extent and design of any low-income rate affordability program should be based on a "needs assessment." Beginning in 2002, the legislature stated that "an assessment of the needs of low-income electricity and gas ratepayers shall be conducted periodically by the commission. . . . The assessment shall evaluate low-income program implementation and the effectiveness of weatherization services and energy efficiency measures in low-income households. The assessment shall consider whether existing programs adequately address low-income electricity and gas customers' energy expenditures, hardship, language needs, and economic burdens."[39]

California's stated goal for its CARE program is to achieve 100% penetration within the low-income population.[40] The CPUC articulated its objective in unequivocal terms: "Simply put, our goal is to reach 100% of low-income customers who are eligible for, and desire to participate in, the CARE program."[41] The commission adopted

---

the following . . .(4) services provided for low-income electricity customers, including, but not limited to, energy efficiency services, education, weatherization, and rate discounts." (emphasis added)

32 The original eligibility guideline was set so that eligibility for LIRA would be the same as eligibility for California's Universal Lifeline Telephone Service (ULTS). California Pub. Utils. Comm'n, Consumer Advisory & Compliance Div., Low-Income Ratepayer Assistance Program (LIRA): Program Report 2 (Sept. 1, 1990).

33 Interim Order Approving Various Emergency Program Changes in Light of Anticipated High Natural Gas Prices in the Winter of 2005–2006, Order Instituting Rulemaking on the Commission's Proposed Policies and Programs Governing Post-2003 Low-Income Assistance Programs at 9, 10, No. D.05-10-044 (Cal. Pub. Utils. Comm'n Oct. 27, 2005).

34 *Id.* at 10.

35 *See* www.cpuc.ca.gov/PUC/energy/Low+Income/care.htm.

36 Cal. Pub. Util. Code § 382(b) (West).

37 Cal. Pub. Util. Code § 382(d) (West).

38 Cal. Pub. Util. Code § 382(d), (f) (West).

39 *Id.* § 382(d).

40 Interim Order Approving Various Emergency Program Changes in Light of Anticipated High Natural Gas Prices in the Winter of 2005–2006, Order Instituting Rulemaking on the Commission's Proposed Policies and Programs Governing Post-2003 Low-Income Assistance Programs at 9, 10, No. D.05-10-044 (Cal. Pub. Utils. Comm'n Oct. 27, 2005).

41 Interim Decision: Status of Rapid Deployment, CARE Penetration Goals, Automatic Enrollment, and Related Program Planning Issues, Order Instituting Rulemaking on the Commission's

a "rapid deployment policy" through which utilities were to take all reasonable efforts to expand the enrollment in CARE.[42] It acknowledged that, while the objective certainly applied statewide, it would be met with varying degrees of success by different utilities.

> We recognize that the utilities will not reach this goal at the same pace, given differences in demographic characteristics and the magnitude of the eligible low-income population within each service territory, as well as differences in where each utility stands today with respect to program penetration. We also recognize that the law of diminishing returns applies to CARE outreach efforts over time, that is, it becomes increasingly difficult to enroll additional customers, the closer the utility moves toward achieving 100% participation.[43]

Each utility submits to the California utility commission a biannual plan on how it intends to implement the CARE program. Since the discount provided by each utility's program in California is identical, the regulatory review is primarily on the level of administrative costs incurred,[44] along with a review of the outreach and enrollment processes utilized by each company.[45] The California utility commission establishes utility-specific expectations on the penetration rate for the CARE program in each service territory[46] and determines whether the utility is adequately addressing those expectations.[47]

Given California's emphasis on reaching 100% of its eligible population, one focus of the state utility commission's review of each utility's biannual plan involves the extent of outreach and ease of enrollment.

The commission also seeks to minimize the extent to which re-certification causes a drop-off in enrollment. In reviewing Southern California Edison's 2005 CARE budget and operating plan, for example, the commission noted:

> SCE states that there is a shrinking pool of remaining CARE-eligible but non-participating customers in its territory, requiring increasingly sophisticated outreach to reach these customers. SCE also believes it needs to reduce the percentage of customers that are removed from the program during the recertification process. After two years in the CARE program, customers must recertify their financial eligibility. The recertification process requires active efforts by customers and thus causes customers who fail to respond to requests for recertification to fall off of the rolls.[48]

The California commission sought to have the automatic enrollment of households from the state Department of Community Services and Development (DCSD) Energy Assistance programs into CARE.[49] Moreover, gas and electric utilities serving the same geographic areas are encouraged to share participant lists to facilitate the enrollment of CARE participants from one utility into the CARE program

Proposed Policies and Programs Governing Low-Income Assistance Programs at 4, No. D.02-07-033 (Cal. Pub. Utils. Comm'n July 17, 2002).

42 *In re* Compliance Application of Pac. Gas & Elec. Co. for Approval of Year 2001 Low-Income Programs et al., No. D.01-05-033, at 41–52 (Cal. Pub. Utils. Comm'n May 3, 2001).

43 *Id.* at 4.

44 *See, e.g.*, Order Approving Utility Budgets for Low Income Energy Efficiency Programs and California Alternative Rate for Energy, No. D.06-12-038 (Cal. Pub. Utils. Comm'n Dec. 15, 2006) ("Each of the applicant utilities has CARE rates that discount electricity and gas by 20%. Although the application of the rate itself requires no particular administrative work, the utilities must conduct targeted outreach and marketing efforts to maximize participation by qualified customers." *Id.* at 46).

45 *See, e.g.*, Order Instituting Rulemaking on the Commission's Proposed Policies and Programs Governing Post-2003 Low-Income Assistance Programs, No. D.05-04-052 (Cal. Pub. Utils. Comm'n Apr. 21, 2005); Energy Division Report on Program Year 2005 California Alternate Rates for Energy (CARE) and Low-Income Energy Efficiency (LIEE) Programs of the Small and Multi-Jurisdictional Utilities 15, app. A (Cal. Pub. Utils. Comm'n Apr. 29, 2005) ("PacifiCorp has done a dismal job of reaching its eligible population and increasing enrollment. Due to the rural and diverse nature of PacifiCorp's territory and their high volume of low-income customers, Energy Division feels it is imperative that PacifiCorp exceed their proposed 2005 penetration benchmark of 39% or a target of 6,000 enrolled. To meet this benchmark and target, PacifiCorp would need to enroll a net of 1,581 new CARE-eligible. Energy Division recommends the Commission require PacifiCorp to increase their efforts to reach the over 15,000 eligible CARE customers. Energy Division recommends that a benchmark of 70% with a target of 10,902 enrolled by set for PacifiCorp for 2005.").

46 *See, e.g.*, Final Opinion: Post-2002 Low-Income Assistance Programs for Small and Multi-Jurisdictional Utilities, No. D.03-03-007 (Cal. Pub. Utils. Comm'n Mar. 14, 2003).

47 Interim Decision: Status of Rapid Deployment, CARE Penetration Goals, Automatic Enrollment, and Related Program Planning Issues, Order Instituting Rulemaking on the Commission's Proposed Policies and Programs Governing Low-Income Assistance Programs at 4, No. D.02-07-033 (Cal. Pub. Utils. Comm'n July 17, 2002). *See also* Energy Division Report on Program Year 2005 California Alternate Rates For Energy (CARE) and Low Income Energy Efficiency (LIEE) Programs of the Small and Multi-Jurisdictional Utilities, app. A, at 10, No. R-04-01-006 (Cal. Pub. Utils. Comm'n Apr. 29, 2005) ("In D.02-07-033, the Commission ordered an overall CARE participation goal of 100%, while acknowledging that it may not be possible to achieve 100% participation right away. In recognition of that, the Commission set benchmark penetration levels for each utility to achieve over the subsequent years. In D.03-03-007, the Commission set the most recent benchmarks for the [small and multijurisdiction utilities—SMJU]. Energy Division recommends that the Commission set higher benchmarks for the SMJU for 2005 and continue to require aggressive outreach and recertification efforts, with the caveat that each utilities' eligible population, benchmarks and budgets may need adjusting depending on the results of the Needs Assessment Study.").

48 Order Instituting Rulemaking on the Commission's Proposed Policies and Programs Governing Post-2003 Low-Income Assistance Programs at 40, No. D.05-04-052 (Cal. Pub. Utils. Comm'n Apr. 21, 2005).

49 *Id.* at 41.

of the corresponding utility providing other fuels.[50] Efforts to automatically enroll MediCal participants into CARE, however, encountered privacy constraints imposed by federal laws regarding use of medical records[51] without the express permission of the customer.[52] Even then, the commission encouraged the state's utilities, along with it own staff, to negotiate a means to routinely obtain the permission of customers to use these MediCal records for automatic enrollment. The commission noted:

> We commend PG&E and the other utilities for efforts they have made to date to accommodate Commission orders regarding automatic enrollment. Automatic enrollment causes large numbers of eligible customers to enroll in the program at limited expense. We plan to continue examining how to expand the program going forward, through arranging for specific customer consent or other methods. In the meantime, the Commission has ordered the IOUs to automatically enroll customers whose data we have received from the DCSD.[53]

In addition to promoting "automatic enrollment," through which a customer is enrolled in CARE without the customer having to apply for the discount, the California commission is also aggressively pursuing ways to implement "categorical eligibility." This enrollment process permits a customer to demonstrate eligibility with documentation of participation in a government means-tested program rather than having to provide evidence of income.[54]

Finally, the commission has both approved and encouraged the development of "a probability model to indicate a customer's likelihood of being eligible for CARE and therefore exempt from the recertification process."[55] In a related vein, the companies have extended the certification period from two years to four years for fixed-income customers "because customers on fixed incomes tend to remain in related programs for long periods. PG&E expects this policy change to mitigate the current high numbers of fixed income CARE customers that do not respond to a request for recertification and are dropped from the program."[56] The commission also noted that Southern California Gas Company reported, in support of its proposal to extend the certification period from two to four years for certain fixed-income households, that "the incomes for those customers on pensions, SSDI, SSI, and Social Security do not change dramatically from year-to-year. Placing these customers on a four-year recertification cycle will ensure that many are not removed from the program because they fail to respond to the recertification request."[57]

Overall, the California rate affordability program is a legislatively-created program designed to deliver moderate benefits to as many eligible customers as possible. Called California Alternate Rate for Energy (CARE), the rate affordability initiative is structured to provide a 20% discount to customers with income at or below 200% of the federal poverty level. While the discount is not substantial, as the commission notes, "it confers a noticeable bill decrease on participating customers."

7.2.2.2.3 Straight discount programs in other states

In Massachusetts, straight discounts were negotiated with electric and gas utilities over the last two decades. Since restructuring, the current mandate for electric discounts is Mass. Gen. Laws ch. 164, § 1 F(4), which effectively locked preexisting discounts into law. Gas discounts are not mandated by statute; however, they are mandated by individual rate case decisions and regulatory commission decisions. The discounts vary by utility from 12% to 30% of the bill.

In September 2008, the Massachusetts Department of Public Utilities (DPU) issued a decision directing electric and gas companies to file new low-income discount rates that restore the percentage value of those discounts as they existed in 1998.[58] The percentage value of the discounts was much higher then because the cents-per-kWh (or per-therm) value of the discount was locked into place as of 1998, but the total cost of electricity and gas has of course risen significantly since then.

The DPU recognized that Massachusetts utilities may not achieve the 1998 discount levels solely by reducing the distribution portion of the bill. In such instances, the companies were directed to reduce the distribution portion of the bill to zero and to develop recommendations, to be filed by December 1, 2008, on how other portions of the bill could be reduced to achieve the 1998 discount level.[59]

The DPU finally ordered Massachusetts utilities to consider the adoption of a "tiered discount," under which

50 Energy Division Report on Program Year 2005 California Alternate Rates for Energy (CARE) and Low-Income Energy Efficiency (LIEE) Programs of the Small and Multi-Jurisdictional Utilities app. A, at 23, 24 (Cal. Pub. Utils. Comm'n Apr. 29, 2005).

51 *See, e.g.*, 42 U.S.C. § 1396a(a)(7)(A); 42 C.F.R. §§ 431.300–431.302.

52 Order Instituting Rulemaking on the Commission's Proposed Policies and Programs Governing Post-2003 Low-Income Assistance Programs at 48, No. D.05-04-052 (Cal. Pub. Utils. Comm'n Apr. 21, 2005).

53 *Id.*

54 Order Approving Utility Budgets for Low Income Energy Efficiency Programs and California Alternative Rate for Energy at 57, NO. D.06-12-038 (Cal. Pub. Utils. Comm'n Dec. 15, 2006).

55 *Id.* at 50.

56 *Id.* at 52.

57 *Id.* at 9.

58 *In re* Investigation into Expanding Low-Income Customer Prots. & Assistance, Including Standards for Arrearage Management Programs, Discount Rate, Serv. Termination & Energy Efficiency Programs, Order Expanding Low-Income Consumer Prots. and Assistance, No. DPU-08-4 (Mass. Dep't of Pub. Utils. Sept. 15, 2008).

59 *Id*, at 36, 37.

households with lower incomes would receive higher discount levels.[60] The DPU order was issued to implement a specific statutory directive.

Also responding to escalating energy prices, the Massachusetts legislature in late 2005 passed a bill that, among other things, permanently raised eligibility levels for the discounts from 175% of federal poverty guidelines to 200%, which is the same as that for the state LIHEAP program. The Massachusetts DPU also recently expanded eligibility for LIHEAP to households at 60% of the median federal poverty level, or households receiving benefits (for example, LIHEAP, TAFDC, EAEDC, food stamps, Medicaid, Supplemental Security Income, Veterans Benefits, public/subsidized housing) administered through the state's Department of Transitional Assistance.[61]

In Montana, a pre-restructuring discount from the largest utility, Northwestern Energy (formerly Montana Power), is now funded through a universal systems benefits charge (SBC). It provides a 15% discount to households qualifying for LIHEAP on their electric and gas bills, and the discount has been periodically raised to 25% during winter months.

Texas's electric restructuring law created a low-income discount rate.[62] From January 2002 through August 2005, low-income customers in areas of retail electric competition were eligible for the discount (called LITE-UP Texas), which ranged from 10% to 17% and averaged about $10 per month. It was funded through a system benefits charge paid by most electric customers. Customers automatically qualified if they received certain benefits from programs such as Food Stamps, Medicaid or Low-Income Medicare, or TANF or if their income was at or below 125% of federal poverty level. At its peak, the discount program enrolled around 800,000 customers.

The Texas discount, however, soon became a target for legislative raids. In late 2003, faced with a budget deficit, the legislature redirected about $183 million from the system benefits charge to the state's general fund. In May 2005, the state legislature shifted all money for the discount to the state general fund to help balance the state budget. Customers were notified that their electric bill discounts under LITE-UP Texas would end as of August 31, 2005. In June 2007, reacting to escalating electric rates, the Texas legislature appropriated $30 million from the SBC for a summer 2007 discount of about 12% and $170 million for a summer discount during the next two years. In 2011, the LITE-UP Texas summer discount was renewed for households at or below 125% of the federal poverty guidelines, for Medicaid or food stamp recipients, and for others with a qualifying income per individuals/household ratio.[63]

7.2.2.3 The Tiered Discount Program

7.2.2.3.1 Overview

One alternative to the straight discount program is the provision of "tiered" discounts. A tiered discount program differs from the "straight" discount in that the level of discount offered a customer depends upon the customer's income or poverty level. Tiered discounts are designed to reduce, on average, a discount recipient's home energy bill to an affordable percentage of income, assuming that the customer uses energy at an average level of consumption.

The discount is "tiered" because, as incomes decrease, it takes a deeper discount to deliver a benefit equal to the difference between an affordable bill and the average bill.[64] To the extent that a household consumes more or less than average, the household will bear a burden either higher or lower (respectively) than the affordable burden. So long as a customer has annual expenditures that are equal to the company's residential average, application of a tiered discount will reduce that customer's annual electricity or natural gas bill to the burden determined to be affordable.

7.2.2.3.2 The Indiana tiered discount program

Two major Indiana natural gas utilities have low-income tiered discount programs. The programs reach tens of thousands of low-income Indiana residents each year, distributing millions of dollars of benefits. The Indiana utilities grounded their low-income programs in response to the flexible regulation afforded the Indiana Utility Regulatory Commission (IURC) by statute.[65] The flexible regulation allowed under this Indiana statute permits the Indiana commission to set aside traditional regulation for all or part of a utility's rates or services.

In response to the statute allowing utilities to propose alternative regulatory plans, the Indiana utilities (Citizens Gas & Coke Utility, Vectren Energy) submitted proposals for a low-income rate affordability programs, called a "universal service program." The Citizens/Vectren program design offers income-eligible customers a discount off the natural gas bill they would otherwise receive from the

60 *Id.*

61 *See* www.mass.gov/?pageID=eoeeahomepage&L=1&L0=Home&sid=Eoeea (click on the "Energy, Utilities & Clean Technologies" link found on the home webpage; then click on the links found on subsequent webpages in the following order: "Electric Power"; "Customer Rights and Information"; "Consumer Assistance"; "Help With Your Winter Bill"; "Am I eligible for a discount rate?").

62 Public Utility Regulatory Act, Tex. Util. Code Ann. § 39.903 (West).

63 *See* www.puc.state.tx.us/consumer/lowincome/Assistance.aspx.

64 The more levels of discount that exist—that is, the more "tiers" that exist—the more highly targeted the discount will be. However, the more tiers there are, the more complex the program becomes and the more difficult to set up and administer. Regulators need to determine, by policy, how many tiers they wish in their tiered discount program.

65 Ind. Code §§ 8-1-2.5-1–.5-12.

respective companies. Both companies divide their low-income customer population into three tiers. Customers are placed in each tier based on the "State Benefit Matrix" used in the distribution of federal fuel assistance through the federal Low Income Home Energy Assistance Program (LIHEAP). Low-income customers must participate in LIHEAP in order to receive the utility discounts. Enrollment in LIHEAP automatically places the customer in the respective utility discount program.

Citizens provides a discount of either 10%, 18%, or 25%; Vectren provides a discount of 15%, 26%, or 32%, applied to their residential gas service bill. When combined with LIHEAP benefits, the combined benefit of the discount tiers and LIHEAP will represent an approximate reduction of 27%, 40%, or 50% in the overall heating costs for Citizens eligible low-income customers. Vectren's low-income customers will experience a reduction in cost of approximately 35%, 50%, or 60%. The highest benefits go to the households with the lowest income. The discount tiers are designed to approximate an affordable home energy burden under average incomes and usage levels.

The Indiana utilities proposed their respective low-income programs pursuant to the Indiana statute allowing an Indiana energy utility to submit a plan to the state utility commission[66] seeking state regulatory approval of a plan for alternative regulation.[67] In setting forth the framework for flexible regulation, the Indiana legislature declared that "the provision of safe, adequate, efficient and economical retail energy services is a continuing goal of the commission in the exercise of its jurisdiction."[68] Moreover, the Indiana legislature stated, "the public interest requires the commission to be authorized to issue orders and to formulate and adopt rules and policies . . . giving due regard to the interest of consumers and the public, and to the continued availability of safe, adequate, efficient, and economical energy service."[69]

According to the Indiana courts, the state Alternative Utility Regulation (AUR) Act was intended to expand,[70] not restrict, the authority that the state utility commission could exercise under its traditional regulatory authority.[71] The statute allows the state commission to issue regulatory decisions, which would not have been possible for the commission to do under the traditional regulatory statute.[72]

When an Indiana utility requests approval of its election to operate under a plan of alternative regulation, the state utility commission must commence a proceeding to determine whether to approve the utility election. The issue in this proceeding is whether the commission should "decline to exercise, in whole or in part, its jurisdiction over either the energy utility or the retail energy service of the energy utility, or both." In deciding that question, the commission is required to consider four factors, including in relevant part:

- Whether . . . operating conditions . . .render the exercise, in whole or part, of jurisdiction by the commission unnecessary or wasteful;
- Whether the commission's declining to exercise, in whole or in part, its jurisdiction will be beneficial for the energy utility, the energy utility's customers, or the state;
- Whether the commission's declining to exercise, in whole or in part, its jurisdiction will promote energy utility efficiency; and
- Whether the exercise of commission jurisdiction inhibits an energy utility from competing with other providers of functionally similar energy services or equipment.[73]

Under the statute, when a utility elects to petition for an alternative regulatory plan, the state utility commission is explicitly authorized to "establish rates and charges that are in the public interest as determined by consideration of the [statutorily-prescribed] factors. . . ."[74] The Indiana supreme court held that the "public interest" under the alternative regulation statute "encompasses a wide range of considerations" and "is not confined to customer interests."[75] The commission is to consider far more than "just the cost effect to consumers."[76]

The Indiana utilities electing to proceed with an alternative regulatory plan for their low-income customers noted a variety of circumstances that justified their proposals under the statute. However, according to their petition, the plan was developed primarily "in recognition of the concerns over price volatility resulting from imbalances between gas supply and demand, as well as weather-related price spikes often occurring during the heating season, and the resulting increased financial needs of the [. . .] low-income customers."[77]

66 The Indiana statute provides that the statutory sections on alternative regulation "do not apply to an energy utility unless the energy utility voluntarily submits a verified petition to the commission stating the energy utility's election to become subject to such section or sections." *Id.* § 8-1-2.5-4. *See also Id.* § 8-1-2.5-8.

67 *Id.* § 8-1-2.5-4.

68 *Id.* § 8-1-2.5-1(1).

69 *Id.* § 8-1-2.5-1(6).

70 The court speaks of "supplementing" the existing commission regulatory authority.

71 United States Gypsum, Inc. v. Indiana Gas Co., 735 N.E.2d 790 (Ind. 2000).

72 *Id.* at 800.

73 Ind. Code § 8-1-2.5-5.

74 *Id.* § 8-1-2.5-6(a)(1).

75 United States Gypsum, Inc. v. Indiana Gas Co., 735 N.E.2d 790, 804 (Ind. 2000).

76 *Id.*

77 Verified Joint Petition of Indiana Gas Company, Inc., Southern Indiana Gas and Electric Company and the Board of Directors for Utilities of the Department of Public Utilities of the City of Indianapolis, as Successor Trustee of a Public Charitable Trust, d/b/a Citizens Gas & Coke Util., Pursuant to Ind. Code § 8-1-2.5, *et seq.*, for Approval of an Alternative Regulatory Plan

7.2.2.3.3 The New Hampshire tiered discount program

A second major tiered discount program in the United States involves the New Hampshire Electric Assistance Program (EAP). The New Hampshire EAP did not begin as a tiered discount program. In 1996, the New Hampshire state legislature directed state regulators to adopt an electric affordability program intended to "enable residential customers with low incomes to manage and afford essential electricity requirements."[78] The Legislature directed the state Public Utilities Commission (PUC) to design low-income programs "in a manner that targets assistance and has high operating efficiency, so as to maximize the benefits that go to the intended beneficiaries of the low income program."[79] In response, the PUC's plan, called the Final Plan on Restructuring New Hampshire's Electric Utility Industry, authorized the development of a low-income assistance program that was to address three goals: "first, to bring bills into the range of affordability; second, to encourage conservation and the use of energy efficiency mechanisms to make electric bills manageable; and third, to make the most effective use of limited funding."[80]

In August 1998, a "Low-Income Working Group" operating under the auspices of the state PUC submitted its report, Electric Assistance Program Policy Recommendations, to the commission for a statewide percentage-of-income program. In Order 23,573, dated November 1, 2000, the PUC approved the policy recommendations for the EAP. The order established that the EAP was to be a fixed-credit payment program customized to each participant to bring the low-income customer's electric bill into the range of affordability (either 4% of annual income for general-use customers or 6% for space-heat customers). The EAP was selected because the PUC determined that it makes "the most effective use of limited dollars by targeting the most amount of assistance to those consumers with the least ability to pay."[81]

The program was modified to its current tiered discount structure in 2002.[82] In directing the change to the tiered discount program, the New Hampshire PUC ordered that "the concepts of the original EAP should be mirrored in any [tiered discount program] so that the tiers are structured to provide qualified low-income customers with a monthly payment equal to 4% or 6% of the average income within the tier, depending on whether the customer is an electric baseload or space heating customer."[83]

Ultimately, the New Hampshire PUC found that both the original percentage-of-income program that the PUC had adopted for EAP and the tiered discount program that it was considering targeted assistance to low-income customers, and that the percentage-of-income program "target[s] benefits more precisely than the [tiered discount program] does." However, "the targeting of assistance is not the only criterion that we must consider when designing a low-income program. High operating efficiency must also be considered."[84] The PUC continued: "the basic decision facing us is whether customers will benefit more if we adopt a program that has higher estimated administrative costs but more finely targets benefits or if we adopt a program with lower estimated administrative costs that does not as finely target benefits."[85]

Noting that the tiered discount program "is designed to reduce the bill to 4% or 6% of income, assuming that the household consumes at the average level of consumption," the PUC decided that, "on the record before us, the [tiered discount program] strikes the best balance between cost efficiency and program efficiency."[86]

7.2.2.4 Consumption-Based Discounts

A third alternative to providing low-income rate discounts involves programs that operate on a consumption-based matrix. With such programs, the percentage discount varies depending on the level of usage.

The rationale behind basing the discount on consumption is typically to prevent unnecessary "overuse" by the customer. The theory here is that customers are more inclined to conserve if they know that they will get a smaller discount on the second kWh bracket and thus end up paying more for the excess units of energy consumed. For example, most Arizona utilities have a graduated discount on the consumption rate. For limited income customers, Arizona Public Service offers discounts of 40% for consumption falling between 0–400 kilowatt hours (kWh), 26% for 401–800 kWh, and 14% for 801–1200 kWh and a credit of $13 for 1201 kWh and higher.[87]

The PECO Energy Company Customer Assistance Program (CAP) Rate Discount[88] blends elements of a consump-

Which Would Establish a Pilot Universal Service Program, Verified Joint Petition at 4, Case No. 42590 (Ind. Util. Regulatory Comm'n Mar. 4, 2004) (hereafter 2004 ARP Petition).

78 N.H. Rev. Stat. Ann. § 374-F:3 V(a).

79 *Id.* § 369-B:1 XIII.

80 Order No. 22,514, at 95 (N.H. Pub. Utils. Comm'n Feb. 28, 1997) (Final Plan).

81 Order 23,573, at 13, 14 (N.H. Pub. Utils. Comm'n Nov. 1, 2000) (EAP Order).

82 N.H. Pub. Utils. Comm'n, Order 23,980 (N.H. Pub. Utils. Comm'n May 30,2002) (Tiered Discount Order).

83 *Id.* at 2.

84 *Id.* at 43.

85 *Id.* at 44.

86 *Id.* at 47.

87 The Arizona Public Service website on Residential Service/ Low Income Plans is at www.aps.com/main/services/residential/ assistance/assist_6.html.

88 The acronym "CAP" refers to the Customer Assistance Program (CAP) adopted by most Pennsylvania utilities. The PECO "CAP Rate" is a variation on that broader genre of low-income programs.

tion-based discount with elements of a tiered discount program. Under the electric PECO CAP Rate program, PECO primarily serves residential customers in the city of Philadelphia; different discounts are provided to customers based on the ratio of the customer's household income to the federal poverty level. While the discounts are "tiered," unlike in the Indiana and New Hampshire programs, the tiers are not explicitly designed to reduce bills to an affordable percentage of income. PECO offers four tiers, with discounts ranging from 85% for the lowest income tier to 25% for the highest income tier. These discounts are offered for the first 650 kWh of electric consumption and, for the two lowest income tiers during certain months of the year, a discount of 30% is offered for the next 100 kWh (up to 750 kWh).[89]

The Washington Gas Light Residential Essential Services Rate (ResRate) in Maryland is an example of a consumption-based discount offered on a seasonal basis. Washington Gas Light Company operates a natural gas rate affordability program in the state of Maryland.[90] Approved in 2004, the Residential Essential Services Rate (ResRate) program has since been twice extended, for one year in October 2005[91] and again for two more years in September 2006.[92]

The ResRate program provides a credit of 17.7¢ per therm of usage (up to a maximum level of therms/credits specified for each month) for a total maximum credit of $135 per heating season. To be eligible for the credit, customers must be eligible for federal fuel assistance and be current on their bill. Other firm service customers pay for the program.

In recommending approval of the continuation of the ResRate program in August 2006, the staff of the Maryland Public Service Commission (PSC) noted the program's impact on reducing arrearages.[93] In recommending approval, the PSC staff noted:

> Company data for the 2005–2006 heating season as compared to the 2004–2005 heating season indicated that commodity costs associated with gas have increased between 42 and 65%. Although this is a substantial increase in costs to all firm service customers, the number of RES customers in arrearage decreased by 29% or 281 customers. The Company believes that this further illustrates the effectiveness of the program.
>
> * * *
>
> Staff has had the opportunity to thoroughly review this filing and discuss all components of this filing with Washington Gas. Staff noticed that the average arrearage for RES eligible customers increased by over $400, and the total number of RES customers in arrearages decreased significantly. There is a correlation between an increase in customer arrearage and an increase in commodity gas prices. The decrease in number of RES program participants in arrearage shows that the program is effective and is actually reaching its goals of keeping low-income customers on service and promoting positive payment patterns which in turn trickles to other firm customers by lowering collection costs and other costs associated with charge-offs and slow-payment patterns.[94]

The company continues to file annual reports with the Maryland PSC documenting the impacts of the ResRate program.[95]

7.2.2.5 Customer Charge Waiver

The customer charge is the flat or constant charge applied to each residential bill to cover costs that are fixed, such as billing and meter reading. Customer charge-waiver programs can be easy to implement and maintain when eligibility is based on participation in other benefit programs and the utility accepts verification of eligibility from the state agency that runs the benefit program. In such a case, the utility need not independently verify an applicant's income. The benefit for low-income customers from these waiver programs is a lower customer bill.

In Alabama, the major electric utility and two natural gas utilities waive the monthly customer service charge (around $8.00) for customers on supplemental security income, Medicaid, or TANF.[96] These utilities have been providing the customer service charge waiver since 1991 and recover

89 PECO Energy, Three Year Universal Service Plan, No. M-00061945 (Pa. Pub. Util. Comm'n 2008) (submitted to Pennsylvania Public Utility Commission).

90 After the program disapproval discussed further below, the Washington Gas Light filed a proposal (Mail Log No. 91662) to initiate a pilot ResRate program (submitted Feb. 26, 2004). That proposal was adopted without discussion by the commission.

91 Letter Order, ML No. 98963 (Md. Pub. Serv. Comm'n Oct. 19, 2005), *available at* http://webapp.psc.state.md.us/intranet/maillog/maillogitems.cfm (enter mail log number in appropriate space) (approving extension of ResRate through 2005–2006 heating season and directing company to file report with the Commission by June 30, 2006).

92 Letter Order, ML No. 102219 (Md. Pub. Serv. Comm'n Sept. 6, 2006), *available at* http://webapp.psc.state.md.us/intranet/maillog/maillogitems.cfm (enter mail log number in appropriate space) (extending ResRate for two years and directing company to continue providing annual reports).

93 *Id.*

94 *Id.* at 2, 3.

95 *See, e.g.*, 2006 ResRate Annual Report, ML No. 102219 (Md. Pub. Serv. Comm'n June 30, 2006); 2005 ResRate Annual Report, ML No. 98693 (Md. Pub. Serv. Comm'n Sept. 29, 2005).

96 National Ctr. for Appropriate Tech., LIHEAP Clearinghouse, 2006 State-by-State Supplements to Energy Assistance and Energy Efficiency (2006), *at* www.liheap.ncat.org/Supplements/2006/alud.htm. *See also* www.alagasco.com/My-Account/Assistance-Programs/Bill-Assistance-Progrmas-72.html (Alagasco Bill Assistance Programs website).

the cost through their residential ratepayers (estimated to be between 4¢ to 6¢ a month per customer).[97]

In 1987, the Georgia Public Service Commission mandated that major gas and electric utilities waive their monthly service charge for customers age 65 or over who earn less than $10,000 per year. Since then, the Georgia PSC has made several increases to the income limit and the amount of the service charge waiver. Based on changes made during 2005 and early 2006, the income limit has gone from $12,000 to $14,355 and the waivers from $10.50 to $14 per month. Other utilities have smaller discounts. At least 55,000 seniors receive the electric discount yearly, and approximately 35,000 receive the gas discount.

7.2.3 Percentage of Income Payment Plans

7.2.3.1 Overview

One type of program that specifically addresses the actual burden of energy costs on low-income households is the Percentage of Income Payment Plan (PIPP).[98] The basic premise of a PIPP is to have the low-income household pay a pre-determined "affordable" percentage of its monthly income towards its bill. The remainder of the bill is then covered by other energy assistance such as LIHEAP funds, through dollars generated from other utility customer rates or, quite commonly, through a combination of both.

PIPPs are particularly feasible if the utility is seeking to reduce customer arrearages, shut-offs, and reconnections, the majority of which have historically been problems for low-income customers. The costs of terminating energy service, repeated billing for late payments/arrearages, and consequent re-establishment of service in customer homes can be quite costly to a utility and can be avoided through implementing a PIPP to aid those needy customers in paying their bills to avoid these costs of service.

The following discussion sets forth brief descriptions of the major types of PIPPs operating throughout the country.

7.2.3.2 Straight PIPP

7.2.3.2.1 Overview

The straight PIPP identifies an affordable percentage of income for the customer to contribute towards energy costs. The program then looks at household income and calculates the affordable percentage of this income that the customer will be able to pay. For example, if the affordable percentage of income is 5%, and household income is $12,000 annually, the household would be required to pay $600 a year, or $50 monthly. If the household's actual energy bill is $900 annually, the difference of $300 would be provided through LIHEAP and /or other energy assistance funds. A household with the same energy bill of $900, but with a higher income of $15,000 (again, still considered "low income"), would pay $750 annually, and energy assistance funds would pay the remaining $150.

Through this joint household/energy assistance payment process, benefits are distributed so that, if the customer payments are kept at an affordable level, a household's entire energy bill is paid each month, even though the household's payment is set at a percentage of income that may not cover the entire current bill.

7.2.3.2.2 The Ohio PIPP

The Ohio Public Utilities Commission initiated the first straight PIPP in the United States. The Ohio PIPP was developed by the Public Utility Commission of Ohio (PUCO). There were two distinct programs, one for natural gas and one for electricity. The electric program is now under the administration of the Ohio Department of Development (ODOD). Both programs operated under the framework established by the PUCO prior to the transfer to ODOD. However, statutes granted ODOD the authority to redesign the electric program through the regulatory process.[99]

Under PUCO regulations, in addition to regulations of ODOD,[100] eligibility for the Ohio PIPP extends to households with incomes at or below 150% of the federal poverty level.[101] To remain in the program, participating customers must re-verify their income at least once every twelve months.[102]

The incorporation of the Ohio electric PIPP into statute and regulation culminated a nearly two-decade-long initiative to address the problems of low-income Ohio residents who could not afford to pay their home energy bills. The Public Utility Commission of Ohio created the Ohio PIPP in 1983 in response to an emergency arising from the inability of low-income Ohio residents to maintain their home energy service.[103] The PUCO found that the disconnection of utility

97 National Ctr. for Appropriate Tech., LIHEAP Clearinghouse, 2006 State-by-State Supplements to Energy Assistance and Energy Efficiency (2006), *at* www.liheap.ncat.org/Supplements/2006/alud.htm.

98 For more information see NCLC's Models of Low-Income Rates (1991) and Percentage of Income Payment Plans As an Alternative Distribution of LIHEAP Benefits: Good Business, Good Government, Good Social Policy from the Energy and the Poor (1991) series.

99 Ohio Rev. Code Ann. § 4928.53(B)(3) (West).

100 Ohio Admin. Code 122:5-3-02(A).

101 Ohio Admin. Code 122:12-5-3-02 (electric PIPP income eligibility), 4901:1-18-12(B)(6) (gas PIPP income eligibility).

102 Ohio Admin. Code 122:12-5-3-03(C) (electric PIPP re-verification required), 4901:1-18-12(D)(1) (gas PIPP re-verification required).

103 *In re* Investigation into Long-Term Solutions Concerning Disconnection of Gas & Elec. Serv. in Winter (Phase I) Emergen-

service for nonpayment by those who are financially unable to pay constituted an "emergency" as described by Ohio statute.[104]

The Ohio PIPP, as initially conceived by the PUCO, did not represent a discounted rate for low-income customers. Instead, the PIPP was designed to enable low-income customers to retain their utility service by entering into an agreement pursuant to which the customer would make a utility bill payment equal to a prescribed percentage of income. A customer entering into such agreements, however, would not be relieved of paying bills in excess of the percentage of income. Rather, the customer would continue to be liable for those arrears. Those accrued arrears would be subject to repayment by the customer when he or she leaves the PIPP.

In its 1983 decision, the PUCO found that there were both legal and "practical" reasons to adopt the proposed PIPP. According to PUCO, no legal impediment existed to the adoption of PIPP:

> Contrary to the arguments of those who oppose the percentage of income payment plan, the plan adopted by the Commission . . . does not constitute income redistribution, and is reasonable and lawful. This plan does not constitute income redistribution because those customers who qualify for the plan are still liable for any arrearages on their bills. There is no debt forgiveness. The Commission is just foreclosing one method by which a utility may exercise its rights to collect for the debt. The utility still has available to it all of its other remedies at law. Because the customer is still liable for his/her arrearages, the Commission's percentage of income payment plan does not constitute free service or a rebate as charged by opponents to the plan. The plan is not confiscatory. After the plan is in effect the utility will be able, as it has always been able, to recoup its bad debts through a rate case as provided in Chapter 4909 Revised Code. Nor does the plan adopted by the Commission unlawfully discriminate. All residential consumers similarly situated can take advantage of this plan. The policy of this Commission to prevent those without the present ability to pay their utility bills from freezing is a valid state purpose and is the basis upon which the Commission has established this plan. We believe it to be a rational basis.[105]

The PUCO proceeding that gave rise to Ohio's PIPP in 1983 did not exclusively concern establishment of the PIPP. Instead, the proceeding considered a broad range of issues relating to payment plans, deposits, and voluntary fuel check-offs as a means to generate energy assistance funding. The proceeding was initiated by Columbia Gas, who filed a proposal to allow for the reconnection of service to customers upon payment by those disconnected customers of one-half of the outstanding arrears and entry into an agreement through which the remaining half would be paid in equal monthly installments. PUCO expanded the proceeding first to include an investigation into the reconnection procedures of all natural gas utilities and, ultimately, into the reconnection procedures of all electric utilities as well.

Early in the proceeding, the PUCO declared that an "emergency" existed because of the number of residential gas and/or electric customers who were unable to obtain service for the winter heating season because of disconnection for nonpayment attributable to economic recession, increases in the cost of gas and electric service, and a decrease in the level of governmental assistance. Based on this emergency, the PUCO prohibited the disconnection of gas or electric service during the ensuing winter season and ordered the reconnection of service to customers who paid either one-third of their outstanding balance or $200, whichever was less. This is commonly referred to as the Winter Reconnect Order. This order is still issued annually as an "emergency" measure, though the payment requirement has been changed to $175, with customers using the rule required to enroll in a payment plan; PIPP is one of the optional payment plans.[106] Ohio sets the emergency benefit at $175 under the Low Income Home Energy Assistance Program. PUCO staff indicate that roughly 20% of those customers using the Winter Reconnect Order qualify for low-income assistance programs. The remainder have incomes over 175% of the federal poverty line.

Consideration of the PIPP arose out of *utility* objections to the PUCO's "failure to take into consideration a customer's ability to pay before imposing the moratorium. . . ." At least in partial response to that objection, the PUCO docketed an investigation into "long-term solutions to the problems arising from the winter emergency situations."

The PUCO rejected arguments by Ohio's utilities that proposals such as the PIPP were not "long-term solutions" to the general problem of customers' inability to pay in winter. The PUCO noted that "the utility position in this proceeding is that the only long-term solution to the problem is economic assistance and that all other proposals, falling short of being long-term solutions, are outside of the scope of this proceeding."

In dismissing this argument, the PUCO agreed that "the legislature needs to adequately fund energy assistance and weatherization and conservation programs for low income

---

cies, No. 83-303-GE-COI (Ohio Pub. Utils. Comm'n Nov. 23, 1983).

104 Ohio Rev. Code Ann. § 4909.16 (West).

105 Opinion and Order at 14, *In re* Investigation into Long-Term Solutions Concerning Disconnection of Gas & Elec. Serv. in Winter (Phase I) Emergencies, No. 83-303-GE-COI (Ohio Pub. Utils. Comm'n Nov. 23, 1983).

106 Investigation into Disconnection of Gas & Elec. Serv. in Winter Emergencies, Entry, No. 06-1075-GE-UNC (Ohio Pub. Utils. Comm'n Sept. 6, 2006).

consumers. That does not mean that such aid is the *only* ingredient of a comprehensive solution to the problem, only that it is a necessary ingredient." (emphasis added) Moreover, the PUC said it sought to "assure itself that its rules are not *barriers* to those who need utility service during the winter months." (emphasis added)

Finally, the PUCO found that the proposed Ohio PIPP best accomplished the goals the commission sought relative to other available alternatives. The goal, PUCO noted, involves protection of the interests of two disparate groups of ratepayers:

> We are not willing to stand by while others, too poor to pay for utility service during the winter, freeze. At the same time, we are ever mindful of protecting the vast majority of customers of utilities under our jurisdiction who pay their bills in full from responsibility for greatly increasing uncollectibles.

The proposed PIPP, according to the PUCO, best served both of those goals given available alternatives:

> We have in this proceeding looked at such alternatives to the percentage of income plan as maintaining the status quo, extending payment plans from six months to twelve or more months, and having another moratorium. All things considered, the percentage of income plan adopted by the Commission today will do the most to assist those in need to maintain utility service while protecting the companies' remaining rate payers.

In sum, the PUCO found that "from our perspective, the true long-term solution to the problem is three-fold: adequate tax funded energy assistance programs, adequate tax funded weatherization and conservation programs, and adequate commission rules. Of those, only the first, energy assistance, is totally outside of this PUCO's jurisdiction."

The PUCO's decision to adopt the PIPP for Ohio was affirmed by the Ohio Supreme Court, even though the court disapproved the original cost-recovery mechanism. The supreme court found that the PUCO's approval of the recovery of electric and natural gas PIPP costs through an "electric fuel component" (EFC) and "gas cost recovery" (GCR) rider respectively was unlawful.[107] These two rate rider mechanisms, the court said, were statutorily limited to recovery of fuel costs.

Despite this disapproval of the PIPP cost recovery,[108] the supreme court approved the lawfulness of the underlying PIPP decision. The court noted:

> Pursuant to its emergency powers under R.C. 4909.16, the PUCO created the PIP plan as a response to growing concern "about the number of residential gas . . . [and] electric customers unable to obtain service as a result of disconnection for nonpayment of bills because of the economic recession, increases in the cost of gas and electric service, and a decrease in the level of governmental assistance. . . ." [I]t is the opinion of this court that it is clearly within the PUCO's emergency powers under R.C. 4909.16 to fashion such relief as that provided by the PIP plan and we find the plan of the commission to be manifestly fair and reasonable as a solution to the crisis.[109]

The court relied on the broad grant of authority to PUCO under PUCO's emergency powers statutory provision. The court noted that it previously had "recognized that the PUCO's discretionary emergency powers include authority to impair contractual provisions as needed to alleviate an emergency, if it bears a real and substantial relation to the health, safety, morals or general welfare of the public, and if it is not unreasonable or arbitrary."[110]

In sum, while the Ohio electric PIPP is embedded in statute, its original development occurred under the general regulatory authority of the Ohio state utility commission. In Ohio, the commission has authority to take action under circumstances that it deems to be an "emergency." Having declared that emergency, the commission was authorized to develop payment plans responding to that emergency. As originally adopted, the Ohio PIPP was simply one type of payment plan. The commission stated that there is no debt forgiveness and, thus, no income distribution. Electric utilities were banned from disconnecting service to customers who made their percentage-of-income payment. "The Commission is just foreclosing one method by which a utility may exercise its rights to collect the debt. The utility still has available to it all of its other remedies at law." Moreover, since customers continued to remain responsible for their entire bill, there was no free service or rebate.

Ultimately, the Ohio PIPP was embedded into statute and a statutory funding mechanism was created. Program funding was obtained through all retail electric distribution service rates. Administration of the funding was maintained in the Public Utility Commission of Ohio, while program administration was placed with the Ohio Department of Development (ODOD). Natural gas PIPP programs remain under PUCO regulation.

---

107 Montgomery County Bd. of Comm'rs v. Public Util. Comm'n of Ohio, 503 N.E.2d 167, 171 (Ohio 1986).

108 The court informed the PUCO that, "while we cannot condone the recovery of arrearages through the EFC rate in light of the specific statutory language of R.C. 4905.01 and 4909.191, we do not express the opinion that the PUCO would be precluded from fashioning an alternative accelerated recovery mechanism which is not contrary to statute, including recovery of arrearages on a more current basis rather than only after a twelve-month delinquency." *Id.* at n.4.

The PUCO quickly approved an alternative cost recovery mechanism. Income Payment Plan Arrearages, No. 87-244-GE-UNC (Ohio Pub. Utils. Comm'n 1987).

109 Montgomery County Bd. of Comm'rs v. Public Util. Comm'n of Ohio, 503 N.E.2d 170 (Ohio 1986) (internal footnotes omitted).

110 *Id.* at 172.

More than twenty years after PIPP was implemented in Ohio, the program was changed, and PIPP Plus was introduced. Eligible customers are those with household incomes at or below 150% of the federal poverty level and who apply for all energy assistance and weatherization programs for which they are eligible.[111] Under PIPP Plus, gas heating customers pay 6% and 5% of their monthly household income to their gas company and electric company, respectively. Electric heating customers pay 10% of their monthly household income to their electric company.[112] So long as a PIPP customer is current on his or her PIPP payments, the customer may not be disconnected based on arrearages while on the PIPP program[113] Additionally, Ohio offers Graduate PIPP Plus, an arrearage management and credit program for PIPP Plus customers with arrearages who are in good standing and who leave PIPP Plus due to income ineligibility or other reason.[114]

The PUCO rules distinguish between two seasons of the year in its PIPP regulations: the heating season and the non-heating season. The regulations are presented in terms of restrictions on the disconnection of service for nonpayment. They provide that "a PIPP customer who is current on his/her PIPP payments shall not be disconnected, refused reconnection, or denied a transfer of service to a new address, based solely on outstanding arrearages accrued while in the PIPP program" so long as specified payments are made by the customer.[115]

7.2.3.2.3 *The Pennsylvania Customer Assistance Program (CAP)*

Other examples of straight PIPPs can be found in Pennsylvania. The rate affordability programs operated by Pennsylvania natural gas and electric utilities for their low-income customers began nearly twenty years ago with a small pilot project by Columbia Gas Company.[116] Since that time, the universal service concept has expanded for Pennsylvania's energy utilities such that the companies now devote more than $240 million each year to supporting their low-income customers.[117] While the genesis of the Pennsylvania universal service programs can be found in the Pennsylvania Public Utility Commission's (PUC) generic authority over the operations of energy utilities, the preservation of those programs has since been written into statute.

Two utilities in Pennsylvania pioneered the use of affordable rates as a means to address the payment troubles experienced by low-income customers. Columbia Gas Company responded with a willingness to pursue a program first proposed by the state Office of Consumer Advocate. Equitable Gas Company also proposed an income-based rate for its low-income customer population.

The Pennsylvania Office of Consumer Advocate (OCA) proposed that Columbia Gas Company adopt an "Energy Assurance Program" (EAP) as part of Columbia's 1990 rate case. According to the OCA, the issue was one of collection efficiency. "The issue in this proceeding," OCA said, "is not to devise a social response to the broad inability to pay problems of low-income households. The issue is one of what is the most cost-effective means of collection. It is the same issue as whether a utility should pursue a new central station capacity, cogeneration or conservation. . . . The requirement that utilities provide least-cost service should govern utility collection activities too."[118] The OCA also stated that "the issue is this: how can Columbia Gas most effectively and least expensively collect as much as possible from households [that] cannot afford to pay?"[119]

Columbia Gas did not completely oppose the OCA's proposal given its experience with the Ohio Percentage of Income Payment plan (PIPP). "Columbia reiterated its policy position that it is not philosophically opposed to percentage of income payment plans, provided that the plan fully recognizes the costs of such a program and provides for the timely and full recovery of such costs."[120]

The Pennsylvania PUC agreed. The PUC found that "it is incumbent upon us to initiate a pilot project to test empirically some of the claims made by [OCA] for an EAP. Hopefully, the results of the pilot will prove [OCA's] thesis that EAP will enable more customers to avoid termination and collection actions, while also reducing the uncollectible expense that can be anticipated if existing approaches remain unchanged."[121] The PUC then articulated its philosophy that would govern Pennsylvania's regulatory policy for the next two decades:

> We, in conjunction with utilities, and social service agencies, have all worked hard to devise ways to insure that low-income Pennsylvanians have utility services which really are necessities of life as the tragic fire deaths associated with the loss of utility service underlined. . . .

111 Ohio Admin. Code 122:5-3-02 (electric PIPP eligibility requirements), 4901:1-18-12 (gas PIPP eligibility requirements), *available at* www.development.ohio.gov/Community/ocs/pippplus (Ohio Pipp Plus website).

112 *See* www.development.ohio.gov/Community/ocs/pippplus (Ohio Pipp Plus website).

113 Ohio Admin. Code 4901:1-18-15(A).

114 *Id.*

115 Ohio Admin. Code 4901:1-18-15(A).

116 Final Order at 150–160, Pennsylvania Pub. Util. Comm'n v. Columbia Gas of Pa., No. R-891468 (Sept. 19, 1990).

117 Pennsylvania Pub. Utils. Comm'n, Bureau of Consumer Serv., 2005 Report on Universal Service Programs and Collections Performance of the Pennsylvania Electric Distribution Companies and Natural Gas Distribution Companies 48, 49 (2005) (electric CAP delivered benefits of $104 million in 2005; natural gas CAP delivered benefits of $138 million in 2005).

118 Ohio v. Gilmore, 503 N.E.2d 152 (Ohio 1986).

119 *Id.* at 153.

120 *Id.* at 157.

121 *Id.* at 158.

> However, for the poorest households with income considerably below the poverty line, existing initiatives do not enable these customers to pay their bills in full and to keep their service. . . . Consequently, to address realistically these customers' problems and to stop repeating a wasteful cycle of consecutive, unrealistic payment agreements that cannot be kept, despite the best of intentions, followed by service termination, then restoration, and then more unrealistic agreements, we believe that new approaches like PECO's CAP program and the OCA's proposed EAP program should be tried.[122]

Based on this analysis, the Pennsylvania PUC directed Columbia Gas to begin a 1000-customer pilot EAP.

Shortly after directing Columbia Gas to implement a pilot low-income rate affordability program, the PUC further approved a proposal by Equitable Gas Company to pursue a similar program.[123] Unlike the Columbia Gas program, which had been proposed by the state Office of Consumer Advocate (and not opposed by Equitable Gas Company), the Equitable Gas program originated with the gas utility itself.[124] According to the company, the proposed program was

> [n]eeded to (1) remove these customers from the discouraging and expensive collection cycle, (2) motivate them to increase conservation, (3) increase their annual participation in available funding assistance programs, and (4) encourage consistent bill-payment efforts.[125]

The proposed Equitable Gas program would be available to customers with incomes at or below 150% of the federal poverty level. The program would require participants to not exceed their pre-program level of consumption, to apply annually for low-income energy assistance, and to pay at least 8% of their household income toward their gas service.[126]

The Equitable Gas program was, at first, disapproved by the hearing examiner who decided the Equitable Gas rate case. While the program was "an apparently well-intentioned attempt to assist those of Equitable's ratepayers who most need assistance in paying their bills," the hearing examiner "concluded that this Commission is without authority to approve a program such as the EAP." The hearing examiner reasoned that, if the commission "were to approve the subject [energy affordability] program, our action would be tantamount to authorizing a utility to collect money from one group of ratepayers and to use that money for another group of ratepayers for a reason completely unrelated to the ratemaking process (the subsidization of low-income individuals who are unable to pay their utility bills)."[127] The hearing examiner finally concluded that "neither judicial precedent nor the Public Utility Code discuss our statutory authority for the implementation of utility rates based solely on 'ability to pay.' "[128]

The Pennsylvania PUC, however, reversed the hearing examiner's disapproval of the proposed Equitable Gas low-income program. Noting that "we are aware that this Commission's main function in ratemaking is to assure that every rate made, demanded, or received by any public utility shall be just and reasonable," the PUC found that the Pennsylvania statute prohibits only *unreasonable* preferences or advantages to any person. The statute, the PUC said, prohibits any *unreasonable* difference as to rates between classes of service.[129] "The relevant question, therefore, is whether or not the funding of Equitable's proposed [energy affordability] program results in the 'unreasonable' rate discrimination prohibited by the Public Utility Code."[130]

Whether any particular classification or preference is reasonable is a question of fact, the PUC said. "A mere difference in rates does not violate" the Pennsylvania statute.[131] The PUC then found, on a number of bases, that "the record in this proceeding clearly demonstrates that any 'preference' that EAP would yield to program participants is reasonable, and further, the creation of EAP is in the best interest of all Equitable ratepayers, not just program participants."[132]

The PUC stated that Equitable Gas Company's "total costs of service will be less with implementation of [the program] than they would be in the program's absence." While the company currently collects approximately 7.5% of the household income of prospective EAP participants, the PUC found, the program requires a payment of 8% of income toward their gas bill, thus increasing revenues.[133] The requirement that each EAP participant apply for LIHEAP and designate Equitable Gas as the beneficiary will also ensure greater revenue collection, since only one-third of eligibility customers traditionally apply for LIHEAP. Third, the PUC said, the program cost is substantially less than the uncollectible expense associated with the program participants. Customers who are eligible for the Equitable Gas program and "who currently have payment arrangements either negotiated by BCS or the Company pay on average little more than 50 percent of the presubscribed amount." In sum, the commission concluded that

122 *Id.* at 159.

123 Final Order at 63–74, Pennsylvania Pub. Util. Comm'n v. Equitable Gas Co., No. R-901595 (Nov. 21, 1990).

124 Equitable Gas had been working with the state Bureau of Consumer Services (BCS), a bureau of the state utility commission, to develop an appropriate program design. *Id.* at 63.

125 *Id.* at 63.

126 *Id.* at 64.

127 *Id.* at 66.

128 *Id.*

129 *Id.* at 69 (emphasis in original).

130 *Id.* at 69.

131 *Id.* at 70.

132 *Id.* at 70.

133 *Id.* at 71.

> [t]his analysis suggests that the $1.8 million future test year [program] expenses should result in an overall reduction to the Company's cost of service, through its uncollectible expense and savings in credit and collection expenses.[134]

In sum, the PUC commended Equitable Gas "for taking the initiative to propose the [energy affordability] pilot. This program could make it one of the leaders among utilities in the uncollectible arena."[135]

Only two years after initiating the Columbia Gas pilot, the Pennsylvania PUC decided to expand the use of universal service programs to the state's other natural gas and energy utilities.[136] Consistent with its view of the function of such programs as expressed in the early Columbia Gas decision, the policy decision of the PUC was that low-income rate affordability programs were a necessary tool for utilities to use in combating the problem of nonpayment. Indeed, the decision to implement what would become known as Pennsylvania's Customer Assistance Programs (CAPs) arose out of the PUC's investigation into the control of uncollectible accounts.[137] Through that investigation, the Pennsylvania PUC's Bureau of Consumer Services developed recommendations for implementation of CAPs:

> CAPs provide alternatives to traditional collection methods for low-income, payment troubled customers. Generally, customers enrolled in a CAP agree to make monthly payments based on household family size and gross income. These regular monthly payments, which may be for an amount that is less than the current bill, are made in exchange for continued provision of utility service.[138]

The PUC went on to say that,

> [a]s a result of our investigation, the Commission believes that an appropriately designed and well implemented CAP, as an integrated part of a company's rate structure, is in the public interest. To date, few utilities have implemented CAPs. The purpose of this Policy Statement is to encourage expanded use of CAPs and to provide guidelines to be followed by utilities who voluntarily implement CAPs. These guidelines prescribe a model CAP which is designed to be a more cost effective approach for dealing with issues of customer inability to pay than are traditional collection methods.[139]

While the implementation of CAPs in 1992 was left to the discretion of the state's energy utilities, the PUC made clear that it believed "alternative programs must be supported as clearly being in the public interest":[140]

> [T]he commission will request that a utility which chooses to use an alternate program design, or chooses to continue using traditional collection practices and not implement a CAP, address in rate proceedings its overall level of arrearages, collection costs and write-off of bad debt. The utility will also be requested to address the question of whether implementation of a CAP in accordance with commission guidelines could produce net economic benefits to the utility and its ratepayers relative to the alternative program, or in the absence of a CAP.[141]

The original Pennsylvania CAPs were directed toward "low-income negative ability to pay customers."[142]

The Pennsylvania PUC revised its CAP Policy Statement in 1999, both in response to legislation providing for the restructuring of Pennsylvania's electric utility industry and in response to the experience with CAPs to date. In 1996, the Pennsylvania legislature had enacted a statute relating to the restructuring of the electric utility industry.[143] That statute contained three important universal service provisions:

- It provided that the state's electric utilities were to continue, at a minimum, the protections, policies, and services that now assist low-income customers to afford electric service;

---

134 *Id.* at 71.

135 *Id.* at 73.

136 The PUC directed that utilities adopt pilot projects. The PUC decision was based on the BCS recommendation that CAP pilots "should be large enough to provide some relief to the low-income, payment-troubled customer problem and at the same time small enough that changes can be made to the programs without incurring major costs." Final Report on the Investigation of Uncollectible Balances 115, No. I-900002 (Pa. Pub. Utils. Comm'n Feb. 1992).

The commission directed that pilot programs were to involve either 1000 customers or 2% of a company's residential customer base, whichever was greater.

137 *In re* Investigation into the Control of Uncollectible Accounts, No. I-900002 (Pa. Pub. Utils. Comm'n, initiated Oct. 11, 1990).

138 Policy Statement on Customer Assistance Programs (CAP) 2, No. M-00920345 (Pa. Pub. Utils. Comm'n July 2, 1992).

139 *Id.* at 2.

This PUC decision was supported by the BCS Final Report, which indicated that "[t]he Bureau's position is that ratepayers are already bearing significant costs attributable to the problems of payment troubled customers and uncollectible balances. Further, BCS believes that incorporating the following recommendations into utility operations will lead to a more rational and cost effective use of existing resources. Over time, proper implementation of the recommendations may result in a reduction of total utility costs." Final Report on the Investigation of Uncollectible Balances 120, No. I-900002 (Pa. Pub. Utils. Comm'n Feb. 1992).

140 *Id.* at 3.

141 *Id.* at 3.

142 *Id.* at Annex A, § 69.264.

A "negative ability to pay customer" was one whose "financial condition is such that expenses exceed income" as determined through application of factors prescribed by regulation. *Id.* § 69.262 (citing 52 Pa. Code § 56.97(b)).

143 66 Pa. Cons. Stat. §§ 2801–2812.

- It specifically defined "universal service and energy conservation policies" to include customer assistance programs (CAPs);[144] and
- It required the PUC to ensure that universal service and energy conservation policies, activities, and service would be "appropriately funded and available" in each electric utility service territory.[145]

As the Pennsylvania PUC found in promulgating new regulations to implement the electric restructuring act, "the [Public Utility] Code, as now amended by the Act, for the first time imposes a *mandate* for universal service and energy conservation policies, programs and protections that are 'appropriately funded and available in each electric distribution territory.' "[146] Accordingly, rather than merely implementing "pilot" programs, utilities should implement programs, the participation limit on which should

> [r]eflect a needs assessment, consideration of the estimated number of low-income households in the utility's service territory, the number of participants currently enrolled in the pilot CAP, participation rates for assistance programs, and the resources available to meet the needs of the targeted population.[147]

The PUC refused to adopt spending or participation guidelines for Pennsylvania's utilities, holding that to do so would be contrary to statute. "We note," the PUC said, "that neither the Act nor these guidelines specify any particular spending level for universal service and energy conservation as a whole. No inherent increase or decrease in spending is mandated, provided the total level of resources directed to universal service and energy conservation is 'appropriate' and the benefits are made 'available.' "[148]

In considering revisions to the CAP Policy Statement to conform it to policies articulated in response to the electric restructuring statute, the Pennsylvania PUC reported that it would be guided not simply by the statute but by the experience with CAPs that Pennsylvania utilities had had to date. The PUC reported that, at the time of the revision, twelve of the state's fifteen utilities had voluntarily implemented CAPs, with a participation of approximately 50,000 customers. In deciding to direct the state's utilities to adopt CAPs (or pre-approved CAP alternative designs), the PUC noted that the experience to date documented that "participants enrolled in a CAP increase the number of payments they make while maintaining the same level of energy usage."[149]

In addition to program operation details not discussed here, the Pennsylvania PUC made several substantive changes in the CAP program design in its 1999 revisions to the CAP Policy Statement. One of the primary program design changes was in the scope of the program. Rather than being directed toward "negative ability to pay customers," the PUC said that CAPs would henceforth be directed toward "payment troubled customers."[150] The PUC then defined "payment-troubled customer" as any low-income customer who has "failed to maintain one or more payment arrangements."[151] The PUC continued to say, however, that utilities should focus their outreach on *particular* payment-troubled customers.

> Eligibility criteria: The CAP applicant should meet the following criteria for eligibility: . . .(iii) The applicant is a low-income, payment-troubled customer. When determining if a CAP applicant is payment troubled, a utility should select one of the following four options to prioritize the enrollment of eligible payment-troubled customers: (a) a household whose housing and utility costs exceed 45% of the household's total income. Housing and utility costs are defined as rent or mortgage/taxes and gas, electric, water, oil, telephone, and sewage; (b) a household who has $100 or less disposable income after subtracting all household expenses from all household income; (c) a household who has an arrearage. The utility may define the amount of the arrearage; or (d) a household who has received a termination notice or who failed to maintain one payment arrangement.[152]

The PUC had previously made clear that its intent was to distinguish between making all payment-troubled customers (as defined by the PUC) *eligible* for CAP, while allowing utilities to target *outreach* to specific sub-groups of payment-troubled customers.[153]

Finally, the PUC changed the allowed response to non-payment of CAP bills. Under the original CAP Policy Statement, nonpaying CAP customers were removed from the rate affordability program and returned to the basic residential rate. According to the revised PUC policy, however, "the consequences for nonpayment should be loss of

144 *Id.* § 2803.

145 *Id.* § 2804(9).

146 *In re* Guidelines for Universal Serv. & Energy Conservation Programs, 178 Pub. Util. Rep. 4th 508 (Pa. Pub. Utils. Comm'n July 11, 1997) (No. M-00960890).

147 Final Report on the Investigation of Uncollectible Balances § 69.261, No. I-900002 (Pa. Pub. Utils. Comm'n Feb. 1992) (revised).

148 178 Pub. Util. Rep. 4th 512 (Pa. Pub. Utils. Comm'n July 11, 1997).

149 *In re* Revisions to the Customer Assistance Program Policy Statement Made Pursuant to 52 Pa. Code, ch. 69, at 2, No. M-00991232 (Pa. Pub. Utils. Comm'n Apr. 9, 1999).

150 Final Report on the Investigation of Uncollectible Balances § 69.264, No. I-900002 (Pa. Pub. Utils. Comm'n Feb. 1992) (revised).

151 *Id.* § 69.262 (revised).

152 *Id.* § 69.265(4)(iii) (revised).

153 178 Pub. Util. Rep. 4th 516 (Pa. Pub. Utils. Comm'n July 11, 1997).

service; therefore, we recommend that utilities return participants who do not make payments to the regular collection cycle. . . . The changes to this section will allow a utility to immediately start the termination process."[154]

One issue that the PUC did *not* address in its CAP Policy Statement was the size of a CAP as measured by numbers of participants or amount of expenditures. In promulgating regulations to implement the statutory universal service language of the restructuring statute, the PUC had considered proposals to impose both floors and ceilings on universal service expenditures. In refusing to impose specific funding levels, the PUC explained that funding should depend on each utility service territory. The statute was "clear," the PUC said, "that universal service and energy conservation programs are to be appropriately funded and available."[155] Each company's programs must be "fully examined," the commission continued, to determine whether that statutory mandate is being fulfilled. However, the PUC indicated that the pilot project stage of CAPs had come to an end:

> In order to meet our charge under the statute, it is necessary that the needs of the [electric distribution utilities] territory be assessed. Such a study of the community is necessary to ensure that programs are well directed to meet the greatest need in the community for affordable energy. The needs assessment should examine the market for and acceptance of universal service programming in the territory. Current CAP pilots serve a limited number of customers. Given the results of impacts evaluations already reviewed, we expected that [electric utilities] will choose to enhance their CAPs as a cost effective strategy for serving low-income customers.[156]

In its revised CAP Policy Statement, as well as the guidelines for Universal Service Programs promulgated in response to the electric restructuring statute, the Pennsylvania PUC allowed the state's electric and natural gas utilities considerable flexibility in defining the percentage of income that would be considered "affordable" under a CAP program design. The purpose of CAP, the PUC indicated, is directed toward the collection of utility bills, not exclusively to improving affordability. The PUC explained:

> As evaluations are completed, each utility should have a better idea about what is an affordable payment for their CAP customers and can make adjustments to their payment plans to reflect the evaluation findings. However . . . we reject the arguments to lower the payment ranges. . . . As utilities and the Commission have gained experience from the CAP pilots, it seems that some CAP participants' payments have been set too low and could be raised without negatively influencing affordability. The Commission does not believe it is appropriate for customers, as participants of CAP, to make payments that are significantly less than what they have historically been paying. The independent evaluation of Equitable Gas Company's Energy Assistance Program found that EAP participants could afford to pay 8% of their income for gas energy. The evaluation also recommended that EAP participants whose incomes were between 51% and 150% of the federal poverty guidelines could afford to pay 10% of their income for gas energy.[157]

The PUC then articulated its affordability policy: "Our goal in establishing payment ranges is to maximize customer payments, maintain affordable payments, and limit the CAP credits as much as possible."[158]

The most recent consideration of, and general revisions to, the policies governing the development and administration of Pennsylvania's CAP programs came in the PUC's 2006 decision regarding CAP funding levels and cost recovery mechanisms.[159] In this proceeding, the PUC had not undertaken a generic review of the design of CAPs overall but rather a more limited review of how to ensure that CAPs were "appropriately funded" under the Pennsylvania statutes. In addition, the PUC sought to develop policy to implement the statutory directive that utilities be allowed to "fully recover" their universal service costs (including CAP costs).

The PUC determined in 2006 that utility CAP programs in Pennsylvania could not have enrollment ceilings if they were to satisfy the statutory requirement that they be "available."[160] Participation rates, the PUC said, "will fluctuate based on economic conditions, weather and utility prices." In eliminating participation ceilings, however, the PUC warned that utilities must be ensured of full cost recovery. "The Commission may not enforce the availability requirement of the Acts without also recognizing the right of utilities to full cost recovery."[161]

---

154 *In re* Revisions to the Customer Assistance Program Policy Statement Made Pursuant to 52 Pa. Code, ch. 69, at 4, No. M-00991232 (Pa. Pub. Utils. Comm'n Apr. 9, 1999). *See also* Final Report on the Investigation of Uncollectible Balances § 69.265(7), No. I-900002 (Pa. Pub. Utils. Comm'n Feb. 1992) (revised).

155 178 Pub. Util. Rep. 4th 518 (Pa. Pub. Utils. Comm'n July 11, 1997).

156 *Id.*

157 *Id.* at 521.

158 *Id.* at 522.

"CAP credits" refer to the dollar difference between CAP bills at income-based rates and customer bills at full residential rates. Hence, if the full residential bill is $150 and the CAP bill is $80, the CAP credit would be $70 ($150 – $80 = $70).

159 Final Investigatory Order, *In re* Customer Assistance Programs: Funding Levels & Cost Recovery Mechanisms, No. M-00051923 (Oct. 19, 2006).

160 *Id.* at 6.

161 *Id.*

In sum, the development of the Pennsylvania CAP programs provides considerable insight into most of the major issues facing utility-funded percentage-of income programs at the state level. While preservation and expansion of the CAP programs was eventually written into statute as part of the restructuring of the electricity and natural gas industries, the Pennsylvania CAP programs were initiated by the state PUC without explicit statutory authorization. Instead, the PUC found that CAPs should be an "integrated part of a company's rate structure." The purpose of these programs, the PUC found, was not a social purpose. Rather, the CAPs represent "a more cost effective approach for dealing with issues of customer inability to pay than are traditional collection methods."

The focus of the Pennsylvania CAPs as a tool to respond to low-income payment troubles has continued throughout the years. CAPs were considered to be an *alternative* to a way of doing business that simply was not working. The objective of CAP was "to stop repeating a wasteful cycle of consecutive, unrealistic payment agreements that cannot be kept, despite the best of intentions, followed by service termination, then restoration, and then more unrealistic agreements. . . ."

Despite the focus on CAPs as a more effective, and more cost-effective, tool to use in addressing payment troubles, the Pennsylvania PUC adopted a broad perspective on when customers should be considered to be "payment troubled." Payment troubles were not simply to be measured in terms of the level (or presence) of arrears. While the definition incorporated the concept of breaching a payment agreement, the PUC went on to recognize that payment troubles, by definition, exist when total shelter costs overburden the customer; when disposable income was insufficient to cover basic needs; or when certain utility nonpayment characteristics (for example, arrears, defaulted payment plans) were evident.

The Pennsylvania PUC decided *not* to implement a uniform statewide administered program for its CAPs. Instead, each of the state's natural gas and electric utilities were allowed to implement programs designed specifically for their service territories. While companies were required to stay within basic "design guidelines" promulgated by the PUC, their burden—should they choose to deviate from the PUC-identified "model"—was to document that their proposal "could produce net economic benefits to the utility and its ratepayers relative to the alternative program, or in the absence of a CAP."

The Pennsylvania CAP program structure emphasizes the need of each utility to make empirically-based decisions, not only on the design of the program but on the size of the program as well. Rather than adopting program limits by policy or fiat, the PUC directed that utility programs should "reflect a needs assessment," which should examine not only the estimated number of low-income customers, but the expected participation (based on participation rates in other programs) and the "resources available to meet the needs of the target population." Because those needs assessments could vary widely, both by utility territory and by time period, the PUC directed that there should be no ceiling on program participation.

One reason that the Pennsylvania PUC could forego participation ceilings, of course, is because there is an explicit statutory directive that programs not only be "available" in each service territory, but that the implementing utility would be allowed to "fully recover" all universal service costs. Holding that "full recovery" could not occur through a base-rate case, since base rates allow only an "opportunity to recover" those costs deemed to be "normal" in the rate case, the PUC approved recovery of CAP costs through a rate rider that is either reconcilable or is adjusted sufficiently frequently to reflect all universal service costs.

Finally, the Pennsylvania PUC recognized that providing low-income affordability assistance was not the exclusive objective to be sought through CAP. Harking back to the basic philosophy underlying the origin of the program, and the low-income population toward whom the programs are directed, the PUC held that "our goal . . .is to maximize customer payments, maintain affordable payments, and limit the CAP credits as much as possible."[162]

7.2.3.3 The Fixed Credit Model

7.2.3.3.1 Overview

One modification of the straight PIPP is the fixed credit model. This program, like the straight PIPP, begins with an income-eligibility requirement but adds a second provision to its eligibility requirement: the household's actual energy bill. The bill must be over a certain pre-established percentage of household income in order for the household to receive the fixed credit benefits. Once established as eligible, the household payment will vary (possibly in a tiered arrangement) relative to the household's relationship to the poverty guidelines.

The basic premise of the fixed credit approach is to equate the household's energy bill with a designated percentage of income, with a credit on the bill to be provided to make up the difference. The tiered approach would calculate a lower percentage of income required as payment for those whose income is a lower percentage of the poverty level (for example, 50% or 75% of the federal poverty level) and a higher percentage of income for those at higher poverty levels (such as 125% or 150% of the federal poverty level). This method involves first calculating the household's PIPP payment, then calculating the household's annual home

162 As noted above, the "CAP credits" are those dollars that make up the difference between what a participant's bill is at CAP rates and what the bill would have been in the absence of CAP.

energy bill, and finally calculating the amount required to lower the household bill to the original percentage of income calculated. The final step establishes the "fixed credit" amount that the utility pays through the program towards the household's bill.

7.2.3.3.2 The New Jersey program

Since October of 2003, New Jersey has operated a fixed-credit percentage-of-income payment plan under which participants are required to pay no more than 6% of their annual income toward electric and gas bills. The benefit calculation takes the difference between a qualifying low-income customer's previous twelve months of electric and/or gas billing, net of any benefits from LIHEAP or the state Lifeline program (a state-funded energy assistance payment for elderly or disabled households), and 3% (one service) or 6% (two services) of the eligible customer's income.

The New Jersey Universal Service Fund (USF) is a creature of statute. In directing the state to move to retail choice,[163] the New Jersey legislature also provided that "there is established in the Board of Public Utilities a non-lapsing fund to be known as the Universal Service Fund."[164] The legislation provided that the Board of Public Utilities was to determine:

- The level of funding and appropriate administration of the USF;
- The "purposes and programs" to be funded with monies from the fund;
- Which "social programs" should be provided by an electric utility "as part of the provision of its regulated services";
- How to integrate the other state funds available for low-income energy assistance with the USF;[165]
- How to integrate federal energy assistance provided through the Low Income Home Energy Assistance Program (LIHEAP) with the USF;
- How to offset funds already included in rates for uncollectible electricity and natural gas bills against the USF; and
- Whether "new charges should be imposed to fund new or expanded programs."[166]

The New Jersey Board of Public Utilities (BPU) established the Universal Service Fund through a proceeding devoted exclusively to this issue.[167] The New Jersey BPU further determined that the implementation of the USF should occur in two steps, with the first step involving an "interim" program for the immediate heating season[168] and the second step involving a "full" program during the next heating season.[169]

---

163 The Electric Discount and Energy Competition Act, N.J. Stat. Ann. §§ 48:3-49–48:3-98.4 (West) (EDECA).

164 N.J. Stat. Ann. § 48:3-60(b) (West).

165 Two primary programs existed. First, New Jersey funded the "Lifeline Credit Program" established pursuant to Public Law 1979, Chapter 197 (N.J. Stat. Ann. §§ 48:2-29.15 to 48:2-29.30 (West)).

In addition, New Jersey funded the "Tenants' Lifeline Assistance Program," established pursuant to Public Law 1981, Chapter 210 (N.J. Stat. Ann. 48:2-29.31 to 48:2-29.46 (West)).

166 N.J. Stat. Ann. § 48:3-60(b) (West).

167 *In re* Establishment of a Universal Serv. Fund Pursuant to Section 12 of the Electric Discount & Energy Competition Act of 1999, No. EX00020091 (N.J. Bd. of Pub. Utils. 1999).

The commission considered whether the proceeding to determine the design of the USF should be a "fully litigated" proceeding. The commission determined not. "In view of the participation of other State agencies and non-profit groups that may have limited legal resources and experience with administrative proceedings before the Board, we believe a less formal approach, yet one that still provides for the filing of initial and reply comments, the issuance of discovery, and the holding of Public/Legislative hearings at which testimony can be filed, is warranted." Order Establishing Procedural Schedule, at 1, *In re* Establishment of a Universal Serv. Fund Pursuant to Section 12 of the Electric Discount & Energy Competition Act of 1999, No. EX00020091 (N.J. Bd. of Pub. Utils. June 7, 2000).

168 The commission adopted an "interim" program that substantively differed from the final program design. *See* Interim Order at 20, *In re* Establishment of a Universal Serv. Fund Pursuant to Section 12 of the Electric Discount & Energy Competition Act of 1999, No. EX00020091 (N.J. Bd. of Pub. Utils. Oct. 25, 2001).

The commission found that "the record in this USF proceeding clearly indicates that additional resources need to be made available to assist customers who are unable to afford their utility bills." The commission continued to find that, "in order to quickly establish an interim program, the Board orders that the interim Universal Service Fund be in the form of a one-time fixed credit to customers." *Id.* at 20, 21.

These fixed credits in the interim order would be provided to existing LIHEAP customers. "The Board finds that a two-phased approach will provide for immediate funding to meet the needs of this heating season, while providing additional time to develop a permanent plan." *Id.* at 21.

The commission utilized this interim approach to adopt other discrete program components, ordering temporary measures while allowing the development of permanent processes. *See, e.g.*, Order, *In re* Establishment of an Interim Portability Policy for Universal Serv. Fund Credits, No. EX00020091 (N.J. Bd. of Pub. Utils. Dec. 17, 2003); Decision and Order Approving Working Group Recommendations, *In re* Establishment of a Universal Serv. Fund Pursuant to Section 12 of the Elec. Discount & Energy Competition Act of 1999—Interim Arrears Policy, No. EX00020091 (N.J. Bd. of Pub. Utils. Sept. 24, 2003).

169 In the first "full" year of the program, the New Jersey USF enrolled roughly 133,000 accounts (or about 100,000 households, since some households have separate natural gas and electric accounts). According to the commission, "this extremely high enrollment for a new program was attributable both to the success of the automatic enrollment process and the high energy burdens that thousands of low-income customers had to pay each month. Specifically, the data indicates that roughly 22,000 of the initial households were paying more than 20% of their pre-tax income on energy bills, even after LIHEAP and Lifeline credits were applied. Another roughly 35,000 families were paying between 15% and 20% of their pre-tax income on energy. Without USF, it would be very difficult for any of these customers to consistently pay their energy bills."

The purpose of the USF, the BPU said, was to "ensure that low-income customers have access to affordable energy" under the terms of the statute.[170] Stating that the USF would be "an ongoing, evolving program, subject to review and amendment as necessary,"[171] the BPU determined that the program design should:

- Operate on a statewide basis;
- Be funded through a uniform volumetric charge;
- Be funded through the electric and natural gas bills of all customers;[172]
- Be available to households with income at or below 175% of the federal poverty level; and
- Be available to customers "with automatic screening for eligibility from means-tested financial assistance programs."[173]

The commission considered establishing a "crisis" component for the USF but rejected that idea for the early years of the program.

The basic affordability benefits provided through the New Jersey USF are delivered through an income-based "fixed credit" program.[174] "No actual monetary benefit will be given to ensure that the benefit is utilized specifically for utility expenses."[175] The fixed credit provided through the New Jersey USF was designed to reduce participants' natural gas and electric bills to an affordable percentage of income, deemed to be 6%. For customers receiving natural gas and electric service from different utilities, no more than 3% of income would be devoted to each service respectively.[176] According to the New Jersey BPU, through this approach,

> the Percentage of Income Payment Plan (PIPP) will be designed to provide low-income customers with a credit based on assessments of income and consumption that reflect their ability to make affordable monthly payments to the utility... The PIPP will be structured on the premise that eligible customers with lower incomes and higher energy burdens will receive a higher credit than those with higher incomes and a lower energy burden.[177]

The benefit is calculated by estimating what a participant's annual energy bill would be. The participant's LIHEAP (and Lifeline) payment is subtracted from the bill, and the credit necessary to reduce the bill to an affordable percentage of income is calculated. Under the New Jersey program, the credit rather than the customer payment is fixed. If bills increase, either due to price increases or weather that deviates from the norm, the customer bears the burden of paying the increased bill.[178]

The BPU capped allowable credits at $1800 per household. However, "utilities are expected to make every effort to include low-income customers with bills exceeding $1,800 in their weatherization programs."[179] Eligible participants with an annual bill of over $1800, the BPU stated, "will be referred to the New Jersey Comfort Partners part of the New Jersey Clean Energy Program for free weatherization measures."[180]

The New Jersey commission finally approved an arrearage forgiveness component for the state's Universal Service Fund. The commission noted that approximately 54,000 participants, or about 40% of the USF enrollees, entered the USF program with an arrearage.[181] Noting that these cus-

---

Universal Service Fund Order Approving New USF Program Year Rates and New Lifeline Rates at 1–2, *In re* Establishment of a Universal Serv. Fund Pursuant to Section 12 of the Elec. Discount & Competition Act of 1999, No. EX00020091 (N.J. Bd. of Pub. Utils. June 23, 2004).

170 *In re* Establishment of a Universal Serv. Fund Pursuant to Section 12 of the Elec. Discount Universal & Energy Competition Act of 1999, No. EX00020091, at 3 (N.J. Bd. of Pub. Utils. Mar. 20, 2003) (citing N.J. Stat. Ann. § 48:3-51 (2007)).

171 *Id.*

172 The BPU decided, however, that "some large industrial customers have special existing contracts limiting their rate exposure, and these will be honored until their expiration. This issue may be raised in future renegotiations pertaining to these particular contracts." *Id.* at 4.

173 The BPU said that "a one-stop application process is the long-term goal for the USF, and other assistance programs." *Id.* at 3.

174 "Eligibility will be determined based on one's income and their relative energy burden (under the PIPP). Participants will receive their USF benefit in the form of a credit on their electric or gas bills." *Id.* at 3.

175 *Id.* at 4.

176 *Id.* at 5.

177 *Id.* at 5.

178 The New Jersey commission deviated from this approach in response to Katrina-related spikes in natural gas prices. At the request of all stakeholders, the BPU approved a mid-year adjustment in benefits to account for the increase in natural gas bills attributable to Hurricane Katrina. *See generally In re* 2006/2007 Annual Compliance Filings for the Universal Serv. Fund Program Factor Within the Societal Benefit Charge Rate Pursuant to Section 12 of the 1999 Elec. Discount and Competition Act, Order Approving Interim USF Rates & Lifeline Rates, No. ER06070525, at 2 (N.J. Bd. of Pub. Utils. Oct. 23, 2006) ("In its June 22, 2005, Order in Docket No. EX00020091, the Board approved the 2005/2006 USF and Lifeline rates.... Shortly after the June 22, 2005, Board Order, Hurricane Katrina and Rita struck the Gulf Coast contributing to a rapid and significant increase in wholesale natural gas costs.... [T]he Board approved a recalculation of gas benefits on February 15, 2006, for all customers who were enrolled in USF as of December 14, 2005, and screened for USF eligibles for all current USF beneficiaries and all Low-Income Home Energy Assistance Program (LIHEAP) applicants for the November 1, 2005, through December 14, 2005, period. This one-time adjustment was done in order to reflect the most recent gas increase in the calculation of USF benefits.").

179 *In re* Establishment of a Universal Serv. Fund Pursuant to Section 12 of the Elec. Discount Universal & Energy Competition Act of 1999 No. EX00020091, at 5, (N.J. Bd. of Pub. Utils. Mar. 20, 2003).

180 *Id.* at 6.

181 Order at 1, *In re* Establishment of an Arrearage Payment Program for the Universal Serv. Fund, No. EX00020091 (N.J. Bd. of Pub. Utils. Feb. 18, 2004).

tomers brought roughly $17 million of pre-program arrears into the USF, the commission acknowledged the "need to address this problem":

> The primary goals of the [Arrearage Payment Program—APP] are to give customers an opportunity to get out of debt and to create an incentive structure to become regular bill payers. The basic premise of the APP is that any customer who pays his/her bills for one year will receive full forgiveness of any remaining pre-USF arrearages.[182]

The New Jersey BPU established an arrearage program through which USF participants with arrears greater than $60 could participate. Under the program, if a program participant pays his or her monthly utility bill for a twelve-month period, then all of his or her remaining arrears will be forgiven at the end of the twelve months. The program does not require a customer to make twelve consecutive on-time payments. Instead, customers will be evaluated at the end of the twelve-month period to see if they have made the required payments. Customers that do not receive forgiveness after the twelve-month period will have a three-month grace period to make up the payments.[183]

The New Jersey BPU allows utilities to grant forgiveness for periods less than a full twelve months. Under such an approach, utilities are allowed to grant forgiveness credits on either a monthly or quarterly basis.[184] According to the BPU,

> [u]tilities will grant partial forgiveness periodically as customers work toward the goal of full forgiveness at the end of the year. It is anticipated that more frequent forgiveness awards will positively reinforce consistent payments by customers and allow customers to start seeing the "light at the end of the tunnel" with respect to their arrears.[185]

Utilities awarding arrearage credits on a monthly basis will forgive one-twelfth of the customers' pre-program arrears, up to a maximum of $100 per month. Utilities that award quarterly forgiveness credits may forgive one quarter of the total pre-program arrearage each quarter, up to a maximum of $300. Whether the utility grants partial forgiveness on a monthly or quarterly basis is not to be decided by policy, the BPU stated, but would be "based on the different capacities of utilities' billing and computer systems."[186] If a customer does not receive forgiveness in any given month or quarter, the forgiveness is not foregone but simply delayed until the account is current.[187] At the end of the twelve-month period, any unpaid or unforgiven arrears are subject to forgiveness, with no cap on the forgiveness amount.[188]

The BPU found that the arrearage forgiveness program will result in positive benefits to the utility in both the near and long term. According to the BPU:

> this program will encourage bill payment by USF customers; will reduce the amount of write-offs and expenses on collections that ratepayers were already paying for, and will give customers who have faced unaffordable bills prior to USF a way to eliminate their pre-USF arrearages.[189]

The New Jersey BPU approved the collection of universal service costs through a system benefits charge (SBC). Under the SBC, the difference between actual SBC costs and SBC recoveries will be subject to deferral. The SBC will be reset annually to amortize the over- or under-recovered balances and to provide for current program cost recovery over the ensuing year.[190]

New Jersey's utilities have repeatedly asked for the authority to establish "self-implementing" intra-year changes in the SBC, through which the SBC can be changed on thirty days' notice. The utilities argued that "it has been difficult to arrive at the proper level for USF rates because a number of variables that impact the calculations have a high degree of uncertainty. These uncertain variables include the rate at which customers will be successful in earning forgiveness under the arrearage payment program, known as the Fresh Start program; the number of customers who will be enrolled during the final automatic enrollment sweep; and the rate at which customers will apply for the program once the direct application system, formerly called the manual enrollment system, is complete."[191] The New Jersey BPU has yet to approve that self-implementing cost-recovery mechanism.[192]

---

182 *Id.* at 2.

183 *Id.* at 4.

184 *Id.*

185 *Id.* at 2.

186 *Id.*

187 *Id.* at 5.

188 *Id.* at 4, 5.

189 *Id.* at 3.

190 *See, e.g.*, Final Decision and Order at 34, 63, *In re* Rockland Elec. Company's Rate Unbundling, Stranded Cost & Restructuring Filings, Nos. EO97070464, EO97070465, and EO97070466 (consolidated) (N.J. Bd. of Pub. Utils. July 22, 2002); Final Decision and Order at 111, *In re* Public Serv. Elec. & Gas Company's Rate Unbundling, Stranded Costs and Restructuring Filings, Nos. E097070461, E097070462, and E097070463 (consolidated) (N.J. Bd. of Pub. Utils. Aug. 24, 1999).

191 *In re* Establishment of a Universal Serv. Fund Pursuant to Section 12 of the Elec. Discount & Energy Competition Act of 1999 Universal Serv. Fund Order Approving New USF Program Year Rates & New Lifeline Rates, No. EX00020091, at 2 (June 23, 2004).

192 *See, e.g.*, Order Approving Interim USF Rates and Lifeline Rates, at 9, *In re* 2006/2007 Annual Compliance Filings for the Universal Serv. Fund Program Factor Within the Societal Benefits Charge Rate Pursuant to Section 12 of the 1999 Elec. Discount & Energy Competition Act of 1999, No. ER06070525 (N.J. Bd. of Pub. Utils. Oct. 23, 2006).

"The Board is not convinced that there is any reason why an

Finally, the BPU decided that it would "segregate the USF revenues and benefits for gas and electric customers such that the total USF recoveries from gas customers will be used to provide payment assistance to gas customers and the total revenue recoveries from electric customers will be used to provide payment assistance to electric customers."[193]

In sum, the New Jersey Universal Service Fund is a creature of statute. However, while the legislature directed the state utility commission to create such a program, the Board of Public Utilities has relied heavily on a collaborative "work group" process to generate operating details. The BPU established the overall direction of the program. The New Jersey USF includes both a rate affordability component, based on percentage-of-income principles, and an arrearage forgiveness program. While the low-income energy efficiency program operates as a separate and distinct program, the BPU has ensured that the rate affordability and usage reductions programs work in collaboration with each other.

New Jersey has focused not only on developing appropriate benefit levels—the rate affordability benefits are designed to reduce home energy bills to no more than 6% of household income—but also on developing the mechanisms needed to promote widespread availability of the USF program. New Jersey has implemented an automatic enrollment program for LIHEAP participants and a categorical eligibility for recipients of other public assistance programs such as the Food Stamp Program.

The New Jersey USF program is available statewide to both electric and natural gas customers and is paid for by all customer classes.

7.2.3.3.3 The Maine program

Central Maine Power (CMP) has had a fixed credit plan for over a decade. Called the Electric Lifeline Program, participating customers receive a flat monthly credit on their electric bill. For participants with incomes at or below 75% of the federal poverty guidelines, the percentage of income to be used when calculating the credit amount is 4% when the estimated annual usage is 5000 kWh or less and 9% when the estimated annual usage is 14,000 kWh or more. For those with incomes above 75% of the federal poverty guidelines, the percentage of income to be used when calculating the credit amount is 5.1% when the estimated annual usage is 5000 kWh or less and 10.1% when the estimated annual usage is 14,000 kWh or more.

Maine's low-income rate affordability programs were adopted pursuant to explicit statutory authorization enacted in 1990 after the Maine Public Utilities Commission had rejected an affordability proposal on the grounds of lack of jurisdiction.[194] In response to that decision, the legislature enacted language providing that:

> [t]he Commission, as it determines appropriate, . . . shall order electric utilities to develop and submit specific . . . proposals that provide for the development and implementation of: (G) rates or bill payment assistance programs for residential customers who have been certified eligible for state or federal fuel assistance that take into account the difficulty these customers have in paying in full for electric service or that target assistance to these customers in the most efficient manner, taking into account the necessity of maintaining electric service.[195]

This language resulted in programs promulgated by the state's three major electric utilities: Central Maine Power Company, Maine Public Service Company, and Bangor Hydro. The discussion below focuses on the Central Maine Power (CMP) program, since this program was later to serve as the model upon which a statewide program was promulgated.

The Maine Electric Lifeline Program finds its origins in an experimental low-income program adopted by Central Maine Power Company in 1991. The CMP program was expanded to a full low-income rate affordability assistance program by order of the Maine Public Utilities Commission (PUC) in 1992.[196] Presented to the PUC by stipulation,[197]

adjustment would need to be self-implementing. If the [electric distribution companies] or [gas distribution companies] believe it is necessary to adjust USF rates prior to the annual July 1st filing period, they may make appropriate filings with the Board, with a copy to Rate Counsel, and the Board will consider such adjustment." *Id.* at 9.

193 "Any excess or deficient revenues for either sector based on the benefits paid out would be carried forward to the subsequent year's budget for the corresponding group of customers, which would more directly match payments made to gas customers with the associated recoveries from gas customers." *In re* Establishment of a Universal Serv. Fund Pursuant to Section 12 of the Elec. Discount Universal & Energy Competition Act of 1999, No. EX00020091, at 7 (N.J. Bd. of Pub. Utils. Mar. 20, 2003).

194 Final Order, *In re* Central Maine Power Co. Proposed Increase in Rates & Rate Design, No. 89-68 (Oct. 31, 1990). *See also In re* Commission Inquiry into Establishment of Low Income Discount Rate for Residential Households & to Allocate Water Supply Costs Among Customer Classes on a Volumetric Basis, No. 94-430 (Me. Pub. Utils. Comm'n Sept. 1, 1998) ("unlike electric and telephone companies, there is no legislative authority for water utilities to consider income of customers in establishing rates. . . . Utility rates cannot be designed to give preference to any particular person or class of customers").

195 Maine Rev. Stat. Ann. tit. 35-A, § 3153-A(1)(G), *as amended by* 1991 Me. Legis. Serv. ch. 253 (H.P. 983) (L.D. 1428) (West).

196 Summary of Decision and Short Order, *In re* Investigation into Development of Proposals for Pilot Low-Income Programs for Central Maine Power Co., No 91-151-C (Me. Pub. Utils. Comm'n Oct. 1, 1992).

197 The stipulation was agreed to by the commission staff, the Public Advocate, the state association of Community Action Agencies, the American Association of Retired Persons (AARP),

the program proposal was designed to extend the CMP Electric Lifeline Program (ELP) to an average of 18,000 electric customers. The Maine PUC, however, found that, "while the record in this case supports an expansion of the existing ELP, CMP's general body of ratepayers cannot afford the doubling of current program costs. . . ."[198] The PUC thus rejected the proposed stipulation.

The PUC directed the implementation of a scaled-down version of the ELP. While the original stipulation had proposed to extend the program to all customers *eligible* for the federal Low Income Home Energy Assistance Program (LIHEAP), the PUC-ordered program extended only to customers actually participating in the program. Contracting the program in this manner reduced the program cost from $5 million to $4 million. The PUC found that this participation level "constitutes approximately 0.52% of CMP's annual retail revenues [and] is a reasonable balance between the interests of affected low-income ratepayers and the general body of ratepayers."[199] However, the PUC subsequently noted that the 0.5% figure was merely a guide to determining the reasonableness of program costs.[200] It was neither a floor nor a ceiling on funding.

The CMP participant population was divided into two income tiers. The lowest income tier included customers with incomes at or below 75% of the federal poverty level.[201] A second tier reached customers up to 150% of the federal poverty level.[202] In turn, these income tiers were divided into heating and non-heating customers. Any customer with an estimated annual usage of 12,000 kWh or more was deemed to be a heating customer. Not only did these heating customers pay a higher percentage of income as their co-payment under the ELP, but the utility-provided ELP benefits for these customers were reduced by the participant's LIHEAP benefit whether or not that benefit was applied to his or her CMP account.[203] Customers were required to enter into a levelized budget payment plan.[204] Customers whose percentage-of-income payment would yield a benefit of less than $50 were not enrolled in the ELP.

The CMP Electric Lifeline Program was the first program in the country to distribute percentage-of-income-based benefits on a fixed credit basis. Under the program design presented by stipulation and adopted by the Maine PUC, a household co-payment was calculated by applying the required percentage-of-income payment to the customer's income. This household co-payment was subtracted from the customer's expected bill (estimated by applying current rates against projected usage) to determine the annual benefits necessary to reduce the bill to the affordable percentage of income. Those benefits were provided on an equal monthly basis, thus reducing the total bill to an affordable amount as long as the customer's consumption remained at its past levels.

The CMP ELP did not incorporate an arrearage forgiveness program. Rather, pre-program arrears were subject to a twelve-month deferred payment arrangement; the payments made under this arrangement were added to the customer's percentage-of-income-based co-payments. The monthly arrears payment, however, could not exceed the participant's co-payment amount. Any arrearage still remaining at the end of the twelve-month payment arrangement would be subject to a second payment arrangement for which the customer would be eligible at that time.

---

and a coalition of community-based low-income advocacy groups.

198 Summary of Decision and Short Order at 1, *In re* Investigation into Development of Proposals for Pilot Low-Income Programs for Central Maine Power Co., No 91-151-C (Me. Pub. Utils. Comm'n Oct. 1, 1992).

199 *Id.* at 2.

200 "When the Commission established 0.5% of annual jurisdictional revenues as the 1991/92 ELP benefit level, we were designing a program from scratch. The Commission viewed the 0.5% as a reasonable balance between providing assistance to low-income customers and the expense to the general body of ratepayers. We believe that future growth in ELP benefit levels will be a function of changes in federal poverty guidelines as well as changes in CMP's revenues. There is little justification to tie ELP benefit levels exclusively to CMP's revenue increases and decreases. To do so would create undesirable volatility in the ELP from year to year." Order at 8, *In re* Modifications to Central Me. Power Company's Elec. Lifeline Program for the 1993–94 Program Year, No. 93-156 (Me. Pub. Utils. Comm'n Oct. 22, 1993).

201 It is important to remember, however, that the program was limited to the LIHEAP participant population.

202 These two tiers represented a change from the original CMP program. The original CMP program, approved by the Maine PUC in October 1991, was directed exclusively to customers with incomes at or below 75% of the federal poverty level. Summary of Decision and Short Order, *In re* Investigation into the Dev. of Proposals for Pilot Low-Income Programs for Central Maine Power Co., No. 91-151-C (Me. Pub. Utils. Comm'n Oct. 23, 1991).

203 This program requirement was subsequently eliminated. Order at 14–16, *In re* Modifications to Central Me. Power Company's Elec. Lifeline Program for the 1993–94 Program Year, No. 93-156 (Me. Pub. Utils. Comm'n Oct. 22, 1993).

The Maine LIHEAP program had adopted program regulations assigning LIHEAP benefits to the primary heating provider. "The policy of imputing HEAP benefits began in the first year of the Electric Lifeline Program. The Company was concerned that, in principle, ELP benefits should not duplicate benefits provided under HEAP." *Id.* at 15.

Given the change in LIHEAP assignment policy, however, and the fact that the imputation of benefits was preventing some customers from entering the program, the PUC eliminated this requirement with the proviso that, should LIHEAP change its policy back, the PUC would revisit the issue.

204 This requirement was subsequently limited only to customers who entered the program with greater-than-thirty-day arrears. Order at 10–11, *In re* Modifications to Central Me. Power Company's Elec. Lifeline Program for the 1993–94 Program Year, No. 93-156 (Me. Pub. Utils. Comm'n Oct. 22, 1993).

Central Maine Power Company estimated that roughly 33% of its 9100 total ELP customers, or about 3000, had arrears of this magnitude.

Finally, the PUC held that CMP was authorized by statute to use some part of its rate affordability benefits to fund energy-usage reduction efforts (other than fuel switching) for high-use ELP customers. "The Commission agrees," the PUC stated, "with the Company and the other parties that using ELP benefits to fund measures that reduce electric usage for ELP customers is in keeping with our legislative directive to implement low-income programs in an efficient manner, and the Commission's goal of operating least-cost low-income programs."[205] Additionally, the PUC noted:

> Expending ELP benefits to finance electric reduction measures may reduce the long-term costs of the ELP, make electric bills more affordable for low-income customers, and cause less adverse rate impacts for the general body of ratepayers than continuing to provide high ELP benefits. CMP, [Bangor Hydro], and [Maine Public Service] are all entering into their third year of operating low-income programs. While we may modify one or more of the low-income programs, the Commission has no plans to discontinue the programs. This is another reason why it makes sense to use ELP funds to finance energy efficiency measures that reduce electric consumption over a number of years.[206]

While the CMP program served as the model for the subsequent proposed statewide program, the initial programs run by Maine's other two investor-owned utilities substantially differed.

The Maine Public Service (MPS) program, known as PowerPACT, was directed exclusively toward electric heating and electric water heating customers, with the purpose of excluding low-use customers from receiving benefits.[207] Under the PowerPACT program, the utility would provide a fixed benefit to low-income customers who made agreed-upon payments throughout the winter heating season. In order to participate in the program, customers were required to negotiate individual payment plans for their winter bills. These payment plans often resulted in bills smaller than what those bills at full rates would be. If the customer made his or her payments, the utility would then grant a bill credit for the customer's account.

The bill credit provided through PowerPACT was not explicitly designed to yield an affordable bill to program participants. While customers with lower incomes received larger credits—a participant with income below 75% of the federal poverty level received a credit of $160 while a customer with income between 125% and 150% of the federal poverty level received a credit of $85—the credit did not vary based upon actual income or customer consumption.

Rather than seeking to promote affordability, as measured by energy burden, the purpose of the PowerPACT program was to provide incentives for low-income customers to maintain current winter bill payments. As originally proposed, a customer was required to make each of his or her winter bill payments in a full and timely fashion in order to receive PowerPACT benefits. for example, if a customer missed his or her December payment, the benefit would not be granted whether or not the December payment was subsequently made and irrespective of the payment pattern during the remainder of that winter. However, the program was quickly modified to provide that, as long as the winter payments had been made by the time the credits were granted in May, program participants would receive their PowerPACT credits.[208]

Early in the program development, the state Office of Public Advocate's (OPA) office recommended that the program be changed to a burden-based program. "The OPA argues that all three utility-sponsored programs should be similarly designed, except to the extent that demonstrably different customer needs exist. In addition, the OPA argues that as a general matter of policy the percentage-of-income approach that targets benefits to customers as a function of income and usage is a more efficient use of program dollars."[209] However, the Maine PUC rejected that argument, holding that, "while continued experience may lead us to decide to institute a uniform program for each of the three major electric utilities in the State at some point in the future, for now we are satisfied that MPS's PowerPACT Program adequately responds to the requirements of the Electric Rate Reform Act."[210]

Bangor Hydro-Electric Company (BHE) adopted a "low-income rate" (LIR) in response to the Maine PUC's directive to promulgate low-income assistance programs. Under the BHE program, the utility offered four tiers of discounts based upon the income of participating customers.[211] Participants with incomes at or below 50% of the federal poverty level received a 33% discount on monthly consump-

205 Order at 30, *In re* Modifications to Central Me. Power Company's Elec. Lifeline Program for the 1993–94 Program Year, No. 93-156 (Me. Pub. Utils. Comm'n Oct. 22, 1993).

206 *Id.*

207 *See* Order at 2, *In re* Investigation of Modifications to Me. Pub. Serv. Company's PowerPACT Program for the 1993–1994 Program Year, No. 93-158 (Me. Pub. Utils. Comm'n 1993).

208 The company had argued that no benefits should be paid if all payments had not been made in a timely fashion, since "the original purpose of this program was to improve payment behavior." The Public Advocate had argued that a "residual benefit" should be paid, after subtracting the missed payments from what benefits would otherwise have been provided. The commission ultimately accepted staff's recommendation that the "customer be allowed to cure a default on winter payments at any time prior to the award of the credit in the Spring." *Id.* at 8.

209 *Id.*

210 *Id.*

211 Order at 7–10, *In re* Investigation of Modifications to Bangor Hydro-Elec. Company's Low Income Rate Program for the 1993–1994 Program Year, No. 93-157, 1993 Me. PUC LEXIS 118 (Me. Pub. Utils. Comm'n Oct. 21, 1993).

tion above 100 kWh; participants with incomes between 50% and 75% of the federal poverty level received a 25% discount on monthly consumption over 100 kWh; participants with incomes between 75% and 100% of the federal poverty level received a 17% discount on usage above 100 kWh; and participants with incomes between 100% and 150% of the federal poverty level received a 10% discount on usage above 100 kWh. Currently, while Bangor has maintained separate tiers based on household income, the differences between the discounts for customers in each tier appear to have greatly diminished.[212]

While the BHE program was designed to provide higher benefits to lower-income customers, the company did not seek to tie its discounts to any determination of what was required to achieve affordability.

Despite the statutory language directing the PUC to develop "rates or bill payment assistance programs" for LIHEAP recipients "that take into account the difficulty these customers have paying in full for electric service . . . [and] taking into account the necessity of maintaining electric service," Bangor Hydro-Electric asked the PUC to terminate its LIR program for "business-based reasons."[213] BHE argued that "the impact of LIR's cross-subsidies on its rates in a competitive environment are undesirable."[214] Bangor Hydro-Electric argued that low-income rate affordability programs must have one of two mutually exclusive goals. According to BHE:

> The goal of the Program must either be: (1) to pay for itself and therefore be justified on cost-effectiveness grounds, or (2) to provide assistance to low-income ratepayers and therefore be justified as a "social program." The Company insists that the Program can have no overlap or mixing of goals.[215]

The Maine PUC rejected this argument, cautioning BHE not to "let its distaste for what it views as a social program cloud its judgment." The PUC indicated its understanding "that the Company would prefer to discontinue its LIR Program" but warned that "the legislature has directed the Commission to pursue assistance programs for low-income electric ratepayers. The Commission has ordered Bangor Hydro to implement and modify its LIR Program. These are facts that the Company must accept."[216]

The PUC told Bangor Hydro-Electric that the goals of Maine's low-income programs are two-fold:

- "One goal is to provide assistance to low-income residential electric ratepayers"; and
- "Another goal is to deliver that assistance in as efficient a manner as possible."

The PUC noted further that "these goals are not at all times consistent and must, in certain contexts, be weighed and balanced by the Commission."[217] Parties must be careful not to confuse "the exercise of *identifying* goals with the act of *balancing* these goals." Ultimately, the PUC informed BHE that "we expect Bangor Hydro to design and implement its LIR Program in a cost-effective way that targets benefits to low-income residential ratepayers that most need assistance while maintaining Program delivery costs to the overall body of ratepayers."[218] Currently, it appears that Bangor Hydro has changed its eligibility requirements, basing them on total yearly household income limits based on household size. For example, for a family of four to be eligible for LIR, the family's total yearly household income must not exceed $33,075. The income allowed for eligibility is greater if the household includes members who are under the age of twenty-four months or are at least sixty years old.[219]

The Maine regulatory approach to low-income bill payment assistance substantively changed when the state legislature approved the restructuring of Maine's electric industry in 1997. In that restructuring statute, the legislature explicitly directed the Maine PUC to implement a statewide assistance program. The legislation was directed not simply toward the state's three investor-owned electric utilities but to Maine's consumer-owned electric utilities as well.[220]

The Maine electric restructuring statute set forth several basic policy directions for the PUC to pursue in implementing the new low-income assistance programs. The legislation made the following provisions:

- The new program was to "continue existing levels of financial assistance for low-income households";
- The new program was to provide "comparable benefits for electric customers throughout the State";[221]
- A single administrative entity (the Maine State Housing Authority) for a statewide program, using a common set of rules and administrative procedures, would be

212 *See* www.bhe.com/rates/rates_schedule.cfm (Bangor Hydro T&D Rate Schedules).

213 Order at *6–*7, *In re* Investigation of Modifications to Bangor Hydro-Electric Company's Low Income Rate Program for the 1993–1994 Program Year, No. 93-157, 1993 Me. PUC LEXIS 118. (Me. Pub. Utils. Comm'n Oct. 21, 1993).

214 *Id.*

215 *Id.* at 4.

216 *Id.*

217 *Id.* at 5.

218 *Id.* at 12.

219 *See* www.bhe.com/residential/low_income.cfm (explaining eligibility requirements for low income assistance).

220 The PUC ultimately exempted three "island" utilities from the "statewide" program. The PUC found that these utilities had been exempted from the electric restructuring generally and approved their exemption from the low-income program requirement as well. Notice of Rulemaking at 3, Rulemaking to Create the Electric Lifeline Program (Ch, 314), No. 2001-42 (Me. Pub. Utils. Comm'n Feb. 6, 2001).

221 *Id.* at 4 (quoting section 3214(1) as articulating a policy that "electricity is a basic necessity to which all residents of the State should have access. . . .").

more efficient than alternative administrative structures;[222]

- The program was to be paid for by "funds collected by all transmission and distribution utilities in the State."[223]

While not directed by legislation to adopt a percentage-of-income approach to the "new" statewide Electric Lifeline Program, the Maine PUC initially chose to pursue such a design. The basic decision to make, the PUC stated, was whether to adopt a percentage-of-income model such as the existing Central Maine Power (CMP) program or to adopt a tariffed rate discount such as the existing Bangor Hydro-Electric program. The Maine PUC noted that "the discount rate model and the percentage of income model each contain many aspects similar to the other; the major difference is the targeting of funds under the percentage of income model to customers with the greatest need."[224] The PUC reasoned thus:

> We prefer the percentage of income model for several reasons. First, under the percentage of income model, eligible customers will receive a benefit that is directly related to the customer's annual electricity bill as a function of their household income. Second, the percentage of income model better targets limited benefits dollars to those customers who need it most. We acknowledge that the statewide application of the percentage of income model will produce fewer eligible customers and larger average benefits than would the statewide application of a tariffed discount rate. However, such a distribution of limited program dollars is the best way to provide the assistance required by section 3214. Finally, while a statewide program employing a targeted rate discount design would be somewhat simpler and less costly to administer, the superior results of the deployment of a percentage of income model more than justify the associated administrative costs.[225]

The PUC proposed adopting the fixed credit approach of the CMP program.

Moreover, the PUC set the "affordable" payment levels at 6% of income for households at or below 75% of the federal poverty level and 11% for households with income between 75% and 150% of the federal poverty level. The PUC noted that the percentage-of-income-based customer payment involved a balancing of customer affordability and program cost:

> The percentage of income used to calculate the customer's co-payment directly affects the overall cost of the ELP. We have considered a variety of percentage of income combinations and assessed their corresponding benefit levels and costs. Based on the Needs Assessment and our additional analysis to date, the percentage of income structure in the proposed rule will provide financial assistance levels consistent with section 3214 and will do so within an affordable framework.[226]

Finally, the proposed statewide Maine program incorporated an arrearage-forgiveness program for the first time. None of the three utility low-income programs had provided for the forgiveness of pre-program arrears. Nonetheless, the PUC found that an arrearage-forgiveness program was necessitated by statute:

> If a customer enters the program with a high arrears balance, the risk of nonpayment and resulting collection activity is increased. The impact of a large arrears balance can totally wipe out the "affordability" of a participant's required co-payment under a percentage of income program design, sometimes doubling the required payment amount so that the participant is paying more than 20% of his or her income to maintain electric service. Payments of such magnitude are incompatible with the 35-A §3214(1) requirement of "adequate" financial assistance to "all residents of the State."
>
> Under the proposed rule, an eligible customer's pre-program arrears will be deferred during the term of the payment plan. This is a change from CMP's program which provided for pre-program arrears to be included in the calculation of the customer's payment plan up to a point where the customer's expected monthly payments are doubled what the amount would have been without the inclusion of the pre-program arrears. The inclusion of pre-program arrears in the customer's payment plan defeats the purpose of the PIP program, that is, to establish a customer's co-payment that is affordable based on that customer's income level.[227]

The PUC directed each transmission and distribution utility "to offer a participating customer with deferrable pre-program arrears the option to obtain a forgiveness of some or all of the participant's deferred arrears balance." The PUC proposed a matching program, under which the utility would forgive $2 for every $1 of deferrable pre-program arrears paid by the participant.[228]

---

222 The PUC noted, however, that it could not direct the state LIHEAP agency to administer the program. The MSHA would need statutory authority to become the program administrator. *Id.* at 4.

223 *Id.* (citing Me. Rev. Stat. tit. 35-A, § 3214(2)(A)).

224 Notice of Rulemaking at 5, Rulemaking to Create the Electric Lifeline Program (Ch, 314), No. 2001-42 (Me. Pub. Utils. Comm'n Feb. 6, 2001).

225 *Id.* at 5, 6.

226 *Id.* at 6.

227 *Id.* at 10.

228 *Id.*

In response to comments on its initial program proposal,[229] the Maine PUC substantially altered its approach to the low-income program designs. The PUC noted that, while its rulemaking setting forth a statewide program would be completed in the spring, it had established a deadline of having new programs online for the coming winter heating season. Bowing to the pressure of that impending deadline, rather than mandating a uniform statewide program, the PUC adopted regulations providing that each utility could promulgate a program specific to its service territory so long as the program was consistent with PUC-prescribed standards. Moreover, rather than looking at needs on an aggregated statewide basis, the PUC indicated that

> [t]he purpose of the Statewide Low-Income Assistance Plan and the LIAPs is to establish a series of bill payment assistance programs for low-income residential customers that will (1) make participants' electric bills more affordable; (2) make assistance available to low-income customers throughout the State; and (3) ensure that each of Maine's transmission and distribution utilities has the funds necessary to implement a LIAP that addresses the need that exists in that particular utility's service territory.[230]

Noting that the statute "does not require a single, uniform statewide low-income assistance program," the revised rule allowed each of the state's three investor-owned utilities to continue their existing programs.[231] The PUC stated that "we expect that each of the new LIAPs will be modeled after one existing low-income programs, although the amended rule does not require this."[232] However, the PUC did include "several basic design features that all [low-income assistance programs] must incorporate."[233] Amongst those design features were:

- That benefits be designed so that participants with the greatest needs receive the highest benefits;
- That benefits be tiered so that higher benefits will be paid to households with incomes that place them at lower levels of poverty;
- That each program that does not employ a percentage-of-income benefit structure must have a minimum of four separate benefit categories that are based on the federal poverty guidelines; and
- That each program must include a provision that tracks changes in the federal LIHEAP program that may affect a customer's eligibility for the program (such as an increase in LIHEAP eligibility).[234]

The new PUC regulations dropped any requirement of an arrearage-forgiveness program, "primarily because of a lack of information regarding the cost to utilities, and ultimately to ratepayers."[235] The PUC subsequently noted that, "while the concept of arrears forgiveness has been discussed in this rulemaking, the details regarding design and cost have not been sufficiently developed in this proceeding. Therefore, we are not prepared to incorporate a provision into the adopted rule that requires transmission and distribution utilities to implement a pilot preprogram arrears forgiveness program."[236]

In sum, the state of Maine was one of the early pioneers in implementing rate affordability programs for low-income utility customers. In many ways, the state helped to create a framework for what other states would emulate for years, if not decades, to come. Many of the decisions reached, as well as the rationales utilized, helped to define future discussions about low-income rate affordability programs. The Maine PUC's use of 0.5% of revenue as a touchstone for balancing the interests of low-income program participants and the ratepayer population as a whole has been since cited. The Maine percentage, of course, was on total retail revenue and not merely on residential revenue.

The Maine program adopted requirements, both for participating customers and participating utilities, that deserve emulation. On the one hand, Electric Lifeline Program (ELP) participants were required to enter into a levelized budget payment plan, a not unreasonable requirement in exchange for substantial affordability discounts. On the other hand, the ELP, while ultimately not adopting an arrearage-forgiveness program, set a cap on the monthly payment amounts that utilities could require from low-income customers as part of any deferred payment plan.

The Maine PUC recognized that combining energy efficiency with the affordability program could be justified over the course of time. Noting that it had no plans to discontinue the programs, the PUC found that it made sense to finance efficiency programs that reduce electric consumption over a number of years.

229 The PUC noted that its ultimate program design "represents a series of compromises that were necessitated, in part, by the need to get the statewide program in place by October 1, 2001." Order Adopting Rules at 2, *In re* Rulemaking to Create a Statewide Low-Income Assistance Plan (Chapter 314), No. 2001-42, (Me. Pub. Utils. Comm'n July 31, 2001).

230 Order Adopting Rules at 2, *In re* Rulemaking to Create a Statewide Low-Income Assistance Plan (Chapter 314), No. 2001-42, (Me. Pub. Utils. Comm'n July 31, 2001); Notice of Further Rulemaking and Request for Comments at 8, *In re* Rulemaking to Create a Statewide Low-Income Assistance Plan (Chapter 314), No. 2001-42 (Me. Pub. Utils. Comm'n July 31, 2001).

231 Notice of Further Rulemaking and Request for Comments at 5, *In re* Rulemaking to Create a Statewide Low-Income Assistance Plan (Chapter 314), No. 2001-42, (Me. Pub. Utils. Comm'n July 31, 2001).

232 *Id.*

233 *Id.*

234 *Id.* at 9.

235 *Id.* at 3.

236 *Id.* Order Adopting Rules, at 3.

While not ultimately adopted, the Maine program generated an observation from the state Office of Public Advocate (OPA) that could serve other states well. A common debate within states considering rate affordability programs is whether to adopt a single statewide program or to allow utilities to adopt individual programs. According to the OPA, there should be a rebuttable presumption that single statewide program design is appropriate. The OPA argued that "all three utility sponsored programs should be similarly designed, except to the extent that demonstrably different customer needs exist." The ultimate decision to allow different program designs for each utility within the context of state-prescribed standards, including prescribed design features, was not entirely inconsistent with the OPA proposal.

The Maine PUC also acknowledged that its role was to balance the goal of providing affordability assistance with its role of protecting the interests of non-participating customers. That balance might occur in defining the participant tiers (and the corresponding percentage-of-income contributions). Whether to promulgate an arrearage forgiveness program as well was addressed.

7.2.3.4 The Supplemental Energy Assistance Model

7.2.3.4.1 Overview

One form of rate assistance provided by public utilities involves the utility providing supplemental assistance to the state LIHEAP program, which in turn either distributes additional benefits to existing program participants or expands the population of recipients to be served. Two examples of such programs include the Maryland Electric Universal Service Program (EUSP) and the Washington state Low-Income Rate Assistance (LIRA) programs.

7.2.3.4.2 The Maryland EUSP

Maryland's Electric Universal Service Program (EUSP) is a creature of statute.[237] Mandated by the statute directing the state to move to retail choice,[238] the EUSP was statutorily established to deliver bill payment assistance,[239] low-income weatherization, and arrearage retirement to low-income[240] customers.[241] The statute generally provides that the Maryland Public Service Commission (PSC) (1) shall order a universal service program to be made available on a statewide basis to benefit low-income customers;[242] (2) shall establish a universal service program;[243] and (3) shall have oversight responsibility for the universal service program.[244] In addition, the Maryland PSC is charged with making annual recommendations to the legislature with regard to the total amount of funding to be used for the universal service program.[245]

In contrast, the state Department of Human Resources, which is the state agency that administers the federal Low Income Home Energy Assistance Program (LIHEAP) (also known as the Maryland Energy Assistance Program—MEAP), was statutorily charged with the responsibility for administering the EUSP[246] as well as disbursing EUSP funds (with oversight by the PSC).[247]

The design of the specific program components of the EUSP was assigned to a "Universal Service Working Group" (USWG) by the Maryland PSC.[248] In delegating the responsibility to develop a program design, the Maryland PSC articulated several minimum considerations for the USWG to take into account. The USWG was charged with assuming the continuation of existing customer protections, the continuing availability of federal LIHEAP funds, and the availability of low-income weatherization programs. In addition, the PSC indicated that the design of the EUSP should include a continuation of restrictions on winter terminations and the continuation of the state's Utility Service Protection Program (USPP).[249]

The USWG could not reach consensus on how the electric rate affordability program should operate. In response, the Maryland PSC allowed individual parties to advance implementation proposals through a hearing process. The primary constraints, the PSC found, were that non-utility proposals "must demonstrate reasonable efforts by the proponents to work with the utilities' billing systems." Moreover, any utility proposal "must demonstrate reasonable

237 Md. Code Ann., Pub. Util. Cos. § 7-512 (West).

238 This statute was known as the Electric Customer Choice and Competition Act of 1999 and was enacted in April 1999.

239 Md. Code Ann., Pub. Util. Cos. § 7-512.1(a) (West).

240 "Low-income" was statutorily defined to include customers at or below 150% of the federal poverty level, later increased to 175%. *Id.* § 7-512.1(a)(1).

241 *Id.* § 7-512.1(a)(2).

242 *Id.* § 7-505(b)(2).

243 *Id.* § 7-512.1(a)(1).

244 *Id.* § 7-512-1.1(a)(6).

245 *Id.* § 7-512.1(c).

246 *Id.* § 7-512.1(a)(3).

247 *Id.* § 7-512.1(h)(4).

248 The Working Group was comprised of representatives from the state LIHEAP office, the Office of Peoples Counsel, the state energy office, the commission Staff, the state association of Community Action Agencies, each electric utility, industrial and commercial customer groups, and various community-based organizations.

249 The USPP is a payment program established by commission regulation. It allows MEAP-eligible households to enter into a year-round even-monthly-payment program with their utility company. An equal-monthly-payment plan based on the estimated cost of the customer's average annual utility usage minus the MEAP benefit is used to determine the even monthly payments for participants in the USPP. *See* Md. Code Regs. 20.31.05.

efforts to modify existing systems to accommodate reasonable USP proposal objectives."[250]

In addition, the PSC articulated ten principles that were to be incorporated into the statutorily prescribed EUSP. These principles included directives that the EUSP must, in addition to complying with the requirements of the statute,

- encourage customers to conserve energy;
- provide "integrated mechanisms" for bill assistance, weatherization, and arrearage retirement;
- provide that bill assistance benefits be "graduated based on a participant's income level";
- provide that EUSP participants "pay a portion of their own funds in order to remain eligible for bill assistance"; and
- cap bill assistance "at an appropriate level to ensure fund availability."[251]

Early in the process of developing a specific program design through which to implement the statutory EUSP, the Maryland PSC was faced with deciding the objectives of the program. The state LIHEAP agency proposed to incorporate into EUSP a series of services including conservation education, energy conservation through appliance replacement, and "teaching self-help strategies to encourage customers to promptly and regularly pay their electric bills."[252] The PSC rejected these additional services as being beyond the scope of the statute:

> The program as proposed by [the state LIHEAP office] establishes a much broader and more comprehensive effort to assist low-income customers in their ability to pay their electric bills than is set forth in the Act. Conservation measures are worthwhile activities that the commission believes would be beneficial to low-income customers in managing their electric bills. Nevertheless, the commission believes it is paramount that the USP first accomplish the legislatively-mandated components of bill payment assistance, low-income weatherization, and retirement of arrearages.[253]

To that end, the PSC held that "any ancillary activities of the USP should be directly related to the three components of the program."[254]

In particular, the Maryland PSC decided that, while the delivery of energy audits was an integral part of providing weatherization under the EUSP statute, the delivery of energy-efficient appliances was not. The PSC determined, for example, that

> energy audits are undoubtedly within the scope of any weatherization programs. Indeed, the Commission views energy audits as critical to any weatherization program.[255]

In contrast,

> the commission does not view appliance replacement as within the scope of a weatherization program. The commission acknowledges that some measures defined as 'energy conservation' are appropriate in the context of a weatherization program. The Commission's interpretation of the Act compels us to hold that the law did not envision appliance replacement as part of a weatherization program.[256]

The PSC noted that the statute creating the EUSP explicitly referred to funding weatherization as one of the three mandatory program components. Weatherization, the PSC held, was a defined term: "By definition, 'weatherization' is the 'systematic application of insulation materials to a structure to retard the loss of heated or cooled air within that structure.'[257] The Commission views low-income weatherization to include structural or shell repairs or upgrades."[258] The PSC then emphasized that its narrow construction was driven as much by resource constraints as by statutory constraints:

> The commission recognizes that there are other measures that also may reduce energy consumption but do not fall within the parameters of weatherization. Energy conservation . . . may come within the scope of 'universal service program,' as defined and may be desirable. However, [the statute] speaks to low-income weatherization and not the broader category of energy conservation.
>
> The commission notes that the USP has finite resources. The Act requires arrearage retirement and bill payment assistance in addition to low-income weatherization. With the limited amount of money that can be directed toward weatherization at this time, it is appropriate that the measures undertaken meet the narrower parameters defined above. Nevertheless, as funds become available with arrearage retirement completion, it would be appropriate to consider a redistribution of funds to broader low-income energy conservation measures.[259]

---

250 Order No. 75401, at 3, *In re* Commission's Inquiry into the Provision & Regulation of Elec. Serv. (Universal Serv.), No. 8738 (Md. Pub. Serv. Comm'n Aug. 3, 1999).

251 *Id.* at 4.

252 Order No.75935, at 8, *In re* Commission's Inquiry into the Provision & Regulation of Elec. Serv. (Universal Serv.), No. 8738 (Md. Pub. Serv. Comm'n Jan. 28, 2000).

253 *Id.* at 10.

254 *Id.*

255 *Id.* at 11.

256 *Id.*

257 Citing Md. Code Ann., art. 41, § 6-402 (repealed).

258 Order No. 76049, at 2–3, *In re* Commission's Inquiry into the Provision & Regulation of Elec. Serv. (Universal Serv.), No. 8738 (Md. Pub. Serv. Comm'n Apr. 4, 2000).

259 *Id.* at 3.

Because of the benefits that arise from appliance replacements, the PSC said it would "revisit this issue when it is appropriate to do so."

The Maryland PSC devoted considerable thought to the design of an arrearage-retirement program to be implemented as part of the EUSP. Arrearage retirement was one of the three statutorily mandated program components to be included in EUSP. The discussion occurred within the context of how to allocate the statutorily prescribed funding of $34 million amongst the three program components: (1) rate assistance; (2) arrearage retirement; and (3) weatherization. In deciding to fund arrearage retirement at $5.1 million of the $34 million program, the PSC reasoned that "one of the most critical elements for the success of the USP in the future is the arrearage retirement for those low-income customers who either have struggled in the past to maintain their electric service or lost such service altogether."[260]

Arrearage retirement was made broadly available under the EUSP. Having recognized the fundamental role that arrearage retirement plays in maintaining affordability within the EUSP, for example, the PSC held that the program would not "differentiate between on- and off-service customers with respect to arrearage retirement."[261] The PSC held that "active electric customers, as well as applicants for electricity service, including persons who are off-service, are eligible to apply for and receive arrearage assistance from USP."[262]

Even though broadly available, not every EUSP participant will be allowed complete forgiveness of their pre-program arrears. Two limits were placed on the retirement of arrears. First, the PUC established a cap on the amount of arrears that would be subject to retirement under EUSP for off-system customers. The PSC stated that it would

> adopt the [Baltimore Gas & Electric—BG&E] proposal, which establishes $2,000 as the cap for arrearage recovery. In this case, BG&E is willing to forego any recovery over and above that amount. While the Commission does not direct any utility at this time to adopt a similar level as full and complete payment, the fact that the utility with the greatest amount of arrears is willing to adopt this approach suggests that other utilities should be able to accomplish a similar outcome on a voluntary basis. The Commission encourages them to do so.[263]

However, the PSC rejected a proposal to limit the arrears subject to collection (and thus to forgiveness through the EUSP) to those arrears incurred within the three years immediately preceding a customer's entry into the program.[264]

Second, the PSC initially determined that the arrearage retirement program should not offer to pay, under all circumstances, the entire pre-program arrears for program participants. Noting the objection of some parties, the PSC nonetheless also believed that, under certain circumstances, a customer payment contribution toward retiring arrears was warranted and appropriate:

> Financial participation by customers in the retirement of their arrearages will encourage fiscal responsibility while also maximizing the use of funds available under the program. Accordingly, the Commission directs [the state LIHEAP agency] to develop a customer payment plan that requires on-service and off-service customers above 100% of the federal poverty level to contribute toward their arrearage retirement. The amount of contribution should be set within affordability limits and be based on a sliding scale, so that the amount of required contribution correspondingly increases with the level of an individual's income.[265]

The PSC subsequently reversed this decision, however. Noting that it had not changed its mind about the validity of the principle, the PUC simply noted that a detailed review by the stakeholders in seeking to implement the decision found that the decision's complexity outweighed its benefits.[266]

---

260 Order No. 75935, at 14, *In re* Commission's Inquiry into the Provision & Regulation of Elec. Serv. (Universal Serv.), No. 8738 (Md. Pub. Serv. Comm'n Jan. 28, 2000).

261 *Id.* at 20.

262 *Id.*

263 *Id.* at 21.

264 The existing "statute of limitations" on the collectability of arrears is seven years.

265 Order No.75935, at 21, *In re* Commission's Inquiry into the Provision & Regulation of Elec. Serv. (Universal Serv.), No. 8738 (Md. Pub. Serv. Comm'n Jan. 28, 2000).

266 Order 76139, at 5, *In re* Commission's Inquiry into the Provision & Regulation of Elec. Serv. (Universal Serv.), Case No. 8738 (Md. Pub. Serv. Comm'n May 8, 2000) ("these parties have participated in extended review and discussion of the implementation of our directive in work sessions convened since the issuance of Order No. 75395. While these parties still support the general reasonableness and efficacy of this approach, the parties nonetheless now view the administrative complexity and burden for the Department of Human Resources, local administering agencies, and/or the utilities in implementing this requirement as possibly outweighing potential benefits of the requirement and impeding the legislative goals in establishing the arrearage retirement component of the USP. For these reasons, the parties now request the commission to eliminate the customer payment contribution toward arrearage retirement as a design requirement of the program. The Commission is reluctant to eliminate the customer payment contributions toward arrearage retirement. . . . However, since numerous parties, including the original advocates for customer payment contributions, now find that requiring customer payment contributions toward arrearage retirement would be administratively burdensome, as well as a possible impediment to customer participation in the Universal Service Program, the commission modifies its previous determination and therefore will not require such design requirement at this time.").

The PSC determined that customers participating in the Maryland EUSP would be required to obtain service under a levelized budget billing payment plan in order to receive EUSP benefits.[267] This use of budget billing was subsequently reconsidered by the Universal Service Working Group (USWG). The recommendation was that the use of budget billing continue for several reasons.[268] First, the USWG decided that, given how new the EUSP was in Maryland, the program design should not change so quickly. Such changes would be confusing not only to customers but to "enrollment personnel," both of whom are "critical stakeholders." Second, making such a change would require computer programming time and expense not only by the utilities but by the program administrator as well. Finally, the USWG decided that the average payment plan process worked best for most customers:

> Although a few customers may prefer another option, the program should be implemented in a manner that is best for the overall population. The average payment plan meets the overall goal of the EUSP, to make payments by low-income customers affordable. It averages their payments over the year and is especially helpful to customers with fixed incomes. Customers know their monthly payment and are able to fit it into their overall budget process.[269]

The recommendation was accompanied with a disclaimer that the recommendation "is not intended to preclude a utility from voluntarily using a method by which 1/12th of the annual benefit is applied each month for 12 months against actual bills." Continuing into the present, low-income customers must agree to be placed on budget billing in order to participate in and receive benefits through the EUSP.

The Maryland PSC focused on the creation of a statewide program. This focus manifested itself in several ways. First, the allocation of arrearage assistance funds should be statewide. "A customer's location should neither assure coverage nor prove a detriment to coverage," the PSC stated. "This [arrearage retirement] program shall apply Statewide with no geographic allocation and be available on a first-come, first-served basis."[270]

In addition, the PSC mandated that the cost-recovery mechanism should be uniform statewide. The statute not only provided for a fixed program budget for the first three years of the EUSP[271] but also a fixed contribution toward that budget to be obtained from each customer class.[272] The residential charge was set at a uniform, statewide monthly fee of $4.97 to $5.00 annually (41¢ to 42¢ monthly).[273] A multi-step charge was established for commercial and industrial customers.[274] However, the PUC explained that it sought

> . . . a funding methodology that results in sets of uniform Statewide fees for commercial and industrial customers that apply irrespective of the service territory in which the customers are located. The use of Statewide fees should not preclude the differentiation of charges by customer size or electric usage, as long as the methodology proposed includes an appropriate cap. . . . The commission's primary interest in a proposal of this type is (i) to have flat fees that do not vary each month, thereby avoiding customer confusion, and (ii) to ensure that similarly-situated customers that happen to be located in different service territories pay the same charge, thereby avoiding any questions of competitive advantage.[275]

The statute prohibited collecting the universal service charges on a per-kilowatt-hour basis.[276] In adopting a fixed monthly fee, the PSC agreed with the argument by commercial and industrial representatives that the universal service charge "is similar to a utility 'customer charge,' which is traditionally designed and intended to recover a cost that bears no relationship to a customer's consumption."[277]

7.2.3.4.3 The Washington LIRA

Washington State does not have a statewide universal service program, nor does it have a comprehensive package of utility-funded programs. Pursuant to legislation enacted

267 Order 76595, at 2–3, *In re* Commission's Inquiry into the Provision & Regulation of Elec. Serv. (Universal Serv.), No. 8738 (Md. Pub. Serv. Comm'n Nov. 30, 2000).

268 *Id.* Report of the Universal Service Working Group on Supplemental Issues at 2 n.2 (Md. Pub. Serv. Comm'n Mar. 14, 2001).

269 *Id.* at 2–3.

270 Order No. 75935, at 22, *In re* Commission's Inquiry into the Provision & Regulation of Elec. Serv. (Universal Serv.), No. 8738 (Md. Pub. Serv. Comm'n Jan. 28, 2000).

271 Md. Code Ann., Pub. Util. Cos. § 7-512.1(e), provided that the universal service fund collect $34 million each year. As of 2011, the amount is $37 million. *See* Md. Code Ann., Pub. Utils. Cos. § 7-512.1e(2) (West).

272 Md. Code Ann., Pub. Util. Cos. § 7-512.1(e)(2), provides that $9.6 million of the budget should be obtained from residential customers. Section 7-512.1(e)(1) provides that $27.4 million be collected from commercial and industrial customers.

273 Order No. 75935, at 23, *In re* Commission's Inquiry into the Provision & Regulation of Elec. Serv. (Universal Serv.), No. 8738 (Md. Pub. Serv. Comm'n Jan. 28, 2000).

274 Known as the "23-step" fee structure, the commercial and industrial universal service charge imposes a fixed monthly fee ranging from a $3.00-per-month (or $36-per-year) fee to a $3500-per-month (or $42,000-per-year) fee.

275 Order No. 75401, at 5, *In re* Commission's Inquiry into the Provision & Regulation of Elec. Serv. (Universal Serv.), No. 8738 (Md. Pub. Serv. Comm'n Aug. 3, 1999).

276 Md. Code Ann., Pub. Util. Cos., § 7-512.1(b)(7) (West).

277 Order No. 75935, at 28, *In re* Commission's Inquiry into the Provision & Regulation of Elec. Serv. (Universal Serv.), No. 8738 (Md. Pub. Serv. Comm'n Jan. 28, 2000).

in 1999, the Washington Utilities and Transportation Commission (WUTC) has statutory authority to approve a low-income program only if approval of such a program is sought by the utility. According to the WUTC, it may not only not direct a utility to promulgate a low-income affordability program, it may not even direct a utility—unless it receives a request from that utility—to enter a collaborative process to consider whether a potential program design could be generated through discussions with other Washington stakeholders.

The Washington statute provides as follows:

> Upon request by an electrical or gas company or other party to a general rate case hearing, the commission may approve rates, charges, services and/or physical facilities at a discount for low-income senior customers and low-income customers. Expenses and lost revenues as a result of these discounts shall be included in the company's cost of service and recovered in rates to other customers.[278]

The limitations placed upon the WUTC by this statute were perhaps most evident in a 1999 rate case involving Avista Corporation.[279] In that proceeding, a local community-based low-income advocacy organization (Spokane Neighborhood Action Program: or SNAP) proposed a two-part low-income customer program. According to SNAP, Avista should be required to implement a system benefits charge of 1% of total revenues to fund low-income programs. In addition, SNAP recommended that responsibility for the specific design of the low-income interventions be assigned to a working group charged with developing and presenting the program design to the WUTC within a time-certain.[280]

The SNAP proposal was supported both by the Public Counsel and by the Northwest Energy Coalition (NWEC). According to Public Counsel, the WUTC should direct Avista to engage in a collaborative planning process to develop a low-income assistance filing in time for the onset of the winter heating season. NWEC recommended that Avista's energy efficiency programs to low-income customers be combined with "meaningful programs supported by a guaranteed level of investment in low-income energy assistance."[281]

Avista opposed the proposal. If a collaborative process were to be ordered by the WUTC, Avista stated, it should be a statewide process that should be "for the purpose of examining low-income issues, as the same may be affected by existing Commission collection and disconnection rules and practices."[282]

278 Wash. Rev. Code § 80.28.068.

279 Third Supplemental Order, Washington Util. & Transp. Comm'n v. Avista Corp., Nos. UE-991606, UG-991607 (Wash. Utils. & Transp. Comm'n 1999).

280 *Id.* at ¶ 399.

281 *Id.* at ¶ 400.

282 *Id.* at ¶ 401.

The WUTC held that it did not have authority to grant the relief requested by SNAP, the Public Counsel, and NWEC:

> The Commission values and encourages continued dialogue among the various parties with regard to low-income energy efficiency and assistance efforts. However, [the statute] grants no latitude to the Commission to order such rates in the absence of a company request. . . . Therefore, the Commission cannot act on SNAP's proposed one percent wires charge and collaborative process. In our view, the legislature has granted us authority to order a surcharge only if the Company requests it.[283]

Since the *Avista* decision, a variety of utilities have proposed limited low-income assistance programs to be presented by stipulation to the WUTC.

Pacific Power operates the Low-Income Bill Assistance (LIBA) program.[284] LIBA provides a per-kWh discount for families at or below 125% of the federal poverty level (the Washington state LIHEAP eligibility standard). LIBA provides three different discounts, with households at the lowest poverty levels receiving the largest discount. Participation in the PacifiCorp program is quite limited, however. While in 2006 participation was capped at 2618 customers, allowable annual participation in 2011 is 4720 customer.[285]

The PacifiCorp low-income commitment arose out of the acquisition of PacifiCorp by Scottish Power Company.[286] The stipulation[287] sought to resolve all low-income issues presented by the PacifiCorp merger. It involved a commitment by Scottish Power/PacifiCorp to provide $300,000 annually of shareholder funds for the implementation of bill payment assistance and energy efficiency programs "that have been identified, developed and financially structured to ensure they are cost-effective and meet all regulatory and business requirements." The funding commitment was to continue for three years, by which time an evaluation of the spending would be completed. According to the stipulation, "this analysis will form an important factor when deciding the appropriate level of funding going forward."[288] The stipulation provided finally that all of the parties would agree to support company efforts "to recover through rates[] any program costs that are recoverable under Commission rules and Washington law."[289]

283 *Id.* at ¶¶ 402, 403.

284 This program is included in Tariff Schedule 17.

285 *See* www.pacificpower.net/about/rr/wri.html (Pacific Power Low Income Bill Assistance tariff schedule).

286 *In re* Application of PacifiCorp & Scottish Power, P.L.C., No. UE-981627 (Wash. Utils. & Transp. Comm'n 2005).

287 The stipulation was agreed to by the Company, Public Counsel, NWEC, and the Energy Project (a program of the local community action agency).

288 Stipulation at § 2, *In re* Application of PacifiCorp & Scottish Power, P.L.C., No. UE-981627 (Wash. Utils. & Transp. Comm'n 2005).

289 *Id.*

The parties in the case of *Washington Utilities and Transportation Commission v. Puget Sound Energy, Inc.*, addressed the level of funding for the LIBA program.[290] After settlement negotiations bogged down, the Energy Project (a local community action agency project) filed testimony advocating that the utility bring its funding up to a level commensurate with the other invester-owned electric utilities in Washington. This would be an increase from 0.26 % of revenues to somewhere between 0.4%–0.7%. The utility had proposed a much smaller increase but stated in cross-examination that it would do whatever the WUTC instructed.

Puget Sound Energy's (PSE) low-income electric customers would receive benefits under an agreement initiated in discussions with the Energy Project in 2001 but stipulated in the settlement of its electric rate case in 2002.[291] In exchange for agreement to a two-part rate increase generating roughly $58.3 million dollars annually in new revenues, Puget Sound Energy would require a surcharge to cover the new low-income assistance program. The surcharge would add roughly 25¢ per month to a typical monthly homeowner bill. The stipulation provided that overall annual funding for the low-income assistance program would be set at $8.6 million, or approximately 0.50% of pro forma retail revenues.[292] Roughly two-thirds (67.4%) of the funding would be distributed to electric customers with the remainder being allocated to gas customers (32.6%).

The Puget Sound Energy stipulation provided that the costs of the low-income program would be borne by all electric and natural gas customer classes, with the exception that no allocation would be made to natural gas special contract customers.[293] The program was proposed without a termination date.[294] The rate case completed in 2006 added another $1.7 million to the energy assistance funding.

The PSE program is directed toward customers who would otherwise qualify for federal LIHEAP assistance but do not receive such assistance because LIHEAP funds are exhausted.[295]

The PSE program provides benefits to income-qualified customers, with the benefit amount calculated through a pre-determined formula based on a household's actual energy use derived from services the household receives from PSE.[296] Annual benefits are capped at $750.[297] Finally, PSE agreed to "coordinate the creation of a working group that will advise the Company on low income issues."[298] The stipulation provided, however, that "any modifications to PSE's tariffs or schedules must be initiated by PSE and approved by the Commission."[299]

Avista's Low-Income Rate Assistance Program (LIRAP) was approved by the WUTC in May 2001.[300] The purpose of LIRAP is to "reduce the energy cost burden among those customers least able to pay energy bills."[301] Through LIRAP, Avista collects new revenue from both its natural gas and electric customers. In the 2005/2006 program year, the Avista collected roughly $2.9 million from customers ($1.85 million from electric customers; $1 million from natural gas customers), which was then matched with a contribution of $300,000 by Avista's shareholders.

Avista chose to use a different format to fund two programs. One is a single lump-sum grant (originally $200, now $300, per year) for seniors. The other is a "LIHEAP-lookalike" program that provides a lump-sum payment based on a formula considering income level and consumption. Money is distributed to low-income Avista customers in much the same manner as funds are distributed through the federal LIHEAP program. For clients receiving "regular" assistance, the eligibility determination is the same as for the federal LIHEAP program. The amount of assistance for these households is based on the state LIHEAP office's benefit calculation. For clients receiving "emergency" assistance, the process is similar to the local fuel fund (Project Share). Emergency assistance is made available to households in imminent danger of disconnection; the amount of assistance is determined on a case-by-case basis, with a maximum of $300.

While Avista *eligibility* is determined in the same way as other existing low-income assistance programs, the *marketing* of the program is directed toward payment-troubled customers. These include customers receiving shut-off notices and who have large arrears, among other things.

Additional low-income assistance dollars were provided in a 2005 settlement of a general natural gas/electric rate increase request.[302] In this proceeding, Avista agreed to

290 Washington Util. & Transp. Comm'n v. Puget Sound Energy, Inc., Nos. UE-011570, UG-011571 (consolidated), 2002 Wash. UTC LEXIS 329 (Wash. Util. & Transp. Comm'n Aug. 28, 2002) (approving settlement).

291 *Id.* Twelfth Supplemental Order: Rejecting Tariff Filing; Approving and Adopting Settlement Stipulation Subject to Modifications, Clarifications and Conditions; Authorizing and Requiring Compliance Filing (Wash. Util. & Transp. Comm'n June 20, 2002).

292 This funding level was argued to be consistent with Avista's and PacifiCorp's commitment of 0.79% and 0.30%, respectively, of retail revenues.

293 Settlement Stipulation Exhibit G, Settlement Terms for Low Income at ¶¶ 4–5, Washington Util. & Transp. Comm'n v. Puget Sound Energy, Inc., Nos. UE-011570, UG-011571 (consolidated) (Wash. Util. & Transp. Comm'n June 7, 2002).

The settlement stipulation was adopted by the WUTC without comment on the low-income issues.

294 *Id.* at ¶ 7

295 *Id.* at ¶ 14.

296 *Id.* at ¶ 15.

297 *Id.* at ¶ 8.

298 *Id.* at ¶ 21.

299 *Id.*

300 Nos. UE-010436 and UG-010437 (Wash. Utils. & Transp. Comm'n May 2001).

301 Avista Utils., Low-Income Rate Assistance Program (LIRAP): Fifth Annual Report, for the Period May 2005 Through Apr. 2006, at 1 (Aug. 23, 2006).

302 Order No. 05, Approving and Adopting Settlement Agreement with Conditions ¶¶ 141–47, Washington Utils. & Transp.

provide an additional $600,000 per calendar year (for two calendar years) of funding for its Low-Income Rate Assistance Program (LIRAP). The total LIRAP funding would thus reach $3 million per year.[303] The funding was generated through a combination of tax credits and a reallocation of natural gas demand side management funding. The WUTC approved this stipulation, noting that it "is especially important during the current period of rapidly increasing and volatile energy prices."[304]

Cascade Natural Gas Corporation is the most recent Washington utility to agree, by stipulation, to the creation of a low-income rate assistance program. In the stipulated settlement of its 2006 rate case, Cascade agreed to provide $800,000 in bill assistance to low-income customers.[305] In addition, Cascade agreed to add all public utility tax credits obtained from the state of Washington—discussed in more detail below—to this base amount. Cascade expects to receive an additional $107,000 in tax credits based on its $800,000 expenditure.

The Cascade Natural Gas program is based on a design proposed by the Energy Project, a program of Washington's community action agencies.[306] In this program design, the Cascade would distribute energy assistance based on a matrix similar to that used by the LIHEAP office in Washington. Some differences would exist. Rather than using the state's eligibility of 125% of the federal poverty level, Cascade's program would use 150% of the poverty level. Funding would be provided as an annual lump-sum payment similar to LIHEAP. Cascade would use the same community-based agencies as intake points for its program. Cascade committed to modeling its program after other Washington utility programs that had previously been approved by the WUTC.

The Washington legislature has created a supplemental funding source for utilities agreeing to provide rate affordability assistance to their low-income customers. Created in 2001, the legislature provides matching tax credits for dollars provided in rate affordability assistance.[307] Although not required to do so, each Washington utility claiming credits under the program has agreed to devote those credits to supplementing their low-income funding.

The tax credits are provided as an incentive for the state's utilities to increase their funding of low-income affordability assistance. In order to claim the tax credit, the assistance provided must exceed 125% of the qualifying contributions made in 2000.[308] A "qualifying contribution" is low-income assistance funding that is given to an organization under contract to distribute LIHEAP funds.[309] In addition, a tax credit can be obtained for providing "billing discounts" so long as the discount is greater than 125% of any discount that had been provided in 2000.[310] A "bill discount" is defined to include any "reduction in the amount charged for providing service" to a qualified low-income household by an electric or natural gas utility.[311]

The Washington tax credit program allows for a tax credit equal to 50% of any contribution or billing discount provided by a Washington utility.[312] The maximum total credits allowed statewide, however, is set by statute.[313] If the tax credits for which Washington utilities qualify exceed the annual ceiling, the credits are distributed on a formula basis.[314] The ceiling amount is now being substantially exceeded by Washington utilities, thus impeding the tax credit's function as an incentive.

In sum, while not mandating energy affordability programs for its state's utilities, the Washington state legislative and regulatory regime has generated a series of limited programs by each of the state's natural gas and electric utilities. The Washington statutory approach is unique, allowing the state utility commission to approve low-income affordability programs only when such programs are requested by the utility. In contrast, unlike most other state utility commissions, the Washington Utilities and Transportation Commission (WUTC) has taken the narrowest possible path under the statute, holding that the statute "grants no latitude to the Commission . . ."

The programs that have been proposed and approved in Washington have been developed in collaboration with low-income stakeholders. Not only has the low-income energy advocacy community been involved, but service providers (such as community action agencies) and the state LIHEAP office have been part of the collaborations, which have resulted in the submission of stipulated program designs to the WUTC for approval.

In Washington, the utilities serve primarily as a funding agent, generating a revenue stream to be distributed through those agencies already involved with distributing LIHEAP funds. The rate affordability programs are not tied explicitly to producing any particular level of affordability, as measured by home energy burdens, but rather are tied to extending the ability of the LIHEAP program to reach customers who might otherwise go unserved because of limited resources.

Comm'n v. Avista Corp. d/b/a Avista Utilities, Nos. UE-050482, UG-050483 (Wash. Utils. & Transp. Comm'n Dec. 21, 2005).

303 *Id.* at ¶ 141.

304 *Id.* at ¶ 145.

305 Order No. 05 ¶¶ 41–44, Washington Util. & Transp. Comm'n v. Cascade Natural Gas Co., No. UG-060256 (Wash. Utils. & Transp. Comm'n Jan. 12, 2007).

306 *Id.* at ¶ 42.

307 Wash. Rev. Code § 82.16.0497.

308 *Id.* § 82.16.0497(2)(a)(1).

309 *Id.* § 82.16.0497(1)(e)–(g).

310 *Id.* § 82.16.0497(2)(b).

311 *Id.* § 82.16.0497(1)(b).

312 *Id.* § 82.16.0497(2)(b).

313 *Id.* § 82.16.0497(3)(a).

314 *Id.* § 82.16.0497(1)(a).

However, the Washington programs explicitly recognize the difference between establishing eligibility standards and undertaking targeted outreach. While the Avista program, for example, is made available to customers found to be eligible under the state LIHEAP program standards, the company *markets* its program to payment-troubled customers, including those in danger of imminent service disconnection and those with large arrears.

The tax credit program offered in Washington State appears to be unique. The state expands the resources that its utilities are willing to generate through a rate surcharge by matching those resources with state tax credits. Each utility, while seemingly not *required* to do so, has agreed to use those state-matching tax credits as additional resources to expand their low-income programs.

7.2.3.4.4 The Oregon OLGA

Oregon's universal service program is a creature of statute. The state's electric and natural gas utilities operate under separate statutory authority. Funding electric affordability programs in Oregon is mandatory. Funding for natural gas programs is not. The electric and natural gas statutory provisions are discussed separately below.

As part of the legislative approval of a move to electric restructuring in Oregon, the state legislature enacted statutory language explicitly creating a universal service fund.[315] The legislature declared that the program was created:

> . . . for the purpose of providing low-income bill payment and crisis assistance, including programs that effectively reduce service disconnections and related costs to retail electricity customers and electric utilities. Priority assistance shall be directed to low-income electricity consumers who are in danger of having their electricity service disconnected.[316]

The statute created a universal service fund. After the first few years of the law, the funding level was set at $10 million annually beginning in 2002.[317] The statute was amended in 2007 to increase the funding level to $15 million annually and to allow subsequent changes in the level of funding as the number of residential customers and business kWh sales increase.[318]

The Oregon fund applies only to the state's two investor-owned electric utilities: Portland General Electric and PacifiCorp. Funding is collected from all retail customers of these investor-owned electric companies.[319] Residential customers pay a monthly meters charge, while non-residential customers pay a per-kWh charge.[320] The contribution of any individual non-residential customer, however, is capped at $500 per year per "site" for each customer.[321] The Oregon Public Utilities Commission (OPUC) is charged with the responsibility of setting both the meters charge and kWh charge to generate the annual funding of $15 million.[322] The OPUC determines the distribution of the $15 million between the residential and non-residential customer classes as well as the individual charges. In reaching this decision each year, the OPUC considers periodic filings by the two utilities based on the utilities' most recent load forecasts.[323]

Under the Oregon low-income assistance program, low-income customers of the contributing electric companies can receive one regular assistance payment per year toward their electric bill. Under "special circumstances," these customers may also receive an additional "crisis" payment.[324] These assistance amounts can reach a maximum of $300 and $500 respectively.[325] A single grant is made to customers each year.

As with most such low-income programs, while administration of the funding of the program was placed under the supervision of the state utility commission, the program administration was placed within the state LIHEAP agency. The Department of Housing and Community Services (OHCS) set the eligibility for the Oregon program equal to 60% of state median income, believing median income "better represents local conditions" than does the federal poverty level.[326] The utilities collect the funding each month and pay it to OHCS. OHCS contracts with a network of community-based organizations to identify and enroll qualified electric customers.

At roughly the same time the legislature was mandating an electric affordability initiative for the state of Oregon, it

---

315 Popularly known as Senate Bill 1149, the Oregon low-income program was codified at Or. Rev. Stat. § 757.612(1)–(9).

316 Or. Rev. Stat. § 757.612(7)(d).

317 *Id.* § 757.612(7)(b).

318 *See Id.* § 757.612(7)(b); S.B. 461, 74th Legis. Assemb., 2007 Reg. Sess. (Or. 2007).

319 *See generally* Oregon Hous. & Cmty. Servs., Oregon Energy Assistance Program, Report to the 74th Legislative Assembly, 74th Legis. Assemb. (2006).

The statute provides that "the Oregon Housing and Community Services Department shall prepare a biennial report to the Legislative Assembly describing program spending and needs for low-income bill assistance." Or. Rev. Stat. § 757.612(2).

320 Under the statute, the commission shall determine each electric company's proportionate share of the total amount and the rate to be charged to retail electricity consumer. Or. Rev. Stat. § 757.612(7)(b).

321 *Id.* § 757(7)(b).

322 *Id.* § 757.612(7)(b).

323 *See generally* Or. Rev. Stat. § 757.205 (2007). *See, e.g.*, Portland General Electric's Advice No. 02-25 and PacifiCorp's Advice No. 02-028 (Dec. 2, 2002) (effective Jan. 1, 2003; setting meters charge at 38¢ per month and kWh charge at 38¢/kWh); Portland General Electric's Advice 05-002 and PacifiCorp Advice 05-003 (effective Apr. 1, 2005) (setting meters charge at 38¢ and kWh charge at 3¢/kWh).

324 Sami Khawaja & Sharon Baggett, Oregon Hous. & Cmty. Servs., Oregon Energy Assistance Program Evaluation 1-1 (Jan. 2002).

325 *Id.* at 1-4.

326 *Id.* at 1-4.

was also authorizing natural gas companies to develop and propose individual company Oregon Low-Income Gas Assistance (OLGA) programs for approval by the Oregon state utilities commission. In 2001, the legislature amended the state's public utility law to provide that:

> The Public Utility Commission may authorize a natural gas public utility, upon application of the utility, to include in rates for residential customers of the utility amounts for the purpose of generating funds to be used for bill payment assistance to low-income residential customers of the utility.[327]

The statute was written to be an explicit exemption from the statutory ban on discriminatory ratemaking. Oregon's basic public utility law provides that "a public utility may not charge a customer a rate or an amount for a service that is different from the rate or amount the public utility charges any other customer for a like and contemporaneous service under substantially similar circumstances."[328] Moreover, the statute provides that "a public utility may not charge a customer a rate or an amount for a service that is different from the rate or amount prescribed in the schedules or tariffs for the public utility."[329]

The Oregon natural gas statute differs sharply from its electric counterpart. First, while the electric statute mandates an electric affordability program, the natural gas statute merely authorizes the state utility commission to approve such a program should it so choose. In addition, the Oregon statute, mirroring its Washington counterpart, allows the state utility commission to approve a natural gas affordability program only if the program is first proposed by the gas utility.

There is ambiguity in the natural gas statute. It is not clear, for example, whether the statute requires an "all or nothing" approach to OPUC approval. Once a utility proposes a program, the statute is not clear if the OPUC must approve that program *as proposed* or if the OPUC may order modifications in the proposal whether or not the proposing company consents to those modifications. Moreover, it is not clear whether a natural gas utility is authorized, outside of this statute, to provide a low-income affordability program so long as the utility does not seek to "include in rates for residential customers of the utility amounts for the purpose of generating funds to be used for bill payment assistance."[330] Under such a program, the statutory rate discrimination proscription would not be violated, since the low-income bill would be paid in full (albeit from different funding sources).

The precise construction of the statutory wording for Oregon's natural gas statute, however, was rendered moot as the state's natural gas utilities sought approval for affordability programs pursuant to the statute. In March 2002, Avista Utilities submitted a proposal to create a Residential Low-Income Rate Assistance Program (LIRAP) for its residential gas customers.[331] Under the Avista program proposal, the company would seek increased funding equal to roughly one-half of 1% of a residential customer's natural gas billing rate ($0.00438 per therm). The company calculated that residential customers would pay roughly 25¢ at an average usage of 56 therms, compared to the 35¢ assessment on electric customers. In recommending approval of the program, the OPUC staff reported that:

> Avista'a application identifies a need for additional low-income bill payment assistance in the company's Oregon service territory, citing Oregon Housing and Community Services data, showing that Community Action Agencies currently providing low-income bill payment assistance in Avista's Oregon service territory are presently limited by funding to serving less than 14% of the households in need of low-income bill payment assistance.
>
> Avista's own internal data also identifies an increased need for low-income bill assistance within its Oregon service area. Notable among the company's statistics are a 65% increase in payment arrangements, a 26% increase in field collection orders and an increase of 21% in the number of customer accounts written off, resulting in a 93% increase in the amount written off.[332]

The proposed LIRAP program was designed to be used by local community action agencies "in conjunction with and in addition to existing" federal fuel assistance funds "to expand the reach of existing energy assistance." Avista estimated that it would serve an additional population of between 500 and 1000 households. Households would receive winter assistance, with the "potential for assistance in non-winter months."[333] Program participants would be allowed, but not required, to enroll in the company's levelized monthly billing program.

Northwest Natural Gas soon proposed an OLGA program similar to the LIRAP that had been approved for Avista Utilities. Northwest Natural Gas began collecting a monthly OLGA charge of 25¢ in October 2002. In February 2006,

327 Or. Rev. Stat. § 757.315(3).

328 *Id.* § 757.310(2).

329 *Id.* § 310.310(1).

One additional exemption provided by statute is that a utility may offer "an optional schedule or tariff for the provision of energy service that takes into account a customer's past energy usage and provides price incentives designed to encourage changes in the customer's energy usage that correspond to changes in the cost of providing energy." *Id.* § 757.310(3)(c).

330 For example, see the initiatives in Missouri and Colorado under which arguably external funding sources (for example, transportation gas refunds, unauthorized pipeline usage charges) were proposed as funding sources.

331 Avista Utils., Advice No. 02-2-G (Mar. 8, 2002).

332 Avista Utils., Staff Report, Advice No. 02-2-G (Apr. 2, 2002).

333 *Id.* at 5.

the company requested an increase in its OLGA charge to 31¢. While representing an increase of 25%, in recommending approval of the increase, the OPUC staff observed that it was "less than the company's 2004 and 2005 gas cost increases."[334] The proposed increase would result in a total of roughly $1.9 million in low-income assistance in the next year.

In addition, the company's 2006 filing indicated that Northwest Natural Gas "plans to propose a mechanism in its 2006 Purchased Gas Cost filing that will provide a more systematic way to adjust the OLGA charge (up or down) as residential billing rates increase or decrease."[335] The need to modestly increase the charge supporting the gas affordability program resulted not merely from a 35% increase in local distribution gas rates, but from increased experience with the dynamics of the charge. According to the OPUC staff:

> The OLGA charge has not been increased since its inception in 2002. Over the last two years, two gas costs increases have raised NW Natural residential rates by about 35 percent. During the 2004–2005 program year, NW Natural collected about $1.5 million and served 4,996 low-income customers with an average payment per household of $309. The OLGA program served 59 fewer customers than the prior program year (2003–2004) and the average payment per household increased by $27. NW Natural believes this demonstrates that the current growth in OLGA revenues of three percent per year due to customer growth does not provide sufficient funding to meet current program needs, given the higher gas costs and resulting higher bills per customer.[336]

In approving the 2006 NW Natural request for an increase in its OLGA charge, the OPUC found that there was a need to develop more specific standards on when, and to what extent, future changes in the OLGA charge would be approved. Those standards would involve measuring the need for increased funding along with the availability of other sources of energy assistance in each natural gas company's service territory. Each of the three investor-owned gas utilities, along with service providers such as the Community Action Directors of Oregon (CADO), would be invited to participate in promulgating those standards.

In 2006, as part of a decoupling docket, Cascade Natural Gas agreed to fund two new public purpose programs.[337] One of these programs provides bill payment assistance. Under the new program, Cascade Natural Gas would implement a "public purpose charge" equal to 0.75% of its current revenues.[338] That charge would be expected to generate no less than $500,000 per year as "public purpose funds." Cascade Natural Gas agreed to transfer 20% of those funds to local community action agencies to support low-income weatherization and bill assistance programs. Three quarters of the low-income funds would be devoted to weatherization programs, with the remainder devoted to bill assistance. Funding not distributed in any given year would be carried forward to the next year.

The Cascade Natural Gas bill assistance program is tied closely to the state administration of the federal LIHEAP program. Cascade Natural Gas agreed to distribute these bill assistance funds among the community action agencies serving its territory in the same proportion as LIHEAP funds are distributed. The funds, to be provided only to Cascade Oregon customers, would then be distributed based on the LIHEAP payment matrix most currently in use by the state LIHEAP office. The local community action agencies doing LIHEAP intake would have sole responsibility to screen and approve applicants for eligibility. As is evident, the impact of the Cascade Natural Gas program is to extend the LIHEAP program to households that might otherwise not be served due to the lack of federal funding.

Not all utility rate affordability programs in Oregon operate under the statutory framework discussed above. In adopting the electric affordability program in 1999, the Oregon legislature also authorized Oregon electric utilities to provide their own company-specific affordability programs. Under the statute, the state utility commission was explicitly authorized to "allow an electric company to provide reduced rates or other payment or crisis assistance or low-income program assistance to a low-income household eligible for assistance" under the federal LIHEAP program.[339] Programs adopted pursuant to this authorization would be in addition to the electric affordability funding administered through the state LIHEAP office.

In August 2006, Portland General Electric Company proposed an arrearage forgiveness program under the authority of this statute.[340] Called the New Start Pilot, the arrearage program would be made available to the first 600 residential customers who qualified for the federal LIHEAP program and had an outstanding balance of at least $100 (or a balance of at least $100 on an existing payment agreement).

New Start program participants would be placed on a twenty-four-month levelized payment agreement. When a participant makes twelve consecutive monthly payments on time and in full (and attends one "energy awareness class"), the company would waive 50% of the customer's arrearage.

334 Northwest Natural Gas, Staff Report, Advice No. 06-4 (Apr. 20, 2006).

335 *Id.* at 2.

336 *Id.*

337 Stipulation ¶¶ 10 and 11, *In re* Cascade Natural Gas Corp. Request for Authorization to Establish a Decoupling Mechanism, No. UG-167 (Or. Pub. Util. Comm'n Apr. 2006).

338 The level of the public purpose charge would be subject to change upon review.

339 Or. Rev. Stat. § 757.612(7)(f).

340 Portland Gen. Elec., Advice 06-17 (Aug. 4, 2006) (proposed to be effective September 6, 2006).

According to the company, its intent was to "test several hypotheses," including those that test whether

> [t]he requirements for participating in the New Start Pilot will improve customers' payment habits; timely payments will reduce the costs associated with payment delinquency; and the 24-month, levelized time payment agreement will provide customers with stable and predictable monthly bills, which should reduce the likelihood that the participants will become delinquent in the future.[341]

In addition to citing the OPUC's statutory authority under §757.612, Portland General Electric cited its authority under the OPUC's payment plan regulations to enter into "alternate payment arrangements."[342]

The OPUC staff recommended approval of the New Start Pilot. According to the its staff, Portland General Electric:

> . . . developed the New Start Pilot in response to the inevitable accrual of monies resulting from customer accounts that are not paid and eventually booked to the utility's accounts as uncollectible funds. The Pilot is structured to encourage the modification of customer behavior that is related to bill payment, through a combination of education and financial reward.[343]

The OPUC staff noted further that all administrative costs for the program, as well as the portion of a customer's account that may be written off, would be booked below the line. After one year, the staff said, Portland General would review the program and recommend modifications or termination of the program as appropriate.

While it appears that the New Start program is no longer effective, recently the Oregon legislature passed Senate Bill 863, instituting a public purpose charge for the state's electric utilities through January 1, 2026.[344] Thirteen percent of funds collected through this charge would be allocated to low-income weatherization assistance.[345]

In sum, the past and present Oregon statutes present opportunities to gain insights into the limits and potential of utility affordability programs. The basic Oregon ratemaking statute seems to have been used, historically, to foreclose the opportunity for rate assistance programs. The reading of this statute appears to have been too narrow in this regard. The statute, by its very terms, is limited to prohibiting utilities from *charging* one customer a different rate from the one charged to another. Moreover, the statutory language is limited to prohibiting a utility from *charging* a rate different than that prescribed in its rates or tariffs. Under such a statute, it would be possible to charge all customers the same rate (and a rate that does not differ from the tariff). In contrast, the utility can collect funds that would be used as energy assistance to supplement the *payment* of low-income bills. In other words, as it currently stands, while the low-income charges would be the same, the low-income utility customer can receive supplemental funding from a utility revenue source. Such a program would not run afoul of the Oregon statute's plain language.

Enactment of the present-day statutory framework, however, renders this analysis moot. The statute mandates electric low-income assistance funding and authorizes natural gas rate affordability programs. Moreover, the statute explicitly authorizes electric companies to provide rate relief that goes beyond the generation of funds for energy assistance.

Oregon's electric assistance statute, however, does not purport to take on the issue of energy affordability. Rather, this statute focuses on the prevention of utility arrears and service terminations. "Priority assistance," the statute specifically says, is to be provided to customers in danger of having their service disconnected.

The existing Oregon customer assistance programs are closely integrated with the state's LIHEAP office.[346] For the most part, eligibility is set at the same level, intake is done through the same network of community-based agencies, and benefit levels are tied to existing federal LIHEAP benefit levels.

7.2.4 Budget Billing

Spiraling fuel prices at various times and in various states have resulted in state utility regulatory commissions facing public health and safety crises and ordering public utilities in their jurisdiction to take action in response. Such action has been undertaken in the name of assisting consumers who find it difficult to pay their utility bills and in helping these customers to preserve their utility services.

Billing for fuels used to heat residential homes have seen a spike over the past twenty years, placing regulators in the position of deciding how to balance the competing interests of utilities seeking full compensation for high fuel prices with the interests of consumers trying to avoid being overburdened by the high cost of a life necessity. Billing spikes can occur because of (1) high prices or (2) severe hot or cold weather. These two occurrences are often combined and strengthen the threat of unaffordable energy bills.

---

341 Portland Gen. Elec., New Start Pilot, Advice No. 06-17 (Aug. 4, 2006).

342 Or. Admin. R. 860-021-0415(4).

343 Portland Gen. Elec., Staff Report, New Start Pilot, Aug. 24, 2006.

344 *See* S. Bill 863, 76th Legislative Sess., (Or. 2011), *available at* www.leg.state.or.us:8765 (select "2011 Legislative Measures"; type "863" in search box and click on "search"); Or. Rev. Stat. § 757.612(2)(a).

345 Or. Rev. Stat. § 757.612(3)(b)(C).

346 *See* LIHEAP Clearinghouse, State PBF/USF History, Legislation, Implementation: Oregon (Aug. 2010), *at* http://liheap.ncat.org/dereg/states/oregon.htm.

Actions taken by state utility regulatory commissions in response to these billing spikes are frequently directed toward preserving service during cold-weather months.

Budget billing programs provide assistance to low-income (and, in many states non-low-income) customers by restructuring their payments in such a manner that the household pays a set amount each month towards its bill.[347] This plan makes bills more "affordable" to low-income households, by not burdening low-income households with particularly high bills in months when usage is necessarily higher—bills that they simply cannot afford. When slapped with extra high bills, households are less likely to make *any* sort of payment—whether it be partial *or* the entire payment (this is the case with any bill, energy or not). Budget billing thus relieves the low-income customer from the devastating shock of extra high bills. It does not, however, relieve them of the annual burden of energy costs on their incomes, as no discounts or reduced rates are provided.

The Tennessee state utility regulatory commission faced such circumstances in 2005. In the winter of 2005, states were faced with possibility that, due to a "fly-up" in natural gas prices, home heating bills would be as much as 50% higher than during the previous winter. In response, the Tennessee Regulatory Authority (TRA) "approved a budget billing plan under which a natural gas customer who cannot pay his or her monthly bill in total will be enrolled automatically in an equal payment plan."[348] Based on the customer's historical usage, the company divided the customer's bill into twelve equal monthly payments; the payments are then "trued up" annually with the customer's actual bill. The TRA also reinforced its moratorium on winter service disconnections.[349]

The Massachusetts Department of Telecommunications and Energy (DTE) also responded to the high fuel prices of 1999 and 2000. In response to "substantial increases in fuel costs which have driven up the price of electric generation," the DTE stated that utilities should "expand their budget billing and consumer payment plans during the winter heating season . . . to lessen the effects of rate increases on consumers this winter . . ."[350] The DTE found that this need was driven by "steep and significant increases in the prices of natural gas and fuel oil—fuels commonly used for generating electricity in New England."[351]

Not all regulatory action addresses natural gas utilities alone, nor do such actions deal only with *cold* weather problems. The Public Utility Commission of Ohio (PUCO), for example, approved an "extended payment option to residential customers who are having difficulty paying August 1995 electric bills due to the effect of extreme August weather conditions." The PUCO order directed that the company was to allow for customers to "make payments of August bills, without interest, through December 1995."[352]

In some instances, these budget billing plans are combined with some level of rate assistance, even if limited in nature. The Baltimore Gas and Electric Company (BG&E) Customer Assistance Maintenance Program (CAMP) is one such program. The Maryland state utility commission approved BG&E's proposed CAMP initiative in 1994. CAMP[353] was again reviewed and approved by the Maryland Public Service Commission (PSC) in 1997.[354] Under CAMP, low-income customers making current bill payments will receive CAMP credits toward future bills. A program participant can qualify to earn monthly bill credits ranging from $7 to $12 depending upon the customer's annual income.

In reviewing CAMP within the context of the proposed merger of BG&E with Constellation, the Maryland PSC noted that its approval of the program was based on its ability to generate positive impact for non-participating ratepayers. " . . . CAMP was approved in part due to a showing that the financial assistance to low-income customers provided by the program could lead to reductions in uncollectibles."[355]

Because of these benefits, the state Office of Peoples Counsel (OPC) argued, the normal statutory language prohibiting undue preferences did not apply. According to the OPC:

> People's Counsel concludes that low income programs address real needs. In response to some parties' contentions that it is inappropriate to use ratepayer funds for charitable-type purposes, OPC stresses the programs being proposed can be cost-effective. In particular, OPC asserts that CAMP is cost-effective. OPC stresses that the Commission approved CAMP in 1994 based on findings that the program will operate to reduce uncollectibles from low income customers, thereby providing a net benefit to other ratepayers. Thus, while OPC argues that the Commission possesses the authority to engage in income redistributive ratemaking, it contends that that authority is unnecessary to deal with the proposed low income programs.[356]

347 *See* § 6.3.3.1, *supra*.

348 Normally, a customer is allowed to enter into a levelized budget-billing plan only during the warm weather months in order to pre-pay some portion of the expected heating bills for the forthcoming winter.

349 Winter Heating Bills, 3747 Util. Reg. News 6 (Dec. 9, 2005); Order, No. 05-00281 (Tenn. Reg. Auth., issued Oct. 17, 2005).

350 *In re* Standard Offer Serv. Fuel Adjustments, 206 Pub. Util. Rep. 4th 122, 124, 126 (Mass. Dep't of Telecomms. & Energy 2000).

351 *Id.* at 124.

352 *In re* Ohio Edison Co., 165 Pub. Util. Rep. 4th 22 (Pub. Utils. Comm'n of Ohio 1995).

353 CAMP was originally known as the Limited Income Customer Incentive Plan.

354 *In re* Baltimore Gas & Elec. Co., 88 Md. P.S.C. 47 (1997).

355 *Id.* at 91.

356 *Id.* at 90.

The Maryland PSC agreed that "the financial assistance to low income customers provided by the program could lead to reductions in uncollectibles." Accordingly, the commission continued, "these benefits redound to all customers, thereby making ratepayer funding of at least a portion of the costs of these programs appropriate"[357]

The fact that the CAMP program was not "self-supporting" hinder regulatory approval of the program. Instead, the fact that the program would still have some costs was relevant to the way programs costs were allocated. The Maryland PSC stated:

> We disagree with the Joint Applicants' proposal for 100 percent funding of these programs by customers. The Joint Applicants did not show that the low income programs . . . are self-supporting. Thus, while all customers will benefit from the programs, it has not been shown that they will benefit to the extent of the costs that they would bear. Moreover, shareholders also benefit from the operation of these programs, so it is seemly that shareholders pay some of the costs. Therefore, under these circumstances, we find that it is appropriate to direct ratepayer funding of the proposed expense levels for the low income programs . . . at the 50 percent level.

The Maryland PSC noted that the source of funding was appropriate to take into account. "Flowing through a portion of the merger savings directly to the low income programs," the PSC held, "ensures that low income customers receive some tangible benefits from the merger."[358]

7.2.5 Arrearage Forgiveness

7.2.5.1 Overview

In basic terms, *arrearage forgiveness* is relieving a customer from the obligation to pay past (owed) bills. Forgiveness may come in many forms: up-front forgiveness of pre-program arrears (Maryland Electric Universal Service Program, or EUSP); "crisis" grants to prevent the disconnection of service (Wisconsin or the Northern Indiana Public Service Company "Winter Warmth" program); grants that match customer payments with corresponding multipliers of bill credits, such as the $3 of credit that Equitable Gas (Pennsylvania) pays for each $1 of customer payment (up to $20 of arrearage retirement each month); provide bill credits preconditioned upon payment of a certain number of current bills (New Jersey Fresh Start program). These are arrearage forgiveness programs found in Maryland, New Jersey, Ohio, Wisconsin, and Pennsylvania. The discussion below will discuss the arrearage forgiveness programs in Connecticut and Missouri.

357 *Id.* at 91.

358 *Id.*

7.2.5.2 Connecticut

7.2.5.2.1 Overview

Connecticut has a long history of providing regulatory assistance to low-income customer who cannot afford to pay their home energy bills. For example:

- Connecticut's investor-owned utilities may not refuse service to low-income customers due to the inability to pay a cash security deposit as a condition for providing service;[359]
- Gas and electric service disconnections for nonpayment may not occur if a lack of utility service would create a life-threatening situation and the customer lacks the resources to pay off the entire account;[360]
- Gas heating and electric utilities may not terminate service to "hardship" customers[361] between November 1 and May 1 for nonpayment;[362]
- Electric companies must reinstate service to hardship customers without requiring any payment between November 1 and May 1,[363] while gas companies must reinstate service with certain limitations.[364]

359 Conn. Gen. Stat. § 16-262j(a) ("No public service company and no electric supplier shall refuse to provide electric, gas or water service to a residential customer based on the financial inability of such customer to pay a security deposit for such service.").

360 *Id.* § 16-262c(b)(1).

361 *Id.* § 16-262c(b)(3)(B). (" 'hardship case' includes, but is not limited to: (i) A customer receiving local, state or federal public assistance; (ii) a customer whose sole source of financial support is Social Security, Veterans' Administration or unemployment compensation benefits; (iii) a customer who is head of the household and is unemployed, and the household income is less than three hundred per cent of the poverty level determined by the federal government; (iv) a customer who is seriously ill or who has a household member who is seriously ill; (v) a customer whose income falls below one hundred twenty-five per cent of the poverty level determined by the federal government; and (vi) a customer whose circumstances threaten a deprivation of food and the necessities of life for himself or dependent children if payment of a delinquent bill is required"). *See also* Conn. Agencies Regs. § 16-3-100.

Functionally, companies treat as hardship cases anyone who qualifies for energy assistance. In most years, this is limited to households with income up to 200% of the federal poverty level, but companies tend to treat households with income up to 60% of state median income as eligible for moratorium protection during those periods when the state provides energy assistance to such households.

362 Conn. Gen. Stat. § 16-262c(b)(1); An Act Concerning Electricity and Energy Efficiency, Conn. Pub. Act 07-242, § 67 (June 4, 2007).

363 *Id.*

364 Conn. Gen. Stat. § 16-262c(b)(1). *See generally* Decision, Joint Investigation of the Department of Public Utility Control and the Department of Income Maintenance into the Procedures and Practices of the Connecticut Light and Power Co. in Reinstating Electric and Gas Serv., No. 86-II-04 (Conn. Dep't of Pub. Util. Control Apr. 19, 1988).

Each of the protections identified above is means-tested.

Despite the protections offered to low-income customers as described above, the primary utility-funded low-income rate assistance program in Connecticut is the "arrearage forgiveness" program operated by each regulated gas and electric utility.

Connecticut General Statute §16-262c provides that a residential customer using electricity or gas for heat may be eligible to have monies due and owing deducted from the customer's delinquent account, provided the customer meet certain criteria. That customer must:

> a. Apply for and be eligible for benefits available under the Connecticut Energy Assistance Program (CEAP). . . .[365]
>
> b. . . .
>
> c. Enter into and comply with an amortization agreement, which agreement is consistent with the decisions and policies of the Department.[366]

Connecticut General Statute §16-262c provides that such an amortization agreement will result in a reduction of a customer's payments by the amount of the benefits reasonably anticipated from energy assistance.

Mandated by statute,[367] the arrearage forgiveness programs are divided into separate winter and summer components:[368]

- The winter component provides that, if a customer receives benefits through the energy assistance program, enters into a payment agreement for his or her arrears, *and* makes all required payments pursuant to that payment agreement by April 30, the utility will match the amount the customer paid (including the amount of energy assistance) with a bill credit of equal amount.
- The summer program provides that, if a customer has participated in the winter program (and successfully completed his or her winter payments), and if the customer makes all summer payments by October 30, the utility will provide a matching credit of equal amount.

Matching bill payments can reduce pre-program arrears to zero but cannot result in a credit on the customer's account.

7.2.5.2.2 *The basic natural gas utility hardship customer arrearage forgiveness plan*

The arrearage amortization plans offered by the three Connecticut natural gas utilities (Connecticut Natural Gas, Yankee Gas Services, Southern Connecticut Gas) follow a fundamentally similar design.[369] Under these plans:

- A customer is required to make a monthly payment equal to one-twelfth of the annual gas consumption minus the anticipated energy assistance benefit, plus an affordable payment amount toward the arrearage.
- A hardship customer must apply to become a part of the program. Existing customers who applied prior to or during November-would be required to make a total of six personal payments between November 1 and April 30 and an additional six payments between May 1 and October 31.
- Customers who entered the plan after November would be required to make a number of payments equal to the number of months remaining in the applicable six-month period.
- After each six-month period of the plan, the utility company would credit the customer account of each plan participant who has successfully complied with their budget arrangement an appropriate amount reflect-

365 In some instances, as described in more detail below, a customer may receive protections if he or she received assistance through a non-state source of energy assistance, for example, a fuel bank for heat.

366 Decision, Application of the Connecticut Light and Power Company, the United Illuminating Company, the Connecticut Natural Gas Corp., the Southern Connecticut Gas Company, and the Yankee Gas Services Company, for Approval of the Arrearage Forgiveness Program for 2006–2007, No. 06-03-11 (Conn. Dep't of Pub. Util. Control Sept. 27, 2006).

367 Electric non-heating programs are voluntary. Mandatory programs are directed only toward "a residential customer of a gas or electric distribution company using gas or electricity for heat." Conn. Gen. Stat. § 16-262c(b)(4).

368 Connecticut's natural gas utilities are mandated to file annual "implementation plans" on or before July 1 of each year. Conn. Gen. Stat. § 16-262c(b)(5).

The state Department of Public Utility Control (DPUC), in consultation with the Office of Policy and Management, shall, after hearing, approve or modify such plans within ninety days of receipt.

369 Indeed, while each gas utility filed a separate plan in the early years following enactment of the legislation, by 2002 the three utilities (Connecticut Natural Gas Corporation, Southern Connecticut Gas Company, and Yankee Gas Services) had sufficiently uniform plans that the companies filed a "Joint Plan Submission." Decision, Joint Application of Connecticut Natural Gas Corporation, the Southern Connecticut Gas Company, and Yankee Gas Services for Approval of Arrearage Forgiveness Program for 2002–2003, No. 02-07-01 (Conn. Dep't of Pub. Util. Control Sept. 26, 2002). *See also* Decision, Joint Application of the Connecticut Natural Gas Corporation, the Southern Connecticut Gas Company, and Yankee Gas Service Company for Approval of the Arrearage Forgiveness Program for 2003–2004, No. 03-07-03 (Conn. Dep't of Pub. Util. Control Sept. 17, 2003) ("In the future, the Companies will submit a joint plan to ensure that the Plan's policies, procedures and practices are identical for each company"); Decision, Joint Application of Connecticut Natural Gas Corporation, the Southern Connecticut Gas Company, and Yankee Gas Services Company for Approval of Arrearage Forgiveness Program 2004–2005, No. 04-07-01 (Conn. Dep't of Pub. Util. Control Sept. 15, 2004) ("The Companies submitted a joint Plan that is identical in its policies, procedures and practices for each company").

ing their own customer payments and any energy assistance benefits paid or committed on their behalf.

- Customers who enroll in the program, and who *also* qualify for company-sponsored efficiency investments, will be provided free conservation services.[370]

According to the Connecticut Department of Public Utility Control (DPUC), the similarity in plans was an issue of equity. As early as 1993, the DPUC found that "representatives of the Companies and Department staff compared the Companies' respective plans and found that for a given customer the plans resulted in monthly payments that were significantly different."[371] In not approving that approach, the DPUC said:

> The Department is concerned that the relative ease or difficulty of a customer's participation in an arrearage forgiveness plan should not depend on the customer's address. For reasons of equity, a customer's monthly payment amount should depend on the amount of the arrearage and the fuel assistance benefit, not on whether he or she happens to live in Hartford, Meriden or Bridgeport. We conclude that there should be uniformity in the formulas used by the Companies in determining a customer's monthly payment amount, and, by extension, the formulas used in calculating the forgiveness applied to a customer's arrearage.[372]

Given Connecticut's statutory reliance on the successful completion of designated deferred payment plans as the trigger for receipt of matching payments, the DPUC devoted substantial attention to defining the parameters of payment-plan compliance. Compliance with winter payment terms received the greatest attention.

If a customer enrolls in a payment plan subsequent to November, that customer may not be *required* to make payments retroactive to November 1.[373] In not approving the Southern Connecticut Gas proposal to require hardship customers to make six winter payments prior to April 30 as a prerequisite to obtaining a matching grant—irrespective of when such customers entered the program—the DPUC held that any retroactive payments made by customers must be made on a strictly voluntary basis. If a customer voluntarily makes such payments, he or she may earn the matching credit for them. The payment plan that must be successfully completed to earn matching credits at all may not include a requirement for retroactive payments. In rejecting a renewed request by Southern Connecticut Gas to impose a retroactive-payment requirement in 1992, the DPUC explained:

> This Act was passed in an attempt to assist both hardship customers and the Companies by providing payment incentives. The Act encourages indebted customers who have found themselves in a vicious cycle of service termination and reconnection to make affordable monthly payments and receive not only the benefit of continued year-round service but also the benefit of a reduced arrearage.
>
> Additional burdens on these customers may well discourage them from trying to reduce their arrearages at all. The Act is intended to reduce the levels of arrearages. By proposing mandatory retroactive payments, the Company is seeking to raise the monthly payment amount for some customers at a time when energy assistance may be reduced. The energy assistance reductions are enough of a deterrent without making participating in this program more difficult.
>
> SCG apparently believes that participants who were eligible from November 1 should be penalized with retroactive payments if they are not signed up by November 1 on the grounds that if late signers are not charged retroactively, it is unfair to the customers that did start from November 1. The Authority rejects this argument. Customers already have an incentive to sign up for the program early because customers who participate for a shorter period of time receive reduced benefits. . . .[374]

The DPUC further found that Southern Connecticut Gas "is not precluded from encouraging customers who sign up after November 1 and who were eligible at that time from making voluntary retroactive payments, thereby increasing

370 *See, e.g.*, Corrected Decision, Application of Yankee Gas Services Company for Approval of an Implementation Plan for Hardship Customers Arrearage Amortization Policy Pursuant to Public Act 91-150, No. 91-07-01 (Part B) (Conn. Dep't of Pub. Util. Control Sept. 25, 1991); Decision, Application of the Connecticut Natural Gas Company for Approval of an Implementation Plan for Hardship Customers Arrearage Amortization Policy Pursuant to Public Act 91-150 (Conn. Dep't of Pub. Util. Control Sept. 25, 1991).

371 Decision, Applications of the Connecticut Natural Gas Company, the Southern Connecticut Gas Company, and the Yankee Gas Services Company for Approval of Implementation Plans for Hardship Customers Arrearage Amortization Policy Pursuant to Public Act 91-150, Nos. 93-06-20, 93-06-21, 93-07-03 (consolidated) (Conn. Dep't of Pub. Util. Control Sept. 29, 1993).

372 *Id.* at 6.

373 Decision Application of Southern Connecticut Gas Company for Approval of Implementation Plan for Hardship Customers Arrearage Amortization policy Pursuant to Public Act 91-50, Reopened Proceeding (Conn. Dep't of Pub. Util. Control Feb. 26, 1992).

374 Decision, Applications of the Yankee Gas Services Company, The Connecticut Natural Gas Company, and The Southern Connecticut Gas Company for Approval of Implementation Plans for Hardship Customers Arrearage Amortization Policy Pursuant to Public Act 91-150, Nos. 92-07-15, 92-07-24, 92-07-25 (consolidated) (Conn. Dep't of Pub. Util. Control Sept. 28, 1992).

the benefit of the program to them." Ultimately, however, the DPUC approved a proposal requiring "existing eligible customer who may sign up for the Program in March or April . . . to make a minimum of the equivalent of three monthly payments by April 30."[375]

The DPUC approved deductions from a customer's arrearage of all energy assistance benefits committed to the customer, along with a matching payment based on that commitment, irrespective of whether the energy assistance benefits have actually been paid. The DPUC agreed with the representation of the Department of Social Services (DSS), the state agency that administers the federal energy assistance money, that "the commitment is a guarantee of payment when the Federal funds become available."[376]

This decision is necessary, the DPUC said, in order to protect the customer regarding actions over which he or she has no control. According to the DPUC, the proposed policy of Connecticut Light and Power Company (CL&P) "of only matching payments or CEAP commitments in the Phase in which they are received penalizes the customer who has no control over when their CEAP application is processed and is contrary to the intent of the Program."[377] Moreover, this decision addressed problems caused by the high mobility that exists in the low-income population. A low-income customer may have done everything he or she was supposed to do but moved during the summer; in those instances, DSS paid the customer benefit in the fall, but the customer never got that benefit matched.

One of the most critical aspects of the Connecticut arrearage forgiveness program involves efforts to ensure that plan payments for preexisting arrears are offered at affordable rates. In order for a customer to receive *any* matching grants, in other words, the customer must make his or her budget billing payment for current usage *plus* an "affordable" payment toward his or her arrears. According to the DPUC, it is the responsibility of each utility to ensure that payment plan calculations take customer-specific circumstances into account.

> The Department inquired as to why the Companies do not include a customer's income in calculating a payment arrangement in their Arrearage Forgiveness Programs. The company replied that the customer's income is not taken into consideration because in the past some customers have objected to supplying that information to the Companies. The monthly payment amount is determined according to the calculations provided to the Companies. However, if it is determined that the customer is not able to pay the calculated amount, the Company may adjust the amount to the level that is within the customer's ability to pay and in compliance with Regulations of Connecticut State Agencies, §16-3-100(3)A.[378] The Department looks to the Companies to take into consideration a customer's income when that customer indicates an arrangement may be inappropriate for their income.[379]

The DPUC established a range of arrearage payments permitted under the statute, with a minimum payment of $1 per month and a maximum monthly arrearage payment of $50.[380]

Despite the attention to income in the calculation of the arrearage payment plan, the DPUC has held that a customer must pay his or her entire budget billing amount. The company arrearage forgiveness plans calculate a monthly payment "which can be derived by taking the prior actual twelve months for gas service, minus the estimated future energy assistance payments, divided by twelve months, plus a payment towards the arrearage."[381] It is the payment toward the arrearage, not the overall amortization agreement, that is to be based on "the monthly income of the customer after other indicated expenses have been deducted." The statute creating the arrearage forgiveness programs, the DPUC found, requires that an amortization agree-

375 Decision, Joint Application of Connecticut Natural Gas Corporation, the Southern Connecticut Gas Company, and Yankee Gas Services Company for Approval of Arrearage Forgiveness Program 2005–2006, No. 05-07-01 (Conn. Dep't of Pub. Util. Control Sept. 14, 2005).

376 *Id.* at 5, 7.

377 *Id.* at 5.

378 Section 16-3-100(b)(3)(A) reads in relevant part: "no utility company shall: (A) terminate service to any gas or electric residential customer whose service is subject to termination for a delinquent amount until the company first offers the customer an opportunity to enter into a reasonable amortization agreement. The specifics of the reasonable amortization agreement may vary according to the particular case and shall be determined by both utility company and customer receiving residential utility service. Such agreement shall be subject to change upon the showing by the customer of a change in financial circumstances. . . ."

379 Decision, Joint Application of Connecticut Natural Gas Corporation, the Southern Connecticut Gas Company, and Yankee Gas Services for Approval of Arrearage Forgiveness Program for 2002–2003, No. 02-07-01 (Conn. Dep't of Pub. Util. Control Sept. 26, 2002).

380 Decision, Joint Application of Connecticut Natural Gas Corporation, the Southern Connecticut Natural Gas Company, and Yankee Gas Services Company for Approval of Arrearage Forgiveness Program 2005–2006, No. 05-07-01 (Conn. Dep't of Pub. Util. Control Sept. 14, 2005). *See also* Joint Application of Connecticut Natural Gas Corporation, the Southern Connecticut Natural Gas Company, and Yankee Gas Services Company for Approval of Arrearage Forgiveness Program 2005–2006, No. 05-07-05 (Conn. Dep't of Pub. Util. Control Oct. 5, 2005) ("The Department will order the electric Companies to adjust the amount that may be requested toward the delinquent balance to $1.00 to $50.00 so that the policy followed by both the Gas Companies and the Electric Companies are similar.").

381 Decision, Application of the Southern Connecticut Gas Company for Approval of an Implementation Plan for Hardship Customers Arrearage Amortization Policy Pursuant to Public Act 91-150, No. 91-06-09 (Pt. A) (Conn. Dep't of Pub. Util. Control Sept. 10, 1991).

ment include an "affordable increment" to be paid toward arrears. That "affordable increment" may not be waived. Benefits under the program should not be extended "beyond their intended scope."[382]

Beginning in the winter of 2007, the DPUC authorized operation of a payment program that may be below actual cost of service in the arrearage forgiveness program.[383] Social service agencies contract with the utilities to calculate the amount a household can afford under a fixed budgeting system.[384] If the customer complies with the agreement during the winter, his or her reduced payments can continue during the summer without risking loss of service. This program allows households to earn forgiveness on an ongoing basis when heating costs exceed the ability of the household to meet this expense.[385] These below-budget payment agreements are not available to all hardship customers but only to those who are served by designated social service agencies that contract with the utilities to calculate affordable payment amounts.[386]

The DPUC decided that customers could amend the terms of their underlying payment arrangement with a gas utility should the customer experience a "change in their financial situation."[387] In addition, the DPUC agreed that, "when a customer misses a payment, he/she be advised that a missed payment must be made up in order to maintain eligibility [for matching grants], unless the customer can demonstrate that the change in financial circumstances caused the default, in which case the payment may be reduced."[388]

The DPUC rejected a company proposal that any amendment to a payment plan be limited to circumstances constituting an "emergency." The DPUC reasoned:

> The Authority believes the language as presently written would send a message to the customer that they may only amend the agreement, or indeed contact the Company, if there is an "emergency." Different people may interpret the word emergency differently. The participants, especially the ones in danger of losing status in the plan, should be encouraged to engage in open discourse with the Company on issues of their financial situations. The Company will be ordered below to amend the language of its reminder letter to state if customers have experienced a change in their financial circumstances they should notify the Company, and that said change might alter the terms of their payment arrangement thereby avoiding a default.[389]

At the request of the Connecticut Natural Gas Company, the DPUC clarified that customers have the right to cure any missed payments during the winter period so long as those payments are made before April 31. In other words, rather than requiring "a total of" six payments between November and the end of April, the Connecticut programs require only "the equivalent of" six payments. As Connecticut Natural Gas noted, "the amended language would more effectively encompass customers who miss a payment and make it up."[390]

In 2003, the DPUC changed its policy regarding missed *summer* payments. Historically, the utilities had required summer payments to be made by the due date in order to generate matching payments. According to the DPUC, "[t]his practice has been accepted by the Department in the past; however, the Department believes that, regardless of whether it occurs during Phase One[391] or Phase Two,[392] applicants who fall behind in payments should be subject to the same requirements. This change should result in an increase in the amount of Matching Payment Program ben-

382 *Id.* (citing Office of Consumer Counsel brief).

The DPUC held that the amortization agreement itself is to be structured in the same way as it would be under existing law and department policy. *Id.* (citing Decision, Rotko v. Southern Conn. Gas Co., No. 83-05-28 (Conn. Dep't of Pub. Util. Control Feb. 19, 1985); Decision, Rogers v. Southern Conn. Gas Co., No. 83-07-18 (Conn. Dep't of Pub. Util. Control Feb. 19, 1985)).

The only change made by the statute, according to the DPUC, was the provision for matching credits once customer payments on such an agreement had been made. *Id.*

383 *See* Correspondence from Louise Rickard, Acting Executive Secretary, Connecticut Dep't of Pub. Util. Control, to Stephen Gibelli, Senior Counsel, Northeast Utility Serv. Co. (as agent for Connecticut Light & Power Company and Yankee Gas Company).

384 According to the DPUC's Dec. 11, 2006, approval letter, "the Income/Expense Sheet will require specific information from customers to determine what they can afford to pay. Using the approved Income/Expense Sheet, the dollar figure that results after reducing the customer's monthly income by their monthly expenses shall serve as the maximum monthly payment . . . that the company can require of a hardship customer under a payment arrangement plan."

385 The arrearage forgiveness program continues in 2011. Application of The Connecticut Light and Power Company, the United Illuminating Company, Connecticut Natural Gas Corporation, the Southern Connecticut Gas Company and Yankee Gas Services Company for Approval of Arrearage Forgiveness Program, No. 11-06-14, 2011 Conn. PUC LEXIS 185 (Conn. Pub. Util. Regulatory Auth. Sept. 28, 2011).

386 For the 2007–2008 program year, low-income advocates have pushed for referrals—to social service agencies authorized to set below-budget payments—that are not dependent on a consumer happening to visit such a social service agency or knowing to ask for a referral to one.

387 Corrected Decision at 7, Application of Yankee Gas Services Company for Approval of an Implementation Plan for Hardship Customers Arrearage Amortization Policy Pursuant to Public Act 91-150, No. 91-07-01 (Pt. B) (Conn. Dep't of Pub. Util. Control Sept. 25, 1991).

388 *Id.* at 5.

389 Decision, Application of the Connecticut Natural Gas Company for Approval of an Implementation Plan for Hardship Customers Arrearage Amortization Policy Pursuant to Public Act 91-150, No. 91-07-03 (Conn. Dep't of Pub. Util. Control Sept. 25, 1991).

390 *Id.* at 7.

391 Phase One is the winter program component.

392 Phase Two is the summer program component.

efit that flow to the participants and at the same time reduces the number of terminations during the non-moratorium season."[393]

Despite this requirement for natural gas companies, the DPUC approved a *different* cure policy for summer electric payments. Under electric company policies, a customer who has been disconnected will be subject to normal reconnection requirements and will no longer qualify for the summer matching credits; such a customer may re-enroll the following year. This electric company policy applies only to disconnected accounts, however. "If an electric customer makes up a late payment prior to being terminated, CL&P and [United Illuminating] shall allow that customer to stay on Phase II and be eligible for a matching payment."[394]

The difference between the treatment of disconnected natural gas and electric customers was predicated on natural gas companies having specific concerns about their ability to keep customers in their respective systems during warm weather months.

> The gas companies believe that many hardship gas customers who heat with gas choose to go without gas service in the summer months and maintain their electric service which is more of a necessity. The gas distribution companies believe that their catch-up policy is appropriate because it provides gas heating customers with an additional incentive needed to continue payments and service throughout the summer.[395]

The Department approved both approaches, with the difference being the treatment of disconnected customers by electric utilities.

At the request of Yankee Gas Services, the DPUC approved a proposal to expand the definition of "energy assistance" payments beyond the basic LIHEAP grants that hardship customers receive. According to the Yankee Gas Services 1995/1996 plan, the company would "accept energy assistance payments from traditional sources such as Community Action Agencies and Operation Fuel[396] as well as non-traditional sources such as the Salvation Army, Red Cross, churches and religious and civic organizations."[397]

However, the DPUC rejected a company proposal that would require both traditional and non-traditional sources of energy assistance payments to be equal to or greater than the minimum CEAP award. According to the DPUC,

> [e]ligible customers who apply too late for CEAP funds or after funds have run out often find themselves in a position where they must rely on a number of traditional and non-traditional sources for assistance. Traditional and non-traditional sources often operate with limited funding which limits the amount of assistance they can provide. Requiring these payments to be equal to or greater than the CEAP award would reduce the effectiveness of the Program and limit the number of eligible customers who receive benefits from the Program. It would also unfairly punish customers who are unable to get CEAP benefits that they qualify for but are unable to participate because funds are no longer available. The Department considers non-traditional and traditional programs to be an extension of CEAP, and therefore orders the Companies to accept without limitations traditional and non-traditional sources when CEAP funding is no longer available.[398]

The DPUC stated, however, that its requirements in this regard were not intended to permit "alternative funding sources whether or not CEAP payments are available. . . ."[399] Moreover, the DPUC decided that income verification would need to be provided to the company when customers receive energy assistance from non-traditional agencies.[400]

7.2.5.2.3 *The basic electric utility hardship customer arrearage forgiveness plan*

In 2003, Connecticut amended its statutory basis for an arrearage forgiveness program to provide for the participation of electric companies in offering such programs.[401] The statutory amendment provided that a residential customer using electricity for heat[402] may be eligible to have monies

393 Decision, Joint Application of the Connecticut Natural Gas Corporation, the Southern Connecticut Gas Company, and Yankee Gas Service Company for Approval of the Arrearage Forgiveness Program for 2003–2004, No. 03-07-03 (Conn. Dep't of Pub. Util. Control Sept. 17, 2003).

394 Decision at 6, Joint Application of the Connecticut Light and Power Company, the United Illuminating Company, the Connecticut Natural Gas Corporation, the Southern Connecticut Gas Company and Yankee Gas Services Company for Approval of Arrearage Forgiveness Program Year 2006–2007, No. 06-03-11 (Conn. Dep't of Pub. Util. Control Dec. 11, 2006).

395 *Id.*

396 Operation Fuel is Connecticut's statewide fuel fund.

397 Decision, Application of Connecticut Natural Gas Corporation, Southern Connecticut Gas Company and Yankee Gas Services Company for Approval of the Winter Protected Customer Arrearage Forgiveness Policy, No. 95-06-32 (Conn. Dep't of Pub. Util. Control Sept. 29, 1995).

398 Decision at 3, Joint Application of the Connecticut Light and Power Company, the United Illuminating Company, the Connecticut Natural Gas Corporation, the Southern Connecticut Gas Company and Yankee Gas Services Company for Approval of Arrearage Forgiveness Program Year 2006–2007, No. 06-03-11 (Dec. 11, 2006).

399 *Id.*

400 Decision at 1, Joint Application of Connecticut Natural Gas Corporation, the Southern Connecticut Gas Company, and Yankee Gas Services Company for Approval of Arrearage Forgiveness Program 2005–2006, No. 05-07-01 (Conn. Dep't of Pub. Util. Control Sept. 14, 2005).

401 Conn. Gen. Stat. §§ 16-262c(b)(4), (5), *amended by* Conn. Pub. Act 03-47 (effective Oct. 1, 2003) (An Act Concerning the Filing of Information Regarding Amortization Agreements).

402 Under the statute, electric companies may, but are not required

due and owing deducted from the customer's delinquent account, provided the customer meets prescribed criteria. The prescribed criteria mirror those criteria for the natural gas utility arrearage forgiveness programs.[403]

In approving the electric companies' implementation plans, the DPUC held that, upon a review of the legislative history of the electric legislation, "the anticipation was that the electric amortization programs would mirror and achieve parity with the existing gas utility programs."[404] According to the DPUC, its "examination and analysis of the Companies Programs in this proceeding are intended to make the Programs as homogenous as possible so that each ratepayer in Connecticut is subject to the same policies and guidelines."[405] The DPUC ordered the electric companies' annual filings to include "a joint plan annually to insure that the Program's policies, procedures and practices are as analogous as possible for each company."[406]

The only statutory difference between natural gas and electric company programs is that, while the expenditures of natural gas companies are booked to a deferred account[407] and recovered in each company's next rate proceeding,[408] the statute created a System Benefits Charge (SBC) for electric company programs to recover their costs. "The Department agrees with the Companies that the matching payment costs as well as the costs to administer the Program such as the cost of advertising and additional staffing that are not presently included in Operations and Maintenance expense in rates should be recovered through the SBC."[409] Cost recovery is reviewed in the annual reconciliation of electric company SBC collections and expenditures.

7.2.5.2.4 *The relationship between energy efficiency and arrearage forgiveness*

While not mandated by statute or regulation, Connecticut's natural gas utilities offered participants in their respective arrearage forgiveness programs energy efficiency services from the inception of their programs.[410] Southern Connecticut Gas, for example, reported to the DPUC that its list of arrearage forgiveness program participants would be "used by its Conservation Department to provide likely candidates for its CPRU [Conservation Program to Reduce Uncollectibles]. . . ."[411] The integration of the arrearage forgiveness and low-income efficiency programs was not extensive in these early years.

That changed in 2003. In the joint plan they filed, the DPUC noted that "[t]he Companies briefly discussed their weatherization programs but did not provide any details about that program."[412] The DPUC wanted more:

> The Department would like the Companies to continue their efforts in addressing the problem involving the significant impact energy costs have on low-income households, by targeting those customers for conservation and weatherization programs. The Department will require the Companies to file a report describing in detail the conservation and weatherization programs they offer low-income customers, along with copies of any written materials that are used to educate and inform customers about those services.[413]

The report was to include "a description of the benefits that customers can expect to derive from the programs, the number of applicants who participated in the conservation or weatherization programs and the number of applicants

to, promulgate an arrearage forgiveness program for non-heating electric customers. The same is true for gas utilities, which are allowed but not required to extend their arrearage forgiveness programs to non-heating gas customers.

403 Decision, Joint Application of the Connecticut Light and Power Company and the United Illuminating Company for Approval of an Arrearage Forgiveness Program for 2004–2005, No. 04-04-15 (Conn. Dep't of Pub. Util. Control Aug. 18, 2004).

404 *Id.* at 5.

405 *Id.* at 7.

406 *Id.*

407 *See, e.g.*, Application of the Southern Connecticut Gas Company for Approval of an Implementation Plan for Hardship Customers Arrearage Amortization Policy Pursuant to Public Act 91-150, No. 91-06-09 (Pt. A) (Conn. Dep't of Pub. Util. Control Sept. 10, 1991) ("The recovery of the amounts to be forgiven will be determined in future rate proceedings. . . . The Accounts Receivable arrearages to be forgiven shall be deferred and recorded in Account No. 186. The Company shall maintain sufficient records on these deferred amounts and shall submit said data with its next general rate application.") *Accord* Decision, Application of the Connecticut Natural Gas Company for Approval of an Implementation Plan for Hardship Customers Arrearage Amortization Policy Pursuant to Public Act 91-150, No. 91-07-03 (Conn. Dep't of Pub. Util. Control Sept. 25, 1991).

408 *See, e.g.*, Application of the Yankee Gas Services Company for Approval of an Implementation Plan for Hardship Customers Arrearage Amortization Policy Pursuant to Public Act 91-150, No. 91-07-01 (Pt. B) (Conn. Dep't of Pub. Util. Control Sept. 25, 1991) ("The Public Act provide that the Department shall allow the amounts deducted from the customer's account pursuant to the implementation plan to be recovered by the company in its rates as an operating expense.").

409 Decision at 6, Joint Application of the Connecticut Light and Power Company and the United Illuminating Company for Approval of an Arrearage Forgiveness Program for 2004–2005, No. 04-04-15 (Conn. Dep't of Pub. Util. Control Aug. 18, 2004).

410 1991 Yankee Gas Plan Approval ("Customers who sign up for this Plan and who also qualify for the Company's 'Attic Insulation Plan' will be given free conservation services.").

411 Decision, Application of Connecticut Natural Gas Corporation, Southern Connecticut Gas Company and Yankee Gas Services Company for Approval of the Winter Protected Customer Arrearage Forgiveness Policy, No. 95-06-32 (Conn. Dep't of Pub. Util. Control Sept. 29, 1995).

412 Decision, Joint Application of the Connecticut Natural Gas Corporation, the Southern Connecticut Gas Company, and Yankee Gas Service Company for Approval of the Arrearage Forgiveness Program for 2003–2004, No. 03-07-03 (Conn. Dep't of Pub. Util. Control Sept. 17, 2003).

413 *Id.*

eligible for the conservation or weatherization program." This order came despite the DPUC's finding that "all of the Companies list weatherization as something they offer as a benefit to all Applicants."[414] The DPUC noted that, with respect to natural gas utilities, "the Companies reported that they continue to offer conservation programs. The Conservation services include energy audits, blower door testing, weatherization, and insulation work."[415]

When the Connecticut electric utilities began their arrearage forgiveness programs, the DPUC noted that these companies, too, extended efficiency services to program participants. "The Companies provide conservation services within the authorized funding levels to all eligible customers who sign up for the Forgiveness Plan. The Companies work with the local community action agencies in assisting them in identifying customers and landlords who may be eligible."[416] The DPUC noted that "participants in the Plan will be eligible for all conservation and weatherization programs offered by the Companies."[417]

While utility conservation programs may be "offered" to all participants in the respective arrearage forgiveness program, the DPUC expressed concern about the extent to which arrearage forgiveness program participants were also participating in the conservation programs. In its most recent approval of the utility arrearage forgiveness programs, the DPUC directed "the gas distribution utilities . . . to establish a goal to increase participation by Arrearage Forgiveness Program customers in low-income conservation programs."[418]

In sum, each regulated natural gas and electric utility in Connecticut offers a statutorily mandated arrearage forgiveness program directed toward hardship customers. These programs provide matching grants equal to the sum of customer payments and energy assistance directed to the customer's bill. The forgiveness programs are divided into a summer and winter program component. In order to receive *any* matching grant, a program participant must make *all* required payments during the program period. The Connecticut Department of Public Utility Control has observed that the forgiveness program did not change preexisting policies regarding the structure and affordability of payment plans. Instead, the program simply provided for the matching grant aspect of the program. Both natural gas and electric utilities are ensured of cost recovery through two separate streams of revenue for whatever matching grant is provided.

There is no formal integration of the energy efficiency and arrearage forgiveness programs offered by Connecticut utilities. While these utilities report that any participant in the arrearage forgiveness program is also eligible to receive energy efficiency services, the DPUC has expressed concern over the lack of participation by customers receiving arrearage forgiveness in the respective utility efficiency programs. In its most recent approval of the arrearage forgiveness program, the DPUC directed the state's natural gas utilities to establish a goal of increasing the participation of arrearage forgiveness recipients in the utilities' respective conservation and weatherization programs.

7.2.5.3 Missouri

7.2.5.3.1 Overview

While the state of Missouri has no statewide utility-funded low-income affordability initiative, the state's electric and gas utilities have experimented with pilot programs to generate information about the operation and outcomes of improving affordability. Authority for the approval of such programs is found in their experimental nature. The Missouri state utility commission has, however, consistently asserted that it lacks statutory authority to order (or even approve) a broad-scale program. The discussion below will review the pilot programs developed in recent years, along with the state public utility commission's rationale when programs have been both approved and disapproved. The focus of this discussion is on Laclede Gas Company and its arrearage forgiveness program.

7.2.5.3.2 The disapproved Laclede Gas Catch-Up/ Keep-Up pilot program

In September 2002, Laclede Gas Company filed a proposed arrearage forgiveness program with the Missouri Public Service Commission (PSC). Under the proposed "Catch-up/Keep-up Plan," the company would use discounts obtained through its transportation gas rates, in part, to fund the reduction of arrears for low-income customers. According to the Missouri PSC, the Catch-up/Keep-up tariff

> . . . would increase customers' costs for transportation of natural gas by $6 million by diverting up to that amount from the transportation discounts

414 *Id.*

415 Decision, Joint Application of the Connecticut Natural Gas Corporation, the Southern Connecticut Gas Company, and Yankee Gas Services Company for Approval of Arrearage Forgiveness Program 2005–2006, No. 05-07-01 (Conn. Dep't of Pub. Util. Control Sept. 14, 2005).

In this 2005 plan decision, as well, the DPUC explicitly noted that "all of the Companies list weatherization as being offered to benefit all applicants." *Id.*

416 Decision, Joint Application of the Connecticut Light and Power Company and the United Illuminating Company for Approval of an Arrearage Forgiveness Program for 2004–2005, No. 04-04-15 (Conn. Dep't of Pub. Util. Control Aug. 18, 2004).

417 *Id.*

418 Decision, Application of the Connecticut Light and Power Company, the United Illuminating Company, the Connecticut Natural Gas Corporation, the Southern Connecticut Gas Company, and the Yankee Gas Services Company for Approval of the Arrearage Forgiveness Program for 2006–2007, No. 06-03-11 (Conn. Dep't of Pub. Util. Control Sept. 27, 2006).

> that would otherwise be returned to Laclede's customers. These diverted moneys would be placed in an escrow account to fund an arrearage forgiveness program. Currently, 100% of any pipeline discounts received by Laclede are flowed through to all non-transportation customers. Under Laclede's proposal, only 70% of the pipeline discounts would be flowed through to Laclede customers. The other 30% would be placed in an escrow account and used to reduce the arrearages of Laclede's low-income consumers.[419]

Under Laclede's proposed program, as qualifying customers made payments toward three months of their current bills (billed on a levelized monthly budget-billing basis), one-fourth of the outstanding arrearages for such customers (or $375, whichever was less) would be forgiven.[420] As those arrearages were forgiven, funds would flow from the escrow account holding the pipeline discount into Laclede's accounts receivables.[421]

While the Missouri PSC rejected the Laclede program proposal, it did not base its rejection on jurisdictional grounds. Indeed, the PSC noted that "a properly designed low-income assistance program should benefit all stakeholders by promoting conservation and by assisting low-income consumers in reducing their energy burden. The low-income customers may then be able to pay their utility bills, thereby reducing utility costs for all ratepayers."[422]

The PSC did, however, find "numerous problems with the design" of the proposed Catch-up/Keep-up program. The program, for example, "is not properly designed to address the low-income consumer needs for rate affordability and usage reduction." Even though "the success of the Program is dependent on the modification of the behavior of the low-income customer," the PSC stated, "the expectation that low-income customers in the Program will become better able to pay their bills may be unrealistic." One problem noted by the PSC staff was that the proposed arrearage forgiveness program "does not provide any means to assist participants with payment of *current* gas bills. . . ."[423]

Moreover, the Catch-up/Keep-up program proposal allowed broad discretion to third-party community action agencies (CAA) to "excuse" the three-consecutive-payment requirement if an agency found that the program participant faced "extenuating circumstances." This discretion was bounded neither by a definition of "extenuating circumstances" nor by any limitation on the CAA exercise of discretion. "Regularly granting waivers for extenuating circumstances," the PSC found, "could mean that low-income customers would receive arrearage forgiveness without ever developing regular payment habits, which is a stated Program goal."[424]

The PSC further posited that the real impact of Laclede's proposed Catch-up/Keep-up program would be simply to improve the Company's financial condition.

> Although the program is not well-designed to meet the needs of low-income customers, it is likely to have a positive impact on the Company's current financial condition by improving cash flow and replacing income lost when the Commission denied Laclede's request to extend its Gas Supply Incentive Plan (GISP). The Program allows Laclede to divert a portion of the pipeline discounts that would otherwise be passed on to all ratepayers, and to then use those discounts to reduce the company's bad-debt expense. Thus, Laclede would receive a double recovery because bad-debt expense is already included in permanent rates.[425]

Moreover, the PSC noted, the program allows Laclede to delay write-offs.

> Customers who would otherwise have been written off because they were unable to make the necessary payment to come on-line under the Cold Weather Rule provisions[426] will have the "payment" made for them through the arrearage Program. By reactivating the Program participant's account, Laclede would also delay making any further write-offs on that account.[427]

Aside from the substantive frailties of the proposed Catch-up/Keep-up program, the PSC disapproved of several aspects of the proposed program's cost recovery. The PSC noted that diverting the pipeline refunds would violate the rate cap approved by stipulation in an immediately preceding Laclede base-rate case proceeding. The proposal would divert $6 million to fund the program that "would otherwise be used to offset the transportation cost of gas and reduce the amount that all Laclede customers would pay on a per-unit basis." Moreover, the program, in its essence, requires all customers "to fund, in advance, bad debts that

419 Report and Order at 4, *In re* Tariff Filing of Laclede Gas Co. to Implement an Experimental Low-Income Assistance Program Called Catch-up/Keep-up, No. GT-2003-0117 (Mo. Pub. Serv. Comm'n Jan. 16, 2003).

420 Accordingly, the total arrears would be forgiven over a twelve-month period.

421 Report and Order, at 4, *In re* Tariff Filing of Laclede Gas Co. to Implement an Experimental Low-Income Assistance Program Called Catch-up/Keep-up, No. GT-2003-0117 (Mo. Pub. Serv. Comm'n Jan. 16, 2003).

422 *Id.* at 5.

423 *Id.* (emphasis added).

The program proposal required eligible customers to apply for assistance "from available sources." *Id.*

424 *Id.* at 5.

425 *Id.* at 6–7.

426 *See generally* Mo. Code Regs. Ann tit. 4, § 240-13.055(9)(B), (10)(C).

427 Report and Order at 7, *In re* Tariff Filing of Laclede Gas Co. to Implement an Experimental Low-Income Assistance Program Called Catch-up/Keep-up, No. GT-2003-0117 (Mo. Pub. Serv. Comm'n Jan. 16, 2003).

would normally be considered in future rate cases to the extent that the bad debts actually materialize."[428]

These cost-recovery problems, the PSC held, resulted in an improvement in Laclede's financial condition at the expense of Company's ratepayers.

> The Commission finds that under the Program, Laclede would likely experience higher reported earnings as a result of the double recovery, prepayment or deferred recognition of its bad debt expense. Laclede would also benefit to the extent that it has access to the excess funds accumulated by the Program that permit it to meet its other cash flow requirements, regulated or non-regulated, with funds otherwise used for bad debt. Thus, Laclede would experience an increased cash flow and an increase in income that would flow directly to Laclede's bottom line and consequently to shareholders.[429]

To pay for these benefits to shareholders, "under the Program, all customers, including low-income customers, would forego the benefit of pipeline discounts on their natural gas bills."

The PSC finally determined that Laclede's recovery of its proposed Catch-up/Keep-up costs through the purchase gas adjustment clause (PGA)was unlawful. The pipeline discounts would normally have been passed through to ratepayers via the PGA clause, which is to be "limited in nature to the cost of obtaining the gas itself" and may not include "margin costs; in other words, the costs of doing business, such as labor or materials costs."[430] According to the PSC:

> The Commission is unwilling to adopt a policy that allows the collection of bad debt through the [purchase gas cost recovery] process. PGA costs are limited to recovery of natural gas costs necessary to bring the commodity from the production areas to the Company's city gate. City-gate delivered costs include the cost of the commodity itself, interstate pipeline transportation charges, and interstate storage charges, all of which are subject to a later prudence review. Margin costs such as payroll, depreciation, customer service, bill collection and bad debt expenses are considered in the context of a general rate case and not subject to an adjustment process. Laclede's Program proposes to include margin costs in the [purchase gas cost recovery] process. Such a use of [this mechanism] is unlawful and could be the downfall of this process.[431]

The PSC concluded that "a rate case would have been an appropriate place to consider the Program." It then determined that "the concept of an arrearage forgiveness program is worthy of review. The Commission hereby encourages the parties to establish a collaborative to meet and attempt to develop a possible alternative to the Catch-up/Keep-up Plan."[432]

In issuing such "encouragement," the PSC "acknowledges that there is the issue of whether the law permits a utility to charge, directly or indirectly, customers within the same class a different rate for the same service. As the commission is rejecting the tariff on other grounds, it need not address this question." The PSC stated that

> [t]he Commission appreciates the plight of low-income ratepayers and has previously authorized, and continues to support, a variety of other low-income support projects. The Commission has authorized an experimental pilot program for MGE that is similar to Laclede's proposal. That program, however, was implemented in the confines of a rate case where the Commission explored all relevant factors.[433]

7.2.5.3.3 The approved Laclede Gas Catch-up/Keep-up pilot program

Subsequent to the Missouri PSC's rejection of Laclede's proposed Catch-up/Keep-up program, Laclede Gas, PSC staff and the Office of Public Counsel stipulated in Laclede's 2005 rate case that "a low-income energy assistance program . . . should be approved by the Commission."[434] The settlement of the 2005 rate case included a natural gas rate increase of roughly $8.5 million, compared to the $39 million originally requested by Laclede Gas. The PSC approved the low-income sections of the stipulation without discussion.

The PSC subsequently approved the substantive design of Laclede's low-income program in May 2006,[435] noting in its order that "[s]taff states that the purpose of the Low-Income Energy Affordability Program is to provide a mechanism whereby certain customers of Laclede can pay off their past-due balances and maintain current payments of their gas usage through Laclede's winter months (November-April)." The PSC noted further that its staff had posited that "successful participation in the program should result in a greater number of Laclede customers becoming full-time current-paying customers."[436]

---

428 *Id.* at 7.
429 *Id.* at 8.
430 *Id.* at 10.
431 *Id.* at 10–11.
432 *Id.* at 11–12.
433 *Id.* at 13–14.
434 Order Approving Stipulation and Agreement and Order Approving Tariff, *In re* Laclede Gas Company's Tariff to Revise Natural Gas Rate Schedules, No. GR-2005-0284 (Mo. Pub. Serv. Comm'n Sept. 30, 2005).
435 The original approval of the commission was simply to have the company develop a program in collaboration with commission staff and the Public Counsel. This later approval was of the program design developed through that process.
436 Order Approving Tariff Sheets Filed in Compliance with Commission Order, No. GR-2005-0284 (Mo. Pub. Serv. Comm'n May 5, 2006).

Under the Laclede program,[437] the company would devote bill credits in the sum of $550,000 annually to be made available during the months of November through April. Credits would be distributed to households with incomes at or below 150% of the federal poverty level. To participate in the Winter Bill Payment Assistance Program, a customer would be required to make a minimum monthly payment of $40 during the six-month winter period. Winter Bill Payment Assistance Program funds would be allocated in the following percentages and distributed in the following manner:

- 20% of the funds would be distributed to households with incomes at or below 50% of the federal poverty level. These customers would receive a $60 average monthly credit, to be applied in the amounts of $60 in November and December, $80 in January, and $40 in March and April;
- 40% of funds would be distributed to households with incomes between 50% and 125% of the federal poverty level. These customers would receive a $60 average monthly credit, to be applied in the amounts of $60 in November and December, $80 in January and February, and $40 in March and April.
- 40% of funds would be distributed to households with incomes between 125% and 150% of the federal poverty level. These customers would receive an average $70 monthly credit, to be applied in the amounts of $40 in November, $70 in December, $100 in January and February, $70 in March, and $40 in April.

The program design noted that the higher-income tier receives a higher benefit amount because these customers do not qualify for federal LIHEAP assistance in Missouri.

In addition to the bill credits toward current bills, the Low-Income Energy Affordability Program incorporated an arrearage repayment program as well. Funded at $350,000 annually, this program makes available benefits for households up to 185% of the federal poverty level. In order to qualify for arrearage credits, households with incomes at or below 125% of the federal poverty level must not only pay their current bill on time and in full but must make a minimum $10 monthly arrearage payment. Customers with incomes between 125% and 185% of the federal poverty level must make a minimum $15 monthly arrearage payment. Customers with incomes at or below 50% of the federal poverty level are not required to make the minimum arrears payments during the winter months; instead, these minimum payments are made from program funds.

The arrearage program will match 100% customer arrearage payments so long as both the current bill and the minimum arrears payment are made in full and on time. Customers may also pay *more* than the minimum arrearage payment and obtain a correspondingly higher match. In addition, late fees are waived for any arrearages subject to the arrearage repayment program as long as the customer is making his or her required payments.

In 2010, the Missouri PSC approved a pilot low-income program for AmerenUE customers, as a result of the parties' agreement in a rate case. Under the pilot program, eligible customers can receive tiered bill credits and arrearage forgiveness. The pilot is anticipated to run for two years.[438]

7.2.5.4 Other States

In August 2003, low-income utility consumer advocates filed a brief with the Massachusetts Department of Transportation and Energy (DTE) to support an arrearage management program proposed by KeySpan Gas called On Track. Approved by the Department, and now underway, On Track provides up to $400 of credit to customers enrolled in the program who keep up with their payment plan obligations.[439]

7.2.6 Line Extension Assistance

New customers in new residences seeking to connect to existing utility infrastructure may be faced with covering the costs of connecting, which can amount to thousands of dollars. In Maine, however, Central Maine Power offers a new power line program, which provides a credit of up to $2800 for wire and pole installation charges.[440] To qualify for this program, among other requirements the total household income must be less than 115% of HUD's area median income based on family size, and the home must be the primary residence.[441]

7.2.7 System Benefit Charges in Restructured States

7.2.7.1 Overview

As of 2010, twenty-two states and the District of Columbia had enacted some form of electric and/or gas utility restructuring legislation.[442] However, no state has adopted

437 Tariff PSC Mo. No. 5, Consolidated, Original Sheet Nos. R-49 to R-52 (eff. May 13, 2006).

438 *See* Press Release, Missouri Pub. Serv. Comm'n, Pilot Program to Help AmerenUE Low-Income Customers with Electric Bills (Aug. 9, 2010); http://liheap.ncat.org/news/aug10/mo.htm.

439 The brief is available on NCLC's energy and utility website at www.nclc.org/initiatives/energy_and_utility/index.shtml.

440 *See* http://wmca.org/energy-utilities/cmp-electric-bill-assistance-liapelp (Western Maine Community Action website, describing New Power Line Program).

441 *Id.*

442 *See* Mine Yucel & Adam Swadley, Did Residential Electricity Rates Fall After Retail Competition?, at 18 (Federal Reserve Bank of Dallas, working Paper No. 1105, May 2011), *available*

restructuring legislation since 2000, and seven states that had initially passed restructuring legislation have retreated through legislation or regulation (Arizona, New Mexico, Nevada, California, Arkansas, West Virginia, and Oklahoma).[443]

Twenty-two of the restructured states included in their restructuring legislation a public benefits charge (also known as a wires charge, system benefits charge, societal benefits charge, or universal service charge) as a means of providing initial funding or, in some cases, preserving or expanding existing funding for low-income energy assistance and weatherization programs in addition to other public benefits that have been historically provided by the regulated utilities.

Public benefits charges typically are non-bypassable charges on electricity or gas usage which are paid by one or more classes of utility customers. The charges are often measured in mills (1 mill is $0.001) per kilowatt hour or per therm (gas) and are a part of the customers' utility bill. The distribution company usually collects and transfers the fees to the agency administering the public benefits programs in the state. Rate affordability programs operating as a result of state system benefits charges are described in previous sections for states such as New Hampshire,[444] New Jersey,[445] Pennsylvania,[446] Ohio,[447] and Maryland.[448]

7.2.7.2 Nevada's System Benefits Charge Program

The Nevada universal service program is one example of a system benefits (or wires) charge used to fund low-income assistance. Legislatively authorized in 2001, the Fund for Energy Assistance and Conservation was set aside as a "special revenue fund" in the state treasury. Out of this fund, the legislature created a bill payment assistance program, administered by the state's Division of Welfare and Supportive Services (DWSS),[449] and an energy efficiency program, administered by the Housing Division.[450]

The Nevada program is designed to be comprehensive in nature. In addition to using funds generated by the state's "universal energy charge," under the statute, "all money received from private or public sources to carry out the purposes of this chapter must be deposited in the state treasury for credit to the Fund."[451] The DWSS is directed to ensure, to the extent practicable, "that the money in the Fund is administered in a manner which is coordinated with all other sources of money that are available for energy assistance and conservation, including, without limitation, money contributed from private sources, money obtained from the Federal Government and money obtained from any agency or instrumentality of this State or political subdivision of this State."[452]

The legislature directed the DWSS, the Department of Health and Human Services (for bill payment assistance), and the Housing Division of the Department of Business and Industry (for weatherization and efficiency assistance) to "coordinate with other federal, state and local agencies that provide energy assistance or conservation services to low-income persons. . . ."[453]

The Nevada program provides no discretion in how the universal service funding is to be utilized. According to the statute, 75% of the money in the Fund *must* be distributed to the DWSS "for programs to assist eligible households in paying for natural gas and electricity."[454] This funding requirement, however, is both a floor and a ceiling. The DWSS, in other words, does not have the discretion to use more than 75% for such purposes.[455] The legislature further provides that 25% of the funds *must* be distributed to the Housing Division for programs of "energy conservation, weatherization and energy efficiency for eligible households."[456]

The statute provides that, out of its funding, the DWSS may use its universal service money "*only* to . . . assist eligible households in paying for natural gas and electricity."[457] In addition, the funds can be used for the related purposes of engaging in consumer outreach, program design, and program evaluation. The Housing Division is authorized to use its funding only to provide an eligible household with services of basic home energy conservation and home energy efficiency or to assist an eligible household to acquire such services."[458] The legislature explicitly included "services of load management" under the rubric of these programs.[459] The Housing Division may also "pay for appropriate improvements associated with energy conserva-

at http://dallasfed.org/research/papers/2011/wp1105.pdf (map showing Status of Electric Market Restructuring as of September 2010); National Ctr. for Appropriate Tech., State-By-State Overview Of Low-Income Restructuring Legislation & Implementation, LIHEAP Clearinghouse (2007), *at* www.liheap.ncat.org/dereg.htm.

443 Barbara Alexander, Managing Default Service to Provide Consumer Benefits in Restructured States: Avoiding Short-Term Price Volatility (June 2003).

444 *See* § 7.2.2.3.3 and text accompanying notes 77–85, *supra.*

445 *See* § 7.2.3.3.2 and text accompanying notes 162–192, *supra.*

446 *See* § 7.2.3.2.3 and text accompanying notes 110–161, *supra.*

447 *See* § 7.2.3.2.2 and text accompanying notes 98–109, *supra.*

448 *See* § 7.2.3.4.2 and text accompanying notes 236–276, *supra.*

449 Nev. Rev. Stat. § 702.250(1).

450 *Id.* § 702.270(1).

451 *Id.* § 702.250(2).

452 *Id.* § 702.250(3).

453 *Id.* §§ 702.260(8)(c) (Welfare Division), 702.270(6)(c) (Housing Division).

454 *Id.* § 702.260(1) (emphasis added).

455 The requirement that the DWSS "must" use 75% of the funding for bill payment assistance normally carries with it the implication that the DWSS "may" use more than 75% should it choose.

456 Nev. Rev. Stat. § 702.270(1).

457 *Id.*§ 702.260(2)(a) (emphasis added).

458 *Id.* § 702.270(2).

459 *Id.* § 702.270(2)(a).

tion, weatherization and energy efficiency," engage in consumer outreach, and pay for program design and evaluation.

Though similar in structure, the purpose of bill payment assistance in Nevada differs somewhat from the assistance distributed under related programs in other states. Like many states, Nevada pays percentage-of-income-based benefits to its program participants. But the Nevada program is not aimed at making bills affordable. Instead, it puts greater emphasis on equity. Rather than tying bill payment assistance to an affordable percentage of income, the Nevada statute provides that the amount of assistance provided to each household shall, to the extent practicable, be "sufficient to reduce the percentage of the household's income that is spent on natural gas and electricity to the median percentage of household income spent on natural gas and electricity statewide."[460] In other words, the percentage of income home energy burden for the median-income household is the program's objective regardless of whether that median income burden is above, below, or precisely equal to what is affordable.

The Nevada low-income energy assistance programs are funded through a legislatively imposed "universal energy charge."[461] The universal energy charge is imposed on "each retail customer,"[462] explicitly defined to include "without limitation, a residential, commercial or industrial end-use customer that purchases natural gas or electricity for consumption" in the state.[463] While customers of certain types of utilities are exempt from paying the universal energy charge,[464] those customers are also prohibited from receiving any "money or other assistance" from the universal energy fund.[465]

The Nevada statute is specifically designed to impose the universal energy charge on customers that have bypassed the distribution systems of the state's electric and/or natural gas utilities. In the event that a customer uses the distribution system of a local public utility, the utility is directed to collect the universal service charge as a separately stated line item on each customer's distribution bill.[466] However, if a retail customer does *not* use the local distribution utility, the statute states that it is the retail customer's responsibility to remit the appropriate funds to the state.

The Nevada program is designed so that the level of program funding is set by statute, rather than fluctuating to meet the required needs of program participants. A uniform charge of 3.30 mils per therm of natural gas, and 0.39 mils per kilowatt hour (kWh) of electricity, is imposed on each retail customer.[467] Statutory caps were created on the quarterly payment required of any single customer or "multiple retail customers under common ownership and control."[468] The only role played by the Nevada Public Utilities Commission (PUC) in the state's universal service program is in administering the collection of funds.

Given the limited funding provided under the Nevada statute, program administrators are given flexibility in defining both what population they are to serve and precisely what amount of assistance—as opposed to the *type* of assistance—should be provided. The DWSS may provide assistance to households with annual incomes of "not more than 150% of the federally designated level signifying poverty. . . ."[469] Thus, in times of constrained funding, it would appear that the DWSS can limit eligibility to those households with incomes below this level if needed to stay within budget. Moreover, the DWSS has the obligation only to distribute bill payment assistance "to the extent practicable," in order to reduce home energy burdens to that of the statewide median.[470] To achieve this statutory objective may not be "practicable" during periods of reduced funding.[471] Finally, while the DWSS is "*authorized* to render emergency assistance to a household if an emergency related to the cost or availability of natural gas or electricity threatens the health or safety of one or more of the members of the household,"[472] it is not *required* to render such emergency assistance. It may thus choose not to take action that is authorized but not mandated by the program's statutory charter. The DWSS is not allowed complete discretion in its decision-making, however. The statute specifically provides that it must prepare, and must work with a general oversight group in preparing, an annual plan.[473]

Similar observations can be made about the administration of energy efficiency funding provided pursuant to the statute.[474]

460 *Id.* § 702.260(6)(a).

461 *Id.* §§ 702.100, 702.160.

462 *Id.* § 702.160(1).

463 *Id.* § 702.090(2).

464 For example, customers of rural electric cooperatives (RECs) do not pay the universal service charge. This statutory mandate, however, was largely rendered irrelevant by program provisions that allowed customers of such utilities to receive greater LIHEAP benefits, with the reduction in LIHEAP benefits in the rest of the state being made up with universal service funds.

465 Nev. Rev. Stat. § 702.150.

466 *Id.* § 702.160(3).

467 *Id.* § 702.160(1).

468 Quarterly payments exceeding $25,000 are subject to refund under the statute. *Id.* § 702.160(5).

469 *Id.* § 702.260(3).

470 *Id.* § 702.260(6)(a).

471 How the Welfare Division would actually respond to funding constraints is, of course, speculative. Whether the DWSS would reduce benefit levels (by increasing the percentage-of-income burden), reduce eligibility, or engage in some other action cannot be determined in the abstract. This discussion only identifies what the DWSS is authorized to do.

472 Nev. Rev. Stat. § 702.260(4).

473 *Id.* § 702.280.

474 *Id.* § 702.270(3), (4).

7.2.7.3 Wisconsin's System Benefits Charge Program

Wisconsin's home energy affordability program was created by statute. Mandated by Act 9 of the 1999 Wisconsin General Assembly,[475] the Wisconsin public benefits fund supports two affordability initiatives:[476] (1) low-income energy assistance[477] and (2) low-income energy efficiency.[478]

The objective of the low-income components of the Wisconsin public benefits program "is to deliver services in a manner that contributes to making households energy self-sufficient within the constraints of state and federal limits for eligibility."[479] To this extent, the energy efficiency component of the low-income assistance programs funded by the public benefits fund differs from other efficiency components supported by the public benefits fund that, rather than focusing on improving affordability, "revolve around market development of energy efficient products and services and energy savings."[480]

The long-term goal of the low-income assistance programs supported by the public benefits fund is to improve the "energy sustainability" of households. "In this context, 'sustainability' is defined as the ability of a household to make full and timely payments of energy bills over an extended period of time without resorting to actions that cannot be maintained or are otherwise undesirable."[481]

The Wisconsin public benefits fund is unique in that it aggregates the various streams of dollars spent on low-income energy initiatives into a single fund for integrated distribution and targeting. The public benefits fund is derived from: (1) funds from investor-owned utilities through the public benefits charge established each year by the state utility commission; (2) a fee added to electric bills starting in October 2000 that participating utilities collect and remit to the state; (3) funds contributed by participating electric cooperatives and municipal electric utilities;[482] (4) federal funds provided through the Low Income Home Energy Assistance Program (LIHEAP) and Weatherization Assistance Program (WAP) programs; and (5) voluntary contributions.[483]

The use of state public benefits funds, and the programs funded through their use, are not dictated by statute. Instead, the state Department of Administration (DOA), in consultation with the state Council on Utility Public Benefits,[484] annually determines the "new or continued programs" that will provide "low-income assistance" each year.[485] The DOA has determined that public benefits funds collected in Wisconsin will be used to supplement federal LIHEAP funds to allow the state to provide an electric benefit in addition to a home heating benefit. According to the DOA,[486]

> heating assistance is provided entirely with federal funds. . . . The Public Benefits funds have enabled the program to expand services to assist with non-heating electric costs. This assistance is intended to help pay a portion of the electric costs of a household, not to cover the entire annual cost of electricity for the household.[487]

Public benefits funds are also used to provide crisis assistance to a limited number of low-income households.[488] In fiscal year 2006, the public benefits fund energy assistance program provided an average electric benefit of $159 to 137,502 households; the program distributed an average crisis assistance benefit of $220 to 8220 households.[489]

In addition to voluntary contributions made to the public benefits fund under the statute, the state of Wisconsin generates two streams of non-federal funding: (1) low-income assistance funds currently embedded in utility rates,

475 1999 Assemb. Bill 133, 1999 Wis. Act 9, § 109 (Wis. eff. Oct. 29, 1999).

476 The Wisconsin Home Energy Plus program also has a lead-abatement component. This lead hazard reduction program is funded with dollars provided by the U.S. Department of Housing and Urban Development. It is not considered further below. *See generally* Steven Tryon, Wisconsin Home Energy Plus Program: Overview for Public Benefits Council (Jan. 20, 2005).

477 Wisconsin's energy assistance program is called the Home Energy Plus program.

478 The Wisconsin low-income energy efficiency program is part of the state's broader efficiency program called Focus on Energy.

479 Bobbi Tannebaum, Energy Ctr. of Wis., Wisconsin LIHEAP Performance Measures: Working Group Report (Dec. 2000).

480 Wisconsin Dep't of Admin., Division of Energy, Focus on Energy Public Benefits Evaluation: Quarterly Summary Report, Contract Year 3, First Quarter, Final Submission, at 16 (Dec. 2, 2003).

481 Lark Lee et al., Wisconsin Dep't of Admin., Division of Energy, Low-Income Public Benefits Evaluation: Year 2 Low-Income Program Evaluation, Vol. 1—Final Report, at 1-1 (2003) (citing LIHEAP Performance Measures).

482 Cooperatives and municipal electric utilities may, but are not required to, participate in the public benefits fund program. If they do not, they must operate their own "commitment to community" programs. *See* Wis. Stat. § 16.957(1)(c).

483 *Id.* § 16.957. *See also* Wisconsin Dep't of Admin., Division of Energy, Wisconsin Public Benefits Programs Annual Reports (2003/2004); *id.* (2004/2005); *id.* (2005/2006).

484 Wis. Stat. § 15.107(17).

485 Wis. Admin. Code Dep't of Admin. § 45.06.

486 DOA is the agency charged with administering the state public benefits fund programs.

487 Wisconsin Dep't of Admin., Division of Energy, Wisconsin Public Benefits Programs Annual Reports 30 (2003/2004), *available at* www.focusonenergy.com/About-Us/Annual-Reports.aspx.

488 *Id.* at 31.

In fiscal year 2004, LIHEAP provided an average crisis assistance payment of $301 to more than 34,000 households, while the public benefits fund provided an average crisis assistance payment of $168 to 6346 households. *Id.*

489 Wisconsin Dep't of Admin., Division of Energy, Wisconsin Public Benefits Programs Annual Reports 318 (2005/2006), *available at* www.focusonenergy.com/About-Us/Annual-Reports.aspx.

and (2) a state low-income assistance fee in an amount determined by the administrator of the public benefits fund.[490]

The Wisconsin statute which created the public benefits fund originally provided that investor-owned utilities transfer to the fund an amount equal to what each utility spent for public benefits programs in 1998; however, these companies are now required to spend 1.2% of their annual operating revenues, but the Commission may require more.[491] The state utility commission is charged with determining the amount spent by each utility.[492]

The Wisconsin statute's intent was to transfer financial support for the state's low-income assistance programs from each utility to the state public benefits fund. From 2001 through 2002, the Public Service Commission (PSC) of Wisconsin was charged with requiring each utility to spend "a decreasing portion of the amount determined" to have been previously used for low-income assistance, with the remaining portion of the determined assistance to be transferred to the public benefits fund. After 2002, each utility was required to transfer the *entire* amount of low-income assistance.

In a 2000 proceeding, the PSC developed an inventory and valuation of the dollars expended by Wisconsin utilities for low-income energy assistance.[493] According to the PSC, Wisconsin utilities provided $21.3 million on low-income assistance, including "low-income weatherization, low-income uncollectibles and arrearages, and low-income Early Identification Programs (EIP)."[494] In making this determination, the commission found that "the historical assumption that 50 percent of total uncollectibles is attributable to low income households is not determinative." In addition, the PSC found, "it is not reasonable to base an estimate of low-income uncollectibles solely on participation in the federal Low-Income Home Energy Assistance Program."[495] According to the PSC, "a LIHEAP participation rate of 28 percent in 1998 is too low to fairly represent all low-income households that may be in arrearage or incur bad debt expense with the utility."[496]

The PSC ultimately determined that some issues relating to uncollectibles and arrearages may need to be resolved by a working group process. It left to the state Department of Administration (DOA), which administers the public benefits funds, the discretion to determine whether a work group would be helpful to address issues which include who benefits from the use of the uncollectibles/arrearages dollars transferred to the public benefits fund; which programs should be financially supported by those funds; and how programs could be designed "to be most effective in reducing arrearages and uncollectibles."[497]

In its 2000 Act 9 proceeding, the PSC decided that some programs operated by Wisconsin's utilities in 1998 would continue to be operated by the utilities even after the emergence of public benefits funds. Rather than transferring to the fund dollars used on those programs, those dollars would remain with the utilities to continue the program. The Early Identification Program (EIP) was one such program. "Utilities will continue to be the first point of contact for their customers and the utilities will have to continue to assist these customers through EIP services."[498] Until ordered by the commission to do otherwise, "each utility shall continue to spend annually, at a minimum, a level of funding equivalent to the retained portion of its 1998 EIP expenditures."[499] If funds were not spent on "appropriate EIP-related activities," the PSC said, the funds should be transferred to the PSC and deposited into the utility public benefits fund.[500]

The PSC also found that "voluntary customer and corporate contributions to utility-sponsored customer assistance programs are not considered utility public benefits expenditures for purposes of establishing 1998 utility ex-

490 That administrator is the Department of Administration (DOA), which administers the federal LIHEAP funds.

491 Wis. Stat. § 196.374(2), (3).

492 *See, e.g.*, Wis. Stat. §§ 196.03, 196.37.

Public benefits programs included not only low-income assistance but also energy conservation and efficiency, environmental research and development, and renewable resources. *Id.* § 196.374(2)(a)–(d).

493 Decision, Investigation on the Commission's Own Motion of Appropriate Measures to Maintain or Enhance the Existing Levels of Energy Efficiency, Services to Low-Income Customers, Renewable Resources and Research and Development ("Public Benefits") in Restructured Electric and Natural Gas Industries, No. 05-BU-100 (Pub. Serv. Comm'n of Wis. Aug. 17, 2000).

494 *Id.* at 3.

495 *Id.* at 4.

496 *Id.* at 10.

Having said what it would *not* use in making its determination, the PSC did not explain the basis for the determination it *did* make in its final decision. One commissioner (Mettner) "dissented on the method for identifying uncollectible accounts receivable associated with low-income customers, contending that the approved method exceeded the plain meaning of the statute." *Id.* at 16.

That "method," however, was never identified or discussed, let alone rationalized, in a commission order.

497 Final Order at 7–8, Investigation on the Commission's Own Motion of Appropriate Measures to Maintain or Enhance the Existing Levels of Energy Efficiency, Services to Low-income Customers, Renewable Resources, and Research and Development ("Public Benefits") in Restructured Electric and Natural Gas Industries, No. 05-BU-100 (Pub. Serv. Comm'n of Wis. Jan. 4, 2001).

498 Decision at 11, Investigation on the Commission's Own Motion of Appropriate Measures to Maintain or Enhance the Existing Levels of Energy Efficiency, Services to Low-Income Customers, Renewable Resources and Research and Development ("Public Benefits") in Restructured Electric and Natural Gas Industries, No. 05-BU-100 (Pub. Serv. Comm'n of Wis. Aug. 17, 2000).

499 *Id.*

500 *Id.* at 15.

penditures levels."[501] Finally, the PSC determined that "customer service activities are distinct from utility public benefits programs."[502]

In Wisconsin, cost-recovery of funds transferred to the public benefits fund by each utility is accomplished through base rate case proceedings.[503] According to the PSC, "if a utility requests rate recovery for public benefits-related costs that they are required to transfer to DOA, the utility will need to justify the need for rate recovery in its rate case proceeding."[504]

Finally, the Wisconsin public benefits fund is supported by a "low-income assistance fee" included on all customer bills.[505] While the amount of the fee is determined by the Department of Administration each year, the statute states that it must be a fixed charge[506] and that customers are to receive an annual summary of the low-income assistance fees they have paid and the programs supported by those fees.[507] All customer classes are required by statute to pay the fee, with 70% of the total revenue being collected from residential customers and 30% being collected from nonresidential customers.[508]

The low-income assistance fee should be in an amount that, when combined with other low-income resources (identified above), equals the state's "low-income need" target.[509] "Low-income need" is defined as the "amount obtained by subtracting from the total low-income energy bills in a fiscal year the product of 2.2% of the estimated average annual income of low-income households in this state in that fiscal year multiplied by the estimated number of low-income households in this state in that fiscal year."[510] Estimates of low-income home energy bills are based on data obtained from the state energy agency.[511]

In sum, the Wisconsin public benefits fund aggregates all sources of low-income home energy affordability funding into a single trust fund and places those funds under a single administrator. The fund incorporates the multiple streams of revenue—including federal dollars, private contributions, utility dollars generated from preexisting low-income initiatives, and ratepayer dollars generated by a statutorily imposed low-income assistance charge—for the benefit of low-income households.

The amount of funding varies annually, with aggregated revenue streams matched against an annual determination of "low-income need." This determination takes into account home energy bills and the number of low-income households in Wisconsin.

The distribution of aggregated funding streams is determined by the state LIHEAP agency in consultation with the state's Public Benefits Council. An annual program proposal is developed and released, articulating how the funding is divided between fuel assistance, energy efficiency, and crisis assistance. The objective of the combined program is to improve "energy sustainability" within the low-income community.

7.3 Developing and Administering an Affordability Program

7.3.1 Outreach and Administrative Issues

Outreach and administration can be crucial in the success of a low-income affordability program. The costs to perform these will be a primary consideration in establishing the program.

Administrative procedures should keep the following goals in mind:

1. Outreach should be reasonably calculated to make the low-income program known to low-income residents, including renters, people of color, monolingual speakers of languages other than English, the uneducated or functionally illiterate, and seniors;
2. Application sites, hours and procedures that are accessible to low-income residents, as enumerated in the preceding sentence;
3. Objective and complete standards for evaluating eligibility and answering questions such as the following:
    - What is a household (for example, when several families live in a single dwelling)?
    - What income will be considered in determining eligibility?
    - How will in-kind income be evaluated?
4. Effective but minimally intrusive measures for verifying eligibility (for example, ascertaining that applicants have not misstated income);

501 *Id.* at 8.

502 *Id.* at 5.

503 Final Order at 12, Investigation on the Commission's Own Motion of Appropriate Measures to Maintain or Enhance the Existing Levels of Energy Efficiency, Services to Low-income Customers, Renewable Resources, and Research and Development ("Public Benefits") in Restructured Electric and Natural Gas Industries, No. 05-BU-100 (Pub. Serv. Comm'n of Wis. Jan. 4, 2001).

504 *Id.* at 13 ("it is reasonable to address the specific rate recovery issues identified by the utilities and any others yet to be identified in future rate case proceedings").

505 Wis. Stat. § 16.957(2)(a)(4), (5)(a).

506 *Id.* § 16.957(4)(b).

The fees shall be established by DOA regulation and shall not be imposed on a per-kilowatt-hour basis. *Id.* § 16.958(4)(b).

507 *Id.* § 16.957(4)(am).

508 *Id.* § 16.957(4)(b)(2).

509 *Id.* § 16.957(4)(c).

510 *Id.* § 16.957(1)(n).

In turn, "low-income energy bills" and "total low-income energy bills" mean the total estimated amount that all low-income households are billed for residential electricity, natural gas, and heating fuel in a fiscal year. *Id.* § 16.957(1)(u).

511 Wis. Admin. Code Dep't of Admin. § 43.04(1).

5. Measures to process applications within defined, short time-frames, and to furnish eligibility retroactively to the date of application;
6. Protections to ensure confidentiality of applicants and beneficiaries;
7. Measures to ensure the prompt receipt of rebates, no later than fifteen days after normal due date for rent;
8. Notice to applicants and beneficiaries of adverse determinations; and
9. Fair hearings that are in accord with procedural due process, when applicants and beneficiaries contest such determinations.

7.3.2 *Costs in Establishing an Affordability Program*

7.3.2.1 Start-up Costs

Staff time (or consulting fees) will need to be expended to identify the scope of the affordability program, to set goals for the particular utility's affordability response, to review options for rate and program design, and to test selected options to see how well in theory they meet the utility's goals.

New billing arrangements must be made, either using the manual billing system, or by adding new programming to the data processing system. To the extent the affordability program is large enough to require new staff, the hiring process will require management time and some minimal advertising expenses. It may be necessary or desirable to bring the proposal before the public, or to a city council or regulatory body. If so, time spent educating ratepayers and others with an interest in the proposal will be valuable in anticipating questions and concerns and, if necessary, adjusting the proposal to improve it in light of these concerns. The time required for these tasks is another start-up cost.

7.3.2.2 Ongoing Administration Costs

Once the program is adopted and is up and running, there are continuing costs of administration. To the extent that the utility chooses to perform its own in-house means-testing (and has chosen an affordability model in which rate discounts or special services are only available to those of limited income), staff time must be devoted to taking and processing applications. If a self-verification of income system is used, this time may be minimal. While experience counsels that self-verification will, in practice, lead to only a few cases of error or outright fraud, the use of self-verification may not be acceptable to regulators or to the general public. Alternatively, some Pennsylvania utilities randomly re-verify households that have self-verified to ensure that these households have not enrolled fraudulently through self-verification.

To meet concerns about the integrity of the application of means-tested availability clauses while keeping processing costs down, the best solution is often to piggy-back eligibility for the rate on to the customer's receipt of or proven eligibility for some means-tested public benefit open only to low-income households. This is called categorical eligibility.

Thus, many gas, electric and telephone utilities which offer affordability rates and low-income rate discounts use an availability clause that opens the rate to customers who are receiving such forms of means-tested assistance as:

- Temporary Assistance to Needy Families (TANF);[512]
- Supplemental Security Income (SSI);[513]
- Low-Income Home Energy Assistance (LIHEAP);[514]
- Food Stamps;[515]

---

512 The Personal Responsibility and Work Opportunities Reconciliation Act of 1996, Pub. L. No. 104-193, 110 Stat. 2105 (Aug. 22, 1996), *codified at* 42 U.S.C. § 601–619, abolished AFDC, JOBS, and Emergency Assistance grants (EA) and replaced them with TANF, a block grant to the states. Formerly, AFDC was an entitlement; it was available to any eligible family in the form of a cash grant, and the federal government, with a state match, provided the necessary funding to serve those families. Under TANF, states will receive a fixed amount of federal funds each year, regardless of need. Through a state plan, which must be approved by HHS, states will establish their own eligibility criteria and determine what form the benefits will take. States are not obligated to provide cash assistance or to serve every family that is deemed eligible.

513 Supplemental Security Income (SSI) is a means-tested, federally administered income assistance program established by the 1972 amendments to the Social Security Act, Pub. L. No. 92-603, 86 Stat. 1329, 1415 (1972), that began in 1974. SSI provides monthly cash payments in accordance with uniform, nationwide eligibility requirements to needy aged, blind, and disabled persons. U.S. House of Reps. Comm. on Ways & Means, U.S. Gov't Printing Office, Overview of Entitlement Programs ("Green Book") (2002).

514 42 U.S.C. § 8624(a)–(*l*).

The largest federal government assistance program for the payment of utility bills for low-income people, in terms of number of households served with direct benefits, is the Low Income Home Energy Assistance Program (LIHEAP). This program is known by various acronyms in different states; on a national basis it is referred to as "LIHEAP." The statute authorizing the program is found at 42 U.S.C. § 8621(a)–(e). LIHEAP provides cash benefits for a number of purposes: assistance with heating bills; assistance with cooling bills; crisis benefits—only available to deal with an emergency relating the energy. *See* ch. 8, *supra*.

515 The Food Stamp Program is designed to increase the food purchasing power of eligible low-income households. Upon receiving food stamps, households are supposed to be able to buy a nutritionally adequate low-cost diet. The amount of money provided for this low-cost diet is derived from the U.S. Department of Agriculture's lowest-cost food plan (the Thrifty Food Plan), varied by household size, and adjusted annually for inflation. U.S. House of Reps. Comm. on Ways & Means, U.S.

- Social Security.[516]

A good source of information on means-tested programs is the local or state welfare office and any Community Action Association or Legal Services office.

However, the administrative efficiency comes at the price of missing those households that have fallen through the tattered safety net of programs. Many poor households are not enrolled in the public assistance programs for which they are eligible. In 2010, there were approximately 305.6 million people in the United States living at or below the poverty level.[517] As noted in NCLC's comments to the FCC on increasing the program-based eligibility and adding income-based eligibility for the federal Lifeline telephone assistance program, the penetration rates for many public assistance programs have declined, and penetration rates have never been as high as they should be in the first place.[518] Welfare rolls have declined by more than 50%

Gov't Printing Office, Overview of Entitlement Programs ("Green Book") 923 (1998)).

As of 2006, approximately 25.6 million people living in 11.3 million households were participating in the Food Stamp Program. As reported for 2006, the following were reported as characteristics of the food stamp population: 87% of food stamp recipient households were below the federal poverty levels (gross monthly income). In 2006, 58% of Food Stamp recipients had income less than 75% of the Federal Poverty Level, while 39% had income less than 50% of the Poverty Level. Most (84%) had a child under age 18, an elderly person, or a disabled person in the household. The average Food Stamp recipient household had a gross monthly income in 2006 of $673 and a net monthly income of $328. They had countable resources of $137. U.S. Dep't of Agric., Food & Nutrition Servs., Characteristics of Food Stamp Households: Fiscal Year 2006 (Sept. 2007).

To be eligible for the Food Stamp Program, recipients cannot have a gross income of more than 130% of the Federal Poverty Level. (The gross income limit does not apply to elderly/disabled household members.) In addition, a recipient's resources or "counted liquid assets" must be less than $2000 or $3000 for elderly/disabled. For purposes of the Food Stamp program, "elderly" persons are those age 60 and older. U.S. House of Reps. Comm. on Ways & Means, U.S. Gov't Printing Office, Overview of Entitlement Programs ("Green Book") (2004).

Recipients in the two primary Federal/State cash welfare programs, the TANF and SSI programs, as well as state general assistance programs, generally are automatically eligible for food stamps. *Id.*

There are non-financial requirements as well. All non-elderly adults receiving benefits who are able to work are required to be employed or to register for employment.

516 Unlike the other programs discussed in this chapter, the Social Security Program is not need-based. In other words, once a person has participated in the work force and met other eligibility requirements (such as age and/or disability) they become eligible for social security benefits, regardless of other (unearned) income or other resources.

Description of Program. The Social Security Program consists of two programs: The Old-Age and Survivors Insurance (OASI) program and the Disability Insurance (DI) program. The OASI program provides monthly benefits to retired workers and their dependents and to survivors of insured workers. U.S. House of Reps. Comm. on Ways & Means, U.S. Gov't Printing Office, Overview of Entitlement Programs 5 (1998) ("1998 Green Book").

The disability insurance (DI) program provides monthly cash benefits for disabled workers under age 65 and their dependents. 1998 Green Book, at 12.

The purpose of both the OASI and DI programs is to replace income when the wage earner is no longer able to work. 1998 Green Book, at 5.

While the OASI program insures a worker and his dependents against loss of income due to retirement or death, the DI program insures against the loss of income due to the worker's physical or mental disability.

Benefit Levels. Benefit levels vary depending on the worker's salary, length of employment, among other things. The average OASDI benefit for retired workers in December 1996 was $745; The average monthly benefit for disabled workers was $704. The average monthly benefit for spouses of retired workers was $384. For widows and widowers (non-disabled), it was $707. For children of retired workers, $337; children of deceased workers, $487; and children of disabled workers, $194. 1998 Green Book, at 3.

Participation Rates. An estimated 96% of the country's paid work force is covered either voluntarily or mandatorily by the Social Security System. 1998 Green Book, at 7.

In December 1997, there were 43.7 million beneficiaries in the OASI and DI programs who in "current-payment" status for that month. 1998 Green Book, at 6.

The population receiving benefits is as follows:

- Retired workers—61.5%
- Wives and husbands of retired workers—6.8%
- Children of retired workers—1.0%
- Disabled workers—10.0%
- Wives and husbands of disabled workers—0.5%
- Surviving children—4.3%
- Widows and widowers—11.5%

1998 Green Book, at 17.

Eligibility. Benefits can only be paid to workers, their dependents or survivors if the worker is "insured." 1998 Green Book, at 12.

A worker earns one quarter of coverage, up to a total of four quarters, for each $700 of annual earnings. Workers are "fully insured" for benefits for themselves and their families if they have one quarter of coverage for every four quarters upon reaching age 21, up until the year in which they reach age 62 (which will be gradually increased to 67 beginning in 2000), become disabled, or die. Workers are "currently insured" who have six quarters of coverage during the thirteen calendar quarters ending with the quarter in which they died. 1998 Green Book, at 12.

To be eligible for the DI program, a person must meet the definition of disability, which is generally "an inability to engage in substantial gainful activity by reason of a physical or mental impairment." 1998 Green Book, at 13.

517 U.S. Census Bureau, Income, Poverty and Health Insurance in the United States: 2010 Tables and Figures, at tbl. 4 (Sept. 2011), *available at* www.census.gov/hhes/www/poverty/data/incpovhlth/2010/table4.pdf (People and Families in Poverty by Selected Characteristics: 2009 and 2010).

518 Comments of the National Consumer Law Center on Behalf of the Massachusetts Union of Public Housing Tenants Re: Proposed Rules, 47 C.F.R. pt. 54 Lifeline and Link Up Program,

during the past decade; food stamp enrollment has declined by one-third; only a small percentage of income-eligible households actually live in public housing because the waiting lists are so long and the federal energy assistance program has been so under-funded that, in fiscal year 2008 only 16% of eligible households received LIHEAP assistance.[519] Only 12% and 11% of households with very young or elderly members, respectively, received LIHEAP assistance.[520]

If receipt of aid under any of these means-tested programs is the primary eligibility criterion to identify a low-income customer, then the work of processing eligibility information for households is done by other agencies. This relieves the utility of the obligation to duplicate this effort.

If a goal is to reach all the low-income families in the service area, there are basically two approaches to take. On the one hand, a utility might use a massive outreach and advertising campaign.[521] Relying excessively on a media campaign for consumer outreach, however, is not likely to be successful. In a 1999 report presented to the California Public Utility Commission, Dr. Brenda Dervin,[522] author of the report, found that one "well-established premise of public communication/education campaign design [is] that mass mediated messages are rarely effective."[523] According to Professor Dervin, media-based campaigns tend to have low penetration levels, with a typical public service announcement campaign producing awareness rates that can be as low as 5%–10%. In a similar vein, very little consumer awareness of a low-income energy assistance program in New York state was found to be generated through media advertising. "[T]he CSA weatherization program . . . had relatively low visibility despite extensive advertising and outreach campaigns."[524]

On the other hand, for the purposes of administering their affordability programs, a number of gas, electric, and telephone utilities today identify the majority of their low-income customers by matching their billing computer tapes with the computerized listings of welfare recipients maintained by the state and federal government (SSI benefits are administered by the federal Social Security Administration). Better effort can be made to target eligible households with very young and elderly members.[525]

The utility can contact the state departments of welfare, public assistance, health and human services, or transitional assistance, among others, to make more formal arrangements for using electronic database sharing to verify whether customers have received their benefits. Similar electronic data-sharing arrangements can be made with the federal Social Security Administration, which administers SSI. Data-sharing can also be arranged with LIHEAP agencies (typically local community action agencies), although this information is rarely available in electronic format. Categorical eligibility and automatic enrollment are discussed more extensively in § 7.3.4.6, *infra*.

7.3.2.3 Net Revenue Implications

7.3.2.3.1 General

Revenue reduction is an apparent cost of offering affordability programs, particularly discounted rate programs. This cost is typically estimated by calculating what the billed revenue would have been had participants remained on the regular rate for their class of service, what the billings would be for these customers under the discount, and determining the difference between these two figures. This is a misleading estimate, however, and the shortcomings of such a method of calculation are discussed later in this chapter. Following is an examination of the various ways in which to gather the data necessary to make such estimates.

7.3.2.3.2 Data to estimate take-rate of program

First, it will be necessary to estimate the numbers of customers who are likely to take advantage of the discounted-rate (or other) program. To get a sense of how many customers are likely to be billed at the reduced rate, it is first necessary to develop an estimate of the total number of

---

Before the Fed. Communications Comm'n, No. 03-109 (Aug. 18, 2003).

519 *See* Jessica Bean, *Household Reports of Energy Assistance Receipt Increased 48 Percent During Recession*, Issue Brief No. 27 (Carsey Inst.), Spring 2011, at 2, *available at* www.carseyinstitute.unh.edu/publications/IB-Bean-LIHEAP.pdf.

520 *Id.* at 3.

521 In promoting full enrollments of the CARE program in California, the California Public Utility Commission discourages the use of mass media marketing campaigns. The commission limits mass media expenditures to 10% of total outreach expenditures, emphasizing that they sought, through such funding approval, "a very limited, targeted media campaign to fund non-English radio and print advertising for CARE outreach. . . ." *In re* Application of Southwest Gas Corp. (U 905 G) for Authority to Adjust Pub. Purpose Program Surcharges; In *In re* Application of PACIFICORP for Approval of Post-2002 Low Income Energy Efficiency Program and CARE Program Funding, No. D.03-03-007, 2003 Cal. PUC LEXIS 195, at *69 (Cal. Pub. Util. Comm'n Mar. 13, 2003).

522 Dr. Brenda Dervin is a professor in the School of Communications at Ohio State University.

523 Brenda Dervin, California Pub. Utils. Comm'n, Evaluation of the Pacific Bell Customer Notification and Education Plan on CPN Delivery (1995).

524 Charles Unseld, New York State Energy Office, The Impact of Rising Energy Costs on the Elderly Poor in New York State 61 (Jan. 1978).

525 *See* Jessica Bean, *Household Reports of Energy Assistance Receipt Increased 48 Percent During Recession*, Issue Brief No. 27 (Carsey Inst.), Spring 2011, at 3, *available at* www.carseyinstitute.unh.edu/publications/IB-Bean-LIHEAP.pdf.

households eligible to take service under the rate. Many local organizations will have estimates of the total number of low-income households, as that number changes depending on the cut-off line chosen for the utility's rate. Census data for each state is maintained by a state agency, typically located at a state university or in the capital city, that can provide estimates of the number of households in any given geographic area that come within the relevant range.

The state agency administering the LIHEAP program can help provide the total number of households in the state that qualify for assistance. The agency can also identify the percentage of households that actually apply for and receive this assistance. This ratio can be used to develop estimates of the percentage of households eligible for the rate in a given area and the portion of those eligible who are likely to respond to announcements of the program's availability (assuming the utility does not use the method of computer-tape matching with negative sign-up option (or negative check-off) described in the preceding section).[526] State agencies will also have the number of households receiving various forms of income-based assistance in the state. This data is compiled annually by Congress in what is known as the "Green Book,"[527] which is available at major public libraries and on the website of the U.S. House Ways and Means Committee.

If the utility chooses an aggressive outreach program to ensure that all qualifying customers receive the rate, the key variable that remains is the base of low-income customers who would qualify for the program. A negative check-off outreach is designed to obtain very high levels of customer acceptance of the rate. This is achieved at a modest administrative cost, since much of the work would not be necessary that would other wise be required if the onus for applying for the program fell on the customer.

7.3.2.3.3 Net revenue loss versus gross revenue loss: Avoided costs

Another category of loss is calculated using the difference between billed revenues without and without the discount-rate program. However, this calculation does not produce a valid estimate of the *net* revenue shortfall from applying discounts to the rates of low-income customers.

Merely billing a customer does not mean that the customer will pay the bill. Particularly for low-income consumers, the lack of funds for ordinary household necessities places them at higher risk of not paying their utility bills. This results in higher costs to the utility. Studies by gas and electric utilities show that about half of the customers who fall into default or eventually leave the utility with unpaid bills have incomes so low that they cannot afford to pay their bills in full. In these circumstances, attempting to educate these customers about money management skills misses the point and rarely solves the problem.[528]

Outlined below are some of the costs that accrue to the utility when low-income (or other) customers fall behind or default on their payments:

- *Credit and collection activities.* Customer payment difficulties lead to utility expenses associated with negotiating deferred payment plans; sending shut-off notices; making personal contact; disconnecting and reconnecting service; post-disconnection collection activity; creating lien and tax referral lists, making referrals to tax authorities, perfecting liens and the like.
- *Bad debt.* A percentage of payment-troubled households are unable to pay and, if the utility cannot collect payments due, the accrued unpaid balances become bad debt.
- *Time value/working capital.* Even when the customer eventually pays the bill, the utility incurs working capital expenses associated with the lag between the time service is rendered and the late payment.
- *Regulatory/public agency expenses.* To the extent that unaffordable bills lead to high bill complaints and more organized participation by consumer groups in rate-increase proceedings before regulators or, more likely, public officials such as city councilors, this heightened intervention diverts resources towards conflict resolution rather than bill affordability.
- *Diverted revenue (disconnect costs/reconnect fees).* When a utility uses the disconnection tool, this process costs money. Rather than having a limited-income customer use his or her resources to pay the bill for current consumption, the customer miscellaneous fees instead. Accordingly, the bill for current usage becomes even less affordable.
- *Diverted revenue (forced mobility).* As households are faced with unaffordable utility bills, their residency status tends to be less stable, and household revenue is diverted from paying current monthly bills to paying mobility costs (such as "voluntary" disconnection and

526 The state LIHEAP agency is also the agency most likely to have information on the energy bills and energy burdens of low-income customers. In a program based on reducing bills to an affordable percentage of income, especially, some customers will not participate because their burdens are already at or below the targeted burden. A household, for example, with an income of $10,000 and a home energy bill of $500 (energy burden of 5%) will not participate in a rate affordability program designed to reduce home energy burdens to 6% of income.

527 U.S. House of Reps. Comm. on Ways & Means, U.S. Gov't Printing Office, Overview of Entitlement Programs ("Green Book"), *available at* http://waysandmeans.house.gov.

528 Ron Grosse, Win-Win Alternatives for Credit and Collections (Wis. Pub. Serv. Corp. 1997) (detailed discussion of a "lifestyle survey" conducted to determine why customers do not pay their bills and to develop strategies to reduce nonpayment and arrearages). *See also* Ron Grosse, Regulatory Policy Pertaining to Disconnection for Nonpayment and Potential Issues for Default Providers in the Future (Wis. Pub. Serv. Corp. Aug. 19, 1999).

reconnection at another premise), thus compounding the problem.

- *Spiral of insufficient payments*. If the problem of unpaid and unaffordable bills crosses a certain threshold, the customer may lose all hope of becoming current on the bills and may cease paying altogether.
- *Lost contributions*. Many utilities are capital intensive. Any contribution from a customer above variable costs helps to defray the cost of these investments.
- *Repeated payment plans*. A utility's low-income customers can fall into a constant cycle of negotiating unaffordable payment plans, abandoning such plans upon nonpayment, and negotiating yet another unaffordable plan. This leads to great frustration for both the utility and its customers.

7.3.2.3.4 *Impact of affordable bills: Net revenue increase*

The costs described in the preceding section can either be avoided entirely or reduced substantially by making bills affordable for such payment-troubled households. In some cases, the problem can be viewed as one of semantics or of utility accounting. Take, for example, the expenses associated with delays in payment and working capital. Instead of billing the revenue and booking working capital expense because of the delay in receipt, the utility could bill a reduced revenue level (equal to the working capital on the higher bill). If by reducing the bill to this lower level, the bill became affordable and was paid on time, then the utility would be no worse off (a working capital expense would have been swapped for a billed revenue reduction). Meanwhile the customer would have experienced the relief of being able to pay the amount due and the satisfaction of being able to meet current obligations.

This phenomenon can be illustrated with a simple example for a water utility, depicted in Table 1. Suppose a water utility charges $3 per Ccf, with a customer charge of $20 per quarter. A consumer using 30 Ccf per quarter would be billed $90 for usage and $20 for the customer charge or $110 per quarter. But if that bill represents 5% of the consumer's income, it will be difficult to pay. Say the consumer can only pay $65 toward that current bill. Say the water utility incurred working capital and other credit and collection costs of $10 to get that $65 payment. The billed revenue is $110, but the percentage of bill collected is only [$65/(110 * 100%)], or 59%. The *net* revenue is [$65 collections minus the $10 collection cost], or $55.

However, if the water utility had charged the customer $60 for the quarter, rendering the bill affordable, the customer would be able to pay the entire amount billed. In this case, the percentage of billed revenue collected is 100% and the net revenue is $60, a $5 *improvement* in net revenues over the case in which the bill was *higher*. This is shown in Table 2.

Table 1
High bill, low net revenue

Item	Amount
Billed revenue	$110
Percent collected	59%
Amount collected	$65
Credit and Collection Costs	$10
Net Revenue	$55

Table 2
Low bill, higher net revenue

Item	Amount
Billed revenue	$65
Percent collected	100%
Amount collected	$65
Credit and Collection Costs	$0
Net Revenue	$65

Thus, paradoxically, a lower billed amount can produce a higher net revenue. Most likely, in practice, the net revenue *will* be lower when the billed revenue is reduced, but the reduction in net revenue will be smaller than this reduction in billed revenue. That is, there will not be a dollar-for-dollar reduction in net revenues. This is so because of the offsetting improvements in percentage of billed revenue collected and reductions in credit and collection costs. The lesson learned by utilities offering low-income programs is that it is better to collect 90% of a $60 bill than to collect 60% of an $80 bill. This is even more true if the utility can reduce or eliminate the collection expenses at the same time.

Similar effects are experienced by reducing bills so as to avoid other credit and collection costs. The net expense may not go down if the amount needed to bring the bill to an affordable level exceeds the total of avoided credit and collection costs. But even in this case, the goal of affordability is met and the customer experiences the invaluable ability to pay a bill when rendered, in full. Indeed, some gas and electric utilities have found that bringing the bill within reach of the consumer for the first time produces a phenomenon of *higher* payment amounts than before.[529] In any case,

529 Low Income Customer Payments Climb to Cover Costs of Utility Bill Assistance, N.W. Energy Coalition Report (Oct. 1998) (quoting from study of Clark County's Guarantee of Service Plan); Impact Assessment of the Equitable Gas Company Energy Assistance Program (H. Gil Peach & Assocs. Sept. 1996); Low-Income Usage Reduction Program Historical Report and Program Analysis (Pa. Pub. Util. Comm'n June 1994) (finding improved bill payment performance and reduced arrearages after weatherization); Niagara Mohawk Power Corp., Affordable Payment and Arrearage Program: Evaluation (1992); ICF Res. Inc., Program Evaluation: Weatherization Residential Assistance Partnership (WRAP) Program—Final Report (Northeast Util. 1991); Synergic Res. Corp., Evaluation of the Cost-Effectiveness of a Bad Debt Conservation Program (Com/Elec.

these costs, and the possibility of trading a billed revenue reduction for an expense reduction, should not be ignored.

7.3.3 Data Sharing—Protection of Benefit Recipients' Privacy

The statutes which create means-tested programs strictly protect the privacy of recipients.[530] Some exceptions are provided, however, for disclosures which benefit recipients or aid in the administration of programs. This section will briefly discuss some exceptions and suggest strategies for designing a match program to fit.

Federally supported welfare programs, (that is, TANF, aid to elderly, blind, disabled) may disclose recipients' names to "public officials."[531] A municipal electric or water utility would fit within this exception, as would a water and sewer district or similar political subdivision.[532] Disclosure to others is permissible "for purposes directly connected with the administration of the State plan."[533] The regulations which implement this statute[534] permit disclosure as follows:

1. The administration of the federally approved state plan, including "providing services to applicants and recipients."[535] Because the goal of state plans is to cost-effectively provide eligible persons with the means of subsistence, one can argue that a non-cash benefit program which makes utilities, clearly necessary to subsistence, more affordable will help the program achieve this goal. If a state plan includes crisis assistance for families facing utility termination or eviction, then a program to prevent this crisis should fit neatly within this exception.
2. "The administration of any other Federal or Federally assisted program which provides assistance, in cash or in kind, or services, directly to individuals on the basis of need."[536] An argument can be made that a telephone lifeline program, strongly encouraged by the federal universal service program, fits within this exception.
3. States may, by statute, permit disclosure, provided that use of the information for political or commercial purposes is forbidden.[537] The Massachusetts electric restructuring statute, which requires distribution companies to offer low-income rates and to do outreach, specifically permits a match with lists of recipients of means-tested benefits and a negative option sign-up.[538] The Texas electric restructuring and telephone universal service statutes provide for "automatic enrollment" and require the Department of Human Services to assist the state public utilities commission in developing rules to implement this program.[539] If a state is restructuring its utility industry, low-income advocates should seek to include in the statute a matching plan to provide affordability programs to benefit recipients. Note that the ban on political or commercial use will be a barrier to the offer of certain services, such as aggregation (which would typically include a contract with a free-market supplier and possibly the use of a for-profit aggregator or broker).

Whenever information is disclosed to a utility pursuant to these exceptions, the contract or tariff should clearly limit the use of the information. New York's matching program includes a memorandum of understanding between New York Telephone and the Department of Social Services and a provision in the New York Telephone tariff, specifically describing the purpose for which the data may be used, the requirements for security, including the need to warn all employees handling the data of the criminal penalties for misuse, and a right of inspection by the DSS and the Social Security Administration to ensure that the security practices are being followed.[540] DSS further minimizes privacy concerns by furnishing only a list of "categorically eligible" persons, who may be the recipient of one of several programs, without disclosing which program.

If a computer match and negative option sign-up are not feasible, a mass mailing remains an option. State agencies that administer welfare programs are permitted to send mailings of "materials in the immediate interest of the health and welfare of applicants and recipients, such as

---

1988); Nora Ganim Barnes, R.I. Consumers' Council, A Study of Client Satisfaction: The Percentage of Income Payment Plan (1987).

530 42 U.S.C. §§ 302, 602, 1202, 1352 (aid to elderly, blind, disabled and families); 45 C.F.R. § 205.50 (same); 42 U.S.C. § 1306 (social security and SSI).

531 42 U.S.C. §§ 302, 1202, 1353 (elderly, blind, disabled).
42 U.S.C. § 602 (TANF) requires only that the state "take reasonable steps" to restrict the use and disclosure of information.

532 Note, however, that the status of "quasi-public" or "semi-autonomous" authorities or other such hybrids raises difficult questions of state law, which are beyond the scope of this treatise.

533 42 U.S.C. §§ 302, 1202, 1353 (elderly, blind, disabled).
42 U.S.C. § 602 (TANF) requires only that the state "take reasonable steps" to restrict the use and disclosure of information.

534 45 C.F.R. § 205.50.

535 *Id.* § 205.50(A)(1)(i)(A).

536 *Id.* § 205.50(a)(1)(i)(C).

537 *Id.* § 205.50(a)(1)(iv).

538 Mass. Gen. Laws ch. 164, § 1F(4)(i).

539 Tex. Util. Code Ann. §§ 39.903(j) (electric), 17.004 (customer protection, electric and telephone) (West).

540 Telephone Lifeline Confidential Computer Matching Program Memorandum of Understanding, Between the New York Telephone Company, the New York Department of Social Services, and the N.Y.C. Community Development Agency (July 26, 1994); N.Y. Tel. Co. Tariff, P.S.C. No. 900, revised p.5 (effective Dec. 9, 1994).

announcements of free medical examinations, availability of surplus food, and consumer protection information."[541] This section permits only the sending of information, not the release of names. An appropriate waiver form permitting the release of the consumer's name to the utility could, however, be included with the announcement that a discount is available.

The Social Security Administration, which administers SSI, recognizes "a strong public interest in sharing information with other agencies with programs having the same or similar purposes" and will consider "whether the information will be adequately safeguarded."[542] SSA regulations[543] and the Privacy Act[544] permit disclosure for "routine uses" including "use in other programs which have the same purposes as SSA programs, if the information concerns eligibility. . . ." The Social Security Administration concluded that disclosure of SSI data to the New York DSS for inclusion in the "categorically eligible" list for the Lifeline match was a permissible routine use.[545]

A utility may find it economical to subcontract with a community action agency or other LIHEAP grantee agency to perform outreach and intake for its affordability program, if this is permitted by state law and the contract establishing the program. These agencies have close ties to the target community, and the cost of performing these tasks would be minimal, as it would be an add-on to similar tasks already being performed. The closure of local utility offices also increases the need for community action agencies or other LIHEAP grantee agencies to perform outreach and enrollment for utility low-income programs. In Ohio, the closure of local utility offices has shifted enrollment duties to the community action agencies and non-profits, with utility call centers directing customers to these local agencies.[546] While these agencies are compensated for handling the enrollment of electric PIPP customers, they are not compensated for enrolling natural gas customers due to limited non-profit resources.[547] A coalition of low income consumer advocates has petitioned the Public Utility Commission of Ohio to rectify the shifting of PIPP enrollment costs from the natural-gas companies to the non-profits and to provide better low-income utility consumer protections.[548]

If computer tape matching is used, there are two main approaches to the task of identifying and signing up qualified customers. One is to use the tape matches to generate an informative letter inviting an application for transfer from the regular utility rate to the affordability rate. The other, and more successful method, is one now used by a telephone company in New York State. The independent entity, contracted for the purpose by the telephone company, sends a letter to each matching name that advises the customer that the customer is being placed on the affordability rate and gives the customer thirty days to notify the utility that he or she does NOT wish to be placed on the rate. With this method, the telephone company hopes to get over 80% penetration of their Lifeline basic telephone discount. This negative check-off saves an intermediate step which has turned out to be a barrier to full penetration of affordability efforts. The cost of in-person outreach, then, is limited to reaching those low-income wage earners and others not receiving the means-tested benefits, who cannot be matched by computer tape but qualify for the rate nonetheless.

The Massachusetts Department of Telecommunications and Energy (DTE) recently issued an order that sets up an automatic enrollment program for the low-income discounted gas and electric program and is continuing its investigation into whether to extend the automatic enrollment program to the low-income Lifeline program.[549] Utility companies in Massachusetts are required to provide discount rates to low-income customers,[550] and the utilities are required to conduct substantial outreach that includes automatic enrollment.[551] The department balanced the privacy interests of the customer with the goal of streamlining the application process to increase participation rates in the discount program in its automatic enrollment decision. The Massachusetts Office of Fuel Assistance's enrollment form includes language allowing the customer to voluntary consent to the release of the customer's eligibility information to another utility offering a discount rate. This express consent by the customer to share eligibility information for the purpose of enrollment in a utility discount program avoids customer privacy concerns. The DTE decided to adopt the model and entered into a memorandum of understanding with the Executive Office of Health and Human

541 45 C.F.R. § 205.50(a)(4)(ii).

542 20 C.F.R. § 401.145.

543 *Id.* § 401.150

544 5 U.S.C. § 552a.

545 Letter from Gregory Machler, Director, RSI/SSI Programs Branch, to Jere Fletcher, Public Util. Law Project (Mar. 2, 1994).

546 Comments of AARP, Appalachian People's Action Coalition, Children's Defense Fund—Ohio, Federation for Community Planning, Ohio Association of Community Action Agencies, Ohio Partners for Affordable Energy, the Edgemont Neighborhood Coalition, the Empowerment Center of Greater Cleveland, and the Ohio Association of Second Harvest Food Banks, Before the Public Utilities Commission of Ohio, *In re* Commission's Review of chs. 4901:17 (Establishment of Credit for Residential Utility Service) and 4901:1-18 (Disconnection of Natural Gas or Electric Service to Residential Customers) of the Ohio Administrative Code, No. 03-888-AU-ORD (June 12, 2003).

547 *Id.*

548 *Id.*

549 Investigation by the D.T.E. to Increase the Penetration Rates for Discounted Electric, Gas, and Telephone Service, D.T.E. 01-106-A (Mass. Dep't of Telecomms. & Energy Aug. 2003), *available at* www.state.ma.us/dpu/navigate.htm. *See* appendix F.1.3.4 from the 2008 edition of Access to Utilities, available on the companion website to this treatise.

550 Mass. Gen. Laws ch. 164, § 1F(4)(i); 220 Mass. Code. Regs. § 14.03(2A).

551 Mass. Gen. Laws ch. 164, § 1F(4)(i).

Services (EOHHS) and the Department of Transitional Assistance to incorporate similar voluntary consent language into their applications.[552]

The DTE, in an order dated December 6, 2004, directed the utilities to provide to the EOHHS each residential customer's name, address, and unique identifying number within thirty days of the order so that automatic enrollment could begin. The order does not require the utility to provide the customer's Social Security number to create a computer match to identify customers eligible for a utility discount.[553] Utilities are also to provide a bill insert that provides residential customers an opportunity to opt out of the computer match.[554] The DTE directed the utilities to assume that the computer-matched customers (that is, those eligible for a utility discount because they are currently enrolled in a qualifying benefit program) have agreed to be enrolled in the discount program because they will have received information on their rights and obligations, including their right to withdraw from the discount rate.[555]

Appendix F, *infra*, contains materials on utility discount rate outreach and enrollment from Massachusetts, Texas, and California.

7.3.4 Eligibility Components of Affordability Programs

7.3.4.1 Overview

The usefulness of a low-income rate affordability program depends on the ability of the participating utility company to enroll low-income customers into the program. Enrolling customers involves identifying those customers that are low-income, determining which of those low-income customers meet the non-income eligibility criteria for the program, and then obtaining the documentation necessary to allow the utility to provide the low-income assistance. In this sense, there are three populations to consider: (1) the population of customers who are eligible for the program (the largest population); (2) of the eligible population, the population of customers who apply for the program; and (3) of the applicant population, the population of customers who have been enrolled in the program. Each population gets progressively smaller, the applicant population being a subset of the eligible population, and the enrolled population being a subset of the applicant population.

In designing a low-income affordability program, care must be taken to distinguish between those customers who are "eligible" for the program and those customers whom a utility (or state) "targets" for enrollment. While, for example, the federal Low-Income Home Energy Assistance Program (LIHEAP) sets eligibility for any household at income not to exceed the greater of 150% of the federal poverty level or less than 60% of state median income--and different states may establish narrower ranges of eligibility within that federal band—the LIHEAP program targets "vulnerable" households (including households with the aged, the disabled, and young children). Similarly, a utility rate affordability program may set eligibility based on income and poverty level but target payment-troubled customers. In such instances, nonpayment-troubled low-income customers are still eligible to enroll, but they will not be the target of special enrollment efforts. The distinction between setting eligibility criteria and setting targeting criteria is an important one.

The discussion below considers eligibility criteria. The definition of "low-income" customer is addressed first, followed by any non-income criteria that should be used to define eligibility.

7.3.4.2 Federal Poverty Level

The generally accepted measure of "being poor" in the United States today utilizes the federal poverty level [FPL] published each year by the U.S. Department of Health and Human Services (HHS). The FPL looks at income in relation to household size: for example, it recognizes that a three-person household with an annual income of $6000 is, in fact, "poorer" than a two-person household with an annual income of $6000. The federal government establishes a uniform FPL for the forty-eight contiguous states. A household's level of poverty is the ratio of that household's income to the FPL. For example, the FPL for 2011 for a two-person household was $14,710. A two-person household with an income of $7355 would thus be living at 50% of poverty.[556]

The FPL as a measure has its share of critics—at least with regard to the methodology used, the measure's relevance, and doubts as its accuracy[557]—but it remains the

552 Investigation by the D.T.E. to Increase the Penetration Rates for Discounted Electric, Gas, and Telephone Service, D.T.E. No. 01-106-A (Mass. Dep't of Telecomms. & Energy Aug. 2003), *available at* www.state.ma.us/dpu/navigate.htm. *See* appendix F.1.3.4 from the 2008 edition of Access to Utilities, available on the companion website to this treatise.

553 Investigation by the D.T.E. to Increase the Penetration Rates for Discounted Electric, Gas, and Telephone Service, D.T.E. No. 01-106-A (Mass. Dep't of Telecomms. & Energy Aug. 2003), *available at* www.state.ma.us/dpu/navigate.htm.

554 *Id.*

555 *Id.*

556 2011 HHS Poverty Guidelines, 76 Fed. Reg., 3637, 3638 (Jan. 20, 2011).

557 The Census Bureau maintains a special research collection on the adequacy of the federal poverty level as a measure of "being poor," that can be accessed at www.census.gov/hhes/www/povmeas/povmeas.html. In addition, the U.S. Department of Health and Human Services maintains a special research collection on the federal poverty level, including links to university poverty research institutes financially supported by HHS that can be accessed at http://aspe.hhs.gov/POVERTY.

basic tool used to define poverty. Essentially, the federal poverty level is a measure of how much income a family must have to meet basic needs.[558] The initial level was set in 1955 and, since 1969, has been increased using the Consumer Price Index each year. The table below contains the 2011 federal poverty level guidelines for households of various sizes.[559]

100% of 2011 HHS Poverty Guidelines[560] for All States and for the District of Columbia[561]

Size of family unit	100% of Poverty
1	$10,890
2	14,710
3	18,530
4	22,350
5	26,170
6	29,990
7	33,810
8	37,630

For family units with more than eight members, add $4390 for each additional family member. For Alaska, add $3820 per family member. For Hawaii, add $4780 per family member for Hawaii.

In 2007, when 150% instead of the 100% of FPL is used as a yardstick, the number of people considered to be eligible and "in need" of services rose significantly—from 32 million to 57 million (or 20% of the total U.S. population, as of 2000). In 2011, 46.2 million were below the poverty level.[562] The numbers will increase for those at 150% of poverty. It is widely recognized by decision makers that eligibility for public assistance programs should encompass more than just those considered "poor" by FPL standards and should extend to a larger portion of the population.

7.3.4.3 Median Income

The use of median income is considered by many to be a viable alternative to the federal poverty level (FPL) as a tool for measuring poverty. For example, the federal LIHEAP statute sets the maximum allowable income eligibility at 60% of the state's median income.[563] The federal LIHEAP office annually publishes the range of incomes that is represented using this 60%-of-median-income standard.[564]

For several reasons, the median income is considered by many to be superior to the federal poverty level in determining the scope of "being poor." First, a state's median income better reflects local conditions (economic or otherwise).[565] Not only are median income figures available on a statewide basis but also for individual counties, individual metropolitan areas, and rural/non-metropolitan areas within the state.[566]

Second, state median income estimates published by the U.S. Department of Housing and Urban Development (HUD) are not fixed but may increase or decrease in any given year depending on economic conditions localized to a specific state.[567] This is in contrast to the FPL, which automatically increases each year based on the Consumer Price Index (CPI).

Finally, area median incomes tend to reflect localized cost-of-living indexes. for example, if area A has higher prices for goods and services relative to area B, it is likely that the median income in area A is higher as well. This is true not only inter-regionally (for example, the New England region versus the mountain west region) but also within individual states.[568]

558 *See generally* Measuring Poverty: A New Approach (C. Citro & R. Michaels eds., National Acad. Press, 1995).

Published by the National Academy of Sciences, this study is considered by many to be seminal in its study of the strengths and weaknesses of the poverty level as a measure of "being poor."

559 Links to the Federal Register publication of each year's federal poverty level for the years 1982 to the present can be obtained through the website of the U.S. Department of Health and Human Services at http://aspe.hhs.gov/POVERTY/figures-fed-reg.shtml.

560 76 Fed. Reg. 3637 (Jan. 20, 2011).

561 76 Fed. Reg. 3637, 3638 (Jan. 20, 2011).

562 Annalyn Censky, Poverty Rate Rises in America, http://money.cnn.com/2011/09/13/news/economy/poverty_rate_income/index.htm (Sept. 13, 2011).

563 42 U.S.C. § 8624(b)(2)(B)(ii).

564 *See, e.g.*, U.S. Admin. for Children & Families, State Median Income Estimates for Optional Use in Federal Fiscal Year 2008 LIHEAP Programs and Mandatory Use in Federal Fiscal Year 2009 LIHEAP Programs, LIHEAP Info. Memo. Transmittal No. LIHEAP-IM-2008-5 (Mar. 20, 2008).

565 Separate poverty level figures are published for Hawaii and Alaska.

566 The U.S. Department of Housing and Urban Development uses increments of median income to define households that are poor, very poor, or earn a moderate income. HUD annually publishes area median incomes, which can be found at www.huduser.org/datasets/il.html.

The Census Bureau publishes two-year and three-year rolling averages for state median income.

567 In its FAQs section regarding how it calculates median income, HUD states that "[s]ome area median family incomes changed because incomes are falling in the area. The fiscal year 2008 MFI estimation relies on 2006 American Community Survey (ACS) data as well as 2006 Bureau of Labor Statistics (BLS) wage data. The manner in which the ACS data is used depends on the type of data available, which differs by place size." *See* www.huduser.org/datasets/il/il08/faq_08.html#q2.

For additional details concerning the use of the ACS in HUD's calculations of median family income, see HUD's fiscal year 2008 Income Limits Briefing Materials, attachment 2, at 15–18, which can be found at www.huduser.org/datasets/il/il08/IncomeLimitsBriefingMaterial.pdf.

568 *See, e.g.*, C.A. Christofides et al., Center for Rural Pa., Examining the Rural-Urban Income Gap (Nov. 2006); James A. Kurre, Center for Rural Pa., Differences in the Cost of Living Across Pennsylvania's 67 Counties (July 2000).

7.3.4.4 The Self-Sufficiency Standard

The self-sufficiency standard represents a third definition of "poverty" in the United States. The self-sufficiency standard was developed by an economic "think tank" based in Washington, D.C., called the Women and Poverty Project at Wider Opportunities for Women (WOW). WOW describes its self-sufficiency standard as follows:

> The Self-Sufficiency Standard calculates how much money working adults need to meet their basic needs without subsidies of any kind. Unlike the federal poverty standard, the Self-Sufficiency Standard accounts for the costs of living and working as they vary by family size and composition and by geographic location. *While both the Self-Sufficiency Standard and the official federal poverty measure assess income adequacy, the Standard differs from the official poverty measure in several important ways.*
>
> The Standard defines the amount of income necessary to meet basic needs (including paying taxes) in the regular "marketplace" without public subsidies—such as public housing, food stamps, Medicaid or child care—or private/informal subsidies—such as free babysitting by a relative or friend, food provided by churches or local food banks, or shared housing. The Standard, therefore, estimates the level of income necessary for a given family type—whether working now or making the transition to work—to be independent of welfare and/or other public and private subsidies.[569]

Other organizations also subscribe to the self-sufficiency standard. The Economic Policy Institute offers a "basic family budget" online calculator,[570] while the National Center for Children in Poverty (NCCP)offers both an online "basic needs calculator"[571] and a "family resource simulator."[572] The NCCP and WOW data is not available for all states.

7.3.4.5 Non-Income Eligibility Criteria

The next issue concerns non-income eligibility criteria and whether to impose such criteria in determining eligibility. For programs utilizing non-income eligibility criteria, "being poor" (however defined) is a requirement, although it is not sufficient in itself to make a household eligible for a rate affordability program. An established low-income household must meet certain additional conditions to become eligible.

The most common non-income-eligibility criterion for low-income rate affordability programs is a household's "home energy burden," usually expressed as a percentage of the household's income. That is, not only must a household's income be below a certain level, but the energy burden must exceed a certain percentage of that income. A plan that imposes this requirement is called a Percentage of Income Program (PIPP), and New Jersey, Pennsylvania, Ohio, and Maine have PIPPs, described in more detail in § 7.2.3, *supra*.

The prescribed percentage-of-income burden in PIPPs is used not only to target households with the *highest* home energy burdens for program benefits, but also to eliminate as ineligible households with burdens below the prescribed level. Prescribed home energy burdens differ between states and also differ depending on whether a household uses natural gas or electricity for heating and whether the household is a heating or an electric baseload (non-heating) customer.

Differences exist even within PIPPs that use home energy burdens as an eligibility criterion. Some states (for example, New Jersey) prescribe a uniform affordable burden (for example, 6%, or 3% for natural gas and 3% for electricity). Other states (for example, Pennsylvania) vary the affordable burden based on the household's level of poverty. Households with incomes at the lower levels of poverty not only receive a smaller bill but also use a lower percentage of their income to pay that bill. This "tiered" system, in which affordable home energy burdens differ based on a household's income level, is the exception rather than the rule in rate affordability programs.

Among PIPPs that impose non-income criteria, another common eligibility criterion is whether a low-income customer is considered "payment-troubled." The definition of "payment-troubled" varies. In Pennsylvania, the state PUC defines "payment-troubled" broadly to include customers who have failed to maintain one or more payment plans or who have received termination notices. In Colorado, the Pilot Energy Assistance Program (PEAP) proposed by Public Service Company of Colorado in 2008 defines "payment-troubled" customers as those who have been disconnected from service or who have accumulated a minimum level of arrears.

Some concerns have been expressed, specifically whether or not the imposition of a payment-troubled-eligibility criterion would encourage customers to "develop" troubles with bill payments so as to qualify for the affordability program. However, program evaluations to date have not found this to be evident.

The Center for Rural Pennsylvania is a legislative agency of the Pennsylvania General Assembly.

569 WOW's website can be accessed at www.wowonline.org/ourprograms/fess/sss.asp. *See generally* Wider Opportunities for Women, Bringing the Concept and Measure of Self-sufficiency to Life: A Guide to On-Line Self-Sufficiency Tools, Wider Opportunities for Women (Jan. 2008).

570 The calculator can be accessed at www.epi.org by clicking on the "Resources" tab and scrolling down to "Family Budget Calculator."

571 The calculator can be accessed at http://nccp.org/tools/frs/budget.php.

572 The simulator can be accessed at www.nccp.org/tools/frs.

A non-income-eligibility criterion that has largely been abandoned is a customer's demonstration of a negative ability to pay. This negative ability to pay is measured by comparing the household income and energy burden with what other expenses such a household of that size and composition should have. Such a methodology was found not only to be too administratively complex to implement but also to be virtually impossible to apply with any uniformity or fairness.

The abandonment of the negative-ability-to-pay criterion reflects the recognition—also discussed above with respect to the self-sufficiency standard—that households with incomes below a certain percentage of the federal poverty level or area median income are almost certain to have insufficient income to meet basic needs. Requiring documentation of family expenses, under these circumstances, creates a barrier to program participation without adding value to the eligibility-determination process.

7.3.4.6 Categorical Eligibility

One commonly used alternative to basing eligibility for low-income rate affordability assistance on a direct measurement of income is to use what is known as "categorical eligibility." Sometimes known as "express lane eligibility," this eligibility approach predicates participation in the program—in this case, a utility affordability program—on the household's participation in another program. For example, a utility using categorical eligibility might state that any recipient of the SSI program for poor, elderly, and disabled people would be automatically eligible for its rate affordability program. Using categorical eligibility assumes that there is a high correlation between the income-eligible households the utility seeks to enroll in its affordability program and the households that are already enrolled in the independent programs.

Probably the most administratively simple method of establishing eligibility for a utility rate assistance program—the categorical eligibility approach—pairs those households receiving other public assistance benefits with the eligibility requirements for the low-income affordability program.

Several benefits arise from the use of categorical eligibility to establish eligibility for a rate affordability program. First, using categorical eligibility avoids requiring the utility to engage in the time and expense of certifying income for households. Households participating in another existing public benefits programs have already had their income certified by a social services agency.

Second, using categorical eligibility will increase participation levels. The mere act of requiring a "sign-up process" has been shown to limit program participation, irrespective of the type of program offered (and by whom). To the extent that such processes can be minimized, therefore, participation rates will be maximized.

Finally, requiring low-income households to apply to their local utility for assistance, and to disclose their household income to an institution that has historically been viewed by the low-income population as adversarial, will make the program inherently self-limiting.

Many utilities have recognized the benefits of using categorical eligibility as a method of eligibility determination and have used this approach for many years. For example, eligibility for most low-income energy utility rates in the states of Alabama, Michigan, Mississippi, New York, North Carolina, Rhode Island, and Wisconsin consider eligibility for receiving TANF, SSI, Social Security, or Food Stamps a good indicator of need for energy assistance and use these programs as a guideline for determining customer eligibility.[573] Moreover, eligibility for federal Lifeline telephone affordability assistance is largely based on categorical eligibility considerations.

In addition, other states have utility-funded low-income energy rate assistance programs which use LIHEAP eligibility as a standard. For example, in California, Indiana, Montana, Massachusetts, New Hampshire, and Pennsylvania, customers who receive LIHEAP are automatically enrolled in some or most of these states' utility low-income discount programs. In New Jersey, households receiving food stamps automatically receive LIHEAP payments if they meet program eligibility requirements; LIHEAP recipients, in turn, are automatically enrolled in the state's rate affordability program. In New York, automatic benefits are paid to public assistance, SSI, and food stamp recipients and certain means-tested veterans programs.

In sum, the advantages to categorical eligibility include:

- Relatively low administrative costs in determining initial and ongoing eligibility because another agency is already doing that work.
- Some assurance that a significant proportion of the low-income population who will benefit from the affordability program will participate.

The danger is that using categorical eligibility alone will fail to yield the households who would most benefit from the program. This is because not every household who is eligible for an assistance program participates in it. Using categorical eligibility based on two or more assistance programs may be a way of at least partially addressing this concern.

7.3.4.7 Resources on Outreach and Eligibility

Appendix F, *infra*, has legislation advocacy briefs on outreach and enrollment activities in Massachusetts, Texas, and California. Appendix B, *infra*, has materials concerning

573 *See, e.g.*, N.Y. Comp. Codes R. & Regs. tit. 18, § 393.4(c)(1); appendix E of the 2008 edition of Access, *available on the companion website to this treatise*.

outreach and enrollment activities for the federal Lifeline telephone assistance program.

7.4 Intervenor Funding in Public Utility Regulatory Cases to Encourage Affordability Programs

7.4.1 Introduction

Low-income customers have a big stake in the decisions of public utility regulatory agencies. This section describes resources that may be available to enable low-income consumers and their advocates to participate in the regulatory proceedings that dictate utility rates and practices. NCLC has also developed an intervenors' manual for low-income consumer advocates. The treatise is available on the companion website to this treatise and is also available on the NCLC website on the Energy and Utility Initiatives web page.

By engaging in litigation before public utilities regulatory commissions, advocates have been successful in protecting their clients from the consequences of high utility bills. Vigorous representation of low-income clients in utility regulatory proceedings has produced significant benefits in terms of:

- Discount payment programs;[574]
- Percentage of income payment programs;[575]
- Customer service regulations;
- Targeted conservation funding for low-income customers;[576]
- Utility funding of a Universal Service Access program; and
- Low-income telecommunications training centers.[577]

Legal representation in utility cases is more important today than ever. In the three major industries—electricity, gas, and telephone—radical changes have taken place that have far-reaching consequences for low-income Americans.[578] The industries are evolving from regulated monopolies to more competitive models. However, downward pressure on rates from competition remains elusive for the residential consumer, especially in states that have restructured their electric industry.[579] Recently, the former long-distance giants announced they are pulling out of the residential long-distance market.[580] In the wake of this news, a coalition of telephone carriers has proposed a plan to the Federal Communications Commission that would substantially increase the charge (passed through to the customer) for use of the network infrastructure involved in completing a call.[581] Low-income customers and their representatives need to be at the table, not only to prevent adverse consequences but to have a hand in shaping the new industry models that will dominate these utility services for decades to come.

However, the lack of funds to participate in the regulated utility area prevents many low-income advocacy representatives from offering the full range of representation to their clients in public utility matters. The level of specialized expertise required of counsel and the cost of securing the necessary expert witnesses stand as barriers to many institutions desiring to provide legal assistance to their clients in public utility cases.

In some situations, however, there are specific funds available to support representation of consumers in regulatory proceedings. A number of states allow for the reimbursement of funds expended by representatives who successfully intervene in certain types of proceedings. In the

574 Order, Western Mass. Elec. Co., No. D.P.U. 86-270A (Mass. Dep't Pub. Util. 1987) (approving expansion of elderly and disabled discount to low-income customers generally, relying on presentation by National Consumer Law Center).

575 Opinion and Order on Rehearing, Pennsylvania Pub. Util. Comm'n v. Columbia Gas of Pa., No. R-891468 (Pa. Pub. Util. Comm'n July 6, 1992) (approving stipulation providing for Customer Assistance Plan); Order, Application of Texas Utilities Electric Company for Authority to Change Rates, No. 11735 (Tex. Pub. Util. Comm'n Dec. 1993) (approving maintenance of effort percentage of bill pilot proposed by Texas Legal Services Center, with testimony by National Consumer Law Center).

576 Order, Application of Texas Utilities Electric Company for Authority to Change Rates, No. 11735 (Tex. Dec. 1993) (approving maintenance of effort percentage of bill pilot proposed by Texas Legal Services Center, with testimony by National Consumer Law Center).

577 Order Approving Stipulation, *In re* Application of the Ohio Bell Tel. Co. for Approval of an Alternative Form of Regulation et al., Nos. 93-487-TP-ALT, 93-576-TP-CSS (Pub. Util. Comm'n of Ohio, 1994).

578 As discussed in Chapter 1, *supra*, many states have deregulated various aspects of utility service. To the extent that utility regulation is lifted, ordinary consumer law remedies become increasingly important tools for advocates. Attorney fees may be available to support advocacy under many consumer protection statutes. *See* National Consumer Law Center, Truth in Lending § 11.9 (7th ed. 2010); National Consumer Law Center, Fair Credit Reporting Act § 11.13 (7th ed. 2010); National Consumer Law Center, Unfair Deceptive Acts and Practices § 13.8 (7th ed. 2008 and Supp.); National Consumer Law Center, Credit Discrimination § 11.7.6 (5th ed. 2009 and Supp.); National Consumer Law Center, Fair Debt Collection § 6.8 (7th ed. 2011); National Consumer Law Center, Consumer Class Actions, ch. 18 (7th ed. 2010 and Supp.); National Consumer Law Center, Consumer Law Pleadings (Index Guide with Companion Website).

579 *See, e.g.*, Rebecca Smith, *States Face Fights As Caps Expire on Electric Rates*, Wall St. J., Aug.17, 2004 (residential consumers shouldering more of the fixed costs as residential rate caps expire). *See also* David Cay Johnston, *Competitive Era Fails to Shrink Electric Bills*, N.Y. Times, Oct. 15, 2006.

580 Christopher Stern, *So Long to Long Distance? Calling Packages, Internet Phoning Swiftly Ending a High Cost Category*, Wash. Post, Aug. 5, 2004, at E1.

581 Christopher Stern, *Consumers Would Pay in Phone Proposal*, Wash. Post, Aug. 14, 2004.

absence of state intervenor funding provisions, customers of electric utilities may, in limited instances, be able to use the provisions of the Public Utility Regulatory Policies Act (PURPA) to fund their interventions. This section provides an overview of the law that governs the availability of such funding and the availability of court- or commission-awarded attorney fees to prevailing parties.[582]

7.4.2 State Authority for Intervenor Funding

Intervenor funding for at least some types of public utility proceedings has been explicitly approved by statute,[583] regulation,[584] or court or public utilities commission[585] in a number of states.

Statutory authority for at least some intervenor funding awards has been enacted in several states.[586] In most of these states, the statute authorizes compensation in any matter before the public utilities commission.[587] A few state utility commission rules limit intervenor compensation to proceedings related to PURPA standards.[588] Minnesota has a generally applicable statute[589] and a separate statute for telephone cases.[590] Michigan enacted intervenor funding for fuel cost recovery cases[591] at the same time as it introduced the reconciling fuel cost adjustment charge[592] for the gas and electric utilities.[593]

Courts have found authority to award intervenor funding in the general statutory authority of the public utilities commission. The Utah Supreme Court has exercised its equitable powers to award attorney fees in a constitutional challenge to a commission ruling, under the common fund and private attorney general exceptions to the American rule against fee-shifting.[594] The Indiana Supreme Court has also held that intervenors who successfully litigate a claim for a multi-million dollar refund to ratepayers from a utility are entitled to reasonable attorney fees on a "common fund" theory.[595] However, some other courts have rejected the common fund theory.[596]

In California and Wisconsin, public utilities commission jurisdiction to award funding was upheld in commission and court rulings, even before the passage of state statutes.[597]

582 Grant and contract funding, at least to defray expert witness fees, may be available to local legal services offices seeking to support an intervention, but this chapter will not address these sources of funds.

583 *See* Cal. Pub. Util. Code § 1801 (West); Colo. Rev. Stat. § 40-6.5-105; Idaho Code Ann. § 61-617A; Me. Rev. Stat. tit. 35-A, § 1310; Mich. Comp. Laws §§ 460.6*l* (utility consumer participation board), 460.6m (utility consumer representation fund); Minn. Stat. §§ 216B.16(10), 237.075(10); N.H. Rev. Stat. Ann. § 365:38-a; Wis. Stat. § 196.31.

584 *See, e.g.*, Alaska Admin. Code tit. 3, § 48.115 (compensation for electric consumer intervenors in a proceeding wherein intervenors' position is "related to any" of the PURPA standards).

585 Northern Ind. Pub. Serv. Co. v. Citizens Action Coalition of Ind., Inc., 548 N.E.2d 153 (Ind. 1989); Rodriguez v. Orange & Rockland Util., Inc., 506 N.Y.S.2d 888 (N.Y. App. Div. 1986); Utah State Coalition of Senior Citizens v. Utah Power & Light Co., 776 P.2d 632 (Utah 1989).

586 Cal. Pub. Util. Code § 1801–1802 (West); Colo. Rev. Stat. § 40-6.5-105; Idaho Code Ann. § 61-617A; Me. Rev. Stat. tit. 35-A, § 1310; Mich. Comp. Laws §§ 460.6*l* (utility consumer participation board); § 460.6m (utility consumer representation fund); Minn. Stat. §§ 216B.16(10), 237.075 (10) (telephone proceedings); N.H. Rev. Stat. Ann. § 365:38-a; Wis. Stat. § 196.31.

587 While the Colorado statute contains language that limits compensation to issues "concerning, directly or indirectly, rates or charges," Colo. Rev. Stat. § 40-6.5-105(1)(b), the Colorado Supreme Court has held that the commission is empowered under the state constitution to compensate intervenors in cases other than rate cases. Mountain State Tel. & Tel. Co. v. Public Util. Comm'n, 576 P.2d 544 (Colo. 1978).

588 *See, e.g.*, Alaska Admin. Code tit. 3, § 48.115; Kan. Admin. Regs. § 82-1-239; Tenn. Comp. R & Regs. 1220-04-04-.51; W. Va. Code R. § 150-3-11. *See* § 7.4.5, *infra* (PURPA interventions).

589 Minn. Stat. § 216B.16(10).

590 *Id.* § 237.075 (10).

591 Mich. Comp. Laws § 460.6m (utility consumer representation fund).

592 A reconciling fuel adjustment clause is a rate provision that enables a utility to raise (or lower) its rates if actual fuel charges for a period turn out to be higher (or lower) than were forecast. A reconciling fuel charge insulates the utility from the volatility of fuel price markets.

593 Mich. Comp. Laws §§ 460.6i–460.6k.

594 Stewart v. Utah Pub. Serv. Comm'n, 885 P.2d 759 (Utah 1994). *See also* Barker v. Utah Pub. Serv. Comm'n, 970 P.2d 702 (Utah 1998) (attorney fee award under common fund or private attorney general theory in a telephone-rate proceeding).

595 Northern Ind. Pub. Serv. Co. v. Citizens Action Coalition, 548 N.E.2d 153 (Ind. 1989). *See also* Citizens Action Coalition of Ind. v. PSI Energy, Inc., 664 N.E.2d 401 (Ind. 1996); Citizens Action Coalition of Ind. v. Northern Ind. Pub. Serv. Co., 812 N.E.2d 814 (Ind. Ct. App. 2004).

596 General Tel. Co. v. Alabama Pub. Serv. Comm'n, 356 So. 2d 612 (Ala. 1978); Brandon v. Arkansas Pub. Serv. Comm'n., 992 S.W.2d 834 (Ark. 1999) (commission did not have jurisdiction to award attorney fees under the common fund doctrine); *In re* Illinois Bell Tel. Co., 98 Pub. Util. Rep. 4th 548 (Ill. Commerce Comm'n 1988); Consumers League of Nev. v. Southwest Gas Corp., 576 P.2d 737 (Nev. 1978); Citizens' Util. Bd. Of Or. v. Public Util. Comm'n of Or., 971 P.2d 459 (Or. 1998) (no fund existed from which to recover attorney fees under common fund theory).

597 Consumers Lobby Against Monopolies v. Public Util. Comm'n, 603 P.2d 41 (Cal. 1979) (common fund theory in quasi-judicial proceedings of commission); *In re* Southern Cal. Edison Co., 45 Pub. Util. Rep. 4th 217 (Cal. Pub. Util. Comm'n 1981) (upon adoption of procedures for processing claims, commission has authority to award funds in quasi-legislative as well as quasi-judicial proceedings); Wisconsin's Envtl. Decade v. Wisconsin Pub. Serv. Comm'n, 49 Pub. Util. Rep. 4th 320 (Wis. Cir. 1982) (implied authority arising from fair implication of statutory jurisdiction, and no contrary statute). *See also* Senior Citizens Coal. of Northeastern Minn. v. Minnesota Pub. Util. Comm'n, 355 N.W.2d 295 n.10 (Minn. 1984) (noting, in dictum, potential

The North Dakota Supreme Court has indicated that the state's Equal Access to Justice Act would ordinarily permit fees on an appeal from a commission decision but that the particular costs of the case in question did not qualify for compensation.[598] However, some courts have held that a public utilities commission is without jurisdiction to award intervenor funding absent an express statutory grant of authority.[599] The Utah Supreme Court has held that courts, but not the commission, may exercise their equitable jurisdiction to award attorney fees.[600]

7.4.3 *Specific Conditions for Intervenor Funding Awards*

In those states that allow for intervenor funding, there are many similar requirements for the intervenors to qualify for compensation. These include:

- A showing of financial hardship;
- Substantial or material contribution to the approval, in whole or in part, of a position advocated by the intervenor;
- No duplication of effort; and
- Inadequate representation by publicly funded consumer advocate or public utilities commission staff.

There is a line of intervention cases from the implementation of the Public Utility Regulatory Policies Act of 1978[601] (PURPA) that also cover many of these conditions for intervenor compensation.[602]

Typically, intervention compensation statutes require that the party requesting the funding make a showing of hardship.[603] However, a showing of hardship does not require proof that the party actually incurred expenses. Parties represented by public interest law firms have been granted intervenor funding.[604] The court in *United Tenants of Albany v. Niagara Mohawk Power*[605] reasoned that the denial of such funding would discourage publicly funded law firms from committing their limited resources to highly technical and labor-intensive utility cases and thus reduce or perhaps eliminate this source of representation for low-income consumers. When that issue must be addressed, the mere fact that a party is represented by a public-interest law firm typically will not disqualify the party from receiving intervenor funding.[606]

---

application in utility cases of common fund, substantial benefit, private attorney general and bad faith exceptions to general rule requiring express statutory authority for award of attorney fées in case decided before enactment of intervenor funding statute, but ruling against claim in this case on grounds that commission had not promulgated valid procedures for such claim under Administrative Procedures Act).

598 Shark v. Northern States Power Co., 477 N.W.2d 251 (N.D. 1991) (assuming applicability of the Mini-Equal Access to Justice Act, § 28-32-21.1, N.D. Cent. Code, but holding that no attorney fees are due to an individual who appeared *pro se*).

599 Idaho Power Co. v. Idaho Pub. Util. Comm'n, 639 P.2d 442 (Idaho 1981); Montana-Dakota Util. Co. v. Montana DPSR, 50 Pub. Util. Rep. 4th 481 (Mont. Dist. Ct. 1982); Consumers League of Nev. v. Southwest Gas Corp., 576 P.2d 737 (Nev. 1978); Smith v. Corporation Comm'n of Okla., 225 P. 708 (Okla. 1924), *cited in In re* Okla. Gas & Elec., 58 Pub. Util. Rep. 4th 414 (Okla. Corp. Comm'n. 1984); Belozer Poultry Farms, Inc. v. Portland Gen. Elec. Co., 134 Pub. Util. Rep. 4th 288 (Or. Pub. Util. Comm'n 1992) (Oregon administrative agencies have no power to award attorney fees).

600 Stewart v. Utah Pub. Serv. Comm'n, 885 P.2d 759 (Utah 1994).

601 Pub. L. No. 95-617, 92 Stat. 3117 (Nov. 9, 1978), *codified at* 16 U.S.C. § 2601.

602 *See also* § 7.4.5, *infra* (further discussion of PURPA interventions).

603 Cal. Pub. Util. Code § 1802(g) (West) ("significant financial hardship" means that, in the case of an organization, the economic interest of the members is small in comparison to the costs of effective participation); Idaho Admin. Code r. 31.01.01.162(.04), r. 31.01.01.165(.01(c)) ("significant financial hardship"); Me. Rev. Stat. tit. 35-A, § 1310(1)(A)(3), (1)(B); Minn. Stat. § 216B.16(10) ("when a lack of compensation would present financial hardship"); N.H. Rev. Stat. Ann. § 365:38-a; Wis. Stat. § 196.31(1)(a), (b) ("not be possible without" a grant or "significant financial hardship"). *See also In re* Pacific Gas & Elec. Co., 138 Pub. Util. Rep. 4th 179 (Cal. Pub. Util. Comm'n 1992) (criteria for finding of eligibility for funding); *In re* Pacific Gas & Elec. Co., 123 Pub. Util. Rep. 4th 456 (Cal. Pub. Util. Comm'n 1991) (same PUC considered the relatively small economic interest of the individual members, residential customers, compared to the cost of the proceeding); United Water Idaho, Inc., 187 Pub. Util. Rep. 4th 312 (Idaho Pub. Util. Comm'n 1998) ("Significant financial hardship" to intervenors if funding not awarded; PUC granted one intervenor's request in full, another intervenor's request in part, because hours billed for were "excessive"); *In re* U.S. West Commc'ns, Inc., 179 Pub. Util. Rep. 4th 597 (Idaho Pub. Util. Comm'n 1997) (intervenor funding for AARP, despite challenge that AARP had sufficient funds, and for citizens' coalition); Idaho Power Co., 161 Pub. Util. Rep. 4th 18 (Idaho Pub. Util. Comm'n 1995) (commission first allowed out-of-pocket expenses to each intervenor, then allocated the rest of the statutory maximum $25,000 to group representing low-income residential consumers, on grounds of financial hardship and reasonableness of group's request, compared to large requests from industry groups); Order, *In re* Application of Idaho Power Co., No. IPC-E-92-10, No. 24415, slip. op. (Idaho Pub. Util. Comm'n July 14, 1992) (as between various claimants for intervenor funding, whose aggregate claims exceed the statutory maximum $20,000, Industrial Customers of Idaho "does not have the same degree of financial need" as the other intervenors, and is awarded less than a proportional share of the available funds).

604 *In re* Idaho Power Co., 143 Pub. Util. Rep. 4th 570 (Idaho Pub. Util. Comm'n 1993) (small business group was eligible for funding even though its members had some financial stake in the outcome, that is, would benefit from the proposed conservation lighting program).

605 487 N.Y.S.2d 467, 473 (N.Y. Special Term 1984), *aff'd*, 497 N.Y.S.2d 1019 (N.Y. App. Div. 1985).

606 *In re* Procedure for Compensation of Elec. Consumers, 28 Pub. Util. Rep. 4th 127 (Alaska Pub. Util. Comm'n 1980); Idaho Fair Share v. Public Util. Comm'n, 751 P.2d 107 (Idaho 1988), *overruled on other grounds*, 120 Idaho 849 (1991) (issue of

In states that permit intervenor funding, there is a requirement that the intervenor materially assist the public utilities commission in its deliberations[607] or substantially contribute to the proceedings.[608] Some state statutes and PURPA also require that a party show that it has substantially contributed to the approval, "in whole or in part, of a position advocated by" the consumer.[609] However, in a successful appeal from an adverse commission ruling, appellants were awarded attorney fees on an equitable "private attorney general" theory, despite the commission's rejection of plaintiffs' position below.[610]

Presentations may not be funded if they duplicate the positions or presentations of other parties in the case.[611] PURPA provides that state commissions may require that "persons with the same or similar interests have a common legal representative in [a] proceeding as a condition to receiving compensation."[612] California denies funding for "unproductive or unnecessary participation that duplicates the participation of similar interests. . . ."[613] Other states require a showing that the intervenor's position is not adequately represented by the publicly-funded utility consumer advocate.[614]

---

judicial deference of agency determination); *In re* Washington Water Power Co., 107 Pub. Util. Rep. 4th 261 (Idaho Pub. Util. Comm'n 1989); 487 N.Y.S.2d 467, 473 (N.Y. Special Term 1984), *aff'd*, 497 N.Y.S.2d 1019 (N.Y. App. Div. 1985).

607 Colo. Rev. Stat. § 40-6.5-105(1)(c), (e) (testimony must be of "significant quality" and "materially" assist the commission in rendering its decision); Idaho Admin. Code r. 31.01.01.165(.01)(a) (intervenor must have "materially contributed to the Commission's decision rendered"); Minn. Stat. § 216B.16(10) (commission must find that intervenor "has materially assisted the commission's deliberation"). *See also* Idaho Fair Share v. Public Util. Comm'n, 751 P.2d 107, 111 (Idaho 1988) (economist's and attorney's work on settlement agreement negotiated in related case was "not relevant" to the commission's decision and thus did not "materially contribute" to the decision), *overruled on other grounds*, 120 Idaho 849 (1991) (issue of judicial deference of agency determination); *In re* U.S. West Commc'ns, Inc., 179 Pub. Util. Rep. 4th 597 (Idaho Pub. Util. Comm'n 1997) (intervenors may "materially contribute" to the decision even if the commission does not adopt the position they advocate); Idaho Power Co., 161 Pub. Util. Rep. 4th 18 (Idaho Pub. Util. Comm'n 1995) (detailed discussion of criteria for allocating statutory maximum $25,000 among various intervenors; intervenor's work must have "materially contributed to" the decision); *In re* Application of Northwestern Bell Tel. Co., 386 N.W.2d 723, 725–27 (Minn. 1986) (to determine if intervenor gave material assistance to commission, commission properly considered whether the party prevailed, whether the issues it raised were unique, and whether the intervenor raised matters of more than common knowledge, but award may not be denied merely because party did not prevail).

608 Cal. Pub. Util. Code § 1802(i) (West) ("substantial contribution means that, in the judgment of the commission, the customer's presentation has substantially assisted the commission in the making of its order or decision because the order or decision has adopted in whole or in part one or more factual contentions, legal contentions, or specific policy or procedural recommendations presented by the customer"); Cal. Pub. Util. Code §§ 1801.3(d), 1803 (West); Cal. Pub. Util. Code § 1801.3(f) (West) (no funding for "participation that is not necessary for a fair determination of the proceeding"); Me. Rev. Stat. tit. 35-A, § 1310(1)(A)(2); N.H. Rev. Stat. Ann. § 365:38-a; Wis. Stat. § 196.31(1)(b). *See also* Idaho Power Co., 161 Pub. Util. Rep. 4th 18 (Idaho Pub. Util. Comm'n 1995) (intervenor "materially contributed to decision"); Washington Water Power, 107 Pub. Util. Rep. 4th 261, 300 (Idaho Pub. Util. Comm'n 1989) (boilerplate presentation not tailored to situation of Idaho justified reduction in witness fee hours).

609 16 U.S.C. § 2632(a)(1) (Congress intends that this language be broadly construed. H.R. Rep. No. 1750, *reprinted in* 1978 U.S.C.C.A.N. 7817, *cited in* Utah State Coalition of Senior Citizens v. Utah Power & Light, 776 P.2d 632, 638 (Utah 1989)); Cal. Pub. Util. Code § 1802.3 (West); Me. Rev. Stat. tit. 35-A, § 1310(1)(A)(2), (1)(B); N.H. Rev. Stat. Ann. § 354:38-a.

610 Stewart v. Utah Pub. Serv. Comm'n, 885 P.2d 759 (Utah 1994).

611 *See, e.g.*, Cal. Pub. Util. Code § 1801.3(f) (West) (no duplication of similar interests adequately represented). *But see* Cal. Pub. Util. Code § 1802.5 (West) (intervenor compensation allowed when efforts supplement, complement, or contribute to other's presentations); Southern Cal. Edison Co. v. Public Util. Comm'n of Cal., 12 Cal. Rptr. 3d 441 (2004) (legislature specifically provided for compensation, even if efforts may duplicate to some extent those of the PUC).

612 16 U.S.C. § 2632(a)(3)(B); Appeal of Campaign for Ratepayers' Rights, 634 A.2d 1345 (N.H. 1993) (eligibility properly denied when intervenor did not indicate what position it would take on issues, thus making it impossible to determine if other consumers would "advocate the same or similar positions").

613 Cal. Pub. Util. Code § 1801.3(f) (West); *In re* Pacific Gas & Elec. Co., 123 Pub. Util. Rep. 4th 456 (Cal. Pub. Util. Comm'n 1991) (participation by division of ratepayer advocates does not automatically eliminate need for residential class representation; intervenor representing residential customers was eligible for funding when commission found that customers would not be "adequately represented" without this intervenor).

614 Idaho Admin. Code §§ 31.01.01.162, 31.01.01.165 (proposed finding and recommendation must materially differ from testimony and exhibits of commission staff); Me. Rev. Stat. tit. 35-A, § 1310(1)(A)(1). *See also In re* Pacific Gas & Elec. Co., 123 Pub. Util. Rep. 4th 456 (Cal. Pub. Util. Comm'n 1991) (participation by division of ratepayer advocates does not eliminate need for residential class representation.); *In re* Integrated Res. Planning, 139 Pub. Util. Rep. 4th 379 (Colo. Pub. Util. Comm'n 1992) (commission rejects a proposal to establish a "public participation fund" to fund participation in the planning process, because this would violate the statute when the Office of Consumer Counsel participated in the process; commission notes, however, that it can allow applications for funding if the intervenors propose to address issues in a manner substantially different from OCC); *In re* United Water Idaho, Inc., 187 Pub. Util. Rep. 4th 312 (Idaho Pub. Util. Comm'n 1998) (intervenor funding allowed when intervenors' positions differed materially from those of staff); Idaho Power Co., 161 Pub. Util. Rep. 4th 18 (Idaho Pub. Util. Comm'n 1995) (intervenors' recommendations "differed materially" from staff position); Farmland Indus. v. State Corp. Comm'n, 943 P.2d 470 (Kan. Ct. App. 1997) (PURPA claim denied in part, because publicly funded Citizens Utility Ratepayer Board was party, over challenge by ratepayer of one of two utilities in non-unanimous settlement that CURB had conflict of interest, because interest of CURB in outcome of case versus utility serving applicant for funding was sufficient, although not as great as interest of CURB in outcome of case versus other utility).

An important practical aspect of various intervenor funding arrangements is the extent to which the intervenors can know, going into a case, whether they will secure funding for the work they plan to do.[615] Without such advance assurance, the party will have to do the work "on spec," that is, investing other resources to carry the work and hoping that, after the case is completed, a suit or funding claim will provide funds to reimburse those individuals and firms that contributed their time and resources.

The Wisconsin Public Service Commission has promulgated rules whereby applications for intervenor funding are processed within fifteen days of submission and payment authorizations are made within thirty days of receipt of the claim, when possible.[616] The Michigan Utility Consumers Intervention Board awards contracts for intervention in power supply cost-recovery cases prospectively, based on proposals submitted in advance to the Board.[617]

In general, states with intervenor funding permit the commission to make a case-by-case decision on whether to award intervenor funding.[618] PURPA does not require a determination of eligibility for funding earlier than the end of the proceeding, and funding can be based on the results of the case.[619] Some states have adopted a process by which an intervenor can get a preliminary determination of eligibility, with the actual award to be determined based on the outcome of the proceeding.[620]

The California PUC allows a prospective intervenor to file a request for finding of eligibility for compensation.[621] The application must include evidence of significant financial hardship, a statement of the nature and extent of applicant's planned participation and an itemized estimate of the compensation sought.[622] Approval of this budget gives the parties some assurance that funds will be forthcoming at the conclusion of the case.

7.4.4 *Types of Costs for Which Compensation Is Allowed*

Under some statutes and commission regulations, funding is explicitly available for advocate or attorney fees,[623] expert witness fees,[624] and other reasonable costs.[625] Courts have similarly upheld awards of attorney fees[626] and expert witness fees.[627] A number of statutes allowing funding do not enumerate the types of intervenor costs that qualify for funding.[628]

---

615 Under the Intervenor Funding Project Act, the Ontario Energy Board is authorized to make an award in advance of the proceedings, so long as it does so before the commencement of hearings. *See In re* Consumers' Gas Co., Ltd, 157 Pub. Util. Rep. 4th 291 (Ont. Energy Bd. Nov. 15, 1994).

616 Wis. Admin. Code Pub. Serv. Comm'n §§ 3.05, 3.07.

617 Mich. Comp. Laws § 460.6m.

618 Cal. Pub. Util. Code § 1801.3 (West); Colo. Rev. Stat. § 40-6.5-105; Idaho Admin. Code r. 31.01.01.032; Me. Rev. Stat. tit. 35-A, § 1310; Minn. Stat. § 216B.16(10); N.H. Rev. Stat. Ann. § 365:38-a; Wis. Stat. § 196.31.

619 16 U.S.C. § 2632.

620 Cal. Pub. Util. Code § 1804 (West); Me. Rev. Stat. tit. 35-A, § 1310(2) (determination of intervenor compensation eligibility shall be made at the earliest practicable time in the proceeding). *See also In re* Pacific Gas & Elec. Co., 138 Pub. Util. Rep. 4th 179 (Cal. Pub. Util. Comm'n 1992) (citizens group TURN found eligible (minimal discussion), in natural gas cost allocation proceeding); *In re* Pacific Gas & Elec. Co., 123 Pub. Util. Rep. 4th 456 (Cal. Pub. Util. Comm'n 1991). *But cf.* Stewart v. Utah Pub. Serv. Comm'n, 885 P.2d 759 (Utah 1994) (no need to present attorney fees request to commission which lacked power to approve award).

621 Cal. Pub. Util. Code § 1804 (West).

622 Cal. Pub. Util. Code § 1804(a), (b) (West). *See, e.g., In re* Pacific Gas & Elec. Co., 138 Pub. Util. Rep. 4th 179 (Cal. Pub. Util. Comm'n 1992); *In re* Pacific Gas & Elec. Co., 123 Pub. Util. Rep. 4th 456 (Cal. Pub. Util. Comm'n 1991). *See also In re* Pacific Gas & Elec. Co., 183 Pub. Util. Rep. 4th 181 (Cal. Pub. Util. Comm'n 1997) (intervenor funding request remanded to assigned commissioners to determine whether untimely funding request was excusable; issue was whether the commission's first interim decision so changed the issues that the intervenor could not reasonably be expected to be able to identify issues within thirty days of the pre-hearing conference).

623 Public Utility Regulatory Policies Act, 16 U.S.C. § 2632(a)(1); Cal. Pub. Util. Code §§ 1801, 1802, 1806 (West) (advocate's fees); Idaho Admin. Code r. 31.01.01.162(.01) (legal fees); Me. Rev. Stat. tit. 35-A, § 1310(1)(A), (1)(B); Wis. Admin. Code Pub. Serv. Comm'n § 3.04(2). *But see* Order on Request for Intervenor Compensation, Restructuring Settlement Agreement, DE 99-099, Order No. 24,351 (N.H. Pub. Utils. Comm'n July 16, 2004) (citing commission decision in *In re* Investigation of the Congestion on the Telephone Network Caused by Internet Traffic, which concluded that commission lacked authority to include legal expenses in costs awarded to an intervenor).

624 Public Utility Regulatory Policies Act, 16 U.S.C. § 2632(a)(1); Cal. Pub. Util. Code §§ 1801, 1802, 1806 (West); Idaho Admin. Code r. 31.01.01.162(.01); Me. Rev. Stat. tit. 35-A, §§ 1310(1)(A), (1)(B); Wis. Admin. Code Pub. Serv. Comm'n § 3.04(2). *See also* Order on Request for Intervenor Compensation, *In re* Restructuring Settlement Agreement, DE 99-099, Order No. 24,351 (N.H. Pub. Utils. Comm'n July 16, 2004) (expert consultant fees were costs that were covered by the intervenor compensation statute).

625 Public Utility Regulatory Policies Act, 16 U.S.C. § 2632(a)(1); Cal. Pub. Util. Code §§ 1801, 1802, 1806 (West) (other reasonable costs); Idaho Admin. Code r. 31.01.01.162(.01) (reproduction fees); Me. Rev. Stat. tit. 35-A, § 1310(1)(A), (1)(B) (other reasonable costs); Wis. Admin. Code Pub. Serv. Comm'n § 3.04(2), (3) (clerical services, studies, displays, exhibits, travel and subsistence).

626 *E.g.*, Northern Ind. Pub. Serv. Co. v. Citizens Action Coalition of Ind., Inc., 548 N.E.2d 153, 162 (Ind. 1989).

627 *E.g.*, Shortino v. Illinois Bell Tel. Co., 665 N.E.2d 414 (Ill. App. Ct. 1996); Citizens Action Coalition of Ill. v. PSI Energy, 664 N.E.2d 401 (Ind. App. Ct. 1996); *In re* PSI Energy, Inc., 1996 WL 482655 (Ind. Util. Regulatory Comm'n July 12, 1996) (No. 39498, 39786); Wisconsin's Envtl. Decade v. Wisconsin Pub. Serv. Comm'n., 49 Pub. Util. Rep. 4th, 320, 322 (Wis. Cir. Ct. 1982).

628 *See, e.g.*, Colo. Rev. Stat. § 40-6.5-105; N.H. Rev. Stat. Ann. § 365:38-a.

Courts or commissions have approved funding for expenses incurred before the utility filed its application, when this was preceded by a lengthy period of cooperative effort between the utility and the intervenor groups.[629] Funding has been approved for a non-lawyer who was not a witness but who provided "administrative support" for expert witnesses.[630] Funding has not be allowed for a group's day-to-day expenses[631] but was allowed for out-of-pocket costs.[632]

Attorney fees and other costs may also be available when public utilities commission decisions are appealed to the courts.[633] The American Rule, which generally requires parties to bear their own costs and attorney fees, has several exceptions that may benefit intervenors in public utility cases:

1. Some state statutes define the circumstances under which fee shifting is permitted or required.
2. If a class action creates a "common fund," attorney fees may be available from this fund to prevent a free ride by those class members who benefit from the fund but did not participate in the litigation.[634]
3. When a case vindicates "a strong or societally important public policy," the successful litigant may be awarded attorney fees as a "private attorney general."[635]
4. A losing party that acted "in bad faith, vexatiously, wantonly or for oppressive reasons" may be sanctioned by the imposition of the prevailing party's fees and costs.[636]

Whether awarded by a court or a public utilities commission, attorney fees may be calculated either as a percentage of the recovery or by the lodestar-multiplier method: the number of hours reasonably expended multiplied by reasonable hourly rate, then adjusted for such things as the quality of the legal representation, the novelty or difficulty of the issues, the importance of the results achieved, among other things.[637] In many jurisdictions, the choice between percentage and lodestar calculations is left to the discretion of the trial court or commission.[638] Attorney fee awards are reviewed with a deferential "abuse of discretion" standard.[639] In one case, a fee settlement approved by the public utilities commission in a common fund case included the proviso that approximately one-fifth of the recovery ($3 million) be put into a trust fund to pay for future interventions on behalf of residential ratepayers.[640]

7.4.5 Intervenor Funding Under PURPA

One remote possibility is a mechanism for intervention compensation that has its basis in a 1978 statute. The Public Utility Regulatory Policies Act of 1978[641] (PURPA) provides that utilities must compensate intervenors who "substantially contribute to the approval, in whole or in part, of a position advocated by such consumer[s]," concerning enumerated topics set forth in the statute, when the state has provided no "alternative means" for their representation.[642]

629 *In re* Idaho Power Co., 143 Pub. Util. Rep. 4th 570 (Idaho Pub. Util. Comm'n 1993).

630 *In re* U.S. West Commc'ns, Inc., 179 Pub. Util. Rep. 4th 597 (Idaho Pub. Util. Comm'n 1997).

631 *In re* Idaho Power Co., 143 Pub. Util. Rep. 4th 570 (Idaho Pub. Util. Comm'n 1993).

632 *In re* A Proceeding to Require Energy Util. to Implement Integrated Resource Planning (Haw. Pub. Util. Comm'n 1992); Idaho Power Co., 161 Pub. Util. Rep. 4th 18 (Idaho Pub. Util. Comm'n 1995).

633 Cal. Pub. Util. Code § 1802 (West); N.H. Rev. Stat. Ann. § 365:38-a. *See also* Southern Cal. Edison Co. v. Public Util. Comm'n of Cal., 12 Cal. Rptr. 3d 441 (2004) (intervenor could recover fees and costs of obtaining judicial review of PUC decision).

634 Stewart v. Utah Pub. Serv. Comm'n, 885 P.2d 759, 782–83 (Utah 1994). *See also* Shortino v. Illinois Bell Tel. Co., 665 N.E.2d 414 (Ill. App. Ct. 1996).

635 Stewart v. Utah Pub. Serv. Comm'n, 885 P.2d 759 (Utah 1994).

636 Stewart v. Utah Pub. Serv. Comm'n, 885 P.2d 759, 782 (Utah 1994) (quoting Moore et al., Moore's Federal Practice, § 54.77 (2d ed. 1972)).

637 Shortino v. Illinois Bell Tel. Co., 665 N.E.2d 414 (Ill. App. Ct. 1996); Citizens Action Coalition of Ill. v. PSI Energy, 664 N.E.2d 401 (Ind. App. Ct. 1996).

638 Citizens Action Coalition of Ill. v. PSI Energy, 664 N.E.2d 401 (Ind. App. 1996) (commission did not abuse discretion in rejecting settlement calculated by percentage method, and using lodestar method; remanding to commission because award did not properly compensate intervenors for work in other proceedings arising from same facts). *See also* Shortino v. Illinois Bell Tel. Co., 665 N.E.2d 414 (Ill. App. Ct. 1996) (discussing how to determine reasonableness of hourly rate); Citizens Action Coalition of Ind. et al v. PSI Energy, No. 93A02-9611-EX-721 (Ind. App. Ct. June 5, 1997) (unpublished memorandum opinion) (court clarifies instructions on remand, finds settlement reasonable, orders approval); Petition of PSI Energy, Inc., No. 39498 (Ind. Util. Regulatory Comm'n July 16, 1997) (order on remand; commission approves $14.25 million settlement); *In re* PSI Energy, Inc., Nos. 39498 and 39786 (Ind. Util. Regulatory Comm'n July 12, 1996) (on remand, commission explains how it will calculate both percentage and lodestar figures and compare them before setting fee).

639 Shortino v. Illinois Bell Tel. Co., 665 N.E.2d 414 (Ill. App. Ct. 1996).

640 Petition of PSI Energy, Inc., No. 39498 (Ind. Util. Regulatory Comm'n July 16, 1997) (order on remand).

641 16 U.S.C. § 2601.

642 16 U.S.C. § 2632(a)(1), (b); *In re* A Proceeding to Require Energy Util. to Implement Integrated Resource Planning (Haw. Pub. Util. Comm'n 1992) (commission will allow limited intervenor funding for participation in planning process: nonprofit groups' out-of-pocket expenses, if group can show hardship, good faith effort to obtain other funding, accurate recordkeeping, and "substantial contribution in assisting the commission in arriving at its decision"); Appeal of Campaign for Ratepayers' Rights, 634 A.2d 1345 (N.H. 1993) (intervenor funding is available in proceedings to implement existing PURPA standards and to establish standards; eligibility properly denied when intervenor did not indicate what position it would take on issues, thus making it impossible to determine if other

PURPA was enacted to promote greater efficiency in the use of electricity and to promote certain minimal protections for customers of electric utilities. In 1992, its scope was expanded to include greater competition in the wholesale market for electricity, adoption by states of integrated least-cost planning, and utility investments in conservation and renewables.[643]

While it is possible to argue that the intervention rights in PURPA should be broadly interpreted to include *any* proceeding that involves the consideration of "other concepts which contribute to the achievement of the purposes of PURPA,"[644] courts have been reluctant to allow a broad application of PURPA intervention rights for interventions beyond the initial PURPA standards hearings. The PURPA statute sets a timeline for those standards hearings, and they were to have occurred in the early 1980s and early 1990s.[645]

In *Earle M. Jorgensen Company v. City of Seattle*, 99 Wash.2d 861 (1983), the Supreme Court of Washington in a six-to-three decision limited to the city's ratemaking procedures the PURPA right for electric consumers to intervene and participate in ratemaking proceeding. The dissenting justices focused on the language of 16 U.S.C. § 2631(a), which states:

> In order to initiate and participate in the consideration of one or more standards established by subchapter II of this chapter *or other concepts which contribute to the achievement of the purposes of this chapter*, . . . any electric consumer of an affected electric utility may intervene and participate as a matter of right in *any* ratemaking proceeding or other appropriate regulatory proceeding relating to rates or rate design which is conducted by a State regulatory authority . . . or by a nonregulated electric utility. (emphasis added)

The majority in *Jorgensen*, however, indicated that its restrictive interpretation of the PURPA intervention right was due to concerns about usurpation of state law and the disruptive nature of such a broad application.[646]

In an unpublished decision, a court of appeal in Texas refused to authorize PURPA intervention compensation in a proceeding wherein issues addressed by PURPA standards were raised.[647] The appellate court found that interpreting 16 U.S.C. § 2632(a) to authorize reimbursement for the costs of participating in any proceeding at which the issues addressed by the PURPA standards are considered would be "unduly expansive." The court noted that "[a]lmost any rate proceeding, no matter how limited, involves consideration of one or more of the [PURPA standard issues]. Construing section 2632(a) in the manner suggested by appellants would therefore create a general right of reimbursement for costs incurred in all state ratemaking proceedings."[648] The appellate court limited the right to intervention reimbursement to state proceedings held to consider the adoption or implementation of the PURPA standards. The court noted that "[n]o party requested the hearing be designated a PURPA proceeding or that the PUC consider the appropriateness of implementing PURPA standards at the hearing. . . . At the hearing's conclusion, no request to implement any PURPA standards was made, nor was PURPA referred to in either the PFD or the PUC's final order."[649]

The PURPA standards include, among other topics, use of cost of service to determine rates; declining block rates; time-of-day rates; seasonal rates; interruptible rates; load management techniques; master-metering; automatic adjustment clauses; providing rate information to customers; providing adequate notice of termination and limitations on disconnection when lack of service would be dangerous to health; limits on cost recovery for promotional advertising; lifeline rates; integrated resource planning; investments in conservation and demand management; and assurance of adequate fuel supplies.[650] Thus, PURPA addresses a wide range of current issues involving the setting of rates for electric utilities and the customer service protections afforded to electricity consumers.

Assuming the court applies a broad interpretation of the scope of proceedings eligible for PURPA intervention compensation, intervenors who meet the criteria of the statute may recover the costs of their intervention in either of two ways. If a state[651] has adopted reasonable procedures to compensate intervenors, the intervenors must follow these procedures.[652] In the past, when no such procedures were adopted, intervenors initiated a civil action in state court against the utility.[653]

---

consumers would "advocate the same or similar positions"). *See also In re* Integrated Res. Planning, 139 Pub. Util. Rep. 4th 379 (Colo. Pub. Util. Comm'n 1992).

643 Energy Policy Act of 1992, Pub. L. No. 102-486, 106 Stat. 2776 (Oct. 24, 1992).

644 16 U.S.C. § 2631(a).

645 16 U.S.C. § 2622(b).

646 99 Wash.2d 873 (1083).

647 Texas Ratepayers' Org. to Save Energy Inc. v. Texas Util. Elec. Co., 2000 WL 64157 (Tex. App.—Austin Jan. 27, 2000), *rev. denied*, (Aug. 24, 2000).

Under rule 47.7 of the Texas Rules of Appellate Procedure, unpublished opinions have no precedential value but may be cited with the notation "(not designated for publication)."

648 Texas Ratepayers' Org. to Save Energy Inc. v. Texas Util. Elec. Co., 2000 WL 64157 (Tex. App.—Austin Jan. 27, 2000) (not designated for publication).

649 *Id.*

650 16 U.S.C. §§ 2621(d)(1)–(10), 2624, 2632(a), (b).

651 Or the utility, when it is not regulated by the state agency, as is often the case with rural electric cooperatives. 16 U.S.C. § 2632(a)(2).

652 16 U.S.C. § 2632(a)(2).

653 16 U.S.C. § 2632(a)(2).

In Idaho, Minnesota, and Oklahoma, courts have ruled that, in the absence of the formal adoption of procedures for considering PURPA claims, PURPA intervenors must use the civil litigation method of the statute, 16 U.S.C. § 2632(a)(2), (3), for pursuing funding. Idaho Power Co. v. Idaho Pub. Util. Comm'n,

Most of the litigation under the intervenor funding provisions of PURPA focused on the "alternative means for assuring representation" exception to PURPA's mandate of funding. PURPA provides that compensation of consumer intervenors is not required when the state has "provided an alternative means for assuring representation of electric consumers. . . ."[654]

The conflict generally arose when a state appointed a publicly funded counsel to represent consumer interests in a utility proceeding. The issue raised was whether such publicly funded advocacy satisfies the statutory exception.

One court adopted what amounts to a per se rule that, whenever a publicly funded counsel is involved in the case, there is "an alternative means" sufficient to defeat the claim for funding.[655] Other courts, however, have adopted a case-by-case approach. At least forty-four states plus the District of Columbia have some form of publicly funded utility regulatory advocate for consumers,[656] making this issue a key determiner of the viability of the PURPA funding mechanism.

In *POWER v. Washington Water Power Company*, intervenor POWER argued that a special attorney general appointed to intervene in the case could not adequately represent all classes of consumers, many of whom had interests that were potentially adverse to each other. The court addressed POWER's arguments through a two part analysis: "(1) whether existing statutes provide for adequate representation by a special assistant attorney general of consumer interests; and (2) whether there was adequate representation in this case."[657]

Because the special attorney general was (a) independent of the statute's regulatory authority, (b) empowered to appear and participate in any regulatory proceeding, (c) authorized to retain outside experts, and (d) authorized to hire and retain staff, the court concluded that the office was capable of providing adequate representation of consumers.

The court rejected POWER's argument that conflicts would inevitably arise between various classes of consumers and held that there was no requirement that each class of consumers be represented separately in every case. After examining the facts of the particular case, the court determined that POWER advocated positions that were more or less congruent with those advocated by the special attorney general and was therefore adequately represented in the instant case. Accordingly, the court affirmed the lower court's denial of POWER's request for funding.[658]

By contrast, courts adopting a "case-by-case" approach look to whether there is conflict between the positions of different segments of the public that the publicly funded counsel is mandated to represent.[659] In the first conflicting-interest case, *United Tenants*, the utility argued that the PURPA funding request should be denied because the Consumer's Protection Board (CPB), which was charged with representing the interests of New York consumers in utility proceedings, could adequately represent the United Tenants Association (UTA) in the instant proceedings.

The UTA countered that the CPB was incapable of representing their interests vigorously because of inadequate funding and inherent conflicts of interest between different classes of consumers that the CPB was charged with representing. The court held that a determination had to be made that the particular positions advanced by the UTA were sufficiently similar to those advanced by the CPB to merit the conclusion that UTA was adequately represented by CPB.[660]

The Utah Supreme Court agreed with the New York courts' analysis of how the alternative means provisions of PURPA should be interpreted.[661] In *Utah State Coal. of Sr. Citizens v. Utah Power & Light*, the utility argued that PURPA funding was not available because the state funded a Committee of Consumer Services and the Utah Division of Public Utilities (DPU). The court rejected this argument, which it termed a per se approach to the statutory standard. It would be "impossible," the court reasoned, for the DPU to live up to its obligation to consider the financial health of the utility and fair apportionment of costs among all consumers,[662] while at the same time zealously advocating the

---

639 P.2d 442 (Idaho 1981); Senior Citizens Coal. v. Minnesota Pub. Util. Comm'n, 355 N.W.2d 295 (Minn. 1984); Public Serv. Co. of Okla. v. Oklahoma Corp. Comm'n, 688 P.2d 1274 (Okla. 1983); Smith v. Corporation Comm'n of Okla., 225 P. 708 (Okla. 1924).

These states later passed statutes providing a mechanism for claiming intervenor funding through the regulatory agency.

654 16 U.S.C. § 2632(a)(1). *See also In re* Integrated Res. Planning, 139 Pub. Util. Rep. 4th 379 (Colo. Pub. Util. Comm'n 1992) (commission rejects a proposal to establish a "public participation fund" to fund participation in the planning process because this would violate the statute when the Office of Consumer Counsel participates in the process; commission notes, however, that it can allow applications for funding if the intervenors propose to address issues in a manner substantially different from OCC).

655 POWER v. Washington Water Power Co., 662 P.2d 374 (Wash. 1983) *aff'd and modified on reh'g*, 684 P.2d 716 (Wash. 1984).

656 See the National Association of State Utility Consumer Advocates website at www.nasuca.org.

657 POWER v. Washington Water Power Co., 662 P.2d 374, 376 (Wash. 1983).

658 *Id.*; Farmland Indus. v. State Corp. Comm'n, 943 P.2d 470 (Kan. Ct. App. 1997) (PURPA claim denied in part because publicly funded Citizens Utility Ratepayer Board was party, despite challenge by ratepayer of one of two utilities in non-unanimous settlement in which CURB had conflict of interest).

659 Rodriguez v. Orange & Rockland Util. Inc., 506 N.Y.S.2d 888 (N.Y. App. Div. 1986); United Tenants of Albany, Inc. v. Niagara Mohawk Power Corp., 487 N.Y.S.2d 467 (N.Y. Special Term 1984), *aff'd*, 497 N.Y.S.2d 1019 (N.Y. App. Div. 1985); Utah State Coal. of Senior Citizens v. Utah Power & Light, 776 P.2d 632, 636 (Utah 1989).

660 487 N.Y.S.2d 471 (N.Y. Special Term 1984).

661 Utah State Coalition of Senior Citizens v. Utah Power & Light Co., 776 P.2d 632 (Utah 1989).

662 *See* Utah Code Ann. §§ 54-4a-6, 54-10a-301 (west).

interests of a particular consumer group, such as the elderly and low-income groups represented in these proceedings.[663]

The court also cited a number of reasons why the Committee of Consumer Services failed the alternate means test. The court noted its limited mandate, conflicts between different customer group interests on the committee, and the fact that it was, by its own admission, underfunded.[664]

7.5 The Legality of Utility Affordability Programs

7.5.1 Introduction

In states without statutory language expressly authorizing low-income affordability programs,[665] one of the first questions that utilities ask when contemplating low-income affordability programs is: "Are they legal?" The answer is: "Probably yes, so long as the program is properly designed and properly presented."

Affordability programs in almost every shape and form are in operation in a majority of states across the nation.[666] Commission-regulated gas, electric, and telephone utilities have voluntarily adopted low-income programs, and they have had low-income programs imposed upon them by the state commissions and by legislatures. Municipal utilities of all types are also currently running affordability programs that have not been proclaimed illegal.

On the other hand, a few affordability programs of one type or another have also been struck down as violating a statutory prohibition against unreasonable discrimination in rates. The distinction between those that have been upheld and those that have been struck down is actually quite vague and often has more to do with the issue of how the program is presented, and whether it is challenged as illegal, than with either the specifics of the affordability program or the state in which the challenge was mounted.

A survey of the case law regarding the legality of low-income affordability programs unfortunately yields few lessons. In every state, virtually every type of public utility, whether publicly or privately owned, regulated by a commission or a unit of local government, is governed by the same basic rules prohibiting unjust and unreasonable discrimination in rates and service.[667] The *interpretation* of how this basic legal principle applies to a given affordability program seems to deviate depending upon a variety of factors, including the following:

- Whether the utility is proposing the affordability program itself, or the program is being imposed upon the utility by the regulating body.
- Whether the affordability program is presented as a *cost-based* program that will yield funds necessary for the utility to cover the costs of the program (as opposed to presenting the program as necessary for social policy reasons).
- Whether a group of ratepayers is challenging the program.

The purpose of this section is to explore the issues surrounding the legality of low-income affordability programs. It is interesting and relevant to note that, despite the legal analysis disallowing certain affordability programs found in some states, other affordability programs were permitted in some circumstances.[668]

7.5.2 Utility Rates Cannot Unjustly and Unreasonably Discriminate

One of the basic tenets of utility law is that public utilities are obligated to serve all customers on equal terms—unjust

663 776 P.2d 637 (Utah 1989).

664 *Id.*

665 *See, e.g.*, Cal. Pub. Util. Code § 739.1 (West) (requires commission to establish low-income assistance program for gas and electric customers); Mass. Gen. Laws ch. 164, § 1F(4)(i) (department shall require that electric distribution companies provide discounted rates for low-income customers comparable to low-income discount rate in effect prior to March 1, 1998); 66 Pa. Cons. Stat. §§ 2202, 2203(8), 2802(9)–(10), 2803, 2804(9), (15) (natural gas and electric companies are to maintain, at minimum, protections, policies, and services that assist low-income consumers, and commission is to require that these universal services and energy efficiency programs are adequately funded); Me. Rev. Stat. tit. 35-A, § 3214 (policy of state to ensure adequate provision of financial assistance for low-income electricity customers); Minn. Stat. § 216B.16, subdiv. 14, 15 (directing large electric utilities to target assistance to consumers with lowest incomes and highest energy costs and explicitly stating that commission may consider ability to pay as factor in rate-setting and may establish affordability programs); N.H. Rev. Stat. Ann. § 369-B:1 (directs commission to design low-income programs in matter that targets assistance and has high operating efficiency). *Cf. In re* New Hampshire Natural Gas Utils., 244 P.U.R. 4th 117, 2005 WL 2916368 (N.H. Pub. Util. Comm'n Sept. 1, 2005) (DG 05-076, Order No. 24,508) (commission notes that it has long history of recognizing validity of discounted low-income rates and that, while there is express statutory authority to establish low-income programs as part of restructuring, there is nothing that prohibits commission from establishing such programs as part of their traditional regulatory oversight role).

666 *See* LIHEAP Clearinghouse, 2006 State-by-State Supplements to Energy Assistance and Energy Efficiency, *available at* www.liheap.ncat.org/Supplements/2006/supplement06.htm.

667 *See* Massachusetts Mun. Wholesale Elec. Co. v. City of Springfield, 726 N.E.2d 973 (Mass. App. Ct. 2000); Ohio Edison Co. v. Public Util. Comm'n, 678 N.E.2d 922 (Ohio 1997).

668 *See, e.g., In re* Public Serv. Co. of Colo., 2000 WL 575936 (Colo. Pub. Util. Comm'n Apr. 24, 2000) (No. 99A-337EG, Decision No. C00-393); *In re* PacifiCorp, d.b.a. Utah Power & Light Co. 192 P.U.R. 4th 289, 1999 WL 218118 (Utah Pub. Serv. Comm'n Mar. 4, 1999) (No. 97-035-01); PacifiCorp 1999 Gen. Rate Case Report & Order, No. 99-035-10 (Utah Pub. Serv. Comm'n May 24, 2000).

or undue discrimination among customers is forbidden.[669] As a general rule, a public utility cannot discriminate unjustly in its rates to consumers similarly situated or of the same class for the same service or kind of service.[670] for example, if a utility seeks a rate increase, the burden is on that utility to establish that its proposed schedule of rates is nondiscriminatory; when the increase is spread proportionately across the board among several customer classes, the presumption is that these new rates are reasonable and nondiscriminatory. Conversely, no such presumption arises in favor of an increase that is imposed upon some classes of customers and not upon others.[671] Also, whether a utility's rates or practices are unduly discriminatory is usually a question of fact.[672]

There are several sources for this rule. At common law, the duty of nondiscrimination has been recognized as "a universal principle to protect all who are being served."[673] The reasoning behind the nondiscrimination requirement originally stemmed from the fact that public utilities historically held a monopoly status, and, as C.F. Phillips noted, "[u]nder conditions of near monopoly, discrimination in price and perhaps service may become profitable to a business . . . [and] customers would be helpless in such a situation."[674]

In addition, every state has some statutory enactment applicable to regulated utilities prohibiting discrimination in rates. Statutes governing utility regulation generally prohibit rate discrimination.[675] Similar rules prohibiting discrimination are found in the regulations governing utilities. For example, Florida's administrative rules state that a utility may adopt additional uniform *nondiscriminatory* rules and regulations as it finds necessary.[676]

According to some courts, however, the duty to serve without discrimination does not depend on these statutes or rules:

> We may conclude that in this country, *independently of statutory provisions*, all common carriers will be held to the strictest impartiality in the conduct of their business, and that all privileges or preferences given to one customer, which are not extended to all, are in violation of public duty.[677]

Indeed, some courts have found statutes establishing a duty of nondiscrimination to be merely declarations of the common law. One court points out that an Oklahoma statute "codifies the common law that 'all persons engaged in a public business' have a duty to treat members of all who are similarly situated . . . on equal terms and at reasonable rates."[678] Consequently, this requirement applies even to municipal utilities and rural cooperatives not covered by a state's utility statute.[679]

669 C.F. Phillips, Jr., The Regulation of Public Utilities tbl. 16-2 (1993).

670 Annot., *Public Utilities: Validity of Preferential Rates for Elderly of Low-Income Persons*, 29 A.L.R.4th 615 (1994). *See also* Massachusetts Mun. Wholesale Elec. Co. v. City of Springfield, 726 N.E.2d 973 (Mass. App. Ct. 2000); Ohio Edison Co. v. Public Util. Comm'n, 678 N.E.2d 922 (Ohio 1997). *See generally* 64 Am. Jur. 2d, Public Util. § 33 (2001).

671 Blackstone Valley Chamber of Commerce v. Public Util. Comm'n, 396 A.2d 102, 104 (R.I. 1979).

672 U.S. West Commc'ns, Inc. v. Wyoming Pub. Serv. Comm'n, 988 P.2d 1061 (Wyo. 1999), *reh'g granted*, (Dec. 13, 1999), *rev'd in part on reh'g*, 15 P.3d 722 (Wyo. 2000).

673 Owenboro Gaslight Co. v. Hildebrand, 42 S.W. 351 (Ky. 1897).

674 C.F. Phillips, Jr., The Regulation of Public Utilities 119 (1993).

675 For example, see:

California: "(a) No public utility shall as to rates, charges, facilities, or in any other respect, make or grant any preference or advantage to any corporation or person or subject any corporation or person to any prejudice or disadvantage. . . . (c) No public utility shall establish or maintain any unreasonable difference as to rates, charges, service, facilities, or in any other respect, either as between localities or as between classes of service." Cal. Pub. Util. Code § 453 (West).

Colorado: "No public utility, as to rates, charges, service, or facilities, or in any other respect, shall make or grant any preference or advantage to any corporation or person or subject any corporation or person to any prejudice or disadvantage. No public utility shall establish or maintain any unreasonable difference as to rates, charges, service, facilities, or in any respect, either between localities or as between any class of service. The commission has the power to determine any question of fact arising under this section." Colo. Rev. Stat. § 40-3-106(1)(a).

Illinois: "No public utility shall, as to rates or other charges, services, facilities, or in other respect, make or grant any preference or advantage to any corporation or person or subject any corporation or person to any prejudice or disadvantage. No public utility shall establish or maintain any unreasonable difference as to rates or other charges, services, facilities, or in any other respect, either as between localities or as between classes of service." 220 Ill. Comp. Stat. 5/9-241.

Pennsylvania: "No public utility shall, as to rates, make or grant any unreasonable preference or advantage." 66 Pa. Cons. Stat. § 1304.

Utah: "Except as provided in [telecommunications law] a public utility may not, as to rates, charges, service, facilities or in any other respect, make or grant any preference or advantage to any person, or subject any person to any prejudice or disadvantage; and establish or maintain any unreasonable difference as to rates, charges, service or facilities, or in any other respect, either as between localities or as between classes of service." Utah Code Ann. § 54-3-8 (West).

676 Fla. Admin. Code Ann. r. 25-7.033(1) (gas public utilities), r. 25-6.033 (electric public utilities) (emphasis added).

677 Cook v. Chicago, R.I. & P.R. Co., 46 N.W. 1080 (Iowa 1890) (emphasis added).

678 Hargrave v. Canadian Valley Elec. Coop., 792 P.2d 50, 58 (Okla. 1990) (quoting Consumer's Light & Power Co. v. Phipps, 251 P. 63 (Okla. 1926)).

679 *See* Inland Real Estate v. Village of Palatine, 496 N.E.2d 998, 1002 (Ill. App. Ct. 1986); Dedeke v. Rural Dist. No. 5, 623 P.2d 1324 (Kan. 1981); 64 Am. Jur. 2d Public Utilities §§ 21, 33 (2001).

7.5.3 *Do Affordability Programs Unreasonably Discriminate in Rates?*

7.5.3.1 Courts Taking Literal Interpretation of Duty of Nondiscrimination

A few courts have ruled that rates based solely on age or income of customers violate the principle against unreasonable discrimination.[680] These decisions are a result of the very strict logic applied by some courts in interpreting the duty of nondiscrimination. Some courts take very literally the principle that

> [i]t is axiomatic in rate making that utilities are barred from treating persons similarly situated in a dissimilar fashion.[681]

So long as all residential customers are viewed as being similarly situated, such strict reasoning does not leave much leeway in establishing different rate classifications. The key is to show that a reasonable basis does exist for the differences in the rate divisions between different groups of the same customer class of residential customers. For example, in examining a public service commission's conclusion that a targeted Lifeline rate violated a state statute forbidding a public utility from charging any customer "a greater or less compensation for any service . . . than it charges . . . any other person for a like and contemporaneous service," a court in Indiana simply declared that the statute "prohibits charging different rates for the same services under the same conditions."[682] The court refused to look at the different characteristics between the *targeted* class of customers and the other residential customers.

The Colorado Supreme Court also adopted this line of reasoning, as it concluded that the state statutory scheme prohibits public utilities "from granting preferential rates *to any person*."[683] The public utility commission had ordered the utility companies to provide a lower rate to low-income customers. The court found that the lower rate was "unrelated to the cost or type of the service provided" by merely concluding that this action violated the above-stated prohibition against preferential rates.[684] Along the same lines, the Utah Supreme Court stated that "[i]t is axiomatic in rate making that utilities are barred from treating persons similarly situated in a dissimilar fashion."[685] Such circular reasoning ignores the differences between the groups of customers who will benefit from the low-income program and other residential customers. It is worth noting that the Public Service Commission of Utah did adopt a Lifeline electric rate for low-income customers in 1999.[686]

The Kentucky Public Service Commission denied Kentucky-American Water Company's proposed low-income discounted water program because, while it has statutory authority regarding low-income energy programs,[687] that authorization has not been extended to water utilities.[688] The utility had argued that "[p]ermanently discontinuing water service to the neediest customers is not an acceptable option because potable water is a necessity of life" and that the discount would likely reduce costs to all consumers from disconnections notices, late payments, and bad debt write-offs. The commission's response was that it is a creature of statute and has no express statutory authorization to permit discounts based on income level and thus cannot authorize such discounts.[689]

The Kansas State Corporations Commission recently found that low-income assistance rates in the form of pure discounts are impermissibly discriminatory and unduly preferential. However, it also held that some programs benefiting low-income ratepayers might have system-wide advantages such as weatherization programs.[690] Commission staff had cited *Midwest Gas Users Association v. State Corpora-*

680 *E.g.*, Mountain States Legal Found. v. New Mexico State Corp., 687 P.2d 92, 94 (N.M. 1984).

681 Mountain States Legal Found. v. Utah Pub. Serv. Comm'n, 636 P.2d 1047, 1052 (Utah 1981) (citing to State *ex rel.* Util. Comm'n v. Mead Corp., 78 S.E.2d 290 (N.C. 1953)). *But see* Report and Order, PacifiCorp 1999 Gen. Rate Case, No. 99-035-10 (Utah Pub. Serv. Comm'n May 24, 2000); *In re* PacifiCorp, d.b.a. Utah Power & Light Co., 192 P.U.R. 4th 289, 1999 WL 218118 (Utah Pub. Serv. Comm'n Mar. 4, 1999) (No. 97-035-01).

682 Citizens Action Coal. v. Public Serv. Co., 450 N.E.2d 98, 101 (Ind. Ct. App. 1983) (quoting Ind. Code § 8-1-2-103).

683 Mountain States Legal Found. v. Public Util. Comm'n, 590 P.2d 495, 498 (Colo. 1979) (emphasis added). *See also* Colorado Mun. League v. Public Util. Comm'n, 591 P.2d 577 (Colo. 1979) (decision lowering coin-operated telephone rates in neighborhoods where there was concentration of poor and elderly persons was invalid). *But see In re* Public Serv. Co. of Colo., 2000 WL 575936 (Colo. Pub. Util. Comm'n Apr. 24, 2000) (No. 99A-377EG, Decision No. C00-393) (in approving merger condition regarding extension of Affordable Payment Pilot Program, commission distinguishes *Mountain States Legal Foundation*). *But see also* § 7.5.3.4, *infra*.

684 Mountain States Legal Found. v. Public Util. Comm'n, 590 P.2d 495, 498 (Colo. 1979).

685 Mountain States Legal Found. v. Utah Pub. Serv. Corp., 636 P.2d 1047, 1052 (Utah 1981) (citing to State *ex rel.* Util. Comm'n v. Mead Corp., 78 S.E.2d 290 (N.C. 1953)). *See also* Telluride Power Co. v. Public Util. Comm'n, 8 F. Supp. 341 (D. Utah 1934); Postal Telegraph-Cable Co. v. Associated Press, 127 N.E. 256 (N.Y. 1920); State *ex rel.* Puget Sound Power & Light Co. v. Department of Pub. Works, 38 P.2d 350 (Wash. 1934).

686 *In re* PacifiCorp, d.b.a. Utah Power & Light Co., 192 Pub. Util. Rep. 4th 289, 1999 WL 218118 (Utah Pub. Serv. Comm'n Mar. 4, 1999) (No. 97-035-01); Report and Order, PacifiCorp 1999 Gen. Rate Case, No. 99-035-10 (Utah Pub. Serv. Comm'n May 24, 2000). *See also* § 7.5.3.5, *infra*.

687 Ky. Rev. Stat. Ann. § 278.285(1), (4) (West).

688 *In re* Kentucky-American Water Co., 2005 WL 578209 (Ky. Pub. Serv. Comm'n Feb. 28, 2005) (No. 2004-00103).

689 *Id.*

690 *In re* Low Income Assistance Tariff by Util. Providing Elec. & Natural Gas, 243 Pub. Util. Rep. 4th 509, 2005 WL 267358

tions Commission[691] for the proposition that the mere indicia or potential for subsidization would not rise to the level of undue discrimination. The commission concluded that "[t]here may be legitimate service related distinctions, such as the relative financial inability of low-income ratepayers to make the necessary weatherization improvements, that will provide a rational basis for targeting low-income ratepayers."[692]

7.5.3.2 Most Courts Recognize Differences Between Different Groups of Customers in Same Customer Class

It is quite common for courts and public utilities commissions (PUCs) to conclude that, while public utilities are generally prohibited from discriminating in their rates, this does not mean that every single customer must be charged the same rate. As an Oklahoma court reasoned, the rule requiring nondiscrimination "does not mean a uniformity of rates or prices for services rendered to the public. A 'public business' cannot be required to charge the same rate for services rendered to different classes, or to people differently situated."[693] In other words, if a difference in rates has a *reasonable* basis, it is not an unjust discrimination: "[i]t is 'axiomatic in ratemaking' that 'different treatment for different classes of customers, *reasonably classified*, is not unlawful discrimination.' "[694]

This reasoning is similarly provided by the Hawaii Supreme Court, in a challenge to a declining block rate structure: "It is not any discrimination that is forbidden by the law but only those which are unreasonable. If it were otherwise, there would be only one rate for all customers, for every classification is in effect a discrimination."[695] The court concluded that it could not declare a declining block residential rate structure to be unreasonable as a matter *of law* and remanded the case back to the commission to determine whether this particular declining block residential rate structure was reasonable or whether it was unreasonably discriminatory.[696] Some courts may take the position that the PUC cannot mandate low-income rates, that the utilities can do so voluntarily, and that such discrimination is not illegal.[697]

Some courts and commissions have also noted that other classes of customers have benefited from reduced rates. In a pre-restructuring decision that approved a discounted rate for the first 500 kWh of residential use, a Pennsylvania court noted that

> [t]he law presently permits reduced rates to large industrial and commercial consumers, either because such customers buy a lot of what the utility provides or because they may use another's product if the price factor warrants. (*citations omitted*) We see no reason why in times of stringency the utility might not propose, and the commission might not approve, rates for residential users less than the rates which an allocation of large increases in necessary revenues by a strict application of cost of service studies would suggest.[698]

Similarly, the Public Service Commission of Utah, in approving a low-income Lifeline electric rate also noted that, "each class of service does not pay precisely its 'share' of costs. This is true, for example, of the large customer groups, or special contract customers, according to some views of allocations."[699]

7.5.3.3 Reasonable Discrimination Is Permissible

As explained above, if the difference in rates—the "discrimination"—has a reasonable basis, it is more likely to be found to be legal and not in violation of the prohibition against discrimination in rates. When considering the legality of affordability programs, one needs to be aware of some of the different factors that could potentially make a difference in rates seem "reasonable." For example, one relevant factor might be that the poorest customers cannot afford the standard rate.

(Kan. State Corp. Comm'n Aug. 31, 2005) (No. 04-GIMX-531-GIV).

691 595 P.2d 735 (Kan. Ct. App. 1979).

692 *Id.*

693 Hargrave v. Canadian Valley Elec. Co-op., 792 P.2d 50, 58 (Okla. 1990). *See also* Turpen v. Oklahoma Corp. Comm'n, 769 P.2d 1309 (Okla. 1988) (providing basic telephone service to low-income persons who otherwise would not be able to afford it was within broad discretion of state corporation commission).

694 American Hoechest Corp. v. Department of Pub. Utils., 399 N.E.2d 1, 3 (Mass. 1980) (quoting Boston Real Estate Bd. v. Department of Pub. Utilities, 136 N.E.2d 243, 254 (Mass. 1956) (emphasis added)). *See also* Town Taxi, Inc. v. Police Comm'r of Boston, 387 N.E.2d 129 (Mass. 1979) (error for court to declare discount program involving discount taxi-cab fare for elderly and handicapped persons null and void on ground that it discriminated between classes of passengers); United States Steel Corp. v. Pennsylvania Pub. Util. Comm'n, 390 A.2d 865 (Pa. 1978) (" 'There is no requirement that rates for different classes of service must be either uniform or equal or that they must be equally profitable. Differences in rates between classes of customers based on such criteria as the quantity of electricity used, the nature of the use, the time of the use, the pattern of the use, or based on differences of conditions of service, or cost of service are not only permissible but often are desirable and even necessary to achieve reasonable efficiency and economy of operation.' ").

695 Application of Hawaii Elec. Light Co., 594 P.2d 612, 625, 627 (Haw. 1979).

696 *Id.* at 625–27.

697 Blackstone Valley Chamber of Commerce v. Public Util. Comm'n, 396 A.2d 102 (R.I. 1979); Rhode Island Consumers' Council v. Smith, 302 A.2d 757 (R.I. 1973). *See also* § 7.5.4, *infra.*

698 United States Steel Corp. v. Pennsylvania Pub. Util. Comm'n, 390 A.2d 865 (Pa. 1978).

699 Report and Order, PacifiCorp 1999 Gen. Rate Case, No. 99-035-10 (Utah Pub. Serv. Comm'n May 24, 2000).

Whether or not the difference in rates is reasonable, then, depends on whether there is a reasonable basis for this difference. This reasonable basis may be economically based. For example, it may be possible to demonstrate that, in a particular service area, the cost of providing utility service to low-income customers is less than the cost of providing service to other residential customers, whether this is due to low-income customers using less of the utility service or to other factors. The cost of service to low-income customers includes the cost of collections, terminations, and reconnections necessitated by the difficulties these ratepayers have in paying a rate that may be unaffordable to them.[700] Alternatively, this reasonable basis for the difference in rates may stem from public policy. For example, a municipality may determine that, for public health reasons as well as humanitarian concerns, it does not wish to have its low-income customers go without water and sewer service because of unaffordable rates.

The salient question then becomes what constitutes "reasonable discrimination." Courts give considerable weight to factual evidence in support of these factors. Concrete evidence is often necessary to support preferential rates. "Reasonable classifications between consumers may be made, but there must be adequate findings of fact, supported by evidence, which demonstrates a rational basis for the classification."[701]

7.5.3.4 Cost of Service Principles

In determining whether a difference in rate classification is reasonable, first and foremost, consider the principle articulated by many courts and commissions that, unless there is some evidence that the difference in rates is cost-justified, it is unreasonably discriminatory. Even when the issue of discrimination is not directly addressed, the cost of service principle is of utmost importance.

For example, when the Alabama Public Service Commission rejected a proposed Lifeline rate-design plan based on a percentage of personal income of the ratepayers, it found significant that the complainants "produced no evidence that it costs less to serve low-income customers than other residential customers."[702] Likewise, the Public Utilities Commission of Ohio rejected a proposed Lifeline rate for low-income consumers on the grounds that it was not "cost-justified."[703]

Similarly, in evaluating a public utility commission's decision to *allow* a Lifeline rate, a court relied on the fact that the commission pointed to "no evidence" in the record to support its conclusion and noted that the consensus of expert witnesses was that a cost-of-service study would be required in order to develop a revised rate design to reflect the cost of serving different categories of customers.[704] The court noted that, if there *were* such sufficient evidence, a Lifeline rate *could* be upheld and cited another case in which an exemption of the first 384 kWh from the authorized rate increase *was* supported by evidence in the record.[705]

In 2000 the Colorado Public Utilities Commission approved the extension of a ratepayer-funded affordable payment pilot program as part of a merger proceeding.[706] The program provides a discounted low-income rate and forgives certain arrearages. The commission distinguished *Mountain States Legal Foundation v. Public Utilities Commission*[707] as prohibiting the commission from effecting social policy through preferential ratemaking in favor of a narrow group of customers. A program or rate that has an *economic* justification is a different matter. The particular pilot program at issue was not developed in the name of social policy and has the goal of reducing the utility's lost and uncollectible accounts, effecting a net reduction to all customers' bills. The commission approved the extension of this pilot program because it appeared to not create a subsidy in favor of low-income customers. The commission also approved the continuation of a low-income energy efficiency program because of the uncontradicted evidence that the program was cost-effective.[708]

7.5.3.5 Factors Other Than Cost of Service

As described in the preceding section, cost of service is one of the principle factors in determining whether a rate is reasonable (and, accordingly, *not* unreasonably discriminatory). However, as the Supreme Court of Utah noted in determining whether a rate is just and reasonable as "to each category of customer," while the cost of service should be considered, it is not the sole factor.[709] Other factors to be

700 A commission or court might reasonably conclude that a lower rate to low-income households is justified by the utility's savings realized from the fewer terminations and lower arrearages that will result from the more affordable rate.

701 Mountain States Legal Found. v. Utah Pub. Serv. Comm'n, 636 P.2d 1047, 1054–55, 1057–58 (Utah 1981).

702 Greater Birmingham Unemployed Comm. v. Alabama Gas Corp., 86 Pub. Util. Rep. 4th 218, 224 1987 WL 257976 (Ala. Pub. Serv. Comm'n Sept. 8, 1987), *aff'd*, 539 So. 2d 187 (Ala. 1988).

703 *In re* East Ohio Gas Co., 16 Pub. Util. Rep. 4th 137 (Ohio Pub. Util. Comm'n 1976).

704 Blackstone Valley Chamber of Commerce v. Public Util. Comm'n, 396 A.2d 102, 105–06 (R.I. 1979).

705 *Id.* at 106 (citing Boston Edison Co. v. Department of Pub. Utilities, 375 N.E.2d 305 (Mass. 1978)).

706 *In re* Public Serv. Co. of Colo., 2000 WL 575936 (Colo. Pub. Util. Comm'n Apr. 24, 2000) (No. 99A-337EG, Decision No. C00-393).

707 590 P.2d 495 (Colo. 1979).

708 *Id.*

709 *See also* Public Serv. Co. of N.H., 69 N.H. P.U.C. 67, 88–91 (1984) (the commission found that there were good reasons to consider targeted Lifeline program even though such social ratemaking would vary from traditional ratemaking principles). *Accord* 68 N.H. P.U.C. 603 (1983) (N.H. Public Utilities Commission approves temporary elderly low-income rate); 69 N.H.

considered include the following:[710]

(1) The economic impact of charges on each category of customer;[711]
(2) The safety, health, comfort, and convenience of customers;
(3) The size, location, and nature of the utility's business;
(4) The nature of the use and the benefit obtained from it;
(5) The customer population, and its ability to bear the burden;[712]
(6) Whether a rate classification precipitates a resulting growth in peak load demand; and whether or not the classification is on a small, experimental basis as opposed to a large-scale basis;
(7) Whether a rate classification is designed "to eliminate or palliate past discrimination."[713]

In *Mountain States Legal Foundation*, the court looked at the economic impact of the charges and the safety, health, comfort, and convenience issues (factors 1 and 2) and determined that there were not sufficient facts to support the conclusion that the low-income rates were justifiable.[714]

In 1999, the Public Service Commission of Utah again considered a low-income utility assistance program in a PacifiCorp rate case.[715] The commission noted that, in the *Mountain States Legal Foundation* case, the Lifeline rate for senior citizens failed because of insufficient findings of fact. In *In re PacifiCorp*, the commission concluded that it has the authority to adopt a Lifeline rate and set out four criteria for determining if a Lifeline rate is in the public interest:

(1) The need should be both real and unmet by direct-payment programs, which are the preferred means.
(2) The program must target only low-income households, and it should not raise rates for low-income households that consume above-average amounts of electricity.
(3) The benefits of the program should offset negative impacts on rate-making objectives and should be sufficient to overcome the commission's reluctance to effectuate social policy by means of altered electricity rates.
(4) The program should be easy and inexpensive to administer.[716]

In particular, the commission was persuaded that the proposed Lifeline program was adequately targeted and would not overly burden other customers because only households at or below 125% of poverty would be eligible. They found that 125% of poverty criterion to be discretely defined and that this population bore a higher energy burden than the rest of society and others, who do not face this burden and cannot qualify. The commission was also persuaded that the benefits of the program (approximately a 17% reduction in a low-income bill, reduced uncollectibles, returned checks and service shut offs, among other things) offset the program cost of about 10¢ per average monthly residential bill.[717] In finding that the proposed electric Lifeline program was in the public interest, the commission noted that "[e]xamples abound to demonstrate that one person's improper 'social welfare' program is another person's legitimate regulation of utilities in the 'public interest.' "[718]

The Pennsylvania Public Utility Commission recognized that the size and nature of the utility's business, and "evidence of the general customer population as it relates to the affordability of utility service, is relevant to setting rates."[719]

A Massachusetts court evaluated the resulting growth in peak load demand and whether or not the classification is on a small, experimental (versus large-scale) basis.[720] A Rhode Island court considered relevant whether a rate classification is designed "to eliminate or palliate past discrimination."[721] In this case, the Rhode Island Supreme Court noted that, if there had been proof that the low-income customers were "bearing an unjust portion of the burden of providing the utility with revenue," the proposed Lifeline electric rate in that situation would have been justified.[722] When it allowed a utility-proposed pilot Lifeline rate program, the Arizona Corporation Commission stated that, because "our primary goal is the development of rates and rate relationships which will reflect the utility's total cost of service in a rational manner," any Lifeline rate must be substantially based on

P.U.C. 30 (1984) (N.H. Pub. Util. Commission approves permanent elderly low-income rate).

710 Mountain States Legal Found. v. Utah Pub. Serv. Corp., 636 P.2d 1047 (Utah 1981) (citing to State *ex rel.* Utilities Commission).

711 *Cf. In re* Mountaineer Gas Co., 2004 WL 1091310 (W. Va. Pub. Serv. Comm'n Mar. 10, 2004) (No. 03-1173-G-30C) (regarding utility's gas procurement practices, stating that, "while affordability is not a legitimate ratemaking consideration, it is a practical one. . . . While natural gas companies must recover their reasonable purchased gas costs, if they have no customers, they have no business").

712 *See also In re* United Cities Gas Co., No. 6691-U (Ga. Pub. Serv. Comm'n Nov. 25, 1996) (commission found it reasonable to consider measure to partially alleviate impact of increase in gas rates for low-income elderly customers).

713 Mountain States Legal Found. v. Utah Pub. Serv. Comm'n, 636 P.2d 1047, 1054–55, 1057–58 (Utah 1981) (citing Utah Code Ann. § 54-3-1).

714 *Id.*

715 *In re* PacifiCorp, d.b.a. Utah Power & Light Co., 192 P.U.R. 4th 289, 1999 WL 218118 (Utah Pub. Serv. Comm'n Mar. 4, 1999) (No. 97-035-01); Report and Order, PacifiCorp 1999 Gen. Rate Case, No. 99-035-10 (Utah Pub. Serv. Comm'n May 24, 2000).

716 *In re* PacifiCorp, d.b.a. Utah Power & Light Co., 192 P.U.R. 4th 289, 1999 WL 218118 (Utah Pub. Serv. Comm'n Mar. 4, 1999) (No. 97-035-01).

717 *Id.*

718 Report and Order, PacifiCorp 1999 Gen. Rate Case, No. 99-035-10 (Utah Pub. Serv. Comm'n May 24, 2000).

719 Pennsylvania Pub. Util. Comm'n v. Pennsylvania Gas & Water Co., 1993 WL 193332, 142 Pub. Util. Rep. 4th 302, 304 (Pa. Pub. Util. Comm'n Feb. 25, 1993).

720 American Hoechest Corp. v. Department of Pub. Utilities, 399 N.E.2d 1, 3 (Mass. 1980).

721 Blackstone Valley Chamber of Commerce v. Public Util. Comm'n, 396 A.2d 102 (R.I. 1979).

722 *Id.* at 106.

the cost of service. However, the commission also said that it might permit some non-cost considerations for such a program.[723]

7.5.3.6 Usage

Proof that it costs less to serve the group benefiting from the lower rate can be significant in showing whether a rate classification is nondiscriminatory and thus legal. Flowing directly from this is the relevance of usage. If a court is convinced that there is concrete evidence that low-income customers use less of the utility's service, then the cost of providing them with the service is less, and a lower rate might be construed as *reasonable*, rather than illegal, discrimination.

Using this reasoning, Michigan's utility commission approved a Lifeline rate for elderly customers. The Michigan Public Service Commission had relied on a survey which showed that "low income senior citizens are low users of energy," with the result that low-income senior citizen utility costs are lower than the costs presented to the utility by average residential customers.[724]

However, even this was not sufficient in *Mountain States Legal Foundation*.[725] The Utah court reversed the decision by the Public Service Commission of Utah to allow a "senior citizen rate." The Public Service Commission of Utah had granted a rate increase to the utility, which included an exemption for heads of households over 65 years old as to the first block of 400 kWh per month.[726] The commission had sustained the senior citizen rate partially based on the position that, on average, senior citizens consume less power. However, the court found that the commission lacked adequate facts to support its conclusion[727] and determined that this claim, in conjunction with a claim that senior citizens generally have less income, was insufficient to provide a lawful basis for lower rates.[728]

Insufficient usage data need not necessarily sink a program if the program itself can be designed to provide the data. The District of Columbia Public Service Commission approved a utility's proposed experimental tariff that included a special low rate for customers eligible under LIHEAP or the District of Columbia's complementary energy assistance program.[729] The commission found that the program would facilitate the utility's research in consumption, load patterns, and cost of service of the company's low-income customers.

Another reason that it is important to consider the rate of consumption is that it may be considered in a determination of whether the low-income rate is *efficient*. The Indiana Court of Appeals, for example, considered a challenge to the state utility commission's refusal to require a Lifeline rate. Given that "[o]ne of the justifications advanced for a general Lifeline rate structure is that it is an effective and equitable means of providing assistance to low-income residential electricity consumers," the degree to which the rate structure is equitable and efficient "as an aid to the needy depends in part upon the degree to which the consumption of electricity is related to the level of income."[730]

7.5.3.7 Targeting

In analyzing an affordability program, another important consideration is whether the benefit of the program is narrowly targeted. That is, a program is more likely to be approved by a court or state utilities commission if it is designed to help the most needy customers. If a rate discount ends up benefiting customers who are not the poorest in the service area, the state utilities commission will be less likely to find the discrimination involved in this rate to be justified. For example, in evaluating a Lifeline rate, the Colorado Public Utility Commission noted that "[t]raditional [L]ifeline rate structures are intended to benefit low income residential customers; however, under such rate structures low consumption of electricity, rather than low income consumers, is benefited."[731] The commission went on to conclude that

> [t]he evidence presented in this proceeding has failed to convince this commission that low-usage customers are coextensive with low income consumers. Rather, it is quite probable that many low income persons live in large uninsulated houses, in all electric homes, or if handicapped, require high-usage life-supporting devices, and consequently are large users. Conversely, many affluent customers with well-insulated apartments or

723 *In re* Arizona Pub. Serv. Co., 91 Pub. Util. Rep. 4th 337, 1988 WL 391394 (Ariz. Corp. Comm'n Apr. 1, 1988).

724 *In re* Consumers Power Co., 25 Pub. Util. Rep. 4th 167, 231 (Mich. Pub. Serv. Comm'n 1978). *Accord In re* Consumers Power Co., 151 Pub. Util. Rep. 4th 374, 1994 WL 271541 (Mich. Pub. Serv. Comm'n May 10, 1994) (Michigan Public Service Commission ruled senior citizen discount lawful, pointing out that primary benefit went to senior citizens with low consumption).

725 Mountain States Legal Found. v. Utah Pub. Serv. Comm'n, 636 P.2d 1047 (Utah 1981).

726 *Id.* at 1050.

727 *Id.* at 1057–58.

728 As a general rule, low-income customers do use less energy than their middle income neighbors. *See generally* National Consumer Law Center, Energy and the Poor: The Crisis Continues (1995) (state-by-state analysis of the energy usage and burden of the costs of energy consumption on low-income households).

729 *In re* Potomac Elec. Power Co., 50 Pub. Util. Rep. 4th 500, 3 D.C.P.S.C. 450 (D.C. Pub. Serv. Comm'n 1982).

730 Citizens Action Coal. v. Public Serv. Co., 450 N.E.2d 98, 102 (Ind. Ct. App. 1983).

731 *In re* Generic Hearings Concerning Elec. Rate Structure, 36 Pub. Util. Rep. 4th 6, 76–77 (Colo. Pub. Util. Comm'n 1979).

houses, or second homes, may well benefit from such a Lifeline rate.[732]

In part, the strong need to properly target the population is justified purely on political and policy grounds. If a utility is planning to have a discount rate—which will have, to an extent, a discriminatory effect on other customers—clearly the desired goal is to help only those who are truly in need of assistance.

In evaluating the Indiana Public Service Commission's decision not to mandate a Lifeline rate, the state appeals court relied on the commission's conclusion that,

> although a general [L]ifeline rate structure would benefit low-income consumers who are low users of electricity, it would have the undesirable effects of benefiting many middle and high-income consumers who are low users of electricity and harming a number of low-income consumers who are high users of electricity.[733]

Imprecise targeting led the Rhode Island Public Service Commission to reject a discounted rate for unemployed customers as unreasonable discrimination. The commission feared that the program would allow those with substantial assets or employed relatives living in the same house to receive discounts while customers with lower incomes or financial resources would be ineligible.[734] Similarly the Florida Public Service Commission rejected a proposed Lifeline rate as "not in the public interest" because statistical data showed that it not only would fail to reach a large number of intended beneficiaries but also would reach a large number of unintended beneficiaries and would hamper conservation efforts.[735]

The Public Service Commission of Utah was persuaded that a proposed electric Lifeline program was adequately targeted and would not overly burden other customers because only households at or below 125% of poverty would be eligible. They found that 125% of poverty criterion to be discretely defined and that this population bore a higher energy burden than the rest of society and others who do not face this burden and cannot qualify.[736]

732 *Id.* at 76, 77.
As a general rule, low-income customers do use less energy than their middle-income neighbors. *See generally* National Consumer Law Center, Energy and the Poor: The Crisis Continues (1995) (state-by-state analysis of the energy usage and burden of the costs of energy consumption on low-income households).

733 Citizens Action Coal. v. Public Serv. Co., 450 N.E.2d 98, 102 (Ind. Ct. App. 1983).

734 *In re* Narragansett Elec. Co. 57 Pub. Util. Rep. 4th 120 (R.I. Pub. Util. Comm'n 1983).

735 *In re* Consideration of Lifeline Rates, 43 Pub. Util. Rep. 4th 355, 358–59 (Fla. Pub. Serv. Comm'n 1981).

736 *In re* PacifiCorp, d.b.a. Utah Power & Light Co., 192 P.U.R. 4th 289, 1999 WL 218118 (Utah Pub. Serv. Comm'n Mar. 4, 1999) (No. 97-035-01).

7.5.4 Authority of Public Service Commission to Permit Utility to Have Reduced Rate

In some instances, the courts may find that while *mandating* a reduced rate exceeds the authority of the state utilities commission, it is *within the authority* of the commission to *approve* a discount rate offered by a particular utility. For example, in discussing a telephone rate case, the Rhode Island Supreme Court held that the Rhode Island Public Utilities Commission was not authorized to mandate a $1.00-per-month discount for certain persons 65 years of age or older: "While [the state statutes] . . . generally prohibit preferential treatment of utility customers, they do, by way of exception, authorize the division to *permit* a utility to offer 'free or reduced rate service' to an elderly person."[737] This court relied heavily on that distinction in its decision-making process:

> [T]he authority to grant that limited exception does not carry with it the power to *compel* a utility to afford a reduced rate to senior citizens. Under the statutes, the initiative rests with the utility, and the commission cannot, unless so authorized by the Legislature, compel its exercise.[738]

The highest state court in Massachusetts, for example, has made a clear distinction between whether a state utilities commission can *mandate* the adoption of a reduced utility rate—which it finds illegal—and whether a commission has the authority to *approve* one. "There can be no question that the department's jurisdiction over the entire rate structure includes the authority to approve a reduced rate for certain customers."[739]

737 Rhode Island Consumers' Council v. Smith, 302 A.2d 757, 775 (R.I. 1973) (referring to R.I. Gen. Laws §§ 39-2-2, 39-2-3, 39-2-5).

738 Rhode Island Consumers' Council v. Smith, 302 A.2d 757, 775 (R.I. 1973). *See also* Arkansas Gas Consumers, Inc. v. Arkansas Pub. Serv. Comm'n, 118 S.W.3d 109 (Ark. 2003) (the utility commission did not have statutory authority to impose surcharge to fund temporary low-income gas reconnection policy); Consumer Power Co. v. Association of Bus. Advocating Tariff Equity, 518 N.W.2d 514 (Mich. Ct. App. 1994) (when utility sought rate surcharge to help low-income customers, PSC had authority to approve rate surcharge). *But see* Citizens Action Coal. v. Public Serv. Co., 450 N.E.2d 98, 102 (Ind. Ct. App. 1983) (finding that commission's rate-making power is legislative, thus commission had power to implement general Lifeline rates).

739 American Hoechest Corp. v. Department of Pub. Utilities, 399 N.E.2d 1, 3 (Mass. 1980) (citing to Boston Edison Co. v. Department of Pub. Utilities, 375 N.E.2d 305 (Mass. 1978). *See also In re* United Cities Gas Co., 174 Pub. Util. Rep. 4th 169, 1996 WL 773364 (Ga. Nov. 25, 1996) (approved program for low-income elderly customers that would waive customer charge and monthly service bill); Georgia Power Co. v. Georgia Pub. Serv. Comm'n, 122 Pub. Util. Rep. 4th 214, 1988 WL 391328 (Ga. Super. Ct. July 21, 1988) (upheld discount rate, approved by state PUC, to low-income elderly electric utility customers); New England Tel. & Tel. Co. v. Department of Pub. Utils., 354 N.E.2d 860 (Mass. 1976).

Chapter 8 The Low Income Home Energy Assistance Program (LIHEAP)

8.1 Overview of LIHEAP

8.1.1 LIHEAP Summary

The Low Income Home Energy Assistance Program[1] (hereafter "LIHEAP") is a federal block grant program to the states to help low-income households meet the costs of heating and cooling their homes. Benefits are available to low-income households based on income or to households in which one or more members receive certain means tested benefits, such as SSI.[2] States have flexibility under the LIHEAP statute to use these funds to help vulnerable low-income households through heating and/or cooling assistance grants, and energy crisis intervention; low-cost weatherization and energy-related repair; and other program elements as described in this chapter. In addition to the regular block grant funding for LIHEAP, there is a separate emergency contingency fund from which the President can draw to address home energy needs arising from a natural disaster or other emergency.[3] In such emergency situations, the Secretary of Health and Human Services determines how to allocate the emergency funds to address the emergency that has been identified.[4]

LIHEAP is not a mandatory federal spending program like other entitlement programs such as Social Security and Medicare. LIHEAP is funded annually through the federal appropriations bill for the Departments of Labor, Health and Human Services, and Education as well as related agencies. As a result, the funding level for LIHEAP varies year by year, and advocates must remain ever vigilant to keep the federal appropriation from being cut back. LIHEAP's main weakness is its chronic lack of adequate funding. When states receive severe cuts to their LIHEAP program, they must either reduce the size of their LIHEAP benefits or reduce the number of households served. Outside factors also affect the number and amount of LIHEAP benefits in a particular year. Rising energy prices act to limit the purchasing power of LIHEAP, so larger household benefits are needed to provide an adequate level of assistance. High unemployment rates and increases in the number of people in poverty drive up the demand for LIHEAP assistance, so either a smaller percentage of eligible applicants receive assistance or LIHEAP recipients receive smaller assistance amounts. LIHEAP has been serving between 15% to 20% of the eligible households from the 1990s through 2008, significantly lower than the 36% of eligible households served when the program was first created in the early 1980s.[5] However, in fiscal years 2009, 2010, and 2011, the regular block grant for LIHEAP grew to $4.5 billion. Thus we expect the LIHEAP participation rates to be higher in those years.[6]

All fifty states, many tribes, the District of Columbia, American Samoa, Guam, Puerto Rico, the U.S. Virgin Islands, and the Northern Mariana Islands have chosen to participate in LIHEAP. Each participating state prepares an annual plan, which must be approved by the Secretary of Health and Human Services.[7] State programs are administered by state agencies which frequently contract with local community action programs to administer the program components.

In light of the limited federal funding, the LIHEAP statute requires states to target assistance to the most vulnerable households, those with "the lowest incomes and highest energy costs or needs in relation to income"—in other words, those low-income households with the highest energy burdens and those with vulnerable members including young children, seniors, and people with disabilities.[8] Each state has the flexibility to develop its own eligibility criteria to allocate its limited funds among eligible households.[9] The federal LIHEAP statute prohibits states from limiting LIHEAP to only households in qualifying programs (in other words, states cannot exclude income-eligibility in

1 42 U.S.C. §§ 8621–8630. *See* appx. C, *infra*.
2 42 U.S.C. § 8624(b)(2). *See* § 8.3, *infra*.
3 42 U.S.C. §§ 8621(e), 8622(1) and (7).
4 42 U.S.C. §§ 8621(e), 8623(e).

5 Div. of Energy Assistance, U.S. Dep't of Health & Human Servs., LIHEAP Home Energy Notebook for Fiscal Year 2008, Figure 3-20 (May 2010).
6 *See* appx. C.4, *infra*.
7 42 U.S.C. § 8624.
8 42 U.S.C. § 8624(b)(5). *See also* §§ 8621(a), 8622(4), 8624(b)(1)(A).
9 42 U.S.C. § 8624(b)(2) (parameters for eligibility criteria).

their eligibility criteria) and the statute requires equitable treatment of owners and renters.[10]

Appendix C.3, *infra*, contains a list of the state LIHEAP directors (with websites and numbers for public inquiries about LIHEAP). To learn more about a particular state's program and availability of benefits, contact the state's LIHEAP program, local social service office, the state's utility commission (see Appendix A.8, *infra*, for a listing), or the governor's office to find out which agency in the state runs the LIHEAP program. A utility company is also likely to know about the energy assistance program; many utilities include flyers or information about the local LIHEAP program in their winter newsletters.

Low-income advocates should get involved in the early stages of the planning process. The statute requires states to provide opportunities for public participation in LIHEAP planning.[11] Many state administrative procedure acts or the relevant agencies' enabling acts prescribe agency rulemaking procedures that may include public notice, a comment period, and some kind of public hearing for agency rulemaking. Advocates should begin by contacting the LIHEAP coordinator to have their names placed on the mailing list for notices regarding the LIHEAP plan. They should then follow up with comments or testimony wherever permitted.

The LIHEAP statute requires the provision of fair hearings for applicants challenging a denial.[12] State statutes and regulations often prescribe detailed standards and procedures for agency adjudications. Most states provide for some degree of judicial review of agencies' actions, although this review may be extremely deferential. Some agency actions are not reviewable. If meaningful review of the agency action is not available in state court, the advocate will face the difficult question of what, if any, federal remedy is available.

In the past, some of the most controversial issues have been whether the state plan conforms to the federal targeting requirements, whether the state's definition of "household" is consistent with the federal definition, whether homeowners and all classes of tenants are treated "equitably," and the application of the "income-disregard" provisions, which require LIHEAP payments to be disregarded in determining eligibility for other means-tested programs and available remedies.

8.1.2 History of LIHEAP

As a result of the decontrol of the oil industry and the Iranian Crisis of 1979, a significant increase in heating oil prices occurred during the 1970s. Coupled with a decrease in the energy purchasing power of low-income households, this energy price increase led to the establishment of a major low-income energy assistance program by the federal government.

In 1980, Congress passed the Home Energy Assistance Act as part of the Crude Oil Windfall Profit Act.[13] The stated purpose of this Act was to provide "grants to States to provide assistance to eligible households to offset the rising costs of home energy that are excessive in relation to household income."[14] This program was reauthorized the next year, in Title XXVI of the Omnibus Budget Reconciliation of 1981, as the Low-Income Home Energy Assistance Act of 1981.[15] While the purpose in enacting the Low Income Home Energy Assistance Program (LIHEAP) remained the same, a new emphasis was placed on making block grants to the states and thereby giving states more discretion to administer the program. Over the years, the program has been reauthorized as part of the Human Services Reauthorization Acts of 1984,[16] 1986[17] and 1990.[18] The Augustus F. Hawkins Human Services Reauthorization Act of 1990 (Public Law 101-501) added a leveraging incentive program that sets aside a certain portion of the LIHEAP appropriation to reward states that acquired non-Federal energy resources.[19] In 1993, LIHEAP was included in the National Institutes of Health Revitalization Act[20] with the basic structure of the block grant program remaining unchanged. The program was again reauthorized in 1994 with some important changes included in the Human Services Amendments of 1994.[21] While maintaining the basic purpose to help low-income households meet their immediate home energy needs, the 1994 change targeted assistance to those low-income households with the lowest incomes that pay a high proportion of household income for home energy (that is, those households with the highest energy burdens).[22] Other major changes to the LIHEAP statute include the addition of a new section that authorizes LIHEAP emergency contingency funds; addition of the definitions "energy burden" and "highest home energy needs"; and the addition of a new provision, Assurance 16, that allows states to use up to 5% of their grant to provide services that encourage and enable households to reduce

10 42 U.S.C. § 8624(b)(8).

11 42 U.S.C. §§ 8624(a)(2), (b)(12), (c)(2).

12 42 U.S.C. § 8624(b)(13).

13 Pub. L. No. 96-223, 94 Stat. 229 (1980).

14 *Id.* § 302(8)(b).

15 Pub. L. No. 97-35, tit. XXVI, 95 Stat. 893 (1981).

16 Pub. L. No. 98-558, 98 Stat. 2889 (1984). The reauthorization was for a two-year period (fiscal years 1985 and 1986) in which $2.14 billion was authorized for fiscal year 1985 and $2.275 billion was authorized for fiscal year 1986.

17 Pub. L. No. 99-425, 100 Stat. 973 (1986). This reauthorized LIHEAP for four years, from fiscal years 1987 to 1990.

18 Pub. L. No. 101-501, 104 Stat. 1258 (1990). This reauthorized LIHEAP from fiscal years 1991 through 1994.

19 42 U.S.C. §§ 8621(d), 8626a. *See also* 45 C.F.R. § 96.87.

20 Pub. L. No. 103-43, 107 Stat. 214 (1993). This reauthorization simply extended LIHEAP for one year, from 1994 to 1995, making no changes in policy.

21 Pub. L. No. 103-252, 108 Stat. 637 (1994). LIHEAP was reauthorized through fiscal year 1999.

22 42 U.S.C. §§ 8621(a), 8624(b)(2)(B), (b)(3), (b)(5), (c)(1)(E).

their home energy needs and thereby reduce the need for energy assistance.[23] In 1998, the program was reauthorized through fiscal year 2004, with several amendments including a requirement that LIHEAP weatherization funds be targeted to households with the highest energy burden and an expanded definition of "emergency" for use in allocating contingency funds.[24] The Energy Policy Act of 2005 reauthorized LIHEAP for fiscal years 2005 through 2007 at $5.1 billion for the regular block grant program, providing a substantial increase in the authorization amount.[25] A provision allowing LIHEAP to be used for the purchase of renewable fuels was also added.[26]

8.1.3 LIHEAP Funding

8.1.3.1 LIHEAP Regular Block Grant

While the LIHEAP statute authorizes a funding level for the regular block grant program, emergency contingency funding, and the leveraging component, the actual amount of funding for LIHEAP each fiscal year is determined by the annual federal appropriations process. LIHEAP funding is covered in the Labor, Health and Human Services, Education and Related Agencies appropriations bill for a particular fiscal year.[27]

When Congress fails to pass appropriations bills before the start of the new fiscal year (October 1), Congress usually resorts to a Continuing Resolution (CR) as a stop-gap measure to continue funding federal programs until the spending bills are passed. A government "shut-down" occurs for programs when there is a failure to pass an appropriations bill and/or a stop-gap CR.[28] There have been years during which several short-term CRs were required before all the spending bills were finally passed, and programs were funded pro rata at a prior year's funding level (or another level set by Congress) for the duration of each CR.[29] LIHEAP funding faces several challenges when funded through the CR mechanism. First, the opportunity for increased funding from the prior year is typically not an option because Congress and the Office of Management and Budget (OMB) tend to be conservative with the stop-gap funding levels for programs, often opting for the lower of the prior year's funding level for a particular program or the lower number out of the House and Senate Appropriations committees for that particular program. Second, it is also very important that the wording of the CR allows states to receive enough LIHEAP funding up front, especially in the first CR. Use of a pro rata formula, especially under a short CR, would not provide states with enough funds to adequately start their heating programs. States normally receive their LIHEAP block grant funding from the U.S. Department of Health and Human Services (HHS) in quarterly allotments and states can request up to 100% of their annual block grant in the first quarter. In order to minimize the disruption of a CR on the start of the states' LIHEAP program, it is critical that states be provided with, at a minimum, their full first quarter requests for funding in the first CR.[30]

Funding for the LIHEAP regular program (not including LIHEAP emergency contingency funds or other sources) hit an all-time low of $900 million in fiscal year 1996.[31] Since that low point, funding for the regular LIHEAP program has steadily increased, in part due to increased political pressure from constituents to increase the appropriations for LIHEAP.[32] Between fiscal years 2002 and 2008, with the exception of fiscal year 2006, funding for the regular program hovered between $1.7 to $1.98 billion. In fiscal year 2006, there was an additional $1 billion provided for LIHEAP in March 2006, resulting in $2.48 billion for the regular block grant program[33] In fiscal years 2009 and 2010, the regular LIHEAP program was funded at a record $4.51 billion and LIHEAP emergency contingency funded at $590 million.[34] All of the emergency contingency funding were released in fiscal years 2009 and 2010, so states received a

23 Division of Energy Assistance, U.S. Dep't of Health & Human Servs., Low Income Home Energy Assistance Program Report to Congress for Fiscal Year 1995, at 2–3 (1997).

24 Pub. L. No. 105-285, 112 Stat. 2756 (1998).

25 Pub. L. No. 109-58, 119 Stat. 616 (2005).

26 42 U.S.C. § 8630.

27 The Library of Congress Thomas website tracks appropriations bills. You can access the appropriations bills through the "Appropriations bills" tab at http://thomas.loc.gov/home/thomas.php.

28 For example, in fiscal year 2008, after passing three short-term continuing resolutions, Congress passed a fourth continuing resolution for the remainder of the fiscal year. *See* Pub. L. No. 110-161, 121 Stat 1844 (2007) (covering appropriations for eleven spending bills).

29 For example, in fiscal year 2008, after passing four short-term continuing resolutions, Congress passed a consolidated appropriations bill covering appropriations for eleven out of twelve spending bills. *See* Pub. L. No. 110-161, 121 Stat 1844 (2007).

30 States regularly report their requests to HHS in early September for how much of their upcoming LIHEAP block grant they would like to receive each quarter. If states do not submit this information to HHS, the default is to receive 25% of their block grant each quarter. *See, e.g.*, Estimates of Quarterly Obligations for the Fiscal Year (FY) 2009 Low Income Home Energy Assistance Program (LIHEAP), HHS ACF LIHEAP Action Transmittal No. LIHEAP-AT-2008-6 (July 17, 2008).

31 U.S. Dep't of Health & Human Servs., Administration for Children & Families, Low Income Home Energy Assistance Program Report to Congress for FY 1996, at ii (Sept.2000).

32 *See* appx. C.4, *infra.*

33 Congress had originally appropriated $1.98 billion for the regular program and passed a separate bill to add $1 billion in additional appropriations to the regular and emergency contingency fund (providing an additional $500 million for both). Pub. L. No. 109-204, 120 Stat. 312 (Mar. 20, 2006).

34 *See* Pub. L. No. 111-117, 123 Stat. 3034 (Dec. 16, 2009) (fiscal year 2010 consolidated appropriations act containing LIHEAP funding); Pub. L. No. 110-329, 122 Stat. 3574 (Sept. 30, 2008) (fiscal year 2009 appropriations act containing LIHEAP funding).

record total $5.1 billion in LIHEAP funding and provided heating assistance to an estimated 7.7 million low-income households in fiscal year 2009 and an estimated 8.4 households in fiscal year 2010.[35] Funding for the regular LIHEAP program dipped in fiscal year 2011 to $4.501 billion.[36] Demand for LIHEAP assistance had grown with the recession, persistent unemployment, and growing number of households in poverty.[37]

8.1.3.2 LIHEAP Emergency Contingency Funds

The LIHEAP statute also provides a separate source of LIHEAP funds to address an emergency situation in a state or in several states.[38] These funds are referred to as LIHEAP emergency contingency funds because the release of the funds is contingent upon the Administration identifying an emergency situation and the President's decision to release the funds. An "emergency" is defined to include not only natural disasters and supply shortages but also significant increases in home energy disconnections, participation in certain public benefit programs, unemployment or layoffs, and events meeting other criteria set by the Secretary of Health and Human Services.[39]

For example, during the lethal 1998 heat wave, the president authorized an additional $100,000 to be divided among the eleven Southern and Southwestern states where the heat was most severe,[40] and, in September 2000, the president released $2.6 million in emergency contingency funds to address the extraordinary electricity price increase in Southern California stemming from deregulation.[41] Emergency contingency funds have been released to address severe increases in home energy prices; for example, in February 2008, $40 million in LIHEAP emergency contingency funds were released to eleven states to help low-income households afford record high prices for home heating oil.[42]

Unfortunately, there is a downside to reliance on emergency contingency funds. In any program year, states cannot rely on the release of any or all of the emergency contingency funds. For example, in fiscal year 2002, the Administration steadfastly refused to release any emergency contingency funds despite the downturn in the economy and the huge increase in arrearages and disconnections.[43]

One troubling federal budget maneuver is to increase the amount of the total LIHEAP appropriations that is designated as emergency contingency funding as opposed to the regular program. Depending on the budget rules in place, this accounting maneuver can make the total appropriation for LIHEAP appear larger than it might actually be for the fiscal year. Emergency contingency appropriations (versus the regular appropriation for the program) can sometimes be "scored" differently than regular programs, thus making the overall cost of the spending bill look lower. Unfortunately, this maneuver results in fewer actual dollars to the LIHEAP grantees up front, since the amount and the timing of the release of these emergency funds are within the president's discretion and are dependant upon crisis situations.[44]

35 *See* Press Release, National Energy Assistance Director's Ass'n, Table Illustrating State-by-State Numbers Comparing FY 2009 Actual vs. FY 2010 Projected (Feb. 22, 2010); Press Release, National Energy Assistance Director's Ass'n, Applications for Energy Assistance Again Reach Record Levels (Feb. 8, 2011), *available at* www.NEADA.org.

36 Pub. Law 112-10, 125 Stat 38 (Apr. 15, 2011).

37 National Consumer Law Center, FY 2012 Appropriations for the HHS Low Income Home Energy Assistance Program (Apr. 2011), *available at* www.nclc.org/issues/liheap-a-fuel-assistance.html.

38 42 U.S.C. §§ 8621(e), 8623(e).

39 42 U.S.C. § 8622(1).

40 U.S. Dep't of Health & Human Servs., LIHEAP Allotments Under the FY 1998 Energy Emergency Contingency Fund—Second Distribution, LIHEAP-IM-98-27 (Aug. 20, 1998).

41 U.S. Dep't of Health & Human Servs., LIHEAP Allotments Under the FY 2000 Energy Emergency Contingency Fund—Sixth Distribution, LIHEAP-IM-2000-26 (Sept. 14, 2000).

42 *See* Press Release, U.S. Dep't of Health & Human Servs., HHS Provides $40 Million in Energy Assistance to Low-Income Families (Feb. 22, 2008), *available at* www.hhs.gov/news/press/2008pres/02/20080222a.html.

43 H.R. Rep. No. 107-342, at 103 (2001) (Conf. Rep.).

> The conferees are concerned that the combination of circumstances, according to objective data sources, has left many low income households with utility debts at levels considerably higher than the previous year, while applications for this coming heating season are coming in at rates significantly higher than last year. Therefore, the conferees encourage the Administration to release funds to reduce the energy burden on low income households throughout the nation. The conferees recognize that the contingency fund was authorized to meet the additional home energy assistance needs of one or more States arising from a natural disaster or other emergency, which includes a significant increase in the cost of home energy, a significant increase in home energy disconnections or a significant increase in unemployment, layoffs, or the number of households applying for unemployment benefits. The conferees understand that the latest Department of Labor employment data indicate the unemployment rate has risen almost one full percentage point in the last two months, while payroll employment has fallen by almost 800,000.

See also Letter from NCLC on behalf of Massachusetts Community Action Program Directors Association and the Massachusetts Low-Income Energy Affordability Network to Mitchell Daniels, Director, Office of Management and Budget (Nov. 30, 2001), *available on the companion website to this treatise*); *The Low-Income Energy Assistance Program: Hearing Before the Comm. on Health, Educ., Labor, and Pensions*, 107th Cong. (Oct. 30, 2001) (statement of Senator Kennedy).

44 42 U.S.C. §§ 8621(e) (authorization for LIHEAP emergency contingency funds), 8622(1) (definition of emergency), 8623(e) (allotment of emergency funds).

8.2 Significant LIHEAP Provisions

8.2.1 Purpose

The purpose of the LIHEAP program as stated in the Act is "to assist low-income households, particularly those with the lowest incomes, that pay a high proportion of household income for home energy, primarily in meeting their immediate home energy needs."[45] The statute's definition of "highest home energy needs" takes into account the energy burden of the household (proportion of household income required for home energy) as well as the unique situation of households with vulnerable members, including the frail, the elderly, individuals with disabilities, and very young children.[46]

8.2.2 State Administration of LIHEAP

LIHEAP is administered in thirty states by the state social services agency or welfare department. In twenty-one states, LIHEAP is administered by another agency such as the Department of Housing and Community Development, the Department of Commerce, the State Energy Office, and so forth. In thirty-two states, the agency that administers the LIHEAP program also administers the Department of Energy's low-income weatherization program. In many places, those agencies then contract with local providers, such as community action agencies, that handle LIHEAP intake.[47] LIHEAP is also known by various acronyms in different states (for example, HEAP).

8.2.3 State Plans

In order for states to receive LIHEAP funds, each state must submit an application to the Secretary of Health and Human Services (HHS).[48] Each application must contain assurances by the chief executive officer of each state that the state will meet the sixteen conditions enumerated in the LIHEAP authorizing statute.[49] All of these variables, which are in the discretion of each state, must be addressed in each state's annual application for LIHEAP funds. As part of the annual application, states must submit a plan that provides specific information regarding each of the various types of assistance provided under the program. The information:

> (A) describes the eligibility requirements to be used by the State . . .;
>
> (B) describes the benefit levels to be used by the State . . .;
>
> (C) contains estimates of the amount of funds to be used by the State for each of the programs . . .;
>
> (D) describes weatherization and other energy-related home repair . . .;
>
> (E) describes any steps taken . . . to target assistance to households with high home energy burdens . . .;
>
> (F) describes how the State will carry out the assurances [required by the LIHEAP authorizing statute] . . .;
>
> (G) states . . . the number and income levels of households which apply and the number which are assisted [and the number of households assisted with members over 60, members who were disabled, with young children];
>
> (H) contains any other information determined by the Secretary [of HHS] to be appropriate. . . .[50]

States must be guided by the standards set forth in the LIHEAP authorizing statute in developing their state plans but, because this is a block grant program, they still have a great deal of discretion in implementing the program (for example, in setting eligibility standards within the statutory framework and determining level of benefits for program recipients). This discretion results in LIHEAP programs that vary greatly from state to state.

8.2.4 Public Participation Provisions

The statute provides for public involvement in the state planning and application process. Low-income advocates should take full advantage of this opportunity to participate in designing the LIHEAP program for their particular state.[51] For example, the state must agree to "provide for timely and meaningful public participation in the development of the plan described in subsection (c). . . ."[52]

Another provision of the authorizing statute also clearly demonstrates that Congress intended the public to be involved in the preparation of a state's plan: "Each plan . . . and each substantial revision . . . shall be made available for public inspection within the State . . . in such a manner as will facilitate timely and meaningful review of, and comment upon, such plan or substantial revision."[53]

---

45 42 U.S.C. §§ 8621(a), 8622(4), 8624(b)(1)(A), (b)(5).

46 42 U.S.C. § 8622(4).

47 For more information on state LIHEAP administrative agencies and their subgrantees, visit NCAT's LIHEAP Clearinghouse at www.liheap.ncat.org/admintro.htm.

48 42 U.S.C. § 8624.

49 42 U.S.C. § 8642(b).

50 42 U.S.C. § 8624(c)(1)(A)–(H) (as amended in 1994).
In fiscal year 1998, the U.S. Administration for Children and Families (ACF) issued a streamlined LIHEAP model plan and application process (LIHEAP Information Memorandum Transmittal No. LIHEAP-IM-97-18 (May 15, 1997)). Under the streamlined application process, grantees need to submit a detailed plan only every three years if there are no major changes to their program and submit only an abbreviated application in alternate years.

51 42 U.S.C. § 8624(a)(2), (b)(12), (c)(2).

52 42 U.S.C. § 8624(b)(12).

53 42 U.S.C. § 8624(c)(2).

8.2.5 *Crisis Intervention*

The LIHEAP statute provides for two kinds of emergency assistance, a crisis intervention component in a state's annual program and a separate source of federal LIHEAP funding to provide additional grants to the state(s) in case of natural disaster, economic disruption, or other emergency (discussed in § 7.1.3.2, *supra*). In their annual state LIHEAP plan, states must reserve a reasonable amount of their block grant until March 15 for LIHEAP crisis intervention. States have discretion in defining what constitutes a "crisis" and how that crisis would be addressed by this program component.[54] The statute does set parameters for the crisis intervention component. In a crisis situation, these funds must be made available to an eligible household within eighteen hours if the household is in a life-threatening situation, otherwise within forty-eight hours.[55] The agency must provide a means for physically infirm applicants to either make application without leaving home or travel to the site at which applications are accepted.[56]

8.2.6 *Leveraging and REACH Incentive Programs*

Under the LIHEAP leveraging incentive program, which was first funded in fiscal year 1992, a certain portion of the LIHEAP appropriation may be set aside by Congress each year to reward states that add non-federal resources to meet the heating and cooling needs of low-income households.[57] As part of the 1994 amendments to LIHEAP,[58] the Residential Energy Assistance Challenge option (REACH) was established. Beginning in fiscal year 1996, up to 25% of the leveraging funds may be reserved for the REACH program.[59] The purpose of REACH is to help reduce energy vulnerability in low-income households by providing innovative services through community-based nonprofits that minimize health and safety risks that result from high energy burdens; prevent homelessness as a result of inability to pay energy bills; increase the energy efficiency of low-income families; and target assistance to those most in need.[60]

54 42 U.S.C. § 8623(c).
The LIHEAP Clearinghouse has a chart summarizing the different state crisis components at www.liheap.ncat.org/lhcomp.htm.

55 42 U.S.C. § 8623(c)(1), (c)(2).

56 42 U.S.C. § 8623(c)(3).

57 42 U.S.C. § 8626a. *See also* 45 C.F.R. § 96.87.

58 Human Services Amendments of 1994, Pub. L. No. 103-252, 108 Stat. 623 (1994); 42 U.S.C. § 8626b.

59 42 U.S.C. § 8626b(b)(1).

60 *Id.*

8.2.7 *Low-Cost Residential Weatherization or Other Home Energy-Related Repair*

States may use up to 15% of their annual LIHEAP block grant (or up to 25% with a waiver) for low-cost residential weatherization or other home-energy-related repair.[61] The LIHEAP statute does forbid the use of LIHEAP "for the purchase or improvement of land, or the purchase, construction, or permanent improvement (other than low-cost residential weatherization or other energy-related home repairs) of any building or other facility."[62] In thirty-two states, the same agency administers LIHEAP and the Department of Energy's low-income weatherization program.[63]

8.3 Program Eligibility

8.3.1 *Introduction*

States have wide latitude to establish eligibility and benefit levels based on federal law. The LIHEAP statute targets assistance to households with the highest energy burdens or needs.[64] Eligibility for LIHEAP benefits is determined in two ways: program eligibility, in which families are determined to be eligible based on their participation in another public benefits program, such as TANF, Supplemental Nutrition Assistance Program (or SNAP, formerly Food Stamps), Supplemental Security Income and certain veterans' benefits; and income eligibility. For the income eligibility requirement, Congress set the maximum federal eligibility at the greater of (1) 150% of the federal poverty level or (2) 60% of the state's median income, except that a state may not exclude a household from eligibility if the household income is less than 110% of the poverty level for that state, but the state may give priority to those households with the highest home energy costs or needs in relation to income.[65] In the fiscal year 2009 and fiscal year 2010 appropriations for LIHEAP, Congress allowed states to increase, for the applicable program year, the maximum income eligibility to 75% of state median income.[66]

61 42 U.S.C. § 8624(k).

62 42 U.S.C. § 8628.

63 *See* ch. 9, *infra*; www.liheap.ncat.org/admintro.htm (state LIHEAP components summarized by the LIHEAP Clearinghouse).

64 *See* 42 U.S.C. §§ 8621(a), 8622(4), 8624(b)(1)(A), (b)(5).
The Human Services Amendments of 1994 reauthorized LIHEAP through 1999; Congress amended the purpose of LIHEAP to clarify that LIHEAP is "to assist low-income households, particularly those with the lowest incomes, that pay a high proportion of household income for home energy, primarily in meeting their immediate home energy needs."

65 42 U.S.C. § 8624(b)(2)(B).

66 *See* Pub. L. No. 110-329, 122 Stat. 3574 (Sept. 30, 2008) (fiscal

In fiscal year 2011, forty states set their maximum income eligibility at or near the federal maximum and three states set their eligibility standards for heating assistance at or near 110% of poverty, the federal minimum allowable under the authorizing statute.[67] In fiscal year 2008,when the regular LIHEAP program was funded at $1.98 billion, only 16% of eligible families received LIHEAP heating and/or crisis assistance.[68] The U.S. Department of Health and Human Services estimates that, in fiscal year 2008, there were about 9.4 million households spending over 15% of their income on residential energy and about 4.3 million households spending over 25%.[69]

In the state application, the chief executive officer certifies that the state agrees to make payments *only* with respect to:

> (A) households in which 1 or more individuals are receiving—
> (i) assistance under the State program funded under part A of title IV of the Social Security Act . . .;[70]
> (ii) supplemental security income payments under title XVI of the Social Security Act;
> (iii) supplemental nutrition assistance program benefits under the Food and Nutrition Act of 2008 . . . ; or
> (iv) payments under section 1315, 1521, 1541, or 1542 of title 38, or under section 306 of the Veterans' and Survivors' Pension Improvement Act of 1978; or
> (B) households with incomes which do not exceed the greater of—
> (i) an amount equal to 150% of the poverty level for such State; or
> (ii) an amount equal to 60% of the State median income;
>
> except that a State may not exclude a household from eligibility in a fiscal year solely on the basis of household income if such income is less than 110% of the poverty level for such State, but the State may give priority to those households with the highest home energy costs or needs in relation to household income. . . .[71]

Thus, a state must certify that households participating in the programs listed above, or households falling within the stated income requirement, are the only households receiving LIHEAP assistance.

Among these households, the state must make assurances that it will provide, in a timely manner, "the highest level of assistance . . . to those households which have the lowest incomes and the highest energy costs or needs in relation to income, taking into account family size. . . ."[72] States also may not differentiate in providing assistance between households who are participating in the categorical programs listed in the statute (at 42 U.S.C. § 8624(b)(2)(A)) and those applicants who are eligible based solely on income (under 42 U.S.C. § 8624(b)(2)(B)).[73] States must also provide assurance that they will treat owners and renters "equitably."[74] Assurances must also be made that the state will "provide an opportunity for a fair administrative hearing to individuals whose claims for assistance . . . are denied or are not acted upon with reasonable promptness."[75]

These apparently simple requirements have given rise to some difficult legal issues, including the definition of "household," compliance with "targeting" requirements, equitable treatment of owners and renters, and application of the income-disregard provisions to various combinations of benefits.

8.3.2 "Household" As Determination of Eligibility

8.3.2.1 Definition of Household

One critical eligibility issue arises from a discrepancy between a state program's definition of "household" and that of the LIHEAP statute. The definition of the term "household" is important to the receipt of LIHEAP for two reasons. First, only eligible households can participate in the program.[76] Secondly, the level of assistance is determined by consideration of family size and household income.[77] Under the federal LIHEAP statute, a household is defined as

year 2009 appropriations act containing LIHEAP funding); Pub. L. No. 111-117, 123 Stat. 3034 (Dec. 16, 2009) (fiscal year 2010 consolidated appropriations act containing LIHEAP funding).

67 National Ctr. for Appropriate Tech., LIHEAP Clearinghouse, State Percent of Poverty Guidelines for LIHEAP Components, *available at* www.liheap.ncat.org/tables/FY2011/POP11.htm.

68 U.S. Dep't of Health & Human Servs., Division of Energy Assistance, LIHEAP Home Energy Notebook for FY 2008, fig. 3-20 (May 2010).

69 U.S. Dep't of Health & Human Servs., Division of Energy Assistance, LIHEAP Home Energy Notebook for FY 2008, fig. 3-11 (May 2010).

70 This LIHEAP eligibility provision appears to be unaffected by the change from AFDC to TANF. TANF is a block grant program. States are permitted but not required to provide emergency utility assistance under TANF.

71 42 U.S.C. § 8624(b)(2).

72 42 U.S.C. § 8624(b)(5) (as amended in 1994).

73 42 U.S.C. §§ 8624(b)(5), (b)(8)(A).

74 42 U.S.C. § 8624(b)(8)(B).

75 42 U.S.C. § 8624(b)(13).

76 Eligibility is defined by each state within the parameters of 42 U.S.C. § 8624(b)(2) (regarding categorical and income eligibility of households) and other provisions of the statute, all of which refer to "low-income" households.

77 The state shall "provide, in a timely manner, that the highest level of assistance will be furnished to those households which have the lowest incomes and the highest energy costs or needs in relation to income, taking into account family size. . . ." 42 U.S.C. § 8624(b)(5) (as amended in 1994).

"any individual or group of individuals who are living together *as one economic unit* for whom residential energy is customarily purchased in common or who make undesignated payments for energy in the form of rent."[78] Since states are given broad discretion in administering LIHEAP, some states alter this definition in a way that can negatively impact low-income consumers.

8.3.2.2 Unrelated Boarders

For example, in *Mitchell v. Perales*,[79] the plaintiff claimed that New York's definition of household conflicted with the federal definition by "including the income of an applicant's roomer or boarder in that applicant's income for purposes of determining eligibility."[80] The plaintiff had been denied LIHEAP benefits because, instead of using her income alone to determine eligibility, the state also included the income of her boarder, which put her above the eligibility limit, even though this boarder was unrelated to her and she received no support from him other than payment of rent. This type of income determination was made possible under New York's definition of "household" as:

> all individuals residing in a dwelling unit for which residential space heating is provided by a single heating system and who share common bath and kitchen facilities. For residential dwelling units in multiple-family dwellings, all persons residing in any one unit are considered part of a single household for HEAP purposes.[81]

Unfortunately, the district court denied the plaintiff's request for a preliminary injunction, in part because the regular LIHEAP benefits for that fiscal year had been exhausted, as a result of which the harm claimed by the plaintiff had already transpired.[82]

The Vermont Supreme Court struck down a similar definition, which treated roomers and boarders as part of a "fuel household" regardless of whether they were part of an "economic unit."[83] The court looked to cases defining "economic unit" for purposes of food stamp eligibility.

78 42 U.S.C. § 8622(5) (emphasis added).

79 1988 U.S. Dist. LEXIS 3969 (N.D.N.Y. May 4, 1988).

80 *Id.* at 5, 6.

81 *Id.* at 3.

82 *Id.* at 11. *But see* Mitchell v. Hayt, No. 88-CV-382, slip op. at 20, 21 (N.D.N.Y. Dec, 1988) (fuel-assistance program definition of household that automatically included the income of all persons occupying dwelling unit violated 42 U.S.C. § 8624(b)(5)), *cited in* Dutton v. Dep't of Soc. Welfare, 721 A.2d 109, 113 (Vt. 1998).

83 Dutton v. Dep't of Soc. Welfare, 721 A.2d 109 (Vt. 1998).

8.3.2.3 Separate Living Quarters

In another case, *Brown v. Maine Division of Community Services*,[84] plaintiffs contended that the state's definition of household was more restrictive than that found in the federal Act. Under the state LIHEAP rules, the definition of household included a definition of "separate living quarters," which referred to who may not live in a household and how "separate" quarters must be accessed from the outside.[85] Under this definition, the plaintiffs, who operated as separate economic units but lived in quarters that did not qualify as "separate quarters" under Maine rules, were denied LIHEAP benefits. The parties settled the case by entering into a consent decree in which it was agreed that, while structural characteristics of a building may be one of the relevant criterion used to determine if individuals comprise an "economic unit," it will not be "per se determinative of whether there are separate households within the buildings."[86]

8.3.2.4 Strategies

Advocates challenging a state's definition of household as violating LIHEAP should look to the language of the Act as well as its legislative history. The definition of "household" in the LIHEAP authorizing statute means "any individual or group of individuals who are living together as one economic unit for whom residential energy is customarily purchased in common or who make undesignated payments for energy in the form of rent."[87] In the Act's legislative history, Congress clarified what it meant by individuals "living together as one economic unit":

> In determining what income should be considered in measuring a household's income eligibility for assistance, [Congress] intends that total household cash from all sources be considered—excluding what the State determines as reasonable allowances for income over which the household has no control or does not actually receive. . . .[88]

Thus, advocates could stress that, while other individuals might live with their client, their client has no control over any income except his or her own. The client does not actually receive any of the individuals' income (except rent or room and board, if applicable). Since their client has no control over this money, it should not be considered when deciding LIHEAP eligibility.

The definition of household was amended in 1981[89] and, as cited in *Dutton*, the Senate sponsor of the amendment

84 No. CV-83-276 (Me. Aug. 23, 1983).

85 *Id.* at 2.

86 *Id.*

87 42 U.S.C. § 8622(5).

88 S. Rep. No. 378, at 11 (1979).

89 Prior to 1981, the LIHEAP statute defined household as "all individuals who occupy a housing unit." Pub. L. No. 97-35

explained that the definition of household needed to be changed because "the definition that is now in the Low Income Home Energy Act does not adequately address the needs of low-income owners who have lodgers living in their homes. There was no intent of Congress to exclude these persons and this amendment would cover them by redefining households. . . ."[90]

Advocates should also look at other low-income federal benefit programs to see how "household" is defined and how this definition is interpreted. The legislative history of LIHEAP encourages such comparison: "[Congress] intends this household definition to be comparable to the household definition used for the Food Stamp Program, including the exclusion of residents of institutions, except that roomers and boarders would, under this Act, be treated as renters."[91]

Generally speaking, under the Food Stamp Program,[92] "individuals living together constitute a single food stamp household if they customarily purchase food and prepare meals in common."[93] Under these rules, almost all co-residents, including roomers and live-in attendants, may apply and be treated as separate households as long as they purchase food and prepare meals separately.[94] However, this program makes boarders ineligible for food stamps unless they apply with the household with whom they are boarding.[95]

As the legislative history (stated directly above) shows, Congress intended the definition of a LIHEAP "household" to be comparable to the Food Stamp "household" except in its treatment of boarders and roomers, signaling that they did not intend for this group of individuals to be excluded from eligibility. Advocates, in comparing "household" definitions, should emphasize that the distinguishing factor in determining eligibility for food stamps is whether individuals' incomes are co-mingled in buying food. Following the reasoning of this definition, eligibility for LIHEAP should be based on whether individuals are combining incomes to pay for energy bills. Any state definition that fails to distinguish households according to this "one economic unit" criterion is violating LIHEAP by being more restrictive than the Act allows: "Each state plan shall include assurances that eligibility standards and application and eligibility certification procedures will be no more restrictive than those established by the Secretary under the Act."[96]

§ 2603(2)(a), 95 Stat. 893, 894 (1981).

90 Dutton v. Dep't of Soc. Welfare, 721 A.2d 109, 113 (Vt. 1998); 127 Cong. Rec. 26234 (1981).

91 Dutton v. Dep't of Soc. Welfare, 721 A.2d 109 (Vt. 1998).

92 The Food Stamp Program is now called the Supplemental Nutrition Assistance Program, or SNAP.

93 U.S. House Ways & Means Comm., 2000 Green Book, WMCP 106-14, at 870, 871 (2000).

94 *Id.*

95 *Id.* at 876.

96 S. Rep. No. 378, at 20 (1979).

8.4 Targeting of Benefits

The LIHEAP authorizing statute requires states to "target" assistance to those most in need; that is, the highest level of assistance must be furnished to those households with the lowest incomes and the highest energy costs or needs.[97] Although states must make assurances that they will meet the conditions enumerated in section 8624(b) of the Act, state programs may fail to do so.

A particularly disturbing example of a state's blatant failure to carry out the proportioning requirement was in the case of *Northern Kentucky Welfare Rights Association v. Jones*.[98] Under Kentucky's state LIHEAP plan, eligibility to participate in the subsidy component of the program was limited to only the elderly and the disabled. Many of the neediest households were thus excluded from receiving any subsidy assistance at all.[99] The court, following the precedent laid out in *Cabinet for Human Resources, Commonwealth of Kentucky v. Northern Kentucky Welfare Rights Association*,[100] dismissed the claim on jurisdictional grounds.[101] Although the substantive issue was never resolved by judicial remedy, Kentucky did voluntarily change its state plan so as to include eligible low-income households in accordance with the intention of the Act.[102]

A different targeting requirement was the subject of *Goodwin v. Perales*,[103] in which New York's highest court upheld a state Department of Social Services regulation that, in order to be eligible for emergency LIHEAP funds, the applicant had to be the tenant of record in addition to the customer of record. A tenant of record, under the regulation, was someone who had "primary responsibility for the payment of the monthly rent or mortgage for their dwelling unit."[104] The plaintiff applicant, who along with her three daughters lived with the homeowner and paid him rent, did not qualify even though the utility service was in her name, because the homeowner, and not the plaintiff, was the tenant of record.

The applicant challenged this regulation on the grounds that it violated both LIHEAP and the equal protection clause

97 42 U.S.C. § 8624(b)(5).

In 1994, this provision was amended so that "the highest level of assistance will be furnished to those households which have the lowest incomes and the highest energy costs or needs in relation to income, taking into account family size, except that the State may not differentiate in implementing this section between the households described in clause (2)(A) [categorical eligibility] and (2)(B) [income eligibility] of this subsection."

98 985 F.2d 561 (6th Cir. Jan 19, 1993) (unpublished; use FI CTA6 Rule 28 and FI CTA6 IOP 206 for rules regarding the citation of unpublished opinions).

99 *Id.* at 3.

100 954 F.2d 1179 (6th Cir. 1992).

101 Northern Ky. Welfare Rights Ass'n v. Jones, 1993 U.S. App. LEXIS 1327 (6th Cir. Jan. 19, 1993).

102 *Id.*

103 669 N.E.2d 234 (N.Y. 1996).

104 669 N.E.2d 234, 237 (N.Y. 1996).

of the United States Constitution. Though she was successful at the Appellate Division of the New York Supreme Court, the Court of Appeals reversed and upheld the "tenant of record" requirement against both challenges.

The court started its analysis with a discussion of *Rodriguez v. Cuomo*,[105] pointing out that the Second Circuit "read great significance into the block grant nature of the [LIHEAP] program. So do we."[106] From that philosophical vantage point, the court first addressed the plaintiff's contention that the DSS "tenant of record" requirement violated LIHEAP. The court held that the rule, professed to ensure that DSS made payments only to those most in need of them, was fully consistent with LIHEAP's purpose of assisting those who have the highest energy costs or needs in relation to income and was "not unreasonable, irrational, or clearly erroneous."[107] The court noted that, under a parallel state program, the "tenant of record" requirement was added after local social services districts found themselves paying the utility costs not only of qualified applicants but also of individuals living with them, some of whom were better able to pay and might be otherwise ineligible for public assistance.[108] The tenant of record requirement was enacted to deter this sort of misuse of the system and to distribute state funds as carefully as possible. An important factor in the court's analysis was that the targeting requirement did not categorically exempt the plaintiff's household from receiving emergency utility assistance but simply meant that she was the wrong person to apply for it.[109]

Having upheld the DSS regulation against LIHEAP, the court gave short shrift to the plaintiff's equal protection argument that if she had been the wife of the homeowner she would satisfy the "tenant of record" requirement. The court ruled that DSS' decision to treat married and unmarried persons differently for purposes of determining eligibility for emergency utility benefits was not unreasonable. It was not the fact that she was married, but the fact that she was not the tenant of record, that caused her application to be rejected.

This case shows that, because LIHEAP's nature is that of a block grant of finite funds, courts may be inclined to give states more leeway in targeting benefits, so long as the state can come up with a plausible relationship between the targeting requirement and LIHEAP's purpose of assisting those who have the highest energy costs or needs in relation to income. To combat a targeting requirement, an advocate should distinguish *Goodwin* by showing that the requirement categorically excludes some of the most needy by creating conditions the household cannot possibly meet, thereby violating LIHEAP's purpose.

8.5 Equitable Treatment of Owners and Various Classes of Renters

8.5.1 Introduction

The LIHEAP authorizing statute requires equitable treatment of owners and various classes of renters.[110] One can easily determine how much a homeowner spends for energy. In the case of a tenant, all or part of the energy expenses may be included in rent. If the tenant resides in public or subsidized private housing, a utility allowance may be provided, or the amount he or she spends on utilities may be considered in determining how much income is available to pay rent. A state's efforts to simplify this problem—that is, by excluding all or some public housing tenants—may bear so heavily on some needy families as to violate the requirement of "equitable" treatment.[111]

8.5.2 Public Housing and Section 8 Tenants

8.5.2.1 General

One of the more common recurrent eligibility problems concerns tenants in public or publicly assisted housing who receive a utility allowance. Initial state practices in treatment of these households varied greatly, with some states excluding such tenants from eligibility and other states completely ignoring the existence of the utility allowance. The majority of states, however, provide partial benefits, often unrelated to actual heating expenses. By 2003, at least twenty-two states denied LIHEAP eligibility to subsidized housing residents whose energy costs were included in rent while other states allowed eligibility to those households if the tenants' rental costs were not a fixed percentage of their income or were greater than 30% of their income.[112] When subsidized housing tenants were responsible for some or all heating and cooling costs, several states treated these subsidized renters no differently than other renters, while other states provided reduced benefits.[113] Courts have split over whether the Department of Agriculture could count utility allowances as income, with some courts simply counting

105 953 F.2d 33 (2d Cir. 1992).

106 669 N.E.2d 234, 238 (N.Y. 1996).

107 *Id.*

108 *Id.* at 240.

109 *Id.* at 241.

The court noted that, in order to meet the DSS "customer of record" requirement, the utility service would have to be switched from the plaintiff's name to the homeowner's. *Id.* at 239.

110 42 U.S.C. § 8624(b)(8)(B).

111 *See* § 8.5.2.2, *infra*.

112 National Ctr. for Appropriate Tech., LIHEAP Clearinghouse, Subsidized and Rental Household Eligibility and Benefits, *available at* www.ncat.org/liheap/tables/subtable.htm.

113 *Id.*

them as income[114] and others allowing the utility allowance to be deducted from the calculation of income as long as the household shows it actually incurs out-of-pocket energy costs.[115] Section 927 of the Housing and Development Act of 1992 has been amended to include a special rule for LIHEAP that prohibits the automatic denial of LIHEAP eligibility for tenants responsible for paying some or all heating or cooling costs.[116]

8.5.2.2 Section 927 of the Housing and Development Act of 1992

In 1992, Congress enacted a provision in the Housing and Development Act that addresses this eligibility controversy directly. Section 927 stipulates:

> (a) ELIGIBILITY.—Tenants who—
>
> (1) are responsible for making out-of-pocket payments for utility bills; and
>
> (2) receive energy assistance through utility allowances that include energy costs . . . shall not have their eligibility or benefits under other programs designed to assist low-income people with increases in energy costs since 1978 (including but not limited to the Low-Income Home Energy Assistance Program) reduced or eliminated.
>
> (b) EQUAL TREATMENT IN BENEFIT PROGRAMS.—Tenants described in subsection (a) shall be treated identically with other households eligible for or receiving energy assistance, including in the determination of the home energy costs for which they are individually responsible and in the determination of their incomes.[117]

Basically, this provision states that tenants who have out-of-pocket expenses for utilities shall not have their benefits reduced or eliminated because they also receive assistance through a utility allowance. This amendment reaffirms the principles set forth in *Crawford v. Janklow* and *Clifford v. Janklow*.[118]

In *Crawford*, the Eighth Circuit Court of Appeals ruled that South Dakota's categorical exclusion of people living in subsidized or public housing violated section 8624(b)(5) of the LIHEAP Act:

> [I]f the states wish to narrow the number of persons eligible for assistance, they must exclude persons from the top of the class described by Congress, in terms of income and proportionate energy costs, rather than from the bottom.[119]

In *Clifford*, South Dakota's plan had been modified in accordance with *Crawford* so that subsidized or publicly housed persons were no longer excluded from eligibility. However, the revised plan acted to reduce the benefits these households received based solely on their subsidized/public housing status. The court found that this revised plan violated the income-disregard provision of LIHEAP,[120] which "clearly prohibits the states from reducing a household's entitlement to other forms of public assistance based on its receipt of LIHEAA funds."[121] Although the state's plan technically complied with the income-disregard provision by reducing LIHEAP benefits and not other program benefits, the court found that it contradicted the intent of the provision: "We see no logical reason why it should be permissible for a state to achieve a net effect contrary to Congress's intent merely by subtracting from one side of an equation instead of the other."[122] The *Clifford* court concluded the plan also violated LIHEAP because, by singling out and reducing benefits to subsidized housing residents, it failed to give the highest assistance to those with the lowest incomes and the highest energy costs.[123]

The enactment of section 927 was intended to clarify the decisions of both *Crawford* and *Clifford* by reaffirming that "housing assistance programs are intended to supplement, not replace, help that low-income people receive under energy assistance and other need-based programs."[124] However, it should be noted that controversy exists over section 927 and whether it should apply to all out-of-pocket utility bills, in particular those not related to heating and cooling, such as in the case of subsidized housing tenants who pay for their heat through their rent, as in *Rodriguez v. Cuomo*.[125]

8.5.2.3 Subsidized Housing Tenants Who Pay for Heat Through Rent

In *Rodriguez v. Cuomo*, the plaintiffs were all residents of government subsidized housing whose heat was included in their rent and whose income fell below 110% of the state's poverty level. While these residents were not billed separately for heat, they did pay separately for non-heat-related utilities.[126] An action was brought challenging a New York LIHEAP regulation that excluded from eligibility all tenants of subsidized housing with heat included in their rent.[127]

---

114 *E.g.*, Larry v. Yamauchi, 753 F. Supp. 784 (E.D. Ark. 1990).

115 *E.g.*, West v. Sullivan, 973 F.2d 179 (3d Cir. 1992).

116 Pub. L. No. 103-185, § 927(d), 107 Stat. 2244 (1993).

117 Housing and Development Act of 1992, Pub. L. No. 102-550, § 927(a), (b), 106 Stat. 3885(1992).
The LIHEAP statute includes the provisions of this law. 42 U.S.C. § 8624 (see note, *Clarifications on Utility Allowances*, at the end of the section).

118 138 Cong. Rec. 11,471 (Oct. 5, 1992) (floor statement by Rep. Maxine Waters).

119 Crawford v. Janklow, 710 F.2d 1321, 1327 (8th Cir. 1983).

120 42 U.S.C. § 8624(f)(1).

121 Clifford v. Janklow, 733 F.2d 534, 537 (8th Cir. 1984).

122 *Id.* at 538.

123 *Id.* at 541.

124 138 Cong. Rec. 11,471 (Oct. 5, 1992) (floor statement by Rep. Maxine Waters).

125 953 F.2d 33 (2d Cir. 1992).

126 *Id.* at 35.

127 *Id.*

The Second Circuit Court of Appeals ruled that the LIHEAP provision which states that no household may be excluded from eligibility if its income is less than 110% of poverty level does not ensure that all those falling within this class will receive benefits.[128] Rather, the clause provides that a household cannot be denied benefits if its income falls below 110% of the poverty level *and* it is able to meet other valid, non-income-based eligibility requirements, as determined by the state.[129] The court held that states have great discretion in determining these non-income-based eligibility requirements so long as they act to give the highest assistance to those with the lowest incomes and the highest proportionate energy costs.[130] Consequently:

> [t]he state may therefore rationally determine that tenants of government subsidized housing whose heat is included in their rent do not have "the lowest income and the highest energy costs in relation to income" in comparison with households not occupying such housing.[131]

With this analysis, the court upheld the New York regulation as a valid distribution criterion for LIHEAP funds.

8.5.2.4 Section 927 Amended by Congress

To address continuing concerns from states and others that the 1992 changes did not adequately address the issue of benefits for subsidized housing tenants, new language was added to section 927 in the Housing and Community Development Act of 1993.[132]

A new provision was added, section 927(d), which applies only to LIHEAP. The new "Special Rule for Low-Income Home Energy Assistance Program" applies to tenants in public or publicly assisted housing who are responsible for paying some or all of their heating or cooling costs. These tenants shall not have their eligibility automatically denied, but states are allowed to take into consideration the heating or cooling component of the utility allowance received. Under this revised provision, if states reduce the size of the LIHEAP benefits for these tenants due to the receipt of a utility allowance, the LIHEAP reduction must be "reasonably related" to the amount of the heating or cooling component of the utility allowance received.[133]

Furthermore, in considering the amount of benefits provided to households, states must consider tenants' out-of-pocket heating or cooling costs in relation to their incomes, within the benefit matrix used for all eligible households under 42 U.S.C. § 8624(b)(5).[134]

---

128 *Id.* at 37.

129 *Id.*

130 *Id.*

131 *Id.* at 41.

132 Pub. L. No. 103-185, § 1, 107 Stat. 2244 (1993).

The changes made by both the 1992 and 1993 Housing Acts are found in the historical and statutory notes section at the end of 42 U.S.C. § 8624 under *Clarification on Utility Allowances.*

133 Pub. L. No. 103-185 (codified at the note following 42 U.S.C. § 8624 and reprinted below).

> Clarification on utility allowances. Act Oct. 28, 1992, Pub. L. No. 102-550, Title IX, Subtitle A, § 927, 106 Stat. 3885 (effective and applicable on enactment, as provided by § 2 of such Act, which appears as 42 USCS § 5301 note); Dec. 14, 1993, Pub. L. No. 103-185, § 1, 107 Stat. 2244, provides:
>
> (a) Eligibility. Tenants who—
>
> (1) are responsible for making out-of-pocket payments for utility bills; and
>
> (2) receive energy assistance through utility allowances that include energy costs under programs identified in subsection (c); shall not have their eligibility or benefits under other programs designed to assist low-income people with increases in energy costs since 1978 reduced or eliminated, except as provided in subsection (d).
>
> (b) Equal treatment in benefit programs. Tenants described in subsection (a) shall be treated identically with other households eligible for or receiving energy assistance, including in the determination of the home energy costs for which they are individually responsible and in the determination of their incomes for any program in which eligibility or benefits are based on need, except as provided in subsection (d).
>
> (c) Applicability. This section applies to programs under the United States Housing Act of 1937 [42 U.S.C.S. §§ 1437, *et seq.*], the National Housing Act [12 U.S.C.S. §§ 1701, *et seq.*], section 101 of the Housing and Urban Development Act of 1965 [12 U.S.C.S. § 1701s and 42 U.S.C.S. § 1451], section 202 of the Housing Act of 1959 [12 U.S.C.S. § 1701q], and title V of the Housing Act of 1949 [42 U.S.C.S. §§ 1471, *et seq.*].
>
> (d) Special rule for Low-Income Home Energy Assistance Program. For purposes of the Low-Income Home Energy Assistance Program, tenants described in subsection (a)(2) who are responsible for paying some or all heating or cooling costs shall not have their eligibility automatically denied. A State may consider the amount of the heating or cooling component of utility allowances received by tenants described in subsection (a)(2) when setting benefit levels under the Low-Income Home Energy Assistance Program. The size of any reduction in Low-Income Home Energy Assistance Program benefits must be reasonably related to the amount of the heating or cooling component of the utility allowance received and must ensure that the highest level of assistance will be furnished to those households with the lowest incomes and the highest energy costs in relation to income, taking into account family size, in compliance with section 2605(b)(5) of the Low-Income Home Energy Assistance Act of 1981 (42 U.S.C. § 8624(b)(5)).

134 *See* 139 Cong. Rec. 9516–18 (Nov. 15, 1993) (statement of Congressman Gonzalez and additional members).

8.5.2.5 *Marbley v. Bane*: Interpretation of Section 927 As Amended

In *Marbley v. Bane*,[135] the issue addressed in *Rodriguez* was revisited in light of the 1993 clarification of section 927. The issue, as presented by the court, was whether the state violated federal statutory or constitutional law when it categorically denied HEAP (state energy assistance) to persons whose heating costs were embedded in the rent. In deciding this issue, the court took a narrow reading of the amendment,[136] which protects tenants "who are responsible for paying some or all heating or cooling costs." The court rejected the plaintiffs' argument that they were responsible for paying heating costs even though the costs were embedded in the rent. By relying on the definition in the LIHEAP statute of heating costs as "a source of heating," the court also rejected the argument that out-of-pocket payments to the electric company for warm air blower fixtures constitute heating costs, noting that "warm air blower fixtures channel and direct heat, and they distribute it, but they are not the source of it."[137] Thus, this court's interpretation was that the language in section 927(d) means that "only those tenants who pay separately for the costs of fueling a 'source of heating' are protected from automatic exclusion from HEAP."[138]

8.6 Income-Disregard Provision

8.6.1 General

The LIHEAP authorizing statute also contains directives that must be followed in administering the program. One provision indicates the intent that any LIHEAP assistance be supplemental to any other program benefits. This provision states that:

> [n]otwithstanding any other provision of law unless enacted in express limitation of this paragraph, the amount of any home energy assistance payments or allowances provided directly to, or indirectly for the benefit of, an eligible household under this subchapter shall not be considered income or resources of such household (or any member thereof) for any purpose under any Federal or State law, including any law relating to taxation, supplemental nutrition assistance program benefits, public assistance, or welfare programs.[139]

This section addresses the situation in which a LIHEAP recipient is otherwise eligible for *other* forms of government assistance (for example, SNAP benefits or a housing subsidy). In calculating the person's income to determine eligibility and benefit levels for the *other* program, if LIHEAP assistance is counted as part of that income the individual receives fewer benefits of another sort. This tends to nullify the effect of the LIHEAP assistance and is precisely the result that the income-disregard provision is trying to prevent.

This provision in effect prohibits other federal or state benefits from being reduced because a household receives or benefits from a LIHEAP payment. Most often, this issue arises with respect to the Supplemental Nutrition Assistance Program.[140] However, sometimes other programs are affected. For example, a New York district court relied on the income-disregard provision of the LIHEAP statute in holding that the state had improperly considered federal heating assistance in calculating eligibility for a state-run heating assistance program.[141]

8.6.2 Effect of "Income-Disregard" Provision on Distribution of Benefits

The method by which LIHEAP benefits are distributed can also cause some problems for low-income consumers. In most states, LIHEAP subsidy benefits will be paid directly to the utility supplier. Sometimes, however, LIHEAP benefits are given directly to the eligible households, thus making them responsible for payment to the energy vendor. This usually happens when a household receives emergency energy assistance from LIHEAP. This difference in how assistance is distributed has sometimes led to problems when the LIHEAP recipient also receives assistance from other assistance programs.

8.6.3 Vendor Payments

In *Schmiege v. Secretary of Agriculture of the U.S.*,[142] when food stamp assistance was determined, LIHEAP benefits, as mandated by the income-disregard provision in the Act, were not counted as income. However, those recipients who received the payments individually and then paid the utility vendor were able to declare an energy expense deduction while those whose assistance was paid directly to

135 Marbley v. Bane, 57 F.3d 224 (2d Cir. 1995), *overruled in part on other grounds*, Buckhannon Bd. & Care Home, Inc. v. West Va. Dep't of Health & Human Res., 532 U.S. 598 (2001) (attorney fees).

136 Pub. L. No. 103-185, § 1, 107 Stat. 2244 (1993) (codified at the note following 42 U.S.C. § 8624).

137 57 F.3d 224, 230 (2d Cir. 1995).

138 *Id.* at 231.

139 42 U.S.C. § 8624(f)(1) (as amended in 1994 and 2008).

140 *See* § 8.6.2, *infra* (discussion of income-disregard provision, including impact of new welfare reform legislation).

141 DeAllaume v. Perales, 701 F. Supp. 49 (S.D.N.Y. 1988).

142 693 F.2d 55 (8th Cir. 1982).

the utility vendor could not.[143] The end result of this disparate treatment was that those whose LIHEAP benefits went directly to the vendors received decreased food stamp assistance. The Eighth Circuit Court of Appeals agreed that this reduction in assistance based on the method of distribution ran contrary to the intent of Congress and that benefits should "be computed as if the total cost of the fuel, including the amount of assistance provided, had been paid by the household."[144]

8.6.4 Statutory Clarification

In the 1986 Reauthorization of LIHEAP, section 8624(f) was amended to clarify the income-disregard provision in regard to the Food Stamp Program. Section 8624(f)(2) states that:

> for purposes of determining any excess shelter expense deduction under [7 U.S.C. 2014(e)]—
>
> (A) the full amount of such payments or allowances shall be deemed to be expended by such household for heating or cooling expenses, without regard to whether such payments or allowances are provided directly to, or indirectly for the benefit of, such households; and
>
> (B) no distinction may be made among households on the basis of whether such payments or allowances are provided directly to, or indirectly for the benefit of, any of such households.

This provision explicitly states that no distinction may be made between those LIHEAP recipients who receive their benefits directly and those whose benefits are sent directly to the utility supplier. Thus, the full amount of these energy payments must be included in the energy expense deduction used in determining SNAP benefits.

8.7 LIHEAP's Explicit Remedies

8.7.1 Withholding Provision

The enacting statute contains a withholding provision that provides a means of enforcing its requirements. Specifically, the Secretary of Health and Human Services shall, "after adequate notice and an opportunity for a hearing . . . , withhold funds from any State which does not utilize its allotment substantially in accordance with the provisions of this subchapter and the assurances such State provided" under section 8624(b).[145] However, since LIHEAP is a block grant program, the Secretary would rarely take such a drastic measure so as to deprive a state and its residents of any funds whatsoever to help meet the costs of home energy bills.

143 *Id.* at 56.
144 *Id.*
145 42 U.S.C. § 8627(a)(1).

8.7.2 Administrative Review

Before choosing to litigate a LIHEAP claim, attorneys should remember the efficacy of administrative advocacy. Seeking to resolve your client's problem through the administrative channels already in place might prove successful while, at the same time, avoiding the cost and time associated with litigation.[146] The starting point is a review of the specific provisions of the state's LIHEAP plan. The LIHEAP statute requires the provision of a fair hearing procedure for applicants who have been denied benefits.[147] Also, some states may have their own regulations or appropriations directives under which the program operates, so it is important to find out if such authority exists and, if so, to review those as well. Finally, advocates should review their own state's administrative procedures act.

Becoming involved in the preparation of a state's plan can also be one of the most effective and efficient ways in which low-income advocates can work to avoid problems before they actually occur. As discussed below, there are challenges to using litigation to enforce the LIHEAP statute.

8.8 Enforcement of the LIHEAP Statute

The LIHEAP Act does not contain an express right of action permitting an individual to bring a federal action challenging denial of a LIHEAP application or the state's adoption of a regulation or state plan inconsistent with the Act.

In the past, some courts have implied a right of action under LIHEAP,[148] though others refused to do so.[149] However, in recent years, the Supreme Court has developed such a stringent test[150] for implying rights of action that, without directly saying so, the doctrine of implied rights of action is effectively dead except for those statutes (of which LIHEAP is not one) whose implied rights of action are well established.

146 Appendix C.3, *infra*, has a listing of state LIHEAP directors, which should be a good resource for the state plan.
147 42 U.S.C. § 8624(b)(13).
148 *See* Crawford v. Janklow, 710 F.2d 1321 (8th Cir. 1983).
149 *See* Cabinet for Human Res. v. Northern Ky. Welfare Rights Ass'n, 954 F.2d 1179 (6th Cir. 1992); Hunt v. Robeson County Dep't of Soc. Servs., 816 F.2d 150 (4th Cir. 1987).
150 *See, e.g.*, Alexander v. Sandoval, 532 U.S. 275 (2001).
Though the Supreme Court has not directly stated that it will no longer imply rights of action, Chief Justice Roberts made the point clear in his confirmation proceedings: "[The Supreme Court was] getting case after case after case. And they finally adopted an approach in the early 1980's that said, look, we're not going to imply rights of action anymore. Congress, if you want somebody to have a right of action, just say so." *Confirmation Hearing on the Nomination of John G. Roberts Jr. to Be Chief Justice of the United States Before the S. Comm. on the Judiciary*, 109th Cong. 294 (2005) (response of Judge John G. Roberts Jr. to question of Sen. Tom Coburn).

Advocates have also attempted to enforce LIHEAP using the Civil Rights Act of 1871, 42 U.S.C. § 1983, which creates a cause of action to challenge "the deprivation of any rights, privileges, or immunities secured by the Constitution and laws." In 1980, in *Maine v. Thiboutot*,[151] the Supreme Court held that the phrase "and laws" encompasses statutes. Section 1983 has become the primary vehicle for enforcing public benefit statutes, like the Medicaid Act, that do not contain an express right of action.

In past years, some courts have upheld LIHEAP claims under section 1983,[152] though others have rejected them.[153] Here too, however, the Supreme Court has created increasingly rigorous tests for deciding whether a statute creates "rights" enforceable under section 1983.[154] Section 1983 is still viable, for the moment, as a vehicle for enforcing some provisions (but not all) in statutes that create an entitlement program like Medicaid.[155]

However, LIHEAP is not a mandatory federal program and individuals have no right to LIHEAP funding. Moreover, the statute gives states a great deal of discretion in the administration of the program. Therefore, it is unlikely that a section 1983 claim under the LIHEAP Act would survive today.[156] Moreover, five of the current Supreme Court justices have indicated a willingness to effectively overturn *Thiboutot* by rejecting use of section 1983 to enforce Spending Clause statutes like public benefits statutes.[157] LIHEAP advocates do not want to be the ones who bring a case that becomes a vehicle for ending enforcement of all public benefit statutes.

Thus, if a state denies an individual a LIHEAP grant, the primary mechanism for challenging that denial will be through the state's process for administrative and, if available, judicial review of that decision.[158]

Advocates may also participate in the state's process for developing its state plan under LIHEAP[159] and may have vehicles under state law for challenging the state's rulemaking.

Finally, if a state adopts rules that are inconsistent with the LIHEAP statute, it is possible to bring a claim under the Supremacy Clause of the U.S. Constitution on the grounds that the rules are preempted by the LIHEAP Act. Though preemption is usually a defense to a claim, the affirmative preemption cause of action is well established.[160] The Supreme Court has repeatedly upheld federal jurisdiction over claims seeking injunctive relief against state laws and regulations that are inconsistent with federal law[161] and has gone beyond jurisdiction to rule on the merits of such claims.[162] The Supreme Court has stated in dicta that preemption claims are viable even under statutes that are not enforceable through section 1983.[163]

Lower courts have upheld preemption challenges to state regulations adopted under federal public benefit statutes,[164] even when there is no cause of action under section 1983.[165] Thus, a preemption claim may be a viable way of enjoining a state LIHEAP regulation or policy that violates the federal statute.

---

151 448 U.S. 1 (1980).

152 *See* Kapps v. Wing, 283 F. Supp. 2d 866 (E.D.N.Y. 2003), *aff'd in part and rev'd in part*, 404 F.3d 105 (2d Cir. 2005) (declining to decide if LIHEAA created a private right of action enforceable through section 1983 and vacating that portion of the district court's declaratory judgment that pertained to section 8624(b)(13) relief); State Communities Aid Ass'n v. Regan, 112 A.D.2d 681 (N.Y. App. Div. 1985).

153 *See* Cabinet for Human Res. v. Northern Ky. Welfare Rights Ass'n, 954 F.2d 1179 (6th Cir. 1992); Hunt v. Robeson County Dep't of Soc. Servs., 816 F.2d 150 (4th Cir. 1987); Boyland v. Wing, 487 F. Supp. 2d 161 (E.D.N.Y. 2007) (finding *Cabinet for Human Resources* and *Hunt* cases persuasive and articulating specific reasons "that provide strong support for the conclusion that Congress did not intend to confer Section 1983-enforceable rights in the statute").

154 *See* Gonzaga Univ. v. Doe, 536 U.S. 273 (2002); Suter v. Artist M., 503 U.S. 347 (1992). *See also* City of Rancho Palos Verdes, Cal. v. Abrams, 544 U.S. 113 (2005) (rejecting section 1983 claim).

155 *See, e.g.*, Watson v. Weeks, 436 F.3d 1152 (9th Cir. 2006).

156 In recent years, courts have rejected many section 1983 claims. *See, e.g.*, Arrington v. Helms, 438 F.3d 1336 (11th Cir. 2006); Sanchez v. Johnson, 416 F.3d. 1051 (9th Cir. 2005); Caswell v. City of Detroit Hous. Comm'n, 418 F.3d 615 (6th Cir. 2005).

157 *See* Lauren K. Saunders, *Are There Five Votes to Overrule Thiboutot? The Threat to Enforcement of Federal Medicaid, Housing, Child Welfare, and Other Safety Net Programs*, Clearinghouse Rev. J. of Poverty L. & Policy 380 (Sept.–Oct. 2006).

158 *See* §§ 8.1.1, 8.7.2, *supra*.

159 *See* §§ 8.2.3, 8.2.4, *supra*.

160 *See* Lauren K. Saunders, *Preemption As an Alternative to Section 1983*, Clearinghouse Rev. J. of Poverty L. & Policy 705 (Mar.–Apr. 2005) (describing use of the preemption cause of action to enforce federal public benefit statutes). *See also* Rochelle Bobroff, *Section 1983 and Preemption: Alternative Means of Court Access for Safety Net Statutes*, 10 Loy. J. Pub. Int. L. 27 (Fall 2008).

161 *See, e.g.*, Verizon Md., Inc. v. Public Serv. Comm'n, 535 U.S. 635 (2002); Shaw v. Delta Air Lines, 463 U.S. 85, at 96 n.14 (1983).

162 *See, e.g.*, Watters v. Wachovia Bank, N.A., 550 U.S. 1 (2007); Arkansas Dep't of Health & Human Servs. v. Ahlborn, 547 U.S. 268 (2006) (state collection law preempted by federal Medicaid Act); Engine Mfrs. Ass'n v. South Coast Air Quality Mgmt. Dist., 541 U.S. 246 (2004); Shaw v. Delta Air Lines, 463 U.S. 85, (1983).

163 *See* Golden State Transit Corp. v. City of Los Angeles, 493 U.S. 103, 107, 119 (1989) (Kennedy, J., dissenting).

164 *See, e.g.*, Comacho v. Texas Workforce Comm'n, 408 F.3d 229 (5th Cir. 2005); Planned Parenthood Affiliates v. Engler, 73 F.3d 634 (6th Cir. 1996). *See also* Arkansas Dep't of Health & Human Servs. v. Ahlborn, 547 U.S. 268 (2006) (state collection law preempted by federal Medicaid Act).

165 *See* Independent Living Ctr. of S. Cal. v. Shewry, 543 F.3d 1050 (9th Cir. 2008); Lankford v. Sherman, 451 F.3d 496, 509–10 (8th Cir. 2006); Planned Parenthood of Houston & Southeast Tex. v. Sanchez, 403 F.3d 324 (5th Cir. 2005).

Chapter 9 Weatherization

9.1 Introduction

Home weatherization is a critical step towards making residential energy costs more affordable. Inefficient fuel consumption increases the energy burden of low-income households, which typically inhabit the oldest, most poorly weatherized structures in a community and must consume extra energy just to maintain a habitable temperature. Making these homes more energy efficient allows low-income households to reduce their energy consumption while enjoying the same level of heat, hot water, lighting, and other "end-uses" of gas and electricity as before.

There are three primary funding sources for low-income energy efficiency programs:

- Federal Department of Energy (DOE) Weatherization Assistance Program (WAP)
- Conservation set-asides from the Low Income Home Energy Assistance Program (LIHEAP)[1]
- Utility energy efficiency programs

9.2 Low-Income Weatherization Assistance Program (WAP)

9.2.1 *History and Overview of the Program*

Major oil price increases following the decontrol of oil in the 1970s significantly increased the cost of energy across the economy and substantially added to the "energy burden" (ratio of household energy expenses to household income) borne by low-income households. In 1976, Congress responded to this crisis by enacting the Energy Conservation and Production Act, which includes the Weatherization Assistance Program (WAP).[2] Throughout most of its history prior to 2009, the WAP was a modestly funded program to improve the energy efficiency of homes and apartments owned or rented by low-income households. Funding, which started at $27.5 million in 1977, quickly rose to $199 million in 1979 and generally kept in the range of $150 million to $240 million for the next thirty years.[3] Since the program's inception through 2009, at least 6.4 million houses have received weatherization services.[4] In 2009, the American Recovery and Reinvestment Act of 2009 allocated $5 billion to weatherization to create jobs and promote economic recovery.[5] Currently, there are approximately 38 million homes eligible for the WAP, 15 million of which are good candidates for weatherization.

The WAP is a block grant program, not an individual entitlement. Each state is granted a fixed amount, to be allocated among eligible households according to a state plan.[6] The WAP is administered by the states under the supervision of the U.S. Department of Energy. The states subcontract with local providers or grantees, such as community action agencies or other public or nonprofit agencies, which then enter into agreements with homeowners and landlords to complete the weatherization work. The grantee-landlord agreements spell out the terms under which the weatherization work will be performed and the obligations of the landlord following the weatherization work. These agreements are usually drafted by the state weatherization agency, which then provides them to its subcontractors.

---

1 Up to 15% of a state's LIHEAP block grant may be devoted to "low-cost residential weatherization or other energy-related home repair for low-income households," 42 U.S.C. § 8624(k)(1), although a state may request a waiver, allowing it to use up to 25% of its LIHEAP funds for weatherization, 42 U.S.C. § 8624(k)(2).

In recent years, Hawaii may be the only state that has not devoted any of its LIHEAP dollars to weatherization; approximately three dozen states devoted between 5% and 15% of their funds to weatherization, and a dozen other states devoted specific dollar amounts to weatherization. National Ctr. for Appropriate Tech., Percent LIHEAP Funds by Program Component, *available at* www.liheap.ncat.org/tables/FY2011/components.htm.

2 42 U.S.C. §§ 6861–6873.

3 U.S. Dep't of Energy, Weatherization Assistance Program Funding, *available at* www.waptac.org/data/files/website_docs/briefing_book/2_programfunding_final.pdf.

4 U.S. Dep't of Energy, Weatherization Assistance Program, *available at* www1.eere.energy.gov/wip/wap.html.

5 *Id.* The funding was included in Pub. L. No. 111-5, div. A, tit. IV, 123 Stat. 138 (Feb. 17, 2009).

6 *See* 74 Fed. Reg. 12535 (Mar. 25, 2009) (Department of Energy has expanded the definition of "state" to include the Commonwealth of Puerto Rico and other U.S. territories and possessions).

9.2.2 Program Eligibility

A family unit[7] is eligible for assistance under the WAP if the household income is at or below 200% of the federal poverty level.[8] Alternatively, a family unit can qualify if any of its members has received cash assistance payments under the Social Security Act or an applicable state or local program during the twelve-month period preceding the determination of that family unit's eligibility. A state may also choose to make all of its LIHEAP-eligible households eligible for the WAP.[9] In addition, the statute requires states to establish priorities, including methods to provide priority to elderly and disabled low-income persons.[10] Under the statute, whether to accord priority to families with young children or to "single-family or other high-energy-consuming dwelling units" is left to the discretion of the state.[11] However, the implementing regulations state that weatherization agencies must "implement procedures to ensure that . . . priority is given to . . . families with children . . . and households with a high energy burden."[12]

Obtaining assistance under the WAP is easier for low-income homeowners than it is for tenants, because all weatherization efforts in rented housing must be arranged through the landlord, whose written permission must be secured by the subgrantee agency.[13] With this permission, income-eligible tenants may receive weatherization services for their own units. Depending on the condition and size of the individual unit and the size of the housing complex, these weatherization activities may be sufficient to help reduce the tenant's energy bill.

If the tenant lives in a multi-unit dwelling, especially in a master-metered building, the weatherization contractor may find that the entire building needs to be weatherized (including, for example, the replacement or retrofit of the heating system). In that situation, the statute requires that not less than 66% (50% for duplexes and four-unit buildings) of the units in the landlord's building must be eligible for assistance, based on tenants' income, or will become eligible dwelling units within 180 days.[14]

On January 25, 2010, the Department of Energy issued a final rule to make it easier to determine whether certain multi-unit properties receiving assistance from the Department of Housing and Urban Development (HUD), the Low Income Housing Tax Credit Program, or certain United States Department of Agriculture (USDA) rural housing programs are income-eligible for the WAP.[15] This rule is based on the understanding that the vast majority of the residents in these assisted properties meet the WAP income eligibility criteria and that there are already income-verification procedures for these federal programs. The Department of Energy has coordinated with HUD and USDA to publish lists of multi-unit buildings meeting the income criteria for the WAP.[16] It is important for advocates to bear in mind that many of these same properties may be able to implement energy efficiency measures through use of HUD or USDA funds.

As discussed in § 9.2.5, *infra*, when rental units receive weatherization assistance, the weatherization agency must ensure that the benefit of the weatherization accrues primarily to the tenants.[17] In large multifamily properties, the owner often pays for the heat (and sometimes other utilities), and the primary benefit of weatherization—reduced energy bills—therefore accrues directly to the owner. The owner would therefore have to demonstrate how other substantial benefits accrue to the tenants in order to meet the requirement that the benefits of weatherization accrue primarily to the tenants. For example, the owner may show that a substantial portion of the energy savings will be directed toward new or expanded tenant services, improved security systems, or other capital improvements, after-school programs for residents, among other things. The preamble to this new rule includes some guidance on this requirement.[18] On April 8, 2010, the DOE provided much more detailed guidance on how to comply with the requirement that the benefits of weatherization in rental properties must primarily accrue to tenants.[19]

9.2.3 Assistance Provided

Allowable expenditures on "labor weatherization materials and related matters," previously limited to $2500 per dwelling unit, have been increased to $6500 per dwelling unit under the American Recovery and Reinvestment Act of 2009.[20] This $6500 cap includes (but is not limited to) the following:

7 Defined as "all persons living together in a dwelling unit." 10 C.F.R. § 440.3.

8 42 U.S.C. § 6862(7); 10 C.F.R. § 440.22.

9 42 U.S.C. § 6862(7); 10 C.F.R. § 440.22. *See, e.g.*, Idaho Admin. Code r. 16.004.16.100(01)(c).

10 42 U.S.C. § 6864(b)(2).

11 42 U.S.C. § 6864(b)(2).

12 10 C.F.R. § 440.16 (b).

13 10 C.F.R. § 440.22(b)(1).

14 10 C.F.R. § 440.22(b)(2). *Cf.* Tenn. Comp. R. & Regs. 1240-7-2-.01(3) (building containing more than four dwelling units not eligible for weatherization due to limited funds).

15 75 Fed. Reg. 3847 (Jan. 25, 2010).

16 Weatherization Program Notice 11-09, Updated Guidance on Eligible Multifamily Property Listings for Use in the Weatherization Assistance Program, *available at* www.waptac.org/data/files/website_docs/government/guidance/2011/wpn%2011-09.pdf.

17 42 U.S.C. § 6863(b)(5)(A); 10 C.F.R. § 440.22(b)(3)(i).

18 The relevant guidance appears at 75 Fed. Reg. 3853, 3854 (Jan. 25, 2010).

19 U.S. Dep't of Energy, Guidance Regarding Accrual of Benefits to Low-Income Tenants in Multi-Family Buildings Under the Weatherization Assistance Program, Weatherization Program Notice 10-15a, *reprinted at* appx. D.6.2, *infra*.

20 42 U.S.C. § 6865(c), *as amended by* Pub. L. No. 111-5, div. A, tit. IV, § 407(b), 123 Stat. 146 (Feb. 17, 2009).

(A) The appropriate portion of the cost of tools and equipment used to install weatherization materials for a dwelling unit;
(B) The cost of transporting labor, tools, and materials to a dwelling unit;
(C) The cost of having onsite supervisory personnel;
(D) The cost of making incidental repairs to a dwelling unit if such repairs are necessary to make the installation of weatherization materials effective; and
(E) The cost of making heating and cooling modifications, including replacement.[21]

Up to 10% may be devoted to administrative costs: 5% for the state and 5% for the subgrantee.[22] Up to 10% may be used for "low cost/no cost" weatherization activities, not to exceed $50 per dwelling unit.[23]

9.2.4 States' Annual Weatherization Plans

Federal regulatory standards regarding specific state program designs are minimal. States are required to design and submit annual "state weatherization plans."[24] The state plan is an integral part of a state's yearly application for WAP funding and must be prepared after notice and a public hearing.[25] The state plan must include, among other things, a production schedule; an estimate of the number of dwelling units to be weatherized; climatic conditions; type of work to be done; estimate of energy to be conserved; allocation among areas within the state; sources of labor; amount of non-federal and non-WAP federal resources being applied to weatherization; the state's definition of "low income"; and procedures to ensure that tenants will be protected.[26]

The regulations provide that, before submitting an application, a state "must provide at least ten days' notice of a hearing to inform prospective subgrantees, and must conduct one or more public hearings to receive comments on a proposed State plan."[27] Moreover, the proposed state plan must be made available to the public.[28]

The special problems of low-income tenants and the provisions for their protection are discussed below.

9.2.5 Applicability of the WAP to Tenants

9.2.5.1 Overview

Tenants as well as homeowners are clearly the intended beneficiaries of the Weatherization Assistance Program. In fact, the majority of income-eligible households are renters. Nonetheless, this group has not always been equitably served by federal weatherization money, relative to its size.[29] Some local administering agencies historically have been reluctant to put weatherization resources into rental units, because of their concern that the benefits from weatherization of rental units would ultimately accrue to the landlords and not to the tenants. Other agencies historically focused on single family homes and one- to four-unit rental properties because larger buildings often require a different set of skills and contractors.

In the absence of specific restrictions guarding against rent increases or evictions, tenants may be deprived of the benefits of weatherization or even left worse off than they were before the work was done. For individually metered units, in which tenants pay their own utility bills, landlords can raise the rent to reflect the enhanced habitability following weatherization, thus negating cost savings to the tenant. For master-metered units, in which the tenant pays for utilities as an indistinguishable part of the rent, the landlord (who pays for the utilities) may not pass any energy savings on to the tenants. Even worse, landlords may evict tenants or sell the property and thus take advantage of the increased value of the dwelling after weatherization.

The weatherization of renter-occupied housing thus poses unique challenges for WAP agencies. However, in recognition of this problem, states have adopted provisions for use in weatherization agreements that prohibit landlords from (1) raising rent for any reason for one to five years,[30] and (2) evicting the tenant from the weatherized unit without good cause.[31] States have also conditioned the sale of the weatherized property upon the buyer's agreement to comply with the weatherization agreement[32] and/or required the landlord to reimburse the weatherization agency for the costs of weatherization if the property is sold within a certain time

21 *Id. See, e.g.*, Harvey v. Fresno County Economic Opportunities Comm'n, 2005 WL 2108135 (Cal. Ct. App. Sept. 1, 2005) (discussing scope of allowable weatherization expenditures).
22 42 U.S.C. § 6865(a)(1).
23 10 C.F.R. § 440.20.
24 Requirements for a state weatherization plan are detailed in 10 C.F.R. § 440.14.
25 10 C.F.R. § 440.14(a).
26 10 C.F.R. § 440.22(b)(3)(i)–(iv); 10 C.F.R. §§ 440.14, 440.16.
27 10 C.F.R. § 440.14(a).
28 *Id.*

29 Tenants are unquestionably eligible for the WAP. 42 U.S.C. § 6863(b)(5); 10 C.F.R. § 440.22(b).
30 National Consumer Law Center, State Weatherization Landlord Tenant Agreements (June 26, 2009), *available at* www.nclc.org/images/pdf/energy_utility_telecom/weatherization/state_landlord_weatherization_agreements.pdf.
Washington's agreement prohibits rent increases for any reason for at least one year. Montana prohibits rent increases due to weatherization for five years.
31 *Id.* Alaska, Connecticut, Indiana, Kansas, Massachusetts, Michigan, Nevada, New Mexico, North Dakota, Wisconsin, and Wyoming are examples.
32 *Id.* Michigan is an example.

period.[33] Importantly, some weatherization agreements explicitly provide tenants with a right of enforcement.[34]

The recent Department of Energy rule to facilitate the income-eligibility determination with federally assisted multi-unit buildings also includes some guidance to the states in the preamble to the rule on how to show that the benefits of weatherization accrue primarily to the tenant.[35] Ever since the advent of the $5 billion in weatherization funding contained in the American Reinvestment and Recovery Act, the Department of Energy, along with the Department of Housing and Urban Development, have been striving to open up the WAP to owners of, and tenant living in, multifamily properties.[36]

9.2.5.2 Guidance Found in WAP Statute and DOE Regulations

The WAP statute, as amended during the 1990 reauthorization,[37] sets broad, general standards for tenant protection. States must ensure that:

(A) Benefits of weatherization assistance in connection with such rental units, including units in which the tenants pay for their energy through their rent, will accrue primarily to the low-income tenants residing in such units;

(B) For a reasonable period of time after weatherization work has been completed on a dwelling containing a unit occupied by an eligible household, the tenants in that unit (including households paying for their energy through their rent) will not be subjected to rent increases unless those increases are demonstrably related to matters other than the weatherization work performed;

(C) Enforcement of paragraph (B) is provided through procedures established by the state through which tenants may file complaints and owners, in response to such complaints, must demonstrate that the rent increase concerned is related to matters other than the weatherization work performed; and

(D) No undue or excessive enhancement will occur to the value of such dwelling units.

The current DOE regulations simply quote the statutory language, with the additional provision that states may seek landlord agreement to the placement of a lien or other contract restrictions, in order to protect the federal investment, and address the issues of eviction and sale of property.[38] Compliance with these standards is a "minimum program requirement" for states.[39]

DOE provided some additional guidance when the regulations were amended to conform to the statutory changes. In the comments preceding the 1993 regulations, DOE advised states to adopt a "comprehensive approach to weatherizing rentals" in order to meet their statutory obligations.[40] These suggestions were merely there to provide some direction to grantees and need not be accepted by the states. DOE further suggested that states may want to consider alternative dispute resolution procedures to help them enforce their obligations.[41]

DOE's 2011 weatherization grant guidance[42] notes that states were previously required to develop "rental procedures" that address the needs of tenants in rental housing and were "encouraged to open a dialog with their local agencies to ensure that the procedures are both understood and attainable." However, the same guidance notes that these rental procedures "are not a part of the application [to DOE]."[43] The Guidance encourages states to "address their rental procedures including any changes from the previous year, in a public hearing forum," particularly the required annual hearing on the state plan.[44]

9.2.5.3 State Plan Regulation of Tenant Weatherization

The somewhat skeletal federal provisions concerning weatherization of rented dwellings leave states with broad discretion to craft strong tenant protection plans. The design of the state plan is an ideal starting point for advocacy on mandatory tenant protections. Through the notice and public hearing procedures,[45] low-income tenants and their advocates can argue for the necessary protections to ensure both that tenants are accorded their fair share of WAP benefits and that they are provided with adequate guarantees that these benefits will accrue to them and not to landlords. Low-income advocates should maintain contact with the

33 *Id.* Idaho and Kentucky are examples.

34 *Id.* Alaska, Massachusetts, and Michigan are examples.

35 75 Fed. Reg. 3851–3854 (Jan. 25, 2010). *See also* U.S. Dep't of Energy, Updated Guidance on Eligible Multifamily Property Listings for Use in the Weatherization Assistance Program, Weatherization Program Notice 11-09, *available at* www.waptac.org/data/files/website_docs/government/guidance/2011/wpn%2011-09.pdf.

36 *See, e.g.*, HUD-DOE Weatherization Partnership: Streamlining Weatherization Assistance in Affordable Housing (Mar. 5, 2010), *available at* http://portal.hud.gov/hudportal/documents/huddoc?id=factsheet_doe_weatherize_3.pdf.

37 42 U.S.C. § 6863(b)(5).

38 10 C.F.R. § 440.22(b), (c).

39 10 C.F.R. § 440.16(*i*).

40 *See* Notice of Final Rulemaking, Supplementary Information, 58 Fed. Reg. 12522 (1993).

41 *Id.*; 10 C.F.R. § 440.22(e).

42 *See* Weatherization Program Notice 011-1 § 5.4, *available at* www.waptac.org (click on "Rules and Guidance" tab, select the "2011 Program Guidance" weblink, then click on the document with the notice number "WPN 11-01").

43 *Id.*

44 *Id.*

45 10 C.F.R. § 440.14.

relevant state agency and add their names to the notice list for state plans or any other rulemaking concerning the state weatherization program. The following sections review the issues that must be addressed in state plans and cite examples of states that have strong tenant protections.

9.2.5.4 Rent Increases Following Weatherization

Weatherization increases a rental unit's value, and landlords may respond by raising the rent, meaning that only the landlord, not the tenant, would benefit from the weatherization subsidy. Historically many states dealt with this problem by requiring rent freezes after weatherization. These freezes were often inadequate because they were generally for a limited duration (one year) and because landlords could justify rent increases by citing, as opposed to demonstrating, other reasons for increasing the rents (for example, increased maintenance, capital improvements, and prevailing property values).

The current statutory language mandates a stricter standard. States must provide protection from landlord rent increases that are not "*demonstrably related* to factors other than the weatherization work performed."[46] This statutory language, repeated in DOE's comments and final regulations, is a major improvement over the prior, vague standard that rents could not be increased "because of the increased value of dwelling units *due solely to* weatherization assistance" (emphasis added).

The new language puts the burden on landlords, whose rent increases may be challenged, to demonstrate the basis for the increase.[47] DOE's regulations do not, however, specify what will justify rent increases. Increased property taxes or unforeseen and unavoidable major repairs to the property, which are unrelated to the weatherization work, are two obvious justifications.[48]

Another consideration for states is the length of time during which tenants should be protected from unjustified rent increases. The 1990 statute provided no time limit on the protections to be afforded tenants except to say that rents shall not be increased "for a reasonable period of time," absent a demonstration that the increase is related to matters other than the weatherization work performed. States must set more specific standards, by regulation or in the provisions of weatherization grantee-landlord agreements, to provide effective guidance to their local contracting agencies and participating landlords.

The guiding statutory principle on this and other issues is that tenants are to be the primary (clearly not the sole) beneficiaries of the weatherization work[49] and that there shall be no undue or excessive enhancement to the value of the weatherized property.[50] The benefits, financial and otherwise, of the weatherization resources invested in a particular property accrue over a number of years; therefore, the protections provided for the tenants should also last for more than just one or two years.

States should set some minimum standards, including, as discussed above, protections for tenants from unreasonable rent increases and evictions and restrictions on the sale of weatherized property for more than one year while providing some flexibility for local subgrantees to attach additional protections and/or to increase the duration of time for the restrictions set forth in the agreement. The local subgrantees will have a better sense of how far they can go in protecting tenants under these statutory provisions while maintaining the interest of landlords in having their properties weatherized.[51]

With the above in mind, states could set restrictions on rent increases for a *minimum* of between two to five years, as New York State has done,[52] but allow local subgrantees to add an additional period of years to the protected period of time if the property weatherized contains more than a certain number of units or if other factors are present. The counterbalance to a longer protected period for tenants is the right of landlords to raise rents and, if they are challenged, to demonstrate that the increases are unrelated to the weatherization work performed.

46 42 U.S.C. § 6863(b)(5)(B) (emphasis added).

47 Increased rents following weatherization activities must be challenged by tenants in order to require landlords to demonstrate the basis for such increases.

48 *See, e.g.*, Michigan Weatherization Assistance Program, Landlord Agreement ¶ 2 (effective Jan. 1, 1997) ("significant increases in actual operating costs"); New York 1–4 Unit Owner Agreement ¶ 3 (rev. May 1999) ("actual increases in property taxes or the costs of improving the premises, not resulting from this agreement"); Vermont Weatherization Letter Series 96-5 (matters other than weatherization work performed, including but not limited to "increases in property taxes, insurance, and owners' costs for later building improvements and for operations, maintenance and services such as trash hauling, snow removal, electricity or fuel").

49 42 U.S.C. § 6863(b)(5)(A).

50 42 U.S.C. § 6863(b)(5)(D).

51 *See* § 9.2.5.1, *infra* (New York and other states that have taken this path).

52 N.Y. State Div. of Hous. & Cmty. Dev., New York State Weatherization Assistance Program, Policy and Procedure Manual 88–89 (2009) (minimum two-year term if tenant pays for heat; minimum five-year term if landlord pays for heat), *available at* www.dhcr.state.ny.us/Publications/Weatherization Manual/WAP_Manual.pdf.

While New York state apparently no longer posts its owner agreements on-line, a version of the multifamily agreement (possibly not the current version) can be found at www.enterprisecommunity.org/training_and_events/live_online_events/documents/040909_wap/Owner%20Agreement%20Multi-Family.pdf. *Cf.* Idaho Admin. Code r. 16.04.16.100(02)(d) (rent may not be raised, "for a reasonable period of time," as a result of increased value of unit due solely to weatherization); 12-3-300 Vt. Code R. 2 (titled "Rent Stabilization Agreement"; term of landlord "agreements shall range from 1–10 years" and shall be "at least 2 years" if the work "involve[s] replacement of a heating system").

9.2.5.5 Evictions

Landlords prevented from raising rents may respond instead by evicting the tenant. In the final regulations, DOE focused on the issue of eviction from a weatherized unit, but only in the course of addressing how states must protect the federal (weatherization) investment and the issue of the sale of weatherized property. According to DOE, states "may seek landlord agreement to placement of a lien or to other contractual restrictions."[53]

The most reasonable way to deal with the issue of eviction, however, is to apply the same type of protection against evictions as is applied in prohibiting unreasonable rent increases that may act to obviate the benefits of weatherization for the tenant, the intended primary beneficiary. As DOE suggested, there should be a clear contractual restriction on evictions of tenants in weatherized units. Based on the above discussion, any such restriction should apply for a specified period of time. These restrictions would not prohibit a landlord from evicting a tenant for cause. Michigan, for example specifically allows evictions for nonpayment of rent, maintaining a nuisance or illegal business, serious property damage, and violation of terms of lease.[54]

9.2.5.6 Rent for New Tenant When Existing Tenant Vacates

When the existing tenant, for whatever reason, vacates the weatherized unit, the owner will benefit from the windfall from weatherization if the owner can raise the rent for a new tenant. The statute does not specifically address this issue, but the statutory framework and the legislative history of the DOE WAP statute suggest the intent that any restrictions in grantee-landlord agreements should run with the weatherized units and not simply disappear if an eligible tenant moves out during the period of protection provided under the agreement.

The rationale for extending any restrictions in grantee-landlord agreements to new leases in weatherized units is simple. If new tenants move into a weatherized unit during the protected period and are charged a higher rent than the previous low-income tenant, then the landlord becomes the primary beneficiary of the weatherization. The grantee-landlord agreements should also state clearly that landlords are required to continue to rent such units to eligible low-income tenants.[55]

Occasionally landlords have to make major capital expenditures in improving a unit that was vacant while the weatherization work was being performed or in improving a unit that has become vacant during the protected period. In these situations, if a complaint is raised about an increase in the rent, the landlord need only demonstrate that the increase resulted from factors unrelated to the weatherization of the unit.

9.2.5.7 Sale of Weatherized Property

The weatherization statute clearly provides that DOE must provide guidance to the states on ensuring that the "benefits of weatherization" of rental units "will accrue primarily to the low-income tenants."[56] The regulations provide that:

> [i]n order to secure the Federal investment . . . and address the issues of eviction from and sale of property receiving weatherization materials . . . , States may seek landlord agreement to placement of a lien or to other contractual restrictions.[57]

The rationale regarding protections against unjustified evictions applies also to the sale of properties following the completion of the weatherization work. Without some specific agreement that sets restrictions on such sales for a specified period, only the landlord will benefit from the expenditure of federal resources on his or her property. Placing a lien should be considered as an extreme option for protecting the interests of tenants. States should consider adding other options as well, which would be triggered prior to any lien provisions. For example, states could limit sale of such properties, for a specified period of time, *unless* the new owner explicitly agrees to the terms of the weatherization agreement signed by the previous owner.[58] States could also consider attaching a covenant running with the property

---

53 10 C.F.R. § 440.22(c).

54 Michigan Weatherization Assistance Program, Landlord Agreement ¶ 4 (effective Jan. 1, 1997).

Massachusetts allows eviction for "good cause related to the tenant," that is, serious or repeated violations of terms of tenancy. Massachusetts Standard Weatherization Agreement ¶ 8(b).

North Carolina allows eviction for just cause. North Carolina Weatherization Assistance Program, Building Owner Agreement (1–7) Dwelling Units.

Vermont's Weatherization Letter Series 96-5 forbids landlords to "evict or otherwise remove existing low-income tenants who meet their obligations as tenants."

55 Many states, including Michigan, New York, North Carolina, and Vermont, have considered this issue in their state's building owner agreements.

56 42 U.S.C. § 6863(b)(2)(B), (5)(A).

57 10 C.F.R. § 440.22(c).

58 Most of the local weatherization agencies in Massachusetts employ an owner agreement form that requires the owner, in the event the property is subsequently sold, to obtain the buyer's consent to comply with the rent increase and eviction restrictions of the underlying weatherization agreement or that requires the selling owner to repay the weatherization agency for the cost of the work performed. Vermont requires that "a suitable lien agreement . . . shall be utilized" to secure "funds recapture" if the "rental property shall be sold within three years of the completion of the project," according to an amortizing recapture schedule. 12-3-300 Vt. Code R. 3.

as a way of ensuring that no sale will occur without consideration of the protections set forth in the grantee-landlord agreement. Filing a copy or synopsis of the agreement with the county clerks' office could also ensure that prospective buyers would have notice, during title searches, of the temporary restrictions applying to the property. As with rent increases and evictions, some period of time longer than just one to two years for restrictions on the sale of weatherized properties would be appropriate.

9.2.5.8 Protecting Tenants Who Pay for Heat Through Rent

The weatherization statute and DOE's implementing regulations are both clear that the benefits of weatherization in rental properties must "accrue primarily to the low-income tenants residing in such units," including "units where the tenants pay for their energy through their rent."[59] Unlike tenants who pay for heat separately from their rent, these tenants will not be "the primary beneficiaries of the weatherization," unless some affirmative steps are taken to accomplish that end.

There are a number of options to ensure that the benefits of the weatherization work performed will accrue primarily to these tenants. Landlords can be required to roll back rents, for some fixed period of time, based on the value of the weatherization work and, to some extent, on the energy savings resulting from the weatherization (although the latter may not show up on the landlord's utility bills immediately). Alternatively, landlords could be required to provide quarterly or annual rebates, also for some specified period of time; this would further ensure that there is no unjust enrichment to the value of the landlords' property due solely to the weatherization work performed. At a minimum, states could follow the lead of Vermont, Massachusetts, and New York in considering extending protections against rent increases, evictions, and the like for a longer period of time to tenants who pay for heat through their rent.[60]

9.2.5.9 Owner Agreements

A key element in any state's weatherization efforts is to include strong protection for tenants in owner-agency contracts and flexibility for the local agency officials to add additional protections if they consider them necessary. Another important element is a system for enforcing landlord compliance with these agreements. Massachusetts and New York, among others,[61] provide such protection.

While states may also require the signing of owner-tenant agreements whenever rental property is weatherized, it is most important to include tenant protections in the agreement signed between the state grantee's subcontractor—the local weatherization agency that actually obtains the owner's agreement to perform the weatherization work—and the owner. In most cases, these agreements are drafted by DOE's grantees—the states—that have the primary responsibility for enforcing these protections and other requirements under the statute. The grantees may even have written standards or guidelines governing the weatherization activities so that these agreements become a routine part of the whole weatherization effort.

When strong tenant protections are not already in place, advocates can urge the state grantee to review currently used grantee-owner agreements, or other appropriate documents, to see how they can be strengthened. DOE's regulations specifically allow contractual restrictions, including the placement of liens on the owner's property.[62] Given this authority, states can devise creative means of protecting tenants through agreements that owners must sign. Low-income tenants and their advocates should work with their states to ensure that the grantee-owner agreements address the various issues set forth above (rent freezes, rent rollbacks, evictions, restrictions on sale of weatherized property, and duration for these various protections).

9.2.5.10 Two Instructive State Plans: Massachusetts and New York

In Massachusetts, the rent freeze is ordinarily for one year. A longer freeze may be imposed or owner contribution required at the discretion of the subgrantee. Additional limitations are placed on rent increases when heat is included in the rent. Property owners must agree either (a) not to sell the property unless the buyer agrees to the weatherization agreement or (b) to repay the agency at time of sale for labor and materials installed. The tenant is a party to the agreement, which may be enforced by the tenant or the subgrantee. Community action agency officials, who are the local weatherization providers, have considerable flexibility in adding additional provisions to owner-agency contracts to improve tenant protections when they see fit. Massachusetts

59 42 U.S.C. § 6863 (b)(5)(A). *See also* 10 C.F.R. § 440.22(b)(3)(i).

60 *See* Massachusetts Standard Weatherization Agreement ¶ 10 (no rent increase for one year, not more than specified percentage per year—preferably based on Consumer Price Index—for negotiated period of years, depending on amount of work done, number of units weatherized, and expected savings to owner).

Vermont Weatherization Letter Series 96-5 recommends a term of three to ten years, depending on the amount of the owner co-payment. When tenants pay for heat separately, the recommended term is one to five years.

61 Massachusetts, Michigan, Minnesota, and New York have comprehensive landlord-agency agreements that seem to be successful in protecting renters without discouraging landlord participation in weatherization programs. New York's standard multifamily and one- to four-unit owner agreements are included on the companion website to this treatise.

62 10 C.F.R. § 440.22 (c) ("States may seek landlord agreement to placement of a lien or to other contractual restrictions").

has one of the country's most extensive monitoring programs for owner compliance with weatherization agreements.[63]

The New York State Weatherization Program ensures substantial protections for tenants. The program guidelines require a two- to five-year freeze on rents after weatherization[64] and, for many of the buildings served, a mandatory contribution to weatherization work. Tenants are stated to be "the intended third party beneficiaries of the agreement" and may enforce it. Local flexibility is again an important aspect of the state's program.

New York's program and its grantee-owner agreements have been used as a model by other states.

9.2.5.11 Alternative Dispute Resolution Issues

The DOE regulations advise that "[s]tates should consider requiring use of alternative dispute resolution procedures including arbitration."[65] Although states may want to make available such procedures *in addition to* state court options as an enforcement mechanism, such procedures *must not* be used as the only option available for tenants to enforce their rights under these agreements.

9.2.5.12 Other Execution, Monitoring, and Enforcement Issues

The 1990 statutory changes require that DOE must offer guidance to states in establishing the requisite procedures to provide tenant protections and "a process for monitoring compliance" with the states' obligations under these amendments.[66] The regulations, however, fail to address the question of how states should monitor compliance with the new grantee-owner agreements. In the absence of additional steps, these new agreements, by themselves, will not accomplish the goal of ensuring that the tenants are the main beneficiaries of weatherization activities. Low-income tenants and their advocates should work with their state weatherization agencies to encourage additional steps to help ensure enforcement of these provisions, such as:

- Adding specific language in the grantee-owner agreement, or other appropriate documents, that clearly give tenants rights under the contract, rather than relying on the assumption that courts will rule that tenants are protected as third-party beneficiaries.[67] This would be an important addition since tenants will likely be the main enforcing parties of the statutory and agreement protections.
- Stating clearly that state weatherization agencies also have the right to enforce the weatherization agreement provisions, even if they are not expected to be the primary enforcers of these agreements. While states are not required by statute or in the legislative history to review every agreement or to ensure that every rental unit weatherized with federal funds is in compliance with the terms of the agreement, it is not unreasonable to expect that states would conduct random checks to ensure that the protections they are obligated to enforce are being met. If they find violations of such agreements, the states should enforce such agreements.
- Requiring "effective and explicit" notice to tenants of the contract obligations undertaken by the owner regarding rent increases, evictions, sale of the property, and the tenants' rights to seek enforcement of these obligations.[68] For example, a copy of the grantee-owner agreement (in plain English, if possible) should be given to the tenants in a rental unit being weatherized, and it should be reviewed and discussed with the tenants at that time. Effective notice may also require copies of the agreement be posted in common areas (when a whole building is being weatherized) during the time of the weatherization and during the protected period. Bilingual notices should also be considered.

If a state is willing to take these additional steps, among others, the tenant protection provisions of the 1990 reauthorization of the WAP will be closer to becoming a reality.

9.2.6 Application of Davis-Bacon Rules to WAP

With the passage of the American Recovery and Reinvestment Act on February 17, 2009,[69] the prevailing wage and benefits provisions of the Davis-Bacon Act[70] (DBA) unquestionably became applicable to the weatherization program. "The program ha[d] historically not been subject

63 California and New York also have stringent monitoring programs.

64 The two-year freeze applies to units for which renters pay their own utilities; the five-year freeze applies to rental units for which the landlord pays utilities. N.Y. State Div. of Hous. & Cmty. Renewal, Weatherization Assistance Program Policies and Procedures Manual ch. 4 (2009 rev.), *available at* www.dhcr.state.ny.us/Publications/WeatherizationManual/WAP_Manual.pdf.

65 10 C.F.R. § 440.22(e).

66 42 U.S.C. § 6863(b)(2)(B).

67 *See* § 9.2.5.10, *supra* (discussing helpful language that New York has adopted).

In Massachusetts, tenants are parties to the owner-subgrantee agreement and may recover damages, attorney fees, and costs in case of breach. Massachusetts Standard Weatherization Agreement.

68 New York utilizes Form DHCR #9 (Tenant Synopsis of the Owner Agreement), which is provided to all tenants in weatherized units or dwellings. Form #9 is available at www.nyswda.org/DirManual/A_Manual/A_Regs/NYRegs.htm. Other states have followed New York's lead in this area.

69 Pub. L. No. 111-5, div. A, tit. XVI, § 1606 (Feb. 17, 2009).

70 Bacon-Davis Act, *codified at* 40 U.S.C. §§ 3141–3148.

to the DBA prevailing wage requirements,"[71] and was seen by most state and local WAP agencies as being exempt from those requirements. Since no Davis-Bacon Act wage rates had ever before been established for weatherization workers, this created a great deal of confusion for WAP agencies around the country. For several months, implementation of ARRA-funded WAP ground to a halt in many states.[72] Eventually, the DOE issued formal guidance[73] and the Department of Labor (DOL) determined prevailing wage rates applicable specifically to weatherization workers.[74] By late 2009, the Davis-Bacon Act problems were resolved. While creating quite a barrier at first to the implementation of ARRA-funded WAP, in some states it did provide the benefit of raising up the wages and benefits that weatherization workers received; in other states, the DOL-determined rates simply ratified existing practices.

9.3 Other Government Initiatives

9.3.1 LIHEAP

In fiscal years 2010 and 2011, the Low Income Home Energy Assistance Program (LIHEAP) provided states with approximately $4.5 billion to $5.1 billion to assist low-income households in paying their energy bills. This program is examined in detail in Chapter 8, *supra*. Of special relevance to weatherization, the program allows a state to devote up to 15% of its grant to weatherization programs, using its discretion, and up to 25% if it seeks a waiver.[75]

9.3.2 Department of Agriculture

As part of its loan and grant program for improvement of rural dwellings, the Department of Agriculture is required to develop and conduct a weatherization program for the purpose of making grants to finance the purchase or installation of weatherization materials in dwelling units occupied by low-income families.[76]

9.3.3 State Funding of Weatherization

There are a number of state government programs that provide a significant amount of funding for weatherization assistance.[77]

9.4 Utility-Sponsored Energy Efficiency

9.4.1 Introduction

For several decades now—since the late 1970s—electric and gas utilities have added energy-saving measures to their mix of options for meeting the energy needs of their customers. These investments on the customer's side of the meter[78] not only avoid the need for new supply resources but also help the customer reduce energy bills. An ever-increasing number of utilities are offering a broad array of energy efficiency programs to both residential and business customers. Public utilities commissions have increasingly ordered utilities to include residential energy efficiency investments in their arsenal of demand side management (DSM) efforts.[79]

---

71 U.S. Dep't of Energy, Weatherization Program Notice 09-9 (July 21, 2009), *available at* http://waptac.org/data/files/website_docs/government/guidance/2009/wpn%2009-9%20davis-bacon.pdf.

72 The states that experienced the fewest problems were relatively low-wage states, in which established prevailing wage rates for arguably comparable jobs (carpenter, painter, roofer) were low enough that the WAP could afford to meet those rates. In states with high prevailing wage rates under the Davis-Bacon Act, those rates were simply too high and the local WAP agencies needed the Department of Labor to make new prevailing wage determinations for newly-defined weatherization worker categories.

73 *See* Weatherization Program Notice 09-9 (July 21, 2009), *available at* http://waptac.org/data/files/website_docs/government/guidance/2009/wpn%2009-9%20davis-bacon.pdf.

74 *See* U.S. Dep't of Labor, Davis Bacon Weatherization Wage Rates, *available at* www.dol.gov/whd/recovery/dbsurvey/weather.htm.

75 42 U.S.C. § 8624(k).

Up to 15% of a state's LIHEAP block grant may be devoted to "low-cost residential weatherization or other energy-related home repair for low-income households," 42 U.S.C. § 8624(k)(1), although a state may request a waiver, allowing it to use up to 25% of its LIHEAP funds for weatherization, 42 U.S.C. § 8624(k)(2).

In recent years, Hawaii may be the only state that has not devoted any of its LIHEAP dollars to weatherization; approximately three dozen states devoted between 5% and 15% of their funds to weatherization, and a dozen other states devoted specific dollar amounts to weatherization. National Ctr. for Appropriate Tech., Percent LIHEAP Funds by Program Component, *available at* www.liheap.ncat.org/tables/FY2011/components.htm.

76 42 U.S.C. § 1474(c). For more information on the Department of Agriculture's housing programs, go to www.rurdev.usda.gov/rhs.

77 *See* National Ctr. for Appropriate Tech., 2009 State-By-State Supplements to Energy Assistance and Energy Efficiency, *available at* http://liheap.ncat.org/Supplements/2009/supplement09.htm.

78 These investments are sometimes termed "demand side management" (DSM), as the utility's activities are intended to decrease customer demand for electricity or gas.

79 A number of organizations track utility investments in energy efficiency. One excellent source is the American Council on an Energy-Efficient Economy, www.aceee.org, which publishes an annual energy efficiency scorecard. The most recent is the 2010 scorecard, which reports $4.3 billion in utility energy efficiency expenditures in 2009, American Council on an Energy-Efficient Economy, 2010 Energy Efficiency scorecard, Report E107 (Oct.

When a utility invests in energy efficiency measures in the home of a low-income customer, it performs an important service. Without outside parties paying all or most of the cost, energy efficiency investments are beyond the reach of most low-income households. Low-income households already use less energy than the average household, indicating that they skimp on energy needs to the extent possible.[80] Low-income families too often cannot take advantage of energy efficiency technologies. A utility program directing energy efficiency towards low-income households enables them to reap the benefits of conservation.

Utilities and ratepayers generally also benefit from such investments. When a utility can put off the construction of a costly new plant and reduce the use of expensive fuels to generate electricity, it saves money. In addition, a utility loses money when a customer cannot afford the bill for energy already provided.[81] Making bills affordable for low-income customers not only defers costly resource acquisitions, it also saves credit and collection expenses for the utility. Whenever a utility makes investments in energy efficiency, low-income customers must be given the chance to participate in those programs. In a recent policy paper,[82] NCLC urged utilities to make proportionately much larger energy efficiency investments in affordable multifamily housing. Multifamily buildings, on average, are much older and less energy efficient than other residential properties—thus helping utilities to meet their energy efficiency goals at lower cost per saved kWh or therm. These building also house some of the poorest families in America, which means efficiency investments in these properties reduce the likelihood that utility service will be terminated for nonpayment or that the owners will be unable to afford the costs of operating and maintaining the buildings.

In many states today, investments in energy efficiency and other DSM tools are considered a normal and expected part of a utility company's operations, although support for these programs is generally strongest on the west and east coasts and in parts of the Midwest. Utilities from states as diverse as Georgia and Maine now invest in energy efficiency under mandates from their state utility commissions.

Moreover, among those states that have restructured their electricity markets, a majority have imposed a non-bypassable systems benefits charge to fund various public benefits, which may specifically include weatherization or, more generally, programs to help low-income customers afford utility service.[83] Several of these states specify that the preexisting level of weatherization or other low-income services must be maintained[84] or prescribe in detail the amount of funding.[85] A few of the restructuring statutes specify the use of the current weatherization network[86] or specifically provide for the continuation of company-sponsored DSM.[87]

It is now incontestable that utilities can fashion cost-effective energy efficiency programs targeted to their low-income customers. Energy efficiency investments, together with rate designs crafted to bring bill payments within the reach of low-income customers, can improve the payment patterns of such customers. The result is that the utility saves money on credit and collection activities and low-income customers are able to maintain vital utility services. Also, utility investments in energy efficiency can leverage federal weatherization dollars and fill gaps left by the Weatherization Assistance Program. Not least of all, utility investments in energy efficiency help to reduce the emissions of greenhouse gasses and a range of harmful air pollutants.

2010), *available at* www.aceee.org/sites/default/files/publications/researchreports/e107.pdf.

A second source is the Consortium for Energy Efficiency. *See* M. Nevius, R. Eldridge, & J. Krouk, The State of the Energy Efficiency Program Industry: Budgets, Expenditures and Impacts 2009 (Mar. 2010), *available at* www.cee1.org/files/StaeofEEIndustry2009.pdf.

80 National Consumer Law Center, Energy and the Poor: The Crisis Continues 29 (1995).

81 For example, in Idaho Power's DSM program the utility pays farmers to help it reduce its load by turning off their irrigation pumps for up to fifteen hours a week and pays homeowners to turn off air conditioners during periods of high demand. The utility reasoned that it would be cheaper to pay its customers to conserve than it would be to buy power at high prices. *See* Kate Galbraith, *Why Is a Utility Paying Customers?*, N.Y. Times, Jan. 24, 2010.

82 National Consumer Law Center, Up the Chimney: How HUD's Inaction Costs Taxpayers Millions and Drives Up Utility Bills for Low-Income Families (Aug. 2010), *available at* www.nclc.org/images/pdf/pr-reports/up_the_chimney_082610.pdf.

83 Ariz. Admin. Code § R14-2-1608; Conn. Gen. Stat. § 16-245l; Del. Code Ann. tit. 26, § 1014; 220 Ill. Comp. Stat. 5/16-108(i), 687/6-5; Me. Rev. Stat. tit. 35-A, § 3214; Mass. Gen. Laws ch. 25, § 19; Mont. Code Ann. §§ 69-8-103(31), (32), 69-8-402; N.H. Rev. Stat. Ann. § 374-F:3, ¶VI; N.J. Stat. Ann. § 48:3-60 (West); N.Y. Pub. Serv. Comm'n, Ops. 96-12, 97-16, 98-3 and Competitive Opportunities Regarding Electric Service: Order Approving Systems Benefits Charge Plan with Modifications and Denying Petition for Rehearing (July 2, 1998).

84 Cal. Pub. Util. Code § 382 (West); N.J. Stat. Ann. § 48:3-60 (West); 66 Pa. Stat. Ann. § 2802(10) (West). *See also* Md. Code Ann., Pub. Util. § 7-211 (West).

85 Del. Code Ann. tit. 26, § 1014; Mass. Gen. Laws ch. 25, § 19; Mont. Code Ann. § 69-8-402. *See also* 220 Ill. Comp. Stat. 5/16-108(i); N.Y. Pub. Serv. Comm'n, Competitive Opportunities Regarding Electric Service: Order Approving Systems Benefits Charge Plan with Modifications and Denying Petition for Rehearing (July 2, 1998).

86 Mass. Gen. Laws ch. 25, § 19.

87 Mass. Gen. Laws ch. 25, § 19; Mont. Code Ann. § 69-8-402; N.Y. Pub. Serv. Comm'n, Competitive Opportunities Regarding Electric Service, Order Approving Systems Benefits Charge Plan with Modifications and Denying Petition for Rehearing (July 2, 1998).

9.4.2 Only Utilities May Be Able to Re-Weatherize Certain Units and Also Increase the Number of Households Served

Utilities can promote the melding of the WAP and utility-financed efforts into a program serving more households than either program could serve operating independently. For example, a state that receives $5 million for the WAP and spends an average of $5,000 per household can serve 1,000 homes. If the utility adds in $500,000 of its low-income energy efficiency funding, the WAP in that state can now reach 1,500 homes. The utility dollars, which generally do not have the same restrictions as federal WAP dollars, can also fill in large gaps in the WAP. One especially significant gap is caused by limitations on the use of the WAP to weatherize properties that have been weatherized since late 1994, even if inadequately or incompletely.[88] Weatherization techniques have advanced significantly in the past fifteen years. In many instances, providing a household with additional energy efficiency services would be cost-effective while also making the household's energy bills more affordable.

One substantial increase in weatherization technology has been the rapid expansion of blower door audits. By depressurizing the interior of the house, auditors can determine where significant infiltration leaks are occurring. Interior air sealing has been found to be one of the most efficient as well as cost-effective means of energy conservation. Similarly, infrared scanning and interior sealing have increased the ability of weatherization operators to reduce energy consumption. Through better research and technology, it also has become evident that old weatherization techniques of caulking and storm window/door replacements were not as effective as sidewall insulation alone.

There is clearly a role for utilities to fill in helping to re-weatherize homes that are not eligible for weatherization. In addition, given the perennial inadequacy of funding for the WAP at the federal level,[89] local WAP agencies tend to give higher priority to homes that have never received weatherization services. Many local agencies rely heavily on utility funding sources to fill in gaps in the DOE-funded program, and re-weatherizing homes is one of the gaps that the DOE program still does not fill adequately. Utility funding can also pay for weatherization-related home repairs that are not allowed, or for which there are strict per-household dollar limits, under the WAP.

88 Under 42 U.S.C. § 6865 (c)(2), a state cannot re-weatherize a unit that was only partially weatherized previously, unless the prior work was completed before September 30, 1994.

89 The notable exception is the 2009–2012 period, when "stimulus" funding provided under Pub. L. No. 111-5, div. A, tit. IV, 123 Stat. 138 (Feb. 17, 2009), included $5 billion for the WAP.

9.4.3 Only Utilities May Be Able to Weatherize Certain Multifamily Dwellings

Multifamily dwellings that are not occupied exclusively by low-income households present another gap in WAP services provided to low-income households. DOE regulations dictate that multifamily dwellings must have certain minimum rates of low-income occupancy in order to be eligible for WAP funding:[90]

2- & 4-unit bldgs.	50%
3- & >5- unit bldgs.	66%

Multi-unit dwellings that have fewer low-income households than required by DOE can be targeted for weatherization services pursuant to a utility's residential energy efficiency program. Since utilities generally tend to underserve multifamily properties, relative to the percentage of households that live in these buildings,[91] advocates should work with local WAP agencies to ensure that utilities allocate an equitable share of their funding to this sector of residential properties. Low-income families living in such situations will probably not otherwise receive conservation services.

9.4.4 Only Utilities Can Engage in Certain Types of Weatherization

Use of the WAP funding is generally restricted to improving the heating or cooling efficiency of a low-income program participant's home, although local agencies may also spend limited funds to "eliminat[e] health and safety hazards" when "necessary."[92] The WAP statute sets out a specific list of "weatherization materials" for which federal funds can be used.[93]

90 10 C.F.R. § 440.22(b)(2).

Recently, the Department of Energy issued a final rule to ease the determination of whether a multi-unit building is eligible for weatherization under the WAP, without further evaluation or verification. *See* 75 Fed. Reg. 3847 (Jan. 25, 2010) (adding 10 C.F.R. 440.22(b)(4)).

91 National Consumer Law Center, Up the Chimney: How HUD's Inaction Costs Taxpayers Millions and Drives Up Utility Bills for Low-Income Families (Aug. 2010), *available at* www.nclc.org/images/pdf/pr-reports/up_the_chimney_082610.pdf.

92 10 C.F.R. § 440.18(d)(15). *See, e.g.*, Idaho Admin. Code r. 16.04.16.200(14) (allowable expenditures include "the cost of eliminating health and safety hazards, elimination of which is necessary before, or because of, installation of weatherization materials").

93 42 U.S.C. § 6862(9).

This definition of "weatherization materials," first adopted in 1976 in the form of broad material categories (Pub. L. No. 94-385, § 412, 90 Stat. 1152 (1976)), was amended into a formal list of allowable materials in 1978 (Pub. L. No. 95-619,

There are several measures that would reduce household energy consumption but cannot be installed with DOE funding. For example:

- Lighting measures;
- Appliance efficiency measures, such as refrigerator replacement; and
- Plumbing repairs (for example, repairs of hot water leaks, which can be one of the most cost-effective energy conserving strategies).

Utilities not only are able to fill these gaps, electric utilities often place a high priority in upgrading lighting and appliances to more efficient models. In some states, local WAP agencies coordinate with their local utilities to ensure that a household receives the full range of energy efficiency improvements that are needed, for example, insulation of the building envelope, air infiltration, and upgrading of outdated and inefficient appliances.

9.4.5 Inadequate Federal Funding

The WAP dollars will never be adequate to provide services to all eligible low-income homes needing weatherization within a reasonable period of time. Over its history, the WAP has generally been annually funded in the range of $120 million to $240 million,[94] with the exception of the 2009–2012 period when the American Recovery and Reinvestment Act (ARRA) provided $5 billion in funding over three-years. It appears likely that post-ARRA funding will decline significantly, possibly to a lower level than at any time since 2001.

Since its inception, the WAP has weatherized over six million low-income homes.[95] At this rate, however, the WAP will only make a small dent in the needs of low-income households, as there are likely fifteen to twenty million households eligible for the WAP that have not received any services.

WAP dollars alone will never address the weatherization and conservation needs of low-income households. Utility support is critical. With nationwide utility spending on energy efficiency programs now likely exceeding $5 billion in all customer sectors, and WAP appropriations expected to decline significantly in fiscal year 2012, utility spending in the residential sector will undoubtedly soon exceed federal appropriations for the WAP. Low-income advocates should insist on an equitable share of utility energy efficiency expenditures being devoted to the low-income sector.

§ 231(b), 92 Stat. 3225 (1978)), and further revised in 1984 (Pub. L. No. 98-558, § 402, 98 Stat. 2887 (1984)) and 1990 (Pub. L. No. 101-440, § 7(a), 104 Stat. 1012 (1990)).

94 *See* www.waptac.org/data/files/website_docs/briefing_book /2_programfunding_final.pdf.

95 *Id.*

9.4.6 Overcoming Utilities' "Cost-Effective" Requirement

A utility is constrained in the low-income energy efficiency programs that it offers by the requirement that such programs be "cost-effective." The term "cost-effective" is a term of art, basically meaning that the cost of the energy efficiency measures must be less than what the utility would have spent in providing the service without those measures. A cost-effective program, in other words, must lower the total costs to the utility, or, in some cases, the total costs to the utility and the program participants (when using the "Total Resource Cost Test") or the costs to society as a whole (the "Societal Cost Test").

When evaluating cost effectiveness, low-income advocates should argue for a broad definition of avoided costs. Utilities benefit both by a decrease in demand and a decrease in the costs imposed by payment-troubled customers: collection of past-due bills, termination and reconnection, need for payment plans and low-income rates, among other things. Improvements to old heating equipment, especially gas systems, will have health and safety benefits that accrue both to the utility in the form of fewer emergency calls and to society in the form of decreased risk of fire or carbon monoxide. Additional benefits to society may include reduced medical costs for treatment of heat-or cold-related illnesses and a reduction in homelessness because loss of utility service can give a household the final push towards abandonment of the home. NCLC sought to quantify the non-energy benefits of energy efficiency and DSM investments and recommended a 50% "adder" for non-energy, non-environmental benefits.[96]

9.4.7 Challenges Presented by Low-Income Energy Efficiency Programs

9.4.7.1 High Transaction Costs

A utility will require a minimum amount of energy savings to pay for the fixed costs of program outreach and administration and the direct cost of installing energy efficiency measures. The costs of program outreach and administration do not vary greatly depending upon the amount of savings generated at a particular dwelling unit. The time devoted to intake, oversight, monitoring, and travel is all the same.

Some types of transaction costs for low-income households may be somewhat higher than for moderate-and upper-income households. For example, many low-income households are renters. Given this, there exists a "split incentive"

96 John Howat & J. Oppenheim, National Consumer Law Center, Analysis of Low-Income Benefits in Determining Cost Effectiveness of Energy Efficiency Programs (Apr. 14, 1999).

regarding energy efficiency measures. While the bill savings will go to the low-income tenant, the utility must approach and gain the consent of the property owner before any work can be done on the dwelling. Since the owner has no incentive for the work to occur, the effort required to obtain the necessary consent may be somewhat greater.

These overhead costs related to setting up the arrangement to weatherize a given dwelling are referred to as transaction costs. With the small energy-savings potential for the many low-income households that consume less energy than average,[97] utilities may at times find that there is insufficient potential for savings to overcome the transaction costs of providing the measures to low-income households in the first place.

In some states, the local WAP agencies obviate this problem by "piggybacking" the utility dollars onto a house that is already scheduled to receive weatherization services. Since the local WAP agency already has to conduct outreach to customers and energy audits, this can significantly defray the utility's per-house administrative costs. In addition, by combining WAP and utility dollars, the local WAP agency can take a "whole house" approach so that each household would receive coordinated services addressing consumption of electricity, heating and cooling fuels, and possibly even water and sewer services.

9.4.7.2 Non-Energy-Savings Repairs

A second problem frequently experienced by low-income energy efficiency programs is the need for home repairs to occur before building-envelope energy-saving measures will have any impact. It makes no sense, in other words, to install insulation into a roof when there are holes in the roof that will ruin the insulation. Similarly, installing a new or repaired heating system will have no impact if there are structural problems with the house that eliminate the new system's effectiveness.

This problem can be substantial. Philadelphia's Energy Coordinating Agency (ECA), which is the nonprofit organization that administers the Philadelphia Gas Works (PGW) Conservation Works Program (CWP), reports that in 1992 roughly 40% of the low-income households who would otherwise have been eligible for CWP were rejected from the program because of the need for major roof repair or replacement.

97 Based on data drawn from the 2001 Residential Energy Consumption Survey, tbl. CE1-3c (Total Energy Consumption in U.S. Households by Household Income), it is clear that households with income of less than $10,000 per year use an average of just half the electricity consumed by the average household with an income of $50,000 or more per year. Even looking at other fuels and income brackets, households with incomes below $25,000 per year generally use one-half to one-third the household energy that higher-income households consume.

The problem is that, while these home repairs may be a necessary precondition to the effective installation of energy-saving devices, they do not always save additional energy by themselves. Every dollar spent on such repairs, therefore, adds a dollar of expense that must be offset by the energy savings generated by the energy efficiency measures. Given the initial problem—that low-income households may often present small-savings potential to begin with—it is less likely that the program will test as cost-effective if the cost of home repairs is included in the costs of the energy efficiency measure.

The utility is thus caught in a classic Catch-22 with many low-income households. Without the home repairs, the energy efficiency measures will not be effective and thus cannot meet the cost-effectiveness tests. However, with the home repairs, the overall cost of the program may outstrip the overall savings, again causing the program to fail a cost-effectiveness test.

9.4.7.3 Inadequacy of Low-Interest Loans

Some utilities help finance weatherization and energy efforts by providing their customers with zero or low-cost interest loans. For low-income households who are already living on the edge, the idea of taking on a new loan is not an incentive to make their homes more energy-efficient, which they may desperately need to do.

9.4.7.4 The Solution: Combining Funds

The solution to this dilemma is for WAP dollars to be combined with utility dollars to form a single comprehensive program. Utility funds are used on cost-effective energy-saving measures. In contrast, WAP dollars can be used as the source of financing for the non-energy-saving components of the total program. As WAP funds are not subject to the same narrow cost-effectiveness tests, these funds can also be used for measures such as outreach and intake.

The combination of WAP and utility dollars will eliminate parallel programs by the utility and the government.[98] Instead, a single program will be created serving the combined populations that the two programs would have served separately. The allocation of responsibilities to the WAP or to the utility for particular expenses will be a function of accounting procedures that the low-income household need not be aware of.

98 However, there is some need for "parallel" programs. Utility investments in energy efficiency can help accomplish some efficiency improvements that cannot be funded through the WAP. Moreover, utility investments can reach some low-income households that cannot be reached using WAP dollars.

Chapter 10 Utility Allowances in Subsidized Housing

10.1 Overview of Utility Allowances: What They Are; Who Gets Them; Why They Are Important for Tenants

10.1.1 Introduction

Tenants of "public housing" (housing owned by a public housing authority or "PHA") and many types of "subsidized housing" (privately owned housing units the rent for which the tenant's payment is reduced through a variety of forms of government assistance) enjoy a unique protection that other low-income families do not. The amount that most of these tenants pay as "shelter costs" (the sum of rent and certain utility payments) is limited by federal law. The letter of the federal law guarantees that public housing tenants and many subsidized tenants pay no more than 30% of their adjusted income as rent.[1] The spirit of law is intended to make sure that the tenant's overall shelter costs, including utility costs, are affordable. Tenants who are required to pay for their own utilities therefore receive a "utility allowance," an allowance that is credited against the rent that would otherwise be due.[2] In theory, the more a tenant has to pay out of pocket for reasonable consumption of utilities, the larger the allowance.

But the practice is quite different. Utility allowances are often inadequate, and tenants suffer. If utility allowances are too low, tenants are forced to pay higher rents. Because the rent burden is now higher, tenants may not be able to pay their utility bills and may lose their gas or electric utility due to nonpayment. Public housing and subsidized tenants can also be evicted for not paying their utility bills, leading to a loss of the subsidy and, likely, homelessness.[3]

Tenants of a single housing authority can collectively end up paying tens of thousands of dollars in excess rent or utility charges if allowances are too low. Even if the utility allowance is too low by only $10 per month, this amounts to $120 per year per tenant. In a housing development that has 250 tenants, this means that the tenants are being overcharged $30,000 per year. It is extremely important for publicly assisted tenants and their advocates to determine whether allowances are reasonable and kept up-to-date. This chapter explains how to do so.

10.1.2 Types of Housing with Utility Allowances

While many of the basic concepts regarding utility allowances are broadly applicable in several of the housing programs, there are some differences between programs that are important to understand. Therefore, it is useful to be familiar with the basic types of publicly assisted housing programs. However, mastering the types of subsidized housing programs is like working on an archeological excavation: lots of digging, only to find newer and older housing programs layered on top of each other, with some of those programs still extant, others rare and endangered, and others largely extinct. This chapter will focus on the more common extant forms of housing, occasionally mention some of the dying breeds, and largely ignore extinct forms of housing.[4]

---

1 42 U.S.C. § 1437a(a). This is the so-called "Brooke Amendment," named for Massachusetts Senator Ed Brooke. In rare cases in which adjustments to household income are very large, the tenant would pay 10% of total unadjusted household income as rent if this is greater than 30% of adjusted household income. *Id.*

2 *See, e.g.*, 24 C.F.R. § 965.502(a) (requiring PHAs to offer utility allowances).

The current version of the most relevant public housing regulations, 24 C.F.R. §§ 965.501–965.508, was added through changes published in 61 Fed. Reg. 7971 on February 29, 1996. For prior versions of the regulations, see 24 C.F.R. pt. 865 (1984), 45 Fed. Reg. 59502 (Sept. 9, 1980) and 24 C.F.R. pt. 965 (1992). These prior versions will be indicated throughout this chapter by use of their parenthetical year dates.

3 *See, e.g.*, Crochet v. Housing Auth. of Tampa, 37 F.3d 607 (11th Cir. 1994) (referencing lease requirement that tenants must pay utility bills); Jackson v. Philadelphia Hous. Auth., 1996 WL 363928 (E.D. Pa. June 21, 1996) (PHA brings eviction action for failure to use utility allowance for intended purpose and consequent gas bill arrearage of $5000; eviction dismissed on procedural grounds); McKeel v. Jasper Hous. Auth., 652 So. 2d 315 (Ala. Civ. App. 1994) (PHA brings eviction based, *inter alia*, on failure to pay for utilities; summary judgment for PHA reversed as material facts were in dispute).

4 Advocates, however, may sometimes encounter tenants who receive extant types of assistance—such as the Section 8 Rural Housing Set-Aside—not discussed in detail in this chapter. The National Housing Law Project publishes an excellent housing law treatise that discusses utility allowances in some of the less common forms of subsidized housing, HUD Housing Programs: Tenants' Rights (3d ed. 2004 and 2010 supp.), which is available for purchase on the NHLP website at www.nhlp.org. The

The conventional public housing program is one of the largest housing programs, administered by the Department of Housing and Urban Development (HUD). Approximately 1.2 million low-income households live in units owned by some 3300 PHAs around the country and subsidized by the federal government. These units house more than three million people.[5] Public housing represents almost 20% of the low-income rental housing stock.

HUD also operates the Section 8 Certificate and Housing Choice Voucher programs (hereafter "the Voucher Program"). The Voucher Program largely supplanted the old "Section 8 certificate" program.[6]

Vouchers provide assistance to low-income tenants who live in privately owned housing. Most voucher tenants choose where they live by finding their own apartments, although some vouchers are "project-based," meaning that the PHA contracts with specific willing landlords who agree to accept voucher-eligible tenants referred by the PHA from its waiting list. Some two million tenants receive voucher assistance. There are a number of variants of the Voucher Program, including Vouchers for Homeownership, Mainstream Voucher Program for Persons with Disabilities, Family Reunification Vouchers, and more.[7] However, there are no significant differences among these Voucher Program variants for purposes of understanding the rights of tenants to have reasonable and adequate utility allowances.

HUD has also subsidized the development of a large number of units for low-income families by reducing the mortgage interest that the owner pays. The oldest program is called the "Section 221(d)(3) Below-Market-Interest-Rate (BMIR)" program.[8] Through this program, developers could obtain mortgages at 3% interest, which significantly reduced their costs and allowed them to set below-market rents for tenants. Later, Congress adopted the Section 236 program[9] under which HUD paid the lenders a subsidy that allowed the lenders to reduce the developer's interest rate to 1%, again so that rents would be below market. Another major subsidy program to foster low-income housing, but one not run by HUD, is the Low Income Housing Tax Credit (LIHTC) program.[10]

Public and subsidized housing programs require that tenants have limited incomes to qualify. The maximum income at the time of initial occupancy is 80% of median income ("low-income"), but there are policies that target households with incomes at or below 50% of median income ("very low-income") and 30% of median income ("extremely low-income") for preferences.[11] To ensure that the housing remains affordable, the Brooke Amendment prohibits charging these tenants more than 30% of their adjusted gross income for their shelter-related costs.[12] Congress has since imposed a minimum rent of $50 for all public housing and remaining Section 8 tenants.[13] Utility costs, however, are still relevant in determining the maximum amount of rent tenants should pay. Therefore, a tenant who makes payments directly to the utility should be entitled to count those payments towards the $50-minimum-rent requirement.

10.1.3 The Role of Utility Allowances in Setting Rents

As just noted, the Brooke Amendment limits to 30% of income the amount that families are required to pay as rent. The Voucher Program calculates the amount of assistance provided as if the tenant were paying no more than 30% of income as rent (although the tenant may pay more). But neither the Brooke Amendment nor the Voucher Program statute clearly defines "rent" as including the tenant's actual rent PLUS utility outlays when determining if the 30%-of-income limit has been exceeded.[14] HUD, however, has a long-standing policy that rent includes actual shelter costs

many types of housing programs are described in section 1.3 of *HUD Housing Programs*, while all of Chapter 6 of that book is devoted to utility charges.

5 HUD's Public Housing Program, *available at* http://portal.hud.gov/hudportal/HUD?src=/topics/rental_assistance/phprog.

6 The "Section 8" program refers to section 8 of the revised United States Housing Act of 1937, *added by* Pub. L. No. 93-383, § 201, 88 Stat. 662 (1974), *codified as amended at* 42 U.S.C. § 1437f. The Housing Choice Voucher program is governed by 42 U.S.C. § 1437f(o). PHAs no longer issue certificates, but there may still be some old certificates in use that have not yet been replaced by vouchers.

7 *See* National Hous. Law Project, HUD Housing Programs: Tenants' Rights (3d ed. 2004 and 2010 supp.) (describing in detail the various types of voucher programs).

8 12 U.S.C. § 1715l.

9 12 U.S.C. § 1715z-1.

10 26 U.S.C. § 42(g).

11 42 U.S.C. §§ 1437a(b)(1), (2), 1437n(a)(2); 24 C.F.R. § 5.603.

12 For conventional public housing tenants, the Brooke Amendment applies. The Brooke Amendment, found at 42 U.S.C. § 1437a(a), states that, in the rare cases in which adjustments to household income are very large, the tenant would pay 10% of total unadjusted household income as rent if this is greater than 30% of adjusted household income. The comparable rental payment rules for the Voucher Program can be found at 42 U.S.C. § 1437f(o)(2). Voucher Program tenants often pay more than 30% of their income for rent, as the program sets a maximum amount of assistance based on an assumed rent ("payment standard"), not the actual rent. If the tenant rents an apartment for more than the payment standard, which the Voucher Program rules fully allow, the amount of assistance does not change, and the tenant ends up paying more than 30% of income as rent.

13 42 U.S.C. § 1437a(a)(3).

14 In contrast to the Brooke Amendment, which is itself silent on whether "rent" includes utility costs, the Voucher Program statute explicitly states that housing assistance payments must include "an amount allowed for utilities." *See* Johnson v. Housing Auth. of Jefferson Parish, 442 F.3d 356 (5th Cir. 2006).

plus a reasonable allowance for the utility costs to ensure that total required shelter-cost payments do not exceed 30% of income.[15]

Tenants can be responsible for one or more of the following utilities: gas, electricity, heating fuel, water and sewer service, trash pickup, and telephone. The regulations require public housing authorities (PHAs) to establish allowances for *all* of these utilities, except telephone:

> *Utility Allowance.* If the cost of utilities (except telephone) and other household services for an assisted unit is not included in the tenant rent but is the responsibility of the family occupying the unit, an amount equal to the estimate made or approved by a PHA or HUD of the monthly cost of a reasonable consumption of such utilities and other services for the unit by an energy-conservative household of modest circumstances consistent with the requirements of a safe, sanitary, and healthful living environment.[16]

While tenants are entitled to utility allowances, they are not based on the tenant's *actual* utility costs but instead on the PHA's estimate of the costs that an "energy-conservative household of modest circumstances" would reasonably use, "consistent with the requirements of a safe, sanitary, and healthful living environment." How the PHA actually sets the level of the utility allowance and how frequently the PHA updates or revises the allowance directly affects whether rents remain affordable as required by the Brooke Amendment and related housing laws. Accurate utility allowances help keep total shelter costs affordable, while inadequate utility allowances create the risks of loss of utility service, eviction, and homelessness. It is important for tenants and their advocates to play close attention to the level of these allowances.

15 *See, e.g.*, 24 C.F.R. § 965.502(a) (public housing) ("PHAs shall establish utility allowances for . . . resident-purchased utilities for all utilities purchased directly by residents from the utility suppliers"). *See also* Dorsey v. Housing Auth., 984 F.2d 622, 624 (4th Cir. 1993) ("The Brooke Amendment requires public housing authorities (PHAs) to charge tenants no more than 30% of their income for rent, which is to include a reasonable allowance for utilities."). *Cf.* Johnson v. Housing Auth. of Jefferson Parish, 442 F.3d 356 (5th Cir. 2006) (Section 8 housing choice voucher payments must include "an amount allowed for utilities"); McGann v. United States, 1999 WL 173596 (S.D.N.Y. Mar. 29, 1999) (Section 8 rent includes monthly utility allowance), *aff'd mem.*, 205 F.3d 1323 (2d Cir. 1999) (text at 1999 WL 173596 (Mar. 29, 1999)).

As is explained in § 10.2.5.2, *infra*, participants in the Housing Choice Voucher Program now have the option to pay more than 30% of income for shelter costs if they wish to obtain a preferable unit.

16 24 C.F.R. § 5.603(b) (PHA owned and Section 8 project-based housing). *See* 24 C.F.R. § 982.517 (Housing Choice Voucher Program).

To the extent a tenant would consider cable or high-speed Internet service a "utility," the PHA does not have to provide a utility allowance for these services.

10.1.4 The Three Basic Metering Arrangements in Publicly Assisted Housing

10.1.4.1 Overview

There are three types of metering systems that tenants will encounter: master meters, check meters, and individual retail meters. The manner in which public housing tenants pay for utilities depends upon the metering system,[17] as does the nature of the "allowances" the tenants receive. HUD strongly prefers that PHAs individually meter tenants' utilities, either by providing for retail service or by using check meters.[18] If a PHA uses master-meters, HUD requires it to convert to individual metering unless the conversion would be impractical, not cost-effective, or in the case of check-metering, not permissible under state or local laws or the policies of the utility supplier or service commission.[19]

10.1.4.2 Master-Metered Projects

Master-metered projects have meters which measure consumption for the building as a whole, and the PHA pays the utility company directly from its operating budget. Here the utility costs are included in the tenants' rents. Tenants are generally subject to a surcharge for the use of certain tenant-supplied appliances.[20]

10.1.4.3 Check-Metered Projects

In check-metered projects, the service is supplied by the utility company through the use of a master meter, but each housing unit has individual meters installed by and under the control of the PHA to measure excess consumption by the household. Tenants living in check-metered units are subject to a surcharge for consumption above the "reasonable" allowance ("excess consumption") established by the PHA.[21]

Most utilities charge lower unit rates for higher amounts of consumption, despite policy trends over the past few decades to discourage "declining block rates" and other

17 In any one project, there might be different metering systems for different utilities. For example, electricity is quite often individually metered for each unit, while it is rare for water consumption to be individually metered. Also, PHAs will often have different metering systems for different projects—for example, installing individual meters in family developments while including utilities as part of the rent in senior developments.

18 24 C.F.R. § 965.401.

19 *Id.*

20 24 C.F.R. § 965.501(b) (in master-metered buildings, "residents shall be subject to charges for consumption by resident-owned major appliances, or for optional functions of PHA-furnished equipment, in accordance with § 965.502(e) and 965.506(b), but no utility allowance will be established").

21 24 C.F.R. § 965.506(a).

such volume discounts.[22] Similarly, when residential apartments are classified as commercial accounts because the buildings are master-metered, the unit rate tends to be lower than when such buildings are classified as residential accounts. Both master-metered and check-metered units generally benefit from the declining block rates and/or commercial rates that the PHA is paying for the utility service, relative to the amounts the tenants would have to pay if they were billed separately. This savings is—or should be—passed on to the tenant. On the other hand, tenants with individual retail meters pay residential rates for their energy, and these unit rates are typically higher than rates for larger blocks of energy or for energy usage classified as "commercial."

10.1.4.4 Retail-Metered Units

Retail-metered units are those in which the tenants have a direct relationship with the utility provider, and each tenant is responsible for the payment of the utility bill for the apartment. These households receive a reduction in their rent (the utility allowance) to cover the expected cost of consuming a "reasonable" amount of utilities. The tenant, not the PHA, is responsible for payment of the bills. To the extent actual consumption exceeds the utility allowance provided by the PHA, the tenants are responsible for the excess. Failure to pay the utility bills can result in termination of service just as for any other utility customer. Moreover, this termination of service may be the grounds for termination from public housing under the lease with the PHA and could lead to eviction from public housing.[23]

The methods housing authorities use to determine allowable usage for utilities have a very significant effect on tenants with check meters or retail meters. For master-metered tenants, basic utility costs are included in the rent and, at worst, tenants are exposed to paying surcharges for use of certain appliances or for excess consumption. For all of these tenants, however, it is critical to understand the proper way for housing authorities to set utility allowances.

10.2 Calculation of Utility Allowances in Publicly Assisted Housing

10.2.1 Overview

This section describes the process by which PHAs should calculate fair and reasonable utility allowances in public housing. Utility allowances in the Voucher Program are discussed at § 10.2.5, *infra*. Tenants and advocates should be alert to the likelihood that allowances in any particular public housing development are inadequate. There is little evidence that PHAs routinely collect actual consumption data by project and devise specifically tailored and reasonable utility allowances. The regulations allow PHAs a fair amount of discretion in setting utility allowances, and PHAs can use that discretion to set allowances that are not adequate.[24] PHAs put utility allowance standards into effect without any approval from HUD, and HUD only reviews the allowances "in the course of audits or reviews of PHA operations."[25] In many cases, utility allowances will not meet the standard of "approximat[ing] a reasonable consumption of utilities by an energy-conservative household."[26] For example, the PHA may set a standard for units

22 *See, e.g.*, Maine Electric Rate Reform Act, Me. Rev. Stat. tit. 35-A, § 3153-A (requiring rates to be set so that they reflect the marginal cost of service).

When the "marginal cost" is below the average cost (the usual example being when new power plants are less expensive than the average cost of existing power plants), such a principle will lead to "declining block rates," under which the last block of use (for example, for all consumption greater than 1000 kWh per month) is priced at a lower unit price than other consumption (for example, for usage less than 1000 kWh per month). When marginal costs are high relative to average costs, however, the reverse will be the case—price per kWh will increase as consumption increases, thereby discouraging users from increasing their consumption.

23 *See, e.g.*, Jackson v. Philadelphia Hous. Auth., 1996 WL 363928 (E.D. Pa. June 21, 1996) (lease termination notice alleged violation of lease with PHA by failing to apply monthly utility allowance toward utilities); Long Drive Apartments v. Parker, 421 S.E.2d 631 (N.C. Ct. App. 1992). *But see* Jackson v. Central Tex. Hous. Assistance Program, No. A-90-CA-0060 (W.D. Tex. Oct. 30, 1990), 24 Clearinghouse Rev. 1292 (Mar. 1991) (Clearinghouse No. 46,268) (PHA agrees to discontinue policy of termination of Section 8 certificate when tenant has utilities disconnected); Jack Moritz Mgt. Co. v. Walker, 429 N.W.2d 127 (Iowa 1988) (landlord waived tenant's breach of lease clause requiring tenant to maintain utility service because landlord provided tenant an opportunity to cure, which tenant did).

Note that a recent version of HUD's Public Housing Occupancy Guidebook § 14.1, at 169 (June 2003), suggests that tenants leases include the following language: "Retaining utility service is the resident's obligation under the lease. Failure to retain utility service is grounds for eviction." A prior version of the Guidebook suggested lease language that made the mere failure to pay utility bills, not termination of service, grounds for eviction.

24 24 C.F.R. § 965.502(e) ("The PHA's determination of allowances, scheduled surcharges, and revisions thereof shall be final and valid unless found to be arbitrary, capricious, an abuse of discretion, or otherwise not in accordance with law.").

25 24 C.F.R. § 965.502(d). In a case dating back to the 1970s, a HUD review helped form the basis for a court order increasing tenants' utility allowances. Residents' Cent. Council v. Cuyahoga Metro. Hous. Auth., No. C-73-742 (N.D. Ohio May 9, 1975).

In another case, an independent review of utility allowances helped to evaluate the thoroughness of HUD's own review. *See* J. Stein, Georgia Legal Servs. Program, Newman Public Housing Utility Study (June 1979) (Clearinghouse No. 29,874).

This study was prepared for and used in Leslie v. Mann, No. C77-49N (N.D. Ga. June 20, 1980), 14 Clearinghouse Rev. 776 (Nov. 1980) (Clearinghouse No. 23,320). Both cases may be on file with the National Housing Law Project.

26 24 C.F.R. § 965.505(a).

of a given bedroom size, ignoring the fact that some of those units are on the upper floors of a poorly insulated high-rise building that is exposed to strong winds, while other units in smaller and newer buildings are designed to consume less energy. PHAs perceive that there are incentives, in the way in which HUD funds public housing, to minimize allowances.[27] There is strong evidence that allowances are seldom adequate to meet the needs of public housing tenants.[28]

10.2.2 Method for Establishing and Revising Allowances: Retail- and Check-Metered Tenants

In 1996, HUD adopted substantially revised rules for "Resident Allowances for Utilities."[29] The regulations leave many things to the discretion of the PHA—including the factors required in determining allowances and the amount of time and administrative effort the PHA spends on the determining, revising, and updating of the allowances.

> The complexity and elaborateness of the methods chosen by the PHA, in its discretion, to achieve the foregoing objective will depend upon the nature of the housing stock, data available to the PHA and the extent of the administrative resources reasonably available to the PHA to be devoted to the collection of such data, the formulation of methods of calculation, and actual calculation and monitoring of the allowances.[30]

Now-repealed versions of the regulations recommended, without requiring, the use of certain sources of data for determining the reasonable consumption levels.[31] However, the PHA is still required to consider at least nine enumerated factors when setting allowances. These factors include:

(1) The equipment and functions intended to be covered by the allowance for which the utility will be used. For instance, natural gas may be used for cooking, heating domestic water, or space heating, or any combination of the three;
(2) The climatic location of the housing projects;
(3) The size of the dwelling units and the number of occupants per dwelling unit;
(4) Type of construction and design of the housing project;
(5) The energy efficiency of PHA-supplied appliances and equipment;
(6) The utility consumption requirements of appliances and equipment whose reasonable consumption is intended to be covered by the total resident payment;
(7) The physical condition, including insulation and weatherization, of the housing project;
(8) Temperature levels intended to be maintained in the unit during the day and at night and in cold and warm weather; and
(9) Temperature of domestic hot water.[32]

However, the regulations are silent on the extent to which the PHA must consider these factors and genuinely incorporate them into fair and appropriate usage allowances. There is not even a requirement that the PHA weigh the same factors in the same manner for all of its projects.

The utility allowance for check-metered units and retail-metered units (that is, tenant-paid) are now set in the same manner. The PHA must establish a separate allowance for "each utility and for each category of dwelling units determined by the PHA to be reasonably comparable as to factors affecting utility usage."[33]

The regulations require that utility allowances for each "unit category and unit size" shall:

> . . . approximate a reasonable consumption of utilities by an energy-conservative household of modest circumstances consistent with the requirement of safe, sanitary, and healthful living environment.[34]

While the regulations give the PHA a great deal of discretion in complying with this standard,[35] the PHA must "maintain a record that documents" how the allowances were computed and must make that record "available for inspection by residents."[36] The PHA must also give tenants advance notice of adoption or revision of allowances or surcharges[37] and an opportunity to submit written comments.[38] The PHA is under an obligation to review its utility allowances at least annually and must adjust those allowances if any change in rates, "by itself or together with prior rate changes not adjusted for, results in a change of 10 percent or more from the rates on which such allowances were based."[39] Changes to utility allowances that reflect these price increases must be made "retroactive to the first day of the month following the month in which the last rate change taken into account in such revision became effective."[40] In other words, if a utility rate increase in May

27 This is discussed more fully in § 10.6, *infra*.
28 *See* General Accounting Office, RCED-91-40A, Assisted Housing: 1 Utility Allowances Often Fall Short of Actual Utility Expenses (Mar. 26, 1991).
29 24 C.F.R. §§ 965.501–965.508, *as revised by* 61 Fed. Reg. 7966, 7971 (Feb. 29, 1996).
30 24 C.F.R. § 965.505(c).
31 24 C.F.R. § 965.476(c) (1995).
32 24 C.F.R. § 965.505(d).
33 24 C.F.R. § 965.503.
34 24 C.F.R. § 965.505(a).
35 24 C.F.R. § 965.502(e) ("The PHA's determinations of allowances . . . shall be final and valid unless found to be arbitrary, capricious, an abuse of discretion, or otherwise not in accordance with law.").
36 24 C.F.R. § 965.502(b).
37 Surcharges are imposed on tenants in master-metered buildings where there are no check-meters "for consumption by resident-owned major appliances, or for optional functions of PHA-furnished equipment." 24 C.F.R. § 965.501(b).
38 24 C.F.R. § 965.502(c).
39 24 C.F.R. § 965.507.
40 24 C.F.R. § 965.507(b).

2011, taken alone or together with prior increases, results in rates being 10% or more higher than the rates the PHA relied upon when it last set utility allowances, it must recalculate the utility allowances and make the revisions retroactive to June 2011.

Tenants may petition for relief from "surcharges for excess consumption" or "from payment of utility supplier billings in excess of the allowances for resident-purchased utilities" on "reasonable grounds," including the special needs of the elderly, ill, or disabled.[41]

10.2.3 PHA Discretion, the HUD Guidebook, and Role of Tenant Advocacy

10.2.3.1 PHAs Have Discretion in Setting Allowances

Long-supplanted regulations[42] provided much more guidance and specificity than the current rules about how to establish allowances. The old standard required allowances to cover the consumption of 90% of the tenants living in a check-metered project and actual average consumption for tenants purchasing their own utilities. Utility allowances therefore had to reflect actual consumption. Although HUD eliminated the 90% standard, the introductory comments to the 1984 regulations stated that HUD was not discarding the concept of actual average consumption, provided "there is a reasonable relationship between the average and the energy-conservative standard."[43] HUD allowed that, in the case of retail-metered units, actual average consumption may be appropriate when there is a reasonable presumption that the savings expected through individual accountability had been achieved.[44] However, because HUD considers that, in the case of check-metered tenants, individual accountability may not be achieved, it cautions against setting the allowance at actual average consumption without considering whether average consumption may be unreasonably high.[45]

The regulations create further problems in practice because they are subject to wide interpretation. Under the old standard, once tenants and the PHA agreed upon the relevant actual consumption data, establishing the allowance was merely mechanical. For retail-metered tenants, the allowance was set at average and, for check-metered tenants it was set at a level sufficient to cover 90% of the tenants. Now, a PHA can set allowances based on the theoretical consumption of an "energy conservative household of modest circumstances" and need not consider actual consumption data for tenants living in the buildings covered by the utility allowance.[46] Under these rules, tenants and PHAs can come up with very different lists of actual data that should be considered in setting allowances. For example, even if the tenants and the PHA agree to consider actual consumption, the PHA may claim that the one family or the ten families consuming the least amount of utilities set the standard for an "energy-conservative household," resulting in very low utility allowances. Tenants and their advocates must utilize the limited rights granted in the regulations to review relevant data and to submit written comments on any proposed changes to utility allowances.[47] Tenants should be assertive in demanding that the PHA has considered all the mandated factors set forth in the regulations.[48] PHAs are local political entities that may respond to concerted advocacy efforts. Even when tenants are not successful in raising utility allowances across the board, they should seek "individual relief" in circumstances in which this relief appears merited, especially if the affected tenants are elderly, ill or disabled.[49]

10.2.3.2 HUD Guidebook

A revision to HUD's Public Housing Occupancy Guidebook ("the Guidebook") released in June 2003 provides the best tools for tenants fighting for adequate utility allowances. For example, the Guidebook notes that "[u]tility allowance amounts will vary by . . . size and type of unit . . . climatic location . . . , type of construction, energy efficiency of the dwelling unit, and other factors. . . ."[50] This merely tracks the existing regulations.[51] But the Guidebook also adds this critical language: "Utility allowance amounts will also vary by residential demographic characteristics affecting home energy usage."[52] This language can only be

41 24 C.F.R. § 965.508.
42 24 C.F.R. § 865.470 (1983).
43 Introductory Comments, 49 Fed. Reg. 31399, 31405 (Aug. 7, 1984).
44 *Id.*
45 *Id.*

46 24 C.F.R. § 965.505(a) ("energy-conservative" household standard), (d) (listing of nine factors PHA shall consider, none of which is actual consumption by tenants).
47 24 C.F.R. § 965.502(b), (c).
48 24 C.F.R. § 965.505(d).
49 24 C.F.R. § 965.508. *See* Amone v. Aveiro, 226 F.R.D. 677 (D. Haw. 2005) (certifying, in a case in which disabled plaintiff requiring oxygen machine, nebulizer, and air conditioner alleged gross insufficiency in utility allowance, class of "disabled persons that currently reside, or have resided within the last two years, in an HCDCH public housing project in which residents receive utility allowances, whose special needs arising from their disability require them to consume utilities in excess of the amount provided for in the standard public housing utility allowances"), *subsequent proceeding*, 2007 WL 2479291 (D. Haw. Aug. 27, 2007) (approval of settlement after earlier finding that public housing project failed to provide adjustments to utility allowances of class members).
50 U.S. Dep't of Hous. & Urban Dev., Public Housing Occupancy Guidebook § 10.7, at 138 (June 2003).
51 24 C.F.R. § 965.505(d).
52 U.S. Dep't of Hous. & Urban Dev., Public Housing Occupancy Guidebook § 10.7, at 138 (June 2003).

interpreted to mean that PHAs must consider, for example, whether a family of six is under-housed in a two-bedroom unit and may consume more utility service than the PHA assumes in setting the utility allowances for two-bedroom units. This language also requires a PHA to consider, for example, that a family of five consists of a mother and four young children and that the family's above-average consumption of hot water is perfectly reasonable and conservative, given the demographics of the family. Since the Guidebook does not provide further detail, it is not clear that the PHA would be required to adjust *all* of its utility allowances to reflect unusual family circumstances. But the Guidebook language would fully support petitions for individual relief from inadequate utility allowances, especially because family size and composition are "special factors affecting utility usage not within the control of the resident."[53]

The Guidebook also includes extremely useful language on the desired relationship between actual consumption and utility allowances, urging changes to allowances when consumption routinely exceeds allowances:

> When the actual consumption by tenants routinely exceeds a utility allowance, the PHA shall increase the allowance unless the PHA can provide evidence that the energy consumption can be attributed to a lack of non[sic]-energy conservative consumption. The fact that tenant consumption is routinely in excess of the PHA's utility allowance is material evidence that the PHA allowance is insufficient or that excess consumption may be due to factors not within the control of the tenants.[54]

This single paragraph completely inverts the usual relationship in which the PHA sets an inadequate utility allowance and the tenants bear an often insurmountable burden in proving that the allowances must be raised. The Guidebook is not a legally binding document, and tenants will have a hard time establishing a cause of action for non-compliance with the Guidebook. But the Guidebook language should prove very useful in negotiating with PHAs and could provide additional weight to litigation that is also founded in the Brooke Amendment or other legal theories.

The Guidebook also favorably addresses the distinction between "necessary appliances," use of which should be included in utility allowances, and luxury appliances, usage of which is not covered. The Guidebook urges PHAs to consider "local usage and custom patterns" when drawing this distinction, which might lead to including, for example, consumption of clothes washers and dryers at a development far from any public laundry or significant use of electric fans in hot climates. This language in the Guidebook provides tenants a basis on which to make their arguments that the PHA consider the actual appliances that tenants must use in particular locales and the larger consumption that might be consistent with "local usage and custom."

The Guidebook also provides detail on an issue that may be helpful to tenants seeking to update their allowances in response to price increases. PHAs are required to revise their allowances if "there is a rate change (including fuel adjustments)[55] . . . [and] such change [that], by itself or together with prior rate changes not adjusted for, results in a change of 10 percent or more from the rates on which such allowances were based."[56] The Guidebook makes it clear that price changes in "non-tariffed home energy services" such as home heating oil must be tracked as well:

> If at the end of the current heating season (October 1 through April 30 of each year), the average price of a non-tariffed fuel has increased by 10 percent or more, relative to the price of the same fuel for the winter heating season in or immediately preceding the date on which the resident payment became effective, the PHA shall readjust the resident payment retroactive to the month following the month in which the last change taken into account became effective.[57]

These provisions of in HUD Guidebook reflect a clear policy that utility allowances should be fair, reasonable, and up-to-date. Whenever tenants are negotiating with PHAs over the level of utility allowances, PHAs should be directed to these Guidebook provisions.

10.2.4 Appliances and Uses Covered by and Excluded from Utility Allowances

Utility allowances would appear to cover the consumption of all tenant-paid "utilities" other than telephone,[58] including household-related services such as trash disposal and water or sewer charges.[59] In public housing, allowances must be established for "major equipment" and for "utility functions furnished by the PHA for all tenants (for example, heating furnace, hot water heater), for essential equipment whether or not supplied by the PHA (for example, range and

---

53 24 C.F.R. § 965.508.

54 U.S. Dep't of Hous. & Urban Dev., Public Housing Occupancy Guidebook § 14.1, at 170 (June 2003).

55 HUD's Public Housing Occupancy Guidebook, § 14.3, at 171, reinforces the point that any increase in a fuel adjustment or automatic adjustment clause must be considered "rate changes."

56 24 C.F.R. § 965.507(b).

57 U.S. Dep't of Hous. & Urban Dev., Public Housing Occupancy Guidebook § 14.3, at 171 (June 2003).

58 24 C.F.R. § 5.603(b).

59 *See, e.g.*, 24 C.F.R. § 982.517(a), (b)(2)(ii) (voucher/rental assistance certificate rules).

However, at least in the rental assistance programs, a PHA may not provide an allowance for "non-essential utility costs, such as costs of cable or satellite television." 24 C.F.R. § 982.517(b)(2)(i).

refrigerator), and for minor items of equipment (such as toasters and radios)."[60] However, since 1996, HUD has prohibited PHAs from including air conditioning usage in setting utility allowances for public housing. PHAs are instructed to avoid "whenever possible" air conditioner systems that do "not provide for resident option," that is, built-in systems under management control.[61] Furthermore, "[f]or systems that offer residents the option to choose air conditioning, the PHA shall not include air conditioning in the utility allowances."[62]

HUD's absolute willingness to include utility allowances for all heating sources (fueled by natural gas, electricity, home heating oil, and so forth) and implacable resistance to public housing utility allowances that reflect air-conditioning usage flies in the face of reality and place tenants at great risk of harm. Excessive heat is even more likely to lead to injury and death than extreme cold.[63] It is hard to reconcile HUD's exclusion of air conditioning-related expenditures from public housing utility allowances with its mandate that utility allowances should be established "consistent with the requirements of a safe, sanitary, and healthful living environment."[64]

HUD has not been consistent in its rules regarding allowances for air conditioning usage. HUD's rules for the rental assistance (voucher and certificate) programs require that the "PHA must provide a utility allowance for tenant-paid air-conditioning costs if the majority of housing units in the market provide centrally air-conditioned units or there is appropriate wiring for tenant-installed air-conditioning."[65] In the past, HUD has been open to the argument that PHAs in warm climates should be allowed to reflect air conditioning usage in utility allowances.[66] Furthermore, in a decision issued two years after the current version of the utility allowance rules were adopted in 1996, a federal court in Texas referenced its prior order that the PHA provide a "utility allowance which includes an amount sufficient to allow for the costs of reasonable use of the air conditioning in the family projects."[67] At least in the context of that case, a PHA was required to consider the costs of air conditioning for tenants living in the sweltering heat of east Texas.[68]

Given HUD's contradictory positions over time and across programs (public housing versus rental assistance), public housing tenants should advocate with their local PHAs to consider essential air conditioning usage when setting allowances. The regulations clearly allow tenants to request relief based on any grounds that the PHA finds "reasonable," especially if the tenants are elderly, ill, or disabled.[69] Elderly and ill tenants face grave health risks, including even death, if they live without air conditioning during times of extreme heat.[70] Well-organized tenant efforts, especially if supported by local politicians, could prove successful in getting PHAs to recognize the importance of air conditioning to a "safe, sanitary and healthful living environment."[71]

Housing authorities often do not consider usage of clothes washers, clothes dryers, or food freezers when setting utility allowances. In fact, many PHAs surcharge master-metered tenants who have these appliances, relying on the provisions of 24 C.F.R. 965.506(b). However, use of clothes washers and dryers, may be a virtual necessity in buildings not located near commercial laundries. Use of washers, dryers and freezers is economically reasonable for low-income

60 24 C.F.R. § 965.505(b).

61 24 C.F.R. § 965.505(e).

62 *Id.*

63 For example, during the summer of 2003, the heat in Europe killed an estimated 20,000 to 35,000 people, most of whom were elderly. Camille Feanny and Keisha Porter, Europe Recalls Lethal 2003 Heat Wave (Aug. 3, 2004), *at* www.cnn.com/2004/TECH/science/08/02/heatwave.europe.

The Centers for Disease Control and Prevention estimate that 7421 Americans died of heat-related deaths between 1979 and 1998, with an annual median of 274 deaths and a single-year high of 1700. Centers for Disease Control, *Heat-Related Deaths—Los Angeles County, California, 1999–2000, and United States, 1979–1998*, 50 Morbidity & Mortality Weekly Report 29 (July 27, 2001).

64 24 C.F.R. § 965.505(a).

65 24 C.F.R. § 965.517(b)(2)(ii).

66 *In re* Housing Auth. of Houston, 25 Clearinghouse Rev. 568 (Aug.–Sept. 1991) (Clearinghouse No. 46,718) (letter from Assistant Secretary for Public & Indian Housing to Susan Sere, Gulf Coast Legal Foundation, dated April 4, 1991, in response to administrative complaint, advising that PHAs may consider air conditioning pending further guidance from HUD).

67 National Ass'n for the Advancement of Colored People, City of Commerce Branch v. Housing Auth. of the City of Commerce, 1998 WL 320307, at *1 (N.D. Tex. June 8, 1998). *See also* Armstrong v. Gallia Metro. Hous. Auth., 2000 WL 1505949, at *17–18 (Sept. 29, 2000) (plaintiffs allege PHA improperly failed to take into account "warm-weather related energy consumption"; court finds genuine issues of material fact in dispute over setting of allowances).

68 There are also a few pre-1996 cases that resulted in settlements for tenants who argued that they were entitled to consideration of their air conditioning usage. *See* Giles v. Housing Auth., No. 89-107 (E.D. Ky. May 3, 1990), 24 Clearinghouse Rev. 257 (July 1990) (Clearinghouse No. 45,074); Hubbard v. Metropolitan Dev. & Hous. Agency, No. 3-87-0789 (M.D. Tenn. Dec. 23, 1987), 22 Clearinghouse Rev. 800 (Dec. 1988) (Clearinghouse No. 43,785).

69 24 C.F.R. § 965.508. *See also* Amone v. Aveiro, 226 F.R.D. 677 (D. Haw. 2005) (certifying, in a case in which disabled plaintiff requiring oxygen machine, nebulizer, and air conditioner alleged gross insufficiency in utility allowance, class of "disabled persons that currently reside, or have resided within the last two years, in an HCDCH public housing project in which residents receive utility allowances, whose special needs arising from their disability require them to consume utilities in excess of the amount provided for in the standard public housing utility allowances"), *subsequent proceeding*, 2007 WL 2479291 (D. Haw. Aug. 27, 2007) (approval of settlement after earlier finding that public housing project failed to provide adjustments to utility allowances of class members).

70 Cooling is recognized in the federal Low-Income Home Energy Assistance Program (LIHEAP) as a critical home energy need. "Home energy" is defined as including "a source of heating or cooling," and "energy crisis" in defined to include any "weather-related . . . emergencies." 42 U.S.C. § 8622(3), (6).

71 24 C.F.R. § 965.505(a).

tenants who cannot afford to use commercial laundries and who can reduce their food purchase costs by purchasing large quantities of food products that are on sale. Tenants and their advocates should argue that, at least in certain contexts, electric utility allowances that reflect use of these appliances is in fact "reasonable consumption of utilities by an energy-conservative household of modest circumstances consistent with the requirements of a safe, sanitary, and healthful living environment."[72]

10.2.5 Rules Specific to the Rental Assistance Programs (Vouchers and Certificates)

10.2.5.1 Differences Between Public Housing and Voucher Programs

There are many similarities, but also important differences, between the public housing program and the rental assistance programs ("Section 8" certificates and housing vouchers), both in terms of the housing programs themselves and utility allowance rules.

Public housing units are owned by the PHA. Rents are largely set based on tenants' incomes. Rental assistance units are privately owned and the owners set their own rents but receive financial assistance from the PHA or other governmental entity so that tenants' out-of-pocket payments are below market rates.

In public housing, if utility allowances were adequate in all cases (which is often not the case), each tenant's rent burden (actual rent plus utilities) would be capped at 30% of income.[73] For master-metered tenants who do not pay utility costs directly, the rent is literally set at 30% of adjusted income. For the large numbers of retail-metered tenants who pay for utilities, the rent is set at 30% of income minus a reasonable allowance for utilities. If the allowance is adequate, these tenants end up paying no more than 30% of income for rent plus utilities.

Tenants who receive voucher assistance are exposed to much higher rents, quite often between 30% and 40% of income and sometimes even higher. The tenant's rent share is not even theoretically capped at 30% of income, as in the public housing program. Instead, the amount of assistance the tenant receives is calculated by reference to a "payment standard."[74] The tenant finds an apartment on the open market, applying that amount of assistance against the actual rent. Because tenants are permitted to rent apartments for which the rent is above the payment standard, the tenant's rent burden is not capped.[75] At the time of initial occupancy, the PHA is supposed to ensure that the tenant's share of the rent does not exceed 40% of adjusted income.[76] Subsequently, however, the owner is free to increase the rent, and the tenant's share is completely unlimited by any voucher rules. The simplified example below illustrates these basic differences between the public housing and voucher programs:

	Tenant A Public Housing	Tenant B Voucher
Adj. income	$1200/mo	$1200/mo.
PUBLIC HOUSING		
Tenant's payment (30%[77] of income; util. incl. w/rent)	$360	N.A.
VOUCHER TENANT		
2-bdrm. payment standard[78]	N.A.	$900/mo.
Assumed Tenant payment (at 30% of income[79])	N.A.	$360
Assistance payment	N.A.	$540[80]
Actual rent[81]	N.A.	$1000/mo.
Tenant's payment	N.A.	$460[82]

72 *Id. Cf.* Armstrong v. Gallia Metro. Hous. Auth., 2000 WL 1505949 (S.D. Ohio Sept. 29, 2000) (housing authority charged monthly washer fee on the ground that washer was a luxury), subsequent proceeding, 2001 WL 1842452 (S.D. Ohio Apr. 23, 2001) (settlement including termination of fee for use of tenant-owned washing machine).

73 *See* §§ 10.1.1, 10.1.2, *supra* (discussing the Brooke Amendment and the setting of rents in public housing.

74 24 C.F.R. § 982.4(b) ("*Payment Standard*: The maximum monthly assistance payment for a family assisted in the Voucher Program (before deducting the total tenant payment by the family).").

75 24 C.F.R. § 982.1(a)(4)(ii) ("In the voucher program, the subsidy is based on a local 'payment standard'. . . . If the rent is more than the payment standard, the family pays a larger share of the rent.").

76 24 C.F.R. § 982.508.

77 42 U.S.C. § 1437a(a)(1).

78 As noted above, the concept of a "payment standard" only applies in the Voucher Program. Here, a "payment standard" of $900 means that the PHA would not provide a subsidy of more than $900 per month for a two-bedroom unit even if the tenant has no income. The amount of assistance decreases as income increases. PHAs determine the payment standard at their own discretion but subject to Department of Housing and Urban Development guidelines, 24 C.F.R. § 982.503.

79 While a tenant's rent share is no more than 30% of income if the actual rent plus utilities does not exceed the "payment standard" (42 U.S.C. § 1437f(o)(2)(A)), the tenant's share will exceed 30% of income if the actual rent plus utilities exceeds the payment standard (42 U.S.C. § 1437f(o)(2)(B)).

80 When the rent (here, $1000) is equal to or greater than the "payment standard" (here, $900), the amount of assistance provided by the PHA to the voucher tenant is equal to the payment standard ($900) less 30% of the tenant's income (here, $360) or $540 in this example. 42 U.S.C. § 1437f(o)(2)(B).

81 In the Voucher Program, the tenant finds an apartment and the rent is simply what the landlord chooses to charge, so long as the rent is "reasonable." 24 C.F.R. §§ 982.1(a)(2), 982.507.

82 The tenant's share of the rent in the Voucher Program is equal to the "actual rent" charged by the owner (here, $1000), less the assistance provided by the PHA. The PHA's assistance is calculated not on the actual rent but on the theoretical "rent standard" (here, $900): when the rent is equal to or greater than the "payment standard" (here, $900), the amount of assistance provided by the PHA to the voucher tenant is equal to the

In this example, Tenant A, the public housing tenant, simply pays 30% of income, or $360, as rent. The housing authority does not calculate a "payment standard" and the tenant's rent will not increase unless her income increases.

Voucher Tenant B, with the same income as Tenant A, ends up paying $460 as rent or more than 38% of her income. Because the PHA is free to set the "payment standard" at anywhere between 90% and 110% of the "fair market rent" ("FMR") in the community[83] and also because the tenant can choose any available apartment, tenants quite frequently rent apartments that are above the payment standard. This means that they often pay much more than 30% of their income as rent.

10.2.5.2 Voucher Tenants Face Unique Problems

Voucher Program tenants who pay their own utility bills face some unique problems. Under the Voucher Program's complex rules, the relationships among "payment standards," actual rents, and utility allowances can drive tenant burdens well above 30% or even 40% of income. In some cases, a PHA that increases the utility allowances for voucher tenants will not increase the amount of assistance the tenants receive, and it may make it impossible for tenants to rent certain apartments. It is hard to understand the unique situation of voucher tenants without considering some very realistic examples.

Consider a tenant who has $666.66 of monthly adjusted income and who finds an acceptable two-bedroom apartment that rents for $650 and that has average monthly utility costs (tenant-paid) of $60. Assume that the PHA has set a "payment standard" of $710,[84] so the actual rent is less than the payment standard. Also assume that the PHA keeps its utility allowances up-to-date and accurate so that it offers a $60 utility allowance. In this example, the amount of assistance that the PHA provides to the landlord will be $510, calculated as the "gross rent" of $710[85] minus the "total tenant payment"[86] of $200.[87] Therefore, the tenant will pay the owner only $140 (the actual rent of $650 minus the PHAs assistance of $510 per month) and pay another $60 out-of-pocket for utilities. The tenant's total rent burden will be $200 ($140 directly to owner plus $60 to utility companies).

Surprisingly, the tenant is worse off if the utility costs increase *even if the PHA increases the utility allowance by a commensurate amount*. If everything in the prior example remains the same, except that the actual monthly utility costs increase to $70 and the PHA increases the utility allowance to $70, the tenant ends up paying $210 per month in total, rather than $200:

- The "gross rent" has increased to $720, the sum of the actual rent of $650 plus utility costs of $70.[88]
- The amount of assistance the PHA will provide to the owner does not increase but remains at $510 because the assistance is now calculated in reference to the "payment standard" of $710, not in reference to the "gross rent" of $720.[89]
- The tenant still pays the landlord $140 towards the rent because the assistance payment to the owner remains at $510.
- The tenants now pays $70, not $60, towards utilities, for a total rent burden of $210 ($140 in rent plus $70 in utilities).

As these examples make clear, higher utility allowances do not provide any benefit to voucher tenants unless the "gross rent" (actual rent plus utility payments) remains equal to or less than the "payment standard." Once the gross rent equals or exceeds the payment standard, the PHA's assistance payments will not increase, even if the PHA recognizes that utility costs are increasing. Moreover, higher utility allowances will eventually remove certain apartments from the voucher market. The Voucher Program rules prohibit tenants from renting units for which their share of the rent plus utilities exceeds "40 percent of the family's adjusted income" at the time of initial occupancy.[90] In the example we have been using of a tenant family with $666.67 of monthly income, this means that the family cannot rent a unit for which their share of the costs exceeds $266.67 (40% X $666.67). If the utility costs of the $650 apartment in our example are $128 per month[91] and the PHA in fact offers a utility allowance of $128, the tenant would be prohibited from renting the apartment because the tenant's share would exceed 40% of monthly income. The PHA's assistance payment would still be only $510, as in the prior examples, and the tenant would pay $140 directly to the owner. But the tenant would also pay $128 for utilities,

payment standard ($900) less 30% of the tenant's income. 42 U.S.C. § 1437f(o)(2)(B).

83 24 C.F.R. § 982.503(b).

84 Payment standards are set pursuant to 24 C.F.R. § 982.503 and may be set anywhere between 90% and 110% of the "fair market rent" without any approval from HUD.

85 "Gross rent" is defined in 24 C.F.R. § 982.4 as "[t]he sum of the rent to owner [here, $650] plus any utility allowance [here, $60]."

86 Total tenant payment is determined according to 24 C.F.R. § 5.628(a) and, in most cases, is simply 30% of the tenant's adjusted income.

87 *See* 24 C.F.R. § 982.505(b)(2) (the housing assistance payment is equal to the "gross rent minus the total tenant payment").

88 24 C.F.R. § 982.4(b).

89 *See* 42 U.S.C. § 1437f(o)(2)(B) (specifying that assistance is calculated in reference to the payment standard if the gross rent exceeds the payment standard); 24 C.F.R § 982.505(b) (same).

90 24 C.F.R. § 982.508.

91 A tenant who pays for electricity used for appliances and natural gas used for heating would easily pay $128 per month in utilities.

for a total "family share"[92] of $268 ($140 plus $128). Since $268 is greater than 40% of the tenant's income, the PHA would bar the tenant from renting the unit.

The real problem here is that utilities are so expensive and the "payment standard" does not reflect the impact of utilities on total rents that tenants pay. Tenants and their advocates should pay attention to the importance of raising payment standards in concert with raising utility allowances, so that any increases in the utility allowances provide real rather than illusory benefits.

10.2.5.3 Calculating Utility Allowances for Voucher Tenants

As in public housing, voucher tenants may live in private housing that has master meters (the bill for which the owner pays) or individual retail meters (for which the tenant pays). Unlike public housing tenants, voucher tenants who live in master-metered units are not subject to surcharges. Also, it is highly unlikely that a private owner would employ the use of check meters.[93] Voucher Program tenants who are responsible for paying any utility bills (for example, individually metered for gas or electricity or for heating oil, propane, sewer bills, and so forth) are entitled to utility allowances.

The rules governing the calculation of utility allowances for tenants in the Voucher Program[94] are clearer and, in some instances, more favorable than those in the public housing program.[95] At the outset, the voucher rules make clear that a PHA "must maintain a utility allowance schedule for all tenant-paid utilities (except telephone), for cost of tenant-supplied refrigerators and ranges, and for other tenant-paid housing services (for example, trash collection, that is, disposal of waste and refuse)."[96] The voucher rules are much clearer than the public housing rules that PHAs must consider the costs of refrigerators and ranges.[97] A guidebook released by HUD clarifies that allowances for these tenant-provided appliances "should be based on the lower of the cost of leasing the equipment or the cost of purchasing it on an installment plan."[98]

The rules also make it clear that the "utility allowance schedule must be determined based on the typical cost of utilities and services paid by energy-conservative households . . . in the same locality [using] . . . normal patterns of consumption for the community. . . ."[99] This is a somewhat clearer standard than for public housing by which the PHA need only "take into account" a laundry list of "relevant factors" and has its discretion repeatedly protected by HUD.[100]

The voucher rules also provide needed clarity by specifying that separate utility allowances must be developed for "space heating; air conditioning;[101] cooking; water heater; water; sewer; trash collection (disposal of waste and refuse); other electric; refrigerator (cost of tenant-supplied refrigerator); range (cost of tenant-supplied range); and other specified housing services."[102] The accompanying guidebook provides PHAs with a sample form for tabulating the allowances in each of these categories.[103]

Utility allowances must be calculated separately for apartment size (number of bedrooms) and for each "unit type (for example, apartment, row-house, town house, single-family detached, and manufactured housing) that are typical for the community."[104] This requirement is very helpful because consumption patterns vary significantly among the various building types. Tenants and their advocates should make sure that PHAs comply with this requirement.

Unlike the public housing program, however, there is no requirement in the Voucher Program that the PHA disclose to tenants any of the information relied on or methods used to develop the utility allowances. Rather, PHAs need only prepare and submit their allowance schedules "in accordance with HUD requirements on the form prescribed by

---

92 See 24 C.F.R. §§ 982.4, 982.515(a) (calculation of "family share").

93 *See* § 10.1.4, *supra* (discussing the types of metering arrangements).

94 24 C.F.R. § 982.517.

95 24 C.F.R. § 965.501–965.508.

96 24 C.F.R. § 982.517(a)(1).

97 The Voucher Program rules are also clear that allowances may not reflect "non-essential utility costs, such as costs of cable or satellite television." 24 C.F.R. § 982.517(b)(2)(i).

98 Voucher Program Guidebook—Housing Choice (7420.10G), § 18.3, at 18-7 (Apr. 2001).

Note that the cover page of the guidebook states that it is prepared by the Quadel Consulting Corporation, with the caution: "The contents of this guidebook are the views of the contractor and do not necessarily reflect the views or policy of the Department of Housing and Urban Development." However, this guidebook is available on HUD's website at www.hud.gov/offices/pih/programs/hcv/forms/guidebook.cfm. HUD seemingly adopts this guidebook with the following language on its web page: "The purpose of this guidebook is to advise public housing agencies (PHAs) and other organizations providing services to PHAs, regarding the administration of the tenant-based subsidy programs. . . . The new Housing Choice Voucher Program Guidebook (7420.10g) is enroute to Public Housing Agencies and HUD field offices through the normal HUD distribution process." The binding legal effect of the guidebook, however, is unclear.

99 24 C.F.R. § 982.517(b).

100 24 C.F.R. §§ 965.502 (e) (preserving PHA discretion); § 965.505 (c), (d) (further preserving PHA discretion and not requiring PHAs to even consider "normal patterns of consumption in the community").

101 "The PHA must provide a utility allowance for tenant-paid air-conditioning costs if the majority of housing units in the market provide centrally air-conditioned units or there is appropriate wiring for tenant-installed air conditioners." 24 C.F.R. 982.517(b)(2)(ii).

102 24 C.F.R. 982.517(b)(2)(ii).

103 Voucher Program Guidebook—Housing Choice (7420.10G), at 18-3 (Apr. 2001).

104 24 C.F.R. § 982.517(b)(3).

HUD."[105] Moreover, PHAs may set utility allowances for voucher tenants on an area-wide basis (for example, for a whole town or city), not on a development-specific basis, as many PHAs do for their public housing developments.[106] As a matter of practice, PHAs simply are less likely to gather and analyze consumption data for privately owned buildings where voucher tenants reside than for individual developments that the PHA owns. Area-wide allowances certainly are administratively simpler but mean that the allowances for voucher tenants may be little more than best guesses of typical or reasonable consumption in particular rental units.

Each PHA is required to review its schedules of utility allowances "each year, and must revise its allowances for a utility category" if there has been a "change of 10 percent or more in the utility rate since the last time the utility allowance schedule was revised."[107] HUD's rules emphasize the importance of offering higher allowances when requested by a person with disabilities "if a higher utility allowance is needed as a reasonable accommodation . . . to make the program accessible to and usable by the family member with a disability."[108] However, unlike the public housing rules,[109] the voucher rules do not specifically authorize any route for individual relief for non-disabled tenants. Nevertheless, voucher tenants who believe that the utility allowance schedule has not been properly calculated have a right under 42 U.S.C. § 1983 to challenge it as violating the United States Housing Act and implementing regulations.[110]

The Voucher Program places a very clear obligation on tenants "to pay for any utilities that the owner is not required to provide but which are to be provided by the tenant," and the "PHA may terminate assistance for the family" if the failure to keep utility services on leads to "a breach of the HQS [housing quality standards]."[111] This rule is particularly unfortunate given the frequent inadequacies of utility allowances and the unique problems that voucher tenants face if utility allowances cause the gross rent to exceed the payment standard.[112] The voucher rules permit (but do not require) a PHA to consider "all relevant circumstances" when determining whether to terminate assistance.[113] It is hard to imagine a more compelling set of circumstances for deciding *not* to terminate assistance than a case in which inadequate utility allowances cause a tenant to miss utility payments, resulting in the electric or gas service being terminated.

Finally, at least as explained in the Voucher Program guidebook, there is one other utility allowance concept in the Voucher Program that is favorable compared to the public housing program.[114] The guidebook recognizes that utility rates vary by the volume of consumption, and customers who consume more (for example, heating customers of an electric utility) tend to get lower rates. The guidebook recommends that, "[f]or convenience in calculating the utility allowances for any combination of utilities, . . . that the PHA use the higher rates."[115] However, the guidebook also recommends using "rates at the middle or bottom of the company's rate schedule" for usage that generally lead to higher consumption for a particular utility service—"electric cooking, water heating and space heating."[116]

In rare circumstances, the housing assistance payment calculated by the housing authority may be larger than the rent due to the owner. This will generally occur if the tenant's income is exceedingly low and the PHA utility allowance is relatively large.[117] In those instances, the "the PHA may pay the balance of the housing assistance payment ('utility reimbursement') either to the family or directly to the utility supplier. . . ."[118]

Utility allowances for voucher tenants will often be set too low, particularly because the PHA will almost certainly set allowances based on municipal-wide or even national data that do no reflect reasonable usage within the specific

105 24 C.F.R. § 982.517(b)(4). *Cf.* 24 C.F.R. § 965.502(b) (requiring PHAs to make utility allowance files available to tenants).

106 24 C.F.R. § 982.517(b)(1); Voucher Program Guidebook—Housing Choice (7420.10G), at 18-3, 18-4 (Apr. 2001) (allowing use of national data, adjusted only for bedroom size).

107 24 C.F.R. § 982.517(c)(1). The Voucher Program Guidebook reinforces this point. Voucher Program Guidebook—Housing Choice (7420.10G), at 18-6 (Apr. 2001).

108 24 C.F.R. § 982.517(e).

109 24 C.F.R. § 965.508(requests for relief from surcharges for excess consumption of PHA-purchased utilities).

110 Johnson v. Housing Auth. of Jefferson Parish, 442 F.3d 356 (5th Cir. 2006).

111 24 C.F.R. § 982.404(b).

The HQS are contained in 24 C.F.R. § 982.401 and include a number of standards that could be breached if, for example, the tenant failed to pay the electric bill, leading to a termination of electric service, causing a breach of food storage and preparation standards, the "thermal environment" standard, and the illumination standard.

112 *See* § 10.2.5.2, *supra* (discussing these problems).

113 24 C.F.R. § 982.552(c)(2). *See, e.g.*, Robinson v. District of Columbia Hous. Auth., 660 F. Supp. 2d 6 (D.D.C. 2009) (deferring to agency's interpretation of regulation and determining that hearing officer was under no obligation to consider mitigating circumstances presented at informal hearing on loss of benefits); Gammons v. Massachusetts Dep't of Hous. & Cmty. Dev., 523 F. Supp. 2d 76, 81 (D. Mass. 2007) (because regulation does not mandate consideration of all relevant circumstances, it cannot support a section 1983 claim).

114 Voucher Program Guidebook—Housing Choice (7420.10G) §§ 18.3, 18-6 (Apr. 2001).

115 *Id.*

116 *Id.*

117 The housing assistance payment can be greater than the rent because the assistance payment is equal to "gross rent" (defined in 24 C.F.R. § 982.4 as actual rent to owner plus utility allowance) less the "total tenant payment," with the caveat that, if the gross rent exceeds the payment standard, the assistance payment is equal to the payment standard less the total tenant payment. 24 C.F.R. § 982.505(b). Therefore, if the utility allowance is relatively large and the tenant's payment relatively small, the assistance payment can be larger than the rent.

118 24 C.F.R. § 982.514(b).

buildings where tenants actually reside. Tenants and their advocates should pay very close attention to the utility allowance levels and advocate for increases whenever those allowances are inadequate.[119]

10.2.6 *Utility Allowances in HUD-Subsidized Developments: Section 236 and Project-Based Section 8*

10.2.6.1 Overview

The vast majority of low-income tenants who receive federal housing assistance live in public housing or are voucher tenants. There are, however, a bewildering array of other housing subsidy programs, some of which may require that tenants be granted utility allowances. It is beyond the scope of this section to describe all of these other housing programs in detail or to summarize the utility allowance rules that apply to each program. Those who need to learn more about any particular housing program should consult the third edition of, and 2010 supplement to, *HUD Housing Programs: Tenants' Right*, which describes the many different housing programs and also provides useful guidance on how to identify the program involved.[120] This section will describe the utility allowance rules in the Section 236 program as well as the still-extant Section 8 programs.

10.2.6.2 Section 236 Housing

Congress adopted the so-called Section 236[121] housing program in 1968 to replace the prior Section 221(d)(3) program.[122] Both programs were designed to reduce the interest-driven costs of developing new housing so that the rents would be more affordable to low-income families. Under the 236 program, HUD provided a subsidy to the developer's lender so that the developer's effective interest rate would be 1%. No new 236 projects have been developed since the 1970s, but there are still many low-income, often elderly tenants, living in Section 236-subsidized buildings. Many of the regulations governing the Section 236 program were repealed in the mid-1990s, but the repealed regulations apply to tenants still living in Section 236 housing under a "savings" clause in the current version of the Section 236 regulations. Therefore, advocates representing Section 236 tenants will have to obtain the April 1, 1995, version of 24 CFR Parts 200 to 499 to review the applicable regulations.[123]

Even with low-interest mortgages, the rents in many 236 developments were too expensive for most truly low-income tenants. Rents that are sufficient to cover an owner's operating costs plus mortgage payments at 1% interest will be less prohibitive than market rents but still more than many low-income people can afford. Over the years, Congress and HUD devised additional assistance to provide to Section 236 development owners so that the rents in some or even all of the units in these Section 236 buildings would be affordable, that is, capped at no more than 30% of the tenant's income. These forms of additional assistance include "Rent Supplement"[124] and "Rental Assistance Payments"[125] that allow the developers to charge tenants covered by this assistance no more than 30% of their income as rent. A tenant whose rent is capped at 30% of income is generally entitled to a utility allowance. Utility allowances may also affect the rent calculation even for those tenants whose rents are not capped as a percentage of income.

There are relatively few Section 236 developments that still receive either Rent Supplement or Rental Assistance payments.[126] By the early 1980s, HUD converted almost all of the units in Section 236 developments to project-based Section 8 assistance, including Section 8 Loan-Management Set Aside or Additional Assistance.[127]

A Section 236 tenant who is master-metered for all utilities pays no utility bills directly. The tenant will simply pay rent to the owner, calculated as the greater of the "basic rent" (based on the owner's actual costs, including the low-interest rate mortgage[128]) or 30% of the tenant's in-

---

119 *See* §§ 10.8, 10.9, *infra* (discussing various advocacy routes that can be followed).

120 Copies of *HUD Housing Programs: Tenants' Right* may be obtained from the National Hous. Law Project, (510) 251-9400, www.nhlp.org. Housing program descriptions appear in sections 1.1, 1.2, and 1.3 of *HUD Housing Programs: Tenants' Right*, while Chapter 6 of that book addresses utility charges in federally subsidized housing.

121 Pub. L. No. 90-448, § 201(a) (1968) (U.S.C.C.A.N. 575) added a new section 236 to the National Housing Act, 12 U.S.C. § 1715z-1. The program is known as "Section 236."

122 The 221(d)(3) program is codified at 12 U.S.C. § 1715*l*(d)(3). There are no utility allowance rules specific to the 221(d)(3) program, although certain tenants in 221(d)(3) housing may get other forms of housing assistance, such as "rent Supplement" or "Section 8 Loan Management Set-Aside," that require the provision of utility allowances.

123 24 C.F.R. § 236.1(c) ("Savings provision. Any mortgage approved by the Commissioner for insurance pursuant to sections 236(j) or 236(n) of the National Housing Act is governed by subpart A of this part as in effect immediately before May 1, 1996, contained in the April 1, 1995, edition of 24 C.F.R., parts 220 to 499, and by subparts B through E of this part, except as otherwise provided in this subpart.").

124 12 U.S.C. § 1701s(j)(1)(D).

125 12 U.S.C. § 1715z-1(f)(2).

126 Advocates who represent tenants in units that still receive either form of assistance may have to do additional research, as the discussion of utility allowances in Chapter 236 housing in this section may not apply. The best reference source is National Housing Law Project's *HUD Housing Programs: Tenants' Rights* (3d ed. 2004 and 2010 Supp.).

127 *See* 24 C.F.R. pt. 886.

128 "Basic rent" is defined in 24 C.F.R. § 236.2 (1995) (saved as applicable under 24 C.F.R. § 236.1(c)) as the "HUD-approved monthly rent . . . determined on the basis of operating the

come. For most low-income tenants, the basic rent will exceed 30% of the tenant's income.[129] The owner may be able to impose utility surcharges on tenants who have large optional appliances (for example, freezer or clothes dryer).[130]

Some Section 236 tenants will live in buildings with master meters (paid for by the owner) and individual check meters. The Section 236 handbook allows owners to impose surcharges on tenants for excessive usage, although "excessive" is not defined.[131]

Most Section 236 tenants will live in buildings that have individual retail meters, at least for electricity and possibly for gas services. However, only some of these tenants will benefit from utility allowances. Section 236 tenants who receive no other form of housing assistance pay as rent the greater of: (1) the basic rent (reflecting the owner's actual costs); (2) 30% of the tenant's adjusted income *less* a reasonable utility allowance; or (3) 25% of the tenant's adjusted income.[132] As noted above, the basic rent for most low-income tenants will exceed 30% of the tenant's income, and the tenant's rent will therefore be set equal to the basic rent, without any adjustment for a utility allowance. However, owners will still have to provide utility allowances for tenants with relatively higher income, if 30% of their income is higher than the basic rent. Much as in the public housing program, "utility allowance" is defined as a "reasonable consumption of such utilities [for example, all but telephone] and other services for the unit by an energy-conservative household of modest circumstances consistent with the requirements of a safe, sanitary, and healthful living environment."[133] Unlike in the public housing program, HUD provides little guidance on how PHAs should translate these words into numerical utility allowances.

Section 236 owners must file a request with HUD to increase utility allowances whenever there has been a cumulative increase of 10% or more in utility rates.[134] Section 236 tenants also have some rights when owners seek to reduce any utility allowances (effectively raising the tenant's rent) or switch to individual retail meters. Owners must provide tenants at least 30 days' advance notice before requesting HUD approval. The notice must describe the tenants' rights to review all relevant materials and to comment on the proposed action.[135] The owner must file specified documentation with HUD and obtain HUD's approval before proceeding with any proposed reductions to utility allowances or conversions from master-metering to individual retail meters.[136]

At least some Section 236 tenants are entitled to "utility reimbursements," meaning a check paid by the PHA to the tenant or tenant's utility company[137] if the utility allowance is larger than the tenant's rent, but the rules are contradictory as to whom it applies. Under 24 C.F.R. § 236.2 (1995),[138] the term "utility reimbursement" is "applicable only to the Rental Assistance Program," implying that utility reimbursements are not applicable to Rent Supplement tenants in Section 236 housing. But the most recent version of the relevant HUD Handbook that covers the Section 236 program (including Rent Supplement and Rental Assistance Payments) states:

> When the TTP [Total Tenant Payment] is less than the utility allowance, the tenant receives a utility reimbursement to assist in meeting utility costs. The tenant will pay no tenant rent. The utility reimbursement is calculated by subtracting the TTP from the utility allowance.[139]

---

project with payment of principal and interest at the rate of 1 percent per annum." *See* prior versions of 24 C.F.R. § 236.2, *available on the companion website to this treatise.*

129 For example, a tenant whose income is $1500 per month (assuming no adjustments to income) would have to pay the basic, rather than the income-based, rent in any development where the basic rent was greater than $450.

130 *See* National Hous. Law Project, HUD Housing Programs: Tenants' Rights § 6.3.2, at 6/19 (3d ed. 2004 and 2010 supp.).
Note that one court refused to overturn an increase in the amount of the surcharge imposed for use of air conditioners, even when the owner had admittedly failed to comply with various HUD rules. Feir v. Carabetta Enter., 459 F. Supp. 841 (D. Conn. 1978).

131 U.S. Dep't of Hous. & Urban Dev., Rental and Cooperative Housing for Lower-Income Families, Section 236, Basic Instructions, Handbook 4510.1 ¶ 5-29 (1973).
Paragraph 5-29(a) notes several situations in which it may not make sense to install check-meters: when all of the tenants are elderly; when the utility service (for example, gas) is used only for cooking; and when the cost of installing and operating check-meters outweighs any potential savings in energy consumption. Advocates should check to determine if there have been any more recent changes or updates to this handbook.

132 12 U.S.C. § 1715z-1(f)(1)(B), (C); 24 C.F.R. § 236.55(b)(1) (1995) (saved as applicable under 24 C.F.R. § 236.1(c)); U.S. Dep't of Hous. & Urban Dev., Occupancy Requirements of Subsidized Multifamily Housing Programs, Handbook 4350.3, REV-1, fig. 5-7 (May 2003). *See* prior versions of 24 C.F.R. § 236.55, *available on the companion website to this treatise.*

133 24 C.F.R. § 5.603; 24 C.F.R. § 236.2 (1995) (saved as applicable under 24 C.F.R. § 236.1(c)).
Under 12 U.S.C. § 1715z-1(f)(1)(C), Section 236 tenants who pay their own utilities are entitled to a utility allowance "as the Secretary [of HUD] determines represents a proportionate decrease for the utility charges to be paid for such tenant."

134 24 C.F.R. § 236.55(d) (1995) (saved as applicable under 24 C.F.R. § 236.1(c)).

135 24 C.F.R. §§ 245.410, 245.420.

136 24 C.F.R. §§ 245.405, 245.416.

137 24 C.F.R. § 236.735(e) ("Where applicable, the Utility Reimbursement shall be paid to the Qualified Tenant. If the tenant and the utility company consent, the owner may pay the Utility Reimbursement jointly to the Qualified Tenant and the utility company, or directly to the utility company.").

138 Saved as applicable under 24 C.F.R. § 236.1(c).

139 U.S. Dep't of Hous. & Urban Dev., Occupancy Requirements of Subsidized Multifamily Housing Programs, Handbook 4350.3, REV-1, ch. 5-29 (2003). *See id.* at ch. 1-2, fig. 1-1 (describing the programs that it covers).

Given that there are likely few remaining units receiving Rent Supplement or Rental Assistance Payments, any need to resolve this ambiguity may be moot.

10.2.6.3 Projects Assisted Under Section 8

As noted in § 10.1.2, *supra*, there are no longer individual Section 8 certificates that provide subsidies to individual tenants who find their own apartments. All individual certificates have been converted to Housing Choice Vouchers. However, there is still "project-based" Section 8 assistance of various types that are tied to the building, not the tenant.

For all remaining Section 8 programs, the definition of "utility allowance" is similar to the definition discussed above for the Section 236 program: that is, one based on "reasonable consumption of such utilities and other services for the unit by an energy-conservative household of modest circumstances. . . ."[140] Like the Section 236 program regulations, the Section 8 regulations provide little detail on how a PHA translates this mandate into actual utility allowances. PHAs have discretion over the sources of consumption and other data that are considered in calculating allowances.

However, the project owner must review the utility allowance schedule at least annually. If the applicable utility rates have increased by 10% or more since the previously established or adjusted allowance, the Section 8 owner must increase the allowance accordingly.[141]

The regulations specifically require utility reimbursements when the utility allowance exceeds the tenant's share of the rent. The payment may be made to the tenant or, if the tenant consents, to the utility supplier on the tenant's behalf.[142]

A 2010 survey of administrators of project-based Section 8 properties revealed that "there is a wide disparity among [these] administrators in their utility allowance requirements" and in their compliance with federal statutes and regulations.[143] The same report concluded that "[i]t is likely that a substantial number of residents of housing with project-based Section 8 contracts are paying more than the statutory 30% of adjusted income for gross rent as the result of utility allowances not keeping up with utility cost increases."[144] To the extent that utility allowances are inadequate, tenants may be able to bring a successful legal action under the Brooke Amendment (42 U.S.C. § 1437a(a)), HUD's utility allowance regulations, and other legal authority.[145]

140 24 C.F.R. § 5.603(b).

141 24 C.F.R. §§ 880.610, 881.601.

142 24 C.F.R. § 5.632(b).

143 Housing Preservation Project, Sargent Shriver Nat'l Center on Poverty Law, *Inconsistent Administration of Project-Based Section Utility Allowances Threatens Low Income Families* (Summer–Fall 2010).

144 *Id.*

145 *See* § 10.7, *infra* (discussing utility allowance litigation theories).

10.2.7 *"Fannie Mae" and "Freddie Mac" Utility Allowances*

The Federal National Mortgage Association (known as "Fannie Mae") and Federal Home Loan Mortgage Corporation (known as "Freddie Mac") are "Government Sponsored Enterprises" (GSEs)[146] that purchase home mortgages and that operate under Congressional goals for promoting affordable housing. The Secretary of the Department of Housing and Urban Development is required to establish an annual goal "for the purchase by each enterprise" of purchase-money mortgages "financing owner-occupied housing" in which low-income families live and in low-income areas, and separately to "establish additional requirements for the purchase by each enterprise of mortgages on multifamily housing that finance dwelling units affordable to very low-income families."[147]

In some instances, however, the GSEs do not have actual information regarding the income of tenants and cannot directly determine whether tenants will be paying less than 30% of their income for rent, making those rents "affordable."[148] Instead, the GSEs determine affordability by comparing the total cost of rent and utilities for units that do not include utilities in rent to the income of targeted low-income populations.[149] On September 3, 2002, HUD published utility allowances that the GSEs may use for determining affordability.[150] While these so-called "utility allowances" do not in any way affect the rent or other payments of tenants who live in buildings where the mortgage has been purchased by one of the GSEs, those allowances reflect HUD's thinking as to the actual level of utility costs in 2002 for all utilities (electricity, gas, fuel oil, other fuel, water and sewerage, garbage, and trash removal[151]). The utility allowances for multifamily buildings are: $41 (efficiency unit); $57 (one-bedroom); $80 (two-bedroom); $112 (three-bedroom or more). For single family units, the allowances are: $41 (efficiency); $73 (one-bedroom); $113 (two-bedroom); $155 (three-bedroom). HUD bases these allowances on data it obtains from the American Housing Survey and revises the allowances every few years. However, in the Federal Register notice announcing these allowances, HUD provides no explanation of how it calculates the individual components (for example, the separate costs of electricity, gas, fuel oil, and so forth) nor how it weights each component, given that few tenants pay for the full array of utilities covered by the allowances.

146 12 U.S.C. § 4502(10) (definition of "enterprise").

147 12 U.S.C. §§ 4562(a), 4563(a).

148 12 U.S.C. §§ 4563(c) (definition of "affordability").

149 12 U.S.C. § 4502(14)–(16), (24) (definitions of "low-income," "median income," "moderate-income," and "very low-income.").

150 67 Fed. Reg. 56471–56473 (Sept. 3, 2002).

151 67 Fed. Reg. 56472 (Sept. 3, 2002).

10.3 Meter Conversions in Public Housing[152]

More than one million families live in PHA-owned public housing. The collective gas and electric utility bills for those units exceeds $2 billion. HUD and PHAs are eager to have tenants bear those costs whenever possible; tenants are generally better off whenever the PHA pays the utility bills. If the PHA is responsible for any of the utilities—that is, heating, hot water, miscellaneous lighting and appliances, and so forth—the PHA sees itself as financially at risk for increases in utility costs. Conversely, if tenants are responsible for the utility bills, the PHAs face little financial risk as rates rise, although the PHA will always be responsible for lighting and heating in hallways and other common areas. If the PHA pays the utility bills, the lights will stay on regardless of each tenant's financial circumstances. If the tenants are responsible for the bills, service will be terminated when winter cold or summer heat drives usage beyond the family's ability to pay; when illness or loss of a job wipes out a family's small savings and ability to pay; or when other necessities such as food, clothing, and medical costs eat up a household's meager earnings.

A PHA should be fairly compensated by HUD for its utility expenses, whether the PHA is paying just for a few hallway lights or for the total usage of utility services by tenants in their apartments. Under the current operating fund system, HUD provides funding to a PHA based on the difference between its "formula expense" (including "Utilities Expense Level") and "formula income."[153] If utility rates are increasing, the PHA is entitled to a larger subsidy from HUD.[154] Furthermore, PHAs receive financial rewards if usage decreases due to investments by the PHA in energy conservation measures.[155] The burden on PHAs of paying for all utilities is thus small. In fact, when energy costs rose sharply in the winter of 2000–2001, HUD announced that it had $50 million to assist PHAs, *not* tenants of those PHAs, in paying their rising energy bills.[156] HUD also released a guide for owners of Section 8 units that allowed them to request a one-time lump sum payment to recover excess utility costs.[157] Once again, this assistance was available to owners who pay their tenants' energy costs, but no new assistance was made available to tenants themselves.

By contrast, the burden is quite high on families in low-income public housing who pay their own utility bills. Low-income families with incomes at or below 100% of the federal poverty guideline—which includes most HUD-assisted households—often receive annual energy bills equivalent to 25% to 35% of total household income.[158] While public housing rents are much lower than in private housing, tenants still struggle to pay any utility bills for which they are responsible. Utility allowances are often inadequate.[159] Terminations of service for nonpayment are not uncommon for a number of reasons: tenant incomes are extremely low; utility rates may be rising; allowances are inadequate; and bills surge upward in winter (in cold climates) and summer (in warm climates) even though utility allowances usually remain the same throughout the year.

But HUD has taken a strong stance in favor of switching tenants to individually metered service. HUD regulations require the use of individual retail meters or check meters for tenants unless individual or check meters are impractical or not permitted.[160] Projects that have not converted must reevaluate the costs and benefits of converting at least every five years.[161]

HUD clearly intends to reduce utility costs for PHAs by having PHAs convert to individual metering. PHAs are most likely to see savings from master-metering when utility allowances are inadequate. If utility allowances were perfectly adequate, a metering conversion would reduce the PHA's out-of-pocket payments to utility companies but lead to a commensurate loss of rent revenue by the adoption of utility allowances. HUD intends that the use of individual meters will shift more of the utility costs onto the tenants. Tenants who live in units converted to individual or check meters will see their costs increase either through failure of inadequate utility allowances to cover utility costs previously paid by the PHA or through payment of PHA surcharges.

PHAs may take the position that meter conversions promote energy conservation because tenants will respond to the bills they see by reducing consumption. HUD has a bad track record of simply assuming that meter conversions will lead to large reductions in consumption. In a suit challenging an earlier version of HUD's meter conversion rules, a court of appeals held that there was an insufficient administrative record to review whether HUD's assumption of a

152 *See* National Hous. Law Project, HUD Housing Programs: Tenants' Rights § 6.3.2.7 (3d ed. 2004 and 2010 supp.) (discussing meter conversions in Section 236 housing).

153 24 C.F.R. §§ 990.110(a), 990.160–990.190.

154 24 C.F.R. § 990.170.

155 24 C.F.R. § 990.185.

156 U.S. Dep't of Hous. & Urban Dev., Notice PIH 2001-09 (HA), Funding of Dire Emergency Utility Costs in the Low Rent Public Housing Program (Mar. 19, 2001).

157 U.S. Dep't of Hous. & Urban Dev., Guidance for Processing Rental Adjustments for Escalating Energy Costs (Apr. 20, 2001).

158 Economic Opportunity Studies, The Burden of FY 08 Residential Energy Bills on Low-Income Consumers chart 4 (2008).

159 The last major study of the adequacy of utility allowances was conducted by the General Accounting Office in 1991. General Accounting Office, GAO/RCED-91-40A, Assisted Housing: Utility Allowances Often Fall Short of Actual Utility Expenses, vol. I (Mar. 26, 1991) (due to inadequate allowances, 32% of Section 8 households had rent burdens greater than 40% of income; at the twenty PHAs with highest rent burdens, average rent burden was 74%).

160 24 C.F.R. § 965.401.

161 24 C.F.R. § 965.407.

25% to 35% reduction in heating usage from meter conversions was properly supported.[162] HUD requires PHAs, when evaluating whether to proceed with conversions to individual retail meters, to weigh the savings of not paying utility bills against the costs of having to provide utility allowances. It similarly requires PHAs, when considering a conversion to a check-metering system, to weight the costs of installing and operating check meters against the potential reduction in utility expenditures.[163] But HUD offers no guidance and places no restraints on the assumptions PHAs can make about the reduced energy consumption that may result from meter conversions.

Tenants must be vigilant in tracking any PHA plans to convert to individual or check meters and in challenging fallacious or unsupported assumptions about energy savings. HUD regulations require PHAs to "adopt revised payment schedules, including appropriate [utility] allowances" before converting to retail service. These same regulations require the PHA to "work closely with resident organizations in planning the conversion to individual metering."[164] Another section of HUD's regulations requires PHAs to "maintain a record that documents the basis on which allowances and scheduled surcharges . . . are established and revised"; to make those documents available to tenants; to provide advance notice to tenants of allowances and scheduled surcharges; and to give tenants at least thirty days to comment on the proposed allowances or surcharges.[165] These procedural rights can create the opportunity for tenants and their advocates to derail ill-conceived meter conversions, especially if the proposed allowances are inadequate. Note, however, that at least one court has determined that the shifting of utility costs to tenants will not give rise to a claim that the Brooke Amendment (42 U.S.C. § 1437a(a)(1))—which caps tenant rents at 30% of adjusted income—has been violated, even though tenants may be required to post utility security deposits and clear up past arrearages.[166]

If a PHA converts to check meters, the PHA must provide tenants with a six-month transition period during which they will be advised of their charges but will not have to pay surcharges; this period also serves to test the adequacy of the newly established allowances.[167] However, HUD does not require such a transition period when the PHA converts to retail metering.[168]

One exception to the policy of converting to individual meters arises when the units need substantial weatherization. In this case, HUD forbids PHAs from installing individual utility meters to measure energy or fuel used for space heaters if the meters would result in economic hardship to the tenants. The PHA must weatherize before converting to individual meters.[169]

10.4 Seasonal Utility Allowances and Carryover Credits

In 1996, HUD amended its regulations to provide that utility allowances "may provide for seasonal variations."[170] HUD went on to specifically exclude consumption for air conditioning from the utility allowances for retail-metered public housing tenants and directed PHAs to surcharge check-metered tenants for their use of optional air-conditioning equipment.[171]

Prior to these new regulations, HUD seemed to be relenting on its position that air conditioning was a luxury and should not be included in tenants' utility allowances. In Houston, tenants filed an administrative complaint with HUD, challenging the determination that the PHA was precluded from including air conditioning as a factor when determining tenants' utility allowances. HUD promptly responded to the administrative complaint and advised the PHA that air conditioning may be included in its utility allowance at least until HUD issued further guidelines on this matter.[172] In the Section 8 program, at least two settlements occurred under which tenants were able to obtain increases in utility allowances specifically to provide for air conditioning. In Kentucky, a PHA agreed to revise its electrical and gas allowances to conform specifically to the criteria cited above in the regulations. Under the revised allowance, an electrical allowance for air conditioning is to be provided if the head of household is at least sixty-two years of age or if some member of the household has a

162 Massachusetts Union of Pub. Hous. Tenants v. Landrieu, 656 F.2d 899 (D.C. Cir. 1981) (per curiam remand). *See* Massachusetts Union of Pub. Hous. Tenants v. Pierce, 755 F.2d 177, 178 (D.C. Cir. 1985) (decision on fees; summarizing prior proceedings and noting the insufficient record for HUD's assumption). *See also* Massachusetts Union of Pub. Hous. Tenants v. Pierce, No. 78-1895 (D.D.C. Mar. 3, 1982, May 20, 1983, Aug. 8, 1983, and Oct. 30, 1984) (hearings upon remand); 15 Clearinghouse Rev. 285 (July, 1981) (Clearinghouse No. 31,152); 17 Clearinghouse Rev. 776 (Nov. 1983) (Clearinghouse No. 31,152).

163 24 C.F.R. § 965.402.

164 24 C.F.R. § 965.405.

165 24 C.F.R. § 965.502.

166 Crochet v. Housing Auth. of City of Tampa, 37 F.3d 607 (11th Cir. 1994).

167 24 C.F.R. § 965.405(d).

168 Regardless of the type of conversion, the PHAs are to advise and assist those residents with high utility consumption. 24 C.F.R. § 965.405(e). Such advice and assistance "may include counseling, installation of new energy conserving equipment or appliances, and corrective maintenance." *Id.*

169 24 C.F.R. § 965.304.

170 24 C.F.R. § 965.504(a). A prior version of these regulations more explicitly noted that seasonal allowances benefit tenants who pay for seasonally varying heating and cooling costs.

171 24 C.F.R. § 965.505(e).

172 *See In re* Housing Auth. of Houston, Tex., 25 Clearinghouse Rev. 568 (Apr. 4, 1991) (Clearinghouse No. 46,718) (letter from Department of Housing and Urban Development to Susanne Sere, Gulf Coast Legal Foundation, in response to administrative complaint).

medically documented need for air conditioning.[173] Even broader relief was obtained in a California case involving air conditioning claims that resulted in increases by at least 100% in utility allowances for all Section 8 tenants. Tenants living in the desert in Southern California were able to exact a settlement from HUD affirming that the utility allowance must include the cost of air conditioning.[174]

In the Cranston-Gonzalez National Affordable Housing Act of 1990,[175] Congress mandated HUD to include a cooling degree day adjustment factor—comparable to the adjustment factor for heating degree days—in the performance funding system utility subsidies for PHAs. This mandate makes it clear that Congress fully understands the impact that cooling costs can have on PHAs. This Congressional policy directly opposes HUD's own policy in effectively precluding PHAs from including the costs of reasonable air conditioning usage when calculating utility allowances for tenants whose utility services are individually metered. There is at least one court decision that post-dates the adoption of the current regulations requiring tenants to pay for their own air conditioning usage.[176] In a case out of Texas, the court reaffirmed an earlier 1995 order requiring the "provision of a utility allowance which includes an amount sufficient to allow for the costs of reasonable use of the air conditioning in the family projects."[177] The case arose in the heat of east Texas and in the context of serious racial discrimination claims. It suggests that tenants who are not receiving utility allowances for their air conditioning usage should be aggressive in demanding equitable treatment.[178]

Retail-metered tenants need seasonal allowances in order to keep up with their rent payments and utility bills. The utility allowance acts as a credit against rent, and seasonally adjusted allowances provide larger rent credits at the precise time that utility bills are largest. If allowances are flat throughout the year, tenants will need to save extra money during mild months (for example, April or October) so as to be able to pay larger bills in the coldest winter or hottest summer months. But this simply is not realistic for tenants who are barely scraping by in any given month of the year.

Tenants who have check meters and a schedule of surcharges should also advocate for the carry-over of credits from one utility service to another. For example, a tenant might have a more-than-adequate allowance for a gas stove (because the tenant cooks rarely) but an inadequate allowance for electric heating because the apartment is on the top floor and more exposed to the wind than other units. Nothing prohibits the housing authority from giving the tenant a credit for below-level gas usage to offset any surcharge that might apply for the tenant's "excessive" electricity usage.[179]

10.5 Surcharges and Litigation Relating to Surcharges in Public Housing

10.5.1 Check-Metering Surcharges

PHAs that have check meters must adopt utility allowances and "establish surcharges for utility consumption in excess of the allowances."[180] The dollar amount of surcharges for check-metered tenants is based on "the PHA's average utility rate" if the PHA charge is based on a "straight per unit of purchase basis (for example, cents per kilowatt hour of electricity) or [on] stated blocks of consumption."[181] The regulations do not authorize the PHA to include any additional charge to recover the administrative costs of installing or operating the check-metering system or calculating the surcharges. While the current version of the regulations should preclude housing authorities from passing on to tenants the cost of administering utility surcharges, there appears to be no litigation on point.[182] This conclusion

173 Giles v. Housing Auth. of Frankfurt, No. 89-107 (E.D. Ky. May 3, 1990), 24 Clearinghouse Rev. 257 (July 1990) (Clearinghouse No. 45,074) (settlement also provided for refunds of overcharges for excessive consumption).

174 Walker v. Kemp, No. 2B-84-4370-RSWL (DX) (C.D. Cal. July 18, 1990) (Clearinghouse No. 45,132); *Settlement of Air Conditioning Claims Permits Prospective Increases in Utility Allowances*, 20 Hous. L. Bull. 145 (Sept./Oct. 1990).

175 Pub. L. No. 101-625, § 508, 104 Stat. 4079, 4187 (1990).

176 24 C.F.R. § 965.505(e) (2003) (adopted Feb. 29, 1996, 61 Fed. Reg. 7971).

177 NAACP v. Housing Auth. of the City of Commerce, 1998 WL 320307 (N.D. Tex. June 8, 1998).

178 24 C.F.R. § 965.508 may provide a useful tool in allowing tenants to file for individual relief from either surcharges for excess consumption or from payment of usage in excess of the utility allowances. Nothing in this regulation prohibits a group of tenants from filing a collective request for individual relief, somewhat akin to filing a class action complaint.

179 Tenants in one case successfully obtained such a credit by consent judgment. Brody v. Humes, No. Civil 5-77-102, Clearinghouse No. 22,960 (D. Minn. Oct. 25, 1979) (check-metered public housing tenants must receive credit for consumption of gas below the allowance applied to excess consumption of electricity within the same season and vice versa).

180 24 C.F.R. § 965.506(a).

181 *Id.*

182 Under a previous version of the regulations, Tennessee tenants successfully challenged the PHA's practice of recovering administrative costs of operating check meters and applying surcharges. The local HUD office ruled that the PHA could not bill tenants at a rate higher than it paid for the utility usage. Letter from H. J. Broyles, Assisted Hous. Mgmt. Branch, HUD Nashville Insuring Office, to Dist. Att'y Ettinger, Aug. 13, 1979).

But, in another case, tenants obtained a reduction in the surcharge to the marginal cost of electricity plus a reasonable administrative expense. Residents' Cent. Council v. Cuyahoga Metro. Hous. Auth., No. C73-742, (N.D. Ohio May 9, 1975). *See also* Steven Ferrey, *Energy Needs of the Poor: A Saga of Ongoing Legislative Neglect and Local Abuse*, 11 Clearinghouse Rev. 331, 336 (Aug. 1977).

is reinforced by the requirement that a PHA must weigh the "cost of debt service (interest and amortization) of the estimated installation costs plus the operating costs of the checkmeters" against the potential reduction in utility expenditures when determining whether to install check meters.[183] If PHAs could recover these installation and operating cost from tenants, HUD would probably not require PHAs to consider them as costs when weighing the costs and benefits of meter conversions.

There has been litigation on the issue of utility surcharges, but most of the litigation took place before the current version of the surcharge regulation was adopted in 1996. The cases generally involve surcharges for air conditioning or are part of an overall challenge alleging inadequate utility allowances.[184] One circuit court has taken a very strong position that PHAs must comply with the procedural notice-and-comment provisions of the utility allowance regulations,[185] also noting that courts have the authority and obligation to review the adequacy of those allowances to make sure the requirements of the Brooke Amendment, 42 U.S.C. § 1437a(a)(1), have been met.[186]

10.5.2 Master-Metering Surcharges

The regulations require PHAs to establish schedules of surcharges for tenant-owned major appliances or for optional functions of PHA-furnished equipment in master-metered units.[187] The surcharge schedules must state the equipment or functions for which the surcharges shall be imposed and must list the amount of such charges. The surcharges must be based "on the cost to the PHA of the utility consumption estimated to be attributable to reasonable usage of such equipment."[188] The dollar amount of surcharges is based on utility consumption attributed to tenant-owned major appliances or optional functions of PHA-furnished equipment, such as air conditioning, over and above the cost of utility consumption estimated to be reasonable usage of such equipment.[189]

When PHAs set or revise surcharge schedules for major appliances or optional uses, the problem that tenants most frequently confront is in the determination of which major appliances or optional functions should be surcharged. The regulations provide PHAs with broad discretion. But there is some useful guidance from a HUD guidebook that PHAs should not be able to surcharge for appliances or uses that are a necessity within the context of local usage and custom.[190]

PHAs frequently want to surcharge tenants for usage of clothes washers, clothes dryers, food freezers, and air conditioners. Clothes washers and dryers are certainly no less of a necessity than, for example, toasters or refrigerators, especially for low-income families who cannot afford to use public laundry facilities or are not located close to them. Moreover, the washing and drying of clothes, whether in the tenant's apartment or elsewhere, is fully "consistent with the requirements of a safe, sanitary, and healthful living environment."[191] If PHAs were to consider "local usage and custom," as the HUD guidebook suggests,[192] they would learn that fully 72% of low-moderate income households (those earning between $15,000 and $30,000 per year) have a clothes washer or washer/dryer combination. Even among the lowest income households (those earning less than $15,000 annually), fully 57% have a washer, dryer, or both.[193] Even though a minority of low-income households do not own them, washers and dryers should not be considered luxuries.[194]

183 24 C.F.R. § 965.403.

184 *See, e.g.*, Scott v. Hamlet Hous. Auth., No. C-88-18-R (M.D.N.C. Aug. 2, 1989), 23 Clearinghouse Rev. 745 (Oct. 1989) (Clearinghouse No. 43,152) (prospective utility allowance increase based upon the highest average monthly consumption over the previous three years; individual relief from utility surcharges that are beyond tenants' control; annual review of utility allowance and adjustments for increases in consumption and utility rate increases); Shelton v. Newport Hous. Auth., No. Civ. 2-86-65 (E.D. Tenn. July 26, 1988) (summary judgment on PHA's liability for utility overcharges); Harper v. Johnson City Hous. Auth., No. CIV-2-86-66 (E.D. Tenn. June 29, 1988) (settlement agreement on utility overcharges); Junior v. Housing Auth., No. 85-2172 (E.D. La. May 1, 1986), 20 Clearinghouse Rev. 281 (July 1986) (Clearinghouse No. 39,421) (denying HUD's motion to dismiss).

185 *See, e.g.*, 24 C.F.R. §§ 965.502(b) (PHA must maintain a record documenting development of allowances and surcharges and make it available to tenants), (c) (PHA shall give advance notice to tenants of proposed allowances and surcharges, any revisions, and the opportunity to submit written comments), 965.507 (PHA must review basis of utility allowances annually).

186 Dorsey v. Housing Auth., 984 F.2d 622, 630 (4th Cir. 1993) (tenant's procedural rights regarding utility allowances/surcharges are enforceable; case remanded to consider evidence of reasonableness of allowances).

187 *But see* § 4.5, *supra* (discussing limits on "resale" by landlords of electricity to master-metered apartments).

188 24 C.F.R. § 965.506(b).

189 *Id.*

190 U.S. Dep't of Hous. & Urban Dev., Public Housing Occupancy Guidebook, § 14.3, at 170 (June 2003) ("This distinction [between "necessary" and "luxury" appliances] should reflect local usage and custom patterns.").

191 24 C.F.R. § 965.505(a).

192 *See* Brown v. Diocesan Charitable Trust, No. CA 3 84-1716G (N.D. Tex. Nov. 1, 1984), 18 Clearinghouse Rev. 1440 (Apr. 1985) (Clearinghouse No. 38,524) (preliminary injunction enjoining eviction of Section 8 tenants because of, *inter alia*, their failure to remove washers and/or dryers from their apartments).

193 U.S. Dep't of Energy, Energy Info. Admin., 2001 Residential Energy Consumption Survey, The Effect of Income on Appliances in U.S. Households, fig. 9, *available at* www.eia.doe.gov/emeu/recs/appliances/appliances.html.

194 *See* Brown v. Diocesan Charitable Trust, No. CA 3 84-1716G (N.D. Tex. Nov. 1, 1984), 18 Clearinghouse Rev. 1440 (Apr. 1985) (Clearinghouse No. 38,524) (preliminary injunction enjoining eviction of Section 8 tenants because of, *inter alia*, their failure to remove washers and/or dryers from their apartments).

In the past and under prior versions of the HUD regulations, tenants have argued with some success that they should not be surcharged for air conditioners in certain climates or at certain times of the year because the use of air conditioners is a vital necessity.[195] Prior to the most recent regulations,[196] HUD had been relenting somewhat on its position that air conditioning was a luxury that should not be included in tenants' utility allowances.[197] Litigation had also been successful in this area.[198] In 1996, however, HUD amended its regulations to expressly require tenants to pay for air conditioning if the system offers them the option to choose it.[199] Tenants who argue that air conditioning is a necessity because of the geographic location of the building or because of age, health, or disability, should bring petitions for individual relief under 24 C.F.R. § 965.508. Nothing in this regulation prohibits a group of similarly situated tenants from bringing bundled or consolidated claims for relief, for example, a petition by all the elderly residents of a high-rise in a hot climate to include reasonable air-conditioning usage in the calculation of allowances. PHAs are required to provide tenants with a notice on how to seek individual relief and the criteria upon which individual relief will be granted.[200]

195 *See* NAACP v. Housing Auth., 1998 WL 320307 (N.D. Tex. June 8, 1998) (defendant housing authority ordered to provide a "utility allowance which includes an amount sufficient to allow for the costs of reasonable use of the air conditioning in the family projects").

196 24 C.F.R. §§ 965.501–965.508 (2003).

197 *See In re* Housing Auth. of Houston, Tex., 25 Clearinghouse Rev. 568 (Apr. 4, 1991) (Clearinghouse No. 46,718) (letter from Department of Housing and Urban Development to Susanne Sere, Gulf Coast Legal Foundation, in response to administrative complaint).

198 *See also* Amone v. Aveiro, 226 F.R.D. 677 (D. Haw. 2005) (certifying, in case in which disabled plaintiff requiring oxygen machine, nebulizer, and air conditioner alleged gross insufficiency in utility allowance, a class of "disabled persons that currently reside, or have resided within the last two years, in an HCDCH public housing project in which residents receive utility allowances, whose special needs arising from their disability require them to consume utilities in excess of the amount provided for in the standard public housing utility allowances"), *subsequent proceeding*, 2007 WL 2479291 (D. Haw. Aug. 27, 2007) (approval of settlement after earlier finding that public housing project failed to provide adjustments to utility allowances of class members).

199 61 Fed. Reg. 7966 (Feb. 29, 1996) (adopting 24 C.F.R. § 965.505(e)).

200 24 C.F.R. § 965.508.

10.6 Inadequacy of Utility Allowances

10.6.1 Relationship Between Costs and Allowances

The Arab oil embargo of 1973–1974 triggered a period of rapid inflation in energy costs that took its toll on the American economy and on low-income families especially. More recently, the winter of 2000–2001 saw extraordinary and unprecedented increases in the price of natural gas. But throughout 2003 and the first half of 2004, wholesale natural gas prices were again at record highs, exceeded only by prices during certain months of the winter of 2000–2001.[201] Home heating oil prices in 2004 were also often at historic peaks, spiking up again in late 2010 and early 2011.[202] As prices have increased, HUD policy has shifted more and more of the burden of energy costs onto low-income tenant households. This leaves the poorest households in America vulnerable to fluctuating utility costs. In many cases, this approach is also illegal, because the effect is that tenant households pay more than 30% of their income for rent and utilities, the maximum allowed by law. Worse, a tenant who is unable to pay for utilities will not only suffer termination of utility service but also risk termination of the subsidized lease. Many PHA leases require that the tenant maintain utility service to the dwelling as a condition of the lease, and the failure to abide by this lease clause is grounds for eviction.[203]

In the late 1980s, Congress became so alarmed at the increasing divergence between tenants' utility costs and allowances that it requested a General Accounting Office (GAO) investigation. During the discussion of the Housing

201 *See* U.S. Dep't of Energy, Energy Info. Admin., *U.S. Natural Gas Prices*, *available at* http://tonto.eia.doe.gov/dnav/ng/NG_PRI_SUM_DCU_NUS_M.htm.

202 The northeast is more dependent on oil as a home heating fuel than other regions. For a history of heating oil prices in Massachusetts, go to the website of the Executive Office of Energy and Environmental Affairs at www.mass.gov/?pageID=eoeeahomepage&L=1&L0=Home&sid=Eoeea (once at the website, click first on the "Energy, Utilities & Clean Technologies" weblink, then on the "Home & Auto Fuel Price Information" weblink).

203 *See, e.g.*, Crochet v. Housing Auth. of Tampa, 37 F.3d 607 (11th Cir. 1994) (referencing lease requirement that tenants must pay utility bills); Pondexter v. Allegheny County Hous. Auth., 2007 WL 3120289 (W.D. Pa. Oct. 23, 2007) (Section 8 voucher tenant subject to eviction for nonpayment of utilities), ***aff'd***, 329 Fed. Appx. 347 (3d Cir. 2009); Jackson v. Philadelphia Hous. Auth., 1996 WL 363928 (E.D. Pa. June 21, 1996) (dismissing eviction on procedural grounds in a case in which PHA brought eviction action for failure to use utility allowance for intended purpose and consequent gas bill arrearage of $5000); McKeel v. Jasper Hous. Auth., 652 So. 2d 315 (Ala. Civ. App. 1994) (summary judgment for PHA reversed, as material facts were in dispute in a case in which PHA brought eviction based, *inter alia*, on failure to pay for utilities).

and Community Development Act of 1987 the issue was raised as to whether the "reasonable consumption" standard on which utility allowances are based is sufficiently objective. Tenant advocacy groups maintained that the standard led PHAs to set allowances too low. The conference report expressed concern that many low-income subsidized households, who were not wasteful of utilities, were being unfairly penalized by low allowances and as a result were effectively paying rent in excess of 30% of income.[204] As a result, the GAO was required to report on (1) how utility allowances are provided to subsidized households, (2) the resulting rent burdens incurred by subsidized households, and (3) better alternatives for providing the utility allowances.[205]

10.6.2 GAO's Findings

The GAO conducted a survey and found that about three-fifths of public housing households and four-fifths of Section 8 certificate households receive utility allowances.[206] According to the GAO,

> about 45 percent of public housing households and approximately 70 percent of section 8 households . . . had utility expenses that were higher than their allowances. This results in rent burdens exceeding 30 percent of adjusted income. Because the deviations were so great for some households, paying utility bills can pose financial hardships . . . [Also], because allowances are typically the same each month while utility expenses vary, month-to-month rent burden fluctuations can create cash flow problems for lower-income households despite an overall 30 percent rent burden.[207]

The bottom line, according to the GAO was that the "majority of the . . . households [surveyed] did not pay 30 percent of adjusted income for rent and utilities. . . ."[208] The GAO pointed out what low-income energy advocates have recognized for some time: "The extent of financial hardship a household experiences depends on the dollar size of the difference and on the income of the assisted household. Those with the lowest incomes and the largest disparity between the allowance and their utility expenses experienced the highest rent burdens."[209]

Furthermore, the GAO illustrated the problems arising when utility allowances are computed on a yearly basis, without seasonal adjustments:

> [E]ven when the 30 percent rent burden amount is met over the course of a year, households may experience several months in which expenses exceed allowances. This occurrence is particularly troublesome for assisted households since they are at the low end of the income range. Unless they are on a budget payment arrangement with a utility company, they will likely find it more difficult to pay utility bills in the months when expenses exceed their allowance by a large amount.[210]

The GAO found that both public housing households and Section 8 households were hurt by the excessive rent burdens caused by insufficient utility allowances, with the problems taking on more alarming proportions in Section 8 families. In public housing, the average monthly total income was $454. After paying 30% of adjusted income for rent and utilities, these households had only about $340 a month left to cover other necessities, such as food, clothing, and medical care.[211] Obviously, "households with utility expenses exceeding allowances by a large amount may have difficulty meeting their financial obligations."[212]

In Section 8 housing, the disparities between income and rent burden were even greater. The GAO found that among those Section 8 households which paid more than 30% of adjusted income for rent and utilities, households paid on average $43 more each month than the amount covered by utility allowances. These averages can mask alarmingly high differences between allowances and actual burdens at some projects. For example, at one project households paid an average of $42 per month in excess of their allowance, which was 60% more than the allowance provided. The GAO found that the effective rent burden exceeded 70%.[213] While the GAO report is now two decades old, there has not been a recent study that is comparable in scope, and findings of the GAO report no doubt paint an accurate (though perhaps understated) portrait of the current situation of public housing tenants.

---

204 Housing and Community Development Act of 1987, H.R. Conf. Rep. No. 426, 100th Cong. 1st Sess. 163–64 (Nov. 6, 1987). *See* Housing, Community Development, and Homelessness Prevention Act of 1987, H.R. Rep. No. 122, 100th Cong., 1st Sess. 13–14 (June 2, 1987) (discussing the reasonable consumption standard).

205 Housing and Community Development Act of 1987, Pub. L. No. 100-242, § 102(b), 101 Stat. 1815, 1821 (Feb. 5, 1988).

206 General Accounting Office, RCED-91-40A, Assisted Housing: Utility Allowances Often Fall Short of Actual Utility Expenses, vol. I, at 18 (Mar. 26, 1991).

207 *Id.*

208 *Id.* at 22.

209 *Id.* at 23.

210 *Id.* at 23.

211 The GAO pointed out that their average monthly adjusted income was $379, 30% of which is $114. While PHAs compute household rental contributions on an adjusted income basis, the household has its gross income from which to make spending choices. General Accounting Office, RCED-91-40A, Assisted Housing: Utility Allowances Often Fall Short of Actual Utility Expenses, vol. I, at 24 (Mar. 26, 1991).

212 *Id.*

213 *Id.* at 4 (Mar. 26, 1991) ("For example, the average rent burden was . . . 74 percent for the 20 cases with the highest rent burdens.").

Although HUD regulations then and now allow PHAs to set allowances that vary over the year to reflect seasonal variations in utility usage,[214] none of the PHAs reviewed by the GAO had set such varying allowances.[215] This failure alone has an alarming effect on a household's ability to maintain utility service throughout the year.[216] As the GAO noted, in a study of Section 8 households with an average annual rent burden of 30%, monthly rent burdens varied from 18% to 48% because of the uneven nature of utility usage throughout the year.[217]

10.6.3 *Reasons for the Inadequate Allowances*

The GAO cited a number of reasons that household expenses differ so radically from the allowances set by PHAs:

1. Establishing utility allowances is an inherently imprecise task.
2. HUD has compounded the imprecision by failing to provide PHAs with adequate guidance defining reasonable consumption.
3. Some "PHAs intentionally act to keep allowances lower than amounts representing reasonable consumption. For public housing, these actions are motivated by the (mistaken) desire to minimize potential revenue loss to PHAs resulting from higher allowances. For Section 8 households, raising utility allowances may make assisted housing less available if landlords believe that the maximum rent they can charge after allowing utility allowances is too low."
4. PHAs routinely make errors in allocating allowances and in computing households' rental contributions.
5. Other factors, such as monthly variations in utility expenses and PHA practices which treat check-metered households differently from retail metered households.[218]

The greatest share of the blame for these problems lies with HUD, which has deliberately shifted the burden of utility costs from HUD's budget to subsidized housing tenants. HUD has done this by failing to guarantee to PHAs adequate allowances for each project supervised by a PHA or to provide for proper weatherization of the housing projects.[219] Furthermore, HUD has successfully relieved itself of most of its mandatory oversight of housing authorities' implementation of their utility allowance schemes. These policy changes have resulted in much litigation around the issue of setting the amount of utility allowances.[220]

---

214 The current rule is 24 C.F.R. § 965.504(b).

215 General Accounting Office, RCED-91-40A, Assisted Housing: Utility Allowances Often Fall Short of Actual Utility Expenses, vol. I, at 28 (Mar. 26, 1991).

216 Check-metered tenants suffer the most from the failure to adopt seasonal allowances. These households receive no credit or rebate for usage less than that allowed (for example, in mild spring or fall months when usage may be lowest). Yet they must pay for "excess" usage above the allowance (for example, in high-use summer or winter months).

By contrast, retail-metered tenants receive the full utility allowance each month as a credit against rent. In those months when they consume less energy than the regular monthly allowance assumes, they keep the difference. When these households use more energy than the allowance provides for, they pay for it out of their own pocket. This theoretically allows the household on the retail meter to reap the full benefit of the utility allowance on an annual basis (assuming the allowance is correctly computed).

217 General Accounting Office, RCED-91-40A, Assisted Housing: Utility Allowances Often Fall Short of Actual Utility Expenses, vol. I, at 29 (Mar. 26, 1991).

218 *Id.* at 33.

219 *See* ch. 9, *infra* (discussing weatherization program).

220 *E.g.*, Wright v. City of Roanoke Redevelopment & Hous. Auth., 479 U.S. 418, 107 S. Ct. 766 (1987) (Brooke Amendment allows for enforcement of utility allowance by tenants under 42 U.S.C. § 1983); Johnson v. Housing Auth. of Jefferson Parish, 442 F.3d 356 (5th Cir. 2006) (Section 8 voucher holders have a right under 42 U.S.C. § 1983 to challenge the PHA's utility allowance schedule pursuant to the United States Housing Act and implementing regulations); McDowell v. Philadelphia Hous. Auth., 423 F.3d 233, 241 (3d Cir. 2005) (upholding consent decree which required PHA to recalculate utility allowances when rates increase, just as the regulations do), *subsequent proceeding*, 2007 WL 1847411 (E.D. Pa. June 25, 2007) (denying PHA's renewed motion to vacate consent decree when PHA sought to phase out over two years utility allowance payments to households at or above 80% of area median income and to adjust utility allowance schedules every year to reflect changes in HUD funding and actual utility costs); Dorsey v. Housing Auth., 984 F.2d 622 (4th Cir. 1993); Hill v. Ogburn, 812 F.2d 679 (11th Cir. 1987) (finding section 1983 claims but dismissing claim against HUD); Brown v. Housing Auth., 820 F.2d 350 (11th Cir. 1987); Nelson v. Greater Gadsden Hous. Auth., 802 F.2d 405 (11th Cir. 1986) (upholding tenants' utility allowance claims); Junior v. Housing Auth., No. 85-2172 (E.D. La. May 1, 1986), 20 Clearinghouse Rev. 281 (July 1986) (Clearinghouse No. 39,421) (denying HUD's motion to dismiss implied cause of action, section 1983, third-party beneficiary and APA claims; leave to amend constitutional claim to show HUD action), *subsequent order* (E.D. La. Nov. 23, 1988), 22 Clearinghouse Rev. 1302 (Mar. 1989) (Clearinghouse No. 39,421) (approving consent judgment providing relief to current and former public housing tenants and revising utility allowances); Castleman v. United States Dep't of Hous. & Urban Dev., No. 83-0461-CV-W-8 (W.D. Mo. Feb. 8, 1984) (stipulated preliminary injunction), 18 Clearinghouse Rev. 174 (June 1984) (prospective relief stipulated), *subsequent order*, 1988 WL 220583 (W.D. Mo. Sept. 8, 1988) (PHA liable and HUD's motion to dismiss PHA's cross-claim denied); Stone v. District of Columbia, No. 82-1761 (D.D.C. Mar. 1983) (stipulation regarding prospective relief), *subsequent op.*, 572 F. Supp. 976 (D.D.C. Aug. 15, 1983) (no implied right of action against PHA to challenge insufficient utility allowances as violation of statutory rent-income ratio; claim against HUD moot), *on appeal*, No. 83-1999 (D.C. Cir. June 15, 1984) (order) (urging defen-

HUD's standard for utility allowances is vague, at best:

> The objective of a PHA in designing methods of establishing utility allowances for each dwelling unit category and unit size shall be to approximate a reasonable consumption of utilities by an energy-conservative household of modest circumstances consistent with the requirements of a safe, sanitary, and healthful living environment.[221]

As the GAO points out, this standard is neither precise nor measurable. "Reasonable consumption" is defined operationally, and the regulation provides PHAs with little guidance by which to judge whether allowances are reasonable and meet households' legitimate energy needs.[222]

10.6.4 Public Housing's Performance Funding System Causes Some PHAs to Deliberately Keep Allowances Too Low

Under the performance funding system (PFS), PHAs receive an operating subsidy from HUD for the day-to-day management of the public housing. The subsidy is a major source of operating income for PHAs; their only other source of income, household rental contributions, is generally insufficient to cover operating expenses. The operating subsidy is calculated according to a formula under which the PHA receives the difference between the estimated expenses and the income the PHA expects to receive from the rents.[223]

The PFS provides that a PHA should be fully reimbursed by HUD for the revenue it would lose in almost all cases when the utility allowances are raised. Under the PFS, a PHA annually submits a budget to HUD, showing projected rental and other income and expenses. Once HUD approves the budget, it pays the PHA the difference between expenses and income. With check-metered tenants and tenant-purchased utilities, an increase of the utility allowance to a reasonable level is reflected in the budget by a reduction of the PHA's projected rental income. An increased utility allowance will mean that a PHA will collect less rent. If less rent is collected, the amount of operating subsidies from HUD must increase because the gap between expenses and income widens.[224]

Likewise, a PHA that surcharges check-metered tenants or master-metered tenants with tenant-supplied major appliances will collect less from surcharges if it raises the utility allowance. If that happens, the PHA will have to report less "other income." Since both rents and "other income" are subtracted from expenses to determine the amount of operating subsidy, in most cases the PHA should not be harmed by establishing reasonable utility allowances and surcharges.

Ideally, PHAs should establish or revise their utility allowances or schedules for surcharges prior to the submission of their annual budgets to HUD.

Although a PHA should not be harmed by establishing a reasonable utility allowance, many PHAs feel pressured to establish low allowances and to try to contain their operating subsidy requests. This pressure is felt most intensely when HUD reviews the PHA's annual operating budget.[225]

Moreover, PHAs may also argue that they must make every effort to keep their operating subsidies down so they will be less dependent upon them and thus less vulnerable if operating subsidies are not fully funded in the future. The flaw in this argument, however, is that unless and until a shortfall actually occurs, tenants will illegally be charged excessive rents and surcharges and HUD will profit from that illegality. Even if a shortfall were to occur, an increase in the utility allowance would only require the PHA to cover a very small portion of the reduced rental income resulting from the utility allowance increase. Thus, if the shortfall were, for example, 2%, HUD would still be covering 98% of the rent revenue lost by increasing the utility allowances.

10.6.5 GAO's Recommendations Regarding Inadequate Utility Allowances

The GAO had a number of concrete recommendations to improve the dismal utility allowance situation:

1. HUD should set its performance expectations for PHAs by redefining the "reasonable consumption utility allowance standard."
2. HUD should encourage PHAs to use assisted households' actual experiences with utility allowances to ensure the allowances are reasonable. This should include requiring PHAs to evaluate and reduce households' seasonal vulnerability by encouraging budget

---

dants to consider retroactive payment of rent overcharge), *subsequent order*, 799 F.2d 773 (1986) (Clearinghouse No. 32,924) (vacating district court opinion and remanding case with instructions to dismiss complaint against HUD, to ensure PHA promptly obtains remaining tenant refunds from HUD, and to rule on tenants' application for fees).

221 24 C.F.R. § 965.505(a).

Prior to 1996 the standard continued: "Stated another way, it should be an objective of the Allowance that excess consumption which may result in a Surcharge (or absorption of utility cost in excess of the Allowance) should be an amount of consumption that is reasonably within the control of a tenant household to avoid." 24 C.F.R. § 965.476(a) (1995).

222 General Accounting Office, RCED-91-40A, Assisted Housing: Utility Allowances Often Fall Short of Actual Utility Expenses, vol. I, at 41 (Mar. 26, 1991).

223 24 C.F.R. § 990.170–990.185.

224 24 C.F.R. § 990.170(e).

225 *See* Fletcher v. Housing Auth., 525 F.2d 532 (6th Cir. 1975) (PHA cannot give preference to higher-income applicants merely to improve operating budget and generate larger rents, despite HUD pressure to increase rents); Housing Auth. v. Pierce, No. 88-0495 (D.D.C. Apr. 20, 1989), 16 Hous. & Dev. Rep. (BNA) 1105 (May 15, 1989).

payment plans or adjusting check-metered allowances to correspond to monthly variations in usage.

3. HUD should ensure that PHAs review the reasonableness of their utility allowances annually, as the regulations require.[226]

Alternatively, GAO proposed that all assisted households could be treated as if they are master-metered. This would mean that the PHA would pay the utility bills for all assisted households. This approach would ensure that all households paid exactly 30% of their income for rent and utilities and that all households would pay the same share of their income for housing and utility costs, combined. The downside of this approach is the lack of an incentive for tenants to conserve.[227] Therefore, the GAO concluded, that despite the obvious advantages to this proposal, the approach would increase federal costs.[228]

The bottom line, according to the GAO, was that Congress must decide whether to continue to allow the current inequities, with some modifications, or to put more money into the subsidized housing program and recognize that energy conservation might be discouraged.[229]

The existing data on energy consumption show that low-income families are already conserving energy when compared to the amount of energy consumed by middle-and upper-income households. For example, according to the Energy Information Administration, households with incomes of less than $30,000 per year use approximately 20% less energy than the average household with income between $30,000 and $100,000.[230] Even those households with incomes between $10,000 and $30,000 use 15% less electricity, on average, than households with incomes between $30,000 and $50,000.[231] While these income disparities narrow somewhat when considering natural gas and home heating oil, the poorest households (less than $10,000 of income) still use only two-thirds to three-quarters the amount of these fuels as the highest income households (those earning $50,000 or more).

While the GAO report was completed many years ago, its findings and recommendations remain useful today. As energy costs rise sharply, tenants need protection from unaffordable energy bills, terminations of utility service, and the risk of eviction for failure to maintain utility service.

10.7 Litigation on Inadequate Utility Allowances

10.7.1 Introduction

Over the past three decades, tenants have brought a number of cases against public housing authorities and other parties (including HUD) alleging that the utility allowances were set too low and in violation of applicable laws and regulations. However, most of those cases were brought under versions of HUD's regulations in force prior to 1996.[232] There have been relatively few reported utility allowance cases since the 1996 version of the regulations went into effect.[233] Cases dated before 1996 must be reviewed care-

226 General Accounting Office, RCED-91-40A, Assisted Housing: Utility Allowances Often Fall Short of Actual Utility Expenses, vol. I, at 51 (Mar. 26, 1991).

227 Note, of course, that placing the risk of increasing energy costs on the tenant removes any incentive for the landlord to invest in insulation and other energy-conserving improvements. This is a classic case of the "split incentive" between landlord and tenant in energy conservation. *See* Kenneth Gillingham, Matthew Harding, & David Rapson, Split Incentives in Residential Energy Consumption(2010), *available at* www.stanford.edu/~mch/GillinghamHardingRapson_SplitIncentives.pdf.

228 General Accounting Office, RCED-91-40A, Assisted Housing: Utility Allowances Often Fall Short of Actual Utility Expenses, vol. I, at 64–65 (Mar. 26, 1991).

229 *Id.* at 68.

230 All data in this paragraph are drawn from Dep't of Energy, Energy Info. Admin., 2005 Residential Energy Consumption Survey, tbl. US1, pt. 2 (Total Energy Consumption, Expenditures and Intensities, 2005), *available at* www.eia.doe.gov/emeu/recs/recs2005/c&e/summary/pdf/tableus1part2.pdf.

231 *Id.* Households with incomes of less than $10,000 per year consume 8906 kWh on average; households with incomes of $50,000 or more per year consumer 10,545 kWh on average.

232 The current version of the most relevant public housing regulations, 24 C.F.R. §§ 965.501–965.508, was added through changes published at 61 Fed. Reg. 7971 (Feb. 29, 1996). For prior versions of the regulations, see 24 C.F.R. Part 865 (1984), 45 Fed. Reg. 59502 (Sept. 9, 1980), and 24 C.F.R. pt. 965 (1992).

233 *See, e.g.*, Johnson v. Housing Auth. of Jefferson Parish, 442 F.3d 356 (5th Cir. 2006) (Section 8 voucher holders have a right under 42 U.S.C. § 1983 to challenge the PHA's utility allowance schedule pursuant to the United States Housing Act and implementing regulations); McDowell v. Philadelphia Hous. Auth., 423 F.3d 233, 241 (3d Cir. 2005) (upholding consent decree that required PHA to recalculate utility allowances when rates increase, just as the regulations do), *subsequent proceeding*, 2007 WL 1847411 (E.D. Pa. June 25, 2007) (PHA's renewed motion to vacate consent decree denied when PHA sought to phase out over two years utility allowance payments to households at or above 80% of the area median income and to adjust utility allowance schedules every year to reflect changes in HUD funding and actual utility costs); Shea v. Kahuku Hous. Found., Inc., 2011 WL 1261150 (D. Haw. Mar. 31, 2011) (approving settlement of contract and UDAP claims arising from Section 8 developer's failure to increase utility allowance, resulting in overpayment of rent by senior housing tenants); Galloway v. Southwick Plaza Ltd. P'ship, No. 01-835 (E.D. Pa. Feb. 20, 2001) (approving settlement among tenants, PHA and owner of mixed-income subsidized development that provided, *inter alia*, for adoption of utility allowances in accordance with public housing regulations); Armstrong v. Gallia Metro. Hous. Auth., No. 2:98-CV-373, 2000 WL 1505949 (S.D. Ohio Sept. 29, 2000) (finding that PHA "failed to establish a utility allowance in compliance with federal law and failed to annually review . . . utility allowances"), *order approving settlement* 2001 WL 1842452 (Apr. 23, 2001) (PHA agreed to change method of calculating utility allowances, terminate the clothes washer fee,

fully to evaluate their relevance to cases brought under current rules.

Many utility allowance challenges are settled without litigation.[234] This may result from the fact that PHAs flagrantly ignore their obligation to establish reasonable utility allowances and to review the adequacy of those allowances at least annually, so that PHAs may see the wisdom of settling the case well before final decisions are issued. While tenants in any individual case may well benefit from a PHA's willingness to settle rather than litigate, the relatively large percentage of settled cases means that there are relatively few reported decisions following contested proceedings. The existing precedents are generally favorable but limited in number and depth of analysis.

Complaints that have been filed allege violations of one or more of the following: the Brooke Amendment (42 U.S.C. § 1437a(a)), HUD's utility allowance regulations (and therefore 42 U.S.C. § 1983), the Annual Contributions Contract (ACC) between HUD and the PHA, the housing assistant payment (HAP) contract between the PHA and the landlord, tenant leases, and the Administrative Procedure Act (APA).[235] The most frequent and successful argument is that an inadequate utility allowance violates the Brooke Amendment because tenants' rent plus utility costs exceed the statutorily established rents ceiling of 30% of adjusted income. Some complaints have also alleged that PHAs have violated due process requirements found in the Constitution or HUD's regulations, particularly claims that the PHA has failed to provide adequate notice to tenants of the adoption or revision of utility charges or the right to comment on those changes and has failed to provide notice of the potential imposition of surcharges for specific appliances or uses.

Of the somewhat limited number of cases, both reported and unpublished, many have been successful.[236]

In particular, because of HUD's regulations regarding tenant participation in multifamily housing projects ("Tenant Participation in Multifamily Housing Projects"), tenants in subsidized multifamily housing should consider filing utility allowance claims against HUD under the APA in addition to bringing any Brooke Amendment or other available claims directly against the project owner or manager and suing HUD under any other available theories.[237] The regulations cover a very broad range of multifamily housing, including housing assisted under the Section 221(d)(3) Below Market Interest Rate ("BMIR") program, the Section 236 program, and other HUD programs.[238] Subpart E of those tenant participation rules[239] requires the mortgagor to obtain HUD's approval before converting a project from "project-paid utilities to tenant-paid utilities" and prior to "a reduction in tenant utility allowances."[240] The regulations also require the mortgagee to give prescribed notice to tenants of these types of utility changes and to include specified documentation when seeking HUD's approval.[241]

Given that HUD's approval is required in some cases involving changes to utility allowances,[242] this may make it

---

periodically review and revise allowances, and pay up to $130,000 to injured plaintiffs). *Cf.* Selma Hous. Dev. Corp. v. Selma Hous. Auth., 2005 WL 1981290 (S.D. Ala. Aug. 16, 2005) (no cognizable protected property right for owners in maintaining utility allowances at fixed level; regulations allowing for adjustments of utility allowances are for benefit and protection of low-income residents, not for safeguarding of rent levels for property owners).

234 *See, e.g.*, *Utility Allowance for Public Housing Tenants*, 20 Clearinghouse Rev. 1450 (Mar. 1987) (Seattle Housing Authority negotiated settlement for utility allowances).

235 The Administrative Procedures Act (APA) is codified at 5 U.S.C. §§ 551–559. With respect to suits under the ACC, however, the third-party beneficiary argument has been rendered ineffectual by new standard contractual language prohibiting these claims. *See, e.g.*, Kirby v. Richmond Redevelopment Hous. Auth., 2005 WL 5864797 (E.D. Va. Sept. 28, 2005), *aff'd*, 194 Fed. Appx. 105 (4th Cir. 2006). *See also* Pondexter v. Allegheny County Hous. Auth., 329 Fed. Appx. 347 (3d Cir. 2009); Anderson v. U.S. Dep't of Housing & Urban Dev., 2010 WL 1407983 (E.D. La. Mar. 25, 2010) (finding no specific statutory mandate requiring utility payments for displaced public housing tenants, and that agency's exercise of discretion had legal and factual basis; dismissing claim alleging violation of Fair Housing Act redressable through Administrative Procedure Act), *later decision*, Anderson v. Donovan, 2100 WL 798118 (E.D. La. Feb. 28, 2011) (decertifying class). *Cf.* 24 C.F.R. § 982.456 (housing assistance payment (HAP) between PHA and landlord "shall not be construed as creating any right of the family or other third-party (other than HUD) to enforce any provision of the HAP contract, or to assert any claim against HUD, the PHA, or the owner under the HAP contract").

236 The lead case is the Supreme Court decision in Wright v. City of Roanoke Redevelopment & Hous. Auth., 479 U.S. 418, 107 S. Ct. 766 (1987).

For other utility cases, see: Shea v. Kahuku Hous. Found., Inc., 2011 WL 1261150 (D. Haw. Mar. 31, 2011) (approving settlement of contract and UDAP claims arising from Section 8 developer's failure to increase utility allowance, resulting in overpayment of rent by senior housing tenants); Miller v. Housing Auth., No. 87-1286 (C.D. Ill. Feb. 2, 1990), 24 Clearinghouse Rev. 42 (May 1990) (Clearinghouse No. 43,223) (consent decree establishing an interim utility allowance schedule, until future allowances are set based on actual consumption); Dunn Residents Council v. Dunn Hous. Auth., No. 81-423-CIV-5 (E.D.N.C. July 11, 1983) (Clearinghouse No. 35,361) (consent judgment including retroactive relief); and the cases cited in note 220, *supra*.

237 24 C.F.R. pt. 245 (Tenant Participation in Multifamily Housing Projects).

238 *See* 24 C.F.R. § 245.10 (full range of housing programs covered by the part 245 tenant participation rules).

239 24 C.F.R. §§ 245.405–245.435.

240 24 C.F.R. § 245.405(a).

241 24 C.F.R. §§ 245.410, 245.416.

242 Tenants and advocates will have to research whether HUD's approval was required at the initial adoption of utility allowances for a particular development or at the time allowances may last have been increased. The answer to this question is distinct from what is addressed in 24 C.F.R. § 245.405, which clearly requires HUD approval when utility allowances are reduced or utilities are switched from project-paid to tenant-paid. Whether HUD approval was required at the time allow-

easier for tenants in multifamily properties to bring APA claims against HUD. There is some authority for the proposition that HUD be sued under the APA for failing to make timely adjustments to utility allowances. In *Zellous v. Broadhead Associates*,[243] for example, tenants sued both the project owners and HUD under the APA for "failing to make timely adjustments in their utility allowance."[244] HUD contended that there was no jurisdiction under the APA, but the court clearly held to the contrary, noting that under the APA the court can order compliance with the Brooke Amendment and the obligation to provide adequate utility allowances.[245] Other courts have also found that HUD can be sued under the APA for not providing adequate utility allowances,[246] but some courts have gone the other way, emphasizing the primary role of PHAs (or subsidized owners) in developing allowances in the first instance and the discretionary role of HUD in reviewing or approving those allowances.[247] Advocates will need to carefully review both the case law and the facts regarding HUD's involvement in the review or approval of any specific utility allowances before including APA claims in a court complaint.

10.7.2 Public Housing Authority Defenses

PHAs have argued in the past that tenants have not stated a claim under 42 U.S.C. § 1983, have no implied right of action to enforce the Brooke Amendment and are not third-party beneficiaries of the ACC. HUD has argued that its actions with respect to utility allowances are committed to agency discretion and therefore not reviewable under the APA, that tenants have no implied right of action under the Brooke Amendment, that tenants are not third-party beneficiaries of the ACC and that PHAs, not HUD, are the proper defendants.[248]

In an unambiguous 1987 decision, the Supreme Court held that tenants have a claim for relief under 42 U.S.C. § 1983 to sue local housing authorities.[249] Similarly, a court of appeals has held that Section 8 voucher holders have a right under 42 U.S.C. § 1983 to challenge the PHA's utility allowance schedule pursuant to the United States Housing Act and implementing regulations.[250] Tenants have been far less successful in maintaining claims against HUD, as opposed to the local PHA.[251] Two courts have found that tenants stated a cause of action on their pendent state claim that the housing authority breached its contractual duty to properly calculate utility allowances in accordance with HUD regulations.[252]

---

ances were first adopted (or last increased) may depend on the precise source of the housing subsidy, the date when allowances were first adopted (or last increased), and the version of any applicable regulations then in effect. HUD approval may or may not have been required, based on these factors. There is no broadly applicable rule that requires owners to obtain HUD approval when allowances are adjusted upward.

243 906 F.2d 94 (3d Cir. 1990).

244 906 F.2d 95 (3d Cir. 1990).

245 906 F.2d 96–98 (3d Cir. 1990).

246 *See, e.g.*, Castleman v. U.S. Dep't of Hous. & Urban Dev., No. 83-0461-CV-W-8 (W.D. Mo. Sept. 8, 1988). *See also* Crowder v. Village of Kaufman, Ltd., 2010 WL 2710601 (N.D. Tex. July 7, 2010) (denying HUD's motion to dismiss; issue whether HUD acted arbitrarily and capriciously in denying Section 8 developer's request for increased utility allowance; first request in nine years during which utility rates had greatly increased); Brighton Vill. Nominee Trust v. Malyshev, 2004 WL 594974 (D. Mass. Mar. 23, 2004) (challenge to HUD's approval of prepayment of mortgage by subsidized owner; "the APA has not been construed as narrowly as HUD would like").

247 *See, e.g.*, Dorsey v. Housing Auth. of Balt., 984 F.2d 622, 632 (4th Cir. 1993) (affirming dismissal of claims against HUD and noting that "HUD does not establish utility allowances").

248 *See, e.g.*, Dorsey v. Housing Auth. of Balt. City, 984 F.2d 622 (4th Cir. 1993) (dismissing claims against HUD, as injury of excessive surcharges cannot be fairly traced to HUD; HUD does not establish utility allowances, amend or revise utility allowances, nor approve them before they become effective).

Because third-party beneficiary claims were sometimes successful, HUD amended the standard ACC to bar them.

249 Wright v. City of Roanoke Redevelopment & Hous. Auth., 479 U.S. 418 (1987), *rev'g*, 771 F.2d 833 (4th Cir. 1985) and 605 F. Supp. 532 (W.D. Va. 1984).

For a detailed discussion of the *Wright* decision, see *Justice Prevails: Wright v. Roanoke*, 17 Hous. L. Bull. 1 (Jan./Feb. 1987); *Wright v. Roanoke: Initial Reactions from the Courts of Appeals*, 17 Hous. L. Bull. 85 (Sept./Oct. 1987).

250 Johnson v. Housing Auth. of Jefferson Parish, 442 F.3d 356 (5th Cir. 2006).

This is so even though the Voucher Program, unlike the public housing program at issue in *Wright*, does not limit a family's permissible housing costs to 30% of adjusted monthly income. The absence of such a limit "gives participants even greater flexibility in the housing market as well as access to more expensive units that better meet their needs. Under the current program, participating families *must* contribute *at least* 30% of their adjusted monthly incomes to housing costs, and they *may*—but *need not*—spend more." 442 F.3d at 358. *See* 42 U.S.C. § 1437f(o)(2)(B).

The voucher scheme gives participants increased flexibility, not diminished rights. Nor was the right to enforce the statute and regulations barred simply because "a participant whose rent alone (exclusive of the utility allowance) exceeds the payment standard is not at all affected by [an increase in] the utility allowance." 442 F.3d at 363 n.30.

251 *See, e.g.*, Hill v. Ogburn, 812 F.2d 679 (7th Cir. 1987) (tenants not entitled to relief against HUD, only against PHA).

252 Nelson v. Greater Gadsden Hous. Auth., 802 F.2d 405 (11th Cir. 1986) (decided prior to Wright v. City of Roanoke Redevelopment & Hous. Auth., 479 U.S. 418, 107 S. Ct. 766 (1987)); Sims v. Housing Auth., No. CV-F-86-386 REC (E.D. Cal. Aug. 5, 1988) (decided under earlier version of regulations). *See also* Shea v. Kahuku Hous. Found., Inc., 2011 WL 1261150 (D. Haw. Mar. 31, 2011) (approving settlement of contract and UDAP claims against Section 8 developer; failure to increase utility allowance resulted in over-payment of rent by tenants of senior housing).

10.7.3 Relief Obtained

The relief obtained by tenants both with and without litigation has been substantial. In one case, for example, tenants in Gadsden, Alabama, obtained a court order setting forth new utility allowances and requiring the PHA to update those allowances at least annually. The court ordered the PHA to increase the gas utility allowances for tenants who purchase their own gas. These allowances had formerly been set at $5 to $8 monthly, depending on the number of bedrooms, and were increased to $25 to $36. The court also ordered increases in the utility allowances for tenants who are master-metered.[253] The injunctive relief in this case saved tenants an estimated $150,000 per year. Other litigation has resulted in both prospective relief in terms of increases in utility allowances, as well as restitution to tenants for previously inadequate allowances.[254] Moreover, some courts have granted specific relief in court orders by incorporating plans for future utility allowance adjustments.[255]

One of the most outstanding examples of relief remains that granted by the court in *Stone v. District of Columbia*.[256] In this case, the PHA ultimately reimbursed tenants for prior rent overcharges due to inadequate utility allowances, with HUD providing the PHA the funds to do so, up to a maximum of nearly $2 million.[257] Ultimately, the D.C. Housing Authority did away with utility allowances and now master-meters all tenants, although tenants can be surcharged for use of certain appliances. According to one commissioner, the PHA felt that administration of the utility allowance program was highly arbitrary and difficult for the staff to administer.[258]

Advocates should always investigate the adequacy of past and present utility allowances and seek prospective and retroactive relief when merited. A currently inadequate allowance is likely to be a sign of previous inadequacies. Cash awards for previously inadequate utility allowances should not affect calculation of income and, therefore, should not the amount of rent due.[259] However, large cash awards might influence resource limits for other benefit programs.

10.8 Advocating for Clients: Developing the Facts

10.8.1 Introduction

Advocating for tenants around utility allowance issues is a fact-intensive exercise. Unlike many other areas of law, the legal standard is quite clear. HUD regulations require that tenants in most subsidized units who pay their own utility bills (individually metered tenants) or who face surcharges if they use more than a specified amount of energy (check-metered tenants) be provided "reasonable" utility allowances. But determining whether a particular allowance is "reasonable" requires evaluation and consideration of a number of factors, including: prevailing utility prices; building location and type of construction; local climatic conditions; family size and unique family needs (for example, disability or illness); and types of appliances used, and so forth.

The first step for advocates is to gather information about current utility allowances and tenants' actual utility bills. The means of doing so are described below.[260]

253 Nelson v. Grater Gadsen Hous. Auth., 606 F. Supp. 948 (N.D. Ala. 1985), *aff'd in part, vacated and remanded in part*, 802 F.2d 405 (11th Cir. 1986).

254 *E.g.*, Currey v. Powers, No. 86-C-122 (D. Colo. Nov. 18, 1986), 20 Clearinghouse Rev. 1324 (Feb. 1987) (Clearinghouse No. 41,778) ($86,000 retroactive compensation and $10,000 in attorney fees); Junior v. Housing Auth., No. 85-2172 (E.D. La. May 1, 1986), 20 Clearinghouse Rev. 281 (July 1986) (Clearinghouse No. 39,421) ($250 utility offset per tenant against any debt owed to PHA and $25,000 in attorney fees). *See also* Blake v. Nishimura, 2010 WL 1372420 (D. Haw. Mar. 31, 2010) (settlement required that evictions for rent delinquencies be postponed until after amount of rent overcharges, resulting from failure to increase utility allowance, could be calculated).

255 *E.g.*, Miller v. Housing Auth., No. 87-1286 (C.D. Ill. Feb. 2, 1990), 24 Clearinghouse Rev. 42 (May 1990) (Clearinghouse No. 43,233) (utility allowances prospectively calculated on average monthly utility consumption from each preceding year); Scott v. Hamlet Hous. Auth., No. C-88-18-R (M.D.N.C. Aug. 2, 1989), 23 Clearinghouse Rev. 745 (Oct. 1989) (Clearinghouse No. 43,152) (utility allowance increases based upon highest average monthly consumption over the previous three years; individual relief from utility surcharges beyond tenants' control; annual review of utility allowance; $83,000 in rent credits and refunds; attorney fees).

256 Stone v. District of Columbia, No. 82-1761 (D.D.C. Mar. 1983) (stipulation as to prospective relief), *subsequent op.*, 572 F. Supp. 976 (D.D.C. 1983) (no implied right of action against PHA), *subsequent order*, 799 F.2d 773 (D.C. Cir. 1986) (Clearinghouse No. 32,924).

257 Stone v. District of Columbia, 1988 WL 4239 (D.D.C. Jan. 5, 1988) (No. 82-1761) ("HUD's subsequent obligation of up to $1,949,200 satisfied plaintiffs' claim for retroactive reimbursement."). *See also* Dunn Residents Council v. Dunn Hous. Auth., 81-423-CIV-5 (E.D.N.C. July 11, 1983) (Clearinghouse No. 35,361) (up to $23,200 for inadequate utility allowances); Final Consent Judgment, O'Neal v. Lake Wales Hous. Auth., No. 80-1015-CIV-T-WC(K) (M.D. Fla. Sept. 29, 1982), 16 Clearinghouse Rev. 921 (Feb. 1983) (Clearinghouse No. 30,120) (tenants awarded up to $21,736 to settle utility allowance litigation); Consent Order, Glaze v. Housing Auth., No. C79-246A (N.D. Ga. Dec. 3, 1981), 16 Clearinghouse Rev. 579 (Nov. 1982) (Clearinghouse No. 26,228) (ordering retroactive payments).

258 E-mail from Commissioner Lynn Cunningham to Charles Harak, Esq., National Consumer Law Center (Feb. 27, 2004).

259 Lump-sum additions to family assets, such as inheritances, insurance payments (including payments under health and accident insurance and worker's compensation), capital gains, and settlement for personal or property losses are not included as income. 24 C.F.R. 5.609(c)(3).

260 § 10.8.3, *infra*.

Advocates should be able to determine quite readily whether the allowances appear adequate in relation to actual bills. But the mere fact that many tenant bills are larger than their allowances does not mean that the allowances are illegal and can be overturned. First, PHAs have wide discretion in setting bills. HUD's standard for public housing is that the "PHA's determinations . . . shall be final and valid unless found to be arbitrary, capricious, an abuse of discretion, or otherwise not in accordance with law."[261] Moreover, a PHA faced with the argument that actual usage is greater than that allowed will simply respond by saying that tenants are wasting energy and are not entitled to allowances that cover 100% of the usage of all or even most tenants.

Advocates will therefore have to dig deeper: research and analyze the methods the PHA used to develop the allowances and determine if they comply with the (rather minimal) regulatory requirements and whether the allowances are in fact reasonable. In some cases, advocates may be able to perform the necessary analysis without resorting to expert advice. For example, the local utility may be able to provide data on typical consumption by appliance and by households of various sizes; the local fuel assistance or weatherization agency may have the ability to carefully analyze the reasonableness of the allowances; or there may be graduate students or professors at local engineering or business schools that can offer assistance, possibly at limited or no cost.[262] Advocates may also find useful material and analyses in HUD reviews that have been conducted in the context of an audit or operations review. Advocates should be prepared, however, to retain expert advice, particularly when there are large numbers of affected tenants and the PHA is unwilling to negotiate.

10.8.2 Determining the Need for Weatherization

Many tenants have high and unaffordable bills because their buildings are poorly insulated and poorly maintained. Apartment units may have broken windows, old and inefficient appliances, or defective heating or cooling systems. If these or other factors are the cause of excessive utility charges, the PHA should be urged to seek out funds to insulate and make other necessary repairs. Some PHAs are able to make the necessary improvements by using available modernization funds.[263] Other PHAs may be able to access funds from the Weatherization Assistance Program (WAP).[264] During 2010 and 2011, the Department of Energy, which oversees the WAP, has been emphasizing the importance of local WAP-funded agencies serving multifamily properties and has facilitated the process for determining which buildings are income-eligible.[265] If problems with the physical condition of a building are serious enough, tenants in many states would be able to go to court seeking repair orders or other remedies.[266] If allegedly "excessive" utility consumption is due to poor housing conditions, old appliances, or lack of insulation, the allowances should be increased. Tenants should not have to bear the burden of poor construction, a PHA's myopic procurement process, or substandard maintenance practices.

HUD has adopted rules that encourage PHAs to engage in weatherization activities, at little cost or risk to the PHA, resulting in extensive additional income for the PHA and savings on utility costs to tenants.[267] Tenants and their advocates should work with PHAs to invest in cost-effective weatherization and energy efficiency upgrades.

10.8.3 Documents to Obtain[268]

As noted above, to evaluate the "reasonableness" of the PHA's utility allowance, the actual energy consumption by

261 24 C.F.R. § 965.502(e).

262 *See, e.g.*, J. Stein, Georgia Legal Servs. Program, *Newnan Public Housing Utility Study* (June 1979) (Clearinghouse No. 29,874). The study was prepared for and used in Leslie v. Mann, No. C77-49N (N.D. Ga. June 20, 1980), 14 Clearinghouse Rev. 776 (Nov. 1980) (Clearinghouse No. 23,320).

NCLC staff may be able to make further suggestions.

263 24 C.F.R. pt. 968.

264 42 U.S.C. §§ 6861–6873; 10 C.F.R. pt. 440. *See* appx. D, *infra* (weatherization reference materials).

265 *See* U.S. Dep't of Energy, WAP Notice 11-09, Updated Guidance on Eligible Multifamily Property Listings for Use in the Weatherization Assistance Program (Apr. 1, 2011), *reprinted at* appx. D, *infra*; U.S. Dep't of Energy, WAP Notice 10-15A, Guidance Regarding Accrual of Benefits to Low-Income Tenants in Multi-Family Buildings Under the Weatherization Assistance Program (Apr. 8, 2010), *reprinted at* appx. D, *infra*; U.S. Dep't of Energy, WAP Notice 10-15, Final Rule on Amending Eligibility Provisions to Multifamily Buildings for the Weatherization Assistance Program (Mar. 2, 2010), *reprinted at* appx. D, *infra*.

266 *See, e.g.*, Perez v. Boston Hous. Auth., 400 N.E.2d 1231 (Mass. 1980) (placing PHA in receivership for failure to provide "decent, safe and sanitary" housing); Boston Hous. Auth. v. Hemingway, 293 N.E.2d 831 (Mass. 1973) (adopting warranty of habitability in residential housing and applying it to public housing landlord).

267 PHAs may retain 100% of the energy savings after payment to the contractor who performs the energy efficiency work until the term of the financing agreement is completed. The PHA is also eligible for an additional operating subsidy to amortize the cost of energy conservation measures. 24 C.F.R. § 990.185.

268 HUD has posted on its website a useful overview of the two basic ways—utilizing an "engineering-based methodology" versus a "consumption-based methodology"—in which housing authorities can calculate utility allowances. *See* U.S. Dep't of Housing & Urban Dev., Calculating Utility Allowances, *available at* http://portal.hud.gov/hudportal/HUD?src=/program_offices/public_indian_housing/programs/ph/phecc/allowances2.

Advocates may find it useful to review this discussion as an aid to determining what documents to request. HUD also provides a very useful glossary: Key Utility Terms, at http://

project tenants must be determined. For check-metered units, the PHA preferably would provide the actual utility bills.[269] Alternatively, tenants can obtain Form 52722[270] (Calculation of Utilities Expense Level) and the results from the utility expense level calculator[271] if that was used by the PHA. The HUD area office may have these forms for the project in question. These forms are useful because the PHA uses them to claim its energy and utility expenses as part of receiving its annual operating subsidy. Since PHAs want to obtain the maximum lawful subsidy, they are motivated to state the full extent of their utility expenses in serving check-metered customers.

If the units have direct retail meters, tenants themselves can provide any actual bills that have been saved. Alternatively, the utility company will have bill histories readily available upon request of the tenant-customers. The local utility may also have data available on "typical" consumption.

The PHA's utility allowance schedule will state the allowances in dollar amounts or in consumption units, such as cubic feet or therms for gas[272] or kilowatt hours for electricity. Because of rapidly changing utility rates, it is most useful to first analyze the adequacy of utility allowances on the basis of energy-unit consumption rather than dollar amounts. For retail-metered units for which allowances are stated in dollar amounts, even if the PHA's allowance is adequate in terms of consumption units (for example, kWh or Ccf), the dollar amount of the allowance may be inadequate if the PHA has not adjusted the allowance to reflect *current* utility rates. For these retail-metered tenants, advocates should carefully review both the consumption units allowed and the utility rates assumed by the PHA in setting the dollar allowances.

10.8.4 Factors to Consider

When evaluating utility allowances, check whether the allowance:

(1) Is based on *current* consumption data because average consumption per household may be increasing over time (for example, more households have a larger number of electric appliances and electronic devices);
(2) Reflects current utility rates;
(3) Clearly discloses the assumed amount of energy consumption, rather than just the dollar amounts (this makes it easier to monitor the adequacy of the allowances);
(4) Is based on bedroom or dwelling size, not the number of residents in the unit (this is particularly important for heat-related allowances, which should reflect the amount of space to be heated, not the number of residents);
(5) Is specifically tailored for each project and type of unit within the PHA's jurisdiction (for example, the heating allowance for single family or townhouse units would generally be larger than for high-rise units because the latter units are generally better insulated by adjoining units); and
(6) Is seasonally adjusted.

The absence of any of these features indicates a potentially inadequate allowance that requires further scrutiny. There may be additional factors that merit close attention, not all of which can be listed here.[273] For example, a particular building might have very old and inefficient natural gas-fired water heaters, requiring a higher allowance for gas service; apartments in a high-rise building might be heated by electric fans that draw in heat from central heating ducts, calling for a higher utility allowance for electric service. Advocates should pay close attention to the sources of space-heating and water-heating as well to the types of appliances generally used by tenants in each building.

10.8.5 Using Utility Bills or Meter Readings to Analyze Consumption

In order to analyze the adequacy of current utility allowances, it is important to compare the average consumption for either check-metered or retail-metered units to the consumption assumed by the PHA in setting the allowances. The first step is to obtain the monthly utility bills or meter readings, sorted by building type and bedroom size (for example, sorted by one-, two- and three-bedroom high-rise units; one-, two- and three-bedroom row house units, and so forth). The next steps are as follows:

(1) Add together all of the *consumption amounts* (*not* dollar charges) for one month for each separate size and category of unit (for example, determine that the twelve two-bedroom apartments in a high-rise build-

portal.hud.gov/hudportal/HUD?src=/program_offices/public_indian_housing/programs/ph/phecc/definitions.

269 *See* 24 C.F.R. § 965.502(b) (PHAs must make available to tenants documents that form the basis for utility allowances).

270 *Available at* http://portal.hud.gov/hudportal/documents/huddoc?id=DOC_11783.doc.

Note that the form "is used to calculate the utilities expense level component of eligibility for operating subsidy pursuant to 24 C.F.R. Parts 990.170–990.185. It is used for PHA-owned rental housing projects and PHA units in mixed housing developments . . . this form shall not be used for the Turnkey III and Mutual Help Homeownership Programs, Section and 10(c) Leased Housing Programs, or the Housing Choice Voucher (Section 8) Program."

271 Available at http://portal.hud.gov/hudportal/HUD?src=/program_offices/public_indian_housing/programs/ph/am/of/uel.

272 For gas, one therm equals approximately 100 cubic feet, or one "Ccf."

273 *See* 24 C.F.R. § 965.505(d) (listing factors that PHAs "shall take into account" when setting public housing utility allowances).

ing consumed 6000 kWh of electricity in the month of May);

(2) Divide this figure by the number of units in the category to obtain the average monthly consumption of each category of unit (for example, divide the 6000 kWh by the twelve apartments to determine that the average two-bedroom high-rise unit used 500 kWh of electricity in the month of May);

(3) Compare this average consumption figure to the allowance (if stated in consumption amounts) or to the consumption amount assumed by the PHA in developing the dollar allowance.

(4) Determine how many units in the category exceeded the allowance and the percentage of units that exceeded the allowance. Under the current regulations, there is no explicit percentage trigger for increasing the allowances. Under the prior regulations, if the PHA surcharged more than 25% of the check-metered units, the allowance should have been increased.[274] This prior regulation may still be used as a reasonable yardstick for judging the adequacy of utility allowance schedules.

(5) Examine the amount that tenants pay in excess of the utility allowance. If, on average, tenants pay only a few dollars per month more than the allowance, it may be difficult to get the allowance increased. On the other hand, if (for example) the average tenant is paying $20 per month more than the allowance (especially for a non-heating utility source), this suggests that the allowance was not properly calculated and should be increased. Also, if the utility allowance for just a few units is significantly inadequate, this may indicate maintenance or repair problems (for example, broken windows, defective water heater, and so forth) or a metering problem (for example, two apartments that are cross-metered in some way) that should be corrected.

When utility bills or sufficient meter readings are not available, advocates may need to rely on the PHA's data reported on HUD Form 52722[275] or comparable utility expense forms, or by estimating consumption using data provided by the local utility, fuel assistance agencies, or other sources (for retail-metered tenants).

10.8.6 Using HUD Form 52722

For units that a PHA owns directly, the PHA must fill out Form 52722 (Calculation of Utilities Expense Level).[276] Form 52722 can be very useful in efforts to represent check-metered clients.[277] On Form 52722, the PHA reports actual consumption separately for sewerage and water, electricity, gas, and other fuels (wood, oil, coal, and so forth). The PHA also provides data over the prior three years, allowing advocates to track changes in consumption patterns over time. The PHA separately reports on the rate or price for each fuel. This form provides much, but by no means all, of the data needed to analyze the adequacy of utility allowances for check-metered tenants. The largest flaw in the reported data is that Form 52722 does not require the PHA to sort consumption by unit size or building type. Advocates will have to draw on other sources or consult with experts to determine whether allowances that are set by unit size and type are supported (or contradicted) by the aggregate consumption data reported on Form 52722.

10.8.7 Estimating Consumption When Actual Readings Are Unavailable

10.8.7.1 General

When tenants pay for their own utilities, they may already have copies of their own bills available. Alternatively, almost every utility will produce, at the customer's request, a billing history that covers at least the last twelve months of usage. Only in unusual cases will advocates need to use other means to estimate consumption by retail-metered tenants.

Any estimate will be inherently imprecise. Utility consumption is affected by too many factors and, in the absence of having actual bills, makes it difficult to develop accurate estimates. Estimates may only be useful for negotiating a higher allowance with a PHA willing to negotiate. Moreover, because of dramatic variation in heat loss factors from project to project and even from floor to floor in some buildings, it is quite difficult to accurately estimate space-heating consumption. In most cases, advocates will only be able to estimate consumption for uses and appliances—for example, electrical consumption for non-heating purposes, cooking, and possibly water heating—when there is less variance between households.

The method for estimating non-heat consumption (either of electricity or gas) involves adding up the average consumption level of all of the appliances that a tenant might be expected or permitted to use. These figures can be obtained from the local utility company and from other sources.[278] If

274 *See* 24 C.F.R. § 965; 45 Fed. Reg. 59502 (Sept. 9, 1980).

275 Discussed in §§ 10.8.3, *supra*, 10.8.6, *infra*.

276 *See* www.hud.gov/offices/pih/programs/ph/am/of/uel.xls (spreadsheet); http://portal.hud.gov/hudportal/documents/huddoc?id=DOC_11783.doc (with instructions)). *See also* 24 C.F.R. §§ 990.160–990.190.

277 For retail-metered families, Form 52722 will only reveal information about common-area usage (for example, hallway or exterior lighting, appliance consumption in meeting rooms, and so forth) or centrally provided services (for example, PHA-provided heating or hot water) because tenants will be paying the bills for usage inside individual apartments.

278 *See, e.g.*, U.S. Dep't of Energy, Estimating Appliance and Home Electronic Energy Use, *available at* www.energysavers.gov/your_

the PHA's allowance is stated in monetary (dollar) terms, multiply the total of the estimated kilowatt-hour (kWh) and hundred cubic feet (Ccf) consumption figures by the current utility rates and compare the resulting dollar amounts to the dollar amount of the current allowance. Make sure to add any customer charge (or other fixed monthly charges), as customers are required to pay these charges on top of the actual consumption charges.

10.8.7.2 Utilities for Heat: Specific Issues

Utilities for heat make up one-half or more of the utility bills paid by tenants who live in apartments for which they pay for heat.[279] Any accurately estimated allowance for heat utilities would be based upon the actual data for the unit. This is rarely the case.

The consumption of utilities for heat depends heavily on the physical characteristics of the unit. The quality of insulation and the location of the unit (for example, top floor, corner apartment with northern exposure) are key factors.[280] Under prior versions of the regulations, HUD recognized the importance of the physical characteristics of units and, theoretically, PHAs were required to determine allowances by relying on actual consumption data.[281]

But utility allowances may be determined by using standard formulas that incorporate variables for heat loss (the extent to which a building retains or loses heat, reflecting such factors as its insulation level, average unit size, and age), "degree days" (a measure of the number of days and extent to which outdoor temperatures fall below, for example, 68° Fahrenheit during the winter), and other factors.

Obviously, this formula will rarely result in allowances that accurately match actual consumption. The utility allowance may under-estimate actual consumption for any number of reasons.

When space heating is fueled by natural gas, some PHAs may provide allowances in terms of gas volumes (cubic feet) rather than heat content (therms or BTUs).[282] Since the heat content of a given volume of gas can vary depending on the source of the gas, the advocate should make sure that the allowance accurately reflects the heat content of the gas used, particularly when the local utility supplies a less efficient gas than was provided in the past. Contact the gas supplier to get the average heat content per cubic foot of its gas.

home/appliances/index.cfm/mytopic=10040; Typical Power Consumption, *available at* www.oksolar.com/technical/consumption.html).

Many utilities have web-based calculators or printed materials that can be used to estimate typical consumption and that may prove more useful in accurately reflecting the actual areas in which tenants reside

279 General Accounting Office, RCED-91-40A, Assisted Housing: Utility Allowances Often Fall Short of Actual Utility Expenses, vol. I (Mar. 1991).

280 *See* National Consumer Law Center, Energy and the Poor (May 1989); Steven Ferrey, *The Ghosts of Cold November; An Examination of HUD's Energy Conservation Policy for the Poor*, 11 Clearinghouse Rev. 1 (May 1977).

281 *E.g.*, 24 C.F.R. § 865.477 (1981).

282 One therm of gas energy equals approximately 100 cubic feet.

10.9 Negotiation Strategies for Public Housing Tenants

10.9.1 Allowances in General

Some tenants faced with inadequate utility allowances have negotiated with their PHA to develop a plan to assist the local public housing authority in collecting and evaluating relevant data. Many PHAs lack the time and expertise to establish reasonable utility allowances, and they do not gather the relevant information because no one is "making them" do it. Although PHAs may argue that they have some discretion *not* to collect relevant data,[283] tenants should assert their unquestionable right to obtain whatever documentation the PHA bases the utility allowance on and to submit their own data and comments.[284] It is to the tenants' advantage to present to the PHA as much cumulative data regarding actual usage and other relevant factors as possible. PHAs must retain all comments and data submitted, which HUD may, in its discretion, review at a later date.[285]

Tenants and advocates who work with a local PHA to develop utility allowances should bear in mind that under the performance funding system (PFS), under which HUD provides operating subsidies to PHAs, a PHA should be fully reimbursed by HUD for the rent revenue it may lose in almost all cases when utility allowances are raised.[286] Furthermore, HUD has provided substantial incentives to PHAs that save energy by investing in weatherization and improved energy efficiency.[287] PHAs are allowed to retain the savings generated by energy efficient measures for periods up to twelve years. The rules now facilitate PHA participation in loans, performance contracts, or shared savings agreements with private energy service companies, utility companies or governmental agencies. To date, however, most PHAs are unaware of how to participate and how to maximize the savings potential of these creatively financed packages.[288] If the utility allowances are developed as a

283 *See, e.g.*, 24 C.F.R. §§ 965.502(e) (regarding PHA discretion), 965.505(c) (same).

284 24 C.F.R. § 965.502(b), (c).

285 24 C.F.R. § 965.502(c), (d).

286 24 C.F.R. § 990.170(e).

287 *See, e.g.*, 24 C.F.R. §§ 965.301–965.308 (regarding energy audits and investments in cost-effective energy efficiency); 24 C.F.R. §§ 990.107, 990.110 (regarding reimbursement to PHAs of investments in energy efficiency).

288 *See* National Consumer Law Center, Up the Chimney: How HUD's Inaction Costs Taxpayers Millions and Drives Up Utility Bills for Low-Income Families (2010), *available at* www.nclc.org/images/pdf/pr-reports/up_the_chimney_082610.pdf.

result of a conversion to individual metering from master-metering, resident organizations should ensure that the PHA works with them to reach the conversion's goal of "achieving an equitable structure that will be advantageous to residents who conserve energy," as required by the regulations.[289] Tenants who find, following the conversion, that their utility consumption is high, should seek advice and assistance from the PHA and, if indicated, should request energy conserving equipment and corrective maintenance.[290] When converting to check-meters, tenants should use the six-month transition period to test the established utility allowances and, should they come up short, argue to the PHA that the allowances must be revised upward.[291]

10.9.2 Individual Relief

The regulations provide that PHAs may grant relief from allowances or surcharges "on such reasonable grounds, such as special needs of elderly, ill or handicapped tenants, or special factors affecting utility usage not within the control of the tenant."[292] The PHA must establish "criteria" for granting such relief, as well as "procedures for requesting the relief."[293] Notice of the criteria, the procedures, as well as the name of the PHA representative from whom to request this relief must be provided to all new tenants and to all tenants along with notice of changes in allowances and surcharges.[294] Tenant advocates should consider working on the development of reasonable criteria for individual relief.

Advocates should challenge assumptions by PHAs that tenants' consumption can be controlled by reducing or setting low utility allowances. There is strong evidence that low-income households use far less energy than higher income households.[295] They have fewer ways to reduce their energy consumption. Unlike higher-income households, for example, low-income families generally do not have extra rooms to close off in the effort to reduce their heating bills. Low-income families also do not have an abundance of non-essential electrical appliances.

10.9.3 Using the PHA Plan Process

Federal law now requires PHAs to prepare one-year and five-year agency plans on an ongoing basis.[296] The law requires each PHA to establish "1 or more resident advisory boards" which "shall assist and make recommendations regarding the development of the public housing agency plan."[297] While the required contents of the plan[298] need not address utility allowances per se, the law is clear that PHAs "must consider" recommendations made by resident advisory boards and by tenants during the plan process and must submit a copy of those recommendations, along with the PHA's response, to HUD.[299] Before submitting the plan to HUD, the PHA must also serve notice of and hold a hearing on the plan in addition to making all relevant documents available for inspection.[300]

The PHA plan process thus presents a useful organizing and advocacy opportunity. On the one hand, the PHA is not under a strict obligation to include in its state plan a section, for example, entitled "Calculation of Utility Allowances." On the other hand, the plan process requires PHAs to listen to the views of tenants on a broad range of policy issues. Utility allowances are based, by their very nature, on local facts and developed under the discretion of local PHA commissioners or administrators. Most utility allowance disputes are resolved far short of litigation at the local level. Tenants and their advocates should consider the plan process, including the public hearing, as an annual opportunity—one that is far easier to utilize than litigation—to raise concerns about the adequacy of utility allowances. The plan process may also serve as a means by which advocates can discover, informally, some of the thinking and analysis behind the PHA's development of current utility allowances that would prove useful if litigation become necessary.

10.10 Utility Allowances for Involuntarily Relocated Tenants

Public housing tenants are sometimes involuntarily displaced from a housing development because of a construction project which is federally financed. This occurs, for example, when the public housing authority has decided to re-develop the site as low-and moderate-income housing, using HOPE VI or other federal housing modernization

289 24 C.F.R. § 965.405(c).
However, note that even if the conversion requires residents to ante up cash for deposits to the utility company or to pay accumulated arrearages, one court has held that such sums are not "rent" for purposes of the Brooke Amendment because they are not paid to the housing authority. Crochet v. Housing Auth. of City of Tampa, 37 F.3d 607 (11th Cir. 1994).

290 24 C.F.R. § 965.405(e).

291 24 C.F.R. § 965.405(d).

292 24 C.F.R. § 965.508.

293 *Id.*

294 *Id.*

295 *See* § 10.6.5, *supra* (discussing household energy consumption by income strata).

296 42 U.S.C. § 1437c-1, *added by* Pub. L. No. 105-276, § 511(a), 112 Stat. 2531 (Oct. 21, 1998).
HUD has adopted implementing regulations at 24 C.F.R. part 903, subpart B (§§ 903.3 to 903.25).

297 42 U.S.C. § 1437c-1(e)(1), (2). *See* 24 C.F.R. § 903.13 (companion regulations).

298 42 U.S.C. § 1437c-1(d). *See* 24 C.F.R. §§ 903.6, 903.7 (companion regulations).

299 42 U.S.C. § 1437c-1(e)(2); 24 C.F.R. § 903.13(c).

300 42 U.S.C. § 1437c-1(f).

program funding. These displaced tenants may be entitled to supplemental rent and utility payments to help defray increased costs in their new dwellings.

The Uniform Relocation Assistance and Real Property Acquisition Policies Act of 1970 (URA)[301] entitles all persons who are involuntarily displaced because of a federally financed project to payments "of the amount necessary to enable such person to lease or rent for a period not to exceed 42 months, a comparable replacement dwelling, but not to exceed $5,250."[302] Relocated public housing tenants are often given Section 8 housing choice vouchers to use to find replacement housing. Given the sorry state of most public housing, the Section 8 apartments they rent are likely to meet the statutory requirement of being "comparable" in quality to the public housing from which they were displaced. However, the tenants' shelter costs may be higher than before since these are not capped at 30% of adjusted income, unlike when they were public housing tenants.[303]

Thus, involuntarily displaced former public housing tenants who become voucher holders may be entitled to supplement payments from the PHA for up to forty-two months to compensate them if they are paying higher rent and utilities than previously. With respect to utilities, this is so even if they are receiving a Section 8 utility allowance. As discussed elsewhere in this chapter, utility allowances for Section 8 voucher holders are "based on the typical cost of utilities and services paid by energy-conservative households that occupy housing of similar size and type in the same locality."[304] In contrast, the URA provides for utility payments equal to average estimated future utility costs for the particular displaced individual, with no proviso regarding hypothetically "energy-conserving households."[305] In some jurisdictions, there may be a substantial gap between the payments calculated under these two standards. If so, tenants should be able to enforce their URA rights against a public housing authority in federal court. Moreover, they should be able to do so under 42 U.S.C. § 1983 without first exhausting administrative remedies.[306]

301 42 U.S.C. §§ 4621–4638.

302 42 U.S.C. § 4624(a).

303 *See* § 10.2.5.1, *supra*.

304 24 C.F.R. § 982.517.

305 49 C.F.R. § 24.2.

306 Renfroe v. Housing Auth. of New Orleans, No. 03-3613, 2004 WL 1630496 (E.D. La. July 19, 2004) (Clearinghouse No. 55,715). *See also* Jones v. Department of Hous. Preservation & Dev., 2008 WL 5155725 (S.D.N.Y. Dec. 8, 2009) ("a claim under the APA is the exclusive means for suing in federal court on the basis of a displacing agency's failure to comply with its obligations under the URA"). *Contra* Wallace v. Chicago Hous. Auth., 298 F. Supp. 2d 710 (N.D. Ill. 2003).

Chapter 11 Telecommunications

11.1 Introduction

While the scope of this chapter seeks to address the primary issues surrounding access to basic telephone service, the idea of what constitutes basic service is changing. The telecommunications services that a consumer may consider essential in interacting with employers, social services, medical professionals, family, and friends are drastically different today than they were in the preceding decades.

Today, perhaps more than ever before, laws and regulations regarding telecommunications services struggle to keep up with a rapidly evolving technology landscape. Technology has blurred the traditional distinctions between the types of services available. For example, local and long-distance phone service were traditionally provided by phone companies over copper wires, also called landline or wireline service. Today, telephone service is not only available using wireline but is also available through wireless, cable, fiber optics, and Internet technologies. Twenty percent of the population now relies exclusively on a mobile phone.[1] The providers of telecommunications services are no longer only telephone companies. They now include cable companies that offer "Voice over Internet Protocol" (VoIP) and/or broadband Internet services with cable TV. Today's services are multifaceted. Wireless plans, in addition to offering phone service, allow users to send text messages, surf the Internet, and download documents, music, and video.

Multiple services are often bundled into one product offering. Telecommunications companies bundle and market as one package the combined services of long-distance calling, cable television, and Internet, through both wireless and wireline technologies. Customers may even be offered a variety of rates. For example, there are flat-rate plans and charge-per-use plans. A former chairman of the Federal Communications Commission (FCC) described the current telecommunications evolution as a "digital migration" wherein "[t]raditional telecommunications services are migrating from old circuit-switched networks to new and advanced Internet protocol networks."[2]

As a result of all of these changes, the jurisdictional landscape of what actors and what services fall under state or federal jurisdiction can be confusing.[3] What is considered basic, essential telephone or telecommunications service traditionally regulated by the Federal Communications Commission (FCC) or state commissions is being re-examined. The FCC is reconsidering what constitutes basic service for which low-income customers can receive federal assistance.[4]

For over seven decades, since the enactment of the Communications Act of 1934, this nation has made a commitment to the goal of making essential telecommunications service universally available throughout the nation.[5] For a very long time, essential telecommunications service meant "plain old telephone service" (POTS) provided over copper wires and using the public switched telephone network (PSTN). The goal of universal service was not merely an altruistic gesture. The value of the network was made more valuable as more people were connected. As the FCC noted:

> The absence of telecommunications service in a home puts its occupants at a tremendous disadvantage in today's society. Parents cannot be reached when urgent situations arise at school. Job seekers cannot offer prospective employers a quick and convenient means of communication. People in immediate need of emergency services cannot contact police departments, fire departments, or medical providers. In short, telephone service provides a vital link between individuals and society as a whole. Given the importance of telephone service in modern society, it is imperative that the Commission take swift and decisive action to promote the deployment of facilities to unserved and underserved areas and to provide

1 *See In re* Federal-State Joint Board on Universal Service Lifeline and Link Up, F.C.C. 10-72 ¶ 10 (F.C.C. Apr. 28, 2010), *available at* http://hraunfoss.fcc.gov/edocs_public/attachmatch/FCC-10-72A1.pdf.

2 *Universal Service: Hearing on Universal Service Before the Senate Comm. on Commerce, Science and Transp.*, 108th Cong. (2003) (statement of Michael K. Powell, Chairman of the Federal Communications Commission).

3 This chapter should be read in conjunction with the discussion of the regulated utility in Chapter 1, *supra*.

4 *See* Notice of Proposed Rulemaking, *In re* Lifeline & Link UP Reform & Modernization, Federal-State Joint Bd. on Universal Serv., F.C.C. 11-32 ¶ 9 (F.C.C. Mar. 4. 2011) (C.C. No. 96-45), *available at* http://hraunfoss.fcc.gov/edocs_public/attachmatch/FCC-11-32A1.pdf.

5 *See* 47 U.S.C. § 254.

the support necessary to increase subscribership in these areas.[6]

As noted above, basic telephone service is essential for day-to-day life. Arguably, in today's interconnected world, the basic service that provides the "vital link between individuals and society as a whole"[7] now extends beyond copper lines and by necessity includes mobile services and Internet technologies. Indeed, the FCC is proposing to apply the federal assistance program for low-income consumers to bundled voice and broadband offerings.[8]

The definition of universal telecommunications service (universal services) was envisioned by Congress to evolve as new technologies become commonplace. The Communications Act states, in listing the core principles of universal service, that "[a]ccess to advanced telecommunications and information services should be provided in all regions of the Nation."[9] Low-income consumers have a great stake in the definition of universal service, because support for the availability and affordability of the various services that comprise universal service depends on their inclusion in the definition. Currently, the federal assistance programs to connect low-income households to telecommunications services, such as the Lifeline and Link-Up programs discussed *infra*, apply to wireline and wireless service. They currently do not include access to other advanced telecommunications services (for example, broadband Internet access) for residential customers.[10]

The FCC and Congress are still wrestling with how to comprehensively reform the federal universal services program to address the need to increase broadband capacity and access.[11] In November 2007, the Federal-State Joint Board on Universal Services sent the FCC a recommendation for comprehensive reform of the High Cost Fund support program, a Universal Service Fund (USF) program to bring telecommunications services to areas for which building the necessary infrastructure to serve the area is associated with high costs. The recommendation contained funding for broadband (via a broadband fund) and wireless infrastructure (via a mobility fund) in underserved areas as well as a provider-of-last-resort fund comprised of the existing incumbent wireline high cost support mechanisms.[12] The FCC opened these recommendations up for comment in 2008[13] and has issued an interim cap on competitive eligible telecommunications carrier (ETC) support for each state to remain in effect until the FCC reaches a final decision on comprehensive reform measures.[14]

In 2009, as part of the American Recovery and Reinvestment Act (ARRA), Congress directed that a national broadband program be created by the Assistant Secretary of Commerce for Communications and Information in consultation with the FCC, and established the Broadband Technology Opportunities Program (BTOP) to provide grants for deploying broadband. The program is to establish broadband access in unserved areas and to improve access to underserved areas of the nation.[15] ARRA requires that the national broadband plan "ensure that all people of the United States have access to broadband capability" and "establish benchmarks for meeting that goal."[16] The national broadband plan must include a plan to use broadband infrastructure and services in "advancing consumer welfare."[17]

The FCC sought comments on financing broadband deployment, noting that current federal support to unserved and underserved areas alone is inadequate and economically

6 *In re* Federal-State Joint Bd. on Universal Serv.: Promoting Deployment & Subscribership in Unserved & Underserved Areas, Including Tribal & Insular Areas, F.C.C. 99-204 ¶ 2 (F.C.C. Sept. 3, 1999) (C.C. No. 96-45), *available at* http://hraunfoss.fcc.gov/edocs_public/attachmatch/FCC-99-204A1.pdf.

7 *Id.*

8 Notice of Proposed Rulemaking, *In re* Lifeline & Link UP Reform & Modernization, Federal-State Joint Bd. on Universal Serv., F.C.C. 11-32 ¶ 12 (Mar. 4, 2011) (C.C. No. 96-45), *available at* http://hraunfoss.fcc.gov/edocs_public/attachmatch/FCC-11-32A1.pdf.

9 47 U.S.C. § 254(b)(2).

10 However, the E-rate universal service program provides schools and libraries with discounted rates for advanced telecommunications services so that students and communities are not left behind in the information age.

11 The FCC has stated that it "will undertake comprehensive universal service reform" at the time that it implements the recommendations of the national broadband plan. *See* High-Cost Universal Service Support, 74 Fed. Reg. 68763 ¶ 1 (Dec. 29, 2009) (further notice of proposed rulemaking). For progress on the national broadband plan, visit www.broadband.gov.

12 Recommended Decision, *In re* High-Cost Universal Serv. Support Federal-State Joint Bd. on Universal Serv., 22 F.C.C.R. 20477 (F.C.C. Nov. 19, 2007) (F.C.C. 07J-4, W.C. No. 05-337, C.C. No. 96-45).

13 Notice of Proposed Rulemaking, 23 F.C.C.R. 1467 (F.C.C. Jan. 29, 2008) (F.C.C. 08-4) (Identical Support Rule); Notice of Proposed Rulemaking, 23 F.C.C.R. 1495 (F.C.C. Jan. 29, 2008) (F.C.C. 08-5) (Reverse Auction); Notice of Proposed Rulemaking, 23 F.C.C.R. 1531 (F.C.C. Jan. 29, 2008) (F.C.C. 08-22) (Joint Board Comprehensive Reform).

14 The High Cost Fund had increased from $2.6 billion in universal services support in 2001 to $ 4.3 billion in support in 2007, and the FCC attributed the growth to competitive ETCs (CETCs), with 94% of the CETC support going to wireless carriers. *See* Order, *In re* High-Cost Universal Service Support Federal-State Joint Bd. on Universal Serv., F.C.C. 08-122 ¶¶ 6, 20 (F.C.C. May 1, 2008) (W.C. No. 05-337, C.C. No. 96-45).

15 American Recovery and Reinvestment Act of 2009, Pub. L. No. 111-5, § 6001(b)(1)–(b)(2), 123 Stat. 115; 75 Fed. Reg. 3792 (general policy and application procedures for BTOP).

16 American Recovery and Reinvestment Act of 2009, Pub. L. No. 111-5, § 6001(k)(2), 123 Stat. 115.

For progress on the national broadband plan, visit www.broadband.gov.

17 American Recovery and Reinvestment Act of 2009, Pub. L. No. 111-5, § 6001(k)(2)(D), 123 Stat. 115.

The act also requires a detailed strategy to make broadband affordable and ensure that its infrastructure is of maximum usefulness to the public. *Id.* § 6001(k)(2)(B). For progress on the national broadband plan, visit www.broadband.gov.

unsustainable.[18] Additionally, the FCC sought comments on whether existing universal service programs should support broadband.[19]

Included in the over 60,000 pages of comments from multiple stakeholders were comments from AT&T requesting that the FCC retire the public switched telephone network (PSTN), over which "plain old telephone service" (POTS) operates, by a firm deadline.[20] AT&T's request reflects a movement among the largest companies in the telecommunications industry toward abandoning traditional landline service in favor of new technologies.[21] Indeed, an industry group advising the FCC has characterized a transition from PSTN as "inevitable" and is drafting recommendations that the FCC set a sunset date for PSTN to enable a transition to an "all IP Network and future technologies."[22] Advocates should examine the effect that such proposals may have on low-income clients who depend on POTS as their primary, most reliable, or affordable communications service.[23]

On March 16, 2010, the FCC released the report, *Connecting America: The National Broadband Plan*, in which the FCC recommended that a new fund be established to eventually eliminate the legacy "high-cost" program.[24] In *Connecting America: The National Broadband Plan*, the FCC proposes the establishment of a new fund, called the Connect America Fund, to provide funding to service providers for new broadband construction in unserved areas.

Along with shifting $15.5 billion from the legacy high-cost program to the Connect America Fund,[25] the FCC recommended that the revenue base for universal service contributions be expanded, possibly to include contributions from broadband revenues and/or entities using large amounts of bandwidth.[26] The FCC proposes that some portion of this funding should be used to conduct pilots for a broadband Lifeline program[27] and that federal funding should eventually be ended for wireline telephone service in favor of broadband platforms that support not only voice services but other applications as well.[28] It is important for advocates

18 *See* Comment Sought on Addressing Challenges to Broadband Deployment Financing: NBP Public Notice #28, G.N. Nos. 09-47, 09-51, 09-137 (F.C.C. Dec. 18, 2009), *available at* http://hraunfoss.fcc.gov/edocs_public/attachmatch/DA-09-2610A1.pdf.

19 *See* Notice of Inquiry, *In re* A Nat'l Broadband Plan for Our Future, F.C.C. 09-31 (F.C.C. Apr. 8, 2009) (G.N. No. 09-51), *available at* http://hraunfoss.fcc.gov/edocs_public/attachmatch/FCC-09-31A1.pdf.

20 Comments of AT&T Inc. on the Transition from the Legacy Circuit-Switched Network to Broadband Before the Federal Communications Commission 3, G.N. Nos. 09-47, 09-51, 09-137 (Dec. 21, 2009).

21 *See, e.g.*, Comments of the National Association of State Utility Consumer Advocates and the New Jersey Division of Rate Counsel, *In re* Applications filed by Frontier Communications Corporation and Verizon Communications Inc. for Assignment or Transfer of Control Before the Federal Communications Commission 1, 3, W.C. No. 09-95 (Sept. 21, 2009) (proposed transfer of 4.8 million Verizon access lines in fourteen states to Frontier represents Verizon's unloading of devalued assets that it no longer wants to maintain); Saul Hansel, *Verizon Boss Hangs Up on Landline Phone Business*, N.Y. Times, Sept. 17, 2009, *available at* http://bits.blogs.nytimes.com/2009/09/17/verizon-boss-hangs-up-on-landline-phone-business; Ken Belson, *Alltel to End Local Service As a Spinoff Is Completed*, N.Y. Times, July 17, 2006, *available at* www.nytimes.com/2006/07/17/technology/17phone.html (Alltel and Sprint's spinoffs of their wireline business exemplifies growing number of companies leaving landline business).

22 Technology Advisory Council, Status of Recommendations (June 29, 2011) (presentation discussing TAC's draft proposal to the FCC).

23 Especially in some rural areas, cellular telephone service is not reliable and may be unaffordable or even unavailable. Furthermore, the lack of population density in rural areas deters companies from investing in broadband technologies to serve those customers because of the cost of infrastructure. In terms of emergency services, at the present time POTS over wireline is widely considered the most reliable type of service through which the specific location of a 911 call can be pinpointed. While broadband technologies associated with portability can help locate the origination of a 911 call, such technologies may use less direct means and locate the call with less specificity compared to when an emergency call issues from a wireline number that connects to the nearest public safety answering point and is associated with a specific address. However, the FCC is proposing to redirect universal service funding from phone service to broadband service. *See* Federal Commc'ns Comm'n, Connecting America: The National Broadband Plan (Mar. 16, 2010), *available at* http://hraunfoss.fcc.gov/edocs_public/attachmatch/DOC-296935A1.pdf.

24 *See* Federal Commc'ns Comm'n, Connecting America: The National Broadband Plan (Mar. 16, 2010), *available at* http://hraunfoss.fcc.gov/edocs_public/attachmatch/DOC-296935A1.pdf.

The high-cost program currently subsidizes telecommunications services in areas of the country where costs would otherwise be too high, but it is not designed to make broadband in particular universally available. It does not require carriers to provide any minimal level of broadband service to their service territories. For progress on the national broadband plan, visit www.broadband.gov.

25 Federal Commc'ns Comm'n, Connecting America: The National Broadband Plan 148 (Mar. 16, 2010), *available at* http://hraunfoss.fcc.gov/edocs_public/attachmatch/DOC-296935A1.pdf.

For progress on the national broadband plan, visit www.broadband.gov.

26 Federal Commc'ns Comm'n, Connecting America: The National Broadband Plan 149 (Mar. 16, 2010), *available at* http://hraunfoss.fcc.gov/edocs_public/attachmatch/DOC-296935A1.pdf.

For progress on the national broadband plan, visit www.broadband.gov.

27 Federal Commc'ns Comm'n, Connecting America: The National Broadband Plan 148 (Mar. 16, 2010), *available at* http://hraunfoss.fcc.gov/edocs_public/attachmatch/DOC-296935A1.pdf.

For progress on the national broadband plan, visit www.broadband.gov.

28 Federal Commc'ns Comm'n, Connecting America: The National Broadband Plan 143 (Mar. 16, 2010), *available at* http://hraunfoss.fcc.gov/edocs_public/attachmatch/DOC-296935A1.pdf.

to bear in mind that, until broadband services are both available to and reliable for all low-income and rural populations in the country, wireline service may be the most cost effective and effective connection that some customers have to their community and emergency services. It can be argued that complete abandonment of financial assistance and wireline services to customers who rely upon POTS would be imprudent and premature, unless reliable broadband capability exists and is an adequate and affordable substitute for all consumers.

11.2 Regulatory Authorities

11.2.1 State Utility Commissions

Traditional wireline telecommunications services (as opposed to wireless or information services) fall under a system of dual regulation by state and federal commissions, depending on whether the service is designated as intrastate or interstate. State public utility commissions have jurisdiction over wireline local and in-state long-distance telephone services and rates. Except for a handful of special situations,[29] the FCC does not have jurisdiction over "charge, classifications, practices, services, facilities, or regulations for or in connection with *intrastate* communication service by wire or radio of any carrier. . . ."[30] States have been successful in arguing that, since the detariffing of long-distance rates, the carriers are subject to a state's consumer protection and contract laws.[31]

The Communications Act also provides state utility commissions with jurisdiction over "other terms and conditions" of wireless service. The same provision also prohibits states from regulating "the entry of or the rates charged" by wireless carriers.[32] The following language shows Congressional intent regarding this phrase:

> By "terms and conditions," the Committee intends to include such matters as customer billing information and practices and billing disputes and other consumer protection matters; facilities siting issues (for example, zoning); transfers of control; the bundling of services and equipment; and the requirement that carriers make capacity available on a wholesale basis or such other matters as fall within a state's lawful authority. This list is intended to be illustrative only and not meant to preclude other matters generally understood to fall under "terms and conditions."[33]

Yet the issue of what constitutes a "term and condition" has generated much litigation, including whether states can regulate early termination fees[34] and line items on bills.[35]

The changing telecommunications landscape is complicated, and there has been a trend in many states to move away from traditional regulation of phone rates. The premise behind deregulating phone rates is that competition will regulate the marketplace and rates for telecommunications service. Depending on the state, rates have been deregulated, or states have allowed companies greater pricing flexibility in many cases. In such cases, there is often an exception for basic phone service, which remains subject to consumer protection rules and regulations. However, the protections sometimes function simply as a temporary cap on basic service rates.[36] Deregulation that removes rate

---

For progress on the national broadband plan, visit www.broadband.gov.

29 *See* 47 U.S.C. §§ 201, 205.

In Core Communications, Inc. v. Federal Commc'ns Comm'n, 592 F.3d 139 (D.C. Cir. Jan. 12, 2010), the D.C. Circuit held that, under 47 U.S.C. § 201, the FCC has authority to institute a rate cap system for Internet dial-up calls, including those originating and terminating with local exchange carriers within one state. The court reasoned that dial-up Internet traffic involves interstate communications that are delivered through local calls. *Id.* at 144–45.

The Pennsylvania Public Utility Commission and Core Communications separately filed petitions for a rehearing, asserting that, while the FCC may set pricing methodology, sections 251 and 252 of the Communications Act of 1934, as added by the Telecommunications Act of 1996, make clear that jurisdiction belongs to state commissions in setting specific rates for intrastate calls. The U.S. Supreme Court declined to review the D.C. Circuit's decision. *See* Core Comm'cns, Inc. v. Federal Commc'ns Comm'n 131 S. Ct. 597, 178 L.3d. 2d. 434 (2010); Pennsylvania Pub. Util. Comm'n v. Federal Commc'ns Comm'n, 131 S. Ct. 626, 178 L. Ed. 2d 434 (2010).

Pursuant to 47 U.S.C. § 152, the FCC is not precluded from involvement in intrastate activities covered in 47 U.S.C. §§ 223–227 (obscene or harassing phone calls, regulation of pole attachments, telecommunications services for hearing-impaired and speech-impaired individuals, telephone operator services, and restrictions on the use of telephone equipment); 47 U.S.C. § 332 (mobile services); 47 U.S.C. § 301 (license for radio communication or transmission of energy); and subchapter V-A of chapter 5 (dealing with cable communications). *See, e.g.*, Tex. v. American Blast Fax, Inc., 159 F. Supp. 2d 936 (W.D. Tex. 2001), *judgment entered*, 164 F. Supp. 2d 892 (W.D. Tex. 2001) (section 227 of the Telephone Consumer Protection Act is specifically exempted from the Communications Act's general ban on intrastate regulation). *See also* Hooters of Augusta, Inc. v. Nicholson, 537 S.E.2d 468 (Ga. Ct. App. 2000).

30 47 U.S.C. § 152 (emphasis added).

31 *See* § 11.2.2, *infra* (discussing tariffing).

32 47 U.S.C. § 332 (c)(3).

33 H.R. Rep. No. 103-111, at 261 (1993), *reprinted in* 1993 U.S.C.C.A.N. 378, 588.

34 *See, e.g.*, Cedar Rapids Cellular Tel., L.P. v. Miller, 280 F.3d 874 (Iowa 2002); Phillips v. AT & T Wireless, 2004 WL 1737385 (S.D. Iowa, July 29, 2004).

35 *See, e.g.*, Sprint Nextel Corp. v., National Ass'n of State Util. Consumer Advocates, 552 U.S. 1165 (2008); National Ass'n of State Util. Consumer Advocates v. Federal Commc'ns Comm'n, 457 F.3d 1238 (11th Cir. 2006); Peck v. Cingular Wireless, L.L.C., 535 F.3d 1053 (Wash. 2008).

36 The National Regulatory Research Institute (NRRI) has been tracking this trend for years. *See* Lilia Perez-Chavolla, Ph.D.,

regulation from the responsibility of public utility commissions makes it more difficult for low-income consumer advocates to make arguments that essential telecommunications services must remain affordable. They no longer have the benefit of relying upon an affordability mandate by the state commission.

Regardless of the type of telecommunications service or problem, however, it may still be helpful to contact the state utility commission's consumer division to see if it can assist in resolving the problem. Appendix A.8, *infra*, contains a list of state utility commissions and commissioners. Also, about forty states and the District of Columbia have a ratepayer advocate. The ratepayer advocate operates independently of the state utility commission and, depending on the state, is sometimes a separate organization or part of the state's attorney general's office.[37]

11.2.2 Federal Communications Commission

The Federal Communications Commission (FCC) is a federal agency that regulates interstate and international communications by radio, television, wire, satellite, and cable operations. The FCC has seven bureaus that are organized by function:

- The Wireline Competition Bureau is responsible for rules and policies concerning telephone companies that provide interstate and, under certain circumstances, intrastate telecommunications services to the public through the use of wire-based transmission facilities (as compared to cellular telephone service). Universal Services issues are covered by this bureau.
- The Wireless Telecommunications Bureau oversees domestic wireless issues (for example, cell phones, pagers, and radio). This bureau is also responsible for the auction of spectrum.
- The Consumer and Governmental Affairs Bureau provides information to the public regarding Commission policies, programs, and activities and is also charged with overseeing disability mandates.
- The Enforcement Bureau enforces the Communications Act as well as the FCC's rules, orders, and the terms and conditions of station authorizations.
- The International Bureau handles international telecommunication matters.
- The Media Bureau handles issues related to radio, television, and cable television.
- The Public Safety and Homeland Security Bureau collaborates with community, industry, and government entities regarding public safety communication issues.

The FCC was created "[f]or the purpose of regulating interstate and foreign commerce in communication by wire and radio so as to make available, so far as possible, to all the people of the United States . . . a rapid, efficient, Nation-wide, and world-wide wire and radio communication service with adequate facilities at reasonable charges. . . ."[38] The FCC regulates interstate telecommunications matters such as determining how to recover costs for the use of a common phone line by multiple services (for example, local phone service and long-distance services), implementing the federal universal services programs and performing telecommunication company merger reviews.

Prior to July 2001, inter-state long-distance phone companies filed tariffs at the FCC that set rates and conditions of service. The Communications Act, as amended, had been found to preempt state public utility commission (PUC) jurisdiction over interstate telephone billing disputes that implicated the tariff filed with the FCC.[39] The "filed rate doctrine" provides that the regulated utility shall charge the rate for the service set forth in the tariff that is properly filed with the regulatory authority. The tariff rate is considered the lawful rate.[40] For example, prior to 2001, consumer debts owed to a long-distance company based on a tariff filed with the FCC could be enforced in federal court, and the two-year statute of limitations of the Act would have applied.[41] Even relatively small collection actions for long-distance charges could have been heard by a federal magistrate judge or district judge.[42]

Since July 2001, the FCC has required that interstate long-distance companies set forth their rates and conditions of service through their contracts with consumers, rather than through tariffs traditionally filed with the FCC. Because of this, the filed rate doctrine no longer protects long-distance companies from challenges to long-distance rates, and consumers cannot use the filed rate doctrine to argue that excessive long-distance rates violate an approved tariff rate. In the absence of a governing tariff, consumer protection laws and contract law do apply. In *Ting v. AT&T Corp.*,[43] the Ninth Circuit rejected the carrier's argument

National Regulatory Research Inst., State Retail Rate Regulation of Local Exchange Providers As of December 2006 (Apr. 2007), *available at* http://nrri.org/pubs/telecommunications/07-04.pdf (an overview of state telecommunications rate regulation).

37 A current list of ratepayer advocates offices is available at the National Association of State Utility Consumer Advocates website at www.nasuca.org.

38 47 U.S.C. § 151.

39 *See* Mellman v. Sprint Commc'ns Co., 975 F. Supp. 1458 (N.D. Fla. 1996) (dismissing breach of contract case, regarding termination of promised "Free Friday" calls to China, pursuant to filed rate doctrine and preemption by Federal Communication Act). *See also* 47 U.S.C. § 152(b).

40 AT&T Corp. v. Central Office Tel., Inc., 524 U.S. 214 (1998).

41 International Magazine Serv. v. Allnet Commc'ns, 469 S.E.2d 305 (Ga. Ct. App. 1996) (suit for nonpayment of long-distance charges was subject to Act's statute of limitation, not the state's).

42 MCI Commc'ns Corp. v. Russell, 861 F. Supp. 280 (S.D.N.Y. 1994) (debts owed based on tariff filed with FCC may be enforced in federal court).

43 319 F.3d 1126 (9th Cir. 2003).

that the Federal Communications Act preempts state consumer protections and contract law. In *McKee v. AT&T, Corp.*,[44] the Supreme Court of Washington State also agreed with the Ninth Circuit in Ting that the Federal Communications Act did not preempt state consumer protections and contract law. The Washington Supreme Court reasoned:[45]

> When Congress authorized the FCC to eliminate the filing requirement, it permitted the tariff filing mechanism to be replaced by a market-based mechanism in the form of individual negotiated contracts between carriers and their customers. [cite omitted] Unlike tariff filing, however, this market-based mechanism depends in part on state law. [cite omitted] The market-based method of achieving the act's goals of reasonableness, fairness, and nondiscrimination in carrier contracts does not require a single, federal standard but rather depends in part on state law for the protection of consumers in the deregulated and competitive marketplace. [cite omitted]

As for wireless carriers, the FCC has jurisdiction over key areas; for the Internet-enabled telecommunications technologies, the FCC has been aggressive in claiming jurisdiction.[46] The Communications Act, as amended, provides the FCC with jurisdiction over wireless carriers' rates and market entry but explicitly provides that states can regulate the "other terms and conditions of commercial mobile services."[47] In 2002, the FCC declared that broadband Internet services are not telecommunication services" but rather "interstate information services" and thus fall under the FCC's jurisdiction.[48] In 2004, the FCC issued an opinion and order preempting Minnesota's telephone regulations that the state commission sought to apply to Vonage's voice-over Internet protocol (VoIP). The FCC found that preemption applies when Vonage's services are mixed and it is impractical or impossible to separate the intrastate from interstate aspects of its service such that applying state regulations would effectively regulate commerce outside of the state.[49]

A Fifth Circuit case, *Texas Office of Public Utilities Counsel v. FCC*, highlights some other areas where there have been jurisdictional battles.[50] In *Texas Office of Public Utilities Counsel*, the Fifth Circuit overturned key FCC provisions implementing the federal universal services programs based on jurisdictional grounds. The Fifth Circuit overturned the FCC's prohibition on disconnection of local phone service for Lifeline customers due to unpaid long-distance charges.[51] The Fifth Circuit also reversed a portion of the FCC's formula used to fund discounted rates for advanced telecommunication services for schools and libraries. The court ruled that the FCC could not include a phone company's in-state revenues in calculating the company's contribution to the universal service program for schools and libraries.[52]

The FCC website[53] is a good resource for FCC activity, copies of reports and orders, and copies of comments filed in the various and numerous rulemaking proceedings. The Wireline Competition Bureau,[54] the Enforcement Bureau[55] and the Consumer and Governmental Affairs Bureau[56] are good sites for learning about agency activity on telephone service.

11.2.3 Federal-State Joint Board on Universal Service

The Telecommunications Act of 1996[57] amended the Communications Action of 1934 and created a Federal-State Joint Board on Universal Service (Joint Board)[58] to set specific policies to implement the Act's universal service

44 McKee v. AT&T Corp., 191 P.3d 845 (Wash. Aug. 28, 2008).

45 *Id.*

46 *See* Core Commc'ns, Inc. v. Federal Commc'ns Comm'n, 592 F.3d 139 (D.C. Cir. 2010) (FCC has authority to institute a rate cap system to Internet dial-up calls, including those originating and terminating with local exchange carriers within one state).

Petitions for a rehearing were separately submitted by Core Communications and the Pennsylvania Public Utility Commission on February 26, 2010. A decision on the petitions was pending at the time this supplement went to press.

47 "Notwithstanding sections 152(b) and 221(b) of this title, no State or local government shall have any authority to regulate the entry of or the rates charged by any commercial mobile service or any private mobile service, except that this paragraph shall not prohibit a State from regulating the other terms and conditions of commercial mobile services." 47 U.S.C. § 332(c)(3)(A). *See also* § 11.2.1, *supra*.

48 *In re* Inquiry Concerning High-Speed Access to the Internet Over Cable and Other Facilities; Internet Over Cable Ruling; Appropriate Regulatory Treatment for Broadband Access to the Internet Over Cable Facilities, F.C.C. 02-77 (F.C.C. Mar. 15, 2002) (G.N. No. 00-185, C.S. No. 02-52), *available at* http://hraunfoss.fcc.gov/edocs_public/attachmatch/FCC-02-77A1.pdf.

49 WWC Holding Co. Inc. v. Sopkin, 488 F.3d 1262 (10th Cir. 2007) (explaining and distinguishing the Vonage case).

50 Texas Office of Pub. Util. Counsel v. Federal Commc'ns Comm'n, 183 F.3d 393 (5th Cir. 1999).

51 *Id.* at 421, 424.

52 *Id.* at 446–48.

53 The FCC website address is www.fcc.gov.

54 The home page for the FCC's Wireline Competition Bureau is www.fcc.gov/wcb. The Wireline Competition Bureau used to be the Common Carrier Bureau until it was restructured and renamed in March 2002. *See* News Release, Federal Commc'ns Comm'n, Federal Communications Commission's Common Carrier Bureau Reorganized Along Functional Lines (Mar. 8, 2002), *available at* www.fcc.gov/Bureaus/Common_Carrier/News_Releases/2002/nrcc0205.html.

The FCC's Wireline Competition Bureau's Industry Analysis and Technology Division regularly prepares reports on universal services and the telephone industry and posts them on their website at www.fcc.gov/wcb/iatd/stats.html.

55 The home page for the Enforcement Bureau is www.fcc.gov/eb.

56 The home page for the Consumer and Governmental Affairs Bureau is www.fcc.gov/cgb.

57 Pub. L. No. 104-104, 110 Stat. 56 (1996).

58 47 U.S.C. § 254(a)(1).

mandate. The Joint Board is charged with the responsibility of making recommendations on changes to FCC regulations in order to implement sections of the Act dealing with universal services.[59] The Joint Board is a standing board and periodically reviews the status of universal service, making recommendations to the FCC as needed and triggering FCC consideration of the need to updates or amendments to universal service policies.[60] The statute also expressly requires that "one member of such Joint Board shall be a State-appointed utility consumer advocate nominated by a national organization of State utility consumer advocates."[61]

11.3 Federal Affordability and Access Programs

11.3.1 Introduction

It is important to note that the goal of universal service has been articulated, although not as explicitly, in federal telecommunications policy since 1934, the year the Communications Act was enacted.[62] The Telecommunications Act of 1996, which amends the Communications Act of 1934, states in unequivocal terms Congress's long-standing commitment to universal service.[63] The 1996 Act instructs the FCC and the Joint Board that:

> Consumers in all regions of the Nation, including low-income consumers and those in rural, insular, and high-cost areas, should have access to telecommunications and information services, including interexchange "long-distance" services and advanced telecommunications and information services, that are reasonably comparable to those services provided in urban areas and that are available at rates that are reasonably comparable to rates charged for similar services in urban areas.[64]

In 1985, the FCC, acting pursuant to the 1934 Communications Act, established the Lifeline and Link-Up programs to ensure that low-income consumers have access to local phone service at reasonable rates. The FCC also established the High Cost Fund program to ensure consumers in hard-to-serve areas, such as areas where rough terrain or remote or rural locations make it expensive to connect to the phone network, also have access to reasonable and affordable rates. These programs are still in existence today although they are modified to comply with the 1996 Act.

The 1996 Act also expands the concept of universal services to include support for eligible schools and libraries and rural health care providers.[65]

The Telecommunications Act of 1996 mandates that "[e]very telecommunications carrier that provides interstate telecommunications service *shall contribute, on an equitable and nondiscriminatory basis, to the specific, predictable, and sufficient mechanisms established by the Commission to preserve and advance universal service*."[66] Currently, contributions to the universal service fund are based on all interstate and international end-user telecommunications revenues. However the sustainability of the universal service fund has been called into question as the interstate telecommunications revenues have declined due to the bundling of long-distance service with other telecommunications service packages, the proliferation of flat-rate long-distance plans, and the migration of long-distance calling customers over to non-contributing telecommunications services (such as advanced Internet protocol networks) at the same time the universal service programs have been growing.[67] In particu-

---

59 47 U.S.C. § 254(a)(1).

60 47 U.S.C. § 254(c)(2). *See also* 47 U.S.C. § 254(b).

61 47 U.S.C. § 254(a)(1).

62 48 Stat. § 1064, ch. 652 (June 19, 1934) (47 U.S.C. § 151).

The 1934 Act created the Federal Communications Commission: "For the purpose of regulating . . . commerce in communication . . . so as to make available, so far as possible, to all the people of the United States, without discrimination on the basis of race, color, religion, national origin, or sex, a rapid, efficient Nation-wide, and world-wide wire and radio communication service with adequate facilities at reasonable charges. . . ."

63 47 U.S.C. § 254(b).

> Universal service principles. The Joint Board and the Commission shall base policies for the preservation and advancement of universal service on the following principles:
>
> (1) Quality and rates
>
> Quality services should be available at just, reasonable, and affordable rates.
>
> (2) Access to advanced services
>
> Access to advanced telecommunications and information services should be provided in all regions of the Nation.
>
> (3) Access in rural and high cost areas
>
> Consumers in all regions of the Nation, including low-income consumers and those in rural, insular, and high cost areas, should have access to telecommunications and information services, including interexchange services and advanced telecommunications and information services, that are reasonably comparable to those services provided in urban areas and that are available at rates that are reasonably comparable to rates charged for similar services in urban areas.

64 47 U.S.C. § 254(b)(3).

65 In 1997, the FCC implemented these new provisions in Report and Order Implementing the Provisions of the Telecommunications Act of 1996, which included the creation of rural health care support (for example, "telemedicine") and the "e-rate" to make advanced telecommunications affordable for schools and libraries. *See* 47 U.S.C. § 254(b)(6), (h). *See also* Report and Order, *In re* Federal-State Joint Bd. on Universal Serv., 12 F.C.C.R. 8776 (F.C.C. May 8, 1997) (No. 96-45).

66 47 U.S.C. § 254(d) (emphasis added).

67 *See, e.g., Universal Service: Hearing on Universal Service Before the S. Comm. on Commerce, Science and Transp.*, 108th Cong. (2003) (statement of Michael K. Powell, Chairman of the Federal Communications Commission). *See also* Universal Serv. Admin. Co., Lifeline Participation Rate Study 2008.

In 2008, twenty-four million U.S. households were eligible for Lifeline, with seven million of the households receiving

lar, the High Cost Fund program grew from $2.6 billion in 2001 to $4.3 billion in 2007.[68]

In all, there are currently four universal service programs: High Cost, Low Income, Rural Healthcare, and Schools and Libraries. However, the FCC is examining possible changes that may include the establishment of program and funding for mobility customers.

11.3.2 Federal Low-Income Assistance Programs: Lifeline, Link-Up, and Toll Limitation Service

11.3.2.1 Federal Low-Income Assistance Program Overview

11.3.2.1.1 Introduction

The federal Low Income Program reimburses eligible telecommunication carriers (for example, the local phone company) for providing to qualifying low-income individuals discounted local access service rates, discounted connection costs, and voluntary limited or blocked access to long-distance service to control charges on the bill.[69] The three components of the Low Income Program are Link Up, Lifeline, and Toll Limitation.[70]

The federal Low Income Program support mechanism accounts for only a small percentage of the total federal universal service funding. In 2007, the programs in the Low Income Program support mechanism accounted for about 12% of the federal universal service support compared to the high-cost universal support mechanism, which accounted for 62% of total federal universal support funds, and the Schools and Libraries "E-rate" program, which accounted for about 26%.[71] In 1997, when the FCC adopted its order implementing the universal service provisions under the Telecommunications Act of 1996, it estimated that, assuming all states participated in these programs to an extent that would draw down the maximum federal support, the programs in the Low Income Program support mechanism would amount to $512 million.[72] In 2010, the programs disbursed over $1.3 billion for Lifeline, Link Up and Toll Limitation support, $4.2 billion for the High Cost Fund;[73] 2.2 billion for Schools and Libraries, and almost $86 million for Rural Healthcare.[74]

11.3.2.1.2 Universal Service Administrative Company (USAC)

The Universal Service Administrative Company (USAC), a private not-for-profit corporation, is responsible for administering the federal Universal Service Fund pursuant to regulations promulgated by the FCC. USAC collects the federal universal service contributions from all telecommunications companies that provide interstate telecommunications service, including local and long-distance phone companies, wireless and paging companies, prepaid calling card service providers, and payphone providers.[75] USAC administers four universal service programs: the High Cost Program, the Low Income Program, the Rural Health Care Program, and the Schools and Libraries "E-Rate" Program.[76] In the case of the Low Income Program, Lifeline, Link-Up, and Toll Limitation Service are separate programs with funding that USAC uses to reimburse eligible telecommunications carriers.[77] The High Cost Fund also compensates carriers, subsidizing the high cost of serving rural and other areas.

11.3.2.1.3 Eligible telecommunications carriers (ETCs)

An eligible telecommunications carrier (ETC) is a common carrier (landline or wireless company) that has been approved or is ordered[78] to provide core services[79] and is

Lifeline support. This represented a 3.33% increase in Lifeline subscribership between 2007 and 2008, with twenty-two states experiencing a subscriber increase and eight states experiencing a greater than 50% increase in subscribers.

68 *See* Order, *In re* High-Cost Universal Service Support Federal-State Joint Bd. on Universal Serv., F.C.C. 08-122 ¶¶ 6, 20 (F.C.C. May 1, 2008) (W.C. No. 05-337, C.C. No. 96-45).

69 47 C.F.R. §§ 54.407, 54.413.

70 Universal Serv. Admin. Co., Universal Service Administrative Company 2010 Annual Report 11.

71 Universal Serv. Admin. Co., Universal Service Administrative Company 2007 Annual Report 5.

72 *In re* Federal-State Joint Bd. on Universal Serv. F.C.C. 97-15 ¶ 359, n.903 (F.C.C. May 8, 1997) (C.C. No. 96-45).

73 The High Cost Fund is a Universal Service Fund program to bring telecommunications services to areas for which building the necessary infrastructure to serve the area is associated with high costs. The High Cost Fund applies to compensate carriers for a portion of the cost in providing telecommunications service to consumers in rural and other high-cost areas. In addition to access, the goal of the fund is to allow consumers to pay rates for telecommunications services that are comparable to rates in urban and other lower-cost areas.

74 Universal Serv. Admin. Co., Universal Service Administrative Company 2010 Annual Report 47.

75 Federal Commc'ns Comm'n Fed. & State Staff, Universal Service Monitoring Report, C.C. No. 98-202 ch. 1 (2007).

76 *See generally* Universal Serv. Admin. Co., Universal Service Administrative Company 2010 Annual Report.

77 For more information on the Universal Services Administrative Company, visit the USAC website at www.universalservice.org.

78 *See* 47 U.S.C. § 214(e)(3) (state utility commission or FCC could require common carrier to provide universal services in unserved areas).

79 47 U.S.C. § 214(e) (eligible telecommunication carriers and the provision of universal services). *See also* 47 U.S.C. § 254(c) (services supported by the federal universal services support mechanism); Order and Order on Reconsideration, *In re* Federal-State Joint Bd. on Universal Serv., F.C.C. 03-170 (F.C.C. July 14, 2003) (C.C. No. 96-45), *available at* 68 Fed. Reg. 49707–

eligible for reimbursement from the federal universal service fund. State utility commissions are responsible for designating a phone company as an ETC.[80] When a state commission does not have jurisdiction over a phone company, the FCC is responsible for determining the ETC designation.[81] The ETC designation is required for a provider to be eligible to receive federal support from the USF.[82] The federal universal services support program to lower the cost of phone service in high-cost, rural, or insular areas also works through ETCs. All ETCs must make Lifeline service available and publicize the Lifeline program.[83]

Providers of prepaid cell phone service have sought "limited" ETC designation from the FCC so that they can become eligible for Lifeline reimbursements.[84] Section 214(e)(6) of the Communications Act, as amended, allows carriers to petition the FCC for ETC designation when the state utility commission does not have jurisdiction. In the case of wireless service providers, states vary in their jurisdiction over ETC status designations. TracFone Wireless, Inc., was granted conditional limited ETC status in Alabama, Connecticut, Delaware, the District of Columbia, Florida, Massachusetts, New Hampshire, New York, North Carolina, Pennsylvania, Tennessee, and Virginia.[85] TracFone received forbearance from the requirement that ETCs offer supported services over their own facilities or a combination of their own facilities as they resell other carriers' services.[86]

11.3.2.2 Lifeline

The Lifeline program began in 1984 to help make telephone service affordable for low-income households through a monthly discount. While the federal assistance program was initially only available in states that matched the federal contribution, the program is now administered in two ways. Since 1998, federal assistance has been available to all states; for those states providing matching assistance, even more federal assistance is available.[87] In 2009, the telephone penetration rate for low-income households was 90.4%, a significant increase from the 80.1% penetration rate in 1984, which was the year before FCC instituted the Lifeline program.[88] In 2010, 10.5 million households benefitted from the Lifeline program, a significant increase from the 9.2 million beneficiary households in 2009.[89] Still, many low-income consumers who are eligible for Lifeline assistance are not enrolled.

The problem is an administrative one. At a time when telephone service was mainly carried over wireline, and a residential customer would typically have one phone number at one address, the Lifeline benefit was disbursed to each unique customer to provide support for service to "a single telephone line in a Lifeline subscriber's principal residence."[90] This gave rise to what has been called the one-per-household rule, which operates to exclude from enrollment low-income consumers who would otherwise qualify for Lifeline but for their residence in a group living environment, for example, a homeless or a domestic violence survivor shelter where many different individuals share one address. Solutions to enrolling these consumers have been proposed, such as the recharacterization of the one-per-household rule as a one-per-economic-unit rule. However, solutions have been hampered by fears of fraud and the possibility of duplicate benefits being given to any single customer.[91] After the receipt of comments on these and other issues, a decision from the FCC is pending.[92]

11.3.2.3 Amount of Lifeline Support

The level of Lifeline assistance varies by state, due to the complex rules under which the federal program provides support to carriers in each state and to the fact that states can increase the federal contribution by providing matching

49712 (Aug. 19, 2003) (no new core services added to list in 47 U.S.C. § 254(c)).

80 47 U.S.C. § 214(e)(2), (3).

81 47 U.S.C. § 214(e)(6). *See also* § 11.3.2.8, *infra* (discussing Tribal Lifeline).

82 47 U.S.C. §§ 214(e)(1), 254(e).

83 47 C.F.R. § 54.405.

84 The limited ETC status does not prevent companies from being eligible for other universal service reimbursements such as Link Up and Toll Limitation Service (other components of the Low Income Program support mechanism) and High Cost Fund program support. The number of customers receiving Lifeline wireless service between November 2008 and June 2009 reportedly doubled to 1.4 million. *See* Matt Richtel, *Providing Cellphones for the Poor*, N.Y. Times, June 14, 2009, *available at* www.nytimes.com/2009/06/15/technology/15cell.html.

85 *In re* Federal-State Joint Bd. on Universal Serv.; TracFone Wireless, Inc., Petition to Rescind State 911/E911 Condition, D.A. 10-75, C.C. No. 96-45 (F.C.C. May 3, 2010), *available at* http://hraunfoss.fcc.gov/edocs_public/attachmatch/DA-10-753A1.pdf; *In re* Petition for Limited Designation as Eligible Telecommunications Carrier (ETC) by Virgin Mobile USA, L.P., No. 090245-TP (Order No. PSC-10-0323-PAA-TP), 2010 WL 2022003 (Fla. P.S.C. May 19, 2010) (Florida Public Service Commission approving Virgin Mobile's ETC application).

86 *See* 47 U.S.C. § 214(e)(1)(A).

87 *See* Federal Commc'ns Comm'n, December 2010 Monitoring Report 6-4 (Dec. 2010).

88 *See* Federal Commc'ns Comm'n, December 2010 Monitoring Report (Dec. 2010), *available at* http://transition.fcc.gov/wcb/iatd/monitor.html.

89 *See* Universal Serv. Admin. Co., Universal Service Administrative Company 2010 Annual Report at 12.

90 *See In re* Federal-State Joint Bd. on Universal Serv. Lifeline and Link Up, F.C.C. 10-72 ¶ 21 (F.C.C. Apr. 28, 2010), *available at* http://hraunfoss.fcc.gov/edocs_public/attachmatch/FCC-10-72A1.pdf.

91 *See generally In re* Lifeline and Link Up Reform and Modernization, F.C.C. 11-97 (F.C.C. June 17, 2011).

92 *See* Federal-State Joint Board on Universal Service Seeks Comment on Lifeline and Link-up Eligibility, Verification, and Outreach Issues Referred to Joint Board, 25 F.C.C.R. 7551, (F.C.C. June 15, 2010) (F.C.C. 10J-2) (order requesting comments).

funds.[93] Actual Lifeline support will also vary by carrier because a component of Lifeline reimburses carriers for their subscriber line charge, and this varies by carrier.

In general, eligible customers in states without a Lifeline program can be credited up to $10.00 per month under the federal Lifeline program. In states providing additional support, the benefit to customers could exceed $10.00. Eligible customers living on tribal reservations can save up to an additional $25 in federal Lifeline support,[94] but there is a minimum rate of $1.00 per month.[95] The actual amount of the discount under the Enhanced Lifeline program will vary depending on the amount of the subscriber line charge and the existence of matching funds.[96]

Information about Lifeline and Link-Up programs in the states is also available at USAC's website at www.lifeline support.org (see low-income households). The FCC, the National Association of State Utility Consumer Advocates, and the National Association of Regulatory Utility Commissioners have established a Lifeline website for additional information on the program (www.lifeline.gov).

11.3.2.4 Services Covered Under Universal Services

11.3.2.4.1 General

The federal Low Income Program support mechanism operates as a reimbursement to eligible telecommunications carriers for the discounted rates, discounted connection charges, and toll-limitation services provided to qualified low-income consumers. Eligible telecommunications carriers are also eligible for reimbursement from the federal high-cost support mechanism, a federal universal services program to help keep telecommunications services and rates for consumers in rural, high-cost, and insular areas reasonably comparable to services and rates in urban areas.[97] To date, the FCC has established basic minimum services that eligible telecommunications carriers must provide to qualified low-income consumers and consumers in rural, insular, and high-cost areas (areas where connection to the phone network is very expensive). These services include: single-party service; voice-grade access to the public-switched network; dual-tone multifrequency signaling (DTMF) or its functional equivalent; access to emergency services; access to operator services; access to inter-exchange service; access to directory assistance; and toll-limitation services for qualifying low-income consumers.[98] This list may change, and services such as broadband may eventually be considered a basic minimum service.[99] Some of these services are described in greater detail in § 11.3.2.4.4, *infra.*

When the statutory language is ambiguous, the Fifth Circuit deferred to the FCC's determination that section 254(h) authorizes the FCC to mandate support for discounted Internet services and internal connections to schools and libraries.[100]

11.3.2.4.2 Number-portability charge waiver

The FCC requires local phone companies to allow customers to keep their phone numbers when switching phone companies.[101] It has also allowed local phone companies to pass through to customers the costs of providing number portability in a monthly charge that can exist for five years.[102] It waived the number-portability charge for Lifeline customers in its number portability rules,[103] but the Lifeline regulations did not initially reference these rules.[104] The FCC recently clarified that the number-portability charge is waived for Lifeline customers by cross-referencing, in the definition of Lifeline, the exemptions contained in the number-portability rule.[105]

---

93 *See* 47 C.F.R. § 54.403.

The federal regulations set out four tiers of support: tier 1—the amount of the end-user common line charge (also called the subscriber line charge or access charge), which increased to a cap of $6.50 starting July 2003; tier 2—an additional $1.75 per month for all eligible customers; tier 3—a 50% federal match of state support up to a maximum $1.75; and tier 4—additional support of up to $25 per month for Tribal Lifeline).

94 Tier 3 support of up to $1.75 as a 50% match of state or utility support (that is, $3.50 would draw the maximum federal match).

95 47 C.F.R. § 54.403(a)(4)(i).

96 47 C.F.R. § 54.403. *See also In re* Access Charge Reform; Price Cap Performance Review for Local Exchange Carriers; Low-Volume Long-Distance Users; Federal-State Joint Bd. on Universal Serv., F.C.C. 00-193 ¶¶ 33, 70–104, 185–205 (May 31, 2000) (C.C. Nos. 96-262, 94-1, 99-249, 96-45), *subsequent proceeding*, Errata to F.C.C. 00-193 (F.C.C. June 14, 2000) (D.A. 02-1027).

Customers interested in receiving Enhanced Lifeline rates should contact their local phone company or state utility commission's consumer division for more information. A list of state utility commissions is provided in Appendix A.8, *infra*.

97 47 U.S.C. § 254(b); 47 C.F.R. §§ 54.1, 54.301–54.316.

98 Report and Order, Federal-State Joint Bd. on Universal Serv., 12 F.C.C.R. 8809 ¶ 61, F.C.C. 97-157 (F.C.C. 1997) (C.C. No. 96-45).

99 The National Broadband Plan recommends that FCC expand Lifeline and Link Up to make broadband affordable for low-income consumers. Federal-State Joint Board on Universal Services Seeks Comments on Lifeline and Link Up Eligibility, Verification and Outreach Issues Referred to Joint Board, 25 F.C.C.R. 7551, 75548–59 (F.C.C. July 15, 2010) (F.C.C. 10J-2), *text of order reproduced in* F.C.C. 10-72 ¶ 12.

The National Broadband Plan recommends that FCC expand Lifeline and Link Up to make broadband affordable for low-income consumers. F.C.C. 10-7212 (May 4, 2010).

100 *See* Texas Office of Public Utility Counsel v. F.C.C., 183 F.3d 393, 440–43 (5th Cir. July 30, 1999).

101 47 C.F.R. §§ 52.20–52.99.

102 47 C.F.R. § 52.33.

103 47 C.F.R. § 52.33(a)(1)(i)(C).

104 47 C.F.R. § 54.401.

105 69 Fed. Reg. 34590–34601 (June 22, 2004), *codified at* 47 C.F.R. § 54.401(e).

11.3.2.4.3 No-disconnect rule

The FCC attempted, through issuance of a regulation, to prohibit disconnection of local service to Lifeline customers due to nonpayment of toll (long-distance) charges.[106] However, as discussed in § 11.2.2, *supra*, and § 11.6.2, *infra*, the Fifth Circuit overturned the regulation in July 1999 on the basis of jurisdictional grounds.[107] The FCC, in a subsequent order, amended its rules to eliminate the regulation.[108] The FCC acknowledged that telephone companies often deny service to customers with unpaid local or long-distance bills and, in light of the Fifth Circuit decision, declined to take action on the matter. The FCC merely encourages states to consider implementing rules that would require eligible telecommunications service providers to serve otherwise eligible consumers.[109] A number of states have public utility commission regulations, policies, or case law that prevent disconnection of any residential user's local service because of nonpayment of long-distance charges.[110]

11.3.2.4.4 "Universal Service" is an evolving term

Congress, in defining universal services in the 1996 Act, acknowledged the rapidly changing technological landscape. The Federal-State Joint Board on Universal Services is charged with making recommendations to the FCC, which in turn is charged with periodically establishing a definition of universal service that takes into account "advances in telecommunications and information technologies and services."[111] On July 14, 2003, the FCC released its decision adopting the recommendation of the Federal–State Joint Board on Universal Services[112] to retain the existing list of core services that must be provided by eligible telecommunications carriers.[113]

The Act provides a general framework for determining what services should comprise universal services. The Joint Board, in recommending, and the FCC, in rulemaking

> shall consider the extent to which such telecommunications services—
> (A) are essential to education, public health, or public safety;
> (B) have, through the operation of market choices by customers, been subscribed to by a substantial majority of residential customers;
> (C) are being deployed in public telecommunications networks by telecommunications carriers; and
> [D) are consistent with the public interest, convenience, and necessity.[114]

Thus the Act contemplates a four-part general test to determine what service elements are so fundamental to modern life that they should be accessible and affordable to all consumers. The core services that define universal services must be provided by eligible telecommunications carriers to their customers in order to receive reimbursement from the federal universal services High Cost and Low-Income support mechanisms.[115]

---

106 Formerly found at 47 C.F.R § 54.401(b).

107 Texas Office of Pub. Util. Counsel v. Federal Commc'ns Comm'n, 183 F.3d 393 (5th Cir. 1999).

108 *In re* Federal-State Joint Bd. on Universal Serv., Access Charge Reform, F.C.C. 99-29 (F.C.C. Oct. 8, 1999) (effective Nov. 1, 1999) (C.C. Nos. 96-45, 96-45, 96-262).

109 69 Fed. Reg. 34597 (June 22, 2004).

110 For example, in Washington, residential consumers cannot be disconnected for nonpayment of information service charges (for example, 1-900 numbers) or long-distance charges (the local company may toll-restrict the consumers phone service, however). Wash. Admin. Code § 480-120-172. *See also* N.Y. Comp. Codes R. & Regs. tit. 16, § 606.4(a) (New York has similar protections for local phone service); 16 Tex. Admin. Code § 26.28(a)(4)(E) (Texas prohibits disconnection for nonpayment of non-tariffed charges but allows disconnection for nonpayment of long-distance charges incurred after toll-blocking was imposed).

Massachusetts has opened an informal proceeding seeking to consider modernizing its billing and termination consumer protection regulations. *See* Massachusetts Dep't of Telecomms. & Cable, Notice of Public Informational Forums (June 20, 2011) (notice from Commissioner Geoffrey G. Why accompanying the order closing docket, Investigation by Department of Telecommunications and Energy on its own Motion to Establish Retail Billing and Termination Practices for Telecommunications Carriers, D.T.E./D.T.C. 06-8).

However, Massachusetts currently has an established policy to prohibit disconnection of local service for nonpayment of long-distance charges. *See* Letter from Massachusetts Dep't of Pub. Util. to New England Tel. Co. (Dec. 5, 1985) ("the rights of the consumer to maintain access to the local network remain paramount," and a local phone company's "right to disconnect for nonpayment cannot be transferred to another company by any contractual means"); Letter from Mass. Dep't of Pub. Util. to New England Tel. Co. (June 26, 1987) (phone company can use toll-denial for nonpayment of long-distance charges only if it can selectively deny access to the specific long-distance carrier's network with whom the customer has unpaid charges); Massachusetts Dep't of Telecomm. & Energy, Order on Motion for Reconsideration and Extension of the Judicial Appeal Period by Bell Atlantic-Mass., DPU/DTE 96-AD-9-A (May 25, 2000) (Massachusetts DPU/DTE refuses to reconsider its policy prohibiting all-carrier toll denial), *available on the companion website to this treatise. See also* § 6.4, *supra*; appx. A, *infra* (more information about disconnection protections).

111 47 U.S.C. § 254(c)(1). *See* H.R. Rep. No. 458-104, at 131 (1996). (Joint Explanatory Statement of the Committee of the Conference) ("[t]he Commission is given specific authority to alter the definition from time to time" in order to "take into account advances in telecommunications and information technology").

112 Recommended Decision, *In re* Federal-State Joint Bd. on Universal Serv., F.C.C. 02J-1 (F.C.C. July 10, 2002) (C.C. No. 96-45).

113 Order and Order on Reconsideration, Federal-State Joint Bd. on Universal Serv., F.C.C. 03-170 ¶ 1 (July 14, 2003) (C.C. No. 96-45), *published at* 68 Fed. Reg. 49707–49712 (Aug. 19, 2003).

114 47 U.S.C. § 254(c)(1).

115 47 U.S.C. §§ 214(e), 254(e). *See also* 47 C.F.R. § 54.201–54.207; 47 C.F.R. § 54.405.

In May 1997, the FCC relied on the Joint Board's recommended definition of universal services and its analysis of section 254(c)(1) in the FCC's order implementing the universal services provision of the Telecommunications Act of 1996.[116] The Joint Board and the FCC found that the four criteria "must be considered, but not each necessarily met, before a service may be included within the general definition of universal service, should it be in the public interest."[117] The May 1997 definition of "core" or "designated" universal services that would be supported by universal services support programs covered the following:[118]

- Single-party service: In addition to being widely available and having a majority of residential customers subscribing to it, this service was also found essential to public health and safety because it allows residential consumers to access emergency services without delay.[119]
- Voice grade access to the public switched network: This service includes the ability to place calls and to receive calls.[120] At the end of 1999, the FCC began a proceeding to review the frequency and bandwidth range for this service.
- Dual Tone Multifrequency (DTMF) signaling or its functional equivalent: As opposed to the rotary dial pulses, DTMF allows for rapid call set up and use in automated directory systems.[121] Usually, each phone keypad has twelve tones and the caller can press a particular key to access a menu item in an automated answering system.
- Access to emergency services including, in some circumstances, access to 911 and enhanced 911 (E911):[122] Universal service coverage is limited to support for telecommunications network components necessary for access to 911 and E911 but not the underlying services.
- Access to operator services: The FCC defined operator service to mean "any automatic or live assistance to a consumer to arrange for billing or completion, or both, of a telephone call."[123]
- Access to inter-exchange service: This essentially means access to a long-distance service. Note: Lifeline assistance does not extend to covering the costs of long-distance service, just access to long-distance service.
- Access to directory assistance: The ability to access directory assistance was considered a core service because it enables consumers "to obtain essential information, such as the telephone numbers of government, business, and residential subscribers."[124]
- Toll-limitation services for qualified low-income consumers: Toll limitation includes blocking of long-distance calls or limiting long-distance calls made from the consumer's phone.[125] Free access to this service was considered important in order to keep customers connected to the phone system because "uncontrollable" long-distance charges were found to be a major cause of low telephone subscribership among low-income consumers.[126]

In 2003, the FCC[127] and Federal-State Joint Board on Universal Services[128] rejected as additional core universal services advanced (or high-speed) services and soft dial tone (or warm line) service. Advanced or high-speed services enable customers to access the Internet with faster connections and with more advanced capabilities such as voice, high-speed data, video-on-demand, and interactive delivery services. A warm dial tone, especially in light of the diminishing access to public payphones, could quickly connect a low-income household to life-saving emergency services. However, the FCC felt that the states were in a better position to establish these services and agreed to monitor the state development of these programs. The FCC agreed with the Joint Board that these services, while useful for educational, public health, and public safety purposes, are not essential and are not subscribed to by a majority of residential customers in addition to having negative effects on the pool of eligible telecommunications carriers.[129] Soft dial tone or warm line service allows a consumer without local

116 Report and Order, *In re* Federal-State Joint Bd. on Universal Serv. F.C.C. 97-157 ¶¶ 56–87 (F.C.C. May 8, 1997) (C.C. No. 96-45).

117 Report and Order, *In re* Federal-State Joint Bd. on Universal Serv. F.C.C. 97-157 ¶ 61 (F.C.C. May 8, 1997) (C.C. No. 96-45).

In the same paragraph, the FCC went on to state that "[w]e interpret the statutory language, particularly the word 'consider,' as providing flexibility for the Commission to establish a definition of services to be supported, after it considers the criteria enumerated in section 254(c)(1)(A-D)."

118 Report and Order, *In re* Federal-State Joint Bd. on Universal Serv. F.C.C. 97-157 ¶¶ 56–87 (F.C.C. May 8, 1997) (C.C. No. 96-45).

119 *Id.* ¶ 62.

120 *Id.* ¶¶ 63, 64.

121 *Id.* ¶ 71.

122 Enhanced 911 (E911) service enables emergency service personnel to identify the approximate location of the calling party.

123 Report and Order, *In re* Federal-State Joint Bd. on Universal Serv. F.C.C. 97-157 ¶ 75 (F.C.C. May 8, 1997) (C.C. No. 96-45).

124 *Id.* ¶ 80.

125 47 C.F.R. § 54.400(d).

126 Report and Order, *In re* Federal-State Joint Bd. on Universal Serv. F.C.C. 97-157 ¶ 82 (F.C.C. May 8, 1997) (C.C. No. 96-45).

127 Order and Order on Reconsideration, *In re* Federal-State Joint Bd. on Universal Serv., F.C.C. 03-170 (F.C.C. July 14, 2003) (C.C. No. 96-45).

128 Recommended Decision, *In re* Federal-State Joint Bd. on Universal Serv., F.C.C. 02J-1 (F.C.C. July 10, 2002) (C.C. No. 96-45).

129 Order and Order on Reconsideration, *In re* Federal-State Joint Bd. on Universal Serv., F.C.C. 03-170 ¶¶ 8–13 (F.C.C. July 14, 2003) (C.C. No. 96-45).

service to contact emergency services and the local carrier's central business office.[130]

In November 2007, the Federal-State Joint Board on Universal Services sent the FCC a recommendation for comprehensive reform of the High Cost Fund support program that contains funding for broadband (via a broadband fund) and wireless infrastructure (via a mobility fund) in underserved areas as well as a provide-of-last-resort fund comprised of the existing incumbent wireline high cost support mechanisms.[131] The FCC opened these recommendations up for comment in 2008[132] and has issued an interim cap on competitive ETC support for each state to remain in effect until the FCC reaches a final decision on comprehensive reform measures.[133] The FCC, in its national broadband plan released on March 16, 2010, proposed creating a new broadband account in the Universal Service Fund that is directed toward funding the nation's areas that are currently without high-speed Internet.[134]

However, that view seems to be evolving as, recently, the FCC declared access to mobile systems to be an essential need.[135] As such, the FCC recommended the creation of a mobility fund to provide one-time support of the deployment of 3G networks, with a goal of making available a minimum of 3G mobile service to all states.[136] This position contrasts with the FCC's prior position in which the it noted that the wireless companies were not competing with wireline carriers to provide the supported services covered by the High Cost Fund. Instead, under the current High Cost Fund program rules, they were providing mobility as an additional service, rather than as a substitute for landline service.[137]

11.3.2.5 The Federal Link-Up Program

The Lifeline Connection Assistance (Link-Up) program[138] is a federal universal service program to provide eligible low-income consumers with discounted connection charges for telephone service. Eligible low-income consumers can receive half off the company's installation charges, up to a maximum $30.[139] Eligible customers can also work out a deferred payment schedule (interest-free) on the remaining costs of connection (up to $200) for up to one year.[140] The Enhanced Federal Link-Up plan for eligible customers living on tribal reservations covers half of the first $60 in connection charges ($30) and 100% of the next $70 (up to $100 total). Thus, for example, if the total connection charge is $130, the federal Link-Up program covers $100.[141]

The FCC's Universal Service Order prohibits states from limiting the number of eligible connections made in a year[142] to address the special needs of low-income consumers who may have difficulty maintaining a permanent residence.[143] Under the federal Link-Up regulations, a qualified customer can receive Link-Up assistance for a second or subsequent time when there is a change in the principal place of residence.[144]

11.3.2.6 Eligibility for Lifeline and Link-Up

The eligibility requirements for Link-Up are the same as for Lifeline. In states providing state support for telephone Lifeline programs, the states can determine customer eligibility criteria pursuant to FCC standards.[145] The state's eligibility criteria must be based solely on income factors or factors directly related to income.[146] The eligibility criteria for Enhanced or Tribal Lifeline and Link-Up is discussed in

130 *Id.* ¶¶ 16, 17.

131 Recommended Decision, *In re* High-Cost Universal Serv. Support Federal-State Joint Bd. on Universal Serv., 22 F.C.C.R. 20477, F.C.C. 07J-4 (F.C.C. Nov. 19, 2007) (W.C. No. 05-337, C.C. No. 96-45).

132 Notice of Proposed Rulemaking, 23 F.C.C.R. 1467, F.C.C. 08-4 (F.C.C. Jan. 29, 2008) (Identical Support Rule); Notice of Proposed Rulemaking, 23 F.C.C.R. 1495, F.C.C. 08-5 (F.C.C. Jan. 29, 2008) (Reverse Auction); Notice of Proposed Rulemaking, 23 F.C.C.R. 1531, F.C.C. 08-22 (F.C.C. Jan. 29, 2008) (Joint Board Comprehensive Reform).

133 The High Cost Fund program had increased from $2.6 billion in universal services support in 2001 to $ 4.3 billion in support in 2007, and the FCC attributed the growth to competitive ETCs (CETCs), with 94% of the CETC support going to wireless carriers. *See* Order, *In re* High-Cost Universal Service Support Federal-State Joint Bd. on Universal Serv., F.C.C. 08-122 ¶¶ 6, 20 (F.C.C. May 1, 2008) (W.C. No. 05-337, C.C. No. 96-45).

134 *See* Federal Commc'ns Comm'n, Connecting America: The National Broadband Plan 141–44, *available at* http://hraunfoss.fcc.gov/edocs_public/attachmatch/DOC-296935A1.pdf.

For progress on the national broadband plan, visit www.broadband.gov.

135 *See* Federal Commc'ns Comm'n, Connecting America: The National Broadband Plan 146, *available at* http://hraunfoss.fcc.gov/edocs_public/attachmatch/DOC-296935A1.pdf.

136 *See id.*

137 Order, *In re* High-Cost Universal Service Support Federal-State Joint Bd. on Universal Serv., F.C.C. 08-122 ¶¶ 20, 21 (F.C.C. May 1, 2008) (W.C. No. 05-337, C.C. No. 96-45). *See* § 11.3.2.1.3, *supra* (discussing ETCs).

138 47 C.F.R. §§ 54.411, 54.413, 54.415.

139 47 C.F.R. § 54.411.

140 *Id.*

141 *See id.*

142 *In re* Federal-State Joint Board on Universal Serv., 12 F.C.C.R. 8776 ¶ 382 (May 7, 1997).

143 *Id.*

144 47 C.F.R. § 54.411(c).

145 *In re* Federal-State Joint Bd. on Universal Serv., F.C.C. 97-157 ¶ 373 (F.C.C. May 8, 1997) (C.C. No. 96-45). *See* 47 C.F.R. § 54.409(a). *See also* § 11.3.2.7.1, *infra*.

146 47 C.F.R. § 54.409(a); *In re* Federal-State Joint Bd. on Universal Serv., F.C.C. 97-157 ¶¶ 373, 375 (F.C.C. May 8, 1997) (C.C. No. 96-45). *See also In re* Federal-State Joint Bd. on Universal Serv., D.A. 98-1709 (F.C.C. Aug. 27, 1998) (C.C. No. 96-45) (Minnesota's eligibility criteria for its Telephone Assistance

§ 11.3.2.8, *infra*. The vast majority of states provide state-funded Lifeline discounts.[147]

Lifeline and Link-Up Federal Default Eligibility (As of February 2010)[148]

Consumer must certify in writing under penalty of perjury that he or she participates in one of the following programs:

- Medicaid
- Food Stamps[149]
- Supplemental Security Income
- Federal Public Housing
- Low Income Home Energy Assistance Program
- Temporary Assistance to Needy Families
- National School Lunch Program's Federal Free Lunch Program

OR

- Has an income at or below 135% of the federal poverty guidelines (documentation required)

In those states without additional state Lifeline support, federal default criteria apply.[150] In order to be eligible under the default criteria, the consumer must meet a state-established means test that requires the subscriber to participate in one of the following programs: Medicaid, food stamps,[151] Supplemental Security Income (SSI), federal public housing assistance (Section 8), the Low Income Home Energy Assistance Program, National School Lunch Program's free lunch program, or Temporary Assistance for Needy Families.[152]

The FCC stated that it would revise the default eligibility standard if there was a disproportionately low number of Lifeline participants in states where the default eligibility applies.[153] On October 12, 2001, the FCC initiated a rulemaking proceeding to review the Lifeline and Link-Up programs.[154] A recent analysis of Lifeline enrollment strategies found that states with high Lifeline enrollment rates employ one or more of the following strategies: automatic enrollment of households identified as eligible by government benefits programs, self-certification by eligible households, and aggressive (sometimes well-funded) outreach. States with low penetration rates were ones that relied on bill stuffers and required households to fill out individual application forms.[155]

In April 2004, the FCC adopted the Federal-State Joint Board recommendation for expanding eligibility for the Lifeline and Link-Up programs by adding an income-based criterion and additional programs to the default federal eligibility criteria (which applies in states without a state Lifeline support program).[156] The Joint Board recommended that, in light of the declining participation rate in many public assistance programs since the passage of "The Personal Responsibility and Work Opportunity Reconciliation Act" in 1996, consumers at or below 135% of the Federal Poverty guidelines be eligible for Lifeline and Link-Up assistance.[157] The Joint Board also recommended adding TANF and the federal free lunch program to the list of default federal eligibility criteria because these programs are used in the enhanced Lifeline and Link-Up (Tribal Lifeline and Link-Up) eligibility criteria and will help increase subscribership.[158]

While the FCC expanded the Lifeline federal default eligibility criteria and added federal certification and verification procedures and outreach guidelines, it also issued a notice of proposed rulemaking seeking comment on whether the income eligibility should be increased to 150% of poverty and whether the FCC should adopt rules governing

Program was not in compliance with federal income-only criteria).

147 Federal default states and territories are American Samoa, Delaware, Hawaii, Indiana, Iowa, Louisiana, New Hampshire, North Dakota, South Dakota, and the Northern Mariana Islands. *See* www.usac.org/li/low-income/eligibility/federal-criteria.aspx.

148 47 C.F.R. § 54.409.

149 As of October 1, 2008, the name of the federal program has changed to Supplemental Nutrition Assistance Program (SNAP). *See* www.fns.usda.gov/snap.

150 47 C.F.R. § 54.409(b).

There are currently eight default states: Delaware, Hawaii, Indiana, Iowa, Louisiana, New Hampshire, North Dakota, and South Dakota. In addition, default criteria apply in American Samoa and the Northern Mariana Islands. *See* http://www.universalservice.org/li/tools/frequently-asked-questions/faq-lifeline-linkup-order.aspx#q1 (frequently asked questions on Universal Service Administrative Company (USAC) website about Lifeline Link-Up order).

151 As of October 1, 2008, the name of the federal program has changed to Supplemental Nutrition Assistance Program (SNAP). *See* www.fns.usda.gov/snap.

152 47 C.F.R. §§ 54.409(b), 54.415(b); *In re* Federal-State Joint Bd. on Universal Serv., F.C.C. 97-157 ¶ 374 (F.C.C. May 8, 1997) (C.C. No. 96-45). *See also* § 11.3.2.7.2, *infra*.

153 *In re* Federal-State Joint Bd. on Universal Serv., F.C.C. 97-157 ¶ 374 (F.C.C. May 8, 1997) (C.C. No. 96-45).

154 66 Fed. Reg. 54967–54970 (Oct. 31, 2001).

155 Comments of NCLC on behalf of the Massachusetts Union of Public Hous. Tenants, Before the Federal Commc'ns Comm'n Joint Bd. on Universal Serv., F.C.C. 01-J-2 (Dec. 28, 2001) (C.C. No. 96-45). *See also* Comments of the Universal Serv. Admin. Co., Before the Federal Communications Comm'n *In re* Federal-State Joint Bd. on Universal Serv., C.C. No. 96-45 (Dec. 31, 2001).

156 Federal Commc'ns Comm'n, *In re* Lifeline & Link-Up, 20 F.C.C.R. 1918 (F.C.C. Apr. 29, 2004) (F.C.C. 04-87, W.C. No. 03-109).

157 Federal Commc'ns Comm'n, *In re* Lifeline & Link-Up, 20 F.C.C.R. 1918 ¶¶ 15–19 (F.C.C. Apr. 29, 2004) (F.C.C. 04-87, W.C. No. 03-109)

158 Federal Commc'ns Comm'n, *In re* Lifeline & Link-Up, 20 F.C.C.R. 1918 ¶¶ 20–24 (F.C.C. Apr. 29, 2004) (F.C.C. 04-87, W.C. No. 03-109)

the advertisement of Lifeline and Link-Up.[159] However, as of now, the income eligibility remains at 135%.[160]

11.3.2.7 Certification and Verification for Lifeline and Link-Up

11.3.2.7.1 General

Certification of Lifeline and Link-Up eligibility occurs when a customer is signing up for the program. Verification of continued eligibility occurs periodically after a customer enrolls in Lifeline. There are state and federal default procedures for certification of eligibility. Recently the FCC adopted rules regarding certification of the new income-based eligibility and requiring all states to establish verification procedures.[161] The FCC encourages, but does not mandate, the use of automatic enrollment and on-line verification in its recent order expanding the eligibility criteria for Lifeline and Link Up.[162]

11.3.2.7.2 States with state Lifeline support

In states providing state support for Lifeline programs, the states can establish eligibility criteria as long as they are based solely on income factors or factors directly related to income.[163] For example, Washington State's criteria for Lifeline assistance (called the Washington Telephone Assistance Program (WTAP)) is enrollment in one of nine benefit programs administered by the state Department of Social and Health Services (DSHS).[164] A qualified customer can enroll in WTAP in a matter of minutes by calling the local phone company and providing his or her DSHS client identification number and address. While the customer is on hold, the phone company then places a toll-free call to DSHS to verify that the customer is enrolled in one of the nine programs.[165] The FCC, in its May 1997 Universal Services Report and Order, highlighted California's decision to allow self-certification because studies indicate that the costs for verification would exceed the losses from abuse of self-certification.[166]

The FCC's new rules for certification of income-based eligibility give states with their own Lifeline programs the flexibility to develop their own certification procedures. However, self-certification of income eligibility is not permitted and consumers must provide documentation of income. Consumers who qualify because of income eligibility must certify under penalty of perjury that the documents accurately reflect the household's income and the number of people in the household.[167] An officer of the eligible telecommunications carrier must also certify that the company is in compliance with the state income-certification procedures and that documentation of income was presented.[168]

The FCC now requires states to verify continuing eligibility for the Lifeline and Link-Up programs.[169] In the past the FCC has noted that, because these states are generating matching funds, they have an interest in preventing fraud, waste, and abuse. For example, Minnesota verifies all its Lifeline—called Telephone Assistance Program—customers' eligibility annually (85% through on-line verification using Department of Revenue, public assistance, and LIHEAP databases; the rest of the Lifeline customers are contacted in the mail).[170] In Illinois, phone companies have access to a database of state low-income assistance program participants so that the companies can perform on-line verification of a consumer's eligibility for Lifeline.[171] Florida leaves verification up to the carrier, with some carriers performing periodic verification—either by sending a sample or complete list of participants to the state's Department of Children and Families to identify ineligible participants—and some relying on the consumer to notify the company that they are no longer eligible.[172] The FCC's new rules allow states with their own programs the flexibility to design their own verification procedures, and eligible telecommunications carriers must be able to document compliance with the state's regulations and verification requirements.[173]

159 69 Fed. Reg. 34629–34631 (June 22, 2004).
The FCC has subsequently sought to refresh the record on this docket. *See* 72 Fed. Reg. 40816–40918 (July 25, 2007). *See also* Notice of Proposed Rulemaking, *In re* Lifeline & Link UP Reform & Modernization, Federal-State Joint Bd. on Universal Serv., F.C.C. 11-32 ¶ 12 (Mar. 4, 2011) (C.C. No. 96-45), *available at* http://hraunfoss.fcc.gov/edocs_public/attachmatch/FCC-11-32A1.pdf.

160 47 C.F.R. § 54.409.

161 69 Fed. Reg. 34590–34601 (June 22, 2004).

162 *Id.*

163 47 C.F.R. § 54.409(a); *In re* Federal-State Joint Bd. on Universal Serv., F.C.C. 97-157 ¶¶ 373, 375 (F.C.C. May 8, 1997) (C.C. No. 96-45). *See also In re* Federal-State Joint Bd. on Universal Serv., D.A. 98-1709 (F.C.C. Aug. 27, 1998) (C.C. No. 96-45) (Minnesota's eligibility criteria for its Telephone Assistance Program was not in compliance with federal income-only criteria).

164 Wash. Admin. Code §§ 388-273-0010 to 388-273-0035.

165 Comments of the Staff of the Washington Utilities and Transportation Commission to the Federal-State Joint Bd. on Universal Serv., C.C. No. 96-45, Review of the Lifeline and Link Up Services for Low Income Consumers (Dec. 28, 2001).

166 *See In re* Federal-State Joint Bd. on Universal Serv., F.C.C. 97-157 ¶ 376 (F.C.C. May 8, 1997) (C.C. No. 96-45).

167 69 Fed. Reg. 34590–34601 (June 22, 2004).

168 *Id.*

169 *Id.*

170 *See In re* Federal-State Joint Bd. on Universal Serv., F.C.C. 03J-2, at App. E (F.C.C. Apr. 2, 2003) (C.C. No. 96-45).

171 *Id.*

172 Comments of the Florida Public Service Commission Regarding the Review of Lifeline and Link Up Service for All Low-Income Consumers, C.C. No. 96-45, Review of the Lifeline and Link Up Services for Low Income Consumers (Dec. 28, 2001).

173 69 Fed. Reg. 34590–34601 (June 22, 2004).

However, when a state does not impose its own certification or verification procedures, the federal verification requirements apply.[174]

11.3.2.7.3 States using the federal default eligibility criteria

In states that use the federal default eligibility criteria (that is, when federal eligibility rules apply in states that do not have their own programs), the Federal Communications Commission requires the customers to self-certify. The customer must sign a document that (1) certifies under penalty of perjury that the customer is receiving benefits from either Medicaid, food stamps, Supplemental Security Income, Low Income Home Energy Assistance Program, federal public housing, National School Lunch Program's free lunch program or Temporary Assistance for Needy Families; (2) identifies the federal assistance program(s); and (3) includes an agreement to notify the company if the customer no longer participates in the program(s).[175] However, in an attempt to reduce opportunities for waste, fraud, abuse, and enrollment of ineligible customers, the FCC is seeking comments on its proposal to amend section 54.409(d)(1) of its regulations such that self-certification would no longer be allowed. Instead, the FCC would require that applicants in all states present documentation to establish their eligibility.[176]

The FCC's new rules for certification of income-eligibility in default states requires that consumer provide documentation of income. Documentation may include, for example, state, federal or tribal tax return or three consecutive income statements if documentation covers less than a year (for example, paycheck stubs, a statement of benefits for social security or VA benefits, retirement or pension statements, unemployment, or workers compensation benefits statements; child support and a divorce decree are also listed as examples).[177] The consumer must certify under penalty of perjury that the documentation accurately reflects the household's income and the number of people in the household.[178]

Recently, the FCC granted a local phone company a waiver of the default eligibility requirements listed in 47 C.F.R. § 54.409(b).[179] Pennsylvania has two separate Lifeline programs, one that includes state support and uses the state's DPW database to determine customer eligibility and a second Lifeline program that does not include state support.[180] The second Lifeline option expands the eligibility income to all subscribers at or below 150% of poverty and permits the addition of additional services.[181] Bell Atlantic was granted a waiver of the 47 C.F.R. § 54.409(b) requirement for written certification for those customers listed in the state's DPW database.[182] The FCC noted that "[t]he Commission may exercise its discretion to waive a rule when the particular facts make strict compliance inconsistent with the public interest. In addition, the FCC may take into account considerations of hardship, equity, or more effective implementation of overall policy on an individual basis."[183]

Under the FCC's new rules, eligible telecommunications carriers (ETCs) in default states must verify annually the continued eligibility of a statistically valid sample of their Lifeline subscribers.[184] Lifeline customers who are called upon to verify continued eligibility must present documentation of enrollment in a qualifying public assistance program and self-certify under penalty of perjury that they continue to participate in the qualifying program or, if they qualify under the income-based criteria, submit the documentation and self-certifications under penalty of perjury required to certify eligibility. An officer of the ETC must also certify under penalty of perjury that the company has income verification procedures, was presented with the proper corroborating documentation, and retains these records.[185]

11.3.2.8 Tribal Lifeline and Link-Up: Enhanced Support

11.3.2.8.1 Introduction

On June 30, 2000, the FCC created the Enhanced Lifeline and Link-Up support provision (also called Tribal Lifeline and Link-Up)[186] to achieve the statutory directive of universal service "to make available, so far as possible, to all the people of the United States . . . wire and radio communication service, with adequate facilities at reasonable

174 *In re* Lifeline & Link Up, 2010 FCC LEXIS 700 ¶¶ 9–10 (F.C.C. Jan. 28, 2010).

175 47 C.F.R. §§ 54.409(d), 54.415(b). *See also In re* Federal-State Joint Bd. on Universal Serv., F.C.C. 97-157 ¶ 377 (F.C.C. May 8, 1997) (C.C. No. 96-45).

176 *See* Notice of Proposed Rulemaking, *In re* Lifeline & Link UP Reform & Modernization, Federal-State Joint Bd. on Universal Serv., F.C.C. 11-32 ¶ 12 (Mar. 4, 2011) (C.C. No. 96-45), *available at* http://hraunfoss.fcc.gov/edocs_public/attachmatch/FCC-11-32A1.pdf; 76 Fed. Reg. 16494 (Mar. 23, 2004).

177 69 Fed. Reg. 34590–34601 (June 22, 2004).

178 *Id.*

179 *In re* Federal-State Joint Bd. on Universal Serv. Bell Atlantic-Pennsylvania, Inc., Petition for Waiver of Section 54.409(b) of the Commission's Rules and Regulations, D.A. 00-2899 (F.C.C. Dec. 27, 2000) (C.C. No. 96-45).

180 *Id.* ¶ 3.

181 *Id.* ¶ 3.

182 *Id.* ¶¶ 5–10.

183 *Id.* ¶ 6.

184 69 Fed. Reg. 34590–34601 (June 22, 2004).

185 *Id.*

186 Twelfth Report and Order, Memorandum Opinion and Order, and Further Notice of Proposed Rulemaking, *In re* Federal-State Joint Bd. on Universal Serv., F.C.C. 00-208 (F.C.C. June 30, 2000) (C.C. No. 96-45).

charge."[187] American Indian and Alaska Native communities, on average, have the lowest levels of telephone subscribership in the country, in large part due to low incomes and poverty, high costs of telephone service, inadequate infrastructure, and lack of competitive providers offering alternative technologies.[188] Enhanced Lifeline and Link-Up support provides up to $25 in addition to regular Lifeline support[189] and up to $70 in addition to regular Link-Up support[190] to qualified customers living on federally recognized reservations or Alaskan Native lands.[191] While the types of telephone service covered are the same as those under the regular Lifeline and Link-Up programs, the Enhanced Lifeline and Link-Up support has some additional eligibility criteria for customers and an alternative process for telephone carriers to receive an "eligible telecommunications carrier" designation.

11.3.2.8.2 Geographic areas covered by enhanced Lifeline and Link-Up

At the present time, eligible customers living on tribal lands qualify for the Enhanced Lifeline and Link-Up support.[192] The definition of "tribal lands" has undergone several modifications in the short time the rule has been in effect. Currently, Enhanced Lifeline and Link-Up is limited to eligible customers living on a "reservation" (which is defined as "any federally recognized Indian tribe's reservation, Pueblo, or Colony, including former reservations in Oklahoma, Alaska Native regions established pursuant to the Alaska Native Claims Settlement Act (85 Stat. 688), and Indian allotments").[193] Originally, eligible customers living "near reservations" (as defined by the Bureau of Indian Affairs' regulations) were also eligible for Enhanced Lifeline and Link-Up, but the FCC immediately stayed that portion of the rule because the BIA's definition would encompass regions that do not exhibit the same characteristics that warranted the creation of the Enhanced Lifeline and Link-Up support.[194] The FCC had initially tied the definition of "reservation" and "near reservation" to Bureau of Indian Affairs' regulations; however, BIA changes to the definitions raised the potential for ongoing administrative uncertainty, so the FCC decided that future modifications to the definition of "reservation" and "near reservation" would only take effect upon specific action by the FCC.[195]

In 2003, the FCC published a notice of proposed rulemaking on its rules regarding the availability of Enhanced Lifeline and Link-Up to eligible customers living "near reservations."[196] Recently, the FCC requested comments to its proposed amendment that would remove "near reservation" from its regulations.[197] It is also seeking comments on its proposed new rule that would govern the process by which Tribal groups and communities may seek designation as Tribal lands.[198] In the meantime, households living near reservations can still apply for the regular Lifeline and Link-Up assistance.

11.3.2.8.3 Enhanced Lifeline and Link-Up customer qualifications

The FCC clarified which eligibility requirements (and consequently which tiers[199] of Federal Lifeline support) applied to applicants for Enhanced Lifeline and Link-Up.[200] In states with their own state Lifeline support, low-income consumers living on tribal lands who meet the state's eligi-

187 *In re* Federal-State Joint Bd. on Universal Serv., 15 F.C.C.R. 12208, 12221 ¶ 21, F.C.C. 00-208 (F.C.C. June 30, 2000) (citing 47 U.S.C. § 151).

188 *In re* Federal-State Joint Bd. on Universal Serv.; Promoting Deployment & Subscribership in Unserved & Underserved Areas, Including Tribal and Insular Areas, F.C.C. 03-115 ¶¶ 19, 20 (F.C.C. May 21, 2003) (C.C. No. 96-45).

189 *See* §§ 11.3.2.2–11.3.2.4, 11.3.2.6, 11.3.3, *supra* (more information on regular Lifeline support).

190 *See* §§ 11.3.2.5, 11.3.2.6, *supra* (more information on regular Link Up support).

191 47 C.F.R. §§ 54.400–54.418.

192 68 Fed. Reg. 41936 (July 16, 2003) (amends 47 C.F.R. pt. 54).

193 *Id.*

194 *In re* Federal-State Joint Bd. on Universal Serv.; Promoting Deployment & Subscribership in Unserved & Underserved Areas, Including Tribal & Insular Areas, F.C.C. 03-115 ¶ 4 (F.C.C. May 21, 2003) (C.C. No. 96-45).

195 68 Fed Reg. 41936 (July 16, 2003).

196 68 Fed. Reg. 41996 (July 16, 2003).

The Wireline Competition Bureau issued a notice to refresh the record relating to what constitutes a "near reservation" area. *See* Federal Commc'ns Comm'n, Public Notice, The Wireline Competition Bureau Seeks Additional Comment on Promoting Deployment and Subscribership in Underserved Areas, Including "Near Reservation" Areas, D.A. 07-1239 (Mar. 12, 2007) (C.C. No. 96-45).

197 *See* 76 Fed. Red. 16494 (Mar. 23, 2011); Notice of Proposed Rulemaking, *In re* Lifeline & Link Up Reform and Modernization Federal-State Joint Bd. on Universal Serv., F.C.C. 11-32 (F.C.C. Mar. 4, 2011) (C.C. No. 96-45).

198 *See* 76 Fed. Red. 16494 (Mar. 23, 2011); Notice of Proposed Rulemaking, *In re* Lifeline and Link Up Reform and Modernization Federal-State Joint Bd. on Universal Serv., F.C.C. 11-32 (F.C.C. Mar. 4, 2011) (C.C. No. 96-45).

199 *See* 47 C.F.R. § 54.403 (the federal regulations set out four tiers of support: tier 1, the amount of the end-user common line charge (also called the subscriber line charge or access charge), which increased to a cap of $6.50 starting July 2003; tier 2—an additional $1.75 per month for all eligible customers; tier 3—a 50% federal match of state support up to a maximum of $1.75; and tier 4—additional support of up to $25 per month for Tribal Lifeline).

200 68 Fed. Reg. 41936 (July 16, 2003). *See also In re* Federal-State Joint Bd. on Universal Serv.; Promoting Deployment & Subscribership in Unserved & Underserved Areas, Including Tribal & Insular Areas, F.C.C. 03-115 ¶¶ 12–24 (F.C.C. May 21, 2003) (C.C. No. 96-45).

bility criteria are eligible for full[201] support.[202] Low-income consumers living on tribal lands who do not meet the state eligibility criteria (in states with state Lifeline support) or live in states without a Lifeline support program can still qualify for Enhanced Lifeline and Link-Up support for tiers one, two, and four[203] if they participate in at least one of the following nine programs:

- Bureau of Indian Affairs General Assistance
- Tribally Administered Temporary Assistance for Needy Families
- Head Start (using the income-qualifying standard)
- National School Lunch Program's free lunch program
- Medicaid
- Food Stamps
- Supplemental Security Income
- Federal Public Housing Assistance (Section 8)
- Low-Income Home Energy Assistance Program

Additionally, the FCC recently proposed to amend section 54.409(c) of its regulations, such that residents of Tribal Lands who participate in the Food Distribution Program on Indian Reservations (FDPIR) would also be eligible.[204]

These consumers are still eligible for Tier 3 support (the federal match) if the phone company or the eligible telecommunications carrier provides carrier-matching funds.[205]

201 They are eligible for all four tiers of support listed in 47 C.F.R. § 54.403 (the federal regulations set out four tiers of support: tier 1, the amount of the end-user common line charge (also called the subscriber line charge or access charge), which increased to a cap of $6.50 starting July 2003; tier 2—an additional $1.75 per month for all eligible customers; tier 3—a 50% federal match of state support up to a maximum of $1.75; and tier 4—additional support of up to $25 per month for Tribal Lifeline).

202 68 Fed. Reg. 41936 (July 16, 2003). *See also In re* Federal-State Joint Bd. on Universal Serv.; Promoting Deployment & Subscribership in Unserved & Underserved Areas, Including Tribal & Insular Areas, F.C.C. 03-115 ¶¶ 23, 24 (F.C.C. May 21, 2003) (C.C. No. 96-45).

203 *See* 47 C.F.R. § 54.403 (the federal regulations set out four tiers of support: tier 1, the amount of the end-user common line charge (also called the subscriber line charge or access charge), which increased to a cap of $6.50 starting July 2003; tier 2—an additional $1.75 per month for all eligible customers; tier 3—a 50% federal match of state support up to a maximum of $1.75; and tier 4—additional support of up to $25 per month for Tribal Lifeline).

204 See 76 Fed. Reg. 16494 (Mar. 23, 2011); Notice of Proposed Rulemaking, *In re* Lifeline & Link UP Reform & Modernization, Federal-State Joint Bd. on Universal Serv., F.C.C. 11-32 ¶ 12 (Mar. 4, 2011) (C.C. No. 96-45), *available at* http://hraunfoss.fcc.gov/edocs_public/attachmatch/FCC-11-32A1.pdf.

205 47 C.F.R. § 54.409(c). *See also In re* Federal-State Joint Bd. on Universal Serv.; Promoting Deployment & Subscribership in Unserved & Underserved Areas, Including Tribal & Insular Areas, F.C.C. 03-115 ¶¶ 23, 24 (F.C.C. May 21, 2003) (C.C. No. 96-45).

11.3.2.8.4 *Eligible telecommunications carriers for Tribal Lifeline and Link-Up*

As discussed in § 11.3.2.1.3, *supra*, an eligible telecommunications carrier (ETC) is a common carrier (phone company) that has been approved or ordered to[206] provide core services[207] and is eligible for reimbursement from the federal universal service fund. State utility commissions are responsible for approving phone company requests to be designated as ETCs.[208] When a state commission does not have jurisdiction over a phone company, the FCC is responsible for determining the ETC designation.[209] Tribal sovereignty raises unique jurisdictional issues.

The FCC, in a recent order, clarified its role in a phone company's designation of ETC status to serve tribal lands.[210] Some state utility commissions have asserted jurisdiction over tribal lands, and the FCC stated that it does not believe "that Congress intended the Commission to use section 214(e)(6) to usurp the role of a state commission that has jurisdiction over a carrier providing service on tribal lands."[211] Under the FCC's Tribal ETC framework, carriers seeking ETC designation for service provided on tribal lands can petition the FCC directly (that is, the phone company does not have to first go through the state utility commission).[212] The FCC will then decide if the phone company is subject to the state commission's jurisdiction and, if not, the FCC will then make a determination on the company's request for an ETC designation.[213]

206 *See* 47 U.S.C. § 214(e)(3) (state utility commission or FCC could require common carrier to provide universal services in unserved areas).

207 47 U.S.C. § 214(e) (eligible telecommunication carriers and the provision of universal services). *See also* 47 U.S.C. § 254(c) (services supported by the federal universal services support mechanism); Order and Order on Reconsideration, *In re* Federal-State Joint Bd. on Universal Serv., F.C.C. 03-170 (F.C.C. July 14, 2003) (C.C. No. 96-45), *available at* 68 Fed. Reg. 49707–49712 (Aug. 19, 2003) (no new core services added to list in 47 U.S.C. § 254(c)).

208 47 U.S.C. § 214(e)(2), (3).

209 47 U.S.C. § 214(e)(6).

210 47 C.F.R. § 54.409(c). *See also In re* Federal-State Joint Bd. on Universal Serv.; Promoting Deployment & Subscribership in Unserved & Underserved Areas, Including Tribal & Insular Areas, F.C.C. 03-115 ¶¶ 5, 8–12 (F.C.C. May 21, 2003) (C.C. No. 96-45).

211 *See also In re* Federal-State Joint Bd. on Universal Serv.; Promoting Deployment & Subscribership in Unserved & Underserved Areas, Including Tribal & Insular Areas, F.C.C. 03-115 ¶ 9 (F.C.C. May 21, 2003) (C.C. No. 96-45).

212 *In re* Federal-State Joint Bd. on Universal Serv., 15 F.C.C.R. 12265–67 ¶¶ 115, 120 (F.C.C. June 30, 2000) (F.C.C. 00-208); *In re* Federal-State Joint Bd. on Universal Serv., Promoting Deployment & Subscribership in Unserved & Underserved Areas, Including Tribal & Insular Areas, 18 F.C.C.R. 10958, at *10961–10962 (F.C.C. May 21, 2003) (F.C.C. 03-115 ¶ 5; C.C. No. 96-45).

213 *In re* Federal-State Joint Bd. on Universal Serv., Promoting Deployment & Subscribership in Unserved & Underserved

While wireless carriers have begun offering prepaid wireless services in some states through the Lifeline program, and many wireless carriers have received universal service subsidies from the High Cost Fund, the FCC and Congress are still wrestling with how to comprehensively reform the federal universal services program to address the need to increase broadband capacity and access. In November 2007, the Federal-State Joint Board on Universal Services sent the FCC a recommendation for comprehensive reform of the High Cost Fund support program that contains funding for broadband (via a broadband fund) and wireless infrastructure (via a mobility fund) in underserved areas as well as a provide-of-last-resort fund comprised of the existing incumbent wireline high cost support mechanisms.[214] The FCC opened these recommendations up for comment in 2008[215] and has issued an interim cap on competitive ETC support for each state to remain in effect until the FCC reaches a final decision on comprehensive reform measures.[216] The question of whether the FCC expands the definition of covered services to include broadband and mobility, and whether Lifeline and Link-Up will be expanded to cover these services, may soon be answered.[217]

11.3.2.9 Modifications to the Lifeline Program

Prior to the 1997 Report and Order, for states to participate in the federal Lifeline program, they had to generate a matching reduction in intrastate end-user charges. The Joint Board on Universal Services and the FCC agreed that, consistent with the statutory principles of the Telecommunications Act of 1996, rates should be "affordable" and "low-income consumers" in *all* regions of the nation should have access to telecommunications services.[218] Thus, qualified low-income consumers in any state can enroll in the Lifeline program. States that have their own state Lifeline support can set their own eligibility criteria as long as it is based "solely on income or factors directly related to income."[219] Low-income consumers in states without a state Lifeline support program must meet the federal default criteria for eligibility.[220]

In June 2000, the FCC substantially increased the amount of Lifeline and Link-Up support for qualified low-income residents of tribal reservations.[221] (See § 11.3.2.8, *supra*, for a description of Tribal Lifeline and Link-Up.) Tribal Lifeline consumers could pay rates as low as $1 per month for local phone service under this program.[222]

The maximum amount of federal Lifeline support has also gradually increased due to the increases in one of the reimbursable charges, the Subscriber Line Charge or the End User Common Line Charge.[223] This charge is covered under Tier 1 support in the Lifeline regulations.[224] The FCC created the subscriber line charge after the break-up of AT&T as part of a larger formula that allows local phone companies to recoup the costs of the use of their network by other services, such as long-distance services. Consumer advocacy groups have long argued against the amount and use of the subscriber line charge in the FCC's Access Charge Reform proceedings. Unfortunately, the FCC adopted an industry-based proposal for access charge reform that has increased the amount of the subscriber line charge.[225] As of July 2003, the charge has increased from $3.50 per month for a residential phone line to $6.50.[226] However, there is also language in the FCC order that increases Lifeline support to offset the increases to the residential subscriber line charge.[227]

Areas, Including Tribal & Insular Areas, 18 F.C.C.R. 10958, at *10961–10962 (F.C.C. May 21, 2003) (F.C.C. 03-115 ¶ 5; C.C. No. 96-45).

214 Recommended Decision, *In re* High-Cost Universal Serv. Support Federal-State Joint Bd. on Universal Serv., 22 F.C.C.R. 20477, F.C.C. 07J-4 (F.C.C. Nov. 19, 2007) (W.C. No. 05-337, C.C. No. 96-45).

215 Notice of Proposed Rulemaking, 23 F.C.C.R. 1467, F.C.C. 08-4 (F.C.C. Jan. 29, 2008) (Identical Support Rule); Notice of Proposed Rulemaking, 23 F.C.C.R. 1495, F.C.C. 08-5 (F.C.C. Jan. 29, 2008) (Reverse Auction); Notice of Proposed Rulemaking, 23 F.C.C.R. 1531, F.C.C. 08-22 (F.C.C. Jan. 29, 2008) (Joint Board Comprehensive Reform).

216 The High Cost Fund had increased from $2.6 billion in universal services support in 2001 to $ 4.3 billion in support in 2007, and the FCC attributed the growth to competitive ETCs (CETCs), with 94% of the CETC support going to wireless carriers. *See* Order, *In re* High-Cost Universal Service Support Federal-State Joint Bd. on Universal Serv., F.C.C. 08-122 ¶¶ 6, 20 (F.C.C. May 1, 2008) (W.C. No. 05-337, C.C. No. 96-45).

217 The National Broadband Plan recommends that FCC expand Lifeline and Link Up to make broadband affordable for low-income consumers. Federal-State Joint Board on Universal Services Seeks Comments on Lifeline and Link Up Eligibility, Verification and Outreach Issues Referred to Joint Board, 25 F.C.C.R. 7551, 75548–75559, F.C.C. 10J-2 ¶ 12 (F.C.C. July 15, 2010).

218 47 U.S.C. § 254(b).

219 47 C.F.R. § 54.409(a).

220 47 C.F.R. § 54.409(b).

221 *See In re* Federal-State Joint Bd. on Universal Serv., F.C.C. 00-208 (F.C.C. June 30, 2000) (C.C. No. 96-45), *codified at* 47 C.F.R. §§ 54.400–54.418.

222 Excludes taxes and fees.

223 47 C.F.R. § 54.403(a)(1).

224 *Id.*

225 *In re* Access Charge Reform; Price Cap Performance Review for Local Exch. Carriers; Low-Volume Long-Distance Users Federal-State Joint Bd. on Universal Serv., F.C.C. 00-193 (May 31, 2000) (C.C. Nos. 96-262, 94-1, 99-249, 96-45), *subsequent proceeding*, Errata to F.C.C. 00-193, D.A. 02-1027 (F.C.C. June 14, 2000).

226 *See In re* Access Charge Reform; Price Cap Performance Review for Local Exch. Carriers; Low-Volume Long-Distance Users Federal-State Joint Bd. on Universal Serv., F.C.C. 00-193 ¶¶ 33, 70–104, 185–205 (May 31, 2000) (C.C. Nos. 96-262, 94-1, 99-249, 96-45), *subsequent proceeding*, Errata to F.C.C. 00-193, D.A. 02-1027 (F.C.C. June 14, 2000). *See also* Federal Commc'ns Comm'n, Trends in Telephone Service § 1-3 (Aug. 2003).

227 *In re* Access Charge Reform; Price Cap Performance Review

While the Lifeline and Link-Up programs are effective at increasing low-income consumer telephone subscribership, the Federal-State Joint Board on Universal Service estimates that, in January 2002, only approximately 38% of eligible households subscribed to Lifeline service.[228] On April 29, 2004, the FCC adopted the recommendations of the Federal-State Joint Board on Universal Service which proposed expanding default eligibility for Lifeline and Link-Up to increase subscribership, establishing certification and verification requirements, and creating outreach guidelines.[229]

The FCC issued a notice of proposed rulemaking on June 22, 2004, seeking comment on whether the eligibility criteria should be expanded to 150% of poverty and whether to establish rules for the advertisement of Lifeline and Link-Up.[230] More recently, the FCC issued a notice that they were seeking to refresh the record in this docket.[231]

11.3.2.10 Barriers to Lifeline Service

11.3.2.10.1 Deposits

The FCC adopted a rule prohibiting phone companies from imposing a deposit requirement on customers initiating Lifeline service who voluntarily elect toll-limitation service (the limiting of long-distance calls to a preset number, including toll-blocking).[232] When a qualified consumer elects to have toll-limitation as part of Lifeline service, the ETC can be reimbursed for those costs. The USAC will reimburse carriers for both toll blocking and toll control (limiting long-distance service to a preset amount) under the Toll-Limitation Service component of the Low Income Program.[233] The FCC acknowledged the deterrent effect of high-deposit charges on low-income consumers but did not extend the prohibition on deposits to all Lifeline customers because of concern about the risk of uncollectible long-distance charges. The FCC's rationale for allowing deposit requirements in other instances is primarily to guard against unpaid long-distance charges.[234]

11.3.2.10.2 Outstanding bills

One major barrier to telephone service that is not covered by the Lifeline program is a customer's outstanding phone bills. A household eligible for Lifeline service could be denied service by the local phone company if there are outstanding phone bills. States can help lower this barrier by prohibiting local phone companies from denying a Lifeline customer's request for reconnection when the outstanding balance is for toll (long-distance) or ancillary charges.[235] In Washington State, local phone service providers must restore service for a customer whose basic service was discontinued for nonpayment if the customer was not a participant in the state Lifeline program (Washington Telephone Assistance Program (WTAP)) or the federal tribal Lifeline program at the time of the disconnection and the customer is eligible for WTAP or tribal Lifeline at the time restoration of service is requested. In order to qualify for the restoration, customers must establish eligibility for WTAP or tribal Lifeline, agree to continue to participate in the appropriate Lifeline program, agree to pay the unpaid basic and ancillary services amounts due to the carrier at a monthly rate more than one and one-half times the WTAP rate, and agree to toll limitation and/or ancillary service restriction until the unpaid amounts are paid.[236]

11.3.2.10.3 Local service from predatory carriers

Low-income consumers and their advocates should be cautious about local phone service providers that focus their marketing on low-income consumers who may not be able to get local phone service from the incumbent provider because of credit problems or unemployment. Whenever possible, these consumers should be enrolled in the Lifeline and Link-Up programs. Local phone service providers that promise service to anyone, without requiring proof of employment or good credit, often charge extremely high

for Local Exch. Carriers; Low-Volume Long-Distance Users Federal-State Joint Bd. on Universal Serv., F.C.C. 00-193 ¶¶ 214–17 (May 31, 2000) (C.C. Nos. 96-262, 94-1, 99-249, 96-45), *subsequent proceeding*, Errata to F.C.C. 00-193, D.A. 02-1027 (F.C.C. June 14, 2000).

228 *In re* Federal-State Joint Bd. on Universal Serv., F.C.C. 03J-2 ¶¶ 6–9, 13 (F.C.C. Apr. 2, 2003) (C.C. No. 96-45).

229 *In re* Lifeline & Link-Up, F.C.C. 04-87 (F.C.C. Apr. 29, 2004) (W.C. No. 03-109).

230 69 Fed. Reg. 34629–34631 (June 22, 2004).

231 Notice of Proposed Rulemaking, *In re* Lifeline & Link UP Reform & Modernization, Federal-State Joint Bd. on Universal Serv., F.C.C. 11-32 ¶ 12 (Mar. 4, 2011) (C.C. No. 96-45), *available at* http://hraunfoss.fcc.gov/edocs_public/attachmatch/FCC-11-32A1.pdf (seeking new comments on raising the federal income threshold for program participation to 150% or below of the federal poverty guidelines). *See also* 72 Fed. Reg. 40816–40818 (July 25, 2007).

232 *In re* Federal-State Joint Bd. on Universal Serv., 12 F.C.C.R. 8776 ¶ 398 (F.C.C. May 8, 1997) (F.C.C. 97-157, C.C. No. 96-45). *See also* 47 C.F.R. § 54.401(c).

233 *In re* Federal-State Joint Bd. on Universal Serv., 12 F.C.C.R. 8776 at ¶ 387 (F.C.C. May 8, 1997) (F.C.C. 97-157).

234 *In re* Federal-State Joint Bd. on Universal Serv., 12 F.C.C.R. 8776 ¶¶ 398, 399 (F.C.C. May 8, 1997) (F.C.C. 97-157, C.C. No. 96-45).

The FCC notes in note 1031 that, "in most cases, [long-distance companies] sell their accounts receivable to [local phone service companies] for billing and collection."

235 See the following stipulation approved by the Florida Public Service Commission, Order No. PSC-99-2503-PAA-TL, issued on December 21, 1999 (cited in Comments of the Florida Public Service Commission Regarding the Review of Lifeline and Link Up Service for All Low-Income Consumers, C.C. No. 96-45, at 4 (Dec. 26, 2001)).

236 Wash. Admin. Code § 480-120-174.

monthly rates. In Colorado, the state's supreme court overruled the state's utility commission's decision to allow a competitive local exchange carrier's (CLEC) local phone service plan to avoid the state's $14.74 cap on monthly rates for basic local phone service.[237] Colorado has a residential basic local service rate cap statute that promotes universal service.[238] The CLEC, NOW Communications, Inc., marketed a $36.50-per-month local phone service plan to customers who could not get service from the incumbent local phone company because of credit problems or unemployment. The state's utility commission had originally ruled that the plan was not subject to the cap because it was part of a package of bundled services (in addition to basic service, the plan allowed customers to make payments and change service at payment centers and provided toll restriction). The state supreme court, reviewing the case de novo, found that the plan, even though it was combined with other service, was a residential basic local phone service and thus subject to the statutory rate cap.[239] The court determined that the use of payment centers was a non-telecommunications service and therefore did not change the nature of the basic service.[240] The court also found it incorrect to characterize toll limitations as an addition to basic service for which extra fees are charged, because it actually removes a feature of basic service.[241] On remand, the Colorado Public Utility Commission ordered the CLEC to refund excess charges to customers.[242]

In Washington State, four high-cost competitive local phone service providers sprung up in 2002 to take advantage of the reimbursement structure of the state's Lifeline program. Whereas the incumbent local phone provider, Qwest, which serves approximately 70% of the state's Lifeline customers, charges a monthly rate of $5.00, the four high-cost CLECs charged a monthly rate of approximately $50.00.[243] Due to an oversight in the reimbursement mechanism and poor oversight by the agency running the state Lifeline program, the state fund went from a balance of $5.8 million in June 2002 to balance of $809,289 in June 2003.[244] The four high-cost CLECs were receiving 40% of the state's WTAP fund,[245] essentially raiding the fund to the point at which its continued existence was endangered. The agency running the state Lifeline program proposed to more than double the client's monthly local phone charge from $4.00 to $9.00,[246] arguing that increasing the WTAP excise tax from 13¢ to the statutorily mandated cap of 14¢ would only raise revenue by $400,000 per year. The state agency that administers WTAP capped the local phone reimbursement to the lowest monthly charge in each area as of June 1, 2003, but did so too late to stop the hemorrhaging of the fund.[247]

One way advocates can protect consumers from these predatory carriers is by working to pass rules and policies that allow customers with unpaid bills to have reasonable arrearage payment and forgiveness plans as covered in Chapter 7, *supra*, and described in § 11.3.2.10.2, *supra*.

11.3.2.11 Strategies for Dealing with Pending Termination of Lifeline Service

Notice by the company of pending termination of Lifeline assistance is an essential service for alerting a customer who still qualifies for the benefit. For example, if a phone company terminates Lifeline assistance because enrollment eligibility was based on the customer's receipt of LIHEAP, and the customer no longer receives LIHEAP assistance but receives SSI, an unnecessary interruption or loss of Lifeline assistance could result if no notice is given. The customer would remain eligible for Lifeline through receipt of SSI, which itself is a basis for Lifeline eligibility. The FCC has responded to this gap in protection of Lifeline service by adopting a rule that requires written notice of pending termination. The eligible telecommunications carrier must have a reasonable basis for believing the customer is no longer eligible for Lifeline assistance and must send the notice of pending termination in a letter separate from the bill, whereupon the customer has sixty days to prove continuing eligibility.[248]

When a customer is no longer eligible for Lifeline, there is still no guarantee that the customer can afford local phone service. Florida has attempted to ease the transition from Lifeline assistance by passing a law that requires local phone companies to offer residential service at 70% of the regular rate for up to a year for Lifeline subscribers who are no longer eligible for Lifeline assistance.[249]

237 Office of Consumer Counsel v. Public Util. Comm'n, 42 P.3d 23 (Colo. 2002).

238 Colo. Rev. Stat. § 40-15-502(3) (amended in 2008).

239 Office of Consumer Counsel v. Public Util. Comm'n, 42 P.3d 23, 28–29 (Colo. 2002).

240 *Id.* at 28.

241 *Id.*

242 *In re* NOW Commc'ns, Inc., 2003 WL 21078053 (Colo. Pub. Utils. Comm'n Jan. 23, 2003) (Nos. 98S-363T, C03-0071).

243 Phyllis Lowe, Washington Dep't of Social & Health Serv., Washington Telephone Assistance Program (WTAP)—Proposal to Increase the Client Co-Payment 2 (June 25, 2003).

244 *Id.* at 3.

245 *Id.* at 2.

246 Phyllis Lowe, Wash. Dep't of Social and Health Serv., Washington Telephone Assistance Program (WTAP)—Proposal to Increase the Client Co-Payment 2 (June 25, 2003).

247 *Id.* at 3.

248 69 Fed. Reg. 34590–34601 (June 22, 2004). 47 C.F.R. § 54.405(d).

249 Fla. Stat. § 364.105.

11.3.2.12 Strategies for Increasing Participation in Lifeline and Link-Up

11.3.2.12.1 Lifeline and Link-Up outreach

Eligible telecommunications carriers are required to publicize Lifeline and Link-Up "in a manner reasonably designed to reach those likely to qualify" for the support.[250] A carrier that fails to comply with the advertising requirement could be liable for a forfeiture pursuant to the FCC's authority under 47 U.S.C. § 503(b)(1)(B) of the Communications Act of 1934. In May 2004, the FCC published a Notice of Apparent Liability for Forfeiture in the amount of $25,000 against Pend Oreille Telephone Company for willfully and repeatedly failing to advertise Lifeline and Link-Up to low-income residents on tribal lands.[251]

Some methods relied upon by ETCs to publicize the programs—such as publishing Lifeline information in bill stuffers, telephone directories, and postings on the Internet—are not designed to reach households without phone service.[252] When the Washington Utilities and Transportation Commission held two workshops on Lifeline and Link-Up outreach and publicity in 2000 and 2001, it learned that no ETC used radio or television to publicize the programs.[253]

The FCC recently issued three outreach guidelines for the Lifeline and Link-Up programs. The first recommended guideline is that Eligible Telecommunications Carriers and states should use outreach materials and methods designed to reach households that do not currently have phone service. Examples of methods include mailings, posters in locations likely to be seen by low-income individuals, multimedia outreach, and information booths. The FCC noted that states and carriers should ensure outreach materials accommodate those with disabilities or low-literacy abilities. Methods highlighted as not likely to be effective include sole or over-reliance on the Internet, phonebooks, and hotlines.[254] The second recommended guideline is that states and carriers develop outreach advertising that can be read or accessed by any sizable non-English population in a carrier's service area. Examples of how carriers can accomplish this include toll-free call centers staffed by speakers of languages spoken in the service territory and applications in other languages.[255] The third guideline is for state and carriers to coordinate outreach efforts with other agencies and tribes that administer any of the relevant government assistance programs.[256]

Some states have aggressively engaged in Lifeline outreach. Maine, which has a high Lifeline enrollment rate, has an easy application process and effective targeted outreach. Households enrolled in public assistance programs that qualify them for Lifeline received a letter from the Maine Telecommunications Education Board describing the program benefits and eligibility rules. Households receiving LIHEAP received a flyer from the community action agencies that subcontract with the state LIHEAP office.[257] These letters and flyers resulted in an increase in enrollment from 60% to 71% within six months.[258] Households applying for public assistance are told about Lifeline by the public assistance agencies and customers applying for phone service are also told about the program.[259] To enroll, households just need to tell the phone company that they receive one of the listed benefits and provide either a social security number or a welfare ID number.[260]

Iowa, a state that does not have state Lifeline support, substantially increased Lifeline enrollment by creating a joint LIHEAP/Lifeline form. According to the FCC's 2001 Trends in Telephone Service Report, Iowa had 11,832 customers enrolled in Lifeline in 2000.[261] In the first year of using the joint form, the Iowa Department of Human Rights (the state LIHEAP agency) enrolled 37,000 LIHEAP customers into Lifeline by submitting the Lifeline applications to the customer's local phone company.[262]

The FCC issued a notice of proposed rulemaking to explore whether it should adopt rules governing the advertisement of Lifeline and Link-Up.[263] In July 2007, the FCC issued a notice[264] seeking to refresh the record in this docket. In 2011, the FCC reiterated the importance of outreach and advertising and is seeking comments on whether it should impose specific outreach requirements on

250 47 C.F.R. §§ 54.405(b), 54.411(d).

251 *In re* Pend Oreille Tel. Co. Apparent Liability for Forfeiture, D.A. 04-1447 (F.C.C. May 24, 2004) (File No. EB-03-TC-123, NAL/Acct. No. 200432170001, FRN 0007838568).

252 *See In re* Federal-State Joint Bd. on Universal Serv., F.C.C. 03J-2, at 47–56 (F.C.C. Apr. 2, 2003) (C.C. No. 96-45); Comments of the National Consumer Law Center on Behalf of the Massachusetts Union of Public Hous. Tenants, Before the FCC Joint Board on Universal Service, C.C. No. 96-45/FCC 01J-2 (Dec. 28, 2001); Comments of the Staff of the Washington Utilities and Transportation Commission to the Federal-State Joint Board on Universal Service, Review of the Lifeline and Link Up Services for Low Income Consumers, C.C. No. 96-45 (Dec. 28, 2001).

253 Comments of the Staff of the Washington Utilities and Transportation Commission to the Federal-State Joint Board on Universal Service, Review of the Lifeline and Link Up Services for Low Income Consumers, C.C. No. 96-45 (Dec. 28, 2001).

254 69 Fed. Reg. 34590–34601 (June 22, 2004).

255 *Id.*

256 *Id.*

257 Comments of the National Consumer Law Center on Behalf of the Massachusetts Union of Public Hous. Tenants, Before the FCC Joint Board on Universal Service, C.C. No. 96-45/F.C.C. 01J-2 (Dec. 28, 2001).

258 *Id.*

259 *Id.*

260 *Id.*

261 Federal Commc'ns Comm'n, Trends in Telephone Service Report, tbl. 7.2 (Aug. 2001).

262 *See* Calendar Year 2003 Annual Report of the Iowa Utilities Board 30, *available at* www.state.ia.us/iub/docs/reports/AnnualReport_CY2003.doc (Iowa Util. Board's website).

263 69 Fed. Reg. 34629–34631 (June 22, 2004).

264 72 Fed. Reg. 40816–40818 (July 25, 2007).

ETCs, pursuant to the Joint Board's 2010 recommended decision.[265] In that decision, the Joint Board recommended that the FCC adopt mandatory outreach requirements for all ETCs that receive low-income support from the Universal Service Fund.[266]

11.3.2.12.2 Automatic enrollment

At the same time, the Federal Communications Commission urges states to adopt the most efficient administrative procedure for the Lifeline program and points to New York's automatic enrollment program design.[267] The FCC, while again encouraging states to use automatic enrollment as a means of certifying eligibility, declined to mandate it due to administrative and financial concerns for the states and telephone companies.[268] In order to establish automatic enrollment into the Lifeline program, New York requires the coordination of computer files between the local phone companies and the social service agencies that administer the programs used to determine Lifeline eligibility.[269] Any time customers of Verizon enroll in a program administered by the New York Department of Family Assistance (NYDFA), they are automatically enrolled in Lifeline unless they choose to opt out.[270] Customers of other phone services who have been identified by NDFA as eligible for Lifeline are notified of their eligibility and given a form to request Lifeline.[271] Those customers who, for four consecutive months, stop receiving assistance from a program administered by NYDFA are removed from the Lifeline program.[272] Participation in New York's Lifeline increased from 197,339 in 1987 to 703,001 in 1998.[273] Massachusetts also uses an automatic enrollment program administered through the state's LIHEAP agency, the Massachusetts Department of Housing and Community Development. LIHEAP-eligible households in Massachusetts, as part of their LIHEAP application, can give permission for their information to be used for enrollment in other utility discount programs.[274] A list of LIHEAP-eligible households is then sent to the local phone company for automatic enrollment into the Lifeline program.[275]

11.3.3 Toll (Long-Distance) Limitation

In addition to the basic telephone services covered by the definition of universal service, and in order to further ensure that low-income consumers remain connected to the telecommunications network, the FCC added Toll Limitation Service to the federal low-income universal services program. Toll Limitation Service includes blocking long-distance calls made from the consumer's phone or limiting the number of long-distance calls made from the consumer's phone.[276] According to the FCC, the main reason people lose access to phone service is because of the failure to pay long-distance bills.[277] In its May 1997 order implementing the universal service provisions of the Telecommunications Act of 1996 ("Universal Service Order"), the FCC required local telephone companies to provide toll-limitation service without charge to Lifeline customers.[278]

11.3.4 Other Federal Universal Services Programs

The other federal universal services programs include the High Cost Fund support program that is designed to keep telephone rates in high-cost areas—areas where, due to the terrain or other conditions, it is expensive to connect to the telephone network—and rural areas reasonably comparable among the states.[279]

---

265 *See* 76 Fed. Reg. 16494 (Mar. 23, 2011); Notice of Proposed Rulemaking, *In re* Lifeline & Link UP Reform & Modernization, Federal-State Joint Bd. on Universal Serv., F.C.C. 11-32 ¶ 12 (Mar. 4, 2011) (C.C. No. 96-45), *available at* http://hraunfoss.fcc.gov/edocs_public/attachmatch/FCC-11-32A1.pdf.

266 76 Fed. Reg. 16494 (Mar. 23, 2011); Notice of Proposed Rulemaking, *In re* Lifeline and Link UP Reform and Modernization, Federal-State Joint Bd. on Universal Serv., F.C.C. 11-32 ¶ 12 (Mar. 4, 2011) (C.C. No. 96-45), *available at* http://hraunfoss.fcc.gov/edocs_public/attachmatch/FCC-11-32A1.pdf.

267 *See In re* Federal-State Joint Bd. on Universal Serv., F.C.C. 97-157 ¶ 378 (F.C.C. May 8, 1997) (C.C. No. 96-45).

268 69 Fed. Reg. 34590–34601 (June 22, 2004).

269 *Id.* ¶ 378.

270 *See In re* Federal-State Joint Bd. on Universal Serv., F.C.C. 03J-2, at App. E (F.C.C. Apr. 2, 2003) (C.C. No. 96-45).

271 *Id.*

272 *Id.*

273 *Id.*

274 Comments of the National Consumer Law Center on Behalf of the Massachusetts Union of Public Hous. Tenants, Before the FCC Joint Board on Universal Service, C.C. No. 96-45/FCC 01J-2 (Dec. 28, 2001); Comments of MASSCAP/MEDA 19–28 (Jan. 31, 2001); Reply Comments of MASSCAP/MEDA 2, 3 (Mar. 7, 2002); Additional Comment of MASSCAP/MEDA 2–4 (Nov. 14, 2002).

275 *Id.*

276 47 C.F.R. § 54.400(d).

277 *In re* Federal-State Joint Bd. on Universal Serv., F.C.C. 97-157 ¶¶ 385, 389 (F.C.C. May 8, 1997) (C.C. No. 96-45).

The FCC also looked to states with toll-limitation programs such as Pennsylvania. Bell Atlantic-Pennsylvania offered free toll-limitation service to customers when they started service or lost toll service for nonpayment once all outstanding charges were paid. According to the FCC, Pennsylvania had one of the highest telephone subscribership rates in the nation. *See id.* ¶ 387.

278 *In re* Federal-State Joint Bd. on Universal Serv., F.C.C. 97-157 ¶ 28 (F.C.C. May 8, 1997) (C.C. No. 96-45). *See also* 47 C.F.R. § 54.401(a)(3).

279 Ninth Report and Order and Seventeenth Order on Reconsideration, Federal Commc'ns Comm'n, C.C. No.96-45, FCC 99-306 (Oct. 21, 1999). *See also* www.universalservice.org (Universal Service Administrative Company's webpage has more information about the program).

Through discounted rates for telecommunications services, the Schools and Libraries program and Rural Health Care Program are designed to increase school and library access to advanced telecommunication services and rural health care programs.[280]

11.4 State Universal Service Programs

States opting to establish statewide universal service programs cannot set up programs that are inconsistent with FCC's rules. Furthermore, states that opt to expand the types of services covered in a universal services plan must also find a specific, predictable, and sufficient mechanism to support the program that does not rely on or burden the federal program. Pursuant to 47 U.S.C. § 254(f):

> A State may adopt regulations not inconsistent with the Commission's rules to preserve and advance universal service. Every telecommunications carrier that provides intrastate telecommunications services shall contribute, on an equitable and nondiscriminatory basis, in a manner determined by the State to the preservation and advancement of universal service in that State. A State may adopt regulations to provide for additional definitions and standards to preserve and advance universal service within that State only to the extent that such regulations adopt additional specific, predictable, and sufficient mechanisms to support such definitions or standards that do not rely on or burden Federal universal service support mechanisms.

As discussed in earlier sections, states that have their own state Lifeline support can set their own eligibility criteria and draw additional federal matching dollars for their Lifeline households.[281] Furthermore, states with their own Lifeline support saw the greatest increase in telephone subscribership (an average of 0.61% per year for states pulling down the maximum federal matching support and an average of 0.29% per year for states receiving less than the maximum federal match, compared to an average of 0.21% per year for states that did not provide state support).[282] For the most up-to-date information on a particular state's universal service programs, contact the local phone company or the state utility commission's consumer division. A list of state utility commissions is provided in Appendix A.8, *infra*. There is also a web page on the Universal Service Administrative Company's (USAC's) website that lists information about a particular state's Lifeline programs (www.usac.org/li/low-income/lifelinesupport/browser). The USAC website also has additional information about the other federal telecommunications universal services programs.[283]

11.5 Services for the Disabled Under the Telecommunications Act of 1996

11.5.1 General

The Federal Communications Commission chose to handle access for the disabled in a proceeding separate from the universal services proceeding.[284] It concluded, based on statutory construction, that services for the disabled were not intended by Congress to comprise a specific category of services under the federal universal services program.[285] However, Title IV of the Americans with Disabilities Act of 1990 requires common carriers offering telephone voice-transmission services to also provide functionally equivalent services for individuals with speech or hearing disabilities.[286] The FCC has also extended the disability access requirements to providers of interconnected Voice over Internet Protocol (VoIP) services and manufacturers of equipment designed to provide those services.[287]

---

280 *In re* Federal-State Joint Bd. on Universal Serv., F.C.C. 97-157 ¶¶ 424–607 (F.C.C. May 8, 1997) (C.C. No. 96-45). *See also* www.universalservice.org (Universal Service Administrative Company's webpage has more information about the program).

281 *See* § 11.3.2.3, *supra*.

282 Federal Commc'ns Comm'n, Federal-State Joint Board October 2002 Monitoring Report, tbls. 6.4, 6-19, *cited in* Recommended Decision, *In re* Federal-State Joint Bd. on Universal Serv., F.C.C. 03J-2 ¶¶ 8–9, C.C. No. 96-45 (F.C.C. Apr. 2, 2003).

283 Universal Serv. Admin. Co., 2120 L Street, N.W., Suite 600, Washington, DC 20037; toll-free: (888) 641-8722. Their website is at www.universalservice.org.

284 *In re* Federal-State Joint Bd. on Universal Serv., F.C.C. 97-157 ¶ 405 (F.C.C. May 8, 1997) (C.C. No. 96-45).

The FCC is handling implementation of 47 U.S.C. § 255 through separate proceedings. *See* Notice of Inquiry, Implementation of Section 255 of the Telecommunications Act of 1996, Access to Telecommunications Services, Telecommunications Equipment, and Customer Premises Equipment by Persons with Disabilities, F.C.C. 96-382 (F.C.C. Sept. 19, 1996) (W.T. No. 96-198); Notice of Inquiry, Telecommunications Relay Services, the Americans with Disabilities Act of 1990, and the Telecommunications Act of 1996, F.C.C. 97-7 (F.C.C. Jan. 14, 1997) (C.C. No. 90-571).

285 *In re* Federal-State Joint Bd. on Universal Serv., F.C.C. 97-157 ¶ 405 (F.C.C. May 8, 1997) (C.C. No. 96-45).

Groups such as the United Cerebral Palsy Association and NAD argued that the FCC's section 255 proceeding would not address services important to the consumers with disabilities such as toll-charge parity for TTY users, subsidies for specialized customer premises equipment or telecommuting costs.

286 47 U.S.C. § 225(b).

287 Report and Order, *In re* IP-Enabled Servs., Implementation of Sections 255 and 251(a)(2) of the Communications Act of 1934, As Enacted by the Telecommunications Act of 1996: Access to Telecommunications Serv., Telecommunications Equip. & Customer Premises Equipment by Persons with Disabilities Telecommunications Relay Servs. & Speech-to-Speech Servs. for Individuals with Hearing and Speech Disabilities, the Use of

Telecommunications carriers are required to provide telecommunications relay service (TRS).[288] Initially, TRS calls were made through text telephones (TTY) that connect to the Public Switched Telephone Network, the wireline network for phone calls. TRS has expanded with the introduction of new technologies. Video Relay Service and Internet Protocol (IP) Relay, which use the Internet, have been recognized by the FCC as forms of TRS.[289] IP Captioned Telephone Service (IP CTS) allows someone who can speak and has residual hearing to use a special telephone with a display that shows the text of what the caller is saying in addition to the transmission of the caller's voice.[290] The FCC has recently tentatively concluded that Speech-to-Speech relay service is a form of TRS that is eligible for compensation from the Interstate TRS Fund.[291] Speech-to-Speech relay service assists people with speaking disabilities through the use of a communications assistant who re-voices the conversation.

One critical issue with the Internet-based relay services is the ability of the callers to make emergency calls. While consumers using traditional TTY service can place a call directly to the appropriate public safety answering point (PSAP),[292] calls using a relay service are sent to a Communications Assistant who must place the call to the appropriate PSAP. Relay services using the Internet pose special challenges because of the current difficulty in identifying the location of the caller. In 2008, Congress passed the New and Emerging Technologies 911 Improvement Act of 2008 (Net 911 Improvement Act of 2008) amending the Wireless Communications and Public Safety Act by extending to IP-enabled voice providers the duty to provide 911 service and enhanced 911 service.[293] The Net 911 Improvement Act requires IP-enabled voice service providers to register with the FCC and establish a point of contact for public safety and government officials. It also provides that states may retain jurisdiction over emergency communications when state jurisdiction does not conflict with federal law or FCC requirements.[294]

The Telecommunications Act of 1996 sets forth specific provisions regarding access by persons with disabilities.[295] Manufacturers of telecommunications equipment or customer premises equipment, providers of telecommunications service,[296] "shall ensure that the equipment is designed, developed, and fabricated to be accessible to and usable by individuals with disabilities, if readily achievable."[297]

If the manufacturing of the equipment or the provision of service in a manner accessible and usable by individuals with disabilities is not readily achievable, there is also a compatibility requirement. The manufacturer or service provider is required under the Act to ensure that "the equipment or service is compatible with existing peripheral devices or specialized customer premises equipment commonly used by individuals with disabilities. . . ."[298]

The FCC rules implementing § 255 of the Telecommunications Act of 1996 cover all hardware and software telephone network equipment (the infrastructure for transmitting phone messages) and customer premises equipment (equipment in the home or office such as telephones, fax machines, and answering machines used to send, route, or receive telecommunications).[299] Basic telecommunications services such as local phone service and special telecommunications services such as call waiting and caller ID are also covered in the FCC rules.[300] The FCC recently ruled that anonymous-call rejection, call screening, and preferred call forwarding use the same technologies as caller ID so, when such features are provided by the local carrier and the TRS has the necessary technology, these services must also be offered to the TRS consumer.[301]

N11 Codes & Other Abbreviated Dialing Arrangements, F.C.C. 07-110 (F.C.C. June 15, 2007) (W.C. No. 04-36, W.T. No. 96-198, C.G. No. 03-123, C.C. No. 92-105).

288 47 U.S.C. § 225(c).

289 Improved TRS Order and Further Notice of Proposed Rule Making (F.C.C. Mar. 2000); IP Relay Declaratory Ruling and Further Notice of Proposed Rule Making (F.C.C. Apr. 2002); Report and Order, Order on Reconsideration & Further Notice of Proposed Rule Making, Telecommunications Relay Services and Speech-to-Speech Services for Individuals with Hearing and Speech Disabilities (F.C.C. June 2004).

290 Declaratory Ruling, *In re* Telecommunications Relay Servs., & Speech-to-Speech Servs. for Individuals with Hearing & Speech Disabilities, 18 F.C.C.R. 16121, F.C.C. 03-190 (F.C.C. Aug. 1, 2003) (C.C. No. 98-67); Declaratory Ruling, *In re* Telecommunications Relay Servs., & Speech-to-Speech Servs. for Individuals with Hearing & Speech Disabilities; Internet-Based Captioned Telephone Serv., 22 F.C.C.R. 379, F.C.C. 06-182 (F.C.C. Jan. 11, 2007) (C.G. No. 03-123).

291 Notice of Proposed Rulemaking, *In re* Telecommunications Relay Servs., & Speech-to-Speech Servs. for Individuals with Hearing & Speech Disabilities: Speech-to-Speech and Internet Protocol (IP) Speech-to-Speech Telecommunications Relay Serv., F.C.C. 08-149 (F.C.C. June 24, 2008) (C.G. No. 03-123, C.G. No. 08-15).

292 Title II of the ADA requires that PSAPs be capable of directly receiving TTY calls. *See also* 28 C.F.R. § 35.162.

293 Pub. L. No. 100-283, 122 Stat. 2620 (July 23, 2008).

294 *Id.*

295 47 U.S.C. § 255(a)(1) defines disability as having the same meaning given by § 12102(2)(a) of Title 42.

296 47 U.S.C. § 255(c).

297 47 U.S.C. § 255(b).

As stated in 47 U.S.C. § 255(a)(2). This section defines "readily achievable" as having the meaning given to it by § 12181(9) of Title 42.

298 47 U.S.C. § 255(d).

299 47 C.F.R. § 6.3.

300 47 C.F.R. § 6.3.

301 Report and Order, Order on Reconsideration and Further Notice of Proposed Rule Making, *In re* Telecommunications Relay Serv. & Speech-to-Speech Serv. for Individuals with Hearing & Speech Disabilities (F.C.C. June 2004).

11.5.2 Guidelines

The Architectural and Transportation Barriers Compliance Board, acting in conjunction with the FCC, is charged with developing and updating guidelines for the accessibility of telecommunications equipment and customer premises equipment.[302]

11.5.3 Enforcement of the Provisions Regarding Access by Persons with Disabilities

The Telecommunications Act of 1996 explicitly states that no additional private rights are being created by the provisions described below.[303] The Act also gives the FCC exclusive jurisdiction for complaints arising under this section.[304] Consumers can file a formal or informal complaint with the FCC about a manufacturer's or telecommunications provider's failure to make devices or services accessible or compatible as required under 47 U.S.C. § 255.[305]

11.6 Telephone Customer Service Issues

11.6.1 Deposits

For an in-depth analysis of a utility's right to collect deposits, see §§ 5.2 and 5.3, *supra*. The FCC has adopted a rule prohibiting telephone companies from charging service deposits to Lifeline customers who elect to use toll-blocking services.[306] The FCC made a distinction between service deposits and advanced payment requirements, noting that local phone companies can impose an advance payment requirement in the amount of one month's local charges. However, the FCC also indicated that amounts greater than one month of local charges would be considered improper.[307] Phone companies must wait until the consumer actually incurs the charges covered by the advanced payment before taking action against the consumer (for example, disconnection or collection efforts).[308] The FCC reasons the "[a]ssessing charges on consumers before any overdue payments are owed could make access to telecommunications services prohibitively expensive for low-income consumers."[309]

11.6.2 Shut-Offs

Chapter 6, *supra*, and Chapter 13, *infra*, discuss protections from utility shut-offs. However, with phone service it is still possible to combine billing for different telecommunications service providers—and, in some states, for non-telecommunication services—on the local phone bill. In addition, carriers market bundled packages services (for example, local, long-distance and vertical features). This raises concerns about the customer's ability to preserve access to basic local phone service in the case of underpayments.

As discussed earlier in this chapter, the Commission attempted to prohibit disconnection of local service for Lifeline customers due to nonpayment of toll charges.

The FCC notes that interstate billing and collection have been deregulated since 1986 and that the interstate long-distance market and the local telephone markets have been separated for over a decade.[310] Yet the local phone company "is the only toll charge collection agent that can offer the penalty of disconnecting a customer's *local* telephone service for nonpayment of other charges."[311] The FCC viewed this practice as a "vestige of the monopoly era" and thus prohibited its practice on Lifeline customers, since low-income consumers are most vulnerable to disconnection associated with the payment of long-distance charges.

The FCC left it to the states to extend the prohibition to other consumers.[312] It is important to note that the FCC was not attempting to prohibit *toll service* providers from disconnecting toll service for nonpayment. Nonetheless, as discussed earlier in this chapter, this federal prohibition was overturned on jurisdictional grounds in a recent Fifth Circuit case, *Texas Office of Public Utilities Counsel v. FCC*.[313] It is up to low-income advocates in each state to advocate for this protection at the state level.

302 47 U.S.C. § 255(e).

303 "Nothing in this section shall be construed to authorize any private right of action to enforce any requirement of this section or any regulation thereunder." 47 U.S.C. § 255(f).

304 47 U.S.C. § 255(f).

305 47 C.F.R. §§ 6.16–6.22.

306 47 C.F.R. § 54.401(c); *In re* Federal-State Joint Bd. on Universal Serv., F.C.C. 97-157 ¶¶ 398–402 (F.C.C. May 8, 1997) (C.C. No. 96-45).

The FCC responded to industry objections that limitation on deposits would not provide an incentive for customers to pay outstanding balances by stating: "We have been presented with no evidence, however, to suggest that a carrier would be less likely to charge service deposits to customers with bad payment histories who have paid their arrearages than to such customers who have not. Thus, it is unclear why allowing carriers to charge service deposits would provide customers with any more incentive to pay outstanding balances." *Id.* ¶ 400.

307 *In re* Federal-State Joint Bd. on Universal Serv., F.C.C. 97-157 ¶ 401 (F.C.C. May 8, 1997) (C.C. No. 96-45).

308 *Id.*

309 *Id.*

310 Report and Order, *In re* Detariffing of Billing and Collection Service, 102 F.C.C.2d 1150 (F.C.C. 1986) (C.C. No. 85-88).

311 *In re* Federal-State Joint Bd. on Universal Serv., F.C.C. 97-157 ¶ 391 (F.C.C. May 8, 1997) (C.C. No. 96-45).

312 *Id.* ¶ 392.

313 183 F.3d 393 (5th Cir. 1999).

There are states that have stepped forward to protect access to basic service in this evolving telecommunications landscape. For example, in Pennsylvania, charges for basic phone service must be billed separately from other services.[314] A customer's failure to pay non-basic service charges may not be grounds for termination of basic service unless it is not technically possible to terminate long-distance service without also terminating basic service.[315] When a customer has not provided written instructions regarding a partial payment, Pennsylvania rules have set out which services are to be paid first. When the payment is insufficient to cover telephone service and non-basic phone service (for example, inside wire maintenance plans, premise visit charges for installation), the payment shall first be applied to telephone service. When the funds are insufficient to cover telephone service, the payment shall first be applied to basic phone service.[316]

In North Carolina, local phone service that is provided in a bundle can be disconnected for failure to pay the total amount due. However, before the local service portion of the bundled service is disconnected, the phone company must give the customer the opportunity to retain local service by paying the amount past due for local service. This protection does not apply if the company does not offer local service on an unbundled basis.[317] Unless the customer has provided instructions otherwise, partial payments are first directed to local service and then to other services.[318]

West Virginia prohibits the inclusion of non-telecommunication services charges on a telephone bill absent express permission from the Commission. When non-communication charges have been approved, West Virginia prohibits the denial, interruption, or discontinuance of telecommunications service for nonpayment of a non-telecommunication service.[319] Basic phone service shall not be disconnected or interrupted for nonpayment of non-basic telecommunication service or non-communication services.[320]

11.6.3 Local Phone Company Collection of Long-Distance Bills As Covered by Fair Debt Collection Practices Act

When a local phone company collects delinquent debts owed to a long-distance carrier or other company using the local phone company's billing service, the question arises as to whether the local phone company is a debt collector within the meaning of the Fair Debt Collection Practices Act.[321] The statutory definition of debt collector includes any person "who regularly collects or attempts to collect, directly or indirectly, debts owed or due or asserted to be owed or due another" but exempts collection activity on "a debt which was not in default at the time it was obtained by such person."[322] The application of the Act will therefore depend upon the contractual arrangements between the local phone company and the long-distance carrier or other company using the local phone company's billing service.

The Seventh Circuit found that a local phone company's collection activities were exempt from the Act, when the local phone company purchased the accounts receivable of the long-distance carriers and pay-per-call services and included the amounts owed to these companies in the local phone company's monthly bill.[323] The court concluded that the local phone company acquired the debts "at the moment each telephone call is placed" and thus fell within the statutory exemption.

For more information on fair debt collection practices, see National Consumer Law Center's treatise, *Fair Debt Collection* (7th ed. 2011).

11.6.4 The Telephone Bill As a New Payment Mechanism

While local phone companies have traditionally allowed companies offering other telephone services—for example, long-distance service and 1-900 services—to use their billing systems, the local phone bill may emerge as a payment device for non-telephone-related services. West Virginia prohibits the inclusion of non-telecommunication services charges on a telephone bill absent express permission from the Commission. When non-communication charges have been approved, West Virginia prohibits the denial, interruption or, discontinuance of telecommunications service for nonpayment of a non-telecommunication service.[324] California's legislature passed a law that allows non-communication charges to appear on telephone bills starting July 1, 2001, subject to consumer protection rules adopted by the California Public Utilities Commission.[325] In the realm of

314 52 Pa. Code § 64.21.

315 *See* 52 Pa. Code §§ 64.63 (no suspension of basic service for nonpayment of non-basic charges), 64.121 (termination not authorized until ten days after an authorized suspension of service).

316 52 Pa. Code § 64.17.

317 4 N.C. Admin Code 11.R12-17(b).

318 4 N.C. Admin Code 11.R12-17(c).

319 W. Va. Code R. § 150-6-2.1(a)(1).

320 W. Va. Code R. § 150-6-2.4(e).

321 15 U.S.C. §§ 1692–1692p. *See* National Consumer Law Center, Fair Debt Collection (7th ed. 2011) (discussing debt collection in detail).

322 15 U.S.C. § 1692a.

323 Whitaker v. Ameritech Corp., 129 F.3d 952 (7th Cir. 1997). *See also* Whitaker v. Ameritech Corp., 1996 U.S. Dist. LEXIS 8573 (N.D. Ill. June 19, 1996) (describing contractual arrangements between Ameritech and long-distance companies).

324 W. Va. Code R. § 150-6-2.1(a)(1).

325 Cal. Pub. Util. Code § 2890 (West), *added to the code by* SB 378 (Stats. 1998, ch. 1041), *amended by* AB 1658 (Stats. 1999, ch. 1005), *and* AB 994 (Stats. 2000, ch. 931). *See also* Interim Opinion Adopting Interim Rules Governing the Inclusion of Noncommunications-Related Charges in Telephone Bills, Decision 01-07-030 (Cal. Pub. Util. Comm'n July 12, 2001).

telemarketing practices, there have been indications that telephone and utility companies are using their billing and collection systems for transactions involving other forms of goods and services.[326] These telemarketing practices are covered in the National Consumer Law Center's treatises, *Unfair and Deceptive Acts and Practices* (7th ed. 2008 and Supp.) and *Consumer Banking and Payments Law* (4th ed. 2009 and Supp.).

11.6.5 Overview of Unfair or Deceptive Telecommunications Practices

11.6.5.1 Slamming

11.6.5.1.1 Introduction

Slamming is the illegal practice of switching a customer's telephone service provider without that customer's knowledge or consent. A 2004 Federal Trade Commission survey estimates 13.9 million consumers experienced unauthorized long-distance carrier changes.[327] Most of the slamming activity has involved long-distance service, but this occurs with local telephone service providers, too.[328] Sometimes the unauthorized switch of long-distance service is due to a mistake by the local phone company. In these situations, the local phone companies are liable for slamming under the federal rules.[329]

The Federal Communications Commission (FCC) has jurisdiction over long-distance slamming when long-distance service crosses state lines.[330] The FCC issued a strong rule[331] that went into effect in April 1999 that prevents telephone companies from profiting from slamming (illegal switching of) customers and has since amended the rule several times to increase consumer protections.[332] The FCC's slamming rule is provided in Appendix B.3, *infra*.

Under the FCC's anti-slamming rule, customers who have not yet paid their bill and who call the unauthorized long-distance company must be told that they are not required to pay charges incurred during the first thirty days after the unauthorized switch.[333] Those customers that have already paid the unauthorized company are entitled to have 150% of that payment amount remitted to their authorized company and to have 50% of their payment returned.[334]

Consumers in a majority of states can turn to their state utility commissions for relief if their state commission has opted to administer the federal slamming rules.[335] If the state commission has not chosen to enforce the federal rules, the consumer can file an informal complaint with the Federal Communications Commission for the same remedies.[336]

11.6.5.1.2 Authorization verification requirements to switch long-distance service

Under the FCC anti-slamming rules, long-distance companies must obtain verification of a customer's authorization

326 67 Fed. Reg. 4492, 4495 (Jan. 30, 2002); National Ass'n of Attorneys Gen., Review of the Telemarketing Sales Rule—FTC file No. P994414, at 10 (May 30, 2000); FTC transcript, Telemarketing Sales Rule Forum, Matter No. P994414, vol. 1, 174–76 (July 27, 2000).

327 Keith B. Anderson, Consumer Fraud in the United States: An FTC Survey, FTC Staff Report (Aug. 2004).

328 In areas where customers can choose a local telephone company, the incumbent local phone company is sometimes referred to as the incumbent local exchange carrier (ILEC, pronounced "eye-leck") and the new entrants to the local phone market are referred to as competitive local exchange carriers (CLECs, pronounced "see-lecks"). The FCC's slamming order uses acronyms like LEC (for local exchange carriers or local phone companies) in addition to one for long-distance carriers, also called interexchange carriers (IXCs). See the FCC's recent order modifying the slamming rule, Third Order on Reconsideration and Second Further Notice of Proposed Rulemaking, *In re* Implementation of the Subscriber Carrier Selection Changes Provisions of the Telecommunications Act of 1996, Policies & Rules Concerning Unauthorized Changes of Consumers' Long Distance Carriers, F.C.C. 03-42 (F.C.C. Mar. 17, 2003) (C.C. No. 94-129).

329 47 C.F.R. §§ 64.1160(g), 64.1170(g), *amended by*, 68 Fed. Reg. 19152 (Apr. 18, 2003).

330 47 U.S.C. § 258 prohibits the slamming, and the FCC has implemented § 258 in 47 C.F.R. §§ 64.1100–64.1195, *amended by* 68 Fed. Reg. 19152 (Apr. 18, 2003).

331 47 C.F.R. §§ 64.1100–64.1195, *amended by* 68 Fed. Reg. 19152 (Apr. 18, 2003); 47 C.F.R. § 1.719; 66 Fed. Reg. 12877–12894 (Mar. 1, 2001); 65 Fed. Reg. 47678–47693 (Aug. 3, 2000); First Order on Reconsideration, *In re* Implementation of the Subscriber Carrier Selection Changes Provisions of the Telecommunications Act of 1996; Policies & Rules Concerning Unauthorized Changes of Consumer Long-Distance Carriers, F.C.C. 00-135 (F.C.C. May 3, 2000) (C.C. No. 94-129).

332 *See* National Consumer Law Center, Unfair and Deceptive Acts and Practices § 8.5.3.3 (7th ed. 2008 and Supp.) (additional information on slamming).

333 47 C.F.R. § 64.1140(b)(1). *See also* 47 C.F.R. § 64.1160.

In a recent order modifying the slamming rule, the FCC declined to modify the requirement that unauthorized carriers pay the authorized carrier 150% of the charges paid by the customer (who must then forward 50% of charges paid by the customer back to the customer). *See* 68 Fed. Reg. 19154 ¶ 9 (Apr. 18, 2003).

334 47 C.F.R. §§ 64.1140 (a), (b)(2), 64.1170(c).

335 47 C.F.R. § 64.1110. *See also* Letter from Bob Rowe, NARUC President, Joan Smith NARUC Chair, Telecommunications Committee, and Bob Gillis, NARUC Chairman, Consumer Affairs Committee to William E. Kennard, Chairman of the Federal Communications Commission (Apr. 6, 2000) (over thirty-five state utility commissions have committed to administering the federal slamming rules).

336 47 C.F.R. §§ 1.719 64.1150(b), *amended by* 68 Fed. Reg. 19152 (Apr. 18, 2003) (requirement that phone carrier contacted by subscriber about the slamming must direct consumer to state commission or FCC, whichever may be appropriate, and shall inform the consumer that he or she can seek resolution from the alleged unauthorized carrier and contact the authorized carrier).

to switch long-distance service.[337] There are three ways to verify a customer's authorization of a switch of long-distance service: through use of a Letter of Agency (LOA), which requires a customer's written or electronically signed authorization; electronic authorization, which must be placed from the subscriber's line at issue; and orally.[338] LOAs must not be combined on the same document, screen or web page with inducements of any kind and cannot contain any promotional language or material.[339] The LOA must be limited to authorizing/verifying a switch and must make clear that it is authorizing a switch of long-distance companies.[340]

The Letter of Agency must include:

- The subscriber's billing name and address;[341]
- Each phone number to be covered by the switch;[342]
- A statement of intent to change long-distance companies;[343]
- A statement that the subscriber designates this new company to act as the agent for this change;[344] and
- A statement that the subscriber understands that only one telecommunications carrier can be designated as the subscribers long-distance company for any one number and that, if other types of long-distance service are involved (for example, international service), a separate statement must be made for each of those additional services.[345]
- A statement that the subscriber can ask the carrier whether there is a fee to switch.[346]

The language of the LOA must be clear and unambiguous and in easy to read print and must include full translations if there is more than one language used.[347] The carrier designated in the LOA as the preferred carrier must be the long-distance company directly setting the rates.[348]

Promotions that use checks are exempt from the requirement that LOA language be separate from prizes, contests or other inducements.[349] However, there must also be notice in easy-to-read print on the front of the check that the consumer is authorizing a change of long-distance company.[350] The regular LOA language listed above must also appear near the signature line at the back of the check.[351]

Other forms of verification of customer-initiated switches include electronic authorization (for example, customer calls a toll-free number established for the exclusive purpose of confirming customer's authority to switch carriers) and independent third-party verification.[352] The FCC LOA rules also prohibit "welcome package" opt-out tactics that require customers to act to avoid being switched.[353]

The FCC slamming rules also require verification of a customer's authorization to switch.[354] Phone companies can use the procedure laid out for LOAs.[355] In the case of electronic authorization, the phone company can verify the authorization electronically but must establish toll-free lines exclusively for that purpose.[356] Oral authorizations require verifications by independent third parties.[357] Phone companies must give the customer the option of using any of the authorization and verification procedures described.[358]

11.6.5.1.3 Procedures for resolving a slamming dispute

If the consumer receives one bill for local and long-distance service, they should first contact the local telephone company to notify it of the unauthorized switch in long-distance companies and that the "change charges" for the unauthorized switch, if any, should be removed from the bill. When reporting the slam to any of the phone companies involved, the customer must identify the authorized phone company and the unauthorized phone company.[359]

In all cases, it is a good idea for the consumer to contact the originally authorized long-distance company to report the slam and ask to be reinstated to the same calling plan they had before the slam. Under the federal slamming rules, the slammer is liable to the customer for this switching charge.[360] Next, the consumer should contact the unauthorized long-distance company (the slammer) to remove all charges within thirty days of the switch per the Federal Communications Commission (FCC) rule discussed *infra*.

All the phone service providers involved in the slamming dispute, once notified by a consumer of an unauthorized change in phone companies, are required to direct the consumer to the state utility commission if the state has opted to administer the federal rules or to the FCC for resolution of the complaint if the state has not opted to

337 47 C.F.R. § 64.1120(a). *But see* AT&T Corp. v. Federal Commc'ns Comm'n, 323 F.3d 1081 (D.C. Cir. 2003) (court of appeals held that FCC exceeded its authority by requiring carriers to guarantee that the actual account customer authorized the carrier switch).
338 47 C.F.R. §§ 64.1120(c), 64.1130.
339 47 C.F.R. § 64.1130 (b)–(d).
340 47 C.F.R. § 64.1130(b), (e).
341 47 C.F.R. § 64.1130(e)(1).
342 47 C.F.R. § 64.1130(e)(1).
343 47 C.F.R. § 64.1130(e)(2).
344 47 C.F.R. § 64.1130(e)(3).
345 47 C.F.R. § 64.1130(e)(4).
346 47 C.F.R. § 64.1130(e)(5).
347 47 C.F.R. § 64.1130(e), (h).
348 47 C.F.R. § 64.1130(f).
349 47 C.F.R. § 64.1130(d).
350 47 C.F.R. § 64.1130(d).
351 47 C.F.R. § 64.1130(d).
352 47 C.F.R. § 64.1120(c)(2), (3).
353 47 C.F.R. § 64.1130(g).
354 47 C.F.R. § 64.1120.
355 47 C.F.R. § 64.1120(c)(1).
356 47 C.F.R. § 64.1120(c)(2).
357 47 C.F.R. § 64.1120(c)(3), *amended by* 68 Fed. Reg. 19152 (Apr. 18, 2003) (removes the requirement that the customer identify the long-distance provider that will be replaced).
358 47 C.F.R. § 64.1120(d).
359 47 C.F.R. § 64.1150(a).
360 47 C.F.R. § 64.1140(b)(3).

enforce the federal rules.[361] The FCC recently added another requirement that these phone service providers inform the consumer that he or she may contact and seek resolution from the unauthorized phone company (the slammer) and may also contact the authorized phone company.[362]

In order to receive the protections and remedies under the federal slamming rule, the consumer must then file a complaint with the state utility commission if the state has opted to administer the federal rules. When the state utility commission has not opted to administer the federal slamming rules, the consumer can file an informal complaint with the FCC to obtain the same remedies.[363] As discussed in § 11.6.5.1.5, the FCC has made an initial effort to make it easier to file a complaint. Note, the FCC will not act on a complaint that has been filed concurrently with a state commission.[364] The state commission or the FCC will then investigate, make a determination about whether there was an authorized switch in phone companies and, when a slam is found, order the proper remedy.[365]

Once the appropriate agency has received a slamming complaint, the unauthorized long-distance company must remove all unpaid charges for the first thirty days after the alleged unauthorized switch while the appropriate agency conducts its investigation.[366] The burden is on the alleged unauthorized long-distance company to provide *clear and convincing* evidence that the switch was authorized.[367]

Outside of the slamming procedures pursuant to the federal slamming rule, a district court in Connecticut, in refusing to dismiss a class action slamming case, found that the federal slamming law, 47 U.S.C. § 258, coupled with 47 U.S.C. § 207 (which, along with section § 206, allows persons injured by common carriers to seek redress by filing a complaint with the FCC or bringing suit in district court), provided a private right of action in cases involving unauthorized switching of long-distance service.[368]

361 47 C.F.R. § 64.1150(b), *amended by* 68 Fed. Reg. 19152 (Apr. 18, 2003).

362 47 C.F.R. § 64.1150, *amended by* 68 Fed. Reg. 19152 (Apr. 18, 2003).

363 47 C.F.R. § 1.718. *See* www.fcc.gov/slamming (listing the states that are handling slamming complaints pursuant to the federal rule).

Contact the state's utility commission's consumer division listed in Appendix A.8, *infra*, or the state's attorney general's office for appropriate procedures for filing a slamming complaint.

364 47 C.F.R. § 64.1150(e).

365 47 C.F.R. § 64.1150(d).

366 47 C.F.R. § 64.1150(c).

367 47 C.F.R. § 64.1150(d).

368 Valdes v. Qwest Commc'ns Int'l, 147 F. Supp. 2d 116 (D. Conn. 2001) (applying the *Cort* test, 422 U.S. 66 (1975), and limited Conboy v. AT&T, 241 F.3d 242 (2d Cir. 2001), to different regulations at issue in that case).

11.6.5.1.4 Filing a complaint with the state utility commission

Under the Federal Communications Commission's slamming rules, the state utility commissions have the option of administering the federal rules for slamming. The state commissions must file their administrative procedures with the FCC and also notify the FCC if they opt to stop administering the federal slamming rule.[369] Pursuant to the FCC's slamming rule, "any carrier, executing, authorized, or allegedly unauthorized," once notified by a customer of a slam, must direct that customer to either the state commission or the FCC for resolution of the complaint.[370] Almost three-quarters of the states have opted to administer the federal slamming rules: Alabama, Arkansas, California, Colorado, Connecticut, Florida, Idaho, Indiana, Iowa, Kansas, Kentucky, Louisiana, Maine, Maryland, Massachusetts, Michigan, Minnesota, Mississippi, Montana, Nebraska, Nevada, New Hampshire, New Jersey, New York, North Carolina, North Dakota, Ohio, Oklahoma, Oregon, South Carolina, South Dakota, Tennessee, Texas, Utah, Vermont, Washington, and Wyoming as well as the District of Columbia and Puerto Rico.[371] If the slam occurred in District of Columbia, Puerto Rico, or one of the thirty-seven states that have opted to handle slamming complaints pursuant to the federal rule, contact your state's utility commission or attorney general.

When states have not opted to administer the FCC's slamming rule, consumers may file a complaint with the FCC. Instructions are provided in § 11.6.5.1.5, *infra*.

11.6.5.1.5 Filing a complaint with the FCC

In order to get the relief available under the federal slamming rule, complaints to the FCC must be in writing.[372] The FCC has altered their informal complaint process to be able to provide the remedies available under the slamming rule. If the consumer is not satisfied with the FCC's resolution of the informal complaint, the consumer can file a formal complaint pursuant to 47 C.F.R. §§ 1.720–1.736 with the FCC.[373]

There is no fee to file an informal complaint with the FCC. Consumer may submit a slamming complaint to the FCC by e-mail, fax, or regular mail. The FCC has set up an

369 47 C.F.R. § 64.1110.

370 47 C.F.R. § 64.1150(b), *amended by* 68 Fed. Reg. 19152 (Apr. 18, 2003) (adds a requirement that any phone carrier contacted about the slamming also tell the consumer that he or she can contact and seek resolution from the alleged unauthorized carrier (the slammer) and can contact the authorized carrier).

371 For an updated list, visit the FCC's website at www.fcc.gov/slamming for information on filing a slamming complaint. The FCC's website also links to state slamming complaint websites.

372 47 C.F.R. § 1.719(b).

373 47 C.F.R. § 1.719(d).

e-mail address for informal slamming complaints (slamming@fcc.gov). Consumers must provide the information set out below, but note that, unless the consumer has an electronic copy of the disputed bill or an electronic version of a welcome letter or package showing the name of the alleged unauthorized carrier and the disputed changes, the consumer will need to submit the informal complaint in writing to the following address:

Federal Communications Commission
Consumer and Governmental Affairs Bureau
ATTN: Slam Team, Room CY A257
445 12th Street, S.W.
Washington, DC 20554
Fax: 202-418-0035
E-mail for complaints: slamming@fcc.gov

Written FCC informal slamming complaints must contain the following information:[374]

- Consumer's name, address, telephone number, and e-mail address (if available)
- Phone number(s) involved in the slamming
- Name of the unauthorized long-distance company
- Name of the authorized long-distance company
- Name of the authorized local phone company
- Complete statement of facts showing that the alleged unauthorized long-distance company switched the consumer's long-distance service without permission (include copies of any documentation—for example, phone bills, contest materials, promotions, "checks"—but, unless the consumer has an electronic copy of the disputed bill, the complaint must be filed in writing with a paper copy of the bill attached)
- Statement of whether the consumer paid any of the disputed charges to the alleged unauthorized long-distance service
- The specific relief sought (see § 11.6.5.2, *infra*, for a description of remedies)

The FCC also has an on-line form for slamming complaints, Form 501. It can be accessed at the FCC's website at www.fcc.gov/complaints (see wired telephone complaints). For informal complaints submitted on-line, the FCC specifically requires a few additional pieces of information: the amount of the disputed charge and a copy of any bill about which the complaint is brought.

The state commission or FCC will then issue an order informing the unauthorized phone company, the authorized phone company, and the customer about the agency's findings and the appropriate remedy, if any.[375]

For more information, consumers can call their state's utility commission's consumer division.[376]

374 47 C.F.R. § 1.719(b).
375 47 C.F.R. §§ 64.1150, 1.719(c).
376 *See* appx. A.8, *infra*.

11.6.5.2 Remedies Under the Federal Slamming Rule

11.6.5.2.1 If the consumer has not paid the unauthorized long-distance company[377]

Upon notification by the customer of an unauthorized switch in phone service providers, the alleged unauthorized carrier must remove the first thirty days of charges from the customer's bill while the appropriate agency investigates the slamming allegation.[378] Once the appropriate agency determines that there has been an unauthorized switch in long-distance service, the consumer who has not yet paid any of the disputed charges is absolved of charges incurred during the first thirty days with the unauthorized long-distance service.[379] Neither the authorized nor the unauthorized phone company can pursue collection against the customer for these charges.[380]

If there are charges incurred after the first thirty days with the unauthorized long-distance service, the unauthorized phone company must forward the bill to the consumer's authorized long-distance service. The authorized long-distance service may then bill the consumer what it would have charged for that additional long-distance use[381] or 50% of the unauthorized company's charges for that additional period.[382] After the unauthorized switch, if the consumer paid the unauthorized carrier for services provided after the first thirty days, the rights and remedies of 47 C.F.R. § 64.1170 apply (described in § 11.6.5.2.2, *infra*).

11.6.5.2.2 If the consumer has already paid the unauthorized long-distance company[383]

Once the appropriate agency determines that there has been an unauthorized switch and the consumer has already paid for the unauthorized long-distance company, the unauthorized company is prohibited from benefiting from the illegal practice of slamming. Under the federal rules, the unauthorized long-distance company must forward to the authorized long-distance company 150% of the charges paid by the consumer and copies of the unauthorized company's

Consumers can call the state utility commission's consumer division or the FCC's toll free information line at 1-888-CALL-FCC (1-888-225-5322). The TTY number is 1-888-TELL-FCC (1-888-835-5322).

377 47 C.F.R. §§ 64.1160–64.1195.
378 47 C.F.R. § 64.1160(b).
379 47 C.F.R. § 64.1160(d).
380 47 C.F.R. § 64.1160(d).
381 47 C.F.R. § 64.1160(e)(1).
382 47 C.F.R. § 64.1160(e)(2) (customers can reject this and require a calculation under the authorized carrier's rates).
383 47 C.F.R. § 64.1170–.1170(g), *amended by* 68 Fed. Reg. 19154 (Apr. 18, 2003).

phone bills to that consumer.[384] The authorized long-distance company must refund or credit the consumer 50% of the charges paid to the unauthorized company.[385] The consumer also has the right to have the authorized company re-rate the unauthorized carrier's charges based on the authorized company's rates and, to the extent the re-rated amount exceeds the 50% paid by the consumer, the authorized company, on behalf of the consumer, can seek this additional amount from the slamming company.[386] Note, if the unauthorized company fails to pay the authorized company the consumer is not entitled to receive any refund from the authorized long-distance company.[387] When the unauthorized company fails to pay, the authorized company must inform the agency that issued the slamming order and inform the consumer of his or her right to pursue a claim against the slamming company for a refund.[388] When the unauthorized switch of long-distance service is due to a mistake by the local phone company, the local phone company is liable for the reimbursement under the federal rules.[389]

When possible, and regardless of whether the unauthorized company has forwarded 150% of the paid charges to the authorized company, the authorized phone company must return the consumer to his or her original long-distance calling plan, with any premiums that the consumer would have been entitled to but for the unauthorized switch.[390] These federal remedies are in addition to any appropriate state remedies.[391]

11.6.5.3 Preventive Measures

The FCC anti-slamming rules also allow customers to "freeze" their existing long-distance company through the local phone company.[392] Since freezing accounts with a particular phone company also invites anti-competition abuses, the FCC requires solicitations for such freezes to be clear and include instructions to lifting the freeze. Local phone companies offering preferred carrier freezes must do so in the following manner:[393]

- Offer the freeze on a nondiscriminatory basis to all customers;[394]
- Distinguish the types of phone services subject to a freeze and require a separate authorization in any solicitations and company freeze procedures for each service that is frozen;[395]
- In solicitations and other materials about preferred carrier freezes, provide a clear and neutral explanation of the preferred carrier freeze and which services could be subject to a freeze, a description of how to lift the freeze, and a description of any charges for the freeze;[396] and
- Use authorization and verification procedures similar to those set out in the rule to authorize and verify a change of phone service provider.[397]

A consumer wishing to "freeze" his or her long-distance service should contact the local phone company for instructions.

11.6.5.4 State Slamming Protections

States may have separate verification procedures for intrastate change orders.[398] States may also have additional remedies when a customer has already paid an unauthorized long-distance provider[399] If clients in your state have a choice of local telephone service, you may see the emergence of such slamming cases. Contact the state public utility commissioner's office to see if your state has separate slamming protections.[400] Under Kansas's slamming statute, a customer was awarded $12,500 in statutory penalties and attorney fees (which includes the cost of the appeal).[401] Information on state public utility commissioners is listed in Appendix A.8, *infra*. A state's unfair and deceptive acts and practices law may also be applicable when slamming has occurred.[402] For more information on using state unfair and

384 47 C.F.R. § 64.1170(b).
In an order modifying the slamming rule, the FCC declined to modify the requirement that unauthorized carriers pay the authorized carrier 150% of the charges paid by the customer (who must then forward 50% of charges paid by the customer back to the customer). *See* 68 Fed. Reg. 19154 ¶ 9 (Apr. 18, 2003).

385 47 C.F.R. § 64.1170(c).

386 47 C.F.R. § 64.1170(c).

387 47 C.F.R. § 64.1170(e).

388 47 C.F.R. § 64.1170(e).

389 47 C.F.R. §§ 64.1160(g), 64.1170(g), *amended by* 68 Fed. Reg. 19152 (Apr. 18, 2003).

390 47 C.F.R. § 64.1170(f).

391 47 C.F.R. § 64.1170(b).

392 47 C.F.R. § 64.1190.

393 47 C.F.R. § 64.1190.

394 47 C.F.R. § 64.1190(b).

395 47 C.F.R. § 64.1190(c).

396 47 C.F.R. § 64.1190(d)(1).

397 47 C.F.R. § 64.1190(d)(2).

398 47 C.F.R. § 64.1120(c)(4).

399 47 C.F.R. § 64.1170(b).

400 *See, e.g.*, Ala. Code § 8-19B-1; Ark. Code Ann. §§ 4-88-401 to 4-88-403; Cal. Pub. Util. Code § 2889.5 (West); 220 Ill. Comp. Stat. 5/13-902; 815 Ill. Comp. Stat. 505/2DD; Kan. Stat. Ann. § 50-6,103 (slamming protections in the Kansas Consumer Protection Act); Mich. Comp. Laws § 484.2505.

401 Doty v. Frontier Commc'ns, Inc., 36 P.3d 250 (Kan. 2001). *See also* CEO Commc'ns, Inc. v. Michigan Pub. Serv. Comm'n, 2002 WL 992065 (Mich. Ct. App. May 10, 2002) (affirming compensatory damages award of $10,000 and separate fines of $20,000 and $19,400).

402 *See* F.C.C. Staff Opinion letter to David Gilles, Assistant Attorney General, State of Wisconsin, 13 F.C.C.R. 15344 (Aug. 12, 1998) (staff's opinion that FCC slamming rules do not preempt state consumer protection statutes and regulations designed to protect consumers from deceptive practices related to the marketing of telecommunications services).

deceptive practices laws, see National Consumer Law Center's treatise, *Unfair and Deceptive Acts and Practices* (7th ed. 2008 and Supp.).

11.6.5.5 Cramming

Cramming is the illegal practice of placing unauthorized, misleading or deceptive charges on a phone bill.[403] Cramming is often hard to detect because phone bills are difficult to decipher due to the multitude of federal and state bottom-of-the-bill charges and the fact that the local phone company often provides billing services for other telecommunications companies. The FCC reports that, in two separate investigations, each including over 17,000 consumers, only 0.1% actually used the third-party service or dial-around long-distance service they were being charged for.[404] While cramming is one of the most common landline complaints to the FCC, only a small portion of victims become aware of cramming charges.[405]

The FCC issued a Truth in Billing rule to make phone bills easier to decipher.[406] The rule requires phone bills to contain toll-free numbers for billing inquiries regarding the particular charges on the bill.[407] Phone bills must also be clearly organized with the name of the service provider associated with each charge; the bill must separate the charges according to the different service providers, and the phone bill must clearly and conspicuously identify as new any change in service providers from the last bill and any charges from a new service provider.[408] Phone bills must include clear and non-misleading descriptions of the billed charges[409] and must clearly identify charges for which nonpayment will result in disconnection of local phone service.[410]

On June 16, 2011, the FCC Enforcement Bureau issued "notices of apparent liability," totaling $11.7 million, to four companies for charging consumers a variety of small amounts—ranging from $1.99 to $19.99—every month over a period of months to years for long-distance calls that these consumers did not make.[411]

On July 12, 2011, the FCC proposed cramming rules that would require providers who offer third-party call-blocking services to inform their customers of this option. The proposed rules would also provide that all third-party charges must be separated from landline charges, strengthening existing Truth in Billing rules.[412]

It is a deceptive practice for a company to represent that telephone subscribers are legally obligated to pay billed charges whether or not they used or authorized use of the calls.[413] It is even deceptive for a company to bill the subscriber, without further representation, when it knows there is a high probability that the person initiating the call was not authorized to make the call.[414]

When a tariff and the filed rate doctrine does not apply to telephone services, there is no legal basis to require that subscribers to a phone line pay for services they did not use or authorize.[415] To even charge to the line subscriber, instead of the actual user, for such services is an unfair practice.[416]

For more detailed discussion about using a state's unfair and deceptive acts and practices law to address cramming, see section 9.7.3 of National Consumer Law Center, *Unfair and Deceptive Acts and Practices* (7th ed. 2008 and Supp.).

11.6.5.6 Pay-per-Call or 1-900 Numbers

11.6.5.6.1 General

Consumers can easily accumulate unaffordable charges on their phone bills by using expensive pay-per-call or 1-900 services. Congress passed the Telephone Disclosure and Dispute Resolution Act to protect consumers from abusive pay-per-call services.[417] The Federal Communications Commission and the Federal Trade Commission have written pay-per-call (also called 1-900) regulations pursuant to the Telephone Disclosure and Dispute Resolution Act of 1992.[418] The FCC's regulations[419] focus on the telephone

403 *See, e.g.*, Brown v. SBC Commc'ns, Inc., 2007 WL 684133 (S.D. Ill. Mar. 1, 2007); Micronet, Inc. v. Indiana Util. Regulatory Comm'n, 866 N.E.2d 278 (Ind. Ct. App. 2007) (directory assistance service).

404 Joel Guerin, Consumer and Governmental Affairs Bureau, *Unauthorized Fees: What's Hiding in Your Phone Bill?* (July 12th, 2011), www.fcc.gov/blog/unauthorized-fees-whats-hiding-your-phone-bill (official FCC blog).

405 *Id.*

406 47 C.F.R. §§ 64.2400–64.2401.

407 47 C.F.R. § 64.2401(d).

408 47 C.F.R. § 64.2401(a).

409 47 C.F.R. § 64.2401(b). *See* Beattie v. CenturyTel, Inc., 234 F.R.D. 160 (E.D. Mich. 2006) (charging for optional inside wire maintenance insurance under the heading "non-regulated services" constituted unreasonable practice; however, bills charging for "Inside Wire Maintenance Plan" complied with law), *aff'd and remanded in part on other grounds*, 511 F.3d 554 (6th Cir. 2007).

410 47 C.F.R. § 64.2401(c).

411 Press Release, Federal Commc'ns Comm'n, FCC to Crammers: No More Mystery Fees (June 16, 2010), *available at* www.fcc.gov/document/fcc-crammers-no-more-mystery-fees.

412 Joel Guerin, Consumer and Governmental Affairs Bureau, *Unauthorized Fees: What's Hiding in Your Phone Bill?* (July 12th, 2011), www.fcc.gov/blog/unauthorized-fees-whats-hiding-your-phone-bill (official FCC blog).

413 FTC v. Verity Int'l, Ltd., 124 F. Supp. 2d 193 (S.D.N.Y. 2000).

414 *Id.*

415 *Id.*

416 *Id.*

417 Pub. L. No. 102-556, § 1, 106 Stat. 4181 (1992), *codified at* 15 U.S.C. §§ 5701–5724.

418 Pub. L. No. 102-556, 106 Stat. 4181 (1992) (15 U.S.C. §§ 5701–5724).

419 47 U.S.C. § 228; 47 C.F.R. § 64.1501.

company's behavior while the Federal Trade Commission's regulations[420] focus on the behavior of the pay-per-call provider. The 1-900 legislation and implementing regulations are reprinted in Appendix B.4, *infra.*

1-900 (pay-per-call) numbers are different than toll-free numbers (for example, 1-800 and other toll free numbers). 1-900 services provide information, entertainment and other services at a cost greater than the mere cost of the call.[421] The term excludes directory assistance services provided by the phone companies.[422] Pay-per-call services covered by federal law are limited to 1-900 numbers.[423] Some examples of 1-900 services include chat lines, psychic hotlines, and adult entertainment lines. The 1-900-service companies are also called "information providers" (IPs) and they often provide their services through long-distance companies. Sometimes IPs use a service bureau as a middleman to handle transmission and billing services with the long-distance company. Also, if the 1-900 service advertises that ordinary toll rates apply, the IP's long-distance rates could be much higher than the customer's regular long-distance rates. Furthermore, 1-900 calls to a foreign country could end up in another part of the phone bill, possibly as an international long-distance call, but the call is still a 1-900 call and the rights and remedies for 1-900 calls apply.

11.6.5.6.2 Some key pay-per-call protections in the regulation of phone companies offering pay-per-call services

The authorizing legislation and the implementing regulations in the area of pay-per-call services provide the following consumer protections:

- Phone companies cannot disconnect or interrupt a customer's local or long-distance service because of nonpayment of charges for any interstate pay-per-call service.[424]
- 1-900 charges must be separated from other local and long-distance charges on a bill and the bill must contain information on certain consumer rights such as the right not to be disconnected for nonpayment of 1-900 charges.[425]
- Phone companies shall prohibit the use of any 1-800 telephone number or other number advertised or widely understood to be toll free[426] in a way that results in:
  - a pay-per-call charge for merely completing the call;[427]
  - connection to a pay-per-call service;[428]
  - a return collect call for information to conversation services;[429] or
  - a charge "by virtue of being asked to connect or otherwise transfer to a pay-per-call service."[430]

There are some limited exceptions for written agreements and charges by credit, prepaid, debit, charge or calling cards.[431] The implementing regulations also have additional limitations for: calls using telecommunication devices for the deaf; directory services; the purchase of goods and services that are not information services; and the use of a bypass mechanism for repeat callers.[432]

11.6.5.6.3 Blocking requirement

Phone companies that provide local service shall offer, when technically feasible, complete or limited pay-per-call blocking options for free to new subscribers or otherwise at a reasonable fee.[433] Requests to remove 900-blocking must be in writing.[434]

11.6.5.6.4 Disclosure requirement

Pay-per-call services must provide an introductory disclosure that describes the service, the cost, and fees for the call; explains that the charges begin after the introductory message; and allows the caller to hang up before the end of the introductory message without incurring charges.[435] Pay-per-call services must also inform the caller if the service is providing information about federal programs, but the service is not expressly authorized by a federal agency to provide this information.[436] Phone companies assigning a 1-900 number to an interstate pay-per-call service must provide, for free, a list of pay-per-call numbers it carries with a brief description of each service and cost and fees for service, when asked for this information.[437] Phone companies providing billing and collecting services are also re-

420 15 U.S.C. § 5711; 16 C.F.R. § 308.5.
421 47 C.F.R. § 64.1501(a).
422 47 C.F.R. § 64.1501(a)(4).
423 47 C.F.R. §§ 64.1501(a)(3), 64.1506.
424 47 U.S.C. § 228(c)(4); 47 C.F.R. § 64.1507.
425 47 U.S.C. § 228(d)(2); 47 C.F.R. § 64.1510(a)(2).
426 15 U.S.C.§ 5711(a)(2)(F); 47 U.S.C. § 228(c)(7); 47 C.F.R. § 64.1504; 16 C.F.R. § 308.5(i).
427 47 U.S.C. § 228(c)(7)(a); 47 C.F.R. § 64.1504(a); 16 C.F.R. § 308.5(i)(1).
428 47 U.S.C. § 228(c)(7)(b); 47 C.F.R. § 64.1504(b); 16 C.F.R. § 308.5(i)(2).
429 47 U.S.C. § 228(c)(7)(d); 47 C.F.R. § 64.1504(d); 16 C.F.R. § 308.5(i)(4).
430 47 U.S.C. § 228(c)(e); 47 C.F.R. § 64.1504(e).
431 47 U.S.C. § 228(c)(7)(c); 47 C.F.R. § 64.1504(c)(1), (2); 16 C.F.R. § 308.5(i)(3).
432 47 C.F.R. § 64.1504(f).
433 47 U.S.C. § 228(c)(5); 47 C.F.R. § 64.1508.
434 47 C.F.R. 64.1508(b).
435 15 U.S.C. § 5711(a)(2); 16 C.F.R. § 308.5.
436 15 U.S.C. § 5711(a)(2); 16 C.F.R. § 308.5.
437 47 U.S.C. § 228(c)(2); 47 C.F.R. § 64.1509(a).

quired to disclose the subscriber's rights.[438] Entities offering pay-per-call service must make disclosures regarding costs and the chances of receiving a prize in advertisements and at the beginning of a call and must allow the consumer to hang up with no charge after the introductory disclosures.[439] They must also disclose an alternate free way of entering any game of chance or sweepstakes.[440] They cannot direct advertisements at children under age 12 except for bona fide educational products.[441] Advertisements directed to children under age 18 are allowed but must include a warning that parental permission is necessary for any calls.[442]

11.6.5.6.5 Remedies

Nonpayment of 900-number charges is the simplest and most effective remedy for 900-number fraud. Some consumers may have already paid these charges, however, and may have difficulty recovering the money from fly-by-night 900-number providers. Phone companies are responsible for ensuring that procedures are in place to forgive, refund, or credit charges that violate federal law or the FCC's or FTC's rules.[443] If the phone company also provides billing and collecting services, it has the discretion to make these determinations.[444] Carriers are, however, required to forgive the debt and refund any payment if the FTC, the FCC, or a court finds that the 900-number service violated the federal law or regulations.[445] The FCC can impose sanctions or penalties for violations of the regulations.[446] However, phone companies are not criminally or civilly liable solely because they provide transmission, billing, and collection for a pay-per-call, unless the companies reasonably should have known the service was in violation of the pay-per-call laws.[447] Telephone companies must require that providers of pay-per-call service comply with the statute and must terminate them if they violate it.[448] FCC regulations also forbid a telephone company from billing consumers for pay-per-call services that the telephone company knows or has reason to know violate the regulations.[449] The FTC, the FCC, and state consumer protection officials all have enforcement authority under the federal law.[450] The FTC has filed a number of actions to enforce its rule.[451]

Many state 900-number laws have criminal as well as civil penalties, and many state attorney general offices have given priority to fighting 900-number fraud. Consumers should be encouraged to report 900-number fraud to law enforcement officials and state consumer protection authorities. Not only may the consumer benefit through a restitution order, but information about telephone fraud helps law enforcement authorities locate and prosecute fraudulent providers.

11.6.5.7 State Laws Regulating 1-900 Numbers

The federal pay-per-call law clearly states that other consumer protection laws and complementary state laws are not preempted.[452] While the Act does not give consumers a private cause of action, it should be clear that its standards are enforceable through state UDAP laws.[453]

A number of states have enacted statutes to protect consumers from abusive 900-number practices.[454] In other states,

438 47 U.S.C. § 228(d); 47 C.F.R. § 64.1509(b).

439 15 U.S.C. § 5711(a)(1), (2); 16 C.F.R. §§ 308.3, 308.5. *See* FTC v. Career Info. Serv., 1996 U.S. Dist. LEXIS 21207, 1996-2 Trade Cas. (CCH) ¶ 71,468 (N.D. Ga. June 21, 1996) (issuing preliminary injunction prohibiting pay-per-call service from failing to make required disclosures).

440 16 C.F.R. § 308.3(c).

441 15 U.S.C. § 5711(a)(1)(D); 15 U.S.C. § 5711(a)(2)(c); 16 C.F.R. §§ 308.3(e), 308.5(h).

Even before the 900-number federal legislation, the FTC had accepted a series of consent orders dealing with companies pitching 1-900 numbers to children, offering free gifts and stories, without encouraging parental supervision. Consent Order, Fone Telecommunications, 116 F.T.C. 426 (FTC 1993), 5 Trade Reg. Rep. (CCH) ¶ 23,348 (F.T.C. No. C-3432) (Mar. 17, 1993); Consent Order, *In re* Phone Programs, 115 F.T.C. 977, 1992 FTC LEXIS 298, 5 Trade Reg. Rep. (CCH) ¶ 23,259 (1992); Consent Order, *In re* Teleline, 114 F.T.C. 399, 1991 FTC LEXIS 339, 1991 FTC LEXIS 403 (1991); Consent Order, *In re* Audio Commc'ns, 114 F.T.C. 414, 1991 FTC LEXIS 341, 1991 FTC LEXIS 405 (1991).

442 15 U.S.C. § 5711(a)(1)(E), (a)(2)(c); 16 C.F.R. §§ 308.3(f), 308.5(a)(4).

For examples of 900-number fraud directed at children and the FTC's approach to the problem prior to the current regulations, see Consent Order, *In re* Phone Programs, 115 F.T.C. 977, 1992 FTC LEXIS 298 (1992); Consent Order, *In re* Teleline, 114 F.T.C. 399, 1991 FTC LEXIS 339, 1991 FTC LEXIS 403 (1991); Consent Order, *In re* Audio Commc'ns, 114 F.T.C. 414, 1991 FTC LEXIS 341, 1991 FTC LEXIS 405 (1991).

443 47 U.S.C. § 228(f); 47 C.F.R. § 64.1511(a).

444 47 U.S.C. § 228(f); 47 C.F.R. § 64.1511.

445 47 U.S.C. § 228(f); 47 C.F.R. § 64.1511(a).

446 47 U.S.C. § 228(e).

447 *Id.*

448 47 U.S.C. § 228(c)(3); 47 C.F.R. §§ 64.1502, 64.1503(b).

449 47 U.S.C. § 228(d); 47 C.F.R. § 64.1510.

450 15 U.S.C. §§ 5712–5713, 5723; 47 U.S.C. § 228(b).

451 Proposed Consent Order, FTC v. Gannett Satellite Info. Network, Inc., 5 Trade Reg. Rep. (CCH) ¶ 23,898 (E.D. Va. 1995); American TelNet, Inc., 5 Trade Reg. Rep. (CCH) ¶ 23,723 (S.D. Fla. 1994) (proposed consent decree against service bureau that switched callers from a 1-800 number to a 1-900 number and did not make the required price disclosures); Delta Fin. Serv., Inc., 5 Trade Reg. Rep. (CCH) ¶ 23,685 (FTC File No. X92 0049 1994) (proposed consent decree against 900-number loan brokering service).

452 47 U.S.C. § 228(g); 15 U.S.C. § 5722(a).

453 *See* National Consumer Law Center, Unfair and Deceptive Acts and Practices §§ 9.7.2–9.7.4 (7th ed. 2008 and Supp.).

454 State laws on 900-number abuses are summarized in National Consumer Law Center, Unfair and Deceptive Acts and Practices appx. E (7th ed. 2008 and Supp.). *See also* Colo. Rev. Stat. §§ 6-1-302, 6-1-303 (references to pay-per-call in telemarketing statute); Del. Code Ann. tit. 6, § 2504A (extra recordkeeping

900-number providers are regulated by the public utility commissions. Regulated telephone companies are allowed to provide transmission services (a necessity for the 900-number provider) only if the provider complies with a detailed list of consumer protection laws.[455] Other states simply require that 900-number charges be separately itemized and conspicuously identified on telephone bills, that consumers be advised that basic telephone service may not be refused, terminated, or require a deposit as a result of nonpayment of 900-number bills, and that basic service must include options for blocking 900-number calls.[456] These statutes are important because the federal regulations only cover interstate 900-number services.[457]

Like the federal statutes and regulations, almost all the state laws require cost disclosures in advertisements and during the brief oral preamble after a customer places a call.[458] The typical state statute also restricts prize promotions[459] and prohibits various methods of switching a consumer from a free call to a pay-per-call call.[460]

Louisiana's statute prohibits repetition of material and other gimmicks to prolong the call.[461] It also departs from the typical statute by addressing the value of the information the 900-number provides, prohibiting untimely, out-of-date, or garbled information.[462] Oklahoma's statute prohibits billing for 900-number calls that provide vulgar, violent, obscene, or racist information or false or misleading advertisements.[463] California's statute explicitly includes transactions over the Internet.[464]

A number of state statutes repeat the federal prohibition against disconnection of local or long-distance service because of nonpayment of 900-number charges[465] as well as the federal requirement that telephone bills itemize 900-number charges.[466] Wisconsin requires telephone companies to disclose on the bill that telephone service cannot be disconnected for failure to pay 900-number charges.[467] Vermont and Oregon require full refunds upon request in certain circumstances.[468]

Many state 900-number statutes declare that a violation is a UDAP violation,[469] but a few set forth no private cause of action or list only criminal penalties.[470]

In addition to the laws directed specifically at 1-900 numbers, state laws regulating telephone sales in general may apply depending on their coverage provisions. Advocates should also look to see whether fair debt collection laws may apply, especially if the 900-number provider contracts with an independent billing company or collection agency to recover its charges.[471]

11.6.5.8 Other Entities Liable for a Provider's 900-Number Fraud

Other entities that provided services or technology that facilitated the 900-number fraud may be liable if they knew or should have known of the fraud. For example, a class action was certified against AT&T in a case involving games of chance that people played by calling a 1-900 number.[472]

requirements for prize promotions that invite consumer calls to a 1-900 number); Iowa Code § 535C.2 (regulated loan brokers' "advance fee" defined to include pay-per-call charges); Minn. Stat. § 237.66 (phone companies must advise residential customers of available 900-number blocking options); N.H. Rev. Stat. Ann. § 358-O:4 (requirements for prize promotions); N.C. Gen. Stat. § 66-265 (telemarketing statute forbids prize promotions that include call to 1-900 number).

455 *See, e.g.*, Alaska Admin. Code tit. 3, § 53.500–.599; Fla. Admin. Code Ann. r. 25-4.110; Ill. Admin. Code tit. 83, § 772 (implements pay-per-call statute).

456 *See, e.g.*, 65-407-202 Me. Code R. §§ 1–6 (LexisNexis); N.H. Code Admin. R. Ann. Pub. Utils. Comm'n § 412.01(15) (basic telephone service must include 900-number blocking option); N.J. Admin. Code § 14.3-3A.8(a) (defines pay-per-call as non-basic; basic service may not be terminated or denied for nonpayment of non-basic service charges); Or. Admin. R. 860-021-0620, 860-034-0290 (utilities that provide billing and collection services for 900-number providers must advise consumers of their rights under 900-number statute); S.D. Admin. R. 20:10:05:05, 20:10:09:03, 20:10:10:04, 20:10:10:10; Tenn. Comp. R. & Regs. 1220-4-2-.58 (must offer 900-number blocking); 16 Tex. Admin. Code 26.124.

457 See the FTC's statement of basis and purpose for its 900-number rule at 58 Fed. Reg. 42364, 42367 (Aug. 9, 1993) for a discussion of this issue.

458 *See, e.g.*, Ariz. Rev. Stat. Ann. § 13-2920; Cal. Bus. & Prof. Code § 17539.5 (West) (disclosures in solicitations); Idaho Code Ann. §§ 48-1103, 48-1104; 815 Ill. Comp. Stat. 520/10; Iowa Code §§ 714A.2, 714A.3; La. Rev. Stat. Ann. § 51:1731 (disclosures in ads); Or. Rev. Stat. §§ 759.705, 759.710; Vt. Stat. Ann. tit. 9, §§ 2502, 2503; Va. Code Ann. § 59.1-430; Wash. Rev. Code §§ 19.162.030, 19.162.040.

459 *See, e.g.*, Cal. Bus. & Prof. Code § 17539.5 (West); 815 Ill. Comp. Stat. 520/10(d); Vt. Stat. Ann. tit. 9, § 2507.

460 *See, e.g.*, Cal. Bus. & Prof. Code § 17539.5(b) (West); Vt. Stat. Ann. tit. 9, § 2513.

461 *See, e.g.*, La. Rev. Stat. Ann. § 51:1733(2). *See also* Wis. Stat. § 196.208(5)(b) (prohibits charge for time caller is on hold).

462 La. Rev. Stat. Ann. § 51:1733(6).

463 *See, e.g.*, Okla. Stat. tit. 17, § 140.2.

464 *See, e.g.*, Cal. Bus. & Prof. Code § 17539.5(a)(1) (West).

465 *See, e.g.*, Me. Rev. Stat. tit. 35A, § 802.

466 *See, e.g.*, Vt. Stat. Ann. tit. 9, § 2514; Wis. Stat. § 196.208(7).

467 Wis. Stat. § 196.208(7).

468 Or. Rev. Stat. § 759.720(4) (charges made by children or mentally disabled individuals void and unenforceable); Vt. Stat. Ann. tit. 9, §§ 2505 (credit cards and loans), 2507 (prize promotions), 2508 (use by children), 2509 (charitable donations), 2516 (no sponsor shall bill or collect if there are violations of provisions).

469 *See, e.g.*, Idaho Code Ann. § 48-1105; 815 Ill. Comp. Stat. 520/15; Iowa Code § 714A.5; Me. Rev. Stat. tit. 35A, § 808; Vt. Stat. Ann. tit. 9, § 2516; Va. Code Ann. § 59.1-434. *See also* Or. Rev. Stat. § 759.720 (creating a private cause of action for treble damages or $500, whichever is greater).

470 *See, e.g.*, Ariz. Rev. Stat. Ann. § 13-2920(G) (criminal penalty only).

471 *See* National Consumer Law Center, Fair Debt Collection (7th ed. 2011) (discussing debt collection in detail).

472 Sikes v. American Tel. & Tel. Co., Clearinghouse No. 50,437

Even for those who won, the prize usually was worth less than the 900-number charges they incurred. The consumers allege that AT&T received a substantial portion of the profits from this scheme and knew or should have known of its fraudulent nature.

Entities known as "service bureaus" are also often involved in 900-number schemes. They act as intermediaries between the telephone company and pay-per-call providers, providing access to telephone service and voice storage for the providers.[473] An FTC regulation makes them liable if they know or should know of violations of the FTC's pay-per-call rule by providers.[474] The FTC won a consent order requiring a service bureau to pay $2 million in consumer redress due to its facilitation of a 900-number scam.[475] A "billing aggregator" who acts as an intermediary to enable a service provider to cram a charge onto a consumer's telephone bill can also be held liable for the provider's violations.[476]

11.6.6 Unsolicited Calls

On January 20, 2010, the FCC sought comments on its proposal for new restrictions for prerecorded and autodialed calls, intending to coordinate with the Federal Trade Commission's recent amendment to the Telemarketing Sales Rule and, to some extent, the rule's "Do Not Call" provisions.[477] Under the FCC's proposed rules, callers making a non-sales-related call would not be allowed to autodial or prerecord calls to a wireless number unless the consumer has given prior express consent in writing.[478] Currently, callers with an "established business relationship" are allowed to make prerecorded calls to consumers under the FCC's regulations, while they are prohibited from doing so without express written consumer consent under the 2008 amendments to the FTC's Telemarketing Sales Rule.[479]

11.6.7 Prepaid Telephone Cards

Prepaid telephone cards for long-distance and international calls are one alternative to traditional long-distance service. These cards provide low-income households without traditional long-distance service the ability to make long-distance calls. Prepaid calling cards are also popular for placing international calls. According to AT&T, recent immigrants and low-income customers are the most frequent purchasers of prepaid cards.[480] Users of AT&T's prepaid calling cards are "disproportionately minorities, college students, travelers, people in the military, and people without bank accounts."[481] Unfortunately, not all prepaid calling cards provide quality service and reasonable rates.[482] Clifton Telecard Alliance One, L.L.C., agreed to pay $1.3 million in settlement of a suit filed by the Federal Trade Commission alleging that its calling cards failed to deliver the number of minutes advertised. The settlement was filed in the U.S. District Court for the District of New Jersey.[483] Washington State requires companies providing prepaid calling service in the state to register with the Washington Utilities and Transportation Commission.[484] Washington's prepaid calling card regulations cover customer service requirements for companies, disclosure of rate information,

(S.D. Ga. May 13, 1994). *But see* Andrews v. AT&T, 95 F.3d 1014 (11th Cir. 1996) (declining to certify a nationwide class action relating to hundreds of 900-number telemarketing programs); Zekman v. Direct Am. Marketers, 695 N.E.2d 853 (Ill. 1998) (declining to import common law fraud concepts into UDAP statute, so AT&T not liable for another company's 900-number fraud even if it knowingly received the benefits; no mention of FTC rule). *Cf.* Brown v. SBC Commc'ns, Inc. 2007 WL 684133 (S.D. Ill. Mar. 1, 2007) (fraud claim for relief stated in cramming case in which phone company billed customers for services they never ordered; "role in the alleged fraud is hardly peripheral"); Saltzman v. Enhanced Servs. Billing, Inc., 811 N.E.2d 191 (Ill. App. Ct. 2003) (question of fact exists as to whether practice of billing customers for unauthorized, unverified charges while representing that charges are owed amounts to direct participation in fraud).

473 *See* 16 C.F.R. § 308.2(d)(i) (definition of service bureau); Consent Order, American TelNet, Inc., 5 Trade Reg. Rep. (CCH) ¶ 23,723 (C.D. Cal. 1994) (description of service bureau).

474 16 C.F.R. § 308.5(l).

475 Consent Order, American TelNet, Inc., 5 Trade Reg. Rep. (CCH) ¶ 23,723 (C.D. Cal. 1994).

476 *See* Complaint and Order, FTC v. Hold Billing Serv., Ltd., 5 Trade Reg. Rep. (CCH) ¶ 24,464 (N.D. Ga. 1998); United States v. Enhanced Servs. Billing, Inc., Civ. No. 01 1660 (D.C. filed Aug. 1, 2001) (billing aggregator filed to perform a reasonable investigation into disputed 1-900 charges), *available at* www.ftc.gov/os/2001/08/enhancedbillingstip.pdf. *See also* Stipulated Final Judgment and Order, FTC v. International Telemedia Assoc., Inc., Civ. No. 1:98-CV-1935 (N.D. Ga. 2001), *available at* www.ftc.gov/os/2001/10/itastipfinaljdmt.pdf.

477 *See* Notice of Proposed Rulemaking, *In re* Rules & Relations Implementing the Telephone Consumer Protection Act of 1991, C.G. No. 02-278 (F.C.C. Jan. 20, 2010).

478 *See* Notice of Proposed Rulemaking, *In re* Rules & Relations Implementing the Telephone Consumer Protection Act of 1991, at 16, C.G. No. 02-278 (F.C.C. Jan. 20, 2010).

479 *Id.* ¶¶ 27–28.

480 AT&T, Petition for Declaratory Ruling Regarding Enhanced Prepaid Calling Card Services, W.C. No. 03-133, at 4 (May 15, 2003). *See generally* Julia Marlowe & Martha Rojo, *Deceptive Claims for Prepaid Telephone Cards and the Need for Regulation*, 19 Loy. Consumer L. Rev. 1 (2006).

481 AT&T, Petition for Declaratory Ruling Regarding Enhanced Prepaid Calling Card Services, W.C. No. 03-133, at 4–5 (May 15, 2003).

482 *See* Julia Marlowe & Martina Rojo, Consumer Problems with Prepaid Phone Cards (2004) (study of 236 prepaid phone cards for calls to Spanish-speaking countries found higher than average per-minute cost, rounding of minutes, and inability to contact customer service).

483 Press Release, Federal Trade Comm'n, Prepaid Calling Card Distributor Agrees to Pay $1.3 Million (June 29, 2009).

484 Wash. Admin. Code § 480-120-028 (2004)and Wash. Rev. Code § 80.36.350 (2004). *See also* Cal. Pub. Util. Code § 885; Fla. Admin. Code Ann. r. 25-24.910; 815 Ill. Comp. Stat. 505/2TT; Mo. Code Regs. Ann. tit. 4 § 240-32.150.

and other consumer protections.[485] For information on using unfair and deceptive acts and practices laws to protect consumers from abusive prepaid calling card practices, refer to the National Consumer Law Center's treatise, *Unfair and Deceptive Acts and Practices* § 8.5.3.4 (7th ed. 2008 and Supp.).

11.7 Payphones

11.7.1 Overview

The Telecommunications Act of 1996 takes away from the states some discretion in setting rates for pay telephones. The pricing terms required by the Act have raised pay telephone rates,[486] an outcome which adversely and disproportionately affects low-income individuals. In its order implementing this provision of the Act,[487] the FCC found that the market may not provide payphones in all places that are important to public interest, for example, neighborhoods with low residential phone penetration or phones with high maintenance costs.[488] So states may fund public-interest payphones in a way that is competitively neutral and fairly compensates service providers.[489] States are best equipped to do this.[490] But public-interest payphones must fulfill a health, safety, or public welfare policy objective, may not be in locations with existing payphones, and must not otherwise exist in the marketplace.[491]

Other criteria for placement of public interest payphones may be unrestricted access, specified distance from other payphones, and a minimum of one payphone per exchange.[492] Providers of public interest payphones must be fairly compensated.[493] States had until September 29, 1998, to study the issue,[494] and the FCC entertained petitions asserting that a specific state was not providing for public interest payphones in accordance with the Act and order.[495]

The FCC also found that there are locations where the marketplace competition does not work because of size or caller's lack of time to find substitutes. The result is non-competitive rates, shared with the location provider via commissions.[496] In such cases, regulation may be necessary.[497]

The marketplace shall set coin rates "unless the state can show that there are market failures within the state that would not allow market-based rates."[498] "Such a detailed showing could consist of, for example, a detailed summary of the record of a state proceeding that examines the costs of providing payphone service within that state and the reasons why the public interest is served by having the state set rates within that market."[499] Some recent Bell company studies have shown that rates are substantially above cost.[500] By September 20, 1998, optionally and in conjunction with this required payphone marketplace study, "each state should evaluate whether it needs to take any measures to ensure that payphones serving important public interests will continue to exist. . . ."[501]

> In addition, when states have concerns about possible market failures, such as that of payphone locations that charge monopoly rates, they are empowered to act, for example, by mandating that additional PSPs [payphone service providers] be allowed to provide payphones, or by requiring that the PSP secure its contract through a com-

485 Wash. Admin. Code § 480-120-264. *See also* Alaska Admin. Code tit. 3, § 52.377; Cal. Bus. & Prof. Code § 17538.9 (West); Fla. Admin. Code Ann. r. 25-24.900; 815 Ill. Comp. Stat. 505/2TT; Mo. Code Regs. Ann. tit. 4, § 240-32.170; N.Y. Pub. Serv. Law § 92-f (McKinney); 16 Tex. Admin. Code § 26.34.

486 47 U.S.C. § 276.

For example, Bell companies in the few states with 10¢ local payphone rates have raised them to 25¢ or more. *E.g.*, New England Tel. & Tel. Co., D.P.U. 97-18.

487 Report and Order, *In re* Implementation of the Pay Telephone Reclassification & Compensation Provisions of the Telecommunications Act of 1996, No. 96-388 (F.C.C. Sept. 20, 1996) (C.C. Nos. 91-35, 96-128) (citations are to paragraphs).

488 *Id.* ¶ 7. *Accord Id.* ¶ 264. *See id.* ¶ 277.

489 *Id.* ¶¶ 7, 264, 283–84. *See* 47 C.F.R. § 64.1330(c).

490 Report and Order, *In re* Implementation of the Pay Telephone Reclassification & Compensation Provisions of the Telecommunications Act of 1996, No. 96-388 ¶¶ 7, 278–80 (F.C.C. Sept. 20, 1996) (C.C. Nos. 91-35, 96-128) (citations are to paragraphs).

491 *Id.* ¶ 282. *See id.* ¶¶ 279, 281.

492 Report and Order, *In re* Implementation of the Pay Telephone Reclassification & Compensation Provisions of the Telecommunications Act of 1996, No. 96-388 (F.C.C. Sept. 20, 1996) (C.C. Nos. 91-35, 96-128) (citations are to paragraphs).

493 *Id.* ¶¶ 283, 284. *See id.* ¶ 279; 47 C.F.R. § 64.1330(c).

494 *Id.* ¶ 285. *See* 47 C.F.R. § 64.1330(c). *See also* State of Vt. Pub. Serv. Bd., Generic Investigation into the Transition from Regulation to Competition for Public Telephone Service in Vermont, No. 6012 (Dec. 29, 2000) (Vermont's Public Service Board began a proceeding to reexamine the need for a public-interest payphone program in the state in December 2000).

Wisconsin set up a Public Interest Pay Telephone Fund pursuant to Wis. Admin. Code PSC § 160.073.

495 Report and Order, *In re* Implementation of the Pay Telephone Reclassification & Compensation Provisions of the Telecommunications Act of 1996, No. 96-388 (F.C.C. Sept. 20, 1996) (C.C. Nos. 91-35, 96-128).

496 *Id.* ¶¶ 15, 59.

497 *Id.* ¶ 15.

498 *Id.* ¶ 51.

499 *Id.* ¶ 61.

500 In Massachusetts, the charge rate is 25¢, and the cost is 16.7¢ (D.P.U. 97-18); in New Hampshire, the rate is 35¢ and the cost is 20¢ (D.S. 97-028). *See also* Pradnya Joshi, *Verizon Raises Payphone Rates to 50 Cents*, Newsday, Mar. 11, 2002 (Verizon raises rates for New York payphones to 50¢ in March 2002).

501 Report and Order, *In re* Implementation of the Pay Telephone Reclassification & Compensation Provisions of the Telecommunications Act of 1996, No. 96-388, Report and Order in C.C. 96-128 et al.—Pay Telephones (F.C.C. Sept. 20, 1996) (C.C. Nos. 96-128).

> petitive bidding process that ensures the lowest possible rate for callers. If market failure persists after such action, the state should recommend the matter to the Commission. . . .[502]

Also, the FCC "may review, at our option, the deregulation of local coin rates nationwide and determine whether marketplace dysfunction exist. . . ."[503] But note that the FCC has already determined that competition is the best approach to achieving lower prices and widespread payphone deployment and that "[c]ompetition over time will lead to the more efficient placement of payphones, improved payphone service, and lower prices for consumers."[504] This finding includes the desirability of market-rate local coin rates[505] even though the FCC acknowledges that the deregulated rates so far are 25¢ to 35¢.[506]

11.7.2 Inmate Payphones

The FCC currently has a rulemaking proceeding to look at inmate payphone rulemaking.[507] Families of prisoners are paying incredibly high phone rates to stay connected to incarcerated family members. Due, in large part, to security measures (for example, ability to screen calls and no use of cash or credit cards) inmate calls are restricted to long-distance collect calls from payphones.[508] What has been happening is that the bidding process for prison phone service contracts has resulted in higher prices, not lower. As explained by the FCC:[509]

> Typically, the confinement facility awards a contract to provide calling service by competitive bidding and grants the winning provider a monopoly on all inmate calling services. To have a realistic chance of winning a contract, the bidder must include an amount to cover commissions paid to the inmate facility. In the case of state prisons, which are often located far from major population centers and where consequently most of the traffic is toll traffic and not subject to state ceilings for local calls, the confinement facility monopolies prove sufficiently remunerative to allow the [inmate calling service] provider to offer generous commissions. In fact, under most contracts, the commission is the single largest component affecting the rates for inmate calling service. [footnotes omitted]

The commissions usually range between 20% and 63%, with most states charging over 45%.[510] As the FCC noted, the competition in the bidding process for the prison phone contracts perversely results in higher rates because "the bidder who charges the highest rates can afford to offer confinement facilities the largest location commission. . . ."[511] The National Association of State Utility Consumer Advocates has filed comments with the FCC arguing that the interstate rates for inmate calls is not just and reasonable and urges the FCC to prohibit the commissions and institute rules that will result in lower phone rates for inmate calls.[512]

There have been several challenges to the inmate calling rates brought by the families of inmates. However, for the most part, these cases have not been successful.[513] One case survived a motion to dismiss because the Indiana Court of Appeals characterized the issue, the legality of the inmate

502 *Id.* ¶ 61.

503 *Id.* ¶ 51. *Accord id.* ¶ 61.

504 *Id.* ¶ 55.

505 *Id.* ¶¶ 56, 335.

506 *Id.* ¶ 56. *See also* Pradnya Joshi, *Verizon Raises Pay Phone Rates to 50 Cents*, Newsday, Mar. 11, 2002 (Verizon raises rates for New York payphones to 50¢ in March 2002).

507 Report and Order, *In re* Implementation of the Pay Telephone Reclassification & Compensation Provisions of the Telecommunications Act of 1996, No. 96-388 (F.C.C. Sept. 20, 1996) (C.C. Nos. 91-35, 96-128). *See also* Order on Remand and Notice of Proposed Rulemaking, *In re* Implementation of the Pay Telephone Reclassification & Compensation Provisions of the Telecommunications Act of 1996, F.C.C. 02-39 (F.C.C. Feb. 21, 2002) (C.C. No. 96-128); Comments of the National Association of State Utility Consumer Advocates, *In re* Implementation of Pay Telephone Reclassification & Compensation Provisions of the Telecommunications Act of 1996, D.A. 04-774 (Mar. 24, 2004) (C.C. No. 96-128).

508 Order on Remand and Notice of Proposed Rulemaking, *In re* Implementation of the Pay Telephone Reclassification & Compensation Provisions of the Telecommunications Act of 1996, No. 02-39 ¶ 9 (F.C.C. Feb. 21, 2002) (C.C. No. 96-128).

509 Order on Remand and Notice of Proposed Rulemaking, *In re* Implementation of the Pay Telephone Reclassification & Compensation Provisions of the Telecommunications Act of 1996, No. 02-39 ¶ 10 (F.C.C. Feb. 21, 2002) (C.C. No. 96-128).

510 Order on Remand and Notice of Proposed Rulemaking, *In re* Implementation of the Pay Telephone Reclassification & Compensation Provisions of the Telecommunications Act of 1996, No. 02-39 n.34 (F.C.C. Feb. 21, 2002) (C.C. No. 96-128).

511 Order on Remand and Notice of Proposed Rulemaking, *In re* Implementation of the Pay Telephone Reclassification & Compensation Provisions of the Telecommunications Act of 1996, No. 02-39 ¶ 12 (F.C.C. Feb. 21, 2002) (C.C. No. 96-128).

512 Comments of the National Association of State Utility Consumer Advocates, *In re* Implementation of Pay Telephone Reclassification & Compensation Provisions of the Telecommunications Act of 1996, D.A. 04-774 (Mar. 24, 2004) (C.C. No. 96-128). *See also* Reply Comments of the National Association of State Utility Consumer Advocates, *In re* Implementation of the Pay Telephone Reclassification & Compensation Provisions of the Telecommunications Act of 1996 Petition for Rulemaking or, in the Alternative, Petition to Address Referral Issues in Pending Rulemaking, C.C. No. 96-128 (July 2007); Comment, *The Big Disconnect: Will Anyone Answer the Call to Lower Excessive Prisoner Telephone Rates*, 8 N.C. J. of Law & Tech. 159 (2006); Note, *Is There a Winning Argument Against Excessive Rates for Collect Calls from Prisoners?*, 25 Cardozo L. Rev. 1489 (2004).

513 *See generally* Holloway v. Magness, 2011 WL 204891, at *4 (E.D. Ark. Jan. 21, 2011) (noting that challenges based upon a variety of theories have failed to afford inmates relief for high calling rates).

calling contract, as being within the state's utility commission's jurisdiction.[514] The contracts at issue provided commissions of 53% and 40% and a $262,000 signing bonus. Indiana has a statute that prohibits illegally taxed fees and regulations prohibiting the imposition of licensing fees greater than that reasonably related to the administrative cost of exercising regulatory power. The case was remanded to the trial court to determine whether the sheriff and the State had the authority to enter into these contracts and to reap a profit in accordance with those agreements.[515] In another case challenging the non-disclosure of inmate call rates to the recipients of those long-distance calls, the Court of Appeals in Washington held that the Administrative Procedures Act was the sole means to challenge state utility commission regulations.[516]

The filed rate doctrine has also been held to bar challenges to the payment of rates filed at the state utility commission.[517] Other barriers met by families challenging the inmate calling services include the state's 11th Amendment immunity,[518] the court's holding that the class of persons receiving inmate calls was held not to be similarly situated to those in the general public for equal protection challenge,[519] and the court finding that no due process violations were committed when recipients were free to accept or reject high-cost inmate calls.[520]

514 Alexander v. Cottey, 801 N.E.2d 651 (Ind. Ct. App. 2004), *clarified by* 806 N.E.2d 315 (Ind. Ct. App. 2004).

515 On remand, the trial court granted summary judgment for the defendants, and the judgment was subsequently affirmed on appeal. *See* Alexander v. Marion County Sheriff, 891 N.E.2d 87 (Ind. Ct. App. 2008).

516 Judd v. AT&T Co., 66 P.3d 1102 (2003), *aff'd*, 95 P.3d 337 (2004).

517 Byrd v. Goord, 2005 WL 2086321 (S.D.N.Y. Aug. 29, 2005); McGuire v. Ameritech Servs., 253 F. Supp. 2d 988 (S.D. Ohio 2003); Guglielmo v. WorldCom, Inc., 808 A.2d 65 (N.H. 2002); Bullard v. State of N.Y., 763 N.Y.S.2d 371 (N.Y. App. Div. 2003).

518 McGuire v. Ameritech Serv., 253 F. Supp. 2d 988 (2003).

519 McGuire v. Ameritech Serv., 253 F. Supp. 2d 988 (2003). *But see* Byrd v. Goord, 2005 WL 2086321 (S.D.N.Y. Aug. 29, 2005) (equal protection claim survives motion to dismiss: "the state defendants have offered no rational basis to justify placing the burden of this additional commission solely on the friends and families of inmates, and those individuals providing counseling and professional services, thereby charging them more per call than similarly situated collect call recipients").

520 McGuire v. Ameritech Serv., 253 F. Supp. 2d 988 (S.D. Ohio 2003). *See also* Holloway v. Magness, 2011 WL 204891 (E.D. Ark. Jan. 21, 2011) (denying First Amendment challenge and agreeing with *Walton* court's reasoning); Walton v. New York State Dep't of Correctional Servs., 893 N.Y.S.2d 453 (N.Y. 2009) (inmate calls that generated commission for Department of Correctional Services did not constitute an unlawful tax or unconstitutional taking and was not a violation of the rights to free speech, association, or equal protection), *aff'g* 869 N.Y.S.2d 661 (N.Y. App. Div. 2008). *But see* Byrd v. Goord, 2005 WL 2086321 (S.D.N.Y Aug. 29, 2005) (claims alleging First Amendment, substantive due process, and equal protection violations survive motion to dismiss).

The Maine Public Utilities Commission recently concluded that it has jurisdiction over the state's Department of Corrections in its operation of the Client Phone System for the sate of Maine's prison system. In Maine, the Department of Corrections owns and operates the prison phone system, which includes local and in-state long-distance service.[521] The Minnesota PUC also recently found that inmate payphone service was a regulated service under Minnesota law despite the deregulation of payphone service in the state.[522] Several states have recently enacted laws to address the issue of inmate telephone rates by calling for systems with the "lowest available rates" or "affordable telephone services."[523] However, it remains to be seen whether a meaningful correlation exists between state legislation and lower rates.

In 2007, the Iowa Utilities Board, which has jurisdiction over such services, imposed a $2500 penalty against Evercom System, Inc., finding that the company charged a consumer for unauthorized collect calls. The district court reversed the board's decision. On appeal by the board and the Office of Consumer Advocate, the Court of Appeals of Iowa reversed the district court's decision, finding that the board's determination that Evercom had committed a cramming violation was not irrational or illogical but supported by substantial evidence.[524] However, shortly after this opinion was issued, a media report claimed that Correctional Billing Services, a division of Evercom Systems, Inc., imposed a minimum charge of $31.95 for setting up a billing account to use for inmate calls.[525] This charge consisted of $11.00 for a fifteen-minute call, taxes, and transaction fees before a call to the inmate was ever completed.[526] While states like Iowa may have statutes and case law or a utilities commission to protect consumers against unauthorized charges in telecommunications services, it is sometimes left

521 Barbara Pierce et al., Maine Pub. Utils. Comm'n, Request for Commission Investigation into Unjust, Unreasonable, Discriminatory Rates for Telephone Services Provided by the Maine Department of Corrections and Verizon, No. 2007-467 (Aug. 1, 2008).

522 Minnesota Pub. Utils. Comm'n, *In re* the Petition of the Minnesota Dep't of Commerce Regarding Regulation of Inmate Tel. Serv., No. P-999/DI-07-204 (July 26, 2007).

523 *See, e.g.*, D.C. Code § 24-263.01; N.M. Stat. Ann. § 33-14-1; R.I. Gen. Laws § 42-56-38.1; Vt. Stat. Ann. tit. 28, § 802a; Va. Code Ann. § 53.1-1.1; Wash. Rev. Code § 9.73.095.

In July 2007, the governor of New York signed that state's "Family Connections" law (S. 705-B), which is designed to prevent the Department of Correctional Services from collecting monies over and above the reasonable cost of providing telephone service to inmates. The state currently exacts a 57.5% share of the total profit on inmate calls. The law went into effect on April 1, 2008. *See* N.Y. Correct. Law § 623 (McKinney).

524 Evercom Sys., Inc. v. Iowa Utils. Bd., 2010 WL 447321 (Iowa Ct. App. Feb. 10, 2010).

525 Rekha Basu, *Investigate Iowa Jail Phone Services*, Des Moines Register, Feb. 17, 2010, at 13A.

526 *Id.*

to advocates to use these as enforcement tools and bring violations to light.[527]

11.7.3 Internet As a Regulated Telecommunications or Information Service

In a December 21, 2010, report and order, the FCC promulgated its Open Internet Rules, to be effective sixty days after publication in the Federal Register of the Office of Management and Budget's approval regarding information collection requirements.[528] Along with rules to preserve an open Internet through transparency requirements and prohibitions on blocking access to legal websites,[529] it establishes a formal complaint procedure of violation of the new rules[530] and sets forth the basis of jurisdiction.

Under the rules, any person can file a formal complaint regarding a violation of the rules after giving notice to the defendant.[531] While the FCC reserves the right to adjust the burden of proof, in general the complainant bears the burden to prove the complaint by a preponderance of evidence. A complaint pleaded with specificity, providing facts and possibly providing documentation or an affidavit, will establish a prima facie case, after which the burden shifts to the broadband provider to demonstrate that the challenged practice is reasonable. The complainant then has a chance to rebut.[532] The FCC expects to draw on its engineering, economic, and legal experts to resolve complaints under the Open Internet Rules.[533]

527 *See, e.g.*, Evercom Sys., Inc. v. Iowa Utils. Bd., 2010 WL 447321 (Iowa Ct. App. Feb. 10, 2010) (while the Iowa Utilities Board initially declined to determine whether Evercom had violated a law, the Office of Consumer Advocate successfully petitioned the board and obtained a determination of a legal violation and the imposition of a civil penalty).

528 *In re* Preserving the Open Internet Broadband Industry Practices, 25 F.C.C.R. 17905 at ¶ 161, F.C.C. 10-201 (Dec. 23, 2010), *appeal dismissed*, Verizon v. Federa Commc'ns Comm'n, 2011 WL 1235523 (D.C. Cir. Apr. 4, 2011) (appeal is premature when the order has not yet been published in the Federal Register).

529 *In re* Preserving the Open Internet Broadband Industry Practices, 25 F.C.C.R. 17905 at ¶¶ 97–98, F.C.C. 10-201 (Dec. 23, 2010) (disclosure of network practices required to inform Internet users); *id.* ¶¶ 99–107 (prohibition on blocking guarantees end user's access to legal sites).

530 *Id.* ¶¶ 154–60.

531 *Id.* ¶ 156.

532 *Id.* ¶ 157.

533 *Id.* ¶ 159.

Regarding jurisdiction, the FCC states that its Open Internet Rules are based on its jurisdiction to regulate mobile broadband.[534] Notably, the National Broadband Plan recommends that the FCC expand Lifeline and Link Up to make broadband affordable to low-income consumers.[535] The FCC cites to the Telecommunications Act of 1996 as giving the FCC and states authority to take actions to encourage the deployment of advanced telecommunications capability, which includes broadband Internet access.[536] It also notes that VOIP is being used as a substitute for traditional telephone service and infers that, because the Communications Act of 1934 imposes a duty on all telecommunications carriers to interconnect directly or indirectly, it necessarily has authority to act when degradation or blocked services on VOIP impacts the service of a traditional telephone customer and frustrates the interconnection goals of the network.[537] The agency also found that, pursuant to its authority to oversee orderly local television broadcasting, it has authority to protect competition and ensure that broadband providers do not block or degrade the quality of on-line programming or charge excessive and unreasonable fees.[538]

Already, the FCC order has been challenged by the industry, even before its effective date. The FCC stated in its order that "all the rules we adopt in this Order [shall be] effective 60 days after the date of Federal Register notice announcing the decision of the Office of Management and Budget regarding approval of the information collection requirements."[539] Verizon appealed the Open Internet Order. However, the D.C. Circuit Court of Appeals deemed Verizon's appeal premature when publication in the Federal Register had not yet occurred.[540] The FCC's exercise of jurisdiction to expand Lifeline and Link Up to broadband customers is welcome. However, as the Verizon appeal demonstrates, whether and how the agency will regulate new technologies, and to what degree the states will be involved, will likely be an issue subject to future litigation.

534 *Id.* ¶¶ 94–95.

535 Federal-State Joint Board on Universal Service Seeks Comment on Lifeline and Link-up Eligibility, Verification, and Outreach Issues Referred to Joint Board, 25 F.C.C.R. 7551 ¶ 12, F.C.C. 10J-2 (F.C.C. June 15, 2010) (order requesting comments).

536 *Id.* ¶ 117 (citing 47 U.S.C. § 1302(d)).

537 *Id.* ¶¶ 125–26.

538 *Id.* ¶ 128.

539 *Id.* ¶ 161.

540 Verizon v. Federal Commc'ns Comm'n, 2011 WL 1235523 (D.C. Cir. Apr. 4, 2011) (appeal is premature when the order has not yet been published in the Federal Register).

Chapter 12 Affordable Water Service

12.1 The Growing Problem of Water Affordability

The drinking-water and wastewater industries have not adopted and implemented water affordability programs, policies and rate designs to the extent that the natural gas, electric, and local phone service providers have. Recent research into water affordability programs found that most water utilities take an ad hoc approach to helping their payment-troubled customers.[1] An American Water Works Association 2004 survey found that 64% of water utilities did not view nonpayment of bills as a big problem, but the larger water utilities and those with larger bills were more likely to view nonpayment as a problem.[2] A 2008 Association of Metropolitan Water Agencies survey found that companies tended to rely more on charitable-giving assistance programs over low-income discounts.[3] Similarly, an older industry survey found that only approximately 14% of drinking-water utilities and 13% of wastewater utilities reporting having either rate relief or other subsidies for low-income consumers.[4] Another survey of municipal wastewater utilities also reports that a low percentage of such utilities provide Lifeline rates (7.6%) or collect customer contributions for customer assistance programs (10.7%).[5] Thus, there is much room for improvement.

Unlike the case for low-income home energy needs—which are addressed through the Low Income Home Energy Assistance Program (LIHEAP)—or the case for local phone service—which is addressed by Lifeline and Link-Up—there is no federal assistance program to help low-income households pay their water bills.[6] Yet access to safe and affordable water is currently a problem for low-income households. The problem will likely get much worse as water utilities are faced with the need to comply with water quality regulations and to repair, upgrade, and replace aged infrastructure. The Congressional Budget Office has estimated that drinking water systems will invest between $11.6 billion and $20.1 billion each year during the years 2000 through 2019, while wastewater systems will invest between $13 billion and $20.9 billion each year.[7] From 1996 through 2004, annual rate increases for both water (4.24%) and wastewater (4.09%) were nearly twice the rate of the average annual increase in inflation during the same time period.[8] Driving the increases in the price of drinking water in particular are "new or more stringent drinking water regulations and the replacement and repair of aging, deteriorating water and wastewater infrastructure."[9] How to fund the gap between current funding—consisting of government and ratepayer revenues—and the projected future infrastructure needs potentially is a pressing question for policy makers, the industry, and ratepayers.[10]

Inability to pay for water and sewer services results in the same types of actions taken by other utility services: shutoff, notification of a collection agency, notification of a credit bureau and, because a substantial percentage of water sewer utilities are owned by municipalities, the potential for a lien to be placed on the property.[11] Disconnection of water

1 John E. Cromwell et al., Water Research Found., Best Practices in Customer Payment Assistance Programs (2003).

2 *Id.* at 13.

3 *Id.* at 19.

4 U.S. Gen. Accounting Office, GAO-02-764, Water Infrastructure: Information on Financing, Capital Planning, and Privatization (Aug. 2002).

5 Association of Metro. Sewerage Agencies, 2002 AMSA Financial Survey: A National Survey of Municipal Wastewater Management Financing and Trends 83 (2003).

6 Financial assistance from the USDA Rural Utilities Service and other federal agencies is available to states and local communities to fund water and wastewater infrastructure. Such funding may help reduce the portion of a customer's water bill that is based not on consumption but on fixed costs of service. However, there is no federal funding mechanism comparable to LIHEAP or Lifeline for payment assistance for water utility customers.

7 *Future Investment in Drinking Water Infrastructure, Hearing Before the H. Subcomm. on Environment and Hazardous Materials, Comm. on Energy and Commerce*, 107th Cong. (2002) (testimony of Perry Beider).

8 Howard Hoover & George Faftelis, *How Healthy Are Your Utility's Financial Fundamentals*, Journal AWWA 97:4 (Apr. 2005).

9 Melissa Stanford, National Regulatory Research Inst., Water Affordability Programs Memorandum (Apr. 27, 2007), *available at* http://nrri.org/pubs/water/07-stanford.pdf.

10 *See* American Soc'y of Civil Engineers, 2009 Report Card for America's Infrastructure (2009), *available at* www.asce.org/reportcard; U.S. Gov't Accountability Office, Clean Water Infrastructure: Design Issues and Funding Options for a Clean Water Trust Fund 1 (July 15, 2009).

11 Association of Metro. Sewerage Agencies, 2002 AMSA Financial Survey: A National Survey of Municipal Wastewater Management Financing and Trends 43 (2003).

service may also result in a consumer's house being deemed uninhabitable. In addition to other questionable and harmful practices, a municipality that owned a water utility (Easton Water) in Pennsylvania, automatically declared a house to be uninhabitable once water service was disconnected. The municipality then required a full housing inspection before reconnecting the water service.[12] Reconnection of water service may be accompanied by a reconnection charge, which can be a barrier for low-income customers in reestablishing water service.

12.2 Types of Water Affordability Programs

The low-income affordability rates described for energy utilities can also be applied to water and sewer bills (for example, rate discounts, service charge waivers, and percentage of income payment plans (PIPPs)).[13] The water bill is often comprised of a customer service charge and a usage charge.[14] However, an important factor in affordability rate design is the strong correlation between residential water usage and the number of people in the household. A study by the American Water Works Research Foundation, *Residential End Uses of Water*, found that the larger the household, the greater the usage. Use of toilet, shower, and faucet accounted for 26.7%, 16.8%, and 15.7% of indoor per-capita water usage, respectively.[15] Thus, a "Lifeline" rate that discounts an initial block of water usage for all or a subset of residential customers will likely be inadequate for a large household.

Few state utility commissions report that water companies within their jurisdictions offer water affordability programs. In 2006, the Staff Subcommittee on Water and Consumer Affairs of the National Association of Regulatory Utility Commissioners (NARUC), in collaboration with the National Regulatory Research Institute (NRRI), surveyed utility commissions about the availability of water affordability programs. Twenty-two commissions responded to the survey,[16] with six state utility commissions identifying sixteen utility programs.[17] The six state utility commissions reporting water affordability programs included those in California, Kentucky, New Jersey, Ohio, Pennsylvania, and West Virginia.[18]

In addition, a 2006 American Water Works Association (AWWA) survey found that 34 of 231 water utilities (primarily municipal utilities) offered a low-income program, while twelve more had a low-volume discount program.[19] Existing programs in the fall of 2006 represented an increase of nine programs over the same time period in 2005.

With the exception of the New Jersey Board of Public Utilities, even those state utility commissions reporting existing water affordability programs identified shortcomings in those programs. Pennsylvania and West Virginia both reported that "assistance levels per household were not adequate" and that "total demand for assistance exceeds available funding."[20] Only West Virginia reported a problem with "customers continu[ing] to accrue arrearages."

Despite the growing number of water affordability programs in the country, such programs remain outside the purview of the smallest water utilities. According to the NARUC/NRRI survey, as of 2006, no water utility with fewer than 10,000 customers offered an affordability program,[21] a situation possibly due to the "low capability of small utilities to finance and operate their own affordability programs."[22]

12.3 Examples of Low-Income Water Affordability Rates

1. The Philadelphia Water Department (PWD) offers one of the most extensive water affordability programs in the country. The PWD's low-income rate program can be divided into three basic components: extended payment plans, petitions to the Philadelphia Water Revenue Bureau (WRB), and the PWD's Water Revenue Assistance Program (WRAP) Each component provides progressively greater assistance to low-income customers in arrears.

The first component of the PWD affordability program offers an extended payment plan through which low-income customers (at or below 150% of poverty) can retire arrears.[23] The extended payment plan offers two payment options: a "10/5" payment plan and a "disposable income" payment plan. Under the 10/5 plan, which the PWD will offer initially, a customer is asked to make a downpayment

12 Roger Colton, Fisher Sheehan & Colton, Collecting Water Bills in Easton, Pennsylvania (Sept. 5, 2002).

13 For an extensive examination of water affordability programs, see Margot Saunders et al., American Water Works Ass'n Research Found., Water Affordability Program (1998), and American Water Works Ass'n, M1 Manual, Principles of Water Rates, Fees and Charges ch. 16 (5th ed. 2000) (low-income affordability rates).

14 Margot Saunders et al., American Water Works Ass'n Research Found., Water Affordability Programs 14 (1998).

15 American Water Works Ass'n Research Found., Residential End Uses of Water ch. 5 (1999).

16 These twenty-two commissions represent about half of all state commissions that regulate water. In the United States, forty-four state utility commissions and the Texas Commission on Environmental Quality regulate water utilities.

17 Melissa Stanford, National Regulatory Research Inst., Water Affordability Programs Memorandum 6 (Apr. 27, 2007), *available at* http://nrri.org/pubs/water/07-stanford.pdf.

18 *Id.* at 10.

19 American Water Works Ass'n Research Found., 2006 Water and Wastewater Rate Survey Pt. III, at 9 (2006).

20 *Id.* at 13.

21 *Id.* at 17.

22 *Id.* at 11.

23 Philadelphia Water Department Regulations § 100.9.

of 10% of his or her arrears and pay 5% of the remaining arrears each month (in addition to the current bill). Under this 10/5 plan, arrears would be retired in twenty months.

If payments under the 10/5 plan are not affordable, a low-income customer is offered the PWD's "disposable income" payment plan. In this plan, the PWD calculates the customer's disposable income that is available to pay the customer's water bill. Taking into account this disposable income, the payment plan spreads out payments toward arrears over a term not exceeding thirty-six months.

Should the thirty-six-month disposable income payment plan still be unaffordable, a second component of the PWD program is available. A customer can petition a special "committee" of the PWRB for a special extended payment plan based on ability to pay. The WRB is an agency separate from the Philadelphia Water Department, operates as the "collections" arm of the municipal government, and is part of the Revenue (not Water) Department. All customers with incomes below 100% of the federal poverty level (FPL) are referred to the Water Revenue Bureau Conference Committee (WRBCC). Customers with incomes between 100% and 150% of the FPL must furnish proof of income and expenses to be eligible for a WRBCC agreement. Customers with incomes above 150% of FPL must be referred to the WRBCC by the WRB and only for extraordinary expenses.

The WRBCC has virtually unlimited discretion in establishing the individualized terms of a low-income payment plan. Often called Conference Committee or WRBCC payment plans, such agreements do not deliver debt relief of any kind to Water Department customers with arrears.

Under the third and final component of the PWD program, a low-income customer has the option of applying to the Water Revenue Assistance Program (WRAP). Customers with incomes at or below 175% of the FPL are income-eligible for WRAP.

A low-income customer enrolled in WRAP has his or her arrears suspended by the Philadelphia Water Department. The customer is also entitled to a $200 grant annually, to be used toward paying the customer's current bill. The customer must apply to Philadelphia's local "fuel fund" for assistance in reducing arrears and must also re-certify his or her income on an annual basis.

As of the end of fiscal year 2008, the PWD had roughly 11,300 participants enrolled in its WRAP program. Additionally, the PWD has begun negotiations with the local public advocate on the use of mechanisms that expand participation.

2. The Seattle Human Services Department offers payment assistance and consultation for eligible customers of electric, water, sewer, and garbage services in the city of Seattle. The city provides a utility discount of 50% off of electric and water bills for income-eligible customers, seniors, and adults with disabilities ratepayers.[24] The Human Services Department also provides a one-time payment assistance which pays 50% of past-due balances up to $200 for low-income households at or below 70% of the state median income level. Customers living in federally subsidized housing are ineligible for the program.[25]

3. The Los Angeles Department of Water and Power offers a low-income subsidy that provides eligible households with a discount of up to 15% on electricity, water, and sewer services.[26] The low-income subsidy for water consists of a $5.00-per-month base credit, with an additional $1.00 per month for each additional occupant in excess of three occupants; the subsidy is capped at $10 per month.[27]

4. The District of Columbia Water and Sewer Authority (DC WASA) offers a discount in the form of free service for the first 4 Ccf (or 2992 gallons) per month of the eligible customer's water bill. In 2009, a similar discount also began to be applied to the first 4 Ccf of the eligible customer's sewer bill. DC WASA determined the savings to be an amount greater than the dollar savings offered to Philadelphia customers under PWD's WRAP, discussed above. This program benefitted 5814 customers in 2008 with a total of $344,000 in payment assistance. Approximately 25% of these customers use less than 4 Ccf and therefore pay no water and sewer charges, although they pay for other minimum fees such as metering and payment in lieu of taxes. DC WASA has also invested resources into outreach, such as translating its customer assistance brochure into five languages to reach a diverse customer base, contacting ninety-one agencies (of which forty-four agencies agreed to stock the brochures), and targeting marketing efforts toward agencies with low-income clientele instead of undertaking wider media campaigns.[28]

Other payment restructuring programs offered by energy utilities can help low-income households with their water bills:

Rate Structure Alternatives: One way of making rates more affordable to low-income customers is through the use of "lifeline" rates, which are implemented through a utility's basic rate structure. A "lifeline" rate provides for reduced-cost (though not necessarily below-cost) rates for initial blocks of consumption.

Special lifeline rates are increasingly being authorized by state statutes. Declaring that "access to an adequate supply of healthful water is a basic necessity of human life, and shall be made available to all residents of California at an affordable cost," the California legislature imposed a statu-

24 *See* www.seattle.gov/light/accounts/assistance.

25 *See* Seattle, Wash., Mun. Code 21.76.040 (Low Income Rate Credits). *See also* www.seattle.gov/light/accounts/assistance.

26 *See* www.ladwp.com/ladwp/cms/ladwp004031.jsp.

27 Los Angeles Water Rates, § 3, provision K, June 1, 1995, *amended*, July 28, 1997, and Feb. 4, 2000; Los Angeles Department of Water and Power Ordinance No. 170435, *amended by* Ordinance Nos. 171639, 173017, 175964, 177968, 179802.

28 *See* District of Columbia Water & Sewer Auth., Retail Rates and Low Income Residents: Discount Program and Impacts (Sept. 24, 2009).

tory mandate on the California Public Utilities Commission (CPUC) to consider the propriety of "rate relief for low-income ratepayers." This mandate is limited, however, providing only that the Commission "shall consider and *may* implement" low-income programs.[29] Class A, and some Class B and C, water utilities in California provide low-income rate assistance programs.[30] In an effort to increase participation in the low-income water assistance programs, California's utility commission requires Class A and B water utilities and regulated energy utilities with overlapping service territories to share low-income customer information and automatically enroll eligible customers in the water programs.[31]

There is one limitation to these California programs that should be noted: only "customers" of a water utility may be provided with rate assistance. Households living in multi-family housing, for example, are thus not considered "customers" and are not covered under statute. However, in an effort to get a better understanding of low-income water affordability and program effectiveness, the California utility commission has required the larger, regulated water companies to submit data on disconnections, reconnections, water usage data for large low-income households, the inclusion of low-income consumers in conservation programs, and the number of low-income customers who are ineligible for the low-income water discount due to master-metering.[32]

New Mexico also authorizes, but does not require, utilities to offer special water rates to improve affordability for low-income water consumers. Under New Mexico law, "a utility may provide assistance in the form of reduced or subsidized rates to or on behalf of those individuals who meet the eligibility criteria of one or more need-based assistance programs administered by the [human services] department and who are not living in nursing homes or intermediate care facilities or not living in circumstances that do not require them to pay, directly or indirectly, for water, sewer or solid waste service."[33]

Other water companies have adopted low-income assistance programs without a statutory directive. For example, in 2002, the Pennsylvania American Water Company (PAWC) agreed to implement a low-income water assistance program.[34] In enrolling customers into its program, PAWC agreed to accept automatic income verification from the state Department of Public Welfare or evidence of a household's receipt of assistance through LIHEAP as sufficient to establish eligibility for its water affordability program.[35] At the time the program was adopted, the company provided a 15% reduction in its monthly service charge for customers with incomes at or below 110% of the federal poverty level; the program was subsequently amended to increase the discount to 20% ($2.10 per month versus $10.50 per month in customer charge) for customers at or below 150% of the FPL. The company subsequently expanded its discount to reduce the monthly customer service charge by 65%. In its rate case settlement of November 2009, PAWC agreed that the annual shareholder contribution to its "H20—Help to Others" program would increase from $150,000 to $250,000 annually.[36]

Deferred Payment or Arrearage Management Plans: While a customer of a privately-owned water utility might benefit from the jurisdiction of the state utility commission and its rules, regulations, or policies regarding the provision of deferred payment or arrearage management plans, a customer of a municipally owned water utility may need to look to state contract law and state unfair and deceptive trade practices statutes to argue for the creation of such programs.[37]

Waiver or Lowering of Charges: Low-income customers are in jeopardy of losing water, sewer, and other services because they cannot afford to pay for these services. Charging these customers prohibitive fees for disconnection, reconnection, and late payments further hampers their ability to pay utility bills and only worsens the problem.[38]

29 Cal. Pub. Util. Code § 739.8 (West).

30 *See* Seaneen Wilson, California Pub. Util. Comm'n Div. of Water & Audits, Assessment of Water Utility Low-Income Assistance Programs (Oct. 2007), *available at* www.cpuc.ca.gov/NR/rdonlyres/159B7FB3-D717-41C3-9BCE-27FFE7530AD5/0/dwa_lowincome_research_paper_112507.pdf. *See also* CPUC Decision 11-05-020, Adopting the Guidelines for Sharing of Low-Income Customer Information 12–13 (May 5, 2011).

31 Decision 11-05-020, Adopting the Guidelines for Sharing of Low-Income Customer Information (Cal. Pub. Utils. Comm'n May 5, 2011).

32 Decision 11-05-004, Decision Resolving Phase 2 Conservation Goals and Modifying Tracking of Conservation and Low-Income Data (Cal. Pub. Utils. Comm'n May 5, 2011); Decision 11-05-020, Adopting the Guidelines for Sharing of Low-Income Customer Information (Cal. Pub. Utils. Comm'n May 5, 2011).

33 N.M. Stat. Ann. § 27-6A-4.

34 Opinion and Order, Pennsylvania Pub. Util. Comm'n v. Pennsylvania-American Water Co., No. R-00016339 (Pa. Pub. Util. Comm'n Jan. 25, 2002); Further Recommended Decision, Pennsylvania Pub. Util. Comm'n v. Pennsylvania-American Water Co., No. R-00016339 (Pa. Pub. Util. Comm'n Oct. 23, 2002); Opinion and Order, Pennsylvania Pub. Util. Comm'n v. Pennsylvania-American Water Co., No. R-00016339 (Pa. Pub. Util. Comm'n Jan. 27, 2003).

35 Further Recommended Decision at 5, Pennsylvania Pub. Util. Comm'n v. Pennsylvania-American Water Co., No. R-00016339 (Pa. Pub. Util. Comm'n Oct. 23, 2002).

36 *See* Pennsylvania Pub. Util. Comm'n v. Pennsylvania-American Water Co., No. R-2009-2097323 (order issued Nov. 6, 2009); Press Release, Pennsylvania Pub. Util. Comm'n, PUC Approves Lower Rate Increase Than Requested by PA American Water (Nov. 6, 2009).

37 *See* § 15.4, *infra*. *See also A Municipal Water Utility That Is Not Regulated by a State Public Service Commission Must Still Offer Deferred Payment Plans for Arrears*, FSC's Law & Economics Insights, Issue 02-5 (Sept./Oct. 2002).

38 Margot Saunders et al., American Water Works Ass'n Research Found., Water Affordability Programs ch. 5 (1998). *See generally* Scott Rubin et al., American Water Works Ass'n Research Found., Thinking Outside the Bill: A Utility Manager's Guide to Assisting Low-Income Water Customers (2004).

Modifications to the Way Water Usage Is Billed: Low-income households are less able to weather drastic increases in bill charges simply because they do not have cash reserves on hand to tide them over. Some water utilities bill quarterly or at longer intervals, which can cause hardship for cash-strapped households. Receiving smaller monthly water bills can help low-income households to maintain adequate and timely bill payments. Similarly, as water bills can increase seasonally, budget-billing plans can strengthen the ability of low-income households to budget sufficiently for water services.[39]

39 Margot Saunders et al., American Water Works Ass'n Research Found., Water Affordability Programs ch. 5 (1998). *See generally* Scott Rubin et al., American Water Works Ass'n Research Found., Thinking Outside the Bill: A Utility Manager's Guide to Assisting Low-Income Water Customers (2004).

Chapter 13 Bankruptcy Issues: When Either the Consumer or Landlord Files for Bankruptcy

13.1 Using Bankruptcy to Prevent Utility Shut-Off and Deal with Arrearages

13.1.1 Bankruptcy As a Source of Consumer Protections

13.1.1.1 Introduction

The United States Bankruptcy Code[1] presents one of the most important sources of consumer rights to deal with utility shut-offs and industry unwillingness to restructure utility arrearages. Under the Bankruptcy Code, a consumer may seek to discharge unpayable debts through a variety of mechanisms. Moreover, the bankruptcy court provides a forum in which to challenge liens held by utility companies and to raise consumer defenses against unjustified claims. Some of the potential advantages of the bankruptcy forum are:

- Once a petition is filed, the automatic stay provision of the Bankruptcy Code[2] will prevent shut-off[3] and other efforts to collect the prebankruptcy arrears until the stay is terminated. If a utility company violates the automatic stay by engaging in collection efforts without permission from the bankruptcy court, the Code provides for a damage remedy including attorney fees and costs.[4]
- The Code requires that, upon filing bankruptcy, utility service that has been shut off must be immediately restored.[5] Depending on the circumstances, a utility may be able to demand a reasonable security deposit once service has been restored. That deposit should be no greater than the amount charged to new customers who have no utility arrears.[6]
- Most utility arrearages will be fully dischargeable in the bankruptcy process, even if payments to the utility on the arrears through the bankruptcy process are nominal or nil (and they usually are as discussed below).[7] This means that debtors will be able to avoid entirely the obligation to make payments on the arrears going forward and will have a fresh start in dealing with their utility providers. Efforts by a utility to obtain payment of a discharged debt are prohibited by the Code.[8] (Liens associated with some utility debts are not automatically eliminated by bankruptcy. However, the Code provides a variety of opportunities to avoid liens or repay them on favorable terms to avoid enforcement as discussed below.)
- Most consumers with utility arrears will also have other pressing financial problems, including, for example, pending foreclosures, repossessions, and garnishments. Use of the bankruptcy process creates a forum to deal with all of the consumer's debt problems together rather than on a piecemeal basis.

---

1 11 U.S.C. §§ 101–1532.

2 11 U.S.C. § 362. *See* National Consumer Law Center, Consumer Bankruptcy Law and Practice ch. 9 (9th ed. 2009).

3 Note, however, that shut-off may be possible for unpaid bills arising after the bankruptcy filing. Additionally, a utility is entitled to demand adequate assurance (usually in the form of a small security deposit) to guarantee future payment. 11 U.S.C. § 366(b).

Failure to provide adequate assurance may also be a ground to terminate utility service after a bankruptcy is filed. *See* § 13.1.2.2, *infra*.

4 11 U.S.C. § 362(k)(1). *See, e.g., In re* Coin Phones, Inc., 203 B.R. 184 (Bankr. S.D.N.Y. 1996) (actual and $1 million punitive damages awarded for violation of automatic stay and breach of covenant of good faith and fair dealing against telephone business). *See generally* National Consumer Law Center, Consumer Bankruptcy Law and Practice § 9.6 (9th ed. 2009 and Supp.).

Occasionally such damage awards can be extremely high.

5 11 U.S.C. § 366; *In re* Whittaker, 882 F.2d 791 (3d Cir. 1989).

6 *See* § 13.1.2.3.2, *infra*.

7 11 U.S.C. § 524. *See generally* National Consumer Law Center, Consumer Bankruptcy Law and Practice ch. 15 (9th ed. 2009 and Supp.).

In relatively few instances, a utility may be able to argue that debts incurred by consumers are non-dischargeable for some reason under 11 U.S.C. § 523(a) or 11 U.S.C. § 1328(a). The most common situation in which these issues arise are debts that the utility believes are based on theft of service or other misconduct of the debtor. The burden is on the utility to raise the issue and have the debt determined non-dischargeable.

8 11 U.S.C. § 524(a); National Consumer Law Center, Consumer Bankruptcy Law and Practice ch. 15 (9th ed. 2009 and Supp.).

- The objections to claim process in bankruptcy provides a forum for determining whether debts are valid. This means that most questions about the validity of disputed debts can be resolved in the bankruptcy case.[9] However, since bankruptcy will terminate the consumer's legal liability to pay most utility debts, whether they are valid or not, it may be unnecessary to incur the time and expense of litigating their validity.
- Although liens associated with utility bills are not automatically eliminated by a bankruptcy, the Code does provide several opportunities to avoid or restructure obligations on liens. Both judgment liens that impair exemptions and improperly perfected liens can be avoided in many cases to protect a debtor's exemptions.[10] The underlying debts are then unsecured and dischargeable. If the lien cannot be avoided and there is a realistic concern about enforcement, chapter 13 of the Code creates a variety of opportunities for a consumer debtor to reorganize and pay off the debt secured by the lien over time, provided that the creditor has adequate protection while the lien is being paid.[11]

Some lawyers and advocates think of bankruptcy as a last resort to deal with debt problems, including utility bills, only when all other avenues of relief have failed. In some cases, bankruptcy may be the appropriate choice for consumers even if other, less dramatic, options are never utilized. Indeed, because of the importance of access to utilities, an imminent shut-off alone can justify a bankruptcy. Sometimes bankruptcy is the only way to deal with the debt. At a minimum, whenever utility debts are unmanageable, debtors should be told about their bankruptcy options so that they can make a fully informed choice to address their financial problems.[12]

Learning basic bankruptcy law can appear to be a daunting task. However, as with any area of the law, knowledge can be built over time by learning to answer each question as it arises. The material set out below is intended, for the most part, to cover the intersection between utility obligations and bankruptcy. The discussion here is thus not a comprehensive guide to the bankruptcy process overall. For a more complete discussion readers will need to turn to the National Consumer Law Center's *Consumer Bankruptcy Law and Practice* (9th ed. 2009 and Supp.). Another National Consumer Law Center publication, Bankruptcy Basics (2007), offers a step-by-step guide to current bankruptcy practice for pro bono attorneys, general practitioners, and legal services attorneys.

13.1.1.2 The 2005 Bankruptcy Amendments

Congress made significant changes to the Bankruptcy Code in 2005 under the Bankruptcy Abuse Prevention and Consumer Protection Act (BAPCPA).[13] These changes were effective for bankruptcy cases filed after October 16, 2005. The 2005 amendments did not alter the basic Bankruptcy Code provisions that apply to utility debts in consumer cases. As before the amendments, utility debts can still be discharged or made subject to affordable repayment terms. For consumer debtors, the essential Code provisions ensuring the right to continued or restored utility service after a bankruptcy filing were not changed. However, the amendments did create new paperwork requirements and established other procedural hurdles for obtaining bankruptcy relief. Some of the more important changes are summarized in this section. Although they have not affected the scope of bankruptcy relief available for most consumers, the 2005 amendments have tended to increase the time and expense associated with obtaining a bankruptcy discharge.

The 2005 amendments established a "means test" that requires bankruptcy debtors with significant disposable income to enter into debt repayment plans or otherwise be precluded from chapter 7 relief. Consumers whose household incomes are below the median for their states are completely exempt from this means test.[14] If the debtors do not fall within the below-state-median income "safe harbor," the formula allows certain deductions from income as calculated on an official form to be filed with all chapter 13 and chapter 7 cases.[15] As a result of either the automatic "safe harbor" exclusion or the application of additional deductions from income, the means test system has no effect on the great majority of low- and middle-income consumers seeking bankruptcy relief today. Particularly for debtors who have not had sufficient income to pay for the basic utilities for their homes, it is highly unlikely that the means test will be an obstacle to bankruptcy relief.

The BAPCPA amendments mandate pre-filing and post-filing counseling sessions for all consumer debtors. The debtor must attach to the initial petition a certification that

9 *See generally* National Consumer Law Center, Consumer Bankruptcy Law and Practice ch. 14 (9th ed. 2009 and Supp.).

10 11 U.S.C. §§ 522(f), 544, 545. *See* National Consumer Law Center, Consumer Bankruptcy Law and Practice § 10.4 (9th ed. 2009 and Supp.).

11 National Consumer Law Center, Consumer Bankruptcy Law and Practice chs. 11, 12 (9th ed. 2009 and Supp.).

12 NCLC's book for consumers and debt counselors, Guide to Surviving Debt (2010 ed.), contains helpful information on bankruptcy, managing utility debt, and other strategies to alleviate problems of families facing financial difficulties.

13 Pub L. No. 109-8, 119 Stat. 23 (Apr. 20, 2005).

14 Current median income figures for each state are available on the United States Trustee program website at www.usdoj.gov//ust/eo/bapcpa/meanstesting.htm. The median income cutoffs for the means test safe harbor vary considerably from state to state. For example, the Census Bureau figures applicable to bankruptcy cases filed after March 15, 2011, set the safe harbor cap for a family of four at $53,709 for New Mexico and $103,361 for Maryland.

15 Official Form 22. *See* National Consumer Law Center, Consumer Bankruptcy Law and Practice § 13.4 (9th ed. 2009 and Supp.).

the prebankruptcy session was completed within 180 days of the petition filing date. These sessions can be completed by phone, over the Internet, or in person through approved credit counseling agencies.[16] Approved counseling agencies must waive the fee (typically $30 to $45) for debtors who cannot afford to pay it. Unless the court orders otherwise, within fifteen days of the petition filing the debtor must also file copies of all pay stubs ("payment advices"), if any, or other evidence of payment received from employers within sixty days before the petition was filed.[17]

Another BAPCPA amendment affects the automatic stay in certain cases. The automatic stay is limited for certain repeat filers whose earlier cases were dismissed without a discharge order within a year of the date of filing of a new case.[18] If the debtor had one case dismissed within that one-year period, the automatic stay in the new case will not apply to the debtor thirty days after the new case is filed unless the debtor obtains a timely order for continuation of the stay. The automatic stay will not go into effect at all in the new case if, during the previous year, the debtor filed two or more bankruptcy cases and these were dismissed, unless the debtor obtains an order imposing a stay.[19]

Finally, in a change that could be relevant to some consumers seeking relief from utility debt, the 2005 amendments increased from seven to eight years the time allowed between the filing of successive chapter 7 cases.[20]

13.1.1.3 A Consumer Debtor's Bankruptcy Options

For an individual, there are two types of available bankruptcy relief: liquidation and reorganization. There are advantages and disadvantages to either strategy.

Liquidation under chapter 7 of the Code is sometimes referred to as "straight" bankruptcy.[21] In a chapter 7 case, all of the debtor's non-exempt assets are converted to cash and distributed to creditors according to certain statutory rules.[22] At the end of the proceeding, the individual debtor receives a discharge. This absolves the consumer from any responsibility to pay most debts and also gives various other protections.[23] The discharge does not, however, eliminate creditors' *in rem* rights associated with liens on property that the debtor will retain.

In most chapter 7 cases involving low- and moderate-income consumer debtors, all assets are exempt[24] so that no property is sold and no payments are made to creditors.[25] This is often referred to as a "no asset" chapter 7 case. In a no asset case, the debtor nonetheless obtains a discharge.

The second type of relief is a reorganization of the debtor's financial affairs. Reorganization is open to qualifying individuals under chapters 11, 12, and 13 of the Bankruptcy Code. Chapter 11 bankruptcies are so complicated and expensive that they rarely make sense for individuals.[26] Chapter 12 reorganizations are available only to family farmers and family fishermen.[27] Chapter 13 is the most common form of reorganization for individuals.[28]

In a chapter 13 case, the debtor proposes a plan for payment of some or all of his or her debts within certain statutory guidelines.[29] Usually this involves periodic payments from the debtor's income. The plan is then carried out under court supervision with the court protecting the debtor, and usually all of the debtor's property, from creditors. At the end of the case, as with a chapter 7 proceeding, the debtor receives a discharge from personal liability on most debts, as well as other protections.[30] One purpose of the "means testing" regime instituted under the 2005 BAPCPA amendments was to force higher-income debtors with substantial disposable income into chapter 13 repayment plans and restrict unfettered access to a chapter 7 discharge.

Although neither a chapter 13 nor a chapter 7 discharge, by itself, protects the debtor's property from creditors with valid security interests in the property, a debtor in either

16 11 U.S.C. § 109(h). *See* National Consumer Law Center, Consumer Bankruptcy Law and Practice §§ 3.2.1.4, 7.3.5 (9th ed. 2009 and Supp.).

17 11 U.S.C. § 521(a)(1)(B)(iv). *See* National Consumer Law Center, Consumer Bankruptcy Law and Practice § 7.3.10 (9th ed. 2009 and Supp.).

18 11 U.S.C. § 362(c)(3). *See* National Consumer Law Center, Consumer Bankruptcy Law and Practice § 9.3.3 (9th ed. 2009 and Supp.).

19 11 U.S.C. § 362(c)(4).

20 11 U.S.C. § 727(a)(8).

Shorter time frames apply when the consumer is a repeat filer seeking relief under chapter 13 (four-year bar after prior chapter 7 filing and two-year bar after prior chapter 13 filing. 11 U.S.C. § 1328(f)(1), (f)(2)).

21 *See* National Consumer Law Center, Consumer Bankruptcy Law and Practice ch. 3 (9th ed. 2009 and Supp.).

22 National Consumer Law Center, Guide to Surviving Debt ch. 20 (2010 ed.).

23 *Id.*

24 The exemption scheme under the Bankruptcy Code is complicated by the authority that Congress gave states to create state law exemptions and to opt out of those created by the federal bankruptcy law. A majority of states have done so. In other states debtors have the choice between federal and state exemption law. Each state's exemption scheme is set out in volume 14 of the treatise by Lawrence P. King, Collier on Bankruptcy (16 ed. rev. 2010), which is published by Matthew Bender and is almost universally available in law libraries. *See* National Consumer Law Center, Consumer Bankruptcy Law and Practice ch. 10 (9th ed. 2009 and Supp.).

A summary of state exemption laws is also found in Appendix G of National Consumer Law Center, Collection Actions (2d ed. 2011).

25 In many cases involving small amounts of non-exempt property, the property is not sold. This is because the costs of liquidating the property exceed any potential distribution to creditors.

26 *See generally* National Consumer Law Center, Consumer Bankruptcy Law and Practice § 6.3.4 (9th ed. 2009 and Supp.).

27 *Id.* at ch. 16.

28 *Id.* at chs. 4, 12.

29 *Id.* §§ 12.3–12.6.

30 *Id.* § 4.8.

chapter may seek to challenge the validity of liens.[31] If the lien is invalid, then the creditor is left with a dischargeable unsecured claim. If the lien is valid, the Code offers a number of ways for debtors to obtain full or partial relief, on favorable terms in most cases.[32] However, there are more options for dealing with secured claims in chapter 13 than in chapter 7.

13.1.1.4 The Purposes of Bankruptcy

The purposes of bankruptcy are usually described as two-fold: a fresh start for the debtor and equity among creditors.[33] The "fresh start" concept encompasses the statutory goal of allowing honest individuals who have become mired in debt to free themselves from that morass and to engage in newly productive lives unimpaired by their past financial problems. It avoids the kind of permanent discouragement that might prevent a person from ever becoming reestablished as a hard-working member of society, striving to find the good life and fulfill the American Dream. The Supreme Court has described the fresh start as "a new opportunity in life, unhampered by the pressure and discouragement of preexisting debt."[34] Central to the fresh start concept is preservation of the debtor's exempt property so that the debtor will not be forced to go forward without essential resources.

The goal of equity among creditors is achieved by the fair distribution of the debtor's assets according to established rules, set forth in the statute, which guarantees identical treatment to similarly situated creditors. This guarantee, and various provisions that provide for the forced disgorgement by creditors of assets seized by them shortly before bankruptcy, are meant to discourage creditors from rushing to be the first to seize the property of a struggling individual. Thus, even before a bankruptcy has been filed the specter of the bankruptcy may cause creditors to work with debtors to find a mutually acceptable non-bankruptcy resolution to their financial difficulties. Many creditors realize that aggressive collection could force debtors to seek relief from the bankruptcy court.

13.1.2 Public Utility Bills Under the Bankruptcy Code

13.1.2.1 Introduction

The Bankruptcy Code provides special treatment for public utility arrears. Under the law, a consumer's bankruptcy filing automatically stays a threatened shut-off[35] and requires the utility to immediately reconnect any terminated service.[36] As long as the consumer makes a deposit or provides other adequate assurance of payment[37] for future utility service and makes required payments for postpetition service,[38] utilities may not disconnect service.[39] Moreover, the consumer in bankruptcy will typically pay little or nothing on the past-due utility bills.[40]

Bankruptcy is not only a potent remedy, but the mere existence of the consumer's legal rights in bankruptcy should affect a utility's bill-collecting behavior. It will often be in a utility's self-interest to establish reasonable payment plans with consumers. The alternative is that the consumer files bankruptcy and the utility recovers little or no repayment on arrearages. Moreover, in the event of a bankruptcy, the utility service will remain connected if the consumer can meet the deposit requirements or otherwise provide adequate assurance of payment of ongoing bills. A rational utility should instead accept deferred (and even partial) payments as preferable to no payment at all.

Despite these protections, an issue does exist regarding the applicability of the Bankruptcy Code to some utilities. Before discussing the substantive protections in any detail, this issue is first addressed below.

13.1.2.2 Is a Service Provider a "Utility" Under the Bankruptcy Code?

The key to a consumer's rights to continued utility service after filing bankruptcy is Bankruptcy Code section 366.[41] This sets out special obligations that apply to a "utility." "Utility" is not a defined term in the Bankruptcy Code.

One issue that may arise is whether a utility service provider is covered. The issue arises, for example, with

31 *See* § 13.1.3.2.2, *infra*.

32 National Consumer Law Center, Consumer Bankruptcy Law and Practice ch. 11 (9th ed. 2009 and Supp.).

33 *Id.* § 2.3.

34 Local Loan Co. v. Hunt, 292 U.S. 234, 244 (1934).

35 11 U.S.C. § 362.

36 11 U.S.C. § 366. *See In re* Whittaker, 882 F.2d 791 (3d Cir. 1989).

37 *See* § 13.1.2.3.2, *infra*.

38 *In re* Begley, 41 B.R. 402 (Bankr. E.D. Pa. 1984), *aff'd*, 760 F.2d 46 (3d Cir. 1985).

39 Cheryl Anderson, *Providing Adequate Assurance for Utilities Under Section 366*, 9 Bankruptcy Dev. J. 199, 205–11 (1992); Hicks, Recent Developments in Section 336: Utility Service and the Bankruptcy Code, 1994–1995 Norton Annual Survey of Bankruptcy Law 449; Russell R. Johnson, III, *Adequate Assurance of Payment for Utilities Under 11 U.S.C. § 366(b): The Need for a Legislative Solution*, 4 J. Bankr. Law & Prac. 79 (Nov./Dec. 1994). *See* Annot., *Bankruptcy, Debtor's Protection Under 11 U.S.C. Section 366 Against Utility Service Cutoff*, 83 A.L.R. Fed. 207 (1987). *See generally* National Consumer Law Center, Consumer Bankruptcy Law and Practice (9th ed. 2009 and Supp.).

40 For example, in a chapter 7 case in which the consumer has no assets, the utility would recover nothing. In a chapter 7 or 13 case, if the consumer's assets were almost as large as the outstanding debts, then the utility would recover significantly more.

41 11 U.S.C. § 366.

Rural Electric Cooperatives, which fit part of, but not the entire, profile of a public utility.[42] Similar issues arise with respect to cable television service with nonexclusive contracts in a community.[43]

Case law generally supports finding that providers of gas, electricity, water, and telephone are covered as utilities within the meaning of Code section 366.[44] A supplier is a utility not because of its regulated status but because of its monopoly status. The legislative history of section 366 states:

> This section is intended to cover utilities that have some special position with respect to the debtor, such as an electric company, gas supplier, or telephone company that is a monopoly in the area so that the debtor cannot easily obtain comparable services from another utility.[45]

The financial impracticality of changing existing systems (for example, pipes or wiring) to allow another utility to serve a customer is an indication of the utility's monopoly status.[46]

In the future, the question of coverage under section 366 may become more commonplace and troubling as utilities lose the characteristics of a monopoly in jurisdictions where competition is introduced. If utility restructuring efforts have not produced true competition, especially when the majority of residential customers retain service from a default provider, advocates should argue that section 366 still applies. Moreover, section 366 should continue to apply to the portion of the utility bill attributable to distribution services (the pipes and wiring) when the provider retains monopoly status with respect to those services.

In *One Stop Realtour Place, Inc. v. Allegiance Telecom, Inc.*,[47] a real estate business whose telephone service had been terminated prior to filing bankruptcy claimed that a local exchange carrier had violated section 366 by refusing to restore service. The telephone company argued that, due to deregulation of telephone service and competition brought about by the Telecommunications Act of 1996, the debtor could obtain comparable service from the incumbent local exchange carrier or other companies and that the debtor's president had access to cellular service and her residential telephone service. Thus, the company suggested it was not a provider of a monopoly service and therefore not a "utility" under section 366.

In ruling that the company was subject to section 366, the bankruptcy court adopted a plain language construction of the Code section, noting that the company was a "utility" within the term's ordinary meaning since it "provides telephone service to the public and is subject to regulation by the FCC and the Pennsylvania PUC."[48] Acknowledging that market changes have taken place in the telephone industry and that the legislative history for section 366 does reference the monopoly status of the provider, the court nevertheless felt compelled to give the term a broad meaning that considers the "special position" of the provider to the debtor based on the debtor's inability to "easily obtain comparable service."[49] The court noted that the debtor's testimony was uncontradicted that it would take at least two weeks for her to get service from an alternate provider and that she would not be able to keep her same telephone number, both factors that could be fatal to a small business.

Note that, even if an entity is not found to be a utility within the meaning of section 366, a variety of protections remain including the automatic stay and a potential for discharge. What may not apply is the right to continued service after the case is filed.[50]

---

42 *See, e.g.*, Sun Valley Ranches, Inc. v. Prairie Power Coop. Inc., 856 P.2d 1292 (Idaho Ct. App. 1993). *See generally* National Consumer Law Center, The Regulation of Rural Electric Cooperatives: The Common Law, Consumer Law and a Cornucopia of Consumer Protections (1993). Chapter 1 of that volume discusses a common law basis for defining an REC as a utility.

43 *See In re* Darby 470 F.3d 573 (5th Cir. 2006) (cable provider found not a "utility" subject to section 366 based on debtor's testimony that cable service not a necessity and that similar service is available from satellite provider at same cost as adequate assurance deposit demanded by prepetition cable provider); *In re* Moorefield, 218 B.R. 795 (Bankr. M.D.N.C. 1997) (cable company granted non-exclusive franchise by municipality is not a utility).

44 *In re* Tarrant, 190 B.R. 704 (Bankr. S.D. Ga. 1995) (municipal utility covered by section 366, must restore service after filing); *In re* Gehrke, 57 B.R. 97 (Bankr. D. Or. 1985) (electric coop association is a utility). *See In re* Hobbs, 20 B.R. 488 (Bankr. E.D. Pa. 1982) (condominium owners association that sells electricity to condominium owner treated as a utility for purposes of section 366); *In re* Good Time Charlie's Ltd., 25 B.R. 226 (Bankr. E.D. Pa. 1982) (shopping mall providing electricity is a utility); *In re* Coachlight Dinner Theatre, Inc., 8 B.R. 657 (Bankr. S.D.N.Y. 1981) (radio station not utility, thus not required to continue advertising for debtor who provides adequate assurance); *In re* Robmac, Inc., 8 B.R. 1 (Bankr. N.D. Ga. 1979) (county water service covered by § 366). *See also In re* Monroe Well Serv., Inc., 83 B.R. 317 (Bankr. E.D. Pa. 1988) (electric company is utility even when it supplies service to industrial user); Kiriluk v. Chester Water Auth., 76 B.R. 979 (Bankr. E.D. Pa. 1987); *In re* Coastal Dry Dock & Repair Corp., 62 B.R. 879 (Bankr. E.D.N.Y. 1986).

45 S. Rep. No. 987, 95th Cong. 2d Sess. 60 (1978), *reprinted in* 1978 U.S.C.C.A.N. 5846.

46 *In re* Good Time Charlie's Ltd., 25 B.R. 226 (Bankr. E.D. Pa. 1982).

47 268 B.R. 430 (Bankr. E.D. Pa 2001).

48 268 B.R. 436, 437 (Bankr. E.D. Pa 2001). ("public utility" defined as a "business organization . . . performing a public service and subject to special governmental regulation") (quoting Merriam-Webster's Collegiate Dictionary (10th ed. 2001)).

49 268 B.R. 430 (Bankr. E.D. Pa 2001) (quoting *In re* Good Time Charlie's Ltd., 25 B.R. 226 (Bankr. E.D. Pa. 1982)).

50 Even if an entity is not found to be a utility within the meaning of section 366, an alternative basis for continued service that applies in some situations involving provision of services by government entities is found in 11 U.S.C. § 525(a). That section prohibits government entities from discriminating against debtors on the basis of bankruptcy. *See* § 13.1.2.5, *infra*. *See gen-*

13.1.2.3 Special Bankruptcy Rules for Utility Arrears

13.1.2.3.1 Continuation or reconnection of service

Bankruptcy Code section 366[51] establishes special rules for utility service terminations. Once a consumer files for bankruptcy, the utility may not disconnect (or refuse to reconnect) service because of the bankruptcy filing or because the consumer has not paid for service rendered before the bankruptcy filing.[52] The utility can disconnect service only if it is not paid for postpetition service or if: (1) it waits twenty days after the bankruptcy is filed, and (2) if, by the end of that twenty days, it has not received "adequate assurance of payment" for service rendered after the date of the bankruptcy filing.[53] This statutory section reads as if it is self-executing, and it is generally understood to mean that the utility may terminate service after twenty days without special permission from the court if it does not believe adequate assurance has been provided.[54]

In other words once a bankruptcy is filed, the utility may not disconnect service during the next twenty days; it may only disconnect service after that if the consumer does not provide a deposit or some other assurance of future payments (or again falls in arrears for utility service rendered after the bankruptcy is filed). Service terminations not following these rules can be remedied by swift injunctive relief from the court[55] as well as possible damages,[56] sanctions for violation of the automatic stay or contempt,[57] and attorney fees for the consumer. Standing alone, section 366 does not provide automatically for the prevailing debtor's recovery of attorney fees in an enforcement proceeding.[58] However, the Bankruptcy Code's provision creating remedies for violations of the automatic stay expressly authorizes recovery of the debtor's attorney fees.[59] Governmental units that violate section 366 are also subject to fees shifting under the Civil Rights Attorneys' Fees Act.[60]

Since section 366 states that, after a bankruptcy filing, a utility may not "refuse" to render service because of a preexisting debt, the debtor whose service has already been disconnected should be entitled to a prompt reconnect as well.[61] The Third Circuit has ruled that the utility must immediately reconnect service, even if no security deposit is provided. The consumer then has the statutory twenty days to produce adequate assurance of future payment.[62] Although sanctions for violation of the automatic stay may not be available for a utility's refusal to restore service, compensatory damages may be awarded for violations of section 366 based on the bankruptcy court's authority under 11 U.S.C. § 105.[63]

When a utility conditions restoration or continuation of service on payment of any prepetition charge, this signals a violation of the automatic stay.[64] The utility's application of

---

erally National Consumer Law Center, Consumer Bankruptcy Law and Practice § 15.5.4 (9th ed. 2009 and Supp.).

51 11 U.S.C. § 366.

52 11 U.S.C. § 366(a).

53 11 U.S.C. § 366(b).

54 *See, e.g.*, Collier on Bankruptcy ¶ 366.03 (16th ed. Rev.). *See also In re* Carter, 133 B.R. 110 (Bankr. N.D. Ohio 1991) (water company did not violate automatic stay when it terminated service after chapter 13 debtor did not provide adequate assurance payment within twenty days of filing petition); *In re* Stage Enters., Inc., 1 B.R. 732 (Bankr. M.D. Fla. 1979).

However, a utility may take substantial risks in terminating service when the debtor has tendered what he or she believes to be adequate assurance. Section 366(b) states that a "party in interest" (which presumably includes the utility) may request court notification of the amount necessary to provide adequate assurance.

55 *See In re* Hobbs, 20 B.R. 488 (Bankr. E.D. Pa. 1982). *But see* Johnson v. Philadelphia Elec. Co., 80 B.R. 30 (Bankr. E.D. Pa. 1987).

56 11 U.S.C. § 362(k)(1). *See, e.g., In re* Whittaker, 882 F.2d 791 (3d Cir. 1989) (nominal damages of $20 but no attorney fees); *In re* Tarrant, 190 B.R. 704 (Bankr. S.D. Ga. 1995) ($190 damages for lost food and $32 damages for lodging expenses); *In re* Smith, 170 B.R. 111 (Bankr. N.D. Ohio 1994) (actual damages and attorney fees awarded for willful disconnection of telephone service after notice of bankruptcy); *In re* Tabor, 46 B.R. 677 (Bankr. S.D. Ohio 1985). *See also* 11 U.S.C. § 362(h).

57 *In re* Tabor, 46 B.R. 677 (Bankr. S.D. Ohio 1985) (utility fined $250 as sanctions for contempt of court and $526 in damages for applying amount tendered to prepetition debt and requesting excessive amount as adequate assurance).

58 Whittaker v. Philadelphia Elec. Co., 92 B.R. 110 (E.D. Pa. 1988), *aff'd*, 882 F.2d 791 (3d Cir. 1989); *In re* Bedford Town Condo., 2010 WL 3777826 (Bankr. D. Md. Sept. 20, 2010).

59 11 U.S.C. § 362(k)(1).

60 42 U.S.C. § 1988. *See* Higgins v. Philadelphia Gas Works, 54 B.R. 928 (E.D. Pa. 1985) (attorney fees awarded under Civil Rights Act against municipal utility that violated section 366).

61 *In re* Whittaker, 882 F.2d 791 (3d Cir. 1989). *See also* Robinson v. Michigan Consol. Gas Co. Inc., 918 F.2d 579 (6th Cir. 1990); Citizens Gas & Coke Util. v. Matthews, 2004 WL 2137637 (S.D. Ind. Aug. 13, 2004) (rejecting gas utility's rationale of debtor's alleged "lack of creditworthiness," which included seven shut-offs for nonpayment over four years, as ground for refusal to restore service during initial twenty-day postpetition period); One Stop Realtour Place, Inc. v. Allegiance Telecom, Inc., 268 B.R. 430 (Bankr. E.D. Pa. 2001).

62 *In re* Whittaker, 882 F.2d 791 (3d Cir. 1989).

Not addressed in *Whittaker* is the question of a reconnect charge. At worst, a reconnect charge may not exceed reconnect charges assessed to users who pay their arrearages in full and request a reconnect. At best, there may be no reconnect charge because the debtor should be treated the same as a new customer. The consumer would only have to pay a reconnect charge if new customers pay connect charges. *See* Whittaker v. Philadelphia Elec. Co., 92 B.R. 110 (Bankr. E.D. Pa. 1988), *aff'd on other grounds*, 882 F.2d 791 (3d Cir. 1989).

63 *See In re* Whittaker, 882 F.2d 791 (3d Cir. 1989) (nominal damages of $20 but no attorney fees); One Stop Realtour Place, Inc. v. Allegiance Telecom, Inc., 268 B.R. 430 (Bankr. E.D. Pa. 2001) (following *Whittaker*, only compensatory damages available).

64 11 U.S.C. § 362(a)(6) (prohibiting "any act to collect, assess, or recover a claim against the debtor that arose before the commencement of the case under this title"). *See In re* Parks, 2008

a portion of the debtor's postpetition payments to the prepetition debt violates the automatic stay's broad prohibition against all actions to collect a prepetition debt.[65] The utility provider's good faith belief that it had the right to terminate service due to unpaid prepetition charges is not a defense to a debtor's action under section 362(k) of the Bankruptcy Code for damages to remedy a violation of the automatic stay.[66] A creditor's actions are "willful" for purposes of a stay violation if the creditor intended to take the actions in question.[67] An award of actual damages against the utility is mandatory if the stay violation was willful.[68]

13.1.2.3.2 The obligation to provide adequate assurance

After the twenty-day period following the bankruptcy filing, the utility may disconnect service if it does not have adequate assurance of payment of postpetition utility service. Although what constitutes "adequate assurance" is not defined for purposes of bankruptcy cases filed under chapters 7, 12, or 13, section 366(b) specifically mentions "a deposit or other security." The concept is that so long as the utility is protected as to payment for future service, there may be no disconnection for the failure to pay for prebankruptcy usage.[69] Protection in the form of a security deposit is the most obvious example but not the only form of assurance allowed.[70] When a security deposit is not feasible, there are several other options. One is to grant the utility a voluntary lien on the debtor's property for any amount owed for post-filing usage that is not paid promptly. Although there are obvious problems with giving a utility leverage in the form of a lien on property, this may be preferable to the consumer losing service entirely.[71] When the prepetition debt is small, the debtor and utility may also agree that the debtor will pay the prepetition debt as adequate assurance and waive the automatic stay with respect to that debt.[72]

Another alternative to a security deposit is available in a chapter 12 or 13 filing when significant payments are being made under the plan.[73] The plan could give priority, administrative expense status to an adequate assurance deposit or to any delinquent debt for postpetition utility service.[74] The utility would then be assured of payment for future service because the trustee would first pay the utility before other creditors under the plan.

WL 2003163 (Bankr. N.D. Ohio May 6, 2008) (gas utility willfully violated automatic stay by demanding payment for one year of prepetition service as condition to restoration of postpetition gas service to debtor); *In re* Tarrant, 190 B.R. 704 (Bankr. S.D. Ga. 1995) (utility's refusal to restore electric service unless debtor paid prepetition bill violated automatic stay); *In re* Smith, 170 B.R. 111 (Bankr. N.D. Ohio 1994) (phone company liable for actual damages, attorney fees, and punitive damages after it discontinued service and refused to restore it until payment made); *In re* Tabor, 46 B.R. 677 (Bankr. S.D. Ohio 1985) (violation of stay to terminate service after debtors refused to pay an excessive deposit and utility applied $1 received from trustee to prepetition debt); *In re* Lanford, 10 B.R. 129 (Bankr. D. Minn. 1981) (utility violated stay by refusing to restore debtor's phone service unless debtor paid prepetition charges incurred by other resident of same dwelling).

65 11 U.S.C. § 362(a)(6). *See In re* Nixon, 419 B.R. 281 (Bankr. E.D. Pa. 2009).

66 *In re* Parks, 2008 WL 2003163 (Bankr. N.D. Ohio May 6, 2008) (rejecting utility's defense that it refused to restore service under belief prepetition gas service had been stolen through meter tampering); *In re* Smith, 170 B.R. 111, 116 (Bankr. N.D. Ohio 1994) (rejecting utility creditor's defense of good faith reliance on advice of in-house counsel).

67 *See In re* Nixon, 419 B.R. 281 (Bankr. E.D. Pa. 2009) (rejecting municipal gas utility's clerical mistake defense, finding willful violation of stay in utility's application of debtors' postpetition payments to prepetition bill); National Consumer Law Center, Consumer Bankruptcy Law and Practice § 15.4.3.6 (9th ed. 2009 and Supp.).

68 *In re* Parks, 2008 WL 2003163, at *7 (Bankr. N.D. Ohio May 6, 2008).

69 11 U.S.C. § 366(b) specifically mentions "for service after such date."

70 National Consumer Law Center, Determining the Cost-Effectiveness of Utility Credit and Collection Practices 48–52 (1990) (discussing alternatives to cash deposits).

For example, prepayment of postpetition bills is an option, particularly with telephone service. *See also* Cheryl Anderson, *Providing Adequate Assurance for Utilities under Section 366*, 9 Bankruptcy Dev. J. 199, 205–11 (1992); Russell R. Johnson, III, *Adequate Assurance of Payment for Utilities under 11 U.S.C. § 366(b): The Need for a Legislative Solution*, 4 J. Bankr. Law & Prac. 79 (Nov./Dec. 1994).

71 If this option is pursued in a chapter 13 filing, it should be provided for in the debtor's plan, and it may be necessary to obtain bankruptcy court approval before the debtor grants the lien.

72 *In re* Wells, 280 B.R. 701 (Bankr. S.D. Ala. 2001).

73 11 U.S.C. § 1322(b)(1) allows debtors in a chapter 13 to designate classes of claims, thus treating some claims better than others. *See generally* National Consumer Law Center, Consumer Bankruptcy Law and Practice § 12.4 (9th ed. 2009 and Supp.).

Similar rights are available in a chapter 12 plan. *See* 11 U.S.C. § 1222.

74 *See* H.R. Rep. No. 595, 95th Cong., 1st Sess. 350 (1977).

11 U.S.C. § 366 has no exclusion dealing with administrative expenses as does 11 U.S.C. § 361. *See also* Virginia Elec. & Power Co. v. Caldor, Inc., 117 F.3d 646 (2d Cir. 1997) (administrative expense claim can be a component of adequate assurance; no requirement that court order a cash security deposit); *In re* Steinebach, 303 B.R. 634 (Bankr. D. Ariz. 2004) (debtors delinquent in utility payments may provide for deposit in plan, for which utility may file proof of claim); *In re* Epling, 255 B.R. 549 (Bankr. S.D. Ohio 2000) (approving chapter 13 plan provision requiring utilities seeking a deposit to file an administrative claim to be paid by the trustee); *In re* Hennen, 17 B.R. 720 (Bankr. S.D. Ohio 1982); *In re* George C. Frye Co., 7 B.R. 856 (Bankr. D. Me. 1980). *Compare In re* Statmore, 177 B.R. 312 (Bankr. D. Neb. 1995) (utility can be granted administrative expense status for postpetition service), *with In re* Martinez, 92 B.R. 916 (Bankr. D. Colo. 1988) (section 366 provides sole remedy and precludes administrative expense status for postpetition utility debt).

A third-party surety guaranteeing one or two month's payment should also be sufficient. When the consumer is eligible for federal fuel assistance funds that will go directly to the utility, this should also affect the size of a deposit needed to protect the utility.[75] Adequate assurance can be provided in any way that protects the utility from an unreasonable risk of nonpayment. The assurance, however, does not have to be an absolute guarantee.[76]

Section 366 was amended in 2005 by adding a new subsection (c) that deals with the provision of adequate assurance by a chapter 11 debtor. The provision lists six forms of adequate assurance that are deemed acceptable.[77] It also provides that the treatment of a utility claim as an administrative expense priority shall not constitute an assurance of payment.[78] Significantly, the statutory language is clear that the new provision applies only in chapter 11 cases.[79] This lends further support for the view that forms of adequate assurance that are alternatives to lump-sum payment of a security deposit, including forms not provided for or otherwise prohibited in section 366(c), may be acceptable in chapter 7, 12, and 13 cases.[80]

In any event, a security deposit will likely be the most common form of adequate assurance. However, limits exist on the amount and form of deposit that can be required.[81] If the consumer is not in arrears on a utility bill at the time the bankruptcy is filed and the debtor does not have a history of payment problems on the account, the consumer may argue that no adequate assurance payment is necessary.[82] In addition, it may be helpful to consider that adequate assurance of payment need not be the equivalent of a guarantee of payment.[83] While there are arguments that no deposit should be required if the utility does not seek one from its other customers,[84] particularly if it does not seek a deposit from other customers with poor credit records, the typical practice will be to require a deposit.

The bankruptcy court can review the utility's decision about the size of the deposit and a demand for an unreasonably high deposit can be modified downwards.[85] For example, the bankruptcy court could rule that a utility should not demand a security deposit in excess of what other regulated utilities in the state demand.[86] In such a situation, the bankruptcy court may adopt the state public utility commission's standards.[87] A Wisconsin bankruptcy court followed this principle. A state regulation prohibited utilities from demanding any deposit for service to a household with income under 200% of federal poverty guidelines. The court held that a utility's demand for any deposit from a bankruptcy debtor earning under the guideline amount unlawfully discriminated against the bankruptcy debtor.[88] Similarly, the utility arguably may not demand a security deposit

75 *See In re* Allen, 69 B.R. 867 (Bankr. E.D. Pa. 1987) (debtor can choose whether to apply home energy assistance payment to postpetition bill or as adequate assurance payment).

76 *See In re* Keydata Corp., 12 B.R. 156 (B.A.P. 1st Cir. 1981); *In re* Santa Clara Circuits W., Inc., 27 B.R. 680, 684–85 (Bankr. D. Utah 1982).

77 11 U.S.C. § 366(c)(1)(A) (acceptable forms of adequate assurance are a cash deposit, a letter of credit, a certificate of deposit, a surety bond, a prepayment of utility consumption, or another form of security that is mutually agreed on between the utility and the debtor or the trustee).

78 11 U.S.C. § 366(C)(1)(B).

79 *In re* Astle, 338 B.R. 855 (Bankr. D. Idaho 2006). *See generally* Bertrand Pan & Jennifer Taylor, *Sustaining Power: Applying 11 U.S.C. § 366 in Chapter 11 Post-BAPCPA*, 22 Emory Bankr. Dev. J. 371 (Spring 2006).

80 *In re* Astle, 338 B.R. 855 (Bankr. D. Idaho 2006) (2005 amendments to section 366 did not prevent chapter 12 debtor from providing adequate assurance of payment by extending to utility a first position, secured lien on the debtor's cattle).

81 *See, e.g., In re* Spencer, 218 B.R. 290 (Bankr. W.D.N.Y. 1998) (the sum of the highest two monthly statements without late charges for the year preceding bankruptcy); *In re* 499 W. Warren St. Assoc. Ltd. P'ship, 138 B.R. 363 (Bankr. N.D.N.Y. 1991) (average monthly bill); *In re* Stagecoach Enters., Inc., 1 B.R. 732 (Bankr. M.D. Fla. 1979) (two months billing).

82 *In re* Steinebach, 303 B.R. 634 (Bankr. D. Ariz. 2004) (no deposit necessary under section 366(b) for consumers with no delinquent account balance and no history of two delinquent monthly payments during preceding twelve months).

83 *In re* Steinebach, 303 B.R. 634 (Bankr. D. Ariz. 2004); *In re* Adelphia Bus. Solutions, Inc., 280 B.R. 63 (Bankr. S.D.N.Y. 2002).

84 *See* Whittaker v. Philadelphia Elec. Co., 92 B.R. 110 (Bankr. E.D. Pa. 1989), *aff'd on other grounds*, 882 F.2d 791 (3d Cir. 1989); Kiriluk v. Chester Water Auth., 76 B.R. 979 (Bankr. E.D. Pa. 1987). *See also* National Consumer Law Center, Consumer Bankruptcy Law and Practice § 9.8.2.2 (9th ed. 2009 and Supp.). *But see* Hanratty v. Philadelphia Elec. Co., 907 F.2d 1418 (3d Cir. 1990) (utility may require adequate assurance in bankruptcy even if it does not normally require security deposits from its new non-corporate customers).

85 11 U.S.C. § 366(b) states that "[o]n request of a party in interest . . . the court may order reasonable modification of the amount of the deposit or other security. . . ." *See* Sharon Steel Corp. v. National Fuel Gas Distrib. Corp., 871 F.2d 1217 (3d Cir. 1989) (court, not local regulating authority, has power to set terms under which service must be provided); *In re* Spencer, 218 B.R. 290 (Bankr. W.D.N.Y. 1998) (bankruptcy court has reasonable discretion to determine appropriate amount and form of adequate assurance); *In re* Cunha, 1 B.R. 330 (Bankr. E.D. Pa. 1979).

86 *See In re* Hennen, 17 B.R. 720 (Bankr. S.D. Ohio 1982) (utility could not demand deposit in excess of that set by state regulation without violating section 366(a)).

87 *In re* Steinebach, 303 B.R. 634 (Bankr. D. Ariz. 2004) (state regulation prohibiting deposits for customers not delinquent in payment more than twice during previous twelve months provided guidance supporting court's decision that no deposit necessary under section 366(b)).

Some courts have, however, refused to be bound by state law or PUC rules. *In re* Kiriluk, 76 B.R. 979 (Bankr. E.D. Pa. 1987). *See, e.g.,* Lloyd v. Champaign Tel. Co., 52 B.R. 653 (Bankr. S.D. Ohio 1985); *In re* Houdashell, 7 B.R. 901 (Bankr. W.D. Mo. 1981); *In re* Stagecoach Enters., Inc., 1 B.R. 732 (Bankr. M.D. Fla. 1979) (two months billing).

88 *In re* Cannon, 2008 WL 2553475 (Bankr. E.D. Wis. June 23, 2008).

greater than it seeks from other customers whose service has been disconnected and then reconnected.[89]

When a deposit is more than one month's service usage, the consumer should be allowed to make payments in installments[90] because the utility is not in danger of losing more than a month's deposit during the first month of service. To refuse the installment request would be to demand more than adequate assurance.

Some debtors have attempted to have a prepetition security deposit applied as adequate assurance of postpetition payments pursuant to section 366. Several courts have found that the prepetition deposit is security for prepetition payment and therefore may be applied to the prepetition bill based on state law rights of recoupment.[91] If this argument is not available to the utility, and the prepetition security deposit constitutes exempt property under a specific exemption or under a "wild card exemption," the security deposit can be applied toward a postpetition security deposit, although there may be limitations.[92] On the other hand, a postpetition adequate assurance payment under section 366(b) is assurance for future payments only. If a discharge is entered, the deposit can never be applied to the prepetition debt.[93]

13.1.2.3.3 *Procedure for determining adequate assurance*

The procedure for determining the amount of security deposit or adequate assurance is somewhat unclear. Some utilities will automatically respond to the consumer's notice of bankruptcy by issuing an immediate demand for adequate assurance in a specific amount.[94] If the utility does not do so, local practice should be reviewed either with the utility or with an attorney familiar with local consumer bankruptcy practice. Some utilities do not collect deposits from consumers in bankruptcy. If that is the case, obviously no deposit or other assurance should be offered. On the other hand, if the local utility does expect adequate assurance, the consumer should probably propose a form of adequate assurance to the utility during the twenty-day grace period.[95]

---

89 Actually, one might argue that a consumer who has filed a bankruptcy has a better chance than others of being able to meet all debt obligations. In *In re* Fisher, 29 B.R. 542 (Bankr. D. Kan. 1983), the court discussed the risk to future creditors involved with a chapter 11 reorganization plan. The court held that such a plan "carries with it a statutory presumption it will be completed." 29 B.R. at 545 (Bankr. D. Kan. 1983). *Accord In re* Doud, 74 B.R. 865, 869 (Bankr. S.D. Iowa 1987).

The court noted that "an intelligently developed plan" may result in a debtor:

> who is better able to meet his obligations than is the average debtor to whom a particular creditor normally lends. A plan may result in the debtor having substantially less unsecured debt and, more importantly, a plan will detail a specific budget along with a particular provision for setting aside a sufficient amount of future income to fund plan payments.

Bankruptcy Reform Act of 1978: Chapter 13 Cramdown of the Secured Creditor, 1981 Wis. L. Rev. 333, 357, n.131 (1981) (quoting Comment).

The court also noted that "these factors, along with the debtor's court-imposed obligation to fund the plan, might make payments less risky than the loan repayments of an average debtor." *Bankruptcy Reform Act of 1978: Chapter 13 Cramdown of the Secured Creditor*, 1981 Wis. L. Rev. 333, 357, n.131 (1981). *Accord In re* Steinebach, 303 B.R. 634, 641 (Bankr. D. Ariz. 2004) (bankruptcy filing will make it "more, not less, likely that the debtor will be able to pay postpetition monthly utility bills"); *In re* Wilkinson, 33 B.R. 933, 936–37 (Bankr. S.D.N.Y. 1983). *But see In re* Southern States Motor Inns, 709 F.2d 647, 651–53 (11th Cir. 1983); *In re* Fi-Hi Pizza, 40 B.R. 258, 270 (Bankr. D. Mass. 1984) (rejecting a downward adjustment for the rehabilitative aspects of a reorganization plan).

90 *In re* Robmac, Inc., 8 B.R. 1 (Bankr. N.D. Ga. 1979); *In re* Cunha, 1 B.R. 330 (Bankr. E.D. Va. 1979). *See also In re* Bedford Town Condo., 427 B.R. 380 (Bankr. D. Md. 2010) (interpreting stricter chapter 11 utility deposit requirements under 11 U.S.C. § 366(c), court allows debtor to pay a two-month average usage deposit in affordable installments).

91 *E.g.*, *In re* McMahon, 129 F.3d 93 (2d Cir. 1997).

Similarly, some courts have granted relief from stay to allow a utility company to apply the prepetition utility deposit to the prepetition debt. *See* Brooks Shoe Mfg. v. United Tel. Co., 39 B.R. 980 (E.D. Pa. 1984). *See generally* National Consumer Law Center, Consumer Bankruptcy Law and Practice § 10.4.2.6.7 (9th ed. 2009 and Supp.).

92 *In re* Cole, 104 B.R. 736 (Bankr. D. Md. 1989). *See also In re* Anchor Glass Container Corp., 342 B.R. 872 (Bankr. M.D. Fla. 2005) (to extent prepetition deposit for prepetition service is used for adequate assurance payment, deposit may only be applied to postpetition usage and any unused portion must be refunded to debtor).

This result may be correct when the utility company did not meet the state law prerequisites to obtain a right of set-off or other security interest by, for example, segregating the security deposit funds. *E.g.*, *In re* Voight, 24 B.R. 983, 985 (Bankr. N.D. Tex. 1982) (utility security deposits are property of the estate since prerequisites to state or bankruptcy set-off rights were not met).

93 *See In re* Smiley, 1998 Bankr. LEXIS 392 (Bankr. S.D. Ill. 1998).

The application of a postpetition adequate assurance payment is somewhat less clear if the prepetition debt is not discharged when, for example, the case is dismissed. Arguably, adequate assurance payments made pursuant to the Bankruptcy Code cannot later be treated as a security deposit for other purposes under state utility tariffs.

94 A utility letter demanding a deposit does not violate the automatic stay. *In re* Norsal Indus., 147 B.R. 85 (Bankr. E.D.N.Y. 1992); *In re* Heard, 84 B.R. 454 (Bankr. W.D. Tex. 1987) (utility may make demand for adequate assurance).

95 If the consumer simply sends in a payment, however, he or she should make clear to the utility that the payment is the assurance for future service and that it should *not* be applied to prepetition arrears. Some courts place the burden on the debtor to provide reasonable assurance; the utility need only send the Public Service Commission shut-off notice. *In re* American Investcorp & Dev. Co., 155 B.R. 300 (Bankr. D.R.I. 1993).

In another case in which no communication occurred, the court allowed a shut-off. *In re* Carter, 133 B.R. 110 (Bankr. N.D. Ohio 1991).

In the latter situation, if the consumer must propose the size of the assurance, he or she should inquire first as to the standard amount. It may also be possible to argue that absent a demand for adequate assurance the consumer debtor has no basis on which to pay. The risk in such a course of action is that the provisions of section 366 appear, by their plain language, to place the burden on the debtor.

If the utility and the consumer cannot agree on the form and/or amount of assurance, the safest approach is to give the utility whatever assurance it seeks and then apply to the bankruptcy court to modify the amount of the security deposit.[96] If this is impractical, another safe approach is to apply to the bankruptcy court before the twenty-day period has expired, asking the court to set the type and amount of adequate assurance.[97]

Usually a utility will agree to continue service until the court determines the issue but, if the utility will not agree, the consumer should request a stay of any disconnect from the bankruptcy court until the court rules on the issue of adequate assurance. Frequently, the utility will not even appear at the hearing to modify the amount of security. In many cases, it is not practical for a utility to contest the size of one individual's security deposit. If the utility does not appear, it is likely the court will rule immediately in the consumer's favor or grant temporary relief until it does rule.

Another approach, perhaps more risky, is to offer the utility what the consumer believes to be adequate assurance. If the utility then disconnects service without getting a declaration from the bankruptcy court first as to the reasonableness of the tender of assurance, then the utility arguably is subject to contempt sanctions if the court finds the consumer's tender was reasonable.[98] If the utility continues to provide service and accept monthly payments for an extended period of time after the debtors have made what they considered to be an appropriate adequate assurance payment, the utility's conduct should be construed as a waiver of any objection to the amount of the adequate assurance payment.[99] A variety of pleadings on these issues are contained in NCLC's *Consumer Bankruptcy Law and Practice* appx. G.6 (9th ed. 2009 and Supp.).

96 A form motion is available in National Consumer Law Center, Consumer Bankruptcy Law and Practice appx. G, Form 57 (9th ed. 2009 and Supp.) (Motion for Modification of Security Deposit for Utility Service).

97 11 U.S.C. § 366(b).

98 *See also* § 6.7, *supra* (discussing damage actions that can be brought when a utility engages in an unlawful disconnection of service).

99 *In re* Weisel, 2010 WL 419442 (W.D. Pa. Feb. 1, 2010) (utility waived right to terminate gas service for debtors' failure to make full adequate assurance payment by accepting payments for nearly one-and-one-half years after chapter 13 petition filed, but utility properly terminated service for failure to pay for postpetition service).

13.1.2.3.4 Post-petition termination procedures

Once the debtor has provided adequate assurance to a utility, the involvement of the bankruptcy court normally ends. Absent a contrary procedure specifically ordered by the bankruptcy court or agreed to by the debtor as part of the adequate assurance, state law will govern the treatment of postpetition debts.[100] Thus, any termination procedures required by state law or consumer rights provided by state law are applicable to debts arising after adequate assurance has been provided.

The automatic stay bars creditor actions to collect upon a prebankruptcy debt.[101] The stay does not restrict actions to collect for postpetition utility usage. The automatic stay also prohibits creditors from exercising control over property of the bankruptcy estate.[102] However, courts have rejected the contention that the automatic stay's prohibition on actions against property of the bankruptcy estate bars termination of service to chapter 13 debtors who defaulted on postpetition utility obligations.[103]

13.1.2.4 Utility Has No Service Obligation If Customer Has Tampered with Service

Courts have found no section 366 obligation to restore utility service to a debtor if the utility can show that the debtor, or sometimes someone under the debtor's control or in the debtor's family, has tampered with utility lines or meters or otherwise engaged in illegal use of utility service. This has been dubbed the "tampering exception" to section 366.[104]

100 Robinson v. Michigan Consol. Gas Co. Inc., 918 F.2d 579 (6th Cir. 1990) (section 366 does not preempt state and municipal utility termination regulations); Begley v. Philadelphia Elec. Co., 760 F.2d 46 (3d Cir. 1985) (state termination rights still apply to debtor in bankruptcy).

101 11 U.S.C. § 362(a)(6).

102 11 U.S.C. § 362(a)(3).

103 *In re* Jones, 369 B.R. 745 (B.A.P. 1st Cir. 2007) (utility does not violate bankruptcy stay by terminating gas service and refusing to restore service to chapter 13 debtor for nonpayment of postpetition service charges; noting that modification of chapter 13 plan to cure postpetition utility arrearage would have been an option for debtor to preserve service); *In re* Weisel, 2010 WL 419442 (W.D. Pa. Feb. 1, 2010) (gas utility did not need order for relief from stay to terminate service solely due to debtor's failure to pay for postpetition service; termination of service to chapter 13 debtor was not an action to exercise control over property of the bankruptcy estate in violation of section 362(a)(3)).

104 *See In re* Crome, 2008 WL 5645100 (Bankr. N.D. Ill. Dec. 23, 2008) (no violation of automatic stay or section 366 to terminate service for debtor's unauthorized pre- and postpetition gas usage); Memphis Light, Gas & Water Div. v. Farley, 135 B.R. 292 (W.D. Tenn. 1991) (restitution required before service restored); *In re* Morris, 66 B.R. 28 (E.D. Mich. 1986) (restitution required before service restored); *In re* Webb, 38 B.R. 541 (Bankr. E.D. Pa. 1984) (utility has burden of proving tampering within reasonable time before request to reinstate).

The debtor may contest the allegations of tampering in a proceeding seeking restoration of service as required by section 366. The burden in such a proceeding is on the utility to establish that tampering occurred.[105] If the utility denied service on the basis of what proves to be an erroneous claim of tampering, the utility can be held liable for monetary damages for violation of the bankruptcy stay.[106] "Tampering" and other forms of illegal reconnection must be distinguished from customers' continued receipt of service due to the utility's own lack of oversight. The utility's use of pejorative terms such as "stolen services" or "unauthorized services" cannot transform the utility's own negligence into an act of "tampering."[107] Other non-bankruptcy approaches to restoration of service may also apply as discussed elsewhere in this treatise.[108]

13.1.2.5 The Right to Continued Utility Service Under Section 525(a) for Bankruptcy Debtors Who Are Customers of Utilities That Are "Governmental Units"

Section 525(a) of the Bankruptcy Code prohibits government entities from discriminating against bankruptcy debtors.[109] Specifically, the section bars "governmental units" from denying certain benefits ("a license, permit, charter, franchise, or other similar grant") to a person solely because the person owed a debt to the government, filed for bankruptcy relief, and discharged the debt.[110] The Code defines a "governmental unit" to be a "department, agency, or instrumentality" of federal, state, or local government.[111] A municipal department that provides water, gas, electric, or similar utility services to consumers fits squarely within the definition of a "governmental unit."[112]

Under the Code's anti-discrimination provision, the governmental unit must treat a bankruptcy debtor who discharges debts owed to the government as if the debts never existed.[113] In the context of utility service, if the customer could have retained continued and uninterrupted service if he or she had made timely payments on prepetition bills, the government utility must continue to provide uninterrupted service upon the customer's filing a bankruptcy petition.

A governmental unit utility may terminate service due to nonpayment for postpetition service, using termination procedures as it would for any customer who did not pay bills. The utility also retains the right to enforce prepetition liens that were not avoided through an independent action by the debtor during the bankruptcy case. However, the government utility may not treat the bankruptcy debtor differently solely because the debtor owed an unsecured and dischargeable prepetition debt to the utility. Any demand for a new deposit or other form of payment based on the debtor's having owed a prepetition debt to the utility would violate section 525(a).

There is arguably a conflict between a straightforward application of Code section 366(b) and section 525(a). Section 366(b) on its face expressly allows a utility to discontinue and refuse service if a bankruptcy debtor does not timely comply with the "adequate assurance" requirement, typically payment of a deposit postpetition. On the other hand, section 525(a) mandates that a governmental unit treat the bankruptcy debtor as if the prepetition debt never existed.

Two appellate decisions have strengthened debtors' arguments that the anti-discrimination terms of section 525(a) must prevail over any contrary obligations created under section 366(b).[114] In *Federal Communications Commission v. Nextwave Personal Communications*, the Supreme Court held that section 525(a) barred the Federal Communication Commission (FCC) from revoking a debtor's license for broadband spectrums solely because the debtor had failed to make prepetition installment payments due under an auction financing agreement with the government. In reaching its conclusion, the Court rejected the government's argument that in canceling the licenses it was simply following its regulatory

105 *In re* Broadnax, 37 B.R. 909 (Bankr. E.D. Pa. 1984) (when utility could not meet burden of proving tampering, section 366 applies).

106 *In re* Parks, 2008 WL 2003163 (Bankr. N.D. Ohio May 6, 2008).

107 *Id.* 2008 WL 2003163, at *5–6 (N.D. Ohio May 6, 2008) (distinguishing case in which debtor passively received continued gas service due to utility's billing mistakes from cases in which customers took affirmative steps to reconnect illegally after termination or otherwise directly tampered with meter).

108 *See* Index, *infra* (see under "Meter Tampering").

109 11 U.S.C. § 525(a). *See* National Consumer Law Center, Consumer Bankruptcy Law and Practice § 9.8.2.2.5 (9th ed. 2009 and Supp.).

110 11 U.S.C. § 525(a).

111 11 U.S.C. § 101(27).

112 *See In re* Marcano, 288 B.R. 324 (Bankr. S.D.N.Y. 2003) (section 525(a) looks to whether the entity performs a "public function" or whether there is a "pervasive entwinement" of an organization's activities with those of the government). *See also In re* Stoltz, 315 F.3d 80 (2d Cir. 2002) (local housing authority is a governmental unit subject to section 525(a)); TI Fed. Credit Union v. DelBonis, 72 F.3d 921 (1st Cir. 1995) (credit union is "governmental unit" because it acts as instrumentality of government in carrying out regulated lending activities); *In re* Exquisito Servs., Inc., 823 F.2d 151 (5th Cir. 1987) (concession granted to run business on military base protected by section 525(a)).

113 *See, e.g.*, Nextwave Personal Commc'ns v. Federal Commc'ns Comm'n, 254 F.3d 130, 153 (D.C. Cir. 2001), *aff'd sub nom.* Federal Commc'ns Comm'n v. Nextwave Personal Commc'ns, 537 U.S. 293 (2003) (termination of licenses contrary to section 525(a) if FCC would have allowed licensee to retain licenses if timely installment payments on debt had been made).

114 *See* Federal Commc'ns Comm'n v. Nextwave Personal Commc'ns, 537 U.S. 293 (2003); *In re* Stoltz, 315 F.3d 80 (2d Cir. 2002). *Cf. In re* Heard, 84 B.R. 454 (Bankr. W.D. Tex. 1987) (suggesting that section 366(b) takes precedence over section 525(a)).

guidelines.[115] The Supreme Court noted that the FCC would have allowed the purchaser to retain the licenses had the purchaser timely paid the installments instead of defaulting and filing for bankruptcy relief. The revocation of the licenses was clearly due to nonpayment of a debt. Section 525(a) applied regardless of what the FCC claimed were valid regulatory reasons for refusing to restore the licenses.

The *Nextwave* decision counters a local government utility's argument that it can demand a deposit or similar payment from a bankruptcy debtor because such deposits are allowed under a state or local regulatory scheme. There is no "regulatory purpose" exception to the application of section 525(a). If the government utility would not require the deposit if the customer had not incurred the dischargeable debt, then the termination of service for nonpayment of an adequate assurance deposit or simply because the customer filed for bankruptcy relief violates section 525(a).

In *In re Stoltz*, the Second Circuit held that section 525(a) bars a public housing authority from proceeding to evict a tenant who owed a prepetition rent debt to the housing authority. In *Stoltz*, the housing authority claimed that a different Code section, section 365(b)(1), required that the debtor/tenant promptly cure her rent default or provide adequate assurance of a prompt cure as a condition to maintaining rights under her public housing lease. The housing authority argued that the terms of section 365(b)(1) applied to all leases in bankruptcy. According to the housing authority, the requirements of section 365(b)(1) trumped any duty it might have as a governmental unit under section 525(a). The court of appeals disagreed. The court held that section 525(a) was a specific Code provision that applied to governmental units such as housing authorities. There was a direct conflict between the application of section 525(a) and section 365(b)(1) in this situation, and the specific duties applicable to the housing authority as a governmental unit took precedence over the Code provisions that applied generally to leases in bankruptcy.[116] The analogy to utility service should be clear. Section 366(b) is a Code provision applicable to utility service in bankruptcy in general. Section 525(a) applies to governmental units specifically and sets important limitations on how governmental units may treat bankruptcy debtors. In the event of any conflict between the implementation of section 525(a) and section 366(b), section 525(a) must prevail, provided the utility is a governmental unit.[117]

An action for declaratory and injunctive relief to enforce the debtor's rights under section 525(a) would be the appropriate avenue for relief should a government utility improperly insist on payment of a deposit as a condition to continued service or restoration of service to a bankruptcy debtor.[118] The complaint may also include a claim for damages for violation of the bankruptcy stay.[119]

13.1.3 General Bankruptcy Considerations

13.1.3.1 Treatment of Pre-Bankruptcy Arrearages

When a consumer files a chapter 7 bankruptcy, all debts listed with the bankruptcy court are discharged (with certain specified exceptions, such as debts incurred by fraud).[120] In the typical case involving most low-income households, when the consumer-petitioner has no assets, the utility gets nothing for the amount owed prepetition, and the consumer has no future legal obligation to pay the debts for the prepetition usage.[121] Nor can the utility disconnect service

115 537 U.S. 293, 301–02 (2003).

116 *In re* Stoltz, 315 F.3d 80, 92–95 (2d Cir. 2002).

117 In an early decision, one court reconciled Code sections 525(a) and 366(b) in the opposite way, holding that section 366(b)'s adequate assurance provision took precedence over the governmental unit's duty under section 525(a) to treat debtors without discrimination. *In re* Heard, 84 B.R. 454 (Bankr. W.D. Tex. 1987).

In addition to ruling well before the *Nextwave* and *Stoltz* decisions described above, the *Heard* court relied upon a Second Circuit decision construing section 525(a). *In re* Goldrich, 771 F.2d 28 (2d Cir. 1985). In later amendments to the Bankruptcy Code, Congress expressed disapproval of the *Goldrich* decision. *See In re* Stoltz, 315 F.3d 80, 86 n. 2.

118 *See* National Consumer Law Center, Consumer Bankruptcy Law and Practice appx. G, Form 104 (9th ed. 2009 and Supp.) (form relates to enforcement of section 525(a) against a public housing authority but may be adapted for public utility threatening termination of service or refusing to restore service).

119 11 U.S.C. § 362(k).

In some instances, a state governmental unit may argue that a claim for damages is barred by the Eleventh Amendment to the Constitution. *See* National Consumer Law Center, Consumer Bankruptcy Law and Practice § 14.3.2.2 (9th ed. 2009 and Supp.) (discussing sovereign immunity issues in bankruptcy).

120 *See* 11 U.S.C. §§ 523, 524, 727.

121 If a consumer fraudulently steals utility service, however, such as by tampering with a meter, the utility may argue that this debt was incurred by fraud and is not dischargeable in a chapter 7 or chapter 13 bankruptcy. 11 U.S.C. §§ 523(a)(2), 1328(a)(2).

Alternatively, the utility may argue that theft of service is conversion which creates a non-dischargeable debt for willful and malicious injury under 11 U.S.C. § 523(a)(6). In most such cases, there are questions about whether the debtor is responsible for the alleged theft and about the amount of service which is stolen. The utility should be required to carry the burden of proof that this debtor is actually responsible for the fraudulent behavior. The utility's adversary complaint seeking to have the debt declared non-dischargeable on these grounds must also be timely filed within sixty days of the first date set for the meeting of creditors in the debtor's bankruptcy case. Fed. R. Bankr. P. 4007(c).

In addition, debts that are nondischargeable for willful and malicious injury to property under 11 U.S.C. § 523(a)(6) may be discharged in a chapter 13 bankruptcy. 11 U.S.C. § 1328(a)(2). *See* National Consumer Law Center, Consumer Bankruptcy Law and Practice § 15.4 (9th ed. 2009 and Supp.) (discussing in detail the exceptions to discharge). *See generally* Roger D. Colton, *Heightening the Burden of Proof in Utility Shutoff*

or refuse reinstatement because of nonpayment of these prepetition debts.

In a chapter 7 proceeding, a consumer's non-exempt assets[122] are sold by a trustee to pay creditors.[123] But in many consumer cases, all of a consumer's assets are exempt, meaning the consumer will lose no assets through the chapter 7 filing.[124] For example, a consumer's home is only forfeited to the extent the home's value exceeds the mortgages on the house,[125] and only if this difference is more than the applicable homestead exemption.[126] Thus, for example, a chapter 7 filing has no impact on a $70,000 home with a $50,000 mortgage if the state's homestead exemption is $20,000 or more.[127]

When a consumer has non-exempt assets, or is in arrears on a secured debt, a chapter 13 filing (or a chapter 12 filing for family farmers and family fishermen) is usually preferable to chapter 7. The chapter 13 filing will protect the debtor's unsecured assets. In chapter 13, instead of liquidating assets, a consumer proposes a plan to deal with the secured creditors and also to pay out to unsecured creditors over a period of three to five years a certain percentage of the amount owed.[128]

The amount paid over time to the unsecured creditors will vary depending on the consumer's income and assets. The unsecured creditors must receive at least as much as they would have received in a chapter 7 bankruptcy if the consumer's non-exempt assets were liquidated.[129] Under an alternate test, the unsecured creditors must receive everything the consumer earns over the term of the plan that does not have to go to secured creditors and that is not reasonably necessary for the maintenance or support of the debtor and the debtor's dependents.[130] The unsecured creditors are entitled to be paid under whichever test yields more.

The utility companies will only be general unsecured creditors and will thus receive only a percentage of the amount owed them, again depending on the size of the consumer's non-exempt assets, income, and reasonably necessary expenses.[131] In many cases, the utilities will receive only 10% or less of the arrears and whatever percentage they do receive will be paid in installments over three to five years.

The Bankruptcy Code does not mandate that chapter 13 plan installments be in equal monthly amounts.[132] For example, in northern states, where postpetition utility bills may be highest in winter months, the debtor's attorney could propose a plan whereby installments for prepetition debts are paid only in the warmer months to allow more level utility payments over the whole year. Also, the plan could propose skipping payments the first few months to allow the consumer to produce a security deposit for postpetition service.

13.1.3.2 Status of Utility Claims in Bankruptcy

13.1.3.2.1 Objecting to utility claims for priority treatment

As discussed above, utility arrears are generally unsecured claims without entitlement to priority payment in the bankruptcy process. Prepetition utility debts are thus not entitled to any special treatment in the bankruptcy payment scheme.[133] Occasionally, however, a utility will improperly assert a priority. This utility practice can be especially disadvantageous to a debtor in chapter 13, when priority

Cases Involving Allegations of Fraud, 33 Howard L.J. 137 (1990).

122 *See* National Consumer Law Center, Consumer Bankruptcy Law and Practice ch. 10 (9th ed. 2009 and Supp.) (analysis of what property is exempt).

123 A chapter 7 proceeding is a liquidation of non-exempt assets to pay creditors.

124 Common exemptions include a certain amount of equity in a home, a certain amount of equity in a car, inexpensive household goods, certain property necessary for the debtor to work, and certain benefits such as social security, unemployment compensation, and public assistance.

125 To the extent that the value of property equals the mortgage on the property, the debtor has no equity in that property that could be paid to unsecured creditors. The creditor with the mortgage on the property—"the secured creditor"—has first priority.

126 In most states, the applicable state homestead exemption will apply. In certain states the debtor can choose between the federal bankruptcy homestead exemption of $21,625 per debtor or the state homestead exemption. The basic federal bankruptcy exemptions that are available to debtors at the option of each state are listed in 11 U.S.C. § 522(d). State law homestead exemptions vary greatly in amount from state to state.

127 If there is a small amount of non-exempt equity, generally the trustee will not sell the property because of the costs of sale. These include transfer taxes, realtor fees, capital gains taxes, and other similar costs associated with transfer of property.

128 11 U.S.C. § 1322.

129 11 U.S.C. § 1325(a)(4).

130 11 U.S.C. § 1325(b).

For debtors whose household income is above the state median family income, the amount required to be paid into the plan for disposable income is based on the "current monthly income" formula provided for in section 101(10A) of the Bankruptcy Code. However, the Supreme Court has held that the amount derived through the "current monthly income" formula is only presumptively the correct amount that the above-median income debtor must pay under a chapter 13 plan. Hamilton v. Lanning, 130 S. Ct. 2464 (2010).

At the time of plan confirmation, the bankruptcy court may recognize known or virtually certain changes in the debtor's income and expenses that render the formulistic "current monthly income" calculation inappropriate for certain debtors. In these instances the court may look to the actual income or expenses of the debtors. *See* National Consumer Law Center, Consumer Bankruptcy Law and Practice § 12.3.4 (9th ed. 2009 and Supp.).

131 11 U.S.C. § 1325.

132 *See* 11 U.S.C. §§ 1322, 1325.

133 11 U.S.C. § 507(a). *See* 11 U.S.C. §§ 726 (order of payment of claims in chapter 7), 1322(a)(2) (requirement that priority claims be paid in full under a chapter 13 plan).

debts must be paid in full in order to successfully complete the case.

Debtor's counsel must be careful to review proofs of claim filed by utilities. When a priority is asserted, it is usually asserted in bad faith or in error.[134] An objection to claim should be filed. If the priority claim is frivolous or otherwise in bad faith, sanctions should be available.[135] A form objection to an improper priority claim is contained in another National Consumer Law Center treatise.[136]

13.1.3.2.2 Dealing with secured claims of utilities

There are generally two instances in which utility claims may be secured by a lien.[137] The first of these is when the utility has a judgment lien against property of the debtor obtained in a court process seeking to collect the debt. Depending on the law of the applicable jurisdiction, a judgment can be a lien on various property but, in most cases, use of a judgment as a lien will be limited to attachment on real estate. For the lien to be enforceable it must be valid under state law. Utility liens like other liens may be attacked when they are wholly or partially invalid.[138]

Judgment liens can also be attacked and voided when they impair an exemption to which the debtor would otherwise be entitled.[139] When that avenue is available, a motion may be filed that, if successful, renders the lien void and the claim unsecured. In many cases, the utility will not oppose the motion and an order will be entered by default. Some care should be taken to properly record the order voiding the lien so that it will be indexed with the judgment. This will prevent title problems from arising at a later date.

The other situation in which a utility may have a secured claim is when the utility is a government entity and has a right to a statutory lien for unpaid bills. In many parts of the country water utilities have this right. Often the resulting liens are enforceable as tax liens in the applicable jurisdiction.[140] Under certain circumstances, statutory liens can be avoided by the debtor or the trustee under 11 U.S.C. §§ 544 or 545. The most common use of this provision is when the liens are not properly recorded and so are unenforceable against a bona fide purchaser for value.[141]

A final option for voiding utility liens is stripdown in chapter 13. Under 11 U.S.C. § 506, a secured claim can be no greater than the value of the collateral securing the claim. To the extent the claim exceeds the value of the collateral it is void: this is a stripdown. This can reduce or eliminate liens that have no real economic value to the creditor because even if the collateral were seized and sold, the sale would not yield sufficient proceeds to repay the lien.[142]

If a lien cannot be avoided, then the utility will have to be dealt with as a secured creditor. In chapter 7, this means that the lien will survive the bankruptcy unless it is paid through sale of property or redemption under 11 U.S.C. § 722. In chapter 13, the lien will have to be dealt with in the chapter 13 plan, either by payment in installments or by allowing the creditor to retain the lien and the concomitant enforcement rights. These and other options for dealing with secured creditors are discussed at length in Chapter 11 of National Consumer Law Center, *Consumer Bankruptcy Law and Practice* (9th ed. 2009 and Supp.).

Even if the lien survives the bankruptcy, however, it is important to remember that the debtor's personal obligation to repay the debt is discharged. Since a utility's shut-off remedy emerges from the debtor's personal liability to pay the debt, the shut-off remedy is unavailable to collect the debt even if the lien remains. Thus the lien can be enforced under the appropriate state law procedures, but shut-off cannot be used as an alternative basis to collect the debt.[143]

134 One very unlikely, but possible, priority claim by a utility would be for postpetition services. This might be allowable as an administrative expense under 11 U.S.C. § 507(a)(1). Utilities will rarely assert a claim for postpetition services in the bankruptcy process, preferring instead to utilize their non-bankruptcy remedies such as termination of services.

135 Fed. R. Bankr. P. 9011.

136 *See* National Consumer Law Center, Consumer Bankruptcy Law and Practice appx. G, Form 79 (9th ed. 2009 and Supp.) (Objection to Frivolous Priority Claim and Request for Sanctions).

137 A third situation arises occasionally for utility financed appliances. The utility may retain a purchase money security interest in the appliance after it is sold. In some parts of the country the monthly installment on the appliance will be billed together with the monthly usage charge. There are a variety of strategies for addressing security interests in personal property. However, those issues are beyond the scope of this treatise. *See generally* National Consumer Law Center, Consumer Bankruptcy Law and Practice ch. 11 (9th ed. 2009 and Supp.).

138 11 U.S.C. § 502(b)(1). *See also* 28 U.S.C. § 157(b)(2)(k). *See generally* National Consumer Law Center, Consumer Bankruptcy Law and Practice § 14.4.3 (9th ed. 2009 and Supp.).

139 11 U.S.C. § 522(f). *See* National Consumer Law Center, Consumer Bankruptcy Law and Practice appx. G, Form 92 (9th ed. 2009 and Supp.).

140 The enforcement of tax liens and available defenses are discussed in National Consumer Law Center, Foreclosures ch. 4 (2d ed. 2007 and Supp.).

141 *See* National Consumer Law Center, Consumer Bankruptcy Law and Practice § 10.4.2.6.2 (9th ed. 2009 and Supp.). *See, e.g.*, McLean v. City of Phila., 891 F.2d 474 (3d Cir. 1989).

142 This option is available only in chapter 13. *See* Dewsnup v. Timm, 502 U.S. 410, 112 S. Ct. 773, 116 L. Ed. 2d 903 (1992).
Stripdown is further discussed in National Consumer Law Center, Consumer Bankruptcy Law and Practice § 11.7 (9th ed. 2009 and Supp.). The restriction on stripdown embodied in the Supreme Court's decision in Nobelman v. American Sav. Bank, 508 U.S. 324 (1993) is inapplicable because utility liens are not "security interests" entitled to protection as defined in the Bankruptcy Code since they are not created by agreement. *See, e.g.*, *In re* McDonough, 166 B.R. 9 (Bankr. D. Mass. 1994); *In re* Cullen, 150 B.R. 1 (Bankr. D. Me. 1993).

143 *See generally* National Consumer Law Center, Consumer Bankruptcy Law and Practice ch. 15 (9th ed. 2009 and Supp.).

13.1.3.3 Bankruptcy Rights As Leverage to Establish Voluntary Payment Plans

Utilities that refuse to work out payment plans with low-income customers and instead aggressively disconnect customer service may be acting against their own economic best interest.

In the typical low-income consumer case, the consumer has few, if any, non-exempt assets. A bankruptcy filing would thus permanently eliminate all or most of the debt owed to the utility at the time of filing, with any amount that is to be paid often disbursed in installments over a period of years. In addition, the utility would not be permitted to disconnect service based on the prior debt. In the alternative, the utility could negotiate a payment plan, even if this plan is for payment of only part of the arrearages. Partial payment is better than the little or no payment the utility would receive under the Bankruptcy Code. Utilities might be better off to deal with the consumer informally.

It also may be in the consumer's own interest to negotiate a plan with the utility rather than to file bankruptcy. This would avoid both the cost of bankruptcy and any consumer reluctance associated with such a filing. It does not penalize the consumer in any fashion to avoid bankruptcy; the consumer can always file bankruptcy at a later date, if the arrearages are not brought under control. Moreover, since a consumer may not file for a second chapter 7 bankruptcy for eight years,[144] if any possibility of significant imminent future financial problems exists, the chapter 7 bankruptcy remedy may need to be kept open for future use.[145]

13.1.3.4 Disadvantages to Bankruptcy Filing

A filing fee in the amount of $299 must be paid for a chapter 7 case and $274 for a chapter 13 case, although the fee may be waived in a chapter 7 case and paid in installments in a chapter 7 or 13 case.[146] Based on a requirement imposed by the 2005 amendments, the debtor will also have to obtain a budget and credit counseling briefing from an approved credit counseling agency within the 180 days before the bankruptcy is filed.[147] Filing a chapter 7 bankruptcy will result in the loss of non-exempt assets. Filing a chapter 13 case will require monthly bankruptcy payments for the period of the chapter 13 plan, usually three years. In some cases these amounts will exceed the payments necessary under a voluntary payment agreement.

There is no clear answer to the question whether filing bankruptcy will affect creditors' perceptions of the debtor's creditworthiness. The bankruptcy filing can appear on a credit record for ten years,[148] but since bankruptcy eliminates most obligations on prepetition debts, households should be in a better position to pay current bills and should thus be better able to repay future loans. For this reason some creditors are willing to provide credit to debtors who have filed recent bankruptcies.

Finally, it should be clear to the client that filing bankruptcy is not a panacea. The bankruptcy will only address arrears arising prior to filing. If fundamental utility service remains unaffordable, or if the debtor has other financial priorities, these will lead to postbankruptcy debts and long-term problems with access to service. These fundamental issues are addressed, to the extent possible, in other sections of this book.

13.1.3.5 Timing Issue Related to Filing Bankruptcy

Pursuing relief from unpayable bills through bankruptcy is not a difficult proposition, but there are strategic and tactical decisions to make. One key question is selecting the correct time to file bankruptcy. It is a mistake, for example, to file just before the consumer will incur additional debt; debts incurred after the filing are not dischargeable.[149] Consequently, debtors should try to wait as long as they can before filing bankruptcy. However, it is probably not a good idea to recommend waiting until after disconnection of service to file. The reconnection process can be cumbersome and lack of service while waiting for reconnection can be an extreme hardship.

Sometimes questions arise about whether a debtor should pay a utility bill while waiting to file bankruptcy. If cash can later be exempted, it is better for the consumer, prepetition, to save money rather than to pay a dischargeable utility bill.[150] The money can then be used as a deposit for future

144 11 U.S.C. § 727(a)(8).

145 A discharge cannot be entered in a chapter 13 case if the debtor received a discharge in prior chapter 7, 11, or 12 case that was filed within four years of the chapter 13 filing, or if the debtor received a discharge in a prior chapter 13 case that was filed within two years of the chapter 13 filing. 11 U.S.C. § 1328(f)(1) and (f)(2).

146 11 U.S.C. § 1930.

147 11 U.S.C. § 109(h). *See* National Consumer Law Center, Consumer Bankruptcy Law and Practice §§ 3.2.1.4, 7.3.5 (9th ed. 2009 and Supp.) (discussing the counseling requirement).

148 15 U.S.C. § 1681c(a)(1).

149 Note that a consumer should argue that a utility bill received postpetition for service prepetition is dischargeable because it was incurred prepetition.

150 However, if the money is *not* exempted, such a tactic serves no purpose because the trustee will turn that money over to unsecured creditors including the utility. *See generally In re* Ward, 2010 WL 447326 (Bankr. D. Ariz. Feb. 9, 2010) (debtor may apply Arizona exemption for six months of "fuel" to prepay for estimated six months of future postpetition electric and gas service; prepayment for water/sewer service, garbage pick up, and phone/Internet service are not "fuel" covered by the exemption; however, portions of advance payments for water/sewer, garbage pick-up, and phone/Internet service may be used to cover adequate assurance deposits under section 366 if such deposits are required).

service (or to pay the bankruptcy filing fee), while past-due bills will be discharged by the bankruptcy. Even if the cash cannot be exempted, a soon-to-be bankruptcy debtor usually has more pressing financial needs than paying dischargeable debts.

If a consumer files a chapter 7 and receives a discharge and then continues to have trouble paying utility bills, another chapter 7 filing is not an option. The consumer will have to wait eight years to file chapter 7 again.[151] However, the debtor may obtain a discharge in a chapter 13 case if the case is filed more than four years after the debtor filed a prior chapter 7, 11, or 12 case in which a discharge was granted or more than two years after the debtor filed a prior chapter 13 case in which a discharge was granted.[152]

13.1.3.6 Conversion of Cases and Voluntary Dismissal of Chapter 13 Cases

In most instances a bankruptcy case can be converted from one chapter to another. Absent bad faith by the debtor, a case that has not previously been converted can be converted by the debtor from chapter 7 to chapter 13.[153] A case under chapter 13 can always be converted to chapter 7, regardless of whether it has been converted before.[154]

As a matter of law, conversion of a chapter 13 case to chapter 7 allows a debtor to discharge debts that arose after the case was filed but before conversion.[155] When new utility arrears have arisen postpetition, this can be an important right to expand the discharge. To obtain a discharge of postpetition debt that arose before conversion, a debtor should probably give notice of conversion to the utility.[156] Upon notice, the utility should cease collection activities on the postpetition debt and treat that debt in all ways as if it arose before the bankruptcy case was filed. Failure to do so gives rise to damage claims and attorney fees.[157]

Sometimes a chapter 13 case does not work out because the debtor cannot propose a confirmable plan that meets Bankruptcy Code requirements or because the debtor cannot afford the necessary payments. Chapter 13 cases can be voluntarily dismissed by the debtor if they have not previously been converted from chapter 7.[158] Both chapter 7 and chapter 13 cases can be involuntarily dismissed by the court.[159] In some cases, utilities will not resume collection activities on prepetition debt even if a case is dismissed, due to administrative error or failure to properly log the dismissal in the necessary computer system.

13.1.3.7 Initiating a Bankruptcy Case

The bankruptcy filing itself is not difficult. In an emergency, a bankruptcy can be filed in as few as five minutes, with the debtor's attorney filling out several simple forms. A $299 initial fee must be paid at the outset of a chapter 7 case; $274 for chapter 13.[160] Most debtors, upon application, can pay this fee in installments if no payment to an attorney has been made or can request a waiver of the filing fee in a chapter 7 case.[161] In addition, the debtor will also have to file a certificate from an approved credit counseling agency stating that the debtor has received budget and credit counseling within the 180 days before the bankruptcy is filed.[162] The balance of the forms must be filed within fifteen days. Step-by-step directions on how to file bankruptcy and the relevant forms to do so are found in the National Consumer Law Center's *Consumer Bankruptcy Law and Practice* and *Bankruptcy Basics*.

13.2 Tenant's Right to Utilities When Landlord Files Bankruptcy

13.2.1 Introduction

When real estate markets decline, the owners of rental housing may seek relief under the bankruptcy laws. This can be particularly true for properties leased to low-income tenants. Most of the time, a landlord's bankruptcy filing will have no effect on the tenants. However, if the landlord is responsible for providing utility services such as water or electricity and fails to provide these services, legal issues may arise related to the bankruptcy.

151 11 U.S.C. § 727(a)(8). However, a subsequent chapter 13 case can be filed.

152 11 U.S.C. § 1328(f)(1), (2); National Consumer Law Center, Consumer Bankruptcy Law and Practice § 4.2.3 (9th ed. 2009 and Supp.).

153 11 U.S.C. § 706(a). *But see* Marrama v. Citizens Bank of Mass., 549 U.S. 365 (2007) (debtor's bad faith nondisclosure of assets in initial chapter 7 schedules precludes conversion to chapter 13).

A case can also be converted by the court but only to chapter 11. Involuntary conversions to chapter 13 are not permitted. *See generally* National Consumer Law Center, Consumer Bankruptcy Law and Practice § 13.7 (9th ed. 2009 and Supp.) (discussing conversion of chapter 7 and chapter 13 cases).

154 11 U.S.C. § 1307(a).

The right to convert prevents debtors from being locked into payments under chapter 13 that they cannot or do not want to make.

155 11 U.S.C. § 348(d); National Consumer Law Center, Consumer Bankruptcy Law and Practice § 4.7.4 (9th ed. 2009 and Supp.).

156 *See* National Consumer Law Center, Consumer Bankruptcy Law and Practice appx. G, Form 54 (9th ed. 2009 and Supp.) (Letter to Utility Company Giving Notice of Conversion from Chapter 13 to Chapter 7).

157 11 U.S.C. § 362(k)(1).

158 11 U.S.C. § 1307(b). *See, e.g., In re* Barbieri, 199 F.3d 616 (2d Cir. 1999).

159 11 U.S.C. §§ 707, 1307(c).

160 11 U.S.C. § 1930.

161 11 U.S.C. § 1930(f).

162 11 U.S.C. §§ 109(h), 521(b).

The balance of this section will identify the issues that arise regarding utilities when the landlord files bankruptcy, covering first the issues related to maintaining tenants' utility service. The section will then provide some basic information on collecting damages and other claims from a landlord once a bankruptcy case has been filed.

It is important to note that a landlord's bankruptcy case will proceed differently depending on whether the landlord files under chapter 7, 11, or 13 of the Bankruptcy Code. This chapter does not comprehensively discuss every issue that may arise in a landlord's case in each specific chapter of the Code. Rather, in the interest of demystifying the process, the section covers common issues that will arise under any chapter of the Bankruptcy Code. Distinctions are made only when necessary for a practitioner to understand the basic means by which a tenant may seek relief related to provision of utility service.

In 2005 Congress amended the Bankruptcy Code through the Bankruptcy Abuse and Consumer Protection Act (BAPCPA).[163] These amendments added a number of new requirements that affect primarily consumer debtors. Section 13.1, *supra*, discusses the ways in which the amendments impact upon consumers who file for bankruptcy relief. A few of the BAPCPA changes apply to commercial debtors. For the most part these non-consumer amendments were intended to strengthen accountability in bankruptcy proceedings involving businesses, and particularly to prevent delays and misuse of chapter 11 by debtors who have no serious intention of reorganizing.[164] While not as pervasive as the changes affecting consumer debtors, the BAPCPA amendments related to chapter 11 and small business bankruptcies have at least the potential to serve as tools that consumers may use to better protect their rights as creditors in bankruptcy cases. The National Consumer Law Center treatise, *Consumer Bankruptcy Law and Practice*, summarizes the basic procedures involved in chapter 11 and other bankruptcy cases in which consumers may appear as creditors.[165]

Section 366 of the Bankruptcy Code addresses the provision of utility service to bankruptcy debtors.[166] The BAPCPA amendments added a new subsection (c) to section 366. This amendment does not directly affect consumer debtors or landlords who are debtors in chapter 7 or 13 cases.[167] New subsection (c) of section 366 applies only in chapter 11 cases. It sets more onerous requirements for chapter 11 debtors who must comply with the "adequate assurance" or deposit requirements of section 366 in order to maintain postbankruptcy utility service.[168] Enacted for the benefit of utilities, this new provision could indirectly have a negative impact on residential tenants. The provision limits the forms of deposit and payment that landlords in chapter 11 must provide to a utility in order to maintain service to their tenants.[169] However, even under these new provisions, bankruptcy courts have the power to modify the schedule for payment of an adequate assurance deposit in order to lessen the risk of utility terminations.[170] The deposit requirements set forth in section 366(c) do not preclude courts in chapter 11 cases from setting hearings and ruling on adequate assurance issues during the initial thirty-day period after bankruptcy filing.[171]

In another provision that could play a role in a landlord's bankruptcy, the 2005 amendments designated a new administrative priority claim for the value of "goods" sold to the debtor in the ordinary course of the debtor's business within twenty days of the petition filing.[172] Courts have held that certain utility services constitute "goods" entitled to this administrative priority claim. This priority claim provides a benefit to utilities in addition to the new and more stringent deposit requirements under section 366(c).[173]

163 Pub. L. No. 109-8, 119 Stat. 23 (Apr. 20, 2005).

164 *See* National Consumer Law Center, Consumer Bankruptcy Law and Practice §§ 18.7.4.5, 18.7.10, 18.7.11 (9th ed. 2009 and Supp.) (discussing, respectively, new standards in section 1112(b)(4), which make it easier for party in interest to force dismissal or conversion of chapter 11 case; new section 1104(e), which adds grounds for U.S. trustee to move for appointment of chapter 11 trustee; and new section 1121(e) and 1129(e), which expedite proceedings and create new reporting requirements in small business bankruptcies).

165 National Consumer Law Center, Consumer Bankruptcy Law and Practice ch. 18 (9th ed. 2009 and Supp.).

166 11 U.S.C. § 366.

167 *See In re* Astle, 338 B.R. 855 (Bankr. D. Idaho 2006) (new section 366(c) applicable only in chapter 11 cases).

168 *See* § 13.1.2.3.2, *supra*.

169 *See generally* Geida D. Sanlate, *Tilting the Scale in Favor of Debtors in Light of BAPCPA's Amendment of Section 366*, 4 Rutgers Bus. L.J. 42 (Spring 2007).

170 *In re* Bedford Town Condos., 427 B.R. 380 (Bankr. D. Md. 2010) (requiring adequate assurance deposit equal to two months' average utility payments but allowing debtor to pay deposit in affordable monthly installments).

171 *In re* Bedford Town Condo., 427 B.R. 380 (Bankr. D. Md. 2010) (debtor condominium association not required to pay the adequate assurance deposit demanded by utility as a condition to having a hearing to establish amount and terms of payment of the deposit); *In re* Circuit City Stores, Inc., 2009 WL 484553 (Bankr. E.D. Va. Jan. 14, 2009); *In re* Beach House Prop., L.L.C., 2008 WL 961498 (Bankr. S.D. Fla. 2008); *In re* Syroco, Inc., 374 B.R. 60 (Bankr. D. P.R. 2007). *But see In re* Lucre, Inc., 333 B.R. 151 (Bankr. W.D. Mich. 2005) (chapter 11 debtor must pay utility's adequate assurance demand to maintain service during initial thirty-day postpetition period while seeking any court review of deposit requirements).

172 11 U.S.C. § 503(b)(9).

173 *See* GFI Wis., Inc. v. Reedsburg Util. Comm'n, 440 B.R. 791 (W.D. Wis. 2010) (electricity provided to chapter 11 debtor twenty days before petition date qualified as "good" entitled to administrative expense claim); *In re* Erving Indus., Inc., 432 B.R. 354 (Bankr. D. Mass. 2010) (same); *In re* Pilgrim's Pride Corp., 421 B.R. 231 (Bankr. N.D. Tex. 2009) (natural gas sold to chapter 11 debtor qualified for administrative expense priority under section 503(b)(9) as "goods" sold to debtor in the ordinary course of its business within twenty days before petition date; priority status was in addition to and not a substitute

13.2.2 *Effect of Bankruptcy on State Law Remedies*

An important first question is whether the landlord is obligated by contract (lease), state law or federal regulation to provide utilities for tenants. If so, the landlord's bankruptcy petition does not itself change this obligation. The landlord's obligations remain in effect[174] as do the tenants' right to fit and habitable housing.[175] It is the process by which those rights and duties are enforced that changes with the landlord's bankruptcy.

Typically, when a tenant's utilities are disconnected because of the landlord's failure to pay the utility provider, the tenant has remedies in state court. Although these remedies vary procedurally among the states, they include temporary restraining orders and preliminary injunctions enjoining the landlord from causing the discontinuation of services or ordering him or her to have service reconnected, causes of action under state unfair and deceptive acts or practices statutes and fair debt collection statutes, and claims for actual and consequential damages for breach of contract.[176] In addition, many states provide specific statutory remedies. These rights and remedies still exist after the commencement of the bankruptcy (subject to the automatic stay discussed below).[177] However, the way in which the tenant or tenant's advocate procures those remedies must be considered in light of the Bankruptcy Code and Rules.

Debtors, including landlords and corporations, file bankruptcy cases to obtain protection from their creditors. The tenant seeking to enforce the right to utilities or other services is thrust into the position of "creditor" under the Bankruptcy Code. This puts the attorney, who may be accustomed to representing the debtor, in the position of creditor's attorney. It is important to understand that the Bankruptcy Code, while protecting the debtor from claims of the creditor, also has numerous provisions by which a creditor can enforce claims. In some cases it may even be easier or quicker to enforce tenant claims as a creditor in the bankruptcy process than in state or other federal courts under applicable landlord/tenant laws.

13.2.3 *Keeping the Utilities on During the Bankruptcy Process*

13.2.3.1 The Automatic Stay

When the landlord files a bankruptcy case, an "automatic stay" goes into effect regardless of the chapter under which the case is filed.[178] Virtually all legal proceedings against the landlord must cease and no new cases may be filed until relief (to proceed) is granted by the bankruptcy court.[179] A violation of this stay could result in contempt, actual damages, costs, attorney fees, and possible punitive damages. The tenant's attorney is bound by the stay and may be personally subject to the same restrictions and penalties as the tenant.[180] If the stay applies to a particular action or proceeding, that action or proceeding is automatically enjoined until the stay is terminated by a grant of "relief from stay" or otherwise.[181]

If there is any doubt about whether the stay applies to a contemplated action to enforce tenants' rights, the rule of thumb is to assume that it does. Although this may sometimes be frustrating, remember that the stay applies to utility companies as well. Before terminating service due to the landlord's prepetition arrearages, utility companies must obtain relief from the stay. Tenants may benefit from this protection while these issues are being resolved in the bankruptcy case and may even intervene in the proceedings between the utility company and the landlord.[182]

There are two ways to deal with the automatic stay: (1) raise issues of utilities or repairs with a request for injunctive relief in the bankruptcy court, or (2) seek "relief from stay" to proceed in another forum. Probably the best approach is to follow both courses of action at the same time and see which is successful first.

---

for adequate assurance deposit under section 366); *In re* Plastech Engineered Prods., Inc., 397 B.R. 828 (Bankr. E.D. Mich. 2008) (same). *But see In re* Samaritan Alliance, L.L.C., 2008 WL 2520107 (Bankr. E.D. Ky. June 20, 2008) (sale of electricity is a "service" and not sale of "goods" entitled to administrative priority under section 503(b)(9)). *See generally* William L. Medford & Bruce H. White, *Utilities As Providers of Goods Under § 503(b)(9)*, 28 Am. Bankr. Inst. J. 22 (Jan. 2010).

174 An exception may arise if the landlord or a trustee chooses to reject tenant leases as executory contracts. *See* 11 U.S.C. § 365. In that situation, tenants receive alternate protections. 11 U.S.C. § 365(h).

175 State law governs the landlord's duty and definition of that duty to provide fit and habitable housing. *See* § 3.4, *supra*.

176 *See* § 3.4, *supra*.

177 *See, e.g.*, Robinson v. Michigan Consol. Gas Co. Inc., 918 F.2d 579 (6th Cir. 1990); Begley v. Philadelphia Elec. Co., 760 F.2d 46 (3d Cir. 1985) (state termination rights still apply to debtor in bankruptcy).

178 11 U.S.C. § 362.

179 *Id. See* National Consumer Law Center, Consumer Bankruptcy Law and Practice ch. 9 (9th ed. 2009 and Supp.).

180 11 U.S.C. § 362(h). *See* National Consumer Law Center, Consumer Bankruptcy Law and Practice § 9.6 (9th ed. 2009 and Supp.).

181 *See* National Consumer Law Center, Consumer Bankruptcy Law and Practice § 9.3 (9th ed. 2009 and Supp.) (discussing the duration of the automatic stay).

182 Tenants may intervene in adversary proceedings pursuant to Fed. R. Bankr. P. 7024. The right to intervene in proceedings on motions, such as those for relief from stay, is less clear but may be requested under the discretionary language in Fed. R. Bankr. P. 9014.

13.2.3.2 Seeking Injunctive Relief Against Landlord in Bankruptcy Court

Probably the easiest way to deal with the automatic stay when utility service is off (or illegal shut-off is threatened) is for the tenant to seek an order for injunctive relief in the bankruptcy court. The tenant can seek the same relief from the bankruptcy court as in the state court—to maintain contractually required service. In the bankruptcy court, the tenant files an adversary proceeding[183] requesting injunctive relief.[184]

The bankruptcy system is responsible for administration of the estate consistent with state law.[185] In general, the pleadings to be filed in bankruptcy court are similar to those filed in state court with the changes necessary to accommodate federal bankruptcy practice. The relief requested may be the same. If a trustee is responsible for administering the property in chapter 7 or when a trustee has been appointed, for cause, in chapter 11, that person should be named as a defendant along with the landlord.[186]

In preparing for the hearing, it may be useful to have the appropriate local health or safety agency inspect the building. That authority should be prepared to testify that no heat or electricity is available and that their absence violates local ordinances or state statutes and poses an imminent threat to health and safety. While most judges would probably be willing to take judicial notice that absence of heat and light is a threat to safety, the inspector's testimony about what building or health codes are being violated will satisfy the violation of law requirement of *Midlantic National Bank v. New Jersey Department of Environmental Protection*.[187]

In addition to proving imminent danger, tenants may also have to prove that the resources are available for the debtor-in-possession or third-party trustee to remedy the situation. Tenants should testify about willingness to pay rent. If possible, the local housing authority and the local energy assistance agency should present statements about the availability of Section 8 payments[188] and LIHEAP[189] payments. If an independent trustee has expressed reluctance to become involved in the management of the building, it is also helpful to obtain a statement from a commercial or nonprofit management group expressing a willingness to manage the property and an analysis that the cash flow from the building will be sufficient to provide services and remedy violations.

It is important that the imminent danger part of the tenant's case not prove too much. Testimony that the building is falling down and needs major structural repairs could potentially be harmful because the trustee is then likely to argue that the resources are not available to manage the building.

Given the relatively informal nature of bankruptcy hearings and the request for equitable relief, the tenants' attorney should be prepared to enter into discussions to fashion some agreement among the tenants, the debtor or the trustee, and any lenders with security interests in the property.[190] For example, if management of the building is an issue, the tenants might locate a community housing group that would be willing to be hired by the trustee as an interim manager. Similarly, tenants might encourage a secured lender to pursue foreclosure in order to facilitate a quick and orderly transition to new ownership.

13.2.3.3 Removal of Pending Actions to Bankruptcy Court

As with the filing of other actions for relief in bankruptcy court, actions already pending against the landlord in state or federal court can be removed for decision to the bankruptcy court.[191] Rather than waiting for relief from stay to proceed with a non-bankruptcy cause of action, it may be speedier to remove the case and prosecute it in the bankruptcy forum. In general removal of a pending case must be

---

183 *See* Fed. R. Bankr. P. 7001–7087.

184 *See* Fed. R. Bankr. P. 7065.

185 28 U.S.C. § 959(b). *See* Midlantic Nat'l Bank v. New Jersey Dep't of Envtl. Prot., 474 U.S. 494, 106 S. Ct. 755, 88 L. Ed. 2d 859 (1986).

186 Unless a trustee is appointed in a chapter 11 case, the debtor is permitted to manage property of the estate as the "debtor in possession." *See* 11 U.S.C. §§ 1101, 1107.

In chapter 13, although a trustee is assigned to every case, his or her duties generally do not include managing property of the debtor's estate. *See* 11 U.S.C. §§ 1302, 1306(b).

Whether a chapter 13 trustee must be named in an adversary proceeding seeking restoration of utilities will depend on local practice. If there is any doubt, it is probably better practice to name the trustee.

187 474 U.S. 494, 106 S. Ct. 755, 88 L. Ed. 2d 859 (1986).

188 Under section 8 of the Housing Act of 1937, 42 U.S.C. § 1437f, and the implementing regulations, 24 C.F.R. pt. 800, § 8, eligible low-income tenants receive rent subsidies. These payments are issued by the local housing authority and paid directly to the landlord so that the landlord receives two checks, one from the tenant and the other from the housing authority. The trustee will have to arrange to be named payee by the housing authority in place of the landlord. *See* National Hous. Law Project, HUD Housing Programs: Tenants' Rights (3d ed. 2004 and Supp.) (explaining in detail the Section 8 program).

189 Under the federal Low Income Home Energy Assistance Program (LIHEAP), agencies administering the program in some states may arrange direct payment of energy assistance benefits to landlords when heat or electric services are included as part of the rent. *See* 42 U.S.C. § 8624(b)(7).

When landlords are receiving LIHEAP payments directly, the trustee will have to arrange to receive the payments in place of the landlord.

190 *See, e.g.*, *In re* Armstrong, 96 B.R. 55 (Bankr. E.D.N.C. 1989) (abandonment only permitted conditional upon the debtor setting aside $250,000 for clean up of hazard).

191 28 U.S.C. § 1452; Fed. R. Bankr. P. 9027. *See generally* National Consumer Law Center, Consumer Bankruptcy Law and Practice § 9.7.3.2 (9th ed. 2009 and Supp.).

sought within ninety days after the bankruptcy case is commenced.[192]

13.2.3.4 Seeking Relief from Stay

If the preferred choice is to avoid having substantive issues decided in the bankruptcy court, then it is necessary to seek "relief from the automatic stay." To continue with or begin a new case against the landlord outside the bankruptcy court, a tenant must obtain permission from the bankruptcy court. Under 11 U.S.C. § 362(d)(1), relief from the automatic stay can be granted for "cause."[193]

The current rules specifically provide that the proper way to request relief from stay "shall" be by motion under Bankruptcy Rule 9014.[194] The creditor's attorney must file this motion asking the court's permission to go forward on the matter.

The Code provides for expedited treatment for motions for relief from stay.[195] If that hearing is not completed in a timely fashion, the stay is automatically terminated.

At the hearing for relief from the stay, the tenant as a creditor carries the initial burden of production on the grounds for the motion. The tenant should be ready to present evidence that the landlord is and has been responsible under state law for providing utilities and that the tenant will suffer harm without those utilities. The tenant will also need to convince the court that this matter is best handled in the state court.

As failure to carry such initial burden will result in a denial of the request for relief from stay,[196] the tenant must present evidence proving the alleged grounds for the motion. The health and safety hazards due to lack of utility service should provide a compelling ground for relief from stay.

If relief from stay is granted, the tenant may proceed with the state court litigation. Generally, the creditor gets relief from stay (a) to establish liability and to force the debtor to perform certain duties, or most commonly (b) to proceed to judgment on the claim but not enforce it. Most bankruptcy courts will limit grants of relief from stay so that any money judgment obtained in the non-bankruptcy forum must be enforced through the bankruptcy process. This prevents creditors who obtain relief from stay from seizing assets belonging to the bankruptcy estate to the detriment of creditors who do not have relief from stay.

If the tenant is seeking unfair or deceptive acts and practices (UDAP) damages or other similar relief for a wrongful termination or constructive eviction in the state court proceeding, the tenant should attempt to get specific findings that the landlord's acts were willful. If the landlord's conduct is found to be willful and malicious in state court, these determinations can provide collateral estoppel effect in a subsequent case brought against the landlord to have those damages found "nondischargeable" in bankruptcy.[197] This will allow the tenant to seek to collect from the landlord despite the cancellation of debts normally associated with a bankruptcy discharge.[198]

13.2.3.5 *In Forma Pauperis*

The cost for a creditor-filed adversary proceeding seeking injunctive relief (or a determination of nondischargeability) in the bankruptcy court is $250.[199] The cost for filing a motion for relief from stay is presently $150. If the tenant cannot afford the fee, the tenant can request permission to file *in forma pauperis*.[200] Although 28 U.S.C. § 1930(a) specifically provided, prior to amendments made in 2005, that filing fees could not be waived, most courts had held that its restriction on *in forma pauperis* filing applied only to starting a bankruptcy case and the regular *in forma pauperis* statute, 28 U.S.C. § 1915, applied to other proceedings.[201] The 2005 amendments to section 1930 now make clear that even the fee for filing a chapter 7 bankruptcy case may be waived.[202]

192 *See* Fed. R. Bankr. P. 9027(a)(2).

193 National Consumer Law Center, Consumer Bankruptcy Law and Practice § 9.7.3.2 (9th ed. 2009 and Supp.) (discussing in detail cause for relief from the automatic stay).

194 Fed. R. Bankr. P. 4001(a)(1).

195 11 U.S.C. § 362(e).

196 *See, e.g.*, *In re* Sonnax Indus., Inc., 907 F.2d 1280 (2d Cir. 1990).

197 11 U.S.C. § 523(a)(6). *See, e.g.*, Cohen v. De la Cruz, 523 U.S. 213, 118 S. Ct. 1212 (1998) (actual and punitive damages awarded to tenants based on UDAP for rent overcharges nondischargeable under section 523(a)(2)(A)).

198 *See* National Consumer Law Center, Consumer Bankruptcy Law and Practice §§ 14.4.3.6, 18.5.4 (9th ed. 2009 and Supp.).
Complaints to determine the dischargeability of a debt on these grounds must be brought in the bankruptcy court within sixty days after the first date set for the meeting of creditors. Fed. R. Bankr. P. 4007(c).

199 There is no charge for debtor-filed adversary proceedings.

200 National Consumer Law Center, Consumer Bankruptcy Law and Practice §§ 14.6, 18.6.1, appx. G (9th ed. 2009 and Supp.).

201 Tripati v. U.S. Bankruptcy Court for E. Dist. of Tex., 180 B.R. 160 (E.D. Tex. 1995) (constitution requires that an indigent creditor "be afforded an opportunity to be heard before his claims are disposed of"); *In re* McGinnis, 155 B.R. 294 (Bankr. D.N.H. 1993); *In re* Melendez, 153 B.R. 386 (Bankr. D. Conn. 1993); *In re* Shumate, 91 B.R. 23 (Bankr. W.D. Va. 1988); *In re* Moore, 86 B.R. 249 (Bankr. W.D. Okla. 1988) (leave to appeal); *In re* Sarah Allen Home, Inc., 4 B.R. 724 (Bankr. E.D. Pa. 1980); *In re* Palestino, 4 B.R. 721 (Bankr. M.D. Fla. 1980) (leave to initiate adversary proceeding). *See also In re* Ravida, 296 B.R. 278 (B.A.P. 1st Cir. 2003) (federal in forma *pauperis* statute applies to bankruptcy court fees other than initial petition filing fee, but waiver of fee denied for this appeal as filed in bad faith). *But see In re* Perroton, 958 F.2d 889 (9th Cir. 1992); Countryman v. Prue, 343 B.R. 904 (N.D. Ind. 2006) (following *Perroton*, bankruptcy courts not authorized to grant in forma *pauperis* motions).

202 28 U.S.C. § 1930(f).

To proceed *in forma pauperis*, the tenant must file a motion for leave to proceed *in forma pauperis* along with an affidavit to the bankruptcy court.[203] Although there are jurisdictions in which bankruptcy courts will not waive fees, it might be possible in those jurisdictions to obtain permission from the district court to proceed *in forma pauperis*.[204]

13.2.3.6 Withholding Rent to Maintain Utilities

Whether the landlord files under chapter 7, 11, or 13, the tenants individually or as a group can petition the court to allow them to withhold rent to pay the utility bills themselves to maintain utility service. Withholding rent without permission of the court is prohibited by the automatic stay, as the rent is an asset of the bankruptcy estate.[205]

In addition, section 553 of the Bankruptcy Code offers creditors a limited right to set off "a mutual debt owing by such creditor to the debtor that arose before the commencement of the case under this title against a claim of such creditor against the debtor that arose before the commencement of the case. . . ."[206] If the tenant owes prepetition rent and has paid for utilities that were supposed to be provided by the landlord, the tenant may be entitled to setoff pursuant to section 553.

Alternatively, tenants, at their option, may pay for utilities and then seek repayment for the money expended by filing an administrative expense claim.[207] Administrative costs receive priority but are ordinarily paid after secured claims. There are, however, some circumstances, under which they may be paid before secured claims.[208]

13.2.3.7 Seeking Appointment of a Trustee in a Chapter 11 Bankruptcy

The Bankruptcy Code provides for appointment of a trustee in the event of the debtor's mismanagement of a chapter 11 estate.[209] This is a useful strategy when the landlord is not maintaining the property or is not fulfilling a legal obligation to provide utility service to tenants. Section 1104(a)(1) allows the appointment of a trustee for "cause"[210] that includes "fraud,[211] dishonesty, incompetence[212] or gross mismanagement. . . ."[213]

Alternatively, section 1104(a)(2) provides a more flexible standard for the appointment of a trustee.[214] One approach to having a trustee appointed under section 1104(a)(2) is to allege a breach of the debtor's fiduciary duty to creditors. Several cases have held a breach of fiduciary duty is grounds for a trustee appointment because a debtor-in-possession is a fiduciary for the creditors of the estate and has the same duties as a trustee appointed by the court.[215] In addition, in some states tenants are given specific statutory authority to petition for receivership.

203 *See* National Consumer Law Center, Consumer Bankruptcy Law and Practice appx. G (9th ed. 2009 and Supp.) (sample pleadings).

204 *See* National Consumer Law Center, Consumer Bankruptcy Law and Practice §§ 14.6, 18.6.2 (9th ed. 2009 and Supp.) (discussing in-depth *in forma pauperis*).

205 11 U.S.C. §§ 362(a)(3), 541(a)(6).

206 11 U.S.C. § 553. *See* National Consumer Law Center, Consumer Bankruptcy Law and Practice § 10.4.2.6.7 (9th ed. 2009 and Supp.).

207 This issue is discussed in more detail below and in National Consumer Law Center, Consumer Bankruptcy Law and Practice § 18.5.3 (9th ed. 2009 and Supp.).

208 11 U.S.C. § 506(c).

209 11 U.S.C. § 1104(a) (1). *See* National Consumer Law Center, Consumer Bankruptcy Law and Practice § 18.7.4 (9th ed. 2009 and Supp.) (discussing in detail the appointment of a trustee). *See also In re* Sharon Steel Corp., 871 F.2d 1217, 1226 (3d Cir. 1989); *In re* Ionosphere Clubs, Inc., 113 B.R. 164, 167 (Bankr. S.D.N.Y. 1990); *In re* Sullivan, 108 B.R. 555, 556 (Bankr. E.D. Pa. 1989).

210 *In re* Sharon Steel Corp., 871 F.2d 1217, 1226 (3d Cir. 1989); *In re* Oklahoma Ref. Co., 838 F.2d 1133 (10th Cir. 1988); Tradex Corp. v. Morse, 339 B.R. 823 (D. Mass. 2003) ("cause" need be shown only by preponderance of evidence; debtor's inaccurate financial records met cause standard); *In re* Veblen W. Dairy, L.L.P., 434 B.R. 550 (Bankr. S.D. 2010); *In re* Cardinal Indus., 109 B.R. 755, 765 (Bankr. S.D. Ohio 1990); *In re* V. Savino Oil & Heating Co., 99 B.R. 518, 525 (Bankr. E.D.N.Y. 1989). *See In re* Ngan Gung Restaurant, Inc., 195 B.R. 593 (S.D.N.Y. 1996) (court has power to appoint a trustee to sanction conduct abusive of judicial process); Collier on Bankruptcy ¶ 1104.02[3][d] (16th ed. rev.).

211 *In re* Bibo, 76 F.3d 256 (9th Cir. 1996); *In re* Garman, 625 F.2d 755 (7th Cir. 1980); *In re* PRS Ins. Group, Inc., 274 B.R. 381 (Bankr. D. Del. 2001) (diversion and misuse of corporate accounts sufficient to show fraud and dishonesty); *In re* Russell, 60 B.R. 42 (Bankr. W.D. Ark. 1985); *In re* Colby Constr. Inc., 51 B.R. 113, 116 (Bankr. S.D.N.Y. 1985).

212 *In re* Modanlo, 342 B.R. 238 (D. Md. 2006); *In re* LaSherene, Inc., 3 B.R. 169, 174–76 (Bankr. N.D. Ga. 1980).

213 *In re* Brown, 31 B.R. 583, 585–86 (D.D.C. 1983); *In re* Ionosphere Clubs, Inc., 113 B.R. 164, 167 (Bankr. S.D.N.Y. 1990); *In re* Stein & Day, Inc., 87 B.R. 290, 294 (Bankr. S.D.N.Y. 1988); *In re* Colby Constr. Inc., 51 B.R. 113, 116 (Bankr. S.D.N.Y. 1985); *In re* Anchorage Boat Sales, Inc., 4 B.R. 635, 645 (Bankr. E.D.N.Y. 1980); *In re* LaSherene, Inc., 3 B.R. 169, 174–76 (Bankr. N.D. Ga. 1980).

214 *In re* Taub, 427 B.R. 208 (E.D.N.Y. 2010); *In re* Parker Grande Dev., 64 B.R. 557, 561 (Bankr. S.D. Ind. 1986); *In re* Anchorage Boat Sales, Inc., 4 B.R. 635, 644 (Bankr. E.D.N.Y. 1980).

215 *In re* Nautilus of New Mexico, Inc., 83 B.R. 784, 789 (Bankr. D.N.M. 1988); *In re* Parker Grande Dev., 64 B.R. 557, 561 (Bankr. S.D. Ind. 1986) (breach of fiduciary duty because debtor-in-possession has such poor skills, ability, training and experience in land management, and business acumen, he could not protect and conserve property for benefit of creditors); *In re* Russell, 60 B.R. 42, 47 (Bankr. W.D. Ark. 1985); *In re* Ford, 36 B.R. 501, 504 (Bankr. W.D. Ky. 1983) (co-owner president of debtor was incapable of dealing with debtor as fiduciary and appointed a trustee pursuant to (a)(2)); National Consumer Law Center, Consumer Bankruptcy Law and Practice § 18.7 (9th ed. 2009 and Supp.). *Cf. In re* Cardinal Indus., 109 B.R. 755, 766–68 (Bankr. S.D. Ohio 1990) (debtors had not addressed serious deficiencies in recordkeeping processes; evidence established Unsecured Creditors' Committee's loss of faith in debtor's intentions and abilities to reorganize their affairs; and cost-benefit analysis was met).

An application for appointment of a trustee is by motion and may be made by any party in interest or by the United States trustee.[216] Although the motion can be filed at any time, it may be preferable to wait for evidence of postpetition misconduct.

The application for appointment of a trustee is effective for two reasons. First, the trustee will be likely to maintain the estate better. In addition, the motion itself can be leverage to force the landlord to start paying the utility bills and/or maintain the property.[217] The 2005 BAPCPA amendments broadened the grounds for appointment of a trustee in a chapter 11 case.[218] Generally, any conduct listed as a ground for the court to dismiss a chapter 11 case or convert it to chapter 7 under section 1112 of the Code is now a ground for appointment of a trustee.

As an alternative to seeking appointment of a trustee, a creditor or other interested party may move to have a chapter 11 case dismissed or converted to chapter 7.[219] This alternative will likely leave tenants to their state law remedies sooner than if the case stays in chapter 11. However it will end a chapter 11 proceeding that was filed without any real intent to reorganize. The BAPCPA amendments created new standards that limit the bankruptcy court's discretion to deny a motion for dismissal or conversion of a chapter 11 case.[220]

13.2.3.8 Maintaining Service in a Chapter 7 Bankruptcy

13.2.3.8.1 Abandonment by the trustee

In theory, in a chapter 7 bankruptcy, the chapter 7 trustee takes over management of the assets of the estate and liquidates them for the benefit of the unsecured creditors.[221] In practice, in a typical apartment building bankruptcy, the only assets of the entity filing bankruptcy will be the building and the land on which it is situated. The real estate will frequently be mortgaged well beyond its value so there is no equity remaining for the unsecured creditors.

Section 554 of the Bankruptcy Code[222] permits the trustee to "abandon" property which is burdensome to the estate or is of inconsequential value and benefit to the estate. Because the building will usually have no equity from which the estate will benefit upon foreclosure and because the rents will be insufficient to meet the mortgage payments and other expenses, the trustee is likely to conclude that the building meets the statutory tests for abandonment.[223]

Abandonment by the trustee has the potential for leaving the tenants in legal limbo. The foreclosing creditors may do nothing until they have completed state foreclosure proceedings which, depending on state practice, may take from several weeks to several months. The creditors may believe they have no legal right to manage the building prior to the foreclosure. The debtor in theory remains responsible until the foreclosure but, by filing bankruptcy, the debtor has renounced any intention of continuing management and will have no interest or incentive to continue. Further, continued involvement by the debtor may be the last thing the tenants want.[224]

However, the tenants' attorney has some tools to protect the tenants' interests in this situation. In *Midlantic National Bank v. New Jersey Department of Environmental Protection*,[225] the United States Supreme Court held that a trustee cannot abandon property even though it is burdensome to the estate when abandonment would be "in contravention of a state statute or regulation that is reasonably designed to protect the public health or safety from identified hazards,"[226] and would result in "imminent and identifiable harm."[227] When these two factors can be shown, courts will not permit the trustee to abandon the property.[228]

216 11 U.S.C. § 1104(a).

217 *See* National Consumer Law Center, Consumer Bankruptcy Law and Practice § 18.7.4 (9th ed. 2009 and Supp.) (discussing appointment of a trustee in a chapter 11 case).

218 11 U.S.C. §§ 1104(a)(3),1112(b)(4). *See* National Consumer Law Center, Consumer Bankruptcy Law and Practice § 18.7.4.5 (9th ed. 2009 and Supp.).

219 *See* National Consumer Law Center, Consumer Bankruptcy Law and Practice § 18.7.11 (9th ed. 2009 and Supp.) (discussing 11 U.S.C. § 1112(b), which lists factors court must consider in deciding whether to grant motion to dismiss or convert chapter 11 case).

220 *Id.*

221 11 U.S.C. § 704.

222 11 U.S.C. § 554.

223 *See* National Consumer Law Center, Consumer Bankruptcy Law and Practice §§ 18.8.2.1, 18.8.2.4 (9th ed. 2009 and Supp.) (discussing further abandonment and responses to abandonment).

224 The provisions of the Protecting Tenants at Foreclosures Act, 12 U.S.C. § 5220 (effective May 20, 2009), give most tenants important additional protections once a foreclosure has been completed. The party acquiring the property through foreclosure must continue leases for their existing terms. This includes any landlord obligation to provide utility service under the leases. Section 8 tenancies must continue subject to the Section 8 good cause lease termination rules. In addition, many states have enacted statutes during the current foreclosure crisis that give additional protections to tenants in foreclosed properties. *See, e.g.*, N.Y Real Prop. Acts. Law §§ 1303, 1305 (McKinney); 735 Ill Comp. Stat. 5/15-1508.5; 735 Ill. Comp. Stat. 5/15-1704.

Extensive material discussing federal, state, and local legislation enacted to protect tenants from consequences of their landlords' foreclosures can be found at the website of the National Housing Law Project. http://nhlp.org/foreclosure andtenants.

225 474 U.S. 494, 106 S. Ct. 755, 88 L. Ed. 2d 859 (1986).

226 *Id.*, 474 U.S. 494, 507.

227 *Id.*, 474 U.S. 494, 507, n.9. *See generally* National Consumer Law Center, Consumer Bankruptcy Law and Practice § 18.7.4.5 (9th ed. 2009 and Supp.).

228 *See, e.g.*, *In re* Stevens, 68 B.R. 774 (D. Me. 1987) (chapter 7 trustee could not abandon drums of contaminated oil; cleanup expenses are priority administrative expenses); *In re* American Coastal Energy, Inc., 399 B.R. 805 (Bankr. S.D. Tex. 2009) (chapter 11 trustee may not abandon contaminated estate prop-

While the *Midlantic* case involved the ownership of a dump containing toxic materials and most of the cases following *Midlantic* have involved some sort of environmental hazard, nothing in the language of the case limits its holding to such hazards. In an unreported West Virginia case,[229] for example, a legal services attorney, arguing on the basis of *Midlantic* and 28 U.S.C. § 959(b) (regarding the management of property in the possession of the trustee), obtained an order requiring the trustee to accept payments from the tenants and Section 8 payments from the public housing authority to restore utility service and to continue to manage the property until such time as the secured party presented an acceptable plan for taking over the management.

In a strict sense, the "abandonment" of a lease as part of a bankruptcy case simply means that the lease will not be administered as part of the bankruptcy estate.[230] The term "rejection" of the lease as used in the section of the bankruptcy code dealing with treatment of the debtor's leases has a similar meaning.[231] Neither the "abandonment" nor the "rejection" of the lease by the bankruptcy estate allows the landlord debtor unilaterally to avoid state law obligations to residential tenants as those obligations existed before the bankruptcy filing. While there had been some confusion on this point in the past, 1994 amendments to the Bankruptcy Code clarified the issue.[232] The Code further allows the debtor to offset postbankruptcy rent obligations otherwise owed to the debtor if the tenant incurs costs as a result of the debtor's noncompliance with the lessor's obligations under the lease.[233]

13.2.3.8.2 Loss of services without abandonment

When the trustee has not abandoned the property, he or she may nevertheless not supply needed service. This situation arose in *Saravia v. 1736 18th Street, N.W. Ltd. Partnership*.[234] *Saravia* involved a chapter 11 case in which the debtor-in-possession,[235] having rejected the tenant leases under section 365(a) of the Bankruptcy Code,[236] attempted to cut off municipal services arguing that since the leases were voided, there was no obligation to provide the services required under the lease. The District of Columbia Circuit flatly rejected the debtor's argument. The court ruled that so long as the District of Columbia, where the housing was located, required the provision of heat and other utility services to tenants under its housing regulations, then, especially in light of the Supreme Court's discussion of section 959(b) in the *Midlantic* case, section 959(b) required the debtor-in-possession, as trustee, to comply with the District of Columbia housing regulations and provide the required services.[237] While the trustee in a chapter 7 is unlikely to reject tenant leases,[238] the *Saravia* case is an important precedent illustrating that the principles of *Midlantic* may apply to tenants' rights in housing.[239]

Another useful case in states which allow a debtor to recoup money expended to cure a landlord's default on an obligation to repair and maintain the premises is *In re*

erty but has duty to bring property into compliance with environmental and safety laws); *In re* Chaffee Aggregates, Inc., 300 B.R. 170 (Bankr. W.D.N.Y. 2003) (trustee is bound by local property laws in managing and operating estate property; automatic stay does not bar enforcement of applicable zoning laws); *In re* Peerless Plating Co., 70 B.R. 943 (Bankr. W.D. Mich. 1987) (chapter 7 trustee could not abandon metal plating shop over objections of EPA). *But see In re* Vel Rey Props., 174 B.R. 859 (Bankr. D.D.C. 1994) (trustee not permitted to operate apartment building without compliance with building code in order to maximize return to creditors but could abandon property because public danger from housing code violations was not imminent). *Cf. In re* Armstrong, 96 B.R. 55 (Bankr. E.D.N.C. 1989) (debtor-in-possession in chapter 11 could abandon polluted property only if $250,000 set aside for cleanup).

229 Hemetek v. Standish (*In re* Bush), No. 89-20949 ch. 7, Adv. Pro No. 90-0010, Clearinghouse No. 44,839 (Bankr. S.D. W. Va. Feb. 2, 1990).

230 *See* B.N. Realty Assocs. v. Lichtenstein, 238 B.R. 249, 255 (S.D.N.Y. 1999); *In re* Couture, 225 B.R. 58, 64 (D. Vt. 1998); *In re* Bacon, 212 B.R. 66, 68 (Bankr. E.D. Pa. 1997).

231 11 U.S.C. § 365(d)(1) (in chapter 7 case, lease is deemed "rejected" if trustee does not formally assume responsibilities under it within sixty days of bankruptcy filing). *See In re* Lavigne, 114 F.3d 379, 386–87 (2d Cir. 1997) ("rejection" of lease under section 365 terminology is not termination or repudiation of debtor's obligations and rights under contract but pertains only to bankruptcy estate's obligation).

232 11 U.S.C. § 365(h)(1)(A)(ii). *See In re* Haskell, 321 B.R. 1 (Bankr. D. Mass. 2005) (debtor landlord's proposed sale of property free and clear of debtor's leasehold interests would violate section 365(h)); *In re* Taylor, 198 B.R. 142 (Bankr. D.S.C. 1996); *In re* Churchill Props. III, Ltd. P'ship, 197 B.R. 283 (Bankr. N.D. Ill. 1996). *But see* Precision Indus., Inc. v. Qualitech Steel SBQ, L.L.C., 327 F.3d 537 (7th Cir. 2003) (expresses minority view allowing sale of property by debtor free and clear of prebankruptcy lease obligations).

233 11 U.S.C. § 365(h)(1)(B) (but note that provision is subject to limitation on tenants' rights to sue debtor/landlord for monetary damages arising out of debtor's postbankruptcy breaches of lease).

234 844 F.2d 823 (D.C. Cir. 1988).

235 *In re* Mobile Steel Co., 563 F.2d 692 (5th Cir. 1977); Collier on Bankruptcy ¶ 510.05 (16th ed. rev.).

236 11 U.S.C. § 365(a).

237 Another problem for tenants can arise if the trustee or landlord as debtor-in-possession elects to reject a lease and sell the rental property under an asset sale free and clear of the tenants' possessory or other interests in the property. 11 U.S.C. § 363(f); Precision Indus., Inc. v. Qualitech Steel SBQ, L.L.C., 327 F.3d 537 (7th Cir. 2003). *See* National Consumer Law Center, Consumer Bankruptcy Law and Practice § 18.9.3 (9th ed. 2009 and Supp.).

238 *See* National Consumer Law Center, Consumer Bankruptcy Law and Practice § 18.8.3 (9th ed. 2009 and Supp.) (rejection of leases).

239 *But see In re* Vel Rey Props., 174 B.R. 859 (Bankr. D.D.C. 1994) (trustee not permitted to operate apartment building without compliance with building code in order to maximize return to creditors but could abandon property because public danger from housing code violations was not imminent).

Flagstaff Realty Trust.[240] In *Flagstaff*, the Third Circuit concluded that a tenant that had performed prepetition repairs could recoup any amounts expended from rent even after the debtor filed bankruptcy and rejected the lease. It may also be possible for tenants to work with local government housing code officials and regulatory authorities to enforce building and fire codes. Such enforcement of police and regulatory powers is generally not subject to the automatic stay in the landlord's bankruptcy case.[241]

13.2.4 Enforcing Monetary Claims Against Landlord

13.2.4.1 Filing a Claim Against Landlord

Whether or not the tenant's claim has been reduced to a judgment, the tenant (as creditor) has to file a proof of claim in order to share in the distribution of the bankruptcy estate.[242] "Claim" is defined in the Bankruptcy Code and covers a broad range of creditor rights.[243] When in doubt, the best practice is to file a proof of claim. It is only from the property in the bankruptcy estate that the debtor's (in this case the landlord's) creditors can be compensated.

Therefore, a claim should be filed regardless of whether the tenant (a) has a judgment against the landlord, (b) has not initiated litigation, or (c) is not even certain of the exact amount of the claim. For example, if the tenant has chosen to pay for utilities directly to maintain service, the claim continues to accrue with each payment. Alternatively, a claim may be filed for the damages a tenant suffers by virtue of being left without utilities even if the amount of damages has not been determined in court.[244]

The claim must be filed in the bankruptcy court even if litigation has begun or a judgment has been obtained outside the bankruptcy proceeding. It must be made on Official Form 10[245] or a substantially similar document.[246] It may be filed by the tenant's attorney[247] and should be filed with the court,[248] not with the trustee (although a copy to the trustee may be appropriate) unless there is a local rule to the contrary.[249]

In cases under chapters 7, 12, or 13, the proof of claim must be filed within ninety days after the first date set for the meeting of creditors under section 341(a) of the Code, unless advised otherwise by the court.[250]

Certain claims are entitled to priority.[251] They are paid in order of priority set by the Code before payment to general unsecured creditors.[252] In making a proof of claim, take care to claim any available priorities. Unless there is an objection, a proof of claim is deemed allowed.[253] Therefore, the claim should be for as high an amount and with as high a priority as good faith will permit.[254]

If the claim is for postpetition claims (expenses incurred after the filing of the bankruptcy), the tenant can classify those claims as administrative expenses.[255]

13.2.4.2 Recovering Administrative Costs

To the extent the debtor's claims against the landlord for failing to maintain utilities arise following commencement of the case, these claims may be payable from the bankruptcy estate as administrative expenses.[256] To qualify as an administrative expense, a tenant's claim must be the "actual, necessary costs . . . of preserving the estate. . . ."[257] Since utility service is required as a prerequisite to tenants paying rent on property of the estate, it is not hard to argue that claims related to utility service following commencement of the case should be borne by the estate as a cost of preserving the estate.[258]

240 60 F.3d 1031 (3d Cir. 1995). *See also In re* 105 E. Second St. Assocs., 207 B.R. 64 (Bankr. S.D.N.Y. 1997).

241 11 U.S.C. § 362(b) (4), (5). *See In re* 1820–1838 Amsterdam Equities, Inc., 191 B.R.18 (S.D.N.Y. 1996) (bankruptcy court could not interfere with code enforcement by city against debtor's property).

242 11 U.S.C. § 502.

243 11 U.S.C. § 101(5).

244 In such an instance, the court is empowered to estimate the actual claim under 11 U.S.C. § 502(c). Certainly the debtor should file a claim in the highest good faith amount, which could be available under any theory. At a minimum, this should include consequential damages for breach of contract, together with any statutory damages available in the applicable jurisdiction for illegal shut-off.

245 *See* National Consumer Law Center, Consumer Bankruptcy Law and Practice appx. D.3, Official Form 10 (9th ed. 2009 and Supp.) (sample Proof of Claim form).

246 Fed. R. Bankr. P. 3001(a).

247 Fed. R. Bankr. P. 3000(b).

248 Fed. R. Bankr. P. 3002(b), 5005(a).

249 *See* National Consumer Law Center, Consumer Bankruptcy Law and Practice § 18.4 (9th ed. 2009 and Supp.) (discussing the timing and procedure for filing a proof of claim).

250 Fed. R. Bankr. P. 3002(c).

251 11 U.S.C. § 507.

252 National Consumer Law Center, Consumer Bankruptcy Law and Practice § 12.3.4.3 (9th ed. 2009 and Supp.) (discussing the most likely priorities for consumer creditors are administrative expenses for postpetition claims).

253 11 U.S.C. § 502(a).

254 *See, e.g.*, *In re* Partners Group Fin., L.L.C., 394 B.R. 68 (Bankr. E.D. Pa. 2008) (consumer's proof of claim against mortgage broker properly included treble damages based on unliquidated UDAP claim and attorney fees; portion of claim that included consequential damages for lost income and profits due to debtor's breach of contract disallowed).

255 *See* National Consumer Law Center, Consumer Bankruptcy Law and Practice § 12.3.4.3 (9th ed. 2009 and Supp.).

Alternatively, consumer deposits are entitled to priority under section 507(a)(6) to the extent of $2225. *See generally* National Consumer Law Center, Consumer Bankruptcy Law and Practice § 18.5.5 (9th ed. 2009 and Supp.).

256 11 U.S.C. § 503(b)(1).

257 *Id.*

258 *In re* Boston Reg'l Med. Ctr., 291 F.3d 111 (1st Cir. 2002) (postpetition payments due, in lieu of employer's unemployment compensation fund contributions, qualify as expense for

A request for payment must be filed to recover an administrative expense under 11 U.S.C. § 503. If an administrative claim is allowed, that claim will be paid ahead of all other unsecured claims.[259] As a result, there is a higher likelihood that administrative expense claims will be paid in full.

In certain cases, administrative expense claims may be payable ahead of secured claims as well. Section 506(c) provides that the reasonable and necessary costs of preserving and disposing of property securing an allowed secured claim may be recovered by the party incurring the expenses, to the extent the expenditure benefits the secured creditor.[260]

The usefulness of this provision by tenants is limited, however, by the fact that only the trustee may seek to "tax" a secured creditor for expenses of preserving collateral.[261] Earlier cases allowing the party who provided the service or incurred the expense to recover under section 506(c) from the secured creditor are no longer good law.[262] When tenants have claims for utility expenditures, recovery from the secured creditor will require cooperation of the trustee, who might be willing to invoke section 506(c) to reimburse the tenants if doing so will preserve or increase the value of the property.

Three elements must be shown before an expense qualifies to be paid under section 506(c): (1) the expenditure must be necessary; (2) the amounts expended are reasonable; and (3) the secured creditor benefits from the expenditure.[263]

The burden of proving these elements is on the party claiming the expense.[264] As much evidence as possible addressing how the maintenance of utilities benefits the secured creditor should be introduced. For instance, maintenance of utilities benefits a secured creditor by preventing broken water pipes, slowing deterioration by moisture damage, or ensuring rental income by keeping tenants in their units.

13.2.4.3 Seeking a Determination of Nondischargeability

The main goal of an individual landlord's chapter 7 case will be to obtain a discharge of claims, meaning a bankruptcy court determination that the landlord is no longer liable for certain debts. (Corporate debtors do not receive a discharge.) In a bankruptcy case filed by an individual landlord under chapter 7 or 11, it may be possible to obtain a determination that the debt owed to tenants/creditors for failing to maintain utilities is not dischargeable.

Most often the grounds for such a determination will be available only if the landlord acted willfully or maliciously in turning off the utility services.[265] Such claims arise in many cases when landlords deliberately terminate utility service to achieve an illegal eviction.[266]

It may be possible to obtain a nondischargeability determination in a landlord's chapter 13 case based on a utility shut-off causing personal injury or death. If the tenant has been awarded restitution or damages in a civil action against the landlord, based on willful or malicious injury by the landlord that caused personal injury or death of an individual, the tenant may seek a determination that the civil judgment is nondischargeable in a chapter 13 bankruptcy case filed by an individual landlord.[267]

A determination of nondischargeability must be sought by filing an adversary proceeding.[268] The complaint initiating the adversary proceeding must be filed within sixty days following the first date set for the meeting of creditors. If not

administrative priority); *In re* Friendship Coll. Inc., 737 F.2d 430 (4th Cir. 1987) (the term "estate" as used in section 503(b)(1)(B)(i) implies postpetition liabilities); *In re* Charlesbank Laundry, Inc., 755 F.2d 200 (1st Cir. 1985) (civil fine based on debtor's postpetition conduct granted administrative expense status).

For example, the postpetition right to return of a security deposit, absent rejection of the lease, has been held to be an administrative expense entitled to priority. *In re* Boston Post Road Ltd. P'ship, 21 F.3d 477 (2d Cir. 1994) (tenants who are owed security deposits have administrative claims that are entitled to priority); *In re* Cantonwood Assocs. Ltd. P'ship, 138 B.R. 648 (Bankr. D. Mass. 1992) (same). *See also* Reading Co. v. Brown, 391 U.S. 471, 482, 88 S. Ct. 1759, 20 L. Ed. 2d 751 (1968) (postpetition tort claim is administrative expense).

259 11 U.S.C. § 507(a)(1).

260 *See, e.g., In re* Parque Forestal, Inc., 949 F.2d 504 (1st Cir. 1991).

The First Circuit allowed tenants of a building complex to recover costs for building security under section 506(c) directly from the secured creditor.

261 Hartford Underwriters Ins. Co. v. Union Planters Bank, N.A., 120 S. Ct. 1942, 147 L. Ed. 2d 1 (2000).

262 *See, e.g., In re* Parque Forestal, Inc., 949 F.2d 504 (1st Cir. 1991).

263 *In re* Delta Towers, Ltd., 924 F.2d 74 (5th Cir. 1991); *In re* Trim-X, Inc., 695 F.2d 296 (7th Cir. 1982).

264 *In re* Flagstaff Foodservice Corp., 739 F.2d 73 (2d Cir. 1984); Brookfield Prod. Credit Ass'n v. Borson, 738 F.2d 951 (8th Cir. 1984).

265 11 U.S.C. § 523(a)(6).

The U.S. Supreme Court has ruled that only intentional torts can be found nondischargeable for willful and malicious injury. Torts based on reckless or negligent conduct are not within the scope of the exception. Kawaauhau v. Geiger, 118 S. Ct. 974 (1998). *See also In re* Mills, 73 B.R. 638 (B.A.P. 9th Cir. 1987) (mismanagement of apartment house in bad faith was willful and malicious act, injuring property of trust deed holder), *rev'd*, 841 F.2d 902 (9th Cir. 1988) (holder of deed of trust failed to meet burden of proof that landlord's conduct, in failing to maintain building, was malicious, intentional, or reckless). *See generally* National Consumer Law Center, Consumer Bankruptcy Law and Practice §§ 15.4.3.6, 18.5.4 (9th ed. 2009 and Supp.) (generally discussing challenges to dischargeability and discussing willful and malicious injury discharge exception).

266 *E.g.*, Cohen v. De la Cruz, 523 U.S. 213, 118 S. Ct. 1212 (1998) (actual and punitive damages awarded to tenants based on UDAP for rent overcharges nondischargeable under section 523(a)(2)(A)).

267 11 U.S.C. § 1328(a)(4).

268 Fed. R. Bankr. P. 4007. *See* Fed. R. Bankr. P. 7001–7087.

filed within this deadline or any extension, the claim is permanently discharged.[269]

269 *In re* Medalgia, 52 F.3d 451 (2d Cir. 1995) (creditor's timely, actual notice of filing of bankruptcy petition barred late challenge to discharge despite debtor's failure to properly list debt in schedules); *In re* Green, 876 F.2d 854 (10th Cir. 1989) (actual notice of bankruptcy filing is sufficient); *In re* Price, 871 F.2d 97 (9th Cir. 1989) (knowledge of bankruptcy is sufficient); *In re* Alton, 837 F.2d 457 (11th Cir. 1988); Neeley v. Murchison, 815 F.2d 345 (5th Cir. 1987); *In re* Bucknum, 105 B.R. 25 (B.A.P. 9th Cir. 1989), *aff'd*, 951 F.2d 204 (1991); *In re* Ricketts, 80 B.R. 495 (B.A.P. 9th Cir. 1987); *In re* Walker, 103 B.R. 281 (D. Utah 1989), *rev'd in part on other grounds*, 927 F.2d 1138 (10th Cir. 1991). *But see In re* Eliscu, 85 B.R. 480 (Bankr. N.D. Ill. 1988) (creditor with no notice of case at all not subject to deadline).

13.2.5 Conclusion

When a landlord is having financial problems, failure to maintain utilities and bankruptcy often go hand in hand. Advocates for tenants should not automatically assume that bankruptcy is an obstacle; in many cases careful work in the bankruptcy forum will make it easier rather than more difficult for tenants to obtain a quick and effective legal remedy.

Chapter 14 Manufactured Homes and Utility Service

14.1 Introduction

14.1.1 Importance and Definition of Manufactured Homes

Manufactured homes are an important source of housing for low-income Americans. Eighteen million Americans live in manufactured homes.[1] There are currently over eight million manufactured homes in the United States, almost seven million of which are occupied.[2] Many people choose these units because they seek the security and privacy of homeownership at a fraction of a conventional home's upfront cost.[3] Many others do so because they have few other affordable housing options. The median household income of manufactured-home residents was $30,000 in 2009, as compared with $47,000 for all households.[4] Many United States armed forces personnel live in manufactured-home parks.[5]

The term "manufactured home" refers to homes that are typically constructed in a factory and are designed to meet the specifications of the Department of Housing and Urban Development Code.[6] Manufactured homes are often referred to as mobile homes, but the term "mobile home" should only apply to homes built before 1976 and prior to the creation of the HUD Code. Sometimes the terms "manufactured home" or "mobile home" will be improperly applied to recreational vehicles (RVs) or trailers. While such vehicles are not manufactured homes, they may sometimes be used for permanent housing in a manner similar to housing found in manufactured-home communities.

14.1.2 Unique Utility Issues Generally Apply to Homes Sited on Rented Land

When manufactured homes are sited on land owned by the homeowner, utility issues are generally the same as those applying to site-built homes. One exception is weatherization issues, discussed at § 14.6, *infra*. If the manufactured-home resident rents both the home and the land upon which it sits from one entity, the rules governing utility service are usually the same as for other tenants or for homeowners, depending on whether the landlord or the manufactured-home occupant is contractually responsible for the utilities.

This chapter focuses on the special utility issues that arise when the manufactured-home owner sites the home in a manufactured home community or "park," and the consumer owns the home but rents the lot or "pad" upon which the home sits. These special issues relate in particular to the overwhelming power the park owner has over the community residents—homes are difficult and expensive to relocate and are often damaged in the process, and there often is no other park that will accept the home in any event. The homeowner has little choice if the park owner wishes to increase prices or change the terms of utility service. Consumer protections in this area are found in a patchwork of special manufactured-home park statutes, landlord-tenant law, and other state and federal legislation.

14.2 Community Owner Restrictions on Choice of Utility Provider

Owners of manufactured-home communities may attempt to place restrictions on the homeowners' ability to freely contract with fuel or other utility providers, such as propane

1 *Dream Home . . . or Nightmare?*, Consumer Rep., Feb. 1998, at 30.

2 U.S. Census Bureau, American Housing Survey National Tables: 2009, at tbl. 1-1 (Total Inventory and Vacant Units—All Housing—Introductory Characteristics); tbl. 2-1 (Occupied Units—Total Occupied—Introductory Characteristics), *available at* www.census.gov/housing/ahs/data/national.html.

3 The median purchase price for currently occupied homes was $27,000, not including land. U.S. Census Bureau, American Housing Survey National Tables: 2009, at tbl. 3-14 (Occupied Units—Owners—Value, Purchase Price, and Source of Down Payment), *available at* www.census.gov/housing/ahs/data/national.html.

4 U.S. Census Bureau, American Housing Survey National Tables: 2009, at tbl. 2-12 (Occupied Units—Total Occupied—Income Characteristics), *available at* www.census.gov/housing/ahs/data/national.html.

5 TJAGSA Practice Notes 29, 31, Army Law, July 1997.

6 24 C.F.R. § 3280.

The Standards and the Manufactured Home Procedural and Enforcement Regulations are authorized under the National Mobile Home Construction and Safety Standards Act of 1974, Pub. L. No. 93-383, tit. VI, 88 Stat. 633 (Aug. 22, 1974) (42 U.S.C. § 5401).

or liquid petroleum gas (LPG) vendors, forcing the homeowner to use a provider that brings extra profit to the community owner but higher prices or inferior service to the homeowner. Often the resident is forced to use a submetered utility provided by the community owner or another provider that has a relationship with the community owner.

State law in certain states prohibits a manufactured-home park owner from restricting a tenant's choice of fuel provider.[7] This allows the resident to choose between obtaining gas or electric service from the local utility or from the park, if offered. But residents in other states may not be so fortunate. Wisconsin generally forbids manufactured-home parks to limit tenants' choice of vendors but makes an exception for utility services.[8] A New Jersey court held that a landlord acted reasonably in forbidding oil tanks and requiring tenants to convert, at their own expense, to piped natural gas or electricity.[9] Yet other states allow the park owner to restrict the choice of vendors, but these states also require that prices charges by the park owner for fuel or LPG gas be "competitive" or equal to the average price charged by dealers in the community.[10]

14.3 Utility Billing, Master Metering, and Submetering Arrangements

14.3.1 Restrictions on Master Metering

In many manufactured-home communities, park owners obtain gas and electric service at wholesale rates and resells the utilities to residents using master-meter/submetering arrangements.[11] Master metering and submetering issues in the apartment rental context is discussed in another chapter.[12] This section focuses on such issues in manufactured-home communities.

A number of state statutes specifically regulate a manufactured-home community owner's provision of energy services to manufactured-home residents in order to prevent overcharging and to ensure safety.[13] Some states specifically ban master metering in manufactured-home parks, requiring utilities to be individually metered for each resident or included in the rent,[14] although some bans allow "grandfathering" of existing parks.[15] Other states have general restrictions on master metering that may apply to manufactured-home communities.[16]

A few such master-metering statutes specifically exempt manufactured-home communities from their consumer protections.[17] More commonly, statutes restricting master me-

7 *See, e.g.*, Me. Rev. Stat. tit. 10, § 9095 (fuel oil and bottled gas, unless park has centralized distribution system); Mass. Gen. Laws ch. 140, § 32L(3); R.I. Gen. Laws § 31-44-3 (no restrictions on fuel or other utilities).

8 Northern States Power Co. v. National Gas Co., 606 N.W.2d 613 (Wis. Ct. App. 2000) (park required tenants to purchase "propane or natural gas" service from company that had installed its pipes in park; only propane was available; contract did not violate public policy; note that plaintiff here was natural gas utility that wished to serve certain park residents, and there was no claim that service under contract was inadequate or unreasonably priced).

9 Hanover Mobile Home Owners' Ass'n v. Hanover Vill. Assocs., 720 A.2d 361 (N.J. Super. Ct. App. Div. 1998) (landlord introduced evidence that aging oil tanks posed threat to park water supply).

10 765 Ill. Comp. Stat. 745/19 ("reasonable retail price"); Me. Rev. Stat. tit. 10, § 9095 ("average retail price charged by other retailers in the county"); Mass. Gen. Laws ch. 140, § 32L(3) ("average prevailing price in the locality"); N.H. Rev. Stat. Ann. § 205-A:2(IV) (average prevailing price in the locality for similar goods and services); N.J. Stat. Ann. § 46:8C-2(b)(2) (West) ("competitively priced").

11 *See* Phillip E. Hassman, Annotation, *Landlord Supplying Electricity, Gas, Water, or Similar Facility to Tenant As Subject to Utility Regulation*, 75 A.L.R.3d 1204 (1977) (discussing cases in which states considered landlords, including manufactured-home parks, as utilities).

12 *See* § 4.5, *supra*.

13 Ariz. Rev. Stat. Ann. §§ 33-1401 to 33-1491; Cal. Civ. Code § 798.38 (West) (California has numerous provisions relating to manufactured homes; this is only one of them); Colo. Rev. Stat. §§ 38-12-212.3, 38-12-212.7; Conn. Gen. Stat. §§ 21-64 to 21-84a; Del. Code Ann. tit. 25, §§ 7001 to 7037, 7101 to 7114; Fla. Stat. §§ 723.001 to 723.0861; Idaho Code Ann. §§ 55-2001 to 55-2019; 765 Ill. Comp. Stat. 745/1 to 745/26; Ind. Code §§ 16-41-27-1 to 16-41-27-34; Iowa Code §§ 562B.1 to 562B.32; Kan. Stat. Ann. §§ 58-25,100 to 58-25,126; Me. Rev. Stat. tit. 10, §§ 9091 to 9100; Md. Code Ann., Real Prop. tit. 8A, §§ 101 to 1803 (West); Mass. Gen. Laws ch. 140, §§ 32A to 32S; Mich. Comp. Laws §§ 125.2325, 125.2328, 125.2329; Minn. Stat. §§ 327C.01 to 327C.15; Neb. Rev. Stat. §§ 76-1450 to 76-14,111; Nev. Rev. Stat. §§ 118B.010 to 118B.260; N.H. Rev. Stat. Ann. § 205-A; N.J. Stat. Ann. §§ 46:8C-2 to 46:8C-21, 2A:18-61.1(a) (West); N.J. Admin. Code § 5:23; N.M. Stat. Ann. §§ 47-10-1 to 47-10-23; N.Y. Real Prop. Law §§ 233, 235 (McKinney); N.D. Cent. Code §§ 23-10-01 to 23-10-14; Ohio Rev. Code Ann. §§ 3733.01 to 3733.02 (West); Or. Rev. Stat. §§ 90.505 to 90.840; 68 Pa. Stat. Ann. §§ 398.1 to 398.16 (West); R.I. Gen. Laws §§ 31-44-1 to 31-44-22; S.C. Code Ann. §§ 27-47-10 to 27-47-620; Utah Code Ann. §§ 57-16-1 to 57-16-18 (West); Vt. Stat. Ann. tit. 10, §§ 6201 to 6266; Va. Code Ann. §§ 55-248.41 to 55-248.52; Wash. Rev. Code §§ 59.20.010 to 59.20.901; W. Va. Code R. §§ 37-15-1 to 37-15-8; Wis. Stat. § 710.15; Wis. Admin. Code Agric., Trade & Consumer Prot. §§ 125.01 to 125.09.

14 *See, e.g.*, Ariz. Rev. Stat. Ann. § 33-1413.01 (if landlord charges separately for utilities, each user must have individual meter); Mass. Code Regs. tit. 105, § 410.354 (manufactured-home parks and multiple dwellings must have separate metering if tenants pay utilities separately); Utah Admin. Code r. R746-210-1 to R746-210-5 (manufactured-home parks and multi-unit buildings constructed after 1984); Wis. Admin. Code P.S.C. § 113.0803 (after Mar. 1, 1980, manufactured-home parks, new non-transient multi-unit residential, and commercial buildings).

15 *See, e.g.*, Utah Admin. Code r. R746-210-1 to R746-210-5 (constructed before 1985); Wis. Admin. Code P.S.C. § 113.0803 (constructed before March 1, 1980).

16 *See* § 4.5, *supra* (discussing master metering in detail).

17 *See, e.g.*, Nev. Admin. Code §§ 704.980 to 704.991 (manufactured home parks); Utah Admin. Code r. R746-210-1 to R746-

tering will exempt from their protections transient accommodations, such as campgrounds providing spaces for RVs and similar units. Of course, even RVs in campgrounds are sometimes used for permanent housing. Such residents should, but may not, be afforded the protections given to those in more traditional permanent housing situations.[18]

14.3.2 Other Protections Involving Master Metering

Other common state statutory provisions include requiring the disclosure, before the tenant occupies the site, of utility charges or the method of calculating them,[19] the method of allocating master-metered utilities,[20] limitations on the landlord's power to exact administrative fees,[21] or fees for installation or use of appliances.[22] The landlord may also be required to post the prevailing utility rates,[23] provide itemized utility bills,[24] or use the same billing format as the serving utility.[25]

In addition, many states limit the rates that landlords or landowners of manufactured-home communities can charge for the resale of utilities. These resale charge limitations fall into two main groups: (1) those provisions that allow a park to charge the tenants on a pro rata basis the same amount charged to the park by the utility at the master-meter level without making any profit on the resale ("flow-through")[26]

210-5 (transient facilities such as dormitories, nursing homes, travel trailer parks). *See also* National Consumer Law Center, Unfair and Deceptive Acts and Practices § 8.1.2.5.2 (7th ed. 2008 and Supp.) (statutes).

18 *See, e.g.*, Shepard v. Bonita Vista Props., L.P., 664 S.E.2d 388 (N.C. Ct. App. 2008) (dissent argues that long-term residents living for a number of years on campground are not afforded protections of state Residential Rental Agreement Act, despite Act's inclusion of manufactured-home lot rent situations).

19 Alaska Stat. § 34.03.080; Del. Code Ann. tit. 25, §§ 7006, 7008 (landlord must identify availability, capacity, and connection fee for all utility services); Conn. Gen. Stat. § 21-82(d) (charges for all services must be disclosed in rental agreement); Fla. Stat. § 723.012 (prospectus given to potential tenant must disclose manner in which utility services will be provided, person or entity furnishing services, and fees for any services provided by park); Idaho Code Ann. §§ 55-2007(1)(b), 55-2007(4)(d), (e) (rental agreement must disclose what utilities and services are included in rent; landlord must describe, upon request, all utilities and services available within park); 765 Ill. Comp. Stat. 745/9 (all charges must be itemized in lease); Iowa Code § 562B.14 (must provide explanation of utility rates, charges, and services unless tenant will pay utility charges separately); Me. Rev. Stat. tit. 10, § 9093 (all fees and assessments must be disclosed before tenant occupies site); Md. Code Ann., Real Prop. § 8A-201 (West) (must disclose availability, capacity, and connection fee of all utility services at site and description of each utility service owner will provide); Mass. Gen. Laws ch. 140, § 32P (must disclose before rental an itemized list of all charges and fees); Neb. Rev. Stat. § 76-1482 (landlord must provide written explanation of utility rates, charges, and services before rental agreement signed unless tenant will pay utility charges directly to utility company); Nev. Rev. Stat. § 118B.040 (utilities that are included with lot rental and payment responsibility for them); N.H. Rev. Stat. Ann. §§ 205-A:2 (VII), 205-A:6(I) (must disclose to prospective tenant all terms and conditions of rental, including utility charges); N.J. Stat. Ann. § 46:8C-2(c) (West) (prior to occupancy of site, must disclose in writing all fees, charges, and assessments); Ohio Rev. Code Ann. § 3733.11(B) (West) (all fees must be disclosed in writing); Or. Rev. Stat. § 90.510(1)(i) (rental agreement must disclose what utilities and services are available, by whom furnished, and who is responsible for paying for them); 68 Pa. Stat. Ann. §§ 398.2, 398.6 (West) (charges for, *inter alia*, electricity, gas, sewer, and water must be disclosed in writing before owner accepts any deposit, fee, or rent); Utah Code Ann. § 57-16-4(3)(c) (West) (separate charges for electricity and so forth must be disclosed in lease); Vt. Stat. Ann. tit. 10, § 6236(e)(1) (utility charges must be disclosed in lease); Wash. Rev. Code § 59.20.060(1)(i) (rental agreement must disclose utilities, services, and fees); W. Va. Code R. § 37-15-3 (services provided and fees); Wis. Admin. Code Agric., Trade & Consumer Prot. §§ 125.01, 125.03 (if utilities are billed separately, based on usage, must disclose rate or method of calculation); Herrick d.b.a Tan Tara Mobile Home Park v. Florida Dep't of Bus. Regulation, Div. of Fla. Land Sales, Condominiums & Mobile Homes, 595 So. 2d 148 (Fla. Dist. Ct. App. 1992) (park violated statute when it charged for individual use while prospectus stated that utility charges would be pro-rated; improper rent increase when park began to charge for individual water use while still charging rent that included pro-rated utilities).

20 N.M. Stat. Ann. § 47-10-22 (manufactured-home park that bills separately for utilities but does not submeter must disclose allocation formula); Wis. Admin. Code Agric., Trade & Consumer Prot. §§ 125.01(10), 125.03 (manufactured-home park must disclose either rate or method of allocation).

21 Minn. Stat. § 327C.04 (fees permitted only if landlord would lose money at "hold harmless" rate); N.H. Rev. Stat. Ann. § 205-A:6 (III) (only as permitted by PUC); N.M. Stat. Ann. § 47-10-20 (reasonable fee to offset costs incurred in providing service); R.I. Gen. Laws § 31-44-3 (return on park's investment in costs of bringing service to individual units); Va. Code Ann. § 55-248.45:1 (landlord may not impose meter-reading fee).

22 N.J. Stat. Ann. § 46:8C-2(b)(1) (West) (may not charge fee for installation or use of gas or electric appliance unless charge reflects actual cost to park of installation or use); N.Y. Real Prop. Law § 233(h)(2) (McKinney) (same); Ohio Rev. Code Ann. § 3733.11(E) (West) (same); 68 Pa. Cons. Stat. § 398.7 (same).

23 Ariz. Rev. Stat. Ann. § 33-1432; Cal. Civ. Code § 798.40 (West); R.I. Gen. Laws § 31-44-3 (park operator must post prevailing utility rate schedule).

24 Ariz. Rev. Stat. Ann. § 33-1413.01; Conn. Gen. Stat. § 21-82(d); N.M. Stat. Ann. § 47-10-22 (amount due for each utility and either amount consumed and unit price or allocation formula used); Wis. Admin. Code Agric., Trade & Consumer Prot. § 125.04(3).

25 Ariz. Rev. Stat. Ann. § 33-1413.01.

26 *See, e.g.*, Colo. Rev. Stat. § 38-12-212.7 (manufactured-home park landlord must remit to utility all monies collected from each resident for resident's share of charges to landlord, failing which utility may demand deposit from landlord and may sue and recover attorney fees); Fla. Stat. § 723.045 ("amount charged by the public utility"); Md. Code Ann., Real Prop. § 8A-503 (West) (amount utility charges park owner); Minn. Stat. § 327C.04(3), (4) (manufactured-home parks must hold tenants harmless but, with respect to electricity, if "hold harmless" rate would cause loss to park owner, park owner may bill at rate to avoid loss but may not consider administrative, capital, or other expenses in

and (2) those that require only that the landlord not charge each tenant more than the tenant would have paid had the tenant received service directly from the regulated utility ("hold harmless"), regardless of whether the park makes a profit or not.[27] Some flow-through jurisdictions allow manufactured-home park owners a small service charge to cover the costs of metering and billing.[28]

When community owners in smaller rental communities fail to properly price utilities in a submetering arrangement, these owners may claim a lack of knowledge or ability to correctly calculate the amount to be charged to residents. Most courts have determined that such arguments are without merit.[29]

14.3.3 When Park Switches So That Utilities Are No Longer Included in Rent

If a park switches from utilities that are included in rent to the use of individual meters—but continues to charge the same rent—the result to the residents in real terms will be a rent increase, which may violate state statutes or regulations governing rent.[30] The issue of separate billing versus inclusion in rent for utilities and other charges may also arise under local rent control ordinances or regulation. In reviewing such ordinances, it is important that the local ordinance be analyzed within its relationship to any state requirements regarding the manufactured-home lot rent.[31]

14.3.4 Special Concerns for Water Submetering Arrangements

Submetering of water service in manufactured home communities raises special concerns. Public water systems, often including those in manufactured-home communities, are governed by federal law and may also be regulated by state drinking water and landlord-tenant statutes. These statutes may restrict the landowners' use of submetering or ratio utility billing systems (RUBS). This subsection focuses on specific issues that arise in the use of water service submetering for manufactured-home communities. A general and more complete discussion of submetering issues can be found in § 4.5, *supra*.

While there has been a trend in recent years to increase the use of submetering in apartments and manufactured-home communities (ostensibly to promote conservation), concerns have been raised about the possible dangers of such metering.[32] These issues became increasingly important when the Environmental Protection Agency (EPA), which regulates

calculating cost); Nev. Rev. Stat. § 704.940 (if submetered, may not charge higher rate than charged to landlord; if allocated total charges to tenants, may not exceed cost of service to park); N.M. Stat. Ann. § 47-10-20; R.I. Gen. Laws § 31-44-3(4)(ii) (manufactured home park may not receive directly or indirectly any amount for resale of utilities that exceeds amount charged the park by utility company); Tex. Util. Code Ann. § 184.014(b) (West) (electricity); Tex. Water Code Ann. § 13.503(b) (West) (water); Va. Code Ann. § 55-248.45:1 (manufactured-home park owner must flow-through and may not charge meter-read fee); Wash. Rev. Code § 59.20.070(6) (actual utility costs). *See also* Mich. Comp. Laws § 125.2328 (unfair and deceptive practice to directly or indirectly charge or collect for electric, fuel, or water service without first accurately measuring tenant's use, unless service included in rent). *See also* § 4.5.2.3, *supra* (discussing in detail "flow-through" and "hold harmless" rules).

27 *See, e.g.*, Ariz. Rev. Stat. Ann. § 33-1413.01 (may not charge more than prevailing basic service single-family residential rate charged by serving utility); Minn. Stat. § 327C.04(4) (manufactured-home parks must hold tenants harmless but may only exceed flow-through allocation if landlord suffers loss at flow-through rates); Nev. Rev. Stat. § 704.940 (landlord may assess service charge, but amount may not exceed what tenants would be required to pay directly to utility); Wash. Rev. Code § 59.20.070(6); Allison v. Sherburne Country Mobile Home Park, 475 N.W.2d 501 (Minn. Ct. App. 1991) (manufactured-home park monthly service fee upheld since no higher than that charged by local utility); Shepard v. Bonita Vista Props., L.P., 664 S.E.2d 388 (N.C. Ct. App. 2008) (recreational vehicle campground that submetered electrical services and charged more than actual cost of electricity was public utility, and its ignorance of proper way to calculate charges provided no defense); Allegheny Ctr. Assocs., 228 A.2d 26 (Pa. Super. Ct. 1967) (utility tariff bans resale except when landlord charges tenants same rates utility would have charged "for a like and contemporaneous service"); General Split Corp. v. P. & V. Atlas Corp., 368 N.W.2d 846 (table), 1985 WL 188069 n.1 (Wis. Ct. App. Mar. 18, 1985) (cites 1963 commission rule requiring resellers to hold tenants harmless).

28 Fla. Stat. § 723.045 (actual maintenance and administrative costs of manufactured-home park water system); N.M. Stat. Ann. § 47-10-21 (manufactured-home park may impose reasonable administrative fee to offset actual cost incurred in providing service); R.I. Gen. Laws § 31-44-3(4)(iii) (manufactured-home park that incurs costs in bringing service to tenants' sites may impose service charge sufficient to produce fair return on that investment).

29 *See, e.g.*, Shepard v. Bonita Vista Props., L.P., 664 S.E.2d 388 (N.C. Ct. App. 2008) (community owner's claim that it did not willfully overcharge residents for electricity because it was ignorant of proper way to charge found meritless).

30 Herrick d.b.a. Tan Tara Mobile Home Park v. Florida Dep't of Bus. Regulation, Div. of Fla. Land Sales, Condos. & Mobile Homes, 595 So. 2d 148 (Fla. Dist. Ct. App. 1992); Sargent v. Bethel Props., Inc., 653 N.W.2d 800 (Minn. Ct. App. 2002) (addition of utility charges to existing manufactured-home park rental agreements was new rule that substantially modified agreements and rendered them unenforceable as a matter of law). *See also* Nev. Rev. Stat. § 118B.153 (amount of rent charged to tenant for utility must be reduced proportionately when landlord decreases or eliminates utility).

31 *See, e.g.*, Cacho v. Boudreau, 149 P.3d 473 (Cal. 2007) (local rent control ordinance that allowed landowner to pass property tax to residents outside of rent was not preempted by California's Mobilehome Residency Law that prohibited charging for anything but rent, utilities, reasonable services, and government assessments).

32 *See* National Consumer Law Center, *Soaking Tenant: Billing Tenants Directly for Water and Sewer Services*, Energy and Utility Update (Fall 2003).

water systems under the Safe Drinking Water Act,[33] revised its policy of subjecting submetering—considered under the Act to be "selling water"—to regulation.

The Safe Drinking Water Act governs public water systems, defined as those with more than fifteen service connections or are serving twenty-five or more people. Since many manufactured-home communities have more than twenty-five residents or more than fifteen pads, they are generally governed by the Act. The Act is enforced by the federal government but may also be enforced by states. A state may be granted primary enforcement responsibility and may adopt its own regulations, but those regulations must be at least as stringent as federal regulations.[34]

The EPA has issued a final policy allowing unregulated submetering for residential properties that receive water from regulated public water systems but still requiring that manufactured-home communities be regulated when they submeter.[35] The Manufactured Housing Institute, an industry group of manufacturers and community owners, unsuccessfully challenged this more favorable treatment of apartment buildings over manufactured-home communities.[36] As a result, manufactured-home communities that submeter for water are considered public water systems. Nevertheless, the EPA has indicated that it may allow states to experiment by allowing unregulated submetering on a case-by-case basis for communities that share characteristics of apartment buildings.[37]

14.4 Park Owner's Failure to Provide Utility Service

A park owner often has the affirmative duty to maintain the utilities within a park.[38] If the park owner fails to provide safe and adequate utilities or hook-ups, a tenant's remedies may be found in manufactured-home statutes or in general landlord-tenant law. Alternatively, a warranty of habitability may be applied to the rental of manufactured-home pads.

General state landlord-tenant acts vary in their coverage of manufactured-home communities. The Montana Residential Landlord and Tenant Act defines "dwelling unit" to include "space in a mobile home park." A Montana court interpreting the act held that the warranty of habitability was violated by a park's contaminated water and grossly malfunctioning sewer system.[39] A Pennsylvania court found a "limited warranty of habitability"—that is, a landlord may rent land for a manufactured home without providing utilities but, if the landlord chooses to provide "utilities and other housing services and charges tenants rent in exchange therefor, the landlord impliedly warrants to maintain the services according to applicable state and local regulations."[40]

Although state landlord-tenant laws may specifically cover the relationship between the manufactured-home community owner and the manufactured-home owner who rents a lot or pad, the issue may become more clouded if the community is not a traditional manufactured-home park. Often campgrounds and other communities lease space on a long-term basis to RVs and other shelters that are used as permanent housing. Coverage for these communities may be less defined in states that have exceptions for "transient" shelter communities or campgrounds and that specifically reference manufactured-home communities in their landlord-tenant statutes.[41]

Landlord-tenant law may provide a variety of remedies for failure to provide proper utilities, for example, rent withholding or receivership and injunctions, among other things.[42] State health or environmental laws or regulations may set standards and provide remedies—that is, a state board of health or department of environmental protection may order the repair of a defective water and sewer system and impose substantial penalties.

14.5 Utility Termination As Means to Evict

A few state statutes specifically allow evictions from manufactured-home parks for nonpayment of utility charges.[43] In many other states, the statutes are silent on the subject, and these utility charges are often not considered rent for which summary eviction proceedings are available.

In most states, statutes or landlord-tenant common law prohibit manufactured-home parks from willfully terminat-

33 42 U.S.C. § 300f.

34 42 U.S.C. § 300g-2(a)(1).

35 68 Fed. Reg. 74233–74255 (Dec. 23, 2003). *See also* 68 Fed. Reg. 51778, 51779 (Aug. 28, 2003) (draft EPA memorandum).

36 Manufactured Hous. Inst. v. United States Envtl. Prot. Agency, 467 F.3d 391 (4th Cir. 2006).

37 68 Fed. Reg. 74234, 74235 (Dec. 23, 2003).

38 *See, e.g.*, Neb. Rev. Stat. § 71-4629 (park owner must maintain all utilities according to state standards); Wash. Rev. Code § 59.20.130(6) (all utilities must be maintained and protected within park, including hookups to individual manufactured homes).

39 Mathes v. Adams, 838 P.2d 390 (Mont. 1992) (construing Mont. Code Ann. §§ 70-24-101 to 70-24-109).

40 Staley v. Bouril, 718 A.2d 283 (Pa. 1998) (contaminated water).

41 *See, e.g.*, Shepard v. Bonita Vista Props., L.P., 664 S.E.2d 388 (N.C. Ct. App. 2008) (dissent argues that long-term residents living for a number of years on campground are not afforded protections of state Residential Rental Agreement Act, despite Act's inclusion of manufactured-home lot rent situations).

42 *See, e.g.*, Penrich, Inc. v. Sullivan, 620 A.2d 1037 (N.H. 1993) (electric and sewer violations; remanding because of tenants noncompliance with notice provisions of manufactured home statute; statute provided for injunction and rent withholding).

43 *See, e.g.*, Me. Rev. Stat. tit. 10, § 9097(1)(a); N.H. Rev. Stat. Ann. § 205-A:4(I); N.M. Stat. Ann. § 47-10-6; Utah Code Ann. §§ 57-16-5, 57-16-6 (West).

ing essential services, including utilities, to tenants.[44] Doing so, or evicting the tenant, would subject the landlord to penalties for wrongful eviction, forcible entry or other violations, and possible tort liability for resulting damage.[45] In some states, questions may arise as to the applicability of landlord-tenant protections to a lot lease situation. Typically such a relationship will be covered, although the issue may be less clear if the space is rented for an RV or other structure commonly used for temporary shelter.[46]

14.6 Addressing Inefficient Homes

14.6.1 Overview

There is a broad spectrum of energy efficiency found in manufactured housing, from older, poorly constructed, and very inefficient units to modern efficient models. There are a number of existing ways in which advocates and homeowners are attempting to address older, inefficient homes and increase efficiency of new homes. In addition, various efforts are underway to better address these problems in the future. This section addresses these different existing and expanding efforts.

14.6.2 Weatherization of Existing Homes

14.6.2.1 Overview

The Weatherization Assistance Program,[47] created in 1976 as part of the Energy Conservation and Production Act, was in part a reaction to the energy crisis in the 1970s. The unique challenges and opportunities that manufactured homes present were not the focus of either the Energy Department's programs or most other weatherization programs. Consequently, the programs were not designed to address the needs of some manufactured-home owners. Many of the issues particular to manufactured housing, such as specific problems stemming from the design of pre-HUD Code homes and the complexities of working in land-lease communities, are not addressed by the Energy Conservation and Production Act.

While the energy efficiency of older units can be greatly improved through weatherization, there are challenges and hurdles to the use of these programs for manufactured homes and especially pre-HUD Code homes.

14.6.2.2 Non-Energy Savings Repairs

One issue that often arises with the weatherization of older manufactured homes is the need for repairs.[48] Structural and non-energy saving repairs present special problems for manufactured homes. Use of DOE weatherization funding is generally restricted to improving the heating or cooling efficiency of a low-income program participant's home,[49] though local agencies may also spend limited funds to eliminate health and safety hazards when necessary. Funding from private utility companies is constrained in the low-income conservation programs by the requirement that such programs be "cost-effective." The term "cost-effective," a term of art, means that the cost of the conservation measures must be less than the value of the energy savings. A cost-effective program, in other words, must lower the total energy cost by an amount greater than the cost of the conservation measures.[50]

While funding for these structural or non-energy saving repairs is difficult to obtain under existing programs, these structural defects are often present in older homes, especially those manufactured prior to the implementation of the HUD Code.

14.6.2.3 Specialized Training Requirements

Another issue for weatherizing manufactured homes is the special training and education required. These homes present real weatherization challenges. Some older homes were built with smaller framing using 2x2 dimensional lumber rather than 2x4 dimensional lumber, so wall and ceiling space may be insufficient to permit adding insulation. The underbelly of the home may not have been properly sealed or may have been damaged in transit or setup. To assist in identifying effective weatherization measures, the DOE created the Manufactured Home Energy Audit (MHEA).[51] Some states have also done research on the

44 *See, e.g.*, Ariz. Rev. Stat. Ann. § 33-1475; Nev. Rev. Stat. § 118B.150; Wash. Rev. Code § 59.20.070.

45 *See* § 6.8, *supra*. *See also* Euclid Beach, Ltd. v. Brockett, 1999 Ohio App. LEXIS 5910 (Ohio Ct. App. Dec. 9, 1999) ($30,000 actual, $7500 punitive damages, and $8800 attorney fees to consumer for damage resulting from "retaliatory" shut-off of water).

46 *See, e.g.*, Shepard v. Bonita Vista Props., L.P., 664 S.E.2d 388 (N.C. Ct. App. 2008) (dissent argues that long-term residents living for a number of years on campground are not afforded protections of state Residential Rental Agreement Act, despite Act's inclusion of manufactured-home lot rent situations).

47 *See* ch. 9, *supra*.

48 *See* § 9.4.7.2, *supra*.

49 10 C.F.R. § 440.18.

50 The computation of cost effectiveness can become very complex. Some computational measures examine the cost to the utility, while others consider total costs to the utility and the program participants (using the "Total Resource Cost Test") or to the costs to society as a whole (using the "Societal Cost Test").

51 For more information about the manufactured home energy audit, see Mark P. Ternes, Oak Ridge Nat'l Lab., Validation of the Manufactured Home Energy Audit (Nov. 2007), *available at* http://weatherization.ornl.gov/pdfs/ORNL_CON-501.pdf.

issues of weatherizing manufactured homes.[52] Typically, recommendations include: sealing and repairing the ductwork and underbelly; installing added insulation, a moisture barrier, and new doors or windows; and repairing or replacing heating and cooling systems. Problems may be especially severe in older units or units that were not properly sited. Multi-sectional units are especially prone to problems in the marriage wall connecting the separately constructed units if they were not properly sited.[53]

14.6.2.4 Weatherization of Homes in Communities

Homeowners living in manufactured-home communities—often called parks—face particular challenges when seeking weatherization efforts. Although the homes themselves are rarely moved, a manufactured-home owner does not have the security of knowing that his or her home will remain where it is or that he or she will retain ownership of the home for the long term. Rent increases, eviction, and community closure can eliminate the investment—including any weatherization improvements—they have in their homes. While the DOE weatherization program was not designed with the specific challenges of such communities in mind, the issue of weatherization in rental units has been addressed and can inform the analysis of the weatherization of manufactured homes.

Local administering agencies are often reluctant to put weatherization resources into rental units, due to legitimate concerns that the benefits from weatherization of rental units would ultimately accrue to the landlords and not to the low-income tenants. For example, landlords may raise the rent after weatherization to reflect increased value, or they may sell the property to realize the higher value after weatherization. Likewise, manufactured-home community landowners may raise the lot rent or attempt to limit the homeowner's ability to sell the home to reap the benefit of the increased value of the home.

The DOE weatherization statute attempts to address some of the concerns about rental units by requiring states to ensure that the benefits of weatherization accrue primarily to the low-income residents. The statute requires that:

- The benefits of weatherization accrue primarily to the low-income residents;
- For a reasonable period of time after weatherization, the residents will not be subjected to rent increases unless those increases are demonstrably related to matters other than the weatherization;
- Residents may file a complaint, in response to which the owner must demonstrate that the rent increase relates to matters other than the weatherization;
- No undue or excessive enhancement will occur to the value of such dwelling units.

DOE regulations reiterate the statutory protections and detail ways the program may seek to protect residents. The regulations permit states to seek a landlord agreement to the placement of a lien or other contract restrictions to protect the federal investment and address the issues of eviction and sale of property. DOE advised states to adopt a "comprehensive approach to weatherizing rentals" in order to meet their statutory obligations, leaving states relatively broad discretion to address tenant protection as part of their plans.

States also may address concerns specific to manufactured-home communities. The notice and public hearing procedures described above for the required state plans offer an opportunity for owners and advocates of manufactured housing to seek protections for homeowners in manufactured-home communities. Public hearings and comment periods generally occur in the spring prior to the submission deadline of the state plans. Advocates hoping to better protect homeowners in manufactured-home communities should develop a relationship with the relevant state agency and add their names to the notice list for state plans or any other rulemaking concerning the state weatherization program.

Advocates for traditional rental tenants have had success with this strategy. Some states set restrictions on rent increases for a minimum of three to ten years and allow local sub-grantees to add additional years to the protected period. Other protections were developed to address evictions without cause, increasing the rent for new tenants, and the sale of properties following the completion of the weatherization work.

These same and similar issues also affect homeowners in manufactured-home communities. Although the incentives for the community owner may not be the same as for a traditional landlord when the landlord's own building is being repaired, there is still a real benefit to the landowner when the repairs are made. The improvement of the housing stock in the community greatly increases the value of the community. Because homes are very rarely moved, these weatherized homes are a real "part" of the community itself.

14.6.3 Replacement of Older Homes

14.6.3.1 Overview

Because of needed structural repairs and the age and condition of some units, it may not always be best to weatherize existing homes. Sometimes replacement units

52 *E.g.*, Lyn M. Bartges & Bob Scott, Home Energy, Weatherizing Mobile Homes (July/Aug. 2004) (providing insight in West Virginia manufactured home weatherization program, which weatherizes between 400 and 500 manufactured homes per year).

53 *See* National Consumer Law Center, Consumer Warranty Law ch. 17 (4th ed. 2010 and Supp.) (providing more information about problems common to the placement and construction of manufactured homes).

will provide greater benefits in terms of efficiency and resident satisfaction, as well as improve the community overall by removing deteriorated units. Although the traditional DOE weatherization program may not be useful in such situations, some states are attempting to encourage such replacements and additional energy-saving measures.

14.6.3.2 Barriers to Replacement of Older Manufactured Homes

14.6.3.2.1 Financing

When the owner of an older manufactured home decides that replacing the home with a new or newer model makes more sense than making extensive repairs, he or she will generally need to find financing to support the cost of a new home. While finding an affordable loan may be challenging for any low-income homeowner, finding fair and affordable financing is especially challenging for homeowners in a manufactured home community.

This issue often arises when a community is converted to resident ownership or when policy changes provide more security for homeowners. Prior to conversions or policy improvement, homeowners may have had little motivation to replace an older home because of the danger that the landowner may close the community or raise the rent to a level that forces the homeowner to leave. The homeowner does not wish to take the chance that a large investment in a new home may be put at risk without secure land tenure. But once the community is resident-owned or the homeowner feels secure in the ability to remain in the community at fair terms, replacing the home may make much more sense.

Unfortunately, lenders often do not appreciate the greatly reduced risk of default that is conferred by improved land security—the knowledge that the home may remain where it is sited and be sold to a new purchaser where it is. After a resident purchase or policy improvements, homeowners wishing to replace their home still often face the more costly terms typically offered to those seeking to finance homes on rented land. This reluctance on the part of lenders may make financing the purchase of a new manufactured home to replace a deteriorated home prohibitively expensive, and sources of financing for used homes are limited. Apart from resident-owned communities, homeowners with older homes on resident-owned land often face problems in obtaining fair financing as well.[54]

14.6.3.2.2 Size of replacement units

Early manufactured homes that were intended primarily for recreational purposes were generally built so that they could be easily pulled behind a car. This generally limited the size of such units to eight feet wide or less, and often to less than twenty feet long. When year-round permanent use became more common, the size of the units increased. Ten-foot-wide units became more common, and often the length extended up to fifty or sixty feet. Many manufactured home communities were established when these dimensions were standard.

Today, the manufactured-home market has changed considerably. In the 1960s, manufacturers began to sell two units that would be joined together onsite to form one home, commonly called a "doublewide." These multi-section units proved to be very popular for a number of reasons. Manufacturers and dealers could often make a greater profit selling one of these multi-sectional units than one "single-wide" unit. An often unrecognized factor contributing to the popularity of multi-section units was that many areas of the country placed zoning restrictions, restrictive covenants, and other restrictions on new homes that required these new homes to meet or exceed a particular size. By the 1990s, sales of multi-sectional units were often double that of single-wide homes. That trend has continued to this day, causing many manufacturers to reduce the number of single-wide homes for sale. The single-wide homes that are offered today are typically much bigger than older homes. New single-wide homes are often fourteen or sixteen feet wide and up to eighty feet in length.

Many manufactured-home communities were created when manufactured homes were much smaller. Thus, newer and larger homes will often not fit the dimensions of the existing lot or the pad on which the original home rested. Some manufacturers produce homes that, though larger than the older homes, will still fit the dimensions of the older pads, but these homes are not available everywhere. Even though manufactured homes are now built to national standards—with some variation for particular geographic areas, such as changes that allow the home to survive increased winds in hurricane-prone regions—the availability of manufactured homes is still typically dependent upon regional markets. Manufactured homes are difficult and expensive to transport, so many of these homes are still manufactured in close proximity to where they will ultimately be placed.

Recently, for environmental reasons and reasons of simplicity, there has been an increased interest in smaller homes in general. This trend has extended to manufactured homes.[55] While some manufactured-home makers are exploring this trend, such homes are still not routinely available.

54 *See* National Consumer Law Center, Manufactured Housing Policy Brief: Financing Homes in Communities, *available at* www.nclc.org/issues/manufactured-housing.html (scroll down to section entitled "Titling and Financing of Manufactured Homes" and click on appropriate brief) (discussing in detail manufactured home financing).

55 *See* The Museum of Modern Art, Home Delivery: Fabricating the Modern Dwelling, *available at* www.momahomedelivery.org.

The reluctance of manufacturers to construct smaller units may be due in part to a smaller profit margin on such units and to the lower overall demand for such homes. Hopefully, as more homeowners in the increasing number of resident-owned communities seek to upgrade their homes, and more programs are implemented promoting replacement of old units, the greater demand for smaller units will result in increased availability across the country.

14.6.3.2.3 Lack of security of land tenure

Replacement of manufactured homes in rental communities raises many of the same issues as the weatherization of such homes. Because homeowners in manufactured-home communities seldom have security of land tenure, they are vulnerable to losing their substantial investment in a new or newer replacement home. Accordingly, it makes sense to focus replacement efforts on homeowners who, through state policy protections or resident ownership of the community, have security of land tenure.

Efforts should be made to help landowners understand the benefits of replacing aging homes in the community. Helping landowners to understand that these programs will improve the housing stock in the community due to the presence of newer homes and will make the community a more desirable place to live may persuade landowners to be more amenable to changes in their agreements with homeowners with regard to terms that provide greater security of land tenure.

14.6.3.2.4 Predatory lending

Issues of fairness in financing arise more often in replacement of homes than in weatherization. Replacement will typically require that the homeowner take out a loan to pay for at least a part of the purchase of the newer home. Sometimes, in the effort to obtain financing for the replacement of an older home, too much attention is focused on the need for financing to the exclusion of other important issues, such as the long-term affordability of the loan. For example, even if an upgrade will produce energy savings, financing it with a loan that puts the homeowner beyond a reasonable debt-to-income ratio may do more harm than good. This is particularly so in light of the precarious financial circumstances of some low-income homeowners and the volatile nature of energy prices.

Any replacement program should contain protections to ensure that the financing for a new or newer home is provided to the homeowner at fair terms. The loan should be one that the homeowner can afford. Preferably, such a loan should be a fully amortizing fifteen- or thirty-year mortgage at a fixed rate set in response to the perceived credit risk of the loan, with no prepayment penalties.

14.6.3.2.5 Dealer capture of benefits

Another issue is the risk within replacement programs of the dealer "capturing" benefits intended for the homeowner. Incentives provided by replacement programs are intended to encourage the homeowner to consider replacement of an older home and to make possible a replacement that would otherwise be unaffordable. Without adequate protections, incentives such as rebates, loan guarantees, or other financial incentives may be realized by the manufactured-home dealer selling the home rather than by the homeowner.

In the sale of a manufactured home, the dealer typically controls a number of variables in the transaction. Consumers generally do not have the knowledge, experience, or negotiating skills necessary to obtain a fair deal. Dealers have the incentive to use any program rebate in order to entice consumers into replacing an older home but will then deprive homeowners of the benefit of the rebate. For example, dealers can simply raise the price of the home or other items in the transaction by the same amount as the rebate. In this way, the money intended to help reduce the cost for homeowners in replacing their homes is instead taken as excess profit by the dealer.

14.6.3.3 New Efforts to Assist Replacement

There has been an increased effort, both on a state and local level, to make replacement of older homes a more accessible option. The Oregon Department of Energy assisted in the creation of a focus group consisting of housing providers, community service providers, utilities, manufactured-housing industry representatives, financial institutions, and weatherization contractors to study ways to replace older units and make weatherization subsidies available for down payments on new units. In New York, a community development block grant was used to replace deteriorating and poorly weatherized manufactured homes.[56] In Minnesota, the Apple Valley Mobile Home Replacement Program provides up to $2000 for removing and demolishing older homes, assistance with set-up and moving costs, and 50% of the down payment for the replacement manufactured home.[57]

Some replacement efforts have focused exclusively on replacing homes located on land that the homeowners own.[58]

---

56 William Apgar, Allegra Calder, Michael Collins, & Mark Duda, Neighborhood Reinvestment Corp. & Joint Ctr. for Housing Studies of Harvard Univ., An Examination of Manufactured Housing As a Community- and Asset-Building Strategy (2002), *available at* www.jchs.harvard.edu/publications/community development/W02-11_apgar_et_al.pdf.

57 Information about the program is available at www.dakotacda.org/homeowners.htm.

58 *See, e.g.*, www.northcountryaffordablehousing.com/mhrp/index.html (North Country Affordable Housing's manufactured home replacement program; providing up to $20,000 to help

While such efforts address concerns, discussed below, about the replacement of homes on rented land, they exclude a large number of homeowners on leased land who cannot take advantage of the programs. Although the exclusion of so many homeowners is problematic, these programs can be very useful for those homeowners who are eligible.

Maine Housing has developed a pilot program promoting Energy Star mortgages for manufactured housing replacement in Maine. Maine's pilot program is an effort to create a larger multi-state pilot program with the U.S. Department of Energy. The Energy Star mortgage program, a joint effort by the Department of Energy and the Environmental Protection Agency, is intended to provide financing for home replacement or home improvements that will cut energy expenditure by 20% or more.

An "energy-efficient mortgage" (EEM) is another product that has been offered to help facilitate financing of replacement manufactured homes. The Federal Housing Administration, Fannie Mae, Freddie Mac, and the Department of Veterans Affairs all offer EEMs. These efforts are laudable and will hopefully increase the availability of financing for replacement homes. However, as discussed previously, it is still important to ensure that any financing is affordable and in the homeowner's best interest.

In central Appalachia, Frontier Homes, which serves homebuyers, worked with Clayton Homes to design a new energy-efficient, single-section manufactured home to be affordable for low-income families, allowing them to replace older homes. These homes are constructed using 2x6 dimensional lumber externally and 2x4 dimensional lumber internally—allowing for upgraded insulation levels, upgraded windows, vinyl siding, shutters, and shingled roofs to ensure both a longer lifespan for the unit and increased energy efficiency without sacrificing construction quality for very low-income homebuyers.

In 2007, the Montana Legislature appropriated $350,000 to fund a pilot program for the decommissioning and replacement of older manufactured homes. The appropriation was based on the results of a study commissioned by local community action programs. The study identified nearly 30,000 pre-1976 manufactured homes in Montana, for which the cost of weatherization improvements often exceeded the value of the home. In addition to the funding provided by the state of Montana decommissioning and replacement program, NeighborWorks, Montana's program uses NeighborWorks America funding, HOME funds, and bank financing.

In Arizona, the Primavera Foundation began a replacement program. The program is helping South Tucson families that are earning as little as $15,000 a year to replace homes damaged beyond the point of rehabilitation.

low-income homeowners replace older homes with new, efficient modular homes).

14.6.3.4 Decommissioning of Homes to Be Replaced

When older manufactured homes are replaced with newer more energy-efficient units, something must be done with the replaced units. The first question is whether the replacement program does, or should, mandate the decommissioning of all or only some of the replaced units. The second question is how these units should be decommissioned.

As described above, an older home that is replaced is often in poor condition and is not energy efficient. Such a unit can even be dangerous and, especially after being moved, may not be fit for habitation. If it is replaced, it should be decommissioned so that it cannot be used again for habitation. Unfortunately, these homes often are resold and subsequently used as residential dwellings. While in most places zoning restrictions and community restrictions prohibit the placement of pre-1976 homes, some jurisdictions do not. Older homes are often moved to, and placed in, these less-regulated areas. Pre-1976 homes are also sometimes sited in jurisdictions that prohibit placing such homes, contrary to local rules or restrictions. Even if the replaced unit is not used again as a home, it may not be properly disposed of but rather simply abandoned, since proper disposal of such units can be expensive.

In order to ensure that unsafe replaced homes are not reused as housing, proposed replacement programs often call for the decommissioning of all replaced homes. If effectively enforced, this would certainly resolve the problem of potential reuse of the home. However, this raises two other questions: How will these units be decommissioned? What about units that are not unsafe but would nevertheless be decommissioned under such program requirements?

No one wants to destroy a unit that might still provide a good, safe home for a family. Such destruction would reduce the number of homes available to low-income families and may even be environmentally harmful when the impact and cost of constructing alternative housing for a family that used the home as well as the impact and cost of destroying the old home are considered. And yet, no one wants a family to live in an unsafe or uninhabitable unit that should have been decommissioned after being replaced by a newer unit but instead is being re-used as housing.

Reconciling these goals can be difficult. Conceivably, each home being replaced can be examined and a determination made as to whether the home can be reused. Unfortunately, this practice would be expensive, especially since many units that will be inspected will likely be found to be unfit. If a profit may be made by reselling the replaced units, the opportunity for fraudulent evaluations will undoubtedly arise. The replaced units are also typically not energy efficient, and their continued use may be detrimental to the environment. Finally, the post-decommissioning resale or disposition of replaced units does not constitute the primary goal of replacement programs in general and implementation would be difficult. Such replacement programs are typically not designed to sell or give away replaced units effectively.

While the design of any replacement program must attempt to balance these competing interests, replacement of pre-1976 units will present the strongest case for a mandate that all replaced units be decommissioned. Pre-1976 units are the most likely to be unfit for habitation and the least likely to have any residual value. They are also the units most likely to be moved to other jurisdictions or sited in violation of local laws or restrictions. While there is the chance that a small number of replaced units could be beneficially used elsewhere, it is unlikely that the number is sufficient to outweigh both the cost of inspection of all replaced units as well as the danger that unfit units will be put back into use.

When homes are to be decommissioned, it is important that it is done in an environmentally sound manner. Older units may contain many dangerous materials. Even relatively benign materials can add greatly to solid-waste disposal at local landfills. Merely disposing of the replaced units can be expensive, but safely removing hazardous materials and properly decommissioning the units can be even more expensive. This often results in discarded units being illegally burned or simply abandoned.

Some efforts have been made at recycling old units that are being decommissioned. Programs in North Carolina,[59] Vermont,[60] Wisconsin,[61] and elsewhere are testament to how such programs might work. While recycling units can be expensive, it greatly reduces the negative impact of large amounts of solid waste being placed in landfills and ensures proper disposal of the units.

14.6.3.5 Efficiency of New Manufactured Homes

Energy-efficient manufactured homes are now eligible for the "Energy Star" rating. The Energy Star logo indicates an energy-efficient product rated using a set of national guidelines. It allows consumers to "comparison shop" more easily and understand the likely energy consumption of purchases they make.

To be Energy Star-qualified, a manufactured home must be substantially more energy-efficient than a comparable model. The requirements differ based on the geographic location and climate. The most common improvements made by manufacturers to achieve the necessary energy efficiencies include: using energy-saving products such as low-emittance windows (or "Low-E" windows, which are coated so as to reflect heat, thus saving energy by reflecting indoor heat back inside in the winter and outdoor heat back outside in the summer); using programmable thermostats; increasing wall cavities through the use of 2x6 dimensional lumber rather than 2x4 dimensional lumber; increasing the "R-value" of insulation ("R-value" is the thermal resistance or insulating quality of insulation); installing an efficient crossover that connects the heating and cooling of multi-sectional units; using a better sealant at the marriage line in multi-section units; and installing Energy Star appliances. The research organization for the factory-built-housing industry, Systems Building Research Alliance, manages the Energy Star certification process on behalf of the U.S. Environmental Protection Agency for both the manufactured and modular housing industries.[62] Currently, approximately 123 manufactured-housing plants in the United States are certified to build Energy Star-qualified homes.

In North Carolina, one program pays the cost for purchasers of new manufactured homes to upgrade their electric furnaces and air conditioners to energy-efficient heat pumps.[63] The cost is about $700 per home. Researchers estimate that these upgraded units realize about $643 in savings per year. Funding for the program comes from the settlement of a case involving oil overcharge. Several western states and Canada have joined together to create the Northwest Energy-Efficient Manufactured Home (NEEM) Program. This program provides certification for energy-efficient homes. The homes are certified as "Eco-rated." It is a voluntary program that creates standards to manufacture homes that meet criteria in five areas: energy efficiency, construction practice, material efficiency, indoor air quality, and water efficiency.

14.7 Resident Ownership of Manufactured Home Communities As Solution to Utility Problems

Utility issues may provide additional incentive for conversion of communities to resident ownership. Manufactured home communities are often plagued with failing waste systems and other infrastructure problems that are difficult and expensive to repair. Yet the residents, who are most affected by these problems, have no control over the community infrastructure because they do not own the land on which their homes sit.

---

59 *See* www.alamance-nc.com/d/county-attorney/mobile-home-recycling-program.html (Alamance County's manufactured-home recycling program).

60 *See* Gail D. Johnson, *Vermont Studies Mobile Home Recycling*, Waste Age, Mar. 1, 2001, *available at* http://wasteage.com/mag/waste_vermont_studies_mobile.

61 *See, e.g.*, www.northcountryaffordablehousing.com/mhrp/index.html (Tomorrow's Home Foundation's manufactured home recycling project in Wisconsin).

62 *See* www.research-alliance.org/pages/es_lender.htm.

63 *See* http://apps1.eere.energy.gov/state_energy_program/project_brief_detail.cfm/pb_id=1129.

When homeowners rent a pad or lot for their home from a community owner, they are also vulnerable to unjustified rent increases and utility bill markups. They may even be subject to eviction from the community at the owner's whim. This dynamic can have a negative effect, not only on the homeowners' feeling of security about their homes but also on the value of the home and the residents' interest in maintaining the community.

Resident purchase of the community is a good way to address such problems. The experience in a number of states shows that resident ownership is a realistic option. In New Hampshire, residents have collectively purchased almost 100 communities, bettering the lives of thousands of homeowners. A high percentage of Massachusetts and Rhode Island communities are also resident-owned. California has at least 100 resident-owned communities, and Florida has hundreds. Vermont has converted over forty communities to either resident or nonprofit ownership.

Typically, such conversions are possible because the state has a resident purchase opportunity law that gives residents an opportunity to purchase their community if it is to be sold.[64]

When residents purchase their community, typically they own it as a cooperative. Once they own the land on which their homes sit, they are able to address utility problems in a way that benefits the community. If residents are able to purchase the community, they may be eligible for funds to repair or replace failing systems that would not be available to a private investor community owner. Some communities have been able to obtain Community Development Block Grant, U.S. Department of Agriculture, and other types of funding. Not only does this increase the ability of the residents to purchase their community, but it also results in better living conditions that the residents would not otherwise enjoy.[65]

---

64 *See* www.nclc.org/issues/manufactured-housing.html (information about resident purchase opportunity laws).

65 *See* www.rocusa.org (click on "Resident Owned Communities" weblink) (providing more information about community infrastructure improvement and resident ownership).

Chapter 15 Due Process Protections for Municipal and REC Customers; Unregulated Deliverable Fuels

15.1 Special Due Process Protections for Municipal and REC Customers

15.1.1 Due Process Requirements May Not Apply to Investor-Owned Utilities

In *Jackson v. Metropolitan Edison Company*, the Supreme Court held that state action is *not* present for purposes of liability under 42 U.S.C. § 1983 or the Due Process Clause of the Fourteenth Amendment, when a utility is privately owned, despite both the regulation of the utilities and the grant of a monopoly by the state.[1] This decision overturned earlier decisions that had found that investor-owned utility terminations violated due process because there was sufficient state action and protected property.[2] The general rule now is that the actions of private utilities do not constitute state action unless the state regulator or a public official, such as a building inspector or fire marshal, actually orders the utility's action, or the state utility commission places its imprimatur on the company's procedure.[3]

Even then, some courts have said that a shut-off must be *ordered* by the PUC in order to constitute state action. It is not enough if the PUC considered, acquiesced in, and even encouraged the shut-off.[4]

However, *Jackson* purports to deal only with a challenge to a utility policy that had been submitted to a PUC as part of the utility company's general tariff, in a case in which the PUC approval was *pro forma*. Indeed, the Court found that the policy probably did not require even this *pro forma* approval. Thus *Jackson* leaves room for the advocate to argue that a utility policy constitutes state action in cases in which there is more significant state involvement. For example, one might argue that the utility is a state actor when:

- The PUC has significantly encouraged the policy allowing termination or an act pursuant to that policy;[5]
- The utility terminates service under state regulations specifically authorizing termination in certain limited circumstances and the PUC had adopted the rule authorizing such terminations after considering objections and holding hearings;[6]

1 419 U.S. 345 (1974). *See also* Dial Info. Servs. Corp. v. Thornburgh, 938 F.2d 1535 (2d Cir. 1991); Alabama Power Co. v. Smith, 575 So. 2d 1084 (Ala. 1991); Walton Elec. Membership Corp. v. Snyder, 508 S.E.2d 167, 169 (Ga. 1998).

2 Palmer v. Columbia Gas of Ohio, Inc., 479 F.2d 153 (6th Cir. 1973); Ihrke v. Northern States Power Co., 459 F.2d 566 (8th Cir. 1972); Salisbury v. Southern New England Tel. Co., 365 F. Supp. 1023 (D. Conn. 1973); Davis v. Weir, 359 F. Supp. 1023 (N.D. Ga. 1973); Bronson v. Consolidated Edison Co. of N.Y., 350 F. Supp. 443 (S.D.N.Y. 1972); Hattell v. Public Serv. Co., 350 F. Supp. 240 (D. Colo. 1972); Stanford v. Gas Serv. Co., 346 F. Supp. 717 (D. Kan. 1972). *Contra* Kadlec v. Illinois Bell Tel. Co., 407 F.2d 624 (7th Cir. 1969); Lucas v. Wisconsin Elec. Power Co., 322 F. Supp. 337 (E.D. Wis. 1970).

3 Jackson v. Metropolitan Edison Co., 419 U.S. 345 (1974); Walton Elec. Membership Corp. v. Snyder, 508 S.E.2d 167, 169 (Ga. 1998). *See also* Mathis v. Pacific Gas & Elec. Co., 891 F.2d 1429, 1431 (9th Cir. 1989); Albert v. Carovano, 851 F.2d 561 (2d Cir. 1988); Roberts v. Louisiana Downs, 742 F.2d 221 (5th Cir. 1984); Occhino v. Northwestern Bell Tel. Co., 675 F.2d 220–23 (7th Cir. 1982); Lovell v. People's Heritage Sav. Bank, 776 F. Supp. 578, 583 (D. Me. 1991); Stoutt v. Southern Bell Tel. & Tel. Co., 598 F. Supp. 1000 (S.D. Fla. 1984) (mere fact that utility's operation is subject to state regulation or has quasi-monopoly status does not make utility state actor for section 1983 purposes). *Cf.* Moongate Water Co. v. Butterfield Park Mut. Domestic Water Ass'n, 291 F.3d 1262 (10th Cir. 2002).

4 Iowa Citizen/Labor Energy Coalition v. Iowa State Commerce Comm'n, 335 N.W.2d 178, 183 (Iowa 1983). *See also* Carlin Commc'n v. Southern Bell Tel. & Tel. Co., 802 F.2d 1352, 1357 (11th Cir. 1986) (no evidence that regulatory body was responsible for Southern Bell's decision); Taylor v. Consolidated Edison Co. of N.Y., Inc., 552 F.2d 39 (2d Cir. 1977); Kops v. New York Tel. Co., 456 F. Supp. 1090, 1094 (S.D.N.Y. 1978) (no allegation that state influenced or encouraged the telephone company's decision), *aff'd*, 603 F.2d 213 (2d Cir. 1979); Srack v. Northern Natural Gas Co., 391 F. Supp. 155 (S.D. Iowa 1975); Montalvo v. Consolidated Ed. Co., 460 N.Y.S.2d 784 (N.Y. App. Div. 1983), *aff'd*, 462 N.E.2d 149 (N.Y. 1984). *But see* Comment, *Constitutional Law Notices of Utility Shutoffs Need Not Meet Due Process Standards Where Rules Promulgated by the Iowa State Commerce Commission Do Not Create a State Action by Utility Companies: Iowa Citizen/Labor Energy Coalition v. Iowa State Commerce Commission*, 33 Drake L. Rev. 459 (1983–1984).

5 *See* Gerena v. Puerto Rico Legal Servs., 697 F.2d 447, 449 (1st Cir. 1983); Piampiano v. Central Maine Power Co., 221 F. Supp. 2d 6 (D. Me. 2002).

6 Bronson v. Consolidated Edison Co., 350 F. Supp. 443, 446 (S.D.N.Y. 1972) (pre-Jackson v. Metropolitan Edison Company).

- State law authorizes utility companies to enter premises to terminate service and the service is terminated by means of such an entry;[7] or
- The PUC instructs the utility to terminate service.[8]

15.1.2 Municipal Utility Terminations Must Comply with Due Process

Municipal utilities are cities and towns, or their agencies or departments, which sell utility services to retail customers. The Supreme Court held in *Memphis Light Gas and Water Division v. Craft* that, when state law provided for termination of utility service only "for cause," customers have a claim of entitlement to continued utility service and must be given adequate notice of their rights in accordance with the Due Process Clause.[9] The Due Process Clause comes into play when the state subjects a protected property interest to a more than *de minimis* interference.[10] Receipt of utility service has been held to constitute a constitutionally significant property interest.[11]

15.1.3 Due Process Requirements

15.1.3.1 General

In *Memphis Light, Gas and Water Division v. Craft*,[12] the Supreme Court held that due process requires a municipal utility to provide its customers with at least notice[13] of the disconnection, the reason for the disconnection,[14] a hearing[15] prior to the termination of utility service, and notice of

7 Denver Welfare Rights Org. v. Public Utils. Comm'n, 547 P.2d 239 (Colo. 1976).

8 Palmer v. Columbia Gas of Ohio Inc., 479 F.2d 153 (6th Cir. 1973) (pre-Jackson v. Metropolitan Edison Company); Condosta v. Vermont Elec. Coop., Inc., 400 F. Supp. 358, 364 (D. Vt. 1975).

9 436 U.S. 1 (1978). *See also* DiMassimo v. City of Clearwater, 805 F.2d 1536 (11th Cir. 1986); Pilchen v. City of Auburn, N.Y., 728 F. Supp. 2d 192 (N.D.N.Y. 2010); Heuser v. Johnson, 189 F. Supp. 2d 1250 (D.N.M. 2001); Koger v. Guarino, 412 F. Supp. 1375 (E.D. Pa. 1976); Donnelly v. City of Eureka, Kan., 399 F. Supp. 64 (D. Kan. 1975); Davis v. Weir, 328 F. Supp. 317, 321–22 (N.D. Ga. 1971) (holding that municipal utility has duty under Due Process Clause to provide notice to user of utility service), *aff'd*, 497 F.2d 139 (5th Cir. 1974). *But see* James v. City of St. Petersburg, Fla., 33 F.3d 1304 (11th Cir. 1994) (when neither tenant nor landlord signed up for service and paid deposit, no protected property interest; citing similar holdings in Coghlan v. Starkey, 845 F.2d 566 (5th Cir. 1988) and Sterling v. Village of Maywood, 579 F.2d 1350 (7th Cir. 1978)); Marrero-Garcia v. Irizarry, 829 F. Supp. 523, 529 (D. P.R. 1993) (no property interest in the continued receipt of water services for which they never contracted), *aff'd*, 34 F.3d 117 (1st Cir. 1994).

10 Goss v. Lopez, 419 U.S. 565 (1975).

11 *See, e.g.*, Mansfield Apartment Owners Ass'n v. Mansfield, 988 F.2d 1469 (6th Cir. 1988); Ransom v. Marrazzo, 848 F.2d 398, 409 (3d Cir. 1988); Craft v. Memphis Light, Gas & Water Div., 534 F.2d 684 (6th Cir. 1976), *aff'd*, 436 U.S. 1 (1977); Palmer v. Columbia Gas of Ohio, Inc., 479 F.2d 153 (6th Cir. 1973); Pilchen v. City of Auburn, N.Y., 728 F. Supp. 2d 192, 199 (N.D.N.Y. 2010) (enactment of city's water service ordinance "establishes a property interest and 'legitimate claim of entitlement' in water service," giving rise to Due Process protection); Heuser v. Johnson, 189 F. Supp. 2d 1250 (D.N.M. 2001) (when a state or local law restricts the ability of a municipal utility provider to terminate service, customers of the provider have a protected property interest in the continuation of service); Dawes v. Philadelphia Gas Comm'n., 421 F. Supp. 806, 817 (E.D. Pa. 1976); Koger v. Guarino, 412 F. Supp. 1375, 1386 (E.D. Pa. 1976); Condosta v. Vermont Elec. Co-op., Inc., 400 F. Supp. 358 (D. Vt. 1974); Donnelly v. City of Eureka, Kan., 399 F. Supp. 64 (D. Kan. 1974); Bronson v. Consolidated Edison of N.Y., Inc., 350 F. Supp. 443 (S.D.N.Y. 1972); Hattell v. Public Serv. Co. of Colo., 350 F. Supp. 240 (D. Colo. 1972); Stanford v. Gas Serv. Co., 346 F. Supp. 717 (D. Kan. 1972); Lamb v. Hamblin, 57 F.R.D. 58 (D. Minn. 1972); Davis v. Weir, 328 F. Supp. 317 (N.D. Ga. 1971), *aff'd*, 497 F.2d 139 (5th Cir. 1974); Denver Welfare Rights Org. v. Public Utils. Com., 547 P.2d 239 (Colo. 1978). *See also* Turpen v. City of Corvallis, 26 F.3d 978 (9th Cir. 1994); Bradford v. Edelstein, 467 F. Supp. 1361, 1376–77 (S.D. Tex. 1979) (and cases discussed therein); Dedeke v. Rural Water Dist. No. 5, 623 P.2d 1324, 1328–29 (Kan. 1981); Tucker v. Hinds County, 558 So. 2d 869 (Miss. 1990). *Cf.* Walker v. Brigham City, 856 P.2d 347 (Utah 1993) (no protectable property right in "rates that do not exceed the cost of service"; when municipal's rates were lower than those of IOUs and other municipals and were reasonable, fact that city made a profit, which went into its general fund, did not result in unconstitutional taking of property.). *But see* Midkiff v. Adams County Reg'l Water Dist., 409 F.3d 758 (6th Cir. 2005) (no due process violation when water district terminated service without notice at request of vindictive landlord); Golden v. City of Columbus, 404 F.3d 950 (6th Cir. 2005) (under Ohio law, non-customer has no protected property interest in provision of water service); James v. City of St. Petersburg, Fla., 33 F.3d 1304 (11th Cir. 1994) (because neither tenant nor landlord had complied with the city's requirements for initiating water service, including paying a deposit, tenant had no entitlement to water service sufficient to support her due process claim; "mere users of water do not have a constitutionally protected property interest in continued service"), *distinguished from* DiMassimo v. City of Clearwater, 805 F.2d 1536 (11th Cir. 1986) (property interest entitling the group of tenants to due process was not the expectation of continued water service as water users but the right to prevent the landlord from obtaining a constructive eviction by disconnecting the city water service); Gagliardi v. Clark, 2006 WL 2847409 (W.D. Pa. Sept. 28, 2006) (provision of water and sewer services, whether by municipality or private company, is not a federally protected right); Perez v. City of San Bruno, 616 P.2d 1287, 1295 (Cal. 1980) (because "right" to receive municipal water service should not be classified as a fundamental right, legislative scheme authorizing discontinuation of service is not subject to strict scrutiny).

12 436 U.S. 1 (1978).

13 *See also* Davis v. Weir, 497 F.2d 139, 143 (5th Cir. 1974) (court did not have to consider whether property interest existed because the municipality conceded on appeal that it had a duty to provide the actual user with notice prior to termination).

14 *See* Note, *Fourteenth Amendment Due Process in Terminations of Utility Service for Nonpayment*, 86 Harv. L. Rev. 1477, 1494–95 (1973).

15 Koger v. Guarino, 412 F. Supp. 1375, (E.D. Pa. 1976) (termination procedures that did not provide for hearing prior to termination violated due process clause), *aff'd without op.*, 549

the availability of "a procedure for protesting a proposed termination of utility service as unjustified."[16] All avenues of redress should be divulged to a customer.[17]

But there is still uncertainty as to the exact procedures that are mandated.[18] The Seventh Circuit decision in *Lucas v. Wisconsin Electric Power Company*[19] stands at one end of the spectrum. According to the *Lucas* court, due process requires only a five-day written shut-off notice, joined with an informal utility review, tempered by the availability of formal judicial remedies.[20] Moreover, the *Lucas* court held that requiring the customer to make payment of the disputed portion, subject to refund, was not constitutionally infirm.

A Texas district court decision in *Limuel v. Southern Union Gas Company*[21] stands at the other end of the spectrum, holding that the minimum requirements of due process included: (1) written notice; (2) an opportunity to be heard in person with testimony and documentary evidence; (3) an opportunity to be represented by counsel; (4) the right to confrontation and cross-examination; (5) a "neutral and detached" hearing officer; and (6) a statement of reasons, along with an identification of the evidence relied upon (though formal written "findings of fact" were not required).[22] The due process cases decided over the past twenty years are summarized by the commentator who observed: "Essentially, the demand in the principal cases has been for adequate notice of termination coupled with a right to an impartial hearing where there is a dispute as to the propriety of the charge."[23]

15.1.3.2 Liability for Third Party's Utility Debts

In addition, the imposition of liability on a customer for the debt of a third person violates both the Equal Protection and Due Process Clauses of the Fourteenth Amendment. The seminal case is *Davis v. Weir*,[24] which involved water service provided by the Atlanta Municipal Utility. Davis, a tenant who paid for his water service through his rent, was current on his rent payments. Davis' landlord fell behind in payment of his water bills, which he disputed, and service to Davis was disconnected. Davis then sought to have the water account placed in his own name and to have service restored. The utility refused, however, unless the landlord's arrearage was paid. The court agreed with Davis' contention that the water company's practice violated both equal protection and due process. It found that there was "no rational basis" for the water company's "discriminatory rejection of new applications for water service based on the financial obligations of third parties."[25] The Fifth Circuit declined to

F.2d 795 (3d Cir. 1977). *But see* Rupp v. Grantsville City, 610 P.2d 338, 341 (Utah 1980) (when there was no dispute of fact, plaintiff residents had refused to pay connection fee, city officials discontinued water service pursuant to ordinance allowing such actions for enforcement of mandatory sewer connection ordinance, and plaintiffs were afforded adequate notice of the consequences of their continuing failure to comply, protections do not require right to pre-termination hearing).

16 436 U.S. at 15. *See also* Pilchen v. City of Auburn, N.Y., 728 F. Supp. 2d 192, 201 (N.D.N.Y. 2010) ("Because the City failed to provide written notice to the plaintiff of her right to a hearing prior to deprivation of her property interest in water service . . . as well as the defendant's failure to provide a written explanation for why the plaintiff could not apply for service in her name [sic] are violations of the Due Process Clause of the Fourteenth Amendment.").

17 Hargis v. City of Cookeville, Tenn., 92 Fed. Appx. 190 (6th Cir. 2004) (unpublished) (no due process violation because customer suffered no harm); Bronson v. Consolidated Edison Co. of N.Y., 350 F. Supp. 443 (S.D.N.Y. 1972) (electric company's notice of termination of service held improper on the grounds that the utility failed to comport with the requirements of due process by not advising the customer of all available recourse).

The Supreme Court in *Craft* noted that, in *Palmer*, the comprehensive remedy for a due process violation, including the provision of a hearing before a management official, was in this case fashioned in response to findings, based on uncontradicted evidence, of "hostility and arrogance on the part of the collection-oriented clerical employees." Memphis Light, Gas & Water Div. v. Craft, 436 U.S. 1, at 12 (1978) (citing Palmer v. Columbia Gas of Ohio, Inc., 479 F.2d 168 (6th Cir. 1973)). *See also* Heuser v. Johnson, 189 F. Supp. 2d 1250, 1268 (D.N.M. 2001) (notice of termination did not comport with due process guarantees when notice failed to inform customers how to challenge utility's determination of violations, failed to state a date and time of a hearing, and failed to provide the name of a municipal's employee to hear and address customer's objections). *But see* Huegel v. City of Easton, 2000 U.S. Dist. LEXIS 17119 (E.D. Pa. Nov. 29, 2000) (notice that failed to include notice of hearing or appeal rights, in light of the other information included in the notice, still comported with due process).

18 John Clarke O'Brien, *Protecting the Consumer in Utility Service Terminations*, 21 St. Louis U.L.J. 452, 469 (1977).

19 466 F.2d 638 (7th Cir. 1972).

20 *Id.* at 647–53.

21 378 F. Supp. 964 (W.D. Tex. 1974).

It should be noted that, both this case and Lucas v. Wisconsin Electric Power Company, 466 F.2d 638, involve private, investor-owned utilities and that both cases were decided before Jackson v. Metropolitan Edison Co., 419 U.S. 345 (1974), in which the U.S. Supreme Court stated conclusively that no state action is present when a utility is privately owned. However, these distinctions go to whether the utility's actions come under constitutional scrutiny; once state action is proven, and constitutional protections clearly apply, the types of due process protections required are still open to question.

22 Limuel v. Southern Union Gas Co., 378 F. Supp. 964, 969 (W.D. Tex. 1974).

23 Ilardi, *The Right to a Hearing Prior to Termination of Utility Services*, 22 Buff. L. Rev. 1057, 1067 (1973).

24 497 F.2d 139 (5th Cir. 1974).

25 *Id.* at 144. *See also* Golden v. City of Columbus, 404 F.3d 950 (6th Cir. 2005) (denial of service to tenant-applicant at premises with unpaid bill from previous occupant or owner, while allowing service to other tenant-applicants, was irrational classification and violation of equal protection); Pilchen v. City of Auburn, N.Y., 728 F. Supp. 2d 192, 203 (N.D.N.Y. 2010) (following the *Davis* case, court finds that "[p]reventing access to [water] service because of the actions of an unrelated party is entirely unreasonable"). *But see* Midkiff v. Adams County Reg'l Water Dist., 409 F.3d 758 (6th Cir. 2005) (rule allowing only property owners to apply for water service did not violate equal protec-

extend the substantive due process protection of *Davis* to a landlord, however, when water service was discontinued to a property owner because of a tenant's unpaid bills.[26]

Following *Davis* is the case of *Smith v. Tri-County Electric Membership Corporation*,[27] wherein Smith's electric service was terminated because he lived with someone who owed the electric company on a delinquent account from a former residence. On the other hand, in *Haynsworth v. South Carolina Electric and Gas Co.*,[28] the plaintiff lived with her husband until their separation. Several months after her husband moved out, plaintiff attempted to switch utility service into her own name. The utility company denied the request because the bill, which was in the husband's name, had not been paid since his departure. The court, distinguishing *Craft*, held that the utility policy was justified and found no discriminatory violation of the Equal Credit Opportunity Act. However, *Haynsworth* is distinguishable from *Smith* and *Davis* because the debt in the case was for service to the plaintiff's residence while he or she was living there.[29]

15.1.3.3 Rights of Tenants When Landlord Defaults and Utility Service Is Disconnected

Many courts have also held (usually in the context of municipally-owned utilities) that tenants have a constitutionally protected interest in continued utility service irrespective of whether the service is billed in their name, and therefore they may not be deprived of this service without due process of law.[30] Recognition of property interests within the Due Process Clause is not based so much on undisputed ownership[31] or privity of contract,[32] but rests on some legitimate claim of entitlement to continued utility service.[33]

The determination of whether a tenant has a legitimate entitlement to utility service is based on the extent and reasonableness of a tenant's reliance on the receipt of continued utility service.[34] The court will look to state law and practice to determine the legitimacy of the tenant's claim.[35] One court has identified a related property interest, sufficient to trigger due process protections, in the right of a tenant to pursue legal and equitable relief through court action against a landlord *before* a proposed termination, which right can be given meaning only if the tenant has advance notice of the proposed termination.[36]

Procedural protections based on entitlement to continued utility service have been developed by courts under both due process and equal protection theories.[37] In assessing the appropriate theory to pursue, the practitioner should bear in mind that the due process analysis focuses on pretermination

---

tion); Chatham v. Jackson, 613 F.2d 73 (5th Cir. 1980) (no due process problem when landlord's water service terminated for unpaid water bills of tenant; Davis v. Weir distinguished).

26 *See* Chatham v. Jackson, 613 F.2d 73 (5th Cir. 1980).

27 689 S.W.2d 181 (Tenn. Ct. App. 1985).

28 488 F. Supp. 565 (D.S.C. 1979).

29 *But see* Ransom v. Marrazzo, 848 F.2d 398 (3d Cir. 1988).

The Third Circuit in *Ransom* questioned the Fifth Circuit's analysis in Davis v. Weir, 497 F.2d 139 (5th Cir. 1974). It reviewed a lower court's dismissal of plaintiffs' claims that their due process and equal protection had been violated when the City of Philadelphia denied water service to their properties. The properties were encumbered by liens that attached due to prior owners' arrearages. Water and sewer service would not be provided until the arrearages were paid. The Third Circuit determined that the provision of water and sewer services, whether by municipality or private company, is not a federally protected right to which substantive due process applies. Ransom v. Marrazzo, 848 F.2d 398, 412 (3d Cir. 1988) (citing Koger v. Guarino, 412 F. Supp. 1345, 1386 (E.D. Pa. 1976), *aff'd*, 549 F.2d 795 (3d Cir. 1977)).

30 DiMassimo v. City of Clearwater, 805 F.2d 1536 (11th Cir. 1986); Koger v. Guarino, 412 F. Supp. 1375, 1386 (E.D. Pa. 1976), *aff'd*, 549 F.2d 795 (3d Cir. 1977); Dawes v. Philadelphia Gas Comm'n, 421 F. Supp. 806, 817 (E.D. Pa. 1976); Davis v. Weir, 359 F. Supp. 1023 (N.D. Ga. 1973). *See also* Lamb v. Hamblin, 57 F.R.D. 58, 61 (D. Minn. 1972); Stanford v. Gas Serv. Co., 346 F. Supp. 717, 720–21 (D. Kan. 1972). *But see* Midkiff v. Adams County Reg'l Water Dist., 409 F.3d 758 (6th Cir. 2005) (right to water service not protected property right and no due process violation when water district terminated without notice at request of vindictive landlord); Golden v. City of Columbus, 404 F.3d 950 (6th Cir. 2005) (water service not a protected property right for non-customers); Ransom v. Marrazzo, 848 F.2d 398, 411–12 (3d Cir. 1988) (limiting *Guarino* with respect to its holding regarding equal protection only); Sterling v. Village of Maywood, 579 F.2d 1350 (7th Cir. 1978).

31 Memphis Light, Gas & Water Div. v. Craft, 436 U.S. 1, 11 (1978).

32 *But see* Sterling v. Village of Maywood, 579 F.2d 1350, 1353–54 (7th Cir. 1978).

Even under a purely contractual theory of property interests, a protected interest may arise if the tenants can claim the status of a third-party beneficiary under state (or perhaps federal) common law.

33 Board of Regents v. Roth, 408 U.S. 564, 577 (1972) ("Property interests . . . are not created by the Constitution. Rather, they are created and their dimensions are defined by existing rules or understandings that stem from an independent source such as state law—rules or understandings that secure certain benefits and that support claims of entitlement to those benefits."); DiMassimo v. City of Clearwater, 805 F.2d 1536 (11th Cir. 1986); Koger v. Guarino, 412 F. Supp. 1375, 1386 (E.D. Pa. 1976), *aff'd without op.*, 549 F.2d 795 (3d Cir. Pa. 1977). *See also* Goss v. Lopez, 419 U.S. 565, 572–73 (1975). *But see* Midkiff v. Adams County Reg'l Water Dist., 409 F.3d 758 (6th Cir. 2005) (right to water service not protected property right for non-customer tenants); Golden v. City of Columbus, 404 F.3d 950 (6th Cir. 2005) (water service not a protected property right under Ohio law for non-customers).

34 Craft v. Memphis Light, Gas & Water Div., 534 F.2d 684 (6th Cir. 1976), *aff'd*, 436 U.S. 1 (1978).

35 Memphis Light, Gas & Water Div. v. Craft, 436 U.S. 1, 11–12 (1977). *See generally* Duhamel, *Rights of the Non-Billed Utility User*, 19 Clearinghouse Rev. 247, 253 (July 1985).

36 Turpen v. City of Corvallis, 26 F.3d 978 (9th Cir. 1994) (due process required prior to city's termination of water service when pre-termination notice to tenants not impossible and termination pursuant to established state procedure).

37 *See, e.g.*, Davis v. Weir, 497 F.2d 139 (5th Cir. 1974); Koger v. Guarino, 412 F. Supp. 1375 (E.D. Pa. 1976) (due process and equal protection), *aff'd mem.*, 549 F.2d 795 (3d Cir. 1977).

procedures prior to elimination of utility services;[38] whereas, the equal protection analysis focuses on how pretermination procedures affect the customer after termination.[39]

In most instances, a utility company holds a practical or legal monopoly on a necessary resource and thus creates a legitimate expectation of service. Common law, statutes or regulations in virtually all jurisdictions impose a duty to serve all applicants on an equal basis and ensure a right to continued service so long as bills are paid and reasonable rules are complied with.[40]

Further, the utility holding itself out to the public entices reliance on continued receipt of service, and users of utilities adjust their lives accordingly.[41] Thus, if anything, users of utilities have a greater claim to a legal entitlement than bill payers who may or may not receive the service provided.[42] However in *Sterling v. Village of Maywood*[43] the Seventh Circuit found no property interest in a tenant's continued receipt of utility service when the billed landlord orders a termination of service. The court looked to Supreme Court cases diminishing the importance of the benefit as a touchstone for finding no property interest.[44] The *Sterling* court examined state law to see if state statutes or contract law gave a non-billed tenant a right to continued service. The court found that state law did not confer an interest upon mere users of the service and, further, that there was no contract between the city and the non-billed tenant.[45]

Although most of the cases in which courts found a property interest in the continued receipt of service involved billed customers, and therefore these courts were not confronted with the issue faced by the *Sterling* court, these courts did not universally rely upon a contract or statutory guarantee-of-service rationale.[46] More often, courts based a protected property interest on a consumer's reliance on the expectation of the continued receipt of the service or the state-protected monopoly status of the utility.[47] These rationales are equally applicable to non-billed consumers of utility services.[48]

More relevant to the instant problem, a utility has no legitimate interest in participating in a landlord's self-help eviction of a tenant.[49] The non-billed tenant has a legitimate property interest, protected under the laws in most states, in the continued enjoyment of the premises that he or she occupies, free from interference by the landlord (aside from the procedure prescribed by law by which a landlord may dispossess a tenant). A 1986 decision of the Eleventh Circuit put it succinctly: "tenants have a [constitutionally] sufficient interest in preventing the landlord from unilaterally by-passing statutory eviction procedures."[50]

In that case, the plaintiffs were non-billed tenants who had been disconnected from utility service at the request of their landlord, without notice to the tenants or an opportunity to be heard. In a memorandum opinion, a federal district court found that Florida law gave tenants a right to avoid constructive eviction by a landlord's termination of vital services.[51] A utility acting on the landlord's orders to

38 *See, e.g.*, Memphis Light, Gas & Water Div. v. Craft, 436 U.S. 1 (1978); Walton Elec. Membership Corp. v. Snyder, 487 S.E.2d 613, 616 (Ga. Ct. App. 1997).

39 *See, e.g.*, Davis v. Weir, 497 F.2d 139 (5th Cir. 1974); Koger v. Guarino, 412 F. Supp. 1375 (E.D. Pa. 1976), *aff'd mem.*, 549 F.2d 795 (3d Cir. 1977).

For a discussion on these cases and the due process and equal protection distinction in the municipal utility context, see Note, *Municipal Utility Service As a Property Right: Pre-Termination Notice to Tenant Not Required: Sterling v. Village of Maywood*, 28 DePaul L. Rev. 885, 96–99 (1979).

40 *See* ch. 2, *supra* (right to service); Jim Rossi, *The Common Law "Duty to Serve" and Protection of Consumers in an Age of Competitive Retail Public Utility Restructuring*, 51 Vand. L. Rev. 1233, 1260 (1998).

41 Koger v. Guarino, 412 F. Supp. 1375, 1386 (E.D. Pa. 1976) (although city was not constitutionally obligated to establish and maintain water service for benefit of citizens, once it did so a user had a legitimate claim of entitlement to continued service absent sufficient cause for termination consistent with procedural protections of the Due Process Clause). *See also* Bradford v. Edelstein, 467 F. Supp. 1361, 1368–69 (S.D. Tex. 1979) (electricity and water); Donnelly v. City of Eureka, Kan., 399 F. Supp. 64, 67–68 (D. Kan. 1975) (water); Bronson v. Consolidated Edison, 350 F. Supp. 443 (S.D.N.Y. 1972) (electricity).

42 Donnelly v. City of Eureka, Kan., 399 F. Supp. 64 (D. Kan. 1975).

43 579 F.2d 1350 (7th Cir. 1978).

44 *Id.* at 1353–54.

45 *Id.*

State statutory law must clearly contemplate creating a right in continued service to establish a property interest protected by the Constitution. *See* Marrero-Garcia v. Irizarry, 33 F.3d 117, 123 (1st Cir. 1994) (state regulatory definition alone insufficient to justify a property interest to receive water services); Gorham v. Butto, 667 F.2d 1146 (4th Cir. 1981) (administrative guidelines not sufficient to give rise to a due process interest); Bills v. Henderson, 631 F.2d 1287 (6th Cir. 1980) (procedural rules created by state administrative bodies cannot serve as a basis for a separate protected liberty interest).

46 *But see* Limuel v. Southern Union Gas Co., 378 F. Supp. 964 (W.D. Tex. 1974).

47 Dawes v. Philadelphia Gas Comm'n, 421 F. Supp. 806 (E.D. Pa. 1976); Donnelly v. City of Eureka, Kan., 399 F. Supp. 64 (D. Kan. 1975).

48 *See* Duhamel, *Rights of the Non-Billed Utility User*, 19 Clearinghouse Rev. 247, 253 (July 1985).

49 For a discussion of the "no legitimate interest" grounds of the equal protection and substantive due process doctrines, see Allegheny Pittsburgh Coal v. Webster County, 488 U.S. 336 (1989); Davis v. Weir, 497 F.2d 139, 144–45 (5th Cir. 1974) (city had no valid governmental interest in requiring payment for utility service in landlord's name from a tenant because of landlord's arrearages). *But see* Midkiff v. Adams County Reg'l Water Dist., 409 F.3d 758 (6th Cir. 2005) (no due process violation when water district terminated without notice at request of vindictive landlord; landlord's contract with water district did not make district an agent of landlord or tenants third-party beneficiaries of contract). *See generally* William Cohen, *State Law in Equality Clothing*, 38 UCLA L. Rev. 87 (1990).

50 DiMassimo v. City of Clearwater, 805 F.2d 1536, 1539 (11th Cir. 1986).

51 *Id.*

terminate service without giving sufficient advance notice to the affected tenant deprived that tenant of her right to contest constructive eviction. Hence, the district court ordered the utility to give non-billed utility users five days' prior notice—time enough for the tenant to seek an injunction against the landlord in state court.[52]

The court of appeals affirmed, quoting extensively from the lower court's opinion. Florida law gives tenants the right to receive adequate utility service, as well as the right to be protected from self-help eviction, the court stated.[53] In order for the integrity of these rights to be maintained, a tenant must not be subjected to termination of utility service without adequate notice, even if the landlord, in whose name the service is billed, orders an immediate termination of service.[54]

DiMassimo defined the protected property interest not as the continued receipt of utility service but as the security of tenure in a tenant's leasehold.[55] The court found a state deprivation of that interest in a municipal utility's complicity with the (private) landlord's[56] attempt at self-help eviction.[57]

Some state laws give tenants either the right to occupancy until displaced by a court order or a right to challenge the termination. In such a case, a utility that terminates service would be a party to the landlord's deprivation of the tenant's interest in continued occupancy even if the landlord has tried to terminate the tenancy (as at the end of the lease period or following notice of termination of a tenancy at will) but has not yet obtained the requisite court order.

States with such laws raise expectations of the right to continued utility service. Once a legitimate expectation has been established, the Due Process Clause ensures that governmental deprivations will occur only after meaningful procedural protections have been exhausted.[58]

The base requirement of due process is notice and a meaningful opportunity to be heard.[59] The nature and extent of the procedural niceties required will vary according to: the private interest that would be deprived; the risk involved by the deprivation of that interest; the value of procedural protections in reducing error; and the governmental interests involved.[60] In the case of a utility's termination of service to a tenant at the insistence of a landlord, the deprivation is profound.[61]

The risk of "error" is high, as a user, although willing and able to pay for service and to follow utility rules, will be denied service. The simple procedure of notice and an opportunity to change the account over to the tenant's name will avoid most of the possibility of error.[62] And the cost to the utility is minimal. The utility already has the addresses of the units it serves or could obtain them without undue burden.[63] Actual prior notice is the bare minimum due process requirement.[64]

Further, a utility has no interest in allowing its service to be used as a means for landlords to exploit tenants. Indeed, by offering to serve the tenant, the utility can maintain service and reduce abandonment and subterfuge.[65]

---

52 *Id.*

53 *Id.*

54 *Id.* at 1539–40.

55 *See also* Devines v. Maier, 665 F.2d 138, 141 (7th Cir. 1981) (leaseholds are property interests within the Fourteenth Amendment).

56 Of course, in cases involving public landlords and subsidized units, a tenant will have an undisputed, protected property interest. *See* Thorpe v. Housing Auth. of Durham, 393 U.S. 268 (1969); Jeffries v. Georgia Residential Fin. Auth., 678 F.2d 919 (11th Cir. 1982); McQueen v. Drucker, 438 F.2d 781 (1st Cir. 1971); Swann v. Gastonia Hous. Auth., 502 F. Supp. 362, 364–67 (W.D.N.C. 1980), *aff'd*, 675 F.2d 1342 (4th Cir. 1982). *See also* James DiPriest, *Self-Help Evictions*, 25 Clearinghouse Rev. 798 (1991); Mary Ann Glendon, *The Transformation of America's Landlord Tenant Law*, 23 B.C. L. Rev. 503, 542 (1983).

57 DiMassimo v. City of Clearwater, 805 F.2d 1536 (11th Cir. 1986). *See* § 6.8, *supra* (discussing various state laws that protect a tenant's right to continued occupancy until a valid court order displacing the tenant has been issued).

58 Memphis Light, Gas & Water Div. v. Craft, 436 U.S. 1 (1978).

59 Mathews v. Eldridge, 424 U.S. 319, 335 (1976).

60 To determine what procedures are necessary to protect a particular property interest, courts should consider:

> first, the private interest that will be affected by the official action; second, the risk of an erroneous deprivation of such interest through the procedures used, and the probable value, if any, of additional or substitute procedural safeguards; and finally, the Government's interest, including the function involved and the fiscal and administrative burdens that the additional or substitute procedural requirement would entail.

Mathews v. Eldridge, 424 U.S. 319, 335 (1976).

61 Koger v. Guarino, 412 F. Supp. 1375, 1388 (E.D. Pa. 1976) (noting that, if the utility is the sole source of service in the area, the effect of deprivations are likely to be immediate and irremediable).

62 This will not, of course, be a wholly satisfactory solution in those cases when the premises are master-metered, metering is expensive, and state law requires the landlord to maintain service in the landlord's name, for example, for public health reasons. *See, e.g.*, 105 Mass. Code Regs. §§ 410.354 (gas and electric in landlord's name unless agreement to contrary), 410.180 and 410.190 (owner to supply water and hot water, tenant cannot be required to pay for water without tenant's written consent to submetering), 410.201 (owner to pay for heat between September 1 and June 15 unless contrary agreement), 410.620 (curtailment or termination of such services prohibited).

63 DiMassimo v. City of Clearwater, 805 F.2d 1536 (11th Cir. 1986). *See also* Mullane v. Central Hanover Bank & Trust Co., 339 U.S. 306 (1950) (personal notice is basic due process requirement when the address of a party is reasonably ascertainable; notice must convey the information necessary to apprise party of the pendency of the action and afford party an opportunity to protect his or her rights).

64 DiMassimo v. City of Clearwater, 805 F.2d 1536 (11th Cir. 1986). *See* Tulsa Prof'l Collection Servs. v. Pope, 485 U.S. 478, 108 S. Ct. 1340, 1345–70 (1988).

65 *See* Koger v. Guarino, 412 F. Supp. 1375, 1389 (E.D. Pa. 1976), *aff'd without op.*, 549 F.2d 795. *Cf.* Myers v. City of Alcoa, 752 F.2d 196 (6th Cir. 1985).

As a utility is in most instances a monopoly provider of an essential service, the recipient of the utility's services has no

The required notice should be in plain language,[66] allow enough time for the tenant to take action against the landlord[67] or to obtain service in his or her own name,[68] and inform the customer of the substantive and procedural rights available.[69]

15.1.4 Applicability to RECs

There is no court decision directly on point as to whether service terminations by RECs (rural electric cooperatives) constitute "state action" and are thus subject to the constraints of constitutional due process.[70]

However, the premise that due process and equal protection apply to RECs is indirectly supported by various court holdings, including a Fifth Circuit decision, *Alabama Power Company v. Alabama Electric Cooperative*.[71] In that case, an investor-owned utility raised antitrust claims against the Cooperative.[72] In defense, the Cooperative argued that it was subject to the "state action" exemption to the federal antitrust statutes.[73] The Fifth Circuit agreed, holding that "rural electric cooperatives are more than public utilities; they are instrumentalities of the United States. They were chosen by Congress for the purpose of bringing abundant, low-cost electric energy to rural America."[74] As a result of this governmental purpose of RECs, the court held that RECs are not subject to antitrust challenges.[75]

In a case similar to *Alabama Power Company*, the D.C. Circuit Court also adopted the notion that RECs were instrumentalities of the federal government. In *Salt River Project Agricultural Improvement and Power District v. Federal Power Commission*,[76] the Circuit Court was faced with the question of whether Federal Power Commission jurisdiction extended to cover RECs. The Federal Power Act exempts from Federal Power Commission jurisdiction companies which are not merely "public utilities." The court held that RECs "were exempt from its coverage as instrumentalities of the Government."[77]

Additionally, the Wyoming Supreme Court found that RECs were entities of the federal government in the context of an eminent domain proceeding. In *Tri-County Electric Association v. City of Gillette*,[78] the court considered whether the city of Gillette had the authority to take certain utility land by eminent domain. Noting that Tri-County was an REC,[79] the Wyoming Supreme Court held that such taking was permissible but that the United States "through the Rural Electrification Administration" would be an indispensable party to such a proceeding.[80]

option to find another service provider, seek alternative services, or to do without. Thus the only options available to the disconnected recipient are to move outside of the utility company's jurisdiction, obtain service in the name of another, or engage in some other form of subterfuge. Gregory v. New England Tel. & Tel., 2 Pub. Util. Rep. 4th 92 (D. Vt. 1973).

66 Wagner v. Duffy, 700 F. Supp. 935 (N.D. Ill. 1988); Aguchak v. Montgomery Ward Co., 520 P.2d 1352 (Alaska 1974).

67 Estate of Miner v. Commercial Fisheries Entry Comm'n, 635 P.2d 827, 832 (1981) (notice must be reasonably calculated under all the circumstances to apprise individual of pendency of deprivation and to afford an opportunity to present objection). *See also* Worrall v. Ogden City Fire Dep't, 616 P.2d 598 (Utah 1980).

68 *See* Chicago Cable Commc'ns v. Chicago Cable Comm'n, 879 F.2d 1540, 1546 (7th Cir. 1989); Craft v. Memphis Light Gas & Water Div, 534 F.2d 684, 687–89 (6th Cir. 1976), *aff'd on other grounds*, 436 U.S. 1 (1978); Coughlin v. Regan, 584 F. Supp. 697, 704 (D. Me. 1984).

69 *See* Wagner v. Duffy, 700 F. Supp. 935, 942–43 (N.D. Ill. 1988); Frates v. City of Great Falls, 568 F. Supp. 1330, 1337–38 (D. Mont. 1983). *See also* Coghlan v. Starkey, 845 F.2d 566 (5th Cir. 1988); Freeman v. Hayek, 635 F. Supp. 178, 183 (D. Minn. 1986); Bronson v. Consolidated Edison Co. of N.Y., 350 F. Supp. 443 (S.D.N.Y. 1972).

70 *But see* San Miguel Power Ass'n v. Public Serv. Comm'n, 292 P.2d 511 (Utah 1956) (recognizing that the RECs are acting as agents for the Rural Electrification Administration in pursuing the electrification of rural America).

71 394 F.2d 672 (5th Cir. 1968). *See also* Condosta v. Vermont Elec. Coop., Inc., 400 F. Supp. 358 (D. Vt. 1974); San Miguel Power Ass'n v. Public Serv. Comm'n, 292 P.2d 511 (Utah 1956) (rural electric cooperatives "acting as agents for the REA in pursuing the electrification of rural America"). *But see* McCarthy v. Middle Tenn. Elec. Membership Corp., 466 F.3d 399 (6th Cir. 2006) (no state action; although cooperatives are subject to state regulation and fulfill state objectives, they are not sufficiently "entwined" with state to rise to level of state actor); Mays v. Buckeye Rural Elec. Coop., Inc., 277 F.3d 873 (6th Cir. 2002) ("[a] private utility company such as Defendant [ ] does not amount to a state actor, even if the utility possesses a monopoly over the provision of a service, for Fourteenth Amendment purposes"); Carter v. Buckeye Rural Elec. Coop., Inc., 2001 WL 1681104 (S.D. Ohio Sept. 7, 2001) (plaintiff failed to come forward with a viable theory of state action).

72 Specifically, the power company raised the claim against the "full power requirements" contracts entered into between a generating and transmission (G&T) co-op and its member distribution and transmission (D&T) co-ops. (A G&T typically produces power, or purchases it in the wholesale market, and sells it at wholesale to a retail utility, such as a D&T, which sells it at retail to the end-user.)

73 *See* Parker v. Brown, 317 U.S. 341 (1943).

74 Alabama Power Co. v. Alabama Elec. Coop., 394 F.2d 672, 677 (5th Cir. 1968).

75 *Id.*

76 391 F.2d 470 (D.C. Cir. 1968).

77 *Id.* at 473 (citing *In re* Dairyland Power Coop., 37 F.P.C. 12 (1968)) (concluding that Congress did not . . . intend RECs to be merely generic "public utilities" or, alternatively, even if the REA-financed cooperatives were public utilities under the Act, they were exempt from its coverage as instrumentalities of the government).

Note that, in areas such as rate-making, cooperatives are effectively self-regulating and not subject to restraints by the state. This autonomy may undermine, to some extent, the purported role of RECs as "state actors," although the government's partial control may be enough to constitute state action for the purposes of Constitutional Due Process.

78 584 P.2d 995 (Wyo. 1978).

79 *Id.* at 998.

80 *Id.* at 1008.

Each of these cases helps support an argument to classify RECs as instrumentalities of the federal government, which should then subject their actions to the Due Process Clause. Congress created the Rural Electrification Administration (REA) in 1936 to help advance the process of providing electrification and adequate telephone service to rural America.[81] The government sought to effectuate this policy through a vast federal loan program administered by the REA.[82] By January, 1981, the REA had approved a total of $14.9 billion in loans to over 1000 cooperatives. The local cooperatives, themselves, are considered to be an integral part of this entire federal program.[83]

15.2 Using the Fair Credit Billing Act to Stop Municipal or REC Disconnects

15.2.1 Introduction

The Federal Fair Credit Billing Act (FCBA)[84] provides customers in certain covered "credit" transactions a statutory mechanism by which to contest bills. Should a consumer wish to utilize the remedies that may be available under the FCBA, the key questions are whether the FCBA applies to the particular category of utility company in question (that is, REC or municipal utility) and whether it applies to the particular transactions in question. There are some questions about whether a utility is rendering "credit" when, as is usually the case,[85] it provides the utility service in advance and only renders bills after the fact.[86] Therefore, anyone asserting the FCBA as the basis for seeking resolution of a billing dispute with a utility company will need to carefully consider whether the transaction is a "credit" transaction covered by the FCBA.

A second key question that must be addressed is whether the utility transaction is exempt from coverage under the Truth in Lending Act (TILA), of which the FCBA is but one part.[87] TILA specifically exempts certain public utility transactions from its coverage. The statute provides that it does not apply to:

> transactions under public utility tariffs, if the [Federal Reserve] Board determines that a State regulatory body regulates the charges for the public utility services involved, the charges for delayed payment, and any discount allowed for early payment.[88]

This exemption would likely eliminate coverage under the TILA and the FCBA for most utilities broadly rate-regulated by a state public utility commission, which is the case for most investor-owned utilities in most states, but not for most RECs and municipal utilities.[89]

81 7 U.S.C. §§ 901–918c.

82 7 U.S.C. §§ 904, 922.

83 It has been recognized that the RECs are acting as agents for the REA in pursuing the electrification of Rural America. "In their contracts with [the] Rural Electrification Administration, from whom they have borrowed money, they [RECs] have committed themselves to serve electric energy to all unserved persons who desire such service and meet the reasonable requirements of the cooperatives as condition of such service." San Miguel Power Ass'n v. Public Serv. Comm'n, 292 P.2d 511 (Utah 1956).

In Alabama Power v. Alabama Electric Cooperative, 394 F.2d 672, 677 (5th Cir. 1968), the Fifth Circuit stated: "The Power Company would treat REA simply as a rival public utility. . . . [However], rural electric cooperatives are something more than public utilities; they are instrumentalities of the United States. They were chosen by Congress for the purpose of bringing abundant, low-cost electric energy to rural America." (citations omitted)

84 15 U.S.C. § 1666. *See* National Consumer Law Center, Truth in Lending § 7.9 (7th ed. 2010).

85 It is usually the case that utilities provide their service through a meter without advance payment, but the use of so-called "prepayment meters" and prepaid service is expanding. Service paid for in advance through a prepayment meter or other prepaid method would not be considered a "credit" transaction for purposes of the FCBA. *See* ch. 4, *supra* (discussing prepayment meters and prepaid utility service).

86 There is some authority for the proposition that utilities are rendering "credit" when they bill only after service has already been provided. *See, e.g.*, Telco Commc'ns Group, Inc. v. Race Rock of Orlando, L.L.C., 57 F. Supp. 2d 340, 343 (E.D. Va. 1999) (holding in the context of Regulation Z, which implements the Truth in Lending Act of which the FCBA is a part: "We agree . . . that because a telephone calling card allows the holder to obtain services and delay the payment for those services, it is covered by the protections of Regulation Z.").

Note that the *Telco* court was addressing a dispute over whether Regulation Z covered using a telephone calling card and that the court's reasoning may thus not apply to the provision of electric and gas service through a meter. *See also* Williams v. AT&T Wireless Servs., 5 F. Supp. 2d 1142, 1145 (W.D. Wash. 1998) (claim under the Equal Credit Opportunity Act; applying for AT&T cellular service was covered by ECOA-implementing Regulation B).

Note that the facts in *Williams* did not involve the provision of traditional utility service but instead focused on a dispute over a deposit requirement imposed by AT&T after running a credit report on Williams.

87 The FCBA is chapter 4 (also called "Part D") of the general Truth in Lending Act. 15 U.S.C. §§ 1666–1666j.

88 15 U.S.C. § 1603(4). *See* Aronson v. Pennsylvania Pub. Util. Comm'n, 740 A.2d 1208 (Pa. Commw. Ct. 1999). *See also* National Consumer Law Center, Truth in Lending § 2.4.6 (7th ed. 2010).

89 Note that the court in Huegel v. City of Easton, 2003 WL 22428435, at *6 (E.D. Pa. May 13, 2003), found that the "City [water department] is exempt from the disclosure requirements of TILA" apparently because "Pennsylvania regulates utility rates and requires that a utility file its tariff with the state." It appears that neither the parties nor the court addressed the question of whether the city, a municipal entity, was actually regulated by the state utilities commission. In many states, municipal entities are not rate-regulated by their states, although some do file their tariffs with a state commission.

The language of Regulation Z, which implements the TILA, uses somewhat different wording than the statute and exempts entities whose "charges for service, delayed payment, or any discounts for prompt payment are filed with or regulated by any governmental unit."[90] This regulation may broaden the statutory exemption, quoted above, for "transactions under utility tariffs," as the regulation only requires that tariffs need be "filed with," and need not be "regulated by," *any* "government entity." (The stature refers to regulation by a "State regulatory body").

The decision in *King v. Town of Waynesville*[91] suggests that courts will in fact broadly read the public utility exemption. In that case, the plaintiff King asserted that the defendant had violated the TILA by failing to disclose certain late fees. The court found that the TILA did not apply, due to the public utility exemption. Based on the defendant's affidavit that it is a "political subdivision of the State of North Carolina. . . . governed by a Mayor and Board of Aldermen. . . . [and] that its [c]harges for service rates, late payments, delayed payments, discounts . . . are regulated . . . by the Town," the court found that the plaintiff has "no cause of action pursuant to TILA" on the basis that "[p]ublic utilities which are regulated by the state are exempt from the requirements of TILA."[92] Yet the affidavit did not state that the Town was a "public utility," in the sense of a regulated investor-owned utility (it fully appears to be a municipal utility), and almost directly contradicts the court's apparent conclusion that it is "regulated by the state." The limited case law suggests that courts will read the public utility exemption quite broadly.

Most RECs and municipal utilities are not formerly regulated by a utility commission, but they still may file tariffs that are not investigated or reviewed, depending on the law in the state of the REC or municipal utility. Under these circumstances, Regulation Z appears to broaden the public utility exemption beyond the intent of the statute.[93] A consumer who attempts to use the FCBA to raise a dispute with a utility provider should be aware that the provider may raise objections to the applicability of the FCBA, which could require court litigation to resolve.

Also, if a utility debt is sold to a private collector who offers payment plans to consumers, the exemption no longer applies.[94]

90 12 C.F.R. § 226.3(c).

91 2003 WL 23354657 (W.D.N.C. Apr. 14, 2003), *aff'd mem.*, 70 Fed. Appx. 138 (4th Cir. 2003).

92 2003 WL 23354657, at *1 (W.D.N.C. Apr. 14, 2003).

93 *But see* Aronson v. Peoples Natural Gas Co., 180 F.3d 558 (3d Cir. 1999) (blanket exception for public utilities, including utilities that "file" tariffs, upheld; note, however, that Peoples Natural Gas Company was a pervasively regulated monopoly, with rates set by the commission).

94 Pollice v. National Tax Funding, 225 F.3d 379 (3d Cir. 2000) (payment plans constituted new extensions of credit by private collector; public utility exemption limited to credit extended by utility itself).

15.2.2 FCBA Protections

If the FCBA does apply, it may offer protections to a customer who disputes a bill.[95] The creditor may not impose late charges[96] or attempt to collect the disputed amount until the matter is resolved.[97] This should prevent disconnection as well.

Whenever a consumer notices a billing error on a periodic statement, the consumer should, within sixty days of transmission of the first statement with the billing error,[98] make sure a written notice (not a telephone notice)[99] is received by the creditor (utility) identifying the consumer, the account number,[100] and the billing error, along with the type, date, and amount of the error.[101] A billing error is specifically defined by an "inclusive" list of definitions.[102] Examples of the types of errors a utility might make that may fall within that list include: failing to credit a payment; making a computational error; estimating a bill incorrectly; or sending a statement to the wrong address. Moreover, charging for service in excess of what was actually used might be characterized as delivering the wrong quantity of goods, one of the defined billing errors.[103] The consumercan either withhold the disputed amount[104] or pay it without waiving any rights.[105]

The covered utility must acknowledge receipt of the notice.[106] Further, the utility may not restrict or close the consumer's account.[107] Under these provisions, presumably,

95 *See, e.g.*, Danner v. Discover Bank, 257 S.W.3d 113 (Ark. Ct. App. 2007); Crestar Bank, N.A. v. Cheevers, 744 A.2d 1043 (D.C. 2000); Jacobs v. Marine Midland Bank, N.A., 475 N.Y.S.2d 1003 (N.Y. Sup. Ct. 1984).

For a comprehensive discussion of FCBA's protections, see National Consumer Law Center, Truth in Lending § 7.9 (7th ed. 2010).

96 Official Staff Commentary to Reg. Z, 12 C.F.R. pt. 226, Supp. I § 226.13(d)(1)-3.

97 Official Staff Commentary to Reg. Z, 12 C.F.R. pt. 226, Supp. I § 226.13(d)(1)-1.

98 Reg. Z, 12 C.F.R. § 226.13(b)(1).

99 Payne v. Diner's Club Int'l, 696 F. Supp. 1153 (S.D. Ohio 1988). *But see* Saunders v. Ameritrust of Cincinnati, 587 F. Supp. 896 (D. Ohio 1984) (creditor who reports to credit bureau that account is delinquent after full payment has been made must provide periodic statements to consumer, and failure to do so is billing error even in absence of written notice from consumer).

100 Reg. Z, 12 C.F.R. § 226.13(b)(2).

101 Reg. Z, 12 C.F.R. § 226.13(b)(3). *See generally* Langenfeld v. Chase Bank USA, N.A., 537 F. Supp. 2d 1181 (N.D. Okla. 2008) (discussing written notice "content" and "timeliness" requirements).

102 15 U.S.C. § 1666(b); Reg. Z, 12 C.F.R. § 226.13(a).

103 *See* Reg. Z, 12 C.F.R. § 226.13(a)(3); Official Staff Commentary to Reg. Z, 12 C.F.R. § 226, Supp. I § 226.13(a)(3)-1.

104 Reg. Z, 12 C.F.R. § 226.13(d)(1).

105 Official Staff Commentary to Reg. Z, 12 C.F.R. pt. 226, Supp. I § 226.13(d)(1).

106 Reg. Z, 12 C.F.R. § 226.13(c)(1).

107 *See, e.g.*, Gray v. American Express Co., 743 F.2d 10 (D.C. Cir. 1984).

the utility could not disconnect service based either on the dispute or on the fact that the amount in dispute has not been paid.

The covered utility must then determine whether a billing error occurred based on a reasonable investigation.[108] It has ninety days or two billing cycles, whichever is sooner, to respond.[109] If an error is found, it must correct the bill and notify any credit reporting agencies that had received notice of the delinquency. Conversely, if the utility determines that no error occurred, the consumer must be notified and the consumer must be given at least ten days to pay prior to the utility issuing any adverse credit report. Moreover, the customer must be given the length of the normally applicable free ride period to pay the bill. In each instance, the time begins with the date the consumer is notified that there is no error.[110]

Statutory and actual damages, plus attorney fees, are available for violation of FCBA's provisions.[111] Statutory damages consist of double the finance charge, with a minimum of $100 and a maximum of $1000.[112] Additionally, a creditor who fails to comply with its duties under the FCBA forfeits the right to collect the disputed amount and resulting finance charge, up to a $50 maximum.[113]

15.3 Unregulated Deliverable Fuels

15.3.1 Introduction

About 16 million households in the U.S. use a deliverable fuel (fuel oil, propane, wood or kerosene) as the primary home heating fuel. More than one-quarter of these households may be eligible to receive LIHEAP benefits. Deliverable fuel usage presents a set of particular challenges for low- and moderate-income households. Deliverable fuel dealers are generally not subject to the types of consumer protections or rate-setting procedures that apply to electric and natural gas utility companies under the jurisdiction of state regulatory commissions. In addition, utility ratepayer-funded payment assistance and energy efficiency programs are generally not available to deliverable fuel customers. Finally, prices of home heating oil and other deliverable fuels have risen dramatically over the past several years. Consequently, households that use a deliverable fuel as the primary heating source are typically at greater risk of losing access to service than are regulated utility customers.

Millions of people depend for energy upon a wide variety of "deliverable" fuels, such as propane, heating oil, kerosene, wood, and coal. While the majority of U.S. households use either electricity or natural gas as their primary heat source, almost a fifth of households use deliverable fuels.[114] Deliverable fuels can be very expensive to use as a heating source. For example, AARP calculated that consumers over the age of 65 spent $2010 to heat their homes in the winter of 2009–2010 if they used fuel oil but only $535 if they heated with natural gas.[115] One source estimated that, for the 2008/2009 winter heating season, average heating costs were $2593 for those who used home heating oil, $1967 for propane, $978 for natural gas, and $875 for electricity.[116] Low-income families relying on deliverable fuels often pay a very high percentage of their income for these mostly unregulated products.

Vendors of deliverable fuels are able to set prices and provide service much like any other provider of a non-utility good or service. Customers who have disputes with these businesses do not have any of the regulatory protections that electric and natural gas consumers enjoy.

Because fuel suppliers are not treated as utilities, they are not bound by the traditional common-law duties and obligations of a public utility. They do not have to provide service to all similarly situated customers in their market area and, in fact, often avoid serving low-income consumers. They can charge whatever prices the market will bear rather than offer rates that are determined to be just and reasonable by a PUC.

Solutions to deliverable fuel affordability problems must be viewed somewhat differently than regulated utility problems. Not only are deliverable fuel dealers not subject to regulatory commission jurisdiction, but they are also structured financially very differently than utility companies. Utilities are granted exclusive franchises and are obligated to serve all customers. This structure provides electric and natural gas utilities access to capital resources on terms that are generally more favorable than those that apply to deliverable fuels dealers. Moreover, utilities that deliver approved payment assistance programs are usually guaranteed

108 Reg. Z, 12 C.F.R. § 226.13(f).

109 Reg. Z, 12 C.F.R. § 226.13(c)(2).

110 Reg. Z, 12 C.F.R. § 226.13(g); Official Staff Commentary to Reg. Z, 12 C.F.R. pt. 226, Supp. I § 226.13(g).

111 15 U.S.C. § 1640(a). *See* National Consumer Law Center, Truth in Lending § 7.9.9 (7th ed. 2010).

112 *See* National Consumer Law Center, Truth in Lending § 11.6.3 (7th ed. 2010).

113 15 U.S.C. § 1666(e).

114 Approximately one half of U.S. households use natural gas as their primary heat source. Roughly one-third use electricity, and approximately 17% use deliverable fuels (fuel oil, propane, kerosene, and wood). *See* Energy Info. Administration, Residential Energy Consumption Survey: What's New in Energy Use? (Mar. 28, 2011), *available at* www.eia.gov/consumption/residential/reports/2009overview.cfm.

115 AARP, Winter Heating Costs and Older and Low-Income Households 2 (Dec. 2010), *available at* http://assets.aarp.org/rgcenter/ppi/econ-sec/decchart.pdf.

Note that the average cost figures are distorted by the fact that almost all households that use fuel oil are located in the cold Northeast states, while many gas-heated households are located in much milder climates.

116 National Energy Assistance Directors' Ass'n, Winter Home Prices Projected to Reach Record Levels for All Fuels (June 23, 2008).

recovery of the costs associated with those programs. Deliverable fuel dealers have access to no such guarantee.

15.3.2 Special Issues Relating to Propane Vendors

Households that use propane or liquefied petroleum gas are easily exploited by their propane suppliers. Although the propane industry theoretically operates in a competitive market, the reality is that most dealers operate as near-monopolies in their local markets. Customers cannot readily change propane gas suppliers because vendors usually will not service tanks that are not their own or deliver gas to competitors' tanks.[117]

If customers decide that their existing service is either too expensive or inadequate, they cannot switch their loyalties without the new company putting in its own expensive tank.[118] Moreover, in instances in which small apartment buildings are involved, one tank can typically serve upwards of eight to ten residences.[119] As long as one tenant is unwilling to switch suppliers, it may be difficult for everyone else to switch.

Given both the difficulty inherent in changing propane suppliers as well as their unregulated status, steep price hikes are not uncommon during periods of peak demand. For example, during the winter of 2002–2003, many states around the country saw prices increases of 50% and more.

In addition, propane companies behave in ways very different from how they presumably would behave if they were regulated. For example, vendors have been known to share credit information with each other and to refuse service customers who were delinquent in their payments to their previous vendors. In addition, they have been known to curtail service with little or no advance notice, refuse to accept repayment plans, and delay returning security deposits.

15.3.3 Problems Associated with the Home Heating Oil Vendors

Although oil-heat customers can change suppliers far more easily than those who use propane, they still face some of the same problems. As with propane, oil prices can rise steeply. The prices that consumers pay are heavily influenced by political and economic developments in the Middle East and other distant events. In addition, households must regularly maintain their oil tanks to avoid leaks that contaminate soil and ground water and must perform more frequent tune-ups than are required for gas systems. Routine maintenance is not prohibitively expensive, but it does raise the cost of heating oil compared to other fuels.

15.3.4 Unfair and Deceptive Acts and Practices Regulations Covering Oil or Propane Service; Other UDAP Challenges

The state of Maine has addressed problems in the delivery of oil with an Unfair and Deceptive Acts and Practices (UDAP) regulation which bars heating oil sellers from unreasonably refusing to sell to certain customers, discriminating between customers, and otherwise engaging in unfair delivery practices.[120]

The Vermont Attorney General has enacted a regulation expressly targeting the sale of propane. This rule generally imposes public-utility-like obligations on propane vendors in areas such as giving notice prior to disconnection, repayment agreements, minimum delivery, discrimination, security deposits, and the assessment of fees and charges.[121]

The state of Connecticut prohibits all vendors of "energy goods" (including heating oil, propane, kerosene, coal, and wood) from refusing to sell to any person willing to pay cash, irrespective of the person's credit history and lack of prior dealings with the vendor. The Connecticut regulations also prohibit vendors from discriminating among cash customers in terms of price or other factors and from entering into agreements with property owners or their agents that bind or influence tenants to purchase "energy goods" from that particular vendor.[122]

Those who litigate a consumer dispute with an oil or propane dealer in a state that does not have such an explicit regulation are not necessarily prevented from succeeding on claims against an unscrupulous vendor. While a PUC's regulations may not apply directly to unregulated compa-

117 Susan Youngwood, *Propane Gas Woes Come to Light*, Vt. Bus. Magazine, Mar. 1990, at 31.

118 Courts are familiar with the fact that propane tanks are inextricably tied to the sale of propane gas. For example, propane dealers have been held strictly liable when defects in their tanks have damaged customers' property. Bainter v. Lamoine L.P. Gas Co., 321 N.E.2d 744, 746 (Ill. App. Ct. 1974) ("the furnishing of the tank by the defendant and the use thereof by the plaintiff was an incident of the sale of the gas and the consideration for the sale included the use of the tank"). *See also* Chris Ingle, Att'y Gen., *Inergy Propane Reach Agreement*, Gaylord Herald Times, Mar. 27, 2008 (Michigan's attorney general reached a settlement with a propone company, alleged to have charged excessive prices for propane, that removed the "trap" residential customers generally find themselves in of having to pay inflated prices or risk paying undisclosed amounts in tank and removal fees).

119 Susan Youngwood, *Propane Gas Woes Come to Light*, Vt. Bus. Magazine, Mar. 1990, at 31.

120 26-239-100 Me. Code. R. §§ 1–12 (LexisNexis) (Trade Practices in the Sale of Residential Heating Oil), *available at* http://maine.gov/sos/cec/rules/26/239/239c100.doc.

121 06-031-011 Vt. Code R. §§ 111.01–111.21 (Liquefied Petroleum "Propane" Gas; pursuant to Vt. Stat. Ann. tit. 9, § 2461(b)).

122 Conn. Agencies Regs. § 42-110b-31.

nies or entities, such regulations may be *indirectly* used to enforce some degree of restraint.[123] In many areas, for example, propane dealers closely resemble utilities because they have a *de facto* local monopoly on an essential energy service. The standards developed for utilities should thus provide guidance as to what is "unfair and deceptive" within the meaning of state UDAP statutes.

Every state has some type of UDAP law. Although they differ by state—some ban only specifically enumerated practices, others have intricate and confusing exceptions[124]—they have been effective in protecting the interests of consumers.[125] Under the standards of unfairness set out within these laws, the existing PUC regulations can be used to measure the overall fairness of a supplier's conduct, even if no regulation specifically outlaws the practice.[126]

Depending on where the advocate practices, an act committed by an unregulated fuel seller may be considered "unfair" under one of two standards. The traditional standard for unfairness was articulated in the United States Supreme Court's *Sperry & Hutchinson Co.* decision.[127] Under this standard, a practice is unfair if it: (1) offends public policy by violating an "established concept" of unfairness; (2) is immoral, unethical, oppressive, or unscrupulous; and (3) causes substantial consumer injury.[128]

Rather than this traditional standard, some states have adopted a modified unfairness standard. Under this standard, a practice may be deemed unfair if: (1) there is substantial consumer injury; (2) it is not outweighed by benefits to competition; and (3) consumers cannot reasonably avoid it.[129] This newer standard stems from a 1980 FTC policy statement addressing "unfairness" from a perspective that emphasized unjustified consumer injury.[130]

Regardless of which standard is used, many consumers will be able to bring successful UDAP claims. To the extent that the unregulated vendor enjoys *de facto* monopoly status (for example, a propane dealer in an area where there are no other dealers), this status may be useful in demonstrating that the vendor's practices are oppressive. Similarly, the consumer may be able to establish that the supplier's actions do not serve any legitimate competitive purpose and that the consumer could not reasonably avoid being harmed under the second standard. Whether either standard would be met would ultimately depend, of course, upon the nature of the vendor's practices and the consumer's injury. But UDAP claims at least provide a relevant framework within which to raise facts about the extent of the consumer's harm as well as the oppressive and unfair nature of the vendor's conduct.[131]

15.3.5 State Price Gouging Statutes and Regulations

In an attempt to introduce some price stability into the heating oil and propane market, two states, Connecticut and Massachusetts, have enacted regulations pursuant to their respective UDAP statutes which proscribe "unconscionably excessive" prices for oil products during market disruptions.[132] Both states specifically define "petroleum products" to include heating oil and propane, and "market emergency" to include shortages or price increases caused

123 *See* Press Release, Office of the Att'y Gen., Attorney General Cox Takes Legal Action Against Inergy Propane (Mar. 4, 2008).

The press release notes that, although the Michigan PUC cited average residential prices per gallon in the winter of 2007–2008 as ranging from $2.33 to $2.45, some Michigan consumers reported that Inergy's suppliers charged them as much as $4.39 per gallon. This disparity led to the attorney general's notice of intended action against the propane company. This notice, *In re* Inergy Propane et al., was filed pursuant to Michigan's Consumer Protection Act, which classifies charging practices grossly in excess of those charged by other retailers as an unfair and deceptive practice. The notice is available at www.michigan.gov/documents/ag/Inergy_Propane_NIA_3-4-08_227068_7.pdf.

124 In Ohio, for example, consumers sought to sue propane dealers under the state UDAP law. The intermediate appellate court held that the UDAP statute did not apply because propane dealers are a "natural gas company" specifically exempt from UDAP. Haning v. Rutland Furniture, Inc., 684 N.E.2d 713 (Ohio Ct. App. 1996).

Consumers did not appeal but instead brought a complaint before the public utilities commission, which regulates natural gas companies. The propane dealer successfully argued that it was not a natural or artificial gas company and thus was not under PUCO's jurisdiction. The state supreme court affirmed, explicitly holding that the court of appeals was in error. Haning v. Public Util. Comm'n of Ohio, 712 N.E.2d 707 (Ohio 1999).

The consumers got no relief, but it appears that in Ohio propane dealers are not exempt from UDAP because they are not the type of gas company that can be regulated by the PUC.

125 For example, the Massachusetts UDAP statute grants standing to consumers to sue for an injunction and damages and permits consumer class actions. Mass. Gen. Laws ch. 93A, § 9(2).

126 *See* § 15.4.2, *infra* (discussing in detail bringing UDAP claims on behalf of utility customers).

127 Federal Trade Comm'n v. Sperry & Hutchinson Co., 405 U.S. 233 (1972).

128 *Id.* at 244, 245.

129 Orkin Exterminating Co. v. Federal Trade Comm'n, 849 F.2d 1354, 1364 (11th Cir. 1988).

130 American Fin. Serv. Ass'n v. Federal Trade Comm'n, 767 F.2d 957, 971 (D.C. Cir. 1985).

131 *See, e.g.*, State v. Price-Rite Fuel, Inc., No. CV-08-14 (Me. Super. Ct. Apr. 2, 2009) (finding that defendants' violation of another statutory requirement that they maintain adequate security was evidence of violation of Unfair Trade Practices Act when the companies intentionally deceived customers, failed to disclose the lack of security, and affirmatively misrepresented facts in a case in which the Maine attorney general prevailed in asserting state UDAP claims against defendants when they had sold over $600,000 in prepaid home heating oil contracts to customers but were unable to purchase sufficient supplies to fulfill those obligations).

132 Conn. Agencies Regs. § 42-110b-29; 940 Mass. Code Regs. § 3.18.

by severe weather.[133] Prices are deemed "unconscionably excessive" if they are substantially higher than petroleum prices immediately prior to the onset of the market disruption—unless otherwise justified by higher costs.[134]

An existing New York statute that prohibited price-gouging related to any "consumer goods and services vital and necessary for the health, safety and welfare of consumers"[135] served as the model for the Connecticut and Massachusetts examples. Not only has the New York statute withstood constitutional scrutiny,[136] it has also been used successfully against a seller of electric generators who, following a hurricane, made sales at prices up to 60% above retail.[137] Several other states have statutes or regulations that forbid "price gouging" in emergency situations.[138] Some of these statutes apply only to a declared state of emergency, and not all of them provide a private right of action.[139]

The Connecticut and Massachusetts regulations are expressly aimed at heating oil and propane price gouging. Until more jurisdictions enact legislation against abuses within the deliverable fuels industry, advocates will have to resort to public utility commission regulations as a possible indirect source of legal theories and remedies against the often deleterious practices of petroleum vendors.

133 Conn. Agencies Regs. § 42-110b-29; 940 Mass. Code Regs. § 3.01.

134 940 Mass. Code Regs. § 3.18.

135 N.Y. Gen. Bus. Law § 396-r (1994) (McKinney).

136 People v. Two Wheel Corp., 512 N.Y.S.2d 439 (N.Y. App. Div. 1987), *aff'd on other grounds*, 525 N.E.2d 692 (N.Y. 1988).

137 *Id.*

138 Ark. Code Ann. §§ 4-88-301 to 4-88-305 (declared state of emergency; specifies "home heating oil"; violation is UDAP); Cal. Penal Code § 396 (West) (declared state of emergency; specifies "home heating oil"); Fla. Stat. § 501.160 (declared state of emergency; specifically covers petroleum products; no private right of action); Ga. Code Ann. § 10-1-393.4 (declared state of emergency; violation is UDAP); Ind. Code § 4-6-9.1-2 (declared emergencies; defines price gouging as "charging a consumer an unconscionable amount for the sale of fuel"); Iowa Admin. Code r. 61-31.1(714) (violation is UDAP); La. Rev. Stat. Ann. § 29:732 (declared state of emergency; according to Louisiana Attorney Gen. Op. No. 05-0366 (May 9, 2006), 2006 WL 1670224, the statutory term of "goods" unquestionably includes "gasoline and other fuels"); Mo. Code Regs. Ann. tit. 15, § 60-8.030 (unfair practice to take advantage of "person's physical or mental impairment or hardship caused by extreme temporary conditions"); N.Y. Gen. Bus. Law. § 396-r (McKinney); S.C. Code Ann. § 39-5-145 (specifies petroleum products); Tex. Code Ann. Bus. & Com. § 17.46 (b)(27) (West); Va. Code Ann. §§ 59.1-525 to 59.1-527 (declared state of emergency; specifies "home heating fuel").

139 Fla. Stat. § 501.160(7) (no private right of action); Tex. Code Ann. Bus. & Com. § 17.46 (b)(27) (West); American Petroleum Corp. v. Northville Indus. Corp., 606 N.Y.S.2d 906 (N.Y. App. Div. 1994) (no private right of action for gasoline retailer; whether consumer has such right remains an open question).

15.3.6 Unconscionability Challenges

If disparity of bargaining power is especially great and a contract provision unduly harsh, a court may refuse enforcement on grounds of unconscionability.[140] An Ohio court found unconscionability when a propane dealer sought to exempt itself from liability for negligence or the effects of a consumer's running out of propane.[141] The dealer was not allowed to raise the exculpatory clause as a defense to a consumer's negligent action when the dealer had terminated its automatic fill service as a result of delinquent payments, and low pressure in the tank had caused a valve to fail, allowing gas to fill the consumer's manufactured home.

> The parties in question clearly have unequal positions of power. On the one hand, Texgas, as a supplier of liquid propane gas to the public, assumes a quasi-public function to safely furnish propane to each of its consumers. Meanwhile the . . . consumers of liquid propane for heating and cooking purposes are dependent on Texgas for their living needs. Therefore, allowing a supplier of propane gas . . . to insulate itself from liability as a result of its own possible negligence, is wholly oppressive and unconscionable and against public policy.[142]

15.4 Applying State Consumer Law to Sales by Unregulated, Deregulated, or Inadequately Regulated Utilities

15.4.1 The Uniform Commercial Code (UCC)

15.4.1.1 Introduction

Energy or telecommunications services are commercial services to which the law of contracts applies.[143] Therefore, the unlawful disconnection or denial of service, or other failure to perform as promised, may give rise to an action for breach of contract.[144] To the extent that the utility in

140 National Consumer Law Center, Unfair and Deceptive Acts and Practices § 4.5 (7th ed. 2008 and Supp.).

141 Orlett v. Suburban Propane, 561 N.E.2d 1066 (Ohio Ct. App. 1989).

142 *Id.* at 1069.

143 Williams v. City of Mount Dora, 452 So. 2d 1143, 1146 (Fla. Dist. Ct. App. 1984) (liability for payment for utility services is based on usual contract law). *See generally* 64 Am. Jur. 2d *Public Utilities* § 25 (2001).

144 *See, e.g.,* DeLong v. Osage Valley Elec. Coop. Ass'n, 716 S.W.2d 320, 322 (Mo. Ct. App. 1986) (plaintiffs "clearly had an option to sue in tort or for breach of contract" based on

question is found to be a "good," the contractual obligations of the two parties are in part established by the Uniform Commercial Code (UCC). The common law of contracts, as developed in each state, would apply as well.

15.4.1.2 UCC Applicability to Utility Sales

Article 2 of the Uniform Commercial Code (UCC) sets out the rights of buyers and sellers of "goods." Some courts have held that the UCC does apply to consumer purchases of utilities, but many other courts have not.[145] Practitioners will have to carefully research a particular state's case law to determine whether the consumer's purchase of electricity, gas, water, or sewer service is considered the sale of "goods" in that state. Courts will more readily find the purchase of deliverable fuels such as heating oil, coal, wood, and propane to be the purchase of "goods," given their physical nature and the fact that they are delivered in discrete amounts.

Courts in some states have found that a utility's provision of water[146] and electricity[147] to customers involves the sale of "goods" covered by Article 2, as does the provision of sewer[148] and gas.[149] But in each of these cases regarding the provision of water,[150] electricity,[151]

allegedly wrongful termination). *See also* 64 Am. Jur. 2d *Public Utilities* § 25 (2001).

145 *See also* Jane Mallor, *Utility "Service" Under the UCC: Are Utilities in for a Shock?*, 56 The Notre Dame Lawyer 89 (1980). *See generally* 2 Anderson Uniform Commercial Code § 2-105:158-160, at 239–41 (3d ed. 2004, with annual supplements); 1 Hawkland Uniform Commercial Code Series § 2-105:2, at art. 2-80, 2-81; 1 Thomas Quinn's Uniform Commercial Code Commentary and Digest, § 2-105[A][3] and 2-105[A][4]; Annot., *Electricity, Gas or Water Furnished by Public Utility As "Goods" Within Provisions of Uniform Commercial Code, Article 2 on Sales*, 48 A.L.R.3d 1060 (1973).

146 Archer Daniels Midland Co. v. Brunswick County, N.C., 56 U.C.C. Rep. Serv. 2d 665, at 674, 129 Fed. Appx. 16 (4th Cir. 2005) (applies U.C.C. § 2-208 to sale of water; notes in footnote 10 that water is a good within meaning of U.C.C. § 2-105); Adel v. Greensprings of Vt., Inc., 363 F. Supp. 2d 692 (D. Vt. 2005) (water is a good within meaning of section 2-105; covered by implied warranty of merchantability; extensive collection and analysis of cases for and against); Zepp v. Mayor & Council of Athens, 348 S.E.2d 673, 2 U.C.C. Rep. Serv. 2d 1179 (Ga. Ct. App. 1986); Jones v. Town of Angier, 638 S.E.2d 607, 61 U.C.C. Rep. Serv. 2d 614 (N.C. Ct. App. 2007); Mulberry-Fairplains Water Ass'n v. Town of N. Wilkesboro, 412 S.E.2d 910, 17 U.C.C. Rep. Serv. 2d 48 (N.C. Ct. App. 1992); Dakota Pork Indus. v. City of Huron, 638 N.W.2d 884, 46 U.C.C. Rep. Serv. 2d 326 (S.D. 2002) (finding that the sale of water by a municipality is the sale of goods governed by the UCC and addressing breach of express warranty and breach of implied warranty of fitness for a particular purpose).

147 *See* Kotz v. Hawaii Elec. Light Co., 83 P.3d 743 (Haw. 2004) ("under the circumstances of this case," over-voltage of electricity from fallen power line not a good governed by UCC); Hedges v. Public Serv. Co. of Ind., 396 N.E.2d 933, 27 U.C.C. Rep. Serv. 945 (Ind. Ct. App. 1979); Helvey v. Wabash County REMC, 278 N.E.2d 608, 10 U.C.C. Rep. Serv. 333 (Ind. Ct. App. 1972); Cincinnati Gas & Elec. Co. v. Goebel, 502 N.E.2d 713, 2 U.C.C. Rep. Serv. 2d 1187 (Ohio Mun. Ct. Hamilton Cnty. 1986) (and cases cited therein); Bellotti v. Duquesne Light Co., 44 Pa. D. & C.3d 425, 4 U.C.C. Rep. Serv. 2d 1393 (Pa. Ct. Com. Pl. Allegheny Cty. 1987); Darling v. Central Vt. Pub. Serv. Co., 762 A.2d 826 (Vt. 2000) (noting that most jurisdictions treat electricity as a good; issue not reached here because sale not shown; electricity escaped from fallen powerline and caused fire). *See also* Enron Power Mktg., Inc. v. Nevada Power Co., 2004 WL 2290486 (S.D.N.Y. Oct. 12, 2004) (noting that Utah courts have not decided this issue; other jurisdictions treat electricity as a good); Bamberger & Feibleman v. Indianapolis Power & Light, 665 N.E.2d 933 (Ind. Ct. App. 1996) (electricity is a product within the strict product liability statute only after transmission voltage is reduced to consumption voltage).

148 State of Ga. v. City of E. Ridge, 949 F. Supp. 1571 (N.D. Ga. 1996) (agreement between a water company and its customer is governed by the provisions of the Georgia Commercial Code).

149 Koch Hydrocarbon Co. v. MDU Res. Group, 988 F.2d 1529 (8th Cir. 1993) (North Dakota law); Prenalta Corp. v. Colorado Interstate Gas Co., 944 F.2d 677 (10th Cir. 1991) (Wyoming law); Aurora Natural Gas v. Continental Natural Gas, Inc., 1999 U.S. Dist. LEXIS 7120 (N.D. Tex. May 10, 1999); New Bremen Corp. v. Columbia Gas Transmission Corp., 913 F. Supp. 985 (S.D. Tex. 1995), *aff'd*, 108 F.3d 332 (5th Cir. 1997) (commercial purchase of natural gas); Kansas Mun. Gas Agency v. Vesta Energy Co., 843 F. Supp. 1401 (D. Kan. 1994); BTA Oil Producers v. MDU Res. Group, Inc., 642 N.W.2d 873, 47 U.C.C. Rep. Serv. 2d 1057 (N.D. 2002); Gardiner v. Philadelphia Gas Works, 197 A.2d 612, 2 U.C.C. Rep. 16 (Pa. 1964); Wagner v. Apollo Gas Co., 582 A.2d 364, 13 U.C.C. Rep. 2d 698 (Pa. Super. Ct. 1990); University of Pittsburg v. Equitable Gas Co., 5 Pa. D. & C.3d 303, 24 U.C.C. Rep. Serv. 1131 (Pa. Ct. of Com. Pl. Allegheny Cty. 1978); Howell Crude Oil Co. v. Tana Oil & Gas Corp., 860 S.W.2d 634 (Tex. App. 1993).

150 *See* Mattoon v. City of Pittsfield, 775 N.E.2d 770 (Mass. App. Ct. 2002) (provision of water was predominantly a service because, although city charged for water, rate covered storage, treatment, and distribution); Sternberg v. New York Water Serv. Corp., 548 N.Y.S.2d 247, 10 U.C.C. Rep. Serv. 2d 732 (N.Y. App. Div. 1989) (although furnishing of water was considered sale of goods, no warranties of merchantability or fitness for a particular purpose were implied); Coast Laundry v. Lincoln City, 497 P.2d 1224, 10 U.C.C. Rep. 1379 (Or. Ct. App. 1972); Gall v. Allegheny County Health Dep't, 555 A.2d 786 (Pa. 1989). *See also* Charter Twp. of Marquette v. City of Marquette, No. 268535, 2006 WL 3500896 (Mich. Ct. App. Dec. 5, 2006) (noting in dicta split in authority over whether directly pumping water to end user is primarily sale of goods or service and indicating agreement with latter view). *Cf.* Grace v. Zimmerman, 853 S.W.2d 92 (Tex. App. 1993) (assignment of wastewater capacity was not sale of goods).

151 *See* Encogen Partners, L.P. v. Niagara Mohawk Power Co., 914 F. Supp. 57 (S.D.N.Y. 1996), *amended on other grounds and question certified*, 110 F.3d 6 (2d Cir. 1997), *vacated on other grounds*, 163 F.3d 153 (2d Cir. 1998) (electricity not UCC "goods" under New York law); G & K Dairy v. Princeton Elec. Plant Bd., 781 F. Supp. 485 (W.D. Ky. 1991) (electricity is "service," not "goods," for purpose of alleging strict liability of seller of electricity); Lilley v. Cape Hatteras Elec. Membership Corp., 13 U.C.C. Rep. Serv. 2d 82 (E.D.N.C. 1990) (electricity is not "goods"); Mancuso v. Southern Cal. Edison, Co., 283 Cal. Rptr. 300, 15 U.C.C. Rep. Serv. 2d 49 (Cal. Ct. App. 1991) (lightning-generated electricity is not a "good"); Rural Elec. Convenience Coop. Co. v. Soyland Power Coop., Inc., 606

sewer,[152] and gas,[153] other courts have found that the UCC does not apply. Courts that have found the UCC to apply have done so because the electricity, gas, or water provided is considered a "thing" that "exists" and is " 'fairly identifiable' as movable at the time of identification to the contract of sale."[154]

One court has held that the attempted use of a pay telephone does not involve a "transaction in goods."[155]

The transmission of cable television programming was held not to be a transaction in goods, as the signals transmitted were not "fairly identifiable as movables before the contract [was] performed," and the dominant purpose of the agreement between the company and the customer was the provision of a service.[156]

Even if UCC Article 2 does not apply, however, it is possible that courts will apply Article 2 concepts by way of analogy.[157]

15.4.1.3 "Usage of Trade" Provides Consumers with Protections

Under the UCC "usage of trade" provisions, advocates may be able to use state public utility commission regulations to incorporate implied terms into the contract between a deregulated or unregulated utility (for example, a generation company, marketer, or broker) and its customers.[158] The challenge would be to convince a court that rules which formally apply to a regulated utility (for example, electric and gas) should apply in trade carried on by, for example, now-deregulated generation companies. Given that deliverable fuels such as propane and heating oil are used for similar purposes as gas and electricity, and the fact that deliverable fuels are as essential for households as regulated electricity and gas, advocates may be able to convince a court to apply "usage of trade" provisions in the regulated industries to companies that supply deliverable fuels.

When a customer enters into a contractual agreement with an energy supplier, "the 'agreement' . . . is not just the stark words of [the contract], but is those words as construed in the commercial setting in which they arose and were used. The course of dealing and trade usage supplement, qualify and explain the meaning of the basic standard terms."[159]

The primary role of "usage of trade" is to "fill gaps" in the written agreement between the two parties to the contract.[160] The UCC rejects "any assumption that because a writing has been worked out which is final on some matters, it is to be taken as including all the matters agreed upon."[161] Instead, contracts are to be read "on the assumption that . . . the usages of trade were taken for granted when the document was phrased. Unless carefully negated, they have

---

N.E.2d 1269, 21 U.C.C. Rep. Serv. 2d 905 (Ill. App. Ct. 1992) (sale of electricity from one power company to another not a "transaction in goods" because not a sale to ultimate consumer, even though it passed through meter as buyer received it); Singer Co. v. Baltimore Gas & Elec. Co., 558 A.2d 419 (Md. Ct. Spec. App. 1989); New Balance Athletic Shoe, Inc. v. Boston Edison Co., 29 U.C.C. Rep. Serv. 2d 397 (Mass. Super. Ct. 1996); Citizens Ins. Co. v. Consumers Energy Co., 57 U.C.C. Rep. Serv. 2d 741 (Mich. Ct. App. 2005) (electricity is a service); Williams v. Detroit Edison Co., 234 N.W.2d 702 (Mich. Ct. App. 1975) ("Electricity is a service rather than a 'good' "); Buckeye Union Fire Ins. Co. v. Detroit Edison Co., 196 N.W.2d 316, 10 U.C.C. Rep. Serv. 977 (Mich. Ct. App. 1972); Bowen v. Niagara Mohawk Power Corp., 590 N.Y.S.2d 628, 19 U.C.C. Rep. Serv. 2d 716 (N.Y. App. Div. 1992) (provision of electricity to home was a service); RT Realty, Ltd. P'ship v. Texas Util. Elec. Co., 181 S.W.3d 905, 61 U.C.C. Rep. Serv. 2d 536 (Tex. App. 2006) (UCC warranty and conspicuousness requirements do not apply to electric service that was governed by tariff that disclaimed warranties).

152 *Cf.* Grace v. Zimmerman, 853 S.W.2d 92, 20 U.C.C. Rep. Serv. 2d 1201 (Tex. App. 1993) (temporary reservation of sewer services not a sale of goods).

153 *See* Stanton v. National Fuel Gas Co., 1 Pa. D. & C.4th 223, 4 U.C.C. Rep. Serv. 2d 378 (Pa. Ct. of Com. Pl. Allegheny Cty. 1987) (when gas does not go through meter and there is no sale, not covered by Article 2).

154 Adel v. Greensprings of Vt., Inc., 363 F. Supp. 2d 692 (D. Vt. 2005) (water is a good; extensive collection and analysis of cases); Zepp v. Mayor & Council of Athens, 348 S.E.2d 673, 677–78 (Ga. Ct. App. 1986); Helvey v. Wabash County REMC, 278 N.E.2d 608 (Ind. Ct. App. 1972) (electricity can be sold as goods). *But see* Kotz v. Hawaii Elec. Light Co., 83 P.3d 743 (Haw. 2004) ("under the circumstances of this case," overvoltage of electricity from fallen power line not a good governed by UCC); Darling v. Central Vt. Pub. Serv. Co., 762 A.2d 826 (Vt. 2000) (noting that most jurisdictions treat electricity as a good; issue not reached here because sale not shown; electricity escaped from fallen powerline and caused fire).

155 Whitmer v. Bell Tel. Co., 522 A.2d 584, 3 U.C.C. Rep. Serv. 2d 12 (Pa. Super. Ct. 1987).

156 Kaplan v. Cablevision of Pa., Inc., 671 A.2d 716, 29 U.C.C. Rep. Serv. 2d 425 (Pa. Super. Ct. 1996).

157 *See* Williams v. Detroit Edison Co., 234 N.W.2d 702 (Mich. Ct. App. 1975) ("Electricity is a service rather than a 'good,' but the doctrine of implied warranty has been held to apply to its sale."); Buckeye Union Fire Ins. Co. v. Detroit Edison Co., 196 N.W.2d 316 (Mich. Ct. App. 1972). *See also* Daniel E. Murray, *Under the Spreading Analogy of Article 2 of the Uniform Commercial Code*, 39 Fordham L. Rev. 447 (1971); Note, *The Uniform Commercial Code: Impact on the Law of Contracts*, 65 Columbia L. Rev. 880, 881 (1965). *See generally* National Consumer Law Center, Consumer Warranty Law (2d ed. 2001 and Supp.).

158 The UCC defines "usage of trade" as "any practice or method of dealing having such regularity of observance in a place, vocation or trade as to justify an expectation that it will be observed with respect to the transaction in question." U.C.C. § 1-303(c).

159 Ebasco Serv., Inc. v. Pennsylvania Power & Light Co., 460 F. Supp. 163, 210 (E.D. Pa. 1978). *See also* Advance Process Supply v. Litton Indus. Credit, 745 F.2d 1076, 1079 (7th Cir. 1984) (citing Columbia Nitrogen Corp. v. Royster, 451 F.2d 3, 9, 10 (4th Cir. 1971)).

160 Latex Glove Co. v. Gruen, 497 N.E.2d 466, 470 (Ill. App. Ct. 1986) ("Trade usage is used to fill a gap in the contract, such as terms regarding delivery, credit and quality of performance."). *See also* GNP Commodities v. Walsh Heffernan Co., 420 N.E.2d 659 (Ill. App. Ct. 1985).

161 State *ex rel.* Yellowstone Park Co. v. District Ct., 502 P.2d 23, 26 (Mont. 1972).

become an element of the meaning of the words used. . . ."[162] The theory is that, when "a contract is made as to a matter about which there is a well-established custom, the same is understood as forming a part of the contract."[163]

Raising "usage of trade," if successful, can result in adding terms that are particularly valuable to utility consumers:

> [Trade usages] may also import an additional term imposing a duty on one party to give a notice to the other in a given situation, even though the express agreement is silent on the matter. Or they may foreclose a particular remedy unless it is sought within a given time period, even though the express agreement is silent on remedies.[164]

It should not be necessary for the energy supplier even to be actually aware of the usage of trade in order for that usage to be binding.[165] Such a usage is binding "if it is a usage of the vocation or trade in which the parties are engaged *or* is a usage of which the parties are or *should be* aware."[166]

One important concept in establishing "usage of trade" is that of "trade codes." Proof of a "trade code," by itself, may establish a usage of trade.[167] Government agency regulations may be construed to establish such a trade code. For example, Federal Trade Commission (FTC) regulations, if otherwise applicable, could be relied upon to establish a trade code binding upon merchants.[168]

Whether by a trade code or otherwise, the person seeking to invoke the usage of trade has the burden of proving it.[169]

Through the applicability of the doctrine of "usage of trade," certain responsibilities could be placed upon unregulated utility companies that might not otherwise be obtainable through specific applications of common law principles. Advocates may be able to persuade a court that an energy marketer or recently deregulated generation company, or a company providing deliverable fuels, should be required to comply with the "usage of trade" that regulated companies have long followed, including regularity in meter reading (for example, an unregulated utility company may not rely upon repeated estimates of meter readings when providing bills or demanding payment), and make-up bills for under-payment attributed to slow meters (for example, customers have a right to enter into a payment plan of a length at least equal to the number of months over which the back-bill accrued).

15.4.1.4 The UCC Standard of "Good Faith"

A fundamental policy of the UCC is that all parties must act in good faith. Section 1-304 of the UCC provides that "[e]very contract or duty within [the Uniform Commercial Code] imposes an obligation of good faith in its performance and enforcement." Similarly, courts routinely hold that the law "imposes an obligation of good faith and fundamental fairness in the performance of every contract."[170] PUC regulations may serve to define what is "good faith" within the context of providing energy to consumers.

The "good faith" obligation allows a court to police transactions for unreasonableness and to reach a decision based as much on equities as on the written agreement itself. For all parties, good faith as defined in section 1-201(20) of the UCC means "honesty in fact" in the conduct or transaction concerned.[171] Section 2-103 provides that "[g]ood faith, except as otherwise provided in Article 5, means honesty in fact and the observance of reasonable commercial standards of fair dealing." Merchants must perform their obligations within the spirit as well as the letter of the contract and the law.

The key question for utility customers is whether they have the right to independently enforce the "observance of reasonable commercial standards of fair dealing." Some courts have expressly held that a seller may *not* be sued for failure to act in good faith.[172] This view holds that the principle of good faith merely helps define the standard for executing other obligations, such as warranties and remedies.

162 Campbell v. Hostetter Farms, 380 A.2d 463, 466 (Pa. Super. Ct. 1977) (quoting U.C.C. § 2-202 cmt. 2). *See also* Venturi v. Adkisson, 552 S.W.2d 643, 645 (Ark. 1977).

163 Murphy v. Reed, 193 S.W.2d 947, 949 (Mo. Ct. App. 1946).

164 J. White & R. Summers, Uniform Commercial Code § 3-3, at 116 (4th ed. 1995).

165 "It is not the law . . . that the buyer must know of the custom; if he should have known, he is bound." Western Indus. v. Newcor Canada Ltd., 739 F.2d 1198, 1202 (7th Cir. 1984).

166 J. White & R. Summers, Uniform Commercial Code § 3-3 at 113, 114 (4th ed. 1995) (emphasis added). *Accord* Western Indus. Inc. v. Newcor Canada Ltd., 739 F.2d 1198, 1202 (7th Cir. 1984); U.S. for Use and Benefit of Union Bldg. Materials v. Haas & Haynie Corp., 577 F.2d 568, 573 (9th Cir. 1978); Wright v. Commercial & Sav. Bank, 464 A.2d 1080, 1084 (Md. Ct. Spec. App. 1983); Mieske v. Bartell Drug Co., 593 P.2d 1308, 1313 (Wash. 1979); Mountain Fuel Supply Co. v. Central Eng'g, 611 P.2d 863, 869 (Wyo. 1980).

167 Tomlinson Lumber Sales v. J.D. Harrold Co., 117 N.W.2d 203, 206 (Minn. 1962).

168 Kawin v. Chrysler Corp., 636 S.W.2d 40, 44, 50 (Mo. 1982).

169 Western Indus. Inc. v. Newcor Canada Ltd., 739 F.2d 1198, 1202 (7th Cir. 1984); Tobias v. North Dakota Dep't of Human Serv., 448 N.W.2d 175, 180 (N.D. 1989).

170 Bank of Ind. v. Holyfield, 476 F. Supp. 104, 109 (S.D. Miss. 1979). *See* Schroeder v. Fageol Motors, Inc., 544 P.2d 20, 24 (Wash. 1975) ("the single most important concept intertwined throughout the entire code is that of good faith dealings").

171 Bowling Green, Inc. v. State St. Bank & Trust Co., 425 F.2d 81 (1st Cir. 1970). *See* Corp. Venezolano de Fomento v. Wintero Sales Corp., 452 F. Supp. 1108 (S.D.N.Y. 1978).

172 Cambee's Furniture, Inc. v. Doughboy Recreational, Inc., 825 F.2d 167 (8th Cir. 1987) (applying South Dakota law); Betterton v. First Interstate Bank of Ariz., N.A., 800 F.2d 732 (8th Cir. 1986) (applying Arizona law); Chandler v. Hunter, 340 So. 2d 818 (Ala. Civ. App. 1976); Super Glue Corp. v. Avis Rent A Car Sys., Inc., 517 N.Y.S.2d 764 (N.Y. App. Div. 1987).

Other courts find an independent cause of action for breach of the good faith duty.[173] Section 1-106(2) expressly provides that "[a]ny right or obligation declared by this Act is enforceable by action unless the provision declaring it specifies a different and limited effect."

15.4.2 Unfair and Deceptive Acts and Practices (UDAP)

15.4.2.1 Scope of UDAP Statutes Coverage

All states have enacted statutes, commonly called "UDAP" statutes, generally prohibiting unfair or deceptive acts and practices.[174] In a few states, only practices delineated in the statute are prohibited. But most UDAP statutes provide a flexible standard and effective remedies for challenging practices that are unfair or deceptive.[175] Many of these state statutes are patterned after the language found in § 5(a)(1) of the Federal Trade Commission (FTC) Act,[176] which prohibits "unfair or deceptive acts or practices." UDAP statutes typically apply to the sale of goods[177] or services[178] or practices "in trade or commerce."[179] Some UDAP statutes apply solely to consumer transactions,[180] so that farmers and other rural customers who use electricity primarily for commercial uses will not be covered in these states. However, in some states, UDAP statutes will apply even to these transactions.

Generally, the provision of electricity, gas, or telephone service will fall within the UDAP definitions of covered goods or services. Most UDAP statutes, however, exempt entities or activities regulated by public service commissions or regulatory agencies in general. The construction of these "regulated activity" exceptions raises difficult questions of state law. Do they exempt activities that are forbidden by the regulatory scheme?[181] Does the exemption apply even if the agency does not regulate and has not addressed the challenged act or practice,[182] or if the agency has no power to grant relief?[183]

A Massachusetts court found a UDAP violation in certain improper accounting practices by a gas utility, which deceived both consumers and the Department of Public Utilities, causing the Department to set rates too high. The court held that the violation was not the high rates but the accounting practices which violated DPU rules.[184] A New Jersey court, on similar facts and with no explicit statutory exemption, held that the utility's actions were exempt from UDAP because the purchased gas adjustment was a "tariff mechanism" subject to the control of the public utility commission.[185] A federal court applied the Texas UDAP statute to utility customers' claims of discriminatory rates, retaliation, and misrepresentation, because the commission lacked power

173 *In re* Coin Phones Inc., 203 B.R. 184 (Bankr. S.D.N.Y. 1996) (compensatory and punitive damages awarded to payphone provider for breach by telephone utility of duty of good faith and fair dealing); Gordon v. Planters & Merchants Bancshares, 935 S.W.2d 544 (Ark. 1996) (allowing plaintiff to seek punitive damages); Tribby v. Northwestern Bank of Great Falls, 704 P.2d 409, 419 (Mont. 1985) ("We are not holding that every contract or statutorily imposed obligation, alone, carries with it an implied covenant of good faith and fair dealing, the breach of which permits recovery in tort," but given allegations of defendant's "reckless disregard" of plaintiff's rights, tort claim may go to jury).

174 These state acts are distinct from state anti-trust acts, violations of which could provide the basis for consumer protection claims. *See* Dunlap v. Colorado Springs Cablevision, Inc., 829 P.2d 1286 (Colo. 1992) (consumers stated cause of action against cable television company under state Unfair Practices Act for geographic price discrimination). *See generally* National Consumer Law Center, Unfair and Deceptive Acts and Practices (7th ed. 2008 and Supp.).

175 *See* National Consumer Law Center, Unfair and Deceptive Acts and Practices, appx. A (7th ed. 2008 and Supp.) (setting forth a state-by-state analysis of state UDAP laws).

176 15 U.S.C. § 45(a)(1).

177 The UDAP statute in a particular state may define the term "goods." In those instances when the term is not defined, some courts refer to the definition of "goods" in U.C.C. §§ 1-905 and 2-105. *See, e.g.*, Riverside Nat'l Bank v. Lewis, 603 S.W.2d 169 (Tex. 1980).

178 Many courts will treat electricity as a "good" or, alternatively, as a "service." *See* § 15.4.1.2, *supra*.

State UDAP statutes vary as to the extent to which they cover "goods" and "services." *See* National Consumer Law Center, Unfair and Deceptive Acts and Practices appx. A (7th ed. 2008 and Supp.).

179 National Consumer Law Center, Unfair and Deceptive Acts and Practices § 2.1.4 (7th ed. 2008 and Supp.).

180 *See* National Consumer Law Center, Unfair and Deceptive Acts and Practices § 2.1.8.1 (7th ed. 2008 and Supp.) (discussing interpretation of "personal, family and household use" and similar coverage limitations in UDAP statutes).

181 *See* Shields v. Lefta, Inc., 888 F. Supp. 894, 898 (N.D. Ill. 1995) (if consumer shows defendant violated Truth in Lending Act regulations, claim may be made under UDAP); Nault's Auto Sales v. American Honda Motor Co., 148 F.R.D. 25, 47 (D.N.H. 1993) ("[t]he mere existence of a regulatory board to oversee certain standards of an industry does not remove all acts and practices of that industry from the provisions of the Consumer Protection Act"); Lowell Gas Co. v. Attorney Gen., 385 N.E.2d 240, 244 (Mass. 1979) ("we note that nothing in [the statute governing utilities], either explicitly or implicitly, excludes application of [the UDAP law] to unfair or deceptive acts or practices of gas utility companies"). *But see* Taylor v. Bear Stearns & Co., 572 F. Supp. 667 (N.D. Ga. 1983) (UDAP did not apply to churning, which was forbidden by securities laws); State v. Piedmont Funding Co., 382 A.2d 819 (R.I. 1978).

182 *See* Martin v. Heinold Commodities, Inc., 643 N.E.2d 734 (Ill. 1994) (mere filing of agency-required disclosure form does not immunize party from UDAP claim, especially when information disclosed, taken as a whole, is deceptive). *But see* Averill v. Cox, 761 A.2d 1083 (N.H. 2000) (parties generally regulated by the state are exempt from UDAP claims).

183 *See* Penny v. Southwestern Bell, 906 F.2d 183 (5th Cir. 1990). *See also* Southwestern Bell Tel. v. Nash, 586 S.W.2d 647 (Tex. App. 1979).

184 Lowell Gas. Co. v. Attorney Gen., 385 N.E.2d 240 (Mass. 1979).

185 Daaleman v. Elizabethtown Gas Co., 390 A.2d 566 (N.J. 1978).

to award damages for past misconduct or to hear the misrepresentation claim. The court acknowledged the commission's authority over ratemaking by staying the proceedings to allow the commission to determine whether the rates were discriminatory.[186] Numerous courts have held, however, that state utility regulatory schemes preempt UDAP coverage.[187] (None of these exemptions apply to rural electric cooperatives, however, as they are unregulated.)[188]

When UDAP coverage is denied to regulated activities, the most common rationale is the pervasiveness of the regulatory scheme.[189] With industry restructuring and deregulation, some of the competitive companies will now be covered by UDAP even though they provide the same service or goods that regulated companies previously provided.[190] Although the local distribution utilities will remain pervasively regulated (and generally UDAP-exempt) monopolies, consumers will be confronted with a new array of competitive sellers and marketers. These companies will, in most cases, be subject only to minimal licensure requirements[191] as well as rules governing information disclosure, slamming prevention, and so forth.

If a state's UDAP exemption refers to activities "regulated by" the public service commission, these entities may attempt to slip through the cracks, subject neither to strict type regulation by the PUC nor to the general consumer protection laws which cover other competitive enterprises. During restructuring, consumer advocates should argue for explicit statutory and regulatory language making deregulated service providers subject to UDAP laws.[192] In the absence of explicit statutory or regulatory language, advocates should still argue that energy service providers are in the same position as other competitive businesses that are subject to the UDAP statute. An exemption for activities regulated by the PSC will not, of course, apply to entities such as rural electric cooperatives that are not regulated by the PUC (although other exemptions may apply).

15.4.2.2 UDAP Standards

The "S&H" standard is used by many state courts in determining what is "unfair or deceptive" under their own UDAP laws and was first described in a landmark Supreme Court case of *FTC v. Sperry & Hutchinson Co.*[193] The Supreme Court in *Sperry & Hutchinson Co.* affirmed the authority of the Federal Trade Commission (FTC) to consider the following factors in determining whether a particular challenged practice is unfair:

1. Does the practice offend public policy as it has been established by "statutes, the common law, or otherwise"?
2. Is it "immoral, unethical, oppressive, or unscrupulous"?
3. Does the practice cause substantial consumer injury?[194]

---

186 Penny v. Southwestern Bell, 906 F.2d 183 (5th Cir. 1990). *See also* Southwestern Bell Tel. v. Nash, 586 S.W.2d 647 (Tex. App. 1979).

187 *See, e.g.*, Porr v. Nynex Corp., 660 N.Y.S.2d 440 (N.Y. App. Div. 1997) (filed rate doctrine and doctrine of primary administrative jurisdiction bar all statutory and common law consumer claims, including UDAP); Tanner Elec. v. Puget Sound Power & Light, 911 P.2d 1301 (Wash. 1996) (state consumer protection act exemption for "regulated industries" exempted an electric company, even if its actions violated utility commission rules). *See also* Shepard v. Bonita Vista Props., L.P., 664 S.E.2d 388 (N.C. Ct. App. 2008). *Cf.* People *ex. rel.* Orloff v. Pacific Bell, 80 P.3d 201 (Cal. Ct. App. 2003) (reversing lower court's decision that precluded district attorneys from pursuing false advertising and unfair business practice claims against utility in civil court, and finding civil court remedies would not undermine state utility commission's authority; state utility commission does not necessarily have exclusive jurisdiction over all causes of action against a public utility, and mere possibility of conflict with commission jurisdiction can be insufficient in itself to preclude a civil action against a public utility). *See generally* National Consumer Law Center, Unfair and Deceptive Acts and Practices §§ 2.3.2.1, 2.3.3 (7th ed. 2008 and Supp.) (regarding, respectively, exemptions for utilities and for regulated industries).

188 *See* Granbois v. Big Horn County Elec. Coop., Inc., 986 P.2d 1097 (Mont. 1999).

189 Continental Mobile Tel. Co. v. Chicago SMSA Ltd. P'ship, 587 N.E.2d 1169 (Ill. App. Ct. 1992); Daaleman v. Elizabethtown Gas Co., 390 A.2d 566 (N.J. 1978); Tanner Elec. Coop. v. Puget Sound Power & Light, 911 P.2d 1301 (Wash. 1996). *See also* Taylor v. Bear Stearns & Co., 572 F. Supp. 667 (N.D. Ga. 1983) (securities); Doyle v. Chihoski, 443 A.2d 1243 (R.I. 1982) (real estate); State v. Piedmont Funding Co., 382 A.2d 819 (R.I. 1978) (securities).

190 *See, e.g.*, Ting v. AT&T, 319 F.3d 1126 (9th Cir. 2003).
The court found that plaintiffs' class action claims against AT&T under the California UDAP law could proceed. The plaintiffs' claims were in large part based on unfair and deceptive practices in which AT&T engaged after the Federal Communications Commission "detariffed" long-distance services, that is, required long-distance companies to enter into contracts directly with customers rather than relying on tariffs filed with the Commission. This case well illustrates the risks consumers face when industries are deregulated as well as the opportunity to bring UDAP laws to bear upon those deregulated companies.

191 In other fields, the fact that an agency licenses or minimally regulates an actor or activity has been held insufficient to bring an activity within the "regulated activities" UDAP exemption. *See, e.g.*, State v. O'Neill Investigations, 609 P.2d 520 (Alaska 1980); State *ex rel.* Stratton v. Gurley Motor Co., 737 P.2d 1180 (N.M. Ct. App. 1987); Skinner v. Steele, 730 S.W.2d 335 (Tenn. Ct. App. 1987).

192 Some states have in fact made it clear that competitive companies will be subject to UDAP claims. *See, e.g.*, 940 Mass. Code Regs. § 19.00 (Retail Marketing and Sale of Electricity) (making certain misrepresentations and other acts or omissions UDAP violations); 90-060-004 R.I. Code R. §§ I–IV (LexisNexis).

193 Federal Trade Comm'n v. Sperry & Hutchinson Co., 405 U.S. 233, 92 S. Ct. 898 (1972).

194 *Id.* at 244, 245. *See* National Consumer Law Center, Unfair and Deceptive Acts and Practices § 4.3.3 (7th ed. 2008 and Supp.) (listing states that follow this standard and discussing current FTC standard and standards applied in the several states).

A consumer does not need to establish that all three criteria have been met in order to make a successful UDAP claim.[195] While a court may consider all three criteria, evidence supporting just one may be sufficient to establish a UDAP violation.[196]

Particularly when a practice violates applicable regulations, is oppressive, and causes substantial injury, the practice should be found to be "unfair." In analyzing the unfairness concept, it is always important to keep in mind the monopoly status enjoyed by many utilities. This status makes it easier to argue that the practices are oppressive and capable of causing injury because consumers have no alternative to turn to for energy.

More recently, the FTC and some states have adopted a modified unfairness standard. The FTC unfairness standard evolved so that a practice would be deemed unfair if: (1) there is substantial consumer injury; (2) it is not outweighed by benefits to consumers or to competition; and (3) consumers cannot reasonably avoid.[197] This newer standard stemmed from a 1980 FTC policy statement addressing "unfairness" from a perspective that emphasized unjustified consumer injury.[198]

In 1994, Congress codified the unfairness standard in amending the FTC Act and defined unfairness at 15 U.S.C. § 45(n):

> The Commission shall have no authority under this section or section 57a of this title to declare unlawful an act or practice on the grounds that such act or practice is unfair unless such act or practice causes or is likely to cause substantial injury to consumers which is not reasonably avoidable by consumers themselves and is not outweighed by countervailing benefits to consumers or competition. In determining whether an act or practice is unfair, the Commission may consider public policies as evidence to be considered with all other evidence. Such public policy considerations may not serve as a primary basis for such determination.

The FTC has interpreted this statute to require three findings to demonstrate unfairness: (1) the act or practice has caused or is likely to cause substantial injury to consumers; (2) consumers cannot reasonably avoid the injury; and (3) countervailing benefits to consumers or to competition does not outweigh the injury to consumers.[199]

When utilities remain regulated monopolies, the second prong of the test—that consumers cannot reasonably avoid the injury—may be the easiest prong to demonstrate to a court's satisfaction. When utilities have been restructured or deregulated, arguments can be made that they retain characteristics of a monopoly such that the injury caused cannot be avoided by consumers.

UDAP claims may arise in a number of ways. Consumers may, for example, find themselves saddled with unaffordable bills because they were given confusing, incomplete, or inaccurate information about the costs of various options or packages. They may have committed to a disadvantageous long-term contract because of high pressure tactics of a telemarketer. Unscrupulous market behavior can inflict substantial consumer injury without violating the letter of statutory or common law. UDAP statutes are aimed at just this kind of wrongdoing.

UDAP has less application to utility goods or services provided under filed tariffs. Telecommunications carriers, in particular, have been adept at using the "filed tariff" doctrine as a shield against a broad range of consumer claims.[200]

195 Macomber v. Travelers Prop. & Cas. Corp., 804 A.2d 180 (Conn. 2002); Cheshire Mortgage Serv., Inc. v. Montes, 612 A.2d 1130 (Conn. 1992).

196 *See, e.g.*, Aurigemma v. Arco Petroleum Prods. Co., 734 F. Supp. 1025 (D. Conn. 1990). *See also* National Consumer Law Center, Unfair and Deceptive Acts and Practices §§ 4.3.3, 4.3.3.1 (7th ed. 2008 and Supp.) (discussing the S&H standard). *But see* Golembiewski v. Hallberg Ins. Agency, Inc., 635 N.E.2d 452 (Ill. App. Ct. 1994) (all three criteria must be met).

197 *See* Orkin Exterminating Co. v. Federal Trade Comm'n, 849 F.2d 1354, 1364 (11th Cir. 1988); American Fin. Serv. Ass'n v. FTC, 767 F.2d 957 (D.C. Cir. 1985) (FTC promulgation of rule concerning creditor practices that used unjustified consumer injury standard upheld on judicial review).

198 American Fin. Serv. Ass'n v. Federal Trade Comm'n, 767 F.2d 957, 971 (D.C. Cir. 1985). *See* 104 F.T.C. 1070, 1072 (1984), *available at* www.ftc.gov/bcp/policystmt/ad-unfair.htm.

199 *See* Letter from Timothy J. Muris, FTC Chairman, to U.S. Dep't of Transp. (June 6, 2003), *available at* www.ftc.gov/os/2003/06/dotcomment.htm (FTC providing comment to Department of Transportation in dockets OST-97-2881, OST-97-3014, and OST 98-4775 regarding FTC's unfairness standard).

200 Cahnmann v. Sprint, 961 F. Supp. 1229 (N.D. Ind. 1997), *aff'd*, 133 F.3d 484 (7th Cir. 1998) (charges authorized by an approved tariff may be charged to customers regardless of advertising of lower or different tariffs even if done fraudulently; no UDAP claim, fraud claim, or damages claim allowed); Marcus v. AT&T Corp., 938 F. Supp. 1158 (S.D.N.Y. 1996), *aff'd*, 138 F.3d 46 (2d Cir. 1998) (filed rate doctrine "trumps" UDAP claims, fraud claims, and contract defenses).

Appendix A State Regulation of Utilities

This appendix is also available on the companion website to this treatise. The companion website facilitates keyword searches and allows relevant provisions to be imported as word-processing documents.

A.1 Summary of Utility Commission Regulation

ALABAMA

The Alabama Public Service Commission's regulations are codified in five separate sections: General Rules 1–19, Special Electric Rules E-1 through E-15, Gas Rules G-1 through G-13, Telephone Rules T-1 through T-31, and Water Rules W-1 through W-21. The General Rules govern deposits, termination and termination protections for gas, electric, water, and telephone utilities. The regulations can be found at www.psc.state.al.us/Administrative/administrative_division.htm (last visited in May 2011).

***General Rules*—Ala. Pub. Serv. Comm'n Gen. R. 1–19**

* * *

Rule 4. Customer Service Requirements and Information:

Utilities shall give customers who make requests reasonably possible information and assistance to help customers receive safe and efficient service and to buy properly adapted appliances.

Rule 5. Complaints:

Utilities shall keep records of customer complaints for 3 years after the final disposition of complaints.

* * *

Rule 8. Deposits:

Utilities may require deposits from customers before beginning or continuing service if they judge the deposit is necessary. The amount of the deposit shall not be exceed the amount of an estimated bill for 2 billing periods or for billing in advance the amount of the estimated bill for 1 billing period plus 2 months estimated toll. Interest shall accrue interest at a rate of 7% per annum and be shall be credited on the December bill.

Utilities may require deposits after giving 5 days' written notice from customers if their account is not in good standing or their deposit was refunded or their usage increases. Telephone utilities may require an additional deposit from customers after giving written notice if there is an excessive toll and the customer is a known credit risk. Telephone utilities may use toll blocking if they do not receive a deposit or discontinue local service if they cannot use toll blocking.

Utilities shall keep records of customers' deposits and issue receipts to customers.

Utilities shall refund deposits to customers in December after 24 months if the account is considered to be in good standing. Customers may apply for a refund earlier.

* * *

Rule 10. Meter Reading and Bill Forms—Electric, Gas, Steam, and Water Utilities:

Gas, steam, water and electricity utilities shall explain to customers how to read meters. Utilities shall record actual meter reading at beginning and end of service if customer makes a request. Utilities can issue estimated bills but must tell customers if they have issued more than two estimated bills in a row.

Rule 11. Rate Schedules, Rules and Regulations:

Utilities shall make their rate schedules, rules and regulations available to the public, shall notify their customers that rate schedules are publicly available, and, upon request, shall send customers rate schedule and how the rate applies to the customers' bills.

Rule 12. Collection of Delinquent Accounts and Discontinuance of Service to Customers for Nonpayment:

Telecommunications bills can be due no earlier than 15 days after the billing date. All other utility bills are delinquent if not paid within 10 days of the due date. Utilities may send a collector to the customer's premises to collect an overdue bill and may charge a collection fee.

Utilities shall give 5 days' written notice before discontinuing service for nonpayment of an overdue bill. Customers shall have the right to pay the overdue bill at any point before service is discontinued.

Utilities cannot discontinue service for nonpayment after 3:30 p.m. if the utility will be closed the next day.

Utilities (except for telephone toll service) shall adopt and follow reasonable tariff rules for discontinuing service when life or health may be threatened by termination, the customer requires special consideration because of age or disability, or other circumstances warrant special consideration.

Utilities shall include heading in bold type "Disconnect Notice," "Termination Notice," "Final Notice," or "Cutoff Notice." The notice shall also state that the customer should contact the utility and then the Commission if there is a dispute.

Utilities shall give the power to extend payment deadlines and to enter into installment agreements to at least one employee in each of its offices.

Residential gas and electric utilities shall not discontinue service for nonpayment on a day when the National Weather Service predicts a temperature of below 32° Fahrenheit.

Utilities shall charge a reconnection fee set by the Commission for each utility to restore service. The amount of the reconnection fee shall be added to the amount of the customer's overdue bill.

Utilities may refuse to provide service or terminate service to customers who owe money for similar service at a former location or to members of the customer's household if they apply within 1 year of the overdue bill.

Rule 13. Discontinuance or Suspension of Service for Reasons Other Than Nonpayment of Service Bill:

Utilities may discontinue service without notice and on any day if there is either a hazardous condition on the customer's premises, use of customer equipment with an adverse effect on other customers or tampering or unauthorized use. Utilities may terminate service after giving the customer a reasonable time to comply if the customer does not provide reasonable access or follow the utilities' rules but cannot discontinue service on a day when the utility will be closed or the day before that day.

* * *

Rule 15. Over-Billing and Under-Billing:

Gas and water utilities shall make adjustments to a customer's bill for up to 36 months if a test of the accuracy of the meter shows that it is more than 2% fast or slow. If the customer has been under-billed, gas or water utilities shall give written notice to the customer and shall give the customer a chance to repay the back payment in monthly installments before sending a back bill to the customer unless the undercharge was caused by tampering or unauthorized use. If the customer has been over-billed, gas or water utilities shall refund the amount of the overcharge either as a credit to the customer's next bill or as a lump sum within 45 days of discovery of the overcharge.

***Special Electric Rules*—Ala. Pub. Serv. Comm'n R. E1–E15**

* * *

Rule E-15. Billing Inaccuracies:

Substantially similar to General Rule 15.

* * *

***Gas Rules*—Ala. Pub. Serv. Comm'n R. G1–G13**

* * *

Rule G-7. Meter Tests:

Gas utilities shall upon customer's request test the accuracy of a customer's gas meter once every 5 years without charging the customer. If the test of the accuracy of the meter shows it is more than 2% fast or slow, gas utilities shall follow General Rule 15.

* * *

***Telephone Rules*—Ala. Pub. Serv. Comm'n R. T1–T31**

Beginning January 1, 2011, the Alabama Public Service Commission shall not have jurisdiction to regulate costs, rates, charges, terms, or conditions of basic or optional telephone services, but it shall retain exclusive jurisdiction for complaints regarding billing and the installment or disruption of service. Ala. Code §§ 37-2A-4, 37-2A-8].

* * *

Rule T-1. Application of Rules:

* * *

This rule states that the General Rules on deposits and billing apply to telephone utilities.

* * *

Rule T-3. Records and Reports:

Telephone utilities shall follow the Federal Communication Commission's regulations on maintenance of customer account records.

* * *

Rule T-5. Customer Relations:

Telephone utilities shall explain rates, charges and service connection charges to customers. Telephone utilities shall provide an estimate of the cost of basic monthly service.

Telephone utilities may require customers who are disputing a bill to pay the undisputed portion of a bill to avoid discontinuing service for nonpayment.

Telephone utilities shall credit customers on a pro rata basis if telephone service is interrupted for more than 48 hours due to malfunctioning telephone company equipment.

Local exchange carriers shall issue a bill each month. If the company bills in advance, the delinquent date must be at least 20 days after the due date of the bill.

Local exchange carriers shall bill customers for toll calls no more than 90 days from the date the toll call was made.

Telephone utilities shall not back-bill for undercharges for more than 36 months and must give the customer written notice and the option to pay the undercharge in monthly installments. Telephone utilities shall refund overcharges due to their error for up to 36 months.

Rule T-6. Reasons for Denying Telephone Service:

In addition to the reasons listed in the General Rules, telephone utilities may deny service if customer's use of equipment would adversely effect utilities' equipment or service to others or in extraordinary circumstances which would cause the utility to lose substantial revenue.

Rule T-7. Insufficient Reasons for Denying Telephone Service:

Telephone utilities shall not deny residential service because the customer did not pay for business service for a different telephone number at a different location, non-regulated services, or disputed charges (including directory advertising, other provider services, and Local Dial-it charges).

ALASKA

The Public Utilities Commission's regulations governing telecommunications service are codified at Alaska Admin. Code tit. 3, §§ 52.200–52.340. Regulations governing electric service are within Alaska Admin. Code tit. 3, §§ 52.400–52.500. Access to the regulations can be found at www.state.ak.us/rca/Regulations (last visited in May 2011).

Telephone—**Alaska Admin. Code tit. 3, §§ 52.200–52.340**

* * *

§ 52.210. Business Office:

Telephone utilities must conveniently locate and staff business offices to provide access to qualified employees who can provide information, accept and process applications, explain charges and adjust errors. Telephone utilities shall make reasonable efforts to tell customers about alternate service that may meet customers' requirements.

Telephone utilities shall notify customers of service connection or installation charges in advance and shall tell customers the amount of the estimated bill for local service and other charges.

Telephone utilities shall make reasonable efforts to acknowledge, and if appropriate, to answer correspondence within 10 working days.

* * *

§ 52.230. Subscriber Billing:

Telephone utilities must bill subscribers every month. Bills must clearly list all adjustments and nonrecurring charges. Bills may show one flat monthly charge for all local service provided for the same telephone number; the monthly charge may be billed one month in advance. Bills must itemize toll charges.

Telephone utilities shall grant credit for any toll call when the customer reports as soon as reasonably possible that the customer called the wrong number or that some part of the call was inadequate for communication.

* * *

Electric—**Alaska Admin. Code tit. 3, §§ 52.400–52.500**

* * *

§ 52.405. Business Office Standards:

Electric utilities must conveniently locate and staff business offices to provide access to qualified employees who can accept and process applications explain charges and adjust errors and provide information.

Electric utilities shall include in their tariff and notify customers of all reasonably convenient ways for contacting business offices or service centers.

Electric utilities shall keep accurate records of applications, customer billing history and complaints. Electric utilities shall answer service complaints and customer correspondence within 10 working days and shall state in their answer that customers may file a complaint with the Commission if they are not satisfied with the utilities' answer. Electric utilities shall keep these records for at least 2 years.

§ 52.410. Establishment of Permanent Service:

Electric utility may require new applicants for service to come to apply in person, present proof of identity, and complete an application. New applicants must present specific information including name, service address, billing address, any address where service has already been provided, statement if applicant is tenant at the place service will be provided and name, address, telephone number of landlord or landlord's agent and name and address of any third-party customer wishes to receive copy of termination notice.

Electric utilities shall inform customers of the most economical available class of service when a customer applies for service.

Electric utilities may refuse to begin new service for falsifying required information and failure to correct the falsification, an outstanding amount due for utility service without an acceptable plan for paying the outstanding balance, failure to meet the credit criteria for waiving a deposit and failure to provide a deposit.

§ 52.420. Deposit Requirements:

Electric utilities must describe their deposit and refund procedure in their tariff.

Electric utilities may require a separate deposit for each meter. The amount of the deposit cannot be more than either twice the estimated monthly bill for the location or twice the average monthly bill for the customer class.

Electric utilities shall refund deposits for residential service within 90 days if the applicant has previously established a "good payment record" with the utility providing electric service or can provide documentation from another electric utility that the applicant was on time with payments for the last 12 consecutive payments.

Electric utilities shall issue a written receipt for the amount of the deposit but cannot require customers to produce the receipt to receive a refund of the deposit.

Electric utilities must refund deposits and any accrued interest within 30 days of providing 12 months of continuous service if the customer has not been overdue in paying more than 2 payments, has not been delinquent for 6 months and is not currently overdue. Electric utilities must also refund deposits and accrued interest within 30 days of service termination after deducting any amount due for utility service and late fees.

Electric utilities may ask for or adjust the amount of a deposit up to the maximum listed above if the customer becomes delinquent in payment.

Electric utilities shall provide deferred payment plans for deposits for residential customers who have an economic hardship.

* * *

§ 52.425. Meter Readings:

If an electric utility cannot read a meter for a reason listed in Alaska Admin. Code tit. 3, § 52.435(b)(2) or (b)(3), the electric utility shall issue an estimated bill.

Electric utilities shall only issue two consecutive estimated monthly bills. Utilities must then get an accurate meter reading unless the meter cannot be read due to severe weather or other dangerous conditions.

Electric utilities may allow customers to read their own meters under specific guidelines.

§ 52.430. General Billing and Collection Requirements:

Electric utilities shall bill monthly. Bills must contain specific information. Electric bills are due and payable either on the billing date or on the postmark date. An electric bill is not past due and a late or finance charge cannot be added as long as the bill is paid within 25 days of the billing date or postmark date.

Utility bills must separately identify amounts due for service from a previous billing cycle as past due on subsequent monthly bills. Utility bills must also separately identify late charges and finance charges.

The term delinquent is defined as "all past due amounts and associated late and finance charges from one billing cycle which are not received by the utility as of the close of the following billing cycle." Electric utilities may discontinue service to customers with delinquent charges.

Electric utilities may provide for a finance charge for past-due or delinquent payments in their tariffs. Electric utilities may assess one late charge when an account becomes past due.

§ 52.435. Estimated Billings:

Electric utilities must indicate on the bill when the bill is based on estimated use.

Electric utilities may issue estimated bills only if customers who read their own meters have failed to send the meter reading to the utility during the billing cycle, or the utility is prevented from reading the meter by severe weather conditions or other circumstances.

§ 52.440. Levelized Billing:

A utility shall offer a levelized billing option to its residential electric heating customers and may offer the option to all customers based upon the customer's actual consumption history for the most recent 12 months or other representative period. Levelized billing shall be adjusted annually, or more frequently, according to usage, and any overcharge shall be immediately refunded or credited to the customer's account. A utility may not refuse enrollment in levelized billing to a customer whose current bill at the time of enrollment is past due or delinquent if the customer enters into a deferred payment agreement, as described in Alaska Admin. Code tit. 3, § 52.445.

§ 52.445. Deferred Payment Agreements:

Electric utilities may not discontinue or refuse to restore service to residential customers who show that a financial hardship prevents them from paying a delinquent bill unless the customer either does not agree to or follow a deferred payment plan.

Deferred payment agreements must provide, in writing, that service will continue if the customer pays 1/3 of the outstanding bill when the agreement is entered into, agrees to pay all future bills according to the billing and collection tariffs of the utility, and agrees to pay the remainder of the outstanding balance in installments in less than 12 months.

Electric utilities and customers shall consider the size of the delinquent account, the customer's ability to pay, the customer's payment history, the amount of time account has been delinquent, the circumstances that caused delinquency, and other relevant factors to decide on a reasonable deferred payment schedule.

Deferred payment arrangements can include a finance charge if included in the utility's tariff.

Electric utilities may discontinue service if a customer does not comply with the terms of a deferred payment agreement.

§ 52.450. Disconnection of Service:

Electric utilities may terminate service without written notice for meter tampering or fraud, or if an immediate hazard threatens the health or safety of the customer, the general population or the utilities' employees or facilities.

Electric utilities may terminate service after following the notice requirements described below if the customer has not paid for utility service within 40 days of rendering of the bill, the customer has not followed the utility's deposit requirements, or the customer has not provided the utility with reasonable access to the meter, utility equipment or other utility property.

Notice of intent to discontinue service shall be at least 15 days before the date scheduled for termination, followed by an attempt, by phone or in person at least 3 days prior to termination. Notice shall also be sent to any third party the customer designated on the service application.

Disconnection notices shall be clearly distinguishable, and shall contain the reasons for disconnection, the amount due, date of disconnection, availability of payment plans and assistance, delay option for medical reasons, tariffed charges for disconnection and reconnection, and complaint procedures.

Electric utilities must provide the notice of intent to discontinue service at least 30 days before the scheduled termination date if the electric utility knows that a person who is seriously ill, an elder, disabled, or dependent on life support systems lives in the customer's residence. Electric utilities must postpone the scheduled disconnection date for 15 days and notify the customer if a customer notifies the utility that a person who is seriously ill, an elder, disabled, or dependent on life support systems lives in the customer's residence after the notice of intent to discontinue service is issued.

For individually metered premises where the landlord is the customer, the utility shall notify the tenant in writing, at least 15 days before the scheduled date for disconnection of the service to the landlord, of the option of subscribing for service in the tenant's own name. However, the utility may not attempt to recover from the tenant or condition service to the tenant on the payment of any outstanding bills or other charges due from the outstanding account of the landlord. If the tenant declines to subscribe for individual service, or arrange for payment of the tenant's outstanding balance, if applicable, the utility may disconnect service without further notice, no earlier than the date scheduled for disconnection.

Service may be terminated, without additional notice, within 10 days from the date contained on the "Shut Off" notice between 8:00 a.m. and 5:00 p.m. Monday through Thursday. Utilities cannot discontinue service on Friday or the day before a holiday.

Service shall not be terminated due to nonpayment from past customer from the same location unless previous customer continues to reside there, nonpayment for unregulated service or equipment or for a different class of service at a different location, amounts in dispute still under investigation (but customer may be required to pay any undisputed amount), or the customer is eligible for, in the process of negotiating, or agrees to a deferred payment plan and has entered into a deferred payment plan.

Electric utilities shall restore service within 3 working days after the reason for discontinuing service is corrected.

* * *

§ 52.465. Meter Measurements, Adjustments, and Tests:

If an electric utility tests a meter and finds that the meter over-estimated the amount of service by more than 2%, the utility shall recalculate bills from the date of the error and shall refund or credit the over-registered amount unless it is less than $5. If the beginning date of error is unknown, the utility shall refund or credit the most recent customer of record for the billed error for the period since the meter was last tested, not to exceed 6 months, or the period during which the most recent customer of record received service through the meter, whichever is less.

Electric utilities cannot charge residential customers for underbilling unless there is evidence that the customer tampered with the meter or electric service.

A utility must test a meter at the customer's request and may charge for the test. If, however, the meter is found to over- or under-register by more 2% and there is no evidence of tampering, the utility may not charge for the test.

ARIZONA

The Corporate Commission's regulations governing electric service can found within: Ariz. Admin. Code §§ 14-2-201–14-2-213; gas, Ariz. Admin. Code §§ 14-2-301–14-2-314; water, Ariz. Admin. Code §§ 14-2-401–14-2-411; telephone, Ariz. Admin. Code §§ 14-2-501–14-2-510; sewer, Ariz. Admin. Code §§ 14-2-601–14-2-610. Many of the regulations governing gas, telephone, water, and sewer service are similar in substance and form to the regulations governing electric service. Questions regarding these services may be answered by referencing the electric regulations governing a specific issue. Access to the regulations can be found at www.azsos.gov/public_services/Table_of_Contents.htm (last visited in May 2011).

***Electric*—Ariz. Admin. Code §§ 14-2-201–14-2-213**

* * *

§ 14-2-203. Establishment of Service:

A deposit or guarantee may be required to receive or continue to receive service due to issues related to nonpayment of services (disconnection, late payments, etc.) for past and present utility service. A deposit shall not exceed an actual or estimated average bill for 2 months of service and shall be returned, with interest (see tariff for rate) after 12 consecutive months with less than two late payments. The utility may review the customer's usage after service has been connected and adjust the deposit amount based upon the customer's actual usage. A utility may require a residential customer to establish or reestablish a deposit if the customer becomes delinquent in the payment of two bills within a 12-consecutive-month period or has been disconnected for service during the last 12 months.

A utility shall not require a deposit from a new applicant for residential service if the applicant is able to provide proof of comparable utility service within the past 2 years and was not delinquent in payment more than twice during the last 12 consecutive months or disconnected for nonpayment or credit verification from said utility service.

The utility shall provide the customer with a receipt for their deposit and the means to claim a deposit should the receipt become lost.

Each utility may make a charge as approved by the Commission for the establishment, reestablishment, or reconnection of utility services.

Service may be denied due to a hazardous condition, providing false information, indebtedness to a utility (unless payment arrangements and/or deposits have been made), or violation of utility rules.

§ 14-2-204. Minimum Customer Information Requirements:

Each electric utility must make available information regarding rates, rules, and regulations needed for its customers and applicants to obtain adequate and efficient service, the rights and responsibilities of a utility customer, and usage information.

* * *

§ 14-2-209. Meter Reading:

Meters shall be read monthly on as close to the same day as practical. Utility or customer may read meters, but utility shall get an actual reading at least once every 6 months. In the event the customer fails to submit the reading on time, the utility may issue the customer an estimated bill.

§ 14-2-210. Billing and Collection:

Bills shall be issued monthly and contain the customer's name, address, telephone or account number, billing period, all payment information and amounts due (late payments, charges, taxes, etc.), clear indication of an estimate, information relating to protections and available assistance, full description and itemization of activity and services, payments, adjustments, credits, and contact information for the provider and the Commission concerning inquiries and disputes. See regulation for specific guidelines allowing estimation of customer bills.

All bills are due and payable no later than 15 days from the date of the bill.

A bill shall be adjusted (refunded or back-billed) dating back to the date of the error, if known, but not longer than 3 months if a meter is found to be either fast or slow by at least 3%. If a meter is found to be not registering, back-billing shall not exceed a period of 3 months (1 year if there is evidence of inaccurate, false, or estimated information from a third party).

A utility may offer deferred or levelized payment plans (see regulation for specific requirements) for payment of charges. A utility shall not be required to offer a subsequent plan if a customer is in violation of a payment agreement.

A utility shall be allowed to assess a penalty when payment is returned for insufficient funds.

§ 14-2-211. Termination of Service:

Service may not be terminated due to issues related to nonpayment of another customer's bills, unregulated charges, a different class of service, a disputed bill, or failure to pay for under-billing if the customer agrees to enter into a payment plan.

Service shall not be terminated for nonpayment when termination would be especially dangerous to the health of an occupant of the residence due to medical condition, life support equipment, or weather and the customer is unable to pay. Service to ill, elderly or disabled persons shall not be disconnected until customer is provided with information concerning assistance in paying their bills (government assistance) and any third party designee has been contacted and has not made arrangements to pay. Customer may be required to enter into a reasonable payment plan to avoid termination of service.

Service may be terminated without notice due to a hazardous condition, meter tampering or fraud, or customer's failure to abide by usage curtailment requirements during shortages.

Notice of termination is required when termination is due to issues related to nonpayment for services, denial of access to utility equipment, or breach of a contract between the customer and the utility.

Notice shall be at least 5 days before the scheduled date of termination and shall include the reasons for disconnection, the amount due, date of disconnection, availability of payment plans and assistance, delay option for medical reasons, and complaint procedures. Termination shall be preceded by a personal visit from a utility representative.

For individually metered premises where the landlord is the customer, the utility shall notify the tenant of the option of subscribing for service in the tenant's own name. However, the utility may not attempt to recover from the tenant or condition service to the tenant on the payment of any outstanding bills or other charges due from the outstanding account of the landlord. If the tenant declines to subscribe for individual service or arrange for payment of the tenant's outstanding balance, if applicable, the utility may disconnect service without further notice no earlier than the date scheduled for disconnection.

§ 14-2-212. Administrative and Hearing Requirements:

Each utility shall make a full and prompt investigation of all service complaints. See regulation for specific complaint procedures, rights, and options to appeal utility decisions to the Commission.

* * *

***Gas*, Ariz. Admin. Code §§ 14-2-301–14-2-314; *Water*, Ariz. Admin. Code §§ 14-2-401–14-2-411; *Telephone*, Ariz. Admin. Code §§ 14-2-501–14-2-510; *Sewer*, Ariz. Admin. Code §§ 14-2-601–14-2-610**

Many of the regulations governing gas, telephone, water, and sewer service are similar in substance and form to the regulations governing electric service. Questions regarding these services may be answered by referencing the electric regulations governing a specific issue.

ARKANSAS

Regulations relating to electric, gas and water are located in Arkansas Public Service Commission General Service Rules, 126-03-003 Ark. Code R. §§ 1.01–8.07. Regulations relating to telecommunications are located in Arkansas Public Service Commission Telecommunications Providers Rules, 126-03-014 Ark. Code R. §§ 1.01–16.01. The Rules regarding telecommunications are substantially similar to the General Service Rules, and differences are noted.

Website: http://170.94.29.3/rules_select2.asp (last visited in May 2011).

***Electric, Gas, and Water*, Ark. Pub. Serv. Comm'n Gen. Serv. Rules—126-03-003 Ark. Code R. §§ 1.01–8.07**

§ 2.01. Information on Utility Service:

* * *

§ 2.01.B. Information Requirements:

Utility shall provide in written form to each applicant and upon request the following information based on class of service: rates for basic service, riders, discounts, options, and other information affecting choice of service within the service class; approved fees and charges; available billing plans and options; rules and procedures for deposits; billing and estimated billing rules and procedures; an itemized bill description, if not shown on the bill; procedures for verifying bill accuracy; any automatic adjustment charge; instructions on reading meters; rules and procedures for paying bills, including payment to authorized payment agents; rules and procedures for a delayed payment agreement; rules and procedures for suspension, reconnection, and termination of service; options to avoid shut-off of service when absent for an extended period; third-party notification procedures; rules and procedures for avoiding shut-off in the event of a serious medical condition or to elder or disabled customers; shut-off rules and procedures for landlords and tenants; local and/or toll-free telephone numbers, address of local business offices, and a statement that customer may obtain a list of authorized payment agents; procedures for making a complaint to the utility and PSC; toll-free and local telephone numbers, and mailing and street addresses of PSC; a statement that General Service Rules are available through each utility business office. These brochures must be in plain language, in a format that is easy to read and understand.

§ 2.02. Directory Listing for Utility Billing and Services:

Utility shall list, in the directory of each telecommunications company providing basic local service in any area that the utility serves, a toll-free telephone number (including a collect call accepted by the utility) that customers may call to report problems or ask about bills or services.

§ 2.03. Customer Notice of Rule and Service Changes:

Utilities shall advise customers at least annually of changes to the General Service Rules made by the PSC. If a utility intends to change the character or type of service in a way that would substantially affect service or operation of any device, appliance, or equipment, it shall notify affected customers at least 30 days before the change.

§ 2.04. Service, Usage, and Billing History Information:

Customers or former customers may obtain the following information from local utilities' business offices upon request: statement of account record for at least 2 years; for electric and gas utilities, a clear statement of customer's actual energy consumption for each billing period during the prior 13 months; and information and assistance as is reasonable for the customer to obtain safe and efficient service and appliances properly adjusted to the service provided.

§ 2.05. Customer Service:

Utility shall have personnel available during business hours with authority to make delayed payment agreements and handle customer questions and complaints. Customers shall have toll-free telephone access to the appropriate business office, and a collect call accepted by the utility is considered to be a toll-free call.

When a customer informs a utility of difficulty paying a bill, the utility shall inform the customer of rights and obligations regarding delayed payment agreements and refer the customer to personnel with the authority to make such payment arrangements.

Rule 2.05(D) sets detailed standards for call centers: answer time, percentage of busy-outs, etc. Performance must be measured monthly, using actual performance data. Automated system must offer option to speak with real person, and 80% of such calls should be answered within 30 seconds of customer's election. Automated systems must enable customer to indicate within 25 seconds that they are reporting a condition that is a threat to public safety, and these calls must be given top priority.

§ 2.06. Complaints to the Utility:

Utility shall fully and promptly investigate all complaints and maintain a complaint record as required by General Service Rule 7.04. A customer may not be required to visit the business office to make a complaint. Complaints may be either written or oral. If a customer disputes a reason for shutting off service, service shall not be suspended while the utility or the PSC processes the complaint. A deposit equal to the disputed amount may be required while the complaint is processed if the reason for shutting off service is for: nonpayment after due date; non-compliance with a PSC order, delayed payment agreement, or extension agreement; failure to pay a deposit; unauthorized service or tampering with equipment; nonpayment of a billed Commission-approved charge; or damaging utility property or not paying for same. The customer must pay any undisputed amounts by the date shown on shut-off notice to avoid suspension. If the utility is in error, the deposit will be refunded with interest. Failure to make a deposit does not prevent customer from complaining to PSC, but the utility may suspend service for some other valid reason (set out in Rule 6.01) while the utility or PSC processes the complaint.

A utility shall report the results of its investigation to the complainant by telephone, mail, or in person within 3 business days of its completion. If the complaint is not resolved, the customer shall be advised of right to complain to PSC, including the PSC addresses and telephone numbers.

§ 2.07. Complaints to the Commission:

§ 2.07.A. Informal Complaints:

Informal complaints may be written or oral and should include name, address, name of the utility involved, account number, detailed reason for complaint, and desired result.

Within 3 business days after receipt, PSC shall explain complaint procedures to customer by telephone or in writing and give complaint details to the utility.

The utility shall respond to Commission request for information no later than 15 calendar days after receipt and shall not initiate contact or correspond with the customer unless first authorized by PSC Consumer Services Office.

* * *

§ 2.07.A(6). Effect of Complaint on Suspension:

Substantially similar to General Services Rule 2.06.

§§ 2.07.A(7), (8). Commission Investigation and Report; Disputed Results:

The PSC shall investigate each informal complaint, issue an investigation report to the complainant, and notify the utility of the investigation results. The utility or the complainant may file a formal complaint if not satisfied with the results, and the PSC shall provide information to the complainant explaining formal complaint procedures.

§ 2.07B. Formal Complaints:

Any consumer or prospective consumer of any utility service may complain to the PSC about the service, furnishing of service, or discrimination in service or rates, after first making a complaint to the utility. Complaints made to the PSC shall be filed according to the PSC's Rules of Practice and Procedure.

§ 3.01. Application for Service:

A utility may not unreasonably discriminate in processing applications. It must give priority to applications involving a medical emergency or public health and safety. Time frames for connection are set by Commission's Special Rules.

Requests for new service, additional service, transfer of service, or change in service may be made in writing, or orally at the utility's discretion. Records of written or verbal applications for services shall be maintained as required by General Service Rule 7.01. Gas and water utilities without an allocated territory are not required to consider requests for service when it is not feasible to provide the facilities.

* * *

§ 3.01.E. Information Provided at Time of Application:

Utility shall: offer information about all rates, payment plans, and equipment options available for the applicant's class of service; explain billing cycle and past-due dates; explain requirements and payment options if a cooperative membership fee, security deposit, or guaranty is required; and provide an expected service date.

* * *

§ 3.03. Extension of Service:

Extension of facilities shall be made according to PSC Special Rules, an Extension of Service Agreement if the applicant is required to pay any cost, and the utility's approved extension of facilities tariff. The cost of extension shall be based on the most economically feasible route from the nearest point of connection to the applicant's point of delivery. If service is to be provided, the utility shall provide the Extension of Service Agreement and explain payment options within 30 days of receipt of the application or provide an explanation for delay if additional time is needed. An applicant may be required to sign an Extension of Service Agreement before construction begins if the applicant is required to pay costs. The Extension of Service Agreement shall include the following applicable information: applicant's name and address; date of application; location and description of the service point; engineering study summary; construction route outline; explanation of all costs; estimated construction start and completion dates; payment terms; and any customer reimbursement. Utility shall attempt to identify and notify residents in the general area of a proposed extension of service and provide an opportunity to participate.

§ 3.04. Refusing Service:

A utility may refuse service to an applicant only for: nonpayment of a bill in the applicant's name for the same service at the premises, except for nonpayment for merchandise or non-utility services purchased, rented, or leased from or through the utility; nonpayment of a bill to a former customer at applicant's residence following relocation of the applicant and former customer to new premises; nonpayment of a bill at premises where the former customer, full-time occupant, or full-time user of the service remains at the premises; non-compliance with a PSC order, delayed payment agreement, or extension agreement; failure to pay an approved fee, charge, or deposit; failure to provide adequate assurance of payment for service within 20 days of an order for relief under the United States Bankruptcy Code; unauthorized use of service or tampering with utility equipment; misrepresentation by the applicant regarding conditions under which the applicant may obtain service; failure to provide acceptable identification; non-compliance with all state and/or municipal regulations governing the service applied for or with the utility's tariffs; unfavorable affect upon service to other customers; creation of hazard upon connection of service to the applicant's equipment; causing or threatening injury to a utility employee (or family member) to retaliate for or prevent an act the utility performs in the ordinary course; causing or threatening damage to utility property; or disconnection of party-line service within the previous 12 months because of unreasonable, unlawful, or abusive use of service.

* * *

§ 3.04.B. Notice to Applicant:

Utility shall give an explanation in writing of refusal of service within 7 business days, which shall include: the reason for refusing service; any conditions under which service would be provided; and the applicant's right to complain to the PSC, including the PSC's telephone numbers and addresses.

§ 3.05. Disputed Charge—Providing Service:

If a utility refuses service for nonpayment of a disputed previous bill, the applicant may complain to the PSC. A utility may require a deposit of the disputed amount before providing service, or it may waive the deposit. Upon either receipt or waiver of the deposit, the utility shall provide service pending final disposition of the dispute.

Upon resolution of the complaint, any part of the deposit found to be due the applicant shall be promptly refunded with interest from the date of the deposit.

§ 4.01. Deposits from Applicants:

A utility may not require a deposit as a condition of service unless: applicant cannot provide satisfactory payment history for same kind of service for the previous 12 months; applicant has an undisputed past-due unpaid account for previous utility service; applicant did not pay bills from the utility by the close of business on the due date either twice in a row or three times in the last 12 months; applicant gave the utility two or more checks for previous service within the preceding 12-month period which were returned unpaid for reasons other than bank error; applicant's service from the utility has been suspended during the last 24 months for nonpayment of any undisputed past-due bill(s), misrepresentation of the applicant's identity in obtaining service, failure to reimburse utility for damages due to negligent or intentional acts, or obtaining, diverting, or using service without the utility's authorization or knowledge; or applicant provided materially false information upon application for service or within the preceding 2-year period that is relevant to the conditions of obtaining service.

* * *

§ 4.01.B–C. Amounts; Payment Procedures:

Deposit may not be more than two average bills as defined in General Service Rule 4.03 if payment for service is due after service begins or more than one average bill if payment for service is due before service begins, except that utility may obtain deposit from landlord not exceeding estimated bill for three average billing periods.

If utility discovers that applicant has used service without authorization or tampered with equipment, it may charge applicant a total deposit of not more than six average bills, plus the potential damage to utility equipment. This deposit may not charged if the customer has received more than 2 years of cumulative service since the utility discovered the unauthorized use or tampering.

If utility has proof of a misrepresentation by the applicant relevant to the conditions under which service may be obtained, it may charge that applicant a total deposit of not more than twice the maximum bill. This deposit may not be charged if the customer has received more than 2 years of cumulative service since the utility discovered the misrepresentation.

The utility may require a debtor in bankruptcy to furnish adequate assurance of payment in the form of a deposit or other security in accordance with the United States Bankruptcy Code (11 U.S.C. § 366).

If an applicant has an unpaid bill from previous service from the utility, the utility may require a deposit equal to twice the maximum billing.

An applicant may pay a deposit in two installments, one-half before receiving service and one-half with the first bill, unless the deposit is required because the applicant used service without authorization or tampered with equipment. Receipts for deposits shall be given upon request.

§ 4.02. Deposits from Customers:

Utility may require a new deposit or an increase in deposit for the following reasons: failure to pay a bill before the close of business on the shut-off date within the previous 12 months; two or more checks were returned unpaid in previous 12 months for reasons other than bank error; failure to pay bills by the close of business on the due date twice in a row or three times in previous 12 months; within previous 24 months, customer misrepresented identity or other facts relevant to the conditions under which service was obtained or continued; unauthorized service, equipment tampering, or damage to equipment during previous 2 years; use of more service than the estimate on a deposit was based, except that additional deposit may not be charged after the first 12 months of service unless the customer transfers service to a new location; customer becomes debtor in bankruptcy, in which utility may require in accordance with the United States Bankruptcy Code (11 U.S.C. § 366) that customer furnish adequate assurance of payment in addition to deposits posted before bankruptcy filing.

* * *

§ 4.02.B–E. Amounts; Written Notice; Payment Procedures; Receipts:

If utility charges a new or additional deposit, the total amount on deposit may not exceed the total of the two highest bills during the previous 12 months, unless the reason for the new or additional deposit is for unauthorized use of service or tampering with equipment, in which case the total amount on deposit may not exceed the estimated bill for 6 average billing periods plus the cost of potential damage to equipment. A customer who becomes a debtor in bankruptcy may be required to furnish adequate assurance of payment in addition to deposits posted before bankruptcy.

A utility shall provide written explanation for any new or additional deposit, the amount of the deposit, when the deposit must be paid, and the consequences of nonpayment.

Except for deposits required as a result of unauthorized service or equipment tampering, customers may pay one-half of any new or additional deposit in equal installments with the next two bills, and a receipt shall be provided upon request.

§ 4.03. Calculation of Average Bill:

For seasonal customers, as defined in the utility's tariff, the average bill is the total of the monthly bills during the "season" divided by the number of months of usage during the season. For non-seasonal customers, the average bill is the total of the last 12 months' bills divided by 12. If a customer or an applicant has less than the required number of months' billing history, the average bill may not exceed the average monthly usage for the class and character of the service.

§ 4.04. Guaranty In Place of a Deposit:

Instead of a deposit, a utility shall accept the written guaranty of a qualified third party to pay an amount equal to the deposit. A third party who is a residential customer of the utility and who meets the following conditions is qualified to act as guarantor on one residential account: third party has no deposit on file on his or her own account, has had service for at least 12 months, has not made late payment more than twice in previous 12 months, and has not had service suspended for nonpayment in previous 12 months.

The utility may allow a customer to guarantee more than one account. A guarantor's liability is limited to the amount required for a deposit when the guaranty was made or a new or additional amount agreed to by the guarantor. A guaranty ends when a deposit is refunded or the guarantor's account is closed. The guarantor's agreement shall be in the form set forth in this rule, and the utility shall provide to the guarantor a copy signed by the utility and guarantor which clearly states the amount of the guarantor's liability. A utility may collect the guaranteed amount on the guarantor's account in the same manner as a charge for service.

§ 4.05. Interest Payment on Deposits:

Utilities shall pay simple interest annually at the rate established annually by the PSC pursuant to Ark. Code Ann. § 23-4-206, not to exceed 10%. Interest may not accrue after the date the utility has made and documented a good faith effort to return the deposit.

§ 4.06. Refunding Deposits:

A deposit shall be refunded if a customer has paid all bills by the due date for the previous 12 months, except that the deposit may be refunded when the account is closed if the reason for the deposit is unauthorized service or tampering with equipment, and utility will comply with United States Bankruptcy Code regarding refunding or retaining a deposit in the case of a customer in bankruptcy. Refunds may be made through a credit on the next billing cycle. When an account is closed, any deposit and accrued interest shall be applied to the amount due the utility, with any balance promptly refunded.

§ 4.07. Deposits and Customer Name Changes:

A utility may not require a customer to make or increase a deposit because of a name change, unless one or more of the conditions otherwise authorizing a new or increased deposit (Rule 4.02.A) applies.

§ 4.08. Deposits and Changes in Service Locations:

A utility may not charge an additional deposit if a customer requests that the same kind and class of service be transferred from one location to another serviced by the same utility and the transfer takes 90 days or less, unless one or more of the conditions otherwise authorizing a new or increased deposit (Rule 4.02.A) applies.

§ 5.01. Information on Bill:

Each bill shall contain the following information: name and account number; if non-metered service, the beginning and ending dates of the billing period and the basic rate schedule designation; net amount of all payments and credits made during the billing period; any previous balance due; amount of any "late payment charge" and an explanation of when it will apply; date the bill was mailed; due date; all charges or credits, including deposit installments or refunds, automatic adjustments, customer or minimum charges, taxes, charges for other utility service, and charges for non-utility merchandise, service, or equipment.

Bills based on meter readings must also include: beginning and ending meter readings; dates of meter readings if read by the utility; number of days in billing period if meter is read by the utility; quantity of units consumed and billed; and rate schedule designation.

If used, estimated usage and industry-specific abbreviations for terms that explain the billing must be clearly shown on the bill.

Bills must include a statement that the customer may contact the utility regarding billing or service problems or a delayed payment agreement, including an address and toll-free number.

* * *

§ 5.03. Billing Periods and Standards:

Billing periods shall be no less than 25 days and no more than 35 days, unless it is the first or final bill, and no later than 30 days after a meter reading. If a change in a meter reading route or schedule alters a billing cycle by more than 5 days, the affected customers must be notified 30 days before the change. If payment is made at a business office, billing records shall show the date payment is received. If payment is made to an authorized payment agent before the utility's close of business on the due date, the account record shall show that the payment was not late. Affected customers shall be promptly notified of billing errors.

§§ 5.04, 5.05. Mailing Date; Due Dates:

Bills may not be mailed later than the mailing date shown on the bill. If no late charge is imposed, the due date may not be less than 14 calendar days after mailing date or not less than 22 calendar days if a late payment charge is imposed.

§ 5.06. Late Payment:

Payment may be considered late if received by the utility or its authorized agent after the utility's close of business on the due date. If the utility is not open on the due date, payment is timely if made by the close of business on the next day that the utility's business offices are open. Payment shall be late if a check is postdated beyond the due date or returned unpaid for reasons other than bank error. If late payment results from bank error, utility must correct customer's record to show that payment was not late. A late notice or suspension notice issued to any customer whose payment was received by the utility's close of business on the due date shall be deleted from the customer's account record.

§ 5.07. Late Payment Charges:

Late payment charges may be calculated only on an overdue portion of a bill and may not exceed 10% of the first $30 dollars or 2% of the remainder.

§ 5.08. Estimated Usage for Billing:

A utility may not estimate usage for more than two consecutive bills except when the meter is inaccessible. After a second estimated reading when the meter is inaccessible, the utility must notify the customer in writing that the meter is inaccessible and specify the action required of the customer to correct the situation. If usage is estimated, utility shall use the customer's consumption for the same time during the previous year and may apply a weather-sensitive factor to the consumption in its calculation. If no figures are available for the previous year, a utility shall use the class average to estimate consumption.

§ 5.09. Extended Due-Date Policy:

Utilities must offer an extended due-date policy to: persons receiving Aid to Families with Dependent Children (AFDC) or Aid to the Aged, Blind and Disabled (AABD); persons receiving Supplemental Security Income; or persons whose primary source of income is Social Security or Veterans Administration disability or retirement benefits. The utility may require verification of these income sources. A qualifying customer's utility bill payment due date will be changed to coincide with or follow the customer's receipt of that income. When a customer applies for an extended due date, utilities shall explain the policy and give the explanation in writing.

Customers who qualify and who pay by the new date will not be considered late, but a late payment charge may be imposed on participants who do not pay by the extended due date. Utilities may remove an extended due date for failure to pay bills by the close of business on the due date two times in a row or any three times in the last 12 months, and customers shall be notified in writing when the extended due date has been removed.

§ 5.10. Levelized Billing Plans for Electric and Gas Utilities:

Electric and gas utilities must provide levelized billing plans for qualifying customers. A customer on a levelized billing plan who becomes delinquent may be removed from the plan and, if the customer qualifies, the company may offer a delayed payment agreement if the customer qualifies.

Applicants must be told about levelized billing plans upon application for service, and qualifying customers may enter the plan at any time. A processing fee may be charged if a customer withdraws from a plan more than once in 12 months. Upon withdrawing from a levelized billing plan, the customer shall have the option of paying the account balance in full, or under a delayed payment agreement, if qualified. If a levelized billing customer terminates service, the utility shall refund any net credit by check and if such a customer withdraws from a plan, any credit shall be refunded within 30 days. An overpayment may be refunded by billing credit unless the customer requests otherwise.

§ 5.11. Extended Absence Payment Procedure:

Utilities shall maintain bill payment options to avoid suspension of service for customers who are away for an extended period of time.

§ 5.12. Method of Payment:

Payment may be made in any reasonable manner, including cash or check payable to the utility. Payment by check may be refused if the customer has given the utility two checks in the previous 12 months that were returned unpaid for reasons other than bank error. Utility may refuse second check for the same bill if the first check was returned unpaid for reasons other than bank error.

§ 5.13. Returned Check Charge:

Customer may be charged a PSC-approved handling fee for checks returned for reasons other than bank error.

§ 5.14. Partial Payments:

Partial payment of a bill that includes charges for non-utility service shall be first credited to past charges for utility service unless there is a disputed bill, a delayed payment agreement, or the customer otherwise specifies in writing.

§ 5.15. Overpayments:

Overpayments shall be credited to the account unless the customer requests otherwise.

If a customer requests a refund after being notified of an overpayment, the utility shall refund the overpayment within 30 days.

§ 5.16. Meter Reading Requirements:

If utility allows a customer to read his or her own meter, the utility shall read that customer's meter at least once every 12 months. The utility shall leave a meter reading report at customer's request, and the customer must renew the request before each reading. Customer is allowed two free reports every 12 months or one if the meter is read annually by the utility, and utility may charge for additional reports. Meter reading reports shall include the date and time of the reading and the meter reading either in numbers or as a diagram showing the positions of the hands on the dial at the time of the reading.

§ 5.17. Billing Metered Service:

Service shall be measured by meters (except for minor incidental use where metering is not practical), and bills for metered service must be based on meter readings unless otherwise provided by tariff.

§ 5.18. Meter Tests at Customer or Commission Request:

A utility shall test a meter for accuracy if requested by the customer. The utility must: inform the customer before testing of any fee that will be charged; give the customer opportunity to withdraw the test request before incurring such charge; inform the customer that there will be no charge if the meter is not as accurate as required by PSC rules; identify when metered will be tested; and inform the customer that the customer and the customer's representative may be present. If a meter must be removed to be tested, the utility shall prevent damage or tampering. The utility shall provide a written report within 10 days after a test, which shall include the date of the customer's test request, the location and date of the test, the meter's identification number, the test results, the PSC Special Rules which apply, and whether the meter's accuracy was in compliance with those rules. Substantially the same procedure applies if a customer asks the PSC for a meter test without first asking the utility.

If a test shows a meter to be as accurate as required by PSC rules, the customer may be charged. If the meter is not as accurate as required, no fee may be charged and the utility must correct the customer's bill as required by General Service Rule 5.19. If a utility tests a meter more than once for a single request and any one of the tests shows the meter not meeting PSC's required accuracy, no fee for any such test may be charged.

§ 5.19. Billing Corrections:

A correction to a customer's account shall be made for meter error exceeding the tolerances permitted by the Commission's Special Rules. The period of correction shall be from the date the meter first became inaccurate, if ascertainable, and end on the date the inaccurate meter was removed. If the first date of the period cannot be determined, the period shall begin 6 months prior to the date of removal. If actual usage cannot be determined, the customer's usage for the same period of the previous year shall be used, using the rates effective during the period of correction. A utility may apply a weather-sensitive factor in calculating the estimated usage for the correction period. If no customer usage data is available for the previous year, the utility shall use the class average to estimate consumption.

* * *

§ 5.19.B. Procedures for Correcting an Over-Billing:

When over-billing occurs, the utility shall explain the correction and refund the amount within 30 days after discovering or being notified of the error. The refund shall be credited to the customer's account unless the customer requests otherwise and shall include interest on the over-billed amount if the over-billing was the utility's fault.

§§ 5.19.C–D. Procedures for Correcting an Under-Billing; Tampering:

If a utility discovers an under-billing, it shall explain the error and offer a delayed payment agreement. If the under-billing occurred over one or more billing periods, the customer must be given at least the same period to pay the under-billing under a delayed payment agreement. If the under-billing was the customer's fault, the utility may charge interest for the period of under-billing. The utility does not have to offer a delayed payment agreement if the under-billing was caused by unauthorized use or tampering with equipment. If a customer tampers with equipment, the utility may charge a reasonable amount for damage and for estimated service. The estimated service may be based on the customer's average lawful usage for the most recent 12-month period, or the class average if such figures are not available.

§ 5.20. Separate Metering and Billing:

Premises shall be separately metered and billed if they are on different non-contiguous tracts of land. Premises on the same tract or contiguous tracts of land may be master metered provided that the premises: are operated as one location by an individual customer; are physically integrated with each other; provide a complete service or produce a complete product; are similar in terms of energy use; and are in the same service territory. Tracts of land separated by public streets, public roads, or public alleys are considered contiguous. The customer shall own and pay for all facilities beyond the master meter and shall pay all costs related to the installation, removal, and rearrangement of such facilities necessary to allow service through a single meter.

Utilities shall separately meter and bill separate premises even if commonly owned or under common ownership. Utilities may not combine metering and billing unless otherwise permitted in this rule.

Gas and electric utilities may not install master meters or combine individual bills in any newly constructed residential complexes two stories or less and in manufactured home parks, excluding dormitories, hotels, and motels. Gas and electric utilities shall offer individual meters for all premises not covered by this rule when both multiple individual usage and master metering is possible.

A utility or building owner may apply for an exemption from this rule's limitations on master metering. The criteria for exemption from master-metering requirements include energy efficiency or conservation and accurate price signals to users.

§ 5.21. Transferring Past Due Balances to Other Accounts:

A past-due balance from a customer's closed account may only be transferred to an account of the same customer for the same class of service at any location or to the account of the customer's guarantor as allowed under Rule 4.04.

§ 6.01. Authorized Suspension:

A utility may suspend service only for the following reasons: failure to pay a bill before the close of business on the last day to pay as shown on the most recent shut-off notice; nonpayment of a bill at premises where the former customer, full-time occupant, or full-time user of the service remains at the premises; nonpayment of a bill incurred by former customer at a location during a time when a current customer and the former customer lived together at the former location; non-compliance with PSC order, delayed payment agreement, or extension agreement; failure to pay a required deposit; unauthorized use of service or tampering with equipment; misrepresentation of fact relevant to the conditions under service was obtained or continued; nonpayment of PSC-approved charge; refusing utility reasonable access to equipment; violation of rules regarding interference with service to other customers or the operation of nonstandard equipment or unauthorized attachment, if the customer was first notified and given opportunity to comply; violation of federal, state, or local laws or regulations regarding use of service; abandoning the premises served; causing or threatening injury to a utility employee or employee's family to prevent or to retaliate for an act the utility performs in the ordinary course of business; causing or threatening to cause damage to utility property; not paying for damage to utility equipment on the customer's premises; or the existence of a health or safety hazard.

§ 6.02. Unauthorized Suspension:

Service may not be suspended for nonpayment for: non-utility merchandise or services purchased, rented, or leased from or through the utility; a different kind or class of service; or service received under a separate active account.

§ 6.03. Bankruptcy:

Service may not be suspended to a trustee or debtor in bankruptcy for nonpayment of a bill incurred prior to bankruptcy filing if the trustee or the debtor pays a deposit under Rule 4.02.A. within 20 days of the order for relief in bankruptcy. Service may not be suspended during such 20-day period and, if suspended, must be reconnected upon debtor's request, but service may be suspended after such 20-day period if deposit has not been paid.

§ 6.04.A. Notification of Suspension of Service:

A utility must provide written notice 5 calendar days before it suspends service. If delivered to the customer's premises, the notice must be left in a conspicuous place. If mailed, the 5 days begins 3 calendar days after the date the notice is placed in the U.S. mail and addressed to the customer's last known address.

§ 6.04.B. Suspension Without Prior Written Notice:

Service may be suspended without prior written notice for: non-compliance with PSC order, delayed payment agreement, or extension agreement; unauthorized use or tampering with equipment; causing or threatening injury to a utility employee or employee's family to prevent or to retaliate against an act the utility performs in the ordinary course of business; causing or threatening to cause damage to utility property; not paying for damage to utility equipment on the customer's premises; or the existence of a health or safety hazard.

The utility shall notify the customer of the reason for suspension by first class mail or by leaving a notice at the premises, unless prior written notice has been given. Utility shall otherwise follow suspension requirements of Rule 6.09.B.

* * *

§ 6.06. Third-Party Notification of Suspension:

Customer may name a consenting person or agency to receive a copy of all shut-off notices, and a utility shall mail one copy of all shut-off notices to both the customer and such other person or agency.

§ 6.07. Form and Contents of Shut-Off Notice:

Shut-off notices shall contain the following information: the title "SHUT-OFF NOTICE," "CUT-OFF NOTICE," or "DISCONNECT NOTICE" in type at least one-quarter inch high; customer's name, address, and service address, if different; reason for suspension and any overdue amount; explanation of what to do to avoid suspension; date after which service will be suspended if customer does not take appropriate action; a statement that customer may qualify to pay the bill in installments to avoid shut-off but that the customer must ask for a delayed payment agreement by the close of the last business day shown on the notice to make payment; a statement that a customer who has a serious medical condition, is 65 or older, or is disabled may qualify for delaying suspension; for electric and gas utilities, a statement that the customer contact the utility to obtain the names of federal, state, and local bill payment assistance agencies; the cost and requirements to reconnect service; the charges if utility personnel must go to the premises to collect; telephone number and address of the office to bill, make payment arrangements, or make a complaint; and a statement that any customer with an unresolved complaint may contact the PSC, including the PSC's mailing and street address and local and toll-free numbers.

§ 6.08. Payment Requirements to Prevent Suspension:

To avoid suspension, customer must pay the utility or its authorized agent before the utility's close of business on the last day to pay as shown on the most recent shut-off notice. The utility may require the customer to pay applicable approved collection fees or late charges to prevent suspension. A customer may not be required to pay for usage that has not been billed, or billed but not overdue, to prevent suspension. Payment made within 24 hours after the utility's close of business on the last day to pay shall not prevent the utility from suspending service and charging a reconnect fee if service was suspended. A utility may not refuse payment made on an account after the utility's close of business on the last day to pay, but it is not required to reconnect service if such payment is less than the amount required by the utility before reconnection.

§ 6.09. Suspension Procedures:

Service may be suspended only during normal utility business office hours, excluding the last normal business office hour and a day or the preceding day when the utility does not have employees available to authorize reconnection. If a utility issued more than one shut-off notice, it may not suspend service before the close of business on the last day to pay shown on the most recent shut-off notice, unless the utility may otherwise suspend service without prior written notice under Rule 6.04. A utility must suspend service within 30 days after the last day to pay unless suspension is delayed under PSC rules or the reason for the suspension has been eliminated.

Utility employees suspending service shall identify themselves to the customer or any other adult at the premises, give the reason for being there, and accept payment if offered or honor a receipt from the utility or a canceled check showing payment. Payment in cash may be refused if the customer is given 24 hours to pay at the business office or the customer has given two checks within the last year that were returned for reasons other than bank error. If the customer or other adult is not present or does not respond, the employee must leave a notice in a conspicuous place containing the following: a statement that service has been suspended and the reasons for suspension; the address and telephone number to arrange for reconnection; the amount past due and any approved collection charge; and the action and payment necessary for reconnection.

§ 6.10. Closing Suspended Accounts:

A utility shall not close a suspended account until a customer has been given 7 calendar days to have service reconnected after suspension. Once an account is closed, a utility may treat a former customer who wants service again as an applicant.

§ 6.11. Collection Fees:

A utility may charge a PSC-approved collection fee if the last day to pay printed on the shut-off notice has passed and a utility employee accepts payment at the premises under Rule 6.09 or visits the premises to collect at the customer's request.

§ 6.12. Reconnection of Service:

The utility shall reconnect service at customer's request if all reasons for suspension have been eliminated. Reconnection shall be in the normal course of business if suspension was the customer's fault or immediately if suspension was the utility's fault. Customer may not be required to pay for usage that has not been billed or that has been billed but is not overdue before reconnection. Utility may require payment of any PSC-approved collection, late charge, or reconnection fees if suspension is in accordance with applicable PSC rules. If the suspension is for unauthorized use of service or tampering with equipment, the utility may require a reasonable payment for damage to equipment and estimated usage before reconnection or refuse to reconnect unless the PSC orders otherwise.

§ 6.13. Delayed Payment Agreement and Extension Agreement:

If a customer whose average bill for the most recent 12 months is $200 or less informs the utility that he or she is having difficulty making payment, the utility shall explain that delayed payment agreements are available and inform the customer of his rights and obligations under such an agreement.

If such a customer requests a payment extension of less than 30 calendar days from the payment due date, the utility may offer to enter an extension agreement instead of a delayed payment agreement. The utility shall inform the customer of its rights to suspend service without prior written notice if the customer fails to comply with an extension agreement.

A utility shall offer and enter into a delayed payment agreement if the customer agrees to pay the down payment and all installments by the due dates and pay all bills coming due during the period of the agreement in full by each due date. A utility may not limit the number of delayed payment agreements a customer may enter into if the customer otherwise qualifies.

A utility is not required to enter into a delayed payment agreement: if the customer has not complied with the terms of a delayed payment agreement in the last 12 months, including failure to pay an agreed-upon down payment within 3 business days but excluding when a utility corrects an under-billing; after the last day to pay printed on the most recent shut-off notice has passed except when Rules 6.16 (social service agency payment) or 6.17 (medical necessity) apply; if the customer is bound by a current delayed payment agreement; if the customer has engaged in unauthorized use of service or has tampered with equipment in the last 24 months; or if a customer has misrepresented a fact relevant to the conditions under which service was obtained or continued in the last 24 months.

A utility may require some form of identification of the customer or the person making the agreement and may refuse to enter into the agreement if the information is not provided or is not acceptable evidence of identity.

All delayed payment agreements shall be in writing and, if arranged by telephone, the utility shall send or give the customer a copy of the agreement within 5 business days of receiving the customer's down payment. A utility may require the customer to sign the agreement and return it within 10 calendar days of the making of the agreement, but the customer's signature is not necessary for validity and enforcement of a documented agreement.

The utility may not require more than one-quarter of the overdue bill as the down payment in order to enter into an agreement, and the customer may make at least three monthly installment payments from the date of the down payment to pay the balance. Interest may be charged on delayed payment agreement installment payments.

Down payment and period of installment restrictions do not apply when the agreement is reached as the result of an underbilling.

If a customer can show a change in ability to pay due to a serious medical condition or the loss of a major source of income, the utility must document a good faith effort to renegotiate a delayed payment agreement once during the term. The customer loses the right to renegotiate for failure to keep any term of the agreement if the agreement is not kept.

A utility may suspend service without prior written notice if a customer does not comply with the terms of a delayed payment agreement or extension agreement.

* * *

§ 6.15. Cold Weather Rule:

Electric and gas utilities may not suspend residential service on a day when the National Weather Service forecasts that a temperature of 32° Fahrenheit or lower will occur at any time during the following 24-hour period. The utility must obtain the most current forecast for the customer's weather zone from the National Weather Service reports on the morning of the day that the customer's shut-off is scheduled.

Gas utilities may not shut off service to low-income customers eligible for certain public benefits (including LIHEAP) between November 1 and March 31. Customers must inform the utility and provide written proof within 14 days that they have been approved for the public benefits. Customers must agree to a minimum monthly payment equal to the amount of a levelized billing plan payment and enter into a delayed payment agreement for the deferred amount and any existing arrearage, to be paid off between April and October. In case of fraud, misuse, or failure to make required payments, the utility may initiate Commission-approved suspension procedures. A second suspension moratorium will not be permitted to a customer who owes money on a previous agreement.

§ 6.16. Agency Guaranty of Payment:

If a social service agency agrees to pay at least one-quarter of an overdue bill, service shall be continued—or restored, if suspended for nonpayment—if the customer qualifies for and agrees to pay any remaining overdue amounts and any additional deposit under a delayed payment agreement, with the agency payment deemed the down payment for the delayed payment agreement. The utility may verify any notice received from such agency and require written confirmation of an oral agreement within 10 days of the date of oral agreement. If an account remains unpaid 40 days after an agency notifies a utility that it will be making a payment, service may be suspended after giving the customer an additional 5-calendar-day written notice.

§ 6.17. Medical Need for Utility Service:

Utilities must honor a physician's certificate in the prescribed form attesting that a customer or permanent resident of the household has a serious medical condition and stating that suspension of service would result in a substantial risk of death or grave impairment to the health of the customer or permanent household resident.

Notice of such a serious medical condition may be given in person, by telephone, or in writing by a physician, nurse, nurse practitioner, physician's assistant, or public or private agency providing physical or mental health care services. Upon being notified, a utility must inform the health care professional that a physician's certificate is required within 7 days and shall postpone suspension or reconnect service that has been suspended for 30 days or less. The utility is not required to continue to provide service after 30 days unless the medical certificate is renewed and may suspend service if it does not receive the requested physician's certificate within 7 days.

Upon receipt of the certificate, the utility shall mail or delivery a written notice of its receipt to an adult at the customer's residence that includes the date the certificate was received, the date postponement of suspension or reconnection of service was commenced, the date the postponement of suspension or reconnection will expire, an explanation of the right to renew the certificate, and the last day the customer has to renew the certificate. The notice may be delivered by first class mail or by delivery to an adult person at the residence.

The utility may, at its own expense, seek an opinion from a second physician. Failure to attend the required medical appointment without good cause is grounds for suspension of service. If the second opinion indicates that grounds do not exist for delaying suspension, the utility may suspend, after giving 5 days' notice. The telephone rules include this too.

A customer may renew a certificate once for an additional 30 days by providing a new certificate before the initial 30-day time period expires. A utility does not have to accept more than one physician's certificate per household each year, and delaying suspension or reconnecting service does not excuse the customer from paying for service. Upon expiration of the certification, the utility must provide 5 days' written notice of suspension in accordance with Rule 6.04.

§ 6.18. Elderly and Handicapped:

Utilities shall attempt to identify and inform eligible elder and disabled persons that a program for such qualifying customers exists and—upon request for service, inquiry of options for elder or disabled customers, or when contacted by a customer about suspension—ask such persons if they wish to be registered.

At least 72 hours before suspending service to an identified elder or disabled account, the utility must make two attempts at different times of day to contact in person or by telephone the customer, an adult at the premises, or someone previously designated by the customer. If successful, the utility shall offer to explain what can be done to avoid suspension and the payment and assistance options available. If unsuccessful, the utility must, before suspending service, give 24 hours' written notice explaining what can be done to avoid suspension. If the notice is delivered to the customer's premises, it must be left in a conspicuous place. If mailed, the twenty-four hours begins 3 calendar days after the date the notice is postmarked.

When informed that an identified elder or disabled customer cannot pay a bill on time or upon contacting an identified elder or disabled customer prior to suspension, the utility shall: offer to arrange a delayed payment agreement or, for electric and gas service, arrange for levelized billing; explain the right to a third-party notice before suspension; and provide the names of federal, state, and local bill payment assistance agencies.

* * *

§ 6.18.E. Hot Weather Protection:

An electric or gas utility may not suspend residential service to an elder or disabled customer on a day when the National Weather Service forecasts a temperature of 95° Fahrenheit or higher at any time during the following 24-hour period. For gas utilities, hot weather protection is limited to elder or disabled air conditioning customers. The forecast for the customer's weather zone must be obtained from the National Weather Service reports on the morning of the scheduled shut-off day.

Service may be suspended if a customer gives false information to qualify as elder or disabled.

§ 6.19. Provisions for Landlords and Tenants:

Each utility shall file procedures for identifying accounts when service is provided at an address different from the billing address. The procedures may include requiring landlords to identify themselves as landlords and to identify their tenants by name, address, and account number. Without such identification, a utility is not required to treat a customer as a tenant unless it has actual knowledge or reliable information that the person receiving service is a tenant.

A utility shall not suspend service to an identified tenant for nonpayment without first sending a suspension notice to the landlord. If no response is received from the landlord within 7 days of mailing, the utility shall: post a suspension notice in conspicuous locations or mail a suspension notice to all tenants at least 14 days before suspending service; wait at least 30 days after the due date of the landlord's bill before suspending service; and allow any tenant to apply for service in the tenant's name if separate metering is feasible. A utility may not recover from a tenant, or condition service to a tenant on, payment of any amounts owed by the landlord.

§ 6.20. Stopping Service at Customer Request:

A customer who wants to stop service must notify utility at least 5 days before the requested disconnection date. The notice period begins on the day the customer telephones the utility or personally informs the local business office or three days after the customer mails notice to the utility. The customer is not liable for service after the requested disconnection date if proper notice was given, and utility must confirm disconnection date upon customer's request.

§ 7.01. Application Records:

Each utility must keep a record of every written or verbal application for utility service for at least 2 years unless it is cancelled or withdrawn, except gas and water utilities without allocated territories need not consider a request for service as an application if service is not feasible. An application remaining active after the 2-year period must be kept until service is cancelled or withdrawn. Each application record shall include: name and current address of applicant; address of requested service location; date of request, class of service requested, and date service is desired; estimated service date; availability of facilities; date on which service was provided; or reason for delay or deferral.

§ 7.02. Account Records:

The utility shall keep a record of billings to, and all money paid by, each customer so that costs and payments for separate services can be identified, including customer name, mailing address, service location, account number, dates on which service was provided, meter readings, billed amounts, rate schedules and payment plans, any payment arrangements, and each transaction regarding a deposit. The accounts of elder and disabled customers shall be marked and a record kept of the handling of overdue accounts of such customers.

§ 7.03. Deposit Records:

When a deposit is made, the utility shall keep for at least 2 years a record of the following information for each customer account: the customer's name and service location; the date, amount, and reason for the deposit; each transaction regarding the deposit; and efforts to return the deposit.

§ 7.04. Complaint Records:

The utility shall keep for at least 3 years a record of customer complaints by specific type of complaint and showing the name and address of the complainant, account number, date and character of the complaint, action taken to resolve the complaint, and date of resolution. The record shall be maintained in a manner that allows reporting by name, account number or telephone number, and category.

§§ 7.05–7.07. Test and Inspection, Operating, and Service Records:

Utilities shall make a complete record of every required test or inspection, including the time, date, place, tester, inspector, and the results. Such records shall be kept for at least 2 years or as specified in the General Service Rules or Special Rules applicable to electric, gas, and water service. A utility must keep detailed records of the performance of its customer call center: calls attempted, busy signals, answer time, abandoned calls, etc. Such records shall be kept for at least 3 years. It must also keep records of service outages—date, place, cause, etc. Such records shall be kept for at least 2 years.

***Telecommunications, Telecommunications Providers Rules*—126-03-014 Ark. Code R. §§ 1.01–16.01**

* * *

§ 1.08. Interest Payment on Deposits:

Interest on deposits shall be paid at the rate set annually by the PSC, but in no event at more than 10%. Interest does not accrue after the date that the provider has made and documented a good faith effort to return the deposit.

* * *

§ 2.01. Service Information:

§ 2.01(B). Information Requirements:

Substantially similar to General Service Rule 2.01(B). In lieu of the brochures, the utility may provide the required information at the front of a directory distributed to all customers.

* * *

§ 2.02. Directory Listing for Billing and Services:

Substantially similar to General Service Rule 2.02.

§ 2.03. Customer Notice of Rule and Service Changes:

Substantially similar to General Service Rule 2.03.

§ 2.04. Service, Usage, and Billing History Information:

Substantially similar to General Service Rule 2.04.

§ 2.05. Customer Service:

Substantially similar to General Service Rule 2.05.

§ 2.06. Complaints to the Local Exchange Carrier:

Substantially similar to General Service Rule 2.06.

§ 2.07. Complaints to the Commission:

Substantially similar to General Service Rule 2.07.

§ 3.01. Application for Service:

Substantially similar to General Service Rule 3.01. LEC shall inform applicants that service connection fees may be billed in installments.

* * *

§ 3.03. Extension of Service:

Substantially similar to General Service Rule 3.03.

§ 3.04. Refusing Service:

Substantially similar to General Service Rule 3.04.

§ 3.05. Disputed Charge—Providing Service:

Substantially similar to General Service Rule 3.05.

§ 4.01. Deposits from Applicants:

Substantially similar to General Service Rule 4.01. Deposit may not exceed more than one average bill as defined in Rule 4.03 if payment for service is due before service begins.

§ 4.02. Deposits from Customers:

Substantially similar to General Service Rule 4.02. A customer may pay any new or additional deposit (except such deposits due to using service without authorization, or tampering with or damaging LEC equipment, during the last 2 years) in two installments by the due dates of the next two bills.

§ 4.03. Calculation of Average Bill:

The average bill shall be the total of the previous 4 months' bills divided by four unless the customer or applicant has less than 4 month's billing history, in which case the average bill may not exceed the anticipated amount of 1 month's bill.

§ 4.04. Guaranty In Place of a Deposit:

Substantially similar to General Service Rule 4.04.

§ 4.05. Refunding Deposits:

Substantially similar to General Service Rule 4.06.

§ 4.06. Deposits and Customer Name Changes:

Substantially similar to General Service Rule 4.07.

§ 4.07. Deposits and Changes in Service Locations:

Substantially similar to General Service Rule 4.08.

§ 5.01. Information on Bill:

Substantially similar to General Service Rule 5.01.

* * *

§ 5.03. Billing Periods and Standards:

Substantially the same as General Service Rule 5.03.

§ 5.04. Mailing Date:

Substantially similar to General Service Rule 5.04.

§ 5.05. Due Dates:

Substantially similar to General Service Rule 5.05.

§ 5.06. Late Payment:

Substantially similar to General Service Rule 5.06.

§ 5.07. Late Payment Charges:

Substantially similar to General Service Rule 5.07.

§ 5.08. Extended Due Date Policy:

Substantially similar to General Service Rule 5.09.

§ 5.09. Extended Absence Payment Procedure:

Substantially similar to General Service Rule 5.11.

§ 5.10. Method of Payment:

Substantially similar to General Service Rule 5.12.

§ 5.11. Returned Check Charge:

Substantially similar to General Service Rule 5.13.

§ 5.12. Partial Payments:

If a customer pays part of a bill for LEC service, an LEC shall first credit the payment to earlier charges for telecommunications service. This rule does not apply when there is a disputed bill, delayed payment agreement, or other written instructions.

§ 5.13. Overpayments:

Substantially similar to General Service Rule 5.15.

§ 5.14. Billing Corrections:

If local service is interrupted or out for more than 24 hours, an LEC shall refund a portion of the monthly charge for the number of days without service. Procedures are substantially similar to General Service Rules 5.19(B), (C), and (D).

§ 5.15. Transferring Past Due Balances to Other Accounts:

Substantially similar to General Service Rule 5.21.

§ 6.01. Authorized Suspension:

Substantially similar to General Service Rule 6.01.

§ 6.02. Unauthorized Suspension:

Substantially similar to General Service Rule 6.02, with the addition that an LEC may not suspend service for nonpayment by another telephone customer who has separate telephone service at the same location.

§ 6.03. Bankruptcy:

Substantially similar to General Service Rule 6.03.

§ 6.04. Notification of Suspension of Service:

Substantially similar to General Service Rule 6.04. An LEC may also suspend service without prior written notice for a misrepresentation of fact relating to conditions under which the applicant or customer obtained or continued service.

* * *

§ 6.06. Third-Party Notification of Suspension:

Substantially similar to General Service Rule 6.06.

§ 6.07. Form and Contents of Shut-Off Notice:

Substantially similar to General Service Rule 6.07.

§ 6.08. Payment Requirements to Prevent Suspension:

Substantially similar to General Service Rule 6.08.

§ 6.09. Suspension Procedures:

Substantially similar to General Service Rule 6.09(1)–(4).

§ 6.10. Closing Suspended Accounts:

Substantially similar to General Service Rule 6.10.

§ 6.11. Reconnection of Service:

Substantially similar to General Service Rule 6.12.

§ 6.12. Delayed Payment Agreement and Extension Agreement:

Substantially similar to General Service Rule 6.13. Unless the customer establishes that toll access is required due to medical condition or used to monitor a medical condition, an LEC may restrict toll-calling access as part of a delayed payment agreement if more than $100 is owed in toll charges on the bill for which the agreement is requested and the customer within the previous 12 months: failed to pay a bill before the shut-off date; paid with two or more checks that were returned unpaid for reasons other than bank error; failed to pay twice in a row by the due date or three times; or misrepresented identity or other facts relating to conditions under which service was obtained or continued.

* * *

§ 6.14. Agency Guaranty of Payment:

Substantially similar to General Service Rule 6.16.

§ 6.15. Medical Need for Telecommunications Service:

Substantially similar to General Service Rule 6.17.

§ 6.16. Elderly and Handicapped:

Substantially similar to General Service Rule 6.18.

§ 6.17. Stopping Service at Customer Request:

Substantially similar to General Service Rule 6.20.

§ 7.01. Application Records:

Substantially similar to General Service Rule 7.01.

§ 7.02. Account Records:

Substantially similar to General Service Rule 7.02

§ 7.03. Deposit Records:

Substantially similar to General Service Rule 7.03.

§ 7.04. Complaint Records:

Substantially similar to General Service Rule 7.04.

§ 7.05. Test and Inspection Records:

Substantially similar to General Service Rule 7.05.

* * *

Rule 13.04. Required Billing Information (Inter-Exchange Service):

Bills shall be issued not later than 90 days after service is provided and shall contain the following applicable information: name and telephone or identifying number under which service is billed; previous balance due; ending date of the bill cycle or the invoice date; either the due date or the total payable upon receipt and the date after which a late payment charge will be imposed; itemization of the charges and taxes; and the name of the provider and a toll-free number.

Rule 13.05. Over- and Under-Billing (Inter-Exchange Service):

If a customer is over-billed, the provider shall make a refund or billing credit in a subsequent billing cycle following discovery and computation of the amount. If a customer is billed an amount to correct a previous under-billing that results in undue hardship for the customer, the customer may make special payment arrangements unless the under-billing was caused by unauthorized or fraudulent use or procurement of service.

Rule 13.06. Wrong Number Credit (Inter-Exchange Service):

A provider shall credit a customer's account for a call when a customer reaches a wrong number on an intrastate toll call and promptly notifies the appropriate company representative.

Rule 13.07. Prepaid Services (Inter-Exchange Service):

Prepaid services shall be permitted, and amounts received for prepaid services may not be treated as deposits.

Rule 13.08. Deposits (Inter-Exchange Service):

Providers may require deposits from customers and shall pay interest thereon at the rate prescribed by the PSC.

CALIFORNIA

The law governing electric is found in Cal. Pub. Util. Code §§ 392, 394.2, 394.4, 394.5 and 761.5; the law governing master metering is found in Cal. Pub. Util. Code §§ 739.5, 777, 777.1, and 777.1(e); provisions applicable to electric, gas, heat and water are found in Cal. Pub. Util. Code §§ 761.5, 779, 779.1, 779.2, 779.5, 780, 780.5, and 781; and provisions applicable to telephone service are found in Cal. Pub. Util. Code §§ 779.2, 786, 788, 2889.5, and 2896.

Website: www.cpuc.ca.gov/PUC/documents/go.htm (last visited in May 2011).

***Electric*—Cal. Pub. Util. Code §§ 392, 394.2, 394.4, 394.5**

§ 392. Disclosure of Components of Electric Bills; Customer Education Program; Standard Bill Format:

Utility bill must disclose total charges associated with: transmission and distribution, including charges constituting research, environmental, and low-income funds, and with generation, including competition transition charge.

Bill must include conspicuous notice that customer will continue to be liable for payment of competition transition charge if the customer elects to purchase electricity from another provider.

Before implementing competition transition charge, utility and PUC must institute a customer education program regarding changes to the electric industry that provides customers with information necessary to make choices as to electric service.

The utility shall use the standard bill format specified in § 394.4.

* * *

§ 394.2. Consumer Complaints Regarding Electric Service Providers; Investigation of Abuses; Remedies:

PUC must accept and attempt to informally resolve consumer complaints regarding service providers. PUC may initiate investigations into service providers when it suspects pattern of customer abuses. Consumer complaints regarding service by a public agency within its political boundary or the service territory of a local publicly owned utility shall be resolved by the public agency. Consumer complaints regarding violation of direct access rules adopted by a local publicly owned utility are resolved through that local utility's consumer complaint procedures.

Residential customers also have the option to proceed with a complaint against a provider filed in the court system or with the Commission but not in both forums. PUC has the authority in such proceedings to accept, compile, and resolve complaints and to award reparations but not to award any other damages or to regulate the rates or charges of provider. A party to a conflict before the PUC may pursue an appeal of a decision through the court system if otherwise authorized.

Provider must provide the PUC access to relevant accounts, books, papers, and documents related to California transactions in connection with customer complaints or PUC investigations into customer abuses.

No provider may discontinue service for a disputed amount provided the customer has filed a complaint that is pending with PUC and paid the disputed amount into an escrow account.

* * *

§ 394.4. Minimum Standards; Adoption of Rules:

§ 394.4(a). Confidentiality:

Customer information, including billing, credit, or usage information, is confidential unless the customer consents in writing. The requirement of confidentiality does not include disclosure of generic information regarding general characteristics of a group or rate classification, unless disclosure would reveal customer-specific information.

§ 394.4(b). Physical Disconnects and Reconnects:

Only an electrical corporation, or a publicly owned electric utility, that provides physical delivery service to a customer may physically disconnect or reconnect a customer from the transmission or distribution grid. Physical disconnection by electrical corporation subject to PUC jurisdiction may occur only in accordance with PUC protocols. Disconnection by publicly owned electric utilities may occur only in accordance with protocols established by the governing board of the local publicly owned electric utility.

§ 394.4(c). Change in Providers:

Upon notice supplied by an electric service provider to the electric corporation or local publicly owned electric utility providing service, customers eligible for direct access may change their energy supplier. Suppliers may charge for the change, but any fee or penalty charged for early termination of service must be disclosed in contract or applicable tariff.

§ 394.4(d). Written Notices:

Notices describing the terms and conditions of service (including those described in § 394.5), service agreements, notices of late payment, notices of discontinuance of service, and disconnection notices must be easily understandable and must be provided in the language in which the provider offered the services.

§ 394.4(e). Billing:

All bills must have a standard bill format determined by the PUC or the local governing body and must be in sufficient detail for the customer to recalculate the bill for accuracy. Late fees must be separately stated. A phone number must be provided by which customers may report and resolve billing inquiries and complaints. A provider contacted by a customer regarding a billing dispute must advise the customer at the time of initial contact that the customer may file a complaint with the Commission if the dispute is not satisfactorily resolved by the provider.

§ 394.4(f). Meter Integrity:

Customer must have a reasonable opportunity to have its meter tested to ensure reasonable accuracy of the meter. The PUC or local governing body determines who is responsible for the cost of testing.

§ 394.4(g). Customer Deposits:

Service providers may require customer deposits before commencing service. The amount may not exceed the estimated bill for a 3-month period.

* * *

§ 394.5. Notice of Service to Potential Customers; Contents; Denial of Service:

Before commencing service, provider (except for an electrical corporation as defined in Cal. Pub. Util. Code § 218, or a local publicly owned electric utility as defined in Cal. Pub. Util. Code § 224.3) must provide potential customer with written notice describing the price, terms, and conditions of the service.

The notice must include: a clear description of the price, terms, and conditions of service, including the price of electricity expressed in a format which allows for the customer to compare similar products and services; the total price of electricity on a cents-per-kilowatt-hour basis (or other basis determined by the PUC), including services and charges regulated by the PUC; and estimates of the total monthly bill at varying consumption levels.

The provider must separately disclose all recurring and nonrecurring charges associated with the sale of electricity. If services other than electricity are offered, the provider must itemize the services and charges associated with each.

The provider must provide an explanation of the applicability and amount of the competition transition charge (determined under §§ 367–376).

The provider must provide: a description of the right to rescind the contract without fee or penalty in accordance with § 395; an explanation of the customer's financial obligations, including procedures regarding past-due payments, discontinuance of service, billing disputes, and service complaints; the provider's registration number, if applicable; notification of the right to change providers upon written notice, including any fees or penalties assessed for early termination; and a description of the availability of low-income assistance programs and how to apply.

Any provider who declines to provide services to a consumer must, at the consumer's request, disclose to that consumer the reason for the denial in writing within 30 days. At the time service is denied, the provider must disclose the customer's right to make this request at the time service is denied. Consumers must have at least 30 days from the date of denial to make the request.

§ 395. Cancellation of Contract; Notice of Cancellation:

Customer has right to cancel a contract for electric service until midnight of the third business day following the day customer signs an agreement or offer to purchase.

Cancellation occurs upon customer giving written notice at the address specified in the agreement or offer. Notice by mail is effective when deposited in the mail if the notice is properly addressed and the postage prepaid. However communicated, notice of cancellation is effective if it states intention not to be bound by the contract.

* * *

§ 761.5. Electrical and Gas Corporations; Centralized Credit Check System; Participation; Limitations on Use of Information; Laws Applicable:

If the PUC determines that it would be cost-effective, it may authorize electrical and gas corporations to participate in a centralized credit check system in order to share information on customers. The electrical and gas corporations may also share such information with telephone corporations and publicly owned public utilities. No public utility participating in the centralized credit check system may utilize any such information for internal marketing purposes. A public utility may release information to a collection agency for purpose of collecting an outstanding bill, but it may not otherwise release, transfer, or sell any information obtained through the centralized credit check system.

Every electrical and gas corporation participating in a centralized credit check system is subject to the state Consumer Credit Reporting Agencies Act and the federal Fair Credit Reporting Act.

***Master Metering (Electric, Gas, Heat, and Water)*—Cal. Pub. Util. Code §§ 739.5, 777, 777.1, 777.1(e)**

* * *

§ 739.5. Residential Gas or Electric Service; Provision by Master-Meter Customer Through Submeter Service System; Rates; Rebates; Customer Services; Maintenance; Itemized Billing; Notice; Response to Complaints:

If gas or electric service, or both, is provided by a master-meter customer to tenants of a manufactured home park, apartment building, or similar residential complex, the master-meter customer must charge each user the same rate which would apply if the user were receiving the same service directly from the gas or electrical corporation. A corporation furnishing service to the master-meter customer must establish uniform rates for master-meter service at a sufficient differential to cover the reasonable average costs to master-meter customers of providing sub-meter service, except that such costs may not exceed the average cost to the corporation in providing comparable services directly to the users.

Every master-meter customer of a gas or electrical corporation who receives any rebate from the corporation must make a pro-rata distribution or credit to the account of each user served by the master-meter customer based upon the ratio of gas or electricity, or both, used by the user consumer during the last billing period to the total amount furnished by the corporation to the master-meter customer during that period.

Electrical or gas corporations furnishing service to a master-meter customer must furnish to each user within a sub-metered system every public safety customer service provided to its other residential customers. A list of such service must be provided to the master-meter customer, who must post the list in a conspicuous place accessible to all users. The public safety customer services must be provided without additional charge unless the corporation has included the average cost of the services in the rate differential provided to the master-meter customer on or before January 1, 1984. If so, the PUC must deduct the average cost of providing the public safety services when approving rate differentials for master-meter customers.

Master-meter customers are responsible for maintenance and repair of its sub-meter facilities beyond the master meter, and an electrical or gas corporation is not required to make repairs to or perform maintenance on the sub-meter system.

Every master-meter customer must provide an itemized billing of charges for electricity and/or gas to each individual user, including the opening and closing readings for the meter, and the identification of rates and quantities attributable to each service. The master-meter customer must post in a conspicuous place the prevailing residential gas or electrical rate schedule as published by the gas or electric corporation.

Every electrical and gas corporation must notify each master-meter customer of the customer's responsibilities to end users under this section.

* * *

§ 777. Master Meters Used in Residential Service; Notice of Termination of Service for Nonpayment:

When (1) an electrical, gas, heat, or water corporation provides individually metered residential service to occupants of a detached single-family dwelling, multi-unit residential structure, manufactured home park, or permanent residential structures in a labor camp, (2) the owner, manager, or operator is listed as the customer of record, and (3) the account is in arrears, then the corporation must make every good faith effort to notify the occupants at least 10 days prior to termination that service will be terminate. The notice must inform the occupants that they have the right to become customers and to be billed for service without being liable for any amount on the delinquent account.

A corporation is not required to make service available to the occupants unless each agrees to the terms and conditions of service and meets the requirements of law and the corporation's rules and tariffs. If one or more of the occupants is willing and able to assume responsibility for the entire account to the corporation's satisfaction, or if there is a legal, physical way for the corporation to selectively terminate service to occupants who do not meet the requirements of the corporation's rules and tariffs, the corporation must make service available to the occupants who meet the requirements.

If service for a period of time is a precondition for establishing credit with the corporation, then a satisfactory equivalent is residence and proof of prompt payment of rent or other credit obligation for the same period of time that is acceptable to the corporation.

An occupant who becomes a customer pursuant to this section and whose periodic payments, such as rental payments, included charges for electrical, gas, heat, or water service which were not separately stated, the occupant may deduct from such periodic payment charges paid to the corporation for such services during the preceding payment period.

In the case of a detached single-family dwelling, the corporation may do any of the following: (1) give notice of termination at least 7 days prior to the proposed termination, and (2) in order for the delinquent amount to be waived, require an occupant who becomes a customer to verify that the delinquent account customer of record is or was the landlord, manager, or agent of the dwelling. Verification may include a lease or rental agreement, rent receipts, a government document showing the occupant as renter, or information disclosed pursuant to Cal. Civ. Code § 1962 (West) (disclosures required by owner or agent).

§ 777.1. Master Meters in Residential Service: Written Notice of Termination; Obligation to Furnish Service; Creditworthiness As Condition; Deductions from Periodic Payments; Termination; Rules and Orders; Local Authority; Preemption of Punitive Damage Statutes; Representative of Residential Occupants:

When (1) an electrical, gas, heat, or water corporation furnishes service to occupants through a master meter in a multi-unit residential structure, manufactured home park, or permanent residential structures in a labor camp, (2) the owner, manager, or operator is listed by the corporation as the customer of record, and (3) the account is in arrears, then the corporation must make every good faith effort to inform the residential occupants by written notice posted on the door of each unit at least 15 days prior to termination that service will be terminated on a date specified in the notice. If it is not reasonable or practicable to post the notice in that manner, the corporation must post two copies of the notice in each accessible common area and at each point of access to the premises.

The notice must inform the occupants that they have the right to become customers who will be billed for service without liability for any amount due on the delinquent account. The notice must plainly describe: what the occupants must do to prevent the termination or to reestablish service; the estimated monthly cost of service; the title, address, and telephone number of a representative of the corporation who can assist the occupants in continuing service; and the address and telephone number of a legal services project (defined in § 6213 of the Business and Professions Code) recommended by the local county bar association. The notice must be in English and in any other language that the corporation determines is the primary language spoken by a significant number of the occupants.

A corporation is not required to provide service to the occupants unless each occupant or a representative of the occupants agrees to the terms and conditions of service and meets the requirements of law and the corporation's rules and tariffs. If one or more of the occupants or the occupants' representative (excluding a tenants' association) are willing and able to assume responsibility for subsequent charges to the account, or if there is a legal and physical means of selectively terminating service to those occupants who have not met the requirements of the corporation's rules and tariffs or for whom the occupants' representative is not responsible, then the corporation shall make service available to those occupants who have met the requirements individually or through a representative.

If service for a period of time is a precondition for establishing credit with the corporation, then a satisfactory equivalent is residence and proof of prompt payment of rent or other credit obligation for the same period of time that is acceptable to the corporation.

An occupant who becomes a customer pursuant to this section and whose periodic payments, such as rental payments, included charges for electrical, gas, heat, or water service which were not separately stated, the occupant may deduct from such periodic payment charges paid to the corporation for such services during the preceding payment period.

* * *

§§ 777.1(e)–(l). Termination of Service:

A corporation may not terminate service to master-metered premises subject to § 777.1(a): during the pendency of the corporation's investigation of a customer dispute or complaint; when the customer has been granted an extension of time to pay a bill; for a debt owed by the customer to any other person or corporation, or when the delinquent account or other debt was incurred with a person or corporation other than the electrical, gas, heat, or water corporation demanding payment; when the delinquent account arises from another property owned, managed, or operated by the customer; or when a public health or building officer certifies that termination would result in a significant threat to the health or safety of the occupants or the public.

If an owner, manager, or operator directs, permits, or fails by act or omission to prevent a termination of service under this section while a unit receiving service is occupied, then the occupant or the occupants' representative (excluding a tenants' association) may commence an action to recover: reasonable costs and expenses incurred by occupant or representative and related to restoration of service; actual damages related to the termination of service; and reasonable attorney fees of the occupants or the representative incurred in enforcing this section, including but not limited to enforcement of a lien.

If an owner, manager, or operator directs, permits, or fails by any act or omission to prevent a termination of service while a unit receiving that service is occupied, the corporation may commence an action to recover: delinquent charges accrued prior to the expiration of the termination notice prescribed by § 777.1(a); reasonable costs incurred by the corporation related to the restoration of service; and reasonable attorney fees incurred in the enforcement of this section or in the collection of delinquent charges, including but not limited to enforcement of a lien. If the court finds that the owner, manager, or operator has paid the amount in arrears prior to termination, there shall be no recovery of any charges, costs, damages, expenses, or fees from the owner, manager, or operator.

An abstract of any money judgment entered in the occupant's or corporation's favor shall be recorded pursuant to § 697.310 of the Code of Civil Procedure.

If service subject to this section is terminated without compliance with this section, then any service wrongfully terminated must be restored without charge. If a corporation wrongfully terminates service, then it shall be liable to the occupants or customer for actual damages resulting from the termination and for the costs of enforcing this section, including but not limited to reasonable attorney fees, if the occupants or their representative made a good faith effort to have the service continued without interruption.

This section preempts any statute or ordinance permitting punitive damages against any owner, manager, or operator due to an involuntary termination of residential public utility service or permitting the recovery of costs related to the formation, maintenance, and termination of a tenants' association.

* * *

***Electric, Gas, Heat, and Water*—Cal. Pub. Util. Code §§ 779, 779.1, 779.2, 779.5, 780, 780.5, 781**

§ 779. Termination of Service for Nonpayment of Delinquent Account; Notice; Time; Complaint or Investigation of Dispute; Amortization of Delinquency (Electric, Gas, Heat, or Water):

An electrical, gas, heat, or water corporation may not terminate service for nonpayment without first giving notice of the delinquency and impending termination as specified in § 779.1.

Service may not be terminated for nonpayment under the following circumstances: an investigation is pending by the corporation into a customer or subscriber dispute or complaint; a customer has been granted an extension of time for payment; or, upon certification of a licensed physician and surgeon that termination will be life threatening to the customer, that the customer is financially unable to pay within the normal payment period, and the customer is willing to enter into an amortization agreement for payment pursuant to § 779(e) regarding charges that the customer is unable to pay prior to delinquency.

A customer who has initiated a complaint or requested an investigation within 5 days of receiving the disputed bill, or who has made a request before termination of service for an extension because of an inability to make payment in full by the normal due date, must be given an opportunity for review of the complaint, investigation, or request for extension by a review manager of the corporation. The review must indicate whether the customer will be permitted to amortize any unpaid balance over a period of time, not to exceed 12 months. No termination of service may be effected if the customer complies with an amortization agreement and also keeps the account current as charges accrue in subsequent billing periods.

A customer who provides the certification of a licensed physician and surgeon that termination of service will be life threatening and who is unable to pay for service within the normal payment period shall, upon request, be permitted to amortize, over a period not to exceed 12 months, the unpaid balance of any bill asserted to be beyond the means of the customer to pay within the normal period for payment.

A customer whose complaint or request for an investigation results in an adverse determination by the corporation may appeal the PUC.

§ 779.1. Period Allowed for Payment; Notice of Delinquency; Contact with Resident or Notice Prior to Termination; Third-Party Notification for Elders or Dependent Adults; Contents of Notice (Electric, Gas, Heat, or Water):

Corporation must allow customer at least 19 days from the date of mailing of bill, postage prepaid, for payment. No corporation may terminate residential service for nonpayment of a delinquent account without first giving written notice of the delinquency and impending termination at least 10 days prior to the proposed termination. The notice may not be mailed earlier than 19 days from the date of mailing of the bill, and the 10-day notice of termination does not start until 5 days after the mailing of the notice.

Corporation must make a reasonable attempt to contact an adult person residing at the subject premises by telephone or personal contact at least 24 hours prior to any termination of service. If telephone or personal contact cannot be accomplished, the corporation must give by mail or in person a notice of termination at least 48 hours prior to termination.

Corporation must provide to customers who are 65 years of age or older, or who are dependent adults as defined in § 15610(b)(1) of the Welfare and Institutions Code, a third-party notification service under which the corporation will attempt to notify a person designated by the customer to receive notice when the customer's account is subject to termination. The notice must include information as to what is required to prevent termination of service. The customer must make a request for third-party notice on a form provided by the corporation, and the request must include the third party's written consent. The third-party notification does not obligate the third party to pay overdue charges or to prevent or delay termination of service.

Termination notices must be in a clear and legible format and must include the following: name and address of the delinquent customer; the delinquent amount; the date by which payment or arrangements for payment must be made to avoid termination; the procedure that may be used by the customer to initiate a complaint or request an investigation concerning service or charges; the procedure for requesting amortization of the unpaid charges; the procedure for the customer to obtain information on the availability of applicable financial assistance, including private, local, state, or federal sources; the telephone number of a corporation representative who can provide additional information or institute arrangements for payment; and the telephone number of the PUC to which customer inquiries may be directed.

A customer whose complaint or request for an investigation has resulted in an adverse determination by the corporation may appeal the determination to the PUC. Any subsequent appeal of the dispute or complaint to the Commission is not subject to this section.

If a customer does not comply with an amortization agreement, the corporation shall not terminate service without giving notice at least forty-eight hours prior to cessation of the conditions required to avoid termination. Such notice does not entitle the customer to further investigation by the corporation.

Service terminated without compliance with the section shall be restored without charge, and a notation to that effect shall be mailed to the customer at his or her billing address.

§ 779.2. Termination of Residential Service for Nonpayment of Delinquent Account or Other Indebtedness Owed to Other Person or Corporation; Exceptions (Electric, Gas, Heat, Telephone, and Water):

An electrical, gas, heat, telephone, or water corporation may not terminate service for nonpayment of any delinquent account or other debt owed by the customer to any other person or corporation or when the delinquent account or other debt was incurred with a person or corporation other than the electrical, gas, heat, telephone, or water corporation demanding payment.

This section does not apply to any telephone corporation operating within service areas that furnishes billing services to subscribers of any telephone corporation operating between service areas pursuant to tariffs on file with the PUC which provide for furnishing those billing services. Such tariffs must provide for adequate subscriber notice, review, and appeal procedures prior to any termination of service for nonpayment of a delinquent account.

This section does not apply to any privately owned or publicly owned public utility that collects sanitation or sewerage charges for a public agency pursuant to agreement under § 54346.2 of the Government Code or § 5472.5 of the Health and Safety Code.

* * *

§ 779.5. Requirement for Deposit to Be Based Solely Upon Credit Worthiness of Applicant (Electric, Gas, Heat, or Water):

Requirement of deposit prior to establishing an account and furnishing service shall be based solely upon the creditworthiness of the applicant as determined by the utility.

§ 780. Termination of Services on Weekends, Legal Holidays or Time When Business Office Not Open (Electric, Gas, Heat, or Water):

When the reason for termination is delinquency in payment, termination of service shall not occur on Saturday, Sunday, legal holiday, or at any time during which the business offices are not open to the public.

§ 780.5. Individual Meters for Electrical and Gas Service; Multi-Unit Residential Structures, Condominiums and Mobile Home Parks:

Every unit in an apartment house or similar multi-unit residential structure, condominium, and manufactured home park for which a building permit was obtained on or after July 1, 1982, shall be individually metered for electrical and gas service. Separate metering for gas service is not required for dormitories or other housing provided by a post-secondary educational institution for students or employees, or farm-worker housing, and is not required for units not equipped with gas appliances requiring venting or receiving the majority of energy for water or space heating from a solar energy system or cogeneration technology.

§ 781.5 Water Meters; Continuation of Unmetered Service; If in Existence on January 1, 1979; Exception; Public Hearing; Findings:

The PUC may not require any water corporation not subject to Water Code §§ 526-28 which furnishes water through less than 500 service connections nor any customer of such corporation to install any water meter at any water service connection between the water system of the corporation and the customer if such service connection was unmetered on January 1, 1979, except after a public hearing held within corporation's service area and the following findings are made: metering will be cost-effective within the corporation's service area; metering will result in a significant reduction in water consumption within the service area; and the costs of metering will not impose an unreasonable financial burden on customers within the service area unless it is found necessary to ensure an adequate water supply within the service area.

***Telephone*—Cal. Pub. Util. Code §§ 786, 788, 2889.5, 2896**

§ 786. Residential Telephone Service Listings; Charges Imposed by Rules or Regulations; Public Telephone Service; Methods for Compliance:

Telephone corporations operating within a service area must provide annually to each subscriber in a manner prescribed by the PUC a listing of the services it provides, the rates or charges for those services, and the state or federal regulatory agency or agencies responsible for regulating those services.

Corporations providing public telephone service must also provide a description of that service, the corporation's policies for providing that service (including policies for public need and safety), and how a customer can contact the corporation for additional information concerning the corporation's policies or for assistance regarding a specific public telephone.

This section does not apply to any entity or person owning or operating coin-activated telephone equipment available for public use that is not a telephone corporation.

Changes imposed on subscribers in response to rules or regulations of the Federal Communications Commission must be shown separately from other charges on a bill. A corporation operating within a service area must either identify such charges, by asterisk or other means, with the statement, "THIS CHARGE IS (or THESE CHARGES ARE) IMPOSED BY ACTION OF THE FEDERAL COMMUNICATIONS COMMISSION" or include in the bill a listing of the total charges imposed pursuant to FCC tariff and identified with the statement, "TOTAL CHARGES IMPOSED BY ACTION OF THE FEDERAL COMMUNICATIONS COMMISSION."

The bill must also provide the address and telephone number of the Federal Communications Commission, to which inquiries may be directed.

Compliance with this section must include: an explanation of the configuration of telecommunications services in California; the names, addresses, and telephone numbers of the regulatory agencies responsible for intrastate and interstate telephone service; a general description of the services provided by the telephone corporation or telecommunications provider issuing the explanation, how those services may be obtained, and notice that other providers are available; a description of billing charges that may appear on billing statements; and the procedures by which customers (including customers equipped with telephone devices for the disabled) may protest billed items and contact the provider about those charges.

* * *

§ 788. Notice to Residential Subscribers; Inside Telephone Wiring; Responsibilities of Subscriber and Telephone Corporation:

A telephone corporation that is a provider of local exchange service must issue to each residential customer an annual notice containing the following in a manner and form prescribed by the PUC: a explanation of the corporation's and customer's respective responsibilities regarding a customer's inside telephone wiring (as defined in Civil Code § 1941.4), including an explanation of the respective obligations of a landlord and tenant for such wiring; an explanation of procedures and charges for determining and notifying the customer about whether a malfunction is located in the telephone network or the customer's inside telephone wiring, including customer-provided equipment; a full description of the types of services offered, including the rates, charges, and conditions for maintaining or repairing a subscriber's inside telephone wiring and whether such services are offered by non-utility providers.

* * *

§ 2889.5. Telephone Services for Which Competition Has Been Authorized; Change in Service Provider; Verification; Notice; Records; Disputed Changes:

No telephone corporation or corporation representative may change or authorize a different telephone corporation to make any change in the provider of any authorized competitive telephone service until the corporation or its representative fully informs the customer subscriber of the nature and extent of the offered service, and the corporation or its representative specifically establishes that the customer intends to change his or her telephone service provider, and explains any charges associated with that change.

The customer's decision to change telephone service provider must be confirmed by an independent third-party verification company or by using an electronic means that complies with 47 C.F.R. § 64.1120 in effect as of June 17, 2008. The third-party verification company must: be independent from the corporation seeking to provide the new service; not be directly or indirectly managed, controlled, directed, owned wholly or in part by the corporation seeking to provide new service or by any corporation, firm, or person who directly or indirectly manages, controls, directs, or owns more than 5% of that corporation; operate from facilities physically separate from those of the telephone corporation seeking to provide the new service; and not derive commissions or compensation based upon the number of confirmed sales.

The telephone corporation seeking to verify the sale must do so by either connecting the customer by telephone to the third-party verification company or by arranging for the verification company to call the customer to confirm the sale.

The verification company must obtain the customer's oral confirmation regarding the change, record that confirmation by obtaining appropriate verification information, and make the record available to the customer upon request. Information obtained from the customer may not be used for marketing purposes. Any unauthorized release of such information is grounds for a civil suit by the customer against the telephone corporation or employees responsible for the violation.

A service provider is not required to comply when the customer directly calls the local service provider to change service provider, but a service provider does not avoid the verification requirements by asking the customer to contact a local exchange service provider directly to make any change in service. A local exchange service is required to comply with the verification requirements for its own competitive services (through which subscribers have the ability to pre-subscribe to a telephone service provider) and is not required to perform any verification requirements for any changes solicited by another telephone corporation.

Upon confirmation of transfer of service, the telephone corporation seeking to verify the change in service must notify the customer by U.S. Mail that the customer's service provider has been changed, and the provider that initiated the change must send the notice within 14 days of the date of the change. The notice must clearly and legibly provide notice of change in service provider and include a customer service telephone number to call if the customer did not authorize the change in service.

In a situation in which the telephone corporation obtains a written service order, the order must inform the customer of the nature and extent of the action and the customer must be given a copy. The customer's signature must indicate a full understanding of the relationship being established with the telephone corporation. When a written subscriber solicitation or other document contains a letter of agency authorizing a change in service, the solicitation must include a separate document solely to explain the nature and extent of the solicitation. If any part of a solicitation is in a language other than English, any written authorization contained in that mailing must be in the same language.

The telephone corporation must retain a record of the verification of the sale for at least 1 year, and the record must be made available to the customer, the Attorney General, or the PUC upon request.

If a customer does not sign an authorization and notifies the telephone corporation within 90 days that he or she does not wish to change telephone corporations, the customer shall be switched back to his or her former telephone corporation at the expense of the telephone corporation that initiated the change.

When a customer changes telephone service providers, notice of the change must be conspicuously noted on the subscriber's bill. Notice in the following form is deemed to comply with this subdivision:

> NOTICE: Your local (or long distance) telephone service provider has been changed from (name of prior provider) to (name of current provider).
>
> Cost of change: $ __.

A telephone corporation that violates the verification requirement must refund to a subscriber any charges paid by the subscriber in excess of the amount that the subscriber would otherwise have had to pay had the service not been changed.

No telephone corporation, or entity or person acting on its behalf, may make any change or authorize a different telephone corporation to make any change in the provider of any intrastate service for which competition has been authorized without having (or instituted reasonable steps to obtain) signed and dated orders for service on file from the customers. All orders must be in the form prescribed in federal law for letters of agency. A telephone corporation is responsible for charges associated with any disputed changes in telephone service for which it cannot produce a dated order for service signed by the subscriber. This subdivision applies to all intrastate services for which competition has been authorized.

* * *

§ 2896. Required Customer Services:

Telephone corporations must provide customer service, including but not limited to: providing sufficient information to help subscribers make informed choices about services and providers, including information regarding the provider's identity, service options, pricing, and terms and conditions of service; the ability to access a live operator by dialing "0" without charge; service regarding network technical quality, customer service, installation, repair, and billing; and information concerning the regulatory process and how customers can participate, including the process of resolving complaints.

* * *

COLORADO

The regulations governing telephone, electric, gas, and water are located in 4 Colo. Code Regs. §§ 723-2-2000–723-2-2185, 723-2-2301–723-2-2899, §§ 723-3-3000–723-3-3999, §§ 723-4-4000–723-4-4999, and §§ 723-5-5000–723-5-5420, respectively. Provisions of regulations that are substantially similar to others are indicated accordingly.

***Telephone*—4 Colo. Code Regs. §§ 723-2-2000–723-2-2185, 723-2-2301–723-2-2899**

* * *

§ 2004. Disputes:

If a provider and a customer are unable to resolve a dispute, the provider must give the customer the contact information for the External Affairs Section of the Commission.

Rules 2162 and 2163 define optional and non-optional operator services. Non-optional services include, inter alia, payphone calls, credit card calls, phone service in hotels, etc., calls by disabled persons who require assistance, collect, third-party billed or person to person calls. Optional, i.e., unregulated, services include teleconferencing, travel cards, and services provided to inmates of correctional institutions.

* * *

§ 2164. Regulation of Non-optional Operator Services:

This rule sets "benchmark" maximum rates for non-optional operator services. If the Commission approves charges above the benchmarks, it may require the provider to disclose the rate before completing the call, and allow the customer to disconnect without charge.

§ 2165. Requirements for Providers of Non-optional Operator Services:

An OSP must identify itself at the beginning of each call, and permit the customer to disconnect without charge before the call is completed. Upon request the OSP must disclose its rates, method of billing, and complaint procedure. An OSP may not bill for any uncompleted call. An OSP may not transfer a call to another provider unless the customer consents, after disclosure of any charges.

OSPs must connect emergency calls immediately, and inform the emergency services provider of the location of origin of the call.

OSPs must be capable of providing collect and third party billed calls. Customers may not be billed for such calls unless they agree to accept the charges.

§ 2166. Arrangements with Call Aggregators:

OSPs must require aggregators (such as hotels) to post on or in close proximity to the telephones the name of the OSP, instructions on how to obtain rate information, and the customer's right to obtain service from the carrier of their choice.

Aggregators must assure that a customer is not charged more for using 800/888, 950 or 10XXX or 1010XXX access codes than for calls placed with the pre-subscribed OSP.

§ 2167. Call Blocking Prohibited:

OSPs may not prevent customers from accessing a preferred operator service using 800/888, 950 or 10XXX or 1010XXX access codes.

* * *

§ 2185. Obligations of Provider of Last Resort:

A POLR must offer basic local exchange service to any customer in its area who requests it, unless the customer owes a balance to the POLR and has not made an agreement for repayment. The POLR must advertise the availability of this service in the media, and in its directories.

* * *

§ 2302. Customer Deposits:

§ 2302(a), (b). Customer Deposits; Criteria for Establishment and Amount of Deposits:

Except for sub-section (b)(I) [criteria] this rule applies only to deposits for basic local exchange service. Each LEC must have a written, non-discriminatory policy for determining an applicant's credit status. LECs must process applications made orally, in writing, or via a secure website. It may not refuse service to a customer who refuses to give a Social Security number. LEC may require a deposit if billing records are available and show recent or substantial delinquencies. It must provide at least one non-cash alternative for paying a deposit that does not require use of a Social Security number. The amount of a deposit may not exceed the charges for 90 days local exchange service, including any associated taxes or surcharges.

§ 2302(c). Limitation on the Use of Deposits:

The payment of a deposit does not relieve a customer of the obligation to pay current bills when due. A forfeited deposit may be applied only to the customer's indebtedness.

§ 2302(d). Payment of Deposits:

A deposit must be paid in full, prior to start of service, unless the LEC agrees to an installment plan.

§ 2302(e). Interest and Deposits:

A LEC must pay simple interest on customer deposits, at a rate calculated by the Commission, using the formula provided in this rule, based on the interest rate on United States Treasury constant maturities.

§ 2302(f). Refund of Deposits:

Unless the LEC has sufficient factual information to conclude that the customer is an unsatisfactory credit risk, it must refund the deposit, with interest, after 12 consecutive months of satisfactory payments. Upon discontinuance of service or when customer establishes satisfactory credit, the LEC must refund, with interest, the balance of any deposit in excess of any unpaid bills. Any balance due after discontinuance and final bill is payable without notice or demand from the customer.

§ 2302(g). Deposit Policy Included in the Tariff:

Each LEC must include in its tariffs a detailed explanation of its deposit policy, the conditions under which deposits will be required and returned.

§ 2303 Denial or Discontinuance of Service:

§ 2303(a). Disconnection Without Notice:

Disconnection without notice is permitted only for: condition immediately hazardous to life, physical safety, or property; order of court, commission, or other authorized public authority; unauthorized restoration of properly disconnected service; violation of rule, tariff, law or ordinance that affects physical safety or the integrity of provider's service; failure to give provider reasonable access to facilities; service obtained by fraud, i.e., by use of a false name, or at a location where another person owes an outstanding bill and continues to reside.

§ 2303(b). Disconnection with Notice:

For nonpayment of bill for LEC service, 30 days after due date, which must be at least 15 days after billing date; if service obtained fraudulently or without provider authorization, or used, or suspected of being used, for fraudulent purpose.

§ 2303(c). Restrictions on Denial or Disconnection of Service—Disposition of Payments:

A provider may not disconnect for nonpayment until a customer had been issued a bill that conforms to requirements of § 2304 (*infra*). It may not disconnect for indebtedness of prior occupant, or for services or facilities not ordered by the customer, or for any other indebtedness except that for basic local exchange service, including taxes and surcharges. It may not use its purchase of a customer's indebtedness (i.e., another provider's accounts receivable) to deny or discontinue service to that customer.

* * *

§ 2303(c)(IV). Amortization Agreements:

If a customer pays or is willing to pay all current charges, and has entered into a payment plan for any arrearages, the provider may not disconnect while the customer is current on the payment plan. If a plan is not satisfied, the provider may disconnect without further notice.

§ 2303(c)(V). Timing of Disconnection:

A provider may disconnect only during regular business hours, and not after noon on a day before a day when customer service office will not be open.

§ 2303(c)(VI). Denial of Service by Alternative Provider If Provider of Basic LEC Services Is Permitted to Stop Offering Services:

If a provider of basic LEC service is allowed to stop offering basic LEC service, an alternative provider may refuse service if customer has balance owed to alternative provider and has not made arrangements to pay the outstanding balance to the alternative provider.

§ 2303(c)(VII). Medical Emergencies:

A provider must postpone disconnection for 60 days from the date of a certificate, issued by a Colorado-licensed physician, or a practitioner working under the supervision of a physician, that disconnection would create or aggravate a medical emergency. The 60 days may be increased by 30 days, upon receipt of another certificate. A customer is entitled to only one 90-day extension in any 12-month period. A customer who, before the issuance of the certificate, had broken a payment arrangement, must pay all amounts due up to the date of the certificate, and resume payments. A certificate is uncontestable as to medical judgment, but the provider may use reasonable means to verify its authenticity.

§ 2303(d). Notice Requirements:

A disconnect notice must provide at least 15 days, from the date the notice was issued, to respond, and state clearly the amount due, and the date by which customer must enter into payment arrangement to avoid disconnection. It must notify the customer that basic service may not be discontinued for nonpayment for optional services. If the customer has chosen electronic billing, the notice may be provided electronically. The notice must be in both English and Spanish.

§ 2303(e). Restoration of Service:

Service must be restored without charge if it was not properly disconnected, as required by this rule. It must be restored within 24 hours, or by 5 p.m. on the next business day if the 24-hour period ends on a Saturday, Sunday or holiday, if within 10 days of disconnection the customer pays the amount due, plus any deposit required by tariff, either by paying the provider directly or paying an authorized agent and presenting the provider with evidence of the date and amount of payment; or presents a medical certificate within 24 hours of disconnection; or demonstrates that the cause for disconnection has been cured.

§ 2304. Customer Billing Requirements:

§ 2304(a). Billing Information:

The Commission incorporates by reference the FCC's Truth in Billing rules (47 C.F.R. §§ 64.2400–64.2401, as revised on October 1, 2004. In addition, bills must clearly display the billing date and due date, which must be at least 15 days after the billing date, and where technically feasible, that e-billing is permitted at customer's option.

§ 2304(b). Payment of Bills, Billing Disputes, and Bill Credits or Refunds:

§ 2304(b)(I). Partial Payments:

Partial payments should be applied first to past local exchange service, so as to preserve local exchange service.

§ 2304(b)(II). Billing Disputes:

If a bill is disputed, the provider may require the customer to pay the undisputed portion to avoid disconnection for nonpayment. The provider must investigate, and report promptly to the customer. If the matter is not resolved, the provider must advise the customer that an informal or formal complaint may be filed with the Commission.

§ 2304(b)(III). Adjustments—Over-billing or Under-billing:

In case of over-billing, the provider must offer the customer a refund. If the refund exceeds the charges for 2 months local exchange service, including taxes and surcharges, the provider must offer the customer the choice of a credit or a payment, which must be mailed within 30 days. Refunds shall not be provided for a period of over 2 years. In case of under-billing which exceeds the charges for 2 months local service, including taxes and surcharges, the provider must offer a payment plan over a time period equal to the period over which the under-billing occurred. A customer may not be billed for more than 2 years of under-billing. If a provider collects more than is due as a result of an erroneous payment or electronic transfer, it must give a refund within 5 days of discovering the mistake. If the refund exceeds the amount of 2 months basic service, including taxes and surcharges, the company must offer the customer a choice of a credit or a payment.

§ 2304(b)(IV). Service Interruptions:

If service is interrupted and remains out of order for more than eight hours during a continuous twenty-four-hour period after being reported by the customer or is found to be out of order, an automatic credit will be made, with each loss of service for eight hours or more during a twenty-four-hour period counting as one day.

An adjustment is not required if the loss of service is due to: negligence or willful act of the customer; a malfunction of facilities not under LEC control; natural disasters or similar events; or inability to access customer's premises.

§ 2304(b)(V). Missed Service Calls:

In the event the LEC misses a service call (i.e., an appointment for a premise visit associated with installation of new service or with a re-grade of service) by more than four hours, the LEC shall make a credit to the monthly bill of the customer in the amount of one-third the tariffed rate that was to be charged. This credit shall also apply when the LEC misses scheduled installation work to be done in the central office.

* * *

§ 2305. Refund Plans:

If a provider proposes, or is required, to give a refund to a class of customers, it must present a refund plan, conforming to criteria set forth in detail in this rule, to the Commission.

§ 2306. Public Information:

Each provider must have a business office or customer service center, staffed to provide access, in person or by telephone, to personnel who can provide information, accept applications, explain charges, adjust errors, and generally provide customer service. Toll-free calling must be available to customers calling the service center. At the business offices or customer service centers, the LEC must provide copies of tariffs and price lists, maps of the exchange area, and publicly announced information about available service and proposed changes.

* * *

§ 2311 Changing Provider/Carrier Pre-Subscription (Anti-Slamming):

* * *

§ 2311(b)(I). Verification of Orders for Service:

Carrier may neither submit nor execute a change in a subscriber's authorized carrier, except in accordance with this rule.

* * *

§ 2311(b)(II)(A). Written or electronically signed letter of agency:

Letter must be a separate document or screen and contain nothing except the prescribed authorizing language. It may not include any inducements and is invalid if presented to customer in connection with a game of chance. Checks are permissible, if the check includes an easily readable boldface statement that a change of carrier is being authorized and contains no promotional material. A letter of agency must contain, in readable type, the name, billing address, and telephone number(s) covered by the request; the decision to change from the current carrier to the soliciting carrier; the authority for the submitting carrier to act as subscriber's agent in making this change; the subscriber's understanding that one carrier is permitted but not required to provide local, intra-LATA, and inter-LATA (or any combination thereof) services to one phone number; the subscriber's understanding that the change may result in a charge to the subscriber. A letter of agency may not suggest or require that a subscriber take any action to retain his or her current authorized carrier. If any part of a letter of agency is in a foreign language, then the entire letter must be translated into that language. Letter of agency submitted with electronically signed authorization must include customer disclosures required by § 101(c) of the Electronic Signatures in Global and National Commerce Act.

§ 2311(b)(II)(B). Subscriber-initiated call:

Must confirm name, billing address, decision to change, and understanding of change fee. A carrier that wishes to confirm electronically must provide one or more toll-free numbers that connect to a voice response unit that records the information and confirms the originating number by ANI (automatic number identification).

§ 2311(b)(II)(C). Third-party verification:

The third party must be separate from the carrier, have no financial incentive to confirm changes, and must operate from a separate location. Three-way conference calls are permitted, provided that the carrier or its sales representative drops out as soon as the three-way connection is established. The verification must be carried out in the same language as the sales promotion, be recorded, and provide customer with option to speak with a live person at any time during the call.

* * *

§ 2311(d). Authorized Carrier Freeze:

A LEC may offer freezes if they are provided free of charge, on a non-discriminatory basis, regardless of carrier selection. The procedure must be explained to the customer, and the decision to impose or terminate a freeze must be confirmed by a written or electronic authorization that meets the standards for a letter of agency (described above).

* * *

§ 2311(f). Enforcement:

Upon being notified by a subscriber of an unauthorized change, a carrier must switch the subscriber back to the authorized carrier at no charge to the subscriber. A carrier that initiates an unauthorized change is liable to the subscriber, the authorized carrier, or both, for specified charges incurred by the subscriber during the period of the unauthorized change and to the executing carrier for change fees.

§ 2311(g). Waiver for the sale or transfer of subscribers:

Prescribes a procedure for notice to subscribers if a carrier acquires, through sale or transfer, all or part of another carrier's subscriber base.

* * *

§ 2806. Prohibition on Disconnection:

LITAP (Low-Income Telephone Assistance Program) service may not be disconnected for nonpayment of toll charges. Waiver is possible if the utility can show that it would incur substantial and unjustifiable costs; and it offers toll limitation at no charge; and subscription rate for low-income customers is equal to or greater than the national rate for low-income customers.

§ 2807. Offering of Toll Limitation:

Toll limitation must be offered to low-income customers when they apply for LITAP.

§ 2808. Service Deposit:

The utility may not require a deposit from a LITAP customer who accepts toll limitation. If toll limitation is not feasible, a deposit may be charged.

* * *

Electric—**4 Colo. Code Regs. §§ 723-3-3000–723-3-3999**

* * *

§ 3004. Disputes and Informal Complaints:

A dispute is a problem that a customer or applicant bring directly to the attention of the company, without the involvement of the staff or Commission. A utility should follow the procedures of Rule 1301 of Commission's Rules of Practice and Procedure and make a full and prompt investigation of all disputes and informal complaints. If a customer or applicant is not satisfied with the outcome, the company must inform him or her of the availability of an informal complaint to the Commission, and provide the Commission's address and toll-free telephone number. The utility must keep records of all disputes and informal complaints, which shall be accessible to the complainant, and to Commission and staff.

§ 3005. Records:

A utility must keep, retain for at least 3 years, and make available for inspection, records of, inter alia, disputes and informal complaints, customer billing and deposits, and all tariffs filed with the Commission. If the utility has a website, the tariffs should also be posted on the website.

* * *

§ 3108. Tariffs:

Tariffs must include information about, inter alia, line extension policies, meter testing and equipment, customer deposit policy, installment and other payment plans, collection and service fees, after-hours restoration fees, and rules governing customer relations.

* * *

§ 3300. Service Meters and Related Equipment:

Meters used for billing purposes shall be furnished, installed, and maintained at the utility's expense. Equipment, devices, or facilities furnished or maintained at utility's expense may be removed by utility after discontinuance of service.

The meter must be marked with any constant or factor needed to calculate usage or, if this is too complicated, with instructions on how to contact the utility to obtain this information.

* * *

§ 3305. Meter Testing Upon Request:

The utility furnishing metered electric service shall test the accuracy of any electric service meter free of charge upon request of a customer, provided the meter has not been tested within 12 months prior to request and the customer will accept results of test as basis for settlement of difference claimed. A written report of the test result shall be given to the customer with, the original being kept at the office of the utility for at least 2 years.

A customer who disagrees with the test result may make a written request for an independent test. The company must make the meter available for testing by a qualified independent testing service of the customer's choosing. If the meter is found to be accurate, within the standards set by these rules, the customer must pay for the test; if inaccurate, the utility must pay.

* * *

§ 3309. Meter Reading:

At a customer's request, the utility must provide written documentation of the date of the last meter reading, and the total usage, expressed in kilo-watt hours or other unit of service rendered. The utility must also, upon request, explain to customers its method of reading meters. Tariffs should state when meters will be read, the circumstances, if any, under which customers must read their own meters, and the procedure.

Absent good cause, a utility should read meters monthly. For good cause shown, it may read a meter once every 6 months.

* * *

§ 3401. Billing Information and Procedures:

§ 3401(a). Bill Contents:

All bills shall show: net amount due; dates and meter readings beginning and ending with the period of service; a distinct marking, if an estimated bill; an appropriate rate or rate code identification; date payable after which bill becomes past due; the total amount of payments or credits made to the customer's account during the billing period; any past-due amount; identification of an amount due for unregulated charges, if applicable; any transferred amount from any account other than the customer's current account; and all other essential facts upon which the bill is based, including factors and/or constants when practical.

The due date shall be no earlier than 15 days subsequent to the mailing or delivery of the bill.

§ 3401(b). Partial Payments:

A utility that bills for unregulated goods or services shall allocate partial payments first to regulated charges, then to unregulated or non-tariffed charges, and to the oldest balance due within each category.

§ 3401(c), (d). Transfer of Balances:

If a utility transfers a balance from one person's account to another, pursuant to its benefit of service policy, it must include in its tariffs an explanation of how the utility will verify that the person to be billed actually received the benefit of service. If a utility transfers a customer's prior debt to a current bill, it must inform the customer of the source of the unpaid debt (i.e., the address and time period when services provided).

§ 3401(e). E-billing:

If a utility chooses to offer e-billing, it must obtain the affirmative consent of the customer, and may not charge a fee for the service. Any fee for customer payment options must be the same as for customers who use printed bills. Electronic bills must contain the same disclosures and customer information as printed bills.

§ 3402. Adjustments for Meter and Billing Errors:

If a meter accuracy test shows that the meter is running more than 2% slow, the utility may bill for one-half the weighted average error, for the period from the discovery of the error back to the last meter test, not to exceed 6 months. The customer may elect to enter into a payment arrangement equal in time to the time during which the under-billing lasted. If a meter is found to be running more than 2% fast, the utility must refund one half of the weighted average error, from the time of discovery of the error back to the last meter test, not to exceed 2 years. The customer may elect to receive the refund as a credit on future bills, or as a one-time payment, which must be mailed within 30 days of request.

If a meter has an incorrect register ratio or multiplier, and the error is adverse to the customer, the utility shall refund an amount equal to the excess charged for the period of time the incorrect meter was used in billing, not to exceed 2 years. If the error is adverse to the utility, the utility may charge the customer for the corrected charges for the same period of time, not to exceed 6 months.

If a meter does not register, registers intermittently, or partially registers for any period, the utility shall estimate charges for a period not exceeding 6 months by averaging amounts registered over similar periods.

§ 3403. Applications for Service, Customer Deposits, and Third-Party Guarantee Arrangements:

§ 3403(a)–(g). Deposit Criteria:

A utility must process applications for service made orally or in writing, and use non-discriminatory criteria for requiring a deposit. If billing records are available from the utility for that customer, a deposit may not be required unless the records show recent or substantial delinquencies. No deposit may be required from a customer who presents evidence of 12 months of timely payment for similar service from another utility, which 12 months must have ended within 60 days of the application. Utilities that use credit scoring or prior payment history must disclose in their tariffs the criteria that trigger a deposit requirement. If credit scoring is used, the utility must disclose the scoring model, evaluation criteria, and score that trigger a deposit requirement. If a utility denies an application or requires a deposit, it must inform the customer in writing, within 3 business days, of the reason for its decision.

§ 3403(e), (h). Form of Deposits:

A utility that requires deposits must provide one non-cash alternative for payment that does not require the disclosure of a social security number. No services by or indebtedness to a utility may result in a lien, mortgage or security interest in real or personal property, unless the debt has been reduced to judgment.

§ 3403(*i*). Amount of Deposit:

The deposit may not exceed an estimated 90 days bill, or, for customers who pay in advance, 60 days. A deposit may be required in addition to any advance or guarantee in connection with line extension.

§ 3403(j)–(*l*). Records and Receipts:

A utility receiving cash deposits must maintain records of customer's name, amount and date of deposit, all transactions (i.e., payment of interest), address(es) where customer received service, and date when deposit returned to customer or unclaimed deposit returned to energy assistance organization. The utility must provide a receipt to the customer, but may not refuse to return a deposit for the sole reason that the customer cannot produce a receipt. The utility's tariff must set forth the circumstances under which deposits will be required and returned.

§ 3403(m). Application of Deposits:

The payment of a deposit does not relieve a customer of the obligation to pay current or past-due charges. A utility is not required to apply a deposit to any charges except those due after termination of service.

§ 3403(n). Interest on Deposits:

Interest is payable upon the return of the deposit or annually at the request of the customer. Interest accrues from the time of deposit to the date of payment to the customer or to the date on which an equal amount is credited to the customer's account, at the utility's option. The simple interest rate to be paid on customer deposits shall be determined annually by PUC Staff.

The interest rate is the average monthly interest rate for October 1 through September 30 of the year immediately preceding as quoted for one-year United States Treasury constant maturities published in the Federal Reserve Bulletin by the Board of Governors of the Federal Reserve System.

If the difference between the existing deposit rate and the newly calculated rate is 25 basis points or more, the new rate shall be effective on January 1 of the following year; otherwise, the rate remains the same.

§ 3403(o). Third-Party Guarantees:

In lieu of a cash deposit, a customer or applicant may use a third-party guarantee, if the guarantor is a customer in good standing of the utility. The amount of the guarantee may not exceed the amount of a cash deposit. If the guarantor terminates service or terminates the guarantee before the customer has established 12 consecutive months of satisfactory payment, the utility may require a new guarantee or cash deposit.

§ 3403(p)–(r). Unclaimed Deposits:

If a cash deposit remains unclaimed for 2 years after termination of service, notwithstanding reasonable efforts to locate the customer, the funds should be paid to the energy assistance organization. If a customer later claims the deposit and the utility pays the customer, it may deduct the sum from future funds submitted to the energy assistance organization.

* * *

§ 3404. Installment Payments:

§ 3404(a). Budget Billing:

A utility must make available a budget or levelized payment plan.

§ 3404(b)(I). Arrearage Arising from Events Under Utility's Control:

A customer may be permitted to make installment payments if a bill includes amounts from past billing periods that result solely from events under the utility's control, including meter malfunctions, billing errors, utility meter reading errors, or failure to read the meter. Such installment payments may extend over a period equal to the period of such events and may not bear interest.

§ 3404(b)(II)–(g). Other Installment Plans:

An installment payment plan must be made if a customer: pays at least 10 % of the amount shown on the notice of discontinuance and enters into an installment plan on or before the notice expiration date; pays at least 10% of any amount more than 30 days past due and enters into an installment plan on or before the last day covered by a medical certification or extension thereof; or, after service has been discontinued, pays at least any collection and/or reconnection charges and enters into an installment plan arrangement, unless such an arrangement has already have breached.

Installment arrangements must be made with respect to any and all of the following applicable amounts at the time request for arrangement is made: the unpaid balance shown on the notice; amounts not included on the notice that have since become more than 30 days past due; any bill that is past due but is less than 30 days past due; any bill that has been issued but is not past due; authorized collection fees, whether or not appearing on a regular monthly bill; any deposit billed, billed in part, or required due to discontinuance or delinquency or to establish initial credit, except for deposits required as a condition of initiating service; and any other charges or fees in the utility's tariff, including miscellaneous service charges, investigative charges, or insufficient check charges.

The terms of an installment plan must be explained and offered to each customer who contacts the utility in response to a notice of discontinuance. Customer who agrees to enter into an installment plan arrangement shall be provided a copy of the applicable regulations and a statement of the agreed payment arrangement within 7 days of the agreement.

An installment payment plan may consist of equal monthly installments over a period not to exceed 6 months. The first monthly payment shall be due together with the new bill on the due date of the new bill unless the new bill has already been included in the installment plan. The subsequent monthly installments shall be due together with the new bills on the due date of the new bills.

A customer may choose in the alternative a "budget billing" arrangement, under which the amount owed shall be added to the preceding year's total billing and modified for rate increases or cost adjustments, with the total being billed in 11 equal monthly payments followed by a settlement billing in the twelfth month.

§§ 3405–3406. Service, Rate, and Usage Information; Component and Source Disclosure:

A utility must provide upon request, an explanation of the rate schedule applicable to a customer, the customer's actual consumption or degree-day adjusted consumption for each billing period during the previous year (if reasonably ascertainable) and any other information needed to enable the customer to obtain safe and efficient service. The utility must mail to all customers, in April and October, "electricity facts" including the components of the average delivered price of electricity, and the power supply mix. This rule provides a format for these disclosures.

§ 3407. Discontinuance of Service:

§ 3407(a). Sufficient Reasons for Discontinuance:

Nonpayment of regulated charges; fraud or subterfuge; service diversion; equipment tampering; safety concerns; exigent circumstances; order of appropriate government authority; unauthorized restoration of discontinued service.

§ 3407(b), (e)(I) and (II). Insufficient Reasons for Discontinuance:

Nonpayment of: amounts which have not appeared on monthly bill or are not due; amounts on another account held or guaranteed by the customer which have not been transferred to current account; account on which customer is not or was not customer of record or guarantor, or amounts due from previous occupant of premises, so long as customer did not obtain service through fraud or subterfuge; account established in customer's name by another through fraud and without consent; delinquent amounts for which utility cannot provide billing records; debt for service other than that rendered by utility in Colorado; any unregulated charge. A utility may not disconnect if the customer tenders the full amount due (excluding the charge for a service call) to an employee authorized to receive payment, including the employee dispatched to discontinue service, or pays, on or before the expiration date of the termination notice, 10% of the amount due and enters into an installment plan.

§ 3407 (c), (d). Energy Diversion or Tampering:

If the utility discovers connections or devices of any kind on the premises, including energy-consuming devices connected on the line side of a meter, which would prevent meter from registering actual consumption, utility may give customer a 15-day notice to remove or correct such devices or connections and advise the customer of the possibility of an estimated bill for consumption not properly registered. The utility may opt to remove or correct said devices or connections and, if they do, the interruption of service necessary to do this shall not constitute discontinuance or require advance notice; however, the utility must leave written notice of the violation, the action taken by the utility, and the possibility of an estimated bill. If the utility discovers evidence of tampering or diversion, it must mail notice within 3 days informing the customer of the steps it will take to investigate.

* * *

§ 3407(e)(III). Timing of Disconnection:

Service may not be discontinued between 12:00 p.m. on Friday and 8:00 a.m. the following Monday, or between 12:00 p.m. on the day prior to and 8:00 a.m. of the day following any state or federal holiday, or any day during which utility's local office is closed.

§ 3407(e)(IV). Medical Emergency:

A utility may not disconnect for 60 days after receipt of a certificate from a Colorado-licensed physician, or health-care practitioner working under the supervision of a physician, stating that discontinuance would aggravate an existing condition or create a medical emergency. The certificate may be extended for one 30-day period. A customer may invoke this sub-paragraph only once in any 12-month period. The certificate is incontestable as to medical judgment, but the utility may use reasonable means to verify its authenticity.

§ 3408. Notice of Discontinuance of Service:

§ 3408(a)–(f). Notice Contents and Procedure:

Before termination, a utility must send by first-class mail or hand delivery, 15 days before the discontinuance date, a notice with heading in bold capitals THIS IS A FINAL NOTICE OF DISCONTINUANCE OF UTILITY SERVICE AND CONTAINS IMPORTANT INFORMATION ABOUT YOUR LEGAL RIGHTS AND REMEDIES. YOU MUST ACT PROMPTLY TO AVOID UTILITY SHUTOFF. The notice must disclose: the reason for discontinuance; the amount past due; the date by which an installment plan must be entered into or full payment made, and how and where to do so; the customer's rights if any household member is seriously ill; the right to dispute the discontinuance with the utility or file a formal or informal complaint with the Commission, along with the Commission's address and toll-free number; that if a formal complaint is filed, the Commission may grant a motion to postpone termination; that if service is discontinued, customer will be liable for reconnection and collection charges; information about financial assistance for low-income customers. The utility must also provide notice to any third party designated by the customer. Discontinuance notices must be printed in English and any other language spoken by at least 10% of the residents of the utility's territory, as shown by U.S. Census data. A utility must offer and explain an installment plan to any customer who contacts it in response to a termination notice. At least 24 hours before the proposed discontinuance, the utility must attempt to give notice in person or by telephone to the customer and any designated third party.

§ 3408(g). Notice of Discontinuance for Broken Installment Plan:

In case of a broken installment plan, the notice must be headed in capital letters "notice of broken arrangement," and must advise the customer that the utility may discontinue if it does not receive the installment payment within 10 days after notice or receive the current payment within 30 days after due date; that if service is discontinued utility may refuse to restore until customer pays all amounts more than 30 days past due for regulated service, plus all collection and reconnection charges; that the customer has certain rights in case a household member is seriously ill.

§ 3408(h). Exceptions to Notice Requirement:

Notice is not required termination is required because of safety concerns or exigent circumstances; order of appropriate government agency; energy diversion; or unauthorized restoration of discontinued service.

§ 3408(*i*). Discontinuance of Service to Multiple Dwelling:

When service recorded on a single meter is used directly or indirectly by more than one dwelling unit in a multi-unit dwelling or a cluster of dwellings, the notice period shall be 30 days and the notice may include the current bill.

Prior to the expiration of the 30-day notice period, the utility also shall provide written notice to each individual dwelling unit stating: that a notice of discontinuance has been sent to the party responsible for the payment of utility bills for the dwelling; the proposed date of discontinuance; that the occupants of the dwelling units may avoid discontinuance by paying new bills in full within 30 days of issuance; and how to contact the utility for information or to arrange to receive a copy of the next new bill.

Notice shall be delivered or mailed to the addressee or occupant of each unit and a copy posted to the extent possible in at least one common area.

§ 3409. Restoration of Service:

Service must be restored without charge if discontinuance did not comply with these rules. Unless prevented by safety concerns or exigent circumstances, service must be restored within 24 hours (excluding weekends and holidays) or 12 hours if customer pays after-hours charges if: customer pays in full the amount due for regulated charges and any necessary fees; the customer pays collection and restoration fees, enters into payment arrangement and makes first payment (unless discontinuance was for broken payment arrangement); presents a medical certificate; or demonstrates that the cause for discontinuance, if other than nonpayment, has been eliminated.

§ 3410. Refunds:

A utility that gives refunds to a class of customers must present a refund plan to the Commission, meeting the criteria set forth in this section.

* * *

§ 3803. Exemption Requirements:

A master-meter operator which charges its end users only the actual costs billed to the MMO by the serving utility is exempt from rate regulation. (The MMO may not bill its customers for any other charges and fees.)

* * *

***Gas*—4 Colo. Code Regs. §§ 723-4-4000–723-4-4999**

* * *

§ 4004. Disputes and Informal Complaints:

Substantially similar to § 723-3-3004.

§ 4005. Records:

Substantially similar to § 723-3-3005.

* * *

§ 4108. Tariffs:

Tariffs must include information on, inter alia, all terms, conditions, etc. with respect to regulated products; line extension provisions; meter testing; benefit of service transfer policy; customer deposit policy; payment plans; collection or restoration fees or other miscellaneous charges; any other rules, regulations or policies concerning customer relations.

* * *

§ 4300. Service Meters and Related Equipment:

Substantially similar to § 723-3-3300. If the method of calculating usage is too complicated to be shown on the meter, bills must include step-by-step instructions for converting the meter reading to the billing determination.

* * *

§ 4303. Meter Testing Requirements:

Substantially similar to § 723-3-3303.

* * *

§ 4305. Meter Testing Upon Request:

Substantially similar to § 723-3-3305.

* * *

§ 4309. Meter Reading:

Substantially similar to § 723-3-3309.

* * *

§ 4401. Billing Information and Procedures:

§ 4401(a). Bill Contents:

Substantially similar to § 723-3-3401(a).

§ 4401(b). Partial Payments:

Substantially similar to § 723-3-3401(b).

§ 4401(c), (d). Transfer of Balances:

Substantially similar to § 723-3-3401(c) and (d).

§ 4401(e). E-billing:

Substantially similar to § 723-3-3401(e).

§ 4402. Adjustments for Meter and Billing Errors:

Substantially similar to § 723-3-3402, except that tolerance is 1%.

§ 4403. Applications for Service, Customer Deposits and Third-Party Guarantees.

§ 4403(a)–(g). Deposit Criteria:

Substantially similar to § 723-3-3403(a)–(g).

§ 4403(e), (h). Form of Deposits:

Substantially similar to § 723-3-3403(e) and (h).

§ 4403(*i*). Amount of Deposit:

Substantially similar to § 723-3-3403(i).

§ 4403(j)–(*l*). Records and Receipts:

Substantially similar to § 723-3-3403(j)–(l).

§ 4403(m). Application of Deposits:

Substantially similar to § 723-3-3403(m).

§ 4403(n). Interest on Deposits:

Substantially similar to § 723-3-3404(n).

§ 4403(o). Third-party Guarantees:

Substantially similar to § 723-3-3403(o).

§ 4403(p)–(r). Unclaimed Deposits:

Substantially similar to § 723-3-3403(p)–(r).

§ 4404. Installment Payments:

§ 4404(a). Levelized Payment Plans:

Substantially similar to § 723-3-3404(a).

§ 4404(b)(I). Arrearage Arising from Events Under Utility's Control:

Substantially similar to § 723-3-3404(b)(I).

§ 4404(b)(II)–(g). Other Arrearages:

Substantially similar to § 723-3-3404(b)(II)–(g).

§ 4405. Service, Rate, and Usage Information:

Substantially similar to § 723-3-3405

§ 4406. Itemized Billing Components:

For transportation customers: per-unit and monthly distribution company costs and, if applicable, per-unit and monthly gas cost adjustment transportation costs.

For all other customers: per-unit and monthly local distribution costs, per-unit and monthly gas commodity costs, per-unit and monthly costs of upstream services.

§ 4407. Discontinuance of Service:

§ 4407(a). Sufficient Reasons for Discontinuance:

Substantially similar to § 723-3-3407(a).

§ 4407(b), (e)(I), and (II). Insufficient Reasons for Discontinuance:

Substantially similar to § 723-3-3407(b) and (e)(I) and (II).

§ 4407(c), (d). Energy Diversion or Tampering:

Substantially similar to § 723-3-3407(c) and (d).

§ 4407(e)(III). Time of Discontinuance:

Substantially similar to § 723-3-3407(e)(III).

§ 4407(e)(IV). Medical Emergencies:

Substantially similar to § 723-3-3407(e)(IV).

§ 4408. Notice of Discontinuance:

§ 4408(a)–(f). Notice Contents and Procedure:

Substantially similar to § 723-3-3408(a)–(f).

§ 4408(g). Discontinuance Notice for Broken Installment Plan:

Substantially similar to § 723-3-3408(g).

§ 4408(h). Exceptions to Notice Requirement:

Substantially similar to § 723-3-3408(h).

§ 4408(*i*). Discontinuance of Service to Multiple Dwelling:

Substantially similar to § 723-3-3408(i).

§ 4409. Restoration of Service:

Substantially similar to § 723-3-3409.

§ 4410. Refunds:

Substantially similar to § 723-3-3410.

* * *

***Water*—4 Colo. Code Regs. §§ 723-5-5000–723-5-5410**

§ 5004. Disputes and Informal Complaints:

Substantially similar to § 723-3-3004.

§ 5005. Records:

Substantially similar to § 723-3-3005.

* * *

§ 5108. Tariffs:

Substantially similar to § 723-3-3108.

* * *

§ 5300. Service Meters and Related Equipment:

Substantially similar to § 723-3-3300.

* * *

§ 5305. Meter Testing Upon Request:

Substantially similar to § 723-3-3305.

* * *

§ 5309. Meter Reading:

Substantially similar to § 723-3-3309.

§ 5401. Billing Information and Procedures:

§ 5401(a). Bill Contents:

Substantially similar to § 723-3-3401(a).

§ 5401(b). Partial Payments:

Substantially similar to § 723-3-3401(b)

§ 5401(c)–(d). Transfer of Balances:

Substantially similar to § 723-3-3401(c)–(d).

§ 5401(e). E-billing:

Substantially similar to § 723-3-3401(e).

§ 5402. Adjustments for Meter and Billing Errors:

Substantially similar to § 723-3-3402

§ 5403. Applications for Service, Customer Deposits, and Third-party Guarantee Arrangements:

§ 5403(a)–(f). Deposit Criteria and Procedures:

Substantially similar to § 723-3-3403(a)–(f).

§ 5403(g). Denial of Application:

A utility that denies an application for service or requires a deposit must provide, within 3 business days, a written explanation of the reasons for its action.

§ 5403(h). Limits on Deposits:

No utility may require security other than a cash deposit or a third-party guarantee. No indebtedness to a utility may result in a mortgage, lien, or security interest in real or personal property, unless reduced to judgment.

§ 5403(*i*). Amount of Deposit:

Similar to § 723-3-3403(*i*).

§ 5403(j)–(l). Records and Receipts:

Substantially similar to § 723-3-3403(j)–(l).

§ 5403(m). Application of Deposits:

Substantially similar to § 723-3-3403(m).

§ 5403(n). Interest on Deposits:

Substantially similar to § 723-3-34-3403(n).

§ 5403(*o*). Third-party Guarantees:

Substantially similar to § 723-3-3403(o).

§ 5404. Installment Payments:

§ 5404(a). Levelized Payment Plans:

Substantially similar to § 723-3-3404(a).

§ 5404(b)(I). Arrearage Arising from Events Under Utility's Control:

Substantially similar to § 723-3-3404(b)(I).

§ 5404(b)(II)–(g). Other Installment Plans:

Substantially similar to § 723-3-3404(b)(II)–(g).

§ 5405. Service, Rate and Usage Information:

Substantially similar to § 723-3-3405.

* * *

§ 5407. Discontinuance of Service:

§ 5407(a). Sufficient Reasons for Discontinuance:

Substantially similar to § 723-3-3407(a).

§ 5407(b), (e)(I), and (II). Insufficient Reasons for Discontinuance:

Substantially similar to § 723-3-3407(b), (e)(I) and (II).

§ 5407(c), (d). Energy Diversion or Tampering:

Substantially similar to § 723-3-3407(c) and (d).

§ 5407(e)(III). Timing of Discontinuance:

Substantially similar to § 723-3-3407(e)(III).

§ 5407(e)(IV). Medical Emergency:

Substantially similar to § 723-3-3407(e)(IV).

§ 5408. Notice of Discontinuance:

§ 5408(a)–(f). Notice Contents and Procedure:

Substantially similar to § 723-3-3408(a)–(f).

§ 5408(g). Discontinuance for Broken Installment Plan:

Substantially similar to § 723-3-3408(g).

§ 5408(h). Exceptions to Notice Requirement:

Substantially similar to § 723-3-3408(h).

§ 5408(*i*). Discontinuance of Service to Multiple Dwelling:

Substantially similar to § 723-3-3408(i).

§ 5409. Restoration of Service:

Substantially similar to § 723-3-3409.

§ 5410. Refund Plans:

Substantially similar to § 723-3-3410.

CONNECTICUT

Regulations relating to electric, gas, water and sewage are located in Conn. Agencies Regs. § 16-3-100(a)–(j). Regulations relating to telephone are located in Conn. Agencies Regs. § 16-3-101(A)–(C) and §§ 16-247g-1 to 16-247g-9. Regulations relating to estimated billing are located in Conn. Agencies Regs. § 16-3-102(A)–(D). Regulations relating to security deposits are located in Conn. Agencies Regs. § 16-262j-1(a), (b). Provisions that are substantially similar to others are indicated accordingly.

Website: www.state.ct.us/dpuc/administ.htm

***Electric, Gas, Water, and Sewer*—Conn. Agencies Regs. § 16-3-100(a)–(j)**

§ 16-3-100. Termination of Utility Service

* * *

§ 16-3-100(b)(1). Grounds for Termination Without Notice:

Utility service may be terminated without notice if provision of the service would constitute a hazardous condition as determined by the utility company.

§ 16-3-100(b)(2). Grounds for Termination with Notice:

Service may be terminated with notice for the following reasons: furnishing service would be in contravention of any federal, state, or local orders, ordinances, or law; tampering with water pipes, meters or other utility equipment by the customer of a water company; fraud or material misrepresentation in obtaining service; use of equipment in a manner adverse to the utility or service to others after customer notified; violation of or non-compliance with utility rules filed with PUC; failure to provide reasonable access to utility equipment or if access is obstructed or hazardous; failure or refusal to reimburse utility for repairs or loss of property caused by intentional or negligent acts of customer or customer's agents; failure of the customer to furnish equipment or permission specified as a condition to obtaining service or if such equipment or permissions are withdrawn or terminated; nonpayment of delinquent account, provided the utility has notified the customer and attempted to obtain payment in accordance with this section; unauthorized unmetered service or unauthorized metered service; or failure to provide identification no later than 15 days from opening an account.

Service may be terminated if a customer is paying for a delinquent account under an amortization agreement and either fails to comply with the agreement or to stay current on current charges. If a customer makes payment or payments amounting to 20% of the balance due, then notice is required of the conditions the customer must meet to avoid termination.

Service may not be terminated from November 1 to April 15 to customers receiving electric service and who lack the financial resources to pay the entire account. During the same period, no gas company or municipal utility furnishing gas may terminate or refuse to restore gas service in hardship cases when the customer uses such gas for heat and cannot pay the entire account. A gas company that terminated service between April 16 and October 31 to a customer who uses gas for heat and who, during the previous period of November 1 to April 15, had gas service maintained because of hardship status, may refuse to reinstate service from November 1 to April 15 only if customer has failed since the preceding November 1 to make a payment of the lesser of: (i) 20% of the outstanding principal balance owed as of the date of termination; (ii) $100; or (iii) the minimum payment due under an amortization agreement.

§ 16-3-100(b)(3). Exceptions:

Gas or electric service may not be terminated for a delinquent amount until the company first offers the customer an opportunity to enter into amortization agreement. If such an agreement is reached, the company may charge simple interest on the unpaid balance of the delinquent account at the rate of 6% per annum.

Between November 1 and April 15, a company may not terminate or refuse to reinstate electric or gas service in hardship cases, and no gas company and no municipal utility furnishing gas may terminate or refuse to reinstate residential gas service in hardship cases when the customer uses such gas for heat and lacks the financial resources to pay his or her entire account. However, a gas company that terminated service between April 16 and October 31 to a customer who uses gas for heat and who had service maintained during the previous period between November 1 and April 15 due to hardship may refuse to reinstate the service from November 1 to April 15 only if the customer has failed since the previous November 1 to make a payment of the lesser of: 20% of the outstanding principal balance as of the date of termination; $100; or the minimum payment(s) due under an amortization agreement.

Company may not terminate service: if resident is seriously ill or in a life-threatening situation as certified by a registered physician; pending any complaint, investigation, hearing; or appeal initiated by customer and regarding disputed amounts; or if termination would be violate the Connecticut General Statutes.

Company may not refuse to restore service of former customer if any resident therein becomes seriously ill or a life-threatening situation occurs as certified by a registered physician.

Company may not terminate or deny service for failure to pay for: merchandise purchased from the utility; a different type or class of service at the same or another location or for repair of customer-owned or -rented equipment; the bill of another customer as guarantor; improperly billed charges; or an estimated bill, unless the customer refuses to provide meter access during company's normal working day or to provide a customer reading (and unless the company may otherwise provide estimated bill).

Company may not terminate or deny service for delinquency in payment by a previous occupant.

Company may not terminate service on any Friday, Saturday, Sunday, state or federal holiday, or day before any state or federal holiday when its business offices are not open, or within one hour before closing.

Company may not terminate gas or electric service between November 1 and April 15 for nonpayment of a delinquent account without first giving notice of customer rights in person or by certified mail.

Company may not terminate or refuse to restore gas or electric service provided at interruptible rates to singly metered multi-unit residential buildings when the customer has failed to curtail usage.

§ 16-3-100(c). Notice to Customers of Rights Under This Section:

Utility shall: file with PUC a brief explanation of the rights of customers regarding termination of service; make the explanation available upon request at each company office; send to each customer at least once a year and to new customers upon initiation of a service notice that such explanation is available upon request; include such explanation with every termination notice; and provide the explanation in Spanish and English if a substantial number of Spanish-speaking people reside in its service area.

Gas and electric companies must also provide an explanation of customer rights regarding amortization agreements and hardship.

§ 16-3-100(d). Notice of Termination:

Company may not terminate service prior to 13 days after notice has been sent by first class mail to the customer and to any third party designated by the customer. If a person opening an account does not provide identification, the company shall furnish service and provide notice that the service may be terminated after 15 days if identification is not provided.

If service is not terminated within 120 days of notice, company shall mail another notice at least 13 days before termination. If an electric or gas company issues a notice but fails to terminate service before issuing a new bill, the company shall mail an additional notice of the termination at least 13 days, or at least 7 days by certified mail, prior to termination, stating the delinquent amount and that the termination notice remains in effect. If the electric or gas company provides multiple dates of termination, termination may not occur prior to latest date or for balances that are not delinquent.

* * *

§ 16-3-100(d)(2). Contents of Termination Notice:

Termination notice must provide or include: reasons for termination; conditions required to prevent termination; the date after which service may be terminated unless the conditions are met; the conditions for restoration of service, including fees or deposits; and a brief explanation of the customer's notification rights.

§ 16-3-100(d)(3). Timing of Termination Notice:

Termination notice may not be sent prior to the time a customer has a delinquent account or prior to the existence of grounds for termination.

If, after receipt of termination notice or entering into amortization agreement, the customer makes payment(s) totaling 20% of balance due, service may not be terminated before 13 days after the mailing of a subsequent termination notice. The subsequent notice does not entitle the customer to further or additional notice upon subsequent payment of 20%.

If utility service is terminated without notice, the company shall keep a record of the conditions that caused the termination. The company shall attempt to notify the customer at the time of termination of the conditions causing the termination, the conditions which must be met to have service restored, and the means of contacting the company for restoring service.

* * *

§ 16-3-100(e). Termination and Serious Illness:

Company may not terminate service to the residence of any customer if any resident is seriously ill, provided the serious illness is certified by a licensed physician no later than 13 days after the mailing of the termination notice and the certification is renewed every 15 days if the physician did not specify the length of the illness. Company has the right to contest validity of any certification before the PUC.

A physician's certification is sufficient if initially made by telephone, subject to the company's right to confirm the validity of the physician's call. If the certification is made by telephone, the company shall send the physician a copy of its certification form, and the certifying physician shall complete and return the certification form to the company no later than 7 days after receipt. All certification forms shall contain at least the following information: name and address of the patient; whether the condition is a serious illness or a life-threatening situation; length of the serious illness or life-threatening situation; and physician's office address and telephone number.

If service is continued pursuant to such a certification, the customer shall enter an amortization agreement under which the customer may amortize the unpaid balance, provided the customer simultaneously keeps the account current as charges accrue in subsequent billing periods—the exception being that service which is continued due to a current life-threatening situation certification shall not be terminated for failure to do so—and no such amortization agreement is required between November 1 and April 15 for a customer determined to be a hardship.

Customer is expected to renew the serious illness or life-threatening situation certificate no later than the last day specified by the physician as the length of the applicable situation. If the physician fails to do so or indicates that the length is not readily ascertainable, then the certificate shall be renewed every 15 days.

If service is continued pursuant to a certification and the customer otherwise fails to comply with an amortization agreement or to renew with the certification, the company may terminate service after providing a 13-day notice.

§ 16-3-100(f). Review of Reasonable Amortization Agreements and Hardship Cases:

If a customer and an electric or gas company are unable to reach an amortization agreement or agree as to whether the customer is a hardship case and lacks the financial resources to pay an entire account from November 1 to April 15, the company may not terminate service and shall refer the customer to a specified review officer who shall attempt to reach an amortization agreement with the customer.

If the review officer cannot reach an amortization agreement between November 1 and April 15, the officer shall determine if the customer is a hardship case. The company may request documentation certifying that the customer is a hardship case, including documentation from a social service or other aid agency.

If the customer disagrees with a review officer as to an amortization agreement or as to whether the customer qualifies as a hardship case or not, the officer shall provide a written report to the customer providing the PUC's consumer assistance toll-free telephone number and informing the customer of the right to appeal for an informal PUC investigation within 5 days after the receipt of the report.

If the PUC's consumer assistance division is unable to reach a mutually satisfactory resolution, either the customer or the company may appeal in the form of a formal complaint with the PUC and requesting a hearing before a PUC hearing officer. Service may not be terminated pending such an appeal.

§ 16-3-100(g). Review of Disputed Accounts:

Service shall not be terminated for any reason requiring prior written notice while any matter relating to a reason for termination is in dispute, provided the customer has notified the company of the dispute and is pursuing the procedures for investigation by the company, referral to a review officer, notice, investigation by the PUC, or a formal complaint with the PUC in a timely manner.

§ 16-3-100(h). Notification of Third Parties:

Customer may request that a third person designated by the customer receive copies of all notices regarding termination of service. Such third party shall not be liable for the customer's bills except when the third party has previously agreed to it. Company shall maintain a list of the names and addresses of organizations that have notified the company that they are available as third parties, and such information shall be provided upon the customer's request.

§ 16-3-100(*i*). Termination of Service to Tenants:

A company may not, without a 13-day notice, terminate service to a dwelling unit when it has actual or constructive knowledge that the billed customer or members of his or her household are not the exclusive occupants of the premises. Notice to the occupants subject to termination of their rights to continued service may be by the most practicable means under the circumstances. The notices shall contain: the date of the proposed termination; the right of the tenant in an individually metered unit to establish service in his or her own name without liability for the balance owed or any security deposit; company's intent to seek a receivership or other arrangement if there is a master meter; and the telephone numbers and addresses of the company's local office and of the PUC.

If an occupant in an individually metered unit notifies the company of his or her desire to establish service in his or her own name, the occupant may do so without liability for any portion of the amount previously billed to the premises and without obligation to pay a security deposit as a condition of establishing the service in his or her name. The company shall notify the occupant of the right to deduct the full amount of payment for utility service from his or her rent.

If service is provided through a master meter, the company may, with the written agreement of all occupants, establish service in the name of the occupants pursuant to a plan for billing and payment agreed to by all parties. Service may not be terminated if payment of the agreed share of any of the occupants is received. The company may discontinue this arrangement upon a 13-day written notice or upon the written request of any of the occupants. In the latter case, the company shall promptly provide a 13-day notice to each occupant.

§ 16-3-100(j). Termination of Spouses' and Former Spouses' Utility Service:

Company may not terminate, threaten to terminate, or refuse to provide residential utility service for a period of 90 days for nonpayment of a delinquent account when the person seeking to retain or obtain service is the unnamed customer and is divorced, legally separated, or has an annulled marriage from the named account customer of the delinquent account or when an action regarding the same is pending, provided the unnamed customer: notifies the company at the time of the request and provides corresponding court documentation within 21 days thereof; no longer resides with the spouse or former spouse; provides the current or last known address or place of employment of the named customer; and requests service from the time the company is notified of the divorce, legal separation, annulment, or action seeking the same.

The 90-day period commences on the earlier of the date that the unnamed customer requests service, the date of the judgment file showing the unnamed customer's divorce, legal separation, or annulment, or the date of the summons commencing such an action.

During the 90-day period, the company shall make diligent efforts to collect the delinquent balance from the named customer, including the following: obtaining the named customer's address; sending a final notice of delinquency on the old account to a known address of the named customer; and transferring the delinquent balance to another account of the same type and class of the named customer, if one has been established. If the named customer's account remains delinquent, the company may utilize other collection methods that it deems cost-effective, including referral for collection, sending demands for payment, and legal action.

If the company receives a certified copy of an appropriate court order assigning sole responsibility for the delinquent account to the named customer, it shall not terminate or refuse to provide service, due to the delinquency, to the unnamed customer for 90 days in addition to the 90-day grace period. If the company fails to obtain payment after the 180-day period expires, it shall offer the unnamed customer an opportunity to enter into an amortization agreement.

Once an unnamed customer has become a named customer of an account, service may not be terminated or refused for nonpayment of delinquent balances incurred prior to the earlier of the date of such customer's request for utility service, the date of the judgment file of a divorce or legal separation, certification of annulment, or the writ of summons commencing an action seeking the same.

***Telephone*—Conn. Agencies Regs. § 16-3-101(A)–(C); §§ 16-247g-1 to 16-247g-9**

§ 16-247g-3. Notice of Rates:

Within 30 days of inception of service, company shall confirm in writing to customer the rates and services that the customer has chosen and give a simple and clear description of the rates and services.

§ 16-247g-4. Billing Practices:

At time of initial subscription and annually thereafter, company shall provide customer with a description of its billing practices, including at least the following information: billing period and frequency; deposit requirements; late payment charges; returned check charges; credits for service outages; credits for service outages; and whether the company provides customer credit reports to credit agencies.

§ 16-247g-5. Information on Bills:

Each bill must: identify carrier and include a toll-free telephone number and address of the company to which complaints may be addressed; include a toll-free telephone number and address of the Department of Public Utility Control; conspicuously identify charges for which nonpayment will not result in disconnection of basic, local service; provide the date of service and the basic and non-basic amount due for the current billing period, separately identified from any prior balance; and state the current rates being charged for services and the date by which payment must be received in order to avoid late payment charges.

§ 16-247g-7. Company Complaints:

Company shall promptly acknowledge receipt of complaints relating to services and provide a substantive response within 10 business days of receipt. Records of complaints shall be kept for at least 3 years.

§ 16-3-101. Termination of Telephone Service:

* * *

§ 16-3-101(A)(3). Delinquent Bill:

A bill is delinquent if it is unpaid for more than 30 days from receipt of the bill, with receipt being 33 days from first-class postmarked date. For an account with toll charges accrued but not billed in the amount of over twice the average monthly bill over previous 3 months, bill may issue immediately as delinquent. Bills issued to delinquent accounts are part of delinquency upon receipt. Partial payment of a delinquent account does not affect the delinquent status of the remaining balance.

* * *

§ 16-3-101(B)(1). Grounds for Termination Without Notice:

Telephone service may be terminated without notice: for hazardous conditions; if furnishing service would contravene any federal, state, or local order, ordinance, law or regulation, and such authority either forbids or does not allow time for notice; if customer fails after receipt of termination notice to comply with terms of amortization agreement or to keep current as charges accrue unless the customer makes payment(s) of at least 20% of the delinquent account; if the charges incurred and outstanding after receipt of a termination notice and subsequent to the initiation of any complaint, investigation, hearing, or appeal exceed on a monthly basis the average monthly bill for the previous 3 months or if such charges for an account less than four months old exceed on a monthly basis the average estimated usage and are equal to or exceed the greater of $50 or the customer's deposit, if any.

After termination, the company shall notify the customer in writing of the reason for termination and the conditions that must be met to obtain service.

§ 16-3-101(B)(2). Grounds for Termination with Notice:

Substantially similar to §§ 16-3-100(b)(2)(C)–(M).

§ 16-3-101(B)(3). Exceptions:

Service may not be terminated for nonpayment during such time as any resident is seriously ill as certified to the company by a registered physician, provided the customer agrees to amortize the unpaid balance over a reasonable period of time and keeps the account current as undisputed charges accrue in subsequent billing periods.

Service may not be terminated while any complaint, investigation, hearing, or appeal initiated by a customer is pending provided the customer keeps the account current as undisputed charges accrue in each subsequent billing period and the amount of charges incurred and outstanding subsequent to the initiation of any such proceeding does not exceed the greater of the average monthly bill for the previous 3 months or fifty ($50) dollars (or the greater of $50 or the estimated monthly usage for an account of less than 4 months).

Company may not refuse to reinstall service that is disconnected for nonpayment to the home of any former customer if any resident therein becomes seriously ill as certified to the company by a registered physician, provided the customer agrees to amortize the unpaid balance of the account together with reconnection and installation charges and to comply with any deposit requirements.

* * *

§ 16-3-101(B)(3)(d). Time of Disconnection:

Substantially similar to § 16-3-100(b)(3)(N) (utilities).

* * *

§ 16-3-101(C)(1). Termination, Notices, Generally:

Substantially similar to § 16-3-100(c). If a company has actual knowledge that the user of the service is not the customer to whom the bills are sent then, in addition to the termination notice sent to the customer, the company shall also attempt to provide notice to the user via telephone during the normal business hours of the company.

§ 16-3-101(C)(2). Timing of Termination and Termination Notices:

Substantially similar to § 16-3-100(d). If payment of at least 20% of a delinquent account or payment arrangement is not made subsequent to termination notice, service may be terminated on the scheduled expiration date or within 10 business days thereafter. If a utility does not terminate service within 10 business days of the expiration date, then the notice procedure must be repeated.

If a person opening an account does not provide identification, the company shall service and provide notice that service may be terminated if identification is not provided within 15 days.

§ 16-3-101(C)(3). Termination and Serious Illness:

Substantially similar to § 16-3-100(e)(1)–(e)(5). Failure to renew a serious-illness certificate automatically voids customer's rights under this section, except that any amortization agreement previously made to pay off unpaid balance shall not be voided so long as customer complies with agreement.

§ 16-3-101(C)(4). Company Review Officer; Investigation by Company:

After contacting a customer service representative, a customer may notify the company review officer in writing (in person or by mail) that any related matter is still disputed within 7 days after receipt of a termination notice or 4 days after the notice of customer service representative's decision. The review officer shall investigate the customer's complaint and provide written notice of the officer's determination within 10 days of receipt of the complaint. The notice shall advise the customer of the right to request further investigation by the PUC within 4 days of receipt. The review officer shall also consider entering into an amortization agreement under which the customer may amortize the unpaid balance over a reasonable period of time provided the customer remains current as to undisputed charges accruing in subsequent billing periods.

A customer disputing the legality of a proposed or completed termination for a reason other than a billing error or disputed charge has a right to a review by the company and/or PUC. A customer who demonstrates good cause for not instituting review procedures within the time limit may do so within a reasonable time. The company shall not be required to maintain or reinstall service pending the review unless the PUC so orders.

§ 16-3-101(C)(5). Investigation by PUCA; and Right to Hearing Before PUC Hearing Officer:

Substantially similar to § 16-3-100(g)(2), (g)(3). Customer must pay when due undisputed charges and all undisputed charges accrued and outstanding subsequent to initiation of complaint, investigation, hearing, or appeal, and the company may terminate services for circumstances not the subject of the complaint, investigation, hearing, or appeal.

* * *

§ 16-3-101(C)(7). Customer Contact:

No telephone company shall terminate service to any customer unless such company first makes a good faith effort to contact the customer receiving such telephone service and states that termination of service is imminent. A good faith effort shall be deemed to be an attempt either by telephone or mail in such a manner as is reasonable in light of the circumstances. The telephone company shall be relieved of this requirement to contact the customer in the event that such contact would be in contravention of any orders, ordinances, laws or regulations of the federal government or of the State of Connecticut or any political subdivision or regulatory body thereof.

§ 16-3-101(C)(8). Partial Payment:

If, following the receipt of a termination notice or the initiation of an amortization agreement after receipt of a termination notice, the customer makes payment(s) amounting to 20% of the balance due prior to the notice expiration or the date for the next partial payment due under the amortization agreement, the telephone company shall not terminate service without giving subsequent notice to the customer. Such subsequent notice neither entitles the customer to further investigation, review or appeal by the company or PUC nor lessens the time allowed for initial investigation, review, or appeal of the original notice. If the customer makes such payment(s) on or before the day of actual termination, and termination occurs, the company will reinstate service without any reconnection or installation charges.

* * *

Estimated Billing—Conn. Agencies Regs. § 16-3-102(A)–(C) (Gas, Electric, and Water)

Each company that estimates bills shall file with the PUC and provide to a customer upon request a simple, clear, and concise statement of the formulae used to prepare estimates. Estimated bills given to customers must be clearly marked as such on the face. Codes or symbols designating the bill as being estimated may be used only if a legend clearly explaining the code or symbol appears on the face of the bill. An electric or gas company with a substantial number of Spanish-speaking customers shall provide all information relating to estimated bills in Spanish and English.

§ 16-3-102. Estimated Billing:

* * *

§ 16-3-102(C). Companies' Obligation to Obtain Actual Reading:

Each company shall obtain a reading whenever possible. If a company is unable to do so during any billing period for which a reading was scheduled to be made, it shall provide the customer with a card requesting immediate customer reading, instructing the customer that he or she may provide the reading to the company (by mail, telephone, or both) and warning the customer that an estimated bill will be issued if no reading is received in the time specified to prepare the bill.

If an estimated bill is issued for two consecutive billing periods, the company shall mail a notice of the next scheduled visit by a company representative in order to allow the customer to either make arrangements for a company reading or to make a customer reading on the same date.

§ 16-3-102(D). Amortization Agreements:

If a customer receives an actual bill following one or more estimated bills, and the actual bill is more than 25% larger than the amount of the prior estimated bill due to the inaccuracy of the prior estimated bill, the company shall, upon order of the PUC, arrange for amortization of the excess amount in equal installments at a rate such that the bill will be fully amortized over a period not less than the period during which no actual reading was taken. In cases in which customers request an amortization of bills, the companies shall advise the customer in writing to contact the PUC for an order approving an amortization. Companies shall inform customers of the foregoing availability of amortization agreements.

Security Deposits—Conn. Agencies Regs. § 16-262j-1(a), (b) (Gas or Electric)

§ 16-262j-1. Security Deposits:

* * *

§ 16-262j-1(b)(1). Security Deposit from New Customer:

A company may require a security deposit from a new customer only if the new customer does not provide positive responses to at least three of the following six inquiries: the employer's name, address, and telephone number and the applicant's position; the length of time with present employer and previous employment if less than 18 months; if the applicant rents premises, the duration of any written lease or length of residence at present and preceding residences; types of bank accounts, location of accounts, and how long accounts these have been maintained; banks at which accounts are located and how long accounts have been maintained; whether the applicant has a credit history or references; and whether the applicant has a significant source of income other than from employment.

An applicant shall be given an explanation prior to the inquiry that the questions are being asked only to determine credit standing. Questions are to be asked in the order that they appear in the regulation, and no further questions may be asked when three positive responses are provided. The regulation enumerates responses that are deemed positive responses to each question. Refusal to answer any question or part thereof is deemed a negative response.

§ 16-262j-1(b)(2). Deposits from Other than New Customer:

A company may require a deposit from someone other than a new customer if: the company has terminated the prospective customer's utility service during the past 2 years for nonpayment of a delinquent account; failure to amortize an unpaid account balance in accordance with an agreement; fraud or misrepresentation; or failure to reimburse the company for damages due to customer's intentional or negligent conduct; the company has obtained a judgment against the prospective customer during the past 2 years for nonpayment of a delinquent account; the prospective customer has had a delinquent account for the greater of 3 consecutive months or two consecutive billing cycles during the past 2 years; or the prospective customer has an outstanding delinquent account.

§ 16-262j-1(b)(3). Customer's Inability to Pay Deposit:

A company shall notify a prospective customer whether a security deposit will be required within 5 business days after receiving a request for service and, if applicable, responses to the company's requests for verification of the customer's statements. A customer from whom a security deposit is required shall be informed that service will not be denied if the customer lacks the financial ability to pay the deposit.

* * *

§ 16-262j-1(b)(3)(C). Amount of Security Deposit:

The security deposit shall not exceed 3/12 of a year's estimated billing. Company may opt to allow for installment payments of security deposit.

* * *

§ 16-262j-1(b)(4). Interest on Security Deposits:

Interest on security deposits received from a customer for each calendar year is payable at the rate prescribed in § 16-262j of the Connecticut General Statutes. Interest accrues daily and must be paid or credited to the customer's account annually. Accrued interest must be paid upon return of the deposit if the deposit is returned on a date other than the annual payment date of interest.

Section 16-292j provides that interest on deposits before January 1, 1994, accrue interest at the average rate paid as of December 30, 1992, on savings deposits by insured commercial banks as published in the Federal Reserve Board bulletin and rounded to the nearest one-tenth of one percentage point, but not less than 1.5%. On and after January 1, 1994, the rate for each year shall be no less than the average rate paid on savings deposits by insured commercial banks as published in the Federal Reserve Board bulletin in November of the previous year, but shall not less than one and one-half per cent.

DELAWARE

The regulations relating to telecommunications are located in 26-4000-4003 Del. Code Regs. §§ 1–5. Regulations relating to electric are located in 26-3000-3001 Del. Code Regs. §§ 1–10. Regulations relating to water are located in 26-2000-2001 Del. Code Regs. §§ 1–6. Regulations relating to termination of electric and gas service during the heating season are located in 26-3000-3002 Del. Code Regs. §§ 1–7. Regulations that are substantially similar to others are indicated accordingly.

Website: www.state.de.us/delpsc/legal.shtml (last visited in May 2011).

***Electric*—26-3000-3001 Del. Code Regs. §§ 1–10**

* * *

§ 2.1.1.9. Contracts:

Electric supplier shall provide Commission with either its standard residential contract or a link to it on supplier's website. Such contract is subject to review by Commission Staff which has authority to require changes to make consistent with these Rules. Such contract shall be in clear and plain language and must include the following information: statement of the duration of the contract; price stated in cents per kWh or precise mechanism or formula by which price will be determined; list of any fees, including early termination penalties, late fees, and interest charges which can be imposed, as well as the magnitude of the fees and the conditions under which such fees can be imposed; list of supplier's termination rights explaining the specific conditions under which service may be terminated. Supplier must provide customer with at least 30 days notice of contract termination and procedures to maintain ongoing service; supplier's local or toll-free telephone number and address, and the Commission's address and telephone number; statement that because of relocation outside of their current EDC's service territory, customer may terminate contract without termination fee upon 30-day written notice to supplier.

§ 3.5. Price Terms:

Electric supplier must provide customer with 30 days' written notice of any price term changes.

§ 3.6. Information that Must be Provided to a Customer by the Electric Supplier:

Electric supplier must provide customer with copy of the contract, which includes the terms and conditions of service.

§ 3.11. Record Retention:

Electric supplier must retain customer account records for 2 years.

§ 4.2. Bill Contents:

Bill must contain the following information: name, address, and local or toll-free telephone number of the supplier or the Electric Distribution Company, if different; payment due date; if applicable, an itemized list of each service or product currently billed for (including any applicable charges for the Public Purpose Programs and a Competitive Transition Charge); amount of consumption, including whether consumption is based on actual or estimated usage; actual cents per kWh (or appropriate block charges or other pricing mechanism) charged for actual or estimated usage during the current billing period; total charge for each service or product; amount of payment or credit applied to outstanding balance during the billing period; amount still owed from the previous billing period; applicable taxes and fees; and any late fees as defined in the contract.

***Water*—26-2000-2001 Del. Code Regs. §§ 1–6**

§ 6.0. Customer Relations:

§ 6.1. Application for Service:

All applications for service should be in writing. To the maximum extent possible, the customer should be the individual or entity responsible for payment, and service may not be refused on the basis that the applicant is not the owner of the premises.

§ 6.1.1. Termination of Service:

A customer desiring to terminate or suspend service must notify the utility in writing.

§ 6.1.2. Rate Schedules:

The utility must assist the customer or applicant in selecting the most economical rate schedule.

§ 6.1.3. Customer Notification:

Customers affected by a change in service rates or service schedule classification must be notified in accordance with Del. Code Ann. tit. 26, § 304, which provides in part that no public utility may change an existing rate except after a 60-day notice to the PSC stating the proposed rate change and the effective date of the change. Proposed changes shall be shown by filing new schedules or as otherwise indicated in rate schedules filed, in effect, and open to public inspection. Public notice of proposed changes shall be given as required by PSC, and the PSC may allow a proposed change upon a showing of good cause without requiring 60 days' notice or public notice.

§ 6.1.4. Tariff Notice:

Utility must keep in each office where applications are received a copy of its current tariff for public inspection at any reasonable time.

§ 6.1.5. Meter Reading:

Customers must be informed of the method of meter reading.

§ 6.1.6. Maps/Records:

Utility must maintain current maps, plans, or records of its transmission and/or distribution systems, with such information necessary to inform customers, applicants, and others entitled to the information as to the facilities available to serve customers within its service area.

§ 6.1.7. Deposits:

Utility may require from any applicant or customer a reasonable deposit that will be applied against any unpaid balance due the utility for service at the time service is terminated. If the utility holds a deposit at the time service is terminated then the deposit, plus accrued interest if applicable less any amount owed for service, must be returned to that customer.

The amount of the deposit may not be more than the estimated service charge for two consecutive billing periods. If requested by the applicant or customer, the utility shall provide means whereby a deposit of $35 or more may be paid through installments of at least two billing periods.

Utility shall issue a receipt to each customer from whom a deposit is received and shall provide a method to acquire the deposit if the receipt is lost. The utility shall keep a record of all deposits, including: name and address; date and amount; and all information pertinent to each transaction involving the deposit. A record of each unclaimed deposit must be maintained for at least 7 years, during which the utility shall attempt to return the deposit.

§ 6.1.8. Interest on Deposits:

Utility must pay interest on deposits at the annual rate of 6%. Interest is computed from the date of receipt and is credited to the depositor's account annually, when the deposit is returned, or upon termination of service, whichever first occurs. Interest stops accruing on the date service is terminated, the date the deposit is returned, or the date that notice is sent to the depositor's last known address informing the depositor that the deposit is no longer required.

§ 6.2. Billing Statements:

Billing statements must include: the previous meter reading; the meter reading for the current billing period; the date the meter was read; the amount of consumption during the billing period; the gross and/or net cash amount of the bill; and the due date by which the bill must be paid in order to benefit from any discount or to avoid any penalty.

Statements must also include the applicable rate schedule or identify the applicable rate schedule. If the actual rates are not shown, the bill must include a statement that the applicable rate schedule will be made available for examination upon request.

Any conversions from meter reading units to billing units, calculations of billing units from any other recording devices, or other factors used in calculating the bill must also be included in or with the billing statement.

* * *

§ 6.2.3. Estimated Bills:

No more than two consecutive billing statements may be estimated. Estimated bills shall be made by averaging the amount of water registered over corresponding periods in previous years and adjusting for any known changes in the customer's usage.

* * *

§ 6.3.1. Fast Meters:

If a meter tests more than 2% fast, the utility shall make a refund for the period of incorrectly measured service that does not go beyond the date that the error was determined or, if not determined, the lesser of 3 years or a period equal to one-half of the time since the meter was last tested.

§ 6.3.2. Slow Meters:

If a meter tests more than 2% slow or is stopped, the utility may bill for an unbilled error for a period not greater than 12 months or the period since the meter was last tested. No adjustment shall be made for amounts less than $5.

* * *

§ 6.3.4. Overcharge Adjustment:

If an overcharge occurs due to an incorrect estimated meter reading, incorrect rate schedule application, incorrect meter connection, or other similar reason, the overcharge amount shall either be refunded or credited to the customer's account. Refunds less than $1 shall be credited to the account, and overcharges due to an incorrect meter reading shall be included in a subsequent billing based on a correct meter reading.

§ 6.3.5. Undercharge Adjustment:

If an undercharge occurs due to an incorrect meter reading, incorrect rate schedule application, incorrect meter connection, stopped meter, or other similar reason, the amount may be billed to the customer. The utility may deny service for nonpayment for only that portion of an undercharge applicable to the 12 months immediately preceding its discovery, unless otherwise authorized by the PSC.

§ 6.4. Denial of Service Without Notice:

Utility may discontinue service without notice when: a hazardous condition exists on the customer's premises; the customer's use of equipment adversely affects the utility's equipment or service to other customers; and there is any unauthorized use of the service, including diversion of service to bypass a meter and unauthorized resale of water. Service may not be restored until the cause for disconnection has been corrected.

If allowed by tariff, the utility may impose a reasonable charge for restoring service and also from customers who have been disconnected for unauthorized use of water. A customer whose service was disconnected or interrupted due to damage caused by that customer or the customer's agents to the utility's equipment may be charged the actual cost for repairs required to reconnect service.

§ 6.5. Denial of Service Requiring Notice:

When service has been disconnected for any of the following reasons, a charge may be made for restoring service. Such reconnection charge shall not exceed five dollars ($5), unless a tariff filed with the PSC indicates otherwise.

Service may be discontinued with notice for: violation of or noncompliance with PUC standards, violation of or non-compliance with utility's tariffs, or state, county, and municipal ordinances; failure to fulfill contractual obligations for service or facilities; failure to permit the utility reasonable access to equipment; failure to provide a required deposit; failure to furnish utility with equipment, permits, certificates, or rights-of-way agreed to as a condition for service, or withdrawing or terminating same; willful waste of water, including excessive leakage due to customer's negligible maintenance of pipes and fixtures; and nonpayment if the utility has made a reasonable attempt to obtain payment, no payment resulted, and no bona fide dispute exists (i.e., and no investigation of a complaint by the utility or the PSC is pending, and no formal complaint has been filed with the PSC).

In the case of nonpayment, the utility shall provide at least 5 working days' notice before disconnection. Disconnection may not occur on any day preceding a holiday or other non-working day, or between 12:00 noon on any Friday and 12:00 noon on the following Monday, unless the utility provides facilities for payment and restoration of services at all times during such period. If the Friday is a legal, state or national holiday, the preceding business day shall be substituted and, likewise, if the Monday is a state or national legal holiday, the next succeeding business day shall be substituted.

If service is master metered or the billing address is different than the premises served, the company shall make a good faith effort to notify the occupant(s) in sufficient time to permit them to avoid termination by making payment or arrangements for payment. The company shall keep for 1 year from termination a record of its attempts to so notify such occupants.

§ 6.6. Insufficient Reasons for Denial of Service:

The utility may not refuse service or discontinue service to an applicant or customer for: failure of a prior customer to pay for service rendered at the same premises; failure to pay for merchandise purchased from the utility; failure to pay for any other public utility service, except for jobbing or repair work done on the customer's premises; failure to pay for a different class of service (i.e., nonresidential service); or failure to pay as guarantor the bill of another customer.

§ 6.7. Responsibility of Utility Regarding Disconnection of Service:

The utility shall not be liable for any property damage or inconvenience suffered by the customer as the result of a discontinuance permitted by the applicable regulations or tariffs filed with PUC.

§ 6.7.1. Second-Party Notification:

Each water utility shall maintain a second-party termination notice list, and each customer shall be notified of and offered the opportunity to designate a second party to be notified prior to termination of service for nonpayment of a bill. No water utility shall be required to give notice to any second party unless and until the second party has notified the utility, in writing, of willingness to accept such notice. By accepting second party status, that party shall not incur any obligation to the utility.

Where second party status has been established, service may not be terminated for nonpayment without at least 5 days' oral or written notice to the second party.

The customer designating a second party is responsible for providing the utility with current and accurate information as to the second party's name, address, and telephone number, and the utility shall have no liability for inaccurate or non-current information provided by the customer.

§ 6.8. Restrictions/Curtailments on Water Usage:

Before imposing a restriction on water use, a utility must notify customer and give the PSC written notice if it determines that it is necessary to do so. Such notice must include: the reason for the restriction; the nature and extent of the restriction, i.e., outdoor water usage, etc.; the effective date of the restriction; and the probable date the restriction may be terminated.

If a customer fails to comply with a curtailment on the use of water, service may be denied to that customer provided that the customer has been given notice with a copy sent to the PSC.

§ 6.8.2. Restrictions on Outdoor Use:

A utility may impose reasonable curtailments on the outdoor use of water during periods of supply shortage, excessive demand, or other difficulty that jeopardizes the supply of water to other customers.

§ 6.8.3. Restrictions on Large-Use Customers:

A utility may impose curtailments on customers whose use of large quantities of water hinders adequate service to that customer or other customers.

***Termination of Electric or Natural Gas Service for Nonpayment During Extreme Seasonal Conditions*—26-3000-3002 Del. Code Regs. §§ 1–7**

§ 3. Prohibitions:

§ 3.1. Written and Verbal Notice:

Utility may not terminate service during the heating or cooling season for nonpayment of past-due bill(s) without giving at least 14 days' prior written notice that states the fact of impending termination, the date on or after which termination will occur, and the steps that may be taken to avoid termination. During the heating season, the written notice must also be given to the occupant if the billing address is different than the premises serviced. During the heating season, the utility must also make at least two documented attempts on separate days to contact the customer by telephone before actual termination, and one attempt must be after 6:00 p.m. During the cooling season, the covered utility must make at least one such attempt.

§ 3.2. Content of Notice:

A termination notice must state: the date, no less than 14 days from the date of mailing, on or after which termination will occur unless arrangement is made for the payment of undisputed delinquent bill(s); that termination will not occur pending determination of a good faith dispute of unpaid bill(s) if utility is so notified before actual termination; and the telephone number and address to contact regarding such a dispute and the name of the person or persons authorized to receive notice and resolve disputes.

Delay in termination pending resolution of disputed bill(s) is not required when the undisputed portions would otherwise justify termination or when the customer does not agree to pay current undisputed bills as they become due and undisputed arrearages by installment payments. If termination for nonpayment occurs, service will not be restored on the grounds that a good faith dispute exists unless and until arrangements are made for payment in the event the dispute is resolved in the utility's favor.

If the customer is unable to pay the full undisputed amount, termination may be avoided by entering into an initial installment agreement under which the customer pays both current bills as they become due and the undisputed arrearage in monthly installments over a period not less than the period that the unpaid bills were incurred, with interest as stated in the utility's tariff on the unpaid balance at the next billing date. If a customer fails to comply with an initial installment agreement, the limitation on the minimum duration installment period shall not apply to any subsequent installment agreement. The name, address, and telephone number to contact regarding installment arrangements must be given to the customer.

The termination notice must advise the customer of charitable or governmental organizations or agencies that may be able to assist if the customer is unable to pay the undisputed amount in full or enter into an installment arrangement or of the name and telephone number of an organization that the customer can contact to obtain such information.

The termination notice must state that termination is prohibited if any occupant of the premises is so ill that termination would adversely affect health or recovery, as certified to the utility by a licensed physician or any accredited Christian Science practitioner.

§ 3.3. Final Contact Prior to Termination:

The utility employee who is to disconnect service must make a reasonable good faith attempt to make personal contact at the premises prior to disconnection. If personal contact is made, the employee must: identify himself or herself to the customer or some responsible person at the premises and announce the purpose of his or her presence; identify and record the name of the person contacted; either accept payment of all amounts necessary to avoid disconnection and issue a receipt, or, if the form of payment is unacceptable, make other payment arrangements with the customer; record and report to a supervisor any statements disputing the accuracy of the reasons for termination; record and report to a supervisor statements or other information concerning the existence of any condition that would result in a medical emergency if service were terminated; and receive written certification from a duly licensed physician or accredited Christian Science practitioner that a named occupant is so ill that termination would adversely affect the occupant's health or recovery. The utility may not disconnect service upon receipt of such certification.

§ 4. Third-Party Notice:

§ 4.1. Non-Mandatory Third-Party Notice:

Utilities must inform customers of any third-party notification program offered by the utility in which the customer can designate in writing a third person to receive notice of past-due bills and written notice of termination of service. The designated third party must indicate in writing a willingness to receive such notice, and the third party may not be held liable to the utility in any way by acceptance of such status.

§ 4.2. Termination Notice Without Third-Party Notice Program:

A utility without a third-party notice program may not terminate service to a dwelling unit during the heating or cooling season without giving written notice and having actual face-to-face contact with an occupant over the age of 15 years of age in accordance with § 3.3.

§ 4.3. Information Concerning Third-party Notice:

If a utility adopts a third-party notice program, it must take appropriate steps to make all customers aware of the program.

§ 5. Termination of Service to Multiple Occupancy Dwelling Units Served Through a Master Meter:

§ 5.1. Termination of Service to Master Metered Multiple Dwelling:

No utility may terminate service during the heating or cooling season to any apartment complex, trailer park, or other grouping of individual residential units to which service is provided directly or indirectly through a master meter without individual meters, unless the utility has provided the notice required in §§ 5.2 and 5.3.

§ 5.2. Notice to Owner:

No later than 14 calendar days prior to the scheduled date of termination for nonpayment, written notice pursuant to § 5.1 must be sent by First Class mail to: the owner of the premises; the person, firm, or corporation issued the last preceding bill; or the person, firm, or corporation that has made payment. The notice must include the information required by § 3.2.

§ 5.3. Notice to Occupants:

No later than 10 calendar days prior to termination for nonpayment, the utility must provide notice to the occupants. The notice must state the intended date of termination of service, the amount due, and the procedure by which any tenant or public agency may make or guarantee the amount due in order to avoid termination of service. The notice must either be mailed by first class mail to the "occupant" of each dwelling unit in the building to which service is proposed to be terminated or posted in a conspicuous place at each building subject to termination, including common areas accessible to the utility.

§ 5.4. Notice to State Agencies:

No later than 14 calendar days prior to termination of service to a multiple occupancy dwelling unit, the utility shall give written notice of its intention to do so to the PSC and to the Division of the Public Advocate.

* * *

§ 6. Prohibition of Termination During Extreme Seasonal Temperature Conditions:

§ 6.1. Conditions of Termination:

Utility may not terminate service for nonpayment on a day when the National Weather Service reports that the 8:00 a.m. temperature measured at a location within the state and within fifty miles of the premises is 32° Fahrenheit or below on the morning termination is scheduled.

Utility may not terminate service for nonpayment on a day when the 8:00 a.m. National Weather Service forecast includes a special weather statement or other information predicting that the Heat Index measured at a location in the state and within fifty miles of the premises may equal or exceed 105° Fahrenheit on the date of termination.

§ 6.2. Deferred Termination:

If termination of service has been deferred due to weather in accordance with § 6.1, notice of deferment must be left at the premises on the actual termination date notifying the occupant that service will be terminated thereafter on a day when § 6.1 does not apply unless payment arrangements are made. If termination of service involves an apartment complex, trailer park, or other grouping of individual residential dwelling units to which service is provided directly or indirectly through a master meter without individual meters, notice in accordance with § 5.3 is sufficient.

Telephone—26-4000-4003 Del. Code Regs. §§ 1–5

§ 4.0. Customer Service and Protection:

§ 4.1. Information Available to Customers:

The customer should be the individual or entity responsible for payment, and service may not be refused because the applicant is not the owner of the premises.

Upon a customer's request for service or a transfer of service, the utility shall if requested inform the applicant or customer of its lowest-priced alternatives available at the customer's location. The utility shall post a notice in a conspicuous place in each office that is open to the public of the location where applications for service are received stating that copies of the filed rate schedules and rules relating to service are available for inspection.

A utility shall provide printed material—i.e., a pamphlet or directory of customer information pages, entitled "Customer's Rights and Responsibilities"—to all new customers at the time service is initiated and to all customers on a biennial basis. The material shall state: the right to information about rates and services and to inspect or obtain (upon payment of copying costs) a copy of the applicable tariffs and service rules; the time allowed to pay bills; the grounds for suspension of service and the procedure before a utility may terminate service; how to resolve billing disputes and how disputes affect suspension of service; information on alternative payment plans and the right to request such plans; the steps necessary to reconnect service after involuntary suspension; a statement that a grievance procedure exists, including a supervisory review and the right to file a complaint with the PSC, including the PSC's address and telephone number; that service may not be discontinued due to nonpayment of a disputed amount under investigation by the company, that no notice of discontinuance for nonpayment of such an amount may be sent pending such investigation, and that no deposit may be required on a disputed amount while the dispute is being investigated; the hours, addresses, and telephone numbers of offices where bills may be paid and information obtained; the circumstances under which a deposit or additional deposit may be required, how a deposit is calculated, the interest paid on deposits, and the time frame and requirement for return of the deposit; a statement that services are provided without discrimination as to a customer's race, nationality, color, religion, sex, or marital status, and a summary of the company's policy regarding credit history based upon the credit history of the customer's former spouse; notice of any special services for customers with disabilities; and a toll free number or the equivalent for repair service or billing inquiries.

Utilities shall encourage customers with physical disabilities and those who care for such customers to identify themselves so that action can be taken to inform such persons of their rights, when necessary and appropriate.

§ 4.2. Customer Complaints:

Utility shall promptly investigate customer complaints and advise the customers of the results. If a customer or applicant expresses dissatisfaction with the utility's report after exhausting the utility's internal problem-solving procedures, the utility must advise the person in writing of the right to have the problem considered and reviewed by the PSC and provide the PSC's address and telephone number.

Upon receipt of a complaint from the PSC on behalf of a customer, the utility shall investigate and advise the PSC of the results within 30 days. A utility shall keep a record showing the identity of the complainant, the date and nature of the complaint, and any adjustment or disposition for a period of 2 years after final resolution, except that complaints regarding rates or charges and which required no further action by the utility need not be maintained.

* * *

§ 4.4. Response to Request for Service:

A utility may decline to serve an applicant if: the applicant has not complied with the State and municipal regulations and utility rules and regulations filed with the PSC governing the service applied for; the applicant's installation or equipment is known to be hazardous or such that satisfactory service cannot be given; the applicant is indebted to the utility for the same kind of regulated intrastate service as applied for (unless the indebtedness is in dispute and the applicant complies with the deposit requirement in these rules); or the applicant refuses to make a required deposit. Upon refusal of service, the utility must inform the applicant of the basis for the refusal and that the applicant may file a complaint with the PSC.

* * *

§ 4.4.4.3. Insufficient Grounds for Refusal to Serve:

The following do not constitute sufficient cause for refusing service to a present customer or applicant: delinquency in payment for service by a previous occupant; failure to pay for merchandise or charges for non-utility service; failure to pay a bill caused by previous under-billing due to misapplication of rates more than 6 months before date of application; violation of the utility's rules regarding non-standard equipment or unauthorized attachments which interferes with services of others unless the customer is notified and given opportunity to comply; failure to pay a bill of another customer as guarantor thereof, unless the customer made such a written guarantee as a condition to service; failure to pay the bill of another customer at the same address except when the change of customer identity is made to avoid or evade payment; or refusal to pay charges billed on behalf of another carrier.

§ 4.5. Billing:

§ 4.5.1. Due Date:

The due date for payment of a monthly bill may not be less than 20 days from the date of mailing after issuance. If the last day falls on a Saturday, Sunday, bank holiday, or other day when the utility office which regularly receives payment is not open to the general public, the due date shall be the next business day.

§ 4.5.2. Rendering and Form of Bills:

Bills must show: the date of the bill; the due date on or before payment must be received to avoid being delinquent; the dates of the billing period for local exchange service; charges shown separately for local exchange service, toll service, local usage, taxes and applicable surcharges; an itemized statement of toll charges listing the date, time, destination, duration, and rate period for each call; the total amount of all payments and credits made to the account during the current billing period; the amount of applicable late payment charges; the total amount due; and a statement that a rate schedule, an explanation of how to verify the bill accuracy, and explanation of charges can be obtained from the utility's local business office.

Annually and upon customer's request, utility shall provide an itemization of all service, equipment, and other recurring charges billed.

If service is interrupted other than by customer's negligence or willful act and remains out of order for 24 hours or longer after access to the premises, an appropriate adjustment or refund determined on the basis of the known period of interruption (beginning generally from the time it was reported) shall be made to the customer. The refund amount, which may be made by credit on a subsequent bill, shall be the pro rata portion of the flat-rate charges and that portion of the service facilities rendered useless or inoperative.

§ 4.5.3 Charges for Services:

Utility may not charge disconnection fees, membership fees, application fees, service call fees, or any other type of fee except as provided for in the utility's tariff.

§ 4.5.4.1. Refunds of Overcharges:

If the customer is due a refund, an adjustment shall be made for the entire period of overcharges. If an overcharge is adjusted by the utility within 90 days of the bill in error, interest shall not accrue. If an overcharge is not adjusted within 90 days of the incorrect bill, interest shall be applied to the amount of the overcharge at the rate for payment on deposits (9% per annum unless a different rate is specified in utility's tariff). Interest on overcharges that are not adjusted within 90 days of the incorrect bill shall accrue from the date of payment. Interest shall not apply to payment arrangements.

§ 4.5.4.2. Back-Billing of Undercharges:

If a customer is undercharged, the utility may back bill the customer for the amount which was under-billed. The back-billing may not exceed 6 months unless the utility can produce records to identify and justify the additional amount of back billing. Unless the under billing was the result of deliberate customer action, the utility may not disconnect service if the customer fails to pay charges arising from an under-billing more than 6 months prior to the date the utility initially notified the customer of the amount of the undercharge and the total additional amount due. If the under billing is $25 or more, the utility shall offer the customer a payment arrangement option for the same length of time as that of the under-billed period.

§ 4.5.5. Payment Arrangements:

The utility shall exercise good faith and fair judgment in attempting to enter into a reasonable payment agreement and shall consider the size of the unpaid balance, the customer's payment history, and the length of time that the bill accumulated. The utility may not suspend service for an undisputed delinquent bill while it is negotiating a payment agreement or within 24 hours after negotiations fail.

§ 4.5.6. Disputed Bills:

Substantially similar to Rule 4.2. Service may not be discontinued for nonpayment of disputed portion of a bill pending the completion of the utility's investigation of the dispute, and suspension notices or demands for additional deposits may not be made during such time.

§ 4.5.7. Notification of Alternative Payment Programs or Payment Assistance:

Upon contact by a customer to discuss his or her inability to pay a bill or need for assistance with payment, a utility representative shall inform the customer of all available alternative payment and payment assistance programs that are available, e.g., payment arrangements and suspension moratoriums for the ill, and of the eligibility requirements and procedures for each.

§ 4.6. Deposits and Credit Standards:

If an applicant's credit is not established, a deposit not more than $50 per residence may be required. No deposit may be required if the applicant has had prior telephone service billed in his or her name and is not indebted to the provider for such service, has a history of timely payments, and has not had service suspended for nonpayment. Absent a credit history with a telecommunications utility, a deposit may be required unless the applicant provides satisfactory evidence of employment with the same employer for 1 year prior to the date of application, ownership of the premises, or a written lease of at least 1 year for such premises.

Residential deposits may be retained for 1 year and shall be returned with interest by check after 1 year if the account is not delinquent at that time.

A deposit may be required for an existing customer when a utility determines that the customer's credit is doubtful or service is suspended for nonpayment. The deposit shall not exceed the customer's average 2-month bill, including toll charges, during the preceding 12-month period and may be adjusted to maintain an amount equal to such average bill.

Interest on deposits accrues at the rate of 9% per annum (unless a different rate is specified in the utility's tariff) for the period a deposit is retained and if retained for more than 1 year the interest will be paid annually through a credit to the customer's account.

Each new customer required to pay a deposit shall receive a written description of the utility's deposit policy.

§ 4.7. Discontinuance of Service:

Service may be disconnected if a bill has not been paid or a payment arrangement has not been entered into within 30 days from the date of mailing of a bill and after proper notice has been given. Proper notice consists of a separate mailing or hand delivery at least 10 days prior to a stated date of suspension.

The notice shall contain the following: the words "suspension notice" or similar conspicuous language; the reason for the suspension; a statement of any amounts currently due and of any required deposit; a statement of any applicable reconnection fee required to restore service; a statement that the customer should immediately contact the utility, including the mailing address and telephone number where questions may be answered and payment agreements entered into; and a statement that, if they need assistance with payment or are ill and unable to pay their bill, they may be eligible for alternative payment programs (such as a payment arrangement and should contact the local office of the utility for more information).

Service may not be suspended on a holiday or weekend but shall fall on the next working day after the 10-day notice period. Payment at a utility's authorized payment agency is deemed payment to the utility, and a utility may request customers who pay at payment agencies less than 3 days before the suspension date to call the company with receipt information. Late notices or disconnect notices shall not be issued earlier than the first day the bill becomes delinquent to allow a reasonable time to ascertain receipt of payment by mail or at the utility's authorized payment agency.

* * *

§ 4.7.2. Suspension with Notice:

Utility service may be disconnected after proper notice for: nonpayment of an undisputed delinquent account or undisputed portion of an account when a dispute exists as to part but not all of a bill amount; failure to comply with the terms of a payment arrangement; violation of the utility's rules regarding use of service in a manner that interferes with the service of others or the operation of nonstandard equipment, after a reasonable attempt has been made to provide the customer with an opportunity to remedy the situation; and failure to comply with properly required deposit or guarantee arrangements.

§ 4.7.3. Suspension Without Notice:

Utility service may be disconnected without notice when a dangerous condition exists for as long as the condition exists or when service is connected without authority by a person who has not made application for service or who has reconnected service following suspension of service for nonpayment. When reasonable given the nature of the hazardous condition, a written statement providing notice of and reason for suspension shall be posted at a place of common entry or upon the front door of each affected residential unit as soon as possible after service has been disconnected.

§ 4.7.4. Suspension Prohibited:

Service may not be disconnected for: delinquency in payment by a previous occupant of the premises; failure to pay for merchandise or charges for non-utility service provided by the utility; failure to pay for a different type or class of service unless it is provided by the billing utility and the fee for such service is included on the same bill; failure to pay the account of another customer as guarantor thereof, unless the guarantee was a condition to service; or failure to pay charges from an under-billing resulting from misapplication of rates more than 6 months prior to the current bill.

§ 4.7.5. Suspension on Holidays or Weekends:

Unless a dangerous condition exists or unless the customer requests disconnection, service may not be disconnected on a day, or on a day immediately preceding a day, when personnel of the utility are not available to the public for the purpose of making collections and reconnecting service.

§ 4.7.6. Disconnection Due to Utility Abandonment:

No telecommunications utility may abandon a customer or a certificated service area without written notice to its customers, all similar neighboring utilities, and prior approval from the PSC.

§ 4.7.7. Suspension for Ill and Disabled:

A local exchange carrier may not suspend or refuse to restore service if an occupant is certified by a physician or Christian Science practitioner to be seriously ill and affected with a medical condition which would be aggravated by cessation of service. An LEC may limit the use of service to calls necessary to the health of such an occupant.

If an LEC is informed before suspension of service that such a medical certification will be procured, then suspension shall not occur for at least 3 days, at which time service may be suspended if no certification is produced. Initial certifications may be written or oral, and the LEC has the right to verification by either calling the physician or Christian Science practitioner or requiring written confirmation within 7 days.

Certifications, written or oral, shall include the following information: name, address, and telephone number of the registered account customer; name and address of the afflicted person and the person's relationship to the customer; nature and anticipated length of the affliction; name, office address, and telephone number of the certifying physician or Christian Science practitioner; and the specific reason why access to service must be maintained, including localities in which it is necessary for calls to be made.

Service may not be suspended for the period specified in the medical certification but should not to exceed 30 days. If no time is specified or it is not readily ascertainable, service shall not be suspended for at least 30 days. An initial certification may be renewed for up to 30 days provided the same requirements for the initial certification are met.

If service is required to be restored due to such certification, the LEC shall attempt to have service restored on the date of the certification, and service shall be restored before the end of the next working day.

§ 4.7.8. Resolution of Disputes:

Any customer or applicant for service requesting the opportunity to dispute any action of a utility shall be given an opportunity for a supervisory review by the utility. If the utility is unable to provide a supervisory review immediately following the request for such review, arrangements for the review shall be made for the earliest possible date. Service may not be disconnected pending completion of the review. If a customer chooses not to participate in such review or to make arrangements for such review to take place within 5 days after requesting it, the company may disconnect service, provided notice has been issued under standard disconnect procedures. Any customer who is dissatisfied with the review by the utility must be informed of their right to file a complaint with the PSC. The results of the supervisory review must be provided in writing to the customer within 10 days of the review, if requested.

§ 4.8. Continuity of Service:

If the utility makes any change in the type of service that would adversely affect the efficiency of operation or the adjustment of the customers' equipment, then all affected customers must be notified at least 60 days in advance of the change or as early as feasible if 60 days' notice is not possible. If adjustments or replacements of the utility's standard equipment must be made to permit use under such changed conditions, customers may not be charged for such adjustments or replacements.

* * *

DISTRICT OF COLUMBIA

Source: D.C. Mun. Regs. tit 15, §§ 300–399 and 400–499 (also cited as 15 D.C. Adm. Code §§ 300–399 and 400–499), *available at* www.dcpsc.org/commorders/dcmr15/dcmr15.shtm. *See also* D.C.'s *Consumer Bill of Rights, available at* www.dcpsc.org/pdf_files/commorders/consumerbill/consbillofrights.pdf. The D.C. Commission's website is: www.dcpsc.org.

***Electric, Gas, and Telephone*—D.C. Mun. Regs. tit. 15, §§ 300–399**

§ 300.3. Discrimination:

Consumers shall not be penalized or discriminated against for exercising rights under applicable utility regulations.

* * *

§ 302.1. Utility Meter Reading Requirements:

Gas and electric utilities shall schedule residential meters for regular monthly intervals and read within 3 days of the schedule date unless it is impossible due to inaccessibility or other extraordinary conditions.

* * *

§ 303. Meters Read by Customers:

§ 303.1. Gas and electric utilities shall provide customer with electronic or telephonic means to report a customer reading whenever the company cannot make an actual reading, and shall furnish a customer reading card upon request.

§ 303.6. Any gas and electric utility customer may read s own meter so long as usage is reported accurately and timely to the utility by telephone or telecommunications device, Internet, postage prepaid meter reading card provided by utility or other technological means available to customer and approved by commission.

[*Editor's note: Subsections have been omitted*].

* * *

§ 304. Billing:

§ 304.1. Customer shall be provided a bill at least once during each billing cycle (26–35 days) unless otherwise agreed to.

§ 304.3. Each estimated bill shall be clearly and conspicuously identified as such. Estimated bills may only be rendered only in limited circumstances.

§ 304.4. Whenever three or more estimated bills have been rendered in succession, the utility shall, at customer request, make an actual reading at a mutually agreeable time.

* * *

§ 304.10. A gas or electric utility may, at the election of a customer, bill a customer under a level payment billing program. The utility shall inform the customer of this option.

§ 304.11. The utility shall perform a periodic analysis of the customer's level payment billing plan and notify the customer if actual usage varies significantly from that upon which the plan was based and give the customer an opportunity for revision of the plan.

§ 305. Payments:

§ 305.1. Utility bills shall be due within 20 days after the date they are rendered. If due date falls on a non-business day, due date is next business day.

* * *

§ 305.3. No late payment charge shall be levied on all amounts paid by the due date, or on amounts in dispute before the Commission. Amounts paid after the due date may bear a late payment charge as established by tariffs in accordance with Commission procedure.

§§ 305.4, 305.5. Customer payments shall be applied as follows: first to arrears for utility service, oldest item first; next to arrears for non-regulated charges; next to current utility services; and finally, to current non-regulated charges, unless the utility and agree to different payment terms.

§ 307. Deposits:

§ 307.1. A utility shall not require a cash deposit or guarantee from a person who has never been a customer of the utility.

§ 307.2. A utility may not require a cash deposit for new or continued service on the basis of income level, home ownership, residence location, race, color, creed, sex, age, or national origin.

§ 307.3. A utility shall not require a cash deposit from a person who has been a customer of a utility before, except if:

(a) The service of the customer has been terminated for non-payment within previous 12 months;

(b) The customer has used, interfered with or diverted the service in an unauthorized manner (and certain other conditions apply);

(c) The customer's account has been delinquent for an excess of 60 days within the previous 12 months; or

(d) The customer has an outstanding balance due the utility for utility services. In any event, provision of new service may be conditioned upon payment of the outstanding balance.

* * *

§ 307.5. A utility shall not require a cash deposit as a condition of continued service, except if:

(a) Utility service at the customer's residence has been used, interfered with or diverted in an unauthorized manner within previous 12 months; or

(b) The customer's account has been delinquent for an excess of 60 days within the previous 12 months.

* * *

§ 307.7. No deposit shall exceed the lesser of one hundred dollars ($100) or 2/12ths the estimated annual bill. Deposits more than $35 may be paid in a minimum of three equal monthly installments.

§ 307.8. Each utility shall be liable for interest on deposits held, calculated as simple interest equal to the average one-year Treasury bill rate for September, October and November of the previous year.

§ 307.9. Upon termination of service, the deposit with accrued interest shall be credited to any outstanding final bill and any remaining balance shall be returned to the customer.

§ 307.10. A deposit and accrued interest shall be refunded promptly if the customer pays all utility charges for twelve successive months.

§ 308.1 Use of Customer's Social Security Number:

Upon requesting a customer's Social Security account number, the utility must inform the customer that providing the number is optional.

* * *

§ 310. Grounds for Termination:

§ 310.1. Residential utility service shall not be terminated except after proper notice and in the following cases:

(a) Nonpayment;

(b) Failure to enter into or comply with the terms of a deferred payment plan;

(c) Service is being used but no one has applied for customer status at the premises;

(d) Unauthorized use, interference with or diversion of utility service;

(e) Failure to allow utility access to premises when utility has requested access in writing;

(f) Unsafe condition, adverse effect on delivery systems, or violation of statute, regulation or Commission-approved tariff provision;

(g) Utility has reason to believe there is fraud or customer has misrepresented identity to obtain service;

(h) Application for service was made in name of person not an occupant without disclosing such person's actual address or written consent;

(*i*) Application for service was made in name of third party without disclosing that fact or without authority;

(j) Application for service was made by person for purpose of assisting another occupant to avoid payment of that occupant's outstanding bill;

(k) Application for service was made by individual who cannot legally enter into contract (e.g., unemancipated minor); or

(*l*) failure to comply with Commission order.

§ 310.2. These reasons are not sufficient grounds to terminate gas or electric service:

(a) Failure to pay for residential service at a different location, except for unpaid balances transferred from one residential account to another, or an amount owed for estimated bills, unless utility has attempted to obtain actual reading;

(b) Failure to pay for merchandise, appliances, or nonresidential utility service.

§ 310.3. A gas or electric utility may not terminate service used as the primary source of heating for nonpayment, failure to make a deposit or guarantee, or failure to comply with deferred payment plan on any day when the National Weather Service forecasts the temperature to be 32 degrees Fahrenheit or below during the next 24 hours, or on any day preceding a holiday or weekend when such forecast is that the temperature will be 32 degrees Fahrenheit or below during the holiday or weekend.

§ 311. Procedures for Termination:

§ 311.1. A utility shall postpone termination of service for up to 21 days if the customer provides a physician's certificate or notice from a public health official stating that termination would be detrimental to the health and safety of a bona fide occupant of the premises, provided that the customer enters into a deferred payment plan. The postponement may be extended for additional periods of not more than 21 days by renewal of the certificate or notice.

§ 311.2. A utility shall not terminate service when a dispute involving the account in question has been docketed at the Commission, provided that payments are made for amounts not in dispute.

§ 311.3. A utility shall not terminate residential service unless a written termination notice has been sent to the customer at least 15 days (10 days for telephone) prior to the proposed termination. When the customer has requested, a duplicate copy of the notice shall be sent to a designated third party.

* * *

§ 311.5. [*describing required contents of termination notice*]

§§ 311.7–311.9. Utilities may not terminate service after 5:00 p.m. Thursday and before 8:00 a.m. Monday, on a legal holiday, or on a day utility is closed, with very limited exceptions.

* * *

§ 312. Personal Contact before Termination:

§ 312.1. At least two attempts to contact the customer are required prior to termination.

§ 312.2. At least 2 days before the date set for termination, a utility shall make reasonable efforts to contact the customer in person, by telephone, or by other technological means.

§ 312.3. Immediately preceding the physical disconnection of gas or electric service, the utility representative shall make reasonable effort to identify himself or herself to the customer or other responsible person on the premises and announce the purpose of his or her presence; a telephone utility shall make a second attempt to contact the consumer.

§ 312.4. If prior telephone contact has not been made as provided in § 312.2 and the customer or other responsible person is not on the premises, termination of gas or electric service shall not occur and notice shall be left that service may be disconnected as soon as next business day unless outstanding bills are paid.

§ 313. Adjustment in the Field:

§ 313.2. If, just prior to termination, evidence is presented to the utility's representative which reasonably indicates that the bill has been paid, that a Deferred Payment Plan has been developed, that the bill is currently the subject of a pending proceeding before the Public Service Commission, or there is a medical emergency, service shall not be terminated.

§ 313.3. The field service representative shall be authorized to accept payment. If payment in full of all charges due is tendered, service shall not be terminated.

§ 313.4. The field service representative shall seek authorization from his or her supervisor to accept partial payments, or to override his or her orders to terminate service upon a reasonable explanation by the customer of the delinquency.

§ 314. Disconnection:

§ 314.1. If the two attempts to contact requirement is satisfied, the utility may terminate service to a residential customer.

§ 314.2. When service is terminated, the employee shall leave a notice that service has been terminated and the address and telephone number of the utility where the customer may arrange to have service restored. The notice shall also state procedures to be followed where a medical or safety emergency exists on the premises.

§ 315. Restoration of Service:

A utility must restore service within 24 hours of cure of the cause for termination.

* * *

§ 320. Customer Inquiries and Complaints:

§ 320.1. A utility shall establish procedures which will insure the prompt, efficient, and thorough receipt, investigation and resolution of all customer inquiries, service requests and complaints.

§§ 320.2–320.5. Qualified customer service representatives (CSRs) and supervisory personnel shall be available at all times during normal business, including personnel authorized to entered into deferred payment plans; personnel to address complaints not resolved by the CSRs; and personnel who can address emergency conditions and interruptions or terminations of service. The utility shall make necessary arrangements to insure that foreign language-speaking personnel shall be made available to assist the non-English-speaking public.

§ 320.10. When a complaint cannot be resolved between the utility and a customer, the utility shall refer the customer to the Commission for resolution.

* * *

§ 321. Publication of Consumer Pamphlet:

§§ 321.1–321.4. [*Detailed provisions regarding the content and distribution of the Pamphlet.*]

§ 321.5. The cover of the pamphlet shall indicate conspicuously in Spanish that a Spanish translation is available on request.

* * *

§ 323. Office of Consumer Services:

§§ 323.1–323.8. [*Establishes Offices of Consumer Services and defines its duties, as well as the procedures for making and resolving complaints.*]

* * *

§ 324. Formal Complaints:

§§ 324.1–324.4. [*Describes the procedures for filing a formal complaint.*]

* * *

***Master Metered Apartment Buildings (Electric and Gas)*—D.C. Mun. Regs. tit. 15, §§ 400–499**

§ 400. Purpose and Applicability:

Discussing purpose and applicability in general.

§ 401. Tenants' Rights:

§ 401.1. A gas or electric utility shall not terminate service to any master-metered apartment building on the basis of nonpayment by the owner unless that utility provides an opportunity for the tenants to assume prospective financial responsibility for the utility services in their own names, either individually or collectively, without any liability for the amount due while service was billed directly to the owner.

* * *

§ 402. Notice of Tenants' Rights and Options:

§ 402.1. At least 21 days prior to terminating service, a utility company shall send each tenant whose name is made known to the utility company a Notice of Tenants' Rights and Options. The notice shall contain the following:

(a) A description of the options available to tenants for the provision of utility service:

(1) Individual metering;

(2) Collective payment by a tenant's association;

(3) Individual payment based on a fair and equitable allocation of the total bill; and

(4) The appointment of a receiver;

(b) The telephone number and address of the utility;

(c) The date, time and place for a meeting between the tenants and a field representative from the utility to discuss the available alternatives;

(d) The statement that the tenant has the right to deduct all future payments made by the tenant for utility services from rent owed as provided by § 3 of D.C. Law 3-94; and

(e) A Preliminary Election Card to indicate the each tenant's preferred option.

* * *

§ 405. Notice of Option Selected:

§ 405.1. After the utility has received all of the tenants' Preliminary Election Postcards or after the expiration of the 10-day waiting period (whichever comes first), the utility shall advise all tenants of the option selected by the majority of the tenants for payment of utility service to the building.

* * *

§ 405.4. If the utility company does not find the selected option to be practicable, it shall state its reasons in the notice and advise the tenants of their right to appeal.

§ 406. Tenant Payment of Utility Bill:

§ 406.1. Tenants who elect to have their units individually metered at their own expense and tenants who elect to receive service in their own name pursuant to the utility's fair and equitable share proposal shall pay their utility costs directly to the utility company.

* * *

§ 410. Notice of Utility Charge Paid by Tenant:

The utility must submit to the owner a monthly listing of utility charges made by tenants who have elected to receive service in their own name. The tenant is authorized to reduce his or her rent payment to the owner by an amount equal to the utility charge.

* * *

FLORIDA

The Public Service Commission's regulations governing electric service can be found within the customer relation subsection of the Fla. Admin. Code Ann. r. 25-6.093–25-6.109; gas, Fla. Admin. Code Ann. r. 25-7.079–25-7.091; water and wastewater, Fla. Admin. Code Ann. r. 25-30.310–25-30.360. The customer relations regulations governing telephone service can be found within Fla. Admin. Code Ann. r. 25-4.107–25-4.119. The regulations governing gas and water service are similar in form and substance to the regulation governing electric service, any questions regarding specific issues may be answered by referencing the electric service regulations. Access to the regulations can be found at www.flrules.org/gateway/Browse.asp (last visited in May 2011).

Electric Service—Fla. Admin. Code Ann. r. 25-6.093–25-6.109

25-6.093. Information to Customers:

The utility must provide such information as is necessary to enable the customer to obtain safe and efficient service. Upon request, the utility must explain the method of reading meters and calculating the bill; the billing cycle and approximate meter reading dates; and provide a copy and explanation of the rate schedule. Upon request, the utility must assist the customer to obtain the rate schedule most advantageous to the customer's requirements. Within 60 days of initiation of service, at least annually thereafter, and within 60 days after the approval of a new rate, the utility must provide each customer with a summary of the major rate schedules available to that class of customer. The utility must provide its customers with quarterly reports on the sources of generation, by fuel type for utility generation, or "purchased power" for off-system purchases. Upon request, the utility must provide a customer with a summary of that customer's actual usage over the past 12 months.

25-6.094. Complaints and Service Requests:

A utility must make a full and prompt investigation of customer complaints and service requests. It must provide a method of receiving and responding to emergency calls on a 24-hour basis.

25-6.095. Initiation of Service:

The utility shall undertake to initiate service without unreasonable delay. The utility may charge a reasonable fee to defray the cost of establishing service provided such charge is specified in its filed tariff. A person desiring service may be required to make application in writing.

* * *

25-6.097. Customer Deposits:

A utility's tariff must include its criteria for establishing credit and setting the amount of deposits. Credit will be deemed established if consumer provides a guarantor who is a customer of the utility with a satisfactory payment record or posts a cash deposit or irrevocable letter of credit or surety bond. A utility may, upon 30 days' written notice, request a new or additional deposit. Total deposit may not exceed twice the average charges for actual usage for preceding 12 months, or average actual monthly use if less than 12 months' service. After 23 months, the utility must refund the deposit if the customer has not, during the previous 12 months, had more than one late payment nor paid with a check refused by a bank, been disconnected for nonpayment, tampered with service, or used service in an unauthorized or fraudulent manner. A utility must pay simple interest on deposits of 6% per year. A customer is entitled to receive interest only after 6 months of service, at which point interest is due from the date the deposit was placed. The utility must keep records of deposits, including customer's name, service address, date and amount of deposit, and all transactions. The customer must be given a non-refundable certificate of deposit, and the utility must provide a method to get back deposits if the certificate is lost. The deposit receipt must disclose the right to a refund if, after ninety days, the amount of the deposit proves to be high. After service is discontinued, the amount of the deposit may be credited against the final account and the balance, if any, shall be returned to the customer within 15 days after discontinuance.

* * *

25-6.099. Meter Readings:

Unless special circumstances warrant, meters shall be read at monthly intervals on the approximate corresponding day of each meter-reading period.

25-6.100. Customer Billings:

Bills shall contain information concerning meter-reading dates, a clear indication and explanation (after 3 consecutive estimated bills) if the bill is based on an estimated reading, consumption amounts, due dates, amounts and penalties due, any information that will allow and assist in the computation of charges, and address and telephone number of local office where bill can be paid and questions answered. An actual meter reading shall be taken at least once every 6 months.

25-6.101. Delinquent Bills:

Bills shall not be considered delinquent prior to the expiration of 20 days from the date of mailing or delivery by the utility.

25-6.102. Conjunctive Billing:

Conjunctive billing shall not be permitted. Bills for two or more points of delivery to the same customer shall be calculated separately for each such point of delivery.

25-6.103. Adjustment of Bills for Meter Error:

A bill shall be adjusted dating back to half the time of the last meter reading if a meter is found to be fast by 2%, or the period that it was slow by 2%, but not exceeding a period of 12 months. Meters not registering any reading shall be estimated. Customers shall be provided a payment period equal to that of the under-billing period.

25-6.104. Unauthorized Use of Energy:

In the event of unauthorized or fraudulent use, or meter tampering, the utility may bill the customer on a reasonable estimate of the energy used.

25-6.105. Refusal or Discontinuance of Service by Utility:

Service may be disconnected or refused without notice due to hazardous conditions, fraud, or tampering.

Service may be disconnected or refused with notice for issues relating to nonpayment (except nonpayment of service charge on dishonored check), non-compliance with state or municipal law or regulation, customer's equipment is inadequate or adversely affects others service, denial of reasonable access to equipment, failure to establish credit for initial, current, future, or additional services.

Service may not be disconnected for payment delinquency of a previous occupant, failure to pay bill as guarantor, failure to pay for a different class of service, failure to pay amount in a bona fide dispute according to dispute procedures, or failure to pay other non-regulated charges or for merchandise, or failure to pay NSF charges.

Notice shall not be less than 5 days before the scheduled date of disconnection.

Disconnection notices shall be separate from a bill.

When service has been discontinued for proper cause, each utility may charge a reasonable fee to defray the cost of restoring service.

When notice is required, no utility shall discontinue service to any non-commercial customer between 12:00 noon on a Friday and 8:00 a.m. the following Monday or between 12:00 noon on the day preceding a holiday and 8:00 a.m. the next working day.

Each utility shall submit, as a tariff item, a procedure for discontinuance of service when that service is medically essential.

25-6.106. Under-Billings and Over-Billings of Energy:

Substantially similar to 25-6.103.

* * *

***Gas Service*—Fla. Admin. Code Ann. r. 25-7.079–25-7.091**

***Water and Wastewater Service*—Fla. Admin. Code Ann. r. 25-30.310–25-30.360**

§ 30.310. Initiation of Service:

A utility may require a written application. After applicant's compliance with reasonable rules, the utility should provide service without unnecessary delay. The utility must provide each applicant with the booklet "Your Water and Sewer Service," available from the PSC.

§ 30.311. Customer Deposits:

A utility's tariff must include criteria for deposits. An applicant may establish credit by providing a guarantor, making a deposit, or posting an irrevocable letter of credit or surety bond. Utilities must provide receipts, and an alternative method of claiming the deposit if the receipt is lost. After 6 months' continuous service, the utility must pay interest on deposits at 6% per year, calculated from date of deposit. After 23 months of service with a satisfactory payment record—not more than one late payment in the preceding 12 months, no returned check, disconnection, theft or tampering—either the deposit must be refunded. When service is discontinued, the deposit may be applied to the last bill, and any balance refunded within 15 days.

Upon 30 days' notice, a utility may require a new or additional deposit. The total amount of the old and new deposit may not exceed the average bill for two billing periods for preceding 12 months, or average monthly bill if service period is less than 12 months.

* * *

§ 30.320. Refusal or Discontinuance of Service:

A utility may refuse service if the customer's facilities are inadequate, or the service would unfavorably affect the service of other customers. It may refuse or discontinue service for violation of law, regulation or utility rule; for using service for a different property or purpose than that described in the application; failure to make a deposit; denial of reasonable access; nonpayment of bills after five working-days notice.

The utility may discontinue without notice for hazardous condition, tampering, or unauthorized or fraudulent use of service.

Service must be reconnected when the cause for disconnection has been corrected.

The utility must inform customers in writing of its reasons for refusal or discontinuance, and must provide contact information for the Commission.

Inadequate reasons for denial or discontinuance: delinquency by a prior occupant, unless the current occupant also occupied the premises when the delinquency occurred, and the previous occupant continues to occupy the premises and benefit from the service; failure to pay for appliances or equipment, or a different class of service (unless service of two or more classes is provided to the same customer on the same premises); failure to pay a bill as guarantor; failure to pay a bad check charge.

Service may not be disconnected between noon Friday and 8:00 a.m. Monday, or between noon on the day before a holiday and 8:00 a.m. on the business day following the holiday, except for hazardous condition, tampering or fraud, or a customer-requested disconnection.

§ 30.325. Termination of Service by Customer:

A utility may require reasonable notice if a customer wishes to terminate. The customer remains liable for service provided up to the time notice is received.

§ 30.330. Information to Customers:

A utility must provide customers with its address, and its daytime and after-hours telephone numbers. Upon request the utility must provide information to enable customers to receive safe and efficient service; advise customers how to read meters and compute billing amounts; explain the procedure for obtaining a meter test; provide rate information and assist the customer in obtaining the most advantageous rate.

§ 30.335. Customer Billing:

Bills must be rendered at regular intervals and include the billing period; applicable rate schedule; beginning and ending meter readings; amount of bill; delinquent date or date after which bill becomes past due; any authorized late payment charge. An estimated bill must be clearly identified. Any municipal franchise fees must be listed separately. A bill may not be considered delinquent before the twenty-first day after mailing.

§ 30.340. Adjustment of Bills for Meter Error:

If a meter is fast in excess of the tolerance specified in rule 25-30.262, the utility must refund the overcharge for the lesser of 12 months or one-half the time since the last meter test. If the date of the error can be fixed, the refund should be computed back to that date.

A utility may backbill for the lesser of 12 months, or the actual time the meter was slow (if ascertainable). The backbill may be paid over a period equal to that covered by the backbill. In case of unauthorized use, the utility may bill for a reasonable estimate of the service taken, plus a fee for restoring service.

§ 30.345. Customer Service Charges:

Customer service charges must be specified in the tariff. They may include a reconnection fee for terminated service and a reasonable fee for temporary service.

§ 30.350. Backbilling:

A utility may not backbill for more than 12 months for any undercharge resulting from the utility's mistake. The utility must allow the customer to pay the undercharge over a period equal to the time of the underbilling.

* * *

***Telephone Service*—Fla. Admin. Code Ann. r. 25-4.107–25-4.119**

25-4.107. Information to Customers:

The utility must inform the customer about the installment plan for payment of connection charges. Upon request, the customer must be given the 800 number for placement on the Do-Not-Call list. If enhanced or optional services are discussed, each must be individually identified and the price disclosed.

25-4.109. Customer Deposits:

A utility's tariff must include its criteria for establishing credit and setting the amount of deposits. Credit will be deemed established if the applicant: was a customer of any LEC within the past 2 years and, for the last 12 consecutive months of service, did not have more than one bill paid after becoming delinquent and never had service disconnected for nonpayment; provides a guarantor who is a customer of the utility with a satisfactory payment record; or posts a cash deposit or irrevocable letter of credit or surety bond. A deposit shall not exceed the estimated amount of 1 month's local exchange service plus 2 months toll service, if provided or billed by the LEC. If after 90 days this estimate proves to be high, the LEC must refund upon demand the difference between the estimate and the actual usage. A utility may, upon 15 days' written notice, request a new or additional deposit. The amount of the new deposit must not exceed twice the actual monthly toll provided or billed by the LEC plus 1 months' local service, for the 90 days preceding the notice. If the service period is less than 90 days, then new or additional deposit shall be based on actual average monthly billing. After 23 months of continuous service and a satisfactory payment record, the utility must refund the deposit if the customer has not, during the previous 12 months, had more than one late payment nor paid with a check refused by a bank, been disconnected for nonpayment, or used service in an unauthorized or fraudulent manner. A utility must pay simple interest on deposits of at least 6% per year. A customer is entitled to receive interest only after 6 months of service, at which point interest is due from the date the deposit was placed. The utility must keep records of deposits, including customer's name, service address, date and amount of deposit, and all transactions. The customer must be given a non-refundable certificate of deposit, and the utility must provide a method to get back deposits if the certificate is lost. The deposit receipt must disclose the right to a refund if, after 90 days, the amount of the deposit proves to be high. After service is discontinued, the amount of the deposit may be credited against the final account and the balance, if any, returned to the customer within 45 days after discontinuance.

The limitation on deposits does not apply to "special arrangement agreements covering termination equipment installations, for which the telephone company may require a reasonable deposit."

25-4.110. Customer Billing for Local Exchange Telecommunications Companies:

Bills shall not be considered delinquent prior to the expiration of 15 days from the date of mailing or delivery by the company.

Bills shall contain customer's name, address, telephone or account number, billing period, all payment information and amounts due (late payments, charges, taxes, etc.), information relating to protections and available assistance, full description and itemization of activity and services, payments, adjustments, credits, items for which nonpayment will result in disconnection of basic local service, and contact information of the provider.

25-4.111. Customer Complaints and Service Requests:

Substantially similar to 25-6.094. See regulation for complaint procedure specifics.

25-4.113. Refusal or Discontinuance of Service by Company:

Substantially similar to 25-6.105.

* * *

GEORGIA

The Public Service Commission's General Rules governing electric, gas, and telephone service can be found within Ga. Comp. R. & Regs. 515-3-1.01–515-3-1.11. Electric and gas disconnection of service rules can be found in Ga. Comp. R. & Regs. 515-3-2.01–515-3-2.03 and Ga. Comp. R. & Regs. 515-3-3.01–515-3-3.10, respectively. Additional rules governing gas service billing procedures can be found within Ga. Comp. R. & Regs. 515-7-6.01–515-7-6.05. Specific regulations governing telephone service can be found within Ga. Comp. R. & Regs. 515-12-1.01–515-12-1.34. The regulations governing telephone service are substantially similar to the regulations governing electric and gas service and are indicated accordingly. Access to regulations can be found at http://rules.sos.state.ga.us/cgi-bin/page.cgi?d=1(PDF Format) (last visited in May 2011).

***General Rules (Electric, Gas, and Telephone)*—Ga. Comp. R. & Regs. 515-3-1.01–515-3-1.11**

* * *

515-3-1.10. Accounting Requirements; Deposits:

Utilities may require deposits from customers before beginning or continuing service if they judge the deposit is necessary. The amount of the deposit shall not exceed the amount of an estimated bill for 2 1/2 billing periods (pursuant to 515-7-9.04, gas service deposits shall not exceed $150). Electric and gas utility shall pay interest on deposits held more than 6 months at a rate of 7% per annum. Deposits shall be automatically refunded within 30 days after 24 months of billing without a discontinuance of service, without two or more bills having been past due, or when customer discontinues service. A utility shall review the accounts of customers not meeting this requirement after 12 periods.

* * *

***Electric Service Disconnection Rules*—Ga. Comp. R. & Regs. 515-3-2.01–515-3-2.03**

515-3-2.01. Reasons for Disconnection:

Service may be disconnected due to nonpayment for services not paid within 45 days of billing date, failure to comply with utility rules, by order of Commission, court, or authorized agency, or due to a dangerous condition. Service shall not be terminated due to failure to pay for merchandise or a different class of service, or failure to pay for a previous occupant's service.

515-3-2.02. Limitations on Disconnection:

Notice of intent to discontinue service shall be at least 5 days before the date scheduled for termination, followed by an attempt, by phone or in person at least 2 days prior to termination.

Disconnection notices shall be clearly distinguishable and shall contain the reasons for disconnection, the amount due, date of disconnection, availability of payment plans and assistance, delay options, including for medical reasons, and utility contact information. Disconnection shall occur on a business day when a representative of the utility is available to receive payment from the customer.

Disconnection procedure shall not begin due to nonpayment of 3 or more estimated bills unless the customer was provided an equal amount of time to pay the estimated billing.

515-3-2.03. Disconnection During Illness:

Service shall not be discontinued for nonpayment upon receipt of notice from customer in writing, or orally with written notice within 10 days thereafter, of a serious illness which would be aggravated by discontinuation, and upon receipt within 10 days of such initial notice of a written statement from a physician, county board of health, hospital, or clinic identifying the illness and its expected duration, and certifying that illness would be aggravated by discontinuance. Postponement of service upon such notice shall not exceed 1 month from date of initial notice, and may be extended one additional period.

515-3-2.04. Seasonal Restrictions:

Electric service shall not be disconnected due to nonpayment from November 15 through March 15 if the customer agrees to pay any past-due amount in equal monthly installments between March 15 and October 15, and to make timely payments on subsequent bills, or on a day when the forecasted low for a 24-hour period beginning at 8:00 a.m. on the scheduled date of disconnection is expected to be below 32° Fahrenheit. Service shall not be disconnected on a day that a National Weather Service Heat Advisory or Excessive Heat Warning is in effect prior to 8:00 a.m. on the scheduled disconnection date.

***Gas Service Disconnection Rules*—Ga. Comp. R. & Regs. 515-3-3.01–515-3-3.10**

515-3-3.01. Reasons for Disconnection:

Substantially similar to 515-3-2.03.

515-3-3.02(A). Limitations on Disconnections by a Local Distribution Company (LDC):

Substantially similar to 515-3-2.02.

515-3-3.02(B). Limitations on Disconnections by a Marketer or an Electing Distribution Company (EDC):

Substantially similar to 515-3-2.02.

Notice shall be 15 days. Service shall not be disconnected if the overdue bill is solely comprised of an unpaid deposit, unless it is for a deposit that was assessed either at the commencement of service with the marketer or within 60 days from the commencement date of service. Notice shall contain a statement that qualified low-income consumers may transfer to the regulated provider without termination of service.

515-3-3.03. Disconnection During Illness:

Substantially similar to 515-3-2.03.

515-3-3.04. Seasonal Restrictions:

Gas service shall not be disconnected due to nonpayment from November 15 through March 15 if the customer agrees to pay any past-due amount in equal monthly installments between March 15 and October 15 and agrees to make timely payments on subsequent bills, or on a day when the forecasted low for the 48 hour period beginning at 8:00 a.m. on the scheduled date of termination is expected to be below 32°.

515-3-3.05(A). Disconnections for Multi-Family Dwellings by a Local Distribution Company:

Notice shall be personally served on at least one adult in each dwelling unit or posted conspicuously on the premises when personal service cannot be made. Notice shall be at least 5 days before the scheduled date of disconnection.

515-3-3.05(B). Disconnections for Multi-Family Dwellings by a Marketer or Electing Distribution Company:

Substantially similar to 515-3-3.05(A). Notice shall be at least 15 days before the scheduled date of disconnection.

515-3-3-.06(A). Right of the Consumer (Gas Service):

In the case of a disputed bill, consumers shall have the right, after all remedial measures with the utility or marketer have failed, to request in writing, or orally to be followed by a request in writing, the Georgia Public Service Commission to investigate the dispute either before or after service has been terminated. Any late charges assessed in the case of a disputed bill shall be refunded if it is determined that the consumer does not owe the bill.

* * *

***Billing Procedures (Gas)*—Ga. Comp. R. & Regs. 515-7-6.01–515-7-6.05**

* * *

515-7-6.02. Service Quality Standards for Billing (Gas Service):

Bills shall be mailed or posted electronically within 30 days from the actual meter reading or estimated reading, shall be due no less than 20 days from the mailing or posting date, and shall contain information concerning meter-reading dates, consumption amounts, due dates, amounts and penalties due, any information that will allow and assist in the computation of charges, and utility's contact information for questions or complaints.

Estimated bills are prohibited by marketers, except that, if the distribution company or other person authorized to read meter fails to provide information to marketer, a clearly labeled estimated bill is permitted for not more than two consecutive months.

Competitive retail natural gas service charges shall not exceed marketer's published price. Marketers shall not engage in cramming. Prohibitions and restrictions on marketers' ability to increases natural gas service charge or assessing new or additional charges. Marketer must provide advance written notice of new or additional service charges or fees and notice shall inform consumer of right to cancel service without penalty.

Late fees must be reasonable and may not exceed the greater of $10 or 1.5% of the overdue balance. A late fee may not be imposed for a past-due balance of $30 or less. If a refund or credit is due a customer, it must be applied or issued within 60 days after the overpayment has been acknowledged by the marketer.

Bills must include the Commission's website address, where the customer may obtain pricing information relative to gas marketers.

* * *

515-7-6.04. Consumer Rights and Remedies (Gas Service):

Gas service providers shall correct billing errors within 30 days of discovery. Customers shall be given at least 90 days to pay utility billing errors. The utility shall not impose any penalty or begin disconnection procedures due to billing errors or when a bill is in dispute (customer may be required to pay undisputed portion of bill while dispute is pending).

* * *

515-7-9.04. Disclosure Statement (Gas Service):

The utility shall provide information concerning services, rate schedules and any changes in services and rate schedules, information that will assist in choice of service, and all the rights, remedies, responsibilities, and assistance associated with services (see regulation for disclosure specifics).

515-7-9.05. Right to Rescission (Gas Service):

A customer shall have 3 days to cancel service upon receipt of enrollment materials, notice of a change in terms and conditions of services, or notice of new or additional services.

* * *

***Telephone Service*—Ga. Comp. R. & Regs. 515-12-1.01–515-12-1.34**

The regulations governing telephone service are substantially similar to the regulations governing electric and gas service and are indicated accordingly.

* * *

515-12-1.05. Customer Deposits for Communication Services:

Utilities may require deposits from customers before beginning or to continue receiving service if they judge the deposit is necessary. The utility shall maintain records of deposits and provide customers with a receipt. The amount of the deposit shall not exceed the amount of an estimated bill for 2 1/2 billing periods. Interest shall accrue interest at a rate of 7% per annum. Deposits and interest shall be automatically refunded, minus any amounts due, within 30 days after 12 months of billing without a discontinuance of service, without two or more bills having been past due, or when customer discontinues service. A utility shall review the accounts of customers not meeting this requirement after 12 periods.

A customer can establish credit by paying a deposit or providing a guarantee, being a customer of the same utility for 24 consecutive billing periods without discontinuance for nonpayment or more than one late payment within preceding 12 billing period, or otherwise demonstrating lack of credit risk.

515-12-1.06. Reasons for Denying Service:

Substantially similar to 515-3-2.01.

515-12-1.07. Insufficient Reasons for Denying Service:

Substantially similar to 515-3-2.01.

* * *

515-12-1.28. Telephone Service Disconnection:

No basic residential service shall be disconnected for local service charge until at least 29 days from the date of the bill.

The remainder of this regulation is substantially similar to the rules governing electric and gas service disconnection.

* * *

HAWAII

The regulations regarding gas and electric service are located in Haw. Code R. §§ 6-60-1–6-60-10, and the regulations regarding telecommunications are located in Haw. Code R. §§ 6-80-1–6-80-142. Reference should also be made to Haw. Pub. Util. Comm'n Gen. Order No. 7, Rules 1–8 (Oct. 27, 1972) (electric), Haw. Pub. Util. Comm'n Gen. Order No. 8, Rules 1–8 (Dec. 20, 1972) (telephone), and Haw. Pub. Util. Comm'n Gen. Order No. 9, Rules 1–8 (gas), available at the state website, www.hawaii.gov/budget/adminrules/public-utilities-commission.

***Gas and Electric*—Haw. Code R. §§ 6-60-1–6-60-10**

* * *

§ 6-60-5. Master Metering:

Master-metering provisions for electric or gas services are applicable to new buildings for which building permits were obtained within 6 months after June 19, 1981 (effective date of the regulation). Service to residential units must be supplied through individually-metered service for each unit whether the unit is owner-occupied or rented, except where prohibited by local code or ordinance.

Master metering for apartments, condominiums and multi-unit buildings containing residential units is permitted when the individual occupant does not control a substantial portion of the energy used, e.g., for water heating or air-conditioning, or if master-metered service would encourage conservation or efficient use of energy. Such determinations are made by the utility.

In the event of a dispute, a person may apply to the Commission for modification or exemption by furnishing the facts and circumstances warranting an individual meter. The utility must either join in support or oppose the application, and provide an explanation of its position.

§ 6-60-6. Automatic Adjustment Clause:

A utility's rate schedule may include an automatic rate adjustment clause if previously approved by the PUC. Such a clause provides for increases or decreases without prior hearing of rates incurred by the utility due to changes in fuel (gas) and energy (electric) costs. The changes in fuel and energy costs may not be included in a fuel adjustment clause unless the contracts or prices for those costs have been previously approved or filed with the PUC.

An adjustment shall be effective on the date of change. When a cost change occurs during a billing period, the adjustment shall be prorated for the number of days each it was in effect.

§ 6-60-7. Information to Customers:

A utility must furnish (orally or in writing) available rate schedules for service, consumption information, and available rate options and assist in selecting the most economical rate schedule.

Within 60 days after commencement of service, the utility must provide a written explanation of the existing rate schedule and billing practice, including termination procedures and policy, and keep a record in the customer's file that the explanation was provided.

Within 60 days after filing an application to increase its rates and charges, a utility must, through a billing insert, notify customers of, as well as explain, the amount of increase sought. Customers must be notified by a billing insert within 60 days after approval by the PUC of a change in rates, classification, or service.

At least once bi-annually, a utility must provide customers an explanation of the existing rate schedules available to their respective class of service.

Upon request of a customer, but not more than once per calendar year, a utility must provide a statement of the customer's actual consumption for each billing period during the prior year, if readily available, and such other information as the customer may reasonably request.

§ 6-60-8. Procedures for Termination of Service:

A customer must be given at least 15 days from the date of issuance to pay a bill. A customer may file a complaint or dispute with the utility but must also do so within the 15 days allowed to pay the bill. If the latter, then the utility must make a written response to the customer including its determination as to any errors or adjustments. The customer must be notified of the exact amount due and payable on the bill, which amount must be paid within 7 days of the notice. If the customer pays that amount under protest, the protest is submitted to the PUC for final determination.

Written notice of termination is required and must state: the reason(s) for termination; the date on or after which termination will occur; what the customer must do to avoid termination; and the telephone number(s) of a utility representative to call regarding termination.

Termination may not occur on Saturdays, Sundays, or holidays observed by the utility and must occur during normal utility working hours.

Termination of service to elder or disabled customer may not commence without a written report and investigation by the utility to the PUC submitted not less than 5 days before the intended of termination. Elder customers must show proof of being age 62 years or older by appearing in person at the utility office or by verifying date of birth in a personal written statement. Disabled customers can be qualified by certification of physical condition by either a registered physician or an appropriate state agency.

* * *

***Electric*—Haw. Pub. Util. Comm'n Gen. Orders No. 7, Rules 1–8 (Standards for Electric Utility Service)**

* * *

§§ 3.2, 3.3. Meter Reading Sheets, Cards, or Billing Register; Meter Reading Interval:

Meters must clearly indicate units registered; if dial readings must be multiplied by a constant, this must be clearly marked on customer's bill. Where calculations are needed, company must explain to customer upon request. Residential meters may be read bi-monthly.

* * *

§ 4.2(c). Customer Deposits:

§ 4.2(c)(1). Amount of Deposits:

Deposit may not be less than $10, and no more than twice maximum estimated charge for 2 consecutive months.

§ 4.2(c)(2). Interest on Deposits:

Simple interest payable at 6% per annum, payable annually if requested by the customer or upon return of deposit. Interest accrual stops upon return of deposit, date of service termination, or on date notice is sent to customer that deposit is no longer required.

For electric utility, no interest is due if the refund occurs within 30 days of establishment of credit. If held more than 30 days, then payment of interest is retroactive to date of establishment of credit.

§ 4.2(c)(3). Record of and Receipt for Deposit:

Must issue receipt and provide means to establish claim of refund if receipt is lost, and keep records of name, address, amount, date and all transactions. Must keep record of unclaimed deposit for at least 3 years.

§ 4.3. Customer Bill Forms:

Billing to be done as promptly as possible following meter reading, and include: dates of billing period; beginning and ending meter reading; quantity and kind of units measured; rate schedule; amount of bill; distinct marking on estimated bills; and conversion units for meter readings, fuel adjustments, etc.

§ 4.5. Adjustment of Bills:

Adjustments are to be made for fast or slow meter from time when inaccuracy began (if known) but not more than 3 months for slow meters, 6 months for fast meters. Must refund for overcharges of $1 or more for present customer and $2 or more for past customer.

* * *

§ 6.1(d). Meter Testing on Request of Customer:

Upon customer's request and at no charge, utility shall test customer's meter but not more than once in 12-month period. The customer or a representative may be present. A report of the results shall be provided to the customer, and the utility shall maintain record of the report of each test.

* * *

***Telephone*—Haw. Pub. Util. Comm'n Gen. Order No. 8, Rules 1–8 (Standards for Telephone Service)**

* * *

§ 4.2(c). Customer Deposits:

§ 4.2(c)(1). Amount of Deposits:

Deposit may not be less than $5, and no more than maximum estimated charge for service connection plus 1 month's charge for exchange service and estimated toll charges.

§ 4.2(c)(2). Interest on Deposits:

Simple interest payable at 6% per annum, payable annually if requested by the customer or at time deposit is returned or credited to customer's account. Interest accrual stops upon return of deposit, date of service termination, or on date notice is sent to customer that deposit is no longer required.

No interest is due if the refund occurs within 30 days of establishment of credit. If held more than 30 days, then payment of interest is retroactive to date of establishment of credit.

* * *

***Gas*—Haw. Pub. Util. Comm'n Gen. Order No. 9, Rules 1–8 (Standards for Gas Service)**

§§ 3.2, 3.3. Meter Reading Sheets, Cards, or Billing Register; Meter Reading Interval:

Meters must clearly indicate units registered; if dial readings must be multiplied by a constant, this must be clearly marked on customer's bill. Where calculations are needed, company must explain to customer upon request. Residential meters shall be read monthly unless otherwise ordered by Commission.

* * *

§ 4.2(c). Customer Deposits:

§ 4.2(c)(1). Amount of Deposits:

Deposit may not be less than $5, and no more than twice maximum estimated charge for 2 consecutive months.

§ 4.2(c)(2). Interest on Deposits:

Simple interest payable at 6% per annum, payable annually if requested by the customer or upon return of deposit. Interest accrual stops upon return of deposit, date of service termination, or on date notice is sent to customer that deposit is no longer required. Utility may retain deposit as long as deemed necessary to ensure payment.

§ 4.2(c)(3). Record of and Receipt for Deposit:

Must issue receipt and provide means to establish claim of refund if receipt is lost, and keep records of name, address, amount, date and all transactions. Must keep record of unclaimed deposit for at least 3 years.

§ 4.3. Customer Bill Forms:

Billing to be done as promptly as possible following meter reading, and include: dates of billing period; beginning and ending meter reading; quantity and kind of units measured; rate schedule; amount of bill; distinct marking on estimated bills; and conversion units for meter readings, fuel adjustments, etc.

* * *

§ 4.5. Adjustment of Bills:

Adjustments are to be made for fast or slow meter from time when inaccuracy began (if known) but not more than 3 months for slow meters, 6 months for fast meters. Must refund overcharges of $1 or more for present customer and $2 or more for past customer.

* * *

§ 6.1. Utility Inspections and Tests:

* * *

§ 6.1(d). Meter Testing on Request of Customer:

Upon customer's request, utility shall test customer's meter but not more than once in 12-month period. No deposit or charge is required for a test, except utility may charge specified deposit to cover cost of test from customer whose average monthly bill is less than $50 and who requests test within 6 months of new installation or last test. The customer or a representative may be present. A report of the results shall be provided to the customer, and the utility shall maintain record of the report of each test.

* * *

Telecommunications—**Haw. Code R. § 6-80**

* * *

§ 6-80-64. Directories:

Directories must include emergency numbers (police, fire, etc.); instructions on how to place repair service calls, information or directory assistance calls, intrastate calls and calls to inter-exchange carriers; information on billing, nuisance call, and emergency call procedures, and where carriers' tariffs are available for inspection; information on Caller ID, per call or per line blocking, number to call to verify that per line blocking has been effectuated; name, address and phone number of Commission, and that customer should contact Commission if unsatisfied by carrier's response to customer complaint.

* * *

§ 6-80-99. Rates and Specials Charges Information:

Upon a customer's request, a carrier must provide explanations of its rates, charges, and provisions applicable to service furnished or available under its tariffs.

A carrier must: notify a customer of any service connection charge before it is incurred, and any special charges not specifically stated in the carrier's tariff (e.g., charges for extraordinary construction, maintenance, and replacement, for special installations, equipment, and assemblies, and for overtime work); and provide an estimate of the initial billing for service (including fractional monthly amounts).

§ 6-80-100. Customer Billing:

Carrier must bill on a regular basis. Each bill must itemize: applicable exchange access charges; extended area service charges; enhanced and other local service charges; period of time for which local service and equipment charges apply; telephone number of the carrier's business office; due date of the bill; applicable state and federal taxes; and interstate customer line charges.

If the carrier has assumed responsibility for collecting toll charges, the bill must itemize: toll calls charged to the account; date, time, and length of each call; and destination of each call or point of origin for collect or third-party calls, or both the destination and point of origin.

Any partial payment shall be applied first to amount due for basic service.

§ 6-80-101. Billing Information:

A carrier must maintain an accurate record of each customer's name and address and the class and type or types of service furnished. It may not resell or otherwise make available to any third party any billing name and address information, except to enable another entity to bill and collect for telecommunications services or as otherwise required by law. A carrier providing such information to such a qualified third party must first obtain from that party a signed agreement to adhere to the carrier's procedures concerning customer information, including non-listed and non-published telephone numbers and the requirement that billing name and address information may not be resold or otherwise made available except to such qualified parties. If a carrier determines that a third party is not adhering to such a signed agreement, it must cease providing billing name and address information to that third party after 15 days' notice to its customers and to the PUC together with an explanation why it is ceasing to provide such information.

§ 6-80-102. Billing Disputes:

A carrier may require customer to pay undisputed portion of the bill when a billing dispute arises. The carrier must conduct an investigation of the disputed charge(s) and provide a report to the customer. If the dispute is not reconciled, the carrier shall advise the customer that the customer has the right to file a complaint with the PUC.

A customer must be rebilled under the appropriate tariff schedule if: the customer was not eligible under the billed tariff schedule; the customer was eligible under more than one schedule but was billed under a schedule not elected by the customer; or the customer's election was based on erroneous information provided by the carrier. The carrier need not adjust billings if it acted in good faith based upon available information.

If a carrier under-bills due to its omission or negligence and the amount owed by the customer over a period of one month exceeds $25, the carrier must offer and agree to reasonable arrangements for payment. If a carrier over-bills, it must refund the over-billed amount. The refund may be by a credit on future bills if less than $25, and credit or cash refund at the customer's election if $25 or more.

A bill is not past due unless unpaid for 20 calendar days after the billing date stated on the bill.

§ 6-80-103. Adjustments for Out of Service Conditions:

A carrier must make appropriate adjustments or refunds when service is interrupted for reasons other than the customer's negligence or willful act and remains interrupted for more than twenty-four hours after being reported or found. If service interruption is due to a natural or other disaster beyond the carrier's control, then it shall make adjustments and refunds to affected customers if service is not restored within forty-eight hours.

Any adjustment or refund: shall be based on a known period of interruption, beginning from the time the interruption is first reported or found; shall be the prorated portion of month's charge for the days or portion of days that service was out; and may be made in the form of a credit on a subsequent bill.

§ 6-80-104. Establishment of Credit:

A customer may establish credit by: furnishing satisfactory credit information and references; establishing a record of prompt payment for service for 6 to 12 consecutive months; or furnishing a guarantor.

To determine whether a customer's credit is acceptable, a carrier may consider the customer's credit and payment history rating as reported by a nationally recognized credit reporting organization, ownership interest in the premises; and employment;

If service is discontinued for nonpayment and before service is restored, a carrier may require the customer to pay past-due amounts and connection charges, and to either re-establish credit or provide a deposit.

If a bill is not paid within 5 days of receipt of a notice of discontinuance for nonpayment, the carrier may require the customer to make a cash deposit as provided in § 6-80-105.

§ 6-80-105. Customer Deposits:

A carrier may require a cash deposit to guarantee payment of bills until credit is established. The deposit may not exceed twice the average monthly bill for the same class of service to the same class of customers in the customer's given exchange. An estimate of monthly billings may be used to determine a deposit if the carrier can show that the customer's usage may be substantially different from the average usage for the same class of service.

The deposit must be returned to the customer within 30 days of the customer's establishing credit. If returned within 30 days, the carrier need not pay any interest on the deposit. If not returned within 30 days, simple interest at the rate of at least 6% per annum shall be paid from the date credit was established until: the deposit is returned; service is terminated; or notice is sent to the customer's last known address that the deposit is no longer required.

A carrier must maintain a record of each unclaimed deposit for 3 years, during which time the carrier must make a reasonable effort to return the deposit. Unclaimed deposits and accrued interest are to be credited to the appropriate account.

§ 6-80-106. Denial or Discontinuance of Service:

§ 6-80-106(a). Denial or Discontinuance of Service Without Notice:

A carrier may deny or discontinue service without permission or notice: if there exists a condition immediately dangerous or hazardous to life, physical safety, or property; upon the order of any court, the PUC, or any other duly authorized public authority; or if service was obtained fraudulently or without the carrier's authorization.

§ 6-80-106(b). Denial or Discontinuance of Service with Notice:

A carrier may deny or discontinue service without permission and with notice only for: nonpayment of an undisputed past-due bill not in dispute; failure to provide a required deposit or guarantee; obtaining service by subterfuge; unauthorized interference, diversion, or use of the service situated or delivered on or about premises; violation of any carrier rule filed with the PUC; failure to comply with laws and regulations pertaining to the service; or failure to permit the carrier reasonable access to its facilities or equipment.

§ 6-80-106(c). Contents and Timing of Termination Notice:

Written notice of termination must be provided stating the reasons for and date of scheduled termination and the actions the customer may take to avoid termination. The customer must be given at least 5 days from the date of notice to respond, or 7 days if the notice is mailed.

§ 6-80-106(d). Insufficient Reasons for Denying or Discontinuing Service:

A carrier may not deny or discontinue service for: delinquency in payment by a previous occupant except that service may be denied to a member of the delinquent customer's household; failure to pay directory advertising charges; and failure to pay any disputed amount pending resolution of the dispute.

Basic service to residences may not be discontinued for nonpayment of: inter-island, interstate, or international service; flexibly priced services; fully or partially competitive services; or any service offered by a third party. However, the carrier may refuse to provide inter-island service, flexibly priced services, or fully or partially competitive services for nonpayment even if the debt is to another carrier.

* * *

§ 6-80-107. Customer Complaints:

A carrier shall: receive service trouble reports 24 hours a day and all other complaints during normal business hours, without toll or other charge; handle complaints efficiently and courteously and investigate complaints fully and promptly; advise customers who remain dissatisfied after exhausting carrier's internal procedures of the right to have the complaint considered and reviewed by the PUC, including the PUC's address and telephone number; investigate and respond within 30 days to customer complaints transmitted by the PUC to the carrier; not issue any notice of discontinuance for nonpayment of a disputed amount while a complaint investigation is pending by the carrier or the PUC; and maintain for 2 years following final disposition of the complaint an accurate record of each customer complaint, including the customer's name, the date and nature of the complaint, and its disposition.

* * *

§ 6-80-114. Customer's Entitlement to Information:

Upon request for service, a carrier shall provide the following information: the availability of facilities to provide the requested service at the customer's location; the lowest-priced alternative available; the availability for inspection and copying of the carrier's rate schedules and rules filed with PUC; the circumstances under which a deposit or additional deposit may be required and how it is calculated, the interest paid on deposits; the time frame and requirement for the returning a deposit; the hours, addresses, and telephone numbers of offices where bills may be paid and information obtained; the toll free number for repair service or billing inquiries; the time allowed to pay outstanding bills; how billing disputes may be resolved; alternative payment plans offered; available grievance procedures and the right of the customer to file a complaint with the PUC; grounds for suspension of service; procedure for terminating service; that service cannot be discontinued for nonpayment of a disputed amount during pending carrier investigation; that basic residential service may not be discontinued for nonpayment of inter-island, interstate, or international service, flexibly priced services, fully or partially competitive services, or any telecommunications service offered by a third party, subject to the right of the carrier to refuse to provide inter-island service, flexibly priced services, or fully or partially competitive services based on the nonpayment for any of these services, even if the debt is to another carrier; the customer's right to change carriers and procedures for doing so; the procedure for reconnecting service after involuntary suspension; and information on Caller ID and related services, including information on blocking Caller ID on a per call or per line basis, and a telephone number to dial to verify that a request for per line blocking has been effected.

IDAHO

The Public Utilities Commission's general rules governing electric, gas, and water customer relations can be found within Idaho Admin. Code r. 31.21.01.000–31.21.01.702. The regulations governing telephone customer relations can be found within Idaho Admin. Code r. 31.41.01.000–31.41.01.702. Many of the regulations governing telephone service are similar in substance and form to the general rules governing electric, gas, and water service. Questions regarding telephone service may be answered by referencing the general rules governing a specific issue. Access to the regulations can found at: www.adm.idaho.gov/adminrules/rules/idapa31/31index.htm (requires PDF) (last visited in May 2011).

***General Rules (Electric, Gas, and Water)*—Idaho Admin. Code r. 31.21.01.000–31.21.01.800**

* * *

31.21.01.101. Deposit Requirement:

A deposit shall not be required unless proof that the applicant or customer is a credit risk or is likely to damage utility property. Lack of previous utility service is not per se evidence of a credit risk. A deposit may be required due to: termination of service within previous 4 years for nonpayment, misrepresentation of identity, nonreimbursement for damages caused by customer; obtaining, diverting or using service without authorization; lack of credit history combined with a lack of 12 consecutive months of previous service within the last 4 years; 2 or more final termination notices within the last 12 months; or filing for bankruptcy relief.

31.21.01.102. Other Deposit Standards Prohibited—Residential Customers:

Deposit requirement may not be based on residential ownership or location, employment tenure or type, income level, race, creed, sex, age, religion, national origin, marital status, number of dependents, or other criterion prohibited by Idaho Admin. Code regulations.

* * *

31.21.01.104. Explanation for Requirement of Deposit:

A utility shall immediately provide a customer or applicant with the reason(s) a deposit is required and the rights and procedures for disputing a required deposit.

31.21.01.105. Amount of Deposit:

A deposit shall not exceed 1/6 of the estimated annual usage. When gas is the primary source of space heat, a deposit shall not exceed a total of 2 months of the highest monthly bills from the previous 12 months. Customers shall be allowed to pay a deposit by making an initial payment of half the amount of the deposit followed by a second installment payable in 1 month.

31.21.01.106. Interest on Deposits:

Interest on deposits shall accrue according to the rate for one-year Treasury Bills for the previous November 1 through October 31. Interest accrues from date that deposit or installment is made until refunded or applied to bill. Interest shall not accrue when service is temporarily terminated at customer's request and deposit is held for future application, or after service is terminated and utility is unable to return the deposit.

31.21.01.107. Return of Deposit:

Deposits shall be returned if a customer makes 12 consecutive monthly payments with no more than 1 late payment. Upon termination of service, a utility shall credit the customer's account and shall return any remaining portion to the customer. Deposits may be held during a dispute concerning termination of service.

31.21.01.108. Transfer of Deposit:

Generally, a deposit may only be transferred (customer to customer, location to location, etc.) upon a request by the customer.

31.21.01.109. Receipt for Deposit—Records of Deposit:

The utility shall provide the customer with a receipt for their deposit and maintain records to enable a customer to claim a deposit should the receipt become lost.

* * *

31.21.01.201. Issuance of Bills—Content of Bills:

Bills shall contain: the billing date and billing period; beginning and ending meter readings or clear statement that bill is estimated; comparison with previous consumption; due date; itemization of all charges, transferred amounts, amounts past due, payments and credits, and total due; and address and toll-free telephone number in utility's service territory for billing inquiries.

31.21.01.202. Due Dates of Bills—Delinquent Bills:

A due date shall not be less than 15 days from the date of issuance or 12 days after mailing or delivery if bill is mailed or delivered more than 3 days after billing date. A customer who receives income on a particular date may be eligible for a 15-day hardship extension on a due date, or customer may be billed in cycle corresponding to receipt of funds.

31.21.01.203. Billing Under Inappropriate Tariff Schedule:

Rebilling shall not occur for errors that occurred more than 3 years from the date of discovery. Rebilling shall not be required if the utility acted in good faith and/or provided the customer with proper billing options. Rebilling for undercharges is limited to 6 months unless reasonable person should have discovered inappropriate billing, in which case rebilling may extend up to 3 years. A utility shall offer payment arrangements in proportion to the amount of time the under-billing occurred. A utility shall issue a credit on the next bill, with any remaining credit balance credited against future bills unless the customer requests a refund.

31.21.01.204. Inaccurately Billed Service Under Correct Tariff Service—Failure to Bill for Service:

When the beginning date of the error cannot be determined, adjustments shall not be for more than 6 months; when the date of the error is known, adjustments shall not exceed 3 years. Payment standards for under-billing are identical to Idaho Admin. Code r. 31.21.01.203.

* * *

31.21.01.207. Billing Prohibited:

Utilities shall not bill for non-utility services or merchandise that is not authorized or ordered by the customer. Such charges shall be removed from the customer's bill within 2 billing cycles from notice by customer.

* * *

31.21.01.301. Explanation for Denial of Service to Applicant:

When required under Idaho Admin. Code r. 31.21.01.302, the reasons for denial and the procedures for disputing the denial shall be provided to the customer.

31.21.01.302. Grounds for Denial or Termination of Service with Prior Notice:

Notice shall be given if service is denied or to be terminated for issues related to nonpayment of bills and deposits (including failure to comply with payment arrangement), misrepresentation or providing false information, denial of access to meters, willful waste of service, or service to minors. Utility is not required to connect service for customer or applicant who owes money on existing or previous account if the amount owed is for service provided within previous 4 years.

31.21.01.303. Grounds for Denial or Termination of Service Without Prior Notice:

Notice is not required if service is denied or terminated due to a dangerous condition, illegal use of service, utility is unable to notify customer, or due to an order from an authorized source (Commission, court order, etc.).

31.21.01.304. Requirements for Notice to Customers Before Termination of Service:

A utility shall give at least 7 days initial notice followed by final notices of 3 days and 24 hours before service is terminated. The notice requirements shall be repeated if termination does not occur 21 days after the scheduled date of termination. Additional notice is not required if a customer violates the terms of a payment plan or tenders payment with a dishonored check or from an account with insufficient funds.

31.21.01.305. Contents of Notice of Intent to Terminate Service:

Notice of disconnection, mailed or delivered personally, shall contain the reasons for disconnection, the amount due, date of disconnection, availability of payment plans and assistance, delay option for medical reasons or winter protections, and complaint procedures.

31.21.01.306. Termination of Residential Gas and Electric Service—Winter Protection Plan:

Service shall not be terminated from December through February for nonpayment when customer' declares inability to pay in full and residence includes children, elders, or disabled individuals. Customers who are eligible for winter protection shall be offered but not required to enter into a winter protection payment plan (see Regulation for Payment Plan specifics).

31.21.01.307. Third-Party Notification:

A gas or electric utility shall provide customers with the option of third-person notification concerning termination notice. A third party does not incur any financial liability for services provided.

31.21.01.308. Serious Illness or Medical Emergency:

A utility shall delay disconnection 30 days upon receipt of a certificate from a physician or public health official with medical training that customer, member of customer's family or permanent resident of premises is seriously ill or has a medical emergency, or will become seriously ill or have a medical emergency because of termination. Additional 30 day postponement available upon renewal of certificate. If a customer whose service has been disconnected is eligible for a medical delay, service shall be restored within 24 hours with the limit beginning on the day of restoration.

* * *

31.21.01.310. Insufficient Grounds for Termination or Denial of Service:

Service shall not be terminated due to a bill less than $50 or 2 months charges (whichever is less), a delinquent bill of another customer (unless customer has assumed responsibility), or failure to pay for non-utility goods or services, unpaid bills for service four or more years prior unless customer has promised in writing to pay within prior 4 years, or failure to pay disputed amounts pending complaint with Commission or court action.

31.21.01.311. Times When Service May be Terminated—Opportunity to Avoid Termination of Service:

Generally, service shall only be terminated weekdays from 8:00 a.m.–5:00 p.m. Service shall not be terminated on Friday, the day of or the day before a legal holiday, weekends, or at a time that the utility's office is not open to the public. Service may be terminated Monday–Thursday from 5:00 p.m. through 9:00 p.m. if the utility is unable to gain access during normal business hours; Friday between 8:00 a.m.–5:00 p.m. for illegal use or premises are abandoned; or any time if dangerous condition exists or utility is ordered to do so.

The terminating employee shall accept proof that the reason for terminating service has been remedied, thereby avoiding termination of service, and shall also accept payment at the time of service terminations.

Service shall not be terminated if the reason for termination is the subject of a dispute.

31.21.01.312. Denial or Termination of Services to Master-Metered Accounts and Residents or Occupants Who Are Not Customers:

In addition to the aforementioned notice requirements, a utility shall provide 2 days' written notice, by posting in a common area of a multi-unit building or master-metered dwellings, and by delivery to premises where customer is not a resident or occupant.

31.21.01.313. Payment Arrangements:

Utilities shall offer reasonable payment arrangements to customers who cannot pay a bill (see regulation for payment plan specifics).

* * *

31.21.01.401. Complaint Procedures:

See regulations for specific complaint requirements and procedures.

* * *

31.21.01.701. Summary of Rules:

At the initiation of service, the utility shall provide information concerning deposits, denial or termination of service, postponement of termination due to serious illness or medical emergency, availability of payment arrangements, how to file a complaint with utility and Commission, and that termination of service is prohibited pending a complaint with Commission or in state court. Gas and electric utility must also include information regarding winter payment plan, third party notification and level pay plan.

* * *

***Telephone*—31.41.01.000–31.41.01.702**

Many of the regulations governing telephone service are similar in substance and form to the general rules governing electric, gas, and water service. Questions regarding telephone service may be answered by referencing the general rules governing a specific issue.

ILLINOIS

The Commerce Commission's general regulations governing electric, gas, water, and sewer service can be found within Ill. Admin. Code tit. 83, § 280.10–280.200, Apps. A–D. The regulations governing telephone services can be found within Ill. Admin. Code tit. 83 § 735.10–735.230, Apps. A–C. Many of the regulations governing telecommunication service are similar in substance and form to the general regulations. Questions regarding telecommunication regulations may be answered by referencing the general regulations governing a specific issue. Access to the regulations can be found at www.ilga.gov/commission/jcar/admincode/083/083parts.html (last visited in May 2011).

***General Regulations (Electric, Gas, Water, and Sewage)*—Ill. Admin. Code tit. 83, §§ 280.10–280.200, Apps. A–D**

* * *

§ 280.50. Applicants for Service:

A utility may refuse to provide service if, after a review of its own past service records, it finds that an applicant for residential service has failed to pay for past-due utility service for the same class of service furnished to him or her at the same or at another address; if the applicant owes a past-due bill pursuant to the Rights of Married Persons Act [making both spouses liable for certain family expenses]; or if the credit score of the applicant for residential service does not meet or exceed the pre-determined minimum credit score selected by the utility using a credit scoring system, unless the applicant, at the option of the utility, pays any past-due bill and/or provides a deposit pursuant to § 280.70 and/or enters into a deferred payment agreement pursuant to § 280.110.

A utility shall not require a deposit based on a credit scoring system if the applicant for residential service is eligible for the Low Income Home Energy Assistance Program (LIHEAP) or provides proof of identity fraud.

A bill for one class of service (residential or nonresidential) shall not be transferred to a bill for the other class of service, nor shall the bill for one form of utility service (such as gas) be transferred to a bill for another form of utility service (such as electric). Service shall not be denied for nonpayment of bills for merchandise or non-utility services.

If a utility takes telephone applications from third parties or users who will not be customers, and fails to verify the application with the customer, the customer may disclaim liability.

§ 280.60. Present Customers:

A utility may request a deposit pursuant to § 280.70 from a present residential customer during the first 24 months that the customer receives utility service from the utility if the customer, during any 12-month period, pays late 4 times if billed monthly, 2 consecutive times or 3 times if billed bi-monthly or two times if billed quarterly or semi-annually, or if the customer's wires, pipes, meters or other service equipment have been tampered with and the customer enjoyed the benefit of the tampering. However, the utility shall not be subject to the 24-month limit in instances of tampering.

The utility shall make the request for the deposit within 45 days upon discovery of the event that gave rise to the deposit requirement.

Present residential customers who are indebted to a utility for past-due utility service shall have the opportunity to negotiate a deferred payment agreement pursuant to § 280.110 herein to retire the debt.

§ 280.70. Deposits:

An electric or gas utility shall not require a deposit that exceeds 1/6 of estimated annual charges for service. A water or sewage utility shall not require a deposit that exceeds 1/3 of estimated annual charges for service. A utility may request that a minimum of 1/3 of the amount of a requested deposit be paid within 12 days after the issue date of the request for deposit. At least 2 billing periods shall be allowed by gas utilities and electric utilities in which to pay the balance of the deposit. A period of 30 days shall be allowed by water utilities and sewage utilities in which to pay the balance of the deposit.

Generally, deposits, plus interest, shall be refunded after 12 consecutive months of timely payments for service (dependant on billing terms—monthly, bimonthly, etc.). Generally, A deposit need not be returned if a customer has been delinquent in paying for 6 months of service (4 months for customers who have been receiving service for less than 24 months).

Deposits plus interest need not be refunded until the customer pays any past-due bills for utility service.

Deposits plus interest shall be refunded upon the discontinuance of service for more than 30 days less the amount of unpaid bills, if any, for the service. A transfer of service from one premise to another within the area served by the utility need not be deemed a discontinuance of service by the utility if the character of service remains the same.

The rate of interest will be the same as the rate existing for the average one-year yield on U.S. Treasury securities for the last full week in November.

At the end of every year of service, if the deposit plus interest is not refunded to the customer, the utility shall automatically refund the accrued interest on the deposit to the customer by crediting the customer's account and so stating this credit clearly on the customer's next regular bill.

A utility shall provide the applicant or customer with a Certificate of Deposit for any deposit received.

§ 280.75. Refunds:

Refunds due to overcharging shall accrue interest at the rate pursuant to § 280.70 from the date of the overcharge.

* * *

§ 280.80. Estimated Bills:

If billed on a monthly basis, utility may estimate usage every other billing period provided the bill clearly indicates it is an estimate. A utility may estimate billing for consecutive months if the customer fails to provide access for an actual reading, or circumstances beyond utility's control make actual reading extremely difficult.

§ 280.90. Past Due Bills and Late Payment Charges:

The due date for payment of a bill may be no less than 21 days from the date of transmittal, and shall not be considered delinquent until 2 business days after due date.

Late payment charges shall be set at an amount equal to 1 1/2% per month on any amount, including amounts previously past due, for utility service which is considered past due. A utility shall waive the assessment of a late payment charge for residential customers one time per 12-month period if it bills on a monthly or bi-monthly basis, and for residential customers one time per 24-month period if it bills on a quarterly or semi-annual basis.

A utility may not continue to assess a late payment charge on any final bill which has been outstanding for more than 12 months.

A utility shall not assess a late payment charge bill for a budget or levelized payment plan or for any amount billed which is not for utility service.

Customers whose primary income is received 10 days following their billing due date shall be eligible for the preferred payment date program. Income that qualifies for the preferred payment date program: AFDC, Aid to the Aged, Blind, and Disabled [AADB], SSI, VA benefits, unemployment compensation, general assistance, and supplemental security income.

§ 280.100. Unbilled Service:

A bill for services shall not be rendered more than 1 year from the date the services were provided. A utility shall offer payments plans over a time equal to the amount of time of undercharges for billing errors due to estimated billing, utility billing error, meter failure or leakage.

§ 280.105. Treatment of Illegal Taps:

A customer whose bill appears unreasonably high may request that the utility investigate the possibility of an illegal tap. If one is found, the utility must bill the customer according to a domestic use or degree/day analysis and bill the illegal use to the guilty party if he or she can be found or, if this is not possible, assign the price of the illegal use to a bad debt account.

§ 280.110. Deferred Payment Agreements:

Residential customers who are indebted to a utility for past-due utility service shall have the opportunity to enter into a deferred payment plan unless the customer has failed to make payment under a plan within prior 12 months. When establishing a reasonable repayment plan, the utility shall consider the amount owed, the customer's ability to pay, the size of the arrearage, and the reason for the outstanding bill.

Applicant or customer shall pay an initial payment of 1/4 the amount due followed by minimum 2-month (4-month for gas and electric) and a maximum of a 12-month payment period to retire the outstanding balance.

Gas or electric customers shall have the right to renegotiate a payment plan should their financial circumstances change provided the customers notifies the utility within 14 days from defaulting on the plan.

If a gas or electric customer defaults on a deferred payment agreement but has not yet had service discontinued by the utility, the utility shall permit such customer to be reinstated on the deferred payment agreement if the customer pays in full the amounts which should have been paid up to that date pursuant to the original payment agreement.

§ 280.120. Budget Payment Plan:

When the character of an applicant's or customer's consumption of service causes or is likely to cause a substantial fluctuation among his/her bills over an annual period, the utility shall offer to the applicant or customer a budget payment plan which equalizes his/her payments into monthly installments.

§ 280.130. Discontinuance of Service:

Service may be disconnected, with notice, for issues relating to nonpayment (including deposits and deferred payment plans), denial of reasonable access to equipment, or violation of utility rules or Commission order.

Service shall not be discontinued until at least five days after delivery or 8 days after the mailing of a disconnection notice (see regulation for specific notice requirements).

A disconnection notice shall remain effective for two consecutive 20-day periods, provided that during each such period a call is made at the customer's premises or billing address or telephone contact with the customer is made. If the utility does not discontinue service within the two consecutive 20-day periods, the utility shall not discontinue service until at least 5 days after delivery or 8 days after mailing of a new notice of its intention to discontinue service to the customer. Service shall not be discontinued and shall be restored if discontinued where a customer has established, renegotiates, or is reinstated onto a deferred payment agreement pursuant to § 280.110 and has not defaulted on such agreement, or the reason for termination is in dispute.

Termination of service shall not occur if the gas or electric service is the primary source of heat for a customer and the following 24-hours is predicted to be 32° or lower, or on any day before a holiday or weekend when it is forecast that the temperature will be 32° Fahrenheit or lower during the holiday or weekend.

When certified by either a physician or the Board of Health that termination would aggravate a serious illness of any permanent resident, termination shall be postponed for 30 days, during which customer must enter into agreement to pay the unpaid balance and to keep the account current during the period that the unpaid balance is to be paid. Certification may be renewed for an additional 30-day period.

Service shall not be terminated after 2:00 p.m. or on a holiday or weekend unless utility is prepared to reconnect the same day.

§ 280.135. Discontinuance of Service During the Period of Time from December 1 Through and Including March 31:

Disconnection due to nonpayment during the winter protection months shall not occur unless the utility has offered the customer a deferred payment plan and the customer has refused (see regulation for specific payment and notice requirements), and the utility has provided the contact information for available assistance.

§ 280.136. Energy Act of 1989 Participants Discontinuance Prohibition:

No electric or gas public utility shall disconnect service to any residential customer who is a participant under § 6 of the Energy Assistance Act of 1989 for nonpayment of a bill or deposit where gas or electricity is used as the primary source of space heating or is used to control or operate the primary source of space heating equipment at the premises during the period of time from December 1 through and including March 31 of the immediately succeeding calendar year.

§ 280.138. Reconnection of Former Residential Utility Customers for the Heating Season:

Gas or electric services disconnected due to issues related to nonpayment and that are a primary heat source are eligible for reconnection during the winter protection months (see regulation for specific requirements).

§ 280.140. Discontinuance of Service to Accounts Affecting Master Metered Apartment Buildings:

See 765 Ill. Comp. Stat. 735/1 *et seq.* for the procedures to inform tenants of the pending discontinuance of their utility service and set out their remedies including their right to petition a court for appointment of a receiver to collect rents and remit a portion thereof to the utility for payment of utility bills.

§ 280.150. Service Reconnection Charge:

When service has been discontinued the utility may charge and collect the reconnection charge, if any, set forth in its rules, regulations or terms and conditions of service which are on file with the Commission, and such rules shall provide for automatic waiver of one reconnection charge for each customer for each year.

§ 280.160. Dispute Procedures:

Disputes that cannot be resolved or are resolved to the dissatisfaction of the customer may be reviewed by the Commission and utility shall provide telephone number and address of the Consumer Assistance Section of the Commission.

Service shall not be disconnected during a dispute provided the customer pays the undisputed amount of the bill or an amount equal to last year's bill, pays all future periodic bills by the due date, and enters into bona fide discussions with the utility to settle the dispute.

§ 280.170. Commission Complaint Procedures:

See regulation for specific informal and formal complaint procedures.

§ 280.190. Second Language Notices:

Where there is a "demonstrated need" for a second language in a service area, notices must include this phrase, in the appropriate language: "Important—this notice affects your rights and obligations and should be translated immediately."

§ 280.200. Customer Information Booklet:

Utilities must provide a customer information booklet containing credit and collection practices.

* * *

***Telephone*—Ill. Admin. Code tit. 83 §§ 735.10–735.230, Apps. A–C**

Many of the regulations governing telecommunication service are similar in substance and form to the general regulations. Questions regarding telecommunication regulations may be answered by referencing the general regulations governing a specific issue.

INDIANA

The Utility Regulatory Commission's regulations governing electric service can be found within: 170 Ind. Admin. Code 4-1-1–4-1-30; gas, 170 Ind. Admin. Code 5-1-1–5-1-30; water, 170 Ind. Admin. Code 6-1-1–6-1-28; telecommunications, 170 Ind. Admin. Code 7-1.3-1–7-1.3-9. Many of the regulations governing gas, water, and telephone service are similar in substance and form to the regulations governing electric service. Questions regarding gas, water, and telephone service may be answered by referencing the electric regulations governing a specific issue. Access to the regulations can be found at www.in.gov/legislative/iac/title170.html.

***Electric*—170 Ind. Admin. Code 4-1-1–4-1-30**

* * *

4-1-11. Customer Requests for Tests; Application to Utility

A customer may request a meter test, and a second test after 12 months. Thereafter, if a test is requested at less than 36-month intervals, the customer must bear the expense of the test if no error is found.

* * *

4-1-13. Bills:

All bills shall contain information concerning meter reading dates and consumption amounts, due dates, amounts and penalties due, and any information that will allow and assist in the computation of charges. A bill must clearly indicate that it is an estimated bill. A utility may estimate a customer bill only for good cause, including a customer request, inclement weather, labor or union disputes, inaccessibility of a customer's meter if the utility has made a reasonable attempt to read it, and other circumstances beyond the control of the utility, its agents, and employees.

A utility shall not transfer a bill for nonresidential service to a bill for residential service, nor shall a utility transfer a bill for residential service to a bill for nonresidential service.

A bill is considered delinquent unless payment is received within 17 days after the initial bill is postmarked. A late payment charge may be assessed but shall not exceed 10% of the first $3 and 3% of the excess of $3.

A utility must offer a balanced billing program, in which a bill is averaged over an extended period and the account balanced at the end of that period. Notice of this option must be included in the required customer information pamphlet.

4-1-14. Billing Adjustments:

If a meter is fast by more than 3% for watt-hour meters or 4% for demand meters, the utility must refund or credit the amount of the overcharge for the lesser of 1 year or the period during which the meter was inaccurate (if known). If a meter is stopped or slow, the utility may charge for the lesser of 1 year or one-half the period since the last meter test. Other billing errors (e.g., incorrect tariff applications) may be corrected for the lesser of 1 year or from the known date of the error.

4-1-15. Creditworthiness of Customers; Deposits; Refunds:

A utility shall not consider geographic location or discriminate in any way when determining creditworthiness.

A deposit may be required of a present customer to receive or continue to receive service due to issues related to nonpayment of services (disconnection, late payments, etc.) for past and present utility service.

A deposit shall not be required if an applicant who has not been the customer of any utility within previous 2 years can demonstrate any two of the following: a consistent employment history (or acceptable reasons for unemployment); purchase or long-term rental of residence to be served; a student-graduate; or is being discharged from military service.

A deposit shall not be required of an applicant who has been the customer of any utility with previous 2 years if: no bills are owed for service rendered within previous 4 years; no more than two delinquent bills to any utility within previous 12 months (or one if less than 12 months); and no service disconnection for nonpayment within two previous years.

A deposit shall not exceed 1/6 of estimated annual billing (gas is 1/3). A deposit of more than $70 shall be payable over 2 monthly billing cycles. Deposits held for more than 12 months shall earn 6% per annum interest. A deposit shall be refunded after 9 consecutive months or 10 of 12 months of timely payments, or the creditworthiness can be established by other means. Customers shall receive receipts for deposits and the utility shall provide a method by which a customer can claim a deposit if the receipt is lost.

4-1-16. Disconnection of Service; Prohibited Disconnections; Reconnection:

Service may be disconnected without notice due to emergencies, unauthorized use, tampering, or order of court, Commission, or authorized public authority.

Service may be disconnected with notice for issues relating to nonpayment, denial of reasonable access to equipment, or violation of utility rules or regulations.

Notice of disconnection shall be given at least 14 days before the scheduled date of disconnection and shall be clearly distinguishable. A disconnection notice shall contain the reasons for disconnection, date of disconnection, telephone number of utility office and a reference to customer rights pamphlet furnished under 170 Ind. Admin Code 4-1-18. The disconnecting employee shall not be required to accept payment from the customer, user, or other responsible person in order to prevent the service from being disconnected, but service shall not be disconnected if credible verification is presented that bill has been satisfied or is currently disputed and under review.

Utility shall postpone termination for 10 days if prior to noticed disconnect date customer provides medical statement from licensed physician or public health official that disconnection would be a serious and immediate threat to the health or safety of a designated person in customer's household. Postponement may be continued for an additional 10-day period upon renewal of certificate.

Disconnection may be avoided if the customer agrees to pay a portion of the bill and enter into a payment agreement (see regulation for specific requirements and procedures) or for cause (financial hardship).

A utility may charge a reasonable reconnection charge, not to exceed the charge approved by the Commission in the utility's filed tariffs.

When the reason for disconnection has been remedied, the utility must reconnect the service to the customer or user as soon as reasonably possible but at least within 1 working day after it is requested to do so.

Service shall only be terminated between 8:00 a.m.–3:00 p.m., but not on any day when the utility is closed or after 12:00 when the utility is closed the following day.

Service shall not be denied for nonpayment of bill by a previous customer, failure to pay for merchandise, failure to pay for service at different location if unpaid for less than 45 days, failure to pay for a different form or class of service, or where a customer who has not breached a payment plan within previous 12 months shows inability to pay full amount due (e.g., financial hardship), pays a portion of bill, agrees to pay balance of delinquent bill in 3 months and agrees to pay undisputed future bills as they become due.

A customer who wants to disconnect must give the utility 3 days' notice. The utility must disconnect within 3 working days of the requested date, and customer will not be liable for service used after that time.

* * *

4-1-16.6. Home Energy Assistance; Disconnection of Service to Recipients; Notice Period:

During the period from December 1 through March 15, a utility may not disconnect service to customers who are receiving or have applied to receive low-income or elder assistance.

This rule shall not prevent disconnection due to emergencies, fraud, customer's use of equipment adversely affecting others or service, unauthorized use, or tampering.

4-1-18. Informational Pamphlets and Rate Schedules; Notice of Proposed Rate Change:

Each utility must publish and distribute, without request, to all applicants for service and to all current customers, a comprehensive pamphlet which, in clear language, easily understandable to a layman, fully describes the rights and responsibilities of the customers, and, whenever it petitions the Commission for any change in its residential base rate schedules, it must furnish to each residential customer, within 45 days of such request, a notice which fairly summarizes the nature and extent of the proposed changes.

* * *

4-1.5-2. Master-Metering of New Multi-Unit Structures:

Generally forbidden, except in hotels, motels, or similar transient lodgings, unless applicant can prove that the cost of individual metering would outweigh the benefits and would not serve the objectives of the act.

* * *

***Gas*—170 Ind. Admin. Code 5-1-1–5-1-30**

* * *

5-1-14. Billing Adjustments:

If a meter is fast by more than 2%, the utility must refund the overcharge for the lesser of 1 year or one-half the time since the last meter test. If a meter is stopped, or is more than 2% slow, the utility may back-bill for the lesser of 1 year or one-half the time since the last meter test. For other errors, the bill may be adjusted for the lesser of 1 year or since the time of the error, if known.

5-1-15. Creditworthiness of Customers; Deposit; Refund:

A utility shall not consider geographic location or discriminate in any way when determining creditworthiness.

A deposit may be required to receive or continue to receive service due to issues related to nonpayment of services (disconnection, late payments, etc.) for past and present utility service.

An applicant who has not been the customer of a utility during the past 2 years demonstrates creditworthiness by showing two of the following: a consistent employment history, i.e., not more than two employers in the past 2 years, or recent discharge from military, or recent graduation from school, university, or vocational program; purchase or long-term rental of residence to be served; or bank or commercial credit and a credit check shows that customer has not been in default more than twice in the past 12 months. A utility must inform the customer of the facts on which it bases its decision to require a deposit and give the customer an opportunity to rebut these facts or offer other evidence of creditworthiness.

A deposit shall not exceed 1/6 of estimated annual billing for a new applicant who cannot establish creditworthiness or 1/3 of estimated annual billing for applicants or customers with an unsatisfactory payment history with a utility. (During the winter, LIHEAP-eligible consumers may be required to make only a 1/6 deposit.). A deposit of more than $70 shall be payable over 8 weeks for utilities serving less than 35,000 residential customers. A deposit of more than $150 dollars shall be payable over 12 weeks. Deposits held for more than 30 days by a utility serving more than 35,000 residential customers shall pay interest at a rate to be set by the Commission, based on the interest rate of certain U.S. Treasury securities. Deposits held for 12 months by a smaller utility shall pay interest at 6% per year. A deposit shall be refunded after 12 consecutive months or 12 of 15 months of timely payments (without late payment in 2 consecutive months), or the creditworthiness can be established by other means. Customers shall receive receipts for deposits and the utility shall provide a method by which a customer can claim a deposit if the receipt is lost.

5-1-16. Disconnection of Service; Prohibited Disconnections; Reconnection:

Service may be disconnected without notice due to emergencies, by order of the Commission, any court, or authorized public authority, customer's use of equipment adversely affects others or service, unauthorized use, or tampering.

Service may be disconnected with notice for issues relating to nonpayment or violation of utility rules or regulations.

Notice of disconnection shall be given at least 14 days before the scheduled date of disconnection and shall be clearly distinguishable. A disconnection notice shall contain the reasons for disconnection, date of disconnection, telephone number of utility office, and a reference to customer rights pamphlet furnished under 170 Ind. Admin. Code 5-1-18. The disconnecting employee shall not be required to accept payment from the customer, user, or other responsible person in order to prevent the service from being disconnected, but service shall not be disconnected if credible evidence is presented that bill has been satisfied or is currently disputed and under review.

A utility shall delay disconnection 10 days upon receipt of a certificate from a physician or public health official that disconnection would be a serious and immediate threat to the health or safety of a designated person in customer's household. Termination may be delayed for an additional 10 days upon receipt of a second certificate. Only 20 days postponement per 12-month period is required.

Disconnection may be avoided for cause (financial hardship) if the customer agrees to pay a portion of the bill and enter into a payment agreement (see regulation for specific requirements and procedures).

A utility may charge a reasonable reconnection charge, not to exceed the charge approved by the Commission in the utility's filed tariffs.

When the reason for disconnection has been remedied, the utility must reconnect the service to the customer or user as soon as reasonably possible but at least within 1 working day after it is requested to do so.

Service shall only be terminated between 8:00 a.m.–3:00 p.m., but not on any day that the utility is closed or after 12:00 when the utility is closed the following day.

Service shall not be denied for nonpayment of bill by a previous customer (unless the utility has good reason to believe the customer is attempting to defraud the utility); failure to pay for merchandise; or, for failure to pay an unusually large bill to correct previous under-billing or for inability to pay (e.g., financial hardship), provided that the customer pays a reasonable portion of the under-billed or delinquent amount, agrees to a payment plan as to the balance, and pays undisputed bills as they become due.

* * *

5-1-16.6. Home Energy Assistance; Disconnection of Service to Recipients; Notice Period:

Between December 1 and March 15, a utility may not disconnect service to a consumer who is receiving, is eligible for, or has applied for assistance, except for hazardous condition, fraud, or tampering or court order.

* * *

***Water*—170 Ind. Admin. Code 6-1-1–6-1-28; *Telecommunications*—170 Ind. Admin. Code 7-1.3-1–7-1.3-9**

Many of the regulations governing gas, water, and telephone service are similar in substance and form to the regulations governing electric service. Questions regarding gas, water, and telephone service may be answered by referencing the electric regulations governing a specific issue.

* * *

6-1-16. Disconnection of Service; Prohibited Disconnection; Reconnection:

Substantially similar to §§ 4-1-16 and 5-1-16 except that notice period is 7, rather than 14, days.

IOWA

The Utilities Division's regulations governing gas service can be found within Iowa Admin. Code r. 199-19.1–199-19.17. Specific regulation governing electric, water, and telephone service can be found within Iowa Admin. Code r. 199-20.1–199-20.8, 199-21.1–199-21.9, and 199-22.1–199-22.24, respectively. Although not summarized below, general regulations governing complaint procedures can be found within Iowa Admin. Code r. 199-6.1–199-6.8. Many of the regulations governing electric, water, and telephone service are similar in substance and form to the regulations governing gas service. Questions regarding electric, water, and telephone service may be answered by referencing the gas regulations governing a specific issue. Access to the regulations (in PDF form) can be found at www.legis.state.ia.us/aspx/ACODocs/chapterList.aspx?agency=199 (last visited in May 2011).

***Gas Service*—Iowa Admin. Code r. 199-19.1–199-19.16**

* * *

199-19.3. Disposition of gas:

* * *

199-19.3(1). Multiple Dwellings:

Individual metering is required unless: gas is used for central heating, cooling, or water-heating; the facility is designated for elder or disabled persons; submetering or resale was permitted prior to 1966; or individual metering would be impractical [defined]. If master metering is permitted, utility service may be included as an unidentified portion of the rent or condominium fee. If other allocation is used, the total charged may not exceed the amount charged by the utility for the same period.

* * *

199-19.3(6). Prepayment Meters:

Pre-payment meters may not be set to require a higher rate than a standard meter, except pursuant to a special rate schedule filed under 19.2(4).

199-19.3(7). Meter Reading and Billing Interval:

Readings of all meters used for determining charges and billings to customers shall be scheduled at least monthly and for the beginning and termination of service. A utility may provide a procedure that enables customers to provide meter readings, but shall obtain an actual reading at least once every 12 months or when service is initiated.

A utility may arrange for a meter to be read by electronic means. If the utility does not have a plan to test-check electronic readings, a utility representative must physically read the meter once every 12 months.

199-19.3(8). Readings and Estimates:

Bills may be estimated under certain circumstances, but, unless under extraordinary circumstances or with customer approval, estimated bills shall not be issued for more than 3 consecutive months.

* * *

199-19.4. Customer Relations:

199-19.4(1). Customer Information:

Utilities shall post information at each office and/or provide customers with information concerning bill payment methods and contents, their rights, complaint procedures and contact information, and assist the customer or prospective customer in selecting the most economical rate schedule available for the proposed type of service.

Upon request, the utility must inform customers how to read meters, provide a statement of either customer's actual consumption or degree/day-adjusted consumption for each billing period during the past 12 months, and provide any other information reasonably requested by the customer.

199-19.4(2), (3). Customer Deposits; Interest on Customer Deposits:

A deposit or guarantee may be required as a condition for receiving, or continuing to receive service. A utility shall provide at least 12 days' notice if a new or additional deposit is required as a condition of receiving, or continuing to receive service. A deposit shall not exceed or estimated high-usage bill for 1 month of service for a location that has received service in the previous 12 months, or estimated 1 month's service if no previous service or less than 12 months of service. Interest shall be paid on deposits at the rate of 7.5% per year compounded annually, and shall be returned or refunded when the deposit is returned.

199-19.4(4), (5). Customer Deposit Records; Customer's Receipt for a Deposit:

The utility shall provide the customer with a receipt of deposit, and provide a method to claim a deposit should the receipt be lost.

199-19.4(6). Deposit Refund:

Deposits or guarantee shall be returned after 12 consecutive months of prompt payment of utility bills (including 11 timely payments and one automatic forgiveness of late payment). All accounts, for which a deposit is not returned after 12 consecutive months of service, shall be reviewed at 12-month intervals.

* * *

199-19.4(8). Customer Bill Forms:

Bills shall contain meter readings and reading dates, number of units metered, rate schedule, and conversions or calculations used to determine billing units, all payment information and amounts due (late payments, charges, taxes, etc.), and clear indication of an estimated or minimum bill.

* * *

199-19.4(10). Payment Agreements:

Customers who cannot fully pay for services rendered shall be offered a reasonable payment plan, unless the customer is in default for an existing payment plan. Reasonableness shall be determined by considering the current household income, ability to pay, payment history including prior defaults on similar agreements, the size of the bill, the amount of time and the reasons why the bill has been outstanding, and any special circumstances creating extreme hardships within the household.

A utility must offer a second payment agreement, for a term equal to or longer than the first, to a customer who defaults but has made at least two consecutive payments. The customer shall be required to pay for current service in addition to the monthly payments under the second payment agreement and may be required to make the first payment as a condition of entering into a second payment plan. A utility must provide written reasons for refusal of a proposed payment plan. Within 10 days, the customer may seek the assistance of the board in negotiating a payment plan. Service may not be disconnected while review of this request is in progress.

199-19.4(11). Bill Payment Terms:

Customer shall be given at least 20 days from the date a bill is rendered before it is considered delinquent for nonpayment. The delinquency date for residential customers (whose consumption is less than 250 ccf per month) may be changed for cause, e.g., 15 days after the customer's receipt of income. Under no circumstances may the date be extended more than 30 days from the date of preparation of the previous bill. A utility may asses a 1.5% rate charge for bills not paid within the 20-day due date. Each account shall be granted at least one complete forgiveness of a late payment charge each calendar year. No collection fee other than the late payment may be imposed. This rule does not forbid the cost-related changes in disconnection and reconnection fee.

Utilities must offer residential customers whose consumption is less than 250 ccf per month a levelized payment plan. Consumers must be informed of this when they request service. Consumers may enter or leave the plan at any time of year.

* * *

199-19.4(13). Adjustment of Bills:

Where metering is fast or slow more than 2% a bill shall be adjusted (refund or back-billed).

If a customer has been over- or under-charged for a reason other than meter error, e.g., incorrect application of tariff or incorrect connection of the meter, the amount of the overcharge not exceeding 5 years must be refunded. If the customer was undercharged, the back bill may not exceed the tariffed rate for like charges for the 12 months preceding the error.

* * *

199-19.4(15). Refusal or Disconnection of Service:

Service may be disconnected without notice due to hazardous conditions, customer's use of equipment adversely affects others or service, unauthorized use, or tampering.

Service may be disconnected with notice for issues relating to nonpayment, denial of reasonable access to equipment, or violation of utility rules or regulations.

Notice of disconnection shall be given at least 12 days before the scheduled date of disconnection and shall be clearly distinguishable. A disconnection notice shall contain the reasons for disconnection, the amount due, date of disconnection, availability of payment plans and assistance, delay option for medical reasons, and complaint procedures. Additional notification procedures, including posting notice at the residence to be disconnected and attempted notification by telephone shall be required during the winter protection period (November 1 through April 1). If service to a multiple dwelling is to be disconnected, notice must be posted on the premises at least 2 days before disconnection, stating the date and reason for disconnection.

Low-income customers shall not be subject to disconnection during the winter protection period.

Before November 1 each year, the utility must inform consumers of the availability of energy assistance for low-income households.

Disconnection shall be delayed for 30 days from receipt of written statement from doctor or public health official that shutting off service would pose an especial health danger to permanent resident of premises. Verification by doctor or public health official may be by telephone initially, but written statement must be provided within 5 days.

Service may not be disconnected for nonpayment of a disputed bill, but the utility may require the undisputed amount to be paid pending resolution of the dispute as a condition for continuing to receive service.

Disconnection shall occur from 6:00 a.m. through 2:00 p.m. and shall not occur on a weekend, legal holiday. If gas is the primary method of space heating, disconnection may not take place at a time when the temperature is predicted to be 20° Fahrenheit or lower within the next 24 hours.

Once the reason for disconnection has been remedied the utility shall restore service the same day, or when remedy occurred after 7:00 p.m., by at least 11:00 a.m. the following day.

199-19.4(16). Insufficient Reasons for Denying Services:

Service shall not be denied for nonpayment of bill by a previous customer, failure to pay a deposit during the winter protection months, failure to pay for merchandise or for a different type or class of service, failure to pay for back-billing due to a slow meter, failure to pay a bill to correct previous under-billing due to a misapplication of rates, or delinquency in payment by occupant, if applicant is creditworthy and able to satisfy deposit requirement.

* * *

199-19.4(18). Change in Character of Service:

If a change in character of service necessitates adjustment of customers' appliances, the adjustment shall be made without charge and with a minimum of inconvenience to customers.

199-19.4(19). Customer Complaints:

The utility must promptly investigate and keep records of customer complaints. The tariff shall include a "concise, fully informative" procedure for handling complaints. The utility must take reasonable steps to ensure that customers unable to travel are not denied their right to be heard. The final step of the complaint procedure must be a filing for board resolution.

* * *

***Electric*—Iowa Admin. Code r. 199-20.1–199-20.8; *Water*—Iowa Admin. Code r. 199-21.1–199-21.9; *Telephone*—Iowa Admin. Code r. 199-22.1–199-22.24**

Many of the regulations governing electric, water, and telephone service are similar in substance and form to the regulations governing gas service. Questions regarding electric, water, and telephone service may be answered by referencing the gas regulations governing a specific issue.

KANSAS

The Corporation Commission regulates electric, gas, water, and telephone service providers under their consumer information rules. The regulations governing telephone service is similar in form and substance to the regulation governing electric, gas, and water service, any questions regarding specific issues may be answered by referencing the electric, gas, and water service regulations. Access to the regulations, in PDF format, can be found at www.kcc.ks.gov/pi/billing.pdf (electric, gas and water) and www.kcc.ks.gov/telecom/phonebilling.pdf (telephone) (last visited in May 2011).

***Electric, Natural Gas, and Water*—Billing Standards**

Section I. Standards on Billing Practices:

Bills may be issued on a monthly or other basis, and shall contain information concerning meter-readings and reading dates, consumption amounts, clear indication of an estimated bill, billing adjustments, due dates, amounts and penalties due, any information that will allow and assist in the computation of charges, and contact information of the utility. Meters shall be read in the range between 26 to 36 days.

Customer may be required to read meters and may be charged a reading charge if they fail to provide a reading for 2 consecutive months, but a utility must obtain an actual at least once every 12 months.

Bills shall not be estimated for more than 3 consecutive billing periods or 6 months, whichever is less, and no more than 6 estimated bills may be issued per year. Bills may be estimated if the customer is a participant in a levelized or budgeted payment plan.

Utilities shall annually provide customer with an explanation of Commission's complaint procedures.

A utility shall not refuse or disconnect service (or threaten to), for delinquent bills of more than 5 years old when service agreement is written or 3 years old when an oral agreement.

Section II. Standards on Delayed Payment Charges:

When a utility provides multiple services or utilities combine billing, the customer shall be allowed to designate priority of payment allocation. A delinquent bill may be subject to a 2% service charge on the amount due. Customers may receive a 14 due-date extension in exchange for an assessment of a 1% service charge. Utilities may also charge a disconnection and reconnection fee per tariff.

Customers with delinquent balances shall be offered levelized payment plans allowing equal payments over a 12-month period.

Section III. Standards on Security Deposit Practice:

A new customer may be required to pay a deposit or provide a guarantee of payment if they have insufficient credit due to delinquent bills (past or present), diversion of services, failure to meet the tariff's accepted credit rating, or failure to provide positive identification. Customers may be given up to 4 months to provide positive identification whereupon a deposit shall be refunded. After application for service, customers shall be given at least 5 days' notice if a deposit is required for nonpayment or diversion issues. The amount of the deposit shall not exceed the amount of an estimated bill for 2 billing periods, or 3 billing periods for customers documented to have diverted service. Customers shall be allowed to pay a deposit in monthly installments (see regulation for further deposit amounts and installment specifications). Utility shall maintain records and provide customers with receipts of deposits. Deposits shall accrue interest at a rate determined by the Commission (.50% for 2011), which shall be credited to the customer's account or refunded at least annually.

Deposits shall be returned or credited after 12 consecutive months without more than 3 late payments or when service is disconnected.

Section IV. Standards on Discontinuance of Service Practices:

Services may be discontinued for nonpayment, failure to make deposit or provide guarantee, diversion or interference with service, misrepresentation of identity, refusal of reasonable inspection, when health or safety risk is possible, or violation of utility regulations. Notice shall be sent as a separate mailing and shall be given at least 10 days before discontinuance. Notice shall contain the customer's name, address, and telephone number; reason, date, how to avoid discontinuance and utility contact information, cost of reconnection, winter and medical delay options, and settlement options. A reasonable effort to contact a customer shall be made at least 48 hours preceding discontinuance. Notice of disconnection is valid for 1 month after the scheduled disconnection date.

Service may not be discontinued: for failure to pay for merchandise, services elsewhere, or a delinquent bill of another person or a previous occupant; for failure to pay for a different class of service at same location; for failure to pay a disputed bill; for failure to pay unpaid written service account more than 5 years old or oral account more than 3 years old.

Utility shall either allow payment in reasonable installments or postpone discontinuance for at least 21 days so customer can make arrangements for reasonable installment payments if customer notifies utility and establishes that discontinuance would be especially dangerous to health of customer, resident member of customer's family, or other permanent resident and that customer is either unable to pay for service in accordance with utility's billing or able to pay only in installments.

Notice is not required when disconnection is due to a dangerous condition, denial of access to utility equipment, violation of utility rules, and unauthorized use of service.

Disconnecting employee shall accept payments allowing avoidance of disconnection. Once the reason for disconnection has been remedied, service shall be restored as soon as reasonably possible.

Upon notification that the reason for disconnection is disputed, the utility shall postpone disconnection until the dispute is resolved. If the utility is unable to resolve the dispute it shall inform the customer of Commission review procedures, but may continue disconnection procedures.

Section V. Cold Weather Rule:

Special notification, payment plans, and assistance requirements shall be made available to customers whose heat-related services are subject to termination between November 1 and March 31 or when the temperature is expected to be in the mid-30° (see regulation for requirements).

* * *

***Telephone*—Billing Standards**

The regulations governing telephone service is similar in form and substance to the regulation governing electric, gas, and water service, any questions regarding specific issues may be answered by referencing the electric, gas, and water service regulations.

KENTUCKY

The Public Service Commission's general regulations governing electric, gas, telephone, and water service can be found within 807 Ky. Admin. Regs. 5:006 §§ 1–27. Access to the regulations can be found at www.lrc.ky.gov/kar/title807.htm (last visited in May 2011).

* * *

§ 6. Billings, Meter Readings, and Information:

Bills shall be issued at regular intervals and shall contain information concerning dates and consumption amounts, clear indication of an estimated bill, due dates, amounts and penalties due, and any information that will allow and assist in the computation of charges.

§ 7. Deposits:

A deposit or guarantee that is required as condition of receiving or continuing to receive service shall not exceed 2/12 of the customer's actual or estimated annual bill where bills are rendered monthly, 3/12 when bills are rendered bimonthly, and 4/12 when bills are rendered quarterly. Customers shall be notified if the utility will hold and recalculate the amount of deposit every 18 months. Interest shall accrue on all deposits at the rate prescribed by law, beginning on the date of deposit. Interest accrued shall be refunded to the customer or credited to the customer's bill on an annual basis, except that a utility shall not be required to refund or credit interest on deposits if the customer's bill is delinquent on the anniversary of the deposit date.

§ 8. Special Charges:

A utility may assess additional charges for installation, termination (due to dispatch of utility employee regardless of actual termination but shall not be more than once per billing period), reconnection after termination, late payments, returned checks, and certain customer requested meter re-readings when no error is found.

* * *

§ 10. Bill Adjustment for Gas, Electric, and Water Utilities:

A customer's bill shall be adjusted if their meter is found to registering fast or slow by at least 2%. Except in an instance where a utility has filed a verified complaint with the appropriate law enforcement agency alleging fraud or theft by a customer, the utility shall immediately determine the period during which the error has existed, and shall re-compute and adjust the customer's bill to either provide a refund to the customer or collect an additional amount of revenue from the under-billed customer. In all instances of customer over-billing, the customer's account shall be credited or the over-billed amount refunded at the discretion of the customer within 30 days after final meter test results. Customer accounts shall be considered to be current while a dispute is pending pursuant to this section, as long as a customer continues to make payments for the disputed period.

§ 11. Status of Customer Accounts During Billing Dispute:

With respect to any billing dispute to which § 10 does not apply, customer accounts shall be considered to be current while the dispute is pending as long as a customer continues to make undisputed payments and stays current on subsequent bills.

§ 12. Customer's Request for Termination of Service:

Any customer desiring service terminated or changed from one address to another shall give the utility 3 working days' notice in person, in writing, or by telephone, and shall not be responsible for charges for service beyond the 3-day notice period if the customer provides reasonable access to the meter during the notice period.

§ 13. Utility Customer Relations:

Each utility shall negotiate and accept reasonable partial payment plans at the request of residential customers who have received a termination notice for failure to pay, except for nonpayment of an existing payment plan.

Each gas and electric utility shall develop and offer to its residential customers a budget payment plan based on historical or estimated usage which adjusts accounts so as to bring each participating customer current once each 12-month period.

Each utility must make available at each of its listed business offices information regarding rates, rules, and regulations needed for its customers and applicants to obtain adequate and efficient service, a brochure that explains the rights and responsibilities of a utility customer, and usage information.

§ 14. Refusal or Termination of Service:

Services may be discontinued or refused for issues related to nonpayment of bills (current or past), refusing access to utility equipment, diversion or interference with service, misrepresentation of identity, refusal of reasonable inspection when health or safety risk is possible, or violation of utility regulations or state or federal law.

Electric and gas utilities notice of termination shall be at least 10 days before the scheduled date of termination (telephone, sewage, and water at least 5 days), and shall be no sooner than 27 days after issuance of the bill at issue (20 days for telephone, sewage, and water). A utility may terminate service to a customer without advance notice if it has evidence that a customer has obtained unauthorized service by illegal use or theft.

A termination notice shall contain account identification and address, date of termination, the reason for termination, dispute procedures and contact information, and all information that would assist the customer in avoiding termination of services, including but not limited to, the termination postponement procedures for medical emergencies or payment plan options for low-income families.

A utility shall postpone termination for 30 days if physician, registered nurse, or public health officer certifies in writing that termination will aggravate a debilitating illness or infirmity on the premises. Utility may refuse consecutive extensions beyond initial 30-day period if certificate is not accompanied by agreed partial payment plan.

A gas or electric utility shall not terminate service for 30 days beyond the termination date, during the winter protection months from November 1 through March 31, if the Kentucky Cabinet for Human Resources (or its designee) certifies in writing that the customer is eligible for the cabinet's energy assistance program or household income is at or below 130% of the poverty level, and the customer presents such certificate to the utility. Eligible customers shall be required to make an initial payment to the best of their ability and be required to enter into a payment plan (see regulation for specific eligibility and payment plan requirements).

* * *

LOUISIANA

The Public Service Commission's regulations governing electric, gas, water, sewage, and telephone service are codified and amended in a series of General Orders. These regulations and select General Orders can be at found at the Public Service Commission's website at www.lpsc.org under "Regulations & Applications" (last visited in January 2010) (Although not summarized below, additional regulations can be found within La. Rev. Stat. Ann. §§ 45:845–45:859, 45:1222.)

General Order U 9-10-57. Notice of Disconnection:

Customers shall be given at least 5 days' written notice before the scheduled date of disconnection (bills are considered delinquent if not paid 20 days after issuance). Notice shall be separate from any other utility correspondence and shall specify that service shall be terminated unless payment is made.

General Order U 2-20-73. Late Payment Penalty Charge:

A 5% penalty charge may be assessed if a bill has not been paid within 20 days of it being issued.

General Order 07-11-75. Billing Errors (as amended by General Order U 04-21-1993):

Unless billing error is due to instances of customer fraud (meter tampering, etc.), a utility shall not back-bill a customer for undercharges occurring more than 6 months from the date of discovery.

General Order U 01-21-76. Bill Estimates:

Unless the utility and the customer have an agreement allowing the customer to provide meter readings, billing shall be based on actual meter readings and not estimated.

General Order U 10-18-88. Customer Billing; Tariff and Non-tariff Items:

Tariff and non-tariff items shall be listed separately and explained fully on a customer's bill.

General Order U 09-17-91. Deposits:

A deposit, required to receive or continue to receive service and held longer than 6 months, shall accrue interest at a 5% simple per annum rate. Interest shall be credited to a customer's account or refunded annually.

General Order 12-13-93. Denial or Termination of Service; Past Due Bills:

Service shall not be denied or terminated for an outstanding balance on a previous account that is more than 3 years old.

Ex Parte General Order 3-7-02. Energy Emergency Deferred Billing Program:

Eligible customers (persons with low incomes who are 65 or older, persons who receive public assistance, persons whose sole income consists of Social Security payments, vital government entities, and persons who need life-sustaining electrically operated equipment or treatment that requires electricity) may pre-enroll in a deferred billing program that allows them to defer payment up to 12 months, and utility may not discontinue service to customer enrolled in a deferred payment program as long as customer continues to make required payments.

MAINE

The Public Utility Commission's general regulations governing electric, gas, telephone, and water service can be found within 65-407-81 Me. Code R. §§ 1–17 and 65-407-870 Me. Code R. §§ 1–4. Although not summarized, regulations governing gas and electric transmission and distribution utilities can be found at 65-407-815 Me. Code R. §§ 1-16, additional regulations governing telephone service can be found within 65-407-290 Me. Code R. §§ 1–20, and the telephone anti-cramming regulations can be found within 65-407-297 Me. Code R. §§ 1–7. Access to regulations can be found at www.maine.gov/sos/cec/rules/rules.html (last visited in May 2011).

General Regulations (Electric, Gas, Telephone, and Water Service)—65-407-81 Me. Code R. §§ 1–17

* * *

§ 3. Billing and Payment Standards:

Bills shall be issued regularly and shall contain the billing period, meter readings, all payment information and amounts due (late payments, charges, taxes, etc.), due date, a clear indication of an estimated bill, full description and itemization of activity and services, payments, adjustments, credits. A utility may issue a bill for estimated usage when extreme weather conditions, emergencies, equipment failure, work stoppages or other similar circumstances prevent an actual meter reading by utility employees. A utility must obtain an actual meter reading at least once every 12 months unless procedures are established allowing customers to provide actual reading. A utility cannot issue two consecutive estimated bills for reasons other than those listed, unless the customer has been provided with an opportunity to read the meter and report the actual usage instead of an estimated bill.

A utility shall not render a bill for under-billing occurring more than 12 months from the time of billing unless the under-billing was due to customer fraud or unauthorized use (6-year look-back period). Customers shall be given at least 45 days' notice of pending under-billing charges. A utility shall offer under-billed customers the opportunity to enter into a payment plan.

Due dates falling on a Saturday, Sunday, legal holiday, or day when utility payment office is not open shall be extended to the next business day. When payment is mailed, payment is complete when the utility receives the payment.

Partial payment shall be credited to the oldest balance due unless otherwise required.

* * *

§ 5. Deposits:

A deposit or guarantee may be required due to poor utility payment history (including undisputed nonpayment within the last 6 years), customer is deemed a credit risk (see regulation), lack of employment or income, or bankruptcy filing. Deposits shall not exceed 2 of the highest consecutive billing periods (actual or estimated from other customers average), and shall be refunded or credited, within 30 days, after 12 consecutive months of timely payments. If the customer is still deemed to present a risk under the aforementioned standards, a new deposit may be required.

Deposits may be paid with an initial 50% payment followed by two equal payments in 30-day intervals (utility has discretion to extend payment period and amount). A guarantor may be required to be a customer in good standing with the utility.

§ 6. Payment Arrangements:

A utility shall continue to serve a customer who expresses an inability to pay their bill if the customer is eligible (see regulations for requirements and considerations) and agrees to enter into a reasonable payment plan. If an agreement cannot be reached, service shall not be disconnected until after consultation with the Consumer Assistance Division.

A utility is not required to negotiate a second payment plan if the customer has breached a payment plan.

§ 7. When Disconnection Procedures Can Begin:

Disconnection procedures can begin for issues relating to nonpayment (bills, deposits, guarantee, payment plan), when an undisputed bill of more than $50 is over due, an undisputed bill of less than $50 has been due for more than 90 days, refusing access to utility equipment, unauthorized use, misrepresentation or fraud, or violation of rules or Consumer Assistance Division or Commission decisions.

§ 8. When Disconnection Cannot Occur:

Disconnection shall not occur for nonpayment of non-basic utility service, nonpayment of a different account or account of another (unless it has been determined that the customer is legally responsible), amounts owed from estimated bills (absent reasonable attempt to gain access or a reading from customer), or a medical emergency pursuant to § 65-407-81-11.

Local telephone service shall not be disconnected for nonpayment of toll charges, and Lifeline customers shall not be disconnected for nonpayment of toll charges.

§ 9. Disconnection Notice:

A utility shall give at least 14 days' notice before scheduled disconnection due to nonpayment of bills (due date is 30 days after issuance), refusing access to utility equipment, or fraud or misrepresentation.

A utility shall give at least 3 days' notice before disconnection due breach of payment plan, failure to produce of deposit or guarantee, failure to apply for customer status, failure to comply with Commission decision, or a using a check for payment that is dishonored.

Telephone utilities may issue a disconnection notice 5 days after a bill of $500 or more is render and if the utility has determined, through personal contact, that abandonment or nonpayment may occur.

Notice of disconnection shall be clearly distinguishable and shall contain the reasons for disconnection, the amount due, date of disconnection, availability of payment plans and assistance, winter protections, delay option for medical reasons, and complaint procedures.

Tenants shall be given individual notice if the landlord's account, from which they receive service, is subject to disconnection. Notice shall also be posted in a common area of master-metered multi-unit dwellings. Tenants shall be given the opportunity to receive service in the tenants' names and/or assume responsibility for payment. When a master meter serves a residence, the utility shall be required to make reasonable arrangements for individual metering.

Disconnection notices shall expire 10 days after the scheduled date of disconnection and shall require the utility to repeat notification procedures.

§ 10. Disconnection Procedures:

Service shall only be disconnected Monday through Thursday from 8:00 a.m.–3:00 p.m. Disconnection shall not occur on a Friday, the day of or the day before a legal holiday, or on day that the utility is closed to the public. The utility shall make a reasonable attempt to personally notify a customer prior to and after disconnection and explain the rights and remedies contained in the written disconnection notice. A utility employee is not required to be authorized to accept payment or negotiate a payment plan on the day of disconnection, but if not, then employee must offer opportunity to speak with employee who is authorized before disconnection occurs. A disconnection or reconnection fee, not to exceed $10 may be assessed.

§ 11. Medical Emergency:

No utility shall terminate or refuse to restore service for 3 days when notified by a customer that a medical emergency exists. Disconnection shall be delayed 30 days when a medical emergency, as certified by a medical doctor, orally or in writing (written confirmation is required 7 days after oral notification), exists. If the medical condition is likely to continue beyond the expiration of an initial certification, a certificate may be renewed in intervals of 30 days as long as the condition exists. Customers remain liable for charges incurred while certificate is in effect and shall enter into a payment plan.

§ 12. Reconnection of Service:

Once the reason for disconnection has been remedied, the utility shall make a reasonable effort to restore service on the day reconnection is requested and no later than the next business day.

§ 13. Dispute Resolution:

Service shall not be disconnected for nonpayment of disputed bills or amounts. Customers may be required to pay for amounts not in dispute to continue to receive service (see regulation for a full description of dispute, appellate, and hearing rights and procedures).

* * *

§ 17. Winter Disconnection Rule:

Customers meeting the eligibility requirements shall not have service disconnected from November 1 through March 31. Heightened notice requirements (personal contact) are required, and payment plan options are available during this period (see regulation for a full description of eligibility and notice requirements, and payment plan options).

* * *

***General Regulations (Electric, Gas, Telephone, and Water Service)*—65-407-870 Me. Code R. § 1–4**

§ 1. Late Payment Charge:

Late payment charges on overdue bills (25 days from the date of issue) shall not exceed the Indexed Late Payment Rate, calculated by the Commission, using the formula prescribed in this rule of service. Late payment charges shall not be assessed due to a disputed amount unless the customer fails to pay any amount due after the dispute is resolved. Late payment charges shall not be assessed on payment plans established under the Winter Protection Rules or on overdue amounts that are the sole result of a budget payment plan. At least 30 days before a late payment program is imposed, or existing late payment amount increased, the utility must notify customers. All bills thereafter must disclose the due date and the interest rate for late payments.

§ 2. Interest on Deposits:

All deposits shall accrue interest at a rate equal to the interest rate of a one-year certificate of deposit published in the Wall Street Journal on November 1 or next publication date, rounded to the nearest 1/10 of a percent.

§ 3. Charge for Returned Checks:

A charge for a returned check may be assessed at the greater of $5 per account for which the check is to be applied or what the issuing bank charges the utility, but the charge shall not exceed $15. A utility that charges more than $5 must provide proof of the bank charge.

* * *

MARYLAND

The Public Service Commission's general regulations governing electric and gas service can be found within Md. Code Regs. 20.25.01.01–20.25.01.07 (not reprinted below), 30.02.01–30.04.03, and 31.01.01–31.05.10. The regulations governing telephone service can be found within Md. Code Regs. 20.45.01.01–20.45.09.07. Although not summarized, specific regulations governing electric can be found within: Md. Code Regs. 20.50.01–20.50.08; gas, Md. Code Regs. 20.55.01–20.55.09; water, Md. Code Regs. 20.70.01–20.70.08; sewage, Md. Code Regs. 20.75.01–20.75.07. Many of the regulations governing telephone service are substantially similar to the general regulations governing electric and gas service. Questions regarding telephone service may be answered by referencing the general regulations governing a specific issue. Access to the regulations can be found at www.dsd.state.md.us/comar/subtitle_chapters/20_Chapters.aspx (last visited in May 2011).

***General Regulations (Electric and Gas)*—Md. Code Regs. 20.25.01.01–20.25.01.07, 30.02.01–30.04.03, and 31.01.01–31.05.10**

* * *

30.02.02. Establishment of Credit:

Applicants may be establish credit by showing prior Maryland utility service within the previous 2 years, not currently owing any outstanding bills to a utility doing business in Maryland, and not having service discontinued for nonpayment of a utility bill or 2 or more delinquent payments during the last 12 months. In addition, a utility may require proof of 3-years continuous employment, ownership and occupancy of premises, or furnishing a guarantee of payment to establish credit for receipt of service. Customers who are 60 years of age or older shall not be required to furnish a deposit if they can establish age, intent to be the primary customer of service provided, and the absence of any outstanding bills.

30.02.03. Reestablishment of Credit:

Substantially similar to 30.02.02.

30.02.04. Deposit:

A deposit may not be less than $5 or more in amount than 2/12 of the estimated charges for service for the ensuing 12 months, except that an amount equal to 3/12 of the estimated charge for service for the ensuing 12 months will be permitted for those utilities which bill quarterly. Utility shall issue a receipt of deposit to each customer from whom a deposit is received, and shall provide means by which a depositor may establish his claim if his receipt is lost. A utility shall provide an installment plan for the payment of deposits in excess of $50.

Each utility shall pay simple per annum interest on a deposit equal to the average of the percentage yields of 1-year treasury constant maturities for September, October, and November of the preceding year. Interest shall be paid annually, if requested by the customer, or at the time the deposit is returned.

30.02.04-1. Use of Deposit:

A utility may apply a deposit plus accrued interest, first against any unpaid balance due the utility for that service, and then against any unpaid balance due the utility on any other residential account of that customer.

30.02.05. Refund of Deposit:

Upon discontinuance of service, the utility shall refund the customer's deposit plus accrued interest, or the balance, if any, in excess of the unpaid bills for service furnished by the utility. Deposits, plus any accrued interest, shall be refunded after the first 12 months if no disconnection or more than two late payments, or if credit is established pursuant to 30.02.02. Customers who do not meet the aforementioned requirement for a refund shall have their payment history reviewed every 12 months thereafter.

Customers who are 60 years old or older shall receive a refund of a deposit upon a request, a showing of proof of age, and the absence of any past-due bills.

30.02.06. Appeal by Applicant or Customer:

Utilities shall inform customers, dissatisfied with credit or deposit decisions of the utility, that they have the right to a meeting with a utility supervisor and subsequent review by the Commission.

* * *

30.03.01. Authorization to Impose Late Payment Charges:

A gas, electric or telephone utility may impose a late charge of 1.5%, and subsequent monthly late charges, if the bill has not been paid within 20 days of the date of issue. The total of the late charges should not exceed 5% of the original unpaid amount. Customer receiving monthly Social Security benefits, supplemental security income, disability payments, or other financial aid through government-sponsored assistance programs which constitutes the main source of income shall be offered bill-extender programs to prevent late charges.

* * *

30.04.01–30.04.03. Customers' Rights Pamphlet; Contents of Pamphlet; Delivery to Customer:

Each utility shall prepare and deliver a Customer's Rights pamphlet to every customer annually between the months of August through October. The pamphlet shall contain all the procedures, protections, rights, responsibilities, and remedies associated with service, including a termination policy statement, general summary of alternate payment plans and the Winter Heating Protection Program, and information on the Maryland Energy Assistance Program and on access to other programs to assist low-income customers such as the Utility Service Protection Program under 31.05.01–31.05.10.

* * *

31.01.03. Customer Responsibilities:

Any customer may notify the utility either before the date on which the termination is scheduled or within 14 days of receiving the notice that he or an occupant of the premises is an elder, disabled, seriously ill, or relies upon life-support equipment. Notice to the utility includes sending to the utility a written statement of the status of the individual and sending to the utility the required certifications not later than the scheduled date of termination of service.

* * *

31.01.05. Service Reconnection Charge:

A customer shall be liable for a reconnection charge contained in the utility's tariffs and the past-due amount.

* * *

31.01.07. Third-Party Notification:

Each utility shall inform its customers of the availability of third-party notification, by which the customer can designate a third person to receive notices of termination of service in addition to the customer. The third party is not liable for the account of the customer, but shall be able to initiate action to prevent termination of service.

31.01.08. Alternate Payment Plans:

A utility shall make a good faith effort to negotiate a payment plan with customers and low-income customers who cannot pay for services. When negotiating a plan a utility shall consider the circumstances and financial condition of the customer. If a customer fails to adhere to the alternate payment plan, the utility shall notify the customer that termination procedures may be begin.

A utility is not required to offer a payment plan to customers who have failed to meet the terms and conditions of any alternate payment plan during the past 18 months, committed fraud or theft against the utility, or refused the utility access to equipment at the customer's residence.

* * *

31.02.01. Insufficient Reasons for Terminations:

A utility shall not terminate service due to failure of a previous customer to pay for service at the premises to be served; failure of the customer to pay: for merchandise purchased from the utility; for a public utility service other than the one at issue; the bill of another customer as guarantor of that other customer; a bill which is delinquent for less than 3 months if the security deposit exceeds the amount of the estimated final bill for service; any outstanding bill which is less than $100, and which is delinquent for less than 3 months; any undercharge for the period in excess of 4 months; an outstanding bill that is over 7 years old, unless the customer signed an agreement to pay the outstanding bill before the expiration of this period, or an outstanding bill is for unauthorized service obtained by the customer or services obtained through misrepresentation.

31.02.02. Terminations Requiring Notice:

A utility may terminate service, after providing notice, due to issues related to nonpayment of services or deposits, failure to allow access to utility equipment on customer's property, or violation of utility or Commission rules regarding service.

31.02.03. Terminations Without Notice:

Notice of termination is not required due to hazardous conditions, customer's equipment adversely effects service to customers, tampering with utility equipment, or unauthorized use or access of service.

31.02.04. Termination with 7 Days' Notice:

A utility shall give at least 7 days' notice before terminating service for issues relating to obtaining service for the customer, or another, using fraudulent means or misrepresentation. The notice shall contain the reason and date of termination, amount owed, and the customer's right to dispute termination. The protections concerning life support and the medical necessity of service provided under 31.03.01 shall supersede this regulation.

31.02.05. Termination Procedures:

A utility shall attempt normal collection procedures concerning past-due bills before beginning termination procedures. A utility shall give at least 14 days' notice to the customer or third person designee before the scheduled date of termination. Utility may terminate service if it is prepared to accept payment and reconnect service on both the day of and day after termination.

31.02.06. Text of the Notice of Termination:

Disconnection notices shall be clearly distinguishable, and shall contain the reasons for disconnection, the amount due, date of disconnection, availability of payment plans and assistance, delay option for medical reasons or winter protections, and complaint procedures.

* * *

31.03.01. Restrictions for Serious Illness and Life-Support Equipment

Subject to physician certification, electric or gas service, or both, shall not be terminated for an initial period of up to 30 days beyond the scheduled date of service termination when the termination will aggravate an existing serious illness or prevent the use of life-support equipment of any occupant of the premises. Customers shall enter into payment plan for any past-due bills and current amounts due. Termination may be further delayed upon presentation of additional certificates.

A utility may refuse to honor a certificate that is incomplete, unsigned, or appears to be altered or may petition the Commission to determine the adequacy of the certification. Termination of service to a customer covered by this section may occur only after two attempts at personal contact, by telephone or personal visit. Upon contact, the utility must inform the customer about payment arrangements and sources of financial assistance.

31.03.02. Restrictions for Elderly or Handicapped Individuals:

If a utility is aware that termination is to occur at residence of an elder (65 or older) or disabled person resides the utility shall attempt to make personal contact, either by phone or in person, with the customer on two separate occasions, and shall inform the customer of any and all financial assistance available to avoid termination of service. Contacts shall be attempted during normal business hours or after 6:00 p.m. if contact has not been made. Contact shall include leaving a copy of the termination with a resident of the premises who is at least 18 years old.

31.03.03. Winter Restrictions:

Service shall not be terminated from November 31 through March 31 or when the forecasted temperature is not expected to exceed 32° Fahrenheit for the next 24 hours, for nonpayment unless the utility certifies, at least 24 hours prior to termination, to the Commission, via affidavit, that termination will not constitute a threat to life or health, and the amount due is greater than $200 for a single service utility or $300 for a dual service utility and the total amount due is greater than the amount of the customer's deposit with the utility. Additional contact and payment plan provisions during the winter protection months are substantially similar to 31.03.02.

31.03.06. Tenants in a Master-Metered Building:

Tenants shall be notified at least 14 days before the scheduled date of termination. Notice shall be mailed or delivered to each individual residence and placed in a common area of the dwelling.

* * *

***Telephone Service*—Md. Code Regs. 20.45.01.01–20.45.09.07**

Many of the regulations governing telephone service are substantially similar to the general regulations governing electric and gas service. Questions regarding telecommunications service may be answered by referencing the general regulations governing a specific issue.

* * *

45.04.01. Customer Billing:

Bills to customers shall be rendered at least monthly and shall contain a clear listing of all charges and credits, due dates, amounts due, and any overcharge/undercharge adjustments.

Unless authorized by the Commission, retroactive billing may not be for undercharges which occurred more than 12 months before the discovery of the error. If the total undercharge is more than 35% of the customer's average monthly bill during the preceding 3 months, the customer shall be allowed to enter into an installment plan to pay the total retroactive billing, without interest.

* * *

MASSACHUSETTS

The Department of Telecommunications and Energy's regulations governing electric, gas, and water service billing, termination and protection from termination are codified at 220 Mass. Code Regs. §§ 25.01–25.06. 220 Mass. Code Regs. § 27.00 prohibits utilities from requiring deposits before starting or continuing service. 220 Mass. Code Regs. §§ 29.01–29.13 outlines the refund procedure for tenants whose landlords violate the regulations governing metering. Access to the regulations can be found at www.mass.gov/dte/cmr/cmr220-001-004.htm by clicking on the "Statutes and Regulations" link in the left column.

***Billing and Termination Procedures (Electric, Gas, and Water Service)*—220 Mass. Code Regs. §§ 25.01–25.06**

* * *

§ 25.02. Billing and Termination Procedure for Residential Customers:

Bills shall not be due until at least 45 days after they have been received. Disputed portions of a bill are not "due" while a complaint, investigation or hearing is pending, but a customer may be required to pay any undisputed portion of a disputed bill. A utility may discontinue service for nonpayment only if the bill has not been paid within 45 days of receipt; the utility has sent a second request for payment stating that service will be terminated at least 48 days after the bill was received (gas and electric companies) or 46 1/2 days after the bill was received (water companies); the utility has sent a final notice of termination at least 72 hours but no more than 14 days before gas or electric service is terminated and at least 36 hours before terminating water service, and the bill is still not paid on the termination date.

Estimated bills are permitted if the estimate procedure is approved by the Department, the bill is clearly labeled an estimate, and the company has attempted to schedule meter readings outside of ordinary business hours or furnished card to the customer to read his or her meter and did not render an estimated bill in the immediately preceding billing period. Notwithstanding this rule, estimated bills are permitted if the customer has denied access to the meter or otherwise made reading unreasonably difficult or reading is made unreasonably difficult by circumstances beyond the control of the company. No company may bill a resident of a multiple dwelling based on an estimated allocation of charges made from a reading of a single meter in the multiple dwelling.

Utilities shall terminate service only for nonpayment of a bill and reasons of safety, health, cooperation with civil authorities, or other reason specifically granted under state statute.

Utilities can terminate service only between 8:00 a.m. and 4:00 p.m. from Monday through Thursday. Utilities cannot terminate service on a holiday or the day before a holiday.

Utility bills, second requests for payment, and termination notices shall include or be accompanied by a brief explanation of the customer's rights.

Utilities shall make payment plans and budget plans available to customers.

Utilities shall send customers a notice describing the rate they are charged and telephone number where customers can get additional information on available rates and stating that customers should notify utilities immediately if they are not being charged the most advantageous rate.

When utilities create new accounts, utilities shall send each customer of record a notice stating that the person is a customer of record and the customer's listing on the utilities' record, that the customer of record is liable on all bills and also providing a telephone number for the customer to call and change his or her status or listing.

Customers shall notify utilities of any dispute by phone or mail or in person. Utilities shall investigate, try to resolve complaints and tell customers how the complaint was resolved. Customers may appeal the utilities' decision to the Department.

§ 25.03. Termination of Service to Customers During Serious Illness, Infancy, Winter Months:

Utilities cannot terminate or refuse to restore a customer's service upon certification that: the customer or someone living in the customer's house is seriously ill; or there is a child under the age of 12 months; or all adults are age 65 or older and a minor resides in the home; or between November 15 and March 15, the customer's service provides heat or runs the heating system if the service has not been terminated for nonpayment before November 15;, and the customer cannot pay the overdue bill because of "financial hardship" (customer is eligible for the Low-Income Home Energy Assistance program administered by the Massachusetts Department of Housing and Community Development). A company that received fuel assistance payments from a customer in the preceding winter must protect that customer's account from November 15–January 1 to give the customer time to apply for assistance. For all customers, the company must provide financial hardship forms and instructions before November 15.

Customers may begin claims for infant and winter protection by telephoning the Department. A registered physician, physician assistant, nurse practitioner or local board of health official must telephone the Department for serious illness protection, and provide written certification within 7 days. The Department shall send a written certification form for other claims for protection, and the customer or someone acting for the customer must return the certification form within 7 days.

Customers shall renew the financial hardship and serious illness certifications quarterly unless the illness is certified as chronic, in which case certificates must be renewed every six months.

Utilities shall include prominent written notice of the rule 25.03 protections on all arrearage notices. From November 15 until March 15, utilities shall not send a notice of termination to any customer who has given the utility a statement of financial hardship.

Customers may challenge a utility's decision denying their claim for protection.

Before discontinuing service, the utilities' employee must tell an occupant that service will be discontinued and must give notice of claims for protection and a financial hardship form. Utilities shall leave a notice describing claims for protection and a financial hardship form at the residence if no occupants are there when they discontinue service. Utilities must postpone shutting off service for 72 hours if an occupant claims that he or she is protected, in order to allow time to obtain certification. In addition, heating account customers during the winter protection season must be given personal or telephone notice not less than 3 days before shutoff.

§ 25.04. Termination of Service to Accounts Affecting Tenants:

Utilities shall use procedures reasonably designed to identify tenants who may be affected by discontinuing service to a landlord customer because of nonpayment. Utilities shall give written notice to residential units with affected tenants that shall state the date when service will be discontinued, how service to the affected tenant may be continued, and the rights of a tenant to deduct a direct payment to a utility from rent without retaliation from the landlord. Utilities shall also post this information in common areas of the building. Tenants may ask the utility to continue or resume service and pay the amount of the projected bill for the 30-day period beginning on the later of the date when service will be discontinued or the date service is resumed.

In addition to notifying the landlord and the tenants, the company must notify the Department, which may hold a hearing to determine whether the tenants can pay the arrearage from withheld rent. The department must consider whether, *inter alia*, the tenants are withholding rent for other reasons, whether other companies have a claim on withheld rent, and whether payment would be an undue burden on the tenants.

Before terminating service to a multiple dwelling because of larceny or unauthorized use, the utility must attempt to identify and collect from the proper party and give 30 days' notice to the tenants of the date and reason for termination and that service will continue if a qualified party agrees to pay for it.

This rule does not apply to terminations for reasons of health or safety or cooperation with civil authorities. For health or safety terminations, the utility must post a notice, with the reason for termination and contact information for the utility and the Department, and must notify the Department immediately or at most within 24 hours of termination.

§ 25.05. Termination of Service to Elderly Persons:

Utilities shall use procedures reasonably designed to identify households where all residents are 65 years or older. Customers 65 years or older may choose a third party to receive notices of outstanding bills, service termination and rights to a hearing.

Utilities cannot discontinue service to a household where all residents are 65 years or older unless the Department investigates, makes specific required fact findings and gives written approval. Utilities, customers and third parties may request a hearing.

Utilities shall include a statement about the rights of households in which all residents are 65 years or older with regard to second requests for payment, termination notices, and rights to a hearing.

When a utility employee enters a building to shut off service, he or she must present the occupants with notice of the rights under this section. If informed that all occupants are age 65 or over, termination should be postponed until after Department approval. If no one is home, the employee should leave a written notice of these rights.

§ 25.06. Construction:

The regulations shall be liberally construed, and the notice provisions shall be read in the aggregate.

§ 25.07. Elimination of Practice of Gas and Electric Companies of Requiring Deposit as a Condition to Service:

Gas and electric utilities may not require a deposit before beginning or continuing service to residential customers. Utilities may require payment of an overdue bill before requiring or continuing service if the customer has not paid two consecutive overdue bills.

***Billing Procedures for Residential Rental Property Owners Cited for Violation of State Sanitary Code—*220 Mass. Code Regs. §§ 29.01–29.13**

§ 29.01. Scope and Purpose:

This chapter sets up a procedure for electric and gas utilities to bill property owners for utility service that was improperly billed to tenants when a violation of the metering regulations existed and to refund this amount to the tenants.

* * *

§ 29.04. Citation of Sanitary Code Violation:

Property owners shall not contest sanitary code violations which shall be considered accurate. The date of correction shall be the actual date of re-inspection contained in the written correction notice. Property owners shall give the correction notice to the utility.

§ 29.05. Tenant Customer Responsibility:

Tenant customers who are listed as the customer of record by the utility are assumed to have agreed to pay for gas or electricity in a dwelling unit where there is a sanitary code violation. Tenants who receive a Sanitary Code citation shall give the utility a copy of the citation and the name and address of the property owner within 60 days even if the tenant is no longer occupying the dwelling unit. Tenants who do not shall not receive a refund.

§ 29.06. Utility Company Responsibility:

Utilities that receive a Sanitary Code citation shall determine if the violation is "minimal use," under rule 29.08, what the property owner's time period of responsibility is under rule 29.07 and what amount the tenant customer was billed under rule 29.07 or 29.08. Utilities shall then place the amount paid by the tenant in escrow and transfer the account into the name of the property owner.

Utilities that receive a Sanitary Code citation notice under this section shall provide written notice to the tenant customer and property owner within 30 days.

§ 29.07. Determination of Retroactive Time Period and Amount of Property Owner's Responsibility:

Utilities shall determine the time period of the property owner's responsibility for service billed to the tenant customer by going back 2 years from the effective date of the citation, by using the date the tenant customer became the customer of record or by finding the approximate date the sanitary code violation began whichever is shortest. Utilities shall use the amount paid by the tenant customer during this time period unless the violation is "minimal use" to calculate the amount due from the property owner.

§ 29.08. Determination of Minimal Use Violation:

Utilities shall bill the property owner $10 per month for the time period of the property owner's responsibility for minimal use violations. Tenant customers can challenge the decision to classify a use as a minimal use violation.

§ 29.09. Dispute and Hearing Procedure:

Property owners or tenants can challenge either the time period of responsibility or the amount owed by property owner by contacting the Consumer Division of the Department within 60 days. The Department will investigate the dispute; utilities, property owners and tenant customers can request an informal hearing.

§ 29.10. Tenant Customer Refund:

Utilities must refund the amount incorrectly paid to the tenant customer within 30 days. Utilities may first use the refund as a credit toward any unpaid bill of the tenant customer.

* * *

MICHIGAN

The Public Service Commission's general regulations governing electric and gas service can be found within Mich. Admin. Code r. 460.101–460.169. The regulations governing telecommunications service can be found within Mich. Admin. Code r. 484.1–484.386. Specific regulations governing electric and gas service, although not summarized here, can be found within Mich. Admin. Code r. 460.3101–460.3804 and Mich. Admin. Code r. 460.20101–460.20606, respectively. Many of the substantive issues governing telephone utilities are substantially similar to the general regulations governing electric and gas service and are therefore not summarized. Questions regarding telecommunications service that are not summarized may be answered by referencing the general regulations governing a specific issue. Access to the regulations can be found at www.michigan.gov/mpsc by clicking on the "Documents Library" link in the left column (last visited in May, 2011).

***Electric and Gas*—Mich. Admin. Code r. 460.102–460.169**

460.106. Service Requests:

Applicants for service can request service in person, in writing, on the phone, using the fax or Internet or other means of communication. Applicants shall provide positive identification and pay a deposit if required under 460.109 or 460.110. Utility may require payment of a non-disputed delinquent account in applicant's name if accrued within the past 6 years. Utility shall provide information on the dispute process.

460.107. Applicant Information:

A utility shall not require anyone other than the applicant to assume responsibility for the service. If applicant is a tenant, utility may require confirmation by landlord, manager or owner of the property.

460.108. Prohibited Practices:

A utility shall not require a deposit or a guarantee based on credit score (if customer has a history of utility service within the previous 6 years), income, home ownership, residential location, race, color, creed, sex, age, national origin, or marital or family status, disability or any other criteria not authorized.

460.109. Deposits for New Customer:

A deposit may be required as a condition of receiving service for issues related to nonpayment of undisputed bills (within the last 6 years) from the applicant or if within the past 3 years the applicant lived in a residence with a person who accrued a delinquent account; misrepresentation of identity or credit standing or failure to provide positive identification information; requesting service for location where applicant does not reside; unauthorized access or diversion of service; applicant has filed for bankruptcy within the past 6 years.

A deposit may not be required if the department of human services is responsible for making utility payments, or the applicant secures a guarantor, or the applicant is over 65 and has a satisfactory payment history for the past 3 years with a gas or electric company.

460.110. Deposits for Previous Customers or Continued Service:

Substantially similar to 460.109. A deposit may be required if the utility has shut off service for nonpayment; customer has tendered 1 or more checks for service that have been dishonored by the issuing bank, or has had 1 or more debit card, credit card, or other form of payment denied in the previous 12 months.

460.111. General Deposit Conditions:

A deposit required due to an outstanding account shall not exceed twice the average monthly bill for the premises. If the customer's consumption history for the premises is not available, the deposit shall not exceed twice the utility's average residential monthly bill. Low-income customers will have the option of paying the deposit in 2 monthly installments. A deposit required during the heating season due to nonpayment shall not exceed the utility's average monthly bill for such service. A deposit required for unauthorized use of service shall not exceed 4 times the average peak season monthly bill. If a deposit is required because of an unpaid account in another's name, the utility shall provide notice of the reason and the process for disputing the deposit. The utility shall not require a deposit after a shut-off for nonpayment if it failed to offer an opportunity to enter into a settlement agreement (460.155) prior to the shut-off.

Deposits shall accrue interest at a 7% per annum rate, and shall be semiannually credited to a customer's account, or paid upon return of the deposit, whichever occurs first. Deposit shall be returned with accrued interest upon satisfactory payment for 12 months.

460.112. Guarantee Terms and Conditions:

Guarantees must be in writing and state all terms, including a maximum amount. A guarantee shall be in effect for no more than 36 months. If customer has provided satisfactory payment for 12 consecutive months, credit shall be established and utility shall release the guarantor, unless the guarantee was required because of unauthorized use.

* * *

460.117. Billing Frequency; Method of Delivery:

Bills shall be mailed monthly unless the utility and customer agree to an alternative method of delivery. Seasonal billing shall be delivered per tariff. Customers may designate a third party to receive bills, shut-off notices and other utility correspondence. Customers using on-line billing have the same rights and responsibilities as those using paper billing.

460.118. Equal Monthly Billing:

Customers shall have access to an equal monthly billing program, with any amount billed in excess of $10 at the end of the program year refunded to the customer or credited to customer's account per customer request.

* * *

460.120–121. Payment of Bill:

Billing due dates shall not be less than 21 days from the date of transmission.

460.122. Allowable Charges:

In addition to consumption and other tariff-approved charges, a utility may assess a 2% non-compounded late charge unless the customer payments are made by the department of human services or the customer is a participant in the Winter Protection Program pursuant to 460.148.

460.123. Bill Information:

Bills shall be issued at regular intervals and shall contain information concerning dates and consumption amounts, clear indication of an estimated bill, due dates, amounts and penalties due, any information that will allow and assist in the computation of charges, and utility address and telephone number. On-line payment protections described.

460.124. Separate Bills:

Utility shall transmit a separate bill for each service location. If, however, there is a shutoff or termination at one location, a utility may transfer the balance to any other residential account of the customer.

460.125. Non-tariff Services:

A company may bill for tariff and non-tariff service on the same bill, if the non-tariff services are designated clearly and separately. Failure to pay for unregulated service may result in termination of that service, but not the termination of gas or electric service. Partial payments must be credited first to tariff services.

460.126. Billing Error:

Overcharges to a customer's account, within 3 years from the date of discovery (unless a customer can establish an earlier date), shall be credited to a customer's account plus 7% APR interest or refunded. Upon customer's request, overcharges greater than 10% shall be refunded within 30 days. Undercharges, not due to meter tampering or fraud (restrictions waived), may be back-billed for the amount within a 12-month period from the time of the discovered error, but utility shall offer customer a payment plan.

* * *

460.129 and 460.130. Complaint Procedures and Personnel:

A utility must establish procedures for the prompt and efficient handling of customer inquiries, service requests, and complaints. It must ensure that qualified personnel are available during business hours to answer inquiries, respond to complaints, and enter into settlement agreements. Provision must be made for customers who cannot communicate in English to receive prompt and effective assistance. Qualified personnel must be available at all times to respond to emergency conditions and service shutoffs.

460.131. Publication of Procedures:

All utility procedures (complaint, billing, deposits, shutoff, restoration, etc.) shall be published in easily understood pamphlets and shall be made available at initiation of service, at utility offices and websites, and upon request by a customer.

460.132. Access to Rules and Rates:

Utilities except RECs must provide, within 60 days after commencing service or the issuance of new rates, a clear explanation of the rates for which a customer is eligible and notice of the availability of company assistance in determining the most advantageous rate. (RECs are required to provide certain information annually.) Utilities must notify customers with 60 days (or a reasonable time for RECs) of the filing of a general rate case application. A utility must keep on file, provide access to, and conspicuously post notice of the availability of these rules.

* * *

460.135. Customer Access to Consumption Data:

Upon request, a utility must provide a customer with a statement of the customer's actual or weather adjusted energy usage for each billing period during the past 12 months, if the data is reasonably ascertainable. Customers must be notified annually that this information is available.

* * *

460.137. Shutoff Permitted:

Service may be terminated for issues related to nonpayment of bills (within the previous 6 years, and including failure of a person living at residence to pay an outstanding, undisputed bill within previous 3 years if customer lived at the residence for all or part of the time when the bill was incurred), failure to provide deposits, or guarantee; unauthorized use; breach of settlement agreement; misrepresentation of identity; failure to allow reasonable access to utility equipment; violation of utility rules.

460.138. Notice of Shutoff:

Notice, to the residence and a designated third party, shall be given at least 10 days before the scheduled date of termination. A single-metered residence containing 3 or more separate households (landlord/tenant) shall be given at least 30 days' notice before the scheduled date of termination.

460.139. Form of Notice:

Notice shall include, among other things, the earliest date of disconnection, the reasons for disconnection, customers rights regarding settlement agreements, filing complaints, requesting a hearing and that utility will not shut-off service pending resolution of the complaint, actions to avoid disconnection (medical, economic and winter assistance programs), contact information of service provider, and a statement that disconnection may result in additional reconnection fees.

460.140. Time of Shutoff:

Pursuant to the relevant utility regulations, service may be terminated on the scheduled day or within a reasonable period following that day. Service shall be terminated between 8:00 a.m. to 4:00 p.m., and shall not be disconnected on any day on which the utility cannot reestablish service on the same or following day. Service shall not be terminated on Friday for nonpayment under a winter protection program during the winter months (November 1 through March 31). Service shall not be terminated for nonpayment of disputed amounts.

460.141. Manner of Shutoff:

A utility shall make at least 2 attempts to contact a customer (mail, phone, personal) at least 1 day before scheduled termination. The utility employee, when arriving to terminate service, shall accept, as a means of avoiding termination of service, evidence that the reason for termination has been remedied or disputed, or full payment, including a reasonable charge for sending an employee to the premises, if provided for in the tariff. Payment by any reasonable means shall be accepted, including personal check unless the customer has tender a dishonored check for services within the previous 12 months. Utility shall post notice regarding termination and the available remedies if the customer is not available on the day of termination.

If the utility has not made telephone contact with the customer, and the customer is not at home when the employee arrives to shut off service, the employee must leave a notice that service will be shut off on the next business day. If the utility has provided the required notice and the customer does not respond, the employee may shut off service.

* * *

460.143. Shutoff Prohibited:

Service shall not be terminated for nonpayment of items not approved as integral to service, failure to pay for concurrent service at a separate metering point or location, or failure to pay for a different class of service. Service shall not be terminated if customer or spouse is called to full time active military service.

Tenants shall not be subject to termination due to nonpayment of landlord unless, premises are unoccupied, customer agrees in writing to the shut-off, it is not feasible to provide service to tenant.

460.144. Restoration of Service:

When the reason for termination of services has been remedied, a utility shall, except for reasons beyond the utility's control, promptly restore service on the day requested. A utility may charge a reasonable reconnection fee.

* * *

460.146. Notice of Energy Assistance:

Each year utilities shall inform each customer of all available federal and state energy assistance programs, Winter Protection Programs under 460.148 and 460.149, the military shut-off protection in 460.150 and the Medical Emergency Provisions under 460.147. Notification shall be included as a separate mailing or included within the bill as part of the bill or as an insert. Utility shall provide access to information on federal and state energy assistance programs when a customer receives a past-due notice.

Utilities shall inform customers, within 60 days, of any additional energy assistance or changes in existing programs.

460.147. Medical Emergency:

If customer or member of the household is a critical care customer or has a certificate of medical emergency, termination may not occur for an additional 21 days if it would aggravate an existing medical emergency. Certification may be renewed an additional 21 days, up to a total of 63 days in a 12-month period.

460.148. Winter Protection Plan for Low-Income Customers:

During November 1 through March 31, except where unauthorized use of service, utility shall not disconnect eligible low-income households for nonpayment if customers posts a monthly amount of 7% of the estimated annual bill and customer has applied for state or federal heating assistance. If there is an arrearage, customer shall be allowed to pay it off in equal installments between the date of application and the start of the subsequent heating season.

Failure to pay monthly amounts or failure to comply with the terms and conditions of this winter protection rule could result in shut off of service.

At the conclusion of the space heating season, utility shall reconcile amount due and allow customer to pay it off in equal installments between April 1 and October 31.

Other conditions apply.

460.149. Winter Protection Plan for Senior Citizens:

Utility shall not shut off service to an eligible elder (65 or older who advises utility of his/her eligibility) during the space heating season (November 1 through March 31). If power has been disconnected, services shall be restored without payment of amount due, deposits, reconnection fees or other charges. Amounts due are reconciled at the end of the space heating season and eligible seniors are permitted to pay amounts due in equal monthly installments between April 1 and October 31.

460.150. Military Protections:

Utility shall not shut off service to an eligible military customer for 90 days, and shall continue shutoff protection for at least one additional 90-day period as long as customer remains eligible and requests the utility to do so. After expiration of last 90-day period, utility shall require customer to pay any past due amounts in equal monthly payments over a period of up to 12 months. Utility shall provide eligible customer with information on payment assistance programs.

* * *

460.151. Disputed Claims:

A customer may initiate a claims dispute before shut off date by contacting the utility in writing, in person, or by telephone or through a regulation officer. The utility shall promptly investigate and advise the customer of the results of the investigation, attempt to resolve the dispute informally, and provide an opportunity to enter into a settlement agreement.

460.152. Hearing:

A utility shall offer a customer, who is not satisfied with a dispute resolution, a hearing with a utility officer. Customers shall have 5 days to accept the hearing offer. Customers opting for an informal hearing shall pay the undisputed portions of their bill or if there is no agreement, 50% of the disputed amount not to exceed $100 (or faces disconnection). If dispute is resolved in favor of the customer, in whole or in part, utility shall promptly return any excess amount with interest.

460.153. Notice of Hearing:

Utility shall send or personally serve written notice of the time, date, and location of the hearing on the day the scheduling is determined. Notice shall describe hearing procedures and amount of required payment and due date of 10 business days from the date of notice.

* * *

Telecommunications—Mich. Admin. Code r. 484.1–484.386

Many of the substantive issues governing telephone utilities are substantially similar to the general regulations governing electric and gas service and are therefore not summarized. Questions regarding telecommunications service that are not summarized may be answered by referencing the general regulations governing a specific issue.

484.321. Discrimination Prohibited:

Provider may not discriminate against or penalize a customer for exercising a right granted by these rules.

484.322. Provider Prohibitions:

A provider shall not make a statement or representation, including an omission of material information, regarding the rates, terms, or conditions of providing a basic local exchange service that is false, misleading, or deceptive; charge a customer for a subscribed service for which the customer did not make an initial affirmative order (failure to refuse an offered or proposed service is not an affirmative order for the service); or state to a customer that basic local exchange service will be shut off unless the customer pays an amount that is due in whole or in part for an unregulated service. If a customer has cancelled a service, provider may not charge for service provided after effective date of cancellation.

* * *

484.331. Billing Frequency:

A provider must render a bill during each billing period to every customer.

* * *

484.333. Payment of Bills:

A customer shall have at least 17 calendar days from the date of rendition of the bill to make payment.

484.334. Computation of Payment Period:

The date of rendition of the bill is the date of physical mailing. If the due date falls on a non-business day, then the final payment date is extended to the next business day. The date of payment of a remittance by mail is 2 days before receipt of the remittance.

484.335. Billing Information:

Bills must include beginning and ending dates of billing period, due date, itemized statement of amount due for local exchange service, regulated toll service, all taxes, and contact information for provider for inquiries or complaints.

484.336. Partial Payment:

Unless otherwise specified by the customer, if partial payment of a bill is made, then the provider shall first credit the partial payment to basic local exchange service and regulated toll service.

* * *

484.337. New Services and Changes in Services:

No later than 15 days after the completion of an order for new service or a change in existing service that results in a billing change, the provider shall send a written itemized statement of the services ordered, including all associated charges. A customer shall have the right, within 1 billing period of receiving a bill for new services or changed services, to cancel, reduce, or modify a service or a portion of a service without further service charge.

484.341. Cash Deposit As a Condition of Service; Obligation to Provide Service; Amount of Deposit:

A company may require a deposit only if the applicant refuses to provide identification that can be readily and inexpensively verified or has a history of payment default within 60 months for telecommunications services. A provider may refuse service to a residence under any name, if an outstanding bill exists, and the person responsible for that bill still resides there. A provider may require a deposit of up to $150 per access line.

484.342. Prepayments:

A provider may require the prepayment of 1 billing period's charges for basic local exchange service as a condition of service. If pricing is usage-sensitive, then the pre-payment should be not more than the average charge for similar services in the customer's exchange during the most recent calendar year for which data are available.

484.351. Publication of Procedures:

An LEC must make available to customers a pamphlet (including an audio format for visually impaired customers) that summarizes the rights and responsibilities of customers, including how to understand and verify billings, payment standards, procedure for termination, reconnection, and inquiries and complaints, including complaints to the Commission.

484.353. Public Access to Rules and Rates:

Each directory must prominently include contact information for the LEC and the Commission.

Rules 484.361 through 484.373 set forth the procedures for formal and informal complaints and dispute resolution.

484.373. Payment of Amount Not in Dispute:

A customer may be required to pay the undisputed amount of the bill while a formal complaint with commission is pending.

* * *

484.381. Shutoff of Service; Reasons:

A provider may shut off basic local exchange service to a customer for issues relating to nonpayment, including a delinquent balance of $150 or more for basic local exchange service and regulated toll service in the name of the customer, or for maintaining a delinquent balance of $125 or more for 3 consecutive months; for tampering or unauthorized interference with provider's equipment; for denial of access at reasonable times for inspection, maintenance, or replacement; for misrepresentation of identity for purpose of obtaining local service; for violation of tariff provision; or for other unauthorized use or interference.

484.382. Psychiatric and Medical Emergencies:

Shutoff will be postponed for 15 days upon receipt of physician's certificate certifying that a customer or other permanent resident of the premises suffers from mental or physical illness and will be endangered by a shutoff. One additional 15-day postponement is available if the certificate is renewed. If the provider is notified that a medical or psychiatric emergency exists, shutoff must be postponed for 7 days to allow consumer to obtain a certificate.

484.383. Form and Contents of Notice:

Shutoff notice must include reason for shutoff; date for shutoff; notice of right to file complaint and that service will not be shutoff while complaint is pending; and contact information for LEC where customer may make inquiries or negotiate a settlement agreement.

484.384. Notice of Shutoff of Service:

A provider of basic local exchange service shall not shut off service unless written notice is sent by first-class mail to the customer or personally served not fewer than 5 days before the date of the proposed shutoff. A shutoff notice may not be sent while a formal complaint is pending concerning the bill upon which the notice is based.

484.385. Time of Shutoff:

Basic service may not be shut off on a day, or the day preceding a day, when the provider's personnel are not available to reconnect or when a complaint related to the shutoff is pending.

484.386. Restoration of Service:

A provider shall restore service promptly, but not later than 1 working day after the customer's request, when the cause for the shutoff of service has been cured or credit arrangements have been made. Before restoring service, the provider may require payment of the delinquent account for basic local and regulated toll service or a settlement agreement for the payment of these amounts; a reconnection fee; and a deposit of up to $150 per access line. Payments may be made in any reasonable manner, but provider may refuse a personal check if a check has been dishonored, for reasons other than bank error, within the preceding 3 years.

* * *

MINNESOTA

The Public Utility Commission's general regulations governing electric and natural gas service can be found within Minn. R. 7820.0200–7820.5600. The regulations governing telecommunications service can be found within Minn. R. 7810.0100–7810.8815. Many of the regulations governing telecommunications service are similar in substance and form to the general regulations governing electric and gas service. Questions regarding telecommunications service may be answered by referencing the general regulations governing a specific issue. Access to the regulations can found at www.revisor.mn.gov/rules (last visited in May 2011).

***General (Electric and Gas)*—Minn. R. 7820.0200–7820.5600**

7820.0200. Customer Information:

Utilities shall post information at each office and/or provide customers with information concerning bill payment methods and contents; disconnection and reconnection; deposit and guarantee requirements; meter reading procedures; their rights; complaint procedures; and contact information, including contact information for the Commission. Bills must include contact information for complaints and inquiries to the utility and a notice that customer information is available on request.

7820.0300. Complaint Procedures:

Utilities shall have qualified personnel available during regular business hours to receive and, if possible, resolve all customer inquiries, requests, and complaints. If any complaint cannot be promptly resolved, the utility shall contact the customer within 5 business days and at least once every 14 calendar days thereafter, and advise the customer regarding the status of its investigation until: the complaint is mutually resolved; or the utility advises the customer of the results of its investigation and final disposition of the matter; or the customer files a written complaint with the Public Utilities Commission or the courts.

* * *

7820.1000. Permissible Service Disconnection with Notice:

Pursuant to the notice requirements of 7820.2400, service may be disconnected for issues related to nonpayment (outstanding amount shall equal or exceed deposit); failure to make proper application for service; violation of any of the utility's rules; failure to provide the utility reasonable access to its equipment and property; breach of the contract for service between the utility and the customer; failure of the customer to furnish such service, equipment, and/or rights-of-way necessary to serve the customer as shall have been specified by the utility as a condition of obtaining service; willfully wasting service through improper equipment; when necessary for the utility to comply with any order or request of any governmental authority having jurisdiction.

7820.1100. Permissible Service Disconnection Without Notice:

Service may be disconnected without notice for unauthorized use of or tampering with the utility's equipment, or for a condition that is hazardous to the customer, other customers, to the utility's equipment, or to the public.

* * *

7820.1300. Nonpermissible Reasons to Disconnect Service:

Service shall not be disconnected due to delinquency in payment for services rendered to a previous customer who occupied the premises unless the customer continues to occupy the premises; failure to pay for merchandise, appliances, or services not approved by the Commission as an integral part of the utility service; failure to pay for a different class of service; failure to pay for a bill to correct a previous under-billing due to an inaccurate meter or billing error if the customer agrees to payment over a reasonable period of time.

7820.1400. Landlord-Tenant Rule:

Tenants subject to termination of services due to landlord nonpayment shall be given proper notice under these rules, and the options for receiving individualized service and billing (if feasible). Tenants shall not be required to pay a landlord's past-due amounts as a condition of receiving individualized service.

* * *

7820.1500–7820.2300.

[*Editor's note:* Minnesota's "Cold Weather Rule" protections, which used to be covered under Minn. R. 7820.1500–7820.2300, have been moved into Minn. Stat. §§ 216B.096 (cold weather rule for public utilities) and 216B.097 (cold weather rule for cooperative or municipal utilities), effective September 1, 2008.]

7820.2400. Notice Requirements:

Notice, at least 5 days before disconnection, shall be clearly distinguishable and shall contain the reasons for disconnection, the remedies available for avoiding disconnection, the amount due, date of disconnection, availability of payment plans and assistance, and complaint procedures.

In lieu of mailing, notices may be delivered by a representative of the utility. Such notices must be in writing and receipt of them must be signed by the customer, if present, or some other member of the customer's family of a responsible age or the utility representative must make an affidavit under oath that the representative delivered the notice to the customer or the customer's residence.

7820.2500. Manner of Disconnection:

Service may be disconnected only in conjunction with a personal visit by a representative of the utility in an attempt to make personal contact with the customer at the address. If the address is a building containing two or more dwelling units, the representative shall make a personal visit to the door of the customer's dwelling unit within the building.

The representative of the utility shall at all times be capable of receiving payment, if nonpayment is the cause of the disconnection of service, or the representative shall be able to certify that the cause of disconnection has been remedied by the customer.

7820.2600. Reconnection of Service:

The utility may charge a reconnect fee based on the cost of reconnection as stated in the utility's tariff on file with the Commission.

7820.2700. Disputes:

The utility shall promptly investigate all billing disputes. If the dispute is not resolved to the satisfaction of the customer, the customer must submit the entire payment and may designate the disputed portion to be placed in escrow to the utility. Such payment shall be called an escrow payment.

7820.2800. Escrow Payments for Disputes:

The escrow payment form must provide space for the customer to explain why the utility's resolution of the dispute is unsatisfactory to the customer. Submitting escrow payment form is deemed an informal complaint, and upon settlement of the dispute, any sum to which the customer is found to be entitled must be refunded to the customer and must be supplemented by an 8% per annum interest charge from the date of payment to the date of return by the utility.

7820.2900. Waiving Right to Disconnect; Emergency Status:

The customer may apply to the utility to waive its right to disconnect. If the utility refuses to waive its right to disconnect, the customer may apply to the Commission for emergency status. If the Commission determines the customer has a probable claim in the dispute and that hardship may result in the event of disconnection of service, it may declare an emergency status to exist and order the utility to continue service for a period not to exceed 30 days.

* * *

7820.3200. Billing Basis:

Bills must be based on meter readings or estimated usage. If a customer is eligible for more than one rate schedule, the utility must advise the customer as to the selection of a rate that will result in the lowest cost of projected consumption.

7820.3300. Meter Reading and Billing Periods:

Readings of all meters used for determining charges to customers shall be made each month unless otherwise authorized by the Commission upon petition by the utility. A utility may permit the customer to supply meter readings on a form supplied by the utility, providing a utility representative reads the meter at least once every 12 months or at an interval determined upon petition to the Commission and when there is a change in customers and when requested by the customer.

7820.3400. Estimated Billing:

When access to a meter cannot be gained and the customer fails to supply a meter-reading form in time for the billing operation, an estimated bill may be rendered. Only in unusual cases or when approval is obtained from the customer shall more than two consecutive estimated bills be rendered, unless the customer fails to supply meter readings as provided in part 7820.3300.

7820.3500. Billing Content:

Bills shall be issued at regular intervals and shall contain information concerning dates and consumption amounts, clear indication of an estimated bill, due dates, amounts and penalties due, and any information that will allow and assist in the computation of charges.

* * *

7820.3700 (Electric) and 7820.3900 (Gas). Inaccurate Electric Meters; Inaccurate Natural Gas Meters:

A customer's bill shall be adjusted if their meter is found to registering fast or slow by at least 2%. Adjustment shall be based on 1/2 the time that has passed since the previous reading but shall not exceed 6 months, unless it can be established that the error was due to some cause, the date of which can be fixed with reasonable certainty, in which case the refund or charge shall be computed to that date, but in no event for a period longer than 1 year. An estimated billing may be used when a meter is found to be intermittently or not registering, but shall not exceed 1 year. If the recalculated bills indicate that the amount due the utility exceeds $10, the utility may bill the customer for the amount due. The first billing rendered shall be separated from the regular bill and the charges explained in detail. If a customer notifies a utility of doubts about a meter's accuracy, and the utility fails to respond within a reasonable time, there shall be no back-billing for the period from the customer's notification to the date the meter was checked.

7820.3800 (Electric) and 7820.4000 (Gas). Electric Utility Billing Errors; Natural Gas Utility Billing Errors:

For other billing errors, i.e., incorrect reading or calculation, incorrect connection of meter, etc., provisions substantially similar to rules 7820.3700 and 3900 [inaccurate meter].

* * *

7820.4200. Guarantee of Payment:

A utility shall not require a deposit or guarantee from any customer or applicant who has established good credit. Credit standards must bear a reasonable relationship to the assurance of payment.

7820.4300. New Service:

A utility shall not require a cash deposit or other guarantee of payment as a condition of obtaining new service unless a customer has outstanding, unpaid and undisputed prior utility service account with the utility, the service of a customer or applicant has previously been disconnected for any permissible reason which is not in dispute, or the credit history as provided in this chapter demonstrates that payment cannot be assured.

The determination of an adequate credit history must be determined by objective criteria which shall be filed with the Commission in the utility's tariff. Such criteria must bear a reasonable relationship to the assurance of payment.

7820.4400. Existing Service:

A utility shall not require a cash deposit or other guarantee of payment as condition of continuing existing service unless the service of the customer has been disconnected or has been liable for disconnect for any permissible reason, including nonpayment of a bill which is not in dispute.

7820.4500. When Payment Guarantee Permissible:

When required, a customer may assure payment by submitting a deposit or a written guarantee. Deposits or guarantee shall be returned or credited after 12 consecutive months of prompt payment of utility bills. A deposit shall not exceed an estimated two months' gross bill or existing two months' bill where applicable. Interest shall be paid on deposits in excess of $20 at the rate of 6% per year compounded annually. With notice any deposit may be applied by the utility to a bill when the bill has been determined by the utility to be delinquent. Customers shall receive a receipt for deposits, and the utility shall establish procedures to claim a deposit should the receipt be lost. A utility shall not require a deposit of any customer without explaining in writing why that deposit or guarantee is being required and under what conditions, if any, the deposit will be diminished upon return.

Upon termination of a guarantee contract or whenever the utility deems same insufficient as to amount or surety, a cash deposit or a new or additional guarantee may be required for good cause upon reasonable written notice to the customer.

7820.4600. Good Credit:

A customer, who within the last 12 months has not had service disconnected for nonpayment of a bill and has not been liable for disconnect for nonpayment of a bill which is not in dispute, shall be deemed to have established good credit.

7820.4700. When Deposit or Payment Guarantee Impermissible:

A utility shall not require a deposit or a guarantee of payment based upon income, home ownership, residential location, employment tenure, nature of occupation, race, color, creed, sex, marital status, age, national origin, or any other criterion which does not bear a reasonable relationship to the assurance of payment of which is not authorized by this chapter.

No utility shall use any credit reports other than those reflecting the purchase of utility services to determine the adequacy of a customer's credit history without the permission in writing of a customer. Refusal of a customer to permit use of a credit rating or credit service other than that of a utility shall not affect the determination of the utility as to that customer's credit history.

7820.4800. Information Available to Customers and Public:

A utility must retain records as required by Commission rules. A customer's own billing, complaint, payment, and deposit records shall be retained for at least 3 years and shall be available to that customer. A utility must have available for customers and applicants the information needed to obtain and maintain adequate, timely, and efficient service. A utility must furnish other information that a customer may reasonably request.

7820.4900. Emergency Information:

Each utility must have, and list in the telephone directory, a 24-hour emergency number at which there can be notifications of service deficiencies or other emergencies.

* * *

7820.5200. Billing Terms:

Late payment charges must be designated as late payment charges. The use of the terms "penalty," "discount," or "net-gross" differential is forbidden.

7820.5300. Determination of Delinquency:

If payment is not received by the utility by the next scheduled billing date, which must be not less than 25 days from the current billing date, a late payment charge may be imposed. The current billing date must be no more than 3 working days before the date of mailing of the bill by the utility.

7820.5400. Requirements for Imposing Late Payment Charge:

Utilities must include in their tariffs, which must be approved by the Commission, the terms and conditions of the late payment fee and documents supporting the finance fee and grace period. Bills must state the terms and conditions of the late charge, including the date after which it is due, the amount, and the monthly and annual percentage rates.

7820.5500. Amount of Late Payment Charge:

A late payment charge shall not be imposed on arrearages of under $10 and shall not exceed 1.5% of the monthly amount due. A minimum late charge shall not exceed $1.

7820.5600. Crediting of Payments:

The utility shall credit all payments received against the oldest outstanding account balance before the application of any late payment charge.

***Telecommunications*—Minn. R. 7810.0100–7810.8815**

Many of the regulations governing telecommunications service are similar in substance and form to the general regulations governing electric and gas service. Questions regarding telecommunications service may be answered by referencing the general regulations governing a specific issue.

* * *

7810.1400. Customer Billing:

Bills must be adjusted if service is out for 24 hours or more and did not result from negligent or willful act of customer. Customers or applicants must be provided, upon request, with information enabling them to choose the most economical service that meets their needs.

7810.2100. Manner of Disconnection:

No disconnection on Friday, Saturday, Sunday or holiday, or at any time when utility's business office is not open to the public.

MISSISSIPPI

The Public Service Commission's Rules general rules governing electric, gas, telecommunications, water, and sewer service can be found within Miss. Pub. Service Comm'n Gen. R. 1–15. Access to the regulations can be found at www.psc.state.ms.us/executive/rules.html (last visited in May 2011). *See also* 26-000-002 Miss. Code R. §§ 1 to 15 (LexisNexis).

***General (Electric, Gas, Telecommunications, Water, and Sewer Services)*—Miss. Pub. Service Comm'n Gen. R. 1–15**

* * *

Rule 6. Customer Relations:

Utility shall provide information concerning services, rate schedules and any changes in services and rate schedules, information that will assist in choice of service.

Rule 7. Refusal to Serve Customers:

Utilities shall inform customers of their right dispute a refusal of service to the Commission. Service may be refused for noncompliance with state or municipal regulations, inadequate facilities, hazardous conditions, and indebtedness to utility for same type of service.

Service shall not be refused due to nonpayment of previous customer (not a current household member), or for failure to pay for a different kind of service or for merchandise purchased from the utility. Service shall not be refused due to operation of nonstandard equipment, unless the customer is provided notice and an opportunity to remedy the deficiency.

Rule 8. Discontinuance of Service:

When service is scheduled to be terminated for issues related to nonpayment for service (including failure to make payments under a payment plan) or violation of utility regulations, a customer shall receive at least 5 days' notice through U.S. mail. Customers shall have the right to pay for service, including through the utility representative sent to terminate service, at any time prior to termination. Payment at the time of termination or a reconnection fee may be charged by the utility ($1 and $2 respectively or larger per tariff).

Notice is not required when termination is due to a hazardous condition, or fraudulent, negligent, or unlawful use of service.

If a customer, subject to termination of service, demonstrates an "extreme financial difficulty" or a medical emergency from December through March, the utility shall not terminate service without offering the customer a levelized payment plan. Utilities may require a customer to accept a payment plan that requires payment of amounts due that accrued before November 11 with the remaining balance to paid in installments of 133% (levelized monthly bill plus 33% of past-due amount). However the utility is not prevented from negotiating a plan that is more acceptable to a customer. Customers shall not be allowed to carry forward an unpaid balance beyond December 1 of the following winter season. Customers demonstrating a medical emergency shall not have service terminated after April 1 if the customer agrees to a levelized payment plan for previous utility service and is current in utility bill.

Rule 9. Customer Deposits:

A utility may, after reasonable notice is given, require a deposit from any person, except those who are 60 years or older or those who have made timely payments for 12 months, to guarantee payment for service and to guarantee the return and protection of utility property. Pursuant to Rule 10, a deposit may be required during a billing dispute. The utility shall provide the customer with a receipt of deposit, and provide a method to claim a deposit should the receipt be lost. Pursuant to Miss. Code Ann. § 75-17-1(1), deposits, held for more than 1 year, shall accrue interest at not less than the 12-month average of the 10-year Treasury note yield, but not more than 8% per annum. Interest shall be refunded and/or credited to a customer's account on July 1 of every third year, or when customer initiates disconnection of service. Deposits shall be returned when a customer reaches the age of 60, or when a customer has made timely payments for 12 consecutive months.

A deposit shall not exceed 1 month's estimated bill for residential service (2 months for other customers). Deposits for telecommunications service shall not exceed 1 month's estimated final bill for a similar type of service. A utility may require a customer to pay an additional deposit after a deposit has been refunded and issues of nonpayment arise, or when an existing deposit is deemed inadequate.

Rule 10. Billing:

Bills shall be issued regularly and shall contain the billing period, all payment information and amounts due (late payments, charges, taxes, etc.), full description and itemization of activity and services, payments, adjustments, credits. A customer may be required to pay a deposit in an amount equal to a disputed amount to continue to receive service.

Meters found to be in error of 2%, 3%, or 4% (see regulation for specific meter error minimums), shall result in a refund or adjustment from the time of the error if it can be reasonably determined or from 3 months prior to the last meter-reading when it cannot.

Except for master-metered buildings prior to 1993, master metering is prohibited.

Rule 11. Meters:

Meters shall be read at no less than 25-day and no more than 35-day intervals, and bills for service shall be submitted to customer within 30 days of reading. A utility may implement estimated billing for reasons beyond its control, but the utility shall attempt to get an actual reading after two consecutive estimated readings.

Each utility shall provide, install, and install, at its own expense, all equipment necessary for the delivery, regulation and measurement of service to the point of delivery to its customers. When additional meters or equipment are furnished by the utility only for the convenience of the customer, charges therefore shall be made in accordance with a schedule legally in effect.

Prepayment meters may be used at the utilities discretion and the utility shall make adjustments for estimated and actual usage at least once a year or accordingly for shorter terms of service.

* * *

MISSOURI

The Public Service Commission's general regulation governing electric, gas, and water can be found within Mo. Code Regs. Ann. tit. 4, §§ 240-13.010–240-13.070; the regulation governing telecommunications can be found in Mo. Code Regs. Ann. tit. 4, §§ 240-31.010, 240-33.010–240-33.170. Mo. Code Regs. Ann. tit. 4, § 240-33.150 contains specific regulations governing unauthorized changes in telephone service provider (slamming). Many of the substantive issues within the telecommunications regulations are substantially similar to those dealing with gas, electric, and water and are indicated accordingly. Access to the regulations can found at www.psc.mo.gov/statutes-rules (last visited in May 2011).

***General (Electric, Gas, and Water)*—Mo. Code Regs. Ann. tit. 4, §§ 240-13.010–240-13.070**

* * *

§ 240-13.015. Billing:

Billing periods shall be not less than 26 nor more than 35 days for monthly-billed customers, nor more than 100 days for quarterly-billed, except for initial, corrected of final bills. The delinquency date must be shown on the bill and may not be less than 21 days for a monthly-billed customer or 16 days for quarterly-billed. After that date, a delinquency charge may be imposed in accordance with the tariff.

§ 240-13.020. Billing and Payment Standards:

Billing shall be for actual usage except when weather, emergencies, access to customer's premises, or other similar circumstance requires an estimated reading. All estimates are to be clearly indicated.

Billing may occur cyclically, quarterly, monthly, or, at the customer's request, under an approved equal payment plan. Unless otherwise specified under a preferred payment plan, due dates for quarterly bills shall be at least 16 days from date of billing whereas monthly bills shall be at least 21 days.

Bills shall include the billing period, the due date and late date, previous balance, amount due, total due, and contact information for inquiries and complaints.

§ 240-13.025. Billing Adjustments:

All billing errors, including overcharges for monthly or quarterly billing periods not exceeding 60 or 20 consecutive billing periods respectively shall be adjusted. Undercharges for monthly or quarterly billing periods not exceeding 12 or 4 consecutive billing periods respectively shall be adjusted.

§ 240-13.030. Deposits and Guarantees of Payment:

A new or existing customer may be required to pay a deposit or provide a guarantee of payment if they have insufficient credit due to delinquent bills (past or present), diversion of services, or failure to meet the tariff's accepted credit rating. Deposits and guarantees shall not exceed 1/6 estimated bill for new monthly customers, 1/3 for new quarterly customers, or twice the highest bill in the prior 12 months for existing customers, and, when assessed during November–January, may be paid in 6 monthly installments. All deposits shall accrue interest based on the tariff rate. Deposits, and guarantees, shall be returned or credited to the account after 1 year of timely payments.

Credit can be established with a record of home ownership or purchase, 1-year full time employment or adequate source of income, or references from commercial creditors.

§ 240-13.035. Denial of Service:

A utility may refuse to commence service for: failure to pay undisputed, delinquent charge for services provided by the utility or its affiliate; failure to provide deposit or guarantee; refusal to allow the utility access to for inspection, meter reading, etc. after being given proper notice; misrepresentation of identity; violation of other rules that affect safety or the integrity of the system; failure of a prior owner or occupant to pay a bill, if the prior owner or occupant remains an occupant; noncompliance with settlement agreement; tampering or diversion by the applicant or a previous owner or occupant who remains an occupant. A utility may not refuse service for: failure to pay for merchandise or services not subject to Commission jurisdiction; failure to pay the bill of a prior occupant, unless the utility can prove that the applicant received substantial benefit from the service, i.e., resided at the premises with the customer of record at the time when the bill was incurred, that the bill was incurred in the past 7 years, and that the utility attempted to collect from the customer of record. Notwithstanding any other provisions of the rule, a utility may temporarily refuse to connect for reasons of maintenance, health, safety, or a state of emergency. New service should ordinarily be provided within 3 days of the date specified by the applicant or, in case of new construction, 3 days after the work and all necessary inspections are completed.

§ 240-13.040. Inquiries:

All rights, responsibilities, procedures, and policies shall be made available to all customers in a clear and understandable manner.

§ 240-13.045. Disputes:

Disputes must be received 24 hours before discontinuance of service. Amounts not in dispute must be paid. Service cannot be discontinued until 10 days after the dispute is registered and proper notice of the discontinuance has been given. Frivolous disputes may result in discontinuance of service.

§ 240-13.050. Discontinuance of Service:

Services may be discontinued for nonpayment, failure to make deposit or provide guarantee, diversion or interference with service, misrepresentation of identity, refusal of reasonable inspection when health or safety risk is possible, or violation of utility regulations or state or federal law. Notice shall be given at least 10 days before discontinuance by mail or 96 hours before when hand delivered, and shall contain the customer's name, address, and telephone number; reason, date, how to avoid discontinuance and utility contact information, cost of reconnection, and settlement options. A reasonable effort to contact a customer shall be made at least 24 hours preceding discontinuance.

Service may not be discontinued for failure to pay for merchandise, services elsewhere or a different class of service, delinquent bill of another person or a previous occupant, failure to pay corrected under-billing unless offered a payment when unable to pay. Utility shall postpone discontinuance for not more than 21 days if discontinuance will aggravate an existing medical emergency of the customer, member of the customer's family, or other permanent resident of premises.

§ 240-13.055. Cold Weather Maintenance of Service—Provision of Residential Heat-Related Utility Service During Cold Weather:

Households in which one member is age 65 or older or disabled, as shown by a doctor's certificate or an award letter from a Federal agency, should register annually before October 1. From November 1 through May 31, the utility must mail disconnect notices at least 10 days before disconnection to the customer and, in the case of registered elder or disabled persons, to the designated third party. Within 96 hours before disconnection, the utility must make further efforts to contact the customer either by a second notice, a door hanger, or two telephone attempts. For a registered elder or disabled customer, the utility must make personal contact at the time of discontinuance with the customer or a family member over the age of 15. All notices must disclose the method of calculating the required payments and the availability of assistance from the state and from private charities. The utility may not threaten to disconnect at a time when disconnection would be forbidden by the temperature moratorium. The utility may not disconnect on any day when the temperature is predicted to drop below 32° within 24 hours or, if utility personnel will not be available on the next day to reconnect, during the period when personnel are unavailable; nor for a registered low-income (150% of poverty) elder or disabled customer who has entered into a cold weather period payment plan, made the initial payment, and continued to make payments of the lesser of 50% of the actual bill for the billing period or the levelized payment amount. A utility may not disconnect between November 1 and May 31 if the customer claims an inability to pay, furnishes any requested information to the utility, enters into a payment agreement and makes the first payment, and there is no other lawful reason for discontinuance. A customer who moves during the duration of a payment plan may receive service at the new address if he or she pays all amounts due under the payment plan and any other past-due amounts. A utility may not assess a deposit, or require payment of a deposit previously assessed, from a customer who enters into a payment plan and makes timely payments. Between November 1 and May 31, a utility must reconnect if a customer claims inability to pay, provides required information, agrees to a payment plan and makes payments, and the arrearage was not the result of tampering or diversion. A pledge by the LIHEAP agency of the amount of a required payment is treated as a payment. A payment plan should be a 12-month budget plan, with payments sufficient to cover past arrears, current amounts, and estimated future amounts. If the customer is unable to pay, the customer and utility may negotiate a plan to pay off the arrears over a reasonable period greater than 12 months. A customer who defaults on a payment plan but has not yet been disconnected may reinstate the plan by paying amount due under the payment agreement and any other past-due amounts. The initial payment for a payment agreement is 12% of the budget bill amount for a customer who has never defaulted on a plan or 80% for a customer who has defaulted. Notwithstanding other provisions of this rule, gas companies shall restore service, between November 1 and May 31, upon the payment of the lesser of $500 or 50% of the arrears, with the rest to be paid pursuant to a payment plan, as described above. Any late fee, trip fee, or reconnection fee must be deferred.

* * *

***Telephone*—Mo. Code Regs. Ann. tit. 4, §§ 240-31.010, 240-33.010–240-33.160**

Many of the substantive issues within the telecommunications regulations are substantially similar to those dealing with gas, electric, and water and are indicated accordingly.

* * *

§ 240-31.050. Eligibility for Funding—Low-Income Customers and Disabled Customers:

Those meeting the definitional requirements of "low-income" or "disabled" customers pursuant to § 240-31.010 are eligible to receive essential and/or discounted telecommunication services.

* * *

§ 240-33.040. Billing Payments and Standards for Residential Customers:

When discussing plans with customers and applicants, the utility must provide the name and rates associated with the plan. Written notice of rate increases must be provided 10 days before the increase (30 days for certain small companies). If a utility does not provide a preferred payment date plan, charges will be due not less than 21 days after the rendition of the bill. If the company has a preferred payment date plan, charges are due on that date. Late payment charges are permitted, if specifically stated in the tariff. Each bill must state: the number of access lines; the beginning and ending dates of the billing period; delinquency date; penalty fees and advance payments, if any; the amount due for local service (or the package rate if service is bundled); itemization of the amounts due for other regulated and non-regulated services, including the duration of toll calls; itemization of any other taxes, fees, etc.; a toll-free number for questions and disputes concerning the bill; amount of any deposit held by the company and accrued interest; any other credits and charges; and, during the first billing period, include a bill insert with an itemized account of charges for equipment and service.

§ 240-33.045. Requiring Clear Identification and Placement of Separately Identified Charges on Customers Bills:

Utilities may not misrepresent any charge as governmentally mandated or authorized by disguising it, naming it, or placing it on the bill in a way that implies it is governmentally mandated or authorized or giving it a name confusingly similar to such a charge.

§ 240-33.050. Deposits and Guarantees of Payment for Residential Customers:

Substantially similar to § 240-13.030 except amount of deposit shall not exceed two months of an average estimated bill.

§ 240-33.060. Residential Customer Inquiries:

Bills must disclose each company name and provide a toll-free number that customers may call for billing inquires or to cancel consent to certain services. Utilities must provide personnel during normal business hours to respond to customer inquiries. Upon customer request, and if technically feasible, a utility must restrict: calls from the customer's number to pay-per-call numbers; calls from inmates of state correctional institutions; toll calls without a valid passcode; calls using a dial-around pattern. Customer must be notified of these rights at the initiation of service, annually thereafter, and whenever a customer complains of unauthorized calls on his or her line.

§ 240-33.070. Discontinuance of Service to Residential Customers:

Substantially similar to § 240-13.050. There are no weather-related exceptions. Upon customer request, company may provide written notice of discontinuance in electronic format. Local service may not be disconnected for failure to pay for other than basic local service, but a utility may place global toll-blocking and discontinue any optional, non-basic calling features. Discontinuance must be postponed for at least 21 days if the customer presents reasonable evidence that a household member is under the care of a physician and that telephone service is needed to obtain emergency medical assistance. Payment by personal check may be refused if, within 12 months, a payment has been tendered by check that was dishonored for any reason other than bank error.

§ 240-33.080. Disputes by Residential Customers:

Bills must include a toll-free number for customer disputes. A customer must notify the utility of a dispute before the due date of the bill in question and must pay the undisputed amount. If the customer and the utility cannot agree as to the undisputed amount, the customer must pay, at the utility's option, 50% of the disputed charge or an amount based on usage during a like period under similar conditions. If the dispute cannot be resolved, the utility must inform the customer of the right to file a complaint with the Commission and must provide contact information.

§ 240-33.090. Settlement Agreements with Residential Customers:

When a customer is unable to pay the full amount due, the telecommunications company shall permit the customer to enter into an initial settlement agreement under which the charge may be paid as mutually agreed to by both parties.

* * *

§ 240-33.150. Verification of Orders for Changing Telecommunications Service Provider (Anti-Slamming):

This section sets standards for written authorization, electronic authorization, or third-party verification of requests to change carrier. Written authorization must be by a separate document, containing no inducements (although a check that clearly discloses that cashing it will result in change of carrier is acceptable). Electronic authorization must be made from the telephone number(s) on which the carrier is to be changed and must connect to a unit that records the prescribed information, including automatic identification of the originating phone number. Third-party verifiers must be independent of the carrier seeking a change, must have no financial incentive to verify, and must operate from a location separate from the carrier. All these forms of authorization must indicate the billing name and address of the subscriber, the number of the affected telephone(s); the decision to change carriers; authorization to the submitting carrier to make the change; and various other disclosures. If any part of the letter is in a language other than English, the entire letter must be translated into that language. LECs that offer preferred carrier freezes must do so non-discriminatorily and must clearly explain to customers the effects of a freeze and the procedure for imposing and lifting freezes. A submitting carrier that fails to comply with this rule is liable to the authorized carrier for any charges paid to the submitting carrier after the violation.

* * *

MONTANA

The Department of Public Service's general regulations governing electric, gas, and water can be found within Mont. Admin. R. 38.5.901–38.5.904, 38.5.1101–38.5.1112, 38.5.1401–38.5.1418; privately owned water utilities can be found within Mont. Admin. R. 38.5.2501–38.5.2514; telecommunications service standards can be found within Mont. Admin. R. 38.5.3330–38.5.3371. Many of the regulation governing privately owned water utilities and telecommunications service standards are substantially similar to those governing electric, gas, and water, and are indicated accordingly. Access to the regulations can be found at www.mtrules.org/gateway/ChapterHome.asp?Chapter=38.5 (last visited in May 2011).

***General (Electric, Gas, and Water)*—Mont. Admin. R. 38.5.901–38.5.904, 38.5.1101–38.5.1112, 38.5.1401–38.5.1418**

* * *

38.5.902. Billing Errors:

A corrected bill shall not be submitted to a customer after 6 months from the date the error was discovered unless for theft of service.

* * *

38.5.1101. Establishment of Credit—Residential:

Credit may be established through satisfactory payment of previous services, 12 months consecutive employment or regular income, ownership of significant legal significance in premises to be served, or providing a payment guarantee pursuant to rules 38.5.1111–38.51112 of this title.

* * *

38.5.1103. Deposit Requirements:

Deposits or guarantee may be required if customer failed to meet regulatory requirements, similar service was terminated for nonpayment, prior customer with delinquent bill still resides at premises, or unauthorized interference with service.

38.5.1104. Prohibited Standards for Requiring Cash Deposit or Other Guarantee for Residential Service:

Standards shall be applied pursuant to these regulations in a non-discriminatory manner.

38.5.1105. Amount of Deposit:

The amount of a deposit shall not exceed one-sixth the annual estimated billing, but telephone services may be adjusted if actual charges are more or less than estimation.

38.5.1106. Transfer of Deposit:

Deposits less outstanding balance shall be transferable when location of service is changed within Montana, except that telephone deposit is only transferable within same exchange.

38.5.1107. Interest on Deposits:

Interest on deposits shall accrue at a rate of 6% per year.

38.5.1108. Refund of Deposits:

Deposits or guarantee shall be returned after 12 months of service without disconnection proceedings or more than two notices of delinquency, or upon termination of service.

38.5.1109. Record of Deposits:

Utility shall maintain records and provide customers with receipts of deposits and means to obtain return of deposit if receipt is lost.

* * *

38.5.1402. Grounds for Termination of Service:

Service may be terminated for nonpayment, misrepresentation of identity when obtaining service, unauthorized use or interference, failure to allow utility access to premises when required, or violation of utility rules.

38.5.1403. Prohibited Grounds for Termination:

Termination is prohibited for failure of any other person, other than the customer, to pay any charges due, or failure to pay for merchandise.

38.5.1405. Notice Prior to and at the Time of Termination:

The utility must always make a diligent attempt to contact a customer, either in person, by phone, or by mail before terminating service. If there is no response within 10 days after initial notice of termination is sent, notice shall be given, either in person or by mail, 10 days before termination. If notification has not been possible, a last attempt shall be made the day preceding termination. If a customer's check is returned for insufficient funds, or a customer has breached a payment plan, notice is decreased to 5 days. Individual tenants must be notified 15 days prior to termination and tenant may dispute termination.

At the time of termination and during normal business hours the utility shall have qualified personnel available to reconnect services if reason for termination is rectified.

38.5.1406. Contents of Written Notice:

Notice must contain the termination policy and a summary of all rights and remedies, reason and date of termination, amount of any reconnection fees, instructions on how service may be restored, and particular provisions for landlord customers and tenants.

38.5.1407. Grounds for Termination Without Notice:

No notice is required if a dangerous condition requires termination, termination upon order of a court, commission or authorized public authority, or termination for theft or fraud.

38.5.1408. Customer's Right to Dispute a Termination Notice:

A customer has a right to dispute a termination notice for reasons including but not limited to the extent to which a customer has control of a source of income, i.e., public assistance checks, weather, customer is an elder, medical condition.

38.5.1409. Termination for Nonpayment When Prohibited:

Termination may not occur for nonpayment of disputed portion of a bill during negotiations between customer and utility or if customer has filed a complaint with the Commission.

38.5.1410. Termination of Service During Winter Months:

Termination of services shall be prohibited for nonpayment from November 1 to April 1 unless approved by the Commission.

38.5.1411. Medical Emergencies:

Termination may not occur upon certification by licensed health care professional that it will aggravate an existing medical condition and threaten the health of any permanent resident. Certification is valid for 180 days from date that it is signed and may be renewed semi-annually. Utility and customer shall negotiate payment arrangement and, if customer's failure to pay results in arrearage of $500 or more, customer must enter into payment plan equal to average of last 12 months' billing plus 1/12 of the arrearage. Disconnection may be initiated if customer fails to comply with payment plan, subject to winter months protection under § 38.5.1410.

38.5.1412. Time of Termination:

Service may only be terminated between 8:00 a.m. and 12:00 noon and may not be terminated unless, on the day preceding or the day of termination, the utility is available to receive payment and reconnect.

38.5.1413. Method of Termination:

Substantially similar to rule 38.5.1405.

38.5.1415. Payment Arrangements:

When a customer is unable to pay a bill a utility may negotiate a reasonable payment plan taking into account customer's ability to pay, the size of the unpaid balance, the customer's payment history, and the amount of time and reasons why the debt is outstanding.

* * *

38.5.1503. Optional or Alternative Rate Information:

Within 60 days of establishing service the utilities shall inform customers of alternative or optional rate schedules that may affect them.

* * *

38.5.1602. Prohibition of Master Meters:

Master meters are prohibited for electrical service in all new buildings.

* * *

***Privately Owned Water Utilities*—Mont. Admin. R. 38.5.2501–38.5.2514**

Many of the regulation governing privately owned water utilities are substantially similar to those governing electric, gas, and water, and are indicated accordingly.

* * *

38.5.2504. Consumer Discontinuance of Service:

Customer shall give 24-hour notice and a specific discontinuance date and shall be responsible for all charges unless notice is given.

38.5.2505. Utility Discontinuance of Service:

Substantially similar to R. 38.5.1402–38.5.1418

* * *

R. 38.5.2509. Utility to Provide Meters:

Unless an additional meter is requested by customer or authorized by Commission, meters shall be provided and maintained at utility expense.

* * *

R. 38.5.2511. Meter Reading:

Reading shall occur monthly, bimonthly, or at no less than 6-month intervals for rural customers. Customers may be requested to read meters. Utility may estimate but meter must be read at least once in six months.

* * *

***Telecommunication Service Standards*—Mont. Admin. R. 38.5.3330–38.5.3371, 38.5.3801–38.5.3819, 38.5.3901–38.5.3913**

Many of the regulation governing privately telecommunications service standards are substantially similar to those governing electric, gas, and water, and are indicated accordingly.

* * *

38.5.3332. Customer Billing:

Bills issued monthly and shall contain information needed to determine due date, payment amount, and charges (local, itemized toll charges, and taxes). A payment plan shall be offered for under-billing of more than $25; over-billing shall be reconciled with either a credit to future bills or, upon request by consumer, a cash refund. A utility may require payment of the undisputed portion of bill to avoid discontinuance of service. Adjustments shall be made for interruption of more than 24 hours.

If the bill includes charges from an entity that did not bill the customer for any service during the previous billing cycle, the name of the new provider and the charges billed must be clear and conspicuous.

Local exchange service may not be terminated for nonpayment for toll services, unregulated services, or services provided by another carrier, except when these services are combined in one package at a single rate. Bills must clearly distinguish between regulated and unregulated services.

Partial payments must be applied first to local exchange service.

If services are billed more than 60 days after service was rendered, the utility must offer a payment plan for a period equal to the time it took the carrier to bill the customer, and late payment charges may not be imposed or other collection action taken.

Carriers may not charge for unanswered calls.

* * *

38.5.3334. Customer Deposits for Telecommunications Service:

See R. 38.5.1101–38.5.1112. A telecommunications provider may not require a deposit to initiate service to a subscriber who participates in the Montana Telephone Assistance Program and has subscribed to toll blocking, except that a deposit may be required for optional local calling features and services.

38.5.3335. Complaints and Appeals:

Must be promptly investigated, and consumer shall be notified of outcome and appeals processes.

* * *

38.5.3339. Termination of Service:

Substantially similar to R. 38.5.1402–38.5.1418. Other prohibited grounds for termination are failure to pay for business service at another location, failure to pay an amount in dispute before the Commission, or failure to pay for unregulated service or service provided by other carriers, unless the service is combined with local exchange service in a package at a single rate.

Carriers must provide for third-party notification free of charge.

The notice period for termination is 7 days before termination, except in cases of abnormally high toll usage and risk of nonpayment. Abnormally high toll usage means more than 200% of consumer's monthly average for the past 6 months and an amount greater than $100. Risk of nonpayment means either lack of a deposit when one is permitted or, within the past 12 months, there has been a disconnection for nonpayment, for two or more delinquency notices, or for two or more bad checks. Before terminating pursuant to this provision, the carrier must make at least three attempts to contact customer, and provide an opportunity to supply adequate assurance of payment. If this is not provided, service may terminate after 24 hours; if the customer cannot be reached, may terminate 3 business days after mailing notice.

* * *

38.5.3801. Change in Telecommunications Provider:

A provider shall obtain proper authorization, as required under R 38.5.3802, before initiating a change in a customer's provider and for each individual service sold.

* * *

38.5.3803. Complaints of Unauthorized Switch in Carrier:

Complaints alleging an unauthorized switch shall be initially responded to within 5 working days and the burden of showing proper authorization is on the entity initiating the change.

38.5.3804. Telecommunications Carrier Liability:

A carrier found responsible for an unauthorized switch in service shall be liable to the customer for all charges associated to the unauthorized switch and to the original carrier for charges related to reinstating service.

38.5.3805. Refund of Charges:

Substantially similar to R. 38.5.3804, but refunds are limited to 6 months of consecutive unauthorized service. Refunds or credits shall be given within 60 days of the original complaint.

* * *

38.5.3812. True and Complete Carrier Communications Pertaining to Customer Authorization for Change of Carriers:

Authorization shall be deemed invalid if a carrier makes false, misleading, or deceptive statements, or fails to disclose material information concerning the switch.

* * *

38.5.3901. Customer Authorization Required Prior to Placement of Charges on Customer's Telephone Bill:

Substantially similar to R. 38.5.3801. A provider that is not the customer's selected provider may not initiate the placement of charges on a bill unless it was customer initiated, i.e., accepting a collect call, or unless proper authorization was obtained. Providers must get proper authorization for each individual service sold and must maintain records of authorization for 2 years.

* * *

38.5.3907. Complaints of Unauthorized Charges for Products or Services Being Placed on a Customer's Telephone Bill:

Substantially similar to R. 38.5.3803.

* * *

38.5.3910. Telecommunications Carrier or Other Entity Liability:

Substantially similar to R. 38.5.3804.

* * *

38.5.3913. Credit or Refund of Charges:

Substantially similar to R. 38.5.3805.

NEBRASKA

The Public Service Commission's regulations governing denial and discontinuance of electric, natural gas, and water services are within Neb. Rev. Stat. §§ 70-1601–70-1615. Additional regulations regarding gas are within 291 Neb. Admin. Code §§ 9-011.01–9-011.06, and the regulations governing telecommunications are within 291 Neb. Admin. Code §§ 5-002.01–5-002.51. Regulations governing unauthorized changes in telecommunications service (Slamming) and unauthorized charges (Cramming) are within 291 Neb. Admin. Code §§ 5-004.01–5-004.12. Additional regulations governing telecommunication's slamming practices, although not summarized herein, can be found within Neb. Rev. Stat. §§ 86-201–86-211. Access to the regulations can be found at www.psc.state.ne.us/home/NPSC/rules/rules.htm.

***Denial or Discontinuance of Utility Service (Electric, Natural Gas, and Water)*—Neb. Rev. Stat. §§ 70-1601–70-1615**

§ 70-1601. Applicant for Service; Denial Prohibited, When:

Applicants shall not be denied services due to unpaid bills for similar service that are not collectable at law because of statutes of limitations or due to discharge in bankruptcy.

* * *

§ 70-1603. Municipal Utility; Owned and Operated by a Village; Discontinuance of Service; Notice; Procedure:

A village-owned and operated utility shall provide notice 7 days prior to discontinuance by mail.

§ 70-1604. Municipal Utility; Owned and Operated by a Village; Discontinuance of Service; Conference; Notice; Procedure:

Village-owned and operated utilities are not subject to §§ 70-1608 through 70-1614 but must establish procedure where, prior to discontinuance, a customer may request and shall be given a conference hearing with the village's board of trustees concerning disputes.

§ 70-1605. Discontinuance of Service; Notice; Procedure:

Substantially similar to § 70-1603 except notice shall be given in person or by first class mail. Holidays and weekends are excluded from the 7-day notification limit.

§ 70-1606. Discontinuance of Service; Notice; Content:

Notice of discontinuance shall be clearly marked and distinguishable from bills and shall contain the reason, options for paying the bill, date of discontinuance, restoration costs, conference rights and prohibition against discontinuance until conclusion of conference, and a statement informing the customer that 30-day postponement is available upon certification by a licensed physician that customer or household resident has an existing illness or disability and would suffer an immediate and serious health hazard from disconnection.

* * *

§ 70-1608. Discontinuance of Service; Dispute; Conference:

Conference disputes are heard and resolved by an employee designated by the utility.

§ 70-1609. Discontinuance of Service; Dispute; Statement; Effect:

Written statements concerning disputes and the relief requested shall be accepted by the utility, and discontinuance shall not occur until the conference is completed.

§ 70-1610. Conference; Employee; Duties:

Once a request for a conference is received, the utility must notify the customer and hold a conference within 14 days of the request. If a customer fails to attend a conference without providing a legitimate reason, the utility is relieved from taking any further action prior to discontinuance. Utilities shall make a reasonable effort to reschedule conferences.

§ 70-1611. Conference; Employee; Decision to Terminate, When:

At the conclusion of a conference, discontinuance shall be the last resort after all other remedies have been exhausted.

§ 70-1612. Appeal; Hearing; Procedure:

Utilities shall establish and implement procedures that enable customers to appeal conference decisions.

§ 70-1613. Appeal; Hearing; Domestic Subscriber; Rights:

During an appeal hearing, the customer may be bring legal counsel, have access to relevant utility records, call witnesses and confront and cross-examine witness, and request a record of the proceedings.

* * *

§ 70-1615. Sections; Not Applicable; When:

Sections 70-1602 through 70-1614 are not applicable when disconnection or interruption is for maintenance or to protect the health and safety of the customer or the general public.

***Telephone Service*—291 Neb. Admin. Code §§ 5-002.01–5-002.51; 291 Neb. Admin. Code §§ 5-004.01–5-004.12**

* * *

§ 5-002.16. Refusal of Service:

Service may be refused or disconnected for use of equipment that adversely affects others' service, tampering, violation of or non-compliance with rules or regulations, or for issues relating to nonpayment.

Service shall not be refused for nonpayment of a previous customer (other than a member of the same household), failure to pay for directory advertising, certain operator service charges, or disputed 900, 960, or 976 call charges.

§ 5-002.17. Customer Billing:

Bills shall be issued regularly and shall contain a clear listing of all charges. A written itemized listing of subscribed services and monthly rates shall be provided when service is ordered or as part of the initial bill and upon subsequent request of customer.

Termination shall not occur until a disputed bill is resolved. Disputes not resolved to the satisfaction of the customer, may be brought to the attention and reviewed by the Commission. The Commission may delay termination of service until said review is complete.

§ 5-002.18. Information:

Applicants shall be provided information and assistance in securing the most desirable rate and grade of service.

§ 5-002.19. Rules Governing Credit and Deposits:

Deposits shall not exceed 2 months of local service charges plus 2 months of estimated of toll charges. Deposit amounts may be increased due to increased usage or additional services, or due to untimely payments.

Deposits held in excess of 30 days shall accrue 7% per annum interest, and shall be refunded, upon request by the customer, after 12 months of timely payments, or voluntarily by the provider after 24 months of timely payments. New and existing customers shall be allowed to pay deposits or increased deposits in 3 monthly installment payments. For purposes of interest, a deposit is received on the day the final installment is made.

A guarantor may be furnished in lieu of a deposit and shall be subject to the amount and release requirements of deposits. A guarantor shall be released from liability no less than 10 days after the request is made. Cancellation of a guarantee may require the customer to pay a deposit. A provider is allowed 6 months to notify a guarantor of charges for which he or she is liable.

§ 5-002.20. Complaint Handling Procedures:

Complaints concerning all aspects of service shall be accepted and investigated by the provider. Suspension or termination of service shall be delayed until a dispute is resolved. Service may be terminated or suspended for failure to pay undisputed portions of bills.

* * *

§ 5-004.03. Authorized Change in Subscriber's Carrier:

Unless customer initiated, submission, initiation, or an actual change in a customer's provider shall only occur upon verifiable written, electronic, or oral authorization.

§ 5-004.04. Written Confirmation of Change:

A new provider must send customers a clear and distinguishable notification indicating and explaining the change in provider services within 30 days of the change.

§ 5-004.05. Charges Paid by a Subscriber to an Unauthorized Carrier:

Customers may notify either their original provider or the unauthorized provider concerning unauthorized charges and/or changes in providers. If an unauthorized provider is notified it shall notify the original provider.

An authorized provider shall notify an unauthorized provider of the complaint and, within 10 days, the unauthorized provider shall either furnish proper verification or refund all unauthorized charges.

* * *

NEVADA

The majority of the Public Utility Commission's regulations governing consumer electric and gas services can be found in Nev. Admin. Code §§ 704.302–704.390. Regulations governing the termination of water service are contained in Nev. Admin. Code §§ 704.391–704.3936. Although the majority of regulations concerning consumer telephone services can be found in Nev. Admin. Code §§ 704.395–704.421, many of the substantive issues within the regulations are substantially similar to those dealing with gas and electric and are indicated accordingly. Access to the regulations can be found at http://leg.state.nv.us/nac/chapters.html (last visited in May 2011).

Electric and Gas Services—**Nev. Admin. Code §§ 704.302–704.390**

* * *

§ 704.314. "Satisfactory Credit" Defined:

Satisfactory credit means payment of utility bills for 12 months with not more than 3 late payments (after the issuance of the next month's bill) or one termination.

§ 704.320. Records of Utility:

Utility shall retain records concerning each customer's use, amounts billed, complaints, terminations and reconnections, and deposits collected and returned for 3 years. A utility may not provide any list of names, addresses, telephone numbers or any related information about its customers to any other person for commercial purposes.

* * *

§ 704.322. Form for Complaint by Customer:

Utility shall have complaint forms available at every office.

§ 704.323. Transmittal of Information to Customer:

Utility shall send rate schedule at the time of application for service and in the next bill after a rate change. A clear and concise statement for 1 year of actual usage shall be provided by the utility upon request by the customer.

§ 704.326. Application for Service; Provision of Range of Historical Energy Use at Location of Service:

Applications may be made by mail, except that a person applying for utility service for the first time, or who had not received service from the utility during the preceding 2 years, may be required to apply in person, unless this will cause undue hardship. Upon request by an applicant, the utility shall provide a range of historical energy use at the location where service is to be provided.

§ 704.327. Establishment of Credit:

If required by the utility, a customer can establish credit by paying a deposit, being a customer of the same utility within the last 2 years and has established satisfactory credit, or 12 months of timely payments to another utility during a period of 2 years of service with another utility.

§ 704.328. Deposits—Generally:

A deposit shall not to exceed 150% (or 50% of that amount for an elder customer) of an average estimated monthly bill for an applicant, or 150% of the highest monthly bill for existing customers. An elder customer may be required to pay an additional deposit due to delinquency or termination of service.

§ 704.329. Deposit—Alternatives:

A deposit shall not be required if the customer (a) has established satisfactory credit with the utility or any other municipal or regulated energy utility or (b) uses a satisfactory guarantor or (c) receives benefits from a retirement plan or the Social Security Administration, unless the customer has had a termination or four delinquent payments within a 12-month period. The utility shall provide customers with forms for obtaining credit history from previous utilities or employment verification. Payment history and/or continuous employment for 1 year may be considered when determining if a deposit is required. A guarantor shall not be required to begin service. If a newly divorced or separated applicant is seeking service in his or her own name, the utility may consider previous payment record even if the previous service was not in the applicant's name.

§ 704.330. Deposit—Additional Amount:

An additional deposit, not exceeding the limits pursuant to § 704.328 when combined with the additional deposit, may be required if the customer is subject to termination only if initial deposit has been returned or more than one-half has been applied to customer's account. The amount of the new deposit may be combined with the arrearage and paid pursuant to a deferred payment plan (rule 341).

§ 704.331. Deposit: Notification of Requirement:

A utility must notify a customer after the third late payment if a deposit will be required after the fourth late payment.

§ 704.332. Deposit—Payment Installments:

Subject to a written agreement between the utility and the customer, a utility shall allow a deposit to be paid in installments. An initial payment of 1/3 of the total deposit, if more than $50, may be required before service begins with the remainder being paid in two installments of equal amount in 30-day intervals. Failure to pay deposit installments may result in termination of service without notice.

§ 704.333. Deposit: Return:

Deposits shall be returned after timely payments for 12 consecutive months.

§ 704.334. Guarantors:

A guarantor must be a customer of the utility and shall only be liable for an amount that would equal a required deposit. Liability shall end after customer makes timely payments for 12 consecutive months. A guarantor shall be pay an amount owed within 3 months or be subject to termination of services.

§ 704.336. Basis and Contents of Bill for Service:

Each bill shall include a complete and detailed description of all charges, amounts due, date due, adjustments, meter readings and dates thereof, amounts of consumption, and the telephone number and address of where to direct inquiries and complaints concerning bills.

§ 704.337. Billing Based upon Estimated Use:

Bills may be estimated if circumstances beyond the control of the utility prevent an actual meter reading. Estimated bills must be clearly marked and shall be adjusted after the next actual reading.

§ 704.338. Program for Equalized Billing for Service:

A utility must offer equalized billing to any customer whose service is connected at the time of the request. If the customer has arrears, the utility may require payment of 50% of the arrears before entering the program and payment of the remaining arrearage over a 1-year period. A customer who fails to make two or more consecutive timely payments may be removed from the equalized billing program and may not re-enter without the approval of the utility.

§ 704.339. Billing and Payment for Service:

Due dates shall be at least 15 days after issuance, and if falling on a holiday, a Sunday, or if office for receiving payment is closed, due date is on the next business day. Payments made by first-class mail are timely if received within 4 days of due date. If a utility has the capability to allow customers to choose a due date, it must notify customers annually that they have this choice. If a utility does not have this capability, it must work with a customer upon request to establish a mutually satisfactory due date. Each utility must provide at least one system of payment that allows customers to make payments via the Internet.

The utility may charge a fee, as set forth in its tariff, for late payments or returned checks. The company may charge a fee for the use of a credit card, if this fee is reviewed and approved by the Commission.

§ 704.341. Program for Deferred Payment of Delinquent Bill:

A utility shall provide a customer with a deferred payment plan for a delinquent bill unless it has already done so in the last 11 months. Failure to fulfill a payment plan agreement may result in termination upon 48 hours' notice. A utility shall consider funds, not yet disbursed, committed by a government agency to assist customers in paying their bills.

§ 704.342. Program to Pay Bills of Customers Under Financial Hardship; Coordination with Other Entities Providing Assistance to Lower-Income Customers:

Utilities shall provide a program to assist customers who have difficulty paying their bills due to financial hardship.

§ 704.343. Testing Meters for Accuracy:

A customer is entitled upon request to one free meter test per year. The customer may be present at the test and may request the presence of a Commission representative. The utility must provide the customer in writing of the results of the test and notify the customer if a meter is repaired or replaced.

§ 704.344. Adjustment of Bill When Meter Inaccurate:

A customer who owes money due to an inaccurate meter may pay it over a 3-month period. Overcharges due to inaccuracy shall be credited no later than 30 days after overcharge is discovered.

Adjustments may be made for no more than three months in case of under-billing, unless the under-billing resulted from tampering or unauthorized use, in which case the adjustment will be made for the greater of six months or from the date when the unauthorized use began. In case of over-billing, adjustment should be made for no more than six months.

§ 704.346. Resolution of Dispute Regarding Bill, Charge, or Service:

If a dispute is not resolved to a customer's satisfaction, the utility shall inform the customer of his or her right to file a complaint with the division. A customer may be required to pay any disputed amount pending resolution of the complaint.

§ 704.348. Refusal to Provide Service:

Service may be refused until a customer complies with tariff; or for obtaining or intending to obtain services fraudulently; use of service that is detrimental to the utility, facilities or other customers; or the existence of conditions listed in § 704.350.

§ 704.350. Termination of Service—No Prior Notice:

Service may be terminated without notice due to hazardous conditions, court order, intent to defraud utility, unanticipated events, abandonment of premises, after diligent attempts to provide notice pursuant to §§ 704.360 and 704.365, or if service is obtained without specific credit authorization.

§ 704.355. Termination of Service—Prior Notice:

After proper notice, service may be terminated for: violation of utility rule, or nonpayment of a delinquent bill, a security deposit or guarantee, or an installment plan payment. Service may be terminated at a new location for nonpayment of service from a previous location or at any location the nonpaying customer receives residential service.

§ 704.360. Termination of Service: Provision of Notice:

Notice shall be given, either in person or by first-class mail, at least 10 days before termination. If customer does not respond to initial notice, the utility shall give a second notice either in person, by first-class mail, by phone, by posting notice on a door at the customer's residence, or—if requested by the customer and within the capability of the utility—by electronic notice to the most recent electronic address provided by the customer at least 48 hours before the date of termination. If a customer has failed to comply with a deferred payment agreement, the utility may terminate on 48 hours' notice.

A termination notice shall contain account identification and address, date of termination, the reason for termination, dispute procedures and contact information, and all information that would assist the customer in avoiding termination of services, including but not limited to, the termination postponement procedures for elder and disabled residents.

A utility shall make every effort to contact individual customers at locations (apartment houses and manufactured home parks) using master meters pursuant to § 704.560.

§ 704.365. Termination of Service: Designation and Notification of Third Person:

A utility shall provide elder or disabled customers with the option of third-person notification concerning termination notice. The utility must make a diligent effort to notify the designated third person but does not incur any liability for failure to notify.

§ 704.370. Termination of Service—Postponement When Dangerous to Health:

A utility shall postpone termination for 30 days upon receiving notice from a licensed physician or public health official that termination of service would be especially dangerous to the health of customer or other permanent resident living at the residence. In addition to the medical certificate, the customer must provide a signed statement that the customer is unable to pay or is able to pay only in installments. Before postponement expires, customer must arrange with utility to pay bills. Postponement may be extended an additional 30 days if utility receives a renewed medical certificate before expiration of initial postponement.

The initial notice may be by telephone but must be followed within 5 days by a written statement. If a utility intends to terminate after the postponement, it must notify the Division, the customer, any designated third party, and, for gas, electric and water utilities, any governmental agencies or other organizations that have notified the utility that they can assist in paying utility bills.

§ 704.372. Termination of Service—Postponement upon Agreement to Pay Delinquent Bill:

A utility may postpone termination regardless of a customer's eligibility for a deferred payment plan, if the customer agrees and the utility determines that the customer is able to pay.

§ 704.375. Termination of Service—Miscellaneous Restrictions:

Service may not be terminated on a weekend or holiday or the day before a weekend or holiday. A utility may not terminate if it knows that a customer or a permanent resident of the customer's household is confined to the location where service is provided; is on life support which, to operate at that location, requires services provided by the utility; and is likely to die without the aid of the life support if the utility terminates service. A utility may not terminate for an outstanding amount of $50 or less. A utility must postpone termination if the National Weather Service forecast for the next 24 hours predicts a temperature of 15° Fahrenheit or below, or 105° Fahrenheit or above.

§ 704.380. Termination of Service—Restrictions Regarding Certain Delinquent Bills:

Service shall not be terminated for failure to pay for another class of service, or a delinquent bill of a previous occupant of the residence.

§ 704.383. Resumption of Service:

A utility shall resume service for compliance with requirements of utility's tariff, upon a court order, or receipt of certification of medical emergency under § 704.370. If payment is received before 10:00 a.m., the utility must reconnect on the day payment is received; otherwise within twenty-four hours of payment. In the case of a multi-unit residential complex, the utility shall resume service to each unit "on a priority basis." A utility may charge a fee for resuming a customer's service.

§ 704.385. Written Notice of Special Assistance Available to Elderly Persons and Persons with Disability:

A utility shall notify each new residential customer and all existing customers at least once a year that special assistance is available for elder and disabled persons having difficulty paying their bills on a timely basis.

§ 704.390. Notice of Termination of Service to Customer Who Is Elderly or Who Is Person with Disability:

A utility shall not terminate the service of a residence where an elder or disabled person resides unless it has notified some adult resident, either by phone or in person, at least 48 hours prior to termination. The utility must also notify any governmental agencies or other organizations that have notified the utility that they will assist customers in paying their utility bills.

***Telecommunications*—Nev. Admin. Code §§ 704.395–704.421**

Many of the substantive issues within the regulations governing telecommunications service are substantially similar to those dealing with gas and electric and are indicated accordingly.

* * *

§ 704.4045. Records of Utility:

Substantially similar to § 704.320, but records maintained for only 1 year.

* * *

§ 704.4065. Notice of Programs for Customers with Special Needs:

Provider shall notify each customer of programs that are available to assist customers who are elders, disabled, or have special needs.

* * *

§ 704.408. Application for Service:

May apply for service by mail or telephone, but application may be refused for fraud (past or present), intent to defraud, or for good cause.

§ 704.4085. Establishment of Credit:

Substantially similar to §§ 704.327 and 704.329.

§ 704.409. Deposit—Generally:

Substantially similar to § 704.329. The amount of a deposit shall not exceed twice the average monthly bill when actual usage can be determined, or the lesser of $100 or twice the amount of an average of an estimated monthly bill. Deposit amount is half of the aforementioned limits for elder customers eligible for assistance under the Link-up America program.

§ 704.4095. Payment of Deposit and Connection Fee:

Substantially similar to § 704.332.

§ 704.4105. Deposit Return:

Substantially similar to § 704.333.

§ 704.411. Cosigners and Guarantors:

Substantially similar to § 704.334.

§ 704.412. Contents of Bill for Service:

Substantially similar to § 704.336.

§ 704.4125. Payment of Bill for Service:

Substantially similar to § 704.339, except that a bill paid by mail is timely if received by the utility not more than 3 days after the past-due date. No provision regarding allowing customer to choose due date.

§ 704.413. Agreement for Deferred Payment of Bill:

Substantially similar to § 704.341, but customer must pay at least 40% of the delinquent amount at the time of the agreement and the balance in 3 equal consecutive monthly installments.

§ 704.4135. Apportionment of Partial Payment of Bill:

Partial payments shall be apportioned in a ratio that the charge for local service bears to the charge for toll service, unless customer specifies otherwise.

* * *

§ 704.4145. Resolution of Dispute Regarding Bill, Charge or Service:

Substantially similar to § 704.346.

§ 704.4151. Furnishing Local Service to Customer Who Fails to Pay Disputed Toll Charges and Files Complaint; Action upon Resolution of Complaint:

Customers who have failed to pay a disputed charge and have filed a complaint with the division shall be provided with local service if toll restrictions are available, and all outstanding local charges, fees, or deposits are paid.

* * *

§ 704.416. Grounds for Termination of Service:

Substantially similar to § 704.355, but notice must be given at least 5 days before scheduled termination.

§ 704.4165. Notice of Intended Termination of Service:

Substantially similar to § 704.360.

§ 704.417. Special Notice of Propose Termination When Dangerous to Health:

Substantially similar to § 704.390.

§ 704.4175. Designation and Notification of Third Persons:

Substantially similar to § 704.365.

§ 704.418. Refusal of Service and Termination Without Notice:

Substantially similar to §§ 704.348 and 704.350.

§ 704.4185. Postponement of Termination When Dangerous to Health:

Substantially similar to § 704.370.

§ 704.419. Postponement of Termination upon Agreement to Pay Delinquent Bill:

Substantially similar to § 704.372.

§ 704.4195. Restriction on Termination: Certain Delinquent Bills; Weekends and Holidays

A utility may not terminate for failure to pay for another class of service or for a bill incurred by a previous occupant, unless the customer has a written agreement to pay for this previous service. May not terminate on a weekend, a holiday, or the day before a weekend or holiday unless extraordinary conditions exist or the utility can reestablish service immediately in an emergency.

§ 704.4205. Contesting Propriety of Termination:

A customer may contest the propriety of a termination or scheduled termination to the division. The termination notice must include notice of this right, contact information for the division, notice that customer may be required to pay the disputed amount, with a refund if customer prevails, and notice of deposit and fee requirements for restoration of terminated service. The utility may include this information in its directory and cross-reference the directory in its termination notice.

§ 704.421. Resumption of Service:

Service must be restored if customer has complied with the utility's requirements; upon court or Commission order; in case of nonpayment, within 24 hours after payment, unless payment is received on a Friday, Saturday, Sunday, or legal holiday, in which case service should be restored by the end of the next business day.

Service must be restored immediately upon a determination that failure to resume would be especially dangerous to the health of the customer or a permanent resident of the premises.

NEW HAMPSHIRE

The Public Utility Commission's general regulations governing electric, gas, sewer, telephone, steam, and water can be found in N.H. Code Admin. R. Ann. PUC 1200–1204. Regulations dealing with each specific utility, although not summarized, can be found in N. H. Code Admin. R. Ann. PUC 300–310 (Electric); N.H. Code Admin. R. Ann. PUC 400–469 (Telephone); N.H. Code Admin. R. Ann. PUC 500–513 (Gas); N.H. Code Admin. R. Ann. PUC 600–610 (Water); N.H. Code Admin. R. Ann. PUC 701–708(Sewer); N.H. Code Admin. R. Ann. PUC 1101/-1107 (Steam). Access to the regulations can found at www.puc.state.nh.us/regulatory/rules.htm (last visited in May 2011).

***General (Electric, Gas, Sewer, Telephone, and Water)*—N.H. Code Admin. R. Ann. PUC 1200–1203**

* * *

1202.09. Due Date:

Bills are due no less than 25 calendar days from the bill day when the bill is sent electronically or via first class mail.

* * *

1203.01. Initiation of Basic Utility Service:

A utility may require written application. Service may not be denied to an otherwise qualified applicant based on income, home ownership, race, color, creed, gender, marital status, age (except for unemancipated minors), national origin, or disability.

1203.02. Information to Customers:

Upon receiving a request for new service, the utility shall provide information concerning the most advantageous rate or rates available to that customer. Utilities shall provide a complete description of its billing methods and rate schedules. The information must include the toll-free number for the Commission's consumer affairs division. If 25% or more of the customers in a utility's franchise area speak a particular foreign language, the required information must also be provided in that language. Gas and electric utilities must make available the Commission's pamphlet Consumers' Rights and Responsibilities by displaying copies in business offices, mailing them to any person requesting a copy, and notifying customers at least three times yearly that this pamphlet is available.

1203.03. Deposits:

New applicants may be required to pay a deposit or provide a guarantee or direct debit for issues relating to nonpayment that occurred within 3 years of present application (within 2 years if any utility has obtained judgment against person) or if a customer is unable to show that he or she intends to stay at the service location for at least 12 consecutive months, unless the customer can show six months without delinquency in accounts with similar utilities. When a utility requests a deposit, it must notify the customer that a deposit may be waived if a customer shows proof of financial hardship and has not interfered with or diverted utility service on the customer's premises. The customer must also be informed of the option to provide a guarantee or direct deposit in lieu of a deposit. A guarantor may be a social service organization, a municipal welfare agency, a bank, or a customer in good standing of the utility. In lieu of a deposit, the customer and the utility may arrange for automatic debits from the customer's bank account. If two successive debits are refused for insufficient funds, the utility may require a deposit.

Existing customers may be required to pay a deposit or provide a guarantee or direct deposit for numerous disconnection notices within the previous 12-month period, actual disconnection, or interference or diversion of services. If a customer files for bankruptcy, may require a deposit as permitted by bankruptcy law.

Deposits and guarantees shall be released after 12 consecutive months of timely payments. Deposits shall accrue interest at the prime rate.

A deposit shall be no less than $10 and no more than the total of 2 high-use months of actual or estimated usage. Deposits may be paid in three monthly installments, with the first upon demand, the second after 30 days, and the third after 60 days. A utility must give a customer a receipt for a deposit. A customer who disagrees with a deposit demand may request a conference with the Commission staff. Disconnection for nonpayment of a deposit must be postponed pending the result of this conference. A request for a deposit or guarantee may not be based on the income, home ownership, residential location, race, color, creed, gender, marital status, age, national origin, or disability.

1203.04. Meter Reading:

Meters shall be read at regular intervals. See PUC 300–600 for specific meter regulations concerning electric, gas, and water respectively.

1203.05. Implementation of Rate Changes:

The utility may collect under-billed revenues resulting from failure to implement approved rate changes only after approval from the Commission.

1203.06. Bill Forms:

All utility bills shall be delivered in regular intervals. All bills, except for telephone (see PUC 403.08) shall contain information concerning meter-reading dates, consumption amounts, due dates, amounts and penalties due, any information that will allow and assist in the computation of charges, and contact information of the Commission if a dispute with the utility cannot be resolved. Upon customer request, a utility must provide a clear and concise statement of actual consumption of service by the customer for each billing period during the prior year.

1203.07. Payment Arrangements:

When a customer is unable to pay a bill, a utility shall continue to provide service if the customer agrees to enter into a reasonable payment arrangement. A utility may disconnect without further notice for failure to comply with a payment arrangement, except in case of medical emergency. In case of medical emergency, telephone utility intending to terminate service for failure to enter into or comply with payment arrangement must give Commission 5 business days' notice.

1203.08. Penalties and Charges:

A utility may assess, per tariff and upon approval, penalties and charges for late payments. The Commission will approve a late charge only if the utility can demonstrate that the proposed charge does not exceed the actual costs incurred by the utility due to lateness. A utility may impose a bad-check charge of the greater of $5 or the actual administrative cost of recovery, as specified in the utility's tariff.

Late fees may be assessed only on non-financial-hardship customers. A customer who claims financial hardship must provide evidence to the utility on an annual basis.

* * *

1203.10. Termination of Service:

A utility may require a customer to provide notice of termination. Notice requirement shall not exceed 4 business days before termination. Customer is liable for service until the notice period expires.

1203.11. Disconnection of Service:

Telephone and sewer regulations concerning disconnection can be found at PUC 412.15 and PUC 703.03 respectively. Gas and electric utilities shall notify a customer 14 days prior to termination. The notice must be clear, concise, and conspicuously printed, and shall contain all information concerning the disconnection, consequences of disconnection, and information and methods of avoiding disconnection. Service may be disconnected, with notice, for issues related to nonpayment of past and present charges and bills, and for failure to allow access to residence. A utility may disconnect for a former customer's arrearage only if, during the period when the arrearage accrued, the present customer lived on the premises and received benefit of the service, and both present and former customer continue to reside there and receive the benefit of the service, and the former customer has refused to enter into a payment arrangement.

Disconnection shall only occur between 8:00 a.m. and 3:30 p.m., Monday–Thursday, and shall not occur the day of, or the day before a federal holiday, or when the Commission is not open to the public and the preceding day. Payment that would prevent disconnection at the customer's residence shall be accepted on the day of disconnection.

A utility shall grant a customer a conference to dispute a disconnection if the request is made at least 2 days before the date of disconnection.

Notice of disconnection is not required if service is obtained without utility authorization, a dangerous condition or emergency exists, or the premises are clearly abandoned, i.e., unoccupied and vacant for at least 60 days.

Service shall not be disconnected if the outstanding balance is less than 60 days past due and is less than $50; or if the arrears is due to non-basic utility service (e.g., merchandise, appliances or repairs); or if it is during the winter rule period (November 15–March 31); or if the utility has received certification within 60 days from a licensed physician that a medical emergency exists or would result from a disconnection; or if a municipal welfare office guarantees payment of the bills, and the customer agrees to enter into a payment arrangement for the arrearage. A utility that has received a medical certificate may disconnect only with authorization from the Commission. The rule prescribes detailed criteria for this authorization.

A utility need not accept payment from a customer to an employee, sent to the customer's premises to disconnect service, more than twice in 12 months. A utility may impose a charge for disconnection, if authorized in its tariffs. A utility may use a third-party collector, provided the collector complies with these rules, and the use of a third party is disclosed to the customer.

1203.12. Disconnection of Service in Residential Tenant/ Landlord Situations:

Substantially similar to 1203.11, but when the landlord is listed as the customer of record, each tenant must be notified at least 10 days before disconnection by posting on the premises and by delivery to each tenant through posting on or sliding under unit door, or by mail to named tenant or "occupant" mailed 14 days before disconnection. Tenants must be given an opportunity to take service in their own names, without being required to pay the landlord's arrearage, and must be informed of this option. If a tenant is erroneously disconnected without this notice, the utility must reconnect at no cost to the tenant and proceed to give proper notice.

1203.13. Reconnection of Service:

Service must be reconnected if the cause of disconnection has been corrected. If disconnection was for nonpayment, service must be reconnected if customer pays in full, or enters into payment agreement, or presents evidence of agreement with a welfare official or social services organization to pay the arrearage. The utility shall try to reconnect during business hours on the day of the request. The utility may make connection outside of business hours but is not required to do so except in case of a medical emergency. The Commission may order connection outside of business hours in case of medical emergency, risk of property damage, or other unusual circumstances creating a risk to health, safety, or property.

1203.14. Social Service Assistance:

The utility must provide the names and addresses of social services organizations that can provide assistance with utility bills. The utility must coordinate with these organizations so that it can receive notice, within 4 days of customer's request for assistance, if the organization will assist with the bill. The utility should continue to provide service during that 4-day period. The utility should provide the customer with a monthly accounting of billing and payment history during the period when the social service organization is paying the bill. Notice of disconnection shall not be sent to any customer receiving assistance in paying bills from social service organization unless such assistance has been exhausted or organization has failed to make payments.

1203.15. Denial of Service:

Subject to relevant statutes of limitations, a utility may deny service for outstanding charges or bills. After the statute has run, the utility may deny service if the utility has pursued recovery through the court system, or for a period of 3 years after the statute has run if the utility made reasonable, verifiable, documented collection efforts during the limitations period. New service may be denied upon proof that the application was to avoid payment of past services. Service may be denied for nonpayment by a previous customer only if applicant and former customer resided together and both received benefit of service where the arrearage occurred, both applicant and former customer will benefit from the service being applied for, and the applicant refuses to enter into a payment arrangement.

1203.16. Disconnection Conferences:

A utility shall grant a customer a conference to dispute a disconnection, by phone or in person at the customer's option, if the request has been made 1 or 2 days before the proposed date of disconnection. The utility may not disconnect before the latest of: 5 business days after the conference, 5 business days after the postmarked date of the utility's decision from the conference, or the disconnect date on the disconnect notice. At the conference, the utility must inform the customer of the right to a conference with Commission staff, if customer is dissatisfied with the utility's decision.

1203.17. Conference to Mediate Complaints Other Than Disconnection Complaints:

A conference among the consumer, the utility, and Commission staff may be held at the request of the customer, the utility, or the Commission to mediate complaints other than disconnection complaints.

1203.18. Transfer of Service:

If a utility receives a request to transfer service to a new name, or to add a new name to an account, it must give notice to the new customer within 5 days and may require written confirmation from the new customer. The original customer will remain liable until the new customer has been given the required notice.

* * *

***Winter Rules (Applicable to Electric, Gas, and Steam)*—N. H. Code Admin. R. Ann. PUC 1204.1–1204.6**

1204.1. Scope of Winter Rules:

The requirements of these rules are in addition to PUC 1203.11 and 1203.12.

1204.2. Applicability of Winter Rules:

Arrearages existing prior to the winter period (Nov. 15 through March 31, see 1202.19) will not make a customer eligible for disconnection unless the arrearages exceed, singly or combined with winter arrearages, the amounts specified in PUC 1204.03, below.

1204.03. Protection from Disconnection:

Before a notice of disconnection may be sent, overdue charges must exceed: $125 for gas non-heating customers, $225 for electric non-heating customers, or $450 for electric, gas, or steam heating customers. The utility must obtain Commission approval before disconnecting the service of residential customers known to be age 65 or older. No service may be disconnected during the winter period for nonpayment of a deposit or portion of a deposit.

1204.04. Payment Arrangements:

For non-financial hardship customers, payment plans may require payment of current bills when due and arrearages in equal installments over the winter period and 6 months following the winter period. For financial hardship customers, who must provide evidence of hardship annually, the winter payment plan may require payments of either 10% of the monthly total balance due for the duration of the winter or 10% of the total balance due and the projected future monthly bills. At the end of the winter period, customers with arrearages shall be given the opportunity to make a payment arrangement pursuant to PUC 1203.07, which shall include payment of arrearage in 6 equal monthly installments in addition to payment of current bills.

1204.05. Winter Period Notice of Disconnection:

In addition to compliance with 1203.11 and 1203.12, an adult occupant shall be notified in person or by phone at least 2 days, but not more than 8 days, before disconnection. If the utility is unable to notify an adult occupant, the utility shall seek commission approval pursuant to 201.05 before disconnecting service.

1204.06. Review of Pre-Winter Period Disconnections:

For customers who were disconnected between April 15 and October 15, whose accounts remain inactive on November 1, the utility shall send notice no later than November 7 advising them to contact the utility to arrange for reconnection. During the month of October, the utility must place at least two newspaper advertisements outlining the rights of customers with medical emergency or financial hardship, the availability of payment plans, and contact information for the utility, the Commission, and social service agencies that may provide assistance with utility bills. If a customer contacts the utility and states that there is a medical emergency, the utility must explain the procedure pursuant to Rule 1203.11. A customer who contacts the utility and provides evidence of financial hardship must be offered a payment arrangement whereby payment of 10% of the outstanding balance will be sufficient to restore service and must be provided with contact information for social service organizations that may help if customer cannot make the minimum payment.

NEW JERSEY

The New Jersey Board of Public Utilities' regulations governing all utilities are codified within N.J. Admin. Code §§ 14:3-1.1–14:3-13.3 and contains the basic rules regarding applications for service, payments, deposits, termination of service, resolution of disputes, and related topics. In some cases, it may be important to consult N.J. Admin. Code §§ 14:5-1.1–14:5-9.10 for rules specific to electric service (regarding electric meters); N.J. Admin. Code §§ 14:6-1.1–14:6-7.9 for rules specific to gas service (regarding meters); N.J. Admin. Code §§ 14:9-1.1–14:9-9.1 for rules specific to water and wastewater service; or N.J. Admin. Code §§ 14:10-1.1–14:10-12 App. B for rules specific to telephone service. Access (on a limited basis) to the regulations can be found at www.state.nj.us/bpu/agenda/rules.

***General Rules (All Utilities)*—N.J. Admin. Code §§ 14:3-1.1–14:3-13.3**

* * *

§ 14:3-3.2. Customer Applications for Service:

Customer may apply for service in person, by regular mail, by fax, by e-mail (if available), and by phone. Utilities may require proof of identity and proof of prior address as part of application. The rule lists acceptable forms of identification and proof of former address. A Social Security number may not be required. A utility may not add the name of a second person to a residential account unless specifically requested by that person. Utilities shall usually begin service within 2 business days from receiving application.

§ 14:3-3.3. Providing Information to Customer:

Utilities shall provide customer with "Customer Bill of Rights" either when customer receives first bill or within 30 days of beginning of service.

Utilities must provide customers with information promoting energy conservation.

§ 14:3-3.4. Deposits for Service:

A deposit may be required, taking into account the customer's history regarding payment of utility bills. The amount of the deposit may be determined by adding the average monthly charge (excluding amounts paid in advance) plus 1 month's average bill. If actual bills show the amount to be too high or low, it may be modified. An existing customer may be required to pay (or increase) a deposit upon failing to pay a bill within 15 days of the due date. If a utility requires a deposit or requires applicants to establish a credit record, these requirements must be applied uniformly throughout the utility's territory and must be posted on the company website, if any. The utility must provide a receipt for a deposit. The utility must inform the customer of the interest rate and provide a receipt. Displaying the amount of the deposit on the customer's bill is an acceptable receipt. If a utility other than a telephone utility provides unmetered service for which payment is required in advance, it may not require other guarantees to secure payment.

§ 14:3-3.5. Return of Deposits, Interest on Deposits:

Utilities shall return deposits promptly with interest when an account is closed. Utilities shall offer to refund the deposit in a check or as a credit. Utilities shall review residential accounts every year and nonresidential accounts every other year and refund a deposit if a customer has established satisfactory credit. Utilities shall pay interest at least once on deposits held for 12 months. The interest shall be computed at a rate equal to the average yields on new 6-month Treasury bills.

§ 14:3-3.6. Access to Customer's Premises:

The utility has a right of access to customers' premises at reasonable times for meter reading, inspection, testing, repairing, or removal of utility property.

§ 14:3-3.7. Interruptions of Service:

Utilities shall exercise reasonable diligence to avoid service interruptions and shall keep records of reported service interruptions for 1 year. Telecommunications utilities shall comply with provisions in § 14:10-1A.14.

§ 14:3-3.8. Service Call Scheduling:

If a customer's presence is required for a service call, the company must notify the customer that he or she may request a specific time or, at maximum, a 4-hour block of time during normal business hours. If the utility is unable to keep the appointment, it must notify the customer by the close of business on the business day preceding the scheduled appointment and must reschedule the service call within 24 hours, unless good cause is shown.

14:3-3A.1. Basis of Discontinuance of Service:

Utilities shall give reasonable notice before they terminate service when it can reasonably be given. Utilities may terminate service for a variety of grounds including nonpayment of a valid bill, tampering with a utilities' facility, fraudulent representation relating to use of service, customer moves, providing the utility's service to another without the utility's permission, and refusing to allow reasonable access to customer's premises for necessary purposes connected with service provided by utilities.

Except in a safety-related emergency, utilities may terminate only between 8:00 a.m. and 4:00 p.m. Monday through Thursday and may not discontinue on a state holiday or the day before a state holiday.

If a customer wishes to discontinue service, he or she must give 48 hours' notice to the utility. If this is not done, the customer remains liable for service until the final meter reading is taken.

§ 14.3-3A.2. Discontinuance for Nonpayment:

Except for telephone service, utilities cannot terminate service unless the amount due is more than $100 or the amount due is delinquent for more than 3 months. A utility may not disconnect nor threaten disconnection for nonpayment of charges for repairs, merchandise, installation of conservation measures, optional services, or other non-tariff charges. Residential service may not be disconnected for nonpayment of business service, except in cases of diversion of service.

Before discontinuing residential service for nonpayment, utilities shall follow certain procedures, and electric and gas utility must attempt to notify an adult residing at the premises. If, at time of termination, the customer offers full payment or a reasonable portion thereof, the utility employee must accept the payment, give the customer a receipt, and not disconnect.

Electric and gas utilities cannot terminate service to any residential customer for nonpayment when the high temperature for the next 24 hours is expected to be at or below 32° Fahrenheit. Electric and gas utilities cannot terminate service to customers eligible for the Winter Termination Program (§ 14:3-3A.5) from November 15 through March 15.

Electric utilities cannot terminate service for nonpayment when the customer is eligible for the Winter Termination Program and the high temperature is forecast to be 95° Fahrenheit or more at any time during the following 48 hours.

Utilities cannot terminate residential service for nonpayment for up to 60 days when a medical emergency exists that would be aggravated by discontinuing service. Utility may require customer to provide reasonable proof of inability to pay and written physician's statement stating the emergency, its nature and duration, and that discontinuance will aggravate the emergency. The customer remains liable for the payment of services rendered. The Board may, for good cause shown, extend the 60-day period. The customer must make a written request for extension, accompanied by an updated physician's certificate.

A utility may not discontinue service for nonpayment of a disputed charge if customer has paid the non-disputed amount and requested a Board investigation.

§ 14:3-3A.3. Notice of Discontinuance for Nonpayment:

Before a utility terminates service, it must send the customer notice no earlier than 15 days from the postmark date of the outstanding bill. The notice should provide customers with at least 10 days' written notice of their intent to disconnect. Notice is to be sent first class and in a separate mailing than the bill. Notice shall be available in Spanish upon request. During the heating season, notice must be accompanied by a board-approved Winter Termination Program fact sheet in English and Spanish.

§ 14:3-3A.4. Additional Notice Requirements for Discontinuance of Residential and Special Customers:

Every year, utilities shall tell all residential customers that, if the customer makes a request, notice of intent to terminate service can be sent to a designated third party in addition to customers.

Utilities shall make good faith efforts to notify customers over the age of 65, by telephone in addition to regular mail, of intent to terminate service.

Electric and gas utilities shall solicit information from their customers at least semi-annually about the presence of any life-sustaining equipment on the premises.

The written notice of intent to terminate service for residential customers shall include information concerning how to dispute a charge or the bill and information concerning deferred payment arrangement. Electric and gas utilities shall include additional information on the back of the notice, under the caption "Statement of Customer's Rights," about how to challenge a bill.

§ 14:3-3A.5. Winter Termination Program for Residential Electric and Gas Service:

Electric and gas utilities shall not terminate service for nonpayment from November 15 through April 1 for residential customers who receive Lifeline, HEAP, TANF, SSI, Pharmaceutical Assistance to the Aged and Disabled (PAAD), GA or USF benefits or for customers who cannot pay utility bills because of circumstances beyond their control. Customers who are eligible for, and seek the protection of, the winter protection plan must enroll in a budget payment plan on an annual basis. During the winter protection period, customers must make good faith payments equal to the budget payment amount, if possible, or a lesser amount for those who do not have the ability to pay the full amount. Utilities shall refer disputes about good faith payments to the Utility Commission (BPU). During the heating season, no utility may request a deposit or an increase in a deposit from a customer who is eligible for, and requests participation in, the winter protection program. Residential gas or electric customers who have had their service disconnected and have not reconnected by November 15 can have their service connected if they make a down payment of up to 25% of the outstanding balance. Customers in the Winter Termination Program who receive LIHEAP or other energy assistance shall forward that amount to their electric or gas utility if that utility is the major supplier of heat. Electric or gas utilities can terminate service for tampering with the utility's facilities but shall follow specific procedures.

§ 14:3-3A.6. Discontinuance of Service to Tenants:

Electric, gas, water, and wastewater utilities shall make every reasonable effort to find out if a landlord-tenant relationship exists at a location. Utilities cannot terminate service for nonpayment if the tenants are the end-users but not the customers unless the utilities have given a 15-day notice in writing to the owner and to the tenants. Utilities shall offer the tenant the option to continue individual service. The provision of individual service may not be conditioned on the tenant's payment of outstanding bills due on the account of any other person. If the landlord requests, electric or gas utility must notify the landlord if a tenant's service is being voluntarily or involuntarily discontinued and service will be transferred to the landlord's name.

§ 14:3-3A.7. Notification to Municipalities of Discontinuance of Residential Gas and Electric Service:

Upon request, gas and electric utilities shall provide all municipalities in their service area with a daily list of all customers whose gas or electric service was terminated on the previous day.

§ 14:3-3A.8. Discontinuance of a Residential Customer's Telephone Service:

Basic residential local telephone service (BRLTS) providers may terminate basic local telephone service only for nonpayment of basic local telephone service charges of more than $30. BRLTS providers shall give at least 10 days' written notice before disconnecting basic telephone service and shall tell customers that they can make partial payments. BRLTS providers can deny or block non-basic telephone service (for example, long distance or call waiting) when non-basic charges are more than $20. A local provider may offer consumers a credit limit option for non-basic services, which will be blocked if consumer exceeds that limit. Partial payments by residential customers must be applied first to basic services. If a customer alleges that slamming has occurred, the portion of the bill attributable to the slamming must be treated as disputed. Service may not be discontinued for those charges, nor partial payments applied to them.

§ 14:3-3A.9. Basis for Restoration:

Utilities shall restore service within 12 hours when payment of all charges is received and when conditions causing disconnection of service are corrected. In case of discontinuance for nonpayment, a utility may require a deposit. Payment of the deposit may not be required prior to the restoration; the utility shall bill the customer for the deposit and allow 15 days to pay or make other reasonable payment arrangements with the customer.

* * *

§ 14:3-4.5. Meter Tests at a Customer's Request:

A customer is entitled, upon request, to one free meter testing in a 12-month period. A customer may request a test by a Board inspector. The fee for this test is $5, which will be refunded if the meter tests more than 2% fast (more than 1.5% in the case of water meters).

§ 14:3-4.6. Adjustment of Charges for Meter Error:

If a meter is found to be fast by more than 2% (1.5% for water meters), the utility must refund the overcharge for the period since the meter became inaccurate, if known, otherwise for the shorter of (i) the time the meter has served the customer, (2) one-half the time between the earlier of last meter test or time when meter was taken out of service, or (3) one-half the statutorily allowed time between tests plus the lesser of period from last test or when meter was taken out of service. If the meter is slow, the utility may not back-bill unless there was theft or tampering; the meter wholly failed to register; or the customer reasonably should have known that the bill did not reflect actual usage. In case of tampering, immediate payment may be required; otherwise the payment may be amortized over a period of time equal to the time the customer was undercharged.

* * *

§ 14:3-7.1. Billing General Provisions:

A utility must either provide discontinuance notices in English and Spanish or include on its bills a statement, in Spanish, that customers may request Spanish termination notices and must provide a toll-free number for customers to make this request.

If an overpayment due to billing error is not paid or credited within 2 billing cycles after customer points out the error, the utility must pay interest at the same rate prescribed for deposits.

Late charges may not be imposed on residential customers or on state, county, or municipal government entities.

All bills must include contact information for the Board of Public Utilities.

§ 14:3-7.2. Form of Bill for Metered Service:

Utilities shall include specific information in bill for metered service, including meter readings, date of meter reading, and applicable rate schedule. Bills must clearly indicate the method used to calculate the bill (for example, electronic reading, estimate, or budget billing) and must explain the conversion from meter reading to billing units. Utilities shall read or make a reasonable effort to read meters regularly but may bill residential customers based on estimated usage. Utility must send notice to customer on the fifth and seventh month after 4 months of estimated billing that a meter reading must be obtained at risk of discontinuance upon passage of 8 months since last reading. Customers may amortize if low estimates result in an actual bill that is 25% greater than the estimated bills. If a utility seeks to replace or modify its method of actual meter readings, e.g., by automation, it must obtain Board approval.

§ 14:3-7.3. Form of Bill for Unmetered Service:

Bills must show the time period, applicable rate schedule (or statement that this will be furnished on request), gross and/or net amount of bill, and due date.

§ 14:3-7.4. Method of Billing:

Utilities may bill monthly, bi-monthly, or quarterly either in written or electronic form if the customer requests electronic billing. In ''unusual credit situations,'' bills may be rendered at shorter intervals. A utility furnishing unmetered service, including a telephone utility, may—on uniform, nondiscriminatory terms—require payment in advance for one billing period. Utilities shall prorate bills when service is begun or ended within a billing period.

§ 14:3-7.5. Budget Billing Plans for Residential Accounts:

Gas, electric, water, and wastewater utilities that do not bill according to a flat rate shall have voluntary budget billing and payment plans available upon request for residential customers. Among other things, at least once during the budget year, the monthly budget amount shall be compared with average usage and adjusted if there is an increase or decrease of 25% or more in the monthly budget amount. Budget billing is voluntary, except that gas or electric customers who seek Winter Termination Program protection are required to participate in budget billing.

§ 14:3-7.6. Disputes As to Bills:

A customer who disputes a bill must pay all undisputed charges. If the utility and the customer cannot reach an agreement, the utility must advise the customer that he or she has 5 days to request an investigation by the Board. If the customer requests an investigation, all collection activity must cease until the dispute is resolved. The Board may require the consumer to place the disputed amount in escrow.

§ 14:3-7.7. Deferred Payment Agreements:

The utility must make a good faith effort to provide a customer presently unable to pay with a fair and reasonable deferred-payment plan that takes into account the customer's financial circumstances. The down payment for a residential customer should not exceed 25% of the amount due. If one utility provides more than one service, it must offer a separate plan for each service or the option of having one service discontinued while the customer makes payments on the other. If the customer's circumstances change for reasons beyond his or her control, the utility must renegotiate the plan. If the customer breaches a payment agreement, the utility may discontinue service following the usual notice. If the customer breaches a payment agreement for one kind of service, the utility may discontinue only that kind of service. A utility is not required to offer more than one plan, per type of service, per year (except that the Board may require it to do so "if such action is reasonable").

§ 14:3-7.8. Diversion of Service:

Electric, gas, water and wastewater utilities cannot require tenant-customers (defined to include condominium owners) to pay for diverted service. Tenant-customers may make a request in writing for a diversion investigation if they think the level of consumption reflected in their bill is unreasonably high. Utilities shall investigate, provide a written report to the tenant-customer, landlord, and beneficiary, and try to reach an agreement with the parties.

* * *

NEW MEXICO

The Public Utility Commission's regulations governing electric and gas service can be found at N.M. Code R. §§ 17.5.410.1–17.5.410.44. Regulations governing water and sewer, not summarized below, are substantially similar to the regulations for gas and electric, and are contained in N.M. Code R. § 17.12.760 and § 17.13.960, respectively. Although the majority of regulations governing telecommunications services can be found in N.M. Code R. §§ 17.11.16.1–17.11.16.34, many of the substantive issues within the regulations are substantially similar to those governing gas and electric and are indicated accordingly. The regulation governing unauthorized charges and/or changes in telephone service provider (cramming and slamming) can be found at N.M. Code R. §§ 17.11.8.1–17.11.8.15. Access to the regulations can be found at www.nmcpr.state.nm.us/nmac/_title17/title17.htm.

Electric and Gas—**N.M. Code R. §§ 17.5.410.1–17.5.410.44**

§ 17.5.410. Residential Customer Service by Gas, Electric and Rural Electric Cooperative Utilities:

* * *

§ 17.5.410.8. Application:

Utility shall not unreasonably discriminate or penalize a customer for exercising their rights under this title.

§ 17.5.410.9. Exemption and Variance:

If an unreasonable hardship with no reasonable alternative exists, a customer may request a temporary or permanent exemption from this title.

§ 17.5.410.10. Rendition of Bills:

Bills shall be rendered regularly and shall contain the amount of charges and usage for each service. Utility shall notify customers of rate changes and their impact on customers.

§ 17.5.410.11. Budget Payment Plans:

Budget or levelized payment plans shall be available to customers. A utility may remove a chronically delinquent customer (i.e., one disconnection or three delinquent bills within the past 12 months) from the budget plan and withhold the plan from that customer for up to 12 months.

§ 17.5.410.12. Contents of Bills:

All bills shall contain information concerning dates and itemization of charges, due dates, amounts and penalties due, any information that will allow and assist in the computation of charges, and utility address where customer may inquire or complain regarding bill. Estimated bills must be clearly and conspicuously identified as estimates.

§ 17.5.410.13. Payment Standards:

Due dates shall be at least 20 calendar days from the rendering of a bill and shall be past due at least 15 days before deemed delinquent. The due date shall be the following day if the due date falls on a Sunday, a legal holiday, or a day that the utility's office that receives payment is not open to the public.

§ 17.5.410.14. Finance, Service, Carrying, Penalty and Special Service Charges:

Unless approved by the Commission, a utility shall not assess finance, service, carrying, or penalty charges for outstanding balances. Charges for special services may be included in the same bill as utility charges but must be clearly and separately designated. Partial payments must be applied first to any arrearage for utility charges. Connection and re-connection charges may not exceed the actual cost involved but shall be no less than the minimum allowed in the tariff.

§ 17.5.410.15. Estimated Bills:

Except for a seasonal customer, a utility shall not estimate billing unless the utility is unable to get an actual reading through no fault of its own because the customer makes it unreasonably difficult, a meter is defective or has been tampered with, or other extraordinary conditions exist. A utility may not estimate bills for more than 2 consecutive billing periods absent an agreement with the customer, and it shall get an actual reading at least annually. A utility shall provide a method and instructions by which customers are allowed to read their own meters. Customers shall be offered payment plans for underestimated bills. If a utility underestimates a bill and then seeks to correct it, the customer must be given an opportunity to participate in an installment payment plan for the under-billed amount.

§ 17.5.410.16. Residential Security Deposits or Guarantees:

A deposit may be required for unsatisfactory credit, chronic delinquency (disconnected or 3 delinquent payments in the last year—see § 17.5.410.7), reconnection after discontinuance of service, or unauthorized use of utility services.

§ 17.5.410.17. Methods to Establish Acceptable Credit Rating:

Credit may be established by a customer or a guarantor through home ownership, fulltime employment for at least 1 year, proof a regular source of income, or an adequate credit reference from a commercial source or prior utility. A utility is to consider low-income, elder, or disabled status when determining amount of deposit. If an applicant cannot establish acceptable credit, but previously received service in the name of a spouse, the utility may consider prior utility service to that spouse in determining whether and in what amount to charge a deposit.

§ 17.5.410.18. Amounts of and Accounting of Security Deposits:

A deposit shall not be more than 1/6 of an annual estimated bill or more than 1.5 times the amount of an estimated maximum monthly bill. Utility shall provide a receipt of a deposit and interest shall accrue annually. A utility must provide a procedure by which a customer who cannot produce the receipt may obtain the return of a deposit.

§ 17.5.410.19. Refund of Deposit, Termination of Guarantee:

Deposits or guarantees shall be returned, credited, or terminated after 12 months of service without being chronically delinquent.

* * *

§ 17.5.410.21. Internal Utility Complaint Procedures:

Utility shall establish procedures to receive, investigate, and resolve complaints to both English and non-English-speaking customers. A utility must have qualified personnel available during business hours to respond to questions, complaints, and service requests and to negotiate settlement agreements. Qualified personnel or other reasonable means must be available at all times to respond to customer reports of emergency conditions.

* * *

§ 17.5.410.23. Public Notice of Residential Customer's Rights:

Utility shall make available to customers, in English and Spanish, information concerning rights, responsibilities, remedies, and procedures associated with rates, charges, and services.

* * *

§ 17.5.410.25. Assistance to Customers:

The utility shall assist residential customers in choosing appropriate service. The utility shall maintain customer records for 3 years. Upon a customer's request, the utility shall provide copies of that customer's records to the customer or, in case of a dispute, to any person authorized by the customer. The utility must correct any undisputed mistakes in a customer's payment history that are brought to its attention.

* * *

§ 17.5.410.29. Discontinuance of Service:

A utility may terminate service without notice for unauthorized use of service, tampering or damaging equipment, use that is detrimental to customers, or if a hazardous condition exists.

A utility shall give at least 15 days' notice before discontinuance of service resulting from nonpayment of charges or deposit or noncompliance with a payment agreement.

A utility shall give at least 3 days' notice for discontinuance of service resulting from refusal of access by customer or provisions of required permits.

§ 17.5.410.30. Prohibitions on Discontinuance of Service:

Service shall not be discontinued for nonpayment for special services or services of a different class, disputed charges, amounts due from another account of guarantor, services at another location (although unpaid balances may be transferred to other accounts), or prior occupant's delinquent accounts unless the prior occupant continues to reside at the premises, or a court has found the current occupant liable for the former occupant's debt.

§ 17.5.410.31. Requirements Prior to Discontinuance of Service to Subsection B of 17.5.410.29 NMAC:

Before discontinuance pursuant to § 17.5.410.29 (nonpayment) the utility must send notice at least 15 days before the disconnection date. The notice must be in simple language, in both English and Spanish. Notice shall also contain all information concerning the disconnection, amounts due, consequences of disconnection, and information and methods of avoiding disconnection, including but not limited to winter protection plans (November 15–March 15), remedies, assistance, and postpone of discontinuance for low-income, ill, elder, and disabled customers.

At least 2 days before discontinuance, the utility must make reasonable efforts to remind the customer of the pending discontinuance and of the available of financial assistance and the protections for serious illness. Disconnection will be postponed for 30 days (or service will be reconnected) if the utility receives a certificate from a health professional stating that discontinuance will endanger life or health and a financial certification, and customer enters into a settlement agreement or deferred payment plan. (Forms for medical and financial certification are found in §§ 17.5.410.43 and 17.5.410.44.) The utility must offer customers the right to designate a third party to receive notices. A utility must arrange a payment plan for any customer not chronically delinquent (one disconnection or three late payments within one 12-month period) who claims an inability to afford charges. A utility may disconnect only between 8:00 a.m. and 3:00 p.m. and may not disconnect less than 24 hours prior to a holiday or weekend, unless personnel are available to accept payments and restore service during that holiday or weekend. Between November 15 and March 15, the utility must postpone discontinuance for 15 days if it receives a certification that customer is eligible for low-income heating assistance and that the agency will make payment within 15 days after the scheduled disconnect date.

§ 17.5.410.32. Emergency Discontinuance of Service:

A utility may discontinue without notice for reasons of health, safety, operation, maintenance or state of emergency.

§ 17.5.410.33. Restoration of Service:

A utility shall reconnect services no later than the next business day upon receiving payment, plus any reconnection fees, of the amount owed or an amount curing a default on a payment plan. If a medical certificate and financial certificate are received, the utility must reestablish service within 12 hours.

§ 17.5.410.34. Notice by Residential Customer:

Customer may initially notify utility of a disputed charge but shall provide written notice within 5 days after initial notice. Customers shall pay undisputed portion of charges before discontinuance is scheduled to occur.

* * *

§ 17.5.410.36. Determination of Disputed Amount:

If a customer and a utility cannot agree to the undisputed amount, the customer shall pay an amount based on either yearly or monthly consumption.

* * *

§ 17.5.410.38. Adjustment of Bills:

Incorrect bills due to meter or billing error shall be adjusted pursuant to NMPUC Rules 560.22 and 650.22.

§ 17.5.410.39. Notice of Right to File Complaint with Commission:

When a customer and utility confer to resolve a dispute, the utility must advise the customer of the right to appeal to the Commission within 7 days and provide contact information for the Commission.

§ 17.5.410.40. Settlement Agreements to Be in Writing:

Settlement agreements extending beyond 45 days must be in writing. A utility is not required to enter into a settlement agreement with a chronically delinquent customer (one disconnection or three late payments within 12 months) but should give "special consideration" to customers who are elder, disabled, or low-income in deciding whether to offer plans to chronically delinquent customers.

§ 17.5.410.41. Installment Payments:

This section sets the criteria for determining reasonable installment payments and the information to be provided to installment plan customers.

§ 17.5.410.42. Failure to Comply with Settlement Agreement:

If a customer fails to comply with a settlement agreement, the utility may disconnect upon 7 days' notice, in the form provided for in this section. During the winter heating season, the utility must follow the procedures of § 5.410.31, above.

* * *

***Telecommunications (Slamming and Cramming Protections)*—N.M. Code R. §§ 17.11.8.1–17.11.8.15**

* * *

§ 17.11.8. Slamming and Cramming Protection

* * *

§ 17.11.8.9. Prohibited Acts:

Unless the change in service or charge is customer initiated, submission, initiation, or actual change in a customer's provider or charges to a customer's account shall only occur upon verifiable written or oral authorization.

§ 17.11.8.10. Customer Authorizations:

Authorization of charges or change in service shall be void unless signed by the customer and obtained using a full and complete description of the change or charge that is distinguishable from all other provider correspondence, or a complete recording of an oral agreement that provides the same disclosures, and shall not occur until authorization has been obtained. A customer's authorization is void if obtained using a sweepstakes, contest, or drawing entry form.

§ 17.11.8.11. Information on Customer Telephone Bills:

All bills shall contain information concerning dates and itemization of charges or change in service, due dates, amounts and penalties due, any information that will allow and assist in the computation of charges, contact information of the utility to inquire about or dispute a charge, and information informing customers that they may be absolved from liability for unauthorized changes or charges for a period of 90 days from the date they appeared on the bill.

If a bill includes charges for local exchange services, it must clearly distinguish between charges for which nonpayment will lead to disconnection, and charges that will not. Charges that will not lead to disconnection must be clearly and conspicuously identified. At least twice a year, by bill stuffer or separate mailing, the utility must explain the procedure for resolving complaints about unauthorized charges or changes, including contact information for the Commission.

§ 17.11.8.12. Resolution of Customer Complaints and Disputes:

Customers may register complaints concerning unauthorized changes or charges to the authorized or unauthorized provider, or the local exchange service company. Upon receipt of a complaint, all collection efforts shall immediately cease.

Written complaints must be submitted to Consumer Relations Division of the Commission Staff and shall contain a copy of the bill, a brief description of the unauthorized change or charge and amount, and an outline of any resolution attempts (include names, contact information, and dates of resolution attempts).

Within 14 days of notice from Commission of complaint, the provider at issue shall submit verification to the Commission for review. Customers shall have 30 days to contest Commission findings.

§ 17.11.8.13. Payment of Disputed Charges:

Collection and disconnection efforts shall not occur unless and until a disputed change or charge is resolved in the provider's favor.

A change or charge found to be unauthorized shall be, within 30 days, refunded and/or removed from the customer's bill, credited to a customer's original account, and result in restoration of customer's original service. Any additional cost due to lack of authorization shall be borne by the violating provider.

Complaints not within the initial 90-day absolution period shall be allowed per Commission review.

§ 17.11.8.14. Sale and Verification of Telecommunications Services:

All providers must approve all sales scripts and written materials used by their sellers. Sellers must make adequate inquiry to ensure that the person they are speaking with is the customer. Sellers must identify themselves and the services they are selling and must explain the terms and price and any fees for change of provider. Sellers may not use false or misleading information or "tactics that could be considered by a prudent person to be pressure tactics."

* * *

***Telecommunications*—N.M. Code R. §§ 17.11.16.1–17.11.16.34**

Many of the substantive issues within the regulations governing telecommunications are substantially similar to those governing gas and electric and are indicated accordingly.

* * *

§ 17.11.16. Consumer Protection:

* * *

§ 17.11.16.8. Disconnection of Basic Local Exchange Service (LEC) and Allocation of Partial Payments:

An LEC shall not disconnect local services for failure to pay toll charges or discretionary services. Toll blocking shall be provided at no charge if requested by a customer. Involuntary toll blocking may be imposed for failure to pay toll charges. Partial payments shall be credited to local services unless requested differently, in writing, by the customer.

* * *

§ 17.11.16.11. Access to Service and Rate Information:

Carriers must have a toll-free number for service and rate information; must provide information to disabled customers in a form accessible to them; must provide information in English and Spanish, at the customer's request; and may provide information electronically if the customer agrees in writing. Carriers must provide detailed information about rates, charges, termination procedures, availability of service, charges for repair service, how to subscribe, and prompt notice of any change in rates. Customers must be notified of the availability of low-income assistance, third-party notification, and 900-number blocking.

§ 17.11.16.12. Fair Marketing Practices:

Carriers must provide accurate information, may not describe discretionary services as essential or engage in other unfair, deceptive or unconscionable trade practices, and must assist customers, upon request, to obtain the most economical service. The Commission may require a carrier to submit its sales scripts or other marketing materials for review.

* * *

§ 17.11.16.14. Bills:

Substantially similar to § 17.5.410.12 and must include itemization of any repair charges for work on the customer's side of the interface.

§ 17.11.16.15. Information Required Semi-Annually:

LECs must inform customers semi-annually in English and Spanish that local service will not be disconnected for nonpayment of toll or discretionary service and that third-party notification, low-income assistance, service and rate information are available, among other things.

§ 17.11.16.16. Billing Disputes and Errors, General Refunds and Bill Credits:

A customer may be required to pay undisputed amount. Utility shall offer payment plans for billing resulting from utility error. A credit or refund for over-billing is due no later than the second bill. Under-billing may be added to the customer's next bill but shall be subject to an interest-free payment plan if the amount exceeds the customer's average monthly bill for the previous 6 months.

§ 17.11.16.17. Discontinuance or Interruption of Service:

Substantially similar to § 17.5.410.29.

§ 17.11.16.18. Prohibitions on Discontinuance of Service:

Substantially similar to § 17.5.410.30.

§ 17.11.16.19. Requirements Prior to Discontinuance of Service:

Substantially similar to § 17.5.410.31. The utility must advise the customer of the existence of low-income assistance (LITAP) and how to apply.

§ 17.11.16.20. Payment Plans:

An LEC must attempt to negotiate a payment plan with a customer who has not been chronically delinquent and indicates an inability to pay. The LEC may not discontinue while negotiations are in progress. LECs must provide a procedure for reviewing customer allegations that payment plans are unaffordable, that a charge is not due, or that a customer has not defaulted on a payment plan.

§ 17.11.16.21. Restoration of Services:

Substantially similar to § 17.5.410.33.

§ 17.11.16.22. Complaints and Appeals:

A carrier must make a good faith effort to respond to and resolve customer complaints. If the complaint cannot be resolved, the carrier must provide the customer with contact information, including the toll-free number for the Commission's Consumer Relations Division. Upon receipt of a consumer complaint forwarded by the Commission, a carrier must make an initial response within 10 days.

§ 17.11.16.23. Customer Deposit Policy:

A carrier that requires deposits must have an equitable, nondiscriminatory, written policy for establishment or re-establishment of credit. The decision may not be based on location, income level, source of income, occupation, race, creed, sex, sexual orientation, national origin, marital status, or number of dependents.

§ 17.11.16.24. Criteria for Establishing the Need for and the Amount of Deposit:

An LEC may require a deposit from an existing customer in case of "substantial nonpayment for intrastate services provided by the LEC" twice in the past 6 months or 3 times in the past 12 months. A deposit may be required for restoration of service after nonpayment. In lieu of a deposit, the customer may provide a guarantee for not more than the amount of the deposit. The guarantee will be terminated after 12 months of satisfactory payment. The Commission may authorize an LEC to waive deposit requirements for certain low-income customers. Deposit or amount of guarantee shall not exceed more than 3 months of estimated service. The requirement of a deposit may be disputed.

§ 17.11.15.25. Limitations on the Use of Deposits:

Making a deposit does not relieve a customer of the duty to pay current bills when due. A carrier may not apply a deposit for one carrier's services to services provided by another carrier. An LEC may not require a deposit for or refuse to provide local service because of indebtedness for toll or discretionary services. A carrier may not require any security other than a deposit or a guarantee. No indebtedness to a carrier may result in a mortgage or security interest in any real or personal property, unless that indebtedness has been reduced to judgment by a court.

§ 17.11.16.26. Interest on Deposits:

Deposits shall accrue simple interest at the greater of the rate specified in N.M. Stat. Ann. § 62-13-13 or the rate charged by the carrier for late payment.

§ 17.11.16.27. Deposit Records:

The carrier must provide customers with receipts for deposits and keep records of deposits for 1 year after the deposit is returned.

§ 17.11.16.28. Refund of Deposits:

Substantially similar to § 17.5.410.19.

§ 17.11.16.29. Privacy:

Adopts by reference FCC's rules regarding privacy of consumer proprietary network information.

§ 17.11.16.30. Confidentiality; Operator Assisted Calls:

Operators and employees must regard customer communications as confidential; may not listen, except as necessary to provide operator services; may not divulge any information inadvertently overheard.

§ 17.11.16.31. Trouble Isolation Charge Prohibited:

Upon a customer's report of trouble on a line, the LEC must determine, without charge to the customer, whether the trouble is on the LEC or the customer side of the interface.

* * *

§ 17.11.16.33. Medical Certification Form:

This section provides medical certification form for serious or chronic illness.

§ 17.11.16.34. Financial Certification Form:

This section provides financial certification form for serious or chronic illness.

* * *

NEW YORK

The Public Service Commission's regulation governing electric, gas and steam can be found within N.Y. Comp. Codes R. & Regs. tit. 16, §§ 11.1–11.32; N.Y. Comp. Codes R. & Regs. tit. 16, §§ 14.1–14.20 contains the regulations governing water utilities; N.Y. Comp. Codes R. & Regs. tit. 16, §§ 609.1–609.17 contains the general regulations governing telephone utilities. Many of the substantive issues governing water and telephone utilities are substantially similar to those governing electric, gas, and steam and are indicated accordingly. Access to the regulations can be found at www.dps.state.ny.us/brochures.html (last visited in May 2011).

***General (Electric, Gas, and Steam)*—N.Y. Comp. Codes R. & Regs. tit. 16, §§ 11.1–11.39**

* * *

§ 11.3. Applications for Residential Service:

Utility shall provide service within 5 days upon receipt of a written or oral application. A utility may require reasonable proof of an applicant's identity. A utility may require a written application if there are arrears or evidence of tampering at the premises and may require a lease or other proof of the date when applicant first became responsible for services to the premises. If a customer moves to a new address within the utility's service area and applies for service within 60 days, this must be treated as a continuation of the previous service, provided that prior service was not terminated or suspended for nonpayment, theft, or tampering. Written notice of a denial to provide service shall be made within 3 days and shall contain the reason for denial, the remedy for denial, and information necessary to dispute the denial.

Service may be denied for issues relating to nonpayment and termination of services. Service shall not be denied if the applicant reconciles any payment or termination issues by either paying the full amount owed or enters into a payment plan, is disputing the amount causing the denial, or the applicant is receiving either public assistance or SSI and the utility is notified by the organization providing the assistance.

A utility is not obligated to provide services to a nonresidential seasonal applicant who fails to pay a lawfully required deposit.

If a utility fails to provide services pursuant to this section, the utility may be liable to the applicant for $25 per day of withheld services.

§ 11.4. Termination or Disconnection of Residential Service:

Notice of termination shall be personally served on customer or mailed to customer at the premises no less than 15 days prior to termination, and not before the bill is 20 days past due. If customer has provided an alternative mailing address, then notice must be (i) mailed to the premises and the alternative address or (ii) mailed to the alternate address and either personally served on adult resident of premises served, explained by telephone to adult resident, or posted at premises. If a utility is aware that a customer subject to service termination is receiving public assistance or SSI, from which no guarantee has been provided, it shall notify the assisting organization not more than 5 days, nor no less than 3 days, prior to termination. If utility has received a guarantee, it shall provide at least 15 days' notice of nonpayment stating that payment has not been made and indicating the amount of arrearage to the recipient and to the local social services commissioner. Written notice of a denial to provide service shall contain the reason for termination, the date of termination, the remedies and assistance available for avoiding termination, and information necessary to dispute the termination.

Service may be terminated, with notice, for issues relating to nonpayment of bills and deposits. Service shall only be terminated between the hours of 8:00 a.m.–4:00 p.m., Monday through Thursday, unless the day of or the following day is a holiday or the office to receive payment is closed. Service shall not be terminated during the 2-week period encompassing Christmas and New Years.

Termination shall not occur for nonpayment of bills rendered before the preceding 12 months unless it is the result of excusable conduct on the part of the utility, a billing dispute, adjustment to estimated bills, or culpable conduct on the part of the customer, provided that the utility shall initiate billing within 4 months of the resolution of the dispute, the adjustment, or cessation of the excusable or culpable conduct.

Utility shall verify that account is delinquent at the time of termination, and shall accept payment and cancel termination if customer reconciles the reason for termination. Utility shall provide rapid posting of payments to assist in avoiding unnecessary termination.

A final termination notice from a seller of natural gas or electricity must include a statement that suspension of distribution service may accompany commodity termination, even if the customer's account for distribution service is current.

If an ESCO (a seller of gas or electricity to be distributed via a utility's distribution system) informs a utility that a customer's commodity service has been suspended for nonpayment and demonstrates compliance with the requirements of this rule, the utility should suspend distribution and related services.

§ 11.5. Residential Service—Special Procedures:

No utility shall terminate or refuse to restore service for 30 days when a medical emergency, as certified by a medical doctor or local board of health, orally or in writing, exists. A demonstration of the customer's inability to pay charges for service shall be required before a certificate of medical emergency can be renewed. If the medical condition is likely to continue beyond the expiration of an initial certification, a certificate may be renewed for 60 days or, subject to Commission approval, a longer period. Customers remain liable for charges incurred while certificate is in effect. If a doctor or board of health certifies that a member of the customer's household uses life support that requires a utility's service, and customer shows an inability to pay, the certification shall remain in effect until terminated by the Commission. A utility should maintain a special file of such residential customers. Once the certificate expires, the utility shall abide by the notification and termination requirements of § 11.4.

No utility shall terminate or refuse to restore service where a customer is blind, disabled, or 62 years of age or older, and all the remaining residents of the household are 62 years of age or older, 18 years of age or under, or blind or disabled unless it makes a diligent effort to contact by telephone, or in person, an adult resident at the customer's premises at least 72 hours prior to termination of service for the purpose of devising a plan that would preclude termination and arrange for payment of bills. If a plan cannot be implemented, the utility shall delay termination for 15 days, and notify and request that social services assist in devising a plan. If termination occurs utility shall within 10 days make a diligent effort to contact adult resident at customer's premises to determine whether alternative arrangements for service have been made, and, if not, attempt to devise plan for restoration of service and payment of bills. If termination has occurred and the utility receives notice that the customer is entitled to protections under this title, it shall make a diligent effort to contact the customer within 24 hours to arrange a payment plan, and, if unable to do so, utility shall notify the department of social services.

These notification and assistance requirements shall be made available to customers whose heat-related services are subject to termination between November 1 and April 15. A utility shall, 72 hours before termination, attempt to contact and discern if a resident's health or safety would be deleteriously affected if heat-related service were terminated. Utility shall attempt to contact a customer at least once by telephone and if unsuccessful, by an onsite personal visit.

If a utility does not succeed in making personal contact before termination, and no one contacts it about re-connection by 12:00 noon the following day, the utility must make a site visit to determine whether a serious impairment to health or safety is likely to result. If impairment appears likely, the utility must restore service. If the utility cannot make personal contact, and the premises do not appear vacant, it must contact the local social services agency. In case of theft or tampering, the utility must nonetheless follow procedures to determine if termination would result in impairment of health or safety. If this is impractical because of an unsafe condition (e.g., a gas meter by-pass), it should terminate and specially notify the social services agency on the day of termination. Between September 1 and November 1 of each year, the utility must make a survey of former heat-related customers whose service was terminated during the 12 months preceding November 1 to determine if a serious impairment of health or safety would result from lack of service. If impairment is likely, service must be restored. If the utility cannot make contact, or the customer refuses reconnection, the utility must contact the social services agency. Special protections are available during the heating season for customers who are unable because of mental or physical problems to protect themselves.

§ 11.6. Voluntary Third-Party Notice:

A utility shall provide residential customers with the option of third-person notification concerning termination notice. A third party does not incur any financial liability for services provided.

§ 11.7. Service to Entire Multiple Dwellings:

Notice shall be given to the owner or the superintendent and posted in a common area 15 days (18 days if mailed) prior to termination service. The required notice must also be posted in common areas, mailed to the occupant of each unit, and mailed to the local health officer, social services office, and certain specified municipal officials. Notice shall be increased to 30 days prior to termination during winter protection period (November 1–April 15). If account is reconciled, the utility shall notify residents. Termination shall not occur if residents, per Commission approval, make timely payments. The occupants may be required to pay only current charges, i.e., those for the most recent billing period, defined as the first bill on or after the date of the termination notice, not including arrears. Additional procedures are required in cities during the heating season to ensure that serious impairment of health or safety will not result.

§ 11.8. Service to Two-Family Dwellings:

Substantially similar to § 11.7.

* * *

§ 11.9. Reconnection of Service:

Service shall be restored within 24 hours after reason for termination is reconciled or notice of health, elder, or disability protections. Failure to restore service, without good cause, may result in utility paying a $25 per day penalty to the customer or $50 in cases involving medical emergency; or elder, blind, or disabled customer; or heat-related services during winter season; or actual notice of likelihood of serious impairment of health or safety.

§ 11.10. Deferred Payment Agreements:

A utility shall offer a deferred payment plan and may postpone termination for 10 days to negotiate with customer. Notification shall include information pertaining to available financial assistance for medical, elder, disabled, and low-income customers. A utility may require proof of financial statements (assets and liabilities) in determining payment plan eligibility and amounts. A utility shall not be required to offer payment options below $10 per month if the customer demonstrates financial difficulty in paying for services. Customers demonstrating financial eligibility shall not be required to pay a down payment.

If an initial down payment is required, it shall not exceed 15% of payment agreement amount or 50% of 1 month of estimated usage.

If a customer's plan payments become delinquent, the utility shall send notification of delinquency at least 8 days before final termination notice is sent. Notice shall inform customers that payment is due within 20 days and that the payment plan may be altered if the customer contacts the utility and can demonstrate that their financial situation has changed.

§ 11.11. Budget or Levelized Payment Plans:

Every utility shall offer budget or levelized payment plans based on 12 months of previous or estimated usage.

§ 11.12. Residential Service Deposits:

Customers already receiving service, who are not delinquent in payment or had services terminated within the previous 6 months, shall not be required to pay a deposit. A delinquent payment is two consecutive months of arrears without making reasonable payment, defined as one half of the total arrears, or failure to make a reasonable payment on a bimonthly bill within 50 days after the bill is due.

Applicants shall not be required to pay a deposit unless they are either seasonal or short-term customers, cannot provide reasonable proof of identity, or as an approved method of cost-effectiveness by the Commission.

A utility shall request the payment of a deposit within 2 months of delinquency. Notice of delinquency and the possibility of a required deposit shall be at least 20 days before the deposit payment is due.

Deposits shall not be required of customers or applicants receiving public assistance or SSI. A deposit shall not be required for customers or applicants 62 years or older unless service has been terminated within the previous 6 months.

A deposit shall be a reasonable amount not to exceed two average monthly bills for the calendar year. When heat-related, a deposit shall not exceed two estimated average monthly bills during the heating season. A utility shall allow delinquent customers to pay a deposit in 12 monthly installments.

Interest, at a rate to be set by the Commission, shall be credited to the customer's account on the first billing after 1 year of service, or when the deposit is refunded (including after 12 consecutive months of timely payments).

§ 11.13. Meter Readings and Estimated Bills:

A utility may estimate bills if a reasonable effort has been made to acquire an actual reading, circumstances beyond the control of the utility makes an actual reading difficult, circumstances indicate an actual reading would be erroneous, an estimate is authorized by the Commission, or the customer is seasonal or short term.

After 4 months or 2 billings cycles (whichever is greater) of estimated bills, a utility shall either make a reasonable effort to read the meter, or provide the customer with the means of furnishing an actual reading.

After 6 months or 3 billing cycles (whichever is greater) of estimated bills, a utility shall attempt to make a specific appointment with the customer to read the meter. If no response is received after 8 months or 4 billing cycles (whichever is greater), the utility shall send notice informing the customer that if no appointment is made a $25 penalty charge may be assessed to the account. A utility shall offer payment plans, tailored to the customer's financial needs, for underestimates of more than 50% or $100 (whichever is greater).

§ 11.14. Back-Billing on Residential Accounts:

A utility shall not charge for services of more than 6 months prior to the mailing of the first bill, nor adjust bills upward after 12 months from the date of service unless failure was due to customer conduct and not due to negligence of the utility, or the adjustment was the subject of a dispute. Payment plans shall be allowed for adjusted bills of $100 or more.

§ 11.15. Late Payment and Other Charges:

If a clear explanation relating to a late charge is contained on a bill, a utility may impose a one-time or continuing late payment charge not to exceed 1.5% of the unpaid monthly balance that is delinquent (20 days past due). A late charge shall not be imposed on any bill that is subject to a complaint. Upon resolution of the complaint, the utility may assess a late charge if the entire amount in dispute is due the utility, provided that no such charge may be imposed for more than 2 months of the pendency of the complaint unless authorized by the Commission or its designee. No other charge, penalty, fee, or interest may be imposed for late payment, collection effort, service termination, disconnection, suspension, or deferred payment agreement as a result of failure to make timely payment for services.

Utility shall offer residential customers on fixed incomes the opportunity to pay their bills on a reasonable schedule that is adjusted for such customer's periodic receipt of income without said customers incurring late payment charges.

§ 11.16. Contents of Bills:

Bills shall contain the customer's name, address and account number, billing period, all payment information and amounts due (late payments, charges, taxes, etc.), full description and itemization of activity and services, payments, adjustments, credits, and explanation of how bill may be paid.

§ 11.17. Notification Requirements:

Utility shall make available at the initiation of service and annually thereafter to customers information concerning rights, responsibilities, remedies, protections, and procedures associated with rates, charges, and services. In a county where 20% of the population speaks a language other than English, the utility must offer, at the customer's option, bills and notices in both English and that other language. At least annually, the utility must give notice of this option in the other language. Additional information is required for users billed by time-of-use rates.

§ 11.18. Emergency Disconnections of Residences:

A utility may disconnect service to a residence when an emergency may threaten the health or safety of a person, a surrounding area, or the utility's distribution system.

§ 11.19. Inspection and Examination of Utility Apparatus:

A utility's authorized agent may request access to equipment on a non-holiday workday between 8:00 a.m. and 6:00 p.m. (or 9:00 p.m. in case of theft or tampering), or at such other reasonable times as requested by a customer. The utility employee may not use force or enter locked premises without the consent of the person in control of the premises, except in case of an emergency that threatens the health or safety of a person, or of the surrounding area, or the distribution system, or by court order.

§ 11.20. Complaints to the Utility:

A utility shall provide a clear and easily accessible method for filing and resolving complaints. A utility's resolution of a complaint shall be provided to the complainant, either orally or, upon request, in writing, and shall contain information relating to the procedures of further Commission review.

A utility shall refrain from terminating service during the investigation and for 15 days following the resolution of a complaint. Customer shall be required to pay undisputed portions of bills and/or an amount reasonably related to their estimated service.

§ 11.21. Emergency Hotline:

Inquiries relating to initiation, termination, or reconnection of service may be directed to the Commission by calling 800-342-3355 on any business day between the hours of 7:30 a.m.–7:30 p.m. In response to hotline calls, a Commission employee has the authority to order the continuation, re-connection, or initiation of service, if the health or safety of a person is involved or if there is a reasonable question regarding the termination, disconnection, suspension, or refusal to initiate service. Utilities must provide the Commission with the names and phone numbers of utility employees authorized to direct compliance with such orders.

* * *

§ 11.32. Service to Shared Meter Account:

The utility shall give all customers, whose service may be affected, 15 days' written notice (or 30 days during heating season) of its intention to terminate service to a shared meter account. During heating season, the utility must comply with the requirements of §§ 11.5–11.8, above. Any occupant who would be affected by termination of a shared meter account may prevent termination of service by paying the current charges for such service. An occupant who chooses to pay current charges shall not be liable for any future bills rendered for utility service through the shared meter.

A utility may not discontinue service to an occupied building at the owner's request, unless a new account will be opened and discontinuance of the shared meter account will not result in interruption of service.

* * *

***Water*—N.Y. Comp. Codes R. & Regs. tit. 16, §§ 14.1–14.20**

Many of the regulations governing water service are similar in substance and form to the general regulations (electric, gas, and steam service). Questions regarding water service regulations may be answered by referencing the general regulations governing a specific issue.

***Telephone*—N.Y. Comp. Codes R. & Regs. tit. 16, §§ 609.1–609.17**

Many of the substantive issues governing telephone utilities are substantially similar to those governing electric, gas, and steam and are indicated accordingly.

* * *

§ 609.3. Applicants for Residential Local Exchange Service:

Substantially similar to § 11.3. Service may be denied for nonpayment of services to any telecommunications provider within the last 6 months unless the applicant pays a deposit pursuant to § 609.9 or makes an advance payment of twice the estimated monthly bill for local exchange service (cannot be both). An applicant with previous service from the same provider within the previous 12 months shall be afforded the same type of service, and any type of payment arrangements as a continuation of previous service, unless the applicant's previous service was terminated more than 10 days before the application for new service for issues relating to nonpayment.

§ 609.4. Suspension or Termination of Basic Local Exchange Service:

Substantially similar to § 11.4. Local exchange service shall not be disconnected for nonpayment of services other than local service.

Notice of termination may not be sent until at least 25 days after bill is issued. Bills shall be mailed within 6 days of billing date. After initial notification the utility shall attempt to notify the customer by phone before termination, including at least one attempt made by phone, during non-business hours.

A utility shall make a diligent effort to contact and/or ascertain whether a residence has been abandoned before terminating service for that specific reason. When a check for payment of services is dishonored, the utility shall make at least 2 attempts within 24 hours, one of which must be outside of normal business hours, to contact the customer, unless the customer has had a previous dishonored check within the past 12 months.

Termination shall not occur for nonpayment of bills rendered before the preceding 6 months unless it is the result of a billing dispute or culpable conduct on the part of the customer, provided that the utility shall initiate billing not more than 2 months after resolution of the dispute or cessation of the culpable conduct.

§ 609.5. Suspension or Termination of Residential Basic Local Exchange Service—Special Procedures:

Substantially similar to § 11.5.

§ 609.6. Voluntary Third-Party Notice Prior to Termination of Service:

A utility shall provide customers with the option of third-person notification concerning termination notice. A third party does not incur any financial liability for services provided.

§ 609.7. Reconnection of Service:

Service shall be restored within 24 hours after the reason for termination is reconciled or notice of health, elder, or disability protections is received, unless circumstances beyond utilities' control prevent reconnection, in which case service shall be restored with 12 hours after circumstances cease.

§ 609.8. Deferred Payment Agreements:

Substantially similar to § 11.10 for issues relating to medical, elder, disabled, or public assistance protections. Utility shall not terminate service for nonpayment to customers receiving service for 3 months or less unless a deferred payment plan has been offered and rejected, or violated. Charges may total up to $150 over a 5-month period unless a greater amount and time-span is agreed upon. A down payment shall not exceed the lesser amount of 1/5 the total amount of arrears or 3 months of the customer's average bill plus the difference, if any, between the amount of arrears and the amount being deferred.

§ 609.9. Residential Basic Local Exchange Service Deposits:

Substantially similar to § 11.12, except deposits may be made in installments not to exceed 6 months.

§ 609.10. Back-Billing on Residential Accounts:

A utility shall not charge for services nor adjust bills upward after 24 months from the date of service unless the failure was due to customer conduct. If the delay was not due to customer conduct, payment plans shall be allowed for adjusted bills over a period of time not less than 1 month for each month of late-billed charges.

§ 609.11. Adjusted Payments and Other Charges:

Every telephone corporation shall offer residential customers on fixed incomes the opportunity to pay their bills on a reasonable schedule that is adjusted for such customer's periodic receipt of income.

Unless approved by the Commission, a utility shall not impose any type of additional charge for late payments, payment plans, collection efforts, reconnection of service, or for dishonored negotiable instruments.

§ 609.12. Contents of Bills:

Bills shall contain the customer's name, address, telephone or account number, billing period, all payment information and amounts due (late payments, charges, taxes, etc.), full description and itemization of activity and services, payments, adjustments, credits, and contact information for the provider concerning inquiries and disputes. New customers shall be given 60 days to change the type or grade of service, or change or cancel any non-basic services.

§ 609.13. Notification Requirements:

Utility shall make available to customers, information concerning rights, responsibilities, remedies, and procedures associated with rates, charges, and services.

§ 609.14. Emergency Disconnections of Residences:

A utility may disconnect service to a residence when an emergency may threaten the health or safety of a person, a surrounding area or the utility's distribution system.

§ 609.15. Inspection and Examination of Telephone Corporation Apparatus:

A utility's authorized agent may request access to equipment on a non-holiday workday between 8:00 a.m. and 6:00 p.m., or at such other reasonable times as requested by a customer.

§ 609.16. Telephone Corporation Complaint-Handling Procedures:

Substantially similar to § 11.20.

* * *

NORTH CAROLINA

The Department of Commerce Utilities Commission's general regulations governing electric, gas, water, and telecommunications service providers can be found within 4 N.C. Admin. Code 11.R12-1–11.R12-17. Although not summarized here, 4 N.C. Admin. Code 11.R6-1–11.R6-95 contains specific regulations governing natural gas providers, 4 N.C. Admin. Code 11.R7-1–11.R7-38 contains specific regulations governing water services, 4 N.C. Admin. Code 11.R8-1–11.R8-69.1 contains specific regulations governing electrical service, and 4 N.C. Admin. Code 11.R10-1–11.R10-25 contains specific regulations governing sewer service. 4 N.C. Admin. Code 11.R20-1 contains specific regulations governing unauthorized changes in telephone service provider (slamming) and unauthorized telephone service charges (cramming). Access to the regulations can be found at http://ncrules.state.nc.us/ncadministrativ_/default.htm (last visited in May 2011).

***Water*—4 N.C. Admin. Code 11.R7-1–11.R7-38.**

* * *

11.R7-4. Approval of Rate Schedules, Rules, and Regulations:

Utilities must file a tariff to impose charges for returned checks, in an amount to be approved by the Commission.

* * *

11.R7-8. Service Interruptions:

Insofar as practical, the utility must notify customers in advance of any work that will result in service interruption of long duration. This is not required for interruptions caused by matters beyond the control of the utility, such as accident, weather, public enemies, or strikes.

* * *

11.R7-20. Utility's Discontinuance of Service:

Service may be discontinued for violation of properly filed rules, denial of reasonable access to premises. The utility must diligently try to persuade the customer to correct rule violations. If the customer does not comply, service may be discontinued on 5 business days' notice. Discontinuance without notice is permitted for emergency, dangerous condition, or fraudulent use. In case of dispute, the utility must attempt to resolve the dispute. If this fails, either party may refer the matter to the Commission, and disconnection is not permitted while the matter is pending. The utility may charge a Commission-approved fee, the greater of $15 or actual cost of reconnection, for reconnection after service has been discontinued either for rule violation, nonpayment, or at the request of the customer.

***Electric*—4 N.C. Admin. Code 11.R8-1–11.R8-69.1.**

* * *

11.R8-14. Meter Testing at Request of Consumers:

A consumer is entitled, upon request, to one free meter test per year. For an additional test, the customer must deposit an amount determined by the Commission to cover the reasonable cost of the test. If the meter is found to register more than 2% fast, the deposit must be returned to the consumer. The consumer has a right to be present at the test or to have an expert or other representative (paid for by customer) present. The consumer is entitled to a written report of the results of the meter test.

* * *

11.R8-25. Rate Schedule, Rules and Regulations:

Copies of all rates, rules, and regulations shall be available on request to customers.

* * *

11.R8-44. Method of Adjustment for Rates Varying from Schedule or for Other Billing Errors:

For willful overcharges, the procedure is prescribed by N.C. Gen. Stat. § 62-139(b). For accidental overcharges, the utility will refund the excess amount for the entire period of the overcharge, if that period can be determined, or, if not, for the 12 months preceding the discovery of the overcharge. If the amount cannot be determined, it may be estimated. If an overcharged customer owes a past-due balance, the amount may be applied to that balance. If an undercharge results from theft or tampering during the residency of the consumer, or if the consumer knew of the undercharge and did notify the utility, then same rule for undercharges. In case of other undercharges, the utility may bill for up to 150 days (12 months for a customer with a demand of 50 kilowatts or greater). Estimation is permitted if the exact amount cannot be determined. The customer must be allowed to pay back the under-billing over the same number of billing periods as the interval for which the consumer is being required to pay. Billing adjustments shall not be made for meter errors of 2% or less.

* * *

11.R8-48. Information to Be Provided to New Customers:

Within 60 days of initiation of service, new customers must be provided with a clear and concise explanation of the rate schedules available to that customer and an explanation of procedures by which rates may be increased to adjust for the cost of fuel. Utilities are encouraged but not required to provide information about consumer credit, meter reading and billing, termination and reconnection, reporting power failures, billing information, request for service changes, energy conservation tips, and load management information.

11.R8-49. Notification to Consumers of Tariff Changes:

Utilities seeking a change in tariffs must publish notice in the local news media within 30 days after the Commission requires filing of notice and must provide a bill insert notifying customers of the proposed change within 60 days of that order.

11.R8-50. Notification of Available Rate Schedules and Breakdown of Company Operating Expenses:

At least annually, the utility must notify its customers of the rate schedules available within the customer's classification and must provide a breakdown of the utility's operating expenses.

11.R8-51. Provisions of Past Billing Upon Consumer Request:

A consumer is entitled upon request to one free summary itemizing the consumer's energy use for each billing period (12-month minimum). For an additional summary within a 12-month period, the company may charge $5.

* * *

***General (Electric, Gas, Water, Telecommunications)*—4 N.C. Admin. Code 11.R12-1–11.R12-17**

11.R12-1. Declaration of Public Policy [Deposits]:

Deposit criteria must be applied in an equitable and non-discriminatory manner and be predicated upon the credit risk of the individual, without regard to the area in which he or she lives.

11.R12-2. Establishment of Credit by Customer:

An applicant may establish credit through: ownership of the premises served or other real estate (unless applicant is an unsatisfactory credit risk); credit references that may be easily verified; prior utility service within 24 months without a disconnection, or not more than 2 late payments within 12 months, if the average bill for prior service was at least 50% of the estimated bill for new service, and the credit of the applicant is unimpaired; pay a deposit; or furnish a guarantor. Payment of a deposit does not relieve the customer of the obligation to pay ongoing bills.

11.R12-3. Reestablishment of Service:

Applicants who were previous or existing customers, who were disconnected for nonpayment, may be required to pay the outstanding amount and any reconnection fees and reestablish credit pursuant to 11.R12-2, except that an applicant for residential service may not be denied service for failure to pay for nonresidential service. Existing customers may be required to pay a deposit if customer is disconnected for nonpayment, or fails to pay amount due within 5 days of termination notice regardless of whether payment was made and the conditions of service or the basis on which credit was originally established have materially changed.

11.R12-4. Deposit; Amount; Receipt; Interest:

A deposit (or guarantee) shall not exceed 2/12 of the estimated charge for the next 12 months of service (except for seasonal service).

Customers shall receive receipts of deposits that also indicate that interest shall accrue, at a rate of 8% per annum, if held for more than 90 days.

11.R12-5. Refund of Deposit:

Deposits shall be automatically refunded after 12 months of billing without a discontinuance of service or without two or more bills having been past due, when customer discontinues service, or upon customer's request if credit has been otherwise established under 11R12-2.

11.R12-6. Record of Deposit:

A utility must keep records showing the name and billing address of the customer, the date and amount of the deposit, and all transactions.

11.R12-7. Appeal by Applicant or Customer:

Applicants or customers expressing dissatisfaction concerning establishing or reestablishing credit shall be informed of the rights to appeal to a supervisory panel and the Commission..

11.R12-8. Discontinuance of Service for Nonpayment:

Notice shall be given at least 5 days prior to discontinuance for nonpayment. If a customer has a history of abuse or excessive use of toll or metered service, and the deposit, if any, will not cover use during the 5-day notice period, service may be discontinued on 24 hours' notice. In this situation, a telephone utility may block toll service on 24 hours' notice, but the usual 5 days' notice is still required for local service.

11.R12-9. Uniform Billing Procedure:

Late charges may be assessed at a rate of 1% per month (1.5% for nonresidential accounts) no earlier than 25 days after billing date.

Due dates shall be no less than 15 days after the billing the date, and shall be adjusted, upon the customer's request, due to utility mailing error.

In unusual cases, if a utility has good cause to believe that unusually extensive use of metered or toll service and other factors create a risk that customer will not be able to pay a bill, and the customer's deposit is not sufficient to cover the excess use, the utility may accelerate the due date and proceed with toll limitation or disconnection. The utility must provide a written explanation to the customer and the Commission.

11.R12-10. Disconnection of Residential Customer's Natural Gas Service:

Past-due or delinquent date shall be no less than 25 days after the billing date, and shall be clearly indicated on the bill. Payments within the 25-day period shall maintain or count towards establishing credit.

A customer whose bills vary seasonally (e.g., one who uses gas for heat) may be treated as a seasonal customer for purposes of deposit requirements. The deposit may not exceed 1/3 of the estimated bill for the period of October through March.

A utility must file a tariff setting a charge for returned checks, not to exceed the amount set by N.C. Gen. Stat. § 25-3-506.

Termination shall not occur without the customer receiving at least 10 days' notice that includes the reason and the date of termination and methods of avoiding termination, including but not limited to information concerning the availability of federal, state, or private assistance. At least 24 hours before scheduled termination, the utility must make good faith efforts to contact the customer or designated third party, by phone or personal visit, to warn of termination and explain the alternatives. Service shall not be terminated from Friday through Sunday or the before or day of a federal or state holiday.

The rule prescribes a timetable for billing and terminations. Meters should be read every 30 days and bills sent out 5 days after reading. If a bill is not paid, the bill following the second reading must separately list the arrearages and warn the customer that disconnection will occur if they are not paid within 10 days. Ten days later, accounts must be reviewed by a supervisor. Next day, a utility employee should make a field call to disconnect, or accept payment, or defer disconnection because of death or illness.

Termination shall not occur between November 1 to March 31 without express approval of the Commission if the customer can establish that a household member is elder or disabled, that the customer is unable to pay but is entering into a payment plan, or the local social service office has established that customer is eligible for the Energy Crisis Assistance Program. The utility shall make every effort to contact and accept payment from the customer prior to termination.

Customer may appeal a termination or notice of termination to the Commission if not resolved through the dispute procedures.

Payment plans shall be offered and may require the customer to accept a plan that will bring his account into balance within 6 months.

The utility must offer customers the opportunity to designate a third party to receive notices. The utility must have an internal procedure to flag households in which a person is elder, disabled, seriously or chronically ill, or on life support, so as to identify the household for careful handling in case of delinquency.

11.R12-11. Disconnection of Residential Customer's Electric Service:

Substantially similar to 11.R12-10 except the rule prescribes a timetable for disconnections. For customers with good credit established, disconnect notices will be sent 14 days after the billing date of the third unpaid bill, i.e., 79 days after the billing date of the first unpaid bill. Ten days later, the company must review the account to determine if the customer has taken corrective action. For customers within their first 12 months of service, or those who have not established good credit, the disconnect notices go out 14 days after the billing date of the second unpaid bill, i.e., 49 days after the billing date of the first bill. A utility must have a Commission-approved code for determining whether a customer has established good credit. The customer must be informed of how the code operates and of his or her current classification.

* * *

11.R12-17. Disconnection, Denial, and Billing of Telephone Service:

Local service may not be disconnected for failure to pay for services other than local service, but toll-blocking may be imposed for failure to pay for toll service. (If an LEC offers only bundled local service, it may require payment for the bundled service but not for services billed on behalf of third parties.) A utility may not disconnect local service or impose toll blocking for nonpayment of disputed charges. A utility may disconnect local service if customer subject to toll-blocking contrives by fraud, tampering, etc., to receive toll service with intent to avoid paying. Partial payments must be allocated first to local service, then to other regulated services, and finally to unregulated services. Global toll-blocking may be imposed for nonpayment of toll services *except* calls to 900-numbers or other non-regulated charges other than toll services and international calls to information service providers on the first and second occasion. For 900-number calls, if a customer challenges the charge or is unable to pay, the carrier must remove the charge and offer designated service blocking. If this happens a second time, the carrier must remove the charge and impose designated service blocking. For international calls to information providers, global toll-blocking may be imposed after the second call. Local service may not be denied, nor global toll-blocking imposed, for a debt more than 3 years old unless the company has obtained or is actively pursuing a court judgment. LEC's disconnect notices must show what amount must be paid to maintain local services and what amount must be paid to maintain local and toll services and must explain the customer's alternatives. IXC's disconnect notices must specify the amount required to maintain toll service. Carriers must advise their customers annually as to their disconnect policies. If a utility bills for more than one provider, the name and toll-free phone number of each provider must be shown on the page with the bill for that provider's services. Regulated and non-regulated services must be clearly separated and the consequences of nonpayment of each item clearly explained.

* * *

11.R20-1. Slamming, Cramming, and Related Abuses in the Marketing of Telecommunications Services:

Changes of provider require express authorization from the customer or the customer's representative for each change. Upon a customer's request, any offer to provide telecommunications services must be sent in writing, describing rates, terms, and conditions. A request for this written offer may not be deemed acceptance of the offer. Any telemarketing script or direct mail advertisement must disclose the name of the provider, that the purpose of the contact is to sell telecommunications services, and that the provider may not be changed without the consumer's express authorization.

* * *

NORTH DAKOTA

The Public Service Commission Public Utility Division's Standards of Service Regulations governing natural gas can be found at N.D. Admin. Code 69-09-01-01–69-09-01-30; electric, N.D. Admin. Code 69-09-02-02.1–69-09-02-39; telephone, N.D. Admin. Code 69-09-05-00.1–69-09-05-14. Issues within the three areas of regulations that are substantially similar will be indicated accordingly. Access to the regulations can be found at www.legis.nd.gov/information/acdata/html/69-09.html (last visited in May 2011).

***Natural Gas*—N.D. Admin. Code 69-09-01-01–69-09-01-30**
69-09-01. Standards of Service—Gas:

* * *

69-09-01-17. Deposits and Guarantees:

New applicants or existing customers may be required to pay deposit or furnish a guarantee. Deposits or guarantees shall not exceed 1.5 times the estimate for 1 month of billing. The utility shall pay interest on such deposits at the rate paid by the Bank of North Dakota on a 6-month certificate of deposit. The interest may be paid to the depositor, or may be deducted from the depositor's indebtedness to the utility for gas service. Customers shall receive a receipt for deposit and the utility shall keep a record of all deposits. The payment or deduction for interest must be made during each calendar year or whenever a deposit is refunded or service discontinued. Guarantee contracts are of an indeterminate length but shall be terminated if service if disconnected.

69-09-01-18.1. Discontinuance of Gas Service:

Termination of service may result from nonpayment for services, failure to comply with utility rules, tampering or interfering with service or due to a dangerous condition. Service shall not be terminated due to failure to pay for merchandise or a different class of service, failure to pay for a previous occupant's service, or failure to pay a bill as a guarantor.

Notice of discontinuance to customers or individual tenants by first-class mail, or in person to customers who are disabled or 65 years old or older, shall be at least 10 days prior to termination. Notice shall contain the method and reason for discontinuance, the amount due, and the rights and remedies concerning termination, including but not limited to deferred payments plans, and the availability of a 30-day termination stay if a resident is elder, disabled, or a medical emergency would result from terminating service. Discontinuance may be avoided by paying disputed portion of bill under protest.

Service shall not be disconnected on weekends, Fridays, state holidays, the day before a state holiday, or after noon on any day. A reconnection fee and a deposit or guarantee may be required.

69-09-01-19. Extensions of Service:

When the utility deems the expense justified, it shall provide extensions and maintain master-metered services to customers and authorized manufactured home parks. If the utility deems the expense unjustified, the customer(s) may request a Commission hearing for further determination.

69-09-01-20. Information to Customers:

Utility shall provide information concerning services, rate schedules and any changes in services and rate schedules, information that will assist in choice of service, and information that unless the rate is changed, customers are bound by their choice of rate for 12 months.

69-09-01-21. Billing Basis:

Bills shall be issued monthly unless utility and customer consent to more frequent billing. Bills may be estimated when meter is not read for one or more consecutive billing cycles. Estimates are to be based on normal consumption for the same period during the previous year or preceding months. Upon discovering an overbilling that exceeds the following month's consumption, the correct consumption shall be determined for 2 months and the bill shall be adjusted.

69-09-01-22. Meter Readings on Bills:

Bill shall indicate that the meter was read at the beginning and end of each billing cycle, and shall clearly indicate if the bill was computed using any other method than a per unit charge.

69-09-01-23. Adjustment of Bills for Meter Error:

A bill shall be adjusted dating back to 1/2 the time of the last meter reading if a meter is found to be either fast or slow, but shall not exceed a period of 6 months. Meters not registering any reading shall be estimated.

69-09-01-24. Refunds:

Any claim of a refund may be refused if it is not within 6 years from the date of overpayment.

* * *

***Electric*—N.D. Admin. Code 69-09-02-02.1–69-09-02-39**

69-09-02. Standards of Service—Electric

Many of the regulations governing electric service are similar in substance and form to the regulations governing gas service. Questions regarding electric service regulations may be answered by referencing the electric and gas regulations governing a specific issue.

***Telecommunications*—N.D. Admin. Code 69-09-05-00.1–69-09-05-14**

Many of the substantive issue within the regulations governing telecommunications utilities are substantially similar to the regulations governing gas service and are indicated accordingly.

69-09-05. Standards of Service—Telephone:

69-09-05-01. Lowest Priced Service Alternatives:

Upon a request for service, the provider shall provide information concerning the lowest cost alternatives for service, and assist the customer in choosing them.

69-09-05-02. Discontinuance of Telecommunications Services:

Substantially similar to 69-09-01-18.1. However, local service shall not be disconnected for nonpayment of long-distance service unless it is technically impossible to disconnect long-distance service without disconnecting local service.

69-09-05-02.1. Determination of Delinquency:

If a customer's partial payment on outstanding charges for telecommunications services, excluding payments on a deferred installment agreement, is equal to or greater than the outstanding charges for essential services and federal access charges, the customer is not delinquent in payment for essential services for the purpose of termination or reconnection.

69-09-05-03. Deposits and Guarantees:

Substantially similar to 69-09-01-17, but amount of deposit shall not exceed 2 times the estimate of an average monthly bill. An eligible telecommunications carrier may not collect a service deposit in order to initiate lifeline service if the qualifying low-income consumer voluntarily elects toll blocking from the carrier. If toll blocking is unavailable, the carrier may charge a service deposit.

69-09-05-04. Rules for Resale of Telecommunications Services:

Resellers who require prepayment for their services must either post a bond or maintain an escrow account in a North Dakota bank sufficient to cover the amount of the pre-payments.

* * *

69-09-05-04.2. Unauthorized Service Changes:

A telecommunications company may not change a customer's local or long-distance carrier without authorization from the customer.

69-09-05-05. Rules for the Provision of Operator Services:

Operator services must provide written materials disclosing to the end user the name and toll-free number of the service. Operators must clearly identify the service, provide rate information on request, and provide emergency service equal to that of the local exchange carrier or immediately transfer emergency calls to the local exchange carrier. For billing purposes, operator services must itemize, identify, and rate85 calls; not charge for incomplete calls; and disclose their names on bills that include charges for their services.

* * *

69-09-05-07. Customer Trouble Reports:

When a customer's service is found to be out of order or a customer reports trouble, the local exchange company shall test its facilities to determine if the problem is with the local exchange company's facilities. If there is a problem with the provider's facilities, the local exchange company shall correct the trouble promptly, and shall not charge the customer to test to determine if the problem is on the local exchange company's facilities or to correct a problem on the local exchange company's facilities. A local exchange company shall inform a customer in advance what charges will be assessed to identify or correct a problem located on the customer's facilities.

* * *

69-09-05-12. Eligible Telecommunications Carrier Applications and Advertising:

Eligible telecommunications carriers must advertise, in their directories and in the media, the availability of Lifeline and Link-Up service and the process by which customers may qualify for these services.

* * *

69-09-05-13. Essential Service Provider Bills:

A bill for essential service shall contain the name and contact information of the provider, the essential services for which the bill is issued, all related taxes, fees, and surcharges, and a disclosure that essential service may be discontinued for nonpayment of nonessential services.

* * *

OHIO

Ohio Admin. Code 4901:1-6-01–4901:1-6-37 contains the rules regarding telephone service. Ohio Admin. Code 4901:1-17-01–4901:1-17-09 and 4901:1-18-01–4901:1-18-17 contain the general rules regarding utility service. In some cases it may be important to consult Ohio Admin. Code 4901:1-10-01–4901:1-10-33 for specific rules regarding electric utility service, and Ohio Admin. Code 4901:1-15-01–4901:1-15-35 regarding water and sewer service. Access to the Administrative Code can be found at www.puco.ohio.gov/puco/docketing/docketinginformation.cfm?doc_id=888.

Telephone—Ohio Admin. Code 4901:1-6-01–4901:1-6-37

* * *

4901:1-6-07. Customer Notice Requirements:

Company shall provide at least 15 days' notice to affected customers of any material change in the rates (except for rate decrease), terms and conditions of service, and any change in company's operations that are not transparent and may impact service. The notice shall name the service being changed, a description of the change including rate increases, the effective date of the change, and the company's contact information. Notice shall be provided in any reasonable manner, including bill insert, bill message, direct mail, or electronic means if customers consents.

4901:1-6-12. Service Requirements for BLES:

Basic local exchange service ("BLES") shall be installed within 5 business days of receipt by company of completed application for new service, unless customer requests or agrees to a later date. Payment due date for BLES may not be earlier than 14 consecutive days after the date the bill is postmarked. The postmark may appear on the bill rather than the envelope as long as the postmark date is never earlier than the date that the bill actually enters the mail.

For nonpayment of any amount past due, BLES may be disconnected not earlier than 14 days after the due date, provided customer is given notice 7 days before disconnection. Disconnection notice may be included in customer's next bill provided that bill is postmarked at least 7 days before disconnection date indicated on bill and that disconnection language is clearly highlighted and stands apart from regular bill language. The notice shall identify the total amount that must be paid to avoid disconnection, the earliest date disconnection may occur, and toll-free and website contact information of the Public Utilities Commission and the Ohio Consumer's Counsel.

LEC may require a deposit, not exceeding 230% of 1 month's estimated service charges, for installation of BLES for any person that LEC determines, in its discretion, is not creditworthy.

Unless prevented from doing so by circumstances beyond its control or unless customer requests otherwise, LEC shall reconnect customer whose BLES was disconnected for nonpayment no later than 1 business day after the day the LEC receives full payment of past-due charges or the first payment under a payment plan, whichever first occurs.

4901:1-6-15. Directory Information:

An LEC providing BLES shall make telephone directory available to customer at no additional charge. Directory may be in any reasonable format, including a printed directory, an electronic directory accessible on the Internet, a computer disc, or free directory assistance. The directory shall include all current published numbers in the local calling area, including emergency numbers and those for the local police, the state highway patrol, the county sheriff and fire departments, the Ohio relay service, operator assistance, and directory assistance. BLES customers may request a printed directory at no additional charge.

4901:1-6-17. Truth in Billing Requirements:

Every telephone company shall comply with the FCC's truth in billing requirements (47 C.F.R. § 64.201) and shall clearly and accurately identify on every bill all services rendered, all service providers, and all billed charges, fees, and taxes. Every bill shall state that customers with questions or complaints should contact the company first and shall provide toll-free and website contact information for the Public Utilities Commission and the Ohio Consumers' Counsel.

4901:1-6-18. Slamming and Preferred Carrier Freezes:

This rule incorporates the FCC rules and procedures prescribed by 47 C.F.R. §§ 64.1100 to 64.1170 for authorization, verification and record-keeping for changes of carrier and for preferred carrier freezes. Carriers that provide freezes may not attempt to retain a customer during the process of changing a preferred carrier selection, or provide information to its marketing staff or any affiliate.

4901:1-6-30. Company Records and Complaint Procedures:

Company shall provide the public utilities commission with a contact, including a toll-free number and e-mail address, for complaint resolution and shall respond to public utilities commission and consumer inquiries and complaints in a reasonable and timely manner.

* * *

4901:1-6-31. Emergency and Outage Operations:

This section prescribes standards for reporting and managing outages. Each provider must have an emergency plan, to assure that service will be restored first to priority customers such as police and fire stations, hospitals, individual customers with life-threatening conditions, and customers who have subscribed to the Federal telecommunications service priority program (47 C.F.R. 64, app. A). Providers must have a continuity of operations plan for a major epidemic.

* * *

***Establishment of Credit for Residential Utility Service (Gas, Sewer, Telephone, Water)*—Ohio Admin. Code 4901:1-17-01–4901:1-17-09**

* * *

4901:1-17-02. Written Credit Procedures Required:

Standards for establishing or re-establishing credit must be in writing. They must be administered in a non-discriminatory manner, without regard to race, color, religion, gender, national origin, age, disability, and must be based on the credit risk of the individual, without regard to the collective credit reputation of the area in which the customer or applicant lives. Utility shall make credit procedures available upon request and shall provide information verbally or in writing based upon applicant's or customer's preference. Electronic transactions and notices may be used if both customer and utility agree.

4901:1-17-03. Establishment of Credit:

Credit may be established if applicant: was a previous customer or received the same type of service within 24 consecutive months without a disconnection or without 2 consecutive bills with past-due balances within the last 12 months; provides a guarantor to secure payment of bills for 60 days of service; is financially responsible freeholder of premises to be served or other real estate in the service territory; demonstrates that he or she is a satisfactory credit risk by means that may be quickly and inexpensively checked by utility such as by credit check; or pays a deposit. Previous customer may be required to make a deposit in order to establish financial responsibility.

Unpaid utility bills, either from receipt of service or from serving as guarantor, shall result in unsatisfactory credit.

If a customer with a guarantor fails to pay, the balance (not greater than the amount billed to the defaulting customer for 60 days of service or 2 monthly bills) may be transferred to the guarantor's account. The guarantor will then be subject to disconnection if the transferred sum is not paid within 30 days.

4901:1-17-04. Deposit to Reestablish Creditworthiness:

Customer may be required to make deposit based on customer's credit history with utility, disconnection, or failure to make full payment or payment arrangements for any bill containing a previous balance. Applicant may be required to pay deposit when service was disconnected within preceding 12 months for nonpayment, fraudulent conduct, tampering, or unauthorized reconnection.

4901:1-17-05. Deposit Administration Provisions:

Except for telephone service (§ 4901:1-6-12), deposits shall not exceed 1/12 of estimated annual charges plus 30% of the estimated monthly charge. Telephone deposits shall not exceed 230% of estimated average monthly bill for regulated services.

The utility shall maintain records of deposits, provide customers with a receipt, and shall pay 3% interest on deposits held for more than 180 days. Interest shall not be paid after discontinuance if utility has made reasonable effort to refund deposit.

4901:1-17-06. Refund of Deposit and Release of Guarantor:

Deposits shall be refunded or credited to a customer's account after timely payment of bills for 12 consecutive months, or upon customer's request at any time after customer's credit has otherwise been established. Upon discontinuance of service, deposit shall be applied to final bill, and any remaining deposit balance of at least $1.00 shall be refunded.

* * *

4901:1-17-08. Applicant and/or Customer Rights:

Customers expressing dissatisfaction with deposit requirements shall be informed of the rights and procedures for a supervisory and a public utilities commission review.

***Disconnection of Gas, Natural Gas, or Electric Services*—Ohio Admin. Code 4901:1-18-01–4901:1-18-17**

* * *

4901:1-18-03. Reasons for Disconnection:

Gas or electric providers may disconnect for use of service in a manner detrimental to the service of other consumers; violation of law or court order; customer's move from the location; health or safety hazard; denial of access for a year or more, despite notice and reasonable opportunity to arrange access; fraud or tampering; for scheduled repairs or maintenance, upon 6 hours' notice to consumers; for nonpayment, following the procedures outlined in § 4901:1-18-06 below. If fraud or tampering is shown, service may be reconnected only if consumer gives assurance that the practice has been discontinued, pays for unauthorized use and property damage, and all other fees or charges authorized by tariff.

4901:1-18-04. Delinquent Bills:

Bills are delinquent if a customer has not paid or made arrangements for payment by the due date of a bill containing a previous balance for regulated services; or is in default on an extended payment plan; or fails to make the initial payment on an extended payment plan. The minimum payment to avoid disconnection may not exceed the delinquent amount, i.e., the previous balance for regulated services.

4901:1-18-05. Extended Payment Plans and Responsibilities:

Utility shall offer payment plans to delinquent customers who contact the utility or to customers seeking to avoid a delinquency. Payment plans shall allow a customer to pay either six equal payments on the arrearages plus full payment of the current bill or nine equal monthly payments on the arrearages in addition to an adjustable levelized plan for the projected monthly bills, with the plan ending 9 months from the initial payment. A 3-month payment plan shall be offered during the winter heating season. Utility may disconnect in accordance with § 4901:1-18-06 for failure to make payment under payment plan. Levelized payment plans shall be offered to any customer not in default on payment plans. PIPP plans shall be available to eligible low-income households during heating season if a balance remains after expiration of a 3-month payment plan.

4901:1-18-06. Disconnection Procedures for Natural Gas and Electric Companies:

This section deals only with disconnection for nonpayment for regulated services. Other causes for disconnection are covered in rule 4901:1-18-10, below.

Gas and electric utility shall postpone disconnection for 30 days where: customer provides certification that disconnection would be especially dangerous to health or that disconnection would make operation of necessary medical or life-supporting equipment impossible or impractical; customer establishes an inability to pay; and customer enters into payment plan prior to end of certification period, and makes payment under plan (the initial payment on the plan shall not be due until the end of the certification period). Certifications may be renewed for two additional 30-day periods, and may not exceed a total of 90 days per household in any 12-month period. Disconnection of service is restricted when occurring between November 1 and April 15.

Due dates shall not be less than 14 days from the date of a bill's postmark (4933.122(A)), and notice shall not be less than 14 days before disconnection. Notice shall include the earliest date of disconnection, the reasons for disconnection, actions to avoid disconnection, contact information of service provider, Commission and Ohio Consumer's Counsel, and a statement that disconnection may result in a deposit and reconnection fees. Personal notice shall be given the day of disconnection at the premises to be disconnected, and if neither the customer nor an adult resident is present, written notice shall be conspicuously posted prior to disconnection.

Disconnection may be during normal business hours, but shall not be after 12:30 p.m. on a day preceding a day when all services needed to arrange reconnection are not regularly performed or available.

4901:1-18-07. Reconnection of Service:

Reconnection shall occur upon payment, proof of payment, or agreement to pay for all outstanding amounts and any reconnection fees. 'Service may be reconnected the day of payment if service has been disconnected for fewer than 10 days, the utility is notified before 12:30 the day of payment, and customer agrees to incur any additional costs. If service has been disconnected for more than 10 days, than utility may treat customer as new customer and connect service consistent with new customer timeframes. A utility may impose a reconnection charge only if service has been actually disconnected but may impose a collection charge.

4901:1-18-08. Landlord Tenant Provisions:

To avoid disconnection, tenants whose service is included in rent or who reside in master-metered units must be given separate 10-day notice if landlord/customer has not paid or made payment arrangements by end of prior 14-day notice period and must be informed of procedures allowing payment of an amount at least equal to landlord's current monthly bill. Note that Ohio law also provides a rent-withholding procedure, by which rent may be paid into a court-supervised escrow for payment of utility bills or correction of other housing violations. A utility may not disconnect if it receives notice that tenants have invoked this procedure.

* * *

4901:1-13-11. Residential Natural Gas Bills and Payment:

All bills shall contain information concerning dates and consumption amounts, due dates, amounts and penalties due, any information that will allow and assist in the computation of charges, and contact information for the Commission if a dispute with the utility cannot be resolved. Each bill must disclose the customer's historical consumption during each of the preceding 12 months, with total and average consumption for that 12-month period. The utility must provide a list of its authorized payment centers. The charge for payment at authorized agent locations may not exceed $2.00. Payments to the company directly or to a payment center must be credited the same day. Disconnection is not permitted if payment is made to the company or a payment center by the close of business on the disconnection date listed on the disconnection notice. On-line billing is permitted, but customers may not be required to use on-line billing, nor may enrollment or usage fees be charged. The on-line billing statement must include all the material required for a paper bill.

4901:1-18-09. Combined Utility Companies:

This section prescribes allocation methods for payments to combined utilities. If a customer of a combined utility is facing disconnection, he or she may choose whether to make payment or enter into payment plan for one service or both. Disconnection notices, or a utility's response to a customer who inquires about reconnection, must explain all these options.

4901:1-18-10. Insufficient Reasons for Refusing or Disconnecting Service:

Service may not be refused or disconnected for failure to pay for service to a former customer, unless the former customer and the applicant continue to be members of the same household; for failure to pay a nonresidential account; for failure to pay a disputed amount (but the customer must pay any undisputed amount); for failure to pay any unregulated charges.

* * *

OKLAHOMA

The Corporate Commission's Regulations governing electric utilities can be found within Okla. Admin. Code §§ 165:35-1-1–165:35-41-7. Natural Gas regulations can be found in Okla. Admin. Code §§ 165:45-1-1–165:45-23-7. Telecommunications regulations can be found in Okla. Admin. Code §§ 165:55-1-1–165:55-25-11. Water regulations can be found in Okla. Admin. Code §§ 165:65-1-1–165:65-13-8. The regulations governing natural gas and water are substantially similar to the regulations governing electric and are indicated accordingly. Access to the Administrative Code can be found at www.occeweb.com/rules/rules1.htm (last visited in May 2011).

***Electricity*—Okla. Admin. Code §§ 165:35-1-1–165:35-41-7**

* * *

§ 165:35-15-1. Meters:

Meters shall be furnished, installed, and maintained at the utilities expense. Additional meters may require an additional charge.

§ 165:35-15-2. Meter Reading, Meter Reading Records, Cards, and Charts:

Meters shall be read monthly either by the utility or the consumer. If read by the consumer, the reading must be verified by the utility at least every 6 months. No more than 2 consecutive estimated bills shall be rendered by the utility, unless access is beyond utility's control.

Denial of access to meters, connections, or other utility property is grounds for disconnection, upon 10 days' notice. If the consumer or property owner fails to correct dangerous conditions (including dangerous animals), the utility may relocate the meter to a safe location at the expense of the consumer or property owner. A consumer may request one free special meter reading per year.

* * *

§ 165:35-15-20. Meter Testing on Request of Consumer:

Upon receipt at an office of a utility of a written request of a consumer, the utility shall, at no charge, within 20 days, test the accuracy of the meter through which the consumer is being served.

* * *

§ 165:35-15-22. Adjustment of Bills:

A refund shall be paid to a consumer for a meter in error of more than 2%, but shall not exceed a 6-month period unless the date of error can be determined. If a meter is slow by more than 2%, a utility may collect for a period of 1/2 the time since the previous test, but it shall not exceed 6 months unless the date of error can be determined. Utility shall offer payment plans for under-billing. If necessary, amount of error may be an estimate from the previous year's usage.

* * *

§ 165:35-19-2. Consumer Information:

Utility shall maintain information concerning the locations of it facilities. Utility shall provide consumers with rate schedules, most advantageous rates and services, information regarding actual consumption (upon request), contact information regarding disputes, disconnection information, information concerning customer rights, and a 24-hour telephone number for emergencies.

* * *

§ 165:35-19-10. Deposits and Interest:

Applicants may be required to pay a deposit, not to exceed 1/6 of an estimated annual bill, if they cannot show 12 months of same or similar service, within 18 months prior to application, without a disconnection, more than 2 late payments, or a dishonored check. Existing customers may be required to pay a deposit in case of disconnection, dishonored check, or two or more late payments within a year. Deposits may be made in installments, and after 30 days shall accrue interest at rate determined by the utility based on yields of U.S. Treasury securities.

Accounts shall be reviewed every 12 months, and, if a consumer makes timely payments for 12 months (no disconnection, no more than 2 late payments, no dishonored checks), a deposit shall be returned or credited to a consumer's account.

* * *

§ 165:35-19-30. Information on Bills:

All bills shall contain information concerning dates and consumption amounts, due dates, amounts and penalties due, and any information that will allow and assist in the computation of charges. A bill must clearly indicate that it is an estimated bill. Large utilities (150,000 or more Oklahoma customers) must include a historic usage chart; smaller utilities must inform customers that such a chart is available on request.

§ 165:35-19-31. Average Monthly Payment Plan (AMPP):

Utilities shall offer consumers the option of being billed on an average monthly payment plan.

§ 165:35-19-32. Penalty or Charge for Late Payment of Bills and Negotiable Instruments:

Whether the utility or the consumer reads a meter, a penalty charge, not to exceed 1.5%, may be assessed for late payments. Timely payments, that avoid penalty charges, shall not be described as "prompt payment discounts," or using language of a similar import on any bill.

Residential bills shall be due no earlier than 20 days after being mailed. Checks shall be accepted for payment unless the consumer has tendered 2 or more negotiable instruments for payment in the preceding 12 months that have been dishonored by the issuing institution.

§ 165:35-19-40. Failure to Make Application for Electric Service:

Any person who uses the electrical service of a utility but fails to apply or enter into a contract for said services shall be held liable to the utility for payment.

An electric utility has not consented to a contract or use of service by a new occupant if it elects not to disconnect service after the previous occupant has terminated service (provided the utility reads the meter when service is terminated and when service is initiated to subsequent customer).

* * *

§ 165:35-21-1. Disconnection of Service by a Consumer:

Consumers may be required to give up to at least 5 days written notice (excluding holidays and weekends) for account closure or disconnection, and shall be liable for charges until notice expires.

§ 165:35-21-2. Disconnection of Service by a Utility:

Service may be disconnected for issues relating to nonpayment, denial of reasonable access to equipment, failure to apply for service or unauthorized use or misrepresentation, dangerous conditions, adverse effect on services of utility or consumers, violation of rules or regulations, abandonment of premises, or causing or threatening injury to utility employee, employee's family, or utility property.

Service may not be disconnected: for failure to pay for another type or classification of services, or for an unpaid bill for services outside of the utility's territory; for nonpayment of an unsubstantiated bill more than 3 years old; for failure to pay for under-billing for misapplication of rates unless offered a payment plan; for an unpaid bill of a prior customer (not currently a household member); for failure to pay a disputed portion of a bill or estimated bill; if a current customer in good standing accepts a new household member who owes a previous bill, except if that person is listed on the lease arrangements or another utility as a responsible party, or as shared service with customer at same or different location. Pending verification, service may not be denied or disconnected to a consumer who alleges that service was obtained in his or her name at another location without the consumer's consent.

Disconnection may occur the date of or 30 days after scheduled disconnection, but shall not occur within the last two hours of the business day, on a holiday, or after noon on Friday.

§ 165:35-21-3. Utilities Encouraged to Keep Current Lists of Energy Assistance Programs:

Utilities are strongly encouraged, but not required, to compile a list with contact information for all known payment assistance programs, including information about any bilingual programs, that can help consumers with energy bills, and to give the list to any consumer who asks for assistance.

§ 165:35-21-10. Delays to Disconnection of Residential Service:

Utility shall not disconnect service used for heat if the predicted daytime high is below 32° or the nighttime low will reach 20°, or the utility is used for cooling and the predicted heat index is 101° or higher. Disconnection shall be postponed 30 days upon notification that disconnection would give rise to life-threatening condition (defined as situation where customer or other permanent resident is dependent upon equipment that is prescribed by physician, requires electricity to operate, and is needed to sustain person's life) and upon receipt within 30 days of medical certification. An additional 30 days' delay is required if the medical certificate is renewed within the 30 days. No more than 60 days delay is required pursuant to this rule. Disconnection for nonpayment shall be delayed for at least 20 days if, upon notification to the utility, a consumer has applied and is waiting for financial assistance from a federal, state, or local agency and said agency verifies the application, and the consumer enters into a payment plan for payment of any amount not covered by the assistance.

A utility must offer a deferred payment arrangement to consumers unable to pay. Consumers may accept this arrangement up to but not on the disconnection date. The utility must renegotiate agreements if the consumer initiates renegotiation before breach. If a deferred payment arrangement is breached, the utility may disconnect without further notice if the disconnect date has not been passed or on 24 hours' notice thereafter. Provision of false information pursuant to this section or the sections protecting elder or disabled consumers is grounds for disconnection.

§ 165:35-21-11. Commission Notification Procedure for the Elderly and/or Consumers with Disabilities:

If an elder or disabled persons requests, and is placed on the Commission's notification program, the utility shall notify the Commission, by phone or mail, 10 business days prior to disconnection and, upon the Commission's request, delay disconnection an additional 5 days.

* * *

§ 165:35-21-14. Service Limiters and Other Restrictions on Utility Service:

If a customer is subject to disconnection, the utility may, with the customer's permission, use a service limiter to restrict usage in lieu of disconnection.

* * *

§ 165:35-21-20. Notice of Disconnection of Service:

First notice shall be at least 10 days before disconnection. Additional notice shall be sent 2 business days before disconnection between November 15 and April 15. Second notice may be in writing, in person, or by telephone, but may be oral only after compliance with 10 day written notice requirement.

Notice shall contain a bold and clearly visible indication of disconnection, the customer's account information, any reconnection charges, dispute information, reason and date of disconnection, contact information of utility and statement that customer must first contact utility before contacting Commission's Consumer Services Division, and options for avoiding and delaying disconnection.

Notice to tenants and others subject to master metering shall be placed conspicuously in a common area according to this section.

§ 165:35-21-21. Manner of Disconnection of Service:

During disconnection, utility employee shall accept payment and cancel disconnection, but shall not be required to accept a negotiable instrument from a customer whose account has been verified as not containing sufficient funds. After disconnection, employee shall leave written notice of disconnection that contains the reason for disconnection and information regarding reconnection.

§ 165:35-21-30. Disconnection Without Notice:

A utility may disconnect service without notice if it reasonably believes that a hazardous condition exists, unauthorized use, for repairs, and failure to pay a deposit after a good faith effort by the utility to notify of pending disconnection. Disconnection for unauthorized use may result in additional reconnection charges.

§ 165:35-21-31. Reconnection of Service:

Once the reason for disconnection has been eliminated, the utility shall reconnect service according to its regular workload but no later than 24 hours after the reason has been eliminated if disconnection was fault of customer. The same 24-hour standard applies when disconnection for nonpayment has occurred immediately preceding severe weather (defined in 165:35-21-10C), and a utility receives payment of the past-due bill, confirmation of medical certificate, or a guarantee for payment from a federal, state, or local agency. A utility may charge a reconnection fee.

§ 165:35-21-40. Mediation:

If a customer disputes a bill, a utility shall investigate and seek to resolve the dispute, and, if unsuccessful, the consumer may register a complaint with the Consumer Services Division (CSD). If the dispute remains unresolved after issuance of informal decision, customer can file complaint with Commission.

* * *

§ 165:35-23-1. Denial of Service to a Consumer:

A utility may refuse to provide service to an applicant or consumer from whom there remains owing an unpaid account for service of a similar character previously supplied to such applicant or consumer at any location in Oklahoma by an electric utility, or an applicant or consumer who uses an alias, trade name, business name, the name of a relative or other person as a device to escape payment of an unpaid obligation for utility service. The utility may not otherwise require the payment of unpaid utility bills of another as a condition of furnishing service, unless that other person remains an occupant or user.

* * *

§ 165:35-23-5. Service to Mobile Home Parks:

No utility shall be required to furnish electrical service to a manufactured home park until the utility has been furnished, at no cost to the utility, any necessary easements which may terminate when the property ceases to be used as a manufactured home park. Manufactured home spaces shall be served by the utility through individual meters and billed under the residential rate.

* * *

Natural Gas—**Okla. Admin. Code §§ 165:45-1-1 to 165:45-23-7**

The regulations governing natural gas are similar in form and substance to the regulations governing electric. Questions regarding gas service may be answered by referencing the electric regulation governing a specific issue.

Telecommunications—**Okla. Admin. Code §§ 165:55-1-1 to 165:55-25-11**

The regulations governing telecommunications substantially similar to the regulations governing electric and are indicated accordingly.

* * *

§ 165:55-7-1. Telephone Directories:

Directories shall include the coverage area, emergency information, service, billing, use and provider contact information, and information regarding disputes, inquires, and disconnection. Listings in white pages and directory assistance data base shall be non-discriminatory, regardless of the user's telecommunications service provider.

* * *

§ 165:55-7-3. Trouble Caused by Customer-Provided Equipment (CPE) or Inside Wiring:

A customer may be charged for a premises visit for a trouble report caused by customer-provided equipment or inside wiring. This charge may not be imposed if the customer is not informed of the charge at the time when he or she reports the trouble.

* * *

§ 165:55-9-1. Billing Period:

Bills, unless otherwise authorized, shall be issued monthly. Local service may be billed in advance. Bills must be sent U.S. Mail, unless the customer agrees to another means, such as the Internet.

§ 165:55-9-2. Content of Bills:

Bills must clearly identify each service provider, separate charges by service provider, and itemize previous balance, current service, etc. Bills must include a brief, plain-language explanation of each charge. Any change in service provider must be clearly identified, including the identification of any charges from the new provider. If bills include both local-exchange service and other services, they must clearly indicate charges for which nonpayment can result in disconnection of local service. Telecommunications service providers and inter-exchange carriers must provide a toll-free number where customers can contact a person capable of answering questions and resolving complaints.

§ 165:55-9-2.1. Bills Rendered by a Billing Agent:

Bills rendered by service provider or interexchange carrier as a billing agent for other provider, IXL or reseller shall provide a toll-free number of the rendering agency, or information regarding agent's ability to adjust billing if so authorized.

§ 165:55-9-3. Due Date and Penalty:

Payment shall be due 15 days after mailing or after any deferred payment date. Late payments may be subject to a 1.5% penalty charge unless otherwise provided by approved tariff.

§ 165:55-9-4. Request for Payments Other than Normal Billings:

Utility may bill separately for additional charges not normally billed on regular billing cycle, e.g., for new or additional deposits, high toll charges, or other advance payments.

§ 165:55-9-5. Billing Disputes:

Substantially similar to § 165:35-21-40.

§ 165:55-9-6. Refund for Service Interruptions:

If service is interrupted for more than 24 consecutive hours and is not due to the customer's negligence or willful conduct or is beyond the control of the utility, a provider shall pay upon customer's request a refund based on a prorated part of that month's local exchange service charges and any regulated equipment charges.

* * *

§ 165:55-9-10. Establishment of Credit for Residential Applicants and Customers:

Substantially similar to § 165:35-19-10.

* * *

§ 165:55-9-13. Reestablishment of Credit:

An applicant whose service has been suspended or disconnected for nonpayment shall be required, before service is provided, to pay all amounts due for regulated services, or to execute a deferred payment agreement (if offered), and to establish credit as provided above, or (if permitted by tariff) to apply for less than basic local exchange service.

§ 165:55-9-14. Deposits and Interest:

Substantially similar to § 165:35-19-10. Amount of deposit for local or toll service shall not exceed 2 months of actual or estimated charges for each service. If local service is billed in advance, the deposit may include only 1 month's such charges. A deposit for toll service must be re-evaluated after 4 months if customer so requests and can show that toll charges during the 4 months decreased by 50% or more.

* * *

§ 165:55-11-1. Denial or Termination of Service Without Notice:

Substantially similar to §§ 165:35-21-30, except there is no provision for refusal or disconnection for failure to pay a deposit.

§ 165:55-11-2. Denial or Disconnection of Service After Notice:

Substantially similar to § 165:35-21-2.

§ 165:55-11-3. Responsibility for Accounts:

A provider is not required to provide service to an applicant or end-user who has not paid for prior service in the same or different location provided to the same person or legal entity. A provider is not required to provide service applied for in the name of another person or legal entity, or a fictitious name, or the name of another household member for the purpose of avoiding payment of an unpaid obligation. Customers are not responsible for the payment of another customer's bill unless the customer superseded the service or was a co-applicant or guarantor or shared the service on the unpaid account. Provider must extend payment arrangement to applicant for prior bill unless applicant has not fulfilled payment arrangements within previous 12 months.

§ 165:55-11-4. Insufficient Reason for Denial or Suspension or Disconnection of Service:

Substantially similar to § 165:35-21-2. Local service may not be denied or terminated for nonpayment of non-regulated charges or for disputed charges.

* * *

§ 165:55-11-6. Service Disputes:

Substantially similar to § 165:35-21-40.

* * *

§ 165:55-11-10. Suspension or Disconnection for Nonpayment or Failure to Make Security Deposit:

Substantially similar to § 165:35-21-20, except it includes Internet notice provisions and there is no second notice requirement.

* * *

§ 165:55-11-12. Notice of Disconnection and Notice of Suspension:

Substantially similar to § 165:35-21-20. The notice must disclose whether the past-due amount includes billing for non-deniable or unregulated services, for which local service may not be disconnected, and must include a toll-free number for questions and payment arrangements.

§ 165:55-11-12.1. Emergency Service Following Suspension:

Regardless of the reason for suspension, if the central office is capable of providing emergency service following suspension, the TSP shall also provide access to 911 or E911 service for at least 30 days.

§ 165:55-11-13. Reconnection:

Substantially similar to § 165:35-21-31, but service does not have to be reconnected within 24 hours of account reconciliation.

* * *

§§ 165:55-19-1.1 and 165:55-19-1.2. Slamming; Letter of Agency Form and Content:

Changes to a customer's service or service provider shall be authorized and verifiable (see regulation for verification procedures).

* * *

§ 165:55-19-3. Carrier Liability for Cramming:

Unauthorized charges to a customer's account are prohibited. Disconnection shall not occur until any dispute involving unauthorized charges are resolved.

* * *

***Water Service*—Okla. Admin. Code §§ 165:65-1-1–165:65-13-8**

The regulations governing water are similar in form and substance to the regulations governing electric. Questions regarding water service may be answered by referencing the electric regulation governing a specific issue.

OREGON

The Public Utility Commission's general regulations regarding gas, electric, and telecommunications service can be found in Or. Admin. R. 860-021-0000–860-021-0420; water regulations can be found in Or. Admin. R. 860-036-0001–860-36-0930; regulations for wastewater service and for joint water/wastewater utilities can be found in Or. Admin. R. 860-037-0001–860-037-0630. In some cases it may be important to consult Or. Admin. R. 860-034-0010–860-034-0290 for the rules specific to small telecommunications utilities. Many of the substantive issue regarding water regulations are substantially similar to the general regulations and are indicated accordingly. Access to the administrative rules can be found at http://arcweb.sos.state.or.us/banners/rules.htm (last visited in May 2011).

***General (Gas, Electric, Telecommunications)*—Or. Admin. R. 860-021-0000–860-021-0420**

* * *

860-021-0009. Applications for Utility Service from an Energy or Large Telecommunications Utility:

An application is required from a person who has not previously been served by the utility; or is seeking reconnection after involuntary disconnection; or has voluntarily terminated and did not seek restoration within 20 days. The utility may request name, billing and service addresses, date of birth, day and night telephone numbers, Social Security number and proper identification. Proper identification is either a current Oregon driver's license, or a state or Federal identification with picture, or a combination of certified birth certificate, school, or work picture ID, and name and contact information of a teacher, employer or caseworker who can verify applicant's identity. A large telecommunications utility must protect persons at risk from domestic violence by allowing the use of a modified or alternative name in the directory, or by providing a free non-published number to a customer who presents a copy of a restraining order and an affidavit stating that customer cannot afford to pay for the non-published listing.

860-021-0010. Information for Utility Customers and Applicants:

The utility must assist the consumer in selecting the most advantageous rate. The summary of rights and responsibilities provided to customers must specifically include rights to third-party notification, medical certificates, levelized billing, sources of financial assistance, the availability of notices in languages other than English and, for telecommunications utilities, the telephone solicitation rules.

A utility that provides metered service must, upon request, inform customers how to read meters. Utilities must keep on file, and make available to customers, copies of rate schedules, tariffs, and the utility's and Commission's rules and regulations. Utilities must conspicuously post, in offices where credit matters are transacted, notices explaining customers' rights and responsibilities.

860-021-0011. Multilingual Notices:

All customer's rights shall contain translations into Spanish, Vietnamese, Cambodian, Laotian, and Russian, and disconnection notices shall contain a specified warning regarding shut off in such languages.

860-021-0015. Dispute Resolution:

A customer or applicant dissatisfied regarding a utility's resolution of a dispute may seek redress through the Consumer Service Division, and, if still dissatisfied, may file a complaint with the Commission.

While a formal complaint is pending, the customer is responsible for paying undisputed amounts. The utility must continue or restore service, provided that: service was not terminated for theft of services or failure to establish credit; a bona fide dispute exists; if termination was for nonpayment, customer or applicant makes an arrangement to avoid loss to the utility, such as prepaying estimated charges, and the customer or applicant diligently pursues the dispute-resolution process.

860-021-0017. Designation of Third Party to Receive Notices:

Utility shall offer customers and applicants the option of having a third party receive bills and notices.

860-021-0019 Restrictions on Entering a Customer's Residence:

No employee may enter a customer's residence without proper authority, except in an emergency endangering life or property.

* * *

860-021-0045. Installation of Electric Service:

The electric utility shall furnish, own, operate, maintain, and replace the service connections with the exceptions as may be listed in these rules or its tariff for line extensions. If a single service connection furnishes service to two or more customers, each customer's service must be metered and billed separately.

860-021-0050. Installation of Gas Service:

Substantially similar to 860-021-0045.

* * *

860-21-0057. Connection of Residential Energy Utility Service:

The utility must provide a location where applicants may contact the utility between 8:00 a.m. and 5:00 p.m. on business days to request connection, provide credit information, and pay any applicable fees. Connection should be made within 2 business days (with certain exceptions provided in this rule). For natural gas utilities reconnecting between September 15 and November 15 at address where applicant received service at any time within previous 12 months, connection should be made within 2 business days if service was disconnected between August 15 and November 15 of the current year, or five business days if service was terminated between November 16 of the previous year and August 14 of the current year.

860-021-0120. Meter Reading and Bill Forms:

Bills shall be issued monthly and shall indicate the due date, beginning and ending meter readings, consumption amounts, and a clear indication if the bill is an estimate.

If access to a meter is difficult, the utility may seek the customer's cooperation in obtaining readings; customer's readings must be verified at least every 4 months. Failure to provide access to the meter at reasonable times after reasonable notice is grounds for disconnection.

860-021-0125. Due and Payable Periods:

Due dates and pay periods shall be no less than 15 days from the day after a bill's postmark or postage meter date.

860-021-0126. Late-Payment Charge:

Late payment charges are set by the Commission, shall not be assessed on outstanding amounts less than $200 or carried over for 2 consecutive months, and are not allowed unless the utility offers preferred billing options (customer allowed to choose monthly due date).

* * *

860-021-0130. Meter Test:

A customer is entitled to one free meter test per year, which should be conducted within 20 working days after the customer's request. The customer and a designated representative have a right to be present. The utility may charge for a second test within 12 months, unless the meter is found to register outside the 2% accepted tolerance standard.

860-021-0135. Adjustment of Utility Bills:

Adjustments shall be made when an error (meter reading) is more than 2%. Payment arrangements shall be offered for under-billing. When the beginning date of the error cannot be determined adjustments shall not be for more than 6 months; when the date of the error is known, adjustments shall not exceed 3 years.

860-021-0200. Establishing Credit for Residential Utility Service:

Credit may be established by proof of 12 months of utility service within the past 24 months, if service was terminated voluntarily and all services timely paid for; or by satisfying Commission-approved credit requirements based on a third-party credit report or the utility's own credit scoring formula; or by proof of 1-year employment or income verification; or by paying a deposit or furnishing a guarantor. Telephone utility may not require a deposit if the customer or applicant is eligible for Oregon Telephone Assistance Program and agrees to toll blocking. In lieu of a deposit or guarantee, the customer of an energy utility may agree to use a demand limiter or "pay as you go" metering, if equipment is available.

A deposit or guarantor may be required for prior disconnection, tampering, or theft of service or unpaid balance owed to an Oregon utility at the time of termination, for a similar type of service within the past 24 months.

Deposits for gas and electric service shall not exceed 1/6 annual estimated usage; deposits for phone service, and guarantee generally, shall not exceed 2 months' estimated billing. An increased deposit may be required for theft or tampering; for the discovery that the consumer gave false information in obtaining service or establishing credit; for an energy utility, if the customer moves and the anticipated bill at the new residence is 20% greater than the basis for the existing deposit; or, for a telephone utility, if intra-LATA toll activity exceeds the basis of the prior deposit.

860-021-0205. Deposit Payment Arrangements for Residential Energy Utility Service:

Deposits may be paid in full or in 3 monthly installments, and, except for the last payment, shall be in installments of $30 or 1/3 whichever is greater.

If a customer fails to comply with deposit payment arrangements, the utility may disconnect on 5 days' notice. A customer who has been disconnected for this reason must pay the entire deposit, a reconnection fee, a late fee, and one-half the past-due amount before service is restored. The remaining half must be paid within 30 days.

860-021-0206. Payment Arrangements for Deposit and Installation Charges for Residential Telecommunications Utility Service:

Payment arrangements for deposits shall be paid in 4 monthly installments with one-quarter (1/4) due immediately and, except for the last payment, monthly installments of $20 or one-quarter (1/4) whichever is greater. Disconnection and re-connection provisions substantially similar to gas and electric, above. At the time when a telecommunications utility demands a deposit, it must inform the consumer about Link-up America and the Oregon Telephone Assistance Program.

860-021-0210. Interest on Deposits for Residential and Nonresidential Utility Service:

Interest on deposits shall be based on rates for a 1-year Treasury bill.

860-021-0215. Refund of Deposits for Residential and Nonresidential Utility Service:

A deposit shall be refunded when service is terminated, or customer is current and has not been disconnected and has not had more than two 5-day disconnection notices within previous 12 months.

860-021-0305. Grounds for Disconnecting Utility Service:

Service may be disconnected for issues relating to nonpayment, denial of reasonable access to equipment, failure to apply for service or unauthorized use or misrepresentation, tampering, violation of utility, state, or local rules, or dangerous or emergency conditions.

860-021-0310. Voluntary Disconnection of Utility Service:

A customer who is about to move, or who otherwise wishes service disconnected, must give 5 days' notice. Until such notice is given, customer remains liable for any service provided.

860-021-0315. Emergency Disconnection of Utility Service:

In emergencies endangering life or property, an energy or large telecommunications utility may terminate service without notice.

860-021-0320. Disconnection of Service on Weekends and Holidays:

Service shall not be disconnected for nonpayment on a weekend or a state or utility-recognized holiday. Service may not be disconnected on a Friday, or the day before a state- or utility-recognized holiday without the consent of customer, utility, and Consumer Services Division.

860-021-0325. Accounts Not Related to Residential Utility Service:

Service shall not be disconnected for failure to pay for nonresidential services.

860-021-0326. Disconnection of Gas or Electric Service to Tenants:

Tenants, not responsible for payment, shall be given 5 days' notice of disconnection. A utility shall notify the Commission when disconnection is pending in a master-metered multi-family residence, and it shall make a reasonable effort to notify tenants of pending disconnection and available alternatives.

860-021-0328. Reconnection of Residential Energy Utility Service:

This rule applies to reconnections within 20 days after disconnection, if customer has satisfied all requirements for reconnection. If reconnection is requested on a business day, it should usually be done by 5:00 the next business day. If request is made before 3:00 p.m. on a Friday business day, service shall be restored by 5:00 p.m. the next day. The utility must offer after-hours reconnection and may charge an additional fee for this service.

860-021-330. Reconnection Fee for Utility Service:

A utility may charge a reconnection fee per tariff.

860-021-0334. Transfer Billing:

A customer's balance from previous account may be transferred to an existing account.

860-021-0335. Refusal of Utility Service:

Applicants must be notified of reason for refusal and of Commission's complaint process. Service may be refused for nonpayment of a prior account within Oregon, for overdue balance of person at residence, if applicant resided there when amount became due and continues to live there.

Service may not be denied if applicant pays half the amount of the outstanding balance with the remaining amount to be paid within 30 days.

860-021-0405. Notice of Pending Disconnection of Residential Electric or Gas Utility Service:

Utility shall give an initial notice of at least 15 days before disconnection for nonpayment and a subsequent notice of at least 5 days. Utility shall make every reasonable effort to notify through mail or hand delivery and shall attempt personal notification at the time of disconnection. If a remote disconnect is planned, utility must attempt telephone contact twice a day for three days before the disconnect (one call each day between 8:00 a.m. and 5:00 p.m. and one between 6:00 p.m. and 8:00 p.m.) and must leave a message on the answering machine, if any, each day. "Initial implementation of section 7(b)(B) [the section quoted immediately above] may not occur during the winter heating season (November 1 through April 30)."

Notice of disconnection shall be clearly distinguishable, and shall contain the reasons for disconnection, the amount due, date of disconnection, availability of payment plans and assistance, delay option for medical reasons, and complaint procedures.

If upon making personal or telephone contact, a reasonable person would conclude that the customer or an adult at the residence does not understand the consequences of disconnection, the utility must notify the Department of Human Services and the Commission and must delay disconnection for 5 additional business days.

860-021-0410. Emergency Medical Certificate for Residential Electric or Gas Utility Service:

Disconnection shall be delayed upon oral or written confirmation that disconnection would significantly endanger the physical health of the customer or a member of the customer's household. Oral notification shall be confirmed within 14 days. Delay shall be valid for duration of condition but may not exceed 6 months for non-chronic conditions and 12 months for chronic conditions.

The utility may terminate if a medical certificate customer breaches a payment arrangement, but must first notify the Consumer Services Division of the Commission, which may hold a hearing to determine whether to permit disconnection. A utility may verify the accuracy of a medical certificate and, if it believes the customer does not qualify, may seek Commission permission to disconnect.

Customer shall enter into a payment arrangement for an overdue balance and may renegotiate if a financial hardship is shown.

860-021-0414. Equal-Payment Plans for Residential Electric and Gas Service:

Electric and gas utilities will make equal-payment plans available to residential customers. A customer with no outstanding balance who agrees to remain on an equal payment plan for 12 months may enter into equal-payment agreement at any time during the year. The plan will provide for an annual adjustment between the estimated charge and the actual charges. If a customer changes residences during the term of the agreement, the payments may be adjusted to reflect the anticipated change in usage.

860-021-0415. Time-Payment Agreements for Residential Electric and Gas Service (Non-Medical Certificate Customers):

A gas or electric utility may not disconnect residential service for nonpayment if a customer enters into a written time-payment plan. A utility will offer customers a choice of payment agreements. At a minimum, the customer may choose between a levelized payment plan and an equal-pay arrearage plan. The utility shall review the monthly installment plan periodically. If needed due to changing rates or variations in the amount of service used by the customer, the installment amount may be adjusted to bring the account into balance within the time specified in the original agreement.

860-021-0420. Field Visit Charge:

A utility may charge a Commission-approved fee if an employee visits a residential address to disconnect or re-connect but is unable do so because of customer action.

860-021-0505. Disconnection Procedures for All Commercial Electric and Gas Utility Customers and All Customers of Large Telecommunications Utilities:

Five days' notice is required. Notice must be in bold face, and state in easy-to-understand language the reasons for disconnection; disconnection date; amount to be paid to avoid disconnection; explanation of Commission's complaint process; explanation of medical certificate procedure. An employee who makes a premises visit to disconnect must try to make contact with the customer or other resident at the service address and, failing this, leave a notice in a conspicuous place. In lieu of disconnection, a large telecommunications utility may impose service limitation, i.e., customer may make outgoing local calls but may not receive calls or make toll calls. This temporary curtailment requires 5 days' written notice, which must warn that permanent disconnection will follow after 10 days if the customer does not make full payment. A telecommunications carrier may not discontinue or deny local service for failure to pay for any service not under the LEC's tariff. The utility may, however, limit access to toll or 900-number services. A utility may not deny or discontinue local service to customers eligible for Oregon Telephone Assistance for failure to pay toll charges.

860-021-0510. Emergency Medical Certificate for Residential Telecommunications Utility Service:

Substantially similar to 860-0410. Twelve-month certificate is not available. The customer must enter into a payment agreement satisfying the requirements of 860-021-0575.

860-021-0550. Termination of Local Exchange Residential Service for Telecommunications Customers at Significant Risk:

Customers "at significant risk" are persons at risk for domestic violence or unwanted sexual contact; elders or disabled persons at risk of abuse; stalking victims. Significant risk must be shown by a copy of a restraining order or other relevant court order and an affidavit from the customer stating that termination would place the customer or a household resident at significant risk. A customer who seeks protection under this section must enter into a payment agreement for any overdue balance. Before disconnecting for breach of payment agreement, the utility must give 5 days' notice to the Commission's Consumer Services section.

860-021-0575. Time Payment Agreements for Large Telecommunications Utilities:

Time payments must include a down payment of the greater of $10 or 25% of the amount due for tariffed or price-listed services, followed by full payment within 90 days, and an agreement to keep subsequent bills current. Payments must be made monthly and may not be accelerated if the customer changes residence.

* * *

860-021-0610. Telephone Solicitation Notices by Large Telecommunications Utilities:

Large telecommunications utilities must notify their customers annually, by bill insert or conspicuous notice in directories, about the no-call list and the procedure for adding one's name to it.

860-021-0620. Customer Notification and Information Delivery Services for Large Telecommunication Utilities:

Utilities that provide billing services for information providers must inform customers, in the information for new customers and annually thereafter by bill insert or conspicuous publication in the directory, of the availability of blocking for 900-numbers (if technically feasible); that local or long-distance service will not be suspended or terminated for nonpayment for information services; certain statutory private remedies for misconduct by information providers; the invalidity of information providers' charges incurred by unemancipated minors or certain mentally ill persons.

* * *

***Water*—Or. Admin. R. 860-036-0010–860-036-0250**

The regulations governing water service are similar in form and substance to the general regulations. Questions regarding water service may be answered by referencing the general regulation governing a specific issue.

860-036-0105. Use of Water Meters:

Pre-payment meters are forbidden, except in special cases or for clearly defined classes of service authorized by the Commission.

PENNSYLVANIA

The Public Utility Commission's general regulations governing electric, gas, steam-heat, waste-water and water service can be found within 52 Pa. Code §§ 56.1–56.231. The regulations governing telecommunication service can be found within 52 Pa. Code §§ 64.1–64.213. Many of the regulations governing telecommunication service are similar in substance and form to the general regulations. Questions regarding telecommunication regulations not summarized here may be answered by referencing the general regulations governing a specific issue. Access to the regulations can be found at www.pacode.com/secure/data/052/052toc.html (last visited in May 2011).

***General (Electric, Gas, Steam Heat, Waste-water and Water Service)*—52 Pa. Code §§ 56.1–56.231**

* * *

§ 56.11. Billing Frequency:

A utility shall render a bill once every billing period to every residential customer in accordance with approved rate schedules.

§ 56.12. Meter Reading; Estimated Billing; Customer Readings:

If billed on a monthly basis, utility may estimate usage every other month if the customer is provided the options, instructions, and procedures to read meter. A utility may estimate the bill of a customer if extreme weather conditions, emergencies, equipment failure, work stoppages, or other circumstances prevent actual meter reading. In specific circumstances, a utility may use remote devices for reading meters. Utility shall provide equalized payments plans over 10-, 11-, or 12-month periods.

§ 56.13. Separate Billings for Merchandise, Appliances, and Nonrecurring Services:

Charges for other than basic service shall appear on a separate bill.

§ 56.14. Previously Unbilled Utility Service:

When a utility renders a make-up bill for previously unbilled utility service resulting from billing error, meter failure, leakage that could not reasonably have been detected or loss of service, or four or more consecutive estimated bills, and the make-up bill is at least $50 and exceeds the otherwise normal estimated bill by at least 50%, the utility shall review the bill with the customer and make a reasonable attempt to enter into a payment agreement. Payment periods shall be as long as period during which unbilled amount accrued, or as long as necessary to prevent bill exceeding estimated monthly bill plus 50%.

§ 56.15. Billing Information:

All bills shall contain information concerning dates and consumption amounts, due dates, amounts and penalties due, any information that will allow and assist in the computation of charges, and contact information of the utility that indicated disputes are to be registered before due date. A bill must clearly indicate that it is an estimated bill.

§ 56.16. Transfer of Accounts:

Customers may be required to give up to at least 7 days' notice for account closure or disconnection, and shall be liable for charges until notice expires. A customer's balance from a previous account may be transferred to an existing account. In the event of a termination of service to a residential customer, a utility may transfer to the account of a third-party guarantor any portion of the unpaid balance that is equivalent to the cash deposit requirement of the customer.

* * *

§ 56.21. Payment:

The due date for payment of a bill may be no less than 20 days from the date of transmittal (the date of mailing or physical delivery by the utility to the customer), and shall be the next business day if due date is on a weekend, holiday, or other day when utility payment offices are not open. Payment shall be deemed to have been made on the date of the postmark. The utility shall not impose a late payment charge unless payment is received more than 5 days after the due date.

§ 56.22. Accrual of Late Payment Charges:

Late payment charges shall not exceed 1.5% interest per month, or 18% when annualized, on full unpaid and overdue balance of bill and shall not be imposed for rebilling or on disputed estimated bills unless utility was willfully denied access to the meter.

§ 56.23. Application of Partial Payments Between Utility and Other Service:

Unless specifically instructed, payments that do not fully cover service and non-service charges shall be first applied to service charges.

§ 56.24. Application of Partial Payments Among Several Bills for Utility Service:

In the absence of written instructions, a disputed bill or an amortization agreement payment received by a utility which are insufficient to pay a balance due both for prior service and for service billed during the current billing period shall first be applied to the balance due for prior service.

* * *

§ 56.32. Credit Standards:

A deposit for service shall not be required if the applicant: had a 24 consecutive month payment history for a similar type of service, the periodic bill was at least 50% of new estimated service, service was not terminated for nonpayment in previous 12 months, and applicant has no unpaid balance from that account; or owns or has an agreement to purchase property or a 12-month lease of property. A utility may accept information confirming positive credit but a lack of credit shall not indicate a credit risk. Utility may accept employment history, residency during previous 5 years, letters of reference, source of income, or credit cards as elements of establish credit.

§ 56.33. Cash Deposits; Third-Party Guarantors:

If an applicant fails to meet credit standards, the utility shall provide service when the applicant pays a deposit or furnishes a third-party guarantor that equals the amount of cash deposit required.

* * *

§ 56.35. Payment of Outstanding Balance:

A utility may require, as a condition of the furnishing of residential service to an applicant, the payment of any outstanding residential account with the utility which accrued within the past 4 years for which the applicant is legally responsible and for which the applicant was billed properly.

§ 56.36. Written Procedures:

A utility shall inform and provide applicants and customers with credit-establishment procedures and requirements, and shall notify an applicant or customer of the reason a deposit is required.

§ 56.37. General Rule:

If the investigation and determination of credit status is expected to take, or in fact takes longer than 3 business days commencing the date after the application is made, the utility shall provide service pending completion of the investigation.

§ 56.38. Payment Period for Deposits by Applicants:

An applicant may elect to pay any required deposits in three installments: 50% payable upon the determination by the utility that the deposit is required, 25% payable 30 days after the determination, and 25% payable 60 days after the determination.

§ 56.41. General Rule:

An existing customer may be required to pay a deposit if delinquent in payment for 2 consecutive months or 3 or more bills in the preceding 12 months, delinquency account arising from make-up bill for underbilling, for reconnection of terminated service, or failure to comply with settlement or payment agreement.

§ 56.42. Payment Period for Deposits by Customers:

The due date of a deposit, except for reconnection of service, shall be due no less than 21 days of mailing or service. Deposits may be paid in installments consisting of a 50% initial payment followed by two 25% installments at 30-day intervals.

* * *

§ 56.51. Amount of Cash Deposit:

A deposit from an applicant shall not exceed the average estimated bill of a period equal to one billing period plus 1 additional month's service (shall not to exceed 4 months in the case of water and sewage utilities and 2 months in the case of gas, electric and steam heat utilities), with a minimum deposit of $5. The same amounts are applicable to an existing customer's prior usage if a deposit is required.

* * *

§ 56.53. Refund of Deposit:

A utility shall release a guarantor, refund or credit a deposit to a customer's account, plus accrued interest, if the customer establishes credit or makes timely payments for 12 consecutive months. Deposits shall be returned, with accrued interest if the customer provides a guarantor. When service is terminated or disconnected, the utility may apply a deposit, plus any accrued interest, to any outstanding balance.

* * *

§ 56.55. Periodic Review:

If a customer is not entitled to a refund of a deposit under § 56.53, the customer's account shall be reviewed each billing period.

* * *

§ 56.57. Interest Rate:

Interest at the rate of the average of 1-year Treasury bills for September, October, and November of the previous year is payable on deposits without deductions for taxes thereon unless otherwise required by law.

§ 56.58. Application of Interest:

Interest shall be paid annually to the customer, or, at the option of either the utility or the customer, shall be applied to service bills.

* * *

§ 56.71. Interruption of Service:

A utility may temporarily interrupt service when necessary to effect repairs or maintenance, to eliminate an imminent threat to life, health, safety, or substantial property damage, or for reasons of local, state, or national emergency.

§ 56.72. Discontinuation of Service:

When a customer requests discontinuance of service at a location other than the customer's residence, or at a single meter multi-family residence, 10 days' notice shall be posted at the premises, including posting in common areas of multi-family residence, if the customer fails to certify that premises are unoccupied or the affected occupants do not consent to the discontinuance.

§ 56.81. Authorized Termination of Service:

A utility may terminate service for nonpayment, failure to establish credit, unreasonable denial of access to or tampering with equipment, fraud or material misrepresentation in obtaining service, or violating rules of tariff.

§ 56.82. Days Termination of Service Is Prohibited:

Except in emergencies, service shall not be terminated on Friday through Sunday, on the day of or the day before a holiday observed by bank, the utility, or the Commission, or on a day the utility is closed.

§ 56.83. Unauthorized Termination of Service:

Service shall not be terminated for various reasons relating to nonpayment of services of a different type, of others, or from other locations; nonpayment of charges for utility service furnished more than 4 years prior to the date the bill is rendered; nonpayment of charges calculated on the basis of estimated billings, unless the estimated bill was required because utility personnel were unable to gain access to the affected premises to obtain an actual meter reading on two occasions, or a subsequent and verifying actual reading is obtained; noncompliance with a payment agreement prior to the due date of the bill which forms the basis of the agreement; nonpayment of delinquent accounts: which accrued over two billing periods or more, which remain unpaid in whole or in part for 6 months or less, and which amount to a total delinquency of less than $25; nonpayment of delinquent accounts when the amount of the deposit presently held by the utility is within $25 of account balance. Service shall also not be terminated for nonpayment, in whole or in part: for leased or purchased merchandise, appliances or special services including but not limited to merchandise and appliance installation fees, rental and repair costs; of meter testing fees; of special construction charges; and of other nonrecurring charges that are not essential to delivery or metering of service.

§ 56.91. General Notice Provisions:

Prior to termination of service, the utility shall mail or deliver written notice to the customer at least 10 days prior to the date of the proposed termination.

§ 56.92. Notice When Dispute Pending:

A utility may not mail or deliver a notice of termination if a notice of dispute has been filed and is unresolved and the subject matter of the dispute forms the grounds for the proposed termination.

§ 56.93. Personal Contact:

Except when authorized by §§ 56.71, 56.72 or 56.98 (relating to interruption of service; discontinuation of service; and exception for terminations based on occurrences harmful to person or property), a utility may not interrupt, discontinue or terminate service without personally contacting the customer or a responsible adult occupant at least 3 days prior to the interruption, discontinuance or termination.

§ 56.94. Procedures Immediately Prior to Termination:

A utility shall attempt to make personal contact immediately prior to termination. If evidence of a medical condition or emergency, a dispute is pending, or payment is offered, termination shall not occur. Personal checks shall be accepted for payment unless the customer has submitted a check for payment within past year that was returned for insufficient funds.

§ 56.95. Deferred Termination When No Prior Contact:

When no contact has occurred prior to termination, the utility shall not disconnect service and shall post notice that disconnection will occur no earlier than 48 hours from notice.

§ 56.96. Post-Termination Notice:

When service is actually terminated, notice, that contains the address and telephone number of the utility where the customer may arrange to have service restored as well as a medical emergency notice, shall be conspicuously posted or delivered to responsible adult at customer's residence and to/at the affected premises.

* * *

§ 56.99. Use of Termination Notice Solely As a Collection Device Prohibited:

A utility shall not threaten or use notice of termination unless it has the present and grounds to terminate.

§ 56.100. Winter Termination Procedures:

Utilities shall not terminate heat related service between December 1 and March 31 except as provided in this section or in § 56.98 (relating to exception for terminations based on occurrences harmful to person or property), until it has attempted to reach an agreement with the customer. If an agreement cannot be reached the utility shall seek Commission approval before terminating service. When services have been disconnected prior to December 1 of each year, the utility shall within 90 days prior to December 1 make a reasonable attempt to contact customer and attempt to reach an agreement to restore service.

* * *

§ 56.111. General (Emergency) Provision:

A utility may not terminate, or refuse to restore service to a premise when an occupant therein is certified by a physician to be seriously ill or affected with a medical condition that will be aggravated by a cessation of service or failure to restore service.

§ 56.112. Postponement of Termination Pending Receipt of Certificate:

If, prior to termination of service, the utility employee is informed that an occupant is seriously ill or is affected with a medical condition which will be aggravated by a cessation of service and that a medical certification will be procured, termination may not occur for at least 3 days. Service may be terminated if no certification is produced within that 3-day period.

* * *

§ 56.114. Length of Postponement; Renewals:

A certified medical postponement shall not exceed 30 days but may be renewed for two additional 30-day periods. Pursuant to § 56.118, a utility may contest a renewal.

§ 56.115. Restoration of Service:

Upon receipt of a medical certificate, a utility shall make a diligent effort to restore service that day, but shall have services restored before the end of the next working day.

* * *

§ 56.117. Termination upon Expiration of Medical Certification:

Once an initial and/or renewed medical certificate has expired, service may be terminated without additional notice if notice under § 56.91 has been previously given.

* * *

§ 56.141. Dispute Procedures:

Unless otherwise provided for in this chapter, a disputed termination shall not occur until the dispute is resolved provided the undisputed portions of bill are paid.

§ 56.142. Time for Filing a Termination Dispute or Informal Complaints:

Notice of a dispute shall be filed at least the day before a scheduled termination to be considered timely.

§ 56.143. Effect of Failure to Timely File a Termination Dispute:

Failure to timely file a notice of dispute, except for good cause, shall constitute a waiver of applicable rights to retain service without complying with the termination notice, and may constitute a waiver of rights to file an informal complaint in accordance with this chapter.

§ 56.151. General Rule:

Utility shall not issue termination notice on a disputed matter, shall make a reasonable attempt to investigate, and shall negotiate a reasonable payment arrangement if ratepayer or occupant claims a temporary inability to pay undisputed bill.

* * *

§ 56.181. Duties of Parties; Disputing Party's Duty to Pay Undisputed Portion of Bills; Utility's Duty to Pay Interest Whenever Overpayment Found:

A customer is obligated to pay amounts not in dispute. Resolution of informal complaint of a disputed amount in favor of the provider may be subject to interest pursuant to § 56.22. Resolution of formal complaint of disputed amount in favor of customer shall be reimbursed with interest pursuant to § 56.22. Partial payment of any disputed amount shall not constitute an admission or waiver of rights.

§ 56.191. General Rule:

Once the reason for termination has been resolved, service shall be restored, subject to a reasonable reconnection fee, by the end of the first full working day.

§ 56.192. Personnel Available to Restore Service:

A utility shall have adequate personnel available between 9:00 a.m. and 5:00 p.m. on each working day, or for a commensurate period of 8 consecutive hours, to restore service.

* * *

***Telephone*—52 Pa. Code §§ 64.1–64.213**

Many of the regulations governing telephone service are similar in substance and form to the general regulations. Questions regarding telephone regulations not summarized here, may be answered by referencing the general regulation governing a specific issue.

* * *

§ 64.11. Method of Payment:

Payment may be made in any reasonable manner, including by personal check, unless, within the prior 12 months, the customer has tendered a dishonored check for payment.

* * *

§ 64.16. Accrual of Late Payment Charges:

Late payment charges shall not exceed 1.25% interest per month, or 15% when annualized, on full unpaid and overdue balance of bill or deposit, and shall not be imposed for rebilling or on disputed estimated bills unless utility was willfully denied access to the meter.

* * *

§ 64.23. Standardizing LEC Responses to Customer Contacts Alleging Unauthorized Charges Added to the Customer's Bill (Cramming) and Unauthorized Changes to the Customer's Long Distance Carrier (Slamming):

Upon receipt of a complaint alleging cramming or slamming, the utility shall inform the customer that it will verify the lack of authorization, that any unauthorized changes or charges shall be removed and/or reversed, that the necessary steps shall be taken to prevent future occurrences, the possibility of the violating provider using outside collection methods, and information and procedure for the customer to file a complaint with the Commission.

* * *

RHODE ISLAND

The Public Utilities Commission's regulations governing termination of electric, gas, and water service can be found within 90-060-002 R.I. Code pts. I–X. Standards of service for electric are governed under 90-070-005 R.I. Code R. pts. I–IX; gas, 90-070-021 R.I. Code R. §§ A–K; and water, 90-070-014 R.I. Code R. §§ I–VIII. Specific regulations governing class A&B and C&D electric services are substantially similar in form and substance to the standards of service for electric service providers and may be found at www.ripuc.ri.gov/rulesregs/divrules.html. Regulations governing telephone service can be found within 90-060-007 R.I. Code R. §§ 1.1 to 10.1 (LexisNexis). Questions regarding these specific services may be answered by referencing the standards of service regulations. Additionally, the regulations governing gas, water, and telephone service are similar in form and substance to the regulations governing electric service. Questions regarding gas, water, and telephone service may be answered by referencing the regulations governing electric service. Access to these regulations (without citations) can be found at www.ripuc.ri.gov/rulesregs/divrules.html.

***Termination of Residential Electric, Gas and Water Utility Service*—90-060-002 R.I. Code R. pts. I–X**

Utilities may terminate service after following the notice requirements described below if the customer has not paid for utility service within 40 days of rendering of the bill or 10 days after the due date, the customer has not followed the utility's deposit requirements, or the customer has not provided the utility with reasonable access to the meter, utility equipment or other utility property, and other issues relating to nonpayment. Notice shall be at least 10 days before the scheduled date of disconnection.

Service shall not be terminated due to failure to pay for merchandise or a different class of service, failure to pay for a previous occupant's service, or when the reason for disconnection is in dispute.

Disconnection notices shall be clearly distinguishable, and shall contain the reasons for disconnection, the amount due, date of disconnection, availability of payment plans and assistance, delay options during heating season, for seriously ill, elderly or disabled, and for households with financial hardship and infant, and complaint procedures.

A utility shall postpone termination for 21 days upon receiving certification from a licensed physician that someone living at the residence is seriously ill. Postponement of service may be extended after review.

Service that is the primary source of heat shall not be disconnected due to nonpayment from November 1 through April 15, unless said bill exceeds $500, or when a delinquent bill for services that do not provide heat exceeds $200. During the moratorium period (November 1–April 15), no gas or electric utility shall terminate service for nonpayment where the utility has evidence that the person or persons whose services are scheduled to be terminated is a Protected Status Customer (defined as unemployed and currently receiving unemployment compensation; elderly or handicapped; recipients of LIHEAP; seriously ill; or living in a residence where there is domiciled a person under the age of two (2) years and there is a financial hardship). Disconnection of service is also restricted when services are provided to elder, disabled, or customers eligible under Rhode Island's hardship exception, or when the major wage earner has left the residence due to a marital dispute (see regulation for restrictions specifics).

Customers expressing problems paying utility bills shall be offered reasonable payment plans (water service providers have discretion in offering payment).

Service shall not be disconnected on any Friday, Saturday, Sunday, legal holiday, or day before any legal holiday, or at any time when the public utility's business offices are not open for business. Service may be disconnected only between the hours of 8:00 a.m. and 4:00 p.m. of the date specified in the notice or within a reasonable number of days thereafter. Utility shall not terminate service for nonpayment on days for which the National Weather Service has issued a heat advisory or excessive heat warning for the State.

The utility shall have personnel available until 5:00 p.m. or 3 hours after the time of shutoff, whichever is later, authorized to reconnect service and enter into payment agreements, and disconnecting employee shall accept payments or have the ability to negotiate a payment plan.

When service is disconnected, the individual making the disconnection shall immediately inform a responsible adult that service has been terminated or provide notice.

Once the reason for disconnection has been remedied, service shall be restored as soon as reasonably possible.

***Standards for Electric Utilities*—90-070-005 R.I. Code R. pts. I–IX**

The utility shall provide information concerning services, rate schedules and any changes in services and rate schedules, information that will assist in choice of service, and all the rights, remedies, responsibilities, and assistance associated with services (see regulation for disclosure specifics).

An applicant may be required to make application in writing.

Deposits shall not be more than the estimated bill for 2 normal billing periods. Interest shall be paid on deposits held 6 months or more in accordance with applicable rate schedules or the terms and conditions of the public utility.

Deposits, plus accrued interest thereon, less any amount due the public utility, will be refunded upon termination of service. When a deposit is applied against an account which has been terminated, interest shall cease to be accumulated on the balance at the date of termination.

Bills shall be due no less than 30 days from the mailing date, and shall contain information concerning meter-reading dates, consumption amounts, due dates, amounts and penalties due, any information that will allow and assist in the computation of charges, and contact information of the Commission if a dispute with the utility cannot be resolved.

A customer may request discontinuance upon 24 hours' notice. A utility may discontinue for nonpayment, on 10 days' notice, if a bill remains unpaid 30 days after presentation. In lieu of discontinuance, a utility may require payment at less than monthly intervals. After disconnection, a utility may require a reconnection charge. A utility may disconnect upon 10 days' notice for violation of rules or without notice if continued service would endanger life or property. A utility may disconnect without notice if fraudulent use is detected. A utility may not disconnect on a Friday, a Saturday, or the day before a holiday.

Each public utility shall make a full and prompt investigation of customer complaints made either directly or through the Division.

Meters must be read at regular intervals, so far as practicable, on the corresponding day of each reading period. A customer may request a meter test, which should be performed within 15 days of the request. If the meter has been tested within 36 months, the utility may require a $25 deposit, which will be refunded if the meter proves to be more than 2% inaccurate. A customer's bill shall be adjusted if their meter is found to registering too fast or slow by at least 2%. If the meter is fast, the utility must refund the charge for the excess kilowatt hours billed during the previous 12 months, unless the time when the error occurred can be definitely fixed. Adjustment may not be made if there is evidence of meter tampering. If the meter is slow, the company may charge for excess kilowatt hours billed in the last 12 months or since the date of the last test, whichever is shorter. If there is evidence of tampering, the company may bill for all excess hours since the estimated date of the tampering. If a meter fails to register, the bill may be based on information recorded prior or subsequent to the period of non-registration or on any other pertinent information supplied by the customer or known to the utility.

***Rules and Regulations Prescribing Standards for Telephone Utilities*—90-060-007 R.I. Code R. §§1.1 to 10.1; *Standards for Gas Utilities*—90-070-021 R.I. Code R. §§ A–K; *Standards for Water Utilities*—90-070-014 R.I. Code R. §§ I–VIII**

The regulations governing gas, water, and telephone service are similar in form and substance to the regulations governing electric service.

SOUTH CAROLINA

The Public Service Commission's regulations governing electric utilities can be found within S.C. Code Ann. Regs. 103-300–103-392. The regulations governing gas utilities can be found within S.C. Code Ann. Regs. 103-400–103-494. The regulations governing sewage service can be found within S.C. Code Ann. Regs. 103-500–103-582. The regulations governing telecommunications service can be found within S.C. Code Ann. Regs. 103-600–103-690.1, and the regulations governing water service can be found within S.C. Code Ann. Regs. 103-700–103-782. The regulations governing gas, water and sewage service are similar in form and substance to the regulations governing electric. Questions regarding these services may be answered by referencing the electric regulation governing a specific issue. Access to the regulations can found at www.www.psc.sc.gov/laws/default.asp (last visited in May 2011).

***Electric Utilities*—S.C. Code Ann. Regs. 103-300–103-392**

* * *

103-330. Customer Information:

Utility shall provide applicants, within 60 days of application, a clear and concise explanation of rate schedules. Upon request, the utility shall provide customers with documentation of the previous 12-months usage, complaint procedures, meter-reading information, emergency information, and advice and assistance with choosing service.

103-331. Customer Deposits:

New applicants, who cannot provide satisfactory references, have been previously terminated for issues relating to nonpayment, are applying for reconnection of service, or had service terminated for fraudulent use may be required to pay a deposit. Existing customers with two consecutive late payments of 30 days, or more than two non-consecutive late payments within past 24 months may be required to pay a deposit.

103-332. Deposit Amounts:

A deposit (or guarantee) for a new applicant shall not exceed 2 months (60 days) of estimated billing. Existing customers shall not be required to pay a deposit (or provide a guarantee) in excess of the 2 highest consecutive months from the previous year's service. Deposits may be adjusted according to a customer's billing expenses and payment habits.

103-333. Interest on Deposits:

Deposits held longer than 6 months shall accrue interest, per annum, at a rate set by the Commission. Customers shall receive interest payment refunds every 2 years or when the deposit is returned.

* * *

103-335. Deposit Receipt:

Customers shall receive receipts for deposits and the utility shall provide a method by which a customer can claim a deposit if the receipt is lost.

103-336. Deposit Retention:

Deposits shall be refunded after 2 years of service unless the customer has had 2 consecutive 30-day late payments or more than 2 non-consecutive 30-day late payments within the previous 24 months of service.

103-337. Unclaimed Deposits:

Records of unclaimed deposits shall be maintained for at least 1 year, and the utility shall make a reasonable effort to return all unclaimed deposits. Unclaimed deposits together with accrued interest shall be turned over to State Treasurer.

103-338. Deposit Credit:

A customer's deposit shall not be applied to a bill, and a new deposit shall not be required, unless disconnection has been in effect for at least 72 hours without the customer paying the full amount due and applying for reconnection of service.

103-339. Customer Billing:

Bills shall be issued regularly and shall contain information concerning meter readings and reading dates and itemized charges, due dates, amounts and penalties due, any information that will allow and assist in the computation of charges, and billing period.

Bills may be estimated for good cause but must be clearly marked. A utility shall not estimate a customer's bill more than once in a 60-day period without customer's agreement.

A 1.5% late charge may be added to balances not paid within 25 days of billing date. Payment by check, debit card, credit card or electronic payment shall only be refused as a method of payment for good cause.

When service is terminated for issues relating to nonpayment, violations of rules, or fraudulent use of service, a reasonable disconnection and/or reconnection fee may be assessed.

103-340. Adjustment of Bills:

Utilities shall offer plans for general billing purposes and for charges resulting from under-billing. If a customer's meter is in error more than 2% their bill may be adjusted accordingly, but for no more than the previous 60 days from the time the error is discovered. If a billing error is due to reasons other than meter error or willful conduct by the utility, the adjustment may, if it can be determined, be for the entire duration of the error (not exceeding the applicable statute of limitations) or for a period of 12 months (if the duration of the error cannot be determined).

* * *

103-342. Reason for Denial or Discontinuance of Service:

Service may be denied or terminated, without notice, due to hazardous conditions, use of equipment that adversely affects other customers, or unauthorized or fraudulent use.

Notice shall be required if service is denied or terminated for issues relating to nonpayment, refusal to allow reasonable access to equipment, tampering, or violation of State law, local ordinance, or Commission order. Indebtedness of more than 6 years shall not be grounds for refusing or terminating service.

103-343. Insufficient Reasons for Denying Service:

Service shall not be denied or terminated due to arrearage of prior occupant (unless prior occupant will benefit from service), or for nonpayment of merchandise.

103-344. Right of Access:

Authorized agents of the utility shall have access to equipment and premises, at reasonable hours, for the purpose of reading meters and other necessary and proper utility business.

103-345. Customer Complaints:

Utility shall promptly investigate all complaints. If a utility receives notice from the Commission that it has received a complaint, the utility shall not terminate service until it receives notice from the Commission that the investigation is complete, and the customer fails to make a written request for a Commission hearing within 15 days of the Commission mailing the investigation results.

* * *

103-352. Procedures for Termination of Service:

Notice shall be sent 10 days prior to termination, shall be clearly distinguishable, and shall contain the reasons for disconnection, the amount due, date of disconnection, availability of payment plans and assistance, 30-day delay option for certified medical reasons during the months of December through March, complaint procedures, and the address, telephone number and working hours of utility employee to contact to arrange interview regarding payment or payment arrangements. A second notice, similar in nature shall be given 2 days prior to termination (if in person or by phone), or at least 3 days prior to termination if by mail. Payment, if offered, shall be accepted on the day of termination, by the utility employee responsible for terminating service, as means of continuing service.

Payment plans may require that a customer keep their account current and pay any outstanding balance in 6-month installments. Notice of termination due to a delinquent payment plan account shall be given at least 5 days prior to termination if by mail or at least 3 days if given in person.

Service shall only be terminated Monday–Thursday between 8:00 a.m.–4:00 p.m. provided that the utility is not closed the following day.

Customers for whom disconnection would be dangerous to health may be disconnected in accordance with S.C. Ann. Code § 58-27-2520, et seq. (electric) and § 58-5-1120 (gas), and electric and gas utilities are to publish their termination procedures on their websites.

***Gas*—S.C. Code Ann. Regs. 103-400–103-494; *Sewage*—S.C. Code Ann. Regs. 103-500–103-582; *Water*—S.C. Code Ann. Regs. 103-700–103-782**

The regulations governing gas, water and sewage are similar in form and substance to the regulations governing electric. Questions regarding these services may be answered by referencing the electric regulations governing a specific issue.

***Telecommunications*—S.C. Code Ann. Regs. 103-600–103-690.1**

Many of the substantive issues governing telecommunications are substantially similar to those governing electric and are indicated accordingly.

103-620. Customer Information:

Substantially similar to 103-330.

103-621. Customer Deposits:

Substantially similar to 103-331 through 103-338. A deposit may be required after 2 late payment notices within a 9-month period, or if a check for payment for services has been returned within the previous 6 months.

* * *

103-622. Customer Billing:

Substantially similar to 103-339.

* * *

103-623. Adjustment of Bills:

Substantially similar to 103-340.

* * *

103-625. Reasons for Denial or Discontinuation of Service:

Substantially similar to 103-342. Service may be terminated for excessive use of toll service, if after two days written notice prior to termination, satisfactory payment arrangements are not made, or when the utility has a reasonable belief that illegal or willful misuse of service is occurring.

103-626. Insufficient Reasons for Denying Service:

Substantially similar to 103-342. Service shall not be denied for failure to pay for non-regulated equipment or services.

103-627. Rights of Access:

Substantially similar to 103-344.

103-628. Complaints:

Substantially similar to 103-345.

* * *

103-633. Procedures for Termination of Service:

Substantially similar to 103-352, but notice shall be given 5 days prior to termination of service and cold weather related and medical certification protections do not apply.

* * *

SOUTH DAKOTA

The Public Utilities Commission's regulations governing electric and gas utility service can be found within S.D. Admin. R. 20:10:15:01 through S.D. Admin. R. 20:10:20:11. The regulations governing telecommunications service can be found within S.D. Admin. R. 20:10:05:01–20:10:10:10. Regulations governing unauthorized changes in telecommunications providers (slamming) and unauthorized charges (cramming) can be found within S.D. Admin. R. 20:10:34:01–20:10:34:11. Many of the regulations governing telephone service are similar in substance and form to the regulations governing electric and gas service. Questions regarding telephone regulations, not summarized here, may be answered by referencing the electric and gas regulations governing a specific issue. Winter and medical protection are not applicable to telecommunications service. Access to the regulations can be found at http://legis.state.sd.us/rules/index.aspx (last visited in May 2011).

***Electric and Gas*—S.D. Admin. R. 20:10:15:01–20:10:20:11**

* * *

20:10:16:02. Customer Information:

Utility shall provide, upon request, rate schedules, utilities rules, rights and remedies, deposit or guarantee requirements, and contact information regarding inquiries, emergencies, and disputes.

* * *

20:10:17:01. Billing Basis:

Bills shall be based on actual or estimated usage, but may be based on a combination of both.

20:10:17:02. Meter Readings:

Utility or customer may read meters, but utility shall get an actual reading at least every 12 months.

20:10:17:03. Information on Bills:

All bills shall contain information concerning dates and consumption amounts, date that bill will become delinquent and date by which payment must be made to avoid late fee, amounts and penalties due, and clear indication of estimated bill.

* * *

20:10:17:05. Meter Test by Customer Request:

A customer may request a meter test, but may be required to pay a $10 deposit for a second test within 12 months. The deposit shall be returned if the meter is found to be in error.

20:10:17:06. Adjustments of Bills for Slow or Fast Meter Error—Electric:

A customer's bill shall be adjusted if their meter is found to registering fast or slow by at least 2%. Adjustment shall be based on 1/2 the time that has passed since the previous reading, but shall not exceed 6 months unless the date the error began can be determined with reasonable certainty.

20:10:17:07. Adjustments of Bills for Slow or Fast Meter Error—Gas:

Substantially similar to 20:10:17:06.

20:10:17:08. Adjustments to Bills for Meter Failing to Register:

Bills may be adjusted using estimates of past usage if a meter fails to register.

* * *

20:10:17:10. Equal Monthly Billing:

Upon request, a customer's bills may be provided in equal monthly billing amounts, and the bill shall reflect the difference between the regular and monthly billing.

* * *

20:10:17:12. Disputes:

Disputes shall be promptly investigated and resolved, and, if resolved to the customer's dissatisfaction, the utility shall inform the customer of their right to appeal the resolution to the Commission within 10 days after a disconnection notice is sent. Customers may be required to pay undisputed portion of bills to avoid disconnection.

* * *

20:10:19:01. Nondiscriminatory Credit Policy Required:

Credit policy shall be easily understandable and nondiscriminatory. Redlining, through the use of "economic character of the area," "collective credit reputation," home ownership, or friendly relationships with a bank as means of establishing credit is explicitly prohibited.

20:10:19:02. Establishment or Reestablishment of Satisfactory Credit for Residential Service:

Notice that credit is insufficient shall be given at least 15 days before credit requirement is due.

Credit may be established by paying a deposit or providing a guarantee of no more than 1/6 an annual estimated bill, or agreement to be on the "Early Payment List."

20:10:19:04. Types of Credit Explained:

A previous history of utility service without any disconnection or fewer than 3 disconnection notices in the last year of service shall sufficiently establish credit. Pursuant to 20:10:19:03, a utility may accept other means sufficiently establishing credit by a customer with no previous utility service. Deposits may be paid in installments of 4 equal monthly installments.

* * *

20:10:19:08. Interest on Deposits to Be Paid by Utility:

Interest on a deposit shall accrue at a 7% simple annual rate.

* * *

20:10:19:10. Transfer of Service:

A transfer of service is not a disconnection and shall not require a second deposit unless the initial deposit has been applied to the customer's account.

20:10:19:11. Refund During Service:

Deposits, plus interest, shall be refunded to a customer if, after 12 consecutive months, the customer has not had service disconnected or has had fewer than 3 disconnection notices.

* * *

20:10:20:01. Reasons for Refusal—Use:

Service may be refused due to issues relating to nonpayment for service (past and present accounts), applicant's unwillingness to provide correct information, providing false information, or violation of utility rules or state statutes.

20:10:20:02. Insufficient Reasons for Refusal:

Service shall not be denied for a customer's debt to another utility, nonpayment of guarantor bill, a previous occupant's delinquent bill, or an occupant's debt to utility unless applicant is seeking return of service to indebted household and no attempt is forthcoming to liquidate that household debt.

20:10:20:03. Nonpayment of Past-Due Bills As Reason for Disconnection:

The utility shall give at least 10 days' notice, after the 20-day payment period has expired, before disconnection may occur. Notice requirements shall be waived in cases of fraud, anticipated abandonment of premises, or a refusal to enter into a payment program.

Notice shall be by mail or delivery to billing or service address, but, in cases regarding first-time disconnection, notice shall be by telephone, visit, or certified mail.

Notice shall contain a bold and clearly visible indication of disconnection, the customer's account information, dispute information, reason and date of disconnection, contact information of utility, and options for avoiding and delaying disconnection.

20:10:20:04. Other Reasons for Disconnection:

Disconnection may occur for failure to pay payment plan payments, failure to pay a deposit or an increased deposit, failure to allow access to meters and/or utility equipment, or violation of utility rule or state regulation.

* * *

20:10:20:06. The Disconnecting Act:

Disconnection shall not occur on Friday, weekends, legal holidays, or at a time that the utility's office is not open to the public.

20:10:20:07. Last-Minute Payments:

Payment shall be accepted at any time prior to disconnection. If disconnecting utility employee cannot accept an offer of payment, disconnection shall be delayed until such time that the payment offered can be accepted.

20:10:20:08. Insufficient Reasons for Disconnection:

Service shall not be disconnected for failure to pay for merchandise, a different class of service, or the bill for which customer is a guarantor.

20:10:20:09. Landlord and Tenant Rule:

When the utility knows of a landlord-tenant relationship (mastermetered account), notice, similar to that required under 20:10:20:03, shall be given. Tenants may avoid disconnection of service due to a landlord's nonpayment by accepting an offer to apply for individual service when it is economically feasible. Payment of a landlord's bill shall not be a condition for receiving service.

20:10:20:10. Residential Winter Disconnection:

Customers shall receive an extra 30 days before disconnection from November 1 through March 31.

20:10:20:11. Residential Medical Emergency:

A utility shall delay disconnection an additional 30 days upon receipt of a certificate from a physician or social service agency that a medical emergency exists.

***Telecommunications*—S.D. Admin. R. 20:10:05:01–20:10:10:10**

Many of the regulations governing telecommunications service are similar in substance and form to the regulations governing electric and gas service. Questions regarding telecommunications regulations, not summarized here, may be answered by referencing the electric and gas regulations governing a specific issue. Winter and medical protection are not applicable to telecommunications service.

* * *

20:10:07:03. Transmittal of Bills:

Substantially similar to 20:10:17:03, but bills shall also contain an itemized list of charges at least annually or upon customer's request.

* * *

20:10:07:05. Interruptions and Refunds:

Unless due to the negligent or willful act of the customer, service interruptions of more than 24 hours shall result in a pro rata refund to the customer.

* * *

20:10:08:03. Establishment or Reestablishment of Satisfactory Credit:

Substantially similar to 20:10:19:02, but a customer may also be required to accept toll-restricted service as a condition for service.

* * *

20:10:08:06. Deposit Policy for Applicants with No Past Service:

Applicants with no past service history, who are considered a credit risk, may be required to pay a deposit equaling the lesser of $130 or 2 months' estimated service charges. Applicants with no service history, not deemed to be a credit risk, may be required to pay a deposit of not more than $25.

20:10:08:07. Deposit If Applicant Has Past Experience Without Liability:

A deposit may be based on an applicant's toll service history, but shall be limited to the amounts under this title.

* * *

20:10:10:04. Other Reasons for Disconnection:

Substantially similar to 20:10:20:04, but service shall not be disconnected for failure to pay pay-per-call charges for which company is acting as billing agent.

* * *

20:10:10:08. Early Disconnection:

Service may be disconnected before the 15 day waiting period due to a customer's extraordinarily high bill if the customer has not paid a deposit.

* * *

***Unauthorized Changes in Telecommunications Providers (Slamming) and Unauthorized Charges (Cramming)*—S.D. Admin. R. 20:10:34:01–20:20:34:11**

* * *

20:10:34:02:02. Exception for Acquisition of Subscriber Base—Notification Requirements:

This section provides an exception to the usual rules for authorization of transfers if one carrier acquires the subscriber base of another through sale or transfer. The rule prescribes notice to the Commission and to each subscriber, including the rates, terms, etc., of service, the subscriber's right to choose another carrier, and a toll-free customer service number for the new carrier.

20:10:34:03. Letter of Agency Form and Content:

A letter of agency authorizing a change of service provider shall be written document that clearly, legibly, and completely describes the change, all the rights, responsibilities, and charges associated with the change, and shall contain the name, address, and telephone number(s) to be served.

* * *

20:10:34:04.01. Electronic Authorization:

Electronic authorization for change in service (or charges) shall only occur from the telephone number to be served and shall meet the requirements of 20:10:34:03.

20:10:34:05. Complaints of Unauthorized Changing of a Telecommunications Company:

Upon receipt of an oral or written complaint, the company that initiated the change at issue shall provide verification of the authorization within 30 days. Charges not authorized are invalid.

* * *

20:10:34:07. Refund or Credit of Charges Billed by Unauthorized Telecommunications Company—Payment for Unauthorized Change—Opportunity for Hearing:

Unauthorized charges shall be refunded or credited within 60 days of determination. The violating company shall also be liable for all costs associated with restoring original service.

* * *

20:10:34:10. Notification of Increase in Rates:

Customers must be notified, individually and in writing, at least 30 days in advance of any rate increase or other "materially adverse" change in rates, terms, or conditions of service, defined as a change "making it more burdensome on the customer as determined from the perspective of a reasonable person in the average customer's position."

20:10:34:10.01. Complaints of Unauthorized Billing of Products or Services:

Substantially similar to 20:10:34:05.

20:10:34:11. Refund or Credit of Unauthorized Charges—Payment for Unauthorized Charge—Opportunity for Hearing:

Substantially similar to 20:10:34:07.

TENNESSEE

The regulations governing electric utility service can be found within the rules of the Tennessee Regulatory Authority, Tenn. Comp. R. & Regs. 1220-4-4.01–1220-4-4.54. The regulations governing gas service can be found within Tenn. Comp. R. & Regs. 1220-4-5.01–1220-4-5.48. The regulations governing water service can be found within Tenn. Comp. R. & Regs. 1220-4-3.03–1220-4-3.43. The regulations governing telecommunications service can be found within Tenn. Comp. R. & Regs. 1220-4-2.03–1220-4-2.58. Many of the substantive issues within the gas, telecommunications, and water regulations are substantially similar to the regulations governing electric. Questions regarding gas, telephone, and water regulations not summarized here may be answered by referencing the electric regulations governing a specific issue. Access to the regulations can be found at www.state.tn.us/sos/rules/1220/1220-04/1220-04.htm (last visited in May 2011).

Electric—**Tenn. Comp. R. & Regs. 1220-4-4.01–1220-4-4.54**

* * *

1220-4-4.07. Disposition of Electricity:

Each dwelling and commercial unit in a multi-dwelling unit residential building, manufactured home park or commercial building, the construction of which has commenced after the effective date of this rule, shall have installed a separate electric meter.

* * *

1220-4-4.14. Customer Information:

At the initiation of service, the utility shall provide information concerning services, rate schedules and any changes in services and rate schedules, information that will assist in choice of service, and all the rights, remedies, responsibilities, and assistance associated with services.

1220-4-4.15. Customer Deposits:

Deposits to insure payment of service shall not exceed the lesser of estimated charges for two consecutive billing periods or 90 days. Deposits shall accrue interest at a rate to be set by the Authority. The utility shall provide the customer with a receipt for their deposit and the means to claim a deposit should the receipt become lost.

Deposits may be kept for a length of time necessary to insure payment of bills. Unclaimed deposits shall continue to accrue interest and be held for no less than 3 years, after which, they shall be credited to the appropriate account.

1220-4-4.16. Customer Bill Forms:

Bills shall contain meter readings and reading dates, clear identification of estimated bill, consumption, amount due and date by which bill must be paid to benefit from discount or to avoid penalty, rate schedule, and information used in determining bill.

* * *

1220-4-4.18. Adjustments of Bills:

Unless it can be shown to be beyond the control of the utility, meters that are found to be fast or slow by 2% or more shall result in the customer's bill being adjusted for 1/2 the time elapsed time since the last meter reading, but said time period shall not exceed 6 months.

1220-4-4.19. Reasons for Denying Service:

Service may be denied or terminated, without notice, if a hazardous condition exist, use of equipment adversely affects others' service, or for tampering or unauthorized use.

Service may be denied or terminated, with at least 7 days' notice prior to the date of termination for issues relating to nonpayment, failure to fulfill a contract, violation of rules or regulations, or failure to allow access to utility equipment. Notice may be included in the customer's bill and shall include account identification and address, date of termination, the reason for termination, reconnection charges, dispute procedures and contact information. Utility must provide to new customers, and annually to existing customers, all information that would assist the customer in avoiding termination of services, including but not limited to, the 30-day termination postponement procedures for medical emergencies.

Upon receiving written notification from a physician, public health official, or social service agency that a medical condition would be aggravated due to termination of service, termination shall be postponed for 30 days and the utility shall refer the customer to a social service agency.

Service may not be terminated for failure to pay a portion of a bill that is being disputed. Service shall not be terminated, unless it is for reasons not requiring notice, on a day or a day preceding the utility's office not being open to the public.

1220-4-4.20. Insufficient Reasons for Denying Services:

Service shall not be denied for nonpayment of bill by a previous customer, failure to pay for merchandise or for different type or class of service, failure to pay a bill as guarantor, failure to pay for back-billing due to a slow meter, failure to pay a bill to correct previous under-billing due to a misapplication of rates.

* * *

1220-4-4.23. Customer Complaints:

Complaints concerning the charges, practices, facilities or service of the utility shall be investigated promptly and thoroughly.

* * *

1220-4-4.26. Customer's Discontinuance of Service:

Any customer desiring that service be discontinued shall give at least 3 days' notice to the utility, unless a longer or shorter period shall be incorporated in any standard or special contract mutually agreed upon. Until the utility shall have such notice, the customer may be held responsible for all service rendered.

1220-4-4.27. Access to Property:

The utility shall at all reasonable times have access to meters, service connections and other property owned by it on customer's premises for the purposes of operation and maintenance.

* * *

1220-4-4.30. Request Tests:

Upon request, but not more than once every 12 months, a utility shall test a customer's meter and notify the customer with 10 days.

* * *

Water—**Tenn. Comp. R. & Regs. 1220-4-3.03–1220-4-3.43**

The regulations governing water service are similar in form and substance to the regulations governing electric. Questions regarding water service may be answered by referencing the electric regulation governing a specific issue.

Gas—**Tenn. Comp. R. & Regs. 1220-4-5.01–1220-4-5.48**

The regulations governing gas are similar in form and substance to the regulations governing electric. Questions regarding gas service may be answered by referencing the electric regulation governing a specific issue.

Telecommunications—**Tenn. Comp. R. & Regs. 1220-4-2.03–1220-4-2.58**

Many of the substantive issues within the telecommunications are substantially similar to the regulations governing electric and are indicated accordingly.

* * *

1220-4-2.10. Customer Billing:

Bills shall be issued monthly and shall contain an itemized statement of all charges. Initial bills shall also inform the customer of their right to receive a pro rata refund, based on monthly charges, when, for reasons other than willful or negligent conduct on the part of the customer, service is interrupted for more than 24 hours.

1220-4-2.11. Customer Deposits:

No deposit shall be required as a condition for establishment of service other than as provided in the utility's rules and tariffs on file with the Authority.

1220-4-2.12. Reasons for Denying Service:

Substantially similar to 1220-4-4.19.

1220-4-2.13. Customer Complaints:

Substantially similar to 1220-4-4.23.

* * *

1220-4-2.29. Basic Utility Obligations:

The utility shall inform the customer of any service connection charge to be applied to bill and the monthly charge for the service ordered, with the exception of business customers not requiring this information, prior to undertaking any action to furnish the service ordered. To customers inquiring about new service, the utility shall provide any information and assistance necessary to obtain service conforming to the customer's needs.

* * *

1220-4-2.35. Installations of Service:

Generally, where facilities are available, installations shall occur within 5 working days of receipt of an application.

* * *

1220-4-2.56. Verification of Orders for Changes for Local and Long-Distance Carriers:

Unless customer initiated, submission, initiation, or an actual change in a customer's provider shall only occur upon verifiable written, electronic, or oral authorization (see regulation for verification procedures). Unauthorized changes in service are invalid. This section also prescribes detailed standards for telemarketers soliciting a change of carrier. The Consumer Services Division may demand copies of telemarketing scripts or require that telemarketing calls be recorded.

Service shall not be disconnected during a dispute concerning unauthorized change in service unless the customer has been advised to notify the authority of the alleged slamming and warned that failure to do so within 30 days may result in disconnection.

When a telecommunications service provider is notified by an end user of an unauthorized change, it shall, within one business day, switch the end user back to the end user's preferred carrier; suspend collection of any disputed charges until the dispute is resolved; and inform the end user of the Authority's complaint procedure.

LECs must offer to subscribers, upon request, a freeze for additional protection against slamming. LECs that bill for long-distance carriers must clearly disclose, on the first page of the first bill following a change of carrier, that a change has been made.

* * *

1220-4-2.58. Billing Requirements for Charges on Consumer's Telephone Bills:

Substantially similar to 1220-4-2.10 and 1220-4-2.56. Utility shall offer customers blocking services to prevent unwanted charges from being billed.

TEXAS

The majority of regulations governing consumer electric services can be found in 16 Tex. Admin. Code §§ 25.1–25.43. Although the majority of regulations concerning consumer telephone services can be found in 16 Tex. Admin. Code §§ 26.1–26.87, concerning gas regulations can be found in 16 Tex. Admin. Code §§ 7.45–7.465, and concerning sewer and water regulations can be found in 30 Tex. Admin. Code §§ 291.1–.15, 291.80–291.90, many of the substantive issue within the regulations are substantially similar to the regulations governing electric and are indicated accordingly. Access to Texas' Administrative Code can be found at www.sos.state.tx.us/tac/index.shtml (last visited in May 2011).

Electric—**16 Tex. Admin. Code §§ 25.1–25.43**

* * *

§ 25.22. Request for Service:

All applications for new service, not requiring construction such as line extensions, must be filled within seven business days. If construction is required, the applicant must be notified, and the deadline for service is extended.

§ 25.23. Refusal of Service:

An applicant must be informed of the reason for refusal, and their rights to file a complaint under § 25.30. Service may be refused due to inadequate facilities or equipment; indebtedness for same kind of service; failure to pay guarantee (guarantee must be in writing and it must have been a condition of service); delinquent debt by another customer at the same address, if the change in identity was to avoid or evade payment of the debt; refusal to pay a deposit.

If indebtedness is in dispute, service cannot be refused if a deposit is paid. Service cannot be refused for delinquency of payment for services by a previous occupant, failure to pay for non-regulated services, failure to pay a bill that includes more than the allowed amount of under billing, unless the under billing is the result of theft of service, and failure to pay bill of another customer at same address except where change in identity is to avoid payment.

§ 25.24. Credit Requirements and Deposits:

An applicant or customer, may be required, and shall be notified that they have to pay a deposit if their credit is not sufficiently established. A deposit may be required for issues related to non-payment, for theft of service, or excessive usage. Credit history will be applied equally for 12 months after divorce to spouse or former spouse who shared service for 12 months prior to divorce. Applicants over the age of 65 are assumed to have sufficient credit unless they have an outstanding debt for the same type of service, from the current or another provider, within the last 2 years.

Credit may be established with 1 year without disconnection or more than one late payment, generally accepted credit cards, letters of credit reference that may be quickly and inexpensively contacted by the utility, or ownership of substantial equity that may be easily liquidated.

The total of all deposits, or guarantees, shall not exceed 1/6 of the estimated annual billing, shall be returned upon 1 year of billing without a disconnection or more than two late payments, and shall include interest at a rate set by the Commission. Guarantors must be notified of a default, the consequences of the default, and their rights and responsibilities concerning the default.

§ 25.25. Issuance and Format of Bills:

Unless authorized, bills shall be issued monthly, and calculated by an estimate (no more than twice every 3 months) or a meter reading by the customer or the utility, and shall include the date of reading if read by the utility, total amount due, any penalty for late payment, and other general information.

§ 25.26. Spanish Language Requirements:

When required under § 25.5, the community must be provided information concerning their rights and access to new services, discount programs, promotions, and requests for repair services in Spanish.

§ 25.27. Retail Electric Service Switchovers:

A consumer has the right to switch retail electric service to any electric or municipally owned utility that has the right to provide service in the customer's area.

§ 25.28. Bill Payment and Adjustments:

A due date shall not be less than 16 days from the date of issuance or the next business day if falling on a holiday or weekend, and shall not include any late-payment charges. Overcharges shall be corrected in 3 months or interest is due. Undercharges are not subject to interest, or disconnection for undercharges more than 6 months before date of bill, unless due to theft of service. For undercharges of $50 or more, the utility must offer a deferred payment plan. Failure to pay undercharges may result in disconnection of services.

When an amount is in dispute, the customer shall not be disconnected for nonpayment of a disputed portion of a bill until the dispute is completely resolved.

Utilities shall offer customers, who express an inability to pay their bills, alternative payment plans and information concerning disconnection moratoriums for the ill, and any payment assistance or energy assistance programs.

§ 25.29. Disconnection of Service:

All notices for disconnection shall be a separate mailing or hand delivery, 10 days before disconnection, and contain the words "disconnection notice," or similar language prominently displayed, in English or Spanish, as needed to inform the community. Disconnection notices shall also contain information regarding the availability of payment programs, energy assistance, and disconnection moratoriums for the ill. If electricity is being disconnected for landlord delinquency (master-metered apartments), notice of the intent to disconnect and actual disconnection shall be provided. Disconnection may occur without notice if a dangerous condition exists or for any type of theft of service.

Unless a dangerous condition exists or the customer requests disconnection, service shall not be disconnected on holidays or weekends, or the day immediately preceding a holiday or weekend, unless utility personnel are available on those days to take payments and reconnect service.

Service may be disconnected for issues relating to nonpayment, or interference with the service of others in violation of utility rules.

Services cannot be disconnected for failing to pay for merchandise or non-utility services, under billing (unless for theft), failure to pay an estimated bill not part of an approved meter reading plan, if the customer is an energy assistance grantee (if the granting agency notifies the company of a grant sufficient to pay the bill), or if the customer is in a deferred payment plan. If, upon physician verification, a person, residing in the unit would become seriously ill or more seriously ill, as a result of the disconnection, disconnection shall be delayed for up to 63 days provided a deferred payment plan is entered into. Service shall not be disconnected on a day when the previous day's temperature did not exceed 32° and it is predicted by the National Weather Service to remain at that level for 24 hours, or in zones where an excessive heat alert is in effect.

§ 25.30. Complaints:

Complaints may be filed by telephone, mail, or in person, and the complaint shall be investigated, and the results reported to the complainant within twenty-one days. If a customer is dissatisfied with complaint resolution they may request a supervisory review whose results must be provided to the customer within ten days of its completion. Service may not be disconnected until a review is completed, but failure to participate in a review may result in disconnection pursuant to § 25.29. Customers dissatisfied with a supervisory review shall be informed of their right to file a complaint with the Commission.

§ 25.31. Information to Applicants and Customers:

Utilities must provide a customer with a customer rights manual upon receipt of their request for new or transferred services.

§ 25.41. Price to Beat:

Residential customers meeting the eligibility requirements shall be offered and may choose from available price to beat options.

§ 25.43. Provider of Last Resort (POLR):

A basic standard retail service package must be available at a fixed, non-discountable rate to every requesting customer in areas that are open to competition. Customers must be assured of continuity of service if their REP defaults.

POLR service is intended to be temporary, and the price is set based on cost and risk. POLR service must include: basic service; call center for customer inquiries; standard billing; low-income benefits, as provided by PURA § 39.903; standard metering. The provider must make available to POLR customers the same competitive products and services available to similarly situated non-POLR customers.

Bills must include an explanation of why the customer is receiving POLR service, that POLR service is intended to be temporary, and information about available competitive service, including contact information for power to choose (a website or toll-free number providing information about competitive markets). POLRs must inform new customers of charges and the standard terms of service.

The rule sets forth procedures for choosing POLRs and setting the POLR rate.

If a customer is transitioned to a POLR, the former provider must return the unused portion of the customer's deposit within 7 days of the transition. A POLR may request a deposit, but must initiate service immediately, and may not disconnect without going through disconnection procedure. Deposits must be waived, if this is required under the Security and Billing provisions of the Standard Terms of Service.

The rule sets forth a procedure for mass transitions, which may not be used to eliminate unprofitable contracts while retaining the profitable ones. When a customer is transitioned to a POLR, both the former company and the POLR must provide notices concerning the new service, the availability of competitive services, etc.

A POLR may disconnect only after compliance with the applicable customer service rules in subchapter R (§§ 25.471–25.498).

Starting in the 2007–2008 POLR term, a utility may charge POLR customers a rate lower than the POLR rate, if applied uniformly to all POLR customers.

This rule requires detailed reporting regarding disconnect notices, transfers, or disconnections for nonpayment, including the average amount owed, how many were eligible for rate reductions, etc.

***Retail Electric Providers*—16 Tex. Admin. Code §§ 25.471–25.498**

* * *

§ 25.472(b)(1)(C). Privacy of Customer Information:

Prohibition against retail electric providers disclosing customer's proprietary information does not apply to the release of such information to a consumer reporting agency. *See also* Tex. Util. Code Ann. § 39.107 (West) ("All meter data, including data generated, provided, or otherwise made available, by advanced meters and meter information networks, shall belong to a customer, including data use to calculate charges for service, historical load data, and any other proprietary customer information.").

§ 25.498. Retail Electric Service Using a Customer Prepayment Device or System:

Retail electric providers using prepayment or advanced meters are exempt from specified provisions relating to disconnection, issuance of bills, and bill payments and adjustments. No billing or notice of disconnection is required, levelized and average payment plans need not be offered; payment arrangements, deferred payment plans; and partial payments need not be considered; and electric service may be disconnected for nonpayment of non-electric services.

***Telecommunications*—16 Tex. Admin. Code § 26.1–26.37**

Many of the substantive issue within the regulations governing telecommunication service are substantially similar to the regulations governing electric and are indicated accordingly.

* * *

§ 26.4. Statement of Nondiscrimination:

Substantially similar to § 25.4.

* * *

§ 26.22. Request for Service:

Substantially similar to § 25.22.

§ 26.23. Refusal of Service:

Substantially similar to § 25.23.

§ 26.24. Credit Requirements and Deposits:

Substantially similar to § 25.24. After divorce, credit history for prior 12 months may be applied to both spouses equally for a period of 12 months. However, the requirements for credit are met if the applicant is determined to be a victim of family violence, pursuant to § 71.004 of the Texas Family Code, by a family violence center, by certain law enforcement entities, or by medical personnel providing treatment to the customer.

This rule specifies what may be counted in calculating 1/6 of an estimated annual bill for purposes of setting a deposit amount. May not include long-distance service from another service provider and, if the company provides long-distance service, the deposit amounts for local or long-distance service must be separately identified.

§ 26.25. Issuance and Format of Bills:

Substantially similar to § 25.25.

§ 26.26. Foreign Language Requirements:

Substantially similar to § 25.26.

§ 26.27. Bill Payments and Adjustments:

Substantially similar to § 25.28. However, if a customer's service is interrupted for reasons other than by the negligence or willful act of the customer, and it remains interrupted for 24 hours or longer after being reported and after access to the premises is made available, an appropriate refund shall be made to the customer.

§ 26.28. Suspension or Disconnection of Service:

Substantially similar to § 25.29.

A local service provider shall, upon request by the customer, release the customer's line and telephone number to another local service provider in an expeditious manner and without disruption of service, and, if the customer's service is suspended, a release shall occur within five business days. A provider shall not refuse a release for nonpayment of a bill.

§ 26.29. Prepaid Local Telephone Service (PLTS):

Residential applicants or former customers who may be refused services for indebtedness to any provider, and current residential customers facing suspension or disconnection of services shall be notified of their eligibility to receive, and all information concerning PLTS.

§ 26.30. Complaints:

Substantially similar to § 25.30.

§ 26.31. Disclosures to Applicants and Customers:

Promotions shall be consistent in language translation and shall not be fraudulent, unfair, misleading, deceptive, or anti-competitive under federal or state law.

A provider, before acceptance of service shall provide the applicant with an explanation of services or products offered, charges and how they appear on the bill, minimum contract service terms, any pre-installation charges (refundable and non-refundable), necessary changes in telephone numbers, cancellation policy, customer service contact information, and a detailed description of the terms and conditions governed under this title.

§ 26.32. Protection Against Unauthorized Billing Charges ("Cramming"):

A provider shall inform, and receive consent from the customer for all charges that will appear on a customer's bill, and maintain consent verification records, after consent and verification were obtained, and records concerning all unauthorized charges for 24 months.

Consent and verification consists of the name and telephone number of customer, questions and answers that ensure that consent was given by an authorized customer, an explanation of the product or service offered, charges, cancellation procedures, and how charges will appear on the bill.

Consent and verification shall be obtained in writing that is consistent with the language requirements, or verbal by a recording that is clear, slow, and easy to understand with the conversation occurring between the actual customer and the provider or with a third-party acting as the provider's agent, or any FCC approved method. An electronic signature that complies with Electronic Signatures in Global and National Commerce Act (E-Sign) is acceptable, but customer must be given the option of verifying by other means. Customer's consent is null and void if product or service is not provided within 60 days of consent, and new consent must be obtained before charges may be billed.

Upon notification of unauthorized charges the service provider shall, within forty-five days, cease charging for the unauthorized service, remove the charges from the customer's bill, provide a refund or credit to the consumer, and pay interest on refunds due for at least three billing cycles. A service provider may not disconnect, nor file an adverse credit report, for allegedly unauthorized charges unless a dispute has been resolved adversely to the customer.

Carriers must notify consumers of their rights under this section by notice in their directories and by including, in each bill, Commission contact information for complaints of unauthorized charges. Notice in Spanish must be provided, unless less than 10% of the customers in the service area speak Spanish.

The rule prescribes a procedure for complaints regarding cramming.

§ 26.37. Texas No-Call List:

The list is maintained by the Commission or its designee. Telemarketers must buy a copy of the list and may not call no-call registrants, with certain exceptions, including an established business relationship or debt collection. Misuse of the list is subject to administrative penalties. Certificated telecommunications utilities (CTUs) must inform residential customers of the availability of the no-call list and the registration procedure.

* * *

***Water and Sewer*—30 Tex. Admin. Code §§ 291.1–291.15, 291.80–291.90**

Many of the substantive issue within the regulations governing water service are substantially similar to the regulations governing electric and are indicated accordingly.

* * *

§ 291.22. Notice of Intent to Change Rates:

Subject to Commission approval, all customers must be notified 60 days prior to change. The notice must include information on how to protest a rate change.

* * *

§ 291.81. Customer Relations:

Must inform and provide applicants with all of the cost associated with the initiation of new service or transferring of service. Utility must maintain copies of the Commission's rules and procedures under this title, and contact information about service and complaints. All complaints, once received must be promptly investigated and the results reported to the applicant or customer. Applicants or customers dissatisfied with response are to be provided with information of their recourse through the Texas Commission on Environmental Quality complaint process. The utility must maintain a business office, at which applications for service may be filed and payments made, within the county (or within 20 miles) where customer is located.

§ 291.82. Resolution of Disputes:

Services shall not be disconnected until the resolution of the dispute unless the customer or applicant refuses to participate or allow an inspection within five business days after requesting it.

§ 291.83. Refusal of Service:

Substantially similar to 16 Tex. Admin. Code § 25.23.

§ 291.84. Applicant and Customer Deposit:

Substantially similar to 16 Tex. Admin. Code § 25.24. Applicants over 65 may only be required to pay a deposit if they have a delinquent balance with water or sewer utility. Residential customers may not be required to pay a deposit unless they have been disconnected, and the deposit shall not exceed $50 for water service and $50 for sewer service. Deposits shall be returned, or may be credited to an account after 18 months of billing without a delinquency.

§ 291.85. Response to Requests for Service by a Retail Public Utility Within Its Certificated Area:

Unless a new service tap or additional construction is required, or for good cause, an accepted application shall be filled within one business day. Service requiring a tap shall be filed within five business days. If service requiring construction cannot be completed within thirty days the utility shall provide a written explanation and expected completion date that does not exceed 180 days.

§ 291.86. Service Connections:

The fee charged by a utility for connecting a residential service shall be as stated on the approved tariff. An applicant's fees and responsibilities can vary depending on connection demands.

§ 291.87. Billing:

Substantially similar to 16 Tex. Admin. Code § 25.28. However, a one time late fee of $5 or 10% may be assessed. The utility must offer a payment plan if a customer's monthly bill is more than three times the average bill and the customer has not received more than 2 disconnect notices in the prior 12 months. Utilities are encouraged to offer payment plans to other customers who claim an inability to pay.

In case of over-billing, the customer is entitled to a refund for the entire period of over-billing. In case of under-billing, the utility may back-bill for not more than 12 months, except in case of theft or tampering. If the undercharge is $25 or more, the utility must offer a payment plan with the same duration as the period of under-billing. Estimated bills are permitted, but actual meter reading is required every 2 months.

§ 291.88. Discontinuance of Services:

Substantially similar to 16 Tex. Admin. Code § 25.29. However, water service may be terminated for failure to pay sewer bill.

Service shall be reconnected thirty-six hours after payment for past-due services plus any applicable reconnection fees, or after entering into a payment plan under § 291.87.

§ 291.89. Meters:

Meters shall be provided, installed, and maintained by the utility. Unless authorized in tariff, meters shall be read on monthly basis. The utility is to be given access to meters for overall maintenance and for required monthly readings. A utility shall test a meter upon request by a customer.

* * *

UTAH

The Public Service Commission's general regulations governing electric, gas, water, and sewer services can be found within Utah Admin. Code r. 746-200-1–746-200-10, with specific regulations governing electric service within Utah Admin. Code r. 746-310-1–746-310-10 and gas service within Utah Admin. Code r. 746-320-1–746-320-9. Telecommunication service rules can be found within Utah Admin. Code r. 746-240-1–746-240-8. Regulations that are substantially similar to a regulation already summarized will be indicated accordingly and will not be summarized. Access to the Administrative Code can be found at www.psc.utah.gov/rulesandcode/index.html (last visited in May 2011).

***General (Electric, Gas, Water, and Sewer)*—Utah Admin. Code r. 746-200-1–746-200-10**

746-200-1. General Provisions:

At the initiation of service, the utility shall provide information concerning services, rate schedules and any changes in services and rate schedules, information that will assist in choice of service, and all the rights, remedies, responsibilities, and assistance associated with services. Spanish and English versions of consumer information shall be made available upon request in service areas of over 10,000 customers.

* * *

746-200-3. Deposits, Eligibility for Service, and Shared Meter or Appliance:

A deposit or a guarantee may be required to receive or continue receiving service. Deposits shall accrue interest at a rate set by the Commission, and shall be returned after 12 consecutive months of timely service. Customers shall have the right to pay a deposit in at least 3 monthly installments if the first payment is paid when the deposit is required.

Service may be denied for issues relating to nonpayment of past-due amounts, unsafe conditions, tampering with equipment, providing false information to obtain service, or applicant is living with a previous account holder whose service was terminated for nonpayment and applicant was living with indebted account holder at the time.

Customers unable to pay outstanding balances in full shall be offered payment plans as a method of obtaining or continuing service.

If one meter serves more than one unit, or if appliances serve more than one unit, the utility should recommend that service be in the property owner's name. The account may be in another person's name, if that person acknowledges that the request is made willingly and has knowledge of the account responsibility.

746-200-4. Account Billing:

Due dates shall be at least 20 days from the date the bill is prepared and shall contain customer's name, address, telephone or account number, billing period, all payment information and amounts due (late payments, charges, taxes, etc.), and instruction to contact the utility with any questions. Late charges, returned check charges, and reconnection charges may be imposed. Other finance charges, service charges, or other similar charges are prohibited.

Bills may be estimated, but a utility shall attempt to get an actual reading at least once every 2 months. If attempts to get an actual reading either by making attempts through personal notification or through at least 2 regular route visits are unsuccessful, the utility shall notify the customer that an actual reading is required as condition of continuing to receive service.

Bills or past-due amounts may be disputed and services shall not be terminated for failure to pay disputed amounts. Customers may be required to pay undisputed portions of a bill as a condition of continuing or receiving service. A utility shall not transfer a past-due amount older than 4 years to a customer's current account.

746-200-5. Deferred Payment Agreement:

New, continuing, or reconnection of service shall be provided if the customer enters into a written deferred payment plan to pay all past-due amounts. The customer shall have the right to set the amount of the monthly payment, if the balance, plus interest, will be paid within 12 months with the initial payment being paid at the time of the agreement. Customers shall be allowed to include the current bill and any reconnection charges to be included in the payment plan amount. Termination may proceed after a payment agreement is breached, and a utility is not obligated to renew the agreement. Deferred payment plans need not be offered if the delinquent balance results from unauthorized usage or diversion.

746-200-6. Reconnection of Disconnected Service:

Utilities must have personnel available to reconnect service 24 hours a day. Reconnection should generally take place on the next business day following the request for reconnection and compliance with all conditions, which may include a reconnection fee, or a payment arrangement. A utility may impose an additional charge for reconnection outside of normal business hours.

746-200-7. Termination of Service:

Service may be disconnected for issues relating to nonpayment, denial of reasonable access to equipment, failure to comply with Commission order, unauthorized use or misrepresentation, and adverse effect on services of utility or consumers. Service may be terminated without notice for a hazardous condition or for equipment tampering.

Notice of disconnection shall be provided 10 days before the disconnection date and shall contain the reasons for disconnection, the amount due, date of disconnection, availability of payment plans and assistance, delay option for medical reasons, and complaint procedures. A final attempt at notification shall be made by mail, phone, or in person at least 48 hours prior to termination, and, if termination is scheduled between October 1 through March 31, personal notification shall be delivered to the customer's residence before termination. A customer may designate a third party to receive notice, and the utility must send duplicate notices to, and make reasonable efforts to contact, a third party residing in the service area before disconnection.

Service may not be terminated and will be restored when termination of service will cause or aggravate a serious illness or infirmity of a person living in the residence. Upon receipt of a statement signed by an enumerated provider and identifying the health infirmity or potential health hazard, and how termination of service will injure the person's health or aggravate their illness, a utility will continue or restore service for the period set forth in the statement or 1 month, whichever is less. Termination of service shall be delayed for 30 days when the customer is determined to be from a low-income household and payment is received from a state program. Households in which life-supporting equipment [defined] is in use should register with the utility, after which termination will require specific permission from the Commission.

Tenants shall be given at least 5 days' notice if the landlord's account, from which they receive service, is subject to termination. Tenants may receive 30 days service by paying the past-due amount from the previous 30 days.

Service shall only be terminated Monday through Thursday from 9:00 a.m.–4:00 p.m., and shall not occur on a legal holiday or day that the utility offices are closed to the public.

Service shall not be terminated due to a delinquent account in the name of a spouse that accrued before a divorce, living with a delinquent account holder (unless living with the delinquent account holder at the time the account became delinquent), a delinquent account of $25 or less (unless the account has been delinquent for 2 months), or failure to pay a bona fide disputed amount.

An electric utility may, with the customer's consent, install a load limiter in lieu of disconnection for nonpayment or breach of payment agreement.

A customer who wishes to terminate shall give 4 days' notice. A customer who is not an occupant must give 10 days' notice and sign an affidavit that termination is not sought as a means of evicting tenants. (Disconnection is permitted in 4 days if the owner signs an affidavit that there are no tenants.)

Utah Admin. Code r. 746-200-8 and 746-200-9 set forth the procedures for informal and formal dispute resolution.

* * *

Electric—**Utah Admin. Code r. 746-310-1–746-310-10**

* * *

746-310-02. Customer Relations:

The utility must provide customers with an explanation of the rate schedule within 60 days after commencement of service, annually thereafter, and within 30 days (60 days if it bills bimonthly) of an application for change in the rate schedule. Utility bills must include information on usage during the same billing period the previous year and include contact information for customer questions or concerns. If a customer has once obtained service from an electric utility, that customer may not be served by another electric utility at the same premises without the prior approval of the Commission.

746-310-03. Meters and Meter Testing:

A customer may request a meter test. If the meter has been tested within 12 months, the utility may require a deposit of not more than the cost of the test. If the meter is found to have an error of more than 2%, the deposit is refunded to the customer. If the meter is fast, the utility must provide a refund for up to 6 months of overcharge, unless the error resulted from a cause, the date of which can be ascertained. If the meter is slow, the utility may back-bill for up to 6 months, unless the error resulted from a cause the date of which can be ascertained. If the meter fails to register, the utility may back-bill for estimated use for not more than 3 months.

* * *

746-310-08. Billing Adjustments:

Unless it is for fraud or theft of service, a utility shall not render a back-billing more than 3 months after becoming aware of the error. A utility shall not back-bill for services rendered more than 24 months before the utility became aware of the circumstances, error, or condition that caused it.

Unless the customer knew or should have known of the underbilling, a customer shall have the right to pay the back-billing without interest over a period equal to that of the under-billing period.

746-310-9. Over-Billing:

Over-billing, which occurred less than 24 months from the time of the complaint, shall be credited or offset a customer's subsequent bills if the amount is $50 or less, or less than two average month's bills. A customer shall have a right to refund if the over-billed amount exceeds $50 or 2 average month's bills, but not a customer with a balance owing unless the refund would result in a credit balance. Interest, at the greater of the rate paid on deposits or charged for late payments, shall accrue on over-billed amounts until a full accounting to the customer is accomplished, unless it can be shown that the customer knew or should have known the over-billing was occurring.

* * *

***Gas*—Utah Admin. Code r. 746-320-1–746-320-9**

The regulations governing gas service are similar in form and substance to the specific regulations governing electric. Questions regarding gas service may be answered by referencing the electric regulation governing a specific issue.

***Telecommunications*—Utah Admin. Code r. 746-240-1–746-240-8**

Telecommunication regulations that are substantially similar to a regulation already summarized will be indicated accordingly and will not be summarized.

* * *

746-240-3. Deposits and Eligibility for Service:

Substantially similar to 746-200-3, but deposits need not be refunded after 12 consecutive months of service and may be held until service is terminated or deposit is credited to the account.

746-240-4. Account Billing:

Substantially similar to 746-200-4 and electric regulations regarding under- and over-billing. Unless it is due to willful or negligent conduct on the part of the customer, or for reasons beyond the utility's control, bills shall be adjusted for service interruptions of more than either 24 or 48 hours (as provided in tariff or price lists). If under-billing results from omission or negligence by the utility, it must offer a payment plan for under-billings of more than $25, accumulated over more than 1 month. Over-billings should be refunded by a credit on the bill or by a refund at the customer's option.

746-240-5. Deferred Payment Agreement:

Substantially similar to 746-200-5.

746-240-6. Termination:

Substantially similar to 746-200-6, but service shall not be terminated if the overdue balance is $15 or less unless delinquent for at least 3 months. Additional reasons for termination include: abusive use of service that interferes with another person's service; using service in a manner that causes wrongful billing of charges to another; or fraudulent or unlawful use of service. Notice of termination shall be 7 days prior to termination.

* * *

VERMONT

Vermont's Public Service Board Rules (PSB) governing the deposit requirements for receiving or continuing general utility service (electric, gas, water, telephone, and cable television) can be found within 30-000-003 Vt. Code R. §§ 3.201–3.205. The general regulations governing the disconnection of general services can be found within 30-000-004 Vt. Code R. §§ 3.301–3.308. The general regulations governing telephone services can be found within 30-000-053 Vt. Code R. §§ 7.601–7.623. Specific regulations governing water and gas service, although not summarized below, can be found within Vermont Public Service Board General Order Numbers 29 (30-000-030 Vt. Code R. §§ 1–26) and 43 (30-000-022 Vt. Code R. §§ 1–27), respectively. The regulations can be found at www.psb.vermont.gov/statuterulesandguidelines/current rules.

***Ratepayer Deposits for Gas, Electric, Water, Telephone and Cable Television Service*—30-000-003 Vt. Code R. §§ 3.201–3.205**

* * *

§ 3.202. Conditions for Taking of Deposits:

Customers and applicants shall be informed of the reason a deposit is required and of their right to dispute it to the Board. Deposits may be paid in 3 monthly installments. Interest shall accrue, per annum (pro rated if kept less than 12 months), at 2% below the prime interest rate. Interest shall be credited to a customer's account after 12 months.

§ 3.203. Grounds for Requiring a Deposit:

Applicants or existing customers may be required to pay a deposit or provide a guarantee for service. Existing customers shall only be required to pay a deposit or provide a guarantee if service has been terminated pursuant to 30-000-004 Vt. Code R. §§ 3.301–3.308.

Applicants may be required to pay deposit or provide a guarantee if deemed a credit risk, or have had previous utility service disconnected or sent 2 disconnection notices within the previous 24 months.

Applicants may establish credit by providing bank references or other reasonable demonstrations of creditworthiness, checking account without an overdraft in the previous 12 months, a guarantee from a creditworthy customer, or references from previous utility service. Prior utility providers shall furnish credit references within 3 working days after such request is made.

§ 3.204. Calculation of Deposit Amount:

Deposits or guarantees shall not exceed 2/12 of estimated usage based on the specific residence to be served or a reasonable estimate based on a similar residence.

§ 3.205. Return of Deposits:

Deposits shall be credited or refunded (guarantees released) after 12 consecutive months of service without a disconnection or 3 disconnection notices (2 notices if billed bimonthly or quarterly).

Disconnection of Residential Gas, Electric, Telephone and Water Service—**30-000-004 Vt. Code R. §§ 3.301–3.308**

§ 3.301. Definitions:

A bill is delinquent if payment is not received 30 days after the mailing date. Notice of delinquency and disconnection shall be no more than 40 days after delinquency, but notice shall not be more than 20 days or less than 14 days prior to the first date of disconnection.

§ 3.302. General Rule:

Disconnection for nonpayment, except for deposits, shall not occur if the amount due is less than $50 (unless this exception has been used more than twice in one calendar year), the amount has been due for more than 2 years, the amount is the subject of a dispute or due to failure to pay for certain non-recurring charges, a physician certifies that disconnection may result in immediate and serious harm to the health of customer or household resident, due to a delinquent bill owed by another person unless a person owing a delinquent bill, resulting from service to that household, resides in the same household, or the utility failed to offer the customer a payment plan.

Payment plans shall be based on actual or estimated usage from the previous 12 months of service. The monthly payment due shall not exceed one-twelfth of the annual estimated bill, or the estimated average monthly amount for customers who expect to be in a dwelling for less than 1 year. When establishing a reasonable repayment plan, the company shall consider the income and income schedule of the customer, if offered by the customer, the customer's payment history, the size of the arrearage and current bill, the amount of time and reason for the outstanding bill and whether the delinquency was caused by unforeseen circumstances.

Tenants shall be given at least 3 days' notice if the landlord's account, from which they receive service, is subject to disconnection. Notice shall also be posted in a common area of multi-unit dwellings. Tenants shall be given the opportunity receive service in the tenants name and/or assume responsibility for payment. When a master meter serves a residence, the utility shall be required to make reasonable arrangements for individual metering.

No utility shall terminate or refuse to restore service for the lesser of 30 days or the period provided in the certificate when a medical emergency, as certified by a medical doctor, orally or in writing (written confirmation is required 7 days after oral notification), exists. The use of physician's certificate to prevent disconnection or to restore service is limited to two consecutive 30-day periods and may not exceed three 30-day periods in a calendar year, except by written order of the Board. Customers remain liable for charges incurred while certificate is in effect.

§ 3.303. Disconnection Notice Form:

Notice of disconnection shall be clearly distinguishable and shall contain the reasons for disconnection, the amount due, date of disconnection, availability of payment plans and assistance, delay option for medical reasons, and complaint procedures. Notice shall also inform customers that service shall not be disconnected, between November 1 through March 31 when the temperature will be below 32° during the 48 hour period beginning at the time of disconnection, if someone 62 years or older resides within the residence.

§ 3.304. Winter Disconnections:

In addition to notice requirements of Rule 3.300, utility shall attempt to provide actual oral notice, by phone or in person, during the winter protection months.

§ 3.305. Notice Under Repayment Plan:

If disconnection is due to a failure to abide by the terms of a payment plan extending the time for payment for more than 2 weeks, notice shall be given prior to disconnection either 5 days if by mail, or 72 hours if by telephone. A customer is within substantial compliance of a payment plan if the customer has paid at least 75% of the payment plan payment.

§ 3.306. Time and Notice of Disconnection:

Service shall only be disconnected Monday through Thursday from 8:00 a.m.–2:00 p.m. within 4 days of the date indicated on the disconnection (8 days during winter protection months). Disconnection shall not occur on a legal holiday, or on day that the utility is closed to the public or the preceding day. If utility has personnel available to reconnect and enter into arrangements until 8:00 p.m. of a business day, service may be disconnected until 5:00 p.m.

§ 3.307. Restoration of Service:

Service shall be restored within 24 hours after the reason for disconnection has been eliminated. Upon receipt of a medical certificate, service shall be restored as soon as possible but shall be at least within 24 hours after receipt.

A utility shall restore service if the customer has paid 1/2 of the delinquent amount bill (or a lesser agreed upon amount), and agrees to a payment plan that reconciles the account within 3 months.

* * *

Electric Bill Information—**30-000-011 Vt. Code R. §§ 4.201–4.202**

4.201. Requirement:

Utility shall provide customer at least annually a listing of the price components of customer's rate, and whatever additional information is needed to calculate actual bill.

* * *

Selection of Primary Telecommunications Carrier (Slamming)—**30-000-045 Vt. Code R. §§ 4.701–4.703**

* * *

4.702. Changes to Primary Inter-Exchange Carrier:

Unless customer initiated, submission, initiation, or an actual change in a customer's provider shall only occur upon verifiable written, electronic, or oral authorization (see regulation for verification procedures and content requirements of letter of agency).

4.703. Changes to Primary Local Exchange Carrier:

Substantially similar to § 4.702.

VIRGINIA

The general regulations governing electric and gas service utilities can be found within 20 Va. Admin. Code §§ 5-10-10, 50-10-20, 5-312-90 and for utilities generally within Va. Code §§ 56-232–56.265. Rules governing telecommunications service providers can be found within 20 Va. Admin. Code §§ 5-401-10–5-429-60. Access to regulations can be found at www.virginia.gov/cmsportal/government_881/virginia_1048/index.html (last visited in May 2011).

***General (Electric and Gas Service Utilities)*—20 Va. Admin. Code §§ 5-10-10, 5-10-20, 5-312-90**

§ 5-10-10. Rules on Meter Testing, Bad Check Charges, and Late Payment Charges:

Upon request by a customer, a utility shall conduct 1 free meter test within a 24-month period; an additional test may require a deposit, but said deposit shall be returned if the meter is found to be at least 2% in error.

A service charge for a returned check shall be uniformly applied and shall not exceed $6.

A utility may apply a 1.5% monthly charge on overdue balances. A bill shall not be considered overdue if payment is received within 20 days from the mailing or delivery of the bill.

§ 5-10-20. Rule Governing Utility Customer Deposit Requirements:

A deposit to protect against uncollectible accounts shall not exceed 2 months' estimated usage. A customer shall have the right to pay a deposit that exceeds $40 in 3 consecutive monthly installments.

Deposits held longer than 90 days shall accrue interest at a rate established in December of the preceding year and equal to the average rate of a 1-year Constant Maturity Treasury bill from September through November of the preceding year—nonprofit organizations owned by their customers shall receive an interest rate of 75% of the aforementioned rate.

Deposits should not be held longer than 1 year (residential service) or 2 years (all others) provided the customer establishes satisfactory credit. A utility may refund a deposit at any time.

* * *

§ 5-312-90. Billing and Payment:

Bills shall contain customer's name, address, telephone or account number, billing period, all payment information and amounts due (late payments, charges, taxes, etc.), full description and itemization of activity and services, payments, adjustments, and credits, due date, and billing party address and toll-free telephone number for inquiry or dispute.

Terms and conditions for disconnection of service shall be set forth in each electric or gas local distribution company's approved tariff.

Va. Code Ann. §§ 56-247.1–56-253. Commission to Require Public Utilities to Follow Certain Procedures (§ 56.247.1):

Customers shall be allowed one full billing cycle to pay for 1 month's local or basic service before initiating proceedings for nonpayment.

Utility shall pay customer a rate of interest, as determined by the Commission on deposits, and return the deposit and accrued interest after not more than 1 year of satisfactory credit.

Notice shall be sent by mail at least 10 days prior to termination.

Residential service shall not be terminated for issues related to nonpayment of nonresidential service.

Electric utility may, upon customer's request and pursuant to tariff, install a prepaid metering equipment system that is configured to terminate electric service immediately and automatically when the customer has incurred charges for electric service equal to the customer's prepayments for such service. The foregoing provisions regarding billing cycles, interest, notice, and termination for nonpayment of nonresidential service shall not apply to electric services provided on such a prepaid metering equipment system.

Every public utility shall establish procedures for prompt and effective receipt and investigation of complaints.

***Telecommunications*—20 Va. Admin. Code §§ 5-401-10–5-429-60**

* * *

§ 5-413-10. Disconnection of Local Exchange Service for Failure to Pay:

Local service may be disconnected for failure to pay for local service, for a "basic bundle," or for failure to pay SLC, USF, or TRS fees or surcharges billed by the LEC. These fees and surcharges must be separately identified on the bill. An LEC may disconnect local services not required to be included in its tariff but may disconnect only the non-tariffed services for failure to pay for those services.

§ 5-413-20. Customer Bill and Directory Information:

A bill for local service shall clearly indicate and explain items for which local service may be disconnected for nonpayment and those for which disconnection for nonpayment is prohibited.

LEC white pages directories must include a list of services for which nonpayment may result in disconnection of local service; notice of the right to bring billing disputes to the Commission; and contact information for the Commission.

§ 5-413-30. Access to Inter-Exchange Carriers:

Nonpayment of specific inter-exchange toll charges may result in a local service provider blocking access to that specific inter-exchange provider, but a local service provider shall not block a customer's access to other inter-exchange providers.

* * *

WASHINGTON

The Utilities and Transportation Commission's regulations governing gas service can be found within Wash. Admin. Code 480-90-103–480-90-199; electric, Wash. Admin. Code 480-100-103–480-100-999; water, Wash. Admin. Code 480-110-205–480-110-999; telecommunications, Wash. Admin. Code 480-120-011–480-120-999. Many of the regulations governing electric, telecommunications, and water service are similar in substance and form to the regulations governing gas service. Questions regarding electric, telecommunications, and water service regulations may be answered by referencing the gas service regulations governing a specific issue. Access to the regulations can found at http://apps.leg.wa.gov/wac (last visited in May 2011).

Gas—**Wash. Admin. Code 480-90-103–480-90-199**

480-90-103. Information to Consumers:

Each gas utility must make available at each of its listed business offices information regarding rates, rules, and regulations needed for its customers and applicants to obtain adequate and efficient service, and provide to customers upon application and annually thereafter a brochure that explains the rights and responsibilities of a utility customer.

Upon request, a utility must provide an applicant with the high and low bills for the premises for the previous year. The utility must provide, upon request, a detailed account of customer's usage, if available, and a comparison of the current month's use with that for the same month the preceding year.

480-90-108. Application for Service:

A utility may require an applicant to provide proof of identity. The applicant may be allowed to choose from a list of acceptable sources of identification, which must include at least five alternatives.

No customer may re-meter or sub-meter gas for sale to others.

* * *

480-90-113. Residential Service Deposits Requirements:

A deposit or a guarantee, of an amount not to exceed 2/12 of an estimated annual billing (3/12 for bimonthly billing), may be required from an applicant or existing customer. Deposit payments shall not be due less than 6 days from the date that notice of the deposit is mailed or delivered (9 days if mailed from outside of Washington, Oregon, or Idaho).

Customers and applicants may be required to pay a deposit for 3 or more delinquent payment notices within previous 12 months, disconnection of service, or a person living at the residence owes a past-due bill. Applicants may also be required to pay a deposit if they fail to demonstrate 12 consecutive months of employment or regular source of income, not owning or purchasing the premises to be served, or an unpaid and overdue balance from any gas or electric utility service. Additional deposits may also be required, and, if a guarantor refuses to accept the additional amount, the customer is responsible for paying it.

In lieu of a deposit when customer indicates inability to pay, the utility must offer the option to pre-pay any service initiation fees and estimated charges at the regular billing periods (After 1 year of regular pre-payments, the utility must bill the customer in the usual way), to provide a guarantor, or to provide a utility reference.

A utility shall allow a customer or applicant to pay a deposit in installments consisting of a 50% initial payment with the remaining 50% to be paid in 2 equal monthly installments.

Deposits shall accrue interest, per annum, at rate equal to the one-year Treasury Constant Maturity calculated by the U.S. Treasury, as published in the Federal Reserve's Statistical Release H.15 on January 15 of that year.

Deposits, plus interest, shall be refunded (within 15 days) or credited (on the thirteenth month's bill) after 12 consecutive months of timely payments (no disconnection notices or no more than two delinquent payment notices). When a customer moves to a new address within the utility's territory, the deposit plus interest must be transferred or refunded (less any outstanding balance from the old address).

If service is terminated for nonpayment, deposits are to be returned less any amount owed.

480-90-123. Refusal of Service:

A utility may refuse service if a hazardous condition exists, a customer fails to install safety devices when requested by the utility, issues related to fraud, theft, and tampering, or for failure of responsible party to secure the necessary approval, permits or easements.

A utility may not refuse to provide new or additional service to a residential applicant or residential customer who has a prior obligation. A prior obligation is the dollar amount, excluding deposit amounts owed, the utility has billed to the customer and for which the utility has not received payment at the time the service has been disconnected for nonpayment. The utility must provide service once the customer or applicant has paid all appropriate deposit and reconnection fees (not applicable to customers that have been disconnected for failure to honor the terms of a winter low-income payment program). A utility may not refuse service for a prior occupant's balance, unless the utility can determine, based on objective evidence, that a fraudulent act is being committed, such that the new customer is acting in cooperation with the former customer to avoid payment.

Any applicant or customer who has been refused new or additional service may file with the Commission an informal complaint under 480-07-91 (informal complaints), or a formal complaint under 480-07-391.

480-90-128. Disconnection of Service:

Service shall not be disconnected due to amounts in disputes with either the utility or the Commission, or for amounts that may be owed the utility for non-regulated services. Utilities with combined accounts for both natural gas and electric service will have the option of choosing which service will be disconnected.

Service may be disconnected, with notice, for issues relating to nonpayment, denial of reasonable access to equipment, unauthorized use or adverse effect on services of utility or consumers, or violation of utility, Commission, federal, state, or local rules.

Notice of disconnection, mailed or delivered personally, shall be at least 8 days (11 days if mailed from outside Washington/Oregon/Idaho) prior to disconnection. Disconnection notices shall be clearly distinguishable, and shall contain the reasons for disconnection, the amount due, date of disconnection, how to avoid disconnection, utility's name, address and toll-free number to call regarding disconnection, availability of payment plans (pursuant to 480-90-138), delay option for medical reasons, and winter low-income payment program (pursuant to 480-90-143). A second notice of disconnection shall either be by personal notification delivered 2 days prior to disconnection, by mail at least 3 days (6 days if mailed from outside Washington/Oregon/Idaho) prior to disconnection, or through at least 2 attempts of notification by telephone. A utility shall keep records of attempts to notify by telephone at least 90 days, and shall be required to abide by second notice by mail or delivery requirements if telephone notice is unsuccessful. A disconnection not occurring within 10 days of scheduled date voids the initial notice and requires notice requirements be repeated unless customer and utility have entered into payment plan.

However, if utility provides a second notice within 10 business days of the disconnection date stated in the first notice, the disconnection date is extended an additional two business days from the disconnection date of the second notice. If service is not disconnected within the extended 10-day period, the second notice will be considered void unless the customer and utility have agreed upon a payment arrangement. If void, the utility must repeat the second notice requirement. If the utility provides a second notice after the 10 business days of the first disconnection notice, the second notice will be considered void unless the parties have entered into a payment arrangement. If void, the utility must repeat notice requirements.

Utilities shall accept payment when arriving to disconnect service, but is not obligated to make change for overpayment (overpayment shall be credited to customer's account), and may charge a fee for the disconnection visit.

When a utility is notified of a medical emergency related to disconnection, the utility shall reconnect service at least by the next business day without requiring a deposit or reconnection fee, or disconnection shall be delayed for an additional 5 days pending written physician certification. Written certification shall delay disconnection for 60 days and may be renewed for an additional 60 days. During the delay period, the utility may require the customer to keep account current, pay 10% of any outstanding balance, and enter into a payment plan that reconciles the account within 120 days. If a customer fails to provide written certification, a utility shall abide by the second notice requirements. A customer may claim the benefits of the medical emergency provision only twice in any 120-day period.

When service is provided through a master meter or service and billing address are not the same, a utility shall attempt to identify and notify the actual service user(s). Actual service users shall be provided an additional 5 days beyond the date of disconnection to arrange to receive service.

Disconnection may occur without notice if a dangerous condition exists or for any type of theft, fraud, or tampering related to service, unless the customer immediately pay a deposit and any amounts owed as a result of the theft fraud or tampering. A second occurrence may result in disconnection and a refusal to reconnect service. A dishonored check shall not be considered fraud.

Except in cases of emergency or danger to life and property, service shall not be disconnected Saturdays, Sundays, legal holidays, or on any other day on which the utility cannot reestablish service on the same or following day. The utility may charge for a premises visit if provided for in its tariff.

The utility must offer customers the opportunity to designate a third party to receive notices. If the utility has reason to believe the customer is unable to understand the effect of a disconnection, it must notify the appropriate social services agency. When a third party or social services agency is involved, the utility must delay disconnection for 5 days to give them the opportunity to respond.

When disconnection is customer initiated, the utility may require customers to give at least 3 days' notice prior to the date service is to be disconnected. The customer is not responsible for usage after the requested date for discontinuance of service, provided the customer gave proper notice.

480-90-133. Reconnecting Service After Disconnection:

Utility shall make a reasonable attempt to restore service 24 hours after the reason for disconnection has been reconciled. The Commission may require that the utility reconnect service when the propriety of the disconnection is at issue.

480-90-138. Payment Arrangements:

The utility shall offer all customers an opportunity to enter into equalized payment agreements. The utility may deny the equalized payment plan option to customers who have been removed from a payment plan within the last 6 months for nonpayment or who are more than 2 months past due on their current account.

480-90-143. Winter Low-Income Payment Program:

Customers, subject to disconnection, may continue to receive heat-related services and assistance during the months of November 15 through March 15 if eligible for a low-income payment plan provided by the Department of Community, Trade, and Economic Development or its successor (see regulation for specific rules and procedures). Required payments by income-eligible customers during the winter season may not exceed 7% of the household income plus one-twelfth of any billings from the date application is made until March 15. If the past-due bill is not paid by the following October 15, customer will not be eligible for protection under this section until that past-due bill is paid.

* * *

480-90-168. Access to Premises; Identification:

Utility representatives have a right of access to customer's premises at reasonable times for repairs, maintenance, testing, and meter reading. The customer has a right to see utility-issued identification before granting access.

* * *

480-90-173. Gas Utility's Responsibility for Complaints and Disputes:

A utility must promptly investigate complaints and disputes and provide an appeal to a utility supervisor. If a customer is dissatisfied with the result, the utility must inform the customer of the Commission's complaint procedure and provide contact information.

480-90-178. Billing Requirements and Payment Dates:

Bills shall be issued at intervals not to exceed two 1-month billing cycles, and shall include information concerning dates and itemized charges, due dates, amounts and penalties due, clear indication of an estimated or prorated bill, any information that will allow and assist in the computation of charges, and utility contact information. The minimum time for payment is 15 days from the mailing date (18 days if mailed outside Washington, Oregon, and Idaho). A utility must allow customers to change a designated payment due date for a satisfactory reason, such as the date of receipt of income.

480-90-183. Complaint Meter Tests:

A customer is entitled to one free meter test per year, which should be provided within 20 days of demand. The customer may witness the test or send a designated representative. The utility may charge for additional tests if the meter tests within accepted tolerances. If a meter is found inaccurate, the utility must refund or bill from the date when customer was first billed from a defective meter, if known or, if not known, for 6 months. In case of under-billing, the utility must offer a payment arrangement.

480-90-188. Payment Locations:

A utility must provide payment agencies in locally accessible places, must give the Commission 30 days' notice if a payment location will be closed, and must include on its bills a toll-free number to obtain a current list of payment locations.

* * *

***Electric*—Wash. Admin. Code 480-100-103–480-100-199; *Water*—Wash. Admin. Code 480-110-205–480-110-999; *Telecommunications*—Wash. Admin. Code 480-120-011–480-120-999**

Many of the regulations governing electric, telecommunications, and water service are similar in substance and form to the regulations governing gas service. Questions regarding electric, telecommunications, and water service regulations may be answered by referencing the gas service regulations governing a specific issue.

***Electric*—Wash. Admin. Code 480-100-103–480-100-199**

* * *

480-100-123. Refusal of Service:

Substantially similar to 480-90-123. A utility may refuse to provide service to a master meter if the property has more than one dwelling unit, and the occupants control a significant part of the electricity used in the individual unit, and it is cost-effective in the long run to provide individual metering.

480-100-128. Disconnection of Service:

Substantially similar to 480-90-128. First notice period is 8 days from mailing or delivery of notice (11 days if mailed outside Washington, Oregon, or Idaho).

* * *

***Water*—Wash. Admin. Code 480-110-205–480-110-999**

* * *

480-110-335. Establishing Credit and Deposits:

Substantially similar to 480-90-113, except a deposit may be required if customer had two or more delinquency notices in the prior 12 months.

* * *

480-110-355. Discontinuing of Service:

Substantially similar to 480-90-128. Reasons for disconnection include willful waste of water through defective equipment or otherwise.

* * *

480-110-375. Form of Bills:

Substantially similar to 480-90-178, except company may bill at 3-month intervals and must indicate whether it is billing in arrears or in advance.

* * *

***Telecommunications*—Wash. Admin. Code 480-120-110–480-120-999**

* * *

480-120-104. Information to Consumers:

The utility must provide each new customer with a confirmation or welcome letter with contact information for the utility, type of service and rate, and a reference to additional information provided in the directory. The utility must advise the customer within 15 days of any material change in service. If an LEC is serving as an executing carrier, it must provide the names of the inter-exchange companies to which the customer is currently subscribed and, if available, 6 months' account history. If a customer seeks to change an inter-exchange carrier, the LEC must notify the chosen carrier, or advise the consumer to do so, to confirm that an account has been established.

* * *

480-120-122. Establishing Credit—Residential Services:

Substantially similar to 480-90-113, except a utility may require a deposit if customer has had 2 or more delinquency notices in the prior 12 months. If a deposit is required for inter-exchange service, the customer must be offered the option of toll restriction, if technically feasible. A new or additional deposit may be required if toll charges exceed $30 or exceed average usage for the prior 6 months by the greater of $20 or 20%.

* * *

480-120-147. Changes in Local Exchange and Intrastate Toll Services:

A carrier may not submit a change order unless it is confirmed as provided for in this rule. A letter of agency must be a separate document or screen and may not be combined with inducements. (Checks that conspicuously include the approved letter of agency language, and no other inducements, are permissible.) The rule also prescribes standards for telephone verification or independent third-party verification. LECs must offer, and inform consumers about, a preferred carrier freeze and a procedure for lifting the freeze. This rule provides a separate procedure for carriers acquiring customers as the result of a merger or acquisition.

* * *

480-120-161. Form of Bills:

Substantially similar to 480-90-178, except bills must be issued monthly. If charges for more than one provider appear on the same telephone bill, the charges must be separated by service provider. Any changes of provider must be conspicuously disclosed. If a bill includes local-exchange services, it must clearly identify those charges for which nonpayment may result in disconnection. Bills must clearly identify any change in service provider, and any charges from a new provider.

The utility must accept payments by cash, certified funds, or personal check. Personal checks may be refused, after notice, if two checks are returned NSF within 12 months. Partial payments must be credited first to basic service.

480-120-162. Cash and Urgent Payments:

This rule prescribes standards (depending on the size of the company) for payment stations at which customers may pay cash or make "urgent" payments, i.e., those required to prevent imminent disconnection.

* * *

480-120-164. Pro Rata Credits:

A utility must provide pro rata credits if service is billed monthly and is not available for a total of 24 hours in one billing cycle (except in case of force majeure or a problem caused by customer's equipment or inside wiring).

* * *

480-120-172. Discontinuing Service—Company Initiated:

Substantially similar to 480-90-128. Disconnection for nonpayment: Basic service may be discontinued only for nonpayment for basic service. Ancillary service may be discontinued only for nonpayment of ancillary charges or if basic service is discontinued. Inter-exchange service may be discontinued only for nonpayment of inter-exchange service or if basic service is discontinued. The utility may not charge for toll restriction after toll service is discontinued. First notice period is 8 days from mailing, delivery, or emailing (if customer has consented to such method) of discontinuance notice.

May disconnect if customer is receiving service at an address where a former customer with an overdue balance resides, and there is evidence that customer lived at the address while the balance was incurred and "helped incur the obligation," or if there is evidence of other fraud, such as "rotation of service among roommates . . . for the purpose of avoiding . . . debts."

Medical certificates are valid for up to ninety days.

* * *

480-120-174. Payment Arrangements:

Customers are entitled, once in 5 years, to an option to pay a prior obligation over 6 months. Customers who were eligible for, but not participating in, the Washington Telephone Assistance Program or the Federal enhanced tribal lifeline program at the time of disconnection may be reconnected if they participate in either program and agree to pay amounts due at a rate of not more than 1.5 times the rate required to be paid by WTAP recipients, and agree to toll or ancillary service restriction (or both if required by company).

* * *

480-120-251. Directory Service:

LECs must provide directories, updated at least every 15 months, which include customer information on establishing credit, deposits, delinquency, disconnection, assistance programs, and complaint procedures.

* * *

480-120-255. Information Delivery Services:

LECs that offer information delivery services must offer, and inform customers of, blocking service. LECs must provide this information, along with a summary of customer's rights vis-à-vis information services and contact information for the Commission, by a single-subject bill insert and conspicuous publication in the directory. A company that provides billing or collection services for information providers must require, in its contract with the information service, that the information service conspicuously disclose in its advertising and promotion the cost of the service.

480-120-261. Operator Services:

The operator service must protect the confidentiality of all communication it carries, processes or transmits, unless otherwise authorized by law. OSPs must assure that when automated services are provided customers can reach a live operator, must assure accurate recording of call times for operator-assisted calls, and must assure that operators handling O or E911 calls can route the call to the proper emergency service 24 hours a day.

480-120-262. Operator Service Providers:

Applies to OSPs providing services for pay phones or call aggregators (such as hotels, prisons, hospitals, campuses). On pay-phones, the name and contact information for the OSP, and the contact information for complaints to the Commission, must be conspicuously posted. Before completing an operator assisted call, the OSP must disclose the rate. (In case of a collect call, it must be disclosed to both caller and recipient). If the rate does not exceed the prescribed benchmark the customer may be told how to access a rate quote, by not more than two keystrokes. If the rate exceeds the benchmark, the disclosure must quote the rate. The OSP must identify itself, by the name registered with the Commission, at the beginning of every call. The OSP must provide the billing company with itemized information necessary for billing and with a toll-free number for consumer inquiries, and must assure that customers are not billed for uncompleted calls.

* * *

WEST VIRGINIA

The Public Service Commission's regulations governing electric service provider's customer relations can be found within W. Va. Code R. §§ 150-3-4.1–150-3-4.18; gas, W. Va. Code R. §§ 150-4-4.1–150-4-4.16; sewer, W. Va. Code R. §§ 150-5-4.1–150-5-4.12; telecommunications, W. Va. Code R. §§ 150-6-2.1–150-6-2.9; water, W. Va. Code R. §§ 150-7-4.1–150-7-4.15. Many of the regulations governing gas, sewer, water, and telecommunications service are similar in substance and form to the regulations governing electric. Questions regarding gas, sewer, water, and telecommunications regulations may be answered by referencing the electric regulations governing a specific issue. Access to the West Virginia Code of State Rules can be found at www.wvsos.com/csr (last visited in May 2011).

Electric Service Provider*'s Customer Relations—*W. Va. Code R. §§ 150-3-4.1–150-3-4.18

§ 150-3-4.1. Customer Information:

Each electric utility must make available at each of its listed business offices information regarding rates, rules, and regulations needed for its customers and applicants to obtain adequate and efficient service, a brochure that explains the meter reading procedures, the rights and responsibilities of a utility customer, and usage information.

§ 150-3-4.2. Customer Deposits:

A deposit or guarantee, to secure payment of charges for service, shall not exceed 1/12 of annual estimated charges. Deposits shall accrue interest, per annum, at rate equal to the average of the one-year Treasury Bill rates of October, November, and December of the previous year. Deposits and interest shall be promptly and automatically refunded after 12 consecutive months of timely payments. Customers shall receive a receipt for deposits, and the utility shall establish procedures to claim a deposit should the receipt be lost.

Guarantors must give at least 30 days' notice before rescinding a guarantee.

§ 150-3-4.3. Billing Information:

Bills shall be issued at regular intervals and shall contain information concerning meter readings and reading dates and consumption amounts, due dates, amounts and penalties due, and any information that will allow and assist in the computation of charges.

§ 150-3-4.4. Adjustment of Bills:

A customer's bill shall be adjusted if their meter is found to registering fast or slow by at least 2%. Adjustment shall be based on 1/2 the time that has passed since the previous reading but shall not exceed 6 months.

* * *

§ 150-3-4.7. Customer Discontinuance of Service:

Customers must give at least 3 days' notice, and may be charged a reconnection fee if the customer requests service at the same residence within 8 months.

§ 150-3-4.8. Utility Discontinuance of Service:

Service may be terminated for issues related to nonpayment (10 days after due date), fraud, violation of rules, or failure to allow the utility reasonable access to utility property within the customer's premises. Notice shall not be required if a hazardous condition requires termination. Delinquency in payment for service by a previous occupant of the premises to be served other than a member of the same household shall not be grounds for termination or refusal of service.

Written notice shall be at least 10 days prior to termination date (5 days if for violation of a payment plan), and shall be followed by personal notice at least 24 hours prior to termination, unless it can be reasonably established that the residence is not inhabited. Notice becomes void if service is not terminated within 30 days of notice.

Termination shall be delayed and a payment plan offered in some circumstances if, prior to termination, the utility is notified that the reason for termination is being disputed (customers may be required to pay undisputed portion of bills), termination would be dangerous to the health and safety of a household member (medically or from December through February), or the customer can only pay the bill in monthly installments. When calculating a payment plan, a utility shall consider the amount due, customer's ability to pay, customer's payment history, and the time and reason the bill has not been paid. A utility may assess a 6% carrying fee on a payment plan. Utilities shall renegotiate payment plans should the existing plan create a financial hardship due to a change in the customer's finances.

Medical certification must be received 10 days after utility notification, and shall be renewed every 30 days unless a physician states, to a reasonable degree of medical certainty, that the condition is permanent.

Service shall not be terminated to residential customers 65 years or older or to customers that are physically, mentally or emotionally incapacitated unless a relative or responsible third party is notified and the customer refuses to enter into a payment plan.

If customer of record is (a) a landlord of a master-metered multiple unit dwelling, or (b) a third party who does not reside at the service location, then five (5) days' written notice, using P.S.C. W. Va. Form 14 ME, shall also be posted.

Service shall only be terminated Monday–Thursday from 8:00 a.m.–4:00 p.m., and shall not be terminated the day preceding or the day of a legal holiday or when the utility's payment office is not open to the public.

Payment shall be accepted at the time of termination, but a personal check may be refused if the customer has issued a dishonored check for services within the previous 12 months. A $5 reconnection fee may be assessed. Service shall be restored within 8 hours after receipt of payment.

§ 150-3-4.9. Refusal to Serve Applicant:

Service may be refused for non-compliance with municipal, utility or Commission rules or the applicant's facilities are inadequate.

§ 150-3-4.10. Change in Character of Service:

A utility shall notify all customers who may be affected by a change in service before any change is implemented, and no change for which customer will incur expense may be made without customer's agreement to and understanding of such costs.

* * *

§ 150-3-4.16. Reduced Rates for Low-Income Residential Customers:

Low-income customers may qualify for a 20% reduced rate for December through April (see regulation or contact Commission for specific guidelines and procedures).

* * *

***Gas*—W. Va. Code R. §§ 150-4-4.1–150-4-4.16; *Sewer*—W. Va. Code R. §§ 150-5-4.1–150-5-4.12; *Telecommunications*—W. Va. Code R. §§ 150-6-1–150-6-2.9; *Water*—W. Va. Code R. §§ 150-7-4.1–150-7-4.15**

Many of the regulations governing gas, sewer, water, and telecommunications service are similar in substance and form to the regulations governing electric. Questions regarding gas, sewer, water, and telecommunications regulations may be answered by referencing the electric regulations governing a specific issue.

* * *

§ 150-6-1.7. Definitions:

The definition of basic local exchange service specifies what must be provided, including, inter alia, access to emergency services, a directory, operator service, directory assistance, access to certain long-distance services (unless denied for failure to pay undisputed amounts due), incoming long-distance calls, procedures for reporting problems and resolving disputes, and optional blocking of Caller ID, pay-per-call access, non-local access, collect calls and third-party charges.

* * *

WISCONSIN

The Public Service Commission's regulations governing electric service can be found within Wis. Admin. Code PSC §§ 113.01–113.1010; gas, Wis. Admin. Code PSC §§ 134.01–134.31; telecommunications, Wis. Admin. Code, PSC §§ 165.01–165.10; water, Wis. Admin. Code, PSC § 185.11–185.88. The regulations governing gas, water, and telecommunications service are similar in form and substance to the regulations governing electric. Questions regarding these services may be answered by referencing the electric regulation governing a specific issue. Access to Wisconsin's Administrative Code can be found at www.legis.state.wi.us/rsb/code/psc/psc.html (last visited in May 2011).

***Electric*—Wis. Admin. Code PSC §§ 113.01–113.1010**

* * *

§ 113.0301. Disconnections, Residential:

Service shall not be refused or disconnected due to a disputed bill, past-due charges of a prior occupant not residing at the premises served, failure to pay for merchandise or non-utility services, failure to pay for a different type or class of service, failure to pay another's bill as a guarantor, failure to pay for under-billing occurring of more than 1 year due to misapplication of rates or faulty metering, failure to pay an estimated bill not issued pursuant to approved meter reading plan, or to assist a landlord in evicting a tenant.

Service may be refused or disconnected, with notice, for issues related to nonpayment of past or present charges (including delinquent bills of prior occupant or customer residing in the premises to be served), faulty or nonstandard equipment, interference with service of others, providing false information in obtaining service, failure to supply credit information, or failure to allow the utility to conduct a meter reading (required every 6 months).

Service may be disconnected, without notice, when a dangerous condition exists, unauthorized use or reconnection of service, or use of unsafe equipment.

Notice shall be at least 10 days prior to disconnection, shall be clearly distinguishable, and shall contain the reasons for disconnection, the amount due, date of disconnection, availability of payment plans and assistance, 21 day delay options (for medical, winter, and heat related reasons), and complaint procedures. If service is not disconnected within 20 days after disconnection date, a utility shall provide a second notice, personally delivered to the residence, no more than 48 hours and no less than 24 hours before disconnection.

Disconnection shall be delayed for 21 days, and utility shall negotiate special payment arrangements, when a licensed physician, public health, social service, or law enforcement official certifies that a medical or protective emergency would result from disconnection.

A utility shall provide, or make every reasonable effort, to provide at least 5 days individual notice and notice in a common area for multi-dwelling units, master-metered accounts, or other instances where the billing and service addresses are different. Notice shall also include the procedures for obtaining individualized service and billing.

A utility shall not disconnect service on a day or the day immediately preceding a day when utility's business office is not open to public unless utility personnel are readily available to the occupant 24 hours per day to negotiate restoration of and to restore service.

* * *

§ 113.0303. Reconnection of Service:

Before October 15, a utility shall attempt to contact by mail, phone, or personally, all disconnected households within the previous 12 months. If contact does not result from mail or telephone call, the utility shall attempt personal contact before October 25 (November 1 for households disconnected between October 15 and October 31). Services shall be reconnected, and, if necessary, social services contacted if utility discovers conditions dangerous to human health or safety.

§ 113.0304. Cold Weather Disconnections:

Between November 1 to April 15, a utility may disconnect only those households whose gross quarterly incomes are above 250% of the federal income poverty guidelines and where health and safety would not be endangered because of the infirmities of age, developmental or mental disabilities or like infirmities incurred at any age or the frailties associated with being very young, if service were terminated or not restored.

A utility shall attempt personal contact the day of and the day after disconnection to verify the occupants' well being, ensure there is no danger to health or safety, and to inform the occupants of available assistance and shelter. Service shall be reconnected if utility discovers conditions dangerous to human health or safety.

* * *

§ 113.0402. Deposits Residential:

A deposit or guarantee shall not be required if the customer or applicant provides the utility with information showing that his or her gross quarterly income is at or below 200% of federal income poverty guidelines. A deposit or guarantee shall not be required for service unless a customer has an outstanding account balance with any Wisconsin electric utility which accrued within the last 6 years and for which there is not a payment agreement or dispute.

An applicant shall not be required to pay a deposit or provide a guarantee that exceeds the higher of 2 estimated consecutive billing periods.

Applicants or customers who may be required to pay a deposit or provide a guarantee shall be informed of the availability of payment plans and dispute procedures.

An existing customer may be required to pay a deposit or provide a guarantee, not to exceed the amount of two consecutive high-usage bills within previous 12 months, if service has been disconnected within the previous 12 months for nonpayment or rule violations, false credit information, or, if during winter protection months, account was more than 80 days past-due and customer had the ability to pay for services. If 80 days past-due during winter protections, and customer had the ability to pay for services, deposit or guarantee may be as much as four consecutive high usage bills.

All deposits shall be reasonable and shall consider a customer's ability to pay, amount of and time period of delinquent bill, payment history, and reason for delinquency.

All deposits shall be returned or credited to a customer's account, with interest (per annum) equal to average of one-year U.S. Treasury securities for week ending on or after December 1y, after 12 consecutive months of timely payments.

A utility may apply deposits to past-due amounts and require the customer to bring the deposit back to the required amount within 20 days or be subject to disconnection.

* * *

§ 113.0404. Deferred Payment Agreement:

Deferred payment plans shall be offered to customers having difficulty paying bills and accepted as means of avoiding disconnection of service if the customer agrees to pay a reasonable initial payment followed by reasonable installment payments. All payment plans shall also consider a customer's ability to pay, amount of and time period of delinquent bill, payment history, and reason for delinquency. Customers shall be notified of their right to dispute and appeal the terms and/or reasons for written payment to the Commission. Utilities may, pursuant to §§ 113.0301 and 113.0304, disconnect services for failure to abide by payment plan terms, and are not obligated to renegotiate a payment plan.

§ 113.0405. Meter Readings and Billing Periods:

Meters shall be read by the utility at least once every 2 months, or once every 6 months when the utility has procedures allowing customers to provide readings. Date of reading may be postponed but not more than 5 days from the scheduled reading. A utility shall make a reasonable effort to read meters during non-business hours when requested by customer. Bills shall be rendered within 40 days from the date the meter is read.

§ 113.0406. Billing:

Bills shall be due no less than 20 days from date of issuance, and shall contain the customer's name, address, telephone or account number, billing period, meter readings and reading dates, all payment information and amounts due (late payments, charges, taxes, etc.), full description and itemization of activity and services, payments, adjustments, credits, distinct making if an estimated bill, and date after which late payment shall be applied.

A one-time 3% ($.50 minimum), or 1% per annum, late charge may be assessed on past-due amounts or amounts not billed due to diversion of service or meter tampering. If a bill is in dispute, a late charge may only be assessed against the portion of the disputed bill later found to be correct and payable to the utility. Customers shall receive information pertaining to available reduced rates at least once every 12 months.

Budgeted or equalized payment plans shall be offered to all customers and applicants, and shall be notified of any adjustments for under or over billing. A customer shall have the right to pay under-billed amounts using a deferred payment plan.

§ 113.0407. Dispute Procedures:

Customer disputes shall be initially negotiated between the customer and utility, and if no agreement can be reached, customer has the right to a two-tiered standard of Commission review (formal and informal). Service shall not be disconnected during a dispute, but may be disconnected for nonpayment of undisputed charges. After an informal decision has been reached, a customer must request a formal review within 7 days.

* * *

§ 113.0501. Information Available to Customers:

Each utility shall have available in its offices where payments are received and at area libraries, copies of its rates and rules applicable to the locality. The rates and rules shall be available for customer inspection by electronic, written or telephonic means and reasonable notice as to their availability shall be provided to customers. Directories for each municipality served shall include 24-hour repair and emergency service phone numbers. At service initiation and annually thereafter utility shall provide customer with written notice of all the rights, remedies, responsibilities, and assistance associated with services.

* * *

***Gas*—Wis. Admin. Code PSC §§ 134.01–134.31; *Telecommunications*—Wis. Admin. Code PSC §§ 165.01–165.10; *Water*—Wis. Admin. Code PSC §§ 185.11–185.88**

The regulations governing gas, water, and telecommunications service are similar in form and substance to the regulations governing electric. Questions regarding these services may be answered by referencing the electric regulation governing a specific issue.

WYOMING

The Public Service Commission's general regulations governing electric, gas, and water service can be found within 023-020-2 Wyo. Code R. §§ 201–253; 023-020-3 Wyo. Code R. §§ 301–325 (electric); 023-020-4 Wyo. Code R. §§ 401–420 (gas); 023-020-6 Wyo. Code R. §§ 601–615 (water). Regulations governing telephone service can be found in Wyo. Admin. Code PSC UA Ch. 5, § 504. Specific regulations governing electric shall be included within the general regulations and cited accordingly. The regulations governing gas and water service billing and adjustments are similar in form and substance to the regulation governing electric billing and adjustments, and, any questions regarding these issues may be answered by referencing the electric billing and adjustment regulation. Access to the rules and regulations can be found at http://psc.state.wy.us/htdocs/rules_new.htm (last visited in May 2011).

* * *

§ 239. Information for Customers:

The utility shall provide information concerning services, rate schedules and any changes in services and rate schedules, information that will assist in choice of the most suitable and advantageous service, and all the rights, remedies, responsibilities, and assistance associated with services.

§ 240. Customer Complaints Made to Utility (Except Rail and Motor Common Carriers):

All complaints shall be promptly and fully investigated by the utility either directly or through the Commission, and the utility shall maintain complete records of written complaints received for 3 years from the date of resolution.

§ 241. Customer Deposits, Gas, Electric, and Water Utilities:

An applicant or customer may be required to pay a deposit or provide a third-party guarantee to ensure payments for services if: customer owes an undisputed prior balance to the utility; customer's service from the utility was terminated for nonpayment, failure to reimburse company for damages caused by consumer, fraud, or tampering; provision of false information; consumer is seeking service for the first time from the utility or did not have service for 12 consecutive months during the past 4 years; an applicant cannot pass an objective credit screen; applicant or customer has filed bankruptcy within the past 5 years; a former customer who owes a balance continues to reside at the service location. A deposit may not be required based on property ownership or location, income level, source of income, employment tenure, nature of occupation, race, creed, sex, age, national origin, marital status, number of dependents, or any other criterion not authorized by these rules. Deposits shall not exceed 90 days of estimated or actual billing, and shall be returned or credited, with interest (at a rate assigned by Commission by November 30 of each year) if held for more than 6 months, after 12 consecutive months without disconnection or late payments. Customers shall be given a receipt for deposits and the utility shall establish procedures for claiming a deposit should the receipt be lost.

§ 242. Discontinuance of Service by Gas, Electric, and Water Utilities:

Utility shall give at least 7 days' notice before terminating service for issues relating to nonpayment or violation of rules. Notice shall not be required if termination is due to hazardous conditions, fraud, tampering with service, destruction of utility property, noncompliance with curtailment procedures during supply shortages, or cooperation with civil authorities. Tenants subject to termination of services due to landlord nonpayment shall be given at least 15 days personal notice or notice posted in common area that includes information describing the options for receiving individualized service and billing (if feasible). Tenants shall not be required to pay a landlord's past-due amounts.

Notice of disconnection shall be clearly distinguishable and shall contain the reasons for disconnection, the amount due, date of disconnection, availability of payment plans and assistance, delay option for weather related (November 1 through April 30) or medical reasons, and complaint procedures. During winter protection months, a utility shall attempt personal notification at the residence to be terminated. Utility must notify residence subject to termination of service that an additional 15 day delay is available if it can be documented that a resident is disabled or seriously ill, including persons whose physical health or safety would be seriously endangered if service were discontinued. An additional 30 days' notice is required if household resident is dependent on utility for life support services. If customer has a guarantor, notice must be provided to the guarantor at the same time as to the customer.

Upon request by a customer, a family member, or other responsible person, the company shall notify a third person about overdue bills and termination notices. The utility shall have a procedure to advise customers of this option. If a customer has provided a guarantor in lieu of a deposit, the guarantor must be given notice of disconnection at the same time as the customer. A guarantor's service may not be disconnected for the customer's default. If a landlord requests, the company will notify the landlord of a tenant's impending disconnection and the option to put service in the landlord's name.

Service shall not be terminated due to nonpayment of merchandise or non-utility services, disputed bills or amounts, when customer agrees to a payment plan; if the utility has commenced providing service to a customer without obtaining a payment agreement for bill nonpayment at a customer's previous address, and the customer has paid the utility's bills on time at his new address; if a customer pays a bill on time for a specific service at a specific location, even though the customer is receiving another service that is subject to disconnection for bill nonpayment; if a customer is paying his bills on time, even though a prior customer of the utility, including a spouse who is delinquent, is cohabiting or living in the same house.

A utility may not terminate if this would "especially endanger health," for example, because of extreme weather or if the customer can document inability to pay and that he or she has exhausted government assistance, is actively applying for it, or is able to pay only in installments (the documentation requirement does not apply to elder or disabled persons.)

Service shall only be disconnected Monday through Thursday, 8:00 a.m.–4:00 p.m., and shall not be disconnected the day of, or day before, a legal holiday; when the utility is not able to reconnect service; or between December 24 through January 2. Pre-paid meters are allowed, as permitted by tariff.

If a customer requests disconnection, the utility must make every reasonable effort to disconnect on the day of the request. For disconnection after usual business hours, the utility may charge a fee.

A utility may install a prepaid meter but must strictly comply with PURPA provisions regarding termination, must provide "reasonable and emergency access for the provision of prepaid utility commodity," must inform the consumer of card purchase locations, and must provide an emergency telephone number and written instructions for emergencies and service problems.

§ 243. Reconnection of Disconnected Service:

Service disconnected for nonpayment shall be reconnected immediately or upon day requested by customer when the reason for disconnection has been eliminated. A reconnection charge may be assessed, and customers shall be notified if any additional charges are applicable for non-business connections requested by the customer.

* * *

§ 245. Refusal to Serve New Customers or Expand Existing Service:

Service may be denied due to inadequate facilities, a hazardous condition, adverse affects on other customers' services, indebtedness to utility for in-state services (unless payment arrangements and/or deposit have been made). If indebtedness is in dispute, service may not be denied if a deposit is paid in the amount of normal deposit plus amount equal to disputed amount.

* * *

Electric (Specific)—**023-020-3 Wyo. Code R. §§ 301–325**

* * *

§ 306. Bill Adjustments for Meter Error:

A customer's bill shall be adjusted if their meter is found to be registering fast or slow by more than 2%. Adjustment shall be based on (i) the 6-month period immediately preceding the removal of the meter for the test, or the time since the last test but not exceeding 6 months, or (ii) the date of the error, if it can be definitely fixed.

* * *

***Gas*—023-020-4 Wyo. Code R. §§ 401–420; *Water*—023-020-6 §§ 601–616**

Specific regulations governing electric shall be included within the general regulations and cited accordingly. The regulations governing gas and water service billing and adjustments are similar in form and substance to the regulation governing electric billing and adjustments, and, any questions regarding these issues may be answered by referencing the electric billing and adjustment regulation.

A.2 Background to Utility Consumer Protection Rules

A.2.1 Introduction

Historically, public utility rates have been regulated to protect against monopoly pricing of essential services. Similarly, state utility regulatory authorities and legislatures established provisions pertaining to customer service so that utilities with exclusive franchise rights are precluded from delivering a necessary service in a discriminatory manner. While utility rates are the primary determinant of what consumers pay for utility service, provisions related to late payment fees, security deposits and other charges also determine the affordability of utility costs.

Utility consumer protections are legal provisions dealing with the terms of obtaining and retaining service. The protections and rules of service include requirements to provide consumers with information regarding their utility service, provisions regarding security deposits and advance payment for service, late payment fees, termination and restoration of service, establishment of payment plans, and resolution of disputes between customers and utility companies. Each state has adopted its own structure, and there is considerable variability between provisions state-to-state.[1] Utility consumer protection and customer service rules may be found in state regulations and statutes, and in some cases in regulatory commission orders and utility company tariffs. In many cases, utility commission websites include links to that state's consumer protections and customer service rules.

Utility consumer protections in many states have been adopted to protect society's most vulnerable members—including those with low incomes, the elderly, the very young, and people with disabilities—from loss of necessary service. Many of the existing state utility consumer protection provisions were adopted during the 1970s and 1980s. Today's energy pricing and economic environments are very different, which means that many of the original consumer protection rules are inadequate.

Arguably, states need to establish a stronger link between low-income energy assistance programs and regulatory consumer protections. Both low-income energy assistance programs and components of the regulatory consumer protection structure are intended to ensure against loss of essential services in order to protect health and safety. Inadequate consumer protections and punitive customer service rules run counter to this goal. It is essential for regulatory consumer protections to be designed and implemented in a manner consistent with the goals and objectives of existing payment assistance programs.

A.2.2 Components of the Consumer Regulatory Protection Structure

Provision of Utility Service: All public electric and natural gas utilities, whether they are investor-owned, municipal or cooperative, are subject to legal obligations to serve everyone living within the utility's service area who has applied for service, is willing to pay for the service, and comply with the utility's rules and regulations.[2] This obligation prevents utilities from choosing to serve only those customers and geographic areas on the basis of profit potential.

Denial of Service: Most state customer service rules allow utilities to deny service in cases of noncompliance with rules or regulations, dangerous conditions, or noncompliance with state and local codes. Some states relieve utilities of the duty to serve applicants with outstanding bills. In addition, some states specify that a utility may not refuse to serve a prospective customer under circumstances such as delinquency by a previous occupant or failure to pay for merchandise purchased from the utility.

Provision of Consumer Information and Notification of Consumer Rights: Most states require regulated utility companies to provide information about pricing and utility service to any customer who requests it. Some states require companies to regularly provide information to consumers regarding payment assistance and the right to file a consumer complaint or dispute billing amounts. Several states require companies to inform customers of medical certification procedures and circumstances under which service may not be terminated.

Security Deposits: As utility debt and the write-off of uncollectible accounts increase in response to rapidly rising energy prices, many companies are using security deposits as a means of minimizing risk. However, from the consumer's perspective, onerous security deposit provisions merely increase the overall cost of utility service. In some cases, they make it nearly impossible to obtain service. Customer service rules regarding security deposits vary widely from state to state. While some states allow utility

1 See Appx. A.1, *supra*, for summaries of each state's consumer protection regulations.

2 *See* § 2.1.2, *supra*.

companies to obtain the value of four or more months of service up-front, others allow either none, or minimal security deposits, from new residential customers.

Another aspect of utility security deposits of particular concern involves the use of credit scoring. Increasingly, companies are interested in using third-party credit scores to determine whether new or additional security deposits will be required of particular customers. This is problematic for a number of reasons. First, it is highly inappropriate to use a credit score based on a range of financial transactions to determine the extent to which a prospective customer is likely to pay his or her utility bill. In addition, credit scores are notoriously inaccurate. Finally, individuals that lack an extensive credit history many have poor credit scores that simply do not reflect likelihood to pay for utility service. In short, use of credit scores to determine security deposits or other aspects of utility service should be viewed with great skepticism.[3]

Payments and Due Dates: States vary in their treatment of the time that must expire before a utility bill is considered past due. Some states require payment in as few as ten days after a bill is postmarked. Other states allow as many as forty-five days to expire before a bill is considered to be past due. Payment due dates are important because they have direct bearing on the amount of time which must expire before a customer faces the possibility of disconnection.

Late Payment Fees: In some state, utilities are prohibited from charging residential customers late payment fees. However, in many states companies are allowed to charge a percentage of the most recent bill or a percentage of any outstanding amounts. Similar to security deposits, assessment of late payment charges and fees can significantly increase the cost of service.

Termination and Disconnection of Service: States have adopted widely varying provisions regarding the termination of electric and natural gas utility service. In some states provisions are far more protective than in others. For example, in Massachusetts utilities are prohibited from terminating service in low-income households where occupants are elderly or disabled. In addition, Massachusetts utilities cannot terminate service in households were there is an infant under twelve months of age. Further, Massachusetts utilities are prohibited from terminating service between November 15 and April 15 in households were there is financial hardship. Many other states have adopted some combination of similar protections. However, large numbers of states do very little to protect vulnerable customers from service disconnections.

Restoration of Service: In most cases of disconnection for nonpayment, customers are required to pay part or all of the outstanding billing amount and sometimes enter into a payment plan with the utility company. Terms for restoration of service have become increasingly important since high and volatile energy prices have led to large arrearage amounts in low-income households. Onerous restoration terms effectively preclude some households from restoring service once it has been lost.

Establishment of Payment Plans: Some states have adopted rules that require utility companies to offer customers special payment agreements as an alternative to service termination, or as a means of restoring service. Payment plan terms and requirements vary widely from state to state. Access to reasonable payment plans is a central aspect of the utility consumer protection structure. Some states have adopted a highly punitive approach to payment plan terms where a missed payment—irrespective of the circumstances involved—is followed up with a requirement for a higher monthly payment toward back bills.

A more sensible approach has been adopted in Iowa. There, customers who have received a disconnection notice are offered a payment plan of at least twelve months in duration. In the event that the initial payment plan fails after the customer has demonstrated a good-faith effort to make timely payments, a subsequent payment plan of equal or greater duration must be offered.[4] This rule is based on the assumption that most customers are interested in remaining current on their utility bills, but that difficult financial circumstances often lead to payment troubles.

Disputes and Dispute Resolution: The right to dispute a utility bill or service practice is central to the consumer protection structure. Most states require that customers be informed of that right. In addition, most states specify that companies should investigate an attempt to resolve disputes with customers. When a customer and a company are unable to resolve a dispute, state rules allow formal or informal procedures before regulatory commission administrative staff.

A.2.3 The Need to Strengthen Utility Consumer Protections

During the late-1970s through the mid-1980s many state legislatures and public utility commissions (PUCs) developed new consumer protections to help ensure uninterrupted access to utility service. The new rules were developed largely in response to rapidly-rising electricity prices associated with the 1970s oil embargos and cost overruns on large baseload power plant construction projects across the country.

The steady rise in energy prices and the increased utility interest in adopting advanced metering technologies and dynamic pricing, along with the advances in information technology providing for quick and ready access to consumer credit information, have elevated the importance of effective consumer protections for low-income households.

Unfortunately, many of the consumer protection frameworks of the 1970s and 1980s are no longer effective in providing consumers with reasonable security from loss of vital service. The energy price levels and volatility of today were simply not contemplated when original regulations were adopted nearly four decades ago. In addition, key state utility consumer protection frameworks have come under attack from utility companies facing the pressures associated with increasing customer arrearages and uncollectible accounts. For example, a petition filed with the Illinois Commerce Commission by a consortium of electric and natural gas utilities called for a need to limit credit risk and reduce bad debt. Very often utilities and regulators assume that achievement of such goals may only be accomplished through means that run counter to the universal service goals, and increase the cost of obtaining and retaining electricity and natural gas service.

When consumer protections are inadequate and energy security for those on low incomes is compromised, the protections are actually working counter to the goals and objectives of federal and

3 A complete analysis of credit scoring and reporting may be found in National Consumer Law Center, Fair Credit Reporting (7th ed. 2010).

4 Iowa Admin. Code r. 199-19.4(10).

state payment assistance and energy efficiency programs. For example, when a state LIHEAP office scrambles to cobble together the resources necessary to keep a client from losing utility service, those efforts may be undermined by unreasonable payment plan or new security deposit provisions. What is needed now is a state-by-state re-examination of existing utility consumer protections to ensure that vulnerable customers who demonstrate good faith efforts to make affordable utility payments are protected from loss or degradation of service.

A.3 Selected State Utility Consumer Protection Regulations

A.3.1 Deposits

220 Mass. Code Regs. 27—Elimination of the Practice of Gas and Electric Companies of Requiring a Deposit from Residential Customers As a Condition to Furnishing Utility Service

220 CMR 27.00 is applicable solely to utility service rendered to residential customers by any gas or electric utility company (hereinafter referred to as Company) subject to the jurisdiction of the Department of Public Utilities of the Commonwealth of Massachusetts. All non-residential accounts, including commercial, industrial and municipal accounts, are expressly excluded from the coverage of 220 CMR 27.00.

No Company may require a deposit to secure payment of utility bills in advance of or as a condition to new or continued service. A Company may properly condition new or continued service, subject to law and the Department's regulations on Billing and Termination Procedures for Residential Customers of Gas and Electric Companies, upon payment by the customer of any outstanding bill of that Company; provided however, that if a customer has not failed previously to pay when due and finally determined to be payable two or more consecutive bills of that Company, the Company shall grant or continue service as long as the customer shall pay the overdue bill in full or under an installment payment plan, not to exceed three months in duration. On or before the effective date of 220 CMR 27.00 any Company holding deposits to secure payment of utility bills in advance of or as a condition to new or continued service shall promptly refund all such deposits, together with interest accrued to date of return, in cash or as a credit to its customers' next bills for service.

A.3.2 Payment Plans

Iowa Admin. Code 199-19.4(10)—Payment agreements

a. Availability of a first payment agreement. When a residential customer cannot pay in full a delinquent bill for utility service or has an outstanding debt to the utility for residential utility service and is not in default of a payment agreement with the utility, a utility shall offer the customer an opportunity to enter into a reasonable payment agreement.

b. Reasonableness. Whether a payment agreement is reasonable will be determined by considering the current household income, ability to pay, payment history including prior defaults on similar agreements, the size of the bill, the amount of time and the reasons why the bill has been outstanding, and any special circumstances creating extreme hardships within the household. The utility may require the person to confirm financial difficulty with an acknowledgment from the department of human services or another agency.

c. Terms of payment agreements.

(1) First payment agreement. The utility shall offer customers who have received a disconnection notice or have been disconnected 120 days or less and who are not in default of a payment agreement the option of spreading payments evenly over at least 12 months by paying specific amounts at scheduled times. The utility shall offer customers who have been disconnected more than 120 days and who are not in default of a payment agreement the option of spreading payments evenly over at least 6 months by paying specific amounts at scheduled times.

1. The agreement shall also include provision for payment of the current account. The agreement negotiations and periodic payment terms shall comply with tariff provisions which are consistent with these rules. The utility may also require the customer to enter into a level payment plan to pay the current bill.

2. When the customer makes the agreement in person, a signed copy of the agreement shall be provided to the customer.

3. The utility may offer the customer the option of making the agreement over the telephone or through electronic transmission. When the customer makes the agreement over the telephone or through electronic transmission, the utility shall render to the customer a written document reflecting the terms and conditions of the agreement within three days of the date the parties entered into the oral agreement or electronic agreement. The document will be considered rendered to the customer when addressed to the customer's last-known address and deposited in the U.S. mail with postage prepaid. If delivery is by other than U.S. mail, the document shall be considered rendered to the customer when delivered to the last-known address of the person responsible for payment for the service. The document shall state that unless the customer notifies the utility within ten days from the date the document is rendered, it will be deemed that the customer accepts the terms as reflected in the written document. The document stating the terms and agreements shall include the address and a toll-free or collect telephone number where a qualified representative can be reached. By making the first payment, the customer confirms acceptance of the terms of the oral agreement or electronic agreement.

4. Each customer entering into a first payment agreement shall be granted at least one late payment that is made four days or less beyond the due date for payment and the first payment agreement shall remain in effect.

(2) Second payment agreement. The utility shall offer a second payment agreement to a customer who is in default of a first payment agreement if the customer has made at least two consecutive full payments under the first payment agreement. The second payment agreement shall be for the same term as or longer than the term of the first payment agreement. The customer shall be required to pay for current service in addition to the monthly payments under the second payment agreement and may be required to make the first payment up-front as a condition of entering into the second payment agreement. The utility may also require the customer to enter into a level payment plan to pay the current bill. The utility may offer additional payment agreements to the customer.

d. Refusal by utility. A customer may offer the utility a proposed payment agreement. If the utility and the customer do not reach an agreement, the utility may refuse the offer orally, but the utility must render a written refusal of the customer's final offer, stating the reason for the refusal, within three days of the oral notification. The written refusal shall be considered rendered to the customer when addressed to the customer's last-known address and deposited in the U.S. mail with postage prepaid. If delivery is by other than U.S. mail, the written refusal shall be considered rendered to the customer when handed to the customer or when delivered to the last-known address of the person responsible for the payment for the service.

A customer may ask the board for assistance in working out a reasonable payment agreement. The request for assistance must be made to the board within ten days after the rendering of the written refusal. During the review of this request, the utility shall not disconnect the service.

A.3.3 Prohibition on Termination of Service Where There Is a Serious Illness

Or. Admin. R. 860-021-0410—Emergency Medical Certificate for Residential Electric and Gas Service

(1) An energy utility shall not disconnect residential service if the customer submits certification from a qualified medical professional stating that disconnection would significantly endanger the physical health of the customer or a member of the customer's household. "Qualified medical professional" means a licensed physician, nurse-practitioner, or physician's assistant authorized to diagnose and treat the medical condition described without direct supervision by a physician.

(2) The oral certification to the utility must be confirmed in writing within 14 days by the qualified medical professional prescribing medical care. Written certifications must include:

(a) The name of the person to whom the certificate applies and relationship to the customer;

(b) A complete description of the health conditions;

(c) An explanation of how the person's health will be significantly endangered by terminating the service;

(d) A statement indicating how long the health condition is expected to last;

(e) A statement specifying the particular type of utility service required (for example, electricity for respirator); and

(f) The signature of the qualified medical professional prescribing medical care.

(3) If a medical certificate is not submitted in compliance with sections (1) and (2) of this rule, the energy utility may disconnect service after providing a five-day notice to the customer. The notice shall comply with the requirements of OAR 860-021-0405, except subsection (1)(b), subsection (2)(e), and section (4) of this rule shall not be applicable.

(4) An emergency medical certificate shall be valid only for the length of time the health endangerment is certified to exist, but no longer than six months without renewal for certificates not specifying chronic illnesses and no longer than twelve months for certificates specifying illnesses identified as chronic by a "Qualified Medical Professional" as defined in this rule. At least 15 days before the certificate's expiration date, an energy utility will give the customer written notice of the date the certificate expires unless it is renewed with the utility before that day arrives.

(5) A customer submitting a medical certificate is not excused from paying for electric or gas service:

(a) Customers are required to enter into a written time-payment agreement with the energy utility when an overdue balance exists. Terms of the time-payment agreement shall be those in OAR 860-021-0415 or such other terms as the parties agree upon in writing;

(b) When financial hardship can be shown, a customer with a medical certificate may renegotiate the terms of a time-payment agreement with the energy utility; and

(c) Time-payment arrangements in effect when a medical certificate terminates remain in effect for the balance then owing. If a customer fails to pay charges incurred after the certificate terminates, the provisions of OAR 860-021-0415 (standard time-payment provisions) shall apply to payment of the arrearage incurred after the medical certificate expires. The terms of the medical certificate time-payment plan continue to apply to the arrearage accrued during the disability.

(6) If a medical certificate customer fails to enter into a written time-payment agreement within 20 days of filing the certificate, or to abide by its terms, the energy utility shall notify the Commission's Consumer Services Division of its intent to disconnect service and the reason for the disconnection. The energy utility may disconnect service after providing a notice 15 days in advance of disconnection for nonpayment, or five days before disconnection for failure to enter into a written time-payment agreement. The notice shall comply with the requirements of OAR 860-021-0405, except subsection (2)(e) shall not be applicable. A hearing may thereafter be held to determine whether the energy utility should be permitted to disconnect service to the customer.

(7) An energy utility may verify the accuracy of a medical certificate. If the energy utility believes a customer does not qualify, or no longer qualifies for a medical certificate, the utility may apply to the Commission to terminate the service of the customer.

A.3.4 Prohibition of Termination of Service During Winter Moratorium

Minn. Stat. § 216B.096—Cold Weather Rule; Public Utility

Subd. 5. Cold weather rule.

(a) During the cold weather period [October 15 through April 15], a utility may not disconnect and must reconnect utility heating service of a customer whose household income is at or below 50 percent of the state median income if the customer enters into and makes reasonably timely payments under a mutually acceptable payment agreement with the utility that is based on the financial resources and circumstances of the household; provided that, a utility may not require a customer to pay more than ten percent of the household income toward current and past utility bills for utility heating service.

(b) A utility may accept more than ten percent of the household income as the payment arrangement amount if agreed to by the customer.

(c) The customer or a designated third party may request a modification of the terms of a payment agreement previously entered into if the customer's financial circumstances have changed or the customer is unable to make reasonably timely payments.

(d) The payment agreement terminates at the expiration of the cold weather period unless a longer period is mutually agreed to by the customer and the utility.

(e) Each utility shall use reasonable efforts to restore service within 24 hours of an accepted payment agreement, taking into consideration customer availability, employee availability, and construction-related activity.

* * *

Subd. 7. Prohibitions and requirements.

(a) This subdivision applies during the cold weather period.

(b) A utility may not charge a deposit or delinquency charge to a customer who has entered into a payment agreement or a customer who has appealed to the commission under subdivision 8.

(c) A utility may not disconnect service during the following periods:

(1) during the pendency of any appeal under subdivision 8;

(2) earlier than ten working days after a utility has deposited in first class mail, or seven working days after a utility has personally served, the notice required under subdivision 4 to a customer in an occupied dwelling;

(3) earlier than ten working days after the utility has deposited in first class mail the notice required under subdivision 4 to the recorded billing address of the customer, if the utility has reasonably determined from an on-site inspection that the dwelling is unoccupied;

(4) on a Friday, unless the utility makes personal contact with, and offers a payment agreement consistent with this section to the customer;

(5) on a Saturday, Sunday, holiday, or the day before a holiday;

(6) when utility offices are closed;

(7) when no utility personnel are available to resolve disputes, enter into payment agreements, accept payments, and reconnect service; or

(8) when commission offices are closed.

(d) A utility may not discontinue service until the utility investigates whether the dwelling is actually occupied. At a minimum, the investigation must include one visit by the utility to the dwelling during normal working hours. If no contact is made and there is reason to believe that the dwelling is occupied, the utility must attempt a second contact during non-business hours. If personal contact is made, the utility representative must provide notice required under subdivision 4 and, if the utility representative is not authorized to enter into a payment agreement, the telephone number the customer can call to establish a payment agreement.

(e) Each utility must reconnect utility service if, following disconnection, the dwelling is found to be occupied and the customer agrees to enter into a payment agreement or appeals to the commission because the customer and the utility are unable to agree on a payment agreement.

A.3.5 Limits on Timing of Service Termination

220 Mass. Regs. Code 25.02—Billing and Termination Procedure for Residential Customers

(1) Billing and Payment. All bills shall be payable upon receipt. However, no bill shall be considered "due" under applicable law or 220 CMR 25.00 in less than 45 days from receipt or in the case of gas and electric companies in less time than has elapsed between receipt of such bill and receipt of the most recent previous bill for the company's services, whichever period is greater.

The initial bill after commencement of service shall not be "due" in less than 45 days from receipt, or in less time than has elapsed between receipt of such bill and the day upon which service was initially extended, whichever is greater.

No disputed portion of a bill which relates to the proper application of approved rates and charges, or the company's compliance with 220 CMR 25.00, shall be considered "due" during the pendency of any complaint, investigation, hearing or appeal under 220 CMR 25.00.

* * *

(3) Termination of Service. Except as elsewhere provided in 220 CMP 25.00, service may be terminated only if:

(a) A bill is not paid within 45 days from receipt, or such longer periods as may be permitted by 220 CMR 25.02(1); and

(b) The company, not earlier than 27 days after the rendering of the bill (i.e. first request for payment), renders a second request for payment, stating its intention to terminate on a date not earlier than 48 days after the receipt of the bill in the case of gas and electric companies, and 46 1/2 days in the case of water companies; and

(c) The company renders a final notice of termination not earlier than 45 days after receipt of the bill. Such notice must be rendered at least 72 hours, but in no event more than 14 days, prior to termination in the case of gas and electric companies; and at least 36 hours prior to termination in the case of water companies; and

(d) The bill remains unpaid on the termination date indicated on the notice.

In no event shall service to a customer be terminated for failure to pay a portion of any bill which is the subject of a dispute pursuant to 220 CMR 25.02(4). However, a customer shall be responsible for and accordingly shall be subject to termination for non-payment of any portion of any bill which is not the subject of a dispute pursuant to 220 CMR 25.02(4).

Service shall not be terminated for any reason other than failure to pay a bill, unless the Department certifies its approval after giving both parties an opportunity to be heard. Such a hearing shall not be construed to be an "adjudicatory proceeding" as defined by M.G.L. c. 30A.

Nothing in 220 CMR 25.00 shall be construed to prevent termination for reasons of safety, health, cooperation with civil authorities or any other reason for which termination power is specifically granted in the Massachusetts General Laws.

When service to a customer has been terminated, the Director of the Department's Consumer Division or the Director's designee, may order resumption of service pending an investigation pursuant to 220 CMR 25.02(4).

Termination of service under 220 CMR 25.02 may be effected between the hours of 8:00 A.M. and 4:00 P.M., Monday through Thursday, provided that such day is not a holiday as defined in M.G.L. c. 4, § 7, cl. (18) or the day before such a holiday.

All bills shall contain, or be accompanied by, a brief explanation of the customer's rights pursuant to 220 CMR 25.02(4). All second requests for payment referred to in 220 CMR 25.02(3)(b) and all termination notices referred to in 220 CMR 25.00 shall be accompanied by a brief explanation of the customer's rights pursuant to 220 CMR 25.00.

A.3.6 Other Limitations on Denial of Service

Wis. Admin. Code Pub. Serv. Comm'n § 113.0301—Residential Disconnections

* * *

(1m) Residential utility service may be disconnected or refused for any of the following reasons:

(a) Failure to pay a delinquent account or failure to comply with the terms of a deferred payment, as provided in s. PSC 113.0404.

(b) Violation of the utility's rules pertaining to the use of service in a manner which interferes with the service of others or to the operation of non- standard equipment, if the customer has first been notified and provided with reasonable opportunity to remedy the situation.

(c) Failure to comply with deposit or guarantee arrangements, as specified in s. PSC 113.0402.

(d) Refusal or failure to permit authorized utility personnel to read the meter at least once every 6 months in order to determine actual usage. The 6-month period begins with the date of the last meter reading.

(e) Failure to comply with Wisconsin statute, commission rule or commission order pertaining to conservation or availability of service.

(f) Failure to pay costs or fees incurred by and awarded to the utility by a court of law, for pursuit of collection of bills, or failure to pay extraordinary collection charges as allowed and specified in the utility's tariffs filed with the public service commission.

(g) Failure to comply with applicable requirements of this section, or of the utility's rules, or with s. 101.865, Stats., or if the customer proposes to use a device that is not designed to reasonably minimize interference with communication and signal services.

(h) Delinquency in payment for service received by a previous customer or occupant at the premises to be served, if an account is transferred to a new account holder or customer and the previous account holder or customer continues to be an occupant of the dwelling unit to be served.

(*i*) Failure of an applicant for utility service to provide adequate verification of identity and residency, as provided in sub. (3).

(j) Failure of an applicant for utility service to provide the credit information set out in s. PSC 113.0406 (7)(a).

(k) Refusal or failure to provide authorized utility personnel access to utility equipment.

* * *

(8) Residential utility service may not be disconnected or refused for any of the following reasons:

(a) Delinquency in payment for service by a previous occupant of the premises to be served.

(b) Failure to pay for merchandise or charges for non-utility service billed by the utility, except where authorized by law.

(c) Failure to pay for a different class of utility service, except as provided in sub. (7)(a).

(d) Failure to pay the account of another customer as guarantor thereof.

(e) Failure to pay charges arising from any underbilling occurring more than one year prior to the current billing and due to any misapplication of rates or faulty metering.

(f) Failure to pay an estimated bill other than a bill rendered pursuant to an approved meter reading plan.

(g) A utility to knowingly assist a landlord in the removal or eviction of a tenant from rental property.

* * *

A.3.7 Notice Requirements Relating to Service Termination

65-407-81 Me. Code R. § 9—Disconnection Notice

A. Without Notice. A utility can disconnect a customer without notice in the circumstances described in:

- Section 7(A)(6) (unauthorized use);
- Section 7(A)(8) (dangerous condition); or,
- Section 7(B) (request or abandonment).

B. 14-Day Notice. A utility must provide written notice of the intent to disconnect at least fourteen (14) calendar days before the stated disconnection date in any of the circumstances described in:

- Section 7 (A)(1) (failure to pay);
- Section 7 (A)(5) (refusal of access);
- Section 7 (A)(7) (fraud or material misrepresentation); or
- Section 7(A)(8) (non-dangerous tariff provision concerning utility delivery system)

C. 3-Day Notice. A utility must provide written notice of the intent to disconnect a customer at least three (3) business days before the stated disconnection date in any of the circumstances described in:

- Section 7(A)(2) (broken payment arrangement);
- Section 7 (A)(3) (failure to provide a deposit or guarantor);
- Section 7(A)(4) (failure to apply for customer status);
- Section 7(A)(9) (failure to comply with Commission decision), unless the Consumer Assistance Division or the Commission establishes a different notice period; or
- Section 9(H) (dishonored check).

D. Time of Issuance.

1. A utility cannot issue a disconnection notice for the circumstances described in Section 7(A)(1) (failure to pay an overdue amount) until at least thirty (30) days after the original bill is mailed. See Section 2(J) for when a bill is considered to have been mailed. A utility cannot issue a disconnection notice for the circumstances described in Section 7(A)(2) (broken payment arrangement) and 7(A)(3) (failure to pay a deposit) until at least one (1) business day after the due date of the payment. In either case, a utility that mails disconnection notices from and requires that payment be sent to a location outside Maine must add five (5) calendar days to the time period established by this subsection.

2. A utility can issue a disconnection notice for the other circumstances described in Section 7 at any time after the applicable criteria are met.

3. A telephone utility can issue a disconnections notice no earlier than five (5) business days after the postmark of the original bill (or the date of the bill if it is mailed on that date) if:

a. the customer's account balance includes toll usage that exceeds $500;

b. the customer has been notified of the accelerated collection procedures with or at the same time as the original bill;

c. the telephone utility makes personal contact with the customer or there is clear evidence of abandonment; and,

d. the customer has refused or failed to provide satisfactory evidence of his or her ability to pay or enter into a payment arrangement for the account balance.

E. Disconnection Date. The disconnection date stated in the notice must not be a Friday, weekend, legal holiday, the day before a legal holiday or a day when the utility's office is not open for public business. The term "legal holiday" is defined in 4 M.R.S.A. Section 1051.

F. Period of Effectiveness. A disconnection notice is effective for ten (10) business days after the disconnection date stated in the notice. If a utility fails to properly disconnect service within ten (10) business days after the disconnection date, the disconnection notice procedures must be repeated.

G. Refusal of Access by Customer. If a customer expressly refuses to allow the utility access to the meter or other fixture or device necessary to accomplish disconnection, the ten (10) business day period provided in subsection F can begin on the date of the last refusal by the customer. This provision applies if the utility:

1. records the date, time and manner of each attempt to disconnect service and each express refusal by the customer to allow access; and

2. has no other reasonable means to disconnect the customer other than that refused by the customer.

H. Bad Check. If the customer has paid by a check which was not honored by the bank before the expiration of the disconnection notice, the utility must attempt to obtain payment by alternate means from the customer before disconnecting service. If a check is not honored after the expiration of the disconnection notice, the utility can issue a 3-day disconnection notice and require payment by cash or certified check. A disconnection notice issued as a result of a dishonored check supersedes any other pending disconnection notice.

***I.* Disconnection Notice Procedures for Leased or Rented Property.**

1. A utility cannot disconnect a leased or rented dwelling at the request of a lessor, owner, or agent ("landlord") or because the landlord (as a customer) has failed to pay an overdue amount, unless:

a. the tenant agrees in writing to the disconnection;

b. the landlord signs a notarized statement that the premises are vacant;

c. the utility by personal inspection determines that the premises are vacant; or

d. the utility gives notice as described in paragraph.

2. A utility must make every reasonable attempt to deliver the notice in person to at least one adult occupant of each dwelling unit. With respect to a single meter, multi-unit dwelling, the utility must also post the notice at or near the front and rear entrances to the building or buildings affected. The notice must, in addition to the applicable disclosures of subsection J, inform the tenant how service can be continued. A utility must either offer the tenant the opportunity to obtain service in the tenant's name or otherwise assume responsibility for further payment.

3. The disconnection notice must be mailed or delivered at least ten (10) days before the disconnection date stated in the notice.

4. Before the actual disconnection of service to a single-meter, multi-unit dwelling, a utility must:

a. have a tariff approved by the Commission that:

i. assesses a reasonable fee for the collection of an unpaid account balance from the landlord, in addition to an applicable reconnection fee; and

ii. authorizes the utility to separately meter each dwelling unit, at the landlord's expense, if the dwelling is disconnected for nonpayment of an overdue amount;

b. apply any existing deposit to the current account balance;

c. file the lien authorized by Title 35-A M.R.S.A., Section 706 and seek a writ of attachment; and,

d. notify the Consumer Assistance Division of the actions taken pursuant to this subsection and their results.

5. A utility cannot require the tenant to pay for any charges incurred by the landlord or demand a deposit or advance payment based on the landlord's credit history.

6. This subsection also applies if a municipality requests the utility to disconnect residential service at a dwelling where the municipality has temporarily put the service in its name on behalf of the occupant.

J. Content of Disconnection Notice. A disconnection notice must be in writing and conspicuously contain the following information:

1. the overdue amount or the exact reason for the disconnection if not for an overdue amount;

2. what the customer must do to avoid disconnection;

3. the disconnection date and the period for which the disconnection notice is effective;

4. a statement of the customer's right to postpone disconnection for a medical emergency of the customer or an occupant and a description of now to declare a medical emergency according to Section 11;

5. a statement that the customer can avoid disconnection by negotiating a payment arrangement with affordable monthly or weekly installment payments and that the overdue amount must be paid in a reasonable period of time. This disclosure is not required if the disconnection notice is for a broken payment arrangement;

6. a statement of the customer's right to submit a disputed matter before the disconnection date to: Consumer Assistance Division, Public Utilities Commission, 242 State Street, State House Station #18, Augusta, Maine 04333-0018; telephone 289-3831 or toll free 1-800-452-4699;

7. a statement that the customer cannot submit a dispute to the Consumer Assistance Division until the customer has first tried to resolve the dispute with the utility;

8. the title and telephone number of the appropriate utility representative and a statement that the call may be made collect from within the utility's service area, unless a toll free number is offered or calls within the utility's service area are toll free to the designated telephone number;

9. a statement of the reconnection charge, if any; and,

10. a statement of the utility's policy concerning the requirement of a deposit in the event of disconnection.

K. Plain Language Disconnection Notice. Every utility must use a plain language disconnection notice after February 1, 1989. The disconnection notice must be filed with the Commission, but does not require prior Commission approval before its use. A plain language disconnection notice should reflect the following guidelines:

1. The type size used in texts should be no smaller than 10 points high. The typeface (shape of the letters) should be designed to improve or enhance the visual size of the type. Headlines should be in larger or bold type. All text should be in capitals and lower case as opposed to ALL IN CAPITALS;

2. The color of the disconnection notice and type should avoid problems for persons whose "color deficient" sight makes all colors appear as shades of gray;

3. The use of reverse-blocks in which letters appear as white against a black or dark gray background should be avoided; and,

4. The headline on a disconnection notice should conspicuously be entitled "Disconnection Notice" in at least 12 point type.

L. Designation of Third Party to Receive Notices. Any customer may notify the utility in writing that he or she is designating a third party to receive notices concerning the customer's account. The utility must keep a record of the third party name, address and telephone number. Whenever the utility contacts the customer about matters related to deposits, disconnections, overdue amounts or hazardous conditions of utility service, the utility must make every reasonable effort to contact the third party and provide the same information at the same time it is provided to the customer. Any notice of disconnection provided to the third party must contain the disclosures required by subsection J. Nothing in this subsection obligates the third party to make payment of any amount owed by the customer, unless there is independent evidence of an obligation to pay. Every utility must inform applicants and customers of their right to designate a third party to receive notices.

A.4 Chapter 140, Acts of 2005 (MA)

In November 2005, Massachusetts enacted its so-called "HEAT" (Heating Energy Assistance and Tax Relief) legislation, Chapter 140 of the Acts of 2005. Section 17, reproduced below, requires utility companies to offer payment plans of no less than four months, with directions to the state's utility regulatory body to consider requiring longer payment plans on an individual customer or across-the-board basis. Section 17 also requires every regulated electric and gas company to file an "arrearage management program" under which a portion of the customer's arrears will be written off if the customer keeps up with a negotiated payment plan. Section 2 of Chapter 140 (not reproduced below) appropriated a $20 million state supplement to the federal fuel assistance funds the state received in FY 2006.

2005 Mass. Acts Chapter 140 (Approved November 22, 2005)

AN ACT RELATIVE TO HEATING ENERGY ASSISTANCE AND TAX RELIEF.

Whereas, The deferred operation of this act would tend to defeat its purpose, which is to establish forthwith a heating energy assistance and tax relief program, therefore it is hereby declared to be an emergency law, necessary for the immediate preservation of the public convenience.

Be it enacted by the Senate and House of Representatives in General Court assembled, and by the authority of the same, as follows:

* * *

SECTION 17. **(a)** Notwithstanding any general or special law to the contrary, the department of telecommunications and energy shall initiate a generic proceeding, not later than December 1, 2005 to develop standards that shall apply to each electric and gas company regarding the adoption of an arrearage management program for eligible low-income customers, as defined under chapter 164 of the General Laws. The department shall require each such company to file by December 30, 2005 an arrearage management program that includes all relevant operational details, including a plan to coordinate the arrearage management plan with the low-income weatherization and fuel assistance agencies and services. Upon approval by the department, said company shall implement its program. The department shall review and approve each program with such modifications as the department deems appropriate, no later than February 28, 2006. The department shall conduct an annual review of such programs and may at any time order such revisions or modifications as the department deems appropriate. For purposes of this section, an arrearage management program shall include a plan under which companies work with eligible low-income customers to establish affordable payment plans and provide credits to those customers toward the accumulated arrears where such customers comply with the terms of the program.

(b) The department shall require a company that initially offers a low income customer who has an arrearage, but whose utility service has not yet been terminated, a payment plan of not less than 4 months including the initial down payment of 25 per cent of the balance owed, and the remaining repayment balance amounts shall be divided equally; but, a company that seeks a repayment agreement of less than 4 months shall request approval from the department for good cause shown. A company making such a request shall notify the customer that the request has been made. This paragraph shall not limit the right of a customer to request a payment plan of more than 4 months or limit the authority of the department to order a payment plan of more than 4 months either on an individual basis or through revisions to its billing and termination regulations."

* * *

A.5 State-By-State Extreme Temperature Protections

This summary excludes illness and age-related protections, unless they are a condition of the extreme temperature protections and focuses on state utility commission regulations.

ALABAMA

Ala. Pub. Serv. Comm'n Gen. R. 12(B)(5)

Gas/Electric: Gas and electric.
Covered Group: Residential electric or natural gas customers
Date-Based: No.
Temperature-Based Threshold: No termination for the calendar day in which the temperature is 32° Fahrenheit or below.
Summary of Rules/Seasonal Policy: No terminations on a day when the National Weather Service forecasts that temperature will be 32° Fahrenheit or below.
Additional information: None specified.

ALASKA

No information specified.

ARIZONA

Ariz. Admin. Code §§ 14-2-201, 14-2-211 (electric), 14-2-311 (gas), 14-2-301 (definitions)

Gas/Electric: Gas and electric.
Covered Group: Customers who have an inability to pay.
Date-Based: None specified.
Temperature-Based Threshold: No termination when the temperature is forecast not to exceed 32° Fahrenheit for the next day.
Summary of Rules/Seasonal Policy: None specified.
Additional information: None specified.

ARKANSAS

126-03-003 Ark. Code. R. §§ 6.15, 6.18 (LexisNexis)

Gas/Electric: Gas and electric.
Covered Group: Hot weather protection for elderly and disabled. In addition to temperature-based rule, cold weather rule for low-income gas customers who make regular minimum payments during the winter.
Date-Based: November 1 to March 31 (n. gas cold weather rule).
Temperature-Based Threshold: No termination for the calendar day in which the temperature is 32° Fahrenheit or below or 95° Fahrenheit or higher (for elderly and disabled).
Summary of Rules/Seasonal Policy: No terminations on a day when the National Weather Service forecasts that temperature will be 32° Fahrenheit or below at any time during the following 24-hour period.
Additional information: 7 months to pay balance, from April to October, interest on deferred payments only accrues once repayment begins.

CALIFORNIA

None specified.

Gas/Electric: None specified.
Covered Group: None specified.
Date-Based: None specified.
Temperature-Based Threshold: None specified.
Summary of Rules/Seasonal Policy: None specified.
Additional information: Some utilities include shut-off protections in their tariffs.

COLORADO

No information specified.

CONNECTICUT

Conn. Gen. Stats. § 16-262c(b)(1); Conn. Agencies Regs. §§ 16-3-100(a)(6); 16-3-100(b)(2)(B); 16-3-100(b)(3)(B)

Gas/Electric: Gas and electric.
Covered Group: Gas & electric heat customers with financial hardship who cannot pay entire account.
Date-Based: November 1 to May 1.
Temperature-Based Threshold: None specified.
Summary of Rules/Seasonal Policy: Gas company can refuse to restore service from November 1 to May 1 if service was terminated between May 2 and October 31 and, during the past year from November 1 to May 1, the customer received hardship benefit, and has not paid either 20% of outstanding balance, $100, or payment established by agreement.
Additional information: The Connecticut General Assembly passed legislation in June 2007 extending the winter shut-off period to May 1. (P.A. 07-242, § 67, codified in Conn. Gen. Stat. § 16-262c(b)(1)).

DELAWARE

26-3000-3002 Del. Code Regs. § 6.0 (LexisNexis)

Gas/Electric: Gas and electric.

Covered Group: None specified.
Date-Based: Cooling season: June 1 to Sept. 30. Heating season: November 15 to March 31.
Temperature-Based Threshold: No termination for the calendar day in which the temperature is 32° Fahrenheit or below or exceeds 105° Fahrenheit on the morning of the date when service is scheduled for termination.
Summary of Rules/Seasonal Policy: Measures temperature to within 50 miles of dwelling to be disconnected.
Additional information: None specified.

DISTRICT OF COLUMBIA

D.C. Mun. Regs. tit. 15 § 310.3

Gas/Electric: Gas and electric.
Covered Group: None specified.
Date-Based: None specified.
Temperature-Based Threshold: No termination when the temperature is forecast to be 32° Fahrenheit or below during the next 24 hours.
Summary of Rules/Seasonal Policy: None specified.
Additional information: None specified.

FLORIDA

No information specified.

GEORGIA

Ga. Comp. R. & Regs. 515-3-2-.04 (gas and electric), 515-3-3-.04 (gas)

Gas/Electric: Gas and electric.
Covered Group: Date-based moratoria for customers who agree to pay their arrears in equal installments and agree to pay on time for current service.
Date-Based: November 15 to March 15.
Temperature-Based Threshold: No gas or electric utility may terminate when the forecasted low temperature for a 24-hour period beginning at 8:00 a.m. on the date of disconnection is below 32° Fahrenheit. For a gas local distribution company, electing distribution company, regulated provider or marketer, the forecast period is 48 hours. In addition to cold-weather restriction, electric utility may not terminate if, prior to 8:00 a.m. on date of disconnection, a National Weather Service heat advisory or excessive heat warning is in effect or forecast to be in effect.
Summary of Rules/Seasonal Policy: None specified.
Additional information: The maximum duration of the payment plan begins with the first billing period after March 15 and concludes prior to the following October 15, unless the consumer fails to keep the agreement.

HAWAII

No information specified.

IDAHO

Idaho Admin. Code r. 31.21.01.306

Gas/Electric: Gas and electric.
Covered Group: Any residential customers who declares s/he is unable to pay in full and whose household contains children, elderly, and infirm persons. These customers must also be offered a Winter Payment Plan.
Date-Based: December to February for household with elderly, infirm, or children. November through March for Winter Payment Plan.
Temperature-Based Threshold: None specified.
Summary of Rules/Seasonal Policy: Winter Payment Plan: Protection begins when plan is initiated. Payments are one-half of Level Pay Plan for that customer. A customer who has an outstanding balance must make a plan to pay it on or after April 1 if on the Winter Payment Plan, or March 1 if not.
Additional information: Only qualify for Winter Payment Plan if consumer has paid off prior year's payment plan and owes no more than $75 or last month's balance to the utility on November 1. Consumer who moves to new address from December to February serviced by same utility will be connected no matter the balance owed.

ILLINOIS

Ill. Admin. Code tit. 83, §§ 280.130(i), 280.135(a), 280.136

Gas/Electric: Gas and electric.
Covered Group: None specified.
Date-Based: Between December 1 to March 31, utility cannot disconnect unless the utility has offered a deferred payment plan and informed customer of specific agencies and funds available for payment assistance. May not disconnect customers who are participants under Sec. 6 of the Energy Act of 1989, if service is the primary source of heat or used to operate or control the primary source of heat.
Temperature-Based Threshold: No termination when the temperature is forecast to be 32° Fahrenheit or below during the next 24 hours or on any day preceding a holiday or a weekend when the temperature is forecast to be below 32° Fahrenheit during the holiday or weekend.
Summary of Rules/Seasonal Policy: None specified.
Additional information: None specified.

INDIANA

170 Ind. Admin. Code 4-1-16.6, 5-1-16.6, 8-1-2-121

Gas/Electric: Gas and electric.
Covered Group: Date-based moratoria for customers who are receiving, or who are eligible and have applied for, heating assistance.
Date-Based: December 1 to March 15.
Temperature-Based Threshold: None specified.
Summary of Rules/Seasonal Policy: None specified.
Additional information: None specified.

IOWA

Iowa Admin. Code r. 19.4(15)(d)(7); 19.4(15)(d)(9); 19.4(17); 20.4(15)(d)(8), (10); 20.4(17)

Gas/Electric: Gas and electric.
Covered Group: Date-based moratoria for customers who have been certified as eligible for LIHEAP or WAP by the CAA.
Date-Based: November 1 to April 1.
Temperature-Based Threshold: No disconnection for gas or electric heat customers when National Weather forecast for the following 24 hours is that temperature will be 20° Fahrenheit or below.
Summary of Rules/Seasonal Policy: None specified.
Additional information: None specified.

KANSAS

Kan. Corp. Comm'n, Electric, Natural Gas and Water Billing Standards, Section V ("Cold Weather Rule") (effective July 24, 2007). ***See*** **www.kcc. state.ks.us/pi/billing.pdf.**

Gas/Electric: Gas and electric.
Covered Group: During the date-based moratoria, customers must inform utility of inability to pay, enter into a payment agreement, pay 1/12 of the arrearage, 1/12 of the current bill, disconnection and reconnection fees and deposit (if applicable), enter into an 11-month arrearage plan or other negotiated payment plan for the arrearage, and apply for federal, state and local assistance funds.
Date-Based: November 1 to March 31 (when temperatures are extreme).
Temperature-Based Threshold: No disconnections between November 1 and March 31 when the National Weather Service forecasts temperatures will be 35° Fahrenheit or below or in the mid-30s or colder within the following 48-hour period.
Summary of Rules/Seasonal Policy: None specified.
Additional information: Customers apparently can get disconnected during the cold weather rule period if the temperature is forecast to rise above 35°, and customers cannot get reconnected without paying.

KENTUCKY

807 Ky. Admin. Regs. 5:006, §§ 14, 15

Gas/Electric: Gas and electric.
Covered Group: Customers who are certified by the KY Cabinet for Human Resources (or its designees) that they are eligible for energy assistance. or have a household income at or below 130% of poverty. and who present their certificate to the utility. Customers much show a good faith effort by paying current bills in accordance with their ability to do so. Customers shall also agree on a payment plan to become current by October 15 at latest.
Date-Based: November 1 to March 31 (30-day prohibition on disconnections in certain situations).
Temperature-Based Threshold: None specified.
Summary of Rules/Seasonal Policy: None specified.
Additional information: Reconnection is predicated on payment of 1/3 of outstanding bill or $200, whichever is less.

LOUISIANA

No information specified.

MAINE

65-407-81 Me. Code R. §§ 15, 17 (LexisNexis)

Gas/Electric: Gas and electric.
Covered Group: Customer eligibility established by inability to pay, qualifying for HEAP, having income not exceeding 150% of OMB poverty line, or receiving Supplemental Security Income.
Date-Based: November 15 to April 15.
Temperature-Based Threshold: Commission can determine due to weather or health emergencies that one or more utility disconnections will be prohibited for 10 days at a time, subject to renewal for further 10-day periods.
Summary of Rules/Seasonal Policy: Utilities are encouraged to enter into regular or special payment arrangements with customers who have arrears greater than $50.00. Customers are expected to pay a reasonable portion of their bills when due during the winter months.
Additional information: None specified.

MARYLAND

Md. Code Regs. 20.31.03.03

Gas/Electric: Gas and electric.
Covered Group: None specified.
Date-Based: For the period November 1 to March 31, utilities cannot terminate service unless the utilities first certify to the PSC by affidavit, filed at least 24 hours before the termination, that the termination will not constitute a threat to the life or health of the occupants.
Temperature-Based Threshold: No disconnections when the temperatures are 32° Fahrenheit or below.
Summary of Rules/Seasonal Policy: Utilities may not terminate service when the forecasted temperature at 6:00 a.m. is not expected to exceed 32° Fahrenheit for the next 24 hours.
Additional information: May not terminate unless arrearage is greater than $200 for single-service utility or $300 for dual service, which exceeds the amount of any deposit.

MASSACHUSETTS

220 Mass. Code Regs. § 25.03 (LexisNexis)

Gas/Electric: Gas and electric.
Covered Group: Customers whose service provides heat or operates the heating system and who provide, and periodically renew, evidence of financial hardship.
Date-Based: November 15 to March 15.
Temperature-Based Threshold: None specified.
Summary of Rules/Seasonal Policy: During moratorium period, no termination notice may be sent to financial hardship customer. If customer received fuel assistance the prior winter, the utility will provide this service from November 15 to January 1 to give customer time to apply for program for current season.

Additional information: No right of reconnection if service was terminated prior to November 1. The DPU has extended the moratorium beyond March 15 by sending letter requests to the companies.

MICHIGAN

Mich. Admin. Code r. 460.140; 460.148; 460.149; 460.150

Gas/Electric: Gas and electric.
Covered Group: Senior citizens, military families, and recipients of certain needs-based public aid, and households with income at or below 150% of the federal poverty guidelines.
Date-Based: November 1 to March 31.
Temperature-Based Threshold: None specified.
Summary of Rules/Seasonal Policy: No shut-off during space-heating season if the customer is a senior citizen, has a household income not greater than 150% of the federal poverty guidelines, or is a recipient of needs-based aid who agrees to pay 7% of the projected bill per month and applies for energy assistance. Seniors are not required to enter into the 7% payment plan. At the end of the space-heating season, the utility shall reconcile the accounts and allow customer to pay amount owed in equal installments between April 1 and October 31. No shut-offs for a 90-day period for eligible military customers. Shut-off protection shall apply for at least one additional 90-day period for eligible military customers. After close of last 90-day period, past-due amounts can be paid in equal installments over a period of 12 months.
Additional information: None specified.

MINNESOTA

Minn. Stat. §§ 216B.096 through .098

Gas/Electric: Gas and electric.
Covered Group: Customers whose median income does not exceed 50% of state median income and who enter into a payment plan.
Date-Based: October 15 to April 15.
Temperature-Based Threshold: None specified.
Summary of Rules/Seasonal Policy: During heating season, utility may not disconnect, or must make reasonable efforts to reconnect within 24 hours if customer is already disconnected, if customer enters into payment plan. Customers with household income at or below 50% of state median income may not be required to pay more than 10% of household income. Utility may renegotiate plan if customer shows changed circumstances. Electric utility may not disconnect during period of National Weather Service excessive heat watch, heat advisory, or excessive heat warning.
Additional information: Before heating season, utility must notify customer of cold weather rule, payment plans, sources of aid, etc. After disconnection of residential customer during the winter moratorium, utility must notify the municipality, which must notify police and fire department.

MISSISSIPPI

Miss. Pub. Serv. Comm'n Gen. R. 8.E, 8.F; 26-000-002 Miss. Code R. §§ 8(E), 8(F) (LexisNexis)

Gas/Electric: Gas, electric, telephone, and water.
Covered Group: Customers who are unable to pay the full amount of their bill and agree to pay the amount due before November 11 and enter into a payment plan for future bills.
Date-Based: December 1 to March 31.
Temperature-Based Threshold: Gas or electric may not terminate if National Weather Service has issued a freeze warning as of 8:00 a.m. on disconnection date, and electric utility may not terminate if National Weather Service has issued an excessive heat warning as of such time.
Summary of Rules/Seasonal Policy: None specified.
Additional information: None specified.

MISSOURI

Mo. Code Regs. Ann. tit. 4, §§ 240-13.055 (5), 240-13.055(6); Mo. Rev. Stat. § 660.123

Gas/Electric: Gas and electric.
Covered Group: Customers who are unable to pay, or who are registered low-income elderly or disabled customers, but enter into a payment agreement and pay initial reasonable amount up front.
Date-Based: Heating season November 1 to March 31. Cooling season June 1 to Sept. 30.
Temperature-Based Threshold: No disconnections on any day the 6 a.m.–9 a.m. National Weather Service forecasts temperatures will drop below 32° Fahrenheit or rise above 95° Fahrenheit, or the heat index rise above 105° Fahrenheit, for the following 24 hours or a longer period during which utility personnel are not available to reconnect.
Summary of Rules/Seasonal Policy: No discontinuance of service from November 1 to March 31 if customer states inability to pay or is a registered low-income elderly or disabled customer, enters into payment agreement, and complies with utilities requests for income information.
Additional information: Reconnection between November 1 and March 31 for any customer who enters repayment plan and requests reconnection.

MONTANA

Mont. Admin. R. 38.5.1410

Gas/Electric: Gas and electric.
Covered Group: Customers who have established they are unable to pay or able to pay only in installments, has a member of the household 62 or older or with a disability. During the winter moratorium, utilities need the specific prior approval of the PSC to terminate service.
Date-Based: November 1 to April 1.
Temperature-Based Threshold: No disconnections on any day when the temperature at 8:00 a.m. is at or below freezing or if Weather Service forecasts a snowstorm or freezing temperatures for the succeeding 24-hour period.

Summary of Rules/Seasonal Policy: None specified.
Additional information: None specified.

NEBRASKA

291 Neb. Admin. Code §§ 9-011.05 to 9-011.05C4

Gas/Electric: Gas.
Covered Group: LIHEAP-eligible customers who document eligibility; any customer who enters into payment plan.
Date-Based: November 1 to March 31.
Temperature-Based Threshold: During these winter months, Customers have an additional 30 days to pay their bills. PSC has the authority to order a temporary ban on disconnections during periods of severe weather or when there is danger to the life and health of customers or to property.
Summary of Rules/Seasonal Policy: LIHEAP-eligible customer may not be disconnected during moratorium period. Other customers may be reconnected by paying the current bill, at least 1/4 of the arrearage and any required deposit or reconnection fee, and by entering into a payment plan.
Additional information: None specified.

NEVADA

Nev. Admin. Code § 704.375

Gas/Electric: Gas and electric.
Covered Group: None specified.
Date-Based: None specified.
Temperature-Based Threshold: No termination for a forecasted 24-hour period of extreme temperatures during which the temperature is forecasted to be 15° Fahrenheit or below or 105° Fahrenheit or higher.
Summary of Rules/Seasonal Policy: None specified.
Additional information: None specified.

NEW HAMPSHIRE

N.H. Code Admin. R. Ann. PUC 1204.01-06

Gas/Electric: Gas, electric, and steam.
Covered Group: During the winter, utilities must seek PUC approval before disconnecting service to customers known to be 65 years or older.
Date-Based: November 15 to March 31.
Temperature-Based Threshold: None specified.
Summary of Rules/Seasonal Policy: During the winter, before a utility can send a disconnection notice, arrears shall exceed $125 for gas non-heating customers, $225 for electric non-heating customers, and $450 for electric, gas, and steam heat customers.
Additional information: Reconnection available for winter period for consumers showing financial hardship or medical emergency.

NEW JERSEY

N.J. Admin. Code §§ 14:3-3A.2 and 14:3-3A.5

Gas/Electric: Gas and electric.
Covered Group: Customers receiving income-tested federal or state benefits or are unable to pay their bills because of circumstances such as unemployment, illness' or other circumstances causing financial hardship. Previously disconnected and eligible customers whose service has not been reconnected as of November 15 must pay up to 25% of the outstanding balance, enroll in a budget payment plan, and make good faith payments during the protection period when possible.
Date-Based: November 15 to March 15.
Temperature-Based Threshold: May not disconnect a residential customer if the temperature is forecast to be 32°F or below during the next 24 hours. May not disconnect a customer eligible for the Winter Termination Program if the temperature is forecast to be 95°F or greater within the next 48 hours.
Summary of Rules/Seasonal Policy: None specified.
Additional information: None specified.

NEW MEXICO

N.M. Code R. § 17.5.410.31(F) (LexisNexis)

Gas/Electric: Gas and electric.
Covered Group: Customer must be eligible for LIHEAP or the state's low income utility assistance.
Date-Based: During the period November 15 to March 15, utilities must provide service for at least 15 days or more after the date of disconnection if the HS dept has certified that the customer is eligible for LIHEAP or the state's low income utility assistance and that payment will be made during the 15-day period.
Temperature-Based Threshold: None specified.
Summary of Rules/Seasonal Policy: None specified.
Additional information: None specified.

NEW YORK

N.Y. Comp. Codes R. & Regs. tit.16, § 11.5(c)(2)

Gas/Electric: Gas, electric, and steam.
Covered Group: Customers likely to suffer serious impairment to health or safety as a result of termination due to age, infirmity, mental incapacitation, use of life support systems, serious illness, physical disability, or any other factual circumstances that indicate severe or hazardous health situations.
Date-Based: During the period between November 1 to April 15, utilities must contact customers by phone or in person at least 72 hours before the scheduled disconnection to ascertain if the resident is likely to suffer a serious impairment to health or safety as a result of termination. Utility cannot disconnect if customer is likely to suffer a serious impairment to health or safety, unless social services commissioner informs utility that customer's condition is not likely to result in serious impairment to health or safety or that alternative means of protecting health or safety has been devised.
Temperature-Based Threshold: None specified.
Summary of Rules/Seasonal Policy: None specified.
Additional information: None specified.

NORTH CAROLINA

4 N.C. Admin. Code 11.R12-10, 11.R12-11

Gas/Electric: Gas and electric.
Covered Group: A member of the household is either certified as disabled or 65 years or older, the customer cannot pay for service in full, or the household is certified by the local social service office which administers the Energy Crisis Assistance program or other similar programs as being eligible to receive assistance under such programs.
Date-Based: November 1 to March 31.
Temperature-Based Threshold: None specified.
Summary of Rules/Seasonal Policy: During heating season, may not terminate service to member of covered group without express approval of the commission.
Additional information: None specified.

NORTH DAKOTA

No information specified.

OHIO

Ohio Admin. Code 4901:1-18-04(A), 4901:1-18-05(B)(3), 4901:1 -18-06(B)

Gas/Electric: Gas and electric.
Covered Group: Customer who is in default and can pay 1/3 of the balance due each month of the winter heating season.
Date-Based: November 1 to April 15.
Temperature-Based Threshold: None specified.
Summary of Rules/Seasonal Policy: Company shall not disconnect service unless it has made contact ten days in advance and has informed consumer of right to set up payment plan under Rule 4901:1-18-05.
Additional information: Gas and electric companies must notify customers of the medical certificate procedure before the beginning of the winter heating period, and electric companies must so notify customers before the summer cooling period.

OKLAHOMA

Okla. Admin. Code §§ 165:35-21-10(c), 165:35-21-31(c), 165:45-11-14(c), 165:45-11-19(c)

Gas/Electric: Gas and electric.
Covered Group: Customers using service for heat and/or cooling.
Date-Based: None specified.
Temperature-Based Threshold: No termination if the temperature actually is, or is forecast to be, 32° Fahrenheit or below during the day or 20° Fahrenheit or below at night, or the heat index is, or is forecast to be, 101° Fahrenheit or higher on the day of disconnection.
Summary of Rules/Seasonal Policy: None specified.
Additional information: Right of reconnection when service is disconnected immediately preceding a period of severe weather as described in Okla. Admin. Code 165:35-21-10(c) and 165:45-11-19(c). Customer must either pay the bill or submit a medical certificate or a guarantee from a social service agency to pay the bill directly to the company.

OREGON

Or. Admin. R. 860-021 -0405(9)(b)(B)

Gas/Electric: Gas and electric.
Covered Group: None specified.
Date-Based: None specified.
Temperature-Based Threshold: None specified.
Summary of Rules/Seasonal Policy: Small rule states that the utility cannot remotely disconnect a customer after only attempting to contact customer by telephone during the winter heating season, from November 1 to April 30.
Additional information: None specified.

PENNSYLVANIA

52 Pa. Code § 56.100; 66 Pa. Stat. Ann. § 1406 (West)

Gas/Electric: Gas, electric, steam heat, water, and wastewater.
Covered Group: General eligibility.
Date-Based: December 1 to March 31.
Temperature-Based Threshold: None specified.
Summary of Rules/Seasonal Policy: Utility may not shut off service without contacting consumer and attempting to establish a reasonable agreement. (No detail on what that entails.) If a reasonable agreement cannot be reached, utility must apply to commission for permission to terminate. No termination for households with income at or below 250% of federal poverty guideline (150% for Philadelphia Gas Works customers).
Additional information: Utility must contact consumer within 90 days prior to December 1 and attempt to work out an agreement and restoration of service.

RHODE ISLAND

90-060-002 R.I. Code R. pt. III, § 3(C); pt. VIII (LexisNexis)

Gas/Electric: Gas and electric.
Covered Group: Protected status customers (including elderly, handicapped, infants, low-income heating assistance recipients, seriously ill, and unemployed) or customers with arrearages not exceeding $500 (if service is primary heat source) or $200 (if service is not primary heat source).
Date-Based: November 1 to April 15.
Temperature-Based Threshold: Summer Moratorium: National Weather Service issues heat advisory or excessive heat warning—no termination of service is allowed.
Summary of Rules/Seasonal Policy: Termination during November 15 to April 15 moratorium period is forbidden as to protected-status customers or those with arrears less than the prescribed amounts.
Additional information: None specified.

SOUTH CAROLINA

S.C. Code Ann. Regs. 103-352, 103-452; S.C. Code Ann. §§ 58-27-2520, 58-5-1120

Gas/Electric: Gas and electric.
Covered Group: Customers with a medical certificate stating that termination would be especially dangerous to resident's health.
Date-Based: December 1 to March 31.
Temperature-Based Threshold: None specified.
Summary of Rules/Seasonal Policy: Gas and electrical utilities must submit to the Office of Regulatory Staff their termination procedures for special needs customers at any time and all residential customers in times of extremely hot or cold temperatures. These must include notice provisions and definitions of extremely hot and cold temperatures.
Additional information: None specified.

SOUTH DAKOTA

S.D. Admin. R. 20:10:20:10

Gas/Electric: Gas and electric.
Covered Group: General eligibility.
Date-Based: November 1 to March 31.
Temperature-Based Threshold: None specified.
Summary of Rules/Seasonal Policy: During Winter period, utility must allow an additional 30 days for consumer to pay before disconnecting service.
Additional information: None specified.

TENNESSEE

No information specified.

TEXAS

16 Tex. Admin. Code § 25.29(i)

Gas/Electric: Electric.
Covered Group: None specified.
Date-Based: None specified.
Temperature-Based Threshold: No termination when the previous day's temperature did not exceed 32° Fahrenheit and the temperature is predicted to remain at or below that level for the next 24 hours. No termination when National Weather Service issues a heat advisory for any county in the electric utility's service territory or when such advisory has been issued on one of the preceding two calendar days.
Summary of Rules/Seasonal Policy: None specified.
Additional information: None specified.

UTAH

Utah Admin. R. 195-8-1

Gas/Electric: Gas and electric.
Covered Group: In the month of or the month prior to request, household meets one of the following requirements: (1) gross income less than 125% of poverty, (2) suffered medical or other emergency, (3) loss of employment , (4) 50% drop in income.
Date-Based: November 15 to March 15 (state HEAT Program has power to extend the duration of the moratorium in response to severe weather).
Temperature-Based Threshold: None specified.
Summary of Rules/Seasonal Policy: The moratorium restricts the utility from shutoff during the winter. To qualify for the moratorium, the customer must have a termination notice or refusal to reconnect, have applied for HEAT, have applied for utility assistance through the American Red Cross, is qualified for protection under this rule, and make good faith effort to pay bill during moratorium.
Additional information: Note that Utah Admin.R.746-200-7(E) approves the inclusion in the standard HEAT (LIHEAP) contracts with utility companies that utility will not terminate service for at least 30 days after receipt of a HEAT payment on behalf of the low-income household.

VERMONT

30-000-004 Vt. Code R. § 3.304

Gas/Electric: Gas and electric.
Covered Group: Customers 62 years or older seeking the disconnection protection when temperatures are forecast to fall below 32° Fahrenheit must provide utility with advance written notice of qualification for this protection.
Date-Based: November 1 to March 31.
Temperature-Based Threshold: Disconnections prohibited if temperatures will drop below 10° Fahrenheit during a 48-hour period beginning on the morning of the anticipated disconnection. No disconnections if a resident is 62 years or older and the temperatures are forecasted to fall below 32° Fahrenheit during a 48-hour period beginning on the morning of the anticipated disconnection.
Summary of Rules/Seasonal Policy: None specified.
Additional information: None specified.

VIRGINIA

No information specified.

WASHINGTON

Wash. Admin. Code §§ 480-90-143, 480-100-143

Gas/Electric: Gas and electric.
Covered Group: Space-heating customers who notify the utility of an inability to pay the full bill and any deposit; self-certify income; apply for home energy assistance and low-income weatherization and agree to a percentage-of-income payment plan and pay all amounts owed by the following October 15.
Date-Based: November 15 to March 15.
Temperature-Based Threshold: None specified.
Summary of Rules/Seasonal Policy: None specified.
Additional information: None specified.

WEST VIRGINIA

W. Va. Code R. §§ 150-3-4.8.1, 150-4-4.8.1

Gas/Electric: Gas and electric.
Covered Group: Customers who notify utility of inability to pay and that termination is dangerous to the health and safety of a member of the household.
Date-Based: December 1 to February 28.
Temperature-Based Threshold: None specified.
Summary of Rules/Seasonal Policy: Disconnection during the moratorium period is presumed to be dangerous to health. Any customer who claims inability to pay is entitled to a hearing before a managerial employee, with an appeal to the Commission.
Additional information: None specified.

WISCONSIN

Wis. Admin. Code PSC §§ 113.0301(16), 113.0303, 113.0304, 134.0624, 134.0623

Gas/Electric: Gas and electric.
Covered Group: Households with incomes at 250% of poverty or less whose health and safety would be endangered because of age or disabilities; burden is on utilities to verify household situation.
Date-Based: November 1 to April 15.
Temperature-Based Threshold: Electric utility may not disconnect when a heat advisory, heat warning, or heat emergency issued by National Weather Service is in effect. Utility shall make reasonable attempts to reconnect service to occupied dwelling when an occupant states that there is potential threat to health or life resulting from combination of heat and loss of service. Utility may require occupant to produce physician's statement or notice from public health, social services, or law enforcement official identifying the medical emergency. Upon expiration of advisory warning or emergency, utility may disconnect service that was reconnected during such period without further notice if payment plan has not been established.
Summary of Rules/Seasonal Policy: Between November 1 to April 15, prior to and at the time of disconnection, a utility rep must meet personally with responsible adult member of the household to discover any special circumstances that deserve special attention. On the day after a disconnection, utility must make an in-person visit to ascertain danger to health and life. Utilities required to have a reconnection plan which includes contact with disconnected customers prior to October 25 to inform customers of payment plan options. Personal contact required if household still disconnected after October 25 and, if any danger to health detected, shall immediately reconnect.
Additional information: None specified.

WYOMING

Wyo. Pub. Serv. Comm'n Regs., ch. 2, § 242(c), 242(h)(ii), 242(*i*)

Gas/Electric: Gas, electric, and water.
Covered Group: For extreme weather protection: customers who can document (except for elderly and disabled) they are unable to pay their bill and have exhausted or is actively seeking government assistance or are able to pay only in installments.
Date-Based: December 24 to January 2 (no disconnections for nonpayment); November 1 to April 30 (extreme weather).
Temperature-Based Threshold: None specified.
Summary of Rules/Seasonal Policy: Personal notice before disconnection required November 1 to April 30.
Additional information: None specified.

A.6 State-By-State Summary of Serious Illness Protections

The following state summaries were drawn from state statutory and regulatory provisions. Advocates should carefully review the statutes and regulations cited to determine which customers may benefit from these protections.

Alabama

Ala. Pub. Serv. Comm'n Gen. R. 12(E)

Utilities: Electric, gas, telephone, and water.
Summary of Protection: Utilities (except telephone toll service) shall adopt and follow reasonable tariff rules for discontinuing service when life or health may be threatened by termination.
Covered Group: None specified.
Process to Obtain Protection: None specified.
Duration of Protection: None specified.
Recertification Process (Frequency, Chronic Illness Waiver): None specified.

Alaska

Alaska Admin. Code tit. 3, § 52.450

Utilities: Electric.
Summary of Protection: If utility is informed that occupant is seriously ill, disabled, or dependent on life support system, it must provide termination notice at least 30 days prior to scheduled disconnection date. If utility is so notified after issuance of the termination notice, disconnection shall be extended by 15 days and the utility shall notify the customer of the extension.
Covered Group: Occupant.
Process to Obtain Protection: Notification to utility that occupant is seriously ill, disabled, or dependent on life support system.
Duration of Protection: Utility required to provide 30 days' notice of termination if it is informed that occupant is seriously ill, disabled, or dependent on life support systems. If so notified after issuance of termination notice, then disconnection shall be extended by 15 days.
Recertification Process (Frequency, Chronic Illness Waiver): None specified.

Arizona

Ariz. Admin. Code §§ 14-2-211, 14-3-311

Utilities: Electric and gas.
Summary of Protection: Utility shall not terminate service when

customer is unable to pay and (i) customer can establish through medical documentation and opinion of licensed physician that termination would be especially dangerous to customer or permanent resident of premises, or (ii) life support equipment used in the home is dependent on service. Separate provision provides that service to ill, elderly or disabled may not be terminated until customer is informed of known funds available from government and social assistance agencies, and third-party designee receives notice and has not arranged to pay outstanding bill.
Covered Group: Customer or permanent resident.
Process to Obtain Protection: Customer must either establish through medical documentation and opinion of licensed physician that termination would be especially dangerous to customer or permanent resident of premises, or life support equipment used in the home must be dependent on service.
Duration of Protection: Customer utilizing danger-to-health-or-life-support provision may be required to enter into payment plan within 10 days after scheduled termination date.
Recertification Process (Frequency, Chronic Illness Waiver): None specified.

Arkansas

126-03-003 Ark. Code R. § 6.17 (LexisNexis)

Utilities: Electric, gas, and water.
Summary of Protection: Upon being notified by health care professional that suspension of service would result in substantial risk of death or grave impairment to the health of a customer or permanent resident of household with a serious medical condition, utility shall postpone or reconnect service that has been suspended for 30 days or less.
Covered Group: Customer or permanent resident of household.
Process to Obtain Protection: Notice of such a serious medical condition may be given in person, by telephone, or in writing by a physician, nurse, nurse practitioner, physician's assistant, or public or private agency providing physical or mental health care services. Upon being notified, a utility must inform the health care professional that a physician's certificate is required within 7 days.
Duration of Protection: 30 days.
Recertification Process (Frequency, Chronic Illness Waiver): Certificate may be renewed once for an additional 30 days by providing a new certificate before the initial 30-day time period expires. Utility does not have to accept more than one certificate per household per year.

California

Cal. Pub. Util. Code §§ 777.1; 779 (West)

Utilities: Electric, gas, heat, and water.
Summary of Protection: Utility may not terminate service upon certification of licensed physician and surgeon that disconnection would be life threatening, and the customer is unable to pay within normal payment period and enters into an amortization agreement not exceeding 12 months regarding all charges asserted to be beyond the means of customer to pay prior to delinquency. For master-metered premises, service may not be terminated when a public health or building officer certifies that termination would result in significant threat to the health or safety of residential occupants or the public.
Covered Group: Customer. For master-metered premises, occupants or the public.
Process to Obtain Protection: None specified.
Duration of Protection: None specified.
Recertification Process (Frequency, Chronic Illness Waiver): None specified.

Colorado

4 Colo. Code Regs. §§ 723-2-2303(c)(VII), 723-2-3407(e)(IV), 723-2-4407(e)(IV), 723-2-5407(e)(IV) (LexisNexis)

Utilities: Electric, gas, telephone (local exchange service), and water.
Summary of Protection: Provider must postpone disconnection for 60 days from the date of a certificate issued by a Colorado-licensed physician, or a practitioner under the authority of the physician, that disconnection would create or aggravate a medical emergency.
Covered Group: Customer or permanent resident of household.
Process to Obtain Protection: Certificate issued by Colorado-licensed physician (or practitioner under physician) that disconnection would create or aggravate a medical emergency.
Duration of Protection: 60 days.
Recertification Process (Frequency, Chronic Illness Waiver): The 60 days may be increased by 30 days upon receipt of another certificate. Only one 90-day extension permitted in any 12-month period.

Connecticut

Conn. Agencies Regs. §§ 16-3-100(e)(1) to 16-3-100(e)(5), 16-3-101(C)(3)

Utilities: Electric, gas, sewer, telephone, and water.
Summary of Protection: Utility may not terminate service if it receives certification by licensed physician no later than 13 days after the mailing of termination notice (or within 7 days of receipt for telephone service).
Covered Group: Customer or member of household.
Process to Obtain Protection: Certificate issued by licensed physician that resident is seriously ill or there is life-threatening situation. Initial certification by telephone is sufficient, subject to confirmation, and if made by telephone utility shall send form for completion and return no later than 7 days from receipt.
Duration of Protection: 15 days.
Recertification Process (Frequency, Chronic Illness Waiver): If the physician did not specify the length of the illness or length is not ascertainable, the certification must be renewed every 15 days. For telephone service, failure to renew certificate automatically voids customer's rights under serious illness section except for any amortization agreement.

Delaware

26-4000-4003 Del. Code Regs. § 4.7.7 (LexisNexis)

Utilities: Telephone.

Summary of Protection: Suspension of service shall be postponed at least 3 days if utility is informed that an occupant is seriously ill and affected with a medical condition, which would be aggravated by suspension, and that medical certification will be obtained. Local exchange carrier may not suspend or refuse to restore service if within such time a physician or Christian Science practitioner certifies that occupant is seriously ill and affected with a medical condition that would be aggravated by cessation of service.
Covered Group: Occupant.
Process to Obtain Protection: Certification by physician or Christian Science practitioner that an occupant is seriously ill and affected with a medical condition that would be aggravated by cessation of service. Initial certifications may be written or oral, and the LEC has the right to verify by either calling the physician or Christian Science practitioner or requiring written confirmation within 7 days.
Duration of Protection: Greater of time specified in certification or 30 days.
Recertification Process (Frequency, Chronic Illness Waiver): Initial certification may be renewed for up to 30 days provided the same requirements for the initial certification are met.

District of Columbia

D.C. Mun. Regs. tit. 15, § 311.1; D.C. Consumer Bill of Rights § 311.1 (www.dcpsc.org/pdf_files/commorders/consumerbill/Revised_Consumer_Bill of_Rights.pdf)

Utilities: Electric, gas, and telephone.
Summary of Protection: Utility shall postpone termination for up to 21 days if customer provides a physician's certificate or notice from a public health official stating that termination would be detrimental to the health and safety of a person occupying the premises, and customer enters into a deferred payment plan.
Covered Group: Occupant.
Process to Obtain Protection: A physician's certificate or notice from a public health official stating that termination would be detrimental to the health and safety of a person occupying the premises.
Duration of Protection: Not exceeding 21 days.
Recertification Process (Frequency, Chronic Illness Waiver): Postponement may be extended for additional periods of not more than 21 days by renewal of the certificate or notice.

Florida

Fla. Admin. Code Ann. r. 25-6.105(11), 25-7.089; Fla. Stat. § 366.15

Utilities: Electric and gas.
Summary of Protection: Utility must submit as a tariff item a procedure for discontinuance of service when service is medically necessary. For electric utility, "medically essential" means medical dependence on electric-powered equipment that must be operated continuously or as circumstances require as specified by physician to avoid loss of life or immediate hospitalization of customer or permanent resident. Medically essential service may be recertified once every 12 months.
Covered Group: Customer or permanent resident (electric).
Process to Obtain Protection: For electric utility, customer must complete forms supplied by utility, including form completed by a physician licensed in state which explains in medical and non-medical terms why electric service is medically essential.
Duration of Protection: 12 months (electric).
Recertification Process (Frequency, Chronic Illness Waiver): For electric utility, medically essential service shall be recertified once every 12 months. Electric utility shall send recertification materials to customer by regular mail at least 30 days prior to expiration of customer's certification. The materials shall advise customer that recertification forms must be completed and submitted within 30 days after expiration of existing certification. If recertification forms are not received within the 30-day period, utility may terminate the certification.

Georgia

Ga. Comp. R. & Regs. 515-3-2.03, 515-3-3.03, 515-12-1.28

Utilities: Electric, gas, and telephone.
Summary of Protection: Service shall not be discontinued for nonpayment upon receipt of notice from customer in writing, or orally with written notice within 10 days thereafter, of a serious illness which would be aggravated by discontinuation, and upon receipt within 10 days of such initial notice of a written statement from a physician, county board of health, hospital, or clinic identifying the illness and its expected duration, and certifying that illness would be aggravated by discontinuance.
Covered Group: Customer.
Process to Obtain Protection: Notice from customer in writing, or orally with written notice within 10 days thereafter, of a serious illness that would be aggravated by discontinuation, and upon receipt within 10 days of such initial notice of a written statement from a physician, county board of health, hospital, or clinic identifying the illness and its expected duration, and certifying that illness would be aggravated by discontinuance.
Duration of Protection: The shorter of either the length of the illness or one month from the date of initial notice.
Recertification Process (Frequency, Chronic Illness Waiver): Postponement may be renewed one additional time by repeating procedure for initial postponement.

Hawaii

None specified.

Idaho

Idaho Admin. Code r. 31.21.01.308, 31.41.01.306

Utilities: Electric, gas, sewer, telephone, and water.
Summary of Protection: Utility shall postpone termination for 30 days from receipt of certificate by licensed physician or public health official with medical training that customer, member of customer's family, or permanent resident of premises is seriously ill or has a medical emergency, or will become seriously ill or have a medical emergency because of termination, and that termination would adversely affect health of customer, member or resident.

Covered Group: Customer, member of customer's family, permanent resident of premises.
Process to Obtain Protection: Certificate by licensed physician or public health official with medical training that customer, member of customer's family, or permanent resident of premises is seriously ill or has a medical emergency, or will become seriously ill or have a medical emergency because of termination, and that termination would adversely affect health of customer, member, or resident. Utility may verify authenticity of certificate and may refuse postponement if it is determined that certificate is fraudulent.
Duration of Protection: 30 days.
Recertification Process (Frequency, Chronic Illness Waiver): Second postponement available upon receipt of second certificate stating that serious illness or medical emergency still exists.

Illinois

Ill. Admin. Code tit. 83, §§ 280.130(j), 735.140

Utilities: Electric, gas, telephone, and water.
Summary of Protection: Discontinuance prohibited for up to 60 days upon certification that it will aggravate an existing serious illness of any permanent residence of the premises.
Covered Group: Permanent resident of the premises.
Process to Obtain Protection: Certification must be by registered physician or local board of health and may be by telephone if written certification is forwarded to utility within 5 days.
Duration of Protection: 30 days. Within first 30 days, customer must enter into an agreement to pay unpaid balance and keep current account paid during the time unpaid balance is to be paid.
Recertification Process (Frequency, Chronic Illness Waiver): Certification may be renewed for additional 30 days by providing another certificate.

Indiana

170 Ind. Admin. Code 4-1-16(c), 5-1-16(c), 6-1-16(c)

Utilities: Electric, gas, and water.
Summary of Protection: Utility shall postpone termination for 10 days if prior to noticed disconnect date customer provides medical statement from licensed physician or public health official that disconnection would be a serious and immediate threat to the health or safety of a designated person in customer's household.
Covered Group: Person in customer's household.
Process to Obtain Protection: Certification must be medical statement from licensed physician or public health official.
Duration of Protection: 10 days.
Recertification Process (Frequency, Chronic Illness Waiver): Postponement may be continued for one additional 10-day period by providing additional medical statement.

Iowa

Iowa Admin. Code r. 199-19.4(15), 199-20.4(15), 199-22.4(6)

Utilities: Electric, gas, and telephone.
Summary of Protection: Termination delayed for 30 days from receipt of written statement from doctor or public health official that shutting off service would pose an especial health danger to permanent resident of premises.
Covered Group: Permanent resident of premises.
Process to Obtain Protection: Verification by doctor or public health official may be by telephone initially, but written statement must be provided within 5 days. Service shall be restored if it has been disconnected within 14 days prior to verification.
Duration of Protection: 30 days.
Recertification Process (Frequency, Chronic Illness Waiver): Service may be shut off after 30 days if payment arrangements have not been made.

Kansas

Standards on Discontinuance of Service Practices, Section IV (www.kcc.ks.gov/pi/billing; www.kcc.ks.gov/telecom/phone billing)

Utilities: Electric, gas, telephone, and water.
Summary of Protection: Utility shall either allow payment in reasonable installments or postpone discontinuance for at least 21 days so customer can make arrangements for reasonable installment payments if customer notifies utility and establishes that discontinuance would be especially dangerous to health of customer, resident member of customer's family, or other permanent resident and that customer is either unable to pay for service in accordance with utility's billing or able to pay in installments.
Covered Group: Customer, member of customer's family, or other permanent resident.
Process to Obtain Protection: Customer must establish that discontinuance would be especially dangerous to health of customer, resident member of customer's family, or other permanent resident and that customer is either unable to pay for service in accordance with utility's billing or able to pay in installments.
Duration of Protection: At least 21 days.
Recertification Process (Frequency, Chronic Illness Waiver): None specified.

Kentucky

807 Ky. Admin. Regs. 5.006, § 14

Utilities: Electric, gas, telephone, and water.
Summary of Protection: Termination of service postponed for 30 days if physician, registered nurse, or public health officer certifies in writing that termination will aggravate a debilitating illness or infirmity on the premises.
Covered Group: None specified.
Process to Obtain Protection: Written certification by physician, registered nurse, or public health officer that termination will aggravate a debilitating illness or infirmity.
Duration of Protection: 30 days.
Recertification Process (Frequency, Chronic Illness Waiver): Utility may refuse consecutive extensions beyond initial 30-day period if certificate is not accompanied by agreed partial payment plan.

Louisiana

La. Rev. Stat. Ann. § 45:1222; La. Pub. Serv. Comm'n. General Order (Mar. 7, 2002)

Utilities: Electric and gas.
Summary of Protection: Customer who needs life-sustaining, electrically operated equipment or life-sustaining medical equipment that requires electricity in order to live shall not have service discontinued as long as customer is enrolled in and making required payments under deferred payment program.
Covered Group: Customer.
Process to Obtain Protection: None specified.
Duration of Protection: None specified.
Recertification Process (Frequency, Chronic Illness Waiver): None specified.

Maine

65-407-81 Me. Code R. § 11 (LexisNexis)

Utilities: Electric, gas, telephone, and water.
Summary of Protection: Utility may not disconnect or refuse to restore service for 3 days if customer or occupant gives oral or written notice that medical emergency exists and that certification will be provided by a registered physician within 3 days and before disconnection.
Covered Group: Customer or occupant.
Process to Obtain Protection: Initial notice of medical emergency may be made by customer or occupant, with oral or written certification within 3 days from registered physician that customer or occupant has a medical condition that will be seriously aggravated by lack of service. If oral (which may also be by employee or agent of physician), utility may require written certification within 7 days.
Duration of Protection: Lesser of period specified in certification or 30 days. If no time period specified, then at least 30 days.
Recertification Process (Frequency, Chronic Illness Waiver): Additional periods up to 30 days each as long as medical emergency is certified. Utility may require payment arrangement as condition of renewal, and disconnection can resume upon expiration of certificate if customer has failed to pay or enter into payment arrangement for overdue amount.

Maryland

Md. Code Regs. 20.31.03.01

Utilities: Electric and gas.
Summary of Protection: Electric or gas service, or both, may not be terminated for an initial period of up to 30 days beyond scheduled termination date upon receipt of written physician's certification that termination will aggravate an existing serious illness or prevent the use of life-support equipment of any occupant of the premises.
Covered Group: Occupant.
Process to Obtain Protection: Physician or customer may initially telephone utility regarding intent to obtain certification, and physician's written certificate must be forwarded to utility not later than day before scheduled termination date. Utility may refuse to honor a certificate that is incomplete, unsigned, or appears to be altered, or it may petition the Commission to determine the adequacy of the certification.
Duration of Protection: Up to 30 days beyond the scheduled date of termination. Customer shall enter into payment plan for any past-due bills and current amounts due.
Recertification Process (Frequency, Chronic Illness Waiver): Termination may be further delayed upon presentation of additional certificate. Termination of service to customer covered by regulation may occur only after two attempts at personal contact, by telephone, or personal visit. Upon contact, utility must inform customer about payment arrangements and sources of financial assistance.

Massachusetts

220 Mass. Code Regs. § 25.03 (Weil)

Utilities: Electric, gas, and water.
Summary of Protection: Utility may not shut off or refuse to restore service to home of any customer upon certification that the customer or someone living in customer's home is seriously ill.
Covered Group: Customer or occupant.
Process to Obtain Protection: Initial certification may be made by telephone and must be made by registered physician, physician assistant, nurse practitioner, or local board of health official, who must provide written certificate within 7 days of initial telephone certification.
Duration of Protection: Certification must be renewed quarterly, unless the illness is certified as chronic, in which case certificates must be renewed every six months.
Recertification Process (Frequency, Chronic Illness Waiver): If illness is certified as chronic, certification must be renewed every six months.

Michigan

Mich. Admin. Code r. 460.102, 460.147, 484.382

Utilities: Electric, gas, and telephone.
Summary of Protection: Utility shall postpone shutoff for not more than 21 days if customer or member of customer's household is a critical care customer or has a certificated medical emergency which would be aggravated by service shutoff. For telephone, provider shall postpone shutoff of local exchange service and regulated toll service for not more than 15 days if customer produces physician's certificate stating that customer, member of customer's family, or another permanent resident of the premises is suffering from an existing mental illness or medical condition which will be endangered by shutoff.
Covered Group: Customer or member of household. For telephone, customer, member of customer's family, or another permanent resident of premises.
Process to Obtain Protection: For gas and electric, "medical emergency" is an existing medical condition defined and certified by a physician or public health official on official stationary or company-provided form. For telephone service, customer must produce physician's certificate stating that customer, member of

customer's family, or another permanent resident of the premises is suffering from an existing mental illness or medical condition, which will be endangered by shutoff. For telephone, initial notification may be made by telephone, but customer must produce physician's certificate within 7 days.
Duration of Protection: Not more than 21 days for gas and electric, and not more than 15 days for telephone.
Recertification Process (Frequency, Chronic Illness Waiver): Utility shall extend postponement for further periods of not more than 21 days and not to exceed a total postponement of 63 days within any 12-month period only if customer provides additional certificates. For telephone, postponement may be extended for one additional 15-day period by the renewal and resubmission of certificate.

Minnesota

Minn. R. 7810.2600, 7820.2900, 7820.3000

Utilities: Electric, gas, and telephone.
Summary of Protection: Customer may apply to the utility to waive its right to disconnect. If the utility refuses to waive its right to disconnect, the customer may apply to the commission for emergency status. If the commission determines the customer has a probable claim in the dispute and that disconnection may result in hardship, it may declare an emergency status and order the utility to continue service for up to 30 days.
Covered Group: Customer.
Process to Obtain Protection: Customer must ask utility to waive disconnection and may apply to commission if utility refuses. For gas and electric, utility is not obligated to suspend disconnection upon the filing for review with the commission, unless the customer pays, when due, all current bills issued pending commission decision.
Duration of Protection: Not more than 30 days.
Recertification Process (Frequency, Chronic Illness Waiver): For gas and electric, if the same customer or any other person files for subsequent review by the commission regarding the same account, the subsequent filings do not relieve the customer from the obligation to pay for service rendered after the first filing. If subsequent requests for review are filed during the pendency of the first review, all designated disputed payment or portions thereof made after the first filing are deemed to be made into escrow.

Mississippi

26-000-002 Miss. Code R. § 8 (LexisNexis)

Utilities: Electric, gas, sewer, telephone, and water.
Summary of Protection: Customer's service shall not be discontinued for 60 days when utility receives written notice from a physician licensed in Mississippi or adjoining state certifying that discontinuance of service would create life threatening situation for customer or other permanent resident.

Customer claiming medical emergency exception shall not have service terminated following expiration of mid-winter period (December through March) if by April 1 the customer agrees to pay, and does pay, a sum equal to 133% of levelized billing amount from and after April 1 until all amounts due utility for previous service have been paid and the customer is current in utility bill.
Covered Group: Customer or permanent resident of household.
Process to Obtain Protection: Customer must provide a utility-generated form signed by a licensed physician and certifying that discontinuance of service to the customer would create a life-threatening situation for the customer or other permanent resident.
Duration of Protection: Generally, 60 days. Service may not be terminated from December through March without offering a levelized payment plan, which may require customer to pay amounts due that accrued before November 11 with remaining balance to be paid in installments of 133% (levelized monthly bill plus 33% of past due amount).
Recertification Process (Frequency, Chronic Illness Waiver): Customers demonstrating a medical emergency shall not have service terminated after April 1 if the customer agrees to pay and does pay according to a levelized payment plan and is current in utility bill. Customers are not allowed to carry forward an unpaid balance beyond December 1 of the following winter season.

Missouri

Mo. Code Regs. Ann. tit. 4, §§ 240-13.050(9), 240-33.070(11)

Utilities: Electric, gas, telephone, and water.
Summary of Protection: Utility shall postpone discontinuance for not more than 21 days if: for gas, electric and water, discontinuance will aggravate an existing medical emergency of the customer, member of the customer's family, or other permanent resident of premises; for telephone, service is necessary to obtain emergency medical assistance for a household member who is under care of a physician.
Covered Group: For electric, gas, and water, customer, member of the customer's family, or other permanent resident of premises. For telephone, household member who is under care of a physician.
Process to Obtain Protection: If requested, person who alleges a medical emergency shall provide the utility with reasonable evidence of the necessity.
Duration of Protection: Not more than 21 days.
Recertification Process (Frequency, Chronic Illness Waiver): None specified.

Montana

Mont. Admin. R. 38.5.1411

Utilities: Electric and gas.
Summary of Protection: Service may not be terminated for 180 days from date of certification by licensed healthcare professional (licensed physician, certified physician assistant, advanced practice registered nurse, or registered nurse) that absence of service will aggravate an existing medical condition that would threaten the health of any permanent resident.

Utility may not terminate service to medically protected account from November 1 to April 1 and on any day when the reported ambient air temperature at 8:00 a.m. is at or below freezing or the U.S. Weather Service forecasts a snowstorm or freezing temperatures for succeeding 24-hour period.
Covered Group: Any permanent resident.
Process to Obtain Protection: Written certification by licensed

healthcare professional that termination will aggravate an existing medical condition that would threaten the health of any permanent resident. Utility and customer shall negotiate payment plan consistent with customer's ability to pay. If failure to make payments results in arrearage of $500 or more, customer is required to enter into monthly payment plan equal to the average of the last 12 months' billing plus 1/12 of the arrearage.
Duration of Protection: 180 days.
Recertification Process (Frequency, Chronic Illness Waiver): Certificates may be renewed on a semi-annual basis.

Nebraska

Neb. Rev. Stat. § 70-1606(7)

Utilities: Electric, gas, and water.
Summary of Protection: Disconnection postponed for 30 days upon receipt of physician's certificate that subscriber or household resident has an existing illness or disability and would suffer an immediate and serious health hazard from disconnection.
Covered Group: Subscriber or household resident.
Process to Obtain Protection: Physician's certificate filed with utility within 5 days of receipt of disconnection notice and providing that subscriber or household resident has an existing illness or disability and would suffer an immediate and serious health hazard from disconnection.
Duration of Protection: 30 days.
Recertification Process (Frequency, Chronic Illness Waiver): Only one postponement permitted for each incident of nonpayment of any past-due account.

Nevada

Nev. Admin. Code §§ 704.370, 704.3936, 704.4185

Utilities: Electric, gas, telephone, and water.
Summary of Protection: Disconnection shall be postponed for 30 days upon receipt of both (1) written certification from licensed physician or public health official that termination of service would be especially dangerous to the health of customer or other permanent resident and would constitute an emergency affecting his or her health, and (2) customer's signed statement that he or she is unable to pay or is able to pay in installments.
Covered Group: Customer or other permanent resident.
Process to Obtain Protection: Initial notice may be by telephone, but written certification must be sent within 5 days. In addition to the medical certificate, the customer must provide a signed statement that he or she is unable to pay or is able to pay in installments.
Duration of Protection: 30 days. Before postponement expires, customer must arrange with utility to pay the bills. Gas, electric, and telephone utilities must allow installment plan up to 90 days to pay bills (water utility must allow up to 60 days).
Recertification Process (Frequency, Chronic Illness Waiver): Postponement may be extended an additional 30 days if utility receives a renewed medical certificate before initial period expires. If utility intends to terminate after postponement, it must notify the Division, the customer, any designated third party, and, for gas, electric and water, any governmental agencies or other organizations that have notified the utility that they can assist in paying utility bills.

New Hampshire

N.H. Code Admin. R. Ann. P.U.C. 412.15; 703.04; 1203.11

Utilities: Electric, gas, sewer, telephone, and water.
Summary of Protection: Service shall not be disconnected, and disconnection notice shall not be sent if utility has been notified by a licensed physician or mental health practitioner within 60 prior days that a medical emergency exists or would result from disconnection.
Covered Group: Customer.
Process to Obtain Protection: Notification by the licensed physician or mental health practitioner shall be written or by telephone provided utility receives written confirmation within 7 days of initial telephone notification.
Duration of Protection: 60 days. Customer must also negotiate a payment schedule.
Recertification Process (Frequency, Chronic Illness Waiver): Postponement may be renewed every 60 days. Utility shall not disconnect service to a customer subject to medical emergency postponement without approval from the Commission, and Commission shall not approve disconnection when the customer has made a good faith effort to pay utility bill. For telephone, utility that intends to terminate service for failure to enter into or comply with payment arrangement shall notify the Commission not less than 5 business days prior to termination.

New Jersey

N.J. Admin. Code § 14:3-3A.2

Utilities: All public utilities.
Summary of Protection: Discontinuance prohibited for up to 60 days if a medical emergency exists within the premises that would be aggravated by the discontinuance.
Covered Group: Customer.
Process to Obtain Protection: Utility may require customer to provide written physician's statement stating the emergency, its nature and duration, and that discontinuance will aggravate the emergency.
Duration of Protection: 30 days. Utility may require recertification by physician as to continuing nature of the medical emergency after 30 days.
Recertification Process (Frequency, Chronic Illness Waiver): Upon written request from the customer accompanied by updated physician's certificate, the Board may extend the 60-day period for good cause, and service may not be discontinued pending the Board's decision. At the end of the emergency period, the customer remains liable for all services rendered. For telephone, if customer incurs charges exceeding customer's average bill for the 6 months preceding the first 30-day period, the utility may require the customer to pay the excess charges during the medical emergency.

New Mexico

N.M. Code R. §§ 17.5.410.31, 17.11.16.19 (LexisNexis)

Utilities: Electric, gas, telephone.
Summary of Protection: Disconnection will be postponed for 30

days (or service reconnected) to a residence where a seriously or chronically ill person resides if at least 2 days prior to scheduled discontinuance utility receives a signed medical certification from a medical professional that discontinuance might endanger the customer's life or health and a signed financial certification, and customer enters into settlement agreement or deferred payment plan.
Covered Group: Customer.
Process to Obtain Protection: At least 2 days prior to scheduled discontinuance, utility must receive a signed medical certification from a medical professional that discontinuance might endanger the customer's life or health and a signed financial certification, and customer must enter into settlement agreement or deferred payment plan.
Duration of Protection: 30 days.
Recertification Process (Frequency, Chronic Illness Waiver): Utility has the discretion to delay the continuance for a longer period.

New York

N.Y. Comp. Codes R. & Regs. tit. 16, §§ 11.5, 14.5, 609.5

Utilities: Electric, gas, steam, telephone, and water.
Summary of Protection: Utility shall not terminate, disconnect, suspend or refuse to restore service for 30 days from receipt of certification by medical doctor or local board of health that a resident of customer's residence suffers from a serious illness or medical condition that severely affects his or her well-being. Certification to telephone utility must also include explanation that absence of telephone service would create a serious risk of inaccessibility to emergency medical assistance, assistance relating to medical care, or professional advice.

If customer or resident of premises suffers from medical condition requiring utility service to operate a life-sustaining device (e.g., iron lung or dialysis machine), certification shall remain effective until terminated by commission provided customer demonstrates inability to pay on at least a quarterly basis.
Covered Group: Resident of customer's residence.
Process to Obtain Protection: Initial certification by medical doctor or board of health of the existence of a medical emergency may be made by telephone if written certification is provided to utility within 5 business days.
Duration of Protection: 30 days. Customer must demonstrate inability to pay for service before certificate of medical emergency can be renewed. For telephone, demonstration of inability to pay may be required before a certificate can be renewed. Certification on behalf of customer or resident requiring life-sustaining device is effective until terminated by commission provided customer demonstrates inability to pay on at least a quarterly basis.
Recertification Process (Frequency, Chronic Illness Waiver): A renewed certificate is effective for 30 days except that, in cases certified as chronic, the renewed certificate shall remain in effect for 60 days or a longer period if approved by the Commission. Customer remains liable for payment of service while certification remains in effect and shall make reasonable efforts to pay for service.

North Carolina

4 N.C. Admin. Code 11.R12-10, 11.R12-11

Utilities: Electric, gas.
Summary of Protection: Utility shall establish an internal procedure to attempt to identify by special code a customer whose household is known to have a resident who is either chronically or seriously ill, disabled, or on a life support system, for the purpose of careful handling when service becomes subject to termination due to nonpayment.
Covered Group: Customer or member of household.
Process to Obtain Protection: None specified.
Duration of Protection: Utility has discretion to waive or extend termination, particularly when waiver or extension would prevent undue hardship in situations in which termination would be especially dangerous to health or customer or member of household is elderly or disabled.
Recertification Process (Frequency, Chronic Illness Waiver): None specified.

North Dakota

N.D. Admin. Code 69-09-01-18.1, 69-09-02-05.1

Utilities: Electric, gas.
Summary of Protection: Termination notice must advise customer of the right to stay termination for up to 30 days if the customer informs utility within 10-day termination notice period that dangerous health conditions exist, that customer is 65 years old or older, or that customer is disabled.
Covered Group: Customer.
Process to Obtain Protection: It is the customer's responsibility to notify utility of circumstances, and utility shall annually include a preaddressed, postage-paid postcard for such notice.
Duration of Protection: Up to 30 days.
Recertification Process (Frequency, Chronic Illness Waiver): None specified.

Ohio

Ohio Admin. Code 4901:1-15-27; 4901:1-18-06

Utilities: Electric, gas, sewage, and water.
Summary of Protection: Service shall not be disconnected for nonpayment upon certification that disconnection (i) would be especially dangerous to health, or (ii) would make operation of necessary medical or life-supporting equipment impossible or impractical. If service had been disconnected within 21 days prior to certification of special danger to health, service shall be restored upon proper certification and customer agrees to payment plan.
Covered Group: Permanent resident of premises.
Process to Obtain Protection: Initial certification may be by telephone if written certification is forwarded to utility within 7 days. Certification must be by a licensed physician, physician assistant, clinical nurse specialist, certified nurse practitioner, certified nurse-midwife, or local board of health physician.
Duration of Protection: 30 days.
Recertification Process (Frequency, Chronic Illness Waiver): Cer-

tification may be renewed for two additional 30-day periods. Total medical certification shall not exceed 90 days per household in any 12-month period. Customer must enter into extended payment plan prior to end of medical certification period.

Oklahoma

Okla. Admin. Code §§ 165:35-21-10, 165:45-11-14

Utilities: Electric and gas.
Summary of Protection: Utility shall suspend discontinuance or restore service upon notice from customer that disconnection will cause life-threatening condition for consumer or other permanent resident of household.
Covered Group: Customer or other permanent resident of household.
Process to Obtain Protection: Customer may provide initial notification provided prescribed form of medical certification by medical doctor or osteopath is returned within 30 days of initial notification.
Duration of Protection: 30 days.
Recertification Process (Frequency, Chronic Illness Waiver): Suspension may be extended for additional 30-day period if request and certification is made before the end of initial 30-day period. Utility is not required to furnish service after 60 days without full payment or payment plan. Consumer is not prohibited from claiming life-threatening condition upon full payment of account balance from previous life-threatening claim.

Oregon

Or. Admin. R. 860-021-0410, 860-021-0510

Utilities: Electric, gas, and telephone.
Summary of Protection: Service shall not be disconnected if customer submits written certification from qualified medical professional (licensed physician, nurse-practitioner, or physician's assistant) that disconnection would significantly endanger the physical health of customer or member of customer's household.
Covered Group: Customer or member of customer's household.
Process to Obtain Protection: Initial certification may be oral but must be confirmed in writing within 14 days by qualified medical professional. Utility may verify accuracy, and if it believes customer does not qualify or no longer qualifies, it may apply to Commission to terminate service. Customer is required to enter into payment plan for overdue balance and may renegotiate if financial hardship is shown. If electric or gas customer fails to enter into payment plan within 20 days of filing certificate, or to abide by its terms, utility shall notify Commission's Consumer Services Division of intent to disconnect, and may disconnect for nonpayment after 15 days notice or after 5 days notice for failure to enter into payment plan. Telephone customer must enter into payment plan within 10 days of filing certificate.
Duration of Protection: Certificate is valid for length of time the health endangerment is certified to exist, but no longer than 6 months without renewal for certificates not specifying chronic illness, and no longer than 12 months for chronic illness. Electric and gas utility shall give customer at least 15 days' written notice of a certificate's expiration date unless renewed before expiration date.
Recertification Process (Frequency, Chronic Illness Waiver): None specified.

Pennsylvania

52 Pa. Code §§ 56.111 to 56.118, 64.123, app. A

Utilities: Electric, gas, steam heat, telephone, waste water, and water.
Summary of Protection: If utility is informed prior to termination of service that an occupant is seriously ill or affected with a medical condition which will be aggravated by termination of service and that a medical certification will be obtained, then termination may not occur for at least 3 days. For telephone, if customer contacts utility, has physician certify by phone or in writing that customer or resident is seriously ill and that person will be endangered by termination, and makes equitable arrangement to pay LEC past-due and current bills, then service will not be cut off for up to 30 days.
Covered Group: Occupant.
Process to Obtain Protection: Initial certification may be written or oral, subject to utility's right to verify by calling the physician or requiring written confirmation within 7 days. For telephone, customer must contact utility, have physician certify by phone or in writing that customer or resident is seriously ill, and make equitable arrangement to pay past-due and current bills.
Duration of Protection: Maximum of time specified in medical certificate or 30 days. For telephone, up to 30 days.
Recertification Process (Frequency, Chronic Illness Waiver): Certifications may be renewed for up to 30 days provided ratepayer has met obligation to equitably arrange to make payment on all bills. If obligation is not met, renewals are limited to two 30-day periods. Utility may petition the Commission to contest the validity of a certification, to terminate service prior to expiration, or to contest the renewal of a certification. None specified for telephone.

Rhode Island

90-060-002 R.I. Code R. § III (LexisNexis); 90-060-007 R. § VIII (LexisNexis)

Utilities: Electric, gas, telephone, and water.
Summary of Protection: Utility shall not disconnect service to customer's permanent residence during such time that a licensed physician certifies to the utility or the Division that any resident is seriously ill. For telephone, discontinuance shall be postponed for up to 30 days if physician certifies that continued access to service is required because of serious illness of resident.
Covered Group: Any resident of customer's permanent residence.
Process to Obtain Protection: Licensed physician's initial certification may be made by telephone provided that a written certification is forwarded to the utility or the Division within 7 days. The utility must honor licensed physician's certification but may seek Division review of its validity. For electric, gas, and water, if the certification does not comply with the rule and the utility rejects it, it must immediately inform the customer of the reasons and of the customer's right to Division review of the rejection.
Duration of Protection: Initial postponement shall not be less than 3 weeks from receipt by utility of the written certification. Utility

shall acknowledge receipt of the written certificate and provide written notice to the customer of the date upon which service will be terminated unless the customer arranges for payment, requests a hearing, or enrolls in a payment plan. For telephone, initial postponement shall be for lesser of duration of illness or 30 days. If at end of certification period customer has not paid delinquent bill or agreed to payment plan, company can discontinue service after 5 calendar days' written notice.
Recertification Process (Frequency, Chronic Illness Waiver): If duration of the illness exceeds three weeks, the customer may request a review to determine whether, how long, and under what circumstances the exemption shall continue. For telephone, certification is renewable once with the approval of the Division.

South Carolina

S.C. Code Ann. Regs. 103-352, 103-452

Utilities: Electric and gas.
Summary of Protection: Service will not be terminated from December through March if customer or member of household provides a utility form certificate from a licensed physician no less than 3 days prior to termination or at termination stating that termination would be especially dangerous to such person's health. The certificate must be signed by the customer and state that the customer is unable to pay by installments.
Covered Group: Customer or member of household.
Process to Obtain Protection: Customer or member of household must provide a utility form certificate from a licensed physician no less than 3 days prior to termination or at termination stating that termination would be especially dangerous to such person's health. The certificate must be signed by the customer and state that the customer is unable to pay by installments.
Duration of Protection: 31st day from the date that the certificate is signed by the physician. The customer must conform to a deferred payment plan.
Recertification Process (Frequency, Chronic Illness Waiver): Certificate may be renewed for no more than 3 additional 30-day periods.

South Dakota

S.D. Admin. R. 20:10:20:11

Utilities: Electric and gas.
Summary of Protection: Utility shall postpone disconnection for 30 days from the date of a physician's certificate or a notice from a public health or social services official stating that disconnection will aggravate an existing medical emergency of customer, member of customer's family, or other permanent resident.
Covered Group: Customer, member of customer's family, or other permanent resident.
Process to Obtain Protection: Utility must receive physician's certificate or notice from public health or social services official stating that disconnection will aggravate an existing medical emergency of customer, member of customer's family, or other permanent resident.
Duration of Protection: 30 days.
Recertification Process (Frequency, Chronic Illness Waiver): Postponement is limited to a single 30-day period.

Tennessee

Tenn. Comp. R. & Regs. 1220-4-4.19, 1220-4-5.18

Utilities: Electric and gas.
Summary of Protection: Utility shall postpone termination of service for 30 days upon written certification by physician, public health officer, or social service official that discontinuation will aggravate existing medical emergency of customer or other permanent resident.
Covered Group: Customer or other permanent resident.
Process to Obtain Protection: Utility must receive certificate from physician, public health officer, or social service official stating that discontinuation will aggravate an existing medical emergency of customer or other permanent resident.
Duration of Protection: 30 days. During the 30-day period, utility shall refer customer or other permanent resident to social service agencies for investigation, confirmation of need, and guarantee of payment.
Recertification Process (Frequency, Chronic Illness Waiver): None specified.

Texas

16 Tex. Admin. Code §§ 25.29, 26.28; 30 Tex. Admin. Code § 291.88

Utilities: Electric, telephone, and water and sewer.
Summary of Protection: Service may not be disconnected when customer establishes that disconnection will cause some resident to become seriously ill or more seriously ill. For telephone, customer must establish that suspension or disconnection will prevent customer from summoning emergency medical help for resident who is seriously ill.
Covered Group: Resident of customer's permanent residence.
Process to Obtain Protection: By disconnection date, applicable person's attending physician (any public health official, including medical doctors, doctors of osteopathy, nurse practitioners, registered nurses, and any other similar public health official) must submit a written statement to utility that disconnection will cause some resident to become seriously ill or more seriously ill, and the customer must enter into a deferred payment plan. For telephone, physician must certify that suspension or disconnection will prevent customer from summoning medical help for resident who is seriously ill.
Duration of Protection: Lesser of 63 days from the issuance of bill in question or a shorter period agreed upon by utility and customer or physician. For water and sewer, service may be disconnected if the next month's bill and the past due bill are not paid by due date of the next month's bill, unless customer enters into deferred payment plan.
Recertification Process (Frequency, Chronic Illness Waiver): None specified.

Utah

Utah Admin. Code r. 746-200-7, 746-240-6

Utilities: Electric, gas, telephone, and water and sewer.
Summary of Protection: Service may not be disconnected upon receipt of written statement from defined medical provider identifying the health infirmity or potential health hazard and how termination will injure resident's health or aggravate their illness. For telephone, licensed physician must certify that discontinuance will aggravate an existing medical emergency or create a medical emergency for the customer, family member, or other permanent resident.
Covered Group: Resident. For telephone: customer, family member, or other permanent resident.
Process to Obtain Protection: Defined medical provider must provide a written statement identifying the health infirmity or potential health hazard and how termination will injure resident's health or aggravate their illness. For telephone, licensed physician must certify that discontinuance will aggravate an existing medical emergency or create a medical emergency for the customer, family member, or other permanent resident.
Duration of Protection: Lesser of one month or period stated in the medical provider's written statement. For telephone, lesser of 30 days or period agreed to by utility and account holder. The account holder remains liable for the cost of service but no action may be taken to terminate prior to end of postponement.
Recertification Process (Frequency, Chronic Illness Waiver): The subject person may petition the Commission for an extension of time.

Vermont

30-000-004 Vt. Code R. §§ 3.301 to 3.303; 30-000-053 Vt. Code R. § 7.623

Utilities: Electric, gas, telephone, and water.
Summary of Protection: Utility shall not disconnect or refuse to restore service upon receipt of certification from licensed physician that it would be an immediate and serious hazard to health of customer or resident of household.
Covered Group: Customer or resident of household.
Process to Obtain Protection: Initial notice by telephone or otherwise that a physician's certificate is forthcoming is effective as receipt and is valid for 30 days, provided physician's certification is received within 7 days.
Duration of Protection: Lesser of 30 days or duration of the hazard.
Recertification Process (Frequency, Chronic Illness Waiver): Certification to prevent disconnection or to cause a reconnection is limited to two consecutive 30-day periods, and may not exceed three 30-day periods in any calendar year except by written order of the Board.

Virginia

None specified.

Washington

Wash. Admin. Code §§ 480-90-128, 480-100-128, 480-110-355, 480-120-172

Utilities: Electric, gas, telephone, and water.
Summary of Protection: Utility must postpone disconnection or reinstate service for 5 business days after receipt of verbal or written notice of existence of medical emergency. Gas, electric, and telephone service must be restored by end of business day if request is timely, and not later than noon the following day, and without prior payment of deposit or reconnection fee.
Covered Group: Household resident.
Process to Obtain Protection: Utility may require that customer provide within 5 business days a written certification from a qualified medical professional that disconnection would aggravate an existing medical condition of a household resident (for water and telephone, that discontinuation would endanger physical health). Within 5-day grace period, utility may require customer to pay 10% (for water, 25%; for telephone, greater of 25% or $10) of the delinquent balance, agree to pay remaining delinquent balance within 120 days (for water and telephone, 90 days), and pay subsequent bills when due. If customer fails to provide written certification or percentage of delinquent balance, utility may proceed after providing required notice (for water and telephone, no further notice required).
Duration of Protection: Lesser of 60 days (for telephone, 90 days; for water, 6 months) or length of time that health endangerment is certified to exist.
Recertification Process (Frequency, Chronic Illness Waiver): Certification is valid for no longer than 60 days (for telephone, 90 days; for water, 6 months), unless renewed. For gas and electric, customer may claim medical emergency only twice within any 120-day period.

West Virginia

W. Va. Code R. §§ 150-3-4.8, 150-4-4.8, 150-6-2.2(f)

Utilities: Electric, gas, and telephone.
Summary of Protection: Hearing shall be held with utility managerial employee if customer notifies utility of inability to pay in accordance with utility's bill and that termination would be especially dangerous to health or safety of member of customer's household. Termination shall be postponed upon receipt within 10 days of hearing of written certification from licensed physician that termination would be especially dangerous.
Covered Group: Member of customer's household.
Process to Obtain Protection: Hearing is required if prior to termination customer notifies utility of inability to pay and that termination would be especially dangerous to health of safety of household member. Termination shall be postponed if utility received written certification from physician within 10 days of meeting.
Duration of Protection: 30 days. Customer must be offered a deferred payment plan if customer can only pay arrearage in installments.
Recertification Process (Frequency, Chronic Illness Waiver): Certificates must be renewed every 30 days (starting from the date certification is sent to utility) unless physician can state to a

reasonable degree of certainty that the condition is permanent.

Wisconsin

Wis. Admin. Code P.S.C. §§ 113.0301, 134.062(11), 185.37

Utilities: Electric, gas, and water.
Summary of Protection: Utility shall postpone disconnection or reconnect for up to 21 days to enable customer to arrange for payment if customer produces statement from licensed Wisconsin physician or notice from a public health, social services, or law enforcement official identifying a medical or protective services emergency and the length of time that disconnection would aggravate the circumstances.
Covered Group: Customer. For water service, occupant, member of customer's family, or other permanent resident.
Process to Obtain Protection: Customer must produce statement from licensed Wisconsin physician or notice from a public health, social services, or law enforcement official identifying medical or protective services emergency and length of time that disconnection would aggravate the circumstances.
Duration of Protection: 21 days. Customer remains responsible for the cost of service during period that service is continued.
Recertification Process (Frequency, Chronic Illness Waiver): Postponement may be extended by renewal of statement or notice if there is evidence of reasonable communications between the parties to make payment arrangements. In the event of a dispute as to an emergency, either party may request informal review by Commission staff. Pending a decision, service shall be continued provided customer has submitted the statement or notice.

Wyoming

023-020-2 Wyo. Code R. § 242 (LexisNexis)

Utilities: Electric, gas, and water.
Summary of Protection: Utility must grant an additional 15 days from termination date for bill payment if customer can provide written health care documentation that a member of customer's household is disabled or seriously ill and whose physical health or safety would be seriously endangered if service were disconnected.
Covered Group: Member of customer's household.
Process to Obtain Protection: Customer must provide written health care documentation that a member of customer's household is disabled or seriously ill and whose physical health or safety would be seriously endangered if service were discontinued.
Duration of Protection: 22 total days (7-day termination notice period plus 15 additional days).
Recertification Process (Frequency, Chronic Illness Waiver): None specified.

A.7 State-By-State Summary of Customer Contact and Notification Procedures Prior to Disconnection of Service

The following state summaries were drawn from state statutory and regulatory provisions. Advocates should carefully review the statutes and regulations cited to determine which customers benefit from the referenced contact and notice provisions. For example, in some states, special classes of customers such as the elderly or seriously ill may benefit from additional protections compared to those customers who do not fall within these groups.

Alabama

Ala. Pub. Serv. Comm'n Gen. R. 12, 13 *(electric, gas, water, telephone)*

Utilities Covered: *Electric, gas, telephone, and water.*
Contact Requirements:
On-Site Personal Contact: None specified.
Telephone Contact: None specified.
Other Personal Notice/Contact: None specified.
Social Service Agency Contact: None required.
Notice Requirements:
Timing and Delivery of Written Notice: 5-day written notice of intention to discontinue service after delinquency. Telecommunications bill is delinquent not earlier than 15 days after the billing date; bills for other utilities are delinquent if not paid within 10 days from the due date. Ala. Pub. Serv. Comm'n Gen. R. 12(A), (B). Notice shall be deemed given to customer when a copy is left with customer, left at the service address, or posted in the United States mail addressed to the customer's last known post office address. If the notice is mailed, it shall be delivered to the Post Office at least 5 calendar days before disconnection date. Ala. Pub. Serv. Comm'n Gen. R. 12(G).
Content of Written Notice: Specific heading in bold letters of "Disconnect Notice," "Termination Notice," "Final Notice," or "Cutoff Notice" required, along with statement that, in the event of a dispute, the customer should first contact utility, and then the Alabama Public Service Commission if dispute remains unresolved. Ala. Pub. Serv. Comm'n Gen. R. 12(C).

Alaska

Alaska Admin. Code tit. 3, §§ 52.445, 52.450 *(electric)*

Utilities Covered: Electric.
Contact Requirements:
On-Site Personal Contact: Utility must attempt personal contact by telephone or visit to premises at least 3 working days before disconnection. If by telephone, the utility shall attempt to make contact no less than three times at various periods in the day or make other reasonable attempts to contact the customer. If by visit to the premises, the utility's authorized representative shall hand-deliver a "Shut-Off Notice" to the customer or, if no personal contact is possible, leave the notice in a prominent place. If the

premises are 25 or more miles from the nearest location from which the utility delivers notices and if telephone contact cannot be made, a first class, postage-prepaid letter may serve as an alternative to a hand-delivered "Shut-Off" notice. The notice must be mailed no less than 5 working days before the scheduled disconnection date. The "Shut-Off Notice" or completed telephone call must provide customer with the following information: (A) the customer's name and address, and the service address, if different; (B) concise reasons for the impending disconnection; (C) the date on or after which service will be disconnected; (D) the business office telephone number, after-business-hours telephone number if applicable, and the utility address where the customer may pay the delinquent bill, enter into a deferred payment agreement, or file a bill dispute complaint; and (E) the amount of the charges for disconnection and reconnection of service. 3 Alaska Admin. Code tit. 3, § 52.450(c)(3).
Telephone Contact: Utility must attempt personal contact by telephone or visit to premises least 3 working days before disconnection. If by telephone, the utility shall attempt to make contact no less than three times at various periods in the day or make other reasonable attempts to contact the customer. 3 Alaska Admin. Code tit. 3, § 52.450(c)(3).
Other Personal Notice/Contact: None specified.
Social Service Agency Contact: None required, but see Content of Written Notice (utility notice required to provide a list of any governmental or social assistance agencies, if known by the utility, that may offer energy assistance).
Notice Requirements:
Timing and Delivery of Written Notice: 15 days before scheduled disconnection, utility shall mail or deliver to customer and any third party designee, written notice of intent to disconnect service. No notice required if immediate hazard, meter tampering, fraud, or failure to comply with curtailment procedures. Alaska Admin. Code tit. 3, §§ 52.450(a), (c). If utility has been informed that resident is seriously ill, elderly, disabled or dependent on life support, initial notice must be at least 30 days before the scheduled disconnection. In the event that utility is notified after issuance of a termination notice that a customer's residence is occupied by a person seriously ill, elderly, with a disability, or dependent on life support systems, the utility shall extend the disconnection date by 15 days and notify the customer of the extension. Alaska Admin. Code tit. 3, § 52.450(c)(2).
Content of Written Notice: For nonpayment, written notice must include the following: (A) customer's name and address, and the service address, if different; (B) the date on or after which service will be disconnected unless the customer takes appropriate action; (C) reason for disconnection, including, the amount of the delinquent bill; (D) a statement advising the customer to contact the utility regarding deferred payment and other procedures to avoid disconnection; (E) a list of any governmental or social assistance agencies, if known by the utility, that may offer energy assistance; (F) a specific request to notify the utility immediately regarding avoiding disconnection if a resident is seriously ill, elderly, with a disability, or dependent on life support systems; (G) a statement that the utility's stated reason for disconnection may be disputed and potentially resolved by contacting the utility at a specific address or telephone number; (H) a statement that the utility retains the right to terminate service, after allowing a customer who disputes a bill the opportunity for a meeting, if the utility continues to find that the reason for the disconnection is just; (I) the telephone number and address of the commission and a statement that the customer may file a complaint with the commission under Alaska Admin. Code §§ 48.120 or 48.130 if not satisfied with the utility's response or resolution of a contested bill; and (J) the amount of the utility's tariffed charges for disconnection and reconnection. Alaska Admin. Code tit. 3, § 52.450(c)(1).

Arizona

Ariz. Admin. Code §§ 14-2-210, 14-2-211 *(electric)*, 14-2-310, 14-2-311 *(gas)*, 14-2-409, 14-2-410 *(water)*, 14-2-508, 14-2-509 *(telephone)*, 14-2-609 *(sewer)*

Utilities Covered: Electric, gas, sewer, telephone, and water.
Contact Requirements:
On-Site Personal Contact: Electric, gas, or water service may only be disconnected "in conjunction with a personal visit to the premises by an authorized representative of the utility." Ariz. Admin. Code §§ 14-2-211(E)(4) (electric); 14-2-311(E)(4) (gas); 14-2-410(E)(4) (water).
Telephone Contact: None specified.
Other Personal Notice/Contact: None specified.
Social Service Agency Contact: None specified.
Notice Requirements:
Timing and Delivery of Written Notice: 5 days' written notice (10 days for water) to customer and, for gas and electric, to third-party designee. Notice is deemed given if posted by first class U.S. Postal Service mail to customers' last known address or left with customer. Ariz. Admin. Code §§ 14-2-211(D), (E) (electric); 14-2-311(D), (E) (gas); 14-2-410(E) (water); 14-2-509(E) (telephone); 14-2-609(E) (sewer).
Content of Written Notice: Written notice shall include the following information: (A) name of the person whose service is to be terminated and the service address; (B) amount of outstanding bill; (C) the date on or after which service may be terminated; (D) a statement advising the customer to contact the utility at a specific address or phone number regarding any deferred payment or other procedures to avoid termination; and (E) a statement that the utility's stated reason for termination service may be disputed by contacting the utility at a specific address or phone number, advising the utility of the dispute and making arrangements to speak with a responsible utility employee who is empowered to resolve the dispute prior to the scheduled termination date. The utility retains the option to terminate service after affording the opportunity for such a meeting and concluding that the reason for termination is just and advising the customer of the right to file a complaint with the Commission. Ariz. Admin. Code §§ 14-2-211(D), 14-2-311(D) (gas); 14-2-410(D) (water); 14-2-609(D) (sewer). Telephone regulation is identical except there is no stated option to arrange for meeting with utility employee. Ariz. Admin. Code § 14-2-509(D) (telephone).

Arkansas

126-03-003 Ark. Code R. §§ 6.01 to 6.19 *(electric, gas, water)* (LexisNexis); 126-03-014 Ark. Code R. §§ 6.01 to 6.16 *(telephone)* (LexisNexis)

Utilities Covered: Electric, gas, telephone, and water.

Contact Requirements:
On-Site Personal Contact: If the customer offers to make a payment at time of disconnection, the utility employee shall accept payment or honor utility receipt or canceled check showing payment. Utility employees may refuse cash payment if they give customer 24 hours to pay at the business office. The employee may refuse payment by check if the customer has given the utility two checks which were returned for reasons other than bank error within the last year. If the customer or other adult is not at the premises or does not respond, the utility employee must leave a notice in a conspicuous place which contains the following: (A) statement that service has been suspended; (B) the reason for the suspension; (C) the address and telephone number where the customer may arrange to have service reconnected; (D) the amount past due; (E) any approved collection charge; and, (F) the action and payment required for reconnection. 126-03-003 Ark. Code R. § 6.09(B) (electric, gas, water).
Telephone Contact: None specified.
Other Personal Notice/Contact: At least 72 hours before suspending service to an identified elderly or disabled account, utility must make two attempts at different times of day to contact the customer, an adult at the premises, or someone previously designated by the customer, either in person or by telephone. If the attempt to contact is successful, the utility shall offer to explain what can be done to avoid suspension and the payment and assistance options (delayed payment agreement, levelized billing for gas and electric, right to third-party notice before suspension of service, and federal, state, and local bill payment assistance agencies). If the attempt to make personal contact is not successful, the utility must give 24 hours' written notice explaining what can be done to avoid suspension. If the 24-hour notice is made by delivery to premises, it shall be left in a conspicuous place. If the utility mails the notice, the 24 hours begins 3 calendar days after the date the notice is postmarked. 126-03-003 Ark. Code R. § 6.18 (electric, gas, water); 126-03-014 Ark. Code R. § 6.16 (telephone).
Social Service Agency Contact: If a social service agency agrees to pay at least 1/4 of an overdue bill, the utility shall continue service or restore service if the customer qualifies and agrees to a delayed-payment agreement. If customer's account remains unpaid for 40 days after the agency notifies a utility that the agency will be making a payment, the utility may suspend service after an additional 5 calendar days' written notice to the customer. 126-03-003 Ark. Code R. § 6.16 (electric, gas, water); 126-03-014 Ark. Code R. § 6.14 (telephone).
Notice Requirements:
Timing and Delivery of Written Notice: 5 calendar days' written notice to customer with copy mailed to third-party designee. If by delivery, utility must leave notice in a conspicuous place. If by mail, the 5 days begins 3 calendar days after the notice is mailed by first-class U.S. Postal Service to the customer's last known address. 126-03-003 Ark. Code R. §§ 6.04, 6.06 (electric, gas, water); 126-03-014 Ark. Code R. §§ 6.04, 6.06 (telephone). Utility must suspend service within 30 days after the last day to pay, as printed on the most recent shutoff notice, unless suspension is delayed under the Rules or the reason for suspension eliminated. 126-03-003 Ark. Code R. § 6.09 (electric, gas, water); 126-03-014 Ark. Code R. § 6.09 (telephone). If customer's account remains unpaid for 40 days after a social service agency notifies a utility that the agency will be making a payment, the utility may suspend service after an additional 5 calendar day written notice to the customer. 126-03-003 Ark. Code R. § 6.16(C) (electric, gas, water); 126-03-014 Ark. Code R. § 6.14(C) (telephone). Written notice, by first class mail or delivery to an adult at the premises, must be given by the utility to a customer subject to protection due to certification of serious medical condition. Such notice shall include the date that postponement of suspension or reconnection of service commenced, the date on which the postponement of suspension or reconnection shall expire, an explanation of the right to renew the certificate, and the specific last date by which the certificate must be renewed. 126-03-003 Ark. Code R. § 6.17(C)(4) (electric, gas, water); 126-03-014 Ark. Code R. § 6.15(C)(4) (telephone).
Content of Written Notice: Shut-off notice shall include the following information: (A) "SHUT-OFF NOTICE," "CUT-OFF NOTICE," or "DISCONNECT NOTICE" in type at least 1/4 inch high; (B) customer's name and address, and service address, if different; (C) reason for suspension and amount overdue; (D) clear statement of what to do to avoid suspension; (E) date after which the utility will suspend service unless the customer takes appropriate action; (F) a statement: "YOU MAY QUALIFY TO PAY YOUR BILL IN INSTALLMENTS AND AVOID SHUT-OFF, BUT YOU MUST CONTACT THE UTILITY'S BUSINESS OFFICE BY THE CLOSE OF BUSINESS ON THE LAST DAY TO PAY PRINTED ON THIS NOTICE AND ASK FOR A DELAYED PAYMENT AGREEMENT"; (G) statement that a customer with a serious medical condition or who is 65 or older or disabled may contact the utility about qualifying for delaying suspension; (H) for electric and gas utilities, statement that the customer may contact the utility for the names of federal, state, and local bill payment assistance agencies; (I) cost and procedure for reconnection; (J) applicable charges if utility personnel must visit premises to collect the bill; (K) utility telephone number and address where customer may pay the bill, make payment arrangements, or make a complaint; and, (L) statement that any customer with an unresolved complaint may contact the Commission, including the Commission's mailing and street address and local and toll-free numbers. 126-03-003 Ark. Code R. § 6.07 (electric, gas, water). Telephone utility notice provision is substantially similar. 126-03-014 Ark. Code R. § 6.07 (telephone).

California

Cal. Pub. Util. Code §§ 777, 777.1, 779 *(electric, gas, water, heat)* (West)

Utilities Covered: Electric, gas, heat, and water.
Contact Requirements:
On-Site Personal Contact: None specified.
Telephone Contact: None specified.
Other Personal Notice/Contact: Every corporation shall make a reasonable attempt to contact an adult resident at premises by telephone or personal contact at least 24 hours prior to termination of service. If telephone or personal contact cannot be accomplished, utility shall give 48 hours' notice of termination by mail or in person. Cal. Pub. Util. Code § 779.1(b) (electric, gas, heat, water).
Social Service Agency Contact: None specified.
Notice Requirements:
Timing and Delivery of Written Notice: 10 days' written notice

mailed to the customer to whom the service is billed, not earlier than 19 days after the bill was mailed, and the 10-day period starts 5 days after mailing of the notice. Cal. Pub. Util. Code § 779.1(a) (electric, gas, heat, and water). Customers who are 65 years of age or older, or who are dependent adults as defined in Welfare and Institutions Code § 15610(b)(1), may designate a third party to receive notice. Cal. Pub. Util. Code § 779.1(c) (electric, gas, heat, and water). If a customer fails to comply with an amortization agreement, utility must give at least 48 hours' notice that includes conditions customer must meet to avoid termination, but such notice does not give customer any right to a further investigation by the utility. Cal. Pub. Util. Code § 779.1(f) (electric, gas, heat, and water).

Content of Written Notice: Written notice shall include: (A) delinquent customer's name and address; (B) the delinquent amount; (C) the date by which payment or arrangements for payment must be made to avoid termination; (D) the procedure to initiate a complaint or request an investigation of service or charges; (E) the procedure to request amortization of the unpaid charges; (F) the procedure to obtain information on the availability of financial assistance, including private, local, state, or federal sources, if applicable; (G) the telephone number of a utility representative who can provide additional information or institute payment arrangements; and (H) the telephone number of the commission for customer inquiries. Cal. Pub. Util. Code § 779.1(d) (electric, gas, heat, and water).

Colorado

4 Colo. Code Regs. §§ 723-2 r. 2303, 723-3 r. 3408, 723-4 r. 4408, 723-5 r. 5408 *(electric, gas, telephone, water)* (LexisNexis)

Utilities Covered: Electric, gas, telephone, and water.

Contact Requirements:

On-Site Personal Contact: At least 24 hours prior to discontinuance of service, a utility shall attempt to give notice of the proposed discontinuance in person or by telephone both to the customer and to any third party the customer has designated in writing to receive such notices. If the utility attempts to notify the customer in person but fails to do so, it shall leave written notice of the attempted contact and its purpose. 4 Colo. Regs. 723-3 r. 3408(f) (electric); 4 Colo. Regs. 723-4 r. 4408(f) (gas); 4 Colo. Regs. 723-5 r. 5408(f) (water).

Telephone Contact: At least 24 hours prior to discontinuance of service, a utility shall attempt to give notice of the proposed discontinuance in person or by telephone both to the customer and to any third party the customer has designated in writing to receive such notices. If the utility attempts to notify the customer in person but fails to do so, it shall leave written notice of the attempted contact and its purpose. 4 Colo. Regs. 723-2 r. 3408(f) (electric); 4 Colo. Regs. 723-4 r. 4408(f) (gas); 4 Colo. Regs. 723-5 r. 5408(f) (water).

Other Personal Notice/Contact: None specified.

Social Service Agency Contact: None specified.

Notice Requirements:

Timing and Delivery of Written Notice: 15 days' written notice of proposed termination date by first class mail or by hand-delivery. 4 Colo. Regs. § 723-3 r. 3408(a) (electric); 4 Colo. 723-4 r. 4408(a) (gas); 4 Colo. Regs. 723-5 r. 5408(a) (water). Telephone: for nonpayment of local exchange service 30 days after due date, which must be at least 15 days after billing date, or if service obtained fraudulently or without authorization, or used or suspected of being used for fraudulent purpose. 4 Colo. Regs. 723-2 r. 2303(b). When a utility knows that the service is used by customers in multi-unit dwellings or in a cluster of dwellings and is recorded on a single meter used either directly or indirectly by more than one unit, the notice period shall be 30 days. The notice may include the current bill, must be provided to each unit stating that a notice of discontinuance has been sent to the party responsible for the payment of utility bills for the unit and that the occupants of the units may avoid discontinuance by paying the next new bill in full within 30 days of its issuance and successive new bills within 30 days of issuance, and must be posted in at least one common area. 4 Colo. Regs. 723-3 r. 3408(i) (electric); 4 Colo. 723-4 r. 4408(i) (gas); 4 Colo. Regs. 723-5 r. 5408(i) (water).

Content of Written Notice: Telephone: clearly state in both English and Spanish the amount due, the date by which payment must be received or customer must enter into payment arrangement to avoid disconnection, and that basic service may not be discontinued for nonpayment for other services, such as wireless or optional services. Notice must be electronic if customer has chosen electronic billing. 4 Colo. Regs. 723-2 r. 2303(d). Electric, gas, water: Notice heading shall contain the following warning in capital letters: "THIS IS A FINAL NOTICE OF DISCONTINUANCE OF UTILITY SERVICE AND CONTAINS IMPORTANT INFORMATION ABOUT YOUR LEGAL RIGHTS AND REMEDIES. YOU MUST ACT PROMPTLY TO AVOID UTILITY SHUT OFF." The body of the notice shall state: the reason for the discontinuance of service and of the particular rule (if any) which has been violated; the amount past due for utility service, deposits, or other regulated charges, if any; the date by which an installment payment plan must be entered into or full payment must be received in order to avoid discontinuance of service; how and where the customer can pay or enter into an installment payment plan prior to the discontinuance of service; that the customer may avoid discontinuance of service by entering into an installment payment plan with the utility pursuant to rule 3404 (electric), 4404 (gas) or 5404 (water) and the utility's applicable tariff; that the customer has certain rights if the customer or a member of the customer's household is seriously ill or has a medical emergency; that the customer has the right to dispute the discontinuance directly with the utility by contacting the utility, and how to contact the utility toll-free from within the utility's service area; that the customer has the right to make an informal complaint to the External Affairs section of the Commission in writing, by telephone, or in person, along with the Commission's address and local and toll-free telephone number; that the customer has the right to file a formal complaint, in writing, with the Commission pursuant to rule 1302 and that this formal complaint process may involve a formal hearing; that, in conjunction with the filing of a formal complaint, the customer has a right to file a motion for a Commission order ordering the utility not to disconnect service pending the outcome of the formal complaint process and that the Commission may grant the motion upon such terms as it deems reasonable, including but not limited to the posting of a cash deposit or bond with the utility or timely payment of all undisputed regulated charges; that, if service is discontinued for nonpayment, the customer may be required, as a condition of restoring service, to pay reconnection and collection charges in accordance with the utility's tariff; and that qualified low-income customers may be able to obtain financial assistance to assist with the payment of the utility bill and that more detailed information on that assistance may be obtained by calling the utility toll-free. The utility shall state its toll-free telephone number. Electric: 4 Colo. Regs. 723-3 r. 3408(a), (b). Gas: 4 Colo. Regs. 723-4 r. 4408(a), (b). Water: 4 Colo. Regs. 723-5 r. 5408(a), (b). In case of breach of installment plan, must be headed "notice of broken arrangement" and must advise customer that utility may discontinue if it does not receive installment payment within 10 days after notice, or the current payment within 30 days after due date; that, if service is disconnected, utility may refuse to restore until customer pays all amounts more than 30 days past due for regulated service, plus collection and reconnection charges; and that customer has certain rights in case a household member is seriously ill. Electric: 4 Colo. Regs. 723-3 r. 3408(g). Gas: 4 Colo. Regs. 723-4 r. 4408(g); Water: 4 Colo. Regs. 723-5 r. 5408(g).

Connecticut

Conn. Agencies Regs. §§ 16-3-100, 16-3-101 *(electric, gas, sewer, telephone, water)*

Utilities Covered: Electric, gas, sewer, telephone, and water.
Contact Requirements:
On-Site Personal Contact: None specified.
Telephone Contact: Telephone: If company has actual knowledge that user is not the customer to whom bills are sent, company shall also attempt to provide notice to the user via telephone during normal business hours. Conn. Agencies Regs. § 16-3-101(C)(1). Service to any customer may not be terminated without first making good faith effort to contact the customer receiving such service stating that termination of service is imminent. A good faith effort is deemed to be an attempt at such contact either by telephone or mail at such contact in such a manner as is reasonable in light of the circumstances. Good faith effort not required when it would be in contravention of any order, ordinance, law, or regulation of the federal government, the State of Connecticut, or any political subdivision or regulatory body. Conn. Agencies Regs. § 16-3-101(C)(7).
Other Personal Notice/Contact: None specified.
Social Service Agency Contact: None specified.
Notice Requirements:
Timing and Delivery of Written Notice: Electric, gas, water, and sewer: 13 days' written notice of proposed termination date sent by first class mail to the customer and to any third-party designee and prior to compliance with section 16-3-100(i). If a person opening an account does not provide identification, the company shall furnish service and provide notice that service may be terminated after 15 days if identification is not provided. If service is not terminated within 120 days of notice, additional 13-day notice is required. If electric or gas company issues a notice but fails to terminate before issuing new bill, it shall mail an additional notice of termination at least 13 days, or at least 7 days by certified mail, prior to termination, stating the delinquent account and that the termination notice remains in effect. If electric or gas company provides multiple dates of termination, termination may not occur prior to latest date or for balances that are not delinquent. Conn. Agencies Regs. § 16-3-100(d). 13-day notice by most practicable means required to dwelling when utility has actual or constructive knowledge that the billed customer or members of customer's household are not the exclusive occupants of premises. Telephone: If company has actual knowledge that user is not the customer to whom bills are sent, company shall in addition to 13-day notice to customer attempt to provide notice to the user via telephone during normal business hours. Conn. Agencies Regs. § 16-3-101(C)(1). If payment of at least 20% of a delinquent account or payment arrangements have not been made subsequent to termination notice, service may be terminated on the scheduled expiration date or within 10 business days thereafter, but notice procedure must be repeated if utility fails to terminate service within 10 business days of the expiration date. Conn. Agencies Regs. § 16-3-101(C)(2).
Content of Written Notice: Electric, gas, water and sewer: a statement of the grounds for the proposed termination; the conditions required to prevent termination of service; the date after which service may be terminated unless the required conditions are met; the conditions for restoration of service if service is terminated, including but not limited to any reconnection fee or the possibility of the requirement of a deposit; and a brief explanation of the customer's rights under section 16-3-100(c) regarding termination of service. Conn. Agencies Regs. § 16-3-100(d)(2). Telephone: a brief explanation of the customer's rights under section 16-3-101(c) regarding termination of service, and notice of utility's right under section 16-3-101(B)(1)(d) to terminate service without notice for excessive charges incurred after receipt of termination notice. Conn. Agencies Regs. § 16-3-101(C)(1). If, after receipt of termination notice or entering into amortization agreement, the customer makes payment(s) totaling 20% of balance due, service may not be terminated before 13 days after mailing of subsequent termination notice, and subsequent notice does not entitle customer to further or additional notice upon subsequent payment of 20%. Conn. Agencies Regs. §§ 16-3-100(d)(4); 16-3-101(C)(8) (telephone). When utility has actual or constructive knowledge that billed customer or members of customer's household are not the exclusive occupants of premises, 13-day notice shall state the date of the proposed termination; the right of the tenant, if the dwelling units are individually metered, to establish service in his or her own name without liability for the balance owed or a security deposit; the intent of the company to request the establishment of a receivership or other arrangement, if there is a master meter; and the telephone number and address of the local office of the company and the telephone number and address of the DPUC. Conn. Agencies Regs. § 16-3-100(i). If service is through a master meter and the occupants agree in writing to a plan for billing and payment, then arrangement can be discontinued upon 13 days' notice by company or upon written request of any occupant, in which case the company shall provide 13-day notice to each occupant. Conn. Agencies Regs. § 16-3-100(i).

Delaware

26-2000-2001 Del. Code Regs. §§ 6.5 6.7 *(water)* (LexisNexis); 26-3000-3002 Del. Code Regs. § 3.1 *(electric, gas)* (LexisNexis); 26-4000-4003 Del. Code Regs. § 4.7 *(telephone)* (LexisNexis)

Utilities Covered: Electric, gas, telephone, and water.
Contact Requirements:
On-Site Personal Contact: Electric and gas: utility employee who

is to disconnect service shall make a reasonable good faith attempt to make personal contact at the premises to be disconnected. If personal contact is made, employee shall: identify self to the customer (or responsible person at the premises) and announce the purpose of visit; identify and record the name of the person contacted; accept payment of all amounts tendered and necessary to avoid termination, and issue receipt. If the form of payment is unacceptable to the utility, employee can make other payment arrangements with the customer; record and report to supervisor any statements disputing the cause for termination of service; record and report to supervisor statements or other information concerning the existence of any condition on the premises which would result in a medical emergency if service were terminated; receive written certification from a duly licensed Delaware physician or accredited Christian Science practitioner that a named occupant of the dwelling unit is so ill that termination of service will adversely affect the occupant's health or recovery. 26-3000-3002 Del. Code Regs. § 3.3. A utility without a third-party notice program may not terminate service during the heating or cooling season without first giving the written notice required by section 3.1, making actual contact on a face-to-face basis with an occupant over the age of 15 years and giving the minimum notice required in § 3.3. 26-3000-3002 Del. Code Regs. § 4.2.
Telephone Contact: Electric and natural gas: During the heating season, utility shall make at least two documented attempts on separate days to contact the customer by telephone prior to actual termination of service, and one such attempt must be made after 6:00 p.m. During the cooling season, utility shall make at least one documented attempt to contact the customer by telephone prior to actual termination. 26-3000-3002 Del. Code Regs. § 3.1.1.
Other Personal Notice/Contact: Electric and natural gas: During the heating season only, and where the billing address is different from the serviced location, 14 days' written notice required by § 3.1.1 must also be given to the occupant of the serviced premises. 26-3000-3002 Del. Code Regs. § 3.1.2.
Social Service Agency Contact: Electric and natural gas: not less than 14 calendar days prior to termination of service to a multiple occupancy dwelling unit, utility shall provide written notice of its intention to terminate to the PSC and to the Division of the Public Advocate. 26-3000-3002 Del. Code Regs. § 5.4.
Notice Requirements:
Timing and Delivery of Written Notice: Water: If termination for nonpayment, utility must send written notice that customer has at least 5 working days in which to make settlement or have service disconnected. 26-2000-2001 Del. Code Regs. § 6.5.4.2.1. If customer has designated a second party to be notified and second-party status is established, utility shall not terminate service without at least 5 days' oral or written notice to the second party. Id. § 6.7.1. Electric and natural gas: utility shall not terminate service during the heating or cooling season for nonpayment of a past-due bill or bills unless at least 14 days' written notice has been given to customer prior to termination. 26-3000-3002 Del. Code Regs. § 3.1. Telephone: 10 days' notice by mail or hand delivery. 26-4000-4003 Del. Code Regs. § 4.7.
Content of Written Notice: Electric and natural gas: During the heating or cooling season, notice shall state fact of impending termination, the date on or after which termination will occur, and the steps that may be taken to avoid termination. 26-3000-3002 Del. Code Regs. § 3.1.1. Telephone: Notice shall prominently display the words "suspension notice" or similar language and state the reason for the threatened suspension of service, the amounts currently due and any required deposit, whether a specific reconnection fee will be required to restore service, and that the customer should immediately contact the utility to attempt to resolve the matter (mailing address and telephone number for inquiry and payment agreements must be included). Statement attached to or on face of notice shall notify customer that they may be eligible for alternative payment programs if they need assistance with payment or are ill and unable to pay their bill and to contact the utility local office for more information. 26-4000-4003 Del. Code Regs. § 4.7.1.

District of Columbia

D.C. Muni. Regs. tit. 15, §§ 311 to 314 *(electric, gas, telephone)*

Utilities Covered: Electric, gas, telephone.
Contact Requirements:
On-Site Personal Contact: None specified.
Telephone Contact: Utility shall make at least two attempts to contact customer prior to termination. At least 2 days before scheduled date, utility shall make reasonable efforts to contact the customer by telephone to advise of the pending action and what steps must be taken to avoid termination. For gas and electric, immediately preceding the physical disconnection, utility representative designated to do so shall make reasonable effort to identify himself or herself to the customer or other responsible person on the premises and announce the purpose of his or her presence. Telephone utility must make a second attempt to contact the consumer. Termination of gas or electric may not occur if prior contact is not made and the customer or responsible person is not on the premises at time of termination, and utility employee shall leave a notice reasonably calculated to be seen by persons residing on the premises stating that service may be terminated as soon as the next business day unless outstanding bills are paid. D.C. Mun. Regs. tit. 15, § 312.
Other Personal Notice/Contact: None specified.
Social Service Agency Contact: None specified.
Notice Requirements:
Timing and Delivery of Written Notice: Written termination notice sent to the customer at the billing address by first class mail or other technological means at least 15 days before date of proposed termination and a duplicate copy sent by first class mail to designated third party requested by customer. D.C. Mun. Regs. tit. 5, § 311.3.
Content of Written Notice: The termination notice shall state the following: the customer's name and address; the address where service is to be discontinued, if different; the reason for the proposed termination of service; the earliest date that service will be terminated absent payment or adjustment; the telephone number and address of the utility, and an invitation to contact the utility to resolve the matter; the customer's right to delay termination of service for medical reasons; the possibility of deferred payments; the right to file a complaint with the Public Service Commission, and the availability of representation and assistance by the People's Counsel. D.C. Mun. Regs. tit. 5, § 311.5. When service is terminated, the utility employee shall leave a notice reasonably calculated to be seen by persons residing on the premises stating that service has been terminated and the address and telephone number

of the utility where the customer may arrange to have service restored. The notice shall also state procedures to be followed when a medical or safety emergency exists on the premises. D.C. Mun. Regs. tit. 5, § 314.2. At least 21 days prior to terminating electric or gas service to a master-metered apartment building, utility company shall send, by registered and regular mail, to each tenant whose name is made known to the utility company a Notice of Tenants' Rights and Options. The notice shall contain the following: (A) a general fact sheet giving the reason for the proposed change in billing, the owner's name, and a description of the following options available to tenants for the provision of utility service: (1) individual metering; (2) collective payment by a tenant's association; (3) individual payment based on an allocation of the total bill; and (4) the appointment of a receiver; (B) the telephone number and address of the utility, the name of the person or persons handling these matters and an invitation to contact the utility for more information; (C) the date, time, and place for a meeting between the tenants and a field representative from the utility to discuss the available alternatives; notice regarding this meeting shall be sent to the District agency which is authorized to represent citizens in utility matters; (D) the statement that the tenant has the right to deduct all future payments made by the tenant for utility services from rent owed as provided by § 3 of D.C. Law 3-94; and (E) a Preliminary Election Card, printed on a postage paid postcard, to be filled out by the tenant indicating the tenant's preference among the following options: (i) Individual metering, if practicable; (ii) collective payment by a tenants' association, if practicable; (iii) Individual payment based on an allocation of the total bill; and (iv) appointment of a receiver. The postcard shall also provide that failure to return the postcard by a stated date, which shall be not less than 10 days from the date the postcard is mailed, shall mean that the tenant does not wish to receive service in his or her own name and desires the appointment of a receiver. D.C. Mun. Regs. tit. 5, § 402.

Florida

Fla. Admin. Code Ann. r. 25-4.113 *(telephone)*, r. 25-6.105 *(electric)*, r. 25-7.089 *(gas)*, r. 25-30.320 *(water)*

Utilities Covered: Electric, gas, telephone, and water.
Contact Requirements:
On-Site Personal Contact: None specified.
Telephone Contact: No later than 24 hours before scheduled disconnection for nonpayment of customer who requires medically essential service, electric utility shall attempt to contact the customer by telephone in order to provide notice of disconnection. If the customer does not have a telephone number listed on the account or if the utility cannot reach the customer or other adult resident of the premises by the specified time, the utility shall send a representative to the residence to attempt to contact the customer no later than 4 p.m. of the day before the scheduled disconnection. If contact is not made, the utility may leave written notice at the residence advising the customer of the scheduled disconnection and the utility may disconnect service on the specified date. Fla. Stat. § 366.15.
Other Personal Notice/Contact: None specified.
Social Service Agency Contact: None specified.
Notice Requirements:
Timing and Delivery of Written Notice: For telephone, water and wastewater, 5 working days' written notice to the customer for nonpayment or noncompliance with utility rules and regulations. Fla. Admin. Code Ann. r. 25-4.113 (telephone), r. 25-30.320 (water, wastewater). For gas and electric, 5 working days' notice and a copy to a designated third party in the utility's service area. Fla. Admin. Code Ann. r. 25-6.105(5)(g) (electric), r. 25-7.089 (gas). Gas and electric notice must advise that persons dissatisfied with decision to discontinue service may register complaint with utility and with Public Service Commission and provide Public Service Commission's toll-free number.
Content of Written Notice: Gas and electric must notify customer at least 5 working days prior to termination that service will cease unless the deficiency is corrected in compliance with utility's regulations, resolved through mutual agreement, or successfully disputed by the customer. Gas, electric, and water utility notice shall also advise that persons dissatisfied with decision to discontinue service may register complaint with utility and with Public Service Commission, and provide Public Service Commission toll-free number. Fla. Admin. Code. Ann. r. 25-6.105 (electric), r. 25-7.089 (gas), r. 25-30.320 (water). Telephone and water utilities shall notify customer of reason for discontinuance. Fla. Admin. Code Ann. r. 25-4.113(2) (telephone), r. 25-30.320(4) (water).

Georgia

Ga. Comp. R. & Regs. 515-3-2.02, 515-3-3.02, 515-3-3.05, 515-3-3.09, 515-12-1.28 *(electric, gas, telephone)*

Utilities Covered: Electric, gas, and telephone.
Contact Requirements:
On-Site Personal Contact: None specified.
Telephone Contact: None specified.
Other Personal Notice/Contact: Gas, electric, and telephone utility must make good-faith effort to make personal contact at least 2 days prior to the proposed disconnection date if personal contact has not been made previously. Ga. Comp. R. & Regs. 515-3-2.02 (electric); 515-3-3.02 (A), (B), 515-3-3.09 (gas); 515-12-1.28 (telephone).
Social Service Agency Contact: None specified.
Notice Requirements:
Timing and Delivery of Written Notice: For gas local distribution company (LDC) and electric, 5 days' written notice delivered to the service address or to the address of any party who utility knows has undertaken the responsibility to pay the bill. Ga. Comp. R. & Regs. 515-3-2.02(A), 515-3-3.02. For gas marketers, gas electing distribution companies, or gas regulated providers, notice shall be 15 days. Ga. Comp. R. & Regs. 515-3-3.02 (B), 515-3-3.09. For LDC gas service to multi-family dwelling where landlord or lessor is responsible for payment for service, 5 days' written notice shall be personally served on at least one adult in each dwelling unit or posted conspicuously on premises when personal service cannot be made. Gas marketers, electing distribution companies, or other regulated providers must provide 15 days' notice. Ga. Comp. R. & Regs. 515-3-3.05(A), (B), 515-3-3.09. For telephone, unless service may be disconnected without notice, local service cannot be terminated without 5 days' written notice to customer and not

before 29 days after date of bill. Ga. Comp. R. & Regs. 515-12-1.28.
Content of Written Notice: For gas (local distribution companies), electric, and telephone, notice shall include the earliest date for the proposed disconnection; the amount due and the reason for the proposed disconnection; a telephone number to call for information about the proposed disconnection; the procedure for preventing disconnection of service, including when a medical emergency may exist; and (except for telephone) information concerning any programs known to the utility that might assist the consumer in paying the past-due bill. Ga. Comp. R. & Regs. 515-3-2.02, 515-3-3.02(A), 515-12-1.28. For gas marketers, gas electing distribution companies, or gas regulated providers, notice shall also state that qualified low-income customers may transfer to the regulated provider without termination of service and that consumer is entitled to at least one reasonable payment arrangement in writing prior to each disconnection, unless the such consumer failed to honor a previous payment arrangement. Ga. Comp. R. & Regs. 515-3-3.02 (B), 515-3-3.09.

Hawaii

Haw. Code R. §§ 6-60-8 *(electric, gas)*, 6-80-106 *(telephone)* (LexisNexis)

Utilities Covered: Electric, gas, and telephone.
Contact Requirements:
On-Site Personal Contact: None specified.
Telephone Contact: None specified.
Other Personal Notice/Contact: None specified.
Social Service Agency Contact: None specified.
Notice Requirements:
Timing and Delivery of Written Notice: For gas and electric, customer must be given reasonable written notice prior to termination of service. Prior to notice, customer must be given 15 days to pay the bill after issuance. Customer may file a complaint or dispute with the utility about the charges within the 15 days and, if so, utility must respond with exact amount due and payable, which must be paid within 7 days. If the amount is paid under protest, the protest is submitted to the Public Utilities Commission for final determination. Haw. Code R. § 6-60-8. For telephone, customer shall be given written notice of the carrier's intention to discontinue service and allowed not less than 5 days from the date of the notification to respond. If the notification is by mail, the customer has 2 additional days to respond. Haw. Code R. § 6-80-106(c).
Content of Written Notice: For gas and electric, notice shall state: reason(s) for termination; the date on or after which termination will occur; the action that the customer must take to avoid termination; and the telephone number(s) of utility representatives available to handle the subject of termination. Haw. Code R. § 6-60-8. For telephone, notice must state the reason for and date of the scheduled discontinuance and actions which the customer may take to avoid discontinuance of service. Haw. Code R. § 6-80-106(c).

Idaho

Idaho Admin. Code r. 31.21.01.300, r. 31.21.01.304, r. 31.21.01.305, r. 31.21.01.306, r. 31.21.01.308, r. 31.21.01.311, r. 31.41.01.303, r. 31.41.01.304 *(electric, gas, sewer, telephone, water)*

Utilities Covered: Electric, gas, sewer, telephone, and water.
Contact Requirements:
On-Site Personal Contact: None specified.
Telephone Contact: Gas, electric, or water: may send 3-day final written notice. At least 24 hours before the proposed date of termination, utility shall attempt to contact customer in person or by telephone and provide information required in initial written notice. Idaho Admin. Code r. 31.21.01.304, 31.41.01.303.
Other Personal Notice/Contact: Gas, electric, or water: may send 3-day final written notice. At least 24 hours before the proposed date of termination, utility shall attempt to contact customer in person or by telephone and provide information required in initial written notice. Idaho Admin. Code r. 31.21.01.304, 31.41.01.303.
Social Service Agency Contact: None specified.
Notice Requirements:
Timing and Delivery of Written Notice: Written notice to customer mailed at least 7 calendar days before the proposed date of termination. Idaho Admin. Code r. 31.21.01.304, 31.41.01.303. Gas, electric, or water utility may mail a final written notice to the customer at least 3 calendar days, excluding weekends and holidays, before the proposed date of termination. At least 24 hours before the proposed date of termination, utility shall attempt to contact customer in person or by telephone and provide information required in initial written notice. Notice requirements must be repeated if termination does not occur within 21 days of scheduled date, except no additional notice required if after receipt of notice customer violates terms of payment plan, tenders payment with a dishonored check, or makes an electronic payment from an account with insufficient funds. Idaho Admin. Code r. 31.21.01.304, r. 31.41.01.303. Written notice may be provided by electronic mail (i.e., e-mail) if the customer is billed electronically and separately consented in writing to receiving electronic notification. Idaho Admin. Code r. 31.21.01.300, r. 31.21.01.304, r. 31.41.01.303.
Content of Written Notice: Written or oral notice of intent to terminate service shall state: reason(s) for termination and proposed date of termination; actions customer may take to avoid termination; that a certificate notifying the utility of a serious illness or medical emergency in the household may delay termination per rule 31.21.01.308 (gas, electric, or water) or rule 31.41.01.306 (telephone); that an informal or formal complaint concerning termination may be filed with the utility or the Commission; that service will not be terminated pending resolution of the complaint, and the Commission's address and telephone number; that the utility is willing to make payment arrangements (in bold print on written notices); that partial payments will be applied toward utility service charges first, unless the customer requests otherwise; and that charges for non-utility services cannot be used as a basis for termination (for telephone, the amount that must be paid to avoid termination and that partial payments will be applied to past-due charges for local exchange service first). Idaho Admin. Code r. 31.21.01.305, r. 31.41.01.304. For gas and electric, during the months of November, December, January and February, oral and written notices shall include an explanation of restrictions on

termination of service and the availability of the Winter Payment Plan under Rule 306. Idaho Admin. Code r. 31.21.01.305.

Illinois

Ill. Admin. Code tit. 83, §§ 280.130, 280.135, 280.136 *(electric, gas, water)*, 735.130, 735.140 *(telephone)*

Utilities Covered: Electric, gas, telephone, and water.
Contact Requirements:
On-Site Personal Contact: Utility shall attempt to advise customer that service is being discontinued by directing the employee making the disconnection to contact the customer at the time service is being discontinued. Ill. Admin. Code tit. 83, § 280.130 (electric, gas, water, sewer). Prior to termination of service for any residential customer or master-metered apartment building between December 1 through March 31, electric and gas utilities shall also notify the customer or an adult residing at the customer's premise either by telephone, a personal visit to the customer's premise, or by First Class mail, informing the customer that: the customer's service is subject to termination for nonpayment; the customer can avoid disconnection by entering into a deferred payment agreement to pay past-due amounts over a period not to extend past the following November; the customer may enter into a levelized payment plan for the payment of future bills; and the customer may apply for any available assistance to aid in the payment of utility bills from any governmental or private agencies from a list of such agencies provided to the customer by the utility. A utility shall be required to make only one such contact with the customer during any such period from December 1 through March 31. Ill. Admin. Code tit. 83, § 280.135.
Telephone Contact: None specified.
Other Personal Notice/Contact: In addition to written notice, telephone utility shall attempt to advise the customer when service is scheduled for discontinuance. Ill. Admin. Code tit. 83, § 735.130.
Social Service Agency Contact: None specified.
Notice Requirements:
Timing and Delivery of Written Notice: Notice separately delivered or mailed to a customer at least 5 or 8 days, respectively, prior to discontinuance of service, with copy to any third-party designee. Notice remains in effect for 2 consecutive 20-day periods, provided that during each such period a call is made at the customer's premises or billing address or telephone contact with the customer is made. Ill. Admin. Code tit. 83, § 280.130 (electric, gas, water, sewer). For telephone, notice remains in effect for 20 days, and there is no third-party designee provision. Ill. Admin. Code tit. 83, § 735.130.
Content of Written Notice: A "Form of Utility Shut Off" is located at Ill. Admin. Code tit. 83, pt. 280, App. A. A form of notice to be inserted with notices of disconnection to gas and electric customers is located at Ill. Admin. Code tit. 83, pt. 280, App. D. Generally, Appendix A shows the scheduled date of discontinuance, the amount owed, the amount required to be paid to avoid discontinuance, the availability of a payment plan, the hours and telephone number of a utility representative, and the amount to be paid to restore service. Appendix D describes the terms and conditions of deferred payment plans, including between December 1 and March 31 (winter rules). For telephone, "Notices of Discontinuance and of Requirements to Avoid Shut Off in the Event of Illness" forms are located at Ill. Admin. Code. tit. 83, pt. 735, Apps. A and B, respectively.

Indiana

170 Ind. Admin. Code §§ 4-1-16, 5-1-16, 6-1-16 *(electric, gas, water)*

Utilities Covered: Electric, gas, and water.
Contact Requirements:
On-Site Personal Contact: Immediately preceding the actual disconnection of service, the utility employee designated to perform such function shall make a reasonable attempt to identify himself to the customer or any other responsible person upon the premises, announce the purpose of his presence, and make a record to be maintained for at least 30 days. The employee shall have sufficient information to inform the customer or other responsible person the reason for disconnection, including the amount of any delinquent bill of the customer, and shall request any available verification that the outstanding bill has been satisfied or is currently in dispute. Upon the presentation of such credible evidence, service shall not be disconnected. I70 Ind. Admin. Code §§ 4-1-16 (electric); 5-1-16 (gas); 6-1-16 (water).
Telephone Contact: None specified.
Other Personal Notice/Contact: None specified.
Social Service Agency Contact: None specified.
Notice Requirements:
Timing and Delivery of Written Notice: 14 days' prior written notice (7 days for water) to customer by either mailing the notice to the customer at the address shown on the records of the public utility, or personal delivery to the customer or a responsible member of customer's household at address of record. I70 Ind. Admin. Code §§ 4-1-16 (electric); 5-1-16 (gas); 6-1-16 (water).
Content of Written Notice: Notice must state: date of proposed disconnection; specific factual basis and reason for proposed disconnection; telephone number of utility office which customer may call during regular business hours in order to question the proposed disconnection or seek information concerning customer; and a reference to the prescribed pamphlet furnished to the customer for information as to customer's rights. 170 Ind. Admin. Code §§ 4-1-16 (electric); 5-1-16 (gas); 6-1-16 (water).

Iowa

Iowa Admin. Code r. 199-19.4, r. 199-20.4, r. 199-21.4, r. 199-22.4 *(gas, electric, water, telephone)*

Utilities Covered: Electric, gas, water, and telephone.
Contact Requirements:
On-Site Personal Contact: None specified.
Telephone Contact: Gas and electric utility must make diligent attempt to contact, by telephone or in person, the customer responsible for payment for service to inform the customer of the pending disconnection and the customer's rights and responsibilities. From November 1 through April 1, if the attempt at customer contact fails, the premises shall be posted at least one day prior to disconnection with a notice informing the customer of the pending disconnection and rights and responsibilities available to avoid disconnection. If an attempt at personal or telephone contact of a

customer occupying a rental unit has been unsuccessful, the landlord of the rental unit, if known, shall be contacted to determine if the customer is still in occupancy and, if so, the customer's present location. The landlord shall also be informed of the date when service may be disconnected. If the disconnection will affect occupants of residential units leased from the customer, the premises of any building known by the utility to contain residential units affected by disconnection must be posted, at least 2 days prior to disconnection, with a notice informing any occupants of the date when service will be disconnected and the reasons for the disconnection. Iowa Admin. Code r. 199-19.4(15) (gas); 199-20.4(15) (electric).
Other Personal Notice/Contact: None specified.
Social Service Agency Contact: None specified.
Notice Requirements:
Timing and Delivery of Written Notice: For nonpayment of electric, gas, or telephone bill or deposit, disconnection date shall not be less than 12 days (5 days for telephone bill and 12 days for telephone deposit) after written notice is rendered. The notice is considered rendered to the customer when addressed to the customer's last-known address and deposited in the U.S. Postal Service mail with postage prepaid. If delivery is by other than U.S. Postal Service, the notice is rendered when delivered to the last-known address of the person responsible for payment for the service. Iowa Admin. Code r. 199-19.4(15) (gas); 199-20.4(15) (electric). For nonpayment of water bill, customer must be given 12 days' written notice, excluding Sundays and holidays. Iowa Admin. Code r. 199-21.4(7)(water).
Content of Written Notice: For gas and electric, the notice shall state the reason for the notice, final date by which the account is to be settled or specific action taken, a written summary of the rights and responsibilities available (including a reasonable payment plan, low-income energy assistance, and postponement due to especial health danger), and a toll-free or collect telephone number at which a utility representative qualified to provide additional information about the disconnection can be reached. Iowa Admin. Code r. 199-19.4(15) (gas); 199-20.4(15) (electric). For water, notice shall state that customer has at least 12 days, excluding Sundays and legal holidays, in which to make settlement of the account. Iowa Admin. Code r. 199-21.4(7) (water). For telephone, notice shall state the reason for the notice, the final date by which the account is to be settled or specific action taken, that local exchange service shall not be denied for failure to pay for deregulated services, and a toll-free or collect telephone number at which a utility representative qualified to provide additional information about the disconnection can be reached. Iowa Admin. Code r. 199-22.4(3), (5).

Kansas

Standards on Discontinuance of Service Practices, Section IV (www.kcc.ks.gov/pi/billing.pdf) *(electric, gas, water)*; www.kcc.ks.gov/telecom/phonebilling.pdf) *(telephone)*

Utilities Covered: Electric, gas, water, and telephone.
Contact Requirements:
On-Site Personal Contact: None specified.
Telephone Contact: Electric, gas, or water utility should notify, or attempt to notify, customers by phone at least 2 days before they are to be disconnected. Standards on Discontinuance of Service Practices, Section IV.
Other Personal Notice/Contact: Immediately preceding disconnection, utility employee who is to disconnect service shall make a reasonable effort to: contact and identify himself or herself to the customer or responsible person upon the premises and announce the purpose of presence; identify and record the name of the person contacted; accept payment of all amounts tendered that are necessary to avert disconnection; record statements disputing the accuracy of the delinquent bill; record statements disputing the accuracy of utility's cause for discontinuance; and record statements concerning the medical condition of any permanent resident of the premises. Standards on Discontinuance of Service Practices, Section IV.
Social Service Agency Contact: None specified.
Notice Requirements:
Timing and Delivery of Written Notice: For nonpayment, 10 days' written notice (7 for telephone), separate from other utility bills, information, or advertising, shall be sent to the account name and address and, in the case of residential occupancy, to the address where service is provided, if different. Service of notice by mail is complete upon mailing. For electric, gas, and water, the notice shall be effective for 1 month after initial date upon which service can be disconnected and, if utility records show that the account serves more than one residential dwelling unit, the utility shall also post a notice in a common area of the residential building served at least 5 days prior to the discontinuance date. Standards on Discontinuance of Service Practices, Section IV.
Content of Written Notice: Notice shall contain the following information: (A) the name and address of the customer and the address, if different, where service is rendered; (B) a clear and concise statement of the reason for the proposed discontinuance of service and the cost and conditions for reconnection; (C) the dates between which service can be discontinued unless the customer takes appropriate action; (D) terms under which the customer may avoid discontinuance; (E) a statement that discontinuance may be postponed or avoided if a customer can demonstrate that special circumstances prevent complete payment and satisfactory credit arrangements are made with the utility for moneys not in dispute; and (F) the availability of a procedure which may be utilized in the event of a dispute or under other circumstances (e.g., especial danger to health and inability to pay); the address, telephone number and name of the utility office or personnel empowered to review and rectify disputed bills; the opportunity to meeting with a designated employee of the utility regarding a bill, the utility's reasons for discontinuance, requesting credit arrangements or requesting a postponement of discontinuance; and, except for telephone utility, the telephone number of the Commission's Consumer Protection Office. Standards on Discontinuance of Service Practices, Section IV.

Kentucky

807 Ky. Admin. Regs. 5.006 § 14 *(electric, gas, sewer, telephone, water)*

Utilities Covered: Electric, gas, sewer, telephone, water.
Contact Requirements:
On-Site Personal Contact: None specified.

Telephone Contact: None specified.
Other Personal Notice/Contact: None specified.
Social Service Agency Contact: None specified.
Notice Requirements:
Timing and Delivery of Written Notice: 10 days' written notice (5 days for water, sewer, and telephone), distinguishable and separate from any bill and mailed or otherwise delivered to the last known address of the customer. Notice shall plainly state the reason for termination, that the termination date will not be affected by receipt of any subsequent bill, and that the customer has the right to dispute the reasons for termination. Termination date may not be fewer than 27 days (20 days for water, sewer, and telephone) from the mailing date of the unpaid bill. 807 Ky. Admin. Regs. 5.006 § 14.
Content of Written Notice: Notice shall plainly state the reason for termination, that the termination date will not be affected by receipt of any subsequent bill, and that the customer has the right to dispute the reasons for termination. For electric and gas utility, notice shall include existence of local, state, and federal programs providing for payment of utility bills under certain conditions and include the address and telephone number of the Department for Social Insurance of the Cabinet for Health and Family Services to contact for possible assistance. 807 Ky. Admin. Regs. 5.006 § 14.

Louisiana

La. Rev. Stat. Ann. § 45:1222; La. P.S.C. General Order (Mar. 7, 2002); La. General Order 9-10-57 *(electric, gas)*

Utilities Covered: Electric and gas.
Contact Requirements:
On-Site Personal Contact: None specified.
Telephone Contact: None specified.
Other Personal Notice/Contact: None specified.
Social Service Agency Contact: None specified.
Notice Requirements:
Timing and Delivery of Written Notice: 5 days' written notice. La. P.S.C. General Order 9-10-57.
Content of Written Notice: None specified.

Maine

65-407-81 Me. Code R. §§ 9, 10, 17 *(electric, gas, water)* (LexisNexis); 65-407-290 Me. Code R. § 14 (LexisNexis); 65-407-291 Me. Code R. § 13 *(telephone)* (LexisNexis)

Utilities Covered: Electric, gas, telephone, and water.
Contact Requirements:
On-Site Personal Contact: Electric, gas, and water utility must make a reasonable effort to contact the customer personally before disconnection occurs by either contacting the customer by telephone prior to disconnection or by attempting personal contact with the customer at the time of a premise visit to disconnect. 65-407-81 Me. Code R. § 10. Electric or gas utility shall attempt to make personal contact in person or by telephone before the proposed disconnection date when disconnection notice is issued between November 1 and March 31. 65-407-81 Me. Code R. § 17.
Telephone Contact: Telephone utility must make a reasonable effort to contact the customer by telephone before disconnection occurs. 65-407-290 Me. Code R. § 14.
Other Personal Notice/Contact: None specified.
Social Service Agency Contact: None specified.
Notice Requirements:
Timing and Delivery of Written Notice: Generally, 14 days' written notice for nonpayment and not before 30 days after issuance of bill. 3 days' written notice for breach of payment arrangement, failure to provide deposit or guarantor, or dishonored check. A telephone utility can issue a disconnection notice 5 business days after the postmark of the original bill (or the date of the bill if mailed on that date) if: the customer's account balance includes toll usage exceed exceeding $500; the customer has been notified of the accelerated collection procedures; the utility makes personal contact with the customer or there is clear evidence of abandonment; and the customer has refused or failed to provide satisfactory evidence of ability to pay or enter into a payment arrangement for the account balance. Disconnection notices are effective for 10 days, after which notice must be repeated. Utility must make every reasonable effort to provide notice to third-party designee or, in the case of a tenant of premises subject to disconnection for customer nonpayment, in person to at least one adult occupant of each dwelling unit. For master-metered premises, there is a 10-day notice period, and notice must also be posted on premises and advise how service can be continued by obtaining service in tenant's name or otherwise assuming responsibility for payment. 65-407-81 Me. Code R. § 9; 65-407-290 Me. Code R. § 14.
Content of Written Notice: Written notice shall state the following: (A) the overdue amount or the exact reason for the disconnection if not for an overdue amount; (B) what must be done to avoid disconnection; (C) the disconnection date and the period for which the disconnection notice is effective; (D) a statement of the customer's right to postpone disconnection for a medical emergency of the customer or an occupant and a description of procedure for doing so; (E) statement that disconnection can be avoided by negotiating a payment arrangement with monthly or weekly installment payments and that the overdue amount must be paid in a reasonable period of time (disclosure is not required if the disconnection notice is for a broken payment arrangement); (F) a statement of the customer's right to submit a disputed matter before the disconnection date to Consumer Assistance Division, along with address and telephone numbers; (G) a statement that the customer cannot submit a dispute to the Consumer Assistance Division until the customer has first tried to resolve the dispute with the utility; (H) the title and telephone number of the appropriate utility representative and a statement that the call may be made collect from within the utility's service area, unless a toll-free number is offered or calls within the utility's service area are toll-free to the designated telephone number; (I) a statement of any reconnection charge; and (J) the utility's policy concerning requiring a deposit in the event of disconnection. 65-407-81 Me. Code R. § 9; 65-407-290 Me. Code R. § 14; 65-407-291 Me. Code R. § 13. Electric or gas utility disconnection notices issued from November 1 through March 31 shall include a prescribed written Notice of Customer Rights regarding winter disconnection rules and eligibility for payment plans. 65-407-81 Me. Code R. § 17.

Maryland

Md. Code Regs. 20.31.02, 20.31.03, 20.31.05 *(electric, gas)*, 20.45.04.06 *(telephone)*, 20.70.04.08 *(water)*

Utilities Covered: Electric, gas, telephone, and water.

Contact Requirements:

On-Site Personal Contact: Gas or electric utility may terminate service to premises covered by serious illness or life-support provisions, occupied by elderly or disabled person, or from November 1 through March 31 only after two attempts at personal contact, by telephone or in person and on different dates between mailing of notice and time of scheduled termination. If personal contact is made, the utility shall inform the customer of possible sources of financial assistance and the availability of alternate payment plans or arrangements offered by the utility. Md. Code Regs. 20.31.03.01, 20.31.03.02, 20.31.03.03.

Telephone Contact: None specified.

Other Personal Notice/Contact: None specified.

Social Service Agency Contact: None specified.

Notice Requirements:

Timing and Delivery of Written Notice: 14 days' written notice delivered in person or sent by first class mail to the name and address of the person in whose name the account is held with a copy to third-person designee. Utility shall advise customer of alternate payment plans offered by the utility and the Utility Service Protection Program offered by the utility in accordance with regulation 20.31.05. Md. Code Regs. 20.31.02.05 (electric, gas). For nonpayment, telephone and water utility shall provide 5 days' written notice, excluding Sundays and holidays, and telephone utility may terminate immediately for failure to comply with payment arrangement. Md. Code Regs. 20.45.04.06, 20.70.04.08. Tenants receiving gas or electric service in a master-metered building shall be given 14 days' notice by individual notice by first class mail, flyers, or "door stuffers" and by posting termination notices in conspicuous locations. Md. Code Regs. 20.31.03.06. Sewer service may not be discontinued for nonpayment of service charges. Md. Code Regs. 20.75.04.07(F).

Content of Written Notice: For electric and gas, notice shall include: customer's name, account number, and service address; reasons for and date of proposed termination; reconnection charges; total amount due; summary of customer's rights and remedies, including dispute procedures, utility address, and telephone numbers of utility representatives; statement that it is the customer's responsibility to notify utility of inability to pay in accordance with utility's billing practices; statement that it is the customer's responsibility to notify the utility that customer or an occupant of the premises is elderly, handicapped, has a serious illness, or relies upon life-support equipment, as well as a brief explanation of the special provisions regarding such persons; and an explanation of notification procedures. Md. Code Regs. 20.31.02.06. Utility shall advise customer of alternate payment plans offered by the utility and the Utility Service Protection Program offered by the utility in accordance with regulation 20.31.05. Md. Code Regs. 20.31.02.05 (electric, gas).

Massachusetts

220 Mass. Code Regs. § 25 *(electric, gas, water)* (LexisNexis)

Utilities Covered: Electric, gas, and water.

Contact Requirements:

On-Site Personal Contact: Upon entering any premises to shut off service to any customer, the company representative must, before shutoff, state to an occupant that service is to be shut off and present occupant with a notice of the protections afforded customers under 220 Mass Code Regs. 25.03(1) and a financial hardship form. If the occupant claims protection, shutoff shall be postponed for 72 hours in order to allow the customer time to submit documentation supporting his/her claim or to obtain telephone certification from a physician, physician assistant, nurse practitioner, governmental agency, or religious institution as provided generally in 220 Mass. Code Regs. 25.03(2). In the case of telephone certification, the company shall inform the calling party of the 7-day deadline for submission of appropriate documentation as provided in 220 CMR 25.03(2). If service is terminated to a home when none of its occupants is present, or when entry is not allowed by the occupant, the company shall leave a notice describing serious illness, infant, and winter protections and a financial hardship notice at or under the occupant's door. 220 Mass. Code Regs. § 25.03. If all of the occupants are 65 years of age or older, termination may not occur until after approval is obtained from the Department. 220 Mass. Code Regs. 25.05.

Telephone Contact: From November 15 through March 15, utility shall give heating account customers telephone or personal notice of the impending shutoff no earlier than 3 days before the shutoff. 220 Mass. Code Regs. § 25.03.

Other Personal Notice/Contact: None specified.

Social Service Agency Contact: None specified.

Notice Requirements:

Timing and Delivery of Written Notice: For nonpayment, utility must, not earlier than 27 days after the rendering of the bill (i.e. first request for payment): (A) render a second request for payment, stating its intention to terminate on a date not earlier than 48 days after the receipt of the bill in the case of gas and electric companies, and 46 1/2 days in the case of water companies; and (B) render final notice of termination at least 72 hours, but in no event more than 14 days, prior to termination in the case of gas and electric companies, and at least 36 hours prior to termination in the case of water companies. 220 Mass. Code Regs. § 25.02. Before terminating service of landlord customers paying for service to a residential building, 30 days' written notice to tenants shall be posted in a common area and mailed or otherwise delivered to the address of each affected tenant. 220 Mass. Code. Regs. 25.04.

Content of Written Notice: All second requests for payment and all termination notices referred to in 220 Mass. Code Regs. 25.00 shall be accompanied by a brief explanation of the customer's rights pursuant to 220 Mass. Code Regs. 25.00, and notices shall advise customers (and in the case of persons 65 years of age or older, third-party designees) of the availability of payment plans for payment of accumulated arrearages and/or prospective billings. Unless otherwise authorized by the Department, no notice threatening termination of service shall be issued between November 15 and March 15 to any customer who has provided the company with a notice of financial hardship in accordance with 220 Mass. Code Regs 25.00. 220 Mass. Code Regs. §§ 25.02, 25.03, 25.05. 30 days' written notice to tenants regarding termination of service of landlord paying for service to a residential building shall contain the following information: (A) the date on which the notice is rendered; (B) the date on or after which service will be terminated; (C) the circumstances under which service to the affected tenant may be continued; (D) the projected bill; (E) the statutory rights of a tenant to deduct the amount of any direct payment to the company from any rent payments then or thereafter due, to be protected against any retaliation by the landlord for exercising such statutory right, and to recover money damages from the landlord for any such retaliation; (F) a telephone number at the company and at the Department which a tenant may call for an explanation of his/her rights. 220 Mass. Code Regs. 25.04. All written communications by a company to a customer regarding bills shall include notice that service cannot be terminated for nonpayment without approval of the Department if all residents are 65 years of age or older, that payment plans are available, and that the customer has a right to a hearing at the Department of Public Utilities before termination (along with telephone numbers of the company and Department of Public Utilities). 220 Mass. Code Regs. § 25.05.

Michigan

Mich. Admin. Code r. 460.102, r. 460.138, r. 460.139, r. 460.141, r. 460.147 to r. 460.150 *(electric, gas)*; Mich. Admin. Code r. 484.382 to r. 484.384 *(telephone) (Rescinded effective June 14, 2011)*

Utilities Covered: Electric, gas, and telephone.

Contact Requirements:

On-Site Personal Contact: Employee designated to shut off service may identify himself or herself and announce purpose of visit. If customer presents evidence that reasonably indicates that the claim has been satisfied or is currently in dispute or offers payment in full together with collection charge (if provided for in tariff), then service shall not be shut off. Mich. Admin. Code r. 460.141.

Telephone Contact: At least 1 day before shutoff of service, utility shall make at least two attempts to contact the customer by telephone, if a telephone number is available to the utility, to advise the customer of the shutoff and what steps the customer must take to avoid shutoff. If utility uses an automated notification system, it shall document the process for ensuring that at least two attempts are made to notify the customer of the pending shutoff. If the telephone number is not available, the customer has no telephone, or the telephone contacts are not made, the utility shall either leave a notice at the premises advising the customer that service will be shut off on or after the next business day or send notice by first-class mail postmarked at least 5 business days before shutoff of service is scheduled. Mich. Admin. Code r. 460.141. If disconnection is to be done remotely, the notice shall conspicuously state that a utility representative will not return to the premises before disconnection. If disconnection is to be done remotely and the utility contacts the customer or other responsible person in the household by telephone on the day scheduled for shutoff, it shall inform such person that shutoff is imminent and the steps necessary to avoid it. Unless the customer makes payment or reasonably demonstrates that the claim is satisfied or in dispute, the employee may disconnect service. If the utility mailed the above-described 5-day notice, and either telephone contact with the customer cannot be made or the customer did not respond to the notice, then no further customer contact is required on the day scheduled for disconnection, and the utility may disconnect service. Mich. Admin. Code r. 460.142.

Other Personal Notice/Contact: None specified.

Social Service Agency Contact: None specified.

Notice Requirements:

Timing and Delivery of Written Notice: 10 days' notice to the customer by first-class mail (to the account name and address and to the address where service is provided if the service address is different and the notice can be delivered at that address) or personal service, with a copy to third-party designee. Mich. Admin. Code r. 460.138. 5 days' notice by mail or personal service for telephone service. Mich. Admin. Code r. 484.384 (rescinded effective June 14, 2011).

Content of Written Notice: Shutoff notice shall contain the following: (A) name and address of the customer, and the address at which service is provided, if different; (B) clear statement of reason for proposed shutoff; (C) date on or after which the utility may shut off service, unless the customer takes appropriate action; (D) that customer has the right to enter into a settlement agreement with the utility if the amount is undisputed and the customer is unable to pay in full; (E) that the customer may file a complaint disputing the claim before the proposed shutoff date; (F) that the customer may request a hearing before a hearing officer if the customer disputes the reasonableness of the settlement agreement offered by the utility or if the complaint cannot be otherwise resolved and that the customer must pay to the utility that portion of the bill that is not in dispute within 10 business days of the date that the customer requests a hearing; (G) that the customer has the right to represent himself or herself, to be represented by counsel, or to be assisted by other persons of his or her choice in the complaint process; (H) that service will not be shut off pending the resolution of a complaint that is filed with the utility or the commission; (I) the telephone number and address of the utility where the customer may make inquiry, enter into a settlement agreement, or file a complaint; (J) that the customer should contact a social services agency immediately if the customer believes he or she might be eligible for an energy assistance program or other emergency economic assistance and should inform the utility of any efforts being made to obtain payment assistance; (K) that customers who may be eligible for an energy assistance program should determine if assistance is available before signing a settlement agreement because many agencies will not provide assistance if shutoff is avoided by signing a settlement agreement; (L) that the utility will postpone shutoff if a certified medical emergency exists at the customer's residence or the customer is an eligible low-income customer who is actively seeking emergency assistance from an energy assistance program; (M) that the utility may require a deposit and restoration charge if the utility shuts off service for nonpayment; and (N) that the customer should contact the utility for information about a shutoff protection program. Mich. Admin. Code r. 460.139. *See also* Mich. Admin. Code r. 484.383 (telephone) (rescinded effective June 14, 2011).

Minnesota

Minn. R. 7810.2300, R. 7810.2600 *(telephone)*, R. 7820.1400, R. 7820.2400, R. 7820.2500, R. 7820.2900 *(gas, electric)*, Minn. Stat. § 216B.096 *(cold weather rule for public utilities)*. *Cf.* Minn. Stat. §§ 216B.097 *(similar cold weather rule for cooperative or municipal utilities)*, 216B.0975 *(heat conditions)*, 216B.098(5) *(medical emergencies)*

Utilities Covered: Electric, gas, and telephone.
Contact Requirements:
On-Site Personal Contact: Service may be disconnected only in conjunction with a personal visit by a utility representative to the address where the service is rendered and an attempt to make personal contact with the customer at the address. Minn. R. 7820.2500 (electric, gas). During cold weather period (October 15 through April 15), electric or gas utility may not discontinue service until it investigates whether the dwelling is actually occupied, and the investigation must include one visit during normal working hours. If no contact is made and there is reason to believe that the dwelling is occupied, the utility must attempt a second contact during non-business hours. If personal contact is made, the utility representative must provide notice under this statute, and, if the utility representative is not authorized to enter into a payment agreement, the telephone number the customer can call to establish a payment agreement. Minn. Stat. Ann. § 216B.096 (cold weather rule for public utilities). *Cf.* Minn. Stat. Ann. § 216B.097 (similar cold weather rule for cooperative or municipal utilities).
Telephone Contact: None specified.
Other Personal Notice/Contact: None specified.
Social Service Agency Contact: None specified.
Notice Requirements:
Timing and Delivery of Written Notice: 5 days' written notice (excluding Sundays and holidays) by delivery or by first class mail to the service address or to the address where the bill is sent if different. If by delivery, utility must obtain receipt signed by customer, if present, or member of the customer's family of responsible age, or the utility representative must make a sworn affidavit that he or she delivered the notice to the customer or the customer's residence. Minn. R. 7820.2400 (gas, electric); Minn. R. 7810.2300 (telephone). If gas or electric service disconnection is scheduled during cold weather period from October 15 through April 15, then 10 days' written notice by mail or 7 days' notice if by personal service. Minn. Stat. Ann. § 216B.096 (cold weather rule for public utility). *Cf.* Minn. Stat. Ann. § 216B.097 (similar cold weather rule for cooperative or municipal utilities).
Content of Written Notice: Disconnection notice shall contain the date on or after which disconnection will occur, reason for disconnection, and methods of avoiding disconnection in normal, easy-to-understand language. Minn. R. 7820.2400 (electric and gas); Minn. R. 7810.2300 (telephone). Each year, between September 1 and October 15, electric and gas utility must provide all customers, personally or by first class mail, a summary of rights and responsibilities under cold weather rule. The summary must also be provided to all new residential customers when service is initiated. Minn. Stat. Ann. § 216B.096 (cold weather rule for public utility). *Cf.* Minn. Stat. Ann. § 216B.097 (similar cold weather rule for cooperative or municipal utilities).

Mississippi

26-000-002 Miss. Code R. § 8 *(electric, gas, sewer, telephone, water)* (LexisNexis)

Utilities Covered: Electric, gas, sewer, telephone, and water.
Contact Requirements:
On-Site Personal Contact: None specified.
Telephone Contact: None specified.
Other Personal Notice/Contact: None specified.
Social Service Agency Contact: None specified.
Notice Requirements:
Timing and Delivery of Written Notice: For nonpayment, 5 days written notice to the customer, and notice is considered to be given to the customer when a copy is left with customer, left at the premises where service is provided, or mailed using U.S. Postal Service, addressed to customer's last known address. Rule 8.
Content of Written Notice: Notice must contain delinquency and date on or after which discontinuance may occur.

Missouri

Mo. Code Regs. Ann. tit. 4, §§ 240-13.050, 240-13.055 *(electric, gas, water)*, 240-33.070 *(telephone)*

Utilities Covered: Electric, gas, telephone, and water.
Contact Requirements:
On-Site Personal Contact: Immediately preceding discontinuance of service, the utility employee designated to perform this function shall (unless the employee's safety is endangered) make a reasonable effort to contact and identify himself/herself to the customer or a responsible person on the premises and announce the purpose of his/her presence. Mo. Code Regs. Ann. tit. 4, § 240-13.050 (electric, gas, water). Between November 1 and March 31, at the time of discontinuance, an electric or gas utility shall make a personal contact on the premises with an elderly or disabled customer registered under the cold weather rule or some member of the family above the age of 15 years. Mo. Code Regs. Ann. tit. 4, § 240-13.055.
Telephone Contact: None specified.
Other Personal Notice/Contact: At least 24 hours before disconnection (96 hours if gas or electric disconnection is scheduled between November 1 and March 31), a utility shall make reasonable efforts to contact the customer to advise him/her of the proposed discontinuance and what steps must be taken to avoid it. Reasonable efforts shall include either a written notice following the 10-day notice pursuant to section 240-13.050(4), a door hanger or at least two telephone call attempts (one attempt for telephone utility) reasonably calculated to reach the customer. Mo. Code Regs. Ann. tit. 4, §§ 240-13.050 (electric, gas, water); 240-13.055 (cold weather rule for gas and electric); 240-33.070 (telephone, but no cold weather rule).
Social Service Agency Contact: None specified.
Notice Requirements:
Timing and Delivery of Written Notice: 10 days' written notice by first class mail or personal delivery to customer at least 96 hours prior to discontinuance. Service by mail is complete upon mailing, and utility shall maintain an accurate record of the date of mailing or delivery. Mo. Code Regs. Ann. tit. 4, §§ 240-13.050 (electric, gas, water); 240-33.070 (telephone). Between November 1 and

March 31, in the case of an elderly or disabled customer registered under cold weather rule, notice shall also be given to the additional party listed on the customer's registration form, and the utility's initial contact with the registered individual shall include two or more telephone call attempts along with the mailing of the notice, Mo. Code Regs. Ann. tit. 4, § 240-13.055 (gas, electric).

Content of Written Notice: Notice of discontinuance shall include the following: the name and address of the customer and the address, if different, where service is rendered; the reason for the proposed discontinuance and the cost for reconnection; the date on or after which service will be discontinued unless appropriate action is taken; how a customer may avoid the discontinuance; the possibility of a settlement agreement if the claim is for a charge not in dispute and the customer is unable to pay the full amount at one time; a toll-free telephone number and the address of the utility where the customer may make an inquiry. Upon customer request, telecommunications company may provide information contained in the written notice of discontinuance in electronic format. Mo. Code Regs. Ann. tit. 4, §§ 240-13.050 (electric, gas, water); 240-33.070 (telephone). Except for telephone, notices shall be: conspicuously posted in public areas of buildings known to the utility to be single-metered multi-dwelling-unit buildings; given to occupant(s) of multi-dwelling-unit building where each unit is individually metered or to occupant of single-family residence if the utility is aware that a single customer is responsible for payment for service to all units in the building or that the occupant of the residence is not the customer. In the case of an individually metered multi-dwelling unit building or of a single-family residence, the notice provided to the occupant of the unit the service to which is about to be discontinued shall outline the procedure by which the occupant may apply in his/her name for the same metered service. Mo. Code Regs. Ann. tit. 4, § 240-13.050(6). Between November 1 and March 31, notices and contacts required under cold weather rule must describe terms for service under rule, including the method of calculating the required payments, the availability of financial assistance from the Division of Family Services, and the identity of social service or charitable organizations that have notified the utility that they provide that assistance. Mo. Code Regs. Ann. tit. 4, § 240-13.055.

Montana

Mont. Admin. R. 38.5.1405, R. 38.5.1406, R. 38.5.1410, R. 38.5.1411, R. 38.5.1413 *(electric, gas)*, 38.5.2505 *(privately owned water utility)*, 38.5.3339 *(telephone)*

Utilities Covered: Electric, gas, telephone, and water (privately owned utility).

Contact Requirements:

On-Site Personal Contact: Prior to termination, utility must make diligent attempt to contact the customer, either in person or by telephone. If telephone or personal contact is not made, the utility employee shall leave notice in a conspicuous place that service will be terminated on the next business day unless the delinquent charges have been paid. Actual termination may not take place until 1 day after personal or telephone notice or, in the alternative, 1 business day after notice has been posted in a place conspicuous to the customer when the customer was not contacted personally or by phone. If contact is made, the employee shall present the occupant with a statement of charges. Upon presentation of evidence which reasonably indicates that the charge has been paid or is subject to a dispute previously registered with the utility or the Commission, or upon payment in full of all delinquent charges, service shall not be terminated. Mont. Admin. R. 38.5.1405, 38.5.1413 (electric, gas). For telephone, on the business day prior to disconnection, carrier representative must make a reasonable effort to contact and notify the customer of the information in the written notice, and carrier must keep a record showing the name of employee, date, and hour of attempted contact and whether the customer was orally notified of disconnection. Mont. Admin. R. 38.5.3339 (telephone).

Telephone Contact: None specified.

Other Personal Notice/Contact: Telephone carriers must establish system of third-party notification of nonpayment and provide service upon customer request and free of charge. Mont. Admin. R. 38.5.3339.

Social Service Agency Contact: None specified.

Notice Requirements:

Timing and Delivery of Written Notice: If no response to first notice is received within 10 days of mailing, utility must send a second notice by first class or certified mail (return receipt requested). The second notice must be mailed to or personally served on the customer at least 10 days prior to proposed termination date. For privately owned water utility, if no response to the second notice is received within 10 days of mailing or service, the utility shall conspicuously post notice that service will be terminated on the next business day unless the delinquent charges have been paid. Mont. Admin. R. 38.5.1405 (gas, electric); 38.5.2505 (privately owned water utility). Landlord customers must be given 30 days' initial notice. Service may be terminated upon serving written notice 5 business days prior to the proposed termination date when a customer remits an insufficient funds check as payment to the utility after receiving the first notice of termination or when customer breaches a payment agreement. Mont. Admin. R. 38.5.1405 (gas, electric). For telephone, 7 days' written notice, and notice may be excused when service is to be terminated for excessive toll usage and an identifiable risk of nonpayment exists. However, carrier shall not terminate service under the provisions of this rule without first contacting or making a diligent effort to contact the customer to (A) notify the customer of the excessive toll usage; (B) notify the customer of the possibility that service can be terminated on an expedited basis; and (C) provide opportunity to supply adequate assurance of payment. Diligent effort shall consist of not less than three distinct attempts at contact either in person or by telephone, and carrier must keep a record showing the name of the employee, date, hour, and type of each attempted contact. If no contact is made, carrier may terminate service 3 days (not including days when there is no mail delivery) after the mailing of notice in the form otherwise required under rule. If contact is made and no adequate assurance is supplied, carrier may terminate service not less than 24 hours after such contact. Mont. Admin. R. 38.5.3339 (telephone).

Content of Written Notice: For gas and electric, notice must contain: (A) utility's termination policy; (B) identification of affected customer and service account; (C) reason(s) for termination; (D) date of proposed termination; (E) amount of any reconnection fee; (F) summary of rights and remedies, including procedures to dispute the termination notice, provisions relating to elderly and disabled consumers and those suffering a medical emergency, and provisions for customers unable to pay, including steps to claim inability to pay, availability of installment payment arrangements, and sources of financial assistance; (G) designation of the bill in question as actual or estimated; (H) except for notice to tenants, amount owed and time period over which amount was incurred; (I) instructions on how service can be restored; (J) in the case of a landlord customer, the date on or after which the utility will notify tenants of the proposed termination; in the case of notification of tenants: (i) the amount of an average monthly bill for utility service to the premises and the largest bill for utility service to the premises in the previous 12 months; (ii) a statement that Commission procedures and the Laws of Montana may give tenant certain rights with respect to which the tenant may wish to consult an attorney or Montana Legal Services. Mont. Admin. R. 38.5.1406 (gas, electric). For telephone, notice must contain: reason for disconnection; corrective and appeal action that customer may take; and any cost of reconnection, deposit, or other costs associated with reconnection. Mont. Admin. R. 38.5.3339 (telephone).

Nebraska

Neb. Rev. Stat. §§ 70-1603 to 1612 *(electric, gas, water)*; 291 Neb. Admin. Code §§ 5-002.17B, 10-006.01F *(telephone)*, 9-011 *(gas)*

Utilities Covered: Electric, gas, telephone, and water.
Contact Requirements:
On-Site Personal Contact: None specified.
Telephone Contact: None specified.
Other Personal Notice/Contact: Each utility subject to section 70-1603 or 70-1605 (village-owned and -operated, public, or private electric, gas, or water utility) shall establish a third-party notice procedure for notifying a designated third party of any proposed discontinuance and shall advise its subscribers, including new subscribers, of the availability of such procedures. Neb. Rev. Stat. § 70-1607; 291 Neb. Admin. Code § 9-011.01 (gas).
Social Service Agency Contact: None specified.
Notice Requirements:
Timing and Delivery of Written Notice: A village-owned and -operated electric, gas, or water utility must provide at least 7 days' written notice. Prior to discontinuance, subscriber, upon request, shall be provided a conference with the board of trustees of the village. Neb. Rev. Stat. §§ 70-1603, 70-1604. Public or private utility must give at least 7 days' notice (excluding holidays and weekends) by conspicuously marked first class mail or in person. Neb. Rev. Stat. § 70-1605. Subscriber to public or private utility may request a conference over a proposed discontinuance before an employee designated by the utility to hear and decide such matters, and disconnection may not occur until the conference is completed. Conference must be held within 14 days of request. Employee shall allow termination of utility service only as a measure of last resort after the utility has exhausted all other less drastic remedies. If subscriber fails to attend without legitimate reason, utility may proceed with discontinuance. Subscriber may appeal adverse decision to utility office or board designated by utility. Neb. Rev. Stat. §§ 70-1608 to 70-1612. In lieu of second utility appeal, gas regulations provide for filing complaint with Commission. Neb. Admin. Code § 9-011.02 (gas).
Content of Written Notice: Public or private electric, gas, or water utility notice must contain: (A) the reason for the proposed disconnection; (B) statement of intention to disconnect unless subscriber either pays the bill or reaches a payment agreement; (C) the date when service will be disconnected if appropriate action is not taken; (D) name, address, and telephone number of utility employee or department to whom subscriber may inquire or complain; (E) subscriber's right, prior to the disconnection date, to request a conference regarding any dispute over proposed disconnection, and a statement that the utility may not disconnect service pending the conclusion of the conference; (F) statement that disconnection may be postponed or prevented upon presentation of a duly licensed physician's certificate stating that disconnection would cause subscriber or resident with an existing illness or disability to suffer an immediate and serious health hazard, that such certificate shall be filed with the utility within 5 days of receiving termination notice, that the certification will prevent disconnection for 30 days from such filing, and that only one postponement is allowed for each incidence of nonpayment; (G) cost to subscriber for restoring service; (H) availability of installment payment plan; and (I) statement that welfare recipients may qualify for assistance in payment and that they should contact their caseworker. Neb. Rev. Stat. § 70-1606; 291 Neb. Admin. Code § 9-011.01 (gas). Gas utility may not disconnect from November 1 to March 31 without adding an additional 30 days for payment of bill before disconnecting that service, and it shall also notify customer within 7-day notice period that the residential customer has additional 30 days until disconnection. 291 Neb. Admin. Code § 9-011.05.

Nevada

Nev. Admin. Code §§ 704.360, 704.365, 704.370, 704.375, 704.390 *(electric, gas)*, 704.393 to 704.3934, 704.3936 *(water)*, 704.4165, 704.417, 704.4185, 704.4205 *(telephone)*

Utilities Covered: Electric, gas, telephone, and water.
Contact Requirements:
On-Site Personal Contact: None specified.
Telephone Contact: None specified.
Other Personal Notice/Contact: Absent extraordinary circumstances, telephone utility which receives notice that termination would be especially dangerous to the health of the customer or other permanent resident shall make a reasonable effort to give additional notice by telephone or in person at least 48 hours before the scheduled time of the termination to the customer or other adult resident. Nev. Admin. Code § 704.417.
Social Service Agency Contact: None specified.
Notice Requirements:
Timing and Delivery of Written Notice: For gas and electric, 10 days' written notice with copy to third-party designee of elder or disabled customer, and 48 hours notice for failure to comply with payment plan. Nev. Admin. Code §§ 704.360, 704.365. For water, 10 days' notice to customer. Nev. Admin. Code § 704.393. For telephone, 5 days' written notice with a copy to guarantor and/or third-party designee. Nev. Admin. Code § 704.4165. If electric, gas, or water utility receives no response to the initial 10-day notice, it shall provide a second notice by a method which ensures that notice is delivered to the customer or the customer's premises at least 48 hours before termination, but gas and electric utility

must contact an adult resident where elderly or disabled person resides by phone or in person at least 48 hours prior to termination and by notifying governmental agencies or other organizations that have notified the utility that they will assist customers in making payment. Initial 10-day notice must be served by personal service, first-class mail to customer's last known mailing address or, if requested by an electric or gas customer and within the capability of the utility, by electronic notice sent via the Internet to the most recent electronic address provided to the utility by the customer. Service of initial notice is deemed complete on date of personal service, mailing, or transmission via Internet. Nev. Admin. Code §§ 704.360, 704.390, 704.393. Except for elderly or disabled customers, subject to notice requirements of section 704.390, a second notice issued by electric or gas utility may be communicated in person, by first class mail, Internet, telephone (if the person receiving the communication is 18 years of age or older and is a resident at the address where service is being provided), or by posting notice on the door if no one is present. If an electric or gas utility intends to change the method it normally uses to communicate a second notice, it shall send a written notice to its customers specifying the new method and the date on which it will begin using that method. Nev. Admin. Code §§ 704.360, 704.365, 704.390 (gas, electric). If a utility intends to terminate service after a customer has obtained a postponement due to danger to health under sections 704.370 (gas, electric); 704.3936 (water); or 704.4185 (telephone), it shall also give written notice to the Division, guarantors or third-party designees if required to do so, and electric, gas, and water utility shall also provide notice to governmental agencies or other organizations which have notified the utility that they will assist customers in paying utility bills. Nev. Admin. Code §§ 704.370, 704.390, 704.3936, 704.4185.
Content of Written Notice: For gas and electric, the 10-day initial notice and any second notice must contain the following information: (A) identification of the affected account; (B) date on or after which the intended termination will occur; (C) address where service will be terminated; (D) reason for termination, including, if for nonpayment, a statement designating the bill as one for actual or estimated use and specifying the total amount owed, the period over which that amount was incurred, and the minimum payment required to avoid termination; (E) procedures that are available to dispute or appeal from the intended termination, specifying the address and telephone number of the utility's office that is responsible for handling complaints or inquiries; (F) a statement that the utility will promptly investigate any complaint or dispute and give the customer its written decision on the matter; (G) a statement that, if the customer wishes to dispute any fact or interpretation of a regulation relied upon by the utility in its decision to terminate service, the customer must communicate with the Division, and with the Division's mailing address, telephone number, and toll-free telephone number; (H) a statement that service will not be terminated before a resolution of the dispute if the customer pays the questioned portion of the bill at the time the dispute arises and pays all subsequent bills; (I) an explanation of any payment arrangements which the utility offers; (J) a list of the names, addresses, and telephone numbers of at least two governmental agencies or other organizations that have notified the utility that they will assist customers in paying their utility bills; (K) an explanation of the postponement available upon receipt of medical certification that termination would be especially dangerous to health of customer or permanent resident; (L) a statement that a customer should notify the utility immediately if any member of the customer's household requires the continuing use of electric or gas appliances to maintain that member's essential health; and (M) an explanation of the utility's fee schedule and procedures for reconnecting service. If a customer or other adult resident of household communicates orally with the utility concerning an initial or second notice, the utility shall explain to the customer or other adult resident each of the foregoing items of information. Nev. Admin. Code § 704.360. The notice requirements for water and telephone utilities are substantially similar. Nev. Admin. Code § 704.393 (water); Nev. Admin. Code §§ 704.4165, 704.417, 704.4205 (telephone).

New Hampshire

N.H. Code Admin. R. Ann. PUC 412.15 to 412.18, 452.01, 452.08 to 452.09 *(telephone)*, 703.03 *(sewer)*, 1203.11 to 1203.12, 1203.14, 1203.16 *(electric, gas, steam, water)*, 1204.3, 1204.5 *(electric, gas, steam)*

Utilities Covered: Electric, gas, sewer, steam, telephone, water.
Contact Requirements:
On-Site Personal Contact: If utility employee or agent visits the premises to disconnect, that employee shall notify an adult occupant or, if no adult is at the premises, leave a note as to how the customer may be reconnected. If the customer tenders payment in full, the employee shall either accept payment, give a receipt, and leave the service connected; or, without disconnecting, direct the customer to go immediately to the utility's nearest office and tender payment there. N.H. Code Admin. R. Ann. PUC 412.17 (telephone); 1203.11 (electric, gas, steam & water).
Telephone Contact: Before disconnecting, telephone utility shall attempt to notify an adult occupant by telephone. N.H. Code Admin. R. Ann. PUC 412.17.
Other Personal Notice/Contact: During winter period (November 15 through March 31), utility shall also provide notice to an adult occupant in person or by telephone at least 2 business days but no more than 8 business days prior to proposed disconnection date. If utility is unable to so notify an adult occupant, it shall first seek commission approval pursuant to rule 201.05 before disconnecting service. N.H. Code Admin. R. Ann. PUC 1204.05. (electric, gas, steam).
Social Service Agency Contact: None specified.
Notice Requirements:
Timing and Delivery of Written Notice: 14 days' written notice, and telephone utility notice may not be mailed fewer than 30 days from the bill date. N.H. Code Admin. R. Ann. PUC 412.17 (telephone); 1203.11 (electric, gas, steam, water). For telephone, notice may be delivered electronically to telephone customers who have elected to receive bills and notices electronically. N.H. Code Admin. R. Ann. PUC 452.01 (telephone). For toll service, no less than 5 nor more than 14 days' verbal or written notice. N.H. Code Admin. R. Ann. PUC 452.08 (telephone).
Content of Written Notice: Written notice shall include: customer name, mailing address, and account number; scheduled disconnection date; reason for disconnection and the overdue amount; possible consequences of disconnection, such as deposit requirement, reconnection fee, and/or any other similar consequences; address and telephone number at which the customer may contact the

utility; toll-free telephone number of the commission's consumer affairs division; and method by which customer may question or contest the disconnection notice, preceded in conspicuous type by the words 'Important Notice—Your Rights'; and, except for telephone, notice of right to postponement upon certification of medical emergency. N.H. Code Admin. R. Ann. PUC 1203.11 (electric, gas, steam, water); 412.17 (telephone). If telephone utility notice includes overdue charges for non-regulated services such as telephone directory advertising, telephone equipment, or Internet connectivity charges, the notice shall also separately list the amount due for regulated services and state that service cannot be disconnected for nonpayment of such services. N.H. Code Admin. R. Ann. PUC 412.17 (telephone).

New Jersey

N.J. Admin. Code §§ 14:3-3A.1 to 14:3-3A.9 *(all public utilities)*

Utilities Covered: All public utilities.
Contact Requirements:
On-Site Personal Contact: After the end of the notice period but before discontinuance of service, the electric or gas utility representative shall personally notify an adult occupant or leave a sealed note, in the event that no adult is on the premises, which includes information as to how service may be reconnected. If a customer offers payment of the full amount or a reasonable portion of the amount due at the time of discontinuance, a utility representative shall accept payment without discontinuance of service. N.J. Admin. Code § 14:3-3A.2.
Telephone Contact: Except for utilities that make good faith efforts to contact all customers by telephone prior to discontinuance and have filed a procedure for doing so with the Board, utility shall make good faith efforts to determine which customers are over 65 years of age and shall make good faith efforts to notify such customers of discontinuance of service by telephone in addition to notice by regular mail. N.J. Admin. Code §§ 14:3-3A.4.
Other Personal Notice/Contact: None specified.
Social Service Agency Contact: None specified.
Notice Requirements:
Timing and Delivery of Written Notice: 10 days' written notice mailed to customer and third-party designee not sooner than 15 days from the postmark of the outstanding bill. The 10 days begin on the postmark date of the notice. The notice shall be sent by first class mail, apart from the bill and as a separate mailing, unless the utility receives an exemption from the Board. Upon previous request of the customer, a utility shall send a Spanish-language version of the notice. During the heating season (November 15 through March 15), electric or gas utility notice shall be accompanied by a Winter Termination Program fact sheet printed in both English and Spanish. No additional notice is required when a customer pays the bill by check after receiving notice of discontinuance and the check is subsequently dishonored. If service is being discontinued both for nonpayment and for nonpayment at a different location or nonpayment of a deposit, then the utility may provide notice under N.J. Admin. Code § 14:3-3A.1, which provides that the utility shall provide reasonable notice to the customer, to the extent reasonably possible. N.J. Admin. Code §§ 14:3-3A.3, 14:3-3A.4, 14:3-3A.7.1. A telephone utility may terminate basic residential local service only when charges for such service exceed $30, and notice of discontinuance must inform customer of ability to make a partial payment and the method of allocating partial payments. N.J. Admin. Code § 14:3-3A.8.
Content of Written Notice: Notice of discontinuance shall include: (A) statement that the utility is subject to the jurisdiction of the New Jersey Board of Public Utilities, including the Boards' address and local and toll-free telephone numbers; (B) statement that customer should contact utility if the customer is either unable to make payment or wishes to contest a bill, including information sufficient for the customer to make appropriate inquiry; and (C) statement that customer may contact the utility to discuss the possibility of entering into deferred payment agreement if unable to pay outstanding bill. If customer receives more than one service from the same utility, the statement shall state that deferred payment agreements are available separately for each service. Notices of discontinuance to electric and gas customers shall also include the following: (A) statement that the customer may dispute a charge in accordance with N.J. Admin. Code § 14:3-7.6, may contact the Board of Public Utilities to request assistance in the resolution of a bona fide disputed charge, and may request a formal hearing; (B) statement that, if within 5 days of disputing the charges, a request is made to the Board of Public Utilities for an investigation of the disputed charge, the customer's service shall not be discontinued for nonpayment of bills, provided all undisputed charges are paid; and (C) statement that a customer may have counsel, or a third party of the customer's choosing, present when appearing before a utility to contest a bona fide disputed charge. Electric and gas utility notices must conform to specific format, font, size, and location requirements. During the heating season (November 15 through March 15), electric or gas notices of discontinuance shall be accompanied by a Winter Termination Program fact sheet, printed in both English and Spanish, and setting forth all terms and conditions of the Winter Termination Program. Water utilities providing service to customers with fire protection service or multi-use service must also provide 30 days' notice to the customer, the Board, and enumerated individuals. N.J. Admin. Code §§ 14:3-3A.3, 14:3-3A.4.

New Mexico

N.M. Code R. §§ 17.5.410.31 *(electric, gas),* 17.11.16.19, 17.11.16.20 *(telephone),* 17.12.760 [Rules 9, 21] *(water),* 17.13.960 [Rules 9, 21] *(sewer)* (Lexis/Nexis)

Utilities Covered: Electric, gas, sewer, telephone, and water.
Contact Requirements:
On-Site Personal Contact: None specified.
Telephone Contact: None specified.
Other Personal Notice/Contact: Each utility shall take reasonable steps to communicate with customer by telephone or personal contact at least 2 days prior to the actual date of discontinuance to remind the customer of the pending date, advise the customer of the availability of financial assistance for utility service payments, and obtain payment of delinquent accounts. The utility employee who personally contacts a residential customer and the utility employee sent to discontinue utility services shall note any information made known to the employee by the residential customer regarding any resident's serious illness or life-endangering health condition, such as whether a resident is physically disabled, frail,

or elderly. Such information shall immediately be reported in writing to a utility employee authorized to prevent discontinuance. That employee shall either delay the discontinuance if it is apparent that the medical and financial certification forms required by this section to obtain a postponement based upon medical emergency will be received or shall state in writing why discontinuance of service will not be delayed. The utility employee sent to discontinue utility service shall be empowered to receive payment of delinquent bills and, upon receipt of payment, to cancel the discontinuance order. N.M. Code R. §§ 17.5.410.31 (gas, electric); 17.11.16.19 (telephone); 17.12.760 [Rule 9] (water); 17.13.960 [Rule 9] (sewer).

Social Service Agency Contact: None specified.

Notice Requirements:

Timing and Delivery of Written Notice: 15 days' written notice in English and Spanish (7 days for failure to comply with electric, gas, water, or sewer utility payment plan), and delivered in person or by U.S. Postal Service mail, postage prepaid, addressed to the last address for the customer known to the utility. For gas, electric, water, and sewer customers who participate in third-party notification program, utility may not discontinue for nonpayment without first contacting the designated person, organization, or governmental agency by phone or in writing at least 15 days prior to the proposed discontinuance date and determining that the designated person, organization, or governmental agency has not made a commitment to assist with payment of the customer's past-due charge within a reasonable period of time. Telephone shall not discontinue service without providing the 15-day notice and the 2-day notice to third-party designee, but it may discontinue after the 2-day notice for failure to comply with payment plan. N.M. Code R. §§ 17.5.410.31 (gas, electric); 17.11.16.19 (telephone); 17.12.760 [Rules 9, 21] (water); 17.13.960 [Rules 9, 21] (sewer).

Content of Written Notice: 15-day notice shall contain: (A) title, address, telephone number, and working hours of utility personnel responsible for administering termination procedures; (B) amount owed and the specific date service shall be discontinued unless the customer pays the amount due or makes other payment arrangements. Upon request, utility shall provide customer information concerning the outstanding charges, including the dates of service during which they were incurred and the date and amount of the last payment; (C) statement that utility will review disputed portion of the bill if customer pays undisputed portion of the bill; (D) statement that a customer may file complaint with the Commission if customer disagrees with the utility's determination concerning discontinuance of service; (E) statement that: (a) service will not be discontinued to residence where a seriously or chronically ill person resides or will reestablish service to such a residence if, at least 2 days prior to the proposed discontinuance date: (i) the utility receives a signed medical certification stating that discontinuance might endanger the customer's life or health; (ii) the utility receives a signed financial certification demonstrating inability to pay or eligibility for financial assistance; and (iii) the customer enters into a written settlement agreement or deferred payment plan with the utility; (b) if service has been discontinued, the utility shall reestablish service within 12 hours after the customer has satisfied the requirements of postponement for medical reasons; (c) the residential customer will not be relieved of the obligation to pay for services rendered if utility service is continued or reestablished under the provisions of this paragraph; and (d) timely delivery to the utility of duly executed medical certification and financial certification forms shall be adequate to delay discontinuance of service for at least 30 days and that the utility may, in its discretion, delay the discontinuance for a longer period; (F) blank copies of the medical certification and financial certification forms prescribed by the Commission, or substantially similar forms; (G) statement in capital letters of the cost of reconnection; and (H) a prescribed statement in capital letters regarding the availability of low-income assistance in paying utility bill. N.M. Code R. §§ 17.5.410.31 (gas, electric); 17.11.16.19 (telephone); 17.12.760 [Rule 9] (water); 17.13.960 [Rule 9] (sewer).

New York

N.Y. Comp. Codes R. & Regs. tit. 16, §§ 11.4 to 11.8, 11.32 *(electric, gas, steam)*, 14.4 to 14.8 *(water)*, 609.4 to 609.6 *(telephone)*

Utilities Covered: Electric, gas, steam, telephone, and water.

Contact Requirements:

On-Site Personal Contact: If a customer offers payment of the full amount at the time of termination or disconnection, the utility representative must accept such payment and shall not terminate or disconnect service. If such payment is made, the representative shall provide a receipt showing the date, account, name, address, and amount received. N.Y. Comp. Codes R. & Regs. tit. 16, §§ 11.4 (electric, gas, steam); 14.4 (water). At time of termination, disconnection, or suspension of heat-related utility service during the cold weather period (from November 1 through April 15), utility shall attempt to contact, in person, the customer or other adult resident to determine whether a resident is likely to suffer a serious impairment to health or safety as a result. The utility's representative shall explain the reasons for termination, disconnection, or suspension and provide customers with information on the protections available for medical emergencies, the elderly, blind, or disabled, and during periods of cold weather. If language barrier prevents communication, the utility shall take steps to ensure communication before termination, disconnection, or suspension. N.Y. Comp. Codes R. & Regs. tit. 16, § 11.5 (electric, gas, steam).

Telephone Contact: After issuing termination notice and before termination date, telephone utility shall attempt at least once to notify customer by telephone call during non-working hours of intended termination and how it may be avoided. N.Y. Comp. Codes R. & Regs. tit. 16, § 609.4. When customer is known to be or identified to telephone utility as being blind, disabled, or 62 years of age or older, and all the remaining residents of the household are 62 years of age or older, 18 years of age or under, blind or disabled, then utility shall not terminate service for an additional 20 days after the noticed termination date and shall make a diligent effort to contact by telephone, or in person if telephone contact is unsuccessful, an adult resident at the customer's premises at least 8 days prior to termination date for the purpose of devising a payment plan. N.Y. Comp. Codes R. & Regs. tit. 16, § 609.5.

Other Personal Notice/Contact: During the cold weather period (from November 1 through April 15), utility shall attempt to contact, by telephone or in person, customer receiving heat-related utility service or an adult resident of the customer's premises at least 72 hours before the intended termination, disconnection, or suspension (and, if unsuccessful, at the time of termination) in order to determine whether a resident is likely to suffer a serious impairment to health or safety as a result. Utility shall attempt telephone contact once during normal business hours and, if unsuccessful, during reasonable non-business hours (6 p.m.–9 p.m. on weekdays or 9 a.m.–5 p.m. on Saturdays and Sundays); and, if both telephone contacts are unsuccessful or the customer does not have a telephone, by an onsite personal visit. During such contacts, the utility's representatives shall explain the reasons for termination, disconnection, or suspension and provide customers with information on the protections available under this Part. If language barrier prevents communication, the utility shall take steps to ensure communication before termination, disconnection, or suspension. N.Y. Comp. Codes R. & Regs. tit. 16, §§ 11.5 (electric, gas, steam); 14.5 (water). No utility shall terminate, disconnect, or suspend or refuse to restore service when a customer is known to be or identified to the utility as being blind, disabled, or 62 years of age or older, and all the remaining residents of the household are 62 years of age or older, 18 years of age or under, or blind or disabled, without making a diligent effort to contact by telephone, or in person if telephone contact is unsuccessful, an adult resident at the customer's premises at least 72 hours prior to termination, disconnection, or suspension of service in order to devise a plan that would preclude termination, disconnection, or suspension and arrange for payment of bills. If utility terminates, disconnects, or suspends service and is subsequently notified that customer would be entitled to the protections for elderly, blind, or disabled, the utility shall within 24 hours of such notification make a diligent effort to contact by telephone or in person an adult resident at the customer's premises in order to devise a plan that would restore service and arrange for payment of bills. If service to elderly, blind, or disabled is terminated, disconnected, or suspended, utility shall within 10 days make a diligent effort to contact, by telephone or in person, an adult resident at the customer's premises to determine whether alternative arrangements for service have been made and, if none have been made, attempt to devise a plan that would restore service and arrange for payment of bills. N.Y. Comp. Codes R. & Regs. tit. 16, §§ 11.5 (electric, gas, steam); 14.5 (water).

Social Service Agency Contact: During the period from November 1 through April 15, no utility shall terminate, disconnect, or suspend heat-related service for nonpayment when the utility determines that a resident is likely to suffer a serious impairment to human health or safety as a result unless the utility complies with cold weather period notice provision, notifies the local social services commissioner orally and within 5 days in writing that a resident is likely to suffer such an impairment, and the local social services commissioner informs the utility that the reported condition is not likely to result in a serious impairment to health or safety or that an alternative means for protecting the person's health or safety has been devised. If a utility terminates, disconnects, or suspends service during the cold weather period, and the customer or a resident 18 years or older was not personally contacted by the utility within previous 72 hours and the customer has not contacted the utility to request reconnection before 12 noon on the following day, the utility shall immediately attempt to determine, by onsite inspection, direct personal contact at the premises with the customer or other adult resident, or other reasonable measures whether there is continuing occupancy and whether a serious impairment to health or safety is likely to result. If the utility determines that a serious impairment would result, it shall immediately restore service. If the utility is unable to obtain personal contact with the customer or an adult resident and does not have reasonable grounds to believe that the customer has vacated the premises, it shall immediately refer the name and address of the customer to the local commissioner of social services. N.Y. Comp. Codes R. & Regs. tit. 16, §§ 11.5 (electric, gas, steam); 14.5 (water). During the cold weather period, electric, gas, or steam utility shall refer to social services a customer who is unable because of mental or physical problems to manage his or her own resources or to protect himself or herself from neglect or hazardous situations without the assistance of others and shall continue service for at least 15 days from date of referral unless notified by the social services office that acceptable payment or other arrangements have been made. If (A) a customer is known to be or identified to the utility as being blind, disabled, or 62 years of age or older, (B) all the remaining residents of the household are 62 years of age or older, 18 years of age or under, or blind or disabled, and (C) either attempts at personal contact are unsuccessful or the utility and customer are unable to devise a plan that would preclude termination, disconnection, or suspension and arrange for payment of bills, the utility shall notify the local department of social services of the customer's name and address and the date of termination, disconnection, or suspension in order that social services may help to develop such a plan. The utility shall continue service for not less than 15 business days from the time it makes the referral, unless notified by social services that acceptable payment or other arrangements have been made. N.Y. Comp. Codes R. & Regs. tit. 16, §§ 11.5 (electric, gas, steam); 14.5 (water).

Notice Requirements:

Timing and Delivery of Written Notice: For electric, gas, and steam utility, 15 days' notice (issued not earlier than 20 days from due date) personally served on customer or mailed to customer at premises served and to any third-party designee. Water utility service by mail must provide 18 days' notice. Telephone utility may not issue notice earlier than 25 days from date of bill and must provide 20 days' notice in person or by mail to premises unless customer has provided an alternative address. If electric, gas, or steam customer has provided an alternative mailing address, then notice must be (A) mailed to the premises and to the alternative address, or (B) mailed to alternate address and either personally served on adult resident of premises, explained by telephone to adult resident of premises, or posted at premises. If water customer has provided an alternative mailing address, then utility must first mail 18-day notice to alternate address and then mail 10-day notice to premises. No additional notice is required when payment by check is dishonored. If electric, gas, or steam utility knows customer is receiving public assistance, SSI, or additional State payments pursuant to the Social Services Law, and utility has not received a guarantee of future payment, utility shall notify an appropriate official of the local social services district not more than 5 days nor less than 3 days before the intended termination or disconnection that payment has not been made. Such notice shall state that the customer has been sent a final notice of termination or disconnection, specify the amount of arrears, and state the earliest date on which termination or disconnection may occur. If such notice is made orally, the utility shall send written notification within 1 business day. If the utility has received a guarantee, it shall send a notice of nonpayment to customer and to local social services commissioner at the time the account would otherwise be subject to a final notice of termination or disconnection (15 days) stating that payment has not been made and the amount of the arrears. Water utility may not terminate service for nonpayment to any person known to be receiving public assistance, if payment for service is made directly to the utility by the department of social services or local social services official. N.Y. Comp. Codes R. & Regs. tit. 16, §§ 11.4, 11.6 (electric, gas, steam); 14.4, 14.6 (water); 609.4, 609.6 (telephone).

Content of Written Notice: Notice must include: (A) earliest date on which disconnection may occur; (B) reasons for disconnection, including the total amount required to be paid, and how disconnection may be avoided; (C) address and phone number of the utility office that the customer may contact; (D) availability of procedures for handling complaints; (E) a summary of the protections available under this Part, together with a notice that any customer eligible for such protections should contact the utility; and (F) statement that it is a final termination notice which should be brought to utility's attention when paid. Water utility notice shall also include: statement that payment by check which is subsequently dishonored may result in termination without additional notice; statement that utility representative at time of termination may require payment by cash, certified check, or money order if customer had check dishonored within previous 12 months; any reconnection charge; and possibility of assistance for social services if customer is a recipient of public assistance. The final notice of termination from an ESCO (a seller of gas or electricity to be distributed via a utility's distribution system) shall inform customer that suspension of the customer's distribution service can accompany the ESCO's commodity termination, even if the customer's account for distribution service is current, and shall state the amounts which must be paid to (A) restore commodity supply; and (B) if different, to end suspension of distribution service. N.Y. Comp. Codes R. & Regs. tit. 16, §§ 11.4 (electric, gas, steam); 14.4 (water); 609.4 (telephone). Notice to residents of two-family dwellings (15 calendar days if mailed, served or posted, except 18 calendar days if mailed by water utility, and 30 days if during cold weather period) shall also state that there are special protections for occupants of two-family dwellings where service is not metered separately, that the commission staff may be contacted for information and advice, and that subdivision (1) of section 235-a of the Real Property Law authorizes occupants to set off against their rents payments to utilities in such circumstances. N.Y. Comp. Codes R. & Regs. tit. 16, §§ 11.8 (electric, gas, steam); 14.8 (water). Similar provisions apply to residents of multiple dwellings (N.Y. Comp. Codes R. & Regs. tit. 16, §§ 11.7, 14.7) and to occupants of premises receiving electric, gas, or steam service through a shared-meter account (N.Y. Comp. Codes R. & Regs. tit. 16, § 11.32).

North Carolina

4 N.C. Admin. Code 11.R7-20 *(water)*, 11.R10-16 *(sewer)*, 11.R12-08, 11.R12-17 *(telephone)*, 11.R12-10 *(gas)*, 11.R12-11, *(electric)*

Utilities Covered: Electric, gas, sewer, telephone, water.

Contact Requirements:

On-Site Personal Contact: Immediately prior to termination of gas or electric service, utility's representative shall attempt to personally contact the customer on the premises. The representative shall either: receive payment from the customer or postpone termination for another 24 hours if the customer is prepared to pay but the utility has determined that its representatives should not be required to accept payments from customers on the premises; make satisfactory credit arrangements; agree to postpone termination during the period November 1 to March 31 if the customer qualifies for postponement under this rule; or, in the absence of any of the arrangements or circumstances listed above, terminate service. If no personal contact is made, a notice indicating that service has been terminated shall be left in a conspicuous location and shall specify that the customer may have immediate recourse to the utility in order to arrange for reconnection of service. 4 N.C. Admin. Code 11.R12-10 (gas); 11.R12-11 (electric).

Telephone Contact: At least 24 hours prior to termination, gas and electric utility shall make good faith attempt to contact a customer and any third party designee either by telephone or by visit to the premises in order to personally inform the customer and any designee that termination is imminent and to explain alternatives that may be available under this rule. 4 N.C. Admin. Code 11.R12-10 (gas); 11.R12-11 (electric).

Other Personal Notice/Contact: None specified.

Social Service Agency Contact: None specified.

Notice Requirements:

Timing and Delivery of Written Notice: Gas and electric service shall not be terminated for nonpayment until utility has given customer and any third-party designee at least 10 days' written notice. 4 N.C. Admin. Code 11.R12-10 (gas); 11.R.12-11 (electric). Water and sewer service may be discontinued only after 5 days' written notice, excluding Sundays and holidays. In the event of a dispute between the customer and the utility regarding any bill, the utility shall make an investigation and report the result to the customer. If the parties cannot resolve the dispute, either party may submit the fact to the Commission for its opinion and, pending such opinion, service shall not be discontinued. 4 N.C. Admin. Code 11.R7-20 (water); 11.R10-16 (sewer). Telephone utility may discontinue service or impose toll denial after 5 calendar days' written notice given by first-class mail, delivery to the premises, or by other legal means of service of process, and the 5-day period runs from the day following deposit in the mail, the day of delivery to the premises, or the day of other legal service. 4 N.C. Admin. Code 11.R12-08.

Content of Written Notice: 10-day notice of termination of gas and electric service shall include: (A) explanation of reasons for proposed termination; (B) date of the proposed termination; (C) statement that service will not be terminated if, before termination date, the customer is able to establish inability to pay account in full and agrees to payment plan to bring the account into balance within six months; (D) statements that customer should first contact the utility regarding bill and that, in cases of dispute, how a proposed termination action may be appealed informally to the Commission; and (E) statement that customer may desire to call local social service agency to determine what federal, state, or private assistance may be available. For bills rendered between November 1 and March 31, the notice shall also state that no termination shall take place without the Commission's approval if the customer can establish all of the following: (A) a member of the customer's household is either certifiably handicapped or elderly (65 years of age or older) or both; (B) the customer establishes inability to pay; and (C) the household is certified by the local social service office that administers the Energy Crisis Assistance

Program or other similar programs as being eligible (whether funds are then available or not) to receive assistance under such programs. 4 N.C. Admin. Code 11.R12-10 (gas); 11.R12-11 (electric). Electric customers with good credit established may be issued disconnect notices 14 days after billing date of third unpaid bill, but customers within first 12 months of service or who have not established good credit may be issued disconnect notices 14 days after billing date of the second unpaid bill. 4 N.C. Admin. Code 11.R12-11 (electric). For local carriers, (A) disconnect notices must state the minimum amount that must be paid to maintain local service and the minimum amount that must be paid in order to maintain both local and toll service, (B) disconnect notices for customers subject to global toll denial shall describe toll blocking that will be imposed if toll charges are not paid, offer the option of maintaining choice of available local service options, and identify what local service will be provided if the customer does not express a preference; and (C) disconnect notices for carriers that offer local service on an unbundled basis shall explain option of maintaining local service by paying the regulated past-due balance owed for local service only and shall specify the amount due to maintain local service. For carriers that offer only bundled local service, disconnect notices shall state the minimum amount that must be paid in order to maintain the bundled local service and shall state that basic local service is available from at least one other provider. 4 N.C. Admin. Code 11.R12-17.

North Dakota

N.D. Admin. Code §§ 69-09-01-18.1 *(gas)*, 69-09-02-05.1 *(electric)*, 69-09-05-02 *(telephone)*

Utilities Covered: Electric, gas, telephone.
Contact Requirements:
On-Site Personal Contact: The utility representative directed to make the disconnection shall be deemed authorized and shall accept payment of the delinquent account if tendered by the customer before actual disconnection of service is made. N.D. Admin. Code §§ 69-09-01-18.1 (gas); 69-09-02-05.1 (electric).
Telephone Contact: None specified.
Other Personal Notice/Contact: None specified.
Social Service Agency Contact: None specified.
Notice Requirements:
Timing and Delivery of Written Notice: 10 days' notice by first-class mail addressed to the customer at the place where service is rendered, except that personal notice by delivery is required for customers 65 years of age or older or for disabled customers. A copy must be mailed to the nearest social service office and to any other appropriate financial assistance agency, providing that prior approval has been given by the customer to do so. If customer enters into payment plan, service may be terminated without further notice if the customer fails to pay the delinquent account on or before the date specified in the notice or in accordance with the payment plan. N.D. Admin. Code §§ 69-09-01-18.1 (gas); 69-09-02-05.1 (electric). Telephone utility notice requirement is substantially similar, except it contains no personal or third-party notice requirement for elderly or disabled. N.D. Admin. Code § 69-09-05-02 (telephone). If delinquent gas or electric customer has tenants with the cost of utility services included in the rent, the utility must also give tenants 10 days' written notice and allow each tenant to apply to become the customer in his or her own name, to have service continued or resumed, and to pay the pro rata share of future bills. N.D. Admin. Code §§ 69-09-01-18.1 (gas); 69-09-02-05.1 (electric).
Content of Written Notice: Notice must: show the amount of the delinquency; include the commission's telephone number; identify rights and remedies, including the right to stay termination for up to 30 days if the utility is advised within the notice period that dangerous health conditions exist or that the customer is 65 years of age or older or disabled; advise customer of the right to work out a payment plan for delinquent accounts and of the opportunity to enter into equal monthly payment plans for future service; state that service will be discontinued if the delinquent account is not paid within 10 calendar days from the date of mailing or personal delivery of the notice or if a payment plan is not made. N.D. Admin. Code §§ 69-09-01-18.1 (gas); 69-09-02-05.1 (electric). Telephone utility notice requirement is substantially similar, except it contains no provision for postponement for dangerous health condition, elderly, or disabled. N.D. Admin. Code § 69-09-05-02 (telephone).

Ohio

Ohio Admin. Code 4901:1-6-12 *(telephone)*, 4901:1-15-27 *(water, sewer)*, 4901:1-18-04, 4901:1-18-06, 4901:1-18-08, 4901:1-18-10 *(gas, electric)*

Utilities Covered: Electric, gas, sewer, telephone, and water.
Contact Requirements:
On-Site Personal Contact: On the day of disconnection, gas and electric utility shall provide customer with personal notice, and if the customer is not at home, to an adult consumer. If neither the customer nor an adult consumer is at home, written notice shall be conspicuously posted prior to disconnecting service. Employees or agents who disconnect service shall be authorized to complete one of the following: (A) accept payment in lieu of disconnection; (B) dispatch an employee to the premises to accept payment; (C) make available to the customer another means to avoid disconnection. Ohio Admin. Code 4901:1-18-06 (gas, electric); 4901:1-15-27(water, sewer).
Telephone Contact: None specified.
Other Personal Notice/Contact: Upon request of a property owner, utility shall provide least 3 days' advance notice when service to property owner's property is to be disconnected either at the request of a residential customer who is a tenant or for nonpayment. Ohio Admin. Code 4901:1-18-06 (gas, electric).
Social Service Agency Contact: Between November 15 and April 15, if customer resides in a county in which the department of job and family services has provided utility with a written request for prior notification of disconnection, then the utility shall provide the appropriate county department of job and family services with a list of customers whose service will be disconnected for nonpayment at least 24 hours before the action is taken. Ohio Admin. Code 4901:1-18-06 (gas, electric).
Notice Requirements:
Timing and Delivery of Written Notice: 14 days' notice to customer and third party or guarantor. Ohio Admin. Code 4901:1-18-06 (gas, electric); 4901:1-15-27 (water, sewer). If a landlord is responsible for payment of water or sewer bill, 10 days' notice shall

be given to the consumer or, in a multi-unit dwelling, posted in a conspicuous place. Ohio Admin. Code 4901:1-15-27 (water, sewer). Telephone utility must provide written notice postmarked at least 7 days prior to the date of disconnection (which may not be earlier than 14 days after account becomes past due). Ohio Admin. Code 4901:1-6-12 (telephone). When individuals have gas or electric services included in rental payments or are tenants in a master-metered, multi-unit dwelling, utility shall give 14 days' notice to the landlord/agent, and, if customer has not paid or made payment arrangement at end of notice period, utility shall then make a good faith effort by mail or otherwise to provide a separate 10-day notice to the landlord/agent, to each tenant receiving master-metered service, and to single occupancy dwellings where utilities are included in the rent. In a multi-unit dwelling, written notice shall also be placed in a conspicuous place. Ohio Admin. Code 4901:1-18-08 (gas and electric). During the period from November 1 through April 15, if payment or payment arrangements are not made before disconnection date stated on the 14-day notice, then gas and electric company shall not disconnect service and shall contact the customer or other adult resident at the premises 10 days prior to disconnection by personal contact, telephone, or hand-delivered notice. Notice may be mailed, but such notice must allow 3 calendar days for mailing. This additional notice extends the disconnection date stated on the 14-day notice by 10 additional days. Additional notice must inform customer or adult consumer that sources of federal, state, and local government aid for payment of bills and weatherization are available and provide sufficient information to enable customer to pursue available assistance. The additional notice must also inform customer of right to enter into payments plans under rule 4901:1-18-05 or to enroll in PIPP (percentage of income payment plan). If the customer does not respond to the additional 10-day notice, refuses to accept a payment plan, or fails to make initial payment under plan, then utility may disconnect service after 10-day notice expires. Ohio Admin. Code 4901:1-18-06.
Content of Written Notice: Notice shall include: (A) the delinquent billing account number, the total amount required to prevent disconnection, and any security deposit owed at the time of the notice; (B) earliest date that disconnection may occur; (C) local or toll-free number and address of the utility office to contact about account; (D) toll-free telephone numbers and websites of the Commission and the Ohio Consumers' Counsel to contact for complaint or inquiry; (E) statement that failure to pay the amount required by the date specified in the notice may result in a security deposit and reconnection charge, and the amount of the deposit and reconnection charge. Ohio Admin. Code 4901:1-18-05 (gas, electric); 4901:1-15-27 (water, sewer). Gas and electric utility notice must also include: (F) if applicable, statement that failure to pay charges for non-tariffed and/or non-regulated products or services may result in the loss of those products and/or services; (G) explanation of the payment plans and options available for delinquent accounts as provided in this rule and rule 4901:1-18-05 (payment plans), rule 4901:1-18-12 (PIPP plans) and, when applicable, rule 4901:1-18-9 (disconnection by combination utility providing more than one service); (H) a statement that a medical certification program and forms are available from the company; and (I) statement that a listing of the company's authorized payment agents is available by calling the company's toll-free customer service number. Ohio Admin. Code 4901:1-18-06 (gas, electric). 10-day notice to tenant receiving master-metered gas or electric service or to single-occupancy dwelling where such utilities are included in the rent shall include a summary of the remedies tenants to prevent disconnection or to have service reconnected and a statement that a list of procedures and forms to prevent disconnection is available upon request. Ohio Admin. Code 4901:1-18-08 (gas, electric) (model form of the tenants' 10-day notice is attached as appendix A to this rule). Telephone utility notice shall include: the total dollar amount that must be paid to maintain basic local exchange service; the earliest date that disconnection may occur; toll-free number and website of PUC for complaints that cannot be resolved after contacting utility or for general utility information; and toll-free number and website for contacting Ohio Consumers' Counsel for assistance with complaints and utility issues. Ohio Admin. Code 4901:1-6-12.

Oklahoma

Okla. Admin. Code §§ 165:35-21-10 to 165:35-21-11, 165:35-21-20, 165:35-21-30 *(electric)*, 165:45-11-13 to 165:45-11-14, 165:45-11-16 to 165:4511-17 *(gas)*, 165:55-11-10, 165:55-11-12 *(telephone)*, 165:65-11-13, 165:65-11-15 *(water)*

Utilities Covered: Electric, gas, telephone, and water.
Contact Requirements:
On-Site Personal Contact: Utility employee responsible for disconnection may receive payment of past-due bills, accept a copy of the customer's payment assistance application, or accept a copy of a cancelled check or a utility receipt showing payment and cancel the disconnection. If disconnection occurs, utility employee shall leave a written statement that service has been disconnected, the reason for the disconnection, and the telephone number and address at which the customer may arrange to have service reconnected. Okla. Admin. Code §§ 165:35-21-21 (electric); 165:45-11-17 (gas).
Telephone Contact: None specified.
Other Personal Notice/Contact: None specified.
Social Service Agency Contact: None specified.
Notice Requirements:
Timing and Delivery of Written Notice: First notice shall provide 10 days' written notice from the date of mailing by first-class mail to billing address and any third-party designee. If returned as undeliverable, notice may be delivered to the premises served. For electric, if notice is for nonpayment of deposit required as a condition of service, the 10-day notice is not required (section 165:35-21-30(4)). Notice is deemed delivered 3 business days after mailing. If a master-metered apartment complex, building, or trailer court is subject to disconnection, the written notice shall also be posted in a common area at least 10 days prior to disconnection. Okla. Admin. Code §§ 165:35-21-20 (electric); 165:45-11-16 (gas); 165:65-11-13 (water). From November 15 through April 15, electric and gas utility shall give a second notice 48 hours (at least 2 business days) prior to disconnection that service will be disconnected unless customer enters into payment plan or unless disconnection would create a life-threatening situation for the consumer or other permanent resident of the premises. The second notice may be in writing, in person, or by telephone but made be made orally only if 10-day written notice requirement has been satisfied. Okla. Admin. Code §§ 165:35-21-20 (electric); 165:45-11-16 (gas). When telephone service is to be disconnected for

nonpayment of a bill after service has been suspended or for failure to make a security deposit, the service provider shall give at least 10 days' notice by: (A) mail or delivery to the end-user's billing address; (B) Internet to the email address provided by the end-user; or (C) telephone to the end-user's assigned telephone number or other number provided by the end-user. Notice of disconnection shall be by mail unless the end-user agreed to receive bills through different means. Mailed notice will be deemed given to the end-user 3 business days after mailing. If mailed notice is returned as undeliverable, notice may be delivered to the premises served. If email notice is returned as undeliverable, notice may be given by mail or delivery. If email notice is not returned, notice shall be deemed given on the date the email was sent. If telephone notice is not confirmed to have reached the end-user's telephone number, notice may be given by mail, delivery, or email. If telephone notice is confirmed, notice shall be deemed given on the date the telephonic notice is confirmed. Okla. Admin. Code §§ 165:55-11-10, 165:55-11-12 (telephone).
Content of Written Notice: 10-day notice shall contain: (A) the words "DISCONNECTION NOTICE" or "CUT OFF NOTICE" in bold print no smaller than one-half inch (1/2") tall; (B) name and address of the consumer; (C) reason for proposed disconnection; (D) date on or after which service will be disconnected unless appropriate action is taken; (E) utility telephone number in bold print at which customer may inquire; (F) approved charges for reconnection; (G) statement that consumer must contact utility regarding the disconnection prior to contacting the Commission's Consumer Services Division; (H) address and telephone number of the Commission's Consumer Services Division, in smaller print size than the print size used for the utility's telephone number; (I) statement regarding availability of payment plan; (J) statement regarding the elderly consumer and/or consumer with disabilities notification; (K) statement regarding the life-threatening certificate; (L) statement regarding availability of 20-day financial aid assistance delay; (M) statement regarding availability of a list of agencies providing assistance for utility bills. Okla. Admin. Code §§ 165:35-21-20 (electric); 165:45-11-16 (gas); 165:65-11-13 (water). Notice requirements for telephone service are substantially similar, and there is no reference to payment plans, elderly/disabled notification, life threatening certificate, or 20-day financial assistance delay. Okla. Admin. Code § 165:55-11-12 (telephone). From November 15 through April 15, electric and gas utility must give a second, 48-hour notice which shall include: (A) reason for disconnection and the amount of the unpaid bills; (B) date on or after which service will be disconnected unless the consumer takes appropriate action; (C) telephone number of utility office at which consumer can ask for assistance, make inquiries, enter into a payment plan, obtain information on utility assistance programs, pay the bill or notify the utility of a life-threatening situation; and (D) telephone number of the Commission's Consumer Services Division. Okla. Admin. Code §§ 165:35-21-20 (electric); 165:45-11-16 (gas).

Oregon

Or. Admin. R. 860-021-0405, 860-021-0410, 860-021-0415 *(gas, electric)*, 860-036-0245 *(water)*, 860-037-0245 *(joint water/wastewater)*, 860-034-0260, 860-034-0270, 860-034-0275 *(small telephone utility)*, 860-021-0505, 860-021-0510, 860-021-0550 *(large telephone utility)*

Utilities Covered: Electric, gas, telephone (small and large), and water/wastewater.
Contact Requirements:
On-Site Personal Contact: On day of connection, utility must make a good faith effort to personally contact the customer or an adult at the residence or, when the service address has remote disconnection capability installed, at least 3 business days prior to disconnection date. If contact is made, either in person or via the telephone, the energy utility must advise the customer or an adult at premises of the proposed disconnection. If contact is not made, utility must leave a notice in a conspicuous place that service has been, or is about to be, disconnected. If contact is not made when remote disconnect capability is installed, contact must be attempted (except from November 1 through April 30) by telephone at least twice a day for the 3 consecutive days prior to the proposed disconnection, and at least one call must be placed during the morning or afternoon (8:00 am to 5:00 pm) and another call placed during early evening (6:00 pm to 8:00 pm). When an answering machine or service is available, the utility must leave a message at the end of each day informing the customer of the proposed disconnection. When utility representative has an in-person or telephone conversation with the customer or an adult at the residence under this rule, and the circumstances indicate that the customer or an adult at the residence does not understand the consequences of disconnection, the utility must: (A) notify the Department of Human Services and the Commission; and (B) delay disconnection for 5 additional business days. A utility representative making personal contact is empowered to accept reasonable partial payment of the overdue balance under the time-payment provisions of Or. Admin. R. 860-021-0415. Or. Admin. R. 860-021-0405 (gas, electric). Regulations for water and joint water/wastewater utilities are substantially similar, except they do not include contact provisions when remote disconnection capability exists. Or. Admin. R. 860-036-0245 (water); 860-037-0245 (joint water/wastewater). For telephone, if a premises visit is required to complete disconnection, utility must make a good faith effort to personally contact the customer or a resident at the premises and, if attempt fails, utility must leave a notice in a conspicuous place informing customer that service has been disconnected. Or. Admin. R. 860-021-0505 (large telecommunications utility); 860-034-0260 (small telecommunications utility).
Telephone Contact: If notice is made by delivery to residence, then utility must attempt personal contact and, if person contact cannot be made with customer or adult resident, notice must be left in a conspicuous place. Or. Admin. R. 860-021-0405 (gas, electric); 860-036-0245 (water); 860-037-0245 (joint water/wastewater).
Other Personal Notice/Contact: None specified.
Social Service Agency Contact: None specified.
Notice Requirements:
Timing and Delivery of Written Notice: 15-day written notice (5 days for telephone) in person or sent by first-class mail to the customer's last known address and any third-party designee. Service is complete on the date of personal delivery or on the day after the date of the U.S. Postal Service postmark or postage metering. Gas and electric utility must provide second written notice in same manner at least 5 business days before disconnection. Or. Admin. R. 860-021-0405 (gas, electric); 860-021-0505 (large telecommunications utility); 860-034-0260 (small telecommunications util-

ity). Water and joint water/wastewater utility must provide 5 days' written notice, unless disconnection is for failure to comply with payment plan, which requires 15 days' written notice followed by 5 days' written notice. Or. Admin. R. 860-036-0245 (water); 860-037-0245 (joint water/wastewater). When gas, electric, water, or joint water/wastewater utility's records show a billing address different from the service address, the utility must provide a duplicate of the 5-day disconnect notice to the occupants and in the same manner, unless the utility has reason to believe that the service address is occupied by the customer. When such utility's records show that a residence is a master-metered multi-family dwelling (including rooming houses), the utility must notify the Commission's Consumer Services Division at least 5 business days before disconnection and must use reasonable efforts to notify occupants of the pending disconnection and available alternatives. Or. Admin. R. 860-021-0326 (gas, electric); 860-036-0230 (water); 860-037-0230 (joint water/wastewater). As alternative to disconnection, telephone utility may temporarily curtail service by preventing incoming calls and/or outgoing toll calls while permitting outgoing local calls. Temporary curtailment of service is permitted only after 5 days' written notice, which shall include statement that permanent disconnection will follow within 10 days unless the customer makes full payment of any overdue amount. Or. Admin. R. 860-021-0505 (large telecommunications utility); 860-034-0260 (small telecommunications utility).

Content of Written Notice: 15-day notice for nonpayment (not including failure to pay a deposit or to comply with deposit payment plan) shall be printed in boldface type and shall include: (A) reason for the proposed disconnection; (B) earliest date for disconnection; (C) explanation of the Commission's complaint process and toll-free number; (D) amount to be paid to avoid disconnection; (E) explanation of the time payment agreement provisions of Or. Admin. R. 860-021-0415; (F) explanation of the medical certificate provisions of Or. Admin. R. 860-021-0410; and (G) name and telephone number of Department of Human Services unit or other agencies that may be able to provide financial assistance. Or. Admin. R. 860-021-0405 (gas, electric). Regulation for 5-day notice for telephone utility is substantially similar, except there is no requirement to include statements regarding payment agreement provisions or agencies able to provide financial assistance. Or. Admin. R. 860-021-0505 (large telecommunications utility); 860-034-0260 (small telecommunications utility). Regulations for water and joint water/wastewater utility notice are substantially similar except that there is no requirement to include statements regarding medical certificate provisions or agencies able to provide financial assistance. Or. Admin. R. 860-036-0245 (water); 860-037-0245 (joint water/wastewater).

Pennsylvania

52 Pa. Code §§ 56.2, 56.72, 56.91 to 56.118, 56.131 *(electric, gas, steam heat, water, wastewater)*, 59.24 *(gas)*, 61.23 *(steam heat)*, 64.71 to 64.74, 64.101 to 64.109, 64.111, 64.121 to 64.123 *(telephone)*

Utilities Covered: Electric, gas, telephone, steam heat, water, wastewater.

Contact Requirements:

On-Site Personal Contact: Immediately preceding termination, a utility employee (who may be the employee designated to terminate service) shall attempt to make personal contact with a responsible person at the ratepayer's residence and at the affected dwelling. Termination shall not occur if evidence is presented that payment has been made, a serious illness or medical condition exists, or a dispute or complaint is pending, or if the employee is authorized to receive payment and payment in full is tendered in any reasonable manner. Payment by personal check need not be accepted if the customer within the past year has tendered a check which has been returned for insufficient funds or for which payment has been stopped. 52 Pa. Code § 56.94. If prior contact is not made with a responsible adult either at the ratepayer's residence or at the affected dwelling, the employee shall not terminate service and shall conspicuously post a termination notice at such locations advising that service will be disconnected not less than 48 hours from the time and date of posting. 52 Pa. Code § 56.95. If service is terminated, notice or a written statement that contains the address and telephone number of the utility where the ratepayer or occupant may arrange to have service restored as well as a medical emergency notice (substantially in the form attached to this chapter as appendix B) shall be conspicuously posted or delivered to a responsible person at the ratepayer's residence and at the affected premises. 52 Pa. Code § 56.96.

Telephone Contact: None specified.

Other Personal Notice/Contact: Utility may not terminate service without personally contacting the customer or a responsible adult occupant at least 3 days prior to termination. 52 Pa. Code § 56.93. "Personal contact" means: (A) contacting the customer or responsible adult occupant in person or by telephone; (B) contacting third-party designee and, if no such designee, contacting a community interest group or other entity, including a local police department, that has previously agreed to receive a copy of the notice of termination and to attempt to contact the customer; and (C) if there is no third-party designee or such a community interest group or other entity, contacting the Commission in writing. 52 Pa. Code § 56.93.

Social Service Agency Contact: None specified.

Notice Requirements:

Timing and Delivery of Written Notice: 10 days' notice (7 days for telephone) mailed or delivered to customer and third-party designee. 52 Pa. Code §§ 56.91, 56.131; 64.71, 64.111 (telephone). See also 52 Pa. Code §§ 59.24 (gas); § 61.23 (steam heat), which provide that service may not be discontinued until after at least 24-hour written notice has been given by the utility that bills are 5 or more days delinquent. Immediately after telephone service is suspended, a termination notice substantially in the form of the suspension notice and indicating how the customer may arrange to have service restored shall be mailed to the customer's billing address. The termination notice shall include the amount past due that customer must pay to avoid termination of basic service, a medical emergency restoration notice substantially in the form set forth in Appendix B, a statement that service will be terminated on or after a specified date, and shall explain that the customer will have to request service as an applicant, subject to additional charges, if termination occurs. When at least 10 days have passed since suspension of service, the company may terminate service for failure to pay a reconnection fee and to remedy the original grounds for suspension. 52 Pa. Code §§ 64.121, 64.123 (telephone).

Content of Written Notice: 10-day written notice shall include the following information: (A) reason for the proposed suspension; (B) amounts currently due, including a required deposit; (C) statement that a specific reconnection fee will be required to have service restored if such fee is contained in approved tariff; (D) date on or after which service will be suspended unless one of the following occurs: (i) payment in full is received, (ii) grounds for suspension are otherwise eliminated, (iii) a payment agreement is entered into, or (iv) a dispute is filed with the utility or Commission; (E) statement that the customer should immediately contact the utility to attempt to resolve the matter, including the mailing address and telephone number where questions may be asked and payment agreements entered into; (F) the following statement: "If, AFTER discussing your problem with the Utility you remain dissatisfied, you may file an informal complaint with the Public Utility Commission. TO AVOID TERMINATION OF SERVICE PENDING RESOLUTION OF A DISPUTE THIS INFORMAL COMPLAINT MUST BE FILED BEFORE THE PROPOSED DATE FOR TERMINATION OF YOUR SERVICE. You may file an informal complaint by telephoning the Public Utility Commission at 1 (800) 692-7380 or by writing to the following address Public Utility Commission, Box 3265, Harrisburg, Pennsylvania 17120": and (G) a medical emergency notice substantially in the form set forth in Appendix A (relating to Medical Emergency Notice). 52 Pa. Code § 56.2. Regulation for telephone 7-day notice is substantially similar except that there is no specific requirement for statement regarding filing informal complaint with Commission. 52 Pa. Code § 64.72 (telephone). If, after the issuance of the initial termination notice and prior to termination, a ratepayer or occupant contacts the utility regarding the termination, an authorized utility employee shall fully explain: (A) the reasons for the proposed termination; (B) all available methods for avoiding a termination, including tendering payment in full or otherwise eliminating the grounds for termination, and entering a settlement or payment agreement; and (C) the medical emergency procedures. If a settlement or payment agreement is not established, the utility shall further explain the following: (A) the ratepayer's right to file a dispute with the utility and, subsequently, an informal complaint with the Commission; (B) the procedures for resolving disputes and informal complaints, including the address and telephone number of the Commission; and (C) the ratepayer's obligation to pay undisputed portions of a bill. 52 Pa. Code § 56.97. Telephone provision is substantially similar. 52 Pa. Code § 64.74 (telephone)

Rhode Island

90-060-002 R.I. Code R. pts. III to V, VIII *(electric, gas, water)* (LexisNexis); 90-060-007 R.I. Code R. §§ 4.1, 4.3, 4.4 *(telephone)* (LexisNexis)

Utilities Covered: Electric, gas, water.

Contact Requirements:

On-Site Personal Contact: If utility sends an employee to disconnect service, and the customer tenders payment of the bill in full or in part in accord with payment plan, service shall not be disconnected. For purposes of this section, utility's field personnel and employees are deemed authorized and shall be required to accept and provide a receipt for such payment but shall not be required to make change or to enter into agreements. Utility employee sent to disconnect service shall bring either a copy of the bill showing the amount outstanding or all the information contained therein. 90-060-002 R.I. Code R. pt. IV. When service is disconnected, the individual making the disconnection shall immediately inform a responsible adult that service has been terminated. If a responsible adult is not present, a note or letter advising that service has been terminated shall be conspicuously placed. A written notice shall also be given to the responsible adult or left on the premises in a conspicuous place advising that service may be restored immediately if (A) the customer was validly protected from shutoff during the moratorium period as described in section 3(C), or (B) if service is necessary to protect the health, welfare, and safety of the residents of the dwelling as described in part VII, or (C) upon the customer's enrollment in a payment plan described in sections 2(A)(4) and 2(A)(5). 90-060-002 R.I. Code R. pt. III (electric, gas, water).

Telephone Contact: None specified.

Other Personal Notice/Contact: None specified.

Social Service Agency Contact: None specified.

Notice Requirements:

Timing and Delivery of Written Notice: Written notice mailed to the billing address in order to be received, under reasonable circumstances, at least 10 days before disconnection date (with a copy to third-party designee of elderly or disabled customer). If service is provided at address other than the billing address or to occupants at the billing address who do not live in the same residential unit as the customer, the utility shall make reasonable effort to notify such users of the pending termination of service at least 10 days prior to termination. In addition to or in lieu of mailing notice to such occupants, utility shall attempt to notify occupants by posting or delivering notice. 90-060-002 R.I. Code R. pt. III (electric, gas, water). For telephone, 15 calendar days' notice by first class mail or hand delivery. 90-060-007 R.I. Code R. § 4.1. During the utility termination moratorium period (November 1 through April 15), no electric, gas, or water utility shall terminate service unless it has, at least 48 hours (not including Saturday, Sunday, or holidays) prior to termination, filed with the Division an employee affidavit in the form approved by the Division (see Forms I, II, and III in Appendix B) which states: (A) that subsequent to the 10-day notice period, the affiant personally visited the premises and spoke directly with the customer or an adult within the residence and that the affiant advised the person that service will be terminated unless within 48 hours the customer makes satisfactory arrangements with the utility or follows the procedures for obtaining a review by the Division, (B) that the person was informed of procedures for obtaining such review, that the person understood the communication, and (C) that the person was advised of the protections available under Sections 3(B), (C), (D) and (E) and the affiant neither observed nor was informed of any circumstances, including illness, which would make termination of service a violation of these rules and regulations. In the alternative, the utility shall file an affidavit which states: that subsequent to the 10-day notice period, the affiant personally visited the residence on at least two occasions, one of which was made on a weekday between 5:00 p.m. and 7:00 p.m. or on a Saturday between 9:00 a.m. and 5:00 p.m.; that on each occasion the affiant was unable to gain admission or if admitted found no adult person at home; and that the affiant left a written notice containing the information set out above in a form approved by the Division (see Form II in Appendix B hereto) prominently tacked or otherwise affixed to the front door of the customer's residence. 90-060-002 R.I. Code R. pt.

III, § 4).
Content of Written Notice: Notice shall include: (A) reason for disconnection; (B) statement that service will be disconnected unless the customer pays the bill, enters into payment plan, or seeks review of the bill pursuant to these regulations; (C) the date on, or within a reasonable time after which, service will be disconnected if the customer does not take appropriate action; (D) the name and telephone number of the utility's office or employee to whom the customer may inquire or complain; (E) the customer's right to submit the matter to a Division of Public Utilities reviewing officer, and a statement that service will not be disconnected pending a review; (F) statement that the customer should not submit the matter to the Division of Public Utilities until after first discussing the case with a utility representative; (G) a statement that disconnection will be postponed upon presentation of a doctor's certificate that there is a seriously ill resident; (H) a statement that, if any resident is disabled and/or all residents of the home are elderly, disconnection may be averted in accordance with section 3E; (I) a statement that, if any resident in the home is under 2 years of age and the customer's service has not been previously shut off for nonpayment before the birth of the child, and there is a financial hardship, disconnection may be averted in accordance with section 3F; (J) a statement regarding availability of protection from disconnection from November 1 and April 15 in accordance with section 3(C)(1) and (C)(2); (K) a statement regarding the right to enroll in a residential payment plan as described in Part V hereof; (L) a statement regarding the availability of LIHEAP assistance to eligible customers; and (M) on all final notices of termination the following statement in English, Spanish, Portuguese, and French: "THIS IS A UTILITY SERVICE TERMINATION NOTICE. TRANSLATE IMMEDIATELY." and the appropriate symbol for termination as set out in Appendix C to these regulations. 90-060-002 R.I. Code R. pt. III (electric, gas, water). Telephone regulations are substantially similar. 90-060-007 R.I. Code R. §§ 4.3, 4.4.

South Carolina

S.C. Code Ann. Regs. 103-352 *(electric)*, 103-452 *(gas)*, 103-735.1 *(water)*, 103-633 *(telephone)*, 103-535.1 *(sewerage)*; S.C. Code Ann. §§ 58-27-2510 to 58-27-2560 *(electric)*, 58-5-1110 to 58-5-1160 *(gas)*

Utilities Covered: Electric, gas, sewerage, and telephone, water.
Contact Requirements:
On-Site Personal Contact: All employees assigned to terminate service shall be authorized to accept payment from customers or, at utility's option, allow such customer at least one full working day beyond the initial termination date to make payment arrangements. In areas where the utility has determined that its employees' safety warrants it, such employees shall not be required to accept payments from customers subject to termination. S.C. Code Ann. Regs. 103-352 (electric); 103-452 (gas).
Telephone Contact: None specified.
Other Personal Notice/Contact: Not more than 2 business days prior to termination, utility shall make reasonable efforts either by telephone or in person (not more than 3 business days if by mail) to notify customer that service is subject to termination for nonpayment. S.C. Code Ann. Regs. 103-352 (electric); 103-452 (gas).
Social Service Agency Contact: None specified.

Notice Requirements:
Timing and Delivery of Written Notice: 10 days' notice mailed to customer and third-party designee. S.C. Code Ann. Regs. 103-352 (electric); 103-452 (gas). Utility shall provide for payment plan when customer is unable to pay the amount due, and service shall not be terminated unless the utility has informed the customer that a payment plan is available. The payment plan shall require customer to maintain account current and pay not less than 1/6 of the outstanding balance for a period not to exceed 6 months. The outstanding balance may include the late payment charge authorized by regulation 103-339(3) (electric) or 103-439(3)(gas). If customer fails to comply with payment plan, utility may terminate service upon 3 days' written notice, if personally delivered, or 5 days' notice by mail. S.C. Code Ann. Regs. 103-352 (electric); 103-452 (gas). For water utility (A) 10 days' notice sent by regular mail to billing address and providing that customer has ten days in which to settle account or have service disconnected, or (B) 30 days' notice for nonpayment of connection charge sent by certified mail with a copy to Office of Regulatory Staff. If the latter, at end of 30-day period water utility shall post a second notice to customer by certified mail advising that, in not less than 10 days nor more than 30 days, service may be disconnected at any time without further notice. Water utility notice must advise that customer can contact the ORS if the customer disputes the discontinuance. S.C. Code Ann. Regs. 103-735.1. Sewerage service provision is substantially similar to water, except 30 days' written notice by certified mail to the customer (unless regulation 103-535.A is applicable when hazardous condition exists), with copies to the appropriate county health department and the Office of Regulatory Staff. S.C. Code Ann. Regs. 103-535.1. For telephone, five days' written notice that customer has 5 days in which to settle account or have service disconnected. S.C. Code Ann. Regs. 103-633.
Content of Written Notice: 10-day notice shall include: (A) address and telephone number of utility contact person to arrange personal interview with utility employee who has authority to accept full payment or make other payment arrangements; (B) total amount owed, date, and amount of last payment, and date by which customer must either pay in full or make payment arrangements; (C) statement that service to customer who qualifies as a special needs account customer (customer for whom termination of service would be dangerous to health or member of household) shall only be terminated in accordance with S.C. Code Ann. §§ 58-27-2510 to 58-27-2560 (electric) or 58-5-1110 to 58-5-1160 (gas); (D) statement that service during the months of December through March will not be terminated when customer or a member of household can furnish to the utility, no less than 3 days prior to termination of service or to the terminating crew at time of termination, a utility form (i) signed by a licensed physician and certifying that termination would be especially dangerous to such person's health and (ii) signed by the customer and stating that such customer is unable to pay by installments; and (E) the availability of investigation and review of any unresolved dispute by the state Office of Regulatory staff, including its toll-free telephone number. S.C. Code Ann. Regs. 103-352 (electric); 103-452 (gas).

South Dakota

S.D. Admin. R. 20:10:20:03, 20:10:20:05, 20:10:20:07, 20:10:20:09 to 20:10:20:11 *(electric, gas)*, 20:10:10:03, 20:10:10:05, 20:10:10:07 to 20:10:10:08, 20:10:10:11 *(telephone)*

Utilities Covered: Electric, gas, and telephone.
Contact Requirements:
On-Site Personal Contact: If the utility representative who enters the premises to disconnect does not have the authority to collect bills, the representative shall arrange for payment and service shall not be disconnected. S.D. Admin. R. 20:10:20:07 (electric, gas); 20:10:10:07 (telephone).
Telephone Contact: None specified.
Other Personal Notice/Contact: None specified.
Social Service Agency Contact: None specified.
Notice Requirements:
Timing and Delivery of Written Notice: 10 days' written notice (5 days for telephone) following 20-day payment period (15-day payment period for telephone), mailed or delivered to the billing or service address, unless it is customer's first disconnection, in which case utility shall provide personal notice by telephone, visit, or certificate of mailing. S.D. Admin. R. 20:10:20:03 (electric, gas); 20:10:10:03 (telephone). If telephone customer has an extraordinarily high bill for which the deposit does not furnish adequate security (as required by subdivision 20:10:10:03(2)), the company may disconnect before the regular 15-day payment period after giving notice and an opportunity to pay the bill. S.D. Admin. R. 20:10:10:08 (telephone). From November 1 to March 31, utility may not disconnect without adding an additional 30 days before disconnection, and it shall notify the customer before the normal disconnection date that the customer has an additional 30 days until disconnection. S.D. Admin. R. 20:10:20:10 (electric and gas).
Content of Written Notice: Notice shall include: (A) reason for proposed disconnection; (B) utility's intention to disconnect service unless the customer takes corrective action; (C) the corrective action which the customer must take to avoid disconnection; and (D) notice of the customer's right to appeal and where to appeal. S.D. Admin. R. 20:10:20:05 (electric, gas). Telephone provision is substantially similar, except there is no specific requirement to state appeal rights. S.D. Admin. R. 20:10:10:05 (telephone). If customer is receiving gas and electric service from the same utility, the utility shall make every reasonable effort to inform the customer that payments may be applied to either the gas or electric portion of a bill in order to avoid the disconnection of that service. S.D. Admin. R. 20:10:20:03 (electric, gas).

Tennessee

Tenn. Comp. R. & Regs. 1220-4-3.19 *(water)*, 1220-4-4.19 *(electric)*, 1220-4-5.18 *(gas)*; Tenn. Code Ann. § 65-32-1104 *(water)*

Utilities Covered: Electric and gas.
Contact Requirements:
On-Site Personal Contact: In counties with metropolitan form of government and population greater than 500,000, electric, gas, or water representative shall make a reasonable, good faith effort to notify user in person that service shall be discontinued on a certain date. Knocking on the door or ringing the doorbell shall constitute a reasonable, good faith effort, except that utility representative need not knock or ring at residence where service has been discontinued within the previous 4 years. Tenn. Code Ann. § 65-32-1104.
Telephone Contact: None specified.
Other Personal Notice/Contact: None specified.
Social Service Agency Contact: In the event that termination is postponed for 30 days upon written certification by a physician, public health officer, or social service official that discontinuation will aggravate an existing medical emergency of the customer or other permanent resident of the premises, the customer or other permanent resident shall be referred to social service agencies for investigation, confirmation of need, and guarantee of payment during such 30-day period, and the utility shall supply customers with names of agencies providing assistance. Tenn. Comp. R. & Regs. 1220-4-4.19 (electric); 1220-4-5.18 (gas).
Notice Requirements:
Timing and Delivery of Written Notice: 7 days' notice by first class mail to customer and third-party designee. Tenn. Comp. R. & Regs. 1220-4-4.19 (electric); 1220-4-5.18 (gas). Water utility must make reasonable attempt to effect collection and give 7 days' written notice to settle account or have service discontinued. Tenn. Comp. R. & Regs. 1220-4-3.19 (water). Absent an emergency, fraudulent use, or a dangerous condition, wastewater utility shall not discontinue service without first providing "adequate" notice to the customer. When service is discontinued under approved tariff provisions, the utility shall promptly notify the customer of the reason and of the Authority's dispute resolution process found in Rule 1220-1-3. A copy of such notification or other documentation shall be sent within 5 business days to the local county health department and the Authority. A customer who has had service discontinued has the right to a contested case hearing. Tenn. Comp. R. & Regs. 1220-4-13.14 (wastewater).
Content of Written Notice: Notice shall include: (A) customer name and address, and service address, if different; (B) clear and concise statement of the reason for proposed termination; (C) date on which service will be terminated unless the customer takes appropriate action; (D) information regarding reconnection fee; (E) utility telephone number and address where customer may inquire, enter into service continuation agreement, or file a complaint; (F) name and address of the Tennessee Regulatory Authority and a statement to the effect that the Authority is the regulatory authority for the service; (G) statement regarding whether the bill is actual or estimated, amount owed, and the time period over which the amount was incurred. Tenn. Comp. R. & Regs. 1220-4-4.19 (electric); 1220-4-5.18 (gas).

Texas

16 Tex. Admin. Code §§ 7.45, 7.460 *(gas)*, 25.29 *(electric)*, 25.483 *(retail electric provider)*, 26.28 *(telephone)* (West); 30 Tex. Admin. Code § 291.88 *(sewer, water)* (West)

Utilities Covered: Electric, gas, retail electric provider, sewer, telephone, and water.
Contact Requirements:
On-Site Personal Contact: None specified.
Telephone Contact: None specified.
Other Personal Notice/Contact: None specified.

Social Service Agency Contact: None specified.
Notice Requirements:
Timing and Delivery of Written Notice: 10 days' written notice separately mailed or hand delivered, and not issued before the first day after the bill is due, to enable the utility to determine whether the payment was received by the due date. 16 Tex. Admin. Code §§ 25.29 (electric); 25.483 (retail electric provider). 10-day notice provision for telephone, water, and sewer, and 5-day notice provision for gas, are substantially similar. Notice for telephone may be sent electronically if requested by customer. 16 Tex. Admin. Code §§ 7.45 (gas); 26.28 (telephone); 30 Tex. Admin. Code § 291.88 (water, sewer).
Content of Written Notice: Notice for each utility must: (A) have a stated date of disconnection with the words "disconnection notice" or similar language prominently displayed; (B) have a disconnection date that is not a holiday or weekend day; (C) be in English and in Spanish; (D) include a statement that, if customer needs assistance paying bill by the due date or is ill and unable to pay, the customer may be able to make some alternate payment arrangement, establish deferred payment plan, or secure payment assistance; and (E) advise the customer to contact the utility for more information. 16 Tex. Admin. Code §§ 25.29 (electric); 25.483 (retail electric provider); 26.28 (telephone). 5-day notice provision for gas and 10-day notice provision for water and sewer are substantially similar. Sewer utility providing service separate from water utility must also notify customer when water service may be discontinued for failure to pay sewer bill. 16 Tex. Admin. Code § 7.45 (gas); 30 Tex. Admin. Code § 291.88 (water and sewer). When electric bill is for a master-metered apartment complex, utility shall also send notice to customer and inform customer that notice of possible disconnection will be provided to the tenants in 6 days if payment is not made before that time. At least 6 days after providing notice to the customer and at least 4 days before disconnecting, the utility shall post at least 5 notices in conspicuous areas in the corridors or other public places of the apartment complex. Language in the notice shall be in large type and shall read: "Notice to residents of (name and address of apartment complex): Electric utility service to this apartment complex is scheduled for disconnection on (date), because (reason for disconnection)." 16 Tex. Admin. Code §§ 25.29 (electric); 25.483 (retail electric provider).

Utah

Utah Admin. Code r. 746-200-7 *(electric, gas, sewer, water)*, r. 746-240-6 *(telephone)*

Utilities Covered: Electric, gas, sewer, telephone, and water.
Contact Requirements:
On-Site Personal Contact: None specified.
Telephone Contact: None specified.
Other Personal Notice/Contact: If third-party designee resides within service area, utility shall make reasonable efforts to personally contact the third party before termination of service. Utah Admin. Code r. 746-200-7(G) (electric, gas, sewer, water); 746-240-6(F)(telephone). At least 48 hours before scheduled termination, utility shall make good faith efforts to notify the account holder or an adult member of the household by mail, telephone, or personal visit to the residence. If personal notification is not been made either directly by the utility or by the customer in response to a mailed notice, the utility shall leave a written termination notice at the residence. Personal notification by visit or telephone is required only during the winter months, October 1 through March 31. During other months of the year, the mailed 48-hour notice can be the final notice before termination. If termination is not accomplished within 15 business days following the 48-hour notice, the utility must follow the same procedures for another 48-hour notice. Utah Admin. Code r. 746-200-7(G) (electric, gas, sewer, water). For telephone, on the business day prior to discontinuance a utility representative shall make a reasonable effort to contact the account holder in person or by telephone to apprise the account holder of the proposed action and steps to take to avoid or delay discontinuance. This oral notice shall include the same information required for written notice. Each local exchange carrier shall maintain clear written records of these oral notices, showing dates and names of employees giving the notices. Utah Admin. Code r. 746-240-6(F) (telephone).
Social Service Agency Contact: None specified.
Notice Requirements:
Timing and Delivery of Written Notice: 10 calendar days' written notice by first class mail or delivery to the account holder and third-party designee. The 10-day time period is computed from the postmark. Utah Admin. Code r. 746-200-7(G) (electric, gas, sewer, water). For telephone, 7-day written notice from the mailing date. Utah Admin. Code r. 746-240-6(F) (telephone). If third-party designee resides within service area, utility shall make reasonable efforts to personally contact the third party before termination of service. Utah Admin. Code r. 746-200-7(G) (electric, gas, sewer, water); 746-240-6(E) (telephone). Prior to termination notice, utility shall issue late notice which shall include the following information: (A) statement that the account is a delinquent account and should be paid promptly; (B) statement that the account holder should telephone the utility's collection department if there is a question concerning the account; (C) statement of the delinquent account balance, using a term such as "delinquent account balance." Utah Admin. Code r. 746-200-7(A) (electric, gas, sewer, water); 746-240-6(A) (telephone). All utilities except telephone utility shall issue a copy of the "Statement of Customer Rights and Responsibilities" referred to in rule 746-200-1(G) of these rules to the account holder with the first notice. Utah Admin. Code r. 746-200-7(A). For rental property where the tenant is not the account holder and that fact is known to the utility, the utility shall post a termination notice on the premises in a conspicuous place and shall make reasonable efforts to give at least 5 calendar days' actual notice to the occupants by personal visits or other appropriate means. The posted notice shall contain the same information required in the 10-day written notice to the account holder. This notice provision applies when the account holder has requested termination of service or the account holder has a delinquent bill. If nonpayment is the basis for termination, the utility shall also advise the tenants that they may continue to receive service for an additional 30 days by paying the charges due for the previous 30-day period. Utah Admin. Code r. 746-200-7(G) (electric, gas, sewer, water).
Content of Written Notice: Notice must include a summary of the following information: (A) statement of customer rights and responsibilities under existing state law and Commission rules; (B) Commission-approved policy on termination of service by utility; (C) availability of deferred payment agreements and sources of

possible financial assistance (e.g., state and federal energy assistance programs); (D) informal and formal procedures for disputing bills and appealing adverse decisions, as well as the Commission's address and telephone number; (E) specific steps, printed in a conspicuous fashion, that may be taken to avoid termination; (F) the date on which payment arrangements must be made to avoid termination; and (G) subject to rule 746-200-1(E) for utilities with more than 10,000 customers, a conspicuous statement, in Spanish, that the notice is a termination-of-service notice and that the utility has a Spanish edition of its customer information pamphlet, and whether it has personnel available during regular business hours to communicate with Spanish-speaking customers. Utah Admin. Code r. 746-200-7(G) (electric, gas, sewer, water). Telephone notice provision is abbreviated, requiring: (A) reasons for and date of scheduled discontinuance; (B) actions that the account holder may take to avoid discontinuance; and (C) statement of the customer's rights and responsibilities under existing state law and Commission rules. Utah Admin. Code r. 746-240-6(A) (telephone).

Vermont

30-000-004 Vt. Code R. §§ 3.301, 3.303 to 3.305 *(electric, gas, water)*; 30-000-053 Vt. Code R. §§ 7.620, 7.622, 7.623 *(telephone)*

Utilities Covered: Electric, gas, telephone, and water.

Contact Requirements:

On-Site Personal Contact: When service is disconnected at the premises (including at a pole at or near the premises), the individual making the disconnection shall immediately inform a responsible adult on the premises that service has been disconnected or, if no responsible adult is present, leave in a conspicuous and secure place a notice that service has been disconnected and what the customer has to do to have service restored. 30-000-004 Vt. Code R. § 3.306 (electric, gas, water).

Telephone Contact: None specified.

Other Personal Notice/Contact: During the winter period (November 1 through March 31), gas and electric utility shall make reasonable attempts to give the ratepayer or other responsible adult at the premises actual oral notice of the information required by section 3.303. If actual oral notice has not been given in any other manner, reasonable attempts shall consist of at least the following: three telephone calls made at least three hours apart to a telephone number provided by the ratepayer for this purpose or, if no such number has been provided, to the ratepayer's number as it appears in the telephone directory or as obtained from directory assistance, and a personal visit to the premises. Actual oral notice given by one of these methods (telephone calls or personal visit) to the ratepayer or to another responsible adult at the premises eliminates the need for further attempts by any other method. If actual oral notification has not otherwise been given, at least one of the telephone calls made to comply with this section shall be placed between the hours of 5:30 p.m. and 9:30 p.m. on a business day. A telephone call to a telephone not removed from service that results in a busy signal or in any other condition preventing communication or in an unanswered call that has not been allowed to ring for at least 60 seconds shall not count toward satisfaction of the requirement of this section. The unavailability of a ratepayer's telephone number excuses compliance with the requirement to attempt notification by telephone. If no responsible adult is at the premises when a personal visit is made pursuant to this paragraph, a notice containing the information required by section 3.303 shall be left in a secure and conspicuous place. When oral notification is given in compliance with this paragraph, in addition to giving the information required by section 3.303, the utility shall advise the ratepayer or other responsible adult that oral notification is not required to be given in connection with any subsequent disconnection which may occur during the same winter season, unless the utility's tariffs provide otherwise. If compliance with this section fails to result in actual oral notification, then, at least 48 hours before disconnection, the utility shall report to the Department of Public Service, in writing or by telephone, the ratepayer's name, address and, if available, telephone number. The utility shall be prepared to provide a description of the observations of the person who attempted to give oral notice by personal visit as to whether the premises appear to be occupied. If the ratepayer has been given actual oral notice during the current winter period with respect to a previous delinquency, compliance with additional actual notice is not required, provided that notice required by section 3.03 is delivered or mailed to the premises (with a copy mailed to the ratepayer's billing address, if different). Delivery by personal service is complete upon actual delivery to the ratepayer or the premises at least 48 hours prior to disconnection (excluding Vermont holidays), and notice by mail is complete by deposit in U.S. Postal Service mail at least 4 days before disconnection (excluding days when the postal service does not make regular deliveries of mail). 30-000-004 Vt. Code R. § 3.304 (electric, gas).

Social Service Agency Contact: None specified.

Notice Requirements:

Timing and Delivery of Written Notice: Written notice on a Board-approved form, mailed or delivered within 40 days after delinquency but not more than 20 days, nor less than 14 days, prior to the first date on which disconnection may occur. If payment has been made by a dishonored check or other instrument, then the number of days between delivery to the utility of the dishonored instrument and receipt by the utility of notice of dishonor may be deducted from the minimum number of days prior to disconnection that notice must be sent, but in no event may the minimum number of days be less than 4. 30-000-004 Vt. Code R. § 3.301(C) (electric, gas, water). If disconnection is for failure to comply with repayment plan, utility shall deliver or mail notice to the service address (with a copy mailed to billing address, if different) stating that service will be disconnected unless the delinquency is paid by a certain date and the date(s) when service may be disconnected if payment is not made. Delivery of notice shall be made at least 72 hours prior to disconnection, and mailing shall be deposited in U.S. Postal Service mail at least 5 days before disconnection. In lieu of written notice, utility may give notice orally, in person, or by telephone at least 72 hours prior to disconnection. This manner of notice after failure to comply with repayment plan is sufficient in the case of disconnection by a gas or electric utility in the winter provided that the utility has given oral notice of the information contained in section 3.303 at the time the repayment plan was entered into and the repayment plan was reasonable. 30-000-004 Vt. Code R. § 3.305 (electric, gas, water). For telephone, 14 days' written notice, and carrier may disconnect after 3 days' written notice for failure to comply with payment plan or payment by dishonored check or other instrument. 30-000-053 Vt. Code R. §§ 7.620, 7.622.

Content of Written Notice: Written notice shall include: (A) statement that account is delinquent, the amount of the delinquency, and a statement that service will be disconnected unless: (i) the delinquency is paid in full by a certain date; (ii) the ratepayer enters into a reasonable repayment plan; (iii) the ratepayer denies the existence of any delinquency in excess of $50.00, submits the dispute to the Board, and the Board advises the utility not to disconnect service; or (iv) the ratepayer presents to the utility (or gives actual notice that he or she will, within seven days, present to the utility) a statement from a duly licensed physician certifying that disconnection will result in an immediate and serious health hazard to the ratepayer or to a resident within the ratepayer's household (with limitation that use of physician's certificate to prevent disconnection or to cause a reconnection is limited to two consecutive 30-day periods and shall not exceed three 30-day periods in any calendar year, except upon written order of the Board); (B) the dates and times of day when service may be disconnected if the ratepayer does not take appropriate action; (C) a statement that the utility will negotiate a reasonable repayment plan and that, if after entering such negotiations the ratepayer does not believe the utility's terms to be reasonable, the ratepayer may request the assistance of the Consumer Affairs Division of the Department of Public Service in conducting further negotiations; (D) the name(s) or title(s), address(es), telephone number(s), and business hours of the company representatives to whom the ratepayer may make any inquiry or complaint, and a statement that telephone calls made from within Vermont for such purposes may be made collect or toll free; (E) the address, telephone numbers, including the toll-free number, and business hours of the Consumer Affairs Division of the Department of Public Service, and a statement that, in addition to providing assistance or advice as to negotiations with utilities, the Division can provide information as to how to submit to the Board a dispute over the existence of a delinquency; (F) the itemized cost that may be charged to the ratepayers for disconnection, collection, and later restoration of service and, if a deposit may be required for restoration of service, an explanation of how the amount will be calculated; (G) in the case of gas and electric utilities, if disconnection is to occur between November 1 and March 31, inclusive, a list as annually compiled and distributed by the Department of Public Service, of the names, addresses and telephone numbers of governmental and private agencies that may provide assistance to ratepayers in paying their utility bills; (H) in the case of gas and electric utilities, an offer to arrange a monthly installment plan for the payment of future bills, provided that such offer need not be made if the account is for service at premises not used as a principal residence; and (I) in the case of gas and electric utilities, a statement that service to households with any member aged 62 or older shall not be disconnected between November 1 and March 31 if outdoor temperatures are forecast to fall below 32° Fahrenheit during a 48-hour period beginning at the anticipated time of disconnection, provided that the account holder furnishes advance written notice to the utility that the household qualifies under this section and, if requested by the utility, furnishes reasonable proof of such qualification. 30-000-004 Vt. Code R. § 3.303 (electric, gas, water). Telephone regulations are substantially similar. 30-000-053 Vt. Code R. §§ 7.620, 7.622, 7.623.

Virginia

Va. Code Ann. §§ 56-247.1 *(electric, gas, water)*, 56-265.13:7 *(small water or sewer utility)*; 20 Va. Admin. Code §§ 5-312-90(G), (I) *(electric, gas)*, 5-413-25 *(telephone)*

Utilities Covered: Electric, gas, sewer, telephone, and water. Commission rules and regulations concerning denial of telephone service for nonpayment shall not apply to services found to be competitive. Va. Code Ann. § 56-247.1.

Contact Requirements:

On-Site Personal Contact: None specified.
Telephone Contact: None specified.
Other Personal Notice/Contact: None specified.
Social Service Agency Contact: None specified.

Notice Requirements:

Timing and Delivery of Written Notice: Electric, gas, and small water or sewer utility shall give 10 days' notice by mail to customer. Va. Code Ann. §§ 56-247.1(A)(4), (A)(6) (electric, gas, water), 56-265.13:7 (small water or sewer utility). Terms and conditions concerning disconnection for nonpayment shall be set forth in each electric or gas local distribution company's approved tariff. 20 Va. Admin. Code § 5-312-90(G). An LEC shall provide, separately from the bill, 10 days' notice to customer by mail, or e-mail if the customer elects to be billed electronically, of the potential disconnection of basic telephone service or a basic bundle. 20 Va. Admin. Code § 5-413-25 (telephone).

Content of Written Notice: If a customer receives consolidated billing service and a competitive service provider is the billing party, the electric or gas local distribution company shall advise the customer directly of any pending disconnection action by 10 days' notice by mail, separate from the consolidated bill. The 10-day notice shall clearly identify the amount that must be paid and the date by which it must be received and provide instructions for direct payment to the local distribution company to avoid disconnection. When a disconnection notice for nonpayment is included on a customer bill issued by the electric or gas local distribution company, the notice shall appear conspicuously on the first page of the bill and shall clearly identify the amount that must be paid and the date by which it must be paid to avoid disconnection. 20 Va. Admin. Code §§ 5-312-90(G), (I) (electric, gas). Water utility notice shall include contact information for customer to use in contacting utility regarding the notice. Va. Code Ann. § 56.247.1. The 10-day notice required for an LEC shall clearly identify the amount that must be paid to prevent disconnection of basic telephone service or a basic bundle, the date by which the payment must be received to avoid disconnection, and the LEC's toll-free number for inquiry or to make payment arrangements. 20 Va. Admin. Code § 5-413-25 (telephone).

Washington

Wash. Admin. Code §§ 480-90-128 *(gas)*, 480-100-128 *(electric)*, 480-110-355 *(water)*, 480-120-172 *(telephone)*

Utilities Covered: Electric, gas, telephone, and water.

Contact Requirements:

On-Site Personal Contact: A utility representative dispatched to disconnect service must accept payment of a delinquent account at the service address but is not required to give change for cash paid

in excess of the amount due and owing. The utility must credit any overpayment to the customer's account. Wash. Admin. Code §§ 480-90-128 (gas); 480-100-128 (electric); 480-110-355 (water).
Telephone Contact: None specified.
Other Personal Notice/Contact: Second notice must be provided by: (A) delivery to the service premises by attaching it to customer's door, stating a scheduled disconnection date not earlier than 5:00 p.m. of the second business day after the date of delivery (for water and telephone, notice which gives customer until 5:00 p.m. of the following business day); (B) for telephone and if consented to by customer, e-mail notice with disconnection date that is not earlier than 5:00 p.m. of the second business day after the date of delivery; (C) by mail with disconnection date for telephone that is not earlier than 5:00 p.m. of the third business day after the date of mailing (excluding date of mailing), or with disconnection date for gas, electric, and water that is not earlier than 3 business days after mailing or 6 business days if mailed from outside the states of Washington (and, for electric and gas, 6 business days if mailed from outside of Oregon or Idaho); or (D) for gas, electric, and telephone, the utility must attempt at least two times to contact the customer by telephone during regular business hours. A log or record of the calls must be kept for a minimum of 90 calendar days showing the telephone number called, the time of the call, and details of the results of each attempted call. Telephone company may not disconnect before 5:00 p.m. of the next business day after the phone calls or attempts. Telephone company need not attempt such personal contact if it has had cause, in any two previous billing periods during a consecutive twelve-month period, to attempt such contact and the company has notified the customer in writing that such contact will not be attempted in the future before disconnecting service. If gas or electric utility is unable to reach the customer by telephone, the written notice must be mailed or delivered in the manner described above. If gas or electric utility provides a second notice within 10 business days of the disconnection date stated in the initial notice, then the disconnection date is extended an additional 10 working days from the disconnection date of the second notice. If service is not disconnected within the extended 10-business-day period, the notice is void unless the customer and the utility have agreed to a payment plan. Absent such an agreement, the utility must repeat the second notice procedure. If the utility provides a second notice more than 10 days after the disconnection date of the first notice, the notice is void unless the customer and the utility have agreed to a payment plan. Absent such an agreement, gas or electric utility must repeat the initial notice procedure. Wash. Admin. Code §§ 480-90-128 (gas); 480-100-128 (electric); 480-110-355 (water); 480-120-172 (telephone).
Social Service Agency Contact: None specified.
Notice Requirements:
Timing and Delivery of Written Notice: Utility must serve written notice to customer by mail or by personal delivery to the customer's address with notice attached to the primary door. Telephone company may deliver notice electronically if the customer has consented, and disconnection date may not be less than 8 business days after notice is mailed, delivered electronically, or delivered. Gas, electric, and water notice must be not less than 8 business days after the date of personal delivery or mailing or not less than 11 business days if mailed from outside the states of Washington (and, for electric and gas, 11 business days if mailed from outside of Oregon and Idaho). The date of mailing is excluded from the notice period. If gas, electric, or telephone service is not disconnected within 10 business days of the stated disconnection date, the initial notice is void unless the customer and the utility have agreed to a payment plan. Absent such an agreement, the initial notice requirements must be repeated. Water utility notice expires 10 business days after the first day that the company may disconnect, unless the utility and customer have agreed otherwise and confirmed in writing. If customer does not comply with mutually accepted arrangements, water utility may disconnect without further notice. Wash. Admin. Code §§ 480-90-128 (gas); 480-100-128 (electric); 480-110-355 (water); 480-120-172 (telephone). Gas and electric utility must provide copy of notice to third-party designee and, if utility believes that a customer is not able to understand the effect of the disconnection, the utility must consider a social agency to be a third party. In either case, utility must delay disconnection for 5 business days past the original disconnection date after issuing a disconnection notice to a third-party designee. The utility must determine which social agencies are appropriate and willing to receive the notice, the name, and/or title of the person able to deal with the disconnection, and provide that information to the customer. Wash. Admin. Code §§ 480-90-128 (gas); 48-100-128 (electric). When the service address is different from the billing address, gas or electric utility must determine if the customer of record and the service user are the same and, if not, the utility must provide notice to the service user. Wash. Admin. Code §§ 480-90-128 (gas); 48-100-128 (electric).
Content of Written Notice: Notice must include: (A) a disconnection date that is not less than 8 business days after the date of personal delivery, electronic delivery by telephone utility if customer consents, or mailing but not less than 11 business days if mailed from outside the states of Washington (and, for electric and gas, 11 business days if mailed outside of Oregon and Idaho); (B) reason for disconnection, the amount owed (and, if utility provides both gas and electric service, the amount owed for each service), and how to avoid disconnection; (C) information about any charges that may be assessed; and (D) the utility's name, address, and telephone number by which customer may contact the utility. For telephone, notice must include information about avoiding disconnection under medical emergency rule. If disconnection notice is for nonpayment during the winter months (November 15 through March 15), gas and electric utility must advise the customer of the payment plan described in Wash. Admin. Code §§ 480-90-138 (gas) and 480-100-138 (electric) and the winter low-income payment program in Wash. Admin. Code §§ 480-90-143 (gas) and 480-100-143 (electric). Wash. Admin. Code §§ 480-90-128 (gas); 480-100-128 (electric); 480-110-355 (water); 480-120-172 (telephone).

West Virginia

W. Va. Code R. 150-3-4.8 *(electric)*, 150-4-4.8 *(gas)*, 150-5-4.8 *(sewer)*, 150-6-2.2(f), 150-6-2.4 *(telephone)*, 150-7-4.8 *(water)*

Utilities Covered: Electric, gas, sewer, telephone, water.
Contact Requirements:
On-Site Personal Contact: Utility shall accept payment at the premises in lieu of discontinuing service. Payment made by personal check may be refused if, within the past 12 months, a check from the customer has been returned for insufficient funds. W. Va.

Code R. §§ 150-3-4.8 (electric); 150-4-4.8 (gas); 150-7-4.8 (water); 150-5-4.8 (sewer).

Telephone Contact: Telephone company shall also make at least two attempts at personal notice by telephone at least 24 hours prior to termination, but inability to effect personal notice shall not prevent termination of service. W. Va. Code R. § 150-6-2.2(f) (telephone).

Other Personal Notice/Contact: For electric and gas utility, personal contact shall be at least 24 hours prior to scheduled termination unless it is reasonably established that the premises are not permanently inhabited. The personal notice becomes void if service is not disconnected within 30 days of such notice. The individual giving personal notice shall present a copy of the original written notice or a document that contains the same information. If personal notice is by telephone, the person shall inform the customer how to obtain a copy of the original written notice. Utility may petition the Commission to waive the personal contact requirement only after making at least three attempts at personal contact. At least one of the attempts at personal contact must be an on-site visit, with the utility leaving a door hanger with relevant information in the event personal contact is not made. At least one attempt must be after normal working hours of 8 a.m. to 6 p.m. A telephone call may be used as an after-hours personal contact attempt. W. Va. Code R. §§ 150-3-4.8 (electric); 150-4-4.8 (gas). At least 24 hours before disconnecting water service for nonpayment of sewer bill, water utility shall make at least two attempts at personal contact, first by either telephone or visit and second by knocking on the customer's door immediately prior to disconnection. The inability to make personal contact shall not prevent the water utility from terminating service. W. Va. Code §§ 150-7.4.8 (water); 150-5-4.8 (sewer).

Social Service Agency Contact: None specified.

Notice Requirements:

Timing and Delivery of Written Notice: 10 days' written notice complying with P.S.C. W. Va. Form No. 14-E (electric), No. 14-G (gas); Water Form No. 1 (water); Sewer Form No. 1 (sewer) or P.S.C. W. Va. Form No. 14-T (telephone) and sent by first class mail. The written notice shall become void if service is not discontinued within 30 days of the termination date indicated on the notice. W. Va. Code R. §§ 150-3-4.8 (electric); 150-4-4.8 (gas); 150-5-4.8 (sewer); 150-6-2.2(f)(telephone); 150-7-4.8 (water). If the customer of record is: (A) a landlord of a master-metered apartment building, motel, hotel, or other multiple unit dwelling, or (B) a third party who is a non-resident of the single service location, then written notice of termination, using P.S.C. W. Va. Form 14-ME (electric); 14-MG (gas); Water Form No. 2 (water) or Sewer Form No. 2 (sewer) shall also be posted at least 5 days prior to the scheduled termination. A sewer utility requesting termination of water service for nonpayment of sewer service shall mail customer 10 days' written notice complying with Sewer Form No. 1 and advising that sewer utility will request termination of service by the water utility if payment is not made in full or a payment schedule is not established as provided by Sewer Rule 4.8.b.10 (W. Va. Code R. § 150-5-4.8.b.10). The sewer utility notice must contain a statement that, in the event water service is terminated, the customer will be responsible for and required to pay the fees charged to the sewer utility by the water utility. Sewer utility shall provide the water utility with a copy of the notice to the customer required by Sewer Rule 4.8.b (W. Va. Code R. § 150-5-4.8.b) and provide water utility with a written request for termination at least 24 hours before the end of the 10-day notice period to the customer. W. Va. Code R. §§ 150-7-4.8 (water); 150-5-4-8 (sewer).

Content of Written Notice: Written notice must comply with P.S.C. W. Va. Form No. 14-E (electric), No. 14-G (gas); Water Form No. 1 (water) or Sewer Form No. 1 (sewer), or P.S.C. W. Va. Form No. 14-T (telephone). Customer shall be informed, at the time a disconnect notice is issued, of the option for a reasonable payment plan, provided customer demonstrates ability to pay only in installments. W. Va. Code R. §§ 150-3-4.8 (electric); 150-4-4.8 (gas); 150-5-4.8 (sewer); 150-6-2.2(f) (telephone); 150-7-4.8 (water). Ten-day notice for sewer utility requesting termination of water service for nonpayment of sewer service shall comply with Sewer Form No. 1, advise that sewer utility will request termination of service by the water utility if payment is not made in full or a payment schedule is not established as provided by Sewer Rule 4.8.b.10 (W. Va. Code R. § 150-4-8.b.10), and contain a statement that customer will be required to pay the fees charged to the sewer utility by the water utility in the event that service is terminated. W. Va. Code R. § 150-7-4.8 (water).

Wisconsin

Wis. Admin. Code PSC §§ 113.0301, 113.0304, 113.0404 *(electric)*, 134.062, 134.0624, 134.063 *(gas)*, 165.052, 165.0525 *(telephone)*, 185.37, 185.38 *(water)*

Utilities Covered: Electric, gas, telephone, and water.

Contact Requirements:

On-Site Personal Contact: During cold weather period (November 1 through April 15), a utility representative shall meet personally with a responsible adult member of the household prior to and again at the time of disconnection of service to discover any circumstances that deserve special attention, such as medical problems or disabilities. The utility shall maintain a record of all contacts with the household from the time that notice of pending disconnection is first given. If the household has previously requested that a specific third party be notified before disconnection, the utility shall contact that third party prior to disconnection. By the end of the work day following the day of disconnection, the utility shall visit the premises to check on the household's well-being and to ensure there is no danger to human health or life. The utility shall again inform the household of the availability of deferred payment or budget billing agreements, shelter assistance and, in the case of a non-customer occupant, the option of accepting responsibility for payment of future bills. If the utility or its representative observes a danger to human health or life due to the disconnection, service shall immediately be restored. Wis. Admin. Code PSC §§ 113.0304 (electric); 134.0624 (gas).

Telephone Contact: Utility shall make a reasonable effort to have a personal or telephone contact with customer before disconnection. Wis. Admin. Code PSC §§ 113.0301 (electric); 134.062 (gas); 165.052 (telephone); 185.37 (water). If a contact is made, the utility shall review the reasons for the pending disconnection and explain what actions must be taken to avoid disconnection. Wis. Admin. Code PSC §§ 113.0301 (electric); 134.062 (gas); 185.37 (water). During cold weather period (November 1 through April 15), utility shall provide its emergency after-hours telephone number to all households scheduled for utility service disconnection. Wis. Admin. Code PSC §§ 113.0304 (electric); 134.0624 (gas).

Other Personal Notice/Contact: During cold weather period (November 1 through April 15), utility shall prior to disconnection provide its emergency after-hours telephone number to all households scheduled for utility service disconnection and inform such households of the availability of deferred payment agreements, budget billing and, in the case of a non-customer occupant, the option of accepting responsibility for future bills. Wis. Admin. Code PSC §§ 113.0304 (electric); 134.0624 (gas).
Social Service Agency Contact: Telephone utility shall not disconnect without notifying county department of health and social services at least 5 calendar days prior to the scheduled disconnection if customer or responsible person has made a written request for this procedure to the utility. The customer shall be informed of this right upon application for service, and the utility shall provide customers with notice of this right in all telephone directories. Wis. Admin. Code PSC § 165.052 (telephone).
Notice Requirements:
Timing and Delivery of Written Notice: 10 calendar days' written notice (8 for gas) mailed to customer by first class mail or personally served on a responsible adult member of the household. If disconnection is not effected within 20 days (15 for gas) after issuance of notice, a subsequent notice shall be left on the premises not less than 24 hours nor more than 48 hours prior to disconnection. Wis. Admin. Code PSC §§ 113.0301 (electric); 134.062 (gas); 185.37 (water). Telephone provision is substantially the same, except that notice period to customer by mail or personal service is 5 calendar days, and, if disconnection does not occur within 15 days of mailing of notice due to customer pursuing dispute procedures, then an additional 5-day notice must be provided before disconnection. Wis. Admin. Code PSC § 165.052 (telephone). If the billing address is different from the service address, or the account is being billed in the name of "occupant," "resident," or other like term, notice shall be posted at each unit of the service address no fewer than 5 days before disconnection. If access is not possible, the 5-day notice shall be posted, at a minimum, to all entrances to the building and in the lobby. Wis. Admin. Code PSC §§ 113.0301 (electric); 134.062 (gas); 185.37 (water).
Content of Written Notice: Written notice shall be in a form approved by the commission and shall contain the following information: (A) name and address of the customer, and the service address, if different; (B) reasons for the proposed disconnection and that disconnection will occur if the account is not paid, a payment plan is not agreed to, or other suitable arrangements are not made, or, if disconnection is for default on a deferred payment agreement, the notice shall include an explanation of the acts that are considered to constitute default; (C) a statement that customer should communicate immediately upon receipt of the notice with the utility's designated office (statement must list a telephone number) if customer disputes the notice of delinquent account, wishes to negotiate a payment plan, or there is a threat to health or safety of a resident because of the infirmities of aging, developmental or mental disabilities, use of life support systems, like infirmities incurred at any age, or the frailties associated with being very young; (D) a statement that service will be continued during serious illness or protective services emergency if the occupant submits a medical certification or notice pursuant to this rule; and (E) a statement that customer may appeal to the commission staff in the event that the reason for disconnection or the amount of any bill remains in dispute after the customer has pursued the available remedies with the utility. Wis. Admin. Code PSC §§ 113.0301 (electric); 134.062 (gas); 185.37 (water). Telephone notice rule is substantially the same except that there is no provision regarding postponement for serious illness or protective services emergency. Wis. Admin. Code PSC § 165.052 (telephone). If the billing address is different from the service address, or the account is being billed in the name of "occupant," "resident," or other like terms, then additional 5-day notice to resident(s) shall state: (A) date of the notice; (B) proposed date of disconnection; (C) that, if feasible, occupants may apply to accept responsibility for future bills and avoid disconnection of service, and (D) that customer should contact utility immediately if disconnection will aggravate an existing medical or protective services emergency. Wis. Admin. Code PSC §§ 113.0301 (electric); 134.062 (gas); 185.37 (water) (same except no specific statement regarding medical or protective services emergency).

Wyoming

023-020-2 Wyo. Code R. § 242 *(electric, gas, water)* (LexisNexis); 023-020-005 Wyo. Code § 504 *(telephone)* (LexisNexis)

Utilities Covered: Electric, gas, telephone, water.
Contact Requirements:
On-Site Personal Contact: None specified.
Telephone Contact: None specified.
Other Personal Notice/Contact: Utility shall attempt to contact the customer personally before disconnecting service during the cold weather period of November 1 through April 30. 023-020-2 Wyo. Code R. § 242 (electric, gas, water).
Social Service Agency Contact: None specified.
Notice Requirements:
Timing and Delivery of Written Notice: 7 days' written notice to customer, with copy to third-party designee and guarantor. Notice is deemed given when a copy is left with the customer or put in the U.S. Postal Service mail, addressed to the customer's last known address. 023-020-2 Wyo. Code R. § 242 (electric, gas, water). When utility knows that it is disconnecting service for nonpayment by a landlord, the utility shall also post, mail, or deliver to each known tenant a written notice informing the tenant only of the impending disconnection and advising that each tenant has 15 days to arrange for the service to be provided directly to the tenant if, and as, permitted by the available facilities. 023-020-2 Wyo. Code R. § 242 (electric, gas, water). Utility must provide 30 days' notice to a household if any resident is dependent on life-support equipment requiring the utility's service. Service will not be disconnected if the customer provides a medical doctor's statement that a member of the household is dependent upon a life-support system, and the customer enters into and complies with a written deferred-payment agreement. If the customer fails to comply with the payment agreement, the utility may then issue a 7-day written disconnect notice. 023-020-2 Wyo. Code R. § 242 (electric, gas, water). Telephone utility must provide at least 7 days' written notice to the customer, and notice is deemed given when a copy is provided to the customer, delivered to the premises where service is rendered, or put in the U.S. Postal Service mail addressed to the customer's last known address. 023-020-005 Wyo. Code § 504 (telephone).
Content of Written Notice: Written notice shall contain the following information: (A) the name of the person whose service is to be terminated, and the service address; (B) the unpaid amount; (C) the

date the notice is delivered or mailed and the exact date on or after which service is to be terminated; (D) a statement advising the customer to contact the utility at a specific address and phone number regarding any budget billing or other procedures that the utility may offer or to work out some other mutually agreeable solution to avoid termination; (E) the name of any government agency or other organizations which have notified the utility that they provide assistance to certain eligible persons who are unable to pay their utility bills and which have requested that their name, address, and phone number be given to any customers facing possible termination of service (such information may be provided on a separate sheet included with the notice of disconnection); and, (F) a statement advising that the customer may contact the Commission in writing or by phone if the customer wishes to dispute the facts or interpretation of the regulation(s) relied upon by the utility to terminate service. Notice of disconnection must also notify customer that the utility must grant 15 days in addition to the 7 days (22 days total) for the bill payment if the customer can provide written healthcare documentation that a member of the customer's household is disabled or seriously ill, including persons whose physical health or safety would be seriously endangered if service were discontinued. 023-020-2 Wyo. Code R. § 242 (electric, gas, water).

A.8 State Utility Commissions

State utility commissions regulate consumer service and rates for gas, electricity, and a variety of other services within your state. These services include rates for telephone calls and moving household goods. In some states, the utility commissions regulate water and transportation rates. Rates for utilities and services provided between states are regulated by the Federal government.

Many utility commissions handle consumer complaints. Sometimes, if a number of complaints are received about the same utility matter, they will conduct investigations.

For more detailed and up-to-date information about each commission (including the names of the current commissioners), visit the websites listed below for each state.

ALABAMA

Alabama Public Service Commission
100 N. Union Street
Suite 850
Montgomery, AL 36104
P.O. Box 304260
Montgomery, AL 36130
General number: 334-242-5218
Fax: 334-242-0509
Website: www.psc.state.al.us

Complaints and Consumer Affairs
Phone: 800-392-8050
Website: www.psc.state.al.us/Complaints/ComplaintForm.htm (for on-line complaint form)

Aquilla Spivey
Consumer Services Manager
Phone: 334-242-5211
Fax: 334-242-0509
E-mail: aquilla.spivey@psc.alabama.gov

ALASKA

Regulatory Commission of Alaska
701 West 8th Avenue
Suite 300
Anchorage, AK 99501-3469
General number: 907-276-6222
Fax: 907-276-0160
Website: http://rca.alaska.gov/RCAWeb/home.aspx

Complaints and Consumer Affairs
Phone: 800-390-2782 (outside of Anchorage)
E-mail: To file a complaint against a regulated utility, please send an e-mail to the Consumer Protection Mailbox at cp.mail@alaska.gov
Website: www.azcc.gov/divisions/utilities/consumerservices.asp (for on-line complaint form)

Grace Salazar
Manager, Consumer Protection
907-263-2134
Fax: 907-276-0160
E-mail: grace.salazar@alaska.gov

ARIZONA

Arizona Corporation Commission
1200 West Washington Street
Phoenix, AZ 85007
General number: 602-542-2237
Fax: 602-542-3977
Website: www.cc.state.az.us

Complaints
Phone: 602-542-4251 (within metro Phoenix); 520-628-6550 (within metro Tucson)
Phone: (if outside the metro Phoenix or Tucson areas but within Arizona): 800-222-7000 (toll-free, Phoenix Office); 800-535-0148 (toll-free, Tucson Office)
Website: www.azcc.gov/divisions/utilities/consumerservices.asp (for on-line consumer assistance form)

Connie Walczak
Consumer Services Manager
E-mail: cwalczak@azcc.gov

Consumer Affairs
Elijah Abinah
Assistant Director, Utilities Division
Phone: 602-542-6935
Fax: 602-364-0888
E-mail: eabinah@azcc.gov

ARKANSAS

Arkansas Public Service Commission
1000 Center Building
Little Rock, AR 72201-0400
P.O. Box 400
Little Rock, AR 72203
General number: 501-682-2051
Fax: 501-682-5731
Website: www.arkansas.gov/psc

Consumer Complaints
Phone: 501-682-1718; 800-482-1164 (toll-free)
E-mail: consumerissues@psc.state.ar.us

Holly Tubbs
Manager, Consumer Services
Phone: 501-682-0390
E-mail: holly_tubbs@psc.state.ar.us

CALIFORNIA

California Public Utilities Commission
California State Building
505 Van Ness Avenue
San Francisco, CA 94102-3298
General number: 415-703-2782
Fax: 415-703-1758
Website: www.cpuc.ca.gov/puc

Complaints
Phone: 415-703-2074; 866-849-8390(toll-free)
E-mail: public.advisor@cpuc.ca.gov
Website: https://ia.cpuc.ca.gov/cimsapp (for on-line complaint form)

Karen A. Dowd
Manager, Consumer Affairs Branch
E-mail: kad@cpuc.ca.gov

COLORADO

Colorado Public Utilities Commission
1560 Broadway, Suite 250
Denver, CO 80202
General number: 303-894-2000
Fax: 303-894-2065
Website: www.dora.state.co.us/puc

Complaints and Consumer Affairs
303-894-2070; 800-456-0858 (toll-free)
Website: www.dora.state.co.us/pls/real/CCTS_oWEB.complaint_form (for on-line complaint form)

Barbara Fernandez
Chief of Staff
Phone: 303-894-2012
Fax: 303-894-2532
E-mail: barbara.fernandez@dora.state.co.us

CONNECTICUT

Connecticut Department of Public Utility Control
10 Franklin Square
New Britain, CT 06051
General number: 860-827-1553
Fax: 860-827-2822
Website: www.ct.gov/dpuc/site/default.asp

Complaints and Consumer Affairs
Phone: 800-382-4586 (toll-free)
E-mail: dpuc.information@po.state.ct.us
Website: www.dpuc.state.ct.us/CAIUI.NSF/RevWebIntake?OpenForm (for on-line complaint form)

Nick Neeley
Director of Advocacy and Operations
E-mail: nick.neeley@po.state.ct.us

DELAWARE

Delaware Public Service Commission
861 Silver Lake Blvd.
Cannon Bldg.
Suite 100
Dover, DE 19904
Main Number: 302-736-7500
General number: 302-739-4247
Fax: 302-739-4849
Website: http://depsc.delaware.gov

Complaints
Website: http://smu.depsc.delaware.gov/cgi-bin/mail.php?frm_cmplnt (for complaint form)
Charmaine Johnson
Complaint Investigator
E-mail: charmaine.johnson@state.de.us

Consumer Affairs
Kevin S. Neilson
Regulatory Affairs Policy Administrator
Phone: 302-736-7514
Fax: 302-739-4849
E-mail: kevin.neilson@state.de.us

DISTRICT OF COLUMBIA

District of Columbia Public Service Commission
1333 H Street, NW
2nd Floor
Washington, DC 20005
General number: 202-626-5100
Fax: 202-638-1785
Website: www.dcpsc.org

Complaints and Public Affairs
Phone: 202-626-5120
Website: www.dcpsc.org/consumerservices/uccmi/forms/util3.shtm (for consumer complaint and inquiry form)
Linda Jordan
Director, Office of Consumer Services
Phone: 202-626-9169
Fax: 202-626-9210
E-mail: ljordan@psc.dc.gov

FLORIDA

Florida Public Service Commission
2540 Shumard Oak Blvd.
Gerald Gunter Building
Tallahassee, FL 32399
General number: 850-413-6344
Fax: 800-511-0809
Website: www.psc.state.fl.us

Consumer Assistance
Phone: 850-413-6100; 800-342-3552 (toll-free)
Website: www.psc.state.fl.us/consumers/complaints/index2.aspx (for utility complaint Form)

Consumer Affairs
Beverlee S. DeMello
Assistant Director of Office of Public Information
Phone: 850-413-6482
Fax: 850-413-6108
E-mail: bdemello@psc.state.fl.us

GEORGIA

Georgia Public Service Commission
244 Washington Street
Atlanta, GA 30334
General number: 404-656-4501
Fax: 404-656-2341
Website: www.psc.state.ga.us

Consumer Affairs
Website: http://crs.psc.state.ga.us/Consumer/Contact/utilityIndustry.aspx?type=Complaint (for on-line complaint form)
Mike Nantz
Assistant to the Director for Enforcement
E-mail: mnantz@psc.state.ga.us

HAWAII

Hawaii Public Utilities Commission
465 South King Street
Kekuanao'a Building
Honolulu, HI 96813
General number: 808-586-2020
Fax: 808-586-2066
Website: http://puc.hawaii.gov

Complaints and Consumer Affairs
Website: http://puc.hawaii.gov/forms/complaints-inquiries (for informal/formal complaints)
E-mail: hawaii.puc@hawaii.gov
William J. Stokes
Investigator
E-mail: william.j.stokes@hawaii.gov

IDAHO

Idaho Public Utilities Commission
472 West Washington Street
P.O. Box 83720
Boise, ID 83720-0074
General number: 208-334-0300
Fax: 208-334-3762
Website: www.puc.idaho.gov

Complaints and Consumer Affairs
Phone: 208-334-0369; 800-432-0369 (toll-free)
Fax: 208-334-4045
Website: www.puc.idaho.gov/forms/cons/cons.html (for consumer assistance form)

Beverly Barker
Consumer Assistance Supervisor
Phone: 208-334-0302
Fax: 208-334-4045
E-mail: beverly.barker@puc.idaho.gov

ILLINOIS

Illinois Commerce Commission
527 East Capitol Avenue
Springfield, IL 62701
General number: 312-814-2850
Fax: 312-814-1818
Website: www.icc.illinois.gov

On-line Complaints
Phone: 800-524-0795; 217-782-2024 (outside of Illinois)
Website: www.icc.illinois.gov/consumer/complaint

Public Affairs
Beth Bosch
Director of Public Affairs
Phone: 217-782-5793
Fax: 217-785-7413
E-mail: bbosch@icc.illinois.gov

INDIANA

Indiana Utility Regulatory Commission
National City Center
101 West Washington Street
Suite 1500 East
Indianapolis, IN 46204
General number: 317-232-2701
Fax: 317-232-6758
Website: www.in.gov/iurc

Complaints and Consumer Affairs
Phone: 800-851-4268
Website: www.in.gov/iurc/consumer/complaint_form.html (for on-line complaints)

Kenya McMillin
Interim Director
Phone: 317-234-0572
Fax: 317-233-2410
E-mail: kmcmillin.urc.in.gov

IOWA

Iowa Utilities Board
1375 E. Court Avenue, Room 69
Des Moines, IA 50319-0069
General number: 515-281-5979
Fax: 515-281-8821
Website: www.state.ia.us/iub

Consumer Affairs
Phone: 877-565-4450
Fax: 515-725-7399
E-mail: customer@iub.iowa.gov
Website: www.state.ia.us/government/com/util/forms/CustServ/form_Complaints.html (for on-

line complaints)

Jane Whetstone
Customer Service Coordinator
E-mail: jane.whetstone@iub.state.ia.us

KANSAS

Kansas Corporation Commission
1500 SW Arrowhead Rd.
Topeka, KS 66604
General number: 785-271-3100
Fax: 785-271-3354
Website: www.kcc.ks.gov

Complaints
Office of Public Affairs and Consumer Protection
Phone: 785-271-3100; 800-662-0027 (toll-free)
E-mail: public.affairs@kcc.ks.gov

Consumer Protection
Steve Boyd
Phone: 785-271-3242
Fax: 785-271-3111
E-mail: s.boyd@kcc.ks.gov

KENTUCKY

Kentucky Public Service Commission
211 Sower Blvd.
Frankfort, KY 40601
P.O. Box 615
Frankfort, KY 40602
General number: 502-564-3940
Fax: 502-564-3460
Website: www.psc.ky.gov

Complaints/Consumer Services Division
Phone: 800-772-4636
E-mail: psc.consumer.inquiry@ky.gov

Consumer Affairs
Virginia L. Smith
Director, Consumer Services
Phone: 502-561-3940
Fax: 502-564-7397
E-mail: virginial.smith@ky.gov

LOUISIANA

Louisana Public Service Commission
Galvez Building, 12th Floor
602 North Fifth Street
P.O. Box 91154
Baton Rouge, LA 70821-9154
General number: 225-342-4404/4999
Phone: 800-256-2397
Fax: 225-342-2831
Website: www.lpsc.org

Complaints: Contact Commissioner's office. If you do not know who your Commissioner is or need contact information for your Commissioner's office, go to www.lpsc.org/commissioners.aspx to see the district map. If you have trouble contacting your Commissioner's office, contact the main office.

Lawrence C. St. Blanc
Secretary
Phone: 225-342-4427
Fax: 225-342-4087
E-mail: lawrence.stblanc@la.gov

MAINE

Maine Public Utilities Commission
101 Second Street
Hallowell, ME 04347
Mailing: 18 State House Station
Augusta, ME 04333-0018
General number: 207-287-3831
Fax: 207-287-1039
Website: www.maine.gov/mpuc

Complaints/Commission's Consumer Assistance Division
Phone: 800-452-4699 (or log onto website and provide all requested information)
Website: www.maine.gov/mpuc/consumer/file_complaint.shtml

Consumer Assistance
Derek D. Davidson
Director
Phone: 207-287-3831
Fax: 207-287-1039
E-mail: derek.d.davidson@maine.gov

MARYLAND

Maryland Public Service Commission
William Donald Schaefer Tower
6 St. Paul Street, 16th Floor
Baltimore, MD 21202-6806
General number: 410-767-8000; 800-492-0474
Fax: 410-333-6495
Website: http://webapp.psc.state.md.us/Intranet/home.cfm

Complaints
Website: http://webapp.psc.state.md.us/Intranet/info/complaintfront_new.cfm; http://webapp.psc.state.md.us/Intranet/capa/complaintform_new.cfm (for on-line complaint form); http://webapp.psc.state.md.us/Intranet/capa/ComplaintNotes_new.cfm(for instructions)

Consumer Affairs
Odogwu Obi Linton, Esq.
Director, Office of External Relations and Retail Market Development
Phone: 410-767-8046
Fax: 410-333-6844
E-mail: olinton@psc.state.md.us

MASSACHUSETTS

Massachusetts Department of Public Utilities
One South Station
2nd Floor
Boston, MA 02110
General number: 617-305-3500
Fax: 617-345-9101
Website: www.mass.gov/dpu

Consumer and External Affairs
Elizabeth A. Cellucci
Director
Phone: 617-305-3610
E-mail: elizabeth.cellucci@state.ma.us

Consumer Affairs and Business Regulation
Phone: 617-973-8787; 1-888-283-3757 (toll-free)
E-mail: Complete on-line contact form at www.mass.gov/?pageID=ocautilities&sid=Eoca&U=oca_contact_form
Website: www.mass.gov (select "State Agencies" link on top left corner of webpage; select "Alphabetic List, All Branches"; select "Consumer Affairs and Business Regulation, Department of" on list of state agencies; select "For Consumers" tab near the top of webpage; finally, select "How to resolve a consumer problem" under Online Services)

Consumer (DTC)
Karen Robinson
Director, Consumer Division
Phone: 617-368-1121
Fax: 617-478-2591
E-mail: karen.robinson@state.ma.us

MICHIGAN

Michigan Public Service Commission
6545 Mercantile Way
Lansing, MI 48911-7721
P.O. Box 30221
Lansing, MI 48909
General number: 517-241-6180
Fax: 517-241-6181
Website: www.michigan.gov/mpsc

Complaints
Phone: 800-292-9555 (informal complaint within Michigan); 517-241-6180 (outside of Michigan)
Fax: 517-241-2400
Website: www.michigan.gov/mpsc/0,1607,7-159-16368_16415—,00.html

Public Affairs
Judy Palnau
Phone: 517-241-3323
Fax: 517-241-6189
E-mail: palnauj@michigan.gov

MINNESOTA

Minnesota Public Utilities Commission
121 7th Place East, Suite 350
St. Paul, MN 55101-2147
General number: 651-296-7124
Toll free: 1-800-657-3782
Fax: 651-297-7073
Website: www.puc.state.mn.us

Complaints
E-mail: consumer.puc@state.mn.us
Website: www.puc.state.mn.us/PUC/consumers/file-a-complaint/000100 (for instructions and complaint form)

Consumer Affairs
Deborah Motz
Manager
Phone: 651-296-0406; 800-657-3782
Fax: 651-297-7073

E-mail: deborah.motz@state.mn.us

MISSISSIPPI

Mississippi Public Service Commission
501 North West Street
Woolfolk State Office Building
Jackson, MS 39201-1174
P.O. Box 1174
201-A
Jackson, MS 39215
General number: 601-961-5400
Fax: 601-961-5842
Website: www.psc.state.ms.us

Complaints
Website: www.psc.state.ms.us/Complaint (for instructions)

Executive Secretary: Brian Ray
Executive Secretary—PSC
Phone: 601-961-5434
Fax: 601-961-5469
E-mail: brian.ray@psc.state.ms.

MISSOURI

Missouri Public Service Commission
200 Madison Street
Governor Office Building
Jefferson City, MO 65101
P.O. Box 360
Jefferson City, MO 65102
General number: 573-751-3234
Fax: 573-751-1847
Website: http://psc.mo.gov

Consumer Service
Phone: 800-392-4211
Website: http://psc.mo.gov/file-a-complaint/file-a-complaint (for instructions and complaint form)

Consumer Affairs
Gay Fred
Manager, Consumer Services Department
573-751-3160
Fax: 573-526-1500
E-mail: gay.fred@psc.mo.gov

MONTANA

Montana Public Service Commission
1701 Prospect Avenue
P.O. Box 202601
Helena, MT 59620-2601
General number: 406-444-6199
Fax: 406-444-7618
Website: www.psc.mt.gov

Consumer Complaints
Phone: 800-646-6150; 406-444-6150

Consumer Affairs
Phillip W. Cooke
Chief, Compliance and Public Information Bureau
Phone: 406-444-6190
Fax: 406-444-7618
E-mail: pcooke@mt.gov

NEBRASKA

Nebraska Public Service Commission
300 The Atrium
1200 N Street
Lincoln, NE 68508
P.O. Box 94927-4927
Lincoln, NE 68509
General number: 402-471-3101
Fax: 402-471-0254
Website: www.psc.nebraska.gov

Complaints and Consumer Affairs
Toll free: 800-526-0017 (Nebraska only)
Website: www.psc.nebraska.gov/home/NPSC/forms/Complaint_Form.htm (for complaint form)

Cheryl Elton
Telecommunications
Phone: 402-471-0238
Fax: 402-471-0254
E-mail: cheryl.elton@nebraska.gov

NEVADA

Nevada Public Utilities Commission
1150 East William Street
Carson City, NV 89701-3109
General number: 775-684-6101
Fax: 775-684-6110
Website: http://pucweb1.state.nv.us/PUCN

Complaints
775-684-6100 (consumer complaints)
Website: http://pucweb1.state.nv.us/PUCN/ConsumerInfo/Form1.aspx (for complaint form)

Andie Arthurholtz
Manager Consumer Complaints Resolution
Phone: 702-486-7231
Fax: 702-486-7206
E-mail: aarthurz@puc.nv.gov

NEW HAMPSHIRE

New Hampshire Public Utilities Commission
21 South Fruit Street
Suite 10
Concord, NH 03301-2429
General number: 603-271-2431
Fax: 603-271-3878
Website: www.puc.state.nh.us

Consumer Assistance
Phone: 800-852-3793
Website: www.puc.state.nh.us/Consumer/complaint.htm (for on-line complaint form)

Consumer Affairs
Amanda Noonan
Director, Consumer Affairs
Phone: 603-271-2431
Fax: 603-271-3878
E-mail: amanda.noonan@puc.nh.gov

NEW JERSEY

New Jersey Board of Public Utilities
Two Gateway Center, 8th Floor
Newark, NJ 07102
General number: 973-648-2026
Website: www.bpu.state.nj.us

Division of Customer Assistance
Phone: 800-624-0241
973-648-2350 (out-of-state callers)
Website: www.bpu.state.nj.us/bpu/assistance/complaints/inquiry.html (for on-line complaint form)

Complaints and Consumer Affairs
Eric Hartsfield
Director, Division of Customer Relations
Phone: 973-648-4436; 973-648-2836
E-mail: eric.hartsfield@bpu.state.nj.us

NEW MEXICO

New Mexico Public Regulation Commission
1120 Paseo De Peralta
PERA Building
Santa Fe, NM 87501-1269
P.O. Box 1269
Santa Fe, NM 87504
General number: 1-888-4ASK-PRC (1-888-427-5772)
Fax: 505-827-4379
Website: www.nmprc.state.nm.us

Complaints
Website: www.nmprc.state.nm.us/crd.htm (for on-line complaint)

Johnny Montoya
Director, Consumer Relations Division
Phone: 505-827-4661 (direct); 505-827-4592
Fax: 505-827-4463
E-mail: john.montoya@state.nm.us

NEW YORK

New York Public Service Commission
Ellicott Square Building
Buffalo, NY 14203-2508
Three Empire State Plaza
Albany, NY 12223-1350
90 Church Street
New York, NY 10007-2919
General number: 518-474-7080
Fax: 518-473-2838
Website: www.dps.state.ny.us

Complaints
Phone: 800-342-3377
Website: www.dps.state.ny.us/complaints.html (for on-line complaints)

Consumer Affairs and Complaints
Sandra Sloane
Director, Office of Consumer Services
Phone: 518-474-3280
Fax: 518-486-7868
E-mail: sandra_sloane@dps.state.ny.us

NORTH CAROLINA

North Carolina Utilities Commission
430 North Salisbury Street
Raleigh, NC 27603-5918

4325 Mail Service Center
Raleigh, NC 27699-4325
General number: 919-733-4249
Fax: 919-733-7300
Website: www.ncuc.net

Complaints/Consumer Services Division
Phone: 866-380-9816; 919-733-9277
E-mail: Consumer.Services@psncuc.nc.gov

Administrative Services
Renne Vance
Chief Clerk
Phone: 919-733-0840
Fax: 919-733-7300
E-mail: vance@ncuc.net

NORTH DAKOTA

North Dakota Public Service Commission
600 E. Boulevard Avenue, Dept. 408
Bismarck, ND 58505-0480
General number: 701-328-2400
Fax: 701-328-2410
Website: www.psc.nd.gov

Complaints
Website: www.psc.nd.gov/public/consinfo/index.php (consumer information)

General Counsel
Illona A. Jeffcoat-Sacco
General Counsel
Phone: 707-328-2407
Fax: 701-328-2410
E-mail: ijs@nd.us

OHIO

Public Utilities Commission of Ohio
180 East Broad Street
Columbus, OH 43215-3793
General number: 614-466-3016
Fax: 614-466-7366
Website: www.puco.ohio.gov/puco

Complaints
Phone: 800-686-7826
Fax: 614-752-8351
Website: www.puc.state.oh.us/secure/PicForm/index.cfm?navitem=righttop (on-line form)

Consumer Affairs
Doris McCarter
Departmental Director, Service Monitoring and Enforcement Department
Phone: 614-995-0137
Fax: 614-752-8351
E-mail: doris.mccarter@puc.state.oh.us

OKLAHOMA

Oklahoma Corporation Commission
Jim Thorpe Office Building
2101 North Lincoln Blvd.
Oklahoma City, OK 73105-2000
P.O. Box 52000
Oklahoma City, OK 73152
General number: 405-521-2211
Fax: 405-522-1623
Website: www.occeweb.com/index.html

Complaints and Consumer Affairs
Website: www.occeweb.com/Complaints/pucomplaints2.html (for on-line complaint form)

Brooks Mitchell
Acting Director, Consumer Services
Phone: 405-521-2307
Fax: 405-522-1623
E-mail: b.mitchell@occemail.com

OREGON

Oregon Public Utility Commission
550 Capitol Street, NE, Suite 215
P.O. Box 2148
Salem, OR 97308-2148
Website: www.puc.state.or.us

Complaints
Website: www.puc.state.or.us/PUC/consumer/comppro.shtml (for complaint procedure); http://apps.puc.state.or.us/consumer/complaint.asp (for on-line complaint form)

Accounting and Consumer Affairs
David Poston
Administrator, Central Services
Phone: 503-378-6661
Fax: 503-373-7950
E-mail: david.poston@state.or.us

PENNSYLVANIA

Pennsylvania Public Utility Commission
P.O. Box 3265
Harrisburg, PA 17105
400 North Street
Commonwealth Keystone Building
Harrisburg, PA 17120-3265
General number: 717-787-5722
Fax: 717-787-4193
Website: www.puc.state.pa.us

Complaints
800-692-7380 (consumer hotline)
Website: www.puc.state.pa.us/general/filecomplaints.aspx (for on-line instructions)

Consumer Affairs
Lenora M. Best
Chief, Policy Division of Bureau of Consumer Affairs
Phone: 717-783-9090
Fax: 717-783-5659
E-mail: lebest@state.pa.us

PUERTO RICO

Puerto Rico Telecommunications Regulatory Board
500 Avenue, Robert H. Todd
(Pda. 18-Santurce)
San Juan, PR 00907-3981
General number: 787-756-0804
Fax: 787-756-0814
Website: www.jrtpr.gobierno.pr

Complaints
Juan Carlos Diaz
Director of Complaints and Customer Service
Phone: 787-756-0804
Fax: 787-765-4968
E-mail: juan.diaz@jrtpr.gobierno.pr

RHODE ISLAND

Rhode Island Public Utilities Commission
89 Jefferson Blvd.
Warwick, RI 02888
General number: 401-941-4500
Fax: 401-941-8827
Website: www.ripuc.org
Secretary: Pat Rossi
401-941-4500
E-mail: prossi@puc.state.ri.us

Complaint
Website: www.ripuc.org/consumerinfo/filecomplaint.html (for on-line complaint form)

SOUTH CAROLINA

South Carolina Public Service Commission
101 Executive Center Dr.
Columbia, SC 29210
General number: 803-896-5100
Fax: 803-896-5246
P.O. Drawer 11649
Columbia, SC 29211
General number: 803-896-5100
Fax: 803-896-5246
Website: www.psc.sc.gov

Complaints/
Phone: 800-922-1531 or 803-737-5230
Fax: 803-896-5199
Website: www.psc.sc.gov/consumer/info1.asp or www.psc.sc.gov/forms.asp (for on-line consumer information and complaint form)

Administrative Services
Charles L. A. Terreni
Chief Clerk/Administrator
Phone: 803-896-5133
Fax: 803-896-5246
E-mail: charles.terreni@psc.sc.gov

SOUTH DAKOTA

South Dakota Public Utilities Commission
State Capitol
500 East Capitol Avenue
Pierre, SD 57501-5070
General number: 605-773-3201
Fax: 866-757-6031
Website: http://puc.sd.gov

Complaints and Consumer Affairs
Fax: 1-800-332-1782
Website: http://puc.sd.gov/consumer/complaint_form.aspx (for on-line complaint form)
Deb Gregg
Consumer Affairs Manager
Phone: 605-773-3201
E-mail: deb.gregg@state.sd.us

TENNESSEE

Tennessee Regulatory Authority
460 James Robertson Parkway
Nashville, TN 37243
General number: 615-741-2904
Fax: 615-741-5015
Website: www.state.tn.us/tra

Complaints
Fax: 615-741-8953
Website: www.state.tn.us/tra/complnt.html (for on-line complaint form)

Consumer Affairs
Lisa Cooper
Chief, Consumer Services Division
E-mail: lisa.cooper@state.tn.gov

TEXAS

Public Utility Commission of Texas
1701 North Congress Avenue
Austin, TX 78711-3326
P.O. Box 13326
Austin, TX 78701
General number: 512-936-7000
Fax: 512-936-7003
Website: www.puc.state.tx.us

Complaints
Fax: 512-936-7003
E-mail: customer@puc.state.tx.us
Website: www.puc.state.tx.us/consumer/complaint/form/ComplaintForm.aspx?type=e (for on-line complaint form)

Consumer Affairs
Mike Renfro
Director, Customer Protection
Phone: 512-936-7145
Fax: 512-936-7003
E-mail: mike.renfro@puc.state.tx.us

UTAH

Public Service Commission of Utah
160 East 300 South
4th Floor
Salt Lake City, UT 84111
General number: 801-530-6716
Fax: 801-530-6796
Website: www.psc.utah.gov

Complaints/Division Of Public Utilities
Phone: 800-874-0904
Website: www.psc.utah.gov/complaints/index.html (for on-line complaint process information)

Rea Peterson
Customer Service Support
Phone: 801-530-6652
Fax: 801-530-6650
E-mail: rpeterson@utah.gov

VERMONT

Vermont Public Service Board
112 State Street
4th Floor
Montpelier, VT 05620-2701
General number: 802-828-2358
Fax: 802-828-3351
Website: http://psb.vermont.gov

General Counsel
Kurk Janson
E-mail: kurt.janson@state.vt.us

VIRGIN ISLANDS

Virgin Islands Public Services Commission
Post Office Box 40
Charlotte Amalie
St. Thomas, VI 00804
General number: 340-776-1291
Fax: 340-774-4971
Website: www.psc.gov.vi

Complaints
Website: www.psc.gov.vi/filecomplaint.html (for on-line complaint information and form)

VIRGINIA

Virginia State Corporation Commission
1300 E. Main Street
Richmond, Virginia 23219
P.O. Box 1197
Richmond, VA 23218
General number: 804-371-9608
Fax: 804-371-9376
Website: www.scc.virginia.gov

Complaints and Consumer Affairs
Phone: 800-552-7945
Website: www.scc.virginia.gov/pue/complaint.aspx (for on-line instructions); www.scc.virginia.gov/pue/ElectricityComplaint.aspx (for on-line form)

Paulette Edmonds
Telecommunications Specialist
Phone: 804-371-9271
Fax: 804-225-5727
E-mail: paulette.edmonds@scc.virginia.gov

WASHINGTON

Washington Utilities and Transportation Commission
1300 S. Evergreen Park Drive
P.O. Box 47250
Olympia, WA 98504-7250
General number: 360-664-1160
Fax: 360-586-1150
Website: www.utc.wa.gov/Pages/default.aspx

Complaints
Phone: 888-333-WUTC (9882)
E-mail: consumer@utc.wa.gov
Website: www.utc.wa.gov/consumers/Pages/ConsumerComplaints.aspx (for on-line complaint information);
www.utc.wa.gov/consumers/Pages/ConsumerComplaintForm.aspx (for on-line complaint form)

Consumer Protection and Public Affairs
Sharon Wallace
Assistant Director, Consumer Protection and Communications
Phone: 306-664-1143
E-mail: swallace@utc.wa.gov

WEST VIRGINIA

Public Service Commission of West Virginia
201 Brooks Street
Charleston, WV 25301
P.O. Box 812
Charleston, WV 25323
General number: 304-340-0300
Fax: 304-340-0325
Website: www.psc.state.wv.us

Complaints
Phone: 800-344-5113
Website: www.psc.state.wv.us (choose "Formal Complaint" from the left of the screen)

Carrier and Consumer Operations
Carla Nelson
Supervisor—Informal Complaints
Phone: 304-340-0424
Fax: 304-340-0452
E-mail: cnelson@psc.state.wv.us

WISCONSIN

Public Service Commission of Wisconsin
610 North Whitney Way
Madison, WI 53705-2729
P.O. Box 7854
Madison, WI 53707-7854
General number: 608-266-5481
Com. Fax: 608-266-1401
Fax: 608-266-3957
Website: www.psc.wi.gov

Complaints and Consumer Affairs
Phone: 800-225-7729; 608-266-2001 (in Madison)
Website: http://psc.wi.gov/consumerInfo/complaints/index-complaints.htm (for on-line complaint information); http://psc.wi.gov/apps40/complaint/consumer/FileComplaint.aspx (for on-line complaint form)

Amelia Ramirez
Administrator
Phone: 608-267-7829
E-mail: amelia.ramirez@wisconsin.gov

WYOMING

Wyoming Public Service Commission
2515 Warren Avenue, Suite 300
Cheyenne, WY 82002
General number: 307-777-7427
Fax: 307-777-5700
Website: http://psc.state.wy.us

Complaints
Phone: 307-777-7427; 888-570-9905 (toll-free)
E-mail: wpsc_complaints@wyo.gov

Consumer Affairs
Bryce Freeman
Administrator
Phone: 307-777-5742
Fax: 307-777-5700
E-mail: bfreem@state.wy.us

Appendix B Telephone and Telecommunications Materials

This appendix is also available on the companion website to this treatise. The companion website facilitates keyword searches and allows relevant provisions to be imported as word-processing documents.

B.1 Universal Service Sections in the Telecommunications Act of 1996

The following sections of the Telecommunications Act of 1996 concern the federal telecommunications universal services programs. The complete Telecommunications Act of 1996 is available through the FCC website at www.fcc.gov/telecom.html. Additional materials can be found on the companion website to this manual.

B.1.1 Telecom Carriers Eligible for Universal Service Support—47 U.S.C. § 214

Sec.

* * *

§ 214 Extension of lines or discontinuance of service; certificate of public convenience and necessity

* * *

47 U.S.C. § 214 Extension of lines or discontinuance of service; certificate of public convenience and necessity

(a) Exceptions; temporary or emergency service or discontinuance of service; changes in plant, operation or equipment

No carrier shall undertake the construction of a new line or of an extension of any line, or shall acquire or operate any line, or extension thereof, or shall engage in transmission over or by means of such additional or extended line, unless and until there shall first have been obtained from the Commission a certificate that the present or future public convenience and necessity require or will require the construction, or operation, or construction and operation, of such additional or extended line: *Provided*, That no such certificate shall be required under this section for the construction, acquisition, or operation of

(1) a line within a single State unless such line constitutes part of an interstate line,

(2) local, branch, or terminal lines not exceeding ten miles in length, or

(3) any line acquired under section 221 of this title: *Provided further*, That the Commission may, upon appropriate request being made, authorize temporary or emergency service, or the supplementing of existing facilities, without regard to the provisions of this section. No carrier shall discontinue, reduce, or impair service to a community, or part of a community, unless and until there shall first have been obtained from the Commission a certificate that neither the present nor future public convenience and necessity will be adversely affected thereby; except that the Commission may, upon appropriate request being made, authorize temporary or emergency discontinuance, reduction, or impairment of service, or partial discontinuance, reduction, or impairment of service, without regard to the provisions of this section. As used in this section the term "line" means any channel of communication established by the use of appropriate equipment, other than a channel of communication established by the interconnection of two or more existing channels: *Provided, however*, That nothing in this section shall be construed to require a certificate or other authorization from the Commission for any installation, replacement, or other changes in plant, operation, or equipment, other than new construction, which will not impair the adequacy or quality of service provided.

(b) Notification of Secretary of Defense, Secretary of State, and State Governor

Upon receipt of an application for any such certificate, the Commission shall cause notice thereof to be given to, and shall cause a copy of such application to be filed with, the Secretary of Defense, the Secretary of State (with respect to such applications involving service to foreign points), and the Governor of each State in which such line is proposed to be constructed, extended, acquired, or operated, or in which such discontinuance, reduction, or impairment of service is proposed, with the right to those notified to be heard; and the Commission may require such published notice as it shall determine.

(c) Approval or disapproval; injunction

The Commission shall have power to issue such certificate as applied for, or to refuse to issue it, or to issue it for a portion or portions of a line, or extension thereof, or discontinuance, reduction, or impairment of service, described in the application, or for the partial exercise only of such right or privilege, and may attach to the issuance of the certificate such terms and conditions as in its judgment the public convenience and necessity may require. After issuance of such certificate, and not before, the carrier may, without securing approval other than such certificate, comply with the terms and conditions contained in or attached to the issuance of such certificate and proceed with the construction, extension, acquisition, operation, or discontinuance, reduction, or impairment of service covered thereby. Any construction, extension, acquisition, operation, discontinuance, reduction, or impairment of service contrary to the provisions of this section may be enjoined by any court of competent jurisdiction at the suit of the United States, the Commission, the State commission, any State affected, or any party in interest.

(d) Order of Commission; hearing; penalty

The Commission may, after full opportunity for hearing, in a proceeding upon complaint or upon its own initiative without complaint, authorize or require by order any carrier, party to such proceeding, to provide itself with adequate facilities for the expeditious and efficient performance of its service as a common carrier and to extend its line or to establish a public office; but no such authorization or order shall be made unless the Commission finds, as to such provision of facilities, as to such establishment of public offices, or as to such extension, that it is reasonably required in the interest of public convenience and necessity, or as to such extension or facilities that the expense involved therein will not impair the ability of the carrier to perform its duty to the public. Any carrier which refuses or neglects to comply with any order of the Commission made in pursuance of this subsection shall forfeit to the United States $1200 for each day during which such refusal or neglect continues.

(e) Provision of universal service

(1) Eligible telecommunications carriers

A common carrier designated as an eligible telecommunications carrier under paragraph (2), (3), or (6) shall be eligible to receive universal service support in accordance with section 254 of this title and shall, throughout the service area for which the designation is received—

(A) offer the services that are supported by Federal universal service support mechanisms under section 254(c) of this title, either using its own facilities or a combination of its own facilities and resale of another carrier's services (including the services offered by another eligible telecommunications carrier); and

(B) advertise the availability of such services and the charges therefor using media of general distribution.

(2) Designation of eligible telecommunications carriers

A State commission shall upon its own motion or upon request designate a common carrier that meets the requirements of paragraph (1) as an eligible telecommunications carrier for a service area designated by the State commission. Upon request and consistent with the public interest, convenience, and necessity, the State commission may, in the case of an area served by a rural telephone company, and shall, in the case of all other areas, designate more than one common carrier as an eligible telecommunications carrier for a service area designated by the State commission, so long as each additional requesting carrier meets the requirements of paragraph (1). Before designating an additional eligible telecommunications carrier for an area served by a rural telephone company, the State commission shall find that the designation is in the public interest.

(3) Designation of eligible telecommunications carriers for unserved areas

If no common carrier will provide the services that are supported by Federal universal service support mechanisms under section 254(c) of this title to an unserved community or any portion thereof that requests such service, the Commission, with respect to interstate services or an area served by a common carrier to which paragraph (6) applies, or a State commission, with respect to intrastate services, shall determine which common carrier or carriers are best able to provide such service to the requesting unserved community or portion thereof and shall order such carrier or carriers to provide such service for that unserved community or portion thereof. Any carrier or carriers ordered to provide such service under this paragraph shall meet the requirements of paragraph (1) and shall be designated as an eligible telecommunications carrier for that community or portion thereof.

(4) Relinquishment of universal service

A State commission (or the Commission in the case of a common carrier designated under paragraph (6)) shall permit an eligible telecommunications carrier to relinquish its designation as such a carrier in any area served by more than one eligible telecommunications carrier. An eligible telecommunications carrier that seeks to relinquish its eligible telecommunications carrier designation for an area served by more than one eligible telecommunications carrier shall give advance notice to the State commission (or the Commission in the case of a common carrier designated under paragraph (6)) of such relinquishment. Prior to permitting a telecommunications carrier designated as an eligible telecommunications carrier to cease providing universal service in an area served by more than one eligible telecommunications carrier, the State commission (or the Commission in the case of a common carrier designated under paragraph (6)) shall require the remaining eligible telecommunications carrier or carriers to ensure that all customers served by the relinquishing carrier will continue to be served, and shall require sufficient notice to permit the purchase or construction of adequate facilities by any remaining eligible telecommunications carrier. The State commission (or the Commission in the case of a common carrier designated under paragraph (6)) shall establish a time, not to exceed one year after the State commission (or the Commission in the case of a common carrier designated under paragraph (6)) approves such relinquishment under this paragraph, within which such purchase or construction shall be completed.

(5) "Service area defined"

The term "service area" means a geographic area established by a State commission (or the Commission under paragraph (6)) for the purpose of determining universal service obligations and support mechanisms. In the case of an area served by a rural telephone company, "service area" means such company's "study area" unless and until the Commission and the States, after taking into account recommendations of a Federal-State Joint Board instituted under section 410(c) of this title, establish a different definition of service area for such company.

(6) Common carriers not subject to state commission jurisdiction

In the case of a common carrier providing telephone exchange service and exchange access that is not subject to the jurisdiction of a State commission, the Commission shall upon request designate such a common carrier that meets the requirements of paragraph (1) as an eligible telecommunications carrier for a service area designated by the Commission consistent with applicable Federal and State law. Upon request and consistent with the public interest, convenience and necessity, the Commission may, with respect to an area served by a rural telephone company, and shall, in the case of all other areas, designate more than one common carrier as an eligible telecommunications carrier for a service area designated under this paragraph, so long as each additional requesting carrier meets the requirements of paragraph (1). Before designating an additional eligible telecommunications carrier for an area served by a rural telephone company, the Commission shall find that the designation is in the public interest.

[48 Stat. 1075, ch. 652, tit. II, § 214 (June 19, 1934); 57 Stat. 11, ch. 10, §§ 2 to 5 (Mar. 6, 1943); Pub. L. No. 93-506, § 1, 88 Stat. 1577 (Nov. 30, 1974); Pub. L. No. 101-239, tit. III, § 3002(d), 103 Stat. 2131 (Dec. 19, 1989); Pub. L. No. 103-414, tit. III, § 304(a)(4), 108 Stat. 4296 (Oct. 25, 1994); Pub. L. No. 104-104, tit. I, § 102(a), 110 Stat. 80 (Feb. 8, 1996); Pub. L. No. 105-125, § 1, 111 Stat. 2540 (Dec. 1, 1997)]

B.1.2 Federal Telecommunications Universal Services—47 U.S.C. § 254

Sec.

* * *

§ 254 Universal service

* * *

47 U.S.C. § 254 Universal service

(a) Procedures to review universal service requirements

(1) Federal-State Joint Board on universal service

Within one month after February 8, 1996, the Commission shall institute and refer to a Federal-State Joint Board under section 410(c) of this title a proceeding to recommend changes to any of its regulations in order to implement sections 214(e) of this title and this section, including the definition of the services that are supported by Federal universal service support mechanisms and a specific timetable for completion of such recommendations. In addition to the members of the Joint Board required under section 410(c) of this title, one member of such Joint Board shall be a State-appointed utility consumer advocate nominated by a national organization of State utility consumer advocates. The Joint Board shall, after notice and opportunity for public comment, make its recommendations to the Commission 9 months after February 8, 1996.

(2) Commission action

The Commission shall initiate a single proceeding to implement the recommendations from the Joint Board required by paragraph (1) and shall complete such proceeding within 15 months after February 8, 1996. The rules established by such proceeding shall include a definition of the services that are supported by Federal universal service support mechanisms and a specific timetable for implementation. Thereafter, the Commission shall complete any proceeding to implement subsequent recommendations from any Joint Board on universal service within one year after receiving such recommendations.

(b) Universal service principles

The Joint Board and the Commission shall base policies for the preservation and advancement of universal service on the following principles:

(1) Quality and rates

Quality services should be available at just, reasonable, and affordable rates.

(2) Access to advanced services

Access to advanced telecommunications and information services should be provided in all regions of the Nation.

(3) Access in rural and high cost areas

Consumers in all regions of the Nation, including low-income consumers and those in rural, insular, and high cost areas, should have access to telecommunications and information services, including interexchange services and advanced telecommunications and information services, that are reasonably comparable to those services provided in urban areas and that are available at rates that are reasonably comparable to rates charged for similar services in urban areas.

(4) Equitable and nondiscriminatory contributions

All providers of telecommunications services should make an equitable and nondiscriminatory contribution to the preservation and advancement of universal service.

(5) Specific and predictable support mechanisms

There should be specific, predictable and sufficient Federal and State mechanisms to preserve and advance universal service.

(6) Access to advanced telecommunications services for schools, health care, and libraries

Elementary and secondary schools and classrooms, health care providers, and libraries should have access to advanced telecommunications services as described in subsection (h) of this section.

(7) Additional principles

Such other principles as the Joint Board and the Commission determine are necessary and appropriate for the protection of the public interest, convenience, and necessity and are consistent with this chapter.

(c) Definition

(1) In general

Universal service is an evolving level of telecommunications services that the Commission shall establish periodically under this section, taking into account advances in telecommunications and information technologies and services. The Joint Board in recommending, and the Commission in establishing, the definition of the services that are supported by Federal universal service support mechanisms shall consider the extent to which such telecommunications services—

(A) are essential to education, public health, or public safety;

(B) have, through the operation of market choices by customers, been subscribed to by a substantial majority of residential customers;

(C) are being deployed in public telecommunications networks by telecommunications carriers; and

are consistent with the public interest, convenience, and necessity.

(2) Alterations and modifications

The Joint Board may, from time to time, recommend to the Commission modifications in the definition of the services that are supported by Federal universal service support mechanisms.

(3) Special services

In addition to the services included in the definition of universal service under paragraph (1), the Commission may designate additional services for such support mechanisms for schools, libraries, and health care providers for the purposes of subsection (h) of this section.

(d) Telecommunications carrier contribution

Every telecommunications carrier that provides interstate telecommunications services shall contribute, on an equitable and nondiscriminatory basis, to the specific, predictable, and sufficient mechanisms established by the Commission to preserve and advance universal service. The Commission may exempt a carrier or class of carriers from this requirement if the carrier's telecommunications activities are limited to such an extent that the level of such carrier's contribution to the preservation and advancement of universal service would be de minimis. Any other provider of interstate telecommunications may be required to contribute to the preservation and advancement of universal service if the public interest so requires.

(e) Universal service support

After the date on which Commission regulations implementing this section take effect, only an eligible telecommunications carrier designated under section 214(e) of this title shall be eligible to receive specific Federal universal service support. A carrier that receives such support shall use that support only for the provision, maintenance, and upgrading of facilities and services for which the support is intended. Any such support should be explicit and sufficient to achieve the purposes of this section.

(f) State authority

A State may adopt regulations not inconsistent with the Commission's rules to preserve and advance universal service. Every telecommunications carrier that provides intrastate telecommunications services shall contribute, on an equitable and nondiscriminatory basis, in a manner determined by the State to the preservation and advancement of universal service in that State. A State may adopt regulations to provide for additional definitions and standards to preserve and advance universal service within that State only to the extent that such regulations adopt additional specific, predictable, and sufficient mechanisms to support such definitions or standards that do not rely on or burden Federal universal service support mechanisms.

(g) Interexchange and interstate services

Within 6 months after February 8, 1996, the Commission shall adopt rules to require that the rates charged by providers of interexchange telecommunications services to subscribers in rural and high cost areas shall be no higher than the rates charged by each such provider to its subscribers in urban areas. Such rules shall also require that a provider of interstate interexchange telecommunications services shall provide such services to its subscribers in each State at rates no higher than the rates charged to its subscribers in any other State.

(h) Telecommunications services for certain providers

(1) In general

(A) Health care providers for rural areas

A telecommunications carrier shall, upon receiving a bona fide request, provide telecommunications services which are necessary for the provision of health care services in a State, including instruction relating to such services, to any public or nonprofit health care provider that serves persons who reside in rural areas in that State at rates that are reasonably comparable to rates charged for similar services in urban areas in that State. A telecommunications carrier providing service under this paragraph shall be entitled to have an amount equal to the difference, if any, between the rates for services provided to health care providers for rural areas in a State and the rates for similar services provided to other customers in comparable rural areas in that State treated as a service obligation as a part of its obligation to participate in the mechanisms to preserve and advance universal service.

(B) Educational providers and libraries

All telecommunications carriers serving a geographic area shall, upon a bona fide request for any of its services that are within the definition of universal service under subsection (c)(3) of this section, provide such services to elementary schools, secondary schools, and libraries for educational purposes at rates less than the amounts charged for similar services to other parties. The discount shall be an amount that the Commission, with respect to interstate services, and the States, with respect to intrastate services, determine is appropriate and necessary to ensure affordable access to and use of such services by such entities. A telecommunications carrier providing service under this paragraph shall—

(i) have an amount equal to the amount of the discount treated as an offset to its obligation to contribute to the mechanisms to preserve and advance universal service, or

(ii) notwithstanding the provisions of subsection (e) of this section, receive reimbursement utilizing the support mechanisms to preserve and advance universal service.

(2) Advanced services

The Commission shall establish competitively neutral rules—

(A) to enhance, to the extent technically feasible and economically reasonable, access to advanced telecommunications and information services for all public and nonprofit elementary and secondary school classrooms, health care providers, and libraries; and

(B) to define the circumstances under which a telecommunications carrier may be required to connect its network to such public institutional telecommunications users.

(3) Terms and conditions

Telecommunications services and network capacity provided to a public institutional telecommunications user under this subsection may not be sold, resold, or otherwise transferred by such user in consideration for money or any other thing of value.

(4) Eligibility of users

No entity listed in this subsection shall be entitled to preferential rates or treatment as required by this subsection, if such entity operates as a for-profit business, is a school described in paragraph (7)(A) with an endowment of more than $50,000,000, or is a library or library consortium not eligible for assistance from a State library administrative agency under the Library Services and Technology Act [20 U.S.C.A. § 9121 *et seq.*].

(5) Requirements for certain schools with computers having internet access

(A) Internet safety

(i) In general

Except as provided in clause (ii), an elementary or secondary school having computers with Internet access may not receive services at discount rates under paragraph (1)(B) unless the school, school board, local educational agency, or other authority with responsibility for administration of the school—

(I) submits to the Commission the certifications described in subparagraphs (B) and (C);

(II) submits to the Commission a certification that an Internet safety policy has been adopted and implemented for the school under subsection (l) of this section; and

(III) ensures the use of such computers in accordance with the certifications.

(ii) Applicability

The prohibition in clause (i) shall not apply with respect to a school that receives services at discount rates under paragraph (1)(B) only for purposes other than the provision of Internet access, Internet service, or internal connections.

(iii) Public notice; hearing

An elementary or secondary school described in clause (i), or the school board, local educational agency, or other authority with responsibility for administration of the school, shall provide reasonable public notice and hold at least one public hearing or meeting to address the proposed Internet safety policy. In the case of an elementary or secondary school other than an elementary or secondary school as defined in section 8801 of Title 20, the notice and hearing required by this clause may be limited to those members of the public with a relationship to the school.

(B) Certification with respect to minors

A certification under this subparagraph is a certification that the school, school board, local educational agency, or other authority with responsibility for administration of the school—

(i) is enforcing a policy of Internet safety for minors that includes monitoring the online activities of minors and the operation of a technology protection measure with respect to any of its computers with Internet access that protects against access through such computers to visual depictions that are—

(I) obscene;

(II) child pornography; or

(III) harmful to minors;

(ii) is enforcing the operation of such technology protection measure during any use of such computers by minors; and

(iii) as part of its Internet safety policy is educating minors about appropriate online behavior, including interacting with other individuals on social networking websites and in chat rooms and cyberbullying awareness and response.

(C) Certification with respect to adults

A certification under this paragraph is a certification that the school, school board, local educational agency, or other authority with responsibility for administration of the school—

(i) is enforcing a policy of Internet safety that includes the operation of a technology protection measure with respect to any of its computers with Internet access that protects against access through such computers to visual depictions that are—

(I) obscene; or

(II) child pornography; and

(ii) is enforcing the operation of such technology protection measure during any use of such computers.

(D) Disabling during adult use

An administrator, supervisor, or other person authorized by the certifying authority under subparagraph (A)(i) may disable the technology protection measure concerned, during use by an adult, to enable access for bona fide research or other lawful purpose.

(E) Timing of implementation

(i) In general

Subject to clause (ii) in the case of any school covered by this paragraph as of the effective date of this paragraph under section 1721(h) of the Children's Internet Protection Act, the certification under subparagraphs (B) and (C) shall be made—

(I) with respect to the first program funding year under this subsection following such effective date, not later than 120 days after the beginning of such program funding year; and

(II) with respect to any subsequent program funding year, as part of the application process for such program funding year.

(ii) Process

(I) Schools with internet safety policy and technology protection measures in place

A school covered by clause (i) that has in place an Internet safety policy and technology protection measures meeting the requirements necessary for certification under subparagraphs (B) and (C) shall certify its compliance with subparagraphs (B) and (C) during each annual program application cycle under this subsection, except that with respect to the first program funding year after the effective date of this paragraph under section 1721(h) of the Children's Internet Protection Act, the certifications shall be made not later than 120 days after the beginning of such first program funding year.

(II) Schools without internet safety policy and technology protection measures in place

A school covered by clause (i) that does not have in place an Internet safety policy and technology protection measures meeting the requirements necessary for certification under subparagraphs (B) and (C)—

(aa) for the first program year after the effective date of this subsection in which it is applying for funds under this subsection, shall certify that it is undertaking such actions, including any necessary procurement procedures, to put in place an Internet safety policy and technology protection measures meeting the requirements necessary for certification under subparagraphs (B) and (C); and

(bb) for the second program year after the effective date of this subsection in which it is applying for funds under this subsection, shall certify that it is in compliance with subparagraphs (B) and (C).

Any school that is unable to certify compliance with such requirements in such second program year shall be ineligible for services at discount rates or funding in lieu of services at such rates under this subsection for such second year and all subsequent program years under this subsection, until such time as such school comes into compliance with this paragraph.

(III) Waivers

Any school subject to subclause (II) that cannot come into compliance with subparagraphs (B) and (C) in such second year program may seek a waiver of subclause

(II)(bb) if State or local procurement rules or regulations or competitive bidding requirements prevent the making of the certification otherwise required by such subclause. A school, school board, local educational agency, or other authority with responsibility for administration of the school shall notify the Commission of the applicability of such subclause to the school. Such notice shall certify that the school in question will be brought into compliance before the start of the third program year after the effective date of this subsection in which the school is applying for funds under this subsection.

(F) Noncompliance

(i) Failure to submit certification

Any school that knowingly fails to comply with the application guidelines regarding the annual submission of certification required by this paragraph shall not be eligible for services at discount rates or funding in lieu of services at such rates under this subsection.

(ii) Failure to comply with certification

Any school that knowingly fails to ensure the use of its computers in accordance with a certification under subparagraphs (B) and (C) shall reimburse any funds and discounts received under this subsection for the period covered by such certification.

(iii) Remedy of noncompliance

(I) Failure to submit

A school that has failed to submit a certification under clause (i) may remedy the failure by submitting the certification to which the failure relates. Upon submittal of such certification, the school shall be eligible for services at discount rates under this subsection.

(II) Failure to comply

A school that has failed to comply with a certification as described in clause (ii) may remedy the failure by ensuring the use of its computers in accordance with such certification. Upon submittal to the Commission of a certification or other appropriate evidence of such remedy, the school shall be eligible for services at discount rates under this subsection.

(6) Requirements for certain libraries with computers having internet access

(A) Internet safety

(i) In general

Except as provided in clause (ii), a library having one or more computers with Internet access may not receive services at discount rates under paragraph (1)(B) unless the library—

(I) submits to the Commission the certifications described in subparagraphs (B) and (C); and

(II) submits to the Commission a certification that an Internet safety policy has been adopted and implemented for the library under subsection (l) of this section; and

(III) ensures the use of such computers in accordance with the certifications.

(ii) Applicability

The prohibition in clause (i) shall not apply with respect to a library that receives services at discount rates under paragraph (1)(B) only for purposes other than the provision of Internet access, Internet service, or internal connections.

(iii) Public notice; hearing

A library described in clause (i) shall provide reasonable public notice and hold at least one public hearing or meeting to address the proposed Internet safety policy.

(B) Certification with respect to minors

A certification under this subparagraph is a certification that the library—

(i) is enforcing a policy of Internet safety that includes the operation of a technology protection measure with respect to any of its computers with Internet access that protects against access through such computers to visual depictions that are—

(I) obscene;

(II) child pornography; or

(III) harmful to minors; and

(ii) is enforcing the operation of such technology protection measure during any use of such computers by minors.

(C) Certification with respect to adults

A certification under this paragraph is a certification that the library—

(i) is enforcing a policy of Internet safety that includes the operation of a technology protection measure with respect to any of its computers with Internet access that protects against access through such computers to visual depictions that are—

(I) obscene; or

(II) child pornography; and

(ii) is enforcing the operation of such technology protection measure during any use of such computers.

(D) Disabling during adult use

An administrator, supervisor, or other person authorized by the certifying authority under subparagraph (A)(i) may disable the technology protection measure concerned, during use by an adult, to enable access for bona fide research or other lawful purpose.

(E) Timing of implementation

(i) In general

Subject to clause (ii) in the case of any library covered by this paragraph as of the effective date of this paragraph under section 1721(h) of the Children's Internet Protection Act, the certification under subparagraphs (B) and (C) shall be made—

(I) with respect to the first program funding year under this subsection following such effective date, not later than 120 days after the beginning of such program funding year; and

(II) with respect to any subsequent program funding year, as part of the application process for such program funding year.

(ii) Process

(I) Libraries with Internet safety policy and technology protection measures in place. A library covered by clause (i) that has in place an Internet safety policy and technology protection measures meeting the requirements necessary for certification under subparagraphs (B) and (C) shall certify its compliance with subparagraphs (B) and (C) during each annual program application cycle under this subsection, except that with respect to the first program funding year after the effective date of this paragraph under section 1721(h) of the Children's Internet Protection Act, the certifications shall be made not later than 120 days after the beginning of such first program funding year.

(II) Libraries without internet safety policy and technology protection measures in place. A library covered by clause (i) that does not have in place an Internet safety policy and technology protection measures meeting the requirements necessary for certification under subparagraphs (B) and (C)—

(aa) for the first program year after the effective date of this subsection in which it is applying for funds under this subsection, shall certify that it is undertaking such actions, including any necessary procurement procedures, to put in place an Internet safety policy and technology protection measures meeting the requirements necessary for certification under subparagraphs (B) and (C); and

(bb) for the second program year after the effective date of this subsection in which it is applying for funds under this subsection, shall certify that it is in compliance with subparagraphs (B) and (C).

Any library that is unable to certify compliance with such requirements in such second program year shall be ineligible for services at discount rates or funding in lieu of services at such rates under this subsection for such second year and all subsequent program years under this subsection, until such time as such library comes into compliance with this paragraph.

(III) Waivers

Any library subject to subclause (II) that cannot come into compliance with subparagraphs (B) and (C) in such second year may seek a waiver of subclause (II)(bb) if State or local procurement rules or regulations or competitive bidding requirements prevent the making of the certification otherwise required by such subclause. A library, library board, or other authority with responsibility for administration of the library shall notify the Commission of the applicability of such subclause to the library. Such notice shall certify that the library in question will be brought into compliance before the start of the third program year after the effective date of this subsection in which the library is applying for funds under this subsection.

(F) Noncompliance

(i) Failure to submit certification

Any library that knowingly fails to comply with the application guidelines regarding the annual submission of certification required by this paragraph shall not be eligible for services at discount rates or funding in lieu of services at such rates under this subsection.

(ii) Failure to comply with certification

Any library that knowingly fails to ensure the use of its computers in accordance with a certification under subparagraphs (B) and (C) shall reimburse all funds and discounts received under this subsection for the period covered by such certification.

(iii) Remedy of noncompliance

(I) Failure to submit

A library that has failed to submit a certification under clause (i) may remedy the failure by submitting the certification to which the failure relates. Upon submittal of such certification, the library shall be eligible for services at discount rates under this subsection.

(II) Failure to comply

A library that has failed to comply with a certification as described in clause (ii) may remedy the failure by ensuring the use of its computers in accordance with such certification. Upon submittal to the Commission of a certification or other appropriate evidence of such remedy, the library shall be eligible for services at discount rates under this subsection.

(7) Definitions

For purposes of this subsection:

(A) Elementary and secondary schools

The term "elementary and secondary schools" means elementary schools and secondary schools, as defined in section 7801 of Title 20.

(B) Health care provider

The term "health care provider" means—

(i) post-secondary educational institutions offering health care instruction, teaching hospitals, and medical schools;

(ii) community health centers or health centers providing health care to migrants;

(iii) local health departments or agencies;

(iv) community mental health centers;

(v) not-for-profit hospitals;

(vi) rural health clinics; and

(vii) consortia of health care providers consisting of one or more entities described in clauses (i) through (vi).

(C) Public institutional telecommunications user

The term "public institutional telecommunications user" means an elementary or secondary school, a library, or a health care provider as those terms are defined in this paragraph.

(D) Minor

The term "minor" means any individual who has not attained the age of 17 years.

(E) Obscene

The term "obscene" has the meaning given such term in section 1460 of Title 18.

(F) Child pornography

The term "child pornography" has the meaning given such term in section 2256 of Title 18.

(G) Harmful to minors

The term "harmful to minors" means any picture, image, graphic image file, or other visual depiction that—

(i) taken as a whole and with respect to minors, appeals to a prurient interest in nudity, sex, or excretion;

(ii) depicts, describes, or represents, in a patently offensive way with respect to what is suitable for minors, an actual or simulated sexual act or sexual contact, actual or simulated normal or perverted sexual acts, or a lewd exhibition of the genitals; and

(iii) taken as a whole, lacks serious literary, artistic, political, or scientific value as to minors.

(H) Sexual act; sexual contact

The terms "sexual act" and "sexual contact" have the meanings given such terms in section 2246 of Title 18.

(I) Technology protection measure

The term "technology protection measure" means a specific technology that blocks or filters Internet access to the material covered by a certification under paragraph (5) or (6) to which such certification relates.

(*i*) Consumer protection
The Commission and the States should ensure that universal service is available at rates that are just, reasonable, and affordable.

(j) Lifeline assistance
Nothing in this section shall affect the collection, distribution, or administration of the Lifeline Assistance Program provided for by the Commission under regulations set forth in section 69.117 of title 47, Code of Federal Regulations, and other related sections of such title.

(k) Subsidy of competitive services prohibited
A telecommunications carrier may not use services that are not competitive to subsidize services that are subject to competition. The Commission, with respect to interstate services, and the States, with respect to intrastate services, shall establish any necessary cost allocation rules, accounting safeguards, and guidelines to ensure that services included in the definition of universal service bear no more than a reasonable share of the joint and common costs of facilities used to provide those services.

(*l*) Internet safety policy requirement for schools and libraries

(1) In general
In carrying out its responsibilities under subsection (h) of this section, each school or library to which subsection (h) of this section applies shall—

(A) adopt and implement an Internet safety policy that addresses—

(i) access by minors to inappropriate matter on the Internet and World Wide Web;
(ii) the safety and security of minors when using electronic mail, chat rooms, and other forms of direct electronic communications;
(iii) unauthorized access, including so-called "hacking," and other unlawful activities by minors online;
(iv) unauthorized disclosure, use, and dissemination of personal identification information regarding minors; and
(v) measures designed to restrict minors' access to materials harmful to minors; and

(B) provide reasonable public notice and hold at least one public hearing or meeting to address the proposed Internet safety policy.

(2) Local determination of content
A determination regarding what matter is inappropriate for minors shall be made by the school board, local educational agency, library, or other authority responsible for making the determination. No agency or instrumentality of the United States Government may—

(A) establish criteria for making such determination;
(B) review the determination made by the certifying school, school board, local educational agency, library, or other authority; or
(C) consider the criteria employed by the certifying school, school board, local educational agency, library, or other authority in the administration of subsection (h)(1)(B) of this section.

(3) Availability for review
Each Internet safety policy adopted under this subsection shall be made available to the Commission, upon request of the Commission, by the school, school board, local educational agency, library, or other authority responsible for adopting such Internet safety policy for purposes of the review of such Internet safety policy by the Commission.

(4) Effective date
This subsection shall apply with respect to schools and libraries on or after the date that is 120 days after December 21, 2000.

[ch. 652, Title II, § 254 (June 19, 1934), *as added* Pub. L. No. 104-104, tit. I, § 101(a), 110 Stat. 71 (Feb. 8, 1996); *and amended* Pub. L. No. 104-208, div. A, tit. I, § 101(e) [tit. VII, § 709(a)(8)], 110 Stat. 3009-313 (Sept. 30, 1996); Pub. L. No. 106-554, § 1(a)(4) [div. B, tit. XVII, §§ 1721(a)–(f), 1732], 114 Stat. 2763, 2763A-343 to 2763A-350 (Dec. 21, 2000); *as amended* Pub. L. No. 107-110, tit. X, § 1076(hh), 115 Stat. 2094 (Jan. 8, 2002); Pub. L. No. 110-385, Title II, § 215, 122 Stat. 4104 (Oct. 10, 2008)]

B.2 Federal Regulations for Universal Services Support for Low-Income Consumers

The following regulations concern the federal universal services program for low-income consumers. The accompanying website to this manual contains the regulations for all of the federal universal services programs.

B.2.1 Telecom Carriers Eligible for Universal Service Support (Eligible Telecommunications Carriers)—47 C.F.R. §§ 54.201–54.209

Sec.

§ 54.201 Definition of eligible telecommunications carriers, generally.
§ 54.202 Additional requirements for Commission designation of eligible telecommunications carriers.
§ 54.203 Designation of eligible telecommunications carriers for unserved areas.
§ 54.205 Relinquishment of universal service.
§ 54.207 Service areas.
§ 54.209 Annual reporting requirements for designated eligible telecommunications carriers.

SOURCE: 62 Fed. Reg. (June 17, 1997); 72 Fed. Reg. 46920 (Aug. 22, 2007), unless otherwise noted.

AUTHORITY: 47 U.S.C. 151, 154(i), 201, 205, 214, and 254 unless otherwise noted.

47 C.F.R. § 54.201 Definition of eligible telecommunications carriers, generally.

(a) Carriers eligible to receive support.

(1) Beginning January 1, 1998, only eligible telecommunications carriers designated under paragraphs (b) through (d) of this section shall receive universal service support distributed pursuant to part 36 and part 69 of this chapter, and subparts D and E of this part.

(2) [Reserved]

(3) This paragraph does not apply to offset or reimbursement support distributed pursuant to subpart G of this part.

(4) This paragraph does not apply to support distributed pursuant to subpart F of this part.

(b) A state commission shall upon its own motion or upon request designate a common carrier that meets the requirements of paragraph (d) of this section as an eligible telecommunications carrier for a service area designated by the state commission.

(c) Upon request and consistent with the public interest, convenience, and necessity, the state commission may, in the case of an area served by a rural telephone company, and shall, in the case of all other areas, designate more than one common carrier as an eligible telecommunications carrier for a service area designated by the state commission, so long as each additional requesting carrier meets the requirements of paragraph (d) of this section. Before designating an additional eligible telecommunications carrier for an area served by a rural telephone company, the state commission shall find that the designation is in the public interest.

(d) A common carrier designated as an eligible telecommunications carrier under this section shall be eligible to receive universal service support in accordance with section 254 of the Act and shall, throughout the service area for which the designation is received:

(1) Offer the services that are supported by federal universal service support mechanisms under subpart B of this part and section 254(c) of the Act, either using its own facilities or a combination of its own facilities and resale of another carrier's services (including the services offered by another eligible telecommunications carrier); and

(2) Advertise the availability of such services and the charges therefore using media of general distribution.

(e) For the purposes of this section, the term *facilities* means any physical components of the telecommunications network that are used in the transmission or routing of the services that are designated for support pursuant to subpart B of this part.

(f) For the purposes of this section, the term "own facilities" includes, but is not limited to, facilities obtained as unbundled network elements pursuant to part 51 of this chapter, provided that such facilities meet the definition of the term "facilities" under this subpart.

(g) A state commission shall not require a common carrier, in order to satisfy the requirements of paragraph (d)(1) of this section, to use facilities that are located within the relevant service area, as long as the carrier uses facilities to provide the services designated for support pursuant to subpart B of this part within the service area.

(h) A state commission shall designate a common carrier that meets the requirements of this section as an eligible telecommunications carrier irrespective of the technology used by such carrier.

(*i*) A state commission shall not designate as an eligible telecommunications carrier a telecommunications carrier that offers the services supported by federal universal service support mechanisms exclusively through the resale of another carrier's services.

[63 Fed. Reg. 2125 (Jan. 13, 1998); 64 Fed. Reg. 62123 (Nov. 16, 1999); 71 Fed. Reg. 65750 (Nov. 9, 2006)]

47 C.F.R. § 54.202 Additional requirements for Commission designation of eligible telecommunications carriers.

(a) In order to be designated an eligible telecommunications carrier under section 214(e)(6), any common carrier in its application must:

(1)(i) Commit to provide service throughout its proposed designated service area to all customers making a reasonable request for service. Each applicant shall certify that it will:

(A) Provide service on a timely basis to requesting customers within the applicant's service area where the applicant's network already passes the potential customer's premises; and

(B) Provide service within a reasonable period of time, if the potential customer is within the applicant's licensed service area but outside its existing network coverage, if service can be provided at reasonable cost by:

(1) Modifying or replacing the requesting customer's equipment;

(2) Deploying a roof-mounted antenna or other equipment;

(3) Adjusting the nearest cell tower;

(4) Adjusting network or customer facilities;

(5) Reselling services from another carrier's facilities to provide service; or

(6) Employing, leasing or constructing an additional cell site, cell extender, repeater, or other similar equipment.

(ii) Submit a five-year plan that describes with specificity proposed improvements or upgrades to the applicant's network on a wire center-by-wire center basis throughout its proposed designated service area. Each applicant shall demonstrate how signal quality, coverage or capacity will improve due to the receipt of high-cost support; the projected start date and completion date for each improvement and the estimated amount of investment for each project that is funded by high-cost support; the specific geographic areas where the improvements will be made; and the estimated population that will be served as a result of the improvements. If an applicant believes that service improvements in a particular wire center are not needed, it must explain its basis for this determination and demonstrate how funding will otherwise be used to further the provision of supported services in that area.

(2) Demonstrate its ability to remain functional in emergency situations, including a demonstration that it has a reasonable amount of back-up power to ensure functionality without an external power source, is able to reroute traffic around damaged facilities, and is capable of managing traffic spikes resulting from emergency situations.

(3) Demonstrate that it will satisfy applicable consumer protection and service quality standards. A commitment by wireless applicants to comply with the Cellular Telecommunications and Internet Association's Consumer Code for Wireless Service will satisfy this requirement. Other commitments will be considered on a case-by-case basis.

(4) Demonstrate that it offers a local usage plan comparable to the one offered by the incumbent LEC in the service areas for which it seeks designation.

(5) Certify that the carrier acknowledges that the Commission may require it to provide equal access to long distance carriers in the event that no other eligible telecommunications carrier is providing equal access within the service area.

(b) Any common carrier that has been designated under section 214(e)(6) as an eligible telecommunications carrier or that has submitted its application for designation under section 214(e)(6) before the effective date of these rules must submit the information required by paragraph (a) of this section no later than October 1, 2006, as part of its annual reporting requirements under § 54.209.

(c) Public Interest Standard. Prior to designating an eligible telecommunications carrier pursuant to section 214(e)(6), the Commission determines that such designation is in the public interest. In doing so, the Commission shall consider the benefits of increased consumer choice, and the unique advantages and disadvantages of the applicant's service offering. In instances where an eligible telecommunications carrier applicant seeks designation below the study area level of a rural telephone company, the Commission shall also conduct a creamskimming analysis that compares the population density of each wire center in which the eligible telecommunications carrier applicant seeks designation against that of the wire centers in the study area in which the eligible telecommunications carrier applicant does not seek designation. In its creamskimming analysis, the Commission shall consider other factors, such as disaggregation of support pursuant to § 54.315 by the incumbent local exchange carrier.

(d) A common carrier seeking designation as an eligible telecommunications carrier under section 214(e)(6) for any part of tribal lands shall provide a copy of its petition to the affected tribal government and tribal regulatory authority, as applicable, at the time it files its petition with the Federal Communications Commission. In addition, the Commission shall send the relevant public notice seeking comment on any petition for designation as an eligible telecommunications carrier on tribal lands, at the time it is released, to the affected tribal government and tribal regulatory authority, as applicable, by overnight express mail.

(e) All eligible telecommunications carriers shall retain all records required to demonstrate to auditors that the support received was consistent with the universal service high-cost program rules. These records should include the following: data supporting line count filings; historical customer records; fixed asset property accounting records; general ledgers; invoice copies for the purchase and maintenance of equipment; maintenance contracts for the upgrade or equipment; and any other relevant documentation. This documentation must be maintained for at least five years from the receipt of funding.

[70 Fed. Reg. 29978 (May 25, 2005); 72 Fed. Reg. 54217 (Sept. 24, 2007); 72 Fed. Reg. 67858 (Dec. 3, 2007); 73 Fed. Reg. 11837 (Mar. 5, 2008)]

47 C.F.R. § 54.203 Designation of eligible telecommunications carriers for unserved areas.

(a) If no common carrier will provide the services that are supported by federal universal service support mechanisms under section 254(c) of the Act and subpart B of this part to an unserved community or any portion thereof that requests such service, the Commission, with respect to interstate services, or a state commission, with respect to intrastate services, shall determine which common carrier or carriers are best able to provide such service to the requesting unserved community or portion thereof and shall order such carrier or carriers to provide such service for that unserved community or portion thereof.

(b) Any carrier or carriers ordered to provide such service under this section shall meet the requirements of section 54.201(d) and shall be designated as an eligible telecommunications carrier for that community or portion thereof.

47 C.F.R. § 54.205 Relinquishment of universal service.

(a) A state commission shall permit an eligible telecommunications carrier to relinquish its designation as such a carrier in any area served by more than one eligible telecommunications carrier. An eligible telecommunications carrier that seeks to relinquish its eligible telecommunications carrier designation for an area served by more than one eligible telecommunications carrier shall give advance notice to the state commission of such relinquishment.

(b) Prior to permitting a telecommunications carrier designated as an eligible telecommunications carrier to cease providing universal service in an area served by more than one eligible telecommunications carrier, the state commission shall require the remaining eligible telecommunications carrier or carriers to ensure that all customers served by the relinquishing carrier will continue to be served, and shall require sufficient notice to permit the purchase or construction of adequate facilities by any remaining eligible telecommunications carrier. The state commission shall establish a time, not to exceed one year after the state commission approves such relinquishment under this section, within which such purchase or construction shall be completed.

47 C.F.R. § 54.207 Service areas.

(a) The term *service area* means a geographic area established by a state commission for the purpose of determining universal service obligations and support mechanisms. A service area defines the overall area for which the carrier shall receive support from federal universal service support mechanisms.

(b) In the case of a service area served by a rural telephone company, *service area* means such company's "study area" unless and until the Commission and the states, after taking into account recommendations of a Federal-State Joint Board instituted under section 410(c) of the Act, establish a different definition of service area for such company.

(c) If a state commission proposes to define a service area served by a rural telephone company to be other than such company's study area, the Commission will consider that proposed definition in accordance with the procedures set forth in this paragraph.

(1) A state commission or other party seeking the Commission's agreement in redefining a service area served by a rural telephone company shall submit a petition to the Commission. The petition shall contain:

(i) The definition proposed by the state commission; and

(ii) The state commission's ruling or other official statement presenting the state commission's reasons for adopting its proposed definition, including an analysis that takes into account the recommendations of any Federal-State Joint Board convened to provide recommendations with respect to the definition of a service area served by a rural telephone company.

(2) The Commission shall issue a Public Notice of any such petition within fourteen (14) days of its receipt.

(3) The Commission may initiate a proceeding to consider the petition within ninety (90) days of the release date of the Public Notice.

(i) If the Commission initiates a proceeding to consider the petition, the proposed definition shall not take effect until both the state commission and the Commission agree upon the definition of a rural service area, in accordance with paragraph (b) of this section and section 214(e)(5) of the Act.

(ii) If the Commission does not act on the petition within ninety (90) days of the release date of the Public Notice, the definition proposed by the state commission will be deemed approved by the Commission and shall take effect in accordance with state procedures.

(d) The Commission may, on its own motion, initiate a proceeding to consider a definition of a service area served by a rural telephone company that is different from that company's study area. If it proposes such different definition, the Commission shall seek the agreement of the state commission according to this paragraph.

(1) The Commission shall submit a petition to the state commission according to that state commission's procedures. The petition submitted to the relevant state commission shall contain:

(i) The definition proposed by the Commission; and

(ii) The Commission's decision presenting its reasons for adopting the proposed definition, including an analysis that takes into account the recommendations of any Federal-State Joint Board convened to provide recommendations with respect to the definition of a service area served by a rural telephone company.

(2) The Commission's proposed definition shall not take effect until both the state commission and the Commission agree upon the definition of a rural service area, in accordance with paragraph (b) of this section and section 214(e)(5) of the Act.

(e) The Commission delegates its authority under paragraphs (c) and (d) of this section to the Chief, Wireline Competition Bureau.

[67 Fed. Reg. 13226 (Mar. 21, 2002)]

47 C.F.R. § 54.209 Annual reporting requirements for designated eligible telecommunications carriers.

(a) A common carrier designated under section 214(e)(6) as an eligible telecommunications carrier shall provide:

(1) A progress report on its five-year service quality improvement plan, including maps detailing its progress towards meeting its plan targets, an explanation of how much universal service support was received and how it was used to improve signal quality, coverage, or capacity, and an explanation regarding any network improvement targets that have not been fulfilled. The information shall be submitted at the wire center level;

(2) Detailed information on any outage, as that term is defined in 47 CFR 4.5, of at least 30 minutes in duration for each service area in which an eligible telecommunications carrier is designated for any facilities it owns, operates, leases, or otherwise utilizes that potentially affect

(i) At least ten percent of the end users served in a designated service area; or

(ii) A 911 special facility, as defined in 47 CFR 4.5(e).

(iii) Specifically, the eligible telecommunications carrier's annual report must include information detailing:

(A) The date and time of onset of the outage;

(B) A brief description of the outage and its resolution;

(C) The particular services affected;

(D) The geographic areas affected by the outage;

(E) Steps taken to prevent a similar situation in the future; and

(F) The number of customers affected.

(3) The number of requests for service from potential customers within the eligible telecommunications carrier's service areas that were unfulfilled during the past year. The carrier shall also detail how it attempted to provide service to those potential customers, as set forth in § 54.202(a)(1)(i);

(4) The number of complaints per 1,000 handsets or lines;

(5) Certification that it is complying with applicable service quality standards and consumer protection rules;

(6) Certification that the carrier is able to function in emergency situations as set forth in § 54.201(a)(2);

(7) Certification that the carrier is offering a local usage plan comparable to that offered by the incumbent LEC in the relevant service areas; and

(8) Certification that the carrier acknowledges that the Commission may require it to provide equal access to long distance carriers in the event that no other eligible telecommunications carrier is providing equal access within the service area.

(b) Filing deadlines. In order for a common carrier designated under section 214(e)(6) to continue to receive support for the following calendar year, or retain its eligible telecommunications carrier designation, it must submit the annual reporting information in paragraph (a) no later than October 1, 2006, and thereafter annually by October 1 of each year. Eligible telecommunications carriers that file their reports after the October 1 deadline shall receive support pursuant to the following schedule:

(1) Eligible telecommunication carriers that file no later than January 1 of the subsequent year shall receive support for the second, third and fourth quarters of the subsequent year.

(2) Eligible telecommunication carriers that file no later than April 1 of the subsequent year shall receive support for the third and fourth quarters of the subsequent year.

(3) Eligible telecommunication carriers that file no later than July 1 of the subsequent year shall receive support for the fourth quarter of the subsequent year.

[70 Fed. Reg. 29978 (May 25, 2005); 72 Fed. Reg. 67858 (Dec. 3, 2007)]

B.2.2 Universal Services Support for Low-Income Consumers (Lifeline and Link-Up)—47 C.F.R. § 54.400–54.418

Sec.

SOURCE: 62 Fed. Reg. 32948 (June 17, 1997); 72 Fed. Reg. 46920 (Aug. 22, 2007), unless otherwise noted.

AUTHORITY: 47 U.S.C. §§ 1, 4(i), 201, 205, 214, and 254 unless otherwise noted.

47 C.F.R. § 54.400 Terms and definitions.

As used in this subpart, the following terms shall be defined as follows:

(a) Qualifying low-income consumer. A "qualifying low-income consumer" is a consumer who meets the qualifications for Lifeline, as specified in § 54.409.

(b) Toll blocking. "Toll blocking" is a service provided by carriers that lets consumers elect not to allow the completion of outgoing toll calls from their telecommunications channel.

(c) Toll control. "Toll control" is a service provided by carriers that allows consumers to specify a certain amount of toll usage that may be incurred on their telecommunications channel per month or per billing cycle.

(d) Toll limitation. "Toll limitation" denotes either toll blocking or toll control for eligible telecommunications carriers that are incapable of providing both services. For eligible telecommunications carriers that are capable of providing both services, "toll limitation" denotes both toll blocking and toll control.

(e) Eligible resident of Tribal lands. An "eligible resident of Tribal lands" is a "qualifying low-income consumer," as defined in paragraph (a) of this section, living on or near a reservation. A "reservation" is defined as any federally recognized Indian tribe's reservation, pueblo, or colony, including former reservations in Oklahoma, Alaska Native regions established pursuant to the Alaska Native Claims Settlement Act (85 Stat. 688), and Indian allotments. "Near reservation" is defined as those areas or communities adjacent or contiguous to reservations which are designated by the Department of Interior's Commission of Indian Affairs upon recommendation of the local Bureau of Indian Affairs Superintendent, which recommendation shall be based upon consultation with the tribal governing body of those reservations, as locales appropriate for the extension of financial assistance and/or social services, on the basis of such general criteria as: Number of Indian people native to the reservation residing in the area; a written designation by the tribal governing body that members of their tribe and family members who are Indian residing in the area, are socially, culturally and economically affiliated with their tribe and reservation; geographical proximity of the area to the reservation, and administrative feasibility of providing an adequate level of services to the area.

Note to paragraph (e): The Commission stayed implementation of paragraph (e) as applied to qualifying low-income consumers living "near reservations" on August 31, 2000 (15 FCC Rcd 17112).

(f) Income. "Income" is all income actually received by all members of the household. This includes salary before deductions for taxes, public assistance benefits, social security payments, pensions, unemployment compensation, veteran's benefits, inheritances, alimony, child support payments, worker's compensation benefits, gifts, lottery winnings, and the like. The only exceptions are student financial aid, military housing and cost-of-living allowances, irregular income from occasional small jobs such as baby-sitting or lawn mowing, and the like.

[63 Fed. Reg. 2128 (Jan. 13, 1998); 65 Fed. Reg. 47905 (Aug. 4, 2000); 65 Fed. Reg. 58662 (Oct. 2, 2000); 68 Fed. Reg. 41941 (July 16, 2003); 69 Fed. Reg. 34600 (June 22, 2004)]

47 C.F.R. § 54.401 Lifeline defined.

(a) As used in this subpart, *Lifeline* means a retail local service offering:

(1) That is available only to qualifying low-income consumers, and no qualifying consumer is permitted to receive more than one Lifeline subsidy concurrently;

(2) For which qualifying low-income consumers pay reduced charges as a result of application of the Lifeline support amount described in § 54.403; and

(3) That includes the services or functionalities enumerated in § 54.101 (a)(1) through (a)(9). The carriers shall offer toll limitation to all qualifying low- income consumers at the time such consumers subscribe to Lifeline service. If the consumer elects to receive toll limitation, that service shall become part of that consumer's Lifeline service.

(b) [Reserved]

(c) Eligible telecommunications carriers may not collect a service deposit in order to initiate Lifeline service, if the qualifying low-income consumer voluntarily elects toll limitation service from the carrier, where available. If toll limitation services are unavailable, the carrier may charge a service deposit.

(d) The state commission shall file or require the eligible telecommunications carrier to file information with the Administrator demonstrating that the carrier's Lifeline plan meets the criteria set forth in this subpart and stating the number of qualifying low-income consumers and the amount of state assistance. Eligible telecommunications carriers not subject to state commission jurisdiction also shall make such a filing with the Administrator. Lifeline assistance shall be made available to qualifying low-income consumers as soon as the Administrator certifies that the carrier's Lifeline plan satisfies the criteria set out in this subpart.

(e) Consistent with § 52.33(a)(1)(i)(C), eligible telecommunications carriers may not charge Lifeline customers a monthly number-portability charge.

[63 Fed. Reg. 2128 (Jan. 13, 1998); 64 Fed. Reg. 60358 (Nov. 5, 1999); 65 Fed. Reg. 47905 (Aug. 4, 2000); 65 Fed. Reg. 49941 (Aug. 16, 2000); 69 Fed. Reg. 34600 (June 22, 2004); 76 Fed. Reg. 38044 (July 29, 2011)]

47 C.F.R. § 54.403 Lifeline support amount.

(a) The Federal Lifeline support amount for all eligible telecommunications carriers shall equal:

(1) Tier One. The tariffed rate in effect for the primary residential End User Common Line charge of the incumbent local exchange carrier serving the area in which the qualifying low-income consumer receives service, as determined in accordance with § 69.104 or §§ 69.152(d)(1) and 69.152(q) of this chapter, whichever is applicable;

(2) Tier Two. Additional federal Lifeline support in the amount of $1.75 per month will be made available to the eligible telecommunications carrier providing Lifeline service to the qualifying low-income consumer, if that carrier certifies to the Administrator that it will pass through the full amount of Tier-Two support to its qualifying, low-income consumers and that it has received any non-federal regulatory approvals necessary to implement the required rate reduction.

(3) Tier Three. Additional federal Lifeline support in an amount equal to one-half the amount of any state-mandated Lifeline support or Lifeline support otherwise provided by the carrier, up to a maximum of $1.75 per month in federal support, will be made available to the carrier providing Lifeline service to a qualifying low-income consumer if the carrier certifies to the Administrator that it will pass through the full amount of Tier-Three support to its qualifying low-income consumers and that it has received any non-federal regulatory approvals necessary to implement the required rate reduction.

(4) Tier Four. Additional federal Lifeline support of up to $25 per month will be made available to a eligible telecommunications carrier providing Lifeline service to an eligible resident of Tribal lands, as defined in § 54.400(e), to the extent that:

(i) This amount does not bring the basic local residential rate (including any mileage, zonal, or other non-discretionary charges associated with basic residential service) below $1 per month per qualifying low-income subscribers; and

(ii) The eligible telecommunications carrier certifies to the Administrator that it will pass through the full Tier-Four amount to qualifying eligible residents of Tribal lands and that it has received any non-federal regulatory approvals necessary to implement the required rate reduction.

(b) For a qualifying low-income consumer who is not an eligible resident of Tribal lands, as defined in § 54.400(e), the federal Lifeline support amount shall not exceed $3.50 plus the tariffed rate in effect for the primary residential End User Common Line charge of the incumbent local exchange carrier serving the area in which the qualifying low-income consumer receives service, as determined in accordance with § 69.104 or § 69.152(d) and (q) of this chapter, whichever is applicable. For an eligible resident of Tribal lands, the federal Lifeline support amount shall not exceed $28.50 plus that same End User Common Line charge. Eligible telecommunications carriers that charge federal End User Common Line charges or equivalent federal charges shall apply Tier-One federal Lifeline support to waive the federal End-User Common Line charges for Lifeline consumers. Such carriers shall apply any additional federal support amount to a qualifying low-income consumer's intrastate rate, if the carrier has received the non-federal regulatory approvals necessary to implement the required rate reduction. Other eligible telecommunications carriers shall apply the Tier-One federal Lifeline support amount, plus any additional support amount, to reduce their lowest tariffed (or otherwise generally available) residential rate for the services enumerated in § 54.101(a)(1) through (a)(9), and charge Lifeline consumers the resulting amount.

(c) Lifeline support for providing toll limitation shall equal the eligible telecommunications carrier's incremental cost of providing either toll blocking or toll control, whichever is selected by the particular consumer.

[63 Fed. Reg. 2128 (Jan. 13, 1998); 65 Fed. Reg. 38689 (June 21, 2000); 65 Fed. Reg. 47905 (Aug. 4, 2000); 65 Fed. Reg. 49941 (Aug. 16, 2000)]

47 C.F.R. § 54.405 Carrier obligation to offer Lifeline.

All eligible telecommunications carriers shall:

(a) Make available one Lifeline service, as defined in § 54.401, per qualifying low-income consumer that is not currently receiving Lifeline service from that or any other eligible telecommunications carrier, and

(b) Publicize the availability of Lifeline service in a manner reasonably designed to reach those likely to qualify for the service.

(c) Notify Lifeline subscribers of impending termination of Lifeline service if the carrier has a reasonable basis to believe that the subscriber no longer meets the Lifeline-qualifying criteria, as described in § 54.409. Notification of impending termination shall be in the form of a letter separate from the subscriber's monthly bill. A carrier providing Lifeline service in a state that has dispute resolution procedures applicable to Lifeline termination, that requires, at a minimum, written notification of impending termination, must comply with the applicable state requirements.

(d) Allow subscribers 60 days following the date of the impending termination letter required in paragraph (c) of this section in which to demonstrate continued eligibility. Subscribers making such a demonstration must present proof of continued eligibility to the carrier consistent with applicable state or federal verification requirements, as described in § 54.410(c). Carriers must terminate subscribers who fail to demonstrate continued eligibility within the 60-day time period. A carrier providing Lifeline service in a state that has dispute resolution procedures applicable to Lifeline termination must comply with the applicable state requirements.

(e) De-enrollment. Notwithstanding § 54.405(c) and (d) of this section, upon notification by the Administrator to any ETC in any state that a subscriber is receiving Lifeline service from another eligible telecommunications carrier and should be de-enrolled from participation in that ETC's Lifeline program, the ETC shall de-enroll the subscriber from participation in that ETC's Lifeline program within 5 business days. An ETC shall not be eligible for Lifeline reimbursement as described in §§ 54.403 and 54.407 for any de-enrolled subscriber following the date of that subscriber's de-enrollment.

[65 Fed. Reg. 47905 (Aug. 4, 2000); 65 Fed. Reg. 49941 (Aug. 16, 2000); 69 Fed. Reg. 34600 (June 22, 2004); 76 Fed. Reg. 38044 (July 29, 2011)]

47 C.F.R. § 54.407 Reimbursement for offering Lifeline.

(a) Universal service support for providing Lifeline shall be provided directly to the eligible telecommunications carrier, based on the number of qualifying low-income consumers it serves, under administrative procedures determined by the Administrator.

(b) The eligible telecommunications carrier may receive universal service support reimbursement for each qualifying low-income consumer served. For each consumer receiving Lifeline service, the reimbursement amount shall equal the federal support amount, including the support amount described in § 54.403(c). The eligible telecommunications carrier's universal service support reimbursement shall not exceed the carrier's standard, non-Lifeline rate.

(c) In order to receive universal service support reimbursement, the eligible telecommunications carrier must keep accurate records of the revenues it forgoes in providing Lifeline in conformity with § 54.401. Such records shall be kept in the form directed by the Administrator and provided to the Administrator at intervals as directed by the Administrator or as provided in this Subpart.

47 C.F.R. § 54.409 Consumer qualification for Lifeline.

(a) To qualify to receive Lifeline service in a state that mandates state Lifeline support, a consumer must meet the eligibility criteria established by the state commission for such support. The state commission shall establish narrowly targeted qualification criteria that are based solely on income or factors directly related to income. A state containing geographic areas included in the definition of "reservation" and "near reservation," as defined in § 54.400(e), must ensure that its qualification criteria are reasonably designed to apply to low-income individuals living in such areas.

(b) To qualify to receive Lifeline service in a state that does not mandate state Lifeline support, a consumer's income, as defined in § 54.400(f), must be at or below 135% of the Federal Poverty Guidelines or a consumer must participate in one of the following federal assistance programs: Medicaid; Food Stamps; Supplemental Security Income; Federal Public Housing Assistance (Section 8); Low-Income Home Energy Assistance Program; National School Lunch Program's free lunch program; or Temporary Assistance for Needy Families.

(c) A consumer that lives on a reservation or near a reservation, but does not meet the qualifications for Lifeline specified in paragraphs (a) and (b) of this section, nonetheless shall be a "qualifying low-income consumer" as defined in § 54.400(a) and thus an "eligible resident of Tribal lands" as defined in § 54.400(e) and shall qualify to receive Tiers One, Two, and Four Lifeline service if the individual participates in one of the following federal assistance programs: Bureau of Indian Affairs general assistance; Tribally administered Temporary Assistance for Needy Families; Head Start (only those meeting its income qualifying standard); or National School Lunch Program's free lunch program. Such qualifying low-income consumer shall also qualify for Tier-Three Lifeline support, if the carrier offering the Lifeline service is not subject to the regulation of the state and provides carrier-matching funds, as described in § 54.403(a)(3). To receive Lifeline support under this paragraph for the eligible resident of Tribal lands, the eligible telecommunications carrier offering the Lifeline service to such consumer must obtain the consumer's signature on a document certifying under penalty of perjury that the consumer receives benefits from at least one of the programs mentioned in this paragraph or paragraph (b) of this section, and lives on or near a reservation, as defined in § 54.400(e). In addition to identifying in that document the program or programs from which that consumer receives benefits, an eligible resident of Tribal lands also must agree to notify the carrier if that consumer ceases to participate in the program or programs. Such qualifying low-income consumer shall also qualify for Tier-Three Lifeline support, if the carrier offering the Lifeline service is not subject to the regulation of the state and provides carrier-matching funds, as described in § 54.403(a)(3).

(d) In a state that does not mandate state Lifeline support, each eligible telecommunications carrier providing Lifeline service to a qualifying low-income consumer pursuant to paragraphs (b) or (c) of this section must obtain that consumer's signature on a document certifying under penalty of perjury that:

(1) The consumer receives benefits from one of the programs listed in paragraphs (b) or (c) of this section, and identifying the program or programs from which that consumer receives benefits, or

(2) The consumer's household meets the income requirement of paragraph (b) of this section, and that the presented documentation of income, as described in §§ 54.400(f), 54.410(a)(ii), accurately represents the consumer's household income; and

(3) The consumer will notify the carrier if that consumer ceases to participate in the program or programs or if the consumer's income exceeds 135% of the Federal Poverty Guidelines.

[65 Fed. Reg. 47905 (Aug. 4, 2000); 65 Fed. Reg. 49941 (Aug. 16, 2000); 68 Fed. Reg. 41942 (July 16, 2003); 69 Fed. Reg. 34600 (June 22, 2004)]

47 C.F.R. § 54.410 Certification and Verification of Consumer Qualification for Lifeline.

(a) Certification of income. Consumers qualifying under an income-based criterion must present documentation of their household income prior to enrollment in Lifeline.

(1) By one year from the effective date of these rules, eligible telecommunications carriers in states that mandate state Lifeline support must comply with state certification procedures to document consumer income-based eligibility for Lifeline prior to that consumer's enrollment if the consumer is qualifying under an income-based criterion.

(2) By one year from the effective date of these rules, eligible telecommunications carriers in states that do not mandate state Lifeline support must implement certification procedures to document consumer-income-based eligibility for Lifeline prior to that consumer's enrollment if the consumer is qualifying under the income-based criterion specified in § 54.409(b). Acceptable documentation of income eligibility includes the prior year's state, federal, or tribal tax return, current income statement from an employer or paycheck stub, a Social Security statement of benefits, a Veterans Administration statement of benefits, a retirement/

pension statement of benefits, an Unemployment/Workmen's Compensation statement of benefits, federal or tribal notice letter of participation in General Assistance, a divorce decree, child support, or other official document. If the consumer presents documentation of income that does not cover a full year, such as current pay stubs, the consumer must present three consecutive months worth of the same types of document within that calendar year.

(b) Self-certifications. After income certification procedures are implemented, eligible telecommunications carriers and consumers are required to make certain self-certifications, under penalty of perjury, relating to the Lifeline program. Eligible telecommunications carriers must retain records of their self-certifications and those made by consumers.

(1) An officer of the eligible telecommunications carrier in a state that mandates state Lifeline support must certify that the eligible telecommunications carrier is in compliance with state Lifeline income certification procedures and that, to the best of his/her knowledge, documentation of income was presented.

(2) An officer of the eligible telecommunications carrier in a state that does not mandate state Lifeline support must certify that the eligible telecommunications carrier has procedures in place to review income documentation and that, to the best of his/her knowledge, the carrier was presented with documentation of the consumer's household income.

(3) Consumers qualifying for Lifeline under an income-based criterion must certify the number of individuals in their households on the document required in § 54.409(d).

(c) Verification of continued eligibility. Consumers qualifying for Lifeline may be required to verify continued eligibility on an annual basis.

(1) By one year from the effective date of these rules, eligible telecommunications carriers in states that mandate state Lifeline support must comply with state verification procedures to validate consumers' continued eligibility for Lifeline. The eligible telecommunications carrier must be able to document that it is complying with state regulations and verification requirements.

(2) By one year from the effective date of these rules, eligible telecommunications carriers in states that do not mandate state Lifeline support must implement procedures to verify annually the continued eligibility of a statistically valid random sample of their Lifeline subscribers. Eligible telecommunications carriers may verify directly with a state that particular subscribers continue to be eligible by virtue of participation in a qualifying program or income level. To the extent eligible telecommunications carriers cannot obtain the necessary information from the state, they may survey subscribers directly and provide the results of the sample to the Administrator. Subscribers who are subject to this verification and qualify under program-based eligibility criteria must prove their continued eligibility by presenting in person or sending a copy of their Lifeline-qualifying public assistance card and self-certifying, under penalty of perjury, that they continue to participate in the Lifeline-qualifying public assistance program. Subscribers who are subject to this verification and qualify under the income-based eligibility criteria must prove their continued eligibility by presenting current income documentation consistent with the income-certification process in § 54.410(a)(2). These subscribers must also self-certify, under penalty of perjury, the number of individuals in their household and that the documentation presented accurately represents their annual household income. An officer of the eligible telecommunications carrier must certify, under penalty of perjury, that the company has income verification procedures in place and that, to the best of his or her knowledge, the company was presented with corroborating documentation. The eligible telecommunications carrier must retain records of these certifications.

[69 Fed. Reg. 34600 (June 22, 2004); 73 Fed. Reg. 42274 (July 21, 2008)]

47 C.F.R. § 54.411 Link Up program defined.

(a) For purposes of this subpart, the term "Link Up" shall describe the following assistance program for qualifying low-income consumers, which an eligible telecommunications carrier shall offer as part of its obligation set forth in §§ 54.101(a)(9) and 54.101(b):

(1) A reduction in the carrier's customary charge for commencing telecommunications service for a single telecommunications connection at a consumer's principal place of residence. The reduction shall be half of the customary charge or $30.00, whichever is less; and

(2) A deferred schedule for payment of the charges assessed for commencing service, for which the consumer does not pay interest. The interest charges not assessed to the consumer shall be for connection charges of up to $200.00 that are deferred for a period not to exceed one year. Charges assessed for commencing service include any charges that the carrier customarily assesses to connect subscribers to the network. These charges do not include any permissible security deposit requirements.

(3) For an eligible resident of Tribal lands, a reduction of up to $70, in addition to the reduction in paragraph (a)(1) of this section, to cover 100 percent of the charges between $60 and $130 assessed for commencing telecommunications service at the principal place of residence of the eligible resident of Tribal lands. For purposes of this paragraph, charges assessed for commencing telecommunications services shall include any charges that the carrier customarily assesses to connect subscribers to the network, including facilities-based charges associated with the extension of lines or construction of facilities needed to initiate service. The reduction shall not apply to charges assessed for facilities or equipment that fall on the customer side of demarcation point, as defined in § 68.3 of this chapter.

(b) A qualifying low-income consumer may choose one or both of the programs set forth in paragraphs (a)(1) and (a)(2) of this section. An eligible resident of Tribal lands may participate in paragraphs (a)(1), (a)(2), and (a)(3) of this section.

(c) A carrier's Link Up program shall allow a consumer to receive the benefit of the Link Up program for a second or subsequent time only for a principal place of residence with an address different from the residence address at which the Link Up assistance was provided previously.

(d) An eligible telecommunications carrier shall publicize the availability of Link Up support in a manner reasonably designed to reach those likely to qualify for the support.

[65 Fed. Reg. 47906 (Aug. 4, 2000); 65 Fed. Reg. 49941 (Aug. 16, 2000)]

47 C.F.R. § 54.413 Reimbursement for revenue forgone in offering a Link Up program.

(a) Eligible telecommunications carriers may receive universal service support reimbursement for the revenue they forgo in reducing their customary charge for commencing telecommunications service and for providing a deferred schedule for payment of the charges assessed for commencing service for which the consumer does not pay interest, in conformity with § 54.411.

(b) In order to receive universal service support reimbursement for providing Link Up, eligible telecommunications carriers must keep accurate records of the revenues they forgo in reducing their customary charge for commencing telecommunications service and for providing a deferred schedule for payment of the charges assessed for commencing service for which the consumer does not pay interest, in conformity with § 54.411. Such records shall be kept in the form directed by the Administrator and provided to the Administrator at intervals as directed by the Administrator or as provided in this subpart. The forgone revenues for which the eligible telecommunications carrier may receive reimbursement shall include only the difference between the carrier's customary connection or interest charges and the charges actually assessed to the participating low-income consumer.

47 C.F.R. § 54.415 Consumer qualification for Link Up.

(a) In a state that mandates state Lifeline support, the consumer qualification criteria for Link Up shall be the same as the criteria that the state established for Lifeline qualification in accord with § 54.409(a).

(b) In a state that does not mandate state Lifeline support, the consumer qualification criteria for Link Up shall be the criteria set forth in § 54.409(b).

(c) Notwithstanding paragraphs (a) and (b) of this section, an eligible resident of Tribal lands, as defined in § 54.400(e), shall qualify to receive Link Up support.

[65 Fed. Reg. 47906 (Aug. 4, 2000); 65 Fed. Reg. 49941 (Aug. 16, 2000)]

47 C.F.R. § 54.416 Certification of consumer Qualification for Link Up.

Consumers qualifying under an income-based criterion must present documentation of their household income prior to enrollment in Link Up consistent with requirements set forth in §§ 54.410(a) and (b).

[69 Fed. Reg. 34601 (June 22, 2004)]

47 C.F.R. § 54.417 Recordkeeping requirements.

(a) Eligible telecommunications carriers must maintain records to document compliance with all Commission and state requirements governing the Lifeline/Link Up programs for the three full preceding calendar years and provide that documentation to the Commission or Administrator upon request. Notwithstanding the preceding sentence, eligible telecommunications carriers must maintain the documentation required in §§ 54.409(d) and 54.410(b)(3) for as long as the consumer receives Lifeline service from that eligible telecommunications carrier. If an eligible telecommunications carrier provides Lifeline discounted wholesale services to a reseller, it must obtain a certification from that reseller that it is complying with all Commission requirements governing the Lifeline/Link Up programs.

(b) Non-eligible-telecommunications-carrier resellers that purchase Lifeline discounted wholesale services to offer discounted services to low-income consumers must maintain records to document compliance with all Commission requirements governing the Lifeline/Link Up programs for the three full preceding calendar years and provide that documentation to the Commission or Administrator upon request. To the extent such a reseller provides discounted services to low-income consumers, it constitutes the eligible telecommunications carrier referenced in §§ 54.405(c), 54.405(d), 54.409(d), 54.410, and 54.416.

[69 Fed. Reg. 34601 (June 22, 2004); 72 Fed. Reg. 54218 (Sept. 24, 2007); 73 Fed. Reg. 11837 (Mar. 5, 2008); 75 Fed. Reg. 15352 (Mar. 29, 2010)]

47 C.F.R. § 54.418 Digital Television Transition Notices by Eligible Telecommunications Carriers.

(a) Eligible telecommunications carriers (ETCs) that receive federal universal service funds shall provide their Lifeline or Link-Up customers with notices about the transition for over-the-air full power broadcasting from analog to digital service (the "DTV Transition") in the monthly bills or bill notices received by such customers, or as a monthly stand-alone mailer (e.g., postcard, brochure), beginning April 1, 2009, and concluding on June 30, 2009.

(b) The notice must be provided as part of an information section on the bill or bill notice itself or on a secondary document mailed with the bill or bill notice, or as part of a monthly stand-alone mailer (e.g., postcard, brochure) in the same language or languages as the customer's bill or bill notice. These notices must:

(1) Be in clear and conspicuous print;

(2) Convey at least the following information about the DTV transition:

(i) The nationwide switch to digital television broadcasting will be complete on June 12, 2009, but your local television stations may switch sooner. After the switch, analog-only television sets that receive TV programming through an antenna will need a converter box to continue to receive over-the-air TV. Watch your local stations to find out when they will turn off their analog signal and switch to digital-only broadcasting. Analog-only TVs should continue to work as before to receive low power, Class A or translator television stations and with cable and satellite TV services, gaming consoles, VCRs, DVD players, and similar products.

(ii) Information about the DTV transition is available from your local television stations, http://www.DTV.gov, or 1-888-CALL-FCC (TTY 1-888-TELL-FCC), and from http://www.dtv2009.gov or 1-888-DTV-2009 (TTY 1-877-530-2634) for information about subsidized coupons for digital-to-analog converter boxes;

(c) If an ETC's Lifeline or Link-Up customer does not receive paper versions of either a bill or a notice of billing, then that customer must be provided with equivalent monthly notices in whatever medium they receive information about their monthly bill or as a monthly stand-alone mailer (e.g., postcard, brochure).

(d) ETCs that receive federal universal service funds shall provide information on the DTV Transition that is equivalent to the information provided pursuant to paragraph (b)(2) of this section as part of any Lifeline or Link-Up publicity campaigns conducted by the ETC between March 27, 2008, and June 30, 2009.

[73 Fed. Reg. 15449 (Mar. 24, 2008); 73 Fed. Reg. 16763 (Mar. 31, 2008); 73 Fed. Reg. 28732 (May 19, 2008); 74 Fed. Reg. 8878 (Feb. 27, 2009)]

B.3 FCC Slamming Regulations—47 C.F.R. §§ 64.1100–64.1195

Sec.

SOURCE: 56 Fed. Reg. 18523 (Apr. 23, 1991); 56 Fed. Reg. 25372 (June 4, 1991); 56 Fed. Reg. 36731 (Aug. 1, 1991); 57 Fed. Reg. 4740, Feb. 7, 1992); 57 Fed. Reg. 21040 (May 18, 1992); 57 Fed. Reg. 48335 (Oct. 23, 1992); 57 Fed. Reg. 54331 (Nov. 18, 1992); 58 Fed. Reg. 44773 (Aug. 25, 1993); 61 Fed. Reg. 24903 (May 17, 1996); 61 Fed. Reg. 50246 (Sept. 25, 1996); 61 Fed. Reg. 52323 (Oct. 7, 1996); 61 Fed. Reg. 59366 (Nov. 22, 1996); 62 Fed. Reg. 39779 (July 24, 1997); 62 Fed. Reg. 45588 (Aug. 28, 1997); 62 Fed. Reg. 47237 (Sept. 8, 1997); 62 Fed. Reg. 64758, Dec. 9, 1997); 63 Fed. Reg. 20338 (Apr. 24, 1998); 63 Fed. Reg. 43041 (Aug. 11, 1998); 64 Fed. Reg. 51469 (Sept. 23, 1999); 64 Fed. Reg. 51718 (Sept. 24, 1999); 65 Fed. Reg. 38435 (June 21, 2000); 65 Fed. Reg. 48396 (Aug. 8, 2000); 65 Fed. Reg. 54804 (Sept. 11, 2000); 67 Fed. Reg. 9616 (Mar. 4, 2002); 67 Fed. Reg. 22007 (May 2, 2002); 68 Fed. Reg. 6355, Feb. 7, 2003); 68 Fed. Reg. 19159 (Apr. 18, 2003); 69 Fed. Reg. 62816 (Oct. 28, 2004); 76 Fed. Reg. 24400 (May 2, 2011); 76 Fed. Reg. 26647 (May 9, 2011); 76 Fed. Reg. 43205 (July 20, 2011, unless otherwise noted.

AUTHORITY: 47 U.S.C. 154, 254(k); Pub. L. No. 104-104, § 403(b)(2)(B), (c), 110 Stat. 56. Interpret or apply 47 U.S.C. 201, 218, 225, 226, 228, 254(k), and 620, unless otherwise noted.

47 C.F.R. § 64.1100 Definitions.

(a) The term *submitting carrier* is generally any telecommunications carrier that requests on the behalf of a subscriber that the subscriber's telecommunications carrier be changed, and seeks to provide retail services to the end user subscriber. A carrier may be treated as a submitting carrier, however, if it is responsible for any unreasonable delays in the submission of carrier change requests or for the submission of unauthorized carrier change requests, including fraudulent authorizations.

(b) The term *executing carrier* is generally any telecommunications carrier that effects a request that a subscriber's telecommunications carrier be changed. A carrier may be treated as an executing carrier, however, if it is responsible for any unreasonable delays in the execution of carrier changes or for the execution of unauthorized carrier changes, including fraudulent authorizations.

(c) The term *authorized carrier* is generally any telecommunications carrier that submits a change, on behalf of a subscriber, in the subscriber's selection of a provider of telecommunications service with the subscriber's authorization verified in accordance with the procedures specified in this part.

(d) The term *unauthorized carrier* is generally any telecommunications carrier that submits a change, on behalf of a subscriber, in the subscriber's selection of a provider of telecommunications service but fails to obtain the subscriber's authorization verified in accordance with the procedures specified in this part.

(e) The term *unauthorized change* is a change in a subscriber's selection of a provider of telecommunications service that was made without authorization verified in accordance with the verification procedures specified in this part.

(f) The term *state commission* shall include any state entity with the state-designated authority to resolve the complaints of such state's residents arising out of an allegation that an unauthorized change of a telecommunication service provider has occurred that has elected, in accordance with the requirements of § 64.1110(a), to administer the Federal Communications Commission's slamming rules and remedies, as enumerated in §§ 64.1100 through 64.1190.

(g) The term *relevant governmental agency* shall be the state commission if the complainant files a complaint with the state commission or if the complaint is forwarded to the state commission by the Federal Communications Commission, and the Federal Communications Commission if the complainant files a complaint with the Federal Communications Commission, and the complaint is not forwarded to a state commission.

(h) The term *subscriber* is any one of the following:

(1) The party identified in the account records of a common carrier as responsible for payment of the telephone bill;

(2) Any adult person authorized by such party to change telecommunications services or to charge services to the account; or

(3) Any person contractually or otherwise lawfully authorized to represent such party.

[60 Fed. Reg. 35853 (July 12, 1995); 62 Fed. Reg. 43481 (Aug. 14, 1997); 62 Fed. Reg. 48787 (Sept. 17, 1997); 64 Fed. Reg. 7759 (Feb. 16, 1999); 64 Fed. Reg. 9219 (Feb. 24, 1999); 65 Fed. Reg. 47690 (Aug. 3, 2000); 66 Fed. Reg. 12892 (Mar. 1, 2001)]

47 C.F.R. § 64.1110 State notification of election to administer FCC rules.

(a) Initial Notification. State notification of an intention to administer the Federal Communications Commission's unauthorized carrier change rules and remedies, as enumerated in §§ 64.1100 through 64.1190, shall be filed with the Commission Secretary in CC Docket No. 94-129 with a copy of such notification provided to the Consumer & Governmental Affairs Bureau Chief. Such notification shall contain, at a minimum, information on where consumers should file complaints, the type of documentation, if any, that must accompany a complaint, and the procedures the state will use to adjudicate complaints.

(b) Withdrawal of Notification. State notification of an intention to discontinue administering the Federal Communications Commission's unauthorized carrier change rules and remedies, as enumerated in §§ 64.1100 through 64.1190, shall be filed with the Commission Secretary in CC Docket No. 94-129 with a copy of such amended notification provided to the Consumer & Governmental Affairs Bureau Chief. Such discontinuance shall become effective 60 days after the Commission's receipt of the state's letter.

[65 Fed. Reg. 47691 (Aug. 3, 2000); 65 Fed. Reg. 66934 (Nov. 8, 2000); 73 Fed. Reg. 13149 (Mar. 12, 2008)]

47 C.F.R. § 64.1120 Verification of orders for telecommunications service.

(a) No telecommunications carrier shall submit or execute a change on the behalf of a subscriber in the subscriber's selection of a provider of telecommunications service except in accordance with the procedures prescribed in this subpart. Nothing in this section shall preclude any State commission from enforcing these procedures with respect to intrastate services.

(1) No submitting carrier shall submit a change on the behalf of a subscriber in the subscriber's selection of a provider of telecommunications service prior to obtaining:

(i) Authorization from the subscriber, and

(ii) Verification of that authorization in accordance with the procedures prescribed in this section. The submitting carrier shall maintain and preserve records of verification of subscriber authorization for a minimum period of two years after obtaining such verification.

(2) An executing carrier shall not verify the submission of a change in a subscriber's selection of a provider of telecommunications service received from a submitting carrier. For an executing carrier, compliance with the procedures described in this part shall be defined as prompt execution, without any unreasonable delay, of changes that have been verified by a submitting carrier.

(3) Commercial mobile radio services (CMRS) providers shall be excluded from the verification requirements of this part as long as they are not required to provide equal access to common carriers for the provision of telephone toll services, in accordance with 47 U.S.C. 332(c)(8).

(b) Where a telecommunications carrier is selling more than one type of telecommunications service (e.g., local exchange, intraLATA toll, and interLATA toll), that carrier must obtain separate authorization from the subscriber for each service sold, although the authorizations may be obtained within the same solicitation. Each authorization must be verified separately from any other authorizations obtained in the same solicitation. Each authorization must be verified in accordance with the verification procedures prescribed in this part.

(c) No telecommunications carrier shall submit a preferred carrier change order unless and until the order has been confirmed in accordance with one of the following procedures:

(1) The telecommunications carrier has obtained the subscriber's written or electronically signed authorization in a form that meets the requirements of § 64.1130; or

(2) The telecommunications carrier has obtained the subscriber's electronic authorization to submit the preferred carrier change order. Such authorization must be placed from the telephone number(s) on which the preferred carrier is to be changed and must confirm the information in paragraph (a)(1) of this section. Telecommunications carriers electing to confirm sales electronically shall establish one or more toll-free telephone numbers exclusively for that purpose. Calls to the number(s) will connect a subscriber to a voice response unit, or similar mechanism, that records the required information regarding the preferred carrier change, including automatically recording the originating automatic number identification; or

(3) An appropriately qualified independent third party has obtained, in accordance with the procedures set forth in paragraphs (c)(3)(i) through (c)(3)(iv) of this section, the subscriber's oral authorization to submit the preferred carrier change order that confirms and includes appropriate verification data (e.g., the subscriber's date of birth or social security number). The independent third party must not be owned, managed, controlled, or directed by the carrier or the carrier's marketing agent; must not have any financial incentive to confirm preferred carrier change orders for the carrier or the carrier's marketing agent; and must operate in a location physically separate from the carrier or the carrier's marketing agent.

(i) Methods of third party verification. Automated third party verification systems and three-way conference calls may be used for verification purposes so long as the requirements of paragraphs (c)(3)(ii) through (c)(3)(iv) of this section are satisfied.

(ii) Carrier initiation of third party verification. A carrier or a carrier's sales representative initiating a three-way conference call or a call through an automated verification system must drop off the call once the three-way connection has been established.

(iii) Requirements for content and format of third party verification. Any description of the carrier change transaction by a third party verifier must not be misleading, and all third party verification methods shall elicit, at a minimum: The date of the verification; the identity of the subscriber; confirmation that the person on the call is authorized to make the carrier change; confirmation that the person on the call wants to make the carrier change; confirmation that the person on the call understands that a carrier change, not an upgrade to existing service, bill consolidation, or any other misleading description of the transaction, is being authorized; the names of the carriers affected by the change (not including the name of the displaced carrier); the telephone numbers to be switched; and the types of service involved (including a brief description of a service about which the subscriber demonstrates confusion regarding the nature of that service). Except in Hawaii, any description of interLATA or long distance service shall convey that it encompasses both international and state-to-state calls, as well as some intrastate calls where applicable. If the subscriber has additional questions for the carrier's sales representative during the verification, the verifier shall indicate to the subscriber that, upon completion of the verification process, the subscriber will have authorized a carrier change. Third party verifiers may not market the carrier's services by providing additional information, including information regarding preferred carrier freeze procedures.

(iv) Other requirements for third party verification. All third party verifications shall be conducted in the same language that was used in the underlying sales transaction and shall be recorded in their entirety. In accordance with the procedures set forth in 64.1120(a)(1)(ii), submitting carriers shall maintain and preserve audio records of verification of subscriber authorization for a minimum period of two years after obtaining such verification. Automated systems must provide consumers with an option to speak with a live person at any time during the call.

(4) Any State-enacted verification procedures applicable to intrastate preferred carrier change orders only.

(d) Telecommunications carriers must provide subscribers the option of using one of the authorization and verification procedures specified in § 64.1120(c) in addition to an electronically signed authorization and verification procedure under 64.1120(c)(1).

(e) A telecommunications carrier may acquire, through a sale or transfer, either part or all of another telecommunications carrier's subscriber base without obtaining each subscriber's authorization and verification in accordance with § 64.1120(c), provided that the acquiring carrier complies with the following streamlined procedures. A telecommunications carrier may not use these streamlined procedures for any fraudulent purpose, including any attempt to avoid liability for violations under part 64, subpart K of the Commission rules.

(1) No later than 30 days before the planned transfer of the affected subscribers from the selling or transferring carrier to the acquiring carrier, the acquiring carrier shall file with the Commission's Office of the Secretary a letter notification in CC Docket No. 00-257 providing the names of the parties to the transaction, the types of telecommunications services to be provided to the affected subscribers, and the date of the transfer of the subscriber base to the acquiring carrier. In the letter notification, the acquiring carrier also shall certify compliance with the requirement to provide advance subscriber notice in accordance with § 64.1120(e)(3), with the obligations specified in that notice, and with other statutory and Commission requirements that apply to this streamlined process. In addition, the acquiring carrier shall attach a copy of the notice sent to the affected subscribers.

(2) If, subsequent to the filing of the letter notification with the Commission required by § 64.1120(e)(1), any material changes to the required information should develop, the acquiring carrier shall file written notification of these changes with the Commission no more than 10 days after the transfer date announced in the prior notification. The Commission reserves the right to require the acquiring carrier to send an additional notice to the affected subscribers regarding such material changes.

(3) Not later than 30 days before the transfer of the affected subscribers from the selling or transferring carrier to the acquiring carrier, the acquiring carrier shall provide written notice to each affected subscriber of the information specified. The acquiring carrier is required to fulfill the obligations set forth in the advance subscriber notice. The advance subscriber notice shall be provided in a manner consistent with 47 U.S.C. 255 and the Commission's rules regarding accessibility to blind and visually impaired consumers, 47 CFR 6.3, 6.5 of this chapter. The following information must be included in the advance subscriber notice:

(i) The date on which the acquiring carrier will become the subscriber's new provider of telecommunications service;

(ii) The rates, terms, and conditions of the service(s) to be provided by the acquiring carrier upon the subscriber's transfer to the acquiring carrier, and the means by which the acquiring carrier will notify the subscriber of any change(s) to these rates, terms, and conditions;

(iii) The acquiring carrier will be responsible for any carrier change charges associated with the transfer, except where the carrier is acquiring customers by default, other than through bankruptcy, and state law requires the exiting carrier to pay these costs;

(iv) The subscriber's right to select a different preferred carrier for the telecommunications service(s) at issue, if an alternative carrier is available;

(v) All subscribers receiving the notice, even those who have arranged preferred carrier freezes through their local service providers on the service(s) involved in the transfer, will be transferred to the acquiring carrier, unless they have selected a different carrier before the transfer date; existing preferred carrier freezes on the service(s) involved in the transfer will be lifted; and the subscribers must contact their local service providers to arrange a new freeze;

(vi) Whether the acquiring carrier will be responsible for handling any complaints filed, or otherwise raised, prior to or during the transfer against the selling or transferring carrier; and

(vii) The toll-free customer service telephone number of the acquiring carrier.

[65 Fed. Reg. 47691 (Aug. 3, 2000); 66 Fed. Reg. 12892 (Mar. 1, 2001); 66 Fed. Reg. 28124 (May 22, 2001); 66 Fed. Reg. 33208 (June 21, 2001); 68 Fed. Reg. 19159 (Apr. 18, 2003); 68 Fed. Reg. 41942 (July 16, 2003); 68 Fed. Reg. 43010 (July 21, 2003); 70 Fed. Reg. 12611 (Mar. 15, 2005); 73 Fed. Reg. 13149 (Mar. 12, 2008); 73 Fed. Reg. 44170 (July 30, 2008)]

47 C.F.R. § 64.1130 Letter of agency form and content.

(a) A telecommunications carrier may use a written or electronically signed letter of agency to obtain authorization and/or verification of a subscriber's request to change his or her preferred carrier selection. A letter of agency that does not conform with this section is invalid for purposes of this part.

(b) The letter of agency shall be a separate document (or an easily separable document) or located on a separate screen or webpage containing only the authorizing language described in paragraph (e) of this section having the sole purpose of authorizing a telecommunications carrier to initiate a preferred carrier change. The letter of agency must be signed and dated by the subscriber to the telephone line(s) requesting the preferred carrier change.

(c) The letter of agency shall not be combined on the same document, screen, or webpage with inducements of any kind.

(d) Notwithstanding paragraphs (b) and (c) of this section, the letter of agency may be combined with checks that contain only the required letter of agency language as prescribed in paragraph (e) of this section and the necessary information to make the check a negotiable instrument. The letter of agency check shall not contain any promotional language or material. The letter of agency check shall contain in easily readable, bold-face type on the front of the check, a notice that the subscriber is authorizing a preferred carrier change by signing the check. The letter of agency language shall be placed near the signature line on the back of the check.

(e) At a minimum, the letter of agency must be printed with a type of sufficient size and readable type to be clearly legible and must contain clear and unambiguous language that confirms:

(1) The subscriber's billing name and address and each telephone number to be covered by the preferred carrier change order;

(2) The decision to change the preferred carrier from the current telecommunications carrier to the soliciting telecommunications carrier;

(3) That the subscriber designates [insert the name of the submitting carrier] to act as the subscriber's agent for the preferred carrier change;

(4) That the subscriber understands that only one telecommunications carrier may be designated as the subscriber's interstate or interLATA preferred interexchange carrier for any one telephone number. To the extent that a jurisdiction allows the selection of additional preferred carriers (e.g., local exchange, intraLATA toll, interLATA toll, or international interexchange), the letter of agency must contain separate statements regarding those choices, although a separate letter of agency for each choice is not necessary; and

(5) That the subscriber may consult with the carrier as to whether a fee will apply to the change in the subscriber's preferred carrier.

(f) Any carrier designated in a letter of agency as a preferred carrier must be the carrier directly setting the rates for the subscriber.

(g) Letters of agency shall not suggest or require that a subscriber take some action in order to retain the subscriber's current telecommunications carrier.

(h) If any portion of a letter of agency is translated into another language then all portions of the letter of agency must be translated into that language. Every letter of agency must be translated into the same language as any promotional materials, oral descriptions or instructions provided with the letter of agency.

(*i*) Letters of agency submitted with an electronically signed authorization must include the consumer disclosures required by Section 101(c) of the Electronic Signatures in Global and National Commerce Act.

(j) A telecommunications carrier shall submit a preferred carrier change order on behalf of a subscriber within no more than 60 days of obtaining a written or electronically signed letter of agency. However, letters of agency for multi-line and/or multi-location business customers that have entered into negotiated agreements with carriers to add presubscribed lines to their business locations during the course of a term agreement shall be valid for the period specified in the term agreement.

[64 Fed. Reg. 7760 (Feb. 16, 1999); 64 Fed. Reg. 9219 (Feb. 24, 1999); 65 Fed. Reg. 47692 (Aug. 3, 2000); 66 Fed. Reg. 12893 (Mar. 1, 2001); 66 Fed. Reg. 16151 (Mar. 23, 2001); 66 Fed. Reg. 17083 (Mar. 29, 2001); 68 Fed. Reg. 19159 (Apr. 18, 2003); 68 Fed. Reg. 41942 (July 16, 2003); 68 Fed. Reg. 43010 (July 21, 2003); 73 Fed. Reg. 13149 (Mar. 12, 2008)]

47 C.F.R. § 64.1140 Carrier liability for slamming.

(a) Carrier Liability for Charges. Any submitting telecommunications carrier that fails to comply with the procedures prescribed in this part shall be liable to the subscriber's properly authorized carrier in an amount equal to 150% of all charges paid to the submitting telecommunications carrier by such subscriber after such violation, as well as for additional amounts as prescribed in § 64.1170. The remedies provided in this part are in addition to any other remedies available by law.

(b) Subscriber Liability for Charges. Any subscriber whose selection of telecommunications services provider is changed without authorization verified in accordance with the procedures set for in this part is liable for charges as follows:

(1) If the subscriber has not already paid charges to the unauthorized carrier, the subscriber is absolved of liability for charges imposed by the unauthorized carrier for service provided during the first 30 days after the unauthorized change. Upon being informed by a subscriber that an unauthorized change has occurred, the authorized carrier, the unauthorized carrier, or the executing carrier shall inform the subscriber of this 30-day absolution period. Any charges imposed by the unauthorized carrier on the subscriber for service provided after this 30-day period shall be paid by the subscriber to the authorized carrier at the rates the subscriber was paying to the authorized carrier at the time of the unauthorized change in accordance with the provisions of § 64.1160(e).

(2) If the subscriber has already paid charges to the unauthorized carrier, and the authorized carrier receives payment from the unauthorized carrier as provided for in paragraph (a) of this section, the authorized carrier shall refund or credit to the subscriber any amounts determined in accordance with the provisions of § 64.1170(c).

(3) If the subscriber has been absolved of liability as prescribed by this section, the unauthorized carrier shall also be liable to the subscriber for any charge required to return the subscriber to his or her properly authorized carrier, if applicable.

[65 Fed. Reg. 47691 (Aug. 3, 2000); 65 Fed. Reg. 66934 (Nov. 8, 2000)]

47 C.F.R. § 64.1150 Procedures for resolution of unauthorized changes in preferred carrier.

(a) Notification of alleged unauthorized carrier change. Executing carriers who are informed of an unauthorized carrier change by a subscriber must immediately notify both the authorized and allegedly unauthorized carrier of the incident. This notification must include the identity of both carriers.

(b) Referral of complaint. Any carrier, executing, authorized, or allegedly unauthorized, that is informed by a subscriber or an executing carrier of an unauthorized carrier change shall direct that subscriber either to the state commission or, where the state commission has not opted to administer these rules, to the Federal Communications Commission's Consumer & Governmental Affairs Bureau, for resolution of the complaint. Carriers shall also inform the subscriber that he or she may contact and seek resolution from the alleged unauthorized carrier and, in addition, may contact the authorized carrier.

(c) Notification of receipt of complaint. Upon receipt of an unauthorized carrier change complaint, the relevant governmental agency will notify the allegedly unauthorized carrier of the complaint and order that the carrier remove all unpaid charges for the first 30 days after the slam from the subscriber's bill pending a determination of whether an unauthorized change, as defined by § 64.1100(e), has occurred, if it has not already done so.

(d) Proof of verification. Not more than 30 days after notification of the complaint, or such lesser time as is required by the state commission if a matter is brought before a state commission, the alleged unauthorized carrier shall provide to the relevant government agency a copy of any valid proof of verification of the carrier change. This proof of verification must contain clear and convincing evidence of a valid authorized carrier change, as that term is defined in §§ 64.1120 through 64.1130. The relevant governmental agency will determine whether an unauthorized change, as defined by § 64.1100(e), has occurred using such proof and any evidence supplied by the subscriber. Failure by the carrier to respond or provide proof of verification will be presumed to be clear and convincing evidence of a violation.

(e) Election of forum. The Federal Communications Commission will not adjudicate a complaint filed pursuant to § 1.719 or §§ 1.720 through 1.736 of this chapter, involving an alleged unauthorized change, as defined by § 64.1100(e), while a complaint based on the same set of facts is pending with a state commission.

[60 Fed. Reg. 35853 (July 12, 1995); 62 Fed. Reg. 43481 (Aug. 14, 1997); 63 Fed. Reg. 13798 (Mar. 23, 1998); 64 Fed. Reg. 7760 (Feb. 16, 1999); 64 Fed. Reg. 9219 (Feb. 24, 1999); 65 Fed. Reg. 47692 (Aug. 3, 2000); 65 Fed. Reg. 66934 (Nov. 8, 2000); 68 Fed. Reg. 19159 (Apr. 18, 2003); 68 Fed. Reg. 41942 (July 16, 2003); 68 Fed. Reg. 43010 (July 21, 2003); 73 Fed. Reg. 13149 (Mar. 12, 2008)]

47 C.F.R. § 64.1160 Absolution procedures where the subscriber has not paid charges.

(a) This section shall only apply after a subscriber has determined that an unauthorized change, as defined by § 64.1100(e), has occurred and the subscriber has not paid charges to the allegedly unauthorized carrier for service provided for 30 days, or a portion thereof, after the unauthorized change occurred.

(b) An allegedly unauthorized carrier shall remove all charges incurred for service provided during the first 30 days after the alleged unauthorized change occurred, as defined by § 64.1100(e), from a subscriber's bill upon notification that such unauthorized change is alleged to have occurred.

(c) An allegedly unauthorized carrier may challenge a subscriber's allegation that an unauthorized change, as defined by § 64.1100(e), occurred. An allegedly unauthorized carrier choosing to challenge such allegation shall immediately notify the complaining subscriber that: The complaining subscriber must file a complaint with a State commission that has opted to administer the FCC's rules, pursuant to § 64.1110, or the FCC within 30 days of either the date of removal of charges from the complaining subscriber's bill in accordance with paragraph (b) of this section, or the date the allegedly unauthorized carrier notifies the complaining subscriber of the requirements of this paragraph, whichever is later; and a failure to file such a complaint within this 30-day time period will result in the charges removed pursuant to paragraph (b) of this section being reinstated on the subscriber's bill and, consequently, the complaining subscriber will only be entitled to remedies for the alleged unauthorized change other than those provided for in § 64.1140(b)(1). No allegedly unauthorized carrier shall reinstate charges to a subscriber's bill pursuant to the provisions of this paragraph without first providing such subscriber with a reasonable opportunity to demonstrate that the requisite complaint was timely filed within the 30-day period described in this paragraph.

(d) If the relevant governmental agency determines after reasonable investigation that an unauthorized change, as defined by § 64.1100(e), has occurred, an order shall be issued providing that the subscriber is entitled to absolution from the charges incurred during the first 30 days after the unauthorized carrier change occurred, and neither the authorized or unauthorized carrier may pursue any collection against the subscriber for those charges.

(e) If the subscriber has incurred charges for more than 30 days after the unauthorized carrier change, the unauthorized carrier must forward the billing information for such services to the authorized carrier, which may bill the subscriber for such services using either of the following means:

(1) The amount of the charge may be determined by a re-rating of the services provided based on what the authorized carrier would have charged the subscriber for the same services had an unauthorized change, as described in § 64.1100(e), not occurred; or

(2) The amount of the charge may be determined using a 50% Proxy Rate as follows: Upon receipt of billing information from the unauthorized carrier, the authorized carrier may bill the subscriber for 50% of the rate the unauthorized carrier would have charged the subscriber for the services provided. However, the subscriber shall have the right to reject use of this 50% proxy method and require that the authorized carrier perform a re-rating of the services provided, as described in paragraph (e)(1) of this section.

(f) If the unauthorized carrier received payment from the subscriber for services provided after the first 30 days after the unauthorized change occurred, the obligations for payments and refunds provided for in § 64.1170 shall apply to those payments. If the relevant governmental agency determines after reasonable investigation that the carrier change was authorized, the carrier may re-bill the subscriber for charges incurred.

(g) When a LEC has assigned a subscriber to a carrier without authorization, and where the subscriber has not paid the unauthorized charges, the LEC shall switch the subscriber to the desired carrier at no cost to the subscriber, and shall also secure the removal of the unauthorized charges from the subscriber's bill in accordance with the procedures specified in paragraphs (a) through (f) of this section.

[65 Fed. Reg. 47692 (Aug. 3, 2000); 65 Fed. Reg. 66934 (Nov. 8, 2000); 68 Fed. Reg. 19159 (Apr. 18, 2003); 68 Fed. Reg. 41942 (July 16, 2003); 68 Fed. Reg. 43010 (July 21, 2003); 73 Fed. Reg. 13149 (Mar. 12, 2008)]

47 C.F.R. § 64.1170 Reimbursement procedures where the subscriber has paid charges.

(a) The procedures in this section shall only apply after a subscriber has determined that an unauthorized change, as defined by § 64.1100(e), has occurred and the subscriber has paid charges to an allegedly unauthorized carrier.

(b) If the relevant governmental agency determines after reasonable investigation that an unauthorized change, as defined by § 64.1100(e), has occurred, it shall issue an order directing the unauthorized carrier to forward to the authorized carrier the following, in addition to any appropriate state remedies:

(1) An amount equal to 150% of all charges paid by the subscriber to the unauthorized carrier; and

(2) Copies of any telephone bills issued from the unauthorized carrier to the subscriber. This order shall be sent to the subscriber, the unauthorized carrier, and the authorized carrier.

(c) Within ten days of receipt of the amount provided for in paragraph (b)(1) of this section, the authorized carrier shall provide a refund or credit to the subscriber in the amount of 50% of all charges paid by the subscriber to the unauthorized carrier. The subscriber has the option of asking the authorized carrier to re-rate the unauthorized carrier's charges based on the rates of the authorized carrier and, on behalf of the subscriber, seek an additional refund from the unauthorized carrier, to the extent that the re-rated amount exceeds the 50% of all charges paid by the subscriber to the unauthorized carrier. The authorized carrier shall also send notice to the relevant governmental agency that it has given a refund or credit to the subscriber.

(d) If an authorized carrier incurs billing and collection expenses in collecting charges from the unauthorized carrier, the unauthorized carrier shall reimburse the authorized carrier for reasonable expenses.

(e) If the authorized carrier has not received payment from the unauthorized carrier as required by paragraph (c) of this section, the authorized carrier is not required to provide any refund or credit to the subscriber. The authorized carrier must, within 45 days of receiving an order as described in paragraph (b) of this section, inform the subscriber and the relevant governmental agency that issued the order if the unauthorized carrier has failed to forward to it the appropriate charges, and also inform the subscriber of his or her right to pursue a claim against the unauthorized carrier for a refund of all charges paid to the unauthorized carrier.

(f) Where possible, the properly authorized carrier must reinstate the subscriber in any premium program in which that subscriber was enrolled prior to the unauthorized change, if the subscriber's participation in that program was terminated because of the unauthorized change. If the subscriber has paid charges to the unauthorized carrier, the properly authorized carrier shall also provide or restore to the subscriber any premiums to which the subscriber would have been entitled had the unauthorized change not occurred. The authorized carrier must comply with the requirements of this section regardless of whether it is able to recover from the unauthorized carrier any charges that were paid by the subscriber.

(g) When a LEC has assigned a subscriber to a non-affiliated carrier without authorization, and when a subscriber has paid the non-affiliated carrier the charges for the billed service, the LEC shall reimburse the subscriber for all charges paid by the subscriber to the unauthorized carrier and shall switch the subscriber to the desired carrier at no cost to the subscriber. When a LEC makes an unauthorized carrier change to an affiliated carrier, and when the customer has paid the charges, the LEC must pay to the authorized carrier 150% of the amounts collected from the subscriber in accordance with paragraphs (a) through (f) of this section.

[64 Fed. Reg. 7761 (Feb. 16, 1999); 65 Fed. Reg. 47693 (Aug. 3, 2000); 65 Fed. Reg. 66934 (Nov. 8, 2000); 68 Fed. Reg. 19159 (Apr. 18, 2003); 68 Fed. Reg. 41942 (July 16, 2003); 68 Fed. Reg. 43010 (July 21, 2003)]

47 C.F.R. § 64.1180 [Reserved]

[68 Fed. Reg. 19159 (Apr. 18, 2003); 68 Fed. Reg. 41942 (July 16, 2003); 68 Fed. Reg. 43010 (July 21, 2003)]

47 C.F.R. § 64.1190 Preferred carrier freezes.

(a) A preferred carrier freeze (or freeze) prevents a change in a subscriber's preferred carrier selection unless the subscriber gives the carrier from whom the freeze was requested his or her express consent. All local exchange carriers who offer preferred carrier freezes must comply with the provisions of this section.

(b) All local exchange carriers who offer preferred carrier freezes shall offer freezes on a nondiscriminatory basis to all subscribers, regardless of the subscriber's carrier selections.

(c) Preferred carrier freeze procedures, including any solicitation, must clearly distinguish among telecommunications services (e.g., local exchange, intraLATA toll, and interLATA toll) subject to a preferred carrier freeze. The carrier offering the freeze must obtain separate authorization for each service for which a preferred carrier freeze is requested.

(d) Solicitation and imposition of preferred carrier freezes.

(1) All carrier-provided solicitation and other materials regarding preferred carrier freezes must include:

(i) An explanation, in clear and neutral language, of what a preferred carrier freeze is and what services may be subject to a freeze;

(ii) A description of the specific procedures necessary to lift a preferred carrier freeze; an explanation that these steps are in addition to the Commission's verification rules in §§ 64.1120 and 64.1130 for changing a subscriber's preferred carrier selections; and an explanation that the subscriber will be unable to make a change in carrier selection unless he or she lifts the freeze.

(iii) An explanation of any charges associated with the preferred carrier freeze.

(2) No local exchange carrier shall implement a preferred carrier freeze unless the subscriber's request to impose a freeze has first been confirmed in accordance with one of the following procedures:

(i) The local exchange carrier has obtained the subscriber's written or electronically signed authorization in a form that meets the requirements of § 64.1190(d)(3); or

(ii) The local exchange carrier has obtained the subscriber's electronic authorization, placed from the telephone number(s) on which the preferred carrier freeze is to be imposed, to impose a preferred carrier freeze. The electronic authorization should confirm appropriate verification data (e.g., the subscriber's date of birth or social security number) and the information required in §§ 64.1190(d)(3)(ii)(A) through (D). Telecommunications carriers electing to confirm preferred carrier freeze orders electronically shall establish one or more toll-free telephone numbers exclusively for that purpose. Calls to the number(s) will connect a subscriber to a voice response unit, or similar mechanism that records the required information regarding the preferred carrier freeze request, including automatically recording the originating automatic numbering identification; or

(iii) An appropriately qualified independent third party has obtained the subscriber's oral authorization to submit the preferred carrier freeze and confirmed the appropriate verification data (e.g., the subscriber's date of birth or social security number) and the information required in § 64.1190(d)(3)(ii)(A) through (D). The independent third party must not be owned, managed, or directly controlled by the carrier or the carrier's marketing agent; must not have any financial incentive to confirm preferred carrier freeze requests for the carrier or the carrier's marketing agent; and must operate in a location physically separate from the carrier or the carrier's marketing agent. The content of the verification must include clear and conspicuous confirmation that the subscriber has authorized a preferred carrier freeze.

(3) Written authorization to impose a preferred carrier freeze. A local exchange carrier may accept a subscriber's written and signed authorization to impose a freeze on his or her preferred carrier selection. Written authorization that does not conform with this section is invalid and may not be used to impose a preferred carrier freeze.

(i) The written authorization shall comply with §§ 64.1130(b), (c), and (h) of the Commission's rules concerning the form and content for letters of agency.

(ii) At a minimum, the written authorization must be printed with a readable type of sufficient size to be clearly legible and must contain clear and unambiguous language that confirms:

(A) The subscriber's billing name and address and the telephone number(s) to be covered by the preferred carrier freeze;

(B) The decision to place a preferred carrier freeze on the telephone number(s) and particular service(s). To the extent that a jurisdiction allows the imposition of preferred carrier freezes on additional preferred carrier selections (e.g., for local exchange, intraLATA toll, and interLATA toll), the authorization must contain separate statements regarding the particular selections to be frozen;

(C) That the subscriber understands that she or he will be unable to make a change in carrier selection unless she or he lifts the preferred carrier freeze; and

(D) That the subscriber understands that any preferred carrier freeze may involve a charge to the subscriber.

(e) Procedures for lifting preferred carrier freezes. All local exchange carriers who offer preferred carrier freezes must, at a minimum, offer subscribers the following procedures for lifting a preferred carrier freeze:

(1) A local exchange carrier administering a preferred carrier freeze must accept a subscriber's written or electronically signed authorization stating his or her intent to lift a preferred carrier freeze; and

(2) A local exchange carrier administering a preferred carrier freeze must accept a subscriber's oral authorization stating her or his intent to lift a preferred carrier freeze and must offer a mechanism that allows a submitting carrier to conduct a three-way conference call with the carrier administering the freeze and the subscriber in order to lift a freeze. When engaged in oral authorization to lift a preferred carrier freeze, the carrier administering the freeze shall confirm appropriate verification data (e.g., the subscriber's date of birth or social security number) and the subscriber's intent to lift the particular freeze.

[64 Fed. Reg. 7761 (Feb. 16, 1999); 64 Fed. Reg. 9219 (Feb. 24, 1999); 66 Fed. Reg. 12893 (Mar. 1, 2001); 66 Fed. Reg. 17083 (Mar. 29, 2001); 73 Fed. Reg. 13150 (Mar. 12, 2008)]

47 C.F.R. § 64.1195 Registration requirement.

(a) Applicability. A telecommunications carrier that will provide interstate telecommunications service shall file the registration information described in paragraph (b) of this section in accordance with the procedures described in paragraphs (c) and (g) of this section. Any telecommunications carrier already providing interstate telecommunications service on the effective date of these rules shall submit the relevant portion of its FCC Form 499-A in accordance with paragraphs (b) and (c) of this section.

(b) Information required for purposes of part 64. A telecommunications carrier that is subject to the registration requirement pursuant to paragraph (a) of this section shall provide the following information:

(1) The carrier's business name(s) and primary address;

(2) The names and business addresses of the carrier's chief executive officer, chairman, and president, or, in the event that a company does not have such executives, three similarly senior-level officials of the company;

(3) The carrier's regulatory contact and/or designated agent;

(4) All names that the carrier has used in the past; and

(5) The state(s) in which the carrier provides telecommunications service.

(c) Submission of registration. A carrier that is subject to the registration requirement pursuant to paragraph (a) of this section shall submit the information described in paragraph (b) of this section in accordance with the Instructions to FCC Form 499-A. FCC Form 499-A must be submitted under oath and penalty of perjury.

(d) Rejection of registration. The Commission may reject or suspend a carrier's registration for any of the reasons identified in paragraphs (e) or (f) of this section.

(e) Revocation or suspension of operating authority. After notice and opportunity to respond, the Commission may revoke or suspend the authorization of a carrier to provide service if the carrier provides materially false or incomplete information in its FCC Form 499-A or otherwise fails to comply with paragraphs (a), (b), and (c) of this section.

(f) Imposition of fine. After notice and opportunity to respond, the Commission may impose a fine on a carrier that is subject to the registration requirement pursuant to paragraph (a) of this section if that carrier fails to submit an FCC Form 499-A in accordance with paragraphs (a), (b), and (c) of this section.

(g) Changes in information. A carrier must notify the Commission of any changes to the information provided pursuant to paragraph (b) of this section within no more than one week of the change. Carriers may satisfy this requirement by filing the relevant portion of FCC Form 499-A in accordance with the Instructions to such form.

(h) Duty to confirm registration of other carriers. The Commission shall make available to the public a comprehensive listing of registrants and the information that they have provided pursuant to paragraph (b) of this section. A telecommunications carrier providing telecommunications service for resale shall have an affirmative duty to ascertain whether a potential carrier-customer (i.e., reseller) that is subject to the registration requirement pursuant to paragraph (a) of this section has filed an FCC Form 499-A with the Commission prior to offering service to that carrier-customer. After notice and opportunity to respond, the Commission may impose a fine on a carrier for failure to confirm the registration status of a potential carrier-customer before providing that carrier-customer with service.

[66 Fed. Reg. 12894 (Mar. 1, 2001); 66 Fed. Reg. 17083 (Mar. 29, 2001)]

B.4 Federal 900-Number Regulations

B.4.1 FCC 900-Number Regulations—47 C.F.R. §§ 64.1501–64.1515

Sec.

§ 64.1501 Definitions.
§ 64.1502 Limitations on the provision of pay-per-call services.
§ 64.1503 Termination of pay-per-call and other information programs.
§ 64.1504 Restrictions on the use of toll-free numbers.
§ 64.1505 Restrictions on collect telephone calls.
§ 64.1506 Number designation.
§ 64.1507 Prohibition on disconnection or interruption of service for failure to remit pay-per-call and similar service charges.
§ 64.1508 Blocking access to 900 service.
§ 64.1509 Disclosure and dissemination of pay-per-call information.
§ 64.1510 Billing and collection of pay-per-call and similar service charges.
§ 64.1511 Forgiveness of charges and refunds.
§ 64.1512 Involuntary blocking of pay-per-call services.
§ 64.1513 Verification of charitable status.
§ 64.1514 Generation of signalling tones.
§ 64.1515 Recovery of costs.

SOURCE: 56 Fed. Reg. 18523 (Apr. 23, 1991); 56 Fed. Reg. 25372 (June 4, 1991); 56 Fed. Reg. 36731 (Aug. 1, 1991); 57 Fed. Reg. 4740, Feb. 7, 1992); 57 Fed. Reg. 21040 (May 18, 1992); 57 Fed. Reg. 48335 (Oct. 23, 1992); 57 Fed. Reg. 54331 (Nov. 18, 1992); 58 Fed. Reg. 44773 (Aug. 25, 1993); 61 Fed. Reg. 24903 (May 17, 1996); 61 Fed. Reg. 39087 (July 26, 1996); 61 Fed. Reg. 50246 (Sept. 25, 1996); 61 Fed. Reg. 52323 (Oct. 7, 1996); 61 Fed. Reg. 59366 (Nov. 22, 1996); 62 Fed. Reg. 39779 (July 24, 1997); 62 Fed. Reg. 45588 (Aug. 28, 1997); 62 Fed. Reg. 47237 (Sept. 8, 1997); 62 Fed. Reg. 64758, Dec. 9, 1997); 63 Fed. Reg. 20338 (Apr. 24, 1998); 63 Fed. Reg. 43041 (Aug. 11, 1998); 64 Fed. Reg. 51469 (Sept. 23, 1999); 64 Fed. Reg. 51718 (Sept. 24, 1999); 65 Fed. Reg. 38435 (June 21, 2000); 65 Fed. Reg. 48396 (Aug. 8, 2000); 65 Fed. Reg. 54804 (Sept. 11, 2000); 67 Fed. Reg. 9616 (Mar. 4, 2002); 67 Fed. Reg. 22007 (May 2, 2002); 68 Fed. Reg. 6355, Feb. 7, 2003); 69 Fed. Reg. 62816 (Oct. 28, 2004); 76 Fed. Reg. 24400 (May 2, 2011); 76 Fed. Reg. 26647 (May 9, 2011); 76 Fed. Reg. 43205 (July 20, 2011, unless otherwise noted.

AUTHORITY: 47 U.S.C. 154, 254(k); secs. 403(b)(2)(B), (c), Pub. L. No.104-104, 110 Stat. 56. Interpret or apply 47 U.S.C. 201, 218, 225, 226, 228, 254(k), and 620, unless otherwise noted.

47 C.F.R. § 64.1501 Definitions.

For purposes of this subpart, the following definitions shall apply:

(a) *Pay-per-call service* means any service:

(1) In which any person provides or purports to provide:

(i) Audio information or audio entertainment produced or packaged by such person;

(ii) Access to simultaneous voice conversation services; or

(iii) Any service, including the provision of a product, the charges for which are assessed on the basis of the completion of the call;

(2) For which the caller pays a per-call or per-time-interval charge that is greater than, or in addition to, the charge for transmission of the call; and

(3) Which is accessed through use of a 900 number;

(4) Provided, however, such term does not include directory services provided by a common carrier or its affiliate or by a local exchange carrier or its affiliate, or any service for which users are assessed charges only after entering into a presubscription or comparable arrangement with the provider of such service.

(b) *Presubscription or comparable arrangement* means a contractual agreement in which:

(1) The service provider clearly and conspicuously discloses to the consumer all material terms and conditions associated with the use of the service, including the service provider's name and address, a business telephone number which the consumer may use to obtain additional information or to register a complaint, and the rates for the service;

(2) The service provider agrees to notify the consumer of any future rate changes;

(3) The consumer agrees to use the service on the terms and conditions disclosed by the service provider; and

(4) The service provider requires the use of an identification number or other means to prevent unauthorized access to the service by nonsubscribers;

(5) Provided, however, that disclosure of a credit, prepaid account, debit, charge, or calling card number, along with authorization to bill that number, made during the course of a call to an information service shall constitute a presubscription or comparable arrangement if an introductory message containing the information specified in § 64.1504(c)(2) is provided prior to, and independent of, assessment of any charges. No other action taken by a consumer during the course of a call to an information service, for which charges are assessed, can create a presubscription or comparable arrangement.

(6) Provided, that a presubscription arrangement to obtain information services provided by means of a toll-free number shall conform to the requirements of § 64.1504(c).

(c) *Calling card* means an identifying number or code unique to the individual, that is issued to the individual by a common carrier and enables the individual to be charged by means of a phone bill for charges incurred independent of where the call originates.

[59 Fed. Reg. 46770 (Sept. 12, 1994); 61 Fed. Reg. 39087 (July 26, 1996)]

47 C.F.R. § 64.1502 Limitations on the provision of pay-per-call services.

Any common carrier assigning a telephone number to a provider of interstate pay-per-call service shall require, by contract or tariff, that such provider comply with the provisions of this subpart and of titles II and III of the Telephone Disclosure and Dispute Resolution Act (Pub. L. No. 102-556) (TDDRA) and the regulations prescribed by the Federal Trade Commission pursuant to those titles.

47 C.F.R. § 64.1503 Termination of pay-per-call and other information programs.

(a) Any common carrier assigning a telephone number to a provider of interstate pay-per-call service shall specify by contract or tariff that pay-per-call programs not in compliance with § 64.1502 shall be terminated following written notice to the information provider. The information provider shall be afforded a period of no less than seven and no more than 14 days during which a program may be brought into compliance. Programs not in compliance at the expiration of such period shall be terminated immediately.

(b) Any common carrier providing transmission or billing and collection services to a provider of interstate information service through any 800 telephone number, or other telephone number advertised or widely understood to be toll-free, shall promptly investigate any complaint that such service is not provided in accordance with § 64.1504 or § 64.1510(c), and, if the carrier reasonably determines that the complaint is valid, may terminate the provision of service to an information provider unless the provider supplies evidence of a written agreement that meets the requirements of this § 64.1504(c)(1).

[61 Fed. Reg. 39087 (July 26, 1996)]

47 C.F.R. § 64.1504 Restrictions on the use of toll-free numbers.

A common carrier shall prohibit by tariff or contract the use of any 800 telephone number, or other telephone number advertised or widely understood to be toll-free, in a manner that would result in:

(a) The calling party or the subscriber to the originating line being assessed, by virtue of completing the call, a charge for a call;

(b) The calling party being connected to a pay-per-call service;

(c) The calling party being charged for information conveyed during the call unless:

(1) The calling party has a written agreement (including an agreement transmitted through electronic medium) that specifies the material terms and conditions under which the information is offered and includes:

(i) The rate at which charges are assessed for the information;

(ii) The information provider's name;

(iii) The information provider's business address;

(iv) The information provider's regular business telephone number;

(v) The information provider's agreement to notify the subscriber at least one billing cycle in advance of all future changes in the rates charged for the information;

(vi) The subscriber's choice of payment method, which may be by direct remit, debit, prepaid account, phone bill, or credit or calling card and, if a subscriber elects to pay by means of phone bill, a clear explanation that the subscriber will be assessed for calls made to the information service from the subscriber's phone line;

(vii) A unique personal identification number or other subscriber-specific identifier that must be used to obtain access to the information service and instructions on its use, and, in addition, assures that any charges for services accessed by use of the subscriber's personal identification number or subscriber-specific identifier be assessed to subscriber's source of payment elected pursuant to paragraph (c)(1)(vi) of this section; or

(2) The calling party is charged for the information by means of a credit, prepaid, debit, charge, or calling card and the information service provider includes in response to each call an introductory message that:

(i) Clearly states that there is a charge for the call;

(ii) Clearly states the service's total cost per minute and any other fees for the service or for any service to which the caller may be transferred;

(iii) Explains that the charges must be billed on either a credit, prepaid, debit, charge, or calling card;

(iv) Asks the caller for the card number;

(v) Clearly states that charges for the call begin at the end of the introductory message; and

(vi) Clearly states that the caller can hang up at or before the end of the introductory message without incurring any charge whatsoever.

(d) The calling party being called back collect for the provision of audio or data information services, simultaneous voice conversation services, or products; and

(e) The calling party being assessed by virtue of the caller being asked to connect or otherwise transfer to a pay-per-call service, a charge for the call.

(f) Provided, however, that:

(1) Notwithstanding paragraph (c)(1) of this section, a written agreement that meets the requirements of that paragraph is not required for:

(i) Calls utilizing telecommunications devices for the deaf;

(ii) Directory services provided by a common carrier or its affiliate or by a local exchange carrier or its affiliate; or

(iii) Any purchase of goods or of services that are not information services.

(2) The requirements of paragraph (c)(2) of this section shall not apply to calls from repeat callers using a bypass mechanism to avoid listening to the introductory message: *Provided*, That information providers shall disable such a bypass mechanism after the institution of any price increase for a period of time determined to be sufficient by the Federal Trade Commission to give callers adequate and sufficient notice of a price increase.

[61 Fed. Reg. 39087 (July 26, 1996); 69 Fed. Reg. 61154 (Oct. 15, 2004)]

47 C.F.R. § 64.1505 Restrictions on collect telephone calls.

(a) No common carrier shall provide interstate transmission or billing and collection services to an entity offering any service within the scope of § 64.1501(a)(1) that is billed to a subscriber on a collect basis at a per-call or per-time-interval charge that is greater than, or in addition to, the charge for transmission of the call.

(b) No common carrier shall provide interstate transmission services for any collect information services billed to a subscriber at a tariffed rate unless the called party has taken affirmative action clearly indicating that it accepts the charges for the collect service.

47 C.F.R. § 64.1506 Number designation.

Any interstate service described in § 64.1501(a)(1)-(2), and not subject to the exclusions contained in § 64.1501(a)(4), shall be offered only through telephone numbers beginning with a 900 service access code.

[59 Fed. Reg. 46770 (Sept. 12, 1994)]

47 C.F.R. § 64.1507 Prohibition on disconnection or interruption of service for failure to remit pay-per-call and similar service charges.

No common carrier shall disconnect or interrupt in any manner, or order the disconnection or interruption of, a telephone subscriber's local exchange or long distance telephone service as a result of that subscriber's failure to pay:

(a) Charges for interstate pay-per-call service;

(b) Charges for interstate information services provided pursuant to a presubscription or comparable arrangement; or

(c) Charges for interstate information services provided on a collect basis which have been disputed by the subscriber.

[59 Fed. Reg. 46770 (Sept. 12, 1994)]

47 C.F.R. § 64.1508 Blocking access to 900 service.

(a) Local exchange carriers must offer to their subscribers, where technically feasible, an option to block access to services offered on the 900 service access code. Blocking is to be offered at no charge, on a one-time basis, to:

(1) All telephone subscribers during the period from November 1, 1993 through December 31, 1993; and

(2) Any subscriber who subscribes to a new telephone number for a period of 60 days after the new number is effective.

(b) For blocking requests not within the one-time option or outside the time frames specified in paragraph (a) of this section, and for unblocking requests, local exchange carriers may charge a reasonable one-time fee. Requests by subscribers to remove 900 services blocking must be in writing.

(c) The terms and conditions under which subscribers may obtain 900 services blocking are to be included in tariffs filed with this Commission.

47 C.F.R. § 64.1509 Disclosure and dissemination of pay-per-call information.

(a) Any common carrier assigning a telephone number to a provider of interstate pay-per-call services shall make readily available, at no charge, to Federal and State agencies and all other interested persons:

(1) A list of the telephone numbers for each of the pay-per-call services it carries;

(2) A short description of each such service;

(3) A statement of the total cost or the cost per minute and any other fees for each such service; and

(4) A statement of the pay-per-call service provider's name, business address, and business telephone number.

(b) Any common carrier assigning a telephone number to a provider of interstate pay-per-call services and offering billing and collection services to such provider shall:

(1) Establish a local or toll-free telephone number to answer questions and provide information on subscribers' rights and obligations with regard to their use of pay-per-call services and to provide to callers the name and mailing address of any provider of pay-per-call services offered by that carrier; and

(2) Provide to all its telephone subscribers, either directly or through contract with any local exchange carrier providing billing and collection services to that carrier, a disclosure statement setting forth all rights and obligations of the subscriber and the carrier with respect to the use and payment of pay-per-call services. Such statement must include the prohibition against disconnection of basic communications services for failure to pay pay-per-call charges established by § 64.1507, the right of a subscriber to obtain blocking in accordance with § 64.1508, the right of a subscriber not to be billed for pay-per-call services not offered in compliance with federal laws and regulations established by § 64.1510(a)(1), and the possibility that a subscriber's access to 900 services may be involuntarily blocked pursuant to § 64.1512 for failure to pay legitimate pay-per-call charges. Disclosure statements must be forwarded to:

(i) All telephone subscribers no later than 60 days after these regulations take effect;

(ii) All new telephone subscribers no later than 60 days after service is established;

(iii) All telephone subscribers requesting service at a new location no later than 60 days after service is established; and

(iv) Thereafter, to all subscribers at least once per calendar year, at intervals of not less than 6 months nor more than 18 months.

[61 Fed. Reg. 55582 (Oct. 28, 1996)]

47 C.F.R. § 64.1510 Billing and collection of pay-per-call and similar service charges.

(a) Any common carrier assigning a telephone number to a provider of interstate pay-per-call services and offering billing and collection services to such provider shall:

(1) Ensure that a subscriber is not billed for interstate pay-per-call services that such carrier knows or reasonably should know were provided in violation of the regulations set forth in this subpart or prescribed by the Federal Trade Commission pursuant to titles II or III of the TDDRA or any other federal law;

(2) In any billing to telephone subscribers that includes charges for any interstate pay-per-call service:

(i) Include a statement indicating that:

(A) Such charges are for non-communications services;

(B) Neither local nor long distances services can be disconnected for non-payment although an information provider may employ private entities to seek to collect such charges;

(C) 900 number blocking is available upon request; and

(D) Access to pay-per-call services may be involuntarily blocked for failure to pay legitimate charges;

(ii) Display any charges for pay-per-call services in a part of the bill that is identified as not being related to local and long distance telephone charges;

(iii) Specify, for each pay-per-call charge made, the type of service, the amount of the charge, and the date, time, and, for calls billed on a time-sensitive basis, the duration of the call; and

(iv) Identify the local or toll-free number established in accordance with § 64.1509(b)(1).

(b) Any common carrier offering billing and collection services to an entity providing interstate information services on a collect basis shall, to the extent possible, display the billing information in the manner described in paragraphs (a)(2)(i), (A), (B), (D) and (a)(2)(ii) of this section.

(c) If a subscriber elects, pursuant to § 64.1504(c)(1)(vi), to pay by means of a phone bill for any information service provided by through any 800 telephone number, or other telephone number advertised or widely understood to be toll-free, the phone bill shall:

(1) Include, in prominent type, the following disclaimer: "Common carriers may not disconnect local or long distance telephone service for failure to pay disputed charges for information services;" and

(2) Clearly list the 800 or other toll-free number dialed.

[58 Fed. Reg. 62044 (Nov. 24, 1993); 59 Fed. Reg. 46771 (Sept. 12, 1994); 61 Fed. Reg. 39088 (July 26, 1996)]

47 C.F.R. § 64.1511 Forgiveness of charges and refunds.

(a) Any carrier assigning a telephone number to a provider of interstate pay-per-call services or providing transmission for interstate information services provided pursuant to a presubscription or comparable arrangement or on a collect basis, and providing billing and collection for such services, shall establish procedures for the handling of subscriber complaints regarding charges for those services. A billing carrier is afforded discretion to set standards for determining when a subscriber's complaint warrants forgiveness, refund or credit of interstate pay-per-call or information services charges provided that such charges must be forgiven, refunded, or credited when a subscriber has complained about such charges and either this Commission, the Federal Trade Commission, or a court of competent jurisdiction has found or the carrier has determined, upon investigation, that the service has been offered in violation of federal law or the regulations that are either set forth in this subpart or prescribed by the Federal Trade Commission pursuant to titles II or III of the TDDRA. Carriers shall observe the record retention requirements set forth in § 42.6 of this chapter except that relevant records shall be retained by carriers beyond the requirements of part 42 of this chapter when a complaint is pending at the time the specified retention period expires.

(b) Any carrier assigning a telephone number to a provider of interstate pay-per-call services but not providing billing and collection services for such services, shall, by tariff or contract, require that the provider and/or its billing and collection agents have in place procedures whereby, upon complaint, pay-per-call charges may be forgiven, refunded, or credited, provided that such charges must be forgiven, refunded, or credited when a subscriber has complained about such charges and either this Commission, the Federal Trade Commission, or a court of competent jurisdiction has found or the carrier has determined, upon investigation, that the service has been offered in violation of federal law or the regulations that are either set forth in this subpart or prescribed by the Federal Trade Commission pursuant to titles II or III of the TDDRA.

[59 Fed. Reg. 46771 (Sept. 12, 1994)]

47 C.F.R. § 64.1512 Involuntary blocking of pay-per-call services.

Nothing in this subpart shall preclude a common carrier or information provider from blocking or ordering the blocking of its interstate pay-per-call programs from numbers assigned to subscribers who have incurred, but not paid, legitimate pay-per-call charges, except that a subscriber who has filed a complaint regarding a particular pay-per-call program pursuant to procedures established by the Federal Trade Commission under title III of the TDDRA shall not be involuntarily blocked from access to that program while such a complaint is pending. This restriction is not intended to preclude involuntary blocking when a carrier or IP has decided in one instance to sustain charges against a subscriber but that subscriber files additional separate complaints.

47 C.F.R. § 64.1513 Verification of charitable status.

Any common carrier assigning a telephone number to a provider of interstate pay-per-call services that the carrier knows or reasonably should know is engaged in soliciting charitable contributions shall obtain verification that the entity or individual for whom contributions are solicited has been granted tax exempt status by the Internal Revenue Service.

47 C.F.R. § 64.1514 Generation of signalling tones.

No common carrier shall assign a telephone number for any pay-per-call service that employs broadcast advertising which generates the audible tones necessary to complete a call to a pay-per-call service.

47 C.F.R. § 64.1515 Recovery of costs.

No common carrier shall recover its cost of complying with the provisions of this subpart from local or long distance ratepayers.

[59 Fed. Reg. 36687 (July 18, 1994)]

B.4.2 FTC 900-Number Regulations—16 C.F.R. §§ 308.1–308.9

Sec.

Authority: Pub. L. No. 102-556, 106 Stat. 4181 (15 U.S.C. 5701 *et seq.*)

Source: 58 Fed. Reg. 42400 (Aug. 9, 1993), unless otherwise noted.

16 C.F.R. § 308.1 Scope of regulations in this part.

This rule implements titles II and III of the Telephone Disclosure and Dispute Resolution Act of 1992, to be codified in relevant part at 15 U.S.C. 5711–14, 5721–24.

16 C.F.R. § 308.2 Definitions.

(a) *Bona fide educational service* means any pay-per-call service dedicated to providing information or instruction relating to education, subjects of academic study, or other related areas of school study.

(b) *Commission* means the Federal Trade Commission.

(c) *Pay-per-call service* has the meaning provided in section 228 of the Communications Act of 1934, 47 U.S.C. 228.[1]

(d) *Person* means any individual, partnership, corporation, association, government or governmental subdivision or agency, or other entity.

(e)(1) *Presubscription or comparable arrangement* means a contractual agreement in which

(i) The service provider clearly and conspicuously discloses to the consumer all material terms and conditions associated with the use of the service, including the service provider's name and address, a business telephone number which the consumer may use to obtain additional information or to register a complaint, and the rates for the service;

(ii) The service provider agrees to notify the consumer of any future rate changes;

(iii) The consumer agrees to utilize the service on the terms and conditions disclosed by the service provider; and

(iv) The service provider requires the use of an identification number or other means to prevent unauthorized access to the service by nonsubscribers.

(2) Disclosure of a credit card or charge card number, along with authorization to bill that number, made during the course of a call to a pay-per-call service shall constitute a presubscription or comparable arrangement if the credit or charge card is subject to the dispute resolution requirements of the Fair Credit Billing Act and the Truth in Lending Act, as amended. No other action taken by the consumer during the course of a call to a pay-per-call service can be construed as creating a presubscription or comparable arrangement.

(f) *Program-length commercial* means any commercial or other advertisement fifteen (15) minutes in length or longer or intended to fill a television or radio broadcasting or cablecasting time slot of fifteen (15) minutes in length or longer.

(g) *Provider of pay-per-call services* means any person who sells or offers to sell a pay-per-call service. A person who provides only transmission services or billing and collection services shall not be considered a provider of pay-per-call services.

(h) *Reasonably understandable volume* means at an audible level that renders the message intelligible to the receiving audience, and, in any event, at least the same audible level as that principally used in the advertisement or the pay-per-call service.

(i) *Service bureau* means any person, other than a common carrier, who provides, among other things, access to telephone service and voice storage to pay-per-call service providers.

---

1 Section 228 of the Communications Act of 1934 states:

(1) The term *pay-per-call* services means any service—

(A) In which any person provides or purports to provide—

(i) Audio information or audio entertainment produced or packaged by such person;

(ii) Access to simultaneous voice conversation services; or

(iii) Any service, including the provision of a product, the charges for which are assessed on the basis of the completion of the call;

(B) For which the caller pays a per-call or per-time-interval charge that is greater than, or in addition to, the charge for transmission of the call; and

(C) Which is accessed through use of a 900 telephone number or other prefix or area code designated by the (Federal Communications) Commission in accordance with subsection (b)(5) (47 U.S.C. 228(b)(5)).

(2) Such term does not include directory services provided by a common carrier or its affiliate or by a local exchange carrier or its affiliate, or any service the charge for which is tariffed, or any service for which users are assessed charges only after entering into a presubcription or comparable arrangement with the provider of such service.

(j) *Slow and deliberate manner* means at a rate that renders the message intelligible to the receiving audience, and, in any event, at a cadence or rate no faster than that principally used in the advertisement or the pay-per-call service.

(k) *Sweepstakes*, including games of chance, means a game or promotional mechanism that involves the elements of a prize and chance and does not require consideration.

16 C.F.R. § 308.3 Advertising of pay-per-call services.

(a) General requirements. The following requirements apply to disclosures required in advertisements under §§ 308.3(b)–(d), and (f):

(1) The disclosures shall be made in the same language as that principally used in the advertisement.

(2) Television video and print disclosures shall be of a color or shade that readily contrasts with the background of the advertisement.

(3) In print advertisements, disclosures shall be parallel with the base of the advertisement.

(4) Audio disclosures, whether in television or radio, shall be delivered in a slow and deliberate manner and in a reasonably understandable volume.

(5) Nothing contrary to, inconsistent with, or in mitigation of, the required disclosures shall be used in any advertisement in any medium; nor shall any audio, video or print technique be used that is likely to detract significantly from the communication of the disclosures.

(6) In any program-length commercial, required disclosures shall be made at least three times (unless more frequent disclosure is otherwise required) near the beginning, middle and end of the commercial.

(b) Cost of the call.

(1) The provider of pay-per-call services shall clearly and conspicuously disclose the cost of the call, in Arabic numerals, in any advertisement for the pay-per-call service, as follows:

(i) If there is a flat fee for the call, the advertisement shall state the total cost of the call.

(ii) If the call is billed on a time-sensitive basis, the advertisement shall state the cost per minute and any minimum charges. If the length of the program can be determined in advance, the advertisement shall also state the maximum charge that could be incurred if the caller listens to the complete program.

(iii) If the call is billed on a variable rate basis, the advertisement shall state, in accordance with §§ 308.3(b)(1)(i) and (ii), the cost of the initial portion of the call, any minimum charges, and the range of rates that may be charged depending on the options chosen by the caller.

(iv) The advertisement shall disclose any other fees that will be charged for the service.

(v) if the caller may be transferred to another pay-per-call service, the advertisement shall disclose the cost of the other call, in accordance with §§ 308.3(b)(1)(i), (ii), (iii), and (iv).

(2) For purposes of § 308.3(b), disclosures shall be made "clearly and conspicuously" as set forth in § 308.3(a) and as follows:

(i) In a television or videotape advertisement, the video disclosure shall appear adjacent to each video presentation of the pay-per-call number. However, in an advertisement displaying more than one pay-per-call number with the same cost, the video disclosure need only appear adjacent to the largest presentation of the pay-per-call number. Each letter or numeral of the video disclosure shall be, at a minimum, one-half the size of each letter or numeral of the pay-per-call number to which the disclosure is adjacent. In addition, the video disclosure shall appear on the screen for the duration of the presentation of the pay-per-call number. An audio disclosure shall be made at least once, simultaneously with a video presentation of the disclosure. However, no audio presentation of the disclosure is required in: (A) An advertisement fifteen (15) seconds or less in length in which the pay-per-call number is not presented in the audio portion, or (B) an advertisement in which there is no audio presentation of information regarding the pay-per-call service, including the pay-per-call number. In an advertisement in which the pay-per-call number is presented only in the audio portion, the cost of the call shall be delivered immediately following the first and last delivery of the pay-per-call number, except that in a program-length commercial, the disclosure shall be delivered immediately following each delivery of the pay-per-call number.

(ii) In a print advertisement, the disclosure shall be placed adjacent to each presentation of the pay-per-call number. However, in an advertisement displaying more than one pay-per-call number with the same cost, the disclosure need only appear adjacent to the largest presentation of the pay-per-call number. Each letter or numeral of the disclosure shall be, at a minimum, one-half the size of each letter or numeral of the pay-per-call number to which the disclosure is adjacent.

(iii) In a radio advertisement, the disclosure shall be made at least once, and shall be delivered immediately following the first delivery of the pay-per-call number. In a program-length commercial, the disclosure shall be delivered immediately following each delivery of the pay-per-call number.

(c) Sweepstakes; games of chance.

(1) The provider of pay-per-call services that advertises a prize or award or a service or product at no cost or for a reduced cost, to be awarded to the winner of any sweepstakes, including games of chance, shall clearly and conspicuously disclose in the advertisement the odds of being able to receive the prize, award, service, or product at no cost or reduced cost. If the odds are not calculable in advance, the advertisement shall disclose the factors used in calculating the odds. Either the advertisement or the preamble required by § 308.5(a) for such service shall clearly and conspicuously disclose that no call to the pay-per-call service is required to participate, and shall also disclose the existence of a free alternative method of entry, and either instructions on how to enter, or a local or toll-free telephone number or address to which consumers may call or write for information on how to enter the sweepstakes. Any description or characterization of the prize, award, service, or product that is being offered at no cost or reduced cost shall be truthful and accurate.

(2) For purposes of § 308.3(c), disclosures shall be made "clearly and conspicuously" as set forth in § 308.3(a) and as follows:

(i) In a television or videotape advertisement, the disclosures may be made in either the audio or video portion of the advertisement. If the disclosures are made in the video portion, they shall appear on the screen in sufficient size and for sufficient time to allow consumers to read and comprehend the disclosures.

(ii) In a print advertisement, the disclosures shall appear in a sufficient size and prominence and such location to be readily noticeable, readable and comprehensible.

(d) Federal programs.

(1) The provider of pay-per-call services that advertises a pay-per-call service that is not operated or expressly authorized by a Federal agency, but that provides information on a Federal program, shall clearly and conspicuously disclose in the advertisement that the pay-per-call service is not authorized, endorsed, or approved by any Federal agency. Advertisements providing information on a Federal program shall include, but not be limited to, advertisements that contain a seal, insignia, trade or brand name, or any other term or symbol that reasonably could be interpreted or construed as implying any Federal government connection, approval, or endorsement.

(2) For purposes of § 308.3(d), disclosures shall be made "clearly and conspicuously" as set forth in § 308.3(a) and as follows:

(i) In a television or videotape advertisement, the disclosure may be made in either the audio or video portion of the advertisement. If the disclosure is made in the video portion, it shall appear on the screen in sufficient size and for sufficient time to allow consumers to read and comprehend the disclosure. The disclosure shall begin within the first fifteen (15) seconds of the advertisement.

(ii) In a print advertisement, the disclosure shall appear in a sufficient size and prominence and such location to be readily noticeable, readable and comprehensible. The disclosure shall appear in the top one-third of the advertisement.

(iii) In a radio advertisement, the disclosure shall begin within the first fifteen (15) seconds of the advertisement.

(e) Prohibition on advertising to children.

(1) The provider of pay-per-call services shall not direct advertisements for such pay-per-call services to children under the age of 12, unless the service is a bona fide educational service.

(2) For the purposes of this regulation, advertisements directed to children under 12 shall include: any pay-per-call advertisement appearing during or immediately adjacent to programming for which competent and reliable audience composition data demonstrate that more than 50% of the audience is composed of children under 12, and any pay-per-call advertisement appearing in a periodical for which competent and reliable readership data demonstrate that more than 50% of the readership is composed of children under 12.

(3) For the purposes of this regulation, if competent and reliable audience composition or readership data does not demonstrate that more than 50% of the audience or readership is composed of children under 12, then the Commission shall consider the following criteria in determining whether an advertisement is directed to children under 12:

(i) Whether the advertisement appears in a publication directed to children under 12, including, but not limited to, books, magazines and comic books;

(ii) Whether the advertisement appears during or immediately adjacent to television programs directed to children under 12, including, but not limited to, children's programming as defined by the Federal Communications Commission, animated programs, and after-school programs;

(iii) Whether the advertisement appears on a television station or channel directed to children under 12;

(iv) Whether the advertisement is broadcast during or immediately adjacent to radio programs directed to children under 12, or broadcast on a radio station directed to children under 12;

(v) Whether the advertisement appears on the same video as a commercially-prepared video directed to children under 12, or preceding a movie directed to children under 12 shown in a movie theater;

(vi) Whether the advertisement or promotion appears on product packaging directed to children under 12; and

(vii) Whether the advertisement, regardless of when or where it appears, is directed to children under 12 in light of its subject matter, visual content, age of models, language, characters, tone, message, or the like.

(f) Advertising to individuals under the age of 18.

(1) The provider of pay-per-call services shall ensure that any pay-per-call advertisement directed primarily to individuals under the age of 18 shall contain a clear and conspicuous disclosure that all individuals under the age of 18 must have the permission of such individual's parent or legal guardian prior to calling such pay-per-call service.

(2) For purposes of § 308.3(f), disclosures shall be made "clearly and conspicuously" as set forth in § 308.3(a) and as follows:

(i) In a television or videotape advertisement, each letter or numeral of the video disclosure shall be, at a minimum, one-half the size of each letter or numeral of the largest presentation of the pay-per-call number. The video disclosure shall appear on the screen for sufficient time to allow consumers to read and comprehend the disclosure. An audio disclosure shall be made at least once, simultaneously with a video presentation of the disclosure. However, no audio presentation of the disclosure is required in: (A) An advertisement fifteen (15) seconds or less in length in which the pay-per-call number is not presented in the audio portion, or (B) an advertisement in which there is no audio presentation of information regarding the pay-per-call service, including the pay-per-call number.

(ii) In a print advertisement, each letter or numeral of the disclosure shall be, at a minimum, one-half the size of each letter or numeral of the largest presentation of the pay-per-call number.

(3) For the purposes of this regulation, advertisements directed primarily to individuals under 18 shall include: Any pay-per-call advertisement appearing during or immediately adjacent to programming for which competent and reliable audience composition data demonstrate that more than 50% of the audience is composed of individuals under 18, and any pay-per-call advertisement appearing in a periodical for which competent and reliable readership data demonstrate that more than 50% of the readership is composed of individuals under 18.

(4) For the purposes of this regulation, if competent and reliable audience composition or readership data does not demonstrate that more than 50% of the audience or readership is composed of individuals under 18, then the Commission shall consider the following criteria in determining whether an advertisement is directed primarily to individuals under 18:

(i) Whether the advertisement appears in publications directed primarily to individuals under 18, including, but not limited to, books, magazines and comic books;

(ii) Whether the advertisement appears during or immediately adjacent to television programs directed primarily to individuals under 18, including, but not limited to, mid-afternoon weekday television shows;

(iii) Whether the advertisement is broadcast on radio stations that are directed primarily to individuals under 18;

(iv) Whether the advertisement appears on a cable or broadcast television station directed primarily to individuals under 18;

(v) Whether the advertisement appears on the same video as a commercially-prepared video directed primarily to individuals under 18, or preceding a movie directed primarily to individuals under 18 shown in a movie theater; and

(vi) Whether the advertisement, regardless of when or where it appears, is directed primarily to individuals under 18 in light of its subject matter, visual content, age of models, language, characters, tone, massage, or the like.

(g) Electronic tones in advertisements. The provider of pay-per-call services is prohibited from using advertisements that emit electronic tones that can automatically dial a pay-per-call service.

(h) Telephone solicitations. The provider of pay-per-call services shall ensure that any telephone message that solicits calls to the pay-per-call service discloses the cost of the call in a slow and deliberate manner and in a reasonably understandable volume, in accordance with §§ 308.3(b)(1)(i)–(v).

(*i*) Referral to toll-free telephone numbers. The provider of pay-per-call services is prohibited from referring in advertisements to an 800 telephone number, or any other telephone number advertised as or widely understood to be toll-free, if that number violates the prohibition concerning toll-free numbers set forth in § 308.5(i).

16 C.F.R. § 308.4 Special rule for infrequent publications.

(a) The provider of any pay-per-call service that advertises a pay-per-call service in a publication that meets the requirements set forth in § 308.4(c) may include in such advertisement, in lieu of the cost disclosures required by § 308.3(b), a clear and conspicuous disclosure that a call to the advertised pay-per-call service may result in a substantial charge.

(b) The provider of any pay-per-call service that places an alphabetical listing in a publication that meets the requirements set forth in § 308.4(c) is not required to make any of the disclosures required by §§ 308.3(b), (c), (d) and (f) in the alphabetical listing, provided that such listing does not contain any information except the name, address and telephone number of the pay-per-call provider.

(c) The publication referred to in § 308.4(a) and (b) must be:

(1) Widely distributed;

(2) Printed annually or less frequently; and

(3) One that has an established policy of not publishing specific prices in advertisements.

16 C.F.R. § 308.5 Pay-per-call service standards.

(a) Preamble message. The provider of pay-per-call services shall include, in each pay-per-call message, an introductory disclosure message ("preamble") in the same language as that principally used in the pay-per-call message, that clearly, in a slow and deliberate manner and in a reasonably understandable volume:

(1) Identifies the name of the provider of the pay-per-call service and describes the service being provided;

(2) Specifies the cost of the service as follows:

(i) If there is a flat fee for the call, the preamble shall state the total cost of the call;

(ii) If the call is billed on a time-sensitive basis, the preamble shall state the cost per minute and any minimum charges; if the length of the program can be determined in advance, the preamble shall also state the maximum charge that could be incurred if the caller listens to the complete program;

(iii) If the call is billed on a variable rate basis, the preamble shall state, in accordance with §§ 308.5(a)(2)(i) and (ii), the cost of the initial portion of the call, any minimum charges, and the range of rates that may be charged depending on the options chosen by the caller;

(iv) Any other fees that will be charged for the service shall be disclosed, as well as fees for any other pay-per-call service to which the caller may be transferred;

(3) Informs the caller that charges for the call begin, and that to avoid charges the call must be terminated, three seconds after a clearly discernible signal or tone indicating the end of the preamble;

(4) Informs the caller that anyone under the age of 18 must have the permission of parent or legal guardian in order to complete the call; and

(5) Informs the caller, in the case of a pay-per-call service that is not operated or expressly authorized by a Federal agency but that provides information on a Federal program, or that uses a trade or brand name or any other term that reasonably could be interpreted or construed as implying any Federal government connection, approval or endorsement, that the pay-per-call service is not authorized, endorsed, or approved by any Federal agency.

(b) No charge to caller for preamble message. The provider of pay-per-call services is prohibited from charging a caller any amount whatsoever for such a service if the caller hangs up at any time prior to three seconds after the signal or tone indicating the end of the preamble described in § 308.5(a). However, the three-second delay, and the message concerning such delay described in § 308.5(a)(3), is not required if the provider of pay-per-call services offers the caller an affirmative means (such as pressing a key on a telephone keypad) of indicating a decision to incur the charges.

(c) Nominal cost calls. The preamble described in § 308.5(a) is not required when the entire cost of the pay-per-call service, whether billed as a flat rate or on a time sensitive basis, is $2.00 or less.

(d) Data service calls. The preamble described in § 308.5(a) is not required when the entire call consists of the non-verbal transmission of information.

(e) Bypass mechanism. The provider of pay-per-call services that offers to frequent callers or regular subscribers to such services the option of activating a bypass mechanism to avoid listening to the preamble during subsequent calls shall not be deemed to be in violation of § 308.5(a), provided that any such bypass mechanism shall be disabled for a period of no less than 30 days immediately after the institution of an increase in the price for the service or a change in the nature of the service offered.

(f) Billing limitations. The provider of pay-per-call services is prohibited from billing consumers in excess of the amount described in the preamble for those services and from billing for any services provided in violation of any section of this rule.

(g) Stopping the assessment of time-based charges. The provider of pay-per-call services shall stop the assessment of time-based charges immediately upon disconnection by the caller.

(h) Prohibition on services to children. The provider of pay-per-call services shall not direct such services to children under the age of 12, unless such service is a bona fide educational service. The Commission shall consider the following criteria in determining whether a pay-per-call service is directed to children under 12:

(1) Whether the pay-per-call service is advertised in the manner set forth in §§ 308.3(e)(2) and (3); and

(2) Whether the pay-per-call service, regardless of when or where it is advertised, is directed to children under 12, in light of its subject matter, content, language, featured personality, characters, tone, message, or the like.

(*i*) Prohibition concerning toll-free numbers. Any person is prohibited from using an 800 number or other telephone number advertised as or widely understood to be toll-free in a manner that would result in:

(1) The calling party being assessed, by virtue of completing the call, a charge for the call;

(2) The calling party being connected to an access number for, or otherwise transferred to, a pay-per-call service;

(3) The calling party being charged for information conveyed during the call unless the calling party has a presubscription or comparable arrangement to be charged for the information; or

(4) The calling party being called back collect for the provision of audio or data information services, simultaneous voice conversation services, or products.

(j) Disclosure requirements for billing statements. The provider of pay-per-call services shall ensure that any billing statement for such provider's charges shall:

(1) Display any charges for pay-per-call services in a portion of the consumer's bill that is identified as not being related to local and long distance telephone charges;

(2) For each charge so displayed, specify the type of service, the amount of the charge, and the date, time, and, for calls billed on a time-sensitive basis, the duration of the call; and

(3) Display the local or toll-free telephone number where consumers can obtain answers to their questions and information on their rights and obligations with regard to their use of pay-per-call services, and can obtain the name and mailing address of the provider of pay-per-call services.

(k) Refunds to consumers. The provider of pay-per-call services shall be liable for refunds or credits to consumers who have been billed for pay-per-call services, and who have paid the charges for such services, pursuant to pay-per-call programs that have been found to have violated any provision of this rule or any other Federal rule or law.

(*l*) Service bureau liability. A service bureau shall be liable for violations of the rule by pay-per-call services using its call processing facilities where it knew or should have known of the violation.

16 C.F.R. § 308.6 Access to information.

Any common carrier that provides telecommunication services to any provider of pay-per-call services shall make available to the Commission, upon written request, any records and financial information maintained by such carrier relating to the arrangements (other than for the provision of local exchange service) between such carrier and any provider of pay-per-call services.

16 C.F.R. § 308.7 Billing and collection for pay-per-call services.

(a) Definitions. For the purposes of this section, the following definitions shall apply:

(1) *Billing entity* means any person who transmits a billing statement to a customer for a telephone-billed purchase, or any person who assumes responsibility for receiving and responding to billing error complaints or inquiries.

(2) *Billing error* means any of the following:

(i) A reflection on a billing statement of a telephone-billed purchase that was not made by the customer nor made from the telephone of the customer who was billed for the purchase or, if made, was not in the amount reflected on such statement.

(ii) A reflection on a billing statement of a telephone-billed purchase for which the customer requests additional clarification, including documentary evidence thereof.

(iii) A reflection on a billing statement of a telephone-billed purchase that was not accepted by the customer or not provided to the customer in accordance with the stated terms of the transaction.

(iv) A reflection on a billing statement of a telephone-billed purchase for a call made to an 800 or other toll free telephone number.

(v) The failure to reflect properly on a billing statement a payment made by the customer or a credit issued to the customer with respect to a telephone-billed purchase.

(vi) A computation error or similar error of an accounting nature on a billing statement of a telephone-billed purchase.

(vii) Failure to transmit a billing statement for a telephone-billed purchase to a customer's last known address if that address was furnished by the customer at least twenty days before the end of the billing cycle for which the statement was required.

(viii) A reflection on a billing statement of a telephone-billed purchase that is not identified in accordance with the requirements of § 308.5(j).

(3) *Customer* means any person who acquires or attempts to acquire goods or services in a telephone-billed purchase, or who receives a billing statement for a telephone-billed purchase charged to a telephone number assigned to that person by a providing carrier.

(4) *Preexisting agreement* means a "presubscription or comparable arrangement," as that term is defined in § 308.2(e).

(5) *Providing carrier* means a local exchange or interexchange common carrier providing telephone services (other than local exchange services) to a vendor for a telephone-billed purchase that is the subject of a billing error complaint or inquiry.

(6) *Telephone-billed purchase* means any purchase that is completed solely as a consequence of the completion of the call or a subsequent dialing, touch tone entry, or comparable action of the caller. Such term does not include:

(i) A purchase by a caller pursuant to a preexisting agreement with a vendor;

(ii) Local exchange telephone services or interexchange telephone services or any service that the Federal Communications Commission determines by rule—

(A) Is closely related to the provision of local exchange telephone services or interexchange telephone services; and

(B) Is subject to billing dispute resolution procedures required by Federal or state statute or regulation; or

(iii) The purchase of goods or services that is otherwise subject to billing dispute resolution procedures required by Federal statute or regulation.

(7) *Vendor* means any person who, through the use of the telephone, offers goods or services for a telephone-billed purchase.

(b) Initiation of billing review. A customer may initiate a billing review with respect to a telephone-billed purchase by providing the billing entity with notice of a billing error no later than 60 days after the billing entity transmitted the first billing statement that contains a charge for such telephone-billed purchase. If the billing error is the reflection on a billing statement of a telephone-billed purchase not provided to the customer in accordance with the stated terms of the transaction, the 60-day period shall begin to run from the date the goods or services are delivered or, if not delivered, should have been delivered, if such date is later than the date the billing statement was transmitted. A billing error notice shall:

(1) Set forth or otherwise enable the billing entity to identify the customer's name and the telephone number to which the charge was billed;

(2) Indicate the customer's belief that the statement contains a billing error and the type, date, and amount of such; and

(3) Set forth the reasons for the customer's belief, to the extent possible, that the statement contains a billing error.

(c) Disclosure of method of providing notice; presumption if oral notice is permitted. A billing entity shall clearly and conspicuously[2] disclose on each billing statement or on other material accompanying the billing statement the method (oral or written) by which the customer may provide notice to initiate review of a billing error in the manner set forth in § 308.7(b). If oral notice is permitted, any customer who orally communicates an allegation of a billing error to a billing entity shall be presumed to have properly initiated a billing review in accordance with the requirements of § 308.7(b).

(d) Response to customer notice. A billing entity that receives notice of a billing error as described in § 308.7(b) shall:

(1) Send a written acknowledgment to the customer including a statement that any disputed amount need not be paid pending investigation of the billing error. This shall be done no later than forty (40) days after receiving the notice, unless the action required by § 308.7(d)(2) is taken within such 40-day period; and

(2)(i) Correct the billing error and credit the customer's account for any disputed amount and any related charges, and notify the customer of the correction. The billing entity also shall disclose to the customer that collection efforts may occur despite the credit, and shall provide the names, mailing addresses, and business telephone numbers of the vendor and providing carrier, as applicable, that are the subject of the telephone-billed purchase, or provide the customer with a local or toll-free telephone number that the customer may call to obtain this information directly. However, the billing entity is not required to make the disclosure concerning collection efforts if the vendor, its agent, or the providing carrier, as applicable, will not collect or attempt to collect the disputed charge; or

(ii) Transmit an explanation to the customer, after conducting a reasonable investigation (including, where appropriate, contacting the vendor or providing carrier),[3] setting forth the reasons why it has determined that no billing error occurred or that a different billing error occurred from that asserted, make any appropriate adjustments to the customer's account, and, if the customer so requests, provide a written explanation and copies of documentary evidence of the customer's indebtedness.

(3) The action required by § 308.7(d)(2) shall be taken no later than two complete billing cycles of the billing entity (in no event later than ninety (90) days) after receiving the notice of the billing error and before taking any action to collect the disputed amount, or any part thereof. After complying with § 308.7(d)(2), the billing entity shall:

(i) If it is determined that any disputed amount is in error, promptly notify the appropriate providing carrier or vendor, as applicable, of its disposition of the customer's billing error and the reasons therefor; and

(ii) Promptly notify the customer in writing of the time when payment is due of any portion of the disputed amount determined not to be in error, which time shall be the longer of ten (10) days or the number of days the customer is ordinarily allowed (whether by custom, contract or state law) to pay undisputed amounts, and that failure to pay such amount may be reported to a credit reporting agency or subject the customer to a collection action, if that in fact may happen.

(e) Withdrawal of billing error notice. A billing entity need not comply with the requirements of § 308.7(d) if the customer has, after giving notice of a billing error and before the expiration of the time limits specified therein, agreed that the billing statement was correct or agreed to withdraw voluntarily the billing error notice.

(f) Limitation on responsibility for billing error. After complying with the provisions of § 308.7(d), a billing entity has no further responsibility under that section if the customer continues to make substantially the same allegation with respect to a billing error.

(g) Customer's right to withhold disputed amount; limitation on collection action. Once the customer has submitted notice of a billing error to a billing entity, the customer need not pay, and the billing entity, providing carrier, or vendor may not try to collect, any portion of any required payment that the customer reasonably believes is related to the disputed amount until the billing entity receiving the notice has complied with the require-

2 The standard for "clear and conspicuous" as used in this section shall be the standard enunciated by the Board of Governors of the Federal Reserve System in its Official Staff Commentary on Regulation Z, which requires simply that the disclosures be in a reasonably understandable form. See 12 CFR part 226, Supplement I, Comment 226.5(a)(1)-1.

3 If a customer submits a billing error notice alleging either the nondelivery of goods or services or that information appearing on a billing statement has been reported incorrectly to the billing entity, the billing entity shall not deny the assertion unless it conducts a reasonable investigation and determines that the goods or services were actually delivered as agreed or that the information was correct. There shall be a rebuttable presumption that goods or services were actually delivered to the extent that a vendor or providing carrier produces documents prepared and maintained in the ordinary course of business showing the date on, and the place to, which the goods or services were transmitted or delivered.

ments of § 308.7(d). The billing entity, providing carrier, or vendor are not prohibited from taking any action to collect any undisputed portion of the bill, or from reflecting a disputed amount and related charges on a billing statement, provided that the billing statement clearly states that payment of any disputed amount or related charges is not required pending the billing entity's compliance with § 308.7(d).

(h) Prohibition on charges for initiating billing review. A billing entity, providing carrier, or vendor may not impose on the customer any charge related to the billing review, including charges for documentation or investigation.

(*i*) Restrictions on credit reporting—

(1) Adverse credit reports prohibited. Once the customer has submitted notice of a billing error to a billing entity, a billing entity, providing carrier, vendor, or other agent may not report or threaten directly or indirectly to report adverse information to any person because of the customer's withholding payment of the disputed amount or related charges, until the billing entity has met the requirements of § 308.7(d) and allowed the customer as many days thereafter to make payment as prescribed by § 308.7(d)(3)(ii).

(2) Reports on continuing disputes. If a billing entity receives further notice from a customer within the time allowed for payment under § 308.7(i)(1) that any portion of the billing error is still in dispute, a billing entity, providing carrier, vendor, or other agent may not report to any person that the customer's account is delinquent because of the customer's failure to pay that disputed amount unless the billing entity, providing carrier, vendor, or other agent also reports that the amount is in dispute and notifies the customer in writing of the name and address of each person to whom the vendor, billing entity, providing carrier, or other agent has reported the account as delinquent.

(3) Reporting of dispute resolutions required. A billing entity, providing carrier, vendor, or other agent shall report in writing any subsequent resolution of any matter reported pursuant to § 308.7(i)(2) to all persons to whom such matter was initially reported.

(j) Forfeiture of right to collect disputed amount. Any billing entity, providing carrier, vendor, or other agent who fails to comply with the requirements of §§ 308.7(c), (d), (g), (h), or (i) forfeits any right to collect from the customer the amount indicated by the customer, under § 308.7(b)(2), to be in error, and any late charges or other related charges thereon, up to $50 per transaction.

(k) Prompt notification of returns and crediting of refunds. When a vendor other than the billing entity accepts the return of property or forgives a debt for services in connection with a telephone-billed purchase, the vendor shall, within seven (7) business days from accepting the return or forgiving the debt, either:

(1) Mail or deliver a cash refund directly to the customer's address, and notify the appropriate billing entity that the customer has been given a refund, or

(2) Transmit a credit statement to the billing entity through the vendor's normal channels for billing telephone-billed purchases. The billing entity shall, within seven (7) business days after receiving a credit statement, credit the customer's account with the amount of the refund.

(*l*) Right of customer to assert claims or defenses. Any billing entity or providing carrier who seeks to collect charges from a customer for a telephone-billed purchase that is the subject of a dispute between the customer and the vendor shall be subject to all claims (other than tort claims) and defenses arising out of the transaction and relating to the failure to resolve the dispute that the customer could assert against the vendor, if the customer has made a good faith attempt to resolve the dispute with the vendor or providing carrier (other than the billing entity). The billing entity or providing carrier shall not be liable under this paragraph for any amount greater than the amount billed to the customer for the purchase (including any related charges).

(m) Retaliatory actions prohibited. A billing entity, providing carrier, vendor, or other agent may not accelerate any part of the customer's indebtedness or restrict or terminate the customer's access to pay-per-call services solely because the customer has exercised in good faith rights provided by this section.

(n) Notice of billing error rights—

(1) Annual statement.

(i) A billing entity shall mail or deliver to each customer, with the first billing statement for a telephone-billed purchase mailed or delivered after the effective date of these regulations, a statement of the customer's billing rights with respect to telephone-billed purchases. Thereafter the billing entity shall mail or deliver the billing rights statement at least once per calendar year to each customer to whom it has mailed or delivered a billing statement for a telephone-billed purchase during the previous twelve months. The billing rights statement shall disclose that the rights and obligations of the customer and the billing entity, set forth therein, are provided under the federal Telephone Disclosure and Dispute Resolution Act. The statement shall describe the procedure that the customer must follow to notify the billing entity of a billing error and the steps that the billing entity must take in response to the customer's notice. If the customer is permitted to provide oral notice of a billing error, the statement shall disclose that a customer who orally communicates an allegation of a billing error is presumed to have provided sufficient notice to initiate a billing review. The statement shall also disclose the customer's right to withhold payment of any disputed amount, and that any action to collect any disputed amount will be suspended, pending completion of the billing review. The statement shall further disclose the customer's rights and obligations if the billing entity determines that no billing error occurred, including what action the billing entity may take if the customer continues to withhold payment of the disputed amount. Additionally, the statement shall inform the customer of the billing entity's obligation to forfeit any disputed amount (up to $50 per transaction) if the billing entity fails to follow the billing and collection procedures prescribed by § 308.7 of this rule.

(ii) A billing entity that is a common carrier may comply with § 308.7(n)(1)(i) by, within 60 days after the effective date of these regulations, mailing or delivering the billing rights statement to all of its customers and, thereafter, mailing or delivering the billing rights statement at least once per calendar year, at intervals of not less than 6 months nor more than 18 months, to all of its customers.

(2) Alternative summary statement. As an alternative to § 308.7(n)(1), a billing entity may mail or deliver, on or with each billing statement, a statement that sets forth the procedure that a customer must follow to notify the billing entity of a billing error. The statement shall also disclose the customer's right to withhold payment of any disputed amount, and that any action to collect any disputed amount will be suspended, pending completion of the billing review.

(3) General disclosure requirements.

(i) The disclosures required by § 308.7(n)(1) shall be made clearly and conspicuously on a separate statement that the customer may keep.

(ii) The disclosures required by § 308.7(n)(2) shall be made clearly and conspicuously and may be made on a separate statement or on the customer's billing statement. If any of the disclosures are provided on the back of the billing statement, the billing entity shall include a reference to those disclosures on the front of the statement.

(iii) At the billing entity's option, additional information or explanations may be supplied with the disclosures required by § 308.7(n), but none shall be stated, utilized, or placed so as to mislead or confuse the customer or contradict, obscure, or detract attention from the information required to be disclosed. The disclosures required by § 308.7(n) shall appear separately and above any other disclosures.

(*o*) Multiple billing entities. If a telephone-billed purchase involves more than one billing entity, only one set of disclosures need by given, and the billing entities shall agree among themselves which billing entity must comply with the requirements that this regulation imposes on any or all of them. The billing entity designated to receive and respond to billing errors shall remain the only billing entity responsible for complying with the terms of § 308.7(d). If a billing entity other than the one designated to receive and respond to billing errors receives notice of a billing error as described in § 308.7(b), that billing entity shall either: (1) Promptly transmit to the customer the name, mailing address, and business telephone number of the billing entity designated to receive and respond to billing errors; or (2) transmit the billing error notice within fifteen (15) days to the billing entity designated to receive and respond to billing errors. The time requirements in § 308.7(d) shall not begin to run until the billing entity designated to receive and respond to billing errors receives notice of the billing error, either from the customer or from the billing entity to whom the customer transmitted the notice.

(p) Multiple customers. If there is more than one customer involved in a telephone-billed purchase, the disclosures may be made to any customer who is primarily liable on the account.

16 C.F.R. § 308.8 Severability.

The provisions of this rule are separate and severable from one another. If any provision is stayed or determined to be invalid, it is the Commission's intention that the remaining provisions shall continue in effect.

16 C.F.R. § 308.9 Rulemaking review.

No later than four years after the effective date of this Rule, the Commission shall initiate a rulemaking review proceeding to evaluate the operation of the rule.

Appendix C The Low Income Home Energy Assistance Program (LIHEAP)

This appendix is also available on the companion website to this treatise. The companion website facilitates keyword searches and allows relevant provisions to be imported as word-processing documents.

C.1 LIHEAP Statute—42 U.S.C. §§ 8621–8630

Sec.

42 U.S.C. § 8621. Home energy grants

(a) Authorization

The Secretary is authorized to make grants, in accordance with the provisions of this subchapter, to States to assist low-income households, particularly those with the lowest incomes, that pay a high proportion of household income for home energy, primarily in meeting their immediate home energy needs.

(b) Authorization of appropriations

There are authorized to be appropriated to carry out the provisions of this subchapter (other than section 8626a of this title), $2,000,000,000 for each of fiscal years 1995 through 1999, such sums as may be necessary for each of fiscal years 2000 and 2001, and $5,100,000,000 for each of fiscal years 2005 through 2007. The authorizations of appropriations contained in this subsection are subject to the program year provisions of subsection (c) of this section.

(c) Availability of appropriations

Amounts appropriated under this section for any fiscal year for programs and activities under this subchapter shall be made available for obligation in the succeeding fiscal year.

(d) Authorization of appropriations for leveraged resources

(1) There is authorized to be appropriated to carry out section 8626a of this title, $30,000,000 for each of fiscal years 1999 through 2004, except as provided in paragraph (2).

(2) For any of fiscal years 1999 through 2004 for which the amount appropriated under subsection (b) of this section is not less than $1,400,000,000, there is authorized to be appropriated $50,000,000 to carry out section 8626a of this title.

(e) Emergency funds

There is authorized to be appropriated in each fiscal year for payments under this subchapter, in addition to amounts appropriated for distribution to all the States in accordance with section 8623 of this title (other than subsection (e) of such section), $600,000,000 to meet the additional home energy assistance needs of one or more States arising from a natural disaster or other emergency. Funds appropriated pursuant to this subsection are hereby designated to be emergency requirements pursuant to section 251(b)(2)(D) of the Balanced Budget and Emergency Deficit Control Act of 1985 (2 U.S.C. § 901(b)(2)(D)), except that such funds shall be made available only after the submission to Congress of a formal budget request by the President (for all or a part of the appropriation pursuant to this subsection) that includes a designation of the amount requested as an emergency requirement as defined in such Act (2 U.S.C. § 900 *et seq.*).

[Pub. L. No. 97-35, tit. XXVI, § 2602, 95 Stat. 893 (Aug. 13, 1981); Pub. L. No. 98-558, tit. VI, § 601, 98 Stat. 2889 (Oct. 30, 1984); Pub. L. No. 99-425, tit. V, § 501, 100 Stat. 973 (Sept. 30, 1986); Pub. L. No. 101-501, tit. VII, §§ 701, 702, 707(b), 104 Stat. 1258, 1261 (Nov. 3, 1990); Pub. L. No. 103-43, tit. XX, § 2011, 107 Stat. 214 (June 10, 1993); Pub. L. No. 103-252, tit. III, §§ 302–304(a), 311(c)(1), 108 Stat. 657, 658, 661 (May 18, 1994); Pub. L. No. 105-285, tit. III, § 302, 112 Stat. 2756 (Oct. 27, 1998); Pub. L. No. 109-58, tit. I, § 121, 119 Stat. 616 (Aug. 8, 2005)]

42 U.S.C. § 8622. Definitions

As used in this subchapter:

(1) The term "emergency" means—

(A) a natural disaster;

(B) a significant home energy supply shortage or disruption;

(C) a significant increase in the cost of home energy, as determined by the Secretary;
(D) a significant increase in home energy disconnections reported by a utility, a State regulatory agency, or another agency with necessary data;
(E) a significant increase in participation in a public benefit program such as the supplemental nutrition assistance program carried out under the Food and Nutrition Act of 2008 (7 U.S.C. § 2011 *et seq.*), the national program to provide supplemental security income carried out under title XVI of the Social Security Act (42 U.S.C. § 1381 *et seq.*), or the State temporary assistance for needy families program carried out under part A of title IV of the Social Security Act (42 U.S.C. § 601 *et seq.*), as determined by the head of the appropriate Federal agency;
(F) a significant increase in unemployment, layoffs, or the number of households with an individual applying for unemployment benefits, as determined by the Secretary of Labor; or
(G) an event meeting such criteria as the Secretary, in the discretion of the Secretary, may determine to be appropriate.

(2) The term "energy burden" means the expenditures of the household for home energy divided by the income of the household.

(3) The term "energy crisis" means weather-related and supply shortage emergencies and other household energy-related emergencies.

(4) The term "highest home energy needs" means the home energy requirements of a household determined by taking into account both the energy burden of such household and the unique situation of such household that results from having members of vulnerable populations, including very young children, individuals with disabilities, and frail older individuals.

(5) The term "household" means any individual or group of individuals who are living together as one economic unit for whom residential energy is customarily purchased in common or who make undesignated payments for energy in the form of rent.

(6) The term "home energy" means a source of heating or cooling in residential dwellings.

(7) The term "natural disaster" means a weather event (relating to cold or hot weather), flood, earthquake, tornado, hurricane, or ice storm, or an event meeting such other criteria as the Secretary, in the discretion of the Secretary, may determine to be appropriate.

(8) The term "poverty level" means, with respect to a household in any State, the income poverty line as prescribed and revised at least annually pursuant to section 9902(2) of this title, as applicable to such State.

(9) The term "Secretary" means the Secretary of Health and Human Services.

(10) The term "State" means each of the several States and the District of Columbia.

(11) The term "State median income" means the State median income promulgated by the Secretary in accordance with procedures established under section 1397a(a)(6) of this title (as such procedures were in effect on August 12, 1981) and adjusted, in accordance with regulations prescribed by the Secretary, to take into account the number of individuals in the household.

[Pub. L. No. 97-35, tit. XXVI, § 2603, 95 Stat. 894 (Aug. 13, 1981); Pub. L. No. 97-115, § 16, 95 Stat. 1609 (Dec. 29, 1981); Pub. L. No. 98-558, tit. VI, § 602, 98 Stat. 2890 (Oct. 30, 1984); Pub. L. No. 103-252, tit. III, §§ 304(b), 311(c)(2), 108 Stat. 658, 662 (May 18, 1994); Pub. L. No. 105-285, tit. III, §§ 303, 304(a), 112 Stat. 2756 (Oct. 27, 1998); Pub. L. No. 110-234, tit. IV, § 4002(b), 122 Stat. 1095 (May 22, 2008); Pub. L. No. 110-246, tit. IV, § 4002(b), 122 Stat. 1857 (June 18, 2008)]

42 U.S.C. § 8623. State allotments

(a) Amount; distribution, computation, etc.

(1)

(A) Except as provided in subparagraph (B), the Secretary shall, from that percentage of the amount appropriated under section 8621(b) of this title for each fiscal year which is remaining after reserving any amount permitted to be reserved under section 8628a of this title and after the amount of allotments for such fiscal year under subsection (b)(1) of this section is determined by the Secretary, allot to each State an amount equal to such remaining percentage multiplied by the State's allotment percentage.

(B) From the sums appropriated therefor after reserving any amount permitted to be reserved under section 8628a of this title, if for any period a State has a plan which is described in section 8624(c)(1) of this title, the Secretary shall pay to such State an amount equal to 100 percent of the expenditures of such State made during such period in carrying out such plan, including administrative costs (subject to the provisions of section 8624(b)(9)(B) of this title), with respect to households described in section 8624(b)(2) of this title.

(2) For purposes of paragraph (1), for fiscal year 1985 and thereafter, a State's allotment percentage is the percentage which expenditures for home energy by low-income households in that State bears to such expenditures in all States, except that States which thereby receive the greatest proportional increase in allotments by reason of the application of this paragraph from the amount they received pursuant to Public Law 98-139 shall have their allotments reduced to the extent necessary to ensure that—

(A)

(i) no State for fiscal year 1985 shall receive less than the amount of funds the State received in fiscal year 1984; and

(ii) no State for fiscal year 1986 and thereafter shall receive less than the amount of funds the State would have received in fiscal year 1984 if the appropriations for this subchapter for fiscal year 1984 had been $1,975,000,000, and

(B) any State whose allotment percentage out of funds available to States from a total appropriation of $2,250,000,000 would be less than 1 percent, shall not, in any year when total appropriations equal or exceed $2,250,000,000, have its allotment percentage reduced from the percentage it would receive from a total appropriation of $2,140,000,000.

(3) If the sums appropriated for any fiscal year for making grants under this subchapter are not sufficient to pay in full the total amount allocated to a State under paragraph (1) for such fiscal year, the amount which all States will receive under this subchapter for such fiscal year shall be ratably reduced.

(4) For the purpose of this section, the Secretary shall determine the expenditure for home energy by low-income households on the basis of the most recent satisfactory data available to the Secretary.

(b) Allotments to insular areas

(1) The Secretary shall apportion not less than one-tenth of 1 percent, and not more than one-half of 1 percent, of the amounts appropriated for each fiscal year to carry out this subchapter on the basis of need among the Commonwealth of Puerto Rico, Guam, American Samoa, the Virgin Islands of the United States, and the Commonwealth of the Northern Mariana Islands. The Secretary shall determine the total amount to be apportioned under this paragraph for any fiscal year (which shall not exceed one-half of 1 percent) after evaluating the extent to which each jurisdiction specified in the preceding sentence requires assistance under this paragraph for the fiscal year involved.

(2) Each jurisdiction to which paragraph (1) applies may receive grants under this subchapter upon an application submitted to the Secretary containing provisions which describe the programs for which assistance is sought under this subchapter, and which are consistent with the requirements of section 8624 of this title.

(c) Energy crisis intervention

Of the funds available to each State under subsection (a) of this section, a reasonable amount based on data from prior years shall be reserved until March 15 of each program year by each State for energy crisis intervention. The program for which funds are reserved by this subsection shall be administered by public or nonprofit entities which have experience in administering energy crisis programs under the Low-Income Energy Assistance Act of 1980, or under this subchapter, experience in assisting low-income individuals in the area to be served, the capacity to undertake a timely and effective energy crisis intervention program, and the ability to carry out the program in local communities. The program for which funds are reserved under this subsection shall—

(1) not later than 48 hours after a household applies for energy crisis benefits, provide some form of assistance that will resolve the energy crisis if such household is eligible to receive such benefits;

(2) not later than 18 hours after a household applies for crisis benefits, provide some form of assistance that will resolve the energy crisis if such household is eligible to receive such benefits and is in a life-threatening situation; and

(3) require each entity that administers such program—

(A) to accept applications for energy crisis benefits at sites that are geographically accessible to all households in the area to be served by such entity; and

(B) to provide to low-income individuals who are physically infirm the means—

(i) to submit applications for energy crisis benefits without leaving their residences; or

(ii) to travel to the sites at which such applications are accepted by such entity.

The preceding sentence shall not apply to a program in a geographical area affected by a natural disaster in the United States designated by the Secretary, or by a major disaster or emergency designated by the President under the Disaster Relief Act of 1974 (42 U.S.C. § 5121 *et seq.*), for so long as such designation remains in effect, if the Secretary determines that such disaster or such emergency makes compliance with such sentence impracticable.

(d) Allotments to Indian tribes

(1) If, with respect to any State, the Secretary—

(A) receives a request from the governing organization of an Indian tribe within the State that assistance under this subchapter be made directly to such organization; and

(B) determines that the members of such tribe would be better served by means of grants made directly to provide benefits under this subchapter;

the Secretary shall reserve from amounts which would otherwise be payable to such State from amounts allotted to it under this subchapter for the fiscal year involved the amount determined under paragraph (2).

(2) The amount determined under this paragraph for a fiscal year is the amount which bears the same ratio to the amount which would (but for this subsection) be allotted to such State under this subchapter for such fiscal year (other than by reason of section 8626(b)(2) of this title) as the number of Indian households described in subparagraphs (A) and (B) of section 8624(b)(2) of this title and residing within the State on the reservation of the tribes or on trust lands adjacent to such reservation bears to the number of all households described in subparagraphs (A) and (B) of section 8624(b)(2) of this title in such State, or such greater amount as the Indian tribe and the State may agree upon. In cases where a tribe has no reservation, the Secretary, in consultation with the tribe and the State, shall define the number of Indian households for the determination under this paragraph.

(3) The sums reserved by the Secretary on the basis of a determination under this subsection shall be granted to—

(A) the tribal organization serving the individuals for whom such a determination has been made; or

(B) in any case where there is no tribal organization serving an individual for whom such a determination has been made, such other entity as the Secretary determines has the capacity to provide assistance pursuant to this subchapter.

(4) In order for a tribal organization or other entity to be eligible for an amount under this subsection for a fiscal year, it shall submit to the Secretary a plan (in lieu of being under the State's plan) for such fiscal year which meets such criteria as the Secretary may by regulations prescribe.

(e) Allotment of emergency funds

Notwithstanding subsections (a) through (d) of this section, the Secretary may allot amounts appropriated pursuant to section 8621(e) of this title to one or more than one State. In determining whether to make such an allotment to a State, the Secretary shall take into account the extent to which the State was affected by the natural disaster or other emergency involved, the availability to the State of other resources under the program carried out under this subchapter or any other program, and such other factors as the Secretary may find to be relevant. Not later than 30 days after making the determination, but prior to releasing an allotted amount to a State, the Secretary shall notify Congress of the allotments made pursuant to this subsection.

[Pub. L. No. 97-35, tit. XXVI, § 2604, 95 Stat. 894 (Aug. 13, 1981); Pub. L. No. 98-558, tit. VI, §§ 603, 604, 98 Stat. 2890 (Oct. 30, 1984); Pub. L. No. 99-425, tit. V, §§ 502(a), 503, 505(b), 100 Stat. 973–975 (Sept. 30, 1986); Pub. L. No. 101-501, tit. VII,

§ 703, 104 Stat. 1258 (Nov. 3, 1990); Pub. L. No. 103-252, tit. III, §§ 304(c), 311(c)(3), 108 Stat. 659, 662 (May 18, 1994); Pub. L. No. 105-285, tit. III, §§ 304(b), 305, 112 Stat. 2757 (Oct. 27, 1998)]

42 U.S.C. § 8624. Applications and requirements

(a) Form; assurances; public hearings

(1) Each State desiring to receive an allotment for any fiscal year under this subchapter shall submit an application to the Secretary. Each such application shall be in such form as the Secretary shall require. Each such application shall contain assurances by the chief executive officer of the State that the State will meet the conditions enumerated in subsection (b) of this section.

(2) After the expiration of the first fiscal year for which a State receives funds under this subchapter, no funds shall be allotted to such State for any fiscal year under this subchapter unless such State conducts public hearings with respect to the proposed use and distribution of funds to be provided under this subchapter for such fiscal year.

(b) Certifications required for covered activities

As part of the annual application required by subsection (a) of this section, the chief executive officer of each State shall certify that the State agrees to—

(1) use the funds available under this subchapter to—

(A) conduct outreach activities and provide assistance to low income households in meeting their home energy costs, particularly those with the lowest incomes that pay a high proportion of household income for home energy, consistent with paragraph (5);

(B) intervene in energy crisis situations;

(C) provide low-cost residential weatherization and other cost-effective energy-related home repair; and

(D) plan, develop, and administer the State's program under this subchapter including leveraging programs,

and the State agrees not to use such funds for any purposes other than those specified in this subchapter;

(2) make payments under this subchapter only with respect to—

(A) households in which 1 or more individuals are receiving—

(i) assistance under the State program funded under part A of title IV of the Social Security Act (42 U.S.C. § 601 *et seq.*);

(ii) supplemental security income payments under title XVI of the Social Security Act (42 U.S.C. § 1381 *et seq.*);

(iii) supplemental nutrition assistance program benefits under the Food and Nutrition Act of 2008 (7 U.S.C. § 2011 *et seq.*); or

(iv) payments under section 1315, 1521, 1541, or 1542 of title 38, or under section 306 of the Veterans' and Survivors' Pension Improvement Act of 1978; or

(B) households with incomes which do not exceed the greater of—

(i) an amount equal to 150 percent of the poverty level for such State; or

(ii) an amount equal to 60 percent of the State median income;

except that a State may not exclude a household from eligibility in a fiscal year solely on the basis of household income if such income is less than 110 percent of the poverty level for such State, but the State may give priority to those households with the highest home energy costs or needs in relation to household income;

(3) conduct outreach activities designed to assure that eligible households, especially households with elderly individuals or disabled individuals, or both, and households with high home energy burdens, are made aware of the assistance available under this subchapter, and any similar energy-related assistance available under subtitle B of title VI (relating to community services block grant program) (42 U.S.C. § 9901 *et seq.*) or under any other provision of law which carries out programs which were administered under the Economic Opportunity Act of 1964 (42 U.S.C. § 2701 *et seq.*) before August 13, 1981;

(4) coordinate its activities under this subchapter with similar and related programs administered by the Federal Government and such State, particularly low-income energy-related programs under subtitle B of title VI (relating to community services block grant program) (42 U.S.C. § 9901 *et seq.*), under the supplemental security income program, under part A of title IV of the Social Security Act (42 U.S.C. § 601 *et seq.*), under title XX of the Social Security Act (42 U.S.C. § 1397 *et seq.*), under the low-income weatherization assistance program under title IV of the Energy Conservation and Production Act (42 U.S.C. § 6851 *et seq.*), or under any other provision of law which carries out programs which were administered under the Economic Opportunity Act of 1964 (42 U.S.C. § 2701 *et seq.*) before August 13, 1981;

(5) provide, in a timely manner, that the highest level of assistance will be furnished to those households which have the lowest incomes and the highest energy costs or needs in relation to income, taking into account family size, except that the State may not differentiate in implementing this section between the households described in clause (2)(A) and (2)(B) of this subsection;

(6) to the extent it is necessary to designate local administrative agencies in order to carry out the purposes of this subchapter, give special consideration, in the designation of such agencies, to any local public or private nonprofit agency which was receiving Federal funds under any low-income energy assistance program or weatherization program under the Economic Opportunity Act of 1964 (42 U.S.C. § 2701 *et seq.*) or any other provision of law on August 12, 1981, except that—

(A) the State shall, before giving such special consideration, determine that the agency involved meets program and fiscal requirements established by the State; and

(B) if there is no such agency because of any change in the assistance furnished to programs for economically disadvantaged persons, then the State shall give special consideration in the designation of local administrative agencies to any successor agency which is operated in substantially the same manner as the predecessor agency which did receive funds for the fiscal year preceding the fiscal year for which the determination is made;

(7) if the State chooses to pay home energy suppliers directly, establish procedures to—

(A) notify each participating household of the amount of assistance paid on its behalf;

(B) assure that the home energy supplier will charge the eligible household, in the normal billing process, the difference between the actual cost of the home energy and the amount of the payment made by the State under this subchapter;

(C) assure that the home energy supplier will provide assurances that any agreement entered into with a home energy supplier under this paragraph will contain provisions to assure that no household receiving assistance under this subchapter will be treated adversely because of such assistance under applicable provisions of State law or public regulatory requirements; and

(D) ensure that the provision of vendored payments remains at the option of the State in consultation with local grantees and may be contingent on unregulated vendors taking appropriate measures to alleviate the energy burdens of eligible households, including providing for agreements between suppliers and individuals eligible for benefits under this subchapter that seek to reduce home energy costs, minimize the risks of home energy crisis, and encourage regular payments by individuals receiving financial assistance for home energy costs;

(8) provide assurances that (A) the State will not exclude households described in clause (2)(B) of this subsection from receiving home energy assistance benefits under clause (2), and (B) the State will treat owners and renters equitably under the program assisted under this subchapter;

(9) provide that—

(A) the State may use for planning and administering the use of funds under this subchapter an amount not to exceed 10 percent of the funds payable to such State under this subchapter for a fiscal year; and

(B) the State will pay from non-Federal sources the remaining costs of planning and administering the program assisted under this subchapter and will not use Federal funds for such remaining costs (except for the costs of the activities described in paragraph (16));

(10) provide that such fiscal control and fund accounting procedures will be established as may be necessary to assure the proper disbursal of and accounting for Federal funds paid to the State under this subchapter, including procedures for monitoring the assistance provided under this subchapter, and provide that the State will comply with the provisions of chapter 75 of title 31 (commonly known as the "Single Audit Act");

(11) permit and cooperate with Federal investigations undertaken in accordance with section 8627 of this title;

(12) provide for timely and meaningful public participation in the development of the plan described in subsection (c) of this section;

(13) provide an opportunity for a fair administrative hearing to individuals whose claims for assistance under the plan described in subsection (c) of this section are denied or are not acted upon with reasonable promptness;

(14) cooperate with the Secretary with respect to data collecting and reporting under section 8629 of this title;

(15) beginning in fiscal year 1992, provide, in addition to such services as may be offered by State Departments of Public Welfare at the local level, outreach and intake functions for crisis situations and heating and cooling assistance that is administered by additional State and local governmental entities or community-based organizations (such as community action agencies, area agencies on aging, and not-for-profit neighborhood-based organizations), and in States where such organizations do not administer intake functions as of September 30, 1991, preference in awarding grants or contracts for intake services shall be provided to those agencies that administer the low-income weatherization or energy crisis intervention programs; and

(16) use up to 5 percent of such funds, at its option, to provide services that encourage and enable households to reduce their home energy needs and thereby the need for energy assistance, including needs assessments, counseling, and assistance with energy vendors, and report to the Secretary concerning the impact of such activities on the number of households served, the level of direct benefits provided to those households, and the number of households that remain unserved.

The Secretary may not prescribe the manner in which the States will comply with the provisions of this subsection. The Secretary shall issue regulations to prevent waste, fraud, and abuse in the programs assisted by this subchapter. Not later than 18 months after May 18, 1994, the Secretary shall develop model performance goals and measurements in consultation with State, territorial, tribal, and local grantees, that the States may use to assess the success of the States in achieving the purposes of this subchapter. The model performance goals and measurements shall be made available to States to be incorporated, at the option of the States, into the plans for fiscal year 1997. The Secretary may request data relevant to the development of model performance goals and measurements.

(c) State plan; revision; public inspection

(1) As part of the annual application required in subsection (a) of this section, the chief executive officer of each State shall prepare and furnish to the Secretary, in such format as the Secretary may require, a plan which—

(A) describes the eligibility requirements to be used by the State for each type of assistance to be provided under this subchapter, including criteria for designating an emergency under section 8623(c) of this title;

(B) describes the benefit levels to be used by the State for each type of assistance including assistance to be provided for emergency crisis intervention and for weatherization and other energy-related home repair;

(C) contains estimates of the amount of funds the State will use for each of the programs under such plan and describes the alternative use of funds reserved under section 8623(c) of this title in the event any portion of the amount so reserved is not expended for emergencies;

(D) describes weatherization and other energy-related home repair the State will provide under subsection (k) of this section, including any steps the State will take to address the weatherization and energy-related home repair needs of households that have high home energy burdens, and describes any rules promulgated by the Department of Energy for administration of its Low Income Weatherization Assistance Program which the State, to the extent permitted by the Secretary to increase consistency between federally assisted programs, will follow regarding the use of funds provided under this subchapter by the State for such weatherization and energy-related home repairs and improvements;

(E) describes any steps that will be taken (in addition to those necessary to carry out the assurance contained in paragraph (5) of subsection (b) of this section) to target assistance to households with high home energy burdens;

(F) describes how the State will carry out assurances in clauses (3), (4), (5), (6), (7), (8), (10), (12), (13), and (15) of subsection (b) of this section;

(G) states, with respect to the 12-month period specified by the Secretary, the number and income levels of households which apply and the number which are assisted with funds provided under this subchapter, and the number of households so assisted with—

(i) one or more members who had attained 60 years of age;

(ii) one or more members who were disabled; and

(iii) one or more young children; and

(H) contains any other information determined by the Secretary to be appropriate for purposes of this subchapter. The chief executive officer may revise any plan prepared under this paragraph and shall furnish the revised plan to the Secretary.

(2) Each plan prepared under paragraph (1) and each substantial revision thereof shall be made available for public inspection within the State involved in such a manner as will facilitate timely and meaningful review of, and comment upon, such plan or substantial revision.

(3) Not later than April 1 of each fiscal year the Secretary shall make available to the States a model State plan format that may be used, at the option of each State, to prepare the plan required under paragraph (1) for the next fiscal year.

(d) Expending of funds

The State shall expend funds in accordance with the State plan under this subchapter or in accordance with revisions applicable to such plan.

(e) Conduct of audits

Each State shall, in carrying out the requirements of subsection (b)(10) of this section, obtain financial and compliance audits of any funds which the State receives under this subchapter. Such audits shall be made public within the State on a timely basis. The audits shall be conducted in accordance with chapter 75 of title 31.

(f) Payments or assistance not to be deemed income or resources for any purpose under Federal or State law; determination of excess shelter expense deduction

(1) Notwithstanding any other provision of law unless enacted in express limitation of this paragraph, the amount of any home energy assistance payments or allowances provided directly to, or indirectly for the benefit of, an eligible household under this subchapter shall not be considered income or resources of such household (or any member thereof) for any purpose under any Federal or State law, including any law relating to taxation, supplemental nutrition assistance program benefits, public assistance, or welfare programs.

(2) For purposes of paragraph (1) of this subsection and for purposes of determining any excess shelter expense deduction under section 5(e) of the Food and Nutrition Act of 2008 (7 U.S.C. § 2014(e))—

(A) the full amount of such payments or allowances shall be deemed to be expended by such household for heating or cooling expenses, without regard to whether such payments or allowances are provided directly to, or indirectly for the benefit of, such household; and

(B) no distinction may be made among households on the basis of whether such payments or allowances are provided directly to, or indirectly for the benefit of, any of such households.

(g) Repayment of funds expended improperly; offset

The State shall repay to the United States amounts found not to have been expended in accordance with this subchapter or the Secretary may offset such amounts against any other amount to which the State is or may become entitled under this subchapter.

(h) Periodic evaluation of expenditures by Comptroller General

The Comptroller General of the United States shall, from time to time evaluate the expenditures by States of grants under this subchapter in order to assure that expenditures are consistent with the provisions of this subchapter and to determine the effectiveness of the State in accomplishing the purposes of this subchapter.

(*i*) Certain recipients of supplemental security income ineligible for payments or assistance

A household which is described in subsection (b)(2)(A) of this section solely by reason of clause (ii) thereof shall not be treated as a household described in subsection (b)(2) of this section if the eligibility of the household is dependent upon—

(1) an individual whose annual supplemental security income benefit rate is reduced pursuant to section 1611(e)(1) of the Social Security Act (42 U.S.C. § 1382(e)(1)) by reason of being in an institution receiving payments under title XIX of the Social Security Act (42 U.S.C. § 1396 *et seq.*) with respect to such individual;

(2) an individual to whom the reduction specified in section 1612(a)(2)(A)(i) of the Social Security Act (42 U.S.C. § 1382a(a)(2)(A)(i)) applies; or

(3) a child described in section 1614(f)(2) of the Social Security Act (42 U.S.C. § 1382c(f)(2)) who is living together with a parent, or the spouse of a parent, of the child.

(j) State verification of income eligibility; policies and procedures applicable

In verifying income eligibility for purposes of subsection (b)(2)(B) of this section, the State may apply procedures and policies consistent with procedures and policies used by the State agency administering programs under part A of title IV of the Social Security Act (42 U.S.C. § 601 *et seq.*), under title XX of the Social Security Act (42 U.S.C. § 1397 *et seq.*), under subtitle B of title VI of this Act (relating to community services block grant program) (42 U.S.C. § 9901 *et seq.*), under any other provision of law which carries out programs which were administered under the Economic Opportunity Act of 1964 (42 U.S.C. § 2701 *et seq.*) before August 13, 1981, or under other income assistance or service programs (as determined by the State).

(k) Limitation on use of funds; waiver

(1) Except as provided in paragraph (2), not more than 15 percent of the greater of—

(A) the funds allotted to a State under this subchapter for any fiscal year; or

(B) the funds available to such State under this subchapter for such fiscal year; may be used by the State for low-cost residential weatherization or other energy-related home repair for low-income households, particularly those low-income households with the lowest incomes that pay a high proportion of household income for home energy.

(2)

(A) If a State receives a waiver granted under subparagraph (B) for a fiscal year, the State may use not more than the greater of 25 percent of—

(i) the funds allotted to a State under this subchapter for such fiscal year; or

(ii) the funds available to such State under this subchapter for such fiscal year; for residential weatherization or other energy-related home repair for low-income households, particularly those low-income households with the lowest incomes that pay a high proportion of household income for home energy.

(B) For purposes of subparagraph (A), the Secretary may grant a waiver to a State for a fiscal year if the State submits a written request to the Secretary after March 31 of such fiscal year and if the Secretary determines, after reviewing such request and any public comments, that—

(i)

(I) the number of households in the State that will receive benefits, other than weatherization and energy-related home repair, under this subchapter in such fiscal year will not be fewer than the number of households in the State that received benefits, other than weatherization and energy-related home repair, under this subchapter in the preceding fiscal year;

(II) the aggregate amounts of benefits that will be received under this subchapter by all households in the State in such fiscal year will not be less than the aggregate amount of such benefits that were received under this subchapter by all households in the State in the preceding fiscal year; and

(III) such weatherization activities have been demonstrated to produce measurable savings in energy expenditures by low-income households; or

(ii) in accordance with rules issued by the Secretary, the State demonstrates good cause for failing to satisfy the requirements specified in clause (i).

(*l*) State tax credits to energy suppliers who supply home energy at reduced rates to low-income households

(1) Any State may use amounts provided under this subchapter for the purpose of providing credits against State tax to energy suppliers who supply home energy at reduced rates to low-income households.

(2) Any such credit provided by a State shall not exceed the amount of the loss of revenue to such supplier on account of such reduced rate.

(3) Any certification for such tax credits shall be made by the State, but such State may use Federal data available to such State with respect to recipients of supplemental security income benefits if timely delivery of benefits to households described in subsection (b) of this section and suppliers will not be impeded by the use of such data.

[Pub. L. No. 97-35, tit. XXVI, § 2605, 95 Stat. 896 (Aug. 13, 1981); Pub. L. No. 98-558, tit. VI, § 605, 98 Stat. 2891 (Oct. 30, 1984); Pub. L. No. 99-425, tit. V, § 504, 100 Stat. 974 (Sept. 30, 1986); Pub. L. No. 101-501, tit. VII, §§ 704, 705, 104 Stat. 1259 (Nov. 3, 1990); Pub. L. No. 102-83, § 5(c)(2), 105 Stat. 406 (Aug. 6, 1991); Pub. L. No. 103-252, tit. III, §§ 305–309, 311(a)(1), (b), (c)(4), (5), 108 Stat. 659–662 (May 18, 1994); Pub. L. No. 104-66, tit. I, § 1072(c), 109 Stat. 721 (Dec. 21, 1995); Pub. L. No. 104-193, tit. I, § 110(p), 110 Stat. 2175 (Aug. 22, 1996); Pub. L. No. 105-285, tit. III, § 306, 112 Stat. 2758 (Oct. 27, 1998); Pub. L. No. 110-234, tit. IV, § 4002(b), 122 Stat. 1095 (May 22, 2008); Pub. L. No. 110-246, tit. IV, § 4002(b), 122 Stat. 1857 (June 18, 2008)]

42 U.S.C. § 8625. Nondiscrimination provisions

(a) Prohibitions

No person shall on the ground of race, color, national origin, or sex be excluded from participation in, be denied the benefits of, or be subjected to discrimination under, any program or activity funded in whole or in part with funds made available under this subchapter. Any prohibition against discrimination on the basis of age under the Age Discrimination Act of 1975 (42 U.S.C. § 6101 *et seq.*) or with respect to an otherwise qualified handicapped individual as provided in section 794 of title 29 also shall apply to any such program or activity.

(b) Procedures applicable to secure compliance

Whenever the Secretary determines that a State that has received a payment under this subchapter has failed to comply with subsection (a) of this section or an applicable regulation, he shall notify the chief executive officer of the State and shall request him to secure compliance. If within a reasonable period of time, not to exceed 60 days, the chief executive officer fails or refuses to secure compliance, the Secretary is authorized to (1) refer the matter to the Attorney General with a recommendation that an appropriate civil action be instituted; (2) exercise the powers and functions provided by title VI of the Civil Rights Act of 1964 (42 U.S.C. § 2000d *et seq.*), the Age Discrimination Act of 1975 (42 U.S.C. § 6101 *et seq.*), or section 794 of title 29, as may be applicable; or (3) take such other action as may be provided by law.

(c) Maintenance of civil actions

When a matter is referred to the Attorney General pursuant to subsection (b) of this section, or whenever he has reason to believe that the State is engaged in a pattern or practice in violation of the provisions of this section, the Attorney General may bring a civil action in any appropriate United States district court for such relief as may be appropriate, including injunctive relief.

[Pub. L. No. 97-35, tit. XXVI, § 2606, 95 Stat. 900 (Aug. 13, 1981)]

42 U.S.C. § 8626. Payments to States; fiscal year requirements respecting availability, etc.

(a)

(1) From its allotment under section 8623 of this title, the Secretary shall make payments to each State in accordance with section 6503(a) of title 31, for use under this subchapter.

(2) Each State shall notify the Secretary, not later than 2 months prior to the close of a fiscal year, of the amount (if any) of its allotment for such year that will not be obligated in such year, and, if such State elects to submit a request described in subsection (b)(2) of this section, such State shall submit such request at the same time. The Secretary shall make no payment under paragraph (1) to a State for a fiscal year unless the State has complied with this paragraph with respect to the prior fiscal year.

(b)

(1) If—

(A) the Secretary determines that, as of September 1 of any fiscal year, an amount allotted to a State under section 8623 of this title for any fiscal year will not be used by such State during such fiscal year;

(B) the Secretary—

(i) notifies the chief executive officer of such State; and

(ii) publishes a timely notice in the Federal Register; that, after the 30-day period beginning on the date of the notice to such chief executive officer, such amount may be reallotted; and

(C) the State does not request, under paragraph (2), that such amount be held available for such State for the following fiscal year;

then such amount shall be treated by the Secretary for purposes of this subchapter as an amount appropriated for the following fiscal year to be allotted under section 8623 of this title for such following fiscal year.

(2)

(A) Any State may request that an amount allotted to such State for a fiscal year be held available for such State for the following fiscal year. Such request shall include a statement of the reasons that the amount allotted to such State for a fiscal year will not be used by such State during such fiscal year and a description of the types of assistance to be provided with the amount held available for the following fiscal year. Any amount so held available for the following fiscal year shall not be taken into account in computing the allotment of or the amount payable to such State for such fiscal year under this subchapter.

(B) No amount may be held available under this paragraph for a State from a prior fiscal year to the extent such amount exceeds 10 percent of the amount payable to such State for such prior fiscal year. For purposes of the preceding sentence, the amount payable to a State for a fiscal year shall be determined without regard to any amount held available under this paragraph for such State for such fiscal year from the prior fiscal year.

(C) The Secretary shall reallot amounts made available under this paragraph for the fiscal year following the fiscal year of the original allotment in accordance with paragraph (1) of this subsection.

(3) During the 30-day period described in paragraph (1)(B), comments may be submitted to the Secretary. After considering such comments, the Secretary shall notify the chief executive officer of the State of any decision to reallot funds, and shall publish such decision in the Federal Register.

[Pub. L. No. 97-35, tit. XXVI, § 2607, 95 Stat. 900 (Aug. 13, 1981); Pub. L. No. 98-558, tit. VI, § 606, 98 Stat. 2892 (Oct. 30, 1984); Pub. L. No. 101-501, tit. VII, § 706, 104 Stat. 1260 (Nov. 3, 1990); Pub. L. No. 103-252, tit. III, § 310, 108 Stat. 661 (May 18, 1994); Pub. L. No. 105-285, tit. III, § 307, 112 Stat. 2758 (Oct. 27, 1998)]

42 U.S.C. § 8626a. Incentive program for leveraging non-Federal resources

(a) Allotment of funds

Beginning in fiscal year 1992, the Secretary may allocate amounts appropriated under section 8621(d) of this title to provide supplementary funds to States that have acquired non-Federal leveraged resources for the program established under this subchapter.

(b) "Leveraged resources" defined

For purposes of this section, the term "leveraged resources" means the benefits made available to the low-income home energy assistance program of the State, or to federally qualified low-income households, that—

(1) represent a net addition to the total energy resources available to State and federally qualified households in excess of the amount of such resources that could be acquired by such households through the purchase of energy at commonly available household rates; and

(2)

(A) result from the acquisition or development by the State program of quantifiable benefits that are obtained from energy vendors through negotiation, regulation or competitive bid; or

(B) are appropriated or mandated by the State for distribution—

(i) through the State program; or

(ii) under the plan referred to in section 8624(c)(1)(A) of this title to federally qualified low-income households and such benefits are determined by the Secretary to be integrated with the State program.

(c) Formula for distribution of amounts

(1) Distribution of amounts made available under this section shall be based on a formula developed by the Secretary that is designed to take into account the success in leveraging existing appropriations in the preceding fiscal year as measured under subsection (d) of this section. Such formula shall take into account the size of the allocation of the State under this subchapter and the ratio of leveraged resources to such allocation.

(2) A State may expend funds allocated under this subchapter as are necessary, not to exceed 0.08 percent of such allocation or $35,000 each fiscal year, whichever is greater, to identify, develop, and demonstrate leveraging programs. Funds allocated under this section shall only be used for increasing or maintaining benefits to households.

(d) Dollar value of leveraged resources

Each State shall quantify the dollar value of leveraged resources received or acquired by such State under this section by using the best available data to calculate such leveraged resources less the sum of any costs incurred by the State to leverage such resources and any cost imposed on the federally eligible low-income households in such State.

(e) Report to Secretary

Not later than 2 months after the close of the fiscal year during which the State provided leveraged resources to eligible households, as described in subsection (b) of this section, each State shall prepare and submit, to the Secretary, a report that quantifies the leveraged resources of such State in order to qualify for assistance under this section for the following fiscal year.

(f) Determination of State share; regulations; documentation
The Secretary shall determine the share of each State of the amounts made available under this section based on the formula described in subsection (c) of this section and the State reports. The Secretary shall promulgate regulations for the calculation of the leveraged resources of the State and for the submission of supporting documentation. The Secretary may request any documentation that the Secretary determines necessary for the verification of the application of the State for assistance under this section.

[Pub. L. No. 97-35, tit. XXVI, § 2607A, *as added by* Pub. L. No. 101-501, tit. VII, § 707(a), 104 Stat. 1260 (Nov. 3, 1990); *amended by* Pub. L. No. 103-252, tit. III, § 311(a)(2), (c)(6), 108 Stat. 661, 662 (May 18, 1994)]

42 U.S.C. § 8626b. Residential Energy Assistance Challenge option (R.E.A.Ch.)

(a) Purpose
The purpose of the Residential Energy Assistance Challenge (in this section referred to as "R.E.A.Ch.") program is to—

(1) minimize health and safety risks that result from high energy burdens on low-income Americans;
(2) prevent homelessness as a result of inability to pay energy bills;
(3) increase the efficiency of energy usage by low-income families; and
(4) target energy assistance to individuals who are most in need.

(b) Funding
(1) Allocation
For each fiscal year, the Secretary may allocate not more than 25 percent of the amount made available pursuant to section 8621(d) of this title for such fiscal year to a R.E.A.Ch. fund for the purpose of making incentive grants to States that submit qualifying plans that are approved by the Secretary as R.E.A.Ch. initiatives. States may use such grants for the costs of planning, implementing, and evaluating the initiative.
(2) Reservation
The Secretary shall reserve from any funds allocated under this subsection, funds to make additional payments to State R.E.A.Ch. programs that—

(A) have energy efficiency education services plans that meet quality standards established by the Secretary in consultation with the Secretary of Energy; and
(B) have the potential for being replicable model designs for other programs.

States shall use such supplemental funds for the implementation and evaluation of the energy efficiency education services.

(c) Criteria
(1) In general
Not later than May 31, 1995, the Secretary shall establish criteria for approving State plans required by subsection (a) of this section, for energy efficiency education quality standards described in subsection (b)(2)(A) of this section, and for the distribution of funds to States with approved plans.
(2) Documentation
Notwithstanding the limitations of section 8624(b) of this title regarding the authority of the Secretary with respect to plans, the Secretary may require a State to provide appropriate documentation that its R.E.A.Ch. activities conform to the State plan as approved by the Secretary.

(d) Focus
The State may designate all or part of the State, or all or part of the client population, as a focus of its R.E.A.Ch. initiative.

(e) State plans
(1) In general
Each State plan shall include each of the elements described in paragraph (2), to be met by State and local agencies.
(2) Elements of State plans
Each State plan shall include—

(A) an assurance that such State will deliver services through community-based nonprofit entities in such State, by—
(i) awarding grants to, or entering into contracts with, such entities for the purpose of providing such services and payments directly to individuals eligible for benefits; or
(ii) if a State makes payments directly to eligible individuals or energy suppliers, making contracts with such entities to administer such programs, including—
(I) determining eligibility;
(II) providing outreach services; and
(III) providing benefits other than payments;
(B) an assurance that, in awarding grants or entering into contracts to carry out its R.E.A.Ch. initiative, the State will give priority to organizations that—
(i) are described in section 9902(1) of this title, except where significant geographic portions of the State are not served by such entities;
(ii) the Secretary has determined have a record of successfully providing services under the Low-Income Home Energy Assistance Program; and
(iii) receive weatherization assistance program funds under part A of title IV of the Energy Conservation and Production Act (42 U.S.C. § 6861 *et seq.*);
except that a State may not require any such entity to operate a R.E.A.Ch. program;
(C) an assurance that, subject to subparagraph (D), each entity that receives a grant or enters into a contract under subparagraph (A)(i) will provide a variety of services and benefits, including—
(i) payments to, or on behalf of, individuals eligible for residential energy assistance services and benefits under section 8624(b) of this title for home energy costs;
(ii) energy efficiency education;
(iii) residential energy demand management services, including any other energy related residential repair and energy efficiency improvements in coordination with, or delivered by, Department of Energy weatherization assistance programs at the discretion of the State;
(iv) family services, such as counseling and needs assessment, related to energy budget management, payment plans, and related services; and

(v) negotiation with home energy suppliers on behalf of households eligible for R.E.A.Ch. services and benefits;

(D) a description of the methodology the State and local agencies will use to determine—

(i) which households will receive one or more forms of benefits under the State R.E.A.Ch. initiative;

(ii) the cases in which nonmonetary benefits are likely to provide more cost-effective long-term outcomes than payment benefits alone; and

(iii) the amount of such benefit required to meet the goals of the program;

(E) a method for targeting nonmonetary benefits;

(F) a description of the crisis and emergency assistance activities the State will undertake that are designed to—

(i) discourage family energy crises;

(ii) encourage responsible vendor and consumer behavior; and

(iii) provide only financial incentives that encourage household payment;

(G) a description of the activities the State will undertake to—

(i) provide incentives for recipients of assistance to pay home energy costs; and

(ii) provide incentives for vendors to help reduce the energy burdens of recipients of assistance;

(H) an assurance that the State will require each entity that receives a grant or enters into a contract under this section to solicit and be responsive to the views of individuals who are financially eligible for benefits and services under this section in establishing its local program;

(*I*) a description of performance goals for the State R.E.A.Ch. initiative including—

(i) a reduction in the energy costs of participating households over one or more fiscal years;

(ii) an increase in the regularity of home energy bill payments by eligible households; and

(iii) an increase in energy vendor contributions towards reducing energy burdens of eligible households;

(J) a description of the indicators that will be used by the State to measure whether the performance goals have been achieved;

(K) a demonstration that the plan is consistent with section 8622 of this title, paragraphs (2), (3), (4), (5), (7), (9), (10), (11), (12), (13), and (14) of section 8624(b) of this title, subsections (d), (e), (f), (g), (h), (i), and (j) of section 8624 of this title, and section 8625 of this title;

(L) an assurance that benefits and services will be provided in addition to other benefit payments and services provided under this subchapter and in coordination with such benefit payments and services; and

(M) an assurance that no regulated utility covered by the plan will be required to act in a manner that is inconsistent with applicable regulatory requirements.

(f) Cost or function

None of the costs of providing services or benefits under this section shall be considered to be an administrative cost or function for purposes of any limitation on administrative costs or functions contained in this subchapter.

[Pub. L. No. 97-35, tit. XXVI, § 2607B, *as added by* Pub. L. No. 103-252, tit. III, § 312, 108 Stat. 662 (May 18, 1994); *amended by* Pub. L. No. 105-285, tit. III, § 308(c), (d), 112 Stat. 2758 (Oct. 27, 1998)]

42 U.S.C. § 8627. Withholding of funds

(a) Improper utilization of funds; response to complaints respecting improprieties

(1) The Secretary shall, after adequate notice and an opportunity for a hearing conducted within the affected State, withhold funds from any State which does not utilize its allotment substantially in accordance with the provisions of this subchapter and the assurances such State provided under section 8624 of this title.

(2) The Secretary shall respond in writing in no more than 60 days to matters raised in complaints of a substantial or serious nature that a State has failed to use funds in accordance with the provisions of this subchapter or the assurances provided by the State under section 8624 of this title. For purposes of this paragraph, a violation of any one of the assurances contained in section 8624(b) of this title that constitutes a disregard of such assurance shall be considered a serious complaint.

(b) Investigations; conduct, etc.

(1) The Secretary shall conduct in several States in each fiscal year investigations of the use of funds received by the States under this subchapter in order to evaluate compliance with the provisions of this subchapter.

(2) Whenever the Secretary determines that there is a pattern of complaints from any State in any fiscal year, the Secretary shall conduct an investigation of the use of funds received under this subchapter by such State in order to ensure compliance with the provisions of this subchapter.

(3) The Comptroller General of the United States may conduct an investigation of the use of funds received under this subchapter by a State in order to ensure compliance with the provisions of this subchapter.

(c) Inspection of books, documents, etc.

Pursuant to an investigation conducted under subsection (b) of this section, a State shall make appropriate books, documents, papers, and records available to the Secretary or the Comptroller General of the United States, or any of their duly authorized representatives, for examination, copying, or mechanical reproduction on or off the premises of the appropriate entity upon a reasonable request therefor.

(d) Request for information not readily available

In conducting any investigation under subsection (b) of this section, the Secretary may not request any information not readily available to such State or require that any information be compiled, collected, or transmitted in any new form not already available.

[Pub. L. No. 97-35, tit. XXVI, § 2608, 95 Stat. 901 (Aug. 13, 1981); Pub. L. No. 98-558, tit. VI, § 608, 98 Stat. 2893 (Oct. 30, 1984); Pub. L. No. 101-501, tit. VII, § 708, 104 Stat. 1261 (Nov. 3, 1990)]

42 U.S.C. § 8628. Limitation on use of grants for construction

Grants made under this subchapter may not be used by the State, or by any other person with which the State makes arrangements to carry out the purposes of this subchapter, for the purchase or improvement of land, or the purchase, construction, or permanent improvement (other than low-cost residential weatherization or other energy-related home repairs) of any building or other facility.

[Pub. L. No. 97-35, tit. XXVI, § 2609, 95 Stat. 902 (Aug. 13, 1981)]

42 U.S.C. § 8628a. Technical assistance, training, and compliance reviews

(a) Grants and contracts
Of the amounts appropriated under section 8621(b) of this title for any fiscal year, not more than $300,000 of such amounts may be reserved by the Secretary—

(1) to—

(A) make grants to State and public agencies and private nonprofit organizations; or

(B) enter into contracts or jointly financed cooperative arrangements or interagency agreements with States and public agencies (including Federal agencies) and private nonprofit organizations;

to provide for training and technical assistance related to the purposes of this subchapter, including collection and dissemination of information about programs and projects assisted under this subchapter, and ongoing matters of regional or national significance that the Secretary finds would assist in the more effective provision of services under this subchapter; or

(2) to conduct onsite compliance reviews of programs supported under this subchapter.

(b) Private nonprofit organizations and business concerns
No provision of this section shall be construed to prevent the Secretary from making a grant pursuant to subsection (a) of this section to one or more private nonprofit organizations that apply jointly with a business concern to receive such grant.

[Pub. L. No. 97-35, tit. XXVI, § 2609A, *as added by* Pub. L. No. 99-425, tit. V, § 505(a), 100 Stat. 975 (Sept. 30, 1986); *amended by* Pub. L. No. 103-252, tit. III, § 311(a)(3), 108 Stat. 661 (May 18, 1994); Pub. L. No. 105-285, tit. III, § 309, 112 Stat. 2759 (Oct. 27, 1998)]

42 U.S.C. § 8629. Studies and reports

(a) The Secretary, after consultation with the Secretary of Energy, shall provide for the collection of data, including—

(1) information concerning home energy consumption;

(2) the amount, cost and type of fuels used for households eligible for assistance under this subchapter;

(3) the type of fuel used by various income groups;

(4) the number and income levels of households assisted by this subchapter;

(5) the number of households which received such assistance and include one or more individuals who are 60 years or older or disabled or include young children; and

(6) any other information which the Secretary determines to be reasonably necessary to carry out the provisions of this subchapter.

Nothing in this subsection may be construed to require the Secretary to collect data which has been collected and made available to the Secretary by any other agency of the Federal Government.

(b) The Secretary shall, no later than June 30 of each fiscal year, submit a report to the Congress containing a detailed compilation of the data under subsection (a) of this section with respect to the prior fiscal year, and a report that describes for the prior fiscal year—

(1) the manner in which States carry out the requirements of clauses (2), (5), (8), and (15) of section 8624(b) of this title; and

(2) the impact of each State's program on recipient and eligible households.

[Pub. L. No. 97-35, tit. XXVI, § 2610, 95 Stat. 902 (Aug. 13, 1981); Pub. L. No. 98-558, tit. VI, § 607, 98 Stat. 2893 (Oct. 30, 1984); Pub. L. No. 99-425, tit. V, § 506, 100 Stat. 976 (Sept. 30, 1986); Pub. L. No. 103-252, tit. III, § 311(c)(7), 108 Stat. 662 (May 18, 1994)]

42 U.S.C. § 8630. Renewable fuels

In providing assistance pursuant to this title, a State, or any other person with which the State makes arrangements to carry out the purposes of this title, may purchase renewable fuels, including biomass.

[Pub. L. No. 109-58, tit. I, § 121, 119 Stat. 616 (Aug. 8, 2005)]

C.2 LIHEAP Regulation—45 C.F.R. §§ 96.80–96.89

Sec.

96.80 Scope.
96.81 Carryover and reallotment.
96.82 Required report on households assisted.
96.83 Increase in maximum amount that may be used for weatherization and other energy-related home repair.
96.84 Miscellaneous.
96.85 Income eligibility.
96.86 Exemption from requirement for additional outreach and intake services.
96.87 Leveraging incentive program.
96.88 Administrative costs.
96.89 Exemption from standards for providing energy crisis intervention assistance.

SOURCE: 46 Fed. Reg. 48587 (Oct. 1, 1981); 47 Fed. Reg. 29486 (July 6, 1982); 52 Fed. Reg. 4625 (Feb. 13, 1987); 52 Fed. Reg. 37965 (Oct. 13, 1987); 57 Fed. Reg. 1977 (Jan. 16, 1992); 58 Fed. Reg. 17070 (Mar. 31, 1993); 58 Fed. Reg. 60128 (Nov. 15, 1993); 62 Fed. Reg. 45963 (Aug. 29, 1997); 69 Fed. Reg. 42592 (July 16, 2004), unless otherwise noted.

AUTHORITY: 31 U.S.C. §§ 1243 note, 7501 to7507; 42 U.S.C. §§ 300w to 300w-10, 300x to 300x-13, 300y to 300y-10, 701 to 731, 1397 to 1397h, 8621 to 8630, 9901 to 9009; 5 U.S.C. § 301.

Subpart H—Low-income Home Energy Assistance Program

45 C.F.R. § 96.80. Scope.

This subpart applies to the low-income home energy assistance program.

45 C.F.R. § 96.81. Carryover and reallotment.

(a) Scope. Pursuant to section 2607(b) of Public Law 97-35 (42 U.S.C. 8626(b)), this section concerns procedures relating to carryover and reallotment of regular LIHEAP block grant funds authorized under section 2602(b) of Public Law 97-35 (42 U.S.C. 8621(b)).

(b) Required carryover and reallotment report. Each grantee must submit a report to the Department by August 1 of each year, containing the information in paragraphs (b)(1) through (b)(4) of this section. The Department shall make no payment to a grantee for a fiscal year unless the grantee has complied with this paragraph with respect to the prior fiscal year.

(1) The amount of funds that the grantee requests to hold available for obligation in the next (following) fiscal year, not to exceed 10 percent of the funds payable to the grantee;

(2) A statement of the reasons that this amount to remain available will not be used in the fiscal year for which it was allotted;

(3) A description of the types of assistance to be provided with the amount held available; and

(4) The amount of funds, if any, to be subject to reallotment.

(c) Conditions for reallotment. If the total amount available for reallotment for a fiscal year is less than $25,000, the Department will not reallot such amount. If the total amount available for reallotment for a fiscal year is $25,000 or more, the Department will reallot such amount, except that the Department will not award less than $25 in reallotted funds to a grantee.

[48 Fed. Reg. 52060 (Nov. 16, 1983); 49 Fed. Reg. 27146 (July 2, 1984); 52 Fed. Reg. 37967 (Oct. 13, 1987); 57 Fed. Reg. 1977 (Jan. 16, 1992); 60 Fed. Reg. 21357 (May 1, 1995); 64 Fed. Reg. 55858 (Oct. 15, 1999)]

45 C.F.R. § 96.82. Required report on households assisted.

(a) Each grantee which is a State or an insular area which receives an annual allotment of at least $200,000 shall submit to the Department, as part of its LIHEAP grant application, the data required by section 2605(c)(1)(G) of Public Law 97-35 (42 U.S.C. 8624(c)(1)(G)) for the 12-month period corresponding to the Federal fiscal year (October 1–September 30) preceding the fiscal year for which funds are requested. The data shall be reported separately for LIHEAP heating, cooling, crisis, and weatherization assistance.

(b) Each grantee which is an insular area which receives an annual allotment of less than $200,000 or which is an Indian tribe or tribal organization which receives direct funding from the Department shall submit to the Department, as part of its LIHEAP grant application, data on the number of households receiving LIHEAP assistance during the 12-month period corresponding to the Federal fiscal year (October 1-September 30) preceding the fiscal year for which funds are requested. The data shall be reported separately for LIHEAP heating, cooling, crisis, and weatherization assistance.

(c) Grantees will not receive their LIHEAP grant allotment for the fiscal year until the Department has received the report required under paragraph (a) or (b) of this section.

[47 Fed. Reg. 29486 (July 6, 1982); 47 Fed. Reg. 43062 (Sept. 30, 1982); 52 Fed. Reg. 37967 (Oct. 13, 1987); 64 Fed. Reg. 55858 (Oct. 15, 1999)]

45 C.F.R. § 96.83. Increase in maximum amount that may be used for weatherization and other energy-related home repair.

(a) Scope. This section concerns requests for waivers increasing from 15 percent to up to 25 percent of LIHEAP funds allotted or available to a grantee for a fiscal year, the maximum amount that grantees may use for low-cost residential weatherization and other energy-related home repair for low-income households (hereafter referred to as "weatherization"), pursuant to section 2605(k) of Public Law 97-35 (42 U.S.C. 8624(k)).

(b) Public inspection and comment. Before submitting waiver requests to the Department, grantees must make proposed waiver requests available for public inspection within their jurisdictions in a manner that will facilitate timely and meaningful review of, and comment upon, these requests. Written public comments on proposed waiver requests must be made available for public inspection upon their receipt by grantees, as must any summaries prepared of written comments, and transcripts and/or summaries of verbal comments made on proposed requests at public meetings or hearings. Proposed waiver requests, and any preliminary waiver requests, must be made available for public inspection and comment until at least March 15 of the fiscal year for which the waiver is to be requested. Copies of actual waiver requests must be made available for public inspection upon submission of the requests to the Department.

(c) Waiver request. After March 31 of each fiscal year, the chief executive officer (or his or her designee) may request a waiver of the weatherization obligation limit for this fiscal year, if the grantee meets criteria in paragraphs (c)(2)(i), (c)(2)(ii), and (c)(2)(iii) of this section, or can show "good cause" for obtaining a waiver despite a failure to meet one or more of these criteria. (If the request is made by the chief executive officer's designee and the Department does not have on file written evidence of the designation, the request also must include evidence of the appropriate delegation of authority.) Waiver requests must be in writing and must include the information specified in paragraphs (c)(1) through (c)(6) of this section. The grantee may submit a preliminary waiver request for a fiscal year, between February 1 and March 31 of the fiscal year for which the waiver is requested. If a grantee chooses to submit a preliminary waiver request, the preliminary request must include the information specified in paragraphs (c)(1) through (c)(6) of this section; in addition, after March 31 the chief executive officer (or his or her designee) must submit the information specified in paragraphs (c)(7) through (c)(10) of this section, to complete the preliminary waiver request.

(1) A statement of the total percent of its LIHEAP funds allotted or available in the fiscal year for which the waiver is requested, that the grantee desires to use for weatherization.

(2) A statement of whether the grantee has met each of the following three criteria:

(i) In the fiscal year for which the waiver is requested, the combined total (aggregate) number of households in the grantee's service population that will receive LIHEAP heating, cooling, and crisis assistance benefits that are provided from Federal LIHEAP allotments from regular and supplemental appropriations will not be fewer than the combined total (aggregate) number that received such benefits in the preceding fiscal year;

(ii) In the fiscal year for which the waiver is requested, the combined total (aggregate) amount, in dollars, of LIHEAP heating, cooling, and crisis assistance benefits received by the grantee's service population that are provided from Federal LIHEAP allotments from regular and supplemental appropriations will not be less than the combined total (aggregate) amount received in the preceding fiscal year; and

(iii) All LIHEAP weatherization activities to be carried out by the grantee in the fiscal year for which the wavier is requested have been shown to produce measurable savings in energy expenditures.

(3) With regard to criterion in paragraph (c)(2)(i) of this section, a statement of the grantee's best estimate of the appropriate household totals for the fiscal year for which the wavier is requested and for the preceding fiscal year.

(4) With regard to criterion in paragraph (c)(2)(ii) of this section, a statement of the grantee's best estimate of the appropriate benefit totals, in dollars, for the fiscal year for which the waiver is requested and for the preceding fiscal year.

(5) With regard to criterion in paragraph (c)(2)(iii) of this section, a description of the weatherization activities to be carried out by the grantee in the fiscal year for which the wavier is requested (with all LIHEAP funds proposed to be used for weatherization, not just with the amount over 15 percent), and an explanation of the specific criteria under which the grantee has determined whether these activities have been shown to produce measurable savings in energy expenditures.

(6) A description of how and when the proposed wavier request was made available for timely and meaningful public review and comment, copies and/or summaries of public comments received on the request (including transcripts and/or summaries of any comments made on the request at public meetings or hearings), a statement of the method for reviewing public comments, and a statement of the changes, if any, that were made in response to these comments.

(7) To complete a preliminary waiver request: Official confirmation that the grantee wishes approval of the waiver request.

(8) To complete a preliminary waiver request: A statement of whether any public comments were received after preparation of the preliminary waiver request and, if so, copies and/or summaries of these comments (including transcripts and/or summaries of any comments made on the request at public meetings or hearings), and a statement of the changes, if any, that were made in response to these comments.

(9) To complete a preliminary waiver request: A statement of whether any material/substantive changes of fact have occurred in information included in the preliminary waiver request since its submission, and, if so, a description of the change(s).

(10) To complete a preliminary waiver request: A description of any other changes to the preliminary request.

(d) "Standard" waiver. If the Department determines that a grantee has meet the three criteria in paragraph (c)(2) of this section, has provided all information required by paragraph (c) of this section, has shown adequate concern for timely and meaningful public review and comment, and has proposed weatherization that meets all relevant requirements of title XXVI of Public Law 97-35 (42 U.S.C. 8621 *et seq.*) and 45 CFR part 96, the Department will approve a "standard" waiver.

(e) "Good cause" waiver.

(1) If a grantee does not meet one or more of the three criteria in paragraph (c)(2) of this section, then the grantee may submit documentation that demonstrates good cause why a waiver should be granted despite the grantee's failure to meet this criterion or these criteria. "Good cause" waiver requests must include the following information, in addition to the information specified in paragraph (c) of this section:

(i) For each criterion under paragraph (c)(2) of this section that the grantee does not meet, an explanation of the specific reasons demonstrating good cause why the grantee does not meet the criterion and yet proposes to use additional funds for weatherization, citing measurable, quantified data, and stating the source(s) of the data used;

(ii) A statement of the grantee's LIHEAP heating, cooling, and crisis assistance eligibility standards (eligibility criteria) and benefits levels for the fiscal year for which the waiver is requested and for the preceding fiscal year; and, if eligibility standards were less restrictive and/or benefit levels were higher in the preceding fiscal year for one or more of these program components, an explanation of the reasons demonstrating good cause why a waiver should be granted in spite of this fact;

(iii) A statement of the grantee's opening and closing dates for applications for LIHEAP heating, cooling, and crisis assistance in the fiscal year for which the waiver is requested and in the preceding fiscal year, and a description of the grantee's outreach efforts for heating, cooling, and crisis assistance in the fiscal year for which the waiver is requested and in the preceding fiscal year, and, if the grantee's application period was longer and/or outreach efforts were greater in the preceding fiscal year for one or more of these program components, an explanation of the reasons demonstrating good cause why a waiver should be granted in spite of this fact; and

(iv) If the grantee took, or will take, other actions that led, or will lead, to a reduction in the number of applications for LIHEAP heating, cooling, and/or crisis assistance, from the preceding fiscal year to the fiscal year for which the waiver is requested, a description of these actions and an explanation demonstrating good cause why a waiver should be granted in spite of these actions.

(2) If the Department determines that a grantee requesting a "good cause" waiver has demonstrated good cause why a waiver should be granted, has provided all information required by paragraphs (c) and (e)(1) of this section, has shown adequate concern for timely and meaningful public review and comment, and has proposed weatherization that meets all relevant requirements of title XXVI of Public Law 97-35 (42 U.S.C. 8621 *et seq.*) and 45 CFR part 96, the Department will approve a "good cause" waiver.

(f) Approvals and disapprovals. After receiving the grantee's complete waiver request, the Department will respond in writing within 45 days, informing the grantee whether the request is approved on either a "standard" or "good cause" basis. The Department may request additional information and/or clarification from the grantee. If additional information and/or clarification is requested, the 45-day period for the Department's response will start when the additional information and/or clarification is received. No waiver will be granted for a previous fiscal year.

(g) Effective period. Waivers will be effective from the date of the Department's written approval until the funds for which the waiver is granted are obligated in accordance with title XXVI of Public Law 97-35 (42 U.S.C. 8621 *et seq.*) and 45 CFR part 96. Funds for which a weatherization waiver was granted that are carried over to the following fiscal year and used for weatherization shall not be considered "funds allotted" or "funds available" for the purposes of calculating the maximum amount that may be used for weatherization in the succeeding fiscal year.

[57 Fed. Reg. 1977 (Jan. 16, 1992); 60 Fed. Reg. 21358 (May 1, 1995); 60 Fed. Reg. 33260 (June 27, 1995)]

45 C.F.R. § 96.84. Miscellaneous.

(a) Rights and responsibilities of territories. Except as otherwise provided, a territory eligible for funds shall have the same rights and responsibilities as a State.

(b) Applicability of assurances. The assurances in section 2605(b) of Public Law 97-35 (42 U.S.C. 8624(b)), as amended, pertain to all forms of assistance provided by the grantee, with the exception of assurance 15, which applies to heating, cooling, and energy crisis intervention assistance.

(c) Prevention of waste, fraud, and abuse. Grantees must establish appropriate systems and procedures to prevent, detect, and correct waste, fraud, and abuse in activities funded under the low-income home energy assistance program. The systems and procedures are to address possible waste, fraud, and abuse by clients, vendors, and administering agencies.

(d) End of transfer authority. Beginning with funds appropriated for FY 1994, grantees may not transfer any funds pursuant to section 2604(f) of Public Law 97-35 (42 U.S.C. 8623(f)) that are payable to them under the LIHEAP program to the block grant programs specified in section 2604(f).

[57 Fed. Reg. 1978 (Jan. 16, 1992); 60 Fed. Reg. 21357 (May 1, 1995); 64 Fed. Reg. 55858 (Oct. 15, 1999)]

45 C.F.R. § 96.85. Income eligibility.

(a) Application of poverty income guidelines and State median income estimates. In implementing the income eligibility standards in section 2605(b)(2) of Public Law 97-35 (42 U.S.C. 8624(b)(2)), grantees using the Federal government's official poverty income guidelines and State median income estimates for households as a basis for determining eligibility for assistance shall, by October 1 of each year, or by the beginning of the State fiscal year, whichever is later, adjust their income eligibility criteria so that they are in accord with the most recently published update of the guidelines or estimates. Grantees may adjust their income eligibility criteria to accord with the most recently published revision to the poverty income guidelines or State median income estimates for households at any time between the publication of the revision and the following October 1, or the beginning of the State fiscal year, whichever is later.

(b) Adjustment of annual median income for household size. In order to determine the State median income for households that have other than four individuals, grantees shall adjust the State median income figures (published annually by the Secretary), by the following percentages:

(1) One-person household, 52 percent;

(2) Two-person household, 68 percent;

(3) Three-person household, 84 percent;

(4) Four-person household, 100 percent;

(5) Five-person household, 116 percent;

(6) Six-person household, 132 percent; and

(7) For each additional household member above six persons, add three percentage points to the percentage adjustment for a six-person household.

[48 Fed. Reg. 52060 (Nov. 16, 1983); 49 Fed. Reg. 27146 (July 2, 1984); 53 Fed. Reg. 6827 (Mar. 3, 1988); 64 Fed. Reg. 55858 (Oct. 15, 1999)]

45 C.F.R. § 96.86. Exemption from requirement for additional outreach and intake services.

The requirement in section 2605(b)(15) of Public Law 97-35 (42 U.S.C. 8624(b)(15)), as amended by section 704(a)(4) of the Augustus F. Hawkins Human Services Reauthorization Act of 1990 (Pub. L. 101-501)—concerning additional outreach and intake services—does not apply to:

(a) Indian tribes and tribal organizations; and

(b) Territories whose annual LIHEAP allotments under section 2602(b) of Public Law 97-35 (42 U.S.C. 8621(b)) are $200,000 or less.

[52 Fed. Reg. 37967 (Oct. 13, 1987); 57 Fed. Reg. 1978 (Jan. 16, 1992); 60 Fed. Reg. 21357 (May 1, 1995)]

45 C.F.R. § 96.87. Leveraging incentive program.

(a) Scope and eligible grantees.

(1) This section concerns the leveraging incentive program authorized by section 2607A of Public Law 97-35 (42 U.S.C. 8626a).

(2)(i) The only entities eligible to receive leveraging incentive funds from the Department are States (including the District of Columbia), Indian tribes, tribal organizations, and territories that received direct Federal LIHEAP funding under section 2602(b) of Public Law 97-35 (42 U.S.C. 8621(b)) in both the base period for which leveraged resources are reported, and the award period for which leveraging incentive funds are sought; and tribes and tribal organizations described in paragraphs (a)(2)(ii) and (a)(2)(iii) of this section.

(ii) Indian tribes that received LIHEAP services under section 2602(b) of Public Law 97-35 (42 U.S.C. 8621(b)) through a directly-funded tribal organization in the base period for which leveraged resources are reported, and receive direct Federal LIHEAP funding under section 2602(b) in the award period, will receive leveraging incentive funds allocable to them if they submit leveraging reports meeting all applicable requirements. If the tribal organization continues to receive direct funding under section 2602(b) in the award period, the tribal organization also will receive incentive funds allocable to it if it submits a leveraging report meeting all applicable requirements. In such cases, incentive funds will be allocated among the involved entities that submit leveraging reports, as agreed by these entities. If they cannot agree, HHS will allocate incentive funds based on the comparative role of each entity in obtaining and/or administering the leveraged resources, and/or their relative number of LIHEAP-eligible households.

(iii) If a tribe received direct Federal LIHEAP funding under section 2602(b) of Public Law 97-35 (42 U.S.C. 8621(b)) in the base period for which resources leveraged by the tribe are reported, and the tribe receives LIHEAP services under section 2602(b) through a directly-funded tribal organization in the award period, the tribal organization will receive leveraging incentive funds on behalf of the tribe for the resources if the tribal organization submits a leveraging report meeting all applicable requirements.

(b) Definitions—

(1) *Award period* means the fiscal year during which leveraging incentive funds are distributed to grantees by the Department, based on the countable leveraging activities they reported to the Department for the preceding fiscal year (the base period).

(2) *Base period* means the fiscal year for which a grantee's leveraging activities are reported to the Department; grantees' countable leveraging activities during the base period or base year are the basis for the distribution of leveraging incentive funds during the succeeding fiscal year (the award period or award year). Leveraged resources are counted in the base period during which their benefits are provided to low-income households.

(3) *Countable loan fund* means revolving loan funds and similar loan instruments in which:

(i) The sources of both the loaned and the repaid funds meet the requirements of this section, including the prohibitions of paragraphs (f)(1), (f)(2), and (f)(3) of this section;

(ii) Neither the loaned nor the repaid funds are Federal funds or payments from low-income households, and the loans are not made to low-income households; and

(iii) The benefits provided by the loaned funds meet the requirements of this section for countable leveraged resources and benefits.

(4) *Countable petroleum violation escrow funds* means petroleum violation escrow (oil overcharge) funds that were distributed to a State or territory by the Department of Energy (DOE) after October 1, 1990, and interest earned in accordance with DOE policies on petroleum violation escrow funds that were distributed to a State or territory by DOE after October 1, 1990, that:

(i) Were used to assist low-income households to meet the costs of home energy through (that is, within and as a part of) a State or territory's LIHEAP program, another Federal program, or a non-Federal program, in accordance with a submission for use of these petroleum violation escrow funds that was approved by DOE;

(ii) Were not previously required to be allocated to low-income households; and

(iii) Meet the requirements of paragraph (d)(1) of this section, and of paragraph (d)(2)(ii) or (d)(2)(iii) or this section.

(5) *Home energy* means a source of heating or cooling in residential dwellings.

(6) *Low-income households* means federally eligible (federally qualified) households meeting the standards for LIHEAP income eligibility and/or LIHEAP categorical eligibility as set by section 2605(b)(2) of Public Law 97-35 (42 U.S.C. 8624(b)(2)).

(7) *Weatherization* means low-cost residential weatherization and other energy-related home repair for low-income households. Weatherization must be directly related to home energy.

(c) LIHEAP funds used to identify, develop, and demonstrate leveraging programs.

(1) Each fiscal year, States (excluding Indian tribes, tribal organizations, and territories) may spend up to the greater of $35,000 or 0.08 percent of their net Federal LIHEAP allotments (funds payable) allocated under section 2602(b) of Public Law 97-35 (42 U.S.C. 8621(b)) specifically to identify, develop, and demonstrate leveraging programs under section 2607A(c)(2) of Public Law 97-35 (42 U.S.C. 8626a(c)(2)). Each fiscal year, Indian tribes, tribal organizations, and territories may spend up to the greater of two (2.0) percent or $100 of their Federal LIHEAP allotments allocated under section 2602(b) of Public law 97-35 (42 U.S.C. 8621(b)) specifically to identify, develop, and demonstrate leveraging programs under section 2607A(c)(2) of Public Law 97-35 (42 U.S.C. 8626a(c)(2)). For the purpose of this paragraph, Federal LIHEAP allotments include funds from regular and supplemental appropriations, with the exception of leveraging incentive funds provided under section 2602(d) of Public Law 97-35 (42 U.S.C. 8621(d)).

(2) LIHEAP funds used under section 2607A(c)(2) of Public Law 97-35 (42 U.S.C. 8626a(c)(2)) specifically to identify, develop, and demonstrate leveraging programs are not subject to the limitation in section 2605(b)(9) of Public Law 97-35 (42 U.S.C. 8624(b)(9)) on the maximum percent of Federal funds that may be used for costs of planning and administration.

(d) Basic requirements for leveraged resources and benefits.

(1) In order to be counted under the leveraging incentive program, leveraged resources and benefits must meet all of the following five criteria:

(i) They are from non-Federal sources.

(ii) They are provided to the grantee's low-income home energy assistance program, or to federally qualified low-income households as described in section 2605(b)(2) of Public Law 97-35 (42 U.S.C. 8624(b)(2)).

(iii) They are measurable and quantifiable in dollars.

(iv) They represent a net addition to the total home energy resources available to low-income households in excess of the amount of such resources that could be acquired by these households through the purchase of home energy, or the purchase of items that help these households meet the cost of home energy, at commonly available household rates or costs, or that could be obtained with regular LIHEAP allotments provided under section 2602(b) of Public Law 97-35 (42 U.S.C. 8621(b)).

(v) They meet the requirements for countable leveraged resources and benefits throughout this section and section 2607A of Public Law 97-35 (42 U.S.C. 8626(a)).

(2) Also, in order to be counted under the leveraging incentive program, leveraged resources and benefits must meet at least one of the following three criteria:

(i) The grantee's LIHEAP program had an active, substantive role in developing and/or acquiring the resource/benefits from home energy vendor(s) through negotiation, regulation, and/or competitive bid. The actions or efforts of one or more staff of the grantee's LIHEAP program—at the central and/or local level—and/or one or more staff of LIHEAP program subrecipient(s) acting in that capacity, were substantial and significant in obtaining the resource/benefits from the vendor(s).

(ii) The grantee appropriated or mandated the resource/benefits for distribution to low-income households through (that is, within and as a part of) its LIHEAP program. The resource/benefits are provided through the grantee's LIHEAP program to low-income households eligible under the grantee's LIHEAP standards, in accordance with the LIHEAP statute and regulations and consistent with the grantee's LIHEAP plan and program policies that were in effect during the base period, as if they were provided from the grantee's Federal LIHEAP allotment.

(iii) The grantee appropriated or mandated the resource/benefits for distribution to low-income households as described in its LIHEAP plan (referred to in section 2605(c)(1)(A) of Public Law 97-35) (42 U.S.C. 8624(c)(1)(A)). The resource/benefits are provided to low-income households as a supplement and/or alternative to the grantee's LIHEAP program, outside (that is, not through, within, or as a part of) the LIHEAP program. The resource/benefits are integrated and coordinated with the grantee's LIHEAP program. Before the end of the base period, the plan identifies and describes the resource/benefits, their source(s), and their integration/coordination with the LIHEAP program. The Department will determine resources/benefits to be integrated and coordinated with the LIHEAP program if they meet at least one of the following eight conditions. If a resource meets at least one of conditions A through F when the grantee's LIHEAP program is operating (and meets all other applicable requirements), the resource also is countable when the LIHEAP program is not operating.

(A) For all households served by the resource, the assistance provided by the resource depends on and is determined by the assistance provided to these households by the grantee's LIHEAP program in the base period. The resource supplements LIHEAP assistance that was not sufficient to meet households' home energy needs, and the type and amount of assistance provided by the resource is directly affected by the LIHEAP assistance received by the households.

(B) Receipt of LIHEAP assistance in the base period is necessary to receive assistance from the resource. The resource serves only households that received LIHEAP assistance in the base period.

(C) Ineligibility for the grantee's LIHEAP program, or denial of LIHEAP assistance in the base period because of unavailability of LIHEAP funds, is necessary to receive assistance from the resource.

(D) For discounts and waivers: eligibility for and/or receipt of assistance under the grantee's LIHEAP program in the base period, and/or eligibility under the Federal standards set by section 2605(b)(2) of Public Law 97-35 (42 U.S.C. 8624(b)(2)), is necessary to receive the discount or waiver.

(E) During the period when the grantee's LIHEAP program is operating, staff of the grantee's LIHEAP program and/or staff assigned to the LIHEAP program by a local LIHEAP administering agency or agencies, and staff assigned to the resource communicate orally and/or in writing about how to meet the home energy needs of specific, individual households. For the duration of the LIHEAP program, this communication takes place before assistance is provided to each household to be served by the resource, unless the applicant for assistance from the resource presents documentation of LIHEAP eligibility and/or the amount of LIHEAP assistance received or to be received.

(F) A written agreement between the grantee's LIHEAP program or local LIHEAP administering agency, and the agency administering the resource, specifies the following about the resource: eligibility criteria; benefit levels; period of operation; how the LIHEAP program and the resource are integrated/coordinated; and relationship between LIHEAP eligibility and/or benefit levels, and eligibility and/or benefit levels for the resource. The agreement provides for annual or more frequent reports to be provided to the LIHEAP program by the agency administering the resource.

(G) The resource accepts referrals from the grantee's LIHEAP program, and as long as the resource has benefits available, it provides assistance to all households that are referred by the LIHEAP program and that meet the resource's eligibility requirements. Under this condition, only the benefits provided to households referred by the LIHEAP program are countable.

(H) Before the grantee's LIHEAP heating, cooling, crisis, and/or weatherization assistance component(s) open and/or after the grantee's LIHEAP heating, cooling, crisis, and/or weatherization assistance component(s) close for the season or for the fiscal year, or before the entire LIHEAP program opens and/or after the entire LIHEAP program closes for the season or for the fiscal year, the resource is made available specifically to fill the gap caused by the absence of the LIHEAP component(s) or program. The resource is not available while the LIHEAP component(s) or program is operating.

(e) Countable leveraged resources and benefits. Resources and benefits that are countable under the leveraging incentive program include but are not limited to the following, provided that they also meet all other applicable requirements:

(1) Cash resources: State, tribal, territorial, and other public and private non-Federal funds, including countable loan funds and countable petroleum violation escrow funds as defined in paragraphs (b)(3) and (b)(4) of this section, that are used for:

(i) Heating, cooling, and energy crisis assistance payments and cash benefits made in the base period to or on behalf of low-income households toward their home energy costs (including home energy bills, taxes on home energy sales/purchases and services, connection and reconnection fees, application fees, late payment charges, bulk fuel tank rental or purchase costs, and security deposits that are retained for six months or longer);

(ii) Purchase of fuels that are provided to low-income households in the base period for home energy (such as fuel oil, liquefied petroleum gas, and wood);

(iii) Purchase of weatherization materials that are installed in recipients' homes in the base period;

(iv) Purchase of the following tangible items that are provided to low-income households and/or installed in recipients' homes in the base period: blankets, space heating devices, equipment, and systems; space cooling devices, equipment, and systems; and other tangible items that help low-income households meet the costs of home energy and are specifically approved by the Department as countable leveraged resources;

(v) Installation, replacement, and repair of the following in the base period: weatherization materials; space heating devices, equipment, and systems; space cooling devices, equipment, and systems; and other tangible items that help low-income households meet the costs of home energy and are specifically approved by the Department;

(vi) The following services, when they are an integral part of weatherization to help low-income households meet the costs of home energy in the base period: installation, replacement, and repair of windows, exterior doors, roofs, exterior walls, and exterior floors; pre-weatherization home energy audits of homes that were weatherized as a result of these audits; and post-weatherization inspection of homes; and

(vii) The following services, when they are provided (carried out) in the base period: installation, replacement, and repair of smoke/fire alarms that are an integral part, and necessary for safe operation, of a home heating or cooling system installed or repaired as a weatherization activity; and asbestos removal and that is an integral part of, and necessary to carry out, weatherization to help low-income households meet the costs of home energy.

(2) Home energy discounts and waivers that are provided in the base period to low-income households and pertain to generally applicable prices, rates, fees, charges, costs, and/or requirements, in the amount of the discount, reduction, waiver, or forgiveness, or that apply to certain tangible fuel and non-fuel items and to certain services, that are provided in the base period to low-income households and help these households meet the costs of home energy, in the amount of the discount or reduction:

(i) Discounts or reductions in utility and bulk fuel prices, rates, or bills;

(ii) Partial or full forgiveness of home energy bill arrearages;

(iii) Partial or full waivers of utility and other home energy connection and reconnection fees, application fees, late payment charges, bulk fuel tank rental or purchase costs, and home energy security deposits that are retained for six months or longer;

(iv) Reductions in and partial or full waivers of non-Federal taxes on home energy sales/purchases and services, and reductions in and partial or full waivers of other non-Federal taxes provided as tax "credits" to low-income households to offset their home energy costs, except when Federal funds or Federal tax "credits" provide payment or reimbursement for these reductions/waivers;

(v) Discounts or reductions in the cost of the following tangible items that are provided to low-income households and/or installed in recipients' homes: weatherization materials; blankets; space heating devices, equipment, and systems; space cooling devices, equipment, and systems; and other tangible items that are specifically approved by the Department;

(vi) Discounts or reductions in the cost of installation, replacement, and repair of the following: weatherization materials; space heating devices, equipment, and systems; space cooling devices, equipment, and systems; and other tangible items that help low-income households meet the costs of home energy and are specifically approved by the Department;

(vii) Discounts or reductions in the cost of the following services, when the services are an integral part of weatherization to help low-income households meet the costs of home energy: installation, replacement, and repair of windows, exterior doors, roofs, exterior walls, and exterior floors; pre-weatherization home energy audits of homes that were weatherized as a result of these audits; and post-weatherization inspection of homes; and

(viii) Discounts or reductions in the cost of installation, replacement, and repair of smoke/fire alarms that are an integral part, and necessary for safe operation, of a home heating or cooling system installed or repaired as a weatherization activity; and discounts or reductions in the cost of asbestos removal that is an integral part of, and necessary to carry out, weatherization to help low-income households meet the costs of home energy.

(3) Certain third-party in-kind contributions that are provided in the base period to low-income households:

(i) Donated fuels used by recipient households for home energy (such as fuel oil, liquefied petroleum gas, and wood);

(ii) Donated weatherization materials that are installed in recipients' homes;

(iii) Donated blankets; donated space heating devices, equipment, and systems; donated space cooling devices, equipment, and systems; and other donated tangible items that help low-income households meet the costs of home energy and are specifically approved by the Department as countable leveraged resources;

(iv) Unpaid volunteers' services specifically to install, replace, and repair the following: weatherization materials; space heating devices, equipment, and systems; space cooling devices, equipment, and systems; and other items that help low-income households meet the costs of home energy and are specifically approved by the Department;

(v) Unpaid volunteers' services specifically to provide (carry out) the following, when these services are an integral part of weatherization to help low-income households meet the costs of home energy: installation, replacement, and repair of windows, exterior doors, roofs, exterior walls, and exterior floors; pre-weatherization home energy audits of homes that were weatherized as a result of these audits; and post-weatherization inspection of homes;

(vi) Unpaid volunteers' services specifically to: install, replace, and repair smoke/fire alarms as an integral part, and necessary for safe operation, of a home heating or cooling system installed or repaired as a weatherization activity; and remove asbestos as an integral part of, and necessary to carry out, weatherization to help low-income households meet the costs of home energy;

(vii) Paid staff's services that are donated by the employer specifically to install, replace, and repair the following: weatherization materials; space heating devices, equipment, and systems; space cooling devices, equipment, and systems; and other items that help low-income households meet the costs of home energy and are specifically approved by the Department;

(viii) Paid staff's services that are donated by the employer specifically to provide (carry out) the following, when these services are an integral part of weatherization to help low-income households meet the costs of home energy: installation, replacement, and repair of windows, exterior doors, roofs, exterior walls, and exterior floors; pre-weatherization home energy audits of homes that were weatherized as a result of these audits; and post-weatherization inspection of homes; and

(ix) Paid staff's services that are donated by the employer specifically to: install, replace, and repair smoke/fire alarms as an integral part, and necessary for safe operation, of a home heating or cooling system installed or repaired as a weatherization activity; and remove asbestos as an integral part of, and necessary to carry out, weatherization to help low-income households meet the costs of home energy.

(f) Resources and benefits that cannot be counted. The following resources and benefits are not countable under the leveraging incentive program:

(1) Resources (or portions of resources) obtained, arranged, provided, contributed, and/or paid for, by a low-income household for its own benefit, or which a low-income household is responsible for obtaining or required to provide for its own benefit or for the benefit of others, in order to receive a benefit of some type;

(2) Resources (or portions of resources) provided, contributed, and/or paid for by building owners, building managers, and/or home energy vendors, if the cost of rent, home energy, or other charge(s) to the recipient were or will be increased, or if other charge(s) to the recipient were or will be imposed, as a result;

(3) Resources (or portions of resources) directly provided, contributed, and/or paid for by member(s) of the recipient household's family (parents, grandparents, great-grandparents, sons, daughters, grandchildren, great-grandchildren, brothers, sisters, aunts, uncles, first cousins, nieces, and nephews, and their spouses), regardless of whether the family member(s) lived with the household, unless the family member(s) also provided the same resource to other low-income households during the base period and did not limit the resource to members of their own family;

(4) Deferred home energy obligations;

(5) Projected future savings from weatherization;

(6) Delivery, and discounts in the cost of delivery, of fuel, weatherization materials, and all other items;

(7) Purchase, rental, donation, and loan, and discounts in the cost of purchase and rental, of: supplies and equipment used to deliver fuel, weatherization materials, and all other items; and supplies and equipment used to install and repair weatherization materials and all other items;

(8) Petroleum violation escrow (oil overcharge) funds that do not meet the definition in paragraph (b)(4) of this section;

(9) Interest earned/paid on petroleum violation escrow funds that were distributed to a State or territory by the Department of Energy on or before October 1, 1990;

(10) Interest earned/paid on Federal funds;

(11) Interest earned/paid on customers' security deposits, utility deposits, etc., except when forfeited by the customer and used to provide countable benefits;

(12) Borrowed funds that do not meet the requirements in paragraph (b)(3) above (including loans made by and/or to low-income households), interest paid on borrowed funds, and reductions in interest paid on borrowed funds;

(13) Resources (or portions of resources) for which Federal payment or reimbursement has been or will be provided/received;

(14) Tax deductions and tax credits received from any unit(s) of government by donors/contributors of resources for these donations, and by vendors for providing rate reductions, discounts, waivers, credits, and/or arrearage forgiveness to or for low-income households, etc.;

(15) Funds and other resources that have been or will be used as matching or cost sharing for any Federal program;

(16) Leveraged resources counted under any other Federal leveraging incentive program;

(17) Costs of planning and administration, space costs, and intake costs;

(18) Outreach activities, budget counseling, case management, and energy conservation education;

(19) Training;

(20) Installation, replacement, and repair of lighting fixtures and light bulbs;

(21) Installation, replacement, and repair of smoke/fire alarms that are not an integral part, and necessary for safe operation, of a home heating or cooling system installed or repaired as a weatherization activity;

(22) Asbestos removal that is not an integral part of, and necessary to carry out, weatherization to help low-income households meet the costs of home energy;

(23) Paid services where payment is not made from countable leveraged resources, unless these services are donated as a countable in-kind contribution by the employer;

(24) All in-kind contributions except those described in paragraph (e)(3) of this section; and

(25) All other resources that do not meet the requirements of this section and of section 2607A of Public Law 97-35 (42 U.S.C. 8626a).

(g) Valuation and documentation of leveraged resources and offsetting costs.

(1) Leveraged cash resources will be valued at the fair market value of the benefits they provided to low-income households, as follows. Payments to or on behalf of low-income households for heating, cooling, and energy crisis assistance will be valued at their actual amount or value at the time they were provided. Purchased fuel, weatherization materials, and other countable tangible items will be valued at their fair market value (the commonly available household rate or cost in the local market area) at the time they were purchased. Installation, replacement, and repair of weatherization materials, and other countable services, will be valued at rates consistent with those ordinarily paid for similar work, by persons of similar skill in this work, in the grantee's or subrecipient's organization in the local area, at the time these services were provided. If the grantee or subrecipient does not have employees performing similar work, the rates will be consistent with those ordinarily paid by other employers for similar work, by persons of similar skill in this work, in the same labor market, at the time these services were provided. Fringe benefits and overhead costs will not be counted.

(2) Home energy discounts, waivers, and credits will be valued at their actual amount or value.

(3) Donated fuel, donated weatherization materials, and other countable donated tangible items will be valued at their fair market value (the commonly available household cost in the local market area) at the time of donation.

(4) Donated unpaid services, and donated third-party paid services that are not in the employee's normal line of work, will be valued at rates consistent with those ordinarily paid for similar work, by persons of similar skill in this work, in the grantee's or subrecipient's organization in the local area, at the time these services were provided. If the grantee or subrecipient does not have employees performing similar work, the rates will be consistent with those ordinarily paid by other employers for similar work, by persons of similar skill in this work, in the same labor market, at the time these services were provided. Fringe benefits and overhead costs will not be counted. Donated third-party paid services of employees in their normal line of work will be valued at the employee's regular rate of pay, excluding fringe benefits and overhead costs.

(5) Offsetting costs and charges will be valued at their actual amount or value.

(i) Funds from grantees' regular LIHEAP allotments that are used specifically to identify, develop, and demonstrate leveraging programs under section 2607A(c)(2) of Public Law 97-35 (42

U.S.C. 8626a(c)(2)) will be deducted as offsetting costs in the base period in which these funds are obligated, whether or not there are any resulting leveraged benefits. Costs incurred from grantees' own funds to identify, develop, and demonstrate leveraging programs will be deducted in the first base period in which resulting leveraged benefits are provided to low-income households. If there is no resulting leveraged benefit from the expenditure of the grantee's own funds, the grantee's expenditure will not be counted or deducted.

(ii) Any costs assessed or charged to low-income households on a continuing or on-going basis, year after year, specifically to participate in a counted leveraging program or to receive counted leveraged resources/benefits will be deducted in the base period these costs are paid. Any one-time costs or charges to low-income households specifically to participate in a counted leveraging program or to receive counted leveraged resources/benefits will be deducted in the first base period the leveraging program or resource is counted. Such costs or charges will be subtracted from the gross value of a counted resource or benefit for low-income households whose benefits are counted, but not for any households whose benefits are not counted.

(6) Only the amount of the net addition to recipient low-income households' home energy resources may be counted in the valuation of a leveraged resource.

(7) Leveraged resources and benefits, and offsetting costs and charges, will be valued according to the best data available to the grantee.

(8) Grantees must maintain, or have readily available, records sufficient to document leveraged resources and benefits, and offsetting costs and charges, and their valuation. These records must be retained for three years after the end of the base period whose leveraged resources and benefits they document.

(h) Leveraging report.

(1) In order to qualify for leveraging incentive funds, each grantee desiring such funds must submit to the Department a report on the leveraged resources provided to low-income households during the preceeding base period. These reports must contain the following information in a format established by the Department.

(i) For each separate leveraged resource, the report must:

(A) Briefly describe the specific leveraged resource and the specific benefit(s) provided to low-income households by this resource, and state the source of the resource;

(B) State whether the resource was acquired in cash, as a discount/waiver, or as an in-kind contribution;

(C) Indicate the geographical area in which the benefit(s) were provided to recipients;

(D) State the month(s) and year(s) when the benefit(s) were provided to recipients;

(E) State the gross dollar value of the countable benefits provided by the resource as determined in accordance with paragraph (g) of this section, indicate the source(s) of the data used, and describe how the grantee quantified the value and calculated the total amount;

(F) State the number of low-income households to whom the benefit(s) were provided, and state the eligibility standard(s) for the low-income households to whom the benefit(s) were provided;

(G) Indicate the agency or agencies that administered the resource/benefit(s); and

(H) Indicate the criterion or criteria for leveraged resources in paragraph (d)(2) of this section that the resource/benefits meet, and for criteria in paragraphs (d)(2)(i) and (d)(2)(iii) of this section, explain how resources/benefits valued at $5,000 or more meet the criterion or criteria.

(ii) State the total gross dollar value of the countable leveraged resources and benefits provided to low-income households during the base period (the sum of the amounts listed pursuant to paragraph (h)(1)(i)(E) of this section).

(iii) State in dollars any costs incurred by the grantee to leverage resources, and any costs and charges imposed on low-income households to participate in a counted leveraging program or to receive counted leveraged benefits, as determined in accordance with paragraph (g)(5) of this section. Also state the amount of the grantee's regular LIHEAP allotment that the grantee used during the base period specifically to identify, develop, and demonstrate leveraging programs under section 2607A(c)(2) of Public Law 97-35 (42 U.S.C. 8626a(c)(2)).

(iv) State the net dollar value of the countable leveraged resources and benefits for the base period. (Subtract the amounts in paragraph (h)(1)(iii) of this section from the amount in paragraph (h)(1)(ii) of this section.)

(2) Leveraging reports must be postmarked or hand-delivered not later than November 30 of the fiscal year for which leveraging incentive funds are requested.

(3) The Department may require submission of additional documentation and/or clarification as it determines necessary to verify information in a grantee's leveraging report, to determine whether a leveraged resource is countable, and/or to determine the net valuation of a resource. In such cases, the Department will set a date by which it must receive information sufficient to document countability and/or valuation. In such cases, if the Department does not receive information that it considers sufficient to document countability and/or valuation by the date it has set, then the Department will not count the resource (or portion of resource) in question.

***(i)* Determination of grantee shares of leveraging incentive funds.** Allocation of leveraging incentive funds to grantees will be computed according to a formula using the following factors and weights:

(1) Fifty (50) percent based on the final net value of countable leveraged resources provided to low-income households during the base period by a grantee relative to its net Federal allotment of funds allocated under section 2602(b) of Public Law 97-35 (42 U.S.C. 8621(b)) during the base period, as a proportion of the final net value of the countable leveraged resources provided by all grantees during the base period relative to their net Federal allotment of funds allocated under that section during the base period; and

(2) Fifty (50) percent based on the final net value of countable leveraged resources provided to low-income households during the base period by a grantee as a proportion of the total final net value of the countable leveraged resources provided by all grantees during the base period; except that: No grantee may receive more than twelve (12.0) percent of the total amount of leveraging incentive funds available for distribution to grantees in any award period; and no grantee may receive more than the smaller of its net Federal allotment of funds allocated under section 2602(b) of Public Law 97-35 (42 U.S.C. 8621(b)) during the base period, or two times (double) the final net value of its countable leveraged resources for the base period. The calculations will be based on data contained in the leveraging reports submitted by grantees under paragraph (h) of this section as approved by the Department, and allocation data developed by the Department.

(j) Uses of leveraging incentive funds.

(1) Funds awarded to grantees under the leveraging incentive program must be used to increase or maintain heating, cooling, energy crisis, and/or weatherization benefits through (that is, within and as a part of) the grantee's LIHEAP program. These funds can be used for weatherization without regard to the weatherization maximum in section 2605(k) of Public Law 97-35 (42 U.S.C. 8624(k)). However, they cannot be counted in the base for calculation of the weatherization maximum for regular LIHEAP funds authorized under section 2602(b) of Public Law 97-35 (42 U.S.C. 8621(b)). Leveraging incentive funds cannot be used for costs of planning and administration. However, in either the award period or the fiscal year following the award period, they can be counted in the base for calculation of maximum grantee planning and administrative costs under section 2605(b)(9) of Public Law 97-35 (42 U.S.C. 8624(b)(9)). They cannot be counted in the base for calculation of maximum carryover of regular LIHEAP funds authorized under section 2602(b) of Public Law 97-35 (42 U.S.C. 8621(b)).

(2) Grantees must include the uses of leveraging incentive funds in their LIHEAP plans (referred to in section 2605(c)(1)(A) of Public Law 97-35) (42 U.S.C. 8624(c)(1)(A)) for the fiscal year in which the grantee obligates these funds. Grantees must document uses of leveraging incentive funds in the same way they document uses of regular LIHEAP funds authorized under section 2602(b) of Public Law 97-35 (42 U.S.C. 8621(b)). Leveraging incentive funds are subject to the same audit requirements as regular LIHEAP funds.

(k) Period of obligation for leveraging incentive funds. Leveraging incentive funds are available for obligation during both the award period and the fiscal year following the award period, without regard to limitations on carryover of funds in section 2607(b)(2)(B) of Public Law 97-35 (42 U.S.C. 8626(b)(2)(B)). Any leveraging incentive funds not obligated for allowable purposes by the end of this period must be returned to the Department.

[60 Fed. Reg. 21359 (May 1, 1995); 60 Fed. Reg. 33260, (June 27, 1995); 60 Fed. Reg. 36334 (July 14, 1995)]

45 C.F.R. § 96.88. Administrative costs.

(a) Costs of planning and administration. Any expenditure for governmental functions normally associated with administration of a public assistance program must be included in determining administrative costs subject to the statutory limitation on administrative costs, regardless of whether the expenditure is incurred by the State, a subrecipient, a grantee, or a contractor of the State.

(b) Administrative costs for territories and Indian tribes. For Indian tribes, tribal organizations and territories with allotments of $20,000 or less, the limitation on the cost of planning and administering the low-income home energy assistance program shall be 20 percent of funds payable and not transferred for use under another block grant. For tribes, tribal organizations and territories with allotments over $20,000, the limitation on the cost of planning and administration shall be $4,000 plus 10 percent of the amount of funds payable (and not transferred for use under another block grant) that exceeds $20,000.

[52 Fed. Reg. 37967 (Oct. 13, 1987)]

45 C.F.R. § 96.89. Exemption from standards for providing energy crisis intervention assistance.

The performance standards in section 2604(c) of Pub. L. 97-35 (42 U.S.C. 8623), as amended by section 502(a) of the Human Services Reauthorization Act of 1986 (Pub. L. 99-425)—concerning provision of energy crisis assistance within specified time limits, acceptance of applications for energy crisis benefits at geographically accessible sites, and provision to physically infirm low-income persons of the means to apply for energy crisis benefits at their residences or to travel to application sites—shall not apply under the conditions described in this section.

(a) These standards shall not apply to a program in a geographical area affected by (1) a major disaster or emergency designated by the President under the Disaster Relief Act of 1974, or (2) a natural disaster identified by the chief executive officer of a State, territory, or direct-grant Indian tribe or tribal organization, if the Secretary (or his or her designee) determines that the disaster or emergency makes compliance with the standards impracticable.

(b) The Secretary's determination will be made after communication by the chief executive officer (or his or her designee) to the Secretary (or his or her designee) of the following:

(1) Information substantiating the existence of a disaster or emergency;

(2) Information substantiating the impracticability of compliance with the standards, including a description of the specific conditions caused by the disaster or emergency which make compliance impracticable; and

(3) Information on the expected duration of the conditions that make compliance impracticable.

If the communication is made by the chief executive officer's designee and the Department does not have on file written evidence of the designation, the communication must also include:

(4) Evidence of the appropriate delegation of authority.

(c) The initial communication by the chief executive officer may be oral or written. If oral, it must be followed as soon as possible by written communication confirming the information provided orally. The Secretary's exemption initially may be oral. If so, the Secretary will provide written confirmation of the exemption as soon as possible after receipt of appropriate written communication from the chief executive officer.

(d) Exemption from the standards shall apply from the moment of the Secretary's determination, only in the geographical area affected by the disaster or emergency, and only for so long as the Secretary determines that the disaster or emergency makes compliance with the standards impracticable.

[52 Fed. Reg. 4625 (Feb. 13, 1987); 53 Fed. Reg. 6827, (Mar. 3, 1988)]

C.3 2011 State LIHEAP Directors

The directory below is reprinted from information found at www.acf.hhs.gov/programs/ocs/liheap/grantees/states.html#AL. Households seeking more information about LIHEAP in their state should contact the National Energy Assistance Referral (NEAR) project. NEAR is a free service for persons who want information on where to apply for LIHEAP help. NEAR can be contacted by e-mail at energyassistance@ncat.org (please include your city, county, and state along with your e-mail message) or by using NEAR's toll-free phone number, 1-866-674-6327 or 1-866-NRG-NEAR. A number of State LIHEAP offices also have toll-free numbers (listed in the directory below).

Mr. Gareth D. Whitehead
Energy Section Supervisor
Alabama Department of Economic and Community Affairs
Community Services Division
P.O. Box 5690
Montgomery, Alabama 36103-5690
Tel.: (334) 242-4909
Fax: (334) 353-4311
E-mail: willie.whitehead@adeca.alabama.gov
Website: http://216.226.178.189/txtlstvw.aspx?LstID=d9aead61-987c-4dae-a648-c48bcff32da9
Public Inquiries: (800) 392-8098

Ms. Susan Marshall
LIHEAP Program Coordinator
Alaska Department of Health and Social Services
Division of Public Assistance
400 Willoughby, Suite 301
Juneau, Alaska 99801-1700
Tel.: (907) 465-3099
Fax: (907) 465-3319
E-mail: susan.marshall@alaska.gov
Website: www.hss.state.ak.us/dpa/programs/hap
Public Inquiries: (800) 470-3058

Ms. Sandra Mendez
LIHEAP Coordinator
Community Services Administration
Arizona Department of Economic Security
1789 W. Jefferson, Site Code 086Z
P.O. Box 6123
Phoenix, Arizona 85007
Tel.: (602) 542-6607
Fax: (602) 364-1756
E-mail: smendez@azdes.gov
Website: https://egov.azdes.gov/cmsinternet/intranet.aspx?id=2328&menu=34
Public Inquiries: (800) 582-5706

Ms. Cathy Rowe
Manager, Home Energy Assistance Program
Office of Community Services
Department of Human Services
P.O. Box 1437/Slot 1330
Little Rock, Arkansas 72203-1437
Tel.: (501) 682-8726
Fax: (501) 682-6736
E-mail: cathy.rowe@arkansas.gov
Website: www.arkansas.gov/dhs/dco/ocs
Public Inquiries: (800) 482-8988

Ms. Kathy Andry
Senior Manager
Department of Community Services and Development
P.O. Box 1947
Sacramento, California 95812-1947
Tel.: (916) 576-7109
Fax: (916) 263-1406
E-mail: kandry@csd.ca.gov
Website: www.csd.ca.gov
Public Inquiries: (866) 675-6623

Mr. Todd Jorgensen
LIHEAP Director
Colorado Department of Human Services
789 Sherman Street, Suite 440
Denver, Colorado 80203
Tel.: (303) 861-0325
Fax: (303) 861-0275
E-mail: todd.jorgensen@state.co.us
Website: www.cdhs.state.co.us/leap
Public Inquiries: (866) 432-8435 or (303) 861-0269

Ms. Carlene Taylor
Program Administration Manager
Community, Energy & Refugee Services
Department of Social Services
25 Sigourney Street, 10th Floor
Hartford, Connecticut 06106
Tel.: (860) 424-5889
Fax: (860) 424-4952
E-mail: carlene.taylor@ct.gov
Website: www.ct.gov/staywarm
Public Inquiries: (800) 842-1132

Ms. Leslie Lee
Energy Program Manager
Department of Health and Social Services
Division of State Service Centers
1901 N. DuPont Highway
New Castle, Delaware 19720
Tel.: (302) 255-9875
Fax: (302) 255-4463
E-mail: leslie.lee@state.de.us
(800) 464-HELP (4357)
New Castle County: (302) 654-9295
Kent County: (302) 674-1782
Sussex County: (302) 856-6310
Website: www.dhss.delaware.gov/dssc/liheap.html
Public Inquiries: (800) 464-HELP (4357)

Ms. Denise Watson
Supervisory Energy Program Specialist
District Department of the Environment
Energy Administration
2000 14th Street NW, Suite 300 East
Washington, D.C. 20009
Tel.: (202) 673-6709
Fax: (202) 673-6725
E-mail: denise.watson@dc.gov
Website: http://ddoe.dc.gov/ddoe/site/default.asp
Public Inquiries: (202) 673-6750 or 6700

Ms. Hilda Frazier
Community & Social Services Operations Manager
Department of Community Affairs
Bureau of Housing and Community Development
Community Assistance Section
2555 Shumard Oak Boulevard
Tallahassee, Florida 32399-2100
Tel.: (850) 488-7541
Fax: (850) 488-2488
E-mail: floridaliheap@dca.state.fl.us
Website: www.floridacommunitydevelopment.org/liheap/index.cfm
Public Inquiries: (850) 488-7541

Ms. Lynne Boring
Director
DHS/DFCS/State Office of Family Independence
2 Peachtree Street NW, Suite 21-440
Atlanta, Georgia 30303
Tel.: (404) 651-8701
Fax: (770) 357-8580
E-mail: laboring@dhr.state.ga.us
Website: www.heatga.org/assistance/assistance.asp
Public Inquiries: (800) 869-1150

Ms. Doreen Harada
Acting LIHEAP Coordinator
BESSD/FAP/LIHEAP
Benefit, Employment, and Support Services Division
Financial Assistance Office
820 Mililani Street, Suite 606
Honolulu, Hawaii 96813
Tel.: (808) 586-5734
Fax: (808) 586-5744
E-mail: dharada@dhs.hawaii.gov
Website: www.hawaii.gov/health/disability-services/neurotrauma/key-services-finance.html#liheap
Public Inquiries: (808) 586-5740

Ms. Genie Sue Weppner
Program Manager
Division of Welfare
Idaho Department of Health and Welfare
450 West State Street, 2nd Floor
Boise, Idaho 83702
Tel.: (208) 334-5656
Fax: (208) 334-5817
E-mail: weppnerg@dhw.idaho.gov
Information on applying for energy assistance: czamora@capai.org
Website: www.idahocommunityaction.org/programs/programsenergyassistance
Public Inquiries: (208) 442-9991 or (208) 442-9987

Mr. Larry Dawson
Deputy Director
Department of Commerce and Economic Opportunity
Office of Energy Assistance
100 West Randolph, Suite 3-400
Chicago, Illinois 60601
Tel.: (312) 814-2606
Fax: (312) 793-2798
E-mail: larry.dawson@illinois.gov
Website: www.ildceo.net/dceo/Bureaus/Energy+Assistance
Weatherization website: www.ildceo.net/dceo/Bureaus/Energy+Assistance/Illinois+Weatherization
Public Inquiries: 1-877-411-WARM (9276)

Mr. Tom Scott
Energy Assistance Program Manager
Indiana Housing and Community Development Authority
30 South Meridian Street, Suite 1000
Indianapolis, Indiana 46204
Tel.: (317) 232-7015
Fax: (317) 232-7778
E-mail: tscott@ihcda.in.gov
Website: www.in.gov/ihcda/2523.htm
Public Inquiries: (800) 872-0371

Mr. Jerry McKim
Chief, Bureau of Energy Assistance
Division of Community Action Agencies
Department of Human Rights
Lucas State Office Building
321 E. 12th Street, 2nd Floor
Des Moines, Iowa 50319
Tel.: (515) 281-0859
Fax: (515) 242-6119
E-mail: jerry.mckim@iowa.gov
Website: www.dcaa.iowa.gov/bureau_EA/index.html
Public Inquiries: (515) 281-3861

Ms. Winona Dickson
LIHEAP Program Manager
Kansas Social & Rehabilitation Services
915 SW Harrison Street, Suite 580
Topeka, Kansas 66612
Tel.: (785) 368-8122
Fax: (785) 296-6960
E-mail: winona.dickson@srs.ks.gov
Website: www.srskansas.org/ISD/ees/lieap.htm
Public Inquiries: (800) 432-0043

Ms. Sharon Vinyard
Policy Analyst
Department for Community Based Services
Division of Family Support
Human Resources Building
275 East Main Street, 3E-I
Frankfort, Kentucky 40601
Tel.: (502) 564-3440, Ext. 3023
Fax: (502) 564-0405
E-mail: sharon.vinyard@ky.gov
Website: http://chfs.ky.gov/dcbs/dfs/liheap.htm
Public Inquiries: (800) 456-3452

Ms. Darleen Okammor
Program Manager
Louisiana Housing Finance Agency
Energy Assistance Department
2415 Quail Drive
Baton Rouge, Louisiana 70808
Tel.: (225) 763-8700, Ext. 205
Fax: (225) 763-8752
E-mail: dokammor@lhfa.state.la.us
Website: www.lhfa.state.la.us/programs/energy_assistance/low_income_energy.php
Public Inquiries: (888) 454-2001

Ms. Jo-Ann Choate
LIHEAP Coordinator
National Energy Policy Advisor
Maine State Housing Authority
353 Water Street
Augusta, Maine 04330
Tel.: (207) 624-5708
Fax: (207) 624-5780
E-mail: jchoate@mainehousing.org
Website: www.mainehousing.org/ENERGYProgramsDetail.aspx?ProgramID=37
Public Inquiries: (800) 452-4668

Mr. Ralph Markus
Director
Office of Home Energy Programs
Department of Human Resources
311 West Saratoga Street
Baltimore, Maryland 21202
Tel.: (410) 767-7415
Fax: (410) 333-0079
E-mail: rmarkus@dhr.state.md.us
Website: www.dhr.state.md.us/ohep
Public Inquiries: (800) 352-1446

Mr. Gerald Bell
Director
Community Services Programs
Division of Community Services
Department of Housing and Community Development
100 Cambridge Street, Suite 300
Boston, Massachusetts 02114-2524
Tel.: (617) 573-1438
Fax: (617) 573-1460
E-mail: gerald.bell@state.ma.us
Website: www.mass.gov/dhcd/components/cs/Fuel/default.htm
Winter Heating Helpline website: www.mass.gov/?pageID=ocaconstituent&L=2&L0=Home&L1=Consumer&sid=Eoca
Public Inquiries: (800) 632-8175

Ms. Barbara Anders
Director, Adult and Family Services
Michigan Department of Human Services
Grand Tower Suite 1306
P.O. Box 30037
Lansing, Michigan 48909
Tel.: ((517) 335-6358
Fax: (517) 335-7771
E-mail: andersb@michigan.gov
Website: www.michigan.gov/dhs
Public Inquiries: (800) 292-5650

Mr. John Harvanko
Director, Office of Energy Assistance Programs
Minnesota Department of Commerce
85 7th Place East, Suite 500
St. Paul, Minnesota 55101-2198
Tel.: (651) 284-3275
Fax: (651) 297-7891
E-mail: john.harvanko@state.mn.us
Website: www.state.mn.us/portal/mn/jsp/content.do?id=-536881374&agency=Commerce
Public Inquiries: (800) 657-3710

Mr. Sollie Norwood
Director
Division of Community Services
Mississippi Dept. of Human Services
750 N. State Street
Jackson, Mississippi 39202-4772
Tel.: (601) 359-4768
Fax: (601) 359-4370
E-mail: sollie.norwood@mdhs.ms.gov
Website: www.mdhs.state.ms.us/cs_info.html
Public Inquiries: (800) 421-0762

Ms. Heather Jones
LIHEAP Manager
Family Support Division
Department of Social Services
615 Howerton Court
P.O. Box 2320
Jefferson City, Missouri 65102
Tel.: (573) 751-6789
Fax: (573) 526-5592
E-mail: heather.jones@dss.mo.gov
Website: www.dss.mo.gov/fsd/liheap.htm

Mr. Jim Nolan
Chief
Intergovernmental Human Services Bureau
Department of Public Health
and Human Services
1400 Carter Drive
Helena, Montana 59620
Tel.: (406) 447-4260
Fax: (406) 447-4287
E-mail: jnolan@mt.gov
Website: www.dphhs.mt.gov/programsservices/energyassistance/index.shtml
Public Inquiries: (800) 332-2272

Mr. Mike Kelly
Program and Planning Specialist
Program Assistance Unit
Department of Health and Human Services
301 Centennial Mall South, 4th Floor
P.O. Box 95026

Lincoln, Nebraska 68509
Tel.: (402) 471-3121
Fax: (402) 471-9597
E-mail: mike.kelly@nebraska.gov
Website: www.dhhs.ne.gov
Public Inquiries: (402) 471-3121

Ms. Lori Wilson
Chief, Employment & Support Services
Division of Welfare & Supportive Services
1470 College Parkway
Carson City, Nevada 89706
Fax: (775) 684-0617
E-mail: lwilson@dwss.nv.gov
Website: http://dwss.nv.gov/index.php?option=com_content&task=view&id=116&Itemid=279
Public Inquiries: (800) 992-0900 (EXT. 4420)
Las Vegas area: (702) 486-1404
Reno/Carson City: (775) 684-0730

Ms. Celeste Lovett
Fuel Assistance Program Manager
Office of Energy & Planning
4 Chennel Drive
Concord, New Hampshire 03301-8501
Tel.: (603) 271-2155
Fax: (603) 271-2615
E-mail: celeste.lovett@nh.gov
Website: www.nh.gov/oep/programs/fuelassistance/index.htm

Mr. Jose Sanchez
LIHEAP Coordinator
Department of Community Affairs
Division of Community Resources
Office of Low-Income Energy Conservation
101 South Broad Street
P.O. Box 811
Trenton, New Jersey 08625-08111
Tel.: (609) 984-6670
Fax: (609) 292-9798
E-mail: JSanchez@DCA.state.nj.us
Website: www.energyassistance.nj.gov
Public Inquiries: (800) 510-3102

Ms. Lori Williams
LIHEAP Program Manager
New Mexico Human Services Department
Income Support Division
Work & Family Support Bureau
P.O. Box 2348
Santa Fe, New Mexico 87504-8501
Tel.: (505) 383-2495
Toll-free: (888) 523-0051
Fax: (505) 383-2551
E-mail: loretta.williams@state.nm.us
Website: www.hsd.state.nm.us/isd/liheap.html
Public Inquiries: (800) 283-4465

Ms. Paula Cook
LIHEAP Coordinator
Division of Employment and Transitional Supports
New York State Office of Temporary and Disability Assistance
40 North Pearl Street
Albany, New York 12243-0001
Tel.: (518) 473-0332
Fax: (518) 474-9347
E-mail: NYSHEAP@dfa.state.ny.us
Website: http://otda.ny.gov/main/programs/heap
Public Inquiries: (800) 342-3009

Ms. Erica Jennings
Program Consultant
NCDHHS, Division of Social Services
Economic and Family Services Section
Food & Nutrition Servs. & Energy Programs
325 North Salisbury Street
Raleigh, North Carolina 27603-5905
Tel.: (919) 334-1224
Fax: (919) 334-1266
E-mail: erica.jennings@dhhs.nc.gov
Website: www.ncdhhs.gov/dss
Public Inquiries: (800) 662-7030 (CARE LINE)

Mr. Ron Knutson
Assistant Director of Energy & Nutrition
Department of Human Services
State Capitol Building, Judicial Wing
600 E. Boulevard, Dept. 325
Bismarck, North Dakota 58505-0250
Tel.: (701) 328-4882
Fax: (701) 328-1060
E-mail: rknutson@nd.gov
Website: www.nd.gov/dhs/services/financialhelp/energyassist.html
Public Inquiries: (800) 755-2716

Mr. Nick Sunday
Chief, OCS/HEAP
Ohio Department of Development
P.O. Box 1001
77 South High, 25th Floor
Columbus, Ohio 43216
Tel.: (614) 644-6846
Fax: (614) 728-6832
E-mail: nick.sunday@development.ohio.gov
Website: www.odod.state.oh.us/cdd/ocs/heap.htm
Public Inquiries: (800) 282-0880 (TDD: (800) 686-1557)

Ms. Kathie Wright
Program Field Representative
Oklahoma Department of Human Services
Family Support Services Division-SNAP/LIHEAP Section
P.O. Box 25352
Oklahoma City, Oklahoma 73125
Tel.: (405) 521-3444
Fax: (405) 521-4158
E-mail: LIHEAP2@okdhs.org
Website: www.okdhs.org/programsandservices/liheap
Public Inquiries: (866) 411-1877 or (405) 521-3444

Ms. Melissa Torgerson
LIHEAP Program Coordinator
Oregon Housing and Community Services
North Mall Office Building
725 Summer Street NE, Suite B
Salem, Oregon 97301-1266
Tel.: (503) 986-2094
Fax: (503) 986-2006
E-mail: melissa.torgerson@hcs.state.or.us
Website: www.oregon.gov/OHCS/SOS_Low_Income_Energy_Assistance_Oregon.shtml
Public Inquiries: (800) 453-5511

Mr. Edward J. Zogby
Director
Bureau of Policy
Office of Income Maintenance
Department of Public Welfare
P.O. Box 2675
Harrisburg, Pennsylvania 17105
Tel.: (717) 787-4081
Fax: (717) 787-6765
E-mail: LIHEAPMAIL@state.pa.us
Website: www.dpw.state.pa.us/foradults/heatingassistanceliheap/index.htm
ONLINE APPLICATION: www.humanservices.state.pa.us/compass/CMHOM.aspx
Public Inquiries: (866) 857-7095

Mr. Lewis Babbitt
Fiscal Management Officer
Office of Energy Resources
Department of Administration
One Capitol Hill
Providence, Rhode Island 02908-5850
Tel.: (401) 574-9103
Fax: (401) 574-9125
E-mail: lbabbitt@energy.ri.gov
Website: www.energy.ri.gov
Public Inquiries: (401) 574-9100

Ms. Bertie McKie
Senior Manager
Governor's Office of Economic Opportunity
1205 Pendleton Street, Suite 358
Columbia, South Carolina 29201
Tel.: (803) 734-0662
Fax: (803) 734-0356
E-mail: bmckie@oepp.sc.gov
Website: www.oepp.sc.gov/oeo/programs.htm

Mr. David Gall
Program Administrator
Office of Energy Assistance
Department of Social Services
206 West Missouri Avenue
Pierre, South Dakota 57501-4517
Tel.: (605) 773-4131
Fax: (605) 773-6657
E-mail: david.gall@state.sd.us
Website: http://dss.sd.gov/energyassistance/index.asp
Public Inquiries: (800) 233-8503

Ms. Pam Davenport
Director for Community Services
Department of Human Services
Citizens Plaza Building
400 Deaderick Street
Nashville, Tennessee 37248-9500
Tel.: (615) 313-4762
Fax: (615) 532-9956
E-mail: pam.davenport@tn.gov
Website: http://tennessee.gov/humanserv/adfam/afs_hea.html
Public Inquiries: (615) 313-4766

Ms. Cate Taylor
Planner, Energy Assistance
Texas Department of Housing & Community Affairs
Energy Assistance Section
P.O. Box 13941
Austin, Texas 78711-3941
Tel.: (512) 475-1435
Fax: (512) 475-3935
E-mail: cate.taylor@tdhca.state.tx.us
Website: www.tdhca.state.tx.us/ea/index.htm
Public Inquiries: (877) 399-8939
Lite-Up Texas: (866) 454-8387
PUBLIC UTILITY COMMISSION COMPLAINTS: (888) 782-8477

Mr. Sherman Roquiero
Director, State Energy Assistance & Lifeline (SEAL) Office
Division of Housing & Community Development
Utah Department of Community & Culture
324 South State, Suite 500
Salt Lake City, Utah 84111
Tel.: (801) 538-8644
Fax: (801) 538-8615
E-mail: shermr@utah.gov
Website: http://housing.utah.gov/seal/index.html
Public Inquiries: (877) 488-3233

Mr. Richard Moffi
Fuel Assistance Program Chief
Office of Home Heating Fuel Assistance
Department for Children and Families
103 South Main Street
Waterbury, Vermont 05676
Tel.: (802) 241-1097
Fax: (802) 241-4327
E-mail: richard.moffi@ahs.state.vt.us
Website: http://dcf.vermont.gov/esd/fuel_assistance
Public Inquiries: (800) 479-6151 or (802) 828-6896

Ms. Andrea Gregg
Program Manager
Virginia Department of Social Services
Energy Assistance Program
801 E. Main Street
Richmond, Virginia 23219
Tel.: (804) 726-7368
Fax: (804) 726-7358
E-mail: andrea.gregg@dss.virginia.gov
Website: www.dss.virginia.gov/benefit/ea/index.html
Public Inquiries: (800) 230-6977

Mr. Cinque R. Finnie
LIHEAP Contract Manager
Department of Commerce
906 Columbia Street, S.W.
P.O. Box 48350
Olympia, Washington 98504-8350
Tel.: (360) 725-2855
Fax: (360) 586-0489
E-mail: cinque.finnie@commerce.wa.gov
Website: www.liheapwa.org

Ms. Danita Jones
LIHEAP Director
Division of Family Assistance
West Virginia Department of Health and Human Resources
350 Capitol Street, Rm B-18
Charleston, West Virginia 25301-3704
Tel.: (304) 558-8290
Fax: (304) 558-2059
E-Mail: danita.d.jones@wv.gov
Website: www.wvdhhr.org/bcf/family_assistance/utility.asp
Public Inquiries: (800) 642-8589

Ms. Susan Brown
Deputy Administrator
Wisconsin Department of Administration
Division of Energy Services
P.O. Box 7868
Madison, Wisconsin 53707-7868
Tel.: (608) 267-3680
Fax: (608) 267-6931
E-mail: heat@wisconsin.gov
Website: www.homeenergyplus.wi.gov
Public Inquiries: (866) 432-8947

Ms. Brenda Ilg
Program Manager
LIHEAP/Weatherization Programs
Department of Family Services
2300 Capitol Avenue
Hathaway Building, 3rd Floor
Cheyenne, Wyoming 82002-0490
Tel.: (307) 777-6346
Fax: (307) 777-6276
E-mail: BILG@state.wy.us
Website: http://dfsweb.state.wy.us/economic-assistance/lieap/index.html
Public Inquiries: (800) 246-4221

C.4 LIHEAP Profile

The information in this table is from documents and preliminary estimates by the U.S. Department of Health and Human Services (DHHS), Administration for Children and Families, Division of Energy Assistance. DHHS documents include the annual reports to Congress on LIHEAP for fiscal years 1985–2007, the LIHEAP Home Energy Notebook for fiscal years 1995–2008, and DHHS LIHEAP appropriations summaries.
For purposes of analysis, the projected average heating benefit assumes no decline in the number of households served, and the projected total number of households assisted assumes no decrease in average benefit.

Fiscal Year	Funding[1] in Billions of $$[2]	Avg. Benefit (heating/crisis)[3]	Avg. Benefit (cooling; summer crisis)[4]	Number of Households Served (heating/crisis)	Number of Households at the Maximum Income Eligibility Standard
1981	$1.850 ($1.850)	$213	$129	7.1 million	19.7 million
1982	$1.752 ($1.875)	$202	N/A	6.3 million	22 million
1983	$1.975 ($1.975)	$225	$62	6.8 million	22.2 million
1984	$1.875 ($2.075)	$236	N/A	6.8 million	22.7 million
1985	$2.100 ($2.100)	$242	$57	6.8 million	22.8 million
1986	$2.010 ($2.010)	$231	N/A	6.7 million	23.4 million
1987	$1.825 ($1.825)	$216	$79	6.8 million	24.1 million
1988	$1.532 ($1.532)	$217	N/A	6.2 million	24.8 million
1989	$1.383 ($1.383)	$204	$97; $95	5.9 million	25.2 million
1990	$1.393 ($1.443)	$209	$70	5.8 million	25.4 million

Fiscal Year	Funding[1] in Billions of $$[2]	Avg. Benefit (heating/crisis)[3]	Avg. Benefit (cooling; summer crisis)[4]	Number of Households Served (heating/crisis)	Number of Households at the Maximum Income Eligibility Standard
1991	$1.415 ($1.610)	$215	$73; $105	6.1 million	25.9 million
1992	$1.475 ($1.500)	$190	$59; $137	6.2 million	27.5 million
1993	$1.321 ($1.346)	$201	$141	5.6 million	28.4 million
1994	$1.412 ($1.737)	$211	$171; $95	6.1 million	29 million
1995	$1.289 ($1.419)	$198	$129; $202	5.5 million	24 million
1996	$0.878 ($1.080)	$203	$137; $106	4.2 million	27.8 million
1997	$0.975 ($1.215)	$213	$136	4.3 million	29 million
1998	$0.975 ($1.160)	$213	$235	3.9 million	29.1 million
1999	$1.073 ($1.275)	$237	$137	3.6 million	29.2 million
2000	$1.072 ($1.844)	$271	$206	3.9 million	29.4 million
2001	$1.372 ($1.856)	$364	$211	4.8 million	30.4 million
2002	$1.673 ($1.800)	$291	$145	4.4 million	32.7 million
2003	$1.761 ($1.988)	$312	N/A	4.8 million	34.7 million
2004	$1.762 ($1.889)	$277	$192	5 million	35.4 million
2005	$1.858 ($2.182)	$304	$197	5.3 million	34.8 million
2006	$2.453 ($3.080)	$317	$223	5.5 million	34.4 million
2007	$1.98 ($2.188)	$320	$171	5.3 million	33.6 million
2008	$1.980 ($2.591)	N/A	N/A	N/A	N/A
2009	$4.48 ($5.1)	N/A	N/A	N/A	N/A
2010	$4.48 ($5.1)	N/A	N/A	N/A	N/A
2011	$4.5 ($4.7)	N/A	N/A	N/A	N/A

1 The amount appropriated for the regular LIHEAP block grant to the states and, in parenthesis, the total appropriated for LIHEAP when adding in amounts appropriated for the Leveraging/REACH funds and LIHEAP emergency contingency funds. The LIHEAP emergency contingency funds are released at the discretion of the President in response to a legislatively defined set of crises.

2 Administration for Children & Families, U.S. Dep't of Health & Human Servs., LIHEAP Appropriations Chart, *available at* www.acf.hhs.gov/programs/ocs/liheap/funding/total09.

3 This information is taken from the U.S. Department of Health and Human Services annual reports to Congress on LIHEAP for fiscal years 1985–2006 and the U.S. Department of Health and Human Services' LIHEAP Home Energy Notebooks for FY 1995–2007.

4 This information is taken from the U.S. Department of Health and Human Services annual reports to Congress on LIHEAP for fiscal years 1985–2006 and the U.S. Department of Health and Human Services' LIHEAP Home Energy Notebooks for FY 1995–2007. The combined average benefit level for cooling plus summer crisis assistance were not provided until the FY 2000 report to Congress. There may be households that received both forms of assistance.

Appendix D The Department of Energy's Weatherization Assistance Program

This appendix is also available on the companion website to this treatise. The companion website facilitates keyword searches and allows relevant provisions to be imported as word-processing documents.

D.1 Weatherization Assistance Program Legislation—42 U.S.C. §§ 6861–6873

ELECTRIC UTILITY RATE DESIGN INITIATIVES

42 U.S.C. § 6861. Congressional findings and purpose

(a) Findings
The Congress finds that—

(1) a fast, cost-effective, and environmentally sound way to prevent future energy shortages in the United States while reducing the Nation's dependence on imported energy supplies, is to encourage and facilitate, through major programs, the implementation of energy conservation and renewable-resource energy measures with respect to dwelling units;

(2) existing efforts to encourage and facilitate such measures are inadequate because—

(A) many dwellings owned or occupied by low-income persons are energy inefficient;

(B) low-income persons can least afford to make the modifications necessary to provide for efficient energy equipment in such dwellings and otherwise to improve the energy efficiency of such dwellings;

(3) weatherization of such dwellings would lower shelter costs in dwellings owned or occupied by low-income persons as well as save energy and reduce future energy capacity requirements; and

(4) States, through Community Action Agencies established under the Economic Opportunity Act of 1964 (42 U.S.C. § 2701 *et seq.*) and units of general purpose local government, should be encouraged, with Federal financial and technical assistance, to develop and support coordinated weatherization programs designed to alleviate the adverse effects of energy costs on such low-income persons, to supplement other Federal programs serving such low-income persons, and to increase energy efficiency.

(b) Purpose
It is, therefore, the purpose of this part to develop and implement a weatherization assistance program to increase the energy efficiency of dwellings owned or occupied by low-income persons, reduce their total residential energy expenditures, and improve their health and safety, especially low-income persons who are particularly vulnerable such as the elderly, the handicapped, and children.

[Pub. L. No. 94-385, tit. IV, § 411, 90 Stat. 1151 (Aug. 14, 1976); Pub. L. No. 101-440, § 7(j), 104 Stat. 1015 (Oct. 18, 1990)]

42 U.S.C. § 6862. Definitions

As used in this part:

(1) The term "Secretary" means the Secretary of Energy.

(2) The term "Director" means the Director of the Community Services Administration.

(3) The term "elderly" means any individual who is 60 years of age or older.

(4) The term "Governor" means the chief executive officer of a State (including the Mayor of the District of Columbia).

(5) The term "handicapped person" means any individual (A) who is an individual with a disability, as defined in section 705 of title 29, (B) who is under a disability as defined in section 1614(a)(3)(A) or 233(d)(1) of the Social Security Act (42 U.S.C. §§ 1382c(a)(3)(A), 423(d)(1)) or in section 102(7) of the Developmental Disabilities Services and Facilities Construction Act (42 U.S.C. § 6001(7)), or (C) who is receiving benefits under chapter 11 or 15 of title 38.

(6) The terms "Indian," "Indian tribe," and "tribal organization" have the meanings prescribed for such terms by section 102 of the Older Americans Act of 1965 (42 U.S.C. § 3002).

(7) The term "low-income" means that income in relation to family size which (A) is at or below 200 percent of the poverty level determined in accordance with criteria established by the Director of the Office of Management and Budget, except that the Secretary may establish a higher level if the Secretary, after consulting with the Secretary of Agriculture and the Director of the Community Services Administration, determines that such a higher level is necessary to carry out the purposes of this part and is consistent with the eligibility criteria established for the weatherization program under section 2809(a)(12) of this title, (B) is the basis on which cash assistance payments have been paid during the preceding 12-month period under titles IV and XVI of the Social Security Act (42 U.S.C. §§ 601 *et seq.*, 1381 *et seq.*) or applicable State or local law, or (C) if a State elects, is the basis for eligibility for assistance under the Low-Income Home Energy Assistance Act of 1981 (42 U.S.C. § 8621), provided that such basis is at least 200 percent of the poverty level determined in accordance with criteria established by the Director of the Office of Management and Budget.

(8) The term "State" means—

(A) a State;

(B) the District of Columbia;

(C) the Commonwealth of Puerto Rico; and

(D) any other territory or possession of the United States.

(9) The term "weatherization materials" means—

(A) caulking and weatherstripping of doors and windows;

(B) furnace efficiency modifications, including, but not limited to—

(i) replacement burners, furnaces, or boilers or any combination thereof;

(ii) devices for minimizing energy loss through heating system, chimney, or venting devices; and

(iii) electrical or mechanical furnace ignition systems which replace standing gas pilot lights;

(C) clock thermostats;

(D) ceiling, attic, wall, floor, and duct insulation;

(E) water heater insulation;

(F) storm windows and doors, multiglazed windows and doors, heat-absorbing or heat-reflective window and door materials;

(G) cooling efficiency modifications, including, but not limited to, replacement air-conditioners, ventilation equipment, screening, window films, and shading devices;

(H) solar thermal water heaters;

(I) wood-heating appliances; and

(J) such other insulating or energy conserving devices or technologies as the Secretary may determine, after consulting with the Secretary of Housing and Urban Development, the Secretary of Agriculture, and the Director, of the Community Services Administration.

[Pub. L. No. 94-385, tit. IV, § 412, 90 Stat. 1152 (Aug. 14, 1976); Pub. L. No. 95-602, tit. I, § 122(e), 92 Stat. 2987 (Nov. 6, 1978); Pub. L. No. 95-619, tit. II, § 231(a)(1), (b)(2), 92 Stat. 3224, 3225 (Nov. 9, 1978); Pub. L. No. 96-294, tit. V, § 577(1), (2), 94 Stat. 760 (June 30, 1980); Pub. L. No. 98-558, tit. IV, §§ 401, 402, 98 Stat. 2887 (Oct. 30, 1984); Pub. L. No. 100-242, tit. V, § 570(d), 101 Stat. 1950 (Feb. 5, 1988); Pub. L. No. 101-440, § 7(a), 104 Stat. 1012 (Oct. 18, 1990); Pub. L. No. 102-486, tit. I, § 142(b), 106 Stat. 2843 (Oct. 24, 1992); Pub. L. No. 105-220, tit. IV, § 414(f), 112 Stat. 1242 (Aug. 7, 1998); Pub. L. No. 109-58, tit. I, § 122(b), 119 Stat. 616 (Aug. 8, 2005); Pub. L. No. 109-365, 120 Stat. 2522 (Oct. 17, 2006); Pub. L. No. 110-140, tit. IV, § 411(a), 121 Stat. 1600 (Dec. 19, 2007); Pub. L. No. 111-5, div. A, tit. IV, § 407(b), (e), 123 Stat. 146 (Feb. 17, 2009)]

42 U.S.C. § 6863. Weatherization program

(a) Development and conduct of program by Secretary; grants to States and Indian tribal organizations

The Secretary shall develop and conduct, in accordance with the purpose and provisions of this part, a weatherization program. In developing and conducting such program, the Secretary may, in accordance with this part and regulations promulgated under this part, make grants

(1) to States, and

(2) in accordance with the provisions of subsection (d) of this section, to Indian tribal organizations to serve Native Americans. Such grants shall be made for the purpose of providing financial assistance with regard to projects designed to provide for the weatherization of dwelling units, particularly those where elderly or handicapped low-income persons reside, occupied by low-income families.

(b) Consultation by Secretary with other Federal departments and agencies on development and publication in Federal Register of proposed regulations; required regulatory provisions; standards and procedures; rental units

(1) The Secretary, after consultation with the Director, the Secretary of Housing and Urban Development, the Secretary of Health and Human Services, the Secretary of Labor, and the heads of such other Federal departments and agencies as the Secretary deems appropriate, shall develop and publish in the Federal Register for public comment, not later than 60 days after August 14, 1976, proposed regulations to carry out the provisions of this part. The Secretary shall take into consideration comments submitted regarding such proposed regulations and shall promulgate and publish final regulations for such purpose not later than 90 days after August 14, 1976. The development of regulations under this part shall be fully coordinated with the Director.

(2) The regulations promulgated pursuant to this section shall include provisions—

(A) prescribing, in coordination with the Secretary of Housing and Urban Development, the Secretary of Health and Human Services, and the Director of the National Institute of Standards and Technology in the Department of Commerce, for use in various climatic, structural, and human need settings, standards for weatherization materials, energy conservation techniques, and balance combinations thereof, which are designed to achieve a balance of a healthful dwelling environment and maximum practicable energy conservation;

(B) that provide guidance to the States in the implementation of this part, including guidance designed to ensure that a State establishes (i) procedures that provide protection under paragraph (5) to tenants paying for energy as a portion of their rent, and (ii) a process for monitoring compliance with its obligations pursuant to this part; and

(C) that secure the Federal investment made under this part and address the issues of eviction from and sale of property receiving weatherization materials under this part.

(3) The Secretary, in coordination with the Secretaries and Director described in paragraph (2)(A) and with the Director of the Community Services Administration and the Secretary of Agriculture, shall develop and publish in the Federal Register for public comment, not later than 60 days after November 9, 1978, proposed amendments to the regulations prescribed under paragraph (1). Such amendments shall provide that the standards described in paragraph (2)(A) shall include a set of procedures to be applied to each dwelling unit to determine the optimum set of cost-effective measures, within the cost guidelines set for the program, to be installed in such dwelling unit. Such standards shall, in order to achieve such optimum savings of energy, take into consideration the following factors—

(A) the cost of the weatherization material;

(B) variation in climate; and

(C) the value of energy saved by the application of the weatherization material.

Such standards shall be utilized by the Secretary in carrying out this part, the Secretary of Agriculture in carrying out the weatherization program under section 1474(c) of this title, and the Director of the Community Services Administration in carrying out weatherization programs under section 222(a)(12) of the Economic Opportunity Act of 1964 (42 U.S.C. § 2809(a)(12)). The Secretary shall take into consideration comments submitted regarding such proposed amendment and shall promulgate and publish final amended regulations not later than 120 days after November 9, 1978.

(4) In carrying out paragraphs (2)(A) and (3), the Secretary shall establish the standards and procedures described in such paragraphs so that weatherization efforts being carried out under this part and under programs described in the fourth sentence of paragraph (3) will accomplish uniform results among the States in any area with a similar climatic condition.

(5) In any case in which a dwelling consists of a rental unit or rental units, the State, in the implementation of this part, shall ensure that—

(A) the benefits of weatherization assistance in connection with such rental units, including units where the tenants pay for their energy through their rent, will accrue primarily to the low-income tenants residing in such units;

(B) for a reasonable period of time after weatherization work has been completed on a dwelling containing a unit occupied by an eligible household, the tenants in that unit (including households paying for their energy through their rent) will not be subjected to rent increases unless those increases are demonstrably related to matters other than the weatherization work performed;

(C) the enforcement of subparagraph (B) is provided through procedures established by the State by which tenants may file complaints and owners, in response to such complaints, shall demonstrate that the rent increase concerned is related to matters other than the weatherization work performed; and

(D) no undue or excessive enhancement will occur to the value of such dwelling units.

(6) As a condition of having assistance provided under this part with respect to multifamily buildings, a State may require financial participation from the owners of such buildings.

(c) Failure of State to submit application; alternate application by any unit of general purpose local government or community action agency; submission of amended application by State

If a State does not, within 90 days after the date on which final regulations are promulgated under this section, submit an application to the Secretary which meets the requirements set forth in section 6864 of this title, any unit of general purpose local government of sufficient size (as determined by the Secretary), or a community action agency carrying out programs under title II of the Economic Opportunity Act of 1964 (42 U.S.C. § 2781 *et seq.*), may, in lieu of such State, submit an application (meeting such requirements and subject to all other provisions of this part) for carrying out projects under this part within the geographical area which is subject to the jurisdiction of such government or is served by such agency. A State may, in accordance with regulations promulgated under this part, submit an amended application.

(d) Direct grants to low-income members of Indian tribal organizations or alternate service organizations; application for funds

(1) Notwithstanding any other provision of this part, in any State in which the Secretary determines (after having taken into account the amount of funds made available to the State to carry out the purposes of this part) that the low-income members of an Indian tribe are not receiving benefits under this part that are equivalent to the assistance provided to other low-income persons in such State under this part, and if he further determines that the members of such tribe would be better served by means of a grant made directly to provide such assistance, he shall reserve from sums that would otherwise be allocated to such State under this part not less than 100 percent, nor more than 150 percent, of an amount which bears the same ratio to the State's allocation for the fiscal year involved as the population of all low-income Indians for whom a determination under this subsection has been made bears to the population of all low-income persons in such State.

(2) The sums reserved by the Secretary on the basis of his determination under this subsection shall be granted to the tribal organization serving the individuals for whom such a determination has been made, or, where there is no tribal organization, to such other entity as he determines has the capacity to provide services pursuant to this part.

(3) In order for a tribal organization or other entity to be eligible for a grant for a fiscal year under this subsection, it shall submit to the Secretary an application meeting the requirements set forth in section 6864 of this title.

(e) Transfer of funds

Notwithstanding any other provision of law, the Secretary may transfer to the Director sums appropriated under this part to be utilized in order to carry out programs, under section 222(a)(12) of the Economic Opportunity Act of 1964 (42 U.S.C. 2809(a)(12)), which further the purpose of this part.

[Pub. L. No. 94-385, tit. IV, § 413, 90 Stat. 1152 (Aug. 14, 1976); Pub. L. No. 95-619, tit. II, § 231(a)(2), (b)(1), 92 Stat. 3224 (Nov. 9, 1978); Pub. L. No. 96-294, tit. V, §§ 573(b), 574, 577(2), 94 Stat. 759, 760 (June 30, 1980); Pub. L. No. 98-479, tit. II, § 201(h), 98 Stat. 2228 (Oct. 17, 1984); Pub. L. No. 100-418, tit. V, § 5115(c), 102 Stat. 1433 (Aug. 23, 1988); Pub. L. No. 101-440, § 7(b), 104 Stat. 1012 (Oct. 18, 1990); Pub. L. No. 103-82, tit. IV, § 405(l), 107 Stat. 922 (Sept. 21, 1993)]

42 U.S.C. § 6864. Financial assistance

(a) Annual application; contents; allocation to States
The Secretary shall provide financial assistance, from sums appropriated for any fiscal year under this part, only upon annual application. Each such application shall describe the estimated number and characteristics of the low-income persons and the number of dwelling units to be assisted and the criteria and methods to be used by the applicant in providing weatherization assistance to such persons. The application shall also contain such other information (including information needed for evaluation purposes) and assurances as may be required (1) in the regulations promulgated pursuant to section 6863 of this title and (2) to carry out this section. The Secretary shall allocate financial assistance to each State on the basis of the relative need for weatherization assistance among low-income persons throughout the States, taking into account the following factors:

(A) The number of dwelling units to be weatherized.
(B) The climatic conditions in the State respecting energy conservation, which may include consideration of annual degree days.
(C) The type of weatherization work to be done in the various settings.
(D) Such other factors as the Secretary may determine necessary, such as the cost of heating and cooling, in order to carry out the purpose and provisions of this part.

(b) Requirements for assistance
The Secretary shall not provide financial assistance under this part unless the applicant has provided reasonable assurances that it has—
(1) established a policy advisory council which (A) has special qualifications and sensitivity with respect to solving the problems of low-income persons (including the weatherization and energy-conservation problems of such persons), (B) is broadly representative of organizations and agencies which are providing services to such persons in the State or geographical area in question, and (C) is responsible for advising the responsible official or agency administering the allocation of financial assistance in such State or area with respect to the development and implementation of such weatherization assistance program;
(2) established priorities to govern the provision of weatherization assistance to low-income persons, including methods to provide priority to elderly and handicapped low-income persons, and such priority as the applicant determines is appropriate for single-family or other high-energy-consuming dwelling units;
(3) established policies and procedures designed to assure that financial assistance provided under this part will be used to supplement, and not to supplant, State or local funds, and, to the extent practicable, to increase the amounts of such funds that would be made available in the absence of Federal funds for carrying out the purpose of this part, including plans and procedures (A) for securing, to the maximum extent practicable, the services of volunteers and training participants and public service employment workers, pursuant to title I of the Workforce Investment Act of 1998 (29 U.S.C. § 2801 *et seq.*), to work under the supervision of qualified supervisors and foremen, (B) for using Federal financial assistance under this part to increase the portion of low-income weatherization assistance that the State obtains from non-Federal sources, including private sources, and (C) for complying with the limitations set forth in section 6865 of this title; and
(4) selected on the basis of public comment received during a public hearing conducted pursuant to section 6865(b)(1) of this title, and other appropriate findings, community action agencies or other public or nonprofit entities to undertake the weatherization activities authorized by this subchapter: *Provided*, Such selection shall be based on the agency's experience and performance in weatherization or housing renovation activities, experience in assisting low-income persons in the area to be served, and the capacity to undertake a timely and effective weatherization program: *Provided further*, That in making such selection preference shall be given to any community action agency or other public or nonprofit entity which has, or is currently administering, an effective program under this subchapter or under title II of the Economic Opportunity Act of 1964 (42 U.S.C. § 2781 *et seq.*).

(c) Annual update of data used in allocating funds
Effective with fiscal year 1991, and annually thereafter, the Secretary shall update the population, eligible households, climatic, residential energy use, and all other data used in allocating the funds under this part among the States pursuant to subsection (a) of this section.

[Pub. L. No. 94-385, tit. IV, § 414, 90 Stat. 1154 (Aug. 14, 1976); Pub. L. No. 96-294, tit. V, §§ 573(c), 577(2), 94 Stat. 759, 760 (June 30, 1980); Pub. L. No. 101-440, § 7(c), (g), 104 Stat. 1012, 1014 (v) (Oct. 18, 1990); Pub. L. No. 105-277, div. A, § 101(f) (tit. VIII, § 405(d)(38), (f)(29)), 112 Stat. 2681-337, 2681-427, 2681-434 (Oct. 21, 1998)]

42 U.S.C. § 6864a. Private sector investments

(a) In general
The Secretary shall, to the extent funds are made available for such purpose, provide financial assistance to entities receiving funding from the Federal Government or from a State through a weatherization assistance program under section 6863 or section 6864 of this title for the development and initial implementation of partnerships, agreements, or other arrangements with utilities, private sector interests, or other institutions, under which non-Federal financial assistance would be made available to support programs which install energy efficiency improvements in low-income housing.

(b) Use of funds

Financial assistance provided under this section may be used for—

(1) the negotiation of such partnerships, agreements and other arrangements;

(2) the presentation of arguments before State or local agencies;

(3) expert advice on the development of such partnerships, agreements, and other arrangements; or

(4) other activities reasonably associated with the development and initial implementation of such arrangements.

(c) Conditions

(1) Financial assistance provided under this section to entities other than States shall, to the extent practicable, coincide with the timing of financial assistance provided to such entities under section 6863 or section 6864 of this title.

(2) Not less than 80 percent of amounts provided under this section shall be provided to entities other than States.

(3) A recipient of financial assistance under this section shall have up to three years to complete projects undertaken with such assistance.

[Pub. L. No. 94-385, tit. IV, § 414A, *as added by* Pub. L. No. 102-486, tit. I, § 142(a), 106 Stat. 2842 (Oct. 24, 1992)]

42 U.S.C. § 6864b. Technical transfer grants

(a) In general

The Secretary may, to the extent funds are made available, provide financial assistance to entities receiving funding from the Federal Government or from a State through a weatherization assistance program under section 6863 or section 6864 of this title for—

(1) evaluating technical and management measures which increase program and/or private entity performance in weatherizing low-income housing;

(2) producing technical information for use by persons involved in weatherizing low-income housing;

(3) exchanging information; and

(4) conducting training programs for persons involved in weatherizing low-income housing.

(b) Conditions

(1) Not less than 50 percent of amounts provided under this section shall be awarded to entities other than States.

(2) A recipient of financial assistance under this section may contract with nonprofit entities to carry out all or part of the activities for which such financial assistance is provided.

[Pub. L. No. 94-385, tit. IV, § 414B, *as added by* Pub. L. No. 102-486, tit. I, § 142(a), 106 Stat. 2842 (Oct. 24, 1992)]

42 U.S.C. § 6865. Limitations on financial assistance

(a) Purchase of materials and administration of projects

(1) Not more than an amount equal to 10 percent of any grant made by the Secretary under this part may be used for administrative purposes in carrying out duties under this part, except that not more than one-half of such amount may be used by any State for such purposes, and a State may provide in the plan adopted pursuant to subsection (b) of this section for recipients of grants of less than $350,000 to use up to an additional 5 percent of such grant for administration if the State has determined that such recipient requires such additional amount to implement effectively the administrative requirements established by the Secretary pursuant to this part.

(2) The Secretary shall establish energy audit procedures and techniques which (i) meet standards established by the Secretary after consultation with the State Energy Advisory Board established under section 6325(g) of this title, (ii) establish priorities for selection of weatherization measures based on their cost and contribution to energy efficiency, (iii) measure the energy requirement of individual dwellings and the rate of return of the total conservation investment in a dwelling, and (iv) account for interaction among energy efficiency measures.

(b) Allocation, termination or discontinuance by Secretary

The Secretary shall insure that financial assistance provided under this part will—

(1) be allocated within the State or area in accordance with a published State or area plan, which is adopted by such State after notice and a public hearing, describing the proposed funding distributions and recipients;

(2) be allocated, pursuant to such State or area plan, to community action agencies carrying out programs under title II of the Economic Opportunity Act of 1964 (42 U.S.C. § 2781 *et seq.*) or to other appropriate and qualified public or nonprofit entities in such State or area so that—

(A) funds will be allocated on the basis of the relative need for weatherization assistance among the low-income persons within such State or area, taking into account appropriate climatic and energy conservation factors; and

(B) due consideration will be given to the results of periodic evaluations of the projects carried out under this part in light of available information regarding the current and anticipated energy and weatherization needs of low-income persons within the State; and

(3) be terminated or discontinued during the application period only in accordance with policies and procedures consistent with the policies and procedures set forth in section 6868 of this title.

(c) Limitations on expenditures; exceptions; annual adjustments

(1) Except as provided in paragraphs (3) and (4), the expenditure of financial assistance provided under this part for labor, weatherization materials, and related matters shall not exceed an average of $6,500 per dwelling unit weatherized in that State. Labor, weatherization materials, and related matter includes, but is not limited to—

(A) the appropriate portion of the cost of tools and equipment used to install weatherization materials for a dwelling unit;

(B) the cost of transporting labor, tools, and materials to a dwelling unit;

(C) the cost of having onsite supervisory personnel;

(D) the cost of making incidental repairs to a dwelling unit if such repairs are necessary to make the installation of weatherization materials effective; and

(E) the cost of making heating and cooling modifications, including replacement.

(2) Dwelling units partially weatherized under this part or under other Federal programs during the period September 30, 1975, through September 30, 1994, may receive further financial assistance for weatherization under this part.

(3) Beginning with fiscal year 2000, the dwelling unit averages provided in paragraphs (1) and (4) shall be adjusted annually by increasing the average amount by an amount equal to—

(A) the limitation amount for the previous fiscal year, multiplied by

(B) the lesser of (i) the percentage increase in the Consumer Price Index (all items, United States city average) for the most recent calendar year completed before the beginning of the fiscal year for which the determination is being made, or (ii) three percent.

(4) The expenditure of financial assistance provided under this part for labor, weatherization materials, and related matters for a renewable energy system shall not exceed an average of $3,000 per dwelling unit.

(5)(A) The Secretary shall by regulations—

(i) establish the criteria which are to be used in prescribing performance and quality standards under paragraph (6)(A)(ii) or in specifying any form of renewable energy under paragraph (6)(A)(i)(I); and

(ii) establish a procedure under which a manufacturer of an item may request the Secretary to certify that the item will be treated, for purposes of this paragraph, as a renewable energy system.

(B) The Secretary shall make a final determination with respect to any request filed under subparagraph (A)(ii) within 1 year after the filing of the request, together with any information required to be filed with such request under subparagraph (A)(ii).

(C) Each month the Secretary shall publish a report of any request under subparagraph (A)(ii) which has been denied during the preceding month and the reasons for the denial.

(D) The Secretary shall not specify any form of renewable energy under paragraph (6)(A)(i)(I) unless the Secretary determines that—

(i) there will be a reduction in oil or natural gas consumption as a result of such specification;

(ii) such specification will not result in an increased use of any item which is known to be, or reasonably suspected to be, environmentally hazardous or a threat to public health or safety; and

(iii) available Federal subsidies do not make such specification unnecessary or inappropriate (in the light of the most advantageous allocation of economic resources).

(6) In this subsection—

(A) the term "renewable energy system" means a system which—

(i) when installed in connection with a dwelling, transmits or uses—

(I) solar energy, energy derived from the geothermal deposits, energy derived from biomass, or any other form of renewable energy which the Secretary specifies by regulations, for the purpose of heating or cooling such dwelling or providing hot water or electricity for use within such dwelling; or

(II) wind energy for nonbusiness residential purposes;

(ii) meets the performance and quality standards (if any) which have been prescribed by the Secretary by regulations;

(iii) in the case of a combustion rated system, has a thermal efficiency rating of at least 75 percent; and

(iv) in the case of a solar system, has a thermal efficiency rating of at least 15 percent; and

(B) the term "biomass" means any organic matter that is available on a renewable or recurring basis, including agricultural crops and trees, wood and wood wastes and residues, plants (including aquatic plants), grasses, residues, fibers, and animal wastes, municipal wastes, and other waste materials.

(d) Supplementary financial assistance to States

Beginning with fiscal year 1992, the Secretary may allocate funds appropriated pursuant to section 6872(b) of this title to provide supplementary financial assistance to those States which the Secretary determines have achieved the best performance during the previous fiscal year in achieving the purposes of this part. In making this determination, the Secretary shall—

(1) consult with the State Energy Advisory Board established under section 6325(g) of this title; and

(2) give priority to those States which, during such previous fiscal year, obtained a significant portion of income from non-Federal sources for their weatherization programs or increased significantly the portion of low-income weatherization assistance that the State obtained from non-Federal sources.

(e) Supplementary financial assistance to grant recipients

(1)

(A) Beginning with fiscal year 1992, the Secretary may allocate, from funds appropriated pursuant to section 6872(b) of this title, among the States an equal amount for each State not to exceed $100,000 per State. Each State shall make available amounts received under this subsection to provide supplementary financial assistance to recipients of grants under this part that have achieved the best performance during the previous fiscal year in advancing the purposes of this part.

(B) None of the funds made available under this subsection may be used by any State for administrative purposes.

(2) The Secretary shall, after consulting with the State Energy Advisory Board referred to in subsection (d)(1) of this section, prescribe guidelines to be used by each State in making available supplementary financial assistance under this subsection, with a priority being given to subgrantees that, by law or through administrative or other executive action, provided non-Federal resources (including private resources) to supplement Federal financial assistance under this part during the previous fiscal year.

[Pub. L. No. 94-385, tit. IV, § 415, 90 Stat. 1155 (Aug. 14, 1976); Pub. L. No. 95-619, tit. II, § 231(c), 92 Stat. 3225 (Nov. 9, 1978); Pub. L. No. 96-294, tit. V, §§ 571, 572, 573(a), 575, 577(2), 94 Stat. 759, 760 (June 30, 1980); Pub. L. No. 98-558, tit. IV, §§ 403, 404, 98 Stat. 2887, 2888 (Oct. 30, 1984); Pub. L. No. 101-440, § 7(d)–(f), (i), 104 Stat. 1013, 1014 (Oct. 18, 1990); Pub. L. No. 106-469, 114 Stat. 2029 (Nov. 9, 2000); Pub. L. No. 109-58, tit. II, § 206(a), 119 Stat. 654 (Aug. 8, 2005); Pub. L. No. 111-5, div. A, tit. IV, § 407(b), (e), 123 Stat. 146 (Feb. 17, 2009)]

42 U.S.C. § 6866. Monitoring and evaluation of funded projects; technical assistance; limitation on assistance

The Secretary, in coordination with the Director, shall monitor and evaluate the operation of projects receiving financial assistance under this part through methods provided for in section 6867(a) of this title, through onsite inspections, or through other means, in order to assure the effective provision of weatherization assistance for the dwelling units of low-income persons. The Secretary shall also carry out periodic evaluations of the program authorized by this part and projects receiving financial assistance under this part. The Secretary may provide technical assistance to any such project, directly and through persons and entities with a demonstrated capacity in developing and implementing appropriate technology for enhancing the effectiveness of the provision of weatherization assistance to the dwelling units of low-income persons, utilizing in any fiscal year not to exceed up to 20 percent of the sums appropriated for such year under this part.

[Pub. L. No. 94-385, tit. IV, § 416, 90 Stat. 1156 (Aug. 14, 1976); Pub. L. No. 96-294, tit. V, § 577(2), 94 Stat. 760 (June 30, 1980); Pub. L. No. 111-5, div. A, tit. IV, § 407(b), (e), 123 Stat. 146 (Feb. 17, 2009)]

42 U.S.C. § 6867. Administration of projects receiving financial assistance

(a) Reporting requirements
The Secretary, in consultation with the Director, by general or special orders, may require any recipient of financial assistance under this part to provide, in such form as he may prescribe, such reports or answers in writing to specific questions, surveys, or questionnaires as may be necessary to enable the Secretary and the Director to carry out their functions under this part.

(b) Maintenance of records
Each person responsible for the administration of a weatherization assistance project receiving financial assistance under this part shall keep such records as the Secretary may prescribe in order to assure an effective financial audit and performance evaluation of such project.

(c) Audit and examination of books, etc.
The Secretary, the Director (with respect to community action agencies), and the Comptroller General of the United States, or any of their duly authorized representatives, shall have access for the purpose of audit and examination to any books, documents, papers, information, and records of any project receiving financial assistance under this part that are pertinent to the financial assistance received under this part.

(d) Method of payments
Payments under this part may be made in installments and in advance, or by way of reimbursement, with necessary adjustments on account of overpayments or underpayments.

[Pub. L. No. 94-385, tit. IV, § 417, 90 Stat. 1156 (Aug. 14, 1976); Pub. L. No. 96-294, tit. V, § 577(2), 94 Stat. 760 (June 30, 1980)]

42 U.S.C. § 6868. Approval of application or amendment for financial assistance; administrative procedures applicable

(a) In general
The Secretary shall not finally disapprove any application submitted under this part, or any amendment thereto, without first affording the State (or unit of general purpose local government or community action agency under section 6863(c) of this title, as appropriate) in question, as well as other interested parties, reasonable notice and an opportunity for a public hearing. The Secretary may consolidate into a single hearing the consideration of more than one such application for a particular fiscal year to carry out projects within a particular State. Whenever the Secretary, after reasonable notice and an opportunity for a public hearing, finds that there is a failure to comply substantially with the provisions of this part or regulations promulgated under this part, he shall notify the agency or institution involved and other interested parties that such State (or unit of general purpose local government or agency, as appropriate) will no longer be eligible to participate in the program under this part until the Secretary is satisfied that there is no longer any such failure to comply.

(b) Notice
Reasonable notice under this section shall include a written notice of intention to act adversely (including a statement of the reasons therefor) and a reasonable period of time within which to submit corrective amendments to the application, or to propose corrective action.

[Pub. L. No. 94-385, tit. IV, § 418, 90 Stat. 1157 (Aug. 14, 1976); Pub. L. No. 96-294, tit. V, § 577(2), 94 Stat. 760 (June 30, 1980)]

42 U.S.C. § 6869. Judicial review of final action by Secretary on application

(a) Time for appeal; jurisdiction; filing of administrative record by Secretary
If any applicant is dissatisfied with the Secretary's final action with respect to the application submitted by it under section 6864 of this title, or with a final action under section 6868 of this title, such applicant may, within 60 days after notice of such action, file with the United States court of appeals for the circuit in which the State involved is located a petition for review of that action. A copy of the petition shall be forthwith transmitted by the clerk of the court to the Secretary. The Secretary thereupon shall file in the court the record of the proceedings on which he based his action, as provided in section 2112 of title 28.

(b) Conclusiveness of findings of Secretary; remand; modified findings by Secretary; certification of record
The findings of fact by the Secretary, if supported by substantial evidence, shall be conclusive. The court may, for good cause shown, remand the case to the Secretary to take further evidence, and the Secretary may thereupon make new or modified findings of fact and may modify his previous action. The Secretary shall certify to the court the record of any such further proceedings. Such new or modified findings of fact shall likewise be conclusive if supported by substantial evidence.

(c) Power of court to affirm or set aside action of Secretary; appeal to Supreme Court
The court shall have jurisdiction to affirm the action of the Secretary or to set it aside, in whole or in part. The judgment of the court shall be subject to review by the Supreme Court of the United States upon certiorari or certification, as provided in section 1254 of title 28.

[Pub. L. No. 94-385, tit. IV, § 419, 90 Stat. 1157 (Aug. 14, 1976); Pub. L. No. 96-294, tit. V, § 577(2), (3), 94 Stat. 760 (June 30, 1980)]

42 U.S.C. § 6870. Prohibition against discrimination; notification to funded project of violation; penalties for failure to comply

(a) Prohibition
No person in the United States shall, on the ground of race, color, national origin, or sex, or on the ground of any other factor specified in any Federal law prohibiting discrimination, be excluded from participation in, be denied the benefits of, or be subjected to discrimination under any program, project, or activity supported in whole or in part with financial assistance under this part.

(b) Notification and enforcement
Whenever the Secretary determines that a recipient of financial assistance under this part has failed to comply with subsection (a) of this section or any applicable regulation, he shall notify the recipient thereof in order to secure compliance. If, within a reasonable period of time thereafter, such recipient fails to comply, the Secretary shall—

(1) refer the matter to the Attorney General with a recommendation that an appropriate civil action be instituted;
(2) exercise the power and functions provided by title VI of the Civil Rights Act of 1964 (42 U.S.C. § 2000d *et seq.*) and any other applicable Federal nondiscrimination law; or
(3) take such other action as may be authorized by law.

[Pub. L. No. 94-385, tit. IV, § 420, 90 Stat. 1158 (Aug. 14, 1976); Pub. L. No. 96-294, tit. V, § 577(2), 94 Stat. 760 (June 30, 1980)]

42 U.S.C. § 6871. Annual report by Secretary and Director to President and Congress on weatherization program

The Secretary and (with respect to the operation and effectiveness of activities carried out through community action agencies) the Director shall each submit, on or before March 31, 1977, and annually thereafter, a report to the Congress and the President describing the weatherization assistance program carried out under this part or any other provision of law, including the results of the periodic evaluations and monitoring activities required by section 6866 of this title. Such report shall include information and data furnished by each State on the average costs incurred in weatherization of individual dwelling units, the average size of the dwellings being weatherized, and the average income of households receiving assistance under this part.

[Pub. L. No. 94-385, tit. IV, § 421, 90 Stat. 1158 (Aug. 14, 1976); Pub. L. No. 96-294, tit. V, § 577(2), 94 Stat. 760 (June 30, 1980); Pub. L. No. 101-440, § 7(h), 104 Stat. 1014 (Oct. 18, 1990)]

42 U.S.C. § 6872. Authorization of appropriations

For the purpose of carrying out the weatherization program under this part, there are authorized to be appropriated—

(1) $750,000,000 for fiscal year 2008;
(2) $900,000,000 for fiscal year 2009;
(3) $1,050,000,000 for fiscal year 2010;
(4) $1,200,000,000 for fiscal year 2011; and
(5) $1,400,000,000 for fiscal year 2012.

[Pub. L. No. 94-385, tit. IV, § 422, 90 Stat. 1158 (v); Pub. L. No. 95-619, tit. II, § 231(d), 92 Stat. 3226 (Nov. 9, 1978); Pub. L. No. 96-294, tit. V, § 576, 94 Stat. 760 (June 30, 1980); Pub. L. No. 98-181, tit. IV, § 464, 97 Stat. 1235 (Nov. 30, 1983); Pub. L. No. 101-440, § 8(c), 104 Stat. 1016 (Oct. 18, 1990); Pub. L. No. 105-388, § 3, 112 Stat. 3477 (Nov. 13, 1998); Pub. L. No. 109-58, tit. I, § 122(a), 119 Stat. 616 (Aug. 8, 2005); Pub. L. No. 110-140, tit. IV, § 411(a), 121 Stat. 1600 (Dec. 19, 2007)]

42 U.S.C. § 6873. Availability of labor

The following actions shall be taken in order to assure that there is a sufficient number of volunteers and training participants and public service employment workers, assisted pursuant to title I of the Workforce Investment Act of 1998 (29 U.S.C. § 2801 *et seq.*) and the Older American Community Service Employment Act (42 U.S.C. § 3056 *et seq.*), available to work in support of weatherization programs conducted under part A of the Energy Conservation in Existing Buildings Act of 1976 (42 U.S.C. § 6861 *et seq.*), section 222(a)(12) of the Economic Opportunity Act of 1964 (42 U.S.C. § 2809(a)(12)), and section 504 of the Housing Act of 1949 (42 U.S.C. § 1474):

(1) First, the Secretary of Energy (in consultation with the Director of the Community Services Administration, the Secretary of Agriculture, and the Secretary of Labor) shall determine the number of individuals needed to supply sufficient labor to carry out such weatherization programs in the various areas of the country.
(2) After the determination in paragraph (1) is made, the Secretary of Labor shall identify the areas of the country in which there is an insufficient number of such volunteers and training participants and public service employment workers.
(3) After such areas are identified, the Secretary of Labor shall take steps to assure that such weatherization programs are supported to the maximum extent practicable in such areas by such volunteers and training participants and public service employment workers.

[Pub. L. No. 95-619, tit. II, § 233, 92 Stat. 3227 (Nov. 9, 1978); Pub. L. No. 105-277, div. A, § 101(f) (tit. VIII, § 405(d)(39), (f)(30)), 112 Stat. 2681-337, 2681-427, 2681-434 (Oct. 21, 1998)]

D.2 Weatherization Assistance Program Regulations—10 C.F.R. 440

SOURCE: 45 Fed. Reg. 13035 (Feb. 27, 1980); 49 Fed. Reg. 3629 (Jan. 27, 1984); 50 Fed. Reg. 49917 (Dec. 5, 1985); 58 Fed. Reg. 12525 (Mar. 4, 1993); 60 Fed. Reg. 29480 (June 5, 1995); 65 Fed. Reg. 77217 (Dec. 8, 2000), unless otherwise noted.

AUTHORITY: 42 U.S.C. § 6861 *et seq.*; 42 U.S.C. § 7101 *et seq.*

10 C.F.R. § 440.1 Purpose and scope

This part implements a weatherization assistance program to increase the energy efficiency of dwellings owned or occupied by low-income persons or to provide such persons renewable energy systems or technologies, reduce their total residential expenditures, and improve their health and safety, especially low-income persons who are particularly vulnerable such as the elderly, persons with disabilities, families with children, high residential energy users, and households with high energy burden.

[58 Fed. Reg. 12525 (Mar. 4, 1993); 65 Fed. Reg. 77217, Dec. 8, 2000); 71 Fed. Reg. 35775 (June 22, 2006)]

10 C.F.R. § 440.2 Administration of grants

Grant awards under this part shall comply with applicable law including, without limitation, the requirements of:

(a) Executive Order 12372 entitled "Intergovernmental Review of Federal Programs," 48 FR 3130, and the DOE Regulation implementing this Executive Order entitled "Intergovernmental Review of Department of Energy Programs and Activities" (10 CFR part 1005);

(b) Office of Management and Budget Circular A-97, entitled "Rules and Regulations Permitting Federal Agencies to Provide Specialized or Technical Services to State and Local Units of Government under Title III of the Inter-Governmental Coordination Act of 1968";

(c) Unless in conflict with provisions of this part, the DOE Financial Assistance Rule (10 CFR part 600); and

(d) Such other procedures applicable to this part as DOE may from time to time prescribe for the administration of financial assistance.

(e)*(1) States, Tribes and their subawardees, including, but not limited to subrecipients, subgrantees, contractors and subcontractors that participate in the program established under this Part are required to treat all requests for information concerning applicants and recipients of WAP funds in a manner consistent with the Federal government's treatment of information requested under the Freedom of Information Act (FOIA), 5 U.S.C. 552, including the privacy protections contained in Exemption (b)(6) of the FOIA, 5 U.S.C. 552(b)(6). Under 5 U.S.C. 552(b)(6), information relating to an individual's eligibility application or the individual's participation in the program, such as name, address, or income information, are generally exempt from disclosure.

(2) A balancing test must be used in applying Exemption (b)(6) in order to determine:

(i) Whether a significant privacy interest would be invaded;

(ii) Whether the release of the information would further the public interest by shedding light on the operations or activities of the Government; and

(iii) Whether in balancing the privacy interests against the public interest, disclosure would constitute a clearly unwarranted invasion of privacy.

(3) A request for personal information including but not limited to the names, addresses, or income information of WAP applicants or recipients would require the State or other service provider to balance a clearly defined public interest in obtaining this information against the individuals' legitimate expectation of privacy.

(4) Given a legitimate, articulated public interest in the disclosure, States and other service providers may release information regarding recipients in the aggregate that does not identify specific individuals. However, a State or service provider must apply an FOIA Exemption (b)(6) balancing test to any request for information that can not be satisfied by such less-intrusive methods.

10 C.F.R. § 440.3 Definitions

As used in this part:

Act means the Energy Conservation in Existing Buildings Act of 1976, as amended, 42 U.S.C. 6851 *et seq.*

Assistant Secretary means the Assistant Secretary for Conservation

* *Editor's note:* 10 C.F.R. § 440.2(e) was added by 75 Fed. Reg. 11422 (Mar. 11, 2010) and adopted as a final rule by 75 Fed. Reg. 32090 (June 7, 1010). However, the Code of Federal Regulations website omits this paragraph from 10 C.F.R. § 440.2 (see www.access.gpo.gov/nara/cfr/waisidx_11/10cfr440_11.html, last visited August 26, 2011). Westlaw appears to indicate erroneously that paragraph (e) was reserved by 75 Fed. Reg. 11422 (Mar. 11, 2010), as amended by 75 Fed. Reg. 32090 (June 7, 1010). Given this contradictory information, users of this treatise are encouraged to conduct further research before referencing paragraph (e).

and Renewable Energy or official to whom the Assistant Secretary's functions may be redelegated by the Secretary.

Base Allocation means the fixed amount of funds for each State as set forth in § 440.10(b)(1).

Base temperature means the temperature used to compute heating and cooling degree days. The average daily outdoor temperature is subtracted from the base temperature to compute heating degree days, and the base temperature is subtracted from the average daily outdoor temperature to compute cooling degree days.

Biomass means any organic matter that is available on a renewable or recurring basis, including agricultural crops and trees, wood and wood wastes and residues, plants (including aquatic plants), grasses, residues, fibers, and animal wastes, municipal wastes, and other waste materials.

CAA means a Community Action Agency.

Capital-Intensive furnace or cooling efficiency modifications means those major heating and cooling modifications which require a substantial amount of funds, including replacement and major repairs, but excluding such items as tune-ups, minor repairs, and filters.

Children means dependents not exceeding 19 years or a lesser age set forth in the State plan.

Community Action Agency means a private corporation or public agency established pursuant to the Economic Opportunity Act of 1964, Pub. L. 88-452, which is authorized to administer funds received from Federal, State, local, or private funding entities to assess, design, operate, finance, and oversee antipoverty programs.

Cooling Degree Days means a population-weighted annual average of the climatological cooling degree days for each weather station within a State, as determined by DOE.

Deputy Assistant Secretary means the Deputy Assistant Secretary for Technical and Financial Assistance or any official to whom the Deputy Assistant Secretary's functions may be redelegated by the Assistant Secretary.

DOE means the Department of Energy.

Dwelling Unit means a house, including a stationary mobile home, an apartment, a group of rooms, or a single room occupied as separate living quarters.

Elderly Person means a person who is 60 years of age or older.

Electric base-load measures means measures which address the energy efficiency and energy usage of lighting and appliances.

Family Unit means all persons living together in a dwelling unit.

Formula Allocation means the amount of funds for each State as calculated based on the formula in § 440.10(b)(3).

Formula Share means the percentage of the total formula allocation provided to each State as calculated in § 440.10 (b)(3).

Governor means the chief executive officer of a State, including the Mayor of the District of Columbia.

Grantee means the State or other entity named in the Notification of Grant Award as the recipient.

Heating Degree Days means a population-weighted seasonal average of the climatological heating degree days for each weather station within a State, as determined by DOE.

High residential energy user means a low-income household whose residential energy expenditures exceed the median level of residential expenditures for all low-income households in the State.

Household with a high energy burden means a low-income household whose residential energy burden (residential expenditures divided by the annual income of that household) exceeds the median level of energy burden for all low-income households in the State.

Incidental Repairs means those repairs necessary for the effective performance or preservation of weatherization materials. Such repairs include, but are not limited to, framing or repairing windows and doors which could not otherwise be caulked or weather-stripped and providing protective materials, such as paint, used to seal materials installed under this program.

Indian Tribe means any tribe, band, nation, or other organized group or community of Native Americans, including any Alaskan native village, or regional or village corporation as defined in or established pursuant to the Alaska Native Claims Settlement Act, Pub. L. 92-203, 85 Stat. 688, which (1) is recognized as eligible for the special programs and services provided by the United States to Native Americans because of their status as Native Americans, or (2) is located on, or in proximity to, a Federal or State reservation or rancheria.

JTPA means the Job Training Partnership Act, 29 U.S.C. 1501 *et seq.*

Local Applicant means a CAA or other public or non profit entity unit of general purpose local government.

Low Income means that income in relation to family size which:

(1) At or below 200 percent of the poverty level determined in accordance with criteria established by the Director of the Office of Management and Budget, except that the Secretary may establish a higher level if the Secretary, after consulting with the Secretary of Agriculture and the Secretary of Health and Human Services, determines that such a higher level is necessary to carry out the purposes of this part and is consistent with the eligibility criteria established for the weatherization program under Section 222(a)(12) of the Economic Opportunity Act of 1964;

(2) Is the basis on which cash assistance payments have been paid during the preceding twelve month-period under Titles IV and XVI of the Social Security Act or applicable State or local law; or

(3) If a State elects, is the basis for eligibility for assistance under the Low Income Home Energy Assistance Act of 1981, provided that such basis is at least 200 percent of the poverty level determined in accordance with criteria established by the Director of the Office of Management and Budget.

Native American means a person who is a member of an Indian tribe.

Non-Federal leveraged resources means those benefits identified by State or local agencies to supplement the Federal grant activities and that are made available to or used in conjunction with the DOE Weatherization Assistance Program for the purposes of the Act for use in eligible low-income dwelling units.

Persons with disabilities means any individual (1) who is a handicapped individual as defined in section 7(6) of the Rehabilitation Act of 1973, (2) who is under a disability as defined in section 1614(a)(3)(A) or 223(d)(1) of the Social Security Act or in section 102(7) of the Developmental Disabilities Services and Facilities Construction Act, or (3) who is receiving benefits under chapter 11 or 15 of title 38, U.S.C.

Program Allocation means the base allocation plus formula allocation for each State.

Relevant Reporting Period means the Federal fiscal year beginning on October 1 and running through September 30 of the following calendar year.

Renewable energy system means a system which when installed in connection with a dwelling—

(1) Transmits or uses solar energy, energy derived from geothermal deposits, energy derived from biomass (or any other form of renewable energy which DOE subsequently specifies through an amendment of this part) for the purpose of heating or cooling such dwelling or providing hot water or electricity for use within such dwelling; or wind energy for nonbusiness residential purposes; and

(2) Which meets the performance and quality standards prescribed in § 440.21 (c) of this part.

Rental Dwelling Unit means a dwelling unit occupied by a person who pays rent for the use of the dwelling unit.

Residential Energy Expenditures means the average annual cost of purchased residential energy, including the cost of renewable energy resources.

Secretary means the Secretary of the Department of Energy.

Separate Living Quarters means living quarters in which the occupants do not live and eat with any other persons in the structure and which have either direct access from the outside of the building or through a common hall or complete kitchen facilities for the exclusive use of the occupants. The occupants may be a single family, one person living alone, two or more families living together, or any other group of related or unrelated persons who share living arrangements, and includes shelters for homeless persons.

Shelter means a dwelling unit or units whose principal purpose is to house on a temporary basis individuals who may or may not be related to one another and who are not living in nursing homes, prisons, or similar institutional care facilities.

Single-Family Dwelling Unit means a structure containing no more than one dwelling unit.

Skirting means material used to border the bottom of a dwelling unit to prevent infiltration.

State means each of the States, the District of Columbia, American Samoa, Guam, Commonwealth of the Northern Mariana Islands, Commonwealth of Puerto Rico, and the Virgin Islands.

Subgrantee means an entity managing a weatherization project which receives a grant of funds awarded under this part from a grantee.

Support Office Director means the Director of the DOE Field Support Office with the responsibility for grant administration or any official to whom that function may be redelegated by the Assistant Secretary.

Total Program Allocations means the annual appropriation less funds reserved for training and technical assistance.

Tribal Organization means the recognized governing body of any Indian tribe or any legally established organization of Native Americans which is controlled, sanctioned, or chartered by such governing body.

Unit of General Purpose Local Government means any city, county, town, parish, village, or other general purpose political subdivision of a State.

Vestibule means an enclosure built around a primary entry to a dwelling unit.

Weatherization Materials mean:

(1) Caulking and weatherstripping of doors and windows;

(2) Furnace efficiency modifications including, but not limited to—

(i) Replacement burners, furnaces, or boilers or any combination thereof;

(ii) Devices for minimizing energy loss through heating system, chimney, or venting devices; and

(iii) Electrical or mechanical furnace ignition systems which replace standing gas pilot lights;

(3) Cooling efficiency modifications including, but not limited to—

(i) Replacement air conditioners;

(ii) Ventilation equipment;

(iii) Screening and window films; and

(iv) Shading devices.

Weatherization Project means a project conducted in a single geographical area which undertakes to weatherize dwelling units that are energy inefficient.

[49 Fed. Reg. 3629 (Jan. 27, 1984), *as amended at* 50 Fed. Reg. 712 (Jan. 4, 1985); 50 Fed. Reg. 49917 (Dec. 5, 1985); 55 Fed. Reg. 41325 (Oct. 10, 1990); 58 Fed. Reg. 12525 (Mar. 4, 1993); 60 Fed. Reg. 29480 (June 5, 1995); 65 Fed. Reg. 77217 (Dec. 8, 2000); 71 Fed. Reg. 35775 (June 22, 2006); 74 Fed. Reg. 12539 (Mar. 25, 2009)]

10 C.F.R. § 440.10 Allocation of funds

(a) DOE shall allocate financial assistance for each State from sums appropriated for any fiscal year, upon annual application.

(b) Based on total program allocations at or above the amount of $209,724,761, DOE shall determine the program allocation for each State from available funds as follows:

(1) Allocate to each State a "Base Allocation" as listed in Table 1.

TABLE 1
Base Allocation Table

State	Base allocation
Alabama	$1,636,000
Alaska	1,425,000
Arizona	760,000
Arkansas	1,417,000
California	4,404,000
Colorado	4,574,000
Connecticut	1,887,000
Delaware	409,000
District of Columbia	487,000
Florida	761,000
Georgia	1,844,000
Hawaii	120,000
Idaho	1,618,000
Illinois	10,717,000
Indiana	5,156,000
Iowa	4,032,000
Kansas	1,925,000
Kentucky	3,615,000
Louisiana	912,000
Maine	2,493,000
Maryland	1,963,000
Massachusetts	5,111,000
Michigan	12,346,000
Minnesota	8,342,000
Mississippi	1,094,000
Missouri	4,615,000
Montana	2,123,000
Nebraska	2,013,000
Nevada	586,000
New Hampshire	1,193,000
New Jersey	3,775,000
New Mexico	1,519,000
New York	15,302,000
North Carolina	2,853,000
North Dakota	2,105,000
Ohio	10,665,000
Oklahoma	1,846,000
Oregon	2,320,000
Pennsylvania	11,457,000
Rhode Island	878,000
South Carolina	1,130,000
South Dakota	1,561,000
Tennessee	3,218,000
Texas	2,999,000
Utah	1,692,000
Vermont	1,014,000
Virginia	2,970,000
Washington	3,775,000
West Virginia	2,573,000
Wisconsin	7,061,000
Wyoming	967,000
American Samoa	120,000
Guam	120,000
Puerto Rico	120,000
Northern Mariana Islands	120,000
Virgin Islands	120,000
Total	171,858,000

(2) Subtract 171,258,000 from total program allocations.

(3) Calculate each State's formula share as follows:

(i) Divide the number of "Low Income" households in each State by the number of "Low Income" households in the United States and multiply by 100.

(ii) Divide the number of "Heating Degree Days" for each State by the median "Heating Degree Days" for all States.

(iii) Divide the number of "Cooling Degree Days" for each State by the median "Cooling Degree Days" for all States, then multiply by 0.1.

(iv) Calculate the sum of the two numbers from paragraph (b)(3)(ii) and (iii) of this section.

(v) Divide the residential energy expenditures for each State by the number of households in the State.

(vi) Divide the sum of the residential energy expenditures for the States in each Census division by the sum of the households for the States in that division.

(vii) Divide the quotient from paragraph (b)(3)(v) of this section by the quotient from paragraph (b)(3)(vi) of this section.

(viii) Multiply the quotient from paragraph (b)(3)(vii) of this section for each State by the residential energy expenditures per low-income household for its respective Census division.

(ix) Divide the product from paragraph (b)(3)(viii) of this section for each State by the median of the products of all States.

(x) Multiply the results for paragraph (b)(3)(i), (iv) and (ix) of this section for each State.

(xi) Divide the product in paragraph (b)(3)(x) of this section for each State by the sum of the products in paragraph (b)(3)(x) of this section for all States.

(4) Calculate each State's program allocation as follows:

(i) Multiply the remaining funds calculated in paragraph (b)(2) of this section by the formula share calculated in paragraph (b)(3)(xi) of this section.

(ii) Add the base allocation from paragraph (b)(1) of this section to the product of paragraph (b)(4)(i) of this section.

(c) Should total program allocations for any fiscal year fall below the total program allocations under Pub. L. 103-332, then each State's program allocation shall be reduced from its allocated amount under Pub. L. 103-332 by the same percentage as total program allocations for the fiscal year fall below the total program allocations under Pub. L. 103-332.

(d) All data sources used in the development of the formula are publicly available. The relevant data is available from the Bureau of the Census, the Department of Energy's Energy Information Administration and the National Oceanic and Atmospheric Administration.

(e) Should updates to the data used in the formula become available in any fiscal year, these changes would be implemented in the formula in the following program year.

(f) DOE may reduce the program allocation for a State by the amount DOE determines cannot be reasonably expended by a grantee to weatherize dwelling units during the budget period for which financial assistance is to be awarded. In reaching this determination, DOE will consider the amount of unexpended financial assistance currently available to a grantee under this part and the number of dwelling units which remains to be weatherized with the unexpended financial assistance.

(g) DOE may increase the program allocation of a State by the amount DOE determines the grantee can expend to weatherize additional dwelling units during the budget period for which financial assistance is to be awarded.

(h) The Support Office Director shall notify each State of the program allocation for which that State is eligible to apply.

[60 Fed. Reg. 29480 (June 5, 1995); 74 Fed. Reg. 12539 (Mar. 25, 2009)]

EFFECTIVE DATE NOTE: At 60 Fed. Reg. 64315 (Dec. 15, 1995), § 440.10 was revised, effective December 15, 1995.

10 C.F.R. § 440.11 Native Americans

(a) Notwithstanding any other provision of this part, the Support Office Director may determine, after taking into account the amount of funds made available to a State to carry out the purposes of this part, that:

(1) The low-income members of an Indian tribe are not receiving benefits under this part equivalent to the assistance provided to other low-income persons in the State under this part; and

(2) The low-income members of such tribe would be better served by means of a grant made directly to provide such assistance.

(b) In any State for which the Support Office Director shall have made the determination referred to in paragraph (a) of this section, the Support Office Director shall reserve from the sums that would otherwise be allocated to the State under this part not less than 100 percent, or more than 150 percent, of an amount which bears the same ratio to the State's allocation for the fiscal year involved as the population of all low-income Native Americans for whom a determination under paragraph (a) of this section has been made bears to the population of all low-income persons in the State.

(c) The Support Office Director shall make the determination prescribed in paragraph (a) of this section in the event a State:

(1) Does not apply within the sixty-day time period prescribed in § 440.12(a);

(2) Recommends that direct grants be made for low-income members of an Indian tribe as provided in § 440.12(b)(5);

(3) Files an application which DOE determines, in accordance with the procedures in § 440.30, not to make adequate provision for the low-income members of an Indian tribe residing in the State; or

(4) Has received grant funds and DOE determines, in accordance with the procedures in § 440.30, that the State has failed to implement the procedures required by § 440.16(6).

(d) Any sums reserved by the Support Office Director pursuant to paragraph (b) of this section shall be granted to the tribal organization serving the individuals for whom the determination has been made, or where there is no tribal organization, to such other entity as the Support Office Director determines is able to provide adequate weatherization assistance pursuant to this part. Where the Support Office Director intends to make a grant to an organization to perform services benefiting more than one Indian tribe, the approval of each Indian tribe shall be a prerequisite for the issuance of a notice of grant award.

(e) Within 30 days after the Support Office Director has reserved funds pursuant to paragraph (b) of this section, the Support Office Director shall give written notice to the tribal organization or other qualified entity of the amount of funds reserved and its eligibility to apply therefor.

(f) Such tribal organization or other qualified entity shall thereafter be treated as a unit of general purpose local government eligible to apply for funds hereunder, pursuant to the provisions of § 440.13.

[49 Fed. Reg. 3629 (Jan. 27, 1984), *as amended at* 58 Fed. Reg. 12529 (Mar. 4, 1993)]

10 C.F.R. § 440.12 State application

(a) To be eligible for financial assistance under this part, a State shall submit an application to DOE in conformity with the requirements of this part not later than 60 days after the date of notice to apply is received from the Support Office Director. After receipt of an application for financial assistance or for approval of an amendment to a State plan, the Support Office Director may request the State to submit within a reasonable period of time any revisions necessary to make the application complete or to bring the application into compliance with the requirements of this part. The Support Office Director shall attempt to resolve any dispute over the application informally and to seek voluntary compliance. If a State fails to submit timely appropriate revisions to complete the application, the Support Office Director may reject the application as incomplete in a written decision, including a statement of reasons, which shall be subject to administrative review under § 440.30 of this part.

(b) Each application shall include:

(1) The name and address of the State agency or office responsible for administering the program;

(2) A copy of the final State plan prepared after notice and a public hearing in accordance with § 440.14(a), except that an application by a local applicant need not include a copy of the final State plan;

(3) The budget for total funds applied for under the Act, which shall include a justification and explanation of any amounts requested for expenditure pursuant to § 440.18(d) for State administration;

(4) The total number of dwelling units proposed to be weatherized with grant funds during the budget period for which assistance is to be awarded—

(i) With financial assistance previously obligated under this part, and

(ii) With the program allocation to the State;

(5) A recommendation that a tribal organization be treated as a local applicant eligible to submit an application pursuant to § 440.13(b), if such a recommendation is to be made;

(6) A monitoring plan which shall indicate the method used by the State to insure the quality of work and adequate financial management control at the subgrantee level;

(7) A training and technical assistance plan which shall indicate how funds for training and technical assistance will be used; and

(8) Any further information which the Secretary finds necessary to determine whether an application meets the requirements of this part.

(c) On or before 60 days from the date that a timely filed application is complete, the Support Office Director shall decide whether DOE shall approve the application. The Support Office Director may—

(1) Approve the application in whole or in part to the extent that the application conforms to the requirements of this part;

(2) Approve the application in whole or in part subject to special conditions designed to ensure compliance with the requirements of this part; or

(3) Disapprove the application if it does not conform to the requirements of this part.

(Approved by the Office of Management and Budget under control number 1904-0047)

[49 Fed. Reg. 3629 (Jan. 27, 1984), *as amended at* 50 Fed. Reg. 712 (Jan. 4, 1985); 55 Fed. Reg. 41325 (Oct. 10, 1990); 58 Fed. Reg. 12529 (Mar. 4, 1993); 60 Fed. Reg. 29481 (June 5, 1995)]

EFFECTIVE DATE NOTE: At 60 Fed. Reg. 64315 (Dec. 15, 1995), § 440.12(b)(4) was revised, effective December 15, 1995.

10 C.F.R. § 440.13 Local applications

(a) The Support Office Director shall give written notice to all local applicants throughout a State of their eligibility to apply for financial assistance under this part in the event:

(1) A State, within which a local applicant is situated, fails to submit an application within 60 days after notice in accordance with § 440.12(a) or

(2) The Support Office Director finally disapproves the application of a State, and, under § 440.30, either no appeal is filed or the Support Office Director's decision is affirmed.

(b) To be eligible for financial assistance, a local applicant shall submit an application pursuant to § 440.12(b) to the Support Office Director within 30 days after receiving the notice referred to in paragraph (a) of this section.

(c) In the event one or more local applicants submits an application for financial assistance to carry out projects in the same geographical area, the Support Office Director shall hold a public hearing with the same procedures that apply under section § 440.14(a).

(d) Based on the information provided by a local applicant and developed in any hearing held under paragraph (c) of this section, the Support Office Director shall determine in writing whether to award a grant to carry out one or more weatherization projects.

(e) If there is an adverse decision in whole or in part under paragraph (d) of this section, that decision is subject to administrative review under § 440.30 of this part.

(f) If, after a State application has been finally disapproved by DOE and the Support Office Director approves local applications under this section, the Support Office Director may reject a new State application in whole or in part as disruptive and untimely without prejudice to submission of an application for the next program year.

(Approved by the Office of Management and Budget under control number 1904-0047)

[49 Fed. Reg. 3629 (Jan. 27, 1984), *as amended at* 58 Fed. Reg. 12525, 12529 (Mar. 4, 1993)]

10 C.F.R. § 440.14 State plans

(a) Before submitting to DOE an application, a State must provide at least 10 days notice of a hearing to inform prospective subgrantees, and must conduct one or more public hearings to receive comments on a proposed State plan. The notice for the hearing must specify that copies of the plan are available and state how the public may obtain them. The State must prepare a transcript of the hearings and accept written submission of views and data for the record.

(b) The proposed State plan must:

(1) Identify and describe proposed weatherization projects, including a statement of proposed subgrantees and the amount of funding each will receive;

(2) Address the other items contained in paragraph (c) of this section; and

(3) Be made available throughout the State prior to the hearing.

(c) After the hearing, the State must prepare a final State plan that identifies and describes:

(1) The production schedule for the State indicating projected expenditures and the number of dwelling units, including previously weatherized units which are expected to be weatherized annually during the program year;

(2) The climatic conditions within the State;

(3) The type of weatherization work to be done;

(4) An estimate of the amount of energy to be conserved;

(5) Each area to be served by a weatherization project within the State, and must include for each area:

(i) The tentative allocation;

(ii) The number of dwelling units expected to be weatherized during the program year; and

(iii) Sources of labor.

(6) How the State plan is to be implemented, including:

(i) An analysis of the existence and effectiveness of any weatherization project being carried out by a subgrantee;

(ii) An explanation of the method used to select each area served by a weatherization project;

(iii) The extent to which priority will be given to the weatherization of single-family or other high energy-consuming dwelling units;

(iv) The amount of non-Federal resources to be applied to the program;

(v) The amount of Federal resources, other than DOE weatherization grant funds, to be applied to the program;

(vi) The amount of weatherization grant funds allocated to the State under this part;

(vii) The expected average cost per dwelling to be weatherized, taking into account the total number of dwellings to be weatherized and the total amount of funds, Federal and non-Federal, expected to be applied to the program;

(viii) The average amount of the DOE funds specified in § 440.18(c)(1) through (9) to be applied to any dwelling unit;

(ix) [*Reserved*];

(x) The procedures used by the State for providing additional administrative funds to qualified subgrantees as specified in § 440.18(d);

(xi) Procedures for determining the most cost-effective measures in a dwelling unit;

(xii) The definition of "low-income" which the State has chosen for determining eligibility for use statewide in accordance with § 440.22(a);

(xiii) The definition of "children" which the State has chosen consistent with § 440.3; and

(xiv) The amount of Federal funds and how they will be used to increase the amount of weatherization assistance that the State obtains from non-Federal sources, including private sources, and the expected leveraging effect to be accomplished.

[49 Fed. Reg. 3629 (Jan. 27, 1984), *as amended at* 50 Fed. Reg. 712 (Jan. 4, 1985); 58 Fed. Reg. 12526 (Mar. 4, 1993); 60 Fed. Reg. 29481 (June 5, 1995); 65 Fed. Reg. 77217 (Dec. 8, 2000); 66 Fed. Reg. 58366 (Nov. 21, 2001)]

10 C.F.R. § 440.15 Subgrantees

(a) The grantee shall ensure that:

(1) Each subgrantee is a CAA or other public or nonprofit entity;

(2) Each subgrantee is selected on the basis of public comment received during a public hearing conducted pursuant to § 440.14(a) and other appropriate findings regarding:

(i) The subgrantee's experience and performance in weatherization or housing renovation activities;

(ii) The subgrantee's experience in assisting low-income persons in the area to be served; and

(iii) The subgrantee's capacity to undertake a timely and effective weatherization program.

(3) In selecting a subgrantee, preference is given to any CAA or other public or nonprofit entity which has, or is currently administering, an effective program under this part or under title II of the Economic Opportunity Act of 1964, with program effectiveness evaluated by consideration of factors including, but not necessarily limited to, the following:

(i) The extent to which the past or current program achieved or is achieving weatherization goals in a timely fashion;

(ii) The quality of work performed by the subgrantee;

(iii) The number, qualifications, and experience of the staff members of the subgrantee; and

(iv) The ability of the subgrantee to secure volunteers, training participants, public service employment workers, and other Federal or State training programs.

(b) The grantee shall ensure that the funds received under this part will be allocated to the entities selected in accordance with paragraph (a) of this section, such that funds will be allocated to areas on the basis of the relative need for a weatherization project by low-income persons.

(c) If DOE finds that a subgrantee selected to undertake weatherization activities under this part has failed to comply substantially with the provisions of the Act or this part and should be replaced, such finding shall be treated as a finding under § 440.30(i) for purposes of § 440.30.

(d) Any new or additional subgrantee shall be selected at a hearing in accordance with § 440.14(a) and upon the basis of the criteria in paragraph (a) of this section.

(e) A State may terminate financial assistance under a subgrant agreement for a grant period only in accordance with established State procedures that provide to the subgrantee appropriate notice of the State's reasons for termination and afford the subgrantee an adequate opportunity to be heard.

[49 Fed. Reg. 3629 (Jan. 27, 1984), *as amended at* 55 Fed. Reg. 41326 (Oct. 10, 1990); 58 Fed. Reg. 12526 (Mar. 4, 1993); 65 Fed. Reg. 77218 (Dec. 8, 2000)]

10 C.F.R. § 440.16 Minimum program requirements

Prior to the expenditure of any grant funds each grantee shall develop, publish, and implement procedures to ensure that:

(a) No dwelling unit may be weatherized without documentation that the dwelling unit is an eligible dwelling unit as provided in § 440.22;

(b) Priority is given to identifying and providing weatherization assistance to:

(1) Elderly persons;

(2) Persons with disabilities;

(3) Families with children;

(4) High residential energy users; and

(5) Households with a high energy burden.

(c) Financial assistance provided under this part will be used to supplement, and not supplant, State or local funds, and, to the maximum extent practicable as determined by DOE, to increase the amounts of these funds that would be made available in the absence of Federal funds provided under this part;

(d) To the maximum extent practicable, the grantee will secure the services of volunteers when such personnel are generally available, training participants and public service employment workers, other Federal or State training program workers, to work under the supervision of qualified supervisors and foremen;

(e) To the maximum extent practicable, the use of weatherization assistance shall be coordinated with other Federal, State, local, or privately funded programs in order to improve energy efficiency and to conserve energy;

(f) The low-income members of an Indian tribe shall receive benefits equivalent to the assistance provided to other low-income persons within a State unless the grantee has made the recommendation provided in § 440.12(b)(5);

(g) No dwelling unit may be reported to DOE as completed until all weatherization materials have been installed and the subgrantee, or its authorized representative, has performed a final inspection(s) including any mechanical work performed and certified that the work has been completed in a workmanlike manner and in accordance with the priority determined by the audit procedures required by § 440.21; and

(h) Subgrantees limit expenditure of funds under this part for installation of materials (other than weatherization materials) to abate energy-related health and safety hazards, to a list of types of such hazards, permissible abatement materials and their costs which is submitted, and updated as necessary at the same time as an annual application under § 440.12 of this part and which DOE shall approve if—

(1) Elimination of such hazards are necessary before, or as a result of, installation of weatherization materials; and

(2) The grantee sets forth a limitation on the percent of average dwelling unit costs which may be used to abate such hazards which is reasonable in light of the primary energy conservation purpose of this part;

(i) The benefits of weatherization to occupants of rental units are protected in accordance with § 440.22(b)(3) of this part.

(Approved by the Office of Management and Budget under control number 1904-0047)

[49 Fed. Reg. 3629 (Jan. 27, 1984), *as amended at* 58 Fed. Reg. 12526 (Mar. 4, 1993); 65 Fed. Reg. 77218 (Dec. 8, 2000)]

10 C.F.R. § 440.17 Policy Advisory Council

(a) Prior to the expenditure of any grant funds, a State policy advisory council, or a State commission or council which serves the same functions as a State policy advisory council, must be established by a State or by the Regional Office Director if a State does not participate in the Program which:

(1) Has special qualifications and sensitivity with respect to solving the problems of low-income persons, including the weatherization and energy conservation problems of these persons;

(2) Is broadly representative of organizations and agencies, including consumer groups that represent low-income persons, particularly elderly and handicapped low-income persons and low-income Native Americans, in the State or geographical area in question; and

(3) Has responsibility for advising the appropriate official or agency administering the allocation of financial assistance in the State or area with respect to the development and implementation of a weatherization assistance program.

(b) Any person employed in any State Weatherization Program may also be a member of an existing commission or council, but must abstain from reviewing and approving activities associated with the DOE Weatherization Assistance Program.

(c) States which opt to utilize an existing commission or council must certify to DOE, as a part of the annual application, of the council's or commission's independence in reviewing and approving activities associated with the DOE Weatherization Assistance Program.

[49 Fed. Reg. 3629 (Jan. 27, 1984), *as amended at* 58 Fed. Reg. 12529 (Mar. 4, 1993); 65 Fed. Reg. 77218 (Dec. 8, 2000)]

10 C.F.R. § 440.18 Allowable expenditures

(a) Except as adjusted, the expenditure of financial assistance provided under this part for labor, weatherization materials, and related matters included in paragraphs (c)(1) through (9) of this section shall not exceed an average of $6,500 per dwelling unit weatherized in the State, except as adjusted in paragraph (c) of this section.

(b) The expenditure of financial assistance provided under this part for labor, weatherization materials, and related matters for a renewable energy system, shall not exceed an average of $3,000 per dwelling unit.

(c) The $6,500 average will be adjusted annually by DOE beginning in calendar year 2010 and the $3,000 average for renewable energy systems will be adjusted annually by DOE beginning in calendar year 2007, by increasing the limitations by an amount equal to:

(1) The limitation amount for the previous year, multiplied by

(2) The lesser of:

(i) The percentage increase in the Consumer Price Index (all items, United States city average) for the most recent calendar year completed before the beginning of the year for which the determination is being made, or

(ii) Three percent.

(3) For the purposes of determining the average cost per dwelling limitation, costs for the purchase of vehicles or other certain types of equipment as defined in 10 CFR part 600 may be amortized over the useful life of the vehicle or equipment.

(d) Allowable expenditures under this part include only:

(1) The cost of purchase and delivery of weatherization materials;

(2) Labor costs, in accordance with § 440.19;

(3) Transportation of weatherization materials, tools, equipment, and work crews to a storage site and to the site of weatherization work;

(4) Maintenance, operation, and insurance of vehicles used to transport weatherization materials;

(5) Maintenance of tools and equipment;

(6) The cost of purchasing vehicles, except that any purchase of vehicles must be referred to DOE for prior approval in every instance.

(7) Employment of on-site supervisory personnel;

(8) Storage of weatherization materials, tools, and equipment;

(9) The cost of incidental repairs if such repairs are necessary to make the installation of weatherization materials effective;

(10) The cost of liability insurance for weatherization projects for personal injury and for property damage;

(11) The cost of carrying out low-cost/no-cost weatherization activities in accordance with § 440.20;

(12) The cost of weatherization program financial audits as required by § 440.23(d);

(13) Allowable administrative expenses under paragraph (d) of this section; and

(14) Funds used for leveraging activities in accordance with § 440.14(b)(9)(xiv); and

(15) The cost of eliminating health and safety hazards elimination of which is necessary before, or because of, installation of weatherization materials.

(e) Not more than 10 percent of any grant made to a State may be used by the grantee and subgrantees for administrative purposes in carrying out duties under this part, except that not more than 5 percent may be used by the State for such purposes, and not less than 5 percent must be made available to subgrantees by States. A State may provide in its annual plan for recipients of grants of less than $350,000 to use up to an additional 5 percent of such grants for administration if the State has determined that such recipient requires such additional amount to implement effectively the administrative requirements established by DOE pursuant to this part.

(f) No grant funds awarded under this part shall be used for any of the following purposes:

(1) To weatherize a dwelling unit which is designated for acquisition or clearance by a Federal, State, or local program within 12 months from the date weatherization of the dwelling unit would be scheduled to be completed; or

(2) To install or otherwise provide weatherization materials for a dwelling unit weatherized previously with grant funds under this part, except:

(i) As provided under § 440.20;

(ii) If such dwelling unit has been damaged by fire, flood, or act of God and repair of the damage to weatherization materials is not paid for by insurance; or

(iii) That dwelling units partially weatherized under this part or under other Federal programs during the period September 30, 1975, through September 30, 1993, may receive further financial assistance for weatherization under this part. While DOE will continue to require these homes to be reported separately, States may count these homes as completions for the purposes of compliance with the per-home expenditure limit in § 440.18. Each dwelling unit must receive a new energy audit which takes into account any previous energy conservation improvements to the dwelling.

[58 Fed. Reg. 12526 (Mar. 4, 1993); 65 Fed. Reg. 77218 (Dec. 8, 2000); 66 Fed. Reg. 58366 (Nov. 21, 2001); 71 Fed. Reg. 35775 (June 22, 2006); 74 Fed. Reg. 12540 (Mar. 25, 2009)]

10 C.F.R. § 440.19 Labor

Payments for labor costs under § 440.18(c)(2) must consist of:

(a) Payments permitted by the Department of Labor to supplement wages paid to training participants, public service employment workers, or other Federal or State training programs; and

(b) Payments to employ labor or to engage a contractor (particularly a nonprofit organization or a business owned by disadvantaged individuals which performs weatherization services), provided a grantee has determined an adequate number of volunteers, training participants, public service employment workers, or other Federal or State training programs are not available to weatherize dwelling units for a subgrantee under the supervision of qualified supervisors.

[49 Fed. Reg. 3629 (Jan. 27, 1984), *as amended at* 50 Fed. Reg. 713 (Jan. 4, 1985); 58 Fed. Reg. 12527 (Mar. 4, 1993); 65 Fed. Reg. 77218 (Dec. 8, 2000)]

10 C.F.R. § 440.20 Low-cost/no-cost weatherization activities

(a) An eligible dwelling unit may be weatherized without regard to the limitations contained in § 440.18 (e)(2) or § 440.21(b) from funds designated by the grantee for carrying out low-cost/no-cost weatherization activities provided:

(1) Inexpensive weatherization materials are used, such as water flow controllers, furnace or cooling filters, or items which are primarily directed toward reducing infiltration, including weather-stripping, caulking, glass patching, and insulation for plugging; and

(2) No labor paid with funds provided under this part is used to install weatherization materials referred to in paragraph (a)(1) of this section.

(b) A maximum of 10 percent of the amount allocated to a subgrantee, not to exceed $50 in materials costs per dwelling unit, may be expended to carry out low-cost/no-cost weatherization activities, unless the Support Office Director approves a higher expenditure per dwelling unit.

[49 Fed. Reg. 3629 (Jan. 27, 1984), *as amended at* 50 Fed. Reg. 713 (Jan. 4, 1985); 58 Fed. Reg. 12529 (Mar. 4, 1993)]

10 C.F.R. § 440.21 Weatherization materials standards and energy audit procedures

(a) Paragraph (b) of this section describes the required standards for weatherization materials. Paragraph (c) (1) of this section describes the performance and quality standards for renewable energy systems. Paragraph (c) (2) of this section specifies the procedures and criteria that are used for considering a petition from a manufacturer requesting the Secretary to certify an item as a renewable energy system. Paragraphs (d) and (e) of this section describe the cost-effectiveness tests that weatherization materials must pass before they may be installed in an eligible dwelling unit. Paragraph (f) of this section lists the other energy audit requirements that do not pertain to cost-effectiveness tests of weatherization materials. Paragraphs (g) and (h) of this section describe the use of priority lists and presumptively cost-effective general heat waste reduction materials as part of a State's energy audit procedures. Paragraph (i) of this section explains that a State's energy audit procedures and priority lists must be re-approved by DOE every five years.

(b) Only weatherization materials which are listed in Appendix A to this part and which meet or exceed standards prescribed in Appendix A to this part may be purchased with funds provided under this part. However, DOE may approve an unlisted material upon application from any State.

(c)(1) A system or technology shall not be considered by DOE to be a renewable energy system under this part unless:

(i) It will result in a reduction in oil or natural gas consumption;

(ii) It will not result in an increased use of any item which is known to be, or reasonably expected to be, environmentally hazardous or a threat to public health or safety;

(iii) Available Federal subsidies do not make such a specification unnecessary or inappropriate (in light of the most advantageous allocation of economic resources); and(iv) If a combustion rated system, it has a thermal efficiency rating of at least 75 percent; or, in the case of a solar system, it has a thermal efficiency rating of at least 15 percent.

(2) Any manufacturer may submit a petition to DOE requesting the Secretary to certify an item as a renewable energy system.

(i) Petitions should be submitted to: Weatherization Assistance Program, Office of Energy Efficiency and Renewable, Mail Stop EE-2K, 1000 Independence Avenue, SW., Washington, DC 20585.

(ii) A petition for certification of an item as a renewable energy system must be accompanied by information demonstrating that the item meets the criteria in paragraph (c)(1) of this section.

(iii) DOE may publish a document in the Federal Register that invites public comment on a petition.

(iv) DOE shall notify the petitioner of the Secretary's action on the request within one year after the filing of a complete petition, and shall publish notice of approvals and denials in the Federal Register.

(d) Except for materials to eliminate health and safety hazards allowable under § 440.18(c)(15), each individual weatherization material and package of weatherization materials installed in an eligible dwelling unit must be cost-effective. These materials must result in energy cost savings over the lifetime of the measure(s), discounted to present value, that equal or exceed the cost of materials, installation, and on-site supervisory personnel as defined by the Department. States have the option of requiring additional related costs to be included in the determination of cost-effectiveness. The cost of incidental repairs must be included in the cost of the package of measures installed in a dwelling.

(e) The energy audit procedures must assign priorities among individual weatherization materials in descending order of their cost-effectiveness according to paragraph (d) of this section after:

(1) Adjusting for interaction between architectural and mechanical weatherization materials by using generally accepted engineering methods to decrease the estimated fuel cost savings for a lower priority weatherization material in light of fuel cost savings for a related higher priority weatherization material; and

(2) Eliminating any weatherization materials that are no longer cost-effective, as adjusted under paragraph (e)(1) of this section.

(f) The energy audit procedures also must—

(1) Compute the cost of fuel saved per year by taking into account the climatic data of the area where the dwelling unit is located, where the base temperature that determines the number of heating or cooling degree days (if used) reasonably approximates conditions when operation of heating and cooling equipment is required to maintain comfort, and must otherwise use reasonable energy estimating methods and assumptions;

(2) Determine existing energy use and energy requirements of the dwelling unit from actual energy bills or by generally accepted engineering calculations;

(3) Address significant heating and cooling needs;

(4) Make provision for the use of advanced diagnostic and assessment techniques which DOE has determined are consistent with sound engineering practices;

(5) Identify health and safety hazards to be abated with DOE funds in compliance with the State's DOE-approved health and safety procedures under § 440.16(h);

(6) Treat the dwelling unit as a whole system by examining its heating and cooling system, its air exchange system, and its occupants' living habits and needs, and making necessary adjustments to the priority of weatherization materials with adequate documentation of the reasons for such an adjustment; and

(7) Be specifically approved by DOE for use on each major dwelling type that represents a significant portion of the State's weatherization program in light of the varying energy audit requirements of different dwelling types including single-family dwellings, multi-family buildings, and mobile homes.

(g) For similar dwelling units without unusual energy-consuming characteristics, energy audits may be accomplished by using a priority list developed by conducting, in compliance with paragraphs (b) through (f) of this section, site-specific energy audits of a representative subset of these dwelling units. For DOE approval, States must describe how the priority list was developed, how the subset of similar homes was determined, and circumstances that will require site-specific audits rather than the use of the priority lists. States also must provide the input data and list of weatherization measures recommended by the energy audit software or manual methods for several dwelling units from the subset of similar units.

(h) States may use, as a part of an energy audit, general heat waste reduction weatherization materials that DOE has determined to be generally cost-effective. States may request approval to use general heat waste materials not listed in DOE policy guidance by providing documentation of their cost-effectiveness and a description of the circumstances under which such materials will be used.

(*i*) States must resubmit their energy audit procedures (and priority lists, if applicable, under certain conditions) to DOE for approval every five years. States must also resubmit to DOE, for approval every five years, their list of general heat waste materials in addition to those approved by DOE in policy guidance, if applicable. Policy guidance will describe the information States must submit to DOE and the circumstances that reduce or increase documentation requirements.

[50 Fed. Reg. 713 (Jan. 4, 1985); 58 Fed. Reg. 12527 (Mar. 4, 1993); 65 Fed. Reg. 77218 (Dec. 8, 2000); 71 Fed. Reg. 35775 (June 22, 2006)]

10 C.F.R. § 440.22 Eligible dwelling units

(a) A dwelling unit shall be eligible for weatherization assistance under this part if it is occupied by a family unit:

(1) Whose income is at or below 200 percent of the poverty level determined in accordance with criteria established by the Director of the Office of Management and Budget,

(2) Which contains a member who has received cash assistance payments under Title IV or XVI of the Social Security Act or applicable State or local law at any time during the 12-month period preceding the determination of eligibility for weatherization assistance; or

(3) If the State elects, is eligible for assistance under the Low-Income Home Energy Assistance Act of 1981, provided that such basis is at least 200 percent of the poverty level determined in accordance with criteria established by the Director of the Office of Management and Budget.

(b) A subgrantee may weatherize a building containing rental dwelling units using financial assistance for dwelling units eligible for weatherization assistance under paragraph (a) of this section, where:

(1) The subgrantee has obtained the written permission of the owner or his agent;

(2) Not less than 66 percent (50 percent for duplexes and four-unit buildings, and certain eligible types of large multi-family buildings) of the dwelling units in the building:

(i) Are eligible dwelling units, or

(ii) Will become eligible dwelling units within 180 days under a Federal, State, or local government program for rehabilitating the building or making similar improvements to the building; and

(3) The grantee has established procedures for dwellings which consist of a rental unit or rental units to ensure that:

(i) The benefits of weatherization assistance in connection with such rental units, including units where the tenants pay for their energy through their rent, will accrue primarily to the low-income tenants residing in such units;

(ii) For a reasonable period of time after weatherization work has been completed on a dwelling containing a unit occupied by an eligible household, the tenants in that unit (including households paying for their energy through their rent) will not be subjected to rent increases unless those increases are demonstrably related to matters other than the weatherization work performed;

(iii) The enforcement of paragraph (b)(3)(ii) of this section is provided through procedures established by the State by which tenants may file complaints, and owners, in response to such complaints, shall demonstrate that the rent increase concerned is related to matters other than the weatherization work performed; and

(iv) No undue or excessive enhancement shall occur to the value of the dwelling units.

(4)(i) A building containing rental dwelling units meets the requirements of paragraph (b)(2), and paragraphs (b)(3)(ii) and (b)(3)(iv), of this section if it is included on the most recent list posted by DOE of Assisted Housing and Public Housing buildings identified by the U.S. Department of Housing and Urban Development as meeting those requirements.

(ii) A building containing rental dwelling units meets the requirements of paragraph (b)(2), and paragraph (b)(3)(iv), of this section if it is included on the most recent list posted by DOE of Assisted Housing and Public Housing buildings identified by the U.S. Department of Housing and Urban Development as meeting those requirements.

(iii) A building containing rental dwelling units meets the requirement of paragraph (b)(2) of this section if it is included on the most recent list posted by DOE of Low Income Housing Tax Credit buildings identified by the U.S. Department of Housing and Urban Development as meeting that requirement and of Rural Housing Service Multifamily Housing buildings identified by the U.S. Department of Agriculture as meeting that requirement.

(iv) For buildings identified under paragraphs (b)(4)(i), (ii) and (iii) of this section, States will continue to be responsible for ensuring compliance with the remaining requirements of this section, and States shall establish requirements and procedures to ensure such compliance in accordance with this section.

(c) In order to secure the Federal investment made under this part and address the issues of eviction from and sale of property receiving weatherization materials under this part, States may seek landlord agreement to placement of a lien or to other contractual restrictions.

(d) As a condition of having assistance provided under this part with respect to multifamily buildings, a State may require financial participation, when feasible, from the owners of such buildings. Such financial participation shall not be reported as program income, nor will it be treated as if it were appropriated funds. The funds contributed by the landlord shall be expended in accordance with the agreement between the landlord and the weatherization agency.

(e) In devising procedures under paragraph (b)(3)(iii) of this section, States should consider requiring use of alternative dispute resolution procedures including arbitration.

(f) A State may weatherize shelters. For the purpose of determining how many dwelling units exist in a shelter, a grantee may count each 800 square feet of the shelter as a dwelling unit or it may count each floor of the shelter as a dwelling unit.

[58 Fed. Reg. 12528 (Mar. 4, 1993); 65 Fed. Reg. 77219 (Dec. 8, 2000); 74 Fed. Reg. 12540 (Mar. 25, 2009); 75 Fed. Reg. 3856 (Jan. 25, 2010)]

10 C.F.R. § 440.23 Oversight, training, and technical assistance

(a) The Secretary and the appropriate Support Office Director, in coordination with the Secretary of Health and Human Services, shall monitor and evaluate the operation of projects carried out by CAA's receiving financial assistance under this part through on-site inspections, or through other means, in order to ensure the effective provision of weatherization assistance for the dwelling units of low-income persons.

(b) DOE shall also carry out periodic evaluations of a program and weatherization projects that are not carried out by a CAA and that are receiving financial assistance under this part.

(c) The Secretary and the appropriate Support Office Director, the Comptroller General of the United States, and for a weatherization project carried out by a CAA, the Secretary of Health and Human Services or any of their duly authorized representatives, shall have access to any books, documents, papers, information, and records of any weatherization project receiving financial assistance under the Act for the purpose of audit and examination.

(d) Each grantee shall ensure that audits by or on behalf of subgrantees are conducted with reasonable frequency, on a continuing basis, or at scheduled intervals, usually annually, but not less frequently than every two years, in accordance with 10 CFR part 600, and OMB Circular 110, Attachment F, as applicable.

(e) The Secretary may reserve from the funds appropriated for any fiscal year an amount not to exceed 20 percent to provide, directly or indirectly, training and technical assistance to any grantee or subgrantee. Such training and technical assistance may include providing information concerning conservation practices to occupants of eligible dwelling units.

[[55 Fed. Reg. 3005 (Jan. 29, 1990); 55 Fed. Reg. 41326 (Oct. 10, 1990); 58 Fed. Reg. 12529 (Mar. 4, 1993); 74 Fed. Reg. 12540 (Mar. 25, 2009)]

10 C.F.R. § 440.24 Recordkeeping

Each grantee or subgrantee receiving Federal financial assistance under this part shall keep such records as DOE shall require, including records which fully disclose the amount and disposition by each grantee and subgrantee of the funds received, the total cost of a weatherization project or the total expenditure to implement the State plan for which assistance was given or used, the source and amount of funds for such project or program not supplied by DOE, the average costs incurred in weatherization of individual dwelling units, the average size of the dwelling being weatherized, the average income of households receiving assistance under this part, and such other records as DOE deems necessary for an effective audit and performance evaluation. Such recordkeeping shall be in accordance with the DOE Financial Assistance Rule, 10 CFR part 600, and any further requirements of this part.

[58 Fed. Reg. 12529 (Mar. 4, 1993)]

10 C.F.R. § 440.25 Reports

DOE may require any recipient of financial assistance under this part to provide, in such form as may be prescribed, such reports or answers in writing to specific questions, surveys, or questionnaires as DOE determines to be necessary to carry out its responsibilities or the responsibilities of the Secretary of Health and Human Services under this part.

[49 Fed. Reg. 3634 (Jan. 27, 1984)]

10 C.F.R. §§ 440.26–440.29 [Reserved]

[58 Fed. Reg. 12529 (Mar. 4, 1993)]

10 C.F.R. § 440.30 Administrative Review

(a) An applicant shall have 20 days from the date of receipt of a decision under § 440.12 or § 440.13 to file a notice requesting administrative review. If an applicant does not timely file such a notice, the decision under § 440.12 or § 440.13 shall become final for DOE.

(b) A notice requesting administrative review shall be filed with the Support Office Director and shall be accompanied by a written statement containing supporting arguments and requesting, if desired, the opportunity for a public hearing.

(c) A notice or any other document shall be deemed filed under this section upon receipt.

(d) On or before 15 days from receipt of a notice requesting administrative review which is timely filed, the Support Office Director shall forward to the Deputy Assistant Secretary, the notice requesting administrative review, the decision under § 440.12 or § 440.13 as to which administrative review is sought, a draft recommended final decision for the concurrence of the Deputy Assistant Secretary, and any other relevant material.

(e) If the applicant requests a public hearing, the Deputy Assistant Secretary, within 15 days, shall give actual notice to the State and Federal Register notice of the date, place, time, and procedures which shall apply to the public hearing. Any public hearing under this section shall be informal and legislative in nature.

(f) On or before 45 days from receipt of documents under paragraph (d) of this section or the conclusion of the public hearing, whichever is later, the Deputy Assistant Secretary shall concur in, concur in as modified, or issue a substitute for the recommended decision of the Support Office Director.

(g) On or before 15 days from the date of receipt of the determination under paragraph (f) of this section, the Governor may file an application, with a supporting statement of reasons, for discretionary review by the Assistant Secretary. On or before 15 days from filing, the Assistant Secretary shall send a notice to the Governor stating whether the Deputy Assistant Secretary's determination will be reviewed. If the Assistant Secretary grants review, a decision shall be issued no later than 60 days from the date review is granted. The Assistant Secretary may not issue a notice or decision under this paragraph without the concurrence of the DOE Office of General Counsel.

(h) A decision under paragraph (f) of this section shall be final for DOE if there is no review under paragraph (g) of this section. If there is review under paragraph (g) of this section, the decision thereunder shall be final for DOE, and no appeal shall lie elsewhere in DOE.

(*i*) Prior to the effective date of the termination of eligibility for further participation in the program because of failure to comply substantially with the requirements of the Act or of this part, a grantee shall have the right to written notice of the basis for the enforcement action and the opportunity for a public hearing notwithstanding any provisions to contrary of 10 CFR 600.26, 600.28(b), 600.29, 600.121(c), and 600.443. A notice under this paragraph shall be mailed by the Support Office Director by registered mail, return-receipt requested, to the State, local grantee, and other interested parties. To obtain a public hearing, the grantee must request an evidentiary hearing, with prior Federal Register notice, in the election letter submitted under Rule 2 of 10 CFR 1024.4 and the request shall be granted notwithstanding any provisions of Rule 2 to the contrary.

[55 Fed. Reg. 41326 (Oct. 10, 1990), *as amended at* 58 Fed. Reg. 12529 (Mar. 4, 1993)]

10 C.F.R. Part 440 Appendix A—Standards for Weatherization Materials

The following Government standards are produced by the Consumer Product Safety Commission and are published in title 16, Code of Federal Regulations:

Thermal Insulating Materials for Building Elements Including Walls, Floors, Ceilings, Attics, and Roofs Insulation—organic fiber—conformance to Interim Safety Standard in 16 CFR part 1209;

Fire Safety Requirements for Thermal Insulating Materials According to Insulation Use—Attic Floor—insulation materials intended for exposed use in attic floors shall be capable of meeting the same flammability requirements given for cellulose insulation in 16 CFR part 1209;

Enclosed spaces—insulation materials intended for use within enclosed stud or joist spaces shall be capable of meeting the smoldering combustion requirements in 16 CFR part 1209.

The following standards which are not otherwise set forth in part 440 are incorporated by reference and made a part of part 440. The following standards have been approved for incorporation by reference by the Director of the Federal Register in accordance with 5 U.S.C. 552(a) and 1 CFR part 51. These materials are incorporated as they exist on April 5, 1993 and a notice of any change in these materials will be published in the Federal Register. The standards incorporated by reference are available for inspection at the Office of the Federal Register Information Center, 800 North Capitol Street, suite 700, Washington, DC.

The standards incorporated by reference in part 440 can be obtained from the following sources:

Air Conditioning and Refrigeration Institute, 1501 Wilson Blvd., Arlington, VA 22209; (703) 524-8800.

American Gas Association, 1515 Wilson Blvd., Arlington, VA 22209; (703) 841-8400.

American National Standards Institute, Inc., 1430 Broadway, New York, NY 10018; (212) 642-4900.

American Society of Mechanical Engineers, United Engineering Center, 345 East 47th Street, New York, NY 10017; (212) 705-7800.

American Society for Testing and Materials, 1916 Race Street, Philadelphia, PA 19103; (215) 299-5400.

American Architectural Manufacturers Association, 1540 East Dundee Road, Palatine, IL 60067; (708) 202-1350.

Federal Specifications, General Services Administration, Specifications Section, Room 6654, 7th and D Streets, SW, Washington, DC 20407; (202) 708-5082.

Gas Appliance Manufacturers Association, 1901 Moore St., Arlington, VA 22209; (703) 525-9565.

National Electrical Manufacturers Association, 2101 L Street, NW, Suite 300, Washington, DC 20037; (202) 457-8400.

National Fire Protection Association, Batterymarch Park, P.O. Box 9101, Quincy, MA 02269; (617) 770-3000.

National Standards Association, 1200 Quince Orchard Blvd., Gaithersburg, MD 20878; (301) 590-2300. (NSA is a local contact for materials from ASTM).

National Wood Window and Door Association, 1400 East Touhy Avenue, Des Plaines, IL 60018; (708) 299-5200.

Sheet Metal and Air Conditioning Contractors Association, P.O. Box 221230, Chantilly, VA 22022-1230; (703) 803-2980.

Steel Door Institute, 712 Lakewood Center North, 14600 Detroit Avenue, Cleveland, OH 44107; (216) 899-0100.

Steel Window Institute, 1230 Keith Building, Cleveland, OH 44115; (216) 241-7333.

Tubular Exchanger Manufacturers Association, 25 North Broadway, Tarrytown, NY 10591; (914) 332-0040.

Underwriters Laboratories, Inc., P.O. Box 75530, Chicago, IL 60675-5330; (708) 272-8800.

More information regarding the standards in this reference can be obtained from the following sources:

Environmental Protection Agency, 401 M Street, NW, Washington, DC 20006; (202) 554-1080.

National Institute of Standards and Technology, U.S. Department of Commerce, Gaithersburg, MD 20899, (301) 975-2000.

Weatherization Assistance Programs Division, Conservation and Renewable Energy, Mail Stop 5G-023, Forrestal Bldg, 1000 Independence Ave, SW, Washington, DC 20585; (202) 586-2207.

Thermal Insulating Materials for Building Elements Including Walls, Floors, Ceilings, Attics, and Roofs

[Standards for conformance]

Insulation—mineral fiber:	
Blanket insulation	ASTM[1] C665-88.
Roof insulation board	ASTM C726-88.
Loose-fill insulation	ASTM C764-88.
Insulation—mineral cellular:	
Vermiculite loose-fill insulation	ASTM C516-80 (1990).
Perlite loose-fill insulation	ASTM C549-81 (1986).
Cellular glass insulation block	ASTM C552-88.
Perlite insulation board	ASTM C728-89a.
Insulation—organic fiber:	
Cellulosic fiber insulating board	ASTM C208-72 (1982).
Cellulose loose-fill insulation	ASTM C739-88.
Insulation-organic cellular:	
Preformed block-type polystyrene insulation.	ASTM C578-87a.
Rigid preformed polyurethane insulation board.	ASTM C591-85.
Polyurethane or polyisocyanurate insulation board faced with aluminum foil on both sides.	FS[2] HH-I-1972/1 (1981).
Polyurethane or polyisocyanurate insulation board faced with felt on both sides.	FS HH-I-1972/2 (1981). And Amendment 1, October 3, 1985.
Insulation—composite boards:	
Mineral fiber and rigid cellular polyurethane composite roof insulation board.	ASTM C726-88.
Perlite board and rigid cellular polyurethane composite roof insulation.	ASTM C984-83.
Gypsum board and polyurethane or polisocyanurate composite board.	FS HH-I-1972/4 (1981).
Materials used as a patch to reduce infiltration through the building envelope.	Commercially available.

1 ASTM indicates American Society for Testing and Materials.
2 FS indicates Federal Specifications.

Thermal Insulating Materials for Pipes, Ducts, and Equipment Such as Boilers and Furnaces

[Standards for conformance]

Insulation—mineral fiber:	
Preformed pipe insulation	ASTM[1] C547-77.
Blanket and felt insulation (industrial type).	ASTM C553-70 (1977).
Blanket insulation and blanket type pipe insulation (metal-mesh covered) (industrial type).	ASTM C592-80.
Block and board insulation	ASTM C612-83.
Spray applied fibrous insulation for elevated temperature.	ASTM C720-89.
High-temperature fiber blanket insulation.	ASTM C892-89.
Duct work insulation	Selected and applied according to ASTM C971-82.
Insulation—mineral cellular:	
Diatomaceous earth block and pipe insulation.	ASTM C517-71 (1979).
Calcium silicate block and pipe insulation.	ASTM C533-85 (1990).
Cellular glass insulation	ASTM C552-88.
Expanded perlite block and pipe insulation.	ASTM C610-85.
Insulation—Organic Cellular:	
Preformed flexible elastomeric cellular insulation in sheet and tubular form.	ASTM C534-88.
Unfaced preformed rigid cellular polyurethane insulation.	ASTM C591-85.
Insulation skirting	Commercially available.

1 ASTM indicates American Society for Testing and Materials.

Fire Safety Requirements for Insulating Materials According to Insulation Use

[Standards for conformance]

Attic floor	Insulation materials intended for exposed use in attic floors shall be capable of meeting the same smoldering combustion requirements given for cellulose insulation in ASTM[1] C739-88.
Enclosed space	Insulation materials intended for use within enclosed stud or joist spaces shall be capable of meeting the smoldering combustion requirements in ASTM C739-88.
Exposed interior walls and ceilings	Insulation materials, including those with combustible facings, which remain exposed and serve as wall or ceiling interior finish, shall have a flame spread classification not to exceed 150 (per ASTM E84-89a).
Exterior envelope walls and roofs	Exterior envelope walls and roofs containing thermal insulations shall meet applicable local government building code requirements for the complete wall or roof assembly.
Pipes, ducts, and equipment	Insulation materials intended for use on pipes, ducts and equipment shall be capable of meeting a flame spread classification not to exceed 150 (per ASTM E84-89a).

1 ASTM indicates American Society for Testing and Materials.

Storm Windows

[Standards for conformance]

Storm windows:	
Aluminum insulating storm windows	ANSI/AAMA[1] 1002.10-83.
Aluminum frame storm windows	ANSI/AAMA 1002.10-83.
Wood frame storm windows	ANSI/NWWDA[2] I.S. 2-87. (Section 3)
Rigid vinyl frame storm windows	ASTM[3] D4099-89.
Frameless plastic glazing storm	Required minimum thickness windows is 6 mil (.006 inches).
Movable insulation systems for windows	Commercially available.

1 ANSI/AAMA indicates American National Standards Institute/American Architectural Manufacturers Association.
2 ANSI/NWWDA indicates American National Standards Institute/National Wood Window & Door Association.
3 ASTM indicates American Society for Testing and Materials.

Storm Doors

[Standards for conformance]

Storm doors—Aluminum:	
Storm Doors	ANSI/AAMA[1] 1102.7-89.
Sliding glass storm doors	ANSI/AAMA 1002.10-83.
Wood storm doors	ANSI/NWWDA[2] I.S. 6-86.
Rigid vinyl storm doors	ASTM[3] D3678-88.
Vestibules:	
Materials to construct vestibules	Commercially available.
Replacement windows:	
Aluminum frame windows	ANSI/AAMA 101-88.
Steel frame windows	Steel Window Institute recommended specifications for steel windows, 1990.
Wood frame windows	ANSI/NWWDA I.S. 2-87.
Rigid vinyl frame windows	ASTM D4099-89.

1 ANSI/AAMA indicates American National Standards Institute/American Architectural Manufacturers Association.
2 ANSI/NWWDA indicates American National Standards Institute/National Wood Window & Door Association.
3 ASTM indicates American Society for Testing and Materials.

Replacement Doors

[Standards for conformance]

Replacement doors—Hinged doors:	
Steel doors	ANSI/SDI[1] 100-1985.
Wood doors:	
Flush doors	ANSI/NWWDA[2] I.S. 1-87. (exterior door provisions)
Pine, fir, hemlock and spruce doors	ANSI/NWWDA I.S. 6-86.
Sliding patio doors:	
Aluminum doors	ANSI/AAMA[3] 101-88.
Wood doors	NWWDA I.S. 3-83.

1 ANSI/SDI indicates American National Standards Institute/Steel Door Institute.
2 ANSI/NWWDA indicates American National Standards Institute/National Wood Window & Door Association.
3 ANSI/AAMA indicates American National Standards Institute/American Architectural Manufacturers Association.

Caulks and sealants:

[Standards for conformance]

Caulks and sealants:	
Putty	FS[1] TT-P-00791B, October 16, 1969 and Amendment 2, March 23, 1971.
Glazing compounds for metal sash	ASTM[2] C669-75 (1989).
Oil and resin base caulks	ASTM C570-72 (1989).
Acrylic (solvent types) sealants	FS TT-S-00230C, February 2, 1970 and Amendment 2, October 9, 1970.
Butyl rubber sealants	FS TT-S-001657, October 8, 1970.
Chlorosulfonated polyethylene sealants	FS TT-S-00230C, February 2, 1970 and Amendment 2, October 9, 1970.
Latex sealing compounds	ASTM C834-76 (1986).
Elastomeric joint sealants (normally considered to include polysulfide, polyurethane, and silicone).	ASTM C920-87.
Preformed gaskets and sealing materials.	ASTM C509-84.

1 FS indicates Federal Specifications.
2 ASTM indicates American Society for Testing and Materials.

Weatherstripping

[Standards for conformance]

Weatherstripping	Commercially available.
Vapor retarders	Selected according to the provisions cited in ASTM[1] C755-85 (1990). Permeance not greater than 1 perm when determined according to the desiccant method described in ASTM E96-90.
Items to improve attic ventilation	Commercially available.
Clock thermostats	NEMA[2] DC 3-1989.

1 ASTM indicates American Society for Testing and Materials.
2 NEMA indicates National Electrical Manufacturers Association.

Heat Exchangers

[Standards for conformance]

Heat exchangers, water-to-water and steam-to-water.	ASME[1] Boiler and Pressure Vessel Code, 1992, Sections II, V, VIII, IX, and X, as applicable to pressure vessels. Standards of Tubular Exchanger Manufacturers Association, Seventh Edition, 1988.
Heat exchangers with gas-fired appliances.[2]	Conformance to AGA[3] Requirements for Heat Reclaimer Devices for Use with Gas-Fired Appliances No. 1-80, June 1, 1980. AGA Laboratories Certification Seal.
Heat pump water heating heat recovery systems.	Electrical components to be listed by UL.[4]

1 ASME indicates American Society of Mechanical Engineers.
2 The heat reclaimer is for installation in a section of the vent connector from appliances equipped with draft hoods or appliances equipped with powered burners or induced draft and not equipped with a draft hood.

3 AGA indicates American Gas Association.
4 UL indicates Underwriters Laboratories.

Boiler/Furnace Control Systems
[Standards for conformance]

Automatic set back thermostats	Listed by UL.[1] Conformance to NEMA[2] DC 3-1989.
Line voltage or low voltage room thermostats.	NEMA DC 3-1989.
Automatic gas ignition systems	ANSI[3] Z21.21-1987 and Z21.21a-1989. AGA[4] Laboratories Certification Seal.
Energy management systems	Listed by UL.
Hydronic boiler controls	Listed by UL.
Other burner controls	Listed by UL.

1 UL indicates Underwriters Laboratories.
2 NEMA indicates National Electrical Manufacturers Association.
3 ANSI indicates American National Standards Institute.
4 AGA indicates American Gas Association.

Water Heater Modifications
[Standards for conformance]

Insulate tank and distribution piping	(See insulation section of this appendix).
Install heat traps on inlet and outlet piping.	Applicable local plumbing code.
Install/replace water heater heating elements.	Listed by UL.[1]
Electric, freeze-prevention tape for pipes	Listed by UL.
Reduce thermostat settings	State or local recommendations.
Install stack damper, gas-fueled	ANS1[2] Z21.66-1988, including Exhibits A&B, and ANSI Z223.1-1988.
Install stack damper, oil-fueled	UL 17, November 28, 1988, and NFPA[3] 31-1987.
Install water flow modifiers	Commercially available.

1 UL indicates Underwriters Laboratories.
2 ANSI indicates American National Standards Institute.
3 NFPA indicates National Fire Prevention Association.

Waste Heat Recovery Devices
[Standards for conformance]

Desuperheater/water heaters	ARI[1] 470-1987.
Condensing heat exchangers	Commercially available components and in new heating furnace systems to manufacturers' specifications.
Condensing heat exchangers	Commercially available (Commercial, multi-story building, with teflon-lined tubes institutional) to manufacturers' specifications.
Energy recovery equipment	Energy Recovery Equipment and Systems Air-to-Air (1978) Sheet Metal and Air-Conditioning Contractors National Association (SMACNA).[2]

1 ARI indicates Air Conditioning and Refrigeration Institute.
2 SMACNA denotes Sheet Metal and Air Conditioning Contractors' National Association.

Boiler Repair and Modifications/Efficiency Improvements
[Standards for conformance]

Install gas conversion burners	ANSI[1] Z21.8-1984, (for gas or oil-fired systems) ANSI Z21.17-1984, ANSI Z21.17a-1990, and ANSI Z223.1-1988. AGA[2] Laboratories Certification seal.
Replace oil burner	UL[3] 296, February 28, 1989 Revision and NFPA[4] 31-1987.
Install burners (oil/gas)	ANSI Z223.1-1988 for gas equipment and NFPA 31-1987 for oil equipment.
Re-adjust boiler water temperature or install automatic boiler temperature reset control.	ASME[5] CSD-1-1988, ASME CSD-1a-1989, ANSI Z223.1-1988, and NFPA 31-1987.
Replace/modify boilers	ASME Boiler and Pressure Vessel Code, 1992, Sections II, IV, V, VI, VIII, IX, and X. Boilers must be Institute of Boilers and Radiation Manufacturers (IBR) equipment.
Clean heat exchanger, adjust burner air shutter(s), check smoke no. on oil-fueled equipment. Check operation of pump(s) and replacement filters.	Per manufacturers' instructions.
Repair combustion chambers	Refractory linings may be required for conversions.
Replace heat exchangers, tubes.	Protection from flame contact with conversion burners by refractory shield.
Install/replace thermostatic radiator valves.	Commercially available. One pipe steam systems require air vents on each radiator. *See* manufacturers' requirements.
Install boiler duty cycle control system.	Commercially available. NFPA 70, National Electrical Code (NEC) 1993 and local electrical codes provisions for wiring.

1 ANSI indicates American National Standards Institute.
2 AGA indicates American Gas Association.
3 UL indicates Underwriters Laboratories.
4 NFPA indicates National Fire Prevention Association.
5 ANSI/ASME indicates American National Standards Institute/American Society of Mechanical Engineers.

Heating and Cooling System Repairs and Tune-ups/Efficiency Improvements

[Standards for conformance]

Install duct insulation	FS[1] HH-I-558C, January 7, 1992 (see insulation sections of this appendix).
Reduce input of burner; derate gas-fueled equipment.	Local utility company and procedures if applicable for gas-fueled furnaces and ANSI[2] Z223.1-1988 (NFPA[3] 54-1988) including Appendix H.
Repair/replace oil-fired equipment	NFPA 31-1987.
Replace combustion chamber in oil-fired furnaces or boilers.	NFPA 31-1987.
Clean heat exchanger and adjust burner: adjust air shutter and check CO_2 and stack temperature.	ANSI Z223.1-1988 (NFPA 54-1988) including Appendix H.
Clean or replace air filter on forced air furnace.	
Install vent dampers for gas-fueled heating systems.	Applicable sections of ANSI Z223.1-1988 (NFPA 54-1988) including Appendices H, I, J, and K. ANSI Z21.66-1988 and Exhibits A & B for electrically operated dampers.
Install vent dampers for oil-fueled heating systems.	Applicable sections of NFPA 31-1987 for installation and in conformance with UL[4] 17, November 28, 1988.
Reduce excess combustion air:	
A: Reduce vent connector size of gas-fueled appliances.	ANSI Z223.1-1988 (NFPA 54-1988) Part 9 and Appendices G & H.
B: Adjust barometric draft regulator for oil fuels.	NFPA 31-1987 and per manufacturers' (furnace or boiler) instructions.
Replace constant burning pilot with electric ignition device on gas-fueled furnaces or boilers.	ANSI Z21.71-1981, Z21.71a-1985, and Z21.71b-1989.
Readjust fan switch on forced air gas or oil-fueled furnaces.	Applicable sections and Appendix H of ANSI Z223.1-1988 (NFPA 54-1988) for gas furnaces and NFPA 31-1987 for oil furnaces.
Replace burners	See power burners (oil/gas).
Install/replace duct furnaces (gas)	ANSI Z223.1-1988 (NFPA 54-1988).
Install/replace heat pumps	Listed by UL.
Replace air diffusers, intakes, registers, and grilles.	Commercially available.
Install/replace warm air heating metal ducts.	Commercially available.
Filter alarm units	Commercially available.

1 FS indicates Federal Specifications.
2 ANSI indicates American National Standards Institute.
3 NFPA indicates National Fire Prevention Association.
4 UL indicates Underwriters Laboratories.

Replacement Furnaces, Boilers, and Wood Stoves

[Standards for conformance]

Chimneys, fireplaces, vents and solid fuel burning appliances.	NFPA[1] 211-1988.
Gas-fired furnaces	ANS1[2] Z21.47-1987, Z21.47a-1988, and Z21.47b-1989. ANSI Z223.1-1988 (NFPA 54-1988).
Oil-fired furnaces	UL[3] 727, August 27, 1991 Revision and NFPA 31-1987.
Liquified petroleum gas storage	NFPA 58-1989.
Ventilation fans:	
Including electric attic, ceiling, and whole house fans.	UL 507, August 23, 1990 Revision.

1 NFPA indicates National Fire Prevention Association.
2 ANSI indicates American National Standards Institute.
3 UL indicates Underwriters Laboratories.

Air Conditioners and Cooling Equipment

[Standards for conformance]

Air conditioners:	
Central air conditioners	ARI[1] 210/240-1989.
Room size units	ANSI/AHAM[2] RAC-1-1982.
Other cooling equipment:	
Including evaporative coolers, heat pumps and other equipment.	UL[3] 1995, November 30, 1990.[4]

1 ARI indicates Air Conditioning and Refrigeration Institute.
2 AHAM/ANSI indicates American Home Appliance Manufacturers/ American National Standards Institute.
3 UL indicates Underwriters Laboratories.
4 This standard is a general standard covering many different types of heating and cooling equipment.

Screens, Window Films, and Reflective Materials

[Standards for conformance]

Insect screens	Commercially available.
Window films	Commercially available.
Shade screens:	
Fiberglass shade screens	Commercially available.
Polyester shade screens	Commercially available.
Rigid awnings:	
Wood rigid awnings	Commercially available.
Metal rigid awnings	Commercially available.
Louver systems:	
Wood louver systems	Commercially available.
Metal louver systems	Commercially available.
Industrial-grade white paint used as a heat-reflective measure on awnings, window louvers, doors, and exterior duct work (exposed).	Commercially available.

[50 Fed. Reg. 713 (Jan. 4, 1985); 58 Fed. Reg. 12529 (Mar. 4, 1993)]

D.3 Consumer Information About Low-Income Weatherization

D.3.1 Frequently Asked Questions About Weatherization Assistance from Low-Income Families

The following information may be found at the U.S. Department of Energy's website at www1.eere.energy.gov/wip/wap_apply.html (last visited March 18, 2011).

Low-income families often have a number of questions for the U.S. Department of Energy (DOE) on how to apply for weatherization assistance or about DOE's role in the process. If you want to apply immediately for weatherization, you'll need to contact your state agency.[1]

If I rent, can I still apply?

Whether you own or rent, live in a single-family home, multifamily housing complex, or a mobile home, you can apply for assistance. If you rent, you must get written permission from your landlord before weatherization services can be performed.

If my income is within these national guidelines, will I be guaranteed to receive weatherization services?

Not necessarily. You will need to check your states particular guidelines. Funding can also be an issue because Congress allocates a certain amount of funding for the program on a national level, and it varies from year to year. Please be patient if you are put on a waiting list. Your home will be weatherized as soon as possible.

If I'm not eligible for this program, whom can I call for help?

- Low-Income Home Energy Assistance Program (LIHEAP)[2]
  Even if you are not approved for DOE-sponsored weatherization assistance, you might still be eligible for short-term assistance on your utility bill from the LIHEAP Program. Funded by the U.S. Department of Health and Human Services, LIHEAP serves low-income families. In addition, states often use LIHEAP funds for weatherization to reduce a family's energy bills over the long term.
- Assistance to Individuals Involved in a Natural Disaster[3]
  The Federal Energy Management Agency (FEMA) provides a number of services to assist individuals who are victims of a natural disaster. These services include low-interest loans, some cash grants, and links to assistance from other agencies such as the Internal Revenue Service and Farm Service Agency.

  FEMA also lists services it makes available to older Americans who live in federally declared disaster areas, including include Small Business Administration loans and FEMA grants.

1 *Editor's note:* See Appendix D.5, *infra*, for a state-by-state list of Weatherization Assistance Program contacts.

2 *Editor's note:* Information about LIHEAP is accessible at www.acf.hhs.gov/programs/ocs/liheap.

3 *Editor's note:* Information about assistance available from FEMA is accessible at www.fema.gov/assistance.

Why can't I call DOE directly to apply for assistance?

Because of the guidelines set down by the U.S. Constitution, the federal government does not provide assistance directly to individuals. Instead, this function is the responsibility of the states. DOE does not have an application form to give to individuals for weatherizing their homes. DOE does not accept applications from individuals. Since each state has a different procedure, all we can do is refer you to your respective state agency.[4]

What happens to my home during the Weatherization Process?

The first step in the process is for your local weatherization agency to carry out an energy audit. This agency is a nonprofit weatherization organization, local governmental agency, or sometimes a contractor trained in home energy services. The energy audit is a computerized assessment of your home's energy use and an analysis of which energy conservation measures are best for your home.

Once the audit is complete, the auditor or inspector from the local weatherization agency will meet with you and your family to explain how the work crews will conduct the work. Depending on your needs, the inspector will recommend more work in some homes than in others.

Throughout the weatherization process, the health and safety of your family remain a priority. Following weatherization, an inspector will return to make certain that everything is working properly and that nothing was missed.

How will I benefit by participating in this program?

Weatherization reduces your energy bills for a long time. Some measures, such as insulating your walls or roof, for example, will continue to provide you savings for the lifetime of your house—30 years or more. Others, such as making your heating or cooling equipment more efficient, will provide savings for 10 to 15 years. On average, the value of the weatherization improvement to your house is 2.2 times greater than the cost of the improvement itself.

D.3.2 What Are Weatherization Services?

The following information is reprinted from the U.S. Department of Energy's website at www1.eere.energy.gov/wip/weatherization.html (last visited on March 24, 2011)

Weatherization as defined by the Weatherization Assistance Program (WAP) differs in many ways from what is commonly called "weatherizing your home." The latter involves low-cost improvements like adding weatherstripping to doors and windows to save energy. These measures made up the services WAP provided in its early years and are likely responsible for the program's name.

Today, WAP's weatherization services consist of cost-effective energy efficiency measures for existing residential and multifamily housing with low-income residents. Under this definition, it includes a wide variety of energy efficiency measures that encompass the building envelope, its heating and cooling systems, its electrical system, and electricity consuming appliances.

4 *Editor's note:* See Appendix D.5, *infra*, for a state-by-state list of Weatherization Assistance Program contacts.

WAP serves low-income families free of charge and limits the amount of money that can be spent on any single residence as determined by federal rules. (The average expenditure is $6500.)[1] As a result, only the most cost-effective measures are included in the upgrade of a particular home. This constant pressure for low-cost energy savings has become the trademark of weatherization and distinguishes it from the larger home retrofit industry.

Another distinguishing feature of weatherization is attention to an all-around safety check. Many buildings receiving attention are old and in need of repair. Weatherization service providers check major energy systems to ensure occupant safety.

Increasingly, weatherization service providers look at the house as a system under the concept of "whole-house weatherization." In recent years, weatherization providers in many states have begun to combine resources from other programs to address other needs of their clients. This expanded approach is referred to as *Weatherization Plus*.[2]

Weatherization today comprises a comprehensive series of energy efficiency measures that are based on sophisticated analyses of individual homes. These analyses take the whole-house approach, which maximizes energy and dollar savings. Because of this rigorous approach and analyses backing it up, weatherization has become a leader in advancing home energy science and in helping spawn a new industry providing home energy efficiency services to the wider public.

1 *Editor's note:* Current average as of fiscal year 2011. It is possible this average will decline in future years.

2 Information about "Weatherization Plus" is available on the DOE's website, at www.waptac.org/WAP-Basics/Weatherization-Plus.aspx (last visited on March 24, 2011).

D.4 2010 Poverty Income Guidelines and Definition of Income

Department of Energy
Washington. DC 20585

WEATHERIZATION PROGRAM NOTICE 10-18
Effective Date: September 20, 2010

SUBJECT: 2010 POVERTY INCOME GUIDELINES AND DEFINITION OF INCOME

PURPOSE: To provide States with the 2010 Poverty Income Guidelines and Definition of Income for use in the Low-Income Weatherization Assistance Program (Weatherization).

SCOPE: The provisions of this guidance apply to all Grantees applying for financial assistance under the Department of Energy (DOE) Weatherization Assistance Program.

LEGAL AUTHORITY: Title IV, Energy Conservation and Production Act. as amended, authorizes the Department of Energy to administer the Low-Income Weatherization Assistance Program. All grant awards made under this Program shall comply with applicable law including regulations contained in 10 CFR Part 440 (issued February I, 2002), the Energy Policy Act of 2005, the Energy Independence and Security Act 0f 2007, the American Recovery and Reinvestment Act of 2009 and other procedures applicable to this regulation.

BACKGROUND: Usually the Poverty Income Guidelines are published in late January to early February of the current year. However, this year legislation enacted in late 2009 and early 2010 prohibited publication of 2010 poverty guidelines before May 31, 2010, and required that the 2009 poverty guidelines remain in effect until publication of updated guidelines. The procedure for updating the 2010 guidelines was modified to take into account the Consumer Price Index (CPI-UP for the period for which their publication was delayed. As a result, the poverty guideline figures for the remainder of 2010 are the same as the 2009 poverty guideline figures.

PROCEDURES: The American Recovery and Reinvestment Act of 2009, Public Law 111-005, signed by the President on February 17, 2009, raised the DOE Weatherization eligibility criterion by striking "150 percent" in both places it appears in Section 412(7) of the Energy Conservation and Production Act (42 U.S.C. 6862(7)) and inserting "200 percent." The annual revision of the poverty income guidelines was published in the Federal Register Volume 75, Number 148/Wednesday, August 3, 2010, pages 45628–45629. Attached is a table displaying the guidelines showing income eligibility limits at 200 percent of poverty. Guideline tables for Alaska and Hawaii are also included. These guidelines are effective as of August 3, 2010, and apply to both farm and non-farm families. States should distribute these tables immediately to their subgrantees for their use. Additionally, this notice provides grantees with a definition of income for use in the Weatherization Program. This definition is updated from the previous year's guidance. Clarifications on income and eligibility issues are discussed in the Program Year 2010 Weatherization Grant Guidance, in section 5.9, Determining Eligibility Levels and Defining Income, of WPN-IO-1.

Tobias Russell
Acting Program Manager Office of Weatherization and
Intergovernmental Program
Energy Efficiency and Renewable Energy

DEFINITION OF INCOME

A. INCOME: Income means Cash Receipts earned and/or received by the applicant before taxes during applicable tax year(s) *but not* the Income Exclusions listed below in *Section C.*

B. CASH RECEIPTS: Cash Receipts include the following:

1. money, wages and salaries before any deductions;
2. net receipts from non-farm or farm self-employment (receipts from a person's own business or from an owned or rented farm after deductions for business or farm expenses);
3. regular payments from social security, railroad retirement, unemployment compensation, strike benefits from union funds, worker's compensation, veteran's payments, training stipends, alimony, and military family allotments;
4. private pensions, government employee pensions (including military retirement pay), and regular insurance or annuity payments;
5. dividends and/or interest;
6. net rental income and net royalties;
7. periodic receipts from estates or trusts; and
8. net gambling or lottery winnings.

C. INCOME EXCLUSIONS: The following Cash Receipts *are not* considered sources of Income for the purposes of determining applicant eligibility:

1. capital gains;
2. any assets drawn down as withdrawals from a bank;
3. money received from the sale of a property, house, or car;
4. one-time payments from a welfare agency to a family or person who is in temporary financial difficulty;
5. tax refunds;
6. gifts, loans, or lump-sum inheritances;
7. college scholarships;
8. one-time insurance payments, or compensation for injury;
9. non-cash benefits, such as the employer-paid or union-paid portion of health insurance;
10. employee fringe benefits, food or housing received in lieu of wages;
11. the value of food and fuel produced and consumed on farms;
12. the imputed value of rent from owner-occupied non-farm or farm housing;
13. Federal non-cash benefit programs such as Medicare, Medicaid, Food Stamps, school lunches, and housing assistance;
14. combat zone pay to the military; and
15. Child Support, as defined below in *Section E.*

D. PROOF OF ELIGIBILITY: Grantees and subgrantees are reminded that, to the maximum extent practicable, proof of income eligibility and the associated documentation should be included in the client file.

1. **Eligibility Determined by Outside Agency Program:** If income eligibility is determined by an outside agency or program, i.e. Low-Income Home Energy Assistance Program (LIHEAP) or the U.S. Department of Housing and Urban Development (HUD), then copies of the eligibility documentation can be a statement of LIHEAP eligibility or a copy of the HUD building list, included in the client file.

2. **Self-Certification:** After all avenues of documenting income eligibility are exhausted, self-certification is allowable, but evidence of the various attempts at proving eligibility must be contained in the client file, including a notarized statement signed by the potential applicant indicating that he has no other proof of income.

E. CHILD SUPPORT: Child Support payments, whether received by the Payee or paid by the Payor, are not considered sources of Income for the purposes of determining applicant eligibility.

1. **Payee:** Where an applicant receives child support from any state program or individual during an applicable tax year, such assistance is not considered Income for the purposes of determining eligibility.
2. **Payor:** Where an applicant pays child support through a state program and/or to an individual, such assistance is not considered Income for the purposes of determining eligibility (i.e., where an applicant pays Child Support, he or she may not deduct said assistance for the purposes of determining eligibility).

F. ANNUALIZATION OF INCOME: Where an applicant receives Income for a part of the applicable tax year, their partial Income may be annualized to determine eligibility. (Example: Applicant A received income during January, February and March. The method of annualizing income to determine eligibility could be multiplied by four the amount of income received during those three months). The method of calculating annualization of Income is to be determined by the Grantee.

G. RE-CERTIFICATION: An applicant who is deemed ineligible based on Income may be re-certified *if* ineligibility is due to the length of time that expired while the applicant was waiting to receive weatherization services. As a reminder, recertification of eligibility should occur at least every 12 months. The method of determining Re-Certification is to be determined by the Grantee.

2009 POVERTY INCOME GUIDELINES
CONTIGUOUS U.S. GRANTEES
Effective January 23, 2009

	INCOME LEVELS	
Size of Family Unit	**Threshold**	**200%**
1	$10,830	$21,660
2	14,570	29,140
3	18,310	36,620
4	22,050	44,100
5	25,790	51,580
6	29,530	59,060
7	33,270	66,540
8	37,010	74,020
Each additional member add	3,740	7,480

2009 POVERTY INCOME GUIDELINES
ALASKA
Effective January 23, 2009

	INCOME LEVELS	
Size of Family Unit	**Threshold**	**200%**
1	$13,530	$27,060
2	18,210	36,420
3	22,890	45,780
4	27,570	55,140
5	32,250	64,500

6	36,930	73,860
7	41,610	83,220
8	46,290	92,580
Each additional member add	4,680	9,360

2009 POVERTY INCOME GUIDELINES
HAWAII
Effective January 23, 2009

	INCOME LEVELS	
Size of Family Unit	**Threshold**	**200%**
1	$12,460	$24,920
2	16,760	33,520
3	21,060	42,120
4	25,360	50,720
5	29,660	59,320
6	33,960	67,920
7	38,260	76,520
8	42,560	85,120
Each additional member add	4,300	8,600

D.5 State Weatherization Assistance Program Contacts

The list of weatherization contacts in this appendix is reprinted from information found on the Department of Energy website at www1.eere.energy.gov/wip/project_map (last accessed January 18, 2011). For updated or additional information, please visit the website listed above.

ALABAMA

Alabama Department of Economic and Community Affairs
401 Adams Avenue
P.O. Box 5690
Montgomery, AL 36103-5690
Phone: 334-242-4909
Fax: 334-353-4203

ALASKA

Alaska Housing Finance Corporation
Rural Research & Development Department
P.O. Box 101020
Anchorage, AK 99510-1020
Phone: 907-330-8192
Fax: 907-338-1747

ARIZONA

Arizona Department of Commerce
Energy Office
1700 W. Washington
Suite 220
Phoenix, AZ 85007
Phone: 602-771-1216
Fax: 602-771-1203

ARKANSAS

Arkansas Department of Human Services
Division of County Operations
P.O. Box 1437, Slot# S-330
Little Rock, AR 72203-1437
Phone: 501-682-8715
Fax: 501-682-6736

CALIFORNIA

Department of Community Services and Development
P.O. Box 1947
Sacramento, CA 95812-1947
Phone: 866-675-6623
Fax: 916-341-4376

COLORADO

Governor's Energy Office
1580 Logan Street
Suite 100
Denver, CO 80203
Phone: 303-866-2791
Fax: 303-866-2930

CONNECTICUT

Connecticut Department of Social Services
25 Sigourney Street
Hartford, CT 06106-5033
Phone: 1-800-842-1508
Fax: 860-424-5129 or 4952

DELAWARE

Delaware Office of Community Services
Charles Debnam Building, Herman Holloway Campus
1401 North Dupont Highway
New Castle, DE 19720
Phone: 302-255-9894
Fax: 302-255-4465

DISTRICT OF COLUMBIA

District of Columbia Energy Office
2000 14th Street, NW, Suite 300 East
Washington, DC 20009
Phone: 202-671-3306
Fax: 202-673-6725

FLORIDA

Department of Community Affairs
2555 Shumard Oak Boulevard
Tallahassee, FL 32399-2100
Phone: 850-922-1844 or 1846
Fax: 850-488-2488

GEORGIA

Georgia Environmental Facilities Authority
Energy Division
233 Peachtree Street, NE, Suite 900

Peachtree Center—Harris Tower
Atlanta, GA 30303
Phone: 404-584-1107
Fax: 404-584-1069 or 1050

HAWAII

Department of Labor and Industrial Relations
Office of Community Services
830 Punchbowl Street, Room 420
Honolulu, HI 96813
Phone: 808-586-8675
Fax: 808-586-8685

IDAHO

Community Action Partnership Association of Idaho
5400 W. Franklin Street
Suite G
Boise, ID 83705
Phone: 208-375-7382

ILLINOIS

Department of Commerce and Economic Opportunity
400 North Fifth Street
Springfield, IL 62702
Phone: 217-785-6135
Fax: 217-524-5904

INDIANA

Indiana Housing & Community Development Authority
30 South Meridian Street
Suite 1000
Indianapolis, IN 46204
Phone: 317-233-5372
Fax: 317-232-7778

IOWA

Department of Human Rights
Division of Community Action Agencies
Lucas State Office Building
321 East 12th Street
Des Moines, IA 50319
Phone: 515-281-3268
Fax: 515-242-6119

KANSAS

Kansas Development Finance Authority
555 South Kansas Avenue
Topeka, KS 66603
Phone: 785-296-2262
Fax: 785-296-8985

KENTUCKY

Kentucky Housing Corporation
1231 Louisville Road
Frankfort, KY 40601
Phone: 502-564-7630

LOUISIANA

Louisiana Housing Finance Agency
2415 Quail Drive
Baton Rouge, LA 70808
Phone: 225-763-8700, ext. 222 or 234
Fax: 225-763-8710

MAINE

Energy and Housing Services
Maine State Housing Authority
353 Water Street
Augusta, ME 04330-4633
Phone: 207-626-4600
Fax: 202-626-4678

MARYLAND

Maryland Department of Housing and Community Development
100 Community Place
Crownsville, MD 21032-2023
Phone: 410-514-7489
Fax: 410-514-4070 or 7191

MASSACHUSETTS

Massachusetts Department of Housing and Community Development
100 Cambridge Street, Suite 300
Boston, MA 02114-2524
Phone: 617-573-1431
Fax: 617-573-1460

MICHIGAN

State of Michigan Department of Human Services
Weatherization Unit
235 South Grand Avenue, Suite 1314
P.O. Box 30037
Lansing, MI 48909
Phone: 517-335-6070
Fax: 517-335-5042

MINNESOTA

Minnesota Office of Energy Security
85 7th Place East, Suite 500
St. Paul, MN 55101-2198
Phone: 651-296-5175
Fax: 651-297-7891

MISSISSIPPI

Mississippi Department of Human Services
Division of Community Services
750 North State Street
Jackson, MS 39202
Phone: 601-359-4771
Fax: 601-359-4370

MISSOURI

Department of Natural Resources
Energy Center
1101 Riverside Drive
P.O. Box 176
Jefferson City, MO 65102-0176
Phone: 573-751-7657
Fax: 573-751-6860

MONTANA

Department of Public Health and Human Services
P.O. Box 4210
Helena, MT 59601
Phone: 406-447-4260
Fax: 406-447-4287

NEBRASKA

Nebraska Energy Office
P.O. Box 95085
Lincoln, NE 68509-5085
Phone: 402-471-3347
Fax: 402-471-3064

NEVADA

Nevada Department of Business and Industry
Housing Division
1535 Old Hot Springs Road, Suite 50
Carson City, NV 89706-0666
Phone: 775-687-2036 or 2037
Fax: 775-687-4040

NEW HAMPSHIRE

New Hampshire Office of Energy and Planning
4 Chenell Drive
Second Floor
Concord, NH 03301-8501
Phone: 603-271-2615
Fax: 603-271-2615

NEW JERSEY

New Jersey Department of Community Affairs
P.O. Box 811
101 South Broad Street
Trenton, NJ 08625-0806
Phone: 609-984-3301
Fax: 609-292-9798

NEW MEXICO

New Mexico Mortgage Finance Authority
344 4th Street, SW
Albuquerque, NM 87102
Phone: 505-767-2274
Fax: 505-243-3289

NEW YORK

New York State Division of Housing and Community Renewal
38–40 State Street
Hampton Plaza
Albany, NY 12207
Phone: 518-474-5700
Fax: 518-474-9462 or 9907

NORTH CAROLINA

North Carolina Department of Health and Human Services
Office of Economic Opportunity
2013 Mail Service Center
Raleigh, NC 27699-2013
Phone: 919-715-5850
Fax: 919-715-5855

NORTH DAKOTA

North Dakota Department of Commerce
Division of Community Services
Century Center
1600 East Century Ave.
Bismarck, ND 58503
Phone: 701-227-7415 or 7416
Fax: 701-328-5395

OHIO

Ohio Department of Development
77 South High Street, 26th Floor
P.O. Box 1001
Columbus, OH 43216-1001
Phone: 614-466-6289
Fax: 614-466-1864

OKLAHOMA

Oklahoma Department of Commerce
Office of Community Development
P.O. Box 26980
Oklahoma City, OK 73126-0980
Phone: 405-815-5339 or 5370
Fax: 405-815-5344

OREGON

Oregon Housing and Community Services
725 Summer Street N.E.
Suite B
Salem, OR 97301
Phone: 503-986-2016
Fax: 503-986-0996

PENNSYLVANIA

Pennsylvania Department of Community and Economic Development
Center for Community Empowerment
Commonwealth Keystone Building, 4th Floor
Harrisburg, PA 17120
Phone: 717-720-7439
Fax: 717-214-5399

RHODE ISLAND

Rhode Island Office of Energy Resources
One Capitol Hill, 2nd Floor
Providence, RI 02908-5890
Phone: 401-574-9119
Fax: 401-574-9125

SOUTH CAROLINA

Governor's Office of Economic Opportunity
1205 Pendleton Street
Edgar A. Brown Building, 3rd Floor
Columbia, SC 29201
Phone: 803-734-0356 or 9861
Fax: 803-734-0356

SOUTH DAKOTA

Department of Social Services
Office of Energy Assistance
206 West Missouri Avenue
Pierre, SD 57501-4517
Phone: 605-773-4131
Fax: 605-773-6657

TENNESSEE

Department of Human Services
Citizens Plaza Building, 14th Floor
400 Deaderick Street
Nashville, TN 37248-9500
Phone: 615-313-4762
Fax: 615-741-4165

TEXAS

Texas Department of Housing and Community Affairs
P.O. Box 13941
Austin, TX 78711-3941
Phone: 512-475-2125
Fax: 512-475-3935

UTAH

Utah Division of Housing & Community Development
324 South State Street, Suite 500
Salt Lake City, UT 84111-2321
Phone: 801-538-8657
Fax: 801-538-8888

VERMONT

Department for Children & Families—AHS
Office of Economic Opportunity
103 South Main Street
Waterbury, VT 05671
Phone: 802-241-2452 or 2454
Fax: 802-241-2407 or 1225

VIRGINIA

Virginia Department of Housing and Community Development
600 East Main Street
Richmond, VA 23219
Phone: 804-371-7102
Fax: 804-371-7091

WASHINGTON

Washington Department of Community, Trade, and Economic Development
P.O. Box 42525
Olympia, WA 98504-2525
Phone: 360-725-2948
Fax: 360-586-5880

WEST VIRGINIA

Office of Economic Opportunity
Weatherization
950 Kanawha Boulevard, East
Charleston, WV 25301
Phone: 304-558-8860, ext. 221 or 333
Fax: 304-558-4210

WISCONSIN

Office of Recovery and Reinvestment
Wisconsin Department of Administration
101 E. Wilson Street
Sixth Floor
Madison, WI 53703
Phone: 608-266-2035

WYOMING

Wyoming Department of Family Services
2300 Capitol Avenue, 3rd Floor
Cheyenne, WY 82002-0490
Phone: 307-777-6346
Fax: 307-777-7747

D.6 Documents Regarding Use of Weatherization Assistance Program Funding in Multi-Family Buildings

D.6.1 Final Rule on Amending Eligibility Provisions to Multi-Family Buildings for the Weatherization Assistance Program

WEATHERIZATION PROGRAM NOTICE 10-15
Effective Date: March 2, 2010

SUBJECT: FINAL RULE ON AMENDING ELIGIBILITY PROVISIONS TO MULTI-FAMILY BUILDINGS FOR THE WEATHERIZATION ASSISTANCE PROGRAM

PURPOSE: To issue guidance on implementing recent changes to the Weatherization Assistance Program (WAP) requirements for determining eligibility of certain multi-family buildings as identified by the Department of Housing and Urban Development (HUD) and the Department of Agriculture (USDA).

LEGAL AUTHORITY: Title IV, Energy Conservation and Production Act, as amended, authorizes the DOE to administer the WAP. All grant awards made under this Program shall comply with applicable laws including regulations contained in 10 CFR Part 440.

BACKGROUND: Vice-President Biden announced "An Opportunity for Agencies to Collaborate and Help Working Families Weatherize Their Homes in Multi-Unit Buildings" Memorandum of Understanding (MOU) between DOE and HUD signed at Cabinet Meeting on May 06, 2009. As a result, Secretaries Chu and Donovan committed to lowering the hurdles to coordinating the efforts of WAP and the HUD programs for assisted housing. DOE published a final rule in the Federal Register on January 25, 2010, amending 10 CFR Part 440.22, Eligible dwelling units. (75 Fed. Reg. 3847)

See Website at: www.gpo.gov/fdsys/pkg/FR-2010-01-25/html/2010-1300.htm

GUIDANCE:

What the final rule does—

DOE has posted three lists of properties supplied by HUD and USDA. Properties identified on these lists have been determined to meet certain eligibility criteria under WAP. The lists will reduce the review and verification necessary to weatherize the identified buildings through WAP.

List #1—Properties identified on list #1 have been determined to comply with the requirements that—

- A minimum of 66% of the dwelling units in the building are occupied by a family unit that meets the income requirement (as required under 10 CFR 440.22(b)(2));
- For a reasonable period of time after weatherization work has been completed, the eligible dwelling unit will not be subject to rent increases as a result of the weatherization (as required under 10 CFR 440.22(b)(3)(i)); and
- No undue or excessive enhancement has occurred to the value of the dwelling unit (as required under 10 CFR 440.22(b)(3)(i)).
  See Website at: www.eere.energy.gov/wip/docs/10_cfr_440_22_b_4_i_list.xls

List #2—Properties identified on list #2 have been determined to comply with the requirements that—

- A minimum of 66% of the dwelling units in the building are occupied by a family unit that meets the income requirement (as required under 10 CFR 440.22(b)(2)); and
- No undue or excessive enhancement has occurred to the value of the dwelling unit (as required under 10 CFR 440.22(b)(3)(i)).
  See Website at: www.eere.energy.gov/wip/docs/10_cfr_440_22_b_4_ii_list.xls

The buildings identified on the lists must still meet all other applicable eligibility requirements.

What the final rule does not do—

The final rule *does not* result in automatic eligibility for the identified buildings. As indicated above, the final rule only addresses a subset of the eligibility requirements.

The final rule *does not* establish a priority for the weatherization of the identified buildings. States are not required to establish a particular prioritization with regard to the weatherization of multi-family buildings.

CONCLUSION: Weatherization of buildings in the public housing market provides greater opportunities for local agencies to serve even more low-income persons in their communities. The final rule published on January 25, 2010, reduces the procedural obstacles to determining the eligibility of such buildings.

If there are additional questions or concerns, Grantees should contact their PMC Project Officer. DOE appreciates your cooperation and patience as we work together to achieve the Administration's goal of creating jobs and increasing the number of people who benefit from Recovery Act funded weatherization projects.

Claire Broido Johnson
Acting Program Manager Office of Weatherization and Intergovernmental Program
Energy Efficiency and Renewable Energy

D.6.2 Guidance Regarding Accrual of Benefits to Low-Income Tenants in Multi-Family Buildings Under the Weatherization Assistance Program

WEATHERIZATION PROGRAM NOTICE 10-15A
Effective Date: April 8, 2010

SUBJECT: GUIDANCE REGARDING ACCRUAL OF BENEFITS TO LOW-INCOME TENANTS IN MULTI-FAMILY BUILDINGS UNDER THE WEATHERIZATION ASSISTANCE PROGRAM

PURPOSE: To issue guidance for Grantees on establishing procedures to ensure that the benefits of weatherization assistance in connection with multi-family buildings comprised of rental units will accrue primarily to the low-income tenants residing in such units.

LEGAL AUTHORITY: Title IV, Energy Conservation and Production Act, as amended, authorizes the DOE to administer the Weatherization Assistance Program (WAP). All grant awards made under this Program shall comply with applicable laws including regulations contained in 10 CFR Part 440 and other authorities applicable to WAP.

BACKGROUND: A local weatherization agency may weatherize a building containing rental units (e.g., multi-family buildings) using financial assistance for dwelling units eligible for weatherization assistance under WAP if certain conditions are met. 10 CFR 440.22(b). DOE published a final rule in the Federal Register on January 25, 2009, amending 10 CFR Part 440.22. (75 FR 3847). As a result of the final rule, if a multi-unit building is under an assisted or public housing program and is identified by the U.S. Department of Housing and Urban Development (HUD) or the U.S. Department of Agriculture (USDA), and included on a list published by DOE, that building will meet certain income eligibility requirements, and may also satisfy one or both of the procedural requirements to protect against rent increases and undue or excessive enhancement of the weatherized building, as indicated by the list, under WAP without the need for further evaluation or verification.

On March 2, 2010, DOE posted listings of eligible properties to the DOE web page at: http://apps1.eere.energy.gov/wip/eligibility_hud.cfm.

As noted in the January 25, 2009 final rule, inclusion on the published lists does not require the weatherization of the properties, nor does it require a prioritization of these properties. Additionally, the final rule noted that a request for weatherization of a multi-unit building that is on a published list, as with any multi-family building, would still need to demonstrate to the Grantee (or subgrantee administering the program) that the benefits of the weatherization work accrue primarily to the low-income tenants. 75 FR at 3853. This guidance primarily addresses how Grantees can ensure that the benefits of weatherizing a building which consists of rental units will accrue primarily to the low-income tenants of that property.

GUIDANCE: Under the WAP regulations, a Grantee must ensure that for multi-unit buildings the benefits of weatherizing a building that consists of rental units, including rental units where the tenant pays for energy through rent, accrue primarily to the low-income tenants. (42 U.S.C. 6863(b)(5)(A); 10 CFR 440.22(b)(3)(i)).

DOE is not promulgating prescriptive guidance, but wants to provide examples to Grantees of how to address the accrual of benefits. DOE encourages Grantees to establish procedures that will ensure that all owners of multi-unit buildings submit sufficient detail and explanation to allow a determination that the accrual of benefit requirements in 10 CFR 440.22 have been met.

In instances in which tenants of multi-family buildings pay directly for energy, the accrual of benefits requirement can be assured by demonstrating a reduction in the tenants' energy bills. However, DOE recognizes that there are instances in which a tenant does not pay directly for energy (e.g., energy costs are paid through rent, or under certain housing assistance programs, energy costs are paid for through vouchers).

In instances in which a tenant does not pay for energy directly, a combination of several categories of benefits could be used to demonstrate that the benefits of the weatherization accrual primarily to the tenant. Benefits that could be combined, include, but are not limited to:

- longer term preservation of the property as affordable housing;
- continuation of protection against rent increases beyond that required under the WAP regulations (10 CFR 440.22(b)(3)(ii));
- Investment of the energy savings in facilities or services that offer measurable direct benefits to tenants;
- Investment of the energy savings from the weatherization work in specific health and safety improvements with measurable benefits to tenants;
- Improvements to heat and hot water distribution, and ventilation, to improve the comfort of residents; and
- Establishment of a shared savings programs.

Generic assertions such as "tenant services will be improved" or "weatherization will improve health and safety" are not sufficient to demonstrate that the accrual of benefits requirement is met. Procedures established by the Grantee must require significant additional information quantifying the outcomes and benefits to present building residents. Any request for weatherization of eligible multi-unit buildings needs to demonstrate in sufficient detail to the grantee/subgrantee that the benefits of weatherization work accrue primarily to the low-income tenants.

CONCLUSION: Expanding weatherization into the multi-family housing sector, including the public housing market, will provide greater opportunities for local agencies to serve even more low-income persons in their communities. If there are additional questions or concerns, Grantees should contact their PMC Project Officer. DOE appreciates your cooperation and patience as we work together to achieve the Administration's goal of creating jobs and increasing the number of people who benefit from Recovery Act funded weatherization projects.

Claire Broido Johnson
Acting Program Manager
Office of Weatherization and Intergovernmental Program
Energy Efficiency and Renewable Energy

D.6.3 Updated Guidance on Eligible Multi-Family Property Listings for Use in the Weatherization Assistance Program

DEPARTMENT OF ENERGY
Washington, DC 20585

WEATHERIZATION PROGRAM NOTICE 11-09
Effective Date: April 1, 2011

SUBJECT: UPDATED GUIDANCE ON ELIGIBLE MULTI-FAMILY PROPERTY LISTINGS FOR USE IN THE WEATHERIZATION ASSISTANCE PROGRAM

PURPOSE: To notify interested parties of supplemental listings of properties that have been determined to meet certain eligibility criteria under the Weatherization Assistance Program (WAP). Also to provide guidance for accessing current listings and future supplemental listings at the website for the Department of Energy (DOE), Office of Energy Efficiency and Renewable Energy (EERE).

SCOPE: The provisions of this guidance apply to Grantees or other entities named in the Notification of Grant Award as the recipient of financial assistance under the DOE WAP. This guidance applies to all sources of funds in use—American Recovery and Reinvestment Act of 2009 (Recovery Act) and regular appropriated DOE Weatherization funds in 2009, 2010 and beyond.

LEGAL AUTHORITY: Title IV, Energy Conservation and Production Act, as amended, authorizes the DOE to administer the WAP. All grant awards made under this Program shall comply with applicable law including regulations contained in 10 CFR Part 440, the Energy Policy Act of 2005, the Energy Independence and Security Act of 2007, and the Recovery Act.

BACKGROUND: On March 2, 2010, DOE issued Weatherization Program Notice 10-15, titled "Final Rule on Amending Eligibility Provisions to Multifamily Buildings for the Weatherization Assistance Program" (WPN 10-15), in which DOE posted two lists, supplied by HUD, of properties that have been identified to meet certain income eligibility criteria under WAP. The lists reduce the review and verification necessary to weatherize the identified buildings through WAP. WPN 10-15 may be accessed at website: http://waptac.org/Program-Guidance/2010002D2006-Program-Guidance-Documents.aspx.

The two lists posted in WPN 10-15 were:

List #1—Properties identified on list #1 have been determined to comply with the requirements that—

- A minimum of 66% of the dwelling units in the building are occupied by a family unit that meets the income requirement (as required under 10 CFR 440.22(b)(2));
- For a reasonable period of time after weatherization work has been completed, the eligible dwelling unit will not be subject to rent increases as a result of the weatherization (as required under 10 CFR 440.22(b)(3)(i)); and
- No undue or excessive enhancement has occurred to the value of the dwelling unit (as required under 10 CFR 440.22(b)(3)(i)).

List 1 consists of properties that are:

- Public Housing for which 100% of buildings in the identified properties meet the necessary qualifications;
- Public Housing for which only specified buildings in the identified properties meet the necessary qualifications qualify; and
- Assisted Multifamily for which properties meet the necessary qualifications, in part, by having 3 or more years remaining on affordability agreements.

List #2—Properties identified on list #2 have been determined to comply with the requirements that—

- A minimum of 66% of the dwelling units in the building are
- occupied by a family unit that meets the income requirement (as required under 10 CFR 440.22(b)(2)); and
- No undue or excessive enhancement has occurred to the value of the dwelling unit (as required under 10 CFR 440.22(b)(3)(i)).

  List 2 consists of Qualified Assisted Housing Properties that have less than 3 years remaining under the affordability agreement and that meet the income eligibility threshold.

Additionally, WAP regulations provide for a third list. The third list is for properties that have been determined to comply with the requirement that a minimum of 66% of the dwelling units in the building are occupied by a family unit that meets the income requirement (as required under 10 CFR 440.22(b)(2)). At the time WPN 10-15 was issued, no properties were identified for the third list.

GUIDANCE: Since DOE issued WPN 10-15, additional properties have been identified by HUD and USDA. DOE has determined that these additional properties meet the requirements of one of the three lists identified above. As of this notice DOE has posted these additional properties under the appropriate listing. The updated listing can be found at http://www1.eere.energy.gov/wip/multifamily_guidance.html. Below is a brief description of the properties, as added to each list.

LIST 1

Supplemental List 1A: Eligible Multifamily Buildings 10-CFR-440.22(b)(4)(i)

Supplemental List 1A was added on November 15, 2010.

Supplemental List 1A consists of two sub-lists:

Public Housing—Only specified buildings in the identified properties meet the necessary qualifications qualify; and

Assisted Multifamily—Properties meet the necessary qualifications, in part, by having 3 or more years remaining on affordability agreements.

Supplemental List 1B: Eligible Multifamily Buildings 10-CFR-440.22(b)(4)(i)

Supplemental List 1B was added on March 15, 2011.

Supplemental List 1B consists of Assisted Multifamily—Properties meet the necessary qualifications, in part, by having 3 or more years remaining on affordability agreements.

LIST 2

Supplemental List 2A: Eligible Multifamily Buildings 10-CFR-440.22(b)(4)(ii)

Supplemental List 2A was added on November 15, 2010.

Supplemental List 2A consists of Qualified Assisted Housing Properties that have less than 3 years remaining under the affordability agreement and that meet the income eligibility threshold.

Supplemental List 2B: Eligible Multifamily Buildings 10-CFR-440.22(b)(4)(ii)

Supplemental List 2B was added on March 15, 2011.

Supplemental List 2B consists of Qualified Assisted Housing Properties that have less than 3 years remaining under the affordability agreement and that meet the income eligibility threshold.

LIST 3

List 3-1: USDA List of Multifamily Housing Units

List 3-1 was added on March 15, 2011.

The USDA supplied this list of multifamily housing units that meet the income eligibility requirement and that is organized by postal address for use by weatherization service providers.

List 3-2: Low-Income Housing Tax Credit (LIHTC) Buildings

List 3-2 was added on March 15, 2011.

List 3-2 consists of LIHTC properties provided by HUD that met the income eligibility requirement.

Supplemental List 3-2A: Eligible LIHTC Buildings 10-CFR-440.22(b)(4)(iii)

Supplemental List 3-2A was added on March 15, 2011.

Supplemental List 3-2A consists of LIHTC properties provided by HUD that met the income eligibility requirement.

Buildings identified on the lists above and on the DOE/EERE website must still meet all other applicable eligibility requirements in order to receive WAP services. Further, the final rule published in the Federal Register on January 25, 2010, amending 10 CFR Part 440.22, Eligible Dwelling Units (75 Fed Reg. 3847) *does not* result in automatic eligibility for the identified buildings. The final rule only addresses a subset of the eligibility requirements. Nor does the rule require grantees or local WAP providers to set aside WAP funds for these properties. Lastly, the final rule also *does not* establish a priority for the weatherization of the identified buildings. States are not required to establish a particular prioritization with regard to the weatherization of multi-family buildings.

FUTURE POSTINGS: HUD and USDA may from time to time identify additional eligible properties that meet the income eligibility criteria under WAP. DOE will post additional supplemental lists as they become available on the DOE/EERE website at: http://www1.eere.energy.gov/wip/multifamily_guidance.html and issue a Weatherization Program Notice identifying the additional supplemental lists.

CONCLUSION: Weatherization of buildings in the public housing market provides greater opportunities for local agencies to serve even more low-income persons in their communities. The final rule published on January 25, 2010, reduces the procedural obstacles to determining the eligibility of such buildings. If there are additional questions or concerns, Grantees should contact their PMC Project Officer. DOE appreciates your cooperation and patience as we work together to achieve the Administration's goal of creating jobs and increasing the number of people who benefit from Recovery Act funded weatherization projects.

LeAnn M. Oliver
Program Manager
Office of Weatherization and Intergovernmental Program Energy Efficiency and Renewable Energy

D.6.4 Memorandum of Understanding Between HUD and DOE (May 6, 2009)

Memorandum of Understanding
Between
Department of Energy
And
Department of Housing and Urban Development

Coordinating Recovery Act Funds for Home Energy Retrofits

This Memorandum of Understanding ("MOU") is made this_______ day of May, 2009, by and between the U.S. Department of Energy ("DOE") and the U.S. Department of Housing and Urban Development ("HUD").

RECITALS:

R-1. The American Recovery and Revitalization Act of 2009, P.L. No. 111-5 (Recovery Act), provides $16 billion to HUD and DOE that may be used in whole or in part to improve the energy efficiency of existing homes, which includes rental units. HUD's programs include $4.5 billion to renovate and upgrade public and Native American housing (a significant portion of which will be invested in energy improvements), as well as $250 million for energy retrofits of privately owned federally assisted housing. DOE has been provided $5 billion in weatherization funds; $3.2 billion for Energy Efficiency and Conservation Block Grants that cities, counties, states, and Indian Tribes can use to retrofit homes, among other uses; $3.1 billion for the State Energy Program; and other programs. Coordinated use of these funds will help achieve the President's goal of weatherizing one million homes annually.

R-2. On February 27, 2009, HUD and DOE agreed to coordinate the use of the Weatherization Assistance Program, Energy Efficiency and Conservation Block Grant ("EECBG") and other Recovery Act funds in local communities. The two Departments agreed to explore ways to increase the use of weatherization funds in public housing and assisted housing, and to coordinate the use of Community Development Block Grant and EECBG funds in local communities. The purpose of the HUD/DOE collaboration is to help catalyze a home performance/energy retrofit industry nationwide.

R-3. DOE's Weatherization Assistance Program (under part A of Title IV of the Energy Conservation and Production Act (42 U.S.C. 6861 *et seq.*)) is the largest residential energy conservation program in the Nation and operates in all 50 states, the District of Columbia, the U.S. Territories, and on several Native American reservations (collectively, "States").

R-4. The Weatherization Assistance Program provides funding for the improvement of the energy efficiency of low-income dwellings, often employing advanced technologies, thereby reducing our country's carbon footprint and dependence on foreign oil, while decreasing the cost of energy for American families in need.

R-5. Pursuant to the Recovery Act, DOE's Weatherization Assistance Program was allocated $5 billion of funding to achieve the purposes set forth in the Recovery Act.

R-6. The Weatherization Assistance Program presently provides weatherization assistance to more than 100,000 homes each year, but with the substantial funding increase under the Recovery Act, significantly more weatherization projects may be undertaken in an effort to achieve the President's goal.

R-7. HUD's public housing and assisted housing programs (for the purposes of this MOU, sometimes collectively defined as "HUD Qualified Housing"[1]) operate in the same juris-

1 For the purposes of this MOU, "HUD Qualified Housing" includes public housing projects, and assisted housing projects that receive project-based Section 8 assistance, under the U.S. Housing Act of 1937, as amended (42 U.S.C. 1437, *et seq.*), except for projects also benefitting from assistance under Sections

dictions, and benefit the same low-income populations, as the Weatherization Assistance Program. HUD data show that, typically, residents of HUD Qualified Housing largely meet the income requirement for the Weatherization Assistance Program.

R-8. The income verification process applied by HUD for HUD Qualified Housing is rigorous, and owners or public housing authorities participating in HUD Qualified Housing must determine each participating family's income before the family is permitted to move into a HUD Qualified Housing rental unit, and must verify continuing eligibility at least annually thereafter. HUD developed and has implemented a sophisticated system of third-party income verifications, originally designated as the Upfront Income Verification ("UIV") system, now known as the Enterprise Income Verification or EIV system for such purposes.

R-9. For Low Income Housing Tax Credit Program ("LIHTC") projects, State Housing Finance Agencies ("HFAs") follow the income verification processes set forth in HUD Handbook 4350.3 REV1, IRS Code Section 42, and IRS Handbook 8823 (Chapter 5), and incorrect eligibility determinations may adversely affect the utilization of the tax credits. LIHTC owners/agents are required to recertify each low-income household at least annually, within 120 days of the anniversary date of the original occupancy. HFAs are required to review all tenant recertifications and all supporting documentation. State HFAs are required to perform an on-site inspection and a review of 20 percent of tenant files at least every 3 years. DOE expects these procedures will meet requirements of the Weatherization Assistance Program.

R-10. HUD and DOE wish to facilitate the use of Weatherization Assistance Program funds in HUD Qualified Housing and in the LIHTC projects, where such assistance is consistent with the Weatherization Assistance Program and can benefit residents. This may also help achieve economies of scale, public housing, assisted housing, and LIHTC projects to lower energy costs, train and increase the industry workforce, and further the purposes of the Recovery Act.

R-11. DOE and HUD desire to resolve or offer pathways to a resolution, to the extent practicable, of the issues that may hinder DOE, its grantees, and HUD from realizing the benefit of such economies of scale and lower administrative costs through the interaction of HUD's programs and LIHTC projects with the Weatherization Assistance Program. Specifically, not only has the income verification process for multi-unit buildings been burdensome to grantees, but the Weatherization Assistance Program requirements for the states to demonstrate satisfactory rent controls, that there will be no undue or excessive building enhancements, and that the benefits accrue primarily to the low-income tenants resulting from the work performed under the Weatherization Assistance Program, all must be addressed.

I. Purpose.

Consistent with the above recitals:

A. HUD has provided and DOE has reviewed the procedures utilized by HUD or its grantees, and owners/agents, for determining the income eligibility for residents of HUD Qualified Housing and the LIHTC projects, respectively.

B. DOE recognizes that the HUD and LIHTC programs rely on robust procedures to verify participants' income. DOE has determined that these procedures are sufficiently robust to rely on in demonstrating income eligibility requirements of the Weatherization Assistance Program.

C. HUD will provide DOE with a list of the HUD Qualified Housing projects and the LIHTC projects that, based on HUD data, would meet the income eligibility requirements under the Weatherization Assistance Program.

221(d)(3) and (d)(5) and 236 of the National Housing Act (12 U.S.C. 1715l (d)(3)and (d)(5), and 12 U.S.C. 1715z-1, respectively), Supportive Housing for the Elderly projects receiving HUD assistance under section 202 of the Housing Act of 1959 (12 U.S.C. 17012), or Supportive Housing for Persons with Disabilities under Section 811 of the Cranston-Gonzales National Affordable Housing Act, as amended (42 U.S.C. 8013).

D. HUD and DOE will continue to work together to develop guidance for states on evaluating the eligibility of HUD Qualified Housing and LIHTC Housing under the Weatherization Assistance Program.

E. DOE and HUD intend to provide joint guidance within 60 days of this MOU to all affected entities, including states, local governments, and nonprofit and for-profit partners, describing how these programs can be further aligned.

F. DOE and HUD also intend to conduct a series of joint forums throughout the country to facilitate implementation of this MOU and educate stakeholders on how to make this MOU operational.

G. DOE and HUD intend to provide a structure for the necessary technical assistance to assure successful execution, including suggested training, subject matter expertise, and performance measurement.

H. DOE and HUD agree to work cooperatively to explore more highly leveraged and innovative approaches to weatherizing low-income homes.

II. Authorities.

DOE's Weatherization Assistance Program (under part A of Title IV of the Energy Conservation and Production Act (42 U.S.C. 6861 *et seq.*); The American Recovery and Reinvestment Act of 2009, P.L. No. 111-5.

Public housing projects, and assisted housing projects that receive project-based Section 8 assistance, under the U.S. Housing Act of 1937, as amended (42 U.S.C. 1437, *et seq.*), Supportive Housing for the Elderly projects receiving HUD assistance under section 202 of the Housing Act of 1959 12 U.S.C. 17012), or Supportive Housing for Persons with Disabilities under Section 811 of the Cranston-Gonzales National Affordable Housing Act, as amended (42 U.S.C. 8013).

III. Expenses of Each Party.

This MOU does not obligate funds, personnel, services, or other resources of either Department to the other. Each party to the MOU will bear its own expenses in connection with the preparation, negotiation, and execution of the MOU, and neither party shall be liable to the other party for such expenses.

This MOU is an expression of intent only, that each party acts as an independent party with respect to the performance of duties under the MOU and does not represent that it is an employee or agent of another party to the MOU.

This MOU does not give a third party any benefit, legal or equitable right, remedy, or claim under any agreement contained herein.

This Agreement in no way restricts either of the Parties from participating in any activity with other public or private agencies, organizations, or individuals.

This Agreement is strictly for internal management purposes for each of the Parties. It is not legally enforceable and shall not be construed to create any legal obligation on the part of either Party.

IV. Effective Date, Duration, and Amendments.

The effective date of this MOU shall be from the latest date of the signatures below. This MOU shall remain in effect until the termination by either party, which termination shall be effective thirty (30) days after the sending of written notice to the other party. Amendments to this MOU will be effected by the mutual consent of the parties in writing.

V. Implementation

DOE and HUD intend to: (i) provide joint guidance within 60 days after the execution of this

MOU to stakeholders in the Weatherization Assistance Program and HUD's housing programs, and (ii) conduct a series of joint forums to facilitate the implementation of this MOU.

DOE and HUD will comply with all statutory and regulatory requirements in carrying out this MOU, and will identify and work to reconcile issues, in order to achieve the realization of the mutual benefits under this MOU.

DOE and HUD will coordinate all public statements and other disclosures with regard to this MOU, and neither DOE nor HUD may enter into any publicity regarding this MOU, unless the agencies consult in advance on the form, timing, and contents of any such publicity, announcement, or disclosure.

VI. Points of Contact.

Designated points of contact between the agencies will be determined by mutual agreement of the two agencies within 30 days of signature.

VII. Dispute Resolution Mechanism.

In the event of any disagreement arising under this MOU, the parties shall attempt to resolve the disagreement through negotiations in good faith. If the parties are unable to resolve the disagreement, this MOU may be terminated, which termination shall be effective thirty (30) days after the sending of written notice to the other party.

VIII. Signatures.

The following officials agree to the terms and conditions of this MOU:

HUD:

____

Shaun Donovan, Secretary

Date: _______

DOE:

____

Steven Chu, Secretary

Date: _______

Appendix E

Energy Assurance Programs

This appendix is also available on the companion website to this treatise. The companion website facilitates keyword searches and allows relevant provisions to be imported as word-processing documents.

Many states supplement federal Low Income Home Energy Assistance Program (LIHEAP) and Weatherization Assistance Program (WAP) funding through delivery of low-income energy benefits from utility rate assistance and energy efficiency programs, state appropriations, or voluntary "fuel funds." (See Chapter 8, supra, for information regarding the design and implementation of utility energy affordability programs.)

The table below summarizes non-federal low-income energy assurance programs and funding from 2009. We acknowledge the efforts of Kay Joslin and Sherry Vogel of the National Center for Appropriate Technology's LIHEAP Clearinghouse in compiling and distributing this information. Further information regarding this table and specific energy assurance programs may be found at the LIHEAP Clearinghouse website at www.liheap.ncat.org.

2009 State-by-State Supplements to Energy Assistance and Energy Efficiency
Compiled by the LIHEAP Clearinghouse

Visit http://liheap.ncat.org/Supplements/2009/supintro2009.htm for an explanation to the state-by-state supplements table

Shaded states' supplements are public benefits/universal service funds

State	State Local	Ratepayer Funds		Fuel Funds Church Comm	Bulk Fuel Discount	Misc.	Total
		Rate Assistance	Energy Efficiency				
AL		$ 3,537,832		$ 1,288,693			$ 4,826,525
AK	$38,561,158						$ 38,561,158
AZ	$ 4,915,632	$ 19,778,919	$ 5,172,410	$ 1,980,649			$ 31,847,610
AR			$ 644,874	$ 1,736,612			$ 2,381,486
CA	$ 496,524	$940,000,000	$178,000,000	$ 4,687,351		$3,770,134	$1,126,954,009
CO	$ 9,043,166	X	$ 2,300,000	$ 8,929,238			$ 20,272,404
CT	$ 2,280,386	$ 14,935,677	$ 7,903,707	$ 5,926,522	$5,210,955		$ 36,257,247
DE	$ 1,532,000	$ 1,306,656		$ 631,070	$ 223,200		$ 3,692,926
DC		$ 6,300,000	$ 6,500,000				$ 12,800,000
FL				$ 1,085,800			$ 1,085,800
GA		$ 18,564,447	$ 2,000,000	$ 997,721			$ 21,562,168
ID			$ 1,826,695	$ 223,417		$ 19,870	$ 2,069,982
IL	$ 1,000,000	$ 60,405,932	$ 9,066,177	$ 577,304			$ 71,049,413
IN	$13,000,221	$ 13,852,992		$ 4,424,241		$ 25,094	$ 31,302,548
IA	$ 297,500		$ 5,000,000	$ 971,126			$ 6,268,626
KY	$ 1,245,057	$ 2,901,388	$ 319,306	$ 815,143			$ 5,280,894
ME		$ 9,200,000	$ 2,542,165				$ 11,742,165
MD	$27,800,000	$ 34,000,000	$ 1,824,900	$ 5,923,266	$ 778,501	$1,975,347	$ 73,202,014
MA	$ 9,964,000	$ 68,432,648	$ 20,965,000	$ 2,035,057	$8,336,062		$ 109,732,767
MI		$ 55,000,000	$ 14,000,000	$20,486,189			$ 89,486,189
MN	$ 2,077,469	$ 11,485,049	$ 3,962,058	$ 3,983,837	$ 19,171	$ 155,409	$ 21,682,993

MS		$ 513,345		$ 1,928,136		$ 824,388	$ 3,265,869
MO		$ 3,600,000	$ 1,500,000	$ 2,600,000			$ 7,700,000
MT	$ 3,082,488	$ 4,577,268	$ 2,705,362	$ 1,424,056	$ 1,051	$ 176,980	$ 11,967,205
NE				$ 452,000			$ 452,000
NV	$ 313,066	$ 12,241,692	$ 3,590,000	$ 727,779			$ 16,872,537
NH	$ 3,358,079	$ 15,288,366	$ 2,521,459	$ 818,959	$ 651,907		$ 22,638,770
NJ	$ 16,600,000	$ 237,350,721	$ 20,121,577	$ 432,802			$ 284,383,523
NM	$ 306,459			$ 393,608			$ 700,067
NY	$ 98,774,889	$ 82,600,000	$ 20,500,000	$ 1,129,918		$13,173,997	$ 216,178,804
NC		$ 145,009		$ 3,885,758			$ 4,030,767
OH		$ 153,747,400	$ 7,000,761	$ 1,917,000			$ 162,665,161
OK		$ 6,835,019					$ 6,835,019
OR		$ 15,154,107	$ 9,961,685	$ 4,649,435		$ 843,639	$ 30,608,866
PA	$ 238,000	$ 450,000,000	$ 37,000,000	$ 8,035,365			$ 495,273,365
RI		$ 9,263,540	$ 3,610,000	$ 600,000			$ 13,473,540
SC				$ 1,306,589			$ 1,306,589
SD	$ 256,350			$ 335,050		$ 147,160	$ 738,560
TN				$ 1,000,000			$ 1,000,000
TX		$ 85,000,000	$ 1,082,873	$ 6,845,000			$ 92,927,873
UT		$ 2,000,000					$ 2,000,000
VT	$ 7,209,402		$ 1,347,269	$ 737,920	$ 840,472	$ 10,050	$ 10,155,113
VA	$ 154,500			$ 5,021,368			$ 5,175,868
WA	$ 2,835,379	$ 12,112,032	$ 5,421,940	$ 7,661,541		$ 1,408,004	$ 29,438,896
WV	$ 3,000,000			$ 437,000			$ 3,437,000
WI	$ 10,985,503	$ 40,111,280	$ 50,756,828	$ 2,212,475		$ 2,154,826	$ 101,220,912
WY				$ 80,000			$ 80,000
Totals	**$260,237,228**	**$2,390,241,319**	**$434,025,469**	**$121,334,195**	**$16,081,189**	**$24,665,028**	**$3,246,584,428**

Appendix F Utility Discount Rate Outreach and Enrollment—Sample Legislation and Other Material

This appendix is also available on the companion website to this treatise. The companion website facilitates keyword searches and allows relevant provisions to be imported as word-processing documents.

F.1 Massachusetts Materials

F.1.1 Mass. Gen. Laws ch. 164 § 1F(4)(i) [Portion]

The department shall require that distribution companies provide discounted rates for low income customers comparable to the low-income discount rate in effect prior to March 1, 1998. Said discount shall be in addition to any reduction in rates that becomes effective pursuant to said subsection (b) of said section 1B on March 1, 1998, and to any subsequent rate reductions provided by a distribution company after said date pursuant to said subsection. The cost of such discounts shall be included in the rates charged to all other customers of a distribution company. Each distribution company shall guarantee payment to the generation supplier for all power sold to low-income customers at said discounted rates. Eligibility for the discount rates established herein shall be established upon verification of a low-income customer's receipt of any means tested public benefit, or verification of eligibility for the low-income home energy assistance program, or its successor program, for which eligibility does not exceed 200 per cent of the federal poverty level based on a household's gross income. Said public benefits may include, but are not limited to, assistance which provides cash, housing, food, or medical care, including, but not limited to, transitional assistance for needy families, supplemental security income, emergency assistance to elders, disabled, and children, food stamps, public housing, federally-subsidized or state-subsidized housing, the low-income home energy assistance program, veterans' benefits, and similar benefits. The division of energy resources shall make available to distribution companies the eligibility guidelines for said public benefit programs. Each distribution company shall conduct substantial outreach efforts to make said low-income discount available to eligible customers and shall report to said division, at least annually, as to its outreach activities and results. Outreach may include establishing an automated program of matching customer accounts with lists of recipients of said means tested public benefit programs and based on the results of said matching program, to presumptively offer a low-income discount rate to eligible customers so identified; provided, however, that the distribution company, within 60 days of said presumptive enrollment, informs any such low-income customer of said presumptive enrollment and all rights and obligations of a customer under said program, including the right to withdraw from said program without penalty.

In a program year in which maximum eligibility for the low-income home energy assistance program, or its successor program, exceeds 200% of the federal poverty level, a household that is income-eligible for the low-income home energy assistance program shall be eligible for the low-income discount rates required by this subparagraph.

F.1.2 Selected Case Materials, D.T.E. 01-106, Investigation to Increase the Penetration Rate for Discounted Electric, Gas, and Telephone Service

F.1.2.1 D.T.E. 01-106-A, Investigation by the Department of Telecommunications and Energy to Increase the Penetration Rate for Discounted Electric, Gas, and Telephone Service

I. INTRODUCTION

On December 17, 2001, pursuant to G.L. c. 159, § 105 and G.L. c. 164, § 76, the Department of Telecommunications and Energy ("Department") issued an Order opening an investigation into increasing the penetration rate for discounted electric, gas and telephone service. *Order Opening Investigation into Discount Penetration Rate*, D. T.E. 01-106 (December 17, 2001) ("*Order Opening Investigation*").[1] We stated that the primary objectives of this investigation are to: (1) minimize barriers in determining subscriber eligibility; and (2) ensure that eligible customers are enrolled in available discount programs. The Department expressed its commitment to taking all appropriate steps to bring the benefits of available discount programs to all eligible customers.

1 The penetration rate is determined by the percentage of eligible households in Massachusetts that are enrolled in discount rate programs.

Order Opening Investigation at 5. The Department also indicated that its purpose in initiating this investigation was to increase the penetration rate for discount service to eligible customers in a cost-effective manner while minimizing the administrative costs of providing such service. *Id.*, at 2.

The Department requested comments from interested parties on the effectiveness of current outreach programs and enhancing enrollment procedures for eligible customers. *Id.*, at 1. Comments were filed by the Office of the Attorney General of the Commonwealth ("Attorney General"), the Division of Energy Resources ("DOER"), the Department of Transitional Assistance ("DTA"), the Massachusetts Community Action Program Directors Association and the Massachusetts Energy Directors' Association (together, "CAPs"), Verizon New England Inc. d/b/a/ Verizon Massachusetts ("Verizon"), Boston Edison Company, Cambridge Electric Light Company and Commonwealth Electric Company d/b/a NSTAR Electric Company, and NSTAR Gas Company (together, "NSTAR"), Fitchburg Gas and Electric Light Company ("Fitchburg"), Western Massachusetts Electric Company ("WMECo"), Massachusetts Electric Company and Nantucket Electric Company (together, "MECo"), Cape Light Compact ("Compact"), Bay State Gas Company ("Bay State"), Blackstone Gas Company ("Blackstone"), The Berkshire Gas Company ("Berkshire"), Fall River Gas Company and North Attleboro Gas Company (together, "New England Gas Company") and Keyspan Energy Delivery–New England ("Keyspan").[2] Reply comments were filed by CAPs and Verizon.

On July 16, 2002, the Department established Working Groups, consisting of representatives from utilities, state agencies, advocacy groups and Department staff, to identify issues and recommend proposals for increasing the penetration rate for discounted electric, gas and telephone service. The Working Groups focused on the following issues: (1) privacy concerns; (2) data format; (3) outreach and eligibility; and (4) on/off rate standards. On September 17, 2002, the Working Groups submitted recommendations to the Department. On October 31, 2002, based on the Working Groups' recommendations, the Department sought another round of comments from interested parties. On November 14, 2002, comments were filed by Bay State, DOER, Verizon, CAPs, NSTAR, Keyspan, New England Gas Company and WMECo.

Based on the written comments received and the Working Groups' recommendations, the Department identifies the following issues: (1) streamlining the application process; (2) establishing a central entity to collect information; and (3) implementing a computer matching program.

II. ISSUESA. *Streamlining the Application Process*

1. Introduction

The Department stated that it intended to review programs and explore those actions the Department can take to increase subscribership. *Id.*, at 5. The Working Groups noted that utilities are dependent upon the appropriate state benefit agency to verify customer eligibility for discount rate programs. The Working Groups suggested modifying the application process for public benefits to increase the penetration rate for discount electric, gas and telephone service. Given the varying income requirements for public benefit programs,[3] the verification process differs depending on the governmental agency involved in qualifying the customer for those assistance programs. State benefit agencies, such as DTA, the Division of Medical Assistance ("DMA") and the Massachusetts Office of Fuel Assistance ("MOFA"), play a critical role in the eligibility verification process for qualifying customers for discount programs. State benefit agencies and utilities are prevented by law from sharing confidential, customer-specific information without the express written consent of the customer. G.L. c. 66A, § 2; G.L. c. 118A, § 6; G.L. c. 118E, § 49; G.L. c. 271, § 43. For customers applying for the discount through DTA, the utilities use an independent mailing firm to send an application to customers for participation in the discount rate program. For applicants qualifying for discount programs based on fuel assistance benefits, MOFA's application includes language authorizing the release of information to a gas, electric, or phone company offering a discount rate. Therefore, fuel assistance agencies can share their client lists directly with utilities. The Working Groups cited MOFA's application process as the more efficient method and suggested incorporating this application process with other public benefit agencies. The Working Groups recommended that DTA and DMA incorporate language on their applications that would give the agencies authorization to release eligibility information to utilities.

2. Summary of Comments

Bay State argues that the best strategy for increasing the penetration rate for discounted service is to devise the simplest and most efficient application process possible (Bay State Comments at 1). Bay State notes that many applicants for discounted service are ill-equipped to deal with a complex application process due to their limited proficiency in the English language, functional illiteracy or various disabilities (*Id.*). DOER supports the use of a check box to inform customers of the availability of the utility discounts and to streamline the enrollment of those customers (DOER Comments at 2). DOER recommends the check box be expanded to all state agencies offering qualifying benefits (*Id.*, at 2). WMECo argues that the use of a check box would facilitate the verification process by eliminating privacy concerns (WMECo Comments at 2).

CAPs recommended using the MOFA approach of including release authorization language on DTA and DMA application forms, with the application serving as acknowledgment of the customer's consent to release eligibility information (CAPs Com-

2 Initial comments were filed on January 24, 2002. Reply comments were filed on March 7, 2002.

3 Eligibility for the electric and gas residential discount rate shall be established upon verification of a customer's receipt of any means tested public benefit program, or verification of eligibility for the low-income home energy assistance program, or its successor program for which eligibility does not exceed 175 percent of the federal poverty level based on a household's gross income. G.L. c. 164, § 1F (4)(i) and 220 C.M.R. § 14.03 (2A). The Lifeline Program ("Lifeline") is a local monthly telephone discount service for qualifying customers and the Linkup Program ("Linkup") provides qualified customers with a discount on initial connection charges. Eligibility for Lifeline and Linkup is established upon verification of a low-income customer's participation in one of five federal programs: Medicaid, food stamps, Supplemental Security Income ("SSI"), federal public housing assistance, or the Low-Income Home Energy Assistance Program ("LIHEAP"). 47 C.F.R. § 54.409 (b).

ments at 6). In response to the Department's inquiry whether it would be more effective to require applicants to authorize the release of eligibility information as a condition to applying for public benefit programs, CAPs argued that there is almost no advantage, in terms of greater discount rate enrollment, but a substantial risk of legal disputes or controversy (CAPs Comments at 5). Bay State maintained that a requirement for applicants to authorize the release of eligibility information would be more effective than the use of a voluntary check box (Bay State Comments at 2). The majority of commenters suggested that the Department work with DTA and DMA to revise the application process to include language authorizing the release of eligibility information without making it a prerequisite to receiving public benefits (Keyspan Comments at 2; Verizon Comments at 5; MECo Comments at 1; NSTAR Comments at 5; Fitchburg Comments at 2). Keyspan noted the success of fuel assistance agencies and suggested that a similar computer-matching program with the DTA and DMA would increase subscribership with minimal costs to utilities (Keyspan Comments at 2). NSTAR stated that it currently has procedures to communicate with DTA and DMA on behalf of customers that apply through NSTAR for the discount rate; therefore, the check box option would not result in significant incremental costs (NSTAR Comments at 5).

3. Analysis and Findings

The Department already requires gas and electric distribution companies to provide discounted rates for low-income customers. G.L. c. 164, § 1(F)(4)(i); 220 C.M.R. § 14.03(2A). Furthermore, G.L. c. 164, § 1(F)(4)(i) directs each distribution company to conduct substantial outreach efforts to make low-income discounts available to eligible customers. These efforts may include:

> establishing an automated program of matching customers accounts with lists of recipients of said mean tested public benefit programs and based on the results of said matching program, to presumptively offer a low-income discount rate to eligible customers so identified. . . .

GL c. 164, § 1(F)(4)(i). In addition, the Department previously identified Eligible Telecommunication Carriers ("ETC") who must provide discount telephone service to qualifying customers. *Universal Service Programs*, D. T.E. 97-103 (1997).

The Department has carefully reviewed and considered all comments received in the course of this proceeding. In addition, it is clear that gas and electric distribution companies have a legislative directive to participate in this matching program. The Department agrees with the Working Groups and commenters that the application process employed by fuel assistance agencies is a more efficient and reliable process of verifying customer eligibility for discount programs than the current process used by utilities. While the Department believes it appropriate for ETCs to take part in this program, we believe that further investigation is in order to more fully develop the record regarding how to maximize participation by the telecommunications industry in the computer matching program. Therefore, the Department shall implement enrollment of gas and electric eligible customers into the customer eligibility verification process immediately while withholding the implementation for ETCs until the Department is able to further explore this issue in Phase II of this proceeding as described below in Section IV.

B. Establishing a Central Entity to Collect Information

1. Introduction

The Working Groups further suggested that the Department explore the use of a central entity to collect eligibility information from public benefit agencies and to match that information with utility customer lists. The Working Groups cited the success of the State of Texas with utilizing a third-party administrator to identify eligible customers and enroll them in discount rate programs. On October 31, 2002, the Department requested comments regarding the possibility of using MassCARES, a technology-based initiative of the Executive Office of Health and Human Services ("EOHHS"), in order to determine whether EOHHS's MassCARES state beneficiary database could be used to facilitate enrollment of customers in discount programs.

2. Summary of Comments

CAPs fully supports the model of a central entity gathering information that can be shared with utilities in order to facilitate higher enrollment in the discount rate programs (CAPs Comments at 6). CAPs maintains that any new costs of moving to a third-party administrator model in Massachusetts would be outweighed by the savings utilities would realize by reducing the resources they currently devote to identifying and enrolling eligible households (*Id.*, at 7). CAPs and DOER cite the Texas model where a third-party administrator has succeeded in identifying eligible households and enrolling them into discount rate programs (*Id.*, at 6, DOER Comments at 5).

Verizon opposes the establishment of a central entity with a common database for administering these programs (Verizon Comments at 7). Verizon argues that it would be administratively costly and raise serious privacy issues (*Id.*). Verizon and WMECo note that the implementation of a new application procedure obtaining client permission to release eligibility information may eliminate the need for a central entity to gather this information (*Id.*; WMECo Comments at 2). WMECo and Fitchburg favor the check box approach because it should achieve the goal of increasing eligible customer enrollment without the substantial expense of establishing a central data-gathering entity (WMECo Comments at 3; Fitchburg Comments at 2). Fitchburg also argues that a third-party clearinghouse raises issues concerning the costs and cost recovery that have not been fully addressed at this time (Fitchburg Comments at 2).

Keyspan supports exploring the possibility of using MassCARES (Keyspan Comments at 3). Keyspan notes that this would obviate the need to set up separate matching programs with DTA and DMA, as both agencies are within EOHHS (*Id.*). NSTAR and New England Gas maintained that MassCARES may provide utility companies with access to the DTA's and DMA's customer information without the costs of creating a separate database through a third-party administrator (NSTAR Comments at 7; New England Gas Comments at 2). MECo agreed that if MassCARES would allow the utilities access to client information through a secure, web-based system, there would be no need to set up a separate central entity (MECo Comments at 2). Bay State maintains that the EOHHS is a logical choice for maintaining such a central repository of information (Bay State Comments at 2).

3. Analysis and Findings

G.L. c. 164, § 1F(4)(1) provides for establishing an automated program of matching customer accounts of electric distribution companies with lists of recipients of public benefit programs. With respect to discount telephone service, the Federal Communications Commission ("FCC") observed that New York, among other states, has substantially cut Lifeline overhead by mandating the exchange of computer files between social service agencies, which administer participation in other public assistance programs that constitute Lifeline eligibility. *Universal Service Order*, CC Docket No. 96-45, 12 FCC Rcd at 8976 (1996). Further, the FCC has recently proposed a rulemaking to address, among other things, verification procedures and outreach guidelines for Lifeline and Link-Up. *In the Matter of Lifeline and Linkup*, FCC 03-120 (2003).

The Department recognizes that the central entity model has potential to increase the penetration rate for discount service. While the Texas third-party administrator experience has proven successful, it is important to note that Texas did not have a discount rate program prior to the establishment of the central entity. Commenters expressed interest in pursuing the possibility of using the MassCARES state beneficiary database for a computer matching program. The majority of commenters preferred exploring a computer matching program with MassCARES to avoid the set-up costs and technical uncertainties of establishing an independent central entity to gather eligibility information. Based on the comments received in this investigation, the Department concludes that employing a computer matching program, such as the MassCARES database, would increase the penetration rate for all available discount programs. We find that a computer matching program with EOHHS would be the most effective approach for identifying and enrolling eligible customers on discount programs. The Department has entered into a Memorandum of Understanding ("MOU") with EOHHS and DTA to incorporate language on their applications that would give the agencies authorization to release customer eligibility information.[4] The Department directs utilities to exchange customer information with EOHHS for the sole purpose of enrolling eligible customers in discount programs. The Department recognizes that it will take approximately one year from the date agencies begin using applications with language authorizing the release of eligibility information to utilities to implement the computer matching program. In the interim, the Department will require utilities to continue current enrollment procedures.

C. Implementation of Computer Matching Program

1. Introduction

On April 29, 2003, the Department met with interested persons and proposed a computer matching program with EOHHS exchanging customer eligibility information with electric distribution companies, gas distribution companies and eligible telecommunications carriers for the sole purpose of enrolling eligible customers in discount programs. On July 9, 2003, the Department received a final round of comments on any legal impediment and legal justification for utility participation in a computer matching program with EOHHS for the sole purpose of identifying customers eligible for discounted service with subsequent destruction of non-matching data.

Overall, commenters were supportive of the Department's proposal to implement a computer matching program. Several commenters however, noted privacy and rate design concerns. With respect to privacy concerns, the Department notes that the Massachusetts Public Records Law protects disclosure which "may constitute an unwarranted invasion of personal privacy." G.L. c. 66, § 10. In particular, G.L. c. 4 § 7, cl. 26 (c) prevents disclosure of records relating to specific individuals. G.L. c. 4 § 7, cl. 26 (g) provides that trade secrets and commercial and financial information voluntarily provided to the government to help in policy development are not public if the government promises the provider that such information will be kept confidential. G.L. c. 66A, § 2 provides further statutory protections for preventing disclosure of personal data maintained by EOHHS.

With respect to privacy issues concerning the disclosure of customer information to EOHHS, WMECo noted that the Department has previously ordered distribution companies to divulge customers' names, addresses and a unique identifying number (WMECo Comments at 2, *citing* D. T.E. 01-54-B (2002)). The Attorney General recommends that utilities notify all residential customers of their intent to release customer information to EOHHS and provide customers the opportunity to prevent disclosure by notifying the utility (AG Comments at 4).

2. Analysis and Findings

The Department finds that a computer matching program with appropriate safeguards will streamline the enrollment of eligible customers on discount programs in a cost-efficient manner. The privacy waiver set forth on DTA applications will permit the exchange of identifying information between EOHHS and utilities. Applicants and those customers re-certifying eligibility for public benefits will have given their express written permission to share their information with utilities for the purpose of enrolling on the discount rates. In this investigation, the Department will not require utilities to divulge social security numbers, but directs utilities to provide EOHHS with each residential customer name, address and a unique identifying number. The Department directs utilities to provide, by way of a bill insert, all customers with the opportunity to opt out of having their information released to EOHHS. Therefore, residential customers not receiving public benefits will have the opportunity to opt-out of having their information released to EOHHS. Further, consistent with the legislative intent expressed in G.L. c. 164, § 1F(4)(i), we direct utilities to provide for presumptive enrollment on the discount rate provided that the customer is notified within 60 days of all rights and obligation, including the right to withdraw from the discount rate. The Department concludes that such protections will adequately address customers' privacy interests. Finally, the Department will require each electric distribution company, gas distribution company and ETC to file annual updates on the status of discount programs.

---

4 While DTA has committed to include language on future applications authorizing the agencies to share eligibility information with utilities, DTA has not specified the manner in which the new language will be presented on applications. The Department defers to the expertise of DTA in regard to the appropriate manner of notifying beneficiaries of the confidential transfer of data to utility companies.

III. CONCLUSION

At this time, we find that establishing a computer matching program with EOHHS is an appropriate step to bring the benefits of available discount programs to all eligible customers. The Department will continue to meet with Working Groups in the future to evaluate the success of the computer matching program and determine what appropriate steps, if any, are needed to increase the penetration rate for discounted electric, gas and telephone service as well as identify any problems and recommend improvements in the computer matching process. The Department intends to incorporate other means tested programs in the computer matching program and directs utilities to include other state benefit agencies in their matching programs once the Department and the relevant agency have entered into a MOU.

IV. SECOND PHASE OF INVESTIGATION

There are issues related to cost recovery that the Department intends to address by means of a separate proceeding. The Department is aware that utilities may incur a decrease in revenue relating to the computer matching program resulting from higher participation in discount rates. The Department will consider proposals for rate recovery based on increased expenses resulting from the computer matching program in a second phase. Additionally in this phase, the Department will continue to explore how to maximize participation by the telecommunications industry in the computer matching program. Interested parties will have an opportunity to discuss these and other issues at a technical session to be held at the Department's offices at 10:00 a.m. on October 9, 2003.

V. ORDER

Accordingly, after due notice, it is

ORDERED: That all electric distribution companies and gas distribution companies shall electronically transfer residential customer account information on a quarterly basis to EOHHS for an electronic matching program with the MassCARES database for the sole purpose of enrolling eligible customers in discount rate programs, and it is

FURTHER ORDERED: That each electric distribution company and local gas distribution company organized and doing business in the Commonwealth of Massachusetts shall provide presumptive enrollment with subsequent opt out notice to customers, and it is

FURTHER ORDERED: That each electric distribution company and local gas distribution company doing business in the Commonwealth of Massachusetts shall file a report on the status of their computer matching programs six months from the commencement of the computer matching program, and it is

FURTHER ORDERED: That each electric distribution company and local gas distribution company doing business in the Commonwealth of Massachusetts comply with the directives regarding increasing the penetration rate for discounted service contained in this Order.

By Order of the Department,

Paul B. Vasington, Chairman

Eugene J. Sullivan, Jr., Commissioner

Deirdre K. Manning, Commissioner

Appeal as to matters of law from any final decision, order or ruling of the Commission may be taken to the Supreme Judicial Court by an aggrieved party in interest by the filing of a written petition praying that the Order of the Commission be modified or set aside in whole or in part.

Such petition for appeal shall be filed with the Secretary of the Commission within twenty days after the date of service of the decision, order or ruling of the Commission, or within such time as the Commission may allow upon request filed prior to the expiration of twenty days after the date of service of said decision, order or ruling. Within ten days after such petition has been filed, the appealing party shall enter the appeal in the supreme Judicial Court sitting in Suffolk County by filing a copy thereof with the Clerk of said Court. (Sec. 5, Chapter 25, G.L. Ter. Ed., as most recently amended by Chapter 485 of the Acts of 1971).

F.1.2.2 Order on Motion of Boston Edison Company et al. for Reconsideration or, in the Alternative, Clarification

The Commonwealth of Massachusetts Department of Telecommunications and Energy

D.T.E. 01-106-B

Investigation by the Department of Telecommunications and Energy on its own motion, pursuant to G.L. c. 159, § 105 and G.L. c. 164, § 76 to increase the participation rate for discounted electric, gas and telephone service.

ORDER ON MOTION OF BOSTON EDISON COMPANY, CAMBRIDGE ELECTRIC LIGHT COMPANY AND COMMONWEALTH ELECTRIC COMPANY, D/B/A NSTAR ELECTRIC AND NSTAR GAS COMPANY FOR RECONSIDERATION OR, IN THE ALTERNATIVE, CLARIFICATION

I. INTRODUCTION AND PROCEDURAL HISTORY

On August 8, 2003, the Department of Telecommunications and Energy ("Department") issued an Order establishing a computer-matching program for electric distribution companies and local gas distribution companies to facilitate the enrollment of eligible customers in utility discount rate programs. *Investigation re: Discount Program Participation Rate*, D.T.E. 01-106-A (2003). The Department directed electric and gas companies to electronically transfer customer account information on a quarterly basis to the Executive Office of Health and Human Services ("EOHHS"). Subsequently, EOHHS will match this account information with information in its database of recipients of means tested public benefit programs in order to identify customers who are eligible for discount rate programs. D.T.E. 01-106-A at 12. The Department further directed the electric and gas companies to presumptively enroll all eligible customers in applicable discount rate programs, with subsequent notice to customers of their right to unenroll. *Id.* Finally, the Department stated that issues related to cost recovery would be addressed in a separate proceeding. *Id.* at 13.

On August 28, 2003, Boston Edison Company, Cambridge Electric Light Company and Commonwealth Electric Company, d/b/a NSTAR Electric and NSTAR Gas Company (collectively,

"NSTAR") filed a motion to reconsider or, in the alternative, to clarify certain issues related to the timing of the implementation of the computer-matching program established by the Department's Order ("Motion"). On September 12, 2003, Bay State Gas Company ("Bay State"), Blackstone Gas Company ("Blackstone"), KeySpan Energy Delivery New England ("KeySpan"), the Massachusetts Community Action Program Director's Association and the Massachusetts Energy Director's Association (together, "MASSCAP"), New England Gas Company ("New England"), and Western Massachusetts Electric Company ("WMECo") filed responses to the Motion.

II. MOTION FOR RECONSIDERATION/ CLARIFICATION

A. POSITIONS OF THE COMMENTERS

1. NSTAR

NSTAR seeks reconsideration of the Department's directive to implement the computer-matching program without first: (1) investigating the costs and bill impacts for customers who will subsidize the discount rates including the establishment of a cost recovery mechanism; and (2) finalizing certain logistical details of the program[1] (Motion at 1). In the alternative, NSTAR requests that the Department clarify that electric and gas companies need not implement the directives in the Order until the above-referenced issues have been resolved (*id.* at 2).

First, because the program is likely to result in an increase in discount rate participation, NSTAR argues that the Department should either reconsider or clarify its Order and delay implementation of the computer-matching program until an evidentiary record is developed on the expense, revenue, and bill impacts for residential customers (*id.* at 4, 8). In addition, NSTAR argues that the Department should delay implementation of the computer-matching program until all issues related to cost recovery are resolved in order to avoid having electric and gas companies incur costs that may not be recoverable (*id.* at 5). To the extent that electric and gas companies incur costs prior to approval of a recovery mechanism, NSTAR argues that the companies will be assuming a risk that the Department will deny the recovery of some or all of those costs (*id.* at 9).

Second, NSTAR requests that the Department reconsider or clarify its Order and delay implementation of the computer-matching program until EOHHS has revised the applications for income-eligible governmental programs under its jurisdiction[2] and has received permission from its clients to disclose information to electric and gas companies (*id.* at 5–7). Finally, to avoid an inefficient use of resources, NSTAR requests that the Department clarify that electric and gas companies need not begin notifying customers of the opportunity to opt-out of sharing their data with EOHHS until EOHHS has received permission to share client information (*id.* at 7).

2. MASSCAP

MASSCAP opposes NSTAR's request for reconsideration to the extent that it seeks to postpone implementation of the computer-matching program until resolution of a cost recovery mechanism (MASSCAP Response at 1–2). MASSCAP does not oppose clarification of the timetable for the logistical steps that electric and gas companies must take to implement the program (*id.* at 2).

With respect to NSTAR's request for reconsideration, MASSCAP argues that NSTAR has not met the Department's standard of review (*id.* at 3). Specifically, MASSCAP argues that NSTAR has not specified any "extraordinary circumstances" nor has it brought to light any "previously unknown or undisclosed facts" that would warrant reconsideration (*id.* at 4).

Even if the Department were to reconsider its Order, MASSCAP argues that NSTAR's request should be denied as unfounded in law (*id.*). MASSCAP maintains that NSTAR has provided no legal authority for the proposition that the Department cannot implement an order that may have a cost impact in the future unless it first quantifies the costs and develops a cost-recovery mechanism (*id.*). Instead, MASSCAP argues that the Department may adopt policies that apply to all electric and gas companies that will impose costs, without first establishing a cost recovery mechanism (*id.* at 5, *citing Cambridge Electric Light Company v. D.P.U.*, 363 Mass 474, 487 (1973)). As support, MASSCAP cites several instances where the Department has issued orders that may impose costs without first adopting cost recovery mechanisms (*id.* at 5, *citing Service Quality Standards*, D.T.E. 99-84 (2000); *Response of Western Massachusetts Electric Company to the Storm of July 15, 1995*, D.P.U. 95-96 (1995)).

3. Electric and Gas Companies

Bay State supports NSTAR's Motion and requests that the Department clarify that all costs resulting from the implementation of the computer-matching program, including bill impacts and lost revenues resulting from an increase in participation in the discount program, may be deferred for later recovery (Bay State Response at 3, 4). Blackstone also supports NSTAR's Motion and argues that the failure to create a proper cost recovery mechanism will have a significant adverse effect on Blackstone (Blackstone Response at 1–2).

Like NSTAR, Keyspan argues that the Department should not implement the computer-matching program until it has investigated the cost to utilities and established a cost-recovery method (KeySpan Response at 2). New England supports NSTAR's Motion and maintains that, due to its small size, it is particularly sensitive to potential increased costs resulting from the Department's directives (New England Response at 1). WMECo supports NSTAR's Motion in full (WMECo Response at 1). Finally, the electric and gas companies support NSTAR's request to clarify the timeline of logistical steps for program implementation (Bay State Response at 4–5; Blackstone Response at 1; Keyspan Response at 2; New England Response at 2; WMECo Response at 1).

1 Specifically, NSTAR contends that, until EOHHS has received proper authorization from its clients to share information with the electric and gas companies, it should not be required to begin (1) sharing data with EOHHS pursuant to the computer-matching program, and (2) notifying customers of the ability to opt-out of having their information shared with EOHHS (Motion at 4–7).

2 These include the Department of Transitional Assistance ("DTA") and the Division of Medical Assistance ("DMA") programs.

III. STANDARD OF REVIEW

The Department's procedural rule, 220 C.M.R. § 1.11(10), authorizes a party to file a motion for reconsideration within 20 days of service of a final Department order. The Department's policy on reconsideration is well settled. Reconsideration of previously decided issues is granted only when extraordinary circumstances dictate that we take a fresh look at the record for the express purpose of substantively modifying a decision reached after review and deliberation. *North Attleboro Gas Company*, D.P.U. 94-130-B at 2 (1995); *Boston Edison Company*, D.P.U. 90-270-A at 2–3 (1991); *Western Massachusetts Electric Company*, D.P.U. 558-A at 2 (1987).

A motion for reconsideration should bring to light previously unknown or undisclosed facts that would warrant a material change to a decision already rendered. It should not attempt to reargue issues considered and decided in the main case. *Commonwealth Electric Company*, D.P.U. 92-3C-1A at 3–6 (1995); *Boston Edison Company*, D.P.U. 90-270-A at 3 (1991); *Boston Edison Company*, D.P.U. 1350-A at 4 (1983). The Department has denied reconsideration when the request rests on an issue or updated information presented for the first time in the motion for reconsideration. *Western Massachusetts Electric Company*, D.P.U. 85-270-C at 18–20 (1987); *but see Western Massachusetts Electric Company*, D.P.U. 86-280-A at 16–18 (1987). Alternatively, a motion for reconsideration may be based on the argument that the Department's treatment of an issue was the result of mistake or inadvertence. *Massachusetts Electric Company*, D.P.U. 90-261-B at 7 (1991); *New England Telephone and Telegraph Company*, D.P.U. 86-33-J at 2 (1989); *Boston Edison Company*, D.P.U. 1350-A at 5 (1983).

Clarification of previously issued orders may be granted when an order is silent as to the disposition of a specific issue requiring determination in the order, or when the order contains language that is sufficiently ambiguous to leave doubt as to its meaning. *Boston Edison Company*, D.P.U. 92-1A-B at 4 (1993); *Whitinsville Water Company*, D.P.U. 89-67-A at 1–2 (1989). Clarification does not involve reexamining the record for the purpose of substantively modifying a decision. *Boston Edison Company*, D.P.U. 90-335-A at 3 (1992), *citing Fitchburg Gas & Electric Light Company*, D.P.U. 18296/18297, at 2 (1976).

IV. ANALYSIS AND FINDINGS

In D.T.E. 01-106-A at 13, the Department directed the electric and gas companies to "electronically transfer residential customer account information on a quarterly basis" to EOHHS for the purpose of enrolling eligible customers in discount rates. However, NSTAR contends that the Order does not state specifically when the companies must begin transferring such information (Motion at 4–5). As a result, NSTAR seeks reconsideration or clarification of the Department's Order, arguing that, prior to implementing the computer-matching program, the Department must (1) investigate the costs and bill impacts for customers who will subsidize the discount rates including the establishment of a cost recovery mechanism and (2) finalize certain logistical details (Motion at 1).

The Department has reviewed NSTAR's Motion and finds that it fails to demonstrate any mistake or inadvertence by the Department; nor does NSTAR set forth any previously unknown or undisclosed facts that would warrant a material change in the Order. Moreover, the Department finds that NSTAR has failed to demonstrate extraordinary circumstances that would require substantively modifying the Order. Specifically, with respect to cost recovery issues, the Department stated that we would address these issues subsequent to our approval of the program. *See* D.T.E. 01-106-A at 13. The establishment of a cost recovery mechanism is not, as NSTAR suggests, a condition precedent to the implementation of the computer-matching program (Motion at 3; *see Cambridge Electric Light Co. v. D.P.U.*, 363 Mass. 474, 498–499 (1973)).[3] In addition, as discussed below, all logistical prerequisites to the establishment of the computer-matching program have now been met. Therefore, NSTAR's Motion for reconsideration is denied.

Notwithstanding the foregoing, however, we find that the Order does contain language regarding the timing of the implementation of the computer-matching program that is sufficiently ambiguous to leave doubt as to its meaning. Therefore, clarification is warranted.

With respect to NSTAR's request to clarify the cost recovery mechanism, by statute, the costs of the low-income discount must be included in the rates charged to all distribution company customers. G.L. c. 164, § 1F(4)(i). Currently, any lost revenues from the low-income discount program are recovered from all customers through base rates. *Boston Gas Company*, D.T.E. 03-40, at 385 (2003); *The Berkshire Gas Company*, D.T.E. 01-56, at 131–134 (2002). We have recognized that distribution companies may incur a decrease in revenues from increased participation in discount rates once the computer-matching program begins. D.T.E. 01-106-A at 13. Customarily, this new revenue shortfall might be addressed in the context of a future rate proceeding. But the need to effect both the subsidy and the revenue-recovery purposes of G.L. c. 164, § 1F(4)(i) counsel a different approach. With the onset of the winter heating season, at a time when fuel prices are particularly high, the Department must take all appropriate steps to bring the benefits of available utility discount programs to all eligible customers. D.T.E. 01-106, at 6; D.T.E. 01-106-A at 12. To ensure that G.L. c. 164, § 1F(4)(i) is satisfied, we determine that it is reasonable in this instance to modify our method of recovering the low-income discount.

On October 9, 2003, the Department held a technical conference to receive comments on cost recovery mechanisms. Based on the comments received, we find that it is appropriate to establish a reconciliation mechanism to recover any resulting revenue shortfall. Therefore, until a company's next rate case, the electric and gas companies may recover revenues lost as a result of the low-income subsidy in their next reconciliation filing for electric companies or local distribution adjustment factor filing for gas companies. This result is consistent with the legislative intent expressed in G.L. c.

3 In matters where discretion may properly be exercised, the Department has established policies that may impose costs without first adopting a cost-recovery mechanism. For example, in *Service Quality Standards*, D.T.E. 99-84 (2000), the Department required all electric and gas companies to meet new standards for customer service, safety, and reliability and imposed related data collection and reporting obligations. *See also Western Massachusetts Electric Company to the Storm of July 15, 1995*, D.P.U. 95-96 (1995); *Kings Grant Water Company*, D.P.U. 87-228, at 32 (1988); *Boston Edison Company*, D.P.U. 86-91, at 9 (1986); *Boston Edison Company*, D.P.U. 86-71, at 15–16 (1986).

164, § 1F(4)(i). When calculating lost revenues associated with the low-income subsidy, the companies should propose a reconciliation factor based on the difference between the total forecasted lost revenues associated with the low-income discount and the amount of the low-income subsidy that was approved in the company's last rate case or settlement, adjusted for any changes in sales and the number of low-income customers as of the effective date of the computer-matching program.[4]

With respect to NSTAR's request to clarify the logistical details, the Department recognized that it would take approximately one year from the date the agencies under EOHHS' jurisdiction began using applications with language authorizing the release of eligibility information for utilities to implement the computer-matching program. D.T.E. 01-106-A at 10. The Department did not intend that electric and gas companies begin sharing data with EOHHS pursuant to the computer-matching program and notifying customers of the ability to opt-out of having their information shared with EOHHS until EOHHS received authorization from its clients to share such information. In fact, during this interim, we directed electric and gas companies to continue using their current discount rate enrollment procedures. *Id.*

On September 15, 2003, DTA implemented the change on its application to include a privacy waiver that gives the agency authorization to release customer eligibility information (Tr. at 44). One year has passed and EOHHS is now authorized to share DTA client information with electric and gas companies. *See* D.T.E. 01-106-A at 10. Therefore, the Department directs the electric and gas companies to commence sharing data with EOHHS within 30 days of the date of this Order. In addition, the electric and gas companies shall notify customers of the ability to opt-out of having information shared with EOHHS in December 2004 bill inserts.[5]

Finally, pursuant to G.L. c. 164, § 1F(4)(i), each distribution company is required to conduct "substantial outreach efforts" to make the low-income discount program available to eligible customers. As part of these outreach efforts, we direct the electric and gas companies to meet quarterly to evaluate the success and resolve any potential problems with the computer-matching program, evaluate best practices, and work to increase the number of public benefit programs included in the computer-matching program.[6]

IV. ORDER

Accordingly, after due consideration it is:

ORDERED: That Boston Edison Company, Cambridge Electric Light Company, and Commonwealth Electric Company, d/b/a NSTAR Electric and NSTAR Gas Company's Motion for Reconsideration (in Part), or in the Alternative, Motion for Clarification is *DENIED*, in part, and *GRANTED*, in part in accordance with this Order; and it is

FURTHER ORDERED: That all electric distribution companies and local gas distribution companies begin the exchange of customer information with EOHHS for the sole purpose of enrolling eligible customers in discount programs within 30 days of the date of this Order; and it is

FURTHER ORDERED: That all electric distribution companies and local gas distribution companies include opt-out notices in December 2004 bill inserts; and it is

FURTHER ORDERED: That all electric distribution companies and local gas distribution companies comply with all other directives contained in this Order.

By Order of the Department,

____

Paul G. Afonso, Chairman

____

James Connelly, Commissioner

____

W. Robert Keating, Commissioner

____

Eugene J. Sullivan, Jr., Commissioner

COMMISSIONER MANNING, concurring in part and dissenting in part:

I agree with the majority that the implementation of automated enrollment for low-income utility discount rates is appropriate. Implementation of the computer-matching program will make enrolling in the discount program more efficient and effective. I also agree with the majority's finding that the establishment of a cost recovery mechanism is not a prerequisite to the establishment of the computer-matching program. I disagree, however, with the majority's order implementing a cost recovery mechanism without first assessing the impact of the program on company revenues, vetting proposals and allowing comment by the parties. This program is a scaled-down version of the one originally proposed and, therefore, may not result in a dramatic increase in the numbers enrolled in the discount program and associated costs. In addition, the automated program should result in administrative savings. An approach that better serves the interests of ratepayers would have involved ordering companies to file reports after six months indicating numbers enrolled pre- and post-implementation and then soliciting proposals for cost recovery, if warranted.

____

Deirdre K. Manning, Commissioner

4 In each company's next rate case, the Department will consider whether to establish a fully-reconciling mechanism to collect the entire revenue shortfall from discount rates or whether it is more appropriate to resume collecting this shortfall from all customers through base rates.

5 We recognize that the implementation of the computer-matching program within 30 days of the date of this Order combined with an opt-out notice in December 2004 bills will mean that certain customers on later bill cycles will not have an opportunity to opt-out of the first round of data sharing with EOHHS. Although this timing is unfortunate, it is necessary in order to ensure that the computer-matching program is available to assist all low-income customers this winter heating season.

6 For example, public benefit programs include Women Infants and Children, Medicaid, and Free/Reduced Lunch Programs.

F.1.2.3 D.T.E. 01-106-C, Order on Discount Rate Cost Recovery (Oct. 14, 2005)

The Commonwealth of Massachusetts
Department of Telecommunications and Energy

October 14, 2005

D.T.E. 01-106-C

Investigation by the Department of Telecommunications and Energy on its own motion, pursuant to G.L. c. 159, § 105 and G.L. c. 164, § 76, to increase the participation rate for discounted electric, gas and telephone service.

D.T.E. 05-55

Investigation by the Department of Telecommunications and Energy on its own motion as to the propriety of the rates and charges set forth in the following tariffs: (Residential Assistance Adjustment Clause) M.D.T.E. No. 110—Boston Edison Company; M.D.T.E. No. 210—Cambridge Electric Light Company; M.D.T.E. No. 310—Commonwealth Electric Company, filed on August 16, 2005, to be come effective September 1, 2005, by Boston Edison Company, Cambridge Electric Light Company and Commonwealth Electric Company, d/b/a NSTAR Electric.

D.T.E. 05-56

Investigation by the Department of Telecommunications and Energy on its own motion as to the propriety of the rates and charges set forth in the following tariff: M.D.T.E. No. 1089—Residential Assistance Adjustment Provision, filed on July 25, 2005, to become effective September 1, 2005, by Massachusetts Electric Company and Nantucket Electric Company.

I. INTRODUCTION

On August 8, 2003, the Department of Telecommunications and Energy ("Department") established a computer matching program to exchange information regarding customer eligibility for certain means tested public benefits for the sole purpose of increasing[1] the participation of eligible low-income customers in discounted electric and gas service. *Low-Income Discount Participation Rate*, D.T.E. 01-106-A (2003). Because electric and gas distribution companies may incur a decrease in revenues from increased participation in the computer matching program, the Department found that it was appropriate to establish a reconciliation mechanism to recover any resulting revenue shortfall. *Low-Income Discount Participation Rate*, D.T.E. 01-106-B at 9 (2004); D.T.E. 01-106-A, at 18–19.

On August 16, 2005, Boston Edison Company, Cambridge Electric Light Company, and Commonwealth Electric Company (together, "NSTAR Electric"), in compliance with D.T.E. 01-106-B, filed proposed tariffs, M.D.T.E. Nos. 110, 210, and 310, which would allow it to recover costs related to the low-income discount rate computer matching program.[2] On July 25, 2005, Massachusetts Electric Company and Nantucket Electric Company (together, "MECo") filed a similar proposed tariff, M.D.T.E. No. 1086. The proposed tariffs have an effective date of September 1, 2005. On August 23, 2005, the Department suspended the tariffs for investigation until November 1, 2005. The NSTAR Electric tariff filing was docketed as D.T.E. 05-55. The MECo tariff filing was docketed as D.T.E. 05-56.

In order to establish a uniform cost recovery mechanism for all electric and gas distribution companies for costs related to the low-income discount rate computer matching program, the Department consolidated the investigation of D.T.E. 05-55 and D.T.E. 05-56 with its investigation of electric and gas distribution company compliance with the directives contained in D.T.E. 01-106-B. *Low-Income Discount Participation Rate*, D.T.E. 01-106-B/D.T.E. 05-55/D.T.E. 05-56, Notice of Filing and Public Hearing (August 30, 2005). The Department held a public hearing on September 16, 2005.

Immediately after the public hearing, the Department held a technical conference with interested persons to discuss the establishment of a uniform cost recovery mechanism. Following the technical conference, the Department sought comment on an alternative cost recovery mechanism ("Alternative Mechanism") designed to compensate electric and gas distribution companies for revenues lost as a result of increased participation in the low-income discount. *Low-Income Discount Participation Rate*, D.T.E. 01-106-B/D.T.E. 05-55/ D.T.E. 05-56, Hearing Officer Memorandum (September 27, 2005). Comments were filed by the Attorney General of the Commonwealth ("Attorney General"), Bay State Gas Company ("Bay State"), The Berkshire Gas Company ("Berkshire"), Blackstone Gas Company ("Blackstone"), Fitchburg Gas and Electric Light Company d/b/a/ Unitil ("Unitil"), KeySpan Energy Delivery New England ("Keyspan"), MECo, the Massachusetts Community Action Program Directors' Association and the Massachusetts Energy Directors' Association (together, "MASSCAP"), New England Gas Company ("New England Gas"), NSTAR Electric and NSTAR Gas Company (together, "NSTAR"), and Western Massachusetts Electric Company ("WMECo").

II. DESCRIPTION OF PROPOSED COST RECOVERY MECHANISMS

A. NSTAR and MECo

Under the NSTAR and MECo proposed cost recovery mechanisms, the companies would track individual customers enrolled on the discount rate as a result of the computer matching program (MECo Cover Letter, D.T.E. 05-56, at 1; NSTAR Cover Letter, D.T.E. 05-55, at 2). NSTAR and MECo would calculate the difference between the distribution revenue for the usage of these customers under the discounted rate and the regular residential rate to establish a fully-reconciling adjustment factor applicable to all of the companies' customers (*id.*). MECo proposes to accumulate this revenue difference for a twelve-month period and accrue interest costs at the customer deposit rate. MECo would begin

1 Discounted rates for low-income gas and electric customers are available upon verification of a customer's receipt of any means tested public benefit or verification of eligibility for the low-income home energy assistance program, for which eligibility does not exceed 175 percent of the federal poverty level based on a household's gross income. *See, e.g.*, G.L. c. 164, § 1F(4)(i).

2 On September 15, 2005, as part of its peak seasonal cost of gas adjustment filing, NSTAR Gas Company filed a proposed cost recovery mechanism similar to the mechanism filed by NSTAR Electric in D.T.E. 05-55.

recovering this revenue difference through a Residential Assistance Adjustment Factor ("RAAF") after accumulating twelve months of actual data (MECo Cover Letter, D.T.E. 05-56, at 1). Alternatively, NSTAR Electric proposes to begin collecting this estimated revenue difference through a RAAF immediately, with any over- or under-recoveries to accrue interest costs at the prime interest rate (NSTAR Cover Letter, D.T.E. 05-55, at 2).

B. Alternative Mechanism

Under the Alternative Mechanism, all electric and gas distribution companies would establish a baseline amount of low-income discount that is collected through base rates for the twelve months ending June 30, 2005. The baseline amount would be calculated as the difference between the base rate revenues that would have been collected from customers receiving the low-income discount during the year ending June 30, 2005, had no low-income discount existed and the actual base rate revenues collected from low-income customers for the twelve months ending June 30, 2005. *Low-Income Discount Participation Rate*, D.T.E. 01-106-B/D.T.E. 05-55/D.T.E. 05-56, Hearing Officer Memorandum at 2–3 (September 27, 2005).

On or after July 1, 2005, any amount of low-income discount (whether customers are enrolled in the low-income discount rate through traditional outreach or the computer matching program) in excess of the baseline amount would be eligible for recovery through a RAAF. The adjustment factor would be calculated on a prospective basis, similar to the method proposed in the tariffs that were filed by NSTAR Electric in D.T.E. 05-55. Companies would forecast the expected low-income shortfall for the next twelve months. Any subsequent over- or under-recovery would be reconciled in the following year, with interest costs to be accrued at the prime interest rate. *Id.* In the event that a company's total low-income discount in a given year is below the baseline amount, no refund of any baseline amount will be due to ratepayers. *Id.*

III. POSITION OF THE COMMENTERS

A. Electric and Gas Distribution Companies

The electric and gas distribution companies are generally supportive of the Alternative Mechanism and its prospective calculation of the adjustment factor (Bay State Comments at 1–3, Berkshire at 2, Blackstone Comments at 1, KeySpan Comments at 1, MECo Comments at 2–4, New England Gas Comments at 1, NSTAR Comments at 1, Unitil Comments at 1, WMECo Comments at 2–4). While MECo does not oppose a prospective recovery mechanism, it argues that a retrospective mechanism is the simplest approach to comply with the Department's directives in D.T.E. 01-106-B (MECo Comments at 2).

With respect to the interest rate to be applied to any RAAF over- or under-recoveries, most distribution companies support using the prime interest rate (Bay State Comments at 2, Blackstone Comments at 1, New England Gas Comments at 1, NSTAR Comments at 2, Unitil Comments at 1, WMECo Comments at 3). However, MECo argues that the interest rate should be the same as each company's other reconciliation mechanisms accruing interest costs (in MECo's case, the interest rate on customer deposits) (MECo Comments at 3).

Likewise, most distribution companies support the calculation of the baseline amount and operation of the RAAF in the Alternative Mechanism (Berkshire Comments at 2, Blackstone Comments at 1, New England Gas Comments at 1, NSTAR Comments at 2, Unitil Comments at 1, WMECo Comments at 3–4). However, MECo proposes that the calculation of the baseline amount should be revised to reflect the revenue collected through base rates, rather than the amount of the discount provided to low-income customers (MECo Comments at 2–3). Bay State recommends that it be permitted to establish its baseline amount as of December 31, 2004, consistent with the end of the test year used to establish its proposed rates in its open rate case investigation, *Bay State Gas Company*, D.T.E. 05-27 (Bay State Comments a 2). Finally, Blackstone, New England Gas and WMECo suggest that weather normalized sales be used to establish the baseline amount (Blackstone Comments at 1, New England Gas Comments at 1, WMECo Comments at 3).

B. Attorney General

The Attorney General contends that two elements of the Alternative Mechanism should be amended, arguing that they are not in the best interest of customers (Attorney General Comments at 2). First, the Attorney General argues that the baseline for calculating the amount of low-income discount eligible for recovery through a RAAF should be the low-income discount amount currently included in non-low-income customers' base rates, adjusted for any change in billing determinants from the test year until the twelve months ending June 30, 2005 (*id.*). The Attorney General contends that this method will prevent distribution company shareholders from being harmed, while ensuring that the companies do not profit from the number of low-income customers (*id.* at 2–3).

Second, the Attorney General argues that, in order to ensure that the cost recovery mechanism is revenue-neutral, the Department should require the companies to refund to ratepayers any over-recoveries created when a company's total low-income discount is below the baseline amount (*id.* at 3).

C. MASSCAP

MASSCAP supports several of the terms of the Alternative Mechanism, including prospective calculation of the adjustment factor and use of the prime interest rate (MASSCAP Comments at 2, n.1). However, MASSCAP states that any cost recovery mechanism should leave gas and electric distribution companies economically indifferent to whether the total enrollment on the low-income discount rate increases or declines (*id.* at 2). While MASSCAP agrees that the Alternative Mechanism adequately ensures that distribution company shareholders will not be harmed if low-income discount rate enrollment increases, MASSCAP argues that the Alternative Mechanism creates a financial incentive for companies to tolerate declines in total low-income discount rate enrollment (*id.* at 2–3). To remove this incentive, MASSCAP argues that, in the event that a company's total low-income discount is below the baseline amount, a refund should be due to ratepayers (*id.* at 2–4).

IV. ANALYSIS AND FINDINGS

Currently, lost revenues from the traditional low-income discount program are designed to be recovered from all customers through base rates. *See, e.g.*, *Boston Gas Company*, D.T.E. 03-40, at 385 (2003). In establishing the computer matching program, the Department recognized that distribution companies may incur a decrease in revenues from increased enrollment in discount rates. D.T.E. 01-106-A at 13.

In D.T.E. 01-106-B at 9 (2004), the Department stated that "it is appropriate to establish a reconciling mechanism to recover any resulting revenue shortfall" from increased participation in discount rates once the computer matching program begins. Until a company's next rate case, the Department stated that electric and gas companies "may recover revenues lost as a result of the low-income subsidy in their next reconciliation filing for electric companies or local distribution factor filing for gas companies." *Id.* When calculating lost revenues associated with the low-income subsidy, the Department directed the companies to propose a reconciliation factor based on the difference between the total of forecast lost-revenues associated with the low-income discount and the amount of the low-income subsidy that was approved in the company's last rate case or settlement, adjusted for any changes in sales and the number of low-income customers as of the effective date of the computer matching program." *Id.* at 9–10. To this end, the Department offered an Alternative Mechanism for consideration.[3]

There was widespread support for several elements of the Alternative Mechanism, including the establishment of a baseline amount of low-income discount that is collected through base rates, above which electric and gas distribution companies will be permitted to recover lost revenues from additional enrollment, whether through the computer matching program or through traditional means. We address other aspects of the Alternative Mechanism below.

MECo and the Attorney General request that the Department revise the Alternative Mechanism's calculation of the baseline amount of low-income discount that is collected through base rates. Rather than calculating the baseline amount as the difference between the base rate revenues that would have been collected from customers receiving the low-income discount during the fiscal year ending June 30, 2005, had no low-income discount existed and the actual base rate revenues collected from low-income customers for the year ending June 30, 2005, MECo and the Attorney General suggest that the baseline amount be set at the amount of the low-income discount that was included in base rates in each company's last rate case, adjusted for any increase in sales (MECo Comments at 3; Attorney General Comments at 2–3).

We are not convinced that this proposed change would improve the accuracy of the calculation of the baseline amount.[4] In addition, the method described in the Alternative Mechanism is easier to implement in that it does not require that each company determine what level of discount was approved in its last base rate proceeding (which was nearly 15 years ago for some companies). Therefore, the Department directs all electric and gas distribution companies to calculate the baseline amount of low-income discount described in the Alternative Mechanism.

The Alternative Mechanism does not require companies to refund any amounts to ratepayers if a company's total low-income discount in a given year is below the baseline amount. Both the Attorney General and MASSCAP request that the Department change this provision, stating that it creates a financial benefit for company shareholders when there are declines in the total low-income discount rate enrollment (Attorney General Comments at 3; MASSCAP Comments at 2).

The Alternative Mechanism is not intended to displace the ebb and flow of traditional ratemaking where revenues from the low-income discount program are designed to be recovered from all customers through base rates. Rather, the Alternative Mechanism addresses the short-term concern of a potential revenue shortfall from increased participation in discount rates, resulting from a change in Department policy, that was neither known nor measurable when base rates were established. Companies will recover costs through the RAAF until their next general distribution base rate case.[5] As we stated in D.T.E. 01-106-B at 10, n.4, in each company's next rate case, we will consider whether to establish a fully-reconciling mechanism to collect the entire revenue shortfall from discount rates or whether it is more appropriate to resume collecting the entire shortfall from all customers through base rates. Accordingly, we decline to adopt the Attorney General's and MASSCAP's proposed change.

The Alternative Mechanism includes a prospective calculation

3 The Alternative Mechanism comprises the following elements:
- All RAAF tariffs will have an effective date of November 1, 2005.
- The adjustment factor will be calculated on a prospective basis, similar to the method proposed in the tariffs that were filed by NSTAR Electric in D.T.E. 05-55. Companies shall forecast the expected low-income shortfall for the next twelve months. Any subsequent over- or under-recovery will be reconciled in the following year.
- For gas companies, the reconciliation will occur concurrently with peak/winter LDAF filings. For electric companies, the reconciliation will occur concurrently with annual transition charge reconciliation filings.
- Over- or under-recoveries will accrue interest at the prime rate consistent with Department regulations. See 220 C.M.R. § 6.08(2).
- Companies shall establish a baseline amount of low-income discount that is collected through base rates for the twelve months ending June 30, 2005. The baseline amount shall be calculated as the difference between the base rate revenues that would have been collected from customers receiving the low-income discount during the year ending June 30, 2005, had no low-income discount existed and the actual base rate revenues collected from low-income customers for the twelve months ending June 30, 2005.
- On or after July 1, 2005, any amount of low-income discount (whether customers are enrolled in the low-income discount rate through traditional outreach or the computer matching program) in excess of the baseline amount will be eligible for recovery through the RAAF.
- In the event that a company's total low-income discount in a given year is below the baseline amount, no refund of any baseline amount will be due to ratepayers.

Low-Income Discount Participation Rate, D.T.E. 01-106-B/D.T.E. 05-55/D.T.E. 05-56, Hearing Officer Memorandum at 2–3 (September 27, 2005).

4 When rates were designed and the low income discount shortfall was allocated in each company's last distribution rate case, it was done using a rate base allocator, rather than allocated evenly across all rate classes.

5 We note that G.L. c. 164, § 94 rate proceedings are well underway or are pending filing for Bay State and NSTAR, respectively. Some flexibility, we anticipate, may be necessary to reflect the instant Order as it affects those companies' rate proceedings.

of the low-income revenue shortfall. MECo suggests that the Department instead adopt a retrospective calculation of the low-income revenue shortfall (MECo Comments at 2). While we agree that the prospective method requires an additional reconciliation, the effort entailed is not burdensome. Therefore, we are not persuaded to adopt a retrospective calculation.

We expect that each distribution company will add a significant number of customers to the low income discount rate at the start of the computer matching program. The prospective method will allow companies to recover any resulting revenue shortfall immediately, as opposed to waiting up to one year to begin recovery with interest costs accruing every month. Therefore, to reduce the amount of deferrals accruing interest costs, the Department directs the companies to calculate the low-income revenue shortfall on a prospective basis as described in the Alternative Mechanism.

The Alternative Mechanism applies the prime interest rate to any over- or under-recovery of the low-income revenue shortfall. MECo suggests that the Department instead apply the interest rate on customer deposits for electric distribution companies (MECo Comments at 3). While it is correct that the Department's regulations at 220 C.M.R. § 6.08(2) concerning the prime interest rate only apply to gas distribution companies, the Department has in certain circumstances allowed electric distribution companies to apply the prime interest rate to over- and under-recoveries. *See, e.g., Boston Edison Company*, D.P.U. 85-1C at 14 (1985). So that every distribution company calculates interest costs on a uniform basis, the Department directs all electric and gas companies to use the prime interest rate consistent with 220 C.M.R. § 6.08(2) when applying interest to any RAAF over- or under-recovery.

Blackstone, New England Gas, and WMECo raise the issue of weather normalizing the billing determinants used to calculate the low-income discount rate revenue shortfall (MECo Comments at 3; Blackstone Comments at 1; New England Gas Comments at 1). The Alternative Mechanism did not address adjustment for weather normalization. Such an adjustment would result in more accurate calculations for those energy sources that are substantially subject to the annual variability of weather. Therefore, the Department directs all gas distribution companies to weather-normalize the billing determinants used to calculate the low-income revenue shortfall. Weather normalizing the billing determinants is consistent with the Department's ratemaking precedent for the setting of gas rates. Because billing determinants for electricity are not weather normalized, the Department finds that such an adjustment is not appropriate for electric distribution companies.

Bay State Gas Company requests that it be allowed to use December 31, 2004 as the cutoff date for calculating its baseline low-income revenue shortfall to correspond to the test year amounts included in its rate case filing which is presently under consideration by Department (Bay State Comments at 2–3). It is essential that the cutoff date for the baseline amount be as close as possible to the start of the computer matching program. As discussed below, all distribution companies will begin enrolling eligible customers in the low-income discount rate using computer matching data from the second quarter of this year. The cutoff date of June 30, 2005, as specified in the Alternative Mechanism, corresponds to the end of the second quarter of 2005. Therefore, we deny Bay State's request for an alternative cutoff date and instead direct it to apply the cutoff date as specified in the Alternative Mechanism.[6]

The Department is aware and appreciates that certain gas and electric distribution companies already have begun enrolling low-income discount rate eligible customers identified as a result of the computer matching program. We take this opportunity to confirm that these companies will not lose revenues by their decision to enroll eligible customers before the finalization of a cost recovery mechanism because, although the RAAF tariffs will have an effective date of November 1, 2005, any amount of low-income discount in excess of the baseline amount on or after July 1, 2005, will be eligible for recovery through the RAAF. For any gas and electric distribution companies that have not yet begun enrolling eligible customers identified as a result of the computer matching program on the low-income discount rate, the Department directs them to do so immediately, using the computer matching data generated as a result of the second quarter of this year. With the clarification regarding weather normalization of gas billing determinants discussed above, the Department adopts the Alternative Mechanism and directs each gas and electric distribution company to submit a Residential Assistance Adjustment Factor compliance tariff, consistent with the Alternative Mechanism, on or before October 17, 2005.

V. ORDER

Accordingly, after due notice, hearing and consideration, it is

ORDERED: That the tariffs M.D.T.E. No. 110, M.D.T.E. No. 210, and M.D.T.E. No. 310, filed on August 16, 2005, to be come effective September 1, 2005, by Boston Edison Company, Cambridge Electric Light Company and Commonwealth Electric Company, d/b/a NSTAR Electric, are *DISALLOWED*; and it is

FURTHER ORDERED: That the tariff M.D.T.E. No. 1089, filed on July 25, 2005, to become effective September 1, 2005, by Massachusetts Electric Company and Nantucket Electric Company, is *DISALLOWED*; and it is

FURTHER ORDERED: That on or before October 17, 2005, all electric and gas distribution companies shall file Residential Assistance Adjustment Factor tariffs in compliance with this Order; and it is

FURTHER ORDERED: That all electric and gas distribution companies shall comply with all other orders and directives contained herein.

By Order of the Department,

Paul G. Afonso, Chairman

James Connelly, Commissioner

W. Robert Keating, Commissioner

Judith F. Judson, Commissioner

Brian Paul Golden, Commissioner

6 A Department Order in D.T.E. 05-27 will be issued on or before December 1, 2005. Bay State's recovery of any low-income revenue shortfall on a going-forward basis will be addressed in that Order.

An appeal as to matters of law from any final decision, order or ruling of the Commission may be taken to the Supreme Judicial Court by an aggrieved party in interest by the filing of a written petition praying that the Order of the Commission be modified or set aside in whole or in part. Such petition for appeal shall be filed with the Secretary of the Commission within twenty days after the date of service of the decision, order or ruling of the Commission, or within such further time as the Commission may allow upon request filed prior to the expiration of the twenty days after the date of service of said decision, order or ruling. Within ten days after such petition has been filed, the appealing party shall enter the appeal in the Supreme Judicial Court sitting in Suffolk County by filing a copy thereof with the Clerk of said Court. G.L. c. 25, § 5.

F.2 Texas Materials

F.2.1 System Benefit Fund—Tex. Util. Code § 39.903 [Portions]

(a) The system benefit fund is an account in the general revenue fund. Money in the account may be appropriated only for the purposes provided by this section or other law. Interest earned on the system benefit fund shall be credited to the fund. Section 403.095, Government Code, does not apply to the system benefit fund.

(b) The system benefit fund is financed by a nonbypassable fee set by the commission in an amount not to exceed 65 cents per megawatt hour. The system benefit fund fee is allocated to customers based on the amount of kilowatt hours used.

(c) The nonbypassable fee may not be imposed on the retail electric customers of a municipally owned utility or electric cooperative before the sixth month preceding the date on which the utility or cooperative implements customer choice. Money distributed from the system benefit fund to a municipally owned utility or an electric cooperative shall be proportional to the nonbypassable fee paid by the municipally owned utility or the electric cooperative, subject to the reimbursement provided by Subsection (i). On request by a municipally owned utility or electric cooperative, the commission shall reduce the nonbypassable fee imposed on retail electric customers served by the municipally owned utility or electric cooperative by an amount equal to the amount provided by the municipally owned utility or electric cooperative or its ratepayers for local low-income programs and local programs that educate customers about the retail electric market in a neutral and nonpromotional manner.

(d) The commission shall annually review and approve system benefit fund accounts, projected revenue requirements, and proposed nonbypassable fees. The commission shall report to the electric utility restructuring legislative oversight committee if the system benefit fund fee is insufficient to fund the purposes set forth in Subsection (e) to the extent required by this section.

(e) Money in the system benefit fund may be appropriated to provide funding solely for the following regulatory purposes, in the following order of priority:

(1) programs to:

(A) assist low-income electric customers by providing the 10 percent reduced rate prescribed by Subsection (h); and

(B) provide one-time bill payment assistance to electric customers who are or who have in their households one or more seriously ill or disabled low-income persons and who have been threatened with disconnection for nonpayment;

(2) customer education programs, administrative expenses incurred by the commission in implementing and administering this chapter, and expenses incurred by the office under this chapter;

(3) programs to assist low-income electric customers by providing the targeted energy efficiency programs described by Subsection (f)(2);

(4) programs to assist low-income electric customers by providing the 20 percent reduced rate prescribed by Subsection (h); and

(5) reimbursement to the commission and the Health and Human Services Commission for expenses incurred in the implementation and administration of an integrated eligibility process created under Section 17.007 for customer service discounts relating to retail electric service, including outreach expenses the commission determines are reasonable and necessary.

(f) Notwithstanding Section 39.106(b), the commission shall adopt rules regarding programs to assist low-income electric customers on the introduction of customer choice. The programs may not be targeted to areas served by municipally owned utilities or electric cooperatives that have not adopted customer choice. The programs shall include:

(1) reduced electric rates as provided by Subsections (h)–(l); and

(2) targeted energy efficiency programs to be administered by the Texas Department of Housing and Community Affairs in coordination with existing weatherization programs.

(g) Until customer choice is introduced in a power region, an electric utility may not reduce, in any manner, programs already offered to assist low-income electric customers.

(h) The commission shall adopt rules for a retail electric provider to determine a reduced rate for eligible customers to be discounted off the standard retail service package as approved by the commission under Section 39.106, or the price to beat established by Section 39.202, whichever is lower. Municipally owned utilities and electric cooperatives shall establish a reduced rate for eligible customers to be discounted off the standard retail service package established under Section 40.053 or 41.053, as appropriate. The reduced rate for a retail electric provider shall result in a total charge that is at least 10 percent and, if sufficient money in the system benefit fund is available, up to 20 percent, lower than the amount the customer would otherwise be charged. To the extent the system benefit fund is insufficient to fund the initial 10 percent rate reduction, the commission may increase the fee to an amount not more than 65 cents per megawatt hour, as provided by Subsection (b). If the fee is set at 65 cents per megawatt hour or if the commission determines that appropriations are insufficient to fund the 10 percent rate reduction, the commission may reduce the rate reduction to less than 10 percent. For a municipally owned utility or electric cooperative, the reduced rate shall be equal to an amount that can be fully funded by that portion of the nonbypassable fee proceeds paid by the municipally owned utility or electric cooperative that is allocated to the utility or cooperative by the commission under Subsection (e) for programs for low-income customers of the utility or cooperative. The reduced rate for municipally owned utilities and electric cooperatives under this section is in addition to any rate reduction that may result from local programs for low-income customers of the municipally owned utilities or electric cooperatives.

(*i*) A retail electric provider, municipally owned utility, or electric cooperative seeking reimbursement from the system benefit fund may not charge an eligible low-income customer a rate higher than the appropriate rate determined under Subsection (h). A retail electric provider not subject to the price to beat, or a municipally owned utility or electric cooperative subject to the nonbypassable fee under Subsection (c), shall be reimbursed from the system benefit fund for the difference between the reduced rate and the rate established under Section 39.106 or, as appropriate, the rate established under Section 40.053 or 41.053. A retail electric provider who is subject to the price to beat shall be reimbursed from the system benefit fund for the difference between the reduced rate and the price to beat. The commission shall adopt rules providing for the reimbursement.

(j) The commission shall adopt rules providing for methods of enrolling customers eligible to receive reduced rates under Subsection (h). The rules must provide for automatic enrollment as one enrollment option. The Texas Department of Human Services, on request of the commission, shall assist in the adoption and implementation of these rules. The commission and the Texas Department of Human Services shall enter into a memorandum of understanding establishing the respective duties of the commission and the department in relation to the automatic enrollment.

(j-1) The commission shall adopt rules governing the bill payment assistance program provided under Subsection (e)(1)(B). The rules must provide that a customer is eligible to receive the assistance only if the assistance is necessary to prevent the disconnection of service for nonpayment of bills and the electric customer is or has in the customer's household one or more seriously ill or disabled low-income persons whose health or safety may be injured by the disconnection. The commission may prescribe the documentation necessary to demonstrate eligibility for the assistance and may establish additional eligibility criteria. The Health and Human Services Commission, on request of the commission, shall assist in the adoption and implementation of these rules.

(k) A retail electric provider is prohibited from charging the customer a fee for participation in the reduced rate program.

(*l*) For the purposes of this section, a "low-income electric customer" is an electric customer:

(1) whose household income is not more than 125 percent of the federal poverty guidelines; or

(2) who receives food stamps from the Texas Department of Human Services or medical assistance from a state agency administering a part of the medical assistance program.

[*Added by* Acts 1999, 76th Leg., ch. 405, § 39, eff. Sept. 1, 1999. *Amended by* Acts 2001, 77th Leg., ch. 1466, § 19(a), eff. June 15, 2001; Acts 2001, 77th Leg., ch. 1394, § 3, eff. Sept. 1, 2001; Acts 2001, 77th Leg., ch. 1451, § 3, eff. Sept. 1, 2001; Acts 2003, 78th Leg., ch. 211, § 2.02, eff. June 16, 2003; Acts 2003, 78th Leg., ch. 1296, § 4(a), eff. June 20, 2003; Acts 2005, 79th Leg., ch. 412, § 17, eff. Sept. 1, 2005; Acts 2005, 79th Leg., ch. 728, § 21.001, eff. Sept. 1, 2005; Acts 2005, 79th Leg., ch. 797, §§ 11, 12, eff. Sept. 1, 2005; Acts 2005, 79th Leg., ch. 899, § 14.01, eff. Aug. 29, 2005]

F.2.2 Rate Reduction Program—Tex. Admin. Code tit. 16, § 25.454

§ 25.454. Rate Reduction Program.

(a) Purpose. The purpose of this section is to define the low-income electric rate reduction program, establish the rate reduction calculation, and specify enrollment options and processes.

(b) Application. This section applies to retail electric providers (REPs) that provide electric service in an area that has been opened to customer choice, or an area for which the commission has issued an order applying the system benefit fund or rate reduction. This section also applies to municipally owned electric utilities (MOUs) and electric cooperatives (Coops) on a date determined by the commission, but no sooner than six months preceding the date on which an MOU or a Coop implements customer choice in its certificated area unless otherwise governed by § 25.457 of this title (relating to Implementation of the System Benefit Fee by Municipally Owned Utilities and Electric Cooperatives).

(c) Funding. The rate reduction requirements set forth by this subchapter are subject to sufficient funding and authorization to expend funds. In the event that funding and authorization to expend funds are not sufficient to administer the rate reduction program or fund rate reductions for customers, the following shall apply:

(1) The requirements of subsections (e), (f) and (g) of this section are suspended until sufficient funding and spending authority are available.

(2) The requirements of the following sections of this title, insofar as they relate to the rate reduction benefit, are suspended when sufficient funding and spending authority are not available:

(A) § 25.451(j) of this title (relating to Administration of the System Benefit Fund);

(B) § 25.457(i)-(j) of this title;

(C) § 25.475(g)(4)(L) of this title (relating to General Retail Electric Provider Requirements and Information Disclosures to Residential and Small Commercial Customers); and

(D) § 25.43(d)(3)(D), (q)(1)(A)-(B), (q)(2)(A), and (q)(3)(A) of this title (relating to Provider of Last Resort (POLR)).

(3) The requirements of § 25.480(c) of this title (relating to Bill Payments and Adjustments), insofar as they relate to the rate reduction benefit, are suspended if an eligibility list is not available as provided in subsection (i) of this section.

(d) Definitions. The following words and terms when used in this subchapter, shall have the following meanings, unless the context clearly indicates otherwise.

(1) Discount factor—The amount of discount an eligible low-income customer must be provided by any REP, or MOU or Coop, when applicable, in the customer's area, expressed as cents per kilowatt-hour (kWh).

(2) Discount percentage—The percentage of discount established by the commission and applied to the lower of the price to beat (PTB) or minimum provider of last resort (POLR) rate in a particular service territory.

(3) Low-Income Discount Administrator (LIDA)—A third-party vendor with whom the commission has a contract to administer the rate reduction program.

(4) Rate reduction—The total discount to be deducted from a customer's electric bill. This reduction is derived from the discount factor and total consumption in accordance with subsection (e)(3) of this section.

(5) REP—For the purposes of this section, a retail electric provider and an MOU or Coop that provides retail electric service in an area that has been opened to customer choice.

(6) Minimum POLR rate—For the purposes of this section, the minimum POLR rate shall be the POLR rate posted on the commission's website on the Electricity Facts Label for each service territory for 1,000 kWh of usage.

(e) Rate reduction program. In each month for which funds are available for the low-income discount, all eligible low-income customers as defined in § 25.5 of this title (relating to Definitions) are to receive a rate reduction, as determined by the commission pursuant to this section, on their electric bills from their REP.

(1) Discount factors shall be determined in accordance with this paragraph, as the lower of the PTB or minimum POLR rate for each service territory multiplied by the approved discount percentage.

(A) The commission shall periodically establish the discount percentage. The discount percentage may be set at a level no greater than 20%.

(B) The commission staff shall calculate a discount factor for each service territory and post the discount factors on the commission website (www.puc.state.tx.us).

(C) Each discount factor based on the minimum POLR rate shall be in effect from May through October or November through April, subject to revision pursuant to paragraph (2) of this subsection.

(D) Each discount factor based on the PTB shall be recalculated when the PTB rate changes or the commission revises the discount percentage. The discount factor based on the PTB shall reflect any seasonal variation in the PTB.

(2) The commission may revise the discount factors set pursuant to paragraph (1) of this subsection through a change to the discount percentage because of one of the following occurrences:

(A) The commission staff determines that there are sufficient remaining appropriations for the fiscal year to support an increase in the discount percentage without exceeding available appropriations for the fiscal year. This determination may be triggered by the routine review by commission staff of disbursements and remaining appropriations, or by a fluctuation of five percent or more of the minimum POLR rate.

(B) The commission staff determines that there are insufficient remaining appropriations for the fiscal year, and a decrease to the discount percentage is necessary to ensure that funds spent do not exceed appropriations for the fiscal year.

(C) The commission determines that a change in the discount percentage is consistent with the objectives of this section and the public interest.

(3) All REPs shall provide the rate reduction to eligible low-income customers.

(A) The discount factors posted on the commission's website shall be used to calculate the rate reduction for each eligible low-income customer's bill. If the discount factor changes for any area, REPs shall implement the resulting change in the discount factor in their billings to customers within 30 calendar days of the date the commission posts the revised discount factor to its website, or on the effective date of the discount factor, whichever is later.

(B) The rate reduction shall be calculated by multiplying the customer's total consumption (kWh) for the billing period by the discount factor (in cents/kWh) in effect during the billing cycle in which the bill is rendered. If an eligible customer is rebilled, the discount that was in effect during the affected billing cycle will be applied.

(C) The customer's discount amount shall be clearly identified as a line item on the electric portion of the customer's bill, including the description "LITE-UP Discount." If a monthly bill is not issued as provided by § 25.498 of this title (relating to Retail Electric Service Using a Customer Prepayment Device or System), the customer's receipt or confirmation of payment, or detailed information accessed by confirmation code, as described by § 25.498 of this title, shall indicate that the discount was applied to the customer's charges with the words "LITE-UP" or "LITE-UP Discount."

(D) REPs are entitled to reimbursement under § 25.451(j) of this title for rate reductions they provide to eligible low-income customers.

(f) Customer enrollment. Eligible customers may be enrolled in the rate reduction program through automatic enrollment or self-enrollment.

(1) Automatic enrollment is an electronic process to identify customers eligible for the rate reduction by matching client data from the Texas Health and Human Services Commission (HHSC) with customer-specific data from REPs.

(A) HHSC shall provide client information to LIDA in accordance with subsection (g)(1) of this section.

(B) REPs shall provide customer information to LIDA in accordance with subsection (g)(3) of this section.

(C) LIDA shall compare the customer information from HHSC and REPs, create files of matching customers, enroll these customers in the rate reduction program, and notify the REPs of their eligible customers.

(2) Self-enrollment is an alternate enrollment process available to eligible electric customers who are not automatically enrolled and whose combined household income does not exceed 125% of federal poverty guidelines or who receive food stamps or medical assistance from HHSC. The self-enrollment process shall be administered by LIDA. LIDA's responsibilities shall include:

(A) Distributing and processing self-enrollment applications, as developed by the commission, for the purposes of initial self-enrollment, and for re-enrollment of self-enrolled and automatically enrolled customers;

(B) Maintaining customer records for all applicants;

(C) Providing information to customers regarding the process of enrolling in the low-income discount program;

(D) Determining customers' eligibility by reviewing information submitted through self-enrollment forms and determining whether the applicant meets the program qualifications; and

(E) Matching customer information submitted through self-enrollment forms with customer data provided by REPs, creating files of matching customers, enrolling matching customers in the rate reduction programs, and notifying the REPs of their eligible customers.

(3) In determining customers' eligibility in the self-enrollment process, LIDA shall require that customers submit with a self-enrollment form proof of income in the form of copies of tax returns, pay stubs, letters from employers, or other pertinent information and shall audit statistically valid samples for accuracy.

If a person who self-enrolls claims to be eligible because of participation in a qualifying program, LIDA shall require the customer to submit a copy of proof of enrollment or eligibility letter that indicates enrollment of the applicant in the qualifying program.

(4) The following procedures govern a customer's re-enrollment.

(A) A self-enrolled customer may re-enroll by submitting a completed self-enrollment form.

(B) A customer who was formerly, but is no longer, automatically enrolled may re-enroll through self-enrollment.

(C) LIDA shall send a customer who is eligible to re-enroll a self-enrollment form which specifies a date for submitting the completed form that is not more than 30 days after the date the form is mailed. If the customer submits a completed form before the date specified on the form and LIDA determines that the customer is eligible for re-enrollment, the customer shall receive the rate reduction without interruption.

(D) If a customer does not return a properly completed form before the time specified by LIDA, the customer's rate reduction may be interrupted until LIDA determines that the customer is eligible.

(5) The eligibility period of each customer will be determined by the customer's method of enrollment.

(A) The eligibility period for self-enrolled customers is seven months from the date of enrollment.

(B) Automatically enrolled customers will continue to be eligible as long as the customers receive HHSC benefits. Once a customer no longer receives HHSC benefits, the customer will continue to receive the rate reduction benefit for a period of no more than 60 days, during which the customer may self-enroll.

(6) A customer who believes that a self-enrollment application has been erroneously denied may request that LIDA review the application, and the customer may submit additional proof of eligibility.

(A) A customer who is dissatisfied with LIDA's action following a request for review under this paragraph may request an informal hearing to determine eligibility by the commission staff.

(B) A customer who is dissatisfied with the determination after an informal hearing under subparagraph (A) of this paragraph may file a formal complaint pursuant to § 22.242(e) of this title (relating to Complaints).

(g) Responsibilities. In addition to the requirements established in this section, program responsibilities for LIDA may be established in the commission's contract with LIDA; program responsibilities for tasks undertaken by HHSC may be established in the memorandum of understanding between the commission and HHSC.

(1) HHSC shall:

(A) assist in the implementation and maintenance of the automatic enrollment process by providing a database of customers receiving HHSC benefits as detailed in the memorandum of understanding between HHSC and the commission; and

(B) assist in the distribution of promotional and informational material as detailed in the memorandum of understanding.

(2) LIDA shall:

(A) receive customer lists from REPs on a monthly basis through data transfer;

(B) retrieve the database of clients from HHSC on a monthly basis;

(C) conduct the self-enrollment, automatic enrollment, and re-enrollment processes;

(D) establish a list of eligible customers, by comparing customer lists from the REPs with HHSC databases and identifying customer records that reasonably match;

(E) make available to each REP, on a date prescribed by the commission on a monthly basis, a list of low-income customers eligible to receive the rate reduction;

(F) notify customers that have applied for the rate reduction through the self-enrollment process of their eligibility determination and notify automatically enrolled and self-enrolled customers of their expiration of eligibility, and opportunities for re-enrollment in the rate reduction program;

(G) answer customer inquiries regarding the rate reduction program, and provide information to customers regarding enrollment for the rate reduction program and eligibility requirements;

(H) resolve customer enrollment problems, including issues concerning customer eligibility, the failure to provide discounts to customers who believe they are eligible, and the provision of discounts to customers who do not meet eligibility criteria; and

(I) protect the confidentiality of the customer information provided by the REPs and the client information provided by HHSC.

(3) A REP shall:

(A) provide residential customer information to LIDA through data transfer on a date prescribed by the commission on a monthly basis. The customer information shall include, to the greatest extent possible, each full name of the primary and secondary customer on each account, billing and service addresses, primary and secondary social security numbers, primary and secondary telephone numbers, Electric Service Identifier (ESI ID), service provider account number, and premise code;

(B) retrieve from LIDA the list of customers who are eligible to receive the rate reduction;

(C) upon commission request, monitor high-usage customers to ensure that premises are in fact residential and maintain records of monitoring efforts for audit purposes. A customer with usage greater than 3000 kWh in a month shall be considered a high-usage customer;

(D) apply a rate reduction to the electric bills of the eligible customers identified by LIDA within the first billing cycle in which it is notified of a customer's eligibility, if notification is received no later than seven days before the end of the billing cycle, or, if not, apply the rate reduction within 30 calendar days after notification is received from LIDA;

(E) notify customers three times a year about the availability of the rate reduction program, and provide self-enrollment forms to customers upon request;

(F) assist LIDA in working to resolve issues concerning customer eligibility, including the failure to provide discounts to customers who believe they are eligible and the provision of discounts to customers who may not meet the eligibility criteria; this obligation requires the REP to employ best efforts to avoid and resolve issues, including training call center personnel on general LITE-UP processes and information, and assigning problem resolution staff to work with LIDA on problems for which LIDA does not have sufficient information to resolve; and

(G) provide to the commission copies of materials regarding the rate reduction program given to customers during the previous 12 months upon commission request.

(h) Confidentiality of information.

(1) The data acquired from HHSC pursuant to this section is subject to a HHSC confidentiality agreement.

(2) All data transfers from REPs to LIDA pursuant to this section shall be conducted under the terms and conditions of a standard confidentiality agreement to protect customer privacy and REP's competitively sensitive information.

(3) LIDA may use information obtained pursuant to this section only for purposes prescribed by commission rule, including use in determining eligibility for assistance under § 25.455 of this title (relating to One-Time Bill Payment Assistance Program).

(*i*) Eligibility List for Continuation of Late Penalty Waiver Benefits.

(1) In the event that funding and authorization to expend funds are not sufficient to provide rate reductions for low-income customers that can be reimbursed from the system benefit fund, the commission may, in its discretion, require LIDA to maintain a list of low-income customers who would otherwise be eligible for automatic enrollment in the rate reduction program under subsection (f)(1) of this section if funds were available. The procedures set forth in subsection (f)(1) of this section will be used to the extent practicable. In addition to the requirements in this section, program responsibilities for LIDA may be established in the commission's contract with LIDA; and program responsibilities for tasks undertaken by HHSC may be established in a memorandum of understanding between the commission and HHSC. To assist the commission in implementing this provision, REPs shall upon request:

(A) provide residential customer information to LIDA through data transfer on a date prescribed by the commission on a monthly basis. The customer information shall include, to the greatest extent possible, each full name of the primary and secondary customer on each account, billing and service addresses, primary and secondary social security numbers, primary and secondary telephone numbers, ESI ID, service provider account number, and premise code;

(B) retrieve from LIDA the list of customers who would be eligible for automatic enrollment in the rate reduction program if funds were available;

(C) monitor high-usage customers to ensure that premises are in fact residential and maintain records of monitoring efforts for audit purposes. A customer with usage greater than 3,000 kWh in a month shall be considered a high-usage customer;

(D) assist LIDA in working to resolve issues concerning customer eligibility; this obligation requires the REP to employ best efforts to avoid and resolve issues, including training call center personnel on general processes and information, and assigning problem resolution staff to work with LIDA on problems for which LIDA does not have sufficient information to resolve; and

(E) provide other information and assistance, upon request of the commission, to assist in implementation of this section.

(2) If funding is available to include self-enrollees in the list of eligible customers, the commission may, in its discretion, require LIDA to include self-enrollees in the list of eligible customers consistent with subsection (f)(2) of this section or set forth processes for determining eligibility in a procedural guide. The processes, to the extent feasible, will be consistent with subsections (f) and (g) of this section.

(3) If pursuant to subsection (i) of this section, the commission, through the LIDA or other means, provides the REPs with a list of eligible customers § 25.480(c) of this title, which requires that a customer receiving a low-income discount pursuant to the Public Utility Regulatory Act § 39.903(h) may not be assessed a late penalty, shall be continued based on the customer's eligibility for the discount, rather than the customer's receipt of the discount.

(j) Deposit Installment Benefits.

(1) If LIDA is maintaining a list of eligible customers as described in subsection (f) or subsection (i) of this section, then a customer or applicant who qualifies for the rate reduction program is eligible to pay deposits over $50 in two installments, pursuant to § 25.478(e)(3) of this title (relating to Credit Requirements and Deposits).

(A) A REP who requires a customer or applicant to provide sufficient information to the REP to demonstrate that the customer or applicant qualifies for the rate reduction program may request the following information:

(i) a letter from the customer's or applicant's current or prior REP stating that the applicant is on the list of customers who would be eligible for the rate reduction if funds were available;

(ii) a bill from the current or prior REP that demonstrates that the customer or applicant is enrolled in the rate reduction program; or

(iii) other documentation that the REP determines to be appropriate and requests on a non-discriminatory basis.

(B) Upon the request of a customer, a REP shall provide a letter stating that the customer is on the list of customers who would be eligible for the rate reduction if funds were available. This letter may be combined with a letter issued to a customer regarding bill payment history.

(2) If LIDA is not maintaining a list of eligible customers as described in subsection (f) or subsection (i) of this section, a REP shall extend the option to pay deposits over $50 in two installments to any residential customers or applicants who qualify for the rate reduction program. The REP may, on a non-discriminatory basis, require the customer or applicant to provide documentation of eligibility that the REP determines to be appropriate. The REP shall provide notice of this option in any written notice requesting a deposit from a customer. This paragraph supersedes the provisions of § 25.478(c)(3) and (d)(3) of this title that require payment of the entire amount of a deposit within ten days.

(k) Voluntary Programs. Nothing in this section is intended to impair a REP's ability to voluntarily provide a low-income discount or other benefits to low-income customers.

(1) The list of low-income customers who would be eligible for the rate reduction if funds were available, or other non-discriminatory criteria, may be utilized by a REP as evidence of a customer's eligibility for the REP's voluntary low-income program, if offered.

(2) In the event a REP chooses to voluntarily offer a discount or other benefits to low-income customers, the REP shall treat any information obtained regarding the customer's financial status or enrollment in a government program as confidential information and shall not disclose the information to any other party or use the information for any purpose other than enrollment in a voluntary low-income program.

(*l*) Effective date. The effective date of this section is December 1, 2010.

[26 Tex. Reg. 106 (effective Jan. 10, 2001); *amended by* 29 Tex. Reg. 939 (effective Feb. 5, 2004); *amended by* 31 Tex. Reg. 2143 (effective Mar. 23, 2006); *amended by* 33 Tex. Reg. 2299 (Mar. 19, 2008); *amended by* 35 Tex. Reg. 9232 (effective Dec. 1, 2010)].

F.3 California Materials

F.3.1 Cal. Pub. Util. Code § 739.1

Reprinted from www.legaltips.org/california/california_public_utilities_code/727-749.aspx.

§ 739.1. California Alternate Rates for Energy program.

(a) The commission shall establish a program of assistance to low-income electric and gas customers, the cost of which shall not be borne solely by any single class of customer. The program shall be referred to as the California Alternate Rates for Energy or CARE program. The commission shall ensure that the level of discount for low-income electric and gas customers correctly reflects the level of need.

(b) The commission shall work with the public utility electrical and gas corporations to establish penetration goals. The commission shall authorize recovery of all administrative costs associated with the implementation of the CARE program that the commission determines to be reasonable, through a balancing account mechanism. Administrative costs shall include, but are not limited to, outreach, marketing, regulatory compliance, certification and verification, billing, measurement and evaluation, and capital improvements and upgrades to communications and processing equipment.

(c) The commission shall examine methods to improve CARE enrollment and participation. This examination shall include, but need not be limited to, comparing information from CARE and the Universal Lifeline Telephone Service (ULTS) to determine the most effective means of utilizing that information to increase CARE enrollment, automatic enrollment of ULTS customers who are eligible for the CARE program, customer privacy issues, and alternative mechanisms for outreach to potential enrollees. The commission shall ensure that a customer consents prior to enrollment. The commission shall consult with interested parties, including ULTS providers, to develop the best methods of informing ULTS customers about other available low-income programs, as well as the best mechanism for telephone providers to recover reasonable costs incurred pursuant to this section.

(d) The commission shall improve the CARE application process. To the extent possible, the commission shall develop a CARE application process using the existing ULTS application process as a model. The commission shall work with public utility electrical and gas corporations and the Low-Income Oversight Board established in Section 382.1 to meet the low-income objectives in this section.

(e) The commission's program of assistance to low-income electric and gas customers shall, as soon as practicable, include nonprofit group living facilities specified by the commission, if the commission finds that the residents in these facilities substantially meet the commission's low-income eligibility requirements and there is a feasible process for certifying that the assistance shall be used for the direct benefit, such as improved quality of care or improved food service, of the low-income residents in the facilities. The commission shall authorize utilities to offer discounts to eligible facilities licensed or permitted by appropriate state or local agencies, and to facilities, including women's shelters, hospices, and homeless shelters, that may not have a license or permit but provide other proof satisfactory to the utility that they are eligible to participate in the program.

(f) It is the intent of the Legislature that the commission ensure CARE program participants are afforded the lowest possible electric and gas rates and, to the extent possible, are exempt from additional surcharges attributable to the current energy crisis.

F.3.2 California's Moore Universal Telephone Service Act

§ 871. This article shall be known and may be cited as the Moore Universal Telephone Service Act.

§ 871.5. The Legislature finds and declares all of the following:

(a) The offering of high-quality basic telephone service at affordable rates to the greatest number of citizens has been a longstanding goal of the state.

(b) The Moore Universal Telephone Service Act has been, and continues to be, an important means for achieving universal service by making basic telephone service affordable to low-income households through the creation of a lifeline class of service.

(c) Every means should be employed by the commission and telephone corporations to ensure that every household qualified to receive lifeline telephone service is informed of and is afforded the opportunity to subscribe to that service.

(d) The furnishing of lifeline telephone service is in the public interest and should be supported fairly and equitably by every telephone corporation, and the commission, in administering the lifeline telephone service program, should implement the program in a way that is equitable, nondiscriminatory, and without competitive consequences for the telecommunications industry in California.

§ 871.7. The Legislature finds and declares all of the following:

(a) The Moore Universal Telephone Service Act, enacted in 1987, was intended to offer high quality basic telephone service at affordable rates to the greatest number of California residents, and has become an important means of achieving universal service by making residential service affordable to low-income citizens through the creation of a lifeline class of service.

(b) Factors such as competition and technological innovation are resulting in the convergence of a variety of telecommunications technologies offering an expanded range of telecommunications services to users that incorporate voice, video, and data. These technologies have differing regulatory regimes and jurisdictions.

(c) It is the intent of the Legislature that the commission initiate a proceeding investigating the feasibility of redefining universal telephone service by incorporating two-way voice, video, and data service as components of basic service. It is the Legislature's further intent that, to the extent that the incorporation is feasible, that it promote equity of access to high-speed communications networks, the Internet, and other services to the extent that those services provide social benefits that include all of the following:

(1) Improving the quality of life among the residents of California.

(2) Expanding access to public and private resources for education, training, and commerce.

(3) Increasing access to public resources enhancing public health and safety.

(4) Assisting in bridging the "digital divide" through expanded access to new technologies by low-income, disabled, or otherwise disadvantaged Californians.

(5) Shifting traffic patterns by enabling telecommuting, thereby helping to improve air quality in all areas of the state and mitigating the need for highway expansion.

(d) For purposes of this section, the term "feasibility" means consistency with all of the following:

(1) Technological and competitive neutrality.

(2) Equitable distribution of the funding burden for redefined universal service as described in subdivision (c), among all affected consumers and industries, thereby ensuring that regulated utilities' ratepayers do not bear a disproportionate share of funding responsibility.

(3) Benefits that justify the costs.

§ 872. As used in this article, "household" means a residential dwelling that is the principal place of residence of the lifeline telephone service subscriber, and excludes any industrial, commercial, or other nonresidential building.

§ 873. (a)(1) The commission shall annually do all of the following:

(a) Designate a class of lifeline service necessary to meet minimum communications needs.

(b) Set the rates and charges for that service.

(c) Develop eligibility criteria for that service.

(d) Assess the degree of achievement of universal service, including telephone penetration rates by income, ethnicity, and geography.

(2) This information shall be annually reported to the Legislature by the commission in a document which can be made public.

(b) Minimum communications needs includes, but is not limited to, the ability to originate and receive calls and the ability to access electronic information services.

§ 874. The lifeline telephone service rates and charges shall be as follows:

(a) In a residential subscriber's service area where measured service is not available, the lifeline telephone service rates shall not be more than 50 percent of the rates for basic flat rate service, exclusive of federally mandated end user access charges, available to the residential subscriber.

(b) In a residential subscriber's service area where measured service is available, the subscriber may elect either of the following:

(1) A lifeline telephone service measured rate of not more than 50 percent of the basic rate for measured service, exclusive of federally mandated end user access charges, available to the residential subscriber.

(2) A lifeline flat rate of not more than 50 percent of the rates for basic flat rate service, exclusive of federally mandated end user access charges, available to the residential subscriber.

(c) The lifeline telephone service installation or connection charge, or both, shall not be more than 50 percent of the charge for basic residential service installation or connection, or both. The commission may limit the number of installation and connection charges, or both, that may be incurred at the reduced rate in any given period.

(d) There shall be no charge to the residential customer who has filed a valid eligibility statement for changing out of lifeline service.

(e) The commission shall assess whether there is a problem with customers who fraudulently obtain lifeline telephone service. If the commission determines that there is a problem, it shall recommend and promulgate appropriate solutions. This assessment and the solutions determined by the commission shall not, in and of themselves, change the procedures developed pursuant to Section 876.

§ 875. (a) In addition to Section 874, every lifeline telephone service subscriber shall be given an allowance, reduced by the amount of any credit or allowance authorized by the Federal Communications Commission, equal to the then current or announced federally mandated residential end user access charges.

(b) The commission may, in a separate proceeding, establish procedures necessary to ensure that the lifeline telephone service program qualifies for any federal funds available for the support of those programs.

§ 876. The commission shall require every telephone corporation providing telephone service within a service area to file a schedule of rates and charges providing a class of lifeline telephone service. Every telephone corporation providing service within a service area shall inform all eligible subscribers of the availability of lifeline telephone service, and how they may qualify for and obtain service, and shall accept applications for lifeline telephone service according to procedures specified by the commission.

§ 877. Nothing in this article precludes the commission from changing any rate established pursuant to Section 873, either specifically or pursuant to any general restructuring of all telephone rates, charges, and classifications.

§ 878. A lifeline telephone service subscriber shall be provided with one lifeline subscription, as defined by the commission, at his or her principal place of residence, and no other member of that subscriber's family or household who maintains residence at that place is eligible for lifeline telephone service.

An applicant for lifeline telephone service may report only one address in this state as the principal place of residence.

§ 879. (a) The commission shall, at least annually, initiate a proceeding to set rates for lifeline telephone service. All telephone corporations providing lifeline telephone service shall annually file, on a date set by the commission, proposed lifeline telephone service rates and a statement of projected revenue needs to meet the funding requirements to provide lifeline telephone service to qualified subscribers, together with proposed funding methods to provide the necessary funding. These funding methods shall include identification of those services whose rates shall be adjusted to provide the necessary funding.

(b) The commission shall commence a proceeding within 30 days after the date set for the filings required in subdivision (a), giving interested parties an opportunity to comment on the proposed rates and funding requirements and the proposed funding methods. The commission may change the rates, funding requirements, and funding methods proposed by the telephone corporations in any manner necessary, including reasonably spreading the funding among the services offered by the telephone corporations, to meet the public interest. Within 60 days of the annual filing, the commission shall issue an order setting lifeline telephone service rates and funding methods for each telephone corporation making a filing as required in subdivision (a). The commission may establish a lifeline service pool composed of the rate adjustments and surcharges imposed by the commission pursuant to this section for the purpose of funding lifeline telephone service.

(c) Any order issued by the commission pursuant to this section shall require telephone corporations providing lifeline telephone service to apply the funding requirement in the form of a surcharge to service rates which may be separately identified on the bills of customers using those services. The commission shall not allow any surcharge under this section on the rates charged by those telephone corporations for lifeline telephone service.

(d) The commission shall permit telephone corporations operating between service areas to adjust the rates of any service which may be affected by any surcharge imposed by this section.

§ 879.5. Notwithstanding Section 879, the commission shall issue its initial order adopting required rates and funding requirements not later than October 31, 1987, and prior to the issuance of that order, may fund lifeline telephone service through the use of an interim surcharge on service rates for telephone service provided by telephone corporations operating between service areas. The interim surcharge shall not exceed 4 percent of the service rates.

§ 880. The commission may determine any question of fact in its administration of this article.

§ 882. (a) The Public Utilities Commission shall, as soon as practicable, open a proceeding or proceedings to, or as part of existing proceedings shall, consider ways to ensure that advanced telecommunications services are made available as ubiquitously and economically as possible, in a timely fashion, to California's citizens, institutions, and businesses. The proceeding or proceedings should be completed within one year of commencement.

(b) The proceeding or proceedings shall develop rules, procedures, orders, or strategies, or all of these, that seek to achieve the following goals:

(1) To provide all citizens and businesses with access to the widest possible array of advanced communications services.

(2) To provide the state's educational and health care institutions with access to advanced communications services.

(3) To ensure cost-effective deployment of technology so as to protect ratepayers' interests and the affordability of telecommunications services.

(c) In the proceeding or proceedings, the commission should also consider, but need not limit its consideration to, all of the following:

(1) Whether the definition of universal service should be broadened.

(2) How to encourage the timely and economic development of an advanced public communications infrastructure, which may include a variety of competitive providers.

§ 883. (a) The commission shall, on or before February 1, 2001, issue an order initiating an investigation and opening a proceeding to examine the current and future definitions of universal service. That proceeding shall include public hearings that encourage participation by a broad and diverse range of interests from all areas of the state, including, but not limited to, all of the following:

(1) Consumer groups.

(2) Communication service providers, including all providers of high-speed access services.

(3) Facilities-based telephone providers.

(4) Information service providers and Internet access providers.

(5) Rural and urban users.

(6) Public interest groups.

(7) Representatives of small and large businesses and industry.

(8) Local agencies.

(9) State agencies, including, but not limited to, all of the following:

(a) The Business, Transportation and Housing Agency.

(b) The State and Consumer Services Agency.

(c) The State Department of Education.

(d) The State Department of Health Services.

(e) The California State Library.

(10) Colleges and universities.

(b) The objectives of the proceeding set forth in subdivision (a) shall include all of the following:

(1) To investigate the feasibility of redefining universal service in light of current trends toward accelerated convergence of voice, video, and data, with an emphasis on the role of basic telecommunications and Internet services in the workplace, in education and workforce training, access to health care, and increased public safety.

(2) To evaluate the extent to which technological changes have reduced the relevance of existing regulatory regimes given their current segmentation based upon technology.

(3) To receive broad-based input from a cross section of interested parties and make recommendations on whether video, data, and Internet service providers should be incorporated into an enhanced Universal Lifeline Service program, as specified, including relevant policy recommendations regarding regulatory and statutory changes and funding options that are consistent with the principles set forth in subdivision (c) of Section 871.7.

(4) To reevaluate prior definitions of basic service in a manner that will, to the extent feasible, effectively incorporate the latest technologies to provide all California residents with all of the following:

(a) Improved quality of life.

(b) Expanded access to public and private resources for education, training, and commerce.

(c) Increased access to public resources enhancing public health and safety.

(d) Assistance in bridging the "digital divide" through expanded access to new technologies by low income, disabled, or otherwise disadvantaged Californians.

(5) To assess projected costs of providing enhanced universal lifeline service in accordance with the intent of this article, and to delineate the subsidy support needed to maintain the redefined scope of universal service in a competitive market.

(6) To design and recommend an equitable and broad-based subsidy support mechanism for universal service in competitive markets in a manner that conforms with subdivision (c) of Section 871.7.

(7) To develop a process to periodically review and revise the definition of universal service to reflect new technologies and markets consistent with subdivision (c) of Section 871.7.

(8) To consider whether similar regulatory treatment for the provision of similar services is appropriate and feasible.

(c) In conducting its investigation, the commission shall take into account the role played by a number of diverse but convergent industries and providers, even though many of these entities are not subject to economic regulation by the commission or any other government entity.

(d) The recommendations of the commission shall be consistent with state policies for telecommunications as set forth in Section 709, and with all of the following principles:

(1) Universal service shall, to the extent feasible, be provided at affordable prices regardless of linguistic, cultural, ethnic, physical, financial, and geographic considerations.

(2) Consumers shall be provided access to all information needed to allow timely and informed choices about telecommunications products and services that are part of the universal service program and how best to use them.

(3) Education, health care, community, and government institutions shall be positioned as early recipients of new and emerging technologies so as to maximize the economic and social benefits of these services.

(e) The commission shall complete its investigation and report to the Legislature its findings and recommendations on or before January 1, 2002.

§ 884. (a) It is the intent of the Legislature that any program administered by the commission that addresses the inequality of access to high-speed broadband services by providing those services to schools and libraries at a discounted price, provide comparable discounts to a nonprofit community technology program.

(b) Notwithstanding any other law or existing program of the commission, but consistent with the purposes for which those funds were appropriated from the California Teleconnect Fund Administrative Committee Fund in Item 8660-001-0493 of Section 2.00 of the Budget Act of 2003 (Chapter 157 of the Statutes of 2003), and reappropriated in Item 8660-491 of Section 2.00 of the Budget Act of 2006 (Chapter 47 of the Statutes of 2006), the commission may expend up to two million dollars ($2,000,000) of the unencumbered amount of those funds for the nonrecurring installation costs for high-speed broadband services for community organizations that are eligible for discounted rates pursuant to Section 280.

(c) For the purpose of this section:

(1) "High-speed broadband services" means a system for the digital transmission of information over the Internet at a speed of at least 384 kilobits per second.

(2) "Nonprofit community technology program" means a community-based nonprofit organization that is exempt from taxation under Section 501(c)(3) of the Internal Revenue Code and engages in diffusing technology into local communities and training local communities that have no access to, or have limited access to, the Internet and advanced telecommunications technologies.

§ 884.5. (a) This section shall apply to all customers eligible to receive discounts for telecommunications services under the federal Universal Service E-rate program administered by the Schools and Libraries Division of the Universal Service Administrative Company that also apply for discounts on telecommunications services provided through the California Teleconnect Fund Administrative Committee Fund program pursuant to subdivision (a) of Section 280.

(b) A teleconnect discount shall be applied after applying an E-rate discount. The commission shall first apply an E-rate discount, regardless of whether the customer has applied for an E-rate discount or has been approved, if the customer, in the determination of the commission, meets the eligibility requirements for an E-rate discount.

(c) Notwithstanding subdivision (b), the teleconnect discount shall be applied without regard to an E-rate discount for a school district that meets the conditions specified for compensation pursuant to Article 4 (commencing with Section 42280) of Chapter 7 of Part 24 of Division 3 of Title 2 of the Education Code, unless that school district has applied for, and been approved to receive, the E-rate discount.

(d) In establishing a discount under the California Teleconnect Fund Administrative Committee Fund program, the commission shall give priority to bridging the "digital divide" by encouraging expanded access to state-of-the-art technologies for rural, inner-city, low-income, and disabled Californians.

(e) As used in this section:

(1) "E-rate discount" means an actual discount under the E-rate program, or a representative discount figure as determined by the commission.

(2) "E-rate program" means the federal Universal Service E-rate program administered by the Schools and Libraries Division of the Universal Service Administrative Company.

(3) "Teleconnect discount" means a discount on telecommunications services provided through the California Teleconnect Fund Administrative Committee Fund program set forth in subdivision (a) of Section 280.

F.3.3 Interim Opinion on Scope and Schedule for CARE Program Evaluations and Energy Division Audit of PG&E's Low Income Energy Efficiency Program, Cal. P.U.C. D. 03-02-070 (Feb. 7, 2003)

The full text of the interim opinion may be found on the companion website to this treatise.

Appendix G Sample Petitions and Letters Certifying Serious Illness

This appendix is also available on the companion website to this treatise. The companion website facilitates keyword searches and allows relevant provisions to be imported as word-processing documents.

This appendix comprises sample documents to be filed with a state utility regulatory commission or a utility company when seeking protection against disconnection of electric or natural gas service in the event of a serious illness. Please note that these samples come from specific states and that state provisions pertaining to utility consumer protections and rules of practice before regulatory commissions vary widely. Advocates using the templates provided in this appendix should carefully review state law and modify the templates as necessary and appropriate.

G.1 Sample Petition to Intervene with Appearance of Counsel

COMMOMWEALTH OF MASSACHUSETTS DEPARTMENT OF PUBLIC UTILITIES

	)	
Fitchburg Gas and Electric Co.	)	
	)	
General Increase in Rates	)	D.P.U.11-01
(Electric)	)	
	)	

PETITION TO INTERVENE OF THE LOW-INCOME WEATHERIZATION AND FUEL ASSISTANCE PROGRAM NETWORK, THE MASSACHUSETTS ENERGY DIRECTORS ASSOCIATION, AND MONTACHUSETT OPPORTUNITY COUNCIL

1. This is the Petition to Intervene in this docket, pursuant to 220 CMR 1.03 and 1.01(4), of the low-income weatherization and fuel assistance program network (the Network), the Massachusetts Energy Directors Association (MEDA), and Montachusett Opportunity Council (MOC). It requests that the Network, MEDA, and MOC be granted intervenor status in the above-captioned proceeding, in which Petitioner proposes a general increase in rates, including low-income rates.
2. As the only representatives of the low-income customer sector in this proceeding, the Network, MEDA, and MOC are in unique possession of information that can help inform the Department's deliberations in this proceeding. Low-income consumers are finding it increasingly difficult to afford their energy bills due to both (a) volatile but generally increasing energy prices and (b) the general economic crisis, which is causing falling incomes. Rate and bill increases proposed in this proceeding would playa critical role in making energy less affordable for low-income consumers.
3. Petitioners possess relevant and material information regarding the subject matter of this docket, including direct experience of low-income customers, MOC, and other member agencies of the Network and MEDA. Petitioners' participation in this docket will therefore materially assist the Department in its investigation and determinations herein by providing information about the situation of low-income customers as well as about impact of the proposed rates.
4. G.L. c. 25, sec. 19(c) (Green Communities Act, St. 2008, c. 169, sec. 11) provides that "The low-income residential demand side management and education programs shall be implemented through the low-income weatherization and fuel assistance program network and shall be coordinated with all electric and gas distribution companies in the commonwealth with the objective of standardizing implementation." The Network is the organization of agencies that make up the low-income weatherization and fuel assistance program network that implement programs under the Act, as well as the federal fuel assistance program administered by the Department of Housing and Community Development. The Network includes the agency, MOC, that implements these programs in the Company's territory as well as the lead agencies that cover each other utility service territory. MEDA is the association of energy directors of those agencies.
5. Members of the Network, MEDA, and MOC counsel customers of the Company about rates and payment options, and arrange rate payment assistance (including fuel assistance, arrearage management, and other forms of assistance) for Company

customers. As noted, many of the Company's customers, especially the low-income customers served by members of the Network, MEDA, and MOC are currently having an especially difficult time paying their bills, despite a temporary increase in funding of the fuel assistance program, increased funding of energy efficiency plans, and expansion of the arrearage management program.

6. Petitioners are thus substantially affected by this proceeding because the efficiency, weatherization, education, assistance, and counseling services they (or their members) offer are dependent on or affected by the outcome of this proceeding. Petitioners are also substantially affected by this proceeding because its clients (or those of its members) depend on the aforementioned efficiency, weatherization, education, assistance, and counseling services, which will be determined or affected by this proceeding. Further, Petitioners are substantially affected by the level of the Company's rates and bills because (a) their clients (or clients of their members) are more likely to require assistance as rates and bills rise, (b) the efficiency, weatherization, education, counseling and payment assistance services they (or their members) offer are less likely to result in affordable utility bills for their clients as rates and bills rise, (c) they (or their members) will be increasingly called upon to secure other means of assistance with utility bills as rates and bills rise, (d) they (or their members) will be increasingly called upon to assist clients who have had utility service terminated for nonpayment, and (e) they will be called upon by their members to assist them in helping members' clients as rates and bills rise. Petitioners also represent the interest of their (or their members) clients in reasonable and stable rates that they can afford to manage and pay; clients are substantially affected by rates and bills that they cannot afford to pay because they are unreasonably high.
7. The Petitioners have questions about the Company's proposed low-income discount rate, rate design, rate structure (allocation among customer classes), rate base, and expenses with respect to the above-captioned filing.
8. If settlement is not attainable in this proceeding, Petitioners expect to file documentary, and perhaps oral, evidence on the topics described above. Relief sought would include review of proposed rates, rate design, rate structure, rate base, and expenses to mitigate adverse impacts on low-income customers of the Company.

Wherefore, The Low-income Weatherization and Fuel Assistance Program Network, Massachusetts Energy Directors Association, Montachusett Opportunity Council, and their other member agencies, respectfully request intervenor status in this Docket.

Respectfully submitted,

The Low-income Weatherization and Fuel Assistance Program Network,
Massachusetts Energy Directors Association, and
Montachusett Opportunity Council

By their attorney,

[*Attorney name and address*]

Dated: [*Date*]

THE COMMONWEALTH OF MASSACHUSETTS
DEPARTMENT OF PUBLIC UTILITIES

D.P.U. No. 11-01

Fitchburg Gas and Electric Co.
General Increase in Rates (Electric)

APPEARANCE OF COUNSEL

In the above-entitled proceeding, I hereby appear for and on behalf of The Low-income Weatherization and Fuel Assistance Program Network, the Massachusetts Energy Directors Association, and Montachusett Opportunity Council.

[*Attorney name and address*]
Dated: [*Date*]

G.2 Sample Petition to Initiate a Proceeding

THE VERMONT PUBLIC SERVICE BOARD

	)	
In re Application of AARP	)	
Pursuant to 30 V.S.A. § 218(e)	)	
for Establishment of Reduced	)	
Rates for Low Income	)	Docket No.
Consumers of Green Mountain	)	
Power Company and Central	)	
Vermont Public Service Corp.	)	
	)	

PETITION PURSUANT TO 30 V.S.A. § 218(e)

Now comes AARP and it petitions the Board pursuant to 30 V.S.A. § 218(e) to establish reduced rate for low-income residential consumers of Green Mountain Power Company and Central Vermont Public Service Corporation.

1. Section 13(a) of Act No. 92 of the Laws of 2008 created 30 V.S.A. § 218(e). That subsection authorizes the Board to approve a "rate schedule, tariff, agreement, contract or settlement" that sets reduced rates for residential customers with household income at or below 150% of the Federal Poverty Level. It also authorizes any person to submit a petition to the Board to approve of such a rate schedule, tariff, agreement, contract or settlement.
2. AARP is a membership organization with over 130,000 members in Vermont, almost all of whom are residential electricity customers.
3. GMP is a regulated electric utility with a service territory that includes over 96,000 Vermont customers, including residential, commercial and industrial customers.
4. CVPS is a regulated electric utility with over 159,000 Vermont customers, including residential, commercial and industrial users.
5. GMP and CVPS together provide service to the majority of Vermont electric service customers.
6. AARP proposes that the Proposed Order set forth in Appendix A, attached to and incorporated into this Petition, be adopted and issued by the Board.

7. AARP therefore asks that the Board open a docket for this matter, provide statutory notice, schedule a hearing or hearings in this matter, and issue an order substantially as set forth in Appendix A.

Date: May 19, 2009
AARP
By
[*Attorney name and address*]

G.3 Sample Serious Illness Letters

G.3.1 Temporary Illness

A. Template

To Whom It May Concern:

[*Name of patient*] who resides at [*address*] is a patient of mine [*or:* is under my care]. [*Name of patient*] is being treated for [*describe illness or condition*], a serious illness.

Sincerely,

[*Doctor's name and contact information*]

B. Sample

To Whom It May Concern:

Joe Smith, who resides at 123 ABC Street in Anytown, is currently under my care. I am treating him for bronchitis, a serious illness.

Sincerely,

Jane Jones, MD
456 DEF Street
Anytown, USA
508-555-5555

G.3.2 Chronic Illness

A. Template

To Whom It May Concern:

[*Name of patient*] who resides at [*address*] is a patient of mine [*or:* is under my care]. [*Name of patient*] is being treated for [*describe illness or condition*], a chronic illness.

Sincerely,

[*Doctor's name and contact information*]

B. Sample

To Whom It May Concern:

Joe Smith, who resides at 123 ABC Street in Anytown, is currently under my care. I am treating him for chronic depression, an illness of indefinite duration.

Sincerely,

Jane Jones, MD
456 DEF Street
Anytown, USA
508-555-5555

Appendix H Finding Pleadings, Primary Sources on the Companion Website

This appendix is also available on the companion website to this treatise. The companion website facilitates key-word searches and the importing of relevant provisions into a word-processing document.

H.1 Introduction

Access to Utility Service includes free access to its companion website, which remains free with continued subscription to this title. The companion website includes all appendices found in *Access to Utility Service* plus many sample pleadings and over a hundred other primary source documents—statutes, regulations, federal and state agency interpretations, and practice aids—that are easily located with flexible, powerful search tools. Documents are in Adobe Acrobat Portable Document Format (PDF), and the pleadings are also in Microsoft Word format.

This appendix describes the documents found on the companion website, how to access these documents, and how to print the documents, download them onto your computer, or copy-paste them into a word processing file.

H.2 Pleadings and Primary Sources Found on the Companion Website

The companion website to *Access to Utility Service* contains summaries of state utility regulations and state energy assurance programs, as well as numerous pleadings relating to utility law. The site also includes federal statutes and regulations on telecommunications, the LIHEAP program, and the Department of Energy's Weatherization Assistance Program.

The website does *not* contain the full text of this treatise's chapters. See H.5, *infra*, for information on how to use Internet-based keyword searches to pinpoint page numbers in the treatise where topics are discussed.

H.3 How to Access the Website

One-time registration is required to access the companion website. Once registered, a user subsequently logging in will be granted immediate access to all the websites he or she is authorized to use. For example, one username and password allows a subscriber to four NCLC titles to access all four companion websites.

To register for the first time, go to **www.nclc.org/webaccess** and click on "New users click here to register." Enter the Companion Website Registration Number found on the packing statement or invoice accompanying this publication. Then enter the requested information and click on "Enter." An e-mail address may be used for the username, or a different username may be chosen.

Subscribers do *not* need to register more than once. If subscribers purchase additional NCLC treatise titles later, they will automatically be given access to the corresponding companion websites. Registering a second time with the same registration number overrides a prior username and password. (Note that, if users allow all their subscriptions to lapse and then subsequently purchase a treatise, they will have to register again.)

Once registered, click on the login link at **www.nclc.org/webaccess**, enter the username and password, and select the *Access to Utility Service* website from the list of authorized websites.

An alternate login method may be particularly useful for libraries, legal aid offices, or law firms that subscribe to the entire set of NCLC treatises. Simply e-mail publications@nclc.org with a list or range of static IP addresses for which access should be permitted. Users from those addresses can then go to www.nclc.org/ipaccess to be granted access *without* entering a username and password.

Once logged in, users can click the "My Account" link on the left toolbar to change their personal information. We also encourage users who find any mistakes to notify us using the "Report Errors" button, also on the left toolbar. At minimum, **use of the companion websites with Internet Explorer requires Adobe Reader 7.0 or Adobe Acrobat 7.0 (or later versions of the software). Users of other browsers, or those experiencing problems with the websites, should download the latest version of the free Adobe Reader (currently 10) from Adobe's website at www.adobe.com.** A link to Adobe's site is provided on the NCLC companion website login page.

Login

Please take a moment to log in:

Username

Password

☐ Remember my credentials

Login

New Users Click Here Register.

Forgot Your Password and/or User Name?

Access Via IP Address

Important:
Internet Explorer users: This site requires Adobe Acrobat or Reader 7.0 or higher.
Firefox and Safari users: This site requires Adobe Acrobat or Reader 9.0 or higher.
Click Here to download the latest version of Adobe Reader
(Use of earlier Reader versions may result in documents showing as blank pages)

H.4 Locating Documents on the Website

The companion website provides two options to locate documents.

1. The search page (the home page) uses keyword searches to find documents—full text searches of all documents on the website or searches only of the documents' titles.

- Narrow the search to documents of a certain type (such as federal regulations or pleadings) by making a selection from the "Document Type" menu, and then perform a full text or document title search.
- To locate a specific appendix section, select the appendix section number (for example, "A.2.3") or a partial identifier (for example, "A") in the search page's "Appendix" drop-down fields.
- Click on "Search Hints" for a quick reference to special search operators, wildcards, shortcuts, and complex searches. Read this closely, as syntax and search operators may be slightly different from those of other websites.

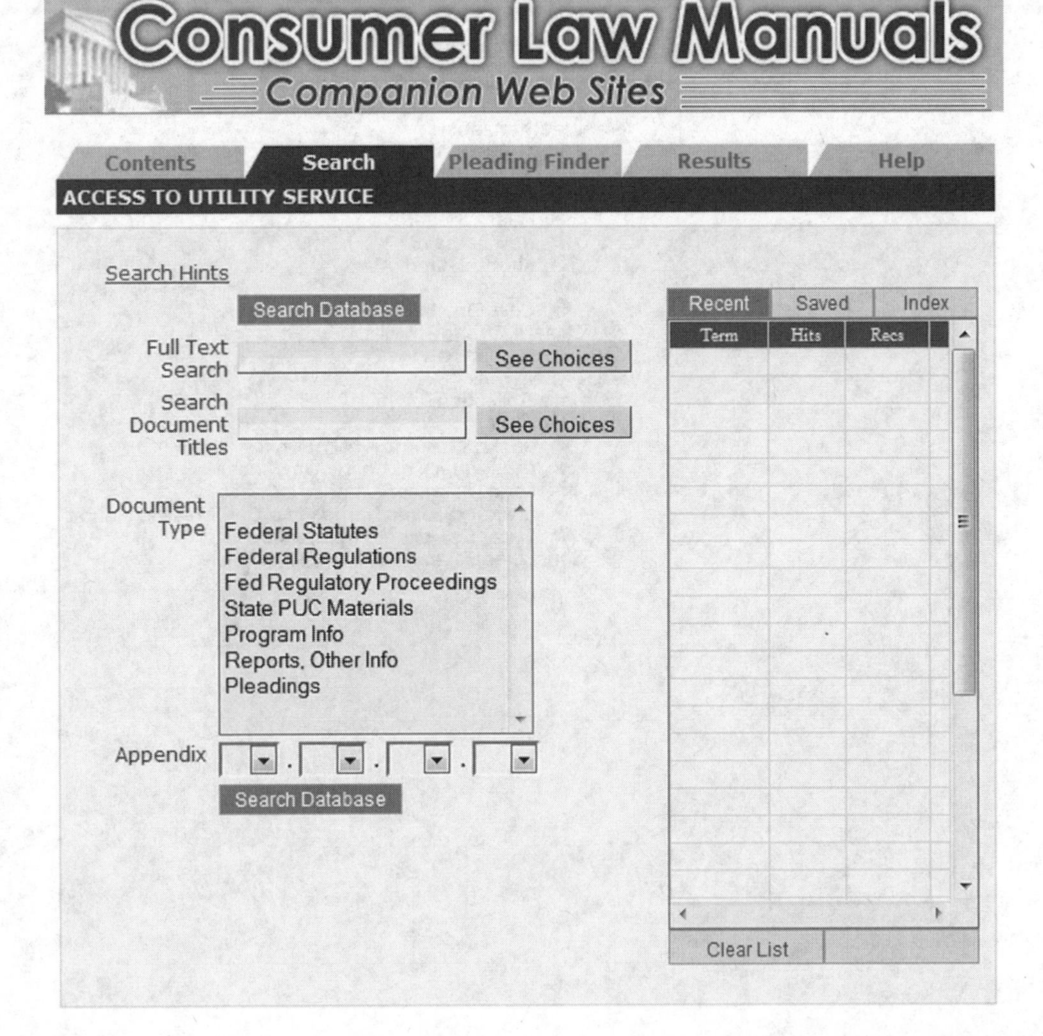

2. The contents page (click on the "Contents" tab at the top of the page) is a traditional "branching" table of contents. Click a branch to expand it into a list of sub-branches or documents. Each document appears once on this contents tree.

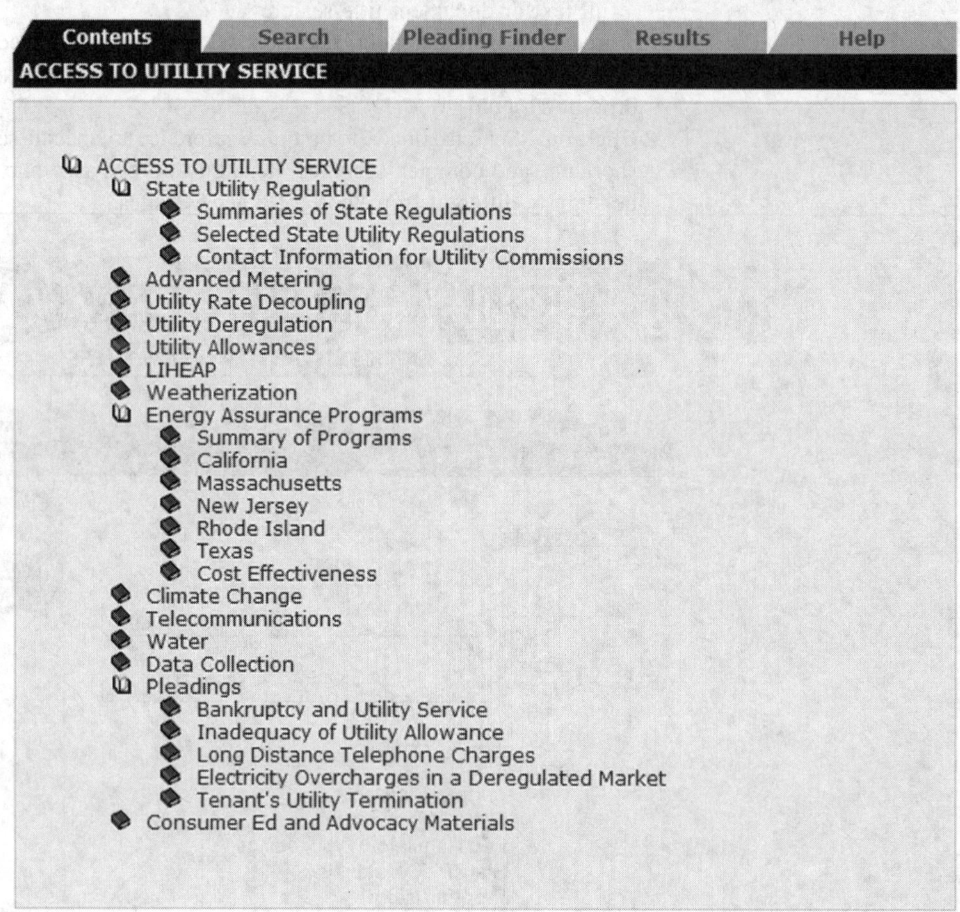

H.5 How to Use the Documents, Find Microsoft Word Versions, and Locate Additional Features

All documents on the website are in Adobe Acrobat PDF format and can be printed, downloaded onto your computer, or cut and pasted into a word processing document. Pleadings and certain other documents also are available in Microsoft Word format, facilitating the opening of entire documents in a word processor. After opening the selected PDF file, click at the top of the page on "Word Version, if available" link. If a Word version is listed as available, click on "DOC Download Document" to save the Word file to your computer.

Links on the left hand toolbar bring you to credit math software, search tips, other websites, tables of contents and indices of all NCLC treatises, and other practice aids. Links to especially important new developments will be placed toward the bottom of the "Search" page.

H.6 Electronic Searches of This and Other NCLC Titles' Chapters

Completely separate from the treatises' companion websites, NCLC offers a handy on-line utility to search the full text of this treatise's chapters and appendices. This free search utility is found at www.nclc.org/keyword and requires no registration or log-in.

While the chapters' text is not available on-line, this web-based search engine will find a word or phrase that can then easily be located in the printed treatise. Select this title, enter a search term or combination of search terms—such as a case name, a regulation cite, or other keywords—and the page numbers containing those terms will be listed. Search results are shown in context, facilitating selection of the most relevant pages.

The full text of other NCLC treatises and supplements, *NCLC REPORTS*, and other publications can also be electronically searched to locate relevant topics at www.nclc.org/keyword. Just select the desired title or search across all NCLC titles.

Current tables of contents, indices, and other information for all eighteen titles in the NCLC consumer law series can be found at www.nclc.org/shop. Click on the "Publications for Lawyers" link and scroll down to the book you want. The PDF documents found there can be quickly searched for a word or phrase.

The Quick Reference at the back of this volume lets you pinpoint the correct NCLC title and section within the title that discuss over 1000 different subject areas. These subject areas are listed in alphabetical order and can also be electronically searched at www.nclc.org/qr.

H.7 Finding Additional Pleadings

Pleadings specifically relating to this title are found in Adobe Acrobat PDF and Microsoft Word formats on the companion website. Over 2000 other pleadings are available in NCLC's *Consumer Law Pleadings* and can be found on the *Consumer Law Pleadings* companion website using the same search techniques discussed above. These 2000 pleadings can also be pinpointed using the *Consumer Law Pleadings* index guide, which organizes pleadings by type, subject area, legal claim, title, and other categories identical to those on the website.

Index

References are to sections

References are to sections

References are to sections

References are to sections

References are to sections

References are to sections

References are to sections

References are to sections

References are to sections

References are to sections

References are to sections

References are to sections

References are to sections

References are to sections

Quick Reference to the Consumer Credit and Sales Legal Practice Series

References are to sections in *all* manuals in NCLC's Consumer Credit and Sales Legal Practice Series. References followed by "S" appear only in a supplement.

Always use the most recent version of this Quick Reference (e.g. use the Quick Reference found in a current supplement instead of that in the main edition). The safest way to insure use of the most current Quick Reference is to use the version available at www.nclc.org/qr.

Readers should also consider another search option available at ***www.nclc.org/keyword***. There, users can search all eighteen NCLC treatises for a case name, party name, statutory or regulatory citation, or *any* other word, phrase, or combination of terms. The search engine provides the title, page number and context of every occurrence of that word or phrase within each of the NCLC treatises. Further search instructions and tips are provided on the website.

Abbreviations

AUS	=	Access to Utility Service (5th ed. 2011)
Auto	=	Automobile Fraud (4th ed. 2011)
Arbit	=	Consumer Arbitration Agreements (6th ed. 2011)
Coll	=	Collection Actions (2d ed. 2011)
CBPL	=	Consumer Banking and Payments Law (4th ed. 2009 and 2011 Supp.)
Bankr	=	Consumer Bankruptcy Law and Practice (9th ed. 2009 and 2011 Supp.)
CCA	=	Consumer Class Actions (7th ed. 2010 and 2011 Supp.)
CLP	=	Consumer Law Pleadings, Numbers 1 Through 17 (2011)
COC	=	The Cost of Credit (4th ed. 2009 and 2011 Supp.)
CD	=	Credit Discrimination (5th ed. 2009 and 2011 Supp.)
FCR	=	Fair Credit Reporting (7th ed. 2010 and 2011 Supp.)
FDC	=	Fair Debt Collection (7th ed. 2011)
Fore	=	Foreclosures (3d ed. 2010 and 2011 Supp.)
Repo	=	Repossessions (7th ed. 2010 and 2011 Supp.)
Stud	=	Student Loan Law (4th ed. 2010 and 2011 Supp.)
TIL	=	Truth in Lending (7th ed. 2010 and 2011 Supp.)
UDAP	=	Unfair and Deceptive Acts and Practices (7th ed. 2008 and 2011 Supp.)
Warr	=	Consumer Warranty Law (4th ed. 2010 and 2011 Supp.)

The Quick Reference to the Consumer Credit and Sales Legal Practice Series pinpoints where to find specific topics analyzed in the NCLC treatises. References are to individual treatise or supplement sections. For more information on these volumes, see *What Your Library Should Contain* at the beginning of this volume, or go to www.nclc.org.

This Quick Reference is a speedy means to locate key terms in the appropriate NCLC treatise. More detailed indexes are found at the end of the individual NCLC volumes. Both the detailed contents pages and the detailed indexes for each treatise are also available on NCLC's website, www.nclc.org.

NCLC *strongly recommends,* when searching for PLEADINGS on a particular subject, that users refer to the *Index Guide* accompanying *Consumer Law Pleadings*, and *not* to this Quick Reference. Another option is to search for pleadings directly on the *Consumer Law Pleadings* website, using the finding tools that are provided there.

The finding tools found on NCLC's companion websites are also an effective means to find statutes, regulations, agency interpretations, legislative history, and other primary source material found in manual appendices and on NCLC's companion websites. Other search options are detailed at page ix, *supra*: *About the Companion Website, Other Search Options*.

References are to sections in *all* manuals in NCLC's Consumer Credit and Sales Legal Practice Series

References are to sections in *all* manuals in NCLC's Consumer Credit and Sales Legal Practice Series

References are to sections in *all* manuals in NCLC's Consumer Credit and Sales Legal Practice Series

References are to sections in *all* manuals in NCLC's Consumer Credit and Sales Legal Practice Series

References are to sections in *all* manuals in NCLC's Consumer Credit and Sales Legal Practice Series

References are to sections in *all* manuals in NCLC's Consumer Credit and Sales Legal Practice Series

References are to sections in *all* manuals in NCLC's Consumer Credit and Sales Legal Practice Series

References are to sections in *all* manuals in NCLC's Consumer Credit and Sales Legal Practice Series

References are to sections in *all* manuals in NCLC's Consumer Credit and Sales Legal Practice Series

References are to sections in *all* manuals in NCLC's Consumer Credit and Sales Legal Practice Series

References are to sections in *all* manuals in NCLC's Consumer Credit and Sales Legal Practice Series

NOTES

NOTES

NOTES

NOTES

NOTES

NOTES

NOTES

NOTES

NOTES

NOTES

NOTES